Index to the *Lahaina News* (1979–2003), the *Lahaina Sun* (1970–1973), and the *Lahaina Times* (1980–1983, limited issues)

Index to
the *Lahaina News*
(1979–2003)
the *Lahaina Sun*
(1970–1973)
and
the *Lahaina Times*
(1980–1983, limited issues)

Compiled and Edited by

Brian Richardson

North Beach-West Maui
Benefit Fund Inc.

Lahaina, Maui, Hawai'i

ISBN: 978-0-578-95374-8

Published by the North Beach-West Maui Benefit Fund, Inc.
PO Box 11329
Lahaina, Hawai'i 96761

Every effort has been made to trace copyright holders and to obtain their
permission for the use of copyright material. The publisher apologizes for any
errors or omissions and would be grateful if notified of any corrections that
should be incorporated in future reprints or editions of this book.

In memory of
Richard Woods
He ʻōpū hālau

Contents

Foreword

West Maui is very fortunate, compared to some communities, in that over thirty years of its community newspapers were microfilmed. Both the producers of newspapers and their readers rarely consider a community newspaper to have any value after being read. For a long time, professional historians also looked at newspapers suspiciously as a legitimate primary historical source. Librarians and other archivists who have recognized their value have had difficulty in preserving the newspapers. Despite these obstacles, West Maui community newspapers were archived starting in the year 1970.

As Hawaiʻi has seen with the scanning and open access to nineteenth and early twentieth century Hawaiian language newspaper archives, newspapers are a valuable source for historical information. Newspapers retain a sense of the time in which the newspaper was printed and the society from which it was published.

In 2017, the Board of the Directors of the HK West Maui Community Fund agreed to fund two research projects: (1) to index and translate a representative sample of nineteenth century Hawaiian language newspaper articles related to West Maui and (2) to index the contemporary English language West Maui community newspapers. Somewhat uncertain and cautious, they broke the second project into two phases. The first phase was to index the *Lahaina Sun* (1970–1973) and what was available of the *Lahaina Times* (1976–1984). After reviewing the work of the first phase, the Board enthusiastically funded the second phase to index the more substantial *Lahaina News* (1979–2003).

The first project, related to nineteenth century Hawaiian language newspapers, was published last year by the North Beach West Maui Benefit Fund as *Malu ʻUlu o Lele: Maui Komohana in Ka Nupepa Kuokoa* (distributed by the University of Hawaiʻi Press).

This project is being provided in a slightly different form. It is being made available online publicly in a text searchable PDF through the University of Hawaiʻi. At the same time, a limited number of printed copies are being distributed to libraries and other institutions that can serve as repositories of those with limited access to the internet. It will also be available for purchase online at cost through print on demand so that historians and others interested may obtain a printed copy.

The North Beach West Maui Benefit Fund is honored to support the publication of another work directly related to the history and current life of West Maui, its lands and its people.

Lance D. Collins
Wainalu, Honokōwai

Preface

This publication provides an index to the *Lahaina News* from its inception in July 1979 to the October 9, 2003 issue. The *Lahaina News* began as a monthly publication, changed to a bi-monthly publication in 1980, and then a weekly publication in September, 1983. The paper was accessed through microfilm copy available through the University of Hawai'i at Mānoa. Roughly 1100 issues of the newspaper, spanning 25 years, are included in this index. An additional six issues are absent because they were missing from the microfilm set: June 29, 1988, August 31, 1988, February 2, 1989, February 27, 1992, July 3, 1997, and December 16, 1999.

The publication also includes an index of the *Lahaina Sun* from 1970 to 1973 and issues of *Lahaina Times* published between 1980 and 1983 that were available on the microfilm collection. Only five of an estimated 40 issues of the *Lahaina Times* were available for indexing. Hopefully the remaining issues can be somehow recovered in the future.

Access to the microfilm was obtained from Hamilton Library at the Univerisity of Hawai'i at Mānoa with the help of Jodie Mattos, Hawaiian Collection librarian.

The entries in the index are arranged alphabetically by main header and then by date. When the newpaper included a supplemental publication, the pagination provided reflects that supplement's pagination or an appropriate alternative.

Most of the articles in the newspaper have been indexed in some form. Common entries include local sports and music, government meetings, developments, crime, business, etc. Events occuring outside of West Maui were also included if the story was judged to be relevant to the readers of the newspaper.

Sports articles were a significant part of the *Lahaina News* and attempts were made to index personalities, events, and results. Specific players and the results of league play are seldom indexed. The newspaper would often print team membership lists or detailed competition results.

An exception to the broad inclusion is the various "events and gossip" columns often included in the *Lahaina News*, which made passing mention of many people and events. These mentions were seldom indexed.

Determining whether people or events are signficant depends in part on the whether the people or events were given a separate entry in the newspaper. If an upcoming event is announced multiple times, not all of the announcements are indexed.

In addition, the status for different entries in the newspaper changed from time to time. Upcoming musical events, for instance, would often have separate paragraphs, but this changed in the late 1980s when the newspaper began publishing a simple calendar that only provided the performer's name. The musical groups were thus indexed in earlier issues, but rarely in later ones. A similar change can be noted with crime. Where a crime or an accident was the focus of a particular article, it was indexed. At times, the *Lahaina News* would include a quick summary of multiple crimes, often petty, that occurred in the area. These passing mentions were seldom indexed.

Attempts have been made to standardize the names of organizations, people, and places, even if those names changed over time. Where the names of people vary, the name has been standardized. However, if people had similar or the same names but could have been different people, the entries were left separate. Attempts have been made to include "see also" entries for names with significant variations.

Photographs and advertisements are seldom indexed. Exceptions included photographs and advertisements that provided additional details on events described elsewhere in the newspaper. The *Lahaina News* typically reprinted the graduation pictures of students at Lahainaluna High School, which are referenced collectively under the heading of Lahainaluna High School but not individually indexed.

For Hawaiian terms, diacritical marks were seldom, inconsistently, and sometimes incorrectly used in the newspapers. They have generally been included to the headers but the descriptions, which are based more closely on the text in the newspaper, have typically not been changed.

Finally, obvious typographical errors have been corrected.

The scope of the index allows users to trace responses to the influx of hippies in the early 1970s, unsuccessful efforts to restore Malu'ulu O Lele, and Linda Lingle's early political activities, with the first mention in 1984. While hotels, tourism, and real estate figure prominently, sporatic mention is also made of land rights, Hawaiian sovereignty, poverty, and social issues. Infrastructure issues, and especially sewage and roads, are pervasive. The Lahaina Bypass is first mentioned in 1986 and by 2003 work is still said to be years away.

The index thus provides a snapshot of West Maui through the editorial and corporate lens of the local newspaper. Of course, a more critical use of the index would also consider what was not included in the newspaper, or what was treated with cursory attention.

Brian Richardson

100TH BATTALION
— featured, Lahaina News, May 21, 1992: 3.

1959 PINK THUNDERBIRD [PLAY]
— to be presented by Theatre Theatre Maui, Lahaina News, April 16, 1992: 17.
— held over, Lahaina News, May 7, 1992: 19.

1STDOMAIN.NET [BUSINESS]
— becomes first certified multilingual registrar, Lahaina News, November 2, 2000: 12.

2 HIP [MUSICAL GROUP]
— to perform at Kobe Japanese Steak House, Lahaina News, October 18, 1989: 12.

20TH CENTURY MASTERS
— gallery opens, Lahaina News, May 16, 1990: 6.

28 BY 4 [MULTI-MEDIA EXHIBIT]
— on display at Dan's Frame and Art, Lahaina News, October 8, 1986: 3.

3521 CORPORATION [BUSINESS]
— Maui County Council's Planning Committee considering request for development on Kahana Ridge, Lahaina News, June 8, 1995: 1,2.

3D BUILDERS AND DESIGN [BUSINESS]
— featured, Lahaina News, June 1, 2000: 13.
— featured, Lahaina News, September 21, 2000: 15.
— to open Sales and Design Center, Lahaina News, January 4, 2001: 13.
— creating custom homes, Lahaina News, March 1, 2001: 7.
— opens new Design Center, Lahaina News, April 26, 2001: 7.

4 HIM [MUSICAL GROUP]
— to perform at Maui Arts and Cultural Center, Lahaina News, June 29, 2000: 20.

4-H CLUBS
— to meet, Lahaina News, September 9, 1993: 3.
— seeks members, volunteers, Lahaina News, November 17, 1994: 4.
— to hold market day, Lahaina News, February 11, 1999: 16.
— Nutrition Fair and Poster Contest to be held, Lahaina News, February 24, 2000: 17.
— seeking youth, Lahaina News, October 5, 2000: 7.

42ND STREET [PLAY]
— performed by Maui Community Theatre, Lahaina News, January 27, 1988: 3.

4TH OF JULY
— see July 4th

5 A RENT-A-SPACE
— see AAAAA Rent-A-Space

505 FRONT STREET
— shopping mall opens, Lahaina News, April 29, 1987: 1,10.
— announce new tenants, Lahaina News, March 23, 1988: 18.
— occupancy at 97 percent, Lahaina News, November 9, 1988: 20.
— new swimwear shop to open, Lahaina News, April 25, 1990: 7.
— Mark Kirkeby named general manager, Lahaina News, June 20, 1991: 7.

5TH OF JULY [PLAY]
— to be performed by Maui Community Theater, Lahaina News, June 1, 2000: 16.
— to be performed by Maui Community Theater, Lahaina News, June 8, 2000: 20.

7-11 [BUSINESS]
— acquire license to sell liquor, Lahaina News, May 23, 1984: 3.

808 STATE [MUSICAL GROUP]
— to perform at Blue Tropix, Lahaina News, May 20, 1993: 9.

88 CENT VIDEO STORE [BUSINESS]
— opens, Lahaina News, June 20, 1990: 7.

9TH LIFE CAT RESCUE
— to hold benefit whale watch, Lahaina News, February 26, 1998: 13.

A

A SWEET DREAM BAR
— opens at The Bay Lounge, Lahaina News, April 1, 1993: 12.

A TASTE OF LAHAINA
— see Taste of Lahaina, A

A TOUCH OF MAUI [BUSINESS]
— opens, Lahaina News, December 13, 1989: 6.

A.J.A. VETERANS CLUB
— West Maui club sponsoring students to visit Washington DC, Lahaina Sun, February 3, 1971: 1.
— Howard Nakamura speaks to, critical of environmentalists, Lahaina Sun, February 21, 1973: 12,13.
— to meet, Lahaina News, June 6, 1991: 4.
— new officers and board elected, Lahaina News, July 25, 1991: 5.
— to meet, Lahaina News, May 28, 1992: 4.
— elects new officers, Lahaina News, November 11, 1993: 3.
— co-sponsoring Chrysanthemum Ball, Lahaina News, November 20, 1997: 3.
— to host Memorial Day services, Lahaina News, May 14, 1998: 1.
— sponsors Chrysanthemum Ball, Lahaina News, November 25, 1999: 7.
— to hold Chrysanthemum Ball, Lahaina News, December 2, 1999: 16.
— Edward Seiya Watanabe new president of, Lahaina News, August 3, 2000: 5.
— hosting Chrysanthemum Ball, Lahaina News, November 9, 2000: 13.
— West Maui club has new officers, Lahaina News, July 12, 2001: 2.
— West Maui club to hold annual Memorial Day Service, Lahaina News, May 23, 2002: 2.
— West Maui club announces new officers, Lahaina News, July 11, 2002: 9.
— West Maui club featured, Lahaina News, July 18, 2002: 1,20.
— West Maui club to host talk by Brigadier General Clarence Merton Agena, Lahaina News, May 22, 2003: 1,18.

A&B COMMERCIAL
— sold to Monarch Building Supply, Lahaina News, December 10, 1986: 3.

A+ PROGRAM
— afterschool program sought by some residents in West Maui, Lahaina News, January 10, 1990: 1,3.
— described, Lahaina News, February 14, 1990: 1,10.
— registration underway at Princess Nahienaena Elementary School, Lahaina News, August 7, 2003: 2.

AAAAA RENT-A-SPACE [BUSINESS]
— opens, Lahaina News, December 2, 1987: 3.
— featured, Lahaina News, May 18, 1988: 16.
— offering wine storage, Lahaina News, January 23, 1992: 11.
— opens, Lahaina News, November 28, 1996: 14.
— donates use of units to American Red Cross, Lahaina News, June 19, 1997: 6.
— blessing held for new storage facility, Lahaina News, October 31, 2002: 6.

AABREY, KENNY [COMEDIAN]
— to perform at Comedy Club and the Sports Page, Lahaina News, February 20, 1991: 9,11.

AARON CHANEY REALTY
— opening in Whaler's Village, Lahaina Sun, November 25, 1970: 3.

ABAY-ABAY, ANDREA
— finalist in Hawaii National Teenager Pageant, Lahaina News, March 12, 1992: 3.

ABBOT, ROY AND WENDY
— presented check to West Maui Little League, Lahaina News, January 12, 1995: 7.

ABBOTT, ISABELLA AIONA
— discusses likely explanation for seaweed overgrowth, Lahaina News, August 16, 1989: 1.
— to speak to The Native Hawaiian Plant Society, Lahaina News, February 18, 1993: 4.
— to lecture at Bailey House Museum, Lahaina News, April 10, 1997: 12,13.

ABC STORES [BUSINESS]
— acquire license to sell liquor, Lahaina News, May 23, 1984: 3.
— rezoning requested to allow building of, Lahaina News, June 18, 1986: 3.
— opens at The Shops at Wailea, Lahaina News, January 25, 2001: 14.
— opens store, Lahaina News, February 22, 2001: 8.

ABDER, ERIC
— director of Wetscreams [film], Lahaina Times, August, 1980 volume 4 number 7: 5.

ABE, AIONA [COUNCIL MEMBER]
— asks for law to allow County to haul away junk automobiles, Lahaina News, October 9, 1985: 8.

ABE, GEORGE
— named chairman of American Cancer Society's annual crusade, Lahaina News, February 20, 1985: 7.

ABE, HIDEO
— to be part of Patsy Mink's Congressional staff, Lahaina News, June 14, 2001: 2.

ABE, HOWARD
— Department of Transportation representative discusses possible improvements to Honoapi'ilani Highway, Lahaina News, December 26, 1984: 3.
— Maui's district engineer of the highway division of the state's Department of Transportation promoted, leaving Maui, Lahaina News, October 9, 1985: 1,20.

ABE INTERNATIONAL VENTURES CORP [BUSINESS]
— sells Embassy Suites Resort to partnership including Mike McCormack, Lahaina News, August 6, 1992: 6.

ABEL, MILT [COMEDIAN]
— to perform at Comedy Club and the Sports Page, Lahaina News, September 24, 1992: 14,17.

ABELLA, DAVID
— chef at Roy's Kahana Bar and Grill to hold cooking demonstrations, Lahaina News, October 1, 1992: 15.

ABELLA, SISTER LEONA
— saved by Richard Loomis after being swept off a rock near Napili, Lahaina Sun, April 12, 1972: 9.
— dies 10 days after being taken from the water off Napili, Lahaina Sun, April 26, 1972: 6.

ABERCROMBIE, NEIL [POLITICIAN]
— sworn in as representative, Lahaina News, January 9, 1991: 4.

ABORIGINAL LANDS OF HAWAIIAN ANCESTRY (ALOHA)
— convention on Moloka'i described, Lahaina Sun, April 18, 1973: 15.
— holds convention on Moloka'i, Lahaina Sun, April 18, 1973: 9.
— President Maxwell discusses situation and plans, Lahaina Sun, July 11, 1973: 14.
— testify at Honokohau Study Advisory Commission concerning land rights, Lahaina Sun, August 8, 1973: 4.

ABORTION
— Donald Billman speaks against, at Maui Community College, Lahaina Sun, October 27, 1971: 4.
— pro-life supporters hope Republican Party will oppose abortion, Lahaina News, February 6, 1992: 1.

— legislative bill supporting RU-486 progresses, Lahaina News, March 19, 1992: 3.
— expected to be an issue in upcoming election, Lahaina News, April 30, 1992: 1.

ABOUT ADAM [FILM]
— to be shown at Maui Arts and Cultural Center, Lahaina News, July 12, 2001: 16.

ABRAMS [FAMILY]
— connection to the sea described, Lahaina Sun, December 27, 1972: 13.

ABREU, JOSEPH
— police officer sues Abraham Aiona [police chief] for violation of his right to free speech, Lahaina Sun, February 10, 1971: 4.
— police officer hearing set for reinstatement, Lahaina Sun, December 15, 1971: 8.
— police officer has been dismissed, Lahaina Sun, December 22, 1971: 15.
— police officer granted Civil Service Commission hearing, Lahaina Sun, January 12, 1972: 8.
— County Civil Service hearing continues for police officer, Lahaina Sun, January 26, 1972: 5.
— County Civil Service hearing suggests self-imposed "gag rule" in the police department, Lahaina Sun, February 2, 1972: 3.
— County Civil Service Commission hearing on police officer updated, Lahaina Sun, February 23, 1972: 18.
— details on police officer termination and lawsuit, Lahaina Sun, March 29, 1972: 6.
— hearing becomes tense, Lahaina Sun, April 5, 1972: 4.
— Civil Service Commission decision on police officer announced, Lahaina Sun, May 24, 1972: 9.
— police officer granted appearance before Maui police commission, Lahaina Sun, November 8, 1972: 9.
— police officer battles police board, Lahaina Sun, November 15, 1972: 9.
— hearing for police officer set, Lahaina Sun, December 27, 1972: 6.
— hearing date set for police officer, Lahaina Sun, January 17, 1973: 3.
— potential fairness of hearing for police officer discussed, Lahaina Sun, February 7, 1973: 10.
— hearing for police officer likely to start soon, after continuances, Lahaina Sun, February 14, 1973: 5.
— new delay for police officer, Lahaina Sun, February 28, 1973: 10.
— outlook of legal battle for police officer discussed, Lahaina Sun, April 18, 1973: 10.
— hearings for police officer continue to be postponed, a middleman is now involved, Lahaina Sun, July 25, 1973: 7.

ABUNDANT HEALTH CENTER
— opens, Lahaina News, September 10, 1992: 9.

ABUSE
— shelter operated by Women Helping Women featured, Lahaina News, April 15, 1987: 1,18.

ABUT, JOEL
— Lahainaluna High School graduate honored at Universal Technical Institute, Lahaina News, December 12, 1991: 5.

AC808 [MUSICAL GROUP]
— featured, Lahaina News, January 2, 1992: 10.
— to perform at Longhi's, Lahaina News, January 9, 1992: 10.
— continues to perform at Longhi's, Lahaina News, January 16, 1992: 12.
— continues to perform at Compadres Mexican Bar and Grill, Lahaina News, August 27, 1992: 14.

ACADEMIE DE DANSE [TROUPE]
— Alaska group to hold annual "Showcase and Dinner Dance" with Andry Dance Studio, Lahaina News, July 30, 1998: 17.

ACADEMY OF PERFORMING ARTS, THE MAUI
— see Maui Academy of Performing Arts, The

ACADEMY OF TRAVEL AND TOURISM
— selects Lahainaluna High School for tow-year program, Lahaina News, March 18, 1993: 3.
— impact on Lahainaluna High School discussed, Lahaina News, September 30, 1993: 2.
— seeking internship positions for students, Lahaina News, February 18, 1999: 11.
— graduate class pictured, Lahaina News, June 7, 2001: 8.
— Advisory Board awards scholarships to students, Lahaina News, June 14, 2001: 10.
— Advisory Board awards scholarships to Elissa Kahahane and Collette Cardoza, Lahaina News, July 10, 2003: 2.

ACCENTS [BUSINESS]
— opens in Mariner's Alley, Lahaina News, February 3, 1988: 3.

ACCIDENTS
— three auto accidents on Honoapi'ilani Highway, Lahaina Sun, July 21, 1971: 1.
— accident on Kuihelana Highway two hours after it opens, Lahaina Sun, September 1, 1971: 16.
— Nelson Kekiwi in automobile accident at the detour on Honoapi'ilani Highway, Lahaina Sun, September 8, 1971: 5.
— cars damaged when driver loses control, Lahaina Sun, March 15, 1972: 3.
— girl hit by boat while swimming off Mala Wharf [correction added on August 26, 1987, page 1], Lahaina News, August 19, 1987: 3.
— Sister Claudia Cabral dies after fall, Lahaina News, December 9, 1987: 3.
— school bus collides with "Sugar Cane" train, Lahaina News, February 16, 1995: 5.
— Sugar Cane Train crash with school bus blamed on faulty light, Lahaina News, March 2, 1995: 1,16.
— car crashes into The Gecko Store, Lahaina News, July 20, 2000: 8.

ACE HARDWARE [BUSINESS]
— to move locations, Lahaina News, June 1, 1995: 10.
— Kula Ace Hardware and Nursery to demonstrate how to grow roses, Lahaina News, January 2, 1997: 10.
— Dave Mulkey named new manager at Lahaina, Lahaina News, April 3, 1997: 10.
— offering "Ultimate Tailgate Sweepstakes", Lahaina News, September 16, 1999: 11.
— offering "Ultimate Tailgate Sweepstakes", Lahaina News, September 16, 1999: 11.
— creates "Ace Helpful Hardware Club", Lahaina News, May 25, 2000: 16.
— to be JC Penny catalog center, Lahaina News, March 20, 2003: 8.

ACES
— child support seminar to be held, Lahaina News, February 19, 1998: 12.

ACKERMAN, JACK
— recounting discovery of black coral, Lahaina News, January 30, 1985: 7,8,9.

ACT NOW!
— sponsoring stage performance with Richard Hatch, Lahaina News, June 20, 1991: 11,12.
— acting classes to be offered, Lahaina News, September 12, 1991: 3.

ACTIVITIES ON MAUI
— program to be formally launched, highlighting vocational education, Lahaina News, February 10, 1994: 4.

ACTIVITIES OWNERS ASSOCIATION
— offering kama'aina rate, Lahaina News, September 25, 1997: 15.

ACTIVITY LINK SYSTEMS [BUSINESS]
— develops software for activity providers, Lahaina News, October 17, 2002: 8.

ACTIVITY OWNERS ASSOCIATION
— to begin publishing "Maui Action" magazine, Lahaina News, January 31, 1990: 5.
— supports bill to regular tour desks, Lahaina News, February 14, 1990: 3.
— offering cheaper tickets for Maui events, Lahaina News, October 9, 1997: 11.

ACTS
— coupon book debuts, Lahaina News, September 14, 1988: 14.

ACUTE CARE FACILITY
— Maui County Council approves establishing facility in West Maui, Lahaina News, October 24, 2002: 3.

ADACHI, OSAMU
— dies in traffic accident, Lahaina Sun, August 25, 1971: 2.

ADAMS, BARTON
— found guilty of sexual assault, Lahaina News, February 6, 1992: 5.

ADAMS, BRYAN [MUSICIAN]
— opens for the Police in concert in Maui, Lahaina News, March 7, 1984: 11.

ADAMS, CARMEN
— radio personality featured, Lahaina News, June 1, 1988: 7.

ADAMS, CONNIE [ARTIST]
— to offer watercolor workshop, Lahaina News, December 12, 2002: 20.

ADAMS, KIPLING "KIP"
— joins Alexander and Baldwin, Lahaina News, April 24, 1991: 7.

ADAMS, ROBERT
— repainting Queen Theater in Lahaina, Lahaina Sun, February 17, 1971: 2.
— fight to end smell from Kihei Wastewater Treatment Plant likely successful, Lahaina News, July 2, 1992: 8.

ADDY, OBO [MUSICIAN]
— Ghanian drummer to perform, Lahaina News, January 11, 1996: 14.

ADENA, RICHARD
— hired as advertising sales representative for the Lahaina News, Lahaina News, May 31, 1989: 15.
— appointed as account manager at Pioneer Printers, Lahaina News, December 26, 1990: 7.

ADJUSTMENTS AND APPEALS, BOARD OF
— reputation as efficient and reasonable, Lahaina Sun, December 6, 1972: 4.

ADLER JEWELRY STORE [BUSINESS]
— robbed, Lahaina News, December 10, 1986: 3.

ADLER, LARRY
— appointed treasurer of The Gardiner Group [owner of Kobe Japanese Steakhouses], Lahaina News, September 6, 1989: 2.

ADMIRAL NEVELOSKY [BOAT]
— to compete in Bud Cup Regatta, Lahaina News, August 29, 1990: 7.

ADOLF, KATEY
— Scholar/Athlete of the Week, Lahaina News, January 20, 2000: 6.

ADOLPHO, GLENN
— new sales manager at Ka'anapali Beach Hotel, Lahaina News, October 25, 2001: 8.

ADONIS [SHIP]
— featured, Lahaina Sun, July 18, 1973: 9.

ADOPT-A-HIGHWAY
— groups sought to participate in, Lahaina News, August 1, 1991: 5.
— new groups added, Lahaina News, April 9, 1992: 5.

ADULT DAY CARE CENTER
— see Maui Adult Day Care Center

ADVANCED TELEPRODUCTION NETWORK [BUSINESS]
— owner Peter Benoit passes away, Lahaina News, June 19, 2003: 3.

ADVENTURERS CLUB
— part of Amfac, Inc.'s development plans, Lahaina News, September 21, 1988: 1.

ADVENTURES OF PEER GYNT, THE [PLAY]
— to be performed at Seabury Hall, Lahaina News, November 28, 1991: 18.

ADVERTISEMENT
— importance of logos discussed, Lahaina News, May 17, 1989: 8.

ADWORKS PUBLIC RELATIONS [BUSINESS]
— to represent Hawaii Dodge Chrysler Plymouth Dealers Association, Lahaina News, July 23, 1992: 17.

AEQUALIS [MUSICAL GROUP]
— to perform at Upcountry Community Center, Lahaina News, April 1, 1993: 15.

AEROBIC, CO. [BUSINESS]
— opens at Kahana Gateway, Lahaina News, June 27, 1991: 9.
— hold grand opening, Lahaina News, July 4, 1991: 4.

AESTHETICA MAUI [BUSINESS]
— featured, Lahaina News, May 22, 1997: 7.

AFFILIATE ARTISTS, INC.[BUSINESS]
— to sponsor musicians, Lahaina News, April 1, 1987: 1,9.

AFFORDABLE HOUSING
— Maui County Council reading bill to allow zero lot line subdivisions to support, Lahaina News, January 9, 1992: 9.
— see also Affordable Housing Corporation of Maui

AFFORDABLE HOUSING CONFERENCE
— to be hosted by Maui Economic Opportunity Inc., Lahaina News, May 1, 2003: 8.

AFFORDABLE HOUSING CORPORATION OF MAUI
— proposing affordable housing off Lahainaluna Road, Lahaina News, September 29, 1994: 1,2.
— residents critical of project proposed for Wainee Village, Lahaina News, February 23, 1995: 1.
— rethinking plans for Lahainaluna Road Project, Lahaina News, March 23, 1995: 1,16.
— proposes elderly rental project for Kelawea Mauka, Lahaina News, November 16, 1995: 3.
— plans for affordable housing ready for council review, Lahaina News, January 11, 1996: 4.

AFFORDABLE HOUSING, MAUI COUNTY COUNCIL SUBCOMMITTEE ON
— to meet with Maui Contractors Association, Lahaina News, August 8, 1990: 4.

AFFORDABLE HOUSING TASK FORCE
— to discuss availability of water, Lahaina News, September 4, 2003: 8.

AFRICA
— West African dance and music to be featured at Haiku Community Center, Lahaina News, November 2, 1988: 3.

AFRICAN HERITAGE CULTURAL FOUNDATION
— to host soul food potluck, Lahaina News, May 30, 1991: 10.

AFTER SCHOOL PROGRAM
— registration begins, Lahaina News, October 22, 1986: 3.
— seeking families to help, Lahaina News, August 24, 1988: 3.

AGACHE, BERNARD
— honored as "Hotelier of the Year", Lahaina News, March 28, 1990: 6.

AGAINST THE TIDE [PLAY]
— to be performed by Theatre Theatre Maui, Lahaina News, July 17, 1997: 16.
— to be produced by Theatre Theatre Maui, Lahaina News, July 24, 1997: 16.
— reviewed, Lahaina News, July 31, 1997: 5.

AGAPAY, JO-ANN
— receives scholarship from The Fun Factory, Inc., Lahaina News, July 23, 1992: 4.

AGAPAY, JUDITH ALAMON
— Lahainaluna High School prom queen, Lahaina News, April 6, 1995: 4.
— receives scholarship from International Airlines Travel Agent Network, Lahaina News, September 5, 1996: 2.

AGAPE INTERNATIONAL CHOIR [MUSICAL GROUP]
— to perform at Maui Arts and Cultural Center, Lahaina News, April 4, 2002: 17.
— to perform at Maui Arts and Cultural Center, Lahaina News, October 2, 2003: 16.

AGASLOG, DANNY
— to chair Maui WalkAmerica 2001 for March of Dimes, Lahaina News, March 1, 2001: 10.

AGAWA, ALVIN
— names fireman of the year, Lahaina News, June 1, 1980: 15.
— coach and family featured, Lahaina News, February 4, 1993: 6.
— Lahainaluna High School softball coach dies, Lahaina News, September 7, 1995: 2.

AGAWA, JANE
— retires from Lahaina Post Office, Lahaina News, November 7, 2002: 1.

AGCAOILI, IRIS
— named Island Manager for Aloha Festivals, Lahaina News, June 24, 1999: 2.

AGENA, CLARENCE MERTON
— "Mayor of Lahaina" interviewed, Lahaina News, February 27, 1985: 1,6,7.
— journalist remembered, Lahaina News, August 12, 1987: 1,12.
— selected as Outstanding Older Americans of Maui County, Lahaina News, May 25, 1988: 10,12.
— Brigadier General to speak to West Maui AJA Veterans Club, Lahaina News, May 22, 2003: 1,18.
— Brigadier General speaks to West Maui AJA Veterans Club for Memorial Day, Lahaina News, May 29, 2003: 1,18.

AGING
— see health

AGING, MAUI COUNTY OFFICE OF
— seeking nominations for Outstanding Older American award, Lahaina News, April 15, 1987: 12.
— hosting health events for seniors, Lahaina News, March 29, 1989: 14.
— relocates office, Lahaina News, April 24, 1991: 5.
— relocates office, Lahaina News, April 24, 1991: 5.
— accepting nominations for outstanding older American award, Lahaina News, March 12, 1992: 5.
— accepting nominations for Outstanding Older Americans, Lahaina News, March 2, 1995: 3.
— to conduct public hearing, Lahaina News, July 20, 1995: 5.
— program cuts should be expected, Lahaina News, August 3, 1995: 3.
— to hold informational session, Lahaina News, January 30, 1997: 10,11.
— Information, Assistance and Outreach team to survey seniors, Lahaina News, May 15, 1997: 13.
— to hold information sessions, Lahaina News, July 10, 1997: 17.
— offering information session, Lahaina News, February 19, 1998: 13.

— canvassing Napili neighborhoods to identify older adult residents, Lahaina News, April 23, 1998: 16.

— accepting applications for booth space for Maui County Senior Citizen's Fair, Lahaina News, October 1, 1998: 8.

— to assist seniors with "circuit breaker" applications, Lahaina News, August 29, 2002: 15.

— to hold training for family caregivers, Lahaina News, June 5, 2003: 9.

— to offer family caregiver training, Lahaina News, June 19, 2003: 9.

AGRICLO, RON

— acts as auctioneer during Whalers Village auction, Lahaina News, January 16, 1991: 10.

AGRICULTURAL AND BUSINESS WORKSHOP COALITION

— planning Small Business Financing workshop, Lahaina News, February 20, 2003: 8.

AGRICULTURAL DISTRICT ZONING ORDINANCE

— Maui County Council plans to reform agriculture bill, Lahaina News, July 25, 2002: 1,24.

AGRICULTURAL TRADE SHOW AND SAMPLING, MAUI COUNTY

— see Maui County Agricultural Trade Show and Sampling

AGRICULTURE

— experimental papaya cultivation project initiated, Lahaina Sun, May 5, 1971: 5.

— pineapple production discussed, Lahaina Sun, July 7, 1971: 5.

— U.S. Department of Agriculture purchases pineapple, Lahaina Sun, July 14, 1971: 2.

— West coast dock strike hurting sugar and pineapple companies, Lahaina Sun, August 18, 1971: 1.

— plans for agriculture development discussed, Lahaina Sun, September 22, 1971: 15.

— sugar and pineapple industries concerned with new air pollution rules, Lahaina Sun, January 19, 1972: 9.

— Olinda farmer critical of Maui County Water Master Plan, Lahaina Sun, January 26, 1972: 8.

— Haleakala Dairy adding more cows, Lahaina Sun, February 2, 1972: 9.

— attempts to get U.S. Department of Agriculture to purchase canned pineapples, Lahaina Sun, March 15, 1972: 14.

— State Department of Agriculture urges federal approval to import Unshu (Mandarin) oranges into Hawaii, Lahaina Sun, March 29, 1972: 10.

— students needed to work pineapple fields in the summer, Lahaina Sun, March 29, 1972: 3.

— Mayor Cravalho suggests importing agricultural workers , Lahaina Sun, April 26, 1972: 3.

— Maui County Agricultural Development Conference to be held, Lahaina Sun, May 10, 1972: 6.

— plan for Maui discussed at Maui County Agricultural Development Conference in Kahului, Lahaina Sun, May 17, 1972: 6.

— seed corn grown in Kihei, Lahaina Sun, May 31, 1972: 4.

— world's first pineapple planting machine to be introduced , Lahaina Sun, May 31, 1972: 5.

— cattle ranch at Hana described, Lahaina Sun, June 7, 1972: 9.

— Senator Hiram Fong pleas that agriculture remain emphasis of state's economy, Lahaina Sun, June 14, 1972: 10.

— papayas discussed, Lahaina Sun, June 14, 1972: 15.

— quality of papayas on Maui discussed, Lahaina Sun, June 21, 1972: 6,7.

— new method of irrigation to be installed in some sugar fields, Lahaina Sun, June 28, 1972: 14.

— Miss Papaya competition announced, Lahaina Sun, July 5, 1972: 11.

— current conditions in Maui discussed, Lahaina Sun, October 4, 1972: 25.

— Maui Land & Pineapple announces it is closing pineapple operations on Moloka'i, Lahaina Sun, October 18, 1972: 3,4.

— proposal to use cane waste for cattle feed, Lahaina Sun, November 1, 1972: 19.

— papaya production in Hawaii increases, Lahaina Sun, November 22, 1972: 11.

— rules controlling agricultural burning to be tightened, Lahaina Sun, January 3, 1973: 10.

— threat of foreign competition to pineapple industry, Lahaina Sun, January 17, 1973: 7.

— unemployment in pineapple industry rises, Lahaina Sun, February 7, 1973: 10,11.

— papaya production on Maui expected to increase, Lahaina Sun, March 7, 1973: 11.

— bill to increase tariff on foreign pineapples introduced, Lahaina Sun, May 23, 1973: 10.

— unit pricing and dating of foods to be discussed by the State Agriculture Department, Lahaina Sun, May 23, 1973: 11.

— possible future discussed, Lahaina Sun, June 13, 1973: 6,7,8,9,10,12.

— possible future of pineapple discussed, Lahaina Sun, June 13, 1973: 8,9.

— papaya production increases, Lahaina Sun, June 20, 1973: 8.

— federal trade bills may help pineapple industry, Lahaina Sun, July 11, 1973: 6.

— production in Hawaii expected to exceed 3 million pounds, Lahaina Sun, August 15, 1973: 7.

— special cargo rates for pineapples from Hawaii to Houston Texas, Lahaina Sun, August 22, 1973: 5.

— Cannery to close, Lahaina News, May 1, 1983: 10.

— Del Monte will continue pineapple production on Moloka'i, Lahaina News, December 28, 1983: 16.

— lots available at Kula Agriculture Park, Lahaina News, May 16, 1984: 17.

— Pioneer Mill lays off workers because of lack of water, Lahaina News, October 10, 1984: 3.

— editorial opposing use of malathion, Lahaina News, January 2, 1985: 2.

— Maui Vegetable Grower's Cooperative Association featured, Lahaina News, January 30, 1985: 18.

— Marijuana second largest crop in United States according to the National Oragnization for Reform of Marijuana Laws (NORML), Lahaina News, August 7, 1985: 9.

— cocoa plants tested for Lahaina, Lahaina News, August 27, 1986: 1,2.

— value of lilikoi and guava discussed, Lahaina News, November 19, 1986: 3.

— Hawaii Cocoa expands operation above Pu'ukoli'i, Lahaina News, June 10, 1987: 1.

— recipes for mangos, Lahaina News, July 8, 1987: 6.

— cocoa failed in Ka'anapali, Lahaina News, November 29, 1989: 1.

— Amfac, Inc. opens landscape tree nursery in Ka'anapali, Lahaina News, November 29, 1989: 1.

— Eleventh Farm Credit District reports positive earnings, Lahaina News, December 6, 1989: 5.

— Pioneer Mill has planted two acres of coffee, Lahaina News, December 13, 1989: 3.

— Wailuku Agribusiness using inmates to pick pineapples, Lahaina News, August 27, 1992: 10.

— sugar harvesting underway, Lahaina News, March 18, 1993: 8.

— 4-H to meet, Lahaina News, September 9, 1993: 3.

— importance of to Maui's economy, Lahaina News, September 23, 1993: 7.

— burning fees to rise, Lahaina News, October 7, 1993: 1.

— new burning fees proposed, Lahaina News, November 18, 1993: 1,3.

— George Kahumoku raising pigs, Lahaina News, October 13, 1994: 14.

— disease and trade hinder major fruit crops, Lahaina News, December 15, 1994: 5.

— description of current situation West Maui Committee of Maui Chamber of Commerce, Lahaina News, February 16, 1995: 12.

— pineapple outlook positive, sugar outlook negative, Lahaina News, July 13, 1995: 10.

— training program to be held on native Hawaiian landscape plants, Lahaina News, August 17, 1995: 4.

— Aloha Friday Fair and Farmers Market organized by Bob McCarthy, Lahaina News, October 5, 1995: 4.

— Aloha Friday Fair and Farmers Market organized by Bob McCarthy, Lahaina News, October 12, 1995: 6.

— Pioneer Mill expecting coffee harvest, Lahaina News, November 2, 1995: 10.

— taro farmers in Honokohau Valley unhappy about plans, Lahaina News, February 1, 1996: 3.

— James Tavares to speak on common landscape problems, Lahaina News, May 16, 1996: 11.

— pineapple and sugar crops feeling effects of drought, Lahaina News, October 31, 1996: 5.

— coffee discussed, Lahaina News, January 2, 1997: 1,16.

— cane harvesting to start, Lahaina News, May 22, 1997: 16.

— students tour Kapalua Land Company, Lahaina News, July 17, 1997: 12.

— Hawaii Tropical Fruit Growers to hold conference, Lahaina News, October 16, 1997: 12.

— Maui County Agricultural Trade Show and Sampling to be held at Ulupalakua Ranch, Lahaina News, April 9, 1998: 13.

— Maui County Agricultural Trade Show and Sampling to be held at Ulupalakua Ranch, Lahaina News, April 23, 1998: 13.

— students taught facets of agriculture, Lahaina News, July 2, 1998: 1,2.

— Ka'anapali Estate Coffee opens new processing facility, Lahaina News, November 5, 1998: 15.

— Maui County Council seeking input on, Lahaina News, December 10, 1998: 14.

— Amfac/JMB announces that Pioneer Mill to stop growing sugar, Lahaina News, March 4, 1999: 1.

— Pioneer Mill discusses plans once sugar ends, Lahaina News, March 11, 1999: 1,11.

— agriculture pesticide workshop to be held, Lahaina News, March 25, 1999: 13.

— Ka'anapali Estate Coffee reports harvest, Lahaina News, March 25, 1999: 13.

— Maui County Agricultural Trade Show and Sampling to begin, Lahaina News, April 22, 1999: 12.

— Kimo Falconer discusses future of agriculture in former sugar fields, Lahaina News, June 1, 2000: 1,6.

— Hawaiian Commercial and Sugar to close Paia Mill, Lahaina News, September 21, 2000: 16.

— Hawaiian Organic Farmers Association to meet, Lahaina News, October 19, 2000: 20.

— Sacred Gardens' Farm, Flower and Food Fairs continue to be held, Lahaina News, January 18, 2001: 17.

— Hawaii To Go conference to be held, Lahaina News, March 1, 2001: 8.

— Maui Pineapple Festival to be held, Lahaina News, August 2, 2001: 18.

— Ka'anapali Estate Coffee closes, Lahaina News, October 4, 2001: 1,20.

— Olowalu home to Jon Applegate's tomato farm, Lahaina News, March 21, 2002: 8.

— Maui Agricultural Trade Show and Sampling to be held at Ulupalakua Ranch, Lahaina News, April 25, 2002: 16.

— Lahainaluna High School offering education in, Lahaina News, May 23, 2002: 1,20.

— Maui County Council plans to reform agriculture bill, Lahaina News, July 25, 2002: 1,24.

— Island Grows Festival to be held, Lahaina News, July 25, 2002: 18.

— councilmember Alan Arakawa seeks approval for improved agriculture bill, Lahaina News, August 22, 2002: 1,2.

— U.S. Department of Agriculture's Farm Service Agency to hold elections for local County Committee, Lahaina News, August 7, 2003: 8.

AGRICULTURE, STATE DEPARTMENT OF

— dedicates renovated and expanded building, Lahaina News, October 24, 1990: 7.

— produced booklet on products for export, Lahaina News, December 12, 1990: 1,2.

AGRICULTURE, U.S. DEPARTMENT OF

— to hold meeting on Farm Bill, Lahaina News, October 17, 1996: 14.

— to hold elections for local County Committee, Lahaina News, August 14, 2003: 8.

AGUAYO, ROBERT [COMEDIAN]

— to perform at Comedy Club and the Sports Page, Lahaina News, April 9, 1992: 19.

— to perform at Comedy Club, Lahaina News, September 16, 1993: 16.

AGUIRRE, CECILIA [ARTIST]

— to exhibit at The Art Center of Maui, Lahaina News, September 24, 1998: 13.

AGUIRRE, GUY

— appointed to information technology coordinator at Od Lahaina Luau, Lahaina News, October 28, 1999: 15.

AGUON, MARSHA [ARTIST]

— to teach class on "Ipu Pawehe—Making Designs on the Ipu", Lahaina News, October 14, 1999: 13.

AGUSTIN, SERGIA

— passes away, Lahaina News, June 17, 1999: 15.

AH HEE, ABRAHAM "SNAKE"

— experience on Hokule'a described, Lahaina News, August 3, 1995: 9.

— waterman on Hokule'a featured, Lahaina News, January 25, 2001: 3.

AH HEE, MYRNA

— to coordinate Aloha Festivals, Lahaina News, June 14, 2001: 18.

AH TIM [MUSICAL GROUP]

— to perform at Moose McGillycuddy's, Lahaina News, May 9, 1990: 18.

— to perform at Polli's On the Beach, Lahaina News, January 9, 1991: 7.

AHA HUI KA'AHUMANU

— Maui chapter celebrating 80th anniversary, Lahaina News, July 10, 2003: 3.

'AHA HULA

— to be held, Lahaina News, July 17, 2003: 16.

AHA HULA 2001

— to be held at Maui Arts and Cultural, Lahaina News, August 23, 2001: 16.

AHA KULAMA

— "A Gathering to Rekindle Light" to be held at Hana Ball Park, Lahaina News, July 2, 1998: 17.

— "A Gathering to Rekindle Light" to be held at Hana Ball Park, Lahaina News, July 9, 1998: 17.

AHA KUPUNA

— hosts conference on Hawaiian independence, Lahaina News, March 10, 1994: 1.

AHA MELE LUAU

— to feature Olomana, Lahaina News, September 20, 1989: 3.

AHA PUNANA LEO
— taking applications, Lahaina News, July 9, 1998: 7.
— Hawaiian language immersion preschool growing, Lahaina News, August 15, 2002: 1.

AHAHUI KA'AHUMANU
— commemorate Queen Ka'ahumanu, Lahaina News, June 14, 2001: 5.
— Sisters of celebrate 80th anniversary, Lahaina News, July 31, 2003: 5.

AHARONI, IDO
— to speak at "L'Chaim Unplugged! - The Soul of Jewish Music", Lahaina News, May 28, 1998: 13.

AHIA, HOWARD [MUSICIAN]
— to perform at Villa Restaurant, Lahaina News, August 13, 1992: 15.
— to perform at Compadres Mexican Bar and Grill, Lahaina News, October 28, 1993: 10.
— to perform at Sansei Restaurant, Lahaina News, May 30, 1996: 2.
— to perform at Sansei Restaurant, Lahaina News, June 20, 1996: 12.

AHIA, SAM [MUSICIAN]
— featured, Lahaina News, October 24, 1991: 16.
— to perform at Pacific'O, Lahaina News, December 16, 1993: 19.
— to perform at "Music on the Beach", Lahaina News, May 20, 1999: 14.

AHIA, SAM AND CONRAD [MUSICIANS]
— to perform at Cook's at the Beach at the Westin Maui, Lahaina News, January 9, 1992: 11.

AHIHI BAY
— plan to create a nature reserve at, Lahaina Sun, August 25, 1971: 11.

AHIHI-KINA'U NATURAL AREA RESERVE
— state to hold meeting to discuss management plans for, Lahaina News, March 19, 1998: 13.

AHPUCK, HARDEY
— owner of roosters indifferent to neighbor complaints about his roosters, Lahaina News, April 9, 1992: 1,13.

AHUE, CLIFF [PERFORMER]
— awarded Maui Philharmonic Society scholarship, Lahaina News, June 20, 1984: 3.
— "Kahiko O Hawaii" show reviewed, Lahaina News, May 6, 1987: 4.
— Ho'oulu Productions to present at Whalers Village, Lahaina News, June 11, 1998: 16.
— kumu's halau to perform at Ka'anapali Beach Hotel, Lahaina News, July 24, 2003: 16.

AI, KAPONO
— to teach forest protocol, Lahaina News, May 16, 2002: 16.

AIDS
— reported on Maui, Lahaina News, April 23, 1986: 1,16.
— corrections to story from April 23rd, Lahaina News, May 7, 1986: 3.
— Maui AIDS Foundation activities since being formed in January, Lahaina News, September 17, 1986: 1,18.
— pennies collected for victims of, Lahaina News, May 4, 1988: 3.
— free testing available, Lahaina News, June 8, 1988: 14.
— update on situation, Lahaina News, August 3, 1988: 17.
— seminar to be held at Maui Inter-Continental Wailea, Lahaina News, November 1, 1989: 8.
— conference to be held at Maui Memorial Hospital, Lahaina News, August 29, 1990: 4.
— "Common Threads: Stories from the Quilt" to be shown, Lahaina News, September 12, 1990: 19.
— services grow, Lahaina News, October 31, 1990: 6.
— hotline for teens created, Lahaina News, May 1, 1991: 3.
— support group to meet at Iao Congregational Church, Lahaina News, June 6, 1991: 3.

— support group to meet at Iao Congregational Church, Lahaina News, June 13, 1991: 6.
— support group meeting to be held, Lahaina News, August 1, 1991: 5.
— support group to meet, Lahaina News, August 15, 1991: 3.
— support group to meet at Holy Innocents Episcopal Church, Lahaina News, October 17, 1991: 7.
— new services offered for Native Hawaiians with, Lahaina News, January 18, 1996: 4.

AIDS EDUCATION PROJECT
— sponsoring workshop for health-care professionals, Lahaina News, September 12, 1990: 11.
— to hold conference, Lahaina News, May 21, 1992: 4.

AIEA HIGH SCHOOL
— Honolulu school updating alumni list, Lahaina News, January 16, 1991: 4.

AIKANE II [CATAMARAN]
— visits Maui, Lahaina Sun, May 5, 1971: 6.

AIKIDO
— demonstration held on Maui, Lahaina Sun, December 6, 1972: 1,15,16,17,18.
— see also martial arts

AIKIDO-KI SOCIETY
— to hold yard sale, Lahaina News, June 18, 1998: 17.
— plans yard sale, Lahaina News, June 25, 1998: 12.

AILETCHER, MICAH
— receives United States National Award, Lahaina News, May 16, 1996: 6.

AIN'T MISBEHAVIN' [PLAY]
— to be performed by Maui Community Theatre, Lahaina News, February 24, 1988: 18.

A'IOLA [MUSICAL GROUP]
— to perform at Molokini Lounge at the Maui Prince Hotel, Lahaina News, May 1, 1991: 16.

AIONA, ABE
— to run for Maui County Council, Lahaina News, May 1, 1980: 7.
— cleared of wrongdoing for political contribution, Lahaina News, June 15, 1980: 3.

AIONA, ABRAHAM
— police chief involved in creating a brochure to deter hippies from coming to Maui, Lahaina Sun, December 9, 1970: 1.
— police chief speaking of National Guard being trained to respond to rioting, Lahaina Sun, December 16, 1970: 4.
— police chief criticized for exaggerating violence on Maui, Lahaina Sun, December 16, 1970: 6.
— police chief discusses increase in crime, Lahaina Sun, January 20, 1971: 8.
— police chief requests increase pay for police , Lahaina Sun, February 10, 1971: 4.
— police chief sued by Joseph Abreu for violation of his right to free speech, Lahaina Sun, February 10, 1971: 4.
— police chief sued by George Ferreira Jr., Lahaina Sun, February 17, 1971: 5.
— police chief proposes changes in parking spaces to alleviate traffic congestion, Lahaina Sun, May 19, 1971: 8.
— police chief discusses nudity on beaches, Lahaina Sun, June 16, 1971: 10.
— police chief appointed Director of Community Relations for Baldwin Pacific Corporation, Lahaina News, April 1, 1987: 12.
— police chief named as vice chair of Office of Hawaiian Affairs, Lahaina News, February 13, 1992: 3.
— police chief become vice chair of the Office of Hawaiian Affairs, Lahaina News, May 21, 1992: 4.
— see also police

AIRLINES [BUSINESS]
— store opens, Lahaina News, July 24, 1997: 12.

AIRPLANES
— Mark Blase lost in plane crash off Hana, Lahaina News, January 11, 1984: 5.
— seaplane crashes on beach near Launiupoko Beach Park, Lahaina News, April 23, 1986: 1.
— noise level for jets tested, Lahaina News, September 23, 1987: 1.
— fund started for families who lost loved ones in Moloka'i air disaster, Lahaina News, November 8, 1989: 2.
— memorial service planned for victims of crash on Moloka'i, Lahaina News, November 7, 1996: 1.

AIRPORT OPERATORS COUNCIL INTERNATIONAL
— to meet with William Carroll, appealing firing from Department of Public Works, Lahaina News, September 3, 1992: 8.

AIRPORTS
— improvements to Kahului airport announced, Lahaina Sun, August 18, 1971: 11.
— proposed West Maui Airport has been postponed indefinitely, Lahaina Sun, December 15, 1971: 5.
— Kahului Airport master plan does not include jumbo jets, Lahaina News, November 1, 1982: 11.
— attempts to establish an airport in West Maui discussed, Lahaina News, December 15, 1982: 15.
— County Councilman Rick Medina suggests new airport for Maui, Lahaina News, January 15, 1983: 2.
— hearing on proposed Mahinahina airstrip held, Lahaina News, December 21, 1983: 3,5.
— West Maui residents favor airport in Mahinahina, Lahaina News, March 21, 1984: 4.
— editorial on proposed airstrip in West Maui, Lahaina News, April 4, 1984: 2.
— continuation of public hearings have been postponed, Lahaina News, April 4, 1984: 5.
— Maui Land & Pineapples withdraws from agreement discussed, Lahaina News, April 11, 1984: 4.
— Hawaiian Airlines looking for land from Maui Land & Pineapple for West Maui airport, Lahaina News, April 25, 1984: 3.
— new terminal planned for Kahului airport, Lahaina News, May 2, 1984: 17.
— editorial on proposed West Maui airport, Lahaina News, May 2, 1984: 2.
— editorial on planned West Maui airport, Lahaina News, June 6, 1984: 2.
— Hawaiian Airlines plan to build airport in Mahinahina, Lahaina News, June 6, 1984: 3.
— editorial on recent developments, Lahaina News, July 11, 1984: 2.
— Hawaiian Airlines officially announces intention to develop airport in West Maui, Lahaina News, September 5, 1984: 3.
— featured discussion of the pros and cons of proposed airport in West Maui, Lahaina News, October 10, 1984: 7,8,9.
— hearing set to change district boundary for airport in West Maui, Lahaina News, November 21, 1984: 3.
— State of Hawaii backs new airport in West Maui, Lahaina News, November 28, 1984: 3.
— editorial on State Land Use Commission hearing, Lahaina News, December 5, 1984: 2.
— report on hearings for airport in West Maui, Lahaina News, December 5, 1984: 6,7,8,9,10.
— proposed site reclassified, Lahaina News, April 10, 1985: 9.
— Mahinahina residents at hearing do not want proposed, Lahaina News, May 22, 1985: 1,11.
— planning group delays decision on Mahinahina airport, Lahaina News, May 29, 1985: 1.

— Maui County Planning Commission approves airport in Mahinahina, Lahaina News, June 12, 1985: 1.
— battle over proposed airport heating up, Lahaina News, August 21, 1985: 1,8.
— Ka'anapali airport to close January 25, 1986, Lahaina News, September 11, 1985: 1.
— Hawaiian Airlines provides their position on proposed West Maui airport, Lahaina News, September 11, 1985: 1,10,11.
— Federal Aviation Administration rules that limits on flights for proposed Mahinahina airport are not legal, Lahaina News, September 25, 1985: 1.
— discussion of impact of imminent Ka'anapali airport closure, Lahaina News, September 25, 1985: 1,9.
— editorial encouraging people to attend public hearings, Lahaina News, October 9, 1985: 2.
— Hawaiian Airlines officials tour proposed site for Mahinahina Airport, Lahaina News, October 16, 1985: 1.
— Hawaiian Airlines promise to stand by airstrip promises, Lahaina News, October 23, 1985: 1,20.
— public hearing held, homeowners oppose proposed airport, seniors support it, Lahaina News, October 30, 1985: 1,9.
— editorial urging people to attend public hearing, Lahaina News, October 30, 1985: 2.
— Aloha Airlines opposes proposed airport at Mahinahina, Lahaina News, November 6, 1985: 1,20.
— public hearing on proposed airport in Mahinahina described, Lahaina News, November 13, 1985: 1,20.
— editorial on the debate concerning proposed airport, Lahaina News, November 20, 1985: 1.
— councilman Howard Kihune seeks options for proposed airport in West Maui, Lahaina News, November 20, 1985: 1,20.
— Maui County Council Planning, Land Use and Economic Development committee decision due before Christmas, Lahaina News, November 27, 1985: 1.
— Howard Kihune to propose Honolua as new site, Lahaina News, December 4, 1985: 1,20.
— proposed Mahinahina airport could include county control of the facility, Lahaina News, December 18, 1985: 1.
— Maui County Council to consider proposed airport in Mahinahina on January 6, Lahaina News, December 25, 1985: 3.
— editorial supporting airport in West Maui, but opposing one in Mahinahina, Lahaina News, January 1, 1986: 1.
— proposed airport in Mahinahina a top story in 1985, Lahaina News, January 8, 1986: 1.
— report on public hearing, Lahaina News, January 15, 1986: 1,20.
— last plane departs from Ka'anapali airstrip, Lahaina News, January 22, 1986: 1,14.
— notice of public hearing on proposed airport, paid for by West Maui Taxpayers Association, Lahaina News, January 22, 1986: 16.
— editorial urging people to attend public hearing on proposed Mahinahina airport, Lahaina News, January 22, 1986: 2.
— report on public hearing, general opposition to proposed Mahinahina airport, Lahaina News, January 29, 1986: 1,14.
— test vote suggests Maui County Council may approve airport in Mahinahina, Lahaina News, February 19, 1986: 1.
— editorial urging pressure to resist approval of in Mahinahina, Lahaina News, February 19, 1986: 2.
— Maui County Council approves airport in Mahinahina, Lahaina News, February 26, 1986: 1,16.
— editorial on political process connected to proposed airport in Mahinahina, Lahaina News, February 26, 1986: 2.
— decision on proposed Mahinahina airport delayed, Lahaina News, March 12, 1986: 1.
— editorial on current situation on proposed airport in Mahinahina, Lahaina News, March 12, 1986: 2.

— Maui County Council waiting for mayor's opinion on proposed airport at Mahinahina, Lahaina News, March 19, 1986: 1.

— aui County Council approves proposed airport at Mahinahina, lawsuits likely, Lahaina News, March 26, 1986: 1,12.

— editorial lamenting continuing issues over proposed airport in Mahinahina, Lahaina News, March 26, 1986: 2.

— editorial criticizing Bob Nakasone on changing mind concerning proposed airport in Mahinahina, Lahaina News, April 2, 1986: 2.

— proposal for airport to be county-owned is filed away, Lahaina News, April 2, 1986: 3.

— Hawaiian Airlines planning blessing of airport in Mahinahina, Lahaina News, April 30, 1986: 3.

— Hawaiian Airlines bless airport in Mahinahina, Lahaina News, May 7, 1986: 1,20.

— legal challenges to proposed airport in Mahinahina detailed, Lahaina News, May 7, 1986: 1,20.

— legal challenges to proposed airport in Mahinahina detailed, Lahaina News, May 21, 1986: 1,11.

— status of legal challenges described, Lahaina News, June 11, 1986: 1.

— proposed Kahului Airport expansion debated, Lahaina News, July 2, 1986: 18.

— Aloha Airlines considering appeal on West Maui airport decision, Lahaina News, July 16, 1986: 1.

— public expressed concerns over proposed development at Kahului Airport, Lahaina News, July 23, 1986: 1.

— West Maui airport delayed, Lahaina News, November 19, 1986: 1.

— Hawaiian Airlines licenses general aviation companies to operate out of Mahinahina airport, Lahaina News, December 31, 1986: 3,12.

— Kapalua West Maui Airport set to open on March 1, Lahaina News, January 14, 1987: 1.

— commuter terminal opens at Kahului airport, Lahaina News, January 21, 1987: 10.

— cost of parking infractions increased, Lahaina News, February 11, 1987: 11.

— construction of Kapalua West-Maui Airport continues, Lahaina News, February 18, 1987: 11.

— Hawaiian Airlines makes first flight to Kapalua-West Maui Airport, Lahaina News, March 4, 1987: 1.

— Mid Pacific Air to service Kapalua-West Maui airport, Lahaina News, March 11, 1987: 3.

— correction to story that Mid Pacific Air will begin service to Kapalua West Maui Airport, Lahaina News, March 18, 1987: 3.

— Kapalua West Maui Airport after one year, Lahaina News, March 16, 1988: 1.

— clarification on status of Hawaiian Airlines lease for lands near Kapalua West Maui Airport, Lahaina News, March 23, 1988: 1.

— public hearing on results regulating tour aircraft operations to be held, Lahaina News, May 24, 1989: 2.

— Noise Compatibility Program at Kahului to be discussed, Lahaina News, November 1, 1989: 6.

— hearing regarding controls for public areas at Kahului Airport, Lahaina News, November 15, 1989: 2.

— Elmer Cravalho claims Kahualui airport will become international, Lahaina News, December 13, 1989: 36.

— debate over state purchasing Kapalua-West Maui airport, Lahaina News, May 30, 1990: 1,12.

— debate over Kapalua-West Maui airport continues, Lahaina News, June 20, 1990: 1.

— state promises no expansion of Kapalua-West Maui Airport, Lahaina News, October 3, 1990: 1.

— second terminal opens at Kahului Airport, Lahaina News, October 24, 1990: 7.

— State Department of Transportation moving forward with plans to buy Kapalua-West Maui airport, Lahaina News, December 5, 1990: 1.

— State Department of Transportation to hold hearing on Kahului Airport, Lahaina News, December 19, 1990: 5,6.

— West Maui Taxpayers Association opposes use of federal money to purchase Kapalua-West Maui Airport, Lahaina News, January 23, 1991: 1.

— public meeting to be held for Kahului Airport Master Plan, Lahaina News, February 13, 1991: 4.

— groundbreaking for Kahului Airport Terminal building, Lahaina News, February 13, 1991: 4.

— new phone numbers for Kahului Airport, Lahaina News, February 27, 1991: 6.

— State likely to condemn Kapalua-West Maui Airport in order to obtain it, Lahaina News, May 15, 1991: 1.

— Howard Kihune says extension of Kahului Airport unlikely, Lahaina News, May 23, 1991: 1.

— Maui County Council votes against extending Kahului Airport runway, Lahaina News, September 12, 1991: 11.

— councilmember Wayne Nishiki concerned over who controls Kapalua airport, Lahaina News, September 19, 1991: 2.

— Kapalua-West Maui Airport study criticized, could delay Lahaina Bypass, Lahaina News, December 12, 1991: 1.

— West Maui Taxpayers Association conducting poll on extending Kahului Airport runway, Lahaina News, January 9, 1992: 1.

— Ka'anapali Taxi wins taxi concession at Kahului airport, Lahaina News, January 16, 1992: 8.

— Aircraft Rescue and Fire Fighting Station proposed for Kahului Airport, Lahaina News, January 30, 1992: 11.

— director of Department of Transportation Rex Johnson to conduct dedication ceremony for new terminal at Kahului airport, Lahaina News, February 20, 1992: 10.

— West Maui Taxpayers Association divided on whether to lengthen runway at Kahului, Lahaina News, March 5, 1992: 1.

— Senator Daniel Inouye to seek federal waiver to maintain restrictions at Kapalua-West Maui Airport, Lahaina News, June 4, 1992: 1.

— Department of Transportation to hold meeting on new fuel handling procedures at public airports, Lahaina News, July 2, 1992: 4.

— Maui Pueo Coalition to advocate to complete Kahului runway extension, Lahaina News, July 9, 1992: 14.

— public hearing to be held concerning extension of runway at Kahalui airport, Lahaina News, August 6, 1992: 3.

— Kihei residents complain about stunt planes, Lahaina News, August 20, 1992: 14.

— meeting to consider runway extension rescheduled, Lahaina News, August 20, 1992: 4.

— Maui County Planning Commission asked to review extension of runway at Kahului, Lahaina News, August 27, 1992: 6.

— overflights and stunts over Maui being investigated, Lahaina News, September 24, 1992: 1.

— Department of Transportation awards contract to modify Moloka'i Airport, Lahaina News, October 1, 1992: 11.

— residents drop suit to allow purchase of Kapalua-West Maui Airport to move ahead, Lahaina News, October 8, 1992: 1.

— Maui County Council votes to eliminate subcommittee reviewing Kahului Airport extension, Lahaina News, October 22, 1992: 4.

— public hearing to consider expansion of Kahului Airport, Lahaina News, October 29, 1992: 7.

— Councilman Dennis Nakamura to seek changes to bill to discourage lengthening of Kapalua-West Maui airport, Lahaina News, January 14, 1993: 1.

— state Department of Transportation to hold public hearing on new rules, Lahaina News, March 25, 1993: 4.

— state takes over Kapalua-West Maui airport, Lahaina News, April 1, 1993: 1.

— corrections on earlier story about state purchasing Kapalua-West Maui airport, Lahaina News, April 8, 1993: 3.

— state seeking input on rules for Kapalua-West Maui Airport, Lahaina News, October 14, 1993: 1,4.

— state intends to keep current airport rules, Lahaina News, October 21, 1993: 1.

— rules to be maintained, Lahaina News, August 11, 1994: 4.

— Mahalo Airlines' attempt to fly into Kapalua-West Maui Airport limited by berm bordering runway, Lahaina News, March 23, 1995: 1,16.

— Mahalo Air ending service to Kapalua-West Maui airport, Lahaina News, September 7, 1995: 3.

— Trans Hawaii-Maui, Inc. awarded contract for Kahului Airport, Lahaina News, December 28, 1995: 10.

— pros and cons of airport expansion discussed, Lahaina News, May 16, 1996: 1,3.

— Hawaiian Airlines partners with Mahalo Air in West Maui, Lahaina News, June 27, 1996: 13.

— Sierra Club to hold update on Kahului Airport, Lahaina News, April 9, 1997: 16.

— Dugied Construction to install Automated Weather Observing Systems at Kapalua-West Mui Airport, Lahaina News, July 30, 1998: 7.

— plans to extend Kahului Airport runway, Lahaina News, September 3, 1998: 1.

— Land Use Commission to hold public hearing on reclassifying land from agriculture to urban use for Kahului Airport expansion, Lahaina News, April 15, 1999: 13.

— disaster drill planned, Lahaina News, May 13, 1999: 1.

— Hawaii Helicopters submitted proposal to change rules at Kapalua-West Maui Airport, Lahaina News, April 13, 2000: 1,16.

— County Council urges legislators to oppose measure to strip counties of authority to approve airport improvements, Lahaina News, May 3, 2001: 3.

— commentary on FAA closing Kapalua-West Maui Airport, Lahaina News, November 21, 2002: 14.

AITKEN, ROBERT
— director for Maui ACLU, Lahaina Sun, January 13, 1971: 6.

AIWOHI, GARY
— becomes acting police captain at Lahaina station , Lahaina News, May 6, 1993: 2.

AIZAWA, HERMAN
— superintendent presents results of new testing method, Lahaina News, December 22, 1994: 2.

— superintendent speaks of expected budget cuts, Lahaina News, January 25, 1996: 1,16.

AJIFU, RALPH
— named branch manager of FKS Rentals and Sales, Lahaina News, March 4, 1993: 8.

AJJA TROPICAL ARTWEAR [BUSINESS]
— opens on Front Street, Lahaina News, August 21, 1985: 3.

AKADA, JEAN
— defeated at U.S. Open, Lahaina News, September 3, 1998: 1.

AKAKA, DANIEL [POLITICIAN]
— receives petition from Pacific Whale Foundation to stop slaughter of dolphins in driftnets, Lahaina News, October 18, 1989: 3.

— attends ceremony on completion of Kahoma Flood Control Project, Lahaina News, June 6, 1990: 1.

AKAKU: MAUI COMMUNITY TELEVISION
— to produce "Cooking with Longhi" show, Lahaina News, March 23, 1995: 11.

— taping "Speak ut Saturday" show, Lahaina News, June 22, 1995: 4.

— to produce sneior issues talk show, Lahaina News, March 7, 1996: 10.

— has openings for Summer Video Camp, Lahaina News, August 14, 1997: 16.

— to offer PSAs to non-profit groups, Lahaina News, October 9, 1997: 20.

— to show Tess Cartright's "Mewes" musical, Lahaina News, January 15, 1998: 13.

— holding production orientation, Lahaina News, March 12, 1998: 11.

— to teach television production skills to youth with Theatre Theatre Maui, Lahaina News, May 7, 1998: 16.

— community television to feature candidates, Lahaina News, September 3, 1998: 18.

— offer to show short announcements from candidates, Lahaina News, September 10, 1998: 8.

— to hold PSA Day, Lahaina News, December 31, 1998: 13.

— to hold PSA Day, Lahaina News, January 7, 1999: 17.

— to hold "Speak Out" taping session, Lahaina News, May 13, 1999: 17.

— to offer youth video production camp, Lahaina News, June 17, 1999: 15.

— to hold "PSA Day" and "Speak Out Maui County" taping session, Lahaina News, August 26, 1999: 17.

— to offer video production class for youth, Lahaina News, September 23, 1999: 5.

— to hold video classes for youth, Lahaina News, October 21, 1999: 16.

— to air Maui County Council meetings, Lahaina News, November 4, 1999: 5.

— seeking performers, Lahaina News, November 25, 1999: 15.

— plans "Day of Holiday Greetings", Lahaina News, December 9, 1999: 20.

— to offer course on services, Lahaina News, December 30, 1999: 13.

— to hold "Speak Out" taping, Lahaina News, March 2, 2000: 12.

— to show "Giving Hawai'i Style", Lahaina News, March 30, 2000: 12.

— offering production class for youth, Lahaina News, April 6, 2000: 17.

— to show "Na Leo o Na Wahine: Women's Voices", Lahaina News, May 25, 2000: 18.

— to host "Talk Politics", Lahaina News, August 24, 2000: 3.

— airing political coverage, Lahaina News, August 31, 2000: 8.

— to offer courses for youth, Lahaina News, October 5, 2000: 16.

— to hold orientation, Lahaina News, November 16, 2000: 17.

— Maui County News show seeks reporters, Lahaina News, February 1, 2001: 17.

— offers TV production courses, Lahaina News, February 1, 2001: 9.

— to hold "Speak Out Maui", Lahaina News, May 3, 2001: 20.

— to hold PSA Day, Lahaina News, May 17, 2001: 21.

— offering courses on video production, Lahaina News, December 20, 2001: 2.

— to hold production classes, Lahaina News, May 9, 2002: 16.

— Surfrider Foundation documentary "Save Ma'alaea: A Cry for Help" to be shown on, Lahaina News, July 11, 2002: 12.

— to offer classes on television production, Lahaina News, September 12, 2002: 20.

— to hold orientation, Lahaina News, February 20, 2003: 17.

— show explores affordable housing issues, Lahaina News, June 12, 2003: 7.

— to air coverage of West Maui Taxpayers Association, Lahaina News, September 4, 2003: 17.

AKAMAI TRIO [MUSICAL GROUP]
— featured, Lahaina News, January 14, 1987: 8.

— to play at Royal Ocean Terrace Lounge at Royal Lahaina Hotel, Lahaina News, October 4, 1989: 9.

AKANA, AKONI
— to present "The Restoration of Moku'ula", Lahaina News, April 22, 1999: 12.

— to discuss research on Moku'ula , Lahaina News, May 27, 1999: 12.

— Executive Director of Friends of Moku'ula discusses organization, Lahaina News, January 16, 2003: 3.

AKANA, BERNARD
— Big Island mayor to speak at Maui Republican Party's Lincoln Day dinner, Lahaina News, February 8, 1989: 5.

AKANA, ELIZABETH [ARTIST]
— to demonstrate Hawaiian quiltmaking, Lahaina News, February 25, 1993: 9.

AKANA, TONY
— kumu hula's halau to compete in California, Lahaina News, September 21, 1988: 2,15.

AKASH, JASMIN
— to speak on "Holographic Meditation", Lahaina News, July 5, 2001: 16.
— to present "Forever Young" at 'Ohana Connections, Lahaina News, September 26, 2002: 17.

AKEN, GORDON
— appointed as banquet and beverage manager at Embassy Suites, Lahaina News, June 16, 1994: 10.

AKI, JO-ANN
— top producer tor Kehalani Broker Referral Program, Lahaina News, May 23, 1996: 16.

AKIMA, ADRIAN LUCKY
— pastor featured, Lahaina News, May 27, 1993: 2.

AKIMA, TRENTON KAPILI
— Lahainaluna High School student is runner-up in "Brown Bags to Stardom", Lahaina News, February 22, 2001: 1.

AKIMEKA [BUSINESS]
— Native Hawaiian-owned information technology company donates equipment to Maui Memorial Medical Center, Lahaina News, February 14, 2002: 8.

AKIMOTO, ARLET
— Scholar/Athlete of the Week, Lahaina News, October 24, 1996: 12.

AKINA, ALLEN [ARTIST]
— featured, Lahaina News, March 1, 1981: 13.

AKINA ALOHA TOURS
— to partner with Maui County to create mass transit system for Maui, Lahaina News, August 29, 2002: 2.

AKINA BUS SERVICE AND ALOHA TOURS [BUSINESS]
— begins local bus service in Kihei, Lahaina News, August 23, 1989: 3.
— offering new shuttle service, Lahaina News, August 11, 1994: 7.

AKINA EXPRESS [BUSINESS]
— begins new bus service, Lahaina News, July 13, 1995: 5.

AKINA, JUDEE MAE
— promoted to food and beverage manager of Old Lahaina Luau, Lahaina News, October 28, 1999: 15.

AKINI, ARNUBI
— killed in automotive accident, Lahaina Sun, August 11, 1971: 11.

AKIU, HERBERT RICHARD KEAHIKULAPALAPAKEOLAOKALANI
— king of Aloha Week, Lahaina News, August 30, 1989: 1.

AKIYAMA, BARBARA
— community volunteer featured, Lahaina News, November 14, 1991: 3.

AKIYAMA, CLIFTON
— appointed operations manager at Lahaina Cannery Shopping Center, Lahaina News, March 11, 1987: 18.
— Boy Scouts honor leader, Lahaina News, May 25, 2000: 15.
— chaired West Maui Cub Scout Fishing Derby, Lahaina News, May 30, 2002: 2.

AKIYAMA, ETHEL
— wins shopping spree at Lahaina Shopping Center, Lahaina News, December 26, 1991: 3.

AKIYAMA, PAT
— appointed temporary-vice principal due to absence of Robert Deaton, Lahaina News, March 20, 1991: 3.

AKIYAMA, TAMMY
— Lahainaluna High School valedictorian, Lahaina News, June 6, 2002: 1.

AKO, MICHAEL
— named new manager of Royal Lahaina Resort, Lahaina News, August 3, 1995: 8.

AKO, SAM AND SHARON
— to organize luau at Sheraton Maui, Lahaina News, July 18, 1990: 12.

AKU CUP
— sporting event to be held in May, Lahaina News, May 14, 1986: 4.

AKU MEMORIAL CELEBRITY GOLF TOURNAMENT
— details, Lahaina News, May 29, 1985: 4.

AL AND KIMO [MUSICAL GROUP]
— to perform at Ritz-Carlton's Lobby Lounge, Lahaina News, September 23, 1993: 11.

ALA HOU COUNSELING CENTER
— offering mental health counseling services, Lahaina News, January 10, 2002: 2.

ALA LANI PRESCHOOL
— to hold "Festival of Sorts", Lahaina News, February 25, 1993: 12.
— to hold "Festival of Sorts", Lahaina News, February 20, 1997: 10.
— to host "Festival of Sorts" fundraiser, Lahaina News, February 25, 1999: 12.

ALA LANI UNITED METHODIST CHURCH
— leases land for new assisted-living project to be operated by Ali'i Community Care, Lahaina News, October 26, 2000: 19.

ALABAMA
— Letter from, by Brett Riley, Lahaina Sun, May 5, 1971: 4.

ALADDIN [PLAY]
— to be performed by the Maui Academy of Performing Arts, Lahaina News, November 28, 1991: 18.
— to be performed, Lahaina News, December 5, 1991: 26.

ALADDIN AND THE WONDERFUL LAMP [PLAY]
— to be performed by Maui Academy of Performing Arts, Lahaina News, May 18, 1995: 11.

ALAELOA
— 270 homes are planned by Maui Land and Pineapple, Lahaina Sun, January 27, 1971: 1,2.
— zoning for houses approved, Lahaina Sun, April 14, 1971: 2.
— Mayor's Beach Access Advisory Committee to meet concerning beach access, Lahaina News, February 18, 1993: 1.
— residents divided on proposed beach access, Lahaina News, February 25, 1993: 2.
— algae particularly bad at, Lahaina News, June 15, 1995: 3.
— development featured, Lahaina News, May 10, 2001: 7.
— development featured, Lahaina News, July 5, 2001: 7.

ALA'ILIMA, PIULA
— United Methodist pastor records songs, Lahaina News, November 8, 1989: 3.
— party held for pastor, Lahaina News, September 15, 1994: 6.
— minister at Lahaina United Methodist Church leaving for spirtual journey, Lahaina News, May 18, 2000: 1,6.

ALAKAI'I [MUSICAL GROUP]
— to perform at Molokini Lounge at the Maui Prince Hotel, Lahaina News, February 6, 1991: 9.

ALAKAI'I, PALAKA
— report from KPOA, Lahaina News, June 13, 1996: 2.

ALAMIDA, CHARLES "ALAN"
— named operations manager at Makena Resort, Lahaina News, November 28, 1990: 8.

ALANO CLUB OF LAHAINA
— needs space to meet, Lahaina News, March 1, 1989: 2.
— moving, Lahaina News, December 31, 1992: 4.
— moves location, Lahaina News, February 25, 1993: 3.
— helping people in recovery, Lahaina News, July 4, 1996: 1,2.
— to hold yard sale, Lahaina News, October 3, 1996: 14.
— to meet, Lahaina News, July 15, 1999: 12,13.
— to open, Lahaina News, November 23, 2000: 20.

ALANUI O MAKENA
— honored by Sierra Club as Conservationists of the Year, Lahaina News, November 11, 1987: 11.

ALASKA AIRLINES [BUSINESS]
— hires Chanell Lehuanani Peters, Lahaina News, August 19, 1999: 13,14.

ALATEEN
— members to meet, Lahaina News, December 20, 2001: 2.
— continues to meet, Lahaina News, December 27, 2001: 16.
— continues to meet, Lahaina News, May 23, 2002: 17.

ALAYA UNLIMITED [BUSINESS]
— Ohana Luncheon and Trade Fair scheduled, Lahaina News, September 10, 1992: 11.
— to host Terry Braverman at Ohana Luncheon and Trade Fair, Lahaina News, March 11, 1993: 11.
— presenting monthly Ohana Luncheon and Trade Fair, Lahaina News, July 15, 1993: 3.
— Ohana Luncheon to feature Andrea Smith, Lahaina News, January 12, 1995: 11.
— psychic fair to be held, Lahaina News, July 27, 1995: 12.

ALAZRAQUI, CARLOS [COMEDIAN]
— to perform at Comedy Club, Lahaina News, September 5, 1991: 9.

ALBERSTEIN, NATHAN
— purchases Kaleakala Motors, Lahaina News, August 8, 1990: 6.
— president of Haleakala Motors, Ltd. receives Time Magazine Quality Dealer Award, Lahaina News, March 6, 1991: 9.

ALBERT C. KOBAYASHI, INC. [BUSINESS]
— likely contractor for Maui Community Arts and Cultural Center, Lahaina News, March 19, 1992: 9.

ALBRITTON, TERRY
— career and Olympics competition described, Lahaina News, September 23, 1987: 10.

ALCHEMIST'S GARDEN
— plans to close, Lahaina News, December 13, 1989: 7.

ALCOHOL
— drinking age raised to 21, Lahaina News, October 1, 1986: 12.
— wine tasting to be held at Luau Gardens, Lahaina News, November 19, 1986: 16.
— Maui Blush debuts from Tedeschi Vineyards, Lahaina News, December 3, 1986: 11.
— court ruling could undermine DUI alcohol assessments, Lahaina News, June 8, 1995: 3.

ALCOHOLICS ANONYMOUS
— moved to Honolua United Methodist Church, Lahaina News, February 22, 1989: 3.
— to meet, Lahaina News, July 18, 1996: 12.
— continues to meet, not always indexed, Lahaina News, October 16, 1997: 16.
— continues to meet, Lahaina News, February 19, 1998: 13.
— meets on Wednesdays, Lahaina News, July 18, 2002: 17.

ALCONCEL, ROSE MARIE
— killed by her husband, who then kills himself, Lahaina News, February 20, 1992: 1,7,8.

ALCOTT, AMY
— golfer participates in Women's Kemper Open, Lahaina News, March 14, 1984: 15.
— golfer's career described, Lahaina News, March 6, 1985: A6.

ALCYONE [SHIP]
— Cousteau research vessel off Maui, Lahaina News, April 22, 1987: 1.
— report on recent whale research undertaken on, Lahaina News, May 20, 1987: 1,10.

ALDEN, LORNA LOUI
— named sales manager for Hilo Hatties, Lahaina News, November 9, 1995: 10.

'ALE'A [MUSICAL GROUP]
— to perform at Ka'anapali Beach Hotel's Tiki Courtyard, Lahaina News, February 6, 2003: 16.

'ALE'A AND PURE HEART [MUSICAL GROUP]
— to perform at Jaycees Summer Jam, Lahaina News, June 24, 1999: 12.

ALESSIO [ARTIST]
— to exhibit at Lahaina Galleries, Lahaina News, March 19, 1998: 13.
— to exhibit at Lahaina Galleries, Lahaina News, February 18, 1999: 12.

ALEXANDER ACADEMY BALLET [TROUPE]
— to perform at Maui Arts and Cultural Center, Lahaina News, March 29, 2001: 17.
— to perform at Maui Arts and Cultural Center, Lahaina News, April 5, 2001: 20.

ALEXANDER ACADEMY OF PERFORMING ARTS [TROUPE]
— to present Ballet Maui 1997, Lahaina News, January 30, 1997: 10.

ALEXANDER AND BALDWIN [BUSINESS]
— leasing money for shrimp aquaculture project, Lahaina Sun, January 20, 1971: 4.
— expected to give land to United States International University once merger with Mauna Olu College is completed, Lahaina Sun, March 10, 1971: 1.
— initiates experimental papaya cultivation project, Lahaina Sun, May 5, 1971: 5.
— gifts 12 acres of land for stadium in Wailuku, Lahaina Sun, June 30, 1971: 3.
— gives 70 acres of land to Maui County, Lahaina Sun, September 6, 1972: 14.
— urges permission to build resort in Wailea, Lahaina Sun, January 24, 1973: 3.
— to raise rates in Kahului Industrial area, Lahaina News, June 1, 1982: 11.
— profits increase, Lahaina News, August 15, 1982: 11.
— Harry Weinberg increases holdings in, Lahaina News, January 4, 1984: 14.
— swaps land in Lihue, Kaua'i with Harry Weinberg for land in Honokowai, Lahaina News, April 4, 1984: 13.
— donates to Maui Community Arts & Cultural Center, Lahaina News, April 22, 1987: 10.
— awarded "U.S. Productivity Award", Lahaina News, August 30, 1989: 5.
— plans to sell Maui Lani residential parcel, Lahaina News, February 21, 1990: 5.
— announces nominations to board of directors, Lahaina News, February 21, 1990: 5.
— donates to Hawaii Public Radio stations, Lahaina News, April 4, 1990: 7.
— announces first quarter earnings, Lahaina News, May 9, 1990: 8,9.

— Ronald Yoda named senior vice president and chief financial officer at, Lahaina News, September 26, 1990: 9.
— R.J. Pfeiffer continues as chairman and chief executive officer of, Lahaina News, November 7, 1990: 8.
— holds groundbreaking for Kahului Town Terrace, Lahaina News, December 26, 1990: 7.
— presents Weslia Whitfield at Stouffer Wailea Beach Resort, Lahaina News, January 16, 1991: 10,11.
— presents Michael Greenfield at Stouffer Wailea Beach Resort, Lahaina News, January 16, 1991: 10,11.
— reorganizes, Lahaina News, March 6, 1991: 10.
— Kipling "Kip" Adams joins, Lahaina News, April 24, 1991: 7.
— planning subdivision in Makana, Lahaina News, May 8, 1991: 6.
— evicts homeless from Ma'alaea, Lahaina News, December 26, 1991: 4.
— has development plans for Ma'alaea, Lahaina News, January 2, 1992: 5.
— appoints Stanley Kuriyama as executive vice president, Lahaina News, January 23, 1992: 13.
— income report, Lahaina News, February 6, 1992: 11.
— donates to Ka Hale Ake Ola Maui Homeless Resource Center, Lahaina News, March 12, 1992: 5.
— employee changes announced, Lahaina News, April 9, 1992: 12,13.
— profits rise, Lahaina News, April 23, 1992: 16.
— plans for Ma'alaea described, Lahaina News, May 28, 1992: 6.
— planning 600-acre project in Ma'alaea, Lahaina News, June 11, 1992: 8.
— proposes new road for Ma'alaea, Lahaina News, June 18, 1992: 15.
— crown opposed proposed development, Lahaina News, June 18, 1992: 4.
— Ma'alaea Community Association seek environmental impact statement for proposed project, Lahaina News, June 25, 1992: 6.
— to hold public meeting to explain proposed development in Ma'alaea, Lahaina News, August 13, 1992: 9.
— proposed Ma'alaea project called premature, Lahaina News, September 3, 1992: 12.
— personnel changes, Lahaina News, October 15, 1992: 8.
— Linda Howe now manager of community relations, Lahaina News, December 31, 1992: 10.
— appoints Donne Dawson as manager of publications, Lahaina News, March 11, 1993: 12.
— plans to purchase California and Hawaiian Sugar Company, Lahaina News, March 11, 1993: 12.
— negotiating with Maui Electric over site of new power plant, Lahaina News, May 6, 1993: 6,7.
— promotes Richard Cameron to vice-president, Lahaina News, May 13, 1993: 7.
— completes acquisition of California and Hawaiian Sugar, Co., Lahaina News, June 24, 1993: 9.1.
— earnings report for second quarter, Lahaina News, August 12, 1993: 9.
— gives money to Ka Lima O Maui, Lahaina News, November 4, 1993: 7.
— Richard Cameron given responsibility over agribusiness activities, Lahaina News, January 27, 1994: 5.
— Mercer "Chubby" Alexander promoted to vice president of Maui Office, Lahaina News, February 3, 1994: 7.
— Foundation gives grant to Maui Academy of Performing Arts, Lahaina News, June 23, 1994: 12.
— W. Allen Doane appointed president, Lahaina News, May 11, 1995: 10.
— to hold fair, Lahaina News, July 27, 1995: 12.
— personnel changes, Lahaina News, February 8, 1996: 6.
— to hold Community Fair, Lahaina News, July 11, 1996: 12,13.
— to hold Community Fair, Lahaina News, July 10, 1997: 17.
— Community Fair to begin, Lahaina News, July 17, 1997: 16.

— Glenn Rogers promoted to executive vice-president of, Lahaina News, July 24, 1997: 13.
— Foundation to help victims of Typhoon Paka on Guam, Lahaina News, January 8, 1998: 11.
— Community Fair to be held, Lahaina News, August 13, 1998: 9.
— Stanley Krasniewski joins, Lahaina News, August 20, 1998: 13.
— Fair to be held, Lahaina News, August 27, 1998: 16.
— appointments at, Lahaina News, September 10, 1998: 11.
— Foundation to sponsor "Technology and the World of Learning", Lahaina News, April 8, 1999: 11.
— Community Fair to be held, Lahaina News, August 26, 1999: 15.
— Steven Walker joins, Lahaina News, February 10, 2000: 14.
— James Andrasick appointed senior vice president, Lahaina News, May 25, 2000: 16.
— donates money to Junior Achievement of Hawaii, Lahaina News, October 5, 2000: 14.
— Foundation presents grant to Kaunoa Senior Services Nutrition Program, Lahaina News, August 2, 2001: 8.
— Foundation donating to nonprofit organizations, Lahaina News, January 17, 2002: 8.
— Foundation provides grant to Maui Memorial Medical Center Foundation, Lahaina News, May 23, 2002: 8.
— Foundation launches website, Lahaina News, August 22, 2002: 8.
— Foundation awards grant to Maui Food Bank, Lahaina News, October 10, 2002: 8.
— Foundation awards grant to Maui Community College, Lahaina News, January 30, 2003: 8.
— Foundation awards grant to Nisei Veterans Memorial Center, Lahaina News, June 19, 2003: 8.
— see also Hawaiian Commercial and Sugar Co.

ALEXANDER AND BALDWIN SUGAR MUSEUM
— see Sugar Museum

ALEXANDER, ARTHUR
— president of Japan Economic Institute of America to speak to Maui Japanese Chamber of Commerce, Lahaina News, August 5, 1993: 7.

ALEXANDER, PAM
— to plan activities for Front Street, Lahaina News, June 27, 1996: 2.

ALEXIA BY GEORGIOU [BUSINESS]
— opens, Lahaina News, April 8, 1993: 6.

ALEX'S HOLE IN THE WALL [RESTAURANT]
— reviewed, Lahaina News, January 18, 1984: 13.
— reviewed, Lahaina News, September 19, 1991: 20,21.
— celebrating 20 years in business, Lahaina News, April 29, 1993: 11.
— moves , Lahaina News, October 7, 1993: 13.

ALFORD'S FINE RESORTWEAR [BUSINESS]
— featured, Lahaina News, March 30, 1988: 3.

ALFRED SHAHEEN [BUSINESS]
— fashion designer featured, Lahaina News, April 11, 1984: 17.

ALGAE
— clean-up study on hold due to lack of funds, Lahaina News, June 15, 1995: 3.
— particularly bad at Alaeloa, Lahaina News, June 15, 1995: 3.

ALGAE BLOOM TASK FORCE
— meets, hears calls from divers to halt injection wells, Lahaina News, June 11, 1992: 1.
— expected to issue report, Lahaina News, July 30, 1992: 3.

ALICE IN WONDERLAND [PLAY]
— to be performed by Maui Youth Theatre, Lahaina News, June 28, 1989: 8.

ALICE THROUGH THE LOOKING GLASS ... HAWAIIAN STYLE [PLAY]
— to be performed by Maui Youth Theatre, Lahaina News, January 16, 1985: 3.

ALI'I COMMUNITY CARE
— to operate new assisted-living project, Lahaina News, October 26, 2000: 19.

ALII DESIGNS [BUSINESS]
— Natalie and Ronnie Babajko open jewelry store, Lahaina News, April 18, 2002: 8.

ALII DRY CLEANERS
— opens, Lahaina News, March 31, 1994: 9.

ALII GARDENS-NANEA A'O KULA
— to teach Holiday Wreath Making, Lahaina News, December 5, 2002: 21.
— to hold Haku Lei Making Tours, Lahaina News, January 9, 2003: 16.
— to host Valentine's Lavender Garden Tour, Lahaina News, February 13, 2003: 16.

ALI'I MOCHA [RESTAURANT]
— opens, Lahaina News, February 3, 2000: 11.

ALIKI WAY APARTMENTS
— renovated, Lahaina News, December 27, 1989: 4.

ALIX, WILBERT
— director of the Natale Institute for Neo-Shamanic Studies to lead "Soul Hunting: Finding Lost Pieces of Self", Lahaina News, September 21, 2000: 20.

ALL FAMILY BOAT SHOW
— to held at Maui Mall in June, Lahaina News, June 4, 1986: 3.

ALL IN THE TIMING [PLAY]
— to be performed by Maui OnStage, Lahaina News, January 31, 2002: 16.
— to be performed by Maui OnStage, Lahaina News, February 7, 2002: 16.

ALL LAHAINA LOCK [BUSINESS]
— featured, Lahaina News, May 23, 1984: 17.

ALL LIGHTS SUPPLY [BUSINESS]
— owner Stu Allen featured, Lahaina News, September 12, 1991: 12.

ALL MY SONS [PLAY]
— to be performed by Maui Academy of Performing Arts, Lahaina News, September 9, 1993: 12.
— to be performed, Lahaina News, September 16, 1993: 16.
— presented by Maui Academy of Performing Arts, Lahaina News, September 30, 1993: 13.

ALL SAINTS DAY
— service to be held at United Church of Christ, Lahaina News, October 29, 1998: 28.

ALL STAR VIDEO [BUSINESS]
— opening, Lahaina News, January 18, 1996: 10.

ALL THAT IS SACRED [PLAY]
— auditions being held for, Lahaina News, March 6, 2003: 17.

ALL THE WAY HOME [PLAY]
— to be performed by Baldwin High School's Performing Arts Learning Center, Lahaina News, April 4, 1996: 16.
— last weekend to see, Lahaina News, April 11, 1996: 13.

ALL-AMERICAN HALL OF FAME BOARD
— Lahainaluna High School students named to, Lahaina News, June 3, 1987: 3.

ALLAIRE, DAVID
— becomes chair of Lahaina Town Action Committee, Lahaina News, January 9, 1991: 5.
— supports "The Restaurant Service Professional" classes, Lahaina News, October 14, 1999: 11.

ALLAIRE, JACKIE
— to compete in Mrs. Hawaii USA, Lahaina News, May 21, 1992: 4.

ALLAIRE, NICOLE
— Scholar/Athlete of the Week, Lahaina News, January 31, 2002: 12.

ALLAN, BETTY
— praised, Lahaina News, June 1, 1981: 13.

ALLAN G. SANFORD GORILLA PRESERVE
— auction to be held to benefit, Lahaina News, August 31, 1995: 7.

ALLAN, GEORGE [ARTIST]
— featured, Lahaina News, March 28, 1984: 7.
— to appear at Upstart Crow Bookstore, Lahaina News, December 11, 1985: 9.
— work reviewed, Lahaina News, September 30, 1987: 9.
— work on display at Village Gallery, Lahaina News, March 9, 1988: 17.
— success at selling art while on location in Vancouver, Canada, Lahaina News, August 3, 1988: 15.
— work chosen for poster by Lahaina Town Action Committee , Lahaina News, February 21, 1990: 14.
— publishes poster of "Maui Symphony" painting, Lahaina News, August 15, 1990: 17.
— exhibits at Village Galleries, Lahaina News, March 6, 1991: 16.
— to hold reception at Village Galleries, Lahaina News, March 12, 1992: 21.
— to exhibit at Maui Arts and Cultural Center, Lahaina News, February 12, 1998: 16.
— to exhibit at Village Gallery, Lahaina News, March 4, 1999: 12.
— to demonstrate painting light, Lahaina News, April 8, 1999: 12.
— to exhibit "Hidden Places" at Village Gallery, Lahaina News, March 9, 2000: 12.
— to exhibit at Village Gallery, Lahaina News, March 8, 2001: 16.
— to lead plein air painting workshop, Lahaina News, October 4, 2001: 16.
— to teach Plein Air painting workshop, Lahaina News, January 3, 2002: 3.
— to exhibit at Village Galleries, Lahaina News, March 7, 2002: 17.
— to exhibit at Village Galleries, Lahaina News, May 23, 2002: 16.
— to be featured at Village Galleries, Lahaina News, March 6, 2003: 15.
— to exhibit at Village Galleries, Lahaina News, March 6, 2003: 16.

ALLEN, CHALON
— finalist for Hearst Foundation Youth Senate Program, Lahaina News, November 21, 1991: 3.

ALLEN, HENRY KALEIALOHA [MUSICIAN]
— to perform with Gabe Balthazar, Lahaina News, June 28, 1989: 15.
— produces album, Lahaina News, April 25, 1990: 14.
— featured, Lahaina News, February 13, 1992: 3.
— teaching steel guitar as part of Folk Arts Apprenticeship Award, Lahaina News, July 1, 1993: 2.
— to perform at Moondoggies, Lahaina News, May 19, 1994: 16.
— to perform at Hawaii Guitar Festival, Lahaina News, June 15, 1995: 11.
— to offer classes on steel guitar, Lahaina News, June 12, 1997: 16.
— to teach steel guitar lessons, Lahaina News, June 19, 1997: 16.
— continues to offer steel guitar lessons, Lahaina News, August 7, 1997: 12.
— to perform at big band event at Ritz-Carlton, Lahaina News, May 7, 1998: 16.
— to perform with Gabe Batazar at the Hawaiian All-Stars Maui Music Festival, Lahaina News, May 27, 1999: 13.
— publishes "America", Lahaina News, August 19, 1999: 15.
— to perform at Fleming's On the Greens, Lahaina News, December 7, 2000: 7.
— to perform at Summer Music Festival, Lahaina News, June 28, 2001: 18.
— to perform at Fleming's on the Greens, Lahaina News, August 2, 2001: 15.
— featured, Lahaina News, July 11, 2002: 1,20.
— to perform, Lahaina News, April 10, 2003: 16.

ALLEN, KYLE
— student athlete featured, Lahaina News, August 15, 2002: 12.

ALLEN, MICHAEL
— running for president as part of New Age Synthesis Party, Lahaina News, September 15, 1980: 11.

ALLEN, RAY [MUSICIAN]
— to perform at Borders Books, Lahaina News, September 16, 1999: 13.
— to perform at Borders Books, Lahaina News, October 21, 1999: 16.

ALLEN, SCOTT [MUSICIAN]
— to perform at Pioneer Inn, Lahaina News, May 15, 1997: 7.
— to perform at Il Bucaniere, Lahaina News, September 4, 1997: 13.

ALLEN, STU
— featured, Lahaina News, September 12, 1991: 12.

ALLEN, WOODY
— film "Everyone Says I Love You" to be shown at Maui Arts and Cultural Center, Lahaina News, April 10, 1997: 13.

ALLISON, MOSE [MUSICIAN]
— blues singer to perform, Lahaina News, July 12, 1989: 12.

ALLISON, MRS. JOSEPH
— president of Lahaina Art Society, Lahaina Sun, January 13, 1971: 7.

ALLTON, DON [MUSICIAN]
— featured, Lahaina News, May 14, 1992: 14.

ALLTON, MARY ELLEN KAPP [ARTIST]
— to exhibit at Lahaina Arts Society Gallery, Lahaina News, September 3, 1998: 21.

ALMASON, BEN [MUSICIAN]
— to perform at Villa Lounge, Lahaina News, August 13, 1992: 15.

ALMEIDA, ANTOINETTE M.
— Franciscan Sister honored, Lahaina News, November 14, 1990: 3.

ALOHA
— see Aboriginal Lands of Hawaiian Ancestry [group]

ALOHA 2001 HOMELESS SHELTER BENEFIT
— fundraiser to be held, Lahaina News, December 27, 2001: 14.

ALOHA ACTIVITIES CENTER
— John Roche appointed manager of, Lahaina News, February 4, 1987: 11.
— to handle ground , Lahaina News, May 13, 1987: 3.

ALOHA AGAIN FROM HAWAII—A TRIBUTE TO ELVIS
— Elvis Wade to stage, Lahaina News, August 14, 2003: 17.

ALOHA AIRGROUP INC. [BUSINESS]
— delaying public stock offering, Lahaina News, July 22, 1993: 7.
— president A. Maurice Myers resigns, Lahaina News, January 6, 1994: 5.

ALOHA AIRLINES [BUSINESS]
— carried more passengers than Hawaiian in October, 1981, Lahaina News, December 1, 1981: 7.
— considering appeal on West Maui airport decision, Lahaina News, July 16, 1986: 1.
— offering free show of Disney's "World on Ice", Lahaina News, July 29, 1987: 3.
— employees begin wearing new uniform, Lahaina News, June 28, 1989: 7.
— to offer collector cans of Maui Chip potato chips, Lahaina News, July 26, 1989: 6.
— expands, Lahaina News, October 11, 1989: 5.
— may assume Air Moloka'i's lease , Lahaina News, October 25, 1989: 10.
— plans to increase passenger traffic, Lahaina News, December 13, 1989: 7.
— increases fares, Lahaina News, January 10, 1990: 6.

— sponsoring Hula Pakahi and Lei Festival at Maui Inter-Continental Wailea, Lahaina News, February 28, 1990: 11.
— teams with Foodland to provide "Fly a Friend" certificates, Lahaina News, October 17, 1990: 12.
— adopts new schedule, Lahaina News, January 16, 1991: 4.
— increases fares, Lahaina News, June 13, 1991: 10.
— first class travelers to receive choice of journal or address book featuring local artist Mamo Howell, Lahaina News, February 13, 1992: 13.
— to lease two Boeing 737-300QCs, Lahaina News, March 5, 1992: 10.
— interisland fares matched by Hawaiian Airlines, Lahaina News, July 9, 1992: 14.
— offering drive-thru check-in, Lahaina News, August 26, 1993: 10.
— launches promotion, Lahaina News, September 30, 1993: 8.
— slashes interisland fares, Lahaina News, December 9, 1993: 6.
— publishes new schedule, Lahaina News, April 14, 1994: 10.
— offering promotion with free tickets, Lahaina News, June 9, 1994: 12.
— publishes new schedule, Lahaina News, July 7, 1994: 8.
— to distribute stationary illustrated by Pegge Hopper, Lahaina News, July 28, 1994: 9.
— ranked highly in consumer satisfaction, Lahaina News, October 13, 1994: 15.
— announces new timetable, Lahaina News, January 26, 1995: 13.
— ranked number one in U.S. Department of Transportation Office of Consumer Affairs' Air Travel consumer complaint Report, Lahaina News, February 2, 1995: 7.
— ranked first with no consumer complaints, Lahaina News, February 23, 1995: 6.
— offering coupon books, Lahaina News, November 9, 1995: 10.
— launches "Rediscover the Island" Sweepstakes, Lahaina News, September 11, 1997: 12.
— to equip planes with automatic external defibrillators, Lahaina News, July 2, 1998: 12.
— to offer group promotion, Lahaina News, August 20, 1998: 13.
— enters code share relationship with Pacific Wings, Lahaina News, September 23, 1999: 11.
— bolsters in-flight medical care program, Lahaina News, December 2, 1999: 13.
— Yvonne Boissoneau promoted to director of the Kahului station of, Lahaina News, August 10, 2000: 14.
— begins direct flights between southern California and Maui, Lahaina News, June 7, 2001: 8.

ALOHA AIRLINES JUNIOR TENNIS CHAMPIONSHIPS
— to be held, Lahaina News, October 25, 1989: 11.

ALOHA AND MAHALO AWARDS
— announced at Kapalua Bay Hotel and Villas, Lahaina News, March 27, 1991: 9.

ALOHA BALLROOM DANCE ACADEMY
— continues to hold dance classes, Lahaina News, April 10, 2003: 21.
— to hold classes, Lahaina News, June 12, 2003: 21.
— to host "A Midnight Summer's Dream" Ball to benefit the American Cancer Society, Lahaina News, July 3, 2003: 9.

ALOHA BUSINESS SYSTEMS [BUSINESS]
— hires Bob Cable and Jack Torrey, Lahaina News, October 17, 1990: 12.

ALOHA CANTINA [RESTAURANT]
— to open, Lahaina News, August 12, 1993: 7.
— opens, Lahaina News, November 4, 1993: 10.
— now serving breakfast, Lahaina News, May 19, 1994: 16.
— names Mark Ringlein as general manager, Lahaina News, October 6, 1994: 11.
— to become Woody's, Lahaina News, December 10, 1998: 1.

ALOHA DESTINATIONS [BUSINESS]
— opens new location, Lahaina News, August 12, 1993: 9.

ALOHA EARTH UNITY DAY
— to hold beach clean-up, Lahaina News, August 13, 1992: 4.
— to be held, Lahaina News, August 20, 1992: 5.

ALOHA FAMILY CHIROPRACTIC AND WELLNESS CENTERS
— new locations added, Lahaina News, January 17, 2002: 8.

ALOHA FAMILY PRACTICE CLINIC [RESTAURANT]
— to open, Lahaina News, September 30, 1999: 11.

ALOHA FESTIVALS
— 45th annual scheduled for October, Lahaina News, July 11, 1991: 11.
— details given, Lahaina News, July 25, 1991: 12.
— theme is "E Pupukahi", Lahaina News, August 8, 1991: 13.
— Ka'anapali Beach Hotel to hold hula competition for children, Lahaina News, August 22, 1991: 10.
— seeking performers for 'Oli and Hawaiian Falsetto Festival, Lahaina News, August 29, 1991: 13.
— scheduled, details given, Lahaina News, August 29, 1991: 14.
— to be offered, Lahaina News, September 5, 1991: 17.
— looking for chanters and singers, Lahaina News, September 12, 1991: 3.
— details given, Lahaina News, September 26, 1991: 12,14.
— details given, Lahaina News, October 3, 1991: 1,15,16,17,24.
— ribbons now on sale, Lahaina News, October 3, 1991: 5.
— details of events, Lahaina News, October 10, 1991: 14,17,22.
— to include Hula O Na Keiki competition, Lahaina News, July 30, 1992: 4.
— seeking support from local businesses, Lahaina News, August 20, 1992: 13.
— to include Hula O Na Keiki competition, Lahaina News, September 3, 1992: 15.
— details, Lahaina News, October 1, 1992: 17.
— details for, Lahaina News, October 8, 1992: 13.
— details for, Lahaina News, October 15, 1992: 15,16.
— to include Hoolaulea O Kai, Lahaina News, October 15, 1992: 3.
— events, Lahaina News, October 22, 1992: 15.
— applications now accepted for Royal Court, Lahaina News, June 24, 1993: 4.
— details of, Lahaina News, October 14, 1993: 12.
— events, Lahaina News, October 21, 1993: 15.
— to be held, Lahaina News, October 13, 1994: 16.
— new board installed, Lahaina News, February 16, 1995: 13.
— to be celebrated at Kapalua Bay Hotel and Villas, Lahaina News, October 12, 1995: 14.
— Royal Ball tribute to King David Kalakaua to be held at Ritz-Carlton, Lahaina News, October 19, 1995: 9.
— to include wood carving competition, Lahaina News, October 2, 1997: 18.
— Royal Court to appear, Lahaina News, October 2, 1997: 20.
— events to be held, Lahaina News, October 2, 1997: 3.
— Royal Court of Maui seeks volunteers, Lahaina News, March 12, 1998: 18.
— seeking volunteers, Lahaina News, March 19, 1998: 2.
— Falsetto Contest to be held, Lahaina News, August 13, 1998: 8.
— Royal Court to appear at Wharf Cinema Center, Lahaina News, September 24, 1998: 16.
— Banyan Tree Ho'olaule'a to be part of, Lahaina News, October 1, 1998: 3.
— to be held at Lahaina Cannery Mall, Lahaina News, October 8, 1998: 6.
— taking contestants for Ho'okuku Hua'olelo, Lahaina News, May 13, 1999: 15.
— to include Banyan Tree Park, Lahaina News, September 30, 1999: 1.

— to include activities at Banyan Tree Park, Lahaina News, October 7, 1999: 1,20.
— to be held, Lahaina News, October 7, 1999: 14.
— to include Maui Polynesian Tahiti Fete, Lahaina News, August 10, 2000: 16.
— to begin, Lahaina News, October 12, 2000: 19.
— to be held, Lahaina News, October 19, 2000: 19.
— Ho'olaule'a to showcase Hawaiian culture, Lahaina News, October 26, 2000: 1.
— to be held, Lahaina News, October 26, 2000: 2.
— royal court visits Wharf Cinema Center, Lahaina News, November 9, 2000: 3.
— new Maui leadership announced, Lahaina News, June 14, 2001: 18.
— Royal Court Investiture to be held, Lahaina News, August 16, 2001: 16.
— to include Falsetto Contest, Lahaina News, September 27, 2001: 16.
— to be held, Lahaina News, October 4, 2001: 1.
— to begin, Lahaina News, October 11, 2001: 14.
— events set, Lahaina News, October 18, 2001: 14.
— searching for new court members, Lahaina News, March 28, 2002: 5.
— royal court to be coronated, Lahaina News, August 1, 2002: 16.
— to host Royal Court, Lahaina News, August 8, 2002: 17.
— events scheduled for, Lahaina News, September 26, 2002: 14.
— to begin, Lahaina News, October 3, 2002: 1,17.
— to be held, Lahaina News, October 10, 2002: 14.
— events to be held, Lahaina News, October 17, 2002: 9.
— seeking volunteers for Aloha Festivals Maui Royal Court, Lahaina News, August 14, 2003: 9.
— seeking crafters for Lahaina Banyan Tree Ho'olaule'a, Lahaina News, August 28, 2003: 5.
— to be celebrated at Wharf Cinema Center, Lahaina News, October 2, 2003: 2.
— Maui Mall to hold Ukulele Festival and Competition, Lahaina News, October 9, 2003: 17.
— to be held, Lahaina News, October 9, 2003: 9.

ALOHA HOUSE, INC. [BUSINESS]
— providing rehabilitation services, Lahaina News, January 17, 2002: 2.
— fundraiser to be held for at Dunes Restaurant, Lahaina News, November 21, 2002: 13.

ALOHA INTERNATIONAL EMPLOYMENT SERVICES [BUSINESS]
— opens branch in Portland, Oregon, Lahaina News, April 25, 1990: 7.
— renamed The Ryan Company, Inc., Lahaina News, March 26, 1992: 11.

ALOHA ISLAND AIR [BUSINESS]
— renamed from Princeville Airways, Lahaina News, June 22, 1988: 3.
— expand on Maui, Lahaina News, July 20, 1988: 3.
— adds more flights, Lahaina News, July 5, 1989: 3.
— to honor tickets made with Air Moloka'i, Lahaina News, October 18, 1989: 7.
— adds to management personnel, Lahaina News, October 24, 1990: 7.
— purchases new planes, Lahaina News, July 2, 1992: 16,17.
— see also Island Air [business]

ALOHA JOE [RADIO SHOW]
— records live show at Whalers Village, Lahaina News, May 25, 2000: 16.

ALOHA LANES [BUSINESS]
— changes name to Wailuku-Royal Lanes Bowling Alley, Lahaina News, August 22, 1990: 13.

ALOHA LASER CARTRIDGE [BUSINESS]
— opens, Lahaina News, June 13, 1990: 7.

ALOHA LUAU
— announces special children's price, Lahaina News, July 8, 1987: 16.
— announces special children's price, Lahaina News, June 15, 1988: 6.
— to return to Sheraton Maui, Lahaina News, June 14, 1989: 17.
— closes, Lahaina News, June 28, 1989: 7.

ALOHA MANA MASSAGE [BUSINESS]
— opens, Lahaina News, April 6, 1995: 6.

ALOHA MELE LUNCHEON
— to be held at the Maui Lu Resort, Lahaina News, September 1, 1981: 16.
— to be held at Maui-Intercontinental Hotel, Lahaina News, March 8, 1989: 3.
— to be held at Lokelani Ballroom at the Maui Inter-Continental Resort, Lahaina News, March 13, 1991: 14.
— to be held at Lokelani Ballroom at the Maui Inter-Continental Resort, Lahaina News, March 20, 1991: 10.
— to be held at Lokelani Ballroom at the Maui Inter-Continental Resort, Lahaina News, April 10, 1991: 12.
— to be held at Lokelani Ballroom at the Maui Inter-Continental Resort, Lahaina News, April 17, 1991: 14.
— continues to be held, Lahaina News, May 1, 1991: 16.

ALOHA MIXED PLATE [RESTAURANT]
— opened by Hoaloha Na Ehā, Lahaina News, February 6, 1997: 9.
— opens, Lahaina News, May 8, 1997: 7.

ALOHA PARTY
— to celebrate 25 years, Lahaina News, July 17, 1997: 17.

ALOHA PLASTIC RECYCLING INC. [BUSINESS]
— resumes recycling, Lahaina News, June 8, 2000: 16.

ALOHA SHARES NETWORK
— helping non-profits, Lahaina News, January 17, 2002: 2.

ALOHA SPIRIT AWARDS
— nominations requested for, Lahaina News, June 5, 1985: 9.
— nominations now being accepted, Lahaina News, April 8, 1987: 3.
— to be held at Kobe Japanese Steak House, Lahaina News, July 16, 1998: 13.
— winners announced, Lahaina News, June 21, 2001: 9.

ALOHA SUMMER
— continues at Lahaina Cannery Mall, Lahaina News, August 15, 1990: 15.

ALOHA TENTS [BUSINESS]
— opens, Lahaina News, December 13, 1989: 6.

ALOHA TOY STORE [BUSINESS]
— opens, Lahaina News, March 25, 1999: 13.
— expands to The Shops at Wailea, Lahaina News, June 28, 2001: 9.

ALOHA VOYAGES [BUSINESS]
— described, Lahaina News, September 16, 1987: 4.
— Circuit Court ruling allows to offer tours, Lahaina News, January 13, 1988: 1,16.
— caught by rules governing ocean usage, Lahaina News, February 3, 1988: 1,22.
— lease scrutinized, Lahaina News, February 24, 1988: 1.

ALOHA WEEK
— events detailed, Lahaina Sun, September 29, 1971: 3.
— Hawaii Visitors Bureau event to be held next week, Lahaina Sun, August 8, 1973: 6.
— begins Sunday, October 14, Lahaina News, October 10, 1984: 3.
— continues, Lahaina News, October 17, 1984: 3.
— committee seeking applicants for Royal Court, Lahaina News, August 21, 1985: 3.
— schedule listed, Lahaina News, October 2, 1985: 1.
— events summarized, Lahaina News, September 17, 1986: 5.
— registration opens for Monarchy Ball, Lahaina News, September 24, 1986: 3.
— activities described, Lahaina News, September 16, 1987: 3.
— schedule corrected, Lahaina News, September 23, 1987: 3.
— events described, Lahaina News, September 23, 1987: 4.
— to be held, Lahaina News, October 12, 1988: 6.
— events listed, Lahaina News, October 19, 1988: 1,6.
— seeking help in producing pageant, Lahaina News, August 30, 1989: 1.
— supported by Roberts Hawaii, Lahaina News, September 6, 1989: 1.
— Lahaina News to special souvenir edition, Lahaina News, September 13, 1989: 1.
— detailed, Lahaina News, September 20, 1989: 3.
— events detailed; insert included with issue of newspaper, Lahaina News, October 4, 1989: 1,12.
— photographs from Keiki hula, Lahaina News, October 25, 1989: 9.
— looking for volunteers, Lahaina News, July 11, 1990: 2.
— events, Lahaina News, October 10, 1990: 13.
— events described, Lahaina News, October 17, 1990: 13,14,15.
— schedule, Lahaina News, October 24, 1990: 13.
— to be held at Lahaina Cannery Mall, Lahaina News, September 28, 1995: 11.
— to be held, Lahaina News, September 26, 1996: 15.
— to be celebrated, Lahaina News, October 3, 1996: 1,18.
— parade to be held, Lahaina News, October 10, 1996: 14.

ALOHA: THE MAGAZINE OF HAWAII AND THE PACIFIC
— to suspend publication, Lahaina News, August 6, 1998: 17.

ALOHA. WELCOME AND HELLO … OR GOODBYE. THE CHOICE IS YOURS [BROCHURE]
— see hippie brochure

ALONZO, RENE [PIANIST]
— performance reviewed, Lahaina News, July 1, 1987: 7.

ALOY, GEORGE
— patrolman honored by Maui Police Department, Lahaina News, November 12, 1986: 3.

ALOY, LOUISE
— family wins Family of the Year from Child and Family Services, Lahaina News, November 20, 1997: 1.

ALPHA BLOODY [MUSICAL GROUP]
— to perform at Lahaina Civic Center Amphitheater, Lahaina News, February 18, 1999: 12.

ALTERNATIVES TO VIOLENCE
— group to meet, Lahaina News, January 7, 1993: 4.
— Teen Girls' Victim Group to educate teen girls on breaking cycle of violence, Lahaina News, November 17, 1994: 4.
— to hold educational workshops, Lahaina News, December 8, 1994: 3.
— funds raised for by Whale Discovery at Whalers Village, Lahaina News, June 8, 1995: 2.
— seeking child care volunteer, Lahaina News, July 13, 1995: 5.
— seeking child care volunteers, Lahaina News, October 26, 1995: 2.
— seeking volunteers, Lahaina News, February 22, 1996: 10.

ALTFELD, DON
— music promoter featured, Lahaina News, October 24, 1984: 18.

ALTMAN, STEVE [COMEDIAN]
— to perform at Comedy Club, Lahaina News, August 8, 1990: 13.
— to perform at Comedy Club, Lahaina News, July 11, 1991: 10.
— to perform at Comedy Club and the Sports Page, Lahaina News, July 9, 1992: 17,21.
— to perform at Maui Comedy Club, Lahaina News, July 6, 1995: 11.

ALU LIKE, INC. [BUSINESS]
— provides Hawaiiana videos, Lahaina News, April 12, 1989: S13.
— sponsors display at Lahaina Public Library, Lahaina News, January 24, 1990: 2.

— offering entrepreneurship training program, Lahaina News, May 13, 1993: 5.
— youth group planning teen activities, Lahaina News, May 26, 1994: 1,4.
— sponsoring youth dance, Lahaina News, June 2, 1994: 3.
— Entrepreneurship Training Program to be held, Lahaina News, April 27, 1995: 10.
— to host "How To Start a Business" course, Lahaina News, February 27, 1997: 10.
— Youth Alcohol, Tobacco and Other Drugs Prevention Project to hold youth dance, Lahaina News, June 26, 1997: 16.
— offering Entrepreneurial Training Program, Lahaina News, September 11, 1997: 12.
— entrepreneurship training program planned, Lahaina News, April 23, 1998: 13.
— to offer "How to Start a Business" class, Lahaina News, August 13, 1998: 13.
— Ke Ola Pono No Na Kupuna to perform at Senior Fair, Lahaina News, October 29, 1998: 24.
— Entrepreneurship Training Program to be held, Lahaina News, February 11, 1999: 13.
— to host Entrepreneurship Training Program, Lahaina News, February 18, 1999: 11.

ALUELA, JOE
— first Valley Isle man to finish Maui Marathon, Lahaina News, March 19, 1998: 2.

ALULI, NANE
— named general manager of The Mauian Hotel, Lahaina News, April 27, 2000: 11.

ALULI, PIA [MUSICIAN]
— featured, Lahaina News, February 20, 1992: 12.
— to perform at Villa Lounge, Lahaina News, August 13, 1992: 15.
— to perform at Embassy Suites Hotel, Lahaina News, December 31, 1992: 13.
— see also Ke'ia [musical group]

ALUMINUM MAN/WOMAN
— triathlon to be held, Lahaina News, May 4, 1995: 8.
— biathlon continues, Lahaina News, June 22, 1995: 6.
— biathlon to be held, Lahaina News, July 13, 1995: 7.
— biathlon continues, Lahaina News, August 31, 1995: 6.
— biathlon concludes, Lahaina News, December 28, 1995: 7.
— biathlon to be held, Lahaina News, January 4, 1996: 6.
— first biathlon of the year to be held, Lahaina News, January 18, 1996: 6.
— biathlon continues, Lahaina News, February 1, 1996: 6.
— biathlon continues, Lahaina News, March 21, 1996: 6.
— biathlon to be held, Lahaina News, April 2, 1998: 15.
— biathlon series continues, Lahaina News, April 16, 1998: 7.
— "Aluminum Man Not-so-serious Series" biathlon to be held, Lahaina News, January 21, 1999: 7.
— biathlon series continues, Lahaina News, February 25, 1999: 7.
— biathlon to be held, Lahaina News, March 25, 1999: 14.
— biathlon to be held at North Beach, Lahaina News, August 3, 2000: 6.

ALVARADO, KRISTA
— wins Na Mele O Maui scholarship, Lahaina News, May 15, 2003: 2.

ALVAREZ, AUDREY MAE
— Lahainaluna High School senior awarded scholarship to Hawaii Pacific University, Lahaina News, March 30, 2000: 3.

ALVIN AILEY REPERTORY ENSEMBLE
— to perform at Baldwin Auditorium, Lahaina News, March 27, 1985: 3.

ALVIN, BETH
— married at Nautilus Center, Lahaina News, January 4, 1989: 2.

ALZHEIMER'S ASSOCIATION
— to hold caregivers workshop, Lahaina News, March 5, 1998: 16.
— sponsoring workshop on planning for the future, Lahaina News, August 27, 1998: 16.
— to hold Memory Walk, Lahaina News, September 17, 1998: 18.
— Warren and Annabelle's hosted magic fundraiser for, Lahaina News, February 3, 2000: 11.
— to hold "Memory Walk", Lahaina News, September 14, 2000: 9.
— to hold registration for "Safe Return" program, Lahaina News, July 26, 2001: 5.
— to hold Memory Walk, Lahaina News, August 30, 2001: 2.
— to hold Memory Walk, Lahaina News, September 20, 2001: 2.
— to hold workshop on dementia, Lahaina News, October 17, 2002: 14.
— to hold workshop on dementia, Lahaina News, October 24, 2002: 9.
— to sponsor workshop on "The Difference: Medicare and Medicaid", Lahaina News, October 31, 2002: 12.
— to offer Safe Return Program, Lahaina News, July 24, 2003: 2.

ALZHEIMER'S KULA HOSPITAL SUPPORT GROUP
— to meet, Lahaina News, October 8, 1998: 17.
— continues to meet, Lahaina News, January 20, 2000: 12.

ALZHEIMER'S LAHAINA SUPPORT GROUP
— to meet, Lahaina News, July 30, 1992: 4.
— to meet, Lahaina News, August 13, 1992: 9.
— to meet, Lahaina News, September 17, 1992: 8.
— to meet, Lahaina News, September 24, 1992: 2.
— to meet, Lahaina News, October 8, 1992: 2.
— support group to meet, Lahaina News, October 22, 1992: 12.
— to hold meeting, Lahaina News, February 18, 1993: 5.
— continues to meet, Lahaina News, June 3, 1993: 3.
— to meet, Lahaina News, September 9, 1993: 3.
— to hold Memory Walk, Lahaina News, October 21, 1993: 4.
— continues to meet, Lahaina News, August 4, 1994: 4.
— to meet, Lahaina News, May 1, 1997: 16.
— to meet, Lahaina News, August 6, 1998: 21.
— continues to meet, Lahaina News, July 1, 1999: 13.
— continues to meet, Lahaina News, May 11, 2000: 21.
— continues to meet, Lahaina News, September 14, 2000: 21.
— continues to meet, Lahaina News, November 16, 2000: 16.

ALZHEIMER'S UPCOUNTRY SUPPORT GROUP
— continues to meet, Lahaina News, April 29, 1999: 16.
— continues to meet, Lahaina News, September 30, 1999: 13.

AMADEUS [PLAY]
— opens at Iao Theatre, Lahaina News, August 16, 1989: 13.
— ending, Lahaina News, August 30, 1989: 3.

AMALGAMATED LAND, INC.[BUSINESS]
— selling property in the New Hebrides, Lahaina Sun, April 7, 1971: 5.
— sale of property in the New Hebrides criticized, Lahaina Sun, May 19, 1971: 2.

AMANO, GREGORY
— chosen to study in Japan by Foundation for Study in Hawaii, Lahaina News, June 7, 1989: 3.

AMARAL, ALVIN
— appointed director of community and governmental relations on Maui by McCormack Properties, Lahaina News, April 3, 1991: 4.

AMARAL, SARA
— life remembered, Lahaina News, January 9, 1997: 3.

AMATEUR BALLROOM DANCER'S ASSOCIATION, UNITED STATES
— to hold monthly dances at Wailuku Community Center, Lahaina News, July 25, 1991: 4.
— to hold dance, Lahaina News, August 26, 1993: 8.

AMATEUR POETS AND SONGWRITERS SOCIETY OF HONOKOWAI
— to meet, Lahaina News, July 17, 1997: 16.
— to meet, Lahaina News, August 14, 1997: 17.
— to meet at Picasso's, Lahaina News, September 25, 1997: 17.
— continues to meet, Lahaina News, October 30, 1997: 16,17.
— continues to meet, Lahaina News, November 27, 1997: 13.

AMBRE, PAULA
— named executive director of The Maui Farm, Inc., Lahaina News, November 5, 1992: 8.

AMBROSE, HARRIDEAN
— honored as educator of the month by Leilani's on the Beach, Lahaina News, March 7, 2002: 5.

AMBROSE, STEPHAN
— assists in Tijuana River Valley, Lahaina News, March 4, 1993: 3.

AMBROSIO, DARCY
— first graduate of Westin Hotels and Resorts Apprenticeship program, Lahaina News, October 24, 1990: 6.

AMERICA
— "Black Tie and Blue Jeans" fundraiser to be held, Lahaina News, August 22, 2002: 20.

AMERICA [MUSICAL GROUP]
— to perform at Royal Lahaina Tennis Stadium, Lahaina News, June 15, 1983: 12.

AMERICAN AIRLINES, INC. [BUSINESS]
— seeks permission to fly directly to Maui, Lahaina News, April 4, 1984: 13.
— to begin flights between Maui and the mainland in December, Lahaina News, July 4, 1984: 18.
— direct flights between Maui and Mainland sold out, Lahaina News, December 19, 1984: 3.
— offering Maui AAdvantage Passport with Maui Visitors Bureau, Lahaina News, October 6, 1994: 11.

AMERICAN ASSOCIATION FOR STATE AND LOCAL HISTORY
— Maui Nei "A Journey Through Lahaina's Past" wins Certificate of Commendation, Lahaina News, July 24, 2003: 8.

AMERICAN ASSOCIATION OF RETIRED PERSONS (AARP)
— December meeting detailed, Lahaina News, January 15, 1981: 14.
— the Maui chapter detailed, Lahaina News, March 1, 1981: 16.
— elect officers for Lahaina chapter, Lahaina News, November 30, 1983: 5.
— Lahaina Chapter to meet, Lahaina News, May 2, 1984: 5.
— hold Christmas dinner at Coconut Grove Restaurant, Lahaina News, December 5, 1984: 3.
— hosting presentation by Marie Johnson on Social Security, Lahaina News, February 27, 1985: 3.
— sets Lei Day fundraiser to May 1, Lahaina News, April 24, 1985: 7.
— bingo night organized at the Lahaina Civic Center, Lahaina News, May 1, 1985: 4.
— celebrating 25 years, Lahaina News, October 2, 1985: 3.
— installs new officers, Lahaina News, December 4, 1985: 3.
— to hold meeting at Lahaina Civic Center, Lahaina News, January 1, 1986: 3.
— to hold February meeting at Lahaina Civic Center, Lahaina News, February 5, 1986: 3.
— meeting at Lahaina Civic Center, Lahaina News, February 26, 1986: 3.
— meeting set for Lahaina Civic Center, Lahaina News, March 26, 1986: 3.
— to hold membership drive, Lahaina News, April 30, 1986: 3.
— regular meeting set for June 2, Lahaina News, May 28, 1986: 3.
— hosting Circus of Hobbies, Lahaina News, August 20, 1986: 15.
— changes meeting date, Lahaina News, November 5, 1986: 3.
— to host State Senator Rick Reed, Lahaina News, December 31, 1986: 12.
— Valentine potluck set, Lahaina News, January 28, 1987: 3.
— to hold dinner and theatre, Lahaina News, February 11, 1987: 3.
— to hold meeting, Lahaina News, April 29, 1987: 3.
— holds seminar on avoiding common frauds, Lahaina News, May 27, 1987: 16.
— to meet for bingo, Lahaina News, July 1, 1987: 3.
— hosting presentation by Thomas Bodden, Lahaina News, October 7, 1987: 3.
— to host speaker Bill Lazell, Lahaina News, October 28, 1987: 3.
— to hold December meeting, Lahaina News, December 2, 1987: 3.
— to host speaker Jim Luckey, Lahaina News, January 6, 1988: 3.
— to host mayor Tavares, Lahaina News, March 2, 1988: 22.
— Jerome Mill named assistant state director, Lahaina News, July 6, 1988: 11.
— to host talk by Jane Ann Covington, Lahaina News, September 28, 1988: 18.
— to hold Christmas dinner, Lahaina News, November 23, 1988: 5.
— to host author Robert Ness, Lahaina News, December 21, 1988: 13.
— changes mailing address, Lahaina News, January 25, 1989: 16.
— members sew and sell lei during May Day, Lahaina News, May 10, 1989: 7.
— to sell lei as fundraiser, Lahaina News, November 8, 1989: 3.
— to host talk by Jim Luckey of the Lahaina Restoration Foundation, Lahaina News, February 28, 1990: 3.
— to offer tax help to elderly, Lahaina News, March 7, 1990: 3.
— to host speech by mayor Linda Lingle, Lahaina News, April 2, 1992: 4.
— to host mayor Linda Lingle, Lahaina News, April 16, 1992: 3.
— to meet, Lahaina News, April 29, 1993: 5.
— to meet, Lahaina News, September 30, 1993: 4.
— Beth Ross elected as new president, Lahaina News, December 22, 1994: 6.
— receives new American flag, Lahaina News, June 22, 1995: 5.
— presents funds to Maui Memorial Hospital, Lahaina News, September 28, 1995: 2.
— members to make and sell lei, Lahaina News, February 15, 1996: 12.
— to hold holo-holo day, Lahaina News, April 4, 1996: 2.
— to hold dinner, Lahaina News, September 26, 1996: 15.
— to celebrate eighteen years, Lahaina News, November 7, 1996: 15.
— to meet, Lahaina News, February 27, 1997: 11.
— sponsoring panel on Maui women, Lahaina News, March 6, 1997: 10.
— recruiting volunteers, Lahaina News, March 6, 1997: 11.
— seeking volunteers to staff information center at county Office of Aging, Lahaina News, March 27, 1997: 13.
— to offer an evening of music, Lahaina News, May 1, 1997: 16.
— to hold grand opening of information center, Lahaina News, September 25, 1997: 6.
— Lahaina Information Center opens, Lahaina News, October 2, 1997: 3.
— to host presentation by Keoki Freeland of the Lahaina Restoration Foundation, Lahaina News, January 1, 1998: 16.
— to hold conference, Lahaina News, April 30, 1998: 17.
— to survey members with State, Lahaina News, June 25, 1998: 11.
— Theo Morrison of LahainaTown Action Committee to speak to, Lahaina News, August 27, 1998: 9.
— Major William Kirk to speak at, Lahaina News, October 1, 1998: 16.
— elects officers, Lahaina News, November 19, 1998: 2.
— to celebrate "Women's Month", Lahaina News, February 25, 1999: 13.
— continues to meet, Lahaina News, May 27, 1999: 12.
— CEO of Maui Memorial Medical Center William Boyd Kleefisch to speak to, Lahaina News, September 30, 1999: 13.

— to hold Christmas dinner, Lahaina News, December 2, 1999: 17.
— author of "Tongue Fu" Sam Horn to speak at meeting of, Lahaina News, December 23, 1999: 3.
— to host talk by mechanic Jim Lytle, Lahaina News, January 27, 2000: 13.
— to hold Bingo Night, Lahaina News, August 24, 2000: 19.
— to hold Christmas luncheon, Lahaina News, November 30, 2000: 16.
— to hold meeting on disaster planning, Lahaina News, January 25, 2001: 16.
— Information Center opens, Lahaina News, January 25, 2001: 7.
— Information Center opens, Lahaina News, February 1, 2001: 17.
— to host "Home Grown Treats" at monthly meeting, Lahaina News, February 22, 2001: 16.
— seeking volunteers for Information Center, Lahaina News, February 22, 2001: 2.
— to host Linda Decker, Lahaina News, March 15, 2001: 18.
— Johanna Bergman to speak on life in Indonesia, Lahaina News, June 28, 2001: 16.
— to meet, Lahaina News, September 20, 2001: 18.
— Lahaina Chapter to hold field trip to Kalama Heights Retirement Residence, Lahaina News, February 21, 2002: 2.
— to hold monthly meetings at Lahaina Civic Center, Lahaina News, April 18, 2002: 2.
— Lahaina chapter to meet, Lahaina News, May 16, 2002: 3.

AMERICAN ASSOCIATION OF UNIVERSITY WOMEN (AAUW)

— to host speech by Nancy Worth, Lahaina News, March 11, 1987: 18.
— to hold meeting, Lahaina News, January 17, 1990: 5.
— to hold fashion show fundraiser, Lahaina News, May 1, 1991: 15,16.
— to host luncheon and fashion show, Lahaina News, April 23, 1992: 7,8.
— to hold "Spring Fling", Lahaina News, May 7, 1992: 4.
— to hold Fashion show and luncheon, Lahaina News, January 21, 1993: 11.
— to hold public presentation on educational opportunities for women, Lahaina News, October 21, 1993: 4.
— presents dramatic oral reading of real life histories, Lahaina News, August 25, 1994: 15.
— to host "Thriving in Changing Times" by Therese Godfrey, Lahaina News, January 26, 1995: 13.
— to hold art exhibit and sale, Lahaina News, February 9, 1995: 11.
— to hold presentation on "Taking Charge of Your Life", Lahaina News, March 2, 1995: 7.
— to hold garage sale, Lahaina News, January 25, 1996: 4.
— to hold Tex-Mex Fiesta-Fashion Show and silent auction, Lahaina News, February 22, 1996: 14.
— to meet, Lahaina News, July 18, 1996: 12.
— to hold fundraiser, Lahaina News, November 14, 1996: 14.
— to hold New Membership Tea, Lahaina News, September 3, 1998: 21.
— selling holiday candy as a fundraiser, Lahaina News, September 24, 1998: 7.
— to hold whale watch fundraiser, Lahaina News, February 25, 1999: 13.
— to hold membership tea, Lahaina News, September 9, 1999: 12.
— to hold lunch at Pacific'O Restaurant, Lahaina News, March 9, 2000: 13.
— to host writer Liz Janes, Lahaina News, March 23, 2000: 12.

AMERICAN AUTOMOBILE ASSOCIATION (AAA)

— Hyatt Regency Maui receives Five Diamond Award from, Lahaina News, February 10, 1988: 11.
— awards Westin Maui Hotel four diamonds, Lahaina News, June 6, 1991: 6.

— awards Hyatt Regency Maui Five Diamond Award, Lahaina News, December 19, 1991: 13.
— recognizes Maui Marriott Resort, Lahaina News, February 18, 1993: 10.
— awards Maui Marriott with Four Diamond accommodation rating, Lahaina News, February 10, 1994: 6.

AMERICAN BAR ASSOCIATION

— to hold annual convention in Honolulu, Lahaina News, July 26, 1989: 6.

AMERICAN BUSINESS WOMEN'S ASSOCIATION, HO'O NA'AUAU CHAPTER

— to hold benefit breakfast and silent auction, Lahaina News, June 6, 1990: 7.
— to hold benefit breakfast for scholarship fund, Lahaina News, June 13, 1990: 7.
— to meet, Lahaina News, July 9, 1992: 13.
— to hold rummage sale, Lahaina News, October 8, 1992: 7.
— to hold rummage sale, Lahaina News, October 15, 1992: 12.

AMERICAN CANCER SOCIETY

— benefit fashion show held, Lahaina Sun, March 31, 1971: 4.
— Maui unit receives the highest per capita donations in the country, Lahaina Sun, October 13, 1971: 4.
— educational drive detailed, Lahaina Sun, May 2, 1973: 6.
— residential drive ends, Lahaina News, June 1, 1980: 14.
— Cancer Shootout event held, Lahaina News, May 1, 1981: 16.
— holds golf tournament fundraiser, Lahaina News, July 15, 1983: 10.
— to hold Great American Smokeout, including workshops, Lahaina News, November 13, 1985: 7.
— to hold fundraiser "A Royal Christmas at the Baldwin Manor", Lahaina News, December 11, 1985: 9.
— names Pat Esclito Jr. as chairman of Residential Crusade, Lahaina News, March 19, 1986: 3.
— to hold first annual Keiki Fun Run, Lahaina News, May 28, 1986: 3.
— to hold Jailathon fundraiser, Lahaina News, July 23, 1986: 3.
— holds benefit concert featuring Melveen Leed, Lahaina News, August 13, 1986: 3.
— offering quit smoking clinics, Lahaina News, October 22, 1986: 3.
— hosts Great American Smokeout, Lahaina News, November 12, 1986: 3.
— Smokeout event to be held November 20, Lahaina News, November 19, 1986: 3.
— hosting talk by Dr. Eli Glatstein, Lahaina News, February 25, 1987: 3.
— sponsoring smoking cessation clinic, Lahaina News, July 15, 1987: 3.
— to hold workshop for mastectomy patients, Lahaina News, October 21, 1987: 3.
— sponsoring "Great American Smokeout", Lahaina News, November 15, 1989: 5.
— to offer smoking cessation classes, Lahaina News, November 5, 1992: 5.
— to hold Maui Midnight Marathon fundraiser, Lahaina News, April 21, 1994: 6.
— to hold Community Crusade, Lahaina News, May 12, 1994: 4.
— to hold Community Crusade, Lahaina News, May 19, 1994: 6.
— looking for volunteers to help senior citizens make out their wills, Lahaina News, April 6, 1995: 4.
— holds Jailathon fundraiser, Lahaina News, August 29, 1996: 2.
— to hold "Wild West Side Jailathon", Lahaina News, July 31, 1997: 2.
— results of "Wild West Side Jailathon" fundraiser, Lahaina News, August 7, 1997: 3.
— to meet, Lahaina News, April 16, 1998: 13.
— to hold "Relay for Life", Lahaina News, July 16, 1998: 6.
— Tiffany and Co.to host benefit for, Lahaina News, April 29, 1999: 2.

— "Relay for Life" to raise money for, Lahaina News, July 8, 1999: 1.

— "Relay for Life" to raise money for, Lahaina News, July 22, 1999: 1,16.

— to bless refurbished Program and Service Center, Lahaina News, October 7, 1999: 16.

— held relay for life, Lahaina News, August 10, 2000: 8.

— to hold "Relay for Life", Lahaina News, May 31, 2001: 2.

— to hold Relay for Life, Lahaina News, July 5, 2001: 5.

— new support group for women and families affected by breast cancer, Lahaina News, August 2, 2001: 1,20.

— to hold "Look Good, Feel Better", Lahaina News, November 8, 2001: 17.

— Relay for Life to be held, Lahaina News, June 6, 2002: 5.

— Honolua Wahine Surf Classic "Surfing for a Cure" to be held, Lahaina News, July 11, 2002: 12.

— holds Youth Relay for Life, Lahaina News, March 13, 2003: 9.

— to hold Relay for Life, Lahaina News, March 27, 2003: 2.

— to hold Relay for Life, Lahaina News, April 3, 2003: 18.

— Relay For Life held, Lahaina News, April 24, 2003: 2.

— Aloha Ballroom Dance Academy to host "A Midnight Summer's Dream" Ball to benefit, Lahaina News, July 3, 2003: 9.

— to hold "Celebrity Power Walk", Lahaina News, September 11, 2003: 16.

AMERICAN CIVIL LIBERTIES UNION (ACLU)

— opposition to Mayor Cravalho's request for emergency powers, Lahaina Sun, December 23, 1970: 1,5.

— opposition to Mayor's request for emergency powers, Lahaina Sun, January 13, 1971: 6.

— recommends that Governor Burns veto Public Defender Bill, Lahaina Sun, May 19, 1971: 8.

— organize panel discussion, Lahaina Sun, June 16, 1971: 3.

— new officers announced, Lahaina Sun, June 23, 1971: 10.

— protests inadequate announcement of hearing concerning proposed camping laws, Lahaina Sun, August 4, 1971: 11.

— told that students receiving more personal freedom than ever, Lahaina Sun, December 22, 1971: 5.

— celebrates one-year anniversary, Lahaina Sun, February 2, 1972: 13.

— accuses Maui County Attorney of ignorance of constitutional principles, Lahaina Sun, June 28, 1972: 3.

AMERICAN DIABETES ASSOCIATION

— to hold support group, Lahaina News, April 10, 1991: 4.

AMERICAN DIRECT INDUSTRIES [BUSINESS]

— mail order firm defaults, Lahaina News, January 3, 1990: 4.

AMERICAN DIVERS, INC. [BUSINES]

— to work on Mala Wharf, Lahaina News, June 24, 1993: 1.

AMERICAN EXPRESS FINANCIAL SERVICES [BUSINESS]

— opening at Wharf Shopping Center, Lahaina News, April 17, 1985: 3.

— to hold financial planning seminar, Lahaina News, April 27, 1995: 10.

AMERICAN FINANCIAL SERVICES ASSOCIATION INDEPENDENTS CONFERENCE AND EXPOSITION

— convention to be held, Lahaina News, April 1, 1993: 8.

AMERICAN HAWAII CRUISES [BUSINESS]

— State Department of Health to test water in harbors while vessels of anchored, Lahaina News, May 13, 1987: 14.

— offering whale watching cruises, Lahaina News, March 21, 1990: 18.

— to no longer dock in Lahaina, Lahaina News, March 30, 1995: 1,16.

— Community Service Scholarships awarded, Lahaina News, May 22, 1997: 6.

AMERICAN HEART ASSOCIATION

— organizes food festival, Lahaina News, September 7, 1988: 3.

— organizing rope jumping benefit, Lahaina News, December 14, 1988: 16.

— name Marcus Kanahele and Cis George as co-chairs of residential campaign, Lahaina News, January 18, 1989: 5.

— to distribute heart health material to residents, Lahaina News, January 25, 1989: 5.

— warns public to beware of mail requests for donations, Lahaina News, April 5, 1989: 14.

— to hold home tour as fundraiser, Lahaina News, November 29, 1989: 36.

— begins "Neighbor-Neighbor" Campaign", Lahaina News, January 24, 1990: 2.

— to raise funds with door-to-door campaign, Lahaina News, February 7, 1990: 2.

— Sheldon Hanks raises most money in jump rope event, Lahaina News, May 15, 1991: 5.

— seeking volunteers for American Heart Month Drive, Lahaina News, October 29, 1992: 7.

— to host Upcountry Christmas Tour, Lahaina News, December 3, 1992: 3.

— presents Upcountry Christmas Tour of Homes and Christmas Craft Fair, Lahaina News, December 1, 1994: 16.

— to hold "Dance for Heart" benefit, Lahaina News, May 18, 1995: 4.

— to host "Dance for Heart", Lahaina News, June 6, 1996: 15.

— to teach Cardio Pulmonary Resuscitation, Lahaina News, October 24, 1996: 15.

— to hold Upcountry Christmas Tour of Homes, Lahaina News, December 3, 1998: 11.

— hosting events for American Heart Month, Lahaina News, January 28, 1999: 6.

— hosting activities for American Heart Month, Lahaina News, February 4, 1999: 9.

— to hold activities for "Stroke Awareness and National High Blood Pressure Month", Lahaina News, May 13, 1999: 15.

— to hold "Old Wailuku Town Christmas House Tour", Lahaina News, December 2, 1999: 17.

— to hold Heart Walk and Health Fair, Lahaina News, January 20, 2000: 7.

— Valley Isle Masters Swimmers to hold annual benefit for, Lahaina News, February 10, 2000: 9.

— Heart Walk and Health Fair to be held, Lahaina News, February 10, 2000: 9.

— to conduct free blood pressure screenings, Lahaina News, February 17, 2000: 16.

— to hold Heart Walk and Health Fair, Lahaina News, February 24, 2000: 6.

— to hold Hawaii Heart Walk Maui 2001, Lahaina News, February 1, 2001: 15.

— to hold Hawaii Heart Walk Maui 2001, Lahaina News, February 15, 2001: 13.

— to hold Hawaii Heart Walk Maui, Lahaina News, February 22, 2001: 16.

— to hold "Black Tie and Blue Jeans—A Tropical Night", Lahaina News, August 9, 2001: 16.

— to hold CPR class, Lahaina News, November 15, 2001: 16,17.

— to hold "Black Tie and Blue Jeans" fundraiser, Lahaina News, August 15, 2002: 3,9.

— to hold Heart Walk, Lahaina News, February 13, 2003: 2.

— King and Queen of Hearts Campaign to benefit, Lahaina News, July 31, 2003: 18.

— to hold "A Night in the Garden of Magic and Music", Lahaina News, August 21, 2003: 2.

AMERICAN HERITAGE HOMES [BUSINESS]

— construction company featured, Lahaina News, February 10, 2000: 13.

AMERICAN INDIAN DANCE THEATRE [TROUPE]
— to perform at the Maui Inter-Continental Wailea Resort, Lahaina News, March 18, 1993: 12.
— to perform traditional and modern Native American dances, Lahaina News, January 18, 2001: 17.

AMERICAN INDIANS
— Intertribal Council of Hawaii Maui Powwow to be held, Lahaina News, May 22, 1997: 17.

AMERICAN INSTITUTE OF ARCHITECTS, MAUI CHAPTER
— announces scholarship, Lahaina News, March 9, 1988: 17.
— to host bridge building contest, Lahaina News, April 5, 1989: 3.
— offering scholarships, Lahaina News, April 19, 1989: 13.
— awards scholarships, Lahaina News, August 2, 1989: 9.
— to hold seminar on neotraditional town planning and affordable housing, Lahaina News, September 5, 1990: 6.
— offers scholarships, Lahaina News, April 17, 1991: 7.
— to hold golf tournament, Lahaina News, June 6, 1991: 9.
— hosting golf tournament, Lahaina News, June 20, 1991: 4.
— looking for teams to play in golf tournament fundraiser, Lahaina News, April 30, 1992: 7.
— new officers installed, Lahaina News, February 4, 1993: 10.

AMERICAN ISUZU MOTORS [BUSINESS]
— will sponsor Kapalua International golf tournament, Lahaina News, October 3, 1984: 13.
— no longer title sponsor of Isuzu Kapalua International Golf Tournament, Lahaina News, November 14, 1990: 11,12.

AMERICAN LAND TITLE ASSOCIATION
— to hold convention, Lahaina News, October 8, 1992: 8.
— to hold convention in West Maui, Lahaina News, October 15, 1992: 8.

AMERICAN LEGION
— to meet, seeking members, Lahaina News, February 23, 1995: 2.
— to hold meeting, Lahaina News, March 30, 1995: 6.
— to hold meeting, Lahaina News, July 20, 1995: 5.
— Lahaina post to hold pancake breakfast, Lahaina News, November 23, 1995: 4.

AMERICAN LUNG ASSOCIATION
— planning "Superkids" Day, Lahaina News, February 10, 1988: 3.
— offers smoking cessation program, Lahaina News, September 14, 1988: 3.
— offering scholarships, Lahaina News, January 18, 1989: 5.
— to hold discussion on drug use, Lahaina News, March 8, 1989: 17.
— to host classes on emphysema and chronic bronchitis, Lahaina News, March 29, 1989: 14.
— to hold annual dinner, Lahaina News, May 31, 1989: 3.
— program on controlling asthma, Lahaina News, June 7, 1989: 5.
— sponsoring "Bike Trek", Lahaina News, August 30, 1989: 3.
— offering "Freedom From Smoking" program, Lahaina News, September 20, 1989: 3.
— encouraging bicyclists to complete in fall Trek on the island of Hawaii, Lahaina News, October 3, 1990: 7.
— to hold Superkids fundraiser, Lahaina News, February 20, 1991: 5.
— to host Dr. Richard Ando, Jr. to speak on asthma treatment, Lahaina News, April 3, 1991: 4.
— to hold annual meeting at Chart House, Lahaina News, May 23, 1991: 3.
— to offer Kokua Na Keiki (Help the Children) classes, Lahaina News, June 6, 1991: 5.
— to hold classes on asthma, Lahaina News, June 13, 1991: 6.
— to hold cycling fund-raiser, Lahaina News, October 10, 1991: 8.
— Jacqueline Frost joins staff of, Lahaina News, October 17, 1991: 7.
— selling "Entertainment '92" books, Lahaina News, December 26, 1991: 4.

— selling "Entertainment '92" books, Lahaina News, January 2, 1992: 5.
— to hold Senior Stroll, Lahaina News, February 11, 1993: 5.
— to sponsor Office Olympics, Lahaina News, June 17, 1993: 3.
— to sell Entertainment Books for fundraiser, Lahaina News, September 8, 1994: 5.
— offering Golf Privilege Card fundraiser, Lahaina News, December 15, 1994: 8.
— to hold Weekend Neighbor Island Bike Trek, Lahaina News, August 24, 1995: 6.
— Lahaina Refrigeration and Services selling Entertainment '96 coupon book for, Lahaina News, October 12, 1995: 14,15.
— selling Entertainment Book, Lahaina News, December 14, 1995: 14.
— offering Golf Privilege Card, Lahaina News, December 28, 1995: 7.
— Superkids event to be held, Lahaina News, January 18, 1996: 6.
— to hold fund-raiser, Lahaina News, February 6, 1997: 15.
— to sell Entertainment Book, Lahaina News, September 11, 1997: 2.
— to organize Office Olympics, Lahaina News, June 4, 1998: 9.
— to hold "Office Olympics", Lahaina News, June 11, 1998: 17.
— continues to seek entrants for Office Olympics, Lahaina News, June 18, 1998: 16.
— asthma program to be shown, Lahaina News, June 18, 1998: 17.
— to sell Entertainment Book, Lahaina News, September 17, 1998: 25.
— to hold Crazy Cannery Olympics benefit, Lahaina News, November 5, 1998: 16.
— to host "Great American Smokeout", Lahaina News, November 19, 1998: 16.
— to hold Winter Ball fundraiser, Lahaina News, December 17, 1998: 11.
— to host "Winter Ball" fundraiser, Lahaina News, January 14, 1999: 12.
— organizing "Office Olympics", Lahaina News, May 6, 1999: 15.
— holds Office Olympics, Lahaina News, June 10, 1999: 13.
— to hold seminar on indoor air quality, Lahaina News, September 9, 1999: 13.
— raising money with "Viva Las Vegas Sweepstakes", Lahaina News, October 14, 1999: 5.
— holding "Viva Las Vegas Sweepstakes", Lahaina News, October 21, 1999: 16.
— hosting "Superkids" day of athletic events, Lahaina News, February 10, 2000: 9.
— to hold "Viva Las Vegas Sweepstakes" fundraiser, Lahaina News, June 22, 2000: 16.
— to hold Last Chance Auto Roundup fundraiser, Lahaina News, December 28, 2000: 16.
— selling Entertainment Book, Lahaina News, May 24, 2001: 3.
— to sell Entertainment Book as fundraiser, Lahaina News, July 4, 2002: 2.
— Hawaii Ballroom Dance Association to hold "Spring Ball" fundraiser for, Lahaina News, February 27, 2003: 9.
— to hold "Spring Ball" fundraiser, Lahaina News, March 6, 2003: 16.
— to hold Golf Ball Drop, Lahaina News, April 3, 2003: 13.

AMERICAN MARKETING ASSOCIATION
— Maui Chapter to meet, Lahaina News, May 16, 1984: 17.
— to hold luncheon, Lahaina News, October 17, 1984: 9.
— Maui Chapter meeting set, Lahaina News, November 28, 1984: 3.
— to meet in January at Maui Beach Hotel, Lahaina News, January 23, 1985: 3.
— Products and Media Auction to begin, Lahaina News, October 23, 1985: 20.
— Frank Blackwell to speak to Maui Chapter, Lahaina News, January 22, 1986: 3.

AMERICAN MASSAGE THERAPY ASSOCIATION
— to hold national education conference at Westin Maui, Lahaina News, May 27, 1993: 3.

AMERICAN MEDICAL RESPONSE
— to hold open house, Lahaina News, May 23, 1996: 2.
— ambulance crews to hold open houses, Lahaina News, May 11, 2000: 3.

AMERICAN RED CROSS
— cardio classes to be offered by, Lahaina News, April 9, 1986: 3.
— offering disaster response course, Lahaina News, September 24, 1986: 3.
— offering courses in CPR, First-Aid and water safety, Lahaina News, February 4, 1987: 11.
— to offer first aid training, Lahaina News, September 9, 1987: 3.
— to offer courses, Lahaina News, September 30, 1987: 3.
— to hold bachelor auction fundraiser, Lahaina News, May 23, 1990: 11.
— offering swimming lessons, Lahaina News, June 20, 1990: 8.
— offering swimming lessons, Lahaina News, June 11, 1992: 6.
— training to be held, Lahaina News, October 1, 1992: 4.
— to hold "Mak-Kap Bicycle Challenge", Lahaina News, May 27, 1993: 9.
— to hold a "Get to know us" party, Lahaina News, March 17, 1994: 4.
— to offer HIV/AIDS Educator training with Maui AIDS Foundation, Lahaina News, September 1, 1994: 7.
— to conduct training for disaster volunteers, Lahaina News, October 6, 1994: 7.
— to hold disaster volunteer training, Lahaina News, January 19, 1995: 4.
— announces "Emergency Management Guide for Business and Industry", Lahaina News, March 16, 1995: 10.
— golf tournament to benefit, Lahaina News, April 13, 1995: 9.
— to host "Disaster in Paradise" display, Lahaina News, March 7, 1996: 10.
— to hold swimming lessons, Lahaina News, July 11, 1996: 11.
— to teach CPR, Lahaina News, February 20, 1997: 10.
— offering CPR and First Aid classes, Lahaina News, June 12, 1997: 16.
— offering disaster training, Lahaina News, June 26, 1997: 17.
— Dee Brown discusses disaster preparedness, Lahaina News, June 10, 1999: 1,20.
— training disaster response volunteers, Lahaina News, May 3, 2001: 21.
— Wailea Golf Club and Valley Isle Timing Association to hold fundraisers for, Lahaina News, October 4, 2001: 13.
— Tesoro Hawaii raises money for, Lahaina News, October 4, 2001: 9.
— Enrique Ortiz new director of, Lahaina News, July 25, 2002: 2.

AMERICAN SAVINGS BANK [BUSINESS]
— opens in Ka'ahumanu Shopping Center, Lahaina News, January 5, 1995: 6.
— names new managers, Lahaina News, February 16, 1995: 13.
— Sharon Osato named manager of Lahaina branch, Lahaina News, May 18, 1995: 6.
— appoints Ida Ferris as branch manager, Lahaina News, July 10, 1997: 12.
— begins MortgageLine service, Lahaina News, March 18, 1999: 13.
— launches MortgageLine, Lahaina News, April 1, 1999: 13.

AMERICAN SEMINAR INSTITUTE [BUSINESS]
— opens office in Whalers Market Place, Lahaina News, October 16, 1985: 3.

AMERICAN SOCIETY OF MECHANICAL ENGINEERS
— to hold convention at Westin Maui, Lahaina News, April 2, 1992: 12.

AMERICAN SOCIETY OF TRAVEL AGENTS (ASTA)
— 1972 convention may be held in Ka'anapali, Lahaina Sun, April 7, 1971: 1.
— will meet in Ka'anapali in 1972, Lahaina Sun, April 21, 1971: 2.
— to hold convention in Ka'anapali in April 1972, Lahaina Sun, July 7, 1971: 2.
— Hawaii Chapter concerned that airline issues will not be addressed, Lahaina News, October 26, 2000: 20.

AMERICAN SOCIETY OF TRAVEL WRITERS
— 50 members visiting Ka'anapali, Lahaina Sun, April 21, 1971: 5.
— writers hosted in Maui, Lahaina Sun, May 12, 1971: 6.

AMERICAN UROLOGICAL ASSOCIATION
— post graduate course to meet, Lahaina News, October 8, 1992: 8.

AMERICAN WATER WORKS ASSOCIATION, HAWAII SECTION
— to hold workshop on current water technology and issues, Lahaina News, March 6, 1991: 5,7.

AMERICAN YOUTH AMBASSADORS
— hosted youth from the Soviet Union, Lahaina News, October 11, 1989: 3.

AMERICAN YOUTH SOCCER ASSOCIATION
— to hold registration, Lahaina News, May 17, 2001: 14.

AMERICANS ON EVEREST [FILM]
— to be shown at public libraries in Maui, Lahaina Sun, April 5, 1972: 14.

AMERICANS WITH DISABILITIES
— Act may not be expensive to implement, Lahaina News, June 2, 1994: 10.

AMERICA'S CUP
— results, Lahaina News, February 4, 1987: 10.
— Rocky Sargent piloting boat in, Lahaina News, March 18, 1987: 6.
— Hawaiian Electric supporting Hawaii effort, Lahaina News, August 5, 1987: 6.

AMERICORPS
— seeking volunteers to provide community service, Lahaina News, August 9, 2001: 2.

AMERSONS [FILM]
— presented by Wailea Shopping Complex, Lahaina News, February 18, 1987: 3.

AMFAC/JMB [BUSINESS]
— obtains permission to build apartments for low income families in Lahaina, Lahaina Sun, October 6, 1971: 5.
— sold land to Quality Pacific to build apartments, Lahaina Sun, December 8, 1971: 4.
— denies rumors it plans to purchase Lahaina-Ka'anapali & Pacific Railroad, Lahaina Sun, February 2, 1972: 5.
— promises to fight civil suit for alleged violations of price control rules, Lahaina Sun, May 31, 1972: 14.
— expansion to California described, Lahaina Sun, September 6, 1972: 17.
— Representative C. Earl Stoner responds to criticisms of project, Lahaina Sun, January 31, 1973: 7.
— profits rose in 1972, Lahaina Sun, February 7, 1973: 11.
— profits projected to rise, Lahaina Sun, June 6, 1973: 22.
— profits over the last decade were good, Lahaina News, April 1, 1980: 14.
— history of detailed, Lahaina News, July 15, 1980: 3.
— may sell hotels, including the Royal Lahaina, Lahaina News, April 15, 1982: 11.
— donates land to county for park and housing, Lahaina News, February 15, 1983: 6.
— planning development mauka of Honoapi'ilani Highway, Lahaina News, March 15, 1983: 10.
— donates $100,000 to West Maui Youth Center, Lahaina News, July 1, 1983: 6.
— reports loss for second quarter, Lahaina News, August 1, 1983: 11.
— opposes creating gas station and fast food restaurants at Kekaa Drive, Lahaina News, September 14, 1983: 5.
— public opposition to proposed fast food and gas station, Lahaina News, November 2, 1983: 14.
— submits plans for Hawaiian Sea Village, Lahaina News, February 6, 1985: 3.

— plan to develop "Hawaiian Sea Village", Lahaina News, April 17, 1985: 1.

— plans 600 acres of additional development in Ka'anapali, Lahaina News, September 25, 1985: 9.

— to develop North Beach with Tobishima Corp., Lahaina News, January 1, 1986: 3.

— to develop North Beach with Tobishima Corp., Lahaina News, January 1, 1986: 3.

— announces management appointments, Lahaina News, April 30, 1986: 3.

— considering cutting number of hotels planned for North Beach, Lahaina News, August 13, 1986: 3.

— requests delay in Sea Village timetable, Lahaina News, November 5, 1986: 3.

— donates to UH Foundation, Lahaina News, September 2, 1987: 3.

— extends reduced rates hotels for hotel in Los Angeles and San Francisco for, Lahaina News, December 16, 1987: 15.

— names Burt Hatton vice-president of land administration, Lahaina News, March 16, 1988: 3.

— appoints Charleen Ikeda as Senior Vice President, Lahaina News, April 27, 1988: 3.

— Maui County Planning Commission grants intervenor status to groups concerning North Beach Project, Lahaina News, June 1, 1988: 1.

— Sea Village receives extension of Special Management Area permit, Lahaina News, June 22, 1988: 3.

— donates to West Maui Youth Center, Lahaina News, July 13, 1988: 2,3.

— donates to United Way, Lahaina News, September 7, 1988: 3.

— Amfac to be purchased by JMB Realty Corp., Lahaina News, September 14, 1988: 1,20.

— details on planned developments, Lahaina News, September 21, 1988: 1,14.

— Amfac Distribution Hawaii, Inc to distribute General Electric products, Lahaina News, July 26, 1989: 6.

— offering relocation land for residents affected by Lahaina Bypass , Lahaina News, August 9, 1989: 1.

— Chris Kinard named vice president of human resources, Lahaina News, September 6, 1989: 2.

— moving ahead on Hawaiian Sea Village, Lahaina News, November 8, 1989: 1.

— names Bert Hatton vice president, sugar, Lahaina News, November 15, 1989: 9.

— appoints Paul Nelson as president of engineering and construction, Lahaina News, November 22, 1989: 5.

— opens landscape tree nursery in Ka'anapali, Lahaina News, November 29, 1989: 1.

— names Jan Kagehiro as Vice President of Corporate Communications, Lahaina News, December 13, 1989: 7.

— donates for scholarships at University of Hawaii, Lahaina News, January 3, 1990: 4.

— to convert 1800 acres of sugarcane production to development, Lahaina News, January 24, 1990: 1.

— creates diversified agriculture and planning department, Lahaina News, January 31, 1990: 5.

— Scott Yamauchi promoted to vice president of operations for Amfac Garden Hawaii, Lahaina News, April 4, 1990: 7.

— Michael Burke appointed manager of land administration, Lahaina News, April 11, 1990: 5.

— Amfac Distribution Hawaii, Inc reorganizes management structure, Lahaina News, May 16, 1990: 8.

— plans for West Maui to be discussed at West Maui Taxpayers Association annual meeting, Lahaina News, May 30, 1990: 5.

— puts Maui Ocean Center and Sea Village projects on hold, Lahaina News, June 13, 1990: 1.

— editorial thanking for sponsoring July 4th symphony, Lahaina News, July 4, 1990: 10.

— growing hedges along Honoapi'ilani Highway; editorial opposing, Lahaina News, August 1, 1990: 2,8.

— to submit revised offer to help develop swimming pool complex, Lahaina News, August 8, 1990: 1.

— mixed response to hedges being planted along Honoapi'ilani Highway, Lahaina News, August 8, 1990: 2.

— opinions on hedges along Honoapi'ilani Highway vary, Lahaina News, August 15, 1990: 3.

— shifting strategy for resort homes, Lahaina News, October 10, 1990: 1.

— appoints Corey Moriyama as manager of human resource development, Lahaina News, October 17, 1990: 12.

— loses money in second quarter, Lahaina News, October 31, 1990: 12.

— State Land Use Commission to hold public hearing on request to reclassify agricultural land, Lahaina News, December 5, 1990: 3.

— State Land Use Commission to hold public hearing on request to reclassify agricultural land, Lahaina News, December 12, 1990: 4.

— reports loss for third quarter, Lahaina News, December 19, 1990: 7.

— proposes "South Beach Mauka" housing project, Lahaina News, December 26, 1990: 1.

— to provide public parks in North Beach as part of development project, Lahaina News, December 26, 1990: 1.

— correction on story from December 19, 1990, Lahaina News, December 26, 1990: 7.

— redefining its development goals, Lahaina News, January 2, 1991: 1.

— Amfac Distribution Hawaii, Inc appoints Jeffrey Ashmore as senior vice president, Lahaina News, January 16, 1991: 5.

— reports profit, Lahaina News, July 18, 1991: 6.

— names Hale Makua as beneficiary of First Development Ka'anapali Classic Senior PGA tour event, Lahaina News, August 8, 1991: 6.

— may face new water rules due to TCP, Lahaina News, September 5, 1991: 1,2.

— partnering with The Nature Conservancy on pilot program to protect native forests above Honokowai, Lahaina News, January 16, 1992: 1.

— holds groundbreaking for park at North Beach, Lahaina News, January 16, 1992: 3.

— conducts survey of West Maui concerning development, Lahaina News, March 12, 1992: 1.

— changes in management announced, Lahaina News, March 19, 1992: 10.

— reports profits, Lahaina News, April 23, 1992: 15.

— to sell water to Maui County following landslide, Lahaina News, May 21, 1992: 1.

— donates to Hale Makua, Lahaina News, June 11, 1992: 4.

— planning to expand Pu'ukoli'i Village development, Lahaina News, July 9, 1992: 3.

— to host Ka'anapali Classic golf tournament, Lahaina News, August 20, 1992: 10.

— plans 1600 units in Pu'ukoli'i, Lahaina News, September 3, 1992: 3.

— to hold opening ceremony for Kahekili Park, Lahaina News, October 15, 1992: 3.

— threatens lawsuit to change designation for Camp Pecusa, Lahaina News, October 22, 1992: 3.

— shocked by Lahaina Community Plan advisory committee designates land at North Beach to park, Lahaina News, October 29, 1992: 1.

— proposes development in Pu'ukoli'i, Lahaina News, January 28, 1993: 3.

— to close Oahu operations, Lahaina to remain open, Lahaina News, August 12, 1993: 4.

— forms Labor-Management Committee with ILWU, Lahaina News, September 9, 1993: 7.

— profits rise, Lahaina News, September 16, 1993: 10.

— to restructure, Lahaina News, November 18, 1993: 7.

— Ka'anapali Coffee successful, Lahaina News, January 20, 1994: 6.

— installs new phone system, Lahaina News, May 19, 1994: 13.

— to host Ka'anapali Keiki Fishing Derby, Lahaina News, July 14, 1994: 9.

— plans luxury neighborhood in Ka'anapali, Lahaina News, October 27, 1994: 7.

— chooses Whalers Realty as listing agent for Ka'anapali Golf Estates, Lahaina News, November 3, 1994: 23.

— Affordable Housing Corp. rethinking plans for Lahainaluna Road Project on property owned by, Lahaina News, March 23, 1995: 1,16.

— to discuss plans for North Beach with West Maui Mayor's Advisory Committee, Lahaina News, April 27, 1995: 5.

— proposing controversial projects, Lahaina News, May 11, 1995: 16.

— request for strip mall before Maui County Council, Lahaina News, June 8, 1995: 5.

— Maui Council not ready to vote on mall proposed by, Lahaina News, July 27, 1995: 1,16.

— Ka'anapali Estate Coffee to open, Lahaina News, July 27, 1995: 10.

— Maui County Council changes position on shopping center proposed by , Lahaina News, November 23, 1995: 1,12.

— energy crops not ruled out, Lahaina News, January 18, 1996: 14.

— submits preliminary design plan for park mauka of West Maui Recreational Center, Lahaina News, January 25, 1996: 7.

— Jim Shimozono appointed general manager at, Lahaina News, April 25, 1996: 12.

— allowing sunset picnickers at Kahekili Park, Lahaina News, May 2, 1996: 3.

— to begin work on Pu'ukoli'i Village, Lahaina News, June 20, 1996: 2.

— may build time share at North Beach, Lahaina News, July 25, 1996: 1,16.

— plans for North Beach discussed, Lahaina News, July 25, 1996: 2.

— to hold meeting on proposed time share development at North Shore, Lahaina News, October 10, 1996: 1.

— to hold meeting on time share development at North Beach, Lahaina News, October 10, 1996: 14.

— may contribute land to expansion of Hanaka'o'o Beach Park, Lahaina News, October 17, 1996: 1,20.

— holds public meeting on proposed time share at North Beach, Lahaina News, October 24, 1996: 3.

— to donate land for homeless shelter, Lahaina News, November 28, 1996: 1,2.

— seeking approval for traffic mitigation plan at North Beach, Lahaina News, December 5, 1996: 1,20.

— seeking public support for highway widening, Lahaina News, January 16, 1997: 1,16.

— Maui Planning Commission to hold meeting to discuss request from, Lahaina News, January 23, 1997: 11.

— promotes expansion of Honoapi'ilani Highway, Lahaina News, January 23, 1997: 3.

— submits new plan for time share resort at North Beach, Lahaina News, April 10, 1997: 1.

— opens Ke Alii Subdivision, Lahaina News, June 12, 1997: 14.

— golf courses and resort area to use reclaimed water, Lahaina News, June 26, 1997: 3.

— president Chris Kanazawa discusses need for new visitor project, Lahaina News, June 26, 1997: 4.

— appoints Kimo Falconer as vice president of Ka'anapali Coffee and Pioneer Mill Company, Lahaina News, July 17, 1997: 13.

— appoints Dave Gleason as president of Hawaii golf division, Lahaina News, July 17, 1997: 13.

— Fishing Derby held, Lahaina News, July 24, 1997: 15.

— Alan Arakawa urges administration to purchase land at Olowalu, Lahaina News, January 22, 1998: 1,16.

— Amfac Property Development Corp sells parcel to mainland developer, Lahaina News, July 2, 1998: 12.

— says 733-acre lot in Olowalu under contract to be sold, Lahaina News, August 13, 1998: 1.

— Amfac Property Development Corp to install irrigation and sprinkler system at Ka'anapali North Course, Lahaina News, August 13, 1998: 13.

— concern over using cane haul as detour while highway is widened, Lahaina News, November 5, 1998: 1.

— announces that Pioneer Mill to stop growing sugar, Lahaina News, March 4, 1999: 1.

— future plans for Pioneer Mill discussed, Lahaina News, March 11, 1999: 1,11.

— update on financial situation on Pioneer Mill, Lahaina News, March 11, 1999: 11.

— to open 10-acre open space in Keka'a, Lahaina News, May 27, 1999: 3.

— plans to demolish Wainee Village homes, Lahaina News, August 19, 1999: 1,20.

— temporarily closes access to Keka'a, Lahaina News, September 23, 1999: 1,3.

— holding public meeting to help future planning, Lahaina News, November 11, 1999: 1,16.

— to diversify crops in Ka'anapali fields, Lahaina News, December 23, 1999: 1,2.

— petition circulated by Sophie Mataafa with request to plant and irrigate former Pioneer Mill sugar fields , Lahaina News, April 20, 2000: 1,8.

— break ground at expansion of Wainee Park, Lahaina News, June 22, 2000: 6.

— "Making it Pono" group pitches courses and project mix in Ka'anapali, Lahaina News, July 20, 2000: 1,9.

— members of "Ka'anapali 2020: Making it Pono" explain vision, Lahaina News, January 18, 2001: 1,7.

— Gary Nickele new president, Lahaina News, March 15, 2001: 9.

— responds to resident concern for dust, Lahaina News, April 26, 2001: 1,22.

— residents ask about Ka'anapali 2020 report, Lahaina News, May 24, 2001: 1,22.

— changes name to Ka'anapali Development Corp, Lahaina News, October 24, 2002: 1,16.

— developing master plan for area above Lahaina, Lahaina News, October 24, 2002: 1,16.

— see also Island Holidays, Whaler's Village, specific businesses and projects

AMILIO'S SUB SHOP [RESTAURANT]

— featured, Lahaina News, December 14, 1983: 16.

AMONCIO, KANAAN

— to perform in The Wizard of Oz, Lahaina News, July 19, 2001: 3.

AMONG, MIKAHALA

— high school outreach counselor featured, Lahaina News, April 11, 1984: 16.

AMOS TECHNICAL CONFERENCE

— to be held, Lahaina News, August 26, 1999: 14.

AMOS, WALLY

— cookie maker to be guest speaker at Unity Church of Maui, Lahaina News, July 8, 1987: 24.

— founder of Famous Amos cookie company to speak, Lahaina News, April 3, 1997: 13.

— cookie maker to sign his book "The Cookie Never Crumbles", Lahaina News, November 22, 2001: 20.

AMOUR, SCOTT [ARTIST]

— to exhibit at Lahaina Arts Society, Lahaina News, November 15, 2001: 16.

AMPAC MORTGAGE LENDING CORPORATION [BUSINESS]
— offering residential mortgage program, Lahaina News, January 30, 1985: 18.

AMPONG, FOSTER
— joins group working on Mo'o Kiha canoe, Lahaina News, April 4, 1996: 2.

AN DIE MUSICK [MUSICAL GROUP]
— to perform at Makawao Union Church, Lahaina News, January 11, 1996: 14.

ANAKA [TRAIN]
— refurbishment completed, Lahaina News, September 10, 1986: 16.
— operational, Lahaina News, November 19, 1986: 16.

ANASTASIS [SHIP]
— arrives in Maui with missionaries from Youth With a Mission, Lahaina News, January 18, 1984: 10.

ANCHETA, GAYLE
— Scholar/Athlete of the Week, Lahaina News, February 1, 1996: 7.

ANCHETA, KAREN
— appointed to Mayor Linda Lingle's Youth Advisory Council, Lahaina News, January 25, 1996: 4.

ANCHETA, KAREN AND GAYLE
— success of local students , Lahaina News, January 10, 2002: 1,18.

ANCHOR SQUARE
— improvements being made, Lahaina News, July 25, 1996: 7.

ANCIENT MARINER'S CLASSIC YACHT RACE
— see San Diego-Maui yacht race

AND A NIGHTINGALE SANG [PLAY]
— to be performed by Seabury Hall Performing Arts, Lahaina News, February 15, 2001: 16.
— being performed, Lahaina News, February 22, 2001: 16.

ANDAGAN, STACIA
— Sylvan Learning Center director featured, Lahaina News, July 9, 1992: 13.

ANDAYA, HERMAN [POLITICIAN]
— to hold public meeting, Lahaina News, September 5, 2002: 5.

ANDELIN, LINDA [ARTIST]
— exhibiting at Royal Art Gallery, Lahaina News, November 22, 1989: 14.

ANDELIN, PAMELA [ARTIST]
— to offer classes, Lahaina News, March 13, 1985: 24.
— featured at The Village Galleries, Lahaina News, January 14, 1987: 3.
— featured at Village Galleries, Lahaina News, February 7, 1990: 15.
— to exhibit at Village Galleries, Lahaina News, February 2, 1995: 11.
— to display work at Kapalua Bay Hotel, Lahaina News, July 16, 1998: 17.
— to exhibit new work at Village Gallery Contemporary, Lahaina News, March 16, 2000: 12.
— to exhibit at Village Galleries, Lahaina News, January 23, 2003: 16.

ANDELLA, LINDA [ARTIST]
— exhibiting at Royal Art Gallery, Lahaina News, March 27, 1991: 18.

ANDERSON, ANDY [POLITICIAN]
— gubernatorial candidate discusses government waste, Lahaina News, September 1, 1982: 4.
— opens campaign headquarters, Lahaina News, August 6, 1986: 20.
— campaign headquarters described [with photographs], Lahaina News, August 20, 1986: 1,3.
— attends ceremony for Research and Technology Park, Lahaina News, October 8, 1986: 1.
— Republican Party chair to attend fundraiser for Linda Lingle, Lahaina News, September 6, 1989: 24.

— gubernatorial candidate to speak, Lahaina News, July 25, 2002: 16.
— shares gubernatorial platform, Lahaina News, August 8, 2002: 9.

ANDERSON, BRUCE
— deputy director of the Department of Health wants larger ocean study, Lahaina News, September 2, 1993: 1,12.
— returns to head state's environmental programs, Lahaina News, March 30, 1995: 2.

ANDERSON, BUD [COMEDIAN]
— to perform at Comedy Club and the Sports Page, Lahaina News, November 5, 1992: 14,17.

ANDERSON, CRAIG
— new manager of The Westin Maui, Starwood Hotels and Resorts, Lahaina News, January 17, 2002: 8.

ANDERSON, D. G. "ANDY" [POLITICIAN]
— gubernatorial candidate to speak to Maui Chamber of Commerce, Lahaina News, March 28, 2002: 15.

ANDERSON, ELIZABETH
— historic cemeteries researcher to offer tours with Jim Luckey, Lahaina News, April 3, 1991: 3.

ANDERSON, JOHN
— presidential candidate opens office in Maui, Lahaina News, August 1, 1980: 6.

ANDERSON, JUDY
— joins staff at Oihana Property Management & Sales, Inc. as office manager of bookkeeping department, Lahaina News, October 3, 1990: 9.

ANDERSON, LAURIE [MUSICIAN]
— to perform at Maui Arts and Cultural Center, Lahaina News, February 21, 2002: 16,17.

ANDERSON, LUCIE [ARTIST]
— to exhibit at Lahaina Art Society show, Lahaina News, July 15, 1993: 12.

ANDERSON, MAL [TENNIS PLAYER]
— wins Grand Master's Tournament on Maui, Lahaina News, April 17, 1985: 4.

ANDERSON, MARK
— wins Hobie-Kimo Jerry Boser Memorial Longboard Contest, Lahaina News, August 1, 1990: 14.
— surfer featured, Lahaina News, August 31, 1995: 1.

ANDERSON, PAMELA
— taping MTV sports special at Studio 505, Lahaina News, July 23, 1992: 19.

ANDERSON, R. ALEX
— composer profiled on Hawaii Public Television, Lahaina News, December 12, 1991: 24.

ANDERSON, SCOTT [MUSICIAN]
— to perform at Maui Community College, Lahaina News, March 18, 1993: 12.

ANDERSON, STEPHANIE [MUSICIAN]
— to perform at Honolulu Coffee Co., Lahaina News, August 29, 2002: 20.

ANDERSON, WILLIS
— discusses stoppage of hotel construction in Kahana, Lahaina Sun, May 12, 1971: 2.

ANDO, RICHARD, JR. [DOCTOR]
— hosted by American Lung Association to speak on asthma treatment, Lahaina News, April 3, 1991: 4.

ANDRADE, ALBERTO
— appointed assistant general manager of Stouffer Wailea Beach Resort, Lahaina News, March 21, 1984: 17.

ANDRADE, RICHARD [POLITICIAN]
— candidate profiled, Lahaina News, September 12, 1990: 6.

ANDRASICK, JAMES
— appointed senior vice president at Alexander and Baldwin, Lahaina News, May 25, 2000: 16.

ANDREWS, FRANK [ARTIST]
— to paint at Village Galleries, Lahaina News, June 12, 2003: 20.

ANDREWS, JOSEPH
— promoted to branch manager at Bank of Hawaii, Lahaina News, March 26, 1992: 10.
— promoted to branch manager at Bank of Hawaii's Pukalani Branch, Lahaina News, December 3, 1992: 4.

ANDRION, ALMA
— killed in automotive accident on Kahekili highway near Waihee, Lahaina Sun, August 4, 1971: 11.

ANDRION, RODOLFO
— killed in automotive accident on Kahekili highway near Waihee, Lahaina Sun, August 4, 1971: 11.

ANDRION, SAMSON
— killed in automotive accident on Kahekili highway near Waihee, Lahaina Sun, August 4, 1971: 11.

ANDRUS, DONALD
— wins grand prize in "Jingle Balls Rock" promotion at Lahaina Cannery Mall, Lahaina News, January 3, 2002: 8.

ANDRY DANCE STUDIO [BUSINESS]
— to hold annual "Showcase and Dinner Dance", Lahaina News, July 30, 1998: 17.

ANESTHESIA [MUSICAL GROUP]
— featured, Lahaina News, May 7, 1992: 19.
— to release new album, Lahaina News, January 28, 1993: 13.
— to perform at Maui Tropical Plantation, Lahaina News, May 5, 1994: 16.

ANGEL, WENDY [ARTIST]
— to exhibit at Maui Sculpture Gallery, Lahaina News, July 30, 1992: 18.

ANGELO, ROBERT [ACTOR]
— featured, Lahaina News, April 12, 1989: 9.
— to offer writing workshops, Lahaina News, August 20, 1992: 14.
— play to be performed, Lahaina News, May 13, 1993: 10.
— performs in "Mad Cloak", Lahaina News, September 25, 2003: 2.

ANHEUSER-BUSCH [BUSINESS]
— Jana Satterfield promoted to marketing manager, Lahaina News, October 2, 2003: 8.

ANHEUSER-BUSCH FOUNDATION
— donates money for conservation of the nene, Lahaina News, November 16, 2000: 12.

ANIMAL ALOHA PROGRAM
— Maui Humane Society holds fundraiser with Maui restaurants, Lahaina News, May 3, 2001: 9.

ANIMAL FARM
— occupants of building on Front Street evicted, Lahaina Sun, January 27, 1971: 1,5.
— photograph of building on Front Street, Lahaina Sun, January 27, 1971: 4.
— building on Front Street discussed by Steve Omar, Lahaina Sun, February 3, 1971: 6.
— eviction notice for building on Front Street given, Lahaina Sun, February 24, 1971: 7.
— Jeffrey "Hulk" Zaugg reflects on living in building on Front Street, Lahaina News, October 2, 2003: 1,20.

ANIMAL PLANET [TELEVISION SHOW]
— to hold keiki game "Animal Planet Zooventure", Lahaina News, August 23, 2001: 16.

ANIMALS
— State Department of Agriculture issues warning on prolific pets, Lahaina Sun, February 16, 1972: 9.
— parrot at Whaler's Village described, Lahaina Sun, February 23, 1972: 15.
— three pair of nene on exhibit at Haleakala National Park, Lahaina Sun, March 22, 1972: 10.
— rubber crocodile causes concern, Lahaina Sun, March 29, 1972: 3.
— State Board of Agriculture approves importation of exotic animals to Moloka'i, Lahaina Sun, April 5, 1972: 14.
— experiences with local pets described, Lahaina Sun, August 2, 1972: 17.
— description of death of a cow, Lahaina Sun, July 18, 1973: 5.
— leash law proposed, Lahaina Sun, July 25, 1973: 4.
— Nene goose established in Haleakala crater, Lahaina Sun, August 15, 1973: 7.
— 1224 dogs killed on Maui, Lahaina News, May 15, 1980: 14.
— nene at Volcanoes National Park killed by a stray dog, Lahaina News, May 15, 1980: 7.
— Navy kills goats with machine guns on Kaho'olawe, Lahaina News, June 15, 1980: 19.
— Maui Dog Wardens issuing citations, Lahaina News, July 1, 1980: 14.
— unleashed dogs seen as potential cause of traffic accidents, Lahaina News, July 1, 1980: 7.
— dog owners lose fight against citations for loose dogs, Lahaina News, August 1, 1980: 7.
— Maui County kills dogs and cats, Lahaina News, August 15, 1980: 10.
— County Human Concerns director Velsa Santos seeks power to deputize dog wardens, Lahaina News, September 1, 1980: 8.
— cost to board dogs going up, Lahaina News, January 1, 1981: 1.
— discussion of common pet ailments, Lahaina News, January 15, 1981: 16.
— procedures for catching stay dogs detailed, Lahaina News, March 1, 1981: 15.
— care and feeding of wild birds detailed, Lahaina News, May 1, 1981: 8,9.
— Furs and Feathers column begins in Lahaina News, Lahaina News, September 1, 1981: 4.
— mayor urges police and judges to act on leash laws, Lahaina News, April 15, 1982: 12.
— leash law citations up, Lahaina News, May 1, 1982: 10.
— care and feeding of wild birds detailed, Lahaina News, May 1, 1982: 9.
— breeding pen for Nene to be created at Haleakala National Park, Lahaina News, May 15, 1983: 6.
— fines for loose dogs increased, Lahaina News, July 1, 1983: 6.
— horseback riding on Maui described, Lahaina News, June 6, 1984: 7,8,9.
— brochure on dog control available at County Animal Shelter, Lahaina News, September 11, 1985: 3.
— fashion show for pets to benefit Maui Humane Society, Lahaina News, November 5, 1986: 3.
— Furs and Feathers column starts again in Lahaina News, printed sporadically, Lahaina News, May 27, 1987: 12.
— Pet Day at Ka'ahumanu Center, Lahaina News, January 18, 1989: 6.
— poisonings in Kihei and Upcountry reported, Lahaina News, March 19, 1992: 4.
— deer rescued from waters off Lahaina, Lahaina News, October 15, 1992: 1.
— debilitated calves found, died, Lahaina News, September 23, 1993: 6.
— wild boar frequenting Napili neighborhood, Lahaina News, September 30, 1999: 1,16.

ANNA, KAREN [ARTIST]
— work of photographer to be exhibited in Makawao, Lahaina News, July 10, 1985: 3.

ANNENBERG, ANDREW [ARTIST]
— work displayed at Wyland Galleries, Lahaina News, August 9, 1989: 13.
— to be guest at Wyland Galleries, Lahaina News, April 25, 1990: 17.
— opens exhibit at Metropolitan Gallery, Lahaina News, July 18, 1991: 13.
— to exhibit at Sea Side Fine Art, Lahaina News, April 4, 1996: 15,16.
— featured, Lahaina News, August 22, 1996: 17.
— work with Élan Vital featured, Lahaina News, February 27, 1997: 14,16.

ANNEXATION
— Na Kupuna o Maui to demonstrate against, Lahaina News, October 9, 1997: 20.
— Noenoe Silva to speak on petitions opposing annexation, Lahaina News, August 27, 1998: 3.
— remembered, Lahaina News, September 26, 2002: 2.

ANNIE [MUSICAL]
— to be performed by Maui Youth Theatre, Lahaina News, February 27, 1985: 3.
— to be performed at Baldwin Theatre Guild, Lahaina News, August 1, 1996: 21.
— to open at Baldwin High School, Lahaina News, August 8, 1996: 16.

ANNIE GET YOUR GUN [PLAY]
— performed by Maui Community Theatre, Lahaina News, January 14, 1987: 3.
— schedule set, Lahaina News, January 28, 1987: 3.

ANNIE JR. [MUSICAL]
— to be held by Maui Academy of Performing Arts, Lahaina News, August 2, 2001: 16.

ANNO, KELBY
— windsurfer featured, Lahaina News, April 4, 1984: 4.

ANN'S PLACE [BUSINESS]
— featured, Lahaina News, January 18, 1984: 14.

ANOGIANAKIS, MARIA
— to teach candle making at The Art School at Kapalua, Lahaina News, July 26, 2001: 17.

ANONSEN, WILLIAM
— becomes Harbors District Engineer for Maui, Lahaina News, June 19, 1997: 15.

ANSAI, TOSHI
— elected president of Maui County Unit of the Hawaii Heart Association, Lahaina Sun, June 30, 1971: 3.

ANSWERING SERVICE
— opens in Kihei, Lahaina News, February 27, 1991: 8.

ANTARCTICA
— Helen Reed recounts visit to, Part I, Lahaina News, July 18, 2002: 1,9.
— Helen Reed recounts visit to, Part II, Lahaina News, July 25, 2002: 10,11.

ANTES, ROBERT
— promoted to director of finance at Grand Hyatt Bali, Lahaina News, September 26, 1990: 9.

ANTHEM [MUSICAL GROUP]
— to perform at Polli's On the Beach, Lahaina News, February 20, 1991: 11.
— formerly called "Keep the Secret", Lahaina News, February 20, 1991: 11.

ANTHONY, ARLENE MARCO [ARTIST]
— wins Lahaina Town Action Committee poster contest, Lahaina News, September 30, 1993: 4.
— to sign 1994 Lahaina poster during Art Night, Lahaina News, December 30, 1993: 10.

ANTHONY, JOHN
— joins Maui Community Television, Lahaina News, August 12, 1993: 6.

ANTHONY NOVAK-CLIFFORD PHOTOGRAPHY [BUSINESS]
— relocates, Lahaina News, January 27, 1994: 5.
— receives Pele award, Lahaina News, March 2, 1995: 7

ANTHURIUMS
— report on numbers shipped to mainland, Lahaina Sun, June 27, 1973: 7.

ANTOHIN, ANATOLY [ARTIST]
— work described, Lahaina News, July 1, 1981: 17.

ANTOINETTE'S FINE GIFTS [BUSINESS]
— opens at Wharf Cinema Center, Lahaina News, August 24, 1995: 10.

ANTONE, DESMON [MUSICIAN]
— to perform at Makai Bar Maui Marriott Resort, Lahaina News, April 21, 1994: 15.
— to perform at Makai Bar, Lahaina News, March 28, 1996: 13.
— to perform at Makai Bar, Lahaina News, April 4, 1996: 15.

ANTOSCH, MARC
— documentary "Ma'alaea Under Fire" to be shown, Lahaina News, May 13, 1999: 17.

ANTOSIK, ANDY
— Pearl Harbor survivor living in Puamana, Lahaina News, December 6, 2001: 1,18.

ANTOSIK, EUNICE
— president of Hawaii Federation of Garden Clubs, Lahaina News, June 27, 1991: 4.

ANUENUE ROOM [RESTAURANT]
— Ritz-Carlton restaurant featured, Lahaina News, May 6, 1999: 6,7.

ANURADHA
— to teach Sacred Dance Workshop, Lahaina News, August 21, 2003: 16.

ANZAI, EARL
— State Finance Director to speak to Maui Chamber of Commerce, Lahaina News, November 2, 1995: 2.
— Budget Director to discuss legislative proposals, Lahaina News, February 27, 1997: 11.

ANZALONE, TOM [COMEDIAN]
— to perform at Comedy Club and the Sports Page, Lahaina News, April 3, 1991: 7,8.

AOAO FINANCIAL SERVICES
— sponsors seminar on reducing pollution, Lahaina News, December 15, 1994: 2.

'AO'AO O NA LOKO I'A O MAUI
— hires Joseph Farber to assist in planning for fishpond restoration project, Lahaina News, September 13, 2001: 9.
— Association of the Fishponds of Maui seeking volunteers, Lahaina News, May 29, 2003: 9.
— Association of the Fishponds of Maui seeking volunteers, Lahaina News, June 26, 2003: 8.

AOKI, JOSLYN
— surfer wins Rookie of the Year, Lahaina News, October 22, 1998: 18.
— wins Roxy Girls Jam surfing contest, Lahaina News, June 15, 2000: 12.

AOKI, LEE
— lures described, Lahaina News, June 13, 1990: 9,24.
— designer of lures featured, Lahaina News, November 26, 1992: 6.

AOKI, ROCKY
— opens Benihana restaurant, Lahaina News, January 17, 1990: 12.

APAKA, JEFFREY [MUSICIAN]
— featured, Lahaina News, August 15, 1981: 4.

APANA, JAMES "KIMO" [POLITICIAN]
— to take questions live on television, Lahaina News, October 29, 1998: 6.
— Mayor-elect to meet with Maui Portuguese Chamber of Commerce, Lahaina News, November 26, 1998: 16.
— new Mayor to speak to LahainaTown Action Committee, Lahaina News, January 7, 1999: 3.
— to speak to Kihei Community Association, Lahaina News, January 14, 1999: 12.
— to speak to LahainaTown Action Committee, Lahaina News, January 14, 1999: 3.
— meets with residents to hear requests for county budget, Lahaina News, January 21, 1999: 1,16.
— to speak at LahainaTown Action Committee town meeting, Lahaina News, January 21, 1999: 3.
— Mayor discusses ways to improve parking in Lahaina, Lahaina News, January 28, 1999: 1,16.
— to introduce cabinet, Lahaina News, March 11, 1999: 11.
— attends ground breaking at Napili Park, Lahaina News, June 3, 1999: 1.
— approved grants based on recommendations from Grants Review Committee, Lahaina News, July 8, 1999: 5.
— to lead Mayor's Ball, Lahaina News, August 19, 1999: 14.
— discusses Complete Business Solutions, Inc (CBSI) helping modernize operations, Lahaina News, September 16, 1999: 3.
— to hear county budget requests, Lahaina News, October 7, 1999: 1.
— taking budget requests, Lahaina News, October 14, 1999: 1,16.
— forming regional panels, Lahaina News, October 21, 1999: 14.
— forming district advisory committees, Lahaina News, October 28, 1999: 13.
— hears concerns from Lahaina residents, Lahaina News, November 4, 1999: 1,16.
— seeking people interested in serving on county boards, commissions, and advisory committees, Lahaina News, November 4, 1999: 3.
— visits mainland for economic development campaign, Lahaina News, December 9, 1999: 6.
— budget is easy on cuts and taxes, Lahaina News, March 23, 2000: 1,16.
— to speak at Memorial Day Service, Lahaina News, May 18, 2000: 9.
— announces that Maui County found location for "A Taste of Lahaina", Lahaina News, June 22, 2000: 1,15.
— launches initiative to boost computer literacy, Lahaina News, July 27, 2000: 14.
— observes "9-1-1 Emergency Number Day", Lahaina News, September 14, 2000: 11.
— working to secure Warrior football game at War Memorial Stadium, Lahaina News, September 21, 2000: 11.
— Maui County to hold hearings on budget, Lahaina News, October 5, 2000: 7.
— to hold hearings on budget, Lahaina News, October 12, 2000: 6.
— announces need for resident to serve on county boards, commissions, and advisory committees, Lahaina News, October 19, 2000: 11.
— to hold hearing on budget, Lahaina News, October 19, 2000: 17.
— taking budget requests, Lahaina News, October 26, 2000: 14.
— recruiting residents for county boards, commissions, and advisory committees, Lahaina News, October 26, 2000: 14.
— extends applications for county boards and commissions, Lahaina News, November 30, 2000: 5.
— discusses parking problems in Lahaina, Lahaina News, January 25, 2001: 1.
— unveils plan to improve parking in Lahaina, Lahaina News, February 8, 2001: 1,22.
— announces choices for vacancies on county boards and commissions, Lahaina News, February 8, 2001: 3.
— meetings to target traffic issues, Lahaina News, February 22, 2001: 3.
— shares vision for West Maui, Lahaina News, March 22, 2001: 1,18.
— West Maui Senior Center included in budget, Lahaina News, March 22, 2001: 3.
— address on budget to be replayed on Akaku: Maui Community Television, Lahaina News, April 5, 2001: 20.
— signs proclamation for "James Manness Memorial 2001 Dance Odyssey" Day, Lahaina News, April 12, 2001: 17.
— met with West Maui Taxpayers Association, Lahaina News, April 26, 2001: 10.
— honors students for peace poetry, Lahaina News, June 14, 2001: 17.
— announces that recycling will continue, Lahaina News, July 26, 2001: 8.
— to hold District Town meetings, Lahaina News, August 16, 2001: 2.
— to offer District Town Meetings, Lahaina News, August 23, 2001: 16.
— to explain new Historic District Sign Design Guidelines, Lahaina News, September 13, 2001: 9.
— to hold meeting at Lahaina Civic Center on Historic District Sign Design Guidelines, Lahaina News, September 20, 2001: 9.
— responds to financial fallout of the September 11th attack, Lahaina News, September 27, 2001: 1,8.
— to hold meeting on budget, Lahaina News, October 11, 2001: 2.
— hosting hearing on county budget, Lahaina News, October 25, 2001: 1.
— holds blessing at Countywide Service Center, Lahaina News, November 15, 2001: 2.
— to speak to Maui Non-Profit Directors' Legislative Breakfast, Lahaina News, November 29, 2001: 17.
— visits New York City Police with Ambassadors, Lahaina News, November 29, 2001: 3.
— to speak at Maui Chamber of Commerce, Lahaina News, November 29, 2001: 8.
— honors county workers, Lahaina News, December 13, 2001: 8.
— reports on increases in direct crisis assistance to Maui County through Hawaii Emergency Laulima Partnership (HELP), Lahaina News, December 27, 2001: 8.
— announces funding for the West Maui Skatepark Association, Lahaina News, January 10, 2002: 1,18.
— to present "State of the County Address", Lahaina News, February 7, 2002: 1.
— seeking nominations for Outstanding Older Americans Awards for Maui County, Lahaina News, March 21, 2002: 2.
— visits injection well sites in Kaua'ula Valley, Lahaina News, May 2, 2002: 1,20.
— mayor urges continued involvement in budget process, Lahaina News, May 2, 2002: 5.
— organizing District Town Hall Meetings, Lahaina News, June 6, 2002: 1,20.
— announces District Town Hall Meetings, Lahaina News, June 13, 2002: 2.
— begins reelection campaign, Lahaina News, June 20, 2002: 20.
— to hold fundraiser, Lahaina News, July 11, 2002: 8.
— endorsed by the Hawaii State Fire Fighters Association, Lahaina News, July 18, 2002: 2.
— to hold fundraiser for Tech Ready initiative, Lahaina News, July 18, 2002: 8.
— signs agreement with Maui Electric to support solar roofs, Lahaina News, September 19, 2002: 8.
— announces start of county's recruitment drive for county boards, commissions and committees, Lahaina News, October 17, 2002: 14.
— seeking commission members, Lahaina News, October 24, 2002: 15.
— to host the Mayor's Ball, Lahaina News, November 14, 2002: 17.
— Mayor's Ball to be held, Lahaina News, November 28, 2002: 16.
— recognizes County employees, Lahaina News, January 9, 2003: 8.

APANA, ROGER
— Maui Scrap Metal expecting metal shredder, Lahaina News, May 24, 1989: 1.

APERTO, JOHN [ARTIST]
— woodcarvings displayed by Lahaina Arts Society, Lahaina News, September 7, 1988: 14.
— holds "Ho'olokahi" exhibit with Susan Belle Jenson, Lahaina News, March 13, 1991: 13.

APIO, ALANI [WRITER]
— play "Kamau" to be read at Gallerie Ha, Lahaina News, October 31, 2002: 28.

APIO, KERMET [COMEDIAN]
— to perform at Comedy Club and the Sports Page, Lahaina News, February 4, 1993: 13,15.

APO, JAN K.
— attorney opens office, Lahaina News, January 26, 1995: 13.

APOLIONA, NICOLE MALIA
— doctor joins Kula Clinic, Lahaina News, August 15, 2002: 8.

APPLE ANNIE'S [RESTAURANT]
— will not be torn down as part of development of Hawaiian Sea Village, Lahaina News, May 8, 1985: 1.

APPLE HILL CHAMBER PLAYERS [MUSICAL GROUP]
— to perform at St. Anthony Church Center, Lahaina News, March 6, 1991: 17.

APPLE, RUSSEL
— research on Hale Pa'ahao, the old prison, Lahaina News, June 27, 1984: 7,8.

APPLE TREE, THE [PLAY]
— to be performed by The Maui Academy of Performing Arts, Lahaina News, April 24, 1991: 11.
— to be held the Maui Lu, Lahaina News, May 1, 1991: 16.
— presented by Maui Academy of Performing Arts, Lahaina News, May 8, 1991: 21.

APPLEBEY, GREGG [ARTIST]
— jewelry discussed, Lahaina News, August 1, 1984: 4.

APPLEBY, GAYLE BRIGHT [ARTIST]
— jewelry discussed, Lahaina News, August 1, 1984: 4.
— creates bronze sculpture for Iao Valley, Lahaina News, June 12, 1985: 11.

APPLEGATE, HAKU
— appointed general manager of Basil Tomatoes Italian Grille, Lahaina News, March 15, 2001: 8.

APPLEGATE, JON
— runs tomato farm at Olowalu, Lahaina News, March 21, 2002: 8.

APPLETON, JOY
— to discuss chemical sensitivity, Lahaina News, November 1, 1989: 6.

APPLEXION, USA
— develops technology with Hawaiian Commercial and Sugar Co. to recover additional sucrose from sugar cane juice, Lahaina News, October 20, 1994: 13.

APRIL FOOLS
— joke articles printed, not included in this index, Lahaina Sun, April 4, 1973: .
— 1982 edition, Lahaina News, April 1, 1982: .

AQUACULTURE
— finds only minimal interest in public hearing, Lahaina Sun, March 29, 1972: 4.
— possible future discussed, Lahaina Sun, June 13, 1973: 17.
— University of Hawai'i Sea Grant Extension to offer workshop on, Lahaina News, April 25, 1996: 6.
— Aquaculture Development Program continues, Lahaina News, September 4, 1997: 15.

AQUATIC CONTINENT CONFERENCE
— longlining criticized at, Lahaina News, August 25, 1994: 2.

AQUINO, EMALIA KAHILI
— discusses situation of native Hawaiian leadership, Lahaina Sun, June 7, 1972: 3.

AQUINO, MARC
— new loan officer at Charter Funding, Lahaina News, February 3, 2000: 11.

AQUINO, RHONDA [ARTIST]
— to paint at Hawai'i Nature Center Gift Shop, Lahaina News, April 5, 2001: 21.

AQUINO, RICHARD
— completes Marine Corp training, Lahaina News, August 1, 2002: 9.

ARABESQUE [BUSINESS]
— moves to Lahaina Center, Lahaina News, July 22, 1993: 7.

ARAKAKI, CHARLES
— appointed to State Public Utilities Commission, Lahaina Sun, January 26, 1972: 14.

ARAKAWA, ALAN [POLITICIAN]
— to host public meeting, Lahaina News, October 10, 1996: 14.
— urges administration to purchase land at Olowalu, Lahaina News, January 22, 1998: 1,16.
— opens campaign headquarters, Lahaina News, July 16, 1998: 9.
— opens headquarters, Lahaina News, July 23, 1998: 16.
— candidate for mayor to hold rally at Kula Community Center, Lahaina News, October 8, 1998: 7.
— to take questions live on television, Lahaina News, October 29, 1998: 6.
— candidate for Kahului County Council Seat, Lahaina News, November 2, 2000: 23.
— seeks approval for improved agriculture bill, Lahaina News, August 22, 2002: 1,2.
— mayor-elect names cabinet appointments, Lahaina News, December 12, 2002: 2.
— to be sworn in as mayor, Lahaina News, January 2, 2003: 1,20.
— recruiting members for boards, Lahaina News, January 23, 2003: 2.
— details Tech Ready campaign, Lahaina News, February 6, 2003: 8.
— to speak to Maui Chamber of Commerce, Lahaina News, February 20, 2003: 9.
— to speak to Maui Chamber of Commerce, Lahaina News, February 27, 2003: 8.
— to be guest speaker at Lahaina Restoration Foundation annual breakfast meeting, Lahaina News, March 20, 2003: 1.
— to speak to Lahaina Restoration Foundation, Lahaina News, March 27, 2003: 9.
— Kokua Fund accepting applicants, Lahaina News, April 24, 2003: 2.
— to speak to Haiku Community Association, Lahaina News, April 24, 2003: 20.
— message supporting International Festival of Canoes, Lahaina News, May 8, 2003: insert3.
— attends welcoming 'awa ceremony for International Festival of Canoes, Lahaina News, May 15, 2003: 1,3.
— Mayor to establish West Maui Advisory Committee, Lahaina News, June 12, 2003: 14.
— battling with Maui Council over budget, Lahaina News, June 12, 2003: 9.
— to establish Maui Mall Advisory Committee, Lahaina News, June 19, 2003: 9.
— to attend grand opening of Wailuku Police Resource Center, Lahaina News, July 24, 2003: 8.
— provides grant to Friends of Moku'ula, Lahaina News, August 28, 2003: 8.
— Mayor pledges to act on advice from West Maui Advisory Committee, Lahaina News, September 4, 2003: 1,20.

— Mayor plans public hearings on Maui County budget, Lahaina News, September 11, 2003: 9.

— invites participation in Maui County budget, Lahaina News, September 18, 2003: 2.

— hosts Masaru Funabashi who ran the Maui Marathon, Lahaina News, September 25, 2003: 3.

ARAKAWA, BRIAN

— coach featured, Lahaina News, January 9, 2003: 1.

ARAKAWA CHINESE FOOD [RESTAURANT]

— opens, Lahaina News, January 2, 1991: 5.

ARAKAWA, JORDAN

— chosen as celebrity bat boy, Lahaina News, September 10, 1998: 3.

ARAKAWA, MIKE

— Lahainaluna High School football coach featured, Lahaina News, October 31, 1991: 5.

ARAKI, FRED

— county highways chief speaks of solution to Wainee flooding issues, Lahaina News, October 25, 1989: 5.

ARAKI, LYNN A.S.

— wins Young Careerist Competition, Lahaina News, October 9, 1997: 14.

ARBITRON COMPANY [BUSINESS]

— releases report rating popularity of radio stations, Lahaina News, March 19, 1998: 11.

ARBOR DAY

— State to hold a tree sale to celebrate, Lahaina News, November 6, 1997: 16.

— community clean-up to be held at Maui Botanical Gardens, Lahaina News, November 13, 1997: 20.

ARBOR WEEK

— to be chaired by Apolonia Day, Lahaina News, November 5, 1992: 13.

— to be celebrated, Lahaina News, November 5, 1998: 8.

ARBY'S [RESTAURANT]

— planned for Lahaina, Lahaina News, August 1, 1984: 14.

— to open, Lahaina News, June 19, 1985: 8.

ARC OF MAUI

— running group home, Lahaina News, March 7, 1996: 4.

— has opening in its home in Napili, Lahaina News, February 22, 2001: 2.

— formerly called Maui Association for Retarded Citizens, Lahaina News, February 22, 2001: 2.

— seeks people with disabilities for lawsuit, Lahaina News, July 5, 2001: 5.

— featured, Lahaina News, June 20, 2002: 1,20.

— receives grant from Atherton Family Foundation, Lahaina News, February 27, 2003: 9.

— see also Maui Association of Retarded Citizens (MARC)

ARCANGEL, JENA

— Lahainaluna High School student wins Maui District "Brown Bags to Stardom", Lahaina News, March 10, 1994: 3.

— Heald Business College presents scholarship to Lahainaluna High School senior, Lahaina News, May 19, 1994: 5.

ARCANGEL, LISA

— Scholar/Athlete of the Week, Lahaina News, May 22, 1997: 13.

ARCANGLE, MICHAEL

— presided over May Day celebrations, Lahaina Sun, May 5, 1971: 2.

ARCHAEOLOGY

— Bishop Museum to study archaeological sites, Lahaina Sun, August 11, 1971: 5.

— County Planning Department maps significant sites on Maui, Lahaina News, December 1, 1981: 16.

— D.T. Fleming Park to be studied, Lahaina News, July 15, 1993: 1.

— Malu'ulu O Lele Park users asked not to play softball, Lahaina News, November 16, 1995: 1,20.

— state archaeologist Theresa Donham to speak on Wailuku Sand Dune, Lahaina News, February 13, 1997: 11.

— project to unearth old capital may begin in 2001, Lahaina News, September 30, 1999: 1,16.

— proposed subdivision delayed by disagreements over archaeological study of, Lahaina News, April 26, 2001: 1,22.

ARCHITECTURAL DESIGN AND CONSTRUCTION INC (ADC INC.) [BUSINESS]

— opens, Lahaina News, July 6, 2000: 9.

ARCHITECTURAL STYLE BOOK FOR LAHAINA [BOOK]

— published by the Maui Historic Commission, Lahaina Sun, November 25, 1970: 1.

ARCHITECTURE

— "Brick Palace" considered the first western-style building in Hawaii, Lahaina Sun, December 16, 1970: 6.

— a round house being built in Ka'anapali, Lahaina Sun, March 29, 1972: 9.

— exhibit at Bailey House Museum featuring plantation-era, Lahaina News, July 6, 1995: 11.

ARCONADO, JENIFER

— chosen as Hoku of the Year by Media Systems, Inc., Lahaina News, January 11, 1996: 11.

AREA PLAN ON AGING

— to be held, Lahaina News, March 27, 2003: 9.

ARF [AGAINST REGULATION AND FINES ORGANIZATION]

— see leash laws

ARGEL, GENE [MUSICIAN]

— interviewed about jazz, Lahaina News, May 15, 1985: 10.

— place in local music scene described, Lahaina News, November 5, 1986: 8.

— to perform at Villa Lounge, Lahaina News, August 13, 1992: 15.

— to perform at Cabana Café, Lahaina News, May 13, 1993: 12.

ARGENTINA TURNER MEMORIAL BLUES BAND [MUSICAL GROUP]

— to perform at Lopaka's Grill and Bar, Lahaina News, January 16, 1992: 18.

— continues to perform at Lopaka's Grill and Bar, Lahaina News, January 30, 1992: 21.

— to perform at Casanova's, Lahaina News, February 4, 1993: 15.

ARICAYAS, KEPA

— wins karaoke competition, Lahaina News, July 13, 2000: 9.

ARICAYOS, AUNTY DOLL

— organizer discusses King Kamehameha Day Parade, Lahaina News, June 13, 2002: 1,18.

ARICAYOS, CAROLEEN "AUNTY DOLL"

— kumu hula featured, Lahaina News, May 21, 1992: 13.

— hula teacher featured, Lahaina News, February 18, 1999: 1,16.

ARISUMI, ANTHONY "BUTCH"

— attempts to build low income housing described, Lahaina Sun, November 29, 1972: 4.

— Maui Planning Commission rejects request to build affordable housing, Lahaina Sun, December 13, 1972: 3.

— granted permission to build moderate cost housing in Kihei, Lahaina Sun, February 14, 1973: 3.

ARISUMI BROTHERS, INC. [BUSINESS]

— begins construction on Ma'alaea Harbor Village, Lahaina News, October 14, 1999: 11.

ARISUMI, JOHN

— union representative speaks of union demands in hotel strike, Lahaina Sun, November 11, 1970: 1.

ARISUMI, MITS AND HIROSHI
— purchase painting at fundraiser for Maui Filipino Community Council, Lahaina News, December 12, 1991: 17.

ARIYOSHI, GEORGE [POLITICIAN]
— lieutenant governor visits Maui, Lahaina Sun, November 24, 1971: 13.
— governor will not debate rivals Andy Anderson and Frank Fasi, Lahaina News, October 1, 1982: 11.
— editorial praising governor for vetoing proposed whale sanctuary, Lahaina News, July 18, 1984: 2.
— releases money for Honoapi'ilani Highway improvements, Lahaina News, September 10, 1986: 3.
— former governor on Japan Foundations Advisory Committee, Lahaina News, August 15, 1991: 7.

ARIYOSHI, HENRY "BRUNO"
— Lahainaluna High School principal requests portable classrooms, Lahaina News, May 23, 1990: 1,6.
— Lahainaluna High School principal receives check from McDonald's, Lahaina News, February 6, 1992: 5.
— named Principal of the Year, Lahaina News, July 16, 1992: 3.
— Lahainaluna High School principal receives award from Milken Family Foundation National Educator Award, Lahaina News, October 28, 1993: 1,12.
— Lahainaluna High School principal collects Milken Family Foundation National Educator Award, Lahaina News, March 10, 1994: 4.
— principal of Lahainaluna High School featured, Lahaina News, March 31, 1994: 1,5.
— Lahainaluna High School principal to retire, Lahaina News, June 1, 1995: 1,3.
— Lahainaluna High School principal to be honored, Lahaina News, June 15, 1995: 2.
— Lahainaluna High School principal to be honored, Lahaina News, June 29, 1995: 4.
— tickets available for celebration honoring, Lahaina News, August 3, 1995: 4.
— to be liaison for Senator Roz Baker, Lahaina News, December 12, 1996: 1.

ARKANSAW BEAR, THE [PLAY]
— to be performed by Maui Academy of Performing Arts, Lahaina News, December 30, 1993: 12.
— auditions continue, Lahaina News, January 6, 1994: 12.

ARLEDGE, TOM
— new pastor at Harvest Chapel Church, Lahaina News, March 27, 1991: 3.

ARLEN, LIZ
— to manage Nancy Emerson School of Surfing in Maui, Lahaina News, June 24, 1993: 10.

ARMORY PARK
— history recounted by Pua Lindsey, Lahaina News, November 19, 1986: 1.
— illegal campers at, Lahaina News, August 4, 1994: 2.
— pavilion closed because roof and support falling apart, Lahaina News, October 19, 1995: 1.

ARMSTRONG, DOUG
— selected as general manager for KHNL/13, Lahaina News, December 27, 1989: 5.

ARMSTRONG, RAMSEY
— member of Lahaina Kamaakina Fishing Association, Lahaina Sun, December 23, 1970: 11.

ARMY CORPS OF ENGINEERS, U.S.
— studying ocean floor of Lahaina, Lahaina Sun, November 18, 1970: 4.
— responds to recent flooding, Lahaina Sun, February 3, 1971: 1.

— improvements to Iao stream undertaken, Lahaina Sun, August 18, 1971: 11.
— seeking comments on proposed storm drain in Central Maui, Lahaina Sun, May 10, 1972: 11.
— plans for Kahului and Lahaina detailed, Lahaina Sun, October 25, 1972: 3.
— sets date for public meetings, Lahaina Sun, November 15, 1972: 11.
— create aerial photographs of Maui, Lahaina Sun, February 28, 1973: 12,13.
— recommends converting part of Kahoma stream to concrete channel as part of flood plan, Lahaina Sun, March 21, 1973: 1.
— studies Maui shoreline, Lahaina Sun, March 21, 1973: 9.
— agrees with Maui County to ease traffic bottleneck in Lahaina, Lahaina News, April 8, 1987: 1.
— to build moorings in West Maui, Lahaina News, January 6, 1988: 3.
— to improvement drainage at North Beach, Lahaina News, November 16, 1988: 1.
— authorizes drainage channel and desilting basin for Mahinahina Stream, Lahaina News, April 5, 1989: 1.
— endorses small boat launching ramp at Kahului Harbor, Lahaina News, August 30, 1989: 3.
— finds ancient Hawaiian remains while working on Kahoma Stream Flood Control project, Lahaina News, October 25, 1989: 3.
— estimates savings from flood damages by Kahoma Stream, Lahaina News, January 3, 1990: 2.
— completes Kahoma Flood Control Project, Lahaina News, June 6, 1990: 1.
— grants federal permit to Longs Drug Stores, Inc. to fill in wetlands, Lahaina News, November 28, 1990: 8.
— to study Lahaina Harbor, Lahaina News, May 28, 1992: 1.
— to complete study to expand Ma'alaea Harbor, Lahaina News, July 2, 1992: 7.
— may construct vertical reef at Keawakapu, Lahaina News, July 16, 1992: 7.
— to hold meeting to discuss plans for Ma'alaea Harbor, Lahaina News, December 10, 1992: 9.
— planning flood basins, Lahaina News, December 31, 1992: 1.
— studying possible harbor in West Maui, Lahaina News, October 27, 1994: 6.
— studying possible wetlands , Lahaina News, March 2, 1995: 16.
— studying wetlands at North Beach, Lahaina News, April 6, 1995: 1,16.
— concludes that wetland in development proposed by JGL will not be regulated, Lahaina News, May 11, 1995: 2.
— decision on Napili housing project to be challenged by Environmental Protection Agency, Lahaina News, July 6, 1995: 3.
— to hold public hearing on wetlands, Lahaina News, June 20, 1996: 13.

ARMY, U.S.
— to hold public hearing on chemical weapons disposal facility on Johnson Island, Lahaina News, July 27, 2000: 20.

ARNETTE, NICK [COMEDIAN]
— to perform at Honolulu Comedy Club, Lahaina News, March 28, 1996: 12.

ARNOLD, CEA
— wins prize at F.W. Woolworth, Lahaina News, February 7, 1990: 3.

ARNOLD, DOUG [WRITER]
— West Maui resident writes books on winning video games, Lahaina News, October 10, 1991: 3.
— publishes second book, "Awesome Sega Genesis Secrets", Lahaina News, January 23, 1992: 13.

ARNOLD, JOAN [ARTIST]
— to exhibit with Lahaina Arts Society, Lahaina News, May 9, 1996: 17.
— golf paintings featured, Lahaina News, August 8, 1996: 17.
— local artist and publisher passes away, Lahaina News, October 7, 1999: 1,2.

ARNOLD, STEPHEN
— promoted to director of sales at Atlantis Submarines, Lahaina News, March 19, 1992: 11.

ARNOLD, TERA
— teaches yoga, Lahaina News, May 31, 2001: 16.
— teaches yoga, Lahaina News, June 7, 2001: 20.

ARNOLD, TOM [ACTOR]
— reads "'Twas the Night Before Christmas" at private lunch at Planet Hollywood, Lahaina News, January 1, 1998: 5.

ARORA, RADHA
— new general manager at Four Seasons Resort Maui, Lahaina News, June 14, 2001: 8.

ARQUETTE, CLIFF
— discusses pollution in Maui, Lahaina Sun, February 3, 1971: 4.

ARRAUNT, ED
— developer given permission to build professional building on Wahie Lane, Lahaina News, May 23, 1991: 1.

ARRON, HANK
— baseball player participates in Legends of Baseball game, Lahaina News, December 26, 1984: 4.

ARROW AIRWAYS
— to start direct flights to Maui from the mainland, Lahaina News, June 1, 1982: 5.
— direct flights between Maui and mainland sold out, Lahaina News, June 15, 1982: 3.

ART
— gallery opening in Whaler's Village, Lahaina Sun, November 25, 1970: 3.
— macrame workshop held, Lahaina Sun, March 3, 1971: 4.
— exhibit of William Longyear at Lahaina Art Society Gallery, Lahaina Sun, March 3, 1971: 6.
— exhibit of Robert Schuman at Lahaina Art Society Gallery, Lahaina Sun, March 3, 1971: 6.
— opinions offered by Robert Kelsey, Lahaina Sun, April 7, 1971: 6.
— black velvet paintings by Jack Fisher displayed at Kula Lodge, Lahaina Sun, April 14, 1971: 8.
— tie-dying discussed, Lahaina Sun, April 21, 1971: 6.
— review of Skip Helling's work, Lahaina Sun, April 28, 1971: 7.
— 14-foot koa-wood tiki dedicated at Maui Community College, Lahaina Sun, May 19, 1971: 5.
— discussion of art as an investment, Lahaina Sun, June 16, 1971: 8.
— sculpture classes offered by Lahaina Art Society, Lahaina Sun, July 14, 1971: 10.
— program at Whalers Village announced, Lahaina Sun, September 1, 1971: 7.
— Paul Bryant's works exhibited at Edsco Laundromat, Lahaina Sun, September 8, 1971: 2.
— Jerome [artist] discussed, Lahaina Sun, September 15, 1971: 14.
— Lahaina Art Society offering courses, Lahaina Sun, September 22, 1971: 10.
— artists can sign up to sell items at the Diamond Head Crater Celebration, Lahaina Sun, November 17, 1971: 4.
— mural by John St. John to be destroyed, Lahaina Sun, January 12, 1972: 7.
— wood carver Bruce Turnbull offering classes, Lahaina Sun, January 19, 1972: 17.
— Tadashi Sato will create a mural in Lahaina, Lahaina Sun, January 19, 1972: 18.
— paintings by John St. John stolen, Lahaina Sun, March 22, 1972: 11.
— exhibit of watercolors of Hawaiian medicinal herbs by Nils Larsen at Lahaina Library, Lahaina Sun, March 29, 1972: 14.
— John St. John has left Maui due to lack of support for art in Lahaina, Lahaina Sun, April 19, 1972: 6.

— free classes offered this summer by the Lahaina Art Society, Lahaina Sun, June 7, 1972: 10.
— leather crafts described, Lahaina Sun, June 7, 1972: 21.
— Art Faire at Lahaina Prison planned, Lahaina Sun, April 25, 1973: 3.
— Old Lahaina Towne Art Faire planned, Lahaina Sun, June 6, 1973: 5.
— reflection on the artist's mind, Lahaina Sun, August 15, 1973: 21.
— Ho'olaulima Kuaina Weaving Guild to hold workshops, Lahaina Sun, August 15, 1973: 9.
— scrimshaw described, Lahaina News, July, 1979: 10.
— scrimshaw factory described, Lahaina News, August, 1979: 6.
— tattooing discussed, Lahaina News, July 1, 1980: 5.
— ceramics classes offered, Lahaina News, August 1, 1980: 6.
— Mayor's Advisory Committee for Culture and the Arts meets, Lahaina News, September 15, 1980: 7.
— jazz instructor Kila Lau teaches dance classes, Lahaina News, September 15, 1980: 8.
— work of Henry Vander Velde described, Lahaina News, October 15, 1980: 2.
— quilting workshop held , Lahaina News, March 1, 1981: 15.
— Hui No'eau offering workshops on oil pastels, printmaking, and batik, Lahaina News, February 15, 1982: 8.
— Arts and Craft Fair to be held at Banyan Tree, Lahaina News, October 1, 1982: 2.
— Art as a Verb show opens at Kaluanui, Lahaina News, December 1, 1982: 15.
— Art Gallery opens on Front Street, Lahaina Times, August 20, 1983 volume 7 number 8: 1.
— Lahaina News begins a regular column on Art, Lahaina News, September 21, 1983: 12.
— Crazy Shirts and t-shirt design discussed, Lahaina News, December 28, 1983: 19.
— exhibit to open in the Lahaina Arts Society's Old Jail Gallery, Lahaina News, January 25, 1984: 5.
— Maui Marine Art Expo '84 opens at Hotel Inter-Continental Maui, Lahaina News, February 1, 1984: 3.
— Art Maui '84 opens, Lahaina News, March 7, 1984: 14.
— Lahaina News criticized by Bishop Museum for use of photograph, Lahaina News, March 7, 1984: 2.
— Art Maui '84 featured, Lahaina News, April 4, 1984: 7,8,9.
— applications for Artist-In-The-Schools being accepted, Lahaina News, April 11, 1984: 5.
— greeting card designs discussed, Lahaina News, April 11, 1984: 7.
— students from Lahainaluna High School win prizes, Lahaina News, April 18, 1984: 3.
— whale art displayed at Kapalua Bay Hotel, Lahaina News, April 18, 1984: 3.
— artist Bill Bagley's career described, Lahaina News, April 25, 1984: 10.
— Mayor's 16th Invitational Art Exhibit to be held, Lahaina News, May 16, 1984: 7.
— juried art show held at Lahaina Arts Society gallery, Lahaina News, May 30, 1984: 22.
— "Summer of '67 and Other Sorrows" art show at the Lahaina Arts Society., Lahaina News, June 13, 1984: 4.
— sand sculptor Norman Richard Kraus at Maui Surf Hotel, Lahaina News, September 26, 1984: 10.
— art as investment discussed, Lahaina News, September 26, 1984: 13.
— "Landscapes" exhibit to be held at Village Gallery, Lahaina News, October 24, 1984: 4.
— Maui Children's Theater described, Lahaina News, November 7, 1984: 10.
— "Wearable Art and Crafts" exhibit at Lahaina Arts Society Main Gallery, Lahaina News, December 12, 1984: 3.
— kapa making detailed, Lahaina News, December 19, 1984: 10.

— photographs to be exhibited at Koho Grill and Bar, Lahaina News, February 6, 1992: 10,11.

— some current shows detailed, Lahaina News, February 6, 1992: 19.

— Maui County Council may rewrite rules on the use of public facilities for craft fairs, Lahaina News, February 13, 1992: 3.

— Lahaina Arts Society offering art appreciation classes to children, Lahaina News, February 13, 1992: 4.

— Seabury Hall to host Craft Fair, Lahaina News, February 13, 1992: 4.

— Lahainaluna High School students are finalists in National Golden Key Art Competition, Lahaina News, February 13, 1992: 7.

— Hawaiian gourds workshop to be offered, Lahaina News, February 20, 1992: 17.

— Mayor's Invitational Art Exhibit to be held, Lahaina News, April 9, 1992: 21.

— Kaha Ki'i Congressional Arts Competition winners announced, Lahaina News, April 23, 1992: 5.

— Kapalua Bay Hotel to exhibit "Pohaku, Through Hawaiian Eyes" photographs., Lahaina News, April 23, 1992: 7.

— Art in the Park juried show to be held, Lahaina News, April 30, 1992: 18.

— exhibition of works by handicapped students to be held, Lahaina News, April 30, 1992: 4.

— wood exhibit to open at Hui No'eau Visual Arts Center, Lahaina News, May 7, 1992: 26.

— Friday Night is Art Night continues, Lahaina News, May 21, 1992: 16,17.

— Art in the Park to be held, Lahaina News, June 11, 1992: 4.

— Kapalua Bay Hotel and Villas to exhibit "Pohaku: Through Hawaiian Eyes", Lahaina News, June 11, 1992: 5.

— update on events for the weekend, Lahaina News, June 18, 1992: 17.

— wood carvers Bruce and Steve Turnbull to be featured at Lahaina Galleries, Lahaina News, June 18, 1992: 19.

— "More Summer Madness" opens at Foundation Galleries, Lahaina News, July 2, 1992: 22.

— photos of sacred stone sites still exhibited at Kapalua Bay Hotel, Lahaina News, July 9, 1992: 5.

— reservations being accepted for Maui Prince Resort's Na Ohana O Makena, Lahaina News, August 13, 1992: 9.

— Maui Choreographer's Forum offering dance demonstration, Lahaina News, August 20, 1992: 4.

— Janice Lally to lecture on art in Australia, Lahaina News, August 27, 1992: 6.

— space available for craftspeople at Na Ohana O Makena, Lahaina News, September 17, 1992: 8.

— Ocean Art Festival to open, Lahaina News, January 21, 1993: 14.

— "Portraits of the Wild" to open at Foundation Gallery, Lahaina News, March 11, 1993: 14.

— Celebration of the Arts to be held, Lahaina News, April 1, 1993: 12,13.

— "Celebration of the Arts" to be held at Ritz-Carlton, Lahaina News, April 8, 1993: 9.

— "Inner Vision" juried art exhibition to be held, Lahaina News, May 13, 1993: 12.

— photographs of contemporary Hawaiian culture to be exhibited, Lahaina News, June 10, 1993: 10.

— Art Night Celebration to be held in Lahaina, Lahaina News, June 10, 1993: 11.

— Art Night to be held in Lahaina, specially designed milk caps available, Lahaina News, June 17, 1993: 13,14.

— "Arts and Crafts Extravaganza" to be held, Lahaina News, June 24, 1993: 4.

— culture-based art increasingly important, Lahaina News, July 1, 1993: 10.

— juried show to be held at Ka'ahumanu Center, Lahaina News, July 8, 1993: 12.

— Foundation Gallery to hold "Smallest Show on Maui", Lahaina News, August 5, 1993: 10.

— galleries suffering in new economic climate, Lahaina News, August 5, 1993: 6.

— Ka'ahumanu Center to present "Maui Seen, The Artist's Perspective", Lahaina News, August 12, 1993: 14.

— Hawaii Bead Society to meet, Lahaina News, September 2, 1993: 2.

— "Art Accents" column begins, Lahaina News, September 9, 1993: 10.

— printmakers to exhibit at Lahaina Cannery, Lahaina News, September 16, 1993: 17.

— Village Galleries to feature abstract art show, Lahaina News, September 30, 1993: 12.

— Trinity Church By the Sea seeking crafters for Christmas Prelude Sale, Lahaina News, September 30, 1993: 6.

— Hawaiian Fish Printers present "The New Gyotaku", Lahaina News, October 28, 1993: 11.

— ice carving competition to be held at Lahaina Cannery Mall, Lahaina News, November 25, 1993: 9,11,12.

— results of ice carving competition, Lahaina News, December 2, 1993: 11.

— 15-foot monkey pod statue of King Kamehameha I completed, Lahaina News, December 2, 1993: 14.

— poster signing by Arlene Marcoe Anthony at Lahaina Art Society, Lahaina News, January 6, 1994: 11.

— exhibit on whales to be held at Four Seasons Resort, Lahaina News, January 20, 1994: 12.

— Russian Art Expo to be held at Metropolitan Art Gallery, Lahaina News, February 3, 1994: 11.

— crafters ask that Lahaina Civic Center hold fairs every week, Lahaina News, February 10, 1994: 1,4.

— Kea Lani resort to feature "Art a la Carte", Lahaina News, February 17, 1994: 12.

— Lahaina Town Action Committee receives grant to support Art Night, Lahaina News, February 17, 1994: 2.

— Art School at Kapalua to open, Lahaina News, February 24, 1994: 1.

— Celebration of the Arts to be held at the Ritz-Carlton, Lahaina News, February 24, 1994: 11,12.

— "The Russian Art Expo Season End" to be exhibit at Metropolitan Art Gallery, Lahaina News, February 24, 1994: 9.

— artists input sought for Art School of Kapalua, Lahaina News, March 17, 1994: 9.

— "Fun with Trash" workshop to be held, Lahaina News, March 17, 1994: 9.

— artists promise to aid the Hawaiian rain forests, Lahaina News, March 24, 1994: 14.

— Art School at Kapalua to hold first formal meeting, Lahaina News, March 24, 1994: 14.

— Foundation Art Gallery to host Marine Art Show, Lahaina News, March 24, 1994: 15.

— Celebration of the Arts held, Lahaina News, March 31, 1994: 13.

— Tess Cartwright using recycled materials, Lahaina News, April 21, 1994: 2.

— Art of Plastic Bottle Sculpturing to be held, Lahaina News, April 21, 1994: 5.

— Lahaina Town Action Committee seeking artists to facilitate "Art in Action" projects, Lahaina News, May 5, 1994: 15.

— volunteers sought for Hawaiian Quilt Research Project , Lahaina News, May 19, 1994: 15,16.

— Lahaina Town Action Committee seeking artists for "Art in Action" project, Lahaina News, May 26, 1994: 15.

— youth art on display at Maui Arts and Cultural Center, Lahaina News, June 30, 1994: 15.

— Kazuma International Gallery to feature "Tobu: To Soar to New Heights", Lahaina News, July 7, 1994: 15.

— Art Night Block Party held, Lahaina News, July 7, 1994: 4.

— "Art Night" to be held, Lahaina News, November 13, 1997: 15.
— Contemporary Museum's exhibition featuring Hawaii artists, Lahaina News, November 13, 1997: 20.
— ice carving event to be held at Lahaina Cannery Mall, Lahaina News, December 4, 1997: 24.
— Arts of Life For Maui Youth Exhibit, Lahaina News, December 4, 1997: 24.
— Maui's Best Craft Fair to be held, Lahaina News, December 25, 1997: 12.
— Sean Kaumeheiwa wins ice carving contest, Lahaina News, December 25, 1997: 7.
— Lahaina Cannery Mall to exhibit student work, Lahaina News, January 1, 1998: 16.
— Maui's Best Craft Fair to be held, Lahaina News, January 15, 1998: 13.
— work of Maui youth on display at Ka'ahumanu Center, Lahaina News, January 29, 1998: 15.
— "Hawaiian Music and Crafts Festival" to be held at Lahaina Cannery Mall, Lahaina News, February 26, 1998: 12.
— Art Maui '98 to be held at Maui Arts and Cultural Center, Lahaina News, March 12, 1998: 21.
— Art Maui '98 to be held at Maui Arts and Cultural Center, Lahaina News, March 19, 1998: 12.
— "Aloha Friday Art Night" to be held, Lahaina News, April 2, 1998: 16.
— "Celebration of the Arts" to be held at Ritz-Carlton, Lahaina News, April 9, 1998: 1,9.
— Vision of Hawaii offers classes on sculpture, Lahaina News, April 9, 1998: 16,17.
— Lahaina Cannery Mall to host art classes by Visions of Hawaii, Lahaina News, April 16, 1998: 13.
— lei makers to compete, Lahaina News, April 30, 1998: 16.
— Matthew Nohara takes second place in Patsy Mink's Second Congressional District Art Contest, Lahaina News, May 21, 1998: 1.
— ice carving competition to be held at Lahaina Cannery Mall, Lahaina News, June 4, 1998: 9.
— Ice Carving Competition to be held, Lahaina News, June 18, 1998: 2.
— Wood Carving Contest to be held at Lahaina Cannery Mall, Lahaina News, July 2, 1998: 17.
— "Through a Liquid Mirror" exhibit to be held, Lahaina News, July 9, 1998: 16.
— Wood Carving Contest to be held at Lahaina Cannery Mall, Lahaina News, July 9, 1998: 16.
— collection of vintage Hawaii-Pacific graphics arts displayed at Old Lahaina Book Emporium, Lahaina News, July 16, 1998: 7.
— "Friday Night is Art Night" continues, Lahaina News, October 15, 1998: 16.
— "Feast or Famine II" exhibit to be held at Maui Arts and Cultural Center, Lahaina News, October 29, 1998: 27.
— "Playing with Fire" to be held at Longhi's, Lahaina News, October 29, 1998: 28.
— "Feast or Famine II" exhibit to be held at Maui Arts and Cultural Center, Lahaina News, November 5, 1998: 14.
— Festival of Art and Flowers to be held, Lahaina News, November 19, 1998: 5.
— ice carving to be demonstrated, Lahaina News, December 3, 1998: 20.
— "Friday Night is Art Night" continues, Lahaina News, December 17, 1998: 24.
— artists to demonstrate at Lahaina Arts Society, Lahaina News, December 24, 1998: 12.
— "Postcards from Maui" by Margaret Leach and Kathleen MacDonald to be held, Lahaina News, December 24, 1998: 13.
— "Contemporary Coordinates/Painting in Hawaii" to be held at Hui No'eau, Lahaina News, January 7, 1999: 16.

— Ka'anapali Beach Hotel hosts Lahaina Arts Society artists, Lahaina News, March 18, 1999: 13.
— "Art Night" held, Lahaina News, March 18, 1999: 16.
— "Maui's Best Craft Fair" to be held, Lahaina News, March 25, 1999: 16.
— "Celebration of the Arts" to be held, Lahaina News, April 1, 1999: 1,20.
— "Friday Night is Art Night" continues, Lahaina News, April 29, 1999: 16.
— printmakers featured at Village Gallery, Lahaina News, May 13, 1999: 16.
— Polynesian artists carving at Banyan Tree Park, Lahaina News, May 27, 1999: 16.
— fairs being held, Lahaina News, June 3, 1999: 16.
— film course to be offered by University of Southern California, Lahaina News, June 10, 1999: 15.
— "Friday Night is Art Night" continues, Lahaina News, June 24, 1999: 12.
— "Currents II: Kaua'i Artists" to be held, Lahaina News, June 24, 1999: 12.
— Na Kupuna O Maui He'ui Cultural Arts Festival to be held, Lahaina News, July 29, 1999: 11.
— John Carr of the John F. Kennedy Center for the Performing Arts to lead workshops for artist educators, Lahaina News, August 26, 1999: 14.
— Lahaina Cannery Mall to hold "Artists in Action", Lahaina News, September 2, 1999: 13.
— Children's Art Exhibit to be held at Hui No'eau Visual Arts Center, Lahaina News, September 2, 1999: 15.
— Gayle Miyaguchi to hold class on making 'Uli'uli, Lahaina News, September 2, 1999: 17.
— "Huc Luquien's Hawai'I: Prints 1918-1950" to exhibit at Maui Arts and Cultural Center, Lahaina News, September 23, 1999: 12.
— "Artists in Action" to be held at Lahaina Cannery Mall, Lahaina News, October 7, 1999: 17.
— Lahaina Center to offer "Art Walk", Lahaina News, November 18, 1999: 15.
— ice carving contest to be held at Lahaina Cannery Mall, Lahaina News, November 25, 1999: 2.
— "Christmas Break Arts Enrichment Camp" to be held, Lahaina News, December 9, 1999: 6.
— "Friday Night is Art Night" continues, Lahaina News, January 6, 2000: 12.
— "Art of Trash, Maui 2000" juried exhibition to be held, Lahaina News, February 17, 2000: 15.
— "Art Walk" to be held at Lahaina Center, Lahaina News, March 9, 2000: 12.
— all-media juried exhibition to be held at Maui Arts and Cultural Center, Lahaina News, March 16, 2000: 13.
— "Upcountry ArtFest" to be held, Lahaina News, April 6, 2000: 16.
— Kihei Art Show to be held, Lahaina News, May 11, 2000: 21.
— master carvers to attend "In Celebration of Canoes" festival, Lahaina News, May 11, 2000: 6.
— printmakers to exhibit at Village Gallery Contemporary, Lahaina News, May 18, 2000: 20.
— "Artwalk" continues to be held at Lahaina Center, Lahaina News, May 25, 2000: 19.
— Na Kupuna O Maui's He'ui Cultural Arts Festivals continue to be held at Banyan Tree Park, Lahaina News, May 25, 2000: 19.
— Hawaii Consortium for the Arts to discuss Hawaii Arts Census, Lahaina News, June 22, 2000: 6.
— "Artwalk" continues to be held at Lahaina Center, Lahaina News, June 29, 2000: 20.
— "90 Degrees" to feature paintings of Evan Asato, William Bartlett, and Akira Iha, Lahaina News, July 6, 2000: 16.

ART FORCE GALLERY [BUSINESS]
— opens, Lahaina News, July 11, 1991: 14.

ART HAWAII
— to be held, Lahaina News, February 22, 1996: 13.

ART LEDUC TRIO, THE [MUSICAL GROUP]
— to perform at Kobe Japanese Steak House, Lahaina News, January 23, 1992: 16.

ART MAUI
— competition to begin, Lahaina News, January 16, 1985: 3.
— jurors to give presentation, Lahaina News, March 20, 1985: 7.
— planned, Lahaina News, February 4, 1987: 8.
— Ninth annual event scheduled, Lahaina News, March 25, 1987: 12.
— presents SFCA Retrospective with Momi Cazimero and Tom Klobe, Lahaina News, January 13, 1988: 16.
— celebrates 10 year anniversary, Lahaina News, April 6, 1988: 4.
— prospectus available, Lahaina News, February 8, 1989: 13.
— to be held at Hui No'eau Visual Arts Center, Lahaina News, February 15, 1989: 5.
— 12th annual, to be held at Hui No'eau Visual Arts Center, Lahaina News, March 7, 1990: 15.
— continues, Lahaina News, March 21, 1990: 14.
— to be held, Lahaina News, January 9, 1991: 8.
— symposium to be held, Lahaina News, January 23, 1991: 9.
— juried exhibition to be held, Lahaina News, March 20, 1991: 13.
— continues, Lahaina News, March 27, 1991: 18.
— on view at Hui No'eau Visual Arts Center, Lahaina News, April 10, 1991: 13.
— to be held at the Kaluanui estate in Makawao, Lahaina News, February 13, 1992: 4.
— to open, Lahaina News, April 2, 1992: 22.
— held at Hui No'eau Visual Arts Center, Lahaina News, April 16, 1992: 21.
— works from selected by State Foundation on Culture and the Arts, Lahaina News, April 23, 1992: 29.
— to be held at the Hui No'eau Visual Arts Center, Lahaina News, February 25, 1993: 11.
— prospectus available, Lahaina News, February 16, 1995: 15,16.
— exhibition of juried works to be held, Lahaina News, March 9, 1995: 12.
— to be held, Lahaina News, March 30, 1995: 12.
— prospectus available, Lahaina News, December 14, 1995: 14.
— to hold general meeting, Lahaina News, May 7, 1998: 20.
— to be held, Lahaina News, March 18, 1999: 2.

ART NIGHT
— details given, Lahaina News, May 23, 1991: 13.
— to be held, Lahaina News, May 30, 1991: 7.
— block party celebration to be held, Lahaina News, June 30, 1994: 12.
— celebration to be held, Lahaina News, July 13, 1995: 5.

ART OF HAWAII
— Village Gallery Contemporary to hold exhibit, Lahaina News, August 14, 2003: 9.

ART OF RICE TRAVELING THEATRE, THE
— to be staged at Maui Arts and Cultural Center, Lahaina News, September 18, 2003: 17.

ART OF THE CHANTER, THE
— show to feature Keali'i Reichel, Lahaina News, January 11, 2001: 3.

ART OF THE SOLO 'UKULELE, THE
— to be held at the Maui Arts and Cultural Center, Lahaina News, March 28, 2002: 19.

ART OF TRASH
— to be held, Lahaina News, February 1, 1996: 12.
— to be held, Lahaina News, March 30, 2000: 12.

ART SCHOOL AT KAPALUA, THE
— to open, Lahaina News, February 24, 1994: 1.
— consultants offer positive feedback, Lahaina News, March 31, 1994: 2.
— to offer free classes, Lahaina News, May 5, 1994: 11.
— art classes by William Rogers to be offered, Lahaina News, May 19, 1994: 15.
— to offer still life art class, Lahaina News, May 26, 1994: 11.
— to hold summer classes, Lahaina News, May 26, 1994: 14,15.
— continues to offer classes, Lahaina News, June 2, 1994: 12.
— to offer drawing classes, Lahaina News, June 16, 1994: 11.
— to host yoga classes, Lahaina News, June 23, 1994: 11.
— to hold free sand painting and watercolor classes, Lahaina News, July 7, 1994: 13,14.
— publishes survey in Lahaina News, Lahaina News, July 7, 1994: 16.
— to host "Teach the Children", Lahaina News, July 28, 1994: 13.
— celebrate donors, Lahaina News, August 4, 1994: 16.
— classes and workshops announced, Lahaina News, September 29, 1994: 12.
— offering classes and workshops, Lahaina News, October 27, 1994: 19.
— offering classes, Lahaina News, January 5, 1995: 11,12.
— to break ground, Lahaina News, January 12, 1995: 11.
— construction of facility near completion, Lahaina News, March 9, 1995: 12.
— seeking volunteers to teach art, Lahaina News, April 6, 1995: 12.
— new directors added to Board, Lahaina News, April 6, 1995: 6.
— offering classes, construction almost completed, Lahaina News, April 13, 1995: 16.
— opens facility, Lahaina News, July 20, 1995: 3.
— to open, Lahaina News, August 10, 1995: 4.
— offering painting and drawing classes, Lahaina News, August 24, 1995: 4.
— to hold bonsai class, Lahaina News, September 14, 1995: 6.
— classes ongoing, Lahaina News, October 12, 1995: 14.
— Lahaina Galleries to host benefit for, Lahaina News, November 2, 1995: 11,12.
— to hold activities for children, Lahaina News, November 16, 1995: 15.
— grand opening to be held, Lahaina News, November 30, 1995: 11.
— Scott de Montluzin joins staff, Lahaina News, February 22, 1996: 14.
— to hold studio classes, Lahaina News, March 14, 1996: 11.
— to offer free art classes, Lahaina News, March 21, 1996: 12.
— offering summer options for youth, Lahaina News, May 23, 1996: 15.
— to offer Silk Painting for Fun workshop, Lahaina News, June 20, 1996: 12.
— fall schedule announced, Lahaina News, September 19, 1996: 16.
— to offer deep-breathing exercise classes, Lahaina News, April 3, 1997: 12.
— to hold lecture and workshop Impressionist Plein-Art Color Theory, Lahaina News, April 10, 1997: 13.
— registration for summer program, Lahaina News, April 24, 1997: 12.
— to offer summer enrichment program, Lahaina News, June 5, 1997: 3.
— to offer summer classes, Lahaina News, July 17, 1997: 16.
— Tess Cartwright to exhibit as part of Art of Trash, Lahaina News, July 24, 1997: 17.
— offering discounted family memberships, Lahaina News, November 6, 1997: 14.
— offering family membership, Lahaina News, November 13, 1997: 2.
— to display work by Carleton Kinkade, Lahaina News, March 26, 1998: 2.
— Jenny Kosenka is new executive director, Lahaina News, April 23, 1998: 13.
— offering Summer Enrichment Program, Lahaina News, June 4, 1998: 2.
— new director Jenny Kosenka featured, Lahaina News, July 9, 1998: 7.

— Children's Summer Camp Program ends, Lahaina News, September 3, 1998: 17.

— seeking models for drawing classes, Lahaina News, September 3, 1998: 8.

— fall classes to begin, Lahaina News, September 17, 1998: 24.

— offering new classes, Lahaina News, September 24, 1998: 7.

— "Paradise/Paradox" exhibit to include photographs, Lahaina News, October 1, 1998: 16.

— to offer spinning, muscle sculpting and other fitness classes, Lahaina News, November 12, 1998: 15.

— to offer fitness classes, Lahaina News, November 26, 1998: 15.

— hosting feather artistry workshop, Lahaina News, December 3, 1998: 7.

— to host lei makers from Niʻihau, Lahaina News, December 31, 1998: 5.

— starting new winter programs, Lahaina News, January 7, 1999: 2.

— featuring art by Ronaldo Macedo, Lahaina News, February 4, 1999: 9.

— announces summer program, Lahaina News, March 18, 1999: 8.

— to offer art classes, Lahaina News, April 22, 1999: 5.

— planning summer program, Lahaina News, May 6, 1999: 3.

— summer program offered, Lahaina News, May 27, 1999: 5.

— to host "Summer… Solstice: A Distinguished Group of Working Artists", Lahaina News, July 1, 1999: 13.

— seeking models, Lahaina News, September 2, 1999: 15.

— to offer classes in the Fall, Lahaina News, September 16, 1999: 5.

— to hold "Arts on the Move" trip, Lahaina News, November 18, 1999: 15.

— expanding curriculum, Lahaina News, November 25, 1999: 15.

— to hold "Keiki Holiday Fun Program", Lahaina News, December 9, 1999: 19.

— to host show of instructor and student art, Lahaina News, December 23, 1999: 7.

— to hold student art show, Lahaina News, January 13, 2000: 12.

— Mick Kolodgy to exhibit "Masked", Lahaina News, February 10, 2000: 17.

— hosting drawing workshop with Liz Singer, Lahaina News, February 17, 2000: 8.

— to offer courses, Lahaina News, February 24, 2000: 9.

— to hold workshop on Feng Shui, Lahaina News, March 2, 2000: 13.

— to show works by Kit Gentry, Lahaina News, March 9, 2000: 13.

— to hold summer enrichment program for children, Lahaina News, May 4, 2000: 3.

— offering summer classes, Lahaina News, June 22, 2000: 6.

— Summer Enrichment Program for children begins, Lahaina News, July 6, 2000: 3.

— offering interim classes, Lahaina News, September 7, 2000: 19.

— offering fall classes, Lahaina News, September 21, 2000: 17.

— to exhibit work of Michael Nees, Lahaina News, September 28, 2000: 17.

— to exhibit Michael Nees, Lahaina News, October 5, 2000: 16.

— to hold after school classes, Lahaina News, December 7, 2000: 9.

— to hold Arts Fair, Lahaina News, January 4, 2001: 2.

— receives grant from The McInerny Foundation, Lahaina News, March 22, 2001: 9.

— to hold Kid's Camp, Lahaina News, March 29, 2001: 18.

— to hold Kid's Camp, Lahaina News, April 5, 2001: 20.

— to hold summer program, Lahaina News, May 24, 2001: 10.

— receives grant from Atherton Family Foundation, Lahaina News, July 19, 2001: 2.

— to host Maria Anogianakis, Lahaina News, July 26, 2001: 17.

— to hold retrospective of the work of Patti Stepp, Lahaina News, October 4, 2001: 16.

— to sell potted Norfolk Christmas trees, Lahaina News, November 15, 2001: 17.

— chef of Chez Paul Patric Callarec to host benefit dinner, Lahaina News, November 29, 2001: 15.

— to offer Winter Art Camp for Kids, Lahaina News, November 29, 2001: 2.

— offering Winter Art Camp for Kids, Lahaina News, December 27, 2001: 2.

— to hold Spring Art Camp, Lahaina News, March 28, 2002: 22.

— receives grant from McInerny Foundation, Lahaina News, April 4, 2002: 14.

— to hold Children's Summer Enrichment Program, Lahaina News, May 2, 2002: 14.

— offering classes, Lahaina News, August 22, 2002: 15.

— to host "Something's Fishy" featuring works by Karen Domingo and Jennifer Holt, Lahaina News, September 19, 2002: 22.

— hosting "Something's Fishing" exhibit, Lahaina News, September 26, 2002: 17.

— to hold Christmas tree fundraiser, Lahaina News, November 21, 2002: 13.

— selling Christmas trees as a fundraiser, Lahaina News, December 5, 2002: 16.

— Andrea Smith to exhibit at, Lahaina News, December 5, 2002: 18.

— plans holiday programs, Lahaina News, December 12, 2002: 17.

— planning holiday programs, Lahaina News, December 19, 2002: 2.

— to host artist Claire Verbiest, Lahaina News, January 9, 2003: 15.

— offering classes, Lahaina News, February 13, 2003: 16.

— classes to be offered, Lahaina News, February 20, 2003: 16.

— offers after school classes, Lahaina News, April 3, 2003: 9.

— offering classes, Lahaina News, April 10, 2003: 16.

— to hold Children's Summer Enrichment Art Program, Lahaina News, May 1, 2003: 15.

— to host Capoeira classes, Lahaina News, June 19, 2003: 13.

— to offer belly dance classes, Lahaina News, July 10, 2003: 18.

— to hold "Green Haliconia—Mixing Clean Clear Greens", Lahaina News, July 31, 2003: 16.

— to offer yoga classes, Lahaina News, August 21, 2003: 18.

— preparing for Fall and Winter season, Lahaina News, September 4, 2003: 5.

ART SEARCH '94
— to be held, Lahaina News, June 9, 1994: 16.

ART TEE GALLERY [BUSINESS]
— opens, Lahaina News, January 24, 1990: 6.

ARTBEAT [MUSICAL GROUP]
— performing at Longhi's, Lahaina News, December 20, 1989: 8.

— to perform at Longhi's, Lahaina News, February 14, 1990: 15.

ARTER, WILLIAM
— named general manager of Maui Park, Lahaina News, January 30, 1991: 5.

ARTFUL DODGER FEED AND READ [BUSINESS]
— hosting musical group Seventh Wave, Lahaina News, March 18, 1987: 18.

— hosting open mike night, Lahaina News, July 8, 1987: 24.

— specials at, Lahaina News, August 12, 1987: 18.

— presents work of Michelle Benz, Lahaina News, January 13, 1988: 16.

— Ron Silliman visits, Lahaina News, February 10, 1988: 11.

ARTHRITIS
— featured, Lahaina News, April 2, 1992: 3.

ARTHRITIS FOUNDATION
— to hold drawing for "Jingle Bears" as fundraiser, Lahaina News, December 7, 1988: 16.

— sponsoring Craft and Gifts Fair, Lahaina News, August 23, 1989: 3.

— holds craft fair, Lahaina News, October 18, 1989: 6.

— to hold Christmas crafts and gifts fair, Lahaina News, November 15, 1989: 5.

— to hold benefit concert, Lahaina News, November 29, 1989: 21.
— to hold golf tournament fundraiser, Lahaina News, March 14, 1990: 11.
— to hold golf tournament at Wailea Blue Course, Lahaina News, March 28, 1990: 9.
— offering free booklet, Lahaina News, August 22, 1990: 5.
— to hold nationwide call-in, Lahaina News, September 12, 1990: 8.
— golf tournament begins, Lahaina News, March 20, 1991: 5,20.
— golf tournament to be held, Lahaina News, April 3, 1991: 16.
— telethon scheduled for The Ward Warehouse in Honolulu, Lahaina News, April 17, 1991: 1.
— telethon held, winners of karaoke announced, Lahaina News, May 1, 1991: 1,3.
— to hold Christmas Crafts and Gifts Fair, Lahaina News, December 19, 1991: 4.
— to offer course on self-management, Lahaina News, December 19, 1991: 5.
— hoping to secure donation of letter quality printer, Lahaina News, December 19, 1991: 6.
— sponsoring course on self-management, Lahaina News, January 2, 1992: 5.
— still looking for donation of printer, Lahaina News, January 2, 1992: 5.
— offering course on self-management, Lahaina News, January 9, 1992: 5.
— to hold telethon, Lahaina News, March 5, 1992: 3.
— to hold telethon from The Wharf Cinema Center, Lahaina News, March 12, 1992: 19.
— to host karaoke competition as fundraiser, Lahaina News, March 19, 1992: 3.
— telethon to be held, will include karaoke contest, Lahaina News, April 2, 1992: 3,4.
— telethon this weekend, details given, Lahaina News, April 9, 1992: 3.
— Dr. Francis Dega to present updates, Lahaina News, July 30, 1992: 5.
— to hold Reindeer Run and Walk for Arthritis, Lahaina News, December 4, 1997: 24.
— support group continues to meet, Lahaina News, November 8, 2001: 17.
— support group continues to meet, Lahaina News, February 21, 2002: 16.
— to hold Joints in Motion Training Team run or walk, Lahaina News, April 11, 2002: 17.
— support group continues to meet, Lahaina News, July 11, 2002: 17.
— working with Health-South Rehabilitation of Wailuku to offer warm water arthritis exercise class, Lahaina News, June 26, 2003: 10.

ARTHUR T. UEOKA MCBA SCHOLARSHIP
— Maui County Bar Association seeking nominations for, Lahaina News, May 17, 2001: 17.

ARTISANS OF HAWAII [BUSINESS]
— featured, Lahaina News, March 20, 1985: 9.

ARTIST IN PARADISE [BUSINESS]
— opened by Robert Bedard, Lahaina News, August 7, 2003: 3.

ARTIST IN THE SCHOOLS
— participant Henry Kaleialoha Allen featured, Lahaina News, February 13, 1992: 3.

ARTISTS GROUP, THE
— exhibiting at Village Gallery, Lahaina News, November 23, 1988: 3.

ARTISTS OF HAWAII EXHIBITION
— at Honolulu Academy of Arts includes artists from Maui , Lahaina News, November 27, 1985: 11.

ARTS EDUCATION FOR CHILDREN GROUP (AECG)
— to perform "The Three Little Pigs", Lahaina News, May 15, 1997: 12.
— offering summer arts enrichment program, Lahaina News, May 29, 1997: 1.
— group to hold "Aloha Fun Days", Lahaina News, June 26, 1997: 3.
— to hold benefit jazz concert at Longhi's Restaurant, Lahaina News, July 24, 1997: 7.
— to hold fundraiser at Maui Marriott Resort, Lahaina News, July 31, 1997: 6.
— to offer summer classes, Lahaina News, May 14, 1998: 2.
— students to perform at Ritz-Carlton, Lahaina News, July 30, 1998: 17.
— offer free hula lessons, Lahaina News, October 8, 1998: 2.
— to present Titanic Casino Masquerade Ball, Lahaina News, October 29, 1998: 22.
— to hold hula lessons, Lahaina News, November 5, 1998: 8.
— to offer "Sounds of Christmas" and Christmas Fair, Lahaina News, December 10, 1998: 9.
— Soroptimists International supporting, Lahaina News, March 25, 1999: 6.
— to offer art classes, Lahaina News, April 29, 1999: 14.
— to hold "Summer Music Camp Showcase", Lahaina News, July 15, 1999: 12.
— receives grant from Soroptimists International, Lahaina News, July 22, 1999: 5.
— Maui Myth and Magic Theatre to hold benefit for, Lahaina News, May 4, 2000: 1.
— to hold auditions for Broadway-style production, Lahaina News, June 29, 2000: 3.
— students to perform concert, Lahaina News, July 27, 2000: 1,17.
— to hold music and performing arts camp, Lahaina News, May 17, 2001: 18.
— to hold art camp, Lahaina News, May 24, 2001: 10.
— Summer Music Festival to support, Lahaina News, June 28, 2001: 18.
— The Shops at Wailea to hold "WOW!—Wailea On Wednesdays", Lahaina News, June 28, 2001: 21.
— Shuichi Komiyama new artistic director, Lahaina News, January 10, 2002: 14.
— to hold summer camp, Lahaina News, May 30, 2002: 3.
— to hold Lahaina Music and Performing Arts Summer Camp, Lahaina News, June 13, 2002: 2.
— to stage "One World" musical, Lahaina News, July 18, 2002: 14.
— featured, Lahaina News, April 17, 2003: 14.
— update on program, Lahaina News, June 12, 2003: 16.

ARTTECH MAUI EXPO
— Paul Hugel to exhibit at, Lahaina News, November 10, 1994: 15.
— to be held at Maui Inter-Continental Resort, Lahaina News, October 26, 1995: 12.

ARTWORK
— continues to be held at Lahaina Center, Lahaina News, September 7, 2000: 20.

AS IS [PLAY]
— to be performed by Maui Community Theatre, Lahaina News, February 4, 1993: 15.

ASAHI BEER-OHASHI KYOSEN GOLF TOURNAMENT
— held at Wailea Golf Course, Lahaina News, January 7, 1987: 3.
— to be held at Wailea Blue golf course, Lahaina News, January 9, 1992: 7.
— details given, Lahaina News, January 23, 1992: 8.

ASATO, EVAN [ARTIST]
— exhibiting at Hui No'eau Visual Arts Center, Lahaina News, February 13, 1991: 13.
— part of "90 Degrees" exhibit at Maui Arts and Cultural Center, Lahaina News, July 6, 2000: 16.

ASCENDANCE
— dance revue to be held, Lahaina News, December 11, 1997: 18.

ASHDOWN, INEZ MACPHEE [WRITER]
— Ka Alaloa O Maui book published, Lahaina Sun, December 27, 1972: 7.
— receives award from Historic Hawaii Foundation, Lahaina News, June 1, 1980: 3.
— recovering from illness, Lahaina News, November 30, 1988: 6.

ASHER, MAXINE
— Claim to have found Atlantis, Lahaina Times, August, 1980 volume 4 number 7: 2.

ASHFIELD, STEVE "SPECS"
— umpire featured, Lahaina News, April 20, 1995: 10.
— baseball coach featured, Lahaina News, August 23, 2001: 1,8.

ASHLEY'S YOGURT AND ICE CREAM SHOPPE [RESTAURANT]
— opens at Kahana Gateway Shopping Center, Lahaina News, April 29, 1993: 9.
— celebrates second anniversary, Lahaina News, May 18, 1995: 11.

ASHLOCK, BRYAN
— director of Sheraton Maui's director of food and beverage receives Chairman's Award, Lahaina News, March 22, 2001: 8.

ASHMORE, JEFFREY
— appointed senior vice president at Amfac Distribution Hawaii, Lahaina News, January 16, 1991: 5.

ASHTON EN L'AIR [BUSINESS]
— dancers to perform, Lahaina News, April 4, 2002: 14.
— to perform, Lahaina News, April 11, 2002: 16.

ASHWORTH KAPALUA CLAMBAKE PRO-AM INVITATIONAL
— golf tournament to be held, Lahaina News, June 25, 1998: 7.
— to raise money for Special Olympics, Lahaina News, July 2, 1998: 15.

ASIAN AND PACIFIC ISLANDER SUPPORT NETWORK
— to hold social event, Lahaina News, January 23, 2003: 16.
— planning cruise, Lahaina News, February 6, 2003: 16.
— hosting weekly meetings with Maui AIDS Foundation, Lahaina News, March 6, 2003: 17.

ASIAN BLEND [MUSICAL GROUP]
— to perform at Montessori Gala, Lahaina News, March 18, 1993: 8.

ASIMUS, DAN
— to talk on "Achieving Optimal Health, Happiness and Success" at 'Ohana Connection, Lahaina News, May 2, 2002: 17.

ASPEN SANTA FE BALLET [TROUPE]
— to perform at Maui Arts and Cultural Center, Lahaina News, February 27, 2003: 17.
— to perform at Maui Arts and Cultural Center, Lahaina News, March 6, 2003: 16.

ASPER, GERRY
— wins gold at Paradise Cup Bodybuilding Championship, Lahaina News, December 3, 1992: 6.

ASSATEGUE [SHIP]
— ran aground off Kaunakakai Harbor, Moloka'i, Lahaina News, October 28, 1993: 4.

ASSEMBLY OF GOD
— to meet in Kahului, Lahaina News, October 8, 1986: 3.

ASSOCIATED LANDSCAPE CONTRACTORS OF AMERICA
— announces Michael Buchanan passed Certified Landscape Technician (Exterior) exam, Lahaina News, October 3, 2002: 8.

ASSOCIATION FOR CHILDREN WITH LEARNING DISABILITIES
— Psychologist Douglas Treadway to speak, Lahaina Sun, June 6, 1973: 11.

ASSOCIATION FOR RESEARCH AND ENLIGHTENMENT INC. [BUSINESS]
— Edgar Cayce Foundation to present lectures in Lahaina, Lahaina News, October 15, 1981: 16.

ASSOCIATION OF MAUI VIDEOGRAPHERS AND FILM-MAKERS
— to hold general meeting, Lahaina News, March 4, 1987: 8.

ASSOCIATION OF TRIAL LAWYERS OF AMERICA
— to meet on Maui, Lahaina News, May 30, 1984: 5.

ASTIER, MARIE PIERRE
— raises money for environmental causes, Lahaina News, July 4, 1990: 5.

ASTON HOTELS AND RESORTS [BUSINESS]
— changes name from Hotel Corporation of the Pacific, Lahaina News, February 12, 1986: 3.
— operating Holo Honokowai as hotel, Lahaina News, December 7, 1988: 1,15.
— to help people evicted from Holo Honokowai, Lahaina News, December 14, 1988: 1.
— offering discounts to kama'aina traveling to outer islands, Lahaina News, May 9, 1990: 15.
— Jerry Fellows appointed regional manager of West Maui for, Lahaina News, December 5, 1990: 4.
— Craig Leeper named regional manager of South Maui for, Lahaina News, December 12, 1990: 6.
— announces promotions, Lahaina News, January 23, 1991: 5.
— names J.W. Ellsworth as president, Lahaina News, April 23, 1992: 15.
— appoints Shirley Tsukano to sales manager-kama'aina market, Lahaina News, July 2, 1992: 18.
— names Jerry Fellows as area vice president for West Maui, Lahaina News, September 25, 1997: 12.
— now managing The Whaler, Lahaina News, June 22, 2000: 9.
— now managing Paki Maui and Kahana Beach Resort Condominium, Lahaina News, September 14, 2000: 15.
— working with Making Memories Breast Cancer Foundation to grant family wish, Lahaina News, October 26, 2000: 20.
— promotes Mike Sands, Monica Schiffer, and Hamilton Toledo, Lahaina News, January 11, 2001: 14.
— Norman Berg named director of sales for Maui for, Lahaina News, April 5, 2001: 9.

ASTON KA'ANAPALI SHORES [BUSINESS]
— see Ka'anapali Shores Hotel [business]

ASTON KA'ANAPALI SHORES HAWAIIAN SAILING CANOE REGATTA
— to be held, Lahaina News, May 29, 1997: 12.
— to be held, Lahaina News, September 28, 2000: 9.

ASTON KAHANA REEF [BUSINESS]
— Kelly Mitchell appointed manager, Lahaina News, September 16, 1999: 11.

ASTON MAUI ISLANDER, THE
— see Maui Islander [business]

ASTON WAILEA RESORT [BUSINESS]
— joins Inter-Continental's Global Partner Hotels and Resorts division, Lahaina News, April 25, 1996: 12.
— Hula Bowl open headquarters in, Lahaina News, August 7, 1997: 5.
— restaurant and sports bar opens, Lahaina News, July 2, 1998: 12.
— to be headquarters for Hooters Hula Bowl, Lahaina News, November 12, 1998: 13.

ASTROGIN [MUSICAL GROUP]
— to perform at Maui Brews, Lahaina News, June 6, 2002: 15.

ASTROLOGY
— course to be offered, Lahaina News, October 21, 1993: 3.

ASTRONOMY
— Hokule'a to appear overhead, Lahaina News, July 4, 1990: 11,24.
— partial eclipse to take place, Lahaina News, July 18, 1990: 14.
— Scorpius, also known as Maui's fish hook, easily viewed in night sky, Lahaina News, August 29, 1990: 20.
— comet Hale-Bopp to be visible, Lahaina News, March 27, 1997: 3.
— stargazing to be held at Hosmer Grove Campground on Haleakala, Lahaina News, May 29, 1997: 16.
— Clive Ruggles to discuss "Ancient Hawaiian Astronomy", Lahaina News, June 13, 2002: 17.
— public can view Mars from roof of Hyatt Regency Maui Resort and Spa, Lahaina News, August 28, 2003: 8.

AT&T WIRELESS SERVICES [BUSINESS]
— consolidates retail centers, Lahaina News, April 2, 1998: 13.
— provides grant to Child and Family Services, Lahaina News, November 5, 1998: 17.
— opens new retail location, Lahaina News, December 3, 1998: 17.
— donates phones to Child and Fancy Services-Maui, Lahaina News, December 24, 1998: 11.
— presents grant to Maui Arts and Cultural Center, Lahaina News, January 7, 1999: 13.
— donates to Maui Arts and Cultural Center, Lahaina News, February 17, 2000: 14.
— opens new site in Kihei, Lahaina News, June 15, 2000: 14.
— expanded, Lahaina News, September 21, 2000: 16.
— donates to Maui Arts and Cultural Center, Lahaina News, April 5, 2001: 8.
— joining with KITV 4 collecting unused wireless phones to reduce domestic violence, Lahaina News, July 5, 2001: 9.

ATA DAMASCO [MUSICAL GROUP]
— to perform at "Live on the Beach", Lahaina News, August 28, 1997: 11.

ATAKAWA, BRIAN
— West Maui Little League Baseball president featured, Lahaina News, April 19, 2001: 12.

ATHENA [SHIP]
— rescued off Maui waters, Lahaina News, January 20, 1988: 18.

ATHERTON FAMILY FOUNDATION
— awards grant to Holy Innocents Preschool, Lahaina News, May 7, 1998: 18.
— awards grant to Art School at Kapalua, Lahaina News, July 19, 2001: 2.
— awards grant to ARC of Maui, Lahaina News, February 27, 2003: 9.

ATHERTON PERFORMING ARTS
— series to present Jeff Linsky, Lahaina News, May 30, 1996: 2.

ATKINSON, ROBERT
— developer proposes marina near Lahaina, Lahaina News, September 2, 1987: 1,4.

ATLANTIC [SHIP]
— sailing to Lahaina from New Jersey, Lahaina Sun, November 15, 1972: 3.

ATLANTIS [CITY]
— speculation that it has been discovered, Lahaina Sun, July 25, 1973: 3.
— research discussed, Lahaina Times, August, 1980 volume 4 number 7: 2.

ATLANTIS CONSPIRACY [BOOK]
— alleged censorship by the government, Lahaina Times, August, 1980 volume 4 number 7: 2.

ATLANTIS SUBMARINES [BUSINESS]
— plan for submarines in West Maui resisted by residents, Lahaina News, June 17, 1987: 1,20.
— plan for submarines in West Maui rejected, Lahaina News, June 24, 1987: 1.
— editorial praising opposition to proposed Atlantis submarine, Lahaina News, June 24, 1987: 2.
— to begin operating in Lahaina Harbor, Lahaina News, October 10, 1990: 8.
— to add a new submarine in Maui, Lahaina News, June 6, 1991: 6.
— Tony Beaumont appointed dive operator, Lahaina News, July 18, 1991: 6.
— appoints Jillian Francis and John Goolsby, Lahaina News, November 21, 1991: 11.
— appoints John Thompson and Jackie Boskoff as managers, Lahaina News, November 28, 1991: 7.
— creates Kama'aina Club, Lahaina News, March 19, 1992: 4.
— has no plan to sink the salvaged Tawny-D to create fish sanctuary, Lahaina News, December 17, 1992: 2.
— names Fei Barber as senior sales manager, Lahaina News, March 4, 1993: 9.
— donates to Swift Hawaiian Aquatic Craft Specialists, Lahaina News, July 1, 1993: 1.
— acquires new shuttle vessels, Lahaina News, June 16, 1994: 10.
— offering free whale watching to Maui odyssey guests, Lahaina News, January 19, 1995: 11.
— appoints Ronald Williams as regional general manager of Maui and Oahu, Lahaina News, March 7, 1996: 11.
— offering kama'aina specials, Lahaina News, October 22, 1998: 17.
— Ronald Williams becomes chief operating officer, Lahaina News, April 5, 2001: 9.
— Brenda Baroso joins as sales manager, Lahaina News, October 31, 2002: 6.

ATLAS TRAVEL [BUSINESS]
— opens office in Azeka Place, Lahaina News, November 19, 1992: 5.

ATTCO [BUSINESS]
— reviewed, Lahaina News, November 23, 1983: 16.

ATTITUDINAL HEALING
— discussed, Lahaina News, October 19, 1988: 1,17.

AU, WHITLOW
— researcher at Marine Mammal Research Program to speak on "Acoustic Recording of Humpback Whales", Lahaina News, February 8, 2001: 20.

AUBRY, KENNETH [COMEDIAN]
— to perform at Comedy Club and the Sports Page, Lahaina News, September 3, 1992: 14,15,18.

AUBURN, TOM [MAGICIAN]
— career and magic skills featured, will perform on Maui, Lahaina News, January 23, 1985: 7,8,9.

AUERSWALD, EDGAR
— named head of Maui Mental Health Service, Lahaina Sun, February 2, 1972: 14.

AUGER, BRIAN [MUSICIAN]
— to perform at Embassy Suites Resort, Lahaina News, September 12, 1991: 13.
— to perform at Embassy Suites Resort with Eric Burdon, Lahaina News, September 19, 1991: 16.

AULDRAMES, CHEYENNE
— wins Keiki Fishing Derby, Lahaina News, August 1, 1990: 14.

AUNTIE EMMA
— see Sharpe, "Auntie" Emma Kapiolani Farden [artist]

AUNTIE EMMA FARDEN SHARPE HULA FESTIVAL
— to be held, Lahaina News, November 26, 1998: 1.

AUNTIE MAME [PLAY]
— to be performed by Maui Community Theatre, Lahaina Sun, August 9, 1972: 7.
— opening day, with photographs, Lahaina Sun, August 16, 1972: 1,19.

AURELIO'S [RESTAURANT]
— features Hawaiian entertainment, Lahaina News, January 30, 1992: 22.

AUS CERTIFIED PUBLIC ACCOUNTANCY CORP. [BUSINESS]
— merges with Ronald A. Kawahara & Co., Lahaina News, August 15, 1990: 11.

AUS, DON
— receives Maui Chamber of Commerce T.S. Shinn service award, Lahaina News, September 28, 1988: 2.

AU'S SHAOLIN ARTS SOCIETY [TROUPE]
— to perform at Chinese New Year, Lahaina News, February 14, 2002: 1,20.

AUSTIN, BILL
— part owner of Aloha Voyages reacts to criticism of special use permit for commercial tourist operation, Lahaina News, November 18, 1987: 1,11,12.

AUSTIN, BRYAN
— named front desk manager at Four Seasons Resort Wailea, Lahaina News, April 9, 1992: 13.

AUSTIN TSUTSUMI & ASSOCIATES
— to work on subdivision on agricultural land between Wailuku and Kahakuloa, Lahaina News, January 31, 1990: 1.

AUSTIN, TSUTSUMI AND ASSOCIATES [BUSINESS]
— to undertake island-wide survey of traffic, Lahaina News, August 24, 1988: 1.
— perform traffic study of West Maui, Lahaina News, December 14, 1988: 1,24.

AUSTRALIA ENSEMBLE [MUSICAL GROUP]
— to perform, Lahaina News, February 25, 1993: 11.

AUTOMOBILES
— large number of unlicensed vehicles, Lahaina Sun, March 10, 1971: 8.
— accident at oceanside cliff at Kawiki, Lahaina Sun, April 7, 1971: 2.
— new license laws come into effect, Lahaina Sun, June 30, 1971: 12.
— drag racing at Pu'unene described, Lahaina Sun, April 5, 1972: 21.
— classic cars seen in Lahaina , Lahaina Sun, June 7, 1972: 6.
— Model A seen being driven on Maui, Lahaina Sun, April 25, 1973: 1,5.
— event at Maui drag strip at Pu'unene airstrip, Lahaina Sun, May 16, 1973: 3.
— Bobby Hartman purchases first Delorean car on Maui, Lahaina News, February 15, 1982: 4.
— description of high-end rental market, Lahaina News, August 6, 1986: 4.
— editorial praising lower speed limits, Lahaina News, October 8, 1986: 2.
— car clinic offered by Maui Community College, Lahaina News, November 23, 1988: 5.
— trends on Maui, Lahaina News, November 29, 1989: 11,16.
— advice if you purchase a lemon, Lahaina News, November 29, 1989: 15.
— car insurance bills to be killed, Lahaina News, February 18, 1993: 10.
— Maui Custom Show to be held at Lahaina Civic Center, Lahaina News, October 28, 1999: 3.
— Maui Classic Cruisers to hold Car Show at Azeka Place II, Lahaina News, September 26, 2002: 16.

AUTOMOTIVE TRADE SHOW AND CAR SHOW
— to be held, Lahaina News, January 16, 1992: 4,5.

AVALENE GALLERY [BUSINESS]
— opens, Lahaina News, November 1, 2001: 8.

AVALON [RESTAURANT]
— reviewed, Lahaina News, February 24, 1988: 9.
— featured, Lahaina News, July 27, 1988: 7.
— planning renovations, Lahaina News, August 23, 1989: 3.
— Mark Ellman becomes sole proprietor, Lahaina News, November 29, 1989: 4.
— featured, Lahaina News, July 22, 1993: 11.
— to open restaurant in California, Lahaina News, April 7, 1994: 12.
— featured, Lahaina News, December 4, 1997: 18.
— featured; adds sushi bar, Lahaina News, March 5, 1998: 6.
— sold by Mark Ellman to FlamCom, Inc., Lahaina News, December 10, 1998: 11,17.
— to hold benefit for Punana Leo O Maui, Lahaina News, December 10, 1998: 20.

AVEIRO, STEPHANIE
— selected as Maui County director of Department of Human Concerns, Lahaina News, January 16, 1991: 9.
— warned to avoid conflict of interest, Lahaina News, November 26, 1992: 3.

AVERILL, HARRY
— named general manager of Lahaina Divers, Lahaina News, September 3, 1992: 8.

AVERY, ALEXANDRA
— offering facials, Lahaina News, February 18, 1999: 12.

AVERY, PAUL
— to represent Hawaiian Airlines Magazine on Maui, Lahaina News, March 20, 1991: 7.

AVERY, STEVE [ATHLETE]
— playing for the University of Arkansas Razorbacks, featured, Lahaina News, August 13, 1986: 4.

AVIS RENT-A-CAR [BUSINESS]
— offering cellular service, Lahaina News, December 26, 1990: 7.
— promotes Linda Walton to Maui agency manager, Lahaina News, March 27, 1991: 9.
— to partner with Kea Lani Hotel, Lahaina News, June 13, 1991: 18.

AWESOME BLOSSOM [BUSINESS]
— plans parties, Lahaina News, November 14, 1996: 8.

AXELSON, JENNY
— Scholar/Athlete of the Week, Lahaina News, May 9, 2002: 12.

AXUM PACIFICA GALLERY [BUSINESS]
— to exhibit works of Val Baldwin, sales to support Maui Humane Society, Lahaina News, July 26, 2001: 16.

AYANA [MUSICIAN]
— to perform at Casanova's, sponsored by Maui Jazz Society, Lahaina News, June 13, 1991: 13.
— to perform at Casanova's, Lahaina News, June 20, 1991: 11.

AYAT, HAROLD
— member of Polynesian Voyaging Society to talk on "The Making of a Voyaging Canoe", Lahaina News, August 9, 2001: 16.

AYAU, HENRY KEAWE, JR.
— elected president of Moloka'i Chamber of Commerce, Lahaina News, August 13, 1992: 12.

AYCOCK, DON
— to speak at West Maui Christian Men's Camp, Lahaina News, September 18, 2003: 5.

AYERS, DAVID
— says marketing data should guide proposed convention center, Lahaina News, May 6, 1993: 1.

AYERS, TOM [COMEDIAN]
— to perform at Comedy Club and the Sports Page, Lahaina News, May 6, 1993: 15,17.
— to perform at Comedy Club and the Sports Page, Lahaina News, May 13, 1993: 10.

AZAD, FARZAD AND KATHRYN
— opens Java Jazz at Honokowai Marketplace, Lahaina News, November 4, 1999: 11.

AZEKA, BILL "KUSUO"
— to speak with son Tyler to "The Young Entrepreneurs Seminar" at Maui Community College, Lahaina News, October 31, 1991: 10.
— honored by mayor Linda Lingle, Lahaina News, March 26, 1992: 5.
— to celebrate 43 years of business, Lahaina News, March 11, 1993: 10.
— to host barbecued ribs competition, Lahaina News, August 19, 1993: 7.
— to sell Azeka Place Shopping Center, Lahaina News, July 27, 1995: 10.
— to hold award for best barbecued ribs, Lahaina News, August 8, 1996: 16.

AZEKA BUILDING CORPORATION [BUSINESS]
— proposes developing land near Azeka Place I and II, Lahaina News, September 3, 1992: 13.

AZEKA PLACE [BUSINESS]
— holds anniversary celebration, Lahaina News, April 15, 1987: 12.

AZEKA PLACE II [BUSINESS]
— construction resumes, Lahaina News, November 14, 1990: 11.
— shopping center to hold grand opening, Lahaina News, July 30, 1992: 12.
— to hold grand opening, Lahaina News, August 6, 1992: 9.
— grand opening held, Lahaina News, August 13, 1992: 9.

AZEKA PLACE SHOPPING CENTER [BUSINESS]
— to hold Halloween costume contest, Lahaina News, October 24, 1991: 22.
— to hold Halloween costume contest, Lahaina News, October 14, 1993: 7.
— to hold Summer Family Fun Day, Lahaina News, August 18, 1994: 16.
— sold to corporation owned by Tom Enomoto, Lahaina News, November 14, 1996: 8.
— to hold "Junior Achievement Day", Lahaina News, June 4, 1998: 13.

AZEKA'S MARKET [BUSINESS]
— to close, Lahaina News, June 30, 1994: 8,9.

AZMAN, BEN [POLITICIAN]
— doctor running for senate seat, Lahaina News, August 8, 2002: 1,20.

AZMAN, ROSIANA (NANI)
— earns Master of Arts in Psychology, Lahaina News, September 14, 2000: 19.

AZMAN, SHARITA
— earns M.D. Degree from John A. Burns School of Medicine, Lahaina News, June 19, 1997: 2.

AZUSA PACIFIC COLLEGE DYNAMICS CHORALE
— perform at Lahaina Baptist Mission, Lahaina Sun, June 16, 1971: 3.

B

B., STEPHEN [COMEDIAN]
— to perform at Comedy Club, Lahaina News, January 23, 1992: 16,17,18.

B.J.'S CHICAGO PIZZERIA [RESTAURANT]
— to move into former Blue Max space, Lahaina News, February 24, 1994: 3.
— to open , Lahaina News, June 30, 1994: 8.

— featured, Lahaina News, July 21, 1994: 10.
— history of building described, Lahaina News, May 25, 1995: 3.
— changes menu, Lahaina News, June 5, 1997: 1,6,7.
— Sons of Hawaii performs at, Lahaina News, September 4, 1997: 2.
— Sons of Hawaii to perform at for documentary, Lahaina News, January 7, 1999: 1,20.

B.M.X. GIRLS [MUSICAL GROUP]
— to perform at benefit concert at Maui Brews, Lahaina News, August 5, 1999: 14.

B&C DELI KITCHEN [RESTAURANT]
— opens, Lahaina News, January 30, 2003: 9.
— Linda Diep is new owner of, Lahaina News, July 24, 2003: 8.

BA-LE [RESTAURANT]
— to open in Lahaina Cannery Mall, Lahaina News, June 1, 2000: 14.

BABA B [MUSICAL GROUP]
— to perform at "A Taste of Lahaina", Lahaina News, September 2, 1999: 18.

BABAJKO, NATALIE AND RONNIE
— open Alii Designs jewelry store, Lahaina News, April 18, 2002: 8.

BABAR THE ELEPHANT [MUSICAL]
— to be performed by Maui Symphony Orchestra, Lahaina News, April 20, 1995: 12.

BABES IN TOYLAND [PLAY]
— cast announced, Lahaina News, November 4, 1987: 3.
— to be performed by Theatre Theatre Maui, Lahaina News, December 10, 1992: 15.

BABY BEACH
— to be cleaned by Boy Scouts, Lahaina News, April 25, 1990: 2.
— volunteers to clean, Lahaina News, October 12, 2000: 1.

BABY FAIR
— to be held at Maui Mall, Lahaina News, April 26, 2001: 20.

BABY HUI, THE [BUSINESS]
— support group network created, Lahaina News, February 5, 1998: 2.

BABY SIGN LANGUAGE
— workshop to be held, Lahaina News, August 7, 2003: 16.
— workshop to be offered, Lahaina News, September 25, 2003: 16.

BACALSO, JUSTIN IKAIKA
— Lahainaluna High School student dies in automobile accident, Lahaina News, February 9, 1995: 7.

BACALSO, LEIMOMI
— Miss Hawaii USA 1990 to appear at Miss Lahaina Pageant, Lahaina News, June 13, 1990: B1.

BACH, JOHANN SEBASTIAN [MUSICIAN]
— music to be performed by Maui Symphony Orchestra, Lahaina News, September 27, 1989: 2.

BACKSTAGE PRODUCTIONS, INC. [BUSINESS]
— opens, Lahaina News, June 27, 1991: 7.

BACKWELL, FRANK
— Maui Visitors Bureau director speaks of projections for tourism on Maui, Lahaina News, February 22, 1989: 13.

BACKYARD [MUSICAL GROUP]
— to perform at Borders Books, Lahaina News, July 1, 1999: 12.

BACON, DICK
— discusses Na Mele O Maui music festival, Lahaina News, November 5, 1986: 1.

BAD MAN'S TERRITORY [FILM]
— to be shown at Lahaina Courtroom by James Warren, co-star with Randolph Scott, Lahaina News, May 22, 1985: 20.

BAD RELIGION [MUSICAL GROUP]
— to perform at Blue Tropix, Lahaina News, February 16, 1995: 15.

BADUA, KELIS AND KAILEE
— sisters compete in Grand National beauty pageant finals, Lahaina News, May 15, 2003: 3.

BADURA-SKOKA, PAUL [MUSICIAN]
— pianist to perform at Maui Arts and Cultural Center, Lahaina News, April 2, 1998: 16.

BAEGNE, MABIBA [DANCER]
— performance hosted by Maui Dance Council, Lahaina News, April 28, 1994: 15.

BAGLEY, BILL [ARTIST]
— career described, Lahaina News, April 25, 1984: 10.
— exhibit at Kaluani, Lahaina News, August 15, 1984: 3.
— work featured, Lahaina News, February 19, 1986: 16.
— offering workshops sponsored by Lahaina Arts Society, Lahaina News, November 26, 1986: 12.
— featured at Old Jail Gallery, Lahaina News, February 11, 1987: 3.
— works featured at Old Jail Gallery, Lahaina News, February 10, 1988: 11.
— to exhibit at Lahaina Arts Society, Lahaina News, January 28, 1993: 14.

BAGOYO, VINCE [POLITICIAN]
— country water director warns of water supply, Lahaina News, May 10, 1989: 1.
— announces candidacy for Maui County Council seat, Lahaina News, May 9, 1990: 2.
— Maui County council member hoping to turn proposed North Beach resort into park, Lahaina News, October 17, 1991: 1.
— returns campaign contribution from Sports Shinko Co., Lahaina News, February 13, 1992: 4.
— Maui County Council Member fears dumping will increase once Makani Landfill closes, Lahaina News, April 2, 1992: 6.
— concerned about source assessment proposed by water board, Lahaina News, September 24, 1992: 6,7.

BAHA'I
— support of West Maui Youth Center, Lahaina Sun, January 6, 1971: 7.
— faith described, Lahaina Sun, January 6, 1971: 7.
— observes Human Rights Day, Lahaina News, December 4, 1985: 3.
— to meet every Friday, Lahaina News, January 23, 1992: 4.
— Institute to support the needy, Lahaina News, September 24, 1998: 7.
— Institute continues to meet, Lahaina News, October 15, 1998: 17.
— to show "Navajo Sand Painting: A Healing Tradition", Lahaina News, November 26, 1998: 16.
— continue to meet, Lahaina News, February 25, 1999: 13.
— to hold Ho'olaule'a Maui Inter-Cultural Festival, Lahaina News, March 4, 1999: 12.
— Institute continues to meet, Lahaina News, May 20, 1999: 17.
— to hold free car wash, Lahaina News, June 17, 1999: 16.
— Youth Dance Workshop to be held, Lahaina News, November 18, 1999: 17.
— gathering to be held, Lahaina News, May 17, 2001: 10.

BAHAMAS
— travel to described, Lahaina News, September, 1979: 7.

BAHENA, CECELIA [ARTIST]
— leading painting workshop, Lahaina News, January 25, 2001: 15.

BAHOUTH, CHIP
— Sheraton Maui manager dives from Black Rock for Visitor Industry Charity Walk, Lahaina News, May 18, 2000: 16.

BAHOUTH, GERALD
— promoted to general manager of Sheraton Maui, Lahaina News, January 16, 2003: 9.

BAILES DE PILIPINAS DANCE TROUPE
— to present "Kalayaan", Lahaina News, November 5, 1998: 20.

BAILEY, ANDREW
— beaten at Makena Beach, Lahaina Sun, April 12, 1972: 9.

BAILEY, BREN [WRITER]
— publishes "Maui Remembers: A Local History", Lahaina News, November 3, 1994: 9.

BAILEY HOUSE MUSEUM
— to open, Lahaina News, October 14, 1987: 3,17.
— closed for fumigation, Lahaina News, October 12, 1988: 3.
— to hold fundraiser, Lahaina News, November 2, 1988: 18.
— Maui Historical Society sponsoring tours of, Lahaina News, November 14, 1991: 3.
— now called Maui Historical Museum, Lahaina News, August 11, 1994: 4.
— to hold open house, Lahaina News, May 11, 1995: 2.
— to feature exhibit on plantation-era architecture, Lahaina News, July 6, 1995: 11.
— to host lecture by Hokulani Padilla on "Hawaiian Language and Social Structure", Lahaina News, February 8, 1996: 4.
— to hold benefit, Lahaina News, October 31, 1996: 18.
— to host lecture on holua sledding, Lahaina News, May 15, 1997: 12.
— celebrates 40 years, Lahaina News, August 21, 1997: 16.
— offering gifts for the holiday, Lahaina News, October 30, 1997: 16.
— has Hawaiian gifts, Lahaina News, December 4, 1997: 24.
— seeking volunteers, Lahaina News, January 29, 1998: 16.
— to host talk by Deborah Pope, Lahaina News, September 3, 1998: 21.
— to celebrate "Living Traditions", Lahaina News, November 19, 1998: 16.
— seeking volunteers, Lahaina News, February 18, 1999: 13.
— to offer class on Genealogy, Lahaina News, April 15, 1999: 12.
— offering Hawaiiana courses, Lahaina News, June 3, 1999: 2.
— archaeology classes to be held, Lahaina News, July 1, 1999: 13.
— archaeology class "Heiau and the Political History of Maui" to be held, Lahaina News, July 15, 1999: 12.
— tour of gardens offered, Lahaina News, August 12, 1999: 17.
— to hold genealogy class, Lahaina News, August 19, 1999: 16.
— Sol Kawaihoa continues to present on Slack Key , Lahaina News, September 2, 1999: 16.
— George Manulani Maimiola to discuss Hawaiian artifacts, Lahaina News, September 16, 1999: 12.
— to offer class on "Hawaiian Weapons—Making Pahoa/Dagger", Lahaina News, September 16, 1999: 13.
— to host class on making Ipu Heke, Lahaina News, September 30, 1999: 13.
— to offer course on weaving lauhala baskets, Lahaina News, October 14, 1999: 12.
— Makahiki season to begin at, Lahaina News, October 14, 1999: 12.
— to host class on making 'uli'uli, Lahaina News, November 4, 1999: 13.
— to host Clifford Nae'ole speaking on "Honokahua Preservation and Hawaiian Unification", Lahaina News, November 4, 1999: 13.
— to show documentary "Kahului Railroad Stories", Lahaina News, June 1, 2000: 17.
— George Manulani Kaimiola to give tour of, Lahaina News, September 6, 2001: 16.
— Victoria Pula to lead "Talk (Hawaiian) History with Victoria", Lahaina News, September 20, 2001: 16.
— Kapiohookalani Lyons Naone to teach class on Hawaiian Moon Calendar at, Lahaina News, September 27, 2001: 17.
— to offer "the Hat Exhibit", Lahaina News, May 23, 2002: 16.
— Bob Hobdy to lead class on "Ahupua'a—Traditional Hawaiian Land Divisions" , Lahaina News, May 30, 2002: 16.
— George Kaimiola to lead tour of, Lahaina News, June 6, 2002: 17.
— to hold demonstration on making poi, Lahaina News, July 25, 2002: 21.

— "E Ho'oulu Aloha: To Grow in Love" benefit to be held, Lahaina News, November 21, 2002: 18.

— concert to benefit, Lahaina News, November 28, 2002: 18.

— to hold kama'aina day, Lahaina News, August 28, 2003: 16.

BAILEY, MATTHEW

— named resident manager of Kapalua Bay Hotel, Lahaina News, March 7, 1990: 7.

BAILEY, MICHAEL

— comments on proposed thrillcraft corridor, Lahaina News, February 24, 1988: 1.

— Earthtrust activist frees dolphins from holding pen in Taiwan, Lahaina News, April 18, 1990: 3.

— see also Earthtrust

BAILEY, ROSELLE

— Waiola Church to offer Hawaiian Culture Series, Lahaina News, February 3, 2000: 12,13.

— blesses new community park at North Beach, Lahaina News, January 24, 2002: 3.

BAILY, MICHAEL

— Director of Greenpeace Hawaii moves to Lahaina, Lahaina News, January 14, 1987: 1,9.

BAIRD, ROBIN

— Pacific Whale Foundation's director of research to speak on whale tagging, Lahaina News, January 27, 2000: 13.

BAIRD, SCOTT [MUSICIAN]

— to perform at Pioneer Inn, Lahaina News, September 19, 1991: 16.

— continues to perform at El Crab Catcher, Lahaina News, October 3, 1991: 13.

— to perform at Pioneer Inn, Lahaina News, February 6, 1992: 18.

— to perform at Moondoggies, Lahaina News, November 25, 1993: 12.

— to perform at Chico's Cantina, Lahaina News, February 3, 1994: 12.

— featured, Lahaina News, July 7, 1994: 12.

— has formed band "Crazy Fingers", Lahaina News, December 8, 1994: 14.

— to perform at Chico's Cantina and Cafe, Lahaina News, July 20, 1995: 11.

— continues to perform at Chico's Cantina, Lahaina News, July 27, 1995: 11.

— to perform at Chico's Cantina and Cafe, Lahaina News, August 24, 1995: 12.

— to perform at Moose McGillycuddy's, Lahaina News, October 2, 1997: 18.

BAJEUX, RENE

— named executive chef at Four Seasons Resort Wailea, Lahaina News, February 6, 1991: 6.

BAKER, ROZ [POLITICIAN]

— to run for 10th District House of Representatives, Lahaina News, February 19, 1986: 3.

— files nomination papers for 10th house district, Lahaina News, May 7, 1986: 3.

— reacts to tort bill, Lahaina News, August 6, 1986: 18.

— candidacy for State Representative featured, Lahaina News, October 29, 1986: 1,11.

— announces run for State House of Representatives, Lahaina News, March 2, 1988: 12.

— meets with voters, Lahaina News, July 20, 1988: 3.

— featured, Lahaina News, October 26, 1988: 1,15.

— to hold community meeting, Lahaina News, February 15, 1989: 14.

— reports on her House bills, Lahaina News, February 22, 1989: 9.

— bill to ban advances in House of Representatives, Lahaina News, March 8, 1989: 1.

— reports on Volunteer Information and Referral Service, Lahaina News, March 15, 1989: 14.

— bill to ban thrillcrafts dead in the legislature, Lahaina News, March 29, 1989: 1.

— reports on some house resolutions, Lahaina News, April 19, 1989: 14.

— reports on thrillcraft ban, likely to result in compromise, Lahaina News, May 3, 1989: 5.

— to hold golf tournament fundraiser, Lahaina News, July 26, 1989: 2.

— to introduce bill to regulate tour activities, Lahaina News, November 15, 1989: 1.

— to seek state funds to study park improvements, Lahaina News, November 29, 1989: 1.

— reviews survey of constituents, Lahaina News, January 3, 1990: 9.

— introduces bill to give King Kamehameha III School a vice principal, Lahaina News, January 24, 1990: 3.

— planning to introduce legislation to stop mansion development at Hawea, Lahaina News, February 14, 1990: 1.

— confident of thrillcraft ban, Lahaina News, February 21, 1990: 4.

— bills to regular tourist activity industry debated, Lahaina News, February 28, 1990: 1.

— King Kamehameha III School will get vice principal, Lahaina News, May 2, 1990: 1.

— requesting portable classrooms for Lahainaluna High School, Lahaina News, May 23, 1990: 1,6.

— sponsors bill to study erosion at Honolua Bay, Lahaina News, June 13, 1990: 1.

— to seek reelection, Lahaina News, July 4, 1990: 3.

— appraises State budget, Lahaina News, January 16, 1991: 1,9.

— appointed vice chair of House Transportation Committee, Lahaina News, January 23, 1991: 4.

— seeks public opinion through survey in Lahaina News, Lahaina News, February 27, 1991: 1,3.

— summarizes results of survey, Lahaina News, April 3, 1991: 5.

— evaluates legislative session, comments on funding of projects in West Maui, Lahaina News, May 15, 1991: 1.

— raises money for Lahainaluna High School athletics department through golf fundraiser, Lahaina News, September 19, 1991: 3.

— to seek tighter law on thrillcraft ban, Lahaina News, January 9, 1992: 1.

— to give weekly 5 minute updates on legislature on KPOA-FM, Lahaina News, January 16, 1992: 3.

— discusses funds approved by legislature, Lahaina News, May 7, 1992: 1.

— files papers to run in reapportioned district , Lahaina News, June 25, 1992: 2.

— to hold benefit for re-election campaign, Lahaina News, August 27, 1992: 3.

— appointed majority leader of the state House, Lahaina News, November 12, 1992: 4.

— medical center a priority, Lahaina News, January 7, 1993: 3.

— discusses legislative concerns, Lahaina News, January 28, 1993: 1,5.

— to hold public session at Lahaina Public Library, Lahaina News, February 25, 1993: 2.

— asks that Mala Wharf dredging be sped up, Lahaina News, March 11, 1993: 2.

— seeks sanity in time share industry, Lahaina News, May 13, 1993: 1,3.

— appointed to senate seat vacated by Russell Blair, Lahaina News, December 2, 1993: 1.

— to hold community forum, Lahaina News, December 30, 1993: 3.

— discusses funding for road improvement in Lahaina, Lahaina News, February 24, 1994: 1.

— updates residents on legislative session, Lahaina News, March 3, 1994: 1,2.

— to offer legislative update, Lahaina News, May 5, 1994: 2.

— community forum held, Lahaina News, May 19, 1994: 1,20.

— to sit on education committee, Lahaina News, July 28, 1994: 4.

— race with Jan Yagi Buen detailed, Lahaina News, September 8, 1994: 2.

— says State risk report to help lawmakers plan, Lahaina News, December 15, 1994: 1.

— to hold community forum, Lahaina News, January 5, 1995: 4.

— discusses issues faced by state legislature, Lahaina News, January 19, 1995: 1,16.

— to focus on thrill craft and road bills, Lahaina News, February 9, 1995: 1,16.

— wants to reduce county liability for recreational facilities, Lahaina News, February 16, 1995: 1,3.

— hold public meeting, Lahaina News, March 16, 1995: 1,4.

— updates on legislative session, Lahaina News, March 30, 1995: 3.

— to meet with West Side Committee, Lahaina News, May 4, 1995: 4.

— to receive Distinguished Alumna Award from Southwest-Texas State University, Lahaina News, October 26, 1995: 2.

— to speak at Maui County Century Club, Lahaina News, December 14, 1995: 19.

— discusses upcoming legislative session, Lahaina News, December 28, 1995: 1,12.

— to hold community forum with Mike White, Lahaina News, January 4, 1996: 4.

— to speak at Democratic Century Club, Lahaina News, December 12, 1996: 8.

— trying to restore subsidy for Moloka'i ferry service, Lahaina News, February 6, 1997: 3.

— announces that funds released for cafeteria at Princess Nahienaena Elementary School, Lahaina News, June 19, 1997: 2.

— participates in "Wild West Side Jailathon" fundraiser for the American Cancer Society, Lahaina News, August 7, 1997: 3.

— Lahaina to Moloka'i ferry a priority, Lahaina News, January 22, 1998: 1,16.

— files for reelection, Lahaina News, June 11, 1998: 9.

— to run Office of Economic Development after loss in primary, Lahaina News, December 10, 1998: 1,2.

— seeking return to State Senate, Lahaina News, June 27, 2002: 1,2.

— to hold fundraiser at Maui Tropical Plantation, Lahaina News, July 18, 2002: 2.

— to hold fundraiser, Lahaina News, July 25, 2002: 16.

— to hold public meeting, Lahaina News, December 5, 2002: 1,22.

— to hold Town Meeting, Lahaina News, December 12, 2002: 2.

— held community forum, Lahaina News, December 19, 2002: 1.

— to hold public meeting with Brian Blundell, Lahaina News, February 20, 2003: 1,20.

— names Maui liaisons, Lahaina News, February 20, 2003: 8.

— held public meeting, Lahaina News, March 6, 2003: 1,20.

— to discuss 2003 legislative session, Lahaina News, May 15, 2003: 1.

— to meet with State Director of Transportation Rodney Haraga, Lahaina News, June 19, 2003: 3.

— critical of Governor Linda Lingle not signing helicopter air ambulance bill, Lahaina News, July 3, 2003: 2.

— to help Business and Professional Women Club celebrate 60 years, Lahaina News, August 21, 2003: 9.

BAKERY, THE [RESTAURANT]
— owner Harold Hardcastle featured, Lahaina News, August 1, 1991: 6.

BAL, EUGENE
— named director of Maui High Performance Computer Center, Lahaina News, December 12, 1996: 13.

BAL, NEIL
— fire inspector discusses threat of summer fires, Lahaina News, July 19, 1989: 1.

BALAGSO, HEATHER
— to represent Maui at Miss Teen Hawaii competition, Lahaina News, July 27, 1995: 3.

BALANGITAO, JOE, JR.
— special education teacher moves from Baldwin High School to Lahainaluna High School, Lahaina News, August 30, 2001: 1,8.

BALAZS, GEORGE
— to discuss sea turtle research, Lahaina News, September 19, 2002: 19.

BALBOA, CINDY
— promoted to account executive in the sales office of the Ka'anapali Beach Hotel, Lahaina News, September 3, 1992: 8.

BALBOA, MARCELO
— World Cup soccer player presents clinic, Lahaina News, August 11, 1994: 6.

BALDACCI, DAVID [WRITER]
— to attend Maui Writers Conference, Lahaina News, August 19, 1999: 2.

BALDWIN, BILL
— new chair of Maui Chamber of Commerce , Lahaina News, June 27, 1996: 12.

BALDWIN, ETHEL [ARTIST]
— to exhibit at Hui No'eau, Lahaina News, March 4, 1999: 12.

BALDWIN HIGH SCHOOL
— students won All-State Speech Tournament, Lahaina Sun, March 29, 1972: 10.

— commended by Western Association of Schools and Colleges, Lahaina Sun, May 31, 1972: 14.

— accreditation successful, Lahaina Sun, September 13, 1972: 3.

— receives computer donation from Maui Marriott, Lahaina News, April 13, 1988: 12.

— class of 1981 to hold reunion, Lahaina News, April 17, 1991: 18.

— to hold commencement exercises, Lahaina News, June 4, 1992: 7.

— class of 1983 to hold reunion, Lahaina News, November 12, 1992: 5.

— teachers request support of URSA program, Lahaina News, December 16, 1993: 6.

— class of 1968 to hold reunion, Lahaina News, October 23, 1997: 20.

— to celebrate May Day, Lahaina News, April 30, 1998: 16.

— class of 1979 planning a reunion, Lahaina News, May 28, 1998: 12.

— class of 1979 to hold reunion, Lahaina News, June 18, 1998: 17.

— student group succeeds in CNBC Student Stock Tournament, Lahaina News, March 18, 1999: 13.

— students participate in stock tournament, Lahaina News, April 29, 1999: 13.

— International Thespian Troupe to hold fundraiser, Lahaina News, January 25, 2001: 7.

— to hold Brown Bags to Stardom, Lahaina News, February 8, 2001: 20.

— students clean up Keka'a Beach, Lahaina News, March 8, 2001: 3.

— to perform "Joseph and The Amazing Technicolor Dreamcoat", Lahaina News, January 17, 2002: 17.

— to perform "Joseph and The Amazing Technicolor Dreamcoat", Lahaina News, January 24, 2002: 16.

— class of 1972 planning reunion, Lahaina News, May 2, 2002: 2.

— class of 1983 to hold reunion, Lahaina News, September 12, 2002: 2.

— class of 1983 to hold reunion, Lahaina News, June 26, 2003: 8.

BALDWIN HOUSE
— tours given as part of annual Thanksgiving Hoolaulea, Lahaina Sun, November 18, 1970: 4.

— historical marker for, discussed , Lahaina Sun, December 16, 1970: 6.

— featured, Lahaina News, December 14, 1983: 9,10,11.

BALDWIN, JOHN
— appointed Maui representative on the state Maritime Authority Commission, Lahaina News, October 8, 1998: 13.

BALDWIN PACIFIC CORPORATION [BUSINESS]
— Abraham Aiona appointed Director of Community Relations for, Lahaina News, April 1, 1987: 12.
— plans for residential development near Maui Research and Technology Park, Lahaina News, October 22, 1992: 12.

BALDWIN PERFORMING ARTS LEARNING CENTER
— to host Broadway Babes, Lahaina News, March 12, 1992: 21,22.
— to host "The Wiz", Lahaina News, January 23, 2003: 17.

BALDWIN, PETER
— elected to board of Bancorp Hawaii, Lahaina News, May 15, 1991: 8.
— to be honored by Boy Scouts as Distinguished Citizen, Lahaina News, May 23, 1991: 3.
— awarded Distinguished Citizen Award by Boy Scouts, Lahaina News, June 6, 1991: 3.

BALDWIN THEATRE GUILD
— staging USO-themed show, Lahaina News, January 7, 1987: 3.
— presents "Play It Again Sam", Lahaina News, March 18, 1987: 18.
— to perform "Diamond Lil Review", Lahaina News, May 6, 1987: 3.
— to perform "The Wiz", Lahaina News, October 21, 1987: 12.
— to perform Diamond Lil Revue, Lahaina News, January 20, 1988: 3.
— sets season, Lahaina News, October 19, 1988: 17.
— to perform "Diamond Lil" fifties cabaret show, Lahaina News, November 29, 1989: 18.
— to present "A Salute to America", Lahaina News, April 4, 1990: 13.
— to perform "The Imaginary Invalid", Lahaina News, May 9, 1990: 18.
— to perform "Once Upon a Mattress", Lahaina News, November 7, 1991: 20.
— to perform "Barefoot in the Park", Lahaina News, February 13, 1992: 22.
— "Joseph, and the Technicolor Dreamcoat" performances continued, Lahaina News, August 13, 1992: 18.
— to perform "Chicago", Lahaina News, November 5, 1992: 17.
— "Chicago" to open, Lahaina News, November 19, 1992: 13.
— to perform "Waiting for the Parade", Lahaina News, January 14, 1993: 15.
— to perform "The Restaurant at the End of the Universe", Lahaina News, April 21, 1994: 16.
— to perform Richard Sheridan's "The Rivals", Lahaina News, November 3, 1994: 28.
— to perform Rogers and Hammerstein's "Carousel", Lahaina News, January 5, 1995: 12.

BALDWIN, VAL [ARTIST]
— to exhibit at Axum Pacifica Gallery, sales to support Maui Humane Society, Lahaina News, July 26, 2001: 16.

BALGAS, ANTHONY
— being sought by police, Lahaina News, February 26, 1998: 2.

BALI
— report of surf at, Lahaina Times, August, 1980 volume 4 number 7: 1.
— dancers and musicians of to perform at Maui Arts and Cultural Center, Lahaina News, March 11, 1999: 13.
— dancers and musicians of to perform, Lahaina News, March 18, 1999: 17.

BALI, ZACH
— Scholar/Athlete of the Week, Lahaina News, November 7, 2002: 11.

BALINBIN, ERIC
— Lahainaluna High School basketball coach featured, Lahaina News, November 28, 2002: 12.

BALINBIN, JOE
— chef receives culinary award, Lahaina News, July 14, 1994: 13.

BALINBIN, RUDY
— joins staff of International Savings and Loans Association, Lahaina News, November 19, 1986: 3.
— joins United Mortgage as loan officer, Lahaina News, May 9, 1990: 9.

BALINBIN, WILLIAM
— Lahainaluna High School graduate recognized by National Academy Foundation, Lahaina News, July 19, 2001: 8.

BALL, BAILEY
— Scholar/Athlete of the Week, Lahaina News, December 7, 2000: 12.

BALL, CAROL [POLITICIAN]
— running for Wailuku-, Lahaina News, February 5, 1998: 3.
— to hold golf tournament fundraiser, Lahaina News, July 23, 1998: 16.
— to hold public meeting, Lahaina News, October 8, 1998: 7.

BALL, CODY
— Scholar/Athlete of the Week, Lahaina News, August 30, 2001: 13.

BALL, EMILY [ARTIST]
— art show "One Canoe, Earth" to be exhibited at Miracles Bookery, Lahaina News, October 12, 2000: 20.

BALL, KIM
— ends his sports column in Lahaina News, Lahaina News, October 17, 1984: 4.
— Lahainaluna High School wrestling coach interviewed, Lahaina News, June 18, 1986: 4.
— president of Hi-Tech Maui named Maui County Small Business Person of the Year, Lahaina News, April 20, 1995: 7.
— owner of Tech Surf Sports and Shapers featured, Lahaina News, February 20, 1997: 6.
— helps to increase inventory of beach access parking, Lahaina News, February 1, 2001: 1,22.
— advocates to add surfing to school sports, Lahaina News, July 31, 2003: 12.

BALL, LINDSAY
— new principal at King Kamehameha III Elementary School, Lahaina News, October 4, 2001: 1,20.
— named "Educator of the Month" by Hula Grill, Lahaina News, May 9, 2002: 2.

BALL, PATRICK [MUSICIAN]
— Celtic harp player to perform at Kahului Public Library, Lahaina News, May 25, 2000: 18.
— Celtic harp player to perform at Makawao Union Church, Lahaina News, April 18, 2002: 16.

BALLENGER, PATRICK
— purchases Lahaina Fish Market, Lahaina Sun, January 31, 1973: 13.

BALLESTEROS, FRANK
— to discuss micro-enterprises, Lahaina News, August 31, 2000: 1.

BALLET
— classes to be offered, Lahaina News, January 30, 1992: 4.

BALLET CONCIERTO DE PUERTO RICO [TROUPE]
— to be presented by Maui Philharmonic Society, Lahaina News, March 23, 1995: 11,12.

BALLET FOLCLORICO DO BRASIL [TROUPE]
— to perform, Lahaina News, April 18, 1996: 16.

BALLET HISPANICO
— to be performed at Baldwin Auditorium, Lahaina News, November 15, 1989: 14.

BALLETS AFRICAINS OF GUINEA [TROUPE]
— to perform at Iao Theatre, Lahaina News, May 16, 1996: 11.

BALLOONS GALORE [BUSINESS]
— featured, Lahaina News, November 14, 1984: 18.
— purchased by David Gardner and Nancy Sing, Lahaina News, June 26, 1985: 20.

BALLOONS N' THINGS [BUSINESS]
— opens, Lahaina News, December 5, 1991: 12.

BALLROOM DANCE
— see Hawaii Ballroom Dance Association

BALLROOM DANCE THEATRE
— held at Baldwin Auditorium, Lahaina News, March 25, 1987: 12.

BALLROOM DANCING
— see dancing

BALOG, DAWN
— opens hypnotherapy practice, Lahaina News, April 18, 1996: 8.

BALTAZAR, GABE [MUSICIAN]
— show to benefit Father Damien church, Lahaina News, June 24, 1987: 7,10.
— to perform with Henry Allen, Lahaina News, June 28, 1989: 15.
— to perform at Blackie's Bar, Lahaina News, December 6, 1989: 15.
— featured, Lahaina News, December 27, 1989: 15.
— featured on Hawaii Public Television "Spectrum Hawaii", Lahaina News, January 30, 1992: 19.
— to perform, Lahaina News, January 21, 1993: 16.
— to perform jazz concert, Lahaina News, January 26, 1995: 16.
— to perform in "Sounds of the Big Band Era" to be held at Maui Lu Resort, Lahaina News, March 30, 1995: 12.
— to perform at big band event at Ritz-Carlton, Lahaina News, May 7, 1998: 16.
— to perform at Maui Symphony Orchestra's "Best of Both Worlds", Lahaina News, May 14, 1998: 8.
— to perform with Henry Allen at the Hawaiian All-Stars Maui Music Festival, Lahaina News, May 27, 1999: 13.
— to receive Legends of Jazz Award from Maui Jazz Society, Lahaina News, June 24, 1999: 14.
— to perform with Maui Symphony Orchestra, Lahaina News, January 13, 2000: 14.
— to perform at "I Love Lahaina", Lahaina News, November 9, 2000: 23.

BALTER, LAURENCE
— member of Edward Jones to present "Perspective and Investment Strategies for an Uncertain Time", Lahaina News, October 4, 2001: 8.
— to discuss managing retirement income, Lahaina News, November 8, 2001: 8.
— to offer seminar on investing, Lahaina News, January 3, 2002: 8.
— holds grand opening for Edward Jones office, Lahaina News, February 14, 2002: 8.
— to lead seminar on estate planning, Lahaina News, February 28, 2002: 8.
— wins Winner's Circle and Partner's Awards from Edward Jones, Lahaina News, July 11, 2002: 8.
— to offer seminar on Social Security benefits, Lahaina News, September 5, 2002: 8.
— to offer seminar on Social Security benefits, Lahaina News, September 12, 2002: 9.
— to open Maui office of Linsco/Private Ledger, Lahaina News, March 13, 2003: 8.
— to discuss "Investing the Warren Buffett Way", Lahaina News, June 5, 2003: 8.

BAMBOO—PLANT OF A THOUSAND USES [FILM]
— shown at Lahaina Library, Lahaina Sun, May 5, 1971: 3.

BANANA MOON [LOUNGE]
— installs new video music system, Lahaina News, September 12, 1984: 3.
— to begin big band performances, Lahaina News, May 1, 1985: 4.
— reviewed, Lahaina News, November 27, 1985: 8.
— now has no cover charge, Lahaina News, October 31, 1991: 14.

BANANA PATCH [BUILDING]
— see hippies

BANCORP FINANCE OF HAWAII, INC. [BUSINESS]
— opens branch in Lahaina, Lahaina News, November 1, 1981: 16.

BANCORP HAWAII, INC. [BUSINESS]
— profits up, Lahaina News, October 26, 1983: 14.
— gives Hawaii staff inter-island tickets, Lahaina News, July 23, 1992: 17.
— earnings up, Lahaina News, August 12, 1993: 9.
— earnings announced, Lahaina News, November 4, 1993: 7.
— earnings up, Lahaina News, February 24, 1994: 10.
— earnings rise, Lahaina News, November 3, 1994: 23.

BANEY & ASSOCIATES INC. [BUSINESS]
— retained as advertising firm by Napili Kai Beach Club, Lahaina News, July 25, 1984: 14.

BANG BANG YOU'RE DEAD [PLAY]
— to be performed by Baldwin High students, Lahaina News, January 13, 2000: 13.
— to be performed by Baldwin High students, Lahaina News, January 20, 2000: 12.

BANG-BANG BOXING PRODUCTIONS
— plans amateur boxing event, Lahaina News, July 12, 2001: 13.
— planning open house, Lahaina News, February 21, 2002: 13.
— to hold "Thunder in the Tropics", Lahaina News, June 27, 2002: 12.

BANGERTER, BOB [MUSICIAN]
— to perform at Longhi's Restaurant, Lahaina News, September 12, 1996: 16.

BANK OF HAWAII [BUSINESS]
— opening in Whaler's Village, Lahaina Sun, November 25, 1970: 3.
— begins annual charge for Visa cards, Lahaina News, December 15, 1981: 16.
— joins national ATM network, Lahaina News, June 1, 1982: 11.
— closing Ka'anapali Branch, Lahaina News, June 18, 1986: 3.
— sponsoring small business seminar, Lahaina News, June 6, 1990: 5.
— to provide interim financing for Napili Fire and Ambulance Station, Lahaina News, August 1, 1990: 4.
— to include Korean language instructions on ATMs, Lahaina News, November 14, 1990: 13.
— sponsoring high school community service program, Lahaina News, November 28, 1990: 2,3.
— to offer seminar on time management, Lahaina News, February 6, 1991: 7.
— appoints Charles Keyes as vice president and manager of Maui Region Business Banking Center, Lahaina News, February 27, 1991: 8.
— sponsoring Kayak Challenge, Lahaina News, March 20, 1991: 5.
— proposes to expand bank at Lahaina Shopping Center, Lahaina News, April 10, 1991: 1.
— to open branch at Kahana Gateway Center, Lahaina News, September 5, 1991: 6.
— announces promotions, Lahaina News, December 12, 1991: 17.
— Alton Kimura appointed assistant vice president at, Lahaina News, February 13, 1992: 12.
— to publish report on Pacific isle economies, Lahaina News, February 20, 1992: 10.
— named "1991 Marketer of the Year", Lahaina News, March 19, 1992: 11.
— survey indicates businesses are pessimistic, Lahaina News, April 2, 1992: 13.
— opens branch at Kahana Gateway Shopping Plaza, Lahaina News, July 2, 1992: 16.
— branch to open at Kahana Gateway, Lahaina News, July 16, 1992: 4.
— Joseph Andrews promoted to branch manager at Pukalani Branch, Lahaina News, December 3, 1992: 4.

— Susan Takeda promoted to vice president of, Lahaina News, October 27, 1994: 15.

— gives gift to Light Bringers Mission, Lahaina News, January 19, 1995: 4.

— to issue credit card with Continental Airlines, Lahaina News, February 2, 1995: 7.

— Chad Van Story, Norman Kalani Kaui, and Scott Temkin indicted for bank robbery, Lahaina News, August 28, 1997: 1,3.

— offering workshop on student loans, Lahaina News, February 19, 1998: 13.

— sponsoring Slack Key Guitar Festival, Lahaina News, June 10, 1999: 14.

— raises lending rate, Lahaina News, September 2, 1999: 13.

— promoted Alvin Imada to vice president and district manager for Maui, Lahaina News, December 14, 2000: 18.

— Angela Isaac joins as executive vice president, Lahaina News, August 9, 2001: 8.

— Timothy Young appointed Vice President and manager of real estate investment banking unit, Lahaina News, October 11, 2001: 9.

— Liane Fukumoto promoted to vice president, Lahaina News, November 15, 2001: 8.

— appointed Kevin Baptist senior vice president and neighbor island regional sales manager at, Lahaina News, February 21, 2002: 8.

— James Hawkins new senior vice president, Lahaina News, August 1, 2002: 8.

— promotes James Ewing to executive vice president, Lahaina News, September 26, 2002: 8.

— John Gray joins as executive vice president, Lahaina News, November 7, 2002: 8.

— Ann Sakamoto joins as new residential loan officer, Lahaina News, November 21, 2002: 9.

— Linda Lewis appointed as community development officer, Lahaina News, November 28, 2002: 8.

— appoints Vanessa DeLima to assistant vice president, Lahaina News, February 20, 2003: 8.

— Bill Glassman new loan officer at, Lahaina News, July 24, 2003: 8.

BANK OF MAUI [BUSINESS]

— sues Aloha National Bank to change its name, Lahaina News, December 15, 1981: 7.

BANKING

— First Hawaiian Inc. to merge with First Interstate of Hawaii, Lahaina News, February 14, 1990: 5.

BANKOH HINANO MOLOKA'I HOE OUTRIGGER CHAMPIONSHIP

— to be held, Lahaina News, October 7, 1999: 9.

BANKOH KAYAK CHALLENGE

— to be held, Lahaina News, April 11, 1990: 7.

— results of, Lahaina News, May 30, 1990: 6.

BANKOH MOLOKA'I HOE

— canoe race to be held, Lahaina News, October 8, 1998: 15.

BANKRUPTCIES

— column begins, occurring most weeks, and is not otherwise indexed, Lahaina News, November 28, 1991: 24.

BANKS, CARL [COMEDIAN]

— to perform at Comedy Club and the Sports Page, Lahaina News, March 12, 1992: 15,18.

— to perform at Comedy Club, Lahaina News, July 8, 1993: 11.

BANYAN ARTS AND CRAFTS FESTIVAL

— application deadline approaching, Lahaina News, April 29, 1993: 3.

BANYAN INN [RESTAURANT]

— reviewed, Lahaina News, October 1, 1980: 10.

— closes, Lahaina News, September 10, 1986: 6.

— purchased by Maui Venture Capital Company, remodeled, Lahaina News, January 28, 1987: 3.

BANYAN INN MARKETPLACE

— Fantasy Island Activity and Tours, Inc.'s plan to build booth in trouble, Lahaina News, March 7, 1990: 1.

— purchased by Duddle International, Ltd., Lahaina News, August 22, 1990: 9.

BANYAN SQUARE ASSOCIATION

— Dona Early new director of, Lahaina News, December 17, 1986: 1.

— new director introduces herself, Lahaina News, December 17, 1986: 4.

— considers installing lights on banyan tree, Lahaina News, September 16, 1987: 1.

BANYAN TREE

— historical marker for, discussed , Lahaina Sun, December 16, 1970: 6.

— plans discussed, Lahaina Sun, February 3, 1971: 7.

— plans discussed by Maui Historic Commission, Lahaina Sun, March 15, 1972: 5.

— little opposition to proposed plans to renovate courtyard, Lahaina Sun, May 17, 1972: 6,7.

— committee formed to plan 1973 centennial celebration of planting of banyan tree, Lahaina Sun, July 19, 1972: 11.

— birthday celebration planned, Lahaina Sun, November 8, 1972: 12.

— questions about actual date of tree being planted, Lahaina Sun, December 6, 1972: 5.

— confusion over actual date of planting, Lahaina Sun, January 31, 1973: 5.

— one hundredth anniversary celebration set for April 24, Lahaina Sun, March 14, 1973: 3.

— celebration detailed, Lahaina Sun, April 18, 1973: 12,13.

— described, Lahaina News, January 15, 1981: 7.

— history of courtyard described, Lahaina News, September 15, 1981: 11.

— healthy, but needs support, Lahaina News, February 27, 1985: 1.

— in good health, Lahaina News, March 6, 1985: 1,16.

— new lights to be installed, Lahaina News, July 31, 1985: 1.

— to be spruced up, Lahaina News, March 19, 1986: 1,3.

— lights installed, Lahaina News, June 4, 1986: 1.

— banyan tree tended to by tree physician, Lahaina News, October 15, 1986: 1.

— is 114 years old, Lahaina News, April 22, 1987: 4.

— celebration of tree held, Lahaina News, May 13, 1987: 4,12.

— debate over whether to install lights on, Lahaina News, September 16, 1987: 1,2.

— to get lights for Christmas, Lahaina News, September 23, 1987: 16.

— may be dark for Christmas, Lahaina News, October 21, 1987: 1,2.

— lights will not be displayed on, Lahaina News, October 28, 1987: 1.

— editorial opposing decision to not put lights on, Lahaina News, October 28, 1987: 2.

— Lahaina Arts Society to hold arts and crafts, Lahaina News, April 5, 1989: 17.

— debate over plans to put lights on, Lahaina News, June 27, 1990: 5.

— Hare Krishna group granted to operate in, Lahaina News, February 6, 1991: 1.

— pruned by Trees of Hawaii contractor, Lahaina News, May 11, 1995: 3.

— parks permit granted for art display, Lahaina News, June 22, 1995: 1,16.

— commemorated for being 123 years old, Lahaina News, April 18, 1996: 4.

— birthday celebrated, Lahaina News, May 2, 1996: 1.

— turns 124, Lahaina News, April 17, 1997: 2.

— police plan to monitor, Lahaina News, June 11, 1998: 1,20.

— Ho'olaule'a to be part of Aloha Festivals, Lahaina News, October 1, 1998: 3.

— to be lit for holiday, Lahaina News, December 3, 1998: 1,6.

— lit for Christmas, Lahaina News, December 17, 1998: 2.

— turning 126, Lahaina News, April 22, 1999: 1,16.

— He'ui Cultural Arts Festivals to be held at, Lahaina News, August 19, 1999: 16.

— LahainaTown Action Committee and Lahaina Arts Society clashing over use of, Lahaina News, August 26, 1999: 1,20.

— Maui County Arborist Committee rejects art fairs, Lahaina News, September 9, 1999: 1,16.

— Na Kupuna O Maui to hold He'ui Cultural Arts Festival, Lahaina News, September 16, 1999: 12.

— to be part of Aloha Festivals, Lahaina News, September 30, 1999: 1.

— to be included in Aloha Festivals, Lahaina News, October 7, 1999: 1,20.

— Na Kupuna O Maui to hold He'ui Cultural Arts Festivals , Lahaina News, March 16, 2000: 12.

— tree to celebrate 127th birthday, Lahaina News, April 6, 2000: 1.

— birthday party held for tree, Lahaina News, April 13, 2000: 13.

— Na Kupuna O Maui's He'ui Cultural Arts Festivals to be held at, Lahaina News, May 25, 2000: 19.

— art festivals continue to be held at, Lahaina News, June 22, 2000: 17.

— Na Kupuna O Maui's He'ui Cultural Arts Festivals continue to be held at Banyan Tree Park, Lahaina News, July 20, 2000: 17.

— festival to be held at, Lahaina News, August 17, 2000: 16.

— Taiko drummers to perform at, Lahaina News, November 23, 2000: 7.

— Lahaina Arts Society continues to hold arts and crafts fairs, Lahaina News, January 25, 2001: 16.

— turning 128, Lahaina News, April 12, 2001: 16.

— celebrating 128 anniversary, Lahaina News, April 19, 2001: 1.

— crafters sought for celebration of 129th birthday of, Lahaina News, March 21, 2002: 18.

— 129th birthday to be celebrated, Lahaina News, April 11, 2002: 1.

— 129th birthday to be celebrated, Lahaina News, April 18, 2002: 14,20.

— project to improve lighting in, Lahaina News, November 7, 2002: 3.

— to be lit for holidays, Lahaina News, December 5, 2002: 2.

— turning 130, Lahaina News, April 3, 2003: 3.

— urning 130, Lahaina News, April 10, 2003: 1,24.

BANYAN TREE [RESTAURANT]
— featured, Lahaina News, March 7, 2002: 9.

BANYAN TREE GALLERY [BUSINESS]
— to hold poster signing reception for Arlene Marcoe Anthony, Lahaina News, December 30, 1993: 10.

BANYAN TREE SQUARE PRESERVATION COMMITTEE
— editorial on activities, Lahaina News, May 23, 1984: 2.

— formed, Lahaina News, May 23, 1984: 3.

— meeting set, Lahaina News, June 27, 1984: 3.

— officers named, Lahaina News, August 8, 1984: 3.

— meeting today, Lahaina News, August 29, 1984: 3.

— editorial supporting the group's activities, Lahaina News, September 12, 1984: 2.

— votes to begin cleanup of Campbell Park, Lahaina News, October 3, 1984: 3.

— editorial urging support of, Lahaina News, October 17, 1984: 2.

— meeting set, Lahaina News, October 17, 1984: 3.

— general membership meeting held, Lahaina News, October 31, 1984: 3.

— meeting set, Lahaina News, February 20, 1985: 3.

— celebrates 1st anniversary, Lahaina News, May 15, 1985: 3.

— told by police captain Solomon Lee that drug crackdown needed, Lahaina News, May 22, 1985: 1.

— reports on accomplishments over last year, Lahaina News, July 31, 1985: 1.

— holds general membership meeting, Lahaina News, October 2, 1985: 3.

— to hold general membership meeting, Lahaina News, March 12, 1986: 12.

— information on how to join, Lahaina News, March 19, 1986: 1.

— editorial urging people to join, Lahaina News, March 19, 1986: 2.

— to begin beautification project near banyan tree, Lahaina News, May 21, 1986: 1.

BANZAI PAINTBALL DISTRIBUTORS [BUSINESS]
— opens, Lahaina News, May 3, 2001: 9.

BAPTIST, CHRIS
— wins Longhi's Par Buster Tournament, Lahaina News, October 29, 1992: 11.

BAPTIST, KEVIN
— appointed senior vice president and neighbor island regional sales manager at Bank of Hawaii, Lahaina News, February 21, 2002: 8.

BAR AND GRILL [RESTAURANT]
— described, Lahaina News, August 19, 1987: 9,10.

BAR, LEBBY [COMEDIAN]
— to perform at Comedy Club, Lahaina News, October 24, 1991: 20.

BARANGAY FOLD DANCERS
— participate in opening of Lahaina Amphitheatre, Lahaina Sun, August 16, 1972: 9.

BARAOIDAN, CORY
— Scholar/Athlete of the Week, Lahaina News, July 23, 1998: 15.

BARAOIDAN, NICOLE
— Scholar/Athlete of the Week, Lahaina News, January 25, 2001: 8.

BARBARIAN BROTHERS
— wrestlers to hold autographing session, Lahaina News, July 23, 1992: 10,25.

— wrestlers to appear at Lahaina Center, Lahaina News, July 23, 1992: 3.

BARBE, CYNTHIA
— Ka'anapali Estate Coffee marketing coordinator discusses new venture, Lahaina News, July 27, 1995: 10.

BARBECUE COOK-OFF
— contestants sought for, Lahaina News, July 4, 1991: 3.

— to be held at Ka'ahumanu Center, Lahaina News, August 1, 1991: 3.

BARBER, KANARA FEI
— named sales representative at Atlantis Submarine, Lahaina News, April 16, 1992: 13.

— named senior sales manager of Atlantis Submarines, Lahaina News, March 4, 1993: 9.

— now regional national sales manager for Embassy Suites Resort, Lahaina News, October 27, 1994: 15.

BARBIER, JOHN
— comments on proposed thrillcraft corridor, Lahaina News, February 24, 1988: 1.

BARBIER, SHERRY
— Mrs. Hawaii featured, Lahaina News, June 6, 1991: 1.

— promotes Mrs. Hawaii Pageant, Lahaina News, April 23, 1992: 4.

BARBIERI, JOHN [MUSICIAN]
— to perform at Courtyard Restaurant, Lahaina News, September 26, 1996: 16.

BARBIN, RY
— Maui Council candidate profiled, Lahaina News, September 15, 1980: 4.

— elected chair of Maui County Democratic Party, Lahaina News, September 18, 1997: 9.

— elected chair of Democratic Party, Lahaina News, May 14, 1998: 7.

BARBOSA, MARILYN
— librarian interviewed for C-SPAN School Bus, Lahaina News, June 12, 1997: 15.

— Princess Nahienahea Elementary School librarian featured, Lahaina News, May 16, 2002: 1,20.

BARBOZA, TROY
— marathon in name of to be held to support Special Olympics, Lahaina News, April 25, 1990: 12.
— First Hawaiian Bank Troy Barboza Law Enforcement Torch Run to be held for Special Olympics, Lahaina News, April 1, 1999: 15.

BARCENA, BARBARA
— Maui Genealogical Society executive director discusses upcoming fundraiser, Lahaina News, July 12, 1989: 3.

BARDWELL, JOHN [ARTIST]
— to conduct watercolor workshops, Lahaina News, November 26, 1986: 12.
— to hold classes on watercolor, Lahaina News, January 21, 1987: 3.
— paintings featured by Lahaina Art Society, Lahaina News, February 25, 1987: 3.

BAREFOOT IN THE PARK [PLAY]
— to be performed by Baldwin Theatre Guild, Lahaina News, February 13, 1992: 22.
— continues, Lahaina News, February 20, 1992: 18.
— to perform at Casanova's, Lahaina News, February 25, 1993: 9.
— to perform at Longhi's, Lahaina News, March 4, 1993: 9.
— to perform, Lahaina News, March 11, 1993: 13.

BARKENTINE BAR
— to be renamed "On the Rocks", Lahaina News, February 20, 1985: 3.

BARKER, JAMES [ARTIST]
— sculptures featured at Wyland Galleries, Lahaina News, August 6, 1998: 15.
— to appear at Wyland Galleries, Lahaina News, August 13, 1998: 16.

BARKLEY, "CHICAGO STEVE" [COMEDIAN]
— to perform at Comedy Club, Lahaina News, April 11, 1990: 15.

BARNES, BRETT
— general manager of Planet Hollywood, Lahaina News, December 12, 1996: 13.

BARNHARD, DON [COMEDIAN]
— to perform at Honolulu Comedy Club, Lahaina News, April 4, 1996: 14.

BARNHARD, SHERRIE [ARTIST]
— to exhibit at Lahaina Arts Society, Lahaina News, June 5, 1997: 18.
— elected president of the Lahaina Arts Society, Lahaina News, July 1, 1999: 3.

BARNHARD, SPANKY AND DON [COMEDIAN]
— to perform at The Sports Page, Lahaina News, January 2, 1991: 7,8.

BARNHART, DON [COMEDIAN]
— to perform at Comedy Club and the Sports Page, Lahaina News, October 8, 1992: 10.
— to perform at Comedy Club, Lahaina News, December 16, 1993: 19.
— to perform at Comedy Club, Lahaina News, December 30, 1993: 11.
— to perform at Honolulu Comedy Club, Lahaina News, December 15, 1994: 18.

BARONET, WILLIE
— being investigated for owing money to investors, Lahaina News, February 6, 1992: 1,7.
— claims that her debts due to law designed to put activity desks out of business, Lahaina News, February 20, 1992: 3.
— Water Activities and Vacation Entertainment, Inc operator indicted on theft and racketeering charges, Lahaina News, October 6, 1994: 11.

BAROSO, BRENDA
— joins Atlantis Adventures as sales manager, Lahaina News, October 31, 2002: 6.

BARR, ALLEN [POLITICIAN]
— discusses Mayor's request for emergency powers, Lahaina Sun, January 13, 1971: 6.
— director for Maui ACLU, Lahaina Sun, January 13, 1971: 6.
— accuses Maui County Council of ignoring its own charter, Lahaina Sun, November 24, 1971: 4.
— will sue Mayor Cravalho again, Lahaina Sun, January 5, 1972: 13.
— clashes with Mayor Cravalho, Lahaina Sun, February 9, 1972: 3.
— files suit against Mayor Cravalho over funds given to parents of children in private schools, Lahaina Sun, June 14, 1972: 3.
— critical of payments to volunteer firemen, Lahaina Sun, August 23, 1972: 9.
— mayor Cravalho reacts to charge against County Council, Lahaina Sun, August 30, 1972: 10.
— suit against mayor Cravalho set for spring 1973, Lahaina Sun, November 8, 1972: 7.
— chosen as delegate to Republican Party convention, Lahaina News, April 1, 1980: 6.
— to run for Maui County Council, Lahaina News, June 18, 1992: 4.
— see also Maui Justice Foundation

BARR, KENNETH
— Kihei taxi company owner receives award from International Taxicab Associates, Lahaina News, October 23, 1985: 20.
— favors moratorium on development, Lahaina News, April 1, 1987: 1,20.
— planning commissioner recounts vote to develop land near Kamaole, Lahaina News, November 25, 1993: 6.

BARRETT, PATRICK
— challenges of Article XII of the Hawaii State Constitution, Lahaina News, February 8, 2001: 3.

BARRIENTOS, TOMAS
— contractor reaches settlement with Department of Commerce and Consumer Affairs, Lahaina News, September 9, 1993: 7.

BARRIO FESTIVAL
— to be held, Lahaina News, May 23, 1990: 13.
— to be held at Wailuku Memorial soccer field, Lahaina News, May 23, 1991: 16.

BARROMEO, EMMANUEL
— Scholar/Athlete of the Week, Lahaina News, April 25, 1996: 8.

BARRON, RONALD
— announces run for County Council, Lahaina News, August 1, 1980: 7.
— Maui council candidate featured, Lahaina News, August 15, 1980: 4.

BARROW, HELEN
— to teach "Awareness Through Movement", Lahaina News, July 11, 2002: 17.
— to hold "Awareness through Movement", Lahaina News, July 18, 2002: 16.

BARTELS, JURGEN
— chairman and chief executive officer of Westin Hotels and Resorts meets with employees, Lahaina News, November 30, 1995: 10.

BARTHOLOMEW, GAIL [WRITER]
— publishes "Maui Remembers: A Local History", Lahaina News, November 3, 1994: 9.

BARTLETT, RANDY
— manager of Maui Land and Pineapple's Pu'u Kukui Watershed discusses threats to ecosystem, Lahaina News, December 10, 1998: 3.
— working to protect Pu'u Kukui Reserve, Lahaina News, July 6, 2000: 1,14.

BARTLETT, WILLIAM [ARTIST]
— part of "90 Degrees" exhibit at Maui Arts and Cultural Center, Lahaina News, July 6, 2000: 16.

BARTLEY, ROSE [ARTIST]
— to exhibit at Banyan Tree Gallery, Lahaina News, April 27, 1995: 11.

BARYSHNIKOV, MIKHAIL [DANCER]
— to perform "Past Forward" with White Oak Dance Project, Lahaina News, October 12, 2000: 21.

BASEBALL
— Iolani High School plays Maui teams, Lahaina Sun, February 10, 1971: 7.
— results of Maui Interscholastic league discussed, Lahaina Sun, February 17, 1971: 7.
— Little League sign-up begins, Lahaina News, February 7, 1990: 9.
— University of Hawai'i Rainbows to play Nitaidai university, Lahaina News, March 14, 1990: 11.
— Lahainaluna High School team begins season well, Lahaina News, March 21, 1990: 9.
— Eddie Feigner to play in exhibition game, Lahaina News, March 28, 1990: 9.
— season ends, Lahaina News, May 30, 1990: 6.
— results of Red Sox tournament, Lahaina News, June 6, 1990: 6.
— AJA tournament to be held, Lahaina News, April 9, 1992: 10.
— Hawaiian Winter League to be broadcast on radio, Lahaina News, April 23, 1992: 15,22.
— Lahaina Cardinals tied for first, Lahaina News, May 7, 1992: 13.
— updates on Winter League, Lahaina News, May 21, 1992: 10.
— update on Tee Ball and Coach Pitch Leagues, Lahaina News, May 21, 1992: 10.
— Lahaina Cardinals lose, Lahaina News, May 21, 1992: 11.
— Aina Kohler pitches no-hitter, Lahaina News, June 4, 1992: 8.
— Kaholo Rickard pitches no-hit shutout, Lahaina News, June 4, 1992: 8.
— Yankees win t-ball, Lahaina News, June 4, 1992: 8.
— local results, Lahaina News, June 11, 1992: 11.
— Upper Deck Hawaiian Winter League to be broadcast, Lahaina News, June 18, 1992: 12,13.
— all-stars picked by Kihei Little League, Lahaina News, June 25, 1992: 11.
— West Maui Pony League team The Plebes finish season, Lahaina News, July 2, 1992: 11,15.
— Kiwanis Maui Little League to begin, Lahaina News, July 9, 1992: 12.
— Upper Deck Hawaiian Winter League season canceled, Lahaina News, July 16, 1992: 4.
— East Maui All Stars win District III Little League, Lahaina News, July 23, 1992: 14.
— Lahaina Red Sox Little League to meet Waiakea-Uka Tigers, Lahaina News, August 6, 1992: 6.
— West Maui Little League Baseball Association to meet, Lahaina News, August 27, 1992: 9.
— Little League organization taking shape, Lahaina News, September 10, 1992: 8.
— update on local games, Lahaina News, October 15, 1992: 10.
— Roger Clemens to offer pitching demonstration, Lahaina News, November 5, 1992: 12.
— State Little League Baseball Tournament to be held in Kihei, Lahaina News, December 10, 1992: 8.
— Little League sign-ups underway, Lahaina News, January 14, 1993: 9.
— Kihei Little League to hold coaching seminar, Lahaina News, January 28, 1993: 7.
— Little League tryouts to be held, Lahaina News, February 25, 1993: 4.
— Little League clinic to be held, Lahaina News, March 11, 1993: 9.
— West Maui Little League to meet, Lahaina News, April 1, 1993: 4.
— West Maui Little League to begin, Lahaina News, April 15, 1993: 8.

— West Maui Little League underway, Lahaina News, April 22, 1993: 8.
— West Maui Little League begins, Lahaina News, April 29, 1993: 6.
— update on Little League, Lahaina News, May 6, 1993: 10.
— current standings in Little League, Lahaina News, June 10, 1993: 8.
— West Maui Little League needs funds to send team to Moloka'i and Kaua'i tournament, Lahaina News, June 24, 1993: 11.
— all-stars named for West Maui Little League, Lahaina News, July 1, 1993: 8.
— West Maui Little League to meet, Lahaina News, September 9, 1993: 9.
— West Maui Little League to evaluate last season, Lahaina News, September 16, 1993: 11.
— results of Hawaii Winter Baseball League, Lahaina News, October 14, 1993: 10.
— Hawaii Winter Baseball League continues, Lahaina News, December 2, 1993: 10.
— member of the Maui Stingrays named to Major League Baseball teams, Lahaina News, December 16, 1993: 11.
— registration begins for Kihei Little League, Lahaina News, January 6, 1994: 8.
— Little League registration to be held, Lahaina News, January 20, 1994: 9.
— West Maui Little League registration extended, Lahaina News, February 3, 1994: 9.
— West Maui Little League tryouts begin, Lahaina News, March 10, 1994: 6.
— West Maui Little League to hold tryouts, Lahaina News, March 24, 1994: 12.
— Maui Community College to sponsor basketball tournament, Lahaina News, March 31, 1994: 8.
— results of West Maui Little League games, Lahaina News, April 14, 1994: 7.
— update on Little League results, Lahaina News, April 28, 1994: 6,7.
— update on local games, Lahaina News, May 5, 1994: 8.
— results of games, Lahaina News, May 12, 1994: 6.
— update on West Maui Little League, Lahaina News, May 19, 1994: 9.
— Lahainaluna High School students named to All-Star Team, Lahaina News, May 26, 1994: 9.
— update on league events, Lahaina News, June 9, 1994: 9.
— little league results, Lahaina News, June 16, 1994: 7.
— West Maui Little League updates, Lahaina News, June 23, 1994: 6.
— all-star teams announced, Lahaina News, June 30, 1994: 6.
— clinic to be held at Malu'ulu O Lele Park, Lahaina News, July 28, 1994: 6.
— Randy Montalvo will play in Hawaii Winter Baseball League, Lahaina News, October 6, 1994: 9.
— Maui Stingrays of Hawaii Winter Baseball League travel to Kaua'i for games, Lahaina News, October 27, 1994: 11.
— West Maui Little League to hold annual general meeting, Lahaina News, October 27, 1994: 8.
— update on Hawaii Winter Baseball League, Lahaina News, November 24, 1994: 8.
— West Maui Little League to hold general meeting, Lahaina News, December 1, 1994: 9.
— Maui Stingrays lead Hawaii Winter Baseball League, Lahaina News, December 1, 1994: 9.
— West Maui Little League to hold registration, Lahaina News, January 26, 1995: 8.
— West Maui Little League seeking sponsors, Lahaina News, March 23, 1995: 7.
— Little League umpires needed, Lahaina News, April 6, 1995: 7.
— goodwill series to be held between Lahaina and Katcukshika-Ku, Japan, Lahaina News, May 25, 1995: 5.
— Little League heating up, Lahaina News, June 8, 1995: 6.

— players sought for game with teams travelling to Katsushika-ku, Japan, Lahaina News, June 8, 1995: 6.

— Maui Stingrays need bat technicians, Lahaina News, June 29, 1995: 7.

— West Maui Little League All-Stars announced, Lahaina News, July 6, 1995: 7.

— West Maui Junior Division Little League All-Stars win District III championship, Lahaina News, July 13, 1995: 7.

— West Maui Youth Baseball Association to hold goodwill game with Katsushika City Youth Baseball Team, Lahaina News, August 10, 1995: 7.

— West Maui Little League to hold annual meeting, Lahaina News, October 19, 1995: 6.

— West Maui Little League registration begins, Lahaina News, January 25, 1996: 10.

— update on local baseball team, Lahaina News, February 15, 1996: 7.

— West Maui Little League registration begins, Lahaina News, March 28, 1996: 7.

— coach Earle Kukahiko featured, Lahaina News, May 2, 1996: 20.

— title races soon, Lahaina News, June 13, 1996: 1,12.

— Cardinals featured, Lahaina News, June 13, 1996: 12.

— local teams competing to go to Little League World Series, Lahaina News, June 27, 1996: 16.

— West Maui Little League Baseball Association to hold annual meeting, Lahaina News, November 21, 1996: 18.

— West Maui Little League Baseball Association registration underway, Lahaina News, January 30, 1997: 7.

— Little League to begin, Lahaina News, April 3, 1997: 5.

— West Maui Little League tournament to be held, Lahaina News, June 19, 1997: 14.

— Maui Stingrays to offer Youth Baseball Clinic, Lahaina News, November 13, 1997: 21.

— Little League seeking people to run organization, Lahaina News, November 27, 1997: 6.

— parents support West Maui Little League, Lahaina News, January 1, 1998: 1,2.

— Lahaina Pony Baseball Team to hold Portuguese Sausage fundraiser, Lahaina News, February 5, 1998: 12.

— West Maui Little League to hold registration for upcoming season, Lahaina News, February 5, 1998: 3.

— clinics set, Lahaina News, March 19, 1998: 7.

— West Maui Little League to begin play, Lahaina News, March 26, 1998: 6.

— clinic to be held, Lahaina News, March 26, 1998: 7.

— Little League baseball series played, Lahaina News, August 20, 1998: 14.

— West Maui Youth Baseball Group to hold rummage sale, Lahaina News, September 10, 1998: 15.

— West Maui Little League holding umpire clinic, Lahaina News, March 11, 1999: 7.

— Little League to begin, Lahaina News, April 15, 1999: 6.

— youth program held, Lahaina News, May 20, 1999: 6.

— Cardinals win West Maui Little League, Lahaina News, June 10, 1999: 7.

— results of Little League Baseball, Lahaina News, July 1, 1999: 6.

— Na Kamaliʻi O Ke Akua to hold One Pitch Men's Mixed Softball Tournament, Lahaina News, August 19, 1999: 6.

— Waiakea Uka Tigers and Lahaina Red Sox Little League to hold annual series, Lahaina News, August 19, 1999: 7.

— kids to travel to Japan for goodwill baseball series, Lahaina News, September 9, 1999: 6.

— West Maui Youth Baseball to hold huli chicken sale, Lahaina News, November 18, 1999: 8.

— Maui Bronco Baseball League to hold general meeting, Lahaina News, November 18, 1999: 8.

— George "Manju" Nitta to teach, Lahaina News, January 13, 2000: 7.

— West Maui Little League Baseball registration begins, Lahaina News, January 20, 2000: 7.

— Maui Bronco Baseball League seeking coaches, Lahaina News, January 20, 2000: 7.

— Little League season to begin, Lahaina News, March 30, 2000: 6.

— Lahaina softball program featured, Lahaina News, April 6, 2000: 6.

— PONY Baseball League continues, Lahaina News, May 18, 2000: 14.

— results of Maui Little League play, Lahaina News, June 1, 2000: 9.

— West Maui Little League season won by The Orioles, Lahaina News, June 15, 2000: 13.

— Little League Baseball all-starts to play at World Series, Lahaina News, July 6, 2000: 12.

— Molokaʻi Little League Baseball Majors Division All-Star Team defeats West Maui, Lahaina News, July 20, 2000: 6.

— Blaine Bernades on Maui PONY All-Star Baseball Team, Lahaina News, August 3, 2000: 6.

— Lahaina Red Sox to play Waiakea Uka Tigers, Lahaina News, August 24, 2000: 6.

— West Maui Little League Baseball to hold registration, Lahaina News, January 25, 2001: 9.

— West Maui Little League Baseball to hold registration, Lahaina News, February 1, 2001: 14.

— West Maui Little League Baseball registration to begin, Lahaina News, February 8, 2001: 14.

— West Maui Little League Baseball looking for umpires, Lahaina News, March 29, 2001: 12.

— West Maui Little League Baseball president Brian Atakawa featured, Lahaina News, April 19, 2001: 12.

— Lahaina Girls Softball Program underway, Lahaina News, April 26, 2001: 14.

— Lahainaluna High School team featured, Lahaina News, May 17, 2001: 14.

— Little League champion crowned, Lahaina News, June 14, 2001: 14.

— Maui PONY League baseball season ends, Lahaina News, June 14, 2001: 14.

— all-stars to compete in tournament, Lahaina News, July 19, 2001: 12.

— Lahaina Red Sox-Waiakea Uka Tigers to play, Lahaina News, August 2, 2001: 13.

— Lahaina Red Sox and Waiakea Uka Tigers to play, Lahaina News, August 9, 2001: 13.

— West Maui Little League to hold clinic for umpires, Lahaina News, March 28, 2002: 11.

— West Maui Little League season to begin, Lahaina News, April 18, 2002: 12.

— Little League to field new team, Lahaina News, May 16, 2002: 12.

— Maui Little League game to be played between White Sox and Orioles, Lahaina News, June 13, 2002: 12.

— West Maui Little League preparing for 2003 season, Lahaina News, January 2, 2003: 12.

— West Maui Little League to hold registration, Lahaina News, January 16, 2003: 13.

— West Maui Little League to hold registration, Lahaina News, January 23, 2003: 13.

— West Maui Little League to hold clinic for umpires, Lahaina News, March 27, 2003: 12.

— umpire clinic planned, Lahaina News, April 3, 2003: 12.

— West Maui Little League season to begin, Lahaina News, April 24, 2003: 10.

— West Maui Little League completes regular season play, Lahaina News, July 10, 2003: 12.

— Lahaina Red Sox to play Waikea-Uka Tigers, Lahaina News, August 14, 2003: 12.

— see also West Maui Little League, West Maui Youth Baseball

BASH ON THE BEACH
— to be held at Kalama Park Pavilion, Lahaina News, April 20, 1988: 6.
— to be held, Lahaina News, April 26, 1989: 3.

BASIL, HARRY [COMEDIAN]
— to perform at Comedy Club, Lahaina News, June 13, 1990: 15.
— to perform at Comedy Club and the Sports Page, Lahaina News, June 10, 1993: 10.
— to perform at Honolulu Comedy Club, Lahaina News, November 16, 1995: 15,16.

BASIL TOMATOES ITALIAN GRILLE [RESTAURANT]
— opens facility, Lahaina News, August 3, 1995: 16.
— celebrating first birthday, Lahaina News, July 4, 1996: 13.
— Haku Applegate appointed general manager of, Lahaina News, March 15, 2001: 8.

BASKET COMPANY, THE [BUSINESS]
— to open, Lahaina News, January 23, 1991: 5.
— purchased by Julie Mohler, Lahaina News, December 24, 1992: 10.

BASKETBALL
— report on high school games, Lahaina Sun, January 20, 1971: 7.
— University of Alaska team to visit Maui in February, Lahaina Sun, January 20, 1971: 7.
— results, Lahaina Sun, January 27, 1971: 7.
— results of Maui Interscholastic league, Lahaina Sun, February 3, 1971: 7.
— results of high school games, Lahaina Sun, February 10, 1971: 7.
— results discussed, Lahaina Sun, February 17, 1971: 7.
— discussed, Lahaina Sun, February 24, 1971: 7.
— Lahainaluna loses to Iolani and Kamehameha, Lahaina Sun, December 29, 1971: 18.
— Maui Classic college tournament to be played, Lahaina News, November 9, 1988: 13.
— Lahaina Cannery to present "Crazy George", Lahaina News, November 23, 1988: 3.
— Westin Maui sponsoring Magic Johnson//Jerry West Executive Basketball Camp, Lahaina News, June 28, 1989: 9.
— Maui Classic to be held, Lahaina News, July 5, 1989: 2.
— Maui Classic to played over Thanksgiving weekend, Lahaina News, November 8, 1989: 24.
— Early Tournament to be held at Lahaina Civic Center, Lahaina News, November 15, 1989: 3.
— Maui Classic to played over Thanksgiving weekend, Lahaina News, November 15, 1989: 6.
— applications being accepted for youth league, Lahaina News, November 15, 1989: 6.
— Maui Classic to be held at Lahaina Civic Center, Lahaina News, November 22, 1989: 9.
— University of Hawai'i Rainbows to play pre-season game, Lahaina News, November 22, 1989: 9.
— University of Hawai'i basketball team to host tournament at Lahaina Civic Center, Lahaina News, December 6, 1989: 7.
— Missouri Tigers win Maui Classic, Lahaina News, December 6, 1989: 7.
— Lahainaluna High School basketball team to compete in Maui Interscholastic League, Lahaina News, December 13, 1989: 8.
— Curt Hold beat Ted St. Martin in free throw competition, Lahaina News, December 13, 1989: 8.
— Rainbows win tournament at Lahaina Civic Center, Lahaina News, December 20, 1989: 6.
— Lahainaluna High School basketball team described, photographed, Lahaina News, January 3, 1990: 6,7,10.
— Lahainaluna High School has good start to season, Lahaina News, January 10, 1990: 5.
— Lahainaluna High School team to play, Lahaina News, January 31, 1990: 9.
— Lahainaluna High School basketball team in state tournament, Lahaina News, February 7, 1990: 8.
— varsity basketball tournament to start, Lahaina News, February 21, 1990: 8.
— training camp to be held, Lahaina News, May 23, 1990: 10.
— clinic to be held with NBA pro James Worthy, Lahaina News, June 20, 1990: 8.
— Maui County Basketball Clinic to be held, Lahaina News, June 27, 1990: 7.
— Earvin "Magic" Johnson to hold basketball camp, Lahaina News, July 11, 1990: 24.
— Salvation Army Mini Camp registration begins, Lahaina News, July 25, 1990: 14.
— Maui Invitational to be held, Lahaina News, September 26, 1990: 14.
— Maui Invitational to be held, Lahaina News, October 3, 1990: 7.
— Maui Invitational to be held, Lahaina News, October 10, 1990: 18.
— Maui Invitational to be held at Lahaina Civic Center, Lahaina News, October 17, 1990: 9.
— Maui Invitational to be held, Lahaina News, October 24, 1990: 12.
— Maui Invitational to be held, Lahaina News, November 14, 1990: 10.
— Tournament to be held over Thanksgiving weekend, Lahaina News, November 21, 1990: 24.
— Harlem Crowns to play in Celebrity Basketball Challenge, Lahaina News, January 23, 1991: 16.
— Lahaina Rainbows defeat Kihei, Lahaina News, January 23, 1991: 16.
— Lahaina Rainbows having winning season, Lahaina News, February 20, 1991: 20.
— Lahaina Rainbows finish first in Menehune basketball league, Lahaina News, February 27, 1991: 1.
— Magic Johnson/Jerry West Executive Basketball Camp to be held at Westin Maui, Lahaina News, May 30, 1991: 4.
— "Fabulous Five" to give clinic at Maui High Gym, Lahaina News, June 6, 1991: 9.
— summer league to begin, Lahaina News, June 13, 1991: 17.
— summer camp to be offered at Westin Maui, Lahaina News, June 13, 1991: 17.
— applications for summer league being accepted, Lahaina News, June 20, 1991: 4.
— Westin Maui hosting "Magic Johnson/Jerry West Executive Basketball Camp", Lahaina News, June 20, 1991: 4.
— Magic Johnson/Jerry West Executive Basketball Camp to be held at Westin Maui, Lahaina News, June 27, 1991: 7.
— Salvation Army to organize camps, Lahaina News, July 18, 1991: 7.
— Magic Johnson/Jerry West Executive Basketball Camp held, Lahaina News, July 25, 1991: 9.
— Salvation Army to offer camp, Lahaina News, August 8, 1991: 6.
— Lahainaluna High School alumni tournament to be held, Lahaina News, December 19, 1991: 9.
— summer league to be held, Lahaina News, June 4, 1992: 8.
— summer league to begin, Lahaina News, June 18, 1992: 12.
— Magic Johnson/Jerry West Executive Basketball Camp to be held, Lahaina News, July 16, 1992: 11.
— Maui Invitation to be held, Lahaina News, October 15, 1992: 10.
— results of Kalama Invitational Basketball Tournament, Lahaina News, December 10, 1992: 6.
— Maui Invitational to be held, Lahaina News, December 17, 1992: 11.
— Lahainaluna High School team begins season, Lahaina News, January 7, 1993: 1,5.
— results of Makawao Menehune Basketball tournament, Lahaina News, January 7, 1993: 5.
— youth league to begin, Lahaina News, January 7, 1993: 5.

— Al Dasago, Lahaina Rainbows menehune basketball coach, praised, Lahaina News, January 14, 1993: 8.
— Lahainaluna High School team to play Moloka'i Farmers, Lahaina News, January 14, 1993: 9.
— West Maui Youth Athletic Association season ending soon, Lahaina News, February 4, 1993: 6.
— update on Menehune Basketball League, Lahaina News, February 4, 1993: 6.
— Open League to start soon, Lahaina News, February 11, 1993: 9.
— update on West Maui Youth Athletic Association, Lahaina News, March 4, 1993: 5.
— update on local game, Lahaina News, March 18, 1993: 5.
— Magic Johnson to hold Executive Baseball Camp again, Lahaina News, June 10, 1993: 8.
— Maui Invitational to be held, Lahaina News, August 12, 1993: 10.
— West Maui Youth Athletic Association league to begin, Lahaina News, December 30, 1993: 8.
— results of league play, Lahaina News, January 6, 1994: 9.
— Lahaina Rainbows compete, Lahaina News, January 20, 1994: 9.
— West Maui Youth Athletic Association league to begin, Lahaina News, February 3, 1994: 9.
— Menehune Basketball League results, Lahaina News, February 3, 1994: 9.
— youth league season now half complete, Lahaina News, February 10, 1994: 11.
— West Maui Youth Athletic Association basketball season winds down, Lahaina News, February 17, 1994: 8.
— youth league season to end, Lahaina News, March 10, 1994: 7.
— outstanding players recognized, Lahaina News, March 17, 1994: 6.
— Maui Community College Associated Students sponsoring collegiate tournament, Lahaina News, March 24, 1994: 12.
— Lahainaluna High School coach discusses season, Lahaina News, March 24, 1994: 9.
— Earvin "Magic" Johnson to hold to play in Best of Maui Charity Basketball Game, Lahaina News, May 19, 1994: 8.
— Maui Invitational tournament to be held, Lahaina News, September 8, 1994: 6.
— University of Hawai'i basketball team plays Australian All-Star team, Lahaina News, November 3, 1994: 21.
— registration begins for youth league, Lahaina News, November 24, 1994: 8.
— update on West Maui Youth Athletic Association league, Lahaina News, January 12, 1995: 7.
— Lahainaluna High School team featured, Lahaina News, January 19, 1995: 6.
— update on Lahaina Rainbows, Lahaina News, February 2, 1995: 6.
— West Maui Youth Athletic Association all-star team named, Lahaina News, March 9, 1995: 7.
— Magic Johnson and Jerry West continue basketball camp, Lahaina News, May 25, 1995: 5.
— Tribe wins basketball league, Lahaina News, June 22, 1995: 6.
— Maui Invitational Basketball Tournament to be held, Lahaina News, August 24, 1995: 6.
— Maui Invitational Basketball Tournament to be held, Lahaina News, August 31, 1995: 6.
— UCLA Bruins to play in Maui Invitational, Lahaina News, November 16, 1995: 9.
— Maui Invitational held, Lahaina News, November 30, 1995: 7.
— update on Lahaina Rainbows, Lahaina News, January 18, 1996: 6.
— West Maui Youth Athletic Association All-Star Game and Awards to be held, Lahaina News, March 14, 1996: 7.
— Lahainaluna High School to offer camp, Lahaina News, August 15, 1996: 13.
— Maui Invitational NCAA Basketball Tournament held, Lahaina News, November 14, 1996: 13.

— West Maui Youth Basketball continues registration, Lahaina News, November 21, 1996: 14.
— Maui invitational NCAA Basketball Tournament to be held, Lahaina News, November 21, 1996: 14,15.
— update on upcoming season at Lahainaluna High School, Lahaina News, November 21, 1996: 7.
— Lahaina Rainbows Menehune team featured, Lahaina News, January 30, 1997: 7.
— West Maui Youth Association league play, Lahaina News, April 10, 1997: 17.
— West Maui Youth Basketball League to begin registration, Lahaina News, November 6, 1997: 9.
— West Maui Parks looking for women's basketball teams, Lahaina News, December 11, 1997: 17.
— West Maui Youth Athletic Association league begins, Lahaina News, January 1, 1998: 12.
— free clinic to be held, Lahaina News, June 11, 1998: 15.
— tickets available for Maui Invitational tournament, Lahaina News, October 15, 1998: 1,20.
— Susan Figg to be stage manager for ESPN at Maui Invitational, Lahaina News, October 22, 1998: 17.
— tickets for Maui Invitational tournament available, Lahaina News, October 22, 1998: 19.
— Lahaina Girls Menehune League team to form, Lahaina News, October 29, 1998: 19.
— West Maui Youth Basketball League to begin, Lahaina News, October 29, 1998: 19.
— Maui Invitational college basketball game to be held, Lahaina News, October 29, 1998: 19.
— West Maui Youth Basketball League to begin, Lahaina News, November 5, 1998: 19.
— Maui Invitational college basketball tournament to be held, Lahaina News, November 5, 1998: 19.
— Maui Invitational college basketball tournament to be held, Lahaina News, November 12, 1998: 15.
— Maui Invitational to begin Monday, Lahaina News, November 26, 1998: 1.
— West Maui Youth Athletic Association league expands, Lahaina News, January 7, 1999: 14.
— Maui Menehune Basketball League to practice, Lahaina News, February 4, 1999: 14,15.
— league wrapping up season, Lahaina News, March 4, 1999: 6.
— West Maui Youth Basketball concludes season, Lahaina News, March 18, 1999: 15.
— West Maui Parks and Recreation to offer clinic, Lahaina News, July 8, 1999: 6.
— summer clinic to be held by West Maui Parks and Recreation, Lahaina News, July 15, 1999: 7.
— NBA stars playing in "Who's Got Game Challenge", Lahaina News, August 26, 1999: 7.
— Lahaina Girls Menehune League tryouts to be held, Lahaina News, October 21, 1999: 9.
— West Maui Youth Basketball League seeks volunteers and coaches, Lahaina News, October 21, 1999: 9.
— West Maui Youth Basketball League registration begins, Lahaina News, October 28, 1999: 9.
— Lahaina Girls Menehune League tryouts to be held, Lahaina News, October 28, 1999: 9.
— West Maui Youth Basketball League registration begins, Lahaina News, November 4, 1999: 7.
— Heels and Gators compete in Maui Invitational, Lahaina News, November 18, 1999: 1,2.
— West Maui Youth Basketball accepting applications, Lahaina News, November 25, 1999: 9.
— West Maui Youth Basketball accepting applications, Lahaina News, December 2, 1999: 9.

— Lahainaluna High School to host Lahainaluna Invitational Basketball Tournament, Lahaina News, December 9, 1999: 9.

— West Maui Youth Basketball begins season, Lahaina News, January 6, 2000: 6.

— Maui County Menehune Basketball League featured, Lahaina News, January 27, 2000: 6.

— West Maui Youth Basketball League season concluding, Lahaina News, March 9, 2000: 6.

— West Maui Youth Basketball League to hold ceremony, Lahaina News, March 23, 2000: 7.

— West Maui Parks and Recreation to hold meeting for league, Lahaina News, May 4, 2000: 14.

— Lahaina Rainbows of Maui County Menehune League Basketball program win championship, Lahaina News, July 6, 2000: 13.

— Menehune Girls Basketball to hold tryouts, Lahaina News, October 19, 2000: 9.

— West Maui Youth Basketball League to hold registration, Lahaina News, October 26, 2000: 11.

— West Maui Youth Basketball League to hold registration, Lahaina News, November 2, 2000: 9.

— West Maui Youth Basketball games held, Lahaina News, January 18, 2001: 9.

— Lahaina Rainbows teams complete regular seasons, Lahaina News, March 8, 2001: 12.

— West Maui Youth Basketball League celebrates successful season, Lahaina News, March 15, 2001: 10.

— results of Lahainaluna High School girls varsity team, Lahaina News, March 22, 2001: 12.

— NFL stars playing charity basketball game, Lahaina News, March 29, 2001: 12.

— charity game to be played featuring Jerry Rice and other NFL stars, Lahaina News, April 5, 2001: 20.

— Junior Lunas Basketball Camp to be held, Lahaina News, June 28, 2001: 15.

— Junior Lunas Basketball Camp to be held, Lahaina News, July 5, 2001: 13.

— Lahaina players competing in Youth Basketball Tournament, Lahaina News, July 26, 2001: 12.

— West Maui Youth Basketball Program to hold registration, Lahaina News, October 25, 2001: 13.

— West Maui Youth Basketball Program to hold registration, Lahaina News, November 8, 2001: 13.

— West Maui Youth Basketball League successful, Lahaina News, January 24, 2002: 12.

— Lahaina Rainbows coach Al Dasugo steps down, Lahaina News, February 21, 2002: 12.

— West Maui Youth Basketball League season concludes, Lahaina News, March 7, 2002: 12.

— West Maui Youth Basketball League concludes all-star games, Lahaina News, March 21, 2002: 13.

— World Youth Basketball Tournament to be held, Lahaina News, August 1, 2002: 14.

— West Maui Youth Basketball Program to hold registration, Lahaina News, October 31, 2002: 10.

— Maui Invitational NCAA tournament to be held, Lahaina News, November 14, 2002: 11.

— Maui Invitational NCAA tournament to be held, Lahaina News, November 21, 2002: 11.

— clinic to be held, Lahaina News, February 6, 2003: 12.

— Lahaina Rainbows successful, Lahaina News, February 13, 2003: 12.

— clinics to be held, Lahaina News, February 13, 2003: 13.

— Lahaina Locals successful, Lahaina News, February 20, 2003: 12.

— Lahainaluna High School coaches hold clinics, Lahaina News, February 20, 2003: 12.

— West Maui Youth Basketball season to end, Lahaina News, March 6, 2003: 12.

— World Youth Basketball Tournament to be held, Lahaina News, July 17, 2003: 12.

— World Youth Basketball Tournament to be held, Lahaina News, July 24, 2003: 13.

— see also West Maui Youth Basketball

BASKIN-ROBBINS [BUSINESS]

— may have to pay for overcharging customers, Lahaina News, August 17, 1995: 3.

BASQUES, SAMANTHA

— basketball player key to Knick's success in Pee Wee division, Lahaina News, February 10, 1994: 12.

BASSIL, BECHARA [ARTIST]

— woodwork to be exhibited during Friday Night is Art Night, Lahaina News, June 22, 1995: 11.

BASTILLE DAY

— to be celebrated at La Bretagne French restaurant, Lahaina News, July 4, 1984: 4,7.

— celebrated, Lahaina News, July 12, 1989: 11.

BATCHELOR, KATE

— realtor joins Lowson and Associates, Lahaina News, August 19, 1999: 12.

BATEMAN, CHANCE SHANE

— trial to begin for alleged beating, Lahaina News, July 9, 1992: 7.

BATWHACKERS

— wins Hyatt Regency Maui Employee Softball Tournament, Lahaina News, July 5, 2001: 13.

BAUSTON, GENE

— to speak on "The Dangers of Factory Farms", Lahaina News, June 5, 2003: 9.

BAXTER, WILLIAM

— appointed resident manager at Kapalau Bay Hotel, Lahaina News, March 5, 1986: 3.

BAY CLUB AT KAPALUA BAY HOTEL [RESTAURANT]

— offering kama'aina specials, Lahaina News, September 17, 1992: 14.

— features new menu, Lahaina News, February 5, 1998: 5.

— new menu, Lahaina News, October 1, 1998: 7.

— to hold dinner featuring Cakebread Winery, Lahaina News, February 6, 2003: 16.

— to feature jazz, Lahaina News, February 20, 2003: 14.

— to host dinner with Chehalem and Rex Hill wineries, Lahaina News, April 17, 2003: 16.

— to hold Winemaker's Dinner, Lahaina News, August 28, 2003: 16.

— see also Bay Club at Kapalua Bay Hotel, Kapalua Bay Hotel

BAY VILLAS AT KAPALUA, THE

— featured, Lahaina News, April 26, 2001: 6.

— development featured, Lahaina News, May 23, 2002: 6.

BAYBAYAN, CLINTON

— Scholar/Athlete of the Week, Lahaina News, May 8, 1997: 15.

BAYBROOK, JENNIFER

— to lead yo-yo retreat, Lahaina News, July 17, 2003: 18.

BAYS, VALERIE CARTWRIGHT

— named Maui Project Development Coordinator for The Nature Conservancy, Lahaina News, October 10, 1991: 5.

BAYSA, REY

— hired by Embassy Suites Resorts as executive chef, Lahaina News, August 8, 1991: 8.

BAYWATCH HAWAII [TELEVISION SHOW]

— to film on Maui, Lahaina News, July 29, 1999: 11.

BEACH ACCESS ADVISORY COMMITTEE
— favors beach access at Alaeloa, Lahaina News, September 3, 1992: 1,17.
— recommends campgrounds near Olowalu, Lahaina News, July 14, 1994: 5.

BEACH ACTIVITIES OF MAUI [BUSINESS]
— expands operations, Lahaina News, February 8, 1996: 6.
— opens new location, Lahaina News, January 6, 2000: 11.
— to provide beach concession and ocean recreation services at Outrigger Reef, Lahaina News, October 5, 2000: 14.

BEACH BROS., THE [MUSICAL GROUP]
— to perform at Kahana Keyes Restaurant, Lahaina News, January 9, 1992: 11.
— continue to perform at Kahana Keyes Restaurant, Lahaina News, March 26, 1992: 14.
— continue to perform at Kahana Keyes Restaurant, Lahaina News, April 9, 1992: 18.
— continues to perform at Kahana Keyes Restaurant, Lahaina News, May 21, 1992: 17.
— continues to perform at Kahana Keyes Restaurant, Lahaina News, July 9, 1992: 21.
— to perform at Maui Arts and Cultural Center, Lahaina News, April 29, 1999: 9.

BEACH CLUB, THE [RESTAURANT]
— reviewed, Lahaina News, November 9, 1983: 13.
— at Ka'anapali Villas, reviewed, Lahaina News, May 18, 1988: 10.
— featured, Lahaina News, August 24, 1988: 11.
— featured, Lahaina News, August 15, 1991: 13.

BEACH DOGS [MUSICAL GROUP]
— to perform at Moose McGillycuddy's, Lahaina News, June 30, 1994: 15.

BEACH, DONN
— proposed new seawall for Lahaina, Lahaina Sun, June 9, 1971: 3.

BEACHCOMBERS [RESTAURANT]
— opens at the Royal Lahaina Resort, Lahaina News, April 22, 1993: 15.
— awarded Golden Platter by International Food, Wine and Travel Writers Association, Lahaina News, July 24, 1997: 6.
— featured, Lahaina News, September 2, 1999: 6,7.

BEACHES
— Cravalho discusses need for public access to, Lahaina Sun, January 20, 1971: 2.
— Public beach park proposed for West Maui, Lahaina Sun, February 24, 1971: 1,8.
— public access discussed, Lahaina Sun, March 17, 1971: 1.
— discusses Maui County's slow expansion of public access, Lahaina Sun, March 31, 1971: 6.
— Major Cravalho authorized to proceed with acquiring rights-of-way, Lahaina Sun, April 7, 1971: 8.
— enforcement of indecency laws discussed, Lahaina Sun, June 16, 1971: 10.
— cleanup of Makena Beach proposed, Lahaina Sun, June 30, 1971: 1.
— cleanup of Makena Beach netted three truckloads of trash, Lahaina Sun, July 14, 1971: 10.
— Maui County Council studying mayor Cravalho's proposal to increase beach access, Lahaina Sun, October 20, 1971: 6.
— requested change to beach access at Napili denied , Lahaina Sun, December 15, 1971: 14.
— slowness of acquiring beach access criticized, Lahaina Sun, April 19, 1972: 21.
— law discussed, Lahaina Sun, August 9, 1972: 26.
— dynamics of changes to, and role of breakwall, Lahaina Sun, December 13, 1972: 24,25.

— Army Corps of Engineers studies Maui shoreline, Lahaina Sun, March 21, 1973: 9.
— Makena beach cleanup planned, Lahaina Sun, March 28, 1973: 1.
— law guaranteeing public access signed by governor Burns, Lahaina Sun, May 30, 1973: 10.
— legal status of access discussed, Lahaina Sun, June 20, 1973: 9.
— new right of ways opened near Sheraton-Maui Hotel, Lahaina News, July 15, 1982: 3.
— "Sandbox" to become Hanaka'o'o Beach Park, Lahaina News, August 1, 1982: 10.
— Maui County discusses extending beach inland from Lahaina to Kapalua, Lahaina News, June 15, 1983: 6.
— Ka'anapali shore water rules discussed, Lahaina News, February 15, 1984: 3.
— Maui Planning Department to hold public meeting on shoreline access, Lahaina News, February 19, 1986: 3.
— information sought by Maui County for shoreline access plan, Lahaina News, March 19, 1986: 3.
— Maui's reputation for nudity on, Lahaina News, February 11, 1987: 1,10.
— public hearing held on access by Maui County Council, Lahaina News, August 9, 1989: 3.
— access to surfing sites to be shut down, Lahaina News, December 19, 1990: 1,2.
— residents discuss creating beach access in Napili, Lahaina News, January 9, 1991: 1.
— West Maui Taxpayers Association supports keeping beach access to the "Little Makaha" surfing site, Lahaina News, January 23, 1991: 3.
— Maui County Council Public Works Committee to consider improvements of at Napili, Lahaina News, April 24, 1991: 1.
— county to fight coastal erosion, Lahaina News, May 30, 1991: 1.
— vegetation encroaching on, Lahaina News, July 11, 1991: 1,9.
— Maui County to study access in Napili, Lahaina News, July 11, 1991: 8.
— no violation found in growth of naupaka by resorts along Ka'anapali Beach, Lahaina News, August 1, 1991: 1.
— Community Work Day to hold clean-up of, Lahaina News, September 26, 1991: 7.
— County fights erosion of, Lahaina News, November 21, 1991: 1,10.
— mayor Linda Lingle creates Beach Access Advisory Committee, Lahaina News, November 21, 1991: 4.
— senator Inouye to seek federal money to purchase land near Big Beach at Makena, Lahaina News, January 9, 1992: 5.
— mayor-appointed Beach Access Advisory Committee seeks to improve access, Lahaina News, April 2, 1992: 1,6.
— citizens advisory committee wants more shoreline protection, Lahaina News, June 18, 1992: 14.
— Dr. Diane Shepherd to speak to Kihei Kiwanis Club on access issues, Lahaina News, July 16, 1992: 6.
— Mayor Linda Lingle submits beach access plan, Lahaina News, July 23, 1992: 10.
— Aloha Earth Unity Day to hold beach clean-up, Lahaina News, August 13, 1992: 4.
— clean-up organized for Aloha Earth Unity Day, Lahaina News, August 20, 1992: 4.
— Mayor Linda Lingle forms advisory committee to advice on beach access, Lahaina News, August 20, 1992: 4.
— clean up to be held, Lahaina News, August 27, 1992: 4.
— Mayor Linda Lingle's Beach Access Advisory Committee favors access at Alaeloa, Lahaina News, September 3, 1992: 1,17.
— Get the Drift and Bag It to be held, Lahaina News, September 24, 1992: 6.
— Maui County plans to improve safety at, Lahaina News, December 10, 1992: 3.
— Mayor's Beach Access Advisory Committee to meet concerning Alaeloa access, Lahaina News, February 18, 1993: 1.

— residents divided on proposed Alaeloa beach access, Lahaina News, February 25, 1993: 2.

— County may seek limited access to Little Makaha beach from Alaeloa Condominium Resort, Lahaina News, March 25, 1993: 3.

— Rick Reed introduces resolution to clean algae from beaches, Lahaina News, March 25, 1993: 3.

— Puamana residents blocked from beach by rocks, Lahaina News, April 22, 1993: 3.

— algae removal may lead to more erosion, Lahaina News, May 6, 1993: 6,7.

— algae cleanup hampered by lack of beach access, Lahaina News, July 1, 1993: 6.

— "Get the Drift and Bag It!" to be held, Lahaina News, September 30, 1993: 4.

— safety tips and warning of dangerous surf, Lahaina News, October 21, 1993: 2.

— Kapalua Bay Hotel and Kapalua Bay Villas criticized for limiting access to Hawea Point, Lahaina News, September 15, 1994: 1,2.

— officials investigation access dispute at Hawea Point, Lahaina News, September 29, 1994: 1,3.

— County seeking access to Little Makana, Lahaina News, October 6, 1994: 1.

— issues over signage following injury of visitor at Ka'anapali Beach, Lahaina News, November 10, 1994: 1,3.

— Maui Council seeking safer path to Slaughterhouse Beach, Lahaina News, February 2, 1995: 1,16.

— Army Corps of Engineers studying wetlands at North Beach, Lahaina News, April 6, 1995: 1,16.

— state and county unclear about jurisdiction for harbor sea wall near Lahaina Public Library, Lahaina News, April 6, 1995: 4.

— trail to Slaughterhouse Beach may be improved, Lahaina News, July 6, 1995: 1,12.

— public trail to Hawea Point opens, Lahaina News, July 13, 1995: 1.

— geologist Charles Fletcher says can be restored, Lahaina News, July 27, 1995: 1,16.

— legal protection sought for surfer stairway at Lahaina Harbor, Lahaina News, July 27, 1995: 4.

— fence at Slaughterhouse Beach eliminates two access trails, Lahaina News, October 26, 1995: 1,16.

— County looking for ways to protect, Lahaina News, February 15, 1996: 1.

— changes at S-Turns Park, Lahaina News, February 15, 1996: 2.

— Honokowai Beach sand project being designed, Lahaina News, May 2, 1996: 19.

— erosion noted near Launiupoko Park, Lahaina News, May 30, 1996: 1,14.

— Mayor Linda Lingle hears about access issues, Lahaina News, July 25, 1996: 2.

— seaweed continues to be an issue, Lahaina News, August 8, 1996: 9.

— West Maui Advisory Committee to discuss access, Lahaina News, October 17, 1996: 4.

— access closed to Nakalele Point, Lahaina News, December 12, 1996: 2.

— Napili beach wall needs to be monitored, Lahaina News, December 19, 1996: 1,28.

— issues with monitoring access of, Lahaina News, December 19, 1996: 28.

— access for surfers at Lahaina Harbor to be finished in mid-August, Lahaina News, July 10, 1997: 9.

— access part of pact for North Beach resort, Lahaina News, October 8, 1998: 1,20.

— state explains plan to restore beach fronting Honokowai Park, Lahaina News, January 14, 1999: 1.

— residents want more details on plan to restore beach at Honokowai Park, Lahaina News, January 21, 1999: 1,16.

— "Between White and Blue on Maui" show to explore restoration of, Lahaina News, March 18, 1999: 17.

— Surfrider Foundation to hold meeting on protecting, Lahaina News, February 17, 2000: 17.

— Maui Pineapple Co gates access to Punalau or "Windmills Beach", Lahaina News, April 5, 2001: 1.

— according to Pacific Whale Foundation, cigarette butts seen as problem on Maui beaches, Lahaina News, June 21, 2001: 2.

— see also specific beaches

BEACHLEY, LAYNE

— surfer wins ASP World Championship, Lahaina News, November 9, 2000: 9.

— surfer wins fourth world title, Lahaina News, December 6, 2001: 1.

— surfer wins fourth world title, Lahaina News, December 13, 2001: 12.

BEACON MAUI

— scheduled, Lahaina News, March 4, 1993: 12.

— to be held, Lahaina News, March 11, 1993: 12.

BEAD HEAVEN [BUSINESS]

— opens, Lahaina News, February 6, 1997: 18.

BEAD SOCIETY OF HAWAII, MAUI CHAPTER

— offering free jewelry workshop, Lahaina News, April 24, 1991: 13.

— to hold Chinese knotting workshop, Lahaina News, October 24, 1991: 4.

— to meet, Lahaina News, October 8, 1992: 2.

— to offering demonstration at Wharf Cinema Center, Lahaina News, December 3, 1992: 16.

— to meet, Lahaina News, March 4, 1993: 4.

— to meet, Lahaina News, November 4, 1993: 6.

— to meet, Lahaina News, December 2, 1993: 4.

— to meet, Lahaina News, February 24, 1994: 11.

— to host Leslie Perles, Lahaina News, August 18, 1994: 5.

BEADLES, LYNN EDGAR [MUSICIAN]

— to perform at Polli's Mexican Restaurant, Lahaina News, December 26, 1990: 11.

BEAL, TANDY [PERFORMER]

— to perform at Castle Theater, Lahaina News, February 1, 1996: 12.

BEALL, EDWARD CARSON

— architect's design work on Whaler's Village, Lahaina Sun, November 25, 1970: 1.

— architect discusses creation of Whaler's Village, Lahaina Sun, December 16, 1970: 5.

— architect worked on Master Plan for west Maui with John Warnecke, Lahaina Sun, December 16, 1970: 5.

BEAM, CROSBY

— new year pastor at Kumulani Chapel, Lahaina News, May 20, 1999: 15.

BEAMER, KAPONO [MUSICIAN]

— releases "Cruisin' On Hawaiian Time" with Dave Jenkins, Lahaina News, December 15, 1994: 16.

— new album "Great Grandmother, Great Grandson" discussed, Lahaina News, September 24, 1998: 9.

BEAMER, KEOLA [MUSICIAN]

— new album reviewed, Lahaina News, August 23, 1989: 12.

— to perform with family at Castle Theatre, Lahaina News, October 24, 1996: 14.

— to perform at Music on the Beach, Lahaina News, September 17, 1998: 27.

— to perform at Music on the Beach, Lahaina News, September 24, 1998: 9.

— to participate in Hawaiian Ki ho'alu (slack key) Workshop, Lahaina News, June 3, 1999: 17.

— to perform at Maui Arts and Cultural Center, Lahaina News, October 7, 1999: 18.

— to perform at Maui Arts and Cultural Center, Lahaina News, October 14, 1999: 13.

— releases CD "Island Born", Lahaina News, February 22, 2001: 14.

— to play songs from new CD "Island Born", Lahaina News, March 15, 2001: 20.

— to play songs from new CD "Island Born", Lahaina News, March 22, 2001: 16.

— publishes "The Shimmering—ka 'oliili", Lahaina News, January 23, 2003: 1,18.

— to perform at Maui Arts and Cultural Center, Lahaina News, July 31, 2003: 15.

BEAMER, NONA [MUSICIAN]

— to perform at Music on the Beach, Lahaina News, September 17, 1998: 27.

— to perform at Music on the Beach, Lahaina News, September 24, 1998: 9.

BEAN, ANDY

— wins Isuzu-Kapalua International tournament, Lahaina News, November 19, 1986: 6,7.

BEANIE BABY SWAP

— to be held, Lahaina News, July 9, 1998: 16.

— raises money for Big Brothers/Big Sisters of Maui, Lahaina News, July 30, 1998: 7.

BEAR HUGS IN HAWAII [BUSINESS]

— reviewed, Lahaina News, June 13, 1990: 14.

BEARD, PAT

— offer puppet show at Lahaina Public Library, Lahaina News, January 2, 1991: 3.

BEARDS

— not acceptable in most restaurants in Lahaina and Ka'anapali, Lahaina Sun, July 14, 1971: 1,12.

BEAT THE FUTURE [SHOW]

— performed by Up With People group, Lahaina News, October 16, 1985: 20.

BEATLES [MUSICAL GROUP]

— "A Hard Day's Night" to be shown at Maui Arts and Cultural Center, Lahaina News, February 1, 2001: 21.

BEATTY, JULIANN

— named top sales producer at Westin Maui, Lahaina News, February 3, 1994: 7.

— promoted to national sales manager, Lahaina News, March 31, 1994: 12.

BEAUMONT, TONY

— named dive operation for Atlantis Submarine, Lahaina News, July 18, 1991: 6.

BEAUSOLEIL [MUSICAL GROUP]

— to perform at Maui Arts and Cultural Center, Lahaina News, November 18, 1999: 11.

— to perform at Maui Arts and Cultural Center, Lahaina News, November 18, 1999: 16.

BEAUTIFUL HOMES OF MAUI

— fundraiser for Napili Fire and Ambulance Station to be held, Lahaina News, December 12, 1990: 4,5.

BEAUTY CONTEST

— Miss Alii 1980 contest held, Lahaina News, March 1, 1980: 7.

BEAUTY QUEEN OF LEENANE, THE [PLAY]

— Maui Community Theatre to produce, Lahaina News, January 27, 2000: 12.

— concluding, Lahaina News, February 3, 2000: 12.

BEAUX ART BALL

— to be held at Maui Hilton, Lahaina Sun, January 27, 1971: 2.

— described, Lahaina Sun, February 24, 1971: 8.

— event described, Lahaina Sun, March 8, 1972: 13.

— to be held by Lahaina Arts Society, Lahaina News, April 24, 1991: 10.

— to be held, Lahaina News, May 1, 1991: 15.

— details of, Lahaina News, May 15, 1991: 12.

— details given, Lahaina News, May 23, 1991: 14.

— to be held by Lahaina Arts Society, Lahaina News, May 30, 1991: 10.

— details provided, Willy K to perform, Lahaina News, June 6, 1991: 18.

BEAZ, KILLER [COMEDIAN]

— to perform at Comedy Club and the Sports Page, Lahaina News, June 11, 1992: 18,19,21.

BEBE SPORT [BUSINESS]

— opens on Front Street, Lahaina News, July 6, 1988: 3.

— featured, Lahaina News, July 20, 1988: 2.

— opens new store, Lahaina News, August 10, 1988: 3.

BEBOP [CLOWN]

— at Lahaina Public Library, Lahaina News, June 10, 1987: 3.

BECK, MICHAEL

— receives Aqua awards from International Bottled ater Association at recent convention, Lahaina News, December 15, 1994: 15.

— to be included in "Who's Who in Executives and Professionals", Lahaina News, March 2, 1995: 7.

BECK, ROBERT

— promoted to General Manager of H&R Block, Lahaina News, January 20, 1988: 18.

BECKER, ROB [COMEDIAN]

— to perform at Comedy Club and the Sports Page, Lahaina News, November 28, 1990: 9,10.

BECKER, THOMAS

— see Flower, Toni

BECKWITH, MICHAEL

— reverend to hold meditation at Unity of Maui, Lahaina News, October 2, 2003: 17.

BECVAR, BRUCE [MUSICIAN]

— to perform at Mandala's, Lahaina News, August 21, 2003: 16.

BEDARD, ROBERT [ARTIST]

— opens "Artist in Paradise", Lahaina News, August 7, 2003: 3.

BEDELL, MARGARET [ARTIST]

— works shown at Village Gallery, Lahaina News, February 10, 1988: 3.

— to exhibit at Coast Gallery Wailea, Lahaina News, February 17, 1994: 12.

— to hold watercolor workshop, Lahaina News, January 23, 2003: 16.

— to exhibit at Village Galleries, Lahaina News, February 6, 2003: 16.

BEDNOB, GERRY [COMEDIAN]

— to perform at Comedy Club, Lahaina News, August 15, 1990: 15.

BEDOYA, JOSEPH

— new tennis professional at Hyatt Regency Maui, Lahaina News, March 25, 1993: 6.

BEEBE, MARINA [ARTIST]

— to present at Village Galleries, Lahaina News, April 11, 1990: 17.

BEEBE, ROXANNE

— recognized as "Designer of the Year" by Hawaii Jewelers Association, Lahaina News, December 28, 2000: 16.

BEEMER, JAN

— appointed operations manager of commercial leases for Kapalua Land Company, Ltd., Lahaina News, July 18, 1990: 7.

BEER

— Oktoberfest to feature Hawaii-made, Lahaina News, October 2, 1997: 9.

BEERER, GAGE
— appointed marketing representative for Xerox Hawaii Maui office, Lahaina News, June 21, 2001: 9.

BEETHOVEN, LUDWIG [MUSICIAN]
— Maui Symphony Orchestra to perform 9th Symphony, Lahaina News, April 26, 2001: 20.

BEGA, MAURICE [MUSICIAN]
— to perform at Longhi's Restaurant, Lahaina News, September 19, 1996: 18.
— to perform at B.J.'s Chicago Pizzeria, Lahaina News, November 21, 1996: 15.
— to perform at Luaus, Lahaina News, March 27, 1997: 11.
— to perform at B.J.'s Chicago Pizzeria, Lahaina News, June 19, 1997: 18.
— to perform at B.J.'s Chicago Pizzeria, Lahaina News, October 9, 1997: 19.
— to perform at Hula Grill, Lahaina News, May 7, 1998: 22.
— to perform at B.J.'s Chicago Pizzeria, Lahaina News, March 1, 2001: 19.
— to perform at B.J.'s Chicago Pizzeria, Lahaina News, April 12, 2001: 19.

BEGGS, WEBB
— discusses mayor's request for emergency powers, Lahaina Sun, December 23, 1970: 5.
— biography, Lahaina Sun, February 10, 1971: 2.

BEHM, DEBBIE LEE
— discusses upcoming Hawaiian Sovereignty vote, Lahaina News, April 13, 1995: 5.

BEIJING ACROBATS
— to perform at Maui Community College, Lahaina News, May 10, 1989: 16.

BEKEART, EDNA PUALANI FARDEN [MUSICIAN]
— music to be shared with students, Lahaina News, December 12, 2002: 1,22.
— participated in Celebration of the Arts at Ritz-Carlton, Lahaina News, April 24, 2003: 1,22.

BEKOFSKY, NOAH
— new executive chef at Kapalua Bay Hotel and Open Villas, Lahaina News, May 1, 2003: 8.

BELA FLECK AND THE FLECKTONES [MUSICAL GROUP]
— to perform at Maui Arts and Cultural Center, Lahaina News, December 12, 2002: 20,21.

BELAFONTE, HARRY [MUSICIAN]
— to perform at Maui Arts and Cultural Center, Lahaina News, May 1, 1997: 17.

BELEZOS, DEBORAH
— coordinator of Big Brothers/Big Sister featured, Lahaina News, December 26, 1991: 3.

BELJAN, PAUL
— opens Maui Psychological Associates, Lahaina News, March 27, 1997: 10.

BELL, ART
— radio talk show host featured, Lahaina News, March 20, 1997: 18,20.

BELL, MARVIN [COMEDIAN]
— to perform at Comedy Club and the Sports Page, Lahaina News, May 28, 1992: 14,16.

BELL, MARY [ARTIST]
— exhibiting at Village Galleries, Lahaina News, April 4, 1990: 15.

BELL, RANDY
— police sergeant speaks of concern for unmarked police vehicles, Lahaina News, August 29, 1991: 1.

BELLAMY, RICHARD [WRITER]
— author of "12 Secrets for Manifesting Your Vision, Inspiration and Purpose" to appear, Lahaina News, October 8, 1998: 16.

BELLAMY, VIVIEN
— career and life described, Lahaina News, November 23, 1983: 9,10,11.

BELLAROS, VICTOR
— Light Bringers Mission co-founder recognized with JC Penny Golden Rule Award, Lahaina News, May 18, 1995: 3.
— director of Light Bringers Rescue Mission thanks Mike Tyson for donating money to organization, Lahaina News, May 9, 2002: 12.

BELLE, SUSAN [ARTIST]
— featured, Lahaina News, February 15, 1982: 10.

BELT, COLLINS, & ASSOCIATES [BUSINESS]
— presents plan for Front Street, Lahaina News, November 21, 1990: 1.

BELUSHI, JIM [COMEDIAN]
— hosts blessing ceremony for Planet Hollywood, Lahaina News, January 20, 1994: 6.
— purchases art, Lahaina News, February 24, 1994: 9.

BELZER, ARNOLD MARK
— Rabbi to speak at Jewish Library of Maui, Lahaina News, January 15, 1998: 12.
— Rabbi to review Alan Dershowitz "The Vanishing American Jew", Lahaina News, February 5, 1998: 12.

BEMROSE, LARRY
— joins Monarch Building Supply, Lahaina News, January 2, 1991: 5.

BEMROSE, SUSAN
— to present research on whales, Lahaina News, February 8, 1996: 7.

BEN ABIERA MEMORIAL
— sponsored by Kihei Canoe Club, Lahaina News, May 23, 1990: 10.

BEN FRANKLIN [BUSINESS]
— to open in Ka'ahumanu Shopping Center, Lahaina Sun, June 21, 1972: 11.

BEN, GLENN AND FRIENDS [MUSICAL GROUP]
— to perform at Marriott's Makai Bar, Lahaina News, January 26, 1995: 14.

BENANTO, LOUIS, JR. [ARTIST]
— carving featured, Lahaina News, March 11, 1993: 3.
— carving of Kamehameha I pictured, Lahaina News, September 30, 1993: 15.

BENATOVICH, DEANNA [ARTIST]
— to exhibit at Lahaina Arts Society, Lahaina News, March 28, 1996: 12.
— to exhibit photographs at Maui Arts Society, Lahaina News, June 6, 2002: 17.

BENCH, JOHNNY
— to play at Isuzu Kapalua International, Lahaina News, October 17, 1990: 9.

BENCOMO, DEREK [ARTIST]
— woodturner to exhibit at Lahaina Cannery Mall, Lahaina News, December 3, 1992: 3.
— to exhibit at Village Galleries, Lahaina News, April 20, 1995: 11.
— work to be part of traveling museum exhibition , Lahaina News, May 18, 1995: 11.
— State Foundation on Culture and the Arts purcahses work by, Lahaina News, December 14, 1995: 18.
— woodturner to exhibit at Maui Crafts Guild, Lahaina News, May 2, 1996: 16.
— featured, Lahaina News, October 17, 1996: 17.
— accepted by Art Maui judges, Lahaina News, March 6, 1997: 13.

BENDON FAMILY FOUNDATION
— donates money to Lahaina Intermediate School library, Lahaina News, September 5, 2002: 3.

BENEDETTI AND SVOBODA [MUSICAL GROUP]
— guitarists to perform at Borders Books, Lahaina News, July 1, 1999: 12,13.
— to perform at Maui Community Theater, Lahaina News, July 15, 1999: 12.

BENEFIT COUNTRY JAMBOREE
— to be held at Haleakala Ranch Racetrack, Lahaina News, May 1, 2003: 16.

BENETTON [BUSINESS]
— to open in Lahaina Cannery Shopping Center, Lahaina News, January 23, 1991: 5.
— to hold clothing drive to support Women Helping Women, Lahaina News, April 22, 1993: 3.
— reopens after renovations, Lahaina News, August 5, 1993: 7.

BENIHANA [RESTAURANT]
— picketed by Maui Carpenter's union, Lahaina News, May 3, 1989: 1.
— opens, Lahaina News, January 17, 1990: 12.
— to offer Valentine's special, Lahaina News, February 14, 1990: 15.
— celebrates first birthday, Lahaina News, May 23, 1990: 8.
— celebrates first anniversary, Lahaina News, August 15, 1990: 11.
— to celebrate National Grandparent's Day, Lahaina News, August 29, 1990: 14.
— to host fundraiser for Napili Fire and Ambulance Station, Lahaina News, September 19, 1990: 4.
— to host Celebrity Chef Dinner, Lahaina News, October 10, 1990: 6.
— hosting Celebrity Chef Dinner, Lahaina News, October 17, 1990: 6.
— to celebrate birthday party, Lahaina News, October 31, 1990: 14.
— Celebrity Chef fundraiser attracted about 200 people, Lahaina News, November 14, 1990: 4.
— to hold twentieth anniversary celebration, Lahaina News, May 15, 1991: 10.
— to celebrate anniversary, Lahaina News, May 23, 1991: 11.
— offering kama'aina rates, Lahaina News, August 8, 1991: 13.
— reviewed; offers kama'aina specials, Lahaina News, September 19, 1991: 18,19.
— offering Thanksgiving Dinner, Lahaina News, November 14, 1991: 15.
— featured, Lahaina News, January 30, 1992: 22.

BENNETT, TONY [MUSICIAN]
— to perform at Maui Arts and Cultural Center, Lahaina News, March 23, 1995: 12.

BENNETT, WILLIAM
— to present "The Joy of Dowsing", Lahaina News, July 27, 2000: 21.

BENOIT, PETER
— passes away, Lahaina News, June 19, 2003: 3.

BENSON, GEORGE [MUSICIAN]
— reviewed, Lahaina News, October, 1979: 5.
— opens recording studio in Lahaina Square, Lahaina News, August 1, 1982: 4.
— playing free concerts in Maui, Lahaina Times, August 20, 1983 volume 7 number 8: 1.
— created Lahaina Sound recording studio, Lahaina News, September 20, 1989: 9.
— to perform at Maui Arts and Cultural Center, Lahaina News, February 24, 2000: 3.
— to perform at Maui Arts and Cultural Center, Lahaina News, March 2, 2000: 12.

BENSON, TY
— Maui Electric engineer discusses plans for underground wiring in Front Street, Lahaina Sun, December 9, 1970: 7.
— engineer discusses Maui Electric Company's new transmission line, Lahaina Sun, January 20, 1971: 8.
— Maui Electric engineer discusses power poles running along highway, Lahaina Sun, February 3, 1971: 1.

BENTO, WILLIAM
— to lead "Envisioning the Destiny of our Future Generations", Lahaina News, May 27, 1999: 12.

BENTON, JAMES GRANT [MUSICIAN]
— to perform at "I Love Lahaina", Lahaina News, October 25, 2001: 15.

BENZ, MICHELLE [ARTIST]
— photographs displayed at Artful Dodger's, Lahaina News, January 13, 1988: 16.

BEPPU, SANFORD
— Department of Education inspector discusses unsafe playground at King Kamehameha III Elementary School, Lahaina News, November 4, 1999: 1,16.

BERENSOHN, PAULUS [ARTIST]
— to offer ceramics classes, Lahaina News, April 3, 1991: 10.
— to speak on "finding one's way with clay", Lahaina News, April 10, 1991: 13.
— to offer workshop on making journals, Lahaina News, February 6, 1992: 4.

BERG, KARL
— elected president of the Hawaiian Sugar Planters' Association, Lahaina Sun, December 30, 1970: 7.
— president of Hawaiian Sugar Planters Association discusses pollution, Lahaina Sun, February 17, 1971: 5.
— president of Hawaiian Sugar Planters Association discusses west coast dock strike hurting sugar and pineapple companies, Lahaina Sun, August 18, 1971: 1.

BERG, NORMAN
— named director of sales for Maui for Aston Hotels and Resorts, Lahaina News, April 5, 2001: 9.

BERG, PAMILLE
— to present "Art, Craft, & Architecture", Lahaina News, April 3, 1991: 10.

BERGER, ANNA MARIE
— wins Maui's Little Miss of America Pageant, Lahaina News, June 5, 1997: 3.

BERGER, JAIOM "ALUMINUM MAN"
— participates in Aluminum Run, Lahaina News, January 4, 1996: 6.
— qualifies for Ironman, Lahaina News, September 19, 1996: 13.
— dies in motorcycle accident; remembered, Lahaina News, December 3, 1998: 3.
— remembered, Lahaina News, December 10, 1998: 1,2.

BERGER, LIA
— Scholar/Athlete of the Week, Lahaina News, December 11, 1997: 16.

BERGER, SAMALIA
— semifinalist in "Teen Magazine's 1997 Athlete of the Year" program, Lahaina News, June 20, 1996: 10.
— semi-finalist for TEEN Magazine's Athlete of the Year, Lahaina News, September 19, 1996: 13.

BERGLUND, ERIK [MUSICIAN]
— to perform at Iao Valley Lodge, Lahaina News, January 3, 1990: 16.
— to perform with Irish harp at Iao Valley Lodge, Lahaina News, January 10, 1990: 12.

BERGMAN, JOHANNA
— to speak to the American Association of Retired Person on life in Indonesia, Lahaina News, June 28, 2001: 16.

BERGSON, CHUCK
— purchases share of KPOA FM radio, Lahaina News, April 11, 1990: 5.
— begins as president of Rotary Club of Lahaina, Lahaina News, July 13, 1995: 5.

BERMAN, CHRIS
— ESPN announcer visits Maui, Lahaina News, February 24, 1988: 6.
— ESPN anchor to be grand marshal for St. Patrick's Day Parade, Lahaina News, March 9, 1995: 11.

BERMAN CHRISTINE
— chiropractor opens office, Lahaina News, January 20, 1994: 6.

BERMAN, HILDEGARD
— creates Spender Menders to help people who overspend, Lahaina News, March 9, 1988: 3.

BERMAN, PETER [COMEDIAN]
— to perform at Comedy Club and the Sports Page, Lahaina News, April 24, 1991: 7,11.
— to perform at Comedy Club and the Sports Page, Lahaina News, April 16, 1992: 17.
— to perform at Honolulu Comedy Club, Lahaina News, November 23, 1995: 11,12.

BERMAN REPORT
— on education to be discussed, Lahaina News, March 15, 1989: 1.

BERMUDEZ, RAUL
— chef at Canoes Oceanfront featured, Lahaina News, July 5, 2001: 14.

BERNADES, BLAINE
— Scholar/Athlete of the Week, Lahaina News, June 4, 1998: 14.
— on Maui PONY All-Star Baseball Team, Lahaina News, August 3, 2000: 6.

BERNARD, HANNAH
— discusses hawkbill turtles nesting at North Beach, Lahaina News, January 30, 1997: 1,16.
— Hawai'i Wildlife Fund to speak on sea turtles and dolphins, Lahaina News, April 15, 1999: 12.
— to speak on "Humpback Whales: The Most Watchable Whales", Lahaina News, March 9, 2000: 1.
— to speak on "Humpback Whales: The Most Watchable Whales", Lahaina News, March 9, 2000: 12,13.
— appointed education director at Maui Ocean Center, Lahaina News, April 19, 2001: 8.
— to give talk on "Would you turn your lights off for a turtle?", Lahaina News, May 8, 2003: 2.

BERNARD, PATRICK [MUSICIAN]
— to perform at Mandala's, Lahaina News, August 21, 2003: 16.

BERNARD, STEVE [COMEDIAN]
— to perform at Honolulu Comedy Club, Lahaina News, February 8, 1996: 13.

BERNARD, WILLIAM "RAY"
— crashes seaplane on beach near Launiupoko Beach Park, Lahaina News, April 23, 1986: 1.

BERNICE INOUYE MUSIC STUDIO
— to hold Japanese Karaoke Spring Festival, Lahaina News, April 4, 2002: 16.

BERRERA, MICHAEL
— Small Business Administration Ombudsman accepting comments on federal regulatory enforcement, Lahaina News, January 23, 2003: 8.

BERRY, CINDY
— to manager sales staff at Westin Maui, Lahaina News, March 26, 1992: 11.

BERTELMANN, SHAWNA
— Scholar/Athlete of the Week, Lahaina News, January 28, 1999: 7.

BERUBE, ALLEN
— to present lecture on oppression of lesbians and gays in World War II, Lahaina News, April 10, 1985: 9.

BERZABAL, WILHEMINA
— Lahainaluna High School student wins scholarship from Cannon's Business College, Lahaina News, August 16, 1989: 3.
— named to Dean's List at Cannon's Business College, Lahaina News, December 13, 1989: 4.
— named to Dean's list at Cannon's Business College, Lahaina News, May 30, 1990: 5.
— graduates from Cannon's Business College, Lahaina News, November 14, 1990: 4.

BESS, BENJAMIN
— owner of Bess Press to lead workshop "The 7 Secrets of Creating and Publishing Children's Books" with Bruce Hale, Lahaina News, November 16, 2000: 16.

BESSIE, THE BANDIT'S BEAUTIFUL BABY [PLAY]
— to be performed by the Valley Isle Players, Lahaina Sun, July 11, 1973: 6.

BEST CHRISTMAS PAGEANT EVER, THE [PLAY]
— to be performed at Lahainaluna High School, Lahaina News, December 12, 1984: 3.
— to be performed, Lahaina News, November 27, 1985: 20.
— to be performed by Maui Youth Theatre, Lahaina News, December 4, 1985: 3.

BEST IN SHOW [BUSINESS]
— to open, Lahaina News, November 28, 2002: 8.

BEST OF MAUI [BOOK]
— published by Sandwich Island Publishing, Lahaina News, August 7, 1997: 5.

BEST OF MAUI CASSETTE TOURS [BUSINESS]
— purchased by Scott Golladay, Lahaina News, December 26, 1990: 7.

BEST OF MAUI HAWAIIAN FESTIVAL, THE
— to benefit Community Clinic of Maui, Lahaina News, June 27, 2002: 16.

BEST OF MAUI: SPORTS, RECREATION, SHOPPING AND DINING [BOOK]
— published, Lahaina News, July 4, 1996: 2.

BEST OF THE SECOND CITY, THE [TROUPE]
— to perform, Lahaina News, January 30, 2003: 16.

BEST PUBLISHING [BUSINESS]
— publishes Lahaina Dining Magazine, Lahaina News, March 18, 1999: 13.

BETRAM, JOE III
— Kihei resident promotes bikeway system, Lahaina News, June 25, 1992: 6.

BETSILL BROTHERS CONSTRUCTION [BUSINESS]
— appoints Alvin Takahashi as principal broker and Jeanne Trusty as director of marketing communications, Lahaina News, July 19, 2001: 9.
— developer featured, Lahaina News, August 16, 2001: 7.
— building the Villas at Kenolio, Lahaina News, August 22, 2002: 6.
— to develop Kenolio Mauka, Lahaina News, October 10, 2002: 6.
— new Kihei community featured, Lahaina News, December 5, 2002: 6.

BETTENCOURT, JEFF
— joins Koho Grill and Bar restaurant as operating partner, Lahaina News, June 3, 1993: 7.

BETTER BUSINESS BUREAU
— seeking nominations for Better Business Award, Lahaina News, April 30, 1992: 11.
— selects L.B. Woffinden as president, Lahaina News, June 4, 1992: 9.
— adds 1-800 line, Lahaina News, February 25, 1993: 6.
— offering toll-free line, Lahaina News, November 19, 1998: 13.
— warns people of "Property Tax Reduction" scam, Lahaina News, January 14, 1999: 11.

— appoints Heather Findley as Maui County membership representative, Lahaina News, January 4, 2001: 14.

— to offer seminar on customer service, Lahaina News, March 8, 2001: 8.

BETTER GARDENS FOR BETTER LIVING [FILM]
— shown at Lahaina Library, Lahaina Sun, July 28, 1971: 11.

BETTINO'S [RESTAURANT]
— reviewed, Lahaina News, August, 1979: 3.

BETTY BOOP
— look-a-like competition to be held, Lahaina News, October 21, 1993: 15,16.

— results of Look-a-like contest, Lahaina News, November 4, 1993: 11.

BEVERLY GANNON AWARDS
— Maui Community College students wins awards for Women in the Culinary Arts, Lahaina News, July 11, 2002: 8.

BEVERLY, PAM [ARTIST]
— to exhibit at Hui No'eau Visual Arts Center, Lahaina News, July 23, 1998: 16.

BEVILACQUA, DIANE
— promoted to manager, industrial engineering and operations analysis at Hawaiian Commercial and Sugar Company, Lahaina News, March 27, 1991: 9.

BEY, DENISE
— to dance at West African dance and music performance, Lahaina News, November 2, 1988: 3.

BEYBLADE BATTLING TOP COMPETITION
— to be held, Lahaina News, August 14, 2003: 16.

BEYOND HEAVEN [BUSINESS]
— to hold "Rejuvenation Facial Workshop", Lahaina News, May 23, 2002: 16.

BEYOND THERAPY [PLAY]
— to be performed by Maui Community Theatre, Lahaina News, January 23, 1991: 8.

— continues at Maui Community Theatre, Lahaina News, January 30, 1991: 7.

— to finish, Lahaina News, February 6, 1991: 9.

BEYOND WORDS [BUSINESS]
— public relations partnership formed, Lahaina News, September 17, 1986: 11.

BEYONDANANDA
— Swami to appear in Maui, Lahaina News, December 28, 1988: 2.

BFI WASTE SYSTEMS [BUSINESS]
— resumes aluminum recycling with Safeway, Lahaina News, October 12, 1995: 6.

— awarded a county contract to haul county recycling dropboxes, Lahaina News, December 14, 1995: 19.

BHAERMAN, STEVE
— Swami to present at Ohana Luncheon and Trade Faire, Lahaina News, January 3, 1990: 16.

BIANCARDI, MARCO
— acupuncturist office opens, Lahaina News, November 28, 1991: 7.

BIATHLON
— see Aluminum Man

BICENTENNIAL
— John Pincetich, chair of Hawaii Bicentennial commission, to speak, Lahaina Sun, July 18, 1973: 7.

BICYCLING
— police urge owners to protect bicycles from theft, Lahaina Sun, January 20, 1971: 8.

— bike path from Lahaina to Ka'anapali suggested, Lahaina Sun, August 18, 1971: 9.

— bicycle path between Lahaina and Ka'anapali proposed, Lahaina Sun, September 22, 1971: 8,9.

— Mayor Cravalho asks for study of possible bicycle paths , Lahaina Sun, October 6, 1971: 3.

— bicycle path discussed, Lahaina Sun, October 13, 1971: 2.

— discussion of House resolution on paths for, Lahaina Sun, March 8, 1972: 17.

— race from Wailuku to Ka'anapali, Lahaina Sun, March 29, 1972: 16.

— Maui Norman K. Tamanaha Hawaiian Marathon and Cycle Race held, Lahaina Sun, April 5, 1972: 17.

— Maui Norman K. Tamanaha Hawaiian Marathon and Cycle Race results, Lahaina Sun, April 12, 1972: 21.

— paths being studied by Maui County, Lahaina Sun, May 10, 1972: 21.

— bicycle group organized, Lahaina Sun, May 31, 1972: 7.

— Rusty Harpoon-Winsock Great Bicycle Race planned, Lahaina Sun, June 28, 1972: 10.

— bicyclist assaulted, Lahaina Sun, July 5, 1972: 14.

— questions raised about funding allocated to create plan for paths, Lahaina Sun, August 2, 1972: 11.

— paths planned for Lahaina, Lahaina Sun, September 27, 1972: 10.

— planning underway for West Maui bike path, Lahaina Sun, November 8, 1972: 11.

— Stanley DeLima and Francis Ornellas cycle from Wailuku to Hana, Lahaina Sun, December 20, 1972: 23.

— Master plan for bike paths on Maui proposed, Lahaina Sun, February 7, 1973: 12,13.

— Haleakala ride described, Lahaina Sun, February 28, 1973: 15.

— work on paths to begin in July, Lahaina Sun, February 28, 1973: 3.

— down Haleakala described, Lahaina Sun, May 23, 1973: 6.

— race to raise money for American Cancer Society planned, Lahaina Sun, June 6, 1973: 5.

— race to raise money for American Cancer Society described, Lahaina Sun, June 27, 1973: 3.

— bike path in Lahaina set to open, Lahaina Sun, August 1, 1973: 3.

— Pacific Island Cruisers begins renting bicycles, Lahaina News, November 15, 1982: 11.

— Maui Bicycle Club to hold events, Lahaina News, July 1, 1983: 3,6.

— Bob Kiger advocating for bike path around Maui, Lahaina News, January 6, 1988: 1,14.

— editorial supporting bike lanes, Lahaina News, February 21, 1990: 16.

— state to expand bike routes, Lahaina News, March 21, 1990: 1.

— bill introduced to encourage, Lahaina News, February 27, 1991: 5.

— "Cycle to the Sun '92" to be held, Lahaina News, July 9, 1992: 12.

— plans for bikeways discussed, Lahaina News, August 6, 1992: 3.

— Cycle to the Sun '92 to be held, Lahaina News, September 10, 1992: 8.

— Maui Bike Expo to be held, Lahaina News, October 22, 1992: 4.

— American Red Cross to hold "Mak-Kap Bicycle Challenge", Lahaina News, May 27, 1993: 9.

— West Maui Cycles to hold Honolua Bay Mountain Bike Classic, Lahaina News, March 24, 1994: 12.

— Ka Lima Cross Country Cycle to be held, Lahaina News, April 28, 1994: 7.

— cycling tour of Kaua'i to be held, Lahaina News, May 12, 1994: 7.

— million dollars allotted for bikeway for West Maui, Lahaina News, May 18, 1995: 1,12.

— Labor Day Weekend Neighbor Island Bike Trek to be held, Lahaina News, August 31, 1995: 6.

— Maui racing team forms, Lahaina News, September 7, 1995: 4.

— bike lanes sometimes sacrificed for infrastructure projects, Lahaina News, December 5, 1996: 3,18.

— plan to enhance bicycle safety in Pali Tunnel, Lahaina News, January 9, 1997: 2.

— state establishing Lahaina to Ma'alaea bikeway, Lahaina News, July 2, 1998: 8.

— "Paradise Bike Ride" to be held in Hilo, Lahaina News, August 6, 1998: 19.

— Neighbor Island Bike Trek to be held, Lahaina News, October 29, 1998: 19.

— Neighbor Island Bike Trek to be held, Lahaina News, November 5, 1998: 19.

— Maui County Council concerned about safety of, Lahaina News, September 2, 1999: 1,20.

— Paradise Ride bicycle ride to benefit Hawaii AIDS organizations, Lahaina News, January 25, 2001: 9.

— Paradise Ride seeking volunteers, Lahaina News, May 30, 2002: 12.

— Gay, Lesbian and Bisexual Monthly Hike to be held, Lahaina News, July 11, 2002: 16,17.

BIG BAND BASH FOR CASH
— fundraiser for musician Tommy Hall held at Stouffer's Wailea Beach Hotel, Lahaina News, January 29, 1986: 8.

BIG BEACH
— development challenging, Lahaina News, February 8, 1984: 9,10,11.

— editorial opposing rural subdivision near, Lahaina News, January 28, 1987: 2.

— senator Inouye to seek federal money to purchase land near, Lahaina News, January 9, 1992: 5.

— appraisal finished, Lahaina News, June 4, 1992: 6.

BIG BROTHERS/BIG SISTERS
— helping isle youth, Lahaina Sun, March 10, 1971: 4.

— fundraising drive underway, Lahaina Sun, May 19, 1971: 7.

— events described, Lahaina Sun, March 15, 1972: 10.

— 4th of July golf tournament raised funds for, Lahaina Sun, July 19, 1972: 11.

— to hold five-mile fun-run-walk fundraiser, Lahaina News, August 15, 1984: 3.

— recruiting volunteers, Lahaina News, January 16, 1985: 3.

— looking for volunteers, Lahaina News, February 19, 1986: 3.

— to hold bowling fundraiser, Lahaina News, May 27, 1987: 16.

— held pledge campaign, Lahaina News, July 15, 1987: 3.

— Chart House holds 10K fun run fundraiser to support, Lahaina News, March 9, 1988: 3,17.

— to hold bowlathon , Lahaina News, July 27, 1988: 6.

— to hold bowling fundraiser, Lahaina News, November 23, 1988: 5.

— to hold benefit run, Lahaina News, March 1, 1989: 2.

— gives Bill Kohne award to Al Terry, Lahaina News, April 12, 1989: 5.

— to host Mardi Gras, Lahaina News, January 31, 1990: 2.

— seeking volunteers, Lahaina News, March 14, 1990: 3.

— to hold bowlathon fundraiser, Lahaina News, July 11, 1990: 9.

— to hold Mardi Gras fundraiser, Lahaina News, February 20, 1991: 3.

— to hold fundraiser at Gerard's, Lahaina News, May 15, 1991: 5.

— to hold Bowlathon fund-raiser, Lahaina News, July 11, 1991: 7.

— Bowlathon to be held, Lahaina News, July 25, 1991: 9.

— Lahaina Rotary Club raises $600 for at Bowlathon, Lahaina News, August 29, 1991: 7.

— coordinator Deborah Belezos featured, Lahaina News, December 26, 1991: 3.

— to hold Mardi Gras fundraiser, Lahaina News, January 9, 1992: 3.

— to hold Mardi Gras fundraiser, Lahaina News, January 30, 1992: 4.

— to hold Mardi Gras fundraiser, Lahaina News, February 6, 1992: 3.

— attend cooking classes at Lahaina Grill, Lahaina News, May 28, 1992: 4.

— Bowlathon fundraiser to be held, Lahaina News, July 30, 1992: 8.

— Kai Hoopii wins volunteer appreciation contest, Lahaina News, August 27, 1992: 3.

— to hold Mardi Gras fundraiser , Lahaina News, February 25, 1993: 8.

— to hold fundraiser at Plantation House Restaurant, Lahaina News, March 18, 1993: 12.

— Mardi Gras fundraiser successful, Lahaina News, April 1, 1993: 4.

— benefit run to be held, Lahaina News, April 8, 1993: 8.

— to hold fashion show as fundraiser, Lahaina News, August 5, 1993: 9.

— to hold Maui Run , Lahaina News, April 6, 1995: 2.

— to hold Chart House Fun Run, Lahaina News, April 6, 1995: 7.

— to hold "Bowl for a Kids Sake" fundraiser, Lahaina News, July 27, 1995: 6.

— receives grant from Chart House fun run, Lahaina News, August 17, 1995: 4.

— NFL Alumni Association hold fundraiser for, Lahaina News, November 16, 1995: 15.

— receives grant from Lahaina Chart House, Lahaina News, May 8, 1997: 15.

— Kay Ryan recognizes as "Big Sister of the Year", Lahaina News, May 29, 1997: 3.

— wireless phones donated to, Lahaina News, December 25, 1997: 3.

— Chart House 5K/10K Fun Run and Walk to benefit, Lahaina News, April 2, 1998: 1.

— Beanie Baby Swap and Trade raises money for, Lahaina News, July 30, 1998: 7.

— Chart House to host 5K/10K Fun Run/Walk fundraiser, Lahaina News, April 1, 1999: 14.

— clothes collected for, Lahaina News, October 28, 1999: 13.

— Lahainaluna High School students mentoring in After School Mentoring Program organized by, Lahaina News, April 13, 2000: 2.

— to benefit from event at David Paul's Lahaina Grill, Lahaina News, April 20, 2000: 16.

— NFL players to compete in charity basketball for, Lahaina News, April 20, 2000: 16.

— to hold "Bowl for Kids' Sake" fundraiser, Lahaina News, August 3, 2000: 6.

— to hold "Bowl for Kids' Sake", Lahaina News, August 10, 2000: 7.

— sponsoring clothing donation bins, Lahaina News, January 10, 2002: 8.

— to hold 5k Run, Lahaina News, March 14, 2002: 13.

— to hold 5K Run, Lahaina News, March 21, 2002: 13.

— to hold 5K Run, Lahaina News, March 28, 2002: 11.

— to hold Fun Run, Lahaina News, April 17, 2003: 12.

— to hold "Bowl for Kids' Sake" fundraiser, Lahaina News, July 17, 2003: 13.

— "Bowl for Kids' Sake" fundraiser to be held for, Lahaina News, July 24, 2003: 13.

— to hold "Bowl for Kids' Sake" fundraiser, Lahaina News, July 31, 2003: 13.

— collecting clothing and items for garage sale, Lahaina News, September 25, 2003: 18.

BIG DOGS [BUSINESS]
— to take over Luana's space , Lahaina News, July 9, 1998: 15.

BIG HUMAN JUICER [MUSICAL GROUP]
— to perform at Longhi's, Lahaina News, December 26, 1990: 8.

— to perform at Moose McGillycuddy's, Lahaina News, January 2, 1991: 7.

BIG ISLAND
— featured as a tourist destination, Lahaina News, June 19, 1997: 3.

BIG MELE, THE
— concert to be held, Lahaina News, July 17, 1997: 16.

— to be held, Lahaina News, July 31, 1997: 16.

BIG MIKE'S DELI [BUSINESS]
— featured, Lahaina News, June 12, 1985: 7.

BIG MOUNTAIN [MUSICAL GROUP]
— reggae band to perform, Lahaina News, January 2, 2003: 15.

BIG RIVER [PLAY]
— Baldwin Theatre Guild to perform music based on the writings of Mark Twain, Lahaina News, August 1, 1991: 18.

BIGA, LILEA
— wins talent show, Lahaina News, February 11, 1993: 15.

BIGA, VERNA
— appointed Food and Beverage director at Sea House Restaurant, Lahaina News, August 26, 1999: 13.

BIGA, WILLIE [MUSICIAN]
— to perform at Taco Joe's Cantina, Lahaina News, December 30, 1993: 11.

BIGLER, JEFF
— mayor Hannibal Tavares awards certificate of merit to, Lahaina News, September 10, 1986: 3.

BIHO, PHILLIPO, III
— Lahainaluna High School boxer featured, Lahaina News, January 27, 1994: 6.

BIHO, REGINA
— returns from Gulf War, Lahaina News, June 27, 1991: 6.

BIKE SHOP, THE [BUSINESS]
— moves into Triangle Square, Lahaina News, June 27, 1996: 12.

BIKE-O-RAMA
— to be held at Lahaina Cannery Mall, Lahaina News, June 4, 1998: 16.

BIKEWAYS MAUI [BUSINESS]
— to hold meeting on bikeway for West Maui, Lahaina News, March 24, 1994: 7.
— to sponsor ride in celebration of National Trails Day, Lahaina News, May 26, 1994: 9.
— endorsed by West Maui Advisory Committee, Lahaina News, April 13, 1995: 1,20.
— stylists to raise money for, Lahaina News, April 25, 1996: 6.
— launches Greenway Initiative, Lahaina News, March 27, 2003: 12.

BILL, DONALD
— ketch Rainbow Goddess sinks, Lahaina News, January 30, 1997: 3.

BILL KOHNE BIG BROTHERS/BIG SISTERS
— award given to Al Terry, Lahaina News, April 12, 1989: 5.

BILL PANEY DIXIE FIVE [MUSICAL GROUP]
— to perform at Maui Philharmonic Society's wine and cheese concert, Lahaina News, September 26, 1984: 3.

BILLABONG GIRLS
— surfing tournament held at Honolua Bay, won by Layne Beachley, Lahaina News, November 9, 2000: 9.
— World Champion Tour to be held at Honolua Bay, Lahaina News, October 11, 2001: 13.

BILLABONG PRO MAUI
— surfing tournament to be held, Lahaina News, December 5, 2002: 1.
— Jacqueline Silva wins, Lahaina News, December 19, 2002: 1,12.

BILLBOARDS
— proposal to ban political signs set to vote, Lahaina Sun, May 12, 1971: 6.

BILLFISH TOURNAMENT
— results described, Lahaina News, September 17, 1986: 9,12.

BILLIANOR, JIMMY
— to be evicted from Honolua Bay, Lahaina News, June 18, 1992: 6.

BILLING SERVICES OF HAWAII [BUSINESS]
— Tori Bence and Robin Lindsey form business, Lahaina News, October 8, 1998: 13.

BILLY TAYLOR TRIO [MUSICAL GROUP]
— to perform at Maui Prince Hotel, Lahaina News, April 18, 1990: 11.
— sponsored by Maui Philharmonic Society, Lahaina News, April 25, 1990: 15.

BILOG, JASON
— Scholar/Athlete of the Week, Lahaina News, June 27, 2002: 12.

BILOXI BLUES [PLAY]
— to be performed by Maui Community Theatre, Lahaina News, February 22, 1989: 3.

BILYEU, MALANI [MUSICIAN]
— to perform "unplugged" at Maui Arts and Cultural Center with Cecilio and Kapono, Lahaina News, August 19, 1999: 16.

BIRCH, GERRY
— surfer featured in Wetscreams [film], Lahaina Times, August, 1980 volume 4 number 7: 5.

BIRDS
— discussion of endangered birds, Lahaina Sun, July 26, 1972: 22.
— talk on fossilized extinct flightless birds sponsored by Maui Historical Society, Lahaina News, March 23, 1988: 14.

BIRDS, THE [PLAY]
— to be performed by Maui Youth Theatre, Lahaina News, April 22, 1987: 10.

BIRO, BRIAN
— leading workshop on "Beyond Success", Lahaina News, February 20, 1997: 10.

BISHOP, ELVIN [MUSICIAN]
— playing at the Keg, Lahaina News, June 25, 1986: 8.
— performance reviewed, Lahaina News, April 22, 1987: 10.
— to play at opening of Sam's Beachside Grill, Lahaina News, April 22, 1987: 8.
— to perform at Maui Marriott for Halloween, Lahaina News, October 24, 1991: 18,19.
— to perform at Westin Maui for New Years, Lahaina News, December 26, 1996: 11.

BISHOP INSURANCE OF HAWAII [BUSINESS]
— featured, Lahaina News, February 1, 1984: 16.

BISHOP MUSEUM
— beginning to survey historical sites on Maui, Lahaina Sun, May 9, 1973: 7.
— field team set up at Mauna Olu college to search island for historic sites, Lahaina Sun, May 30, 1973: 5.
— to present a program on solar eclipse, Lahaina News, June 6, 1991: 3.
— archaeologist Paul Klieger to discuss Moku'ula, Lahaina News, November 9, 1995: 3.
— archaeologist reports on Moku'ula, Lahaina News, May 27, 1999: 1,16.

BISHOP, WANDA
— to lead workshop on "Peaceful Parenting", Lahaina News, March 13, 2003: 16.

BISSEN, RICHARD
— nominated by Mayor Linda Lingle as County Prosecuting Attorney, Lahaina News, July 27, 1995: 4.

BISTRO BOULEVARD, A
— to be held as first part of A Taste of Lahaina, Lahaina News, September 5, 1996: 4.

BIZARRE, JOHN [COMEDIAN]
— to perform at Comedy Club, Lahaina News, August 22, 1991: 10.

BLACK, A. DUANE
— elected chairman of Maui County Tri-Isle Comprehensive Health Planning Council, Lahaina Sun, January 24, 1973: 7.

BLACK CORAL
— recounting discovery by Jack Ackerman, Lahaina News, January 30, 1985: 7,8,9.

BLACK ELVIS [MUSICIAN]
— to perform at Polli's On the Beach, Lahaina News, October 3, 1990: 11.
— to perform at Polli's On the Beach, Lahaina News, November 7, 1990: 11.

BLACK PEARL GALLERY [BUSINESS]
— to host Tahitian Black Pearl Expo, Lahaina News, July 31, 2003: 8.

BLACK ROCK
— see Pu'u Keka'a

BLACK ROCK ILLUSIONS [SHOW]
— magic show to be held at Ka'anapali Beach Hotel, Lahaina News, February 15, 2001: 16.
— continues to be held at Ka'anapali Beach Hotel, Lahaina News, March 1, 2001: 20.
— continues to be held at Ka'anapali Beach Hotel, Lahaina News, April 19, 2001: 17.
— continues to be held, Lahaina News, May 24, 2001: 20.

BLACK SANDS [MUSICAL GROUP]
— to perform at Lopaka's Grill and Bar, Lahaina News, August 20, 1992: 22.
— to perform at Lopaka's Grill and Bar, Lahaina News, October 29, 1992: 20.

BLACK, STEVEN
— candidate for Maui Council discusses positions, Lahaina Sun, August 23, 1972: 9.

BLACK TOP BLUES TOUR
— to be held at Maui Arts and Cultural Center, Lahaina News, August 1, 1996: 21.

BLACK UHURU [MUSICAL GROUP]
— performance reviewed, Lahaina News, July 25, 1984: 12.
— presented by Maui Beer Co., to perform at Maui Tropical Plantation, Lahaina News, April 14, 1994: 12.

BLACK UMFOLOSI [MUSICAL GROUP]
— to perform Maui Arts and Cultural Center, Lahaina News, April 24, 1997: 13.

BLACK UNLIMITED, THE [MUSICAL GROUP]
— to perform at Casanova's, Lahaina News, August 27, 1992: 18.

BLACKABY, HENRY
— to discuss spiritual leadership, Lahaina News, September 20, 2001: 17.

BLACKBEARD'S GALLEY AND GROG [RESTAURANT]
— reviewed, Lahaina News, September, 1979: 3.
— changes under new manager, Lahaina News, August 1, 1983: 14,15.
— support of local music recounted, Lahaina News, June 20, 1984: 12.

BLACKBURN, PATRICIA
— named director of sales and marketing for Tri-Star Restaurant, Lahaina News, August 23, 2001: 9.

BLACKFIELD HAWAII CORPORATION [BUSINESS]
— wins awards at Parade of Homes, Lahaina News, October 25, 1989: 10.
— sells land to Bill Mills, Lahaina News, December 27, 1989: 5.

BLACKFORD, MANSEL [WRITER]
— to lecture on "Fragile Paradise—The Impact of Tourism on Maui, 1959-2000", Lahaina News, December 20, 2001: 16.

BLACKIE'S BAR [RESTAURANT]
— featured, Lahaina News, July 15, 1987: 7,9.
— hosting Emil Richards, Lahaina News, July 13, 1988: 7.
— owner Blackie Gadarian recovering from pneumonia, Lahaina News, August 29, 1990: 1.
— to celebrate 10th anniversary, Lahaina News, December 12, 1991: 18,19.
— to feature Latin music, Lahaina News, December 30, 1993: 10.
— reopens, featured, Lahaina News, January 6, 1994: 10.
— mementos up for sale, Lahaina News, April 27, 1995: 2.

BLACKIE'S MACHINE SHOP [BUSINESS]
— awards scholarships, Lahaina News, June 4, 1998: 13.

BLACKSTREET BLUES BAND [MUSICAL GROUP]
— to perform at Moose McGillycuddy's, Lahaina News, November 23, 1995: 12.

BLACKWELL, FRANK, SR.
— named chair of committee to encourage more filming on Maui, Lahaina News, July 25, 1984: 15.
— to speak to American Marketing Association's Maui Chapter, Lahaina News, January 22, 1986: 3.
— Maui Visitors Bureau chief supports focus on upscale visitors, Lahaina News, January 21, 1987: 5.
— executive director of Maui Visitors Association advocates for funds to market Maui to tourists, Lahaina News, January 9, 1991: 1,5.
— named as "Bank of America Charity Cup Volunteer of the Year", Lahaina News, June 29, 2000: 16.

BLACKWELL, MARY
— named sales manager for Royal Lahaina Resort, Lahaina News, March 9, 1995: 6.

BLAHUTA, JOHANN
— starts Hawaiian-European Connection travel agency specializing in European visitors, Lahaina News, October 31, 1990: 11.
— A Hawaiian European Connection now offering courtesy phones for German speakers, Lahaina News, April 30, 1992: 11.

BLAIR, JEFFREY
— supports banning people in stores entrances from calling out to pedestrians, Lahaina News, August 10, 1995: 1,16.

BLAIR, JOSEPHINE
— teacher retiring from Princess Nahienaena Elementary School, Lahaina News, May 4, 1995: 7.

BLAIR, MACK
— Lahainaluna High School librarian receives funds from the Soroptimists International, Lahaina News, April 16, 1992: 4.

BLAIR, RUSSELL [POLITICIAN]
— to run for Congress, Lahaina News, October 24, 1991: 10.11.
— objections raised by Republican Party district chair to Russell Blair becoming state Senator due to reapportionment, Lahaina News, November 7, 1991: 1,9.
— Republican Party seeks to oust due to reapportionment, Lahaina News, November 21, 1991: 1.
— lieutenant governor Ben Cayetano responds to request to prevent from assuming senatorial seat, Lahaina News, January 9, 1992: 2.
— new state senator supports term limits, Lahaina News, February 13, 1992: 3.
— State Senator calls for solution to algae problem, Lahaina News, January 21, 1993: 10.
— to seek ideas from the community, Lahaina News, January 28, 1993: 1,5.
— state senator to resign, Lahaina News, November 4, 1993: 1,3.

BLANCHETTE, PATRICIA
— to lecture on Alzheimer's, Lahaina News, February 20, 1992: 4,5.

BLANDO, MONIQUE
— Scholar/Athlete of the Week, Lahaina News, October 9, 2003: 12.

BLANDO, RANDY
— Pop Warner football player given Levi Kahahane Scholarship Award, Lahaina News, December 24, 1992: 8.

BLANE, DAVID
— county Planning Director talks of efforts to protect beaches, Lahaina News, February 15, 1996: 1.
— County Planning Director discusses changes to signage and downtown parking, Lahaina News, September 26, 1996: 4.
— leaves position as County Planning Director to work at Chris Hart and Partners, Lahaina News, June 4, 1998: 9.

BLANK, LES
— filmmaker presented by Maui Community College, Lahaina News, March 28, 1996: 13,14.

BLASÉ, MARK
— lost in plane crash off Hana, Lahaina News, January 11, 1984: 5.

BLASINGHAM, KEN AND DONNA
— owners of Happy Days Café interviewed, Lahaina News, July 2, 1986: 7.

BLAYER, URI [ARTIST]
— to exhibit at Village Galleries, Lahaina News, May 29, 2003: 14.

BLAZ, MICHAEL
— to present workshop on "Network Marketing: Business in the 21st Century", Lahaina News, June 6, 1996: 15.

BLEARS, LAURA
— surfer and paddler featured, Lahaina News, February 3, 1994: 8.

BLESSMAN, DEBORAH
— discussed medicinal value of herbs, Lahaina News, April 27, 1988: 18.

BLEVINS, SOLOMON KAWIKA
— police looking for suspect, Lahaina News, June 14, 2001: 3.

BLIND DATE [TELEVISION SHOW]
— episodes to be taped in Maui, Lahaina News, November 15, 2001: 8.

BLITHE SPIRIT [PLAY]
— auditions to be held, Lahaina News, October 28, 1993: 11.
— auditions being held for, Lahaina News, December 30, 1993: 12.
— opens at Iao Theatre, Lahaina News, January 27, 1994: 8.
— featured, Lahaina News, February 3, 1994: 9.

BLOCH [FAMILY]
— featured, Lahaina News, December 3, 1992: 7.

BLOCH, CHELSEA
— wins Keiki Gymnastics season, Lahaina News, January 28, 1993: 7.
— wins gymnastic title, Lahaina News, December 22, 1994: 6.
— Scholar/Athlete of the Week, Lahaina News, March 14, 1996: 7.
— Scholar/Athlete of the Week, Lahaina News, April 6, 2000: 7.

BLOCH, CHEYNE
— successes at swimming competitions, Lahaina News, June 30, 1994: 6.
— success at swimming competition, Lahaina News, December 1, 1994: 9.
— strong showing at Sakamoto Invitational Swim Meet, Lahaina News, June 22, 1995: 6.

BLOCKBUSTER VIDEO [BUSINESS]
— to open first store on Maui, Lahaina News, May 8, 1991: 6.
— participating in World Video Game Championship, Lahaina News, June 22, 1995: 12.

BLODER, MARY
— Lahainaluna High School teacher featured, Lahaina News, October 7, 1999: 3.

BLOOD BANK OF HAWAII
— drive to be held at Hyatt Regency Maui, Lahaina News, August 12, 1987: 3.
— looking for donations, Lahaina News, February 28, 1990: 2.
— to hold blood drive, Lahaina News, May 28, 1992: 3.
— blood drive to be held at Stoffler Wailea Beach Resort, Lahaina News, July 30, 1992: 7.
— to hold drive at Maui Community College, Lahaina News, January 28, 1993: 4.
— blood drive to be held, Lahaina News, July 22, 1993: 6.
— elects new board of trustees, Lahaina News, September 1, 1994: 13.
— Bloodmobile to make a trip to Maui, Lahaina News, September 28, 1995: 2.
— to hold blood drives, Lahaina News, November 30, 1995: 4.

— to hold blood drive, Lahaina News, January 25, 1996: 4.
— to hold drive, Lahaina News, May 30, 1996: 2.
— to hold blood drive, Lahaina News, October 12, 2000: 20.
— continues to hold drives, Lahaina News, December 28, 2000: 16.
— continues to hold blood drives, Lahaina News, February 1, 2001: 20.
— drives continue, Lahaina News, April 5, 2001: 20.
— blood drive to be held, Lahaina News, May 31, 2001: 2.
— blood drives continue to be held, Lahaina News, June 7, 2001: 20.
— continues to offer blood drives, Lahaina News, August 9, 2001: 2.
— to hold Blood Drive, Lahaina News, December 20, 2001: 17.

BLOOD QUANTUM [MUSICAL GROUP]
— to perform at Lahaina Cannery Mall, Lahaina News, December 23, 1999: 16.

BLUDAU, ED
— appointed general manager of Napilikai Beach Club, Lahaina News, August 29, 1990: 8.
— installed as Lahaina Rotary Club president, Lahaina News, July 9, 1992: 3,9.

BLUE GINGER DESIGN [BUSINESS]
— featured, Lahaina News, August 15, 1984: 14.

BLUE HAWAII [SONG]
— history and success discussed, Lahaina News, September 11, 1985: 8.

BLUE HAWAIIAN HELICOPTERS [BUSINESS]
— receives SBA Small Business Person of the Year Award from the U.S. Small Business Administration, Lahaina News, May 29, 1997: 5.

BLUE LAGOON TROPICAL BAR AND GRILL [RESTAURANT]
— reviewed, Lahaina News, February 8, 1989: 8.
— to be renovated, Lahaina News, July 4, 1996: 8,9.
— appoints Joseph Chouinard as new chef, Lahaina News, January 29, 1998: 20.

BLUE LIGHT EMERGENCY PROGRAM
— begins, Lahaina News, December 21, 1995: 4.

BLUE, MARVE [MUSICIAN]
— to perform at Canoes Restaurant, Lahaina News, January 24, 2002: 15.

BLUE MAX [RESTAURANT]
— reviewed, Lahaina Times, July, 1980 volume 4 number 6: 4.
— closes, Lahaina News, June 27, 1984: 12.
— sold in 1984, history recounted, Lahaina News, March 5, 1986: 12.
— employee reunion to be held, Lahaina News, March 10, 1994: 3.

BLUE OCEAN PRESERVATION SOCIETY
— formed, Lahaina News, September 21, 1988: 3.
— holds membership drive, Lahaina News, December 7, 1988: 24.
— hosts discussion of sea mining, Lahaina News, April 26, 1989: 3.

BLUE OYSTER CULT [MUSICAL GROUP]
— to perform at Maui Brews, Lahaina News, May 6, 1999: 21.

BLUE ROOSTER PRODUCTIONS
— bringing John Mayall to perform at Maui Arts and Cultural Center, Lahaina News, January 4, 2001: 17.

BLUE TROPIX [RESTAURANT]
— featured with owner Mark Dirga, Lahaina News, January 30, 1992: 10.
— Mark Ellman to be executive chef, Lahaina News, February 13, 1992: 13.
— new menu and look, Lahaina News, April 1, 1993: 14.
— holds fundraiser for Maui Community Theatre, Lahaina News, February 17, 1994: 9.
— benefit concert held for Bobbie Rocha at, Lahaina News, November 3, 1994: 25.

— to host Roy Allen Reed Memorial Costume Ball, Lahaina News, April 20, 1995: 11.

— to close, Lahaina News, October 3, 1996: 1,18.

BLUEBEARD'S [RESTAURANT]

— purchased by Spencercliff Corporation, Lahaina News, October 24, 1984: 3.

BLUEGILL [SUBMARINE]

— now sunk off Lahaina, history detailed, Lahaina Sun, May 2, 1973: 7.

— Navy seeking to raise ship to move it further off shore, Lahaina News, October 12, 1983: 3,5.

— details of attempts to raise it, Lahaina News, November 16, 1983: 7,8,9,10.

BLUES, BREWS AND BBQ

— music festival to be held, Lahaina News, May 9, 2002: 17.

BLUES BROTHERS [FILM]

— Casanova's to host party themed on, Lahaina News, June 4, 1992: 18.

BLUESBREAKERS [MUSICAL GROUP]

— to perform at with John Mayall, Lahaina News, May 13, 1999: 17.

— to perform with John Mayall at the Maui Arts and Cultural Center, Lahaina News, January 11, 2001: 18.

BLUESTEIN, STEVE [COMEDIAN]

— to perform at Comedy Club and the Sports Page, Lahaina News, May 30, 1991: 7.

— to perform at Comedy Club and the Sports Page, Lahaina News, August 6, 1992: 11,13.

— to perform at Comedy Club and the Sports Page, Lahaina News, April 29, 1993: 10,11.

— to perform at Honolulu Comedy Club, Lahaina News, August 25, 1994: 14.

BLUM, RALPH

— to speak on "Living an Oracular Life", Lahaina News, June 28, 2001: 21.

BLUNDELL, ANDREA

— spearheaded drive for King Kamehameha III School to have a vice-principal, Lahaina News, May 16, 1990: 1,10.

BLUNDELL, BRIAN [POLITICIAN]

— believes West Maui too shallow for harbor, Lahaina News, October 27, 1994: 6.

— to run for State House District 7, Lahaina News, June 4, 1998: 1.

— to seek Board of Education seat, Lahaina News, October 12, 2000: 6.

— candidate for Board of Education, Lahaina News, October 26, 2000: 23.

— running for Hawaii Representative District 10 seat, Lahaina News, September 19, 2002: 3.

— to push for acute care facility and roadway solutions, Lahaina News, November 14, 2002: 1,24.

— to hold public meeting, Lahaina News, December 5, 2002: 1,22.

— to hold Town Meeting, Lahaina News, December 12, 2002: 2.

— held community forum, Lahaina News, December 19, 2002: 1.

— to hold public meeting with Roz Baker, Lahaina News, February 20, 2003: 1,20.

— held public meeting, Lahaina News, March 6, 2003: 1,20.

— hosts Lahainaluna High School student Vanesa Sanchez at State Capitol, Lahaina News, April 3, 2003: 2.

— critical of long-term care legislation, Lahaina News, May 8, 2003: 9.

— to discuss 2003 legislative session, Lahaina News, May 15, 2003: 1.

— meets with Friends of Moku'ula at Malu'ulu O Lele Park, Lahaina News, June 26, 2003: 1.

BLUNDELL, BRIAN AND KIM

— receives Valley Isle Business Award, Lahaina News, October 17, 1996: 1,20.

BLYTH, ANDY [PERFORMER]

— presenting Children's Hour at Artful Dodger's Feed and Read, Lahaina News, June 17, 1987: 3.

BLYTH-KEMP [FAMILY]

— to reunite in Olowalu, Lahaina News, June 5, 1985: 1.

BLYTH-KEMP, ROSE

— service to honor, Lahaina News, February 20, 2003: 3.

BOARD OF REALTORS, MAUI

— see Maui Board of Realtors

BOARD OF TAXATION REVIEW CONFERENCE

— to be held, Lahaina News, June 18, 1992: 4.

BOAR'S HEAD CHRISTMAS FEAST

— to be held, Lahaina News, December 14, 1995: 15.

BOAT DAYS

— see Lahaina Harbor

BOAT HARBOR, SMALL [LAHAINA]

— wooden wharf built around, Lahaina Sun, November 11, 1970: 4.

— projects desired by West Maui Business Association, Lahaina Sun, December 23, 1970: 2.

— improvements completed, Lahaina Sun, February 24, 1971: 1.

— plans to move showers discussed, Lahaina Sun, May 12, 1971: 4.

— plans to flush polluted water from, Lahaina Sun, May 26, 1971: 2.

— problems with discussed, Lahaina Sun, August 18, 1971: 10.

— Warren Hinton critical of signage at, Lahaina Sun, October 20, 1971: 15.

— conflict over who is responsible for collecting garbage at harbor, Lahaina Sun, March 1, 1972: 3.

— issue of garbage collection updated, Lahaina Sun, March 8, 1972: 13.

— plans to improve water quality, Lahaina Sun, March 22, 1972: 4.

— Dave Hudson quits as Harbormaster, Lahaina Sun, April 12, 1972: 7.

— Governor Burns releases funds to develop master plan for, Lahaina Sun, May 17, 1972: 14.

— aspects described, Lahaina Sun, August 30, 1972: 7.

— conflict with State Harbors division, Lahaina Sun, September 27, 1972: 11.

— yachtsmen appeal ruling against liveaboards, Lahaina Sun, October 4, 1972: 9.

— Maui Historic Commission anticipating battle on location of new harbor, Lahaina Sun, October 18, 1972: 12.

— liveaboards file petition, Lahaina Sun, October 18, 1972: 12.

— meeting to discuss plans, Lahaina Sun, October 25, 1972: 9.

— new harbor debated, Lahaina Sun, November 1, 1972: 3.

— boat owners object to new rules, Lahaina Sun, December 27, 1972: 3.

— plans to auction commercial slips put on hold, Lahaina Sun, March 14, 1973: 3.

— visiting yachts not welcome, Lahaina Sun, June 20, 1973: 7.

— trash cleanup described, Lahaina Sun, June 27, 1973: 9.

— funding released for, Lahaina News, April 25, 2002: 3.

— concern over traffic congestion, Lahaina News, October 9, 2003: 1,2.

BOAT LAUNCH

— proposed for Wahikuli, Lahaina Sun, December 23, 1970: 1.

BOAT SHOW

— to be held by Maui Mall and Valley Isle Marine Center, Lahaina News, July 27, 2000: 7.

BOATING

— meeting to discuss proposed rules planned, Lahaina Sun, March 3, 1971: 4.

— hearings set for small boat harbor, Lahaina Sun, March 10, 1971: 7.

— owners unhappy about fee increase, Lahaina Sun, June 23, 1971: 1,12.

— Army Corps of Engineers to hold public meeting to discuss ship harbor for Ma'alaea Bay., Lahaina Sun, July 7, 1971: 10.

— plans to improve Mala wharf, Lahaina Sun, August 25, 1971: 10,12.

— Cartblanche [boat] runs aground near Lahaina small boat harbor, Lahaina Sun, November 3, 1971: 4.

— boat capsizes, two missing, Lahaina Sun, April 26, 1972: 6.

— Kennedy-King Dream II [ship] wrecked on Lahaina seawall, Lahaina Sun, April 26, 1972: 6.

— yachtsmen expected at end of Vancouver to Lahaina yacht race, Lahaina Sun, May 10, 1972: 5.

— Victoria to Maui Yacht Race looking for volunteers, Lahaina Sun, June 7, 1972: 6.

— new outrigger canoes to be used by Lahaina Canoe Club, Lahaina Sun, June 7, 1972: 7.

— yacht races occurring off Lahaina, Lahaina Sun, June 14, 1972: 10.

— Victoria-Maui race underway, Lahaina Sun, July 5, 1972: 7.

— Zig Freilands building a cement boat, Lahaina Sun, August 9, 1972: 21.

— Lahaina Canoe Club committed to preservation of Hawaiian culture, Lahaina Sun, August 30, 1972: 9.

— discussion of the value of sailing, Lahaina Sun, September 20, 1972: 17.

— Steve Elkins' design compared to Hobie Cat design, Lahaina Sun, October 4, 1972: 30.

— Atlantic [ship] sailing from New Jersey to Lahaina, Lahaina Sun, November 15, 1972: 3.

— Ivo Van Laake sails in to Lahaina on the slope Vlaag, Lahaina Sun, November 22, 1972: 1.

— Fujio Matsuda rejects request for people to live aboard their boats, Lahaina Sun, November 22, 1972: 6.

— John Alford's experiences as skipper of the Ola Loa, Lahaina Sun, November 29, 1972: 7.

— Carte Blanche repaired after running aground in 1971, Lahaina Sun, December 6, 1972: 11.

— public hearing set for changes in small boat harbor regulations, Lahaina Sun, December 6, 1972: 22.

— water skiing behind a sailboat described, Lahaina Sun, December 6, 1972: 24.

— story of Bill Becker and the Merriman, Lahaina Sun, December 13, 1972: 11.

— life at the Lahaina small boat harbor described, Lahaina Sun, December 20, 1972: 11.

— life of Nancy Clarke highlighted, Lahaina Sun, January 10, 1973: 13.

— Coast Guard activities in Lahaina detailed, Lahaina Sun, January 17, 1973: 13.

— discussion of seagoing women, Lahaina Sun, February 14, 1973: 15.

— visiting sailors from Tahiti described, Lahaina Sun, February 21, 1973: 7.

— history of the trimaran detailed, Lahaina Sun, April 25, 1973: 12,13.

— Milk Carton Boat Race planned, Lahaina Sun, May 9, 1973: 11.

— sail boats servicing tourists along beach in Ka'anapali described, Lahaina Sun, May 9, 1973: 15.

— report on sailing trip to Honolulu, Lahaina Sun, May 16, 1973: 14.

— new catamarans on Maui, Lahaina Sun, May 16, 1973: 7.

— power ski introduced, Lahaina Sun, July 4, 1973: 20.

— Russian submarine sighted off of the Ka'anapali coast, Lahaina Sun, July 18, 1973: 8.

— Scotch Mist II first to finish Lahaina-to-Honolulu race, Lahaina News, September 14, 1983: 5.

— Pacific Maritime Academy of Honolulu to offer Ocean & Motorboat Operators course, Lahaina News, February 12, 1986: 3.

— training schooner Californian visits Maui, Lahaina News, August 6, 1986: 1,11.

— Department of Land and Natural Resources to hold public hearings on proposed commercial mooring, Lahaina News, August 26, 1987: 3.

— privately-owned marina proposed near Lahaina, Lahaina News, September 2, 1987: 1,4.

— issues with offshore moorings, Lahaina News, September 9, 1987: 1,16.

— Lahaina Yacht Club endorses private marina, Lahaina News, October 14, 1987: 18.

— issues over marine in the past year recounted, Lahaina News, December 30, 1987: 13.

— rules to be enforced off Ka'anapali, Lahaina News, December 30, 1987: 3.

— moving thrillcraft away from Ka'anapali recommended, Lahaina News, January 6, 1988: 3.

— U.S. Army Corps of Engineers to build moorings in West Maui, Lahaina News, January 6, 1988: 3.

— Department of Transportation to hold hearing on rules, Lahaina News, January 13, 1988: 16.

— jet skiers and parasailers harassing whales, Lahaina News, January 20, 1988: 1.

— Athena [ship] rescued off Maui waters, Lahaina News, January 20, 1988: 18.

— temporary mooring installed at Molokini, Lahaina News, January 27, 1988: 3.

— editorial on jet ski harassment, Lahaina News, February 3, 1988: 2.

— ban of thrillcrafts off Mala Wharf to be sought , Lahaina News, February 10, 1988: 1.

— local resistance to thrillcraft corridor plan, Lahaina News, February 24, 1988: 1,20.

— residents call for thrillcraft ban, Lahaina News, March 2, 1988: 1.

— Department of Transportation accepting applications for off-shore mooring permits, Lahaina News, March 2, 1988: 22.

— Department of Transportation takes over mooring permits, Lahaina News, March 9, 1988: 1.

— Councilman Wayne Nishiki asks booking agents to not sell thrillcraft rides, Lahaina News, March 16, 1988: 1.

— thrillcraft issues discussed, Lahaina News, March 16, 1988: 6.

— Department of Transportation considers limiting thrillcraft to four locations, Lahaina News, March 30, 1988: 1.

— Rick Reed not worried about lawsuits if thrillcrafts banned, Lahaina News, May 11, 1988: 1,4.

— fees for Small Harbors increased, Lahaina News, June 1, 1988: 19.

— Victoria-Maui International Yacht Race to take begin, Lahaina News, June 15, 1988: 1.

— parasail mooring okayed by U.S. Army Corps of Engineers, Lahaina News, June 15, 1988: 6.

— Hobie Cat 17 World Championships to take place in Lahaina, Lahaina News, August 10, 1988: 14,15.

— Department of Transportation gets control of near-shore waters off Ka'anapali, Lahaina News, August 10, 1988: 18.

— refueling issue at Lahaina Harbor may be solved, Lahaina News, June 14, 1989: 1.

— summer regatta organized, Lahaina News, July 19, 1989: 5.

— State Canoe Racing Championships to be held, Lahaina News, August 2, 1989: 1.

— Maui Onion wins Bud Cup Regatta, Lahaina News, September 13, 1989: 24.

— state proposes increasing commercial boat fees, Lahaina News, October 25, 1989: 3.

— shuttle boat swamped by huge wave, tourists saved, Lahaina News, February 28, 1990: 1.

— yacht race to be held Sunday, Lahaina News, May 9, 1990: 3.

— yacht "An" salvaged after sinking during Kenwood Cup race, Lahaina News, August 29, 1990: 1.

— Department of Land and ?Natural Resources to replace missing buoys, Lahaina News, October 31, 1990: 9.

— National Marine Fisheries officer describes rules when near humpback whales, Lahaina News, December 26, 1990: 14.

— Flotilla 26 to hold classes and sailing and seamanship, Lahaina News, February 20, 1991: 5.

— search for missing kayaker Lawrence Whitehead called off, Lahaina News, April 10, 1991: 4.

— San Diego-Maui yacht race held, Lahaina News, June 27, 1991: 7.

— San Diego-Maui yacht race results, Lahaina News, July 4, 1991: 7.

— Launiupoko favored by some for marina, Lahaina News, August 1, 1991: 1.

— recreational vessel fee mandated, Lahaina News, August 15, 1991: 4.

— whale season begins, Lahaina News, January 30, 1992: 9.

— Valley Isle Marine Center to hold show, Lahaina News, June 18, 1992: 4.

— Todd Hasensplug and Chris Mueller rescued after boat sinks, Lahaina News, July 16, 1992: 6.

— Victoria-Maui Yacht Race held, first into Lahaina Harbor was Merlin, Lahaina News, July 23, 1992: 15.

— results of Victoria-Maui Yacht Race, Lahaina News, July 30, 1992: 9.

— suit filed against Catamaran Express, Inc., Lahaina News, September 10, 1992: 12.

— commercial mooring area to be installed at Kamaole Beach, Lahaina News, September 24, 1992: 2.

— Haiku residents and visiting relative rescued by Coast Guard, Lahaina News, September 24, 1992: 4.

— concern over proposed marine mammal regulations, Lahaina News, November 19, 1992: 3.

— Tawny-D salvaged off Lahaina Shores, Lahaina News, December 10, 1992: 1.

— classes to be offered by Flotilla 28, Lahaina News, December 31, 1992: 5.

— Mala boaters allowed to use Lahaina Harbor during dredging, Lahaina News, January 21, 1993: 3.

— United States Coast Guard Auxiliary Flotilla 26 to conduct vessel examinations, Lahaina News, February 18, 1993: 4.

— concerns raised over whale sanctuary, Lahaina News, March 25, 1993: 1.

— Kahana Canoe Club sponsoring Hotel/Resort Canoe Championship Regatta, Lahaina News, March 25, 1993: 6.

— safety class to be held, Lahaina News, April 8, 1993: 5.

— Kihei Shoreline Race won by Kimo Knutson, Lahaina News, April 15, 1993: 8.

— public notice on proposed changes to Hawaii Revised Statutes, Lahaina News, June 17, 1993: 7.

— state has plan to keep anchors off the reef, Lahaina News, November 25, 1993: 1,3.

— state firm on plans to increase number of outside permits allowed at Ma'alaea Harbor, Lahaina News, December 2, 1993: 5.

— strong market expected, Lahaina News, December 30, 1993: 5.

— new launching ramp user fees to take effect, Lahaina News, March 10, 1994: 4.

— NAVATEK II to begin operations, Lahaina News, March 17, 1994: 8.

— three people stranded in Au Au Channel, Lahaina News, May 19, 1994: 3.

— the ship "Raven" breaks mooring, Lahaina News, February 2, 1995: 1.

— Maui Boat and Yacht Club to hold second race of season, Lahaina News, April 13, 1995: 9.

— one-day moorings may be installed at high-traffic reefs, Lahaina News, July 27, 1995: 2.

— Maui Boat and Yacht Club to hold race, Lahaina News, August 10, 1995: 7.

— Lahaina Yacht Club Keiki Fishing Tournament held, Lahaina News, September 28, 1995: 6.

— boat days for Lahaina Harbor, Lahaina News, January 25, 1996: 12.

— courses offered by U.S. Coast Guard Auxiliary Flotilla, Lahaina News, January 25, 1996: 4.

— Steinlager Ho'omana'o Challenge to be held, Lahaina News, May 23, 1996: 7,8,9,12,13,14.

— Pyewacket may break Victoria-Maui race record, Lahaina News, July 11, 1996: 1.

— U.S. Coast Guard to enforce safe boating laws, Lahaina News, October 24, 1996: 4.

— tropical storm Delores moves towards Transpacific Yacht Race, Lahaina News, July 10, 1997: 15.

— Sea Explorer Ship continues to offer course, Lahaina News, September 4, 1997: 15.

— "What Boaters Can Do To Be Environmentally Friendly" published by the West Maui Watershed Management Project, Lahaina News, September 11, 1997: 15.

— Victoria-Maui race underway, Lahaina News, July 6, 2000: 13.

— catamaran "Shangri-La" to offer charters, Lahaina News, July 27, 2000: 14.

— Maui Mall to hold "Sea Fest 2001" boat show, Lahaina News, July 26, 2001: 16.

— Sea Fair boat show to be held, Lahaina News, July 25, 2002: 20.

— National Safe Boating Week to be held on theme of "Boat Smart! Boat Safe!", Lahaina News, May 15, 2003: 13.

— see also Lahaina Harbor, Lahaina Yacht Club, paddling, Victoria-Maui Yacht Race

BOATING AND OCEAN RECREATION, DIVISION OF

— starting Adopt-A-Harbor Program, Lahaina News, May 22, 1997: 9.

— provides list of ships to visit Lahaina Harbor, Lahaina News, August 27, 1998: 13.

BOB [PLAY]

— comedy to open at Seabury Hall, Lahaina News, February 12, 1998: 16.

BOBAL, NEHL [COMEDIAN]

— to perform at Honolulu Comedy Club, Lahaina News, January 25, 1996: 14.

BOCHNIAK, PANTA

— to host open mike night at Cafe Makawao, Lahaina News, June 19, 1997: 17.

BODDEN, THOMAS

— to speak at AARP meeting, Lahaina News, October 7, 1987: 3.

— named realtor of the year by the Hawaii Association of Realtors, Lahaina News, November 7, 1990: 7,8.

BODDEN, TOM

— to offer seminar on estate planning, Lahaina News, November 30, 1988: 3.

— attorney to speak to Maui Alzheimer's Support Group, Lahaina News, April 9, 1992: 8.

BODINUS, KELLA

— to exhibit at the Art School at Kapalua, Lahaina News, April 10, 2003: 17.

BODY AND SOIL FARM HEALTH CONFERENCE

— to be held at Maui Tropical Plantation, Lahaina News, July 12, 2001: 9.

BODY SHOP [BUSINESS]

— opens in Whalers Village, Lahaina News, August 18, 1994: 8.

BOES, KIRK [ARTIST]

— featured, Lahaina News, October 4, 1989: 10.

— featured by Lahaina Art Society at Banyan Tree Gallery, Lahaina News, July 11, 1990: 18.

— opens show at Old Jail Gallery, Lahaina News, July 18, 1990: 13.

— surfer critical of lack of beach access to surfing sites, Lahaina News, December 19, 1990: 1,2.

BOHANNON & KELLY, INC. [BUSINESS]

— real estate company featured, Lahaina News, February 29, 1984: 17.

BOHN, DOUGLAS
— promoted to head professional at Kapalua Village Course, Lahaina News, December 26, 1996: 8.

BOISSONEAU, YVONNE
— promoted to director of the Kahului station of Aloha Airlines, Lahaina News, August 10, 2000: 14.

BOLL, LEATRICE
— confirmed as vice principal of Lahainaluna High School, Lahaina News, August 22, 1990: 4.

BOLSHOI BALLET
— to perform at Blaisdell Arena on Oahu, Lahaina News, May 23, 1990: 13.

BOMB-DIGGITY
— concert to be staged at Maui Arts and Cultural Center, Lahaina News, March 29, 2001: 16.

BONAR, DALE
— appointed executive director of Maui Coastal Land Trust, Lahaina News, July 4, 2002: 2.

BONES, BILLY [MUSICIAN]
— to perform at Whalers Village, Lahaina News, March 13, 2003: 14.

BONET [MUSICIAN]
— to perform with John Moriarty Jazz Trio at Ritz-Carlton, Lahaina News, January 6, 1994: 11.

BONGO BOB [MUSICIAN]
— to perform at Greek Zorba, Lahaina News, May 25, 1995: 12.

BONKER
— history of the toy, Lahaina Sun, May 19, 1971: 4.

BONNELL, JACOB [ARTIST]
— sculptor to exhibit at Lahaina Arts Society, Lahaina News, June 5, 2003: 18.

BONNET, CHARLES [POLITICIAN]
— running for Maui County Council seat against Howard Kihune, Lahaina News, July 18, 1990: 4.
— candidate profiled, Lahaina News, September 12, 1990: 7,12.

BONNET, STEPHEN
— Scholar/Athlete of the Week, Lahaina News, March 30, 2000: 7.

BONSAI
— Art School at Kapalua to hold classes on, Lahaina News, September 14, 1995: 6.
— Gordon Feist to begin class on, Lahaina News, October 2, 1997: 18.
— classes offered, Lahaina News, February 19, 1998: 13.

BOOHER, MARK [ACTOR]
— actors from Oregon Shakespeare Festival to hold classes, Lahaina News, December 15, 1994: 19.

BOOKMOBILE
— to make stops in West Maui, Lahaina News, August 1, 2002: 9.

BOOKS
— The Earthquake Generation (Geffery Goodman), Lahaina Times, June, 1980 volume 4 number 5: 2.
— Seth Speaks (Jane Roberts), Lahaina Times, June, 1980 volume 4 number 5: 2.
— suggestions for Christmas, Lahaina News, December 6, 1989: guide10.
— discussion group on romance novels to be held, Lahaina News, June 17, 1999: 17.

BOONE, CHICO [ARTIST]
— work displayed at Artful Dodger Reed and Read, Lahaina News, April 1, 1987: 3.

BOOTMEN [FILM]
— to be shown at Maui Arts and Cultural Center, Lahaina News, November 16, 2000: 17.

BORCHERS, JON [COMEDIAN]
— to perform at Comedy Club, Lahaina News, July 25, 1991: 10.
— to perform at Comedy Club and the Sports Page, Lahaina News, September 10, 1992: 17,19.

BORDERS BOOKS AND MUSIC [BUSINESS]
— to hold "Sanctuary Awareness Day" to support Hawaiian Islands Humpback Whale National Marine Sanctuary, Lahaina News, September 10, 1998: 16.
— to host discussion group on mystery books, Lahaina News, June 24, 1999: 13.
— holds "Teacher Appreciation Weekend", Lahaina News, October 11, 2001: 8.
— honoring educators, Lahaina News, October 24, 2002: 20.
— to hold Educator Appreciation Weekend, Lahaina News, March 27, 2003: 8.

BORGES, JIMMY [MUSICIAN]
— to perform at "I Love Lahaina", Lahaina News, November 9, 2000: 23.

BORGLUM, DALE
— offers workshop on healing, Lahaina News, January 18, 1989: 3.

BORISKIN, MICHAEL [MUSICIAN]
— to perform at Royal Lahaina Resort, Lahaina News, November 4, 1987: 10.

BORN, BARRY
— memorial scholarship established at Maui Community College, Lahaina News, May 29, 1997: 2.

BORN IN PARADISE [BOOK]
— by Armine von Tempsky is published, Lahaina News, May 22, 1985: 3.

BORN JAMERICANS [MUSICAL GROUP]
— to perform at Maui Summer Jam, Lahaina News, June 18, 1998: 17.

BORNHORST, MARILYN
— State Democratic Party chair to speak, Lahaina News, September 18, 1997: 17.

BOROWSKI, STEVE
— named race director of Ironman Triathlon World Championship, Lahaina News, January 16, 1991: 20.

BORROMEO, KYRA
— Scholar/Athlete of the Week, Lahaina News, February 7, 2002: 13.
— selected for Naval Academy Prep School and Merchant Marine Academy, Lahaina News, April 11, 2002: 2.

BORUNDA, XERPHA
— appointed administrative assistant at Lahaina Printsellers, Lahaina News, June 27, 1990: 8.

BOSA PACIFIC HAWAII
— proposes residential project in Kihei, Lahaina News, October 15, 1992: 13.

BOSE, JOHN
— chosen as secretary for Maui ACLU, Lahaina Sun, January 13, 1971: 6.
— named present of Maui American Civil Liberties Union , Lahaina Sun, June 23, 1971: 10.

BOSER, JERRY
— surfer remembered, Lahaina News, August 16, 2001: 12.

BOSKOFF, GEORGE
— long-time surfer featured, Lahaina News, July 14, 1994: 8.

BOSKOFF, JACKIE
— named office manager for Atlantis Submarines, Lahaina News, November 28, 1991: 7.

BOSKOFF, NICKY
— appointed general manager of Aloha Mixed Plate, Lahaina News, October 28, 1999: 15.

BOSKOFF, TARA
— named sales and marketing manager for Maui Divers, Lahaina News, August 14, 1997: 12.

BOSLEY, BRUCE
— football player dies, Lahaina News, May 4, 1995: 4.
— memorial golf tournament to be held, Lahaina News, November 30, 1995: 7.

BOSOM BUDDIES
— West Maui Breast Cancer Support Group to meet, Lahaina News, November 15, 2001: 17.
— West Maui breast cancer support group to meet, Lahaina News, January 17, 2002: 16.

BOSTWICK, JERI
— appointed public relations director for LahainaTown Action Committee, Lahaina News, January 25, 1989: 16.

BOSTWICK, SUSAN HULL
— leads conference helping women to use intuition, Lahaina News, October 22, 1992: 10.

BOTEILHO, AL
— new president of Maui Contractors Association, Lahaina News, November 28, 1991: 6.
— to be honored by Maui Chamber of Commerce, Lahaina News, October 16, 1997: 12.

BOTELHO, ALBERT
— suspect is injured in police chase, Lahaina News, October 29, 1998: 3.

BOTH SIDES NOW
— meeting of lesbian/gay/bisexual group organized, Lahaina News, March 14, 1984: 8.
— gay and lesbian ohana group to hold dance, Lahaina News, March 26, 1998: 13.

BOTTLES
— collecting in Lahaina, Lahaina News, January 10, 1990: 11.

BOTTOMS, JAMES [WRITER]
— to exhibit at Village Galleries, Lahaina News, March 23, 2000: 13.

BOUCHARD, ROBERT "WALLY GATOR"
— featured, Lahaina News, February 17, 1994: 7.

BOULTON, ROBERT
— attorney rebuilding practice after James Gaylor left bills unpaid, Lahaina News, June 21, 1989: 6.

BOUTIQUE, THE [BUSINESS]
— opens, Lahaina News, April 17, 1991: 9.

BOUZOUKI BROTHERS [MUSICAL GROUP]
— to perform at Traditional Acoustic Christmas Concert, Lahaina News, December 19, 1996: 10.

BOWIE, IRENE
— new marketing manager at Pacific Whale Foundation, Lahaina News, February 7, 2002: 8.

BOWL FOR KIDS' SAKE
— to help Big Brothers/Big Sisters, Lahaina News, July 24, 2003: 13.

BOWMAN, BRUCE
— to participate in Fumigation Leaders Forum in California, Lahaina News, November 1, 1989: 9.

BOWMAN, JOHN [COMEDIAN]
— to perform at Comedy Club and the Sports Page, Lahaina News, May 1, 1991: 14,16.
— to perform at Comedy Club and the Sports Page, Lahaina News, June 18, 1992: 18,21.

BOX CANYON BAND
— reviewed, Lahaina Times, August, 1980 volume 4 number 7: 3.

BOXING
— on Maui, Lahaina News, March 20, 1997: 13.
— fight be held at Lahaina Civic Center, Lahaina News, May 14, 1998: 14.
— results of fights, Lahaina News, October 1, 1998: 15.
— Hawaii Junior Olympic State Championships to be held, Lahaina News, May 13, 1999: 7.
— residents win Hawaii Junior Olympic titles, Lahaina News, May 27, 1999: 7.
— Kihei Boxing Club offering lessons by Johnny "Bang-Bang" Jackson, Lahaina News, December 28, 2000: 6.
— "Boxing At the Hut" to be held, Lahaina News, May 17, 2001: 15.
— "Thunder in the Tropics—Island Pride, Hawaii vs. Las Vegas" to be held, Lahaina News, August 23, 2001: 13.
— "Knockouts at Kalama" to be held, Lahaina News, January 24, 2002: 13.
— match to raise money for Kihei Youth Center, Lahaina News, July 17, 2003: 13.

BOY AND HIS POI DOG, A [PLAY]
— to be performed as part of "Theatre in the Schools", Lahaina News, February 16, 1995: 16.
— to be performed by Maui Academy of Performing Arts, Lahaina News, March 23, 1995: 12.

BOY SCOUTS
— meeting held in Kahului, Lahaina Sun, January 20, 1971: 7.
— Scout-o-Rama tickets go on sale, Lahaina Sun, February 17, 1971: 4.
— hike in Haleakala National Park planned, Lahaina Sun, June 30, 1971: 2.
— presented Maui Council with resolutions, Lahaina Sun, February 9, 1972: 3.
— recruiting, Lahaina News, September 23, 1987: 3.
— collecting canned food for the hungry, Lahaina News, November 1, 1989: 6.
— launch food drive, Lahaina News, November 8, 1989: 3.
— sponsoring exhibit baseball game between Hawaii Rainbows and Nittaidai University, Lahaina News, March 7, 1990: 8.
— selling tickets to Scout-O-Rama, Lahaina News, March 28, 1990: 2.
— to help clean Baby Beach, Lahaina News, April 25, 1990: 2.
— Boyd Mossman reelected as president of Maui County Council of the, Lahaina News, February 13, 1991: 5.
— scouts receive awards, Lahaina News, February 27, 1991: 5.
— Nelson Okumura named general chairman of Scout-O-Rama, Lahaina News, March 13, 1991: 5.
— looking to expand ties in West Maui, Lahaina News, April 3, 1991: 1.
— to honor Peter Baldwin as Distinguished Citizen, Lahaina News, May 23, 1991: 3.
— to hold "Scout O'Rama", Lahaina News, April 9, 1992: 8.
— awards Heroism Medal to Joseph Alan Souza, Lahaina News, November 12, 1992: 10,11.
— collect old American flags for disposal, Lahaina News, July 15, 1993: 3.
— to hold recognition dinner for new Eagle Scouts, Lahaina News, February 3, 1994: 4.
— to hold Scout-O-Rama, Lahaina News, March 17, 1994: 4.
— honor Maui residents Clyde Hamai and Evelyn Nitahara, Lahaina News, March 9, 1995: 4.
— collecting food for the needy, Lahaina News, November 16, 1995: 4.
— washing cars in exchange for children's books, Lahaina News, May 2, 1996: 16.
— begins fundraising drive to increase use of Camp Maluhia, Lahaina News, August 22, 1996: 2.

— receives grant from First Hawaiian Bank, Lahaina News, October 31, 1996: 2.

— to hold pinewood derby, Lahaina News, April 17, 1997: 14.

— to hold pie sale, Lahaina News, May 8, 1997: 16.

— picks up litter at Canoe Beach, Lahaina News, April 22, 1999: 5.

— to hold Distinguished Citizen Dinner, Lahaina News, June 10, 1999: 15.

— collecting quilts for Kosovar refugees, Lahaina News, August 26, 1999: 9.

— Walk-A-Thon successful, Lahaina News, May 18, 2000: 7.

— West Side leaders honored, Lahaina News, May 25, 2000: 15.

— collecting food, Lahaina News, November 2, 2000: 3.

— improves Moku'ula, Lahaina News, August 16, 2001: 3.

— Roger MacArthur and David "Buddy" Nobriga to receive Distinguish Citizen recognition, Lahaina News, May 16, 2002: 3.

— scouts in Cub Scout Pack 74 graduate to Boy Scouts, Lahaina News, June 19, 2003: 9.

BOYD, RON
— co-skipper wins Victoria-to-Maui race, Lahaina News, July 18, 1984: 7.

BOYDEN, LINDA [WRITER]
— Cherokee storyteller to share Native American stories at Lahaina Public Library, Lahaina News, November 9, 2000: 25.

— to sign "The Blue Roses" at Maui Child Toys and Books, Lahaina News, May 2, 2002: 16.

— to share "Stories Around the Campfire", Lahaina News, April 3, 2003: 3.

BOYFRIEND, THE [PLAY]
— to be presented at Seabury Hall, Lahaina News, November 5, 1992: 17.

BOYS AND GIRLS CLUB
— Youth Vision 2001 to be held, Lahaina News, March 29, 2001: 3.

— to exhibit "Art of Trash", Lahaina News, April 5, 2001: 18.

— hosting "Art of Trash, Maui 2001", Lahaina News, April 12, 2001: 20.

— to hold Teen Dance, Lahaina News, November 29, 2001: 16.

— visit Lahaina Adult Day Care Center, Lahaina News, December 27, 2001: 1,18.

— Safeway donates to, Lahaina News, January 3, 2002: 8.

— to hold teen dance, Lahaina News, January 24, 2002: 16.

— to hold dance for youth, Lahaina News, February 21, 2002: 3.

— to hold Teen Dance, Lahaina News, March 28, 2002: 2.

— held fieldtrip to meet Chef James McDonald, Lahaina News, April 18, 2002: 2.

— delivers homemade cupcakes to grandparents, Lahaina News, May 30, 2002: 9.

— to hold teen dance, Lahaina News, June 27, 2002: 16.

— Richard Hatch visits, Lahaina News, July 11, 2002: 18.

— to complete in regional meet in San Diego, California, Lahaina News, August 1, 2002: 17.

— to hold Punt, Pass and Kick competition, Lahaina News, September 5, 2002: 13.

— David Smith wins Punt, Pass and Kick contest, Lahaina News, September 12, 2002: 1,22.

— successes highlighted, Lahaina News, November 14, 2002: 1,22.

— unveils Tech Center, Lahaina News, February 20, 2003: 9.

— holds Career Launch Program, Lahaina News, April 10, 2003: 9.

— participates in Art of Trash exhibit, Lahaina News, May 15, 2003: 14.

— to hold teen dance, Lahaina News, May 29, 2003: 16.

BOYS IN THE HOOD [PLAY]
— to be performed by Maui Academy of Performing Arts, Lahaina News, January 16, 1992: 13.

BOYS NEXT DOOR, THE [PLAY]
— auditions to be held, Lahaina News, October 24, 1991: 4.

— to be performed by Maui Academy of Performing Arts, Lahaina News, January 9, 1992: 14.

BRACKEN, PEG
— author of "The I Hate to Cook Book" to speak to Maui Authors' Guild, Lahaina News, April 3, 1985: 3,16.

BRADDIX, DANNY [ARTIST]
— to paint at Hawaii Nature Center Gift Shop, Lahaina News, August 19, 1999: 17.

BRADEN, KEITH
— named senior vice president for marketing and sales at Hawaiian Airlines, Lahaina News, August 26, 1993: 10.

BRADLEY, BRIAN [COMEDIAN]
— to perform at Comedy Club, Lahaina News, March 21, 1990: 13.

— to perform at Comedy Club and the Sports Page, Lahaina News, May 15, 1991: 11.

— to perform at Comedy Club, Lahaina News, October 31, 1991: 14.

— to perform at Comedy Club and the Sports Page, Lahaina News, April 30, 1992: 13,15.

— to perform at Comedy Club, Lahaina News, October 14, 1993: 14.

BRADLEY, DAN [COMEDIAN]
— to perform at Comedy Club and the Sports Page, Lahaina News, February 13, 1991: 9,11.

— to perform at Comedy Club and the Sports Page, Lahaina News, August 13, 1992: 15,16.

— to perform at Comedy Club, Lahaina News, September 23, 1993: 11.

— to perform at Honolulu Comedy Club, Lahaina News, August 18, 1994: 15.

BRADLEY, PAT
— golfer participates in Women's Kemper Open, Lahaina News, March 14, 1984: 16.

— career in golfing described, Lahaina News, March 6, 1985: A7.

BRADSHAW, KEN
— discussion with surfer recounted, Lahaina Times, July, 1980 volume 4 number 6: 7.

BRADY, CHUCK
— promoted to director of corporate sales at Maui Marriott, Lahaina News, August 15, 1991: 6.

— director of corporate sales at the Maui Marriott Resort named manager of the year, Lahaina News, March 5, 1992: 10.

BRAGA, DENNIS AND LISA
— expand chiropractic office, Lahaina News, July 23, 1992: 17.

BRANDT, JACK
— promoted to Maui retail division manager at Monarch Home Center, Lahaina News, August 10, 1988: 17.

BRANIFF AIRLINES [BUSINESS]
— sponsoring music performance in South America, Lahaina Sun, January 20, 1971: 7.

BRAUN, RANDY JAY [ARTIST]
— to exhibit photographs at Old Jail Gallery, Lahaina News, February 25, 1993: 9.

— to exhibit at Lahaina Art Society, Lahaina News, April 7, 1994: 12.

— to sign prints of photographs, Lahaina News, May 21, 1998: 16.

BRAVE ACTS
— festival of one-act plays to be held, Lahaina News, June 8, 1995: 12.

BRAVERMAN, TERRY
— to speak at Ohana Luncheon and Trade Fair, Lahaina News, March 11, 1993: 11.

— to share comedy techniques, Lahaina News, November 21, 1996: 14.

— comic to speak at Maui Church of Religious Science, Lahaina News, May 21, 1998: 16.

— minister and author of "When the Going Gets Tough, the Tough Lighten Up!" to speak at Unity Church, Lahaina News, June 21, 2001: 16.

BRAXTON BROTHERS [MUSICAL GROUP]

— to perform at Maui Music Festival, Lahaina News, April 22, 1999: 3.

BRAY, KEKULA

— discusses conference on Hawaiian independence, Lahaina News, March 10, 1994: 1.

BREADFRUIT

— early story of, in Maui, Lahaina Sun, April 26, 1972: 19.

BREAKDANCING

— featured, Lahaina News, May 19, 1994: 4.

BREAST AND CERVICAL CANCER CONTROL PROJECT

— to meet, Lahaina News, January 8, 1998: 12.

BRECKELS, CHRIS

— Safe Communities working to address problems, Lahaina News, January 17, 2002: 1,20.

BREDEHOFT, RICHARD

— wedding to Cynee Gillette announced, Lahaina Sun, January 20, 1971: 6.

BREEDEN, MAGGIE AND JERRY

— owners of Royal Hawaiian Heritage Jewelry purchase Hawaiian House of Adler stores, Lahaina News, June 30, 1994: 8.

BREEDERS, THE [MUSICAL GROUP]

— to perform at The Big Mele, Lahaina News, July 31, 1997: 16.

BREEZE BROTHERS, THE [MUSICAL GROUP]

— featured, Lahaina News, December 27, 1989: 14.

— to perform at Pioneer Inn, Lahaina News, March 7, 1990: 13.

— to perform at Whale's Tale, Lahaina News, March 21, 1990: 13.

— to perform at Whale's Tale, Lahaina News, April 4, 1990: 13.

— to perform at Whale's Tale, Lahaina News, April 11, 1990: 15.

— to perform at Pioneer Inn, Lahaina News, July 4, 1991: 12.

— continues to perform at Pioneer Inn, Lahaina News, July 25, 1991: 12.

— continues to perform at Pioneer Inn, Lahaina News, September 5, 1991: 10.

— to perform at Pioneer Inn, Lahaina News, September 19, 1991: 16.

— reform and are playing at Aloha Cantina, Lahaina News, February 10, 1994: 2.

BREGEDA, VICTOR [ARTIST]

— to exhibit at Sargent's Fine Art, Lahaina News, July 10, 2003: 17.

BRENSINGER, BARBARA

— named programming and sales coordinator by Maui Today photoadvertising channel, Lahaina News, June 13, 1991: 9.

BRETAGNE, LA [RESTAURANT]

— to celebrate Bastille Day, Lahaina News, July 4, 1984: 4,7.

— reviewed, Lahaina News, July 25, 1984: 13.

— described, Lahaina News, March 2, 1988: 4.

— reviewed, Lahaina News, November 16, 1988: 8.

— reviewed, Lahaina News, January 25, 1989: 10.

— reviewed, Lahaina News, August 9, 1989: 11.

BRETT, JOHN

— brother of baseball George Brett interviewed, Lahaina News, March 26, 1986: 4.

BREWBAKER, PAUL

— Bank of Hawaii economist to speak to Maui Chamber of Commerce, Lahaina News, February 20, 1997: 11.

— Bank of Hawaii Chief Economist to speak on "Maui Talks Money", Lahaina News, February 18, 1999: 11.

— Bank of Hawaii chief economist to speak, Lahaina News, February 17, 2000: 14.

— Bank of Hawaii Chief Economist to discuss economy, Lahaina News, November 22, 2001: 8.

BREWER HOMES, INC. [BUSINESS]

— see C. Brewer Homes, Inc. [business]

BRIAN COMO QUARTET [MUSICAL GROUP]

— performs at Sam's Upstairs, Lahaina News, August 16, 1989: 17.

— to perform at Blackie's Bar with Jon Nagourney, Lahaina News, March 21, 1990: 13.

— to perform at Blackie's Bar, Lahaina News, October 10, 1990: 13.

— to perform at Blackie's Bar, Lahaina News, November 7, 1990: 10.

— continues to perform at Blackie's Bar, Lahaina News, April 10, 1991: 9.

— continues to perform at Blackie's Bar, Lahaina News, May 23, 1991: 12,13.

BRIAN COMO TRIO [MUSICAL GROUP]

— performs at Pacific'O Restaurant, Lahaina News, October 5, 1995: 10.

BRICK PALACE

— exhibit to be created near Lahaina library, Lahaina Sun, December 16, 1970: 6.

BRICKMAN, JIM [MUSICIAN]

— to perform at Maui Arts and Cultural Center, Lahaina News, March 1, 2001: 20.

BRIDAL FAIRE

— to take place at Ka'ahumanu Shopping Center, Lahaina News, December 26, 1990: 7.

— to be held, Lahaina News, March 19, 1992: 6.

— to be held, Lahaina News, December 30, 1993: 10.

— to be sponsored by Maui Chamber of Commerce and Westin Maui, Lahaina News, January 6, 1994: 11,12.

— to include honeymoon giveaway from Westin Maui, Lahaina News, January 20, 1994: 11.

BRIDE STRIPPED BARE [FILM]

— shown at Princess Theatre in Paia, Lahaina Sun, May 5, 1971: 2.

BRIDES

— Bridal Fair scheduled, Lahaina News, January 24, 1990: 28.

BRIDGERS, DEBRA [WRITER]

— to discuss "Make My Day", a celebration of the life of Eric MacCammond, Lahaina News, November 26, 1998: 1,8.

BRIDGES, CHANNING

— new sales and marketing director at Kapalua Bay Hotel and Ocean Villas, Lahaina News, October 2, 2003: 8.

BRIDGES, HARRY

— play of life to be performed, Lahaina News, October 11, 2001: 14.

— show explores legacy of, Lahaina News, October 25, 2001: 16.

BRIDGES, LLOYD, JEFF AND BEAU [ACTORS]

— appear at Planet Hollywood, Lahaina News, December 15, 1994: 17.

BRIDGES YOUTH GROUP

— panel to be held, Lahaina News, January 25, 2001: 17.

— to be held, Lahaina News, May 10, 2001: 21.

BRIGHT, TERESA [MUSICIAN]

— to perform at Molokini Lounge at the Maui Prince Hotel, Lahaina News, April 24, 1991: 11.

— to perform at Hula Grill, Lahaina News, March 27, 1997: 12.

— to perform at "Music on the Beach", Lahaina News, May 20, 1999: 14.

BRIGHTON, ALEXANDRIA

— to offer aromatherapy workshop, Lahaina News, June 1, 2000: 16.

BRIGHTON BEACH MEMOIRS [PLAY]
— to be performed by Seabury Hall Performing Arts Department, Lahaina News, February 16, 1995: 16.

BRINDLE, GRAHAM JOHN
— named director of engineering at Kapalua Bay Hotel, Lahaina News, April 2, 1986: 3.

BRINKMAN, STEVE [ARTIST]
— photographs displayed at Lahaina Cannery Shopping Center, Lahaina News, December 21, 1988: 13.

BRINNER, GEORGE [ARTIST]
— to be featured at Village Gallery Contemporary, Lahaina News, August 17, 2000: 17.

BRISQUE, GINGER [MUSICIAN]
— to perform at Polli's Mexican Restaurant, Lahaina News, July 4, 1991: 14.

BRITAIN, CYNTHIA [ARTIST]
— offering plein air painting workshop, Lahaina News, March 1, 2001: 11.

BRITISH COLUMBIA
— Langley Ukulele Ensemble to perform with Lahaina Intermediate School at Sheraton Maui, Lahaina News, July 27, 2000: 3.

BRITO, ROBERTO
— allowed to steer catamaran as part of Dream Foundation, Lahaina News, February 24, 2000: 3.

BRITTON, LYNN [POLITICIAN]
— resigning as president of Maui Hotel Association, Lahaina News, November 5, 1992: 9.
— Maui County Council member to seek more project districts, Lahaina News, December 31, 1992: 8.
— named catering sales manager at Westin Maui, Lahaina News, August 3, 1995: 8.
— appointed as new manager of Lahaina News, Lahaina News, November 23, 1995: 1,2.
— candidate for South Maui County Council, Lahaina News, November 2, 2000: 18.

BROADBENT, JOHN
— passes away, Lahaina News, October 7, 1999: 2.

BROADCAST MUSIC, INC (BMI)
— to enforce music copyright laws on Maui, Lahaina News, November 12, 1992: 1,17.

BROADHURST, ALICE
— acting Maui district health officer discusses outbreak of dysentery is contained, Lahaina Sun, January 27, 1971: 1.
— appointed Maui District Health Officer, Lahaina Sun, April 28, 1971: 4.
— acting Maui district health officer discusses smallpox vaccinations on Maui, Lahaina Sun, October 20, 1971: 11.

BROADWAY BABES—A REVUE [SHOW]
— to be performed by Baldwin Theatre Guild, Lahaina News, December 9, 1987: 26.
— to be held at The Performing Arts Learning Center, Lahaina News, March 12, 1992: 21,22.
— to be held at Baldwin High School auditorium, Lahaina News, February 3, 1994: 12.
— performances continue, Lahaina News, February 24, 1994: 12.
— to be performed by Baldwin High School Performing Arts, Lahaina News, March 2, 1995: 12.

BROKEN RAINBOW [FILM]
— to be screened at Maui Community College, Lahaina News, May 6, 1987: 3.

BROKOVICH, ERIN
— Sophie Mataafa receives scholarship to meet, Lahaina News, July 3, 2003: 9.

BROOKFIELD, CHARLES
— promoted to senior vice president of planning and development at Aston Hotels and Resorts, Lahaina News, August 8, 1990: 6.

BROOKS, BILL
— Interisland Resorts representative speaks of the proposed Lahaina Hotel, Lahaina Sun, November 11, 1970: 3.

BROOKS, C.W.
— planning to develop 470-room hotel in Lahaina, Lahaina Sun, January 20, 1971: 1.

BROOKS, JEAN
— awarded the Certified Residential Specialist designation, Lahaina News, February 6, 1992: 10.

BROOKS, PAUL
— former editor-in-chief of Houghton Mifflin to be honored , Lahaina News, March 23, 1995: 11.

BROOKS, RICK
— new basketball coach at Lahainaluna High School, Lahaina News, September 20, 2001: 1,18.

BROOKSBY, JANETHA
— Fur & Feathers columnist moves off island, will continue to write, Lahaina News, April 23, 1986: 8.

BROTHER NOLAND [MUSICIAN]
— to perform at Maui Community College Ho'olaule'a, Lahaina News, April 11, 1984: 5.
— to headline summer concerts, Lahaina News, June 13, 1984: 4.
— to perform at "Year of the Hawaiian" concert, Lahaina News, May 27, 1987: 3.
— to perform, Lahaina News, February 8, 1989: 9.
— to perform at Maui Marriott, Lahaina News, March 27, 1991: 12.
— to perform at Maui Lu Resort on New Year's Eve with Pacific Bad Boys, Lahaina News, January 2, 1992: 12.
— to perform at Casanova's, Lahaina News, May 21, 1992: 17.
— to perform at Whalers Village, Lahaina News, November 21, 1996: 14.
— to perform at A Taste of Lahaina, Lahaina News, September 10, 1998: 16.
— performed at A Taste of Lahaina, Lahaina News, September 17, 1998: 1.
— to perform at Hana 'Imi Na'auao Ho'olaule'a, Lahaina News, August 12, 1999: 18.
— to perform at Hana 'Imi Na'auao Ho'olaule'a, Lahaina News, August 19, 1999: 16.
— performs at Ki-Ho'alu 2000 Hawaiian Slack Key Guitar Festival, Lahaina News, June 15, 2000: 3.
— to perform at "I Love Lahaina", Lahaina News, October 18, 2001: 14.
— to perform at MauiFest, Lahaina News, September 18, 2003: 18.

BROTHERS CAZIMERO, THE [MUSICAL GROUP]
— reviewed, Lahaina News, June 1, 1980: 3.
— performance and career reviewed, Lahaina News, November 2, 1983: 4.
— to perform at Baldwin Auditorium, Lahaina News, October 8, 1986: 5.
— to perform at Baldwin Auditorium, Lahaina News, November 4, 1987: 3.
— reviewed, Lahaina News, August 17, 1988: 9,11.
— to perform to benefit Maui Philharmonic Society, Lahaina News, February 22, 1989: 9.
— to perform at Old Lahaina Luau grounds, Lahaina News, April 3, 1991: 6,7.
— to perform at Old Lahaina Cafe and Luau, Lahaina News, April 10, 1991: 1,8.
— to perform at Maui Inter-Continental, Lahaina News, August 15, 1991: 15.
— to perform at Old Lahaina Luau, Lahaina News, November 14, 1991: 15.

— to perform at Aloha Festival, Lahaina News, October 8, 1992: 11.

— to perform benefit concert at the Four Seasons, Lahaina News, October 15, 1992: 18.

— to perform benefit concert for Punana Leo O Maui Hawaiian Language School, Lahaina News, September 30, 1993: 12.

— to perform benefit concert for Punana Leo O Maui Hawaiian Language School, Lahaina News, October 14, 1993: 15.

— to perform benefit concert for Punana Leo O Maui Hawaiian Language School, Lahaina News, October 13, 1994: 19.

— to perform at A Taste of Lahaina, Lahaina News, September 4, 1997: 3.

— to perform at maui Arts and Cultural Center, Lahaina News, November 27, 1997: 13.

— to perform at Maui Arts and Cultural Center, Lahaina News, December 4, 1997: 25.

— new CD featured, Lahaina News, October 8, 1998: 9.

— to perform at Kihei Baptist Church, Lahaina News, February 25, 1999: 12.

— to perform at Whalers Village, Lahaina News, June 17, 1999: 14.

— to perform at "Music on the Beach", Lahaina News, June 24, 1999: 13.

— to perform at Maui Arts and Cultural Center, Lahaina News, April 27, 2000: 12.

— to perform at Maui Arts and Cultural Center, Lahaina News, April 26, 2001: 20.

— to perform as part of Ho'onanea Hawaiian Series, Lahaina News, May 2, 2002: 17.

— to perform at "I Love Lahaina", Lahaina News, October 17, 2002: 15.

— to perform at Ho'onanea Hawaiian Series, Lahaina News, April 24, 2003: 19.

— to perform May Day show, Lahaina News, May 1, 2003: 16.

BROTHERS JOHNSON, THE [MUSICAL GROUP]
— to perform at Casanova's, Lahaina News, September 5, 1991: 18.

BROWN, ARZA
— pastor at Grace Baptist Church featured, Lahaina News, August 28, 2003: 1,18.

BROWN BAGS TO STARDOM
— contest to be held, Lahaina News, February 1, 1996: 12.

— to be held, Lahaina News, February 11, 1999: 17.

— talent competition to be held, Lahaina News, March 16, 2000: 12.

BROWN, BOB [MAGICIAN]
— to perform at Villa Restaurant, Lahaina News, September 3, 1992: 14,15.

BROWN, BOYCE
— lawyer retained by West Maui Taxpayers Association to head fight against proposed airport in West Maui, Lahaina News, August 21, 1985: 1.

BROWN, BRENDA [MAGICIAN]
— to perform at Villa Restaurant, Lahaina News, September 3, 1992: 14,15.

BROWN, CLARENCE "GATEMOUTH" [MUSICIAN]
— to perform at Casanova's, Lahaina News, February 6, 1997: 16.

BROWN, DEE
— American Red Cross discusses disaster preparedness, Lahaina News, June 10, 1999: 1,20.

BROWN, DONNA
— Marine Option Program coordinator to present on limu, Lahaina News, May 3, 2001: 21.

— Marine Option Program coordinator hosting fish identification seminar by Reef Environmental Education Foundation, Lahaina News, December 6, 2001: 13.

BROWN, "DOWNTOWN" FREDDIE
— basketball player visits Maui, Lahaina News, July 9, 1986: 4.

BROWN, ERIC
— member of panel discussing hippies on Maui, Lahaina Sun, December 2, 1970: 1.

— discusses place of hippies on Maui, Lahaina Sun, December 16, 1970: 7.

— director for Maui ACLU, Lahaina Sun, January 13, 1971: 6.

— member of Hawaii Institute of Marine Biology to speak on reefs, Lahaina News, February 14, 2002: 2.

— to present "Status of Hawaii's Coral Reefs: Should We Celebrate or Give Up", Lahaina News, May 9, 2002: 1.

BROWN, GEORGE
— windsurfer featured, Lahaina News, December 14, 1988: 2.

BROWN, IKAIKA [MUSICIAN]
— to perform at Ka'ahumanu Center's center stage, Lahaina News, July 4, 1996: 15.

— to promote new CD "Three Generations" at Borders Books, Lahaina News, July 22, 1999: 12.

— to perform at "I Love Lahaina", Lahaina News, November 14, 2002: 3.

— to perform at Slack Key Guitar and Junior Ukulele Festival, Lahaina News, February 27, 2003: 18.

BROWN, IRENE
— hired by Myers Advertising as account manager, Lahaina News, May 31, 2001: 8.

BROWN, JACKSON [MUSICIAN]
— to perform at Maui Arts and Cultural Center, Lahaina News, April 25, 1996: 17.

BROWN, JILL
— connected to Maui County Committee on Ecology, Lahaina Sun, January 20, 1971: 6.

BROWN, JOLENE
— joins Guest Informant as Hawaiian Islands publisher, Lahaina News, February 11, 1993: 11.

BROWN, JOYCE
— elected president of No Ka Oi Chapter of International of Administrative Professionals, Lahaina News, May 31, 2001: 8.

BROWN, KATHERINE
— Lahaina Intermediate School teacher to become school assessment liaison, Lahaina News, November 2, 2000: 1,2.

BROWN, MACK
— to coach a team at the Hula Bowl, Lahaina News, January 16, 2003: 13.

BROWN, PAUL
— Maui District Schools Superintendent to speak to Republican Party E Komo Mai Club dinner, Lahaina News, December 9, 1999: 20.

BROWN, RONALD [DANCER]
— to perform at Maui Arts and Cultural Center with Evidence, Lahaina News, October 31, 2002: 29.

BROWN, RUSSELL
— benefit concert to be held, Lahaina News, November 25, 1999: 7.

— recovery detailed, Lahaina News, March 9, 2000: 1,16.

BROWN, SHANNON
— murder trial to begin, Lahaina News, February 13, 1992: 4.

BROWN, SUSAN
— named Maui manager of ASK 2000, Lahaina News, December 26, 1990: 3.

BROWNIES
— now accepting orders for cookies, Lahaina News, December 31, 1992: 1.

— looking for troupe leader, Lahaina News, January 28, 1993: 4.

— Lahaina troupe to hold car wash fundraiser, Lahaina News, April 6, 1995: 4.

BROWNING-FERRIS INDUSTRIES OF HAWAII, INC. (BFI) [BUSINESS]
— acquired by Horizon Waste Services, Inc., Lahaina News, April 20, 2000: 13.

BROWNSTEIN, ARTHUR [WRITER]
— author of "Healing Back Pain Naturally" to appear at Borders Books, Lahaina News, April 1, 1999: 16.

BROZ, JERRY
— named executive assistant manager of food and beverage division at Hyatt Regency Maui, Lahaina News, July 25, 1991: 7.

BRUBECK, DAVE [MUSICIAN]
— to play at Baldwin Auditorium, Lahaina News, February 19, 1986: 8.

BRUCE BOSELY MEMORIAL TOURNAMENT
— to be held, Lahaina News, October 5, 1995: 7.

BRUCE, JACK [MUSICIAN]
— to perform in "A Walk Down Abbey Road" celebration of the Beatles, Lahaina News, June 13, 2002: 17.

BRUCE, JIM
— owner of Ka'anapali Kau Lio announces closure of company, Lahaina News, July 18, 1991: 14.
— "Mr. Aloha" to relocate to Rarotonga, Lahaina News, July 26, 2001: 1,18.

BRUCE, ROBERT
— President of Maui chapter of Conservation Council of Hawaii criticizes planned power plant, Lahaina Sun, July 21, 1971: 12.

BRUDDAH WALTAH AND ISLAND AFTERNOON [MUSICAL GROUP]
— to perform at Casanova's, Lahaina News, February 6, 1991: 9.
— to perform at Casanova's, Lahaina News, July 4, 1991: 14.
— to perform at Casanova's, Lahaina News, March 26, 1992: 17.

BRUGIROUX, ANDRE
— to speak on "The Earth is But One County", Lahaina News, March 2, 1995: 11.

BRUMMETT, RAYMOND
— named officer for Lahaina Yacht Club, Lahaina Sun, December 23, 1970: 8.

BRUNETTE, RICK
— named director food and beverage for two Rockresort hotels, Lahaina News, December 20, 1989: 4.

BRUNISH, ROBERT
— supported for provost position by Maui Community College faculty, Lahaina Sun, April 14, 1971: 3.
— ideas for Maui Community College summarized, Lahaina Sun, April 21, 1971: 5.

BRUNS, JOHN
— appointed assistant general manager of Stouffer Wailea Beach Resort, Lahaina News, May 28, 1986: 3.

BRUNSON, ROY
— named head professional at Royal Lahaina Tennis Ranch, Lahaina News, March 21, 1990: 4.

BRUVEL, GIL [ARTIST]
— to exhibit at Metropolitan Art Gallery, Lahaina News, August 20, 1992: 20.
— to visit Sargent's Fine Art, Lahaina News, March 27, 2003: 17.
— to visit Lahaina Galleries, Lahaina News, October 2, 2003: 17.

BRYNER, JOHN [COMEDIAN]
— films "Home and Family", Lahaina News, May 22, 1997: 14.

BRYON, HELEN [ARTIST]
— work displayed at Kula Lodge, Lahaina Sun, January 5, 1972: 5.

BUBBA GUMP SHRIMP [RESTAURANT]
— to open on Maui, Lahaina News, November 20, 1997: 20.
— donates to Lahaina public schools, Lahaina News, December 4, 1997: 17.
— collecting toys for Toys for Tots, Lahaina News, December 18, 1997: 11.

— featured, Lahaina News, January 1, 1998: 6,7.
— opens, Lahaina News, November 4, 1999: 2.
— to support Lahaina public schools, Lahaina News, December 9, 1999: 20.
— donates money to Lahaina public schools, Lahaina News, January 20, 2000: 5.
— to donate percentage of sales from Friday to Friends of Moku'ula, Lahaina News, January 27, 2000: 1,16.
— promotes Robert Caldwell to director of operations, Lahaina News, April 6, 2000: 8.
— requests to create new lanai and canoe display, Lahaina News, May 4, 2000: 2.

BUCHANAN, BUCK
— disk jockey fired from KNUI, Lahaina Sun, February 14, 1973: 4.
— football player visits Maui, Lahaina News, October 9, 1985: 8.
— community activism described, Lahaina News, April 3, 1997: 1,16.

BUCHANAN, MICHAEL
— passes Certified Landscape Technician (Exterior) exam from Associated Landscape Contractors of America, Lahaina News, October 3, 2002: 8.

BUCHNOWSKI, DONALD "BUCKY"
— joins Ka'anapali Beach Properties, Inc., Lahaina News, June 1, 2000: 13.

BUCK, CARI
— new head professional at Royal Lahaina Tennis Ranch, Lahaina News, May 9, 1990: 8.
— tennis pro featured, Lahaina News, December 19, 1991: 8.

BUCK, DAVID
— qualifies for Chotokan black belt, Lahaina News, July 15, 1987: 6.
— qualifies for United States Olympic kayak team, Lahaina News, September 21, 1995: 7.
— wins first place in final leg of Chart House Kayak and Canoe Racing Series, Lahaina News, April 29, 1999: 7.

BUCK, DOT [ARTIST]
— to display watercolors, Lahaina News, August 20, 1986: 3.

BUCKET DANCE THEATRE
— to perform at Baldwin High School Auditorium, Lahaina News, January 31, 1990: 13.
— to perform at Baldwin High School Auditorium, Lahaina News, February 21, 1990: 13.

BUCKLE, WILLIAM
— Captain of Daniel, a whaling ship, Lahaina Sun, January 6, 1971: 8.

BUCKLEY, KATHY [COMEDIAN]
— to perform at Comedy Club, Lahaina News, July 4, 1990: 18.
— to perform at Comedy Club, Lahaina News, August 22, 1991: 10.

BUCKY, CARL
— president of Hawaii Jewelers Association discusses jewelry industry, Lahaina News, December 13, 1989: 15,16,20.

BUD LIGHT [BUSINESS]
— to air commercials made on Maui, Lahaina News, November 24, 1994: 9.

BUD THE BIRDMAN
— releases 30-minute video, Lahaina News, February 1, 1996: 11.

BUDDHISM
— Buddha statue erected at Lahaina Jodo Mission, Lahaina Sun, March 10, 1971: 4.
— Zen Buddhism colony near Haleakala described, Lahaina Sun, March 17, 1971: 4.
— celebration of birth of Buddha planned, Lahaina Sun, April 7, 1971: 3.
— seminar offered by Alfred Bloom, Lahaina Sun, April 21, 1971: 2.
— Buddhist convention held on Maui, Lahaina Sun, October 27, 1971: 6.

— Masaichi Kawaguchi Nembutsu Seminar to be held, Lahaina News, August 2, 1989: 9.

— Hanamatsuri to be celebrated by, Lahaina News, April 3, 2003: 3.

BUDGET

— see Maui County Budget

BUDGET AND FINANCE COMMITTEE, MAUI COUNTY COUNCIL

— to meet, Lahaina News, March 13, 1997: 16.

— to hold budget hearing, Lahaina News, March 12, 1998: 1.

— to hold meeting on county budget, Lahaina News, March 26, 1998: 12.

— discusses County budget at meeting chaired by G. Riki Hokama, Lahaina News, March 29, 2001: 1.

— residents seek funding for various projects, Lahaina News, April 5, 2001: 1,24.

— chair Riki Hokama to hold public meeting, Lahaina News, March 14, 2002: 1,20.

— holds public meeting, Lahaina News, April 4, 2002: 1,2.

— to hold public hearing, Lahaina News, April 4, 2002: 17.

— to hold public hearing, Lahaina News, April 11, 2002: 16.

BUDGET RENT-A-CAR [BUSINESS]

— donates to America's Cup Yacht Race, Lahaina News, September 2, 1987: 3.

— personnel changes announced, Lahaina News, May 21, 1992: 9.

— Hawaii residents eligible for refunds, Lahaina News, February 2, 1995: 7.

— to hold benefit car wash for Give Kids the World, Lahaina News, August 15, 1996: 14.

— recognizes employees, Lahaina News, April 17, 1997: 7.

— holds drawing for HawaiianMiles, Lahaina News, December 20, 2001: 9.

BUDNICK, RICH

— publishes "Stolen Kingdom: An American Conspiracy", Lahaina News, November 26, 1992: 3.

BUDWEISER SUPER JAM

— to feature "The Best", which includes John Entwistle, Jeff Baxter, and Joe Walsh, Lahaina News, October 3, 1990: 12.

BUENCONSEJO, MARVIN

— appointed director of catering at Hyatt Regency Maui, Lahaina News, May 13, 1987: 3.

BUETZER, TATIANA

— Scholar/Athlete of the Week, Lahaina News, February 25, 1999: 7.

BUFFALO, NORTON [MUSICIAN]

— to perform at Maui Marriott for Halloween, Lahaina News, October 24, 1991: 18,19.

BUFFET, GUY [ARTIST]

— career described, Lahaina News, February 1, 1981: 15.

— exhibits at Lahaina Gallery, Lahaina News, July 5, 1989: 13.

— to exhibit paintings about the French Revolution, Lahaina News, August 16, 1989: 1,15.

— presents Governor Waihee a bas relief commemorating the Bicentennial of the French Revolution, Lahaina News, September 27, 1989: 9.

— to hold reception at Lahaina Galleries, Lahaina News, March 28, 1990: 17.

— featured at Westin Maui, Lahaina News, August 26, 1993: 15.

— to sign copies of newest book "The World of Guy Buffet", Lahaina News, May 18, 1995: 10,11.

— opens store in Lahaina Cannery Mall, Lahaina News, June 22, 1995: 10.

— to exhibit at Lahaina Galleries, Lahaina News, October 23, 1997: 20.

— unveils new series of watercolors, Lahaina News, March 26, 1998: 13.

— unveils new series of watercolors, Lahaina News, April 2, 1998: 2.

— to exhibit at Lahaina Galleries, Lahaina News, May 14, 1998: 16.

— to exhibit at Lahaina Galleries, Lahaina News, October 22, 1998: 20.

— to exhibit at Lahaina Galleries, Lahaina News, November 19, 1998: 16.

— to exhibit at Lahaina Galleries, Lahaina News, February 4, 1999: 16.

— to make final appearance at Lahaina Galleries, Lahaina News, April 8, 1999: 12.

— appearing at Lahaina Galleries, Lahaina News, April 20, 2000: 16.

— to exhibit at Lahaina Galleries, Lahaina News, February 22, 2001: 14.

— to exhibit at Lahaina Galleries, Lahaina News, August 2, 2001: 18.

— to appear at Lahaina Galleries, Lahaina News, August 9, 2001: 16.

— to paint for Whale Mania Maui, Lahaina News, August 15, 2002: 14.

BUFFET, GUY AND LAURENCE [ARTISTS]

— to hold benefit for Maui Symphony Orchestra, Lahaina News, November 24, 1994: 11.

BUFFET, LAWRENCE

— ballerina to hold stretch classes, Lahaina News, July 19, 2001: 13.

— ballerina to offer stretch classes at The Art School at Kapalua, Lahaina News, August 2, 2001: 13.

BUFFETT, JIMMY [MUSICIAN]

— concert on Oahu reviewed, Lahaina News, November, 1979: 4.

— to perform at Lahaina Civic Center, Lahaina News, May 15, 1983: 6.

— to perform at Royal Lahaina Tennis Stadium, Lahaina News, August 13, 1986: 8.

— to perform at Royal Lahaina Tennis Stadium, Lahaina News, October 29, 1992: 18.

— to perform, Lahaina News, November 5, 1992: 14.

— concert this Saturday, Lahaina News, November 12, 1992: 18.

BUGAGIAR, ALESSO AND MARCELLO [ARTISTS]

— to exhibit at Lahaina Galleries, Lahaina News, October 1, 1998: 16.

— to visit Lahaina Galleries, Lahaina News, September 4, 2003: 17.

— to appear at Lahaina Galleries, Lahaina News, September 25, 2003: 16.

BUILDING AND NEW PRODUCTS TRADE SHOW

— organized by Maui Contractors Association, Lahaina News, August 16, 1989: 6.

BUILDING CODES

— discussed by Maui County Council, Lahaina Sun, January 13, 1971: 6.

BUILDING INDUSTRY ASSOCIATION OF HAWAII

— selects James Zweedyk as chair of Hawaii Renaissance program, Lahaina News, February 28, 1990: 4.

— announces Sutton Candia Partners winner of Hawaii Renaissance contest, Lahaina News, October 3, 1990: 9.

— Gerald Onaga named chairman of Remodelers Council, Lahaina News, March 6, 1991: 10.

— offering course on basic blueprint reading, Lahaina News, August 15, 1991: 7.

— to host Parade of Homes, Lahaina News, August 15, 1991: 7.

— to hold Parade of Homes, Lahaina News, March 29, 2001: 8.

BUILDING MATERIAL PRODUCT SHOW

— booths still available, Lahaina News, May 30, 1991: 3.

— to be held this weekend, Lahaina News, June 13, 1991: 9,10.

BUILDING NUMBERS

— building owners asked to apply for new numbers, Lahaina Sun, May 19, 1971: 3.

BUILDING PERMITS

— 12-story buildings allowed in Kahana, Wailea, Kamaole, and Ka'anapali, Lahaina Sun, November 11, 1970: 4.

BUILDING PRODUCTS EXPO
— to take place on Big Island, Lahaina News, August 1, 1991: 11.

BUKOSKI, JOSEPH, III
— new pastor at Maria Lanakila Church, Lahaina News, September 10, 1998: 1,24.
— former Father at Maria Lanakila Catholic Church, Lahaina News, September 19, 2002: 18.

BUKOSKI, KIKA [POLITICIAN]
— representative to discuss legislative session, Lahaina News, June 12, 2003: 20,21.

BULGO, JOE [POLITICIAN]
— member of Maui County Council, Lahaina Sun, December 30, 1970: 8.
— councilmember assists in conflict over signage, Lahaina Sun, January 13, 1971: 1,2.
— councilmember submits petition asking state and county to deal with hippies, Lahaina Sun, February 24, 1971: 6.
— councilmember position criticized by William Poulson in editorial, Lahaina Sun, March 3, 1971: 2.
— attitudes towards hippies discussed by councilmember, Lahaina Sun, March 17, 1971: 8.
— councilmember part of informal group responding to hippies, Lahaina Sun, March 24, 1971: 1,5.
— councilmember requests that welfare recipients be finger-printed, Lahaina Sun, June 2, 1971: 6.
— councilmember condemns Maui County Council committee system, Lahaina Sun, July 7, 1971: 1,2.
— councilmember discusses with Edward Kennedy the possibility of creating a national shrine, Lahaina Sun, August 25, 1971: 5.
— councilmember seeks recreational site for motorcycles, Lahaina Sun, September 1, 1971: 12.
— councilmember supporting leash laws, Lahaina Sun, November 24, 1971: 1.
— councilmember supports proposed JFK memorial in Iao Valley, Lahaina Sun, December 29, 1971: 4.
— councilmember introduced resolution supporting cockfighting, Lahaina Sun, March 8, 1972: 5.
— councilmember sued by Jack Stephens and James Franklin, publisher of the New Newspaper, Lahaina Sun, December 6, 1972: 5.
— councilmember critical of environmentalists, Lahaina Sun, February 21, 1973: 4.
— councilmember concerned over how Civil Air Patrol is spending money, Lahaina Sun, February 28, 1973: 4.
— councilmember named vice-chair of Maui County Council, Lahaina Sun, August 8, 1973: 5.

BULLARD, RONNIE [COMEDIAN]
— to perform at Comedy Club and the Sports Page, Lahaina News, March 6, 1991: 11,13.
— to perform at Comedy Club and the Sports Page, Lahaina News, September 3, 1992: 14,18.
— to perform at Comedy Club, Lahaina News, August 5, 1993: 10.

BULLDOZED AMERICA [FILM]
— shown at Lahaina Library, Lahaina Sun, July 28, 1971: 11.

BUMANGLAG, ARSENIA
— killed in car accident, Lahaina News, March 18, 1993: 3,4.

BUMANGLAG, JANICE
— Lahaina Intermediate School student named a United States National Award winner in mathematics, Lahaina News, July 20, 1995: 5.

BUMATAI, ANDY [COMEDIAN]
— to open show for Kool & the Gang, Lahaina News, March 13, 1985: 16.
— to perform at Studio 505, Lahaina News, July 23, 1992: 20.
— to perform at Studio 505, Lahaina News, October 8, 1992: 10.
— to perform at Maui Arts and Cultural Center, Lahaina News, July 26, 2001: 16.

BUNTING, EVE [WRITER]
— to speak "Cross the Bridge to Dreams", Lahaina News, June 4, 1998: 17.

BURCH, LAUREL
— to expand, Lahaina News, September 17, 1992: 10.

BURDON, C.J. [MUSICIAN]
— to perform at Casanova's, Lahaina News, October 24, 1991: 22.

BURDON, ERIC [MUSICIAN]
— to perform at Embassy Suites Resort, Lahaina News, September 12, 1991: 13.
— to perform at Embassy Suites Resort with Brian Auger, Lahaina News, September 19, 1991: 16.

BURGER, CHARLES
— Reverend discusses Christmas services at Holy Innocents' Church, Lahaina Sun, December 23, 1970: 8.
— Reverend assisting Doylene Larson, who lost her house in a fire, Lahaina Sun, December 30, 1970: 1.
— Reverend resigns from Holy Innocents Episcopal Church to return to the mainland, Lahaina News, June 15, 1983: 6.

BURGER KING [RESTAURANT]
— plans to expand in Hawaii, Lahaina News, April 1, 1980: 14.

BURGESS, ROD
— OHA trustee discusses issues faced, Lahaina News, July 13, 1988: 1,12.

BURGEVIN, DIANE
— to compete in Maui Channel Swim, Lahaina News, September 2, 1993: 8.

BURKE, AMY
— top producer for Coldwell Bankers, Lahaina News, March 13, 1991: 7.

BURKE, DAVID
— appointed Director of Sales at Hyatt Regency Maui, Lahaina News, December 16, 1987: 3.

BURKE, MICHAEL
— appointed manager of land administration at Amfac/JMB, Lahaina News, April 11, 1990: 5.

BURKET, JAN
— wins prize for recycling aluminum cans, Lahaina News, November 29, 1989: 36.

BURMA
— Maui Community College offering workshop "Burma: The Golden Land", Lahaina News, September 21, 1988: 3,20.

BURNES, KENT
— to speak on small business success, Lahaina News, August 31, 1995: 10.

BURNETT, IRIS
— passes away, Lahaina News, August 12, 1999: 9.

BURNETT, RANDY
— Sportsman of the Year for West Maui, Lahaina News, December 31, 1986: 6.

BURNS, DON
— fundraiser to be held to support medical expenses of, Lahaina News, April 20, 1995: 6.

BURNS, JIMMY [COMEDIAN]
— to perform at Comedy Club and the Sports Page, Lahaina News, January 9, 1992: 10.

BURNS, SCOTT [ARTIST]
— to exhibit at Viewpoints Gallery, Lahaina News, September 17, 1992: 17.

BURNT BY THE SUN [FILM]
— to be shown by Maui Arts and Cultural Center, Lahaina News, September 28, 1995: 11.

BURR, STEPHEN [ARTIST]
— winner of LahainaTown poster competition, Lahaina News, October 31, 1991: 13.
— to exhibit at Lahaina Cannery Mall Village Gallery, Lahaina News, January 13, 1994: 8.
— to exhibit at Lahaina Cannery Mall village Gallery, Lahaina News, January 20, 1994: 11.
— to exhibit, Lahaina News, January 5, 1995: 12.
— to exhibit at Village Galleries Maui, Lahaina News, April 19, 2001: 17.
— to exhibit at Village Galleries, Lahaina News, April 18, 2002: 16.
— to exhibit at Village Galleries, Lahaina News, April 17, 2003: 16.

BURRELL, KENNY [MUSICIAN]
— to perform at Maui Arts and Cultural Center, Lahaina News, April 30, 1998: 17.

BURTON, C.J. [MUSICIAN]
— to perform at Embassy Suites Resort, Lahaina News, July 11, 1996: 13.
— to perform at Embassy Suites Resort, Lahaina News, August 29, 1996: 12.

BURTON, HENRY
— engineer discusses pollution at Wailuku Sugar mill, Lahaina Sun, November 25, 1970: 4.

BUSES
— new buses introduced to Lahaina and Ka'anapali, Lahaina Sun, May 26, 1971: 5.
— need for local bus system discussed, Lahaina Sun, November 29, 1972: 13.
— Jack Edwards' attempt to operate two buses detailed, Lahaina Sun, January 3, 1973: 11.
— recommended in Wailuku-Kahului plan, Lahaina Sun, January 24, 1973: 1.
— Joe Souki urges that buses for elderly remain in operation, Lahaina Sun, March 7, 1973: 5.
— reconstructed 1925 Packard touring bus being used by Lahaina Restoration Foundation, Lahaina Sun, March 21, 1973: 3.
— Jack Edwards granted permission to run buses Wailuku to Kahului and from Wailuku to Lahaina, Lahaina Sun, April 18, 1973: 3.
— still not in operation, Lahaina Sun, May 23, 1973: 4.
— back in service after being seized by the Internal Revenue Service, Lahaina Sun, May 30, 1973: 3.
— off to a quiet start, Lahaina Sun, June 6, 1973: 18.
— Gray Line bus crashes, Lahaina Sun, June 6, 1973: 19.
— proposal to restrict tour buses in front of Pioneer Inn, Lahaina Sun, July 25, 1973: 3.
— new buses for senior citizens arrive, Lahaina News, May 1, 1980: 14.
— state representative David Morihara asks the county if school bus system could be used for mass transit, Lahaina News, September 26, 1991: 1,3.
— funding sought by residents, Lahaina News, October 23, 1997: 1,2.
— E Noa Corporation running trolley service between South and West Maui, Lahaina News, October 30, 1997: 13.
— new system to begin, Lahaina News, August 29, 2002: 2,9.
— new system to begin, Lahaina News, September 5, 2002: 8.
— see also Shoreline Transportation

BUSH [MUSICAL GROUP]
— to perform, Lahaina News, October 2, 1997: 21.
— to perform at Maui Arts and Cultural Center, Lahaina News, November 13, 1997: 21.

BUSH, GEORGE H.W. [POLITICIAN]
— U.S. President designates Volunteer Action Division as a point of light, Lahaina News, December 26, 1990: 5.
— president recognizes Ka'anapali Beach Hotel as 648th Daily Point of Light, Lahaina News, January 2, 1992: 5.
— honors Ka'anapali Beach Hotel as a point of light, Lahaina News, January 14, 1993: 2.

BUSINESS
— Japanese investors visit West Maui, Lahaina Sun, February 3, 1971: 7.
— Japanese investors visit West Maui, Lahaina Sun, February 3, 1971: 7.
— Bank of Hawaii office opens in Whaler's Village, Lahaina Sun, March 10, 1971: 7.
— Chuck's Steak House opening in July, Lahaina Sun, March 24, 1971: 2.
— Japanese executives who control travel agency business in Japan to visit Maui, Lahaina Sun, April 21, 1971: 1.
— co-op gas station opening in Makawao, Lahaina Sun, June 23, 1971: 3.
— State of Hawaii streamlines loan application procedure for businesses affected by dock strike, Lahaina Sun, September 29, 1971: 15.
— Hawaii Wood Preserving Company given permission to build wood treating plant in Kahului, Lahaina Sun, October 27, 1971: 5.
— the first Longs in Maui opens at the Maui Mall in Kahului, Lahaina Sun, December 8, 1971: 16.
— Maui Eldorado Management Corporation files for bankruptcy, Lahaina Sun, June 7, 1972: 4.
— possible future discussed, Lahaina Sun, June 13, 1973: 20.
— shopping centers in Lahaina described, Lahaina News, September, 1979: 2.
— conditions in September-October, Lahaina Times, October, 1980 volume 4 number 9: 1.
— impact of holidays on restaurants reported, Lahaina News, January 15, 1981: 5.
— improved in Lahaina, Lahaina News, November 1, 1982: 2.
— businesses evicted from old Baldwin Packers Cannery, Lahaina News, February 1, 1983: 4.
— evictions from old Baldwin Packers Cannery delayed, Lahaina News, February 15, 1983: 10.
— poll suggests Hawaii does not make it easy for business, Lahaina News, April 15, 1983: 15.
— discussion of tipping, Lahaina Times, August 20, 1983 volume 7 number 8: 2.
— governor's committee claims Hawaii unsympathetic to, Lahaina News, February 8, 1984: 16.
— editorial discussing future of on Maui, Lahaina News, February 22, 1984: 2.
— potential impact of general strike of Hawaii's public workers detailed, Lahaina News, February 22, 1984: 3.
— request made to increase number of liquor licenses in Lahaina, Lahaina News, February 29, 1984: 17.
— Konokowai-Napili-Kapaha taxpayers meet, Lahaina News, March 7, 1984: 4.
— sports contributed $6 million to Maui economy in 1983, Lahaina News, March 7, 1984: 4,5.
— editorial complaint against posters, Lahaina News, March 21, 1984: 8.
— Hawaiian Electric Industries to meet with shareholders, Lahaina News, April 18, 1984: 17.
— editorial responding to Hawaii labelled "purgatory" for business, Lahaina News, June 20, 1984: 2.
— editorial on Robert Pfeiffer, president of Alexander & Baldwin, calling Maui the most anti-business county in Hawaii, Lahaina News, September 19, 1984: 2.
— editorial on speaking "Hawaiian Business", Lahaina News, February 27, 1985: 1.
— changes detailed, Lahaina News, April 10, 1985: 1,7.
— Harry Weinberg plans for fast food, fast gas shopping plaza limited, Lahaina News, May 15, 1985: 1.
— Maui Community College offering non-credit class on the financial health of your business, Lahaina News, July 3, 1985: 3.

— beach concession in front of Lahaina Shores Shopping Center purchased by Jack and Marcia Seabern, Lahaina News, August 14, 1985: 3.

— realtor firms Jack Huddleston, Inc. and Maui Realty, Inc. merging, to be called Maui Realty, Co., Lahaina News, August 21, 1985: 3.

— businesses using Kaʻanapali Beach fined for peddling in an unlawful area, Lahaina News, September 4, 1985: 3,8.

— editorial warning of the decline of sugar, Lahaina News, October 2, 1985: 2.

— Maui product mail-order catalog printed, Lahaina News, October 16, 1985: 20.

— new businesses listed, Lahaina News, November 13, 1985: 11.

— the process of using a travel agent described, Lahaina News, January 1, 1986: 7.

— video rental companies pull x-rated videos, Lahaina News, February 12, 1986: 1,16.

— Hawaii Capital Loan Program offering loans to small businesses, Lahaina News, March 26, 1986: 3.

— speculation on oldest business in Lahaina, likely Pioneer Mill, Lahaina News, April 9, 1986: 6.

— editorial supporting Pacific Business News' criticism of business developments on Maui, Lahaina News, April 16, 1986: 2.

— Wholesale Produce Dealers Association of Hawaii admits to price fixing, Lahaina News, April 23, 1986: 2.

— editorial urging high school graduates to go into business, warns of difficulties, Lahaina News, May 28, 1986: 2.

— conditional zoning to allow a furniture store on Lahainaluna Road, Lahaina News, May 28, 1986: 3.

— "Great Lahaina Reunion" planned for former plantation workers, Lahaina News, June 25, 1986: 1.

— High Tech park planned for Kihei, Lahaina News, July 2, 1986: 18.

— sales are up for Front Street businesses, Lahaina News, October 8, 1986: 1,16.

— editorial on new businesses opening, Lahaina News, January 14, 1987: 2.

— club to support mayor's Motion Picture Coordination Committee formed, Lahaina News, January 28, 1987: 3.

— "neighborhood businesses" may be allowed in Lahaina Community Plan, Lahaina News, February 25, 1987: 20.

— investment seminar offered at Lahaina Civic Center, Lahaina News, April 1, 1987: 3.

— Harry Weinberg's Lahaina shopping complex nears completion, Lahaina News, September 30, 1987: 3.

— Joanna Jeronomo to offer workshop on power selling, Lahaina News, February 15, 1989: 3.

— rental spaces limited in Lahaina, Lahaina News, June 7, 1989: 1.

— Lahaina News offering free advertising space to promote jobs for youths, Lahaina News, June 7, 1989: 7.

— seminar offered on negotiating with business people from Japan, Lahaina News, June 14, 1989: 7.

— West Maui may face labor shortage, Lahaina News, September 20, 1989: 1.

— advice on resolving appliance disputes, Lahaina News, November 29, 1989: 16.

— consumer hotline created, Lahaina News, December 6, 1989: 3.

— Small Business Hawaii Conference to held with theme "Small Business in the '90s", Lahaina News, December 20, 1989: 4.

— new rules on sale of "penny stocks" now in effect, Lahaina News, January 3, 1990: 4.

— classes on investment to be offered, Lahaina News, January 31, 1990: 5.

— Maui Community College to offer business training classes, Lahaina News, April 4, 1990: 7.

— Bank of Hawaii sponsoring small business seminar, Lahaina News, June 6, 1990: 5.

— "Consumer Watch" column begins, only West Maui entries are typically indexed, Lahaina News, August 8, 1990: 9.

— complaints about car rental insurance frequent, Lahaina News, August 22, 1990: 5.

— Wyland mural causes controversy as potential advertisement, Lahaina News, January 30, 1991: 1,3.

— small business conference to be held at Maui Inter-Continental Wailea, Lahaina News, June 13, 1991: 10.

— accounting offices move location, Lahaina News, June 13, 1991: 10.

— Hawaii Federation of Business and Professional Women's Clubs to honor local, Lahaina News, October 17, 1991: 9.

— Royal Lahaina to offer customer service seminar, Lahaina News, October 24, 1991: 9.

— Royal Lahaina to offer customer service seminar, Lahaina News, October 31, 1991: 10.

— new businesses listed, Lahaina News, December 26, 1991: 8.

— fruit stand in Haiku permitted to sell sundries, Lahaina News, January 23, 1992: 5.

— Business and Environment Conference to be held, Lahaina News, March 5, 1992: 9.

— price of light industrial space to remain high, Lahaina News, March 26, 1992: 12.

— pizza restaurants compete, Lahaina News, April 16, 1992: 13.

— "Pulling Through the 90s" conference for small businesses to be held, Lahaina News, July 2, 1992: 17.

— Maui Research and Technology Park designated as foreign trade zone, Lahaina News, July 2, 1992: 7.

— merchants annoyed at tour guides leading tourists to stores that "grease the palm" of the drivers, Lahaina News, August 13, 1992: 12.

— hotel employment expected to jump, Lahaina News, September 24, 1992: 8.

— restaurant revenues up 20% in Lahaina, Lahaina News, October 8, 1992: 8.

— seminar on Japan and tourism to be held, Lahaina News, October 22, 1992: 10.

— Dain Bosworth Money Manager Symposium to be held, Lahaina News, November 19, 1992: 5.

— Georja Skinner sees increase in film industry, Lahaina News, December 3, 1992: 4.

— census to be filled out by, Lahaina News, December 10, 1992: 10.

— Lahaina Town Bazaar cited for allowing vendors to do business in parking lot, Lahaina News, December 17, 1992: 1,2.

— fiber optic complex to be built on Maui, Lahaina News, December 17, 1992: 8.

— hotels expect slow year, Lahaina News, December 31, 1992: 10.

— interest rates expected to rise, Lahaina News, January 7, 1993: 6.

— Hawaiian Insurance and Guaranty Company (HIG) can resume paying workers compensation benefits, Lahaina News, January 7, 1993: 7.

— Jim Channon consulting to offer "Visualization Your Strategy", Lahaina News, February 4, 1993: 9.

— mild recovery predicted, Lahaina News, February 25, 1993: 6.

— Davis-Bacon Act to be suspended, Lahaina News, March 4, 1993: 8,12.

— Communications Techniques unlimited to hold seminar "Satisfying Difficult Customers", Lahaina News, March 25, 1993: 10.

— Maui Job Service Employer committee to host seminar on labor law, Lahaina News, March 25, 1993: 11.

— Maui Chamber of Commerce to host marketing seminar, Lahaina News, April 15, 1993: 7.

— "Pulling Through the '90s" conference to be held at Maui Inter-Continental Resort, Lahaina News, May 6, 1993: 8,9.

— marketing seminars offered by Maui Chamber of Commerce, Lahaina News, May 13, 1993: 5.

— new officers named by various companies, Lahaina News, May 20, 1993: 7.

— county to begin enforcing codes in Lahaina Historic District, Lahaina News, June 3, 1993: 7.

— Made in Maui display at Wailea Shopping Village, Lahaina News, June 17, 1993: 12.
— small business and marketing workshops to be held, Lahaina News, June 17, 1993: 12.
— law to ban sale of activities below cost to deter timeshares, Lahaina News, July 1, 1993: 1,12.
— small town economic development conference to be held, Lahaina News, July 15, 1993: 6.
— marketing seminar offered by Maui Chamber of Commerce, Lahaina News, July 22, 1993: 7.
— tourism revenues slump in Lahaina, Lahaina News, August 5, 1993: 1,12.
— Strategic Positioning Analysis seminar to be held, Lahaina News, August 19, 1993: 13.
— timeshare booths continue to be criticized, Lahaina News, August 26, 1993: 1,5.
— adopting aloha spirit; some capitalizing on native culture and hospitality, Lahaina News, August 26, 1993: 9.
— lack of parking affects consumer spending, Lahaina News, September 9, 1993: 6.
— Chamber of Commerce of Hawaii publishes manual on Labor and Employment Law, Lahaina News, September 16, 1993: 9,10.
— sidewalk sales pitches to be banned, Lahaina News, September 23, 1993: 1,12.
— telephone marketing seminar to be offered, Lahaina News, September 23, 1993: 7.
— "Marketing Magic" seminar to be held, Lahaina News, October 21, 1993: 11.
— Hawaii employers owe record amount of back pay, Lahaina News, October 21, 1993: 11.
— Lahaina Historic District fines to be assessed for cheap signage and roving salespeople, Lahaina News, October 21, 1993: 5.
— Wailea Shopping Center to host "Made in Maui" display, Lahaina News, October 21, 1993: 8.
— Prudential Securities found to have duped Hawaii investors, Lahaina News, October 28, 1993: 7.
— Hawaii Chamber of Commerce seeking to reduce cost to workers compensation, Lahaina News, January 27, 1994: 5.
— Phoenix Organizational Consulting Services announces search for "Most Disorganized Home Office on Maui" announces search for "Most Disorganized Home Office on Maui", Lahaina News, January 27, 1994: 5.
— hotels in Maui stay out of discount wars, Lahaina News, February 3, 1994: 6.
— West Maui Committee of the Chamber of Commerce to host seminar "Staying Alive Until '85", Lahaina News, February 17, 1994: 6.
— micro breweries may be opening soon, Lahaina News, February 24, 1994: 10.
— unemployment rate drops, Lahaina News, February 24, 1994: 10.
— Department of Occupational Safety reminds employers to post OSHA form, Lahaina News, February 24, 1994: 10.
— ban on street vending still unresolved, Lahaina News, April 7, 1994: 1,16.
— Maui County negotiating with One World, One Family t-shirt vendor, Lahaina News, April 21, 1994: 1,20.
— state and insurance companies at odds over proposed insurance bill, Lahaina News, April 28, 1994: 2.
— debate over Hawaii Hurricane Relief Fund will affect residential insurance, Lahaina News, May 5, 1994: 1,6.
— Cultural Resources Committee to hold hearing on t-shirt venders in historic district, Lahaina News, May 12, 1994: 1,3.
— Americans with Disabilities Act may not be expensive to implement, Lahaina News, June 2, 1994: 10.
— stock investment options discussed, Lahaina News, June 16, 1994: 10.

— Governor John Waihee signs "flawed" occupational safety bills, Lahaina News, June 23, 1994: 10.
— hotel liability law passes, Lahaina News, June 30, 1994: 4.
— issue of t-shirt vending goes to Maui County Council, Lahaina News, July 14, 1994: 5.
— crackdown on tour boat industry, Lahaina News, July 21, 1994: 7.
— proposal to increase number of liquor licenses, Lahaina News, July 28, 1994: 8.
— representative Avery Chumbley discusses how government can help small businesses, Lahaina News, August 4, 1994: 8.
— directory of international business being developed by state Department of Business, Economic Development and Tourism, Lahaina News, August 4, 1994: 8.
— Made in Maui outlet opens, Lahaina News, August 4, 1994: 8,9.
— seminar to be offered on labor law, Lahaina News, August 4, 1994: 9.
— jobless rate jumps, Lahaina News, August 18, 1994: 9.
— merchant Tom Lilledal not happy about proposed improvements to Front Street, Lahaina News, September 8, 1994: 1,7.
— wage and hour laws seen as minefield to employers, Lahaina News, September 8, 1994: 10.
— ocean industries seen as viable for Maui, Lahaina News, September 15, 1994: 13.
— offering crime prevention seminars, Lahaina News, September 29, 1994: 10.
— smoke-free workplace supported, Lahaina News, November 3, 1994: 22.
— Maui County Council forming a panel to investigate possible vending areas, Lahaina News, December 8, 1994: 7.
— kiosk space opening in Kahana Gateway, Lahaina News, January 5, 1995: 6.
— Phoenix Organizational Consulting Service to hold "In Search for the Most Disorganized Home Office on Maui", Lahaina News, January 12, 1995: 6.
— strip mall proposed near Dickenson Street, Lahaina News, February 2, 1995: 1.
— Kihei rental and office space opens, Lahaina News, February 2, 1995: 7.
— importance of work relationships discussed, Lahaina News, February 9, 1995: 6.
— Ka'anapali hotels except increase in tourism in 1995, Lahaina News, February 23, 1995: 6.
— workshop on "Starting a Venture in Hawaii" to be held, Lahaina News, March 2, 1995: 7.
— women's clubs offering "Financial Planning for Women", Lahaina News, March 16, 1995: 10.
— Small Business Development Center offering "Developing Business Plans and Proposals" workshop, Lahaina News, April 13, 1995: 12.
— new noise rules may keep bar music off streets, Lahaina News, April 13, 1995: 3.
— new regulations affecting bars, Lahaina News, April 27, 1995: 10.
— film and television prospects for Maui look good, Lahaina News, May 4, 1995: 12.
— success of wedding industry discussed, Lahaina News, May 4, 1995: 13.
— Labor Law Employer Seminar to be held , Lahaina News, May 18, 1995: 6.
— State Securities Commissioner orders Sasha international Trading Co. to cease and desist investment scam, Lahaina News, May 18, 1995: 6.
— Maui Chamber of Commerce to hold forum on worker's compensation, Lahaina News, May 25, 1995: 10.
— officials want billboards kept off the roads, Lahaina News, July 6, 1995: 2.
— Maui County may do away with accessory use permits for commercial boat operators at Ka'anapali Beach, Lahaina News, July 20, 1995: 1.

— Smart Shopper details, Lahaina News, July 9, 1998: 6.

— companies make Pacific Business News "Fastest 50 List", Lahaina News, August 6, 1998: 17.

— Governor Ben Cayetano announces search for Hawaii's best exporter, Lahaina News, August 6, 1998: 17.

— smart shopper details, Lahaina News, August 13, 1998: 6,7.

— Judy McCorkle to offer workshop on financial planning, Lahaina News, September 3, 1998: 11.

— report from State of Hawaii explores retailing in Hawaii, Lahaina News, October 1, 1998: 13.

— Maui Research and Technology Center to host business evaluation workshop, Lahaina News, October 8, 1998: 13.

— "Starting a Venture in Hawaii" to be held at Maui Research and Technology Center, Lahaina News, November 12, 1998: 13.

— Jerry MacDonald reflects on restaurant business in Lahaina, Lahaina News, December 24, 1998: 1,16.

— Maui Research and Technology Center to host "Increasing Value While Cutting Cost" workshop, Lahaina News, February 18, 1999: 11.

— Business Recycling workshop to be held, Lahaina News, February 18, 1999: 13.

— Business Recycling Workshop to be held, Lahaina News, March 18, 1999: 13.

— Maui Research and Technology Center to host "Creating Winning Business Plans and Loan Proposals" workshop, Lahaina News, April 1, 1999: 13.

— Maui Retailer of the Year nominations sought, Lahaina News, April 8, 1999: 11.

— overview of launching business in Hawai'i to be held, Lahaina News, April 15, 1999: 11.

— course on restaurant management to be offered by Maui Chamber of Commerce, Lahaina News, April 15, 1999: 11.

— "Increasing Value While Cutting Costs" workshop to be held at Maui Research and Technology Center, Lahaina News, April 22, 1999: 11.

— course on restaurant management to be offered by Maui Chamber of Commerce, Lahaina News, April 29, 1999: 13.

— workshop to cover ADA for businesses, Lahaina News, May 13, 1999: 13.

— workshops held on ADA, Lahaina News, May 20, 1999: 13.

— Maui Community College to host "Creating Winning Business Plans and Loan Proposals", Lahaina News, May 27, 1999: 11.

— "How to Become a More Effective Supervisor" training to be held, Lahaina News, May 27, 1999: 11.

— "Get Free Press" training to be held, Lahaina News, May 27, 1999: 11.

— Junior Achievement program success, Lahaina News, May 27, 1999: 11.

— "How to Become a More Effective Supervisor" training to be held, Lahaina News, June 3, 1999: 13.

— International Council of Shopping Centers to be held, Lahaina News, July 1, 1999: 11.

— Hawaii Hotel and Restaurant Expo to be held at Blaisdell Center, Lahaina News, July 1, 1999: 11.

— introduction to the Baldridge Criteria, Lahaina News, July 22, 1999: 11.

— "Creativity in Business" workshop to be held, Lahaina News, August 5, 1999: 11.

— "Starting a Venture in Hawaii" workshop to be offered, Lahaina News, August 19, 1999: 13.

— Labor Law Employer Seminar to be held, Lahaina News, September 2, 1999: 13.

— "Developing Fast Growth Ventures" workshop to be held, Lahaina News, September 9, 1999: 11.

— Pacific Island business leaders to speak at "The Role of Business Associations in Pacific Island Economic Growth", Lahaina News, October 7, 1999: 13.

— "Preparing Maui for the Future" to be held, Lahaina News, October 7, 1999: 13.

— The Restaurant Service Professional classes, Lahaina News, October 14, 1999: 11.

— "Using Common Sense In Your Defense Against Costly Litigation" to discuss Americans with Disabilities Act and Fair Housing regulations, Lahaina News, October 28, 1999: 15.

— "Developing Fast-Growth Ventures" to be held at Maui Community College, Lahaina News, October 28, 1999: 17.

— Maui Pacific Center to host "The Role of Business Associations in Pacific Island Economic Growth", Lahaina News, November 4, 1999: 11.

— workshop on "Creating Winning Business Plans and Loan Proposals", Lahaina News, November 25, 1999: 13.

— local businesses begin Loyalty Card Program, Lahaina News, November 25, 1999: 13.

— "Creating Winning Business Plans and Loan Proposals" workshop to be held at Maui Community College, Lahaina News, February 3, 2000: 11.

— vendor ban sought on Laalo Street following child's death, Lahaina News, February 24, 2000: 1,2.

— Maui Community College to host "Quality is Free" business workshop, Lahaina News, March 23, 2000: 12.

— "Creating Winning Business Plans and Loan Proposals" workshop to be held at Maui Community College, Lahaina News, April 6, 2000: 16.

— "Starting a Venture in Hawaii" workshop to be held, Lahaina News, April 20, 2000: 17.

— "Restaurant Waste Minimization and Pollution Prevention Training" to be held, Lahaina News, April 27, 2000: 11.

— Valley Isle Motors president James Falk II receives Maui County's 2000 Entrepreneurial Success Award, Lahaina News, June 1, 2000: 14.

— Hawaii Technology Trade Association to launch Maui Chapter, Lahaina News, June 15, 2000: 14.

— Maui Community College to host "Getting Organized for Quality", Lahaina News, June 15, 2000: 14.

— advice for online investors, Lahaina News, June 15, 2000: 14.

— venture capitalists to speak at Investors Choice International Equity Conference, Lahaina News, June 15, 2000: 17.

— "Starting a Venture in Hawaii" workshop to be held, Lahaina News, June 22, 2000: 8.

— "Getting Organized for Quality" workshop to be held, Lahaina News, June 22, 2000: 9.

— nominations open for "2000 Governor's Exporter of the Year", Lahaina News, June 22, 2000: 9.

— "Starting a Venture in Hawaii" workshop to be held, Lahaina News, July 20, 2000: 14.

— Frank Ballestros to discuss micro-enterprises, Lahaina News, August 31, 2000: 1.

— "Starting a Venture in Hawaii" workshop to be held, Lahaina News, October 12, 2000: 16.

— "Starting a Venture in Hawaii" workshop to be held, Lahaina News, October 19, 2000: 16.

— Labor Law Employer Seminar to be held, Lahaina News, November 2, 2000: 12.

— commercial real estate discussed, Lahaina News, November 9, 2000: 17.

— jobless rate remains unchanged, Lahaina News, November 9, 2000: 18.

— "Business Plans Made Easy" to be held at Maui Community College, Lahaina News, November 30, 2000: 12.

— state awarding economic development grants, Lahaina News, November 30, 2000: 12.

— Kim Spangler to offer "The Secrets of Investing in a Chaotic Market", Lahaina News, March 15, 2001: 8.

— "Starting a Venture in Hawaii" to be held at Maui Community College, Lahaina News, March 22, 2001: 8.
— results of survey of small businesses, Lahaina News, April 19, 2001: 8.
— nominations being accepted for "Governor's Exporter of the Year" awards, Lahaina News, May 24, 2001: 8.
— miser for entrepreneurs to be held at Westin Maui, Lahaina News, June 21, 2001: 9.
— "Retirement Planning for Young Adults" to be held, Lahaina News, July 5, 2001: 9.
— Maui Made Product Show to be held at Lahaina Cannery Mall, Lahaina News, July 26, 2001: 17.
— Maui Community College to hold "Create Business Plans and Proposals", Lahaina News, September 20, 2001: 9.
— North American Securities Administrators Association offers tips for online investing, Lahaina News, September 20, 2001: 9.
— investment opportunities discussed, Lahaina News, October 18, 2001: 8.
— "Starting a Venture in Hawaii", Lahaina News, November 1, 2001: 8.
— Maui merchants offering products online, Lahaina News, November 1, 2001: 8.
— Janis Casco and Valentina Stewart Watson to hold "The Tax Relief Act of 2001" seminar, Lahaina News, December 6, 2001: 8.
— "Starting a Venture in Hawaii" workshop to be authored, Lahaina News, January 10, 2002: 8.
— retail space in Lahaina available, Lahaina News, January 31, 2002: 7.
— Maui Executives Association welcoming new members, Lahaina News, January 31, 2002: 8.
— West Maui businesses win 2002 Keep It Hawai'i award, Lahaina News, April 18, 2002: 1,5.
— Securities Industry Association releases guide to account statements, Lahaina News, May 9, 2002: 8.
— "Fund-raising Basics: How to Create or Expand an Individual Donor Base" to be offered by Hawai'i Community Foundation, Lahaina News, July 11, 2002: 9.
— Maui Young Business Roundtable to meet, Lahaina News, July 25, 2002: 9.
— "Doing Your Business Better" conference to be held, Lahaina News, September 26, 2002: 8.
— "Doing Your Business Better" conference to be held, Lahaina News, October 3, 2002: 8.
— merchants to "West Maui Business Pau Hana", Lahaina News, October 24, 2002: 21.
— Maui Young Business Roundtable seeking members, Lahaina News, January 16, 2003: 8.
— Leighton Chong to discuss product licensing, Lahaina News, February 20, 2003: 8.
— class to cover tax incentives, Lahaina News, February 20, 2003: 9.
— Lynne Woods offering class on office etiquette, Lahaina News, March 13, 2003: 8.
— "Starting a Venture in Hawaii" to be held, Lahaina News, March 20, 2003: 8.
— Department of Business, Economic Development and Tourism launches website to support, Lahaina News, April 24, 2003: 14.
— seminar to focus on labor law, Lahaina News, May 15, 2003: 8.
— workshop on intellectual property and patent to be held at Maui Economic Opportunity, Lahaina News, May 15, 2003: 8.
— quiz released to help consumers avoid financial fraud, Lahaina News, May 15, 2003: 8.
— seminar to focus on labor law, Lahaina News, May 22, 2003: 8.
— Governor Linda Lingle announces search for Hawaii's best exporters, Lahaina News, June 5, 2003: 8.

BUSINESS AFTER HOURS
— to be held at Bailey House Museum, Lahaina News, May 9, 1990: 8.

BUSINESS AND ENVIRONMENT CONFERENCE
— theme is "Moving Toward Sustainability", Lahaina News, March 12, 1992: 12.

BUSINESS AND INDUSTRIAL DEVELOPMENT SERVICES
— Maui Community College to offer non-credit business classes, Lahaina News, January 2, 1991: 5.
— to offer business classes, Lahaina News, January 16, 1991: 5.

BUSINESS AND PROFESSIONAL WOMEN'S CLUBS OF MAUI
— to present fashion show, Lahaina News, February 8, 1984: 16.
— sponsoring working entitled "We Get What We Settle For!", Lahaina News, November 14, 1984: 3.
— installs new officers, Lahaina News, June 11, 1986: 3.
— Maui chapter hosting luncheon on "Women in Transition", Lahaina News, October 25, 1989: 10.
— to hold fashion show for educational scholarships, Lahaina News, November 15, 1989: 9.
— to hold meeting, Lahaina News, January 17, 1990: 4.
— hosting competition for young Maui careerists, Lahaina News, March 14, 1990: 6.
— to hold Young Careerist Competition, Lahaina News, February 20, 1991: 7.
— seeking competitors for Young Careerist Competition, Lahaina News, February 27, 1991: 4.
— Alicia Ann Davis wins Young Careerist Competition, Lahaina News, April 17, 1991: 9.
— to celebrate National Business Women's Week, Lahaina News, October 5, 1995: 4.
— to hold meeting, Lahaina News, July 11, 1996: 13.
— offering Maui Young Careerist Program, Lahaina News, August 22, 1996: 5.
— accepting applications for scholarships, Lahaina News, April 3, 1997: 10.
— recognizes scholarship recipients, Lahaina News, June 19, 1997: 6.
— E. Moani Machado wins first place in competition, Lahaina News, July 17, 1997: 13.
— to host youth competition , Lahaina News, August 28, 1997: 12.
— Young Careerist Competition to be held, Lahaina News, July 30, 1998: 13.
— presenting "Dispelling the Myths—Women and Depression", Lahaina News, September 17, 1998: 13.
— holds annual Scholarship Fashion Show, Lahaina News, November 5, 1998: 17.
— to hold Scholarship Fashion Show, Lahaina News, November 12, 1998: 13.
— accepting applications for scholarships, Lahaina News, February 25, 1999: 11.
— to hold "Getting Somewheres" luncheon, Lahaina News, March 18, 1999: 13.
— to hold "Getting Somewheres" luncheon, Lahaina News, March 25, 1999: 13.
— offering Maui Young Careerist Program, Lahaina News, September 2, 1999: 13.
— seeking applicants for Maui Youth Careerist Program, Lahaina News, September 9, 1999: 11.
— Scholarship Fashion Show and Luncheon to be held, Lahaina News, November 18, 1999: 13.
— organizing "2000 Maui Young Careerist Program", Lahaina News, August 31, 2000: 14.
— to hold Maui Young Careerist Program, Lahaina News, September 21, 2000: 16.
— celebrates 60 years, Lahaina News, August 21, 2003: 9.

BUSINESS AND THE ENVIRONMENT, CONFERENCE
— to be held, sponsored by Maui Inc. Magazine and others, Lahaina News, February 6, 1991: 7.

BUSINESS, ECONOMIC DEVELOPMENT AND TOURISM, STATE DEPARTMENT OF
— offering training program with Pacific Imaging Center, Lahaina News, August 4, 1994: 9.
— wraps up plans for Foreign Trade Zone for proposed state convention center, Lahaina News, August 18, 1994: 9.
— state Data Book and disk is available, Lahaina News, September 15, 1994: 13.
— publishes "State of Hawaii Data Book 2000", Lahaina News, November 1, 2001: 8.
— offering loan program in response to September 11th, Lahaina News, December 20, 2001: 9.
— seeks input on Sustainable Tourism Study, Lahaina News, September 26, 2002: 8.
— state seeking input for Sustainable Tourism Study, Lahaina News, October 3, 2002: 8.
— to hold workshop on ethanol, Lahaina News, November 7, 2002: 8.
— offering funding for community-based economic development, Lahaina News, November 7, 2002: 9.
— launches new website, Lahaina News, April 24, 2003: 14.

BUSINESS EDUCATION ALERT TRAINING (BEAT)
— police hold lecture on lesser-known laws, Lahaina News, March 2, 1995: 3.
— summarized, Lahaina News, April 6, 1995: 2.
— moving to Ka'anapali, Lahaina News, April 27, 1995: 3.
— trainings continue at Hyatt Regency, Lahaina News, May 4, 1995: 5.
— to begin again in mid-August, Lahaina News, July 20, 1995: 5.

BUSINESS EXPO AND FOOD FAIR
— to be held, Lahaina News, May 16, 1990: 6.
— to be held by Maui Chamber of Commerce, Lahaina News, May 30, 1990: 6.
— to be held by Maui Chamber of Commerce, Lahaina News, April 16, 1992: 15.

BUSINESS RECYCLING WORKSHOP
— to be held, Lahaina News, March 11, 1999: 11.
— to be held, Lahaina News, April 8, 1999: 11.

BUSINESS TRAINING PROGRAM
— Pat Nelson to present workshops at Maui Community College, Lahaina News, October 31, 1990: 12.

BUSSARD, CHRISTY
— swimming coach featured, Lahaina News, October 20, 1994: 8.

BUTIHI, ROSHELLE
— Scholar/Athlete of the Week, Lahaina News, September 19, 2002: 12.

BUTLER, CHRIS
— Jagad Guru to speak, Lahaina News, December 25, 1985: 3.

BUTLER, GERARD
— retired Speakers Bureau Director for Pan American Airways featured, Lahaina News, April 12, 1989: 2.

BUTLER, GRANT [WRITER]
— appointed Lahaina District director for Maui United Way, Lahaina News, April 11, 1990: 3.
— to speak on world affairs, Lahaina News, May 13, 1993: 3.
— reflects on career, Lahaina News, March 12, 1998: 1,17.
— to speak at International Lecture Forum in Washington, Lahaina News, December 31, 1998: 3.
— to be recognized by Lahaina Rotary Club, Lahaina News, January 13, 2000: 3.
— recognized by Rotary Club of Lahaina for service, Lahaina News, September 12, 2002: 2.

BUTRICK, LARRY
— Maui's drug prosecutor discusses problems, Lahaina News, January 18, 1989: 1,20.
— to head County's Prosecuting Attorney's Office, Lahaina News, April 17, 1991: 7.

— confirmed as head of Maui County's Prosecuting Attorney's Office, Lahaina News, June 6, 1991: 3.
— sworn in as Prosecuting Attorney, Lahaina News, July 18, 1991: 4.
— Maui County Prosecutor says prosecuting homicides is first priority, Lahaina News, January 9, 1992: 1.

BUTTELING, ROY
— named accounts director at Ritz-Carlton, Lahaina News, July 10, 2003: 8.

BUTTERFLY HULA
— exhibit to be held at Lahaina Arts Society, Lahaina News, February 4, 1999: 16.

BUTTWINICK, ED AND LINDA
— consulting on proposed Art School at Kapalua, Lahaina News, March 31, 1994: 2.

BUZZ'S WHARF [RESTAURANT]
— reviewed, Lahaina News, June 14, 1989: 15.
— featured, Lahaina News, November 22, 1989: 13.
— new menu, Lahaina News, May 1, 1997: 1,6,7.

BYE BYE BIRDIE [MUSICAL]
— to be performed by Maui Youth Theatre, Lahaina News, March 14, 1990: 3.
— cast selected, Lahaina News, April 11, 1990: 15.
— to begin next week, Lahaina News, April 18, 1990: 11.
— to open, Lahaina News, April 25, 1990: 15.

BYPASS
— see Lahaina Bypass

BYRDS OF PARADISE, THE [TELEVISION SHOW]
— producer Steven Bachco to cast, Lahaina News, September 16, 1993: 17.

BYRON VINEYARD AND WINERY [BUSINESS]
— to be featured at Prince Court, Lahaina News, February 20, 1991: 11.

C

C. BREWER HOMES, INC. [BUSINESS]
— plans to develop below Wailuku Heights, Lahaina News, February 27, 1991: supplement7.
— proposed planned community approved, Lahaina News, May 7, 1992: 6.
— homes in Wailuku built by set to open in 1993, Lahaina News, June 25, 1992: 16.
— to permit access to Lahaina Trail, Lahaina News, August 6, 1992: 9.
— earnings increased, Lahaina News, July 28, 1994: 9.
— creates sales force for The Villages of Leiali'i, Lahaina News, September 15, 1994: 13.
— issues with Villages of Leiali'i continue, Lahaina News, December 29, 1994: 1,3.
— Rod Gilliland joins, Lahaina News, January 26, 1995: 13.
— ruling expected soon on ceded land intended for housing project, Lahaina News, March 23, 1995: 2.
— holds Mother's Day, Lahaina News, June 27, 1996: 12.

C. JOELLE [ARTIST]
— to demonstrate printmaking, Lahaina News, April 26, 2001: 20.

C.J. CHENIER AND THE RED HOT LOUISIANA BAND [MUSICAL GROUP]
— to perform at Maui Arts and Cultural Center, Lahaina News, November 27, 1997: 13.

CABACUNGAN, DENISE
— named Host of the Year at Westin Maui, Lahaina News, September 26, 1990: 9.

CABACUNGAN, RODERICK
— mayor Hannibal Tavares awards certificate of merit to, Lahaina News, September 10, 1986: 3.

CABAIS, JERRY
— new front manager at The Mahana, Lahaina News, May 8, 2003: 8.

CABANA, MATTHEW
— graduates from Navy's Basic Nuclear Power School, Lahaina News, March 7, 2002: 5.

CABANILLA SHELL [BUSINESS]
— closing, Lahaina News, September 30, 1999: 1.

CABARET [MUSICAL]
— to be performed by Maui Community Theatre, Lahaina News, January 23, 1991: 4.
— to be performed by Maui Community Theatre, Lahaina News, March 6, 1991: 17.
— being performed by Maui Community Theatre, Lahaina News, March 13, 1991: 14.
— opens Friday, plot summarized, Lahaina News, March 20, 1991: 11.
— continues, Lahaina News, March 27, 1991: 16.
— to be performed by Maui Community Theatre, Lahaina News, March 4, 1999: 12.
— to be performed by Maui Community Theatre, Lahaina News, March 11, 1999: 12.
— to be performed by Maui Community Theatre, Lahaina News, March 18, 1999: 16.
— production to conclude, Lahaina News, March 25, 1999: 16.

CABARET LOUNGE
— to open at Westin Maui, Lahaina News, May 30, 1991: 7.
— actors include Marsha Kelly, Lisa Porter, Tim Weber, and Magnus Hellberg, Lahaina News, June 6, 1991: 14.

CABATBAT, JOLENE
— Scholar/Athlete of the Week, Lahaina News, September 19, 1996: 13.

CABEBE, AGRIFINA "AGGIE"
— community leader to be honored, Lahaina News, December 9, 1999: 16.

CABELL, JOEY
— demonstrating longboard surfing, Lahaina Times, June, 1980 volume 4 number 5: 9.
— designs canoe for Lahaina Canoe Club, Lahaina News, May 22, 1985: 4.

CABLAY, YVONNE
— appointed director of marketing at Westin Maui, Lahaina News, December 3, 1992: 4.
— appointed director of marketing at Westin Maui, Lahaina News, December 17, 1992: 8.

CABLE, BOB
— hired as sales manager by Aloha Business Systems, Lahaina News, October 17, 1990: 12.

CABLEVISION
— Kihei man convicted for illegal hookups, Lahaina News, July 15, 1982: 4.
— Hawaiian Cable Vision Company sues Robert Giso and GKW Electronics, Inc., Lahaina News, October 15, 1982: 2.
— Kahana Villa apartment charged with theft of service, Lahaina News, November 1, 1982: 12.
— Oceanic Cablevision gives grant to Maui Philharmonic Society, Lahaina News, December 28, 1988: 3.
— public hearings to be held, Lahaina News, October 10, 1990: 3.
— public hearing scheduled, Hawaiian Cable Vision Company seeking to renew cable franchise in West Maui, Lahaina News, October 17, 1990: 6.
— rates raised, Lahaina News, January 9, 1991: 3.
— mayor Linda Lingle proclaims April as "National Cable Month", Lahaina News, April 17, 1991: 3.
— see also Chronicle Cablevision, Hawaiian Cablevision, Oceanic Cablevision, and West Side Cable

CABRAL, SISTER CLAUDIA
— dies after fall, Lahaina News, December 9, 1987: 3.

CABRERA, HANNALORE
— Scholar/Athlete of the Week, Lahaina News, October 21, 1999: 8.
— Scholar/Athlete of the Week, Lahaina News, July 20, 2000: 6.

CABRERA, TONY
— Scholar/Athlete of the Week, Lahaina News, October 21, 1999: 8.

CABUCO, MARIA
— passes away, Lahaina News, August 12, 1999: 9.
— passes away, Lahaina News, August 26, 1999: 14.

CACAL, JONATHAN
— Scholar/Athlete of the Week, Lahaina News, May 29, 2003: 12.

CADANAS, LEHUA BISSEN [MUSICIAN]
— to perform at Maui Arts and Cultural Center, Lahaina News, December 28, 1995: 8.

CADDY, PETER
— co-founder of garden in Findhorn (Scotland), Lahaina Times, June, 1980 volume 4 number 5: 5,6.

CADETTES [MARCHING BAND]
— perform near Pioneer Inn, Lahaina News, August 27, 1986: 24.

CAFÉ ALLEGRO [RESTAURANT]
— featured, Lahaina News, January 11, 1984: 14.

CAFCO, RANDY
— tae kwon-do expert featured, Lahaina News, July 31, 1985: 4.

CAFE DE PARIS [RESTAURANT]
— vegetarian cafe opens, Lahaina News, April 1, 1993: 8.

CAFE KULA
— staff and suppliers to hold fundraiser for Gabrielle Dunn, Lahaina News, September 16, 1993: 8.

CAFE MAESTRO [RESTAURANT]
— featured, Lahaina News, July 23, 1992: 24.

CAFE MAKAWAO [RESTAURANT]
— to host open mike night, Lahaina News, May 22, 1997: 16.
— to host open mike night with Panta Bochniak and Richard LaFond, Lahaina News, June 19, 1997: 17.

CAFE O'LEI LAHAINA [RESTAURANT]
— opens, Lahaina News, August 22, 2002: 8.

CAFE SAUVAGE [RESTAURANT]
— featured, Lahaina News, April 4, 2002: 9.
— chef Dean Luis hosted by Lahainaluna High School Food Service Program, Lahaina News, September 11, 2003: 9.

CAFFE CIAO [RESTAURANT]
— featured, Lahaina News, December 2, 1999: 14,15.

CAGE AUX FOLLES, LA [PLAY]
— to be performed by Maui Community Theatre, Lahaina News, November 22, 1989: 12.

CAGLAYAN, SAIM [ARTIST]
— founder of Laguna Beach Plein Air Painters Association to conduct workshop, Lahaina News, December 6, 2001: 15.
— to conduct Plein Air Oil Workshop, Lahaina News, January 10, 2002: 16.

CAIN, GAIL
— named personnel director for Royal Lahaina Hotel, Lahaina News, December 26, 1984: 3.

CAIN, MATT [MUSICIAN]
— to perform at Seabury Hall, Lahaina News, November 21, 1991: 22.

CAIRES, JOSEPH
— to perform at Maui Sun Hotel, Lahaina News, February 20, 1992: 16.
— to perform at Maui Sun, Lahaina News, June 18, 1992: 21.
— to host talent show at the Maui Sun Hotel, Lahaina News, November 5, 1992: 14.

CAIRES, JOSEPH
— injured , Lahaina Sun, March 3, 1971: 1.

CAIRES, MICHAEL
— awarded employee of the year by Maui County, Lahaina News, November 11, 1999: 11.

CAIRO
— report on travel to Egypt, Lahaina Sun, December 20, 1972: 22.

CAISERMAN, NINA
— Scholar/Athlete of the Week, Lahaina News, April 4, 1996: 17.
— Scholar/Athlete of the Week, Lahaina News, October 10, 1996: 12.

CAJODOY, LATISHA
— Scholar/Athlete of the Week, Lahaina News, December 19, 2002: 10.

CAKEBREAD WINERY [BUSINESS]
— to be featured at dinner at Bay Club restaurant, Lahaina News, February 6, 2003: 16.

CALAGNA, MARIE [ARTIST]
— to teach class on acrylic painting, Lahaina News, January 4, 2001: 16.

CALAPINI-DOMINGO, ESTHER
— named director of Holy Innocents Preschool, Lahaina News, July 18, 2002: 8.

CALDICOTT, HELEN
— to speak to Maui Peace Action, Lahaina News, June 19, 2003: 16.

CALDITO, RICHARD
— member of Maui County Council, Lahaina Sun, December 30, 1970: 8.
— reacts to number of resolutions at Maui County Council meeting, Lahaina Sun, January 20, 1971: 8.

CALDWELL, ROBERT
— promoted to director of operations at Bubba Gump Shrimp Co, Lahaina News, April 6, 2000: 8.

CALENDARMAUI.COM
— website launched, Lahaina News, October 18, 2001: 9.

CALGARY FIDDLERS, THE [MUSICAL GROUP]
— to perform free concerts at Ka'anapali Resort, Lahaina News, July 26, 2001: 14.
— to perform at Royal Lahaina Resort, Lahaina News, August 2, 2001: 17.

CALIFORNIA AND HAWAIIAN SUGAR COMPANY [BUSINESS]
— to be purchased by Alexander and Baldwin-Hawaii, Inc [business], Lahaina News, March 11, 1993: 12.

CALIFORNIA GUITAR TRIO [MUSICAL GROUP]
— to be presented by Maui Philharmonic Society, Lahaina News, April 18, 1996: 16.
— to perform, Lahaina News, April 25, 1996: 16.

CALIFORNIA SUITE [PLAY]
— Neil Simon comedy to be performed by Theatre Theatre Maui, Lahaina News, January 18, 1996: 12.
— to open, Lahaina News, February 8, 1996: 13.
— opens Friday, reviewed, Lahaina News, February 29, 1996: 13.
— reviewed, Lahaina News, March 7, 1996: 13.
— to return to the stage, Lahaina News, March 28, 1996: 14.
— to be performed, Lahaina News, April 4, 1996: 14.

CALIFORNIAN [SHIP]
— training schooner visits Maui, Lahaina News, August 6, 1986: 1,11.
— to sail to Lahaina, Lahaina News, July 5, 2001: 3.

CALIMA [MUSICAL GROUP]
— to perform at Maui Arts and Cultural Center, Lahaina News, August 14, 2003: 16.

CALLAREC, PATRICK
— chef to participate in Kapalua Wine Symposium, Lahaina News, July 15, 1993: 10.
— chef joins Light Bringers to serve Christmas dinners, Lahaina News, December 30, 1999: 15.
— chef at Chez Paul to host benefit dinner for The Art School at Kapalua, Lahaina News, November 29, 2001: 15.
— chef at Chez Paul to host benefit dinner for Light Bringers Mission, Lahaina News, January 24, 2002: 9.
— chef at Chez Paul featured, Lahaina News, January 2, 2003: 9.

CALLEY, WILLIAM
— Maui County Council requests pardon for lieutenant, Lahaina Sun, April 7, 1971: 4.

CALLING, THE [MUSICAL GROUP]
— performs at West Fest Summer Jam, Lahaina News, August 30, 2001: 1.

CALLIOPE [MUSICAL]
— to be performed at Makawao Union Church, Lahaina News, January 1, 1986: 3.

CALVERT, RON
— franchise owner of Subway Sandwiches on Maui featured, Lahaina News, January 23, 1992: 11.

CAMANSE, KAINALU
— Scholar/Athlete of the Week, Lahaina News, November 21, 2002: 11.

CAMELOT [PLAY]
— auditions for upcoming Baldwin Theatre Guild beginning, Lahaina News, February 6, 1985: 3.
— Baldwin Theatre Guild to perform, Lahaina News, April 3, 1985: 3.
— to be performed at Maui Community Theatre, Lahaina News, January 8, 1998: 12.
— to be performed at Iao Theatre, Lahaina News, March 19, 1998: 12.

CAMERON [FAMILY]
— may purchase acreage from Maui Land and Pineapple near Pohaku Park, Lahaina News, February 25, 1999: 1,16.

CAMERON CENTER
— see J Walter Cameron Center

CAMERON, COLIN
— president of Maui Pineapple discusses 270 homes planned in Alaeloa, Lahaina Sun, January 27, 1971: 1,2.
— chairman of Mauna Olu Board of Trustees supports merger of Mauna Olu College with United States International University, Lahaina Sun, March 3, 1971: 1,4.
— merger okayed by Board of Trustees, Lahaina Sun, March 10, 1971: 6.
— head of Maui Land & Pineapple purchases Lahaina News, Lahaina News, August 27, 1986: 1.
— ends presidency of Kapalua Land Company, Lahaina News, August 12, 1987: 18.
— developer comments on delay to approve Ritz-Carlton hotel after bones found, Lahaina News, February 8, 1989: 20.
— praises mayor Tavares for intervening when ancient Hawaiian remains found at Ritz-Carlton development, Lahaina News, March 1, 1989: 1,16.
— awarded Oak Leaf from Nature Conservancy, Lahaina News, October 4, 1989: 5.
— to chair Business and Environment Conference, Lahaina News, March 5, 1992: 9.
— remembered, Lahaina News, June 18, 1992: 1,3.
— see also Hawaiian Airlines, Maui Land & Pineapple

CAMERON, FRANCIS [ARTIST]
— to exhibit at Hui No'eau, Lahaina News, March 4, 1999: 12.

CAMERON, J. WALTER
— praised for creating rehabilitation center, Lahaina Sun, November 15, 1972: 6,7.

CAMERON, MARGARET
— benefit auction for Maui Community Arts and Cultural Center held in memory of, Lahaina News, September 7, 1988: 9.

CAMERON, RICHARD
— developer advocates for changes in Honoapi'ilani Highway, Lahaina News, April 22, 1987: 3.
— developer discusses housing with Hawaii Housing Authority, Lahaina News, September 16, 1987: 1,9.
— Kapalua Land Company details new hotel development, Lahaina News, June 15, 1988: 1.
— raising funds to help homeless, Lahaina News, March 19, 1992: 3.
— promoted to vice-president of Alexander and Baldwin-Hawaii, Lahaina News, May 13, 1993: 7.
— given responsibility over Alexander and Baldwin-Hawaii agribusiness activities, Lahaina News, January 27, 1994: 5.
— vice president of Maui Land and Pineapple discusses providing more water to Honokohau Valley, Lahaina News, September 21, 1995: 1.

CAMINITI, STEVE [COMEDIAN]
— to perform at Comedy Club and the Sports Page, Lahaina News, January 16, 1991: 10.
— to perform at Maui Comedy Club, Lahaina News, May 11, 1995: 12.

CAMP FOR CHILDREN WITH CANCER
— held at Camp Mokuleia, Lahaina News, July 23, 1986: 14.

CAMP IMUA
— rummage sale being held by Maui Animal Aloha Center and Imua Rehab to support, Lahaina News, November 17, 1994: 6.

CAMP KAENAE
— YMCA accepting reservations for, Lahaina News, August 21, 1985: 3.
— see also YMCA

CAMP PECUSA
— location of Krishna Festival, Lahaina Sun, April 19, 1972: 6.
— vote to designate as beach park fails at Lahaina Community Plan Citizen Advisory Committee, Lahaina News, October 15, 1992: 1.

CAMP PIIHOLO
— Girl Scouts camp at, Lahaina News, May 24, 1989: 7.
— location of writing camp hosted by Gamekids, Lahaina News, May 7, 1998: 18.

CAMPAIGN RECYCLE MAUI [BUSINESS]
— formed, Lahaina News, September 19, 1991: 4.
— Charles Davidson claims resorts are key to success of recycling, Lahaina News, August 25, 1994: 12.
— featured, Lahaina News, December 7, 1995: 13.
— celebrates 5th anniversary, Lahaina News, April 9, 1998: 13.

CAMPANILE, DARIO [ARTIST]
— to exhibit at Lahaina Galleries, Lahaina News, August 22, 1991: 13.
— to offer classes on still life oil painting, Lahaina News, April 8, 1999: 13.
— to appear at Lahaina Galleries, Lahaina News, April 15, 1999: 13.
— to appear at Lahaina Galleries, Lahaina News, December 23, 1999: 16.
— featured at Lahaina Galleries, Lahaina News, March 19, 1992: 18.

CAMPBELL, ELIZABETH
— joins Hill and Knowton/Skinner Communication, Lahaina News, October 1, 1992: 11.

CAMPBELL ESTATE
— announces Don Reaser as Maui asset manager, Lahaina News, January 14, 1993: 6.

CAMPBELL, ESTATE OF JAMES
— announces that Pacific Museums, Inc. to design and build new exhibit at Whalers Village Shopping Center, Lahaina News, February 20, 1991: 7.
— appoints Ostrander-Chu as advertising agency for Whalers Village, Lahaina News, December 18, 1997: 21.

CAMPBELL, HAL
— harbor chief discusses Department of Transportation taking over mooring permits, Lahaina News, March 9, 1988: 1.

CAMPBELL, HAROLD
— harbor chief discusses changes to Lahaina Harbor, Lahaina News, October 19, 1988: 24.

CAMPBELL, "MAUI LOU"
— wife of Reverend Alexander Campbell dies, Lahaina News, December 1, 1994: 7.

CAMPBELL PARK
— Christmas community party planned at, Lahaina News, December 11, 1997: 3.

CAMPING
— rules and number of accessible parks on Maui change, Lahaina Sun, May 19, 1971: 1.
— new law supported by Mayor Cravalho, Lahaina Sun, June 2, 1971: 1,2.
— ACLU protests inadequate announcement of hearing, Lahaina Sun, August 4, 1971: 11.
— Sierra Club criticizes strict camping rules, Lahaina Sun, December 29, 1971: 18.
— theft of possessions described, Lahaina Sun, May 24, 1972: 21.
— campers at country beaches to be fined for extended stays, Lahaina News, June 16, 1994: 1,3.

CAMPOS, ANDY
— returned lost money, Lahaina Sun, December 23, 1970: 2.

CAMPOS, DANIEL
— Lahaina Intermediate School featured, Lahaina News, October 25, 2001: 3.

CAMPOS, HERB
— Fire Chief discusses need for fire sprinklers, Lahaina News, August 10, 1988: 1,24.

CAMPOS, JESSICA
— Lahaina Intermediate School student wins state writing contest, Lahaina News, May 3, 1989: 3.
— Lahainaluna High School student finalist in National Golden Key Art Competition, Lahaina News, February 13, 1992: 7.

CAMPOS, SU [POLITICIAN]
— to run for West Maui county council seat, Lahaina News, July 21, 1994: 3.
— speaks of candidacy, Lahaina News, June 18, 1998: 1,20.

CANADA
— identified as new tourist market, Lahaina Sun, October 13, 1971: 5.
— navy vessel St. Anthony to arrive on Maui to celebrate end of Victoria-Maui yacht race, Lahaina Sun, July 19, 1972: 14.
— Canadians visiting Maui, Lahaina Sun, March 7, 1973: 15.
— 40% of buyers for new condominium project in north Ka'anapali are Canadian, Lahaina Sun, May 2, 1973: 11.

CANADA 3000 AIRLINES [BUSINESS]
— to begin operations between Vancouver and Honolulu, Lahaina News, November 12, 1992: 12.
— begins flying to Honolulu, Lahaina News, November 19, 1992: 5.
— celebrating 18 months of service to Maui, Lahaina News, February 24, 1994: 10.

CANADA, JERRY
— murder of described, Lahaina News, January 30, 1992: 1,6.
— Roy Kalama, Jr. to be retried for death of, Lahaina News, May 28, 1992: 9.

CANADIAN BRASS [MUSICAL GROUP]
— to perform at Wailea Tennis Stadium, Lahaina News, March 22, 1989: 9.

CANADIAN PACIFIC (CP) AIR [BUSINESS]
— to begin direct flights between Kahului airport and Vancouver, British Columbia, Lahaina News, October 9, 1985: 3.

CANAL, KITTI [ARTIST]
— offering art classes, Lahaina Sun, September 6, 1972: 10.

CANCER INFORMATION SERVICE
— offering free comic book about effects of sun on skin, Lahaina News, July 11, 1984: 3.

CANE BURNING
— example of pollution on Maui, Lahaina Sun, February 3, 1971: 5.
— potentially eliminated by 1980 by new pollution laws, Lahaina Sun, December 22, 1971: 6.
— criticized at public meeting, Lahaina News, November 11, 1987: 1.
— health impact to be discussed , Lahaina News, March 9, 1988: 1.

CANHAM, ROD
— winner of Parade-Fuji National Photo Contest, Lahaina News, September 7, 1988: 1.

CANJA, SUZANNE
— to discuss "Hawksbill Sea Turtle Habitat Study—Honu 'Ea Watch", Lahaina News, August 13, 1998: 15.

CANNERY
— interviews with workers at, Lahaina News, March 11, 1987: 10.

CANNON, BEVERLY
— chef to offer demonstration, Lahaina News, December 4, 1997: 25.

CANNON, CHUCK AND SHIRLEY
— clergy couple from Holy Innocents' Episcopal Church featured, Lahaina News, March 15, 2001: 3.

CANNON'S INTERNATIONAL BUSINESS COLLEGE
— accepting scholarship applications, Lahaina News, November 9, 1988: 20.
— to award Excellence in Business Education Teaching Award, Lahaina News, February 15, 1989: 3.
— now accepting applications for scholarships, Lahaina News, November 1, 1989: 6.
— Wilhemina Berzabal and Rowena Dellatan graduate from, Lahaina News, November 14, 1990: 4.
— to present Business Education Teaching Award, Lahaina News, January 2, 1991: 4.
— bought by Link Corporation, Lahaina News, April 2, 1992: 13.
— Alumni Association seeking alumni, Lahaina News, February 25, 1993: 6.
— offering scholarships, Lahaina News, March 11, 1993: 12.

CANO, JAVIER
— new general manager at Ritz-Carlton, Lahaina News, April 24, 2003: 14.

CANO, JOE [MUSICIAN]
— featured, Lahaina News, August 3, 1988: 8.
— performs around Lahaina, Lahaina News, November 23, 1988: 9.
— to perform at Casanova's, Lahaina News, September 5, 1990: 15.
— continues to perform at Longhi's, Lahaina News, September 12, 1991: 13.
— continues to perform at Longhi's, Lahaina News, November 7, 1991: 14.
— featured, Lahaina News, January 30, 1992: 16.
— continues to perform at Spats at the Hyatt Regency Maui, Lahaina News, March 12, 1992: 16.

— to perform during Arthritis Telethon, Lahaina News, April 2, 1992: 17.
— to perform at Villa Lounge, Lahaina News, August 13, 1992: 15.
— to perform, Lahaina News, November 4, 1993: 12.
— to perform at Magical Maui International Music and Craft Festival, Lahaina News, April 11, 1996: 12.
— see also Joe Cano and Da Talk of Da Town [musical group]

CANOE BEACH
— dedicated, Lahaina News, November 9, 1983: 5.
— ancient grinding stones resurface at, Lahaina News, November 16, 1995: 1.
— to host state championship regatta, Lahaina News, April 22, 1999: 1,16.
— ready for paddling competition, Lahaina News, April 29, 1999: 15.
— see also Hanaka'o'o Beach Park

CANOE CLUBS
— Lahaina Canoe Club opening soon, Lahaina Sun, December 22, 1971: 18.
— begin new season, Lahaina News, March 19, 1986: 18.
— races and fundraising efforts detailed, Lahaina News, April 16, 1986: 16.
— awarded permit to construct canoe house, Lahaina News, May 14, 1986: 3.
— update on events, Lahaina News, May 14, 1986: 4.
— recent results listed, Lahaina News, June 11, 1986: 4.
— Maui County Championships set for July 7, Lahaina News, June 25, 1986: 4.
— paddlers spend summer in Tahiti, Lahaina News, July 30, 1986: 18.
— see also specific clubs

CANOE HALAU [FACILITY]
— history and plans detailed, Lahaina News, June 20, 1984: 7,8,9.
— editorial supporting construction of, Lahaina News, July 4, 1984: 2.

CANOEING
— see paddling

CANOES OCEANFRONT [RESTAURANT]
— featured, Lahaina News, July 5, 2001: 14.

CANTORNA, VIRGINIA
— to leave Kula Hospital for doctorate degree, Lahaina News, August 23, 2001: 9.

CANVAS AND SAIL [BUSINESS]
— locates to Lahaina Industrial Area, Lahaina News, November 7, 2002: 8.

CANVASBACK [CATAMARAN]
— to have open house, Lahaina News, November 21, 1990: 3.
— large sailing catamaran to visit, Lahaina News, November 28, 1990: 3.

CAPE CORWIN [SHIP]
— Coast Guard cutter to be commanded by Lieutenant Ann Fleck, Lahaina News, May 28, 1986: 3.
— U.S. Coast Guard cutter decommissioned, Lahaina News, October 31, 1990: 1.

CAPOEIRA
— Fabio Maximinio to each, Lahaina News, January 3, 2002: 17.
— classes to be offered at Art School at Kapalua, Lahaina News, June 19, 2003: 13.

CAPONI, DONNA
— golfer's career described, Lahaina News, March 6, 1985: A10.

CAPPS, MYKE
— named "Employee of the Year" at Nai'a Properties, Lahaina News, April 25, 2002: 8.

CAPT. NEMO [BUSINESS]
— offering drawing for free scuba certification, Lahaina News, September 21, 1988: 3.

CAPTAIN NEMO'S [RESTAURANT]
— collect trash at Mala Wharf and under water, Lahaina News, December 10, 1986: 6.

CAPTAIN NEMO'S OCEAN EMPORIUM [BUSINESS]
— featured, Lahaina News, May 9, 1984: 13.

CAPT'N CREW TOY SHOP [BUSINESS]
— opening in Whaler's Village, Lahaina Sun, November 25, 1970: 3.

CARD AND CRAFT BOUTIQUE [BUSINESS]
— featured, Lahaina News, July 9, 1992: 14.

CARDEN ACADEMY OF MAUI
— elementary school to open, Lahaina News, June 14, 2001: 3.
— to hold Benefit Country Jamboree, Lahaina News, May 1, 2003: 16.
— plans summer camps, Lahaina News, May 1, 2003: 2.
— to host May Day Ho'olaule'a and fundraiser, Lahaina News, May 15, 2003: 2.
— plans summer camps, Lahaina News, June 5, 2003: 9.

CARDEN, SHERRY [ARTIST]
— works featured at Banyan Tree Gallery, Lahaina News, October 3, 1991: 12.
— works featured at Banyan Tree Gallery, Lahaina News, October 17, 1991: 16.
— works to be featured at Banyan Tree Gallery, Lahaina News, November 7, 1991: 16.
— compiling Maui Eco Directory, Lahaina News, May 13, 1993: 7.
— to exhibit at Roy's Kahana Bar and Grill, Lahaina News, November 4, 1993: 10.

CARDEW, SIMON
— public relations director at Makai Corp. speaks to West Maui Business Association regarding tourism in Lahaina, Lahaina Sun, December 9, 1970: 4.
— public relations director at Makai Corp. will tour the country and distribute new Lahaina press kit to mainland writers and travel agents, Lahaina Sun, December 23, 1970: 8.
— public relations director at Makai Corp. discusses Lahaina press kit, Lahaina Sun, January 13, 1971: 5.
— public relations director at Makai Corp. discusses press kit for Lahaina, Lahaina Sun, January 27, 1971: 7.
— public relations director at Makai Corp. discusses press kit for Lahaina, Lahaina Sun, January 27, 1971: 7.

CARDIGANS, THE [MUSICAL GROUP]
— to perform at The Big Mele, Lahaina News, July 31, 1997: 16.

CARDONE, MARIO
— joins Century 21 First Pacific Properties, Lahaina News, August 1, 1991: 11.
— fined by Real Estate Commission, Lahaina News, August 5, 1993: 7.

CARDOZA, COLLETTE
— Scholar/Athlete of the Week, Lahaina News, February 24, 2000: 7.

CARDWELL, REED [ARTIST]
— to appear at Village Gallery Contemporary, Lahaina News, April 1, 1999: 16.

CAREERTRACK SEMINARS
— to hold "Management Skills for Secretaries, Administrative Assistants, and Other Office Professionals", Lahaina News, November 23, 2000: 16.

CARELLI, GERARD [MUSICIAN]
— to perform at Blackie's Bar, Lahaina News, October 31, 1990: 13.

CAREY, BOB
— photograph of diver with black coral tree recovered off of Maui, Lahaina Sun, December 23, 1970: 2.
— diver rescued by Coast Guard helicopter, Lahaina Sun, June 9, 1971: 5.

CARIBBEAN
— travels to described, Lahaina Sun, April 11, 1973: 22.

CARLE, MONICA
— win radio contest, Lahaina News, November 22, 1989: 3.

CARLIN, JACKIE PIAS [ARTIST]
— to exhibit at Maui Community College, Lahaina News, September 26, 1991: 17.
— "Off the Wall" to be performed at Maui Community College, Lahaina News, October 3, 1991: 18.
— featured at Mayor's Invitational Art Exhibit, Lahaina News, April 11, 1996: 13.

CARLOS, MYRON
— Lahainaluna High School music teacher discusses program, Lahaina News, October 31, 2002: 3.
— Lahainaluna High School music director to lead Concert and Symphonic Bands, Lahaina News, December 12, 2002: 1.

CARLSON, BARRY
— appointed mortgage loan officer of Maui office of Home Financial Services, Inc., Lahaina News, March 6, 1991: 9,10.
— joins Island Mortgage Corporation, Lahaina News, June 18, 1992: 10.
— appointed branch manager of First Federal Savings and Loan Association, Lahaina News, May 29, 1997: 5.

CARLSON, FRANK [MUSICIAN]
— life as surfer featured , Lahaina Sun, April 5, 1972: 6.
— featured, Lahaina News, March 11, 1987: 8.
— career described, Lahaina News, March 9, 1988: 8.

CARMAC, JERRY [MUSICIAN]
— to perform at Lopaka's Grill and Bar, Lahaina News, January 28, 1993: 16.
— to perform at Lopaka's Grill and Bar, Lahaina News, February 11, 1993: 15.

CARMEL
— booklet on hippies produced in California to be used as model for one created in Maui , Lahaina Sun, December 9, 1970: 1.

CARMEN, ERIC [MUSICIAN]
— to perform in "A Walk Down Abbey Road" celebration of the Beatles, Lahaina News, June 13, 2002: 17.

CARMINA BURANA [MUSIC]
— to be performed, Lahaina News, May 5, 1994: 16.
— soprano Maria Fortuna featured, Lahaina News, May 12, 1994: 12.

CARNABUCI, ANTHONY [ARTIST]
— to be featured at Lahaina Art Society, Lahaina News, March 6, 2003: 17.

CARNAHAN, STEPHANIE
— Scholar/Athlete of the Week, Lahaina News, June 24, 1999: 6.

CARNER, JOANNE
— golfer participates in Women's Kemper Open, Lahaina News, March 14, 1984: 20.
— golfing career described, Lahaina News, March 6, 1985: A8.

CARNEY, MARK
— joins Coldwell Banker McCormack Real Estate, Lahaina News, April 9, 1992: 13.

CAROL BROTHERS [MUSICAL GROUP]
— to perform at Longhi's, Lahaina News, October 7, 1993: 12.
— to perform at Moose McGillycuddy's, Lahaina News, December 8, 1994: 16.

CAROLE KAI BED RACE
— route detailed, Lahaina News, February 22, 1984: 3.
— results discussed, Lahaina News, February 29, 1984: 6.
— deadline to enter is February 1, Lahaina News, January 23, 1985: 3.
— set for February, Lahaina News, February 13, 1985: 3.
— results detailed, Lahaina News, February 27, 1985: 4.
— 9th annual set for February 15, Lahaina News, January 29, 1986: 3.
— to take place in Ka'anapali, Lahaina News, February 19, 1986: 3.

— 10th annual to be held, Lahaina News, March 4, 1987: 3.
— entries now being accepted, Lahaina News, February 24, 1988: 18.
— planned, Lahaina News, March 15, 1989: 2,14.
— 13th annual, to be held, Lahaina News, February 21, 1990: 4.
— to be held at Ka'anapali Parkway, Lahaina News, March 14, 1990: 3.

CAROLL, ELAINE [ARTIST]
— to present "The Mirror of Light" multi-image audio visual concert, Lahaina News, April 23, 1986: 3.

CAROUSEL [MUSICAL]
— to be performed by Baldwin Theatre Guild, Lahaina News, January 5, 1995: 12.

CARPE DIEM [MUSICAL GROUP]
— to perform at Polli's On the Beach, Lahaina News, August 8, 1990: 13.

CARPENTER, CHRIS AND CORAL
— students at Shotokan Karate-Do advance, Lahaina News, June 27, 2002: 12.

CARPENTER, JACK [ARTIST]
— featured, Lahaina News, October 31, 1996: 21.

CARPENTER, KIM DAVID
— promoted to director of marketing and tournament operations at Kapalua Land Co. Ltd., Lahaina News, October 28, 1999: 15.
— promoted to vice president of marketing, Lahaina News, March 30, 2000: 11.

CARPENTER, SCOTT
— astronaut to speak for Earth Day, Lahaina News, February 28, 1990: 3.
— astronaut promoting Earth Day, Lahaina News, April 18, 1990: 4.

CARPET CONCEPTS [BUSINESS]
— appoints Mark Harlow , Lahaina News, May 13, 1999: 13.

CARR, JOHN
— leading workshops for artist educators, Lahaina News, August 26, 1999: 14.

CARREIRA, JOSEPHINE [DANCER]
— to teach dances of Portugal, Lahaina News, March 5, 1992: 4.

CARROLL, BILL
— lawsuit continues, Lahaina News, February 4, 1993: 1.

CARROLL, BOB [POLITICIAN]
— candidate for East Maui County Council, Lahaina News, November 2, 2000: 16.

CARROLL, DAVE [MUSICIAN]
— to perform at Makai Bar, Lahaina News, September 19, 1996: 18.

CARROLL, JO ANN
— opens Old Lahaina Book Emporium, Lahaina News, July 16, 1998: 1,20.

CARROLL, JOHN
— challenges of Article XII of the Hawaii State Constitution, Lahaina News, February 8, 2001: 3.

CARROLL, MIKE [ARTIST]
— Lahaina Arts Society featured artist, Lahaina News, December 6, 2001: 3.
— to exhibit at Lahaina Arts Society, Lahaina News, December 20, 2001: 15.

CARROLL, WILLIAM
— charges that County is not pursuing reclamation aggressively, Lahaina News, May 14, 1992: 1.
— union and Lahaina News editor advocate for reinstatement of, Lahaina News, August 20, 1992: 1,3,16.
— appeals firing, to meet with Mayor Linda Lingle, Lahaina News, August 27, 1992: 1.
— Mayor Linda Lingle denies UPW grievance over firing of, Lahaina News, September 24, 1992: 6.

— former county employee sues mayor Linda Lingle and others, Lahaina News, November 26, 1992: 1.
— civil lawsuit continues, Lahaina News, July 15, 1993: 1,3.

CARSON, BERT
— present "Prosperity Plus" workshop, Lahaina News, June 8, 1988: 13.

CARTE BLANCHE [SHIP]
— repaired after running aground in 1971, Lahaina Sun, December 6, 1972: 11.

CARTER, JACK [COMEDIAN]
— dines at Chez Paul, Lahaina News, January 9, 2003: 18.

CARTER, MICHAEL
— football player promoting upcoming Bruce Bosely Memorial Tournament, Lahaina News, October 5, 1995: 7.

CARTER, TY
— Scholar/Athlete of the Week, Lahaina News, June 7, 2001: 14.

CARTER, VONNIE
— appointed store buyer for Maui Ocean Center Store, Lahaina News, January 31, 2002: 8.

CARTHAGINIAN [SHIP]
— reception held for travel writers, Lahaina Sun, May 12, 1971: 6.
— sinking due to worm infestation, Lahaina Sun, June 9, 1971: 1,8.
— photograph, Lahaina Sun, September 8, 1971: 10.
— runs aground, Lahaina Sun, April 5, 1972: 5.
— discussion of recent accident, Lahaina Sun, April 12, 1972: 2,3,4,5.
— Lahaina Restoration Foundation plans to replace, Lahaina Sun, April 19, 1972: 3.
— reaction to its sinking, Lahaina Sun, April 19, 1972: 5.
— Lahaina Restoration Foundation might auction salvaged parts of, Lahaina Sun, April 26, 1972: 6.
— Lahaina Restoration Foundation begins fundraising to replace, Lahaina Sun, June 14, 1972: 11.
— Lahaina Restoration Foundation announces possible replacement for, Lahaina Sun, August 23, 1972: 3.
— search for replacement continues, Lahaina Sun, October 18, 1972: 13.
— replacement likely found by Earl Callicutt, Lahaina Sun, November 8, 1972: 3.
— a replacement has been found in Sweden named the Komet, Lahaina Sun, November 22, 1972: 1.
— crew set to move Carthaginian II from Denmark to Lahaina, Lahaina Sun, February 28, 1973: 3.
— crew of new ship named, Lahaina Sun, March 21, 1973: 11.
— sinking and aftermath detailed, Lahaina Sun, April 18, 1973: 7.
— photographs and account of sinking, Lahaina News, February 15, 1981: 7,10.
— history of the ships recounted, Lahaina News, February 1, 1984: 9,10,11.
— renovations completed, Lahaina News, July 24, 1985: 1,9.
— plans to move from Mala Wharf, Lahaina News, June 3, 1987: 1.
— caretaker Wally Kmentt featured, Lahaina News, May 25, 1988: 3.
— floating museum to be relocated, Lahaina News, August 10, 1988: 16.
— heads for repairs, new berth, Lahaina News, September 21, 1988: 1.
— repairs to be completed soon, Lahaina News, January 4, 1989: 1.
— to return from drydock, Lahaina News, April 19, 1989: 1.
— returns to Lahaina Harbor, Lahaina News, May 31, 1989: 1.
— to host Stan Hugill singing sea shanteys, Lahaina News, June 14, 1989: 16.
— lost 20 years ago, Lahaina News, April 23, 1992: 17,19,10.
— sinking of recounted, Lahaina News, April 20, 1995: 2.
— future of discussed, Lahaina News, August 20, 1998: 1.
— history of, Lahaina News, December 9, 1999: 10,11.
— rigging repaired on, Lahaina News, March 15, 2001: 1.

— deteriorating, to be replaced, Lahaina News, September 12, 2002: 1,24.

— closed for repair, Lahaina News, October 24, 2002: 14.

CARTHAGINIAN II [SHIP]

— exhibit on whales to be installed below ship, Lahaina Sun, May 2, 1973: 5,13.

— still in Denmark, Lahaina Sun, May 23, 1973: 3.

— has set sail from Denmark, Lahaina Sun, May 30, 1973: 10.

— celebrates 60 year anniversary, Lahaina News, May 15, 1980: 7.

— to be sunk Launiupoko and replaced, Lahaina News, July 31, 2003: 1,2.

CARTRIGHT, TESS

— musical "Mewes" to be shown on Akaku cable channel, Lahaina News, January 15, 1998: 13.

CARTWRIGHT, BOB AND TESS

— realtors featured, Lahaina News, June 3, 1999: 12.

— realtors attend groundbreaking for Na Hale O Makena development, Lahaina News, December 7, 2000: 21.

— sponsor a whale for the Soroptimist Club, Lahaina News, December 12, 2002: 6.

CARTWRIGHT, RACHEL

— researcher at Keiki Kohala Project to speak, Lahaina News, May 6, 1999: 21.

— whale naturalist to offer "The Keiki Kohola Project—Caring for Humpback Whale Calves in Maui Waters", Lahaina News, February 28, 2002: 16.

CARTWRIGHT, ROBERT

— receives Certificate of Service from Ka'anapali Shores Annual Home-owners Meeting, Lahaina News, January 10, 2002: 6.

— featured in National Realtor Magazine, Lahaina News, September 18, 2003: 6.

CARTWRIGHT, TESS [PERFORMER]

— to perform at Ka'anapali Beach Hotel, Lahaina News, March 21, 1996: 12.

— to perform "The Garden of BE", Lahaina News, March 28, 1996: 12.

— to exhibit as part of Art of Trash, Lahaina News, July 24, 1997: 17.

— creates television show on Akaku, Lahaina News, February 24, 2000: 15.

— to show how to make character "Bud Burrid" from plastic jugs, Lahaina News, December 21, 2000: 2.

— produces show "Artist Workshop with Ronaldo" on Ronaldo Macedo, Lahaina News, January 24, 2002: 16.

CARVALHO, GLENN

— boxer wins at Hawaii Junior Olympic Championships, Lahaina News, May 21, 1992: 12.

CARVER, E.C. [WRITER]

— to sign book "Last Reunion", Lahaina News, December 13, 2001: 17.

CASALE, MARIA [MUSICIAN]

— harpist to perform at St. Anthony Church Center, Lahaina News, July 16, 1992: 22.

CASANOVA'S [RESTAURANT]

— to hold benefit for Heather Castellanos, Lahaina News, February 6, 1992: 20.

— to celebrate birthday along with KAOI radio, Lahaina News, June 25, 1992: 22.

— to serve lunch again , Lahaina News, December 24, 1992: 18.

— to host Congolese drum and dance artists, Lahaina News, November 5, 1998: 21.

CASAY, ANTHONY [ARTIST]

— work reviewed, Lahaina News, June 1, 1980: 5.

CASCADES GRILLE AND SUSHI BAR [RESTAURANT]

— featured, Lahaina News, July 3, 2003: 14,18.

CASCO [FAMILY]

— featured as sports family, Lahaina News, March 11, 1999: 6.

CASCO, CHRISTIAN

— Lahainaluna High School coach wins Wendy's High School Heisman Program, Lahaina News, November 25, 1999: 8.

CASCO, CLIFFANE

— Lahaina native to play football with Northern Colorado Bears, Lahaina News, February 13, 1997: 13.

— football players featured, Lahaina News, December 11, 1997: 3.

CASCO, CLIFFORD

— baseball coach returns after heart surgery, Lahaina News, May 26, 1994: 9.

CASCO, HERMAN "EDOT" HERMOHINEZ

— services to be held for, Lahaina News, April 23, 1998: 8.

— editorial tribute to, Lahaina News, April 30, 1998: 4.

— to be remembered at Memorial Golf Tournament, Lahaina News, September 10, 1998: 19.

— donates organs, Lahaina News, February 25, 1999: 3.

CASCO, JANIS

— executive director for The Whaler on Ka'anapali Beach, Lahaina News, March 6, 1991: 9.

CASCO, KAINOA

— Scholar/Athlete of the Week, Lahaina News, October 3, 1996: 13.

— Scholar/Athlete of the Week, Lahaina News, March 5, 1998: 14.

CASCO, KALE

— coach of Lahaina Pop Warner football featured, Lahaina News, August 26, 1993: 11.

— director of Lahaina Chiefs Pop Warner football program featured, Lahaina News, September 28, 1995: 7.

— hoping to bring unity to Pop Warner organization, Lahaina News, July 17, 2003: 1,20.

CASCO, KARL

— selected as an Outstanding Young Man of America, Lahaina News, January 18, 1989: 3.

CASCO, KAVIKA

— Princess Nahienaena School student featured, Lahaina News, May 27, 1993: 9.

CASCO, KING BART-THOMAS KAINOA

— King of Junior Promenade court, Lahaina News, May 31, 2001: 3.

CASCO, LAKE

— Scholar/Athlete of the Week, Lahaina News, December 12, 2002: 10.

CASCO, RANDY

— honored as Security Officer of the Year, Lahaina News, April 11, 1990: 5.

— Tae Kwon Do master to instruct, Lahaina News, June 25, 1998: 6.

— receives Loyalty Award from Tae Kwon Do Grandmaster C.E. Sereff, Lahaina News, June 8, 2000: 15.

— achieves rank of 5th Dan black belt in Tae Kwon-Do, Lahaina News, August 7, 2003: 12.

CASCO, RANDY AND STACY

— honored on 20th wedding anniversary, Lahaina News, March 14, 2002: 1,20.

CASCO, RYAN YOSHIO

— Lahainaluna High School prom king, Lahaina News, April 6, 1995: 4.

CASCO, STACY

— recognized for work at Maui Marriott Resort, Lahaina News, October 10, 1991: 7.

— earned Certified Human Resource Executive designation, Lahaina News, October 10, 1996: 8.

CASCO, TIM
— recognized for work at Maui Marriott Resort, Lahaina News, October 10, 1991: 7.

CASE & LYNCH [BUSINESS]
— Gregory Dolton joins, Lahaina News, November 14, 1990: 11.

CASE, DAN
— attorney discusses stoppage of hotel construction in Kahana, Lahaina Sun, May 12, 1971: 2.

CASE, ED [POLITICIAN]
— discusses upcoming legislative session, Lahaina News, February 8, 2001: 9.
— holds "talk story" in West Maui, Lahaina News, February 13, 2003: 1,18.
— to visit Maui, Lahaina News, July 3, 2003: 2.
— discusses West Maui legislation before Congress, Lahaina News, July 10, 2003: 1,20.

CASEBEER, DOUG
— to teach pottery at Hui Noʻeau Center, Lahaina News, May 7, 1998: 21.

CASEY, PHIL
— report on travel/surf adventure, Lahaina News, August 17, 1995: 7.

CASH, ALICE
— to present on "The Healing Power of Music" to ʼOhana Connection, Lahaina News, July 11, 2002: 17.

CASICAS, MICHAEL
— honored by governor Ben Cayetano for volunteerism, Lahaina News, May 2, 1996: 2.
— Patrol Officer named as "Police Officer of the Month by Leilani's on the Beach, Lahaina News, April 13, 2000: 2.
— police officer resigns in frustration, Lahaina News, October 12, 2000: 1,24.

CASLIN, JIM
— finds WWII unexploded mine while diving for lobsters, Lahaina News, April 2, 1986: 1.

CASTAWAY CAFE [RESTAURANT]
— featured, Lahaina News, February 6, 1997: 8.
— featured, Lahaina News, June 3, 1999: 8,9.
— receives Award of Excellence from Wine Spectator magazine, Lahaina News, September 30, 1999: 11.
— opens, Lahaina News, February 24, 2000: 14.
— offering award-winning wine list, Lahaina News, April 19, 2001: 8.
— featured, Lahaina News, October 4, 2001: 14,15.

CASTELLANOS, LENNY [MUSICIAN]
— to perform at Makai Bar, Lahaina News, March 28, 1996: 13.
— to perform at Makai Bar, Lahaina News, September 19, 1996: 18.

CASTENADA, CARLOS [WRITER]
— to hold workshop on "Tensegrity", Lahaina News, March 23, 1995: 2.

CASTILLO, JOICE
— Scholar/Athlete of the Week, Lahaina News, October 12, 2000: 8.

CASTILLO, OCTAVIO
— participates in Earth Maui Nature Summit 5K Run, Lahaina News, June 18, 1998: 1.

CASTILLO, RICK
— honored by PGA of America, Lahaina News, October 5, 2000: 14.

CASTLE & COOKE [BUSINESS]
— new vice presidents elected, Lahaina News, June 1, 1982: 8.
— terminates banana operations in Nicaragua, Lahaina News, November 15, 1982: 11.
— stock offering, Lahaina News, May 15, 1983: 11.
— planning resort on Lanaʻi, Lahaina News, October 19, 1983: 14.
— ownership of Lanaʻi described, Lahaina News, October 3, 1984: 7,8,9.

— open Lodge at Koele, Lahaina News, January 17, 1990: 24.
— to hold annual shareholder's meeting, Lahaina News, May 28, 1992: 11.

CASTLE COUNSELING SERVICES
— offering screening and consultation for alcohol programs, Lahaina News, April 8, 1999: 12.

CASTLE GROUP, INC. [BUSINESS]
— purchases Hawaiian Pacific Resorts, Lahaina News, January 6, 1994: 5.
— acquires management contract for Maui Park, Lahaina News, July 25, 1996: 7.

CASTRO, TOMMY [MUSICIAN]
— to perform at Borders Books and Music, Lahaina News, April 17, 1997: 11.

CASTROVERDE, MILDRED
— second-in-command at Maui Chamber of Commerce to join Aloha Airlines, Lahaina Sun, July 4, 1973: 3.

CASWELL, JAMES
— promoted to assistant vice president, Consumer Service Center at First Hawaiian Bank, Lahaina News, January 30, 1992: 12.

CAT ON A HOT TIN ROOF [MUSICAL]
— auditions to be held by Maui Community Theatre for, Lahaina News, April 18, 1996: 16.
— to be performed by Maui Community Theatre, Lahaina News, October 10, 1996: 14.
— continues, Lahaina News, October 17, 1996: 14.
— reviewed, Lahaina News, October 17, 1996: 18.
— to end run, Lahaina News, October 24, 1996: 14.
— to be performed, Lahaina News, November 14, 2002: 20.
— to be performed, Lahaina News, November 21, 2002: 20.

CATALANO, MAREE [COMEDIAN]
— to perform at Comedy Club, Lahaina News, January 24, 1990: 14.
— to perform at Comedy Club and the Sports Page, Lahaina News, April 8, 1993: 9,11.

CATALINA, BRIAN [COMEDIAN]
— to perform at Comedy Club, Lahaina News, August 5, 1993: 10.

CATALUNA, DON
— discusses installation of statue in Iao Valley, Lahaina News, June 26, 1985: 1.

CATALUNA, LEE [WRITER]
— play "Da Mayah" to be performed, Lahaina News, January 21, 1999: 12.
— play "Da Mayah" to be performed at Iao Theatre, Lahaina News, October 12, 2000: 20.

CATAMARAN EXPRESS, INC. [BUSINESS]
— suit filed against, Lahaina News, September 10, 1992: 12.

CATAPULT PRODUCTIONS [BUSINESS]
— named advertising agent for Whaler's Market Place, Lahaina News, January 8, 1986: 3.
— new PR firm for Excel Fishing Charters, Lahaina News, December 3, 1986: 11.
— to be advertising agent for Napili Kai Beach Club, Lahaina News, October 17, 1990: 11.
— named advertising agent for Resorts of Aloha, Lahaina News, March 5, 1992: 10.
— retained by Kiahani Resort Management, Lahaina News, April 16, 1992: 14.
— retained by Destination Lanaʻi, Lahaina News, June 4, 1992: 9.
— retained by Kahana Gateway, Lahaina News, September 17, 1992: 11.
— hires Cheryl Keefe as account coordinator, Lahaina News, May 25, 1995: 10.

CATE, BRUCE
— wins Great Halloween Costume Contest, Lahaina News, November 9, 1995: 12.

CATFISH JOHN [MUSICIAN]
— to perform at Borders Books, Lahaina News, July 22, 1999: 12.

CATHOLIC DIOCESE OF HONOLULU
— honors volunteers, Lahaina News, June 7, 2001: 2.

CATHOLICS
— see Maria Lanakila Catholic Church

CATLETT, MARY JO
— to perform in "Soulmates, A Rock Opera", Lahaina News, August 21, 2003: 18.

CATO INSTITUTE
— gives Governor Ben Cayetano a grade of "B", Lahaina News, September 10, 1998: 8.

CAVALOTTO, ANDREW
— chef named winner of Sam Choy Poke Recipe contest, Lahaina News, October 23, 1997: 15.

CAVAN, BRUCE
— appointed to conference services manager at Westin Maui, Lahaina News, March 26, 1992: 10.

CAYETANO, BEN [POLITICIAN]
— attends gala function honoring mayor Hannibal Tavares, Lahaina News, December 26, 1990: 5.
— asked by Republican Party to void appointment of senators not chosen by voters due to reapportionment, Lahaina News, January 2, 1992: 1.
— responds to request to prevent Russell Blair from assuming senatorial seat, Lahaina News, January 9, 1992: 2.
— to speak at Democratic Party Presidents Day event, Lahaina News, February 17, 1994: 4.
— announces cabinet appointments, Lahaina News, December 22, 1994: 6.
— offers legislative package, Lahaina News, February 2, 1995: 4.
— releases funds for Hawaii public schools and libraries, Lahaina News, October 5, 1995: 4.
— seeking nominations for outstanding volunteers, Lahaina News, December 19, 1996: 5.
— Lahainaluna High School Traffic Safety Team recognized by, Lahaina News, April 24, 1997: 1.
— to decide on Hawaiian Islands Humpback Whale National Marine Sanctuary, Lahaina News, May 8, 1997: 1.
— accepts whale sanctuary for five years, Lahaina News, June 12, 1997: 12.
— to speak at Maui Chamber of Commerce, Lahaina News, June 19, 1997: 6.
— approves bill to cut automobile insurance premiums, Lahaina News, June 26, 1997: 1.
— signs bill to target delinquent taxes, Lahaina News, July 10, 1997: 2.
— awards Lahaina Yacht Club from Sport Tourism Program, Lahaina News, July 31, 1997: 9,15.
— discusses Hula Mae mortgage program, Lahaina News, August 21, 1997: 9.
— to hold public meeting, Lahaina News, October 9, 1997: 1,3.
— to hold public meeting on plans for Hawaii, Lahaina News, October 9, 1997: 20.
— confident that legislature will pass tax reductions, Lahaina News, December 18, 1997: 1,2.
— refers to Ka'anapali Beach Hotel as innovative Hawaii employer, Lahaina News, January 29, 1998: 1.
— announces Kilohana awardees for Outstanding Volunteerism, Lahaina News, May 7, 1998: 18.
— state plans to restore Lahaina to Kaunakakai ferry, Lahaina News, May 14, 1998: 1.
— funds for school capital improvement released, Lahaina News, May 14, 1998: 7.
— announces search for Hawaii's best exporter, Lahaina News, August 6, 1998: 17.
— receives a "B" from Cato Institute, Lahaina News, September 10, 1998: 8.
— presents Hawaii Youth Medal of Honor to Chase Oshiro for volunteerism, Lahaina News, September 17, 1998: 18,19.
— campaigns on Front Street, Lahaina News, November 5, 1998: 15.
— issues comments on impeachment of President Bill Clinton, Lahaina News, December 24, 1998: 2.
— Governor releases money for electrical system at King Kamehameha III Elementary School, Lahaina News, August 26, 1999: 14.
— to speak at Maui Chamber of Commerce, Lahaina News, October 7, 1999: 14.
— releases funds for the Lahainaluna School Library, Lahaina News, March 30, 2000: 5.
— recognizes volunteers, Lahaina News, April 20, 2000: 15.
— proclaims 2000 as "Year of the Aloha Shirt", Lahaina News, June 8, 2000: 16.
— advocates for health care for every child, Lahaina News, August 31, 2000: 17.
— releases funds for early childhood center on Maui, Lahaina News, October 12, 2000: 19.
— Governor holds ceremony for Kilohana Awards for Outstanding Volunteerism, Lahaina News, May 10, 2001: 2.
— signs bill targeting speeders in school areas, Lahaina News, June 7, 2001: 2.

CAYETANO, VICKY
— to speak to Maui Chamber of Commerce "Entrepreneur and Humanitarian Luncheon", Lahaina News, October 15, 1998: 13.

CAZIMERO, MOMI [ARTIST]
— presents SFCA Retrospective for Art Maui, Lahaina News, January 13, 1988: 16.

CAZIMERO, ROBERT [MUSICIAN]
— to perform at "Starry Night Four Hula", Lahaina News, January 29, 1998: 15.
— see also Brothers Cazimero, The [musical group]

CAZIMERO, ROLAND [MUSICIAN]
— to perform at Concert of the Stars to benefit Kina'u Ministry, Lahaina News, August 22, 1996: 15.
— see also Brothers Cazimero, The [musical group]

CB RICHARD ELLIS HAWAII [BUSINESS]
— G. Warren Freeland heads new brokerage division at, Lahaina News, December 26, 2002: 8.

CECILIO AND KAPONO [MUSICAL GROUP]
— reviewed, Lahaina News, August, 1979: 4.
— playing in Lahaina, Lahaina Times, September, 1980 volume 4 number 8: 2.
— to perform on Maui, Lahaina News, August 15, 1984: 12.
— performance reviewed, Lahaina News, September 5, 1984: 12.
— to perform at Lahaina Amphitheatre, Lahaina News, July 10, 1985: 10.
— to perform, Lahaina News, September 23, 1987: 3.
— to perform at Royal Lahaina Stadium, Lahaina News, December 12, 1991: 18,21.
— featured, Lahaina News, December 19, 1991: 18,19.
— cancels Christmas reunion concert, Lahaina News, March 26, 1992: 10.
— to perform, Lahaina News, August 14, 1997: 16.
— to hold autograph session, Lahaina News, August 20, 1998: 16.
— to perform "unplugged" at Maui Arts and Cultural Center with Malani Bilyeu, Lahaina News, August 19, 1999: 16.

— to perform at Maui Arts and Cultural Center, Lahaina News, October 3, 2002: 16.

— see also Kapono, Henry [musician]

CEDED LAND

— price set for purchase for housing project, Lahaina News, July 28, 1994: 1.

— sale of approved for housing development, Lahaina News, August 18, 1994: 3.

— ruling expected soon on land for housing project, Lahaina News, March 23, 1995: 2.

— dispute goes to Hawaii Supreme Court, Lahaina News, January 18, 1996: 1,14.

— case delayed until April, Lahaina News, February 15, 1996: 1,11.

CEISLER, RICH [COMEDIAN]

— to perform at Comedy Club, Lahaina News, March 17, 1994: 10.

— to perform at Honolulu Comedy Club, Lahaina News, February 22, 1996: 13.

CELEBRATION OF AGING

— exhibits and workshops to be held, Lahaina News, August 10, 1988: 17.

CELEBRATION OF THE ARTS

— to be held, Lahaina News, April 1, 1993: 12,13.

— to be held at Ritz-Carlton, Lahaina News, March 20, 1997: 1,15.

— to be held at Ritz-Carlton, Lahaina News, March 27, 1997: 12.

— to be held at Ritz-Carlton, Lahaina News, March 25, 1999: 1,20.

— to be held at Ritz-Carlton, Lahaina News, April 20, 2000: 3.

— to be held at Ritz-Carlton, Lahaina News, April 12, 2001: 1,11.

— to feature Hawaiian culture, Lahaina News, March 28, 2002: 17.

— held "Cafe U.S.A." annual breakfast program, Lahaina News, April 4, 2002: 1.

— to be held, Lahaina News, April 17, 2003: 3.

— held at Ritz-Carlton, Lahaina News, April 24, 2003: 1.

CELEBRATION OF THE HUMAN BODY, A [EXHIBIT]

— opens at Hui No'eau Visual Arts Center, Lahaina News, April 16, 1986: 3.

CELEBRATION OF YOUTH AND ARTS

— to feature children's art, Lahaina News, December 31, 1998: 12.

CELEBRITIES GALLERY [BUSINESS]

— to host Judith Ripka Trunk Show, Lahaina News, December 26, 2002: 16.

CELEBRITY POWER WALK

— to be benefit American Cancer Society, Lahaina News, September 11, 2003: 16.

CELL TECH [BUSINESS]

— sponsoring seminar on algae, Lahaina News, March 16, 1995: 4.

CELSLER, RICH [COMEDIAN]

— to perform at Comedy Club and the Sports Page, Lahaina News, October 29, 1992: 18,22.

CELTIC/HAWAIIAN GUITAR SUMMIT: A MEETING OF HEARTS

— to be held, Lahaina News, November 2, 2000: 25.

CEMETERIES

— disinternments planned for graves near Jodo Mission, Lahaina News, April 1, 1987: 3.

— remains to be moved from eroding coastal cemetery, Lahaina News, July 8, 1987: 1.

— Nanette Napoleon Purnell to offer workshops on studying, Lahaina News, August 17, 1988: 3,14.

— disinternment necessary for widening of Wainee Street, Lahaina News, November 16, 1988: 1.

CENERENTOLA, LA [OPERA]

— presented by Maui Philharmonic Society, Lahaina News, December 5, 1984: 14.

CENSUS

— importance of, Lahaina News, January 3, 1990: 28.

— begins, Lahaina News, June 27, 1990: 5.

— to be held, Lahaina News, June 15, 2000: 5.

CENSUS BUREAU, U.S.

— hiring census workers, Lahaina News, August 27, 1998: 9.

— apprehensions of census discussed, Lahaina News, March 30, 2000: 1,2.

CENTER CUP GOLF TOURNAMENT

— to be held at Wailea Resort, Lahaina News, May 13, 1987: 12.

CENTER FOR ATTITUDINAL HEALING

— activities described, Lahaina News, October 19, 1988: 1,17.

CENTER FOR COMPUTER TECHNOLOGY TRAINING

— offers computer training, Lahaina News, January 25, 1996: 4.

— offering computer classes, Lahaina News, February 1, 1996: 4.

CENTER FOR DEVELOPING MASTERY

— to hold "Lighten Up" lecture, Lahaina News, March 8, 1989: 16.

— expands facilities, Lahaina News, September 20, 1989: 6.

CENTER FOR HAWAIIAN STUDIES

— to host "An Act of War: The Overthrow of the Hawaiian Nation", Lahaina News, June 17, 1993: 3.

CENTRAL CABINETS OF HAWAII [BUSINESS]

— opens, Lahaina News, June 27, 1991: 7.

CENTRAL MAUI DESTINATION ASSOCIATION

— attempting to create the longest lei, Lahaina News, August 10, 2000: 17.

CENTRAL MAUI SANITARY LANDFILL

— new hours for, Lahaina News, May 13, 1999: 15.

CENTRAL MAUI YOUTH CENTER

— to hold teen dance, Lahaina News, September 23, 1987: 3.

— to present Chalangalang Festival, Lahaina News, March 27, 1991: 16.

— to hold Chalangalang Festival, Lahaina News, April 10, 1991: 12.

— to hold kid's swap meet, Lahaina News, November 14, 1991: 3.

— to hold "Party Palace Dance Club", Lahaina News, November 14, 1991: 3.

— to hold Kids Mart, Lahaina News, January 2, 1992: 5.

— to hold teen dance, Lahaina News, April 24, 1997: 12.

— to hold teen dance, Lahaina News, June 12, 1997: 16.

CENTRAL PACIFIC BANK [BUSINESS]

— to hold "Light Up a Child's Life" campaign, Lahaina News, December 4, 1997: 21.

— appoints Mark Nishino as assistant vice president at Kahului Branch, Lahaina News, March 15, 2001: 8.

— creates team to serve Maui, Lahaina News, February 7, 2002: 8.

CENTRAL PACIFIC CHIROPRACTIC CENTER [BUSINESS]

— sponsoring Eric Sigmund talking about fulfillment, Lahaina News, December 14, 1988: 16.

CENTRAL PACIFIC DIVE CLUB

— adopts a reef, Lahaina News, May 9, 1990: 1.

CENTRAL PACIFIC DIVERS OF LAHAINA [BUSINESS]

— opening new shops, Lahaina News, February 14, 1990: 5.

— purchased by Lahaina Divers, Lahaina News, May 1, 1991: 7.

CENTRAL PACIFIC HURRICANE CENTER

— director Jim Weyman to talk about hurricane preparedness, Lahaina News, July 1, 1999: 13.

CENTRAL PACIFIC MARINE [BUSINESS]

— featured, Lahaina News, August 1, 1984: 14.

CENTRO CRISTIANO BETEL ASSEMBLIES OF GOD
— Hispanic Church opens, Lahaina News, June 10, 1999: 15.
— joins forces with Light Bringers to help Spanish-speaking residents, Lahaina News, February 20, 2003: 3.

CENTURION SECURITY [BUSINESS]
— establishes office on Maui, Lahaina News, September 5, 1990: 6.

CENTURY 21 [BUSINESS]
— begins "Seller's Service Pledge", Lahaina News, August 8, 1991: 11.
— moves Lahaina office, Lahaina News, February 18, 1993: 9.
— announces top sales associates, Lahaina News, August 3, 1995: 8.
— announces top associates, Lahaina News, August 24, 1995: 10.

CENTURY DEVELOPMENT, INC. [BUSINESS]
— owner Jim Patterson proposes Lighthouse Building as retail development, Lahaina News, November 7, 1990: 1.

CERNOSIA, ART
— attorney to present "Hawaii Application of Special Education Law", Lahaina News, April 24, 2003: 20.

CERTIFICHECKS.COM [BUSINESS]
— gift certificate company to open, Lahaina News, August 12, 1999: 13.

CERTIFIED PEST CONTROL AND FUMIGATION SERVICES, INC. [BUSINESS]
— celebrates 10 year anniversary, Lahaina News, May 18, 1988: 18.
— donates equipment to Maui Youth and Family Shelter, Lahaina News, April 4, 1990: 7.
— offering new chemical free pest control method, Lahaina News, May 19, 1994: 12.
— announces scholarship, Lahaina News, January 19, 1995: 6.
— presents scholarships, Lahaina News, January 26, 1995: 9.
— announces scholarship winners, Lahaina News, March 28, 1996: 7.

CERTIFIED PUBLIC ACCOUNTANTS
— continuing education available, Lahaina News, October 5, 1988: 20.

CHA, SONG JA
— luau manager at the Maui Marriott Resort, Lahaina News, February 22, 1996: 11.

CHADBOURN, LLOYD
— elected president of the Kihei Community Association, Lahaina Sun, December 2, 1970: 4.

CHADWICK HAWAII GROUP [BUSINESS]
— acting as wholesaler, Lahaina News, December 13, 1989: 7.

CHAFETZ, STUART
— to conduct Maui Symphony Orchestra, Lahaina News, March 13, 2003: 16.

CHAKA DEMUS AND THE PLIERS [MUSICAL GROUP]
— to perform, Lahaina News, September 3, 1998: 20.

CHALANGALANG FESTIVAL
— to be held at Central Maui Youth Center, Lahaina News, April 10, 1991: 12.

CHALLENGER
— controversy over John Perry independently lowering post office flag to half-staff following explosion of space shuttle, Lahaina News, February 26, 1986: 1,16.

CHAMBER OF COMMERCE
— see Maui Chamber of Commerce

CHAMBER SINGERS
— performing at Baldwin High School, Lahaina Sun, March 17, 1971: 1.

CHAMBERLAIN, BOB [ARTIST]
— "Summer of '67 and Other Sorrows" art show at the Lahaina Arts Society., Lahaina News, June 13, 1984: 4.

CHAMELEONS, THE
— to perform at Maui Arts and Cultural Center, Lahaina News, October 26, 1995: 11.

CHAMINADE UNIVERSITY
— to offer courses on Maui, Lahaina News, January 1, 1986: 3.
— seminars on college aid offered, Lahaina News, February 12, 1986: 3.
— signs cooperative agreement with University of Hawaii, Lahaina News, October 31, 1990: 7.
— to host Maui Invitational, Lahaina News, October 8, 1992: 4.
— see also basketball

CHAMPAGNE [RESTAURANT]
— reviewed, Lahaina News, September 14, 1988: 6,10.

CHAMPION, DENISE [ARTIST]
— work to be featured at Viewpoints Gallery, Lahaina News, February 10, 2000: 16.

CHAN, CYRUS
— appointment by mayor Linda Lingle as Corporation Counsel criticized, Lahaina News, January 9, 1991: 1,5.
— Maui County Council delays confirmation of, Lahaina News, February 20, 1991: 3.

CHANDLER, AUDREY [MUSICIAN]
— to perform at Benihana, Lahaina News, March 7, 1990: 13.
— featured, Lahaina News, April 30, 1992: 13.

CHANDLER, HAUNANI
— Ka'anapali Beach employee wins "Concierge of the Year Award", Lahaina News, February 17, 2000: 14.

CHANDLER, SUSAN
— participated in Maui Youth Council, Lahaina Sun, January 13, 1971: 5.

CHANDLER, WAIKALANI
— Scholar/Athlete of the Week, Lahaina News, May 27, 1999: 6.

CHANEL FASHION BOUTIQUE
— to open at Whalers Village, Lahaina News, May 11, 1995: 10.

CHANEY, BROOKS AND COMPANY [BUSINESS]
— to offer seminar for resident managers, Lahaina News, May 17, 1989: 9.
— to discontinue ERA franchise, Lahaina News, April 23, 1992: 16.
— opens full-service office on Maui, Lahaina News, February 24, 2000: 13.
— Jenny Schroder appointed general manager of, Lahaina News, November 23, 2000: 16.

CHANEY, DONALD
— Lahainaluna High School physics teacher featured, Lahaina News, September 19, 1991: 3,5.

CHANG, PETER
— appointed vice president of hotel operations for Kapalua Bay Hawaii Corporation, Lahaina News, June 20, 1991: 7.

CHANG, RICHARD
— named general manager of Ka'ahumanu Shopping Center, Lahaina Sun, May 23, 1973: 11.

CHANNEL AND HARBOR DREDGING [BUSINESS]
— contracted for construction of new docking facility in Lahaina Boat Harbor, Lahaina Sun, December 30, 1970: 8.

CHANNUKAH
— celebration scheduled, Lahaina News, December 16, 1987: 3.

CHANT [MUSICAL GROUP]
— to perform at "A Taste of Lahaina", Lahaina News, September 2, 1999: 18.
— to perform at Borders Books, Lahaina News, September 9, 1999: 12.

CHANTICLEER [MUSICAL GROUP]
— to perform at Maui Arts and Cultural Center, Lahaina News, November 9, 2000: 24.

CHAO, JANE [ARTIST]
— work displayed at Larry Dotson Gallery, Lahaina News, January 27, 1988: 3.

CHAO, LINUS [ARTIST]
— work displayed at Larry Dotson Gallery, Lahaina News, January 27, 1988: 3.

CHAPLICK, NANCY
— appointed commercial development manager at Hawaiian Cablevision, Lahaina News, March 28, 1990: 7.
— appointed area governor of Maui's four Toastmasters Clubs, Lahaina News, September 23, 1999: 5.

CHAPMAN, BRYAN
— promoted to head of design at Lahaina Printsellers, Lahaina News, July 14, 1994: 13.

CHAPMAN'S MEN'S WEAR [BUSINESS]
— opening in Whaler's Village, Lahaina Sun, November 25, 1970: 3.
— opening at Lahaina Cannery Shopping Center, Lahaina News, April 25, 1990: 7.

CHAPPELL, KATSY [COMEDIAN]
— to perform at Comedy Club and the Sports Page, Lahaina News, January 14, 1993: 12,14.
— to perform at Comedy Club, Lahaina News, February 17, 1994: 11.
— to perform at Comedy Club, Lahaina News, March 17, 1994: 10.

CHAR, VERNON
— attorney for Aloha Airlines says firm now opposes airport in Mahinahina, Lahaina News, November 6, 1985: 1.

CHARBONNEAU, JAY [COMEDIAN]
— to perform at Comedy Club, Lahaina News, August 26, 1993: 16.

CHARBONNIER, LUCIEN
— interests include music production, Lahaina News, April 2, 1992: 12.

CHARITY BALL
— to celebrate Visitor Industry Charity Walk, Lahaina News, July 27, 1988: 11.
— to be held by Maui Hotel Association, Lahaina News, September 13, 1989: 5.

CHARITY WALK
— exceeds fundraising goals, Lahaina News, July 12, 1989: 4.

CHARITY WALK BASH AND RUMMAGE SALE
— to be held at Ashton Ka'anapali Shores, Lahaina News, May 10, 2001: 20.

CHARLES, BOB
— wins Senior Stats Match, Lahaina News, December 20, 1989: 6.
— seeking fourth win in Ka'anapali Classic golf tournament, Lahaina News, October 9, 1997: 16.
— plays in EMC Ka'anapali Classic golf tournament, Lahaina News, September 30, 1999: 6.

CHARLES, FRED [COMEDIAN]
— to perform at Comedy Club and the Sports Page, Lahaina News, January 23, 1991: 7.
— to perform at Comedy Club and the Sports Page, Lahaina News, January 30, 1991: 7.
— to perform at Comedy Club and the Sports Page, Lahaina News, January 30, 1992: 17.
— to perform at Comedy Club and the Sports Page, Lahaina News, July 1, 1993: 11.

CHARLEY [SHIP]
— success in Victoria-Maui Yacht Race, Lahaina News, June 27, 1984: 4.

CHARLEY'S JUICE STAND [BUSINESS]
— will be cut off from public view by construction, Lahaina Sun, November 29, 1972: 10.

CHARLIE AND THE GREAT GLASS ELEVATOR [PLAY]
— to be performed by Maui Youth Theatre, Lahaina News, March 7, 1990: 13.

CHARLIE CHAN [FILMS]
— watched in Makawao, Lahaina Sun, January 6, 1971: 6.

CHARLIE, SEALSKIN
— visits Maui, Lahaina Sun, March 22, 1972: 7.

CHARLIE'S LOCK & KEY [BUSINESS]
— opens, Lahaina News, June 27, 1990: 8.

CHARLOTTE'S WEB [PLAY]
— to be performed by Maui Youth Theatre, Lahaina News, April 23, 1986: 3.
— to be performed at Maui Academy of Performing Arts, Lahaina News, August 3, 2000: 16.

CHART HOUSE [RESTAURANT]
— featured, Lahaina News, August 5, 1987: 7.
— hosts 10K fun run, Lahaina News, March 9, 1988: 3.
— holds blessing as remodeling completed, Lahaina News, August 29, 1990: 8.
— to host American Lung Association annual meeting, Lahaina News, May 23, 1991: 3.
— celebrates 20th anniversary, Lahaina News, November 12, 1992: 12.
— grant from fun run given to Big Brothers/Big Sisters, Lahaina News, August 17, 1995: 4.
— hosting Fun Run and Walk, Lahaina News, March 13, 1997: 13.
— Fun Run and Walk to be held, Lahaina News, March 27, 1997: 7.
— provides grant to Big Brothers/Big Sisters, Lahaina News, May 8, 1997: 15.
— kayaking series to be held, Lahaina News, January 7, 1999: 15.
— 5K/10K Fun Run/Walk, Lahaina News, March 25, 1999: 14.
— to hold fun run to support Big Brothers/Big Sisters, Lahaina News, April 1, 1999: 14.

CHART HOUSE KAYAK AND CANOE RACE
— series continues, Lahaina News, March 7, 1996: 7.
— continues, Lahaina News, March 21, 1996: 6.
— final leg to be held, Lahaina News, April 11, 1996: 7.
— to begin, Lahaina News, January 8, 1998: 6.
— series continues, Lahaina News, February 25, 1999: 7.
— continues, Lahaina News, March 4, 1999: 7.

CHARTER COMMISSION, MAUI COUNTY
— to hold last round of public hearings, Lahaina News, May 1, 1982: 7.
— considering replacing office of the mayor with appointed city manager, Lahaina News, November 14, 1991: 1.
— to meet, Lahaina News, February 6, 1992: 3.
— to meet, Lahaina News, June 4, 1992: 7.
— to hold hearing, Lahaina News, June 11, 1992: 4.
— to hold hearing in Kihei, Lahaina News, June 11, 1992: 8.
— to hold public hearings on changing Maui Charter, Lahaina News, June 21, 2001: 3.
— posting meeting schedules on website, Lahaina News, July 12, 2001: 2.
— reviewing charter and recommending amendments, Lahaina News, September 6, 2001: 16.
— to meet, Lahaina News, September 20, 2001: 17.
— to meet, Lahaina News, October 4, 2001: 16.
— to review charter and recommend amendments, Lahaina News, January 31, 2002: 17.
— to hold public meeting, Lahaina News, February 21, 2002: 17.
— continues to hold meetings, Lahaina News, March 7, 2002: 17.
— to discuss proposals, Lahaina News, March 21, 2002: 2.
— hearings to be held on budget by G. Riki Hokama, Lahaina News, March 21, 2002: 3.

CHARTER FUNDING OF HAWAII [BUSINESS]
— relocates to Alexander and Baldwin Building in Kahului, Lahaina News, December 9, 1999: 15.
— adds new loan consultants, Lahaina News, June 27, 2002: 8.
— Tessie Dumalanta closes record amount of loans for, Lahaina News, December 26, 2002: 8.

CHARTER FUNDING OF MAUI [BUSINESS]
— honors top loan officers, Lahaina News, September 26, 2002: 8.
— honors top loan officers, Lahaina News, October 17, 2002: 8.

CHARTER, MAUI COUNTY
— penalties for violation of, passed by Maui County Council, Lahaina Sun, January 26, 1972: 15.
— revised to provide for nonpartisan election, Lahaina News, September 14, 2000: 1,24.

CHASE, GLENN [ARTIST]
— to exhibit at Lahaina Arts Society, Lahaina News, March 6, 1991: 16.

CHASIE, ROXANNE
— Scholar/Athlete of the Week, Lahaina News, December 9, 1999: 8.

CHASTAIN, JANE
— to speak to Concerned Women for America conference, Lahaina News, October 18, 1989: 3.

CHATEAU DU LOUP [RESTAURANT]
— reviewed, Lahaina News, December 15, 1980: 16.
— new menu reviewed, Lahaina News, July 15, 1981: 4.
— closing, Lahaina News, August 15, 1981: 2.

CHEAP TICKETS INC. [BUSINESS]
— opens, Lahaina News, June 19, 1997: 6.

CHEE KUNG TONG SOCIETY BUILDING
— historical marker for, discussed , Lahaina Sun, December 16, 1970: 6.

CHEEAH AND FAIROH
— to lead presentation on "How to write scripts, large and small", Lahaina News, September 20, 2001: 16.

CHEERLEADING
— to perform at Whalers Village, Lahaina News, November 22, 1989: 8.
— developing as a sport, Lahaina News, October 12, 2000: 8.
— compete in Maui Pop Warner Football Federation Competition, Lahaina News, November 16, 2000: 10.
— Lahaina Chief squad wins major contest, Lahaina News, December 20, 2001: 1,18.
— Lahaina Chiefs Peewee team wins regional title, Lahaina News, January 2, 2003: 12.

CHEESEBURGER IN PARADISE [RESTAURANT]
— to open, Lahaina News, October 25, 1989: 10.
— reviewed, Lahaina News, November 8, 1989: 12.
— opens, Lahaina News, November 22, 1989: 5.
— celebrates first year in business, Lahaina News, October 24, 1990: 6.
— reviewed, Lahaina News, November 28, 1990: 11.
— owner of to open Aloha Cantina in Lahaina, Lahaina News, October 21, 1993: 9.
— promotes Alex Lavery as director of operations, Lahaina News, June 30, 1994: 9.
— hosts roundtable on Front Street Improvement Project, Lahaina News, February 22, 1996: 10.
— featured, Lahaina News, April 4, 1996: 12.
— wins "Beef Backer" award, Lahaina News, April 17, 1997: 7.
— opens at The Shops at Wailea, Lahaina News, August 16, 2001: 8.
— celebrating 13th year, Lahaina News, December 19, 2002: 8.

CHEN, EUGENE
— appointed to General Surgery department at Maui Medical Group, Lahaina News, August 14, 2003: 8.

CHENG, JI [ARTIST]
— work displayed at Dyansen Gallery, Lahaina News, January 27, 1988: 3.

CHENIER, C.J. [MUSICIAN]
— to perform at Casanova's, Lahaina News, July 25, 1990: 11.
— to perform at Casanova's, Lahaina News, September 17, 1992: 17.
— to perform at Maui Arts and Cultural Center, Lahaina News, November 27, 1997: 13.

CHENOWETH, DAVE
— comments on proposed thrillcraft corridor, Lahaina News, February 24, 1988: 1.
— featured, Lahaina News, September 16, 1993: 1,19.

CHEROKEE [SHIP]
— wins Victoria-Maui yacht race, Lahaina Sun, August 2, 1972: 4.

CHERRY, DERON [FOOTBALL PLAYER]
— career featured, Lahaina News, February 18, 1987: 6.

CHERRY POPPIN' DADDIES [MUSICAL GROUP]
— to perform at Maui Arts and Cultural Center, Lahaina News, April 30, 1998: 16.
— to perform at Maui Arts and Cultural Center, Lahaina News, April 30, 1998: 18.

CHESIS, LINDA [MUSICIAN]
— flutist to perform as part of Maui District Intermediate Music Festival, Lahaina News, April 20, 1988: 11.

CHESS
— Maui Chess Club to meet at Artful Dodger, Lahaina News, December 23, 1987: 3.
— Maui Chess Club to meet at Artful Dodger, Lahaina News, February 3, 1988: 3.
— Maui Chess Club to hold youth competition, Lahaina News, March 14, 1996: 11.
— tournament to be held, Lahaina News, March 11, 1999: 12.
— tournament sponsored by Sir Wilfred to be held, Lahaina News, April 1, 1999: 8.
— tournament to be held, Lahaina News, November 18, 1999: 16.
— tournament to be held at Sir Wilfred's, Lahaina News, November 9, 2000: 24.
— Sir Wilfred's Coffee Shop to hold tournament, Lahaina News, September 12, 2002: 21.

CHEZ PAUL RESTAURANT FRANCAIS [RESTAURANT]
— featured, Lahaina News, July 8, 1987: 9.
— reviewed, Lahaina News, April 20, 1988: 9.
— featured, Lahaina News, November 2, 1988: 8.
— reviewed, Lahaina News, April 12, 1989: 8.
— reviewed, Lahaina News, July 12, 1989: 13.
— featured, Lahaina News, November 29, 1989: 19.
— interior renovated, Lahaina News, February 7, 1990: 12.
— featured, Lahaina News, June 6, 1990: 16,18.
— hosts dinner for artists donating works for environmental causes, Lahaina News, March 13, 1991: 1.
— featured, Lahaina News, September 10, 1992: 21.
— to hold benefit for Light Bringers Mission, Lahaina News, January 24, 2002: 9.
— raises money for Light Bringers, Lahaina News, February 28, 2002: 5.
— featured, Lahaina News, January 2, 2003: 9.

CHEZ-VOUS [BUSINESS]
— restaurant delivery service starts, Lahaina News, November 7, 1990: 8.

CHI GUNG
— Kurt Miyajima to teach, Lahaina News, January 10, 2002: 16.

CHICAGO [MUSICAL]
— to be performed by Baldwin Theatre Guild, Lahaina News, November 5, 1992: 17.
— to open, Lahaina News, November 26, 1992: 26.
— to be performed by Maui OnStage, Lahaina News, March 28, 2002: 20.

CHICAGO BRASS [MUSICAL GROUP]
— to perform at Wailea Shopping Village, Lahaina News, February 11, 1987: 11.

CHICAGO DANCE THEATRE [TROUPE]
— to perform at War Memorial Gym, Lahaina News, January 21, 1993: 14,15,16.

CHICHEPORTICHE, JOELLE [ARTIST]
— featured at the Old Jail Gallery, Lahaina News, November 5, 1986: 3.
— to hold classes at Malu'ulu O Lele Cultural Arts Center, Lahaina News, April 8, 1987: 12.
— to hold workshop on acrylic painting, Lahaina News, March 9, 1988: 18.
— show at Gallery Hana, Lahaina News, July 27, 1988: 3.
— students of exhibiting works at Lahaina Arts Society, Lahaina News, December 28, 1988: 13.
— featured, Lahaina News, August 11, 1994: 12.

CHICOINE, PAUL
— appointed area director of marketing sales for Marriott and Renaissance Resorts Hawaii, Lahaina News, August 26, 1999: 13.

CHIEF EXECUTIVE ORGANIZATION
— to hold conference at the Four Seasons Resort, Lahaina News, February 18, 1993: 10.

CHIEMSEE WINDSURFING WORLD CUP
— to be held, Lahaina News, March 17, 1994: 7.

CHIHARA, AUDREY
— Scholar/Athlete of the Week, Lahaina News, June 19, 1997: 14.
— wins Pacific Asian Affairs Council, Lahaina News, February 13, 2003: 2.

CHIHARA, CARSON
— Scholar/Athlete of the Week, Lahaina News, April 1, 1999: 15.

CHIHULY, DALE [ARTIST]
— to appear at Elizabeth Doyle Galleries, Lahaina News, April 12, 2001: 20.

CHILD AND FAMILY SERVICES
— benefit to be held at Embassy Suites Resort Ka'anapali, Lahaina News, February 22, 1989: 1.
— to offer orientation for couples interested in adopting a child, Lahaina News, September 1, 1994: 7.
— seeking nominations for "Hawaii Family of the Year", Lahaina News, September 8, 1994: 5.
— to hold orientation on the adoption process, Lahaina News, March 2, 1995: 3.
— to hold information session on adopting children from China and the Philippines, Lahaina News, July 18, 1996: 13.
— seeking nominations for "Hawaii Families of the Year", Lahaina News, August 22, 1996: 5.
— hosts children at Maui Marriott Resort luau, Lahaina News, January 29, 1998: 8.
— seeking nominations for "Hawaii Families of the Year", Lahaina News, August 6, 1998: 8.
— to recruit foster parents, Lahaina News, October 1, 1998: 8.
— receives grant from AT&T Wireless Services, Lahaina News, November 5, 1998: 17.
— to celebrate centennial, Lahaina News, December 10, 1998: 11.
— organizing support groups, Lahaina News, September 27, 2001: 17.
— to begin Men's Anger Management and Women's Anger Transportation Programs in Lahaina, Lahaina News, October 25, 2001: 2.

— offers anger management programs, Lahaina News, December 6, 2001: 2.
— offering anger management programs, Lahaina News, December 27, 2001: 2.
— coordinating support groups, Lahaina News, April 18, 2002: 17.
— continues to coordinate support groups, Lahaina News, July 25, 2002: 21.
— continues to coordinate support groups, Lahaina News, October 31, 2002: 29.

CHILD MOLESTATION
— Sexual Assault Crisis Center's response to, described, Lahaina News, May 16, 1984: 11.

CHILD PROTECTIVE SERVICES
— to be investigated by lawmakers, Lahaina News, July 31, 2003: 1,2.
— to be investigated by lawmakers, Lahaina News, August 7, 2003: 2.

CHILD SAFETY DAY
— sponsored by Kiwanis Club, Lahaina News, August 11, 1994: 4.

CHILD SAFETY DAY AND BIKE SAFETY RODEO
— to be held by State Farm Insurance Company, Lahaina News, May 16, 2002: 16.

CHILDCARE
— offered free by Lahaina Baptist Church to allow mothers to shop, Lahaina Sun, December 9, 1970: 4.
— single parents seeking, Lahaina News, December 6, 1989: 1,2.
— editorial in support of, Lahaina News, December 6, 1989: 16.
— Lahaina Baptist Church to hold seminar on parenting, Lahaina News, March 14, 1990: 3.
— state strategic plan to be discussed, Lahaina News, May 23, 1990: 5.
— sponsored at Sheraton Maui Hotel; needed in West Maui, Lahaina News, February 13, 1991: 3.
— Diana Day to present on disciplining, Lahaina News, October 27, 1994: 8.
— PARENTS support group to meet, Lahaina News, April 17, 1997: 12.
— classes to be held, Lahaina News, December 25, 1997: 3.
— classes starting, Lahaina News, December 25, 1997: 3.
— free child seat inspections to be offered by Maui Police, Lahaina News, April 23, 1998: 16.
— breastfeeding class to be held, Lahaina News, June 25, 1998: 12.
— "Kids a.m." group for kids and parents to meet, Lahaina News, February 18, 1999: 13.
— Keiki Play Morning to be held, Lahaina News, September 2, 1999: 16.
— "Keiki Play Morning" to be held, Lahaina News, September 23, 1999: 13.
— state releases funds for early childhood center on Maui, Lahaina News, October 12, 2000: 19.

CHILDREN
— supplement for children on computers, Lahaina News, January 11, 1984: A,B,C,D.
— Easter activities, Lahaina News, April 11, 1984: A,B,C,D.
— Supplement focusing on 1984 World's Fair in New Orleans, Lahaina News, May 16, 1984: A,B,C,D.
— "Aloha Liberty Foundation" to hold coloring contest, Lahaina News, December 11, 1985: 9.
— children's supplement features Mother Goose, Lahaina News, February 26, 1986: A,B,C,D.
— workshop on foster parenting offered by Terri Lum, Lahaina News, October 24, 1991: 5.
— Maui's credit unions to sponsor Keiki Fingerprinting, Lahaina News, October 10, 1996: 15.
— Lahaina Recreational Center to host playgroup for , Lahaina News, January 16, 1997: 14.

— Children's Fair to be held at Lahaina Cannery Mall, Lahaina News, July 16, 1998: 17.
— Lahainaluna High School to use "Baby Think It Over" parenting dolls, Lahaina News, August 5, 1999: 3.
— Honokowai Play Group to be held, Lahaina News, February 17, 2000: 17.

CHILDREN AND YOUTH, GOVERNOR'S OFFICE OF
— looking for nominations, Lahaina News, January 27, 1994: 3.

CHILDREN FOR CHILDREN [ENTERTAINMENT GROUP]
— return to Lahaina after performances in California, Lahaina News, June 27, 1984: 10.

CHILDREN OF THE RAINBOW
— nursery to hold open house, Lahaina News, January 7, 1999: 16.
— summer program offered, Lahaina News, May 27, 1999: 5.
— nursery to hold silent auction, Lahaina News, November 28, 2002: 1.
— silent auction to benefit nursery, Lahaina News, December 5, 2002: 20.

CHILDREN OF THE TURNING TIDE [PLAY]
— to be performed at Baldwin High School Performing Arts Learning Center, Lahaina News, February 11, 1993: 15.
— to be performed at Baldwin High School Performing Arts Learning Center, Lahaina News, February 18, 1993: 16.

CHILDREN'S ADVOCACY CENTER OF MAUI
— Friends of to receive proceeds from Hoedown organized by Rotary Clubs of Maui, Lahaina News, September 26, 1990: 7.
— Rotary Clubs of Maui to host Hoe Down to raise funds for, Lahaina News, October 17, 1990: 6.
— to hold Stars for Kids fundraiser, Lahaina News, March 26, 1992: 4.
— fundraiser to be held for by Arica and Harold Keyer, Lahaina News, April 2, 1992: 22.
— Friends of to hold fundraiser, Lahaina News, April 2, 1992: 3.
— Friends of the Children's Advocacy Center of Maui to hold "Stars for Kids" fundraiser, Lahaina News, March 25, 1993: 3,4.
— Friends of to hold "Stars for Kids" fundraiser, Lahaina News, March 25, 1993: 3,4.
— Friends of to hold fundraiser, Lahaina News, April 28, 1994: 5.
— Friends of to raise funds from Maui Stingrays tickets, Lahaina News, November 6, 1997: 14.
— Maui Chamber of Commerce to collect presents for, Lahaina News, December 10, 1998: 9.
— "The Chef and The Maui Child" food fair to benefit, Lahaina News, April 15, 1999: 12.

CHILDREN'S BOOK WEEK
— to be held, Lahaina News, November 14, 1996: 15.
— to be held, Lahaina News, November 12, 1998: 16.

CHILDREN'S CHORUS OF MAUI
— to perform at Maui Inter-Continental Wailea this weekend, Lahaina News, December 18, 1985: 3.

CHILDREN'S DAY
— to be held at Lahaina Cannery Mall, Lahaina News, September 8, 1994: 12.

CHILDREN'S FAIR
— to be held by Hawaii Association for the Education of Young Children, Lahaina News, January 13, 1994: 2.
— to be held by Hawaii Association for the Education of Young Children, Lahaina News, January 19, 1995: 4.
— to be held at Lahaina Cannery Mall, Lahaina News, January 16, 1997: 10.
— to be held, Lahaina News, April 22, 1999: 1.
— to be held at Lahaina Cannery Mall, Lahaina News, February 24, 2000: 16.

CHILDREN'S GARDEN PRESCHOOL
— vandalized, Lahaina News, October 21, 1999: 6.

CHILDREN'S PARADE
— to be held October 31, Lahaina News, October 28, 1987: 3.

CHILDREN'S PLACE, THE
— non-profit seeks funds to recover from fire, Lahaina News, February 7, 1990: 1.

CHILDREN'S RIGHTS
— global demonstration to be held, Lahaina News, September 12, 1990: 9.

CHILE
— naval ship visits Lahaina, Lahaina Sun, March 1, 1972: 5.

CHILI'S GRILL AND BAR [RESTAURANT]
— to open in the Lahaina Center, Lahaina News, June 27, 1991: 7.
— opens in Lahaina, Lahaina News, September 12, 1991: 15.

CHIN, LEAH
— named spa director at Hyatt Regency Maui, Lahaina News, July 26, 2001: 8.

CHINA BOAT [RESTAURANT]
— reopens, Lahaina News, March 7, 1990: 7.

CHINA BOAT SEAFOOD RESTAURANT [RESTAURANT]
— featured, Lahaina News, May 21, 1992: 14.

CHINA CHEF RESTAURANT [RESTAURANT]
— opens in Ka'ahumanu Center, Lahaina News, July 4, 1991: 4.

CHINA, CHINESE
— Senator Spark Matsunaga recommends U.S. diplomatic recognition with Red China, Lahaina Sun, March 17, 1971: 3.
— travel to described, Lahaina News, November, 1979: 10.
— Year of the Chinese celebrations planned, Lahaina News, February 15, 1989: 6.
— Hawaii Heritage Center presenting "Myriad Worlds: 200 Years of the Chinese in Hawaii", Lahaina News, April 12, 1989: 3.

CHINESE CHAMBER OF COMMERCE
— searching for contestants for Narcissus Queen Pageant, Lahaina News, August 8, 1990: 5.

CHINESE MOON FESTIVAL
— to be held by Lahaina Restoration Foundation and Wo Hing Society, Lahaina News, September 19, 2002: 1,22.
— to be held, Lahaina News, September 19, 2002: 22.
— to be hosted by Wo Hing Society of Lahaina, Lahaina News, August 28, 2003: 3.
— Wo Hing Society of Lahaina to teach history of China at, Lahaina News, September 4, 2003: 3.
— to be held by Wo Hing Society and Lahaina Restoration Foundation, Lahaina News, September 11, 2003: 14.

CHINESE NEW YEAR
— Lion Dance to highlight "China in Lahaina", Lahaina News, January 21, 1987: 3.
— events for Lahaina detailed, Lahaina News, January 28, 1987: 4.
— celebration scheduled, Lahaina News, February 17, 1988: 18.
— discussed, Lahaina News, February 17, 1988: 4.
— to begin, Lahaina News, January 24, 1990: 5.
— events detailed, Lahaina News, January 31, 1990: 13.
— food for, Lahaina News, January 31, 1990: 6.
— to be celebrated at Kapalua Shops, Lahaina News, February 20, 1991: 3.
— Lion Dancers from Honolulu to attend celebration, Lahaina News, February 20, 1991: 8.
— events to be held, Lahaina News, January 30, 1992: 16.
— celebrations to be held, Lahaina News, January 30, 1992: 3.
— events detailed, Lahaina News, February 6, 1992: 3.
— Four Seasons Resort Wailea to celebrate, Lahaina News, January 21, 1993: 15.

— events, Lahaina News, February 10, 1994: 1,7,9.10.

— Year of the Boar to be celebrated, Lahaina News, January 26, 1995: 14.

— to be celebrated at Napili Plaza, Lahaina News, February 2, 1995: 11.

— Year of the Rat to be celebrated, Lahaina News, February 15, 1996: 13.

— celebrated, Lahaina News, February 22, 1996: 1.

— celebrated at Wo Hing Temple, Lahaina News, March 7, 1996: 10.

— to be celebrated, Lahaina News, January 30, 1997: 11.

— Year of the Ox celebrated, Lahaina News, February 6, 1997: 1,20.

— to be celebrated, Lahaina News, January 22, 1998: 1,13.

— to be celebrated, Lahaina News, January 29, 1998: 16.

— to be celebrated, Lahaina News, January 29, 1998: 3.

— Year of the Rabbit to be celebrated, Lahaina News, February 11, 1999: 2.

— to be celebrated, Lahaina News, February 18, 1999: 3.

— year of the dragon to be celebrated, Lahaina News, January 27, 2000: 12.

— to be celebrated, Lahaina News, February 3, 2000: 1,16.

— celebration set for Friday, Lahaina News, February 10, 2000: 1.

— to be celebrated, Lahaina News, February 10, 2000: 16.

— to be held, Lahaina News, January 4, 2001: 3.

— Year of the Snake to be celebrated, Lahaina News, January 18, 2001: 1.

— to be celebrated, Lahaina News, January 18, 2001: 7.

— to be celebrated at Lahaina Cannery Mall, Lahaina News, January 25, 2001: 16.

— to be celebrated, Lahaina News, January 25, 2001: 2.

— to be celebrated, Lahaina News, February 1, 2001: 1.

— to be celebrated, Lahaina News, February 1, 2001: 18,20.

— to be celebrated by Wo Hing Society and The Lahaina Restoration Foundation, Lahaina News, January 31, 2002: 14.

— to be celebrated, Lahaina News, February 7, 2002: 1,3.

— Year of the Horse to be celebrated, Lahaina News, February 14, 2002: 1,20.

— celebrated, Lahaina News, February 28, 2002: 15.

— to be celebrated, Lahaina News, January 23, 2003: 1,14,17,20.

— to be celebrated, Lahaina News, January 30, 2003: 1,17,20.

— to be celebrated, Lahaina News, February 6, 2003: 14,16.

CHINESE YEAR YEAR

— celebration of Year of the Rooster, Lahaina News, January 21, 1993: 1.

CHING, DYLAN

— to play in Hula Bowl, Lahaina News, January 20, 2000: 6.

CHING JUNE

— to present on dynamics of child sexual abuse, Lahaina News, October 13, 1994: 7.

CHING, LINDA [WRITER]

— to discuss her book "Hawaiian Goddesses, Alua, Second Generation", Lahaina News, May 9, 2002: 16.

CHING, PATRICK [ARTIST]

— wildlife artist to demonstrate technique, Lahaina News, September 21, 2000: 20.

— to lead oil painting workshop, Lahaina News, October 11, 2001: 17.

— to hold oil painting workshop at The Art School at Kapalua, Lahaina News, October 18, 2001: 16.

— to lecture on "Turtles, Monk Seals and Other Marine Life", Lahaina News, January 17, 2002: 9.

— to conduct painting workshops for The Art School at Kapalua, Lahaina News, January 24, 2002: 17.

— to present on "Turtles, Monk Seals and Other Marine Life", Lahaina News, January 24, 2002: 17.

— author of "Sea Turtles of Hawaii" to sign books at Natural Selections Coffee Co., Lahaina News, February 13, 2003: 17.

CHING, PHILIP

— promoted to vice chairman at First Hawaiian Bank, Lahaina News, January 30, 1992: 12.

CHING, SONNY

— dancer performs in Halau Na Mamo O Pu'uanahulu Ho'oulu I Ka Na'auao, Lahaina News, November 15, 2001: 17.

CHIRANJIVA

— films on spiritual leader shown at Maui Community College, Lahaina Sun, September 20, 1972: 10.

CHIRANJIVA, FATHER

— visits Maui, Lahaina Sun, March 28, 1973: 5.

CHISELERS DIVE TOURNAMENT

— to be held, Lahaina News, August 7, 1997: 11.

CHLOROMATIC HAWAII

— products to be distributed by Pure Image Pools, Lahaina News, June 9, 1994: 12.

CHO, HENRY [COMEDIAN]

— to perform at Maui Marriott Resort, Lahaina News, December 13, 1989: 20.

CHO, JOE AND SUKI

— purchased Napili Subway, Lahaina News, August 22, 2002: 8.

CHO, MARGARET [COMEDIAN]

— to perform at North Beach Brille , Lahaina News, December 29, 1994: 7.

— "Notorious C.H.O." tour to be held at Maui Arts and Cultural Center, Lahaina News, November 22, 2001: 21.

— to perform at Maui Arts and Cultural Center, Lahaina News, November 29, 2001: 16.

— to perform at Maui Arts and Cultural Center, Lahaina News, April 10, 2003: 21.

CHOCK, CHARLENE

— promoted at Four Seasons Resort in Wailea, Lahaina News, January 16, 1991: 5.

CHOCK, CHONG

— passes away, Lahaina Sun, March 24, 1971: 5.

CHOCK, DON

— named director of sales at Ritz-Carlton, Lahaina News, July 10, 2003: 8.

CHOCKY AND JEANIE [MUSICAL GROUP]

— performs at the Royal Ocean Terrace and Royal Lahaina Resort, Lahaina News, February 6, 1991: 8.

— continues to perform at Royal Lahaina Resort, Lahaina News, April 3, 1991: 7.

— continues to perform at Royal Ocean Terrace at Royal Lahaina Resort, Lahaina News, April 24, 1991: 10.

CHOE, JAY

— opens Connie Prince Galleries, Lahaina News, June 29, 2000: 16.

CHONG, BENNY [MUSICIAN]

— to perform at "The Art of the Solo 'Ukulele", Lahaina News, March 28, 2002: 19.

CHONG, LEIGHTON

— to discuss product licensing, Lahaina News, February 20, 2003: 8.

CHOPIN, DAN [COMEDIAN]

— to perform at Comedy Club, Lahaina News, June 13, 1991: 12.

CHOPSTICKS EXPRESS [RESTAURANT]

— featured, Lahaina News, August 5, 1987: 9.

— to hold canned food drive, Lahaina News, November 14, 1991: 15.

— to hold canned food drive, Lahaina News, November 21, 1991: 16.

— featured, Lahaina News, January 2, 1992: 13.

— opens, Lahaina News, November 5, 1998: 17.

CHOQUETTE, SONIA [WRITER]
— author of "The Psychic Pathway and Your Heart's Desire" to visit Unity Church of Maui, Lahaina News, April 3, 2003: 16.

CHORDETTES, THE [MUSICAL GROUP]
— to perform at 1950s concert, Lahaina News, August 23, 1989: 3.

CHORUS LINE, A [MUSICAL]
— auditions to be held, Lahaina News, November 20, 1985: 11.
— performed by Maui Community Theatre, Lahaina News, January 8, 1986: 3.
— auditions being held by Maui Community Theatre, Lahaina News, October 14, 1993: 16.
— to be performed at Iao Theatre, Lahaina News, February 24, 1994: 12.
— performance to benefit health care programs for seniors, Lahaina News, March 3, 1994: 12.
— to be performed, Lahaina News, June 11, 1998: 18.
— to be performed at Maui Arts and Cultural Center, Lahaina News, July 30, 1998: 16.

CHORUS, LTD [BUSINESS]
— executive computer network formed, Lahaina News, January 19, 1995: 10.

CHOSEN FEW [MUSICAL GROUP]
— to perform at Lopaka's Grill and Bar, Lahaina News, May 21, 1992: 18.

CHOTZEN, TAMAR
— executive director discusses Hawaii Nature Center, Lahaina News, January 16, 1992: 3.
— receives United Nations Environmental Leadership Award, Lahaina News, February 25, 1993: 6.

CHOUTEAU, AZBY
— announces candidacy for East Maui set of Maui County Council, Lahaina News, June 1, 1988: 3,19.

CHOY, RUDY
— owner of Aikane II [catamaran] visits Maui, Lahaina Sun, May 5, 1971: 6.

CHOY, SAM [CHEF]
— to join chef Scott Sibley for special dinner, Lahaina News, June 25, 1992: 18,19.
— to open first Maui restaurant, Lahaina News, January 22, 1998: 12,13.
— chef opens Lahaina Restaurant, Lahaina News, December 17, 1998: 17.
— featured, Lahaina News, April 1, 1999: 6,7.
— chef to hold Sam Choy Poke Festival, Lahaina News, July 29, 1999: 11.
— Donna Williams-Crane wins Sam Choy Poke Festival, Lahaina News, September 30, 1999: 5.
— Donna Williams-Crane wins "Best in Show" award at Poke Contest, Lahaina News, December 27, 2001: 10.

CHRIS HART AND PARTNERS [BUSINESS]
— architectural firm created, Lahaina News, February 6, 1992: 11.
— consultants to propose plan to improve Front Street, Lahaina News, June 30, 1994: 1,20.
— seeking to replace existing Harbor Village with new structure, Lahaina News, January 11, 2001: 1,15.

CHRIS' SMOKEHOUSE [RESTAURANT]
— reviewed, Lahaina News, February 15, 1984: 13.
— featured, Lahaina News, July 29, 1987: 9.
— reviewed, Lahaina News, July 6, 1988: 9.
— reviewed, Lahaina News, November 9, 1988: 8.
— reviewed, Lahaina News, May 10, 1989: 17.
— reviewed, Lahaina News, August 30, 1989: 9.
— moves location, Lahaina News, October 11, 1989: 5.
— reopens at new location, Lahaina News, April 4, 1990: 16.

— reopens, Lahaina News, April 11, 1990: 14.
— reviewed, Lahaina News, September 26, 1991: 18.

CHRIST THE KING CHURCH
— to hold "Great American Yard Sale" to benefit the homeless, Lahaina News, August 8, 1990: 4.

CHRIST THE KING SCHOOL
— to host "Keiki Fest 2000", Lahaina News, February 3, 2000: 12.

CHRISTENSEN, NELSON LLOYD
— license suspected, Lahaina News, February 15, 1996: 4.

CHRISTENSEN, PAUL
— recognized for presenting outstanding paper at Hawaiian Sugar Technologists conference, Lahaina News, January 23, 1992: 13.

CHRISTENSON, FLOYD
— named officer for Lahaina Yacht Club, Lahaina Sun, December 23, 1970: 8.

CHRISTIAN, BILL [ARTIST]
— works on display at Lahaina Galleries, Lahaina News, September 20, 1989: 4.

CHRISTIAN COALITION OF WEST MAUI
— to meet, Lahaina News, August 12, 1993: 4.

CHRISTIAN HOME EDUCATORS OF MAUI
— Home School Conference and Curriculum Fair, Lahaina News, March 30, 2000: 12.

CHRISTIAN RECORD BRAILLE FOUNDATION
— to provide services for the blind, Lahaina News, July 17, 1985: 3.

CHRISTIAN RIESE LASSEN ALOHA FOUNDATION
— sponsoring Reindeer Run and Walk, Lahaina News, December 1, 1994: 9.

CHRISTIAN SCIENCE
— lecture to be shown on television, Lahaina News, February 22, 1989: 13.

CHRISTIANITY
— West Maui churches to distribute "Jesus Video", Lahaina News, November 27, 1997: 8.
— West Maui Christian Men's Camp to be held, Lahaina News, September 26, 2002: 18.
— see also specific churches, etc.

CHRISTINE, LOU [WRITER]
— signing "Kill 'Em With Kindness", Lahaina News, March 31, 1994: 4.

CHRISTMAN, HELEN
— named to Liquor Control Commission by Mayor Linda Lingle, Lahaina News, July 23, 1992: 10.
— to be honored by Maui League of Republican Women, Lahaina News, March 11, 1999: 13.
— to be honored by Maui League of Republican Women, Lahaina News, March 18, 1999: 16.

CHRISTMAN, RANDY
— to present "Energize Your Eyes" at 'Ohana Connection, Lahaina News, May 23, 2002: 16.
— to present on "BodyTalk System" to 'Ohana Connection, Lahaina News, February 13, 2003: 17.

CHRISTMAS
— lights donated to Lahaina, Lahaina Sun, December 23, 1970: 1.
— party planned for children, Lahaina Sun, December 23, 1970: 1.
— early history of in Hawaii detailed, Lahaina Sun, December 22, 1971: 14.
— celebrations announced, Lahaina Sun, December 22, 1971: 15.
— Lahaina Jaycees offer prize for best decorated house, Lahaina Sun, December 22, 1971: 4.
— concern over improperly prepared or stored turkey, Lahaina Sun, December 22, 1971: 4.

— tree recycling to be held at Maʻalaea Garden, Lahaina News, January 6, 1994: 7.
— Mall Ball begins at Kaʻahumanu Center, Lahaina News, November 17, 1994: 18,19.
— Santa to visit Pukalani Terrace Center, Lahaina News, November 17, 1994: 19.
— Wailuku Main Street Association to sponsor contests, Lahaina News, November 17, 1994: 4.
— Kapalua Bay Hotel sponsoring progressive tree lighting program, Lahaina News, December 1, 1994: 15.
— events, Lahaina News, December 22, 1994: 1,14,15,16.
— trees can be recycled, Lahaina News, December 22, 1994: 6.
— tree recycling held, Lahaina News, January 5, 1995: 1.
— Ritz-Carlton holds "Tree of Lights" tree lighting ceremony, Lahaina News, November 30, 1995: 11.
— Festival of Lights Celebration to be held, Lahaina News, December 7, 1995: 7,14.
— drawing contests to be sponsored by Maui Mall, Lahaina News, December 14, 1995: 14.
— Adopt-A-Keiki program sponsored by Royal Lahaina Resort, Lahaina News, December 14, 1995: 18,19.
— gift ideas, Lahaina News, December 21, 1995: 4.
— service to be held at Emmanuel Lutheran Church of Maui, Lahaina News, December 21, 1995: 6.
— tree recycling offered, Lahaina News, December 28, 1995: 2.
— tree recycling to be held, Lahaina News, January 4, 1996: 4.
— bazaar to be held at St. Anthony Church, Lahaina News, November 7, 1996: 14.
— Hui Noʻeau Visual Arts Center to host Christmas House, Lahaina News, November 21, 1996: 14.
— gift ideas, Lahaina News, November 28, 1996: 7,8,9.
— Festival of Lights to be held, Lahaina News, December 5, 1996: 14.
— Kaʻanapali Kalikimaka to be held at Kaʻanapali Station of the Sugar Cane Train, Lahaina News, December 5, 1996: 15.
— gift ideas, Lahaina News, December 12, 1996: 16,17,20.
— Longhi's Restaurant to hold benefit for arts education, Lahaina News, December 12, 1996: 24.
— events to be held at Wharf Cinema Center, Lahaina News, December 12, 1996: 26.
— Festival of Lights to be held, Lahaina News, December 19, 1996: 10.
— Santa to arrive at Hula Grill Restaurant, Lahaina News, December 19, 1996: 10.
— restaurant options, Lahaina News, December 19, 1996: 19.
— World Cafe to hold toy drive, Lahaina News, December 19, 1996: 2.
— tree recycling to be held, Lahaina News, January 2, 1997: 10.
— Red Palms I.E. to hold "Christmas in Lahaina", Lahaina News, November 27, 1997: 12.
— Lahaina Cannery Mall sponsoring events, Lahaina News, November 27, 1997: 12.
— Kaʻanapali Kalikimaka to be held at Sugar Cane Train's Kaʻanapali Station, Lahaina News, November 27, 1997: 3.
— Lahaina Town to celebrate, Lahaina News, December 4, 1997: 1,2.
— to be celebrated at Wharf Cinema Center, Lahaina News, December 4, 1997: 22.
— Lahaina Arts Society to hold Christmas Miniature and Holiday Gift Show, Lahaina News, December 4, 1997: 3.
— Kaʻanapali Beach Resort Association and Lahaina-Kaʻanapali and Pacific Railroad celebrates, Lahaina News, December 11, 1997: 1.
— events to be held at Lahaina Cannery Mall, Lahaina News, December 11, 1997: 18.
— Bailey House Museum to celebrate, Lahaina News, December 11, 1997: 18.
— events, Lahaina News, December 11, 1997: 19.
— community party planned at Campbell Park, Lahaina News, December 11, 1997: 3.

— pictures of Santa available, Lahaina News, December 18, 1997: 1.
— Lahaina Cannery Mall holding toy drive, Lahaina News, December 18, 1997: 18.
— services to be held, Lahaina News, December 18, 1997: 19.
— holiday dining, Lahaina News, December 18, 1997: 9.
— events, Lahaina News, December 25, 1997: 12.
— gift and dining guide, Lahaina News, December 10, 1998: 6,7.
— events and community drives planned, Lahaina News, December 10, 1998: 8,9.
— projects to benefit the needy, Lahaina News, December 17, 1998: 1,28.
— gifts, events, and services, Lahaina News, December 17, 1998: 6,7,8,9,10,11.
— Kaʻanapali Kalikimaka to begin, Lahaina News, December 2, 1999: 7.
— Kaʻanapali Kalikimaka underway, Lahaina News, December 9, 1999: 11.
— restaurant offerings, Lahaina News, December 9, 1999: 18,19.
— Kaikuaʻana Ne Kaikuahine Hula Halau to offer Recital, Lahaina News, December 23, 1999: 16.
— religious services scheduled, Lahaina News, December 23, 1999: 16.
— craft fairs to be held, Lahaina News, December 23, 1999: 16.
— tree recycling to be offered, Lahaina News, December 30, 1999: 16.
— tree recycling to be held, Lahaina News, January 6, 2000: 12.
— Kaʻanapali Beach Resort Association to hold food drive, Lahaina News, November 23, 2000: 21.
— Keiki Christmas Karaoke Talent Contest to be held, Lahaina News, December 7, 2000: 23.
— Lahaina Cannery Mall planning events, Lahaina News, December 7, 2000: 24.
— Christmas Break Arts Enrichment Camp to be held, Lahaina News, December 7, 2000: 8.
— Lahaina Cannery Mall planning events, Lahaina News, December 14, 2000: 20.
— activities, Lahaina News, November 29, 2001: 16.
— Santa Claus to arrive at Wharf Cinema, Lahaina News, November 29, 2001: 17.
— activities planned for, Lahaina News, December 6, 2001: 16.
— Jingle Balls Rock to be held at Lahaina Cannery Mall, Lahaina News, December 6, 2001: 20.
— to be celebrated at Maui Mall, Lahaina News, December 13, 2001: 16.
— Na Kamaliʻi Te Mea O Te Atua wins tree decorating contest at Lahaina Cannery Mall, Lahaina News, January 10, 2002: 8.
— events to be held, Lahaina News, December 12, 2002: 20.

CHRISTMAS BREAK ARTS ENRICHMENT CAMP
— to be held, Lahaina News, December 9, 1999: 6.

CHRISTMAS CAROL, A [PLAY]
— to be performed at Maui Community Theatre, Lahaina News, December 12, 1996: 8.
— run at Maui Community College to conclude, Lahaina News, December 19, 1996: 10.

CHRISTMAS CLASSIC CONCERT
— offered by Maui Symphony Orchestra, Lahaina News, November 23, 1988: 5.

CHRISTMAS COUNTRY FAIR
— scheduled, Lahaina News, November 30, 1988: 3.

CHRISTMAS CRAFT FAIR
— to be held at Kalama Heights Retirement Residence, Lahaina News, November 23, 2000: 20.

CHRISTMAS FAIR AND SUPER SWAP WEEKEND
— booths being rented, Lahaina News, October 10, 1984: 3.
— to be held at Kahului Fairgrounds, Lahaina News, December 4, 1985: 3.

CHRISTMAS HOUSE
— fundraiser of Holy Innocents Church, Lahaina Sun, November 25, 1970: 4.
— details of bazaar announced, Lahaina Sun, November 10, 1971: 12.
— Holy Innocents' Episcopal church sale to begin, Lahaina Sun, November 29, 1972: 10.
— Holy Innocent Church organizing, Lahaina News, November 14, 1984: 3.
— opens, Lahaina News, November 9, 1988: 20.
— bazaar planned by Holy Innocents Church, Lahaina News, November 16, 1988: 6.
— fundraiser for Hui No'eau Visual Arts Center, Lahaina News, November 29, 1989: 22.
— to be held, Lahaina News, November 14, 1991: 2.
— to be held this weekend, Lahaina News, November 21, 1991: 2.
— Hui No'eau Visual Arts Center seeking items for, Lahaina News, October 1, 1992: 4.
— to open, Lahaina News, November 12, 1992: 22.
— to be held this weekend, Lahaina News, November 19, 1992: 13.
— to be held at Holy Innocents' Episcopal Church, Lahaina News, November 11, 1993: 3.
— to open, Lahaina News, November 10, 1994: 7.
— Hui No'eau Visual Arts Center to present, Lahaina News, November 5, 1998: 21.
— returns, Lahaina News, November 18, 1999: 16.
— to be held by Hui No'eau Visual Arts Center, Lahaina News, November 16, 2000: 16.
— to open, Lahaina News, November 30, 2000: 1.
— bazaar to be held, Lahaina News, November 21, 2002: 20.

CHRISTMAS IN JULY
— to be held, Lahaina News, July 23, 1992: 4.
— to support the needy, Lahaina News, July 30, 1992: 5.

CHRISTMAS KARAOKE TALENT CONTEST
— to be held at Lahaina Center, Lahaina News, November 26, 1992: 22,23.
— rescheduled, Lahaina News, December 10, 1992: 16.
— finals held, Lahaina News, January 1, 1998: 13.

CHRISTMAS MAUI COUNTY PRODUCTS AND TRADE SHOW
— to be held, Lahaina News, December 10, 1998: 8.

CHRISTMAS NIGHTINGALE [PLAY]
— to be performed by Maui Youth Theatre, Lahaina News, October 25, 1989: 8.
— begins, Lahaina News, December 6, 1989: 12.

CHRISTY, STEVE
— comments on KLHI radio station owners contesting ruling stripping them of control of the station, Lahaina News, January 6, 1994: 1,3.

CHRONICLE CABLEVISION
— offering Digital Music Express (DMX) service, Lahaina News, May 27, 1993: 7.

CHRYSANTHEMUM BALL
— contestants for queen listed, Lahaina News, October 21, 1993: 3.
— Suzanne Okuba crowned queen of, Lahaina News, December 9, 1993: 2.
— to be held, Lahaina News, November 28, 1996: 3.
— to be held, Lahaina News, November 20, 1997: 3.
— to be held, Lahaina News, November 25, 1999: 7.
— to be held, Lahaina News, November 9, 2000: 13.
— to be held, Lahaina News, November 30, 2000: 16.

CHRYSLER [BUSINESS]
— has worst record for Hawaii's "Lemon List", Lahaina News, January 9, 1991: 3,4.

CHU, BARRY
— hired at Westin Maui, Lahaina News, August 24, 1995: 10.

CHUBBY CHARRIER AND THE BAYOU BAND [MUSICAL GROUP]
— to perform at Casanova's, Lahaina News, November 21, 1990: 15.

CHUCK, ROBERT
— director of State Division of Water and Land Development discusses water contamination issues at Napili, Lahaina Sun, November 11, 1970: 1.
— director of State Division of Water and Land Development discusses access to clean water in Napili, Lahaina Sun, February 3, 1971: 4.
— director of State Division of Water and Land Development discusses water program for Kihei and Makena, Lahaina Sun, March 3, 1971: 3.

CHUCK'S STEAK HOUSE [RESTAURANT]
— opening in Whaler's Village, Lahaina Sun, November 25, 1970: 3.
— opening in July, Lahaina Sun, March 24, 1971: 2.

CHUMBLEY, AVERY [POLITICIAN]
— discusses priorities for upcoming legislative session, Lahaina News, December 24, 1992: 6.
— discusses how government can help small businesses, Lahaina News, August 4, 1994: 8.
— to hold community forums on Maui, Lahaina News, December 15, 1994: 6.
— names J. Kalani English as Chief of Staff, Lahaina News, January 26, 1995: 6.
— discusses state of education, Lahaina News, December 14, 1995: 3.

CHUMS RESTAURANT AND CLUB [RESTAURANT]
— to host karaoke, Lahaina News, September 10, 1992: 19.
— offering karaoke, Lahaina News, December 24, 1992: 17.
— to feature karaoke, Lahaina News, March 11, 1993: 15.

CHUN, BINA
— chair of State Reapportionment Commission responds to criticism to redistricting proposal, Lahaina News, June 13, 1991: 1.

CHUN, CHARMAINE
— awarded Hawaii Hotel Association Na Po'e Pa'ahana Award, Lahaina News, February 9, 1995: 6.

CHUN, DOUGLAS [ARTIST]
— new member of Viewpoints Gallery, Lahaina News, March 24, 1994: 16.
— watercolorist to exhibit at Viewpoints Gallery, Lahaina News, January 19, 1995: 12.
— to demonstrate watercolor, Lahaina News, June 20, 2002: 16.

CHUN, KELLENE
— to compete in Miss American Starlet pageant, Lahaina News, June 5, 2003: 3.

CHUN, LAU [ARTIST]
— painter to visit Lahaina, Lahaina News, November 1, 1989: 15.
— impressionist painter to exhibit at Lahaina Galleries, Lahaina News, March 3, 1994: 12.
— unveils latest works, Lahaina News, May 26, 1994: 15.
— to present at Lahaina Galleries, Lahaina News, January 1, 1998: 16.
— to exhibit at Lahaina Galleries, Lahaina News, February 18, 1999: 12.
— impressionist to appear at Lahaina Galleries, Lahaina News, May 27, 1999: 12.
— to exhibit at Lahaina Galleries, Lahaina News, December 23, 1999: 17.
— to exhibit at Lahaina Galleries, Lahaina News, December 30, 1999: 16.

CHUN, PAM [WRITER]
— author of "The Money Dragon" to speak at Na Mea Hawai'i Store, Lahaina News, May 23, 2002: 17.
— author of "The Money Dragon" to speak at Na Mea Hawai'i Store, Lahaina News, May 30, 2002: 16.

CHUNG, CATHY
— appointed Associate Director of Sales at Hyatt Regency Maui, Lahaina News, December 16, 1987: 15.

CHUNG DHO AHN
— preparing plans for central Maui sewage treatment plant, Lahaina Sun, December 9, 1970: 2.

CHUNG, MEL
— to teach Chinese history at Moon Festival with Wo Hing Society of Lahaina, Lahaina News, September 4, 2003: 3.

CHUNG, RINA
— recipient of Rotary Ambassadorial Scholarship, Lahaina News, January 6, 1994: 2.

CHURCH BAZAAR
— planned by Lahaina Methodist Church, Lahaina Sun, April 7, 1971: 3.

CHURCH OF JESUS CHRIST OF LATTER-DAY SAINTS
— to hold bazaar at Lahaina Armory, Lahaina News, October 30, 1985: 3.
— to hold bazaar, Lahaina News, October 29, 1986: 3.
— hosting Family History and Family Preparedness Fair, Lahaina News, September 7, 2000: 20.

CHURCH OF THE NAZARENE
— expanding to Lahaina, Lahaina News, May 21, 1986: 3.

CHURCHES
— Maui County Council may pass bill requiring county to pay for road improvements for church developments, Lahaina News, July 23, 1992: 9.

CIA, GARY AND TJ
— realtors discuss Puamana development, Lahaina News, June 7, 2001: 7.
— opens new real estate company, Lahaina News, September 27, 2001: 7.

CIARAMELLO, RICHARD
— named contractor sales division manager of Hana Highway, Lahaina News, January 2, 1991: 5.

CIBOROWSKI, ROBERT
— chef at Banyan Tree featured, Lahaina News, March 7, 2002: 9.

CIMA, ELAINE [ARTIST]
— to exhibit at Viewpoints Gallery, Lahaina News, April 30, 1992: 18.

CINCO DE MAYO
— celebrations planned, Lahaina News, May 2, 1990: 15.
— events, Lahaina News, April 30, 1992: 13.
— to be celebrated, Lahaina News, April 27, 1995: 11.
— celebrated, Lahaina News, May 2, 1996: 10.
— celebration to be held by La Familia Unida de Maui, Lahaina News, May 1, 1997: 16.

CINDERELLA [PLAY]
— auditions to be held, Lahaina News, October 1, 1986: 12.
— to be presented by the Maui Academy of Performing Arts, Lahaina News, July 21, 1994: 12.
— to be performed by Maui Academy of Performing Arts, Lahaina News, July 28, 1994: 14.

CINDERELLA MISS DIVISION
— Abcde Ka'eo Kiyoko Shibao wins, Lahaina News, April 11, 2002: 3.

CINEMAUI [FILM SERIES]
— sponsored by Maui Community College, Lahaina News, August 13, 1986: 3.

CIRCADIAN RHYTHMS [MUSICAL GROUP]
— to perform at Moose McGillycuddy's, Lahaina News, April 20, 1995: 11.

CIRCLE GALLERY [BUSINESS]
— opens at Westin Maui in Ka'anapali Resort, Lahaina News, January 13, 1988: 3.
— to open, Lahaina News, August 1, 1990: 7.
— grand opening of, Lahaina News, October 31, 1990: 17.

CIRCLE K [BUSINESS]
— to open, is hiring, Lahaina News, November 2, 1988: 3.
— purchased, changed to Texaco, Lahaina News, January 2, 1991: 5.

CIRCLE OF WOMEN
— ceremony honoring Maui county women to be held, Lahaina News, October 21, 1993: 2.

CIRCLE OF WOMEN AWARDS
— announced, Lahaina News, March 22, 1989: 13.
— nominations sought, Lahaina News, February 14, 1990: 2.
— nominations sought for, Lahaina News, February 27, 1991: 4.

CIRCUS
— Starr Brothers Circus to perform at Wailuku War Memorial, Lahaina News, December 24, 1998: 12.

CIRQUE ELOIZE [TROUPE]
— to perform comedic acrobatics at Maui Arts and Cultural Center, Lahaina News, November 2, 2000: 24.
— to perform at the Maui Arts and Cultural Center, Lahaina News, January 16, 2003: 17.
— to be held at Maui Arts and Cultural Center, Lahaina News, January 23, 2003: 16.

CITIUS [BOAT]
— wins Victoria-Maui yacht race, Lahaina News, July 16, 1986: 4.

CITIZEN KANE [FILM]
— to be shown at Wailea Shopping Center, Lahaina News, December 30, 1987: 3.

CITIZENS
— new citizens announced, Lahaina Sun, May 10, 1972: 5.

CITIZENS ADVISORY COMMITTEE ON THE WAILUKU-KAHULUI GENERAL PLAN
— see Wailuku-Kahului General Plan, Citizens Advisory Committee on the

CITIZENS FOR A HEALTHY ENVIRONMENT (CHEM)
— hold meeting at Lahaina Civic Center, Lahaina News, September 21, 1983: 5,6.
— asks Health Department for testing data, Lahaina News, October 12, 1983: 3.
— receives response from Sidney Clark, Maui's state health officer, Lahaina News, October 19, 1983: 6.
— editorial criticizing Sidney Clark's response to group's concern, Lahaina News, October 26, 1983: 2.

CITIZENS' PATROL
— having impact, Lahaina News, August 15, 1996: 1.
— County plans to expand, Lahaina News, August 22, 1996: 1,20.
— program to begin at Front Street, Lahaina News, July 17, 1997: 1.
— to begin, Lahaina News, July 24, 1997: 16.
— needs volunteers, Lahaina News, October 16, 1997: 9.
— begins, Lahaina News, November 6, 1997: 1,13.
— seeking more members, Lahaina News, December 25, 1997: 1,2.

CITRUS COLLEGE BAND [MUSICAL GROUP]
— performing at Hyatt Regency Maui, Lahaina News, July 18, 2002: 16.

CITRUS SINGERS [MUSICAL GROUP]
— to perform at Ka'anapali Hotel, Lahaina News, June 27, 1984: 3.
— to perform at Maui Marriott Resort, Lahaina News, July 25, 1990: 11.
— to perform fundraiser to benefit Rotary Peace Park, Lahaina News, July 22, 1993: 6.

CITY BANK [BUSINESS]
— sponsoring Maui Invitational Golf Tournament, Lahaina News, May 15, 1991: 7.

CIVIL AIR PATROL
— concerns over how organization is spending money, Lahaina Sun, February 28, 1973: 4.

CIVIL DEFENSE AGENCY, MAUI COUNTY
— organizing emergency cattle feeding program due to drought, Lahaina Sun, January 19, 1972: 19.
— practicing for real disaster, Lahaina Sun, November 22, 1972: 4.
— siren triggered by lizard, Lahaina News, July 1, 1993: 5.
— disaster plan almost completed by, Lahaina News, February 3, 1994: 4.
— disaster preparedness guides ready, Lahaina News, June 30, 1994: 4.
— seeking volunteers, Lahaina News, May 29, 1997: 1.
— role during crises, Lahaina News, August 6, 1998: 3.
— seeks volunteers, Lahaina News, August 13, 1998: 9.
— seeking volunteers, Lahaina News, August 20, 1998: 8.
— residents awoken by false alarm, Lahaina News, February 4, 1999: 1.
— reports that funds are available to help flood victims, Lahaina News, December 14, 2000: 8.
— adds information distribution system, Lahaina News, September 27, 2001: 3.

CIVIL DISTURBANCES
— police training to respond to, Lahaina Sun, December 16, 1970: 1,4.

CIVIL SERVICE COMMISSION
— grants hearing to former police officer Joseph Abrea, Lahaina Sun, January 12, 1972: 8.
— to conduct public hearings, Lahaina News, April 25, 2002: 17.

CIVILISATION [DOCUMENTARY]
— shown in Lahaina, Lahaina Sun, November 11, 1970: 4.

CIVILIZATION
— ancient found in Ecuador, Lahaina Times, October, 1980 volume 4 number 9: 3, 4.

CJ'S DELI AND DINER [RESTAURANT]
— to open, Lahaina News, January 2, 2003: 8.
— featured, Lahaina News, February 6, 2003: 9.
— extends hours, Lahaina News, July 17, 2003: 18.
— featured, Lahaina News, September 4, 2003: 9.

CLAIR, GERALD
— appointed branch manager of First Hawaiian Bank's Lahaina Branch, Lahaina News, August 7, 1997: 5.
— promoted to vice president and manager of Lahaina, Napili, and Lana'i branches, Lahaina News, December 31, 1998: 11.

CLAMS, THE [MUSICAL GROUP]
— performing at Moose's, Lahaina News, January 28, 1987: 8,13.
— to perform at Moose McGillycuddy's, Lahaina News, May 27, 1987: 3.
— perform at Penguin Palace Boogie Band, Lahaina News, May 27, 1987: 8.

CLARK, BERNARD
— joins Lahaina Broadcasting Company, Lahaina News, March 27, 1997: 10.

CLARK, CAROL
— appointed as vice president of public relations at Gilbert and Associates, Lahaina News, November 13, 1997: 11.

CLARK, GOLDSMITH GREGORY
— opens jewelry gallery, Lahaina News, March 15, 2001: 8.
— goldsmith opens, Lahaina News, May 3, 2001: 8.

CLARK, JOEY
— Scholar/Athlete of the Week, Lahaina News, October 3, 1996: 13.

CLARK, JOHN
— to speak to Hotel Sales and Marketing Association, Lahaina News, May 8, 1991: 6.
— to speak at Hotel Sales and Marketing Association, Lahaina News, May 15, 1991: 8.
— new librarian at Lahaina Public Library, Lahaina News, January 25, 2001: 1,20.

CLARK, JOYCE [ARTIST]
— work described, Lahaina News, October 1, 1980: 10.
— work discussed, Lahaina News, February 22, 1984: 7.
— featured at Village Galleries Cannery, Lahaina News, February 17, 1988: 3.
— to exhibit at Village Galleries, Lahaina News, January 25, 1996: 14.
— to exhibit at Village Galleries Maui, Lahaina News, March 26, 1998: 12.
— "To Soothe the Spirit" exhibit to be shown, Lahaina News, March 30, 2000: 12.
— to exhibit at Village Gallery, Lahaina News, March 29, 2001: 16.
— to exhibit "String of Pearls … crashing waves to reflecting tidepools", Lahaina News, March 28, 2002: 20.

CLARK, LARRY [COMEDIAN]
— to perform at Comedy Club, Lahaina News, November 14, 1990: 14.

CLARK, PAUL [MUSICIAN]
— free concert by, Lahaina News, February 17, 1988: 18.

CLARK, SIDNEY
— criticized in editorial for response to Citizens for a Healthy Environment (CHEM), Lahaina News, October 26, 1983: 2.

CLARK, TERRY [MUSICIAN]
— performance to be hosted by Calvary Chapel, Lahaina News, January 5, 1995: 12.

CLARK, TERRY AND DUANE [MUSICIANS]
— to perform at Maui Arts and Cultural Center, Lahaina News, November 2, 1995: 12.

CLARKE, IVAN [ARTIST]
— to exhibit at Lahaina Galleries, Lahaina News, July 9, 1998: 16.

CLARKE, NANCY
— life sailing highlighted, Lahaina Sun, January 10, 1973: 13.

CLASSIC AUCTION CO. [BUSINESS]
— to hold liquidation auction, Lahaina News, April 11, 1996: 6.
— to hold auction at Westin Maui, Lahaina News, April 18, 1996: 8.
— to hold auction at Sheraton Maui, Lahaina News, March 27, 1997: 12.

CLASSIC SMALL HOTELS & RESORTS [BUSINESS]
— to operate Paki Maui resort, Lahaina News, September 12, 1990: 10.

CLASSROOM ORGANIZATION AND MANAGEMENT PROGRAM {COMP)
— workshop to be held at Lahaina Intermediate School, Lahaina News, January 27, 1994: 3.

CLAYTON, NICHOLAS
— becomes general manager of Ritz-Carlton Mauna Lani, Lahaina News, February 18, 1993: 10.

CLEAN AND GREEN LANDSCAPE SERVICES [BUSINESS]
— opens, Lahaina News, January 29, 1998: 13.

CLEAN HAWAII CENTER
— to publish "Y2K Directory of Environmental Businesses in Hawaii", Lahaina News, July 20, 2000: 14.

CLEAN WATER ACT
— Rick Reed requests probe to determine if local government complying with, Lahaina News, September 19, 1991: 1.

CLEARLY MAUI INC. [BUSINESS]
— real estate brokerage opens, Lahaina News, June 21, 2001: 7.

CLEMENS, ROGER
— to play at Isuzu Kapalua International, Lahaina News, October 17, 1990: 9.
— holds pitching clinic, Lahaina News, November 19, 1992: 7.
— baseball pitcher competes as amateur at Lincoln-Mercury Kapalua Challenge, Lahaina News, November 12, 1998: 1.

CLEMENTS, ALAN
— to perform spoken word at Maui Arts and Cultural Center, Lahaina News, January 9, 2003: 14.
— to stage "Spiritually Incorrect", Lahaina News, January 16, 2003: 17.
— continues to offer "Spiritually Incorrect" show, Lahaina News, January 23, 2003: 16.

CLEMMENS, GINNI [MUSICIAN]
— to hold vocal workshop at Unity Church, Lahaina News, April 6, 1988: 20.
— to perform at Ka'ahumanu Center, Lahaina News, August 15, 1991: 15.

CLEVELAND, HARLAND
— University of Hawai'i President visits Maui to discuss provost search, Lahaina Sun, May 19, 1971: 1.
— University of Hawai'i President speaks to Maui Community College, Lahaina Sun, November 8, 1972: 3.

CLEVELAND, MIKE
— chairman of Life of the Land in Maui discusses project to determine pollution sources , Lahaina Sun, November 18, 1970: 1.
— chairman of Life of the Land in Maui offers opinions on water pollution control, Lahaina Sun, December 30, 1970: 6.
— director for Maui ACLU, Lahaina Sun, January 13, 1971: 6.
— elected president of Maui chapter of Life of the Land, Lahaina Sun, May 19, 1971: 3.
— chairman of Life of the Land in Maui to appear in court on change of growing marijuana, Lahaina Sun, July 11, 1973: 6.

CLIFF HOUSE COVE
— described, Lahaina Sun, May 23, 1973: 9.

CLIFF, JIMMY [MUSICIAN]
— charter bus available for attendees, Lahaina News, July 16, 1992: 17.

CLIFFHANGER [PLAY]
— comedy to be staged at Maui Arts and Cultural Center, Lahaina News, June 20, 2002: 15.

CLINTON, BILL [POLITICIAN]
— directs creation of Northwestern Hawaiian Islands Coral Reef Ecosystem Reserve, Lahaina News, December 14, 2000: 9.
— signs Executive Order to establish Northwestern Hawaiian Islands as a Coral Reef Ecosystem Reserve, Lahaina News, January 4, 2001: 2.

CLIO BLUE [BUSINESS]
— to open in Whalers Village, Lahaina News, October 26, 2000: 20.

CLOTHING
— innovative swimwear featured at Banana Moon disco, Lahaina News, November 12, 1986: 3.

CLOUD 9 [PLAY]
— auditions to be held for, Lahaina News, April 8, 1999: 12.
— opening, Lahaina News, June 3, 1999: 16.
— to be held this weekend, Lahaina News, June 10, 1999: 16.
— to hold final shows, Lahaina News, June 17, 1999: 16.

CLOUDBURST [MUSICAL GROUP]
— to perform at Inu Inu Lounge at Maui-Intercontinental Wailea, Lahaina News, July 1, 1987: 3.
— to perform at Iao Valley Lodge, Lahaina News, August 22, 1990: 13.

CLOWN
— troupe to perform, Lahaina News, January 3, 2002: 16.

CLUB D-LITE [BUSINESS]
— producing fashion show for Maui AIDS Foundation, Lahaina News, November 14, 1991: 15.
— opens, Lahaina News, November 21, 1991: 14,15.

CLUB LAHAINA
— offering free whalewatching to schoolchildren, Lahaina News, February 8, 1989: 3.

CLUB LANA'I [RESTAURANT]
— reviewed, Lahaina News, August 5, 1987: 4.
— Stardust Dinner Cruise reviewed, Lahaina News, September 9, 1987: 4.
— dinner yacht reviewed, Lahaina News, July 19, 1989: 11.
— to offer "Oceans Alive" educational program, Lahaina News, December 27, 1989: 5.

CLUB RODEO [NIGHT CLUB]
— reviewed, Lahaina News, October 17, 1984: 17.

CLUTE, EVE
— to offer massage classes, Lahaina News, October 5, 1988: 20.
— therapist featured, Lahaina News, April 30, 1992: 10.
— receives University of Hawai'i "Maui Regents Award", Lahaina News, May 28, 1992: 4.
— receives subpoena in connection to William Carroll's lawsuit for wrongful termination, Lahaina News, July 15, 1993: 1,3.
— receives grant to study algae, Lahaina News, November 4, 1993: 3.
— to run for State House of Representatives, Lahaina News, December 9, 1993: 1,12.
— discuss likely cost to clean beaches $1 million, Lahaina News, February 3, 1994: 1.
— organizing mammography study focusing on west side women, Lahaina News, August 19, 1999: 1.
— mammography researcher seeking women's stories, Lahaina News, October 21, 1999: 6.

CO-DEPENDENT'S ANONYMOUS
— to meet, Lahaina News, July 29, 1999: 12.

COALITION FOR A TOBACCO FREE HAWAII
— to organize new anti-smoking campaign, Lahaina News, September 7, 2000: 20.

COALITION FOR ECONOMIC ACTION
— companies supporting Economic Revitalization Task Force, Lahaina News, March 19, 1998: 1,16.

COALITION OF HAWAII AGAINST OCEAN STRIP-MINING (CHAOS)
— to hold information meeting, Lahaina News, June 8, 1988: 14.

COAST GALLERY [BUSINESS]
— opens store in Hyatt Regency Maui, Lahaina News, July 9, 1992: 14.
— Sabrina Taylor opens, Lahaina News, August 28, 1997: 12.

COAST GUARD AUXILIARY, UNITED STATES
— boating courses held, Lahaina News, March 4, 1987: 8.
— offers boating courses, Lahaina News, November 22, 1989: 6.
— offering classes on boating skills and seamanship, Lahaina News, November 29, 1989: 36.
— offering boating skill courses, Lahaina News, August 15, 1990: 7.
— to hold boating classes at Maui Economic Opportunity Building, Lahaina News, October 24, 1990: 5.
— to hold boating classes at Maui Economic Opportunity Building, Lahaina News, October 31, 1990: 8.
— Flotilla 26 to hold classes and sailing and seamanship, Lahaina News, March 20, 1991: 3.
— Flotilla 26 to hold classes and sailing and seamanship, Lahaina News, March 27, 1991: 3,4.
— to hold classes, Lahaina News, April 10, 1991: 4.
— offering free boat examinations, Lahaina News, May 21, 1998: 15.
— to offer courses on Seamanship, Lahaina News, June 4, 1998: 15.
— to offer boating course, Lahaina News, September 10, 1998: 17.
— Flotilla 26 offering class on Boating Safely, Lahaina News, January 6, 2000: 7.
— Flotilla 26 offering free boating classes, Lahaina News, May 4, 2000: 14.

— to offer safe boating classes, Lahaina News, February 13, 2003: 13.

— to offer safe boating classes, Lahaina News, February 20, 2003: 12.

— to conduct free vessel examinations, Lahaina News, April 17, 2003: 13.

— to hold safety checks, Lahaina News, June 19, 2003: 12.

— to hold boating course, Lahaina News, July 3, 2003: 12.

— to teach basic boating and safety skills, Lahaina News, July 10, 2003: 13.

— to offer vessel safety checks, Lahaina News, August 14, 2003: 13.

— to offer free boat safety checks, Lahaina News, August 21, 2003: 12.

COAST GUARD, UNITED STATES

— rescue two black coral divers, Lahaina Sun, June 9, 1971: 5.

— offering classes on boating skills and seamanship, Lahaina News, April 25, 1990: 3.

— cutter Cape Corwin decommissioned, Lahaina News, October 31, 1990: 1.

— discourages use of cellular phones, Lahaina News, August 8, 1991: 4.

— to offer classes on boating skills and seamanship, Lahaina News, September 5, 1991: 3.

— warns boaters to anchor with proper lights, Lahaina News, February 20, 1992: 3.

— Auxiliary Flotilla 26 to conduct vessel examinations, Lahaina News, February 18, 1993: 4.

— rescues windsurfer Michael Dieter, Lahaina News, August 12, 1993: 6.

— rescues five people from sailboat, Lahaina News, January 20, 1994: 3.

— decides not to charge captain of Navatek II after the boat hit a reef, Lahaina News, February 23, 1995: 2.

— search for distress signal removed from boat, Lahaina News, September 26, 1996: 3.

— oil response team forming at Lahaina Harbor, Lahaina News, April 17, 1997: 3.

— encouraging use of life jackets, Lahaina News, May 22, 1997: 9.

— to offer course on boating, Lahaina News, August 7, 1997: 11.

— emergency number changed, Lahaina News, November 27, 1997: 8.

— finds that 80% of boating accidents involve operator-controlled factors, Lahaina News, May 7, 1998: 11.

— to offer free boating course, Lahaina News, August 5, 1999: 12.

— Auxiliary offering basic seamanship and safety classes, Lahaina News, August 10, 2000: 17.

— Auxiliary offering basic seamanship and safety classes, Lahaina News, August 17, 2000: 6.

— to offer Basic Seamanship and Safety Classes, Lahaina News, September 14, 2000: 21.

— Auxiliary to meet, Lahaina News, March 1, 2001: 21.

— Auxiliary to offer safe boating course, Lahaina News, April 12, 2001: 2.

— offering free vessel examinations, Lahaina News, July 12, 2001: 13.

— Auxiliary to meet at Ma'alaea Harbor, Lahaina News, July 26, 2001: 17.

— Auxiliary, Flotilla 3-26 to hold Operation Exercise, Lahaina News, June 6, 2002: 18.

COASTAL GEOLOGY GROUP

— member John Rooney to discuss "Historical Changes and Future Beach Preservation Along West Maui and Kihei Shorelines", Lahaina News, June 6, 2002: 17.

COASTAL HERITAGE DAY

— to be held by Sierra Club, Lahaina News, October 28, 1999: 6.

— to be held to benefit Sierra Club of Maui, Lahaina News, November 4, 1999: 12.

COASTAL ZONE MANAGEMENT

— Doug Tom to speak on ocean issues around Maui, Lahaina News, November 7, 1991: 4.

COASTERS, THE [MUSICAL GROUP]

— to perform at 1950s concert, Lahaina News, August 23, 1989: 3.

— to perform at Maui Marriott Resort, Lahaina News, August 30, 1989: 11.

COASTWEEK

— to be celebrated by Maui Ocean Center, Lahaina News, September 18, 2003: 8.

COATES, BRADLEY [WRITER]

— to promote book "Divorce with Decency", Lahaina News, October 21, 1999: 16.

COATS OF ARMS INTERNATIONAL [BUSINESS]

— featured, Lahaina News, September 14, 1988: 2.

COBALT

— see sea mining

COBO, RICHARD [MUSICIAN]

— to perform at Hawai'i Guitar Festival, Lahaina News, June 12, 1997: 17.

COCAINE

— prevalent in Lahaina, Lahaina Times, July, 1980 volume 4 number 6: 4.

COCHIARELLA, LOU

— organizes first kayak event, Lahaina News, January 30, 1992: 8.

COCHRAN, ANGELA

— win Hard Rock Cafe World Cup of Windsurfing, Lahaina News, May 23, 1991: 10.

COCHRAN, J. WESLEY

— promoted to branch manager at First Federal Savings and Loan, Lahaina News, January 10, 1990: 7.

COCHRAN, REGINA ANN

— fugitive caught, Lahaina News, April 2, 1998: 2.

COCKETT [FAMILY]

— reunion detailed, Lahaina News, August 14, 1985: 8.

— reunion scheduled, Lahaina News, August 24, 1988: 14.

COCKETT, KAWAI [ENTERTAINER]

— to perform at benefit concert for Piilani School of Hula, Lahaina News, August 23, 1989: 3.

— to perform at Hoolaulea fundraiser, Lahaina News, November 15, 1989: 5.

COCKFIGHTING

— photographs and discussion, Lahaina Sun, January 6, 1971: 4,5.

— Maui County Council supports cockfighting, Lahaina Sun, March 8, 1972: 5.

COCOA PLANTS

— tested as possible agricultural crop in Lahaina, Lahaina News, August 27, 1986: 1,2.

COCONUT GROVE [RESTAURANT]

— holds Sweetheart Banquet, Lahaina Sun, February 10, 1971: 6.

— reviewed, Lahaina News, December 1, 1982: 4.

— featured, Lahaina News, October 3, 1996: 8,9.

— pre-sales begin, Lahaina News, September 16, 1999: 11.

— groundbreaking for, Lahaina News, November 11, 1999: 3.

— construction monitored by Kapalua project, Lahaina News, November 18, 1999: 1,2.

— condominium project taking shape, Lahaina News, September 14, 2000: 7.

COCONUT WIRELESS

— reminiscences of, Lahaina News, June 15, 2000: 3.

CODY, COMMANDER [MUSICIAN]

— to perform at Ludwig's, Lahaina News, November 10, 1994: 16.

CODY, LAURA BLEARS CHING

— surfer featured, Lahaina News, December 19, 1984: 4.

COFFEE
— featured, Lahaina News, January 2, 1997: 1,16.
— Ka'anapali Estate Coffee reports high yield, Lahaina News, January 29, 1998: 13.

COFFEE FESTIVAL
— to be held at Lahaina Cannery Mall, Lahaina News, August 2, 2001: 9.

COFFEE PARTNERS HAWAII
— promotes Mary Yacks to district manager, Lahaina News, September 19, 2002: 8.

COFFEE STORE, THE [BUSINESS]
— opens third outlet, Lahaina News, April 15, 1993: 6.
— to hold benefit for Maui Academy of Performing Arts, Lahaina News, March 27, 1997: 13.

COFFELT, NANCY [ARTIST]
— to exhibit at Village Gallery, Lahaina News, July 11, 1990: 18.
— to exhibit at Village Galleries, Lahaina News, December 15, 1994: 16.

COHEN, ALAN [WRITER]
— to present workshop, Lahaina News, June 3, 1987: 3.
— to present to Soroptimists International, Lahaina News, June 10, 1987: 18.
— to hold writing workshop, Lahaina News, September 23, 1987: 9.
— to speak at Alaya Unlimited's Ohana Luncheon, Lahaina News, December 12, 1996: 9.
— author to speak on "Freeing the Fire Within: Living the Vision", Lahaina News, January 8, 1998: 12.
— to hold workshop on psychic powers at Haiku Community Center, Lahaina News, June 6, 2002: 16.

COHEN, DHARMA [ARTIST]
— to exhibit at Lahaina Arts Society Gallery, Lahaina News, July 2, 1998: 17.

COHEN, MORRIE
— named chair of committee to explore alternatives for Maui's economic future, Lahaina Sun, May 23, 1973: 5.
— on Investigation and Complaints Committee of the Maui Chamber of Commerce, Lahaina Sun, July 18, 1973: 3.

COHEN, NORMAN
— bible scholar to speak at the Jewish Library, Lahaina News, January 2, 1997: 11.

COHN, ROBERT AND DEBBIE
— owners of Gold Fantasy attend 2000 JCK International Jewelry Show and Business Conference in Las Vegas, Lahaina News, July 13, 2000: 14.

COKE WHORES
— prevalent in Lahaina, Lahaina Times, July, 1980 volume 4 number 6: 4.
— editorial response to article, Lahaina Times, August, 1980 volume 4 number 7: 3.
— discussion continued, Lahaina Times, August, 1980 volume 4 number 8: 3.

COKER, LARRY
— to coach a team at the Hula Bowl, Lahaina News, January 16, 2003: 13.

COLD STONE CREAMERY [RESTAURANT]
— opens, Lahaina News, April 26, 2001: 9.

COLDWELL BANKER ISLAND PROPERTIES [BUSINESS]
— opens real estate information center at Grand Wailea Resort, Lahaina News, March 16, 2000: 11.
— expands, Lahaina News, February 8, 2001: 8.

COLDWELL BANKER MCCORMACK REAL ESTATE [BUSINESS]
— honors top salespeople, Lahaina News, April 18, 1990: 5.
— awards top producers, Lahaina News, July 25, 1990: 7.
— appoints William Woods as branch manager, Lahaina News, October 31, 1990: 12.
— names top sellers, Lahaina News, October 31, 1990: 12.
— sponsoring car wash for King Kamehameha III School, Lahaina News, March 20, 1991: 3.
— retains Myers Advertising, Inc., Lahaina News, March 27, 1991: 10.
— donates money to King Kamehameha III School for playground, Lahaina News, May 1, 1991: 1.
— announces new realtors, Lahaina News, January 30, 1992: 12.
— announces top salespeople, Lahaina News, April 30, 1992: 11.
— names top employees, Lahaina News, June 18, 1992: 11.
— employee awards announced, Lahaina News, July 23, 1992: 17.
— employees recognized, Lahaina News, October 1, 1992: 10.
— to combine sales operations on Maui, Lahaina News, November 19, 1992: 2.
— employee awards announced, Lahaina News, December 31, 1992: 10.
— announces top employees, Lahaina News, January 28, 1993: 8.
— employees recognized, Lahaina News, February 25, 1993: 6.
— announces employee winners, Lahaina News, July 22, 1993: 8.
— top employees named, Lahaina News, August 26, 1993: 10.
— hires new sales associates, Lahaina News, November 18, 1993: 7.

COLE, CHRIS
— wins Whipple Memorial Golf Tournament, Lahaina News, October 3, 1990: 6.

COLE, HAPPY [COMEDIAN]
— to perform at Comedy Club and the Sports Page, Lahaina News, June 17, 1993: 14.
— to perform at Honolulu Comedy Club, Lahaina News, April 18, 1996: 16.

COLE, RITCHIE [MUSICIAN]
— to perform at Maui Lu, Lahaina News, March 19, 1986: 12.

COLEMAN, JAMES [ARTIST]
— to exhibit at Wyland Galleries, Lahaina News, October 8, 1992: 12.
— to be guest artist at Galerie Lassen, Lahaina News, March 3, 1994: 12.
— Disney artist to exhibit at Wyland Galleries, Lahaina News, August 11, 1994: 12.
— to exhibit at Dolphin Galleries, Lahaina News, March 22, 2001: 16.

COLLARD, JOHN-PHILLIPE
— pianist to perform with Maui Symphony Orchestra, Lahaina News, October 11, 2001: 17.

COLLEGE ASSISTANCE [BUSINESS]
— to offer financial aid counseling, Lahaina News, February 6, 1997: 14.

COLLEY, ROBERT
— awarded Certified Residential Specialist designation, Lahaina News, November 28, 1991: 10.

COLLIER, KATHERINE [MUSICIAN]
— to perform at Maui Chamber Music Festival, Lahaina News, June 12, 1997: 9.

COLLIERS MONROE AND FREELANDER [BUSINESS]
— Todd Hedrick to lead Shopping Center Division at, Lahaina News, September 18, 2003: 8.

COLLINS, DEITRE
— volleyball player unable to compete in the 1984 Olympics, Lahaina News, March 21, 1984: 6.

COLLINS, JAMES [MUSICIAN]
— to perform at Taco Jo's Cantina, Lahaina News, September 16, 1993: 16.

COLLINS, KATHY
— to co-host "Maui Mornings" on FM 101, Lahaina News, March 18, 1987: 18.

COLLINS, LANCE
— running for Board of Education, Lahaina News, August 6, 1998: 14.
— Board of Education candidate shares ideas, Lahaina News, October 22, 1998: 1,2.

COLLINS, PEARL
— becomes general manager of Kahana Sunset, Lahaina News, August 16, 2001: 8.

COLLINS, SHERRY
— crowned Mrs. Hawaii, Lahaina News, June 18, 1992: 4.

COLLINS, STEPHEN
— appointed golf courses superintendent at Kapalua Land Co., Lahaina News, March 30, 2000: 6.

COLONY CAPITAL INC. [BUSINESS]
— may purchase Kapalua Bay Hotel, Lahaina News, March 28, 1996: 10.

COLONY HOTELS AND RESORTS
— celebrating 20th anniversary, Lahaina News, March 26, 1992: 6.

COLORFUL HAWAIIAN FISH [BOOK]
— reviewed, Lahaina Sun, September 8, 1971: 3.

COLSON, CHUCK [MUSICIAN]
— to participate in pre-concert conversation, Lahaina News, January 26, 1995: 15.

COLUCCIO CONSTRUCTION [BUSINESS]
— completes wastewater line replacement project, Lahaina News, August 18, 1994: 5.

COLUMBARIUM
— opens at Hale Aloha Cemetery, Lahaina News, January 23, 1992: 4.

COMAROW, AUSTINE WOOD [ARTIST]
— to exhibit at Village Gallery Contemporary, Lahaina News, April 4, 2002: 16.

COMBATTIMENTO CONSORT AMSTERDAM
— to be hosted by Maui Philharmonic Society, Lahaina News, October 13, 1994: 20.

COMBS, CINDY [MUSICIAN]
— promoting new CD "Slack Key Lady", Lahaina News, September 20, 2001: 17.

COME BACK TO THE FIVE AND DIME JIMMY DEAN, JIMMY DEAN [PLAY]
— to be performed at Maui Community Theatre, Lahaina News, June 10, 1987: 3.

COMEDY
— featured, Lahaina Times, August, 1980 volume 4 number 7: 6.
— comedy club coming to Embassy Vacation Resort, Lahaina News, September 10, 1998: 2.
— see also Comedy Club, Maui Comedy Club, and specific comedians

COMEDY CLUB [BUSINESS]
— opening at Maui Marriott, Lahaina News, October 25, 1989: 14.
— upcoming shows described, Lahaina News, November 15, 1989: 17.
— shows will resume after Christmas, Lahaina News, December 17, 1992: 19.

COMMANDER CODY [MUSICIAN]
— reviewed, Lahaina News, November, 1979: 5.

COMMANDER CODY AND HIS LOST PLANET AIRMEN [MUSICAL GROUP]
— to perform, Lahaina News, July 2, 1992: 20.

COMMERCE AND CONSUMER AFFAIRS, DEPARTMENT OF
— cracking down on unlicensed contractors, Lahaina News, December 12, 1991: 1,17.
— reaches settlement with contractor Tomas Barrientos, Lahaina News, September 9, 1993: 7.
— disciplines two Maui businesses, Lahaina News, June 9, 1994: 12.

— fines Maui businesses , Lahaina News, October 6, 1994: 11.
— cites Maui businesses, Lahaina News, November 24, 1994: 9.
— issues warning about bogus IRA Approved investments, Lahaina News, December 29, 1994: 6.
— Real Estate Commission hosting condominium specialist, Lahaina News, January 5, 1995: 6.
— disciplines Maui businesses, Lahaina News, February 16, 1995: 12,13.

COMMERCE AND CONSUMER AFFAIRS, STATE DEPARTMENT OF
— publishes landlord-tenant handbook, Lahaina News, August 1, 1990: 5.

COMMERCE, U.S. DEPARTMENT OF
— data indicates fastest growing industries in Hawaii, Lahaina News, March 26, 1992: 10.

COMMERCIAL PROPERTIES OF MAUI
— lots are available at Lahaina Business Park, Lahaina News, February 22, 2001: 8.

COMMISSION ON ACCREDITATION FOR LAW ENFORCEMENT AGENCIES
— to rate Maui Police Department, Lahaina News, May 13, 1999: 15.

COMMISSION ON ACCREDITATION FOR LAW ENFORCEMENT AGENCIES [BUSINESS]
— to assess Maui Police Department, Lahaina News, April 4, 2002: 5.

COMMISSION ON CULTURE AND THE ARTS
— see Maui County Commission on Culture and the Arts

COMMISSION ON PERSONS WITH DISABILITIES
— to host seminar on rights connected to renting and managing housing, Lahaina News, October 11, 1989: 3.
— to co-host forum entitled "The Americans with Disabilities Act", Lahaina News, September 26, 1990: 7.

COMMISSION ON THE HANDICAPPED
— sponsoring annual awards contest, Lahaina News, July 15, 1987: 3.

COMMITTEE FOR A HEALTHFUL ENVIRONMENT ON MAUI (CHEM)
— members meet to talk about issues with the organization, Lahaina News, July 25, 1984: 3.

COMMITTEE ON ENDING LITTER, GOVERNOR'S
— to hold reception, Lahaina News, March 27, 1997: 12.

COMMITTEE ON PERSONS WITH DISABILITIES
— seeking volunteers, Lahaina News, January 24, 1990: 4.

COMMITTEE ON THE STATUS OF WOMEN
— seeking nominations for Circle of Women Awards, Lahaina News, September 21, 1995: 4.

COMMODORES, THE [MUSICAL GROUP]
— to perform on Maui, Lahaina News, July 4, 1984: 14.
— to perform at Maui Arts and Cultural Center, Lahaina News, August 29, 2002: 8.
— to perform at Maui Arts and Cultural Center, Lahaina News, September 5, 2002: 16.

COMMUNITY ASSOCIATIONS INSTITUTE (CAI), HAWAII CHAPTER
— to hold seminar on "ABCs of Condominium Fee Conversion", Lahaina News, November 25, 1993: 7.
— to hold workshop on communication, Lahaina News, September 1, 1994: 13.
— to hold "A Guide to Contract Administration for Community Associations", Lahaina News, November 3, 1994: 23.
— offering course "ABC's: A Basic Course for Association Leaders", Lahaina News, March 23, 1995: 10.

COMMUNITY CLEAN UP DAY
— scheduled, Lahaina News, November 19, 1986: 16.

COMMUNITY CLINIC OF MAUI
— opens, Lahaina News, April 18, 1996: 6.
— to offer free mammograms, Lahaina News, July 9, 1998: 7.
— continues to offer health tests, Lahaina News, August 6, 1998: 7.
— continues to offer free health tests, Lahaina News, August 27, 1998: 9.
— to hold "Wishing Well for Health" benefit, Lahaina News, September 30, 1999: 12.
— receives grant from Susan G. Komen Breast Cancer Foundation, Lahaina News, October 17, 2002: 14.
— provides screen services for breast and cervical cancer, Lahaina News, October 31, 2002: 12.
— providing cancer screening, Lahaina News, December 5, 2002: 16.
— continues to offer cancer screenings, Lahaina News, December 26, 2002: 2.

COMMUNITY COLLEGES
— receive grant to train teachers, Lahaina Sun, January 27, 1971: 4.
— see also Maui Community College, University of Hawaii

COMMUNITY FRIENDS VOLUNTEERS
— to hold training, Lahaina News, September 12, 1984: 3.

COMMUNITY ORIENTED POLICING PROGRAM
— included in Mayor Linda Lingle's budget, Lahaina News, March 23, 1995: 1,16.

COMMUNITY PEACE OBSERVANCE
— marks anniversary of atomic bombing, Lahaina News, July 31, 2003: 9.

COMMUNITY PLAN, LAHAINA
— see Lahaina Community Plan

COMMUNITY SWIMMING POOL
— compromise with Mayor Hannibal Tavares may be necessary, Lahaina News, March 29, 1989: 1,12.
— editorial in support of, Lahaina News, March 29, 1989: 4.
— support from Governor John Waihee expected, Lahaina News, May 3, 1989: 5.
— Senator Mamoru Yamasaki introduces bill to fund, Lahaina News, February 28, 1990: 1.
— committee to meet, Lahaina News, April 16, 1992: 4.

COMMUNITY VOICES PROJECT
— seeking community input on proposed change to student drop-off system, Lahaina News, February 10, 2000: 3.
— to hold meeting to discuss aging and long-term care, Lahaina News, February 17, 2000: 16.

COMMUNITY WORK DAY PROGRAM
— described as success, Lahaina News, August 27, 1986: 15.
— organizes "Get the Drift and Bag it", Lahaina News, October 14, 1987: 17.
— looking for volunteers, Lahaina News, January 27, 1988: 3.
— scheduled, Lahaina News, April 19, 1989: 3.
— photographs from, Lahaina News, August 2, 1989: 7.
— scheduled, Lahaina News, November 8, 1989: 3.
— scheduled, Lahaina News, November 15, 1989: 5.
— volunteers honored, Lahaina News, February 28, 1990: 3.
— to be held, Lahaina News, April 25, 1990: 3.
— planned, Lahaina News, July 25, 1990: 12.
— to be held, Lahaina News, November 14, 1990: 5.
— scheduled, Lahaina News, July 18, 1991: 4.
— to hold beach clean-up, Lahaina News, September 26, 1991: 7.
— to host clean-up events, Lahaina News, November 14, 1991: 3.
— sponsoring Keep America Beautiful Day, Lahaina News, April 23, 1992: 4.
— to hold final clean-up of the year, Lahaina News, November 12, 1992: 5.
— officials to intensify enforcement of Uncovered Truck Law, Lahaina News, March 25, 1993: 4.

— bikers clean up areas, Lahaina News, May 6, 1993: 4.
— appointed general manager of Safeway, Inc., Lahaina News, May 6, 1993: 9.
— to be held, Lahaina News, July 15, 1993: 3.
— to schedule clean up, Lahaina News, November 18, 1993: 5.
— to coordinate with Keep America Beautiful, Lahaina News, April 21, 1994: 5.
— to be held, Lahaina News, April 20, 1995: 6.
— to be held, Lahaina News, November 16, 1995: 4.
— to be held, Lahaina News, February 8, 1996: 4.
— to be held, Lahaina News, April 24, 1997: 12.
— to be held, Lahaina News, January 14, 1999: 12.
— to organize clean-up over holiday, Lahaina News, November 18, 1999: 1.
— to hold cleanup, Lahaina News, January 20, 2000: 1.
— to plant trees near Mala Wharf, Lahaina News, February 10, 2000: 1.
— to coordinating "Keep Hawaii Beautiful Day", Lahaina News, April 20, 2000: 1.
— coordinating "Litter Bugs Me", Lahaina News, July 13, 2000: 16.
— to distribute recycled paint, Lahaina News, August 24, 2000: 19.
— to hold beautification events over the holiday season, Lahaina News, November 16, 2000: 1.
— to host countywide clean-up, Lahaina News, January 18, 2001: 2.
— improves Pu'upiha Cemetery area, Lahaina News, March 1, 2001: 22.
— to coordinate "Great American Cleanup", Lahaina News, April 26, 2001: 1.
— to hold "Drop and Swap" paint exchange, Lahaina News, April 26, 2001: 2.
— to coordinate "Holiday Gift to Maui Nui", Lahaina News, November 15, 2001: 3.
— to pick up tires to combat dengue fever, Lahaina News, January 10, 2002: 2.
— to pick-up bulky trash items, Lahaina News, April 4, 2002: 5.
— to hold "Litter Bugs Me", Lahaina News, July 11, 2002: 3.
— to hold "Litter Bugs Me", Lahaina News, July 18, 2002: 18.
— to help pick up bulky items, Lahaina News, August 29, 2002: 15.
— to pick up bulky refuse items, Lahaina News, October 31, 2002: 12.
— to pick up bulky refuse items, Lahaina News, December 5, 2002: 16.

COMO, BRIAN [MUSICIAN]
— to perform at Raffle's Restaurant, Lahaina News, November 21, 1991: 19,22.
— continues to perform at Raffle's Restaurant at Stouffer Wailea, Lahaina News, January 16, 1992: 17.
— continues to perform at Raffle's Restaurant at Stouffer Wailea, Lahaina News, April 16, 1992: 19.
— continues to perform at Raffle's Restaurant, Lahaina News, August 27, 1992: 18.

COMO, PERRY [ENTERTAINER]
— filmed part of his Christmas special in Lahaina, Lahaina News, November 13, 1985: 7.

COMPADRES KAYAK RACING SERIES
— continues to be held, Lahaina News, February 9, 1995: 7.
— second leg won by Edmund "the Machine" Mitchell, Lahaina News, February 16, 1995: 9.

COMPADRES MEXICAN BAR AND GRILL [RESTAURANT]
— to open in Lahaina, Lahaina News, May 2, 1990: 4.
— Miles Worrell to manage Lahaina branch, Lahaina News, January 9, 1991: 5.
— to open in late March, Lahaina News, March 20, 1991: 6,7.
— owner Rick Enos speaks of success of opening day, Lahaina News, April 24, 1991: 7.

— to hold Balloonefit for the Lahaina Restoration Foundation, Lahaina News, May 1, 1991: 14.

— Balloonefit a success, Lahaina News, May 23, 1991: 6.

— forms for chili cookoff now available, Lahaina News, July 11, 1991: 18.

— to hold eclipse photo contest, Lahaina News, July 11, 1991: 4.

— to hold South Pacific Chili Cookoff, Lahaina News, July 18, 1991: 12.

— begins hosting happy hour, Lahaina News, August 8, 1991: 12.

— reviewed, Lahaina News, October 10, 1991: 20.

— names Tim McCarthy as general manager, Lahaina News, December 12, 1991: 16.

— featured, Lahaina News, July 16, 1992: 19,21.

— to sponsor Kayak racing with Maui Kayak Club, Lahaina News, January 21, 1993: 7.

— to hold kayaking event, Lahaina News, February 4, 1993: 6.

— results of Kayak Racing series, Lahaina News, February 11, 1993: 8.

— to host Chili Cookoff, Lahaina News, October 7, 1993: 13.

— to hold Chili Cookoff, Lahaina News, November 11, 1993: 12.

— presents Kayak Racing Series, Lahaina News, January 27, 1994: 6.

— to sponsor benefit for Maui Arts and Cultural Center, Lahaina News, March 24, 1994: 16.

— to hold benefit for Lahaina High School football team, Lahaina News, August 11, 1994: 4.

— to hold benefit for Protect Ma'alaea Coalition, Lahaina News, August 25, 1994: 14.

— to celebrate Cinco de Mayo, Lahaina News, April 30, 1998: 16.

— to hold salsa dancing, Lahaina News, February 7, 2002: 16.

— to hold salsa dancing, Lahaina News, March 21, 2002: 16.

— to host karaoke and dancing, Lahaina News, April 18, 2002: 16.

— continues to hold salsa dancing, Lahaina News, July 11, 2002: 16.

— continues to offer salsa dancing, Lahaina News, November 7, 2002: 21.

— continues to hold salsa dancing, Lahaina News, February 20, 2003: 17.

COMPANY [MUSICAL]
— Maui Community Theatre to hold auditions for, Lahaina News, April 16, 1998: 12.

— to be performed by Maui Community Theatre, Lahaina News, May 28, 1998: 13.

— to open in Honokowai, Lahaina News, June 4, 1998: 16.

COMPANY KIDS OF ORANGE COUNTY [TROUPE]
— to perform "Salute to America", Lahaina News, July 31, 1997: 16,17.

COMPANY OF WAYWARD SAINTS, A [PLAY]
— auditions held by Maui Academy of Performing Arts, Lahaina News, October 28, 1993: 11.

— featured; playing at Kahului Community Center Playhouse, Lahaina News, January 20, 1994: 10.

COMPEHOS, TED [MUSICIAN]
— featured, Lahaina News, July 2, 1992: 20.

COMPLEAT KITCHEN, THE [BUSINESS]
— opens, Lahaina News, November 17, 1994: 10.

COMPLETE BUSINESS SOLUTIONS, INC. [BUSINESS]
— to help modernize Maui County Operations, Lahaina News, September 16, 1999: 3.

COMPLETE CHIROPRACTIC AND MASSAGE [BUSINESS]
— to hold Toys for Tots drive, Lahaina News, December 12, 2002: 2.

COMPLEXIONS
— to perform at Maui Arts and Cultural Center, Lahaina News, September 25, 2003: 17.

COMPUSWAP
— to be held at War Memorial Gym, Lahaina News, July 18, 2002: 20.

— to be held, Lahaina News, July 10, 2003: 8.

— to be held, Lahaina News, July 17, 2003: 8.

COMPUTERS
— Macintosh computer users group to meet, Lahaina News, November 22, 1989: 5.

— Macintosh users group to meet, Lahaina News, November 22, 1989: 5.

— Christmas gift ideas, Lahaina News, November 29, 1989: 9.

— graphics business opens, Lahaina News, January 3, 1990: 4.

— MacConcepts to offer free seminar on graphics software, Lahaina News, February 28, 1990: 4.

— Macintosh Users Group to meet, Lahaina News, April 4, 1990: 7.

— Macintosh workshops to be held at Seabury Hall, Lahaina News, January 2, 1991: 5.

— Maui Mac Mania conference for Macintosh computers to be held, Lahaina News, July 2, 1992: 18.

— Maui Mac Mania conference to be held, Lahaina News, August 6, 1992: 6,8.

— Maui Mac Mania conference to be held, Lahaina News, August 13, 1992: 12.

— Maui Mac Mania II to be held, Lahaina News, September 2, 1993: 7.

— Maui Mac Mania II to be held, Lahaina News, September 2, 1993: 7.

— scamming activities on the internet, Lahaina News, July 14, 1994: 4.

— PC Currents Computer Newsmagazine now online, Lahaina News, February 16, 1995: 13.

— Maui High Performing Computing Center to offer workshop "Getting Wired for Business", Lahaina News, May 18, 1995: 6.

— Roger Stout discusses importance of internet to Maui businesses, Lahaina News, August 3, 1995: 8.

— Center for Computer Technology Training offers computer training, Lahaina News, January 25, 1996: 4.

— Maui Chamber of Commerce offering workshop on online business, Lahaina News, March 21, 1996: 10.

— Maui Apple User Society to meet, Lahaina News, July 18, 1996: 12.

— concerns for the year 2000, Lahaina News, July 10, 1997: 13.

— Harvest Chapel-Church of God to offer training, Lahaina News, February 26, 1998: 13.

— Maui Apple User Society to meet, Lahaina News, May 21, 1998: 16.

— Maui Apple Users Society to meet, Lahaina News, May 21, 1998: 16.

— Small Business Administration warns of Y2K issues, Lahaina News, October 29, 1998: 20.

— threat of Y2K discussed, Lahaina News, November 19, 1998: 1.

— Maui Chamber of Commerce to host presentation on Y2K, Lahaina News, November 26, 1998: 16.

— resources available for Y2K, Lahaina News, January 28, 1999: 11.

— Y2K seminar to be held at Bank of Hawaii Quarterly Luncheon, Lahaina News, February 4, 1999: 13.

— Maui County Y2K Task Force providing information, Lahaina News, February 25, 1999: 11.

— U.S. Small Business Administration urges people to take Y2K seriously, Lahaina News, April 1, 1999: 3.

— installing email in a company discussed, Lahaina News, August 5, 1999: 11.

— installing email in a company discussed, part 2 of 3, Lahaina News, August 19, 1999: 13.

— installing email in a company discussed, part 3 of 3, Lahaina News, August 26, 1999: 13.

— Dial-up compared to ADSL, part 3, Lahaina News, September 9, 1999: 11.

— George Gordon to discuss Y2K, Lahaina News, November 25, 1999: 13.

— Maui Net lowers price for ADSL accounts, Lahaina News, December 9, 1999: 15.

— Local ISP pros and cons, Lahaina News, January 20, 2000: 6.

— Lahainaluna High School receives money for computer learning center, Lahaina News, January 27, 2000: 1,16.

— how to search smarter, Lahaina News, February 3, 2000: 11.

— program internet access in support of Junior Achievement, Lahaina News, May 25, 2000: 16.

— workshop to focus on E-commerce, Lahaina News, August 24, 2000: 14.

— workshop to cover internet marketing, Lahaina News, September 14, 2000: 16.

— "Market Your Health and Wellness Business on the Net", Lahaina News, September 21, 2000: 16.

— Maui Professional Photographers Association to hold seminar on Photoshop 5.5, Lahaina News, September 21, 2000: 20.

— Maui Apple User Society to meet, Lahaina News, January 17, 2002: 16.

— Digital Crossroads Hawaii conference to be held, Lahaina News, October 31, 2002: 6.

— Karen Hue Sing-Ledesma demonstrates Miracle Mouse, Lahaina News, November 7, 2002: 8.

— Maui TechOhana to meet, Lahaina News, November 14, 2002: 8.

— swap meet to be held at the War Memorial Gym, Lahaina News, January 16, 2003: 8.

— CompuSwap to be held, Lahaina News, January 23, 2003: 8.

— Mayor Arakawa details Tech Ready campaign, Lahaina News, February 6, 2003: 8.

— Lahaina Intermediate School technology coordinator Rob Siarot discusses programs, Lahaina News, May 22, 2003: 1,18.

— Y2Tech Maui classes set, Lahaina News, June 5, 2003: 9.

— CompuSwap to be held at the War Memorial Gym, Lahaina News, July 10, 2003: 8.

— CompuSwap to be held at the War Memorial Gym, Lahaina News, July 17, 2003: 8.

CONAGRA FOODS CHAMPIONS SKINS GAME

— to be played at Wailea Golf Course, Lahaina News, January 23, 2003: 13.

CONANT, JOSEPH

— executive director of state Housing Finance and Development Corporation disagrees with mayor Linda Lingle on implications of legislation, Lahaina News, April 3, 1991: 1.

CONCERNED PARENTS AND TEACHERS OF PRINCESS NAHIENAENA SCHOOL

— worried about walk to school, hoping to beautify school, Lahaina News, February 15, 1989: 1.

CONCERNED WOMEN FOR AMERICA

— to hold conference, Lahaina News, October 18, 1989: 3.

CONCERT OF SHARING

— concert to be held at War Memorial, Lahaina News, May 15, 1985: 20.

CONCERT OF THE STARS

— to be held by Kina'u Ministries, Lahaina News, July 13, 1995: 12.

— benefit to be held for Kina'u Ministries, Lahaina News, August 22, 1996: 12.

CONCHING, LEE

— appointed regional director of sales-Eastern Region for Kapalua Bay Hotel and Villas, Lahaina News, February 27, 1991: 8.

CONCIERGE ALOHA PEOPLE OF SERVICE [CAPS]

— formed, Lahaina News, July 13, 1988: 10.

CONCIERGE O' MAUI [BUSINESS]

— to provide custom itineraries for visitors via the internet, Lahaina News, November 26, 1998: 13.

CONCORD STRING QUARTET

— opens Maui Philharmonic Society's season, Lahaina News, August 27, 1986: 12.

CONCRETE

— Concrete Industries Maui seeks to relocate batch plant, Lahaina Sun, September 29, 1971: 13.

— Maui Planning Commission recommends Concrete Industries Maui be allowed to move to a site near Honokowai Stream, Lahaina Sun, October 27, 1971: 11.

CONCRETE INDUSTRIES MAUI [BUSINESS]

— seeks to relocate its batch plant to near Honokowai Stream, Lahaina Sun, September 29, 1971: 13.

CONCUBINE [SHIP]

— breaks rudder, Lahaina Sun, February 28, 1973: 14.

CONDE NAST TRAVELER

— lists Hawaiian Airlines among top 10 in nation, Lahaina News, November 7, 1991: 9.

— Maui voted "Best Island in the World" in Reader's Choice poll, Lahaina News, October 22, 1998: 17.

— Maui is "Best Island in the World" in Readers' Choice Awards Poll, Lahaina News, November 8, 2001: 9.

CONDOMINIUM COUNCIL OF MAUI

— to hold annual luncheon, Lahaina News, March 26, 1998: 11.

— to hold annual luncheon featuring John Morris and Gordon Arakaki, Lahaina News, March 14, 2002: 8.

— to sponsor "Condo Rage" video, Lahaina News, April 11, 2002: 17.

— to discuss conflicts of interest, Lahaina News, November 14, 2002: 8.

— to hold Condo Owners Forum, Lahaina News, June 12, 2003: 7.

— to hold workshop on developing code of ethics, Lahaina News, August 14, 2003: 8.

CONFERENCE ON LITERATURE AND HAWAII'S CHILDREN

— to be held, Lahaina News, June 13, 1996: 10.

CONFERENCE ON QUALITY GROWTH

— to begin, Lahaina Sun, December 13, 1972: 7.

CONFRERIE DE LA CHAINE DES ROTISSEURS, LA

— hosted by Stouffer Wailea Beach Resort, Lahaina News, August 20, 1986: 3.

CONGER, JEAN

— appointed director of development at Maui Arts and Cultural Center, Lahaina News, May 29, 1997: 5.

CONGOLESE AFRICAN DANCE AND DRUM WORKSHOP

— planned for Camp Keanae, Lahaina News, October 29, 1998: 21.

CONJUGACION, TONY [MUSICIAN]

— to perform at Hoolaulea fundraiser, Lahaina News, November 15, 1989: 5.

CONKLIN, DANIEL

— named sales manager for Royal Lahaina Resort, Lahaina News, June 24, 1993: 10.

— director of sales at Napili Kai Beach Club, Lahaina News, October 10, 1996: 8.

CONNECTICUT GENERAL LIFE INSURANCE COMPANY [BUSINESS]

— opens Maui Surf hotel, Lahaina Sun, July 28, 1971: 5.

CONNELL, MARY [ARTIST]

— to offer watercolor demonstration, Lahaina News, January 16, 2003: 16.

CONNER, JOANNA [MUSICIAN]

— to perform at Maui Arts and Cultural Center, Lahaina News, May 1, 1997: 13.

CONNERS, JEFF

— named port captain by Young Brothers and Hawaiian Tug and Barge, Lahaina News, May 29, 2003: 8.

CONNIE PRINCE GALLERIES [BUSINESS]
— to host Mermaid Costume Party, Lahaina News, June 1, 2000: 17.
— Mermaid Art Contest held, Lahaina News, June 29, 2000: 16.

CONNORS, ED "THE PROFESSOR" [MUSICIAN]
— interviewed, Lahaina News, April 17, 1985: 12.
— reviewed, Lahaina News, October 14, 1987: 9,10.

CONO, JOE [MUSICIAN]
— to perform at Maui Inter-Continental Wailea this weekend, Lahaina News, January 1, 1986: 8.

CONRAD, CYNTHIA [ARTIST]
— donates art Maui Historical Society's Bailey Art Project, Lahaina News, June 1, 1988: 19.
— featured artist, Lahaina News, April 5, 1989: 15.
— poster used as fundraiser for Maui Academy of Performing Arts musical, Lahaina News, November 28, 1990: 9.
— to sign shirts at Reyn's, Lahaina News, May 4, 1995: 14.
— curates "Feast or Famine II" art show, Lahaina News, November 5, 1998: 14.

CONRAD, JONATHAN
— Lahainaluna High School athletic trainer featured, Lahaina News, October 28, 1999: 8.

CONSCIOUS BREATHING SUPPORT GROUP
— to meet, Lahaina News, February 13, 2003: 16.

CONSERVATION
— see environment

CONSIDER THE EARTH A SANCTUARY, LTD. [BUSINESS]
— to hold mountain bike race, Lahaina News, January 16, 1992: 7.

CONSOLIDATED AMUSEMENT COMPANY, LTD. [BUSINESS]
— to open in Maui, Lahaina News, May 21, 1992: 8,9.
— opens movie complex at Ka'ahumanu Center, Lahaina News, November 17, 1994: 18.

CONSOLIDATED THEATRE
— opens in Kukui Mall in Kihei, Lahaina News, November 19, 1992: 4.

CONSORTIUM FOR TEACHING ASIA AND THE PACIFIC IN SCHOOLS
— offers workshop on the double-hulled voyaging canoes, Lahaina News, October 31, 1996: 1,22.

CONSTANTINE, MILDRED [ARTIST]
— to jury annual Hawaii Craftsmen show, Lahaina News, September 18, 1985: 3.

CONSTITUTION [SHIP]
— entered Hawaii cruise market, Lahaina News, May 1, 1982: 6.
— American Hawaii ship offering whale watching cruises, Lahaina News, March 21, 1990: 18.

CONSTRUCTION
— home construction announced for Maui, with support of County, Lahaina Sun, January 20, 1971: 3.
— building code violations referred to county attorney, Lahaina Sun, March 17, 1971: 5.
— started on Maui County Building in Wailuku, Lahaina Sun, April 7, 1971: 1.
— hotel in Kahana stopped due to developer's financial troubles, Lahaina Sun, May 12, 1971: 2.
— a record number of building permits issued, Lahaina Sun, June 16, 1971: 1.
— Bank of Hawaii reports on, Lahaina News, July 1, 1981: 11.

CONSUMER DIAL
— telephone service operational again, Lahaina News, July 28, 1994: 8,9.

CONSUMER LAWYERS OF HAWAII
— offering referral service, Lahaina News, May 13, 1999: 15.

CONSUMER PROTECTION AGENCY, STATE
— revising advertising rules, Lahaina News, January 3, 1990: 5.
— legislators crack down on timeshare sales practices, Lahaina News, March 25, 1993: 1.
— recommends banning smoking n fast-food restaurants, Lahaina News, January 20, 1994: 7.
— warns people of "Property Tax Reduction" scam, Lahaina News, January 14, 1999: 11.
— warns residents of internet scams, Lahaina News, October 4, 2001: 2.

CONSUMER PROTECTION COMMISSION, SENATE
— to discuss bills on Front street and timeshares, Lahaina News, March 4, 1993: 3.

CONSUMERS
— emerald scam described, Lahaina News, May 1, 1980: 7.
— issues with garage repair work, Lahaina Times, June, 1980 volume 4 number 5: 1,10.
— right to refunds, Lahaina News, December 6, 1989: guide4.
— jewelry trademark ensures quality, Lahaina News, December 13, 1989: 12.
— "Consumer Watch" column begins, only West Maui entries are typically indexed, Lahaina News, August 8, 1990: 9.
— gas prices at various stations surveyed weekly, not otherwise indexed, Lahaina News, August 15, 1990: 2.
— alleged fraud at auto dealers discussed, Lahaina News, August 29, 1990: 3,5.
— State Senate to study gasoline price fixing, Lahaina News, September 19, 1990: 1,2.
— telemarketing scams, lemon laws discussed, Lahaina News, September 19, 1990: 20.
— House Consumer Protection Committee to look at used car lemon laws again, Lahaina News, October 10, 1990: 2.
— lemon laws apply to bad paint jobs, Lahaina News, October 17, 1990: 1.
— scams from tree trimmers discussed, Lahaina News, October 31, 1990: 4.
— refund rights discussed, Lahaina News, November 14, 1990: 6.
— concern for rising automotive insurance rates, Lahaina News, April 17, 1991: 9.
— discussion of rust proofing of automobiles, Lahaina News, May 30, 1991: 16.
— can now use computerized automated ticket kiosk, Lahaina News, June 20, 1991: 1.
— lack of lemon laws discussed, Lahaina News, February 13, 1992: 8.

CONTINENTAL AIRLINES [BUSINESS]
— to issue credit card with Bank of Hawaii, Lahaina News, February 2, 1995: 7.

CONTRACTORS CONVENTION, 1991 STATE-WIDE
— to be held at Pagoda Hotel in Honolulu, Lahaina News, March 13, 1991: 7.

CONVENTION CENTER AUTHORITY (CCA)
— creates fact sheet and packet with plans, Lahaina News, December 14, 1995: 16.

CONVERSATIONS WITH GOD [BOOK]
— discussion to be held, Lahaina News, August 6, 1998: 20.

CONVINGTON, JANE ANN
— to offer stress management course, Lahaina News, May 11, 1988: 3,14.

CONWAY, RUSTY
— hired as technical director for Maui Arts and Cultural Center, Lahaina News, March 24, 1994: 8.

CONWAY, SUSAN [ARTIST]
— to exhibit at Village Galleries, Lahaina News, December 15, 1994: 18.

CONWAY, TIM [COMEDIAN]
— to perform at Maui Arts and Cultural Center with Harvey Korman, Lahaina News, December 12, 2002: 19.
— tickets on sale for show, Lahaina News, December 26, 2002: 17.

CONYERS, MAHA [ARTIST]
— to present "Painting the Light: Out of Color Worlds Arise", Lahaina News, May 8, 2003: 16.
— to talk on "The Art of Rejuvenation: Chinese Emperor's Chi Gong" at 'Ohana Connection, Lahaina News, August 21, 2003: 17.

CONYOS, MAHA
— to speak on "Tibetan Pulsing Healing", Lahaina News, November 7, 2002: 21.

COOK, DARCY AND HOWARD
— owners of Bebe Sport featured, Lahaina News, July 20, 1988: 2.

COOK, JAMES
— death of recounted, Lahaina News, April 1, 1981: 7,10.
— "Hulihia Hawaii" to be performed, Lahaina News, January 2, 1991: 8.

COOK, PHYLLIS [ATHLETE]
— competed in Valley Isle Triathlon, Lahaina News, May 23, 1984: 6.

COOK, ROBIN [WRITER]
— to attend Maui Writers Conference, Lahaina News, August 19, 1999: 2.

COOK, SUNNY KOBE
— Sleep Country USA founder to sign book "Common Things, Uncommon Ways", Lahaina News, June 20, 2002: 17.
— to sign book "Common Things Uncommon Ways", Lahaina News, June 27, 2002: 16.

COOKE, MARY [WRITER]
— visits Maui bookstore, Lahaina Sun, March 17, 1971: 3.

COOKIN' [TROUPE]
— Korean theater troupe to perform at Maui Arts and Cultural Center, Lahaina News, December 5, 2002: 21.

COOKING
— youth classes to be offered by Sally J. Brown, Lahaina News, January 9, 1997: 11.

COOKING MAUI STYLE
— Sally Brown to offer cooking classes, Lahaina News, November 28, 1996: 11.

COOKS AT THE BEACH [RESTAURANT]
— presents Hawaiian music, Lahaina News, June 4, 1992: 18.

COOL CAT CAFE [RESTAURANT]
— featured, Lahaina News, April 24, 2003: 17.

COOL CATS [MUSICAL GROUP]
— featured, Lahaina News, June 4, 1992: 13.

COOL FLAVOR, A [MUSICAL GROUP]
— to perform at Lopaka's Grill and Bar, Lahaina News, June 25, 1992: 22.

COON BROS, INC. [BUSINESS]
— reorganized, Lahaina News, October 16, 1997: 12.

COON, JIM AND RANDY
— managing beach activities for Ka'anapali Beach Hotel, Lahaina News, January 1, 1998: 15.

COONEN, CLAUDIA [ARTIST]
— to exhibit at Lahaina Arts Society, Lahaina News, August 8, 2002: 15.

COOPER, ALICE [MUSICIAN]
— vacations on island, Lahaina News, March 6, 1985: 7.

COOPER, MALCOLM
— to discuss "Hawaiian Sea and Sky" at Maui Ocean Center, Lahaina News, March 21, 2002: 17.

COOPER, NORA
— journalist participating in Girl Scout program were scouts watch women executives in action, Lahaina News, April 10, 1991: 3.
— journalist to be interviewed by mayor Linda Lingle, Lahaina News, November 28, 1991: 2.

COOPERS AND LYBRAND VICTORIA-MAUI INTERNATIONAL YACHT RACE
— to be held, Lahaina News, July 9, 1998: 15.

COPPERFIELD, DAVID
— discusses shrimp aquaculture project, Lahaina Sun, January 20, 1971: 4.

COPPERS, JEAN
— restaurant manager at Ruby's Diner, Lahaina News, January 16, 2003: 8.

CORAGGIO, PETER [MUSICIAN]
— pianist to perform with Maui Symphony Orchestra, Lahaina News, January 19, 1995: 11.
— to perform with Maui Symphony Orchestra, Lahaina News, January 26, 1995: 15.

CORAL REEF [RESTAURANT]
— featured, Lahaina News, August 3, 2000: 8.

CORAL REEF CELEBRATION
— to honor International Year of the Reef, Lahaina News, September 4, 1997: 15.

CORBY, CHASE
— Scholar/Athlete of the Week, Lahaina News, September 28, 2000: 8.

CORCORAN, JOE [COMEDIAN]
— to perform at Comedy Club, Lahaina News, July 11, 1991: 10.

CORDEIRO, ROBERT "ACE"
— police officer featured, Lahaina News, November 21, 1991: 3.

CORDEN, JEANETTE
— promoted to branch manager of Standard Title and Escrow, Lahaina News, July 8, 1993: 8.

CORDES, MARK [COMEDIAN]
— to perform at Comedy Club, Lahaina News, September 26, 1990: 10.
— to perform at Comedy Club, Lahaina News, September 5, 1991: 9.
— to perform at Comedy Club and the Sports Page, Lahaina News, July 30, 1992: 13,15.
— to perform at Comedy Club, Lahaina News, February 17, 1994: 11.

CORDI, MICHAEL
— named director of marketing and promotions for Lasting Impressions, Lahaina News, August 26, 1993: 10.
— to teach courses on using the internet, Lahaina News, February 15, 1996: 10.

CORN, ALFRED [POET]
— to read at Pukalani Community Center, Lahaina News, May 6, 1993: 17.

CORRALES, FAITH
— Educator of the Month at Kimo's Restaurant, Lahaina News, February 21, 2002: 3.

CORREA, GLENN
— named new deputy director of the county Department of Parks and Recreation, Lahaina News, December 27, 2001: 8.

CORTESE, DAN
— taping MTV sports special at Studio 505, Lahaina News, July 23, 1992: 19.

CORTEZ, JACKSON
— painting exhibited at Ka'ahumanu Shopping Center, Lahaina News, August 6, 1998: 21.

CORVELLE, SEAN [COMEDIAN]
— to perform at Comedy Club, Lahaina News, February 3, 1994: 12.

CORYELL, LARRY [MUSICIAN]
— to perform at Hawaii International Jazz Festival, Lahaina News, July 24, 2003: 14.

COS BAR [RESTAURANT]
— opens at The Shops at Wailea, Lahaina News, January 10, 2002: 8.
— opens at The Shops at Wailea, Lahaina News, April 25, 2002: 8.

COSBY, BILL
— returns to television, Lahaina News, October 10, 1984: 11.

COSBY, JOHN [ARTIST]
— work chosen for LahainaTown Action Committee's poster, Lahaina News, October 13, 1994: 18.

COSCI, RICK [ARTIST]
— to exhibit at Village Galleries, Lahaina News, February 2, 1995: 11.
— to exhibit at Lahaina Arts Society, Lahaina News, November 6, 1997: 16.

COSMETICS, THE [TROUPE]
— to perform comedy at Blue Tropix, Lahaina News, June 24, 1993: 14.
— to perform comedy during Halloween, Lahaina News, October 21, 1993: 16.

COST OF GOVERNMENT COMMISSION
— exploring possibility of replacing Citizen Advisory Committees with Neighborhood Boards, Lahaina News, November 2, 1995: 3.

COSTA, ALEX
— fundraiser for lifeguard suffering from cancer, Lahaina News, August 1, 2002: 5.
— birthday party to be held for, Lahaina News, August 8, 2002: 5.

COSTCO [BUSINESS]
— to open in Kahului, Lahaina News, January 12, 1995: 6.
— Maui Chamber of Commerce to meet at, Lahaina News, October 17, 1996: 15.
— hosting Maui Chamber of Commerce, Lahaina News, October 29, 1998: 13.
— to hold "Miracle Tournament" for Kapi'olani Children's Miracle Network, Lahaina News, May 20, 1999: 6.

COSTELLO, JEFF [MUSICIAN]
— to perform at Borders Books, Lahaina News, June 15, 2000: 16.

COSTELLO, MICHAEL
— recognized as Employee of the Month at Ka'anapali Golf Courses, Lahaina News, June 3, 1999: 13.

COSTELLO, ROBERT
— appointed director of retail operations at Kapalua Land Company, Lahaina News, December 3, 1986: 11.

COSTUME BALL
— to benefit Maui Dance Council, Lahaina News, October 22, 1998: 21.
— to be held, Lahaina News, October 29, 1998: 28.

COTE, JOHN
— realtor describes his life on Maui, Lahaina News, June 28, 2001: 7.

COUCH, DONALD [POLITICIAN]
— to run for state Senate, Lahaina News, June 20, 2002: 1.

COUCH, JOHN
— named chief executive officer at Alexander and Baldwin, Inc., Lahaina News, April 9, 1992: 12.

COUGHLIN ASSOCIATES [BUSINESS]
— expands line of water filtration systems, Lahaina News, July 22, 1993: 7.

COULTRUP, JENNIFER
— wins Camp Hyatt Career Day Essay Contest, Lahaina News, June 11, 1992: 4.

COUNCIL FOR NATIVE HAWAIIAN ADVANCEMENT
— to offer grant workshops, Lahaina News, June 26, 2003: 8.

COUNCIL, JEANNE AND LARRY [MUSICIANS]
— featured, Lahaina News, April 2, 1992: 16.

COUNCIL, LARRY [MUSICIAN]
— to perform at Makai Bar, Lahaina News, September 19, 1996: 18.

COUNCIL OF COMMUNITY ASSOCIATIONS
— meetings to focus on 1992 election and candidate's forum, Lahaina News, July 16, 1992: 5.

COUNSELING
— juvenile counseling program expands, Lahaina Sun, July 7, 1971: 12.

COUNTRY JAM
— to be held, Lahaina News, July 23, 1992: 25.

COUNTRY KARAOKE COMPETITION
— to be held at Lahaina Cannery Mall, Lahaina News, July 8, 1999: 12.

COUNTRY KITCHEN [RESTAURANT]
— reviewed, Lahaina News, March 21, 1990: 12.
— reviewed, Lahaina News, April 18, 1990: 12.
— chef Claude Gaty joins, Lahaina News, August 22, 1991: 4.

COUNTRY ROCK [MUSICAL GROUP]
— to perform at Westin Maui, Lahaina News, February 25, 1993: 10.

COUNTRY TOWN DESIGN GUIDELINES
— draft available from Planning Department, Lahaina News, December 26, 1990: 5.

COUNTRY WESTERN DANCE
— to be held to benefit Lyn Nava, Lahaina News, November 18, 1993: 3.

COUNTRYMAN, BILL
— director of Food and Beverage of Maui Marriott, Lahaina News, April 20, 1988: 13.
— new general manager at Maui Marriott Resort and Ocean Club, Lahaina News, May 8, 2003: 8.

COUNTRYMAN, CHANDLER
— Scholar/Athlete of the Week, Lahaina News, August 20, 1998: 14.

COUNTY ATTORNEY'S OFFICE
— current situation discussed, Lahaina Sun, January 12, 1972: 18.

COUNTY CIVIL SERVICE COMMISSION
— set to announce hearing regarding the reinstatement of Joseph Abreu [police officer], Lahaina Sun, November 24, 1971: 5.
— hearing updated, Lahaina Sun, February 23, 1972: 18.

COUNTY COUNCIL
— see Maui County Council

COUNTY FAIR
— see Maui County Fair

COUNTY OF MAUI BUDGET FOR FISCAL YEAR 1971-1973 [BOOK]
— reviewed, Lahaina Sun, April 5, 1972: 15.

COUNTY YOUTH TRANSPORTATION
— Summer Schedule not available, Lahaina News, August 26, 1993: 8.

COUPLES, FRED
— wins Lincoln-Mercury Kapalua International golf tournament, Lahaina News, November 10, 1994: 1.
— golfer to compete in Lincoln-Mercury Kapalua International tournament, Lahaina News, October 10, 1996: 13.

COURSE IN MIRACLES, A
— support group to meet, Lahaina News, December 23, 1999: 17.

COURT HOUSE, OLD
— see Old Courthouse

COURTER, MARCIE
— opens counseling service, Lahaina News, April 1, 1999: 13.

COURTER, SHARRON
— joins Campbell Estate, Lahaina News, June 11, 1992: 13.
— accountant opens office, Lahaina News, February 25, 1999: 11.
— to offer tips against identity theft, Lahaina News, September 18, 2003: 9.

COURTHOUSE
— State judiciary wants to regain control of, Lahaina News, July 1, 1983: 3.
— to house Lahaina Visitor's Center, Lahaina News, August 11, 1994: 1,3.

COURTNEY, DEL
— to perform at Soroptimists International annual Sweetheart's Ball Dinner Dance, Lahaina News, February 4, 1987: 11.

COURTNEY, LARRY [ARTIST]
— to exhibit at Village Galleries, Lahaina News, March 22, 2001: 16.

COUSTEAU, JEAN-MICHEL
— appearing at Maui Marine Art Expo, Lahaina News, March 4, 1987: 8.
— researching whales off Maui, Lahaina News, April 22, 1987: 1.
— to speak at Maui Marine Expo, Lahaina News, January 13, 1988: 16.
— to speak at world premiere of "Australia: The Last Barrier", Lahaina News, March 1, 1989: 1.
— presents on environment, Great Barrier Reef, Lahaina News, March 15, 1989: 1,13.
— to narrate film at Marine Art Expo, Lahaina News, February 21, 1990: 14.
— to appear at Maui Marine Art Expo, Lahaina News, February 28, 1990: 12.
— to premier film "Australia: Fortunes in the Sea" at Maui Marine Art Expo, Lahaina News, February 27, 1991: 12.
— to speak at Maui Marine Art Expo, Lahaina News, February 25, 1993: 5.
— to present at Maui Marine Art Expo, Lahaina News, February 16, 1995: 16.
— to speak on whales, Lahaina News, March 6, 1997: 1,16.
— attends "Whale Tales for Keiki", Lahaina News, March 27, 1997: 3.
— attends "show and tell" at Whalers Village, Lahaina News, March 5, 1998: 17.
— to speak at WhaleFest, Lahaina News, March 5, 1998: 8.
— to attend opening of Maui Ocean Center, Lahaina News, March 12, 1998: 1.
— shares views of the planet and environment, Lahaina News, March 19, 1998: 1,16.
— to visit Maui Ocean Center, Lahaina News, January 21, 1999: 13.
— to celebrate National Marine Sanctuary Day, Lahaina News, January 28, 1999: 12.
— WhaleFest to end with presentation by, Lahaina News, March 11, 1999: 5.
— participates in WhaleFest, Lahaina News, March 18, 1999: 1.
— students to attend Ambassadors of the Environment summer camp, Lahaina News, September 23, 1999: 3.
— to speak to WhaleFest, Lahaina News, March 23, 2000: 1,16.
— to participate in WhaleFest, Lahaina News, February 22, 2001: 1,14.
— attending WhaleFest, Lahaina News, March 1, 2001: 11.
— to hold whale watching trips with Trilogy Excursions, Lahaina News, March 14, 2002: 5.

COUSTEAU SOCIETY, THE
— co-hosting A Marine Art Expo, Lahaina News, February 14, 1990: 16.
— to show film at Maui Marine Art Expo, Lahaina News, January 23, 1992: 20.
— to receive donations from Domino's Pizza, Lahaina News, February 13, 1992: 13.
— to show "The Great White Shark: Lonely Lord of the Sea", Lahaina News, February 20, 1992: 16.

COUTTS, WILMA [ARTIST]
— exhibit at Kaluani, Lahaina News, August 15, 1984: 3.

COVENANT DANCE THEATRE [TROUPE]
— to stage "Nisei Project", Lahaina News, July 10, 2003: 17.

COVENANT PLAYERS [TROUPE]
— to perform at Lahaina Baptist Church, Lahaina News, January 15, 1998: 12.

COVERUP—THE IRAN-CONTRA AFFAIR [FILM]
— to be shown as fundraiser for medical supplies for Nicaragua, Lahaina News, October 26, 1988: 17.

COVIC, AL
— acquires lease for Olowalu General Store, Lahaina News, August 11, 1994: 7.

COVINGTON, JANE ANN
— new president of Lahaina Arts Society, Lahaina News, October 21, 1987: 3.
— calls emergency meeting concerning Lahaina Arts Society's potential eviction from Old Lahaina Court House, Lahaina News, January 20, 1988: 18.
— hypnotherapist offers weight-loss class, Lahaina News, August 3, 1988: 3.
— to speak to American Association of Retired People, Lahaina News, September 28, 1988: 18.
— clinical hynotherapist to speak to Alaya Unlimited's Ohana Luncheon, Lahaina News, January 9, 1997: 10.

COVINGTON, KELLY [MUSICIAN]
— to perform at Villa Lounge, Lahaina News, July 2, 1992: 22.
— to perform at Villa Lounge, Lahaina News, August 13, 1992: 15.
— to perform at Villa Lounge, Lahaina News, September 17, 1992: 14.
— to perform at SeaWatch Restaurant, Lahaina News, August 18, 1994: 16.
— see also Kelly Covington Band [musical group]

COVINGTON, PHILLIP [COMEDIAN]
— to perform at Comedy Club, Lahaina News, September 23, 1993: 11.

COWAN, CHRISTINA [ARTIST]
— ceramic work featured, Lahaina News, October 24, 1984: 10.
— joins Maui Community Arts and Cultural Center as assistant coordinator of the Art/Craft program, Lahaina News, October 31, 1991: 10.
— named acting general manager at the Maui Arts and Cultural Center, Lahaina News, December 25, 1997: 11.
— president of Maui Arts and Cultural Center, Lahaina News, July 16, 1998: 13.

COWBOY ACTION SHOOTERS OF MAUI
— to host Aloha State Games at Ukumehame Firing Range, Lahaina News, June 4, 1998: 15.

CPR [MUSICAL GROUP]
— to perform at Maui Arts and Cultural Center, Lahaina News, September 27, 2001: 17.
— to perform, Lahaina News, October 11, 2001: 15.

CRADDICK, DAVID
— appointed county water director, Lahaina News, January 30, 1992: 5.
— Maui County water director states that problem with muddy water resolved, Lahaina News, May 28, 1992: 4.
— explains water assessment proposal, Lahaina News, July 30, 1992: 6.
— county water director says that cleaner water to go to Kelawea Mauka, Lahaina News, October 29, 1992: 3.
— Maui County Water Board director to ask for water rebate, Lahaina News, December 17, 1992: 1.
— discusses farmer Hans Michel request that county to pay for land usage, Lahaina News, February 4, 1993: 2.
— Water Director says water notices will not be needed, Lahaina News, June 9, 1994: 1.
— Department of Water Supply Director discusses Mahinahina Water Treatment Plant, Lahaina News, August 31, 1995: 7.
— Director of Water Supply discusses impact of new water plant, Lahaina News, September 11, 1997: 3.

CRAFT AND CARD BOUTIQUE [BUSINESS]
— opens, Lahaina News, May 28, 1992: 11.

CRAFT AND FOOD FAIR
— to be held at Wailuku Hongwanji Mission grounds, Lahaina News, October 24, 1990: 5.

CRAFT, G. ROBERT
— pharmacist honored by Hawaii Pharmaceutical Association, Lahaina News, July 2, 1986: 3.

CRAFTS
— see art

CRAIG D. NEWNAN SCHOLARSHIP COMMITTEE
— awards scholarships, Lahaina News, July 19, 2001: 2.

CRAIG MACDONALD
— Ocean Resources Branch chief speaks of impact of sea-bed mining, Lahaina News, July 6, 1988: 12.

CRAIG, SCOTT
— new pastor at Kumulani Chapel, Lahaina News, May 20, 1999: 15.

CRAMER, JIM
— discusses campaign for swimming pool, Lahaina News, March 23, 1988: 1.

CRAMER, KEANA
— named "Miss Keiki Hula 2001", Lahaina News, July 26, 2001: 5.

CRATER BOUND [BUSINESS]
— providing camping gear, Lahaina News, June 13, 1990: 8.

CRAVALHO, ELMER [POLITICIAN]
— Maui county mayor will ask for funds to construct sewage treatment plants, Lahaina Sun, November 18, 1970: 1.
— Maui county mayor in public meeting in Wailuku with State Department of Transportation to discuss needs, Lahaina Sun, December 2, 1970: 1.
— Maui county mayor prepares booklet for hippies, Lahaina Sun, December 9, 1970: 1.
— Maui county mayor discussing end of ocean dumping of sewage by county, Lahaina Sun, December 9, 1970: 2.
— Maui county mayor discusses who pays for planned underground wiring in Front Street, Lahaina Sun, December 9, 1970: 7.
— Maui county mayor seeks authority to use emergency powers, Lahaina Sun, December 16, 1970: 1.
— Maui county mayor seeking emergency powers, Lahaina Sun, December 16, 1970: 1.
— opposition to Maui county mayor request for emergency powers, Lahaina Sun, December 23, 1970: 1.
— Emergency powers for Maui county mayor opposed, Lahaina Sun, December 23, 1970: 1,5.
— Maui county mayor discusses use of treated sewage for irrigation, Lahaina Sun, December 23, 1970: 11.
— Maui county mayor received list of desired projects from West Maui Business Association, Lahaina Sun, December 23, 1970: 2.
— Maui county mayor discusses pollution programs, Lahaina Sun, December 23, 1970: 4.
— Maui county mayor opposing airport for West Maui, Lahaina Sun, December 30, 1970: 1,8.
— Maui county mayor supports economic growth in inaugural address, Lahaina Sun, January 6, 1971: 1.
— Maui county mayor plans for trip to Far East, Lahaina Sun, January 6, 1971: 1,2.
— Maui county mayor appoints Ichiro Maehara as director of parks and recreation, Lahaina Sun, January 6, 1971: 2.
— Maui county mayor sworn in for second two-year term as Mayor, Lahaina Sun, January 6, 1971: 2.
— Maui county mayor may name teenager to County Planning Commission, Lahaina Sun, January 13, 1971: 1.
— Maui county mayor present at public meeting on ecology, Lahaina Sun, January 13, 1971: 1,2.

— Maui County Council discusses list of improvement projects from Maui county mayor, Lahaina Sun, January 13, 1971: 2.
— Maui county mayor stresses "quality of life" as goal, Lahaina Sun, January 20, 1971: 2.
— Maui county mayor leaves for Far East to stimulate tourism, Lahaina Sun, January 20, 1971: 3.
— Maui county mayor discusses planned Lahaina Whaling Spree, Lahaina Sun, February 3, 1971: 2.
— Maui county mayor participates in welcoming ceremony for Navy fleet tender Bryce Canyon, Lahaina Sun, February 24, 1971: 1.
— Maui county mayor unveils capital improvement projects, Lahaina Sun, March 3, 1971: 1,8.
— Maui county mayor's budget criticized, Lahaina Sun, March 31, 1971: 2.
— Maui county mayor career analyzed by Robert Aitken, Lahaina Sun, April 14, 1971: 4.
— Maui county mayor responds to criticism that Kihei is being favored over Lahaina, Lahaina Sun, April 28, 1971: 1,3.
— Maui county mayor visits Japan, Lahaina Sun, May 19, 1971: 4.
— Maui county mayor skeptical of development plans for Kahului, Lahaina Sun, June 30, 1971: 9.
— Maui county mayor sues to stop bombing of Kaho'olawe, Lahaina Sun, August 4, 1971: 1,2.
— Maui county mayor criticized for absence from office, Lahaina Sun, September 1, 1971: 11.
— Maui county mayor returns after a 12-day absence, Lahaina Sun, September 8, 1971: 4.
— Maui county mayor evaluated in the Hawaii Business magazine, Lahaina Sun, September 8, 1971: 4.
— Maui county mayor claims that sugar land is being under-assessed, Lahaina Sun, September 29, 1971: 5.
— suit against Maui county mayor dismissed, Lahaina Sun, October 6, 1971: 11.
— Maui county mayor discusses attempts to create a Youth Center, Lahaina Sun, November 3, 1971: 14.
— Maui county mayor agrees to look at concerns about Hawaiian Homes Commission, Lahaina Sun, November 10, 1971: 14.
— Maui county mayor may be leaving for two-week trip to the Philippines and Japan, Lahaina Sun, November 17, 1971: 1.
— Maui county mayor on two-week trip to the Philippines, Lahaina Sun, December 1, 1971: 5.
— Maui county mayor critical of rate increase by Hawaiian Telephone Company, Lahaina Sun, January 12, 1972: 1.
— Maui county mayor declares January "Big Brother Month", Lahaina Sun, January 12, 1972: 16.
— Maui county mayor clashes with Allen Barr, Lahaina Sun, February 9, 1972: 3.
— Maui county mayor presents pared-down budget to Maui County Council, Lahaina Sun, March 8, 1972: 3.
— Maui county mayor criticizes labor statistics, Lahaina Sun, March 29, 1972: 4.
— calls for action over pollution at Launiupoko Point, Lahaina Sun, April 12, 1972: 10.
— Maui county mayor suggests importing agricultural workers, Lahaina Sun, April 26, 1972: 3.
— Maui county mayor objects to request for skydiving drop zone, Lahaina Sun, May 10, 1972: 5.
— Maui county mayor praises success of his administration, Lahaina Sun, May 17, 1972: 3.
— Maui county mayor discusses Filipino immigrants, Lahaina Sun, May 24, 1972: 3.
— Maui county mayor responds to accusation of conflict of interest, Lahaina Sun, July 5, 1972: 3,4.
— Maui county mayor says he is voting for McGovern, Lahaina Sun, July 5, 1972: 4.

— interview with Maui county mayor by Rob Kelsey, Lahaina Sun, September 6, 1972: 7.

— re-election campaign of Maui county mayor described, Lahaina Sun, October 4, 1972: 6.

— discussion of mayor's campaign style, Lahaina Sun, October 11, 1972: 5.

— Maui county mayor creates task force to respond to closing of pineapple operations on Moloka'i, Lahaina Sun, October 18, 1972: 5.

— suit filed by Allen Barr against Maui county mayor set for spring 1973, Lahaina Sun, November 8, 1972: 7.

— Maui county mayor accused of not paying a bet on election outcome, Lahaina Sun, November 15, 1972: 3.

— Maui county mayor claims Wailuku-Kahului general plan is good, Lahaina Sun, December 27, 1972: 14.

— Maui county mayor responds to rumors he will run for governor in 1974, Lahaina Sun, February 14, 1973: 3.

— Maui county mayor wins gag order against newspaper publishers James Franklin and Jack Stephens, Lahaina Sun, February 28, 1973: 4.

— Maui county mayor appoints people to Citizens Advisory Committee for new Lahaina Community Development plan, Lahaina Sun, June 13, 1973: 27.

— Maui county mayor discusses his vision of the future of Maui, Lahaina Sun, June 13, 1973: 4.

— supports Bob Nakasone as mayor, Lahaina News, November 15, 1982: 2.

— Maui county mayor schedules political gatherings, Lahaina News, December 6, 1989: 1.

— Maui county mayor claims Kahualui airport will become international, Lahaina News, December 13, 1989: 36.

— Maui county mayor to hold fundraiser, Lahaina News, June 20, 1990: 8.

— campaign to do no sign waiving this election, Lahaina News, September 5, 1990: 4.

— Maui county mayor speaks of career of Colin Cameron, Lahaina News, June 18, 1992: 1,3.

— receives University of Hawai'i Distinguished Alumni Award, Lahaina News, December 9, 1999: 11.

CRAVER, BOB

— named race director for Maui Bud Light Triathlon Championship, Lahaina News, June 3, 1993: 6.

CRAWFORD, EMILY [MUSICIAN]

— pianist to perform at "Cabaret Night" at United Church of Maui, Lahaina News, February 10, 1988: 3.

CRAY, ROBERT [MUSICIAN]

— to perform, Lahaina News, March 26, 1998: 12,13.

— to perform at Maui Arts and Cultural Center, Lahaina News, April 2, 1998: 16.

— to perform at Maui Arts and Cultural Center, Lahaina News, February 24, 2000: 17.

CRAYCE, COLLON

— to discuss fats, oils, and health, Lahaina News, September 17, 1998: 25.

CRAZY CANNERY OLYMPICS

— to benefit American Lung Association, Lahaina News, November 5, 1998: 16.

— to be held, Lahaina News, November 12, 1998: 13.

CRAZY FINGERS [MUSICAL GROUP]

— formed by Scott Baird, Lahaina News, December 8, 1994: 14.

— to perform at World Café, Lahaina News, April 18, 1996: 16.

— to perform at World Café, Lahaina News, June 20, 1996: 12.

— to perform at World Cafe, Lahaina News, July 25, 1996: 13.

— to perform at Hapa's Brew Haus, Lahaina News, May 8, 1997: 17.

— performing at Leilani's, Lahaina News, July 17, 1997: 18.

— to perform at World Cafe, Lahaina News, October 23, 1997: 19.

— to perform at Maui AIDS Foundation's James Manness Memorial "Dance Party Xtreme", Lahaina News, March 26, 1998: 2.

— to perform at Lahaina Civic Center Amphitheater with Alpha Bloody, Lahaina News, February 18, 1999: 12.

— to perform at benefit concert at Maui Brews, Lahaina News, August 5, 1999: 14.

— to perform at Borders Books, Lahaina News, October 21, 1999: 16.

CRAZY FOR YOU [MUSICAL]

— to be performed at Maui Academy of Performing Arts, Lahaina News, March 20, 1997: 16.

CRAZY HORSE [MUSICAL GROUP]

— show at Lahaina Civic Center reviewed, Lahaina Sun, December 6, 1972: 6.

CRAZY KAMP [PLAY]

— to be performed at Theatre Theatre Maui Summer Stock, Lahaina News, July 18, 1996: 10.

CRAZY SHIRTS [BUSINESS]

— opening in Whaler's Village, Lahaina Sun, November 25, 1970: 3.

— featured, Lahaina News, December 28, 1983: 19.

— history of recounted, Lahaina News, January 7, 1987: 4.

— searching for calendar girl, Lahaina News, July 1, 1987: 3.

— 1991 calendar described, Lahaina News, January 2, 1991: 10.

— featured, Lahaina News, April 1, 1993: 8.

— names Ann Tanaka as retail trainer, Lahaina News, May 13, 1993: 6.

— artists Laura Fujikawa to visit, Lahaina News, June 29, 1995: 12.

— to hold sale, Lahaina News, October 2, 1997: 15.

CREATIVE CAKES [BUSINESS]

— featured, Lahaina News, April 25, 1984: 13.

CREATIVE CUTS [BUSINESS]

— closes temporarily , Lahaina News, October 1, 1998: 13.

— Terri Anbe Pascual to close for maternity leave, Lahaina News, May 9, 2002: 8.

CREATIVE DINING [BUSINESS]

— featured, Lahaina News, January 2, 1985: 18.

CREATIVE MEMORIES [BUSINESS]

— offers help organizing photographs, Lahaina News, October 24, 1996: 14.

— to hold workshop on organizing photo albums, Lahaina News, October 9, 1997: 21.

CREDIT ASSOCIATES OF MAUI (BUSINESS)

— to hold "Collection Seminar for Creditors" workshop, Lahaina News, July 4, 2002: 8.

CREDITCARD KEYS

— available locally, Lahaina News, July 19, 1989: 2.

CRENSHAW, BEN

— golfer to play at Isuzu Kapalua International, Lahaina News, October 17, 1990: 9.

CREW, SPENCER

— to present on exhibits at the National Museum of American History, Lahaina News, August 14, 1997: 17.

CRIBBAGE

— to be played at Lahaina Civic Center, Lahaina News, September 10, 1998: 20.

— continues to meet at Lahaina Civic Center, Lahaina News, October 1, 1998: 17.

CRIME

— increased in Maui County in from previous year, Lahaina Sun, January 20, 1971: 8.

— Kenneth Meyerson attacked while sleeping in his car, Lahaina Sun, June 23, 1971: 12.

— theft of potted coco-nut palm reported, Lahaina Sun, June 23, 1971: 5.

— Operation Identification is hoping to cut down number of home burglaries, Lahaina Sun, June 23, 1971: 9.

— has increased substantially, Lahaina Sun, July 21, 1971: 11.

— engines of six Playtime Rentals jet boats damaged, Lahaina Sun, August 25, 1971: 9.

— value of stolen goods has risen this year, Lahaina Sun, November 17, 1971: 4.

— Vederine Edward Mara III sentenced for murder of Monica Pagasian, Lahaina Sun, November 17, 1971: 6.

— Lahaina Deli robbed, Lahaina Sun, December 8, 1971: 17.

— theft of holiday flags along Fort Street reported, Lahaina Sun, December 8, 1971: 4.

— counterfeit checks, Lahaina Sun, December 29, 1971: 5.

— Sheriff seizes sailboat, Lahaina Sun, January 5, 1972: 13.

— history of crime in Lahaina discussed, Lahaina Sun, January 5, 1972: 16.

— three Wailuku men charged with burglaries, Lahaina Sun, January 5, 1972: 17.

— papayas stolen and plants damaged at Waianapanapa Park, Lahaina Sun, January 5, 1972: 7.

— Lahaina Crazy Shirts robbed, Lahaina Sun, January 12, 1972: 17.

— George Mowatt arrested for drunk driving, resulting in death of Beoren Barr, Lahaina Sun, January 12, 1972: 7.

— Maui County Jail officially closed, Lahaina Sun, January 12, 1972: 8.

— murder of Tom and Wendy Day discussed, Lahaina Sun, January 19, 1972: 5.

— many major crimes solved in last year, Lahaina Sun, February 9, 1972: 15.

— police arrest group engaged in cockfighting, Lahaina Sun, February 23, 1972: 9.

— Moloka‘i Joe Warren charged with stealing try-pot, Lahaina Sun, March 1, 1972: 7.

— tourist beaten at Makena Beach, Lahaina Sun, March 15, 1972: 3.

— three people charged with drug possession in Kula, Lahaina Sun, March 15, 1972: 3.

— paintings by John St. John stolen, Lahaina Sun, March 22, 1972: 11.

— three arrested in Makena beating, Lahaina Sun, March 29, 1972: 4.

— Joey Uvalle attacked by three men, Lahaina Sun, April 5, 1972: 3.

— another beating reported at Makena Beach, Lahaina Sun, April 12, 1972: 9.

— recent attacks at Makena Beach discussed, Lahaina Sun, April 19, 1972: 1,7.

— West Maui youth assaults bicyclist, Lahaina Sun, July 5, 1972: 14.

— public seminars on counterfeit money offered, Lahaina Sun, September 20, 1972: 10.

— police clear 18 burglaries, Lahaina Sun, September 27, 1972: 7.

— bogus "Maui diamonds" being sold in local shops, Lahaina Sun, February 21, 1973: 3.

— Jerry Engebritson charged in three deaths in automobile accident, Lahaina Sun, February 28, 1973: 3.

— Emerson Stant sentenced for killing his wife at Kahului airport, Lahaina Sun, March 21, 1973: 10.

— Jerry Engerbritson sentenced for traffic accident resulting in death of three people, Lahaina Sun, July 18, 1973: 6.

— former police officer Calvin Young Hu charged with breaking into sporting goods store, Lahaina Sun, August 1, 1973: 3.

— state investigating prison breaks, Lahaina News, April 1, 1980: 6.

— fire and theft at Nagasako Supermarket, Lahaina News, April 15, 1980: 7.

— Marilyn Moniz, new prosecuting attorney added to County staff, Lahaina News, May 1, 1980: 14.

— police arrest vandals, Lahaina News, August 1, 1980: 7.

— motorists arrested for drunk driving, Lahaina News, August 15, 1980: 7.

— car break-ins on Maui discussed, Lahaina News, September 1, 1980: 6.

— shopping cart thefts reported, Lahaina News, September 15, 1980: 7.

— increased on Maui by 10%, Lahaina News, October 15, 1980: 4.

— Peggy Peacon charged with theft and forgery, Lahaina News, October 15, 1980: 9.

— restitution program discussed, Lahaina News, November 1, 1980: 3.

— major endorses program where victims of crime are flown back to Hawaii, Lahaina News, December 1, 1980: 11.

— current statistics, Lahaina News, March 1, 1981: 15.

— ways to prevent shoplifting discussed, Lahaina News, October 15, 1981: 12.

— police attempt to curb vandalism, Lahaina News, December 1, 1981: 16.

— David Frederick Darling indicted for burglary, Lahaina News, June 15, 1982: 3.

— 70 people arrested in undercover operation on Front Street, Lahaina News, July 1, 1982: 11.

— summary of recent trends, Lahaina News, July 15, 1982: 3.

— scuba tanks stolen, Lahaina News, September 15, 1982: 2.

— man flees while being sentenced in court, Lahaina News, February 1, 1983: 2.

— increased in Hawaii in 1982, Lahaina News, July 1, 1983: 6.

— two found dead in Lahaina, Lahaina News, September 14, 1983: 5.

— Anthony Nicholas Graffafiori arrested in connection to murder of woman and her daughter, Lahaina News, September 28, 1983: 5.

— 107 drunks arrested, Lahaina News, February 29, 1984: 3,4.

— editorial on the New Bedford rape trial, Lahaina News, April 18, 1984: 2,8.

— Sexual Assault Crisis Center's work described, Lahaina News, May 16, 1984: 9,10,11,12.

— 115 drunk drivers arrested in March, Lahaina News, May 23, 1984: 17.

— AWOL Australian sailor charged, Lahaina News, July 4, 1984: 4.

— Australian sailor faces additional charges, Mayor Tavares seeks Australian support, Lahaina News, July 11, 1984: 3.

— Australian government to pay for damages caused by Australian sailor, Lahaina News, August 1, 1984: 13.

— editorial on Australian government agreeing to pay for damages caused by Australian sailor, Lahaina News, August 1, 1984: 2.

— anti-drunk driving efforts during New Year's Eve described, Lahaina News, December 26, 1984: 7,8,9.

— rate declined, Lahaina News, January 9, 1985: 3.

— DUI arrests up 205% from last year, Lahaina News, January 16, 1985: 3.

— breath-tests credited with lowering rate of drunk driving, Lahaina News, January 23, 1985: 3.

— editorial praising Hawaii Supreme Court decision allowing roadblocks, Lahaina News, January 30, 1985: 2.

— police captain Solomon Lee tells Banyan Tree Square Preservation Committee that drug crackdown needed, Lahaina News, May 22, 1985: 1.

— department of the prosecuting attorney looking for help with Return Witness Program, Lahaina News, June 5, 1985: 9.

— editorial opposing frivolous negligence lawsuits, Lahaina News, September 4, 1985: 2.

— National Guard helicopters take part in "Green Harvest" raids on marijuana farming, Lahaina News, September 25, 1985: 20.

— police catch 73 people in fencing operation, Lahaina News, October 9, 1985: 1.

— video store owners worry about vice raids over adult material, Lahaina News, October 16, 1985: 1,20.

— editorial criticizing police raids of video stores renting X-rated movies, Lahaina News, January 22, 1986: 2.

— new patrol boat helping enforce ski boat rules, Lahaina News, May 7, 1986: 3.

— dogs and agents to fight drugs, Lahaina News, July 16, 1986: 1.

— illegal drug enforcement increased, Lahaina News, August 13, 1986: 1,14.

— discussed by Wayne Hedani of Amfac, Lahaina News, November 5, 1986: 1,16.

— editorial critical of light sentence given to Nephi Hanneman for drunk driving, Lahaina News, November 19, 1986: 2.

— Adler jewelry store robbed, Lahaina News, December 10, 1986: 3.

— Lahaina Automotive and Towing in violation of zoning laws, Lahaina News, January 28, 1987: 3.

— U.S. stolen from Front Street, Lahaina News, April 1, 1987: 3.

— 25-pound Bible missing from Holy Innocents Church, Lahaina News, March 23, 1988: 18.

— increased in West Maui in 1987, Lahaina News, March 30, 1988: 1.

— Crime Watch campaign to begin, Lahaina News, June 15, 1988: 1,20.

— Maui Community College hosting teleconference on shoplifting, Lahaina News, October 26, 1988: 17.

— Business Crime Watch deemed successful by Maui Police Chief Howard Tagamori, Lahaina News, November 23, 1988: 1,16.

— criminal drug use in Lahaina a problem, Lahaina News, January 18, 1989: 1,20.

— police issuing set belt citations, Lahaina News, May 17, 1989: 1.

— Jim Ramsay offering reward for arrest of people responsible for killing two Hawaiian ducks, Lahaina News, September 20, 1989: 3.

— thefts have increased, Lahaina News, November 15, 1989: 1.

— Maui Police offers tips, Lahaina News, November 15, 1989: 3.

— stolen surf boards recovered, Lahaina News, February 28, 1990: 2.

— break-ins declining, Lahaina News, March 7, 1990: 1.

— police investigating vandalism, Lahaina News, March 14, 1990: 2.

— Lahaina News to publish weekly report of in West Maui, Lahaina News, May 23, 1990: 1.

— Westin Maui to train employees to recognize potential drunk drivers, Lahaina News, July 4, 1990: 5.

— attempt to cheat Lahaina restaurants unmasked, Lahaina News, August 8, 1990: 1,3.

— assault being investigated, Lahaina News, August 15, 1990: 5.

— attacks on homeless described, Lahaina News, August 22, 1990: 1.

— donated clothes stolen from Salvation Army, Lahaina News, September 26, 1990: 1.

— businesses targeted by imposter, Lahaina News, September 26, 1990: 1.

— children seen leaving area before fire above Lahainaluna High School, Lahaina News, January 9, 1991: 4.

— fight between liquor control inspector and resident classified as misdemeanor, Lahaina News, January 30, 1991: 4.

— John Cuccia recovering from attack, Lahaina News, January 30, 1991: 4.

— drug arrests double on Maui, Lahaina News, October 24, 1991: 1.

— police expect decline with new unit positioned in Lahaina, Lahaina News, October 24, 1991: 1.

— people arrested, including U.S. Postal employees for football gambling pools, Lahaina News, November 14, 1991: 9.

— Maui County Prosecutor Larry Butrick says prosecuting homicides is first priority, Lahaina News, January 9, 1992: 1.

— police investigating alleged sexual assault, Lahaina News, January 16, 1992: 3.

— burglary rate rises in Lahaina, Lahaina News, January 23, 1992: 1.

— murder of Jerry Canada described, Lahaina News, January 30, 1992: 1,6.

— Willie Baronet being investigated for owing money to investors, Lahaina News, February 6, 1992: 1,7.

— Richard Kajihiro arrested for burglary, Lahaina News, February 13, 1992: 1.

— murder trial of Shannon Brown to begin, Lahaina News, February 13, 1992: 4.

— murder suicide involving Rose Marie Alconcel and Frank Alconcel Jr., Lahaina News, February 20, 1992: 1,8.

— Richard Kajihiro indicted for burglaries, Lahaina News, March 5, 1992: 1.

— burglaries up, Lahaina News, March 26, 1992: 4.

— Leroy Tupulua and Jack Dutro III arrested for robbery, Lahaina News, April 2, 1992: 5.

— Leone Helekahi arrested for shooting arrows into a home, Lahaina News, April 23, 1992: 8.

— Mental Health Association and Maui County Alliance for the Mentally Ill to present recommendations on mentally ill criminal offenders, Lahaina News, May 21, 1992: 4.

— Crime Watch listings continues, Lahaina News, June 4, 1992: 17.

— woman abducted from Konokowai Park and raped, Lahaina News, June 11, 1992: 3.

— residents concerned about increase in thefts, police inactivity, Lahaina News, June 18, 1992: 1,3.

— concerns expressed that police are not recovering stolen property , Lahaina News, June 25, 1992: 1.

— thief arrested, Lahaina News, July 9, 1992: 3.

— Arata "Ralph" Yoshitake charged with multiple thefts, Lahaina News, July 30, 1992: 3.

— Wailuku Agribusiness using inmates to pick pineapples, Lahaina News, August 27, 1992: 10.

— police investigating robbery at T-Shirt Factory, Lahaina News, September 10, 1992: 12.

— suspected rapist at large, Lahaina News, October 29, 1992: 3.

— Makena Homeowners Association asks for more police patrols, Lahaina News, December 10, 1992: 8.

— statistics for 1992 released, Lahaina News, January 21, 1993: 10.

— rape increases in West Maui, Lahaina News, January 21, 1993: 3.

— program seeks to stem youth violence, Lahaina News, February 11, 1993: 6.

— murderer William Forsyth was on anti-depressants, Lahaina News, March 11, 1993: 1.

— conference to be held, Lahaina News, March 11, 1993: 11.

— conference on to be held in Kihei, Lahaina News, March 18, 1993: 8.

— reduced with better youth programs, Lahaina News, March 25, 1993: 8.

— homeless man attacked, Lahaina News, April 29, 1993: 3.

— police say that youth gang activity a problem, Lahaina News, May 27, 1993: 5,6.

— roadblocks during Memorial Day lead to two arrests, Lahaina News, June 3, 1993: 3.

— roadblocks resulted in arrest and citations, Lahaina News, June 10, 1993: 4.

— residents mad at police who let moped thieves, Lahaina News, July 1, 1993: 1,8.

— split-second car thefts often unsolved, Lahaina News, July 1, 1993: 1,9.

— police investigating stabbing of cabdriver, Lahaina News, August 12, 1993: 4.

— sexual assaults reported, Lahaina News, September 2, 1993: 2.

— reward offered for information on "La Branche Rockefeller" sculpture missing from the Grand Wailea, Lahaina News, September 2, 1993: 6.

— Crime Watch column summarizes recent events, not usually indexed otherwise , Lahaina News, September 9, 1993: 3.

— police seek help stopping drug pushers, Lahaina News, September 23, 1993: 1.

— equipment stolen from Kihei School portables, Lahaina News, October 14, 1993: 7.

— McGruff the Crime Dog visits Lahaina schools, Lahaina News, October 28, 1993: 4.

— arrests made during traffic checkpoint, Lahaina News, November 4, 1993: 3.

— key concern at Maui Meadows Homeowners Association meeting, Lahaina News, December 9, 1993: 5.

— police officer Lanny Tihada discusses pro-active approach to crime, Lahaina News, December 16, 1993: 1,4.

— program helping to find missing children to be implemented, Lahaina News, January 6, 1994: 1.

— fake $20 bills circulating, Lahaina News, January 20, 1994: 1.

— police report rate is declining, Lahaina News, February 17, 1994: 1.

— police report that arrests are up, Lahaina News, March 24, 1994: 1.

— Honokowai man robbed, Lahaina News, April 28, 1994: 4.

— investigation underway over Friend's Network pyramid scheme, Lahaina News, April 28, 1994: 9.

— Wailuku Main Street Association to hold meeting on, Lahaina News, May 12, 1994: 4.

— scammers on the internet, Lahaina News, July 14, 1994: 4.

— drug related arrests, Lahaina News, August 4, 1994: 2.

— police seek volunteers for anti-crime network, Lahaina News, October 20, 1994: 1,6.

— warning of Nigerian email scam, Lahaina News, November 17, 1994: 10.

— Lahaina Town business anti-crime network established, Lahaina News, December 15, 1994: 1,20.

— investors misled by Prudential Securities Incorporated need to file, Lahaina News, December 15, 1994: 15.

— Drug Liability Act to target small-time drug dealers, Lahaina News, January 19, 1995: 10.

— Lahaina businesses implement anti-crime network, Lahaina News, January 26, 1995: 12.

— Secret Service to provide information to help solve , Lahaina News, February 23, 1995: 1.

— man robs convenience store, Lahaina News, April 20, 1995: 16.

— counterfeit currency found in Lahaina, Lahaina News, June 1, 1995: 2.

— court ruling could undermine DUI alcohol assessments, Lahaina News, June 8, 1995: 3.

— police searching for sex assault suspect, Lahaina News, June 15, 1995: 1,12.

— Honokowai Park regulars say drinking is self-policed, Lahaina News, August 3, 1995: 1,20.

— bans on park drinking and hawking pass first reading at Maui County Council, Lahaina News, August 24, 1995: 1,16.

— illegal aliens arrested by Immigration and Naturalization Service, Lahaina News, September 7, 1995: 1.

— more illegal aliens face deportation, Lahaina News, September 14, 1995: 1,16.

— legalized gambling resisted by West Maui Taxpayers Association, Lahaina News, September 21, 1995: 2.

— police using peddling rule to target drug dealer, Lahaina News, September 21, 1995: 3.

— report on arrests of illegal aliens, Lahaina News, October 19, 1995: 3.

— domestic violence discussed, Lahaina News, October 19, 1995: 3.

— vandalism of Ludwig's of Maui may be vendetta, Lahaina News, February 15, 1996: 1.

— opinions of residents sought, Lahaina News, March 14, 1996: 2.

— Citizens' Patrol to begin soon, Lahaina News, March 28, 1996: 3.

— Valerie Tsutsui calls for criminal probe of son's drug death, Lahaina News, April 11, 1996: 14.

— machete attack described, Lahaina News, April 25, 1996: 1,18.

— shooting followed argument, Lahaina News, May 2, 1996: 1.

— accused machete attacker has new charges added, Lahaina News, May 2, 1996: 1,22.

— Citizens Patrol deterring crime on beaches, Lahaina News, June 6, 1996: 6.

— traffic homicide investigators bogged down, Lahaina News, June 27, 1996: 4.

— police seeking help identifying body found at Nakalele, Lahaina News, July 18, 1996: 1.

— police looking for help finding robbers, Lahaina News, August 15, 1996: 3.

— illegal aliens arrested, Lahaina News, August 22, 1996: 5.

— police seeking information on recent robberies, Lahaina News, January 30, 1997: 3.

— residents nab thief, Lahaina News, April 17, 1997: 2.

— suspect in car thefts arrested while out on bail, Lahaina News, May 1, 1997: 1,3.

— bill would allow crime victims to testify via television feed, Lahaina News, May 15, 1997: 1.

— internet scams, Lahaina News, May 15, 1997: 5.

— State guide targets workplace violence, Lahaina News, July 24, 1997: 12.

— Citizens' Patrol to begin soon, Lahaina News, August 14, 1997: 1.

— Chad Van Story, Norman Kalani Kaui, and Scott Temkin indicted for bank robbery, Lahaina News, August 28, 1997: 1,3.

— crime of the week, Lahaina News, December 4, 1997: 3.

— counterfeit $50 bills in Lahaina, Lahaina News, December 25, 1997: 5.

— authorities warn of scam, Lahaina News, January 15, 1998: 11.

— Crime Stoppers seeks information on wanted fugitive Wayne Kainoa Wa'a, Lahaina News, January 15, 1998: 3.

— Harry Pahukoa III being sought by police, Lahaina News, March 5, 1998: 2.

— residents warned of telephone scam, Lahaina News, May 7, 1998: 15.

— state has tips on mail fraud, Lahaina News, October 15, 1998: 13.

— most car seats installed incorrectly., Lahaina News, April 29, 1999: 1,20.

— tip leads to raids and felony drug arrests, Lahaina News, October 7, 1999: 5.

— Federal Bureau of Investigation targeting phone fraud, Lahaina News, January 6, 2000: 11.

— Geshell Law Office looking for female victims of domestic violence, Lahaina News, February 24, 2000: 3.

— drug trafficking ring dismantled, Lahaina News, May 11, 2000: 1,8.

— police ask for helping locating thieves, Lahaina News, July 20, 2000: 3.

— Drug Court explained at meeting, Lahaina News, August 3, 2000: 1,20.

— car stolen, Lahaina News, October 26, 2000: 13.

— police seeking help finding a male robber, Lahaina News, November 2, 2000: 4.

— nautical items stolen from Wharf Cinema Center, Lahaina News, February 1, 2001: 8.

— police seeking sexual assault suspect, Lahaina News, February 15, 2001: 9.

— Lahaina Crime Watch patrol expanding, Lahaina News, February 22, 2001: 1,3.

— police seeking suspect Brian Garcia, Lahaina News, March 1, 2001: 9.

— property managers form group to fight crime, Lahaina News, March 15, 2001: 1,22.

— two break-ins reported at Lahaina Intermediate School, Lahaina News, May 31, 2001: 1,18.

— Governor Ben Cayetano signs bill targeting speeders in school areas, Lahaina News, June 7, 2001: 2.

— police looking for Solomon Kawika Blevins, Lahaina News, June 14, 2001: 3.

— thieves target community non-profits, Lahaina News, February 21, 2002: 1,20.

— community meeting to focus on reducing crime in Lahaina, Lahaina News, July 18, 2002: 1.

— meeting to focus on reducing, Lahaina News, July 25, 2002: 2.

— domestic violence awareness events to be held, Lahaina News, October 3, 2002: 3.

— surfboards stolen from Hi-Tech Surf Sport, Lahaina News, January 16, 2003: 18.

— identity theft prevention discussed, Lahaina News, January 23, 2003: 7.

— Sharron Courter to offer tips against identity theft, Lahaina News, September 18, 2003: 9.

— Sharron Courter to offer tips against identity theft, Lahaina News, September 25, 2003: 9.

CRIME STOPPERS
— seeking culprit in theft of televisions and computers, Lahaina News, October 25, 1989: 2.

— crime of the week featured, Lahaina News, March 26, 1998: 2.

— trying to locate Theresa Maureen Elliott, Lahaina News, April 16, 1998: 2.

— trying to locate missing house, Lahaina News, April 23, 1998: 3.

— seeking Sataki Tuifua, Lahaina News, May 21, 1998: 8.

— crime of the week, Lahaina News, July 2, 1998: 8.

— to hold Invitational Golf Tournament, Lahaina News, September 16, 1999: 7.

— reports on activities, Lahaina News, March 15, 2001: 2.

— celebrates 22 years, Lahaina News, October 31, 2002: 21.

— launches website, Lahaina News, December 5, 2002: 16.

— has website, Lahaina News, January 16, 2003: 2.

— releases statistics, Lahaina News, April 24, 2003: 2.

CRIME WATCH
— program presented with new manual, Lahaina News, March 25, 1987: 12.

— campaign to begin, Lahaina News, June 15, 1988: 1,20.

— West Maui committee to meet, Lahaina News, November 16, 1988: 5.

— expands, Lahaina News, June 21, 1989: 1,12.

CRIMES OF THE HEART [PLAY]
— to be produced by Maui Community Theatre, Lahaina News, September 21, 1988: 20.

CRIMINAL JUSTICE CLUB
— see Maui Community College

CRISTE, MARILYN
— Lahainaluna High School student wins scholarship from Cannon's Business College, Lahaina News, May 3, 1989: 3.

CRIVELLO, STACY HELM [POLITICIAN]
— running for Moloka'i seat on Maui County Council, Lahaina News, July 25, 2002: 16.

CROCKETT, DAVID [ARTIST]
— to exhibit at Lahaina Arts Society, Lahaina News, August 8, 2002: 15.

CROCKETT, WILLIAM
— rejected as Maui Charter Commissioner, Lahaina News, May 8, 1991: 8.

— named new leasing manager at Ka'ahumanu Center, Lahaina News, January 11, 1996: 11.

CROCKETT-LINGLE, LINDA
— see Lingle, Linda

CROCKFORD, SCOTT
— manager of 505 Front shopping mall discusses grand opening, Lahaina News, April 29, 1987: 1,12.

CROMWELL, DARREN
— raises money for victims of September 11th, Lahaina News, September 27, 2001: 2.

CRONKITE, WALTER
— visits Lahaina, Lahaina News, February 6, 1992: 1.

CROP CIRCLES
— discussed, Lahaina News, July 25, 1996: 14.

CROSBY, DAVID [MUSICIAN]
— to perform at Maui Arts and Cultural Center with band CPR, Lahaina News, September 27, 2001: 17.

— to perform with band CPR, Lahaina News, October 4, 2001: 17.

— to perform, Lahaina News, October 11, 2001: 15.

— to perform, Lahaina News, October 11, 2001: 16.

CROSBY, JOHN [ARTIST]
— to exhibit at Addi Galleries, Lahaina News, September 12, 1996: 16.

CROSBY, STILLS, AND NASH [MUSICAL GROUP]
— to perform at Royal Lahaina Tennis Stadium, Lahaina News, March 20, 1991: 9.

— to perform at Royal Lahaina Tennis Stadium, Lahaina News, March 27, 1991: 12,14.

— to perform at Royal Lahaina Tennis Stadium, Lahaina News, April 10, 1991: 10.

— to perform this week, Lahaina News, April 24, 1991: 7.

CROSS, CHRISTOPHER [MUSICIAN]
— to perform in "A Walk Down Abbey Road" celebration of the Beatles, Lahaina News, June 13, 2002: 17.

CROSS, NANCY
— appointed tournament director for Mercedes Championships, Lahaina News, April 6, 2000: 7.

CROSS, ORRIN
— named as general manager at Hula Grill, Lahaina News, July 7, 1994: 9.

CROSSLEY, DON [ARTIST]
— carver offering services, Lahaina News, March 8, 1989: 2.

— to etch one-of-a-kind bottle, Lahaina News, February 7, 1990: 14.

— to exhibit at Lahaina Arts Society, Lahaina News, April 8, 1993: 11.

CROSSROADS [RESTAURANT]
— reviewed, Lahaina News, February 1, 1984: 15.

CROUTHER, LANCE [COMEDIAN]
— to perform at Comedy Club and the Sports Page, Lahaina News, November 26, 1992: 22,26.

CROVO, ED
— named general manager of Hyatt Regency Maui, Lahaina News, June 27, 1996: 12.

— named general manager of the year of Hyatt Hotels and Resorts, Lahaina News, May 28, 1998: 11.

CROW, CARLA [ARTIST]
— work displayed at Artful Dodger's Reed and Read, Lahaina News, November 11, 1987: 6.

— to be featured at Miracles Bookery, Lahaina News, January 21, 1999: 12.

CROW, JERRY
— Waikiki Aquarium Acting Curator to present "Sharks and Rays of Hawaii", Lahaina News, February 20, 2003: 2.

CROWE, JIM
— director of Teen Challenge speaks of the need for dormitories, Lahaina News, October 31, 1991: 1.

CROWFOOT [TELEVISION SHOW]
— pilot completes production, Lahaina News, May 12, 1994: 2.

CROWLEY, ZOEE
— to discuss "Body Talk—Finding Your Comfort Zones", Lahaina News, November 29, 2001: 17.

CROWN OF THORNS
— starfish found of Lana'i, Lahaina News, June 27, 1990: 1.

CROWN PRINCESS [SHIP]
— to visit Lahaina Harbor, Lahaina News, March 18, 1999: 13.

CROZIER, MIKE [POLITICIAN]
— to meet with Maui Contractors Association, Lahaina News, July 25, 1990: 7.

CRUCIBLE, THE [PLAY]
— to be performed by Seabury Hall Performing Arts, Lahaina News, January 21, 1993: 15.
— to be performed by Seabury Hall Performing Arts, Lahaina News, February 4, 1993: 15.
— performances continue, Lahaina News, February 25, 1993: 12.

CRUISE, DONNIE [ARTIST]
— featured by Lahaina Arts Society, Lahaina News, February 24, 1988: 18.

CRUISE SHIPS
— see Lahaina Harbor, Tourism

CRUZ, CELIA [MUSICIAN]
— to perform at Maui Arts and Cultural Center with her band Yari Moré y Su Orquesta, Lahaina News, July 18, 2002: 15.
— to perform, Lahaina News, July 25, 2002: 20.

CRUZ, JOHN [MUSICIAN]
— to perform at Maui Arts and Cultural Center, Lahaina News, August 7, 1997: 12.

CRYSTAL SYMPHONY [SHIP]
— arrives at Lahaina Harbor, Lahaina News, January 29, 1998: 15.

CUB SCOUTS
— hold Pinewood Derby, Lahaina News, April 27, 1995: 5.
— to hold fishing derby, Lahaina News, May 30, 2002: 2.
— holds "Scouting for Food", Lahaina News, November 28, 2002: 5.

CUCCIA, JOHN
— man paralyzed after assault needs money for rehabilitative care, Lahaina News, September 5, 1990: 2.
— recovering from attack, Lahaina News, January 30, 1991: 4.

CULINARY INSTITUTE OF AMERICA
— to hold job fair at Embassy Vacation Resort, Lahaina News, May 3, 2001: 20.

CULLINEY, JOHN
— biology professor at Hawaii Pacific University to talk on "Ecosystems: Past, Present and Future", Lahaina News, November 2, 2000: 24.

CULTURAL RAINBOW PARADE
— to be held, Lahaina News, September 30, 1993: 4.

CULTURAL RESOURCES COMMISSION, MAUI COUNTY
— Mayor Hannibal Tavares plans to appoint members from Maui Historical Society, Lahaina News, February 21, 1990: 3.
— to host Maui Heritage Series, Lahaina News, May 21, 1992: 4.
— grants permit to improve Malu'ulu O Lele park, Lahaina News, June 25, 1992: 2.
— calls for Lahaina Public Library to be remodeled, Lahaina News, October 8, 1992: 1.
— to hold hearing on design guidelines for Front Street, Lahaina News, December 10, 1992: 4.
— to meet, Lahaina News, February 4, 1993: 4.
— tells Lassen Publishing Company to cover or remove marble entryway, Lahaina News, April 15, 1993: 3.
— recommends approval of Lahaina Town Action Committee's request to renovate rooms at Old Courthouse, Lahaina News, December 8, 1994: 1.
— defers decision on art displays under banyan tree, Lahaina News, February 9, 1995: 1.
— recommends land swap to preserve Moku'ula, Lahaina News, May 11, 1995: 1,6.
— wants idling buses in Lahaina Historic District to be ticketed, Lahaina News, May 11, 1995: 1,6.
— panel to tour archaeological sites at proposed subdivision, Lahaina News, March 5, 1998: 1,20.
— to consider plans for Lahaina Visitor Center, Lahaina News, August 27, 1998: 1,20.
— seeks information on Lahaina Visitor Center, Lahaina News, September 10, 1998: 1,24.
— to hold meeting on proposed Front Street shopping complex, Lahaina News, October 14, 1999: 1,11.
— Commissioners cannot decide on proposed Harbor Village complex, Lahaina News, January 13, 2000: 1,3.
— to hold a site inspection in Lahaina Historic Districts, Lahaina News, July 13, 2000: 13.
— tour Front Street, Lahaina News, July 27, 2000: 19.
— held meeting to discuss razing historic home of D.T. Fleming, Lahaina News, May 8, 2003: 1,18.
— awards contract to Winter and Company for production Lahaina Historic District Architectural Style Book, Lahaina News, September 4, 2003: 1,8.

CULTURAL RESOURCES COMMITTEE
— to hold hearing on t-shirt venders in historic district, Lahaina News, May 12, 1994: 1,3.

CULTURAL VALUES IN THE AGE OF TECHNOLOGY
— symposium to be held at Kapalua Pacific Center, Lahaina News, June 20, 1991: 1.
— conference to feature speech by Senator Daniel Inouye, Lahaina News, March 12, 1992: 3,4.

CULTURE AND ARTS DAY
— to be held at Ka'ahumanu Center, Lahaina News, March 19, 1998: 12.

CULTURE SHOCK [MUSICAL GROUP]
— to perform at Moose McGillycuddy's, Lahaina News, April 17, 1991: 11.
— to perform at Moose McGillycuddy's, Lahaina News, July 18, 1991: 9.
— continues to perform at Moose McGillycuddy's, Lahaina News, August 22, 1991: 10.

CUMMING, STACI
— to be a delegate to the National Federation of Republican Women's Convention, Lahaina News, September 25, 1997: 6.

CUMMINGS, KATHLEEN
— named Desk Person of the Year by the Hawaii Hotel Association, Lahaina News, February 28, 2002: 8.

CUMMINGS, REVEREND GEORGE
— ashes committed to the sea, Lahaina Sun, November 22, 1972: 7.

CUNNINGHAM, FRANK
— describes capturing live whales, Lahaina Sun, December 15, 1971: 18.

CUNNINGHAM, LILLIAN
— doctor to talk on "Understanding Childhood Ear Infections", Lahaina News, July 22, 1999: 13.

CUNNINGHAM, SCOTT
— named harbors district manager for Maui, Lahaina News, December 18, 1997: 3.
— discusses Lahaina-Moloka'i ferry, Lahaina News, January 28, 1999: 1.

CUOMO, BRIAN [MUSICIAN]
— to perform at SeaWatch Restaurant, Lahaina News, August 18, 1994: 16.
— to perform at Longhi's Restaurant, Lahaina News, September 19, 1996: 18.

CURCIO, DAVID
— new chef at Grand Wailea Resort Hotel and Spa, Lahaina News, November 23, 2000: 16.

CURIMAO, DONALEE
— receives Thurston Dupar Inspirational Award, Lahaina News, October 13, 1994: 15.

CURIMAO, KEITH [ARTIST]
— paints mural West Maui Youth Center, Lahaina News, March 9, 1995: 4.

CURIMAO, MICAH
— Scholar/Athlete of the Week, Lahaina News, October 28, 1999: 7.

CURRAN, TOM
— journalist joins the Lahaina Sun, Lahaina Sun, June 28, 1972: 19.
— reporter reflects on U.S. president meeting with Japan's Prime Minister in Honolulu, Lahaina Sun, September 6, 1972: 5.
— Lahaina Sun reporter takes post at United Nations, Lahaina Sun, January 24, 1973: 3.
— letter announcing his move away from Maui, Lahaina Sun, January 24, 1973: 8.

CURREN, TOM
— surfer to visit Local Motion store, Lahaina News, November 3, 1994: 21.
— featured, Lahaina News, November 17, 1994: 8.

CURRENT FACTS AND FIGURES ABOUT HAWAII [BOOK]
— source of information on Hawaiian land ownership, Lahaina News, July 15, 1982: 4.

CURRY, KEVIN [MUSICIAN]
— winner of talent contest at Wharf Cinema Shops and Restaurant, Lahaina News, June 7, 1989: 13.

CURTIS, BRUCE
— new manager of Marriott on Maui, Lahaina News, July 1, 1981: 8.

CURTIS, CHRISTOPHER
— to talk on "Principles of Aikido", Lahaina News, September 4, 2003: 17.

CURVES FOR WOMEN [BUSINESS]
— opens, Lahaina News, June 27, 2002: 8.

CUSICK, GEORGE
— named managing partner at Koho Grill and Bar, Lahaina News, December 12, 1991: 16.

CUSP [MUSICAL BAND]
— to play at Moose McGillycuddy's, Lahaina News, January 11, 1984: 12.

CUSTOM BUILDERS
— opening in Whaler's Village, Lahaina Sun, November 25, 1970: 3.

CUSTOM CYCLE AND HOT ROD SHOW
— to be held, Lahaina News, October 23, 1997: 20.

CUSTOM TAILORING [BUSINESS]
— opens, Lahaina News, August 3, 1995: 8.

CUTTER OF MAUI [BUSINESS]
— hosting "Christmas in Summertime" charity drive, Lahaina News, July 23, 1998: 13.

CUVAISON WINERY [BUSINESS]
— to be featured at Kapalua Bay Hotel and Villas, Lahaina News, May 8, 1991: 19.

CW RESTAURANTS CONSULTANTS, INC. [BUSINESS]
— purchases Denny's franchise for Maui, Lahaina News, December 12, 1991: 16.

CY MAUI/MANIKIN [BUSINESS]
— opens at The Shops at Wailea, Lahaina News, January 25, 2001: 14.

CYCLE TO THE SUN
— to benefit Ka Lima O Maui, Lahaina News, November 15, 2001: 13.

CYCLING
— see bicycling

CYPRIANO, NOHELANI [MUSICIAN]
— to perform at Hotel Inter-Continental in Wailea, Lahaina News, December 28, 1983: 7.
— to perform at "Local Divas in Concert", Lahaina News, September 23, 1999: 12.
— to perform at Lahaina Cannery Mall, Lahaina News, December 19, 2002: 17.

CYRANO DE BERGERAC [PLAY]
— to be performed at Maui Academy of Performing Arts, Lahaina News, February 24, 1994: 12.
— presented by Maui Academy of Performing Arts, Lahaina News, April 21, 1994: 16.

CYRUS, BILLY RAY [MUSICIAN]
— to perform at Maui Arts and Cultural Center, Lahaina News, May 15, 1997: 13.

CZERWINSKI, ROMAN [ARTIST]
— featured at Sunset Galleries, Lahaina News, July 11, 1991: 14.
— to exhibit at Sunset Gallery, Lahaina News, January 30, 1992: 17.
— to be featured at Sunset Galleries, Lahaina News, March 12, 1992: 15.
— to participate in karate international competition, Lahaina News, July 4, 1996: 16.

D

D.E. EASTMAN LOOK GOOD, FEEL GREAT FAMILY DAY
— fundraiser to be held for Maui AIDS Foundation, Lahaina News, August 17, 1995: 6.
— to benefit Maui AIDS Foundation, Lahaina News, August 14, 1997: 17.
— to be held as benefit for Maui AIDS Foundation, Lahaina News, August 24, 2000: 18,20.

D.E.M.O [BUSINESS]
— Ka'ahumanu Center, Lahaina News, August 26, 1999: 14.

D.T. FLEMING BEACH PARK
— pollution detected at, Lahaina News, December 26, 1990: 1.
— County parks director Charmaine Tavares seeks to redo, Lahaina News, February 20, 1991: 1.
— to be studied by archaeologists, Lahaina News, July 15, 1993: 1.
— pre-construction work to begin on, Lahaina News, March 9, 1995: 4.
— new restrooms almost completed, Lahaina News, November 23, 1995: 4.
— closed due to dangerous surf, Lahaina News, November 14, 1996: 1.
— Peace Celebration Day to be held at, Lahaina News, April 30, 1998: 16.
— new lifeguard tower built, Lahaina News, May 20, 1999: 3.
— Maui Watercolorists Association to plein air paint at, Lahaina News, August 21, 2003: 17.

DA BUGGAS [MUSICAL GROUP]
— reviewed, Lahaina News, September 14, 1983: 12.
— move to California, Lahaina News, March 14, 1984: 9.

DA CAPO CHAMBER PLAYERS [MUSICAL GROUP]
— to perform at St. Anthony's Church, Lahaina News, January 24, 1990: 14.

DA DOO RON RUN
— benefit walk/run to be held for Maui Community Theatre, Lahaina News, August 6, 1992: 5.

DA MAYAH [PLAY]
— to be performed at Maui Community Theatre, Lahaina News, January 14, 1999: 13.
— Lee Cataluna's play to be performed, Lahaina News, January 21, 1999: 12.
— Lee Cataluna play to be performed at Iao Theatre, Lahaina News, October 12, 2000: 20.
— opens in the Kapalua Village Clubhouse, Lahaina News, October 26, 2000: 26,28.
— continues to be performed, Lahaina News, November 2, 2000: 24.

DA STING [BUSINESS]
— nightclub in Waikiki, discussed, Lahaina Times, July, 1980 volume 4 number 6: 3.

D'ABITIBI, DANNY [MUSICIAN]
— to perform at Greek Zorba, Lahaina News, May 25, 1995: 12.

DAENEN, ARSENE
— appointed new priest at Maria Lanakila Church, Lahaina News, July 11, 1991: 4.

DAHMS, PAGE
— wins Gummy Bear contest held by Ritchie's Roasted Nuts, Lahaina News, September 25, 1985: 1.

DAIMON, KELSEY
— wins "Mayor for a Day" contest, Lahaina News, December 25, 1997: 1.

DAIRME, KIRA
— Scholar/Athlete of the Week, Lahaina News, January 2, 2003: 12.

DAIRY QUEEN [RESTAURANT]
— opens in Lahaina Cannery Mall, Lahaina News, November 25, 1999: 13.

DAISE, VASHTI
— Lahaina Intermediate School teacher starts publishing business, Lahaina News, September 10, 1992: 9.

DALE, CHARLES
— chef to be featured at David Paul's Lahaina Grill, Lahaina News, October 22, 1992: 17.

DALIA, VERA [WRITER]
— author of "My Precious Legacy" to speak at Borders Books, Lahaina News, July 20, 2000: 16.

DALTON, DEBBIE
— opposed to sea-bed mining, Lahaina News, July 6, 1988: 1,12.
— claims to have been misquoted, Lahaina News, July 20, 1988: 1,4.

DALTON, JOHN
— secretary of the U.S. Navy to speak to Navy League, Lahaina News, March 27, 1997: 13.
— Secretary of the U.S. Navy to speak to Navy League, Lahaina News, April 3, 1997: 12.

DAMES, THE [MUSICAL GROUP]
— to perform at Moondoggies, Lahaina News, November 25, 1993: 12.
— continues to perform at Aloha Cantina, Lahaina News, September 1, 1994: 15.
— to perform at Aloha Cantina, Lahaina News, December 15, 1994: 18.
— continues to perform at Cheeseburger in Paradise, Lahaina News, April 27, 1995: 12.
— to perform at Aloha Cantina, Lahaina News, July 6, 1995: 11.
— to perform at Aloha Cantina, Lahaina News, July 20, 1995: 12.
— to perform at Aloha Cantina, Lahaina News, February 22, 1996: 13.
— continues to perform at Aloha Cantina, Lahaina News, March 14, 1996: 12.
— continues to perform at Aloha Cantina, Lahaina News, August 8, 1996: 16.

DAMIEN, FATHER
— life detailed, Lahaina Sun, May 9, 1973: 12,13.
— plaque attached to statue of in Washington DC, Lahaina Sun, May 16, 1973: 10.
— exhibit on to open at Lahaina Cannery, Lahaina News, December 12, 1991: 3.

DAN HICKS AND THE ACOUSTIC WARRIORS [MUSICAL GROUP]
— to perform at Embassy Suites Resort, Lahaina News, May 30, 1991: 7.

DANA, BILL [COMEDIAN]
— to speak at West Maui Taxpayers Association meeting, Lahaina News, May 17, 1989: 2.

DANCE ODYSSEY
— to be performed as benefit for Maui Community Theatre, Lahaina News, April 6, 1988: 3.

DANCE RIOT III
— to be held by Maui AIDS Foundation, Lahaina News, July 29, 1999: 12.

DANCE RIOT—MAUI PRIDE 2000
— to be held, Lahaina News, June 8, 2000: 21.

DANCE SHOWCASE 2001
— to be performed by Seabury Dance Ensemble, Lahaina News, March 15, 2001: 20.

DANCE TIME
— to hold dance party, Lahaina News, June 24, 1999: 12.

DANCEQUAKE
— to hold Christmas Party fundraiser, Lahaina News, December 12, 1996: 8.
— Festival to be held, Lahaina News, March 13, 1997: 17.
— Festival to be held at Seabury Hall, Lahaina News, March 20, 1997: 16.
— David Ward to offer, Lahaina News, May 13, 1999: 16.
— to be held, Lahaina News, May 20, 1999: 16.

DANCERS AND MUSICIANS OF BALI
— to perform, Lahaina News, March 18, 1999: 17.

DANCES WE DANCE COMPANY [TROUPE]
— to perform at Maui Youth Theatre, Lahaina News, January 2, 1985: 3.
— joined by Douglas Nielsen and Melanie Bates in performance at Baldwin High School Auditorium, Lahaina News, April 2, 1986: 3.

DANCING
— West African dance and music to be featured at Haiku Community Center, Lahaina News, November 2, 1988: 3.
— "Marathon Café, and Evening of Dancing the Day Away" to be held, Lahaina News, June 6, 1990: 13.
— Michelle Ecole to perform at Ka'anapali Beach Hotel, Lahaina News, June 6, 1990: 13.
— "Dance in the Island" television show featuring ballroom dancing to be broadcast, Lahaina News, September 12, 1990: 9.
— folkdancing to be held at Paia School, Lahaina News, July 18, 1991: 5.
— Japanese Classical dancing fatured at Ka'ahumanu Center, Lahaina News, August 29, 1991: 13.
— circle, square, line, and contra dancing offered, Lahaina News, December 5, 1991: 26.
— circle, square, line, and contra dancing offered, Lahaina News, February 6, 1992: 22.
— country dance lessons to be offered, Lahaina News, December 10, 1992: 17.
— classes being offered at Ka'anapali Westin Hotel Health Club, Lahaina News, March 25, 1993: 3.

— folk dancing held at Paia grade school, Lahaina News, April 1, 1993: 13.
— tango classes to be offered, Lahaina News, June 17, 1993: 16.
— country dance lessons to be offered, Lahaina News, December 2, 1993: 14.
— breakdancing featured, Lahaina News, May 19, 1994: 4.
— Maui Paniolo Posse presents weekly country-western dancing, Lahaina News, May 26, 1994: 11.
— "Dance Extravaganza 1994" to be held, Lahaina News, June 9, 1994: 16.
— Maui Ballet School planning summer dance activity, Lahaina News, July 21, 1994: 12.
— Maui Paniolo Posse continues to offer country western dancing, Lahaina News, August 11, 1994: 11.
— "Pieces XII" to be performed, Lahaina News, August 11, 1994: 11.
— Pieces XII to be performed, Lahaina News, August 18, 1994: 14.
— County Western Benefit Dance to be held to support couple who lost home, Lahaina News, August 18, 1994: 15.
— Rhonda Holtz offering modern dance classes, Lahaina News, October 13, 1994: 18.
— classical ballet classes to be held, Lahaina News, October 13, 1994: 19.
— Middle Eastern Dance Festival to be held at Longhi's, Lahaina News, January 19, 1995: 11.
— Judy's "Get on Your Feet" annual dance review to be held, Lahaina News, January 26, 1995: 16.
— New York Express Roller Dance Company to perform, Lahaina News, February 2, 1995: 10.
— Maui Dance Council Community Concert to feature David Ward, Lahaina News, March 16, 1995: 12.
— dance troupe Pilobolus to perform, Lahaina News, April 20, 1995: 12.
— U.S. Amateur Ballroom Dancers Association to hold monthly social dance, Lahaina News, July 6, 1995: 11.
— Pieces XIII to be held at Castle Theatre, Lahaina News, August 10, 1995: 12.
— U.S. Amateur Ballroom Dancers Association to hold monthly social dance, Lahaina News, October 12, 1995: 15.
— U.S. Amateur Ballroom Dancers Association to hold social dance, Lahaina News, December 14, 1995: 14.
— Maui Dance Council to hold concert, Lahaina News, May 30, 1996: 2.
— Mischelle Ecole d Ballet Maui to begin fall session, Lahaina News, September 26, 1996: 15.
— Stars of the Moscow Ballet to perform, Lahaina News, November 14, 1996: 14.
— Moca School of New World Dance to perform, Lahaina News, January 23, 1997: 10.
— Maui Inaugural Anniversary Ball Dinner and Dance to be held, Lahaina News, May 22, 1997: 17.
— Mischelle Ecole D'Ballet Maui to hold dance extravaganza, Lahaina News, June 5, 1997: 16.
— choreographer Terrie Robinson to hold dance workshops, Lahaina News, July 17, 1997: 9.
— lessons to be held at Kihei Community Center Open Room, Lahaina News, July 31, 1997: 16.
— "Pieces XV" to be held, Lahaina News, July 31, 1997: 17.
— Pieces XV to be held, Lahaina News, August 7, 1997: 12.
— ballet classes to be offered by Mischelle Ecole D'Ballet, Lahaina News, October 9, 1997: 9.
— country dances continue to be offered, Lahaina News, January 8, 1998: 12.
— West Hawaii Dance Theatre to perform "Meeting of the Spirits" ballet, Lahaina News, January 22, 1998: 12.
— TILT Dance Company to hold auditions, Lahaina News, January 22, 1998: 12.

— "Tonight is the Night" tap and jazz dance review to be held, Lahaina News, February 5, 1998: 12.
— line dancing continues at Lahaina Civic Center, Lahaina News, February 12, 1998: 16.
— line dancing to be held Upcountry, Lahaina News, June 18, 1998: 17.
— Academie de Danse of Alaska to hold annual "Showcase and Dinner Dance" with Andry Dance Studio, Lahaina News, July 30, 1998: 17.
— "Year of the Paniolo" to be celebrated, Lahaina News, August 6, 1998: 21.
— country line dancing continues to be held, Lahaina News, August 13, 1998: 17.
— Free Polynesian dancing to be held at Lahaina Cannery Mall, Lahaina News, August 20, 1998: 17.
— Mischelle Ecole D Ballet to offer courses, Lahaina News, October 1, 1998: 8.
— "Kalayaan" by Bailes De Pilipinas Dance Troupe to be held, Lahaina News, November 5, 1998: 20.
— line dancing continues to be held, Lahaina News, November 19, 1998: 16.
— New Year's Eve dance party to be held at Iao Theater, Lahaina News, December 24, 1998: 12.
— Virginia Holte to appear in "Ballet Spectacular", Lahaina News, January 21, 1999: 13.
— "An Evening of Classical Ballet" to be held at Maui Arts and Cultural Center, Lahaina News, January 28, 1999: 12.
— Judy Ridolfino to hold "I Just Wanna Be Happy", Lahaina News, January 28, 1999: 13.
— Maui Mixers square dancing continues to be held, Lahaina News, June 3, 1999: 17.
— country dance lessons continue at Upcountry Community Center, Lahaina News, June 17, 1999: 16.
— West Hawaii Dance Theatre to perform "Ballet 2000", Lahaina News, January 27, 2000: 12.
— Shirley Martin and Mike Lewis to hold "Mood Swings" at Casanova's, Lahaina News, April 6, 2000: 18.
— International Hawaii Multicultural Music and Dance Conference, Lahaina News, April 13, 2000: 12.
— "Marathon Cafe XI (Lightning Strikes)" to be held, Lahaina News, June 15, 2000: 17.
— line dancing continues to be offered at Lahaina Civic Center, Lahaina News, June 22, 2000: 17.
— Norman Powers Dance Productions to hold dance at Auntie Aloha's Hawaiian Hut, Lahaina News, August 10, 2000: 16,17.
— Hawaii Ballroom Dance Association continues to hold classes, Lahaina News, August 17, 2000: 16.
— Maui Paniolo Dance Association continues to offer free lessons, Lahaina News, November 9, 2000: 25.
— Maui Paniolo Posse continues to offer western dance lessons, Lahaina News, November 9, 2000: 25.
— dancers from Kochi City, Japan perform at John Manjiro "Izanai Yosakoi Festival of the Future", Lahaina News, March 22, 2001: 1.
— International Irish Dance Company to perform "Spirit of the Dance", Lahaina News, March 22, 2001: 17.
— Alexander Academy Ballet to perform at Maui Arts and Cultural Center, Lahaina News, March 29, 2001: 17.
— lessons sponsored by county Parks Department, Lahaina News, April 26, 2001: 20,21.
— "Marathon Cafe XIII (Spies)" to be held, Lahaina News, June 14, 2001: 20.
— "Marathon Cafe XIII (Spies)" to be held, Lahaina News, June 21, 2001: 16.
— lessons continue to be sponsored by Parks Department, Lahaina News, July 12, 2001: 17.
— Pieces XIX to be held, Lahaina News, August 2, 2001: 16.

— lessons to be offered by county Parks Department, Lahaina News, August 30, 2001: 17.

— Hawaii Ballroom Dance Association to hold ball, Lahaina News, September 27, 2001: 14.

— lessons continue to be offered, Lahaina News, November 8, 2001: 17.

— lessons to be held at Lahaina Civic Center, Lahaina News, December 13, 2001: 17.

— Hubbard Street Dance Chicago to perform at Maui Arts and Cultural Center, Lahaina News, February 28, 2002: 16.

— "Dance Showcase 2002" to be held, Lahaina News, March 7, 2002: 16.

— Ashton en l'air dancers to perform, Lahaina News, April 4, 2002: 14.

— Hot Salsa Dancing Hawaii to hold demonstration, Lahaina News, April 4, 2002: 15.

— Tahitian Dance Presentations to be offered at Whalers Village, Lahaina News, April 11, 2002: 16.

— Polynesian dancing continues to be held at Lahaina Cannery Mall, Lahaina News, May 16, 2002: 16.

— Iona Contemporary Dance Theatre to stage "Destiny", Lahaina News, June 6, 2002: 16.

— "A Dancing Salute to America" to be held, Lahaina News, June 13, 2002: 17.

— Pieces XX to be held, Lahaina News, August 1, 2002: 20.

— Lifou Island Dance Theatre to perform at Maui Arts and Cultural Center, Lahaina News, September 12, 2002: 21.

— Maui Hawaii Ballroom Dance Association to hold Holiday Ball, Lahaina News, November 28, 2002: 14.

— Judy Ridolfino's dance troupe to stage "Dancing from A to Z", Lahaina News, February 6, 2003: 15.

— Tamango's Urban Tap to perform "In Full Cycle", Lahaina News, March 20, 2003: 17.

— Na Kamali'i O Ke Akua attends Tahiti Fete on Oahu, Lahaina News, March 27, 2003: 3,18.

— Polynesian dancing continues to be held at Lahaina Cannery, Lahaina News, April 3, 2003: 16.

— Maui Academy of Performing Arts to hold Dance Extravaganza, Lahaina News, May 15, 2003: 16.

— Rita O'Connor to teach samba, Lahaina News, July 10, 2003: 17.

— Latin Dance Party benefit to be held, Lahaina News, September 25, 2003: 17.

— Complexions to be perform at Maui Arts and Cultural Center, Lahaina News, September 25, 2003: 17.

— Tom Stermitz to lead class on Argentine Tango, Lahaina News, October 2, 2003: 16.

DANG, MARGARET

— promoted to vice president of Bank of Hawaii's Client Experience Department, Lahaina News, September 27, 2001: 9.

DANIEL [SHIP]

— involved in conflict in Lahaina in the 1820s, Lahaina Sun, January 6, 1971: 8.

DANIEL, BETH

— golfer's career described, Lahaina News, March 6, 1985: A10.

DANIELLS, TRENNA [ARTIST]

— to host reception at Collectors Fine Arts, Lahaina News, August 28, 1997: 10.

DANIELS, AMOS

— studio manager discusses Lahaina Sound Studio, Lahaina News, February 17, 1988: 7.

DANIELS, EDDIE [MUSICIAN]

— to perform at Kapalua Music Festival Benefit Concert, Lahaina News, March 18, 1993: 10.

DANIELS, SALLY [ARTIST]

— to offer comedy improvisation playshops, Lahaina News, May 2, 1996: 18.

DANKO, GARY

— chef to participate in Kapalua Wine Symposium, Lahaina News, July 15, 1993: 10.

— San Francisco chef to star in the Kea Lani Food and Wine Masters, Lahaina News, October 11, 2001: 17.

— San Francisco chef to star in the Kea Lani Food and Wine Masters, Lahaina News, October 18, 2001: 16.

DANKWORTH, JACKIE [MUSICIAN]

— presented by Maui Philharmonic Society, Lahaina News, October 28, 1993: 11.

DANNY AND THE DEEP BLUE SEA [PLAY]

— to be performed at the Maui Arts and Cultural Center, Lahaina News, April 18, 1996: 16.

— reviewed, Lahaina News, April 25, 1996: 15.

DAN'S FRAME AND ART [BUSINESS]

— featured, Lahaina News, October 3, 1984: 14.

DANTO, ARTHUR

— philosopher discusses censorship in art at Honolulu of Academy of Art, Lahaina News, August 8, 1990: 15.

DAPITAN, JAN [POLITICIAN]

— coordinator of Community Work Day described it as success, Lahaina News, August 27, 1986: 15.

— named coordinator of Martin Luther King Jr. holiday, Lahaina News, December 28, 1988: 3.

— announces candidacy for state senator for 5th district, Lahaina News, April 18, 1990: 2.

— fundraiser scheduled, Lahaina News, August 8, 1990: 4.

— to hold rally at Kalama Park, Lahaina News, September 5, 1990: 4.

— candidate profiled, Lahaina News, September 5, 1990: 8.

— to hold rally at Kalama Park, Lahaina News, September 12, 1990: 8.

DARE (DRUG AWARENESS RESISTANCE EDUCATION)

— see Drug Awareness Resistance Education (DARE)

DARIAN, RON [COMEDIAN]

— to perform at Comedy Club, Lahaina News, January 23, 1992: 16,18.

DARISAY, PAULETTE "IWA"

— retires from Wharf Cinema Center Shops and Restaurants, Lahaina News, November 14, 2002: 9.

DARK AT THE TOP OF THE STAIRS [PLAY]

— to be performed by Baldwin High School's Performing Arts Learning Center, Lahaina News, March 18, 1993: 12.

DARKSTAR [MUSICAL GROUP]

— appearing in Lahaina, Lahaina News, December 15, 1981: 6.

— have reformed, Lahaina News, November 16, 1983: 12.

— performance in Maui reviewed, Lahaina News, February 29, 1984: 14.

— becomes first rock group to play on Lana'i, Lahaina News, April 18, 1984: 14.

DARLING, CONSTANTINE

— to present "Sex, Gravity and Immortality" with David Leonard, Lahaina News, November 2, 2000: 25.

DARLING, JIM

— studying whales off West Maui, Lahaina News, April 1, 1987: 1,8,10,20.

— to autograph book "Wild Whales" at Whaler's Book Shoppe, Lahaina News, January 20, 1988: 18.

— discuss status of whales in the Pacific, Lahaina News, May 11, 1988: 1,12,13.

— to discuss humpback whale songs, Lahaina News, January 18, 2001: 17.

DAS, KRISHNA [MUSICIAN]
— to perform at Maui Arts and Cultural Center, Lahaina News, March 6, 2003: 17.

DASAGO, AL
— basketball coach to retire, Lahaina News, March 8, 2001: 12.

DASHEFSKY, HOWARD
— news anchor to host Terry Fox "Day of Hope", Lahaina News, October 19, 2000: 18.

DASILVA, LEN
— promoted to chief operating officer at Hilo Hatties, Lahaina News, September 19, 2002: 8.

DASS, RAM [MUSICIAN]
— to perform at Maui Arts and Cultural Center, Lahaina News, March 6, 2003: 17.

DASUGO, AL
— volunteer work described, Lahaina News, July 11, 1991: 7.
— Lahaina Rainbows menehune basketball coach praised, Lahaina News, January 14, 1993: 8.
— becomes basketball coach at Lahainaluna High School, Lahaina News, September 27, 2001: 12.
— Lahaina Rainbows coach steps down, Lahaina News, February 21, 2002: 12.

DATA BOOK
— see Maui County Data Book, Native Hawaiian Data Book, State of Hawaii Data Book

DAUENHAUER, DAKOTA
— Scholar/Athlete of the Week, Lahaina News, November 22, 2001: 10.

DAVE STEFFAN BAND [MUSICAL GROUP]
— to perform at World Cafe, Lahaina News, February 27, 1997: 12.

DAVID, LYNN
— teaching "Identification and Care of Historic Photographs", Lahaina News, July 23, 1998: 17.

DAVID MALO DAY
— celebration postponed until 1972 [this story retracted the following issue], Lahaina Sun, April 21, 1971: 1.
— details of celebration announced, Lahaina Sun, April 12, 1972: 7.
— plans for celebration detailed, Lahaina Sun, April 26, 1972: 5.
— celebrations detailed, Lahaina Sun, May 10, 1972: 7.
— planning in progress, Lahaina Sun, March 21, 1973: 10.
— preparations described, Lahaina Sun, April 25, 1973: 3.
— events listed, Lahaina Sun, May 9, 1973: 1.
— description of event, Lahaina Sun, May 23, 1973: 7.
— planned for April 24, 1982, Lahaina News, April 15, 1982: 10.
— Set for April 15, Lahaina News, April 4, 1984: 3.
— editorial supporting , Lahaina News, April 11, 1984: 2.
— described, Lahaina News, April 11, 1984: 9,10,11.
— tickets on sale, Lahaina News, April 3, 1985: 3.
— set for April 20, Lahaina News, April 10, 1985: 3.
— biography of, Lahaina News, April 24, 1985: 1.
— event described, Lahaina News, April 24, 1985: 1,8,9.
— 15th annual celebration set, Lahaina News, April 16, 1986: 1.
— sponsored by Lahainaluna High School, Lahaina News, March 25, 1987: 3,12.
— reviewed, Lahaina News, April 1, 1987: 4.
— to be celebrated, Lahaina News, April 6, 1988: 3,11.
— 20th celebration to be held at Lahainaluna High School, Lahaina News, March 22, 1989: 13,14.
— to be held, Lahaina News, March 29, 1989: 3.
— souvenir insert with history and details of events, Lahaina News, April 12, 1989: S1-S16.
— program described, Lahaina News, April 26, 1989: 1.
— to be held April 21st, Lahaina News, March 21, 1990: 7.
— tickets now on sale, Lahaina News, March 28, 1990: 15.
— tickets available, Lahaina News, April 4, 1990: 3.
— featured, Lahaina News, April 11, 1990: B1,B2,B3,B4,B5,B6,B7,B8,B9,B10,B11,B12.
— to take place, Lahaina News, April 18, 1990: 11.
— king and queen named, Lahaina News, February 27, 1991: 3.
— set for April 20, details given, Lahaina News, March 27, 1991: 3.
— tickets available, Lahaina News, April 3, 1991: 4.
— Lahainaluna High School to present, Lahaina News, April 10, 1991: 8.
— events described, Lahaina News, April 17, 1991: 11.
— insert with schedule, history, Lahaina News, April 17, 1991: B1,B2,B3,B4,B5,B6,B7,B8.
— to be held, Lahaina News, April 2, 1992: 17.
— to be held, Lahaina News, April 9, 1992: 17.
— to be held, Lahaina News, April 23, 1992: 1,25,B1,B2,B3,B4,B5,B6,B7,B8.
— to be held, Lahaina News, April 22, 1993: 9,10,11,12,13.
— results described, Lahaina News, May 6, 1993: 3.
— to be held, Lahaina News, February 10, 1994: 3.
— Lahainaluna High School seeking alumni to help with, Lahaina News, March 31, 1994: 4.
— to celebrate 25th anniversary, Lahaina News, April 21, 1994: 4.
— to be held, Lahaina News, April 20, 1995: 3.
— held, Lahaina News, April 27, 1995: 1.
— to be held, Lahaina News, April 11, 1996: 6.
— being held, Lahaina News, April 18, 1996: 1,18.
— Lahainaluna High School readying for, Lahaina News, April 10, 1997: 3.
— Lahainaluna High School preparing for, Lahaina News, April 9, 1998: 2.
— tickets available, Lahaina News, April 16, 1998: 2.
— to be celebrated, Lahaina News, April 23, 1998: 1,20.
— tickets available, Lahaina News, March 18, 1999: 1.
— tickets on sale, Lahaina News, April 1, 1999: 8.
— preparations, Lahaina News, April 8, 1999: 3.
— to be held, Lahaina News, April 22, 1999: 1,13,16.
— Byron Cook and Shannon Li are royalty for, Lahaina News, April 13, 2000: 3.
— to be held by Lahainaluna High School, Lahaina News, April 18, 2002: 1.
— to be held, Lahaina News, April 3, 2003: 1.
— to be held by Lahainaluna High School, Lahaina News, April 10, 2003: 1,24.
— held, Lahaina News, April 17, 2003: 1,18.
— see also Malo, David

DAVID NELSON BAND [MUSICAL GROUP]
— Grateful Dead spin-off band to perform , Lahaina News, February 11, 1999: 9.

DAVID PAUL'S LAHAINA GRILL [RESTAURANT]
— reviewed, Lahaina News, March 7, 1990: 14.
— featuring non-alcoholic drink options, Lahaina News, August 15, 1990: 16.
— chef David Paul featured, Lahaina News, August 8, 1991: 18.
— to celebrate anniversary, Lahaina News, February 6, 1992: 17.
— new menu at, Lahaina News, February 13, 1992: 26.
— celebrating anniversary, Lahaina News, February 20, 1992: 13.
— offers Summer/Fall menu, Lahaina News, August 27, 1992: 16.
— expanding, Lahaina News, September 17, 1992: 11.
— expands, Lahaina News, December 3, 1992: 4.
— to be smoke-free, Lahaina News, February 4, 1993: 13,14.
— new hires announced, Lahaina News, April 8, 1993: 6.
— offering dining classes, Lahaina News, April 15, 1993: 10.
— pianist Victoria donating tips to American Lung Association, Lahaina News, December 30, 1993: 11.

— continues Winemaker's dinners, Lahaina News, February 17, 1994: 11.

— special events announced, Lahaina News, December 1, 1994: 16.

— awarded "Best Maui Restaurant" from Hale 'Aina award, Lahaina News, January 12, 1995: 11.

— voted "Best Maui Restaurant" by Honolulu Magazine, Lahaina News, January 11, 1996: 14.

— celebrating holidays, Lahaina News, December 18, 1997: 10.

— offering reward help finding robbers, Lahaina News, December 18, 1997: 14.

— praised for ads, Lahaina News, October 1, 1998: 7.

— featured, Lahaina News, November 5, 1998: 6.

— celebrating ninth anniversary, Lahaina News, March 18, 1999: 17.

— to celebrate ninth anniversary, Lahaina News, March 25, 1999: 16.

— to offer special dinner with Iron Horse Vineyards, Lahaina News, May 27, 1999: 13.

— purchased by Jurg Munch's Mutual Unlimited, Lahaina News, January 20, 2000: 11.

— to hold "Champagne Celebration", Lahaina News, April 13, 2000: 12.

— featured, Lahaina News, May 2, 2002: 9.

— offering kama'aina invitation for September, Lahaina News, September 4, 2003: 8.

— featured, Lahaina News, October 2, 2003: 14.

— extends kama'aina special, Lahaina News, October 9, 2003: 8.

DAVID WARREN SCHOLARSHIP

— applications available through TILT Dance Company, Lahaina News, March 8, 2001: 2.

DAVIDSON, CHARLES

— Campaign Recycle Maui representative claims resorts are key to success of recycling, Lahaina News, August 25, 1994: 12.

DAVIDSON, DAN

— comments on planning problems on Maui, Lahaina News, December 28, 1988: 12.

— executive director of Land Use Research Foundation promotes Developer's Agreement Bill, Lahaina News, March 23, 1995: 3.

DAVIDSON, KAREN [ARTIST]

— to exhibit at Village Gallery-Lahaina, Lahaina News, September 2, 1993: 11.

— general merchandise creative director for Harley-Davidson reports new store to open in Maui, Lahaina News, May 10, 2001: 9.

— to exhibit at Village Gallery Contemporary, Lahaina News, February 20, 2003: 16.

DAVIDSON, RAMESH

— new assistant controller at the Maui Marriott, Lahaina News, September 30, 1993: 8.

DAVIDSON, TOMMY [MUSICIAN]

— to perform at Maui Arts and Cultural Center, Lahaina News, July 19, 2001: 17.

— to perform at Maui Arts and Cultural Center, Lahaina News, July 26, 2001: 16.

DAVIES, DEBBIE [MUSICIAN]

— to perform at Casanova's, Lahaina News, April 3, 1997: 11.

DAVIS, ALICIA ANN

— wins Young Careerist Competition, Lahaina News, April 17, 1991: 9.

— named first runner-up Young Careerist at the Hawaii Federation of Business and Professional Women's Clubs convention, Lahaina News, May 23, 1991: 8.

DAVIS, ANTONIO

— wins state karaoke contest, Lahaina News, August 21, 1997: 9.

DAVIS CUP

— Maui Junior team tryouts planned, Lahaina News, November 2, 1988: 18.

DAVIS, JANET [ARTIST]

— to exhibit at Longhi Gallery, Lahaina News, August 25, 1994: 15.

— to exhibit at Longhi Gallery, Lahaina News, September 1, 1994: 16.

— works exhibited at Longhi Gallery, Lahaina News, October 13, 1994: 18.

DAVIS, JILL

— Scholar/Athlete of the Week, Lahaina News, December 3, 1998: 18.

DAVIS JR., SAMMY [ENTERTAINER]

— attends Aku Memorial Celebrity Golf Tournament, Lahaina News, May 29, 1985: 4.

DAVIS, LYNN ANN

— to present to Maui Historical Society on Bishop Museum visual collections, Lahaina News, February 8, 1989: 3.

— to teach "Identification and Care of Historic Photographs", Lahaina News, July 30, 1998: 16.

DAVIS, MICHELE MAHEALANI

— wins Miss Lahaina Pageant, Lahaina News, June 27, 1991: 1.

— Miss Lahaina interviewed, to enter Miss Hawaii USA Pageant, Lahaina News, October 10, 1991: 1,5.

DAVIS, MIKE

— report on basketball player, Lahaina Sun, January 20, 1971: 7.

DAVIS, MIKE [POLITICIAN]

— candidate for Kahului County Council Seat, Lahaina News, November 2, 2000: 23.

DAVIS, MILES [ARTIST]

— to exhibit at Celebrities Gallery, Lahaina News, March 4, 1999: 12.

DAVIS, RON [POLITICIAN]

— Maui County Fire Chief responds to concern that fire department unaware of fire hazards, Lahaina News, May 8, 1991: 1.

— candidate for State House Representative, District 7, Lahaina News, October 26, 2000: 22.

— freshman representative lists legislative priorities, Lahaina News, January 4, 2001: 1,15.

— to discuss news from legislature, Lahaina News, March 22, 2001: 1.

— meets with residents, Lahaina News, March 29, 2001: 2.

— to hold "talk story" session, Lahaina News, April 19, 2001: 2.

— introduces bill to use DNA to identify pollution sources, Lahaina News, February 14, 2002: 2.

— announces funding released to Lahaina Intermediate School, Lahaina News, February 21, 2002: 2.

DAVIS, SUZANNE

— joins staff at Maui United Way, Lahaina News, July 11, 1990: 6.

DAVIS-BACON ACT

— to be suspended, Lahaina News, March 4, 1993: 8,12.

DAVO [ARTIST]

— work to be shown at Lahaina Arts Society's Old Jail Gallery, Lahaina News, September 28, 1988: 3.

— to exhibit at Lahaina Arts Society, Lahaina News, July 9, 1992: 19.

— to exhibit neo-expressionist work, Lahaina News, October 14, 1993: 14.

— to display at Banyan Tree Gallery, Lahaina News, March 9, 1995: 11.

— work to be exhibited at Lahaina Arts Society, Lahaina News, February 1, 1996: 12.

— to be exhibited at Village Gallery Contemporary, Lahaina News, July 11, 1996: 12.

— reviewed, Lahaina News, August 29, 1996: 13.

— to exhibit at Village Gallery-Contemporary, Lahaina News, February 20, 1997: 13.

— to demonstrate painting at Festival of Art and Flowers, Lahaina News, November 19, 1998: 1.

— to exhibit at Village Gallery Contemporary, Lahaina News, March 11, 1999: 12.

— creates portrait of Dionne Warwick, Lahaina News, September 30, 1999: 3.

— to exhibit at Village Gallery Contemporary, Lahaina News, January 11, 2001: 3.

— to exhibit at Lahaina Arts Society, Lahaina News, August 9, 2001: 14.

— featured, Lahaina News, February 21, 2002: 14.

DAWES, DAVID
— appointed assistant vice president of Island Mortgage Corporation, Lahaina News, June 27, 1990: 8.

DAWSON, DONNE
— appointed manager of publications at Alexander and Baldwin-Hawaii, Lahaina News, March 11, 1993: 12.

DAWSON, DOUG [ARTIST]
— offering plein air painting workshop, Lahaina News, October 11, 2001: 17.

DAY, APOLONIA
— to chair Arbor Week celebration, Lahaina News, November 5, 1992: 13.

DAY THEY SHOT JOHN LENNON, THE [PLAY]
— to be performed at Iao Theater, Lahaina News, November 30, 2000: 16.

— to be performed at Iao Theater, Lahaina News, December 7, 2000: 24.

DAY, TOM AND WENDY
— murder of discussed, Lahaina Sun, January 19, 1972: 5.

DE ANKO'S JEWELRY [BUSINESS]
— opening in Whaler's Village, Lahaina Sun, November 25, 1970: 3.

DE GRASSI, ALEX [MUSICIAN]
— guitarist to perform at Stouffer Wailea Beach Resort, Lahaina News, October 26, 1988: 16.

DE LA GARZA, CHEYNE
— Scholar/Athlete of the Week, Lahaina News, May 16, 2002: 12.

DE LIMA, ABNER KANEHALAUKALUAHINUI
— chairman for Kamehameha Day festivities, Lahaina Sun, June 2, 1971: 3.

DE LOACH VINEYARDS [BUSINESS]
— featured at Kapalua Bay Hotel and Villas Vintner's Dinner, Lahaina News, April 17, 1991: 11.

DE MAESTRA, PAULETTE
— to speak to Lahaina Arts Society, Lahaina News, July 23, 1992: 22.

DE MELLO, JOHN
— candidate for Maui Council discusses positions, Lahaina Sun, August 23, 1972: 9.

DE RENZY, ALEX
— pornographer visits Lahaina in his boat Marysville, Lahaina Sun, December 29, 1971: 15.

DE ROSNAY, ARNAUD
— plan to windsurf from Marquesas to Hawaii, Lahaina Times, August, 1980 volume 4 number 7: 1.

DE SCHIRLEY, PEPPI
— offers free gun classes to young people, Lahaina Sun, January 6, 1971: 3.

DE VERA, MIRIAM
— to talk on the "Philosophy of the Fool" at 'Ohana Connection, Lahaina News, July 24, 2003: 17.

DEAF
— Hawaii State Vocational Rehabilitation and Blind Division to hold meetings to discuss needs for, Lahaina News, May 17, 2001: 17.

DE'ALBERICH, MICHELLE [ARTIST]
— reception to be held at Provenance Gallery, Lahaina News, February 15, 1989: 14.

DEAN, GRAYCE
— Boy Scouts honor leader, Lahaina News, May 25, 2000: 15.

— Boy Scout leader featured, Lahaina News, October 26, 2000: 1,15.

DEAN, LOVE [WRITER]
— creates exhibit on the history of the Hawaiian lighthouse, Lahaina News, March 27, 1991: 16.

DEAN, NICOLE [WRITER]
— author of "Fever" to speak at Borders, Lahaina News, January 14, 1999: 13.

DEAN, SCOTT
— franchise owner of Subway Sandwiches on Maui featured, Lahaina News, January 23, 1992: 11.

DEAN WITTER REYNOLDS [BUSINESS]
— senior vice president to hold seminar on investment market in Hawaii, Lahaina News, July 26, 1989: 6.

— offering seminars on tax deferrals, Lahaina News, September 20, 1989: 6.

— hosting seminar on financial planning, Lahaina News, October 17, 1990: 12.

— to host seminar on financial planning, Lahaina News, October 24, 1990: 7.

— holds seminar on responsible investing, Lahaina News, September 5, 1991: 6.

— to hold seminar on retirement, Lahaina News, December 2, 1993: 9.

— to offer financial seminars, Lahaina News, January 13, 1994: 5.

— to hold workshop on retirement planning, Lahaina News, September 22, 1994: 13.

DEARDEN, NIMBLE MAKALANI
— appointed manager of Ka Piko O Lele, Lahaina News, September 23, 1999: 2.

DEARDORFF, GARY
— opens real estate brokerage, Lahaina News, August 15, 1990: 11.

DEATH
— see injuries and deaths

DEATH AND LIFE OF SHERLOCK HOLMES, THE [PLAY]
— Maui Academy of Performing Arts to hold auditions for, Lahaina News, August 29, 1991: 3.

— to open this week at Kahului Community Center, Lahaina News, October 24, 1991: 22.

DEATON, ROBERT
— vice-principal temporarily replaced by Pat Akiyama, Lahaina News, March 20, 1991: 3.

DEB AND JER'S SANDCASTLE BROADWAY DINNER THEATER REVUE [MUSICAL]
— to be performed at Sandcastle Restaurant, Lahaina News, June 29, 2000: 20.

DEB AND MIKE [COMEDIANS]
— to perform at Comedy Club, Lahaina News, November 25, 1993: 12.

DEBARGE, CHANTAL
— hired as assistant food and beverage manager Embassy Suites Resort Maui, Lahaina News, January 18, 1996: 10.

DEBNAM, JEFF [CAMP SUPERVISOR]
— discusses Teen Challenge program for Maui youth, Lahaina Sun, January 27, 1971: 6.

DEBRIS, BRYAN [ARTIST]
— smoke painting described, Lahaina News, May 26, 1994: 14,15.

— to exhibit carbon and watercolor image "Rape of the Forest", Lahaina News, February 18, 1999: 11.

DEBRUNNER, JAMIE
— joins Whalers Village as new sales representative, Lahaina News, September 24, 1998: 13.

DECISIONS MAUI
— group formed to respond to draft of Lahaina Community Plan, Lahaina News, June 21, 1989: 3.
— group critical of state Legislature for lack of facilities in West Maui, Lahaina News, July 5, 1989: 1.
— group to hold a public workshop on community issues, Lahaina News, February 14, 1990: 2.

DECKER, JOHN AND LINDA
— to hold "Wine, Dine and Fine Music" fundraiser for Maui Chamber of Commerce, Lahaina News, April 16, 1998: 12.

DECKER, LINDA
— to give lecture "What did Edward Bailey See?", Lahaina News, March 6, 1997: 10.
— Maui Historical Society president to give lecture "What did Edward Bailey See?", Lahaina News, June 12, 1997: 17.
— nurse from Senior Medication Management and Wellness Program to discuss medications, Lahaina News, November 2, 2000: 25.
— nurse from Senior Medication Management and Wellness Program to discuss medications, Lahaina News, November 9, 2000: 24.
— to speak at American Association of Retired Persons meeting, Lahaina News, March 15, 2001: 18.

DECLERCQ, ARNOLD
— appointed restaurant manager at Plantation House Restaurant, Lahaina News, June 3, 1993: 7.
— appointed new manager of Lokelani Restaurant, Lahaina News, November 10, 1994: 13.

DECOITE, ALAN
— Maui Military Museum curator to host Christian Home Educators, Lahaina News, January 24, 2002: 1,2.
— owner of Maui Military Museum says must leave its current position, Lahaina News, June 5, 2003: 1,2.

DEEE-LITE [MUSICAL GROUP]
— to perform at Blue Tropix, Lahaina News, November 10, 1994: 16.

DEEP BEACH CLEAN UP
— to be held, Lahaina News, September 24, 1992: 3.

DEER
— hunting out of season, Lahaina News, September 18, 1997: 9.

DEESE, HOWARD
— wins Year of the Ocean Award, Lahaina News, August 13, 1998: 15.

DEFENSE THREAT REDUCTION AGENCY
— taking public comments on Johnston Atoll cleanup, Lahaina News, March 7, 2002: 17.

DEHART, JEFF [COMEDIAN]
— to perform at Comedy Club, Lahaina News, May 23, 1990: 13.
— to perform at Comedy Club and the Sports Page, Lahaina News, July 23, 1992: 20,22,23.

DEL MAR PACIFIC MAUI
— to hold a grand opening for Maui Park Condominiums, Lahaina News, October 5, 2000: 13.

DEL MONTE CORPORATION [BUSINESS]
— agrees to delay closing of Moloka'i pineapple operations, Lahaina News, January 1, 1983: 4.
— laid off 29 works at Kalapuu Plantation on Moloka'i, Lahaina News, February 1, 1983: 4.

DEL ROCCO, DAVE
— to conduct children's story times at public libraries, Lahaina News, August 27, 1998: 17.
— storyteller to perform "Hawaiiana Story Time", Lahaina News, November 18, 1999: 17.

DELA CRUZ, ALBERTO
— Scholar/Athlete of the Week, Lahaina News, November 8, 2001: 12.

DELA CRUZ, JEFF
— county Land Use and Codes plans examiner critical of Lahaina parking plan, Lahaina News, October 25, 1989: 1,4.

DELA CRUZ, KIMO
— to play at Pineapple Hill Restaurant, Lahaina News, December 12, 1991: 19.

DELA CRUZ, RON [POLITICIAN]
— to hold fundraiser, Lahaina News, September 7, 1988: 3.
— featured, Lahaina News, October 26, 1988: 1,14.

DELA ROSA, ALFRED
— labor negotiator consulting the Police Officers Association of Hawaii, Lahaina Sun, December 16, 1970: 1.

DELATORI, ARLENE
— wants derelict vehicles removed from side streets, Lahaina News, December 19, 1996: 5.

DELAWARE DAY CELEBRATION
— to be held, Lahaina News, December 6, 2001: 16.

DELEONARDIS, RICHARD
— appointed as director of conventions and catering at Maui Marriott Resort, Lahaina News, June 19, 1985: 8.

DELIMA, CAROLYN CZAR
— hairstylist relocates, Lahaina News, June 9, 1994: 12.

DELIMA, FRANK [COMEDIAN]
— performs during Wharf Shops and Restaurants 10 year anniversary, Lahaina News, September 28, 1988: 1,20.
— to perform at Zoofest '90, Lahaina News, April 11, 1990: 2.
— performs at King Kamehameha III school, Lahaina News, May 25, 1995: 4.
— to hold community benefit concert, Lahaina News, February 15, 1996: 2.
— heads benefit concert, Lahaina News, February 29, 1996: 4.
— keynote speaker at benefit luncheon, Lahaina News, March 14, 1996: 11.
— to headline "Frankly Speaking: Lunch with Frank DeLima" to benefit West Maui Taxpayers Association and Lahainaluna High School, Lahaina News, April 17, 1997: 13.
— attends "Frankly Speaking: Lunch with Frank DeLima", Lahaina News, May 29, 1997: 2.
— to perform at Lahaina Cannery Mall's celebration on completion of renovation, Lahaina News, February 4, 1999: 5.
— "Sights and Sounds of Ma'alaea" radio show to feature, Lahaina News, November 30, 2000: 16.
— to perform at benefit for Hawaii Firefighters, Lahaina News, September 19, 2002: 25.

DELIMA, VANESSA
— new president of Soroptimists International, Lahaina News, July 22, 1999: 5.
— promoted to assistant vice president at Bank of Hawaii, Lahaina News, February 20, 2003: 8.

DELLATAN, ROWENA
— graduates from Cannon's Business College, Lahaina News, November 14, 1990: 4.

DELMAR, SHARON
— killed in automobile accident, Lahaina News, May 19, 1994: 3.

DELOS PIANOQUARTET [MUSICAL GROUP]
— to perform, Lahaina News, May 18, 2000: 20.

DELOS REYES, DIANE
— appointed new director of Lahainaluna High School Foundation, Lahaina News, April 10, 2003: 15.

DELTA AIRLINES [BUSINESS]
— offering plane tickets as grand price for Halloween costume contest, Lahaina News, August 29, 1991: 9.

DEMAREST, MARIA
— recognized by Media Systems, Inc., Lahaina News, November 4, 1993: 7.

DEMARKE, KAREN
— named "Manager of the First Quarter" at Westin Maui, Lahaina News, June 30, 1994: 9.

DEMELLO, ANDREW
— Planning Commission defers request for special use permit, Lahaina News, November 14, 1990: 4.

DEMELLO, RAY
— elected president of West Maui Youth Center, Lahaina News, July 15, 1982: 3.
— receives T.S. Shinn Award, Lahaina News, July 22, 1993: 8.

DEMILLE, LESLIE [ARTIST]
— featured, Lahaina News, March 28, 2002: 18.

DEMOCRATIC CENTURY CLUB
— to discuss issues, Lahaina News, January 2, 1997: 10.
— to host lawmakers discussing session, Lahaina News, May 22, 1997: 16.
— to open Democratic Information Center, Lahaina News, December 11, 1997: 11.
— to feature candidates at meeting, Lahaina News, July 25, 2002: 16.

DEMOCRATIC PARTY
— controlled by "old guard", Lahaina Sun, May 31, 1972: 21.
— report on 1972 convention, Lahaina Sun, May 31, 1972: 21.
— to meet, Lahaina News, November 4, 1987: 3.
— Dukakis campaign looking for volunteers, Lahaina News, September 21, 1988: 20.
— to hold fundraiser, Lahaina News, May 23, 1990: 6.
— to hold annual Unity Rally, Lahaina News, October 29, 1992: 4.
— to meet, Lahaina News, November 11, 1993: 6.
— to hold grassroots meetings, Lahaina News, November 18, 1993: 3.
— to hold Presidents Day event to begin election year, Lieutenant Governor Ben Cayetano to speak, Lahaina News, February 17, 1994: 4.
— to hold meeting, Lahaina News, March 24, 1994: 7.
— new officers elected, Lahaina News, May 19, 1994: 6.
— to meet, Lahaina News, August 4, 1994: 4.
— to host gubernatorial candidate Ben Cayetano, Lahaina News, September 29, 1994: 5.
— candidates pictured, Lahaina News, November 3, 1994: 32.
— to hold President's Day dinner with Governor-elect Ben Cayetano as keynote speaker, Lahaina News, February 23, 1995: 2.
— to hold organizational meeting, Lahaina News, May 4, 1995: 4.
— Ry Barbin elected as chair of Maui County, Lahaina News, September 18, 1997: 9.
— new leadership elected, Lahaina News, May 14, 1998: 7.
— of Maui names Senator Daniel Inouye as "Man of the Century", Lahaina News, December 9, 1999: 20.
— women to hold buffet luncheon, Lahaina News, May 24, 2001: 20,21.

DEMOGRAPHICS
— stereotypes of Hawaii's people challenged, Lahaina News, February 1, 1983: 16.

DENAIE, LUCIENNE
— honored by Sierra Club, Lahaina News, October 3, 2002: 9.

D'ENBEAU, MADELYN
— running for Board of Education, Lahaina News, August 6, 1998: 14.

DENECKE, HEIDE
— promoted to sales manager at Ritz-Carlton, Lahaina News, December 26, 1996: 8.

DENGUE FEVER
— state's strategy to respond to, Lahaina News, October 18, 2001: 5.

DENGUE RESPONSE TEAM
— honored at Governor's Awards Ceremonies, Lahaina News, October 24, 2002: 8.

DENISEWICZ, ROGER
— to present on "Kaua'i Flower and Gems Essences", Lahaina News, May 7, 1998: 20.
— Kinesiologist to lecture on "Brain Gym", Lahaina News, September 16, 1999: 12.
— demonstrating kinesiology, Lahaina News, December 9, 1999: 21.

DENITZ, HERM
— life to be remembered, Lahaina News, August 1, 2002: 9.

DENNING, RICHARD
— denied building permit, Lahaina Sun, February 9, 1972: 5.
— actor to narrate "Carnival of the Animals" for Maui Symphony Orchestra, Lahaina News, September 15, 1994: 15.

DENNIS, DIANE
— new principal of Lahaina Intermediate School, Lahaina News, August 26, 1993: 4.
— Lahaina Intermediate School principal featured, Lahaina News, April 21, 1994: 1,2.

DENNIS MANAWAITI JAZZ DUO [MUSICAL GROUP]
— to perform at Sound of the Falls, Lahaina News, September 23, 1993: 11.

DENNIS, PAT
— secretary of Lahaina Art Society, Lahaina Sun, January 13, 1971: 7.

DENNY'S [RESTAURANT]
— set to return to Hawaii, Lahaina News, August 1, 1981: 5.
— drug use of employees discussed at, Lahaina Times, August 20, 1983 volume 7 number 8: 2.
— franchise for Maui purchased by CW Restaurants, Lahaina News, December 12, 1991: 16.
— featured, Lahaina News, May 7, 1992: 25.
— may have to pay for overcharging customers, Lahaina News, August 17, 1995: 3.

DENT, JIM
— senior tour golfer featured, Lahaina News, November 22, 1989: 9.

DENT, RALPH
— efforts to help kids featured, Lahaina News, October 19, 2000: 1,7.

DENT, ZACHARY
— receives scholarship from the Environmental and Spatial Technology (EAST) program, Lahaina News, June 28, 2001: 1,22.

DENTON-NELSON, JEANNE [ARTIST]
— to exhibit at Village Gallery Contemporary, Lahaina News, May 16, 2002: 16.
— featured, Lahaina News, May 23, 2002: 18.

DENVER, JOHN [MUSICIAN]
— to perform on Maui, calls for end to world hunger, Lahaina News, November 11, 1987: 1.

DEPARTMENT OF BUSINESS, ECONOMIC DEVELOPMENT AND TOURISM, DEPARTMENT OF
— publishes "State of Hawaii Data Book 1999", Lahaina News, December 7, 2000: 19.

DEPARTMENT OF ECONOMIC DEVELOPMENT
— data on tourism, Lahaina Sun, February 17, 1971: 5.

DEPARTMENT OF TRANSPORTATION
— see Transportation, Department of

DERBY, JOHN
— nominated as new president of West Maui Business Association, Lahaina Sun, May 19, 1971: 7.
— new president of West Maui Business Association, Lahaina Sun, June 23, 1971: 10.

DEREK TRUCKS BAND [MUSICAL GROUP]
— to perform at Rhythm and Blues Mele, Lahaina News, May 8, 2003: 17.
— to perform at Rhythm and Blues Mele, Lahaina News, May 15, 2003: 16.

DEROCHES [MUSICIANS]
— to perform flute and tell Native American stories, Lahaina News, May 13, 1999: 16.

DERTNER, ERIN [ARTIST]
— wins Lahaina Poster Contest, Lahaina News, July 24, 2003: 1,9.

DESAI, PANDIT MUKESH [MUSICIAN]
— to perform at St. John's Church, Lahaina News, June 10, 1999: 17.
— to perform, Lahaina News, June 17, 1999: 16.

DESANTOS, BARRETT
— new national sales manager of the Embassy Suite Resort, Lahaina News, July 8, 1993: 8.

DESERT SHIELD
— song produced to honor, Lahaina News, January 2, 1991: 4.

DESHAZO, WILLIAM [ARTIST]
— featured at Galerie Lassen, Lahaina News, March 24, 1994: 15.
— to appear at Wyland Galleries, Lahaina News, September 6, 2001: 16.

DESIGN CLASSICS—OPTICAL SERVICES INTERNATIONAL ASSOCIATION
— to hold convention, Lahaina News, January 21, 1993: 8.

DESIGN NETWORK [BUSINESS]
— receives Pele Award, Lahaina News, April 16, 1992: 14.

DESLAURIERS, PAUL [WRITER]
— to lead workshop on his book "In the High Energy Zone: The Six Characteristics of Highly Effective Groups", Lahaina News, April 3, 2003: 3.

DESOTO, TURSTEE "FRENCHY"
— to represent OHA on the Kahoʻolawe Island Conveyance Committee, Lahaina News, November 14, 1990: 4,5.

DESPINS, BERNARD
— wins contract for work at Kahului Harbor, Lahaina News, August 2, 1989: 6.

DESSINAS, GEORGE
— Saint Constantine and Helen Greek Orthodox Church father to bless Greek Zorba restaurant, Lahaina News, June 29, 1995: 12.

DESTEFANO, F. DENNIS
— joins National Center for Financial Education, Lahaina News, August 3, 1995: 8.
— to hold "Retirement Planning for Young Adults" to be held, Lahaina News, July 5, 2001: 9.

DESTEFANO, KAY
— veterinarian featured, Lahaina News, February 6, 1997: 2.

DESTEPHANO WEALTH MANAGEMENT
— conducting seminar "Total Retirement Planning Workshop", Lahaina News, August 7, 1997: 12.

DESTINATION MAUI INC. [BUSINESS]
— fined for failing to register as a condominium hotel operator registration, Lahaina News, August 11, 1994: 7.
— now designated as an Accredited Management Organization, Lahaina News, May 21, 1998: 13.

DETTLOFF, JACK
— manager of the Kaʻanapali Beach Hotel, Lahaina Sun, August 25, 1971: 5.

DEVELOPERS
— impact on Lahaina discussed, Lahaina Times, August 20, 1983 volume 7 number 8: 2.

DEVELOPER'S AGREEMENT BILL
— would help fund environmental programs, Lahaina News, March 23, 1995: 3.

DEVELOPMENT
— Cravalho discusses need to control, Lahaina Sun, January 20, 1971: 2.
— Rand Hawaii Ltd. Planning for 34 condominium units in Lahaina, Lahaina Sun, January 27, 1971: 3.
— discussion to develop banyan tree area, Lahaina Sun, January 27, 1971: 4.
— fine sought for Wailea Land Corporation, Lahaina Sun, February 10, 1971: 2.
— proposal for apartment house in agricultural area in Olowalu protested, Lahaina Sun, April 14, 1971: 2.
— 3000 hotel rooms planned by Maui Land & Pineapple, Lahaina Sun, April 21, 1971: 1,8.
— rezoning approved, Lahaina Sun, April 28, 1971: 3.
— a record number of building permits issued, Lahaina Sun, June 16, 1971: 1.
— rezoning approved for 20-acre parcel of Hana Ranch, Lahaina Sun, June 23, 1971: 2.
— 52-unit condominium near Honokowai and Napili okayed by County Planning Commission, Lahaina Sun, June 23, 1971: 3.
— Maui County Council approves rezoning in Napili, Lahaina Sun, June 30, 1971: 12.
— planned hotel not being made public, Lahaina Sun, June 30, 1971: 2.
— construction of Lahaina hotel delayed, Lahaina Sun, July 7, 1971: 1,11.
— The Kahana Sunset, a new condominium, is being constructed between Kaʻanapali and Napili, Lahaina Sun, July 7, 1971: 3.
— Wailuku redevelopment plan discussed, Lahaina Sun, July 14, 1971: 1.
— buildings in Lahaina limited to 6 stories, Lahaina Sun, July 21, 1971: 8.
— Maui County Planning Commission defers decision for low and moderate income housing in Napilihau, Lahaina Sun, July 28, 1971: 12.
— Maui Surf hotel opening, Lahaina Sun, July 28, 1971: 5.
— rezoning in Pukalani okayed by Maui County Planning Commission, Lahaina Sun, August 4, 1971: 1,3.
— temporary height limit to construction passed by Maui County Council, Lahaina Sun, August 11, 1971: 12.
— Maui County Planning Commission approves 324 hotel rooms on Molokaʻi, Lahaina Sun, August 11, 1971: 3.
— Amfac Communities building subdivision in Lahaina, Lahaina Sun, August 18, 1971: 11.
— planned J. Walter Cameron Center seeking bids for construction, Lahaina Sun, September 1, 1971: 11.
— concern for development in Kihei, Lahaina Sun, September 8, 1971: 3.
— Wailea project described, Lahaina Sun, September 15, 1971: 12.
— plans approved for Mana Kai condominium in Kihei, Lahaina Sun, September 15, 1971: 5.
— construction has fallen off in the first half of the year, Lahaina Sun, September 22, 1971: 10.
— Amfac Communities seeking approval for 120-unit apartment in Lahaina, Lahaina Sun, September 22, 1971: 13.
— hotel construction near Keawanui Fishpond on Molokaʻi approved, Lahaina Sun, October 20, 1971: 5.
— construction of restaurant and shopping complex begins in from of Lahaina Shopping Center, Lahaina Sun, November 10, 1971: 1.
— restoration to begin on prison and banyan tree area, Lahaina Sun, November 17, 1971: 1.

— new shopping center for Lahaina, Lahaina Sun, December 1, 1971: 1.

— new apartments for low-income families to be owned by Quality Pacific Ltd to be built in Lahaina, Lahaina Sun, December 8, 1971: 4.

— decision on proposed housing project in Napilihau deferred by Maui Planning Commission, Lahaina Sun, December 15, 1971: 7.

— Maui County Board of Realtors complains that housing subdivision laws are unfair, Lahaina Sun, December 29, 1971: 17.

— large condominium project begins in Napili, Lahaina Sun, January 5, 1972: 6.

— plan to move Lahaina library from downtown location protested, Lahaina Sun, January 19, 1972: 6.

— Maui County wants Alexander & Baldwin land near Maui Memorial Gym, Lahaina Sun, January 19, 1972: 9.

— housing lots in Lahaina to be sold, Lahaina Sun, January 26, 1972: 15.

— Richard Denning denied building permit, Lahaina Sun, February 9, 1972: 5.

— approval asked to convert ranch in Moloka'i to African safari, Lahaina Sun, March 8, 1972: 3.

— groundbreaking ceremonies at commercial building near Lahaina Shopping Center, Lahaina Sun, March 8, 1972: 9.

— Ka'ahumanu Shopping Center near to beginning, Lahaina Sun, March 15, 1972: 5.

— housing development for low and moderate income families will be constructing, Lahaina Sun, March 22, 1972: 14.

— Land survey by County Planning Department planned, Lahaina Sun, March 29, 1972: 4.

— contractor responds to Maui County Planning Commission report on proposed apartment building in Olowalu, Lahaina Sun, April 19, 1972: 10.

— residential construction increasing on neighbor islands, Lahaina Sun, May 10, 1972: 11.

— local workers describe impact of new development, Lahaina Sun, May 17, 1972: 3.

— hotel proposed for Kapalua Beach, Lahaina Sun, May 24, 1972: 9.

— Maui County seeks federal money to create plans for Lahaina, Lahaina Sun, June 7, 1972: 4.

— construction of new shopping center in Lahaina to begin soon, Lahaina Sun, June 7, 1972: 6.

— report on building permits for May, Lahaina Sun, June 14, 1972: 11.

— Planning Commission okays relocation of road in Wailea, Lahaina Sun, June 14, 1972: 9.

— pace of development in Kihei discussed, Lahaina Sun, June 14, 1972: 9.

— criticisms of proposed renewal project in Wailuku discussed, Lahaina Sun, June 28, 1972: 9.

— opposition to Wailea development discussed, Lahaina Sun, July 5, 1972: 5.

— plan for Wailuku-Kahului approved by Citizens Advisory Committee, Lahaina Sun, July 19, 1972: 7.

— groundbreaking for shopping center near Waianae street and Honoapi'ilani highway, Lahaina Sun, August 30, 1972: 11.

— moratorium on building servants' quarters and guest cottages passed, Lahaina Sun, September 6, 1972: 11.

— Alexander & Baldwin gives 70 acres of land to Maui County, Lahaina Sun, September 6, 1972: 14.

— Alexander & Baldwin praised for social values, Lahaina Sun, October 4, 1972: 12.

— Wailuku redevelopment plans criticized, Lahaina Sun, October 4, 1972: 3.

— questions raised in public forum on redevelopment, Lahaina Sun, October 11, 1972: 3.

— Wailuku redevelopment plans criticized, Lahaina Sun, October 25, 1972: 1,14.

— Maui General Plan criticized, Lahaina Sun, October 25, 1972: 22.

— Wailuku-Kahului general plan discussed, Lahaina Sun, October 25, 1972: 5.

— public meeting on Wailuku redevelopment plan expected to be contentious, Lahaina Sun, November 1, 1972: 13.

— Wailuku-Kahului general plan discussed, Lahaina Sun, November 1, 1972: 3.

— Wailuku redevelopment plans public meeting is calm, Lahaina Sun, November 8, 1972: 6,7.

— public hearing on shoreline setback law to be held, Lahaina Sun, November 15, 1972: 10.

— tension between Maui Redevelopment Agency and Wailuku residents has subsided, Lahaina Sun, December 13, 1972: 4.

— construction of hotel that would be the largest building in Lahaina set to begin, Lahaina Sun, December 13, 1972: 5.

— federal money to help pay for future plan for central Maui, Lahaina Sun, December 20, 1972: 15.

— large hotel proposed for Lahaina discussed , Lahaina Sun, December 20, 1972: 3.

— illegal grading and fence construction at hotel site detailed, Lahaina Sun, December 20, 1972: 3.

— Maui general plan outlined, Lahaina Sun, December 20, 1972: 5.

— opposition to new large hotel in Lahaina, Lahaina Sun, December 27, 1972: 1,4.

— Mayor Cravalho claims Wailuku-Kahului general plan is good, Lahaina Sun, December 27, 1972: 14.

— editorials opposing proposed large hotel in Lahaina, Lahaina Sun, December 27, 1972: 5.

— editorials opposing proposed large hotel in Lahaina, Lahaina Sun, January 3, 1973: 7.

— editorials opposing proposed large hotel in Lahaina, Lahaina Sun, January 10, 1973: 4,5.

— Wailea Development Corporation seeks zoning changes, Lahaina Sun, January 17, 1973: 3.

— editorial on the McNeil Building proposed for Lahaina, Lahaina Sun, January 17, 1973: 4.

— editorials opposing proposed large hotel in Lahaina informally referred to as the McNeil Building, Lahaina Sun, January 17, 1973: 5.

— Maui County Council studying ways to stall proposed McNeil Building in Lahaina, Lahaina Sun, January 24, 1973: 4.

— editorials opposing proposed large hotel in Lahaina informally referred to as the McNeil Building, Lahaina Sun, January 24, 1973: 5.

— Wailea tourist project approved by Planning Commission, Lahaina Sun, January 31, 1973: 3.

— last chance to comment on Wailuku-Kahului general plan, Lahaina Sun, January 31, 1973: 6.

— resort apartment complex in Kahana discussed, Lahaina Sun, February 7, 1973: 4.

— moratorium on highrise buildings reviewed by Maui County Council, Lahaina Sun, February 7, 1973: 7.

— Hololani condominium proposed at Kahana, Lahaina Sun, February 14, 1973: 1,12,13.

— Mike Resnick planning to build Kahana Beach hotel, Lahaina Sun, February 14, 1973: 12,13.

— condominium planned at Honokowai, Lahaina Sun, February 14, 1973: 13.

— plans for housing in Kula criticized due to lack of water, Lahaina Sun, February 14, 1973: 3.

— Butch Arisumi granted permission to build moderate cost housing in Kihei, Lahaina Sun, February 14, 1973: 3.

— housing planned at Makawao, Lahaina Sun, February 14, 1973: 5.

— land rezoned at Pauwela to allow low to moderate housing, Lahaina Sun, February 21, 1973: 4.

— proposed golf course in Waihee receives tentative approval, Lahaina News, December 26, 1991: 5.

— Alexander and Baldwin plans for Ma'alaea, Lahaina News, January 2, 1992: 5.

— federal money released for Environmental Impact Statement to study proposed road between Kihei and Ulupalakua, Lahaina News, February 6, 1992: 4.

— non-compliance with federal financing regulations leads to withholding of development funds for Wailuku, Lahaina News, February 6, 1992: 4.

— proposal to enlarge Wailea 670 project recommended for approval, Lahaina News, February 6, 1992: 5.

— proposed subdivision at Kanakanui Road to be discussed, Lahaina News, February 6, 1992: 5.

— conflict over value of ceded land in Wahikuli slated for development, Lahaina News, February 20, 1992: 1.

— plans to build baseball stadium, Lahaina News, March 5, 1992: 3.

— Amfac/JMB Hawaii, Inc. conducts survey of West Maui concerning, Lahaina News, March 12, 1992: 1.

— Maui Eldorado reaches agreement with Royal Court Corp. to develop upscale shopping center, Lahaina News, March 12, 1992: 12.

— fund available for Wailuku businesses, Lahaina News, March 12, 1992: 13.

— Wailea 670 project poised to be approved, Lahaina News, March 12, 1992: 4.

— two-story restaurant planned for Paia, Lahaina News, March 19, 1992: 10.

— court action threatened over variance to Wailea 10 project, Lahaina News, March 26, 1992: 5.

— bill to transfer shoreline permit power to County Councils dies in legislature, Lahaina News, March 26, 1992: 5.

— planned community proposed by C. Brewer Properties approved, Lahaina News, May 7, 1992: 6.

— building permits for commercial developments in South Maui on hold, Lahaina News, May 21, 1992: 4.

— building activity expected to decrease, Lahaina News, May 21, 1992: 8.

— ground breaking ceremony held at Plantation Club Estates, Lahaina News, May 28, 1992: 12.

— developer Jim Patterson asks for extension of special management area permit, Lahaina News, May 28, 1992: 4.

— seawall proposed at Spreckelsville by Sugar Cove Condominium and Cyrus Monroe, Lahaina News, May 28, 1992: 5.

— public meeting to be held to discuss Wailea 670 project, Lahaina News, May 28, 1992: 6.

— discussion on building along slopes, Lahaina News, June 4, 1992: 6.

— Big Beach appraisal finished, Lahaina News, June 4, 1992: 6.

— public meeting to discuss Wailea 670, Lahaina News, June 4, 1992: 7.

— 600-acre project planned in Ma'alaea by Alexander and Baldwin, Lahaina News, June 11, 1992: 8.

— public hearing to discuss Wailea 670 project, Lahaina News, June 11, 1992: 8.

— decision to grant shoreline setback variance appealed, Lahaina News, June 11, 1992: 8.

— Maui County Planning Commission defers hearing on subdivision proposed by Kyushu and Toyo Corporation, Lahaina News, June 11, 1992: 8.

— citizens advisory committee wants more shoreline protection, Lahaina News, June 18, 1992: 14.

— Uwe Schulz, architect helping to restore historic Lahaina, featured, Lahaina News, June 18, 1992: 3.

— crowd opposes Alexander and Baldwin proposal, Lahaina News, June 18, 1992: 4.

— flood control project goes forward without an Environmental Impact Study, Lahaina News, June 25, 1992: 1.

— lawsuit considered against Wailea 670, Lahaina News, June 25, 1992: 6.

— developer of Wailea 10 seeks shoreline setbacks, Lahaina News, June 25, 1992: 8.

— meeting to discuss future of North Beach held, Lahaina News, July 2, 1992: 1.

— public to be held regarding subdivision at Waiakoa, Lahaina News, July 2, 1992: 6.

— moratorium on new hotels may expand across Maui, Lahaina News, July 9, 1992: 1.

— Amfac/JMB planning to expand Pu'ukoli'i Village development, Lahaina News, July 9, 1992: 3.

— C. Brewer Properties seeking to reclassify c. 20,000 acres of land in Ma'alaea, Lahaina News, July 9, 1992: 6,7.

— developers to present to Kihei Community Association, Lahaina News, July 16, 1992: 7.

— C. Brewer Properties proposes 169-acre development in Ma'alaea, Lahaina News, July 23, 1992: 10.

— debate continues over future building mauka of Piilani Highway, Lahaina News, July 23, 1992: 11.

— program to teaching builders about bidding process to be offered, Lahaina News, July 23, 1992: 17.

— subdivision sought for parcel in Makawao at Miner Tract, Lahaina News, July 23, 1992: 7.

— Maui County Council may pass bill requiring county to pay for road improvements for church developments, Lahaina News, July 23, 1992: 9.

— Jesse and Joyce Spencer seeking use permit to subdivide at Keonekai Heights, Lahaina News, July 30, 1992: 7.

— Azeka Place II to hold grand opening, Lahaina News, August 6, 1992: 9.

— residents express concern about dust and density, Lahaina News, August 13, 1992: 9.

— business space increases in Kihei, Lahaina News, August 20, 1992: 13.

— developers to present to Kihei-Makena Community Plan citizen's advisory committee, Lahaina News, August 20, 1992: 14.

— parking lot sought by Towashinyo Maui, Lahaina News, August 20, 1992: 14.

— meeting scheduled for Jesse and Joyce Spencer's request for use permit to subdivide at Keonekai Heights, Lahaina News, August 20, 1992: 15.

— request to develop golf courses at Wailea 670 passes first reading, Lahaina News, August 27, 1992: 13.

— Maui Meadows Homeowners Association requests buffer from Walia 670, Lahaina News, August 27, 1992: 13.

— public hearing to be held to consider KCOM Corporation's proposed shopping center, Lahaina News, August 27, 1992: 3.

— Alexander and Baldwin Properties proposed project in Ma'alaea called premature, Lahaina News, September 3, 1992: 12.

— proposal to turn residential lots into office complex, Lahaina News, September 3, 1992: 12.

— Japan Grand Prix proposes golf course in Makena, Lahaina News, September 3, 1992: 13.

— Kihei Community Plan Citizen's Advisory Committee opposes restaurants between Kamaole II and III Beach Parks, Lahaina News, September 3, 1992: 13.

— Azeka Building Corporation proposes developing land near Azeka Place I and II, Lahaina News, September 3, 1992: 13.

— public hearing to be held for proposed subdivision at Keonekai Heights, Lahaina News, September 10, 1992: 12.

— Wailea 670 nears approval, Lahaina News, September 24, 1992: 2.

— long-term moratorium on hotel construction discussed, Lahaina News, September 24, 1992: 9.

— proposal to sell lots mauka of the Silversword Golf Course, Lahaina News, October 1, 1992: 13.

— Harriman estate to sell to hold on Front Street, Lahaina News, July 22, 1993: 1.

— proposed developments scaled back in Kihei-Makena Community Plan, Lahaina News, July 22, 1993: 6.

— proposed supermarket lacks support, Lahaina News, July 22, 1993: 6.

— county bringing Lahaina up to code, Lahaina News, August 5, 1993: 1,12.

— Tri-Isle Main Street coordinator Jocelyn Perreira speaks of importance of small business, Lahaina News, August 5, 1993: 1,3.

— discussed in supplement published in Lahaina News by West Maui Taxpayers Association, Lahaina News, August 5, 1993: A2,A3.

— state agencies sponsoring public meeting on coastal water and land use, Lahaina News, September 9, 1993: 3.

— Japan Grand Prix of Hawaii, Ltd proposes golf course in Makena, Lahaina News, September 23, 1993: 6.

— residents concerned about JGL Enterprises' rezoning request at Napilihau Villages, Lahaina News, November 25, 1993: 1,3.

— Kenny Barr only planning commissioner to vote against request to develop land near Kamaole, Lahaina News, November 25, 1993: 6.

— Obayashi Hawaii Corp. offering program for remaining homes in Waiehu Terrace Increment B development, Lahaina News, December 9, 1993: 6.

— Linda Lingle talks about funding to improve Front Street, Lahaina News, January 27, 1994: 1,2.

— proposed Maui Ocean Center may lure eco-tourists, Lahaina News, March 3, 1994: 6.

— JGL Enterprises' project approved by Maui County Council, Lahaina News, March 24, 1994: 1,20.

— Subcontractors Association of Hawaii to hold conference, Lahaina News, July 14, 1994: 12.

— hearing to be held to determine details on proposal by, Lahaina News, August 11, 1994: 1,3.

— issues arise connected to Front Street Improvement project, Lahaina News, September 22, 1994: 1,2.

— hearing on apartment complex in Napili proposed by JGL Enterprises Inc. finishes, Lahaina News, September 22, 1994: 6.

— value of proper landscaping discussed, Lahaina News, October 6, 1994: 10.

— Kahana Ridge under construction, Lahaina News, October 13, 1994: 15.

— strip mall proposed near Dickenson Street, Lahaina News, February 2, 1995: 1.

— state Land Use Commission to review plan for commercial park planned in West Maui, Lahaina News, February 16, 1995: 3.

— Maui Planning Commission to consider request for hotel developments at North Beach, Lahaina News, March 9, 1995: 1,16.

— project manager Karen Seddon discusses Front Street construction, Lahaina News, March 16, 1995: 1,4.

— councilman Tom Morrow met with Lahaina Citizen Advisory Committee members, Lahaina News, March 16, 1995: 2.

— LahainaTown Action Committee skeptical of plans for strip mall near swimming pool, Lahaina News, March 16, 1995: 3.

— ruling expected soon on ceded land intended for housing project, Lahaina News, March 23, 1995: 2.

— Environmental Research Corps to study Napilihau Villages and Waihee Golf Course, Lahaina News, March 30, 1995: 1.

— Maui Planning Commission approves strip mall proposed at Dickenson Street and Honoapi'ilani Highway, Lahaina News, April 6, 1995: 4.

— Ka'anapali North Beach Joint Venture seeks clarification from Maui Planning Commission on project's required contributions, Lahaina News, April 13, 1995: 2.

— Amfac/JMB to discuss plans for North Beach with West Maui Mayor's Advisory Committee, Lahaina News, April 27, 1995: 5.

— holds informational hearing concerning North Beach proposal, Lahaina News, May 11, 1995: 1,16.

— Sheraton Maui breaks ground on redevelopment, Lahaina News, May 18, 1995: 6.

— Maui County Council's Planning Committee considering request by Corporation 3521 for development on Kahana Ridge, Lahaina News, June 8, 1995: 1,2.

— request for strip mall before Maui County Council, Lahaina News, June 8, 1995: 5.

— Environmental Protection Agency to be asked by Kahana Sunset Owners Association to protect wetland at JBL development, Lahaina News, June 15, 1995: 1,12.

— bids for Front Street Improvement Project to go out, Lahaina News, June 22, 1995: 4.

— Napili Trade Center not meeting county building codes, Lahaina News, June 29, 1995: 1.

— no position to light industrial park proposed on former sugar cane land, Lahaina News, June 29, 1995: 2.

— Mayor Linda Lingle names task force to decide renovations and future of Courthouse, Lahaina News, June 29, 1995: 4.

— Maui County Council Planning Committee to hold meetings to discuss West Maui Community Plan, Lahaina News, July 6, 1995: 5.

— residents urge slow growth, Lahaina News, July 13, 1995: 1,16.

— Pat Sullivan abandon attempt to rezone property, Lahaina News, July 20, 1995: 1,16.

— Maui Council not ready to vote on mall proposed by Amfac/JMB, Lahaina News, July 27, 1995: 1,16.

— Napilihau Joint Ventures has reservations for first phase, Lahaina News, August 3, 1995: 4.

— Housing Finance and Development Corp. Preparing Draft Environmental Assessment for Villages of Leiali'i proposal, Lahaina News, August 24, 1995: 2.

— demonstration held on ceded land, Lahaina News, August 31, 1995: 1.

— Maui Land and Pineapple Co plan for Honokohau approved by Council Planning Committee, Lahaina News, September 21, 1995: 1,16.

— Maui USA, Inc. to begin construction of Kahana Ridge water tank and pipeline, Lahaina News, October 5, 1995: 4.

— "Designing Our Community" forum to be held by Maui Tomorrow, Lahaina News, October 19, 1995: 4.

— Maui County Council changes position on shopping center proposed by Amfac/JMB Hawaii, Lahaina News, November 23, 1995: 1,12.

— Maui County Council holds public hearing on West Maui Community Plan, Lahaina News, December 7, 1995: 1,20.

— Villages of Leiali'i project cleared by Office of Environmental Quality Control, Lahaina News, December 7, 1995: 3.

— ceded land dispute goes to Hawaii Supreme Court, Lahaina News, January 18, 1996: 1,14.

— ceded land case delayed until April, Lahaina News, February 15, 1996: 1,11.

— merchants concerned about construction on Front Street, Lahaina News, March 14, 1996: 1,16.

— light industrial park sent back to Planning Committee, Lahaina News, March 28, 1996: 1,16.

— Kahana Ridge project planned, Lahaina News, March 28, 1996: 10.

— state can build homes at Villages of Leiali'i regardless of court dispute, Lahaina News, April 18, 1996: 1,18.

— industrial zoning request for Lahaina Business Park is up for final approval, Lahaina News, May 9, 1996: 8.

— Front Street Improvement Project begins, Lahaina News, May 23, 1996: 1,20.

— Planning Department creating a Lahaina Task Force, Lahaina News, June 20, 1996: 14.

— Amfac to begin work on Pu'ukoli'i Village, Lahaina News, June 20, 1996: 2.

— Department of Health investigating runoff from Sheraton Maui construction site, Lahaina News, July 11, 1996: 1.

— Amfac/JMB Hawaii may build time share at North Beach, Lahaina News, July 25, 1996: 1,16.

— parking stall and road improvement projects cleared by Office of Environmental Quality Control, Lahaina News, August 22, 1996: 1.

— controversy over rock wall along Honoapi'ilani Highway, Lahaina News, September 19, 1996: 2.

— plans for North Beach timeshare open to public comment, Lahaina News, October 3, 1996: 3.

— Amfac/JMB Hawaii holds public meeting on proposed time share at North Beach, Lahaina News, October 24, 1996: 3.

— Amfac/JMB Hawaii seeking approval for traffic mitigation plan at North Beach, Lahaina News, December 5, 1996: 1,20.

— Maui Islander Hotel seeking zoning changes, Lahaina News, December 19, 1996: 12.

— decision on North Beach traffic delayed, Lahaina News, December 19, 1996: 3.

— zero-lot-line housing planned for Honokowai by K & H Kahana, Lahaina News, February 27, 1997: 3.

— zoning issues discussed, Lahaina News, March 20, 1997: 2,20.

— conference to be held on cooling impact of trees, Lahaina News, April 10, 1997: 13.

— county to patrol Front Street for code violations, Lahaina News, May 8, 1997: 1.

— Front Street improvements probably to finish next month, Lahaina News, May 15, 1997: 1.

— Amfac Maui opens Ke Alii Subdivision, Lahaina News, June 12, 1997: 14.

— utility work to be done on Front Street, Lahaina News, June 19, 1997: 1.

— Maui County Council to discuss proposed development in North Beach, Lahaina News, July 10, 1997: 1.

— update on Front Street improvements, Lahaina News, July 17, 1997: 3.

— Front Street Improvement Project continues, Lahaina News, August 21, 1997: 6.

— Tri-Isle Resource Conservation and Development Council to pinpoint Hawaiian division of lands, Lahaina News, August 28, 1997: 1.

— Mayor Linda Lingle announces new agreement between Maui County and Amfac concerning North Beach, Lahaina News, September 25, 1997: 2,3.

— County allowing work on Napilihau Villages, Lahaina News, December 4, 1997: 1,2.

— hearing officer recommends construction permit for North Beach, Lahaina News, January 8, 1998: 1,2.

— Honokowai resort seeks conversion to time share, Lahaina News, January 15, 1998: 1,16.

— Maui Planning Commission to consider proposed Napilihau Village, Lahaina News, March 5, 1998: 1,20.

— Na Kupuna O Maui begins vigil opposing Villages of Leiali'i, Lahaina News, March 26, 1998: 12.

— Hawaiians hold vigil to raise concerns for land issues, Lahaina News, April 2, 1998: 1,9.

— plans for future phases of Napilihau withdrawn, Lahaina News, April 16, 1998: 1,16.

— Maui USA's Kahana Ridge featured, Lahaina News, June 25, 1998: 10.

— Department of Land and Natural Resources to discuss South Maui beach issues, Lahaina News, July 16, 1998: 15.

— new time share badge law passed, Lahaina News, August 6, 1998: 1.

— Amfac says 733-acre lot in Olowalu under contract to be sold, Lahaina News, August 13, 1998: 1.

— walkers asked to use Akahele St. to access Kapalua Airport, Lahaina News, August 27, 1998: 1.

— Kahana Sunset featured, Lahaina News, September 24, 1998: 12.

— North Beach resort pact planned, Lahaina News, October 8, 1998: 1,20.

— Maui Lani Homes designing homes, Lahaina News, October 8, 1998: 13.

— condominium planned near coconut grove at Kapalua Bay, Lahaina News, November 12, 1998: 1,20.

— partnership to protect acreage in West Maui mountains, Lahaina News, November 26, 1998: 5.

— light industrial park planned for Lahaina, Lahaina News, December 31, 1998: 11.

— Maui Land and Pineapple suit explained, Lahaina News, February 18, 1999: 1,5.

— Maui Land and Pineapple questions ability of Judge Bertram to hear application for development at Mahinahina, Lahaina News, February 25, 1999: 1,16.

— Department of Land and Natural Resources to hold meeting to discuss management strategies, Lahaina News, February 25, 1999: 12.

— Kahana Ridge house building surging, Lahaina News, April 1, 1999: 12.

— Mahinahina Beach Condominium featured, Lahaina News, April 8, 1999: 10.

— Napili Village Center proposed, conceptual drawing printed, Lahaina News, June 24, 1999: 1,11.

— option for Maui County to purchase land from Amfac/JMB at Keka'a expired, Lahaina News, July 1, 1999: 1.

— Wainee Office Building proposed, Lahaina News, July 1, 1999: 11.

— LahainaTown Action Committee, Hui O Wa'a Kaulua, and Friends of Moku'ula working on Lahaina Interpretive Plan, Lahaina News, August 5, 1999: 1,16.

— shopping center proposed near Malu'ulu O Lele Park, Lahaina News, September 23, 1999: 1,3.

— Cultural Resources Commission to hold meeting on proposed Front Street shopping complex, Lahaina News, October 14, 1999: 1,11.

— construction begins on Ma'alaea Harbor Village, Lahaina News, October 14, 1999: 11.

— shared ownership available at Sands of Kahana, Lahaina News, October 21, 1999: 12.

— Kapalua Land Co, Ltd. breaks ground at The Coconut Grove on Kapalua Bay, Lahaina News, November 11, 1999: 3.

— construction at The Coconut Grove monitored by Kapalua project, Lahaina News, November 18, 1999: 1,2.

— new homes available at Kahana Ridge, Lahaina News, January 6, 2000: 10.

— Whalers Realty, Inc. and Kirkland Development Company held ground breaking for Kahua Kai subdivision, Lahaina News, January 20, 2000: 11.

— sales at The Whaler strong, Lahaina News, February 17, 2000: 12.

— lots available at Lahaina Business Park, Lahaina News, May 25, 2000: 11.

— Terra Pacific Development, Co. LLC named as project developer for The Vintage at Ka'anapali, Lahaina News, June 8, 2000: 11.

— history of issues related to described, Lahaina News, July 6, 2000: 5.

— construction begins at Lahaina Business Park, Lahaina News, July 20, 2000: 13.

— construction of Lahaina Business Park continues, Lahaina News, September 14, 2000: 15.

— coastal land trust forming, Lahaina News, September 28, 2000: 7.

— Kahua Kai in Ka'anapali Golf Estates includes innovative drainage system, Lahaina News, December 7, 2000: 20.

— groundbreaking held for Na Hale O Makena development, Lahaina News, December 7, 2000: 21.

— The Summit at Ka'anapali breaks ground, Lahaina News, December 14, 2000: 10.

— Napili Villas townhouses to be built, Lahaina News, December 14, 2000: 11.

— JDI Limited Partners seeking to replace existing Harbor Village with new structure, Lahaina News, January 11, 2001: 1,15.

— "Ka'anapali 2020: Making it Pono" share conceptual vision for Amfac/JMB Hawaii Inc., Lahaina News, January 18, 2001: 1,7.

— commentary on Maui County Council approval of power plant in Waena, Lahaina News, February 8, 2001: 17.

— Mayor James Apana shares vision for West Maui, Lahaina News, March 22, 2001: 1,18.

— JoAnne Johnson to introduce building moratorium bill, Lahaina News, April 5, 2001: 2.

— officials discussing building moratorium, Lahaina News, April 5, 2001: 8.

— model homes, Lahaina News, April 19, 2001: 6.

— JDI Limited Partners proposing Harbor Village shopping complex, Lahaina News, June 7, 2001: 1,9.

— State Historical Preservation Conference offers suggestions offered for making historic districts work better, Lahaina News, June 14, 2001: 1,22.

— County to enforce historic district rules, Lahaina News, August 16, 2001: 1,9.

— new condo construction in Naplii, Lahaina News, August 23, 2001: 7.

— "Smart Growth for Our Communities—Envisioning Maui County in 2020" to be held, Lahaina News, August 23, 2001: 9.

— meeting to explain new Historic District Sign Design Guidelines to be held, Lahaina News, September 13, 2001: 9.

— mayor James "Kimo" Apana to hold meeting at Lahaina Civic Center on Historic District Sign Design Guidelines, Lahaina News, September 20, 2001: 9.

— Maui Pacific Center to host "Smart Growth for Our Communities—Envisioning Maui County in 2020", Lahaina News, September 27, 2001: 9.

— LoKo Maui to renovate 744 Front Street, Lahaina News, March 28, 2002: 3.

— residents share ideas for future of Lahaina, Lahaina News, April 11, 2002: 1,20.

— Oceanfront Marketplace featured, Lahaina News, May 23, 2002: 7.

— affordable condominiums proposed at Kahana, Lahaina News, June 20, 2002: 6.

— Maui Land and Pineapple moving forward with plans for Kapalua Mauka, Lahaina News, July 4, 2002: 1,20.

— Maui Land and Pineapple breaks ground on Kapua Village subdivision , Lahaina News, August 1, 2002: 8.

— Department of Land and Natural Resources to hold hearings on Maui Land and Pineapple application for land use within Conservation District, Lahaina News, August 1, 2002: 8.

— Hawaiians to raise concerns for bill to force sale of Queen's personal land holdings, Lahaina News, August 29, 2002: 3.

— changes to subdivision by Olowalu Elua Associations triggers hearing, Lahaina News, October 3, 2002: 1,20.

— state seeking input for Sustainable Tourism Study, Lahaina News, October 3, 2002: 8.

— Planning Department permits oceanfront building without public review, Lahaina News, October 17, 2002: 1,17.

— county seeks to acquire property in response to protests, Lahaina News, October 31, 2002: 1,2.

— Department of Planning to prepare master plan for relocating Honoapi'ilani Highway, Lahaina News, October 31, 2002: 1,30.

— Kuleana Ku'ikahi files lawsuit over approval of Kaua'ula project, Lahaina News, November 7, 2002: 1,24.

— Betsill Brothers Construction's new Kihei community featured, Lahaina News, December 5, 2002: 6.

— commentary critical of new shoreline rules, Lahaina News, January 23, 2003: 5.

— Maui County prohibits construction on shoreline lot in Mala, Lahaina News, January 30, 2003: 1,18.

— Sam Ka'ai blesses the Pinnacle Ka'anapali's Kai nehe, Lahaina News, May 29, 2003: 6.

— above Launiupoko Beach Park featured, Lahaina News, May 29, 2003: 7.

— Landtec, Inc. unveils plan for Napili project, Lahaina News, June 19, 2003: 1,18.

— public hearing to be held on Kapalua Mauka, Lahaina News, July 17, 2003: 1,2.

— Maui Planning Department to consider request from Doug White to build residence over storm drainage culvert, Lahaina News, September 18, 2003: 1,20.

— West Maui Taxpayers Association to hold informational forum on shoreline setbacks, Lahaina News, October 9, 2003: 1,3.

— see also Lahaina Community Plan, Makena Community Association, specific plans, projects, and developers

DEVELOPMENT OF HUMAN CONCERNS, MAUI COUNTY

— requesting proposals for 107-acre site in Kihei, Lahaina News, January 9, 1991: 5.

— see Housing and Human Concerns, Maui County Department of

DEVIL IS A WOMAN, THE [PLAY]

— performed at Iao Theatre, Lahaina News, March 14, 1990: 15.

DEVITO, LAURIE [DANCER]

— to present "Jazz Dance Master Class", Lahaina News, February 2, 1995: 12.

DEVO, DEARCA [ARTIST]

— to exhibit at Banyan Tree Gallery, Lahaina News, June 30, 1994: 13.

DEYBRA [ARTIST]

— to exhibit at Jovian Gallery, Lahaina News, June 30, 1994: 12.

DEYOUNG, BRUCE

— appointed general manager for Royal Hawaiian Cruises Maui vessels, Lahaina News, September 4, 1997: 12.

DIABETES

— free tests offered in Lahaina, Wailuku and Hana, Lahaina Sun, December 2, 1970: 1.

DIAGSOFT [BUSINESS]

— opens, Lahaina News, May 13, 1993: 7.

DIAMOND APPROACH, THE

— to hold "Journeying in the Compassionate Heart of Inquiry", Lahaina News, May 21, 1998: 17.

DIAMOND, BARRY [COMEDIAN]

— to perform at Comedy Club and the Sports Page, Lahaina News, May 7, 1992: 21,24.

DIAMOND LIL REVUE

— to benefit scholarship fund, Lahaina News, May 15, 1985: 8.

— Third annual presented by Baldwin Theatre Guild, Lahaina News, May 7, 1986: 3.

— to be performed by Baldwin Theatre Guild, Lahaina News, May 6, 1987: 3.

— presented by Baldwin Theatre Guild, Lahaina News, January 20, 1988: 3.

— to be performed by Baldwin Theatre Guild, Lahaina News, December 6, 1989: 12.

— to be performed by Baldwin High School Theatre Guild, Lahaina News, December 1, 1994: 16.

DIAMOND, MOANA [MUSICIAN]

— to teach singing, Lahaina News, December 31, 1998: 13.

DIAMOND RESORTS OF JAPAN [BUSINESS]

— planning to open resort in Wailea, Lahaina News, February 14, 1990: 5.

— private members club resort opens in Wailea, Lahaina News, September 5, 1990: 5.

DIANA [HURRICANE]
— threatens the islands, Lahaina Sun, August 23, 1972: 1.

DIANA AND LAURENCE CHERNIAK ART GALLERY [BUSINESS]
— to open in Lahaina Market Place, Lahaina News, May 22, 1985: 20.

DIAVOLO [PERFORMER]
— to perform at Maui Arts and Cultural Center, Lahaina News, September 19, 2002: 24.

DIAZ, JOHN DAVE
— Navy Airman Apprentice serving on aircraft carrier, Lahaina News, November 15, 2001: 2.

DICHTER, MISCHA [PIANIST]
— to play at Baldwin Auditorium with the Honolulu Symphony Orchestra, Lahaina Sun, October 20, 1971: 13.

DICHTER, MISHA AND CIPA [MUSICIANS]
— to offer piano concert, Lahaina News, February 17, 2000: 17.
— to perform, Lahaina News, February 24, 2000: 16.

DICK NELSON [ARTIST]
— to give classes, Lahaina News, October 1, 1980: 3.

DICK TRACY [FILM]
— to premiere at Lahaina Cinemas, Lahaina News, June 13, 1990: 18.

DICKENSON SQUARE
— announces new tenants, Lahaina News, September 17, 1986: 11.
— tenants added, Lahaina News, October 29, 1986: 3.
— adds shops, Lahaina News, April 22, 1987: 3.
— more tenants confirmed, Lahaina News, July 8, 1987: 24.
— signs additional tenants, Lahaina News, November 18, 1987: 3.
— concert to be held at, Lahaina News, June 21, 1989: 1.

DICK'S PLACE
— to hold billiards contest, Lahaina News, November 8, 2001: 13.

DIEGO, LAWRENCE
— details of his election campaign for 7th district of the State House, Lahaina Sun, September 27, 1972: 5.

DIEGUEZ, SHARLEE [WRITER]
— singing copies of "The Bearded Lady" at Borders Books, Lahaina News, June 17, 1999: 16.
— to sign copies of "The Bearded Lady", Lahaina News, June 24, 1999: 12.

DIEP, LINDA
— new owner of B&C Deli Kitchen, Lahaina News, July 24, 2003: 8.

DIESEL [MUSICIAN]
— to perform at Border's Books, Lahaina News, August 1, 2002: 20.
— to perform at Lahaina Cannery Mall, Lahaina News, September 19, 2002: 23.

DIGANT [ARTIST]
— featured at Larry Dodson Gallery, Lahaina News, August 3, 1988: 3.

DIGITAL CROSSROADS HAWAII
— conference to be held, Lahaina News, October 31, 2002: 6.
— conference to be held, Lahaina News, November 7, 2002: 9.

DIGITAL MUSIC EXPRESS (DMX)
— option available from Chronicle Cablevision, Lahaina News, May 27, 1993: 7.

DIGNAN, CHASE
— wins television from Super Bowl weekend drawing at Lahaina Center, Lahaina News, February 13, 1992: 21.

DIK BENSON'S SALON [BUSINESS]
— to raise funds for Women Helping Women Shelter, Lahaina News, July 28, 1994: 8.

DIKON, ROGER
— to demonstrate holiday dishes, Lahaina News, November 29, 1989: 21.
— executive chef of the Maui Prince Hotel to reintroduce "Chef's Table", Lahaina News, January 23, 1992: 18,20.
— details on "Chef's Table", Lahaina News, January 30, 1992: 18.

DILLERY, PAUL [COMEDIAN]
— to perform at Comedy Club and the Sports Page, Lahaina News, March 20, 1991: 10.
— to perform at Comedy Club and the Sports Page, Lahaina News, August 20, 1992: 18,20.
— to perform at Maui Comedy Club, Lahaina News, July 6, 1995: 11.

DILLINGHAM CORPORATION
— sold to a group of investors, Lahaina News, April 1, 1983: 11.

DILLON, ASHLEY
— completes Marine Corps basic training, Lahaina News, November 7, 2002: 17.

DINAMATION DINOSAUR EXHIBIT
— opens at Ka'ahumanu Center, Lahaina News, September 5, 1996: 16.

DINER, JERRY [COMEDIAN]
— to perform at Comedy Club and the Sports Page, Lahaina News, November 5, 1992: 14,15,17.

DINING IN [BUSINESS]
— chef Alyce Ostler cooks restaurant-quality meals for customers, Lahaina News, October 19, 2000: 16.
— featured, Lahaina News, February 22, 2001: 9.

DINOSAURS
— replicas to be displayed at Kahului Armory, Lahaina News, August 24, 1988: 9.
— Biology professor to discuss age of, Lahaina News, October 26, 1988: 3,16.

DIOSO, RICARDO [MUSICIAN]
— to perform at Longhi's with John Lewis, Lahaina News, November 25, 1999: 6.

DIPAOLA, JAKE
— wins Shapers Pohai Na Keiki Nalu titles, Lahaina News, June 25, 1998: 7.

DIPIAZZA, GREG [MUSICIAN]
— to perform at Casanova's, Lahaina News, December 19, 1990: 13.
— to perform at Polli's, Lahaina News, June 20, 1991: 11.
— continues to perform at Polli's Mexican Restaurant, Lahaina News, July 4, 1991: 14.
— to perform at Polli's Mexican Restaurant, Lahaina News, November 7, 1991: 20.
— to perform at Honolulu Coffee Co., Lahaina News, August 22, 2002: 20.

DIRGA, MARK
— owner of Blue Tropix featured, Lahaina News, January 30, 1992: 10.

DIRKS, LISA
— hired as events coordinator for LahainaTown Action Committee, Lahaina News, June 10, 1999: 15.

DISABILITIES
— child care for handicapped children now available at Kahului Church, Lahaina Sun, April 18, 1973: 5.
— Orchidland accessible to people with, Lahaina News, October 7, 1987: 16.
— businesses hiring, Lahaina News, January 24, 1990: 7.
— ARC of Maui seeks people with disabilities for lawsuit, Lahaina News, July 5, 2001: 5.

DISADVANTAGED BUSINESS ENTERPRISES
— Maui County Office of Economic Development seeks companies that qualify as, Lahaina News, June 5, 2003: 8.

DISASTER
— Lahaina unprepared, Lahaina News, November 1, 1989: 1,3.
— training begins for hurricane season, Lahaina News, June 17, 1993: 1.
— Maui County plan almost completed by Civil Defense Agency, Lahaina News, February 3, 1994: 4.

— management plan discussed, Lahaina News, July 16, 1998: 1.

— King Kamehameha III Elementary School to hold tsunami drill, Lahaina News, May 9, 2002: 16.

DISASTER PREPAREDNESS

— plan to be available, Lahaina News, June 9, 1994: 2.

— guides ready, Lahaina News, June 30, 1994: 4.

DISCO

— present in Oahu, Lahaina Times, July, 1980 volume 4 number 6: 3.

DISCO DAVE [ENTERTAINER]

— to perform on the ship Stardancer, Lahaina News, March 13, 1991: 11.

DISCO NIGHT

— at Casanova's, Lahaina News, January 9, 1991: 7.

DISCOVERY AIRWAYS

— hires Starr Seigle McCombs as advertising agent, Lahaina News, September 13, 1989: 6.

— to begin interisland operations in May, Lahaina News, November 1, 1989: 8.

DISCOVERY CHANNEL

— Hawaiian Teleproductions, Inc. completes production for, Lahaina News, February 27, 1991: 8.

DISHER, MARK

— Lahaina Intermediate School student honored for returning lost wallet, Lahaina News, February 14, 1990: 3.

— serving in submarine force, Lahaina News, July 29, 1999: 3.

DISNEY [BUSINESS]

— to promote The Magic Kingdom and Fantasmic tour, Lahaina News, May 21, 1992: 15,16.

— to parade through Lahaina, Lahaina News, May 28, 1992: 14.

DISNEY, ROY

— wins Victoria-Maui yacht race, to donate money to local charities, Lahaina News, August 8, 1996: 1,20.

— yacht is first monohull to break eight days in the Transpacific Yacht Race, Lahaina News, July 17, 1997: 15.

DISTRIBUTED ENERGY RESOURCES (DER)

— state to hold forum on, Lahaina News, July 4, 2002: 8.

DISTRIBUTIVE EDUCATION CLUBS OF AMERICA

— hold Employer's Appreciation Luncheon, Lahaina News, May 21, 1992: 5.

DITTMAN, TINA

— contestant in Mrs. Hawaii USA pageant, Lahaina News, June 4, 1992: 4.

DIVE MAUI [BUSINESS]

— moves location, Lahaina News, December 26, 1991: 8.

DIVING

— history of Bluegill [submarine], now sunk off Lahaina, detailed, Lahaina Sun, May 2, 1973: 7.

— danger of the bends detailed, Lahaina Sun, August 22, 1973: 4.

— night access at North Beach an issue for divers, Lahaina News, April 18, 1996: 7.

DIXON, ARNE

— yo-yo expert demonstrates skills at Princess Nahienaena School, Lahaina News, February 28, 1990: 3.

DIXON, BOYD

— state archaeologist to give lecture on Kahikinui Mauka, Lahaina News, April 3, 1997: 12.

— archaeologist to speak at Bailey House Museum, Lahaina News, April 2, 1998: 16.

DIXON BROADCASTING [BUSINESS]

— requests permit to build transmitter at Waiakoa Road, Lahaina News, July 16, 1992: 5.

DIXON, GEORGE

— and first Christmas celebration in Hawaii described, Lahaina Sun, December 22, 1971: 14.

DIXON, IVAN

— to present jazz concert with Maui Philharmonic Society, Lahaina News, May 29, 1997: 16.

DIXON, JIM

— acupuncturist to speak on "Inner Traditions of Traditional Oriental Medicine", Lahaina News, November 15, 2001: 18.

DIZON FAMILY

— featured, Lahaina News, May 17, 1989: 4,5.

DO IT [MUSICAL GROUP]

— to perform at Moose McGillycuddy's, Lahaina News, March 28, 1990: 15.

— to perform at Moose McGillycuddy's, Lahaina News, April 4, 1990: 13.

DOANE, ALAN

— Chief Executive Officer of Alexander and Baldwin to speak to Maui Chamber of Commerce, Lahaina News, November 26, 1998: 17.

DOANE, W. ALLEN

— appointed president of Alexander and Baldwin, Inc, Lahaina News, May 11, 1995: 10.

DOCKTOR, MILTON

— teaching non-credit class at Maui Community College on the financial health of your business, Lahaina News, July 3, 1985: 3.

DOCTORS

— blamed for spread of venereal disease by not willing to treat hippies, Lahaina Sun, February 23, 1972: 3.

DODGERS, LOS ANGELES

— shortshop fined for assault charges at Moose McGillycuddy's, Lahaina News, January 6, 2000: 1.

DODS, WALTER, JR.

— elected chairman and chief executive officer of First Hawaiian Bank, Lahaina News, September 27, 1989: 5.

— named Hawaii chairman of Japan-Hawaii Economic Council, Lahaina News, November 1, 1989: 8.

— announces reorganization of First Hawaiian Bank, Lahaina News, November 1, 1989: 9.

— on executive panel for Senior Management Conference, Lahaina News, September 12, 1990: 12.

DODSON, LEE

— appointed county budget director, Lahaina News, December 5, 1990: 3.

DODSON, PAMELA

— joins Maui Arts and Cultural Center, Lahaina News, March 25, 1999: 13.

DOFA, KERILYN

— Scholar/Athlete of the Week, Lahaina News, July 19, 2001: 13.

DOG DAY AFTERNOON

— to be held at the Maui Animal Shelter and Adoption Center, Lahaina News, April 23, 1992: 8.

DOG WASH

— fundraiser to benefit Maui Friends of the Animals Pet Adoption Home Building Fund, Lahaina News, October 12, 1988: 3.

DOGS

— hearing to discuss leash law announced, Lahaina Sun, October 20, 1971: 14.

— issue of stray dogs discussed, Lahaina Sun, October 20, 1971: 2.

— editorial on proposed dog leash law, Lahaina Sun, November 10, 1971: 2.

— responses to proposed leash law, Lahaina Sun, November 10, 1971: 3.

— proposed leash laws discussed, Lahaina Sun, November 17, 1971: 5.

— featured in children's supplement, Lahaina News, February 8, 1984: A,B,C,D.

DOGWOOD [MUSICAL GROUP]

— punk band to perform at Lahaina Civic Center Amphitheatre, Lahaina News, July 4, 2002: 14.

— to perform with other punk bands at Lahaina Cannery Mall, Lahaina News, July 11, 2002: 16.

DOI, HERMAN [OMBUDSMAN]

— interviewed, Lahaina Sun, December 23, 1970: 2.

DOLAN, JACK

— joins Blue Hawaii Realty, Lahaina News, April 9, 1992: 12.

DOLAN, LAURIE

— dies of drug overdose, Lahaina News, April 1, 1993: 3.

DOLEZAL, ELIZABETH

— competes in Starbucks Solo Kayak and Canoe World Championship, Lahaina News, June 10, 1999: 2.

D'OLIER, MITCH

— Hawaiian Airlines president resigns, Lahaina News, May 27, 1993: 8.

DOLIN, LOREN

— chairman of State Public Utilities Commission discusses proposed barge rate increase, Lahaina Sun, August 4, 1971: 1.

DOLLAR RENT-A-CAR

— opens first office in Lahaina, Lahaina News, June 14, 1989: 7.

DOLLIES PUB AND CAFE [RESTAURANT]

— featured, Lahaina News, January 23, 1985: 10.

— reviewed, Lahaina News, January 20, 1988: 6.

— showing NBA playoffs, Lahaina News, May 2, 1996: 15.

— opens, serves breakfast and offers live sports, Lahaina News, September 25, 2003: 8.

DOLPHIN ENCOUNTER NETWORK

— to host lecture, Lahaina News, October 14, 1987: 17.

DOLPHIN GALLERIES

— donates sculpture for EarthTrust program, Lahaina News, May 30, 1990: 6.

— to hold reception for Thomas Pradzynski, Lahaina News, August 8, 2002: 16.

DOLPHIN SHOPPING CENTER

— groundbreaking ceremony for, Lahaina News, January 21, 1987: 3.

DOLTON, GREGORY

— joins Case & Lynch, Lahaina News, November 14, 1990: 11.

DOMESTIC VIOLENCE

— to be examined, Lahaina News, October 23, 1997: 20.

— candlelight vigil to be held, Lahaina News, October 8, 1998: 17.

— awareness events to be held, Lahaina News, October 3, 2002: 3.

DOMESTIC VIOLENCE AWARENESS MONTH

— "You Can't Beat a Kid" play to be performed at Iao Theater, Lahaina News, October 1, 1998: 16.

— candlelight vigil to be held, Lahaina News, October 1, 1998: 17.

DOMINGO, KAREN [ARTIST]

— to exhibit at "Fish Textile Art" at the Art School at Kapalua, Lahaina News, January 31, 2002: 16.

— to exhibit at Art School at Kapalua, Lahaina News, September 19, 2002: 22.

DOMINGO, MARILYN AND ISAIAS

— Scholar/Athlete of the Week, Lahaina News, March 16, 2000: 6.

DOMINICK [MUSICIAN]

— to perform at Polli's Mexican Restaurant, Lahaina News, November 28, 1990: 10.

— to perform at Polli's Mexican Restaurant, Lahaina News, July 25, 1991: 13.

DOMINICK AND MARIO [MUSICAL GROUP]

— continues to perform at Aloha Cantina, Lahaina News, September 1, 1994: 15.

DOMINO'S PIZZA [RESTAURANT]

— expanding, Lahaina News, May 24, 1989: 8.

— Kory Spiroff becomes new owner, Lahaina News, December 19, 1991: 13.

— donates to The Cousteau Society, Lahaina News, February 13, 1992: 13.

— new store to open, Lahaina News, March 26, 1992: 10.

DON, MEGAN

— to present "Dancing with the Divine Inner Lover", Lahaina News, March 20, 2003: 17.

DON QUIXOTE [BALLET]

— to be performed by Maui Academy of Performing Arts, Lahaina News, May 25, 2000: 18.

DONAGHY, JOE

— becomes president of Maui Contractors Association, Lahaina News, January 9, 1991: 5.

— president of Maui Contractors Association discusses housing situation, Lahaina News, February 27, 1991: supplement15.

DONAHUE, BETH [COMEDIAN]

— to perform at Comedy Club and the Sports Page, Lahaina News, May 15, 1991: 11.

— to perform at Maui Comedy Club, Lahaina News, June 29, 1995: 12.

— to perform at Honolulu Comedy Club, Lahaina News, January 11, 1996: 14.

DONHAM, THERESA

— state archaeologist to speak on Wailuku Sand Dune, Lahaina News, February 13, 1997: 11.

DONOHUE, MAXINE

— celebration of life to be held for, Lahaina News, September 11, 2003: 2.

DONOVAN, CAROL

— to discuss "Six Stages of Disease", Lahaina News, August 8, 1996: 14.

DOOBIE BROTHERS, THE [MUSICAL GROUP]

— to perform, Lahaina News, February 24, 1994: 11.

— to perform, Lahaina News, February 1, 1996: 10.

— to perform, Lahaina News, August 7, 1997: 12.

— to perform at Maui Arts and Cultural Center, Lahaina News, March 23, 2000: 13.

— to perform at Maui Arts and Cultural Center, Lahaina News, March 30, 2000: 13.

— to perform, Lahaina News, April 6, 2000: 16.

DORAN, MAGGIE MORGAN [WRITER]

— wins Maui Authors Guild Writing Contest, Lahaina News, June 22, 1988: 10.

DORCY, LAURENCE

— discusses Hawaiian Chieftain [ship] coming to Lahaina, Lahaina News, April 6, 1988: 1,20.

DORENZO, DIANA [ARTIST]

— to exhibit, Lahaina News, September 24, 1992: 18.

— to exhibit at Lahaina Galleries, Lahaina News, August 18, 1994: 15.

— to exhibit at Viewpoints Gallery, Lahaina News, June 8, 2000: 20.

DORSETT, TONY

— football player meets fans at Whalers Village, Lahaina News, January 27, 2000: 6.

DOSLAND, TOM

— surfer competes in National Scholastic Surfing Association's Summer Spray-Offs, Lahaina News, July 6, 2000: 1,14.

DOTMAUI [RESTAURANT]

— internet cafe opens, Lahaina News, April 26, 2001: 9.

DOTSON, LARRY [ARTIST]
— work discussed, Lahaina News, May 23, 1984: 7.
— signing at Maria Lanakila Church, Lahaina News, April 8, 1987: 12.
— opens gallery, Lahaina News, May 13, 1987: 3.

DOTSON, PATTI
— announce winner of Lahaina Town Action Committee poster contest, Lahaina News, November 15, 1989: 1,19.

DOTTERER, ERIC [MUSICIAN]
— to perform at Smokehouse BBQ, Lahaina News, April 11, 1996: 12.

DOTY, KEITH
— dentist recounts trip to Nepal, Lahaina News, June 14, 1989: 9.

DOUBLE TAKE [MUSICAL GROUP]
— to perform at Casanova, Lahaina News, April 25, 1990: 15.
— to perform at Longhi's, Lahaina News, May 16, 1990: 12.
— to perform at Longhi's, Lahaina News, July 11, 1990: 15.

DOUG TIHADA MEMORIAL REGATTA
— to be held at Hanaka'o'o Beach Park, Lahaina News, July 5, 1989: 6.
— photographs from, Lahaina News, July 19, 1989: 7.
— to be held, Lahaina News, July 4, 1990: 6.

DOUG WHITE GROUP, THE [MUSICAL GROUP]
— to perform at Longhi's Restaurant, Lahaina News, September 19, 1996: 18.

DOUG WHITE TRIO [MUSICAL GROUP]
— to perform at Pacific'O, Lahaina News, July 7, 1994: 14.
— to perform at Pacific'O, Lahaina News, October 20, 1994: 16.

DOUG WHITE-SAL GODINEZ JAZZ DUO [MUSICAL GROUP]
— to perform at Raffle's Restaurant, Lahaina News, February 20, 1992: 17.
— continues to perform at Raffle's Restaurant at Stouffer Wailea, Lahaina News, May 14, 1992: 18.
— to perform at Raffle's Restaurant, Stouffer Wailea, Lahaina News, December 24, 1992: 17.

DOUGHERTY, SCOTT
— appointed manager of Paki Maui, Lahaina News, September 28, 2000: 13.

DOUGLAS, ROBERT
— chair of Maui County Commission on Persons with Disabilities to speak to Republican Party, Lahaina News, January 6, 2000: 13.

DOWN TO EARTH NATURAL FOODS [BUSINESS]
— to hold cooking class, Lahaina News, February 5, 1998: 12.
— to hold "Healthy Heart Fitness Fair", Lahaina News, February 5, 1998: 13.
— offering vegetarian cooking class, Lahaina News, March 5, 1998: 16.
— to celebrate "Great American Meat Out", Lahaina News, March 12, 1998: 20.
— continues to offer cooking classes, Lahaina News, April 2, 1998: 16.
— to host "Women's Wellness Day", Lahaina News, May 14, 1998: 16.
— to hold "Cooking with Keikis", Lahaina News, July 9, 1998: 16.
— to host "National Relaxation Day", Lahaina News, August 13, 1998: 16.
— continues to offer cooking courses, Lahaina News, September 3, 1998: 20.
— to offer free Indian Cooking class, Lahaina News, September 24, 1998: 17.
— offering "Vegetarian breakfast ideas", Lahaina News, October 22, 1998: 21.
— to hold workshop on mehndi henna tattoos, Lahaina News, November 12, 1998: 16.
— to hold vegetarian cooking class, Lahaina News, December 3, 1998: 21.
— to celebrate birthday, Lahaina News, December 31, 1998: 13.
— to offer Thai cooking class, Lahaina News, January 21, 1999: 12.

— to hold vegetarian Italian cooking class, Lahaina News, April 1, 1999: 17.
— to offer classes on Chinese Cooking, Lahaina News, April 8, 1999: 12.
— to offer class on wheat-free cooking, Lahaina News, April 15, 1999: 13.
— to hold class on Thai cooking, Lahaina News, May 6, 1999: 20.
— offering Y2K cooking class on meals to be made during a disaster, Lahaina News, June 3, 1999: 17.
— to hold free meditation sessions, Lahaina News, July 15, 1999: 13.
— to hold vegetarian Indian cooking class, Lahaina News, August 26, 1999: 16.
— to host "Cooking with Stevia", Lahaina News, September 9, 1999: 13.
— to host "Excellent Entrees" cooking class, Lahaina News, September 23, 1999: 12.
— to offer "Japanese Cuisine Made Easy", Lahaina News, October 7, 1999: 17.
— to offer "Harvest Pumpkin Fun" cooking class, Lahaina News, October 21, 1999: 17.
— to offer class on Chinese cooking, Lahaina News, February 3, 2000: 13.
— to offer class on "Tasty Meatless Entrees", Lahaina News, March 23, 2000: 12.
— to offer "Bach Flower Essence Training" class, Lahaina News, March 30, 2000: 13.
— Diane Means to present on "Feng Shui Basics", Lahaina News, April 6, 2000: 16.
— to hold "Wellness Wednesday", Lahaina News, April 19, 2001: 17.
— to host Wellness Wednesday, Lahaina News, April 26, 2001: 21.
— to hold "Wellness Wednesday", Lahaina News, May 17, 2001: 21.
— offers "Wellness Wednesday", Lahaina News, August 2, 2001: 17.
— to hold "Tasting of the Greens", Lahaina News, March 13, 2003: 17.
— offering health product samples, Lahaina News, April 3, 2003: 16,17.
— to offer herb workshop, Lahaina News, May 29, 2003: 17.

DOWNER, PHIL
— to be featured speaker at West Maui Christian Men's Camp, Lahaina News, September 19, 2002: 19.

DOWNER, PHIL AND SUSY
— to offer Marriage and Family Enrichment Weekends, Lahaina News, February 28, 2002: 5.

DOWNEY, HELEN
— to give Sunday morning "Aloha Spirit Ministry Services", Lahaina News, July 16, 1998: 16.
— to give Sunday morning "Aloha Spirit Ministry Services", Lahaina News, July 23, 1998: 16.

DOWNS, CLYDE
— appointed account executive for Destination Maui, Inc., Lahaina News, December 31, 1992: 10.

DOWSETT, TERRY
— installed as president of Aloha Festivals, Lahaina News, February 16, 1995: 13.

DR. JOHN THE NIGHT TRIPPER [MUSICIAN]
— to perform at Maui Arts and Cultural Center, Lahaina News, November 28, 1996: 12.
— to perform, Lahaina News, December 5, 1996: 14.

DR. ROCK AND THE KATS [MUSICAL GROUP]
— to perform during Arthritis Telethon, Lahaina News, April 2, 1992: 17.

DRACULA [PLAY]
— Maui Community Theatre to perform, Lahaina News, August 16, 1989: 3.

DRACULA DASH
— footrace set for October 28, Lahaina News, October 17, 1984: 3.
— footrace set for October 27, Lahaina News, October 16, 1985: 20.

DRACULA: THE MUSICAL? [PLAY]
— to be performed by Maui Community Theatre, Lahaina News, September 27, 1989: 3.
— to open, Lahaina News, October 11, 1989: 10.

DRAG RACING
— races to be held, Lahaina News, August 18, 1994: 7.
— Valley Isle Timing Association to hold, Lahaina News, April 12, 2001: 14.

DRAGON FLY HAWAII [BUSINESS]
— opens at Lahaina Center, Lahaina News, October 3, 1990: 9.

DRAKE, JIM
— swimming-pool maker featured, Lahaina News, November 23, 1988: 2.

DRAMA
— Theatre Theatre Maui to hold registration for summer program, Lahaina News, May 31, 2001: 14.

DRAVECKY, DAVE
— baseball player to speak to Lahaina Rotary Club, Lahaina News, June 11, 1992: 6.

DREAD, MARTY [MUSICIAN]
— to perform on the ship Stardancer, Lahaina News, March 6, 1991: 14.
— featured, Lahaina News, June 2, 1994: 11.
— releases new music, Lahaina News, July 14, 1994: 14.
— to perform at Blue Tropix, Lahaina News, October 27, 1994: 18.
— to perform at Mexico Caliente, Lahaina News, February 22, 1996: 14.
— to perform at Blue Tropix, Lahaina News, March 14, 1996: 12.
— to play at Magical Maui International Music and Craft Festival, Lahaina News, April 4, 1996: 15.
— birthday bash to be, Lahaina News, June 6, 1996: 12.
— featured, Lahaina News, August 1, 1996: 22.
— to perform at World Cafe, Lahaina News, June 26, 1997: 18.
— to perform at Makai Bar, Lahaina News, December 25, 1997: 13.
— to perform at benefit concert at Maui Brews, Lahaina News, August 5, 1999: 14.
— to perform at Maui Brews, Lahaina News, September 20, 2001: 15.
— see also Marty Dread ....

DREADED SEWER RATS [MUSICAL GROUP]
— featured, Lahaina News, September 30, 1993: 11.

DREADLOCK ROCK [MUSICAL GROUP]
— to perform at Maui Lu Resort, Lahaina News, December 11, 1985: 8.

DREAM OF KITAMURA, THE [PLAY]
— to be performed at Maui Community College, Lahaina News, May 27, 1987: 16.

DREPUNG LOSELING MONASTERY
— lamas from to perform, Lahaina News, July 20, 1995: 12.

DRESSER, THE [PLAY]
— to be performed at Maui Academy of Performing Arts, Lahaina News, May 16, 1996: 7.

DREW, ROBERT
— member of Lahaina Kamaakina Fishing Association, Lahaina Sun, December 23, 1970: 11.

DREWRY, LEIGH
— appointed sales manager for Ritz-Charlton, Lahaina News, September 24, 1992: 9.

DRIESBACH DATA [BUSINESS]
— expands at Kahului Industrial Area, Lahaina News, July 25, 2002: 8.

DRIESBACH, FRANCES
— to discuss "Reliable High-Tech Solutions for Small Businesses", Lahaina News, June 22, 2000: 8.

DRIFTERS, THE [MUSICAL GROUP]
— to perform to benefit Hawaii Firefighters Association, Lahaina News, November 13, 1997: 21.
— to perform at Golden Oldies Revue, Lahaina News, October 19, 2000: 21.

DRINKING
— editorial in favor of raising the drinking age, Lahaina News, January 1, 1983: 9.
— Senator Mary George suggests raising drinking age to 21, Lahaina News, January 15, 1983: 2.

DRINKING FOUNTAIN
— plans to repair fountain in the Pioneer Inn arcade, Lahaina Sun, September 1, 1971: 12.

DRISCOLL-MILLER, DIANE
— joins Wailea Golf Resort, Lahaina News, August 19, 1999: 14.

DRIVING MISS DAISY [PLAY]
— to be performed by Maui Community Theatre, Lahaina News, June 18, 1992: 21,22.
— opens, Lahaina News, June 25, 1992: 21,22.
— continues at Iao Theatre, Lahaina News, July 9, 1992: 22.

DROP AND SWAP PAINT EXCHANGE
— to be held, Lahaina News, April 20, 2000: 2.

DROUGHT
— Maui suffering from, Lahaina Sun, September 1, 1971: 1,16.
— rain brings relief, Lahaina Sun, September 8, 1971: 5.
— water use restrictions relaxed in Hana and Kula, Lahaina Sun, September 15, 1971: 4.
— rainfall statistics given, Lahaina Sun, September 29, 1971: 15.
— appears to have ended, Lahaina Sun, December 29, 1971: 14.
— Charles Fullerton discusses cloud seeding as method for weather control, Lahaina Sun, January 12, 1972: 2.
— emergency cattle feeding program undertaken, Lahaina Sun, January 19, 1972: 19.
— severe drought anticipated for this year, Lahaina Sun, June 21, 1972: 11.
— predictions offered for summer of 1972, Lahaina Sun, June 28, 1972: 3.
— most of Maui suffering from, Lahaina Sun, March 28, 1973: 10.
— irrigation of Kula farmlands limited, Lahaina Sun, August 29, 1973: 15.

DROWN, DAVE
— paddler featured, Lahaina News, June 3, 1987: 6.
— seeing to have thrillcraft banned from Mala Wharf, Lahaina News, February 10, 1988: 1.
— comments on proposed thrillcraft corridor, Lahaina News, February 24, 1988: 1.

DRUG ADDICTION SERVICES OF HAWAII
— discusses rise in use of ecstasy, Lahaina News, August 29, 1991: 1.

DRUG AWARENESS RESISTANCE EDUCATION (DARE)
— program expands, Lahaina News, September 18, 1997: 6.
— Lahaina students to design t-shirt for, Lahaina News, June 12, 2003: 3.

DRUG COURT
— explained at meeting, Lahaina News, August 3, 2000: 1,20.

DRUG-FREE COALITION
— to meet, Lahaina News, April 13, 1995: 4.

DRUG-FREE HAWAII AWARENESS MONTH
— to be held, Lahaina News, February 8, 1996: 14.

DRUGS
— drug abuse conference to be held at Maui Community College, Lahaina Sun, February 24, 1971: 1.
— conference on drug abuse held at Maui Community College, Lahaina Sun, March 10, 1971: 6.

— arguments for legalization of marijuana discussed, Lahaina Sun, April 28, 1971: 2.

— Maui County Pharmacists Association condemns doctors dispensing drugs themselves, Lahaina Sun, May 12, 1971: 1,3.

— three Lahaina men charged with smuggling hashish, Lahaina Sun, October 13, 1971: 14.

— men charged with smuggling hashish turned over to grand jury, Lahaina Sun, October 20, 1971: 4.

— hashish smugglers arrested, Lahaina Sun, October 27, 1971: 6.

— students at Baldwin High School fight paint sniffing among teenagers, Lahaina Sun, December 1, 1971: 11.

— county advisory council to be formed, Lahaina Sun, August 9, 1972: 11.

— Teen Challenge's rehabilitation facility in Olowalu described, Lahaina Sun, August 16, 1972: 7.

— Maui Council discusses drug problem, Lahaina Sun, September 27, 1972: 1.

— Bob Kelsey interviews drug spy, Lahaina Sun, May 9, 1973: 9.

— Michael Cleveland to appear in court on charges of growing marijuana, Lahaina Sun, July 11, 1973: 6.

— Robert Olson arrested for possession of marijuana, Lahaina Sun, July 25, 1973: 6.

— reactions to Operation Green Harvest offered, Lahaina News, December, 1979: 13.

— discussion of pakalolo use in Hawaii, Lahaina Times, June, 1980 volume 4 number 5: 8.

— police report marijuana growers leaving their fields, Lahaina News, June 15, 1980: 18.

— Drug Bust Song by Danny Paradise, Lahaina Times, August 20, 1980 volume 4 number 7: 1.

— three men arrested for possession of marijuana, Lahaina News, July 15, 1982: 11.

— Hawaii's pot crop estimated to be worth $750 million, Lahaina News, August 15, 1982: 4.

— Alaska couple arrested for cocaine, Lahaina News, November 1, 1982: 11.

— drug use in restaurants, Lahaina Times, August 20, 1983 volume 7 number 8: 2.

— drug and alcohol treatment project set for Lahainaluna High School, Lahaina News, August 28, 1985: 1.

— enforcement increased, Lahaina News, August 13, 1986: 1,14.

— addiction services described, Lahaina News, August 20, 1986: 1,8.

— enforcement plan for pushers announced , Lahaina News, September 3, 1986: 1.

— Deputy Police Chief Harold Tagomori requests more officers to fight, Lahaina News, September 10, 1986: 1.

— education pilot program set for high school, Lahaina News, February 18, 1987: 8.

— Maui Chamber of Commerce sponsoring public seminar on marijuana eradication, Lahaina News, March 2, 1988: 3.

— results of school drug survey, Lahaina News, March 23, 1988: 1,17.

— addicts blamed for rise in crime, Lahaina News, March 30, 1988: 1.

— parents meet to discuss use in children, Lahaina News, April 13, 1988: 1.

— Vice cops help addicts, Lahaina News, November 23, 1988: 1,24.

— problems connected to criminal use discusses, Lahaina News, January 18, 1989: 1,20.

— drug abuse linked to childhood abuse, Lahaina News, January 25, 1989: 1,14.

— Students Staying Straight to host overnight lock-in at Lahainaluna High School, Lahaina News, January 25, 1989: 16,17.

— Sacred Hearts School to sponsor public drug informational meeting, Lahaina News, January 17, 1990: 5.

— police to discuss substance abuse, Lahaina News, January 24, 1990: 5.

— "Go Ask Alice" to be performed by Baldwin Theatre Guild's, Lahaina News, February 7, 1990: 14.

— ecstasy use increases among youth, Lahaina News, August 29, 1991: 1.

— arrests double on Maui, Lahaina News, October 24, 1991: 1.

— Lahaina Intermediate school to teach dangers of abuse of, Lahaina News, November 7, 1991: 4.

— 14 people arrested in Lahaina, Lahaina News, March 26, 1992: 4.

— use prevalent at Lokelani Intermediate School according to survey, Lahaina News, November 12, 1992: 11.

— heroin and ice in West Maui, Lahaina News, September 15, 1994: 1,2.

— Drug Liability Act to target small-time drug dealers, Lahaina News, January 19, 1995: 10.

— Hawaii Drug Free Month to be held, Lahaina News, February 9, 1995: 3.

— Officer David Lake to speak on, Lahaina News, February 23, 1995: 2.

— Drug Free Awareness Month kicks off, Lahaina News, February 1, 1996: 4.

— cocaine and heroin found in recent deaths, Lahaina News, April 11, 1996: 1,14.

— editorial on need for detox center, Lahaina News, April 18, 1996: 5.

— drug-related deaths not easy to track, Lahaina News, May 16, 1996: 1,2.

— Imi I Loko I Kou Piko (Investing in Our Future) to hold meeting on substance abuse, Lahaina News, November 21, 1996: 15.

— "Drug-Free Hawaii Awareness Month" to be held, Lahaina News, January 15, 1998: 5.

— Parents for Drug Prevention group forming, Lahaina News, September 3, 1998: 8.

— Hui Nalu O Ke Kai program at Lahainaluna High School opposes drug use, Lahaina News, February 18, 1999: 5.

— march planned against, Lahaina News, April 1, 1999: 1,20.

— march held opposing, Lahaina News, April 8, 1999: 1.

— Maui Substance Abuse Training Collaborative seeking counselors, Lahaina News, June 1, 2000: 7.

— Maui Drug Court to be explained by Shackley Raffetto, Lahaina News, July 20, 2000: 1,9.

— new laws will not affect marijuana regulation, Lahaina News, August 17, 2000: 7.

DRUKER, STEVEN
— public interest attorney to speak, Lahaina News, April 10, 2003: 20.

DRUMMOND, LEINA'ALA TERUYA
— declares as Republican candidates, Lahaina News, February 13, 1992: 3.

DRYER, KRISTINE
— becomes Hawaii's first female firefighter, Lahaina News, September 15, 1982: 10.

DUAL JUSTICE [MUSICAL GROUP]
— featured, Lahaina News, December 26, 1991: 12.
— continues to perform at El Crab Catcher, Lahaina News, March 12, 1992: 18.

DUARTE, JOHN
— details of his election campaign for 6th district of the State House, Lahaina Sun, September 20, 1972: 7.

DUARTE, PAT
— awarded "Manager of the Fourth Quarter" at the Westin Maui, Lahaina News, March 24, 1994: 8.

DUARTE, THOMAS
— named Maui County Fire Chief, Lahaina News, July 25, 1990: 6.

DUBE, LUCKY [MUSICIAN]
— to perform at Maui Arts and Cultural Center, Lahaina News, October 17, 2002: 18.

DUBIN, ROGER
— executive director of Hawaii Visitor Bureau, Maui nearly ousted, Lahaina News, April 1, 1993: 3.
— Maui Visitors Bureau executive director resigns, Lahaina News, September 1, 1994: 13.

DUCK DERBY RACES
— to be held at Westin Maui to benefit Juvenile Diabetes Research Foundation, Lahaina News, June 19, 2003: 8.

DUCKS UNLIMITED
— Maui members to hold dinner to benefit wetlands, Lahaina News, November 20, 1997: 16.

DUCKWORTH, JAMES
— chair of LahainaTown Action Committee featured, Lahaina News, March 5, 1992: 3.

DUDDLE INTERNATIONAL, LTD.
— purchases Banyan Inn Marketplace, Lahaina News, August 22, 1990: 9.

DUDLEY, KASEN
— Scholar/Athlete of the Week, Lahaina News, February 22, 2001: 13.

DUDLEY, TRACY [ARTIST]
— to exhibit at Village Gallery-Lahaina, Lahaina News, October 21, 1993: 15.

DUENAS, VANESSA
— National Precious Miss Beauty Queen, Lahaina News, July 2, 1992: 4.

DUERFELDT, GREGORY DAVID
— chef of Swan Court featured, Lahaina News, February 3, 2000: 5.

DUGAN, MIKE [COMEDIAN]
— to perform at Comedy Club and the Sports Page, Lahaina News, April 10, 1991: 10,12.
— to perform at Comedy Club, Lahaina News, August 19, 1993: 15.
— to perform at Honolulu Comedy Club, Lahaina News, February 8, 1996: 13.

DUGIED CONSTRUCTION, INC [BUSINESS]
— to install Automated Weather Observing Systems at Kapalua-West Mui Airport, Lahaina News, July 30, 1998: 7.

DUKE, CHARLES, JR.
— former astronaut promoting opening of AAAAA Rent-a-Space, Lahaina News, March 28, 1990: 6.
— astronaut speaks about Earth, Lahaina News, April 18, 1990: 4.

DUKE, THE [PLAY]
— to be performed, starring Joe Moore, Lahaina News, September 29, 1994: 12.

DUKELOW, OLIVER
— hosts Lahainaluna High School Voyaging and Academy of Travel and Tourism students, Lahaina News, December 17, 1998: 23.

DUMADAG, YVONNE
— promoted to service manager to Bank of Hawaii's Lahaina Branch, Lahaina News, December 12, 1990: 6.

DUMALANTA, TESSIE
— closes record amount of loans for Charter Funding of Hawaii, Lahaina News, December 26, 2002: 8.

DUMPS, THE
— report of conditions of surf spot, Lahaina Times, August, 1980 volume 4 number 7: 1.
— surf location featured in Wetscreams [film], Lahaina Times, August, 1980 volume 4 number 7: 5.

DUNCAN, CASEY
— fugitive brought back to Lahaina from Pennsylvania, Lahaina News, May 28, 1998: 3.

DUNE BUGGIES
— rental operation in Ka'anapali criticized, Lahaina Sun, July 28, 1971: 1,9.

DUNES AT MAUI LANI, THE
— golf course opens, Lahaina News, January 21, 1999: 11.
— golf course featured, Lahaina News, July 8, 1999: 7.
— golf course holds grand opening, Lahaina News, July 13, 2000: 7.
— Clubhouse featured, Lahaina News, November 2, 2000: 11.
— to hold grand opening, Lahaina News, August 2, 2001: 8.
— to hold specials, Lahaina News, June 20, 2002: 12.

DUNES CLUBHOUSE [RESTAURANT]
— featured, Lahaina News, August 2, 2001: 7.

DUNKELBECK, DALE
— cook returns from Minnesota, Lahaina News, February 8, 1984: 5.

DUNKERBECK, BJORN
— wins Peter Stuyvesant Travel Aloha Classic, Lahaina News, November 17, 1994: 1.

DUNLOP, COLIN
— hired by Coldwell Banker McCormack Real Estate, Lahaina News, March 27, 1991: 10.

DUNLOP, VIC [COMEDIAN]
— to perform at Honolulu Comedy Club, Lahaina News, March 7, 1996: 14.

DUNN, GABRIELLE
— benefit to be held for, Lahaina News, September 23, 1993: 6.

DUNN, JACKIE
— one of Maui's main surf stars, Lahaina Times, July, 1980 volume 4 number 6: 1.

DUNN, ROY
— to open Plantation House Restaurant, Lahaina News, April 24, 1991: 7.
— to open new restaurant at Wailea Golf Course with Mike Hooks, Lahaina News, September 30, 1993: 8.

DUNN, SCOTT
— DJ to entertain at Moose McGillycuddy's, Lahaina News, October 8, 1992: 10.
— DJ continues at Moose McGillycuddy's, Lahaina News, January 21, 1993: 14.

DUNN, WAYNE [MUSICIAN]
— to perform at Moondoggies, Lahaina News, June 2, 1994: 12.
— to perform at Pioneer Inn, Lahaina News, May 15, 1997: 7.
— to perform at Il Bucaniere, Lahaina News, September 4, 1997: 13.

DUPONTE, HAROLD [POLITICIAN]
— at public meeting in Lahaina, Lahaina Sun, December 23, 1970: 10.
— details of his election campaign for 7th district of the State House, Lahaina Sun, September 27, 1972: 4.

DUQUE, DEAN
— promoted to personal banking officer, Lahaina News, April 22, 1999: 11.

DURAND, PETER [ARTIST]
— featured at Old Jail Gallery, Lahaina News, October 15, 1986: 8.
— displaying art at Old Lahaina Court House, Lahaina News, November 4, 1987: 3.
— work to be displayed at Windfall Koa, Lahaina News, February 15, 1989: 3.

DURHAM, ANN [MUSICIAN]
— to perform at Sandcastle Restaurant, Lahaina News, June 29, 2000: 20.

DURHAM, ANNE
— to teach art of communication, Lahaina News, October 31, 1996: 18.

DURST, WILL [COMEDIAN]
— to perform at Comedy Club, Lahaina News, November 25, 1993: 12.

DUTCHIE KINO MEMORIAL LONG DISTANCE CANOE RACE
— won by Napili Canoe Club, Lahaina News, August 13, 1992: 6.

DUTRO, JACK, III
— arrested for robbery, Lahaina News, April 2, 1992: 5.

DUTY FREE SHOPPERS [BUSINESS]
— opens at Whalers Village, Lahaina News, December 6, 1989: 8.

DUVAL, DAVID
— wins Mercedes Championships, Lahaina News, January 14, 1999: 3.
— plays at Mercedes Championships, Lahaina News, December 30, 1999: 1,6.
— to compete in Mercedes Championship golf tournament, Lahaina News, December 28, 2000: 1,7.
— to play in Mercedes Championship, Lahaina News, January 11, 2001: 8.

DUVALL, FERN
— biologist to discuss native forest birds, Lahaina News, September 12, 2002: 20.
— State wildlife biologist to present "Getting Acquainted with Seabirds of Maui County", Lahaina News, August 7, 2003: 17.

DVORAK, ROBERT REGIS
— to offer drawing classes, Lahaina News, January 16, 1992: 5.

DYANSEN GALLERIES
— opening second location, Lahaina News, March 30, 1988: 20.

DYER, WAYNE
— to speak at Maui Church of Religious Science and Unity Church, Lahaina News, July 22, 1993: 4.
— spoke at Grand Wailea Ballroom, Lahaina News, June 30, 1994: 20.
— to speak, Lahaina News, July 25, 1996: 12.

DYLAN, BOB [MUSICIAN]
— to perform at Royal Lahaina Resort, Lahaina News, March 26, 1992: 16.
— to perform, Lahaina News, August 13, 1998: 16.
— to perform, Lahaina News, September 3, 1998: 20.
— to perform, Lahaina News, September 10, 1998: 21.

DYNAMIC DUO [MUSICAL GROUP]
— to perform at Polli's Mexican Restaurant, Lahaina News, December 26, 1991: 15.

DYSENTERY
— contained, Lahaina Sun, January 27, 1971: 1.

E

E HO'OLOKAHI E NA KUPUNA
— to be held by Na Kupuna O Maui, Lahaina News, November 20, 1997: 16.

E HO'OULU ALOHA: TO GROW IN LOVE
— concert to be held, Lahaina News, November 15, 2001: 16.
— to be held to benefit Bailey House, Lahaina News, November 21, 2002: 18.

E KOMO MAI CLUB
— State Superintendent Paul LeMahieu to speak to, Lahaina News, October 7, 1999: 16.

E NOA CORPORATION [BUSINESS]
— running trolley service between South and West Maui, Lahaina News, October 30, 1997: 13.

E PILI KAKOU (NO NA MEA HAWAII)
— tickets still available, Lahaina News, December 19, 1990: 13.

E-TICKET
— semi-submersible vessel to begin service from Lahaina, Lahaina News, October 31, 1990: 12.
— accepting advanced booking reservations, Lahaina News, December 12, 1990: 6.

E. T. IGE CONSTRUCTION
— accused of taking sand without a permit, Lahaina Sun, May 12, 1971: 8.
— sues Life of the Land for damages, Lahaina Sun, June 2, 1971: 5.
— drops suit against Life of the Land, Lahaina Sun, June 9, 1971: 5.

E.E. BLACK, LTD.
— awarded contract for truck climbing lane on Haleakala Highway, Lahaina News, October 31, 1990: 12.

EAGLE SCOUTS
— honored, Lahaina News, January 31, 1990: 3.
— collecting American flags, Lahaina News, June 24, 1993: 3.

EAGLES [MUSICAL GROUP]
— concert on Oahu reviewed, Lahaina News, November, 1979: 4.

EAGLES DISTRIBUTORS [BUSINESS]
— wins award from Anheuser-Busch, Lahaina News, September 16, 1993: 10.
— to air Bud Light commercials made on Maui, Lahaina News, November 24, 1994: 9.
— moving to new facility, Lahaina News, January 5, 1995: 6.
— acquires Heinecken beer line from Island Beverages, Lahaina News, January 12, 1995: 6.

E'ALA [CANOE]
— launched, Lahaina News, September 10, 1986: 1.
— price changed for trips, Lahaina News, September 17, 1986: 3.

EARFUL PRODUCTIONS [BUSINESS]
— Daryl "DJ Zinn" Gordon launches deejay business, Lahaina News, July 31, 2003: 8.

EARLE, SYLVIA
— author of "Sea Changes, a Message from the Oceans" to speak, Lahaina News, January 9, 1997: 11.
— oceanographer to speak, Lahaina News, January 16, 1997: 11.
— oceanographer to speak, Lahaina News, January 23, 1997: 10.

EARLY, DONA [WRITER]
— begins column with Lahaina News, typically not indexed, Lahaina News, September 24, 1986: .
— new director of Banyan Square Association, Lahaina News, December 17, 1986: 1.
— publishes "Maui and Lana'i", Lahaina News, April 13, 1995: 13.

EARLY, GAYLE
— nurse joins Ohana Physicians Group, Lahaina News, May 27, 1999: 11.

EARLY MUSIC MAUI
— to hold "Boar's Head Feast", Lahaina News, December 4, 1997: 24.
— to perform "Music of the Spanish Armada", Lahaina News, May 7, 1998: 21.
— "All Bach" concert to be held, Lahaina News, April 27, 2000: 12.
— to stage concert "The Virtuoso and Her Concert", Lahaina News, February 8, 2001: 18.
— to stage Festival of Harps, Lahaina News, November 29, 2001: 17.
— to perform "The Play of Daniel", Lahaina News, March 7, 2002: 16.

EARLY PROVISIONS FOR SCHOOL SUCCESS [EPSS]
— test for children, Lahaina News, May 17, 1989: 1.

EARTH AND COMPANY [BUSINESS]
— to open at Wharf Cinema Center, Lahaina News, January 10, 1990: 6.

EARTH DAY
— organizers looking for sponsors, Lahaina News, March 28, 1990: 3.
— events listed, Lahaina News, April 4, 1990: 3.
— events listed, Lahaina News, April 11, 1990: 3.
— events listed, Lahaina News, April 18, 1990: 3.
— to be held, Lahaina News, April 13, 1995: 4.
— Maui Electric Company gives away high-efficiency showerheads in connection to, Lahaina News, April 24, 1997: 7.
— Lahaina Ho'olaule'a to be part of, Lahaina News, April 23, 1998: 7.
— benefit to be held, Lahaina News, April 22, 1999: 12.
— to be celebrated by Hawai'i Nature Center, Lahaina News, April 13, 2000: 13.
— Project S.E.A.-Link to hold "Dive In to Earth Day", Lahaina News, April 19, 2001: 14.
— to be celebrated, Lahaina News, April 19, 2001: 16.
— Pacific Whale Foundation, Lahaina News, April 19, 2001: 17.
— to be celebrated, Lahaina News, April 18, 2002: 17.
— celebrations to be held, Lahaina News, April 10, 2003: 8.
— to be celebrated, Lahaina News, April 17, 2003: 16.

EARTH MAUI NATURE SUMMIT
— to be held by Kapalua Nature Society, Lahaina News, August 15, 1996: 2.
— to be held this weekend, Lahaina News, August 22, 1996: 12.
— to be held, Lahaina News, July 24, 1997: 9.
— to be held, Lahaina News, August 14, 1997: 2.
— to be held, Lahaina News, August 21, 1997: 7.
— to be held, Lahaina News, August 28, 1997: 10.
— reef protection action outlined, Lahaina News, September 4, 1997: 1,2.
— to be held, Lahaina News, May 21, 1998: 2.
— to be held, Lahaina News, June 4, 1998: 1,20.
— to be held, Lahaina News, June 11, 1998: 1.
— to be held with theme "Hawaii's Treasured Islands", Lahaina News, August 26, 1999: 3.
— to be held, Lahaina News, September 16, 1999: 1,16.

EARTHQUAKES
— felt on Maui, no damage, Lahaina Sun, May 2, 1973: 3.
— history of on Maui, Lahaina News, November 1, 1989: 1.

EARTHTRUST
— activist frees dolphins from holding pen in Taiwan, Lahaina News, April 18, 1990: 3.
— seeking volunteers and funds, Lahaina News, May 2, 1990: 3.
— contributes to Whale Spree festival insert, Lahaina News, February 13, 1991: B3.
— to hold benefit whale watching cruise, Lahaina News, April 3, 1991: 8.
— to hold "Whalewatch Benefit" aboard the Maka Kai, Lahaina News, April 9, 1992: 7.
— to host presentation at Ka'ahumanu Center, Lahaina News, February 11, 1993: 5.

EASILY AMUSED [FILM]
— surf film to be shown, Lahaina News, November 14, 2002: 20.

EAST MAUI ANIMAL REFUGE CENTER
— Upcountry Community Center to host benefit auction for, Lahaina News, November 17, 1994: 6.
— to hold auction for animal refuge, Lahaina News, November 14, 1996: 14.
— damaged by fire, seeking help, Lahaina News, September 4, 1997: 4.
— to hold benefit auction, Lahaina News, October 30, 1997: 16.
— to hold annual fund-raiser, Lahaina News, November 8, 2001: 16,17.
— to hold fundraiser at Sandalwood Country Club, Lahaina News, May 16, 2002: 18.
— to hold benefit at Sandalwood Country Club, Lahaina News, May 30, 2002: 14.

EAST MAUI IRRIGATION CO LTD. [BUSINESS]
— promotes Garret Hew to manager and Albert Honokaupu to general superintendent, Lahaina News, February 24, 2000: 13.

EASTER
— sunrise service planned at Ka'anapali Golf Course, Lahaina Sun, April 7, 1971: 3.
— egg hunt to be held at Lahaina Shopping Center, Lahaina Sun, April 7, 1971: 7.
— activities for children, Lahaina News, April 11, 1984: A,B,C,D.
— discussion of relation between bunnies, eggs, and Jesus, Lahaina News, April 18, 1984: 13.
— egg hunt scheduled, Lahaina News, April 18, 1984: 3.
— Liturgy of the Palms and Eucharist celebrated at Holy Innocents' Church, Lahaina News, March 19, 1986: 3.
— children's supplement, featuring the story of chocolate, Lahaina News, March 19, 1986: A,B,C,D.
— egg hunt planned for Kapalua Shops, Lahaina News, March 26, 1986: 3.
— hotels offering brunch, Lahaina News, March 26, 1986: 3.
— event and services held, Lahaina News, April 15, 1987: 3,4,12.
— egg decorating contest winners announced, Lahaina News, May 13, 1987: 12.
— Easter Egg hunt to be held, Lahaina News, March 23, 1988: 14.
— editorial on importance of, Lahaina News, March 30, 1988: 2.
— events detailed, Lahaina News, March 30, 1988: 4,14.
— report on egg decorating contest, Lahaina News, April 6, 1988: 1,20.
— egg decorating winners announced, with photographs, Lahaina News, April 13, 1988: 3.
— Lahaina Cannery announces egg coloring contest winners, Lahaina News, April 27, 1988: 6.
— Soroptimist International to sponsor egg hunt, Lahaina News, March 22, 1989: 13.
— events detailed, Lahaina News, March 22, 1989: 3,6.
— egg hunts scheduled, Lahaina News, April 4, 1990: 3.
— events, Lahaina News, April 11, 1990: 1,3,16.
— events for, Lahaina News, March 27, 1991: 2,3,16.
— events, Lahaina News, June 20, 1991: 3.
— brunches listed, Lahaina News, April 9, 1992: 20.
— children's art contest to be held at The Shops at Kapalua, Lahaina News, April 9, 1992: 5,6,7.
— egg hunt to be held, Lahaina News, April 9, 1992: 8.
— events, Lahaina News, April 16, 1992: 17.
— brunches listed, Lahaina News, April 16, 1992: 20,21.
— events, Lahaina News, April 16, 1992: 4.
— egg hunt to be held by First Assembly of God, Lahaina News, April 1, 1993: 4.
— events to be held, Lahaina News, April 8, 1993: 3,5,10,11.
— Westin Maui to celebrate, Lahaina News, March 24, 1994: 16.
— egg hunt to be held by First Assembly of God Church, Lahaina News, March 24, 1994: 7.
— events held, Lahaina News, March 31, 1994: 14,15.
— church services to be held for, Lahaina News, March 31, 1994: 4.
— to be celebrated at Ritz-Carlton, Lahaina News, March 30, 1995: 11.
— Margy O'Brien to collect for baskets, Lahaina News, March 30, 1995: 6.
— celebrated at Hyatt Regency, Westin Maui, and Ka'anapali Beach Hotel, Lahaina News, April 6, 1995: 12.
— events detailed, Lahaina News, April 13, 1995: 4,14,15.
— egg hunt, service to be held, Lahaina News, March 28, 1996: 4.
— egg hunt sponsored by First Assembly of God Church, Lahaina News, April 4, 1996: 1.
— events, Lahaina News, April 4, 1996: 7,14,15.
— service to be held, Lahaina News, March 20, 1997: 16.
— dining guide, Lahaina News, March 20, 1997: 6,7,20.
— events, Lahaina News, March 27, 1997: 12.

— egg hunt held by West Soroptimists International, Lahaina News, April 3, 1997: 1.
— restaurants offering meals, Lahaina News, April 2, 1998: 8,9.
— events, Lahaina News, April 9, 1998: 16.
— services to be held, Lahaina News, April 9, 1998: 3.
— events scheduled, Lahaina News, April 1, 1999: 7,8,16.
— bunny at Napili Plaza, Lahaina News, April 8, 1999: 1.
— Palm Sunday service planned at Kumulani Chapel, Lahaina News, April 13, 2000: 12.
— dining options, Lahaina News, April 13, 2000: 5.
— egg hunt to be held at Ritz-Carlton, Lahaina News, April 20, 2000: 16.
— churches to celebrate, Lahaina News, April 20, 2000: 8.
— restaurants offering feasts, Lahaina News, April 20, 2000: 9.
— events to be held, Lahaina News, April 5, 2001: 11.
— events to be held, Lahaina News, April 12, 2001: 10.
— Soroptimists International to hold Easter Egg Hunt, Lahaina News, March 21, 2002: 15.
— dinners featured, Lahaina News, March 21, 2002: 9.
— Wharf Cinema Center to celebrate, Lahaina News, March 28, 2002: 15.
— services and celebration planned, Lahaina News, March 28, 2002: 20.
— celebration held at Lahaina Cannery Mall, Lahaina News, April 18, 2002: 14.
— Soroptimist International to hold Easter Egg Hunt, Lahaina News, April 17, 2003: 2.
— services to be held, Lahaina News, April 17, 2003: 2.

EASTER CRAFT AND GIFT FAIR
— to be held at Lahaina Civic Center, Lahaina News, April 20, 2000: 9.

EASTER SEAL SOCIETY OF MAUI
— benefit show held at Maui Hilton, Lahaina Sun, February 10, 1971: 8.
— fundraising luncheon organized, Lahaina Sun, February 23, 1972: 8.
— description of activities, Lahaina Sun, March 15, 1972: 3.
— B. Martin Luna elected as head, Lahaina Sun, June 28, 1972: 11.
— offering infant stimulation program, Lahaina Sun, March 14, 1973: 10.
— wine tasting fundraiser to be held, Lahaina Sun, March 28, 1973: 11.
— Fashion show fundraiser to be held at Maui Surf Hotel, Lahaina Sun, April 18, 1973: 10.
— will host annual telethon, Lahaina News, February 27, 1985: 3.
— chosen as beneficiary of Taste of Lahaina fundraiser, Lahaina News, March 11, 1993: 3.
— drive is underway, Lahaina News, March 16, 1995: 4.
— NFL players to compete in charity basketball for, Lahaina News, April 20, 2000: 16.
— Sprint program collecting used wireless phones to benefit, Lahaina News, July 4, 2002: 8.

EASTERLING, "AMAZON JOHN"
— to share herbal secrets from South American tribes, Lahaina News, May 10, 2001: 20.

EASTLING, ANNEBELL [ARTIST]
— to exhibit at Maui Pizza Cafe, Lahaina News, June 19, 2003: 16.

EASTMAN, D.E.
— "Look Good, Feel Great" event to benefit Maui AIDS Foundation, Lahaina News, August 20, 1998: 17.

EASY GO HAWAII [BUSINESS]
— convenience store opens in Wharf Cinema Center, Lahaina News, August 24, 1995: 10.

EATON, DEBORAH LYN
— appointed guest services manager at Kapalua Bay Hotel, Lahaina News, December 5, 1990: 4.

EBB AND FLOW ENSEMBLE [MUSICAL GROUP]
— to perform at Maui Arts and Cultural Center, Lahaina News, November 21, 2002: 20.

EBERLY, JOHN
— finds sea mine, Lahaina News, September 11, 1997: 2.

EBESU, SANDI
— director of public affairs for Amfac/JMB Hawaii, Inc., discusses survey of West Maui residents concerning development, Lahaina News, March 12, 1992: 1.

EBSEN, BUDDY [ARTIST, ACTOR]
— paintings described, Lahaina News, December 6, 1989: 9,10.

ECKANKAR
— group promoting Ancient Science of Soul Travel to hold meetings, Lahaina News, June 12, 1985: 3.

ECKSTEIN, WARREN
— animal expert to host nationally syndicated talk show on KAOI, Lahaina News, April 24, 2003: 20.

ECLIPSE
— Tedeschi Vineyards introduces wine to celebrate, Lahaina News, July 4, 1991: 3.
— t-shirt designed for, Lahaina News, July 4, 1991: 3.
— Compadres Mexican Bar and Grill to hold photo contest, Lahaina News, July 11, 1991: 4.

ECLIPSE PROJECT
— seeking photographs for possible book , Lahaina News, July 18, 1991: 4,5.

ECO PROPERTIES
— Tim Taylor is top sales performer, Lahaina News, August 7, 2003: 7.

ECO-QUEST
— Hawai'i Nature Center planning, Lahaina News, May 13, 1999: 15.

ECOLE, MICHELLE [DANCER]
— to perform at Ka'anapali Beach Hotel, Lahaina News, June 6, 1990: 13.

ECOLOGY
— seminars held at Maui Community College, Lahaina Sun, March 17, 1971: 2.

ECOLOGY HOUSE [BUSINESS]
— featured, Lahaina News, January 4, 1984: 14.

ECONOMIC CONDITIONS
— Stores in Paia going out of business, Lahaina Times, June, 1980 volume 4 number 5: 1.

ECONOMIC DEVELOPMENT AND ENVIRONMENT COMMITTEE
— to hold Working Group on Recycling, Lahaina News, June 11, 1998: 2.

ECONOMIC DEVELOPMENT COMMITTEE, MAUI COUNTY COUNCIL
— to discuss Maui Electric Co.'s Integrated Resource Plan, Lahaina News, July 20, 2000: 14.

ECONOMIC DEVELOPMENT, MAUI COUNTY OFFICE OF (OED)
— conducting survey on programs and issues, Lahaina News, May 20, 1999: 13.
— to hold tax incentive workshop, Lahaina News, March 9, 2000: 12.
— to hold Business Financing Workshop, Lahaina News, February 13, 2003: 8.
— planning Small Business Financing workshop, Lahaina News, February 20, 2003: 8.
— to hold small business financing workshop, Lahaina News, March 6, 2003: 8.
— to publish "Starting A Business in Maui County", Lahaina News, April 17, 2003: 8.

— seeks companies that qualify as Disadvantaged Business Enterprises (DBE), Lahaina News, June 5, 2003: 8.

— seeking vendors for Maui Nui-Made Products Festival, Lahaina News, July 3, 2003: 8.

— to hold Services Corps of Retired Executives (SCORE), Lahaina News, July 10, 2003: 8.

— forms Business Advocacy Task Force, Lahaina News, July 31, 2003: 8.

ECONOMIC DEVELOPMENT, MAYOR'S OFFICE OF

— seeking ideas to create four-year university on Maui, Lahaina News, November 17, 1994: 4.

— Robbie Ann Kane appointed coordinator, Lahaina News, January 18, 1996: 4.

— to present tourism program at Maui Community College with the Hawaii Tourism Authority, Lahaina News, June 13, 2002: 5.

ECONOMIC REVITALIZATION TASK FORCE

— pinpoints ideas to help improve Hawaii's economy, Lahaina News, October 30, 1997: 1,13.

— lawmakers to discuss, Lahaina News, November 13, 1997: 1.

— public input sought, Lahaina News, November 13, 1997: 2.

— supported by companies, Lahaina News, March 19, 1998: 1,16.

ECONOMY

— goals for Maui articulated by Mayor Cravalho, Lahaina Sun, March 3, 1971: 8.

— expansion of in Hawaii predicted, Lahaina Sun, August 18, 1971: 5.

— Impact of Nixon's economic policies on Maui studied by Howard Nakamura, Lahaina Sun, December 1, 1971: 13.

— Consumer Expenditure Survey conducted in Maui, Lahaina Sun, February 2, 1972: 14.

— unemployment and strikes discussed at Maui Chamber of Commerce, Lahaina Sun, February 16, 1972: 5.

— Senator Hiram Fong pleas that agriculture remain emphasis of state's economy, Lahaina Sun, June 14, 1972: 10.

— Maui economy slowing down, Lahaina Sun, June 28, 1972: 4.

— Lahaina Community Action Program organizing wholesale buying club for food, Lahaina Sun, August 9, 1972: 7.

— need for welfare on the rise, Lahaina Sun, August 16, 1972: 3.

— last year was good, Lahaina Sun, September 6, 1972: 11.

— discussion of current situation of national economy, Lahaina Sun, November 22, 1972: 19.

— impact of West Coast dock strike, Lahaina Sun, November 29, 1972: 3,9.

— consumer protection courses offered at Kahului Library, Lahaina Sun, February 21, 1973: 4.

— Morrie Cohen chairing committee to explore alternatives for Maui's economic future, Lahaina Sun, May 23, 1973: 5.

— possible future of research discussed, Lahaina Sun, June 13, 1973: 21.

— profits for Alexander & Baldwin and Maui Land & Pineapple, and C. Brewer reported, Lahaina Sun, August 1, 1973: 6.

— business down in Lahaina, Lahaina News, July 1, 1980: 15.

— Representative Cecil Heftel advocates limiting imports of Japanese cars, Lahaina News, August 1, 1980: 6.

— conflict over Japanese and American cars discussed, Lahaina News, November 15, 1980: 1.

— critique of occupancy rates as measure of health of tourism, Lahaina News, November 15, 1980: 16.

— Hawaii has 25% more millionaires this year than last, Lahaina News, December 1, 1980: 16.

— report from First Hawaiian Bank, Lahaina News, January 1, 1981: 5.

— Bank of Hawaii predicts moderate growth, Lahaina News, March 1, 1981: 5.

— value of travel sales for tourists discussed, Lahaina News, May 15, 1981: 8,9.

— food co-op forming in Lahaina, Lahaina News, June 1, 1981: 16.

— Canadian dollar falling, Lahaina News, August 15, 1981: 5.

— Japan Tobacco Corp announces plans to market Mild Seven cigarettes in Hawaii, Lahaina News, October 15, 1981: 5.

— Bank of Hawaii begins annual charge for Visa cards, Lahaina News, December 15, 1981: 16.

— improving in Maui, Lahaina News, June 1, 1982: 11.

— Christmas holidays were good for business, Lahaina News, February 1, 1983: 11.

— impact of underground economy discussed, Lahaina News, February 1, 1983: 4.

— Filipino president Marcos orders overseas workers to send money home, Lahaina News, February 15, 1983: 6.

— reaction to Forbes Magazine claiming Hawaii is anti-business, Lahaina News, March 1, 1983: 10.

— roundtable of Hawaii business people formed, Lahaina News, March 15, 1983: 11.

— First Hawaiian Bank predicts recovery of state economy, Lahaina News, May 1, 1983: 11.

— annual update will be provided First Hawaiian Bank, Lahaina News, November 28, 1984: 3.

— editorial that planning needed before sugar industry ends, Lahaina News, May 15, 1985: 2.

— housing and highway seen as having negative impact on, Lahaina News, December 9, 1987: 1,20.

— foul weather increases fish prices, Lahaina News, November 22, 1989: 3.

— employment rate low in West Maui, Lahaina News, June 6, 1991: 1.

— State officials predict good outlook due to strong Japanese visitor market and low interest rates, Lahaina News, January 23, 1992: 5.

— end of recession predicted, Lahaina News, February 20, 1992: 1,9.

— Bank of Hawaii to publish report on Pacific isle economies, Lahaina News, February 20, 1992: 10.

— Bank of Hawaii survey indicates businesses are pessimistic, Lahaina News, April 2, 1992: 13.

— First Hawaiian Bank to host Maui Outlook Forum, Lahaina News, July 30, 1992: 12.

— unemployment rises, Lahaina News, July 30, 1992: 12.

— forecast is that 1993 to look like 1992, Lahaina News, December 3, 1992: 13.

— minimum wage raised to $5.25 an hour, Lahaina News, December 31, 1992: 20.

— job marking tighter in Maui, Lahaina News, June 17, 1993: 11.

— unemployment rate increases, Lahaina News, August 12, 1993: 9.

— importance of agriculture to Maui, Lahaina News, September 23, 1993: 7.

— bankruptcies increase, Lahaina News, October 14, 1993: 8.

— jobless rate improves, Lahaina News, October 14, 1993: 9.

— Labor Department's Rapid Response Team helps displaces workers, Lahaina News, November 4, 1993: 7.

— recession expected to continue, Lahaina News, November 4, 1993: 7.

— personal income increases, Lahaina News, December 16, 1993: 7.

— strong boat market expected in 1994, Lahaina News, December 30, 1993: 5.

— unemployment benefits extended, Lahaina News, December 30, 1993: 5.

— experts expect wedding industry to thrive in 1994, Lahaina News, January 6, 1994: 5.

— local merchants skeptical of 1994 tourist traffic, Lahaina News, January 13, 1994: 5.

— unemployment rate is steady, Lahaina News, March 31, 1994: 9.

— legislation may help long-term unemployed workers find jobs more quickly., Lahaina News, March 31, 1994: 9.

— unemployment rate up, Lahaina News, April 7, 1994: 10.

— unemployment rate down, Lahaina News, July 7, 1994: 8.

— unemployment on the rise, Lahaina News, October 20, 1994: 13.
— strong economy expected for holiday season and beyond, Lahaina News, November 17, 1994: 10.
— Federal Reserve Board decision to raise interest rates debated, Lahaina News, December 1, 1994: 12.
— jobless rate drops, Lahaina News, December 15, 1994: 15.
— paper price increase impacting Maui, Lahaina News, January 12, 1995: 6.
— employment rate falls, Lahaina News, February 16, 1995: 13.
— economists predict upturn, Lahaina News, March 30, 1995: 10.
— jobless rate jumps, Lahaina News, August 17, 1995: 10.
— jobless rate improves, Lahaina News, August 31, 1995: 10.
— unemployment rate remains unchanged, Lahaina News, November 9, 1995: 10.
— unemployment rate drops, Lahaina News, December 7, 1995: 12.
— update on talks between hotels and International Longshoremen's and Warehousemen's Union (ILWU), Lahaina News, January 11, 1996: 10.
— jobless rate drops, Lahaina News, January 18, 1996: 10.
— Bancorp predicts growth, Lahaina News, April 25, 1996: 12.
— Maui Chamber of Commerce to hold meeting on, Lahaina News, July 18, 1996: 13.
— new Maui Trade Dollar to debut, Lahaina News, December 5, 1996: 6.
— state seeking initiatives to improve slumping economy, Lahaina News, August 7, 1997: 1.
— Senator Daniel Inouye to speak on economic impact of Department of Defense, Lahaina News, February 12, 1998: 13.
— jobless rate drops, Lahaina News, February 12, 1998: 13.
— economist Christopher Grandy discusses need for legislature to take action, Lahaina News, March 5, 1998: 13.
— Hawaii economic improving, Lahaina News, June 4, 1998: 13.
— jobless rate declines, Lahaina News, June 4, 1998: 13.
— jobless rate increases, Lahaina News, July 30, 1998: 13.
— jobless rate improves, Lahaina News, September 3, 1998: 11.
— jobless rate drops, Lahaina News, October 1, 1998: 13.
— falling interest rates to impact, Lahaina News, November 26, 1998: 13.
— Maui County Overall Economic Development Plan to be updated, Lahaina News, December 17, 1998: 17.
— jobless rate down, Lahaina News, December 24, 1998: 11.
— jobless rate down, Lahaina News, December 31, 1998: 11.
— jobless rate is lower, Lahaina News, February 4, 1999: 13.
— jobless rate down, Lahaina News, April 1, 1999: 13.
— Maui County Overall Economic Development Plan to be discussed, Lahaina News, April 8, 1999: 11.
— Economist Leroy Laney discusses Maui's outlook, Lahaina News, August 19, 1999: 13.
— Sam Slom critical of State's policies, Lahaina News, August 26, 1999: 1,20.
— Bank of Hawaii raises lending rate, Lahaina News, September 2, 1999: 13.
— ideas for Lahaina discussed at "Mayor's Economic Summit", Lahaina News, November 4, 1999: 1,3.
— unemployment rate dropped, Lahaina News, November 4, 1999: 11.
— jobless rate constant, Lahaina News, December 30, 1999: 13.
— Borders Books to host job finding workshop, Lahaina News, June 22, 2000: 17.
— Lahaina Cannery Mall to host Job Fair, Lahaina News, July 6, 2000: 16.
— unemployment rate rises, Lahaina News, October 5, 2000: 14.
— jobless rate down, Lahaina News, November 30, 2000: 12.
— Ka Lima O Maui offering free job training, Lahaina News, December 7, 2000: 16.
— visitor arrivals down in October, Lahaina News, December 7, 2000: 19.

— jobless rate steady, Lahaina News, January 4, 2001: 14.
— jobless rate rises, Lahaina News, May 31, 2001: 8.
— jobless rate down, Lahaina News, June 28, 2001: 8.
— merchant's view of economy is mixed, Lahaina News, September 20, 2001: 1,8.
— former chief economist of First Hawaiian Bank Leroy Laney to discuss, Lahaina News, September 20, 2001: 9.
— jobless rate rises, Lahaina News, October 4, 2001: 8.
— director of the state Department of Business, Economic Development and Tourism Seiji Naya to discuss economy, Lahaina News, October 18, 2001: 9.
— development grants available for community-based projects, Lahaina News, November 8, 2001: 8.
— Bank of Hawaii Chief Economist Paul Brewbaker to discuss, Lahaina News, November 22, 2001: 8.
— minimum wage, Lahaina News, December 20, 2001: 9.
— slow recovery predicted, Lahaina News, December 27, 2001: 3.
— jobless rate up, Lahaina News, December 27, 2001: 8.
— state offering loans to small businesses hurt by September 11th, Lahaina News, January 3, 2002: 8.
— minimum wage raised to 6.25, Lahaina News, January 9, 2003: 9.

ECRU [MUSICAL GROUP]
— to perform at Moose McGillycuddy's, Lahaina News, February 28, 1990: 11.

ED NISHIMURA'S WHALER'S VILLAGE FLOWER AND GARDEN CENTER [BUSINESS]
— opening in Whaler's Village, Lahaina Sun, November 25, 1970: 3.

EDDIE AND POKI [MUSICAL GROUP]
— to perform at Old Lahaina Cafe and Luau, Lahaina News, April 11, 1990: 15.

EDEN, JONATHAN
— benefit concert to be held for, Lahaina News, September 4, 1997: 17.
— benefit concert to be held for, Lahaina News, September 11, 1997: 16.
— purchases Partygrams, Lahaina News, February 4, 1999: 13.

EDLAO, MARIANO, SR.
— family of to hold reunion, Lahaina News, April 24, 1991: 5.

EDMONDSON, AMY
— presents workshop on work of Buckminster Fuller, Lahaina News, January 13, 1988: 16.
— workshop on Buckminster Fuller detailed, Lahaina News, February 3, 1988: 1,21.

EDO JAPAN [RESTAURANT]
— opens, Lahaina News, May 6, 1999: 15.

E'DRIE, LORRAINE [ARTIST]
— reception at Larry Dotson Gallery, Lahaina News, March 2, 1988: 22.

EDRIS, MATT
— Lahainaluna High School soccer coach featured, Lahaina News, January 11, 1996: 6.

EDUCATION
— Headstart program continuation sought, Lahaina Sun, June 9, 1971: 4.
— school system criticized by valedictorian David Asai, Lahaina Sun, June 16, 1971: 11.
— Mayor Cravalho sued by parents of parochial school children , Lahaina Sun, October 6, 1971: 11.
— portable classrooms at Kamehameha III School not ready soon, Lahaina Sun, October 13, 1971: 1.
— state teacher strike possible, Lahaina Sun, October 13, 1971: 4.
— Mayor Cravalho and Life of the Land sue to stop bombing of, Lahaina Sun, November 24, 1971: 4.
— John Thompson, a UH administrator, says that students receiving more freedom than ever, Lahaina Sun, December 22, 1971: 5.

— description of Hale Keiki by the Methodist Church in Honolua, Lahaina Sun, March 1, 1972: 15.

— schools returning to normal after threat of strike, Lahaina Sun, March 1, 1972: 3.

— open plan for Baldwin High School approved, Lahaina Sun, March 22, 1972: 4.

— chorus students from Hana High School visit mainland, Lahaina Sun, May 10, 1972: 10.

— criticized for not taking risks, Lahaina Sun, May 10, 1972: 6.

— two Maui students selected to help plan Secondary School Students Conference, Lahaina Sun, May 24, 1972: 14.

— confrontation between State Board of Education and Hawaii State Teachers Association, Lahaina Sun, May 24, 1972: 3.

— proposal to develop "land bank" between Kamehameha Schools and the State approved, Lahaina Sun, May 31, 1972: 6.

— United States International University campus in Maui criticized by sister campus in San Diego, Lahaina Sun, June 7, 1972: 4.

— Alan Barr files suit against Mayor Cravalho over funds given to parents of children in private schools, Lahaina Sun, June 14, 1972: 3.

— construction of public swimming pool at Lahainaluna High School approved, Lahaina Sun, June 14, 1972: 3.

— impact of budget cuts discussed, Lahaina Sun, June 21, 1972: 10.

— plans to move Kihei school criticized, Lahaina Sun, July 5, 1972: 15.

— Maui teachers plan to walkout, Lahaina Sun, October 4, 1972: 9.

— Maui teachers vote to strike, Lahaina Sun, October 11, 1972: 3,10.

— school buses debated, Lahaina Sun, December 6, 1972: 5.

— school buses debated, Lahaina Sun, December 13, 1972: 9.

— new intermediate school for Makawao planned, Lahaina Sun, February 14, 1973: 10.

— vocational education promoted at Maui Community College, Lahaina Sun, February 14, 1973: 4.

— teacher's strike begins, Lahaina Sun, April 11, 1973: 1,5.

— teachers vote on arbitration plan, Lahaina Sun, April 18, 1973: 5.

— seniors will graduate despite strike, Lahaina Sun, April 18, 1973: 5.

— teachers return to classroom after strike, Lahaina Sun, April 25, 1973: 3.

— reflection on teacher's strike, Lahaina Sun, April 25, 1973: 9.

— Maui students tour Europe, Lahaina Sun, July 25, 1973: 8.

— sale of soda at school prohibited, Lahaina News, May 1, 1980: 8.

— YMCA sponsoring psychocalisthenics classes, Lahaina News, February 1, 1981: 16.

— advice on choosing a vocational school, Lahaina News, July 1, 1981: 14.

— Adult Employment Fair planned, Lahaina News, July 1, 1981: 8.

— Maui's Educational Opportunity Center receives federal funding, Lahaina News, September 1, 1981: 16.

— classes at Maui Youth Theatre, Lahaina News, September 15, 1981: 16.

— Supercamp opens on the Big Island, Lahaina News, June 15, 1983: 10.

— recommendations on how to teach your child to read, Lahaina News, August 15, 1983: 7,8.

— advice on dealing with a gifted child, Lahaina News, August 15, 1983: 8,10.

— financial aid workshops held, Lahaina News, January 11, 1984: 5.

— program to retrain adult women offered, Lahaina News, February 15, 1984: 5.

— high school outreach counselor Mikahala Among featured, Lahaina News, April 11, 1984: 16.

— applications for Artist-In-The-Schools being accepted, Lahaina News, April 11, 1984: 5.

— editorial on Chaminade University's plan to build a four-year school on Maui, Lahaina News, April 18, 1984: 2.

— students on Principal's List named, Lahaina News, April 18, 1984: 3.

— Lahainaluna High School Class of 1984 scholarship and award winners announced, Lahaina News, May 30, 1984: 18.

— Lahainaluna High School graduating class pictured, Lahaina News, May 30, 1984: 7,8,9,10,11,14,15,16,17.

— pre-school at Kapalua to remain open, Lahaina News, June 6, 1984: 3.

— information session on earn bachelor's degrees to be held at Maui Community College, Lahaina News, June 13, 1984: 4.

— school supplies for King Kamehameha III school listed, Lahaina News, August 8, 1984: 3.

— drug education meeting for parents to be held at Lahikai School, Lahaina News, March 6, 1985: 3.

— entrance exam set for Sacred Hearts School, Lahaina News, April 3, 1985: 16.

— Maui Committee on Government's Conference on Education set to meet, Lahaina News, April 3, 1985: 3.

— workshop on educational kinesiology to be held by Phillip Crockford, Lahaina News, May 8, 1985: 20.

— Lahaina Arts Society grants scholarships, Lahaina News, May 15, 1985: 20.

— program helping parents keep children drug-free, Lahaina News, June 26, 1985: 1,8.

— Maui Community College offering classes in Lahaina, Lahaina News, August 14, 1985: 3.

— Chaminade University to offer courses, Lahaina News, January 1, 1986: 3.

— Chaminade University to offer seminars on student aid, Lahaina News, February 12, 1986: 3.

— Maui Philharmonic Society Scholarship Fund details announced, Lahaina News, March 19, 1986: 3.

— Kalani High School updating list for 10th-year class reunion, Lahaina News, April 16, 1986: 3.

— Lahainaluna student Sean Cleveland to study in Japan this summer, Lahaina News, May 28, 1986: 3.

— Lahaina student Dana Lee Biamonte graduates from St. Anthony High School, Lahaina News, June 4, 1986: 3.

— Lahaina student Julie Aus graduates from Loyola Marymount University, Lahaina News, June 4, 1986: 3.

— Hawaiian resource materials workshop to be held at Maui Community College, Lahaina News, June 11, 1986: 3.

— metric being taught in schools, Lahaina News, August 27, 1986: 1,14.

— exchange student returns from Japan, Lahaina News, September 3, 1986: 3.

— Ka'anapali Beach Hotel offering courses on Hawaiiana, Lahaina News, October 29, 1986: 3.

— Maui Mission School offering kindergarten classes, Lahaina News, November 26, 1986: 10.

— gymnastics courses offered to children, Lahaina News, February 18, 1987: 10.

— drug education program set for Lahainaluna High School, Lahaina News, February 18, 1987: 8.

— foreign study programs available to high school students, Lahaina News, March 18, 1987: 18.

— oncology scholarship offered to nurses, Lahaina News, April 1, 1987: 3.

— Summer School enrollment to begin, Lahaina News, April 15, 1987: 12.

— Maui Portuguese Chamber of Commerce offering college scholarships, Lahaina News, April 15, 1987: 12.

— Na Mele O Maui offers scholarships, Lahaina News, April 22, 1987: 10.

— Department of Education and Kamehameha Schools offer summer enrichment program, Lahaina News, May 6, 1987: 10.

— Lahaina Arts Society offers scholarships to Maui high school seniors, Lahaina News, May 6, 1987: 8.

— Kamehameha III School students learn how to make books, Lahaina News, May 13, 1987: 1,10.

— Maui Hui Malama expanding educational outreach, Lahaina News, May 27, 1987: 1,3.

— Lahaina Intermediate School students taught oceanography on Lin Wa Glass Bottom Boat, Lahaina News, June 24, 1987: 18.

— English classes for immigrants offered by Maui Hui Malama, Lahaina News, July 15, 1987: 12.

— issue of "school refusal" discussed, Lahaina News, August 19, 1987: 22.

— innovations described, Lahaina News, August 26, 1987: 1,16.

— National Association for the Education of Young Children offers advice, Lahaina News, September 2, 1987: 3.

— University of Hawai'i offers Hawaiian Management Program, Lahaina News, September 2, 1987: 3.

— editorial supporting students learning good oral English, Lahaina News, September 23, 1987: 2.

— scholarships from Kokusai Motorcars announced, Lahaina News, December 16, 1987: 3.

— Second language training offered at Maui Hui Malama, Lahaina News, February 24, 1988: 3.

— bridge building contest held for schools, Lahaina News, March 2, 1988: 3,12.

— American Institute of Architects announces scholarship, Lahaina News, March 9, 1988: 17.

— results of school drug survey, Lahaina News, March 23, 1988: 1,17.

— parents meet to discuss drug use in children, Lahaina News, April 13, 1988: 1.

— summer school sign-up begins, Lahaina News, April 13, 1988: 3.

— report on drug program at Lahainaluna High School, Lahaina News, April 20, 1988: 14.

— Punana Leo, a Hawaiian Language Preschool, dedicated, Lahaina News, May 25, 1988: 1,14.

— K.M. Hatano Scholarships announced, Lahaina News, June 1, 1988: 19.

— teacher shortage increases, Lahaina News, June 8, 1988: 1,20.

— Kapalua Land Company offering golf scholarships, Lahaina News, June 8, 1988: 3.

— Maui Community College offering scholarship to honor Aunty Mary Molina, Lahaina News, September 21, 1988: 20.

— continuing education offered to Chartered Professional Accountants, Lahaina News, November 23, 1988: 3.

— editorial in support of Berman Report on grade and high school, Lahaina News, January 4, 1989: 4.

— principal of King Kamehameha III School Don Williams discusses problems faced by, Lahaina News, January 18, 1989: 1,13.

— American Lung Association offering scholarships, Lahaina News, January 18, 1989: 5.

— study abroad programs available to high school students, Lahaina News, February 8, 1989: 13.

— Maui Marriott creates Student Recognition Program, Lahaina News, February 22, 1989: 1.

— Margaret Cameron Scholarship available to music students from Maui Philharmonic Society, Lahaina News, February 22, 1989: 13.

— concerned parents and teachers to hold board meeting, Lahaina News, March 8, 1989: 17.

— Berman Report to be discussed, Lahaina News, March 15, 1989: 1.

— kindergarten registration opens, Lahaina News, March 29, 1989: 1.

— Lahaina Arts Society offering scholarships to graduating high school students, Lahaina News, March 29, 1989: 3.

— American Institute of Architects to host bridge building contest, Lahaina News, April 5, 1989: 3.

— summer session programs set, Lahaina News, April 19, 1989: 13.

— chronic staff shortages a concern, Lahaina News, May 31, 1989: 1.

— Concerned Parents Teacher Association objects to school cuts, Lahaina News, June 7, 1989: 1.

— King Kamehameha III School faces loss of Vice Principal, Lahaina News, June 14, 1989: 1.

— staff shortages remain an issue, Lahaina News, August 30, 1989: 1.

— adult classes added, Lahaina News, August 30, 1989: 2.

— youth celebrate end of summer school, Lahaina News, August 30, 1989: 4.

— seminar on writing effective news releases to be held, Lahaina News, September 13, 1989: 5.

— course on menu planning offered by assistant food and beverage director of the Hotel Hana Maui, Lahaina News, September 20, 1989: 6.

— public hearing on school budget scheduled, Lahaina News, October 18, 1989: 3.

— applications for summer foreign study programs being accepted, Lahaina News, November 22, 1989: 2.

— Amfac, Inc donates to University of Hawai'i for scholarships, Lahaina News, January 3, 1990: 4.

— some residents want A-plus after school program, Lahaina News, January 10, 1990: 1,3.

— John Trelease to lecture on importance of reading aloud, Lahaina News, January 24, 1990: 4.

— A+ program described, Lahaina News, February 14, 1990: 1,10.

— bills introduced in legislature, Lahaina News, February 21, 1990: 4.

— Hotel Sales and Marketing Association of Maui offers scholarships, Lahaina News, March 7, 1990: 7.

— Parent Teacher Association at King Kamehameha III School calls on parents to support bills, Lahaina News, March 21, 1990: 3.

— University of Hawai'i to offer upper and graduate-level Education courses on Maui, Lahaina News, March 28, 1990: 3.

— Hotel Sales and Marketing Association of Maui offering scholarships, Lahaina News, April 11, 1990: 3.

— summer school registration to begin, Lahaina News, April 18, 1990: 3.

— summer school registration deadline nears, Lahaina News, April 25, 1990: 3.

— Maui District High School Music Festival to be held, Lahaina News, May 9, 1990: 5.

— Lahaina Yacht Club raises funds for scholarships, Lahaina News, May 9, 1990: 5.

— Foodland purchases computers for schools, Lahaina News, May 16, 1990: 5,14.

— survey of parents and community leaders undertaken by King Kamehameha III School, Lahaina News, June 6, 1990: 3,17.

— report cards ready, Lahaina News, June 27, 1990: 5.

— Nagasako Variety and Ben Franklin to hold back to school sales, Lahaina News, August 1, 1990: 5.

— first pep rallies to be held at Ka'ahumanu Center, Lahaina News, August 8, 1990: 5.

— parade to celebrate 150 years of public education to be held, Lahaina News, October 10, 1990: 1.

— report on celebration of 150th anniversary of public education, Lahaina News, October 17, 1990: 3.

— 150 years of public education celebrated, Lahaina News, October 24, 1990: 1.

— University of Hawai'i School of Nursing to hold information session, Lahaina News, October 24, 1990: 2.

— National School Lunch Day celebrated, Lahaina News, October 24, 1990: 5.

— 10th graders at Lahainaluna High School perform well in mathematics but poorly in reading, Lahaina News, January 2, 1991: 1.

— Princess Nahienaena School to host workshop on social issues of youth, Lahaina News, January 2, 1991: 4.

— nurse's aide position to not be filled, Lahaina News, January 23, 1991: 2.

— editorial in support of nurse's aide at King Kamehameha III and Lahaina Intermediate schools, Lahaina News, January 30, 1991: 7.

— teachers Vashte Daise and Dawn Ikinrode escort students to Hulapoe Bay for field trip, Lahaina News, February 6, 1991: 1.

— applications being accepted for KM Hatano Scholarship program, Lahaina News, February 6, 1991: 3.

— bills to install prophylactic vending machines in schools to be introduced, Lahaina News, February 13, 1991: 1,8.

— schools participate in Foodland's "Shop for a Better Education", Lahaina News, February 13, 1991: 5.

— Adopt-a-student program implemented at Princess Nahienaena School, Lahaina News, February 20, 1991: 3.

— Hawaiian Cable Vision sponsoring national teleconference "Cable in the Classroom", Lahaina News, March 6, 1991: 4.

— Maui Catholic Schools Spelling Bee held, Lahaina News, March 6, 1991: 4.

— science fair winners announced, Lahaina News, March 6, 1991: 4.

— Lahaina Intermediate School announces scholars list, Lahaina News, March 6, 1991: 5.

— Greater Lahaina Reunion donates to schools in West Maui, Lahaina News, March 20, 1991: 3.

— Safeway and Foodland praised for donating computers to local schools, Lahaina News, March 20, 1991: 5.

— summer school class registration opens, Lahaina News, April 17, 1991: 1.

— scholarships to Lahainaluna High School students, Lahaina News, April 24, 1991: 1.

— Ka'ahumanu Center to host Spotlight on Education, Lahaina News, April 24, 1991: 11.

— Lappert's Ice Cream donates to local schools, Lahaina News, May 1, 1991: 4.

— Science Carnival to be held, Lahaina News, May 1, 1991: 4.

— summer school deadlines approaching, Lahaina News, May 8, 1991: 3.

— students awarded KM Hatano Scholarship Awards, Lahaina News, May 23, 1991: 4.

— Meyer Ueoka opposes condom vending machines on public school campuses, Lahaina News, May 23, 1991: 4.

— "A Career in Real Estate" to be held, Lahaina News, May 30, 1991: 3.

— Foodland's "Shop for Better Education" provides computers for schools, Lahaina News, June 6, 1991: 4.

— "A Career in Real Estate" to be held, Lahaina News, June 6, 1991: 6.

— applications accepted for Margaret Cameron Scholarship from the Maui Philharmonic Society, Lahaina News, June 13, 1991: 4.

— Na Mele O Maui to award scholarships, Lahaina News, June 13, 1991: 5,6.

— Na Mele O Maui awarding scholarships, Lahaina News, June 20, 1991: 3.

— University of Hawai'i classes now available through interactive television, Lahaina News, June 20, 1991: 3,4.

— real estate seminar canceled, Lahaina News, June 27, 1991: 9.

— physicist George Field to lecture on eclipse, Lahaina News, July 4, 1991: 3.

— national sports scholarships available, Lahaina News, July 4, 1991: 5.

— Denise Zack planning to build preschool, Lahaina News, July 11, 1991: 6.

— sports scholarships available, Lahaina News, August 15, 1991: 4.

— State estimates that student population at Lahainaluna High School will double, Lahaina News, September 5, 1991: 1.

— parents may be eligible for preschool aid, Lahaina News, September 19, 1991: 3.

— A+ program a success, Lahaina News, September 26, 1991: 3.

— preschool aid available, Lahaina News, October 3, 1991: 5.

— Montessori School of Maui to hold Children's Fair, Lahaina News, October 31, 1991: 4.

— Lahaina Intermediate school to teach about drug abuse dangers, Lahaina News, November 7, 1991: 4.

— two-day seminar on writing screenplays to beheld at Stouffer Wailea Beach Resort, Lahaina News, November 28, 1991: 4.

— KM Hatano Scholarship Program offering scholarships, Lahaina News, December 19, 1991: 6.

— Hyatt Regency Maui to offer scholarships, Lahaina News, January 2, 1992: 5.

— Lahaina Pre-School and Napili Pre-School sponsoring book fair, Lahaina News, January 23, 1992: 4.

— Lahaina Pre-School and Napili Pre-School sponsoring book fair, Lahaina News, January 30, 1992: 3.

— Hyatt Regency Maui to offer scholarships, Lahaina News, January 30, 1992: 4.

— legislature criticized for lack of security positions at schools , Lahaina News, February 6, 1992: 4.

— foreign study programs available, Lahaina News, February 6, 1992: 5.

— state education superintendent Sharles Togushi announces site for Upcountry high school, Lahaina News, February 20, 1992: 4.

— Maui schools cited for fire code violations, Lahaina News, March 12, 1992: 1,8.

— classes to be offered during Spring Break at Kahului Community Center Playhouse, Lahaina News, March 12, 1992: 5.

— cost of A-Plus After School program may rise, Lahaina News, March 19, 1992: 3.

— projections on number of students reduced, Lahaina News, March 19, 1992: 4.

— Haleakala Waldorf School to hold open house, Lahaina News, March 19, 1992: 4.

— scholarship applications available from Maui Philharmonic Society, Lahaina News, March 19, 1992: 6.

— officials to enforce fire regulations at local schools, Lahaina News, March 26, 1992: 1,4.

— international student exchange organized, Lahaina News, April 9, 1992: 8.

— attempts to ease transition to intermediate school, Lahaina News, April 16, 1992: 6.

— schools still failing to meet fire code, Lahaina News, April 23, 1992: 1,3.

— some parents object to "Impressions" textbook, Lahaina News, April 30, 1992: 1,3.

— corrections to story that schools still failing to meet fire code, Lahaina News, April 30, 1992: 3.

— parents begin petition against "Impressions" textbook, Lahaina News, May 7, 1992: 1,4.

— Maui District High School Music Festival to be held, Lahaina News, May 7, 1992: 24.

— Educators of the Pacific, Inc. scholarship winners announced, Lahaina News, May 21, 1992: 4.

— winners of Success Strategies Scholarships announced, Lahaina News, May 21, 1992: 4.

— Arita Poulson low bidder on proposed school building in Kihei, Lahaina News, May 28, 1992: 12.

— Maui County Planning Commission approves additional buildings at Lokelani Intermediate and Kihei School, Lahaina News, May 28, 1992: 6.

— John Miller says Kihei needs three elementary schools, Lahaina News, May 28, 1992: 7.

— appraisal finished for Kihei school, Lahaina News, June 4, 1992: 7.

— Lahainaluna High School students receive scholarships from Blackie Gadarian, Lahaina News, June 18, 1992: 22.

— students on Dean's List at Cannon's Business College, Lahaina News, June 18, 1992: 4.

— Foodland, Inc. donates computers to local schools, Lahaina News, July 2, 1992: 26.

— Kihei-Makena Community Plan committee member opposes elementary school in the Wailea resort, Lahaina News, July 2, 1992: 7.

— Sylvan Learning Center featured, Lahaina News, July 9, 1992: 13.

— Lahaina Intermediate School to host School/Community-Based Management conference, Lahaina News, August 20, 1992: 9.

— more funds needed, Lahaina News, September 10, 1992: 11.

— Kihei school enrollment dips, Lahaina News, September 10, 1992: 11.

— parents criticized by students, Lahaina News, September 10, 1992: 4.

— teachers criticize school operations, Lahaina News, September 17, 1992: 7.

— Wailea Community Association awards scholarships, Lahaina News, September 17, 1992: 8.

— High School Pep Rally competition to be held, Lahaina News, September 24, 1992: 18.

— Department of Education to hold public hearing, Lahaina News, November 19, 1992: 1.

— residents of South Maui urge building of new school, Lahaina News, November 19, 1992: 4.

— parents want more control of schools, Lahaina News, December 10, 1992: 1.

— concern over how school facilities should be evaluated, Lahaina News, December 17, 1992: 12.

— students visit Washington, D.C., Lahaina News, December 17, 1992: 3.

— Maui District Task Force proposal for Project Ke Au Hou to be discussed at public meeting, Lahaina News, December 24, 1992: 3.

— Hyatt Regency Maui awards KM Hatano scholarships, Lahaina News, December 31, 1992: 4.

— college financial aid workshop to be offered, Lahaina News, December 31, 1992: 5.

— principals wary of lump sum program, Lahaina News, January 7, 1993: 8.

— fire code violations fewer this year at Lahainaluna High School, Lahaina News, January 14, 1993: 1,3.

— Ralph Murakami named as superintendent for Maui District Schools, Lahaina News, January 14, 1993: 3.

— upgrades to fire equipment for South Maui schools needed, Lahaina News, January 21, 1993: 10.

— John Miller calls for more voices to support, Lahaina News, January 21, 1993: 10.

— Kihei school to begin kindergarten registration, Lahaina News, January 28, 1993: 10.

— registration for kindergarten begins, Lahaina News, February 4, 1993: 4.

— student events to be held, Lahaina News, February 11, 1993: 5.

— preschool may teach Hawaiian language, Lahaina News, February 18, 1993: 3.

— may establish school business manager pilot program, Lahaina News, February 18, 1993: 5.

— Lahaina Intermediate School begins School Community Based Management program, Lahaina News, March 4, 1993: 1.

— Hawaii State Commission on Performance Standards sponsoring public hearing, Lahaina News, March 4, 1993: 7.

— air conditioners to be installed in Kihei, Lahaina News, March 4, 1993: 7.

— Cannon's International Business College offering scholarships, Lahaina News, March 11, 1993: 12.

— Office of Hawaiian Affairs Education Division to hold community meetings, Lahaina News, March 18, 1993: 4.

— Honolua Preschool receives grant from Castle Foundation, Lahaina News, March 25, 1993: 3.

— Maui students lack test taking skills, Lahaina News, April 1, 1993: 1,7.

— great need for capital improvement, Lahaina News, April 1, 1993: 3.

— parents seeking immersion program, Lahaina News, April 8, 1993: 3.

— Na Mele O Maui scholarships available, Lahaina News, April 22, 1993: 3.

— state education panel considers alternative funding sources, Lahaina News, April 22, 1993: 4.

— School-Community Based Management Council to implement student recognition program, Lahaina News, May 13, 1993: 2,3.

— Rotary Club awards scholarships, Lahaina News, May 20, 1993: 2.

— new bus route added, Lahaina News, June 3, 1993: 4,5.

— Ke Au Hou not ready to open in September, Lahaina News, June 10, 1993: 4.

— Howard Fukunaga and J.P. Ortmann thanked for helping improve school facilities in Kihei, Lahaina News, June 24, 1993: 7.

— construction delay at Kihei School explained, Lahaina News, June 24, 1993: 7.

— Kihei School principal Doug Holt resigns to work for state Department of Education, Lahaina News, June 24, 1993: 8.

— Owen Yoshino wins scholarship from Disney, Lahaina News, July 8, 1993: 3.

— Waiola Congregational Church to vote on hosting Punana Leo O Maui preschool, Lahaina News, July 22, 1993: 3.

— Development Agreement Bill workshop to be held at Maui Community College, Lahaina News, August 5, 1993: 5.

— issues likely in Kihei given anticipated growth, Lahaina News, August 12, 1993: 6.

— new principals appointed, Lahaina News, August 12, 1993: 6.

— Maui Planning Commission extends permit to operate Lahaina Pre-School, Lahaina News, September 2, 1993: 2.

— life of children in grade 7 described, Lahaina News, September 30, 1993: 3.

— public school students scoring higher, Lahaina News, October 14, 1993: 1,4.

— Partners in Living and Learning offers incentives for students at Lahaina Intermediate School, Lahaina News, October 14, 1993: 2.

— incentive program at Kihei School to begin, Lahaina News, October 21, 1993: 8.

— Lahainaluna High School principal Henry "Bruno" Ariyoshi receives award from Milken Family Foundation National Educator Award, Lahaina News, October 28, 1993: 1,12.

— Messenjah to perform benefit concert for Iao School Renaissance Education Foundation, Lahaina News, October 28, 1993: 10.

— Lahainaluna Distributed Education Clubs of America elects new officers, Lahaina News, October 28, 1993: 3.

— fire inspector finds code violations at Lahainaluna High School, Lahaina News, November 4, 1993: 1,3.

— student survey reveals drug use, Lahaina News, December 23, 1993: 1,3.

— Educational Opportunity Center to hold workshops on financial aid, Lahaina News, December 30, 1993: 3.

— tax increase proposed to fund school facilities, Lahaina News, December 30, 1993: 7.

— West Maui Schools to hold marathon fund-raiser, Lahaina News, December 30, 1993: 8.

— scholarships available from Hyatt Regency, Lahaina News, January 13, 1994: 2.

— West Maui Complex to host West Maui Marathon Madness, Lahaina News, January 20, 1994: 9.

— update on events, Lahaina News, January 27, 1994: 2.

— activities on Maui, to be formally launched, highlighting vocational education, Lahaina News, February 10, 1994: 4.

— West Maui Kumon Center opens, Lahaina News, February 17, 1994: 1,4.

— deadline approaching for federal financial aid, Lahaina News, February 24, 1994: 4.

— students earn honors, Lahaina News, March 3, 1994: 4.

— First Hawaiian Bank to hold college planning workshop, Lahaina News, March 10, 1994: 4.

— students to take SAT, Lahaina News, April 7, 1994: 4.

— advisory committee for Lahaina Complex seeks health center at Lahainaluna Health Center, Lahaina News, April 28, 1994: 1.

— funding for improvements to Princess Nahienaena Elementary School approved, Lahaina News, May 5, 1994: 1.

— peer educators teach anger management, Lahaina News, May 5, 1994: 1,6.

— art an literary contest offered to children ages 5 to 12, Lahaina News, June 2, 1994: 12.

— students honored, Lahaina News, June 2, 1994: 2.

— youth drug and alcohol use on the rise, Lahaina News, August 4, 1994: 1.

— Lahainaluna High School to participate in Project Graduation, Lahaina News, August 18, 1994: 1.

— updates on schools, Lahaina News, September 22, 1994: 4,5.

— project graduation to be held, Lahaina News, October 13, 1994: 5.

— update on local schools, Lahaina News, October 27, 1994: 2.

— Board of Education member Kelly King expresses views on, Lahaina News, November 17, 1994: 1,3.

— Mayor's Office of Economic Development seeking ideas to create four-year university on Maui, Lahaina News, November 17, 1994: 4.

— update on local schools, including honor rolls, Lahaina News, November 24, 1994: 4,5.

— Meyer Ueoka urges new Board of Education to rethink position on controversial issues, Lahaina News, December 1, 1994: 1.

— new testing method results reported by Herman Aizawa, Lahaina News, December 22, 1994: 2.

— update on local schools, including honor rolls, Lahaina News, December 22, 1994: 4,5.

— Project Graduation to meet, Lahaina News, January 5, 1995: 4.

— Hyatt Regency Maui offering KM Hatano Scholarship Program, Lahaina News, January 5, 1995: 4.

— Educational Opportunity Center to hold financial aid workshops, Lahaina News, January 12, 1995: 4.

— student achievement and curriculum top priorities in School Status and Improvement Report, Lahaina News, January 19, 1995: 2.

— Certified Pest Control and Fumigation Services, Inc. announces scholarship, Lahaina News, January 19, 1995: 6.

— student input not included in proposed school conduct code, Lahaina News, January 26, 1995: 3.

— update from local schools, Lahaina News, January 26, 1995: 5.

— kindergarten registration to begin, Lahaina News, February 2, 1995: 4.

— kindergarten registration to begin, Lahaina News, February 9, 1995: 3.

— update on local schools, including honor rolls, Lahaina News, February 23, 1995: 4.

— Zonta Club of Maui announces availability of "Young Women in Public Affairs" scholarship, Lahaina News, March 2, 1995: 3.

— Maui District Schools beginning summer school classes, Lahaina News, March 16, 1995: 4.

— update on local schools, Lahaina News, March 23, 1995: 4.

— Junior prom to be held at Hyatt Regency Hotel, Lahaina News, April 6, 1995: 2.

— update on local schools, May Day and graduation approaching, Lahaina News, April 27, 1995: 4.

— funding for West Maui schools remain in stat budget, Lahaina News, May 4, 1995: 1,20.

— Lahaina Intermediate School Parent Teacher Student Association to hold elections, karaoke contest, Lahaina News, May 11, 1995: 2.

— updates from local schools, Lahaina News, May 25, 1995: 2.

— Lahaina Rotary Club provides scholarships to Lahainaluna High School students, Lahaina News, June 1, 1995: 2.

— Isa-Lei Hinau named a United States National Award winner in English, Lahaina News, June 15, 1995: 2.

— Lahaina Intermediate School releases Partners in Living and Learning Achievement List, Lahaina News, July 13, 1995: 4.

— Hawaii students perform well in college entrance exams, Lahaina News, September 14, 1995: 1.

— State begins planning for new facilities, Lahaina News, September 14, 1995: 3.

— students to collect goods for victims of Hurricane Marilyn, Lahaina News, September 28, 1995: 2.

— update on local schools, Lahaina News, September 28, 1995: 4.

— Project Graduation to hold planning meeting, Lahaina News, October 5, 1995: 4.

— Ed Smith to speak to Lahaina Complex Site-Based Council, Lahaina News, October 19, 1995: 4.

— update on local schools, Lahaina News, October 26, 1995: 4.

— update on local schools, Lahaina News, November 30, 1995: 3.

— student art contest to be held, Lahaina News, December 14, 1995: 18.

— Avery Chumbley discusses state of, Lahaina News, December 14, 1995: 3.

— update on local schools, Lahaina News, December 28, 1995: 4.

— "Celebration of Youth and the Arts" to be held at Lahaina Cannery Mall, Lahaina News, January 18, 1996: 4.

— Maui Multi-Cultural Organization sponsoring Multi-Cultural Fair, Lahaina News, January 18, 1996: 4.

— expecting budget cuts, Lahaina News, January 25, 1996: 1,16.

— Lahaina and Wailuku to share one school specialist, Lahaina News, January 25, 1996: 16.

— Maui Board of Realtors offering scholarships, Lahaina News, January 25, 1996: 4.

— update on local schools, Lahaina News, January 25, 1996: 6.

— Celebration of Youth and the Arts awards ceremony held, Lahaina News, February 1, 1996: 14.

— KM Hatano Scholarship available offered by Hyatt Regency Maui, Lahaina News, February 22, 1996: 10.

— update on local schools, Lahaina News, February 22, 1996: 2.

— students compete in National PTSA Reflections, Lahaina News, March 7, 1996: 10.

— school council to meet, Lahaina News, March 14, 1996: 11.

— Punana Leo O Maui Hawaiian Language Preschool to hold benefit concert, Lahaina News, March 14, 1996: 13.

— Charles Kaupu teaches teachers about Honokahua agreement, Lahaina News, March 21, 1996: 1,14.

— update on local schools, Lahaina News, March 28, 1996: 6.

— Certified Pest Control and Fumigation Services, Inc. announces scholarship winners, Lahaina News, March 28, 1996: 7.

— Raymond Karelitz to offer SAT-prep workshop, Lahaina News, April 11, 1996: 6.

— Lahainaluna High School students receive scholarships, Lahaina News, April 25, 1996: 6.

— James Furukawa to present class, Lahaina News, June 6, 1996: 15.

— debate over uniforms at Lahainaluna High School continues, Lahaina News, July 11, 1996: 1,16.

— Napili Kai Beach Club founder Millar family presents scholarships, Lahaina News, July 18, 1996: 3.

— Hawaiian Language Immersion Preschool Punana Leo o Lahaina planned, Lahaina News, August 15, 1996: 14.

— interest in Punana Leo school, Lahaina News, August 22, 1996: 1,20.

— Aha Punana Leo representatives answer questions on planned school, Lahaina News, August 22, 1996: 20.

— registration for A-Plus begins, Lahaina News, August 22, 1996: 4.

— local schools collecting old phone books as fundraiser, Lahaina News, August 29, 1996: 1.

— health education teachers sought, Lahaina News, September 19, 1996: 14.

— teachers vote in support of the contract, Lahaina News, October 31, 1996: 3.

— KM Hatano Scholarship Program offered by Hyatt Regency Maui, Lahaina News, January 9, 1997: 14.

— Maui District Student Council Organization to hold "Brown Bags to Stardom", Lahaina News, February 13, 1997: 10.

— Lahaina Cannery Mall sponsoring keiki essay contest, Lahaina News, June 5, 1997: 15.

— Lahaina Yacht Club awards scholarships to Lahainaluna High School students, Lahaina News, June 26, 1997: 2.

— Hui Malama Learning Center offering GED test preparation, Lahaina News, July 10, 1997: 2.

— Hunter Education Classes to be held, Lahaina News, July 31, 1997: 14.

— Adult Education Classes to be held, Lahaina News, September 4, 1997: 16.

— Lahaina teachers learn about Hawaiian values, Lahaina News, November 20, 1997: 11.

— work of Maui youth on display at Ka'ahumanu Center, Lahaina News, January 29, 1998: 15.

— Bank of Hawaii offering workshop on student loans, Lahaina News, February 19, 1998: 13.

— Lahaina Complex seeking public input on school schedule, Lahaina News, March 5, 1998: 1.

— Haleakala Waldorf School to hold open house, Lahaina News, March 12, 1998: 20.

— Lahaina Complex to discuss changing public school schedule, Lahaina News, March 12, 1998: 8.

— Maui District School Music Festival to be held, Lahaina News, April 9, 1998: 17.

— Lahaina school committees need volunteers, Lahaina News, April 23, 1998: 3.

— students experience voyaging in Na Kalai Wa'a Moku o Hawai'i, Lahaina News, April 30, 1998: 7.

— Ka'anapali Beach Resort Association offering Na Mele O Maui scholarships, Lahaina News, May 7, 1998: 18.

— Princess Nahienaena Elementary School PTA extends scholarship deadline, Lahaina News, May 7, 1998: 18.

— students of local schools recognized, Lahaina News, May 7, 1998: 9.

— Lahaina Complex selling scrip for fundraiser, Lahaina News, May 14, 1998: 3.

— Hui Malama Learning Center to offer summer classes, Lahaina News, May 21, 1998: 9.

— Parents Supporting Drug Prevention and Education in Our Schools to meet, Lahaina News, May 28, 1998: 12.

— Punana Leo O Lahaina Preschool opening in the summer, Lahaina News, May 28, 1998: 3.

— school year to begin earlier, Lahaina News, June 11, 1998: 1.

— student scholarships, Lahaina News, June 11, 1998: 2.

— information session to be held on University of Hawaii's Business Administration program, Lahaina News, June 18, 1998: 13.

— basic Japanese lessons to be at Wailuku Hongwanji, Lahaina News, June 25, 1998: 2.

— Punana Leo O Lahaina Preschool opening, Lahaina News, July 2, 1998: 1.

— students taught facets of agriculture, Lahaina News, July 2, 1998: 1,2.

— Japanese language school opens, Lahaina News, July 2, 1998: 8.

— scrip fundraiser results, Lahaina News, July 9, 1998: 7.

— Hawaii Association for the Education of Young Children to hold Children's Fair at Lahaina Cannery Mall, Lahaina News, July 16, 1998: 17.

— Traveling Mini-Science Carnival to be held at Ka'ahumanu Center, Lahaina News, July 16, 1998: 2.

— Maui Arts and Cultural Center hosting "Learning Across the Curriculum: A Summer Institute for Teachers", Lahaina News, July 23, 1998: 17.

— Traveling Mini-Science Carnival to be held at Ka'ahumanu Center, Lahaina News, July 30, 1998: 7.

— interns to work at Maui High Performance Computer Center, Lahaina News, August 6, 1998: 17.

— scholarships awarded, Lahaina News, September 10, 1998: 6.

— Foodland donates money for computers in local schools, Lahaina News, September 24, 1998: 6.

— candidate forum to be held for Board of Education candidates Lance Collins and Mike Victorino, Lahaina News, October 1, 1998: 1.

— Board of Education candidates to hold forum, Lahaina News, October 8, 1998: 7.

— Board of Education candidates share ideas, Lahaina News, October 22, 1998: 1,2.

— Archie Kalepa teaches Lahainaluna Voyagers, Lahaina News, October 29, 1998: 11.

— students eligible to travel to Washington, D.C., Lahaina News, October 29, 1998: 15.

— Punana Leo o Lahaina ready for students, Lahaina News, October 29, 1998: 3.

— Kids Voting Hawaii held, Lahaina News, November 12, 1998: 9.

— Lahaina Intermediate School considering year round schedule, Lahaina News, November 19, 1998: 1,20.

— year round schedule debated, Lahaina News, November 26, 1998: 1,20.

— Na Pua Makamae O Waiola immersion program to begin, Lahaina News, December 10, 1998: 11.

— Punana Leo o Lahaina immersion program to begin, Lahaina News, January 14, 1999: 1,16.

— inspection of facilities indicates imitations, Lahaina News, February 4, 1999: 1,3.

— Maui Business and Professional Women's Club accepting applications for scholarships, Lahaina News, February 25, 1999: 11.

— West Maui Consortium for Teaching Asia and the Pacific in the Schools (CTAPS) offering workshop, Lahaina News, March 18, 1999: 2.

— staggered schedule at Princess Nahienaena Elementary School may be unfeasible, Lahaina News, March 25, 1999: 1.

— Masters in Business Administration to be offered by the University of Hawaii, Lahaina News, March 25, 1999: 13.

— Maui High Band to perform, Lahaina News, March 25, 1999: 17.

— Alexander and Baldwin Foundation to sponsor "Technology and the World of Learning", Lahaina News, April 8, 1999: 11.

— Maui District Intermediate School Music Festival to be held, Lahaina News, April 15, 1999: 5.

— Catholic schools form alliance, Lahaina News, April 22, 1999: 3.

— Wailea Hou to open, Lahaina News, April 29, 1999: 14.

— Maui Chemical and Paper Products establishes Kawasaki Scholarship, Lahaina News, May 6, 1999: 2.

— Ka'anapali Beach Resort Association to offer Na Mele o Maui Scholarships, Lahaina News, May 13, 1999: 15.

— workshop on "How the Arts Enhance Learning in Other Subjects" to be held, Lahaina News, May 20, 1999: 17.

— film course to be offered by University of Southern California, Lahaina News, June 10, 1999: 15.

— Maui County Hawaiian Canoe Association offering scholarships, Lahaina News, June 10, 1999: 15.

— scholarship recipients listed, Lahaina News, June 10, 1999: 8.

— Lahaina Intermediate School to go to yeer-round calendar, Lahaina News, June 17, 1999: 1,20.

— donations sought for "Lokahi Back-to-School" supply drive, Lahaina News, July 15, 1999: 5.

— All-Maui County High School Class of 1969 to hold reunion, Lahaina News, July 15, 1999: 5.

— AECG offering free mime workshop, Lahaina News, August 5, 1999: 12.

— Na Lima Paepae O Lele to establish Hawaiian immersion charter school, Lahaina News, August 26, 1999: 1,20.
— University of Hawai'i to present on interdisciplinary Masters of Educations, Lahaina News, September 9, 1999: 12.
— Al and Jane Nakatani to speak on consequences of human denigration, Lahaina News, September 9, 1999: 12.
— Beverly Gannon establishes scholarship for women in culinary arts, Lahaina News, September 16, 1999: 11.
— students to attend Ambassadors of the Environment summer camp, Lahaina News, September 23, 1999: 3.
— restaurant classes continue, Lahaina News, November 11, 1999: 11.
— Longhi's Restaurant to host "Music for Youth" benefit, Lahaina News, December 30, 1999: 18.
— conference to focus on women pursuing careers in science and technology, Lahaina News, January 13, 2000: 11.
— importance of technology discussed, Lahaina News, January 20, 2000: 3.
— SAT criticized, Lahaina News, January 20, 2000: 5.
— recent reform leads to request for charter school for performing arts, Lahaina News, January 27, 2000: 3.
— state rejects funding for Lahaina Public Charter School for the Performing Arts, planning continues, Lahaina News, February 24, 2000: 1,2.
— Christian Home Educators of Maui to hold Home School Conference and Curriculum Fair, Lahaina News, March 30, 2000: 12.
— Theatre Theatre Maui to hold drama classes, Lahaina News, April 20, 2000: 14.
— Lahaina Cannery Mall holds Millennium Essay Contest, Lahaina News, May 11, 2000: 17.
— Maui District High School Music Festival to be held, Lahaina News, May 11, 2000: 20.
— Summer Pals begins enrollment, Lahaina News, May 11, 2000: 20.
— Punana Leo O Lahaina expanding Immersion Program, Lahaina News, May 18, 2000: 1,6.
— Salvation Army to hold "Lokahi Back to School" program to support needy students, Lahaina News, June 8, 2000: 17.
— Nelson Tomas receives Mamoru and Aiko Takitani Foundation scholarship, Lahaina News, June 29, 2000: 7.
— two seniors from Seabury Hall win Paul Wood Performing Arts Awards, Lahaina News, July 6, 2000: 5.
— Environmental and Spatial Technology (EAST) Initiative to begin at Lahainaluna High School, Lahaina News, July 13, 2000: 1,14.
— students receive Department of Hawaiian Home Lands Hawaiian Home Commission Scholarships, Lahaina News, September 7, 2000: 19.
— conference on environmental education to be held at Maui Community College, Lahaina News, October 5, 2000: 16.
— University of Hawai'i at Manoa hoping to bring Masters of Social Work to Maui, Lahaina News, October 19, 2000: 21.
— students win Maui County Bar Association Arthur T. Ueoka Scholarships, Lahaina News, October 26, 2000: 14.
— Lahaina Intermediate School teacher Katherine Brown to become school assessment liaison, Lahaina News, November 2, 2000: 1,2.
— Lahainaluna High School students unveil Environmental and Spatial Technology (EAST) Lab, Lahaina News, November 16, 2000: 13.
— Punana Leo o Lahaina to hold registration, Lahaina News, February 22, 2001: 2.
— teachers and state at odds over pay, Lahaina News, March 22, 2001: 1,18.
— University of Hawai'i School of Social Work offering program, Lahaina News, April 19, 2001: 17.
— Project BEACON (Bilingual Education and Career Opportunities for Neighbor Islands) grant supporting University of Hawai'i students received, Lahaina News, May 3, 2001: 2.
— Senator Jan Yagi-Buen outlines accomplishments from 2001 session, Lahaina News, May 10, 2001: 10.

— Arts Education for Children Group to hold music and performing arts camp, Lahaina News, May 17, 2001: 18.
— new rule pushes students to settle overdue fees and detention hours, Lahaina News, May 31, 2001: 1.
— Maui Academy of Travel and Tourism Advisory Board awards scholarships to students, Lahaina News, June 14, 2001: 10.
— Carden Academy of West Maui elementary school to open, Lahaina News, June 14, 2001: 3.
— Craig Schulz named to National Dean's List, Lahaina News, June 28, 2001: 5.
— Taulia Marie Tu'ua graduates from Lewis and Clark College, Lahaina News, July 5, 2001: 5.
— University of Hawai'i offering new degrees through distance learning, Lahaina News, July 19, 2001: 16.
— Maui Economic Development Board to hold "Excite Camp" to expose girls to technology, Lahaina News, July 19, 2001: 9.
— online high school Hawai'i E-Charter to debut next month, Lahaina News, July 26, 2001: 1,18.
— Margaret Follett Haskins Scholarship Fund awarded to Maui Community College students, Lahaina News, July 26, 2001: 5.
— Ka Imi Naauau o Hawaii Nei to hold educational benefit concert, Lahaina News, August 9, 2001: 16.
— Ryan Michimoto wins Evans scholarship, Lahaina News, August 30, 2001: 3.
— Warren and Annabelle's awards college scholarships, Lahaina News, August 30, 2001: 9.
— Borders Books and Music holds "Teacher Appreciation Weekend", Lahaina News, October 11, 2001: 8.
— Parent Community Networking Center featured, Lahaina News, October 18, 2001: 1,20.
— Service Testing Parent Focus Group to meet, Lahaina News, October 25, 2001: 2.
— Groundhog Job Shadow Day to be held, Lahaina News, November 22, 2001: 8.
— Honolua Preschool accepting applications, Lahaina News, November 29, 2001: 2.
— Hilo Hatties to hold fundraiser for Maui high schools, Lahaina News, December 6, 2001: 8.
— success of local students Karen and Gayle Ancheta , Lahaina News, January 10, 2002: 1,18.
— editorial calling for a four-year college, Lahaina News, February 7, 2002: 4.
— alternative high school working on new home, Lahaina News, February 21, 2002: 1,18.
— Lahaina complex students among winners at National PTA Reflections Awards, Lahaina News, March 7, 2002: 1,18.
— Department of Education officials to discuss Hawaiian immersion program, Lahaina News, March 28, 2002: 1,20.
— meeting to be held on modified school calendar for Lahaina Complex, Lahaina News, April 18, 2002: 3.
— proposed modified calendar discussed at public hearing, Lahaina News, April 25, 2002: 1,2.
— mediators to patrol playgrounds of Princess Nahienaena Elementary School in response to bullying, Lahaina News, May 9, 2002: 1,20.
— modified school calendar to be discussed, Lahaina News, May 9, 2002: 2.
— modified school calendar to be discussed, Lahaina News, May 16, 2002: 1,20.
— "West Maui Education Day" to be held, Lahaina News, May 23, 2002: 17.
— dress codes discussed, Lahaina News, May 23, 2002: 5.
— volunteers sought as tutors for public schools, Lahaina News, May 23, 2002: 9.
— Napili Kai Foundation awards scholarships to college students, Lahaina News, July 4, 2002: 5.

— Maui Community College students wins Beverly Gannon Awards for Women in the Culinary Arts, Lahaina News, July 11, 2002: 8.
— Lahainaluna High School hosting students from Japan, Lahaina News, August 1, 2002: 1,24.
— Realtors Association of Maui awards scholarships, Lahaina News, September 12, 2002: 8.
— "I Love Lahaina" to raise money for West Maui Schools, Lahaina News, November 14, 2002: 3.
— "I Love Lahaina" raises money for local schools, Lahaina News, December 19, 2002: 14.
— "Wednesday is Tutoring Day in Lahaina" competition held, Lahaina News, December 26, 2002: 1,18.
— appreciation luncheon given to volunteer tutors at Lahaina Complex, Lahaina News, December 26, 2002: 2.
— West Maui Education Initiative (WMEI) featured, Lahaina News, February 6, 2003: 1,18.
— Mayor Arakawa details Tech Ready campaign, Lahaina News, February 6, 2003: 8.
— Lahainaluna High School marketing students win awards from Distributive Education Clubs of America , Lahaina News, March 20, 2003: 1,20.
— increased test scores point to effectiveness of "Wednesday is Tutoring Day in Lahaina", Lahaina News, April 3, 2003: 1,20.
— attorney Art Cernosia to present "Hawaii Application of Special Education Law", Lahaina News, April 24, 2003: 20.
— Maui District High School Music Festival to be held, Lahaina News, May 8, 2003: 14.
— Rotary Club of Lahaina awards scholarships, Lahaina News, June 5, 2003: 1,3.
— Realtors Association of Maui (RAM) awards scholarships, Lahaina News, June 26, 2003: 15.
— Academy of Travel and Tourism Advisory Board awards scholarships to Elissa Kahahane and Collette Cardoza, Lahaina News, July 10, 2003: 2.
— REAL Experience Anti-Tobacco Youth Summit to be held, Lahaina News, July 24, 2003: 2.
— Family Fun Festival to benefit Preschool at Kapalua, Lahaina News, July 24, 2003: 5.
— Kim Ball advocates to add surfing to school sports, Lahaina News, July 31, 2003: 12.
— A+ Program available at Princess Nahienaena Elementary School, Lahaina News, August 7, 2003: 2.
— Bruce Moore discusses school improvements in Lahaina, Lahaina News, September 25, 2003: 1,2.

EDUCATION, BOARD OF
— member Kelly King expresses views on, Lahaina News, November 17, 1994: 1,3.
— candidates for Maui seat listed, Lahaina News, August 6, 1998: 14.
— candidates to hold forum, Lahaina News, October 8, 1998: 7.
— candidates share ideas, Lahaina News, October 22, 1998: 1,2.
— candidates featured, Lahaina News, October 26, 2000: 23,25.
— non-voting student members sought, Lahaina News, December 28, 2000: 2.

EDUCATION, STATE DEPARTMENT OF
— decision to relocate Kamehameha III elementary school to Lahainaluna, Lahaina Sun, November 25, 1970: 3.
— requested to introduce surfing into high school curriculum, Lahaina Sun, January 20, 1971: 7.
— to hold budget hearings, Lahaina News, October 14, 1987: 3.
— offers free bus transportation to handicapped students, Lahaina News, September 5, 1990: 4.
— offering adult education classes, Lahaina News, January 16, 1991: 3.
— planning summer program at Princess Nahienaena School, Lahaina News, April 23, 1992: 4.

— to hold meeting on proposed Upcountry High School, Lahaina News, July 23, 1992: 7.
— warned of difficulty getting staff to move to Maui, Lahaina News, May 20, 1993: 1.
— looking to restructure budget and district staffing, Lahaina News, August 12, 1993: 1,15.
— not sure if Lahainaluna Intermediate uniform vote is valid, Lahaina News, August 1, 1996: 1,5.
— seeks input on accountability standards, Lahaina News, November 15, 2001: 2.

EDUCATIONAL OPPORTUNITY CENTERS ON MAUI (EOC)
— hold financial aid workshops, Lahaina News, January 11, 1984: 5.
— history of program on Maui detailed, Lahaina News, May 23, 1984: 16.
— facilitating universities that may offer degrees on Maui, Lahaina News, August 5, 1987: 3.
— offering scholarships to Maui Community College students, Lahaina News, January 10, 1990: 24.
— to hold financial aid workshops, Lahaina News, January 12, 1995: 4.
— to hold open house, Lahaina News, September 19, 1996: 14.
— holding workshop on reentering college, Lahaina News, April 23, 1998: 16.
— Maui Community College offering free financial aid workshops, Lahaina News, January 21, 1999: 2.
— to hold free college entry workshop, Lahaina News, May 31, 2001: 17.
— to hold workshop on college, Lahaina News, June 7, 2001: 20.

EDUCATORS OF THE PACIFIC, INC. [BUSINESS]
— scholarship winners announced, Lahaina News, May 21, 1992: 4.

EDWARD CARSON BEALL AND ASSOCIATES
— contracted to plan movie-house retail store complex at Whaler's village, Lahaina Sun, August 30, 1972: 11.

EDWARD JONES [BUSINESS]
— opens office in Lahaina, Lahaina News, February 11, 1999: 13.
— redesigned account statement receives praise, Lahaina News, June 3, 1999: 13.
— donates to victims of September 11th, Lahaina News, October 4, 2001: 9.
— holds grand opening at Napili Plaza, Lahaina News, February 14, 2002: 8.
— to open in Napili Plaza, Lahaina News, April 4, 2002: 2.
— ranked top by Kiplinger's Personal Finance magazine, Lahaina News, October 10, 2002: 8.
— Karey Anne Oura takes over office at Napili Plaza, Lahaina News, June 19, 2003: 8.

EDWARDS, CRAIG
— new president of Island Property Management, Lahaina News, August 26, 1993: 10.

EDWARDS, ELIZABETH [ARTIST]
— opens gallery, Lahaina News, January 10, 2002: 8.

EDWARDS, JACK
— running for mayor, Lahaina Sun, September 13, 1972: 4.

EDWARDS, NICK
— Member of Mind International, research organization searching for Atlantis, Lahaina Times, August, 1980 volume 4 number 7: 2.

EDWARDS, TONY [COMEDIAN]
— to perform at Comedy Club, Lahaina News, November 14, 1991: 17.
— to perform at Comedy Club and the Sports Page, Lahaina News, May 20, 1993: 9,10.

EFURD, LAURA
— Patsy Mink's legislative director to speak at Democratic Century Club, Lahaina News, August 21, 1997: 16.

EGER, WILLIAM
— announces candidacy for mayor, Lahaina News, July 15, 1982: 9.
— announces candidacy for mayoral race, Lahaina News, March 12, 1986: 12.

EGGED, RICK
— Waikiki Improvement Association President to speak to LahainaTown Action Committee, Lahaina News, January 2, 2003: 3.

EGGELING, DALE
— golfer to represent Royal Ka'anapali Golf Courses as touring pro, Lahaina News, April 11, 1984: 5.
— golfer's career described, Lahaina News, March 6, 1985: A10.

EGI, KAKO
— Scholar/Athlete of the Week, Lahaina News, March 4, 1999: 6.

EGLI, CAROLINE PETERS
— appointed vice president/administration of Kapalua Land Company, Lahaina News, April 30, 1998: 13.

EGYPT
— travel to described, Lahaina News, December, 1979: 10.
— newspaper owner recounts trip to, Lahaina News, September 30, 1987: 1,16.

EHRLICH, NATHAN "NATTIE NAT" [MUSICIAN]
— to perform at Polli's Mexican Restaurant, Lahaina News, June 27, 1991: 13.

EHRLICH, PETER [ARTIST]
— sculptor featured at Wyland Gallery, Lahaina News, February 21, 1990: 15.
— sculptor to begin three-island tour, Lahaina News, December 26, 1990: 12.

EIA MAKOU NA KEIKI O LAHAINA
— to be held at Lahaina Cannery Mall, Lahaina News, May 16, 1996: 4.

EICHERS, SAKURA
— appointed director of Asia and Pacific sales for Ritz-Carlton, Lahaina News, July 14, 1994: 13.

EIDE, KEVIN
— Napili resident invents soccer device, Lahaina News, October 11, 1989: 6.

EISELE, MOANA [ARTIST]
— to demonstrate tapa printing, Lahaina News, November 14, 1996: 14.

EISENBERG, LEWIS
— discusses Whalers Village Museum, Lahaina News, April 27, 1988: 3.

EISLEY, KEN
— named general manager of Lahaina Hotel, Lahaina News, September 20, 1989: 6.

EITING, JERRY [MUSICIAN]
— to perform at Sandcastle Restaurant, Lahaina News, June 29, 2000: 20.
— member of Maui Light Opera Company to perform at Va Bene Italian Beachside Grill, Lahaina News, May 30, 2002: 16.

EKA EHU KAI [MUSICAL GROUP]
— to perform at Lahaina Cannery Mall, Lahaina News, August 28, 2003: 17.

EKAHI SURGERY CENTER
— Hale Nani Partners sue state to establish, Lahaina News, May 26, 1994: 3.

EKE CRATER
— featured, Lahaina Times, August, 1980 volume 4 number 7: 1.

EKERLUND, STEVE [MUSICIAN]
— to perform at Stella Blues Café and Deli, Lahaina News, July 8, 1993: 12.

EKMAN, ROBERT
— appointed director of sales for Maui Marriott, Lahaina News, May 20, 1987: 3.

EKOLU [MUSICAL GROUP]
— to perform at "A Taste of Lahaina", Lahaina News, September 2, 1999: 18.
— to perform at The Westin Maui, Lahaina News, September 25, 2003: 5.

EL CRAB CATCHER [RESTAURANT]
— observing 12th birthday, Lahaina News, December 19, 1990: 12.
— Joe Montana, Lou Rawls, and Bob Seger each seen at, Lahaina News, February 20, 1991: 14.
— hosting musicians to try out new material, Lahaina News, June 27, 1991: 13.
— Bud Light casting for national advertising campaign, Lahaina News, August 19, 1993: 13.
— closes, Lahaina News, September 23, 1993: 7.

EL SALVADOR
— dangers of reporting on surfing in, Lahaina Times, October, 1980 volume 4 number 9: 2.

ELAN VITAL [BUSINESS]
— opens at The Shops at Wailea, Lahaina News, January 25, 2001: 14.

ELASTIC BAND [MUSICAL GROUP]
— to perform at Maui Sun Hotel, Lahaina News, May 19, 1994: 16.

ELDERLY
— hold party at Kalama Park, Lahaina Sun, March 14, 1973: 1,12.
— retirement community planned for Kihei, Lahaina Sun, March 14, 1973: 12,13.
— nursing home planned for Maui Memorial hospital, Lahaina Sun, March 14, 1973: 13.

ELDORADO MARKET
— holds Hawaiian blessing, Lahaina News, August 7, 1997: 5.
— celebrates 1st anniversary, Lahaina News, September 10, 1998: 11.

ELECTIONS
— results of 1970 general election on Maui, Lahaina Sun, November 11, 1970: 2.
— League of Women Voters registering young eligible voters at Lahainaluna High School, Lahaina Sun, September 29, 1971: 14.
— establishment Democrats maintain control, Lahaina Sun, March 22, 1972: 7.
— discussion of who can vote, Lahaina Sun, May 10, 1972: 20.
— Maui County Clerk advises people to register, Lahaina Sun, May 31, 1972: 7.
— Races for Maui County Council begin, Lahaina Sun, June 28, 1972: 21.
— upcoming election for Mayor of Maui County discussed, Lahaina Sun, June 28, 1972: 6,7.
— mayor Cravalho says he is voting for McGovern, Lahaina Sun, July 5, 1972: 4.
— list of candidates provided, Lahaina Sun, August 23, 1972: 11.
— Common Cause releases voting record of federal politicians, Lahaina Sun, August 30, 1972: 11.
— Bob Kelsey reflects on current political situation, Lahaina Sun, August 30, 1972: 19.
— updates on local races, Lahaina Sun, August 30, 1972: 3.
— Democratic candidates opposing Elmer Cravalho for mayoral race discussed, Lahaina Sun, September 13, 1972: 4,5.
— public transportation a topic in upcoming election, Lahaina Sun, September 20, 1972: 4.
— election details in the 6th district of the State House, Lahaina Sun, September 20, 1972: 7.
— election details in the 7th district of the State House, Lahaina Sun, September 27, 1972: 4,5.

— official ballot samples, Lahaina Sun, October 4, 1972: 11,18.

— mayoral primary described, Lahaina Sun, October 4, 1972: 6.

— City Council candidates described, Lahaina Sun, October 4, 1972: 6,7.

— public opinion poll results, Lahaina Sun, October 4, 1972: 8,9.

— results of primaries detailed, Lahaina Sun, October 11, 1972: 4,5,6.

— primary election results discussed, Lahaina Sun, October 18, 1972: 22.

— campaigns heating up, Lahaina Sun, October 25, 1972: 1.

— general election preparations detailed, Lahaina Sun, November 1, 1972: 4,5.

— results from general election, Lahaina Sun, November 8, 1972: 1.

— Manuel Molina speaks about his campaign, Lahaina Sun, November 15, 1972: 3.

— Mayor Cravalho's spending during, Lahaina Sun, December 6, 1972: 3.

— candidates described, Lahaina News, October, 1979: 2,13.

— commentary on value of two-party system, Lahaina News, September 1, 1980: 3.

— early endorsements noted, Lahaina News, June 1, 1982: 8.

— voter count may be down, Lahaina News, September 1, 1982: 2.

— voters allowed to choose which primary election ballot they use, Lahaina News, September 1, 1982: 2.

— Governor Ariyoshi reelection spending, Lahaina News, September 15, 1982: 10.

— editorial calling for the governors to debate, Lahaina News, October 1, 1982: 8.

— clerk explains nonpartisan election, Lahaina News, September 14, 2000: 1,24.

— primary election to be held, Lahaina News, September 21, 2000: 3.

ELECTIONS, OFFICE OF
— reports record number of people registered to vote, Lahaina News, November 5, 1998: 8.

ELECTRICITY
— electric generating station near Kealia Pond nears completion, Lahaina Sun, December 8, 1971: 8.

— Wailuku and West Maui lose power, Lahaina Sun, December 22, 1971: 15.

— Energy Extension Office offers audits for small businesses, Lahaina News, February 22, 1984: 17.

— rates fall, Lahaina News, September 11, 1985: 3.

— prices fall, Lahaina News, April 16, 1986: 3.

— costs fall again, Lahaina News, May 14, 1986: 3.

— costs fall again, Lahaina News, July 16, 1986: 3.

— prices fall, Lahaina News, August 20, 1986: 3.

— prices fall, Lahaina News, September 17, 1986: 11.

— still falling, Lahaina News, October 22, 1986: 5.

— rates rising, Lahaina News, November 26, 1986: 3.

— to cost less, Lahaina News, January 21, 1987: 3.

— Hawaiian Electric Company requests reduction in base rate, Lahaina News, February 4, 1987: 11.

— new rates in effect, Lahaina News, February 8, 1996: 6.

ELEGANT ILLUSIONS [BUSINESS]
— opens at The Shops at Wailea, Lahaina News, January 10, 2002: 8.

ELEGINO, JEWELRICA
— receives McDonald's Employee Scholarship, Lahaina News, July 19, 2001: 8.

ELEVENTH FARM CREDIT DISTRICT
— reports positive earnings, Lahaina News, December 6, 1989: 5.

ELEY, CHARLES
— to speak on Hawaii Model Energy Code at event sponsored by County Planning Department, Lahaina News, January 14, 1993: 3.

ELF, PAT [POLITICIAN]
— featured, Lahaina News, November 2, 1988: 1,15.

ELI, IRWIN
— doctor to speak on "Somatic Stretching for Lower Back Muscles", Lahaina News, May 9, 2002: 17.

— to teach environmental stress management techniques, Lahaina News, August 22, 2002: 20.

— to talk on "Environmental Stress" at 'Ohana Connection breakfast, Lahaina News, January 23, 2003: 17.

ELIES, JOEL
— receives commendation letter from National Merit Scholarship Program, Lahaina News, October 10, 1990: 6.

ELITE MORTGAGE [BUSINESS]
— Rebecca Ross opens, Lahaina News, May 11, 2000: 11.

ELITE PROPERTIES [BUSINESS]
— names Thomas Mitchell as president, Lahaina News, November 21, 1991: 11.

ELKIN, ED "JOR-EL"
— to present "Jor-El's World: Along the Conscious Trail", Lahaina News, February 1, 2001: 21.

— to talk on "Conscious Aging at Any Age" at 'Ohana Connection breakfast, Lahaina News, July 31, 2003: 17.

ELKINS, PAUL
— elected chairman of Republican Party, Lahaina Sun, October 20, 1971: 5.

— seeking Republican nomination for mayoral race, Lahaina Sun, July 19, 1972: 9.

ELKINS, TOM
— purchases KNUI radio station with Norma Phegley Craig, Lahaina News, September 15, 1980: 13.

ELKS CLUB
— racial criteria of membership criticized, Lahaina Sun, August 18, 1971: 10.

— change membership rules to allow non-whites, Lahaina Sun, October 13, 1971: 1.

— Maui lodge attempting to change "whites only" policy of national organization, Lahaina Sun, May 16, 1973: 4.

ELLEN [ARTIST]
— exhibit at Lahaina Arts Society featuring bird feathers and butterflies, Lahaina News, January 5, 1995: 11.

ELLER, BILL [SUPERINTENDENT FOR HAWAIIAN COMMERCIAL AND SUGAR CO.]
— discusses installation of new sugar cane technology , Lahaina Sun, December 2, 1970: 1.

ELLES, DIANA
— to speak at Women's Aglow, Lahaina News, August 19, 1987: 3.

ELLIKER, TERRIE
— appointed co-editor of Maui Press with Robert McCabe, Lahaina News, February 13, 1992: 12.

ELLIN, MARC
— named general manager of Hyatt Regency Maui, Lahaina News, October 14, 1993: 8.

ELLIOTT, JERRY [COMEDIAN]
— to perform at Comedy Club, Lahaina News, July 11, 1990: 15.

ELLIS, RICHARD
— to manage real estate portfolio of Hawaii Omori Corporation, Lahaina News, July 17, 2003: 9.

ELLIS, RICHARD [ARTIST]
— paintings featured at Marine Art Expo '84, Lahaina News, February 8, 1984: 17.

ELLMAN, MARK
— becomes sole proprietor of Avalon Restaurant and Bar, Lahaina News, November 29, 1989: 4.
— to be executive chef at Blue Tropix, Lahaina News, February 13, 1992: 13.
— sold Avalon Restaurant, Lahaina News, December 10, 1998: 17.

ELLSTROM, ROY
— appointed branch manager at First Federal Savings and Loan Association, Lahaina News, June 30, 1994: 9.

ELLSWORTH, J.W.
— named president of Aston Hotels and Resorts, Lahaina News, April 23, 1992: 15.

ELMER AND THE JAM SESSION [MUSICAL GROUP]
— to perform at Lopaka's Grill and Bar, Lahaina News, March 26, 1992: 18.

ELS, ERNIE
— to compete in Mercedes Championship golf tournament, Lahaina News, December 28, 2000: 1,7.
— to play in Mercedes Championship, Lahaina News, January 11, 2001: 8.
— golfer wins Mercedes Championship, Lahaina News, January 16, 2003: 12.

ELSNER, SUSIE
— Maui representative for Greenpeace interviewed, Lahaina News, September 26, 1984: 8,9.

ELVIS
— "The Lahaina Elvis" to perform, Lahaina News, April 24, 1997: 13.

ELVIS, BLACK [MUSICIAN]
— see Black Elvis [musician]

EMBASSY SUITES HOTEL [BUSINESS]
— plans announced, Lahaina News, February 5, 1986: 3.
— groundbreaking for, Lahaina News, December 10, 1986: 16.
— and shoreline erosion, Lahaina News, August 3, 1988: 1,18.
— scheduled to open in December; announces special offers, Lahaina News, October 19, 1988: 18.
— hosting "Maui Summer Music Splash", Lahaina News, August 8, 1991: 13.
— hires Rey Baysa as executive chef, Lahaina News, August 8, 1991: 8.
— purchased by partnership including Mike McCormack, Lahaina News, August 6, 1992: 6.
— to hold fundraiser for Maui United Way, Lahaina News, November 16, 1995: 5.
— employees honored, Lahaina News, November 30, 1995: 10.
— Marivic Padron named employee of the month, Lahaina News, December 7, 1995: 12.
— names Geri Vaughan as employee of the month, Lahaina News, March 7, 1996: 11.
— Anjun Tanveer named food and beverage director at, Lahaina News, March 14, 1996: 10.
— Dennis Quinlan appointed sales manager at, Lahaina News, August 14, 1997: 12.

EMBASSY VACATION RESORTS [BUSINESS]
— to feature comedy club, Lahaina News, September 10, 1998: 2.
— comedy to be held, Lahaina News, September 24, 1998: 16.
— to host Big Island Comedy Club, Lahaina News, October 1, 1998: 16.
— continues to host comedy performances, Lahaina News, March 11, 1999: 12.
— North Beach Grille featured, Lahaina News, June 1, 2000: 15.

EMC KA'ANAPALI CLASSIC
— pros Jim Colbert and Hugh Baiocchi join roster, Lahaina News, August 26, 1999: 7.
— to begin, Lahaina News, October 12, 2000: 3.

EMC KA'ANAPALI CLASSIC SENIOR PGA TOUR
— contest supports Maui non-profits, Lahaina News, April 20, 2000: 5.

EMERALD PLAZA
— Plaza I hold grand opening and Plaza II holds grand breaking, Lahaina News, August 9, 2001: 9.

EMERGENCY POSITION INDICATING RADIO BEACON (EPIRD)
— value for boating discussed, Lahaina News, April 12, 1989: 1,5.

EMERGENCY WORK RELIEF FUND
— lunched by Maui County, Lahaina News, November 15, 2001: 9.

EMERSON, KEN [MUSICIAN]
— offers demonstration at Lahaina Public Library, Lahaina News, November 11, 1987: 11.

EMERSON, NANCY
— reopening school of surfing, Lahaina News, November 26, 1992: 2.

EMERSON STRING QUARTET [MUSICAL GROUP]
— to perform at Maui Arts and Cultural Center, Lahaina News, November 18, 1999: 16.

EMICO FASHIONS [BUSINESS]
— opens at Lahaina Center, Lahaina News, January 14, 1993: 6.

EMK [BUSINESS]
— Radio Shack dealer featured, Lahaina News, July 4, 1984: 17.

EMMANUEL LUTHERAN CHURCH OF MAUI
— to hold Christmas Eve Service, Lahaina News, December 21, 1995: 6.
— to hold Lenten service, Lahaina News, February 19, 1998: 13.
— to hold midweek services, Lahaina News, November 26, 1998: 16.
— to hold Advent service, Lahaina News, December 9, 1999: 21.
— to hold soup supper, Lahaina News, March 9, 2000: 13.
— to hold advent services, Lahaina News, December 7, 2000: 25.
— to hold soup supper, Lahaina News, December 13, 2001: 17.
— to hold soup supper, Lahaina News, February 7, 2002: 17.
— to hold Lenten services, Lahaina News, March 6, 2003: 17.
— to hold Lenten service, Lahaina News, March 13, 2003: 17.

EMMANUEL LUTHERAN SCHOOL
— to hold Spring Carnival, Lahaina News, May 1, 1997: 16.
— to hold mass to celebrate 150th Anniversary, Lahaina News, September 11, 1997: 16.
— children to perform "Rescue in the Night", Lahaina News, May 15, 2003: 16.

EMMA'S ISLAND MOMENTS [MUSICAL]
— to be performed by Emma Tomimbang, Lahaina News, August 25, 1994: 16.

EMMERT, PAUL [ARTIST]
— exhibition to be held at Honolulu Academy of Arts, Lahaina News, September 5, 1990: 17.

EMORY, KENNETH
— discusses archaeological project at Pihana heiau, Lahaina Sun, August 25, 1971: 8.

EMPLOYERS OVERLOAD [BUSINESS]
— opens Lahaina office, Lahaina News, October 25, 1989: 10.
— expands, Lahaina News, August 12, 1993: 9.

EMPLOYMENT
— advice for students 16 years or younger, Lahaina Sun, March 17, 1971: 3.
— unemployment rate is 7.5 for February, Lahaina Sun, March 31, 1971: 1.
— Maui Chamber of Commerce studying creation of job bank for college graduates, Lahaina Sun, May 5, 1971: 5.
— Maui County hiring freeze, Lahaina Sun, September 22, 1971: 15.
— unemployment rate on Maui is 6.4, Lahaina Sun, June 7, 1972: 11.

— Maui Community College seeking part-time positions in Maui, Lahaina Sun, August 23, 1972: 9.

— unemployment rises in July, Lahaina Sun, September 6, 1972: 11.

— unemployment rate jumps, Lahaina Sun, November 1, 1972: 10.

— unemployment rate rises in September, Lahaina Sun, December 6, 1972: 13.

— improving on Maui, Lahaina Sun, January 3, 1973: 11.

— unemployment checks delayed, Lahaina Sun, January 10, 1973: 3.

— unemployment in Moloka'i and Lana'i dramatically higher, Lahaina Sun, March 7, 1973: 10.

— unemployment rate dips on Maui, Lahaina Sun, April 11, 1973: 11.

— unemployment rises in March, Lahaina Sun, May 9, 1973: 10.

— unemployment rate lowers, Lahaina News, May 15, 1980: 14.

— unemployment rose in March, Lahaina News, May 1, 1983: 11.

— residents of Moloka'i seek jobs on Maui, Lahaina News, December 2, 1987: 1,17.

— year's events recounted, Lahaina News, December 30, 1987: 1.

— Lahaina Public Library offering seminar on improving cashier sales skills, Lahaina News, July 6, 1988: 3.

— survey shows many workers live in Kihei, Lahaina News, September 20, 1989: 1.

— Maui Chamber of Commerce sponsoring panel discussion of labor shortage, Lahaina News, October 4, 1989: 5.

— Job Fair to be held, Lahaina News, October 4, 1989: 5.

— Maui Summer Job Fair to be held, Lahaina News, May 16, 1990: 5.

— Lahaina Job Junction job fair to be held, Lahaina News, January 16, 1991: 4.

— low in West Maui, Lahaina News, June 6, 1991: 1.

— warning that teenagers under 17 require Child Labor Certificate, Lahaina News, June 13, 1991: 4.

— Maui Job Junction to be held, Lahaina News, August 22, 1991: 4.

— Ka'anapali Beach Hotel proposing 3-day work week for workers living in Hana and on Moloka'i, Lahaina News, September 12, 1991: 1,2.

— conference on youth employment to be held at Wailuku Community Center, Lahaina News, September 26, 1991: 6.

— Lahaina Job Junction to be held, Lahaina News, January 23, 1992: 4.

— jobless rate improves, Lahaina News, September 10, 1992: 9.

— declined, Lahaina News, October 15, 1992: 8.

— Career and College Fair to be held, Lahaina News, November 12, 1992: 5.

— unemployment rate increases, Lahaina News, July 15, 1993: 6.

— jobless rate dips, Lahaina News, September 9, 1993: 7.

— Hawaii's Job Bank to be held, Lahaina News, November 5, 1998: 17.

— Job Safari to be held, Lahaina News, September 13, 2001: 9.

ENCARNACION, RENA

— new softball coach at Lahainaluna High School, Lahaina News, December 5, 2002: 10,11.

ENCORE CONSIGNMENT [BUSINESS]

— has moved locations, Lahaina News, June 25, 1992: 16.

— moves location, Lahaina News, July 30, 1992: 5,12.

— opens a new store, Lahaina News, December 24, 1992: 10.

— celebrates 10th anniversary, Lahaina News, August 9, 2001: 8.

ENCYCLOPEDIA OF MAUI

— Hawaii Visitors Bureau begins work on, Lahaina Sun, February 17, 1971: 3.

ENDANGERED SPECIES, THE [BUSINESS]

— store features eco-friendly products, Lahaina News, November 14, 1991: 7.

ENDEAVOUR [SHIP]

— crew sought for replica, Lahaina News, August 12, 1999: 7.

ENDING HUNGER WEEK CAMPAIGN

— fundraiser organized by "Hand to Hand", Lahaina News, November 16, 1988: 13.

ENDLESS SUMMER [FILM]

— creator arrested on suspicion of spying, Lahaina Times, October, 1980 volume 4 number 9: 1.

ENDLESS WINTER

— Warren Miller film to be shown, Lahaina News, March 21, 1996: 13.

ENDO, EICHI

— member of 100th Battalion featured, Lahaina News, May 21, 1992: 3.

ENDO, HARRY

— to present on opportunities after retirement, Lahaina News, April 26, 1989: 13.

ENDO, HARU

— to demonstrate flower arranging at Japan Gallery, Lahaina News, October 12, 1988: 3.

ENDO, PATTI

— to present on skin cancer at 'Ohana Connection, Lahaina News, February 20, 2003: 17.

ENDO, RAY

— promoted by First Hawaiian Bank to assistant vice president of the Kahului Branch, Lahaina News, September 12, 1990: 11.

ENDSLEY, PAT

— director of Wednesday is Tutoring Day discusses program, Lahaina News, April 10, 2003: 1.

ENERGY

— gas supplies adequate, Lahaina Sun, May 30, 1973: 3.

— electric power production increases on Maui, Lahaina Sun, May 30, 1973: 3.

— federal grants announced, Lahaina News, February 1, 1981: 16.

— County offers free energy audit, Lahaina News, October 15, 1981: 16.

— solar heating system installed at the Kihei and Lahaina Fire Stations, Lahaina News, July 15, 1982: 11.

— Maui seen as model for alternative energy, Lahaina News, December 20, 1989: 1,3.

— editorial in support of alternative sources of, Lahaina News, December 20, 1989: 28.

— Maui Electric responds to development of geothermal, Lahaina News, January 17, 1990: 14.

— public hearing set to determine environmental impact of geothermal energy transmission from the Big Island, Lahaina News, March 5, 1992: 3.

— Public Utilities Commission to require integrated resource plan, Lahaina News, March 26, 1992: 6.

— International Conference on Cold Fusion held at West Maui, Lahaina News, December 23, 1993: 1,4.

— Maui Electric Co. anticipates customer savings from programs to improve efficiency, Lahaina News, December 30, 1993: 1,12.

— Pioneer Mill planning to use cane to produce energy, Lahaina News, May 4, 1995: 1,20.

— energy crops not ruled out by Amfac/JMB Hawaii, Lahaina News, January 18, 1996: 14.

— "Breach for the Sun" workshop on solar energy to be held, Lahaina News, October 19, 2000: 20.

— state to hold forum on Distributed Energy Resources (DER), Lahaina News, July 4, 2002: 8.

ENGEL, DAVID

— performing in Herb and Scott Rogers Production show "Forever Plaid", Lahaina News, April 6, 1995: 12.

ENGELDORF, STAN

— Marriott International presents Leadership Excellence to, Lahaina News, July 4, 2002: 8.

ENGELDOW, JILL [WRITER]
— publishes book "Maui Magic, The Best of the Island" with M.J. Harder, Lahaina News, December 30, 1987: 3.

ENGELN, GUY
— new controller at Maui Youth and Family Services, Lahaina News, February 7, 2002: 8.

ENGLEDORF, STAN
— appointed as Resident Manager at Maui Marriott, Lahaina News, December 2, 1987: 3.

ENGLEDOW, JILL
— to hold Island Life 101 class, Lahaina News, July 24, 2003: 2.

ENGLEMAN, RICK
— appointed substance abuse program at Maui Youth and Family Services, Lahaina News, March 20, 2003: 8.

ENGLISH, BOBBI [MUSICIAN]
— to perform as part ot Kaleo O Kalani, Lahaina News, February 22, 1989: 9.

ENGLISH, J. KALANI
— named as Chief of Staff to Avery Chumbley, Lahaina News, January 26, 1995: 6.
— concerned with Malu'ulu O Lele, Lahaina News, January 16, 1997: 1,2.
— to speak to Democratic Century Club, Lahaina News, June 19, 1997: 17.

ENGLISH, MYRA
— Lei Day Hula Festival a tribute to, Lahaina News, April 26, 2001: 20.

ENGLISH SECOND LANGUAGE
— classes to be offered at the Maui Language Institute, Lahaina News, January 3, 2002: 16.

ENMARK, CAROLE
— appointed child-care coordinator for Hawaii Association for Education of Young Children, Lahaina News, January 30, 1992: 3.
— to participate in National Beef Cook-Off, Lahaina News, July 30, 1992: 4.

ENOMOTO, DUKE
— to speak at Reinstated Lawful Hawaiian Government meeting, Lahaina News, September 13, 2001: 1,20.

ENOMOTO, TOM
— purchases Azeka Place Shopping Centers, Lahaina News, November 14, 1996: 8.

ENOS, RICK
— owner of Compadres speaks of success of opening day, Lahaina News, April 24, 1991: 7.

ENRIETTO, ROBERT
— appointed to production development manager of State Film Industry Branch, Lahaina News, March 13, 1991: 7.

ENRIGHT, JOHN [ARTIST]
— to visit Sea Side Fine Art Gallery, Lahaina News, March 28, 1996: 12.

ENRIQUES, JOHN WAYNE [POLITICIAN]
— candidate for Makawao-Haiku-Paia Council Seat, Lahaina News, November 2, 2000: 22.

ENRIQUES, ROBERT
— new sales manager at the Ka'anapali Beach Hotel, Lahaina News, November 28, 2002: 8.

ENSERES [BUSINESS]
— opens, Lahaina News, August 27, 1998: 13.

ENTERTAINMENT
— cockroach race organized at Pioneer Inn bar, Lahaina Sun, January 26, 1972: 5.
— Chinese musical to be performed at Baldwin High School , Lahaina Sun, February 16, 1972: 9.
— night clubs and bars busier after legal drinking age lowered to 18, Lahaina Sun, April 5, 1972: 10.
— Kanu [play] shows at Kahului Fairgrounds reviewed, Lahaina Sun, May 31, 1972: 15.
— Jaleen Holm, theatrical director, looking at Maui as possible place for King Dodo Playhouse actors, Lahaina Sun, July 26, 1972: 11.
— Maui night life described, Lahaina Sun, August 9, 1972: 24.
— Barangay Fold Dancers and Nishizaki Dance Team participate in opening of Lahaina Amphitheatre, Lahaina Sun, August 16, 1972: 9.
— value of local pool hall discussed, Lahaina Sun, August 23, 1972: 5.
— Korean group to perform at Baldwin auditorium, Lahaina Sun, November 15, 1972: 10.
— American Indians to perform at the Maui Mall, Lahaina Sun, November 15, 1972: 11.
— caves used by Masa Hokama to store recording equipment described, Lahaina Sun, April 25, 1973: 15.
— belly dancing to be performed at county fair, Lahaina Sun, July 4, 1973: 21.
— Na Mele O Maui to be held, Lahaina Sun, July 11, 1973: 7.
— Disney characters visit Lahaina Farmers Market [ad], Lahaina Sun, August 8, 1973: 2.
— coin show organized by Maui Coin Club, Lahaina News, May 15, 1980: 8.
— autograph collecting discussed, Lahaina News, December 15, 1980: 13.
— annual glider contest held, Lahaina News, May 15, 1982: 7.
— Del Monte Corporation cut Donny and Marie Osmond from TV commercials, Lahaina News, August 15, 1982: 11.
— sales of Ferraris increases due to Magnum P.I., Lahaina News, September 1, 1982: 12.
— Zoo Fest 83 to be held, Lahaina News, March 15, 1983: 6.
— mayor Tavares reverses decision to turn lights off at some West Maui recreational facilities, Lahaina News, April 1, 1983: 6.
— films from the National Film Board of Canada to be shown at Lahaina Civic Center, Lahaina News, April 15, 1983: 6.
— coloring book, Lahaina News, July 1, 1983: 9,10,11.
— Lahaina News begins publishing a four-page supplement for children, which will typically not be indexed, Lahaina News, September 14, 1983: 3,7,8,9,10.
— Keiki section focusing on children in Lahaina, Lahaina News, September 21, 1983: 7,8,9,10.
— Bob Longhi's Total Experience party described, Lahaina News, September 28, 1983: 7,8,9.
— Halloween games printed, Lahaina News, October 12, 1983: A,D.
— Christmas activities section for children, Lahaina News, December 14, 1983: A,B,C,D.
— entrance deadline for Carole Kai Bedrace coming soon, Lahaina News, January 11, 1984: 10.
— Soroptimists International of West Maui to hold "Sweethearts Ball", Lahaina News, January 25, 1984: 5,6.
— song contest at Maui Community College begins, Lahaina News, March 28, 1984: 3,4.
— Maui Community College to host Ho'olaule'a, Lahaina News, April 11, 1984: 5.
— Joffrey II Dancers cancel Hawaii tour, Lahaina News, April 18, 1984: 5.
— pianist Wladimar Jan Kochanski to perform at Baldwin High School auditorium, Lahaina News, April 18, 1984: 5.
— attempt begins to organize 4th of July fireworks, Lahaina News, May 2, 1984: 5.
— Committee for Fireworks thanks contributors for July 4th display, Lahaina News, July 11, 1984: 10.
— benefit concert to be held for Church of Jesus Christ, Lahaina News, August 15, 1984: 3.
— featured article on what to do in September in Lahaina, Lahaina News, September 19, 1984: 7,8,9.

— Tongan luau scheduled at United Methodist Church, Lahaina News, April 10, 1985: 9.

— rise of video rental stores described, Lahaina News, August 14, 1985: 1.

— audience size limited and no alcohol allowed at Lahaina Civic Center Amphitheater, Lahaina News, October 16, 1985: 1.

— video store owners worry about vice raids over adult material, Lahaina News, October 16, 1985: 1,20.

— auditions for ballet to be held, Lahaina News, October 23, 1985: 20.

— public urged to look out for endangered Hawaiian dark-rumped petrel (Uaʻu), Lahaina News, November 13, 1985: 7.

— Hawaii International Film Festival to be held at Hyatt Regency Maui, Lahaina News, November 20, 1985: 3.

— Morca Dance Theatre to perform Flamenco, Lahaina News, January 15, 1986: 10.

— Maui Money Game created, Lahaina News, January 15, 1986: 7.

— Aku Cup celebrity golf and tennis to be held in May, Lahaina News, May 14, 1986: 4.

— Aku Cup celebrity golf and tennis event held, Lahaina News, May 28, 1986: 1,20.

— Keiki section focusing equal opportunities for children, Lahaina News, May 28, 1986: 7,8.

— Mickey Mouse and two original Mouseketeers to appear at luau at Maui Inter-Continental Wailea Hotel, Lahaina News, June 25, 1986: 3.

— Mickey Mouse and two original Mouseketeers appear at Maui Inter-Continental Wailea Hotel, Lahaina News, July 2, 1986: 10.

— West Maui's only movie house closes, Lahaina News, September 24, 1986: 1.

— "Austin on Tap" dance troupe to perform, Lahaina News, November 19, 1986: 16.

— Greater Lahaina Reunion 1987 being planned, Lahaina News, December 10, 1986: 3.

— editorial supporting Maui Motion Picture Coordinating Committee, Lahaina News, December 17, 1986: 2.

— Okinawan dancers and musicians to perform at Baldwin High School, Lahaina News, March 4, 1987: 8.

— day and time for open mike at Artful Dodger Feed and Read changed, Lahaina News, April 8, 1987: 20.

— movies at Wailea Shopping Village scheduled, Lahaina News, April 8, 1987: 20.

— soap stars from "The Young and the Restless" to appear at Wharf Shops and Restaurants, Lahaina News, December 9, 1987: 26.

— Peking Acrobats to perform, Lahaina News, January 13, 1988: 16.

— Panama Dancers to perform at Baldwin High School Auditorium, Lahaina News, February 24, 1988: 3.

— dancers from USSR to perform, Lahaina News, July 20, 1988: 1,4.

— Israeli folk dancing classes offered, Lahaina News, May 10, 1989: 12.

— "Miracle Landing" movie to be filmed at Kahalui Airport, Lahaina News, September 27, 1989: 1.

— events listed, Lahaina News, May 23, 1990: 13,14.

— Soviet acrobatic artists to perform at War Memorial Gymnasium, Lahaina News, January 9, 1991: 7,8.

— Maui Sun Talent Night Showcase to be held, Lahaina News, November 12, 1992: 3.

— 1-900 number available for updates on upcoming events, Lahaina News, December 30, 1993: 11.

— Peking Acrobats to perform, Lahaina News, January 20, 1994: 12.

— Lahaina Cannery Mall to hold "Shoot for the Stars Talent Competition", Lahaina News, October 30, 1997: 16.

ENTERTAINMENT BOOK

— to be sold by American Lung Association, Lahaina News, July 4, 2002: 2.

ENTREKIN/ZUCCO ADVERTISING [BUSINESS]

— to represent Maui Fudge and Ice Cream, Lahaina News, November 22, 1989: 5.

— Valley Isle Lighting a new client of, Lahaina News, August 29, 1990: 8.

— moves location, Lahaina News, February 27, 1991: 8.

ENVIRONMENT

— proposal to create a Committee on Environmental Control within the Maui County Council, Lahaina Sun, February 24, 1971: 6.

— hearings on air quality scheduled, Lahaina Sun, March 24, 1971: 2.

— Lahaina Outdoor Circle organizes meetings, Lahaina Sun, March 24, 1971: 5.

— testimony on air pollution, Lahaina Sun, March 31, 1971: 4.

— schools of dead fish appear off south shore of Maui, Lahaina Sun, April 21, 1971: 1.

— no explanation yet for schools of dead fish appear off south shore of Maui, Lahaina Sun, May 5, 1971: 1.

— U.S. Department of Agriculture approves program to develop natural resources in Maui County, Lahaina Sun, May 5, 1971: 1.

— Mayor Cravalho proposes banning phosphate soaps, Lahaina Sun, May 12, 1971: 1,8.

— seminar on conservation offered at Maui Beach Hotel, Lahaina Sun, June 9, 1971: 7.

— federal Water Pollution Control Advisory Board commends Maui for progressive planning, Lahaina Sun, June 16, 1971: 1.

— discussed in editor's commentary, Lahaina Sun, August 4, 1971: 2.

— illegal burning of refuse discussed, Lahaina Sun, August 18, 1971: 3.

— plan to create a nature reserve at Ahihi Bay, Lahaina Sun, August 25, 1971: 11.

— state to study report on environmental impact of proposed housing development in Napilihau, Lahaina Sun, December 15, 1971: 7.

— Maui County Advisory Committee studying air pollution controls, Lahaina Sun, December 22, 1971: 6.

— dolphin saved off Halfway Beach, Lahaina Sun, March 29, 1972: 9.

— criticism of environmental statements, Lahaina Sun, April 5, 1972: 4.

— discussion of concerns over public access to government information on, Lahaina Sun, April 26, 1972: 21.

— plans to kill star fish threatening coral off Molokaʻi, Lahaina Sun, June 28, 1972: 11.

— discussion of endangered birds, Lahaina Sun, July 26, 1972: 22.

— Mayor Cravalho announces creation of position for environmental scientist, Lahaina Sun, October 18, 1972: 9.

— study of Molokaʻi undertaken, Lahaina Sun, December 6, 1972: 12.

— discussion of importance of environmental quality control, Lahaina Sun, January 3, 1973: 9.

— hearing on limiting use of conservation districts, Lahaina Sun, March 21, 1973: 11.

— Ahihi-Kinaʻu reserve created, Lahaina Sun, June 27, 1973: 3.

— pineapple waste seen as source of energy, Lahaina News, July 1, 1980: 14.

— area on Haleakala set aside as bird sanctuary, Lahaina News, November 1, 1982: 7.

— County reminds property owners to keep frontage areas clean, Lahaina News, August 15, 1984: 3.

— Maui County Council and Maui Chamber of Commerce co-sponsor island-wide clean-up, Lahaina News, December 5, 1984: 3.

— editorial on misuse of pesticides in the State, Lahaina News, February 27, 1985: 2.

— tree planting scheduled along Alamaha Street, Lahaina News, June 26, 1985: 3.

— information sought by Maui County for shoreline access plan, Lahaina News, March 19, 1986: 3.

— Community Clean Up Day scheduled, Lahaina News, November 19, 1986: 16.

— State Representative Pfeil opposes spraying of marijuana plants with glyphosate, Lahaina News, December 10, 1986: 3.

— underwater cleanup scheduled, Lahaina News, August 19, 1987: 3.

— reef cleanup successful, Lahaina News, September 23, 1987: 3.

— Ocean Recreation Management Plan discussed, Lahaina News, October 7, 1987: 1.

— "Get the Drift and Bag It" results reported, Lahaina News, November 4, 1987: 10.

— comments sought for offshore mining environmental impact statement, Lahaina News, December 23, 1987: 3.

— Maui Chamber of Commerce hosting informational meeting "Garbage to Energy for Maui County", Lahaina News, January 13, 1988: 16.

— meeting on sea bed mining sponsored by Maui Chamber of Commerce, Lahaina News, January 13, 1988: 16.

— public hearing on offshore stripmining leases to be held, Lahaina News, May 18, 1988: 3.

— Coalition of Hawaii Against Ocean Strip-mining [CHAOS] to hold information meeting, Lahaina News, June 8, 1988: 14.

— Blue Ocean Preservation Society formed, Lahaina News, September 21, 1988: 3.

— beach clean-ups aid endangered species, Lahaina News, October 12, 1988: 1.

— importance of ocean awareness stressed by Richard Roshon, Lahaina News, November 16, 1988: 12.

— Pacific Ocean described to increase awareness, Lahaina News, November 23, 1988: 17.

— ocean awareness series describes lowest depths , Lahaina News, December 7, 1988: 7.

— ocean awareness series describes legends, Lahaina News, December 21, 1988: 15.

— ocean awareness series focuses on negative human impact, Lahaina News, December 28, 1988: 5.

— ocean awareness series focuses on impact of plastic, Lahaina News, January 18, 1989: 14.

— ocean awareness series describes locomotion among sea animals, Lahaina News, January 25, 1989: 18.

— ocean awareness series focuses on the Antarctic, Lahaina News, February 15, 1989: 12.

— ocean awareness series describes speed ocean animals can achieve, Lahaina News, February 22, 1989: 5.

— ocean awareness series describes Polynesian wayfinding, Lahaina News, March 8, 1989: 13.

— ocean awareness series describes the ocean's role in the food cycle, Lahaina News, March 15, 1989: 12.

— ocean awareness series describes diet of Humpback whales, Lahaina News, March 29, 1989: 5.

— ocean awareness series describes the Sperm whale and the jojoba plant, Lahaina News, April 5, 1989: 18.

— "Adopt an Access" program created, Lahaina News, April 12, 1989: 6.

— issues with fuel pollution at Lahaina Harbor discussed, Lahaina News, April 19, 1989: 1,13.

— sea mining discussion sponsored by Blue Ocean Preservation Society, Lahaina News, April 26, 1989: 3.

— ocean awareness series describes legends of whale graveyards, Lahaina News, April 26, 1989: 5.

— decline of turtle populations discussed, Lahaina News, May 24, 1989: 5.

— ocean awareness series describes damage done to the ocean, Lahaina News, May 31, 1989: 4.

— seminar on nonpoint source pollution, Lahaina News, June 7, 1989: 3.

— ocean awareness series describes impact of currents on travel, Lahaina News, June 7, 1989: 6.

— ocean awareness series describes passage from Okinawa to Japan, Lahaina News, June 14, 1989: 10.

— ocean awareness series describes travel to Bering Sea, Lahaina News, June 21, 1989: 9.

— ocean awareness series returns to Japan after rough seas in Bering Sea, Lahaina News, July 5, 1989: 5.

— conservation officials seek increase in fish population, Lahaina News, July 12, 1989: 1.

— summer fires expected, Lahaina News, July 19, 1989: 1.

— green algae abundant in West Maui, Lahaina News, August 2, 1989: 3.

— Mikel Mesh and Marie-Pierre Astier seeking support to save rain forests in South America, Lahaina News, August 2, 1989: 4.

— sunlight thought to be reason for overgrowth of seaweed, Lahaina News, August 16, 1989: 1.

— editorial urging probe into unusual algae growth, Lahaina News, August 30, 1989: 6.

— television series "NOVA" exploring marine pollution, Lahaina News, September 20, 1989: 24.

— volunteers sought for marine cleanup, Lahaina News, October 4, 1989: 3.

— algae bloom caused by nitrates from the land, Lahaina News, October 18, 1989: 1.

— State Division of Forestry to give away free seedlings, Lahaina News, November 8, 1989: 3.

— erosion in Honolua Bay to be studied, Lahaina News, December 27, 1989: 1.

— residents planning a recycling campaign, Lahaina News, January 17, 1990: 1.

— erosion continues in Honolua Bay, Lahaina News, January 31, 1990: 1.

— astronaut Scott Carpenter to speak for Earth Day, Lahaina News, February 28, 1990: 3.

— editorial listing achievements, Lahaina News, April 18, 1990: 8.

— Maui Hotel Association contracted with Maui Recycling Group, Lahaina News, May 2, 1990: 2.

— Earthtrust seeking volunteers and funds, Lahaina News, May 2, 1990: 3.

— Central Pacific Dive Club adopts a reef, Lahaina News, May 9, 1990: 1.

— sewage and waste oil dumping facilities at Lahaina Harbor planned, Lahaina News, May 23, 1990: 7.

— experts to study erosion at Honolua Bay, Lahaina News, June 13, 1990: 1.

— Crown of Thorns starfish found of Lana'i, Lahaina News, June 27, 1990: 1.

— Environmental Planning Associates, Inc. awarded contract to study coastal scenic resources, Lahaina News, June 27, 1990: 8.

— money raised by Mikel Mesh and Marie Pierre Astier, Lahaina News, July 4, 1990: 5.

— study finds no long-term effect of sediment runoff into Honolua Bay, Lahaina News, August 15, 1990: 1.

— schedule for recycling drop-off at Foodland, Lahaina News, August 29, 1990: 1.

— reef cleanup scheduled, Lahaina News, September 5, 1990: 4.

— Foodland to hold recycling drop-off, Lahaina News, September 19, 1990: 1.

— students to clean Lahainaluna Road, sponsored by Bank of Hawaii, Lahaina News, November 28, 1990: 2,3.

— limits to testing for pesticide residue discussed, Lahaina News, November 28, 1990: 5.

— Christmas tree recycling available, Lahaina News, December 26, 1990: 4.

— Festival of Trees to be held, Lahaina News, January 16, 1991: 4.

— large tree threatened by beach erosion near Honokowai Park, Lahaina News, February 27, 1991: 1.

— Maui Marine Art Expo to feature The Cousteau Society's "Australia: Fortunes in the Sea", Lahaina News, March 6, 1991: 13,14.

— Chez Paul hosts dinner for artists donating works for environmental causes, Lahaina News, March 13, 1991: 1.

— concert by Bill Oliver and Glenn Waldeck to be held at Maui Community College, Lahaina News, March 20, 1991: 11.

— Keep America Beautiful Day to be held, Lahaina News, April 17, 1991: 7.

— mayor Linda Lingle creates recycling/composting program, Lahaina News, April 24, 1991: 4,5.

— seaweed is blooming in Ka'anapali, Lahaina News, May 1, 1991: 1.

— U.S. Soil Conservation Servicing looking to move outlet of proposed Lahaina Flood Control Project, Lahaina News, May 8, 1991: 1.

— county to fight coastal erosion, Lahaina News, May 30, 1991: 1.

— old telephone books can be recycled, Lahaina News, May 30, 1991: 3.

— runoff blamed for shoreline problems at Honokeana Cove, Lahaina News, June 6, 1991: 1.

— telephone books can be recycled, Lahaina News, June 6, 1991: 3.

— termites to swarm soon, Lahaina News, June 6, 1991: 5.

— Honokohau Valley Association seeking to preserve culture, environment, Lahaina News, June 13, 1991: 1,18.

— Hana Steel, head of Maui County recycling, says Maui should recycle more, Lahaina News, June 20, 1991: 1,3.

— R. W. Munson to present to Napilihau Campaign Recycle Maui on recycling, Lahaina News, June 20, 1991: 3.

— Puamana Community Association to sue county and state for inadequate environmental assessment on Lahaina Flood Control Project, Lahaina News, July 18, 1991: 1.

— false kamani tree thought to be dead is growing, Lahaina News, August 1, 1991: 1,13.

— public meeting to discuss proposed National Marine Sanctuary around Kaho'olawe, Lahaina News, August 8, 1991: 7.

— public meeting to be held on proposed Marine Sanctuary for Kaho'olawe, Lahaina News, August 22, 1991: 3.

— Amfac may face new water rules due to TCP, Lahaina News, September 5, 1991: 1,2.

— Maui County recycling coordinator Hana Steel pleased with recycling efforts, Lahaina News, September 12, 1991: 1.

— Pioneer Mill Company plans to burn and harvest cane, Lahaina News, September 12, 1991: 3.

— LahainaTown Action Committee sponsoring "Once is not Enough Trash Bash", Lahaina News, September 12, 1991: 3.

— Reynolds continues to pay for aluminum cans, Lahaina News, September 12, 1991: 5.

— ground termites found in Lahaina, Lahaina News, September 19, 1991: 1.

— Campaign Recycle Maui formed, Lahaina News, September 19, 1991: 4.

— State aid sought to resolve seaweed growth, Lahaina News, October 10, 1991: 1.

— Community Work Day to hold clean-up of beaches, Lahaina News, October 10, 1991: 4.

— to recycle motor oil, Lahaina News, October 10, 1991: 4.

— motor oil drop-off sites available, Lahaina News, October 31, 1991: 4.

— Coastal Management chief Doug Tom to speak, Lahaina News, October 31, 1991: 4.

— state Department of Transportation to hold public hearing on Draft Environmental Impact Statement for Kahului Airport Master Plan, Lahaina News, November 7, 1991: 9.

— channels blamed for algae growth off Lahaina, Lahaina News, November 14, 1991: 1.

— The Nature Conservancy calls on government to help save endangered species, Lahaina News, November 14, 1991: 1.

— State and federal officials leaning against preparing an Environmental Impact Statement for Lahaina Flood Project, Lahaina News, November 28, 1991: 1,4.

— Maui County identify people failing to comply to mandatory cutbacks in water usage, Lahaina News, November 28, 1991: 5.

— appropriateness of shark hunt debated, following death of Marti Morrell, Lahaina News, December 5, 1991: 9.

— Maui Marriott to host Eco-Fair, Lahaina News, December 12, 1991: 5.

— Team Earth Company creates coloring book, Lahaina News, December 12, 1991: 5.

— Maui County to fund research on algae bloom problem, Lahaina News, January 2, 1992: 1.

— artificial reef sought for Puamana by resident Kim Roberts, Lahaina News, January 2, 1992: 3.

— Christmas tree recycling planned, Lahaina News, January 2, 1992: 4,5.

— composting operation starts in Waikapu, Lahaina News, January 9, 1992: 2,3.

— Amfac/JMB and The Nature Conservancy begin pilot program to protect native forests above Honokowai, Lahaina News, January 16, 1992: 1.

— Maui County Council chair Howard Kihune sees closing landfills as priority, Lahaina News, January 16, 1992: 1,4.

— Maui County allocates funds to study algae blooms, Lahaina News, January 16, 1992: 3.

— state representative Roz Baker seeks state funs for algae study, Lahaina News, January 30, 1992: 1.

— County Planning Commission will not require environmental impact statement for residential project in, Lahaina News, February 6, 1992: 1.

— federal money released for Environmental Impact Statement to study proposed road between Kihei and Ulupalakua, Lahaina News, February 6, 1992: 4.

— legislative panel approves study of algae, Lahaina News, February 13, 1992: 1.

— legislative bill seeks shark hunt, Lahaina News, February 13, 1992: 1,6.

— governor John Waihee proposes funding to deal with extinctions, Lahaina News, February 13, 1992: 4.

— treated sewage suspected as trigger for algae bloom, Lahaina News, February 20, 1992: 3.

— assessment of Lahaina Watershed project in Puamana released, Lahaina News, March 5, 1992: 1,4.

— public hearing set to determine impact of geothermal energy transmission from the Big Island, Lahaina News, March 5, 1992: 3.

— Business and Environment Conference to be held, Lahaina News, March 5, 1992: 9.

— mayor Linda Lingle says state recommendations to reduce algae bloom premature, Lahaina News, March 12, 1992: 1.

— Maui County wants rock wall to halt erosion at Honokowai Park, Lahaina News, March 26, 1992: 1,4.

— state court invalidated permit for Treu Geothermal Energy Co. for Big Island project, Lahaina News, March 26, 1992: 5.

— State Attorney General says fines against Maui County possible for effluent spills, Lahaina News, March 26, 1992: 5.

— Joe Souki backs shark hunting bill, Lahaina News, April 16, 1992: 1.

— Daniel Inouye calls for probe of algae bloom, Lahaina News, April 16, 1992: 1,9.

— Rick Reed asks mayor Linda Lingle to clear algae from beaches, Lahaina News, April 30, 1992: 1.

— deadline set for ruling on whether to require Environmental Impact Assessment for Lahaina Watershed project, Lahaina News, April 30, 1992: 4.

— legislature approves funds for algae study, Lahaina News, May 7, 1992: 1,6.

— Environmental Protection Agency warns state Department of Health that wastewater system needs to be operational, Lahaina News, May 7, 1992: 3.

— operator William Carroll at Wailuku-Kahului Reclamation Facility charges that County is not pursuing reclamation aggressively, Lahaina News, May 14, 1992: 1.

— mayor Linda Lingle announces recycling grant, Lahaina News, May 21, 1992: 4.

— State Algae Bloom Task Force to meet, Lahaina News, May 28, 1992: 3.

— State Algae Bloom Task Force to hold final meeting, Lahaina News, June 4, 1992: 4.

— divers call for halt to injection wells, Lahaina News, June 11, 1992: 1.

— alala chick successfully hatches, Lahaina News, June 11, 1992: 6.

— study required before shark hunt, Lahaina News, June 18, 1992: 6.

— flood control project goes forward without an Environmental Impact Study, Lahaina News, June 25, 1992: 1.

— beach cleanup requested, Lahaina News, June 25, 1992: 7,8.

— U.S. Army Corps of Engineers may construct vertical reef at Keawakapu, Lahaina News, July 16, 1992: 7.

— Pioneer Mill blamed for increase in mosquitoes, Lahaina News, July 16, 1992: 9.

— algae reported off Honokowai, Lahaina News, August 13, 1992: 3.

— survey of ocean following hurricane Iniki underway, Lahaina News, September 24, 1992: 1.

— Environmental Protection Agency to conduct own study on algae blooms, Lahaina News, October 1, 1992: 1.

— fishing ban not expected in whale zone, Lahaina News, October 22, 1992: 1.

— Daniel Inouye announces approval of funds to research green algae bloom, Lahaina News, October 22, 1992: 4.

— Surfrider Foundation to battle algae problem in coastal waters, Lahaina News, November 5, 1992: 1.

— wastewater report for South Maui finished, Lahaina News, November 5, 1992: 13.

— paint exchange program to be held, Lahaina News, November 5, 1992: 5.

— Federal environment officials developing study of algae blooms, Lahaina News, December 3, 1992: 1,3.

— guests complain about smell of algae, Lahaina News, December 3, 1992: 3.

— area of Kihei Peace Park to be devoted to growing native Hawaiian plants, Lahaina News, December 31, 1992: 8.

— Earthtrust to host presentation at Ka'ahumanu Center, Lahaina News, February 11, 1993: 5.

— bills being heard concerning algae growth, Lahaina News, February 18, 1993: 4.

— funds out to clear algae, Lahaina News, February 25, 1993: 1.

— Tamar Chotzen receives United Nations Environmental Leadership Award, Lahaina News, February 25, 1993: 6.

— attempts to save reef at Kaopala Bay, Lahaina News, April 29, 1993: 1.

— algae removal from beaches may lead to more erosion, Lahaina News, May 6, 1993: 6,7.

— reef study underway in South Maui, Lahaina News, June 10, 1993: 7.

— Eve Clute calls phosphorus as key to algae growth, Lahaina News, July 8, 1993: 3.

— Project ReefKeeper to conduct workshop on coral reefs, Lahaina News, July 15, 1993: 3.

— nearshore mud deposits inspected, Lahaina News, August 5, 1993: 4.

— brush near Wainee Village, Lahaina News, September 2, 1993: 2.

— dead school of fish found off West Maui coast, Lahaina News, September 9, 1993: 1,12.

— cane and other agriculture burning fees to rise, Lahaina News, October 7, 1993: 1.

— "Get the Drift and Bag It!" to include survey, Lahaina News, October 7, 1993: 3.

— Maui Sunset condominium to clean algae from beach fronting property, Lahaina News, October 7, 1993: 5.

— Maui Electric Co. promoting fluorescent bulbs, Lahaina News, October 7, 1993: 6.

— Kahana Outrigger emergency sea wall concerns residents, Lahaina News, October 14, 1993: 1,4.

— recounting of Kaua'ula wind of 1951, Lahaina News, October 14, 1993: 3.

— green sea turtle comes ashore at Royal Lahaina Resort, Lahaina News, November 11, 1993: 1.

— cleanup and beautification coordinated by Community Work Day, Lahaina News, November 18, 1993: 3.

— state has plan to keep anchors off the reef, Lahaina News, November 25, 1993: 1,3.

— recycling drop boxes installed at Olowalu Convenience Center, Lahaina News, November 25, 1993: 3.

— Sierra Club Legal Defense Fund has not served notice to the county, Lahaina News, December 30, 1993: 3.

— meeting to discuss freeways, Lahaina News, January 20, 1994: 3.

— artists promise to aid the Hawaiian rain forests, Lahaina News, March 24, 1994: 14.

— rules for whale sanctuary to be ready, Lahaina News, March 24, 1994: 2.

— brush fire destroys 250 acres above Ukumehame Rifle Range, Lahaina News, March 24, 1994: 7.

— state conducting ocean tests for injection wells at Lahaina Wastewater Reclamation Facility, Lahaina News, April 21, 1994: 3.

— Atlantis Submarines assisting University of Hawai'i in studying source of algae blooms, Lahaina News, April 21, 1994: 5.

— Community Work Day to coordinate with Keep America Beautiful, Lahaina News, April 21, 1994: 5.

— need for forest protection discussed, Lahaina News, May 19, 1994: 6.

— legislature criticized for eliminating position of deputy director of environmental health, Lahaina News, May 26, 1994: 1,20.

— Environmental Protection Agency inspection of Lahaina Reclamation Facility reservoir not made public, Lahaina News, June 9, 1994: 1.

— Pacific Island Conference to be held, Lahaina News, June 9, 1994: 6.

— National Oceanic and Atmospheric Agency (NOAA) to unveil possible rules for whale sanctuary, Lahaina News, June 23, 1994: 1,16.

— Hawaiian Islands Humpback Whale National Marine Sanctuary may include the entire state, Lahaina News, July 7, 1994: 1,7.

— "Litter Bugs Me" cleanup to be held, Lahaina News, July 7, 1994: 4.

— Project ReefKeeper to host workshops on coral reef conservation, Lahaina News, July 21, 1994: 4.

— heavy hurricane activity expected this year, Lahaina News, September 22, 1994: 3.

— value of proper landscaping discussed, Lahaina News, October 6, 1994: 10.

— restructuring of Department of Health may reduce number of deputy directors in Environmental Health division, Lahaina News, October 13, 1994: 1.

— volunteers sought for storm drain stenciling project, Lahaina News, October 13, 1994: 3.

— dead fish prompt call for conversation at Black Rock, Lahaina News, November 10, 1994: 3.

— workshop to be held at NiFTAL Center on nitrogen fixing trees, Lahaina News, November 17, 1994: 5.

— stagnant water in Kahana Stream moved by rain, Lahaina News, February 2, 1995: 1.

— bill would end roadside pesticide spraying, Lahaina News, February 23, 1995: 3.

— bills working through legislature, Lahaina News, March 9, 1995: 1,16.

— Cell Tech sponsoring seminar on algae, Lahaina News, March 16, 1995: 4.

— Bruce Anderson returns to head state's environmental programs, Lahaina News, March 30, 1995: 2.

— Lynn Hodgson expresses need to start controlling algae soon, Lahaina News, April 13, 1995: 1,20.

— Pioneer Mill planning to use cane to produce energy, Lahaina News, May 4, 1995: 1,20.

— impact of El Niño discussed, Lahaina News, May 4, 1995: 3.

— plans for sea wall at Honokowai Beach Park revisited, Lahaina News, August 10, 1995: 1.

— protection of discussed in hearings on the West Maui Community Plan, Lahaina News, August 10, 1995: 6.

— community-based algae tracking to start, Lahaina News, August 17, 1995: 6.

— West Maui Watershed Management Advisory Committee to spend money on seaweed clean-up, Lahaina News, August 24, 1995: 1,16.

— Hawaiian Islands National Humpback Whale Sanctuary educating residents about Endangered Species Act, Lahaina News, August 31, 1995: 1,2.

— biologists to study sediment in Honolua Bay, Lahaina News, October 5, 1995: 1,16.

— Wendy Wiltse discusses seaweed problem, Lahaina News, October 5, 1995: 3.

— West Maui Watershed Advisory Committee meeting to discuss seaweed monitoring and wastewater re-use, Lahaina News, October 26, 1995: 3.

— seaweed removed from beaches and water, Lahaina News, November 9, 1995: 4.

— Campaign Recycle Maui featured, Lahaina News, December 7, 1995: 13.

— motor oil drop-off program begins, Lahaina News, December 14, 1995: 19.

— state proposes new regulations to allow people to possess and grow endangered plants, Lahaina News, January 4, 1996: 3.

— surfers rescue sick turtle, Lahaina News, January 18, 1996: 2.

— issues shortchanged by media, Lahaina News, February 1, 1996: 3.

— scientists discuss seaweed problem, Lahaina News, March 7, 1996: 1,4.

— turtles plagued by tumors, Lahaina News, May 9, 1996: 1,3.

— Board of Water Supply asks chemical companies to pay for contaminated wells in Napili, Lahaina News, May 30, 1996: 3.

— volunteers sought to monitor nearshore waters, Lahaina News, July 4, 1996: 5.

— need to stop slugs discussed, Lahaina News, July 25, 1996: 6.

— safer way to kill insects, Lahaina News, August 15, 1996: 1,8.

— Michael Wilson discusses need to save threatened ecosystems, Lahaina News, August 29, 1996: 3.

— Lahaina Divers seeking divers to help with reef cleanup, Lahaina News, September 5, 1996: 19.

— algae control showing promise, Lahaina News, September 5, 1996: 4.

— Hono'ea Project to protect hawksbill turtles to meet, Lahaina News, November 7, 1996: 15.

— coral reefs being helped by Maui dive companies, Lahaina News, December 19, 1996: 13.

— oil response team forming at Lahaina Harbor, Lahaina News, April 17, 1997: 3.

— Maui Electric Company gives away high-efficiency showerheads in connection to Earth Day, Lahaina News, April 24, 1997: 7.

— volunteer training to be held for volunteers, Lahaina News, May 22, 1997: 16.

— Jonathan Holtquist awarded grant to study effects of fish feeding at Airport Beach, Lahaina News, July 17, 1997: 15.

— groundwater tied to algae blooms, Lahaina News, July 24, 1997: 1,3.

— Earth Maui Nature Summit to be held, Lahaina News, July 24, 1997: 9.

— Earth Maui Nature Summit to be held, Lahaina News, August 21, 1997: 7.

— Coral Reef Celebration to honor International Year of the Reef, Lahaina News, September 4, 1997: 15.

— Sea Grant at University of Hawai'i to track sediment, Lahaina News, September 4, 1997: 15.

— West Maui Watershed Management Project publishes "What Boaters Can Do To Be Environmentally Friendly", Lahaina News, September 11, 1997: 15.

— Get the Drift and Bag It to be held, Lahaina News, September 11, 1997: 17.

— Keka'a reef to be studied, Lahaina News, September 18, 1997: 1.

— "Get the Drift and Bag It" to be held, Lahaina News, September 18, 1997: 16.

— visitors told to avoid monk seals in Molokini Inlet, Lahaina News, October 2, 1997: 17.

— Department of Land and Natural Resources looking for snakes, Lahaina News, December 11, 1997: 11.

— big waves have eroded beaches in front of Sheraton Maui, Lahaina News, February 12, 1998: 1,3.

— Storm Drain Stenciling project to be held, Lahaina News, February 12, 1998: 17.

— state to hold meeting to discuss management plans for Ahihi-Kina'u Natural Area Reserve, Lahaina News, March 19, 1998: 13.

— State House of Representative passes resolution concerning Naval sound tests, Lahaina News, April 2, 1998: 1,9.

— Earth Day to be celebrated, Lahaina News, April 23, 1998: 7.

— Earth Maui Summit to be held, Lahaina News, May 21, 1998: 2.

— Earth Maui Nature Summit to be held, Lahaina News, June 4, 1998: 1,20.

— nene living near county water plant, Lahaina News, July 2, 1998: 1,20.

— state supporting recycling, Lahaina News, July 9, 1998: 12.

— signs installed to protect reefs, Lahaina News, October 1, 1998: 2.

— meeting to be held to discuss reef protection, Lahaina News, October 8, 1998: 1.

— reef clean up day held, Lahaina News, November 26, 1998: 2.

— partnership to protect acreage in West Maui mountains, Lahaina News, November 26, 1998: 5.

— Lahainaluna High School students remove alien plants, Lahaina News, November 26, 1998: 6.

— Pu'u Kukui Watershed threatened, Lahaina News, December 10, 1998: 3.

— "Between White and Blue on Maui" show to explore restoration of, Lahaina News, March 25, 1999: 16.

— Down to Earth offering to test water, Lahaina News, April 8, 1999: 13.

— "Keep Hawaii Beautiful Cleanup Day" to be held, Lahaina News, April 8, 1999: 3.

— Hapai ia Ka Hana Malama Aina community cleanup held, Lahaina News, May 20, 1999: 13.

— Lahaina Public Library to host presentation on soil and water conservation, Lahaina News, July 1, 1999: 12.

— former manager of Pioneer Mill worried about flooding after plantation closes, Lahaina News, July 15, 1999: 1,2.

— U.S. Navy to describe proposed grid of sonar-based sound transmitters, Lahaina News, August 19, 1999: 15.

— presentation on Pu'u Kukui Watershed to be held at Ritz-Carlton, Lahaina News, September 16, 1999: 1.

— Earth Maui Nature Summit to be held, Lahaina News, September 16, 1999: 1,16.

— Maui Community College to host workshop on propagation and sale of threatened and endangered plants, Lahaina News, January 27, 2000: 12.

— Maui Invasive Species Committee attempts to stop ivy gourd from spreading, Lahaina News, March 30, 2000: 3.

— high storms and dust, Lahaina News, April 6, 2000: 1,2.

— dust cloud photographed, Lahaina News, April 6, 2000: 3.

— petition circulated by Sophie Mataafa requesting Amfac/JMB to plant and irrigate former Pioneer Mill sugar fields , Lahaina News, April 20, 2000: 1,8.

— Drop and Swap Paint Exchange to be held, Lahaina News, April 20, 2000: 2.

— "Hot Topics" television show explore dust and flooding issues in West Maui, Lahaina News, May 18, 2000: 6.

— efforts made to protect Puʻu Kukui, Lahaina News, July 6, 2000: 1,14.

— Community Work Day Program coordinating "Litter Bugs Me", Lahaina News, July 13, 2000: 16.

— Friends of Haleakala National Park seeks volunteers to remove non-native pine trees, Lahaina News, July 13, 2000: 16.

— opposition mounts to U.S. Navy's plan to use LFA sonar, Lahaina News, July 27, 2000: 1,17.

— U.S. Army to hold public hearing on chemical weapons disposal facility on Johnson Island, Lahaina News, July 27, 2000: 20.

— "Exploring Hawaii's Coral Reefs" published by Pacific Whale Foundation, Lahaina News, August 24, 2000: 7.

— turtle freed from net, Lahaina News, September 7, 2000: 3.

— "Environmental Education in Hawaii: Looking Toward the Future" to be held, Lahaina News, September 28, 2000: 7.

— symposium offered on hurricanes, Lahaina News, October 5, 2000: 1,15.

— conference on environmental education to be held at Maui Community College, Lahaina News, October 5, 2000: 16.

— Hawaii Pacific University biology professor John Culliney to talk on "Ecosystems: Past, Present and Future", Lahaina News, November 2, 2000: 24.

— Anheuser-Busch Foundation donates money to help conserve the nene, Lahaina News, November 16, 2000: 12.

— West Maui Soil and Water Conservation District vice chair Wes Nohara discusses interim fix for flooding and dust issues, Lahaina News, December 14, 2000: 1,17.

— hearing to be set to discuss Northwestern Hawaiian Islands Coral Reef Ecosystem Reserve, Lahaina News, December 14, 2000: 9.

— Reef Environmental Education Foundation (REEF) seeks to support reef preservation, Lahaina News, January 25, 2001: 15.

— Department of Health examining use of hazardous materials at Pioneer Mill, Lahaina News, March 15, 2001: 1,22.

— U.S. Fish and Wildlife Service to hold public hearing on critical habitat designations, Lahaina News, March 15, 2001: 2.

— Project S.E.A.-Link offering marine naturalist training to high school students, Lahaina News, April 12, 2001: 20.

— residents planning campaign against Navy sonar, Lahaina News, April 19, 2001: 3.

— Project SEA-Link recruiting divers for "Great American Fish Count 2001", Lahaina News, July 5, 2001: 1.

— algae creating problems, Lahaina News, July 26, 2001: 2.

— U.S. Geological Survey planning reef survey, Lahaina News, December 20, 2001: 3.

— Makila Land Co. ordered by Commission on Water Resource Management to halt drilling in lands above Lahaina, Lahaina News, January 24, 2002: 1,18.

— Eric Brown of Hawaii Institute of Marine Biology to speak on reef health, Lahaina News, February 14, 2002: 2.

— volunteers preserving areas above Kaʻanapali, Lahaina News, March 21, 2002: 1,20.

— Eric Brown to present "Status of Hawaii's Coral Reefs: Should We Celebrate or Give Up", Lahaina News, May 9, 2002: 1.

— George Balazs to discuss sea turtle research, Lahaina News, September 19, 2002: 19.

— Maui Nui Botanical Gardens to hold native tree giveaway, Lahaina News, October 24, 2002: 14.

— director of marine mammal research program Paul Nachtigall to discuss methods for testing dolphin and whale hearing, Lahaina News, November 7, 2002: 3.

— commentary critical of new shoreline rules, Lahaina News, January 23, 2003: 5.

— West Maui Taxpayers Association to hold meeting to discuss proposed ocean setbacks, Lahaina News, February 20, 2003: 2.

— Hanakaʻoʻo Beach Park cleaned by sailors before leaving for Persian Gulf, Lahaina News, March 20, 2003: 3.

— U.S. Fish and Wildlife Service has grants for habitat restoration, Lahaina News, May 15, 2003: 2.

— Lahaina Watershed Flood Control Project draft Environmental Impact Statement to be discussed, Lahaina News, June 12, 2003: 14.

— Project S.E.A.-Link to conduct reef evaluation, Lahaina News, July 10, 2003: 1,20.

— residents helping to monitor reefs through Great Annual Fish Count, Lahaina News, August 14, 2003: 5.

— Maui Community College to host Watershed Forum, Lahaina News, September 4, 2003: 18.

— Zoe Norcross to discuss beach erosion in talk on "Maui's Dynamic Beaches", Lahaina News, October 9, 2003: 3.

— see also cane burning, pollution, sand, sea mining, specific issues and organizations

ENVIRONMENTAL AND SPATIAL TECHNOLOGY (EAST)

— initiative to install computer lab at Lahainaluna High School, Lahaina News, March 9, 2000: 1,16.

— initiative to begin at Lahainaluna High School, Lahaina News, July 13, 2000: 1,14.

— Zachary Dent receives scholarship from, Lahaina News, June 28, 2001: 1,22.

ENVIRONMENTAL COUNCIL

— seeking essays on public's role in protecting natural environment, Lahaina News, January 2, 1997: 3.

ENVIRONMENTAL PLANNING ASSOCIATES, INC. [BUSINESS]

— awarded contract to study coastal scenic resources, Lahaina News, June 27, 1990: 8.

ENVIRONMENTAL PROTECTION AGENCY

— studies proposed sewage treatment plant at Kahana, Lahaina Sun, March 14, 1973: 5.

— interim audit report discussed, Lahaina News, September 15, 1980: 10.

— asked to help solve odor from Lahaina sewage treatment plant, Lahaina News, October 23, 1985: 3.

— tells state to improve enforcement of sewage regulations, Lahaina News, June 18, 1986: 1.

— warns state Department of Health that wastewater system needs to be operational, Lahaina News, May 7, 1992: 3.

— wants bidding for injection well study , Lahaina News, July 2, 1992: 9.

— forbids more injection wells, Lahaina News, September 3, 1992: 1.

— to conduct own study on algae blooms, Lahaina News, October 1, 1992: 1.

— continues to work on algae growth, Lahaina News, May 27, 1993: 1.

— awards grant to Pacific Whale Foundation, Lahaina News, July 15, 1993: 5.

— inspection of Lahaina Reclamation Facility reservoir not made public, Lahaina News, June 9, 1994: 6.

— intends to issue more permits for injection wells, Lahaina News, October 6, 1994: 1.

— classifies second hand smoke as class A carcinogen, Lahaina News, November 3, 1994: 22.

— to hold hearing on injection well permit, Lahaina News, December 1, 1994: 1,16.

— to hold workshop and hearing on injection wells, Lahaina News, January 12, 1995: 4.

— to hold hearings on injection wells, Lahaina News, January 26, 1995: 6.

— hosts meetings on injection wells at Lahaina Wastewater Reclamation Facility, Lahaina News, February 9, 1995: 2.

— halts plans for new injection wells, Lahaina News, February 23, 1995: 2.

— to be asked by Kahana Sunset Owners Association to protect wetland at JBL development, Lahaina News, June 15, 1995: 1,12.

— biologists preparing case on Napili housing project for, Lahaina News, July 6, 1995: 3.

— earmarks money for watershed, Lahaina News, September 21, 1995: 2.

— reverses decision on injection wells, Lahaina News, December 14, 1995: 5.

— taking comments on injection well permit, Lahaina News, December 28, 1995: 12.

— frowns on sewage spill pact between Department of Health and Maui County, Lahaina News, February 22, 1996: 1,16.

— to hold hearing on injection wells, Lahaina News, March 28, 1996: 1,16.

— report indicates banned chemicals found in Maui water wells, Lahaina News, April 11, 1996: 16.

— to hold public hearing on injection wells, Lahaina News, April 11, 1996: 2.

— urged by residents to curb injection wells, Lahaina News, May 2, 1996: 1,3,22.

— issues county injection well permit, Lahaina News, June 27, 1996: 1.

— breast cancer data released by, Lahaina News, June 27, 1996: 3.

— studying algae growth, Lahaina News, July 24, 1997: 3.

— warns that injection well flow may increase, Lahaina News, April 15, 1999: 1,16.

— to hold open house, Lahaina News, February 13, 2003: 3.

— finds elevated levels of arsenic and lead near Pioneer Mill, Lahaina News, June 12, 2003: 1,2.

ENVIRONMENTAL QUALITY CONTROL, STATE OFFICE OF

— evaluating impact of the state buying Kapalua-West Maui Airport, Lahaina News, November 7, 1991: 1.

ENVIRONMENTAL WRITERS WORKSHOP

— to be held as part of Earth Maui Nature Summit, Lahaina News, August 21, 1997: 16.

EONA [ARTIST]

— work on display at Tradewind Gallery, Lahaina News, September 6, 1989: 4.

EPIC VACATION ADVENTURES [BUSINESS]

— opens, Lahaina News, December 17, 1992: 8.

EPILEPTIC FOUNDATION OF MAUI

— to meet, Lahaina News, January 28, 1993: 4.

— to hold Epilepsy Awareness Week, Lahaina News, May 9, 2002: 18.

EPISCOPAL CHURCH OF THE HOLY INNOCENTS

— see Holy Innocents Episcopal Church

EPPIC [MUSICAL GROUP]

— to perform at Lahaina Cannery, Lahaina News, July 12, 1989: 3.

EQUAL RIGHTS AMENDMENT

— Jeri Libner, president of the National Federation of Business and Professional Women's Clubs, speaks of political future of measure, Lahaina News, June 1, 1983: 6.

EQUUS [PLAY]

— to be performed, Lahaina News, October 27, 1994: 19.

— reviewed, Lahaina News, November 3, 1994: 24,26.

ERA MAUI REAL ESTATE, INC [BUSINESS]

— moves to new office, Lahaina News, November 19, 1992: 5.

ERASMUS, UDO

— to discuss "Fats That Heal, Fats That Kill", Lahaina News, February 25, 1999: 12.

ERDMAN, PARDEE

— named to Statewide Committee on New Communities, Lahaina Sun, November 10, 1971: 6.

ERFER, LYNN

— part of new management team at Ka'anapali Beach Resort Association, Lahaina News, February 1, 2001: 8.

ERIC GILLIOM PROJECT

— to perform at the Maui Arts and Cultural Center, Lahaina News, July 28, 1994: 15.

ERICKSON, TARAN [MUSICIAN]

— to perform at Miss Lahaina Pageant, Lahaina News, June 13, 1990: B4.

ERIK'S ON THE BEACH [RESTAURANT]

— reviewed, Lahaina News, June 20, 1984: 13.

ERIK'S SEAFOOD AND SUSHI RESTAURANT AND OYSTER BAR [RESTAURANT]

— opened by chef Christian Jakobsen , Lahaina News, August 7, 2003: 9.

ERIK'S SEAFOOD GROTTO [RESTAURANT]

— featured, Lahaina News, December 5, 1991: 24,25.

— owner Erik Jakobsen dies in automobile accident, Lahaina News, May 19, 1994: 5.

— featured, Lahaina News, November 6, 1997: 6,7.

— featured, Lahaina News, February 7, 2002: 5.

— to relocate, Lahaina News, October 10, 2002: 1,20.

ERLE, PRINSCILLA

— benefit to be held for, Lahaina News, October 9, 1997: 21.

ERLICH, PETER [ARTIST]

— to exhibit at Wyland Galleries, Lahaina News, December 19, 1991: 19.

EROICA TRIO [MUSICAL GROUP]

— to be hosted by Maui Philharmonic Orchestra, Lahaina News, February 20, 1997: 11.

— to perform at Maui Arts and Cultural Center, Lahaina News, April 12, 2001: 20.

ERSKINE, FRED

— discusses State Board of Agriculture plans to develop agriculture, Lahaina Sun, September 22, 1971: 15.

ERSKINE, MARK

— appointed Director of Marketing for Ka'anapali Beach Resort, Lahaina News, April 20, 1988: 3.

— director of marketing for Maui Marriott discusses hotels in Maui staying out of discount wars, Lahaina News, February 3, 1994: 6.

ERTE [ARTIST]

— celebrating 97th birthday; party scheduled at Circle Gallery, Lahaina News, September 26, 1990: 13.

ESCLITO, PAT JR.

— named chairman of American Cancer Society Residential Crusade, Lahaina News, March 19, 1986: 3.

ESCUDERO [SHIP]

— rumored to be heading to Maui, Lahaina Sun, February 7, 1973: 1,5.

ESPELITA, FEBELYN

— joins Cannon's Business College, Lahaina News, October 31, 1991: 10.

ESPERANTO

— lecture to be held on, Lahaina News, September 23, 1999: 12.

ESPINA, CHARLY
— radio personality moves to KPOA, Lahaina News, January 2, 2003: 8.

ESPRESSO CAFÉ [BUSINESS]
— featured, Lahaina News, January 16, 1985: 18.

ESQUER, RUDY [ARTIST]
— homeless coordinator for Department of Human Concerns seeks job training program, Lahaina News, February 10, 1994: 3.
— County Homeless Coordinator visits Light Bringers base, Lahaina News, July 27, 1995: 4.
— cartoonist featured, Lahaina News, January 11, 1996: 12.

ESQUIRE, RUDY [MUSICIAN]
— to perform at Taco Jo's Cantina, Lahaina News, September 16, 1993: 16.

ESQUIRE, VINCE [MUSICIAN]
— to perform at Hard Rock Cafe, Lahaina News, August 21, 2003: 15.

ESTATE OF JAMES CAMPBELL
— promotes Mel Kitagawa to asset manager for Maui, Lahaina News, December 21, 1988: 13.

ESTATE PLANNING
— video on now available at local libraries, Lahaina News, January 31, 1990: 5.
— workshop to be held, Lahaina News, May 12, 1994: 4.

ESTRELLA [PLAY]
— Filipino zarzuela to be performed at Baldwin Auditorium, Lahaina Sun, June 21, 1972: 19.

ETHANOL
— Department of Business, Economic Development and Tourism to hold workshop on, Lahaina News, November 7, 2002: 8.

ETHERIDGF, MELISSA [MUSICIAN]
— to perform, Lahaina News, May 30, 2002: 15.
— to perform at Maui Arts and Cultural Center, Lahaina News, July 18, 2002: 16.

ETHICS. BOARD OF
— clears JoAnne Johnson of complaints, Lahaina News, September 5, 2002: 1,2.

EUBANK, KEA
— wins first place in skateboard competition, Lahaina News, February 4, 1993: 6.

EUBANK, SPRING
— Lahainaluna High School track star featured, Lahaina News, April 21, 1994: 6.

EUBANKS, MARK [COMEDIAN]
— to perform at Comedy Club, Lahaina News, August 1, 1990: 11.
— to perform at Comedy Club and the Sports Page, Lahaina News, August 20, 1992: 18,20.

EUCALYPTUS
— seen as important for lumber industry, Lahaina Sun, June 13, 1973: 22.

EVANS, DAVE
— Records song "Operation Green Harvest" on cultivation of marijuana, Lahaina Times, July, 1980 volume 4 number 6: 1.

EVANS, SHANELLE
— joins SeaWest Designs as account executive, Lahaina News, March 14, 1990: 6.

EVANSON, MARY
— reelected to executive committee of Sierra Club, Lahaina News, February 13, 1991: 5.
— to be honored by the Sierra Club, Lahaina News, November 4, 1999: 12.

EVENING FUN AT W.M.Y.C.
— to be held by West Maui Recreation Department, Lahaina News, November 11, 1999: 12.

EVENING WITH KRISHNA DAS (A CHANTING NIGHT), AN
— to be held at Maui Arts and Cultural Center, Lahaina News, April 25, 2002: 16.

EVENS, LINDA
— hired by Tateishi and Apo as paralegal, Lahaina News, March 6, 1991: 9.

EVERETT, ALEXANDER
— to lecture, Lahaina News, March 25, 1987: 18.

EVERETT, GREG
— new manager of KAOI Radio, Lahaina News, August 19, 1999: 14.

EVERS, DALE [ARTIST]
— marine life sculptor unveiling new works, Lahaina News, January 19, 1995: 12.

EVERY, TANYA
— awarded Professional Community Association Manager designation, Lahaina News, May 13, 1993: 5.

EVERYBODY'S FAMOUS [FILM]
— to be shown at Maui Arts and Cultural Center, Lahaina News, November 1, 2001: 17.

EVIDENCE [TROUPE]
— to perform at Maui Arts and Cultural Center with Ronald Brown, Lahaina News, October 31, 2002: 29.

EVITA [MUSICAL]
— auditions to be held, Lahaina News, January 2, 1992: 5.
— auditions scheduled by Maui Community Theatre, Lahaina News, March 5, 1992: 5.
— to be held at Maui Community Theatre, Lahaina News, May 7, 1992: 24,26.
— continues at Iao Theatre, Lahaina News, May 14, 1992: 18.
— continues, Lahaina News, May 21, 1992: 18.
— last weekend of shows, Lahaina News, May 28, 1992: 18.

EWING, JAMES
— promoted to executive vice president at Bank of Hawaii, Lahaina News, September 26, 2002: 8.

EWING, JEAN
— promoted to personnel director at Hyatt Regency Maui, Lahaina News, April 24, 1991: 7.

EXCEL [FISHING BOAT]
— added to Captain David Hudson's charter boat business, Lahaina News, May 15, 1985: 20.

EXCEL FISHING CHARTERS
— adds another vessel to commercial charter fishing boats, Lahaina News, December 24, 1986: 8.
— adds third vessel to fishing charter operations, Lahaina News, May 6, 1987: 3.

EXCHANGE CLUB OF MAUI
— presenting annual Search for Talent at Iao Theatre, Lahaina News, April 27, 1988: 6.

EXPEDITIONS [BUSINESS]
— to begin Lahaina-Lana'i ferry service, Lahaina News, May 24, 1989: 8.
— ferry now owned by employees, Lahaina News, August 3, 2000: 14.
— ferry wins business award, Lahaina News, October 25, 2001: 3.

EXPLORING HISTORIC LAHAINA [BOOK]
— written by Summer Kupau, Lahaina News, June 7, 2001: 9.

EXTENDED HORIZONS SCUBA [BUSINESS]
— adds new dive vessel, The Extended Horizons II, Lahaina News, July 14, 1994: 13.

EXTERRA
— championship to be held at Aston Wailea Resort, Lahaina News, October 8, 1998: 15.

EXTREME SPORTS FILMS
— to show "Hit and Run" and "The End" surf and skate movies, Lahaina News, September 14, 2000: 9.

EXTREMITIES [PLAY]
— Maui Community Theatre to hold auditions for, Lahaina News, December 26, 1996: 10.
— to be produced by Maui Community Theatre, Lahaina News, January 30, 1997: 11.
— final weekend of, Lahaina News, February 20, 1997: 10.

EXTREMITIES OF EVERYDAY EXPERIENCE [FILM]
— shown at Princess Theatre in Paia, Lahaina Sun, May 5, 1971: 2.

EYECATCHER MAUI INVITATIONAL BEACH VOLLEYBALL CHAMPIONSHIP
— to held at Ka'anapali Beach, Lahaina News, March 1, 2001: 15.

EZAKI, GEORGE
— discusses Mayor's request for emergency powers, Lahaina Sun, December 23, 1970: 1.
— president of Maui County Board of Realtors complains that housing subdivision laws are unfair, Lahaina Sun, December 29, 1971: 17.

EZRA, DAVID
— federal judge rules against longliners, Lahaina News, August 10, 2000: 7.

F

F-53 [MUSICAL GROUP]
— to perform at Lahaina Civic Center, Lahaina News, March 15, 2001: 20.

FAA, CHIEF
— fire dancer returns to Sheraton's Aloha Luau, Lahaina News, September 3, 1986: 3.

FAAUMU, TIVOLI
— named Maui's "Top Cop", Lahaina News, November 28, 2002: 1,2.

FABRAO, LAURENCE
— named assistant front manager at the Royal Lahaina Resort, Lahaina News, March 9, 1995: 6.

FABULOUS THUNDERBIRDS, THE [MUSICAL GROUP]
— to perform at the Maui Marriott, Lahaina News, June 17, 1993: 13.

FACE THE NEWS [MUSICAL GROUP]
— to perform at Moose McGillycuddy's, Lahaina News, August 22, 1990: 13.

FACELESS [MUSICAL GROUP]
— to perform at Ka'ahumanu Center, Lahaina News, March 5, 1998: 16.

FAGAN, GARTH
— Bucket Dance Theatre to perform at Baldwin High School Auditorium, Lahaina News, February 21, 1990: 13.
— offering dance classes, performing at Maui Arts and Cultural Center, Lahaina News, March 29, 2001: 16,17.

FAHRNI, JENNIFER
— to perform in "Mad Cloak", Lahaina News, September 18, 2003: 18.

FAHSHOLTZ, TOM
— photograph of, at opening of Whaler's Village, Lahaina Sun, December 30, 1970: 6.

FAILLA, DON AND NANCY
— to offer seminar on marketing, Lahaina News, August 5, 1993: 7.

FAIR
— see Maui County Fair

FAIR, DEYBRA [ARTIST]
— to exhibit at Village Galleries, Lahaina News, December 15, 1994: 16.

FAIRECHILD, DIANA [WRITER]
— to sign new book "Jet Smart", Lahaina News, September 3, 1992: 18.
— to autograph her book "Jet Smart", Lahaina News, January 21, 1993: 4.
— to hold book signing at Whalers Book Shoppe, Lahaina News, April 1, 1993: 4.
— to sign books at Waldenbooks, Lahaina News, March 10, 1994: 4.

FAIRGROUNDS RELOCATION REPORT
— public input sought for, Lahaina News, March 8, 1989: 16.

FAIRWAY SHOPS [BUSINESS]
— under construction, Lahaina News, May 17, 2001: 8.

FAIRWAY SHOPS AT KA'ANAPALI
— Whalers Realty first business to sign lease at, Lahaina News, May 2, 2002: 6.

FALCONER, JAMES
— to run for West Maui County Council seat, Lahaina News, August 1, 2002: 3.

FALCONER, KIMO
— appointed vice president of Ka'anapali Coffee and Pioneer Mill Company, Lahaina News, July 17, 1997: 13.
— vice president of Ka'anapali Estate Coffee discusses terrace system in former sugar lands, Lahaina News, November 11, 1999: 1,3.
— Amfac/JMB to diversify crops in Ka'anapali fields, Lahaina News, December 23, 1999: 1,2.
— discusses future of agriculture in former sugar fields, Lahaina News, June 1, 2000: 1,6.

FALCONER, WILL
— to lecture on animal nutrition, Lahaina News, June 24, 1993: 8.
— to lecture on animal nutrition, Lahaina News, September 23, 1993: 3.

FALCONER, WILLIAM
— veterinarian offering animal acupuncture, Lahaina News, August 1, 1991: 5.

FALK, JAMES II
— Valley Isle Motors president receives Maui County's 2000 Entrepreneurial Success Award, Lahaina News, June 1, 2000: 14.

FALLA GUITAR TRIO [MUSICAL GROUP]
— to perform at Maui Arts and Cultural Center, Lahaina News, January 17, 2002: 17.
— to perform at Maui Arts and Cultural Center, Lahaina News, January 24, 2002: 17.

FALSETTOS [PLAY]
— to be performed by the Maui Academy Performing Arts and Maui OnStage, Lahaina News, July 21, 1994: 10,12.
— opens, Lahaina News, July 28, 1994: 14.
— reviewed, Lahaina News, August 4, 1994: 15.

FAME: THE MUSICAL [MUSICAL]
— to be formed at Maui Academy of Performing Arts, Lahaina News, May 19, 1994: 16.
— to be performed by the Maui Academy Performing Arts and Maui OnStage, Lahaina News, July 14, 1994: 15.

FAMILIA, LA [RESTAURANT]
— see La Familia [restaurant]

FAMILY COURT OF THE SECOND CIRCUIT
— looking for volunteers for Guardians Ad Litem (VGAL), Lahaina News, August 25, 1994: 5.
— seeking Guardians Ad Litem, Lahaina News, September 20, 2001: 2.

FAMILY DAY AND CONCERT ON THE GREENS
— held Athletic Awards banquet, Lahaina News, June 3, 1999: 13.

FAMILY FUN FESTIVAL
— to benefit Preschool at Kapalua, Lahaina News, July 24, 2003: 5.

FAMILY LIFE MARRIAGE SEMINAR
— to be held, Lahaina News, August 21, 1997: 9.
— to be held, Lahaina News, September 11, 1997: 2.

FAMILY OF THE YEAR
— won by Louise Aloy, Lahaina News, November 20, 1997: 1.

FANKHAUSER, MERRELL [MUSICIAN]
— returns to Maui, Lahaina Times, September, 1980 volume 4 number 8: 2, 3.
— to perform at Iao Valley Lodge, Lahaina News, August 15, 1990: 14,16.

FANTASEA [MUSICAL GROUP]
— to perform at Kula Lodge, Lahaina News, November 14, 1984: 17.

FANTASTICKS [MUSICAL]
— to be performed by Maui Academy of Performing Arts, Lahaina News, February 4, 1993: 7.
— to open, Lahaina News, February 11, 1993: 13.
— performances continue, Lahaina News, February 25, 1993: 12.
— final shows to be held, Lahaina News, March 11, 1993: 16.

FANTASY ISLANDS ACTIVITIES AND TOURS, INC. [BUSINESS]
— featured, Lahaina News, November 28, 1984: 18.
— sponsoring Toys for Tots, Lahaina News, November 22, 1989: 3.
— plans to build booth at Banyan Inn Market Place in trouble, Lahaina News, March 7, 1990: 1.

FANTUZZI [MUSICAL GROUP]
— to perform at Casanova's, Lahaina News, January 9, 1992: 14.

FAR NIENTE WINERY
— to be featured at Hyatt, Lahaina News, April 30, 1992: 14.

FARBER, JOSEPH
— hired by 'Ao'ao O Na Loko I'a O Maui to assist in planning for fishpond restoration project, Lahaina News, September 13, 2001: 9.
— member of 'Ao'Ao O Na Loko I'a O Maui (Association of the Fishponds of Maui) to give talk on "Ancient Hawaiian Fishponds", Lahaina News, October 4, 2001: 17.

FARBERROW, STUART
— police officer honored for saving lives, Lahaina News, June 17, 1999: 3.

FARDEN [FAMILY]
— featured in documentary "Puamana" at the Hawaii International Film Festival, Lahaina News, December 5, 1991: 20,21,22.

FARDEN, PUAMANA
— promoted to associate director of sales at Hyatt Regency Maui Resort and Spa, Lahaina News, October 10, 2002: 8.

FARM BILL
— U.S. Department of Agriculture to hold meeting on, Lahaina News, October 17, 1996: 14.

FARM SANCTUARY
— member Gene Bauston to speak on "The Dangers of Factory Farms", Lahaina News, June 5, 2003: 9.

FARM SERVICE AGENCY
— U.S. Department of Agriculture to hold elections for local County Committee, Lahaina News, August 7, 2003: 8.

FARMER, JOHN
— discusses public relations plan for Lahaina, Lahaina Sun, December 23, 1970: 8.

FARMER'S MARKET
— see Lahaina Farmer's Market

FARMERS MARKET
— to open at Valley Isle Resort, Lahaina News, May 23, 1991: 4.

FARMING
— Eric Brown's criticism of subsidies for farmers who do not grow anything, Lahaina Sun, December 16, 1970: 7.
— emergency cattle feeding program undertaken due to drought, Lahaina Sun, January 19, 1972: 19.
— Hawaii State Farm Fair to hold giant pumpkin contest, Lahaina News, February 27, 1991: 5.
— Honokohau farmers concerned about water, Lahaina News, August 20, 1992: 1.

FARNER, MARK [MUSICIAN]
— to perform in "A Walk Down Abbey Road" celebration of the Beatles, Lahaina News, June 13, 2002: 17.

FARNSWORTH, DIANE
— promoted to direct of Sales and Marketing at Napili Kai Beach Club, Lahaina News, August 12, 1993: 9.
— promoted to assistant general manager at Napili Kai Beach Club, Lahaina News, December 28, 1995: 10.

FASHION
— trend of women not wearing bras, Lahaina Sun, December 9, 1970: 5.
— show held at the Maui Hilton to benefit Easter Seal, Lahaina Sun, February 17, 1971: 8.
— show for men, Lahaina Sun, March 31, 1971: 3.
— benefit show for American Cancer Society held, Lahaina Sun, March 31, 1971: 4.
— David Malo Day pageant scheduled, Lahaina Sun, April 28, 1971: 1.
— debate over wearing bras discussed, Lahaina Sun, May 24, 1972: 7.
— Spring Fashion Show set for the Maui Lu Resort, Lahaina News, April 11, 1984: 3.
— "Styles of the Eighties" to be held at Maui Inter-Continental Wailea, Lahaina News, October 24, 1984: 4.
— description of situation in Maui, Lahaina News, September 4, 1985: 1,9.
— Hyatte Regency Maui to host show, Lahaina News, August 27, 1986: 3.
— Fashion show held at Hyatt Regency Maui, Lahaina News, January 21, 1987: 10.
— show organized by Ming Yuen and Tiger Lily, Lahaina News, February 11, 1987: 11.
— Wharf Shops and Restaurants to host show, Lahaina News, August 10, 1988: 3.
— suggestions for Christmas, Lahaina News, December 6, 1989: guide3.
— comments on the "ethnic" look, Lahaina News, December 13, 1989: 13,14.
— jewelry industry described, Lahaina News, December 13, 1989: 14,15,16,17,20.
— Maui Community College to offer classes on, Lahaina News, January 10, 1990: 7.
— Magic Moments Bridal Fair to be held, Lahaina News, February 21, 1990: 4.
— experts discuss trends, Lahaina News, December 10, 1992: 14.
— current trends discussed, Lahaina News, February 10, 1994: 12,13.
— Maui Community College Fashion Technology Department to hold annual Spring Fashion Show, Lahaina News, April 21, 1994: 13,15.
— swimwear featured, Lahaina News, June 9, 1994: 15.
— available at Lahaina Cannery Mall, Lahaina News, August 18, 1994: 13.

FASHION DISCOVERY [BUSINESS]
— opens, Lahaina News, June 27, 1990: 8.

FASI, FRANK [POLITICIAN]
— discusses campaign contributions, Lahaina News, September 1, 1982: 4.
— to speak to Maui Chamber of Commerce, Lahaina News, August 30, 1989: 5.
— to attend fundraiser for Linda Lingle, Lahaina News, September 6, 1989: 24.

FASTRAK [MUSICAL GROUP]
— to perform in Lahaina, Lahaina News, May 14, 1986: 12.

FATALITIES
— see injuries and deaths

FATHER DAMIEN STORY, THE [FILM]
— to begin production, Lahaina News, September 5, 1990: 6.

FATHER'S DAY
— contest at Lahaina Cannery Shopping Center, Lahaina News, June 15, 1988: 14.
— Kaʻanapali Beach Hotel offering champagne brunch, Lahaina News, June 13, 1990: 18.
— to be celebrated, Lahaina News, June 17, 1999: 16,17.
— to be celebrated at Kaʻanapali Beach Hotel, Lahaina News, June 14, 2001: 20.

FAUGHT & MIYAHSIRO
— advertising agency wins Pele awards, Lahaina News, February 22, 1989: 3.

FAUGHT & MIYASHIRO ADVERTISING
— promotes Sue Potthoff, Lahaina News, February 25, 1987: 3.

FAUGHT, TOM [ARTIST]
— commissioned to create ceramic pieces for Four Seasons Hotel in Tokyo, Lahaina News, January 23, 1992: 13.

FAULKES EDUCATIONAL TELESCOPE
— to be discussed by Jim Heasley, Lahaina News, November 16, 2000: 16.

FAULKNER, MONIQUE
— new food and beverage director at Maui Ocean Center, Lahaina News, December 6, 2001: 8.

FAULKNER, NIGEL
— named sales manager of Hyatt Regency Hotel, Lahaina News, May 29, 1985: 3.

FAURE, MARIO [MUSICIAN]
— to perform at Aloha Cantina, Lahaina News, December 15, 1994: 18.
— to perform at Aloha Cantina, Lahaina News, March 21, 1996: 12.
— to perform at Makai Bar, Lahaina News, September 19, 1996: 18.

FAWCETT-MCDERMOTT ASSOCIATES [BUSINESS]
— appointed to handle advertising for Kaʻanapali Beach Operators Association, Lahaina Sun, February 3, 1971: 7.

FAYE, MARIELIS [ARTIST]
— exhibiting at Sunset Gallery, Lahaina News, January 17, 1990: 13.

FEAST OF LELE, THE [RESTAURANT]
— opens, Lahaina News, May 6, 1999: 15.

FEAST OR FAMINE [PLAY]
— to be performed by Hui Noʻeau Visual Arts Center, Lahaina News, September 30, 1993: 14.

FEAST OR FAMINE II
— exhibit to be held at Maui Arts and Cultural Center, Lahaina News, October 29, 1998: 27.

FEDERAL AVIATION ADMINISTRATION
— approves environmental impact statement for extending runway at Kahului Airport, Lahaina News, September 3, 1998: 1.

FEDERAL BUREAU OF INVESTIGATION (FBI)
— targeting phone fraud, Lahaina News, January 6, 2000: 11.

FEDERAL COMMUNICATIONS COMMISSION
— conflict with local cable companies, Lahaina Sun, December 23, 1970: 6.
— ruling allows sale of KLHI, Lahaina News, September 8, 1994: 1.

FEDERAL GOVERNMENT
— expenditures in Hawaii to exceed $1 billion, Lahaina Sun, April 28, 1971: 4.
— grants from, Lahaina Sun, July 14, 1971: 12.

FEDERAL TRADE COMMISSION
— offers advice finding contractors, Lahaina News, July 31, 2003: 7.
— offers advice on finding reliable contractors, Lahaina News, October 2, 2003: 7.

FEELIN' [MUSICAL GROUP]
— to perform at Embassy Suites Hotel, Lahaina News, September 17, 1992: 15.

FEENSTRA, MARIAN
— new West Maui District Supervisor for the county Department of Parks and Recreation, Lahaina News, September 9, 1993: 3.

FEIGNER, EDDIE
— baseball player to play in exhibition game, Lahaina News, March 28, 1990: 9.
— "King of Fast Pitch Softball" to appear at charity softball game, Lahaina News, October 25, 2001: 13.

FEILD, RESHAD [WRITER]
— autographing at Waldenbooks, Lahaina News, January 27, 1988: 3.

FEIST, GORDON
— to begin class on Bonsai, Lahaina News, October 2, 1997: 18.

FELD BALLET
— to perform at Baldwin Auditorium, Lahaina News, January 13, 1988: 3.

FELECHNER, SHAUN
— junior golf player featured, Lahaina News, August 10, 2000: 6.

FELICIANO, GARRET
— wins football scholarship, Lahaina News, December 2, 1999: 9.

FELICIANO, JOSE [MUSICIAN]
— to perform, Lahaina News, March 20, 1985: 12.

FELICILDA, GORDON
— playing high school basketball, Lahaina Sun, January 20, 1971: 7.

FELICILDA, KAREN [TENNIS PLAYER]
— career described, Lahaina News, September 18, 1985: 4.

FELICILDA, KATHY [TENNIS PLAYER]
— career described, Lahaina News, September 18, 1985: 4.

FELICILDA, TINA
— joins Merle Norman Cosmetics, Lahaina News, November 19, 1992: 5.

FELINE FOUNDATION OF MAUI, THE
— to hold benefit whale watch, Lahaina News, March 16, 2000: 13.
— to hold benefit Whalewatch, Lahaina News, March 1, 2001: 20.

FELLOW TRAVELERS: TWO COLD WAR CONSPIRACY TALES [PLAY]
— to be held at Seabury Hall, Lahaina News, November 4, 1999: 12.
— being performed, Lahaina News, November 11, 1999: 12.

FELLOWS, JERRY
— appointed regional manager of West Maui for Aston Hotels and Resorts, Lahaina News, December 5, 1990: 4.
— named area vice president for West Maui by Aston Hotels and Resorts, Lahaina News, September 25, 1997: 12.

FELTE, KRISTOPHER
— promoted to head of the Kapalua Bay Course, Lahaina News, August 19, 1999: 7.

FENDI [BUSINESS]
— opens in The Shops at Wailea, Lahaina News, May 3, 2001: 9.

FENECK, DANA
— elected president of Ka'anapali Beach Operators Association, Lahaina News, January 30, 1985: 18.

FENG, JIANG TIE [ARTIST]
— work displayed at Dyansen Gallery, Lahaina News, January 27, 1988: 3.

FERGUSON, DAVE
— appointed as executive vice president of Management Consultants of Hawaii, Inc., Lahaina News, June 24, 1993: 10.

FERGUSON, DAWN
— to discuss "Children Singing Peace Around the World", Lahaina News, July 12, 2001: 16.

FERGUSON, SARAH
— Duchess of York visits Lahaina, Lahaina News, February 24, 2000: 14.

FERGUSON-OTA, AMY
— named Executive chef at The Ritz-Carlton, Mauna Lani, Lahaina News, November 19, 1992: 5.

FERLATTE, DIANE [WRITER]
— to speak during Children's Book Week, Lahaina News, November 5, 1998: 8.
— to present at Maui libraries, Lahaina News, November 12, 1998: 7.
— to tell stories at Lahaina Public Library, Lahaina News, June 15, 2000: 17.
— to perform "Have I Got A Story to Tell" at Kihei Public Library, Lahaina News, November 8, 2001: 17.

FERN, WOODY [WRITER]
— to read at Lahaina Public Library, Lahaina News, October 3, 1991: 5.

FERNANDA [HURRICANE]
— may hit Maui, Lahaina News, August 19, 1993: 1,16.

FERNANDEZ, ARTHUR
— appointed county information and complaints officer by Mayor Cravalho, Lahaina Sun, January 6, 1971: 2.
— mayor's public relations officer featured, Lahaina Sun, April 11, 1973: 4.

FERNANDEZ, JOHN
— County Director of Public Works discussing end of ocean dumping of sewage by county, Lahaina Sun, December 9, 1970: 2.
— County Director of Public Works discusses removal of sand from Baldwin Beach Park, Lahaina Sun, May 26, 1971: 8.
— County Director of Public Works named assistant director for 49th Maui County Fair, Lahaina Sun, June 23, 1971: 12.

FERNANDEZ, MARIO
— opens exhibit at Wyland Gallery, Lahaina News, November 29, 1989: 23.

FERNANDEZ, POPS [MUSICIAN]
— to perform in "Beyond Words", Lahaina News, October 4, 2001: 16.

FERRARI, DEBBIE
— see Glockner-Ferrari, Debbie

FERRARI, DOUG [COMEDIAN]
— to perform at Comedy Club, Lahaina News, July 18, 1990: 11.

FERRARI, MARK
— whale research described, Lahaina News, April 18, 1984: 9,10,11.
— additional discussion of research on whales, Lahaina News, April 25, 1984: 7,8,10.
— research described, Lahaina News, March 13, 1985: 11.
— studying whales off West Maui, Lahaina News, April 1, 1987: 1,8,10,22.
— gives update on whale research, Lahaina News, April 22, 1987: 3.
— to present to Maui Whalewatchers, Lahaina News, February 10, 1988: 3.

— comments on proposed thrillcraft corridor, Lahaina News, February 24, 1988: 1.
— discuss status of whales in the Pacific, Lahaina News, May 11, 1988: 1,12,13.
— Lahaina Intermediate School students host program to honor, Lahaina News, May 8, 1991: 3.
— see also whales

FERRARI RENTALS
— state files lawsuit against exotic car rental agency, Lahaina News, June 12, 1997: 15.

FERRARO, GERALDINE
— editorial praising Walter Mondale's choice of Vice-Presidential running mate, Lahaina News, July 18, 1984: 2.

FERREIRA, GEORGE
— proposes shopping center, Lahaina News, October 15, 1992: 14.
— critical of Kihei-Makena Community plan, Lahaina News, December 17, 1992: 12.

FERREIRA JR. GEORGE
— sues Abraham Aiona [police chief] and three newspapers for libel, Lahaina Sun, February 17, 1971: 5.

FERRER, SHERRILEE
— joins Tateishi and Apo, Lahaina News, May 2, 1990: 4.

FERRIES
— criticism of proposed interisland ferry, Lahaina Sun, November 10, 1971: 1.
— proposed ferry protested, Lahaina Sun, November 17, 1971: 12.
— interisland hydrofoil proposal is being student by State Public Utilities Commission, Lahaina Sun, November 24, 1971: 6.
— controversy over proposed interisland ferry dock at Lahaina discussed, Lahaina Sun, December 8, 1971: 14.
— editorial comments on interisland ferry dock for Lahaina, Lahaina Sun, December 8, 1971: 2.
— impact of Nixon's economic policies on Maui studied by Howard impact of interisland ferry dock in Lahaina discussed, Lahaina Sun, December 15, 1971: 4.
— possible landing sites for interisland ferry to be studied, Lahaina Sun, December 22, 1971: 13.
— West Maui Business Association does not take stand on proposed interisland ferry, Lahaina Sun, January 12, 1972: 7.
— plan for interisland ferry system slowed, Lahaina Sun, March 29, 1972: 3.
— hydrofoil service between Maui and Honolulu planned, Lahaina Sun, March 14, 1973: 5.
— update on developments, Lahaina Sun, May 23, 1973: 15.
— Kentron Hawaii Ltd seeking to bring jetfoil service to Maui, Lahaina Sun, May 30, 1973: 5.
— Ma'alaea likely location for terminal, Lahaina Sun, June 27, 1973: 6.
— Pacific Sea Transportation, Inc. to hold public meetings on interisland hydrofoil service, Lahaina Sun, August 22, 1973: 6.

FERRIS, IDA
— appointed branch manager of American Savings Bank, Lahaina News, July 10, 1997: 12.

FERRO, DOMINICK [MUSICIAN]
— to perform at Moondoggies, Lahaina News, June 2, 1994: 12.
— to perform at Moondoggies, Lahaina News, September 15, 1994: 15.
— to perform at Compadres Bar and Grill, Lahaina News, August 22, 1996: 16.
— to perform at Compadres Bar and Grill, Lahaina News, September 19, 1996: 18.

FERRUCCI, MIKE [COMEDIAN]
— to perform at Comedy Club, Lahaina News, October 3, 1991: 12.

FESTIVAL OF ARTS AND FLOWERS
— to be held, Lahaina News, November 6, 1997: 2.
— to be held, Lahaina News, November 12, 1998: 7.

— to be held, Lahaina News, November 19, 1998: 5.
— to be held, Lahaina News, November 18, 1999: 6.
— to be held, Lahaina News, November 25, 1999: 1,20.
— to be held, Lahaina News, December 2, 1999: 1,3.
— held, Lahaina News, December 9, 1999: 1.
— to be held by LahainaTown Action Committee, Lahaina News, November 30, 2000: 16.
— to be held, Lahaina News, November 29, 2001: 1,18.

FESTIVAL OF CANOES
— to be held, Lahaina News, May 7, 1998: 1.

FESTIVAL OF CANOES PARADE
— to be held, Lahaina News, May 27, 1999: 1,16.

FESTIVAL OF CAROLS
— to be held at Kapalua Bay Hotel, Lahaina News, December 11, 1985: 3.
— organized by Kapalua Music Assembly and Maui Community College, Lahaina News, December 3, 1986: 12.

FESTIVAL OF DRUMS
— to be held at Lahaina Cannery Mall, Lahaina News, February 13, 2003: 14.

FESTIVAL OF HARPS
— to be held at Maui Arts and Cultural Center, Lahaina News, December 2, 1999: 16.
— to be held at Maui Arts and Cultural Center, Lahaina News, November 29, 2001: 17.

FESTIVAL OF HULA
— to be held at Lahaina Cannery Mall, Lahaina News, April 3, 1997: 13.
— held at Lahaina Cannery Mall, Lahaina News, February 17, 2000: 15.
— to be held, Lahaina News, January 25, 2001: 17.
— held, Lahaina News, February 1, 2001: 3.
— to be held at Lahaina Cannery Mall, Lahaina News, January 16, 2003: 14.

FESTIVAL OF JOY
— cultural celebration to be held at Maui Dharma Center Temple Fund, Lahaina News, May 31, 2001: 16.

FESTIVAL OF KINGS KARATE TOURNAMENT
— held at Maui Marriott Resort, Lahaina News, October 17, 1990: 8,9.
— held, Lahaina News, August 12, 1999: 6.
— to be held, Lahaina News, July 27, 2000: 6.

FESTIVAL OF LIGHTS
— celebration to be held, Lahaina News, December 7, 1995: 7,14.
— to be held, Lahaina News, December 5, 1996: 14.

FESTIVAL OF PACIFIC ISLAND ARTS AND CULTURE
— to be held, Lahaina News, May 20, 1999: 8.

FESTIVAL OF RUNNING
— results, Lahaina News, November 28, 1990: 20.

FESTIVAL OF THE BANDS
— competition to take place at Maui Mall, Lahaina News, October 24, 1984: 3.
— to be held at Maui Mall, Lahaina News, August 8, 1990: 13.
— event detailed, Lahaina News, November 21, 1990: 15.
— to be held, Lahaina News, November 28, 1990: 10.

FESTIVAL OF THE GREAT MOTHER
— to be held at Kihei Community Center, Lahaina News, October 10, 1991: 4.

FESTIVAL OF TREES
— winners announced, Lahaina News, December 23, 1987: 14.
— to be held at Lahaina Cannery Shopping Center, Lahaina News, December 19, 1990: 3.
— to be held, Lahaina News, January 16, 1991: 4.
— to be held at Lahaina Cannery Mall, Lahaina News, January 13, 2000: 5.

FESTIVAL OF WHEELS
— to be held to benefit the Arthritis Foundation, Lahaina News, April 10, 1997: 13.
— to be held, Lahaina News, April 17, 1997: 12.

FESTIVAL OF WREATHS
— to be held, Lahaina News, December 17, 1992: 4.

FESTIVAL SINGERS [MUSICAL GROUP]
— to perform, Lahaina News, March 16, 1988: 14.

FESTIVAL, THE [MUSICAL]
— to be performed by Up With People, Lahaina News, October 31, 1996: 18,19.

FICARRA, JAMIE
— Scholar/Athlete of the Week, Lahaina News, October 31, 1996: 15.
— Lahaina Swim Club member breaks swim record, Lahaina News, July 2, 1998: 15.
— Marine Corps Private completes basic training at the Marine Corps Recruit Depot, Lahaina News, March 1, 2001: 10.

FIELD, GEORGE
— physicist to lecture on eclipse, Lahaina News, July 4, 1991: 3.

FIELD, MICHAEL
— scientist to speak on reefs, Lahaina News, January 23, 2003: 2.

FIELDING, ANN [WRITER]
— marine biologist to discuss "Uniqueness of Hawaii's Marine Life", Lahaina News, September 21, 2000: 21.
— to speak on Hawaii marine life, Lahaina News, April 10, 2003: 21.

FIELDS, DAN
— to direct "HOT L BALTIMORE", Lahaina News, May 23, 2002: 15.

FIELDS, RICHARD [ARTIST]
— autographs copies of "Haleakala Sunrise" poster, Lahaina News, March 1, 1989: 5.
— exhibit opens at Whalers Village, Lahaina News, January 3, 1990: 16.
— to sign copies of poster "Haleakala Sunrise", Lahaina News, January 17, 1990: 12.
— exhibiting at Lahaina Printsellers Gallery, Lahaina News, February 20, 1991: 12.

FIESTA AND AUCTION
— to be held by Lahaina Rotary Club, Lahaina News, May 13, 1999: 15.
— Rotary Club to hold, Lahaina News, May 18, 2000: 20.

FIFTH AVENUE MIL [BUSINESS]
— featured, Lahaina News, June 15, 1983: 11.

FIFTH OF JULY [PLAY]
— Maui Community Theatre holding auditions for, Lahaina News, April 6, 1988: 3.
— to open at Iao Theatre, Lahaina News, June 1, 1988: 19.

FIGG, SUSAN
— to be stage manager for ESPN at Maui Invitational basketball, Lahaina News, October 22, 1998: 17.

FIJI [MUSICAL GROUP]
— to perform at Alexander and Baldwin Community Fair, Lahaina News, August 26, 1999: 15.
— to perform at benefit concert for Hui O Wa'a Kaulua, Lahaina News, November 8, 2001: 14.
— to perform at Maui Summer Music Festival, Lahaina News, June 27, 2002: 1,2.

FILIPINO CATHOLIC CLUB
— offering special mass to honor military serving in Gulf War, Lahaina News, February 20, 1991: 3.
— to hold Flores de Mayo fundraiser, Lahaina News, April 23, 1998: 16.
— to hold dinner dance fundraiser, Lahaina News, September 23, 1999: 12.

FILIPINO COUNCIL BALL
— to be held, Lahaina News, February 11, 1993: 15.

FILIPINOS
— surveyed by University of Hawaii, Lahaina Sun, October 25, 1972: 9.

FILLAZAR, ART
— Lahainaluna High School teacher featured, Lahaina News, November 7, 1991: 3.
— awarded Warren E. Shull Advisor-of-the-Year for Hawaii, Lahaina News, May 7, 1992: 4.
— wins Maui District's Teacher of the Year and Earl Reum Award, Lahaina News, November 18, 1999: 3.
— Lahainaluna High School student activities coordinator featured, Lahaina News, February 6, 2003: 1,20.

FILMS
— Family Film Festival announced, Lahaina Sun, January 27, 1971: 2.
— filming on Maui coordinated by Diners/Fugazy Travel & Incentive Company, Lahaina Sun, March 31, 1971: 5.
— two films on England shown at Lahaina library, Lahaina Sun, April 7, 1971: 3.
— experimental films shown at Princess Theatre in Paia, Lahaina Sun, May 5, 1971: 2.
— situation in Lahaina discussed, Lahaina Sun, May 12, 1971: 5.
— short films presented in Paia and Lahaina, Lahaina Sun, October 20, 1971: 4.
— Maui public libraries to show films, Lahaina Sun, October 27, 1971: 11.
— collection of experimental films to be shown, Lahaina Sun, October 27, 1971: 14.
— Maui Community College film series announced, Lahaina News, January 15, 1981: 15.
— Wailea Shopping Village hosting movie classic series, Lahaina News, February 4, 1987: 3,11.
— Hawaii International Film Festival extended, Lahaina News, January 13, 1988: 3,16.
— movie theatre breaks ground at Wharf Shops and Restaurants, Lahaina News, May 18, 1988: 1.
— Hawaii International Film Festival to begin on Maui, Lahaina News, November 30, 1988: 10.
— Foreign Film Festival to be presented by Maui Youth Theatre, Lahaina News, June 6, 1990: 13.
— The Father Damien Story to begin production, Lahaina News, September 5, 1990: 6.
— Hawaii International Film Festival to be held at Maui Inter-Continental Wailea, Lahaina News, October 17, 1991: 20.
— Hawaiian International Film Festival to be held in December, Lahaina News, November 7, 1991: 18.
— "Conference on Motion Picture Production, Co-financing—East and West" to be held, Lahaina News, November 14, 1991: 8.
— seminar on screenwriting to be held, Lahaina News, November 14, 1991: 8.
— "Conference on Motion Picture Production, Co-financing—East and West" detailed, Lahaina News, November 21, 1991: 11.
— International Film Festival to be held at Maui Sun Hotel, Lahaina News, November 12, 1992: 22.
— Georja Skinner sees increase in industry for Maui, Lahaina News, December 3, 1992: 4.
— business prospects for Maui look good, Lahaina News, May 4, 1995: 12.
— Maui Arts and Cultural Center to host Critic's Choice Film Series, Lahaina News, March 28, 1996: 14.
— Pacific Island Images Film Festival to be held at Maui Community College, Lahaina News, July 10, 1997: 17.
— "Paniolo O Hawaii—Cowboys of the Far West" to be shown at Maui Arts and Cultural Center, Lahaina News, January 29, 1998: 17.
— "Ho'olawe: Give and Take" being filmed on Maui, Lahaina News, April 6, 2000: 14.
— FirstLight: Academy Screenings on Maui to be held, Lahaina News, December 19, 2002: 18.

FINANCE
— "Life Planning: A Program for Women" to be held, Lahaina News, February 1, 2001: 8.

FINANCE COMMITTEE, MAUI COUNTY COUNCIL
— reschedules meeting concerning Council budget, Lahaina News, April 16, 1986: 3.

FINANCE FACTORS, LTD. [BUSINESS]
— Audie Pascual appointed branch manager, Lahaina News, April 18, 1996: 8.
— to hold open house, Lahaina News, September 30, 1999: 11.
— Haruku Shinsato wins "Kahului Branch Las Vegas Giveaway", Lahaina News, November 18, 1999: 13.
— Karen Inouye joins, Lahaina News, October 17, 2002: 8.
— Mortgage Center announces winners of grand opening draw, Lahaina News, June 5, 2003: 8.
— Tanya Lee-Greig wins Home Improvement Shopping Spree, Lahaina News, August 7, 2003: 8.

FINANCE, MAUI COUNTY DEPARTMENT OF
— to send survey to condominium owners, Lahaina News, May 28, 1992: 1.
— to hold auction of mopeds and bicycles, Lahaina News, June 24, 1993: 4.
— mails bills to property owners, Lahaina News, July 27, 1995: 4.

FINANCE MORTGAGE LTD. [BUSINESS]
— opens, Lahaina News, March 7, 1996: 11.

FINAZZO, PAUL
— Hawaiian Airlines representative provides the company's position on proposed West Maui airport, Lahaina News, September 11, 1985: 1,10,11.

FINGERS, PAUL
— selling protea, Lahaina News, February 24, 1988: 3.

FINIAN'S RAINBOW [PLAY]
— to be performed by Maui Youth Theatre, Lahaina News, February 10, 1988: 9.
— cast announced, Lahaina News, February 17, 1988: 3.

FINN, MARI
— Scholar/Athlete of the Week, Lahaina News, January 15, 1998: 6.

FINNEY, ALBERT [ACTOR]
— visits Avalon Restaurant, Lahaina News, January 2, 1992: 1.

FINNEY, MICHAEL [COMEDIAN]
— to perform, Lahaina News, January 10, 1990: 12.
— to perform at Honolulu Comedy Club, Lahaina News, October 27, 1994: 18.

FINNIGAN, KATIE
— to present on "Women and Investing", Lahaina News, June 3, 1999: 17.

FINS, THE [MUSICAL GROUP]
— featured, Lahaina News, July 8, 1987: 7,10.
— to perform at Cheeseburger's, Lahaina News, February 13, 1992: 20.
— performs at Cheeseburger in Paradise, Lahaina News, September 1, 1994: 15.

FIRAZZO, VINCE
— wins Lahaina Yacht Club race, Lahaina News, March 27, 1991: 8.

FIRE
— house on Dickenson Street destroyed by, Lahaina Sun, December 9, 1970: 1.
— destroyed workshop building behind old Lahaina Cannery, Lahaina Sun, July 7, 1971: 1.
— Lahainaluna High School gymnasium burns to the ground, Lahaina Sun, August 25, 1971: 1,12.
— at Sacred Hearts School being studied by fire department, Lahaina Sun, August 25, 1971: 1,3.

— policy studying recent fires in Lahaina, Lahaina Sun, September 1, 1971: 1.

— arson suspected in school fire, Lahaina Sun, September 22, 1971: 1.

— fire department criticized for slow response to fire at Kamehameha III School, Lahaina Sun, September 22, 1971: 14.

— continued investigation of fire at Kamehameha III School, Lahaina Sun, September 29, 1971: 1,14.

— police stop fire near Baldwin High School, Lahaina Sun, October 6, 1971: 1.

— recent Lahaina fires will have no effect on insurance rates, Lahaina Sun, October 6, 1971: 5.

— three people arrested in connection with recent fires, Lahaina Sun, October 13, 1971: 13.

— fire station requested beside Lahaina Civic Recreation Center, Lahaina Sun, November 10, 1971: 11.

— new station approved at Lahaina Civic Center, Lahaina Sun, May 31, 1972: 7.

— closes Whaler's Tale restaurant, Lahaina Sun, June 14, 1972: 3.

— questions about who is setting fires at Lahaina's refuse disposal ground, Lahaina Sun, August 2, 1972: 22.

— Front Street likely fire hazard, Lahaina Sun, August 9, 1972: 3.

— new firetruck needed for high rises, Lahaina News, June 1, 1982: 5.

— Maui Community Theatre Playhouse destroyed, Lahaina News, September 26, 1984: 3.

— destroys house, Lahaina News, April 17, 1985: 1.

— restaurant damaged, Lahaina News, April 24, 1985: 20.

— suspicious fire in vacant lot on Front Street, Lahaina News, June 26, 1985: 20.

— brush fire in Olowalu spreads, Lahaina News, July 16, 1986: 3.

— Maui County Fire Department training for ocean rescue, Lahaina News, July 30, 1986: 20.

— Kishi Building on Luakini street gutted by, Lahaina News, November 19, 1986: 3,16.

— house burns on Ainakea Road, Lahaina News, September 12, 1990: 3.

— house fire at Pineapple Hill Drive, Lahaina News, March 26, 1992: 4.

— brush fire near Piilani Highway and Kanani Road, Lahaina News, April 2, 1992: 5.

— abandoned house gutted, Lahaina News, February 18, 1993: 3.

— damages Lahaina businesses, Lahaina News, July 15, 1993: 1,3.

— firefighters called to apartment fire, Lahaina News, December 16, 1993: 2.

— condominium at Mahana at Ka'anapali destroyed, Lahaina News, May 5, 1994: 6.

— brush fire in Kahana, Lahaina News, February 5, 1998: 1.

— car fire near transformer for Kapalua Shops, Lahaina News, June 10, 1999: 1.

— house fire at Lower Honoapi'ilani Road, Lahaina News, July 1, 1999: 1.

— prevention demonstrations held, Lahaina News, October 12, 2000: 6.

— ship catches fire at Mala Wharf, Lahaina News, February 15, 2001: 9.

— Kadotani family saves home from, Lahaina News, July 12, 2001: 1,18.

FIRE AND AMBULANCE STATION, NAPILI

— West Maui Taxpayers Association to hold fundraiser for, Lahaina News, August 8, 1990: 4.

— donations still needed, Lahaina News, August 29, 1990: 4.

— West Maui Taxpayers Association to host fundraiser at Banihana's, Lahaina News, September 19, 1990: 4.

— fundraiser to be held touring homes of Maui, Lahaina News, December 5, 1990: 3.

— Beautiful Homes of Maui fundraiser to be held, Lahaina News, December 12, 1990: 4,5.

— almost completed, holds "topping off ceremony", Lahaina News, January 9, 1991: 3.

— swap meet fundraiser to be held for, Lahaina News, January 30, 1991: 4.

— receives money from State, Lahaina News, May 15, 1991: 1.

— to start operations soon, Lahaina News, May 23, 1991: 1.

— debt stalls opening, Lahaina News, June 27, 1991: 1.

— to be turned over to Maui County, Lahaina News, July 25, 1991: 1.

— to open, Lahaina News, August 22, 1991: 3.

— opening delayed until fuel system installed, Lahaina News, September 12, 1991: 3.

— to hold a golf fundraiser at Kapalua Plantation Golf Course, Lahaina News, September 19, 1991: 6.

— golf fundraiser raises $2,000, Lahaina News, October 17, 1991: 11.

— to hold community party to celebrate opening, Lahaina News, November 14, 1991: 2.

— opening to be celebrated, Lahaina News, November 28, 1991: 2.

— improves fire protection classification for Napili, Lahaina News, February 13, 1992: 3.

FIRE DEPARTMENT, MAUI

— expands fire safety program , Lahaina News, December 15, 1981: 16.

— suspects search for Levette Aquino and her son Kapena, last seen crossing flooded Kaua'ula Stream, Lahaina News, March 31, 1994: 1.

— demonstrate rescue techniques, Lahaina News, October 20, 1994: 5.

— Christmas safety tips, Lahaina News, December 23, 1999: 6.

— investigating fire in vacant Pioneer Mill, Lahaina News, January 30, 2003: 1.

— staff attend Kids Day America, Lahaina News, May 22, 2003: 3.

FIRE STATION, LAHAINA

— promotions announced , Lahaina News, May 1, 1985: 8.

— new captains named, Lahaina News, December 5, 1991: 4.

— Captain Bob Shimada discusses danger of parched hills, Lahaina News, September 11, 2003: 18.

FIRE STATION, NAPILI

— more fundraising needed, Lahaina News, May 30, 1990: 1.

FIREFIGHTERS

— Kristine Dryer became Hawaii's first female firefighter, Lahaina News, September 15, 1982: 10.

— Mayor Linda Lingle signs bill to allow departments to use volunteers, Lahaina News, December 2, 1993: 1.

— publish "Rescue Me Maui" calendar, Lahaina News, April 13, 1995: 12.

— assist in Guam plane crash rescue, Lahaina News, September 18, 1997: 6.

— Golden Oldies Revue Show to raise money for, Lahaina News, October 26, 2000: 28.

— trained by Trident Technologies on Sea Patch/ProgMag kit, Lahaina News, November 30, 2000: 12.

— raise money for disaster relief fund, Lahaina News, October 11, 2001: 8.

— new class graduates, Lahaina News, May 30, 2002: 8.

— kept busy responding to fires on parched hillsides, Lahaina News, September 11, 2003: 1,18.

— Kapena to perform at benefit for, Lahaina News, October 9, 2003: 15.

FIREMAN'S BALL

— postponed, Lahaina News, December 19, 1990: 2.

— to raise money for Napili Fire and Ambulance Station, Lahaina News, March 6, 1991: 11.

— to be held, Lahaina News, March 13, 1991: 8.

— to be held, Lahaina News, March 20, 1991: 9.

— benefit for Napili Fire and Ambulance Station to be held, Lahaina News, March 27, 1991: 1.

— to be held, Lahaina News, March 27, 1991: 12.

— described, Lahaina News, April 10, 1991: 1.

FIREMEN, THE [MUSICAL GROUP]
— reviewed, Lahaina News, July, 1979: 4.

FIRESTONE, ROY [COMEDIAN]
— to perform at GTE Ka'anapali Classic awards dinner, Lahaina News, September 5, 1990: 7.

FIREWORKS
— hope to , Lahaina News, May 2, 1984: 5.

FIRST AFFILIATED SECURITIES OFFICE [BUSINESS]
— opens, Lahaina News, November 3, 1994: 23.

FIRST ANNUAL COMMUNITY CHOICE AWARDS
— deadline for entries soon, Lahaina News, October 15, 1992: 3.

FIRST ASSEMBLY OF GOD
— opens new church, Lahaina News, April 19, 2001: 3.

FIRST CHURCH OF CHRIST, SCIENTIST
— to host lecture by Ann Stewart, Lahaina News, February 20, 1991: 8.
— to host talk by Earline Shoemake, Lahaina News, February 25, 1993: 3.

FIRST CLASS [BUSINESS]
— offering sailing trips, Lahaina News, August 7, 1997: 11.

FIRST DEVELOPMENT, INC. [BUSINESS]
— enters into long-term sponsorship agreement with GTE Ka'anapali Classic, Lahaina News, October 31, 1990: 9.

FIRST FEDERAL SAVINGS AND LOANS [BUSINESS]
— renovation and expansion completed, Lahaina News, August 10, 1988: 3.
— sponsoring home construction workshop with Lindsey Building and Co., Lahaina News, June 11, 1992: 6.
— relocates, Lahaina News, May 4, 1995: 13.

FIRST HAWAIIAN BANK [BUSINESS]
— providing loans for moderate income housing development, Lahaina Sun, December 2, 1970: 3.
— earnings up, Lahaina News, November 1, 1989: 9.
— reorganized, Lahaina News, November 1, 1989: 9.
— splits stock, Lahaina News, November 29, 1989: 4.
— Raymond Ono promoted to branch manager at Wailuku branch, Lahaina News, January 24, 1990: 6.
— to merge with First Interstate of Hawaii, Lahaina News, February 14, 1990: 5.
— implementing trial employee child care program, Lahaina News, February 28, 1990: 4.
— Raymond Ono becomes branch manager at Kahului, Lahaina News, March 7, 1990: 7.
— will pay customers for any mistakes discovered, Lahaina News, March 28, 1990: 6.
— offering 20 minute loans, Lahaina News, April 25, 1990: 7.
— announces employee promotions, Lahaina News, July 25, 1990: 7.
— promotes Ernest Magaoay to branch manager of Lana'i Branch, Lahaina News, October 3, 1990: 9.
— signs agreement with JCB, Lahaina News, October 10, 1990: 12.
— owner of First Hawaiian Bank to purchase First Interstate Hawaii, Inc., Lahaina News, December 12, 1990: 6.
— appoints Janice Paney as Kihei branch manager, Lahaina News, January 16, 1991: 5.
— selling five branch offices of First Interstate Bank, Lahaina News, March 27, 1991: 9.
— leads in number of mortgages, Lahaina News, July 4, 1991: 4.
— to present survey of Maui economy, Lahaina News, July 18, 1991: 6.
— to present results on survey of Maui economy, Lahaina News, August 1, 1991: 11.
— presenting results of survey of Maui economy this week, Lahaina News, August 8, 1991: 8.
— rated in top 10 of "U.S. Banker" annual ratings, Lahaina News, August 8, 1991: 8.

— names Gary Iki as senior vice-president and manager of international banking division, Lahaina News, October 24, 1991: 9.
— mandated to sell five First Interstate Bank of Hawaii branches, Lahaina News, January 2, 1992: 8.
— reports record earnings, Lahaina News, January 30, 1992: 11.
— promotes Howard Karr to vice chairman, Lahaina News, January 30, 1992: 12.
— promotes Philip Ching to vice chairman, Lahaina News, January 30, 1992: 12.
— promotes James Caswell to assistant vice president, Consumer Service Center, Lahaina News, January 30, 1992: 12.
— guaranteeing cash for home equity loan within 15 working days, Lahaina News, March 26, 1992: 11.
— profits rise, Lahaina News, April 30, 1992: 11.
— rated among top 10 banks in the country, Lahaina News, April 30, 1992: 11.
— sets dividends for quarter, Lahaina News, June 4, 1992: 9.
— opening branch in Napili, Lahaina News, June 25, 1992: 16.
— proposes to expand parking, Lahaina News, July 9, 1992: 5.
— promotions announced, Lahaina News, July 23, 1992: 17.
— to host Maui Outlook Forum, Lahaina News, July 30, 1992: 12.
— highly ranked in nation, Lahaina News, August 20, 1992: 12.
— 10th in national ranking for safety and profitability, Lahaina News, August 27, 1992: 11.
— five branches to be sold by trustee, Lahaina News, November 5, 1992: 9.
— now selling mutual funds, Lahaina News, November 12, 1992: 12.
— offers new bank plan, Lahaina News, July 1, 1993: 7.
— income announced, Lahaina News, August 19, 1993: 13.
— declares dividends, Lahaina News, September 16, 1993: 10.
— promotions announced, Lahaina News, April 7, 1994: 10.
— president John Hoag to retire, Lahaina News, July 7, 1994: 9.
— introduces over the phone mortgage loan inquiry service, Lahaina News, September 8, 1994: 12.
— sale of Lahaina-Pakui branch not expected to go through, Lahaina News, November 10, 1994: 12.
— survey indicates strong economy expected for holiday season and beyond, Lahaina News, November 17, 1994: 10.
— economist Leroy Laney to discuss outlook, Lahaina News, July 27, 1995: 10.
— announces new branch managers, Lahaina News, January 11, 1996: 11.
— Lahaina-Pakui branch may close, Lahaina News, January 11, 1996: 11.
— offering security for internet credit card purchases, Lahaina News, September 19, 1996: 8.
— presents check to Boy Scouts, Lahaina News, October 31, 1996: 2.
— appoints Gerald Clair as branch manager in Lahaina, Lahaina News, August 7, 1997: 5.
— staff changes at, Lahaina News, December 24, 1998: 11.
— Senior Vice President Steve Williams to supervise Maui region, Lahaina News, January 6, 2000: 11.
— hosting Troy Barboza Law Enforcement Run to benefit Special Olympics, Lahaina News, March 30, 2000: 6.
— former chief economist Leroy Laney to discuss, Lahaina News, September 20, 2001: 9.
— Mike Mulholland joins as loan officer, Lahaina News, November 14, 2002: 8.

FIRST HAWAIIAN MORTGAGE CO. [BUSINESS]
— opens in West Maui, Lahaina News, April 21, 1994: 9.
— to offer custom-tailored mortgages, Lahaina News, May 12, 1994: 10.

FIRST INSURANCE CO. [BUSINESS]
— manager to teach course on customer service, Lahaina News, October 31, 1990: 12.

FIRST INTERSTATE BANK OF HAWAII [BUSINESS]
— appoints Frances Peart as branch manager, Lahaina News, May 29, 1985: 3.
— to move location, Lahaina News, September 6, 1989: 2.
— holds blessing for new location, Lahaina News, January 17, 1990: 4.
— purchased by First Hawaiian Bank, Inc., Lahaina News, December 12, 1990: 6.
— First Hawaiian, Inc. mandated to sell five branches, Lahaina News, January 2, 1992: 8.
— branch in Lahaina to become Royal Pacific Bank, Lahaina News, January 9, 1992: 2.

FIRST LADY'S OUTSTANDING VOLUNTEER AWARDS
— Mrs. George Ariyoshi inviting nominations for, Lahaina News, February 13, 1985: 3.
— seeking nominations, Lahaina News, December 31, 1992: 4.

FIRST LIGHT STUDIOS [BUSINESS]
— to develop half-hour news show "Maui County News", Lahaina News, December 14, 2000: 18.

FIRST NIGHT MAUI
— to be held, Lahaina News, December 28, 1995: 8.
— to be held at Maui Arts and Cultural Center, Lahaina News, December 26, 1996: 1.
— to be held, Lahaina News, August 14, 1997: 2.
— New Year's Eve celebration to be held, Lahaina News, December 17, 1998: 12.
— to be held, Lahaina News, December 31, 1998: 12.
— see also New Years

FIRSTLIGHT 2000
— film festival to be held, Lahaina News, December 21, 2000: 1,9.

FIRSTLIGHT: ACADEMY SCREENINGS ON MAUI
— films to be shown, Lahaina News, December 23, 1999: 2.
— to be held, Lahaina News, December 19, 2002: 18.
— to be held, Lahaina News, January 2, 2003: 16.

FISH AGGREGATION DEVICES (FADS)
— being repaired, Lahaina News, January 25, 1989: 5.
— state to replace missing fishing buoys, Lahaina News, October 6, 1994: 5.
— state to replace, Lahaina News, September 27, 2001: 13.
— see also fishing

FISH AND GAME BREWING COMPANY [RESTAURANT]
— expands, Lahaina News, May 21, 1998: 13.
— featured, Lahaina News, June 4, 1998: 8,9.
— chefs John Peck and Doug Zuk join, Lahaina News, April 8, 1999: 11.
— featured, Lahaina News, January 11, 2001: 7.
— marks eight anniversary, Lahaina News, October 24, 2002: 8.

FISH AND GAMES SPORTS GRILL [RESTAURANT]
— to open in Kahana Gateway Shopping Center, Lahaina News, June 9, 1994: 12.
— featured, Lahaina News, December 29, 1994: 6.

FISH AND WILDLIFE SERVICE, U.S.
— to hold public hearing on critical habitat designations, Lahaina News, March 15, 2001: 2.
— has grants for habitat restoration, Lahaina News, May 15, 2003: 2.

FISH FOR HEART
— fundraiser for Hawaii Heart Association set, Lahaina News, May 20, 1987: 3.

FISH MARKET MAUI, THE [BUSINESS]
— opens, Lahaina News, March 29, 2001: 9.

FISH POND
— threatened by development planned by Bruce McNeil, Lahaina Sun, March 14, 1973: 4.

FISH TEXTILE ART
— show to feature Jennifer Holt and Karen Domingo, Lahaina News, January 31, 2002: 16.

FISHBACK, H. GLEN
— appointed provost of Maui Community College, Lahaina Sun, June 16, 1971: 1.

FISHER, BILL
— joins Maui Community Arts and Cultural Center as controller, Lahaina News, October 31, 1991: 10.
— named interim director of the Maui Community Arts and Cultural Center, Lahaina News, June 18, 1992: 10.

FISHER, BILL AND SYLVIA
— continue their running career after accidents, Lahaina News, October 22, 1992: 8.

FISHER, JACK
— black velvet paintings displayed at Kula Lodge, Lahaina Sun, April 14, 1971: 8.

FISHER, MICHAEL
— joins Island Mortgage as loan officer, Lahaina News, April 15, 1993: 7.

FISHER, STEVE
— windsurfer plans to sail from Los Angeles to Ka'anapali, Lahaina News, June 6, 1990: 6,24.
— applies to Guinness Book of World Records for "longest documented swim by a dog", Lahaina News, October 17, 1996: 4.
— windsurfer sails from Los Angeles to Maui, Lahaina News, September 11, 1997: 1,5.
— boardsails from California to Hawaii in record time, Lahaina News, April 13, 2000: 1,16.

FISHERMAN'S WHARF [RESTAURANT]
— reviewed, Lahaina News, August 12, 1987: 7.
— reviewed, Lahaina News, October 14, 1987: 7.

FISHING
— picture of ulua caught spear fishing, Lahaina Sun, November 18, 1970: 1.
— Lahaina Kamaakina Fishing Association created to support fishing, Lahaina Sun, December 23, 1970: 1.
— reward for tagged fish offered, Lahaina Sun, June 9, 1971: 6.
— State Director of Health clears most fish for market, Lahaina Sun, June 23, 1971: 11.
— First Annual Lana'i Rendezvous is held, Lahaina Sun, July 7, 1971: 11.
— co-op established on Maui, Lahaina Sun, August 4, 1971: 1,11.
— photographs, Lahaina Sun, September 1, 1971: 14.
— Lokahi Corporation beginning commercial production of shrimp, Lahaina Sun, September 1, 1971: 15.
— large white marlin caught by Lynn Erickson, Lahaina Sun, November 3, 1971: 15.
— Maui County co-op organized, Lahaina Sun, November 24, 1971: 13.
— Maui County to give funds to Fish Farms Hawaii for promotional activities, Lahaina Sun, December 8, 1971: 7.
— mullet season ends, Lahaina Sun, December 8, 1971: 8.
— sale of Pacific blue marlin banned in Hawaii, Lahaina Sun, December 15, 1971: 14.
— Hana Sea Land, Inc. dedication ceremony, Lahaina Sun, February 2, 1972: 9.
— Linda Capurro brought in a 960-pound Pacific Marlin, Lahaina Sun, April 19, 1972: 3.
— catfish raised as food , Lahaina Sun, January 31, 1973: 15.
— lobster season begins, Lahaina Sun, June 6, 1973: 11.
— possible future discussed, Lahaina Sun, June 13, 1973: 16,17.
— 875-pound marling caught by Jim Poquette, Lahaina News, April 17, 1985: 20.

— cost of fish licenses to rise, Lahaina News, July 3, 1985: 8.
— monthly column "At the Harbor" is introduced in the Lahaina News, Lahaina News, August 21, 1985: 9.
— successes of fishing boats listed, Lahaina News, August 21, 1985: 9.
— significant catches listed, Lahaina News, September 18, 1985: 9.
— Lahaina Jackpot Fishing Tournament to be held this week, Lahaina News, October 30, 1985: 3.
— proposed rules to be discussed at public hearing, Lahaina News, November 13, 1985: 3.
— October is slow month, Lahaina News, November 27, 1985: 10.
— few marlin caught during November, Lahaina News, December 25, 1985: 7.
— end-of-year harbor statistics given, Lahaina News, February 5, 1986: 10.
— ahi and mahi catch substantial this month, Lahaina News, March 5, 1986: 4.
— update on events from February, including 615-pound marlin, Lahaina News, March 19, 1986: 8.
— Spring Wahine Fishing Tournament organized by Lahaina Yacht Club, Lahaina News, April 9, 1986: 3.
— update on events for April, including 465 marlin, Lahaina News, May 7, 1986: 6.
— Islander II most successful fishing boat in April, Lahaina News, May 21, 1986: 12.
— glass bottom boat catches marlin, Lahaina News, July 30, 1986: 1.
— update on recent events in local fishing, Lahaina News, July 30, 1986: 9,12.
— monthly update on fishing, Lahaina News, September 3, 1986: 14.
— Billfiish Tourney results described, Lahaina News, September 17, 1986: 9,12.
— August activities, Lahaina News, October 15, 1986: 6,16.
— Keiki tourney results announced, Lahaina News, October 29, 1986: 3.
— Lahaina Jackpot Tournament to be held, Lahaina News, October 29, 1986: 6.
— Department of Land and Natural Resources to hold public hearings on management of, Lahaina News, April 22, 1987: 10.
— success of boats from Lahaina Harbor, Lahaina News, April 29, 1987: 8.
— DLNR changes rules change for spiny lobster, Lahaina News, May 20, 1987: 3.
— activity in Lahaina boats summarized, Lahaina News, July 8, 1987: 6.
— Keiki Fishing Tourney planned, Lahaina News, August 26, 1987: 3.
— Department of Land and Natural Resources to maintain State's Fish Aggregating Devices, Lahaina News, April 6, 1988: 20.
— statistics on fish caught last year, Lahaina News, February 15, 1989: 12.
— details of recent significant catches, Lahaina News, May 17, 1989: 3.
— fish cutting competition held at Whalers Village, Lahaina News, July 5, 1989: 10.
— Amfac, Inc holds annual contests, Lahaina News, July 12, 1989: 2.
— Ka'anapali Keiki Fishing Derby held, Lahaina News, August 2, 1989: 10,11.
— fish cutting competition won by Sous Chef at El Crab Catcher, Lahaina News, August 2, 1989: 9.
— editorial supporting continued fishing at Mala Wharf, Lahaina News, August 9, 1989: 8.
— hopes to export to U.S. Mainland discussed, Lahaina News, August 16, 1989: 1.
— largest marlin in 17 years caught, Lahaina News, August 23, 1989: 1.
— large marlin caught, others listed, Lahaina News, September 27, 1989: 24.
— top catches listed, Lahaina News, October 4, 1989: 6.

— changes to seafood inspection program considered, Lahaina News, October 11, 1989: 1.
— update on latest catches, Dracula's Dash featured, Lahaina News, October 11, 1989: 24.
— update on latest catches, record set, Lahaina News, October 18, 1989: 1,24.
— Lahaina Jackpot Fishing Tournament scheduled, Lahaina News, October 18, 1989: 24.
— results of Lahaina Jackpot Fishing Tournament, Lahaina News, October 25, 1989: 1,28.
— large marlin caught, others listed, Lahaina News, November 1, 1989: 3,24.
— results of Lahaina Jackpot Fishing Tournament, Lahaina News, November 8, 1989: 8.
— Wahine Jackpot Fishing Tournament has record number of participants, Lahaina News, November 15, 1989: 28.
— update on latest catches, Absolute featured, Lahaina News, November 22, 1989: 1,10.
— update on latest catches, Exact featured, Lahaina News, December 6, 1989: 24.
— update on latest catches, Islander II featured, Lahaina News, December 13, 1989: 9.
— update on latest catches, Hinatea featured, Lahaina News, December 20, 1989: 5.
— bottomfishing described, Lahaina News, December 27, 1989: 7.
— Hinatea featured, Lahaina News, January 3, 1990: 1.
— mullet season closes, Lahaina News, January 3, 1990: 28.
— details of recent significant catches, Lahaina News, January 10, 1990: 1,4.
— drift nets used within 12-mile limit, Lahaina News, January 17, 1990: 1.
— update on latest catches, the Exact featured, Lahaina News, January 17, 1990: 1,7.
— fishermen upset about longline fishing, Lahaina News, January 24, 1990: 1.
— update on latest catches, Pailolo featured, Lahaina News, January 24, 1990: 9,10.
— report on largest fish caught for 1989, Lahaina News, January 31, 1990: 8.
— update on latest catches, Finest Kind and Putnam the best of 1989, Lahaina News, January 31, 1990: 9.
— update on latest catches, Adventure I featured, Lahaina News, February 7, 1990: 1,10.
— update on latest catches, Pailolo featured, Lahaina News, February 14, 1990: 7,32.
— update on latest catches, mahi mahi active, Lahaina News, February 21, 1990: 10.
— update on latest catches, Salty Dog featured, Lahaina News, February 28, 1990: 1,7.
— update on latest catches; marlin catches increasing, Lahaina News, March 7, 1990: 1,4,28.
— Ma'alaea boat No Ka Oi III catches four marlin, Lahaina News, March 14, 1990: 7.
— custom lure maker Joe Yee featured, Lahaina News, March 14, 1990: 7,28.
— the boat Finest Kind catches marlin, Lahaina News, March 21, 1990: 28.
— commentary by David Grobecker opposing use of driftnets, Lahaina News, March 28, 1990: 11.
— large marlin caught by crew of Pailolo [boat], Lahaina News, March 28, 1990: 28.
— No Ka Oi III successes described, Lahaina News, March 28, 1990: 4.
— update on latest catches, July Ann II featured, Lahaina News, April 4, 1990: 4,24.

— update on latest catches; Hinatea catches 600-pound marlin, Lahaina News, April 11, 1990: 12,28.

— update on latest catches, mahi mahi plentiful, Lahaina News, April 11, 1990: 4.

— update on latest catches; 13-year old Derrin Davis catches 400-pound marlin, Lahaina News, April 18, 1990: 1,6.

— Spring Wahine Fishing Tournament to be held, Lahaina News, April 18, 1990: 7.

— update on latest catches, Mano Kela featured, Lahaina News, April 25, 1990: 10,11.

— update on latest catches; 955-pound marlin caught, Lahaina News, May 2, 1990: 1.

— update on latest catches; fishing results from Lahaina Yacht Club, Lahaina News, May 2, 1990: 28.

— update on latest catches; 700-pound marlin caught, Lahaina News, May 9, 1990: 6.

— update on latest catches; 937-pound marlin caught, second largest brought to the scales, Lahaina News, May 16, 1990: 8,20.

— update on latest catches, Mano Kela, Lahaina News, May 23, 1990: 10,24.

— Memorial Day tournament to take place, Lahaina News, May 23, 1990: 9.

— update on latest catches; 750-pound marlin caught, Lahaina News, May 30, 1990: 14,20.

— update on latest catches; light tackle fishing, Lahaina News, June 6, 1990: 24.

— update on latest catches, Lee lures discussed, Lahaina News, June 13, 1990: 9,24.

— update on latest catches; Maʻalaea, Lahaina News, June 20, 1990: 20.

— update on latest catches, No Ka Oi III catches 710-pound marlin, Lahaina News, June 27, 1990: 6,20.

— update on latest catches; sailfish off Puerto Vallarta, Lahaina News, July 4, 1990: 11,24.

— keiki derby to be held, Lahaina News, July 4, 1990: 6.

— largest fish ever caught from shoreline anywhere in Hawaii immortalized in Gyotaku-style print, Lahaina News, July 4, 1990: 9.

— update on latest catches, Islander II featured, Lahaina News, July 11, 1990: 10,11,24.

— keiki derby to be held, Lahaina News, July 11, 1990: 8.

— update on latest catches, Mano Kela featured, Lahaina News, July 18, 1990: 14,29.

— keiki derby to be held, Lahaina News, July 18, 1990: 6.

— update on latest catches, Finest Kind featured, Lahaina News, July 25, 1990: 14,20.

— Mayor Hannibal Tavares congratulates winners of Keiki Fishing Derby, Lahaina News, August 1, 1990: 1.

— Cheyenne Auldrames wins Keiki Fishing Derby, Lahaina News, August 1, 1990: 14.

— update on latest catches, Islander II featured, Lahaina News, August 1, 1990: 7.

— Light Tackle Tan & Release Tournament to be held, Lahaina News, August 8, 1990: 7.

— update on latest catches, Exact featured, Lahaina News, August 8, 1990: 8.

— update on latest catches, Maka Kai featured, Lahaina News, August 15, 1990: 18.

— update on latest catches, Absolute featured, Lahaina News, August 22, 1990: 8.

— update on latest catches, Mano Kela featured, Lahaina News, August 29, 1990: 20.

— update on latest catches, Captain Doug Barna recognized, Lahaina News, September 5, 1990: 7.

— update on latest catches, Islander II featured, Lahaina News, September 12, 1990: 24.

— update on latest catches, Finest Kind featured, Lahaina News, September 19, 1990: 18.

— update on latest catches, Absolute featured, Lahaina News, September 26, 1990: 14.

— Maui Ohana Keiki Fishing Tournament held, Lahaina News, September 26, 1990: 3.

— Mano Kela places second in Big Island Invitational Marlin Tournament, Lahaina News, October 3, 1990: 6.

— different types of marlin discussed, Lahaina News, October 17, 1990: 7.

— update on latest catches, Finest Kind featured, Lahaina News, October 24, 1990: 11.

— update on latest catches; Kiwi II catches largest fish this week, Lahaina News, October 31, 1990: 9.

— Linda Conner wins Wahine Jackpot Fishing Tournament, Lahaina News, November 7, 1990: 14.

— update on latest catches; results of Lahaina Jackpot Fishing Tournament, Lahaina News, November 14, 1990: 9,10.

— update on latest catches; record number of fish; number of mainland fishing boats up, Lahaina News, November 21, 1990: 9.

— update on latest catches, Finest Kind featured, Lahaina News, November 28, 1990: 7.

— concern that State fishing policy is confusing, Lahaina News, December 5, 1990: 1.

— update on latest catches; Western Pacific Regional Fisheries Council imposes 90-day moratorium on longline fishing fleet, Lahaina News, December 12, 1990: 20.

— Kapalua Hook-up Fishing Tournament raises money for Kumulani Chapel preschool, Lahaina News, December 19, 1990: 18.

— longliners active in Maui waters, Lahaina News, December 19, 1990: 24.

— update on latest catches off Molokaʻi, Lahaina News, December 26, 1990: 20.

— update on longlines issue, Lahaina News, January 2, 1991: 16.

— Department of Land and Natural Resources to re-institute voluntary Fish Buoy Card reporting system, Lahaina News, January 2, 1991: 16.

— update on latest catches; update on longlines, Lahaina News, January 9, 1991: 16.

— update on latest catches, Absolute featured, Lahaina News, January 16, 1991: 20.

— public meeting to held by Longline Task Force, Lahaina News, January 23, 1991: 1,16.

— public hearing on longlining held, Lahaina News, January 30, 1991: 1.

— update on latest catches, The Finest Kind and Islander II featured, Lahaina News, January 30, 1991: 16.

— update on latest catches, summary of previous year, Lahaina News, February 6, 1991: 14,20.

— Atlantic swordfishermen coming to Hawaii, Lahaina News, February 13, 1991: 20.

— longline fishing moratorium recommended by task force, Lahaina News, February 20, 1991: 20.

— update on latest catches; marlin catch increases, Lahaina News, February 27, 1991: 8,20.

— update on latest catches, Hinatea featured, Lahaina News, March 6, 1991: 24.

— update on latest catches, Islander II featured, Lahaina News, March 13, 1991: 20.

— update on latest catches, Judy Ann II featured, Lahaina News, March 20, 1991: 20.

— update on latest catches, Iwa Lele featured, Lahaina News, March 27, 1991: 8.

— update on latest catches, debate over longline fishing, Lahaina News, April 3, 1991: 16.

— update on latest catches, The Finest Kind featured, Lahaina News, April 10, 1991: 5.

— update on latest catches, Kiwi II featured, Lahaina News, April 17, 1991: 24.
— Lahaina Yacht Club to host Spring Wahine Fishing Tournament, Lahaina News, April 24, 1991: 6.
— update on latest catches, Absolute featured, Lahaina News, May 1, 1991: 7,24.
— Sarah Selken wins Lahaina Yacht Club Spring Wahine Tournament, Lahaina News, May 8, 1991: 1.
— Jim Thommen sets Lahaina Harbor record with 150-pound ulua, Lahaina News, May 15, 1991: 20.
— Kona crab season closed, according to Department of Land and Natural Resources, Lahaina News, May 23, 1991: 10.
— update on latest catches, Judy Ann II featured, Lahaina News, May 23, 1991: 9.
— update on latest catches, 84-pound ulua caught on the Kula Manu , Lahaina News, May 30, 1991: 16.
— update on latest catches, the Finest Kind featured, Lahaina News, June 6, 1991: 18.
— netting season ends for spiny lobster, slipper lobster, and moi, Lahaina News, June 6, 1991: 9.
— ciguatera fish poisoning not an issue on Maui, Lahaina News, June 13, 1991: 1.
— netting season ends for spiny lobster, slipper lobster, and moi, Lahaina News, June 13, 1991: 17.
— West Maui Kapalua Hook-Up Shoreline Fishing Tournament to be held, Lahaina News, June 13, 1991: 17.
— update on latest catches, Anticipation featured, Lahaina News, June 13, 1991: 24.
— update on latest catches, the Absolute featured, Lahaina News, June 20, 1991: 4,7.
— update on latest catches, Islander II featured, Lahaina News, June 27, 1991: 7.
— spiny lobster, slipper lobster, and moi seasons end, Lahaina News, June 27, 1991: 7.
— update on latest catches, Aquasport Diver Dan caught 575-pound blue marlin, Lahaina News, July 11, 1991: 24.
— Keiki Fishing Derby to be held, Lahaina News, July 11, 1991: 5.
— Jackpot Derby to be held, Lahaina News, July 11, 1991: 5.
— two marlins caught, Lahaina News, July 18, 1991: 1,2.
— update on latest catches, Chelsea II featured, Lahaina News, July 25, 1991: 1,20.
— update on latest catches; largest ahi of the year caught, Lahaina News, August 1, 1991: 2.
— update on latest catches, Absolute featured, Lahaina News, August 8, 1991: 7.
— update on latest catches, Radon Manawanui featured, Lahaina News, August 15, 1991: 18.
— update on latest catches, Mano Kela featured, Lahaina News, August 22, 1991: 20.
— Bill Holt wins Hawaiian International Billfish Tournament, Lahaina News, August 29, 1991: 1,4.
— update on latest catches, Iwa Lele featured, Lahaina News, September 5, 1991: 24.
— longline closure extended by Western Pacific Regional Fishery Management Council, Lahaina News, September 12, 1991: 6.
— update on latest catches, Aerial III featured, Lahaina News, September 12, 1991: 7.
— update on latest catches, Finest Kind featured, Lahaina News, September 19, 1991: 28.
— update on latest catches; results of Lahaina Yacht Club Keiki fishing tournament, Lahaina News, September 26, 1991: 24.
— Lana'i tournament won by Lu'uwai family, Lahaina News, October 3, 1991: 8.
— update on latest catches, Ehukai catches 178-pound ahi, Lahaina News, October 10, 1991: 11.

— update on latest catches, Reel Hooker featured, Lahaina News, October 17, 1991: 4.
— Lahaina Yacht Club Wahine and Jackpot Tournaments to be held, Lahaina News, October 17, 1991: 4.
— update on latest catches, Trilogy III featured, Lahaina News, October 24, 1991: 7.
— update on latest catches; 576-pound marlin caught, Lahaina News, October 31, 1991: 7.
— Snoopy Too wins Lahaina Jackpot Fishing Tournament, Lahaina News, November 7, 1991: 5,22.
— update on latest catches, Judy Ann II featured, Lahaina News, November 14, 1991: 4,5.
— update on latest catches, Broadbill featured, Lahaina News, November 21, 1991: 9.
— longliners organizing to allow fishing, Lahaina News, November 28, 1991: 24.
— update on latest catches; 22 billfish hooked, Lahaina News, December 5, 1991: 32.
— appropriateness of shark hunt debated, following death of Marti Morrell, Lahaina News, December 5, 1991: 9.
— update on latest catches; 415 pound marlin caught, Lahaina News, December 12, 1991: 4.
— update on latest catches, The Diver Dan featured, Lahaina News, December 19, 1991: 10.
— update on latest catches, Radon Papio featured, Lahaina News, December 26, 1991: 24.
— update on latest catches; 14-year-old catches marlin, Lahaina News, January 2, 1992: 20.
— importance of lures for catching marlin discussed, Lahaina News, January 9, 1992: 20.
— update on latest catches, Silk Purse featured, Lahaina News, January 16, 1992: 7.
— update on latest catches, Aerial III featured, Lahaina News, January 23, 1992: 9.
— update on recent activities, Lahaina News, February 6, 1992: 13.
— update on recent activities, first blue marlin of the year caught, Lahaina News, February 13, 1992: 10.
— update on recent activities, Lahaina News, February 20, 1992: 6.
— update on recent activities, Lahaina News, March 5, 1992: 8.
— Hawaii Light Tackle Tournament to be held in Kona, Hawaii, Lahaina News, March 12, 1992: 10.
— update on latest catches, Hinatea featured, Lahaina News, March 12, 1992: 9.
— update on latest catches; 445-pound marlin largest this year, Lahaina News, March 19, 1992: 8.
— update on latest catches, The Luckey Strike featured, Lahaina News, March 26, 1992: 9.
— update on latest catches, The Reel Hooker featured, Lahaina News, April 2, 1992: 9.
— update on latest catches, The Exact featured, Lahaina News, April 9, 1992: 11.
— update on latest catches, Diver Dan featured, Lahaina News, April 16, 1992: 11.
— update on latest catches, Ariel featured, Lahaina News, April 23, 1992: 23.
— update on latest catches, Finest Kind featured, Lahaina News, May 7, 1992: 14.
— update on latest catches, Lahaina Fish Co. II featured, Lahaina News, May 28, 1992: 8.
— update on latest catches, Reel Hooker featured, Lahaina News, June 4, 1992: 9.
— update on latest catches; 660 pound marlin caught, Lahaina News, June 11, 1992: 10.
— Maui Trailer Boat Club to hold tournament, Lahaina News, June 11, 1992: 10.

— John Livingstone catches 1356-pound marlin off Kona, Lahaina News, June 18, 1992: 12.

— update on latest catches, Finest Kind featured, vice principal Dick Medenwald on board, Lahaina News, June 18, 1992: 13.

— Amfac Ka'anapali Keiki Fishing Derby scheduled, Lahaina News, June 25, 1992: 10.

— update on latest catches, six blue marlins caught in one day, Lahaina News, June 25, 1992: 12.

— Maui Trailer Boat Club to hold tournament, Lahaina News, July 2, 1992: 12.

— 8-year old Ryan Michimoto wins Amfac Ka'anapali Keiki Fishing Derby, Lahaina News, July 2, 1992: 14.

— update on latest catches, 815-pound marlin caught, Lahaina News, July 2, 1992: 14.

— update on latest catches, the Broadbill featured, Lahaina News, July 16, 1992: 12.

— update on latest catches, Bluefin Trevally may be record catch, Lahaina News, July 23, 1992: 13.

— update on latest catches; Bill Holt wins World Cup Blue Marlin Fishing Tournament, Lahaina News, August 6, 1992: 4.

— results of Kona billfish tournament, Lahaina News, August 20, 1992: 11.

— 435 blue marlin caught, Lahaina News, August 20, 1992: 8.

— update on latest catches, Hinatea featured, Lahaina News, August 27, 1992: 7.

— tournaments to be held, Lahaina News, August 27, 1992: 9.

— Lana'i Rendezvous held, won by the Gina Marie, Lahaina News, September 3, 1992: 7.

— Kapalua West Maui Hook-Up Fishing Tournament to be held, Lahaina News, September 17, 1992: 4,6.

— update on latest catches, The Silk Purse featured, Lahaina News, September 17, 1992: 5.

— tournaments to be held, Lahaina News, September 24, 1992: 13.

— update on latest catches, Alohilani featured, Lahaina News, October 8, 1992: 5.

— update on latest catches, The Slightly Perfect featured, Lahaina News, October 15, 1992: 11.

— fishing ban not expected in whale zone, Lahaina News, October 22, 1992: 1.

— update on latest catches, Finest Kind featured, Lahaina News, October 22, 1992: 9.

— Lahaina Jackpot Fishing Tournament held, Lahaina News, October 29, 1992: 1,10.

— Silk Purse catches 770-pound marlin, Lahaina News, October 29, 1992: 11.

— results of Lahaina Jackpot Fishing Tournament, Lahaina News, November 5, 1992: 1,11.

— 133 marlins caught during Lahaina Jackpot Fishing Tournament, Lahaina News, November 12, 1992: 7.

— successful during Halloween, Lahaina News, November 12, 1992: 8.

— update on latest catches, the Arial featured, Lahaina News, November 19, 1992: 8.

— 'ama'ama season ends, Lahaina News, December 24, 1992: 4.

— issues faced by the Western Pacific Regional Fishery Management Council (WPRFMC) summarized, Lahaina News, January 7, 1993: 14.

— update on latest catches, the Hinatea featured, Lahaina News, January 21, 1993: 6.

— report on previous year totals, Lahaina News, January 28, 1993: 6.

— Msui Trailer Boat Club to hold Bottom Fishing Tournament, Lahaina News, January 28, 1993: 7.

— update on latest catches, first blue marlin of the year caught, Lahaina News, February 11, 1993: 9.

— update on latest catches, The Finest Kind featured, Lahaina News, February 18, 1993: 6.

— results of Maui Trailer Boat Club's Bottom Fishing Tournament, Lahaina News, February 18, 1993: 7.

— update on latest catches; NOAA to hold public meeting on Hawaii Islands Humpback Whale National Marine Sanctuary, Lahaina News, March 11, 1993: 8.

— update on latest catches, Islander II featured, Lahaina News, March 18, 1993: 4.

— update on latest catches, The Silk Purse featured, Lahaina News, March 25, 1993: 5.

— update on latest catches, Bertram Desperado featured, Lahaina News, April 1, 1993: 4.

— update on latest catches; Spring Wahine Fishing Tournament to be held, Lahaina News, April 8, 1993: 8.

— update on latest catches, Arial featured, Lahaina News, April 22, 1993: 8.

— update on latest catches, marlins caught, Lahaina News, April 29, 1993: 7.

— results of Lahaina Yacht Club Spring Wahine Tournament, Lahaina News, May 6, 1993: 11.

— update on latest catches. the Alohilani featured, Lahaina News, May 13, 1993: 7.

— longline fishing may change, Lahaina News, May 20, 1993: 2,3.

— update on latest catches, the Finest Kind featured, Lahaina News, May 27, 1993: 10.

— new rules for gill nets, Lahaina News, May 27, 1993: 3,4.

— update on latest catches and issues, Lahaina News, June 10, 1993: 8.

— derbies to be held, Lahaina News, June 10, 1993: 9.

— update on latest catches; Amfac/JMB Ka'anapali Keiki Fishing Derby results, Lahaina News, June 24, 1993: 12.

— update on latest catches, Exact featured, Lahaina News, July 1, 1993: 9.

— Mala Wharf Fishing and Recreation holds "Anything Goes Tournament", Lahaina News, July 8, 1993: 9.

— update on latest catches; fourth largest billfish of year caught, Lahaina News, July 15, 1993: 7.

— update on latest catches, Exact featured, Lahaina News, July 22, 1993: 9.

— update on latest catches, Kaho'olawe Shoals productive, Lahaina News, August 26, 1993: 11.

— update on latest catches, Islander II featured, Lahaina News, September 2, 1993: 9.

— Keiki Fishing Tournament to be held, Lahaina News, September 9, 1993: 9.

— public meeting to be held on commercial longlining, Lahaina News, September 9, 1993: 9.

— results of Hawaiian International Billfish Tournament, Lahaina News, September 16, 1993: 14.

— update on latest catches, the Aerial II featured, Lahaina News, September 30, 1993: 10.

— second largest blue marlin of the year caught, Lahaina News, October 7, 1993: 8.

— longline restrictions approved by Western Pacific Regional Fishery Management Council, Lahaina News, October 14, 1993: 11.

— update on latest catches, blue marlins caught, Lahaina News, October 21, 1993: 13.

— results of Jackpot Fishing Tournament, Lahaina News, October 28, 1993: 8.

— Jackpot Fishing Tournament results, Lahaina News, November 4, 1993: 1.

— update on latest catches, Judy Ann II featured, Lahaina News, November 4, 1993: 8.

— record breaking fish caught in Lahaina Jackpot contest, Lahaina News, November 11, 1993: 9.

— description of billfish (marlin), Lahaina News, November 25, 1993: 10.

— ulua caught by spearfisher, Lahaina News, May 18, 1995: 7.
— Luckey Strike [ship] success at fishing, Lahaina News, May 25, 1995: 4.
— update on latest catches, blue marlin hooked by Finest Kind, Lahaina News, June 1, 1995: 6.
— update on latest catches, Reel Hooker featured, Lahaina News, June 8, 1995: 6.
— The Slightly Perfect crew wins Ma'alaea Boat and Fishing Club's Memorial Day Weekend Tournament, Lahaina News, June 15, 1995: 6.
— update on latest catches, the Desperado, Lahaina News, June 22, 1995: 6.
— update on latest catches; 618-pound marlin caught, Lahaina News, June 29, 1995: 7.
— update on latest catches; 575-pound sunfish caught, Lahaina News, July 6, 1995: 7.
— update on latest catches, Broadbill brings in second largest marlin of the year, Lahaina News, July 13, 1995: 7.
— update on latest catches, Exact featured, Lahaina News, July 20, 1995: 7.
— update on latest catches, Peke Lani featured, Lahaina News, July 27, 1995: 6.
— charters enjoy record-setting ahi run, Lahaina News, August 3, 1995: 9.
— update on latest catches, Desperado catch taken by sharks, Lahaina News, August 17, 1995: 7.
— update on latest catches, Exact featured, Lahaina News, August 31, 1995: 6.
— update on latest catches, Silk Purse hits catch of the year, Lahaina News, September 7, 1995: 4.
— update on latest catches, Reel Hooker featured, Lahaina News, September 14, 1995: 7.
— Pacific Ocean Research Foundation helping to protect gamefish, Lahaina News, September 21, 1995: 7.
— update on latest catches, Desperado featured, Lahaina News, October 5, 1995: 6.
— update on latest catches, Offshore Hunter featured, Lahaina News, October 12, 1995: 8.
— update on latest catches, Desperado featured, Lahaina News, October 26, 1995: 6.
— results of Lahaina Yacht Club Wahine Jackpot Fishing Tournament, Lahaina News, November 2, 1995: 7.
— results of Lahaina Jackpot tournament, Lahaina News, November 9, 1995: 7.
— update on Lahaina Jackpot Fishing Tournament, Lahaina News, November 23, 1995: 6.
— update on latest catches, Finest Kind featured, Lahaina News, December 7, 1995: 4.
— update on latest catches, article author Donnell Tate catches striped marlin, Lahaina News, December 14, 1995: 11.
— update on latest catches, the Exact featured, Lahaina News, December 21, 1995: 8.
— update on longline catch, Lahaina News, December 28, 1995: 6.
— public's help sought in drafting bottom fishing rules, Lahaina News, January 4, 1996: 7.
— concern that Division of Aquatic Resources (DAR) will cut funding, Lahaina News, January 11, 1996: 7.
— update on current market, Lahaina News, January 18, 1996: 6.
— small billfish discussed, Lahaina News, January 25, 1996: 11.
— Captain Steve Cravens is top captain, Lahaina News, February 1, 1996: 6.
— discussion of catch ratio for marlin, Lahaina News, February 8, 1996: 10.
— marlin size linked to reproduction, Lahaina News, February 15, 1996: 6.
— update on latest catches, the Hinatea featured, Lahaina News, February 22, 1996: 6.
— shark hits marline during seven-hour fight, Lahaina News, February 29, 1996: 6.
— update on latest catches, the Desperado featured, Lahaina News, March 7, 1996: 6.
— update on latest catches, the Alohilani featured, Lahaina News, March 14, 1996: 6.
— update on latest catches, Judy Ann II featured, Lahaina News, March 21, 1996: 6.
— update on latest catches, Reel Hooker lands 675-pound blue marlin after five hour battle, Lahaina News, April 25, 1996: 8.
— Silk Purse wins Spring Wahine Tournament, Lahaina News, May 2, 1996: 20.
— update on latest catches, the Silk Purse featured, Lahaina News, May 9, 1996: 6.
— update on latest catches, Judy Ann II, Lahaina News, May 16, 1996: 14.
— update on latest catches, The Broadbill featured, Lahaina News, May 23, 1996: 6.
— update on latest catches, Luckey Strike II featured, Lahaina News, May 30, 1996: 11.
— ghost net hauled in by Gemini Charters, Lahaina News, June 6, 1996: 1.
— results of Ma'alaea Tournament, Lahaina News, June 6, 1996: 17.
— update on latest catches, Desperado featured, Lahaina News, June 13, 1996: 13.
— update on latest catches, Finest Kind featured, Lahaina News, June 27, 1996: 17.
— update on latest catches, Reel Hooker featured, Lahaina News, July 4, 1996: 17.
— update on latest catches, crew from Ma'alaea Harbor hooks marlin off Kona, Lahaina News, July 11, 1996: 11.
— update on latest catches, the Exact featured, Lahaina News, July 25, 1996: 10.
— update on latest catches, Islander II featured, Lahaina News, August 1, 1996: 18.
— update on latest catches, Islander II featured, Lahaina News, August 29, 1996: 6.
— update on latest catches, twelve-year old lands 410-pound marlin, Lahaina News, September 5, 1996: 14.
— ways to distinguish sex of marlins discussed, Lahaina News, September 19, 1996: 12.
— results of Lahaina Yacht Club Keiki Fishing Tournament, Lahaina News, September 19, 1996: 12.
— update on latest catches, Finest Kind featured, Lahaina News, September 26, 1996: 12.
— Lahaina Jackpot Fishing Tournament history, Lahaina News, October 3, 1996: 12.
— update on latest catches, Alohilani featured, Lahaina News, October 10, 1996: 12.
— update on latest catches, Luckey Strike II featured, Lahaina News, October 17, 1996: 12.
— Lahaina Jackpot Fishing Tournament to be held, Lahaina News, October 24, 1996: 1.
— results of Lahaina Yacht Club Wahine Jackpot Fishing Tournament, Lahaina News, October 24, 1996: 12.
— Marlin Mischief wins Lahaina Jackpot Fishing Tournament, Lahaina News, October 31, 1996: 1,3.
— update on latest catches, Hokuloa featured, Lahaina News, October 31, 1996: 16.
— Lahaina Jackpot Fishing Tournament results, Lahaina News, November 7, 1996: 12.
— update on latest catches, Silk Purse featured, Lahaina News, November 14, 1996: 12.
— update on current situation, Lahaina News, November 21, 1996: 6.

— Lahaina Yacht Club Spring Wahine Fishing Tournament, Lahaina News, April 2, 1998: 15.
— mahi featured, Lahaina News, April 9, 1998: 15.
— update on latest catches, Luckey Strike featured, Lahaina News, April 23, 1998: 15.
— Lahaina Yacht Club Spring Wahine Fishing Tournament to be held, Lahaina News, April 23, 1998: 15.
— Lahaina Harbor holds clean-up day, Lahaina News, April 30, 1998: 15.
— wahoo (ono) featured, Lahaina News, May 7, 1998: 11.
— Lahaina Yacht Club Spring Wahine Fishing Tournament to be held, Lahaina News, May 7, 1998: 11.
— lobster season closed, Lahaina News, May 7, 1998: 11.
— Andrea LaBore wins Lahaina Yacht Club Spring Wahine Tournament, Lahaina News, May 14, 1998: 15.
— discussion of spearfish, Lahaina News, May 21, 1998: 15.
— National Fishing Week to be held, Lahaina News, June 4, 1998: 15.
— moi season closed, Lahaina News, June 11, 1998: 15.
— shellfish featured, Lahaina News, July 2, 1998: 15.
— update on latest catches, Debby Baldwin catches 554-pound marlin on board Betram Piper, Lahaina News, July 23, 1998: 15.
— update on latest catches, Reel Hooker successful at Kaho'olawe Shoals, Lahaina News, July 30, 1998: 15.
— Hawaiian International Billfish Tournament to be held, Lahaina News, August 6, 1998: 19.
— productivity of Kaho'olawe Shoals discussed, Lahaina News, August 20, 1998: 15.
— update on latest catches, The Absolute featured, Lahaina News, August 27, 1998: 15.
— update on latest catches, Islander II featured, Lahaina News, September 3, 1998: 15.
— Lahaina Yacht Club Keiki Fishing Tournament to be held, Lahaina News, September 10, 1998: 15.
— damage to fishing caused by longlines discussed, Lahaina News, September 10, 1998: 15.
— update on latest catches, Luckey Strike II catches second largest marlin of the year, Lahaina News, September 17, 1998: 15.
— Lahaina Yacht Club's Keiki Fishing Tournament draws over 100 contestants, Lahaina News, September 24, 1998: 1.
— report on Lahaina Yacht Club Keiki Fishing Tournament, Lahaina News, September 24, 1998: 15.
— update on latest catches, Hinatea catches third-largest marlin of the year, Lahaina News, October 1, 1998: 15.
— Lahaina Jackpot Tournament to be held, Lahaina News, October 8, 1998: 15.
— update on latest catches, Aerial III successful at Kaho'olawe Shoal, Lahaina News, October 8, 1998: 15.
— update on latest catches, No Problem featured, Lahaina News, October 15, 1998: 15.
— Lahaina Yacht Club's Wahine Jackpot Tournament to be held, Lahaina News, October 15, 1998: 3.
— Lahaina Jackpot Tournament to be held, Lahaina News, October 22, 1998: 19.
— results of fights, Lahaina News, October 22, 1998: 19.
— results of Wahine Jackpot Tournament, Lahaina News, October 22, 1998: 19.
— results of Lahaina Jackpot Tournament, Lahaina News, October 29, 1998: 19.
— update on the latest catches, Lahaina News, November 12, 1998: 15.
— update on latest catches, The Marlin Mischief featured, Lahaina News, November 19, 1998: 15.
— update on latest catches, Start Me Up catches 434-pound blue marlin, Lahaina News, November 26, 1998: 15.
— update on latest catches, Offshore Hunter featured, Lahaina News, December 3, 1998: 19.
— billfish featured, Lahaina News, December 17, 1998: 19.

— striped marlin described, Lahaina News, December 24, 1998: 9.
— tips on catching stripers and spearfish, Lahaina News, January 7, 1999: 15.
— update on latest catches, Desperado successful off the MC-Buoy, Lahaina News, February 11, 1999: 15.
— update on latest catches, Finest Kind successful near Lahaina Lighthouse, Lahaina News, February 18, 1999: 7.
— stripers and spearfish discussed, Lahaina News, February 25, 1999: 7.
— update on latest catches, The Finest Kind featured, Lahaina News, March 4, 1999: 7.
— update on latest catches, The Marlin Mischief featured, Lahaina News, March 11, 1999: 7.
— update on latest catches, Hinatea featured, Lahaina News, March 18, 1999: 15.
— update on latest catches, The Finest Kind featured, Lahaina News, March 25, 1999: 15.
— top charter boats at Lahaina Harbor for 1998, Lahaina News, April 1, 1999: 15.
— update on latest catches, Reel Hooker featured, Lahaina News, April 8, 1999: 7.
— shark finning still allowed, Lahaina News, April 15, 1999: 7.
— update on , Lahaina News, April 22, 1999: 7.
— update on latest catches, Start Me Up featured, Lahaina News, April 29, 1999: 7.
— update on latest catches, Reel Hooker featured, Lahaina News, May 6, 1999: 17.
— tuna tagging program discussed, Lahaina News, May 13, 1999: 7.
— update on latest catches, The Exact featured, Lahaina News, May 20, 1999: 7.
— Scholar/Athlete of the Week, Lahaina News, May 27, 1999: 7.
— concern over taking too many sharks , Lahaina News, June 3, 1999: 15.
— Ma'alaea Boat and Fishing Club's tournament held, Lahaina News, June 10, 1999: 7.
— update on latest catches, Force Lucky Deuce featured, Lahaina News, June 17, 1999: 7.
— update on latest catches, The Finest Kind featured, Lahaina News, June 24, 1999: 7.
— Captain Mark Davis judged best of 1998, Lahaina News, July 1, 1999: 7.
— update on latest catches, No Problem featured, Lahaina News, July 8, 1999: 7.
— Donnell "Andy" Tate appointed International Game Fish Association (IGFA) representative, Lahaina News, July 15, 1999: 7.
— update on latest catches, Alohilani featured, Lahaina News, July 22, 1999: 7.
— shark finning a concern, Lahaina News, July 29, 1999: 7.
— update on latest catches, Kukana Kai from Ma'alaea Harbor featured, Lahaina News, August 5, 1999: 7.
— update on latest catches, Finest Kind featured, Lahaina News, August 12, 1999: 7.
— Larry Libres Fishing and Diving Tournament to be held, Lahaina News, August 12, 1999: 7.
— update on latest catches, Hinatea featured, Lahaina News, August 19, 1999: 7.
— update on latest catches, Marlin Mischief featured, Lahaina News, August 26, 1999: 7.
— state increases fees for, Lahaina News, September 2, 1999: 14.
— jet skier hooks marlin, Lahaina News, September 2, 1999: 9.
— Lahaina Yacht Club to hold Keiki Fishing Tournament, Lahaina News, September 2, 1999: 9.
— update on latest catches, The Exact featured, Lahaina News, September 9, 1999: 7.
— update on latest catches, Start Me Up and Judy Ann II featured, Lahaina News, September 16, 1999: 6,7.

— results of Lahaina Yacht Club Keiki Fishing Tournament, Lahaina News, September 23, 1999: 7.

— update on latest catches, seven-year-old lands 708-pound marlin, Lahaina News, September 30, 1999: 7.

— Lahaina Jackpot Fishing Tournament to be held, Lahaina News, October 7, 1999: 9.

— third largest marlin hooked, Lahaina News, October 14, 1999: 7.

— Team Kaimana wins Wahine Jackpot Tourney, Lahaina News, October 21, 1999: 9.

— Tai Pan II2 wins Lahaina Jackpot Fishing Tournament, Lahaina News, October 28, 1999: 9.

— United Fishing Agency to hold fish auctions, Lahaina News, November 11, 1999: 7.

— trends in commercial fishing market described, Lahaina News, November 18, 1999: 9.

— discussion of longliner area closure, Lahaina News, December 23, 1999: 9.

— impact of tuna fishing on other fish, Lahaina News, December 30, 1999: 9.

— Stiped marlin returning to Hawaii waters, Lahaina News, January 6, 2000: 7.

— bait keeps pesky shark busy, Lahaina News, January 13, 2000: 7.

— update on latest catches, Wild Life featured, Lahaina News, January 20, 2000: 7.

— PGA Tour official hooks large marlin of Lana'i, Lahaina News, January 27, 2000: 7.

— usefulness of circle hooks discussed, Lahaina News, February 3, 2000: 7.

— tuna associate with fish aggregate devices, Lahaina News, February 10, 2000: 7.

— update on latest catches, Hinatea featured, Lahaina News, February 17, 2000: 7.

— update on latest catches, The Marlin Mischief featured, Lahaina News, February 24, 2000: 7.

— editorial calling for ban on shark finning, Lahaina News, February 24, 2000: 7.

— update on latest catches, Hinatea featured, Lahaina News, March 2, 2000: 7.

— studies shed light on differences between marlin sexes, Lahaina News, March 9, 2000: 7.

— update on latest catches, Desperado featured, Lahaina News, March 16, 2000: 7.

— summary of 1998 landings, Lahaina News, March 23, 2000: 7.

— summary of 1999, Lahaina News, March 30, 2000: 7.

— update on latest catches, Marlin Mischief featured, Lahaina News, April 6, 2000: 7.

— mahi discussed, Lahaina News, April 20, 2000: 7.

— update on latest catches, Desperado featured, Lahaina News, April 27, 2000: 7.

— update on latest catches, Betram Pipe featured, Lahaina News, May 4, 2000: 15.

— results of Lahaina Yacht Club Spring Wahine tournament, Lahaina News, May 11, 2000: 15.

— update on latest catches, Offshore Hunter featured, Lahaina News, May 18, 2000: 15.

— update on latest catches, Ho'okela featured, Lahaina News, May 25, 2000: 9.

— update on latest catches, The Offshore Hunter featured, Lahaina News, June 1, 2000: 9.

— update on latest catches, Ho'okela featured, Lahaina News, June 8, 2000: 15.

— update on latest catches, Paul Abatie top captain for 1999, Lahaina News, June 15, 2000: 13.

— success in Lahaina Harbor, Lahaina News, June 22, 2000: 12.

— story recounted, Lahaina News, June 22, 2000: 5.

— details on fishing yellowfin tuna, Lahaina News, June 29, 2000: 15.

— update on latest catches, Judy Ann II featured, Lahaina News, July 6, 2000: 13.

— fishing for opelu described, Lahaina News, July 13, 2000: 5.

— update on latest catches, Finest Kind featured, Lahaina News, July 13, 2000: 7.

— update on latest catches, Desperado featured, Lahaina News, July 20, 2000: 7.

— update on latest catches, the Exact featured, Lahaina News, July 27, 2000: 7.

— update on latest catches, The Finest Kind featured, Lahaina News, August 3, 2000: 7.

— longliners criticized following Judge David Ezra's ruling, Lahaina News, August 10, 2000: 7.

— update on latest catches, Marlin Mischief, Lahaina News, August 17, 2000: 7.

— update on latest catches, Hinatea featured, Lahaina News, August 24, 2000: 7.

— estimates of turtles killed by longline hooks, Lahaina News, August 31, 2000: 7.

— Hawaiian cultural practices discussed, Lahaina News, September 7, 2000: 15.

— Lahaina Yacht Club annual Keiki Fishing Tournament to be held, Lahaina News, September 14, 2000: 1.

— update on latest catches, Start Me Up Too catches mahi mahi, Lahaina News, September 14, 2000: 9.

— Lahaina Yacht Club Keiki Fishing Tournament held, Lahaina News, September 21, 2000: 1.

— update on latest catches, Absolute featured, Lahaina News, September 21, 2000: 9.

— update on latest catches, Judy Ann II featured, Lahaina News, October 5, 2000: 9.

— update on latest catches, Hinatea featured, Lahaina News, October 12, 2000: 9.

— update on latest catches, Meleana catches 552-pound marlin, Lahaina News, October 19, 2000: 9.

— "Start Me Up" wins Lahaina Yacht Club Wahine Fishing Tournament, Lahaina News, October 26, 2000: 11.

— results of Lahaina Jackpot Tournament, Lahaina News, November 2, 2000: 9.

— update on latest catches, Luckey Strike II featured, Lahaina News, November 16, 2000: 11.

— study to use computer tags to track billfish, Lahaina News, November 30, 2000: 7.

— update on latest catches, Offshore Hunter featured, Lahaina News, December 7, 2000: 13.

— tips for identifying bigeye tuna, Lahaina News, December 21, 2000: 7.

— update on latest catches, The Finest Kind featured, Lahaina News, December 28, 2000: 7.

— update on latest catches, Ho'okela featured, Lahaina News, January 4, 2001: 9.

— rigging discussed, Lahaina News, January 11, 2001: 9.

— marlin nervous system featured, Lahaina News, January 18, 2001: 9.

— words of writer Zane Grey describes, Lahaina News, January 25, 2001: 9.

— striped marlin featured, Lahaina News, February 1, 2001: 15.

— update on latest catches, Lahaina News, February 8, 2001: 15.

— tags helping to track marlin movement, Lahaina News, February 15, 2001: 13.

— importance of coral reefs for, Lahaina News, February 22, 2001: 13.

— incredible catches related, Lahaina News, March 1, 2001: 15.

— update on latest catches; Judy Ann II featured, Lahaina News, March 8, 2001: 13.

— update on latest catches, Aerial III featured, Lahaina News, March 15, 2001: 11.

— update on latest catches, Hoʻokela featured, Lahaina News, March 29, 2001: 13.

— update on latest catches; Start Me Up 2 sets Lahaina Harbor for mahi mahi, Lahaina News, April 5, 2001: 15.

— update on latest catches, Kanoa featured, Lahaina News, April 12, 2001: 15.

— Lahaina Yacht Club to hold Spring Wahine Fishing Tournament, Lahaina News, April 12, 2001: 15.

— impact of judicial ruling on longliners discussed, Lahaina News, April 19, 2001: 13.

— Lahaina Yacht Club's Spring Wahine Fishing Tournament to be held, Lahaina News, April 26, 2001: 15.

— history of Fish Aggregation Devices, Lahaina News, May 3, 2001: 15.

— results of Lahaina Yacht Club Spring Wahine Tournament, Lahaina News, May 10, 2001: 15.

— update on latest catches, The Exact featured, Lahaina News, May 17, 2001: 15.

— update on latest catches; the Hinatea featured, Lahaina News, May 24, 2001: 15.

— update on latest catches; Thomas Miller new co-captain of The Desperado, Lahaina News, May 31, 2001: 13.

— nine-year-old girl battles marlin, Lahaina News, June 7, 2001: 15.

— locals to share fishing stories, Lahaina News, June 7, 2001: 20.

— update on latest catches; The Offshore Hunter successful, Lahaina News, June 14, 2001: 15.

— update on latest catches; Start Me Up featured, Lahaina News, July 12, 2001: 13.

— update on latest catches, Kia Iokaʻuhane featured, Lahaina News, July 19, 2001: 13.

— update on latest catches, Judy Ann II featured, Lahaina News, July 26, 2001: 13.

— Project SEA-Link to hold "Great American Fish Count 2001", Lahaina News, July 26, 2001: 16.

— update on latest catches, Start Me Up 2 featured, Lahaina News, August 2, 2001: 13.

— update on latest catches, Reel Hooker featured, Lahaina News, August 9, 2001: 13.

— Department of Land and Natural Resources explains fishing regulations, Lahaina News, August 9, 2001: 8.

— update on latest catches, Start Me Up 2 featured, Lahaina News, August 16, 2001: 13.

— update on latest catches, The Absolute featured, Lahaina News, August 23, 2001: 13.

— update on latest catches, Unreel featured, Lahaina News, August 30, 2001: 13.

— update on latest catches, the Absolute featured, Lahaina News, September 6, 2001: 13.

— update on latest catches, the Unreel featured, Lahaina News, September 13, 2001: 13.

— Lahaina Yacht Club to hold Keiki Fishing Tournament, Lahaina News, September 20, 2001: 13.

— update on latest catches, Judy Ann II successful of Palaoa Point Lighthouse, Lahaina News, September 27, 2001: 13.

— state to replace Fish Aggregation Devices (FADS), Lahaina News, September 27, 2001: 13.

— results of Lahaina Yacht Club Keiki Fishing Tournament, Lahaina News, October 4, 2001: 13.

— update on latest catches, Finest Kind featured, Lahaina News, October 11, 2001: 13.

— Lahaina Jackpot Fishing Tournament to be held, Lahaina News, October 18, 2001: 13.

— mahi mahi discussed, Lahaina News, October 25, 2001: 13.

— Wahine Jackpot Tournament results, Lahaina News, November 1, 2001: 13.

— Oahu team wins Lahaina Jackpot Tournament, Lahaina News, November 8, 2001: 13.

— update on latest catches, the Hinatea featured, Lahaina News, November 15, 2001: 13.

— update on latest catches, No Problem featured, Lahaina News, November 22, 2001: 11.

— education specialist at Department of Land and Natural Resources Russel Sparks to speak on "Fisheries Management in Hawaii", Lahaina News, November 22, 2001: 20.

— update on latest catches, the Hinatea featured, Lahaina News, November 29, 2001: 13.

— use of ʻopelu as bait discussed, Lahaina News, December 6, 2001: 13.

— fish parasites discussed, Lahaina News, December 13, 2001: 13.

— skipjacks discussed, Lahaina News, December 20, 2001: 13.

— update on latest spearfish catches, Lahaina News, December 27, 2001: 13.

— birds as sign of fish, Lahaina News, January 10, 2002: 13.

— marlin behaviors discussed, Lahaina News, January 17, 2002: 13.

— marlin behaviors discussed, part II, Lahaina News, January 24, 2002: 13.

— update on latest catches, Desperado featured, Lahaina News, January 31, 2002: 13.

— fishing boat The Piper scores a "Hawaiian Grand Slam", Lahaina News, February 7, 2002: 13.

— update on latest catches, Marlin Mischief featured, Lahaina News, February 14, 2002: 13.

— billfish behavior discussed, Lahaina News, February 21, 2002: 13.

— discussion on whether marlin attack whales, Lahaina News, February 28, 2002: 13.

— discussion of what billfish see, part I, Lahaina News, March 7, 2002: 13.

— discussion of what billfish see, part II, Lahaina News, March 14, 2002: 13.

— new research project to track tuna habits at FADs, Lahaina News, March 21, 2002: 13.

— update on latest catches, The Desperado featured, Lahaina News, March 28, 2002: 11.

— diver spears ono, Lahaina News, April 4, 2002: 13.

— research on pelagic fish described, Lahaina News, April 11, 2002: 13.

— study reveals data on great white sharks, Lahaina News, April 18, 2002: 13.

— update on latest catches, Start Me Up Too, Lahaina News, April 25, 2002: 13.

— Lahaina Yacht Club to hold Spring Wahine Fishing Tournament, Lahaina News, April 25, 2002: 13.

— update on latest catches, Aerial III featured, Lahaina News, May 2, 2002: 13.

— results of Lahaina Yacht Club Spring Wahine Tournament, Lahaina News, May 9, 2002: 13.

— Lahaina Yacht Club to hold Wahine fishing tournament, Lahaina News, May 9, 2002: 13.

— update on latest catches, Start Me Up Too, Lahaina News, May 16, 2002: 13.

— update on latest catches, The Piper, Lahaina News, May 23, 2002: 13.

— update on latest catches, Ikaika Kai featured, Lahaina News, June 6, 2002: 13.

— update on latest catches, the Finest Kind featured, Lahaina News, June 13, 2002: 13.

— update on latest catches, Start Me Up Too featured, Lahaina News, June 20, 2002: 13.

— advantages to single barbless hooks discussed, Lahaina News, June 27, 2002: 13.

— state to set new minimum legal sizes, Lahaina News, July 4, 2002: 1.

— update on latest catches, the Desperado featured, Lahaina News, July 4, 2002: 13.

— update on latest catches, Iwa Lele featured, Lahaina News, July 11, 2002: 13.

— update on latest catches, Start Me Up Too successful at LA-Buoy, Lahaina News, July 18, 2002: 13.

— update on latest catches, Ikaika Kai featured, Lahaina News, July 25, 2002: 15.

— update on latest catches, The Desperado featured, Lahaina News, August 1, 2002: 15.

— update on latest catches, Desperado featured, Lahaina News, August 8, 2002: 13.

— update on latest catches, Reel Hooker featured, Lahaina News, August 15, 2002: 13.

— update on latest catches, Start Me Up Too featured, Lahaina News, August 22, 2002: 11.

— 25th Annual Wahine Jackpot results, Lahaina News, August 29, 2002: 11.

— Lahaina Jackpot Fishing Tournament won by the Pualele, Lahaina News, September 5, 2002: 13.

— update on latest catches, the Absolute featured, Lahaina News, September 12, 2002: 11.

— update on latest catches, the Finest Kind featured, Lahaina News, September 19, 2002: 11.

— results of Keiki Fishing Tournament, Lahaina News, September 26, 2002: 13.

— update on latest catches, Upcountry featured, Lahaina News, October 3, 2002: 13.

— update on latest catches, the Finest Kind featured, Lahaina News, October 24, 2002: 11.

— update on latest catches, The Hinatea featured, Lahaina News, October 31, 2002: 11.

— update on latest catches, The Iwa Lele featured, Lahaina News, November 7, 2002: 11.

— importance of fishing holes to ancient Hawaiians, Lahaina News, November 14, 2002: 11.

— history of the fishing rod, Lahaina News, November 21, 2002: 11.

— shark attacks discussed, Lahaina News, November 28, 2002: 13.

— shark attacks discussed, Lahaina News, December 5, 2002: 11.

— evolution of the spinning reel discussed, Lahaina News, December 12, 2002: 11.

— evolution of Hawaiian fishing, Lahaina News, December 19, 2002: 11.

— tuna featured, Lahaina News, December 26, 2002: 11.

— tuna featured, Lahaina News, January 2, 2003: 13.

— striped marlin featured, Lahaina News, January 9, 2003: 13.

— stock of tuna discussed, Lahaina News, January 16, 2003: 13.

— history of Fish Aggregating Devices, Lahaina News, January 23, 2003: 13.

— American Fisheries Society of Hawaii to hold annual meeting, Lahaina News, January 23, 2003: 2.

— Fish Aggregating Devices (FADs) discussed, Lahaina News, January 30, 2003: 13.

— Fish Aggregating Devices (FADs) discussed, Lahaina News, February 6, 2003: 13.

— update on latest catches, the KuoKoa featured, Lahaina News, February 13, 2003: 13.

— update on latest catches, the Exact featured, Lahaina News, February 20, 2003: 13.

— Fish Aggregating Devices (FADs) discussed, Lahaina News, February 27, 2003: 13.

— update on latest catches, the Desperado featured, Lahaina News, March 6, 2003: 13.

— hammerhead sharks featured, Lahaina News, March 13, 2003: 13.

— update on latest catches, battle with marlin featured, Lahaina News, March 20, 2003: 13.

— update on latest catches, Lahaina Charter Fleet featured, Lahaina News, March 27, 2003: 13.

— choosing the right lure discussed, Lahaina News, April 3, 2003: 13.

— advice on fishing for marlin, Lahaina News, April 10, 2003: 11.

— update on latest catches, Iwa Lele featured, Lahaina News, April 17, 2003: 13.

— update on latest catches, fisherman Jake Miyake featured, Lahaina News, April 24, 2003: 11.

— update on latest catches, Start Me Up Too featured, Lahaina News, May 1, 2003: 13.

— results of Lahaina Yacht Club Spring Wahine Tournament, Kukana Kai featured, Lahaina News, May 8, 2003: 13.

— update on latest catches, Luckey Strike featured, Lahaina News, May 15, 2003: 13.

— update on latest catches, Aerial III featured, Lahaina News, May 22, 2003: 13.

— update on latest catches, Start Me Up Too featured, Lahaina News, May 29, 2003: 13.

— update on latest catches, Kukana Kai featured, Lahaina News, June 5, 2003: 13.

— update on latest catches, Iwa Lele featured, Lahaina News, June 12, 2003: 11.

— update on latest catches, Start Me Up Too and Jamie Carson featured, Lahaina News, June 19, 2003: 13.

— update on latest catches, Start Me Up Too featured, Lahaina News, June 26, 2003: 11.

— update on latest catches, Michelle Havens featured, Lahaina News, July 3, 2003: 13.

— update on latest catches, Start Me Up featured, Lahaina News, July 10, 2003: 13.

— update on latest catches, Iwa Lele featured, Lahaina News, July 17, 2003: 13.

— update on latest catches, Luckey Strike II featured, Lahaina News, July 24, 2003: 13.

— results of Wahine Jackpot Tournament, Lahaina News, July 31, 2003: 13.

— Jeni-K wins Lahaina Yacht Club Jackpot Fishing Tournament, Lahaina News, August 7, 2003: 13.

— Tuna Club featured, Lahaina News, August 14, 2003: 13.

— discussion of game fish speed, Lahaina News, August 21, 2003: 13.

— update on latest catches, Start Me Up featured, Lahaina News, August 28, 2003: 13.

— scientific work classifying billfish discussed, Lahaina News, September 4, 2003: 13.

— importance of gaffs discussed, Lahaina News, September 11, 2003: 13.

— pressure from factory fleets discussed, Lahaina News, September 18, 2003: 13.

— update on latest catches, The Slightly Perfect featured, Lahaina News, September 25, 2003: 13.

— Lahaina Yacht Club's Keiki Fishing Tournament held, Lahaina News, October 2, 2003: 13.

— Western Pacific Fishery Management Council considering conservation efforts, Lahaina News, October 9, 2003: 13.

— see also Lahaina Jackpot Fishing Tournament, longlines

FISHPONDS

— threatened by proposed hotel development on Moloka'i, Lahaina Sun, May 26, 1971: 6.

— see also 'Ao'ao O Na Loko I'a O Maui

FITZGERALD, ERIC

— thanks residents for support after accident, Lahaina News, April 29, 1999: 1,20.

FITZMAURICE, MICHAEL

— promoted to resident manager at the Royal Lahaina Resort, Lahaina News, August 12, 1993: 9.

FITZPATRICK, KEVIN [MUSICIAN]
— to perform at Ocean Terrace, Lahaina News, May 13, 1993: 12.
— to perform at Kea Lani Hotel, Lahaina News, May 20, 1993: 10,11.

FIYAH [MUSICAL GROUP]
— to perform at Moose McGillycuddy's, Lahaina News, May 2, 1996: 15.
— to perform at World Café, Lahaina News, August 1, 1996: 20.

FLAG
— History of Hawaiian flag detailed, Lahaina Sun, July 21, 1971: 8.
— historic flag to return to Lahaina, Lahaina News, September 19, 2002: 1,21.
— 19th century Hawaiian flag preserved at the Old Lahaina Courthouse, Lahaina News, April 10, 2003: 3.

FLAMCOM, INC. [BUSINESS]
— Mark Ellman sells Avalon Restaurant to, Lahaina News, December 10, 1998: 17.

FLANAGAN, BARRY [MUSICIAN]
— to perform at El Crab Catcher in Whaler's Village, Lahaina News, September 5, 1990: 15.
— accompanied Stephen Stills at El Crab Catcher, Lahaina News, May 23, 1991: 11.
— to perform at El Crab Catcher, Lahaina News, October 24, 1991: 21.

FLANAGAN, TRACY
— new owner of Maui Style, Lahaina News, June 13, 1991: 9.

FLEA MARKET
— proposed for Kahului Fairgrounds, Lahaina Sun, May 5, 1971: 7.

FLECK, ANNE T.
— to take command of Coast Guard cutter Cape Corwin, Lahaina News, May 28, 1986: 3.

FLECK, BELA [MUSICIAN]
— to perform at Maui Arts and Cultural Center, Lahaina News, December 12, 2002: 17.
— to perform at Maui Arts and Cultural Center, Lahaina News, December 12, 2002: 20,21.

FLEETHAM, DAVE
— photograph of sand bar sharks on cover of Life Magazine, Lahaina News, August 29, 1991: 2.

FLEETWOOD MAC [MUSICAL GROUP]
— connection to West Maui, Lahaina News, September 9, 1987: 7,8.

FLEETWOOD, MICK [MUSICIAN]
— to play at Lahaina Civic Center, Lahaina News, May 1, 1985: 10.
— update on concert, tickets selling, Lahaina News, May 29, 1985: 20.
— performance reviewed, Lahaina News, June 5, 1985: 10.
— interview with, Lahaina News, February 3, 1988: 7.
— to perform at Maui Marriott Ballroom, Lahaina News, May 31, 1989: 21.
— praises musical group The Penetrators, Lahaina News, June 14, 1989: 16.

FLEMING BEACH
— photographs, Lahaina Sun, May 23, 1973: 1,12,13.
— Lahainaluna High School students learn at, Lahaina News, June 5, 1997: 5.
— see also Kapalua Beach

FLEMING, DAVID THOMAS
— career described, Lahaina News, July 19, 1989: 4.

FLEMING PARK, D.T.
— see D.T. Fleming Beach Park

FLEMING, THERESA
— appointed property manager at Vacation-Maui.com, Lahaina News, February 13, 2003: 8.

FLEMING'S ON THE GREENS [RESTAURANT]
— opens in the Kapalua Village Clubhouse, Lahaina News, October 19, 2000: 16.
— featured, Lahaina News, November 30, 2000: 13.
— open for holding fundraisers, Lahaina News, April 11, 2002: 8.
— to host "An Evening with Sterline Vineyards in a Celebration of Wine and Food", Lahaina News, June 27, 2002: 9.

FLETCHER, CHARLES
— geologist says beaches can be restored, Lahaina News, July 27, 1995: 1,16.
— speaks on need to protect beaches, Lahaina News, October 12, 1995: 1,16.

FLETCHER PACIFIC CONSTRUCTION CO., LTD. [BUSINESS]
— new name of Pacific Construction Co., Ltd., Lahaina News, June 13, 1991: 18.

FLEX [MUSICAL GROUP]
— featured, Lahaina News, January 27, 1988: 6.

FLIRTATIONS, THE [MUSICAL GROUP]
— to perform at Maui arts and Cultural Center, Lahaina News, March 21, 1996: 13.

FLOATING LANTERNS CEREMONY
— to be organized by Lahaina Jodo Mission, Lahaina News, June 29, 2000: 1.

FLOOD, CARLA
— designed t-shirt for the Kihei Community Association, Lahaina News, November 26, 1992: 18.

FLOOD, E. EMMETT
— spoke at Public Utilities Commission meeting, Lahaina Sun, December 23, 1970: 4.

FLOODING
— on Maui, Lahaina Sun, February 3, 1971: 1.
— heroic responses celebrated, Lahaina Sun, February 17, 1971: 5.
— all counties in Hawaii qualify for emergency flood insurance, Lahaina Sun, July 14, 1971: 2.
— Flood Plain and Tsunami Inundation Area ordinance passed by Maui County Council, Lahaina Sun, January 26, 1972: 15.
— damaged houses in Lahaina, Lahaina Sun, March 1, 1972: 3.
— residents ask for relief, Lahaina Sun, March 15, 1972: 4.
— Lahaina householders complain of lack of support, Lahaina Sun, March 22, 1972: 5.
— federal Soil Conservation Service expected to create plan for Wailuku, Lahaina Sun, July 5, 1972: 10.
— suit against Maui County planned for flooding from last year, Lahaina Sun, July 19, 1972: 7.
— reported in Waihee Valley, Lahaina Sun, July 26, 1972: 9.
— appropriation for flood control for Iao Stream, Lahaina Sun, August 16, 1972: 10.
— responsibility discussed, Lahaina Sun, August 16, 1972: 17.
— County denies flood damage claims , Lahaina Sun, September 27, 1972: 11.
— plans discussed by Army Corps of Engineers, Lahaina Sun, November 29, 1972: 10.
— history and future plans for Lahaina and Kihei detailed by Army Corps of Engineers, Lahaina Sun, December 6, 1972: 7.
— suit filed by Piihana residents against Maui County, Lahaina Sun, December 20, 1972: 14.
— preparations for discussed, Lahaina Sun, February 14, 1973: 9.
— control project in Waiuku could begin in 1974, Lahaina Sun, March 7, 1973: 5.
— Army Corps of Engineers recommends converting part of Kahoma stream to concrete channel, Lahaina Sun, March 21, 1973: 1.
— deadline to appeal flood zone boundaries expires soon, Lahaina News, October 1, 1980: 4.

— Wainee Street flooded, Lahaina News, September 11, 1997: 1,5.
— Maui County Council seeking ways to help victims of, Lahaina News, February 5, 1998: 1,2.

FLORAL DECORATING CONTEST
— to be held at Lahaina Cannery Mall, Lahaina News, May 13, 1999: 15.

FLORAL DESIGNS MAUI [BUSINESS]
— chosen by Bon Apetit as top creative florist, Lahaina News, August 8, 1990: 6.

FLORAL GALLERY [BUSINESS]
— opens in The Shops at Wailea, Lahaina News, May 3, 2001: 9.

FLORES, EDDIE
— offering real estate training class, Lahaina News, April 4, 2002: 8.

FLORES, OSCAR [ARTIST]
— paintings described, Lahaina News, May 15, 1985: 11.

FLORIAN, BUCK
— named manager of Plantation House Restaurant, Lahaina News, May 8, 1991: 6.

FLORIBUNDA MAUI [BUSINESS]
— opens, Lahaina News, June 4, 1992: 9.

FLORIDA
— reviewed as travel destination, Lahaina Times, September, 1980 volume 4 number 8: 2.

FLOTTE, EDDIE [ARTIST]
— exhibits watercolors at Lahaina Cannery, Lahaina News, June 10, 1987: 3.
— to demonstrate painting to Hawaii Watercolor Society, Lahaina News, July 25, 2002: 20.

FLOWER DRUM SONG [PLAY]
— to be performed by Maui Youth Theatre, Lahaina News, December 17, 1986: 2.
— formed by Maui Youth Theatre, Lahaina News, February 25, 1987: 3,6.

FLOWER, TONI
— charged with setting fires around Lahaina, Lahaina Sun, June 27, 1973: 6.
— denies charges, Lahaina Sun, July 11, 1973: 6.
— guilty of rape, Lahaina News, July 15, 1980: 6.
— ruled to be insane, Lahaina News, October 15, 1980: 8.

FLOWERS
— Hyatt Regency Maui to hold show, Lahaina News, April 27, 1988: 4.
— Tropical and Exotic Flower Show winners announced, Lahaina News, May 18, 1988: 18.

FLUORIDATION
— positions offered in conflicting editorials, Lahaina Sun, March 14, 1973: 7.
— "Fluoridation in the 21st Century—Yes or No" to be held, Lahaina News, June 7, 2001: 21.

FLYING CLOUD [SHIP]
— featured, Lahaina Sun, March 21, 1973: 14.

FLYING KARAMAZOV BROTHERS
— to perform at Baldwin Auditorium, Lahaina News, February 4, 1987: 11.
— jugglers to perform at Grand Hyatt Wailea Ballroom, Lahaina News, September 24, 1992: 17.
— to perform, Lahaina News, March 25, 1999: 17.

FLYNN, JACKIE [COMEDIAN]
— to perform at Comedy Club and the Sports Page, Lahaina News, December 5, 1990: 9,14.

FLYNN, KEVIN [COMEDIAN]
— to perform at Comedy Club, Lahaina News, October 10, 1991: 14.

FM 100
— hopes to overturn rejection of permit to build radio tower in Ulupalakua, Lahaina News, March 28, 1990: 1.

FM 101
— hires Bill Dawson to air staff, Lahaina News, December 12, 1991: 16.
— radio station, Lahaina News, July 25, 1996: 2.

FOGELBERG, DAN [MUSICIAN]
— to perform at the Royal Lahaina Tennis Stadium, Lahaina News, April 22, 1993: 15.
— to perform, Lahaina News, May 6, 1993: 15.

FOLEY, MIKE [POLITICIAN]
— planner opens West Maui Environment Planning, Lahaina News, January 21, 1999: 11.
— appointed county planning director, Lahaina News, November 28, 2002: 1,2.
— Maui County Planning Director to speak to West Maui Taxpayers Association, Lahaina News, January 9, 2003: 3.
— to speak to West Maui Taxpayers Association, Lahaina News, January 16, 2003: 1.
— County Planning Director to speak at Haiku Community Association, Lahaina News, February 13, 2003: 17.
— County Planning Director to speak at Haiku Community Association, Lahaina News, February 20, 2003: 16.

FOLK ARTS APPRENTICESHIP AWARDS
— application deadline soon, Lahaina News, March 1, 1989: 2.

FOLKDANCE
— Lahaina Public Library to offer program on international, Lahaina News, November 8, 1989: 6.

FOLLIES [MUSICAL]
— performed by Maui Community Theatre, Lahaina News, January 4, 1984: 10.
— performed by Maui Community Theatre, Lahaina News, February 29, 1984: 3.
— final weekend of, Lahaina News, March 14, 1984: 8.

FOLLOWING SEA [BUSINESS]
— for sale by InterIsland Resorts, Ltd., Lahaina News, July 15, 1982: 11.

FONDA, PETER
— met with students of Kam III School, Lahaina Sun, March 24, 1971: 4.

FONG CONSTRUCTION, INC. [BUSINESS]
— building highway from Ma'alaea to Kahului Airport, Lahaina Sun, November 18, 1970: 1.

FONG, DANNY
— becomes president of Maui Chinese Club, Lahaina Sun, May 31, 1972: 10.

FONG, HIRAM [POLITICIAN]
— announces grant for teacher training, Lahaina Sun, January 27, 1971: 4.
— announces that Quality Wiping Rag Co. has been awarded a federal contract, Lahaina Sun, April 14, 1971: 1.
— discusses federal funding for flood control projects, Lahaina Sun, June 2, 1971: 3.
— attends dinner to support Rick Reed's election, Lahaina News, August 13, 1992: 11.

FONSECA, DAVID
— finishes Gatorade Ironman Triathlon World Championship, Lahaina News, October 15, 1992: 10.

FOO FIGHTERS [MUSICAL GROUP]
— to perform at Maui Arts and Cultural Center, Lahaina News, July 27, 2000: 21.

FOOD AND DRINKS

— history of Maui chips described, Lahaina Sun, August 11, 1971: 9.

— Maui Filipino Barrio Fiesta to feature food, Lahaina Sun, May 16, 1973: 10.

— production of Hawaiian Host macadamia nut chocolate candies described, Lahaina Sun, May 16, 1973: 15.

— drinks at Yamamoto's Fountain described, Lahaina Sun, July 18, 1973: 10.

— Jack Edwards plans to offer low price meats, Lahaina Sun, July 25, 1973: 4.

— Lahaina's first tepanyaki Japanese restaurant opens, Lahaina Sun, August 29, 1973: 15.

— Rum and vodka to be made on Maui, Lahaina News, April 1, 1980: 14.

— drug use by restaurant employees, Lahaina Times, June, 1980 volume 4 number 5: 6.

— review of Blackbeard's (restaurant at Wharf Shopping Center), Lahaina Times, June, 1980 volume 4 number 5: 7.

— review of Stakeout (restaurant in Lahaina Square), Lahaina Times, June, 1980 volume 4 number 5: 7.

— review of Charley's (restaurant in Paia town), Lahaina Times, June, 1980 volume 4 number 5: 7.

— review of Stakeout (restaurant in Lahaina Square), Lahaina Times, June, 1980 volume 4 number 5: 7.

— co-op forming in Lahaina, Lahaina News, June 1, 1981: 16.

— South Pacific Lager, from Papua New Guinea, introduced into Hawaii, Lahaina News, September 15, 1982: 10.

— Foremost Dairies sold, Lahaina News, September 15, 1982: 2.

— Castle & Cook terminates banana operations in Nicaragua, Lahaina News, November 15, 1982: 11.

— editorial criticizing Hawaii Board of Agriculture permission to Safeway to import milk, Lahaina News, May 15, 1983: 2.

— column "For the Love of Wine" begins running in Lahaina News, Lahaina News, September 7, 1983: 13.

— James Beard column begins running in Lahaina News, Lahaina News, September 7, 1983: 13.

— review of Kapalua Wine Symposium, Lahaina News, October 5, 1983: 13.

— editorial on Safeway importing mainland milk, Lahaina News, October 19, 1983: 2.

— State Agriculture Director recommends Safeway be allowed to bring milk to the islands, Lahaina News, December 7, 1983: 14.

— Hawaiian champagne discussed, Lahaina News, December 14, 1983: 15.

— Safeway milk decision delayed, Lahaina News, December 28, 1983: 7.

— milk decision delayed again, Lahaina News, February 15, 1984: 2,14.

— Safeway sues State over decision to stop milk imports, Lahaina News, February 29, 1984: 17.

— request made to increase number of liquor licenses in Lahaina, Lahaina News, February 29, 1984: 17.

— state okays 10-day pull date for milk, Lahaina News, March 28, 1984: 17.

— editorial reflecting on court decision to allow Safeway to import milk, Lahaina News, May 16, 1984: 2.

— Safeway receives permission from State to import milk from mainland, Lahaina News, May 23, 1984: 17.

— editorial on Safeway importing mainland milk, Lahaina News, May 23, 1984: 2.

— ABC Stores and 7-11 acquire license to sell liquor, Lahaina News, May 23, 1984: 3.

— sushi bar opens at Maui Inter-Continental Wailea Hotel, Lahaina News, June 13, 1984: 3.

— editorial on high cost of in Hawaii, Lahaina News, June 27, 1984: 2.

— Safeway files suit that "shelf life" law interferes with interstate commerce, Lahaina News, July 4, 1984: 18.

— Safeway and the State reach an agreement on shelf-life bill for milk, Lahaina News, September 26, 1984: 14.

— editorial on milk settlement between Safeway and the State, Lahaina News, September 26, 1984: 2.

— monthly "For Wining and Dining in Style" column begins, is not otherwise indexed, Lahaina News, December 5, 1984: .

— Girl Scout cookies to go on sale February 3, Lahaina News, January 9, 1985: 3.

— Linda Ryan to offer cooking classes, Lahaina News, January 23, 1985: 3.

— Maui Vegetable Grower's Cooperative Association featured, Lahaina News, January 30, 1985: 18.

— value of chocolate discussed, Lahaina News, February 6, 1985: 10.

— editorial on Haleakala Dairy being required to get a license to import milk to Oahu, Lahaina News, April 17, 1985: 2.

— Chef Sabastian offering gourmet workshop, Lahaina News, May 15, 1985: 8.

— Kapalua Wine Symposium offered at Kapalua Resort, Lahaina News, August 7, 1985: 8.

— children's supplement features the milk cow, Lahaina News, January 29, 1986: A,B,C,D.

— Kapalua Wine Symposium to be held at Kapalua Bay Hotel, Lahaina News, July 9, 1986: 3.

— costs in Hawaii compared to other cities, Lahaina News, August 6, 1986: 2.

— Linda Ryan begins "Cooking with Joy" column, Lahaina News, August 6, 1986: 8.

— Stouffer Wailea Beach Resort hosts La Confrerie de la Chaine Des Rotisseurs, Lahaina News, August 20, 1986: 3.

— mini reviews of local restaurants offered, Lahaina News, August 27, 1986: 10.

— Kapalua Wine Symposium organized, Lahaina News, April 1, 1987: 3.

— Pizza Feast held at Inter-Continental Hotel Wailea, Lahaina News, January 27, 1988: 3.

— non-alcoholic drinks described, Lahaina News, August 30, 1989: 9.

— brunches around Lahaina reviewed, Lahaina News, November 1, 1989: 16.

— Salon Le Mesnil to be paired by executive chef Roger Dikon, Lahaina News, November 28, 1990: 10.

— limits to testing for pesticide residue discussed, Lahaina News, November 28, 1990: 5.

— Tuesday is a Taste of Lahaina continues, Lahaina News, July 25, 1991: 12,13.

— Taste of Lahaina to be held, Lahaina News, August 27, 1992: 3.

— "Best of Maui" guest chefs dinner to take place at Plantation House, Lahaina News, September 24, 1992: 14,14.

— Maui Prince Hotel hosting food and wine seminar, Lahaina News, September 24, 1992: 18.

— January proclaimed as Hawaii Regional Cuisine month at Maui Prince Hotel, Lahaina News, January 14, 1993: 14.

— Vegetarian Food Festival to be held, Lahaina News, April 29, 1993: 3.

— changes in Lahaina restaurants, Lahaina News, July 15, 1993: 11.

— update on restaurants, Lahaina News, August 12, 1993: 12.

— "Dining Early" column features summary of restaurants, not always indexed otherwise, Lahaina News, September 2, 1993: 10,11.

— "Maui Chefs Presents" to be held, Lahaina News, September 2, 1993: 11,12.

— "A Taste of Lahaina" to be held, Lahaina News, September 9, 1993: 11,12.

— Maui Foodbank sponsoring food safety class, Lahaina News, September 9, 1993: 5.

— "A Taste of Lahaina" to be held, Lahaina News, September 16, 1993: 1,15.

— "The Wine Press" column begins, not usually indexed, Lahaina News, September 16, 1993: 16.

— results of "A Taste of Lahaina", Lahaina News, September 23, 1993: 11.

— employees at Ka'anapali Beach Hotel following diet developed at Waianae Coast Comprehensive Health Center, Lahaina News, November 25, 1993: 1,3.

— dairies and farmers question use of growth hormone, Lahaina News, February 17, 1994: 1,3.

— micro breweries may be opening soon, Lahaina News, February 24, 1994: 10.

— training offered to liquor servers, Lahaina News, April 21, 1994: 12.

— "A Taste of Lahaina" to be held, Lahaina News, June 2, 1994: 12.

— radio food talk show to be broadcast, Lahaina News, June 23, 1994: 12.

— registration opens for "A Taste of Lahaina", Lahaina News, June 30, 1994: 15.

— "A Taste of Lahaina" details, Lahaina News, July 7, 1994: 14,15.

— Azeka Rib Cook-Off to be held, Lahaina News, July 7, 1994: 16.

— "A Taste of Lahaina" to be held soon, Lahaina News, August 11, 1994: 11.

— "A Taste of Lahaina" planning continues, Lahaina News, August 18, 1994: 15.

— "Just Desserts" to take place Roy's Nicolina Restaurant, Lahaina News, August 18, 1994: 15.

— details of "A Taste of Lahaina", Lahaina News, August 18, 1994: 2.

— "A Taste of Lahaina" planning continues, cook book to be unveiled, Lahaina News, August 25, 1994: 14.

— Lahaina Iced Tea and Lahaina Lemonade successful on the mainland, Lahaina News, September 1, 1994: 12.

— cooking contests to be held at Maui County Fair, Lahaina News, September 15, 1994: 15.

— A Taste of Lahaina featured, Lahaina News, September 15, 1994: 3.

— George Kahumoku raising pigs, Lahaina News, October 13, 1994: 14.

— Four Seasons Resort Maui offering seasonal menu, Lahaina News, November 17, 1994: 19.

— Westin Maui to offer Vegetarian alternatives, Lahaina News, December 15, 1994: 16,17.

— Westin Maui to highlight specialties from Asian countries, Lahaina News, June 22, 1995: 11,12.

— Kapalua Wine and Food Symposium to be held, Lahaina News, July 13, 1995: 11.

— Ka'anapali Estate Coffee to open, Lahaina News, July 27, 1995: 10.

— chocolate carving demonstration to be held, Lahaina News, February 8, 1996: 14.

— Kea Lani program to be held, Lahaina News, March 7, 1996: 12.

— Gentle World sponsoring vegetarian cooking demonstration, Lahaina News, January 23, 1997: 10.

— Maui Arts and Cultural Center to host "Maui Calls", Lahaina News, August 7, 1997: 12.

— "What's Cookin'" column on local restaurants continues, Lahaina News, January 15, 1998: 12.

— "What's Cookin' in the Queen's Market Food Court" to be held, Lahaina News, April 23, 1998: 16.

— Seventh-Day Adventist Vegetarian Food Fair, Lahaina News, May 14, 1998: 16.

— Lahaina Yacht Club to host "Chili Cook-off", Lahaina News, May 14, 1998: 16.

— Kapalua Wine and Food Symposium to be held, Lahaina News, July 9, 1998: 1,20.

— Down to Earth to teach vegan cooking, Lahaina News, July 30, 1998: 16.

— "Maui Calls" wine tasting event to be held, Lahaina News, August 6, 1998: 10.

— Maui Pinoy Chefs to offer cooking demonstrations, Lahaina News, August 27, 1998: 16.

— Ritz-Carlton to Anuenue Room to host Caymus Winemakers Dinner, Lahaina News, June 10, 1999: 16.

— "Grand Chefs on Tour" to be held at Kea Lani Hotel, Lahaina News, September 2, 1999: 16.

— discussion of food safety, Lahaina News, December 9, 1999: 7.

— Food Network chefs to be part of Kea Lani Hotel's "Food and Wine Masters", Lahaina News, March 16, 2000: 12.

— Kea Lani Food and Wine Masters series continues, Lahaina News, August 31, 2000: 20.

— see also wine

FOOD BANK

— see Maui Food Bank

FOOD PANTRY [BUSINESS]

— opening in Whaler's Village, Lahaina Sun, November 25, 1970: 3.

— to open on Front Street, Lahaina News, May 31, 1989: 15.

— to close, Lahaina News, August 20, 1998: 1.

FOOD SERVICE PROGRAM

— offering sanitation program, Lahaina News, March 27, 1985: 3.

FOOD STAMPS

— criticized as encouraging non-producers to come to Hawaii, Lahaina Sun, February 10, 1971: 4.

FOODBANK NETWORK

— Kevin Davison to present to, Lahaina News, February 11, 1993: 5.

FOODLAND [BUSINESS]

— to open at Lahaina Farmers Market center, Lahaina Sun, May 2, 1973: 11.

— to open pantry in Dickerson Square, Lahaina News, April 30, 1986: 1.

— offers program for customers to support local schools, Lahaina News, February 7, 1990: 3.

— purchases computers for schools, Lahaina News, May 16, 1990: 5,14.

— to begin recycling program, Lahaina News, July 11, 1990: 4.

— to offer recycling service, Lahaina News, August 22, 1990: 4.

— schedule for recycling drop-off, Lahaina News, August 29, 1990: 1.

— to hold recycling drop-off, Lahaina News, September 19, 1990: 5.

— teams with Aloha Airlines to provide "Fly a Friend" certificates, Lahaina News, October 17, 1990: 12.

— recycling at, Lahaina News, October 17, 1990: 6.

— provides facsimile service, Lahaina News, October 24, 1990: 6.

— employee awards given, Lahaina News, December 19, 1990: 7.

— praised for donating computers to local schools, Lahaina News, March 20, 1991: 5.

— owner Maurice "Sully" Sullivan honored by Hawaii Chamber of Commerce, Lahaina News, April 24, 1991: 7.

— recycling drop off available, Lahaina News, June 20, 1991: 4.

— recycling drop off held, Lahaina News, July 4, 1991: 3.

— recycling drop off held, Lahaina News, July 11, 1991: 5.

— customers can purchase holiday turkeys and hams for needy local families, Lahaina News, November 21, 1991: 3.

— allowing customers to purchase turkeys and ham for the needy, Lahaina News, December 5, 1991: 4.

— donates computers to local schools, Lahaina News, July 2, 1992: 26.

— named Business of the Year by the Better Business Bureau, Lahaina News, November 12, 1992: 12.

— results of poster contest announced, Lahaina News, April 22, 1993: 3.

— Princess Nahienaena School students placed fifth in "Shop for Better Education" song contest, Lahaina News, March 31, 1994: 3.

— Roger Wall promoted to executive vice president, Lahaina News, February 9, 1995: 6.

— to donate food to Light Bringers, Lahaina News, April 20, 1995: 6.

— Lahaina Pop Warner Association to play games, Lahaina News, October 24, 1996: 12.

— Lahaina Pop Warner Association teams headed to Maui Bowl, Lahaina News, November 7, 1996: 13.

— Maui Pop Warner Federation hopes to use War Memorial Stadium, Lahaina News, July 31, 1997: 1.

— Lahaina Pop Warner Association begins registration, Lahaina News, July 31, 1997: 14.

— Hula Bowl to open headquarters in Aston Wailea Resort, Lahaina News, August 7, 1997: 5.

— Lahaina Chiefs featured, Lahaina News, October 2, 1997: 16.

— Lahaina Chiefs lose to Keaukaha Warriors, Lahaina News, December 4, 1997: 13.

— Lahaina Pop Warner Association to hold registration, Lahaina News, June 18, 1998: 14.

— Maui Pop Warner Football Federation featured, Lahaina News, September 17, 1998: 14,15.

— cheerleaders support Pop Warner Football teams, Lahaina News, October 1, 1998: 1.

— female player on Lahaina Chiefs Midget football team Angela Peters featured, Lahaina News, October 29, 1998: 18.

— sign-up begins for Lahaina Pop Warner Association, Lahaina News, April 29, 1999: 7.

— Lahaina Pop Warner Football Federation to begin season, Lahaina News, October 7, 1999: 8,14.

— Lahainaluna High School Baldwin High football game set, Lahaina News, November 4, 1999: 6.

— Lahaina Pop Warner Football team and cheerleaders to visit mainland, Lahaina News, November 11, 1999: 6.

— football stars appear at Whalers Village, Lahaina News, January 27, 2000: 6.

— Toddy Lilikoi seeks community support for Pop Warner league, Lahaina News, June 22, 2000: 1,15.

— meeting to be held for Lahainaluna High School junior varsity team, Lahaina News, July 20, 2000: 6.

— Maui Interscholastic League featured, Lahaina News, September 7, 2000: 14.

— update on Maui Pop Warner Football, Lahaina News, September 14, 2000: 8.

— Lahainaluna High School student Lawrence Torres injured in game, Lahaina News, October 26, 2000: 4.

— University of Hawai‘i team to play on Maui, Lahaina News, November 23, 2000: 11.

— Maui Interscholastic League training to begin, Lahaina News, May 10, 2001: 14.

— Lahainaluna High School hosts Youth Football Clinic, Lahaina News, June 14, 2001: 16.

— Lahaina Chiefs of Maui Pop Warner Football Federation to hold player and cheerleader registration, Lahaina News, July 26, 2001: 12.

— Lahaina Chiefs prepare for the Maui Pop Warner football season, Lahaina News, August 9, 2001: 12.

— Ikaika Neizman named to Hawaii All-State Football team, Lahaina News, February 14, 2002: 1,20.

— Lahaina Pop Warner Football/Cheerleading Association to hold registration, Lahaina News, June 6, 2002: 12.

— Lahaina Chiefs Pop Warner Football season begins, Lahaina News, September 5, 2002: 1.

— Lahaina Pop Warner football being fun by Gilbert Shibao, Lahaina News, September 26, 2002: 12.

— student David Smith featured, Lahaina News, October 31, 2002: 10.

— cheerleaders to perform at The Wharf Center, Lahaina News, December 19, 2002: 21.

— Pop Warner Football to hold registration, Lahaina News, July 10, 2003: 13.

— see also Hula Bowl, Lahaina Pop Warner Association, specific players and teams

FOOTE, LIZ

— executive director of Project SEA-Link to speak at Maui Ocean Center, Lahaina News, July 25, 2002: 21.

FOOTHILL COLLEGE FANFAIRS [MUSICAL GROUP]

— to perform at St. John's Episcopal Church, Lahaina News, April 9, 1992: 21.

FOOTLOOSE [MUSICAL]

— auditions to b held for, Lahaina News, May 11, 1995: 12.

— produced by Maui Academy of Performing Arts, Lahaina News, July 20, 1995: 12.

FOOTPRINTS MAUI [BUSINESS]

— opens in The Shops at Wailea, Lahaina News, May 3, 2001: 9.

— opens at Lahaina Cannery Mall, Lahaina News, May 1, 2003: 8.

FOR SALE BY OWNER [BUSINESS]

— opens, Lahaina News, August 14, 1997: 9.

FOR SHEAR HAIR DESIGN [BUSINESS]

— featured, Lahaina News, September 19, 1984: 14.

— featured, Lahaina News, May 22, 1985: 7.

— purchased by Sina Talbot, Lahaina News, November 9, 1995: 10.

— opens, Lahaina News, June 27, 1996: 12.

FOR YOUR EYES ONLY [BUSINESS]

— reviewed, Lahaina News, August 1, 1983: 11.

FORBIDDEN BROAD/FORBIDDEN MAUI [PLAY]

— Maui Community Theatre announces auditions, Lahaina News, May 6, 1993: 20.

FORCING THE LIMITS—HAWAII [FILM]

— longboarding movie to be shown at Maui Arts and Cultural Center, Lahaina News, April 4, 2002: 16.

FORD [BUSINESS]

— auto dealers meet on Maui, Lahaina Sun, March 24, 1971: 1.

FORD BLUES [MUSICAL GROUP]

— to perform at Moose McGillycuddy's, Lahaina News, July 25, 1996: 12.

FORD, DIANE [COMEDIAN]

— to perform at Comedy Club, Lahaina News, March 14, 1990: 15.

FOREIGN FILM FESTIVAL

— to be held, Lahaina News, June 13, 1990: 15.

FOREIGN INTRIGUE IMPORTS [BUSINESS]

— to exhibit art from New Guinea, Lahaina News, March 27, 1997: 14.

— to close, Lahaina News, November 21, 2002: 8.

FOREMOST DAIRIES-HAWAII [BUSINESS]

— establishes distribution operation, Lahaina News, January 21, 1999: 11.

FORESTELL, PAUL

— lecture on Whales, Lahaina News, March 8, 1989: 17.

— director of research for Pacific Whale Foundation discusses Senator Daniel Inouye's proposal to change buffer around whales, Lahaina News, December 16, 1993: 20.

FORESTRY, STATE DIVISION OF

— to give away free seedlings, Lahaina News, November 8, 1989: 3.

FOREVER PLAID [PLAY]

— to be performed as part of Herb and Scott Rogers Professional Theatre Series, Lahaina News, March 30, 1995: 12.

FORMA, JOHANNA "RHANJA"

— new operations manager at Catapult Productions, Inc., Lahaina News, September 17, 1992: 11.

FORSBERG, PETER

— managing editor of Lahaina Times, 1978, Lahaina Times, August, 1980 volume 4 number 7: 2.

FORSYTH, SHAINA MARIE

— Lahaina Intermediate School student participates in Honduras HorseBack teen mission, Lahaina News, June 17, 1999: 3.

FORSYTH, WILLIAM
— murderer was on anti-depressants, Lahaina News, March 11, 1993: 1.

FORT GORDON, GEORGIA
— plan to send police officers for public disturbance training, Lahaina Sun, December 16, 1970: 4.

FORTIER, TANIA
— returns lost wallet, Lahaina News, March 7, 1990: 2.

FORTUNA, MARIA [MUSICIAN]
— soprano featured, Lahaina News, May 12, 1994: 12.

FOSTER CARE
— program seeking foster parents, Lahaina News, July 6, 2000: 6.
— shortage of homes for, Lahaina News, November 8, 2001: 3.
— shortage of families in, Lahaina News, December 13, 2001: 2.

FOSTER FREEZE AND FAMOUS AMOS [BUSINESS]
— featured, Lahaina News, May 8, 1985: 7.

FOSTER HOMES
— needed for abused children, Lahaina News, November 18, 1987: 1,8.

FOSTER, LARRY [ARTIST]
— to hold reception at Foundation Galleries, Lahaina News, February 20, 1992: 17.

FOULIS, SUE ANN [ARTIST]
— art to be shown at Roy's Kahana Bar, Lahaina News, August 13, 1992: 16.

FOUNDATION ART GALLERY [BUSINESS]
— "Summer Madness" show opening, Lahaina News, June 11, 1992: 19.
— hosting back to school show, Lahaina News, September 10, 1992: 22.
— to hold "Smallest Show on Maui", Lahaina News, August 5, 1993: 10.
— to host Marine Art Show, Lahaina News, March 24, 1994: 15.

FOUNDATION FOR RESEARCH AND EVOLUTION
— to present transcendence workshop, Lahaina News, July 23, 1992: 7.

FOUNDATION FOR REVELATION [GROUP]
— showing films at Maui Community College, Lahaina Sun, August 23, 1972: 5.

FOUNDATION FOR STUDY IN HAWAII AND ABROAD
— organizing reunion, Lahaina News, July 13, 1988: 10.

FOUNDATION OF WELLNESS
— founder Dr. Elain Willis to speak at Unity Church, Lahaina News, June 28, 2001: 20.

FOUR FRESHMEN [MUSICAL GROUP]
— to play at Sheraton Maui, Lahaina News, August 31, 1983: 4.
— to perform at Maui Marriott Ka'anapali Ballroom, Lahaina News, July 27, 1995: 11.

FOUR SEASONS HOTELS [BUSINESS]
— to open in Tokyo, Lahaina News, January 23, 1992: 13.

FOUR SEASONS RESORT MAUI [BUSINESS]
— names Valerie Rand as sales manager, Lahaina News, November 7, 1990: 8.
— promotes Charlene Chock, Lahaina News, January 16, 1991: 5.
— Rene Bajeux named executive chef, Lahaina News, February 6, 1991: 6,7.
— to hold fundraiser for Montessori education program, Lahaina News, March 27, 1991: 14.
— to host fashion show fundraiser for Maui Philharmonic Society, Lahaina News, April 17, 1991: 12,14.
— offering Pacific-rim food and wine pairings, Lahaina News, September 12, 1991: 17.
— names Donna Miyashira as food and beverage controller, Lahaina News, September 12, 1991: 4.

— announces promotions, Lahaina News, December 12, 1991: 16.
— receives Five Diamond Award from the American Automobile Association, Lahaina News, January 30, 1992: 12.
— awarded Gold Key by Meeting and Conventions Magazine, Lahaina News, October 15, 1992: 8.
— to receive Superior Deluxe classification from the Official Hotel Guide, Lahaina News, November 5, 1992: 8.
— to celebrate Chinese New Year, Lahaina News, January 21, 1993: 15.
— receives Superior Deluxe classification from Official Hotel Guide, Lahaina News, August 5, 1993: 7.
— Randy Morton named general manager, Lahaina News, April 27, 1995: 10.
— Lori Kennedy selected Director of Public Relations at, Lahaina News, February 8, 1996: 6.
— appoints Reinhard Neubert as director of Food and Beverage, Lahaina News, June 27, 1996: 12.
— appoints Yvonne Landavazo as regional director of public relations, Lahaina News, July 9, 1998: 12.
— presents grants to American Cancer Society and Cancer Research Center of Hawaii, Lahaina News, July 13, 2000: 13.
— Radha Arora new general manager, Lahaina News, June 14, 2001: 8.
— Mark Simon new director of marketing, Lahaina News, June 14, 2001: 8.
— promotes employees, Lahaina News, May 30, 2002: 8.

FOUR-PLAY [PERFORMANCE]
— dance concert to be held, Lahaina News, October 11, 2001: 17.
— dance concert to be held, Lahaina News, October 18, 2001: 16.

FOURTH OF JULY
— see July 4th

FOWLER, DANIEL
— to talk on "Hawaiian Health Care Model" at 'Ohana Connection, Lahaina News, January 2, 2003: 17.

FOX, JOHN [COMEDIAN]
— to perform at Comedy Club, Lahaina News, March 28, 1990: 15.
— to perform at Comedy Club, Lahaina News, October 7, 1993: 12.
— to perform at Honolulu Comedy Club, Lahaina News, August 4, 1994: 16.

FOX PHOTO [BUSINESS]
— opens shop in Wharf, Lahaina News, May 3, 1989: 3.
— opens at the Lahaina Center, Lahaina News, November 7, 1990: 7.

FOX, ROBERT
— architect at quarterly meeting of Lahaina Town Action Committee, Lahaina News, September 26, 1990: 9.
— study of Lahaina expected to be completed, Lahaina News, April 16, 1992: 3.

FOX, TERRY
— see Terry Fox Run

FOXY LADY, THE [NIGHTCLUB]
— closes, Lahaina News, July 11, 1984: 12.

FRAMPTON, GARY
— director of Big Brothers discusses attempts to help isle youth, Lahaina Sun, March 10, 1971: 4.

FRAMPTON, RORY
— wins Compadres Kayak Racing Series, Lahaina News, April 8, 1993: 8.
— joins Chris Hart and Partners, Lahaina News, August 26, 1993: 10.
— discusses proposed canoe house and keiki house for Hui O Wa'a, Lahaina News, September 17, 1998: 1,32.

FRANCIS, JILLIAN
— appointed director of sales for Atlantis Submarines, Lahaina News, November 21, 1991: 11.

FRANCIS, STEPHEN
— reinstated as counselor at Maui Community College, Lahaina Sun, April 11, 1973: 4.

FRANCO, JOE
— ILWU Business Agent to speak to Lahaina-Honolua Senior Citizens Club, Lahaina News, February 7, 2002: 3.
— ILWU Business Agent to speak to Lahaina-Honolua Senior Citizens Club, Lahaina News, February 14, 2002: 2.

FRANCO, KATHLEEN
— indicted for embezzlement, Lahaina News, May 1, 1982: 3.

FRANCO, NORMAN CALVIN
— appointed honorary chairman of the Hawaii Delegation of the Business Advisory Council, Lahaina News, May 30, 2002: 8.

FRANCO, STAN
— discusses group helping those seeking housing [article seems incomplete], Lahaina News, April 26, 1989: 13.

FRANCO, STAN AND STEPHANIE
— selected Maui Family of the Year, Lahaina News, November 4, 1993: 6.

FRANDSEN, RICHARD
— promoted to senior vice president-operations at Maui Gas Service, Lahaina News, August 1, 1990: 7.

FRANK, NORMAN
— police officer speaking about formation of Police Association of Hawaii on Maui, Lahaina Sun, December 16, 1970: 1.

FRANKEN, ERNIE
— owner of Adonis [ship], Lahaina Sun, July 18, 1973: 9.

FRANKENSTEIN [FILM]
— to be shown at Hyatt Regency Maui, Lahaina News, October 26, 1995: 11.

FRANKLIN, JAMES
— part of attempt to create second newspaper for Maui, Lahaina Sun, May 17, 1972: 6.
— republican mayoral candidate publishes biography, Lahaina Sun, October 4, 1972: 9.
— cannot reveal content of mayor Cravalho's deposition, Lahaina Sun, February 28, 1973: 4.

FRANZEL, SONIA
— hired as director of public relations at Hotel Hana-Maui, Lahaina News, January 9, 1991: 5.

FRASER, JOELLE
— joins Skinner Communications, Lahaina News, May 31, 1989: 15.

FRAUGHT & MIYASHIRO ADVERTISING
— named by Royal Lahaina Resort to handle food and beverage advertising, Lahaina News, January 8, 1986: 3.

FRAZER, EDWARD
— proposes flea market at Kahului Fairgrounds, Lahaina Sun, May 5, 1971: 7.

FREAS, TERTIA
— becomes partner at Deloitte and Touche, Lahaina News, August 27, 1992: 11.

FRED BALDWIN MEMORIAL FOUNDATION
— makes donation to Nature Conservancy of Hawaii, Lahaina News, December 26, 1990: 4,5.

FRED SANDS REALTORS
— expands to Maui, Lahaina News, August 19, 1999: 14.

FREDERICKS, ROGER
— conducts golf instruction video session with Jack Nicklaus, Lahaina News, February 10, 2000: 9.

FREDERICKSEN, ERIK
— archaeologist recommends preserving pre-contact burial site at Olowalu, Lahaina News, December 17, 1998: 1,28.
— archaeologist to speak on Lower Main Street Rehabilitation Corridor, Lahaina News, April 8, 1999: 13.

FREDERICKSEN, WALTER
— displays piece of Chinese ceramic bowl found during excavation, Lahaina News, May 10, 1989: 1.

FREDRICK'S AUTO DETAILING [BUSINESS]
— relocates, Lahaina News, April 14, 1994: 10.

FREDY, CHARLES
— sommelier to select wine at Sound of the Falls restaurant, Lahaina News, October 20, 1994: 13.

FREE FORM [FILM]
— shown at Kam III school, Lahaina Sun, December 9, 1970: 4.

FREE THOUGHT SOCIETY
— to meet, Lahaina News, March 15, 2001: 18.

FREEDOM FEST
— to be held at Kings Cathedral, Lahaina News, June 28, 2001: 21.
— to be held on Independence Day, Lahaina News, July 3, 2003: 17.

FREEDOM SPORTS' BIPLANE BARNSTORMERS
— offering tours and rides on Maui, Lahaina News, January 9, 1991: 5.

FREELAND, BETTY HAY [ARTIST]
— featured at Old Jail Gallery, Lahaina News, January 28, 1987: 3.
— to display work, Lahaina News, January 13, 1988: 3.
— featured at Village Galleries, Lahaina News, March 11, 1993: 15.
— to exhibit at Village Gallery, Lahaina News, February 24, 1994: 8.
— to exhibit at The Village Gallery, Lahaina News, March 13, 1997: 15.
— to exhibit at Village Galleries Maui, Lahaina News, February 12, 1998: 16.
— to exhibit at Village Gallery, Lahaina News, February 4, 1999: 17.
— to exhibit "Maui Romance" at Village Gallery, Lahaina News, February 13, 2003: 15,16.

FREELAND, G. WARREN
— heads new brokerage division at CB Richard Ellis Hawaii, Inc., Lahaina News, December 26, 2002: 8.

FREELAND, KEOKI
— promoted to vice president and general manager of Amfac/JMB's Pioneer Mill, Lahaina News, October 1, 1992: 10.
— resigns as vice president and general manager of Pioneer Mills, Lahaina News, September 1, 1994: 1,5.
— hired by Lahaina Restoration Foundation, Lahaina News, November 3, 1994: 1,6.
— chair of the Mayor's Task Force on the Old Lahaina Courthouse reviews location, Lahaina News, December 14, 1995: 1.
— to speak to the American Association of Retired Persons, Lahaina News, January 1, 1998: 16.
— Lahaina Restoration Foundation director to review projects and goals, Lahaina News, May 13, 1999: 3.
— Lahaina Restoration Foundation director discusses replacing the Carthaginian, Lahaina News, September 12, 2002: 1,24.

FREELAND, KEOKI AND BETTY HAY
— community work featured, Lahaina News, June 26, 1997: 1,2.

FREELAND, NORMAN
— of U.S. Coast Guard Auxiliary to talk about boating safety, Lahaina News, October 14, 1999: 13.

FREELAND, PETER [WRITER]
— to sign his book "The May Who Loved Lahaina", Lahaina News, December 6, 2001: 16.

FREEMAN GUARDS [BUSINESS]
— awarded security contract for Kahului Harbor, Lahaina News, October 25, 1989: 10.

FREEMAN, JUDITH PEARL [ARTIST]
— latest works presented at Banyan Tree Gallery, Lahaina News, May 8, 1991: 22.

FREEMAN, MARION [ARTIST]
— to appear at Upstart Crow Bookstore, Lahaina News, December 11, 1985: 9.
— show at Village Galleries, Lahaina News, October 28, 1987: 12.
— wins poster contest from Lahaina Town Action Committee, Lahaina News, November 21, 1990: 1.
— to exhibit at Hui Noʻeau Visual Arts Center, Lahaina News, December 31, 1992: 5.
— to exhibit at Village Galleries, Lahaina News, December 15, 1994: 18.
— wins Lahaina Arts Society poster contest, Lahaina News, November 16, 1995: 15.

FREERIDERS [FILM]
— Warren Miller snowboard adventure film to be shown, Lahaina News, January 14, 1999: 12.

FREETHOUGHT SOCIETY OF MAUI
— to meet, Lahaina News, January 18, 2001: 16.
— continues to meet, Lahaina News, June 28, 2001: 20.
— to meet at Old Lahaina Book Emporium, Lahaina News, August 30, 2001: 16.
— continues to meet, Lahaina News, April 4, 2002: 17.

FREITAS, ANDREW
— re-elected chairman of County Police Commission, Lahaina Sun, January 27, 1971: 2.

FREITAS, BEEBE [MUSICIAN]
— to perform at Maui Community College, Lahaina News, March 18, 1993: 12.

FREITAS-OBREGON, BRENDA [WRITER]
— storyteller to visit libraries, Lahaina News, November 21, 2002: 20.

FREMAUX, CHARLOTTE MURRAY [ARTIST]
— work discussed, Lahaina News, August 29, 1984: 13.

FRENCH CANADIAN ASSOCIATION
— to celebrate 10 year anniversary, Lahaina News, December 20, 2001: 17.

FRENCH FESTIVAL
— to be held at Whalers Village, Lahaina News, October 21, 1999: 13.

FRENCH, JAMES [MUSICIAN]
— appointed musical director of Friends of the Maui Symphony, Lahaina News, January 2, 1992: 5.
— to offer organ recital, Lahaina News, December 30, 1993: 12.

FRENCH, RENEE
— win radio contest, Lahaina News, November 22, 1989: 3.

FRENCH, ROBERT
— police asking for help in death of, Lahaina News, May 27, 1999: 1,16.

FRESH ISLAND FISH COMPANY [BUSINESS]
— will move from Maʻalaea Harbor, Lahaina News, February 7, 1990: 5.

FRESH START
— program for youth moving to Maui, Lahaina Sun, March 7, 1973: 5.

FREWER, SANDRA
— appointed public relations director at Ritz-Carlton Hotel Kapalua, Lahaina News, August 22, 1991: 4.

FREY, SUSAN [ARTIST]
— to offer Leather Box workshop at The Art School at Kapalua, Lahaina News, September 18, 2003: 17.

FRIAS, ROBERT AND BEVERLY
— celebrate 50th wedding anniversary, Lahaina News, July 12, 2001: 8.

FRIDAY NIGHT IS ART NIGHT
— celebrates first year, Lahaina News, June 13, 1990: 13,17.
— celebrates first year, Lahaina News, June 20, 1990: 13.

— details of upcoming events, Lahaina News, September 19, 1990: 13.
— continues to grow, Lahaina News, October 3, 1990: 13.
— upcoming program described, Lahaina News, November 28, 1990: 12.
— details of the week's schedule, Lahaina News, January 2, 1991: 9.
— celebrates 1st birthday, Lahaina News, May 23, 1991: 12.
— to be held, Lahaina News, June 13, 1991: 12.
— to celebrate second birthday, Lahaina News, June 20, 1991: 8,13.
— account of 2nd anniversary celebration, Lahaina News, July 4, 1991: 1.
— continues, Lahaina News, March 12, 1992: 21.

FRIED, DAVE
— to box with Lani Kane of West Maui Boxing Club, Lahaina News, July 20, 2000: 16.

FRIEDERICH, BILL
— to hold "Rhythms of our lives and worship", Lahaina News, February 24, 2000: 16.

FRIEDMAN, BONNIE
— chair of Maui Harvest discusses helping homeless, Lahaina News, April 25, 1990: 5.

FRIEDMAN, JOEL [WRITER]
— singing book "Dear Isaac", Lahaina News, November 30, 2000: 16,17.

FRIEDMAN, MILTON
— to speak, Lahaina News, February 14, 1990: 5.
— correction that Friedman is not the noble winning economist, Lahaina News, February 21, 1990: 5.

FRIEND, CHESTER
— Christmas tree grower featured, Lahaina News, December 19, 1991: 12.

FRIEND'S NETWORK
— pyramid scheme being investigated by Attorney General's Office, Lahaina News, April 28, 1994: 9.

FRIENDS OF FATHER DAMIEN
— holds fundraiser at Pau Hana Inn, Lahaina News, September 2, 1987: 3.

FRIENDS OF HALEAKALA NATIONAL PARK
— group formed, Lahaina News, September 13, 1989: 3.
— offering "Adopt-A-Nene" program, Lahaina News, November 27, 1997: 13.
— seeks volunteers to remove non-native pine trees, Lahaina News, July 13, 2000: 16.
— to hold service trips to Haleakala Crater and Kipahulu's Oheʻo Gulch, Lahaina News, August 29, 2002: 15.

FRIENDS OF KEONEʻOʻIO (LA PEROUSE BAY)
— to hold "Clean Up the Bay Day" at Le Perouse, Lahaina News, January 21, 1999: 12.
— to hold "Clean Up the Bay Day", Lahaina News, January 21, 1999: 12.
— recruiting volunteers to train as naturalists at La Perouse Bay, Lahaina News, November 30, 2000: 16.
— recruiting volunteers, Lahaina News, July 12, 2001: 2.
— seeking volunteers, Lahaina News, August 30, 2001: 17.
— to meet, Lahaina News, November 8, 2001: 16.
— to meet, Lahaina News, December 6, 2001: 16.
— to meet, Lahaina News, May 16, 2002: 16.
— to meet, Lahaina News, November 14, 2002: 21.
— to meet, Lahaina News, November 14, 2002: 21.
— to meet, Lahaina News, November 21, 2002: 20.
— to meet, Lahaina News, March 6, 2003: 17.
— continue to care for Keoneʻoʻio (La Perouse Bay), Lahaina News, April 10, 2003: 21.

FRIENDS OF KEOPUOLANI
— celebrate conversion of Queen to Christianity, Lahaina News, November 1, 1982: 2.
— see also Keopuolani, Queen

FRIENDS OF MOKU'ULA, THE
— opposes homeless shelter, Lahaina News, August 1, 1990: 1.
— organizing to restore Moku'ula, Lahaina News, December 19, 1991: 3.
— hoping to protect island, Lahaina News, September 28, 1995: 1,12.
— requests that baseball move from so that island can be better protected and studied, Lahaina News, October 5, 1995: 1,16.
— provides suggestions for moving softball field, Lahaina News, December 7, 1995: 1,20.
— receives grant to begin restoring Moku'ula, Lahaina News, October 1, 1998: 1,20.
— begin work removing park, Lahaina News, November 19, 1998: 1,20.
— to hold "Community Workday", Lahaina News, December 3, 1998: 20.
— working on Lahaina Interpretive Plan, Lahaina News, August 5, 1999: 1,16.
— Reflections of Old Lahaina Luau and Concert benefit to be held, Lahaina News, August 19, 1999: 18.
— editorial supporting, Lahaina News, August 26, 1999: 4.
— benefit held, Lahaina News, September 2, 1999: 2.
— Nimble Makalani Dearden appointed manager of Archival and Gift Center, Lahaina News, September 23, 1999: 2.
— Bubba Gump Shrimp, Co. to donate percentage of sales from Friday, Lahaina News, January 27, 2000: 1,16.
— to hold orientation for volunteers, Lahaina News, March 30, 2000: 3.
— to hold orientation for volunteers, Lahaina News, April 6, 2000: 17.
— to hold "Reflections of Old Lahaina—The Plantation Era" fundraiser, Lahaina News, January 11, 2001: 3.
— Akoni Akana discusses history of the Kamehameha Iki Park area, Lahaina News, March 29, 2001: 1.
— to hold workshop to explain protocol, Lahaina News, April 5, 2001: 3.
— to hold benefit luau, Lahaina News, January 31, 2002: 2.
— to pursue next phase of vision, Lahaina News, November 21, 2002: 1,22.
— "Reflections of Old Lahaina" fundraiser to be held, Lahaina News, January 16, 2003: 3.
— editorial in support of, Lahaina News, January 16, 2003: 4.
— to hold fundraiser, Lahaina News, January 23, 2003: 18.
— meet with elected officials at Malu'ulu O Lele Park, Lahaina News, June 26, 2003: 1.
— to hold benefit concert, Lahaina News, July 10, 2003: 1,20.
— receives grant from Maui County, Lahaina News, August 28, 2003: 8.
— see also Moku'ula

FRIENDS OF RONALD MCDONALD HOUSE
— seeking residents to write letters of support, Lahaina News, September 5, 1984: 3.

FRIENDS OF THE CHILDREN'S JUSTICE CENTER, THE
— to hold "Sunset and Sand Dollars" Beach Party fundraiser, Lahaina News, April 18, 2002: 5.
— to hold "Sunset and Sand Dollars" Beach Party fundraiser, Lahaina News, May 2, 2002: 2.
— "Sunsets and Sand Dollars" beach party to be held to benefit, Lahaina News, July 24, 2003: 5.

FRIENDS OF THE LAHAINA PUBLIC LIBRARY
— see Lahaina Public Library

FRIENDS OF THE LAHAINA RESTORATION FOUNDATION
— see Lahaina Restoration Foundation

FRIENDS OF UPCOUNTRY MAUI
— oppose proposed site for new high school, Lahaina News, March 5, 1992: 4.

FRIETAS, JACK
— birthday described, Lahaina Sun, July 11, 1973: 13.

FRIGHT NIGHT
— to be held, Lahaina News, October 22, 1998: 6,7.

FROHNMAYER, JOHN
— former head of National Endowment for the Arts to speak, Lahaina News, June 18, 1992: 15.

FROM HEAVEN'S THRONE [PLAY]
— to be performed at Lahaina Baptist Church, Lahaina News, December 16, 1993: 18.

FROM THE LAND OF THE LOTUS BLOSSOMS [PLAY]
— to be performed at Maui Youth Theatre, Lahaina News, October 11, 1989: 12.

FRONT STREET
— underground wiring planned for, Lahaina Sun, December 9, 1970: 7.
— West Maui Business Association commended for cleaning up, Lahaina Sun, December 16, 1970: 3.
— projects desired by West Maui Business Association, Lahaina Sun, December 23, 1970: 2.
— discussion of difficulty determining who is responsible for section of road, Lahaina Sun, January 13, 1971: 7.
— current developments described, Lahaina Sun, April 14, 1971: 7.
— new sidewalk proposed, Lahaina Sun, April 21, 1971: 3.
— Ichiki general store, first opened in 1925, closes, Lahaina Sun, June 9, 1971: 1.
— development plans by McNeil Construction Company not yet public, Lahaina Sun, June 30, 1971: 2.
— one-way traffic proposed, Lahaina Sun, July 7, 1971: 1,9.
— Maui County Traffic Safety Council requests that Front Street be one way, Lahaina Sun, July 28, 1971: 10.
— design planned to follow New England-style, Lahaina Sun, August 4, 1971: 1,3.
— sketches of buildings by Jermone, Lahaina Sun, September 29, 1971: 11.
— sketches of buildings by Jermone, Lahaina Sun, September 29, 1971: 6.
— public meeting called to discuss converting Front Street to one-way, Lahaina Sun, October 6, 1971: 1.
— sketches of buildings by Jermone, Lahaina Sun, October 13, 1971: 11.
— proposal for one-way street discussed at public hearing, Lahaina Sun, October 13, 1971: 12.
— merits of one-way street discussed, Lahaina Sun, October 13, 1971: 2.
— sketches of buildings by Jermone, Lahaina Sun, October 13, 1971: 6.
— Canadian couple seek to challenge development laws, Lahaina Sun, February 23, 1972: 3.
— Kishi Market closing, Lahaina Sun, April 19, 1972: 11.
— changes described, Lahaina Sun, June 14, 1972: 6,7.
— fire risks detailed, Lahaina Sun, August 9, 1972: 3.
— conflict over muntins detailed, Lahaina Sun, September 20, 1972: 3.
— proposal to convert to one-way, Lahaina News, April 15, 1980: 7.
— plan for one-way street opposed, Lahaina News, September 1, 1980: 8.
— photographs of, Lahaina News, January 15, 1983: 16.
— to be improved by Maui County, Lahaina News, December 27, 1989: 1.
— plan to restore presented by Ed Kuniyoshi of Belt, Collins, & Associates, Lahaina News, November 21, 1990: 1.

— improvements to begin in April, Lahaina News, October 27, 1994: 4.

— improvement project to be completed, Lahaina News, July 24, 1997: 1.

— improvements to be dedicated, Lahaina News, August 7, 1997: 1.

— history of, Lahaina News, August 21, 1997: 2.

— work continues on improvements of, Lahaina News, September 11, 1997: 9.

— featured, Lahaina News, March 28, 2002: 7.

FRONT STREET [BOAT]

— wins Lahaina Yacht Club regatta, Lahaina News, June 6, 1991: 1.

FRONT STREET AFFORDABLE HOUSING PARTNERS

— completes Front Street Apartments, Lahaina News, June 21, 2001: 3.

FRONT STREET APARTMENTS

— completed, Lahaina News, June 21, 2001: 3.

FRONT STREET IMPROVEMENT PROJECT

— still short of funds, Lahaina News, June 8, 1995: 1.

— begins, Lahaina News, November 2, 1995: 1,16.

— Kiewit Pacific Construction Co. awarded contract, Lahaina News, December 14, 1995: 4.

— detailed, Lahaina News, April 11, 1996: 4.

— kick off party to be held, Lahaina News, April 18, 1996: 6.

— begins "Scholar Athlete of the Week" column, Lahaina News, April 25, 1996: 3.

— continues, Lahaina News, August 22, 1996: 3.

— update on, Lahaina News, January 9, 1997: 14.

— County Public Works Director Charles Jencks updates on, Lahaina News, April 3, 1997: 1.

FRONT STREET THEATRES

— to open in Lahaina Center, Lahaina News, November 3, 1994: 4.

FROST, JACQUELINE

— joins staff of the American Lung Association, Lahaina News, October 17, 1991: 7.

FRY, HOWARD [ARTIST]

— Lahaina Arts Society to feature Sumi-e work, Lahaina News, June 4, 1998: 16.

FRY, LEWIS

— elected president of Lahaina Jaycees, Lahaina Sun, May 12, 1971: 6.

FRYCHEL, ANTJE

— receives Kapalua Land Company Ltd. Scholarship, Lahaina News, August 29, 1996: 6.

FU WAH CHINESE RESTAURANT [RESTAURANT]

— now offering American breakfast, Lahaina News, November 12, 1992: 22.

FUATA, LUI

— Scholar/Athlete of the Week, Lahaina News, February 22, 1996: 6.

— returns to Lahainaluna High School to teach football, Lahaina News, July 26, 2001: 1,20.

— Lahainaluna High School football player featured, Lahaina News, February 6, 2003: 12.

FUETTERER, HORST

— appointed executive chef at Stouffer's Wailea Beach Resort, Lahaina News, May 1, 1985: 4.

FUGAZI [MUSICAL GROUP]

— to perform at Studio Blue nightclub, Lahaina News, October 17, 1996: 14.

FUGIYAMA, HIDEO [ARTIST]

— wins ice carving competition, Lahaina News, December 26, 2002: 8.

FUJIEKI, JOHN

— named chairman of the board of Star Markets, Lahaina News, August 23, 2001: 9.

FUJIHANA, KYODO [BISHOP]

— discussed new temple and pagoda at Lahaina Jodo Mission, Lahaina Sun, March 10, 1971: 1.

FUJII, BRAD

— Lahainaluna High School student takes first place in conservation awareness contest, Lahaina News, January 4, 1996: 4.

FUJII, BUD

— Scholar/Athlete of the Week, Lahaina News, February 8, 1996: 11.

FUJII, DENNIS

— congratulated by Maui County Council for role in Vietnam War, Lahaina Sun, March 10, 1971: 4.

FUJIKAWA, LAURA [ARTIST]

— to visit Crazy Shirts, Lahaina News, June 29, 1995: 12.

FUJIMORI, WANDA

— part of new Central Pacific Bank team, Lahaina News, February 7, 2002: 8.

FUJIMOTO, TOSHIO "TATA"

— named Credit Union Volunteer of the Year, Lahaina News, May 19, 1994: 13.

FUJITA, YOSHIKO [ARTIST]

— teaching oil painting at Kihei Community Complex, Lahaina News, April 24, 1985: 20.

— students of to exhibit at Banyan Tree Gallery, Lahaina News, March 23, 1995: 11.

FUJITSU ASIAN SCHOLARSHIP PROGRAM

— now available, Lahaina News, August 1, 1991: 4,5.

FUJIWARA, BERNICE

— named Division Secretary of the Year, Lahaina News, June 11, 1992: 13,14.

FUJIWARA, MAY

— president of Lahaina Honolua Senior Citizens Club featured, Lahaina News, June 28, 2001: 1,22.

— Lahaina resident recognized by Hawaii Senate, Lahaina News, July 18, 2002: 3.

FUJIWARA, TYLER

— Scholar/Athlete of the Week, Lahaina News, May 2, 2002: 13.

FUJIYAMA [RESTAURANT]

— reviewed, Lahaina News, November, 1979: 3.

— reviewed, Lahaina News, June 1, 1981: 9.

FUKUDA, ROBERT

— critical of gambling liberalization, Lahaina Sun, October 25, 1972: 4.

FUKUMOTO, LIANE

— promoted to vice president at Bank of Hawaii, Lahaina News, November 15, 2001: 8.

FUKUNAGA, ALVIN

— Public Works Director talks about rule changes for landfills, Lahaina News, October 10, 1990: 6.

FUKUNAGA, HOWARD

— thanked for helping improve school facilities in Kihei, Lahaina News, June 24, 1993: 7.

FUKUOKA, MASAMI

— offering courses in conversational Japanese, Lahaina Sun, February 16, 1972: 17.

FUKUSHIMA, MARY

— to hold Maui World Music Workshops, Lahaina News, June 12, 2003: 5.

FUKUYAMA, GWEN

— promoted to trust officer of First Hawaiian Bank's Financial Services Center, Lahaina News, July 7, 1994: 9.

FULL MOON BOOGIE

— to be held, Lahaina News, September 11, 1997: 16.

FULL SHRED [MUSICAL GROUP]
— to perform at Longhi's, Lahaina News, April 25, 1990: 15.
— to perform at Longhi's, Lahaina News, May 2, 1990: 15.
— to perform at Moose McGillycuddy's, Lahaina News, September 26, 1990: 10.
— to perform at Moose McGillycuddy's, Lahaina News, December 5, 1990: 9.

FULLER, BUCKMINSTER
— works featured at workshop by Amy Edmondson, Lahaina News, January 13, 1988: 16.
— workshop detailed, Lahaina News, February 3, 1988: 1,20.

FULTON, STEPHEN
— joins GECC Financial, Lahaina News, May 24, 1989: 8.

FUN DAY FOR MAUI'S FAMILIES
— to mark dedication of new Maui Economic Opportunity Inc. head-quarters, Lahaina News, August 5, 1999: 11.

FUN FACTORY [BUSINESS]
— to host "Garfield", Lahaina News, June 14, 1989: 2.
— to host Batman, Lahaina News, August 23, 1989: 2.
— gives scholarship to Jo-Ann Agapay, Lahaina News, July 23, 1992: 4.

FUNDERBURGH, ANSON [MUSICIAN]
— to perform at Studio Blue nightclub, Lahaina News, September 5, 1996: 17.

FUNKE-D'EGNUFF, STUART
— names Maui liaison for Roz Baker, Lahaina News, February 20, 2003: 8.

FUNNY GIRL [PLAY]
— to be performed at McCoy Studio Theater, Lahaina News, April 27, 1995: 12.
— to be performed, Lahaina News, May 11, 1995: 12.
— featured, Lahaina News, May 18, 1995: 10.

FUNNY STUFF [PLAY]
— to be performed by Maui Philharmonic Society, Lahaina News, February 23, 1995: 11.

FUNNY THING HAPPENED ON THE WAY TO THE FORUM, A [PLAY]
— to be performed by Maui OnStage, Lahaina News, April 28, 1994: 15.

FURBIES
— Sandwich Island Publishing publishes "Furby Training Guide", Lahaina News, December 24, 1998: 11.

FURTADO [FAMILY]
— lease large area of Front Street, Lahaina News, March 25, 1987: 18.

FURTADO, ALFRED [ARTIST]
— to be artist-in-residence at Village Galleries, Lahaina News, May 20, 1999: 17.
— to be artist-in-residence at Village Gallery, Lahaina News, October 18, 2001: 17.

FURTHER [FILM]
— skiing movie to be shown, Lahaina News, November 23, 2000: 20.

FURUKAWA, COLLEEN
— new grants manager at Maui Arts and Cultural Center, Lahaina News, August 16, 2001: 8.

FURUKAWA, JAMES
— educator to present class, Lahaina News, June 6, 1996: 15.

FURUKAWA, RONALD
— named assistant general manager of Kitagawa Motors, Inc., Lahaina News, March 25, 1993: 10,11.

FURUYA, CHUCK
— business trainer to offer "Tools for Effective Communication", Lahaina News, August 14, 2003: 8.
— to hold "Tools for Effective Communication", Lahaina News, August 21, 2003: 8.

FURUYA, GLENN
— to offer leadership seminar, Lahaina News, September 5, 2002: 8.
— to offer seminar on "Teamwork Local Style", Lahaina News, October 9, 2003: 8.

FURYK, JIM
— wins Lincoln-Mercury Kapalua International, Lahaina News, October 31, 1996: 14.

FUSATO, ROY
— director of Maui County Office on Aging says program cuts to be expected, Lahaina News, August 3, 1995: 3.

FUSATO, ROY AND CHARLOTTE
— named family of the year, Lahaina News, November 17, 1994: 4.

FUSHIKOSHI, SANDY
— Foodland employee nominated for excellence in customer service, Lahaina News, December 19, 1990: 7.

FUTURE CLUB
— begins at Lahainaluna High School, Lahaina News, November 16, 2000: 1,2.

FUTURE FARMERS OF AMERICA
— Lahainaluna High School student attends national conference, Lahaina News, August 14, 2003: 2.

G

GABBARD, MIKE
— spokesman for Sexual Responsibility Hawaii, Lahaina News, October 8, 1986: 3.

GABEL'S [RESTAURANT]
— hosts Hawaiian music, Lahaina News, December 19, 1990: 12.
— featuring music, Lahaina News, December 26, 1990: 10.
— reviewed, Lahaina News, February 20, 1991: 14.

GABRIEL, HANK
— to manage Whaler's Village, Lahaina Sun, November 25, 1970: 3.
— manager of Whaler's Village pictured, Lahaina Sun, December 16, 1970: 5.

GACH, MICHAEL
— to discuss "Self Healing Techniques—Acu-Yoga", Lahaina News, June 19, 2003: 17.

GADARIAN, BLACKIE
— owner of Blackie's Bar featured, Lahaina News, November 14, 1991: 14.
— donates drum set to Lahainaluna High School, Lahaina News, February 4, 1993: 3.
— angry about fire hydrant not working, Lahaina News, September 1, 1994: 1,5.
— selling mementos from Balckie's Bar, Lahaina News, April 27, 1995: 2.
— results of auction of mementos, Lahaina News, May 4, 1995: 1.

GAGAKU
— Japanese court music to be performed, Lahaina News, March 11, 1999: 12.

GAGEN, MARILYN
— to lead seminar on estate planning, Lahaina News, February 28, 2002: 8.

GAGNEY, BETSY
— to discuss native ecosystems, Lahaina News, February 12, 1998: 17.
— DLNR staffer to speak on native ecosystems, Lahaina News, February 19, 1998: 12.

GAINES, EDWENE
— present "Prosperity Plus" workshop, Lahaina News, June 8, 1988: 13.

GAJCAK, JULIA
— appointed director of public relations for Westin Maui Hotel, Lahaina News, April 10, 1991: 6.

GALANG, JUNO [ARTIST]
— to exhibit at Diamond Head Gallery-Pictures Plus, Lahaina News, October 17, 2002: 21.

GALAXY OF STARS
— to be held at Maui Community Theatre, Lahaina News, August 19, 1999: 16.

GALDEIRA, EARL
— member of the Hawaiian Homes Commission at meeting between Hawaiian Homes Commission and The Hawaiians, Lahaina Sun, December 23, 1970: 6.

GALERIE LASSEN [BUSINESS]
— to open at Maui Marriott Hotel, Lahaina News, April 24, 1991: 7.
— president Jona Marie Price featured, Lahaina News, October 3, 1991: 3.
— Debbie John promoted to general manager, Lahaina News, October 24, 1991: 8.
— names Rick Iaconetti as director of sales and shows, Lahaina News, October 24, 1991: 8.
— to open fourth gallery, Lahaina News, February 4, 1993: 9.
— to open fifth gallery, Lahaina News, February 25, 1993: 6.
— James Coleman to be guest artist, Lahaina News, March 3, 1994: 12.
— being sued over numbering of prints, Lahaina News, May 15, 1997: 1.

GALLAGHER [COMEDIAN]
— to perform at Maui Arts and Cultural Center, Lahaina News, November 28, 2002: 14.
— to perform at Maui Arts and Cultural Center, Lahaina News, December 5, 2002: 21.
— to perform at Maui Arts and Cultural Center, Lahaina News, December 12, 2002: 20.

GALLAGHER, HUGH
— appointed mortgage loan officer of Maui office of Home Financial Services, Inc., Lahaina News, March 6, 1991: 10.

GALLAGHER, JIM
— rescuing Ko'olau Brewery on Oahu, Lahaina News, November 30, 1988: 2.
— School-Community Based Management (SCBM) Councilmember featured, Lahaina News, August 12, 1993: 2.

GALLAGHER, MICHAEL
— named executive chef at Sea House Restaurant, Lahaina News, July 29, 1999: 3.
— introduces new menu at Sea House Restaurant, Lahaina News, November 11, 1999: 11.
— Sea House Restaurant chef featured, Lahaina News, December 6, 2001: 9.

GALLAGHER, PAULA
— joins Irwin Mortgage, Lahaina News, March 4, 1999: 11.

GALLAGHER, RICHARD [ARTIST]
— art displayed at Village Gallery, Lahaina News, June 13, 1984: 4.

GALLAGHER, SARAH
— account manager at Media Systems, Lahaina News, May 24, 1989: 8.

GALLEN, FRITZ
— Scholar/Athlete of the Week, Lahaina News, August 1, 2002: 14.

GALLERIE HA [BUSINESS]
— to host stories by Jeff Gere, Lahaina News, May 30, 2002: 17.
— to hold "Drum Off" to celebrate first birthday, Lahaina News, July 4, 2002: 16.
— to hold poetry contest, Lahaina News, September 5, 2002: 16.
— to hold "Ha's Fourth Poetry Slam—Round Out 4", Lahaina News, March 6, 2003: 16.

GALLERY PACIFICA [BUSINESS]
— new gallery owned by Lahaina Printsellers opens, Lahaina News, September 8, 1994: 12.
— opens, Lahaina News, August 1, 2002: 8.
— to host Champagne Receptions, Lahaina News, August 29, 2002: 20.

GALLERY, THE, LTD [BUSINESS]
— donates antique to Maui Historical Society benefit auction, Lahaina News, July 25, 1990: 6.
— wins Pineapple Award for best Halloween display, Lahaina News, November 21, 1991: 11.
— moves to Kahului, Lahaina News, August 27, 1998: 1,20.

GALLIARD STRING QUARTET [MUSICAL GROUP]
— to perform with Hawaii musicians at the Honolulu Academy of Arts, Lahaina News, August 22, 1990: 14.

GALLISHAW, PHIL
— presents promotion plans to Lahaina Retail Committee, Lahaina Sun, February 24, 1971: 1.

GALLIVAN, JOE [MUSICIAN]
— to perform at Longhi's Restaurant, Lahaina News, September 19, 1996: 18.

GAMBLING
— opposed by Maui Christian Ministers Association, Lahaina Sun, March 17, 1971: 3.
— Hawaii Episcopal church calls for repeal of gambling laws, Lahaina Sun, October 25, 1972: 11.
— U.S. attorney Robert Fukuda critical of gambling liberalization, Lahaina Sun, October 25, 1972: 4.
— discussed in public forum, Lahaina Sun, March 7, 1973: 10.
— Big Island senator Stanley Hara favors lottery, Lahaina News, April 1, 1980: 6.
— views of state lottery discussed, Lahaina News, March 15, 1982: 2.
— Representative Joseph Souki to hold meeting on legalizing, Lahaina News, September 14, 1995: 6.
— opinions from residents sought, Lahaina News, February 15, 1996: 4.

GAME SHOW MONTH
— to be held, Lahaina News, October 19, 1988: 6.

GAMEKIDS [TROUPE]
— hosting creative writing camp at Camp Piiholo, Lahaina News, May 7, 1998: 18.
— results of Maui County Creative Writing Contest, Lahaina News, June 28, 2001: 5.
— to perform, Lahaina News, June 19, 2003: 14.

GAMEZ, ROBERT
— golfer to play at Isuzu Kapalua International, Lahaina News, October 17, 1990: 9.

GANDHI AND KING: SEASON FOR PEACE AND NONVIOLENCE
— to be performed at the Queen Ka'ahumanu Center, Lahaina News, January 30, 2003: 16.

GANDY, VALERIE
— named Wedding Services Manager at Media Systems, Inc., Lahaina News, December 22, 1994: 13.

GANNON, BEVERLY
— food-and-beverage consultant ends link with Pioneer Inn restoration project, Lahaina News, July 22, 1993: 1.
— chef to appear on "Today" show, Lahaina News, August 12, 1999: 14.
— establishes scholarship for women in culinary arts, Lahaina News, September 16, 1999: 11.

GANNON, BROOKE
— most valuable player on Maui Junior Davis Cup Team, Lahaina News, July 19, 1989: 5.

GANTER, CIARA [WRITER]
— Scholar/Athlete of the Week, Lahaina News, November 12, 1998: 14.
— Lahainaluna High School student wins poetry contest, Lahaina News, June 14, 2001: 17.

GAP, THE [BUSINESS]
— to open at Old Lahaina Center, Lahaina News, July 8, 1999: 11.

GARAN, BILLY [COMEDIAN]
— to perform at Comedy Club, Lahaina News, June 6, 1990: 13.
— to perform at Iao Theater, Lahaina News, June 6, 1991: 14.

GARBAGE
— problem of junk cars noted by Mayor Cravalho, Lahaina Sun, January 20, 1971: 2.
— issue of garbage collection at Lahaina small boat harbor, Lahaina Sun, March 8, 1972: 13.
— dump along coast at Honolua to close, Lahaina Sun, April 5, 1972: 4.
— complaints that collection is too noisy, Lahaina Sun, July 25, 1973: 3.
— fees for commercial haulers have begun, Lahaina News, December 7, 1988: 6.

GARCIA, ALEX
— Yo-Yo champion to hold exhibition, Lahaina News, July 25, 1996: 13.

GARCIA, BRIAN
— police seeking suspect, Lahaina News, March 1, 2001: 9.
— student wins Patsy Mink Congressional Art Award, Lahaina News, May 24, 2001: 1,22.

GARCIA, DANNY
— playing high school basketball, Lahaina Sun, January 20, 1971: 7.
— becomes Maui Interscholastic League top basketball scorer, Lahaina Sun, January 27, 1971: 7.
— see basketball

GARCIA, GEORGE
— to lead Argentine tango workshop, Lahaina News, October 10, 2002: 16.

GARCIA, JON
— report on basketball player, Lahaina Sun, January 20, 1971: 7.

GARCIA, MICHELLE
— finalist for America's National Teenager Pageant, Lahaina News, February 20, 1992: 4.

GARCIA, NORMAN
— see MDG Supply Inc.

GARCIA, RICHIE "GAJATE" [MUSICIAN]
— to offer workshop, Lahaina News, March 24, 1994: 16.

GARCIA, SHELLEY
— key to Lahainaluna High School softball success, Lahaina News, January 13, 1994: 6.

GARCIA, STEPHEN
— lawyer suspended, Lahaina News, June 28, 2001: 8.

GARCIA, SUNNY
— to compete in Vans G-Shock Triple Crown of Surfing, Lahaina News, November 23, 2000: 11.
— survives a near-drowning in preliminary heat in California, Lahaina News, December 14, 2000: 15.
— wins first event in Triple Crown of Surfing, Lahaina News, November 28, 2002: 13.

GARCIA, TIM
— Lahaina Canoe Club coach featured, Lahaina News, May 11, 1995: 7.

GARDEN AND VALLEY ISLE SEAFOOD
— recognized as outstanding business for Year of the Ocean, Lahaina News, August 13, 1998: 15.

GARDEN BEHIND THE MOON, THE [PLAY]
— auditions to be held for, Lahaina News, September 7, 2000: 20.
— to be presented by Maui OnStage, Lahaina News, November 1, 2001: 17.

GARDEN OF BE, THE [MUSICAL]
— Tess Cartwright's piece being performed, Lahaina News, February 3, 1994: 3.
— to be performed, Lahaina News, October 20, 1994: 15.
— to perform during Halloween Keiki Parade, Lahaina News, October 12, 1995: 3.
— to be performed by Tess Cartwright and the Mewes, Lahaina News, March 28, 1996: 12.
— to be performed, Lahaina News, April 4, 1996: 15.
— created by Tess Cartwright, to be shown on Akaku, Lahaina News, February 24, 2000: 15.

GARDEN PARTY
— to be held by The Maui Academy of Performing Arts, Lahaina News, September 10, 1992: 22.
— to be held by Maui Academy of Performing Arts, Lahaina News, September 2, 1993: 12.
— to be held, Lahaina News, September 9, 1993: 11.
— to support Maui Academy of Performing Arts, Lahaina News, August 18, 1994: 15,16.
— more restaurants and artists to take part, Lahaina News, August 25, 1994: 16.
— to be held, Lahaina News, September 3, 1998: 20.
— to be held to benefit Maui Academy of Performing Arts, Lahaina News, September 16, 1999: 12.
— Maui Academy of Performing Arts to hold, Lahaina News, September 13, 2001: 16.
— to be held by Maui Academy of Performing Arts, Lahaina News, September 12, 2002: 20,21.
— to be held by Maui Academy of Performing Arts, Lahaina News, August 21, 2003: 2.
— to be held to support Maui Academy of Performing Arts, Lahaina News, September 4, 2003: 17.

GARDEN RESTAURANT, THE [BUSINESS]
— reviewed, Lahaina News, May 15, 1991: 14.

GARDENIA COURT RESTAURANT [RESTAURANT]
— featured, Lahaina News, February 4, 1999: 6,7.

GARDENING
— anthuriums, Lahaina News, December 15, 1981: 6.
— growing ginger in Hawaii, Lahaina News, February 15, 1982: 5.
— plants to use as windbreaks discussed, Lahaina News, March 15, 1982: 5.
— Maui Organic Gardening Guide published by Oasis Maui, Lahaina News, April 1, 1987: 3.
— University of Hawai'i Cooperative Extension agent James Tavares to offer advice on, Lahaina News, January 14, 1993: 2.
— Ma'alaea community garden featured, Lahaina News, April 8, 1993: 4.
— organic gardening workshops to be held, Lahaina News, June 16, 1994: 4.
— workshop on organic gardening to be held, Lahaina News, July 14, 1994: 6.
— pesticide strategies discussed, Lahaina News, August 15, 1996: 8.
— strategy for growing plants for clipping, Lahaina News, August 22, 1996: 9.
— Joy Webster to offer workshop on composting, Lahaina News, October 15, 1998: 16.

— program on pruning to be held at Maui Community College, Lahaina News, January 27, 2000: 12.

— home composting workshops continued to be held, Lahaina News, August 3, 2000: 16.

— home composting workshop to be held, Lahaina News, April 10, 2003: 2.

GARDENS
— large produce in Findhorn (Scotland), Lahaina Times, June, 1980 volume 4 number 5: 3.

GARDINER, DIANA
— to organize publicity for the Victoria-Maui Yacht Race, Lahaina News, June 22, 1988: 2.

GARDINER, ROD
— purchases Hawaii Kobe Japanese Steak House, Lahaina News, February 3, 1988: 3.

GARDNER, CHUCK
— sells share of KPOA FM radio to Chuck Bergson, Lahaina News, April 11, 1990: 5.

GARDNER, EMILY
— to offer session on how to help monitor seals, Lahaina News, September 24, 1998: 17.

GARDNER, GUY
— astronaut visits Maui, Lahaina News, May 24, 1989: 3.

GARDNER, JANINE [COMEDIAN]
— to perform at Comedy Club, Lahaina News, February 13, 1992: 18.

GARDNER, MARIA
— to lead Ascension Gathering, Lahaina News, August 1, 1996: 21.

— to lead "advanced transformational workshop", Lahaina News, August 6, 1998: 20.

— to head "Advanced Transformational Workshop", Lahaina News, October 1, 1998: 17.

— to lead workshop on "Cellular Release", Lahaina News, January 14, 1999: 13.

— to lead workshop on "Astral/Emotional Body Clearing", Lahaina News, February 25, 1999: 12.

GARDNER, MICHAEL
— named executive chef at Reilley's Steak House, Lahaina News, March 9, 1995: 6.

GARDNER, RULON
— U.S. Olympic heavyweight wrestling champion visits Maui on promotional tour for Extreme Dreams University, Lahaina News, December 14, 2000: 3.

GARFIELD [CARTOON]
— to be featured at Fun Factory, Lahaina News, June 14, 1989: 2.

— photographs of visit, Lahaina News, June 28, 1989: 10.

GARLOCK, CAROL
— joins Wailea Golf Resort, Lahaina News, August 19, 1999: 14.

GARNER, LOYAL [MUSICIAN]
— to play on Seabird Cruises, Lahaina News, January 18, 1984: 12.

— to perform at Lahaina Cannery, Lahaina News, December 2, 1987: 3.

— to perform at Valentine's Day fundraiser for Maui Historical Society, Lahaina News, February 3, 1994: 12.

— to perform at "Local Divas in Concert", Lahaina News, September 23, 1999: 12.

GARRETT, JOHN [ARTIST]
— works displayed at Hui No'eau Visual Arts Center, Lahaina News, April 22, 1987: 10.

GARRISON, TERRI [MUSICIAN]
— to perform at Casanova's, Lahaina News, January 2, 1991: 8.

— to perform at Casanova's, Lahaina News, May 1, 1991: 18.

— to perform at Embassy Suites Resort Ballroom, Lahaina News, June 20, 1991: 9.

— to perform at Casanova's, Lahaina News, July 18, 1991: 12.

— to perform at Casanova's, Lahaina News, November 21, 1991: 22.

— to perform at Pioneer Inn, Lahaina News, February 6, 1992: 18.

— continues to perform at Pioneer Inn, Lahaina News, March 12, 1992: 17.

GARRISON, VERNON
— seeking rezoning for Aala Place property, Lahaina News, August 6, 1992: 3.

GARRISON, ZINA
— local tennis player featured, Lahaina News, December 21, 1983: 6.

GARY PUCKETT AND THE UNION GAP [MUSICAL GROUP]
— to perform at the Maui Marriott Hotel ballroom, Lahaina News, October 2, 1985: 10.

GARYS ISLAND [RESTAURANT]
— opens, Lahaina News, February 4, 1999: 13.

GAS
— prices at various stations surveyed weekly, not otherwise indexed, Lahaina News, August 15, 1990: 2.

— prices jump, Lahaina News, October 10, 1990: 2.

— state Senate to hold public hearing on cost of, Lahaina News, October 17, 1990: 2.

— editorial critical of State government addressing problems of costs, Lahaina News, May 23, 1991: 8.

GAS COMPANY, THE [BUSINESS]
— increasing rates, Lahaina News, February 21, 1990: 5.

— Daniel Lambert joins, Lahaina News, October 3, 1990: 9.

— announces promotions, Lahaina News, December 12, 1990: 6.

— to increase utility rate, Lahaina News, February 6, 1991: 3.

— fixes gas leak at Papalaua and Front streets, Lahaina News, July 30, 1992: 1,3.

— completes testing of gas lines, Lahaina News, August 13, 1992: 1.

— claims that gas system fixed, Lahaina News, August 20, 1992: 3.

— to repave roads following repair of propane leak, Lahaina News, September 17, 1992: 3.

GAS EXPRESS [BUSINESS]
— opens, includes car wash, Lahaina News, July 2, 1992: 16.

GASMAN, JOE
— barber on Front Street, featured, Lahaina Sun, June 14, 1972: 1,6,7.

— barber in downtown Lahaina retires after 40 years, Lahaina Sun, April 11, 1973: 4.

GASPARETTO, LUIZ [ARTIST]
— to give art demonstration, Lahaina News, January 24, 1990: 14.

GASTON, JOY [TEACHER]
— teaches oceanography to Lahaina Intermediate School students on Lin Wa Glass Bottom Boat, Lahaina News, June 24, 1987: 18.

GATCHELL, CLAY "DUKE"
— merchant launches campaign to greet cruise ships, Lahaina News, August 31, 2000: 1,15.

GATE TO HEAVEN, THE [PLAY]
— to be offered by Maui Community College and the Maui Arts and Cultural Center, Lahaina News, February 9, 1995: 11.

GATELY, ROBYN
— appointed general sales manager of KPOA, Lahaina News, July 21, 1994: 7.

GATES, GARY
— hired by Tateishi and Apo, Lahaina News, April 17, 1991: 9.

GATES, JULIE
— Maui Marriott is new director of sales, Lahaina News, April 2, 1998: 13.

GATES, WENDELL [ARTIST]
— connecting to Maui artistic community, Lahaina News, December 5, 1984: 11.
— mentoring relationship with Bruce Turnbull discussed , Lahaina News, October 16, 1985: 11.

GATHERING OF OUR LIVING TREASURES
— kupuna to meet, Lahaina News, August 16, 2001: 1,9.

GATTI, LISA
— returns money found by banyan tree to owner, Lahaina Sun, May 26, 1971: 3.

GATY, CLAUDE [CHEF]
— joins Country Kitchen Restaurant, Lahaina News, August 22, 1991: 4.

GAXIOLA, CESAR
— Director of MEO Inc. Enlace Hispano Program receives Aloha Award from Maui Chamber of Commerce, Lahaina News, June 21, 2001: 2.

GAY AND BISEXUAL MEN'S KAHULUI COFFEE KLUTCH
— to be held, Lahaina News, April 1, 1999: 16.
— continues to meet, Lahaina News, May 13, 1999: 16.
— continues to be held, Lahaina News, September 16, 1999: 13.
— continues to be held, Lahaina News, April 27, 2000: 13.
— to be held, Lahaina News, September 28, 2000: 17.

GAY AND BISEXUAL MEN'S KIHEI COFFEE KLUTCH
— continues to be held, Lahaina News, September 9, 1999: 12.

GAY AND BISEXUAL MEN'S MONTHLY HIKE
— to be held, Lahaina News, November 2, 2000: 24.

GAY ASIA AND PACIFIC ISLANDER SUPPORT NETWORK
— to celebrate Chinese New Year, Lahaina News, February 7, 2002: 16.

GAYLE, CRYSTAL [MUSICIAN]
— to perform, Lahaina News, March 14, 2002: 16.

GAYLORD, JAMES
— attorney sentenced for stealing money from clients, Lahaina News, December 26, 1991: 3.

GAZEBO, THE [RESTAURANT]
— security guard Walter Rozanski extinguishes fire at, Lahaina News, November 7, 1990: 4.
— featured, Lahaina News, August 29, 1991: 11.
— featured, Lahaina News, March 6, 1997: 7,14.
— featured, Lahaina News, April 3, 2003: 14.

GAZMEN, CONNIE
— receives University of Hawaii-Manoa School of Nursing Educator Award, Lahaina News, February 8, 1996: 4.

GAZMEN, ED [POLITICIAN]
— Maui Council candidate profiled, Lahaina News, September 15, 1980: 4.
— re-enters political arena, Lahaina News, August 4, 1994: 3.
— challenges incumbent Dennis Nakamura to debate, Lahaina News, October 13, 1994: 6.

GAZMEN, GLENN
— Lahaina Girls Fastpitch Softball program coordinator featured, Lahaina News, May 2, 2002: 12.

GEANNIE & CHOCKY [MUSICAL GROUP]
— to perform at Royal Ocean Terrace Lounge at the Royal Lahaina Resort, Lahaina News, September 19, 1990: 11.

GEARHART, BILL
— purchases Escudero [ship], Lahaina Sun, February 7, 1973: 1,5.

GECC FINANCIAL CORPORATION [BUSINESS]
— promotes Joanne Sato to loan officer, Lahaina News, July 7, 1994: 9.

GEE, DAVID [COMEDIAN]
— to perform, Lahaina News, January 10, 1990: 12.
— to perform at Comedy Club and the Sports Page, Lahaina News, February 20, 1992: 12.

GEE, NICOLE
— receives Jerry Boser Hobie Sports Memorial Scholarships, Lahaina News, June 2, 1994: 3.

GEMINI [SHIP]
— offering an Aloha Thanksgiving Sail, Lahaina News, November 15, 2001: 10.
— to hold benefit for victims of September 11th, Lahaina News, November 22, 2001: 20.

GEMS OF HAWAII
— jewelry store opens, Lahaina News, October 10, 1991: 6.

GENERAL SERVICES, INC. [BUSINESS]
— developer to build Napili Villas, Lahaina News, December 14, 2000: 11.

GENTLE WORLD
— sponsoring vegetarian cooking demonstration, Lahaina News, January 23, 1997: 10.

GENTRY, KIT [ARTIST]
— to hold "Pastels for Landscape Painting" class, Lahaina News, February 11, 1999: 16.
— to exhibit at Art School at Kapalua, Lahaina News, March 9, 2000: 13.
— to exhibit at Art School at Kapalua, Lahaina News, March 16, 2000: 12.
— to exhibit at Village Gallery, Lahaina News, January 4, 2001: 16.

GEOGRAPHY
— Mountains of West Maui discussed, Lahaina Sun, May 17, 1972: 17.

GEOLOGICAL SURVEY, U.S.
— studying West Maui's water situation, Lahaina News, October 5, 1995: 1,16.
— planning reef survey, Lahaina News, December 20, 2001: 3.

GEORGE BERNARD SHAW'S WOMEN [PLAY]
— to be performed by Maui Youth Theatre, Lahaina News, April 30, 1986: 3.

GEORGE, CIS
— named co-chair of American Heart Association residential campaign, Lahaina News, January 18, 1989: 5.

GEORGE, ELIZABETH [WRITER]
— to lead "A Passion for Prayer—A Hope Chapel Women's Conference", Lahaina News, January 27, 2000: 12.
— to speak at Calvary Chapel, Lahaina News, May 9, 2002: 17.

GEORGE, LEE [MUSICIAN]
— to perform at Moose McGillycuddy's, Lahaina News, February 14, 1990: 15.
— equipment stolen from his vehicle, Lahaina News, March 7, 1990: 3.

GEORGIOU [BUSINESS]
— clothing store opens in Whaler's Village, Lahaina News, December 23, 1993: 7.
— to open, Lahaina News, December 30, 1993: 5.

GERARD, PHILIP
— author of "Secret Soldiers" to sign books at Borders Books, Lahaina News, July 11, 2002: 17.

GERARD'S [RESTAURANT]
— reviewed, Lahaina News, July 1, 1982: 10.
— reviewed, Lahaina News, December 7, 1983: 13.
— reopens at Plantation Inn, Lahaina News, September 2, 1987: 3.
— reviewed, Lahaina News, October 21, 1987: 4,8.
— will offer wild game on Christmas and New Year's, Lahaina News, December 9, 1987: 3.

— reviewed, Lahaina News, March 9, 1988: 7.

— featured, Lahaina News, September 21, 1988: 10.

— receives award from Ford Times Magazine, Lahaina News, January 11, 1989: 11.

— reviewed, Lahaina News, May 17, 1989: 14.

— celebrates 7th anniversary, Lahaina News, June 21, 1989: 6.

— reviewed, Lahaina News, August 23, 1989: 11.

— featured, Lahaina News, November 8, 1989: 11.

— reactions to expanded menu, Lahaina News, December 20, 1989: 17.

— featured, Lahaina News, April 4, 1990: 12.

— purchases escargot locally, Lahaina News, June 27, 1990: 14.

— featured by Lahaina Art Society at Banyan Tree Gallery, Lahaina News, August 8, 1990: 14.

— offering breakfast buffet, Lahaina News, December 19, 1990: 14.

— to hold fundraiser for Big Brothers/Big Sisters, Lahaina News, May 15, 1991: 5.

— hosting Bastille Day dinner, Lahaina News, July 11, 1991: 16.

— offering breakfast, Lahaina News, January 23, 1992: 16.

— to host French Art Night, Lahaina News, April 23, 1992: 29.

— celebrating 10-year anniversary, Lahaina News, June 11, 1992: 19.

— celebrates 10-year anniversary, Lahaina News, June 25, 1992: 18.

— rated best by Restaurant and Activities Review Guide, Lahaina News, July 9, 1992: 18,19.

— new menu, Lahaina News, February 4, 1993: 14.

GERE, JEFF

— to offer "Amazing Tales" at Gallerie Ha, Lahaina News, May 30, 2002: 17.

GERHARD, MARA-KEALA

— to discuss "Breath and Breathing and the Unlimited Power of Huna", Lahaina News, April 18, 2002: 17.

— to present on "huna", Lahaina News, April 10, 2003: 20.

— to lead workshop on "Breathe Your Way to God", Lahaina News, June 5, 2003: 16.

GERRARD, GLEN

— appointed program director at KLHI FM 101, Lahaina News, August 24, 1995: 10.

GERRY N [SHIP]

— sinks off Maui, crew survives, Lahaina Sun, April 11, 1973: 15.

GERSONDE, JON

— appointed Operations Manager of Westin Maui, Lahaina News, June 25, 1998: 11.

— new manager at the Kapalua Bay Hotel, Lahaina News, January 17, 2002: 8.

GERVAN, LENA

— to discuss how marine animals protect themselves with Jayme Perrello, Lahaina News, May 25, 2000: 19.

GESHELL LAW OFFICE [BUSINESS]

— looking for female victims of domestic violence, Lahaina News, February 24, 2000: 3.

— looking for female victims of domestic violence, Lahaina News, April 6, 2000: 14.

GET OFF WITH ME [PLAY]

— to be performed by Maui Community Theatre, Lahaina News, July 11, 1990: 15.

— to be performed by Maui Community Theatre, Lahaina News, July 18, 1990: 11.

GET THE DRIFT AND BAG IT

— planned, Lahaina News, October 12, 1988: 1.

— scheduled, Lahaina News, October 17, 1990: 6.

— to be held, Lahaina News, September 24, 1992: 6.

— to be held, Lahaina News, October 5, 1995: 4.

— to be held, Lahaina News, October 12, 1995: 3.

— to include seaweed clean-up, Lahaina News, October 19, 1995: 4.

— to be held, Lahaina News, September 12, 1996: 3.

— to be held, Lahaina News, September 11, 1997: 17.

— to be held, Lahaina News, September 10, 1998: 18.

— details of, Lahaina News, September 17, 1998: 22.

— to be held, Lahaina News, September 24, 1998: 6.

— planned, Lahaina News, September 9, 1999: 5.

— to be held, Lahaina News, September 16, 1999: 1.

— drivers find unusual junk during cleanup, Lahaina News, September 23, 1999: 1.

— to be held, volunteers sought, Lahaina News, August 31, 2000: 1.

— to be held, Lahaina News, September 7, 2000: 19.

— to be held as part of International Coastal Cleanup, Lahaina News, September 14, 2000: 19.

— to be held, Lahaina News, September 13, 2001: 1.

— to be held, Lahaina News, September 20, 2001: 17.

— to be held, Lahaina News, September 19, 2002: 1,26.

GETMAN, GARY

— manager of Lahaina-Ka'anapali & Pacific Railway receives award for volunteer work following storm, Lahaina News, April 19, 1989: 3.

— general manager of Lahaina-Ka'anapali and Pacific Railroad featured, Lahaina News, August 29, 1991: 6.

GHALLAB, GHALIB

— to perform at the Maui Arts and Cultural Center, Lahaina News, July 28, 1994: 15.

GIAMARIO, DANIEL

— astrology to present at Renaissance Psychic Faire, Lahaina News, January 25, 1989: 5.

GIBSON, ADRIAN

— chosen as chairman for Maui ACLU, Lahaina Sun, January 13, 1971: 6.

GIBSON, HARRY [SUPERINTENDENT OF STATE PARKS FOR MAUI COUNTY]

— proposal to dredge a swimming area in Launiupoko State Park, Lahaina Sun, November 11, 1970: 3.

— discusses construction of ocean pool at Launiupoko State Park, Lahaina Sun, December 23, 1970: 11.

— discusses installation of guardrails in Wahikuli Park, Lahaina Sun, August 18, 1971: 3.

GIBSON, J. GORDON [SAILOR]

— life detailed, Lahaina Sun, March 7, 1973: 14.

GIBSON, JERRY

— named Executive Assistant Manager, Food and Beverage at Hyatt Regency, Lahaina News, September 24, 1992: 9.

GIBSON, THOMAS CLAIR

— photograph of, Lahaina Sun, December 23, 1970: 9.

GIBSON, WARREN

— performs at Warren and Annabelle's , Lahaina News, May 13, 1999: 13.

GIDEON, GARTH

— named chairman of Lahaina Whaling Festival, Lahaina Sun, February 17, 1971: 8.

— to meet with Thomas Hamilton of the Hawaii Visitors Bureau, Lahaina Sun, February 17, 1971: 8.

GIESKING, DAVID

— diver presumed dead, service held, Lahaina News, May 23, 1984: 5.

GIFFORD, GARY

— named president of Kapalua Land Company, Lahaina News, August 12, 1987: 18.

— now president and chief executive officer of Kapalua Land Company, Ltd., Lahaina News, August 27, 1992: 10.

— president of Kapalua Land Co. discusses possible land swap between Maui Land and Pineapple with state for park in Honolua Bay, Lahaina News, January 26, 1995: 1,20.

GIFT BASKET, THE [BUSINESS]
— Ka'ahumanu Center, Lahaina News, August 26, 1999: 14.

GIGI'S FASHION [BUSINESS]
— opens a larger store, Lahaina News, October 17, 1991: 6.

GILBERT AND ASSOCIATES ADVERTISING AGENCY [BUSINESS]
— hired by Trilogy Excursions, Lahaina News, September 4, 1985: 3.
— ad agency to assist AAAAA Rent-a-Space, Lahaina News, May 16, 1990: 8.
— promotes Lu Anne Riley to vice president, Lahaina News, April 25, 2002: 8.

GILBERT, RANDY [WRITER]
— Lahainaluna High School graduate now bestselling author of "Success Bound: Breaking Free of Mediocrity", Lahaina News, December 5, 2002: 3.

GILDERSLEEVE, ROGER
— appointed Research and Development Division at Trilogy Excursions, Lahaina News, September 30, 1999: 11.

GILES, GIGI
— appointed director of astronomy at Hyatt Regency Maui, Lahaina News, May 15, 1991: 8.

GILL, RAY
— elected PTA present for Kamehameha III School, Lahaina Sun, June 9, 1971: 3.
— named to Maui Chamber of Commerce board of directors, Lahaina Sun, August 4, 1971: 10.

GILL, TOM [POLITICIAN]
— to speak to Democratic Century Club, Lahaina News, April 16, 1998: 13.

GILL, VINCE [MUSICIAN]
— to perform at Maui Arts and Cultural Center, Lahaina News, November 7, 1996: 14.
— to perform at Maui Arts and Cultural Center, Lahaina News, November 7, 1996: 18.

GILLESPIE, DIZZY [MUSICIAN]
— to perform at Maui Prince Hotel, sponsored by Maui Jazz Society, Lahaina News, March 6, 1991: 14.
— to perform at Maui Prince Hotel, Lahaina News, March 13, 1991: 14.
— to perform the Maui Prince Hotel, Lahaina News, April 17, 1991: 14.
— to perform for Maui Jazz Society, Lahaina News, April 24, 1991: 11.
— to perform this week, Lahaina News, May 8, 1991: 21.

GILLESPIE, ROSEMARY
— to speak on "Long Jaws and Happy Faces: Adaptive Radiation of Spiders in Hawaii", Lahaina News, June 20, 2002: 16.

GILLETTE, CYNEE [BUSINESSWOMAN]
— elected secretary of Lahaina Retail Board, Lahaina Sun, December 16, 1970: 3.
— wedding to Richard Bredehoft announced, Lahaina Sun, January 20, 1971: 6.

GILLILAND, ROD
— joins C. Brewer Homes Inc., Lahaina News, January 26, 1995: 13.

GILLIOM, AMY HANAIALI'I [MUSICIAN]
— releases "Native Child" album, Lahaina News, January 11, 1996: 14.
— to host "First Step ... Anything Goes" to benefit Maui Community Theatre, Lahaina News, September 5, 1996: 18.
— to perform with Willie K., Lahaina News, April 24, 1997: 11.
— to perform benefit concert for Ronald McDonald House, Lahaina News, December 11, 1997: 19.
— to perform at fundraiser for Hui O Wa'a Kaulua, Lahaina News, December 24, 1998: 13.
— to perform with Willie K., Lahaina News, December 2, 1999: 17.
— to perform with Willie K at Maui Arts and Cultural Center, Lahaina News, November 30, 2000: 18.
— to perform at Hui O Wa'a Kaulua, Lahaina News, November 1, 2001: 15.
— to perform "A Tribute to Hawaiian Musical Treasures", Lahaina News, April 11, 2002: 17.

GILLIOM, ERIC [MUSICIAN]
— to perform at Maui Youth Theatre, Lahaina News, November 19, 1986: 3.
— to perform at fundraiser for Hui O Wa'a Kaulua, Lahaina News, December 24, 1998: 13.
— releases new CD "Like Chow Fun", Lahaina News, January 6, 2000: 14.

GILLIS, MICHAEL
— North Beach Grille executive chef featured, Lahaina News, March 6, 2003: 9.

GILMAN, GORHAM [ARTIST]
— life and career remembered, Lahaina News, January 11, 1984: 7,8,9.
— details on life from his nephew Robert Gilman, Lahaina News, February 22, 1984: 9.10.11.

GILMORE, MARK
— Lahaina Intermediate School band flourishing under, Lahaina News, April 25, 2002: 1.

GILMORE, ROBERT [WRITER]
— to discuss "Alice in Quantumland", Lahaina News, May 20, 1999: 17.

GILMORE, TOM [COMEDIAN]
— to perform at Comedy Club and the Sports Page, Lahaina News, November 28, 1991: 14,15.

GIMA, ELAINE
— opens new boutique, Lahaina News, February 20, 1992: 9.

GIMA, YOSHIMORI & ASSOCIATES
— renamed Gima, Yoshimori, Miyabara, Deguchi Architects, Lahaina News, January 9, 1991: 5.

GIMA YOSHIMORI MIYABARA DEGUCHI ARCHITECTS, INC. [BUSINESS]
— hires Tim Leong as project architect, Lahaina News, November 28, 1991: 10.

GIMMICK [MUSICAL GROUP]
— reviewed, Lahaina News, April 15, 1980: 5.

GIN GAME [PLAY]
— to be performed by Maui Community Theatre/OnStage, Lahaina News, August 26, 1993: 13.

GINGERBREAD
— as Christmas food, Lahaina News, December 23, 1987: 1,24.

GINZBURG, YANKEL [ARTIST]
— to visit Lahaina Galleries, Lahaina News, September 18, 2003: 17.

GIOVANI'S TOMATO PIE ITALIAN AMERICAN RISTAURANTE [RESTAURANT]
— featured, Lahaina News, September 12, 2002: 14,15.

GIOVANNI, JIM [COMEDIAN]
— to perform at Comedy Club and the Sports Page, Lahaina News, March 26, 1992: 13,16.
— to perform at Comedy Club and the Sports Page, Lahaina News, March 4, 1993: 9,12.

GIRAGOSIAN, HELEN
— offering karate lessons, Lahaina News, March 12, 1998: 15.
— to offer karate lessons, Lahaina News, March 26, 1998: 7.

GIRL SCOUTS
— 60th anniversary celebrated, Lahaina Sun, March 22, 1972: 7.
— leaders praised, Lahaina News, April 25, 1984: 3.

— Lahaina troupe makes lei for Girl Scouts attending Scout World Conference in New York City, Lahaina News, August 29, 1984: 10.

— announce poster contest, Lahaina News, May 15, 1985: 8.

— looking for volunteer group leaders, Lahaina News, September 11, 1985: 3.

— registration open, Lahaina News, February 5, 1986: 3.

— to celebrate Girl Scout Week, Lahaina News, March 5, 1986: 3,10.

— troops forming, Lahaina News, September 24, 1986: 3.

— to meet at banyan tree, Lahaina News, March 11, 1987: 4.

— looking for leaders, Lahaina News, August 12, 1987: 18.

— registration organized, Lahaina News, September 2, 1987: 3.

— registration organized, Lahaina News, October 7, 1987: 3.

— local leaders recognized, Lahaina News, April 20, 1988: 6,11.

— bridging recognized, Lahaina News, May 25, 1988: 10.

— selling cookies, Lahaina News, November 23, 1988: 3.

— leaders honored, Lahaina News, April 26, 1989: 3.

— camp at Camp Piiholo, Lahaina News, May 24, 1989: 7.

— cookie drive under way, Lahaina News, November 29, 1989: 36.

— selling cookies, Lahaina News, January 24, 1990: 28.

— to hold car wash, Lahaina News, February 28, 1990: 3.

— volunteer Odetta Moffett-Hurlock dies, Lahaina News, March 14, 1990: 2.

— honored for selling cookies, Lahaina News, May 23, 1990: 6.

— Lynda Roberts named public relations liaison, Lahaina News, November 21, 1990: 12.

— to sell cookies, Lahaina News, November 21, 1990: 3.

— cookies to arrive soon, Lahaina News, January 16, 1991: 3.

— organizes opportunity for scouts to see women executives in action, Lahaina News, April 3, 1991: 3.

— able to view women executives in action, Lahaina News, April 10, 1991: 3.

— gives Andrea Heath-Blundell an Appreciation Pin, Lahaina News, June 6, 1991: 4,7.

— sponsoring adult camp for volunteers, Lahaina News, July 25, 1991: 5.

— to host astronaut Tammy Jernigan, Lahaina News, August 15, 1991: 3.

— begin fall recruitment campaign, Lahaina News, August 22, 1991: 7.

— cookie sales to begin, Lahaina News, November 7, 1991: 20.

— taking orders for cookies, will be available in January, Lahaina News, November 21, 1991: 4.

— looking for professional women to mentor, Lahaina News, February 6, 1992: 3.

— looking for mentors, Lahaina News, February 13, 1992: 3.

— extends application deadline, Lahaina News, March 19, 1992: 3.

— now accepting orders for cookies, Lahaina News, December 31, 1992: 1.

— to hold recognition dinner, Lahaina News, May 13, 1993: 4.

— to hold annual meeting, Lahaina News, August 12, 1993: 6.

— seeking volunteers, Lahaina News, July 7, 1994: 4.

— seeking members, Lahaina News, April 27, 1995: 5.

— to sell cookies, Lahaina News, January 4, 1996: 4.

— selling cookies, Lahaina News, January 22, 1998: 5.

— to begin selling cookies, Lahaina News, January 21, 1999: 2.

— plant avocado tree at Sacred Hearts School, Lahaina News, June 17, 1999: 15.

GISELA [ENTERTAINER]

— to be featured at Sweethearts Ball, Lahaina News, February 8, 1984: 12.

GIVE KIDS THE WORLD

— to hold benefit car wash, Lahaina News, August 8, 1996: 15.

GIVENS, HARRY [BARTENDER]

— featured, Lahaina Sun, August 15, 1973: 3.

GLADNEY, JOSEPH

— attacked, Lahaina News, August 22, 1990: 1.

GLASCO, BRUCE

— named top pro at Plantation course, Lahaina News, February 3, 1994: 7.

GLASS MENAGERIE, THE [PLAY]

— to be performed at Seabury Hall, Lahaina News, February 13, 1997: 10.

GLASS ORCHID [RETAIL]

— reviewed, Lahaina News, July 1, 1983: 15.

GLASS, TODD [COMEDIAN]

— to perform at Comedy Club, Lahaina News, January 31, 1990: 13.

GLASSER, CHELSEA [ARTIST]

— to exhibit at Art School at Kapalua, Lahaina News, December 3, 1998: 7.

GLASSMAN, BARBARA

— directed of Maui Children's Theater featured, Lahaina News, November 7, 1984: 10.

GLASSMAN, BILL

— new loan officer at Bank of Hawaii, Lahaina News, July 24, 2003: 8.

GLATSTEIN, ELI

— doctor to speak on breast cancer, radiation and lymphoma, Lahaina News, February 25, 1987: 3.

GLAUB, DOMINIQUE

— to hold lecture on relationships, Lahaina News, April 9, 1998: 16.

— to speak on mastering relationships and self-awareness, Lahaina News, May 7, 1998: 21.

— continues to offer talks on mastering relationships and self-awareness, Lahaina News, June 11, 1998: 16.

— continues to offer classes on relationships, Lahaina News, August 6, 1998: 21.

— continues to offer classes on relationships, Lahaina News, January 21, 1999: 13.

— continues to offer workshops, Lahaina News, May 6, 1999: 20.

GLAZIER, DAVID

— commander of U.S. Pacific Fleet at Pearl Harbor to speak at Navy League, Lahaina News, January 29, 1998: 8.

GLEASON, DAVID

— Amfac president discusses challenge to land ownership by Native Hawaiians, Lahaina News, December 9, 1987: 17.

— president of Amfac, Inc. discusses purchase by JMB Realty Corp., Lahaina News, September 14, 1988: 1,20.

— speaks of Amfac, Inc.'s development plans, Lahaina News, September 21, 1988: 1,14.

— named head of course management team at Waikele Golf Club, Lahaina News, May 6, 1993: 9.

— appointed president of Amfac/JMB Hawaii golf division, Lahaina News, July 17, 1997: 13.

— appointed general manager of The Dunes at Maui Lani golf course, Lahaina News, December 10, 1998: 17.

GLEASON, TRACEY

— participates in triathlon, Lahaina News, June 22, 1995: 6.

GLEESON, PAT

— Westin Maui director of romance featured, Lahaina News, February 13, 1992: 11.

GLENN MILLER ORCHESTRA

— to perform at Maui Inter-Continental Resort, Lahaina News, April 14, 1994: 12.

GLOCKNER-FERRARI, DEBBIE

— whale research described, Lahaina News, April 18, 1984: 9,10,11.

— additional discussion of research on whales, Lahaina News, April 25, 1984: 7,8,11.

— research described, Lahaina News, March 13, 1985: 11.

— studying whales off West Maui, Lahaina News, April 1, 1987: 1,8,10,21.

— gives update on whale research, Lahaina News, April 22, 1987: 3.

— to present to Maui Whalewatchers, Lahaina News, February 10, 1988: 3.

— comments on proposed thrillcraft corridor, Lahaina News, February 24, 1988: 1.

— discuss status of whales in the Pacific, Lahaina News, May 11, 1988: 1,12,13.

— gives birth, Lahaina News, February 7, 1990: 3.

— Lahaina Intermediate School students host program to honor, Lahaina News, May 8, 1991: 3.

— see also whales

GLORY AND ULYSSES [FILM]

— to be filmed on Maui, Lahaina News, July 27, 1995: 12.

GLOVER, KYRA

— wins baby beauty contest, Lahaina News, November 29, 1989: 20.

GLOVER, RON

— comments on proposed thrillcraft corridor, Lahaina News, February 24, 1988: 1.

GMO-FREE MAUI

— organization to discuss GMOs, Lahaina News, October 9, 2003: 17.

GMOS

— Lorrin Pang to present on, Lahaina News, August 7, 2003: 2.

GNAZZO, GAIL

— reports on needs of Maui Youth and Family Shelter, Lahaina News, September 13, 1989: 1.

— honored by Western States Youth Service Network, Lahaina News, December 6, 1989: 28.

— re-elected executive director of Maui Youth and Family Services, Lahaina News, August 29, 1990: 4.

GO ASK ALICE [PLAY]

— to be performed by Baldwin Theatre Guild's, Lahaina News, February 7, 1990: 14.

— to be performed by Maui High students, Lahaina News, May 13, 1999: 17.

GO JIMMY GO [MUSICAL GROUP]

— to perform at Maui Brews Island Bistro, Lahaina News, February 27, 2003: 18.

GO-KART

— racing to be held, Lahaina News, October 25, 2001: 12.

GO-YUEN [MUSICAL GROUP]

— to perform Chinese classical and folk music, Lahaina News, February 8, 1989: 5.

GOBRECHT, ELEANOR

— account of sailing adventure, Lahaina Sun, June 9, 1971: 2.

GOD IS DOG SPELLED BACKWARDS [FILM]

— shown at Princess Theatre in Paia, Lahaina Sun, May 5, 1971: 2.

GODARD, MICHAEL [ARTIST]

— to exhibit at Sargent's Fine Art, Lahaina News, May 8, 2003: 16.

GODFREY, THERESE

— offers workshop "Wishbusters: Turning Your Dreams Into Reality", Lahaina News, March 9, 1988: 18.

GODINEZ, SAL

— see Sal Godinez

GODSPELL [MUSICAL]

— cast announced, Lahaina News, February 6, 1992: 22.

— opens, Lahaina News, March 5, 1992: 16,18.

— to be performed by West Maui Players, Lahaina News, January 24, 2002: 17.

— sneak peek to be offered at Whalers Village, Lahaina News, April 11, 2002: 14.

— to be performed by West Maui Players, Lahaina News, April 18, 2002: 16.

— to be performed by West Maui Players, Lahaina News, April 25, 2002: 2.

— being staged by West Maui Players, Lahaina News, May 2, 2002: 16.

GOEMANS, JOHN

— details of run against representative Patsy Mink, Lahaina Sun, September 27, 1972: 6.

GOHEEN, PAUL

— withdrew name for House race and endorsed Clayton Hee, Lahaina News, September 15, 1982: 10.

GOHN, MELINDA

— celebrates publication of new book "Maui Muses", Lahaina News, December 26, 1996: 14.

GOHR, MICHAEL [SAILOR]

— owner of Tanqueray II [ship] described, Lahaina Sun, May 30, 1973: 14.

GOING NASHVILLE! [PLAY]

— to be performed by Baldwin Theatre Guild, Lahaina News, May 20, 1993: 11.

GOING PLACES TRAVEL TOURS AND SERVICES

— to hold grant opening celebration, Lahaina News, March 14, 1996: 10.

GOLCH, LISA [COMEDIAN]

— to perform at Honolulu Comedy Club, Lahaina News, November 16, 1995: 15,16.

GOLD, BRUCE [COMEDIAN]

— to perform at Comedy Club and the Sports Page, Lahaina News, June 4, 1992: 13.

— to perform at Comedy Club and the Sports Page, Lahaina News, June 3, 1993: 13.

GOLD FANTASY [BUSINESS]

— opens, Lahaina News, July 2, 1998: 12.

GOLD, HOWIE [COMEDIAN]

— to perform at Comedy Club and the Sports Page, Lahaina News, February 20, 1992: 12.

GOLDBERG, LOUIS

— to be guest speaker at Kosher Erev Shabbat Dinner, Lahaina News, January 1, 1998: 5.

GOLDEN BEAR [SHIP]

— to debark at Lahaina Harbor , Lahaina News, June 3, 1999: 13.

GOLDEN, JEFF

— named top salesperson by Coldwell Banker McCormack, Lahaina News, October 11, 1989: 5.

GOLDEN OLDIES REVUE SHOW

— musicians raise money for Maui firefighters, Lahaina News, October 26, 2000: 28.

GOLDEN PALACE CHINESE RESTAURANT [RESTAURANT]

— to close, Lahaina News, November 27, 1997: 1,11.

— to close, Lahaina News, December 4, 1997: 21.

GOLDEN PINEAPPLE AWARD

— to be presented to best decorated store front, Lahaina News, October 10, 1991: 7.

— to be awarded, Lahaina News, October 17, 1991: 9.

GOLDFARB, JOEL [MUSICIAN]

— see Joel Goldfarb Quartet [musical group]

GOLDMAN, JONATHAN

— sound healing practitioner to lecture on "Harmonics and Healing Sounds", Lahaina News, October 5, 2000: 7.

GOLDMAN, RITA

— to discuss copy editing and proofreading at Maui Writers Guild, Lahaina News, November 5, 1998: 20.

GOLD'S GYM [BUSINESS]
— to hold "Fitness Extravaganza", Lahaina News, February 13, 1997: 11.
— to sponsor boxing competition, Lahaina News, May 8, 1997: 16.
— hosting "Westside Boxing Club", Lahaina News, September 24, 1998: 15.
— offering "Tae Aerobics" class, Lahaina News, July 15, 1999: 7.

GOLDSBOROUGH, U.S.S. [SHIP]
— battleship anchors off Lahaina, Lahaina News, February 13, 1991: 2.

GOLF BASKETS MAUI [BUSINESS]
— to open at Limahana Place, Lahaina News, April 24, 2003: 9.

GOLF DIGEST [MAGAZINE]
— includes Maui golf courses among best courses in Hawaii, Lahaina News, October 25, 1989: 11.

GOLF HAWAII [TELEVISION SHOW]
— to air on ESPN, Lahaina News, December 12, 1996: 13.
— profiles Ka'anapali's history in professional golf, Lahaina News, November 23, 2000: 11.

GOLF IN DA ISLANDS [BUSINESS]
— to hold Father's Day sale, Lahaina News, June 17, 1999: 13.

GOLFING
— damage to van from golfer at the Royal Ka'anapali Golf Course, Lahaina Sun, February 24, 1971: 1.
— 1971 Japanese Top-Six Pro Golfers Tournament to be played at Ka'anapali Golf Course, Lahaina Sun, December 1, 1971: 13.
— tournament to raise money for Sacred Hearts School planned, Lahaina Sun, January 12, 1972: 8.
— fundraiser for Sacred Hearts School, Lahaina Sun, January 19, 1972: 9.
— tournament held at Waiehu Golf Course, Lahaina Sun, March 8, 1972: 17.
— discussion of cancellation of golf tournament, Lahaina Sun, March 15, 1972: 19.
— two American golfers defeat two Japanese golfers at Ka'anapali, seen on Japanese television, Lahaina Sun, April 5, 1972: 11.
— Asahi Beer Kyosen Golf Tournament held at Wailea Golf Course, Lahaina News, January 7, 1987: 3.
— TV coverage of Kapalua International to expand, Lahaina News, June 24, 1987: 6.
— Isuzu Kapalua International to be held, Lahaina News, November 11, 1987: 6.
— photos from Isuzu Kapalua International, Lahaina News, November 18, 1987: 6.
— senior players to compete in Ka'anapali Classic tournament, Lahaina News, December 2, 1987: 4.
— senior players to compete in Ka'anapali Classic tournament, Lahaina News, December 9, 1987: 4.
— J. Walter Cameron Center receives grant from Isuzu Kapalua International golf tournament, Lahaina News, March 16, 1988: 14.
— Bill Pfeil discusses recent legislative changes regarding creation of courses, Lahaina News, March 23, 1988: 10.
— Hawaii Heart Association Golf Tournament to be held, Lahaina News, June 1, 1988: 19.
— Maui Inter-Continental to hold Father's Day brunch, Lahaina News, June 15, 1988: 6.
— 3rd course planned for Kapalua, Lahaina News, July 6, 1988: 3.
— camp offered to junior golfers, Lahaina News, July 6, 1988: 3.
— West Maui Youth Center receives donation from Amfac, Inc. from fundraiser, Lahaina News, July 13, 1988: 2,3.
— Jacob Neizman Memorial Golf Tournament to be held, Lahaina News, July 27, 1988: 3.
— GTE Ka'anapali Classic to be held, Lahaina News, August 24, 1988: 12.

— tournament held by Maui Board of Realtors in honor of Ralph Yagi, Lahaina News, October 5, 1988: 3.
— GTE Ka'anapali Classic to be held, Lahaina News, October 12, 1988: 13.
— Isuzu Kapalua International tournament detailed, Lahaina News, November 2, 1988: 5.
— Silversword Women's Golf Club to hold invitational tournament, Lahaina News, November 9, 1988: 3.
— Isuzu Kapalua International tournament offers spectator package, Lahaina News, November 9, 1988: 3.
— Maui Junior Davis Cup Team picked, Lahaina News, November 30, 1988: 16.
— teams to compete in Kirin Cup, Lahaina News, December 14, 1988: 18.
— Menehune golf club holds first tournament, Lahaina News, January 25, 1989: 13.
— City Bank Helps Maui Invitational Golf Tournament to benefit Maui Community Arts and Cultural Center, Lahaina News, April 26, 1989: 13.
— benefit tournament to be held for Hale Makua, Lahaina News, June 7, 1989: 5.
— Kapalua Clambake Pro-Am Golf Tournament scheduled, Lahaina News, June 14, 1989: 5.
— Hale Makua Golf Tournament rescheduled, Lahaina News, June 14, 1989: 5.
— Barrio Fiesta tournament to be held at Wailea Blue Golf Course, Lahaina News, July 12, 1989: 2.
— Jacob Neizman Memorial Golf Tournament scheduled, Lahaina News, August 2, 1989: 6.
— clinic for kids held at Kapalua Bay Course, Lahaina News, August 2, 1989: 8.
— Kapalua Open to be held, Lahaina News, August 23, 1989: 5.
— GTE Ka'anapali Classic to host Senior PGA Tour event, Lahaina News, September 6, 1989: 5.
— Orville Moody and Bruce Crampton to participate, Lahaina News, September 6, 1989: 5.
— Ryan Ideta and Mark Merrill win divisions at Hawaii State Open Junior Championship, Lahaina News, September 6, 1989: 5.
— results of Silversword Women's Golf Club tournament given, Lahaina News, October 4, 1989: 6.
— Silversword Women's Golf Club's Invitational to be held, Lahaina News, October 11, 1989: 6.
— Isuzu Kapalua International Tournament to be held, Lahaina News, October 18, 1989: 5.
— Senior PGA tournament to be held at Makena Resort, Lahaina News, October 18, 1989: 5.
— five Maui golf courses among top ten in Hawaii according to Golf Digest, Lahaina News, October 25, 1989: 11.
— Isuzu Kapalua International Tournament begins Sunday, Lahaina News, November 1, 1989: 24.
— amateurs can win a million dollars if they make a hole-in-one, Lahaina News, November 22, 1989: 8.
— Epson Senior Stats Match scheduled, Lahaina News, November 29, 1989: 5.
— Senior PGA Tour at Royal Ka'anapali North Course, Lahaina News, December 6, 1989: 6.
— Fujitsu National Team Championship held, Lahaina News, December 6, 1989: 6.
— hole-in-one competition, Lahaina News, December 6, 1989: 7.
— Silversword Women's Golf Club announce Turkey Shoot winners, Lahaina News, December 6, 1989: 7.
— Women's Kemper Open to be held at Wailea Resort in upcoming years, Lahaina News, December 13, 1989: 8.
— Bob Bries wins Senior Stats Match, Lahaina News, December 20, 1989: 6.

- Napili Kai Beach Club presenting Napili Kai Youth Foundation Invitational tournament, Lahaina News, January 9, 1992: 7.
- Asahi Beer-Ohashi Kyosen Golf Tournament to be held at Wailea Blue golf course, Lahaina News, January 9, 1992: 7.
- Hawaii Golf Course Action Alliance invites National Network Against Resort and Golf Course Development, Japanese anti-golf course group visits Maui, Lahaina News, January 30, 1992: 5.
- Senior Skins Game to be held at Mauna Lani, Lahaina News, January 30, 1992: 9.
- Asahi Beer-Ohashi Kyosen Golf Tournament to be held , Lahaina News, February 6, 1992: 9.
- Women's Kemper Open to be held, Lahaina News, February 20, 1992: 6.
- Waihee School Alumni scheduling golf tournament, Lahaina News, February 20, 1992: 6.
- Lincoln-Mercury will sponsor Kapalua International golf tournament, Lahaina News, March 12, 1992: 10.
- junior season begins, Lahaina News, March 12, 1992: 9.
- Trinity Episcopal Church to hold Ho'oaloha Kolepa Golf Tournament, Lahaina News, March 19, 1992: 8.
- Goro Hokama Golf Classic to be held, Lahaina News, March 19, 1992: 8.
- Judy Grover to defend title, Lahaina News, March 26, 1992: 8.
- American Institute of Architects looking for teams to play in golf tournament fundraiser, Lahaina News, April 30, 1992: 7.
- Professional Golfers Association announces GTE Hawaiian Tel Hall of Fame Championship to be held, Lahaina News, April 30, 1992: 7.
- Lahainaluna High School to hold tournament, Lahaina News, May 21, 1992: 11,12.
- Vivian Kekona wins Silversword Women's golf club ACE for April, Lahaina News, May 21, 1992: 12.
- Maui Trojan Club to hold golf tournament, Lahaina News, June 11, 1992: 10,11.
- Maui Invitational Junior Golf Championship to be held, Lahaina News, June 18, 1992: 12.
- LPGA Women's Kemper Open to be held, Lahaina News, June 18, 1992: 13.
- youth clinic to be held at Wailea Golf Club, Lahaina News, June 25, 1992: 12.
- AT&T to become sponsor of Aloha Section of the Professional Golfers Association Club Professional Championship, Lahaina News, June 25, 1992: 12.
- donations given from Shinko Scholarship and Charity Golf Tournament, Lahaina News, July 2, 1992: 12,13.
- Hospitality Sales and Marketing Association tournament to be held, Lahaina News, July 2, 1992: 13.
- Ka'anapali Classic tournament to be held, Lahaina News, July 9, 1992: 12.
- tournaments to be held, Lahaina News, July 9, 1992: 7.
- Lincoln-Mercury Kapalua International tournament to be held, Lahaina News, July 9, 1992: 7.
- Ka Hale Ake Ola Golf charity tournament to be held, Lahaina News, July 16, 1992: 10.
- Kapalua Land Company awards golf scholarship, Lahaina News, July 16, 1992: 10.
- Wailea Golf Club to offer Junior Golf Clinic, Lahaina News, July 16, 1992: 11.
- Lincoln-Mercury Kapalua International tournament to be held, Lahaina News, July 16, 1992: 12.
- Wailea Golf Club to host Asahi Beer-Ohashi Kyosen Golf tournament, Lahaina News, July 23, 1992: 15.
- "Scramble for the Homeless" tournament held at Kapalua Plantation Golf Course, Lahaina News, July 30, 1992: 8,9.
- Hospitality Sales and Marketing Association tournament to be held, Lahaina News, August 6, 1992: 5.
- Ka'anapali Classic scheduled for Ka'anapali North Course, Lahaina News, August 6, 1992: 5.
- Dick McClean wins Aloha Section, PGA Stroke Play Championship, Lahaina News, August 13, 1992: 6.
- Labor Day tournament to be held, Lahaina News, August 20, 1992: 10.
- Amfac/JMB Hawaii to host Ka'anapali Classic golf tournament, Lahaina News, August 20, 1992: 10.
- Ka'alua Open to take place on Labor Day weekend, Lahaina News, September 3, 1992: 6.
- results of Silversword Women's Golf Club, Lahaina News, September 3, 1992: 6.
- Ka'anapali Classic tournament to be held, Lahaina News, September 24, 1992: 13.
- Maui Filipino Golf Tournament to be held, Lahaina News, October 1, 1992: 8.
- tournaments to be held, Lahaina News, October 8, 1992: 4.
- Maui Contractors Association to hold tournament, Lahaina News, October 15, 1992: 10.
- Maui County Cultural Resources Commission opposes proposed Waihee Oceanfront golf course, Lahaina News, October 22, 1992: 4.
- Lincoln-Mercury Kapalua International tournament to be held, Lahaina News, October 29, 1992: 12.
- Hayes Golf Art Expo to be held, Lahaina News, November 5, 1992: 15.
- Royal Ka'anapali Golf Club to hold club championship, Lahaina News, November 19, 1992: 7.
- Rotary Club of Lahaina sponsoring golf fundraiser to support Maui youth, Lahaina News, December 31, 1992: 6.
- David Ishii and Chihiro Nakajima to return to Wailea Blue Golf Course, Lahaina News, February 11, 1993: 9.
- Kihei-Wailea Rotary Club to hold fundraiser tournament, Lahaina News, February 25, 1993: 5.
- Kapalua Golf Club to offer junior golf season, Lahaina News, March 11, 1993: 9.
- Maui Lumber Open Golf Tournament to be held, Lahaina News, March 18, 1993: 5.
- results of Kihei-Wailea Rotary Club tournament, Lahaina News, March 18, 1993: 8.
- "City Bank Helps Maui" fundraiser to be held, Lahaina News, April 29, 1993: 6.
- GTE Hawaiian Telephone Company to hold golf tournament, Lahaina News, May 6, 1993: 10.
- results of Maui County Bar Association's Attorney Golf Tournament announced, Lahaina News, June 24, 1993: 11.
- junior tournament to be held at Wailea Golf Club, Lahaina News, July 15, 1993: 8.
- Junior tournament to be held at Wailea Golf Club, Lahaina News, July 22, 1993: 9.
- Henry's Bar and Grill and Friends of Kalama Park golf tournament to be held, Lahaina News, July 22, 1993: 9.
- Ka'anapali Golf Courses have new family promotion, Lahaina News, August 5, 1993: 8.
- Kapalua Open to be held, Lahaina News, August 26, 1993: 12.
- PING Ka'anapali Classic to be held, Lahaina News, October 21, 1993: 12.
- Lincoln-Mercury Kapalua International Tournament to be held, Lahaina News, October 28, 1993: 8.
- Lincoln-Mercury Kapalua International Tournament to be held, Hale Irwin among participants, Lahaina News, November 4, 1993: 9.
- Maui Hotel Association sponsoring tournament fundraiser, Lahaina News, November 11, 1993: 8.
- Maui Hotel Association sponsoring tournament fundraiser, Lahaina News, November 18, 1993: 12.
- Lana'i Co. sponsoring Lana'i Charity Golf Classic, Lahaina News, November 25, 1993: 10.

— Kapalua Grill and Bar Invitation Golf fundraiser to help West Maui Youth Center and The PreSchool at Kapalua, Lahaina News, December 23, 1993: 9.

— Lahaina Rotary Club to sponsor Scholarship Scramble golf tournament, Lahaina News, January 20, 1994: 9.

— Lions Club to hold benefit tournament, Lahaina News, February 17, 1994: 8.

— Scaroles Village Pizzeria to hold golf tournament to benefit , Lahaina News, March 31, 1994: 8.

— City Bank Invitational Golf Tournament to be held, Lahaina News, April 14, 1994: 7.

— GTE Hawaiian Tel Hall of Fame Championship to be held, Lahaina News, April 21, 1994: 6.

— Ka'anapali Golf Course announces Kama'aina family promotion, Lahaina News, May 26, 1994: 9.

— Kapalua Villas to offer "Eagle Golf Package", Lahaina News, June 23, 1994: 7.

— Kapalua Plantation Course to host "A Scramble for the Homeless", Lahaina News, June 30, 1994: 7.

— results of Ka'anapali Beach Hotel tournament, Lahaina News, June 30, 1994: 7.

— Maui golfer Kurt Watanabe heading to Junior Amateur Golf Championships, Lahaina News, July 7, 1994: 7.

— junior clinic to be held at Wailea Golf Club, Lahaina News, July 14, 1994: 9.

— Maken Resort to host Ka Lima O Maui 100 Holes of Golf, Lahaina News, August 25, 1994: 9.

— Senior PGA Tour to hold Hyatt Maui Ka'anapali Classic, Lahaina News, October 6, 1994: 9.

— Whalers Realty to host tournament, Lahaina News, October 13, 1994: 11.

— Ka'anapali Classic held, Lahaina News, October 27, 1994: 11.

— Lincoln Mercury Kapalua International tournament begins, Lahaina News, November 3, 1994: 21.

— Fred Couples wins Lincoln-Mercury Kapalua International, Lahaina News, November 10, 1994: 1.

— Callaway Hawaii State Open Golf Tournament results, Lahaina News, December 15, 1994: 8.

— Mark Rolfing to host golf television show on KITV , Lahaina News, December 29, 1994: 5.

— Kapalua begins junior golf season, Lahaina News, March 23, 1995: 7.

— Scaroles Village Pizza to hold golf tournament to benefit Light Bringers, Lahaina News, March 30, 1995: 7.

— Kapalua Golf Club junior golf season begins, Lahaina News, April 6, 1995: 16.

— Professional Golfer's Association of America to hold tournament, Lahaina News, April 27, 1995: 7.

— "City Bank Helps Maui" tournament to be held, Lahaina News, May 4, 1995: 8.

— Kiwanis Club to hold golf fundraiser, Lahaina News, August 3, 1995: 9.

— Wailea Golf Club to hold junior classic, Lahaina News, August 3, 1995: 9.

— Ka Lima O Maui tournament to be held, Lahaina News, August 24, 1995: 6.

— instructional packages offered at Royal Lahaina Resort, Lahaina News, August 31, 1995: 6.

— Hyatt Regency Maui Ka'anapali Classic tournament details, Lahaina News, October 19, 1995: 12,13,14,15,16.

— Lincoln-Mercury Kapalua International tournament to be held, Lahaina News, October 19, 1995: 6.

— Hyatt Regency Maui Ka'anapali Classic tournament seeking volunteers, Lahaina News, October 19, 1995: 6.

— Kapalua Plantation Course to host Coca-Cola Classic, Lahaina News, October 26, 1995: 6.

— Lincoln-Mercury Kapalua International Golf Tournament begins, Lahaina News, November 2, 1995: 7.

— PGA Senior tournament held at Hyatt Regency Maui Ka'anapali Classic, Lahaina News, November 2, 1995: 7.

— Maui Hotel Association to hold Golf Fundraiser, Lahaina News, November 9, 1995: 6.

— Whalers Realty Inc. hosting Golf Tournament in memory John E. "Jack" Kelley, Lahaina News, November 23, 1995: 6.

— Bruce Bosley Memorial Golf Classic to be held, Lahaina News, November 23, 1995: 6.

— Joe Namath and Johnny Unitas play at NFL Alumni Bruce Bosely tournament, Lahaina News, December 7, 1995: 4,5.

— U.S. Women's Amateur Public Links Championship to be held at Kapalua Golf Club, Lahaina News, January 4, 1996: 6.

— Napili Kai Beach Club to host Youth Foundation Golf Tournament, Lahaina News, January 11, 1996: 6.

— David Pritchett promoted to head professional at Kapalua Village Course, Lahaina News, January 11, 1996: 6.

— LPGA professionals to compete, Lahaina News, February 8, 1996: 11.

— "On the Fairway" column by Roger Fredericks begins, is not otherwise indexed, Lahaina News, March 28, 1996: 7.

— Hyatt Regency Maui Ka'anapali Classic wins award for marketing and promotion from Golf Magazine, Lahaina News, April 25, 1996: 14.

— Lahainaluna Athletic Department to hold tournament, Lahaina News, May 16, 1996: 11.

— The Golf Channel to premiere, Lahaina News, June 20, 1996: 10.

— Kris Baptist wins division, Lahaina News, June 27, 1996: 16.

— night putting tournament to help Luna Football Team, Lahaina News, July 25, 1996: 10.

— Jack E. Kelley Golf Tournament to be held, Lahaina News, August 15, 1996: 12.

— Jack E. Kelley Golf Tournament to be held, Lahaina News, September 5, 1996: 14.

— Jack E. Kelley Golf Tournament to be held, Lahaina News, September 12, 1996: 18.

— Hyatt Regency Maui Ka'anapali Classic , Lahaina News, October 10, 1996: 12.

— Maui Junior Golf Association honors players, Lahaina News, October 10, 1996: 12.

— Lincoln-Mercury Kapalua International tournament to be held, Lahaina News, October 10, 1996: 13.

— Hyatt Regency Maui Ka'anapali Classic to be held, Lahaina News, October 17, 1996: 12.

— Fred Couples and others to play at Lincoln-Mercury Kapalua International, Lahaina News, October 17, 1996: 12.

— importance of Bermuda Grass, Lahaina News, October 17, 1996: 13.

— John Daly to play at Lincoln-Mercury Kapalua International tournament, Lahaina News, October 24, 1996: 13.

— update on Ka'anapali Classic tournament, Lahaina News, October 24, 1996: 15.

— Jim Furyk wins Lincoln-Mercury Kapalua International, Lahaina News, October 31, 1996: 14.

— Lincoln-Mercury Kapalua International tournament to be held, Lahaina News, November 7, 1996: 1,20.

— Fred Couples places second in Lincoln-Mercury Kapalua International, Lahaina News, November 14, 1996: 13.

— television show "Golf Hawaii" to air on ESPN, Lahaina News, December 12, 1996: 13.

— Napili Kai Youth Foundation Invitational Gold Tournament to be held, Lahaina News, January 2, 1997: 5.

— Lahaina Rotary Club to host Scholarship Scramble Tournament, Lahaina News, January 9, 1997: 6.

— Napili Kai Youth Foundation Invitational Gold Tournament to be held, Lahaina News, January 9, 1997: 7.

— University of Hawai'i Na Koa Football Club Invitational Golf Tournament to be held, Lahaina News, July 1, 1999: 7.

— Ka'anapali Golf Course offering Summer Junior Special, Lahaina News, July 1, 1999: 7.

— Whalers Realty Inc. Jack Kelley Memorial Golf Tournament, Lahaina News, July 29, 1999: 10.

— Ashworth Kapalua Clambake Pro-Am Golf Tournament raises money for Special Olympics, Lahaina News, August 5, 1999: 7.

— Wailea Golf Club to hold women-friendly golf facilities, Lahaina News, August 5, 1999: 7.

— Wailea Golf Club to hold "Putter Demo Day", Lahaina News, August 12, 1999: 7.

— Wilson Kapalua Open to be held, Lahaina News, August 26, 1999: 7.

— Lahaina United Methodist Church to hold Family Ministry Golf Tournament, Lahaina News, August 26, 1999: 7.

— Wailea Golf Course hosting PGA Match Play Championship, Lahaina News, September 9, 1999: 7.

— Jack Kelley Memorial Golf Tournament to be held, Lahaina News, September 16, 1999: 6.

— Mercedes Championship PGA Tour event to be held, Lahaina News, September 16, 1999: 7.

— Jack Kelley Memorial Golf Tournament held, Lahaina News, September 23, 1999: 10.

— EMC Ka'anapali Classic Senior PGA Tour tournament to be held, Lahaina News, October 7, 1999: 9.

— Senior PGA Tour coming to West Maui, Lahaina News, October 14, 1999: 1.

— Mercedes Championship PGA Tour event to be held, Lahaina News, October 14, 1999: 7.

— EMC Ka'anapali Classic Senior PGA Tour tournament to conclude, Lahaina News, October 21, 1999: 9.

— Whalers Realty sponsors Senior Classic All-Amateur Golf Tournament, Lahaina News, November 18, 1999: 12.

— Joey Sindelar wins Kapalua Challenge golf tournament, Lahaina News, November 25, 1999: 9.

— Hawaii State Golf Association offers savings around the state, Lahaina News, November 25, 1999: 9.

— Mercedes Championship PGA Tour tickets on sale, Lahaina News, December 9, 1999: 9.

— PGA Mercedes tournament to be held, Tiger Woods and David Duval to play, Lahaina News, December 23, 1999: 1,15.

— David Duval plays at Mercedes Championships, Lahaina News, December 30, 1999: 1,6.

— details of Mercedes Championship, Lahaina News, December 30, 1999: 1,6,8.

— Mercedes Championship PGA Tour event to be held, Lahaina News, January 6, 2000: 1.

— Mercedes Championship PGA Tour event to be held, Lahaina News, January 6, 2000: 3.

— Mercedes Championship PGA Tour underway, Lahaina News, January 13, 2000: 1.

— Rotary Club of Lahaina to hold "Scholarship Scramble", Lahaina News, January 20, 2000: 7.

— Roger Fredericks conducts golf instruction video session with Jack Nicklaus, Lahaina News, February 10, 2000: 9.

— Mercedes Championship helping local charities, Lahaina News, March 23, 2000: 11.

— City Bank Helps Maui tournament to benefit Maui Arts and Cultural Center, Lahaina News, March 30, 2000: 6.

— City Bank Helps Maui Golf Tournament to benefit Maui Arts and Cultural Center, Lahaina News, April 6, 2000: 7.

— Mark Rolfing inducted into the Hawaii Golf Hall of Fame, Lahaina News, April 13, 2000: 1.

— EMC Ka'anapali Classic Senior PGA Tour contest supports Maui non-profits, Lahaina News, April 20, 2000: 5.

— PING/Kapalua Clubs for Kids held, Lahaina News, April 20, 2000: 7.

— Maui Interscholastic League play held, Lahaina News, April 27, 2000: 6.

— AIA Scholarship tournament to be held, Lahaina News, May 4, 2000: 14.

— AIA Scholarship tournament to be held, Lahaina News, May 11, 2000: 14.

— Clambake golf tourney to help local charities, Lahaina News, July 13, 2000: 6.

— The Dunes at Maui Lani holds grand opening, Lahaina News, July 13, 2000: 7.

— Maui Kiwanis Golf Classic, Lahaina News, August 3, 2000: 6.

— Maui Kiwanis Golf Classic to be held, Lahaina News, August 10, 2000: 7.

— EMC2 Ka'anapali Classic tournament to be played, Lahaina News, August 24, 2000: 6.

— "Golf In the Environment Tournament" to be held, Lahaina News, September 14, 2000: 9.

— "Golf In the Environment Tournament" to be held, Lahaina News, September 21, 2000: 2.

— results of Kapalua Junior Championship, Lahaina News, September 21, 2000: 8.

— more players to compete in EMC Ka'anapali Classic, Lahaina News, September 21, 2000: 9.

— Senior Skins Game to be held, Lahaina News, September 21, 2000: 9.

— Rick Castillo honored by PGA of America, Lahaina News, October 5, 2000: 14.

— EMC Ka'anapali Classic to begin, Lahaina News, October 12, 2000: 3.

— Ka'anapali Classic being held, Lahaina News, October 19, 2000: 10.

— Jack Kelley Memorial golf Tournament to be held by Whalers Realty to benefit St. Francis Medical Center, Lahaina News, October 19, 2000: 14.

— Hale Irwin wins Ka'anapali Classic, Lahaina News, October 26, 2000: 1.

— Lahainaluna High School Foundation Golf Tournament to be held, Lahaina News, November 16, 2000: 11.

— "Golf Hawaii" profiles Ka'anapali's history in professional golf, Lahaina News, November 23, 2000: 11.

— Mercedes Championship to be held, Lahaina News, December 7, 2000: 10.

— Mercedes Championship to be held, Lahaina News, December 28, 2000: 1,7.

— Senior Skins Game include Hale Irwin, Jack Nicklaus, Arnold Palmer, and Gary Player, Lahaina News, December 28, 2000: 6.

— Mercedes Championship to be held, Lahaina News, January 4, 2001: 1,8.

— Mercedes Championship to be held, players listed, Lahaina News, January 11, 2001: 1,8.

— Senior Skins Game to be played at Wailea Gold Course, Lahaina News, January 18, 2001: 9.

— Na Leo Kako'o O Maui to hold golf tournament fundraiser, Lahaina News, February 1, 2001: 15.

— Maui Board of Realtors to host Presidential Scholarship Golf Tournament, Lahaina News, March 29, 2001: 13.

— Maui Arts and Cultural Center to hold "City Bank helps Maui" benefit tournament, Lahaina News, April 5, 2001: 14.

— Maui Board of Realtors to hold Presidential Scholarship Golf Tournament, Lahaina News, April 5, 2001: 14.

— Lahainaluna students successful, Lahaina News, May 10, 2001: 14.

— Lahainaluna High School football team to hold golf tournament, Lahaina News, May 24, 2001: 15.

— Joey Lum Memorial Golf Tournament to be held, Lahaina News, August 23, 2001: 12.

— Wailea Golf Club to hold annual Junior Golf Class, Lahaina News, August 30, 2001: 12.
— West Side golfer earns spot on Junior Ryder Cup Team, Lahaina News, September 6, 2001: 12.
— Kapalua Golf to hold Kama'aina Appreciation Program, Lahaina News, October 18, 2001: 13.
— Kapalua courses now using website for bookings, Lahaina News, November 15, 2001: 13.
— Waiehu Golf Course under construction, Lahaina News, November 15, 2001: 13.
— Mercedes Championships to be held, Lahaina News, January 3, 2002: 1,13.
— Senior Skins Game to be held, Lahaina News, January 10, 2002: 13.
— Senior Skins Game to be held, Lahaina News, January 17, 2002: 13.
— Senior Skins Game to be held, Lahaina News, January 24, 2002: 13.
— Whalers Realty's Jack Kelly Memorial Golf Tournament raises money for transplant institute, Lahaina News, February 14, 2002: 7.
— Wailea Golf Club LPGA Teaching Professional Cathy Torchiana named to 50 To Teachers by Golf for Women magazine, Lahaina News, February 28, 2002: 13.
— Kapalua Junior Golf season to open, Lahaina News, March 28, 2002: 11.
— Mohala Golf Tournament to be held, Lahaina News, April 4, 2002: 13.
— Mercedes Championship raises money for local charities, Lahaina News, April 11, 2002: 3.
— David Rau named head golf professional at Kapalua's Village Course, Lahaina News, May 16, 2002: 8.
— Joey Lum Memorial Foundation to hold tournament, Lahaina News, August 8, 2002: 12.
— tournament to support Maui Chamber of Commerce, Lahaina News, August 22, 2002: 11.
— Kapalua Junior Golf program ends season with Kapalua Junior Golf Championships, Lahaina News, September 12, 2002: 11.
— Princess Nahienaena Elementary School PTA to hold golf tournament to benefit, Lahaina News, October 3, 2002: 2.
— ConAgra Foods Champions Skins Game to be played at Wailea Gold Course, Lahaina News, January 23, 2003: 13.
— tournament to support Na Leo Kako'o O Maui Hawaiian immersion school, Lahaina News, February 13, 2003: 12.
— Kapalua's Junior Golf Program to be held, Lahaina News, April 10, 2003: 10.
— Lahainaluna High School students to compete at Maui Interscholastic League Championship Tournament, Lahaina News, May 8, 2003: 12.
— Lahaina Rotary Club to hold Scholarship Scramble tournament, Lahaina News, June 5, 2003: 12.
— tickets on sale for Mercedes Championships, Lahaina News, September 11, 2003: 12.
— Kapalua Resort golf instructors recognized by Golf Digest as best teachers in Hawaii, Lahaina News, September 11, 2003: 13.
— yoga to be offered to, Lahaina News, September 25, 2003: 13.

GOLIGHLY, GARY [ARTIST]
— to perform at Haiku Ho'olaule'a and Flower Festival, Lahaina News, March 13, 2003: 16.

GOLLADAY, SCOTT
— purchases Best of Maui Cassette Tours, Lahaina News, December 26, 1990: 7.

GOLUB, JEFF [MUSICIAN]
— to perform at Maui Music Festival, Lahaina News, August 22, 1996: 18.

GOMES, CHRIS
— boxer wins at Hawaii Junior Olympic Championships, Lahaina News, May 21, 1992: 12.

GOMES, CLARICE
— promoted to customer sales and service manager at Hawaii Helicopters, Lahaina News, January 2, 1991: 5.

GOMES, FRANCISCO
— to hold deep-breathing exercise classes, Lahaina News, May 29, 1997: 17.
— continues to offer deep-breathing exercise classes, Lahaina News, June 12, 1997: 17.

GOMES, GEORGE, JR.
— becomes corporate chef with Tri-Star Restaurant Group, Lahaina News, December 14, 2000: 18.

GOMEZ, BROTHER EDWARD
— named principal of St. Anthony school, Lahaina Sun, June 6, 1973: 11.

GOMEZ, LORI
— Lahainaluna High School teacher receives Vocational Service Award from Lahaina Rotary Club, Lahaina News, May 11, 1988: 14.
— teacher and organizer of David Malo Day featured, Lahaina News, June 7, 1989: 4.

GOMEZ, PAUL
— appointed assistant manager at The Kapalua Villas, Lahaina News, January 16, 1991: 5.
— appointed general manager of The Maui Kai Resort, Lahaina News, July 24, 1997: 13.

GOMEZ-POLAND, KEALANI
— Lahainaluna High School student wins Mamoru and Aiko Takitani Foundation scholarship, Lahaina News, May 22, 2003: 2.

GON, SAM
— ecologist from The Nature Conservancy to speak, Lahaina News, April 22, 1999: 12.

GONSALVES, JUDY
— presided over May Day celebrations, Lahaina Sun, May 5, 1971: 2.

GONSALVES, RON
— consultant to Sing Out Maui youth singing group, Lahaina Sun, November 1, 1972: 9.

GONZALES, JEANNIE
— padder featured, Lahaina News, April 4, 1996: 17.

GONZALES, WILLIAM
— president of Kahana Canoe Club discusses upcoming competitions, Lahaina News, May 22, 1997: 9.

GONZALEZ, ARNIE
— chef at Lahaina Grill featured, Lahaina News, May 2, 2002: 9.

GONZALEZ, ARTURO
— chef of Erik's Seafood Grotto featured, Lahaina News, February 7, 2002: 5.

GONZALEZ, RUDOLF [ARTIST]
— to exhibit at Diamond Head Gallery-Pictures Plus, Lahaina News, October 17, 2002: 21.

GONZO, DR. [COMEDIAN]
— to perform at Comedy Club and the Sports Page, Lahaina News, April 2, 1992: 16,20.

GOO, APRIL
— promoted to legal assistant, Lahaina News, June 6, 1991: 6.

GOO, SAM
— discusses pollution in Kahului Harbor, Lahaina Sun, February 3, 1971: 5.

GOOD, ANNA [ARTIST]
— to exhibit at Metropolitan Art Gallery, Lahaina News, August 20, 1992: 20.
— to demonstrate painting, Lahaina News, July 27, 1995: 11.
— creates Sculpture Garden Sanctuary , Lahaina News, October 24, 1996: 15.

— to exhibit at Pictures Plus, Lahaina News, July 10, 1997: 16.

— to be artist-in-attendance at Sargent's Fine Art, Lahaina News, October 19, 2000: 6.

— to visit Sargent's Fine Art, Lahaina News, July 11, 2002: 16.

— to exhibit at Sargent's Fine Art, Lahaina News, August 1, 2002: 20.

— to exhibit at Sargent's Fine Art, Lahaina News, November 7, 2002: 22.

GOOD BEGINNINGS MAUI COUNTY

— to celebrate "April is the Month of the Young Child", Lahaina News, April 19, 2001: 16.

GOOD FORTUNE TRADING CO. [BUSINESS]

— opens, Lahaina News, July 29, 1999: 11.

GOOD SAMARITAN SERVICES [BUSINESS]

— expanding to West Maui, Lahaina News, July 25, 1991: 7.

GOOD STROKES BLUES BAND, THE [MUSICAL GROUP]

— to perform at Moose McGillycuddy's, Lahaina News, March 14, 1990: 15.

— to perform at Moose McGillycuddy's, Lahaina News, April 11, 1990: 15.

— to perform at Casanova's, Lahaina News, August 8, 1991: 14.

— continues to perform at Moose McGillycuddy's, Lahaina News, August 22, 1991: 10.

— to perform at Casanova's, Lahaina News, June 11, 1992: 22.

GOOD WOMAN OF SZECHUAN, THE [PLAY]

— to be performed at Seabury Hall, Lahaina News, October 24, 1991: 22.

GOODE, NANCY

— new owner of Maui Style, Lahaina News, June 13, 1991: 9.

GOODFELLOW BROTHERS, INC. [BUSINESS]

— general contractor for major capital improvements on Moloka'i, Lahaina News, July 4, 1991: 4.

— awarded grant to improve Lower Honoapi'ilani Road, Lahaina News, September 1, 1994: 7.

GOODMAN, DAVID [COMEDIAN]

— to perform at Comedy Club, Lahaina News, December 5, 1991: 22.

GOODMAN, LENN

— University of Hawaii faculty member to present "Cruelty: a Hidden Crisis" on ethical issues relating to child neglect, Lahaina News, October 16, 1985: 3.

GOODMAN, SHIVANI

— to discuss "Healing our lives" at 'Ohana Connection, Lahaina News, August 10, 2000: 17.

GOODNIGHT GECKO, THE [BOOK]

— published, Lahaina News, December 5, 1991: 6.

GOODTIME GUIDE

— begins in the newspaper and not indexed, Lahaina Sun, September 8, 1971: .

GOOLSBY, JOHN

— appointed operations manager at Atlantis Submarines, Lahaina News, November 21, 1991: 11.

GORBAN, MICHAEL [ARTIST]

— to be featured at Sargent's Fine Art, Lahaina News, February 20, 2003: 18.

GORDON, DARYL "DJ ZINN"

— launches deejay business, Lahaina News, July 31, 2003: 8.

GORDON, JAMES [ARTIST]

— to exhibit at Lahaina Arts Society, Lahaina News, August 13, 1992: 15.

— theme of art show at Lahaina Arts Society is Hawaiian Sovereignty, Lahaina News, August 20, 1992: 18.

GORDON SAMUELSON JAZZ TRIO [MUSICAL GROUP]

— to perform at Taco Jo's Cantina, Lahaina News, November 11, 1993: 12.

GORDON, SHIRLEY

— to join CBS Olympics team, Lahaina News, December 19, 1991: 15.

GORELICK, KENNETH BRUCE [MUSICIAN]

— see Kenny G

GORILLA FOUNDATION, THE

— to hold auction for Allan G. Sanford Gorilla Preserve, Lahaina News, August 31, 1995: 7.

— to break ground on land provided by Maui Land and Pineapple for a preserve for Koko the gorilla, Lahaina News, October 5, 2000: 3.

GORING, KAUI

— to speak at Maui Authors' Guild, Lahaina News, October 30, 1985: 3.

GORMAN, R.C. [ARTIST]

— Navajo visits Lahaina, signs books, Lahaina News, November 22, 1989: 15.

— guest artist at Sunset Galleries, Lahaina News, May 1, 1991: 17.

— returns to Lahaina, Lahaina News, November 7, 1991: 17.

— to unveil ceramic plaque "Blue Hawaii", Lahaina News, March 19, 1992: 18.

GOSHI, STANLEY

— appointed Maui County director of public works, Lahaina Sun, July 28, 1971: 11.

GOSPEL ACCORDING TO MARK [PLAY]

— performed by Michael Reardon, Lahaina News, October 30, 1985: 3.

GOSPEL MOUNTAIN BAND

— to perform, Lahaina News, November 27, 1985: 3.

GOTELLI, JIM

— surfer's career discussed, Lahaina News, August 15, 1984: 4.

GOTO, GLEN

— awarded manager of the quarter at Maui Marriott, Lahaina News, August 22, 1991: 4.

GOTO, RYO [MUSICIAN]

— to join Maui Symphony Orchestra to play Tchaikovsky, Lahaina News, November 9, 2000: 24.

GOTTLEIB, CARL [WRITER]

— to attend Maui Writers Conference, Lahaina News, July 27, 1995: 4.

GOTTLIEB, DANNY [MUSICIAN]

— to perform at Blackie's Bar, Lahaina News, July 16, 1992: 17,19.

— to perform at Blackie's Bar, Lahaina News, May 20, 1993: 9,10.

GOURDINE, RUSSELL [ARTIST]

— to exhibit at Lahaina Arts Society as part of "Vision, Expression, Spirit", Lahaina News, December 9, 1999: 17.

GOURMET SNAX [BUSINESS]

— now offering macadamia nut caramel corn, Lahaina News, December 13, 1989: 6.

GOVERNMENT

— example of government not caring about public opinion, Lahaina News, December 1, 1982: 13.

— tax revenues rose in March, Lahaina News, May 1, 1983: 3.

— Clayton Hee discusses time demands of legislators, Lahaina News, February 29, 1984: 16.

— West Maui Taxpayers hold annual meeting, Lahaina News, March 14, 1984: 3.

— editorial on poor quality of county planning, Lahaina News, July 25, 1984: 2.

— driver's license examination stations to close temporarily, Lahaina News, April 9, 1986: 3.

— directory of Hawaii state agencies distributed, Lahaina News, September 27, 1989: 3.

— renovations completed on office for county Planning Department and Land Use and Codes Administration, Lahaina News, September 5, 1990: 4.

— toll-free number to contact State offices, Lahaina News, September 26, 1990: 1.

— State delays opening Information Office, Lahaina News, January 2, 1991: 1.

— bills for 1991 legislative session described, Lahaina News, January 30, 1991: 1.

— bills calling for review of fuel prices introduced in Legislature, Lahaina News, February 13, 1991: 7.

— editorial on proposed changes to auto insurance, Lahaina News, February 27, 1991: 7.

— praise for Mazie Hirono and Donna Ikeda for reducing insurance premiums, Lahaina News, May 21, 1992: 7.

— mayors discuss issues at office of Honolulu Mayor Jeremy Harris, Lahaina News, December 15, 1994: 7.

— need to increase communication between government agencies discussed, Lahaina News, December 22, 1994: 1,20.

GOVERNOR'S MAUI ADVISORY COMMITTEE

— created by Governor Linda Lingle, Lahaina News, July 17, 2003: 9.

— to meet, Lahaina News, September 4, 2003: 1.

— to meet, Lahaina News, September 11, 2003: 2.

GOVERNOR'S OFFICE

— accepting nominations to honor volunteerism, Lahaina News, October 30, 1997: 2.

GOWING, MEL

— appointed to Maui County Private Industry Council, Lahaina News, February 22, 1984: 17.

GOYA, GLENN

— vice president and investments and retirement plan coordinator at Dean Witter Reynolds, Inc., Lahaina News, June 27, 1990: 8.

GOYA, LARRY

— hired as attorney for County, Lahaina News, October 1, 1980: 13.

GRACE BAPTIST CHURCH

— offering free Bible school, Lahaina News, August 2, 1989: 3.

— sponsoring free Bible school, Lahaina News, August 8, 1990: 4.

— to host "Building Your Mate's Self-Esteem", Lahaina News, February 4, 1993: 4.

— to hold Bible School, Lahaina News, August 12, 1993: 4.

— to hold Bible School, Lahaina News, August 1, 1996: 21.

— to celebrate 37-year history, Lahaina News, March 27, 2003: 1,18.

— to celebrate 37-year history, Lahaina News, April 3, 2003: 3.

— pastor Azra Brown featured, Lahaina News, August 28, 2003: 1,18.

GRADDIX, DANNY [ARTIST]

— featured at 20th Century Masters Gallery, Lahaina News, August 22, 1990: 14.

GRAFFMAN, GARY [MUSICIAN]

— to perform on Maui, Lahaina Sun, April 5, 1972: 5.

— reviewed, Lahaina Sun, April 12, 1972: 19.

GRAHAM, BILLY

— films about Japan produced by Reverend, shown in Lahaina and Kihei, Lahaina Sun, November 11, 1970: 2.

GRAMUGLIA, MAURO

— new assistant sous chef at Va Bene Italian Beachside Grill, Lahaina News, February 7, 2002: 8.

GRAND FAIRWAYS NORTH

— residential development opens, Lahaina News, August 26, 1999: 13.

GRAND HYATT WAILEA RESORT AND SPA [BUSINESS]

— scheduled to open, Lahaina News, August 2, 1989: 6.

— names Jim Petrus as general manager, Lahaina News, January 23, 1991: 5.

— opens, Lahaina News, September 12, 1991: 4.

— names sales managers, Lahaina News, February 20, 1992: 10.

GRAND PRIX [BUSINESS]

— to meet with Makena Community Association to discuss proposed golf course, Lahaina News, October 22, 1992: 13.

GRAND WAIKAPU COUNTRY CLUB

— to host jazz concert, Lahaina News, February 22, 1996: 14.

GRAND WAILEA RESORT HOTEL AND SPA [BUSINESS]

— La Branche Rockefeller sculpture missing from, Lahaina News, September 2, 1993: 6.

— to hold job fair, Lahaina News, October 28, 1999: 16.

— "top spa resort in the world" in Conde Nast Traveler Magazine, Lahaina News, December 30, 1999: 13.

— Coldwell Banker Island Properties opens real estate information center at , Lahaina News, March 16, 2000: 11.

— remodeling, Lahaina News, June 22, 2000: 9.

— Larry Quirit and David Curcio new chefs at, Lahaina News, November 23, 2000: 16.

— adds new members to food and beverage team, Lahaina News, August 30, 2001: 9.

GRANSBACK, DON

— manager of earthquake preparedness program, says Maui unprepared, Lahaina News, November 1, 1989: 1,3.

GRANT, GLEN

— to present "Grabbing Your Audience: Training for Interpretation Techniques" at Maui Community College, Lahaina News, July 6, 1988: 17.

GRANT, HAL

— report on basketball player, Lahaina Sun, January 20, 1971: 7.

GRANT WRITING

— course to be offered, Lahaina News, July 29, 1999: 11.

GRANTHAM, ROGER

— services to be held to celebrate life of, Lahaina News, April 3, 2003: 2.

— fundraiser to be held to support family of, Lahaina News, April 17, 2003: 1.

GRANTHAM, ROXANNE

— Scholar/Athlete of the Week, Lahaina News, July 4, 2002: 13.

GRANTSMANSHIP CENTER

— offering grant writing course, Lahaina News, October 7, 1999: 3.

GRAPES OF WRATH, THE [PLAY]

— to be performed at the Maui Academy of Performing Arts, Lahaina News, October 15, 1992: 18.

GRAPEVINE PRODUCTIONS [BUSINESS]

— new associates added, Lahaina News, January 24, 1990: 6.

— Scott Waters named computer art director, Lahaina News, June 6, 1991: 6.

— now agent for Pomegranates in the Sun, Lahaina News, January 23, 1992: 12.

GRASBERG, LYNN

— to speak at Ohana Luncheon, Lahaina News, February 22, 1989: 3.

GRATEFUL DEAD [MUSICAL GROUP]

— vacationing on Maui, Lahaina News, June 1, 1980: 4.

— members Bob Weir and Rob Wasserman, Lahaina News, January 3, 1990: 16.

— cover band Scarlet Fire to perform at Moose McGillycuddy's, Lahaina News, October 5, 1995: 10.

— spin-off bands to perform, Lahaina News, February 18, 1999: 13.

GRATTAFIORI, ANTHONY

— convicted of murder, Lahaina News, August 20, 1986: 15.

— given two life terms for murder, Lahaina News, November 26, 1986: 12.

GRATTAFIORI, NICHOLAS
— fighting extradition for murder, Lahaina News, February 8, 1984: 3.

GRAUE, ERIN
— to present "The NIA Technique—Through Movement We Find Health" at 'Ohana Connection breakfast, Lahaina News, May 16, 2002: 17.
— to talk on "The NIA Technique: Getting Fit the Body's Way" at 'Ohana Connection, Lahaina News, January 30, 2003: 17.

GRAVANCE, LOUIS
— to talk on "Taking Metaphysics to the Front Lines of Corporate America" at 'Ohana Connection breakfast, Lahaina News, September 18, 2003: 17.

GRAVES
— see human remains

GRAVES, DAVID [ARTIST]
— featured at Viewpoints Gallery, Lahaina News, July 2, 1992: 26.

GRAY, JOHN
— joins Bank of Hawaii as executive vice president, Lahaina News, November 7, 2002: 8.

GRAY, JOHN [WRITER]
— to speak on "Men are from Mars, Women are from Venus", Lahaina News, August 28, 1997: 5.

GRAY, SPALDING [WRITER]
— to speak at the Manele Bay Hotel library, Lahaina News, April 24, 1997: 12.

GRAZIANO, DOM
— opening new limousine service, Lahaina News, May 10, 1989: 6.

GREAT AMERICAN SMOKEOUT
— organized by American Cancer Society, Lahaina News, November 13, 1985: 7.

GREAT ANNUAL FISH COUNT
— to be held, Lahaina News, August 14, 2003: 5.

GREAT HAWAII CLEANUP
— to be held, Lahaina News, April 25, 2002: 5.

GREAT JANE'S EATERY [RESTAURANT]
— reviewed, Lahaina News, April 6, 1988: 9.
— reviewed, Lahaina News, October 19, 1988: 9.

GREAT KALUA PORK COOK-OFF
— set for July 4 at Royal Lahaina Resort, Lahaina News, June 19, 1985: 20.

GREAT MAHELE, THE
— discussed, Lahaina News, November 28, 1996: 2.

GREAT MAUI ICE CREAM FESTIVAL
— organized by Hawaii Government Employees Association, Lahaina News, May 24, 1989: 2.
— to be held, Lahaina News, August 9, 1989: 3.

GREAT MAUI SUMMER ICE CREAM FESTIVAL
— to be held, Lahaina News, August 3, 1988: 1.
— described, Lahaina News, August 10, 1988: 6,16,17.
— admission and coupon booklets available, Lahaina News, July 25, 1990: 6.
— event to benefit the Maui Special Learning Center, Lahaina News, August 1, 1990: 11.
— to be held, Lahaina News, August 22, 1990: 13.

GREAT MOLOKA'I MULE DRAG
— to be held, Lahaina News, September 19, 1996: 15.

GREAT MOTHER, FESTIVAL OF
— to be held, Lahaina News, October 17, 1991: 7.

GREAT POLLI'S PALI OUTRIGGER CANOE RACE
— scheduled, Lahaina News, February 7, 1990: 9.

GREAT SCOTT, THE [COMEDIAN]
— to perform at Comedy Club and the Sports Page, Lahaina News, March 11, 1993: 13,15.
— to perform at Comedy Club, Lahaina News, April 28, 1994: 14.

GREAT TAKO WEIGH-IN
— contest tako divers, Lahaina News, September 5, 1984: 3.

GREAT TUNA [PLAY]
— to be performed Maui Community Theatre, Lahaina News, January 17, 1990: 12.
— continues at Maui Community Theatre, Lahaina News, January 24, 1990: 14.
— continues at Maui Community Theatre, Lahaina News, January 31, 1990: 13.

GREAT WHALE COUNT
— Pacific Whale Foundation looking for volunteers for, Lahaina News, February 10, 2000: 2.
— count tally, Lahaina News, March 1, 2001: 1,3.
— Pacific Whale Foundation seeking volunteers for, Lahaina News, February 20, 2003: 18.

GREATER LAHAINA REUNION
— reunion of former plantation workers planned, Lahaina News, June 25, 1986: 1.
— set for August, Lahaina News, May 6, 1987: 10.
— events detailed, Lahaina News, June 17, 1987: 1,20.
— Soroptimists International to hold fashion show to celebrate, Lahaina News, June 17, 1987: 3.
— logo designed by Lahaina Arts Society, Lahaina News, July 8, 1987: 24.
— tickets available, Lahaina News, July 15, 1987: 3.
— plans detailed, Lahaina News, August 19, 1987: 1,4,15.
— events described, Lahaina News, August 26, 1987: 1.
— Hekka Party arranged for volunteers, Lahaina News, September 9, 1987: 3.
— time capsule buried, Lahaina News, November 18, 1987: 3.
— surplus money goes to Lahaina Community Swimming Pool Association, Lahaina News, June 8, 1988: 3.
— donates equipment to West Maui Youth Center, Lahaina News, December 27, 1989: 11.
— donates to schools in West Maui, Lahaina News, March 20, 1991: 3.

GREATEST SHOW ON EARTH [FILM]
— to be shown at Lahaina library, Lahaina News, April 10, 1985: 3.

GREEK ZORBA [RESTAURANT]
— features nightly music, Lahaina News, May 25, 1995: 12.
— turns one, Lahaina News, June 29, 1995: 12.

GREEN, ARIADNE [WRITER]
— to speak on "Mythic Foreplay", Lahaina News, August 3, 2000: 16.
— to hold workshop on "Dreams and Creative Expression", Lahaina News, May 1, 2003: 16.

GREEN HARVEST
— helicopters take part in "Green Harvest" raids on marijuana farming, Lahaina News, September 25, 1985: 20.

GREEN, MARSHA
— to discuss effects of acoustic sounds on Hawaii marine mammals, Lahaina News, January 7, 1999: 1.

GREEN PARTY
— sponsoring Community Work Day, Lahaina News, October 1, 1992: 4.
— to present "Carnival of Music and Food Bank Foodraiser", Lahaina News, February 11, 1993: 5.
— to meet, Lahaina News, July 8, 1993: 4.
— to hold meeting, Lahaina News, June 27, 1996: 15.
— to meet, Lahaina News, May 1, 1997: 16.
— Bu La'ia to run for governor, Lahaina News, August 6, 1998: 17.

GREEN, PAT [MUSICIAN]
— to perform at Bay Lounge at Kapalua Bay Hotel, Lahaina News, January 30, 1992: 17.

GREEN, RENATTE [ARTIST]
— work displayed at Artful Dodger Reed and Read, Lahaina News, April 1, 1987: 3.

GREENE, DANIEL [ARTIST]
— to offer classes on portrait painting, Lahaina News, December 28, 1995: 3.

GREENE, DEBRA
— to talk on "Thought-Forms", Lahaina News, August 16, 2001: 17.

GREENFIELD, MICHAEL [MUSICIAN]
— performance at Stouffer Wailea Beach Resort presented by Maui Philharmonic Society and Alexander and Baldwin, Lahaina News, January 16, 1991: 10,11.

GREENING OF AMERICA [BOOK]
— reviewed by Lee Long, Lahaina Sun, December 30, 1970: 2.

GREENLEAF'S GRILLE [RESTAURANT]
— opens at Lahaina Cannery Mall, Lahaina News, March 21, 2002: 8.

GREENPEACE [ORGANIZATION]
— described, Lahaina News, September 26, 1984: 7,8,9.

GREENSTEIN, STEVE [COMEDIAN]
— to perform at Comedy Club and the Sports Page, Lahaina News, November 21, 1991: 15.

GREIG, JIMMIE
— entertains at annual Thanksgiving Hoolaulea, Lahaina Sun, November 18, 1970: 4.
— directing Lahainaluna Boarders' Chorus, Lahaina Sun, December 16, 1970: 2.
— congratulated for staging David Malo Pageant, Lahaina Sun, May 19, 1971: 8.
— talks about Thanksgiving Hoolaulea, Lahaina Sun, November 17, 1971: 12.
— new CD to celebrate community leader, Lahaina News, February 22, 2001: 1,18.

GRIFFEL, LOIS [ARTIST]
— to offer Impressionist landscape workshop, Lahaina News, February 29, 1996: 14.

GRIFFIN, ANNIE
— state archaeologist comments on discovery of ancient Hawaiian remains in Kapalua, Lahaina News, January 4, 1989: 16.

GRIFFITH, ANTHONY [COMEDIAN]
— to perform at Comedy Club and the Sports Page, Lahaina News, May 27, 1993: 12,15.
— to perform at Maui Comedy Club, Lahaina News, May 25, 1995: 12.

GRIFFITH, RUTH NAKAMURA
— hired by Lahaina Town Action Committee as assistant to the director, Lahaina News, April 14, 1994: 3.

GRIGG, RICKY
— surfer to appear at Borders Books, Lahaina News, October 14, 1999: 7.

GRILL AND BAR [RESTAURANT]
— to change name to Jameson/s Grill and Bar, Lahaina News, April 4, 1996: 12.

GRINDLEY, JASON
— doctor joins Westside Wellness-Complete Chiropractic, Lahaina News, August 15, 2002: 8.

GRONQUIEST, PHILIP [ARTIST]
— to offer demonstration at Old Jail Gallery, Lahaina News, December 2, 1987: 3.

GROSSMAN, BOB AND PAM
— owners of Fantasy Islands Tours and Activities, Lahaina News, November 28, 1984: 18.

GROSSMAN, HEATHER
— finalist for Hawaii's Favorite Pre-Teen, Lahaina News, June 25, 1992: 2.

GROSVENOR PROPERTIES, LTD.
— purchases Ka'anapali Beach Hotel, Lahaina News, July 20, 1988: 3.

GROTH, LALI [ARTIST]
— to exhibit at Hui No'eau Visual Arts Center, Lahaina News, June 28, 2001: 20.

GROUP 70
— architectural firm designing T.P. Lim's proposed home, Lahaina News, September 29, 1994: 1,3.

GROWING DREAMS
— benefit for Maui Youth and Family Services to be held, Lahaina News, July 5, 2001: 5.

GRYCNER, GREG AND SYLVIA [ARTISTS]
— to exhibit at Sunset Gallery, Lahaina News, January 23, 1992: 16.

GTE HAWAIIAN TELEPHONE [BUSINESS]
— request to increase rates, Lahaina Sun, December 2, 1970: 2.
— photograph of newly-completed building in Wailuku, Lahaina Sun, November 10, 1971: 13.
— receives approval to construct amplifier station, Lahaina Sun, December 15, 1971: 17.
— rate increase criticized by Mayor Cravalho, Lahaina Sun, January 12, 1972: 1.
— upgrades to system detailed, Lahaina Sun, June 28, 1972: 10.
— requests rate hike, Lahaina News, June 1, 1983: 15.
— to begin repair of phone lines, Lahaina News, May 2, 1984: 4.
— request for rate hike, Lahaina News, October 10, 1984: 3.
— releases survey of top issues, Lahaina News, January 17, 1990: 5.
— participates in Adopt-A-Highway program, Lahaina News, October 17, 1991: 7.
— proposes installing interisland submarine fiber optic cable, Lahaina News, March 18, 1993: 8.
— names Joseph Pontanilla as island manager, Lahaina News, May 20, 1993: 7.
— to recycle phone books, Lahaina News, June 3, 1993: 3.
— to launch new service in yellow pages, Lahaina News, February 24, 1994: 10.
— linking health care professionals around the world, Lahaina News, February 2, 1995: 7.
— lowers interisland rates, Lahaina News, February 23, 1995: 6.
— gives grant to Maui Community College Business Information Center, Lahaina News, March 30, 1995: 10.
— rates would rise with request filed by, Lahaina News, June 8, 1995: 10.
— unveils feature where potential properties to be viewable on computers, Lahaina News, June 22, 1995: 10.
— recycling phone books, Lahaina News, August 24, 1995: 4.
— seeking increase in telephone rates, Lahaina News, November 30, 1995: 10.
— providing high-speed local dial-up access, Lahaina News, September 19, 1996: 8.
— contributes to community agency, Lahaina News, May 29, 1997: 5.
— offering internet services for homes, Lahaina News, December 3, 1998: 17.
— to sponsor Literacy Champions Campaign, Lahaina News, September 2, 1999: 16.
— awards grant to Princess Nahienaena Elementary School, Lahaina News, November 25, 1999: 15.

GTE KA'ANAPALI CLASSIC
— see Ka'anapali Classic

GTE MOBILNET [BUSINESS]
— opens office in Kahului, Lahaina News, August 26, 1993: 10.
— introduces speakers bureau program, Lahaina News, December 16, 1993: 7.

GUAM
— Lahaina's Ladder Company No. 3 helps with crash on, Lahaina News, September 18, 1997: 6.

GUARDIANS AD LITEM (VGAL)
— Family Court of the Second Circuit looking for volunteers, Lahaina News, August 25, 1994: 5.
— seeking volunteers, Lahaina News, May 16, 1996: 10.
— Family Court of the Second Judicial Court seeking, Lahaina News, September 20, 2001: 2.

GUASAVE MUSICAL [MUSICAL GROUP]
— to perform for Grito de Indepedencia holiday, Lahaina News, September 11, 1997: 17.

GUATEMALA
— dangers of reporting on surfing in, Lahaina Times, October, 1980 volume 4 number 9: 2.

GUERIN, BRUCE [MUSICIAN]
— to perform at Swan Court at Hyatt Regency, Lahaina News, January 30, 1992: 17.

GUERRERO, ARMONDO
— to demonstrate cigar-making techniques, Lahaina News, April 11, 1996: 12.

GUERRERO, RODNEY ULUWEHI [MUSICIAN]
— organizing performance of chants at Iao Theatre, Lahaina News, February 17, 1994: 12.
— releases "Ka Manawa Pono" album, Lahaina News, January 11, 1996: 14.
— to teach singing, Lahaina News, February 19, 1998: 13.
— to offer singing classes, Lahaina News, October 29, 1998: 28.
— to perform at Reflections of Old Lahaina Luau and Concert benefit, Lahaina News, August 19, 1999: 18.
— to perform and emcee "Reflections of Old Lahaina", Lahaina News, August 26, 1999: 8.
— to perform at "A Taste of Lahaina", Lahaina News, September 2, 1999: 18.
— to perform at Hale Makua's benefit luau, Lahaina News, July 6, 2000: 17.
— to perform concert "In My Heart" at the Maui Arts and Cultural Center, Lahaina News, July 26, 2001: 15.

GUERRORO, ULUWEHI [MUSICIAN]
— to perform at Maui Arts and Cultural Center, Lahaina News, August 8, 2002: 16.

GUIDI, RONN [DANCER]
— to offer ballet classes, Lahaina News, March 11, 1987: 3.

GUILICO, LOUIS [OPERA SINGER]
— performed Puccini's "Tosca" at Baldwin High School auditorium, Lahaina Sun, February 3, 1971: 8.

GUILLERMO, SAMSON
— boxer to compete in Hawaii Junior Olympic State Championships, Lahaina News, May 13, 1999: 7.

GUINNESS BOOK OF WORLD RECORDS
— Steve Fisher boardsails from California to Hawaii in record time, Lahaina News, April 13, 2000: 1,16.

GUISE, NADYA
— to offer lecture on relationships, Lahaina News, April 30, 1986: 3.

GUITAR SHORTY [MUSICIAN]
— to perform at Kona Brewing Company, Lahaina News, September 7, 2000: 21.

GULF WAR
— opposition and support expressed, Lahaina News, January 30, 1991: 1.
— list of West Maui residents serving, Lahaina News, February 13, 1991: 4.
— Maui Council of the Filipino Catholic Club offering special mass to honor military serving in, Lahaina News, February 20, 1991: 3.

GUMANAS, CRESENT
— Scholar/Athlete of the Week, Lahaina News, October 17, 2002: 10.

GUN CLUB
— formed, Lahaina Sun, February 24, 1971: 7.

GUN RANGE
— construction to begin, Lahaina News, September 7, 1988: 1.

GUNDAKER, WILLIAM LOUIS KAMIKA
— Lahainaluna High School prom king, Lahaina News, April 20, 2000: 14.

GUNS
— free classes for young people offered by Peppi's Hunting Service, Lahaina Sun, January 6, 1971: 3.
— editorial supporting banning of handguns, Lahaina News, March 11, 1987: 2.
— editorial in support of regulatory bill, Lahaina News, March 11, 1987: 2.

GUNTER, VAN [COMEDIAN]
— to perform at Comedy Club, Lahaina News, October 31, 1991: 14.

GUSMAN, BERNARD
— Royal Lahaina Tennis Ranch director ne director of tennis at Punahou School, Lahaina News, May 8, 1991: 6.

GUSTAVSON, AL
— advocates for sports as a deterrent to gangs, Lahaina News, May 28, 1992: 9.

GUSTAVSON, ROGER
— appointed Executive Chef at Hyatt Regency Maui, Lahaina News, July 23, 1986: 3.

GUTH, ISAIAH
— Scholar/Athlete of the Week, Lahaina News, March 11, 1999: 6.

GUTH, JOSHUA
— Scholar/Athlete of the Week, Lahaina News, December 2, 1999: 8.

GUTH-TUIPULOTU, LITEA
— Scholar/Athlete of the Week, Lahaina News, March 18, 1999: 14.
— to preside over Lahainaluna High School homecoming, Lahaina News, November 2, 2000: 3.

GUTHRIE, THOMAS
— joins Remax Maui, Lahaina News, June 24, 1999: 11.

GUTMAN, SAMMY [COMEDIAN]
— to perform at Comedy Club and the Sports Page, Lahaina News, January 16, 1991: 10.

GUY, BUDDY [MUSICIAN]
— to perform at Maui Marriott Grand Ballroom, Lahaina News, April 9, 1992: 16.
— to perform at Maui Arts and Cultural Center, Lahaina News, June 1, 2000: 17.
— to perform at Maui Arts and Cultural Center, Lahaina News, June 8, 2000: 18.

GUY, GEECHI [COMEDIAN]
— to perform at Comedy Club and the Sports Page, Lahaina News, January 14, 1993: 12,14.
— to perform at Comedy Club, Lahaina News, February 3, 1994: 12.

GUYS AND DOLLS [MUSICAL]
— auditions to be held, Lahaina News, March 11, 1993: 16.
— to be performed at Maui Community Theatre Onstage, Lahaina News, May 27, 1993: 12.

— to be performed, Lahaina News, June 3, 1993: 15.

— continues at Iao Theatre, Lahaina News, June 17, 1993: 16.

GUZMAN, MANNY

— teaches chess, Lahaina News, January 16, 2003: 16,17.

— continues to teach chess at The Boys and Girls Club of West Maui, Lahaina News, January 23, 2003: 17.

— continues to teach chess at The Boys and Girls Club of West Maui, Lahaina News, March 13, 2003: 17.

— continues to teach chess at The Boys and Girls Club of West Maui, Lahaina News, May 1, 2003: 17.

— continues to teach chess, Lahaina News, July 31, 2003: 17.

GYMNASIUM

— opens in Lahaina, Lahaina Sun, April 26, 1972: 3.

GYMNASTICS FOUNDATION OF MAUI

— Maui Gymnastics Invitation to be held, Lahaina News, January 8, 1998: 7.

GYORI, MICHAEL

— Maui Hui Malama to train language tutors, Lahaina News, March 16, 1988: 15.

— discusses Hui Malama Learning Center's English classes, Lahaina News, December 24, 1998: 1,16.

GYOTAKU

— to be taught by Erica Kahn at Hui No'eau Visual Arts Center, Lahaina News, July 27, 1988: 11.

— to be offered by Hawaiian Fish Printers, Lahaina News, July 9, 1992: 19.

GYPSY ROSE [MUSICAL GROUP]

— to offer free concert, Lahaina News, February 27, 1997: 10.

GYPSY'S EYES

— to perform at Pacific'O Restaurant, Lahaina News, September 14, 1995: 12.

H

H. S. BOUNTY [RESTAURANT]

— reviewed, Lahaina News, October 28, 1987: 9.

H.E.L.L.O.

— volunteers needed to visit elderly, Lahaina News, March 4, 1987: 10.

H.M. THEATRES [BUSINESS]

— bankruptcy court approves sale of, Lahaina News, November 26, 1992: 20.

H.P. BALDWIN HIGH SCHOOL

— see Baldwin High School

H&R BLOCK

— promotes Robert Beck to General Manager, Lahaina News, January 20, 1988: 18.

H&S PUBLISHING [BUSINESS]

— opens Maui office, Lahaina News, January 26, 1995: 13.

H20 TROPICAL TOURS, INC. [BUSINESS]

— Dean Gilot new employee, Lahaina News, September 1, 1994: 13.

HA'AHEO PROGRAM

— to be offered by Parks and Recreation Department, Lahaina News, June 5, 1997: 3.

HA'AHEO PROGRAM

— students registering for, Lahaina News, June 11, 1998: 2.

— registering students, Lahaina News, June 18, 1998: 2.

HAAKE, ALVIN

— named to advisory council for the Maui County School Board District, Lahaina Sun, September 29, 1971: 13.

HAAKE, RICHARD

— Mayor Linda Lingle defends county Managing Director, Lahaina News, December 31, 1992: 3.

— County Managing Director discusses Citizens' Patrol beginning soon, Lahaina News, March 28, 1996: 3.

— Managing Director of Civil Defense discusses disaster plan, Lahaina News, June 25, 1998: 3.

— discusses renovation of Old Lahaina Courthouse, Lahaina News, December 3, 1998: 1.

HAAR, FRANCIS [ARTIST]

— photographs and calligraphy to be exhibited at Graphics Arts Gallery, Lahaina News, August 8, 1990: 15.

HAAS, WALTER

— to give free lecture on "Hawaii's Sea Shells: A Dynamic Population in a Dynamic Environment", Lahaina News, August 8, 2002: 17.

HABITAT FOR HUMANITY

— seeking volunteers, Lahaina News, September 18, 1997: 16,17.

HACHIOJI KURUMA NINGYO AND SHINNAI [TROUPE]

— to perform with puppets and narrative song, Lahaina News, October 3, 2002: 16.

HACKETT, SANDY [COMEDIAN]

— to perform at Comedy Club and the Sports Page, Lahaina News, August 13, 1992: 15,16.

HADA, WES [ARTIST]

— photographer to hold workshops, Lahaina News, November 28, 2002: 16.

— photographer to hold workshops, Lahaina News, December 26, 2002: 16.

HADDON, SEAN

— executive chef at Fleming's On The Green, Lahaina News, November 30, 2000: 13.

HADEN, SEYMOUR [ARTIST]

— etchings to be featured at Honolulu Academy of Arts, Lahaina News, September 26, 1990: 13.

HAGEDORN, JOSEPH [MUSICIAN]

— to perform with Maui Symphony Orchestra, Lahaina News, September 17, 1998: 29.

HAGEMANN, MATTHEW

— hydrogeologist works on wellhead protection program, Lahaina News, September 5, 1996: 1,2.

— hydrogeologist to discuss groundwater contamination, Lahaina News, November 14, 1996: 6.

HAGI, GUY

— to judge Maui Onion Amateur Recipe Contest, Lahaina News, July 30, 1998: 9.

HAGIST, RON [FEDERAL MEDIATOR]

— connected to hotel strike, Lahaina Sun, November 11, 1970: 1.

HAHN, JORDAN

— magician to perform at Jameson's Grill and Bar, Lahaina News, April 20, 2000: 16.

— magician to perform at Jameson's Grill and Bar, Lahaina News, May 11, 2000: 20.

HAIKU [TOWN]

— low and middle income housing approved, Lahaina Sun, October 4, 1972: 18.

— town and people described, Lahaina Sun, July 25, 1973: 12,13,14,15.

— housing project dedicated, Lahaina News, August 1, 1980: 6.

HAIKU BOGGIE FESTIVAL

— event described, Lahaina Sun, April 5, 1972: 8.

HAIKU COMMUNITY ASSOCIATION
— to hold elections, Lahaina News, March 9, 2000: 13.
— to meet at Haiku Elementary School, Lahaina News, May 18, 2000: 21.
— to meet, Lahaina News, November 8, 2001: 17.

HAIKU HO'OLAULE'A AND FLOWER FESTIVAL
— to be held, Lahaina News, May 22, 1997: 17.
— to be held, Lahaina News, May 29, 1997: 16.
— to be held, Lahaina News, June 18, 1998: 16.
— to hold "Pineapple Amble", Lahaina News, July 22, 1999: 6.
— begins, Lahaina News, August 12, 1999: 7.
— Haiku School Community Bazaar and Flower Festival to be held at Haiku Elementary School, Lahaina News, March 2, 2000: 13.
— to be held, Lahaina News, March 8, 2001: 15.

HAIKU HOUSING ADVISORY COMMITTEE
— proposes plan for low cost housing, Lahaina Sun, June 7, 1972: 5.

HAIKU MILL
— Bob Kiger unearthing abandoned 19th century mill, Lahaina News, August 21, 1985: 1,20.

HAIKU PRIDE
— benefit concert to be held for Haiku Defense Fund, Lahaina News, September 21, 2000: 21.

HAIR [PLAY]
— to be performed by Maui Community Theatre, Lahaina News, June 27, 1990: 12.
— to open, Lahaina News, July 4, 1990: 18.
— tickets available, Lahaina News, July 11, 1990: 15.

HAKU MELE O HANA
— to be held at Hotel Hana Maui's Plantation House, Lahaina News, September 26, 1990: 10.
— to be held at Hotel Hana Maui, Lahaina News, October 3, 1990: 12.
— scheduled, Lahaina News, August 29, 1991: 14.
— scheduled for this week, Lahaina News, September 5, 1991: 18.
— to be held, Lahaina News, September 21, 1995: 11.

HAL "AKU" LEWIS GOLF TOURNAMENT
— opportunity for residents to "golf with the stars", Lahaina News, May 15, 1985: 3.

HAL, INC. [BUSINESS]
— parent company to Hawaiian Airlines, Inc. and West Maui Airport, Inc incurs operating loss, Lahaina News, November 28, 1990: 8.
— common stock terms set, Lahaina News, November 12, 1992: 12.
— parent company of Hawaiian Airlines, Inc. files for bankruptcy, plans to restructure, Lahaina News, September 30, 1993: 7,8.
— receives approval from bankruptcy court, Lahaina News, June 30, 1994: 9.

HALAS, SUSAN
— art dealer to present "Collecting Hawaii Pacific Graphic", Lahaina News, February 23, 1995: 11,12.
— art dealer to present "Collecting Hawaii Pacific Graphic", Lahaina News, March 2, 1995: 12.

HALAU HULA HO'OLU O KA'ULA
— organizing Lei Day celebration, Lahaina News, April 24, 1991: 10.

HALAU HULA KA MAKANA KILI'O'OPU
— to perform at Ka'anapali Beach Hotel, Lahaina News, May 29, 2003: 16.

HALAU HULA LAKOU I KA MALAMA A KEALOHA
— to perform during Aloha Week, Lahaina News, October 5, 1995: 10.

HALAU HULA NA MAILE KU HONUA
— to perform at Ka'anapali Beach Hotel, Lahaina News, July 24, 2003: 16.

HALAU HULA O KA MAKANI WILI MAKAHA O KAUA'ULA
— to present "the Art of the Chanter", Lahaina News, February 3, 1994: 12.
— to perform with Keali'i Reichel at the Maui Arts and Cultural Center, Lahaina News, February 4, 1999: 17.

HALAU HULA PA'U O HI'IAKA
— to begin hula classes, Lahaina News, September 6, 2001: 16.

HALAU KANI KA PAHU O LOHI'AU
— to participate in Maui AIDS Foundation benefit, Lahaina News, July 6, 1988: 17.

HALAU MAUI NUI O KAMA
— to hold fundraiser and silent auction for Bang-Bang's Kihei Boxing Club, Lahaina News, December 13, 2001: 12.

HALAU NA LEI KAUMAKA O UKA
— performing "Nana I Ke Kumu", Lahaina News, May 25, 2000: 18.
— to perform at Ka'anapali Beach Hotel's Tiki Courtyard, Lahaina News, March 27, 2003: 14.
— to perform at Maui Arts and Cultural Center, Lahaina News, September 25, 2003: 16.

HALAU O KEKUHI
— to perform "Holo Mai Pele: The Travels of Pele", Lahaina News, April 27, 1995: 12.
— to present "Kamehameha Pai'ea", Lahaina News, May 18, 2000: 20.

HALBERG, PAUL
— wins best pizza in western United States with "Bleu Hawaii" pizza, Lahaina News, December 5, 1990: 14.

HALE, ALICE
— director for Maui ACLU, Lahaina Sun, January 13, 1971: 6.

HALE ALII BUILDERS, LTD. [BUSINESS]
— wins Hawaii Renaissance Award, Lahaina News, September 10, 1992: 9.

HALE ALOHA
— historic site's possible use discussed, Lahaina News, April 9, 1986: 1,16.
— plans to restore, Lahaina News, February 17, 1988: 1,17.
— leased to Alan Walker of Lahaina Printsellers, Lahaina News, May 25, 1988: 1.
— Lahaina Restoration Foundation approves rebuilding bell tower at, Lahaina News, November 12, 1992: insert1,insert4.
— restoration completed, Lahaina News, January 25, 1996: 3.
— Lahaina Restoration Foundation wins Maui Historical Society award for restoring Bell Tower, Lahaina News, May 16, 1996: 6.

HALE ALOHA CEMETERY
— columbarium opens, Lahaina News, January 23, 1992: 4.

HALE ALOHA CHURCH
— Chris Hart of Maui Planning Department discusses possible purchase of, Lahaina Sun, December 16, 1970: 6.
— restoration planned, Lahaina Sun, May 30, 1973: 7.
— plans to rebuild bell tower , Lahaina News, April 7, 1994: 3.
— Lahaina Restoration Foundation installs bell at, Lahaina News, February 8, 1996: 1.

HALE ALOHA EPISCOPAL CEMETERY
— Reverend Donald Hart breaks group for Columbarium, Lahaina News, February 27, 1991: 4.

HALE, BRUCE [WRITER AND ARTIST]
— to lead workshop "The 7 Secrets of Creating and Publishing Children's Books" with Benjamin Bess, Lahaina News, November 16, 2000: 16.

HALE, GREG [ARTIST]
— to exhibit at Addi Galleries, Lahaina News, August 22, 2002: 18.

HALE KAHIKO
— opens, Lahaina News, January 23, 1997: 16.

HALE KAI
— development featured, Lahaina News, March 14, 1984: 10.

HALE KAU KAU
— looking for kitchens to feed the hungry, Lahaina News, January 28, 1993: 4.
— serving Christmas Day Dinner, Lahaina News, December 25, 1997: 12.

HALE KOHOLA MUSEUM
— Whale Center of the Pacific offers free whale slide presentation, Lahaina News, March 13, 1997: 16.
— Dirk Younkerman to present on whales, Lahaina News, January 29, 1998: 16.

HALE LAHAINA
— supported by Maui Association of Retarded Citizens, Lahaina News, November 20, 1985: 3.

HALE, LILIA WAHINEMAIKA'I
— featured in documentary by Eddie and Myrna Kamae, Lahaina News, November 5, 1998: 2.

HALE LOKO MAIKAI'I SHELTER
— offering support to victims of family violence, Lahaina News, January 18, 1989: 3.

HALE LUNA CHURCH
— current situation described, Lahaina News, June 9, 1994: 2.

HALE MAHAOLU
— Low-income apartments offered by, Lahaina Sun, March 15, 1972: 4.
— still accepting applications to rent unit in Lahaina Surf, Lahaina Sun, August 2, 1972: 10.
— to hold cookie sale fundraiser, Lahaina News, August 21, 1997: 1.

HALE MAHAOLU EONA
— elderly housing complex planned, Lahaina News, December 14, 2000: 1,17.

HALE MAHAOLU-LAHAINA SURF
— to hold yard sale, Lahaina News, March 20, 1997: 16.
— residents to hold yard sale, Lahaina News, November 13, 1997: 20.

HALE MAHINA BEACH RESORT
— now managed by Ka'anapali Vacations, Lahaina News, February 22, 1989: 13.
— featured real estate, Lahaina News, August 21, 2003: 6.

HALE MAKUA FOUNDATION
— receives donation from Ka'anapali Beach Operators Association, Lahaina News, March 23, 1988: 3.
— benefit golf tournament to be held, Lahaina News, June 7, 1989: 5.
— named by AMFAC as beneficiary of First Development Ka'anapali Classic Senior PGA tour event, Lahaina News, August 8, 1991: 6.
— receives check from Studio 505 , Lahaina News, January 2, 1992: 5.
— receives donation from Amfac/JMB Hawaii, Inc, Lahaina News, June 11, 1992: 4.
— forms Maui Comprehensive Rehabilitation Center with Rehabilitation Hospital of the Pacific, Lahaina News, June 18, 1992: 4.
— Benefit Luau to be held at Wailuku Community Center, Lahaina News, July 7, 1994: 4.
— to hold fundraiser, Lahaina News, July 27, 1995: 12.
— to hold financial planning seminar, Lahaina News, April 9, 1998: 17.
— to hold financial planning seminar, Lahaina News, April 16, 1998: 12.
— to hold annual luau, Lahaina News, July 16, 1998: 17.
— to hold luau fundraiser, Lahaina News, July 23, 1998: 16.
— money raised at golf tournament for, Lahaina News, September 17, 1998: 24.
— Ohana Luau successful, Lahaina News, July 1, 1999: 11.
— to hold benefit luau featuring Uluwehi Guerrero, Lahaina News, July 6, 2000: 17.

— to hold Ohana Luau fundraiser, Lahaina News, July 5, 2001: 15.
— Melveen Leed to perform at Ohana Luau, Lahaina News, August 1, 2002: 18.

HALE NOLO
— groundbreaking for residential housing will occur, Lahaina News, June 13, 1984: 4.

HALE O KEIKI PRESCHOOL
— to benefit from Montessori Gala, Lahaina News, April 3, 1991: 8.

HALE PA'AHAO
— historical marker for prison discussed , Lahaina Sun, December 16, 1970: 6.
— Lahaina Restoration Foundation to take over maintenance of, Lahaina News, May 16, 1984: 3.
— history and plans for old prison described, Lahaina News, June 27, 1984: 7,8,9.
— Maui Historic Commission to reconstruct Gate House at, Lahaina News, July 23, 1986: 1.
— stories from, Lahaina News, June 10, 1987: 10.
— featured, Lahaina News, June 1, 1988: 3.

HALE PA'I
— restoration of printing house at Lahainaluna High School almost complete, Lahaina News, June 15, 1982: 11.
— history of printing at, Lahaina News, February 8, 1996: 12.

HALE ROYAL
— development featured, Lahaina News, May 10, 2001: 6.

HALE ROYALE
— development featured, Lahaina News, March 28, 1984: 18.

HALE-BOPP
— comet to be visible, Lahaina News, March 27, 1997: 3.

HALEAKALA
— photographs of snow, Lahaina Sun, January 13, 1971: 1,3.
— described, Lahaina Sun, August 4, 1971: 5.
— attempts to establish nene in, Lahaina Sun, August 11, 1971: 11.
— wilderness plan proposed, Lahaina Sun, October 20, 1971: 12.
— ecological issues discussed, Lahaina Sun, December 22, 1971: 17.
— discussion of current situation, Lahaina Sun, December 29, 1971: 10,11.
— decision on microwave relay for cable TV delayed, Lahaina Sun, August 16, 1972: 9.
— technology on summit described, Lahaina Sun, September 27, 1972: 7.
— request for laser detailed, Lahaina Sun, October 11, 1972: 13.
— criticism of tourism advertising featuring, Lahaina Sun, November 15, 1972: 19.
— bicycle ride down described, Lahaina Sun, February 28, 1973: 15.
— guided hikes offered to park visitors, Lahaina Sun, May 16, 1973: 11.
— UFO reported in, Lahaina Sun, August 29, 1973: 11.
— description of horseback ride to the crater, Lahaina News, May 15, 1981: 11,12.
— featured, Lahaina News, March 21, 1984: 9,10,11.
— biking down, described, Lahaina News, January 16, 1985: 7,8,9.
— tours available at Space Surveillance facility , Lahaina News, February 12, 1998: 2.
— lunar eclipse to viewed from, Lahaina News, January 13, 2000: 13.

HALEAKALA, BLAISE
— see basketball

HALEAKALA CHAMBER MUSIC SOCIETY
— to present spring concert, Lahaina News, May 21, 1992: 18.
— to present The Haleakala Chamber Players, Lahaina News, February 4, 1993: 15.
— to perform, Lahaina News, February 11, 1993: 16.

HALEAKALA DAIRY
— adding more cows to herd, Lahaina Sun, February 2, 1972: 9.
— lowers prices, Lahaina Sun, June 7, 1972: 11.
— sponsors milk carton boat race, Lahaina Sun, July 25, 1973: 11.
— results of Healthy Baby Contest, Lahaina News, October 22, 1998: 15.

HALEAKALA HAWAIIAN CHURCH
— to hold "Ring in the Millennium", Lahaina News, December 30, 1999: 16.

HALEAKALA MOTORS
— purchased by Nathan Alberstein, Lahaina News, August 8, 1990: 6.

HALEAKALA NATIONAL PARK
— expansion of slowed by State's failure to donate land, Lahaina Sun, April 7, 1971: 2.
— changes made to way cabins are reserved, Lahaina News, November 30, 1983: 5.
— offering walks and hikes this summer, Lahaina News, July 18, 1984: 3.
— to celebrate 75th anniversary, Lahaina News, August 1, 1991: 4.
— cabin fees changed, Lahaina News, November 17, 1994: 5.
— to hold hike into Waikamoi Preserve, Lahaina News, June 20, 1996: 13.
— guided hikes to be offered, Lahaina News, August 29, 1996: 11.
— hike to be held at, Lahaina News, January 16, 1997: 10,11.
— crater hike to be held, Lahaina News, January 23, 1997: 10.
— hosting hike in Waikamoi Preserve, Lahaina News, December 18, 1997: 19.
— staff to lead adventure into the crater, Lahaina News, April 16, 1998: 13.
— to hold star gazing event, Lahaina News, May 21, 1998: 17.
— to offer star gazing event, Lahaina News, June 18, 1998: 16.
— to host hike in Waikamoi Preserve, Lahaina News, July 16, 1998: 16.
— staff to lead hike from Sliding Sands to Ka Lu'u o Ka 'O'o, Lahaina News, August 6, 1998: 20.
— to offer Polynesian navigation, Lahaina News, September 10, 1998: 20.
— staff to lead hike to Waikamoi Preserve, Lahaina News, October 21, 1999: 16.
— staff leading five-hour hike into Waikamoi Preserve, Lahaina News, March 16, 2000: 13.
— to hold "Walk on the Wet Side" hike, Lahaina News, May 18, 2000: 20.
— staff to clean hiking trail, Lahaina News, June 8, 2000: 20.
— presentation on history of park to be held, Lahaina News, August 24, 2000: 20.
— staff to offer "Wet Side Hike", Lahaina News, May 17, 2001: 20.
— to hold "Wet Side Hike", Lahaina News, September 13, 2001: 16.
— staff to lead hike into Haleakala Wilderness, Lahaina News, October 11, 2001: 17.
— to offer safe view of solar eclipse , Lahaina News, December 13, 2001: 16.
— staff to lead "Walk on the Wet Side", Lahaina News, March 14, 2002: 17.
— staff to lead walk to Leleiwi Overlook, Lahaina News, April 11, 2002: 16.
— to hold "Kilo Hoku", Lahaina News, July 4, 2002: 16.
— to offer "Kilo Hoku" star gazing event, Lahaina News, July 18, 2002: 16.
— to lead hike to taro patches of Kapahu Farm, Lahaina News, August 1, 2002: 21.
— to offer "Kilo Hoku" star gazing event, Lahaina News, September 5, 2002: 16.
— to offer tours of taro patches at Kapahu Farm, Lahaina News, October 31, 2002: 28.
— continues to offer hikes, Lahaina News, December 19, 2002: 21.
— to offer tour on Sliding Sands, Lahaina News, March 20, 2003: 16.
— to hold hike in Waikamoi, Lahaina News, March 27, 2003: 17.
— to hold programs, Lahaina News, May 8, 2003: 17.
— to hold hikes in Waikamoi, Lahaina News, July 17, 2003: 16.

HALEAKALA OBSERVATORIES
— Friends of Haleakala National Park to discuss Haleakala Observatories, Lahaina News, February 20, 2003: 2.

HALEAKALA RANCH
— paintings created to celebrate 100th anniversary, Lahaina News, June 14, 1989: 18.

HALEAKALA SCHOOL
— imagination-focused school begins second year, Lahaina Sun, July 18, 1973: 21.

HALEAMAU, GARY [MUSICIAN]
— to perform at Old Lahaina Cafe and Luau, Lahaina News, February 14, 1990: 15.
— to perform at Old Lahaina Cafe and Luau, Lahaina News, July 18, 1990: 11.

HALEY, BRYAN
— selected as Maui Marriott's Manager of the Second Quarter, Lahaina News, July 18, 1990: 7.

HALEY, JACK "MIDDLE"
— Spurs basketball player to surf, Lahaina News, June 15, 1995: 6.

HALII MAILE
— featured, Lahaina Sun, August 15, 1973: 12,13,14,15.

HALI'IMAILE FARMER'S AND CRAFTER'S FAIR
— to be held, Lahaina News, February 27, 2003: 16.

HALI'IMAILE GENERAL STORE [RESTAURANT]
— to hold benefit for Maui Philharmonic Society, Lahaina News, April 5, 1989: 17.
— changes to winter dinner menu, Lahaina News, February 6, 1991: 9.
— to hold "Shopping Party", Lahaina News, November 20, 1997: 16.
— searching for someone born on day store first opened, Lahaina News, September 10, 1998: 6.
— to offer "Aloha Night", Lahaina News, May 31, 2001: 8.

HALIM, EDUARDUS [MUSICIAN]
— pianist to perform at the Academy Theatre, Lahaina News, August 15, 1990: 17.

HALIP, NORMAN
— to speak on "From Russia to Wailea", Lahaina News, May 9, 2002: 17.

HALL AND OATES [MUSICAL GROUP]
— cancel show on Maui, Lahaina News, May 22, 1985: 10.

HALL, CHARLES
— appointed deputy chief of police, Lahaina News, September 3, 1998: 8.

HALL, DANA NAONE [WRITER]
— speaking for Hui Alanui O Makena concerning Kapalua Land Company development, Lahaina News, June 15, 1988: 1.
— receives Cades Award for Poetry, Lahaina News, October 3, 1990: 13.

HALL, FREDRICK
— owner of Lahaina Foreign Cars featured, Lahaina News, September 12, 1984: 14.

HALL, GREG
— discusses improvement work on Front Street, Lahaina News, September 11, 1997: 9.

HALL, HARRY
— diver discusses black coral diving, Lahaina Sun, April 25, 1973: 7.

HALL, TOMMY [MUSICIAN]
— fundraiser held for at Stouffer's Wailea Beach Hotel, Lahaina News, January 29, 1986: 8.
— to perform at Longhi's, Lahaina News, June 22, 1988: 7.

— to perform at Polli's On the Beach, Lahaina News, October 31, 1990: 14.

— to perform at Polli's Mexican Restaurant, Lahaina News, January 2, 1991: 8.

— to perform at Polli's Mexican Restaurant, Lahaina News, May 1, 1991: 18.

— continues to perform at Polli's Mexican, Lahaina News, May 15, 1991: 12.

— to perform at Polli's Mexican Restaurant, Lahaina News, November 7, 1991: 20.

HALLOWEEN

— Lahaina Ecumenical Youth Group to collect coins for United Nations Children's Fund, Lahaina Sun, October 27, 1971: 12.

— events detailed, Lahaina Sun, October 27, 1971: 6.

— parade planned for Lahaina, Lahaina Sun, October 25, 1972: 4.

— celebrations in Maui described, Lahaina News, November 9, 1983: 7,8,9.

— parade to be covered live on radio, Lahaina News, October 24, 1984: 3.

— activities for children, Lahaina News, October 24, 1984: A,B,C,D.

— featured, Lahaina News, October 31, 1984: 7,8,9.

— described, featured more onlookers than participants, Lahaina News, November 7, 1984: 3,4.

— parade set for October 31st, sponsored by Soroptimists International and Rotary Club, Lahaina News, October 23, 1985: 3.

— police to be out in force, Lahaina News, October 30, 1985: 1.

— events described, Lahaina News, November 6, 1985: 8,9.

— activities planned, Lahaina News, October 22, 1986: 1,8,16.

— "Fright Night" to be presented at Hyatt Regency Maui, Lahaina News, October 29, 1986: 3.

— restaurant events listed, Lahaina News, October 29, 1986: 4.

— event described, includes photographs, Lahaina News, November 5, 1986: 1.

— celebrated at Lahainaluna High School, Lahaina News, November 5, 1986: 13.

— party to be held at Unity Church of Maui, Lahaina News, October 21, 1987: 12.

— events around Lahaina described, Lahaina News, October 28, 1987: 4,8.

— events listed, Lahaina News, October 26, 1988: 1.

— events at Wharf Shops & Restaurant detailed, Lahaina News, October 26, 1988: 16.

— Keiki Halloween Parade planned, Lahaina News, October 26, 1988: 6.

— Halloween Costume Ball scheduled for Champagne, Lahaina News, October 26, 1988: 8.

— editorial urging a good Halloween, Lahaina News, August 2, 1989: 12.

— Lahaina Town Action Committee planning contest, Lahaina News, September 13, 1989: 1.

— costume contest sponsored by West Maui Taxpayers Association, Lahaina News, September 27, 1989: 3.

— activities planned, Lahaina News, October 4, 1989: 3.

— sponsors listed, Lahaina News, October 18, 1989: 1.

— events detailed, Lahaina News, October 25, 1989: 16.

— Maui Marriott Resort to hold party, Lahaina News, October 25, 1989: 2.

— contest results, Lahaina News, November 8, 1989: 7.

— scheduled, Lahaina News, October 3, 1990: 2.

— events, Lahaina News, October 10, 1990: 5,9,18.

— events described, Lahaina News, October 17, 1990: 1.

— Dracula's Dash and Keiki Fun Run scheduled, Lahaina News, October 17, 1990: 9.

— events described, Lahaina News, October 24, 1990: 11,13,18.

— laser show to be presented at Lahaina Coolers, Lahaina News, October 31, 1990: 13.

— Lahaina Town Action Committee to hold costume contest, Lahaina News, October 31, 1990: 13.

— Wharf Cinema to celebrate, Lahaina News, October 31, 1990: 13.

— events described, Lahaina News, November 7, 1990: 1,3.

— costume contest to grand prize airline tickets from Delta, Lahaina News, August 29, 1991: 9.

— costume contest to be held, Lahaina News, September 12, 1991: 13,14.

— costume contest organized by Lahaina Town Action Committee, Lahaina News, September 19, 1991: 3.

— Golden Pineapple Award to be presented to best decorated store front, Lahaina News, October 10, 1991: 7.

— costume ideas offered, Lahaina News, October 17, 1991: 15.

— Front Street to be closed to traffic for, Lahaina News, October 17, 1991: 3.

— Dracula's Dash to be held, Lahaina News, October 17, 1991: 4.

— costume contest organized by Lahaina Town Action Committee, Lahaina News, October 17, 1991: 5.

— Keiki Halloween Parade sponsored by Rotary Club and Maui Soroptimist International, Lahaina News, October 17, 1991: 6.

— Maui Community College and The Maui Academy of Performing Arts renting costumes, Lahaina News, October 17, 1991: 6.

— Lahaina Coolers to offer laser show, Lahaina News, October 24, 1991: 18.

— Elvin Bishop-Norton Buffalo Blues Band to perform, Lahaina News, October 24, 1991: 18,19.

— costume contest to be held at Azeka Place Shopping Center, Lahaina News, October 24, 1991: 22.

— keiki Halloween Parade sponsored by Rotary Club and Maui Soroptimist International, Lahaina News, October 24, 1991: 4.

— mask making workshop to be held, Lahaina News, October 24, 1991: 4.

— Maui Community Theatre to stage Haunted Theatre, Lahaina News, October 24, 1991: 4.

— costumes available for rent, Lahaina News, October 24, 1991: 5.

— Dracula's Dash to be held, Lahaina News, October 24, 1991: 6.

— details, Lahaina News, October 31, 1991: 2,3,13,15.

— described as a success, Lahaina News, November 7, 1991: 21.

— details of results, Lahaina News, November 14, 1991: 2,4.

— Lahaina Galleries and The Gallery win Pineapple Awards for best display, Lahaina News, November 21, 1991: 11.

— Lahaina Town Action Committee costume contest to be held, Lahaina News, September 24, 1992: 14,15.

— grand prize set for costume contest, Lahaina News, October 1, 1992: 15,16.

— Fright Night to be offered at Maui Sun Hotel, Lahaina News, October 1, 1992: 17.

— prizes added to Lahaina Town Action Committee costume contest, Lahaina News, October 8, 1992: 10.

— Fright Night to be offered at Maui Sun Hotel, Lahaina News, October 15, 1992: 18.

— "Rocky Horror Picture Show" to be displayed, Lahaina News, October 15, 1992: 18.

— events planned, Lahaina News, October 15, 1992: 7.

— events, Lahaina News, October 22, 1992: 16,17,18.

— party being organized by Maui Chamber of Commerce, Lahaina News, October 22, 1992: 4.

— events, Lahaina News, October 22, 1992: insert.

— events listed, Lahaina News, October 29, 1992: 17,18,19,20,21,22.

— Local Motion wins best window display contest, Lahaina News, November 5, 1992: 16.

— results of costume contest, Lahaina News, November 5, 1992: 3,4.

— events, Lahaina News, October 14, 1993: 13,14.

— Maui Academy of Performing Arts renting costumes, Lahaina News, October 14, 1993: 16.

— events planned, Lahaina News, October 21, 1993: 15,16.

— Azeka Place Shopping Center to host costume contest, Lahaina News, October 21, 1993: 7.

— children's parade to be held, Lahaina News, October 28, 1993: 1.

— spooky story, Lahaina News, October 28, 1993: 2.

— events listed, Lahaina News, October 28, 1993: 3,4,9.

— Azeka Place Shopping Center to host costume contest, Lahaina News, October 28, 1993: 6.

— results of, Lahaina News, November 4, 1993: 12.

— police preparing for, Lahaina News, October 6, 1994: 3.

— Azeka Place Shopping Center to host costume contest, Lahaina News, October 13, 1994: 19.

— Keiki Halloween Parade to be held, Lahaina News, October 13, 1994: 6.

— preparations detailed, Lahaina News, October 20, 1994: 3.

— Keiki Halloween Parade to be held, Lahaina News, October 20, 1994: 5.

— results of, Lahaina News, October 27, 1994: 1,16,17.

— an estimated 15,000 people turn out for, Lahaina News, November 3, 1994: 1.

— events to be held in Lahaina, Lahaina News, September 21, 1995: 12.

— LahainaTown Action Committee seeking face painting artists, Lahaina News, October 12, 1995: 14.

— Maui Academy of Performing Arts to rent Halloween costumes, Lahaina News, October 12, 1995: 15.

— "Garden of Be" to perform during Halloween Keiki Parade, Lahaina News, October 12, 1995: 3.

— details of events, Lahaina News, October 12, 1995: 7.

— Honolua Preschool to host Haunted House, Lahaina News, October 19, 1995: 9.

— details of events, Lahaina News, October 26, 1995: insert1,insert2,insert3,insert4,insert5,insert6,insert7,insert8.

— history of in Lahaina, Lahaina News, October 26, 1995: insert2.

— photo from, Lahaina News, November 9, 1995: 1.

— Bruce Cate wins Great Halloween Costume Contest, other results, Lahaina News, November 9, 1995: 12.

— Maui Community Theatre offering help with costumes, Lahaina News, October 10, 1996: 15.

— Honolua Preschool to host Keiki Haunted House, Lahaina News, October 17, 1996: 15.

— costume contest to be held, Lahaina News, October 17, 1996: 2.

— planned for Lahaina, Lahaina News, October 24, 1996: 1,20.

— events, Lahaina News, October 31, 1996: 1,24.

— "Rocky Horror Picture Show" to be displayed, Lahaina News, October 31, 1996: 18.

— results of contest, Lahaina News, November 7, 1996: 5.

— booths available from LahainaTown Action Committee, Lahaina News, October 16, 1997: 9.

— to be held, Lahaina News, October 23, 1997: 1,7.

— Pet Shop to hold Pet Costume Parade, Lahaina News, October 23, 1997: 20.

— Fright Night to be held at Maui Arts and Cultural Center, Lahaina News, October 23, 1997: 21.

— Lahaina police set ground rules for, Lahaina News, October 30, 1997: 1.

— Westin Maui holding Masquerade Madness as fundraiser for Maui AIDS Foundation, Lahaina News, October 30, 1997: 13.

— Ka'ahumanu Center to hold "Halloween Family Night", Lahaina News, October 30, 1997: 16.

— events to be held, Lahaina News, October 30, 1997: 3.

— celebrated, Lahaina News, November 6, 1997: 1.

— winners of Ghoulish Gala Karaoke, Lahaina News, November 13, 1997: 2.

— LahainaTown Action Committee taking applications for booths for, Lahaina News, October 8, 1998: 17.

— events, Lahaina News, October 22, 1998: 1,6.

— readies for Fright Night '98, Lahaina News, October 22, 1998: 6,7.

— police send out reminders; events, Lahaina News, October 29, 1998: 1,22,23.

— "Family Night" to be held; other events, Lahaina News, October 29, 1998: 28.

— police report on incidents, Lahaina News, November 5, 1998: 1,24.

— "Majestic Pumpkin Patch" float wins contest, Lahaina News, November 5, 1998: 11.

— to be held, Lahaina News, October 21, 1999: 1,3.

— expected to draw 25,000 to Lahaina, Lahaina News, October 28, 1999: 1,2.

— Maui Mall to hold Pet Costume Contest to benefit Maui Human Society, Lahaina News, October 28, 1999: 16.

— LahainaTown Action Committee seeking artists for, Lahaina News, October 19, 2000: 1.

— Wharf Cinema Center planning "Monster Halloween Bash", Lahaina News, October 19, 2000: 11.

— Soroptimists International and Lahaina Rotary Club to hold Keiki Halloween Parade, Lahaina News, October 19, 2000: 19.

— Mardi Gras of the Pacific to be held, Lahaina News, October 26, 2000: 1,8,9.

— to be held, Lahaina News, October 26, 2000: 1,8,9.

— results of The Great Halloween Costume Contest, Lahaina News, November 9, 2000: 13.

— preparations underway, Lahaina News, October 11, 2001: 18.

— being planned, Lahaina News, October 25, 2001: 1,14.

— results of costume contest, Lahaina News, November 8, 2001: 3.

— David Induni to hold mask making workshop, Lahaina News, October 17, 2002: 19.

— events planned, Lahaina News, October 24, 2002: 17.

— to be held in Lahaina, Lahaina News, October 31, 2002: 12,26,27,28.

— results of costume contest, Lahaina News, November 7, 2002: 2.

HALLOWEEN BASH
— to be held at Maui Marriott, Lahaina News, October 21, 1987: 3.

HALMAGYI, PETER [ARTIST]
— to exhibit "Israel Mosaci" at the Maui Metropolitan Museum of Modern Art, Lahaina News, February 25, 1999: 12.

HAMAI APPLIANCES [BUSINESS]
— opens store in Lahaina, Lahaina News, May 15, 1982: 2.
— moving location, Lahaina News, July 30, 1992: 12.

HAMAI, GLENN
— to attend National Scout Jamboree, Lahaina News, April 2, 1992: 5.

HAMBLEY, SCOT [TEACHER]
— approach to teaching discussed, Lahaina Sun, May 9, 1973: 4,5.

HAMILTON, JACK [ARTIST]
— to exhibit at Lahaina Arts Society Gallery, Lahaina News, July 2, 1998: 17.
— to exhibit at the Art School at Kapalua, Lahaina News, July 6, 2000: 1.

HAMILTON, SCOTT
— named directed of sales for Maui Marriott Hotel, Lahaina News, February 18, 1987: 3.
— named director of marketing at Marriott, Lahaina News, May 6, 1987: 10.

HAMILTON, SYLVIA CLARK [ARTIST]
— to exhibit at Lahaina Arts Society, Lahaina News, April 1, 1993: 12.
— to exhibit at Old Jail Gallery, Lahaina News, June 29, 1995: 12.

HAMLIN, ERIC [MUSICIAN]
— to perform at Stouffer's Wailea Beach Resort, Lahaina News, January 3, 1990: 16.

HAMMERSMITH BAND, THE [MUSICAL GROUP]
— to perform at Casanova's, Lahaina News, March 20, 1991: 10.

HAMMOND, JOHN [MUSICIAN]
— to perform at Casanova's, Lahaina News, December 12, 1991: 25.

HAMPTON, ROY
— is missing, may have travelled to Maui, Lahaina News, August 31, 2000: 3.

HAN, WU [MUSICIAN]
— to perform at Maui Arts and Cultural Center with Wu Han, Lahaina News, April 3, 2003: 15.

HANA [TOWN]
— tested for pollution, Lahaina Sun, December 16, 1970: 3.
— photographs of waterfalls on road to Hana, Lahaina Sun, February 10, 1971: 5.
— Hawaiian Airlines decides to phase out operations to, Lahaina Sun, May 24, 1972: 9.
— cattle ranch described, Lahaina Sun, June 7, 1972: 9.
— featured, Lahaina Sun, August 1, 1973: 12,13,14,15.
— land grab described, Lahaina News, April 15, 1980: 14.
— bus trip described, Lahaina News, August 1, 1980: 5.
— photographs of, Lahaina News, July 1, 1983: 12,13.
— Community SummerFest to be held, Lahaina News, June 26, 2003: 20.

HANA CANOE CLUB
— to host MauiFest as benefit, Lahaina News, September 18, 2003: 18.

HANA CULTURAL CENTER
— to hold ho'olaule'a, Lahaina News, August 13, 1998: 16.

HANA ELEMENTARY SCHOOL
— student wins Maui Toyota's Pueo Coloring Contest, Lahaina News, June 12, 1997: 15.

HANA FARMER'S AND CRAFTERS MARKET
— to hold Christmas Fair, Lahaina News, December 7, 2000: 24.

HANA HAWAII
— designated "Hawaii's Millennium Legacy Trail" in White House ceremony, Lahaina News, June 1, 2000: 7.

HANA 'IMI NA'AUAO HO'OLAULE'A
— to be held, Lahaina News, August 13, 1998: 17.
— to be held, Lahaina News, August 20, 1998: 16.
— to be held, Brother Noland featured, Lahaina News, August 12, 1999: 18.

HANA MOUNTAIN
— hunting okayed, Lahaina News, May 21, 1986: 3.

HANA RANCH
— attempts to sell large lots requires providing electricity first, Lahaina Sun, December 27, 1972: 13.
— plan to sell large building lots approved, Lahaina Sun, January 24, 1973: 7.

HANA RELAY
— sponsored by Koho Grill and Bar, Lahaina News, September 5, 1990: 7.
— to be held, Lahaina News, September 19, 1990: 18.
— results, Lahaina News, October 3, 1990: 6.

HANA, ROAD TO
— featured, Lahaina News, July 11, 1984: 7,8,9,10.

HANA SCHOOL
— wins Na Mele O Maui, Lahaina News, April 16, 1992: 19.

HANA SEA LAND [BUSINESS]
— dedication ceremony, Lahaina Sun, February 2, 1972: 9.
— see also Lokahi Pacific Corporation

HANABUSA, COLLEEN [POLITICIAN]
— to discuss land trust bills, Lahaina News, October 28, 1999: 1.

HANAKA'O'O BEACH PARK
— land donated to county by Amfac for park, Lahaina News, January 1, 1983: 4.
— featured, Lahaina News, October 19, 1983: 7,8,9.
— Canoe Beach dedicated, Lahaina News, November 9, 1983: 5.
— to officially open, Lahaina News, February 8, 1984: 7.
— Keiki O Maui Regatta to be held at, Lahaina News, June 28, 1989: 9.
— Napili Invitational canoe race scheduled at, Lahaina News, May 8, 1991: 6.
— restroom pump station to be replaced, Lahaina News, December 8, 1994: 3.
— plans to expand, Lahaina News, October 17, 1996: 1,20.
— regatta held at, Lahaina News, August 12, 1999: 1.
— cleaned by sailors before leaving for Persian Gulf, Lahaina News, March 20, 2003: 1,3.

HANAKA'O'O TRIANGLE RACE
— Edmund Mitchell wins, Lahaina News, March 11, 1993: 9.

HANAKO, PRINCESS
— Japanese royal visits Maui with Prince Hitachi, Lahaina News, June 26, 1985: 1,2,9.

HANAMATSURI
— to be celebrated, Lahaina News, April 4, 1990: 3.
— West Maui Buddhist Council to celebrate Buddha's Birthday, Lahaina News, April 11, 2002: 1.
— to be celebrated by West Maui Buddhists, Lahaina News, April 3, 2003: 3.

HANAU KA MOKU: AN ISLAND IS BORN [PERFORMANCE]
— to be performed at Maui Arts and Cultural Center, Lahaina News, August 22, 2002: 17.

HANCE, JOHN
— president of Pioneer speaks of Amfac, Inc. removing land from sugarcane production, Lahaina News, January 24, 1990: 1.

HANCHETT, E. LANI
— Episcopal bishop visits Lahaina, Lahaina Sun, November 11, 1970: 2.

HANCHETT, THOMAS
— discusses plans to bring charter passenger flights to Maui, Lahaina Sun, January 13, 1971: 6.

HANCOCK, HERBIE [MUSICIAN]
— to perform at Maui Marriott Resort with Thelma Houston, Lahaina News, August 2, 1989: 15.

HANDEL, GEORGE FREDERICK [COMPOSER]
— "Young Messiah" to be performed, Lahaina News, December 24, 1992: 15.
— "Messiah" to be performed, Lahaina News, December 15, 1994: 16.

HANDICAPPED
— get less help in West Maui, Lahaina News, January 17, 1990: 1.

HANDICAPPED SCUBA ASSOCIATION
— to offer trainings to persons with handicaps with Lahaina Divers, Lahaina News, July 4, 1991: 5.
— to offer trainings to persons with handicaps with Lahaina Divers, Lahaina News, August 15, 1991: 4.

HANDLEY [FAMILY]
— fundraiser held for following industrial accident, Lahaina News, December 2, 1993: 8.

HANDSOME BUGGA PRODUCTIONS
— to host surf contest, Lahaina News, June 17, 1999: 7.

HANEGRAAFF, HENDRICK "HANK"
— host of "Bible Answer Man" to speak, Lahaina News, June 15, 1995: 2.

HANEY, ROB [COMEDIAN]
— to perform at Comedy Club and the Sports Page, Lahaina News, April 3, 1991: 7,8.

HANGER, BARBARA
— designer at Island Design Center featured, Lahaina News, April 18, 2002: 7.

HANKS, SHELDON
— raises most money for American Heart Association in jump rope event, Lahaina News, May 15, 1991: 5.

HANLEY, PAUL
— appointed general manager of Hyatt Regency Maui, Lahaina News, July 30, 1986: 3.

HANLEY, TERRY
— recognized as "Manager of the Second quarter" at Westin Maui, Lahaina News, August 27, 1992: 11.
— selected manager of the quarter at Westin Maui, Lahaina News, September 10, 1992: 9.

HANLON, MARION
— Maui Memorial Hospital celebrates doctor's retirement, Lahaina News, March 12, 1998: 11.

HANNA, JACK
— to tape "Jack Hanna's Animal Adventures" at Whalers Village Center Stage, Lahaina News, February 24, 2000: 14.

HANNAHS, NEIL
— to discuss lands mauka of Lahaina Town at Lahaina Restoration Foundation's annual meeting, Lahaina News, April 25, 2002: 1.

HANNAY, JACK
— tapes "Jack Hanna's Animal Adventure" at Whalers Village, Lahaina News, March 9, 2000: 1.

HANNEMANN, MUFI [POLITICIAN]
— Congressional candidate to visit Maui , Lahaina News, August 29, 1990: 4.
— State Director of Business/Economic Development and Tourism speaks to business and visitor industry leaders, Lahaina News, July 1, 1993: 7.

HANNEMANN, NEPI [ENTERTAINER]
— to headline show at Ka'anapali Beach Hotel, Lahaina News, July 4, 1984: 7.

HANNES, JAMES
— to operate show and luggage repair shop, Lahaina News, March 19, 1992: 10.

HANO, WILLIAM
— killed in Puamana Park, Lahaina News, July 1, 1982: 7.

HANSEL AND GRETEL [PLAY]
— to be performed by Maui Theatre, Inc., Lahaina News, December 19, 1991: 19,20,22.

HANSEN, DIANA [POLITICIAN]
— state representative calls for investigation of Hawaiian Homes Commission, Lahaina Sun, November 10, 1971: 14.
— negative reaction to state representative's call to investigate Hawaiian Homes Commission, Lahaina Sun, November 24, 1971: 6.

HANSEN, JAMES
— to present "Diabetes Research Update", Lahaina News, April 27, 2000: 13.

HANSEN, SUSAN MCGOVNEY [ARTIST]
— work displayed at Village Gallery, Lahaina News, October 14, 1987: 17.

HANSEN, TOM
— member of Lahaina Kamaakina Fishing Association, Lahaina Sun, December 23, 1970: 11.

HANSON GALLERIES
— plan to renovate, Lahaina News, June 28, 1989: 7.

HANSON, HAROLD "HAL"
— doctor becomes associated with West Maui Healthcare Center, Lahaina News, January 16, 1991: 3.

HANSON, SCOTT [ARTIST]
— Lahainaluna High School basketball player featured, Lahaina News, December 7, 1983: 4.
— to visit Wyland Gallery, Lahaina News, April 22, 1999: 12.

HANUKKAH
— to be celebrated at Four Seasons Hotel, Lahaina News, December 17, 1998: 24.

HAOLE
— discussion of the word, Part I, Lahaina News, January 17, 2002: 9.
— discussion of the word, Part II, Lahaina News, January 24, 2002: 5.

HAPA [MUSICAL GROUP]
— interviewed, Lahaina News, November 7, 1984: 17.
— appearing at El Crab Catcher, Ka'anapali, Lahaina News, December 5, 1984: 21.
— performance reviewed, Lahaina News, May 1, 1985: 10.
— moved from El Crab Catcher to Westin Maui, Lahaina News, January 20, 1988: 8.
— reviewed, Lahaina News, October 5, 1988: 9.
— to perform at Whale's Tale, Lahaina News, July 11, 1990: 18.
— to perform at Kobe's Japanese Steak House, Lahaina News, July 18, 1991: 9.
— to perform with the Doobie Brothers, Lahaina News, February 24, 1994: 11.
— success at Hoku Hanohano Awards, Lahaina News, May 19, 1994: 14,15.
— to perform at Maui Marriott, Lahaina News, June 9, 1994: 16.
— to perform, Lahaina News, June 16, 1994: 11.
— to perform, Lahaina News, June 23, 1994: 11.
— to hold benefit concert for Maria Lanakila Church, Lahaina News, September 29, 1994: 11.
— to perform at Kobe Japanese Steak House, Lahaina News, October 20, 1994: 16.
— performs at benefit concert for Bobbie Rocha, Lahaina News, November 3, 1994: 25.
— to perform at Maui Marriott Grand Ballroom, Lahaina News, December 14, 1995: 14.
— to perform at opening of Sam Choy restaurant, Lahaina News, January 22, 1998: 12,13.
— to perform at Island Harvest and Hukilau, Lahaina News, May 28, 1998: 13.
— to perform at A Taste of Lahaina, Lahaina News, September 10, 1998: 16.
— to perform at "Music on the Beach", Lahaina News, December 17, 1998: 21.
— to perform at "Music on the Beach", Lahaina News, December 24, 1998: 7.
— to perform at benefit concert for Montessori schools, Lahaina News, February 15, 2001: 16.

HAPA'S [RESTAURANT]
— to hold ballroom dance classes, Lahaina News, March 5, 1998: 16.
— to offer beginning Tango class, Lahaina News, April 24, 2003: 21.
— to hold New York Style Hustle and Dance Party, Lahaina News, June 5, 2003: 17.

HAPPY DAYS CAFE [BUSINESS]
— reviewed, Lahaina News, July 2, 1986: 7.
— reviewed, Lahaina News, January 6, 1988: 8.

HAPPY DAZE [MUSICAL]
— to be performed by Theatre Theatre Maui, Lahaina News, June 6, 2002: 14.
— to be performed by Theatre Theatre Maui, Lahaina News, July 25, 2002: 17.

HAPPY TIME SINGERS [MUSICAL GROUP]
— group forming for singers, Lahaina News, February 28, 2002: 16.
— to perform at Lahaina Methodist Church, Lahaina News, April 4, 2002: 16.
— to perform at Lahaina Methodist Church, Lahaina News, May 2, 2002: 16.

HARADA, DAVID
— memorial service held for Lahaina United Methodist Church reverend, Lahaina News, September 5, 1996: 18.

HARADA, NAOYUKI [MUSICIAN]
— to perform at Maui Arts and Cultural Center, Lahaina News, February 24, 2000: 16.

HARAGA, RODNEY
— Representative Roz Baker to meet with State Director of Transportation, Lahaina News, June 19, 2003: 3.
— director of the State Department of Transportation discusses improvements to transportation, Lahaina News, July 3, 2003: 1,18.

HARANO, TETSUO
— discusses Maui Electric Company's new transmission line, Lahaina Sun, January 20, 1971: 8.
— discusses power poles running along highway, Lahaina Sun, February 3, 1971: 1.
— chief of State Highways division says plans to develop are moving forward, tied to airstrip purchase, Lahaina News, January 16, 1991: 1.
— discusses need for consultant for proposed Kihei-Upcountry road , Lahaina News, June 11, 1992: 9.

HARBOR REUNION PARTY
— described, Lahaina News, December 16, 1993: 3.

HARBOR VILLAGE
— request to demolish existing structures under consideration, Lahaina News, January 11, 2001: 1,15.
— proposal to replace cleared by Maui Planning Commission, Lahaina News, January 18, 2001: 1,15.
— County Council Committee on Public Works to visit, Lahaina News, May 24, 2001: 22.

HARBOR VILLAGE SHOPPING CENTER
— Lyons Naona III discusses proposed development, Lahaina News, October 14, 1999: 1.

HARBORFRONT [RESTAURANT]
— reviewed, Lahaina News, December 7, 1988: 10.
— reviewed, Lahaina News, March 8, 1989: 7.
— reviewed, Lahaina News, December 15, 1981: 5,7.
— changes to menu reviewed, Lahaina News, August 1, 1982: 5.
— reviewed, Lahaina News, October 15, 1982: 4.
— reviewed, Lahaina News, August 15, 1983: 14,15.

HARBORS DISTRICT
— William Anonsen becomes engineer, Lahaina News, June 19, 1997: 15.

HARBORS DIVISION, STATE
— having wooden wharf built around small boat harbor, Lahaina Sun, November 11, 1970: 4.
— warns against people living on boats in Lahaina harbor, Lahaina Sun, December 30, 1970: 4.
— to dredge Lahaina Boat Harbor, Lahaina News, May 11, 1988: 3.
— blamed for sewage dump in Lahaina Harbor, Lahaina News, August 8, 1991: 1.

HARBOTTLE, TOMMAY
— Parent Community Network Center (PCNC) featured, Lahaina News, August 21, 2003: 1.

HARBOUR, JAMES
— to play "Scrooge" in Maui Academy of Performing Arts musical, Lahaina News, November 28, 1990: 9.

HARD DAY'S NIGHT, A [FILM]
— to be shown at Maui Arts and Cultural Center, Lahaina News, February 1, 2001: 21.

HARD DRIVE [MUSICAL GROUP]
— to perform at World Café, Lahaina News, July 18, 1996: 12.

HARD ROCK CAFE [RESTAURANT]
— to open, Lahaina News, January 10, 1990: 6.
— to open on July 4th, Lahaina News, March 28, 1990: 7.
— to hold grand opening to benefit American Cancer Society, Lahaina News, June 13, 1990: 18.
— opening celebration described, Lahaina News, June 27, 1990: 10.
— details on opening, Lahaina News, July 4, 1990: 18.
— opening next week, Lahaina News, July 18, 1990: 11.
— starts recycling, Lahaina News, July 25, 1990: 1,2.
— to hold Thanksgiving dinner for homeless and elderly, Lahaina News, November 7, 1991: 19.
— to sponsor World Cup of Surfing, Lahaina News, December 5, 1991: 19.
— to host World Cup of Windsurfing, Lahaina News, March 12, 1992: 10.
— to hold Rock 'n Roll 10K Run, Lahaina News, June 1, 1995: 6.
— 10K run held, Lahaina News, June 8, 1995: 1.
— to host 10K run, Lahaina News, May 23, 1996: 2.
— to host 10K run, Lahaina News, May 30, 1996: 2.
— Scott Jenkins wins Rock 'n Roll 10K run, Lahaina News, June 6, 1996: 16.
— to host Rock 'n Roll 10K run, Lahaina News, May 29, 1997: 16.
— holds Christmas party for Big Brothers/Big Sisters, Lahaina News, January 1, 1998: 7.
— selling tickets to Hooters Hula Bowl, Lahaina News, January 15, 1998: 7.
— to hold "Save Ma'alaea Benefit", Lahaina News, February 4, 1999: 16.
— to host fundraiser for Surfrider Foundation, Lahaina News, November 9, 2000: 7.
— to host Yu-Gi-Oh event to support Big Brothers/Big /Sisters of Maui, Lahaina News, April 3, 2003: 3.

HARDCASTLE, HAROLD
— owner of "The Bakery" featured, Lahaina News, August 1, 1991: 6.
— receives Valley Isle Business Award, Lahaina News, October 17, 1996: 1,20.

HARDEN, HEATHER
— Morgan Stanley Dean Witter financial advisor to speak, Lahaina News, August 31, 2000: 14.

HARDER, M.J. [WRITER]
— publishes book "Maui Magic, The Best of the Island" with Jill Engeldow, Lahaina News, December 30, 1987: 3.

HARDWICK, DICK [COMEDIAN]
— to perform at Comedy Club, Lahaina News, January 3, 1990: 16.

HARE KRISHNA
— criticized in letter to the editor, Lahaina Sun, February 24, 1971: 8.
— granted permit to operate in Banyan Tree, Lahaina News, February 6, 1991: 1.

HARIMA, SYLVIA
— awarded Hawaii Hotel Association Employee of the Year Award, Lahaina News, May 2, 1990: 4.

HARI'S KITCHEN [TELEVISION SHOW]
— local chefs featured, Lahaina News, September 1, 1994: 15.

HARLEM GLOBETROTTERS
— to play at Lahaina Civic Center, Lahaina News, October 3, 1991: 8.
— to perform, Lahaina News, October 10, 1991: 8.

HARLEY-DAVIDSON
— general merchandise creative director Karen Davidson reports new store to open in Maui, Lahaina News, May 10, 2001: 9.

HARMON ARCHITECTS, INC. [BUSINESS]
— opens at Napili Plaza, Lahaina News, March 1, 2001: 8.

HARMON, DENNIS
— contributing to success of Lahainaluna High School football , Lahaina News, September 11, 2003: 12.

HARMON, JEFF
— won contest to predict winner of Isuzu Kapalua International golf tournament, Lahaina News, November 27, 1985: 4.

HARMONIC CONVERGENCE
— ceremonies to be held, Lahaina News, August 12, 1987: 3.
— media said to misunderstand event, Lahaina News, September 30, 1987: 16.

HARP, ISAAC
— local fisherman drafts Northwest Hawaiian Islands Management Plan, Lahaina News, August 17, 2000: 1,20.

HARP, ISAAC AND TAMMY
— to discuss fishing issues, Lahaina News, November 18, 1999: 17.
— dedication to protecting ocean resources featured, Lahaina News, December 2, 1999: 1,2.

HARRIMAN ESTATE
— possible sale of discussed, Lahaina News, August 5, 1993: 2.

HARRIS COLLECTION [BUSINESS]
— art gallery opens, Lahaina News, January 13, 1988: 16.

HARRIS, HARRIET
— Kihei Youth Center executive director to resign, Lahaina News, October 21, 1993: 7.

HARRIS, JIM
— project manager at The Vintage at Ka'anapali, Lahaina News, May 18, 2000: 10.

HARRIS, MONA [ARTIST]
— to exhibit for Lahaina Arts Gallery at the Old Jail Gallery, Lahaina News, October 27, 1994: 17.
— to exhibit at The Art Center of Maui, Lahaina News, September 24, 1998: 13.
— to exhibit at the Art School at Kapalua, Lahaina News, October 26, 2000: 13.
— to hold exhibit "Off the Beaten Path" at the Art School at Kapalua, Lahaina News, November 2, 2000: 24.

HARRIS, RALPH [COMEDIAN]
— to perform at Comedy Club and the Sports Page, Lahaina News, January 28, 1993: 13,14.

HARRIS, REED
— to discuss "Mary Baker Eddy and the Mind/Body Connection", Lahaina News, March 16, 2000: 13.

HARRIS, WALT [ARTIST]
— to exhibit at Ramsay Galleries and Cafe, Lahaina News, January 13, 1994: 8.

HARRISON [SHIP]
— logbook acquired for display at Whaler's Village, Lahaina Sun, December 16, 1970: 5.

HARRISON, BOB [MUSICIAN]
— to perform at Blackie's Bar, Lahaina News, March 20, 1991: 9.

HARRISON, GAVIN
— to speak to Maui's Gay Asian Pacific Islander Support Network, Lahaina News, November 15, 2001: 17.

HARRISON, JOE
— doctor is retiring from Maui Medical Group, Lahaina News, May 20, 1999: 13.
— recently retired doctor featured, Lahaina News, January 11, 2001: 1,15.

HARRY AND JEANETTE WEINBERG FAMILY CENTER
— new Maui Economic Opportunity Inc. headquarters to be dedicated, Lahaina News, August 5, 1999: 11.

HARRY AND JEANETTE WEINBERG FOUNDATION
— established, Lahaina News, November 14, 1990: 11.
— gives grant to Maui Arts and Cultural Center, Lahaina News, November 17, 1994: 6.
— gives grant to Hawaii Special Olympics, Lahaina News, December 14, 1995: 19.
— construction retail center at former Cabanilla Lahaina Shell, Lahaina News, June 28, 2001: 9.

HARRY AND MYRA [TELEVISION PERSONALITIES]
— to read at Kahului Library, Lahaina News, October 29, 1992: 7.
— to read at Kahului Library, Lahaina News, November 5, 1992: 5.

HARRY'S SUSHI BAR [RESTAURANT]
— opens, Lahaina News, June 11, 1992: 13.

HARRY'S SUSHI BAR AND PUPU BAR [RESTAURANT]
— to open in Napili Shores Resort, Lahaina News, November 18, 1993: 7.

HART, CHRIS
— member of Maui Planning Department speaks of Higgins Maddigan's reprimand for tearing down an old building, Lahaina Sun, December 16, 1970: 2.
— member of Maui Planning Department discusses creation of "Brick Palace" exhibit, Lahaina Sun, December 16, 1970: 6.
— member of Maui Planning Department discusses need for clear rules for signage, Lahaina Sun, January 20, 1971: 1.
— member of Maui Planning Department assumes expanded duties at the Maui Historic Commission, Lahaina Sun, September 15, 1971: 1.
— county planner at Maui Planning Department advocates for advanced for Lahaina, Lahaina Sun, April 18, 1973: 4.
— County Planning Director discusses future of Lahaina, Lahaina News, April 2, 1986: 1,16.
— Planning Director discusses Maui Planning Commissions decision to deny request to build heliport, Lahaina News, August 13, 1986: 16.
— opposes proposed halt to development , Lahaina News, January 21, 1987: 9.
— Maui County Planning Director calls for control rather than moratorium, Lahaina News, May 13, 1987: 1,2.
— speaks of decision to evict Lahaina Arts Society from Old Lahaina Courthouse, Lahaina News, January 27, 1988: 1.
— comments on construction at Hale Aloha, Lahaina News, February 17, 1988: 17.
— discusses Kapalua Land Company's new hotel development, Lahaina News, June 15, 1988: 1.
— discusses possible conversion of apartments to hotel rooms at Holo Honokowai, Lahaina News, September 14, 1988: 1,14.
— Maui planning director criticizes Ocean Recreation Management Plan, Lahaina News, November 23, 1988: 1,16.
— Maui Planning director critical of conversion of Holo Honokowai to hotel, Lahaina News, November 30, 1988: 1.
— editorial in support of, Lahaina News, November 30, 1988: 4.
— Maui Planning Director comments on fate of Native Hawaiian remains found in Kapalua, Lahaina News, December 28, 1988: 1,20.
— to speak at pro-life rally, Lahaina News, January 18, 1989: 3,5.
— critical of state Legislature for lack of facilities in West Maui, Lahaina News, July 5, 1989: 1.
— Maui County Planning Director opposes mayor Linda Lingle's idea of hotel development moratorium, Lahaina News, November 28, 1990: 1.
— to speak at conference on assisted living, Lahaina News, June 27, 1996: 15.

HART, ED [COMEDIAN]
— to perform at Comedy Club and the Sports Page, Lahaina News, January 9, 1992: 10.
— to perform at Comedy Club and the Sports Page, Lahaina News, December 31, 1992: 12,14.

HART, FREDDY
— Scholar/Athlete of the Week, Lahaina News, March 14, 2002: 12.

HART, FREDERICK [ARTIST]
— memorial held for, Lahaina News, October 12, 2000: 18.

HART, MATTHEW
— promoted to manager of The Westin Hotel, Lahaina News, September 19, 1991: 6.
— named general manager of Westin Maui, Lahaina News, February 22, 1996: 11.

HART, MYRNA
— joins law firm Tateishi and Apo, Lahaina News, October 31, 1991: 10.

HARTFORD BALLET
— to perform, Lahaina News, September 28, 1988: 18.

HARTMAN, ROBERT
— arrested for brandishing a weapon, Lahaina Sun, September 1, 1971: 15.
— pleads no contest to disorderly conduct charge, Lahaina Sun, October 27, 1971: 14.

HARTOG, EVA DEN
— major in Salvation Army to speak at Lahaina Methodist Church, Lahaina News, April 15, 1981: 15.

HARVANCHIK, MICHAEL
— named sales and marketing manager at Ka'anapali Estate Coffee, Lahaina News, May 18, 2000: 16.

HARVEST CHAPEL-CHURCH OF GOD
— Tom Arledge new pastor at, Lahaina News, March 27, 1991: 3.
— to hold benefit concert with Bob Whalley, Lahaina News, April 20, 1995: 6.
— to offer training on computers, Lahaina News, February 26, 1998: 13.
— continues to offer computer training, Lahaina News, March 19, 1998: 12.
— continues to offer computer training, Lahaina News, April 23, 1998: 17.

HARVEST CRUSADES, THE
— Greg Laurie to speak to, Lahaina News, July 17, 2003: 1,20.

HARVEST FESTIVAL
— to be held, Lahaina News, October 19, 1995: 4.
— to be held at Lahaina United Methodist Church, Lahaina News, October 14, 1999: 5.
— to be held by Kumulani Chapel, Lahaina News, October 24, 2002: 21.

HARVEY MANDEL AND HIS ELECTRIC SNAKE BAND [MUSICAL GROUP]
— to perform at World Cafe, Lahaina News, July 10, 1997: 18.

HARVEY, STEVE [COMEDIAN]
— to perform at Comedy Club and the Sports Page, Lahaina News, November 7, 1990: 10,11.

HARVIS CONSTRUCTION
— building Mana Kai condominium in Kihei, Lahaina Sun, September 15, 1971: 5.

HASEGAWA, FLORENCE
— awarded Outstanding Older Americans, Lahaina News, May 3, 2001: 1,22.

HASEGAWA, GEORGE
— retired judge in hospital, Lahaina Sun, November 24, 1971: 1.
— retired judge given medical treatment in Honolulu, Lahaina Sun, December 22, 1971: 13.
— retired judge passed away at Maui Memorial Hospital, Lahaina Sun, May 24, 1972: 10.

HASELHOFF, DAVID [ACTOR]
— donates autographed pair of trunks from "Baywatch" to Planet Hollywood, Lahaina News, April 25, 1996: 7.

HASHIMOTO, JASON
— appointed Maui station manager for Aloha Airlines, Lahaina News, May 23, 1990: 8.

HASHIRO, BRIAN
— Maui County engineer discusses concerns with Pu'unene landfill, Lahaina News, April 18, 1990: 1,4.

HASHIRO, RALPH
— named deputy director of the county's Public Works Department, Lahaina News, July 10, 1985: 3.

HASSELBACH, MARK [MUSICIAN]
— to perform at Maui Arts and Cultural Center; to appear at Borders Books, Lahaina News, April 13, 2000: 12.

HASTINGS, SANDY
— working with Royal Keiki Tennis Club, Lahaina News, August 14, 1985: 4.

HATANO, YASUJI
— creates KM Hatano Scholarship Fund, Lahaina News, July 22, 1987: 3.

HATCH, AARIKA
— Scholar/Athlete of the Week, Lahaina News, October 10, 2002: 12.

HATCH, ALISE
— Scholar/Athlete of the Week, Lahaina News, October 31, 2002: 10.

HATCH, RICHARD [ACTOR]
— to present workshops on creativity, Lahaina News, July 11, 1990: 4.
— to speak to Ohana Luncheon and Trade Faire, Lahaina News, May 30, 1991: 3.
— to teach women's workshop "Reclaiming Your Power", Lahaina News, June 13, 1991: 16.
— to take place in stage performance, Lahaina News, June 20, 1991: 11,12.
— to offer theatre workshops, Lahaina News, May 26, 1994: 16.
— to head workshop "Acting from the Heart: Connection Passion, Mission and Power", Lahaina News, May 23, 2002: 2.
— visits West Maui Boys and Girls Club, Lahaina News, July 11, 2002: 18.

HATCHER, TERI [ACTOR]
— to perform in "The Vagina Monologues", Lahaina News, May 22, 2003: 14.
— to perform in "The Vagina Monologues", Lahaina News, May 29, 2003: 16.

HATTER, DIANNA
— Salvation Army Envoy speaks about homeless problem, Lahaina News, July 23, 1992: 3.

HATTON, BERT
— named vice-president of land administration for Amfac Hawaii, Inc, Lahaina News, March 16, 1988: 3.
— appointed vice president, sugar at Amfac, Inc., Lahaina News, November 15, 1989: 9.

HAUKALOA, WILLIE [MUSICIAN]
— to perform at Moose McGillycuddy's, Lahaina News, December 12, 1991: 20.
— to perform at Moose McGillycuddy's, Lahaina News, December 19, 1991: 19.

HAUPT, PRENTISS CARL
— member of Vietnam Veterans of Maui County speaks about cuts to disability benefits, Lahaina News, May 23, 1990: 1,6.

HAUPU, HILARY [LANCE CORPORAL]
— returns from Persian Gulf, Lahaina News, April 10, 1991: 4.

HAUSWIRTH, MICHAEL
— passes away, Lahaina News, August 26, 1999: 14.

HAUTZIG, WALTER [MUSICIAN]
— piano recital at Baldwin Auditorium, Lahaina Sun, April 21, 1971: 2.

HAU'ULA [MUSICAL GROUP]
— to perform at Gabel's, Lahaina News, March 13, 1991: 9.
— to perform at "Music on the Beach", Lahaina News, November 19, 1998: 17.

HAVENS, RICHIE [MUSICIAN]
— to perform at Casanova's, Lahaina News, January 23, 1992: 22.

HAWAII ADVANCED BUILDING TECHNOLOGY PROGRAM
— to present workshop on efficiency, Lahaina News, February 18, 1999: 11.

HAWAII AMATEUR SURFING ASSOCIATION QUIKSILVER SURFER CONTEST
— to be held, Lahaina News, February 19, 1998: 12.

HAWAII ARMED FORCES LEAGUE
— report on basketball league results, Lahaina Sun, January 20, 1971: 7.

HAWAII ARMY NATIONAL GUARD
— to use Ukumehame Firing Range, Lahaina News, September 7, 1988: 1.

HAWAII ARTISAN EVENTS
— to be held at Wailea Beach Resort to support Maui Food Bank, Lahaina News, August 8, 2002: 17.

HAWAII ASSOCIATION FOR THE EDUCATION OF YOUNG CHILDREN (HAEYC)
— Carole Enmark appointed child-care coordinator for, Lahaina News, January 30, 1992: 3.
— Maui chapter to meet, Lahaina News, October 29, 1992: 3,4.
— hosts Children's Fair at Lahaina Cannery Mall, Lahaina News, November 5, 1992: 3,4.
— to host Children's Fair, Lahaina News, January 13, 1994: 2.
— sponsoring Children's Fair, Lahaina News, December 29, 1994: 2.
— to hold Children's Fair at Lahaina Cannery Mall, Lahaina News, July 16, 1998: 17.
— to hold Children's Fair, Lahaina News, July 23, 1998: 16.
— to hold Children's Fair, Lahaina News, April 22, 1999: 12.
— to hold Children's Fair, Lahaina News, January 24, 2002: 3.
— to hold Children's Fair, Lahaina News, January 9, 2003: 16.

HAWAII ASSOCIATION OF PUBLIC WORKS
— mayor Linda Lingle to speak at conference of, Lahaina News, May 15, 1991: 8.

HAWAII ASSOCIATION OF REALTORS
— to hold realtor course, Lahaina News, November 1, 1989: 8.
— names Thomas Bodden realtor of the year, Lahaina News, November 7, 1990: 7,8.
— announces officers and directors, Lahaina News, November 28, 1990: 8.
— to offer courses for realtors, Lahaina News, February 6, 1991: 7.
— to sponsor seminar on 1991 Legislative update, Lahaina News, June 13, 1991: 10.
— annual convention to be held at Ritz-Carlton Mauna Lani, Lahaina News, July 11, 1991: 6.
— registration opens for state convention, Lahaina News, August 15, 1991: 7.
— to offer course for realtors, Lahaina News, February 13, 1992: 13.
— to hold 1992 state convention at the Maui Inter-Continental Hotel Wailea, Lahaina News, March 26, 1992: 11.
— offering realtor class, Lahaina News, April 9, 1992: 13.
— to hold seminar on upcoming legislative session, Lahaina News, June 11, 1992: 14.

HAWAII ASSOCIATION OF THE BLIND
— fundraising to support services, Lahaina News, November 1, 1989: 6.

HAWAII AUDUBON SOCIETY
— sues Air Force over laser experiment, Lahaina News, January 6, 1988: 3.

HAWAII BALLROOM DANCE ASSOCIATION
— to offer dance lessons, Lahaina News, January 3, 1990: 16.
— to host Fall dance at Grand Hyatt Wailea, featuring Maui County Dance Band, Lahaina News, October 10, 1991: 21.
— West Maui Chapter to hold event, Lahaina News, July 15, 1999: 1,16.
— continues to teach ballroom dancing, Lahaina News, September 30, 1999: 12.
— continues to meet, Lahaina News, October 14, 1999: 13.
— to hold "Winter Ball", Lahaina News, January 6, 2000: 12.
— to teach ballroom dancing, Lahaina News, March 16, 2000: 13.
— continues to hold ballroom dancing lessons, Lahaina News, April 20, 2000: 16.
— continues to offer classes, Lahaina News, November 16, 2000: 16.
— to hold New Year's Eve Dance Party at Kihei Community Center, Lahaina News, December 28, 2000: 16.
— to hold Valentine's Day ball, Lahaina News, February 8, 2001: 18.
— offering classes, Lahaina News, March 29, 2001: 14.
— begins dance classes at the Lahaina Civic Center, Lahaina News, June 28, 2001: 17.
— to hold ball, Lahaina News, September 27, 2001: 14.
— to hold "Red, White and Blue" social dance, Lahaina News, June 27, 2002: 17.
— to hold Anniversary Ball, Lahaina News, August 15, 2002: 17.
— to hold Holiday Ball, Lahaina News, November 28, 2002: 14.
— to hold Holiday Ball, Lahaina News, December 5, 2002: 21.
— to hold "Spring Ball" fundraiser for American Lung Association, Lahaina News, February 27, 2003: 9.

HAWAII BLOOD BANK
— to hold blood drive, Lahaina News, July 28, 1994: 4.

HAWAI'I BOATER'S HURRICANE MANUAL
— published by Sea Grant College Program, Lahaina News, June 18, 1998: 15.

HAWAII BONE MARROW DONOR REGISTRY
— encouraging public to attend drive, Lahaina News, January 21, 1999: 12.
— to be held, Lahaina News, August 9, 2001: 2.

HAWAII BRASS ENSEMBLE
— performing at Baldwin High School, Lahaina Sun, March 17, 1971: 1.

HAWAII BUSINESS [BUSINESS]
— magazine evaluates mayor Cravalho, Lahaina Sun, September 8, 1971: 4.
— magazine praises developments in Maui, Lahaina Sun, September 6, 1972: 21.
— publishes survival guide for small businesses, Lahaina News, June 28, 1989: 7.

HAWAII BUSINESS PUBLICATIONS CORPORATION [BUSINESS]
— to produce Hawaiian Airlines' monthly magazine, Lahaina News, September 12, 1990: 10.

HAWAII CALLS
— old episodes of radio show to be aired on KPOA-FM, Lahaina News, April 16, 1992: 4.
— radio show to be recorded at Ka'anapali Beach Hotel, Lahaina News, April 1, 1993: 11.
— to broadcast from Maui Inter-Continental Hula Moons, Lahaina News, October 14, 1993: 15.

HAWAII CANCER INFORMATION SERVICE
— offers free comic book explaining dangers of sun exposure, Lahaina News, June 12, 1985: 3.
— publishes free diet book, Lahaina News, July 10, 1985: 3.

HAWAII CAPITAL LOAN PROGRAM
— offering loans to small businesses, Lahaina News, March 26, 1986: 3.

HAWAII CARPENTERS UNION
— form informational picket lines in front of Ritz-Charlton, Lahaina News, September 2, 1993: 2.

HAWAII CATTLEMEN'S COUNCIL
— accepting scholarship applications, Lahaina News, May 24, 2001: 8.

HAWAII CHAMBER OF COMMERCE
— seeking to reduce cost to workers compensation, Lahaina News, January 27, 1994: 5.

HAWAII CHAMBER ORCHESTRA
— to perform Bach and Handel, Lahaina News, June 5, 1985: 8.

HAWAII CHILDREN'S CAMPAIGN
— honors people and groups who advocate for children and youth, Lahaina News, October 24, 1996: 2.

HAWAII CHRISTIAN LEADERS EVENT
— to be held, Lahaina News, January 28, 1999: 11.

HAWAII CITIZEN AMBASSADORS
— to visit the Soviet Union, Lahaina News, December 17, 1986: 2.

HAWAII COFFEE ASSOCIATION
— to offer coffee workshop with Culinary Arts Department at Maui Community College, Lahaina News, July 17, 2003: 8.

HAWAII COMMITTEE FOR THE HUMANITIES
— awards grant to Lahainaluna Hawaiiana Club, Lahaina News, April 15, 1981: 14.
— to hold public meeting, Lahaina News, September 12, 1996: 15.

HAWAII COMMUNITY FOUNDATION
— gives grant to Maui Economic Development Board (MEDB), Lahaina News, September 25, 1997: 12.
— to hold grant proposal writing workshop, Lahaina News, September 30, 1999: 11.
— to hold meeting to explain Neighborhood Grants Program, Lahaina News, October 7, 1999: 3.
— to hold informational meeting, Lahaina News, October 21, 1999: 14.
— sponsoring Community Voices Project to seek community input on proposed change to student drop-off system, Lahaina News, February 10, 2000: 3.
— offers travel funds for non-profits, Lahaina News, June 29, 2000: 7.
— sponsoring workshops on fundraising, Lahaina News, February 15, 2001: 8.
— to hold meeting on accessing tobacco settlement funding, Lahaina News, March 22, 2001: 2.
— opens office in Maui, Lahaina News, September 13, 2001: 2.
— to offer "Fund-raising Basics: How to Create or Expand an Individual Donor Base", Lahaina News, July 11, 2002: 9.
— to offer workshop on encouraging estate gifts, Lahaina News, September 12, 2002: 2.
— local nonprofit organizations receive grants from, Lahaina News, October 17, 2002: 16.
— to offer grants to community groups, Lahaina News, April 3, 2003: 8.

HAWAII CONGRESS OF PLANNING OFFICIALS
— to hold annual conference at Maui Inter-Continental Wailea, Lahaina News, September 14, 1988: 14.
— to hold conference, Lahaina News, July 15, 1993: 6.
— Maui County to host conference, Lahaina News, October 2, 2003: 8.

HAWAII CONGRESS ON SMALL BUSINESS
— to be held, Lahaina News, October 12, 1995: 12.
— makes legislative recommendations, Lahaina News, January 18, 1996: 11.

HAWAII CONSORTIUM FOR THE ARTS
— to discuss Hawaii Arts Census, Lahaina News, June 22, 2000: 6.

HAWAII CORAL REEF NETWORK
— to meet, Lahaina News, September 26, 1996: 15.
— to discuss upcoming events, Lahaina News, October 3, 1996: 14.

HAWAII COUNCIL FOR THE HUMANITIES
— to hold workshop on grant writing, Lahaina News, August 1, 2002: 21.

HAWAII COUNCIL OF ENGINEERING SOCIETY
— awards Engineer of the Year to Airports Administrator Owen Miyamoto, Lahaina News, March 13, 1991: 7.

HAWAII CRAFTSMEN
— annual show to be juried by Mildred Constantine, Lahaina News, September 18, 1985: 3.
— jurying on Maui scheduled, Lahaina News, October 19, 1988: 14.
— to sponsor law and tax seminar for artists, Lahaina News, May 8, 1991: 4.

HAWAII CRAFTSMEN TRAVELING SHOW
— to exhibit at Lahaina Arts Society gallery, Lahaina News, June 12, 1985: 20.

HAWAII DENTAL ASSOCIATION
— officers elected, Lahaina News, July 4, 1990: 7.

HAWAII DISABILITY RIGHTS CENTER
— to hold meeting on disability rights, Lahaina News, July 10, 2003: 3.
— to hold public comment meeting on disability rights, Lahaina News, July 17, 2003: 17.

HAWAII DROUGHT COUNCIL
— drafting Hawaii Drought Plan, Lahaina News, August 3, 2000: 17.

HAWAII E-CHARTER
— online high school to debut next month, Lahaina News, July 26, 2001: 1,18.

HAWAII ELEGANCE FASHION SHOW
— to be held at Ka'anapali Beach Hotel, Lahaina News, November 11, 1987: 11.

HAWAII EMERGENCY LAULIMA PARTNERSHIP (HELP)
— James Apana reports on increases in direct crisis assistance to Maui County through, Lahaina News, December 27, 2001: 8.

HAWAII ESCROW AND TITLE INC. [BUSINESS]
— expanding, Lahaina News, September 27, 2001: 9.

HAWAII EXPERIENCE THEATRE
— opens, Lahaina News, April 20, 1988: 6.

HAWAII FARM BUREAU
— to hold growers' day, Lahaina News, March 18, 1999: 13.
— accepting scholarship applications, Lahaina News, May 24, 2001: 8.

HAWAII FASHION INDUSTRY ASSOCIATION
— names Hilo Hatties General Retailer of the Year, Lahaina News, August 1, 1991: 11.

HAWAII FEDERATION OF BUSINESS AND PROFESSIONAL WOMEN'S CLUBS
— hold annual convention at Maui Inter-Continental Hotel, Lahaina News, May 1, 1985: 8.
— Beverly Williams installed as president, Lahaina News, May 22, 1985: 3.
— to honor local businesses, Lahaina News, October 17, 1991: 9.
— awards "Employer of the Year" to Ka'anapali Beach Hotel , Lahaina News, November 7, 1991: 9.

HAWAII FEDERATION OF DEMOCRATIC WOMEN
— publishing cookbook, Lahaina News, September 23, 1993: 3.
— to hold first meeting, Lahaina News, April 4, 2002: 2.

HAWAII FERTILITY SYMPOSIUM
— to be held, Lahaina News, September 4, 2003: 2.

HAWAII FLOWER AND PROTEA SHOW
— to be held, Lahaina News, April 9, 1998: 17.
— to be held at Lahaina Cannery Mall, Lahaina News, April 15, 1999:
12.

HAWAII FOOD INDUSTRY ASSOCIATION
— to hold convention at Maui Marriott, Lahaina News, June 4, 1992:
9.
— to hold convention, Lahaina News, June 11, 1992: 14.
— to hold convention, Lahaina News, June 18, 1992: 11.

HAWAII GOLF COURSE ACTION ALLIANCE
— invites National Network Against Resort and Golf Course Development, Japanese anti-golf course group visits Maui, Lahaina News,
January 30, 1992: 5.

HAWAII GOVERNMENT EMPLOYEES ASSOCIATION
— seeking to represent state's policemen, Lahaina Sun, December 16,
1970: 1.
— organizing Great Maui Ice Cream Festival, Lahaina News, May 24,
1989: 2.

HAWAII GROMS ASSOCIATION
— to show "Infamous" surfing film, Lahaina News, March 15, 2001:
20.

HAWAII GUITAR FESTIVAL
— to be held at the Maui Arts and Cultural Center, Lahaina News, June
16, 1994: 12.
— to be held at Maui Arts and Cultural Center, Lahaina News, June 15,
1995: 11.

HAWAII HAIR TRANSPLANT CENTER [BUSINESS]
— opens, Lahaina News, March 27, 1997: 10.

HAWAII HEALTH SYSTEMS CORP. [BUSINESS]
— seeks input on health services, Lahaina News, September 14, 2000:
16.
— seeking input on health services, Lahaina News, September 21, 2000:
2.

HAWAII HEART ASSOCIATION
— to hold fundraiser at Maui Marriott Ballroom, Lahaina News, May
16, 1984: 4.
— Maui chapter sponsoring M.G. Paschoal Memorial Fish for Heart
event, Lahaina News, May 23, 1984: 3.
— raises money jumping ropes, Lahaina News, April 22, 1987: 3.
— conducting CPR training, Lahaina News, August 19, 1987: 3.
— Golf Tournament to be held, Lahaina News, June 1, 1988: 19.

HAWAII HELICOPTERS [BUSINESS]
— acquires a new A-Star Jet Turbine Helicopter, Lahaina News, July 28,
1994: 9.
— new employees announced, Lahaina News, December 1, 1994: 13.
— submits proposal to change rules at Kapalua-West Maui Airport,
Lahaina News, April 13, 2000: 1,16.
— seeks permission to provide helicopter transportation from Kapalua-West Maui airport when emergency is declared, Lahaina News,
June 8, 2000: 1,6.
— begins Kapalua Circle Island tour, Lahaina News, February 8, 2001:
8.

HAWAII HERITAGE CENTER
— presenting "Myriad Worlds: 200 Years of the Chinese in Hawaii",
Lahaina News, April 12, 1989: 3.

HAWAII HIGH SCHOOL ATHLETIC ASSOCIATION
— Walter Chihara critical of, Lahaina News, February 12, 1998: 14.

HAWAII HISTORY DAY
— see History Day

HAWAII HORSESHOE PITCHERS ASSOCIATION
— tournament scheduled, Lahaina News, April 16, 1992: 10.

HAWAII HOTEL AND RESTAURANT EXPO
— to be held at Blaisdell Center, Lahaina News, July 1, 1999: 11.

HAWAII HOTEL ASSOCIATION
— Maui chapter sponsoring charity walk, Lahaina News, May 16, 1984:
5.
— announces organizations receiving charity, Lahaina News, October
24, 1984: 3.
— sponsoring Visitor Industry Charity Walk, Lahaina News, May 8,
1985: 3.
— Maui Chapter chooses "When you Come to Maui, Aloha Comes to
You" as slogan, Lahaina News, July 17, 1985: 3.
— Maui chapter elects Paul Peschiera as president, Lahaina News,
January 29, 1986: 3.
— donates money to West Maui Youth Center, Lahaina News, August
5, 1987: 3.
— sponsoring Visitor Industry Charity Walk, Lahaina News, April 26,
1989: 1.
— to host charity walk, Lahaina News, April 2, 1998: 2.
— Sandi Kato-Klutke installed as general manager, Lahaina News,
August 6, 1998: 17.
— to hold Charity Walk, Lahaina News, March 18, 1999: 13.
— awards hotel workers "Na Po'e Pa'ahana", Lahaina News, January 25,
2001: 14.
— names Kathleen Cummings Desk Person of the Year, Lahaina News,
February 28, 2002: 8.

HAWAII HOTEL ASSOCIATION
— Visitor Industry charity walk planned, Lahaina News, March 26,
1998: 2.

HAWAII HOTS [BUSINESS]
— featured, Lahaina News, December 7, 1983: 14.

HAWAII HOUSING AUTHORITY
— asks for proposals for building low-income homes, Lahaina Sun,
January 13, 1971: 4.
— participate in meeting on public housing, Lahaina Sun, March 24,
1971: 1.
— will work with Honolua Plantation Land Inc. to build low and moderate income homes, Lahaina Sun, November 3, 1971: 11.
— studying housing in West Maui, Lahaina News, September 16, 1987:
1,9.

HAWAII HURRICANE RELIEF FUND
— approves reduction in rates, Lahaina News, June 27, 1996: 12.

HAWAII IN STYLE [TELEVISION SHOW]
— to premiere, Lahaina News, November 8, 1989: 5.

HAWAII INNOVATIVE ENGINEERING, INC
— awarded contract to widen Honoapi'ilani Highway, Lahaina News,
September 7, 1988: 3.

HAWAI'I INSTITUTE FOR HUMAN RIGHTS
— to hold a seminar on Indigenous Peoples' Right sand Collection
Rights in International Human Rights, Lahaina News, June 6, 2002:
18.
— to hold Indigenous Peoples' Rights and Collective Rights in International Human Rights Law at Maui Community College, Lahaina
News, June 13, 2002: 2.

HAWAII INSURANCE BUREAU
— Hawaii State Insurance Commissioner Lawrence Reifurth delays decision on workers' compensation filings, Lahaina News, September 1,
1994: 12.

HAWAII INTERNATIONAL FILM FESTIVAL
— to be held at Hyatt Regency Maui, Lahaina News, November 20,
1985: 3.
— to be held, Lahaina News, December 2, 1987: 6,3.
— to show "Restless Natives" as fundraiser, Lahaina News, November
22, 1989: 4.
— running, Lahaina News, December 6, 1989: 15.

— opens, schedule listed, Lahaina News, November 28, 1990: 9.

— continues, schedule listed, Lahaina News, December 5, 1990: 9.

— to be held at Maui Inter-Continental Wailea, Lahaina News, October 17, 1991: 20.

— to host "Conference on Motion Picture Production, Co-financing—East and West", Lahaina News, November 14, 1991: 8.

— featuring documentary "Puamana" on the Farden family, Lahaina News, December 5, 1991: 20,21,22.

— schedule described, Lahaina News, December 5, 1991: 22.

— schedule listed, Lahaina News, December 12, 1991: 20.

— featured, Lahaina News, November 26, 1992: 24.

— details for, Lahaina News, December 3, 1992: 14.

— to host youth film contest, Lahaina News, December 31, 1992: 20.

— to be held, Lahaina News, April 15, 1993: 12.

— needs volunteers, Lahaina News, October 14, 1993: 14.

— seeking volunteers, Lahaina News, October 28, 1993: 10,11.

— schedule, Lahaina News, November 4, 1993: 11,12.

— announces new ticket distribution policy, Lahaina News, July 7, 1994: 14.

— to be held in November, Lahaina News, October 27, 1994: 17.

— details of, Lahaina News, November 3, 1994: 24.

— to be held, Lahaina News, July 18, 1996: 12.

— to be held, Lahaina News, November 14, 1996: 18.

— seeking volunteers, Lahaina News, October 30, 1997: 2.

— to be held, Lahaina News, November 12, 1998: 16.

— to be held, Lahaina News, November 9, 2000: 13.

— to be held at the Ritz-Carlton, Lahaina News, November 7, 2002: 18.

HAWAII INTERNATIONAL JAZZ FESTIVAL

— all-stars to perform at Lahaina Cannery Mall, Lahaina News, July 11, 2002: 17.

— to be held, Lahaina News, July 24, 2003: 14.

— see also Maui Jazz Festival

HAWAII ISLANDS HUMPBACK WHALE NATIONAL MARINE SANCTUARY

— NOAA to hold public meeting on, Lahaina News, March 11, 1993: 8.

HAWAII JEWELERS ASSOCIATION

— president Carl Bucky discusses jewelry industry, Lahaina News, December 13, 1989: 15,16,20.

HAWAII LAND REFORM ACT

— declared unconstitutional, Lahaina News, February 22, 1984: 17.

HAWAII LAWYERS CARE

— to host Neighborhood Legal Clinic, Lahaina News, July 20, 1995: 5.

— sponsoring Neighborhood Legal Clinic with Legal Aid Society, Lahaina News, September 21, 1995: 4.

HAWAII LONGBOARD SURFING ASSOCIATION

— competition scheduled, Lahaina News, April 16, 1992: 10.

HAWAII LUPUS FOUNDATION

— to host Dr. Michael Klaper, Lahaina News, October 23, 1997: 20.

— to begin monthly support meetings, Lahaina News, April 18, 2002: 2.

— to offer class, Lahaina News, January 30, 2003: 17.

— to offer course on "Advanced Directives", Lahaina News, February 6, 2003: 16.

HAWAII MAGAZINE

— names Ka'anapali Beach as "Maui's Best Beach", Lahaina News, July 1, 1999: 3.

HAWAII MATERIALS EXCHANGE

— to encourage reuse of material, Lahaina News, November 18, 1993: 6.

HAWAII MENTAL HEALTH ASSOCIATION

— begins plan to promote mental health, Lahaina Sun, October 11, 1972: 10.

HAWAII NATIONAL BANK

— giving golden dollar coin for new deposit account, Lahaina News, April 20, 2000: 13.

HAWAII NATURE CENTER

— featured, Lahaina News, January 16, 1992: 3.

— receives funds from Ronald McDonald Children Charities, Lahaina News, March 19, 1992: 6.

— sponsoring hike to Kapilau gorge, Lahaina News, April 9, 1992: 8.

— to hold Easter event, Lahaina News, April 16, 1992: 4.

— organizing Earth Day hike, Lahaina News, April 23, 1992: 8.

— to organize hike for Earth Day, Lahaina News, April 30, 1992: 4.

— organizing weekend hike [not all subsequent hikes are indexed], Lahaina News, May 7, 1992: 6.

— to hold Earth Day hike, Lahaina News, May 28, 1992: 9.

— to hold hike to Kipilau, Lahaina News, June 18, 1992: 4.

— to offer hike in Kapilau, Lahaina News, June 25, 1992: 2.

— to organize hike , Lahaina News, August 6, 1992: 3.

— to hold grand opening, Lahaina News, September 10, 1992: 4.

— organizing activities, Lahaina News, October 22, 1992: 4.

— continues to offer activities, not always indexed, Lahaina News, December 3, 1992: 3.

— continues to offer weekend activities, Lahaina News, February 4, 1993: 4.

— activities continue, Lahaina News, March 25, 1993: 4.

— continues to offer events, Lahaina News, June 24, 1993: 4.

— continues to hold activities, Lahaina News, February 24, 1994: 4.

— sponsoring "Enchanted Forest" fundraiser, Lahaina News, October 13, 1994: 18.

— hosting "Keiki Nature Adventures", Lahaina News, July 4, 1996: 15.

— to offer "Keiki Nature Adventures", Lahaina News, July 11, 1996: 13.

— continues to offer events for kids, Lahaina News, August 15, 1996: 14.

— to hold activities for kids, Lahaina News, November 7, 1996: 14,15.

— continues with Keiki Nature Activities, Lahaina News, December 5, 1996: 15.

— seeking exhibit interpreters, Lahaina News, June 12, 1997: 16.

— seeking volunteers to teach environmental education, Lahaina News, August 21, 1997: 9.

— to hold "Maui Spideriffic", Lahaina News, October 23, 1997: 20.

— offering "Slugfest", Lahaina News, December 18, 1997: 18.

— to hold family hike, Lahaina News, January 8, 1998: 12.

— to sponsor "Ways of Water", Lahaina News, March 12, 1998: 21.

— sponsoring "Wiggly Worms", Lahaina News, March 26, 1998: 12.

— to offer "Natural Egg Dyeing" workshop for children, Lahaina News, April 2, 1998: 17.

— to hold "Crusty Crustaceans", Lahaina News, April 30, 1998: 17.

— to hold "Prowling Predators" activity, Lahaina News, June 11, 1998: 16.

— to hold "Ants and Uncles" activity, Lahaina News, July 2, 1998: 17.

— to hold "Sensational Streamlife" activity for children, Lahaina News, July 30, 1998: 16.

— to hold teacher training, Lahaina News, August 13, 1998: 17.

— to hold "Dragonfly Flyers" activity, Lahaina News, February 4, 1999: 16.

— to hold "Pet Pictoglyphs" activity, Lahaina News, April 1, 1999: 16.

— planning Eco-Quest into Haleakala Crater, Lahaina News, May 20, 1999: 15.

— seeking volunteer teachers, Lahaina News, August 12, 1999: 8.

— planning "Petroglyph Rubbings", Lahaina News, September 2, 1999: 16.

— to hold "Delectable Dirt" activity, Lahaina News, November 4, 1999: 12.

— to hold "Iao Camp Over", Lahaina News, November 18, 1999: 16.

— to hold "Wild Wreaths" activity, Lahaina News, December 2, 1999: 17.

— to hold "Birding for Families", Lahaina News, December 9, 1999: 20.

— to hold "Bug Bash" activity, Lahaina News, January 13, 2000: 12.

— to hold "Forest Impressions" activity, Lahaina News, February 17, 2000: 16.

— to hold "Prowling Predators" activity, Lahaina News, March 16, 2000: 13.

— to celebrate Earth Day, Lahaina News, April 13, 2000: 13.

— to hold "Gooey, Goopy, Groovy Creations", Lahaina News, May 18, 2000: 20.

— to offer "Nature Rovers" activity, Lahaina News, June 1, 2000: 16.

— to hold "Daring Decomposers", Lahaina News, June 29, 2000: 20.

— to hold "Spideriffic", Lahaina News, July 13, 2000: 16.

— to hold "Nature Detectives" activity, Lahaina News, August 3, 2000: 16.

— recruiting part-time volunteer teachers, Lahaina News, August 10, 2000: 8.

— to hold "Bubblemania" activity, Lahaina News, August 17, 2000: 16.

— to hold "Bamboo Bounty", Lahaina News, May 17, 2001: 20.

— to hold "On the Go with H2O", Lahaina News, June 7, 2001: 21.

— recruiting volunteer tutors, Lahaina News, August 16, 2001: 2.

— begins Malama 'Aina program, Lahaina News, February 14, 2002: 8.

— working to restore taro patch, Lahaina News, April 18, 2002: 16.

— seeking volunteers, Lahaina News, September 19, 2002: 5.

— to host Kama'aina Appreciation Day, Lahaina News, November 21, 2002: 13.

— offering free admissions to Interactive Nature Museum to seniors, Lahaina News, December 26, 2002: 2.

— offering Senior Sundays, Lahaina News, January 2, 2003: 18.

— seeking volunteer teachers, Lahaina News, January 16, 2003: 2.

— to offer guided tour along Iao Stream, Lahaina News, February 13, 2003: 17.

— to hold "Love of the Land Celebration", Lahaina News, February 13, 2003: 2.

— free to seniors on the first Sunday of the month, Lahaina News, April 3, 2003: 16.

— to hold guided tours of rain forest, Lahaina News, May 8, 2003: 17.

— to offer guided tours of Iao Stream, Lahaina News, June 19, 2003: 17.

— to offer "Fantabulous Fall Festival", Lahaina News, August 21, 2003: 16.

— to hold guided walk along Iao Stream, Lahaina News, September 11, 2003: 16.

— recruiting volunteers, Lahaina News, September 25, 2003: 9.

HAWAII NURSES' ASSOCIATION
— presents Ruth Kemble Award for Volunteer Service to Elain Slavinsky, Lahaina News, June 7, 2001: 8.

HAWAII OCEAN FILM FESTIVAL
— to be held, Lahaina News, June 10, 1999: 16.

HAWAII OMORI CORPORATION [BUSINESS]
— plans to rebuild Lahaina Cannery, Lahaina News, July 25, 1984: 3.

— supports Foundation for Study in Hawaii and Abroad, Lahaina News, June 5, 1985: 20.

— funds expansion of Honoapi'ilani Highway, Lahaina News, August 24, 1988: 1.

— moving to Lahaina Cannery Mall, Lahaina News, September 12, 1990: 10.

— selects Richard Ellis to manage real estate portfolio, Lahaina News, July 17, 2003: 9.

— see also Lahaina Cannery Shopping Center

HAWAII ONLINE [BUSINESS]
— launches Integrated Service Digital Network (ISDN), Lahaina News, January 19, 1995: 10.

HAWAII PACIFIC RESORTS [BUSINESS]
— division of Castle Group, Inc to manage Maui Sun Hotel, Lahaina News, January 20, 1994: 6.

HAWAII PACIFIC UNIVERSITY
— Lahainaluna High School senior Audrey Mae Alvarez awarded scholarship to, Lahaina News, March 30, 2000: 3.

HAWAII PHARMACEUTICAL ASSOCIATION
— honored pharmacist G. Robert Craft, Lahaina News, July 2, 1986: 3.

HAWAII PLAN: EDUCATIONAL EXCELLENCE FOR THE PACIFIC ERA, THE
— see Berman Plan

HAWAII POLICE ATHLETIC FEDERATION
— seeking teams to sponsor, Lahaina News, October 11, 2001: 13.

HAWAII POLLUTION PREVENTION INFORMATION PROJECT
— attempts to reduce non-point pollution, Lahaina News, November 9, 2000: 1,12.

HAWAII PREPARATORY ACADEMY
— hosting meeting on "How a Boarding School Environment Can Enhance Your Child's Education", Lahaina News, December 13, 2001: 9.

— to hold information session, Lahaina News, November 7, 2002: 17.

— to hold "Cannery Kids Night", Lahaina News, November 7, 2002: 20.

HAWAII PRIMARY CARE ASSOCIATION
— to offer services, Lahaina News, January 3, 2002: 1,18.

HAWAII PRINCE [RESTAURANT]
— offering wedding packages, Lahaina News, July 11, 1991: 6.

HAWAII PRINCE HOTEL WAIKIKI
— extending Kama'aina specials, Lahaina News, February 27, 1991: 5,6.

HAWAII PROPERTY INSURANCE ASSOCIATION
— plans to expand coverage, Lahaina News, February 4, 1993: 9.

HAWAII PROTECTIVE AGENCY
— opening in Whaler's Village, Lahaina Sun, November 25, 1970: 3.

HAWAII PSYCHOLOGICAL ASSOCIATION
— seeking nominations for Healthy Workplace Awards, Lahaina News, August 21, 2003: 8.

HAWAII PUBLIC FINANCE OFFICERS ASSOCIATION
— held annual meeting last week, Lahaina News, September 29, 1994: 1,2.

HAWAII PUBLIC HEALTH ASSOCIATION
— seeking papers for annual meeting to be held at Hawaiian Regent Hotel, Lahaina News, January 20, 1988: 18.

HAWAII PUBLIC RADIO (KHPR)
— receives grant for transmitter on Haleakala, Lahaina News, August 8, 1984: 3.

— to hold fund raising drive, Lahaina News, April 17, 1985: 3.

— to broadcast performances from Kapalua Music Festival, Lahaina News, July 24, 1985: 8.

— receives donation from Alexander and Baldwin, Lahaina News, April 4, 1990: 7.

— to celebrate 20th birthday, Lahaina News, November 15, 2001: 16.

HAWAII REAL ESTATE COMMISSION
— to hold seminar on impact of new laws on realtors, Lahaina News, August 24, 1988: 3.

— creates reference kit, Lahaina News, January 6, 1994: 5,6.

— condominium specialists to be available, Lahaina News, January 6, 1994: 6.

HAWAII REGIONAL CUISINE
— charter members to be featured at the Kea Lani Food and Wine Masters, Lahaina News, March 21, 2002: 16.

HAWAII RENAISSANCE
— Building Industry Association of Hawaii announces Sutton Candia Partners as winner of, Lahaina News, October 3, 1990: 9.

HAWAII RESORT DEVELOPERS CONFERENCE
— to be held, Lahaina News, December 4, 1997: 21.

HAWAII RESTAURANT ASSOCIATION
— Maui chapter to meet, Lahaina News, June 12, 1985: 3.

HAWAII RIGHT TO LIFE MAUI CHAPTER
— to hold pro-life rally, Lahaina News, January 18, 1989: 3,5.

HAWAII SMALL BUSINESS ADMINISTRATION
— awards announced, Lahaina News, April 8, 1993: 6.

HAWAII STARS
— karaoke contest to be held, Lahaina News, August 26, 1993: 15.
— karaoke contest to be held, Lahaina News, June 22, 2000: 16.
— competition Maui finals held, Lahaina News, July 13, 2000: 9.

HAWAII STATE ASSOCIATION OF COUNTIES
— to hold Conference on Quality Growth, Lahaina Sun, December 13, 1972: 7.

HAWAII STATE BAR ASSOCIATION
— Young Lawyers Division offering "Legal Line", Lahaina News, January 17, 2002: 2.

HAWAII STATE COMMISSION ON THE STATUS OF WOMEN
— to hold events for Women's History Month, Lahaina News, August 29, 1996: 11.
— continues lecture series, Lahaina News, September 12, 1996: 15.

HAWAII STATE CRIBBAGE CHAMPIONSHIP
— to be held, Lahaina News, August 8, 1991: 4.

HAWAII STATE FARM FAIR
— to hold giant pumpkin contest, Lahaina News, February 27, 1991: 5.

HAWAII STATE FIRE FIGHTERS ASSOCIATION
— endorses James Apana for Maui County mayor, Lahaina News, July 18, 2002: 2.

HAWAII STATE GEOGRAPHY BEE
— Princess Nahienaena Elementary School student Jason Bilog finalist at, Lahaina News, June 10, 1999: 15.

HAWAII STATE INSURANCE COMMISSIONER
— Lawrence Reifurth delays decision on Hawaii Insurance Bureau's workers' compensation filings, Lahaina News, September 1, 1994: 12.

HAWAII STATE PUBLIC LIBRARY
— to present "Many Mini Arts Festival", Lahaina News, April 9, 1992: 4.
— to hold summer reading program, Lahaina News, May 16, 1996: 7.
— Shanon Peters wins Young Adult Summer Reading Program, Lahaina News, September 7, 2000: 1,7.
— see also specific public libraries

HAWAII STATE THEATRE COUNCIL
— sponsoring workshops from Royal Shakespeare Company, Lahaina News, January 9, 1992: 5.
— Maui members to hold general meeting, Lahaina News, October 29, 1992: 4.
— sponsoring audition workshop, Lahaina News, January 28, 1993: 15.

HAWAII STATE VOCATIONAL REHABILITATION AND BLIND DIVISION
— to hold meetings to discuss needs for deaf and hard -of-hearing, Lahaina News, May 17, 2001: 17.

HAWAII STATE WORLD BENCH PRESS AND DEADLIFT (WABDL) CHAMPIONSHIPS
— to be held at Lahaina Civic Center, Lahaina News, April 25, 2002: 13.

HAWAII STATEWIDE UNIVFORM DESIGN MANUAL FOR STREETS AND HIGHWAYS [BOOK]
— available through State Transportation Department, Lahaina News, January 15, 1981: 2.

HAWAII SWIMMING CLUB-LAHAINA
— organizing sessions at Lahaina Aquatic Center, Lahaina News, August 20, 1992: 8.
— seeking coaches, Lahaina News, September 24, 1992: 3.
— compete at Lahaina Aquatic Center, Lahaina News, September 30, 1993: 9.

HAWAII TECHNOLOGY TRADE ASSOCIATION
— to launch Maui Chapter, Lahaina News, June 15, 2000: 14.
— workshop to focus on technology industry, Lahaina News, August 9, 2001: 8.

HAWAII TO GO
— agriculture conference to be held, Lahaina News, March 1, 2001: 8.

HAWAII TOURISM AUTHORITY
— Mark Rolfing appointed to Board of Director, Lahaina News, October 15, 1998: 13.
— considering requests to promote tourism, Lahaina News, March 25, 1999: 13.
— unveils plan, invites public comments, Lahaina News, July 8, 1999: 1,16.
— taking proposals for events, Lahaina News, August 19, 1999: 14.
— posting news on website, Lahaina News, September 16, 1999: 11.
— to hold funding workshop, Lahaina News, April 5, 2001: 8.
— to hold Statewide Community Informational Meeting, Lahaina News, August 9, 2001: 8.
— to share revisions to Tourism Strategic Plan—Ke Kumu", Lahaina News, November 1, 2001: 3.
— to present on revisions to "Tourism Strategic Plan—Ke Kumu", Lahaina News, November 8, 2001: 16.
— to present tourism program at Maui Community College with Office of Economic Development, Lahaina News, June 13, 2002: 5.

HAWAII TROPICAL FRUIT GROWERS
— to hold conference, Lahaina News, October 16, 1997: 12.
— details of conference, Lahaina News, October 23, 1997: 17.

HAWAII TROPICAL PLANTATION
— planned for Wailuku, Lahaina News, June 15, 1982: 3.

HAWAII TUBERCULOSIS AND RESPIRATORY DISEASE ASSOCIATION
— sponsors tuberculosis testing program, Lahaina Sun, January 6, 1971: 2.

HAWAII UNDERSEA RESEARCH LAB
— Brian Midson to lead virtual tour of Lo'ihi, Lahaina News, November 9, 2000: 25.

HAWAII UNINSURED PROJECT
— public testimony to be taken, Lahaina News, October 25, 2001: 2.

HAWAII, UNIVERSITY OF
— see University of Hawaii

HAWAII VALUE CLUB (HVC)
— opens in West Maui, Lahaina News, July 26, 2001: 9.

HAWAII VISITORS AND CONVENTION BUREAU
— selects Maui Prince Hotel's Greg Gaspar for 2000 Master Chefs cuisine program, Lahaina News, November 11, 1999: 11.
— Keep It Hawai'i awards announced, Lahaina News, May 11, 2000: 11.
— accepting entries for "Keep It Hawai'i" awards, Lahaina News, December 14, 2000: 18.
— to explain marketing strategies, Lahaina News, July 19, 2001: 9.

HAWAII VISITORS BUREAU
— announces increase in tourism in 1984, Lahaina News, January 23, 1985: 3.
— produces "The Islands of Hawaii: E Komo Mai", Lahaina News, April 5, 1989: 15.

— distributing 1989 tourist guide, Lahaina News, November 1, 1989: 8.
— tourists surveyed say islands becoming too commercial, Lahaina News, July 18, 1990: 1.
— official Joseph Collins says changes needed to increase level of tourism, Lahaina News, December 5, 1991: 1,16.
— honors Maui businesses, Lahaina News, September 30, 1993: 7.
— Cathleen Johnson appointed as senior vice president of marketing, Lahaina News, June 16, 1994: 10.
— Barbara Tanabe to become chairman of the board, Lahaina News, July 7, 1994: 9.
— to kick off "Keep It Hawaii" program, Lahaina News, July 28, 1994: 9.
— "Keep it Hawaii" begins, Lahaina News, August 18, 1994: 8,9.
— announces Kahili Awards, Lahaina News, November 10, 1994: 13.
— Keep It Hawaii program begins, Lahaina News, November 23, 1995: 10.
— "Keep It Hawaii" program deadline approaching, Lahaina News, January 11, 1996: 11.
— awards Kahili Award to Hyatt Regency Maui, Lahaina News, April 18, 1996: 9.
— Old Lahaina Luau receives "Keep it Hawai'i" Kahili award, Lahaina News, April 22, 1999: 11.
— "Aloha Cities" marketing program sends chef around the world, Lahaina News, April 22, 1999: 3.
— to hold "Culinary 2000" program to promote Hawaii and its cuisine, Lahaina News, December 9, 1999: 15.
— holds Keep It Hawai'i Awards, Lahaina News, April 10, 2003: 14.

HAWAII WATER ENVIRONMENT ASSOCIATION
— Public Works team wins operations challenge, Lahaina News, March 6, 2003: 8.

HAWAII WATER VENDING [BUSINESS]
— installs water vending machine at Lahaina Square Shopping Center, Lahaina News, May 2, 2002: 8.

HAWAII WATERCOLOR SOCIETY
— to hold organizational meeting, Lahaina News, May 23, 2002: 16.
— to paint boats at Ma'alaea Harbor, Lahaina News, June 6, 2002: 16.

HAWAII WEDDING PROFESSIONALS ASSOCIATION
— new board of directors elected, Lahaina News, September 18, 1997: 18.
— to meet, Lahaina News, July 30, 1998: 13.
— Bridal Faire to be held, Lahaina News, January 14, 1999: 11.

HAWAII WHALE SANCTUARY
— creating education projects, Lahaina News, January 14, 1999: 7.

HAWAII WHALEWATCHING ASSOCIATION
— to hold workshop for water-users, Lahaina News, January 15, 1986: 3.
— prefers policing itself to heavier government enforcement, Lahaina News, January 22, 1986: 1.

HAWAII WILDLIFE FUND
— Hannah Bernard to speak on sea turtles and dolphins, Lahaina News, April 15, 1999: 12.
— to certify employees of Trilogy Excursions as naturalists, Lahaina News, August 10, 2000: 14.
— recruiting volunteers to train as naturalists at La Perouse Bay, Lahaina News, November 30, 2000: 16.

HAWAII YOUTH AT RISK
— to hold dinner and auction, Lahaina News, June 6, 1991: 4.

HAWAII YOUTH RISK BEHAVIOR SURVEY
— released, Lahaina News, December 23, 1993: 1,3.

HAWAII YOUTH SOCCER ASSOCIATION
— holds Olympic Development Program, Lahaina News, June 24, 1999: 7.

HAWAII YOUTH SYMPHONY
— to hold concert at Ka'ahumanu Center, Lahaina News, March 6, 1991: 17.
— to perform at Baldwin High School Auditorium, Lahaina News, February 11, 1993: 15.
— to offer free show, Lahaina News, February 17, 2000: 17.
— to perform at Maui Arts and Cultural Center, Lahaina News, March 1, 2001: 20.
— to perform under conductor Henry Miyamura, Lahaina News, March 7, 2002: 16.

HAWAII: THE SUGAR COATED FORTRESS [BOOK]
— reviewed, Lahaina Sun, May 17, 1972: 15.

HAWAIIAN AFFAIRS, OFFICE OF
— signs agreement with Kapalua Land Company and Hui Alanui O Makena concerning Native Hawaiian burials disinterred, Lahaina News, August 19, 1987: 3.
— proposes more housing, Lahaina News, November 11, 1987: 11.
— holds conference of Indigenous Peoples International in Kona, Lahaina News, November 18, 1987: 3.
— announces funds are available, Lahaina News, March 9, 1988: 18.
— Native Hawaiian extended to all descendants, Lahaina News, June 15, 1988: 6.
— description of issues faced by, Lahaina News, July 13, 1988: 1,12.
— dispute over shoreline in Ka'anapali holds up jurisdiction change, Lahaina News, July 20, 1988: 1,14.
— offers training in entrepreneurship, Lahaina News, August 3, 1988: 3.
— holds public informational meetings, Lahaina News, October 19, 1988: 16.
— extends deadline for referendum on blood quantum, Lahaina News, November 16, 1988: 13.
— wants burial grounds protected, Lahaina News, January 18, 1989: 1.
— calls for stop to study of ancient Hawaiian remains, Lahaina News, March 22, 1989: 1,12.
— working with Hui Alanui O Makena to reinter ancient Hawaiian remains, Lahaina News, March 29, 1989: 1.
— recommends no further study of ancient Hawaiian remains, Lahaina News, April 12, 1989: 1.
— protests lead to site of Ritz-Carlton Hotel to be changed, Lahaina News, April 26, 1989: 1.
— to hold meetings seeking federal restitution for seized lands, Lahaina News, September 13, 1989: 3.
— signs agreement on reinternment of ancient Hawaiian bones, Lahaina News, September 13, 1989: 3.
— to conduct referendum on definition of "Native Hawaiian", Lahaina News, November 29, 1989: 36.
— selects Moses Keale as chair, Lahaina News, January 2, 1991: 3.
— Abraham Aiona named vice chair of, Lahaina News, February 13, 1992: 3.
— Abraham Aiona become vice chair of, Lahaina News, May 21, 1992: 4.
— trustees to hold community meetings, Lahaina News, June 25, 1992: 2.
— seeking comments on Biennium Budget, Lahaina News, October 15, 1992: 3.
— Education Division to hold community meetings, Lahaina News, March 18, 1993: 4.
— to hold meeting, Lahaina News, June 17, 1993: 2.
— Trustees to hold community meeting, Lahaina News, June 24, 1993: 3,4.
— nominees sought for Ke Kukui Malamalama awards, Lahaina News, September 23, 1993: 3.
— to hold community meetings, Lahaina News, June 23, 1994: 5.
— race for Maui seat, Lahaina News, July 21, 1994: 1,16.

— chairman of Office of Hawaiian Affairs Board of Trustees discusses state's purchase of ceded land for housing, Lahaina News, July 28, 1994: 1.

— Clayton Hee says ceded lands being purchased for housing development to be reappraised, Lahaina News, October 27, 1994: 1,5.

— to not act against Lahaina Nautilus, Lahaina News, October 27, 1994: 8.

— challenging Housing Finance and Development Corp. over proposed Villages of Leiali'i project, Lahaina News, December 1, 1994: 4,5.

— to discuss proposed budget, Lahaina News, December 1, 1994: 7.

— to discuss proposed budget, Lahaina News, December 8, 1994: 3.

— publishes "The Native Hawaiian Data Book", Lahaina News, January 5, 1995: 1,3.

— Joanne Sterling named to Historic Preservation Council, Lahaina News, January 26, 1995: 6.

— to hold community meetings, Lahaina News, May 18, 1995: 4.

— looking for descendants of property owners in Honokohau Valley, Lahaina News, February 22, 1996: 1,16.

— publishes the Native Hawaiian Data Book, Lahaina News, August 21, 1997: 9.

— ready to negotiate with state over money owed following Supreme Court decision, Lahaina News, July 30, 1998: 1.

— extends deadline to file nomination papers, Lahaina News, September 3, 1998: 18.

— plans meetings on sovereignty, Lahaina News, February 4, 1999: 1.

— elections open to all registered voters, Lahaina News, May 18, 2000: 17.

— new filing deadline for Board of Trustees candidates, Lahaina News, July 4, 2002: 20.

HAWAIIAN AIRLINES [BUSINESS]

— criticized for ending service to Hana, Lahaina Sun, May 24, 1972: 9.

— plan to cut service to Hana backed by federal civil aeronautics board, Lahaina Sun, October 25, 1972: 10.

— call to boycott, Lahaina Times, June, 1980 volume 4 number 5: 6.

— reports good first quarter, Lahaina News, May 15, 1981: 5.

— looking for land from Maui Land & Pineapple for West Maui airport, Lahaina News, April 25, 1984: 3.

— provides their position on proposed West Maui airport, Lahaina News, September 11, 1985: 1,10,11.

— is unwilling to consider location of new airport other than Mahinahina, Lahaina News, December 4, 1985: 20.

— planning blessing of airport in Mahinahina, Lahaina News, April 30, 1986: 3.

— bless airport in Mahinahina, Lahaina News, May 7, 1986: 1,20.

— offering discounted fares to mainland, Lahaina News, January 10, 1990: 6.

— to use Hawaii Business Publications Corporation to produce monthly magazine, Lahaina News, September 12, 1990: 10.

— experiencing higher rates of reliability, Lahaina News, September 12, 1990: 11.

— awarded passenger and cargo service between Honolulu and Fukuoka, Japan, Lahaina News, October 24, 1990: 7.

— celebrating 61st birthday with discounts, Lahaina News, November 21, 1990: 3.

— celebrating 61st birthday with discounts, Lahaina News, November 28, 1990: 3.

— offering discount, Lahaina News, December 5, 1990: 5.

— enters into deal with Northwest Airlines, Lahaina News, December 26, 1990: 7.

— Paul Avery to represent Hawaiian Airlines Magazine on Maui, Lahaina News, March 20, 1991: 7.

— to hold drawing for trips to Las Vegas for Secretaries' Day, Lahaina News, April 10, 1991: 3.

— begins service to Fukuoka, Japan, Lahaina News, May 23, 1991: 8.

— listed by Conde Nast Traveler as among top 10 in nation, Lahaina News, November 7, 1991: 9.

— to introduce non-stop flights between mainland and outer islands, Lahaina News, January 23, 1992: 13.

— Donald Takaki to join board of directors of, Lahaina News, March 19, 1992: 10.

— to offer non-stop flights between Los Angeles and American Samoa, Lahaina News, April 2, 1992: 12.

— complaints decline, Lahaina News, April 23, 1992: 16.

— passenger traffic increases, Lahaina News, June 11, 1992: 14.

— official airline for Upper Deck Hawaiian Winter League, Lahaina News, July 2, 1992: 18.

— begins new route between Honolulu and Ontario, California; to expand further, Lahaina News, July 2, 1992: 18.

— matches interisland fares offered by Aloha Airlines, Lahaina News, July 9, 1992: 14.

— to begin service between Los Angeles and Kona, Lahaina News, July 23, 1992: 17.

— enjoys customer satisfaction, Lahaina News, July 23, 1992: 17.

— announces new fares, Lahaina News, July 30, 1992: 12.

— traffic increases, no complaints, Lahaina News, August 20, 1992: 12,13.

— announces special fares in response to hurricane Iniki, Lahaina News, September 24, 1992: 9.

— plans to operate Kapalua/West Maui Airport before ownership change, Lahaina News, October 15, 1992: 1.

— to offer service to Lana'i, Lahaina News, February 25, 1993: 6.

— new menu introduced, Lahaina News, March 11, 1993: 12.

— announces profits, Lahaina News, April 29, 1993: 9.

— president Mitch D'Olier resigns, Lahaina News, May 27, 1993: 8.

— starts second daily flight between Honolulu and Los Angeles, Lahaina News, July 1, 1993: 7.

— John Ueberroth resigns as president, Lahaina News, July 22, 1993: 8.

— adds Dash-7 aircraft to fleet, Lahaina News, August 12, 1993: 9.

— comes to agreement with union, Lahaina News, August 26, 1993: 10.

— parent company HAL, Inc. files for bankruptcy, Lahaina News, September 30, 1993: 7,8.

— traffic up, Lahaina News, October 21, 1993: 11.

— reduces interisland fares, Lahaina News, January 20, 1994: 6.

— appoints Donald Straight as vice president of flght operations, Lahaina News, February 3, 1994: 7.

— traffic increases, Lahaina News, April 7, 1994: 10.

— participating in AAdvantage, Lahaina News, June 30, 1994: 9.

— traffic increases, Lahaina News, July 14, 1994: 13.

— announces "Maui Shuttle" service, Lahaina News, July 14, 1994: 13.

— records record revenue passenger miles, Lahaina News, August 18, 1994: 9.

— revenue passenger miles reported, Lahaina News, September 1, 1994: 13.

— August statistics announced, Lahaina News, October 13, 1994: 15.

— to triple service between Las Vegas and Honolulu, Lahaina News, October 20, 1994: 13.

— offering sale prices to celebrate 65th anniversary, Lahaina News, November 10, 1994: 13.

— to offer holiday fare promotion, Lahaina News, December 15, 1994: 15.

— to feature artists on print material, Lahaina News, March 30, 1995: 11.

— partners with Hawaiian Airlines in West Maui, Lahaina News, June 27, 1996: 13.

— celebrates joint venture with Mahalo Air, Lahaina News, July 4, 1996: 3.

— offering daily flights between Maui and Los Angeles, Lahaina News, November 2, 2000: 12.

HAWAIIAN AIRLINES SILVERSWORD INVITATIONAL
— basketball tournament held, Lahaina News, November 27, 1985: 4.
HAWAIIAN CABLEVISION [BUSINESS]
— reviewed, Lahaina News, November 30, 1983: 14.
— to be purchased by Daniels & Associates, Lahaina News, March 11, 1987: 1.
— purchased by West Side Cable, Lahaina News, May 27, 1987: 16.
— to hold contest for free advertising for non-profits, Lahaina News, January 27, 1988: 3.
— sold to United Artists, Lahaina News, February 10, 1988: 1.
— adds more channels, hikes rates, Lahaina News, September 14, 1988: 1.
— dealing with damage following gale-force winds in Lahaina, Lahaina News, January 11, 1989: 13.
— costs for cable to rise, Lahaina News, February 8, 1989: 1.
— to hold coloring book contest, Lahaina News, March 7, 1990: 3.
— Nancy Chaplick appointed commercial development manager at, Lahaina News, March 28, 1990: 7.
— offering pay per view service, Lahaina News, April 25, 1990: 7.
— explains changes to basic package, Lahaina News, July 25, 1990: 5.
— seeking to renew cable franchise in West Maui, public hearing to be held, Lahaina News, October 17, 1990: 6.
— to extend franchise license for 5 more years, Lahaina News, December 5, 1990: 5.
— sponsoring national teleconference "Cable in the Classroom", Lahaina News, March 6, 1991: 4.
— to hold teleconference on use of cable programs in education, Lahaina News, March 20, 1991: 1.
— announces changes to TV schedule, Lahaina News, June 27, 1991: 14.
— offering Maui Today, an advertisement channel, Lahaina News, June 27, 1991: 7.
— offering photoadvertising service, Lahaina News, August 1, 1991: 11,12.
— recognized in national sales contest, Lahaina News, September 5, 1991: 6.
— channels adjusted, Lahaina News, October 3, 1991: 5.
— receives complaint over charging structure for HBO and other services, Lahaina News, January 23, 1992: 1,4.
— supporting Foodbank drive, Lahaina News, April 2, 1992: 4.
— adding services, Lahaina News, August 26, 1993: 4.
— may have stop carrying CBS, NBC and ABC, Lahaina News, September 30, 1993: 1.
— negotiations continue to extend station programming, Lahaina News, October 14, 1993: 9.
— adds new channels, Lahaina News, November 4, 1993: 3.
— to offer Digital Music Express (DMX), Lahaina News, November 18, 1993: 7.
— to offer free previews of The Learning Channel, Cartoon Network, Comedy Center, Lahaina News, July 4, 1996: 15.
— providing customer discounts at Warner Bros. Studio Store, Lahaina News, September 11, 1997: 12.
— bringing Disney characters to the Disney Store, Lahaina News, October 30, 1997: 16.
— offering DMX-Digital Music Service, Lahaina News, May 14, 1998: 13.
— to offer free preview of "Comic Relief 8", Lahaina News, June 11, 1998: 13.
— to install fiber optic network, Lahaina News, July 23, 1998: 3.
— offering free preview of Showtime, Lahaina News, September 17, 1998: 13.
— to add new channels, Lahaina News, January 7, 1999: 13.
— to add new channels, Lahaina News, December 23, 1999: 13.
— replacing General Instruments with Pioneer converters, Lahaina News, February 17, 2000: 14.
— offering amnesty for return of unauthorized descramblers, Lahaina News, August 17, 2000: 14.
— accepting unauthorized cable signal descramblers, Lahaina News, August 24, 2000: 14.
— offering Road Runner internet connection, Lahaina News, September 7, 2000: 18.
— see also cablevision
HAWAIIAN CANOE CLUB
— wins Maui County Hawaiian Canoe Association, Lahaina News, July 24, 1997: 15.
— to win county title, Lahaina News, July 9, 1998: 14.
— to hold fashion show fundraiser, Lahaina News, July 26, 2001: 13.
HAWAIIAN CANOE RACING ASSOCIATION
— state races to begin, Lahaina News, July 31, 1997: 14.
— State Championship Regatta to be held, Lahaina News, August 5, 1999: 1.
— regatta held at Hanaka'o'o Beach Park, Lahaina News, August 12, 1999: 1.
— regatta praised, Lahaina News, August 12, 1999: 4.
— Maui paddlers successful at, Lahaina News, August 16, 2001: 1,18.
HAWAIIAN CHIEFTAIN [SHIP]
— to come to Lahaina, Lahaina News, April 6, 1988: 1,20.
— to arrive in Lahaina, Lahaina News, June 8, 1988: 3.
— christened, Lahaina News, June 22, 1988: 1.
HAWAIIAN CIVIC CLUB
— Lahaina branch to meet, Lahaina News, September 17, 1998: 19.
HAWAIIAN CLAIMS OFFICE
— to hold workshops, Lahaina News, February 9, 1995: 3.
HAWAIIAN COLLECTORS ASSOCIATION
— offering scholarships, Lahaina News, December 17, 1998: 12.
HAWAIIAN COMMERCIAL AND SUGAR CO. [BUSINESS]
— Installing Silver Diffuser in plantation near Paia, Lahaina Sun, December 2, 1970: 1,4.
— criticized for removing sand from Baldwin Beach Park, Lahaina Sun, May 26, 1971: 1,8.
— personnel changes, Lahaina News, October 8, 1992: 8.
— develops technology to recover additional sucrose from sugar cane juice, Lahaina News, October 20, 1994: 13.
— to increase efficiency of sugar cane, Lahaina News, January 19, 1995: 10.
— David Morrell appointed vice-president of diversified services, Lahaina News, October 24, 1996: 9.
— vice presidents appointed, Lahaina News, August 19, 1999: 14.
— hires J. Lee Ingamells as directory of agronomy, Lahaina News, September 2, 1999: 13.
— hires Lee Jakeway as project engineer, Lahaina News, September 2, 1999: 13.
— personnel changes, Lahaina News, June 22, 2000: 9.
— closing Paia Mill, Lahaina News, September 21, 2000: 16.
— Lynn Swisher named vice president of , Lahaina News, December 26, 2002: 8.
HAWAIIAN CONSTITUTION CONVENTION
— calls, Lahaina News, April 12, 2001: 1,24.
HAWAIIAN CULTURAL ARTS EXPO
— to be held, Lahaina News, January 28, 1993: 14.
— selects Lama Ho'ike to benefit from, Lahaina News, January 28, 1993: 4.
— to be held, Lahaina News, February 25, 1993: 10.
HAWAIIAN CUSTOM CAMPERS
— to sponsor rummage sale, Lahaina News, December 9, 1987: 26.
HAWAIIAN DIVING ADVENTURES
— to begin third season, Lahaina News, May 27, 1999: 7.

HAWAIIAN DREDGING AND CONSTRUCTION COMPANY [BUSINESS]
— begins work on Lahaina Health Center, Lahaina News, February 6, 1985: 3.
— awarded contract for repais to Pier 2 at Kahului Harbor, Lahaina News, July 31, 1997: 15.

HAWAIIAN DURAGREEN INC. [BUSINESS]
— Anthony Hong new general manager of, Lahaina News, June 15, 2000: 14.

HAWAIIAN ELECTRIC INDUSTRIES, INC. [BUSINESS]
— purchases Young Brothers, Lahaina News, October 8, 1986: 3.

HAWAIIAN ELEGANCE [SHOW]
— held at Lahaina Cannery Shopping Center, Lahaina News, January 13, 1988: 3.

HAWAIIAN EUROPEAN CONNECTION, A [BUSINESS]
— offering courtesy phones for German speakers, Lahaina News, April 30, 1992: 11.

HAWAIIAN FASHION INDUSTRY ASSOCIATION
— names Local Motion as "Hawaii Apparel of the Year - Export Market", Lahaina News, July 25, 1990: 7.

HAWAIIAN FASHION SHOW
— to be held at Hyatt Regency Maui, Lahaina News, October 10, 1996: 14.

HAWAIIAN FISH PRINTERS
— to exhibit at Upstairs Gallery at the Lahaina Arts Society, Lahaina News, November 7, 1990: 13.
— to present "The New Gyotaku", Lahaina News, October 28, 1993: 11.

HAWAIIAN HEALING TRANSFORMATIONAL TOUR
— to be held at Maui Arts and Cultural Center, Lahaina News, December 12, 2002: 21.
— to be held at Paia Community Center, Lahaina News, December 26, 2002: 16.

HAWAIIAN HEART [MUSICAL GROUP]
— to perform at Old Lahaina Cafe and Luau, Lahaina News, November 7, 1990: 10.

HAWAIIAN HERBAL MEDICINE
— discussed as alternative healing method, Lahaina News, April 27, 1988: 1,17.

HAWAIIAN HOME LANDS, DEPARTMENT OF
— Maui County Task Force to hold public meeting, Lahaina News, January 9, 1992: 5.
— proposal to settle land claims, Lahaina News, January 30, 1992: 5.
— to discuss plans at KHET, Lahaina News, February 20, 1992: 3.
— to hold public meetings on transfer of land, Lahaina News, September 8, 1994: 5.
— opens land for Hawaiians in Ka'anapali, Lahaina News, November 10, 1994: 1,7.
— filing deadline for beneficiaries who suffered damages is next week, Lahaina News, August 24, 1995: 3.
— offering grants through Community Development Grants Program, Lahaina News, August 20, 1998: 8.
— offering Community Development Grants, Lahaina News, September 2, 1999: 15.
— opens Waiehu Kou 2 development, Lahaina News, August 17, 2000: 13.
— Hawaiian Home Commission awards scholarships to students, Lahaina News, September 7, 2000: 19.
— to hold community meetings on General Plan, Lahaina News, June 28, 2001: 5.
— planning for future ways to improve housing opportunities, Lahaina News, July 5, 2001: 1,20.
— providing grants, Lahaina News, January 17, 2002: 2.

— Hui Kako'o 'Aina Ho'opulapula to hold informational meeting on, Lahaina News, November 21, 2002: 3.
— Hui Kako'o 'Aina Ho'opulapula to host community meeting on , Lahaina News, March 6, 2003: 3.
— to meet with Hawaiians to discuss Native Hawaiian community in Honokowai, Lahaina News, May 22, 2003: 1,18.

HAWAIIAN HOMELANDS ACTION NETWORK
— to provide educational workshops, Lahaina News, June 5, 1997: 16.

HAWAIIAN HOMES
— Maui County Task Force to meet, Lahaina News, June 4, 1992: 4.

HAWAIIAN HOMES COMMISSION
— meeting with The Hawaiians [group], Lahaina Sun, December 23, 1970: 6.
— state representative Diana Hansen calls for investigation of, Lahaina Sun, November 10, 1971: 14.

HAWAIIAN HOMES COMMISSION ACT
— documentary to be broadcast on KHNL, Lahaina News, October 4, 1989: 3.

HAWAIIAN HOTELS AND RESORTS
— to resume management of the Royal Lahaina Resort, Lahaina News, May 23, 1991: 8.

HAWAIIAN INSURANCE AND GUARANTY COMPANY [BUSINESS]
— update on claims paid, Lahaina News, March 11, 1993: 12.

HAWAIIAN INSURANCE GROUP
— to phase out operations on Maui, Lahaina News, December 10, 1992: 1.

HAWAIIAN INTERNATIONAL FILM FESTIVAL
— seeking volunteers, Lahaina News, October 18, 1989: 4.
— looking for volunteers, Lahaina News, November 8, 1989: 3.
— to feature "Words Earth and Aloha" by Eddie Kamae, Lahaina News, November 9, 1995: 3.

HAWAIIAN INTERNATIONAL MUSIC FESTIVAL
— to be held at the Maui War Memorial Stadium, Lahaina News, August 8, 1991: 14.
— to feature Henry Kapono, Lahaina News, August 29, 1991: 14.

HAWAIIAN ISLAND SURF AND SPORT [BUSINESS]
— collecting food for Salvation Army, Lahaina News, July 17, 1997: 12.

HAWAIIAN ISLANDS
— shown at Family Film Festival, Lahaina Sun, January 27, 1971: 2.

HAWAIIAN ISLANDS HUMPBACK WHALE NATIONAL MARINE SANCTUARY
— may lose state support, Lahaina News, November 4, 1993: 1,3.
— may include entire state, Lahaina News, July 7, 1994: 1,7.
— no new rules for, Lahaina News, September 1, 1994: 1.
— National Oceanic and Atmospheric Administration continues to work towards, Lahaina News, April 20, 1995: 3.
— People Opposed to the Whale Sanctuary (POWS) attempts to stop creation of whale sanctuary, Lahaina News, July 13, 1995: 3.
— educating residents about Endangered Species Act, Lahaina News, August 31, 1995: 1,2.
— draft plan ready, Lahaina News, September 21, 1995: 1,16.
— public meeting to be held, Lahaina News, November 23, 1995: 1,12.
— National Oceanic and Atmospheric Association seeking advice on sanctuary plan, Lahaina News, February 15, 1996: 10.
— plans still being drafted, Lahaina News, April 11, 1996: 3.
— to hold meeting, Lahaina News, July 11, 1996: 12.
— seeking volunteers, Lahaina News, December 12, 1996: 9.
— workshop on ocean regulations to be held, Lahaina News, January 16, 1997: 11.
— to hold meeting on ocean regulations, Lahaina News, January 23, 1997: 11.

— Environmental Impact Statement to be completed soon, Lahaina News, February 6, 1997: 1,20.

— sponsoring "Careers on the Water Education Program", Lahaina News, February 20, 1997: 10.

— governor Ben Cayetano to decide on, Lahaina News, May 8, 1997: 1.

— Governor Ben Cayetano accepts whale sanctuary for five years, Lahaina News, June 12, 1997: 12.

— to hold Sanctuary Awareness Day at Borders Books Shop and Cafe, Lahaina News, June 26, 1997: 16.

— seeking volunteers, Lahaina News, November 20, 1997: 16.

— to be dedicated, Lahaina News, February 12, 1998: 3.

— editorial encouraging people to support, Lahaina News, April 9, 1998: 4.

— selects individuals to serve on sanctuary management advisory group, Lahaina News, September 3, 1998: 17.

— Border's Books and Music to hold "Sanctuary Awareness Day" to support , Lahaina News, September 10, 1998: 16.

— conducting volunteer training, Lahaina News, November 5, 1998: 21.

— seeking volunteers for management advisory group, Lahaina News, December 10, 1998: 11.

— advisory council to meet, Lahaina News, January 28, 1999: 12.

— funding studies, Lahaina News, January 11, 2001: 1,15.

— funds whale research, Lahaina News, January 11, 2001: 3.

— seeks applicants for Sanctuary Advisory Council, Lahaina News, April 26, 2001: 2.

— National Oceanic and Atmosphere Administration (NOAA) to review plan for, Lahaina News, May 2, 2002: 1,18.

— seeks Hawaii residents to serve on Advisory Council, Lahaina News, August 1, 2002: 9.

— volunteers to present on humpback whales, Lahaina News, February 6, 2003: 1.

— council to meet, Lahaina News, March 6, 2003: 2.

— to host Hans Konrad Van Tilburg speaking on "Wrecks to the Northwest: Our Maritime Legacy in the Hawaiian Archipelago", Lahaina News, March 6, 2003: 2.

— to hold public open house, Lahaina News, March 20, 2003: 16.

HAWAIIAN ISLANDS NATURAL BODYBUILDING AND FITNESS CHAMPIONSHIPS

— to be held, Lahaina News, September 27, 2001: 13.

— to be held at Maui Arts and Cultural Center, Lahaina News, October 3, 2002: 13.

HAWAIIAN ISLANDS RHYTHM AND BLUES MELE

— to be held, Lahaina News, May 14, 1998: 18.

— to be held, Lahaina News, May 11, 2000: 21.

— to be held, Lahaina News, April 25, 2002: 15.

HAWAIIAN ISLANDS WINTER RHYTHM AND BLUES MELE

— to be held, Lahaina News, January 31, 2002: 16.

HAWAIIAN JAM MUSIC FESTIVAL

— to be held at Maui Prince Hotel, Lahaina News, May 1, 1991: 16.

— details of, Lahaina News, May 15, 1991: 12.

HAWAIIAN KINE CHRISTMAS CAROL, A [PLAY]

— to be performed at the Maui Arts and Cultural Center, Lahaina News, December 4, 1997: 24.

— to be performed at Iao Theater, Lahaina News, December 11, 1997: 18.

HAWAIIAN LAND MAMMALS [BOOK]

— reviewed, Lahaina Sun, September 8, 1971: 3.

HAWAIIAN LANGUAGE IMMERSION PROGRAM

— successful, Lahaina News, July 12, 2001: 1,18.

HAWAIIAN LEADERSHIP CONFERENCE

— to be held, Lahaina News, March 25, 1999: 7.

HAWAIIAN LIFEGUARD ASSOCIATION

— scheduling contest, Lahaina News, March 12, 1992: 9.

HAWAIIAN LONGBOARD FEDERATION

— to begin season, Lahaina News, April 12, 2001: 14.

— to hold contest at Launiupoko Beach Park, Lahaina News, May 17, 2001: 15.

— to hold contest at Launiupoko Beach Park, Lahaina News, May 24, 2001: 15.

— season to begin, Lahaina News, February 28, 2002: 13.

— Aston No Ka Oi surfing competition held as part of, Lahaina News, July 4, 2002: 12.

— launches website, Lahaina News, November 7, 2002: 11.

— to hold surfing series, Lahaina News, April 10, 2003: 11.

HAWAIIAN LUAU

— to be held at Wailuku Community Center, Lahaina News, November 6, 1997: 17.

HAWAIIAN MANAGEMENT PROGRAM

— offered by University of Hawaii, Lahaina News, September 2, 1987: 3.

— scheduled, Lahaina News, November 11, 1987: 6.

HAWAIIAN MARATHON

— Hawaiian Marathon scheduled, Lahaina Sun, March 24, 1971: 7.

— scheduled for April 17, Lahaina Sun, April 14, 1971: 1.

HAWAIIAN MOONS COMMUNITY MARKET AND DELI [BUSINESS]

— to hold grand opening, Lahaina News, November 19, 1998: 11.

HAWAIIAN MOTORCYCLE MANUFACTURING [BUSINESS]

— expanding operations, Lahaina News, December 28, 1995: 10.

HAWAIIAN MOVING COMPANY [TELEVISION SHOW]

— featured surfer Kaimana Kinimaka, Lahaina News, October 7, 1999: 1.

HAWAIIAN MUSIC FESTIVAL

— to be held at Lahaina Cannery Mall, Lahaina News, June 27, 2002: 2.

HAWAIIAN ORGANIC FARMERS ASSOCIATION

— to meet, Lahaina News, October 19, 2000: 20.

HAWAIIAN PACIFIC RESORTS

— purchased by Castle Group, Inc., Lahaina News, January 6, 1994: 5.

HAWAIIAN PHOTO ARTS [BUSINESS]

— uses high-tech graphics software and printing equipment, Lahaina News, October 25, 2001: 9.

HAWAIIAN PINEAPPLE PLANTATION TOURS

— to be offered by Maui Pineapple Co., Lahaina News, January 23, 1997: 11.

HAWAIIAN QUILT COLLECTION [BUSINESS]

— opens, Lahaina News, March 4, 1999: 11.

— opening in Hyatt Regency Maui, Lahaina News, July 13, 2000: 14.

HAWAIIAN QUILT RESEARCH PROJECT

— volunteers sought for, Lahaina News, May 19, 1994: 15,16.

HAWAIIAN REFLECTIONS [DISPLAY]

— presented by Lahaina Arts Society in Old Jail Gallery, Lahaina News, March 1, 1982: 12.

HAWAIIAN SAFARI [BUSINESS]

— featured, Lahaina News, November 7, 1984: 18.

HAWAIIAN SEA VILLAGE

— Amfac submits new plans, Lahaina News, February 6, 1985: 3.

— editorial in support of, Lahaina News, February 13, 1985: 2.

— Amfac request to rezone approved by county planning commission, Lahaina News, February 27, 1985: 3.

— plans to create an historical recreation of Hawaiian village, Lahaina News, April 17, 1985: 1,8,9.

— receives zoning changes, Lahaina News, October 2, 1985: 9.
— Amfac asks for delay in timetable of, Lahaina News, November 5, 1986: 3.
— scheduled to be opened in 1990, Lahaina News, April 27, 1988: 3.
— receives extension of Special Management Area permit, Lahaina News, June 22, 1988: 3.
— Amfac, Inc. moving ahead on, Lahaina News, November 8, 1989: 1.
— Maui County Planning Commission to hold hearing on, Lahaina News, November 15, 1989: 2.
— Amfac, Inc. puts project on hold, Lahaina News, June 13, 1990: 1.
— land purchased by KM Hawaii, Inc., Lahaina News, July 18, 1990: 7.

HAWAIIAN SOVEREIGNTY
— theme of James Gordon's art show at Lahaina Arts Society, Lahaina News, August 20, 1992: 18.
— vote to be taken by Hawaiian Sovereignty Elections Council, Lahaina News, April 27, 1995: 1,16.
— Moanaliha Uwekoolani discusses Nation of Hawaii leader Dennis "Bumpy" Kanahele, Lahaina News, November 30, 1995: 1,12.
— residents asked opinions on, Lahaina News, May 9, 1996: 4.
— election results to be released, Lahaina News, September 5, 1996: 1.
— demonstration held, Lahaina News, October 24, 1996: 1.
— meeting to discuss, Lahaina News, October 31, 1996: 19.
— to be discussed, Lahaina News, November 7, 1996: 14.
— Poka Laenui to speak, Lahaina News, November 7, 1996: 15.
— to be discussed, Lahaina News, January 9, 1997: 1,16.
— "If You Care, Be There" educational meeting to be held, Lahaina News, January 30, 1997: 10.
— to hold "If You Care, Be There" meeting, Lahaina News, February 20, 1997: 10.
— hearing to be held to discuss Native Hawaiian Autonomy Act, Lahaina News, January 29, 1998: 1,2.

HAWAIIAN SOVEREIGNTY ELECTIONS COUNCIL
— organizing vote, Lahaina News, April 13, 1995: 5.
— vote to be taken, Lahaina News, April 27, 1995: 1,16.

HAWAIIAN STUDIES
— workshops to be held at Ka'anapali Beach Hotel, Lahaina News, October 21, 1987: 3.
— workshops offered at Ka'anapali Beach Hotel, Lahaina News, June 15, 1988: 6.
— Abraham Kawai'I to lecture on Hawaiian bodywork, Lahaina News, July 6, 1988: 3.
— presentation on astronomy offered at Lahaina Public Library, Lahaina News, July 12, 1989: 6.
— editorial supporting continued fishing at Mala Wharf, Lahaina News, September 13, 1989: 12.
— meeting to be held seeking federal restitution for seized lands, Lahaina News, September 13, 1989: 3.
— documentary on Hawaiian Homes Commission Act to be broadcast on KHNL, Lahaina News, October 4, 1989: 3.

HAWAIIAN STYLE AND CREATIONS [BUSINESS]
— to hold grand opening, Lahaina News, July 30, 1992: 12.

HAWAIIAN STYLE BAND [MUSICAL GROUP]
— to perform at Maui Community Arts and Cultural Center, Lahaina News, August 25, 1994: 15.

HAWAIIAN SUGAR PLANTERS ASSOCIATION
— accused of not trying to reduce air pollution, Lahaina Sun, November 18, 1970: 1.

HAWAIIAN SUGAR TECHNOLOGISTS CONFERENCE
— meeting held in Waikiki, Lahaina Sun, November 10, 1971: 6.

HAWAIIAN SUNDAY JAM
— fundraiser for Na Hoaloha O Lele halau at Old Lahaina Cafe, Lahaina News, October 26, 1988: 16.

HAWAIIAN TELEPRODUCTIONS, INC. [BUSINESS]
— grand finalist for producing commercial , Lahaina News, June 28, 1989: 3.
— winner at Cable Advertising Awards, Lahaina News, April 4, 1990: 6.
— completes production for Discovery Channel, Lahaina News, February 27, 1991: 8.

HAWAIIAN TIME [MUSICAL GROUP]
— to perform at A Taste of Lahaina, Lahaina News, September 10, 1998: 16.

HAWAIIAN TROPICAL PLANTATION
— visitor attraction opens near Waikapu Village, Lahaina News, August 8, 1984: 14.

HAWAIIAN TROPICS BIKINI CONTEST
— finals to be held, Lahaina News, July 2, 1992: 21.

HAWAIIAN TRUST CO. LTD [BUSINESS]
— Carolyn Yamasaki joins, Lahaina News, August 18, 1994: 9.

HAWAIIAN TUG AND BARGE [BUSINESS]
— to provide grants to charitable organizations with Young Brothers, Ltd., Lahaina News, August 30, 2001: 9.
— awarding grants with Young Brothers to non-profit community organizations, Lahaina News, June 20, 2002: 8.
— now accepting grant applications for Community Gift Giving Program, Lahaina News, June 26, 2003: 14.

HAWAIIAN WAR CHANT [SONG]
— history and meaning discussed, Lahaina News, July 17, 1985: 7.

HAWAIIAN WINTER LEAGUE
— signs sponsorship deal with The Upper Deck Company, Lahaina News, April 30, 1992: 11.

HAWAIIAN-EUROPEAN CONNECTION [BUSINESS]
— Johann Blahuta starts travel agency specializing in European visitors, Lahaina News, October 31, 1990: 11.

HAWAIIANA MANAGEMENT CO. LTD. [BUSINESS]
— named managing agent for three Maui properties, Lahaina News, August 12, 1999: 13.

HAWAIIANA MONTH
— ends at Lahaina Cannery Shopping Center, Lahaina News, August 24, 1988: 6.
— to be held at Lahaina Cannery Shopping Center, Lahaina News, August 9, 1989: 1.
— events described, Lahaina News, August 16, 1989: 1,5.

HAWAIIANA RESORTS [BUSINESS]
— initiates new concierge service, Lahaina News, May 8, 1991: 6.

HAWAIIANS, HAWAIIAN CULTURE
— meeting between The Hawaiians and the Hawaiian Homes Commission, Lahaina Sun, December 16, 1970: 3.
— political situation discussed, Lahaina Sun, June 7, 1972: 3.
— Stanley McCutcheon, an attorney from Alaska, speaks on illegal occupation , Lahaina Sun, January 17, 1973: 1.
— request release of 9,500 acres of military land, Lahaina Sun, February 7, 1973: 5.
— Stewart Udall, former interior secretary, to support repatriation, Lahaina Sun, March 21, 1973: 3.
— possible responses to injustice detailed, Lahaina Sun, April 11, 1973: 12,13.
— convention on Moloka'i described, Lahaina Sun, April 18, 1973: 15.
— declaration of independence sent to President Nixon, Lahaina Sun, May 9, 1973: 7.
— burial places of Hawaiian royalty described, Lahaina News, May 1, 1980: 6.
— living in Oregon in 1840, Lahaina News, March 15, 1981: 13.
— Na Mele O Maui celebrations held, Lahaina News, November 9, 1983: 6.

— to elect delegates to sovereignty convention, Lahaina News, January 7, 1999: 1,20.

— "Making Ipu Hele" to be held at Bailey House, Lahaina News, March 11, 1999: 13.

— Ritz-Carlton hosting festival on, Lahaina News, March 18, 1999: 9.

— International Hawaii Multicultural Music and Dance Conference to be held, Lahaina News, April 8, 1999: 13.

— featured in local fairs, Lahaina News, July 8, 1999: 1,16.

— project to unearth old capital may begin in 2001, Lahaina News, September 30, 1999: 1,16.

— Na Kupuna O Maui planning overnight vigil asking for divine guidance and spiritual unity, Lahaina News, January 6, 2000: 1.

— vigil held at Pu'u Keka'a, Lahaina News, January 13, 2000: 1,16.

— Punana Leo o Lahaina supporting Hawaiian Language Immersion, Lahaina News, April 6, 2000: 1,2.

— "Native Hawaiian Perspectives in Higher Education, Part I—Empowerment for the Hawaiian Community through Music, Literature and Art", Lahaina News, April 20, 2000: 16.

— "Native Hawaiian Perspectives in Higher Education, Part II" to be held, Lahaina News, April 27, 2000: 12.

— Lahaina Cannery Mall celebrating "Hawaii Traditions", Lahaina News, August 10, 2000: 16.

— how Lahainaluna High School promoted, Lahaina News, August 10, 2000: 5.

— Hawaiian Language Immersion Program to begin at Princess Nahienaena Elementary School, Lahaina News, September 28, 2000: 1,14.

— Aloha Festivals Ho'olaule'a to showcase, Lahaina News, October 26, 2000: 1.

— Hokule'a to visit Lahaina, Lahaina News, January 25, 2001: 1,3.

— Hawaiians to protest court case challenging Article XII of Hawaii State Constitution, Lahaina News, February 1, 2001: 1,22.

— to march from Moku'ula to Black Rock to protest threats to native rights, Lahaina News, February 22, 2001: 1,3.

— to protest , Lahaina News, March 1, 2001: 1,22.

— "Hu'e: Elua—Walk of Aloha" protest march held, Lahaina News, March 8, 2001: 1,20.

— holds protest march Ka'i huaka'i a me ka lokahi (procession for unity), Lahaina News, March 8, 2001: 2.

— to hold "Ho'omalamalama na Kaulike" march, Lahaina News, April 5, 2001: 1,9.

— Friends of Moku'ula to hold workshop to explain protocol, Lahaina News, April 5, 2001: 3.

— to hold Ho'omalamalama 'na Kaulike (Light for Justice) march, Lahaina News, April 12, 2001: 21.

— "Exploring Health Professions: A Native Hawaiian Perspective" to be held, Lahaina News, May 3, 2001: 2.

— Kahu Lyons Kapi'ioho Naone III to discuss "The Hawaiians' Approach to Conservation", Lahaina News, May 24, 2001: 20.

— Department of Hawaiian Homelands planning for future ways to improve housing opportunities, Lahaina News, July 5, 2001: 1,20.

— "Gathering of Our Living Treasures" to be held, Lahaina News, August 9, 2001: 1,18.

— "Gathering of Our Living Treasures" to be held, Lahaina News, August 16, 2001: 1,9.

— Reinstated Lawful Hawaiian Government to hold weekly meetings, Lahaina News, September 13, 2001: 1,20.

— Lahainaluna High School Academy of Travel and Tourism students learn about Polynesian navigation, Lahaina News, October 18, 2001: 3.

— protest water drilling above Lahaina, Lahaina News, January 31, 2002: 1,9.

— meet to discuss issues at assembly sponsored by Na Kupuna o Hawaii Nei, Lahaina News, February 28, 2002: 3.

— Department of Education officials to discuss Hawaiian immersion program, Lahaina News, March 28, 2002: 1,20.

— Na Kupuna O Maui to hold demonstration against Arakaka 2 lawsuit, Lahaina News, August 8, 2002: 5.

— to raise concerns for bill to force sale of Queen's personal land holdings, Lahaina News, August 29, 2002: 3.

— reflection on Hawaii becoming a territory, Lahaina News, September 19, 2002: 21.

— University of Hawai'i to hold informational meeting on degree in Hawaiian Studies, Lahaina News, February 20, 2003: 16.

— 'Ao'ao O Na Loko I'a O Maui (Association of the Fishponds of Maui) seeking volunteers, Lahaina News, May 29, 2003: 9.

— Ritz-Carlton launches cultural series, Lahaina News, August 21, 2003: 9.

— Lahainaluna High School teachers learn about Hawaiian culture, Lahaina News, September 18, 2003: 1,20.

— Waiola Church offering free conversational Hawaiian language classes, Lahaina News, September 18, 2003: 2.

— Waiola Church offering free conversational Hawaiian language classes, Lahaina News, September 25, 2003: 9.

— Waiola Church offering free conversational Hawaiian language classes, Lahaina News, October 2, 2003: 2.

— see also Aboriginal Lands of Hawaiian Ancestry [group]; Malo, David; specific events, groups, people, and places

HAWAIIANS, THE

— activist group meeting with Richard Paglinawan from Hawaiian Homes Commission, Lahaina Sun, December 16, 1970: 3.

— activist group meeting with Hawaiian Homes Commission, Lahaina Sun, December 23, 1970: 6.

— activist group criticized by David Trask, Jr. of the State Association of Hawaiian Civic Clubs, Lahaina Sun, February 10, 1971: 8.

HAWAI'ILOA [CANOE]

— to visit Maui, Lahaina News, September 18, 1997: 9.

— to stop in Lahaina, Lahaina News, September 25, 1997: 1.

— to stop at Lahaina Harbor, Lahaina News, October 2, 1997: 17.

HAWAII'S JOB BANK

— to be held, Lahaina News, November 5, 1998: 17.

HAWEA POINT

— debate on future use as park or hotel, Lahaina News, August 5, 1987: 1.

— land parcel with Light House auctioned, Lahaina News, August 12, 1987: 1.

— Friends of Hawea Point files petition opposing proposed mansion, Lahaina News, December 6, 1989: 1.

— opposition to proposed mansion grows, Lahaina News, February 14, 1990: 1.

— conflict between L.P. Liem and Friends of Hawea Point over development of mansion may be resolved, Lahaina News, November 28, 1990: 3,4.

— Friends of Hawea Point appears to have resolved conflict with L.P. Liem over development of mansion, Lahaina News, November 28, 1990: 3,4.

— officials investigation access dispute at, Lahaina News, September 29, 1994: 1,3.

— Kapalua Bay Hotel discusses liability at Hawea Point, Lahaina News, January 19, 1995: 4.

— public trail to opens, Lahaina News, July 13, 1995: 1.

HAWK, JAMES [ENTERTAINER]

— dies right after performing at Maui Lu, Lahaina News, September 15, 1981: 6.

HAWK, RUTHIE [TEACHER]

— honored by former student mayor Tavares, Lahaina News, March 12, 1986: 12.

HAWKING

— Maui County Council bans people in store entrances from calling out to pedestrians, Lahaina News, August 10, 1995: 1,2,16.

HAWKINS, JAMES
— new senior vice president at Bank of Hawaii, Lahaina News, August 1, 2002: 8.

HAWS, ROBERT
— announces that Royal Hawaiian Air Service going out of business, Lahaina News, May 28, 1986: 3.

HAY FEVER [PLAY]
— to be performed by Theatre Theatre Maui, Lahaina News, February 9, 1995: 11.
— to be performed by Theatre Theatre Maui, Lahaina News, March 16, 1995: 11.
— reviewed, Lahaina News, March 30, 1995: 11.

HAYASE, SHERI-ANN
— completes U.S. Navy basic training, Lahaina News, July 29, 1999: 3.

HAYASHI, HIDEO
— discusses potholes in Lahaina, Lahaina Sun, January 27, 1971: 1.

HAYASHI, YASUAKI
— named as head of Lahaina Hongwanji Buddhist Mission, Lahaina News, November 16, 1983: 5.

HAYDA, PETER
— named director of sales for Maui Marriott Resort, Lahaina News, April 10, 1985: 9.

HAYDEN, JOAN
— to offer music lessons, Lahaina News, September 17, 1986: 3.

HAYES, BRENT [ARTIST]
— work of Lahainaluna High School student praised, Lahaina News, May 10, 1989: 3.
— to exhibit in Los Angeles, Lahaina News, November 15, 1989: 3.
— to exhibit at Friday Night is Art Night, Lahaina News, July 11, 1990: 17.
— to unveil "Legends of Ka'anapali" painting, Lahaina News, September 12, 1990: 19.
— featured at Sunset Galleries, Lahaina News, November 14, 1990: 16.
— to hold show at Sunset Galleries, Lahaina News, December 5, 1990: 12.
— featured at Sunset Galleries, Lahaina News, June 27, 1991: 13.
— featured at Sunset Galleries, Lahaina News, July 25, 1991: 10.
— sports impressionist to be featured artist at Royal Art Galleries, Lahaina News, September 19, 1991: 16.

HAYES, ISAAC [MUSICIAN]
— stays in Maui, Lahaina Sun, August 16, 1972: 3.

HAYES, PAMELA [ARTIST]
— work featured, Lahaina News, December 3, 1986: 11.
— to discuss recent watercolors at Village Galleries, Lahaina News, June 6, 1990: 15.
— to be artist-in-residence at Village Galleries, Lahaina News, June 24, 1999: 12.
— to give workshop to the Hawaii Watercolor Society, Lahaina News, August 22, 2002: 21.

HAYNES, AL
— Rotary Club of Maui Upcountry to host airplane captain, Lahaina News, April 2, 1998: 16.

HAYNES, CHARLES [MUSICIAN]
— to perform at Blackie's Bar, Lahaina News, January 9, 1992: 10.
— to perform at Blackie's Bar, Lahaina News, June 4, 1992: 14,18.
— to perform Latin music at Blackie's Bar, Lahaina News, December 30, 1993: 10.
— to perform at Blackie's Bar, Lahaina News, January 6, 1994: 10.

HAYNES PARTNERSHIP, INC., THE [BUSINESS]
— becomes agency of hotel scheduled to open, Lahaina News, January 16, 1991: 5.

HAYS, HEATHER
— Miss Hawaii to attend Lahaina Center Fashion/Dance Extravaganza, Lahaina News, May 7, 1992: 19.

HAYS, RONALD [ADMIRAL]
— to speak at Maui Council of the Navy League, Lahaina News, January 22, 1986: 3.
— warns of Soviet Navy at presentation to Maui Council of the Navy League, Lahaina News, February 5, 1986: 3.

HAYWARD, THOMAS [ADMIRAL]
— defends navy's use of Kaho'olawe, Lahaina Sun, September 15, 1971: 1.

HAYWOOD, FRED
— sailboarder's career detailed, Lahaina News, April 17, 1985: 4.
— windsurfer's career described, Lahaina News, September 3, 1986: 4.

HAYWOOD, GUY
— selected as Maui County deputy planning director, Lahaina News, January 16, 1991: 2,9.
— appointed Corporation Counsel for Maui County, Lahaina News, May 23, 1991: 6.
— sworn in as Corporation Counsel, Lahaina News, July 18, 1991: 4.

HAYWOOD, ROBIN
— appointed loan officer at First Federal Savings and Loan Association of America, Lahaina News, April 3, 1991: 4.

HAZEN, SACHIN
— to offer tour on Waihee Ridge Trail, Lahaina News, April 19, 2001: 16.

HAZLEHURST, CHARLE [ARTIST]
— featured at Lagunero Gallery, Lahaina News, October 9, 1985: 8.

HE HO'O MAKA HOU
— Ho'olaule'a to support Na Kamali'i O Ke Akua hula halau, Lahaina News, February 20, 2003: 14.

HE PO'AI ALOHA—ENCIRCLED WITH LOVE [MUSICAL]
— Queen Lili'uokalani tribute to be performed, Lahaina News, March 30, 2000: 12.

HEAD START
— funding provided, Lahaina Sun, February 17, 1971: 5.
— new center opens at Maui Community College, Lahaina News, May 26, 1994: 5.

HEAD, TERRY [ENTERTAINER]
— to be featured at Sweethearts Ball, Lahaina News, February 8, 1984: 12.

HEAD, TIM
— director for Maui ACLU, Lahaina Sun, January 13, 1971: 6.
— awarded Frances Davis Memorial award for teaching, Lahaina Sun, June 23, 1971: 12.
— update on attempts to create a Youth Center, Lahaina Sun, November 3, 1971: 14.

HEAD TO TOE BEAUTY SALON [BUSINESS]
— opens, Lahaina News, November 1, 2001: 8.
— to hold "Learn to Love Your Hair" sessions, Lahaina News, July 4, 2002: 16.
— to offer "Learn to Love Your Hair" sessions, Lahaina News, July 11, 2002: 17.
— continues to hold "Learn to Love Your Hair", Lahaina News, August 15, 2002: 17.
— to celebrate first year in business, Lahaina News, October 3, 2002: 8.

HEADCHAIR
— product featured, Lahaina News, October 17, 1984: 18.

HEAGY, RON
— quadriplegic to speak, Lahaina News, December 4, 1997: 24.

HEALD BUSINESS COLLEGE
— presents scholarship to Lahainaluna High School senior Jena Arcangel, Lahaina News, May 19, 1994: 5.

HEALEY, JOHN
— manager of Hawaiian Cable Vision discusses rules of the Federal Communications Commission, Lahaina Sun, December 23, 1970: 6.
— spokesman for Hawaiian Cable Vision Corporation says FM radio reception improved on Maui, Lahaina Sun, December 1, 1971: 6.

HEALING
— workshop by Dale Borglum held by Maui Center for Attitudinal Healting , Lahaina News, January 18, 1989: 3.
— Kai Po Kaneakua to discuss Hawaiian healing, Lahaina News, August 6, 1998: 21.

HEALING FOR THE AGE OF ENLIGHTENMENT
— to hold seminars on Vita Flex, Lahaina News, October 24, 2002: 20.

HEALING TOUCH
— discussed as alternative healing method, Lahaina News, April 20, 1988: 1.

HEALTH
— projects desired by West Maui Business Association, Lahaina Sun, December 23, 1970: 2.
— medical costs in 1865, Lahaina Sun, February 10, 1971: 3.
— rules connected to practicing as a doctor criticized, Lahaina Sun, February 10, 1971: 4.
— free heart screening at Lahaina courthouse organized by Hawaii Heart Association, Lahaina Sun, February 24, 1971: 1.
— free glaucoma detection clinic organized Lion Clubs of Maui, Lahaina Sun, February 24, 1971: 3.
— free clinic for communicable diseases offered by Maui District Health Office, Lahaina Sun, April 28, 1971: 1.
— alcoholism program offered at Mauna Olu College, Lahaina Sun, April 28, 1971: 7.
— referral clinic operating at the former Peahi Chapel, Lahaina Sun, June 23, 1971: 2.
— hospital proposed for Lahaina, Lahaina Sun, July 28, 1971: 1,2.
— electro-cardio-analyzer available in October to detect heart disease, Lahaina Sun, October 6, 1971: 3.
— cases of syphilis found on Maui, Lahaina Sun, October 6, 1971: 4.
— Family planning clinics organized, Lahaina Sun, October 13, 1971: 4.
— smallpox vaccinations continue, Lahaina Sun, October 20, 1971: 11.
— measles reported in Maui , Lahaina Sun, October 20, 1971: 3.
— Conference on alcoholism and rehabilitation held at Maui Beach Hotel, Lahaina Sun, October 20, 1971: 5.
— Diabetes Detection Drive sponsored by Maui Medical Society and the State Department of Health, Lahaina Sun, December 1, 1971: 12.
— Le Leche League meets on Maui to discuss breastfeeding, Lahaina Sun, December 1, 1971: 5.
— State Health Department warns against certain cheeses contaminated by bacteria, Lahaina Sun, December 15, 1971: 14.
— concern over improperly prepared or stored turkey, Lahaina Sun, December 22, 1971: 4.
— free chest x-rays to be offered, Lahaina Sun, January 12, 1972: 17.
— Hospital rate hike contested, Lahaina Sun, January 19, 1972: 16.
— readers encouraged to receive free chest x-ray, Lahaina Sun, February 2, 1972: 14.
— venereal disease spreading across Hawaii, Lahaina Sun, February 23, 1972: 3.
— Le Leche League sponsoring meetings, Lahaina Sun, March 29, 1972: 11.
— discussion of what to do in case of an emergency, Lahaina Sun, March 29, 1972: 5.

— West Maui Emergency Center proposed, Lahaina Sun, March 29, 1972: 5.
— Maui County Unit of Hawaii Heart Association to teach students about heart diseases, Lahaina Sun, March 29, 1972: 9.
— food poisoning spreads in West Maui through tainted meat, Lahaina Sun, May 17, 1972: 10.
— emergency unit planned for Lahaina, Lahaina Sun, June 7, 1972: 4.
— new facility to be built as part of Maui Memorial Hospital, Lahaina Sun, June 14, 1972: 11.
— Maui Memorial Hospital converts to new rate system, Lahaina Sun, July 5, 1972: 9.
— support for Maui Medical Group detailed, Lahaina Sun, July 26, 1972: 3.
— tighter controls announced to prevent spread of tuberculosis, Lahaina Sun, August 2, 1972: 10.
— exercise classes offered at Wailuku YMCA, Lahaina Sun, October 4, 1972: 14.
— Hawaii Mental Health Association begins plan to promote mental health, Lahaina Sun, October 11, 1972: 10.
— issues faced by veterans, Lahaina Sun, October 11, 1972: 12.
— woman complains of civil rights violations in Maui Memorial Hospital psychiatric ward, Lahaina Sun, November 8, 1972: 4.
— death of Haiku woman highlights problem of ambulance services, Lahaina Sun, November 8, 1972: 4,5.
— second complaint against psych ward, Lahaina Sun, November 15, 1972: 4.
— public defender urges reform of psychiatric laws, Lahaina Sun, November 22, 1972: 3.
— mental health law under review by Mental Health Association of Hawaii, Lahaina Sun, December 13, 1972: 4.
— cases of hepatitis reported, Lahaina Sun, December 20, 1972: 15.
— Ka Lima O Maui rehabilitation center described, Lahaina Sun, December 20, 1972: 6.
— impact of fluoridation on Moloka'i studied, Lahaina Sun, December 27, 1972: 6.
— Hawaii Medical Service Association drug policy criticized, Lahaina Sun, December 27, 1972: 7.
— Central Maui deemed safest place to have a heart attack in the United States, Lahaina Sun, January 24, 1973: 17.
— abortion statistics released, Lahaina Sun, February 14, 1973: 10.
— infant stimulation program offered through Maui Easter Seal society, Lahaina Sun, March 14, 1973: 10.
— Medicom Net emergency communication system to be created, Lahaina Sun, April 11, 1973: 3.
— Julian Lipsher named health educator, Lahaina Sun, April 18, 1973: 4.
— danger of sun exposure for skin cancer described, Lahaina Sun, July 4, 1973: 3.
— Charlotte Kuwanoe named Hospice-Maui director, Lahaina News, October 15, 1980: 3.
— juvenile counseling program praised, Lahaina News, November 1, 1980: 4.
— Great American Smokeout planned, Lahaina News, November 15, 1980: 15.
— people of Hawaii live longer, Lahaina News, December 15, 1980: 10.
— home food delivery for homebound expanded, Lahaina News, January 15, 1981: 11.
— Maui County Medical Society continues breast cancer screening program, Lahaina News, March 15, 1981: 14.
— State approves lease of land for West Maui Youth Center, Lahaina News, May 15, 1981: 7.
— large retirement community proposed for Moloka'i, Lahaina News, March 1, 1983: 6.
— value of walking discussed, Lahaina News, July 1, 1983: 8.
— Helping Other Parents Ease Sorrow (HOPE) support group to meet, Lahaina News, October 12, 1983: 4.

— CPR classes offered at Captain Nemo's Ocean Emporium, Lahaina News, June 27, 1984: 3.

— free measle immunization to be held at Lahaina Civic Center, Lahaina News, July 4, 1984: 4.

— Cancer Information Service offering free comic book about effects of sun on skin, Lahaina News, July 11, 1984: 3.

— IMUA Rehab to hold parenting classes, Lahaina News, July 11, 1984: 3.

— parenting course offered at Lahaina Baptist Church, Lahaina News, August 1, 1984: 13.

— lecture series begins on unwanted pregnancies, Lahaina News, September 5, 1984: 10.

— cancer study by American Cancer Society continues, Lahaina News, September 5, 1984: 3.

— free book on breast cancer offered by Hawaii Cancer Information Service, Lahaina News, September 12, 1984: 3.

— editorial on smoking, Lahaina News, November 21, 1984: 2.

— anti-drunk driving efforts during New Year's Eve described, Lahaina News, December 26, 1984: 7,8,9.

— Medic Four service featured, Lahaina News, January 2, 1985: 6,7,8.

— Resolution Run detailed, Lahaina News, January 9, 1985: 4.

— Hawaii ranked #1 in joggers per capita, Lahaina News, January 9, 1985: 4.

— biking in Maui described, Lahaina News, January 16, 1985: 7,8,9.

— classes to be taught at Kaiser Clinic in Wailuku, Lahaina News, January 23, 1985: 3.

— value of aerobics discussed, Lahaina News, February 20, 1985: 4.

— children's supplement features, Lahaina News, February 20, 1985: A,B,C,D.

— impact of alcohol discussed, Lahaina News, March 20, 1985: 1,7.

— alcoholism, Lahaina News, March 27, 1985: 1,6.

— sex education offered at Maui Family Support Services, Lahaina News, March 27, 1985: 3.

— CPR training at Kineh Community Center, Lahaina News, May 8, 1985: 3.

— "Pakalolo: For Parents Only" program to be held at Lahaina Intermediate School, Lahaina News, May 8, 1985: 3.

— benefits of gymnastics discussed, Lahaina News, May 8, 1985: 4.

— Hawaii Cancer Information Service offers free comic book explaining dangers of sun exposure, Lahaina News, June 12, 1985: 3.

— Dr. John Laszlo to talk on smoking and lung cancer, Lahaina News, June 12, 1985: 3.

— Viapssana meditation retreat to be held, Lahaina News, June 12, 1985: 3.

— anti-smoking clinic offered by American Cancer Society, Lahaina News, June 26, 1985: 3.

— editorial on use of Aldicarb in watermelons imported from California, Lahaina News, July 17, 1985: 2.

— Maui Reach to Recovery Program meeting of mastectomies, Lahaina News, July 24, 1985: 8.

— editorial praising Hyatt Regency Maui's decision to add low and no alcohol items to its menu, Lahaina News, July 31, 1985: 2.

— Hyatt Hotels Corporation announces alcohol management training program, Lahaina News, July 31, 1985: 7.

— pesticide paraquat under scrutiny by federal Drug Enforcement Administration, Lahaina News, August 7, 1985: 1,9.

— mayor Tavares appoints citizen's committee to promote public education on dangers of drugs, Lahaina News, August 21, 1985: 3.

— drug and alcohol treatment project set for Lahainaluna High School, Lahaina News, August 28, 1985: 1.

— program for mothers and pre-adolescent daughters to be held at Maui Community College, Lahaina News, September 11, 1985: 3.

— workshops by Diana Wilson offered on managing stress, Lahaina News, September 18, 1985: 3.

— Women's Health Day to be held October 22 and Kahului Clinic, Lahaina News, October 9, 1985: 8.

— "Let's Talk" program for mothers and pre-adolescent daughters, Lahaina News, October 16, 1985: 3.

— "Let's Talk" program for mothers and pre-adolescent daughters scheduled, Lahaina News, November 27, 1985: 20.

— "Making it on Maui" stress workshop to be held at Holy Innocents' Episcopal Church, Lahaina News, December 11, 1985: 3.

— conference to support programs for mentally ill and substance abusers to be held, Lahaina News, January 1, 1986: 3.

— workshops offered on dynamics of addiction, Lahaina News, January 15, 1986: 3.

— Institute of Body Therapeutics to offer classes on massage, Lahaina News, January 15, 1986: 3.

— nurse Cynthia Vaughn speaking at Osteoporosis Forum at Maui Community College, Lahaina News, February 5, 1986: 3.

— Jazzercise of Lahaina to hold open house, Lahaina News, February 5, 1986: 3.

— editorial criticizing state Department of Health's study of birth defects on Lana'i and Moloka'i, Lahaina News, February 12, 1986: 2.

— cardio-pulmonary-resuscitation (CPR) classes to be held, Lahaina News, February 19, 1986: 3.

— seminar "Serving Alcohol with Care" offered at Napili Kai Beach Club's Down-Under Lounge, Lahaina News, February 19, 1986: 3.

— interpersonal relationship workshop to be held at Maui Community College, Lahaina News, February 26, 1986: 3.

— cardio classes to be offered by American Red Cross, Lahaina News, April 9, 1986: 3.

— AIDS reported on Maui, Lahaina News, April 23, 1986: 1,16.

— Quit Smoking clinic offered by American Cancer Society, Lahaina News, April 30, 1986: 3.

— YMCA to offer program for pregnant women, Lahaina News, April 30, 1986: 3.

— editorial asking for revised fire code, Lahaina News, June 4, 1986: 2.

— program for mothers and their pre-adolescent daughters organized by Maui Family Support Services, Lahaina News, June 4, 1986: 3.

— Maui Family Support Services to hold program on how fathers can talk to their sons, Lahaina News, June 11, 1986: 3.

— Lahaina Comprehensive Health Center opens, Lahaina News, July 23, 1986: 1,3.

— quality of drinking water questioned, Lahaina News, August 20, 1986: 1,16.

— addiction services described, Lahaina News, August 20, 1986: 1,8.

— exercise program offered at Civic Center, Lahaina News, August 27, 1986: 3.

— vigil for AIDS victims to be held, Lahaina News, September 3, 1986: 3.

— low impact aerobics offered by YMCA, Lahaina News, September 10, 1986: 3.

— YMCA offering "first responder" first aid course, Lahaina News, September 24, 1986: 3.

— American Red Cross offering disaster response course, Lahaina News, September 24, 1986: 3.

— drinking age raised to 21, Lahaina News, October 1, 1986: 12.

— Maui Youth and Family Services offering class for parents with children from previous marriages, Lahaina News, October 1, 1986: 5.

— physical therapy office featured, Lahaina News, October 1, 1986: 9.

— stress reduction workshop sponsored by Unity Church of Maui, Lahaina News, October 8, 1986: 3.

— Department of Social Services and Housing introduces "Nursing Home Without Walls" program, Lahaina News, October 15, 1986: 3.

— Gestalt workshop offered, Lahaina News, November 5, 1986: 16.

— benefit auction to be held at Wailea Shopping Village, Lahaina News, November 5, 1986: 3.

— stree reduction workshop offered, Lahaina News, November 5, 1986: 3.

— first responder course offered by YMCA, Lahaina News, November 12, 1986: 3.

— Great American Smokeout held, Lahaina News, November 12, 1986: 3.

— Safe Place planned for West Maui youth, Lahaina News, November 19, 1986: 1,7.

— workshop for liposuction surgeons held at Hyatt Regency Maui, Lahaina News, November 19, 1986: 4.

— beauty restoration by Visions discussed, Lahaina News, November 26, 1986: 1,10.

— convention on Medicare to be held, Lahaina News, November 26, 1986: 10.

— Gestalt workshop offered, Lahaina News, December 3, 1986: 11.

— Maui Electric offers tips on holiday safety, Lahaina News, December 3, 1986: 11.

— support groups for the holidays listed, Lahaina News, December 10, 1986: 16.

— editorial opposing focus on fluoridation, Lahaina News, December 31, 1986: 2.

— stress reduction workshop held at Unity Church, Lahaina News, February 4, 1987: 11.

— AIDS crisis in Maui, Lahaina News, February 11, 1987: 1,20.

— Dehypnosis/Existential Life Review offered, Lahaina News, February 25, 1987: 6.

— lost mate support group organized, Lahaina News, March 4, 1987: 10.

— workshops on coping with cancer offered at Maui Memorial Hospital, Lahaina News, March 4, 1987: 10.

— Rick Reed to draft Senate resolution to study impact of cane burning on, Lahaina News, March 4, 1987: 3.

— workshop held by Nancy Shipley Ruben and Aurora [spiritual entity], Lahaina News, March 4, 1987: 8.

— Rick Reed proposes health care facility for West Maui, Lahaina News, March 11, 1987: 3.

— volunteers needed for Helping Elderly Live Life's Opportunities (HELLO), Lahaina News, March 25, 1987: 18.

— Red Cross sponsors CPR classes, Lahaina News, March 25, 1987: 3.

— Health Director John Lewin recommends people who have received blood transfusions get tested for AIDS, Lahaina News, April 1, 1987: 3.

— "Fresh Start" program aimed at stopping smoking, Lahaina News, April 15, 1987: 12.

— free skin exams offered by dermatologists, Lahaina News, April 29, 1987: 3.

— signs your children could be on drugs, Lahaina News, May 20, 1987: 8.

— low impact aerobics class offered, Lahaina News, May 27, 1987: 3.

— Mayor Tavares requests the creation of an emergency medical facility in Lahaina, Lahaina News, June 10, 1987: 3.

— support group for separated, divorced, and widowed to be held, Lahaina News, June 10, 1987: 3.

— "What is Arthritis?" talk to be offered, Lahaina News, June 24, 1987: 3.

— Institute of Body Therapeutics to hold massage classes, Lahaina News, July 15, 1987: 3.

— presentation on detoxification to be held at Ala Lani United Methodist Church, Lahaina News, August 5, 1987: 3.

— senior citizens to be given vaccinations, Lahaina News, August 12, 1987: 3.

— no smoking policy tightened, Lahaina News, September 16, 1987: 3.

— smoking banned in work places, Lahaina News, September 30, 1987: 3.

— seminar for caregivers offered, Lahaina News, September 30, 1987: 3.

— workshops on using unconscious resources, Lahaina News, October 7, 1987: 16.

— workshop on love at Unity Church of Maui Whole Life Center, Lahaina News, October 7, 1987: 16.

— meditation workshop to be offered by Bonnie Newman, Lahaina News, October 21, 1987: 12.

— smoking banned at Kahului Airport, Lahaina News, November 4, 1987: 10.

— "Beginning Experience" organized for people grieving, Lahaina News, November 18, 1987: 3.

— changes in social programs over last year recounted, Lahaina News, December 30, 1987: 1.

— Maui AIDS Foundation to offer trainings, Lahaina News, March 16, 1988: 14.

— Rotary Clubs of Maui funding polio immunizations around the world, Lahaina News, March 16, 1988: 3.

— Cancer Information Service produces guide, Lahaina News, March 23, 1988: 3.

— Kaiser Permanente renovation in Lahaina complete, Lahaina News, April 6, 1988: 1.

— Lahaina News to begin series on healing, Lahaina News, April 6, 1988: 1.

— unorthodox healing methods described, Lahaina News, April 13, 1988: 1,14,20.

— alternative healing methods discussed, Lahaina News, April 20, 1988: 1,20.

— herbs discussed as healing alternative, Lahaina News, April 27, 1988: 1,17,18.

— value of alternative healing methods discussed, Lahaina News, May 4, 1988: 1.

— discussed as alternative healing method, Lahaina News, May 4, 1988: 15,16.

— HIV AIDS testing offered, Lahaina News, May 4, 1988: 3.

— "Relationship 101" workshop held at Unity Church of Maui, Lahaina News, May 18, 1988: 18.

— free skin exams offered by dermatologists, Lahaina News, May 18, 1988: 3.

— Kokua Na Keiki health education program to be held, Lahaina News, June 1, 1988: 19.

— "Grow", a structured mental health support group, is formed, Lahaina News, June 22, 1988: 11.

— 2nd ambulance added to West Maui, Lahaina News, July 13, 1988: 13.

— smoking cessation program offered by the American Lung Association, Lahaina News, September 14, 1988: 3.

— seminar for retirees , Lahaina News, September 28, 1988: 3.

— attitudinal healing discussed, Lahaina News, October 19, 1988: 1,17.

— workshop on self care offered, Lahaina News, October 19, 1988: 18.

— Violence Hotline set up, Lahaina News, November 9, 1988: 12,20.

— meeting of people with allergies organized, Lahaina News, November 16, 1988: 13.

— issues faced by drug addicts, Lahaina News, November 23, 1988: 1,16.

— "Emerging Issues in Aging" to be offered, Lahaina News, November 23, 1988: 5.

— "Be Well" support group for people with environmental illnesses, Lahaina News, December 7, 1988: 16.

— Conference on Aging to be offered at Holy Innocents' Episcopal Church, Lahaina News, January 11, 1989: 5.

— drug abuse linked to childhood abuse, Lahaina News, January 25, 1989: 1,14.

— changes to Medicaid law may make pre-natal medical services more accessible, Lahaina News, February 8, 1989: 5.

— Bill Lazell to offer seminar on aging, Lahaina News, February 15, 1989: 3.

— CPA and first aid courses offered at Lahaina United Methodist Church, Lahaina News, February 15, 1989: 5.

— blood drive to be held at Westin Maui Hotel, Lahaina News, February 22, 1989: 13.

— stress discussed by Dr. Greg LaGoy, Lahaina News, March 8, 1989: 3.

— KSM Professional Group to offer CPR course, Lahaina News, March 15, 1989: 2.

— Maui Office of Aging hosting events, Lahaina News, March 29, 1989: 14.

— CPR training offered, Lahaina News, April 12, 1989: 3,5.

— Harry Endo to present on opportunities after retirement, Lahaina News, April 26, 1989: 13.

— AIDS '89 Maui program to be held, Lahaina News, May 3, 1989: 4.

— workshop on coping with tragedy to be offered by Maui Center for Attitudinal Healing, Lahaina News, May 17, 1989: 2.

— seminar on long-term care insurance to be offered, Lahaina News, June 7, 1989: 2.

— American Lung Association to offer workshop on controlling asthma, Lahaina News, June 7, 1989: 5.

— "Mended Hearts" club formed for survivors of heart attacks and bypass surgery, Lahaina News, August 2, 1989: 3.

— care home beds shortage discussed, Lahaina News, August 16, 1989: 3.

— dialysis center opens, Lahaina News, September 20, 1989: 2.

— American Lung Association offering "Freedom From Smoking" program, Lahaina News, September 20, 1989: 3.

— Maui County Fair to hold Healthy Baby contest, Lahaina News, October 4, 1989: 2.

— Joy Appleton to discuss chemical sensitivity, Lahaina News, November 1, 1989: 6.

— course on OSHA safety to be offered, Lahaina News, November 1, 1989: 9.

— safety course for welders and autobody painters to be offered, Lahaina News, November 1, 1989: 9.

— effects of crystal methamphetamine discussed, Lahaina News, November 8, 1989: 3.

— sex abuse counseling available from Sex Abuse Interventions, Inc., Lahaina News, December 13, 1989: 4.

— alcohol consumption during News Years described, Lahaina News, December 27, 1989: 1,3.

— girl needs bone marrow, Lahaina News, December 27, 1989: 11.

— workshop to be held on spousal abuse, Lahaina News, March 14, 1990: 3.

— Sandra Price seeks donations to help pay for brother's liver transplant, Lahaina News, March 21, 1990: 1.

— cooking demonstration for low-cholesterol, low-fat dishes sponsored by Seventh Day Adventist churches, Lahaina News, March 28, 1990: 4.

— AIDS cases increase in drug addicts, Lahaina News, March 28, 1990: 5.

— seat belt use low in Lahaina, Lahaina News, August 29, 1990: 4.

— Maui needs more hospital beds, Lahaina News, September 5, 1990: 1,9.

— paralyzed after assault, John Cuccia needs money for rehabilitative care, Lahaina News, September 5, 1990: 2.

— tips on emergency preparation, Lahaina News, September 12, 1990: 15.

— Meadowgold sponsoring Healthy Baby Contest, Lahaina News, September 26, 1990: 6.

— Frontline to broadcast "Broken Minds" on schizophrenia, Lahaina News, October 31, 1990: 8.

— state-wide CPR training held, Lahaina News, November 14, 1990: 4.

— Legislative Forum on Aging Issues to be held, Lahaina News, December 19, 1990: 6.

— Dr. Harold Hanson becomes associated with West Maui Healthcare Center, Lahaina News, January 16, 1991: 3.

— Hawaii Optometric Association to offer free vision tests, Lahaina News, January 16, 1991: 4.

— James Vitale to speak to Central Maui Diabetes Support Group on footcare and diabetes, Lahaina News, January 16, 1991: 4.

— CODA to meet, Lahaina News, January 23, 1991: 4.

— bills to install prophylactic vending machines in schools to be introduced, Lahaina News, February 13, 1991: 1,8.

— Na Pu'uwai to provide health services to native Hawaiians, Lahaina News, March 27, 1991: 3.

— Lahaina has lowest rate of seat belt use, Lahaina News, March 27, 1991: 3.

— State publishes booklet on lead poisoning, Lahaina News, March 27, 1991: 5.

— American Lung Association to host Dr. Richard Ando, Jr. to speak on asthma treatment, Lahaina News, April 3, 1991: 4.

— lack of radiation treatment center on Maui discussed, Lahaina News, April 24, 1991: 1.

— conference to be for service providers on HIV, Lahaina News, May 23, 1991: 4.

— ciguatera fish poisoning not an issue on Maui, Lahaina News, June 13, 1991: 1.

— Kaiser Clinic to reduce hours, Lahaina News, July 11, 1991: 4.

— fundraiser to be held for people with muscular dystrophy, Lahaina News, July 18, 1991: 4.

— older people drawn to exercise at health clubs, Lahaina News, July 25, 1991: 9.

— Medcheck of Maui, Inc. to be at Lahaina Shopping Center, Lahaina News, August 8, 1991: 3.

— illegal drug use a health threat, Lahaina News, August 29, 1991: 1.

— State health director John Lewin to speak to Hawaii Pacific Gerontological Society, Lahaina News, September 5, 1991: 3.

— Medcheck of Maui to offer testing at Lahaina Pharmacy, Lahaina News, September 19, 1991: 8.

— Lahaina to have emergency center, Lahaina News, October 17, 1991: 3.

— Bank of Hawaii sponsoring Senior Citizen Fair, Lahaina News, October 17, 1991: 6.

— lifeguards receive jet ski training, Lahaina News, October 24, 1991: 1.

— nutritionists Michael Klaper and Mary Bush present at Ming Yuen Chinese restaurant, Lahaina News, October 24, 1991: 5.

— Soroptimist International sponsoring free cancer exams, Lahaina News, October 31, 1991: 3.

— Soroptimist International sponsoring free classes on breast self-examination, Lahaina News, November 21, 1991: 3.

— Maui County bill proposes creating non-profit hospital, Lahaina News, December 12, 1991: 6.

— state senator Joe Souki plans to review medical care in West Maui, Lahaina News, January 2, 1992: 1,2.

— Maui Childbirth Education Association to hold classes, Lahaina News, January 9, 1992: 3.

— post-holidays weight-loss strategies discussed, Lahaina News, January 9, 1992: 6.

— Volunteer Blood Donor Month declared, Lahaina News, January 16, 1992: 5.

— Maui Memorial Hospital raising rates, Lahaina News, January 16, 1992: 5.

— Maui Childbirth Education Association offering infant care classes, Lahaina News, February 6, 1992: 5.

— Alzheimer stress reduction techniques to be taught, Lahaina News, February 13, 1992: 4.

— lecture on Alzheimer's by Patricia Blanchette to be held, Lahaina News, February 20, 1992: 4,5.

— documentary "Simple Courage" to air on KHET, Lahaina News, March 12, 1992: 22.

— public forum on AIDS and leprosy to be held, Lahaina News, March 19, 1992: 4.

— featured article on arthritis, Lahaina News, April 2, 1992: 3.

— Alzheimer's support group to meet, Lahaina News, April 9, 1992: 4.

— forum focusing on mental health and substance abuse to be held, Lahaina News, April 9, 1992: 8.

— rural health symposium to be held in Kihei, Lahaina News, April 16, 1992: 4.

— Tai Chi classes to be offered by John Ensign, Lahaina News, April 30, 1992: 4.

— Department of Health offering free immunization, Lahaina News, May 7, 1992: 3.

— childbirth series to be offered through grant by Harold K.L. Castle Foundation, Lahaina News, June 11, 1992: 6.

— meeting to discuss mental health to be held, Lahaina News, June 25, 1992: 2.

— Dr. David Rutolo to lecture on skin care, Lahaina News, July 23, 1992: 7.

— Kahuna La'au Lapa'au to demonstrate native Hawaiian medical practices, Lahaina News, July 30, 1992: 4.

— Maui Childbirth Education Association to offer parenting workshops, Lahaina News, August 20, 1992: 4.

— magician Peter Sampson to headline fundraiser for International Diabetes Youth Camp, Lahaina News, August 27, 1992: 14.

— infant care classes to be offered by Maui Childbirth Education Association, Lahaina News, August 27, 1992: 4.

— Maui Childbirth Education Association to offer parenting workshops, Lahaina News, September 10, 1992: 3.

— forum to be held on schizophrenia, Lahaina News, October 1, 1992: 4.

— Kihei Youth Center and Lokelani Intermediate school sponsoring AIDS education event, Lahaina News, October 29, 1992: 17.

— warning issues over permanent eyelash and eyebrow dyes and tints, Lahaina News, October 29, 1992: 4.

— influenza shots available, Lahaina News, October 29, 1992: 4.

— Medcheck continues provide services, Lahaina News, December 24, 1992: 4.

— state funds released for West Maui Acute Care Hospital Feasibility Study, Lahaina News, January 28, 1993: 3.

— Maui Childbirth and Family Education to hold classes, Lahaina News, January 28, 1993: 4.

— Epilepsy Foundation of Hawaii to meet, Lahaina News, January 28, 1993: 4.

— cancer treatment center proposed, Lahaina News, February 18, 1993: 1.

— support for radiology center, Lahaina News, March 4, 1993: 4.

— Life Dance Training Program to be held, Lahaina News, April 1, 1993: 7.

— Bill and Susan Forsyth ask Governor John Waihee to warn people of dangers of Prozac, Lahaina News, April 22, 1993: 1.

— Maui Colon Health Center to hold lectures, Lahaina News, May 13, 1993: 4,5.

— childbirth preparation series to be held by Maui Childbirth and Family Education, Lahaina News, June 3, 1993: 3.

— free screening offered, Lahaina News, June 17, 1993: 2.

— American Lung Association to sponsor Office Olympics, Lahaina News, June 17, 1993: 3.

— Medcheck of Maui offering testing, Lahaina News, June 24, 1993: 4.

— Hawaii Department of Health launches immunization program, Lahaina News, June 24, 1993: 4.

— works on Alcoholics Anonymous by Dick B. featured in display at Kahului Public Library, Lahaina News, August 5, 1993: 5.

— vaccinations required for students entering school, Lahaina News, August 12, 1993: 4.

— family planning services expanded, Lahaina News, August 19, 1993: 4.

— Hawaii Air Ambulance introduces new service, Lahaina News, September 16, 1993: 4.

— Maui District Health Office providing immunizations, Lahaina News, September 23, 1993: 3.

— International Life Support signs contract to provide ambulance service, Lahaina News, October 14, 1993: 5.

— federal funds released for macadamia nutrition study, Lahaina News, October 28, 1993: 7.

— flu vaccinations available, Lahaina News, November 4, 1993: 3.

— urgent care facility plan, Lahaina News, November 11, 1993: 1.

— employees at Ka'anapali Beach Hotel following diet developed at Waianae Coast Comprehensive Health Center, Lahaina News, November 25, 1993: 1,3.

— health checks available at Longs in Lahaina Cannery Mall, Lahaina News, November 25, 1993: 3.

— yoga and meditation classes to be held at Lahaina United Methodist Church, Lahaina News, December 2, 1993: 4.

— Donna McCartney to speak on "Nurture and Care for the Caretaker", Lahaina News, December 2, 1993: 4.

— Hawaii Youth Risk Behavior Survey released, Lahaina News, December 23, 1993: 1,3.

— checks continue at Long's at Lahaina Cannery, Lahaina News, January 6, 1994: 3.

— nurse seeking health care services for children in West Maui complex, Lahaina News, February 10, 1994: 2.

— dairies and farmers question use of growth hormone, Lahaina News, February 17, 1994: 1,3.

— immunization clinic to be held, Lahaina News, February 24, 1994: 4.

— Maui Childbirth and Family Education to hold classes, Lahaina News, February 24, 1994: 4.

— chiropractor Kalua Kaiahua featured, Lahaina News, March 3, 1994: 1,2.

— Project Healthstart applications due soon, Lahaina News, March 3, 1994: 4.

— advisory committee for Lahaina Complex seeks health center at Lahainaluna Health Center, Lahaina News, April 28, 1994: 1.

— child immunization clinic to be held, Lahaina News, April 28, 1994: 4.

— Barbara Mearns moves yoga classes to Lahaina, Lahaina News, May 5, 1994: 3.

— Hale Nani Partners sue state to establish Ekahi Surgery Center, Lahaina News, May 26, 1994: 3.

— Maui Memorial Hospital's chief of surgery supports stand-alone surgery center, Lahaina News, June 30, 1994: 1.

— childbirth classes to be offered at Honolua Methodist Church, Lahaina News, June 30, 1994: 4.

— American Lung Association to hold course on asthma, Lahaina News, July 7, 1994: 4.

— youth drug and alcohol use on the rise, Lahaina News, August 4, 1994: 1.

— fundraiser pays for cancer detection machine, Lahaina News, August 25, 1994: 1,3.

— aging issues to be discuss at White House Conference on Aging, Lahaina News, August 25, 1994: 5.

— childbirth classes to be offered at Honolua Methodist Church, Lahaina News, August 25, 1994: 5.

— heroin and ice in West Maui, Lahaina News, September 15, 1994: 1,2.

— parenting skills class to be held Wailuku Elementary School, Lahaina News, September 15, 1994: 6.

— workshop to focus on child abuse, Lahaina News, October 13, 1994: 7.

— childbirth classes to be offered at Honolua Methodist Church, Lahaina News, October 20, 1994: 5.

— smoke-free workplace supported, Lahaina News, November 3, 1994: 22.

— "Repair the Roof Before it Rains" seminar to be held by Maui County Department of Housing and Human Concerns, Lahaina News, November 10, 1994: 7.

— West Maui Kidney Dialysis Center opens, Lahaina News, December 8, 1994: 3.

— new director Mike Lawrence hoping to reform health care, Lahaina News, December 22, 1994: 3.

— Alternatives to Violence offering support for teen girls, Lahaina News, January 5, 1995: 4.

— childbirth classes to be held at Honolua Methodist Church, Lahaina News, January 12, 1995: 4.

— childbirth classes to be held at Honolua Methodist Church, Lahaina News, January 26, 1995: 6.

— "Building Your Mate's Self-Esteem" to be held at Grace Baptist Church, Lahaina News, February 9, 1995: 3.

— Initial Response Training Center offering CPR and First Aid courses, Lahaina News, March 9, 1995: 4.

— childbirth classes to be held at Honolua Methodist Church, Lahaina News, March 30, 1995: 6.

— forum to be held on early childhood education and care , Lahaina News, May 25, 1995: 4.

— Maui emergency services strained, Lahaina News, June 8, 1995: 1,2.

— HIV testing to resume on West Side, Lahaina News, June 22, 1995: 5.

— Medcheck continues to offer screening, Lahaina News, July 13, 1995: 5.

— Maui District Health Office resumes HIV testing, Lahaina News, July 20, 1995: 5.

— Maui County Office on Aging to conduct public hearing, Lahaina News, July 20, 1995: 5.

— consultant says West Maui does not need hospital, Lahaina News, August 24, 1995: 1,16.

— Medcheck of Maui continues to offer health services, Lahaina News, September 7, 1995: 2.

— CPR and First Aid classes cotinue at Initial Training Center, Lahaina News, October 5, 1995: 4.

— Health Fair to be held at Lahaina Cannery Mall, Lahaina News, November 16, 1995: 4.

— Medcheck continues to offer services at Lahaina Cannery Mall, Lahaina News, December 7, 1995: 3.

— childbirth classes offered at Honolua Methodist Church, Lahaina News, December 28, 1995: 2.

— childbirth classes offered at Honolua Methodist Church, Lahaina News, January 4, 1996: 4.

— Freedom From Smoking Clinic to be held, Lahaina News, January 4, 1996: 4.

— PATCH to offer family child care training program, Lahaina News, January 4, 1996: 4.

— Victoras Kulvinskas to speak on, Lahaina News, January 11, 1996: 2.

— new services offered for Native Hawaiians with AIDS, Lahaina News, January 18, 1996: 4.

— Maui Childbirth and Family Education to hold infant care class, Lahaina News, January 25, 1996: 4.

— Drug Free Awareness Month kicks off, Lahaina News, February 1, 1996: 4.

— childbirth classes to begin at Honolua Methodist Church, Lahaina News, February 29, 1996: 4.

— National Cancer Institute probing high breast cancer rates in Hawaii, Lahaina News, April 11, 1996: 1,16.

— value of strength training, Lahaina News, April 18, 1996: 12.

— Community Clinic of Maui opens, Lahaina News, April 18, 1996: 6.

— National Cancer Institute to study high rate of breast cancer in Hawaii, Lahaina News, April 25, 1996: 1,18.

— childbirth classes to begin at Honolua Methodist Church, Lahaina News, April 25, 1996: 6.

— Chronic Fatigue and Fibromyalgia support group to meet, Lahaina News, June 6, 1996: 15.

— Medcheck continues to offer services, Lahaina News, June 6, 1996: 15.

— conference to be held on assisted living, Lahaina News, June 27, 1996: 15.

— breast cancer data released by Environmental Protection Agency , Lahaina News, June 27, 1996: 3.

— Alano Club helping people in recovery, Lahaina News, July 4, 1996: 1,2.

— Al and Pat Kwiecinski donates defibrillator to Napili fire station, Lahaina News, July 11, 1996: 1,6.

— alcoholic speaks about illness, Lahaina News, July 11, 1996: 5.

— Hoʻomalu Ala Al Anon to meet, Lahaina News, July 18, 1996: 12.

— Carol Donovan to discuss "Six Stages of Disease", Lahaina News, August 8, 1996: 14.

— D.E. Eastman Look Good, Feel Great Family Day to be held, Lahaina News, August 8, 1996: 18.

— "Brain Gym" led by Karen Peterson, Lahaina News, August 8, 1996: 5.

— Alcoholics Anonymous to meet, Lahaina News, August 15, 1996: 14.

— Geriatrician Gary Johnson to speak, Lahaina News, August 15, 1996: 16.

— American Cancer Society to hold meeting on prostate cancer, Lahaina News, August 22, 1996: 15.

— water safety officers practice stabilizing victims, Lahaina News, September 19, 1996: 4.

— childbirth classes to be held, Lahaina News, September 26, 1996: 14,15.

— Wailea/Makena Health Beat '96 to be held, Lahaina News, October 17, 1996: 14.

— nutrition program held at Lahaina Civic Center, Lahaina News, October 24, 1996: 4.

— magnetic field therapy presentation to be held, Lahaina News, November 21, 1996: 18.

— Karen Peterson to present on Brain Gym, Lahaina News, December 5, 1996: 15.

— Hoʻomalu Ala Al Anon to meet, Lahaina News, December 19, 1996: 10.

— meditation session to offered by Stephen Armstrong and Kamala Masters, Lahaina News, December 26, 1996: 11.

— Nancy Kuntz to present on brain development, Lahaina News, April 3, 1997: 12.

— workshop to be held on managed care, Lahaina News, April 17, 1997: 12.

— Kaiser Permanente to offer "Stress Reduction, A Simple Approach", Lahaina News, May 8, 1997: 17.

— free screenings for skin cancer to be offered, Lahaina News, May 8, 1997: 7.

— Executive Office on Aging to hold public hearing, Lahaina News, July 24, 1997: 16,17.

— Women's Health Month to be held, Lahaina News, September 4, 1997: 1.

— Al-Anon continues to meet, Lahaina News, September 25, 1997: 16.

— program on car seat safety to be held, Lahaina News, October 23, 1997: 20.

— nutrition for elders to be held at Kaunoa Senior Services, Lahaina News, October 30, 1997: 16.

— presenting updates on asthma for adults, Lahaina News, October 30, 1997: 17.

— Department of Health offering free hepatitis B immunization, Lahaina News, November 6, 1997: 16.

— state Department of Health to offer free HIV counseling and testing, Lahaina News, November 6, 1997: 17.

— Department of Health offering free HIV counseling and testing, Lahaina News, November 13, 1997: 20,21.

— Kaunoa Senior Services to offer nutrition program, Lahaina News, November 27, 1997: 12.

— Maui Hotel Association donates defibrillators to county Fire Department, Lahaina News, December 18, 1997: 13.

— childbirth classes to be held, Lahaina News, December 18, 1997: 14.

— Hepatitis B clinic set for Foodland, Lahaina News, December 25, 1997: 3.

— Kaunoa Senior Services to offer nutrition program, Lahaina News, January 22, 1998: 12.

— massage training to offered, Lahaina News, January 22, 1998: 5.

— Senior Stroll to be held, Lahaina News, February 12, 1998: 17.

— Ritz-Carlton hosting CPR training, Lahaina News, February 19, 1998: 2.

— Kaunoa Senior Services continues to offer nutrition program, Lahaina News, March 26, 1998: 12.

— Down to Earth to host "Women's Wellness Day", Lahaina News, May 14, 1998: 16.

— PrimeCo Hawaii Health and Fitness Fair to be held, Lahaina News, May 21, 1998: 13.

— Walk for the Cure for Multiple Sclerosis to be held, Lahaina News, June 18, 1998: 16.

— American Lung Association to hold "Asthma Alert for Parents", Lahaina News, July 16, 1998: 16.

— Community Clinic of Maui to offer free mammograms, Lahaina News, July 30, 1998: 7.

— Women's Health Month to be held, Lahaina News, August 27, 1998: 8.

— women's health presentations offered, Lahaina News, September 3, 1998: 8.

— Women's Health Month events to be held, Lahaina News, September 17, 1998: 21.

— Collon Brayce to discuss fats and oils at Down to Earth, Lahaina News, September 17, 1998: 25.

— Maui County responds to Lahaina News "Hawaii Environment and Health News" insert, Lahaina News, September 17, 1998: 3.

— Kenny Redstone to speak on Maui's medicinal plants, Lahaina News, October 1, 1998: 16.

— Grace Baptist Church to offer classes on homeopathic healing, Lahaina News, October 15, 1998: 16.

— PrimeCo Health and Fitness Fair to be held, Lahaina News, October 29, 1998: 28.

— PrimeCo Health and Fitness Fair to be held, Lahaina News, November 5, 1998: 18,20.

— Dr. Wan Soo Kim to discuss Oriental medicine, Lahaina News, November 12, 1998: 17.

— "Brain Gym" to be held, Lahaina News, January 7, 1999: 17.

— American Health Association hosting events for American Heart Month, Lahaina News, January 28, 1999: 6.

— Joan Morris teaches water jogging, Lahaina News, February 18, 1999: 7.

— Udo Erasmus to discuss "Fats That Heal, Fats That Kill", Lahaina News, February 25, 1999: 12.

— "Living Well With Lupus" to be held, Lahaina News, April 8, 1999: 13.

— Harvest Chapel pastor Laki Ka'ahumanu organizes anti-drug march, Lahaina News, April 15, 1999: 1,16.

— stroke awareness activities to be held, Lahaina News, May 6, 1999: 2.

— Maui Childbirth to begin classes, Lahaina News, May 6, 1999: 20.

— American Heart Association to hold activities for "Stroke Awareness and National High Blood Pressure Month", Lahaina News, May 13, 1999: 15.

— free skin cancer screenings, Lahaina News, May 13, 1999: 16.

— Al-Anon continues to meet, Lahaina News, May 20, 1999: 17.

— Prostate Health Educational Forum to be held, Lahaina News, June 3, 1999: 17.

— Healing Touch class to be held at Maui Memorial Hospital, Lahaina News, June 3, 1999: 17.

— Dr. James McKoy to discuss lupus, Lahaina News, June 10, 1999: 17.

— HIV counseling and testing continues to be offered at Lahaina Comprehensive Health Center, Lahaina News, June 24, 1999: 13.

— "First Steps: An Alzheimer's Disease Orientation" to be held, Lahaina News, July 8, 1999: 13.

— west side women focus of mammography study, Lahaina News, August 19, 1999: 1.

— CPR classes to be held at Mayor Hannibal Tavares Center, Lahaina News, August 19, 1999: 17.

— Hawaii Tumor Registry to help women get mammograms, Lahaina News, August 19, 1999: 2.

— CPR classes to be held at Mayor Hannibal Tavares Center, Lahaina News, August 26, 1999: 16.

— workshop on Jin Shin Jyatsu to be held, Lahaina News, September 16, 1999: 12.

— Overeaters Anonymous to meet, Lahaina News, September 23, 1999: 12.

— workshop to be held on Yoga, Qigong, and Tai Chi, Lahaina News, September 23, 1999: 13.

— Hawaii Immunization TEEN VAX Project, Lahaina News, September 23, 1999: 5.

— "Wishing Well for Health" to benefit Community Clinic of Maui, Lahaina News, September 30, 1999: 12.

— Dr. Michael Morrison to lead discussion of health awareness, Lahaina News, September 30, 1999: 13.

— mammography researcher Eve Clute seeking women's stories, Lahaina News, October 21, 1999: 6.

— "Living Well with Lupus" to be held, Lahaina News, February 24, 2000: 16.

— HIV Counseling and Testing Clinic to be held, Lahaina News, April 20, 2000: 17.

— Hui No Ke Ola Pono to provide cancer check, Lahaina News, May 18, 2000: 8.

— free HIV Counseling and Testing Clinic continues to be offered, Lahaina News, May 25, 2000: 19.

— presentation on "Understanding Lupus", Lahaina News, June 15, 2000: 17.

— display and handouts on prostate cnacer available at Lahaina Public Library, Lahaina News, June 29, 2000: 7.

— Hui No Ke Oia Pono Kokua Program offering "Women's Health Awareness Fair 2000", Lahaina News, July 6, 2000: 16.

— family planning services available, Lahaina News, July 6, 2000: 6.

— Maui Memorial Medical Center to open sleep disorder unit, Lahaina News, August 10, 2000: 1.

— prostate support group to be held, Lahaina News, August 31, 2000: 20.

— Health and Fitness Fair to be held at Lahaina Cannery Mall, Lahaina News, September 7, 2000: 14.

— new anti-smoking campaign to be organized by The Department of Health and Coalition for a Tobacco Free Hawaii, Lahaina News, September 7, 2000: 20.

— Women's Health Month to include "Facts of Life for Teen Girls", Lahaina News, September 7, 2000: 21.

— Hawaii Health Systems Corp. seeks input on health services, Lahaina News, September 14, 2000: 16.

— Women's Health Month to include "Facts of Life for Teen Girls", Lahaina News, September 14, 2000: 20.

— Health and Fitness Fair to be held at Lahaina Cannery Mall, Lahaina News, September 14, 2000: 9.

— prostate support group to meet, Lahaina News, September 28, 2000: 17.

— Mark Moyad to speak on role of nutrition in reducing cancer risk, Lahaina News, October 19, 2000: 11.

— Healthy Baby Contest held at Lahaina Cannery Mall, Lahaina News, October 19, 2000: 17.

— Penny Lorence demonstrates aerobics to older adults, Lahaina News, October 19, 2000: 8.

— Maui Diabetes Conference to be held, Lahaina News, October 26, 2000: 14.

— Health Promotion Hui formed by Maui Memorial Center to promote health, Lahaina News, December 14, 2000: 19.

— Health Promotion Hui to hold "Start Healthy Maui!", Lahaina News, January 18, 2001: 2.

— developments in dentistry described, Lahaina News, January 18, 2001: 7.

— Art School at Kapalua to offer ball fitness classes, Lahaina News, February 15, 2001: 13.

— Natalie and John Tyler to speak on prostate cancer, Lahaina News, February 15, 2001: 17.

— "Ways to Feel Better" to be held by Joanne Tanaka of Kaiser Permanente's Wailuku Clinic, Lahaina News, February 22, 2001: 16.

— "Ways to Feel Better" to be held by Joanne Tanaka of Kaiser Permanente's Wailuku Clinic, Lahaina News, March 1, 2001: 10.

— CPR class to be held at Maui Marriott Resort, Lahaina News, April 5, 2001: 2.

— April Health Promotion Hui to be held, Lahaina News, April 12, 2001: 2.

— prostate cancer support group to meet, Lahaina News, April 26, 2001: 21.

— "Exploring Health Professions: A Native Hawaiian Perspective" to be held, Lahaina News, May 3, 2001: 2.

— "Creating a Health and Wellness Tourism Business Plan" to be held, Lahaina News, May 10, 2001: 9.

— "Stroke: What You Should Know About It" to be held, Lahaina News, May 17, 2001: 17.

— "Lupus 101" workshop to be held, Lahaina News, May 17, 2001: 20.

— Martha Noyes to present "Plants in Hawaiian Medicine", Lahaina News, May 17, 2001: 20.

— CPR training to be offered, Lahaina News, May 24, 2001: 2.

— HIV counseling and testing clinic continues to be held, Lahaina News, May 24, 2001: 21.

— "Fluoridation in the 21st Century—Yes or No" to be held, Lahaina News, June 7, 2001: 21.

— Health Promotion Hui to focus on men's health, Lahaina News, June 14, 2001: 10.

— state senators to discuss changes in Public Employees' Health Fund, Lahaina News, June 21, 2001: 9.

— Foundation for Wellness founder Dr. Elain Willis to speak at Unity Church, Lahaina News, June 28, 2001: 20.

— Maui Parkinson's Disease Support Group to meet, Lahaina News, July 19, 2001: 17.

— Health Promotion Hui to focus on "What You Should Know About Cancer", Lahaina News, July 19, 2001: 2.

— new support group for women and families affected by breast cancer, Lahaina News, August 2, 2001: 1,20.

— Hawaii Bone Marrow Donor Registry to be held, Lahaina News, August 9, 2001: 2.

— "Healthy Aging" focus of August Health Promotion Hui, Lahaina News, August 16, 2001: 2.

— Albert Yazawa new medical director at Kula Hospital and Clinic, Lahaina News, August 16, 2001: 8.

— meditation group to meet on the teachings of Paramahansa Yogananda, Lahaina News, September 13, 2001: 16.

— People's Pottery and Tommy Bahama's Tropical Café and Emporium to hold benefit for breast cancer research, Lahaina News, September 27, 2001: 9.

— "Coping with Trauma" meeting to be held at Christ the King Church, Lahaina News, October 4, 2001: 17.

— state's strategy to respond to dengue fever, Lahaina News, October 18, 2001: 5.

— American Heart Association offering CPR training, Lahaina News, November 8, 2001: 2.

— HIV Counseling and Testing Clinic to be held, Lahaina News, November 22, 2001: 21.

— West Maui Taxpayers Association campaigning for 24-hour acute care facility, Lahaina News, November 29, 2001: 1,20.

— Alateen members to meet, Lahaina News, December 20, 2001: 2.

— Hui No Ke Ola Pono program offering health screenings, Lahaina News, December 27, 2001: 2.

— Community Work Day Program to pick up tires to combat dengue fever, Lahaina News, January 10, 2002: 2.

— Maui Memorial Medical Center to add complementary and alternative care providers, Lahaina News, January 17, 2002: 1,18.

— West Maui breast cancer support group Bosom Buddies to meet, Lahaina News, January 17, 2002: 16.

— Alateen continues to meet, Lahaina News, February 7, 2002: 16.

— Borders Books to host Eric Stein speaking on "Continuous Trauma", Lahaina News, February 14, 2002: 16.

— Hui No Ke Ola Pono offering free breast and cervical screenings, Lahaina News, February 21, 2002: 2.

— Benjamin Noid to speak on natural killer cells and hormones, Lahaina News, March 14, 2002: 2.

— headache support group to be formed, Lahaina News, March 14, 2002: 20.

— Maui Medical Group renovating Lahaina Clinic, Lahaina News, April 4, 2002: 3.

— April Health Promotion Hui to focus on child safety, Lahaina News, April 11, 2002: 3.

— Kurt Miyajima continues to offer Chi Gung and Tai Chi classes, Lahaina News, April 18, 2002: 17.

— Maui Parkinson Support Group to meet, Lahaina News, April 18, 2002: 17.

— Hawaii Lupus Foundation to begin monthly support meetings, Lahaina News, April 18, 2002: 2.

— Epileptic Foundation of Maui to hold Epilepsy Awareness Week, Lahaina News, May 9, 2002: 18.

— June Health Promotion Hui to focus on sports medicine, Lahaina News, June 13, 2002: 16.

— Healthy Hawaii Expo to be held, Lahaina News, June 20, 2002: 16.

— Maui Memorial Medical Center adds new radiation therapy procedure, Lahaina News, June 27, 2002: 8.

— Maui Lupus Support Group continues to meet, Lahaina News, July 25, 2002: 2.

— free HIV counseling and testing continues to be available, Lahaina News, July 25, 2002: 21.

— Maui County to hold meetings on mice and typhus, Lahaina News, August 22, 2002: 2.

— Hui No Ke Ola Pono system recruiting participants for Breast and Cervical Cancer Screening Program, Lahaina News, August 29, 2002: 15.

— Hui No Ke Ola Pono system recruiting participants for Breast and Cervical Cancer Screening Program, Lahaina News, September 12, 2002: 2.

— T'ai Chi classes to be offered, Lahaina News, October 3, 2002: 2.

— Alzheimer's Association to hold workshop on dementia, Lahaina News, October 17, 2002: 14.

— Hui No Ke Ola Pono system recruiting participants for Breast and Cervical Cancer Screening Program, Lahaina News, October 17, 2002: 14.

— Maui County Council approves establishing acute care facility in West Maui, Lahaina News, October 24, 2002: 3.

— Community Clinic of Maui providing cancer screenings, Lahaina News, December 5, 2002: 16.

— Sacred Hearts School students raise money for diabetes research, Lahaina News, December 19, 2002: 3.

— smoking to be banned in bars within restaurants and outdoor areas, Lahaina News, December 26, 2002: 9.

— Hui No Ke Ola Pono Native Hawaiian Health Care System offering programs, Lahaina News, January 16, 2003: 2.

— Kaiser Permanente moves care departments from Wailuku Clinic, Lahaina News, February 27, 2003: 8.

— Sacred Hearts School students recognized for superior fitness, Lahaina News, March 27, 2003: 1,18.

— Chinese healer Yu Tian Jianto lecture, Lahaina News, March 27, 2003: 16.

— National Sleep Awareness Week to be held, Lahaina News, March 27, 2003: 8.

— Area Plan on Aging to be held, Lahaina News, March 27, 2003: 9.

— Maui Medical Group to hold diabetes education classes, Lahaina News, April 10, 2003: 20.

— Linda Machado to speak on "Impact of Emotional/Behavioral Disorders on Families", Lahaina News, April 17, 2003: 2.

— doctors to discuss vaccination, Lahaina News, April 17, 2003: 2.

— update on Acute Care Emergency Medical Facility, Lahaina News, April 24, 2003: 18.

— Linda Machado to talk on "Impact of Emotional/Behavioral Disorders on Families", Lahaina News, April 24, 2003: 20.

— checks available as part of , Lahaina News, May 15, 2003: 2.

— Diabetes Support Group to hold educational classes, Lahaina News, May 22, 2003: 16.

— HIV testing day set, Lahaina News, June 26, 2003: 8.

— Representative Roz Baker critical of Governor Linda Lingle not signing helicopter air ambulance bill, Lahaina News, July 3, 2003: 2.

— WeightWatchers group to meet, Lahaina News, July 17, 2003: 17.

— REAL Experience Anti-Tobacco Youth Summit to be held, Lahaina News, July 24, 2003: 2.

— editorial in support of hospital in West Maui, Lahaina News, July 31, 2003: 4.

— land for proposed West Maui acute care facility donated by Ka'anapali Development Co., Lahaina News, August 7, 2003: 1,20.

— Maui Medical Group to hold classes on diabetes, Lahaina News, August 7, 2003: 16.

— presentations on cost of long-term care to be offered at Edward Jones Napili Office, Lahaina News, August 7, 2003: 8.

— Maui County Committee on the Status of Women to hold Women's Health Month, Lahaina News, September 4, 2003: 18.

— Hawaii Fertility Symposium to be held, Lahaina News, September 4, 2003: 2.

— pilates course to be offered, Lahaina News, September 18, 2003: 16.

— doctor James Leroy to present lecture on "Living Well with Arthritis", Lahaina News, October 9, 2003: 5.

— see also AIDS

HEALTH, EDUCATION, ART, RECREATION, AND TECHNOLOGY (HEART)

— to hold fundraiser at Lahaina Civic Center, Lahaina News, November 28, 1991: 14.

HEALTH FAIR FOR THE HOMELESS

— to be held my Maui Community College School of Nursing and the Salvation Army, Lahaina News, November 8, 2001: 2.

— to be held, Lahaina News, November 15, 2001: 16.

HEALTH PROMOTION HUI

— formed by Maui Memorial Center to promote health, Lahaina News, December 14, 2000: 19.

— to hold "Start Healthy Maui!", Lahaina News, January 18, 2001: 2.

— to hold events at Maui Memorial Medical Center, Lahaina News, February 15, 2001: 2.

— to focus on men's health, Lahaina News, June 14, 2001: 10.

— to present "STROKE: Symptoms, Action, Recovery", Lahaina News, May 9, 2002: 18.

— to focus on "Cancer: Everything You Should Know", Lahaina News, July 18, 2002: 1,20.

— to focus on "Healthy Aging—Continued Care Through Your Life", Lahaina News, August 15, 2002: 3.

— to focus on Travel Safety in March, Lahaina News, March 13, 2003: 2.

— theme for June to be "The Healthy Heart", Lahaina News, June 12, 2003: 14.

— to focus on "The Healthy Heart" in June, Lahaina News, June 19, 2003: 9.

— to focus on Women's Health, Lahaina News, September 18, 2003: 2.

HEALTH, STATE DEPARTMENT OF

— says that outbreak of dysentery is contained, Lahaina Sun, January 27, 1971: 1.

— sponsors Diabetes Detection Drive, Lahaina Sun, December 1, 1971: 12.

— will work to improve waste water treatment, Lahaina News, February 25, 1987: 6.

— sponsoring hotline for teens with Maui AIDS Foundation, Lahaina News, May 1, 1991: 3.

— adopts new rules on wastewater, Lahaina News, October 17, 1991: 12.

— creates algae bloom task force, Lahaina News, February 6, 1992: 3.

— launches immunization program, Lahaina News, June 24, 1993: 4.

— urges seniors to immunize, Lahaina News, July 15, 1993: 3.

— listing greatest threats to environment and human health in West Maui, Lahaina News, September 30, 1993: 1,15.

— sponsoring Hawaii Materials Exchange to encourage reuse of material, Lahaina News, November 18, 1993: 6.

— to extend vaccination hours at clinics, Lahaina News, January 6, 1994: 3.

— restructuring may reduce number of deputy directors in Environmental Health division, Lahaina News, October 13, 1994: 1.

— budget cuts expected, Lahaina News, October 20, 1994: 4.

— warns that food vendors should have permits, Lahaina News, January 26, 1995: 6.

— begins telephone line to update people on the environment, Lahaina News, February 16, 1995: 6.

— notified Board of Water Supply of water contamination in Napili, Lahaina News, May 30, 1996: 3.

— continues to offer free HIV counseling and testing, Lahaina News, April 2, 1998: 17.

— fat burning nutrition system to be explained, Lahaina News, April 23, 1998: 16.

— o offer grants to reduce non-point source pollution, Lahaina News, June 3, 1999: 16.

— to organize new anti-smoking campaign, Lahaina News, September 7, 2000: 20.

— examining use of hazardous materials at Pioneer Mill, Lahaina News, March 15, 2001: 1,22.

— sponsoring workshops on watershed protection, Lahaina News, July 12, 2001: 9.

— to hold workshop on watershed, Lahaina News, July 26, 2001: 9.

— threat of dengue fever in East Maui, Lahaina News, October 11, 2001: 3.

— continues to offer free HIV Counseling and Testing, Lahaina News, May 8, 2003: 17.

— offers free HIV, STD, and Hepatitis clinics, Lahaina News, July 24, 2003: 17.

— offering free HIV, STD, and Hepatitis tests and counseling, Lahaina News, August 7, 2003: 17.

— "LifeFest Maui" to be held at Wailea Resort, Lahaina News, September 11, 2003: 9.

— continues to offer HIV, STD, and hepatitis clinics, Lahaina News, September 25, 2003: 17.

HEALTH-SOUTH REHABILITATION OF WAILUKU

— working with Arthritis Foundation to offer warm water arthritis exercise class, Lahaina News, June 26, 2003: 10.

HEALTHCARE TRAINING AND CAREER CONSULTANTS [BUSINESS]

— plans open house, Lahaina News, October 9, 2003: 8.

HEALTHSOUTH REHABILITATION OF WAILUKU

— offering exercise classes with Arthritis Foundation Aquatic, Lahaina News, April 4, 2002: 13.

HEALTHY BABY CONTEST

— held by Meadowgold, Lahaina News, September 26, 1990: 6.

— to be held at Lahaina Cannery Mall, Lahaina News, September 21, 2000: 19.

— held at Lahaina Cannery Mall, Lahaina News, October 19, 2000: 17.

HEALTHY HAWAII EXPO

— to be held at Lahaina Cannery Mall, Lahaina News, October 2, 2003: 12.

HEALTHY WORKPLACE AWARDS

— Hawaii Psychological Association seeking nominations for, Lahaina News, August 21, 2003: 8.

HEALY TIBBITTS CONSTRUCTION

— to dredge channel to Lahaina boat harbor, Lahaina News, July 27, 1988: 11.

HEARNE, JOHN

— promoted to general manager at Lahaina Coolers, Lahaina News, July 23, 1992: 17.

HEART DANCE [TROUPE]

— to hold grand opening, Lahaina News, March 13, 1997: 16.

— to hold dance, Lahaina News, March 13, 1997: 17.

— to hold "Dancin' The Love" event, Lahaina News, May 17, 2001: 20.

— to stage dance show, Lahaina News, May 30, 2002: 16.

HEART IN A BOX [MUSICAL]

— to be performed at Maui Arts and Cultural Center, Lahaina News, October 13, 1994: 18,19.

HEART OF MAUI

— run/walk to take place, Lahaina News, July 23, 1986: 3,14.

HEART OF MUSIC, THE

— to be held at the Maui Arts and Cultural Center, Lahaina News, April 18, 2002: 17.

HEART WALK AND HEALTH FAIR

— to be held by American Heart Association, Lahaina News, February 10, 2000: 9.

HEARTBEAT

— Castle Medical Center's screening program available, Lahaina News, April 19, 1989: 13.

HEASLEY, JIM

— to discuss Faulkes Educational Telescope, Lahaina News, November 16, 2000: 16.

HEATH, GREGORY

— chef at Castaway Cafe featured, Lahaina News, October 4, 2001: 14,15.

HEATH-BLUNDELL, ANDREA

— receives an Appreciation Pin from Girl Scouts, Lahaina News, June 6, 1991: 4,7.

— joins Locations, Inc. as realtor-associate, Lahaina News, December 19, 1991: 17.

— community volunteer featured, Lahaina News, September 7, 1995: 1,12.

HEBBERD, LINDSAY [ARTIST]

— to exhibit "Cultural Portraits of Indonesia", Lahaina News, December 31, 1998: 13.

— to exhibit photographs at Maui Arts and Cultural Center, Lahaina News, January 7, 1999: 16.

HECKATHORN, JOHN

— named new editor of Honolulu Magazine, Lahaina News, July 8, 1993: 8.

HECO, JOSEPH

— featured, Lahaina News, February 8, 1996: 13.

HECOCKS-BY-THE-OCEAN [RESTAURANT]

— featured, Lahaina News, August 1, 2002: 10.

HEDANI, WAYNE

— discusses crime, Lahaina News, November 5, 1986: 1,16.

— comments on proposed thrillcraft corridor, Lahaina News, February 24, 1988: 1.

— Amfac, Inc. property manager speaks of development plans, Lahaina News, September 21, 1988: 1,14.

— appointed president of Maui Chamber of Commerce, Lahaina News, August 29, 1990: 8.

— Maui Trade Dollar popular, Lahaina News, June 11, 1992: 13.

HEDRICK, TODD

— to lead Shopping Center Division at Colliers Monroe and Freelander, Lahaina News, September 18, 2003: 8.

HEE, CLAYTON [POLITICIAN]

— candidate for State House, Lahaina News, September 15, 1982: 3.

— begins regular column in Lahaina News, will not always be indexed, Lahaina News, February 15, 1983: 2.

— State representative asks for improved biek paths, Lahaina News, June 15, 1983: 6.

— representative announces he is moving to Oahu to run for Senate seat in Kaneohe, Lahaina News, May 2, 1984: 2.

— provides summary of 1984 legislative session, Lahaina News, June 13, 1984: 7.

— ceded lands being purchased for housing development to be reappraised, Lahaina News, October 27, 1994: 1,5.

— discusses "The Native Hawaiian Data Book", Lahaina News, January 5, 1995: 3.

HEFTEL, CECIL [POLITICIAN]

— candidate for governor supports room tax and transferring part to counties, Lahaina News, February 19, 1986: 1.

HEILSCHER, EDWIN

— opens Aloha Mana Massage, Lahaina News, April 6, 1995: 6.

HEINZ, PAULA [ARTIST]

— reception at Larry Dotson Gallery, Lahaina News, March 2, 1988: 22.

HELD DISABLED WAR VETERANS

— offering computers to Maui vets, Lahaina News, October 28, 1999: 13.

HELEKAHI, LEONE

— arrested for shooting arrows into a home, Lahaina News, April 23, 1992: 8.

HELICOPTER AIR FAIR

— to be held at Kahului Airport, Lahaina News, April 13, 1988: 13.

— scheduled, Lahaina News, September 6, 1989: 3.

HELICOPTER ENVIRONMENTAL LIAISON OFFICE [HELO]
— received award for "Fly Neighborly" Noise Abatement Program, Lahaina News, February 10, 1988: 3.

HELICOPTERS
— temporary use of landing pad denied, Lahaina News, April 29, 1987: 1.
— plan for site above Ka'anapali discussed, Lahaina News, May 13, 1987: 1.
— argument over proposed West Maui heliport, Lahaina News, May 20, 1987: 1.
— Sunshine Helicopters make precautionary landing, Lahaina News, May 20, 1987: 3.
— county committee to consider possible helicopter landing sites, Lahaina News, February 24, 1988: 18.
— mayor's committee considers heliport unneeded, Lahaina News, March 2, 1988: 1,24.
— editorial supporting decision to oppose heliport, Lahaina News, March 9, 1988: 2.
— debate over proposed heliport, Lahaina News, April 20, 1988: 1.
— Papillon Helicopters seeks to extend special use permit, Lahaina News, September 13, 1989: 1.
— operators complain of confusing rules governing, Lahaina News, November 1, 1989: 3.

HELIPORT
— applications to create submitted, Lahaina News, July 16, 1986: 1,16.
— to be studied by county planning commission, Lahaina News, July 30, 1986: 11.
— Maui Planning Commissions denies request to build, Lahaina News, August 13, 1986: 16.
— debate continues, Lahaina News, September 17, 1986: 1,8.
— editorial on proposed, Lahaina News, September 24, 1986: 2.
— story from September 17 clarified, Lahaina News, October 1, 1986: 5.
— mayor's ad hoc committee meets, Lahaina News, October 15, 1986: 8.
— studied by ad hoc committee, Lahaina News, October 29, 1986: 20.
— ad committee discusses, Lahaina News, November 26, 1986: 1,5.
— complaints fewer, Lahaina News, December 17, 1986: 2.
— 4 of 6 possible sites rejected, Lahaina News, January 21, 1987: 11.
— Mayor's advisory committee looking into possible locations for, Lahaina News, February 25, 1987: 3.
— County seeking public input on possible sites, Lahaina News, March 4, 1987: 1.
— Maui County Planning Department conducting tests for, Lahaina News, August 26, 1987: 3.
— permitting issues with, Lahaina News, September 9, 1987: 1.
— State Department of Transportation and Federal Aviation Administration to hold public meeting, Lahaina News, April 27, 1988: 6.
— planned for site of former Olowalu landfill, Lahaina News, February 24, 2000: 1,2.
— residents concerned that plans were kept quiet, Lahaina News, March 2, 2000: 1,2.
— Senate changes bill to require council review, Lahaina News, March 23, 2000: 1,2.
— fallout of heliport legislation analyzed, Lahaina News, March 30, 2000: 1,2.
— bill dead, Lahaina News, May 4, 2000: 1,2.

HELLER, STEVE
— to design Century Development's proposed Lighthouse Building, Lahaina News, November 7, 1990: 1.

HELLERWORK
— discussed as alternative healing method, Lahaina News, April 20, 1988: 20.

HELLING, SKIP [ARTIST]
— works shown at Village Gallery, Lahaina Sun, April 28, 1971: 7.

HELLIWELL, HARRY
— elected treasurer of the Kihei Community Association, Lahaina Sun, December 2, 1970: 4.

HELLOW MINNESOTA
— reunion scheduled, Lahaina News, February 20, 1991: 8.

HELM, RAIATEA [MUSICIAN]
— to perform at Ka'anapali Beach Hotel's Tiki Courtyard with The Pandanus Club, Lahaina News, October 24, 2002: 22.
— to perform at Lahaina Cannery Mall's 16th anniversary, Lahaina News, March 20, 2003: 9.
— Hale Makua Foundation to hold 'Ohana Luau, Lahaina News, July 17, 2003: 14.
— to perform at Hale Makua Foundation's 'Ohana Luau, Lahaina News, July 24, 2003: 17.
— to perform at Watershed Forum at Maui Community College, Lahaina News, September 4, 2003: 18.

HELMINTOLLER, STUARD [ARTIST]
— featured at Old Jail Gallery, Lahaina News, January 14, 1987: 3.

HELP DISABLED WAR VETERANS [ORGANIZATION]
— introducing program offering computers, Lahaina News, October 21, 1999: 14.

HELPING ALL THINGS (HATS)
— to host luncheon meeting to benefit Maui Youth and Family Services, Lahaina News, August 10, 1995: 4.
— to offer luncheon to benefit the Maui Symphony Orchestra, Lahaina News, May 1, 1997: 16.

HELPING ELDERLY LIVE LIFE'S OPPORTUNITIES (HELLO)
— trains volunteers to help elderly, Lahaina News, August 13, 1986: 3.
— volunteers needed to visit elderly, Lahaina News, March 4, 1987: 10.

HELPING OTHER PARENTS EASE SORROW (HOPE)
— support group to meet, Lahaina News, October 12, 1983: 4.

HELTZEN, CARTER
— swimmer competes in state competition, Lahaina News, February 4, 1999: 15.

HEMMETER, CHRIS
— creates publishing company, Lahaina News, July 26, 1989: 6.

HEMMETER DEVELOPMENT CO.
— owners of Maui Surf Hotel seek permit for renovations, Lahaina News, February 20, 1985: 1.
— reveals expansion plans for Maui Surf Hotel, Lahaina News, June 5, 1985: 3.

HEMMETER INVESTMENT CO. [BUSINESS]
— agrees to purchase Maui Surf and Kaua'i Surf, Lahaina News, November 21, 1984: 3.

HEMMINGS, FRED [POLITICIAN]
— critical of State housing plan, Lahaina News, July 18, 1990: 3.
— surfer to appear at Borders Books, Lahaina News, October 14, 1999: 7.

HEMOPHILIA FOUNDATION OF HONOLULU
— added as a United Way agency, Lahaina News, August 7, 1985: 8.

HEMP
— Longhi's Gourmet Hemp Seed Feast and Help Clothing Show held, Lahaina News, October 5, 1995: 10.

HEMP FESTIVAL
— to be held at Maui Botanical Gardens, Lahaina News, April 17, 1997: 12.
— to be held, Lahaina News, October 30, 1997: 16.

HEMP SEED FEAST AND HEMP EXPO
— to be hosted by Longhi's Restaurant, Lahaina News, July 20, 1995: 5.
— to be hosted by Longhi's Restaurant, Lahaina News, August 3, 1995: 4.
— to be hosted by Longhi's Restaurant, Lahaina News, August 10, 1995: 4.

HENDERSON, BILL
— to teach workshop on "Controlling Cash and Receivables", Lahaina News, March 13, 1997: 16.

HENDERSON, VERYL
— pastor at Lahaina Baptist Church discusses child care at the church, Lahaina Sun, December 9, 1970: 4.

HENDLER, KATHERINE
— elected president of Ka'anapali Beach Resort Association, Lahaina News, April 17, 1991: 9.

HENDRICKS, JON [SINGER]
— to perform at Casanova's, Lahaina News, June 6, 1990: 13.

HENDRICKS, SUSAN
— new principal at Sacred Hearts School, Lahaina News, July 3, 2003: 1,18.

HENDRIX FILM
— showing at Maui Community College, Lahaina Sun, February 10, 1971: 2.

HENDRIX, JEFF [MUSICIAN]
— offering jazz workshop for Maui Academy of Performing Arts , Lahaina News, January 5, 1995: 12.

HENDRIX, JIMI [MUSICIAN]
— account of career and his concert on Maui, Lahaina News, February 24, 1988: 7,10.

HENEGHAN, GREG
— leading Napili Canoe Club, Lahaina News, June 17, 1999: 6.
— president of Napili Canoe Club discusses organization, Lahaina News, June 28, 2001: 14.

HENNESSEY, CELESTINA
— to host toy drive at World Café, Lahaina News, December 19, 1996: 2.

HENRY ALLEN TRIO, THE [MUSICAL GROUP]
— to perform at Maui Inter-Continental's Inu Inu Lounge, Lahaina News, April 2, 1992: 20.
— to perform at Inu Inu Lounge at Maui Inter-Continental, Lahaina News, July 23, 1992: 25.
— to perform, Lahaina News, April 10, 2003: 16.

HENRY, SCOTT [COMEDIAN]
— to perform at Comedy Club, Lahaina News, June 13, 1991: 12.
— to perform at Comedy Club and the Sports Page, Lahaina News, June 18, 1992: 18,21.
— to perform at Honolulu Comedy Club, Lahaina News, August 4, 1994: 16.

HENSON, CHARLES [ARTIST]
— featured, Lahaina News, December 5, 1996: 17.

HENTON, JOHN "HITMAN" [COMEDIAN]
— to perform at Comedy Club, Lahaina News, June 27, 1990: 12.
— to perform at Comedy Club and the Sports Page, Lahaina News, December 26, 1990: 8,10.
— to perform at Comedy Club and the Sports Page, Lahaina News, December 12, 1991: 20,21.

HENTZ, JULIANA
— Scholar/Athlete of the Week, Lahaina News, April 8, 1999: 7.

HEPBURN, PAULINE [ARTIST]
— to hold workshop at Hui No'eau Visual Arts Center, Lahaina News, April 4, 1990: 14.

HEPBURN, TONY [ARTIST]
— to hold workshop at Hui No'eau Visual Arts Center, Lahaina News, April 4, 1990: 14.

HERB AND SCOTT ROGERS PRODUCTIONS, INC. [BUSINESS]
— season tickets available for shows by, Lahaina News, December 15, 1994: 19.
— change curtain time, Lahaina News, January 26, 1995: 14.
— show times changed, Lahaina News, March 2, 1995: 12.

HERB MARKES ORCHESTRA [MUSICAL GROUP]
— to perform at Oktoberfest, Lahaina News, September 30, 1993: 12.

HERBERG, CYNTHIA LITZAU
— appointed new executive director at Ka'anapali Beach Resort, Lahaina News, March 14, 1996: 10.

HERBERT, BARRY
— appointed training manager at Kapalua Bay Hotel, Lahaina News, December 19, 1990: 7.

HERBERT HORITA DEVELOPMENT
— ready to move forward on Maui Lani project, Lahaina News, December 12, 1991: 13.
— Maui County panel recommends approval of project in Kihei, Lahaina News, December 19, 1991: 17.
— proposed project approved by Maui County Council, Lahaina News, December 26, 1991: 4.

HERBIE MANN AND JAXIL BRAZZ [MUSICAL GROUP]
— to perform at Casanova's, Lahaina News, May 15, 1991: 12.

HERBIG, GARY [MUSICIAN]
— saxophonist to perform at Blackie's, Lahaina News, July 3, 1985: 10.
— to perform at Blackie's Bar, Lahaina News, December 26, 1990: 8.
— to perform at Blackie's Bar, Lahaina News, February 13, 1992: 19.

HERBS
— medicinal value discussed, Lahaina News, April 27, 1988: 1,17,18.

HERE IS HAWAII
— show reviewed, Lahaina News, October 1, 1981: 6.
— dinner show reopens at Ka'anapali Beach Hotel, Lahaina News, April 16, 1986: 3.

HERE'S MAUI [MAGAZINE]
— publication featured, Lahaina Times, August, 1980 volume 4 number 7: 1.

HERE'S TO THE HEROES
— fundraiser to benefit firefighters to be held at Queen Ka'ahumanu Center, Lahaina News, September 5, 2002: 14.

HERITAGE COLLEGE OF WASHINGTON
— recruiting students, Lahaina News, December 10, 1998: 20.

HERITAGE SINGERS [MUSICAL GROUP]
— to perform at Kahului Seventh-day Adventist Church, Lahaina News, June 22, 2000: 17.

HERKES, ROBERT
— appointed general manager of Woody's Oceanfront Grill, Lahaina News, June 24, 1999: 11.

HERMAN, LOUIS
— UH researcher receives federal money to study dolphins, Lahaina Sun, February 2, 1972: 8.

HERMAN, PATTIE
— appointed director of international sales at the Westin Maui and Westin Kaua'i, Lahaina News, June 11, 1992: 14.

HERMANN, SANDER
— sponsoring free basketball clinic, Lahaina News, June 4, 1998: 14.
— sponsoring free basketball clinic, Lahaina News, July 9, 1998: 15.

HERNANDEZ, SCOTT [MUSICIAN]
— to perform at Maui Lu Resort, Lahaina News, October 22, 1998: 21.
— to debut his new CD "Boy", Lahaina News, November 18, 1999: 17.

HEROIN
— becoming more common in West Maui, Lahaina News, September 15, 1994: 1,2.

HERR, RON "ROCKET"
— discusses bottle collecting in Lahaina, Lahaina News, January 10, 1990: 11.

HERTEL, GERD
— executive chef at Kapalua Bay Hotel photographed, Lahaina News, August 1, 1991: 14.

HERTZ [BUSINESS]
— has rental desk at Kapalua Villas, Lahaina News, February 18, 1999: 11.

HESTER, WALTER AND JACQUI
— owners of Maui Jim featured, Lahaina News, March 20, 1997: 1.

HETTIE [ARTIST]
— see Saaiman, Hettie [artist]

HE'UI CULTURAL ARTS FESTIVAL
— to be held at Banyan Tree Park, Lahaina News, August 19, 1999: 16.
— celebrates first anniversary, Lahaina News, August 3, 2000: 1.
— held, Lahaina News, August 10, 2000: 1,15.
— to celebrate Queen Lili'uokalani, Lahaina News, September 27, 2001: 2.
— see also Na Kupuna O Maui He'ui Cultural Arts Festival

HEW, GARRET
— promoted to manager of East Maui Irrigation Co. Ltd., Lahaina News, February 24, 2000: 13.

HEWETT, FRANK [MUSICIAN]
— to perform at Maui Arts and Cultural Center, Lahaina News, December 28, 1995: 8.

HI NO KE OLA PONO
— offering health programs, Lahaina News, October 31, 2002: 12.

HI-TECH SAILBOARDS [BUSINESS]
— changes name to Hi-Tech Surf Sports, Lahaina News, August 22, 1990: 9.

HI-TECH SKATE CHALLENGE
— to be held at Keopuolani Skate Park, Lahaina News, January 21, 1999: 7.

HI-TECH SURF SPORTS [BUSINESS]
— new name for Hi-Tech Sailboards, Lahaina News, August 22, 1990: 9.
— to sponsor snowboarding night at Maui Marriott, Lahaina News, October 13, 1994: 11.
— vintage surfboards stolen from, Lahaina News, January 16, 2003: 18.

HIBBARD, JANET
— promoted to vice president at Advertising Works, Inc., Lahaina News, April 23, 1992: 16.

HICKMAN, PAT [ARTIST]
— chair of Fibre Art Department at University of Hawai'i at Manoa to present on collection of contemporary basket artists, Lahaina News, April 3, 1991: 10.
— fiber artist to discuss work, Lahaina News, September 17, 1998: 28.

HICKS, RENEE [COMEDIAN]
— to perform at Comedy Club and the Sports Page, Lahaina News, January 16, 1992: 12,16.

HIDALDO, DENNIS
— Scholar/Athlete of the Week, Lahaina News, November 18, 1999: 8.

HIDALGO, JUVENAL
— salon owner to donate funds to Maui Academy of Performing Arts, Lahaina News, February 9, 1995: 10.

HIEB, RICHARD
— Salvation Army leader sent to post in Arizona, Lahaina News, February 7, 2002: 1,20.

HIEB, RICHARD AND CAROL
— Salvation Army employees featured, Lahaina News, November 23, 1995: 1,2.

HIGA, DAVID
— Harbors Division chief explains plan to move Carthaginian, Lahaina News, June 3, 1987: 1.

HIGA, JULIE
— to rewrite zoning laws, Lahaina News, April 5, 1989: 1,16.
— president of Maui County Alliance for the Mentally Ill to show a video and speak, Lahaina News, March 27, 1991: 4.
— president of Maui County Alliance for the Mentally Ill to present and discuss film on mental health, Lahaina News, April 3, 1991: 3.

HIGA, KASE
— qualifications to be judge questioned by Maui Justice Foundation, Lahaina Sun, January 19, 1972: 7.

HIGASHI, WINONA
— named publisher of the Oahu Drive Guide, Lahaina News, September 1, 1994: 13.

HIGGINBOTHAM, JOAN
— NASA astronaut to speak at conference on women pursuing careers in science and technology, Lahaina News, January 13, 2000: 11.
— NASA astronaut to speak at conference on women pursuing careers in science and technology, Lahaina News, January 20, 2000: 11.

HIGGINS, CRAIG [COMEDIAN]
— to perform at Comedy Club and the Sports Page, Lahaina News, January 21, 1993: 14.

HIGGINS, LUKE
— basketball coach interviewed, Lahaina News, February 26, 1986: 4.

HIGH PERFORMANCE KITES
— to hold yo-yo demonstration, Lahaina News, October 24, 2002: 20.

HIGH SEAS DIXIELAND BAND [MUSICAL GROUP]
— to perform at Maui Lu Resort, Lahaina News, May 18, 1995: 10.

HIGHAM, JOHN
— civil engineer discusses plans to tear down Pioneer Mill, Co., Lahaina News, September 27, 2001: 1,8.

HIGHWAYS
— Kuihelani Highway being constructed from Ma'alaea to Kahului Airport, Lahaina Sun, November 18, 1970: 1.

HIGHWAYS DIVISION, STATE
— planning improvement projects, Lahaina News, February 4, 1993: 3,4,.
— to investigate areas where highway is vulnerable to ocean, Lahaina News, November 14, 1996: 1,20.

HIGUCHI, FREDRICK HARUO
— featured, Lahaina News, September 6, 2001: 1,18.

HIGUCHI, HERBERT [ARTIST]
— photographer dies, Lahaina News, March 12, 1992: 6.

HIKE MAUI [BUSINESS]
— featured, Lahaina News, January 25, 1984: 14.

HIKIJI, WAYNE [MUSICIAN]
— to perform at Gabel's, Lahaina News, January 9, 1991: 7.
— to perform at Gabel's, Lahaina News, January 23, 1991: 8.

HIKING
— trip to Moloka'i described, Lahaina Sun, September 1, 1971: 3.
— account of John and Alan Siemer hiking from Wailuku to Lahaina through Iao and Olowalu Valleys, Lahaina Sun, August 2, 1972: 7.
— proposed for West Maui, Lahaina Sun, September 27, 1972: 1.
— old trails in Maui detailed, Lahaina Sun, November 8, 1972: 14.
— old trails in Maui detailed, Lahaina Sun, November 15, 1972: 14.
— hikes offered through Kapalua Villas, Lahaina News, May 20, 1999: 6.

HILDORFER, MARTINA
— honored as manager of the quarter by Westin Maui, Lahaina News, July 2, 1992: 16.

HILL AND KNOWLTON/COMMUNICATIONS-PACIFIC, INC
— purchases Skinner Communication, Lahaina News, August 1, 1990: 7.

HILL, CHARLIE [COMEDIAN]
— to perform at Comedy Club and the Sports Page, Lahaina News, January 16, 1992: 12,16.

HILL, CHELSEA
— to discuss Origin-The Language Agency's services, Lahaina News, February 15, 2001: 8.

HILL, MYRTLE
— promoted to front desk manager at Royal Kahana Resort, Lahaina News, May 13, 1993: 5.

HILL, TERRY
— to teach coconut palm frond weaving class, Lahaina News, July 24, 2003: 16.

HILLERMAN, TONY [WRITER]
— to attend Maui Writers Conference, Lahaina News, August 19, 1999: 2.

HILO HATTIES [BUSINESS]
— opens store in Lahaina Center, Lahaina News, February 14, 1990: 5.
— named General Retailer of the Year by Hawaii Fashion Industry Association, Lahaina News, August 1, 1991: 11.
— names Bill Waring as creative merchandising director, Lahaina News, May 7, 1992: 10.
— Carlton Kramer named vice president of sales and marketing, Lahaina News, September 14, 1995: 10.
— Barbara Powers appointed store manager at, Lahaina News, December 23, 1999: 13.
— adding new location in South Maui, Lahaina News, November 9, 2000: 18.
— to hold fundraiser for Maui high schools, Lahaina News, December 6, 2001: 8.
— contributes to Lahainaluna High School Foundation, Lahaina News, January 24, 2002: 8.
— Len DaSilva promoted to chief operating officer at, Lahaina News, September 19, 2002: 8.

HILTON [MAUI]
— see Maui Hilton

HILTON HOTELS CORP. [BUSINESS]
— negotiating to take over management of Kapalua Resort, Lahaina News, May 7, 1992: 10.

HIMANI [ARTIST]
— to exhibit at Banyan Tree Gallery, Lahaina News, January 13, 1994: 8.
— hand-colored images of hula to be exhibited, Lahaina News, January 5, 1995: 12.

HIMEX
— Hawaii Materials Exchange to encourage reuse of material, Lahaina News, November 18, 1993: 6.

HINAU, ANNIE
— local resident's life recounted, Lahaina News, August 5, 1987: 1,12.
— life featured, Lahaina News, May 31, 1989: 2.

HINAU, BETSY
— helps organize Na Mele O Maui, Lahaina News, November 2, 1988: 2.

HINAU, GINGER
— named manager of Honolua Store, Lahaina News, October 22, 1986: 5.

HINAU, ISA-LEI
— named a United States National Award winner in English, Lahaina News, June 15, 1995: 2.

HINTON, WARREN
— discusses plans for underground wiring in Front Street, Lahaina Sun, December 9, 1970: 7.
— discusses plans for banyan tree in Lahaina, Lahaina Sun, February 3, 1971: 7.
— critical of signage at Lahaina small boat harbor, Lahaina Sun, October 20, 1971: 15.
— to share Maui Chamber of Commerce's T.S. Shinn Award, Lahaina News, June 26, 1985: 3.
— chair of the Lahaina Yacht Club Golf Tournament presents check to Maui Memorial Hospital, Lahaina News, October 26, 1995: 5.

HIPP, BYRON
— completes Maui Marathon, Lahaina News, July 5, 2001: 13.

HIPPIE BROCHURE
— reaction by tourists, Lahaina Sun, December 23, 1970: 5.
— discussed, Lahaina Sun, December 30, 1970: 4.
— discussed, Lahaina Sun, January 20, 1971: 5.
— now available at Kahului Airport, Lahaina Sun, January 27, 1971: 2.
— photograph of cover, Lahaina Sun, January 27, 1971: 2.
— inspiration for a game, Lahaina Sun, February 24, 1971: 3,4,5.

HIPPIES
— discussed by the West Maui Business Association, Lahaina Sun, December 2, 1970: 1.
— Booklet prepared for by Maui County, Lahaina Sun, December 9, 1970: 1,6.
— discussed at panel organized by the West Maui Business Association, Lahaina Sun, December 16, 1970: 1.
— described as violent by Police Chief Abraham Aiona, Lahaina Sun, December 16, 1970: 6.
— status on Maui discussed, Lahaina Sun, December 16, 1970: 7.
— as victims of crimes, Lahaina Sun, December 16, 1970: 7.
— projects desired by West Maui Business Association, Lahaina Sun, December 23, 1970: 2.
— text of "hippie brochure", Lahaina Sun, December 23, 1970: 5.
— Jack Stephens suggests crating Hippie Visitors Bureau, Lahaina Sun, December 30, 1970: 4.
— not mentioned in Mayor Cravalho's inaugural speech, Lahaina Sun, January 20, 1971: 2.
— evicted from Animal Farm, Lahaina Sun, January 27, 1971: 1.
— blamed for failure of Lahaina Whaling Spree, Lahaina Sun, February 3, 1971: 2.
— criticized by Joe Bulgo, Lahaina Sun, February 24, 1971: 6.
— debated in letter to the editor, Lahaina Sun, March 3, 1971: 2.
— associated with Zendo Zen Buddhist colony, Lahaina Sun, March 17, 1971: 4.
— discussed in meeting between the West Maui Business Association and Mayor Cravalho, Lahaina Sun, March 17, 1971: 6.
— resolution sent to Mayor Elmer Cravalho, Lahaina Sun, March 17, 1971: 8.
— proposal by Marco Meyer to study "the problem of transients", Lahaina Sun, March 24, 1971: 1,5.
— Maui County Council discusses possible responses, Lahaina Sun, March 24, 1971: 5.
— editorial cartoon, Lahaina Sun, March 24, 1971: 8.
— Reverend Charles Burger editorial on harsh treatment of, Lahaina Sun, March 31, 1971: 5.
— discussed at Maui Chamber of Commerce meeting, Lahaina Sun, May 19, 1971: 8.
— issue of discussed by local businessmen, Lahaina Sun, June 23, 1971: 1.
— Banana Patch receives violations, Lahaina Sun, June 30, 1971: 10.
— "Animal Farm" closes, Lahaina Sun, July 14, 1971: 1.

— Maui Chamber of Commerce encouraging businesses to hire, Lahaina Sun, July 21, 1971: 9.
— Banana Patch still being used, Lahaina Sun, September 1, 1971: 4.
— editorial that the problem has faded, Lahaina Sun, September 29, 1971: 2.
— Banana Patch continues with new landlord, Lahaina Sun, October 27, 1971: 15.
— update on attempts to create a Youth Center, Lahaina Sun, November 3, 1971: 14.
— description of impact of closing of Banana Patch , Lahaina Sun, November 10, 1971: 12.
— blamed for spread of venereal disease, Lahaina Sun, February 23, 1972: 3.
— cleared from Makena beach, Lahaina Sun, April 26, 1972: 20.

HIRATA, CHARLES
— police officer honored with Alaka'i Award , Lahaina News, December 13, 2001: 2.

HIRATA, EDWIN
— speaks of Department of Transportation's plans, Lahaina News, January 20, 1988: 1.
— State Director of Transportation discusses Lahaina Bypass, Lahaina News, March 16, 1988: 1.
— State transportation director reconsidering plans to demolish Mala Wharf, Lahaina News, March 21, 1990: 3.
— State Department of Transportation moving forward with plans to buy Kapalua-West Maui airport, Lahaina News, December 5, 1990: 1.
— says Department of Transportation views Lahaina Bypass as top priority, Lahaina News, December 5, 1990: 3.

HIRATA, WAYNE
— missing; searching for in coastal waters, Lahaina News, January 16, 1992: 3.

HIRONAKA, MASAMI
— to hold ukulele lessons at Kam III School, Lahaina Sun, April 14, 1971: 6.

HIRONO, MAZIE [POLITICIAN]
— advocates for leasehold and insurance premium bills, Lahaina News, November 21, 1991: 7.
— Lieutenant Governor to speak at Democratic Century Club, Lahaina News, April 17, 1997: 13.
— Lieutenant Governor takes up Lahaina Library issues, Lahaina News, June 17, 1999: 1,20.
— Lieutenant Governor to speak to West Maui AJA Veterans Club, Lahaina News, May 24, 2001: 1.
— speaks to West Maui AJA Veterans Club to commemorate Memorial Day, Lahaina News, May 31, 2001: 1,18.

HIROSHIMA
— anniversary of atomic bombing observed at Princess Nahienaena School, Lahaina News, August 1, 1990: 3.

HIROSHIMA [MUSICAL GROUP]
— to perform at Lahaina Civic Center, Lahaina News, May 27, 1987: 8.
— to perform at Maui arts and Cultural Center, Lahaina News, September 2, 1999: 17.
— to perform at Maui Arts and Cultural Center, Lahaina News, September 9, 1999: 13.

HIROSHIMA AND NAGASAKI PEACE PRAYER DAY
— hosted by Iao Congregational Church, Lahaina News, July 27, 1988: 11.

HIROSHIMA-NAGASAKI DAY
— to hold commemoration program, Lahaina News, August 8, 1991: 3.
— to be observed at Peace Park, Lahaina News, August 2, 2001: 16.

HIRSCHMANN, GEORGE
— to perform at Comedy Club and the Sports Page, Lahaina News, April 24, 1991: 7,11.

HISPANIC FRATERNITY OF MAUI
— to celebrate Mexican and Central American Independence Day, Lahaina News, September 16, 1993: 16.

HISPANICS
— Mizpa Hispanic Church to hold meeting on "Hispanics in Maui", Lahaina News, August 2, 2001: 1,20.

HISTORIC DISTRICT SIGN DESIGN GUIDELINES
— meeting to explain to be held, Lahaina News, September 13, 2001: 9.

HISTORIC FUN RUN
— Lahaina Coolers seeking volunteers for, Lahaina News, September 12, 1991: 3.
— details given, Lahaina News, October 3, 1991: 14.
— to be held this week, Lahaina News, October 10, 1991: 8.
— to be held, Lahaina News, October 1, 1992: 8.
— to occur at start of Aloha Festival, Lahaina News, October 8, 1992: 4.

HISTORIC HAWAII FOUNDATION
— seeking nominations for Preservation Awards, Lahaina News, January 16, 1985: 3.
— selects R.J. Pfeiffer as Kama'aina of the Year, Lahaina News, November 21, 1990: 13.

HISTORIC LAHAINA FUN RUN
— to be held by Lahaina Coolers, Lahaina News, October 13, 1994: 10.

HISTORIC PRESERVATION
— Hawaii to not receive funds from Interior Department because no request was made, Lahaina Sun, December 8, 1971: 1.
— lecture to be held at Maui Community College, Lahaina News, October 5, 1988: 3.

HISTORIC PRESERVATION DIVISION
— office notified that human remains found at Pukalani Highlands, Lahaina News, January 30, 1992: 5.
— notified of remains found at D.T. Fleming Park, Lahaina News, September 7, 1995: 1.

HISTORICAL PRESERVATION DIVISION
— to hold public meetings on rules for handling ancient burials, Lahaina News, January 26, 1995: 2.

HISTORY
— story of creation of Hale Pa'i and the early history of printing, Lahaina Sun, June 23, 1971: 4.
— history of printing in Hawaii discussed, Lahaina Sun, January 5, 1972: 14.
— history of crime in Lahaina discussed, Lahaina Sun, January 5, 1972: 16.
— photograph of tombstone of Charles Adam from 1861, Lahaina Sun, February 23, 1972: 1.
— presentation on immigrants in Hawaii, Lahaina Sun, March 15, 1972: 10.
— account of early Lahaina to be featured in TWA Ambassador [magazine], Lahaina Sun, March 29, 1972: 9.
— mountains of West Maui discussed, Lahaina Sun, May 17, 1972: 17.
— Battle of Koko o na Moku recounted, Lahaina Sun, May 24, 1972: 17.
— description of Wai-Ha-ha-ke, a stream near Ka'anapali, Lahaina Sun, May 31, 1972: 17.
— legends connected to Na Hono a Pi'ilani recounted, Lahaina Sun, June 7, 1972: 17.
— biography of Ka Hekili-nui 'Ahu-manu, Lahaina Sun, June 14, 1972: 21.
— Kane Hekili [deity] detailed, Lahaina Sun, June 21, 1972: 15.
— story of temple of Ha-lulu-ko'a-ko'a, Lahaina Sun, July 19, 1972: 17.

— story of Haha-kea, north of Lahaina, Lahaina Sun, July 26, 1972: 19.

— stories of Kane and Kanaloa recounted, Lahaina Sun, August 2, 1972: 15.

— Ponds of Kahana described, Lahaina Sun, August 9, 1972: 19.

— historical place names of Haleakala discussed, Lahaina Sun, August 23, 1972: 15.

— story of Chinese cowboy, Lahaina Sun, August 30, 1972: 15.

— legends of Pele recounted, Lahaina Sun, September 6, 1972: 19.

— biography of David Malo, Lahaina Sun, September 13, 1972: 17.

— Maui's historical sites discussed, Lahaina Sun, September 20, 1972: 15.

— Hawaiian stars detailed, Lahaina Sun, September 27, 1972: 15.

— Hawaiian stars detailed, Lahaina Sun, October 4, 1972: 19.

— Hawaiian stars detailed, Lahaina Sun, October 11, 1972: 19.

— legend of Keka'a, the Hiding Woman, Lahaina Sun, October 25, 1972: 19.

— Hawaiian calendar discussed, Lahaina Sun, November 1, 1972: 22.

— old hiking trails in Maui detailed, Lahaina Sun, November 8, 1972: 14.

— old hiking trails in Maui detailed, Lahaina Sun, November 15, 1972: 14.

— history of Keawaike Harbor of Lele described, Lahaina Sun, November 22, 1972: 9.

— Wailea detailed, Lahaina Sun, November 29, 1972: 14.

— story of Wa'ahea the Prophetess, Lahaina Sun, December 6, 1972: 26.

— story of Lua'ehu described, Lahaina Sun, December 13, 1972: 26.

— story of Lua'ehu at Honolua, Lahaina Sun, December 20, 1972: 26.

— Hawaii is only state to not file a development plan to federal government for historic sites , Lahaina Sun, December 27, 1972: 10.

— early Christian influence described, Lahaina Sun, December 27, 1972: 22.

— early Christian influence described, Lahaina Sun, January 3, 1973: 22.

— early history of Lahaina, Lahaina Sun, January 10, 1973: 22.

— Hawaiian constellations detailed, Lahaina Sun, January 17, 1973: 22.

— Hawaiian astronomers and temples described, Lahaina Sun, January 24, 1973: 22.

— Kaho'olawe detailed, Lahaina Sun, January 31, 1973: 22.

— early roadways in West Maui detailed, Lahaina Sun, February 7, 1973: 22.

— story of guardian spirits of Lua'ehu, Lahaina Sun, February 28, 1973: 22.

— Moloka'i described, Lahaina Sun, March 14, 1973: 14.

— 19th century events on Kaho'olawe detailed, Lahaina Sun, March 28, 1973: 22.

— story of Manu-pae described, Lahaina Sun, April 11, 1973: 14.

— prophecies in Hawaii described, Lahaina Sun, May 30, 1973: 22.

— Maui in 1917 described, Lahaina Sun, June 13, 1973: 24,25.

— account of Lonopuha offered, Lahaina Sun, June 27, 1973: 14.

— 1869 account of sea life reprinted, Lahaina Sun, August 29, 1973: 4.

— place names discussed, Lahaina News, January 20, 1994: 2.

— excerpts from journal of William Stenson, Lahaina News, December 18, 1997: 13.

— documents found in Wo Hing Museum, Lahaina News, December 30, 1999: 1,20.

— historic flag to return to Lahaina, Lahaina News, September 19, 2002: 1,21.

HISTORY DAY

— Lahainaluna High School students compete in, Lahaina News, April 8, 1993: 3.

— Lahainaluna High School success at, Lahaina News, March 16, 1995: 2.

— Lahainaluna High School students win state contest, Lahaina News, May 18, 1995: 1,16.

— winners announced, Lahaina News, May 16, 1996: 6.

— West Maui students successful at, Lahaina News, May 18, 2000: 7.

— Lahaina Intermediate School students in national competition, Lahaina News, June 22, 2000: 7.

— Lahaina Intermediate School student essays advance to national contest, Lahaina News, May 2, 2002: 1,18.

— students win, Lahaina News, May 22, 2003: 2.

HISTORY MONTH, NATIONAL

— sponsoring panel on Maui women, Lahaina News, March 6, 1997: 10.

HITACHI, PRINCE

— Japanese royal visits Maui with Princess Hanako, Lahaina News, June 26, 1985: 1,2,9.

HITCHHIKING

— claim that anti-hitchhiking law is unconstitutional, Lahaina Sun, February 10, 1971: 1,7.

— ruling expected on ant-hitchhiking law, Lahaina Sun, February 17, 1971: 3.

— rules expected soon, Lahaina Sun, May 26, 1971: 3.

— call to legalize, Lahaina Sun, April 19, 1972: 21.

HIV/AIDS SUPPORT GROUP

— to meet, Lahaina News, December 5, 1991: 6.

HIYASHI, RALPH

— public works director discusses odor at Olowalu Dump, Lahaina News, January 23, 1985: 3.

HMS PINAFORE [MUSICAL]

— to be performed at Castle Theatre, Lahaina News, October 3, 1996: 14.

HMSA [BUSINESS]

— HMSA seeking nominations for Ola Pono Award, Lahaina News, October 29, 1998: 15.

— Gina Bella Mataafa wins "Name the 5-a-Day Fruits" contest, Lahaina News, December 9, 1999: 11.

HO, DANIEL [MUSICIAN]

— releases CD "Hymns of Hawai'i" with George Kahumoku, Lahaina News, December 9, 1999: 19.

— to exhibit at Maui Ocean Center, Lahaina News, May 31, 2001: 16.

— to perform benefit for Kai Makana, Lahaina News, July 12, 2001: 14.

— to perform songs from CD "Finding My Way", Lahaina News, July 19, 2001: 16.

HO, DON [MUSICIAN]

— to perform at Maui Arts and Cultural Center to benefit Maui Dharma Center, Lahaina News, June 29, 2000: 21.

HO, DOROTHY TAM

— scored hole-in-one, Lahaina News, August 22, 1990: 9.

HO, JOHNNY LUM [MUSICIAN]

— to perform at Maui Community College Ho'olaule'a, Lahaina News, April 11, 1984: 5.

HO, KALANI

— takes management position at Old Lahaina Luau, Lahaina News, September 26, 2002: 3.

HO, KEAHI

— Lahainaluna High School qualifies for Olympic Trials, Lahaina News, April 18, 1996: 12.

HO, LYNN

— receives award from West Maui Soroptimists, Lahaina News, August 12, 1999: 9.

HO, MRS. RON

— discusses Lahaina press kit, Lahaina Sun, December 23, 1970: 8.

HO, NADINE LUM
— awarded scholarships by Hyatt Regency Maui to study at Maui Community College, Lahaina News, July 1, 1987: 10.

HO, RON
— house suffers storm damage, Lahaina Sun, December 30, 1970: 1.

HOAG, JOHN
— president of First Hawaiian Bank to retire, Lahaina News, July 7, 1994: 9.

HOAH, DICK
— appointed sales manager for J.J. Enterprises, Lahaina News, March 12, 1986: 3.

HOAIKANE [MUSICIAN]
— to perform at Old Lahaina Cafe and Luau, Lahaina News, March 14, 1990: 15.

HOALOHA NA EHĀ [BUSINESS]
— opens Aloha Mixed Plate restaurant, Lahaina News, February 6, 1997: 9.

HOAPILI [GOVERNOR]
— involved in conflict with whalers in Lahaina in the 1820s, Lahaina Sun, January 6, 1971: 8.

HOBBIT, THE [PLAY]
— to be performed by Maui Academy of Performing Arts, Lahaina News, June 27, 1990: 12.
— to perform at Iao Theatre, Lahaina News, November 13, 1997: 21.

HOBDY, BOB
— offering class on ahupua‘a, Lahaina News, November 13, 1997: 20.
— to lead class on "Ahupua‘a—Traditional Hawaiian Land Divisions" at Bailey House Museum, Lahaina News, May 30, 2002: 16.
— to discuss "Ahupua‘a: A Land Management System", Lahaina News, September 5, 2002: 17.

HOBDY, DOREEN
— to hold "E Himeni Kakou—Let's Sing the Traditional Spiritual , Lahaina News, December 2, 1999: 17.

HOBIE CAT 17 WORLD CHAMPIONSHIPS
— to take place in Lahaina, Lahaina News, August 10, 1988: 14,15.
— results, Lahaina News, September 21, 1988: 12.

HOBIE SPORTS [BUSINESS]
— grand opening, Lahaina News, December 7, 1988: 24.
— schedule beach volleyball tournament with Kimo's Restaurant, Lahaina News, October 31, 1991: 5.
— to hold Surf Classic, Lahaina News, January 23, 1992: 8.
— now carrying "City Lights" women's active sportswear, Lahaina News, July 9, 1992: 14.
— to hold Keiki Surf Jam, Lahaina News, July 14, 1994: 9.

HOBIE-KIMO JERRY BOSER MEMORIAL LONGBOARD CONTEST
— won by Mark Anderson, Lahaina News, August 1, 1990: 14.

HOBSON, CHARLES
— reverend to lead revival services, Lahaina News, April 5, 1989: 3.

HOCKEY
— in-line hockey featured, Lahaina News, June 9, 1994: 8.

HOCKING, DAVID
— Biblical scholar to speak on September 11th, Lahaina News, August 29, 2002: 1.

HODBY, DOREEN
— to offer singing classes, Lahaina News, December 3, 1998: 21.

HODGES, CATHLEEN
— to present on nene for the Haleakala National Park, Lahaina News, August 28, 1997: 10,11.
— Haleakala National Park wildlife biologist to present "Ua‘a—Hawaii's Endangered Seabird", Lahaina News, April 13, 2000: 13.

HODGES, MARK
— head of coastal seaweed monitoring team to share draft survey results, Lahaina News, October 26, 1995: 3.
— explains Kaho‘olawe Island Reserve Commission plan, Lahaina News, February 4, 1999: 1.

HODGES, TONY
— director of Life of the Land in Honolulu, Lahaina Sun, November 18, 1970: 1.
— present at public meeting on ecology, Lahaina Sun, January 13, 1971: 1,2.
— speaks at Maui Student Science Seminar program, Lahaina Sun, February 3, 1971: 6.
— moving to Maui, Lahaina Sun, August 4, 1971: 2.
— discusses current situation of Life of the Land, Lahaina Sun, October 20, 1971: 14.
— police question campaign workers, Lahaina Sun, September 13, 1972: 19.
— open letter regarding his running for mayor, Lahaina Sun, September 13, 1972: 2.
— running for mayor, Lahaina Sun, September 13, 1972: 5.
— recommends changing flight patterns to reduce aircraft noise pollution, Lahaina Sun, September 27, 1972: 5.

HODGSON, JAMES [U.S. SECRETARY OF LABOR]
— visits Maui, plays golf, Lahaina Sun, March 15, 1972: 19.

HODGSON, LYNN
— expresses need to start controlling algae soon, Lahaina News, April 13, 1995: 1,20.

HOEDOWN
— organized at Pukalani Elementary School, Lahaina News, April 5, 1989: 3.
— Rotary Clubs of Maui to raise money for Friends of the Children's Advocacy Center of Maui, Lahaina News, September 26, 1990: 7.
— Rotary Clubs of Maui fundraiser to include barbecue steak and chicken dinner, Lahaina News, November 7, 1990: 4,5.
— a success, Lahaina News, November 28, 1990: 4.

HOFFMAN, EDWARD
— named manager of Maui Eldorado Resort Condominium, Lahaina News, January 17, 1990: 24.

HOGAN, EVE
— to speak on "Relationships in the 21st Century, the Rules Have Changed", Lahaina News, July 19, 2001: 16.
— to speak on "Relationships in the 21st Century, the Rules Have Changed", Lahaina News, August 23, 2001: 17.
— to present "Organizing your thoughts for a book or presentation" to 'Ohana Connection, Lahaina News, July 25, 2002: 21.
— to talk on "Way of the Winding Path: A Map for the Labyrinth of Life", Lahaina News, April 17, 2003: 17.

HOGAN, GARY
— named president of Pleasant Island Holidays, Lahaina News, May 27, 1993: 8.
— named president of Pleasant Hawaiian Holidays, Lahaina News, June 24, 1993: 10.

HOGUE PUBLICATION, INC. [BUSINESS]
— opens gallery, Lahaina News, May 3, 2001: 9.

HO‘IKE MAUI
— held at Lahaina Cannery Shopping Center, Lahaina News, March 21, 1990: 13.
— continues at Lahaina Cannery Mall, Lahaina News, March 20, 1991: 9.

HOKAMA, G. RIKI [POLITICIAN]
— candidate for Lahaina County Council, Lahaina News, November 2, 2000: 21.
— to chair Maui County Council Budget and Finance Committee meeting, Lahaina News, March 29, 2001: 1.

HOKAMA, GORO [POLITICIAN] (cont.)
— County Council Budget and Finance Committee chair to hold public meeting, Lahaina News, March 14, 2002: 1,20.
— to hold hearings on Maui County budget, Lahaina News, March 21, 2002: 3.

HOKAMA, GORO [POLITICIAN]
— member of Maui County Council, Lahaina Sun, December 30, 1970: 8.
— elected chair of Maui County Council, Lahaina Sun, January 17, 1973: 7.
— announces public hearings to consider rezoning proposals, Lahaina News, July 16, 1986: 3.
— to seek reelection, Lahaina News, June 1, 1988: 19.
— proposes new real property tax relief, Lahaina News, September 5, 1990: 4.
— announces Western Interstate Region of the National Association of Counties will meet on Maui, Lahaina News, May 1, 1991: 4.
— announces retirement from Dole Food Co., Lahaina News, January 16, 1992: 3.
— to seek re-election, Lahaina News, April 23, 1992: 8.
— elected to chair Mau County Council, Lahaina News, January 7, 1993: 4.
— to recommend Tom Morrow as vice chair of the Maui County Council, Lahaina News, September 9, 1993: 1,12.
— to challenge Mayor's decision to hire outside attorneys, Lahaina News, March 17, 1994: 4.
— critical of Mayor Linda Lingle, Lahaina News, October 20, 1994: 1.
— Democratic Party to hold testimonial dinner for, Lahaina News, December 8, 1994: 3.

HOKAMA, MASA
— caves used to store recording equipment described, Lahaina Sun, April 25, 1973: 15.

HOKOANA, LEROY [DEPUTY FIRE CHIEF]
— discusses Maui County Fire Department training for ocean rescue, Lahaina News, July 30, 1986: 20.

HOKOMA, RIKI [POLITICIAN]
— running for Lana'i seat of Maui County Council, Lahaina News, August 10, 2000: 3.

HOKULE'A [CANOE]
— experience of Abraham "Snake" Ah Hee described, Lahaina News, August 3, 1995: 9.
— to visit Lahaina, Lahaina News, January 25, 2001: 1,3.
— Hokule'a waterman Abraham "Snake" Ah Hee featured, Lahaina News, January 25, 2001: 3.
— tour of to be offered, Lahaina News, February 1, 2001: 17.
— to dock at Lahaina Harbor, Lahaina News, February 8, 2001: 1.
— to participate in "In Celebration of Canoes", Lahaina News, May 10, 2001: 11.
— to visit Lahaina, Lahaina News, April 17, 2003: 9.

HOLBROOK, CLIFFORD
— sentenced to 10 years for rape, Lahaina News, July 15, 1982: 3.

HOLBROOK, HAL
— to present "Mark Twain Tonight!" at Maui Arts and Cultural Center, Lahaina News, March 23, 2000: 12.

HOLBROOK, PATTY
— wins "Return to Maui" contest, Lahaina News, April 2, 1992: 20.

HOLDEN, STEVEN
— named vice president and general manager of Sheraton Maui Hotel, Lahaina News, September 19, 1984: 14.

HOLE IN THE WALL [RESTAURANT]
— reviewed, Lahaina News, October, 1979: 3.
— reviewed, Lahaina News, February 1, 1983: 14.

HOLIDAY RETIREMENT CORP. [BUSINESS]
— to preview retirement complex, Lahaina News, May 4, 2000: 13.

HOLIDAY THEATRES [BUSINESS]
— to open at Wharf Shops and Restaurants, Lahaina News, January 25, 1989: 1.
— could be sold following bankruptcy, Lahaina News, August 27, 1992: 11.

HOLLAND, JULIEANN
— to speak at Renew Wellness Center, Lahaina News, May 15, 2003: 17.

HOLLAND, RICHARD
— to discuss "Dr. Fritz, My Miracle Healer in Brazil", Lahaina News, September 21, 2000: 20.

HOLLAND, RON
— teaching at Tang Soo Do Martial Arts Club, Lahaina News, September 25, 1985: 4.

HOLLANDER, LORIN [PIANIST]
— to lecture and perform, Lahaina News, December 12, 1984: 3.

HOLLERAN, PATRICK
— named director of food and beverage at Embassy Suites Resorts, Lahaina News, August 8, 1991: 8.

HOLLEY, MIKEY
— swimmer successful, Lahaina News, November 18, 1999: 8.

HOLLINGSHEAD, VANESSA [COMEDIAN]
— to perform at Honolulu Comedy Club, Lahaina News, October 26, 1995: 11.
— to perform at Honolulu Comedy Club, Lahaina News, November 2, 1995: 12.

HOLLISTER, MILES
— see Lokahi Pacific

HOLLYWOOD'S FAMOUS POETS SOCIETY
— to hold contest, Lahaina News, August 25, 1994: 14.

HOLMAN, VICTORIA [ARTIST]
— exhibits at Metropolitan Gallery, Lahaina News, December 12, 1990: 12.

HOLMBERG, LOREN
— helping fix Maui Youth and Family Shelter in Paia, Lahaina News, September 13, 1989: 1.
— president of Maui Contractors Association interviewed, Lahaina News, February 28, 1990: supplement19,supplement20,supplement21.

HOLMES, JULIE CLAIRE
— to lecture on women and hormones, Lahaina News, February 16, 1995: 6.
— to speak to Hawaii State Commission on the Status of Women, Lahaina News, September 19, 1996: 15.

HOLMES, VICTOR [ARTIST]
— opens Avalene Gallery, Lahaina News, November 1, 2001: 8.

HOLO HONOKOWAI
— accepting applications from renters, Lahaina News, August 19, 1987: 3.
— now renting, Lahaina News, April 13, 1988: 30.
— now renting, Lahaina News, May 4, 1988: 14.
— some apartments may be converted to hotel rooms, Lahaina News, September 14, 1988: 1,14.
— tenants being evicted from, to convert to hotel, Lahaina News, November 30, 1988: 1.
— operated by Aston Hotels, Lahaina News, December 7, 1988: 1,15.
— editorial critical of conversion to hotel, Lahaina News, December 7, 1988: 4.
— Aston Hotels and JDH & Associates to help evicted tenants, Lahaina News, December 14, 1988: 1.
— Maui County Council and Mayor Hannibal Tavares fight conversion to hotel, Lahaina News, December 21, 1988: 1.

— tenants receive reprieve on eviction; mayor supports purchasing, Lahaina News, January 4, 1989: 1.

— evictions will stop at, Lahaina News, February 8, 1989: 1,5.

— may become mixed-use housing, Lahaina News, February 15, 1989: 12.

— some units to stay long term, Lahaina News, February 22, 1989: 1.

— deal may not hold up according to Maui County Council's legal advisor, Lahaina News, March 22, 1989: 12.

— renter allowed to stay until at least 1992, Lahaina News, July 5, 1989: 3.

HOLO MAI PELE: THE TRAVELS OF PELE [PLAY]

— to be performed by Halau O Kekuhi, Lahaina News, April 27, 1995: 12.

— to be performed, Lahaina News, May 4, 1995: 16.

HOLOCAUST

— Day of Remembrance set, Lahaina News, April 24, 1985: 20.

HOLOCAUST IN MY BODY [FILM]

— Steve Sisgold to premiere, Lahaina News, January 11, 2001: 2.

HOLOKU BALL

— held at Ka'anapali Hotel, Lahaina Sun, May 5, 1971: 3.

— planned for June 5, Lahaina Sun, June 2, 1971: 5.

HOLT, BILL

— wins World Cup Blue Marlin Fishing Tournament, Lahaina News, August 6, 1992: 4.

HOLT, CURT

— beat Ted St. Martin in free throw competition, Lahaina News, December 13, 1989: 8.

HOLT, DOUG

— Kihei School principal resigns to work for state Department of Education, Lahaina News, June 24, 1993: 8.

HOLT, HOKULANI PADILLA

— to lecture on Hawaiian topics at Maui Prince Hotel, Lahaina News, July 4, 1990: 4.

HOLT, JENNIFER [ARTIST]

— to exhibit at "Fish Textile Art" at the Art School at Kapalua, Lahaina News, January 31, 2002: 16.

— to exhibit at Art School at Kapalua, Lahaina News, September 19, 2002: 22.

HOLT, LINDA

— awarded Maui District Teacher of the Year, Lahaina News, September 29, 1994: 5.

HOLT-PADILLA, HOKULANI [MUSICIAN]

— explains Kaho'olawe Island Reserve Commission plan, Lahaina News, February 4, 1999: 1.

— to speak on "The Cultural Heritage of Kaho'olawe", Lahaina News, October 19, 2000: 21.

— joins Maui Arts and Cultural Center, Lahaina News, September 6, 2001: 9.

— to perform at Ka'anapali Beach Hotel's Tiki Courtyard, Lahaina News, February 20, 2003: 15.

— kumu hula to speak at Maui Arts and Cultural Center, Lahaina News, February 20, 2003: 2.

— to perform at Tiki Courtyard, Lahaina News, August 28, 2003: 16.

HOLTE, VIRGINIA [DANCER]

— to appear in "Ballet Spectacular", Lahaina News, January 21, 1999: 13.

HOLTER, LANCE [POLITICIAN]

— plans to run for Maui County Council, Lahaina News, July 25, 2002: 16.

HOLTON, MATTHEW

— wins Hard Rock Cafe 10K Rock 'n Roll Run, Lahaina News, June 5, 1997: 13.

HOLTQUIST, JONATHAN

— awarded grant to study effects of fish feeding at Airport Beach, Lahaina News, July 17, 1997: 15.

HOLY FAMILY ECUMENICAL SHELTER

— to hold luau fundraiser, Lahaina News, August 17, 1988: 14.

— officials comment on homeless, Lahaina News, November 22, 1989: 1.

HOLY GHOST CHURCH

— to celebrate 78th anniversary of church's completion, Lahaina Sun, June 6, 1973: 18.

HOLY GHOST FEAST

— to be held at Holy Ghost Church, Kula, Lahaina News, June 4, 1992: 4.

HOLY INNOCENTS EPISCOPAL CHURCH

— Christmas House fundraiser, Lahaina Sun, November 25, 1970: 4.

— special Christmas services scheduled, Lahaina Sun, December 23, 1970: 8.

— women's group collecting food for Teen Challenge center in Olowalu, Lahaina Sun, February 10, 1971: 6.

— organizing Christmas House, Lahaina News, November 14, 1984: 3.

— to hold Christmas House bazaar, Lahaina News, November 13, 1985: 3.

— start program to help people in crisis in West Maui, Lahaina News, November 20, 1985: 3,11.

— community outreach planned, Lahaina News, November 12, 1986: 3.

— to hold Christmas service, Lahaina News, December 17, 1986: 12.

— to hold Lenten services, Lahaina News, February 17, 1988: 3.

— planning Christmas House Bazaar, Lahaina News, November 16, 1988: 6.

— to offer Conference on Aging, Lahaina News, January 11, 1989: 5.

— Christmas House fundraiser scheduled, Lahaina News, November 15, 1989: 5.

— hopes to build columbarium, Lahaina News, February 21, 1990: 3.

— rummage sale to be held, Lahaina News, April 3, 1991: 1.

— to hold Christmas pageant, Lahaina News, December 19, 1991: 4.

— to hold Christmas House sale, Lahaina News, November 5, 1992: 4.

— to hold Christmas House sale, Lahaina News, November 19, 1992: 3.

— to host Christmas House, Lahaina News, November 11, 1993: 3.

— to hold Christmas House sale, Lahaina News, November 10, 1994: 7.

— to hold rummage sale, Lahaina News, November 4, 1999: 12.

— to hold Christmas House, Lahaina News, November 29, 2001: 16.

— to begin community food basket program, Lahaina News, January 31, 2002: 3.

— offers Community Food Basket, Lahaina News, March 21, 2002: 2.

— Alfred Stefanik to run, Lahaina News, July 4, 2002: 3.

— to hold Christmas House bazaar, Lahaina News, November 21, 2002: 20.

HOLY INNOCENTS PRESCHOOL

— to hold rummage sale, Lahaina News, March 4, 1987: 3.

— to hold rummage sale, Lahaina News, April 5, 1989: 3.

— to hold rummage sale, Lahaina News, April 25, 1990: 3.

— to hold auction and rummage sale, Lahaina News, March 3, 1994: 4.

— to hold benefit concert for Maui Arts and Cultural Center, Lahaina News, March 9, 1995: 4.

— to hold rummage sale, Lahaina News, March 16, 1995: 4.

— to hold rummage sale, Lahaina News, March 23, 1995: 2.

— pictures from rummage sale, Lahaina News, March 30, 1995: 16.

— preschool to hold rummage sale, Lahaina News, April 11, 1996: 6.

— preschool to hold rummage sale, Lahaina News, April 18, 1996: 6.

— to hold car wash, Lahaina News, February 20, 1997: 10.

— to hold car wash, Lahaina News, October 16, 1997: 16.

— to hold car wash benefit, Lahaina News, February 26, 1998: 12.

— to hold summer Hawaiian program, Lahaina News, April 2, 1998: 2.

— receives grant from Atherton Family Foundation, Lahaina News, May 7, 1998: 18.

— Hawaiiana program offered, Lahaina News, May 14, 1998: 7.

— planning Hawaiiana program for children, Lahaina News, May 21, 1998: 9.

— organizing a cookbook fundraiser, Lahaina News, October 1, 1998: 8.

— to create cookbook, Lahaina News, October 22, 1998: 15.

— to sell cookbook as fundraiser, Lahaina News, December 17, 1998: 21.

— to hold car wash fundraiser, Lahaina News, November 1, 2001: 16.

— Esther Calapini-Domingo named director of, Lahaina News, July 18, 2002: 8.

HOME AND GARDEN SHOW
— to be held on the Big Island, Lahaina News, July 11, 1991: 6.

HOME DEPOT [BUSINESS]
— to open, Lahaina News, August 31, 2000: 14.

— new store hiring, Lahaina News, March 1, 2001: 8.

— opens in Kahului, Lahaina News, May 31, 2001: 9.

— to hold kids workshops, Lahaina News, August 1, 2002: 8.

HOME RENTAL NETWORK [BUSINESS]
— opens, Lahaina News, May 31, 1989: 15.

HOME SHOW
— reservations being taken for booths, Lahaina News, February 26, 1998: 11.

— to be held by Maui Contractors Association, Lahaina News, June 26, 2003: 20.

HOMELESS
— poem by homeless printed, Lahaina Sun, August 29, 1973: 19.

— Holy Family Ecumenical Shelter to hold luau fundraiser, Lahaina News, August 17, 1988: 14.

— estimated to be at least 800 on Maui, Lahaina News, November 22, 1989: 1.

— "Christmas at Wailea" festival to support, Lahaina News, December 6, 1989: 28.

— editorial supporting shelter, Lahaina News, February 28, 1990: 14.

— lawmakers review shelter bill, Lahaina News, February 28, 1990: 24.

— Salvation Army proposes homeless shelter, Lahaina News, July 18, 1990: 4.

— attacked by teenagers, Lahaina News, August 22, 1990: 1.

— conditions described as terrible for, Lahaina News, October 24, 1990: 1,7.

— many have jobs, Lahaina News, October 24, 1990: 1,8,9.

— donations given to help, Lahaina News, November 21, 1990: 4.

— fundraiser held by Maui Catholic Charities, Lahaina News, December 26, 1990: 4.

— Maui Catholic Charities to hold fundraiser for, Lahaina News, January 2, 1991: 4.

— Maui Catholic Charities to hold fundraiser for, Lahaina News, January 16, 1991: 4.

— benefit to be held for shelter, Lahaina News, February 6, 1991: 3.

— tickets to "Hand in Hand" auction and dinner benefit available, Lahaina News, February 13, 1991: 4.

— Light Bringers organization helping hunger and homelessness, Lahaina News, July 25, 1991: 3.

— offered relocation option from Maʻalaea beach, Lahaina News, December 19, 1991: 6,7.

— family evicted from beach at Maʻalaea, Lahaina News, December 26, 1991: 4.

— mayor Linda Lingle announces grant for shelter to help, Lahaina News, February 6, 1992: 4.

— Mayor's Advisory Committee on the homeless to hold meeting, Lahaina News, March 12, 1992: 5.

— Alexander and Baldwin, Inc. donates to Ka Hale Ake Ola Maui Homeless Resource Center, Lahaina News, March 12, 1992: 5.

— to be discussed by residents, Lahaina News, June 18, 1992: 9.

— some remain in camp off Kenui Street recently bulldozed , Lahaina News, July 2, 1992: 3.

— homeless man drowns, Lahaina News, July 16, 1992: 4.

— more homeless leave vacant field, Lahaina News, July 16, 1992: 8.

— Salvation Army Envoy Dianna Hatter speaks about, Lahaina News, July 23, 1992: 3.

— services needed, Lahaina News, October 1, 1992: 3.

— Salvation Army wants to offer interim shelters, Lahaina News, December 31, 1992: 1.

— Inmates from Maui County Correctional Center to fix Lightbringers rescue mission shelter, Lahaina News, January 28, 1993: 3,4.

— evicted from near Maluʻulu O Lele Park, Lahaina News, March 18, 1993: 1.

— moved off of field near Shaw Street, Lahaina News, April 8, 1993: 3.

— evictions continue, Lahaina News, April 29, 1993: 1.

— man attacked, Lahaina News, April 29, 1993: 3.

— leave area near Shaw street, Lahaina News, May 13, 1993: 3.

— official discusses possible site for shelter, Lahaina News, May 20, 1993: 1.

— Hard Rock Café to host run for homeless, Lahaina News, May 20, 1993: 6.

— search for homes for shelter for, Lahaina News, May 27, 1993: 1.

— access to mental health services brought by Lightbringers Rescue Mission, Lahaina News, July 8, 1993: 1.

— benefit concert to be held for, Lahaina News, August 19, 1993: 15.

— Lightbringers Rescue Mission calls for shelter after alcohol-related death, Lahaina News, January 20, 1994: 1,2.

— Department of Human Concerns homeless coordinator Rudy Esquer seeks job training program, Lahaina News, February 10, 1994: 3.

— Kapalua Plantation Course to host "A Scramble for the Homeless", Lahaina News, June 30, 1994: 7.

— residents asked opinions on, Lahaina News, May 2, 1996: 2.

— Maui County proposes homeless resource center, Lahaina News, January 30, 1997: 2.

— Senator Daniel Inouye seeks funding for center for, Lahaina News, July 24, 1997: 1,3.

— plans for West Side resource facility, Lahaina News, October 9, 1997: 1,3.

— meeting to decide if county to pursue shelter, Lahaina News, February 19, 1998: 1.

— input wanted on proposed center, Lahaina News, April 23, 1998: 1,20.

— Maui County Council to unveil play for resource center, Lahaina News, April 30, 1998: 2.

— Maui County looking for location for resource center, Lahaina News, May 7, 1998: 1,20.

— groups want two parks closed at night to improve safety and reduce vagrancy, Lahaina News, September 24, 1998: 1,20.

— Light Bringers Rescue Mission produces video on problem of, Lahaina News, November 5, 1998: 8.

— Light Bringers Rescue Mission joining Planet Hope, Lahaina News, April 22, 1999: 5.

— Ka Hale A Ke Ola Homeless Resource Center to hold hearing on shelter, Lahaina News, November 2, 2000: 1,2.

— editorial supporting shelter, Lahaina News, November 23, 2000: 4.

— Maui Economic Concerns of the Community intends to break ground on West Side Resource Center for, Lahaina News, March 8, 2001: 1,18.

— Light Bringers Rescue Mission works with Koinonia Pentecostal Church members to feed, Lahaina News, June 21, 2001: 3.

— Aloha 2001 Homeless Shelter Benefit fundraiser to be held, Lahaina News, December 27, 2001: 14.
— see also Ka Hale A Ke Ola Homeless Resource Center

HOMELESS TREASURES
— new name of Ka Hale A Ke Ola Homeless Resource Center's thrift shop, Lahaina News, April 21, 1994: 9,12.

HOMESCHOOL LEARNING NETWORK, INC. [BUSINESS]
— launches website, Lahaina News, September 27, 2001: 9.
— joins with homeschool.com, Lahaina News, April 11, 2002: 9.

HOMOSEXUALITY
— murder of William Hano discussed, Lahaina News, July 1, 1982: 7.
— mayor Tavares reaffirms ban on use of public park for Miss Gay Moloka'i Beauty Pageant, Lahaina News, March 4, 1987: 3.
— murder of Jerry Canada described, Lahaina News, January 30, 1992: 1,6.

HONDA, ALISON
— new reservations manager at The Mahana, Lahaina News, May 8, 2003: 8.

HONDA, HERBERT [POLITICIAN]
— house representative featured, Lahaina News, August 1, 1980: 4.
— to not seek re-election, Lahaina News, June 18, 1992: 4.

HONDA, MARK
— to issue recommendation on apartment complex proposed by JGL Enterprises, Inc., Lahaina News, January 5, 1995: 4.
— recommends approval of Napilihau Villages housing project proposed by JGL, Lahaina News, January 12, 1995: 1,16.

HONDA, ROY
— available at public meeting to discuss Social Security, Lahaina Sun, December 30, 1970: 4.

HONDA, VICTOR
— discusses careers at National Oceanic and Atmospheric Administration, Lahaina News, March 6, 1997: 3.

HONE HEKE CORPORATION [BUSINESS]
— receives permit to operate ferry between Lahaina and Lana'i, Lahaina News, January 2, 1991: 5.

HONEY SWEET YOGURT AND ICE CREAM SHOPPE [RESTAURANT]
— featured, Lahaina News, July 15, 1987: 10.
— featured, Lahaina News, December 2, 1987: 7.
— reviewed, Lahaina News, December 14, 1988: 8.
— reviewed, Lahaina News, March 15, 1989: 8.
— reviewed, Lahaina News, April 26, 1989: 8.
— reviewed, Lahaina News, July 26, 1989: 12.

HONFED BANK [BUSINESS]
— to sell 118 units of Sands of Kahana to Livex Corp. of Japan, Lahaina News, September 12, 1990: 10.

HONG, ANTHONY
— new general manager of Hawaiian Duragreen Inc., Lahaina News, June 15, 2000: 14.

HONG KONG SEAFOOD RESTAURANT [RESTAURANT]
— opens, Lahaina News, August 27, 1998: 13.
— opens, Lahaina News, September 10, 1998: 11.

HONGWANJI MISSION
— celebrates 80th anniversary, Lahaina News, October 17, 1984: 3.
— council sponsoring public lecture by William Masuda, Lahaina News, March 27, 1985: 3.
— celebrates 100th anniversary, Lahaina News, August 16, 1989: 4.
— to offer Japanese language classes, Lahaina News, August 22, 1990: 4.
— applications for crafts booths open for Wailuku Hongwanji Craft and Food Fair, Lahaina News, August 29, 1990: 4.

— to hold Japanese language classes, Lahaina News, August 29, 1990: 4.
— to host food and crafts fair, Lahaina News, October 24, 1991: 5.
— annual Masaichi Kawaguchi Nembutsu Seminar to be held, Lahaina News, September 24, 1992: 3.
— celebrating 90th anniversary, Lahaina News, October 6, 1994: 7.
— to celebrate 90th anniversary, Lahaina News, October 13, 1994: 6,7.
— 90th anniversary celebration held, Lahaina News, October 20, 1994: 1.
— to hold annual bazaar, Lahaina News, November 3, 1994: 4.
— to host O-Bon Festival, Lahaina News, August 1, 1996: 21.
— to host O-Bon Festival, Lahaina News, August 8, 1996: 14.
— Wailuku Hongwanji Mission Fujinkai to host Autumn Craft and Food Fair, Lahaina News, October 23, 1997: 20.
— to hold O-Bon festival, Lahaina News, July 30, 1998: 1,20.
— to host Autumn Craft and Food Fair, Lahaina News, October 22, 1998: 20.
— preparing for O Bon Festival, Lahaina News, June 3, 1999: 17.
— preparing for 95th anniversary, Lahaina News, October 7, 1999: 15.
— turning 95, Lahaina News, October 14, 1999: 12.
— to hold Autumn Craft and Food Fair, Lahaina News, October 19, 2000: 20.
— to hold bazaar, Lahaina News, March 22, 2001: 9.
— to hold O-Bon Festival, Lahaina News, August 2, 2001: 3.
— celebrates ancestors, Lahaina News, August 9, 2001: 15.
— Business Restoration Fund to hold casino night fundraiser for school, Lahaina News, November 1, 2001: 5.
— to hold O-Bon practice, Lahaina News, June 6, 2002: 17.
— to celebrate O-Bon Festival, Lahaina News, July 25, 2002: 3.
— Georg Woodman to teach martial arts at, Lahaina News, January 16, 2003: 13.
— to hold O-Bon dance practices, Lahaina News, June 12, 2003: 21.
— to hold O-Bon Festival, Lahaina News, July 31, 2003: 18.

HONIG, FREDERICK
— to speak on "Experiencing Your Inner Bliss Through Meditation" at 'Ohana Connection, Lahaina News, May 30, 2002: 16.

HONOAPI'ILANI HIGHWAY
— construction projects to begin, Lahaina News, July 4, 1984: 18.
— stretch of dedicated, Lahaina News, September 10, 1986: 1.
— widening of may take longer to complete, Lahaina News, January 28, 1987: 1.
— community seeks overpass on, Lahaina News, December 29, 1994: 1.
— controversy over rock wall along, Lahaina News, September 19, 1996: 3.
— plans available for widening of, Lahaina News, April 3, 1997: 3.
— resurfacing project winding down, Lahaina News, October 1, 1998: 1,20.
— new bridge part of expansion plans, Lahaina News, January 21, 1999: 1.
— traffic study to be done, Lahaina News, April 15, 1999: 1,16.
— new highway lanes to open mid-April, Lahaina News, March 16, 2000: 1,16.
— call to make safer, Lahaina News, March 1, 2001: 2.
— Department of Planning to prepare master plan for relocating, Lahaina News, October 31, 2002: 1,30.

HONO'EA PROJECT
— group to protect hawksbill turtles to meet, Lahaina News, November 7, 1996: 15.

HONOKAHUA
— human remains found at proposed site for Ritz-Carlton development, Lahaina News, March 1, 1989: 1,16.
— public hearing on Maui Land and Pineapple, Co.'s plans to restore burial site at, Lahaina News, April 18, 1990: 3.

— Maui County Planning Commission defers decision on channel at, Lahaina News, February 6, 1992: 5.

— water wells to be cleaned in, Lahaina News, September 9, 1999: 1,16.

HONOKAHUA SCHOOL

— as location of West Maui Youth Center, Lahaina Sun, January 6, 1971: 7.

— West Maui Youth Center can occupy space rent free, Lahaina Sun, May 5, 1971: 6.

HONOKAHUA VILLAGE

— to be cleared for new development, Lahaina Sun, April 21, 1971: 8.

HONOKAOWAI PARK

— Maui County Council considers banning drinking in, Lahaina News, May 18, 1995: 3.

HONOKAU

— beach front property too expensive for county, Lahaina News, September 21, 1995: 3.

— Maui Land and Pineapple criticized for wastewater violations, Lahaina News, October 2, 1997: 1,2.

HONOKAUPU, ALBERT

— promoted to general superintendent of East Maui Irrigation Co. Ltd., Lahaina News, February 24, 2000: 13.

HONOKOHAU

— farmers concerned about water in, Lahaina News, August 20, 1992: 1.

— property owners interested in selling property for park, Lahaina News, September 3, 1992: 3.

— park planned for, Lahaina News, August 24, 1995: 1,16.

— Maul Land and Pineapple Co to provide more water to valley, Lahaina News, September 21, 1995: 1.

— children to participate in Litter Bugs Me, Lahaina News, May 24, 2001: 8.

— property available at, Lahaina News, October 25, 2001: 7.

HONOKOHAU STREAM

— source of water for Napili, Lahaina Sun, November 11, 1970: 3.

— Kimo Apana and Leilani Bronson explore, Lahaina News, September 14, 1995: 1,16.

HONOKOHAU STUDY ADVISORY COMMISSION

— hears testimony from native Hawaiians concerning land rights, Lahaina Sun, August 8, 1973: 4.

HONOKOHAU VALLEY

— listed as a priority area to preserve, Lahaina Sun, February 16, 1972: 15.

— group forms to preserve, Lahaina News, January 24, 1990: 28.

— residents want trash pickup, Lahaina News, November 24, 1994: 1,3.

— taro farmers unhappy about plans, Lahaina News, February 1, 1996: 3.

— Hawaiian descendants seek land in, Lahaina News, February 22, 1996: 1,16.

— residents want better treatment by Water Department, Lahaina News, March 28, 1996: 1,2.

— Board of Water Supply trucking water into, Lahaina News, July 23, 1998: 1,20.

— residents asked to improve drinking water system, Lahaina News, October 28, 1999: 1,2.

HONOKOHAU VALLEY ASSOCIATION

— meeting recounted, Lahaina News, June 13, 1991: 2,18.

— seeking members, Lahaina News, April 18, 1996: 6.

— new officers and president, Lahaina News, March 27, 1997: 3.

HONOKOWAI [TOWN]

— condominium planned, Lahaina Sun, February 14, 1973: 13.

— decline of town detailed, Lahaina Sun, May 2, 1973: 15.

— plans announced for Embassy Suite Hotel, Lahaina News, February 5, 1986: 3.

— study requested before wastewater treatment plant expanded at, Lahaina News, July 11, 1990: 1.

— proposed shopping center to be considered by Maui County Council , Lahaina News, February 11, 1993: 3.

— residents concerned about traffic with proposed shopping center, Lahaina News, March 4, 1993: 1.

— site work on desedimentation basin begins, Lahaina News, September 15, 1994: 6.

— light to be installed at intersection, Lahaina News, November 24, 1994: 3.

— traffic light to be installed in, Lahaina News, February 13, 1997: 3.

— zero-lot-line housing planned for, Lahaina News, February 27, 1997: 3.

— property managers form group to fight crime, Lahaina News, March 15, 2001: 1,22.

— Department of Hawaiian Homelands to meet with Hawaiians to discuss Native Hawaiian community in, Lahaina News, May 22, 2003: 1,18.

HONOKOWAI BEACH PARK

— erosion wall postponed, Lahaina News, June 16, 1994: 1.

— plans for sea wall revisited, Lahaina News, August 10, 1995: 1.

— sand project being designed, Lahaina News, May 2, 1996: 19.

HONOKOWAI COUNTY PARK

— to get picnic tables, Lahaina Sun, June 2, 1971: 1.

HONOKOWAI KAUHALE

— creating mural, Lahaina News, December 19, 1996: 3.

HONOKOWAI MARKETPLACE

— business tenants announced, Lahaina News, February 18, 1999: 11.

HONOKOWAI PARK

— tree on brink of death, Lahaina News, November 28, 1990: 1.

— large tree threatened by beach erosion, Lahaina News, February 27, 1991: 1.

— Maui County wants rock wall to halt erosion at, Lahaina News, March 26, 1992: 1,4.

— regulars say drinking is self-policed, Lahaina News, August 3, 1995: 1,20.

— plans to improve safety, Lahaina News, July 25, 1996: 2.

— residents want more details on plan to restore beach at, Lahaina News, January 21, 1999: 1,16.

— engineers to explain "Beach Nourishment Demonstration Project", Lahaina News, March 25, 1999: 3.

— beach restoration to be held, Lahaina News, April 8, 1999: 1,16.

HONOKOWAI PLAY GROUP

— to meet at Honokowai Beach Park, Lahaina News, June 8, 2000: 21.

— continues to meet, Lahaina News, September 21, 2000: 21.

— continues to organize play at park, Lahaina News, February 8, 2001: 21.

HONOKOWAI RESORT

— seeks conversion to time share, Lahaina News, January 15, 1998: 1,16.

HONOKOWAI STREAM

— potential location of Concrete Industries Maui plant, Lahaina Sun, October 27, 1971: 11.

HONOKOWAI-NAPILI-KAPALUA TAXPAYERS ASSOCIATION

— critical of taxes, Lahaina News, May 1, 1981: 16.

HONOLUA

— description of Hale Keiki by the Methodist Church, Lahaina Sun, March 1, 1972: 15.

— Howard Kihune to propose as new site for airport, Lahaina News, December 4, 1985: 1,20.

— Napili dam repairs almost finished, Lahaina News, March 14, 1990: 28.

HONOLUA BAY
— photograph, Lahaina Sun, January 12, 1972: 14.
— erosion continues in Honolua Bay, Lahaina News, January 31, 1990: 1.
— first phase of subdivision scheduled to be completed by end of year, Lahaina News, May 9, 1990: 1,4.
— experts to study erosion at, Lahaina News, June 13, 1990: 1.
— study finds no long-term effect of sediment runoff, Lahaina News, August 15, 1990: 1.
— state Department of Land and Natural Resources may pursue state park at, Lahaina News, January 26, 1995: 1,20.
— biologists to study sediment, Lahaina News, October 5, 1995: 1,16.
— to receive thorough cleaning, Lahaina News, September 24, 1998: 1.
— meeting to be held to discuss reef protection, Lahaina News, October 8, 1998: 1.
— Billabong World Junior Championship, Lahaina News, November 11, 1999: 1.
— meeting to discuss impact of professional surfing meets, Lahaina News, August 31, 2000: 18.
— discussion of issues connected to holding contests at, Lahaina News, September 7, 2000: 1,2.
— Billabong Girls Pro professional surfing contest to be held at, Lahaina News, November 2, 2000: 1.
— ASP World Championship ends with Billabong Girls tournament, Lahaina News, November 9, 2000: 9.
— Vespa Trails surfing competition to be held at, Lahaina News, December 12, 2002: 11.
— Legends of the Bay contest held, Lahaina News, February 6, 2003: 13.
— volunteers clean up, Lahaina News, October 2, 2003: 5.

HONOLUA BAY SHOOTOUT
— meeting to be held to organize, Lahaina News, July 20, 2000: 1.
— scheduling discussed, concern with overuse of site, Lahaina News, August 3, 2000: 1,20.

HONOLUA DITCH
— Maui Land and Pineapple postpones project to repair, Lahaina News, June 10, 1993: 1.
— Department of Water Supply seeking to draw more water from, Lahaina News, August 1, 1996: 1,5.

HONOLUA KEIKI [BUSINESS]
— opens in Whalers Village, Lahaina News, November 15, 2001: 8.

HONOLUA LAHAINA SENIOR CITIZENS CLUB
— attend public meeting, Lahaina News, October 22, 1992: 1.

HONOLUA METHODIST CHURCH
— to hold childbirth classes, Lahaina News, September 21, 1995: 4.
— to hold childbirth classes, Lahaina News, February 29, 1996: 4.

HONOLUA PLANTATION LAND COMPANY [BUSINESS]
— names John F. Hyer as vice president, Lahaina Sun, February 10, 1971: 6.
— obtains zoning approval for a 34-acre housing development in Alaeloa, Lahaina Sun, April 14, 1971: 2.
— subdivision planned, Lahaina News, June 7, 1989: 1.

HONOLUA PRESCHOOL
— receives grant from Castle Foundation, Lahaina News, March 25, 1993: 3.
— to hold annual bazaar, Lahaina News, June 17, 1993: 2.
— to hold graduation ceremony, Lahaina News, August 12, 1993: 4.
— to hold fund-raising bazaar, Lahaina News, May 19, 1994: 6.
— to hold bazaar, Lahaina News, April 20, 1995: 6.
— graduates biggest class, Lahaina News, June 8, 1995: 4.
— to host Haunted House, Lahaina News, October 19, 1995: 9.
— to present Halloween Keiki Haunted House, Lahaina News, October 26, 1995: 11.
— to hold bazaar, Lahaina News, April 25, 1996: 6.
— to hold bazaar, Lahaina News, May 2, 1996: 16.
— to host Keiki Haunted House, Lahaina News, October 17, 1996: 15.
— bazaar to be held, Lahaina News, April 24, 1997: 13.
— to hold haunted house, Lahaina News, October 16, 1997: 17.
— awarded national accreditation, Lahaina News, January 29, 1998: 9.
— to hold bazaar, Lahaina News, April 23, 1998: 16.
— accepting applications, Lahaina News, November 29, 2001: 2.
— director Barbara Howard passes away, Lahaina News, October 17, 2002: 2.

HONOLUA SENIOR CITIZENS CLUB DAY
— to be held, Lahaina News, May 14, 1998: 1.

HONOLUA SURF COMPANY [BUSINESS]
— held Legends of the Bay Contest, Lahaina News, March 4, 1999: 7.
— Legends of the Bay contest held, Lahaina News, March 2, 2000: 7.

HONOLUA UNITED METHODIST CHURCH
— groundbreaking set, Lahaina News, April 17, 1985: 3.
— to be consecrated, Lahaina News, November 27, 1985: 3.
— to add additional service, Lahaina News, January 9, 1992: 3.
— to hold July 4 prayer breakfast, Lahaina News, June 26, 1997: 17.
— to hold course on childbirth and family, Lahaina News, August 14, 1997: 17.

HONOLUA UNITED METHODIST PRESCHOOL
— appoints Amy Miller as director, Lahaina News, March 10, 1994: 4.

HONOLUA WAHINE SURF CLASSIC
— "Surfing for a Cure" to be held, Lahaina News, July 11, 2002: 12.

HONOLUA WATERSHED PROJECT
— two dams dedicated, Lahaina News, August 17, 1995: 3.

HONOLULU ACADEMY OF ARTS
— Artists of Hawaii Exhibition includes artists from Maui , Lahaina News, November 27, 1985: 11.
— to exhibit historical artefacts, Lahaina News, January 9, 1991: 8.
— to hold clearance sale, Lahaina News, January 30, 1991: 9.

HONOLULU BOYS' CHOIR
— to perform at Lahaina Civic Center, Lahaina News, April 30, 1986: 3.
— to perform at Maui Arts and Cultural Center, Lahaina News, December 4, 1997: 24.

HONOLULU COMEDY CLUB [BUSINESS]
— to feature Sean Morey, Lahaina News, June 23, 1994: 11.

HONOLULU COMPUTERS, INC. [BUSINESS]
— opening fourth gallery, Lahaina News, July 26, 1989: 6.

HONOLULU DANCE THEATRE
— to perform King Kalakaua's Nutcracker Ballet, Lahaina News, November 28, 2002: 16.

HONOLULU GAS COMPANY [BUSINESS]
— new gas line installed in Lahaina, Lahaina Sun, December 9, 1970: 3.
— gas line to be completed along Front Street, Lahaina Sun, February 17, 1971: 3.

HONOLULU HARBOR FESTIVAL
— poster contest won by Sacred Hearts student, Lahaina News, November 22, 2001: 2.

HONOLULU SYMPHONY
— performed Puccini's "Tosca" at Baldwin High School auditorium, Lahaina Sun, February 3, 1971: 8.
— visit described, Lahaina Sun, October 18, 1972: 14.
— to perform at the Maui Inter-Continental Wailea, Lahaina News, October 17, 1984: 3.
— location of concert changed to Baldwin Auditorium, Lahaina News, April 8, 1987: 12.
— to at Baldwin Auditorium, Lahaina News, February 10, 1988: 9.
— "Diamonds to Denims" scheduled, Lahaina News, February 17, 1988: 18.

— to perform at Westin Maui, Lahaina News, April 26, 1989: 9.

— to perform at Hyatt Regency Maui, Lahaina News, November 22, 1989: 12.

— to perform at Hyatt Regency Maui, Lahaina News, November 29, 1989: 18.

— to perform at Grand Ballroom of the Four Seasons Resort-Wailea, Lahaina News, January 16, 1992: 16.

HONOLULU THEATRE FOR YOUTH
— to present "Paniolo Spurs" at Maui Mall, Lahaina News, February 23, 1995: 12.

— to perform "Othello", Lahaina News, March 21, 2002: 16.

HONOLULU UNITED METHODIST CHURCH
— to host fundraiser to build preschool and Sunday school, Lahaina News, June 1, 1988: 19.

HONOOKOWAI KAUHALE
— dedication ceremony held, Lahaina News, August 8, 1990: 5.

HO'O NA'AUAO
— see American Business Women's Association

HO'OHALIEKE KO KAHIKO HOU A LA'AU LAPA'AU
— to hold Kalua Kaiahua Scholarship Fund-raiser, Lahaina News, April 25, 1996: 17.

HOOKANIES [MUSICAL GROUP]
— to perform at Old Lahaina Cafe and Luau, Lahaina News, February 21, 1990: 13.

HO'OKANO, GEORGE KELI'IAUKAI
— police searching for, Lahaina News, February 19, 1998: 2.

HO'OKANO PAVING CO.
— to repave Mala Boat Launch, Lahaina News, February 28, 1990: 3.

HO'OKELE HOLOKAHIKI
— to be held at Kamehameha Iki Park, Lahaina News, June 13, 1996: 10.

HO'OKENA [MUSICAL GROUP]
— to perform at Maui Arts and Cultural Center, Lahaina News, March 27, 2003: 15.

— to perform at Maui Arts and Cultural Center, Lahaina News, April 3, 2003: 16.

HOOKER, SASCHA
— whale researcher to speak, Lahaina News, August 26, 1999: 16.

HO'OKIPA BEACH PARK
— surfing meet held, Lahaina Sun, October 27, 1971: 6.

— Robby Naish wins O'Neill Invitational surfing competition at, Lahaina News, April 18, 1984: 6.

— location of Marui/O'Neill Grand Slam windsurfing tournament, Lahaina News, March 20, 1991: 5.

— Gerry Lopez/Hi-Tech Surfbash VII to be held at, Lahaina News, November 21, 1996: 6.

— cleanup to be held, Lahaina News, July 10, 1997: 17.

— cleanup to be held, Lahaina News, July 17, 1997: 15.

— results of Lopez/Hi-Tech Surfbash IX surfing competition held at, Lahaina News, December 3, 1998: 19.

— to be site of kiteboarder competition, Lahaina News, September 19, 2002: 12.

— surfers to compete, Lahaina News, March 27, 2003: 13.

HOOKIPA PARK ADVISORY COMMITTEE
— to meet to discuss the park, Lahaina News, June 22, 2000: 17.

HOOKS, MICHAEL
— to open Plantation House Restaurant, Lahaina News, April 24, 1991: 7.

— to open new restaurant at Wailea Golf Course with Roy Dunn, Lahaina News, September 30, 1993: 8.

HO'OLAKO: HAWAIIAN LEGENDS [PLAY]
— presented by Maui Youth Theatre and Maui's Academy of Performing Arts, Lahaina News, October 7, 1987: 3.

— produced by Maui Youth Theatre, Lahaina News, November 11, 1987: 6.

HO'OLAKO: THE YEAR OF THE HAWAIIAN
— to be celebrated at Wailea Shopping Village, Lahaina News, October 21, 1987: 12.

— closing ceremony set, Lahaina News, December 2, 1987: 3.

HO'OLANA [MUSICAL GROUP]
— to perform at Ka'ahumanu Center, Lahaina News, February 12, 1998: 16.

HO'OLANA FARMS
— Anna Palomino to lead workshop on Native landscaping, Lahaina News, March 6, 1997: 10.

— benefit concert for Punana Leo O Maui, Lahaina News, March 20, 1997: 16.

HOOLAU [MUSICAL GROUP]
— to perform at Cabana Cafe, Lahaina News, November 14, 1991: 21.

— to perform at Cabana Cafe, Lahaina News, November 28, 1991: 17.

— continues to perform at The Cabana Cafe at The Four Seasons, Lahaina News, March 12, 1992: 19.

HO'OLAULE'A
— annual Thanksgiving event held in Lahaina, Lahaina Sun, November 18, 1970: 4.

— to be held at Ka'anapali Beach Hotel, Lahaina News, October 17, 1991: 15,21,22.

— to benefit Project Graduation, Lahaina News, November 13, 1997: 20.

HO'OLAULE'A AT KA'ANAPALI BEACH HOTEL
— review of music, Lahaina News, May 1, 1985: 10.

HOOLAWA BRIDGE
— work to begin on, Lahaina News, December 24, 1992: 5.

HO'OLAWE: GIVE AND TAKE [FILM]
— being filmed on Maui, Lahaina News, April 6, 2000: 14.

HO'OLI HALE
— new real estate company opens, Lahaina News, August 28, 1985: 8.

HOOLU TRIO, THE [MUSICAL GROUP]
— to perform at Cabana Café, Lahaina News, May 13, 1993: 12.

— to perform at Cabana Café, Lahaina News, July 8, 1993: 12.

HO'OMALAMALAMA NA KAULIKE (LIGHT FOR JUSTICE)
— march to be held, Lahaina News, April 12, 2001: 21.

HO'OMALU ALA AL ANON
— to meet, Lahaina News, July 18, 1996: 12.

HO'OMANA'O CHALLENGE
— to be held, Lahaina News, May 23, 1996: 7,8,9,12,13,14.

HO'OMANA'O CHALLENGE
— to be held, Lahaina News, May 22, 1997: 1.

HO'OMAU [MUSICAL GROUP]
— to perform from their new release "Paradise", Lahaina News, March 16, 2000: 12.

HO'OMAU HAWAIIAN MUSIC FESTIVAL
— to be held, Lahaina News, February 16, 1995: 16.

— to be held, Lahaina News, March 12, 1998: 21.

— to be held, Lahaina News, March 19, 1998: 12.

— benefit concert to be held for Punana Leo o Lahaina, Lahaina News, March 11, 1999: 13.

— benefit concert for Punana Leo O Maui to be held, Lahaina News, March 14, 2002: 15.

HO'ONANEA HAWAIIAN MUSIC SERIES
— to begin with Brothers Cazimero, Lahaina News, November 28, 1996: 10.

HO'ONANEA HAWAIIAN SERIES
— continues at Maui Arts and Cultural Center, Lahaina News, April 24, 2003: 19.

HOʻONANEA HOU HAWAIIAN MUSIC
— Kalapana to perform at, Lahaina News, November 5, 1998: 21.

HOOPER, MARY ELLEN [COMEDIAN]
— to perform at Comedy Club and the Sports Page, Lahaina News, July 9, 1992: 17,21.

HOʻOPIʻI BROTHERS [MUSICAL GROUP]
— to perform at fundraiser to Piʻilani School of Hula, Lahaina News, September 14, 1988: 11.

HOʻOPIʻI ʻOHANA [MUSICAL GROUP]
— to perform at Kaʻanapali Beach Hotel's Tiki Courtyard, Lahaina News, January 30, 2003: 3.
— releases new CD "Ulalani", Lahaina News, June 26, 2003: 3.

HOʻOPIʻI, SOLOMON
— to perform at Kaʻanapali Beach Hotel, Lahaina News, December 18, 1997: 18.

HOʻOPIʻI, SOLOMON [MUSICIAN]
— to perform at Kaʻanapali Beach Hotel's Courtyard Stage, Lahaina News, December 11, 1997: 19.

HOOPILI BROTHERS, THE [MUSICAL GROUP]
— to perform at Lahaina Cannery Mall as part of Aloha Summer, Lahaina News, August 15, 1990: 15.
— to perform at "Hawaii Calls" show at Kaʻanapali Beach Hotel, Lahaina News, April 1, 1993: 11.

HOOTERS HULA BOWL
— see Hula Bowl

HOOTIE AND THE BLOWFISH [MUSICAL GROUP]
— to perform at the Maui Arts and Cultural Center, Lahaina News, October 24, 1996: 15.
— to perform at Maui Arts and Cultural Center, Lahaina News, October 31, 1996: 19.
— to perform at Maui Arts and Cultural Center, Lahaina News, November 7, 1996: 14.
— concert canceled due to rain, play at World Cafe, Lahaina News, November 14, 1996: 9.

HOʻOULU LOKAHI O MAUI LOA
— the theme for Maui Holoku Ball, Lahaina News, September 9, 1999: 12.

HOʻOULU PRODUCTIONS
— to present at Whalers Village, Lahaina News, June 11, 1998: 16.
— to offer Hawaiian music, Lahaina News, August 6, 1998: 20.

HOOVER, J. EDGAR
— criticized by Hale Boggs in the House, Lahaina Sun, May 26, 1971: 4.

HOP TOMATO ITALIAN BISTRO AND BREWERY [RESTAURANT]
— plans to assemble world record pizza, Lahaina News, April 19, 2001: 1,9.
— assembled 300-foot pizza, Lahaina News, April 26, 2001: 1.
— featured, Lahaina News, May 3, 2001: 10,11.

HOPACO OFFICE OUTLET [BUSINESS]
— opening another retail outlet on Maui, Lahaina News, August 15, 1981: 5.
— supporting local schools, Lahaina News, August 28, 1997: 12.

HOPE CHAPEL
— to hold "Dine and Da Kine", Lahaina News, May 22, 1997: 16.
— sponsoring FamilyLife Marriage Seminar, Lahaina News, September 25, 1997: 6.
— to host "Stand in the Gap" prayer, Lahaina News, October 2, 1997: 20.

HOPE CHE, A
— to hold open house, Lahaina News, January 27, 2000: 12.

HOPE, JIM [COMEDIAN]
— to perform at Comedy Club, Lahaina News, March 28, 1990: 15.

HOPKINS, MARY RICE [MUSICIAN]
— to perform at Hope Chapel, Lahaina News, January 11, 1996: 14.
— to perform at Kaʻanapali Beach Hotel, Lahaina News, January 1, 1998: 17.
— to perform at Kaʻanapali Beach Hotel, Lahaina News, January 8, 1998: 12.
— to offer free performance, Lahaina News, January 15, 1998: 13.

HOPPER, PEGGE [ARTIST]
— artwork to be distributed by Aloha Airlines, Lahaina News, July 28, 1994: 9.

HOPWOOD, PAUL
— ultraman world class athlete featured, Lahaina News, May 3, 2001: 14.

HORAN, CLAUDE [ARTIST]
— sculpture of horse at Pukalani Elementary School is decaying, Lahaina News, January 31, 1990: 28.

HORIKAWA, JOYCE
— honored by Soroptimists International, Lahaina News, May 20, 1987: 17.

HORIMOTO, PATRICK [ARTIST]
— to speak at Native Hawaiian Plant Society, Lahaina News, February 13, 1992: 4.

HORITA, HERBERT
— see Herbert Horita Development

HORITA MAUI, INC. [BUSINESS]
— wins awards at Parade of Homes, Lahaina News, October 25, 1989: 10.

HORIUCHI, BARON
— U.S. Fish and Wildlife Service horticulturalist to speak on rare plant propagation, Lahaina News, June 7, 2001: 20.

HORIZON WASTE SERVICES, INC. [BUSINESS]
— acquires Browning-Ferris Industries of Hawaii Inc. (BFI), Lahaina News, April 20, 2000: 13.
— acquires Maui Disposal Co. Inc., Lahaina News, April 20, 2000: 13.

HORIZON WEST ANTIQUES AND ART [BUSINESS]
— opening in Whaler's Village, Lahaina Sun, November 25, 1970: 3.

HORIZONS ACADEMY OF MAUI
— to hold "Putting on the Ritz" benefit, Lahaina News, April 13, 2000: 12.

HORN, DAN [COMEDIAN]
— to perform at Comedy Club, Lahaina News, August 8, 1991: 12.

HORN, KIMBERLEY [MUSICIAN]
— to perform at Iao Theatre, Lahaina News, September 16, 1993: 18.
— to perform at Ritz-Carlton, Lahaina News, March 31, 1994: 15.

HORN, MICHAEL
— comedian to perform at Artful Dodger's Feed and Read, Lahaina News, August 19, 1987: 3.
— to speak on UFOs, Lahaina News, August 13, 1992: 4.
— to teach acting at the Art School of Kapalua, Lahaina News, November 2, 2000: 24.
— to teach acting at the Art School of Kapalua, Lahaina News, November 9, 2000: 24.

HORN, PAUL [MUSICIAN]
— flutist to perform four times on Maui, Lahaina News, April 16, 1992: 19,22.
— to perform at Maui Arts and Cultural Center, Lahaina News, December 28, 1995: 8.
— flutist to perform at Maui Arts and Cultural Center, Lahaina News, October 25, 2001: 16,17.
— to perform at Maui Arts and Cultural Center, Lahaina News, September 11, 2003: 17.

HORN, SAM [WRITER]
— to hold workshop for Visitor Industry Training and Education Center [VITEC], Lahaina News, April 5, 1989: 15.
— to speak to Maui Christian Women's Club, Lahaina News, September 24, 1992: 6.
— to hold leadership seminars, Lahaina News, January 21, 1993: 8.
— offering "Tongue Fu" session on dealing with difficult customers and co-workers, Lahaina News, December 9, 1993: 6.
— details of "Tongue Fu" presentation, Lahaina News, December 16, 1993: 7.
— leading seminars on"ConZentrate" and "Concrete Confidence", Lahaina News, March 5, 1998: 16.
— to speak at Maui Writers Guild, Lahaina News, June 10, 1999: 15.
— author of "Tongue Fu" to speak at meeting of American Association of Retired Persons, Lahaina News, December 23, 1999: 3.
— to speak to American Association of Retired Persons, Lahaina News, December 30, 1999: 17.

HORNIA, DUKE
— manager of Seasons restaurant, Lahaina News, September 5, 1991: 6.

HORNIA, JEANIE
— appointed group sales manager at Maui Ocean Center, Lahaina News, October 12, 2000: 16.

HOROSCOPE
— Chinese horoscope for March, Lahaina News, March 4, 1987: 12.
— Year of the Rooster left out of last issue of newspaper, Lahaina News, March 11, 1987: 18.

HORSE RACING
— proposals discussed, Lahaina Sun, March 24, 1971: 1,8.

HOSKING, RICH
— to lecture on health value of green algae, Lahaina News, October 19, 1995: 4.

HOSMER GROVE
— star gazing to be held at, Lahaina News, August 21, 1997: 16.
— Haleakala National Park staff to hold stargazing at, Lahaina News, July 19, 2001: 16.

HOSPICE MAUI
— organizing "Maui's Salute to Liberty" fundraiser, Lahaina News, June 18, 1986: 14.
— to hold fundraiser, Lahaina News, February 4, 1987: 11.
— to host celebration of Bicentennial of U.S. Constitution, Lahaina News, June 24, 1987: 3.
— "We the People … 1987" celebration participants listed, Lahaina News, July 1, 1987: 10.
— to hold flower show and luncheon as fundraiser, Lahaina News, July 29, 1987: 3.
— to hold trainings, Lahaina News, September 2, 1987: 3.
— Maui AIDS Foundation sponsoring support groups at, Lahaina News, October 5, 1988: 3,20.
— to offer Fourth of July entertainment and fireworks, Lahaina News, June 14, 1989: 2.
— hosting 5K Run/Fun Walk, Lahaina News, June 20, 1990: 8.
— to hold 5K Run/Fun Walk, Lahaina News, June 27, 1990: 6.
— presenting Kihei/Wailea House and Garden Tour, Lahaina News, February 27, 1991: 5.
— to hold Wailea Tour of Homes fundraiser, Lahaina News, March 5, 1992: 4.
— to hold fundraiser with humorist Allen Klein, Lahaina News, January 14, 1993: 3.
— hosting July 4th Celebration, Lahaina News, June 16, 1994: 5.
— Plumeria Resale Boutique raising money for, Lahaina News, August 12, 1999: 14.
— Executive Director R. Gregory LaGoy honored as "Maui's Outstanding Executive Director for a Non-Profit Organization", Lahaina News, July 26, 2001: 8.

— conducting volunteer training, Lahaina News, October 4, 2001: 2.
— to hold workshop on "Starting the Conversation", Lahaina News, November 8, 2001: 2.

HOSPITALITY SALES AND MARKETING ASSOCIATION (HSMA)
— to hold scholarship golf tournament, Lahaina News, July 16, 1992: 11.
— to meet, Lahaina News, March 25, 1993: 10.
— announces scholarship recipients, Lahaina News, April 17, 1997: 7.
— to hold golf tournament, Lahaina News, July 24, 2003: 13.

HOSPITALS
— picture of hospital, now apartment building, on Front Street, Lahaina Sun, November 18, 1970: 2.
— proposed Lahaina Hospital discussed, Lahaina Sun, October 6, 1971: 1.
— petition to build hospital in Lahaina continues to collect signatures, Lahaina Sun, October 27, 1971: 12.
— rate hikes contested, Lahaina Sun, January 19, 1972: 16.
— new facility to be built as part of Maui Memorial Hospital, Lahaina Sun, June 14, 1972: 11.
— Maui Memorial Hospital converts to new rate system, Lahaina Sun, July 5, 1972: 9.
— Memorial Hospital seeking to expand, Lahaina Sun, July 26, 1972: 9.
— situation at Maui Memorial Hospital discussed, Lahaina Sun, November 15, 1972: 5.
— Maui Memorial hospital attempting to organize a round-the-clock doctor, Lahaina Sun, December 27, 1972: 3.
— experience at Tripler Hospital detailed, Lahaina Sun, May 16, 1973: 9.
— see also Maui Memorial Hospital

HOST RESTAURANT [RESTAURANT]
— open to public now that security has changed at Kahului Airport, Lahaina News, May 23, 1991: 3.

HOT CHAKRA [MUSICAL GROUP]
— to perform at Casanova's, Lahaina News, October 8, 1992: 11.

HOT DOG STAND
— re-opens, Lahaina News, January 20, 2000: 11.

HOT L BALTIMORE [COMEDIAN]
— to be performed by Maui OnStage, Lahaina News, April 11, 2002: 16.
— to be performed at Iao Theater, Lahaina News, May 23, 2002: 15.
— to end, Lahaina News, June 6, 2002: 16.

HOT SALSA DANCING HAWAII
— to demonstrate salsa, Lahaina News, April 4, 2002: 15.

HOTEL CORPORATION OF THE PACIFIC
— takes over management of Maui Hilton Hotel in Ka'anapali, Lahaina News, August 31, 1983: 14.
— changes name to Aston Hotels and Resorts, Lahaina News, February 12, 1986: 3.

HOTEL EMPLOYERS ASSOCIATION
— discusses end of hotel strike, Lahaina Sun, December 30, 1970: 5.

HOTEL EMPLOYERS COUNCIL
— see Strike at Ka'anapali and Royal Lahaina Hotel

HOTEL HANA-MAUI
— offering kama'aina rate year-round, Lahaina News, January 18, 1989: 5.
— to be managed ty ITT Sheraton Corporation, Lahaina News, May 30, 1990: 6.
— hires Sonia Franzel as director of public relations, Lahaina News, January 9, 1991: 5.

HOTEL LANA'I
— shut down, Lahaina News, September 19, 1984: 3.
— sold to Ocean Activities Center of Maui, Lahaina News, October 17, 1984: 3.

HOTEL SALES AND MARKETING ASSOCIATION OF MAUI (HSMA)
— elects officers, Lahaina News, August 26, 1987: 3.
— offers scholarships, Lahaina News, March 7, 1990: 7.
— offering scholarships, Lahaina News, April 11, 1990: 3.
— to hold golf tournament, Lahaina News, July 4, 1990: 6.
— to hold golf tournament, Lahaina News, July 11, 1990: 9.
— Vivian Mur appointed vice president of Maui Chapter, Lahaina News, October 3, 1990: 9.
— to host speaker Dr. John Clark, Lahaina News, May 8, 1991: 6.
— to hold golf fundraiser, Lahaina News, July 18, 1991: 7.
— new officers named, Lahaina News, March 26, 1992: 10.
— to hold scholarship fundraiser at North Course, Lahaina News, July 14, 1994: 9.
— elects new Board of Directors, Lahaina News, December 28, 1995: 10.

HOTELS
— Maui Surf Hotel opens in Ka'anapali, Lahaina Sun, December 1, 1971: 13.
— undergo training to mitigate pollution, Lahaina News, October 6, 1994: 1,2.
— see also strikes
— see also specific hotels, tourism

HOUSE AND GARDEN TOUR
— presented by Hospice Maui, Lahaina News, February 27, 1991: 5.

HOUSE AT POOH CORNER [PLAY]
— to be performed at Maui Youth Theatre, Lahaina News, April 17, 1985: 3.

HOUSE COMMITTEE ON EDUCATION, STATE
— to meet with teachers at Baldwin High School, Lahaina Sun, February 3, 1971: 7.

HOUSE OF SUCCESS, THE
— mental illness program to hold open house, Lahaina News, August 12, 1999: 8.

HOUSE OF THE SUN VISITOR CENTER
— see Haleakala

HOUSE OF VIDEO [BUSINESS]
— one of many video rental stores in West Maui, Lahaina News, August 14, 1985: 1.

HOUSE OF YOGA AND ZEN
— offering healing Mandala Dance, Lahaina News, September 7, 1988: 3.

HOUSEKEEPING OLYMPICS
— won by Sheraton Hotel employees, Lahaina News, September 21, 2000: 11.

HOUSING
— moderate income discussed by Robert Ohata, Lahaina Sun, December 2, 1970: 3.
— construction in Lahaina, Lahaina Sun, December 2, 1970: 3.
— Edward Beall, architect of Whaler's Village, developing 1000-acre sites in California, Lahaina Sun, December 16, 1970: 5.
— projects desired by West Maui Business Association, Lahaina Sun, December 23, 1970: 2.
— low and moderate housing project planned in Paia, Lahaina Sun, March 10, 1971: 5.
— low income families encouraged to apply for new homes in Wahikuli Terrace, Lahaina Sun, April 14, 1971: 1,6.
— transient housing plans studied by Maui Christian Ministers Association, Lahaina Sun, May 12, 1971: 2.
— 100-unit apartment building planned for Honokowai and Napili, Lahaina Sun, June 23, 1971: 5.
— rent increases to public housing challenged, Lahaina Sun, June 30, 1971: 1,4.

— house lots to be sold in Wahikuli area, Lahaina Sun, October 6, 1971: 15.
— Amfac Communities obtains permission to build apartments for low income families, Lahaina Sun, October 6, 1971: 5,11.
— decision to approve low income housing in Napilihau deferred, Lahaina Sun, October 13, 1971: 13.
— Hawaii Housing Authority will work with Honolua Plantation Land Inc. to build low and moderate income homes, Lahaina Sun, November 3, 1971: 11.
— variances okayed for two subdivisions in Kahului, Lahaina Sun, November 3, 1971: 11.
— application for low and moderate income housing in Haiku and Central Maui due soon, Lahaina Sun, November 10, 1971: 1.
— Maui County Board of Realtors complains that laws are unfair, Lahaina Sun, December 29, 1971: 17.
— recent subdivisions described, Lahaina Sun, January 19, 1972: 3.
— last person living in Banana Patch ordered to vacate, Lahaina Sun, January 19, 1972: 7.
— drop in interest rate positive for local housing market, Lahaina Sun, February 23, 1972: 8.
— low-income apartments offered, Lahaina Sun, March 15, 1972: 4.
— groundbreaking ceremonies for low and moderate income housing held in Napili, Lahaina Sun, April 12, 1972: 11.
— Hale Mahaolu receives inquiries concerning Lahaina Surf apartment project, Lahaina Sun, April 26, 1972: 15.
— Topsider treehouse in Kihei described, Lahaina Sun, May 10, 1972: 9.
— landlord-tenant code signed by Governor Burns, Lahaina Sun, June 7, 1972: 14.
— Haiku Housing Advisory Committee proposes plan low cost housing, Lahaina Sun, June 7, 1972: 5.
— low and medium income housing project in Paia nears completion, Lahaina Sun, June 7, 1972: 5.
— proposal to restrict renting guest cottages considered by County Planning Commission, Lahaina Sun, June 14, 1972: 3.
— current situation discussed, Lahaina Sun, June 21, 1972: 19.
— new electrical codes criticized, Lahaina Sun, June 21, 1972: 19.
— issues with condominiums discussed, Lahaina Sun, August 9, 1972: 4.
— affordable housing in Haiku discussed, Lahaina Sun, August 9, 1972: 4.
— commentary, Lahaina Sun, August 30, 1972: 15.
— sale of land by auction planned, Lahaina Sun, September 6, 1972: 17.
— land auction planned, Lahaina Sun, September 13, 1972: 11.
— Wahikuli auction delayed, Lahaina Sun, September 27, 1972: 1.
— low and middle income housing approved for Haiku, Lahaina Sun, October 4, 1972: 18.
— auction of building lots in Wahikuli delayed, Lahaina Sun, October 4, 1972: 18.
— auction of building lots in Wahikuli discussed, Lahaina Sun, October 4, 1972: 21.
— moderate cost housing in Napilihau is being constructed, Lahaina Sun, November 22, 1972: 7.
— Anthony Arisumi's attempts to build low income housing described, Lahaina Sun, November 29, 1972: 4.
— a national disgrace, Lahaina Sun, December 6, 1972: 9.
— Maui Planning Commission rejects Anthony Arisumi's request to build affordable housing, Lahaina Sun, December 13, 1972: 3.
— new housing development planned for Kihei, Lahaina Sun, December 27, 1972: 3.
— public hearing to discuss proposed apartment complex in Kahana, Lahaina Sun, January 31, 1973: 6.
— public seeking more house lots, Lahaina Sun, February 7, 1973: 4.
— public comments sought for Kahana project, Lahaina Sun, February 7, 1973: 4.

— pest treatment described, Lahaina News, February 28, 1990: supplement14,supplement15.

— trends in interior design, Lahaina News, February 28, 1990: supplement15,supplement16.

— trends in prices, financing, Lahaina News, February 28, 1990: supplement5,supplement6,supplement7,supplement8,.

— types of loans described, Lahaina News, February 28, 1990: supplement9,supplement10.

— bids to build affordable housing project Homohana Hale too high, Lahaina News, March 7, 1990: 1.

— State officials consider reducing number of houses in affordable project in Lahaina, Lahaina News, March 14, 1990: 1.

— fire destroys home; churches help victims, Lahaina News, April 11, 1990: 1.

— property prices up, Lahaina News, April 11, 1990: 5.

— problems faced by renters described, Lahaina News, May 16, 1990: 1.

— Lahaina News to publish supplement for potential property buyers, Lahaina News, May 16, 1990: 6.

— affordable rentals offered in Honokowai, Lahaina News, May 23, 1990: 5.

— County accepting applications for Komohana Hale, Lahaina News, May 30, 1990: 5.

— Housing Finance and Development Corporation accepting applications for affordable apartments at Honokowai, Lahaina News, May 30, 1990: 5.

— state plans for Lahaina available to review, Lahaina News, June 13, 1990: 5.

— drawing to be conducted to create waiting list, Lahaina News, June 20, 1990: 5.

— workshop sponsored by Maui Board of Realtors to be held, Lahaina News, June 20, 1990: B1,B2,B3,B4,B5,B6,B7,B8,B9,B10,B11,B12,B13,B14,B15,B16,B17,B18,B19,B20,B21,B22,B23,B24.

— lottery draws hundreds of participants, Lahaina News, June 27, 1990: 3.

— Village One development planned, Lahaina News, July 4, 1990: 1.

— models of Village One houses can be viewed, Lahaina News, July 4, 1990: 8.

— applications for Komohana Hale affordable rentals approaching, Lahaina News, July 11, 1990: 4.

— residents generally pleased with models for affordable homes, Lahaina News, July 18, 1990: 1,3.

— gubernatorial candidate Fred Hemmings critical of State housing plan, Lahaina News, July 18, 1990: 3.

— property tax reform may cause issues for homeowners, Lahaina News, July 25, 1990: 1,6.

— State Department of Commerce and Consumer Affairs publishes landlord-tenant handbook, Lahaina News, August 1, 1990: 5.

— Maui County Council's Subcommittee on Affordable Housing to meet, Lahaina News, August 8, 1990: 4.

— Maui Contractors Association members critical of State efforts to build affordable homes, Lahaina News, August 8, 1990: 6.

— timeshare owners becoming targets for mail fraud, Lahaina News, August 8, 1990: 9.

— Konokowai Kauhale project offers housing relief, Lahaina News, August 15, 1990: 1.

— complaints received concerning rent referral companies , Lahaina News, September 5, 1990: 24.

— American Institute of Architects to hold seminar on neotraditional town planning and affordable housing, Lahaina News, September 5, 1990: 6.

— subdivision planned in Kahana, Lahaina News, September 12, 1990: 8.

— Kapalua Realty sells 30 lots at Plantation Estates for $69 million, Lahaina News, September 26, 1990: 9.

— Amfac shifting strategy for resort homes, Lahaina News, October 10, 1990: 1.

— Oihana Property Management & Sales, Inc. sponsoring Condominium Conference and Trade Show, Lahaina News, October 10, 1990: 12.

— Oihana Property Management & Sales, Inc. sponsoring Condominium Conference and Trade Show, Lahaina News, October 17, 1990: 12.

— project begins in Waiehu Terrace, Lahaina News, October 24, 1990: 5.

— Maui Land and Pineapple to start employee housing program, Lahaina News, October 31, 1990: 1.

— Maui Interface Corp. marketing two-acre homesites at The Plantation Estate, Lahaina News, November 7, 1990: 7.

— apartment building proposed by J. Gary Martin, Lahaina News, November 14, 1990: 3,4.

— project near West Maui ball field nearing completion, Lahaina News, December 12, 1990: 1.

— South Beach Mauka project proposed by Amfac, Lahaina News, December 26, 1990: 1.

— governor John Waihee seeking money for housing project, Lahaina News, January 16, 1991: 1.

— third phase of Honokowai Hale to become available, Lahaina News, January 23, 1991: 3.

— prices increase, Lahaina News, January 30, 1991: 1,2.

— occupancy of Komohana Hale delayed, Lahaina News, February 20, 1991: 1.

— trends in prices, financing, Lahaina News, February 27, 1991: supplement12,supplement20.

— ohana zoning described, Lahaina News, February 27, 1991: supplement19,supplement20,supplement21.

— pest treatment described, Lahaina News, February 27, 1991: supplement21.

— packaged homes discussed, Lahaina News, February 27, 1991: supplement22.

— tips for hiring a contractor, Lahaina News, February 27, 1991: supplement23,supplement24.

— prospects for coming year described, Lahaina News, February 27, 1991: supplement7.

— tax laws discussed, Lahaina News, February 27, 1991: supplement9,-supplement10.

— types of loans described, Lahaina News, February 27, 1991: supplement9,supplement15.

— role of color in design discussed, Lahaina News, February 27, 1991: supplement9,supplement15.

— mayor Linda Lingle opposes proposal to make county conform to state plans for planned housing projects, Lahaina News, March 13, 1991: 1.

— Maui County Council chair Howard Kihune concerned that sugar plantations find affordable housing, Lahaina News, March 13, 1991: 1.

— people start moving into Komohana Hale, Lahaina News, March 20, 1991: 1.

— mayor Linda Lingle and Joseph Conant, executive director of state Housing Finance and Development Corporation, disagree on implications of legislation, Lahaina News, April 3, 1991: 1.

— Napili Gardens townhouse project proposed, Lahaina News, April 10, 1991: 1.

— Maui County Council to sponsor conferences on affordable housing, Lahaina News, April 10, 1991: 4.

— market is softening, Lahaina News, April 10, 1991: 6.

— Alexander and Baldwin planning subdivision in Paia, Lahaina News, May 8, 1991: 6.

— Maui County and the U.S. Department of Housing and Urban Development to sponsor seminars on fair housing, Lahaina News, May 23, 1991: 4.

— relocation of Ikena residents for Lahaina Bypass delayed until study done, Lahaina News, July 4, 1991: 1.

— self-help housing expands, Lahaina News, July 4, 1991: 9.

— proposed Wahikuli project expanded to 4,200 units , Lahaina News, July 11, 1991: 1.

— Maui Board of Realtors to publish Real Estate Guide, accepting advertisements, Lahaina News, August 8, 1991: 7.

— Parade of Homes to be held by Building Industry Association of Hawaii, Lahaina News, August 15, 1991: 7.

— real estate housing level, Lahaina News, September 5, 1991: 8.

— Napilihau Community Association to hold homeowners' meeting, Lahaina News, September 12, 1991: 3.

— median price of single family residences rose, Lahaina News, September 19, 1991: 10.

— Plantation Estates to offer 40 additional homesites, Lahaina News, September 19, 1991: 6.

— condominium prices stable, Lahaina News, September 26, 1991: 10.

— condominium leasehold reform debated, Lahaina News, October 3, 1991: 1,6,7.

— market favoring retailers over landlords, Lahaina News, October 3, 1991: 10.

— Ka'anapali Beach Hotel request to build dormitories approved by Maui County Planning Commission, Lahaina News, October 3, 1991: 5.

— mayor Linda Lingle seeks to build affordable housing, Lahaina News, October 10, 1991: 1.

— prices climb, Lahaina News, October 10, 1991: 12.

— no bills pending at Maui County Council on leasehold, Lahaina News, October 17, 1991: 10.

— condominium sales remain low, Lahaina News, October 17, 1991: 12.

— leasehold reform discussed, Lahaina News, October 17, 1991: 28.

— Maui County Council committee recommends upgrading sewage to allow more housing units, Lahaina News, October 24, 1991: 1.

— property tax changes seem likely, Lahaina News, October 24, 1991: 12.

— Kahana project opposed by State and County, Lahaina News, October 31, 1991: 1,3.

— lots under $200,000 in demand, Lahaina News, October 31, 1991: 8.

— equity loans popular, Lahaina News, October 31, 1991: 8.

— reverse mortgages described, Lahaina News, November 7, 1991: 12.

— home prices rise to $300,000, Lahaina News, November 14, 1991: 12.

— businesses take down signs soliciting time shares, Lahaina News, November 21, 1991: 1,10.

— condominium prices rise, Lahaina News, November 21, 1991: 12.

— Mazie Hirono advocates for leasehold and insurance premium bills, Lahaina News, November 21, 1991: 7.

— suggestions to solve affordable homes shortage, Lahaina News, December 5, 1991: 14,32.

— Hula Mae has loan money for first-time home buyers, Lahaina News, December 12, 1991: 13.

— Maui County Planning Commission approves 98-lot project at Kamaole, Lahaina News, December 12, 1991: 13.

— home prices dip, Lahaina News, December 19, 1991: 16,17.

— condominium prices rise, Lahaina News, December 26, 1991: 9.

— builders back using IRAs for home buying, Lahaina News, January 2, 1992: 9.

— lawmakers to back more leasehold reform, Lahaina News, January 9, 1992: 9.

— Maui County Council reading bill to allow zero lot line subdivisions for affordable housing, Lahaina News, January 9, 1992: 9.

— condominium prices drop slightly, Lahaina News, January 16, 1992: 10.

— development in Wahikuli delayed, Lahaina News, January 16, 1992: 3.

— prices rise, Lahaina News, January 23, 1992: 14.

— condominium associations critical of water assessments, Lahaina News, January 30, 1992: 13.

— importance of color in interior design discussed by Robbie Overvold, Lahaina News, February 6, 1992: 12.

— prices decrease, Lahaina News, February 13, 1992: 14.

— condominium management class offered, Lahaina News, February 13, 1992: 4.

— report on condominium sales, Lahaina News, February 20, 1992: 11.

— banks evaluating loans for leased property, Lahaina News, February 20, 1992: 3.

— Coldwell Banker McCormack Real Estate and Kennedy-Wilson, Inc to offer real estate auctions, Lahaina News, March 5, 1992: 10.

— prices level, Lahaina News, March 5, 1992: 11.

— prices increase, Lahaina News, March 12, 1992: 14.

— new affordable housing requirement for new buildings, Lahaina News, March 26, 1992: 12.

— developer James Schuler outlines plans for future housing developments, Lahaina News, April 2, 1992: 11.

— home prices decrease, Lahaina News, April 9, 1992: 14.

— condominium prices rise, Lahaina News, April 16, 1992: 12.

— proposed Villages of Leiali'i on hold, Lahaina News, April 23, 1992: 24.

— KCOM Corporation proposing 62-unit affordable housing project, Lahaina News, April 23, 1992: 3.

— condominium prices decline, Lahaina News, May 7, 1992: 11.

— planned community proposed by C. Brewer Properties approved, Lahaina News, May 7, 1992: 6.

— Upcountry sales doing better than most, Lahaina News, May 21, 1992: 9.

— sales increase in South and Central Maui, Lahaina News, May 28, 1992: 12.

— Maui County looking for residents willing to have water tested regularly, Lahaina News, May 28, 1992: 4.

— subdivision proposed in Kihei by Kyushu and Toyo Corporation, Lahaina News, May 28, 1992: 6.

— public meeting to be held to review condominium laws, Lahaina News, May 28, 1992: 6.

— mix of affordable housing may change at Wahikuli development, Lahaina News, June 4, 1992: 1.

— prices level but volume up, Lahaina News, June 11, 1992: 12.

— condominium volume drops, Lahaina News, June 18, 1992: 11.

— Jimmy Billianor to be evicted from Honolua Bay, Lahaina News, June 18, 1992: 6.

— homes in Wailuku built by Schuler Homes and C. Brewer Properties set to open in 1993, Lahaina News, June 25, 1992: 16.

— Maui Land and Pineapple self-help employee housing almost finished, Lahaina News, June 25, 1992: 2.

— interest rates at near 25-year low, Lahaina News, July 2, 1992: 16.

— Ed Bello voices concern over unlicensed builders, Lahaina News, July 2, 1992: 19.

— KCOM Corp. plans to build affordable housing, Lahaina News, July 2, 1992: 3,4.

— Na Po'e Kokua forms to assist native Hawaiians in housing matters, Lahaina News, July 2, 1992: 4.

— sales of condominiums in West Maui higher than rest of Maui, Lahaina News, July 9, 1992: 15.

— Series II of Kihei-Piilani Village on market, Lahaina News, July 9, 1992: 15.

— Wailea Community Association requests that Wailea 670 project be delayed, Lahaina News, July 9, 1992: 7.

— prices sag, Lahaina News, July 16, 1992: 13.

— prices for Piilani Village houses reduced, Lahaina News, July 23, 1992: 9.

— Kahana Falls timeshares selling well, Lahaina News, July 30, 1992: 12.

— Vernon Garrison seeking rezoning for Aala Place property, Lahaina News, August 6, 1992: 3.

— condominium prices dip, Lahaina News, August 6, 1992: 8.

— prices up, Lahaina News, August 13, 1992: 13.

— realtors course to be held by Hawaii Association of Realtors, Lahaina News, August 13, 1992: 13.

— Housing Finance and Development Corporation to hold public meeting to discuss conveyance of ceded lands, Lahaina News, August 27, 1992: 3.

— Amfac/JMB Hawaii plans 1600 units in Pu'ukoli'i, Lahaina News, September 3, 1992: 3.

— residential subdivision approval in Kahana recommended by Maui County Council, Lahaina News, September 3, 1992: 3.

— prices remain level, Lahaina News, September 10, 1992: 10.

— condominium prices drop, Lahaina News, September 17, 1992: 12.

— timeshare reforms may be needed, Lahaina News, October 1, 1992: 10.

— proposal to sell lots mauka of the Silversword Golf Course, Lahaina News, October 1, 1992: 13.

— Wai'olu Condominium project in Makena approved, Lahaina News, October 1, 1992: 14.

— project in Kahana likely to be approved by Maui County Council, Lahaina News, October 1, 1992: 9.

— South Maui Condominium Council to organize seminar on legal issues, Lahaina News, October 8, 1992: 7.

— condominium prices rise, Lahaina News, October 8, 1992: 9.

— Bosa Pacific Hawaii proposes residential project in Kihei, Lahaina News, October 15, 1992: 13.

— Patsy Mink announces federal funding for elderly housing complex in Kahului, Lahaina News, October 15, 1992: 8.

— home prices drop, Lahaina News, October 15, 1992: 9.

— pricing variations around Maui discussed, Lahaina News, October 22, 1992: 11.

— changes in housing prices around Maui, Lahaina News, October 29, 1992: 14.

— new sales program at Keonekai Villages, Lahaina News, October 29, 1992: 17.

— home prices rise, Lahaina News, November 5, 1992: 9.

— South Maui Condominium Council to organize seminar on legal issues, Lahaina News, November 12, 1992: 10.

— land use approved for Kahana project, Lahaina News, November 12, 1992: 12.

— condominium prices rise, Lahaina News, November 12, 1992: 7.

— advantage of using mortgage broker discussed, Lahaina News, November 26, 1992: 19.

— sales light in November, Lahaina News, December 10, 1992: 10.

— condominium prices fall, Lahaina News, December 17, 1992: 9.

— Hurricane Iniki projected to spur state's economy, Lahaina News, December 24, 1992: 9.

— State to review development proposed at Pu'ukoli'i by Amfac/JMB, Lahaina News, January 7, 1993: 1.

— condominium sales up in December, Lahaina News, January 14, 1993: 4.

— sales begin in Waiehu Terrace, Lahaina News, January 14, 1993: 4.

— State Land Use Commission votes to reclassify land from agricultural to urban in Kahana, Lahaina News, January 21, 1993: 4.

— South Maui leads in housing sales, Lahaina News, January 21, 1993: 9.

— homeowner's insurance costs to rise, Lahaina News, January 28, 1993: 8.

— home prices rose in 1992, Lahaina News, January 28, 1993: 9.

— meeting for condominium and homeowner associations, Lahaina News, February 4, 1993: 9.

— sales increase, Lahaina News, February 11, 1993: 12.

— upcountry leads in housing sales, Lahaina News, February 18, 1993: 10.

— residents oppose proposed townhouse project in Kihei, Lahaina News, February 18, 1993: 8.

— water meters installed near Big Beach, Lahaina News, February 25, 1993: 5.

— hurricane preparedness discussed in "Maui Building Guide 1993", Lahaina News, February 25, 1993: supplement11,supplement12.

— landscaping discussed in "Maui Building Guide 1993", Lahaina News, February 25, 1993: supplement12.

— trends in prices discussed in "Maui Building Guide 1993", Lahaina News, February 25, 1993: supplement16,supplement18.

— directory published in "Maui Building Guide 1993", Lahaina News, February 25, 1993: supplement25,supplement26,supplement27.

— mortgage rates and loans discussed in "Maui Building Guide 1993", Lahaina News, February 25, 1993: supplement4,supplement9,supplement10.

— lumber prices rising discussed in "Maui Building Guide 1993", Lahaina News, February 25, 1993: supplement6,supplement8.

— hiring a contractor discussed in "Maui Building Guide 1993", Lahaina News, February 25, 1993: supplement6,supplement8,supplement13.

— accessory dwellings discussed in "Maui Building Guide 1993", Lahaina News, February 25, 1993: supplement8.

— workers move into self-help housing, Lahaina News, March 4, 1993: 8.

— West Maui leads in condo sales, Lahaina News, March 11, 1993: 6.

— home prices dip, Lahaina News, March 18, 1993: 6.

— Iao Parkside opens for tenants, Lahaina News, April 1, 1993: 9.

— Maxine Davis criticized for rental called "Mango Manor", Lahaina News, May 13, 1993: 1,3.

— Maui County Council Planning Committee approves development near Kahana Gateway, Lahaina News, May 27, 1993: 1.

— Waiolani sells out, Lahaina News, May 27, 1993: 7,8.

— Kihei residents question impact of proposed projects, Lahaina News, June 3, 1993: 4.

— Lokahi Pacific purchases apartment building to provide affordable housing, Lahaina News, June 17, 1993: 6.

— Maui County Council approves zoning change from agriculture to residential for housing project near Kahana Gateway, Lahaina News, June 24, 1993: 4.

— workshop to be held on purchasing homes, Lahaina News, July 8, 1993: 8.

— Self-Help Housing Corp finishes Kapalua Self-Help Housing Project, Lahaina News, July 22, 1993: 1.

— proposals being accepted for Small Cities Community Development Block Grant (CDBG) Program, Lahaina News, September 16, 1993: 3.

— applications for phase II of Iao Parkside to be ready soon, Lahaina News, September 30, 1993: 7.

— Maui Community College to hold workshops on buying a home, Lahaina News, October 14, 1993: 8,9.

— Kulani and Kua'aina recognized at BIA Parade of Homes Awards Banquet, Lahaina News, October 14, 1993: 9.

— JGL Enterprise applies to Maui Planning Commission for zoning change to build townhouses in Napili, Lahaina News, November 4, 1993: 2.

— Hawaii Real Estate Commission creates reference kit, Lahaina News, January 6, 1994: 5,6.

— few affordable houses being built, Lahaina News, January 20, 1994: 4.

— KCOM Corp. to develop affordable rental units along Honoapi'ilani Highway, Lahaina News, January 20, 1994: 7.

— issues connected to affordable housing discussed by West Maui Taxpayers Association Mark Percell, Lahaina News, February 3, 1994: 2.

— South Maui Condominium Council to present "How to Service - The Reserve Controversy", Lahaina News, March 17, 1994: 8.

— landlord-tenant code discussed, Lahaina News, April 14, 1994: 10.

— debate over Hawaii Hurricane Relief Fund will affect residential insurance, Lahaina News, May 5, 1994: 1,6.

— campers at country beaches to be fined for extended stays, Lahaina News, June 16, 1994: 1,3.

— price set for ceded land to be used for project, Lahaina News, July 28, 1994: 1.

— C Brewer Homes creates sales force for The Villages of Leiali'i, Lahaina News, September 15, 1994: 13.

— affordable rental project planned off Lahainaluna Road, Lahaina News, September 29, 1994: 1,2.

— Amfac/JMB planning luxury neighborhood in Ka'anapali, Lahaina News, October 27, 1994: 7.

— Department of Hawaiian Home Lands opens land for Hawaiians in Ka'anapali, Lahaina News, November 10, 1994: 1,7.

— Kaimana, C. Brewer Homes neighborhood, opens, Lahaina News, November 17, 1994: 10.

— workshop on HOME Investment Partnership Program, Lahaina News, December 8, 1994: 3.

— Tom Soeten Realty and Iwado Realty named principal brokers for The Masters at Ka'anapali Hillside, Lahaina News, December 22, 1994: 13.

— Mark Honda recommends approval of Napilihau Villages housing project proposed by JGL Enterprises, Inc., Lahaina News, January 12, 1995: 1,16.

— Lahainaluna rental project to be submitted to Maui County Council, Lahaina News, January 12, 1995: 2.

— Affordable Housing Corp. to hold public hearing, Lahaina News, February 2, 1995: 4.

— Affordable Housing Corp. to hold public hearing, Lahaina News, February 9, 1995: 3.

— residents critical of rental project proposed by Affordable Housing Corp., Lahaina News, February 23, 1995: 1.

— time share bill dies in House, Lahaina News, March 2, 1995: 1,16.

— Affordable Housing Corp. rethinking plans for Lahainaluna Road Project, Lahaina News, March 23, 1995: 1,16.

— potential properties soon to be viewable on computers, Lahaina News, June 22, 1995: 10.

— rate hike at Weinberg Court Apartments questioned, Lahaina News, June 22, 1995: 2.

— Affordable House Corp. of Maui County considering plan for elderly housing project, Lahaina News, July 13, 1995: 5.

— Self-Help Housing Corporation seeking more self-help housing, Lahaina News, July 20, 1995: 2.

— Rental Housing Trust Fund to take applications for low-interest rate loans, Lahaina News, September 28, 1995: 2.

— elderly rental project proposed by Affording Housing Corp. for Kelawea Mauka, Lahaina News, November 16, 1995: 3.

— no resistance to senior project on Lahainaluna Road, Lahaina News, November 30, 1995: 1,12.

— plans for affordable housing ready for council review, Lahaina News, January 11, 1996: 4.

— state begins new home loan program, Lahaina News, March 14, 1996: 10.

— lots available at Kahana Ridge, Lahaina News, April 25, 1996: 12.

— Wailea Realty Corporation offering free tours of private houses, Lahaina News, May 23, 1996: 16.

— cost of hurricane insurance to drop, Lahaina News, June 27, 1996: 12.

— National Kitchen and Bath Association to host annual Kitchen and Bath Tour, Lahaina News, August 22, 1996: 9.

— construction at Kahana Ridge funded, Lahaina News, September 5, 1996: 22.

— JGL Enterprise Inc. wants to change plans for affordable housing project, Lahaina News, September 26, 1996: 1,18.

— Maui Council to re-examine Napilihau Villages, Lahaina News, October 24, 1996: 1,20.

— composting workshop to be held at Upcountry Home Composting Demonstration, Lahaina News, November 21, 1996: 14.

— Maui County proposes homeless resource center, Lahaina News, January 30, 1997: 2.

— plans for Kua 'Aina Ridge available, Lahaina News, April 3, 1997: 12.

— first phase of construction of Napilihau Villages begins, Lahaina News, April 17, 1997: 2.

— sales up, Lahaina News, April 24, 1997: 6.

— Parade of Homes to be held, Lahaina News, June 12, 1997: 16.

— Maui Contractors Association Home Show to be held, Lahaina News, June 19, 1997: 6.

— Kahana Ridge construction almost completed, Lahaina News, July 31, 1997: 8.

— Ka'anapali Golf Estate Ke Alii Place development breaks ground, Lahaina News, August 7, 1997: 14.

— retrofitting condominiums with water sprinklers will not be required, Lahaina News, August 7, 1997: 5.

— ground breaking for Napilihau Townhouses, Lahaina News, September 4, 1997: 9.

— Na Kupuna O Maui and Lahaina Open Space Society demonstrate against, Lahaina News, March 5, 1998: 3.

— Maui Planning Commission may deny housing project proposed by Maui Land and Pineapple, Co., Lahaina News, August 13, 1998: 1.

— Kahana Ridge featured, Lahaina News, August 20, 1998: 13.

— National Kitchen and Bath Association to hold "Great Kitchen and Bath Tour", Lahaina News, October 15, 1998: 13.

— Mark Percell discusses county projects to ease demand for, Lahaina News, October 22, 1998: 3.

— Self-Help Housing Corporation seeks families interested in building their own homes, Lahaina News, October 29, 1998: 15.

— construction resumes on Napilihau Villages, Lahaina News, March 25, 1999: 13.

— Kahana Ridge building surging, Lahaina News, April 1, 1999: 12.

— Mahinahina Beach Condominium featured, Lahaina News, April 8, 1999: 10.

— Kapalua development featured, Lahaina News, April 8, 1999: 11.

— Self-Help Housing Corporation recruiting families for Kihei Project, Lahaina News, April 22, 1999: 11.

— Kapalua Land Co, Ltd. proposes single-family subdivision in Kapalua Resort area, Lahaina News, June 10, 1999: 13.

— shared ownership available at Sands of Kahana, Lahaina News, July 1, 1999: 10.

— Fair Housing laws to be discussed, Lahaina News, August 5, 1999: 11.

— Fair Housing laws to be discussed, Lahaina News, August 12, 1999: 14.

— Wainee Village homes to be demolished, Lahaina News, August 19, 1999: 1,20.

— Grand Fairways North residential development opens, Lahaina News, August 26, 1999: 13.

— Maui County Council evaluating proposed low-income project at Kenui Street, Lahaina News, October 21, 1999: 1,2.

— 20 Kahana Place featured, Lahaina News, November 25, 1999: 12.

— Greg and Carol Booth break ground on their new home, "Twin Palms at Pineapple Hill", Lahaina News, April 13, 2000: 10.

— openings available at Kihei Self-Help Housing Project, Lahaina News, May 18, 2000: 11.

— Terra Pacific Development, Co. LLC named as project developer for The Vintage at Ka'anapali, Lahaina News, June 8, 2000: 11.

— Hawaiian Homelands develops Waiehu Kou 2, Lahaina News, August 17, 2000: 13.

— The Summit at Ka'anapali featured, Lahaina News, August 24, 2000: 10.

— Ka'anapali Hillside executive homes featured, Lahaina News, August 31, 2000: 10.

— Maui Park Condominium to hold reopening, Lahaina News, October 5, 2000: 13.

— Ali'i Community Care to operate new assisted-living project, Lahaina News, October 26, 2000: 19.

— elderly housing complex Hale Mahaolu Eona planned, Lahaina News, December 14, 2000: 1,17.

— first phase of Front Street Apartments nearly completed, Lahaina News, May 24, 2001: 9.

— gated golf course community The Island holds grand opening, Lahaina News, June 14, 2001: 7.

— Front Street Apartments completed, Lahaina News, June 21, 2001: 3.

— Parade of Homes to be held, Lahaina News, October 4, 2001: 8.

— Legal Aid Society of Hawaii to investigate discrimination in, Lahaina News, January 31, 2002: 8.

— training for condominium owners "Everything You Want to Know About Being a Board Member But are Afraid to Ask", Lahaina News, February 21, 2002: 8.

— home buying and selling seminars to be held, Lahaina News, February 20, 2003: 9.

— tips on finding contractors, Lahaina News, February 27, 2003: 7.

— Housing and Community Development Corporation of Hawaii sponsoring housing survey, Lahaina News, March 20, 2003: 8.

— Maui Economic Opportunity Inc. to host Affordable Housing Conference, Lahaina News, May 1, 2003: 8.

— show on Akaku: Maui Community Television explores affordable housing issues, Lahaina News, June 12, 2003: 7.

— Condominium Council of Maui to hold Condo Owners Forum, Lahaina News, June 12, 2003: 7.

— State Housing and Community Development Corporation of Hawaii (HCDCH) awards tax credit for Wailuku affordable rentals, Lahaina News, June 19, 2003: 7.

— Maui Economic Opportunity to present "Making Affordable Housing A Reality: The Successful Vermont Model", Lahaina News, July 17, 2003: 8.

— fast track affordable housing slated above Puamana, Lahaina News, July 24, 2003: 1,18.

HOUSING ACT, FEDERAL
— basis for development of Wahikuli Terrace, Lahaina Sun, December 2, 1970: 3.

HOUSING ADMINISTRATION, FEDERAL
— mortgages for residential development in Lahaina, Lahaina Sun, December 2, 1970: 3.

— support of low and middle income housing, Lahaina Sun, January 20, 1971: 3.

HOUSING AND COMMUNITY DEVELOPMENT CORPORATION OF HAWAII (HCDCH)
— sponsoring housing survey, Lahaina News, March 20, 2003: 8.

— awards tax credit for Wailuku affordable rentals, Lahaina News, June 19, 2003: 7.

HOUSING AND HUMAN CONCERNS, DEPARTMENT OF
— to hold drama classes with Theatre Theatre Maui, Lahaina News, April 20, 2000: 14.

HOUSING AND HUMAN CONCERNS, MAUI COUNTY DEPARTMENT OF
— Robert Agres Jr. appointed head of, Lahaina News, May 28, 1986: 3.

HOUSING AND URBAN DEVELOPMENT, FEDERAL DEPARTMENT OF
— approves funds for J Walter Cameron Center, Lahaina Sun, December 8, 1971: 17.

— provides funds for North Wailuku General Neighborhood Renewal, Lahaina Sun, December 29, 1971: 17.

HOUSING DIVISION, MAUI COUNTY
— to hold drawing for houses, Lahaina News, June 13, 1990: 1.

HOUSING FINANCE AND DEVELOPMENT CORPORATION (HFDC)
— accepting applications for affordable apartments at Honokowai, Lahaina News, May 30, 1990: 5.

— Maui Contractors Association members critical of State efforts to build affordable homes, Lahaina News, August 8, 1990: 6.

— to begin Phase 1-A of Lahaina Master Planned Project, Lahaina News, September 5, 1991: 1.

— to hold public meeting to discuss conveyance of ceded lands, Lahaina News, August 27, 1992: 3,18.

— to hold hearing, Lahaina News, September 10, 1992: 3.

— to hold public hearing, Lahaina News, September 24, 1992: 3,4.

— seeking developers for housing project, Lahaina News, September 30, 1993: 8.

— to purchase ceded land for housing project, Lahaina News, July 28, 1994: 1.

— approves money to purchase ceded land for housing development Villages of Leiali'i, Lahaina News, August 18, 1994: 3.

— Clayton Hee says ceded lands being purchased for housing development to be reappraised, Lahaina News, October 27, 1994: 1,5.

— Villages of Leiali'i project continuing despite legal challenge from Office of Hawaiian Affairs, Lahaina News, December 1, 1994: 4,5.

— wants to move forward with proposed Villages of Leiali'i, Lahaina News, December 29, 1994: 1,3.

— wants policy from governor regarding sale of ceded land, Lahaina News, August 3, 1995: 3.

— Preparing Draft Environmental Assessment for proposed Villages of Leiali'i development, Lahaina News, August 24, 1995: 2.

— John Min appointed as vice chair by Governor Ben Cayetano, Lahaina News, August 31, 1995: 10.

HOUSTON, CANDACE
— promoted to Oahu general manager of Budget Rent-a-Car, Lahaina News, August 13, 1992: 12.

HOUSTON, THELMA [MUSICIAN]
— to perform at Maui Marriott Resort with Herbie Hancock, Lahaina News, August 2, 1989: 15.

HOW THE OTHER HALF LOVES [PLAY]
— Maui Community Theatre to hold auditions, Lahaina News, August 21, 1997: 17.

— Maui Community Theatre to hold auditions for, Lahaina News, August 28, 1997: 10.

— to be performed by Maui Community Theatre, Lahaina News, October 2, 1997: 21.

HOWARD AHIA BAND [MUSICAL GROUP]
— to perform at benefit concert at Maui Brews, Lahaina News, August 5, 1999: 14.

HOWARD AND THE WHITE BOYS [MUSICAL GROUP]
— to perform at World Cafe, Lahaina News, February 15, 1996: 13.

HOWARD, BARBARA
— director of Honolua Preschool passes away, Lahaina News, October 17, 2002: 2.

HOWARD, GREGG
— Native American storyteller to present "Tales of Wonder" at the Maui Arts and Cultural Center, Lahaina News, May 2, 2002: 17.

HOWARD, JEANNE
— promoted to sales manager for resort sales in continental U.S., Lahaina News, September 24, 1992: 9.

HOWARD, STAN [COMEDIAN]
— to perform at Comedy Club, Lahaina News, April 11, 1990: 15.

HOWE, GRANT
— named president of The Commercial Round Table of Maui, Lahaina News, September 13, 1989: 6.

HOWE, LINDA
— manager of community relations at Alexander and Baldwin, Lahaina News, December 31, 1992: 10.

HOWELL, CHARLES III
— golfer to play at Mercedes Championships, Lahaina News, January 9, 2003: 13.

HOWELL, DONNY
— names project director at Marriott Vacation Club, Lahaina News, May 13, 1999: 13.

HOWELL, MAMO [ARTIST]
— work featured on journal and address book printed by Aloha Airlines, Lahaina News, February 13, 1992: 13.

HOWELL, RICHARD MORGAN[ARTIST]
— carver to exhibit at Village Gallery, Lahaina News, September 13, 2001: 8.

HOWELL, ROBERT
— appointed to director sales at Westin Maui, Lahaina News, December 17, 1992: 8.

HUANG, ALFRED
— to teach Tai Chi, Lahaina News, December 26, 1996: 11.

HUBBARD, EDWARD
— retired Air Force Colonel to speak, Lahaina News, January 31, 2002: 1,9.
— retired Air Force colonel spoke to Lahaina Rotary Club, Lahaina News, February 14, 2002: 1,20.

HUBBARD, FREDDIE [MUSICIAN]
— to play at Maui Lu Resort, Lahaina News, October 2, 1985: 10.
— career described, spends half his year in Australia, Lahaina News, October 9, 1985: 10.

HUBBARD STREET DANCE CHICAGO [TROUPE]
— to perform at Maui Arts and Cultural Center, Lahaina News, February 28, 2002: 16.

HUBERT, STEPHEN FITCH [MUSICIAN]
— to perform at David Paul's Lahaina Grill, Lahaina News, April 4, 1996: 15.
— "Stevie Sparks" to celebrate 21st anniversary of Leilani's on the Beach, Lahaina News, June 19, 2003: 15.

HUDDLESTON, SAM
— to speak at West Maui Christian Men's Camp, Lahaina News, September 20, 2001: 3.

HUDSON, DAVID
— quits as harbormaster, Lahaina Sun, April 12, 1972: 7.
— charter fishing boat owner featured, Lahaina News, October 10, 1984: 4.

HUDSON, MAX [ARTIST]
— to exhibit at Hanson Galleries, Lahaina News, February 14, 1990: 16.

HUDSON, STEVE [COMEDIAN]
— to perform at Comedy Club, Lahaina News, September 9, 1993: 12.

HUERTER, JOHN
— opens Material Things, Lahaina News, March 16, 1995: 10.

HUERTER, SAM
— Scholar/Athlete of the Week, Lahaina News, November 28, 2002: 12.

HUEY LEWIS AND THE NEWS [MUSICAL GROUP]
— to perform, Lahaina News, October 30, 1997: 17.

HUFFORD, RANDY [ARTIST]
— photo accepted 100th International Exhibition of Professional Photography in Dallas, Lahaina News, December 12, 1991: 16.
— photograph "The Whiners" part of International Exposition of Professional Photography, Lahaina News, September 16, 1993: 17.

HUGEL, PAUL [ARTIST]
— to present 3D images at ArtTech Maui Expo, Lahaina News, November 10, 1994: 15.

HUGGINS, HAL
— author of "It's All in Your Head: The Link Between Amalgams and Illness" to speak, Lahaina News, May 13, 1999: 17.
— to speak, Lahaina News, May 20, 1999: 16.

HUGGY THE CLOWN
— to appear at Friday Night is Art Night, Lahaina News, June 20, 1991: 8.

HUGHES CORPORATION
— planning to build Hughes Glomar Explorer to mine manganese nodules from the ocean floor, Lahaina Sun, August 8, 1973: 7.

HUGHES, DAVID [FOOTBALL PLAYER]
— career discussed, Lahaina News, July 25, 1984: 4.

HUGHES, DOUGLAS [WRITER]
— author of "The Pyradice Games" to speak at 'Ohana Connection breakfast, Lahaina News, February 7, 2002: 17.

HUGHES, JENNIFER ANNE
— releases first single through Paradise Island Productions, Lahaina News, October 11, 1989: 4.

HUGHES, KAREN SCHULZ
— appointed new director of sales and marketing at Starwood Hotels and Resort, Lahaina News, May 31, 2001: 8.

HUGHES, KEVIN [COMEDIAN]
— to appear at the Maui Prince, Lahaina News, January 20, 1988: 18.
— to perform at Comedy Club and the Sports Page, Lahaina News, March 18, 1993: 9.
— to perform at Comedy Club and the Sports Page, Lahaina News, March 25, 1993: 13,15.
— to perform at Comedy Club, Lahaina News, July 22, 1993: 12.
— to perform at Comedy Club, Lahaina News, March 3, 1994: 12.
— to perform at Honolulu Comedy Club at Maui Marriott, Lahaina News, July 7, 1994: 14.
— to perform at Maui Comedy Club, Lahaina News, July 20, 1995: 11.

HUGHES, LORD MACMILLAN [ARTIST]
— donates portrait of King David Kalakaua to Lahaina Public Library, Lahaina News, December 14, 2000: 2.

HUGHES, NITA
— to present "Past Recall—The Soul as Co-Author" at 'Ohana Connection, Lahaina News, June 12, 2003: 21.

HUGHES, ROBERT
— elected to board of directors of California a& Hawaiian Sugar Company, Lahaina Sun, February 17, 1971: 2.

HUGHES, TONI
— to speak at Kilauea Military Camp, Lahaina News, October 22, 1986: 5.

HUGHES, TORIAN [COMEDIAN]
— to perform at Comedy Club and the Sports Page, Lahaina News, June 10, 1993: 10.

HUGILL, STAN [MUSICIAN]
— to perform sea shanteys on Carthaginian, Lahaina News, June 14, 1989: 16.
— to perform sea shanteys on Carthaginian, Lahaina News, June 21, 1989: 18.

HUH, SEAN
— new retail store manager at AT&T Wireless Kahului location, Lahaina News, August 16, 2001: 8.

HUI ALANUI O MAKENA

— settles conflict with Seibu Hawaii over Makena road closure, Lahaina News, July 29, 1987: 2.
— signs agreement with Kapalua Land Company and Office of Hawaiian Affairs concerning Native Hawaiian burials disinterred, Lahaina News, August 19, 1987: 3.
— concerned with Kapalua Land Company's new hotel development, Lahaina News, June 15, 1988: 1.
— working with Office of Hawaiian Affairs to reinter ancient Hawaiian remains, Lahaina News, March 29, 1989: 1.
— recommends no further study of ancient Hawaiian remains, Lahaina News, April 12, 1989: 1.
— protests lead to site of Ritz-Carlton Hotel to be changed, Lahaina News, April 26, 1989: 1.
— signs agreement on reinternment of ancient Hawaiian bones, Lahaina News, September 13, 1989: 3.

HUI KAKO'O 'AINA HO'OPULAPULA

— to hold community meeting at Malu'ulu O Lele Senior Center, Lahaina News, October 11, 2001: 20.
— to hold informational meeting on Hawaiian Home Lands, Lahaina News, November 21, 2002: 3.
— to host community meeting on Hawaiian Home Lands, Lahaina News, March 6, 2003: 3.

HUI LOA

— plan for Lahaina town discussed, Lahaina News, August 20, 1986: 6.

HUI MALAMA LEARNING CENTER

— seeking tutors for reading , Lahaina News, March 24, 1994: 7.
— offering workshops on phonics, Lahaina News, January 5, 1995: 4.
— Adult Literacy Program seeking volunteers, Lahaina News, May 11, 1995: 2.
— to train tutors for Adult Literacy Program, Lahaina News, May 18, 1995: 4.
— Maui Stingrays to hold charity game, Lahaina News, November 9, 1995: 6.
— Adult Literacy Program seeking volunteers, Lahaina News, April 25, 1996: 6.
— to offer English classes, Lahaina News, January 16, 1997: 10.
— offering GED test preparation, Lahaina News, July 10, 1997: 2.
— to sell Entertainment Book, Lahaina News, November 13, 1997: 2.
— offering test preparation classes, Lahaina News, February 12, 1998: 8.
— seeking volunteers for literacy program, Lahaina News, April 9, 1998: 17.
— looking for volunteers, Lahaina News, April 16, 1998: 12.
— to offer summer classes, Lahaina News, May 14, 1998: 7.
— seeking after-school tutors, Lahaina News, September 10, 1998: 8.
— seeking after-school tutors, Lahaina News, September 17, 1998: 19.
— to offer English classes, Lahaina News, December 24, 1998: 1,16.
— to offer GED test preparation, Lahaina News, December 31, 1998: 12.
— to hold classes, Lahaina News, May 13, 1999: 15.
— to hold summer classes, Lahaina News, June 17, 1999: 15.
— to hold SAT preparation classes, Lahaina News, August 19, 1999: 16.
— to conduct volunteer orientation, Lahaina News, September 2, 1999: 17.
— to hold Literacy Volunteer Orientation, Lahaina News, December 30, 1999: 15.
— Samuel Millington named new executive director of , Lahaina News, March 9, 2000: 5.
— honors GED graduates, Lahaina News, June 29, 2000: 16.
— to offer literacy courses, Lahaina News, September 21, 2000: 19.
— seeking volunteer classroom aides, Lahaina News, November 9, 2000: 11.
— offer Pre-GED classes, Lahaina News, November 30, 2000: 5.
— awarded grant from Victoria S. and Bradley L. Geist Foundation for "Family Literacy—Family Strengthening Model Demonstration Initiative", Lahaina News, March 15, 2001: 8.

— seeking mentors, Lahaina News, April 26, 2001: 2.
— to offer educational programs, Lahaina News, May 24, 2001: 2.
— Napili student earns GED, Lahaina News, June 14, 2001: 11.
— expanding homeschool program , Lahaina News, August 9, 2001: 2.
— offering GED courses, Lahaina News, August 30, 2001: 2.
— offering English as a Second Language class, Lahaina News, September 13, 2001: 16.
— Gary Patrick Robilotta performing benefit concert for, Lahaina News, September 13, 2001: 3.
— to offer SAT preparation course, Lahaina News, January 24, 2002: 17.
— to hold "Helping Kids Succeed" program, Lahaina News, March 7, 2002: 17.
— planning series of English as a Second Language classes, Lahaina News, March 14, 2002: 17.
— to offer "Core Foundations" program for GED, Lahaina News, March 28, 2002: 21.
— seeking volunteers, Lahaina News, May 16, 2002: 17.
— to offer classes for students grades 4 to 7, Lahaina News, June 13, 2002: 16.
— offering GED programs, Lahaina News, August 15, 2002: 9.
— receives grant from McInerny Foundation, Lahaina News, October 17, 2002: 14.
— receives grant from Victoria S. and Bradley L. Geist Foundation, Lahaina News, December 19, 2002: 2.
— to hold training for volunteers, Lahaina News, December 26, 2002: 2.
— offering programs at Maria Lanakila Church, Lahaina News, January 2, 2003: 5.
— offering programs at Maria Lanakila Church, Lahaina News, February 27, 2003: 9.
— offering second language classes, Lahaina News, March 6, 2003: 17.
— continues to offer English as Second Language classes, Lahaina News, June 26, 2003: 21.
— continues to offer ESL classes, Lahaina News, July 24, 2003: 18.

HUI MANU O MAUI

— advocates protecting Kanaha Pond area, Lahaina Sun, February 28, 1973: 4.

HUI NO KE OLA PONO

— to provide cancer check, Lahaina News, May 18, 2000: 8.
— Kokua Program offering "Women's Health Awareness Fair 2000", Lahaina News, July 6, 2000: 16.
— to hold Women's Health Awareness Fair 2001, Lahaina News, August 2, 2001: 2.
— Breast and Cervical Control Program providing exams, Lahaina News, January 17, 2002: 2.
— offering free breast and cervical screenings, Lahaina News, February 21, 2002: 2.
— Native Hawaiian Health Care System offering programs, Lahaina News, January 16, 2003: 2.

HUI NO'EAU VISUAL ARTS CENTER

— hold Christmas Craft Fair, Lahaina News, December 1, 1980: 11.
— annual wine tasting held, Lahaina News, May 15, 1982: 6.
— to hold Easter Basket Show and Open House, Lahaina News, April 4, 1984: 3.
— sponsoring basket workshop, Lahaina News, May 16, 1984: 5.
— planning underway for Christmas Craft Fair, Lahaina News, September 5, 1984: 10.
— Annual Christmas Craft Fair, Lahaina News, November 14, 1984: 3.
— raku demonstration, Lahaina News, February 13, 1985: 11.
— craft classes set for July and August, Lahaina News, July 17, 1985: 3.
— to hold art classes, Lahaina News, September 11, 1985: 3.
— to hold Christmas Fair November 16 and 17, Lahaina News, October 9, 1985: 8.
— to hold Christmas Craft Fair, Lahaina News, November 13, 1985: 3.

— hosting symposium on "The Jurying Process", Lahaina News, January 15, 1986: 10.
— A Celebration of the Human Body exhibit opens at, Lahaina News, April 16, 1986: 3.
— offering classes, Lahaina News, July 23, 1986: 14.
— to hold classes in August, Lahaina News, August 6, 1986: 18.
— Fall art classes listed, Lahaina News, September 3, 1986: 3.
— sponsoring art classes, Lahaina News, October 1, 1986: 5.
— offering classes in printmaking for children, Lahaina News, October 8, 1986: 3.
— to screen entries for Christmas Craft Fair, Lahaina News, October 22, 1986: 3.
— offering classes on jewelry making, Lahaina News, October 22, 1986: 5.
— to hold art classes, Lahaina News, November 19, 1986: 16.
— offering art classes, Lahaina News, December 3, 1986: 11.
— offering art classes, Lahaina News, January 7, 1987: 3.
— art classes, Lahaina News, February 4, 1987: 11.
— exhibits watercolors, Lahaina News, May 20, 1987: 3.
— classes offered, Lahaina News, June 17, 1987: 3.
— to hold exhibition of works by Hui instructors, Lahaina News, June 17, 1987: 3.
— to offer printmaking classes to children, Lahaina News, July 1, 1987: 3.
— art classes continue, Lahaina News, July 8, 1987: 16.
— ongoing art classes, Lahaina News, August 5, 1987: 3.
— to hold Christmas House Sale, Lahaina News, September 30, 1987: 3.
— featuring work of David Warren and Ilene Kratka, Lahaina News, September 30, 1987: 3.
— hosts juried show, Lahaina News, October 14, 1987: 3.
— previews Christmas Fair, Lahaina News, December 2, 1987: 3.
— to host "A View of Kaluanui", Lahaina News, June 15, 1988: 14.
— to host artist Marilyn Wold, Lahaina News, June 22, 1988: 10.
— to offer classes on cloisonne process, Lahaina News, July 6, 1988: 11.
— to present recent works of life drawings, Lahaina News, August 17, 1988: 14.
— offering ceramics classes, Lahaina News, September 7, 1988: 14.
— open exhibit of members, Lahaina News, September 28, 1988: 3.
— offering make-up sessions for Halloween, Lahaina News, October 19, 1988: 14.
— to hold workshop on collograph-making, Lahaina News, November 2, 1988: 18.
— Christmas House party and classes organized, Lahaina News, November 23, 1988: 18.
— offering drawing and painting classes, Lahaina News, December 14, 1988: 16.
— to offer classes in December, Lahaina News, December 21, 1988: 17.
— to offer life drawing class by Archie Brennan, Lahaina News, January 4, 1989: 3.
— offers classes in January, Lahaina News, January 11, 1989: 5.
— to offer class on large scale watercolors, Lahaina News, February 8, 1989: 5.
— to host Art Maui '89, Lahaina News, February 15, 1989: 5.
— exhibiting artwork by Lahainaluna High School students, Lahaina News, May 24, 1989: 3.
— upcoming events detailed, Lahaina News, December 13, 1989: 24.
— to host juried craft show, Lahaina News, January 17, 1990: 12.
— juried craft show continues, Lahaina News, January 24, 1990: 2.
— to hold workshops by Tony and Pauline Hepburn, Lahaina News, April 4, 1990: 14.
— offering class exploring use of trash as medium, Lahaina News, May 2, 1990: 16.
— to exhibit "Visions of the Volcano", Lahaina News, May 9, 1990: 20.
— to hold mixed media exhibition, Lahaina News, June 20, 1990: 11.
— offering kiln firing class, Lahaina News, July 25, 1990: 13.

— to hold juried members exhibition, Lahaina News, September 5, 1990: 17.
— to hold old book sale, Lahaina News, October 24, 1990: 16.
— to host Pacific storytellers, Lahaina News, October 31, 1990: 17.
— to open Victorian Christmas House, Lahaina News, November 28, 1990: 10.
— David Ulrich named first executive director, Lahaina News, January 30, 1991: 9.
— offers course on drawing the head, Lahaina News, February 6, 1991: 12.
— exhibiting work by Evan Asato, Lahaina News, February 13, 1991: 13.
— to hold metal workshop by Claire Sanford, Lahaina News, February 27, 1991: 13.
— hosting Art Maui, Lahaina News, April 10, 1991: 13.
— to organize "Art Affair" fundraiser, Lahaina News, April 17, 1991: 15.
— to hold "Art Affair" fundraiser, Lahaina News, April 24, 1991: 13.
— to hold Scholarship Show, Lahaina News, May 1, 1991: 4.
— to offer ceramics classes, Lahaina News, June 6, 1991: 17.
— to hold garage sale fundraiser, Lahaina News, August 8, 1991: 4.
— to hold attic sale, Lahaina News, September 12, 1991: 5.
— to hold Second Hand Rose Dinner, Lahaina News, September 12, 1991: 5.
— to present Kamaʻaina Christmas House, Lahaina News, October 24, 1991: 5.
— to offer exhibit celebrating 150 years of photography, Lahaina News, November 28, 1991: 18.
— to hold Kamaʻaina Christmas House fundraiser, Lahaina News, December 5, 1991: 6.
— offering Christmas gift store, Lahaina News, December 19, 1991: 7.
— offering holiday showcase, Lahaina News, January 2, 1992: 5.
— Jody Mitchell to teach class in lei making, Lahaina News, January 30, 1992: 5.
— to offer workshop on making journals, Lahaina News, February 6, 1992: 4.
— to present art videos, Lahaina News, March 5, 1992: 18.
— hosting "Furniture as Art" display, Lahaina News, March 5, 1992: 4.
— hosting Art Maui '92, Lahaina News, April 16, 1992: 21.
— wood exhibit to open, Lahaina News, May 7, 1992: 26.
— to offer children's art classes, Lahaina News, May 21, 1992: 4.
— to host author Milton Murayama, Lahaina News, May 28, 1992: 18.
— to hold summer art classes, Lahaina News, June 11, 1992: 6.
— to offer summer classes, Lahaina News, June 18, 1992: 4.
— to offer art classes, Lahaina News, June 25, 1992: 2.
— to present "Country Jam", Lahaina News, July 16, 1992: 22.
— offering adult workshops, Lahaina News, August 20, 1992: 4.
— new courses started, Lahaina News, September 24, 1992: 4.
— offering holiday workshops, Lahaina News, November 5, 1992: 4.
— to exhibit works by Marin Freeman, Lahaina News, December 31, 1992: 5.
— to hold classes, Lahaina News, February 11, 1993: 5.
— to hold membership drive, Lahaina News, February 18, 1993: 4.
— presenting "Feast or Famine", Lahaina News, September 30, 1993: 14.
— to hold juried Summer Open Exhibit, Lahaina News, May 19, 1994: 16.
— inviting submissions for juried Summer Open Exhibit, Lahaina News, May 26, 1994: 16.
— paniolo heritage exhibit to open, Lahaina News, June 30, 1994: 13.
— accepting applications for juried Summer Open Exhibit, Lahaina News, June 30, 1994: 15.
— to host "Masami Teraoka: Future Tense", Lahaina News, March 2, 1995: 12.
— featuring summer solo shows, Lahaina News, June 29, 1995: 12.
— to host Christmas House, Lahaina News, November 21, 1996: 14.

— opening Children's Art Exhibit, Lahaina News, August 21, 1997: 17.
— Christmas House open, Lahaina News, November 13, 1997: 21.
— to show "Crossings '97", Lahaina News, January 8, 1998: 12.
— to host children's art show, Lahaina News, August 27, 1998: 16.
— to present Christmas House, Lahaina News, November 5, 1998: 21.
— to hold art classes, Lahaina News, June 3, 1999: 2.
— to feature works from Kara Taylor and Patricia Wood, Lahaina News, July 8, 1999: 12.
— offering art classes, Lahaina News, August 26, 1999: 14.
— to hold Children's Art Exhibit, Lahaina News, September 2, 1999: 15.
— offering art classes, Lahaina News, October 28, 1999: 13.
— annual Christmas House craft fair to be held, Lahaina News, November 18, 1999: 16.
— to hold art classes, Lahaina News, December 30, 1999: 15.
— to offer tour, Lahaina News, May 18, 2000: 20.
— to offer art shows and classes, Lahaina News, June 29, 2000: 7.
— to host "Transformations and Encounters" show, Lahaina News, July 6, 2000: 16.
— to hold Christmas House, Lahaina News, November 16, 2000: 16.
— Nancy Skrimstad to hold "Unique Holiday Cards" workshop, Lahaina News, November 30, 2000: 17.
— accepting applications for Solo Show, Lahaina News, January 18, 2001: 2.
— to exhibit "Parts" featuring parts from vehicles, Lahaina News, September 27, 2001: 16.
— to hold "Plein Air" juried exhibit, Lahaina News, December 6, 2001: 16.
— to hold Friday Figure Drawing Workshop, Lahaina News, May 2, 2002: 16.
— to hold Art Open House, Lahaina News, May 16, 2002: 16.
— to feature shows by Jacqueline Lee and Katherine Love, Lahaina News, July 4, 2002: 17.
— work from Summer Art Camp to be displayed, Lahaina News, August 15, 2002: 18.
— to exhibit works from Summer Art Camp, Lahaina News, August 22, 2002: 20.
— to hold show "Fire to Form", Lahaina News, December 19, 2002: 18.
— to feature Juried Members' Exhibit, Lahaina News, May 8, 2003: 16.
— to host Vessel Exhibit, Lahaina News, September 25, 2003: 16.

HUI O HONOKOHAU
— group forms to preserve Honokohau Valley, Lahaina News, January 24, 1990: 28.

HUI O POHAKU-WESTSIDE MAUI
— Christmas Party held, Lahaina News, January 4, 2001: 2.
— to hold S-Turns Longboard Keiki Surf Contest, Lahaina News, January 23, 2003: 12.
— to hold longboarding event at S-Turns, Lahaina News, January 30, 2003: 13.
— Longboard contest held, Lahaina News, February 20, 2003: 1.
— held, Lahaina News, February 27, 2003: 1,20.

HUI O WA'A KAULUA
— president of Hui O Wa'a Kaulua supports Hawaiian cultural park at Kamehameha Iki Park, Lahaina News, November 9, 1995: 1,16.
— building canoe, Lahaina News, November 16, 1995: 5.
— raising money for double-hulled sailing canoe, Lahaina News, January 11, 1996: 1.
— artist impression of, Lahaina News, January 18, 1996: 16.
— assembling double-hulled canoe, Lahaina News, March 7, 1996: 2.
— money in Mayor Linda Lingle's budget, Lahaina News, March 21, 1996: 1,14.
— seeks funds from Maui County Council, Lahaina News, April 11, 1996: 1,3.
— seeking funds from county, Lahaina News, April 25, 1996: 7.
— design of Mo'okiha discussed, Lahaina News, May 2, 1996: 6.

— meeting held, Lahaina News, June 6, 1996: 14.
— plans open house, Lahaina News, November 21, 1996: 1,13.
— to hold one-year anniversary, Lahaina News, November 28, 1996: 10.
— featured, Lahaina News, December 5, 1996: 1.
— new board of directors elected, Lahaina News, February 6, 1997: 2.
— offering cultural camp, Lahaina News, June 5, 1997: 3.
— canoe building Keola Sequiera resigns from, Lahaina News, June 12, 1997: 1.
— members raise concerns, Lahaina News, June 19, 1997: 1.
— to resume work on canoe, Lahaina News, March 26, 1998: 1,16.
— receives gift from Ka'anapali Beach Hotel, Lahaina News, April 23, 1998: 2.
— plans canoe house and Keiki Hale at Kamehameha Iki Park, Lahaina News, September 17, 1998: 1,32.
— to begin lashing canoe Mo'okiha, Lahaina News, March 11, 1999: 12.
— working on Lahaina Interpretive Plan, Lahaina News, August 5, 1999: 1,16.
— sponsors students sailing to Moloka'i, Lahaina News, September 23, 1999: 1,16.
— to host "The Legend of the Laughing Gecko" with Queen Lili'uokalani Children's Center, Lahaina News, February 3, 2000: 12.
— sails to Mo'olele to attend Hokule'a , Lahaina News, March 16, 2000: 1.
— Mahina Martin is new executive director, Lahaina News, March 29, 2001: 1,9.
— to hold benefit dinner, Lahaina News, April 26, 2001: 3.
— continues to work on voyaging Mo'okiha (O Pi'ilani), Lahaina News, September 6, 2001: 1,8.
— benefit concert to be held, Lahaina News, November 8, 2001: 14.
— "He Huihui A Kolea, Talk Story With Nainoa Thompson" fundraiser to be held, Lahaina News, June 27, 2002: 16.

HUI OHANA COUNCIL
— to hold fundraiser, Lahaina News, October 10, 1996: 15.
— to hold fundraiser, Lahaina News, October 17, 1996: 14.
— mental health organization seeking volunteers, Lahaina News, August 28, 1997: 5.
— recruiting volunteers, Lahaina News, November 21, 2002: 13.
— recruiting volunteers, Lahaina News, December 5, 2002: 16.

HULA
— history of described, Lahaina News, September 1, 1981: 12.
— Edwin Kayton presents "A Tribute to Hula" at Maui Marriott Resort, Lahaina News, May 8, 1985: 3,20.
— halau to be featured at Lahaina Cannery Shopping Center, Lahaina News, August 5, 1987: 3.
— lecture by Hoakalei Kamauu to be held at Lahaina Public Library, Lahaina News, October 5, 1988: 3.
— keiki hula featured at Lahaina Cannery Shopping Center, Lahaina News, October 19, 1988: 3.
— shows to be hosted at Lahaina Cannery Shopping Center, Lahaina News, February 8, 1989: 3,5.
— contest to be held at Maui Inter-Continental Hotel, Lahaina News, March 8, 1989: 17.
— deadline to Hula Pakahi and Lei Festival approaches, Lahaina News, April 5, 1989: 5.
— keiki hula shows at Lahaina Cannery Shopping Center, Lahaina News, May 31, 1989: 16.
— benefit concert held for Piilani School of Hula, Lahaina News, August 23, 1989: 3.
— new show to debut at Maui Prince Hotel, Lahaina News, December 20, 1989: 8.
— members of Emma Kapiolani Sharpe Hula Halau travel to Oahu, Lahaina News, August 1, 1991: 8.

HULA BOWL

— to be held at War Memorial Stadium, Lahaina News, January 14, 1999: 7.

— Ricky Williams plays at, Lahaina News, January 28, 1999: 1.

— to be played, Lahaina News, January 20, 2000: 6.

— festival to be held at Lahaina Cannery Mall, Lahaina News, January 27, 2000: 5.

— to benefit Ronald McDonald House Charities, Lahaina News, January 18, 2001: 9.

— cheerleaders practice for, Lahaina News, February 1, 2001: 15.

— to be held, Lahaina News, December 27, 2001: 12.

— to hold Mascot Competition with Maui Humane Society, Lahaina News, January 10, 2002: 16.

— quarterback Eric Crouch to play at, Lahaina News, January 17, 2002: 12.

— to be played at War Memorial Stadium, Lahaina News, January 24, 2002: 13.

— to be held, Lahaina News, January 31, 2002: 13.

— announces finalists for Mosi Tatupu Special team Award, Lahaina News, December 12, 2002: 11.

— University of Hawai'i football players to play at, Lahaina News, December 19, 2002: 11.

— to be played, Lahaina News, January 16, 2003: 13.

— local entertainers to perform at, Lahaina News, January 30, 2003: 13.

HULA GIRL [BOAT]

— catamaran to be removed from Mala rocks, Lahaina News, December 4, 1997: 3.

HULA GRILL [RESTAURANT]

— opens in Whalers Village, Lahaina News, July 7, 1994: 8,9.

— names Orrin Cross as general manager, Lahaina News, July 7, 1994: 9.

— George Kobayashi joins as wine and service manager, Lahaina News, August 18, 1994: 9.

— wine list voted best, Lahaina News, October 27, 1994: 14.

— to hold Beer Seminar, Lahaina News, April 27, 1995: 11.

— to hold youth ukulele contest, Lahaina News, June 6, 1996: 15.

— featured, Lahaina News, September 4, 1997: 5,6.

— to host ukulele, Lahaina News, June 25, 1998: 5.

— to host Santa, Lahaina News, December 10, 1998: 9.

— to host "Na Keiki Ho'okuku Ukulele", Lahaina News, June 21, 2001: 14.

— hosting "Na Keiki Ho'okuku Ukulele" Youth contest, Lahaina News, June 28, 2001: 20.

— honors Harold Kaniho and Rick Paul as "Educators of the Month", Lahaina News, June 28, 2001: 8.

— celebrates 7th anniversary, Lahaina News, July 5, 2001: 9.

— to hold fundraiser for Windows of Hope Relief Fund, Lahaina News, October 11, 2001: 16.

— Aloha Friday Keiki Hula Shows continues to be held, Lahaina News, October 11, 2001: 16.

— recognizes King Kamehameha III Elementary School educators, Lahaina News, April 11, 2002: 2.

— recognizes Lindsay Ball as "Educator of the Month", Lahaina News, May 9, 2002: 2.

— to host Santa Claus, Lahaina News, December 19, 2002: 21.

— to host food and wine feast, Lahaina News, January 16, 2003: 16.

HULA HALAU HOOULU O KAULA

— to perform at Lahaina Cannery Mall as part of Aloha Summer, Lahaina News, August 15, 1990: 15.

HULA HALAU O MOLOKA'I

— to perform at Lahaina Cannery Mall as part of Aloha Summer, Lahaina News, August 15, 1990: 15.

HULA HULA CAFE [RESTAURANT]

— opens at Wharf Cinema Center, Lahaina News, June 24, 1999: 11.

HULA IS LIFE [BOOK]

— signing to be held, Lahaina News, August 5, 1999: 12.

HULA KU'I

— to perform at Mele Ho'ike, Lahaina News, February 4, 1999: 17.

HULA LE'A O NA KEIKI

— solo hula festival to be held at Ka'anapali Beach Hotel, Lahaina News, September 12, 1990: 18.

HULA MAE

— has loan money for first-time home buyers, Lahaina News, December 12, 1991: 13.

— mortgage program encouraging family ownership, Lahaina News, August 21, 1997: 9.

— offering house loans, Lahaina News, April 4, 2002: 8.

HULA MOONS [RESTAURANT]

— featuring Hawaiian music, Lahaina News, February 20, 1992: 17.

HULA O NA KEIKI

— contest to be held, Lahaina News, October 15, 1992: 18.

— winners announced, Lahaina News, November 12, 1992: 20.

— festival to be held at Ka'anapali Beach Hotel, Lahaina News, October 14, 1993: 14,15.

— festival to be held, Lahaina News, October 21, 1993: 14.

— results, Lahaina News, November 4, 1993: 11.

— hula competition to be held at Ka'anapali Beach Hotel, Lahaina News, September 8, 1994: 12.

— competition to be held at , Lahaina News, October 12, 1995: 15.

— won by Le'a Pacheco, Lahaina News, October 19, 1995: 8.

— competition to be held, Lahaina News, February 8, 1996: 14.

— to be held, Lahaina News, September 26, 1996: 1,14.

— competition to be held, Lahaina News, October 10, 1996: 15.

— to be held at Ka'anapali Beach Hotel, Lahaina News, August 14, 1997: 3.

— to be held, Lahaina News, September 18, 1997: 3.

— to pay special tribute to Pua Lindsey, Lahaina News, September 25, 1997: 7.

— competition to be held, Lahaina News, October 9, 1997: 21.

— to be held, Lahaina News, October 16, 1997: 1,16.

— details of competition, Lahaina News, October 23, 1997: 16.

— competition to pay tribute to George Na'ope, Lahaina News, October 8, 1998: 1.

— to be held, Lahaina News, October 15, 1998: 1,2.

— held, Lahaina News, October 29, 1998: 25.

— canceled due to renovations at Ka'anapali Beach Hotel, Lahaina News, July 22, 1999: 5.

— hula competition celebrating 10th anniversary, Lahaina News, October 26, 2000: 27.

— to be held, Lahaina News, November 2, 2000: 3.

— to begin on Friday, Lahaina News, November 9, 2000: 2.

— results, Lahaina News, November 16, 2000: 1.

— results of, Lahaina News, November 23, 2000: 9.

— contest to be held, Lahaina News, November 8, 2001: 1,20.

— free shows held at Lahaina Center, Lahaina News, November 15, 2001: 16.

— results of, Lahaina News, November 22, 2001: 15.

— competition to be held, Lahaina News, October 31, 2002: 18.

— to begin, Lahaina News, November 7, 2002: 19.

— results of, Lahaina News, November 14, 2002: 1,15.

HULA PAKAHI AND LEI FESTIVAL

— deadline to compete approaches, Lahaina News, April 5, 1989: 5.

— to be held at Maui Inter-Continental Wailea, Lahaina News, February 28, 1990: 11.

— to be held, Lahaina News, April 24, 1991: 11.

— solo hula competition to be held, Lahaina News, September 15, 1994: 14.

HULDI, ROGER
— named Director of Outlets at Westin Maui, Lahaina News, October 5, 2000: 14.

HULIAU 2000
— to be held, Lahaina News, July 27, 2000: 20.

HULIHIA HAWAII [PLAY]
— presented by Maui Academy of Performing Arts, Lahaina News, January 2, 1991: 8.

HULL, FOSTER
— publisher of Real Estate Maui Style featured speaker at Maui Authors Guild, Lahaina News, December 3, 1986: 12.
— elected chair of Maui Republican Party, Lahaina News, August 29, 1991: 4.
— Republican Party district chair objects to Russell Blair becoming state Senator due to reapportionment, Lahaina News, November 7, 1991: 1,9.
— appointed to Governor's Small Business Advisory Council, Lahaina News, January 16, 1992: 9.
— declares as Republican candidates, Lahaina News, February 13, 1992: 3.

HULTON, JOHN [POLITICIAN]
— state senator announces that contract to build two interisland ferries expected to be signed, Lahaina Sun, October 20, 1971: 6.

HULTQUIST, JOHN
— wins car race, Lahaina News, February 25, 1993: 4.

HULTQUIST, KENNY [ARTIST]
— to exhibit at Lahaina Arts Society, Lahaina News, March 28, 1996: 12.
— to exhibit at Lahaina Arts Society, Lahaina News, November 6, 1997: 16.
— to demonstrate paper making at the Village Gallery Contemporary, Lahaina News, January 13, 2000: 12.
— to demonstrate paper making at the Village Gallery Contemporary, Lahaina News, January 20, 2000: 13.
— to exhibit at Lahaina Arts Society, Lahaina News, March 16, 2000: 12.
— wins Lahaina Coolers Las Vegas Challenge, Lahaina News, August 8, 2002: 18.
— to visit Gallery Pacifica, Lahaina News, August 22, 2002: 17.

HUMAN CONCERNS, MAUI COUNTY DEVELOPMENT OF
— see Housing and Human Concerns, Maui County Department of

HUMAN REMAINS
— Hawaiian, removed from sand dune at Kapalua, Lahaina News, December 7, 1988: 1,24.
— relocation of remains put on hold for Hawaiian , Lahaina News, December 28, 1988: 1,20.
— controversy of disinterring ancient Hawaiian, Lahaina News, January 4, 1989: 1,16.
— Office of Hawaiian Affairs wants burial grounds protected, Lahaina News, January 18, 1989: 1.
— decision to allow Ritz-Carlton Hotel project delayed, Lahaina News, February 8, 1989: 1,20.
— deal reached over Hawaiian remains found at Honokahua, Lahaina News, March 1, 1989: 1,16.
— Kapalua Land Co. makes claim for reimbursement for relocating Ritz-Carlton Hotel, Lahaina News, March 8, 1989: 1,16.
— Kapalua Land Company stops studying ancient Hawaiian, Lahaina News, March 29, 1989: 1.
— Office of Hawaiian Affairs and Hui Alanui O Makena recommend no further study of ancient Hawaiian remains, Lahaina News, April 12, 1989: 1.
— leads to proposed Ritz-Carlton site to be moved, Lahaina News, April 26, 1989: 1.
— agreement signed on reinternment of ancient Hawaiian bones, Lahaina News, September 13, 1989: 3.
— Mayor Hannibal Tavares discusses moving burial site, Lahaina News, October 25, 1989: 2.
— found during Kahoma Stream Flood Control project, Lahaina News, October 25, 1989: 3.
— ancient Hawaiian, reinterred, Lahaina News, May 16, 1990: 5.
— erosion near near Mala Wharf uncovers, Lahaina News, September 5, 1991: 1.
— found at Pukalani Highlands during construction, Lahaina News, January 30, 1992: 5.
— William Waiohu to represent Lahaina on state burial council, Lahaina News, August 13, 1998: 1,20.
— Erik Fredericksen recommends to Maui/Lana'i Islands Burial Council to preserve pre-contact burial site at Olowalu, Lahaina News, December 17, 1998: 1,28.
— burials found at King Kamehameha III Elementary School grounds, Lahaina News, October 19, 2000: 2.

HUMAN RESOURCES, DEPARTMENT OF
— to host public hearing on child abuse and neglect, Lahaina News, February 20, 1997: 11.

HUMAN RIGHTS DAY
— observed, Lahaina News, December 4, 1985: 3.

HUMAN SERVICE, PARKS AND HOUSING COMMITTEE
— seeks input on fairgrounds relocation, Lahaina News, March 8, 1989: 16.

HUMANISTIC FREE THINKER SOCIETY
— to meet at Lahaina Book Emporium, Lahaina News, October 19, 2000: 11.

HUMANITIES, HAWAII COMMITTEE FOR THE
— to hold grant writing workshop, Lahaina News, October 21, 1999: 16.

HUMBLE SOUL [MUSICAL GROUP]
— to perform at Lahaina Civic Center Amphitheater with Alpha Bloody, Lahaina News, February 18, 1999: 12.

HUMPERDINCK, ENGELBERT [MUSICIAN]
— to perform, Lahaina News, December 9, 1999: 20.

HUNGER PROJECT
— John Denver in support of, Lahaina News, November 11, 1987: 1.

HUNT, DEBBIE
— appointed director of public relations for Westin Maui at Ka'anapali Beach, Lahaina News, September 20, 1989: 6.

HUNT GALLERY [BUSINESS]
— opens, Lahaina News, February 9, 1995: 11.

HUNT, KRYSTIE
— Scholar/Athlete of the Week, Lahaina News, May 20, 1999: 6.

HUNT, LINDSAY
— Scholar/Athlete of the Week, Lahaina News, March 6, 2003: 12.

HUNT, TIFFANY
— Scholar/Athlete of the Week, Lahaina News, January 22, 1998: 6.
— to participate in Youth for Christ/USA national internship program, Lahaina News, May 10, 2001: 2.

HUNTER EDUCATION CLASSES
— to be held, Lahaina News, July 31, 1997: 14.

HUNTER, JAMIE
— attorney claims that anti-hitchhiking law is unconstitutional, Lahaina Sun, February 10, 1971: 1.

HUNTER, KRIS
— named director of research and education at Island Marine, Lahaina News, January 14, 1999: 11.

HUNTER, LONG JOHN [MUSICIAN]
— to play at Sheraton Maui, Lahaina News, December 12, 1996: 1,9.
— to perform, Lahaina News, December 12, 1996: 9.

HUNTING
— on Maui and Lana'i, described, Lahaina Sun, January 6, 1971: 3.
— ram and antelope season open on Lana'i, Lahaina Sun, July 14, 1971: 12.
— applications for hunting licenses available, Lahaina Sun, February 2, 1972: 8.
— wild pig in downtown Haiku, Lahaina Sun, December 27, 1972: 9.
— Axis deer season begins next week, Lahaina Sun, January 31, 1973: 11.
— pig hunting described, Lahaina Sun, February 21, 1973: 4.
— pig hunting described, Lahaina News, November 5, 1986: 6.
— Department of Land and Natural Resources taking comments on preserve for, Lahaina News, September 29, 1994: 5.
— licenses available, Lahaina News, July 26, 2001: 13.

HUNZIKAR, ROBERT
— Water Activities and Vacation Entertainment, Inc operator indicted on theft and racketeering charges, Lahaina News, October 6, 1994: 11.

HURLEY, JOHN
— legal troubles detailed, Lahaina News, July 1, 1981: 10.

HURRICANE MARILYN
— Spats Nightclub to hold fundraiser for victims of, Lahaina News, October 19, 1995: 9.

HURRICANES
— Maui County preparedness evaluated, Lahaina News, October 22, 1992: 6.

HUSKE, BRETT
— named director of sales for Kapalua Bay Hotel, Lahaina News, January 1, 1986: 3.
— elected president of the Maui Chapter of Hotel Sales and Marketing Association, Lahaina News, August 26, 1987: 3.
— named general manager of Kapalua Bay Hotel, Lahaina News, September 27, 1989: 5.

HUSSEY, ADRIAN
— reappointed to the planning commission, Lahaina Sun, January 13, 1971: 8.

HUSSEY, LEIMOMI
— Maui News Player of the Year awarded to, Lahaina News, May 27, 1987: 16.

HUSSEY, MAKANALANI
— wins Wharf Cinema Center's Keiki Christmas Karaoke Contest, Lahaina News, December 28, 2000: 3.

HUSTACE, MARIA
— owner of Kaluaaha Cattle Ranch announces run for U.S. Congress for Republican party, Lahaina News, January 22, 1986: 3.

HUTTON'S FINE JEWELERS [BUSINESS]
— introducing line of jewelry by Henry Dunay, Lahaina News, October 2, 1997: 15.
— to host reception, Lahaina News, October 23, 1997: 6.
— adds "Appassionata" line, Lahaina News, December 17, 1998: 17.
— featuring designs by Paul Klecka, Lahaina News, December 14, 2000: 18.
— to exhibit jewelry by Yvel, Lahaina News, February 22, 2001: 16.

HYA [BUSINESS]
— names Nigel Faulkner as sales manager, Lahaina News, May 29, 1985: 3.

HYANNISPORT, MASSACHUSETTS
— bones of whale for Whaler's Village acquired at auction in, Lahaina Sun, December 16, 1970: 5.

HYATT [BUSINESS]
— art by Chris Lassen located at, Lahaina Times, July, 1980 volume 4 number 6: 1.

HYATT REGENCY MAUI [BUSINESS]
— Hyatt Regency Maui opens, Lahaina News, May 1, 1980: 8.
— review of services, Lahaina News, May 15, 1980: 7.
— plans to increase number of parking stalls, Lahaina News, May 2, 1984: 4.
— sold to VMS Realty of Chicago, Lahaina News, September 19, 1984: 14.
— celebrates 5th anniversary, Lahaina News, April 10, 1985: 9.
— alcohol management training program announced, Lahaina News, July 31, 1985: 7.
— names new directors, Lahaina News, October 23, 1985: 20.
— names David Kahn as director of sales, Lahaina News, February 5, 1986: 3.
— Roger Gustavson appointed Executive Chef, Lahaina News, July 23, 1986: 3.
— receives award from Travel Magazine, Lahaina News, November 26, 1986: 10.
— offers Thanksgiving dinner, Lahaina News, November 26, 1986: 12.
— announces holiday events, Lahaina News, December 17, 1986: 12.
— St. Patrick's Day celebrated at, Lahaina News, March 4, 1987: 10.
— names Werner Neuteufel as general manager, Lahaina News, March 25, 1987: 12.
— features Auntie Malia, Lahaina News, April 8, 1987: 3.
— appoints Marvin Buenconsejo as head of catering, Lahaina News, May 13, 1987: 3.
— awards scholarships to local students to study at Maui Community College, Lahaina News, July 1, 1987: 10.
— offering Kamp Ka'anapali for children of tourists, Lahaina News, July 8, 1987: 16.
— offers kama'aina package, Lahaina News, July 8, 1987: 24.
— purchased by Kokusai Motorcars Hawaii, Inc., Lahaina News, July 8, 1987: 3.
— to host blood drive, Lahaina News, August 12, 1987: 3.
— receives Gold Key Award, Lahaina News, October 14, 1987: 3.
— wins Award of Excellence from Corporate and Incentive Travel magazine, Lahaina News, October 28, 1987: 3.
— donated weightlifting equipment to West Maui Youth Center, Lahaina News, November 11, 1987: 11.
— offers "Reach for the Stars" presentation, Lahaina News, December 16, 1987: 15.
— receives Five Diamond Award from American Automobile Association, Lahaina News, February 10, 1988: 11.
— plans to build parking garage, Lahaina News, March 9, 1988: 3.
— to hold flower show, Lahaina News, April 27, 1988: 4.
— highly rated by Corporate Meetings and Incentives magazine, Lahaina News, June 22, 1988: 11.
— hosts arts and crafts fair, Lahaina News, July 27, 1988: 3.
— sponsoring reef cleanup, Lahaina News, September 7, 1988: 14.
— brunch reviewed, Lahaina News, September 7, 1988: 8.
— receives award from Medical Meetings magazine, Lahaina News, September 28, 1988: 3.
— completing renovations, Lahaina News, November 14, 1990: 13.
— to offer scholarships through KM Hatano Scholarship Program, Lahaina News, December 5, 1990: 5,7.
— to reopen Pavilion Restaurant, Lahaina News, June 13, 1991: 10.
— animals displayed at, Lahaina News, July 11, 1991: 18.
— names Don Kelly as director of sales, Lahaina News, July 25, 1991: 7.
— wins Meeting and Conventions Magazine's Gold Key Award, Lahaina News, August 22, 1991: 4.
— awarded Five Diamond Award from American Automobile Association, Lahaina News, December 19, 1991: 13.

— to offer TimesFax service for up-to-date news, Lahaina News, December 26, 1991: 8.

— to offer scholarships, Lahaina News, January 2, 1992: 5.

— receives Five Diamond Award from the American Automobile Association (AAA), Lahaina News, December 31, 1992: 10.

— to host career day for fifth graders, Lahaina News, March 4, 1993: 4.

— building new group function area, Lahaina News, April 8, 1993: 6.

— to donate to UNICEF, Lahaina News, May 6, 1993: 18.

— names Keith Spinden as executive chef, Lahaina News, December 30, 1993: 6.

— offering KM Hatano Scholarships, Lahaina News, January 13, 1994: 2.

— provides grant to King Kamehameha III Elementary School, Lahaina News, January 27, 1994: 2.

— holds thank you barbeque for employees after large convention, Lahaina News, May 12, 1994: 10.

— appointments announced, Lahaina News, August 4, 1994: 9.

— hires Paul McNally as executive assistant manager, Lahaina News, August 18, 1994: 9.

— receives Corporate and Incentive magazine's Award of Excellence, Lahaina News, September 1, 1994: 12,13.

— receives Five Diamond Award from the American Automobile Association, Lahaina News, December 1, 1994: 13.

— offering KM Hatano Scholarship Program, Lahaina News, January 5, 1995: 4.

— Robert Rippee named associate director of sales at, Lahaina News, March 9, 1995: 6.

— planning renovation, Lahaina News, March 16, 1995: 10.

— opens exhibit "Ka Lei: Symbol of Hawaii", Lahaina News, May 4, 1995: 4.

— celebrates 15th anniversary, Lahaina News, June 8, 1995: 10.

— offering Christmas in July for Maui Chamber of Commerce members, Lahaina News, July 20, 1995: 10.

— opens Aloha Services activity desk, Lahaina News, September 14, 1995: 10.

— to hold New Years dance party, Lahaina News, December 21, 1995: 14.

— Hope Williams named director of catering and convention services at, Lahaina News, January 11, 1996: 11.

— KM Hatano Scholarship available, Lahaina News, February 22, 1996: 10.

— Andra Takishita named wedding coordinator at, Lahaina News, February 22, 1996: 11.

— receives Kahili Award from Hawaii Visitors Bureau, Lahaina News, April 18, 1996: 9.

— to hold Hawaiian Fashion Show, Lahaina News, October 10, 1996: 14.

— Christmas Tree Lighting ceremony to be held, Lahaina News, November 28, 1996: 10.

— Gourmet Magazine awards "Best Hotel in Hawaii" to, Lahaina News, July 2, 1998: 12.

— building a spa, Lahaina News, June 24, 1999: 11.

— Barry Lewin new general manager of, Lahaina News, December 7, 2000: 19.

— softball tournament won by Batwhakers, Lahaina News, July 5, 2001: 13.

— names Leah Chin as spa director, Lahaina News, July 26, 2001: 8.

— Hawaiian Quilt Collection to hold quilting lessons, Lahaina News, October 25, 2001: 16.

— joins Whale Mania Maui, Lahaina News, September 19, 2002: 13.

— promotes Puamana Farden to associate director of sales, Lahaina News, October 10, 2002: 8.

— to offer kama'aina rate, Lahaina News, October 17, 2002: 8.

— play "Tony n' Tina's Wedding" to be performed, Lahaina News, October 24, 2002: 18.

— "Tony n' Tina's Wedding" to be performed at, Lahaina News, November 14, 2002: 20.

— Kalani Nakoa new sales and marketing director, Lahaina News, May 1, 2003: 8.

— fifth-graders shadow employees at, Lahaina News, May 22, 2003: 8.

— public can view Mars from roof, Lahaina News, August 28, 2003: 8.

HYDROFEST
— International Catering Concepts awarded catering contract for, Lahaina News, August 20, 1992: 12.

HYER, JOHN. F.
— architect named vice president of Honolua Plantation Land Company, Lahaina Sun, February 10, 1971: 6.

HYMAN, BARRY
— named portfolio manager at Financial and Investment Management Group, Lahaina News, June 12, 1997: 15.

HYPNOSIS
— workshop to be offered by Irv Katz and Kamala Allen, Lahaina News, August 7, 1985: 8.

— as healing method, Lahaina News, April 13, 1988: 20.

I

I DO! I DO! [PLAY]
— to be performed by Maui Youth Theatre, Lahaina News, January 8, 1986: 3.

— being performed at Iao Theater, Lahaina News, December 17, 1998: 25.

I GO FOR YOU [BUSINESS]
— stand-in service started, Lahaina News, July 13, 1988: 2.

I HATE HAMLET [PLAY]
— to be performed by Maui Community Theatre, Lahaina News, June 22, 1995: 12.

— to be performed, Lahaina News, June 29, 1995: 12.

I LOVE LAHAINA
— to be held to benefit Lahaina Schools, Lahaina News, November 9, 2000: 23.

— details of events, Lahaina News, November 16, 2000: 3.

— raises $17,000 for Lahaina Schools, Lahaina News, December 7, 2000: 3.

— to be held, Lahaina News, October 4, 2001: 2.

— to be held, Lahaina News, October 18, 2001: 14.

— to be held, Lahaina News, October 25, 2001: 15.

— to be held, Lahaina News, November 1, 2001: 1,9.

— successfully held, Lahaina News, November 29, 2001: 9.

— to be held, Lahaina News, October 17, 2002: 15.

— to be held, Lahaina News, October 31, 2002: 20.

— to raise money for West Maui Schools, Lahaina News, November 14, 2002: 3.

— raises money for local schools, Lahaina News, December 19, 2002: 14.

I LOVE YOU, YOU'RE PERFECT, NOW CHANGE [PLAY]
— to be performed at Iao Theater, Lahaina News, March 15, 2001: 20.

— produced by Maui OnStage, Lahaina News, March 22, 2001: 16.

'IA OE E KEALA HULA FESTIVAL
— Tony Akana's Pi'ilani School of Hula to compete in California, Lahaina News, September 21, 1988: 2,15.

IACONETTI, RICK
— competed in Valley Isle Triathlon, Lahaina News, May 23, 1984: 6.

— participation in triathlon featured, Lahaina News, May 15, 1985: 4.

— triathlete featured, Lahaina News, May 21, 1986: 4.

— named director of sales and shows for Galerie Lassen, Inc., Lahaina News, October 24, 1991: 8.

IACONETTI, WILLIAM
— complains about water shortage and contamination in Napili, Lahaina Sun, November 11, 1970: 1.
— discusses access to clean water in Napili, Lahaina Sun, February 3, 1971: 4.
— recently retired doctor featured, Lahaina News, January 11, 2001: 1,15.

IAO CONGREGATIONAL CHURCH
— offering children's vacation Bible session, Lahaina News, July 20, 1988: 3.
— to host musician Michael Stillwater, Lahaina News, December 12, 1991: 25.
— sponsoring "Trash 'N Treasure" fundraiser, Lahaina News, June 5, 1997: 17.
— to hold concert and potluck supper, Lahaina News, March 26, 1998: 12.

IAO INTERMEDIATE SCHOOL
— band to perform at Inu Inu Lounge, Lahaina News, March 27, 1985: 3.
— PTSA to meet, Lahaina News, December 31, 1992: 5.
— to hold carnival, Lahaina News, January 29, 1998: 17.
— to hold carnival, Lahaina News, February 4, 1999: 16.
— band to perform, Lahaina News, May 16, 2002: 17.
— band to perform, Lahaina News, May 15, 2003: 17.

IAO STREAM
— pollution in, discussed, Lahaina Sun, February 3, 1971: 5.
— improvements undertaken by Army Corps of Engineers, Lahaina Sun, August 18, 1971: 11.
— Hawaii Nature Center to hold guided walk along, Lahaina News, September 11, 2003: 16.

IAO THEATRE
— Maui Community Theatre to perform "Get Off With Me", Lahaina News, July 11, 1990: 15.
— to host "Camelot", Lahaina News, March 19, 1998: 12.
— "I Love You, You're Perfect, Now Change" to be shown at, Lahaina News, March 15, 2001: 20.
— available as rental, Lahaina News, August 1, 2002: 9.

IAO VALLEY
— Senator Ted Kennedy backs proposed JFK memorial, Lahaina Sun, December 29, 1971: 4.
— description of hike to, Lahaina Sun, February 9, 1972: 6.7.
— added to national registry of natural landmarks, Lahaina Sun, January 10, 1973: 11.
— Japanese prince and princess unveil statue celebrating Japanese immigration, Lahaina News, June 26, 1985: 1,9.

IAUKEA, LESLIE
— wins Mother/Daughter beauty pageant with mother Lianne, Lahaina News, January 30, 1992: 3.

IAUKEA, LIANNE
— wins Mother/Daughter beauty pageant with daughter Leslie, Lahaina News, January 30, 1992: 3.

IAUKEA, SYDNEY
— wins Miss Lahaina, Lahaina News, June 27, 1990: 3.
— competes in Miss Hawaii USA Pageant, Lahaina News, September 12, 1990: 3.
— attends Maui Humane Society benefit, Lahaina News, October 10, 1990: 6.
— Miss Lahaina welcomes Santa, Lahaina News, December 12, 1990: 10.
— Miss Lahaina featured, Lahaina News, June 6, 1991: 1.

ICE [DRUG]
— becoming more common in West Maui, Lahaina News, September 15, 1994: 1,2.

ICE CARVING
— competition held at Lahaina Cannery Mall, Lahaina News, December 3, 1992: 1.
— competition winners announced, Lahaina News, December 17, 1992: 4.
— contest to be held at Lahaina Cannery Mall, Lahaina News, November 23, 1995: 11.
— contest to be held, Lahaina News, November 25, 1999: 2.
— contest to be held, Lahaina News, October 5, 2000: 7.
— contest to be held at Lahaina Cannery Mall, Lahaina News, November 23, 2000: 1.
— contest seeking contestants, Lahaina News, July 5, 2001: 5.
— contest to be held at Lahaina Cannery Mall, Lahaina News, November 22, 2001: 3.
— competition to be held, Lahaina News, November 21, 2002: 18.
— to be held at Lahaina Cannery Mall, Lahaina News, November 28, 2002: 9.
— Hideo Fugiyama wins competition, Lahaina News, December 26, 2002: 8.

ICE CREAM FESTIVAL
— to be held this week, Lahaina News, August 22, 1991: 12.
— to be held, Lahaina News, August 27, 1992: 6.
— to be held by HGEA/AFPSCME, Lahaina News, August 12, 1993: 4,15.

IDETA, RYAN
— tennis player did well at U.S. Tennis Association national tournament, Lahaina News, August 30, 1989: 24.
— wins division at Hawaii State Open Junior Championship in golf, Lahaina News, September 6, 1989: 5.
— candidate for U.S. National tennis team, Lahaina News, January 3, 1990: 10.
— selected to Nissan Hawaii High School Hall of Fame, Lahaina News, May 21, 1992: 11.
— receives tennis scholarship from Kapalua Land Company, Lahaina News, August 6, 1992: 5.
— tennis player competes in Men's Open Singles championship, Lahaina News, September 17, 1998: 25.

IF ANGELS WERE MORTALS [PLAY]
— to be performed at Kumulani Chapel, Lahaina News, December 19, 2002: 3.

IGE, DAVID [POLITICIAN]
— speaks of the creation of Hawaii Area-Wide Information Access Network, Lahaina News, February 21, 1990: 28.

IGE, DIANE
— Lahainaluna High School graduate receives a 4.0, Lahaina News, February 6, 1992: 3.

IGE, EDWIN
— appointed to County Police Commission, Lahaina Sun, January 13, 1971: 8.

IGLESIA NI CHRISTO
— church to break ground on new building, Lahaina News, April 2, 1992: 1,6.

IGUS, DARROW [COMEDIAN]
— to perform at Comedy Club, Lahaina News, February 14, 1990: 15.

IHA, AKIRA [ARTIST]
— part of "90 Degrees" exhibit at Maui Arts and Cultural Center, Lahaina News, July 6, 2000: 16.

IHIMAERA, WITI [WRITER]
— to performed by "Woman Far Walking", Lahaina News, September 27, 2001: 16.

IIDA, DEBORAH [WRITER]
— to present at Maui Writers Guild, Lahaina News, July 29, 1999: 12.
— to read from book "Middle Son", Lahaina News, April 11, 2002: 17.

— to discuss book "Middle Son" at Wailuku Public Library, Lahaina News, April 18, 2002: 16.

— to sign book "Middle Son", Lahaina News, May 9, 2002: 2.

IKE

— fundraiser to be held to help victims of typhoon, Lahaina News, September 26, 1984: 10.

IKEBANA

— demonstration to be held at Hyatt Regency Hotel, Lahaina News, November 28, 1984: 3.

IKEDA, CHARLEEN

— appointed Senior Vice President at Amfac, Inc, Lahaina News, April 27, 1988: 3.

IKEDA, DONNA [POLITICIAN]

— introduces bill to simplify tax returns, Lahaina News, February 14, 1990: 5.

IKEDA, PHIL

— chosen to participate in Hokule'a voyage from New Zealand to Samoa, Lahaina News, April 23, 1986: 3.

IKEDA'S [BUSINESS]

— to close for renovations, Lahaina News, February 2, 1995: 7.

IKEMIYA, MASANOBU [MUSICIAN]

— pianist to perform with Maui Symphony Orchestra, Lahaina News, April 13, 1995: 14.

— Japanese pianist to perform with Maui Symphony Orchestra, Lahaina News, March 21, 1996: 13.

IKENA

— residents to be displaced by Lahaina Bypass, Lahaina News, March 13, 1991: 1.

IKI, GARY

— named by First Hawaiian Bank as senior vice-president and manager of international banking division, Lahaina News, October 24, 1991: 9.

'ILI'ILI [PLAY]

— to be performed by Maui Community Theatre, auditions to be held, Lahaina News, February 6, 1992: 4.

— to be performed by Maui Community Theatre, Lahaina News, April 9, 1992: 21.

ILWU

— Striking at Royal Lahaina and Ka'anapali Beach Hotels, Lahaina Sun, November 11, 1970: 1.

I'M ON A MISSION FROM BUDDHA [SHOW]

— to be performed by Lane Nishikawa, Lahaina News, March 9, 2000: 12.

IMADA, ALVIN

— promoted to vice president of Bank of Hawaii's branch on Maui, Lahaina News, October 17, 1991: 9.

— promoted to vice president and district manager of Bank of Hawaii for Maui, Lahaina News, December 14, 2000: 18.

IMAGE BLACK AND WHITE [BUSINESS]

— opens, Lahaina News, January 3, 1990: 4.

— relocates, Lahaina News, January 27, 1994: 5.

IMAGES OF A SACRED NATURE

— photography exhibit to be held, Lahaina News, May 16, 2002: 15.

IMAGINARY INVALID, THE [PLAY]

— to be performed by Baldwin Theatre Guild, Lahaina News, May 9, 1990: 18.

IMAGO THEATRE IN FROGZ [SHOW]

— to be performed at Maui Arts and Cultural Center, Lahaina News, January 2, 2003: 17.

— to be staged, Lahaina News, January 9, 2003: 16.

IMAMURA, GRANT

— receives Kapalua Land Co. golf scholarship, Lahaina News, July 25, 1990: 14.

IMAMURA, KALOUKEA

— performing in South America, Lahaina Sun, January 20, 1971: 7.

IMCO REALTY SERVICES [BUSINESS]

— changes name to North American Mortgage Co., Lahaina News, September 17, 1992: 10.

IMI I LOKO I KOU PIKO (INVESTING IN OUR FUTURE)

— to hold meeting on substance abuse, Lahaina News, November 21, 1996: 15.

IMI PONO'I

— to air on KPOA-FM, Lahaina News, April 16, 1992: 4.

IMMER, ANDREA

— to host Kapalua Wine Festival, Lahaina News, June 28, 2001: 10.

— sommelier to host Kapalua Wine and Food Festival, Lahaina News, July 4, 2002: 9.

IMMIGRATION

— Mayor Cravalho discusses Filipino immigrants , Lahaina Sun, May 24, 1972: 3.

— U.S. Immigration and Naturalization Service to conduct interviews, Lahaina News, September 23, 1987: 3.

IMMIGRATION AND NATURALIZATION SERVICE

— continues sweep on Maui, Lahaina News, September 14, 1995: 1,16.

IMPERIALS [MUSICAL GROUP]

— to perform at St. Anthony Auditorium, Lahaina News, January 26, 1995: 15.

IMPORTANCE OF BEING ERNEST, THE [PLAY]

— performed by Maui Youth Theatre, Lahaina News, May 31, 1989: 18.

IMUA E HAWAII, HUKI LIKE

— benefit concert for Maui Community College, Lahaina News, May 1, 1985: 3.

IMUA PAUAHI BENEFIT CONCERT

— to be held at Maui Arts and Cultural Center, Lahaina News, November 27, 1997: 12.

IMUA REHABILITATION CENTER

— benefit held, Lahaina News, February 11, 1987: 11.

— results of bed race, Lahaina News, March 27, 1991: 8.

— to hold fundraiser, Lahaina News, February 25, 1993: 5.

— to host "Valentine's Night Dance", Lahaina News, February 13, 1997: 10.

— to hold childbirth classes, Lahaina News, February 13, 1997: 11.

— seeking counselors for Camp Imua, Lahaina News, May 15, 1997: 12.

— to hold benefit Valentine's Dance and Dinner , Lahaina News, February 4, 1999: 17.

— to provide speech and language services, Lahaina News, August 30, 2001: 2.

IN CELEBRATION OF CANOES

— festival to be held, Lahaina News, May 6, 1999: 19.

— master carvers to attend, Lahaina News, May 11, 2000: 6.

— to be held; insert missing from microfilm, Lahaina News, May 18, 2000: 1,7.

— to include cultural events, Lahaina News, May 25, 2000: 1,14.

— ends with luau at Kamehameha Iki Park, Lahaina News, June 1, 2000: 15.

— to be held, Lahaina News, May 3, 2001: 18,19.

— to begin, Lahaina News, May 10, 2001: 11.

— music to include The Brothers Cazimero, Lahaina News, May 10, 2001: 21.

— concludes, Lahaina News, May 24, 2001: 11.

— to conclude, Lahaina News, May 24, 2001: 21.

— to be held, Lahaina News, May 2, 2002: 15.

— to be held, Lahaina News, May 9, 2002: 1.

— to be presented, Lahaina News, May 23, 2002: 1,20.

— held at Kamehameha Iki Park, Lahaina News, May 30, 2002: 1.

INCALIA
— supposed colony of Atlantis, Lahaina Times, August, 1980 volume 4 number 7: 2.

INCARNATION: PHOTOGRAPHY AND INSTALLATIONS BY DAWN
— exhibit to be held at Maui Mall, Lahaina News, March 22, 2001: 16.

INCIONG, KEONI
— Hawaiian Language Immersion Program educational specialist discusses Hawaiian Immersion program, Lahaina News, March 28, 2002: 1,20.

INCITE HEALTH FOOD STORE
— closing to allow expansion of clothing store, Lahaina Sun, August 2, 1972: 3.

INCREDIBLE JOURNEYS [BUSINESS]
— helicopter flight simulator described , Lahaina News, November 24, 1994: 11.

INCUBUS [MUSICAL GROUP]
— to perform at The Big Mele, Lahaina News, July 31, 1997: 16.

INDEPENDENCE, SS [SHIP]
— saves Mickey Weems from ocean, Lahaina News, February 8, 1984: 3.

— to host benefit for whale research, Lahaina News, March 29, 1989: 6.

— American Hawaii ship offering whale watching cruises, Lahaina News, March 21, 1990: 18.

INDEPENDENT THEATRE INC. [BUSINESS]
— to perform "True West", Lahaina News, July 29, 1999: 12.

INDIA IMPORTS
— opening in Whaler's Village, Lahaina Sun, November 25, 1970: 3.

INDIAN AFFAIRS, SENATE COMMITTEE
— to hold hearings to reauthorize Native Hawaiian Education Act, Lahaina News, November 25, 1999: 1.

INDUNI, DAVID [ARTIST]
— to hold mask making workshop, Lahaina News, October 17, 2002: 19.

INDUSTRY NETWORK CORPORATION
— to stage Maui County Products and Trade Show, Lahaina News, October 15, 1998: 13.

INFINITY BALLET COMPANY [TROUPE]
— to perform with West Hawaii Dance Theatre at Maui Arts and Cultural Center, Lahaina News, January 16, 1997: 10.

INFRASTRUCTURE
— discussion of road conditions and responsibility for fixing the roads, Lahaina Sun, January 13, 1971: 7.

— gas line to be completed along Front Street, Lahaina Sun, February 17, 1971: 3.

— Maui County Council seeks to reduce confusion in the number of houses, Lahaina Sun, February 24, 1971: 6.

— Maui County Council plan for infrastructure improvements, Lahaina Sun, March 3, 1971: 8.

— highways to be repaired, Lahaina Sun, April 28, 1971: 4.

— highways paved, Lahaina Sun, May 19, 1971: 8.

— congestion issues along Front Street discussed, Lahaina Sun, May 19, 1971: 8.

— West Maui Business Association seeks money for off-street parking, Lahaina Sun, May 26, 1971: 5.

— flood control projects, Lahaina Sun, June 2, 1971: 2.

— Pu'u Olai - La Perouse Bay State Park and Reserve Area planned, Lahaina Sun, June 9, 1971: 3.

— request for new seawall for Lahaina, Lahaina Sun, June 9, 1971: 3.

— Maui County Council budget details provided, Lahaina Sun, June 9, 1971: 8.

— town plan for Kahului to be unveiled, Lahaina Sun, June 16, 1971: 12.

— historic sidewalk to be installed along Front Street, Lahaina Sun, June 16, 1971: 5.

— Maui County Council approves funds for capital improvement projects, Lahaina Sun, June 23, 1971: 3.

— new microwave link to Honolulu established , Lahaina Sun, June 30, 1971: 12.

— Army Corps of Engineers to hold public meeting to discuss ship harbor for Ma'alaea Bay., Lahaina Sun, July 7, 1971: 10.

— highway markers okayed by State Transportation Department, Lahaina Sun, July 7, 1971: 12.

— Maui Chamber of Commerce supports building of power plant near Ma'alaea, Lahaina Sun, July 7, 1971: 3.

— paving progresses between Honokohau Bay and Poelua Gulch, Lahaina Sun, August 4, 1971: 10.

— Kuihelani Highway to open, Lahaina Sun, August 11, 1971: 12.

— dedication of Kuihelani (Wailuku bypass) highway scheduled, Lahaina Sun, August 18, 1971: 1.

— bike path from Lahaina to Ka'anapali suggested, Lahaina Sun, August 18, 1971: 9.

— sidewalks requested in Lahaina, Lahaina Sun, September 8, 1971: 13.

— criticism of how roads of planned, Lahaina Sun, September 8, 1971: 3.

— interisland hydrofoil proposed, Lahaina Sun, September 15, 1971: 15.

— proposed interisland ferry system debated, Lahaina Sun, September 22, 1971: 4.

— bicycle path between Lahaina and Ka'anapali proposed, Lahaina Sun, September 22, 1971: 8,9.

— West Maui watershed plans discussed, Lahaina Sun, September 29, 1971: 4.

— search for landing site on Maui for proposed ferry, Lahaina Sun, October 13, 1971: 14.

— State Parks administrator Joseph Souza announces plans to condemn private land to create a state park in Makena area, Lahaina Sun, October 13, 1971: 3.

— Councilman Richard Caldito asks to study possible changes to subdivision ordinances, Lahaina Sun, October 20, 1971: 15.

— Statewide Committee on New Communities to study community development, Lahaina Sun, October 20, 1971: 6.

— contract to build two interisland ferries expected to be signed, Lahaina Sun, October 20, 1971: 6.

— Maui County Council studies changes to railroad laws, Lahaina Sun, October 27, 1971: 6.

— criticism of proposed interisland ferry, Lahaina Sun, November 10, 1971: 1.

— a list of restoration and improvement projects for Lahaina being created, Lahaina Sun, November 10, 1971: 4.

— Governor Burns releases funds for capital improvement projects in Maui, Lahaina Sun, November 17, 1971: 1.

— governor Burns releases funds for capital improvement projects in Maui, Lahaina Sun, December 1, 1971: 12.

— highway from Honokowai Stream to Honokahua Bay approved, Lahaina Sun, December 15, 1971: 5.

— U.S. Army Corps of Engineers working on Kahului Harbor breakwater, Lahaina Sun, December 29, 1971: 6.

— State rejects highway markers in Lahaina, Lahaina Sun, January 12, 1972: 15.

— group appointed by Governor Burns to study Kahului Harbor, Lahaina Sun, January 26, 1972: 8.

— corrections to previous story on parking in Lahaina, Lahaina News, January 22, 1986: 3.

— Lahaina projects listed in mayor's budget, Lahaina News, March 26, 1986: 1.

— flood project begins in Napili, Lahaina News, April 16, 1986: 3.

— parking lot may be rezoned for building, Lahaina News, May 14, 1986: 1.

— possible changes to Honoapi'ilani Highway detailed, Lahaina News, May 21, 1986: 1,11.

— Maui Chamber of Commerce asks for bypass around Lahaina, Lahaina News, June 4, 1986: 3.

— editorial supporting Lahaina bypass, Lahaina News, June 11, 1986: 2.

— plan to reduce parking on Front Street proposed, Lahaina News, June 25, 1986: 1.

— mayor's ad hoc committee makes recommendations regarding Honoapi'ilani Highway, Lahaina News, June 25, 1986: 1,16.

— street closures due to construction, Lahaina News, July 30, 1986: 3.

— governor Ariyoshi releases money for Honoapi'ilani Highway improvements, Lahaina News, September 10, 1986: 3.

— Shoreline bus service reviewed, Lahaina News, October 1, 1986: 4.

— funds from Department of Transportation for Honoapi'ilani Highway, Lahaina News, November 5, 1986: 3.

— Shoreline Transportation and Roberts Tours and Transportation fight over busing in West Maui, Lahaina News, November 12, 1986: 1,8.

— request to build fourth lane for Honoapi'ilani Highway sent to legislature, Lahaina News, December 17, 1986: 1.

— need to upgrade, according to Howard Kihune, Lahaina News, January 21, 1987: 1.

— widening of Honoapi'ilani Highway may take longer to complete, Lahaina News, January 28, 1987: 1.

— attempts to secure funding from legislature for Lahaina Bypass and fourth lane for Honoapi'ilani Highway, Lahaina News, February 4, 1987: 1.

— discussion of the need for a new harbor, Lahaina News, February 4, 1987: 1,16.

— widening of Honoapi'ilani Highway on track, Lahaina News, February 4, 1987: 3.

— State legislature provides money to improve local parks, Lahaina News, February 4, 1987: 3.

— council member Howard Kihune seeks money for, Lahaina News, February 18, 1987: 8.

— house Transportation Committee requests funds to expand Honoapi'ilani Highway, Lahaina News, February 25, 1987: 3.

— Kahoma Stream project to tie of traffic, Lahaina News, March 4, 1987: 1.

— editorial supporting detour along Honoapi'ilani Highway as necessary evil, Lahaina News, March 4, 1987: 2.

— Kahoma Stream Flood Control project tied to traffic issues, Lahaina News, April 1, 1987: 1.

— steel curtain installed along Pali stretch of Honoapi'ilani Highway, Lahaina News, April 8, 1987: 12.

— Public Works Committee of Maui County Council to research Honoapi'ilani highway development, Lahaina News, April 22, 1987: 3.

— Public Works Committee approves realignment of Lower Honoapi'ilani Road, Lahaina News, May 6, 1987: 1.

— traffic light planned for Shaw Street and Honoapi'ilani Highway, Lahaina News, May 6, 1987: 3.

— section of Honoapi'ilani Highway to close while Kahoma Stream Flood Control Project begins, Lahaina News, May 27, 1987: 3.

— Lahaina residents critical of proposal to lease Mala Wharf, Lahaina News, July 1, 1987: 1,10.

— Roberts Hawaii Tours ordered to cease route between Ka'anapali and Lahaina Town, Lahaina News, July 8, 1987: 1.

— Burger King parking lot to be expanded, Lahaina News, July 8, 1987: 3.

— traffic light near Post Office activated, Lahaina News, July 22, 1987: 1.

— editorial on settlement of conflict between Hui Alanui O Makena and Seibu Hawaii over Makena road closure, Lahaina News, July 29, 1987: 2.

— letter box moved at Lahaina Community Center, Lahaina News, August 5, 1987: 3.

— Department of Transportation performing road tests, Lahaina News, August 19, 1987: 3.

— new traffic laws come into effect, Lahaina News, August 26, 1987: 3.

— privately-owned marina proposed near Lahaina, Lahaina News, September 2, 1987: 1,4.

— Maui County to stop picking up trash of people with errant accounts, Lahaina News, September 9, 1987: 3.

— part of Hana Highway to be resurfaced, Lahaina News, October 14, 1987: 17.

— Lahaina Yacht Club endorses private marina, Lahaina News, October 14, 1987: 18.

— detour on Honoapi'ilani Road, Lahaina News, November 11, 1987: 11.

— Kahoma Stream Flood Control Project half finished, Lahaina News, November 18, 1987: 1.

— new traffic light sought along Honoapi'ilani Highway, Lahaina News, November 18, 1987: 3.

— Department of Transportation to repair wharf at Lahaina Harbor, Lahaina News, November 18, 1987: 3.

— fourth lane of Honoapi'ilani Highway delayed, Lahaina News, December 2, 1987: 3.

— waterline to be installed along Front Street, Lahaina News, December 16, 1987: 3.

— resident concerns for roadways and ocean use, Lahaina News, December 23, 1987: 3.

— Native Hawaiian resistance to development over past year recounted, Lahaina News, December 30, 1987: 13.

— Bob Kiger advocating for bike path around Maui, Lahaina News, January 6, 1988: 1,14.

— Department of Transportation to speed up Lahaina Bypass and road widening, Lahaina News, January 20, 1988: 1.

— construction of bridge over Kahoma Stream delayed, Lahaina News, January 20, 1988: 1.

— meeting concerning bike lanes to be held, Lahaina News, January 20, 1988: 3.

— Honoapi'ilani Highway to close for construction of bridge, Lahaina News, February 3, 1988: 3.

— road improvements around Lahaina to begin, Lahaina News, February 10, 1988: 1.

— left had turn from Kekaa Drive banned, Lahaina News, February 10, 1988: 3.

— highway closing assessed, Lahaina News, February 17, 1988: 3.

— county committee to consider possible helicopter landing sites, Lahaina News, February 24, 1988: 18.

— detour of Lower Honoapi'ilani Road planned, Lahaina News, March 2, 1988: 3.

— whether developers should pay impact fees debated, Lahaina News, March 9, 1988: 1.

— temporary bridge installed at Kahakuloa, Lahaina News, April 13, 1988: 12.

— possible impact fees discussed, Lahaina News, April 13, 1988: 3.

— possible impact fees discussed, Lahaina News, April 20, 1988: 1.

— Kahoma Stream bridge construction delayed, Lahaina News, May 4, 1988: 1.

— Honokowai detour making residents and merchants unhappy, Lahaina News, May 4, 1988: 1.

— State Commission of Transportation to hold public information meeting, Lahaina News, May 18, 1988: 1.

— Honoapi'ilani Highway to be restriped, Lahaina News, June 1, 1988: 10.

— debate concerning detour around Kahoma Stream, Lahaina News, June 15, 1988: 1,13.

— detour on Front Street to be tested, Lahaina News, July 20, 1988: 1,14.

— Mayor Hannibal Tavares agrees to Front Street detour, Lahaina News, July 27, 1988: 1,4.

— dredging to begin at channel to Lahaina boat harbor, Lahaina News, July 27, 1988: 11.

— Honoapi'ilani Highway repaving planned, Lahaina News, July 27, 1988: 20.

— Maui County budget provides capital improvement funds to West Maui, Lahaina News, August 3, 1988: 1,24.

— timetable for road repairs detailed, Lahaina News, August 10, 1988: 1.

— extension to Kuakini street sought to ease traffic, Lahaina News, August 17, 1988: 1.

— local merchants to lobby for detour around Kahoma Stream bridge, Lahaina News, August 17, 1988: 14.

— merchants supporting bridge detour to push for other changes , Lahaina News, August 24, 1988: 1.

— island-wide survey of traffic under way, Lahaina News, August 24, 1988: 1.

— editorial supporting detour around Kahoma Stream bridge, Lahaina News, August 24, 1988: 4.

— detour around Kahoma Stream considered by Maui County Council, Lahaina News, September 7, 1988: 20.

— highway widening to begin, Lahaina News, September 7, 1988: 3.

— changes to Lahaina Harbor detailed, Lahaina News, October 19, 1988: 1,24.

— Maui County Council approves condemnation of Luakini Street for conversion to parking lot, Lahaina News, October 26, 1988: 1.

— Army Corps of Engineers to improvement drainage at North Beach, Lahaina News, November 16, 1988: 1.

— widening of Wainee Street controversial, Lahaina News, November 16, 1988: 1,20.

— expansion of Honoapi'ilani begins, Lahaina News, November 16, 1988: 3.

— respite areas on Front Street nearly complete, Lahaina News, November 30, 1988: 1.

— traffic survey results, Lahaina News, December 14, 1988: 1,24.

— portable Kahakuloa bridge to become permanent, Lahaina News, December 14, 1988: 16.

— Fish Aggregating Devices [FADs] being repaired, Lahaina News, January 25, 1989: 5.

— Mayor Hannibal Tavares unveils plans, Lahaina News, April 5, 1989: 1,16.

— changes to zoning laws will impact Lahaina, Lahaina News, April 5, 1989: 1,16.

— importance of naming streets properly discussed, Lahaina News, May 10, 1989: 11.

— state seeking consultant for rural transportation plan, Lahaina News, May 10, 1989: 6.

— Expedition to begin Lahaina-Lana'i ferry service, Lahaina News, May 24, 1989: 8.

— Napili Kai Beach Club manager Dorothy Millar selected to lead campaign to develop fire station, Lahaina News, May 31, 1989: 1.

— traffic light to be installed on Kuihelani Highway, Lahaina News, June 14, 1989: 3.

— informational meeting to be held on Lahaina Watershed Flood Control Project, Lahaina News, July 19, 1989: 1.

— seawalls seen as success by some, damaging by others, Lahaina News, July 26, 1989: 1.

— West Maui Soil and Water Conservation Service urges residents to lobby for flood control project, Lahaina News, July 26, 1989: 1.

— detour on Lower Honoapi'ilani Road planned, Lahaina News, July 26, 1989: 3.

— state plans to fix Mala Wharf, Lahaina News, August 2, 1989: 1.

— concerns over planned sidewalk, Lahaina News, August 23, 1989: 1.

— meeting to discuss widening of Wainee Street, Lahaina News, September 20, 1989: 1.

— widening of Wainee Street criticized, Lahaina News, September 27, 1989: 1.

— roadside peddlers required to obtain a license, Lahaina News, September 27, 1989: 3.

— Kapalua Land Company likely to be receive permission to close road, Lahaina News, October 4, 1989: 1.

— opposition to widening Wainee Street, Lahaina News, October 11, 1989: 1.

— bridge opens on Front Street, Lahaina News, October 11, 1989: 2.

— Maui Historic Commission to hold meeting on widening of Wainee Street, Lahaina News, October 18, 1989: 2.

— public hearing on increases in taxi rates, Lahaina News, October 18, 1989: 3.

— parking plan for Lahaina seen as defective, Lahaina News, October 25, 1989: 1.

— Maui County Public Works to continue to push to widen Wainee Street, Lahaina News, October 25, 1989: 1,4.

— solution to Wainee flooding may be near, Lahaina News, October 25, 1989: 5.

— state opens fourth lane of Honoapi'ilani Highway, Lahaina News, November 1, 1989: 3.

— West Maui Taxpayers Association supports building fire station in Napili, Lahaina News, November 1, 1989: 5.

— Mayor Hannibal Tavares supports widening of Wainee Street, Lahaina News, November 15, 1989: 1.

— hearing on Wainee Street right of way to be held, Lahaina News, November 22, 1989: 2.

— Wainee Street to be limited to two lanes, Lahaina News, November 29, 1989: 1,3.

— editorial critical of funds being used to construct H-3 on Oahu, Lahaina News, December 13, 1989: 10.

— taker proposed to refuel boats, Lahaina News, January 3, 1990: 2.

— work to begin on Kahekili Highway, Lahaina News, January 10, 1990: 24.

— state completes study of Mala Wharf, Lahaina News, February 7, 1990: 1.

— free shuttle services expand in West Maui, Lahaina News, February 7, 1990: 5.

— road blockages lead to review of alternative accesses, Lahaina News, February 21, 1990: 1.

— Mayor Hannibal Tavares proposes to ban bicycle tour operations on county highways, Lahaina News, February 21, 1990: 1.

— public works director proposes building parking lot over cemetery, Lahaina News, February 21, 1990: 3.

— toll road from Kihei to Kula proposed, Lahaina News, February 21, 1990: 4.

— Napili dam repairs almost finished, Lahaina News, March 14, 1990: 28.

— Maui Chamber of Commerce recommends loading zone area, Lahaina News, March 14, 1990: 5.

— state to expand bike routes, Lahaina News, March 21, 1990: 1.

— Maui County budget for West Maui projects detailed, Lahaina News, April 4, 1990: 1.

— resurfacing part of Honoapi'ilani Highway scheduled; to be done by Dillingham Construction Pacific, Inc., Lahaina News, May 16, 1990: 5.

— new public parking to be built on Luakini Street, Lahaina News, May 30, 1990: 5.

— County Council discussing intersection at Dickenson and Honoapi'ilani, Lahaina News, May 30, 1990: 5.

— pipe laying along Ka'anapali highway delayed, Lahaina News, June 27, 1990: 1.

— study requested before wastewater treatment plant expanded at Honokowai, Lahaina News, July 11, 1990: 1.

— government maintaining toll-free number to access government services, Lahaina News, July 25, 1990: 6.

— future of parks in West Maui to be discussed at Napilihau Community Center, Lahaina News, August 1, 1990: 4.

— operator of street sweeping machine quits, nee one being trained, Lahaina News, August 8, 1990: 1.

— Maui County Council examining dangerous road crossings, Lahaina News, September 5, 1990: 1.

— crosswalk considered, Lahaina News, September 5, 1990: 1.

— crosswalk put in at Dickenson Street despite concerns, Lahaina News, September 12, 1990: 1.

— crosswalk to get additional light, Lahaina News, September 26, 1990: 1.

— consultants to develop proposals to improve, Lahaina News, October 24, 1990: 1.

— E.E. Black, Ltd. awarded contract for truck climbing lane on Haleakala Highway, Lahaina News, October 31, 1990: 12.

— Lahaina traffic plan unveiled by Maui County Public Works Department, Lahaina News, November 7, 1990: 1.

— State presents road plan for West Maui, Lahaina News, November 21, 1990: 1.

— plan for Front Street proposes restoration of Mokuhinia Pond, Lahaina News, November 21, 1990: 1.

— Maui County Council proposes ban on tour buses from Baker Street, Lahaina News, November 21, 1990: 4.

— flooding issues along Front Street, Lahaina News, December 12, 1990: 1.

— proposed ferry receives permit to operate between Lahaina and Lana'i, Lahaina News, January 2, 1991: 5.

— state approves land swap for former Wailuku Court House and Ukumehame firing range, Lahaina News, January 23, 1991: 3.

— list of construction projects being compiled for Builder Edition of Lahaina News, Lahaina News, January 23, 1991: 5.

— public meeting to discuss flood control to be held, Lahaina News, February 13, 1991: 1.

— Governor John Waihee releases funds for road construction, Lahaina News, February 20, 1991: 8.

— concerns expressed about flood control plans, Lahaina News, March 6, 1991: 1,5.

— new blinking lights near Dickenson Street delayed, Lahaina News, March 20, 1991: 1.

— need for county services in West Maui, Lahaina News, April 10, 1991: 1.

— mayor Linda Lingle opposes parks bill, Lahaina News, April 17, 1991: 3.

— playground sought in West Maui, Lahaina News, April 24, 1991: 4.

— U.S. Soil Conservation Servicing looking to move outlet of proposed Lahaina Flood Control Project, Lahaina News, May 8, 1991: 1.

— Maui County Council Public Works Committee to address road hazard at corner of Dickenson Street and Honoapi'ilani Highway, Lahaina News, May 8, 1991: 1.

— legislature funds building projects, including Lahaina Bypass, Lahaina News, May 15, 1991: 1.

— changes to parking in Lahaina, Lahaina News, May 15, 1991: 1.

— Howard Kihune seeks new regional park, Lahaina News, May 30, 1991: 3.

— Maui may quality for defense highway funds now that Rockwell Power Systems to locate in Kihei, Lahaina News, June 6, 1991: 4.

— mayor Linda Lingle's opposition to transferring state parks to county lessens, Lahaina News, June 13, 1991: 3.

— County to discuss making biking safe, Lahaina News, June 13, 1991: 4.

— debate continues over loading zone on Front Street, Lahaina News, June 27, 1991: 9.

— mopes require safety check certificate, Lahaina News, July 4, 1991: 3.

— mayor Linda Lingle and Council chair Howard Kihune support regional park, Lahaina News, July 11, 1991: 1.

— Napili Park Advisory Committee to hold public meeting on proposed park, Lahaina News, July 11, 1991: 2.

— traffic increases 9% in West Maui, Lahaina News, July 18, 1991: 1.

— state Legislature authorizes money for improvements of Lahaina Harbor, Lahaina News, July 18, 1991: 1.

— Launiupoko favored by some for boat marina, Lahaina News, August 1, 1991: 1.

— flood control option explored, Lahaina News, August 1, 1991: 1.

— sewer repair to cause traffic jams on Front Street, Lahaina News, August 1, 1991: 13.

— Maui Historic Commission recommends widening Luakini Street, Lahaina News, August 8, 1991: 1.

— mayor Linda Lingle rejects subsidized bus system, Lahaina News, August 8, 1991: 7.

— roadwork to begin to realign bridge over Mahinahina drainage channel., Lahaina News, August 15, 1991: 3.

— Napili Parks Committee expecting proposal on park, Lahaina News, August 15, 1991: 9.

— sewage break along Honoapi'ilani Highway, Lahaina News, August 22, 1991: 1.

— State harbors official Dave Parsons reviews lack of restrooms, Lahaina News, August 22, 1991: 1.

— roadwork on Lower Honoapi'ilani Road to begin, Lahaina News, August 22, 1991: 3.

— road closure due to work on Mahinahina Channel, Lahaina News, August 29, 1991: 3.

— state representative David Morihara asks the county if school bus system could be used for mass transit, Lahaina News, September 26, 1991: 1,3.

— sidewalks and parks requested by mayor Linda Lingle, Lahaina News, October 3, 1991: 1.

— U.S. Soil Conservation Service investigating alternative flood control for Lahaina Watershed Project, Lahaina News, October 10, 1991: 12.

— Lahaina to have emergency center, Lahaina News, October 17, 1991: 3.

— Wainee Street improvement tied to Puamana flood control, Lahaina News, October 31, 1991: 1.

— Department of Transportation awards contracts for services at Maui harbors, Lahaina News, October 31, 1991: 10.

— channels blamed for algae growth off Lahaina, Lahaina News, November 14, 1991: 1.

— meeting to be held to discuss Modified Alternative Plan for the Lahaina Watershed, Lahaina News, November 14, 1991: 2.

— road paving on Honoapi'ilani Highway planned, Lahaina News, November 28, 1991: 3.

— sewage fee increases in Kihei, Lahaina News, December 5, 1991: 13.

— highway work announced, Lahaina News, December 5, 1991: 4.

— trolley system proposed for Maui, Lahaina News, December 12, 1991: 1.

— highway work continues, Lahaina News, December 12, 1991: 6.

— businesses hurt by delays in roadwork, Lahaina News, December 19, 1991: 1.

— new traffic signal to be installed, Lahaina News, December 19, 1991: 6.

— closing landfills is priority for mayor Linda Lingle, Lahaina News, December 26, 1991: 1.

— meetings planned on delay of bridge widening in Mahinahina, Lahaina News, December 26, 1991: 3.

— Army Corps of Engineers planning flood basins, Lahaina News, December 31, 1992: 1.

— Maui County money received from Federal Transportation Authority to support new Transportation Coordinator position, Lahaina News, December 31, 1992: 20.

— Department of Public Works announces resurfacing of Hauoli Street to take place, Lahaina News, December 31, 1992: 8.

— Lahaina Recreation Center Playground Equipment Committee receives money for park equipment, Lahaina News, January 7, 1993: 1.

— Olowalu road to be widened, Lahaina News, January 7, 1993: 1.

— Maui ferries see rise in ridership, Lahaina News, January 7, 1993: 6.

— skateboard park sought for Kihei, Lahaina News, January 7, 1993: 8.

— proposed catchment system receives mixed reactions, Lahaina News, January 14, 1993: 1.

— Charles Eley to speak on Hawaii Model Energy Code sponsored by County Planning Department, Lahaina News, January 14, 1993: 3.

— Department of Transportation to hold hearing on Statewide Master Plan for Bikeways, Lahaina News, January 14, 1993: 3.

— road work planned for North Kihei Road, Lahaina News, January 21, 1993: 11.

— State bikeways hearing to be held state Department of Transportation, Lahaina News, January 21, 1993: 4.

— problems persist at Mala Wharf, Lahaina News, February 4, 1993: 1.

— coalition formed to push for bike paths, Lahaina News, February 4, 1993: 11.

— Lahaina Town Action Committee seeks more bikeways, Lahaina News, February 4, 1993: 3.

— state Highway Division planning projects in 1993, Lahaina News, February 4, 1993: 3,4.

— county seeks funds for Front Street, Lahaina News, February 11, 1993: 1,3.

— public to meet about Alaeloa access, Lahaina News, February 18, 1993: 1.

— state to widen Honoapi'ilani Highway near Ka'anapali Parkway, Lahaina News, February 25, 1993: 3.

— road resurfacing in Kihei planned, Lahaina News, February 25, 1993: 5.

— Kihei Community Association conducts traffic survey, Lahaina News, March 11, 1993: 10.

— plans to widen Mokulele Highway, Lahaina News, March 11, 1993: 10.

— traffic slows because of sewer line replacement, Lahaina News, March 11, 1993: 2.

— road work to be done on Baker Street, Lahaina News, March 18, 1993: 4.

— GTE Hawaiian Telephone Company proposes installing interisland submarine fiber optic cable, Lahaina News, March 18, 1993: 8.

— motor vehicle office proposed for Kihei, Lahaina News, March 25, 1993: 8.

— tow-away zone proposed near Kihei Fire Station, Lahaina News, April 8, 1993: 5.

— residents question need for road connecting Kihei and Upcountry, Lahaina News, April 15, 1993: 4.

— funds sought for state park at Makena, Lahaina News, April 15, 1993: 4.

— bike fest to be hosted by Mayor Linda Lingle, Lahaina News, April 22, 1993: 3.

— road improvements planned for Lower Honoapi'ilani Road, Lahaina News, April 29, 1993: 2.

— drainage plan map, Lahaina News, April 29, 1993: 3.

— hearing to be held on drainage plan for Napilihau Villages, Lahaina News, May 6, 1993: 4.

— negotiations continue between Maui Electric and Alexander and Baldwin for site of new power plant, Lahaina News, May 6, 1993: 6,7.

— Kihei residents want more parking and parks, Lahaina News, May 20, 1993: 4,5.

— Lahaina fire company conducting gas tests along Front Street, Lahaina News, May 27, 1993: 2.

— Pioneer Inn closing makes bathrooms harder to find for boaters, Lahaina News, June 3, 1993: 1.

— roadwork on Lipoa Street planned, Lahaina News, June 3, 1993: 5.

— Maui Land and Pineapple postpones project to repair Honolua Ditch, Lahaina News, June 10, 1993: 1.

— funds sought for bathrooms at Mala Wharf, Lahaina News, June 10, 1993: 3,4.

— county parks projects detailed, Lahaina News, June 24, 1993: 8.

— county staring Youth Transportation Pilot Project, Lahaina News, July 8, 1993: 3.

— State Park at Makena (SPAM) marks 10-year struggle to make Big Beach a state park, Lahaina News, July 8, 1993: 6.

— state suggests scrub land near Olowalu be used for game bird hunting area, Lahaina News, July 22, 1993: 4.

— discussed in supplement published in Lahaina News by West Maui Taxpayers Association, Lahaina News, August 5, 1993: A2,A3.

— cars unable to park along Honoapi'ilani Highway during regatta, Lahaina News, August 19, 1993: 4.

— residents discuss flood protection system, Lahaina News, August 19, 1993: 4.

— lack of parking affects consumer spending, Lahaina News, September 9, 1993: 6.

— West Maui Watershed Advisory Committee to meet, Lahaina News, September 16, 1993: 4.

— Army Corps of Engineers representative discusses agency's role in disasters, Lahaina News, September 16, 1993: 4.

— alternate routes for Upcountry-Kihei Highway proposed, Lahaina News, September 16, 1993: 8.

— contract for roadwork on Honoapi'ilani Highway by Olowalu awarded, Lahaina News, September 23, 1993: 3.

— plan to establish super computer at the Research and Technology Park, Lahaina News, September 23, 1993: 6.

— West Maui Watershed Advisory Committee to begin meeting, Lahaina News, September 30, 1993: 1,15.

— Kihei Community Association lists top priorities, Lahaina News, September 30, 1993: 6.

— state seeking input on rules for Kapalua-West Maui Airport, Lahaina News, October 14, 1993: 1,4.

— County Wastewater Reclamation Division to hold public meeting to relocate Lahaina Wastewater Pump Station No. 3, Lahaina News, October 14, 1993: 5.

— pump station to be moved away from surf, Lahaina News, October 28, 1993: 1,12.

— park improvements underway, Lahaina News, October 28, 1993: 4.

— Maui County's Economic Development, Tourism and Environment Committee to hold workshop on ocean resource management, Lahaina News, November 11, 1993: 3.

— Maui Land and Pineapple wants Napili Regional Park moved near Kapalua/West Maui Airport in the West Maui Community Plan, Lahaina News, November 18, 1993: 1,3.

— plan for skateboarding park postponed, Lahaina News, November 18, 1993: 5.

— roads to be resurfaced, Lahaina News, December 16, 1993: 2.

— road worked planned for Olowalu, Lahaina News, December 23, 1993: 3.

— Kiewit Pacific Co. contracting firm files lawsuit against state over Kahului Airport Terminal extension project, Lahaina News, December 23, 1993: 7.

— meeting to discuss freeways, Lahaina News, January 20, 1994: 3.

— Linda Lingle talks about funding to expand parks, Lahaina News, January 27, 1994: 1,2.

— Governor John Waihee releases funds for improvements for Front Street, Lahaina News, February 10, 1994: 3.

— runoff and soil erosion are concerns, Lahaina News, February 17, 1994: 3.

— residents call for halt to concrete channels, Lahaina News, February 24, 1994: 3.

— Maui County's Department of Public Works, Lahaina News, February 24, 1994: 4.

— sections of Honoapi'ilani Highway to be resurfaced, Lahaina News, March 3, 1994: 4.

— JGI Enterprises plan for Napilihau Villages to be challenged, Lahaina News, March 10, 1994: 1,3.

— Department of Public Works and Waste Management selects pump station site, Lahaina News, March 17, 1994: 1,16.

— Lahaina Express expands transportation service, Lahaina News, March 24, 1994: 8.

— waste water line replacement along Honoapi'ilani Highway planned, Lahaina News, April 7, 1994: 4.

— improvements to sewage system to affect traffic, Lahaina News, April 14, 1994: 1.

— park improvements delayed due to lack of funds, Lahaina News, April 14, 1994: 3.

— road work to start at Papawai Lookout in Olowalu, Lahaina News, April 28, 1994: 4.

— meeting held concerning relocation of Lahaina Wastewater Pump Station No. 3, Lahaina News, May 12, 1994: 4.

— wastewater transmission line replacement project resuming, Lahaina News, May 19, 1994: 6.

— Wahikuli residents oppose proposal to relocate pump station, Lahaina News, May 26, 1994: 1,20.

— Lahaina Citizen Advisory Committee requests part at North Beach, Lahaina News, June 9, 1994: 1.

— disaster preparedness plan to be available, Lahaina News, June 9, 1994: 2.

— Honokowai Beach Park erosion wall postponed, Lahaina News, June 16, 1994: 1.

— work continues of wastewater transmission line, Lahaina News, June 23, 1994: 5.

— public meetings to be held on Front Street improvements, Lahaina News, June 30, 1994: 1,20.

— update on roadwork, Lahaina News, July 7, 1994: 4.

— traffic jams on Honoapi'ilani Highway should not last longer than July 30, Lahaina News, July 14, 1994: 1.

— stormwater drainage plan to be created for West Maui, Lahaina News, July 14, 1994: 1,20.

— Front Street improvements to be done quickly, according to Maui County, Lahaina News, July 14, 1994: 1,20.

— wastewater line replacement project underway again, Lahaina News, July 14, 1994: 6.

— Draft Environmental Assessment for proposed Lahaina Wastewater Pump Station 3 available, Lahaina News, July 21, 1994: 4.

— Honolulu to Kahului is nation's busiest city route, Lahaina News, July 21, 1994: 7.

— West Maui desedimentation basin project delayed, Lahaina News, July 28, 1994: 1,16.

— Mala Wharf to have bathrooms installed, Lahaina News, August 4, 1994: 1.

— safety and irrigation top priorities for parks, Lahaina News, August 4, 1994: 1,4.

— Akina Bus Service offering new shuttle service, Lahaina News, August 11, 1994: 7.

— survey of merchants indicates parking and traffic a problem, Lahaina News, August 18, 1994: 1,3.

— Ka'anapali Parkway to be widened, Lahaina News, August 18, 1994: 5.

— wastewater line replacement project finished, Lahaina News, August 18, 1994: 5.

— comments on Front Street needed, Lahaina News, September 1, 1994: 5.

— construction of Lower Honoapi'ilani Road Improvements begins, Lahaina News, September 1, 1994: 7.

— merchant Tom Lilledal not happy about proposed improvements to Front Street, Lahaina News, September 8, 1994: 1,7.

— site work on desedimentation basins in Mahinahina and Honokowai begin, Lahaina News, September 15, 1994: 6.

— housing for people displaced by Lahaina Bypass sought, Lahaina News, September 22, 1994: 6.

— Honoapi'ilani Highway to be resurfaced, Lahaina News, September 22, 1994: 6.

— merchants support longer parking limits and bans on buses, Lahaina News, September 29, 1994: 3.

— Kahana Bridge opens, Lahaina News, October 13, 1994: 15.

— improvements to begin in April, Lahaina News, October 27, 1994: 4.

— Brian Blundell believes West Maui too shallow for harbor, Lahaina News, October 27, 1994: 6.

— candidates for House differ on need for second harbor, Lahaina News, November 3, 1994: 1,7.

— issues over beach signage following injury of visitor at Ka'anapali Beach, Lahaina News, November 10, 1994: 1,3.

— Honokohau residents want trash pickup, Lahaina News, November 24, 1994: 1,3.

— light coming to intersection at Honokowai, Lahaina News, November 24, 1994: 3.

— Small Business Development Center offering workshop on using MauiLink and the internet, Lahaina News, December 1, 1994: 13.

— restroom pump station at Hanaka'o'o Beach Park to be replaced, Lahaina News, December 8, 1994: 3.

— poor water quality seen as biggest threat to human health, Lahaina News, December 15, 1994: 1,20.

— Oahu Convention Center seen as positive for neighbor islands as well, Lahaina News, December 15, 1994: 14.

— community seeks overpass on Honoapi'ilani Highway, Lahaina News, December 29, 1994: 1.

— state Department of Land and Natural Resources may pursue state park at Honolua Bay, Lahaina News, January 26, 1995: 1,20.

— pedestrian-activated light favored at Honoapi'ilani Highway, Lahaina News, January 26, 1995: 1,20.

— Long Distance/USA-Sprint receives approval for interisland outbound services, Lahaina News, January 26, 1995: 13.

— traffic issues discussed, Lahaina News, March 9, 1995: 3.

— officials discuss motorcycle parking, Lahaina News, March 23, 1995: 2.

— work begins on pump station at Wahikuli Terrace Park, Lahaina News, March 23, 1995: 2.

— parks being improved, Lahaina News, March 30, 1995: 1,16.

— residents request funds for parks at Budget Committee hearing, Lahaina News, April 6, 1995: 1,3.

— funds may be available to fix Kahana drainage issue, Lahaina News, May 11, 1995: 4.

— million dollars allotted for bikeway for West Maui, Lahaina News, May 18, 1995: 1,12.

— security guard to monitor bus traffic on Wharf Street, Lahaina News, May 25, 1995: 1,16.

— Maui County Council's Parks and Recreation Committee to discuss regulating drinking in county parks, Lahaina News, May 25, 1995: 4.

— Governor Ben Cayetano cuts funds for Front Street, Lahaina News, June 1, 1995: 1,12.

— funding for improved emergency communication network frozen, Lahaina News, June 1, 1995: 1,12.

— locations for new emergency phones not selected yet, Lahaina News, June 1, 1995: 12.

— use of roller blading and skateboarding restricted, Lahaina News, June 1, 1995: 2.

— Maui emergency services strained, Lahaina News, June 8, 1995: 1,2.

— campsite to be developed at Papalaua Wayside Park, Lahaina News, June 8, 1995: 5.

— Watershed Project Coordinator Wendy Wiltse says county needs to move quickly on new basins, Lahaina News, June 22, 1995: 1,16.

— bill to establish inter-island ferry service at Lahaina Harbor approved by Governor Ben Cayetano, Lahaina News, June 22, 1995: 4.

— new traffic signals in operation, Lahaina News, June 29, 1995: 4.

— officials want billboards kept off the roads, Lahaina News, July 6, 1995: 2.

— public trail to Hawea Point opens, Lahaina News, July 13, 1995: 1.

— Lahaina Bypass may be delayed due to state funding, Lahaina News, July 13, 1995: 1,16.

— Papalaua Wayside Park may be ready for public camping soon, Lahaina News, July 13, 1995: 2.

— County Parks Director Charmaine Tavares proposes double the park land, Lahaina News, July 13, 1995: 4.

— Akina Express begins new bus service, Lahaina News, July 13, 1995: 5.

— highway to be resurfaced, Lahaina News, July 27, 1995: 1.

— options explored for new harbor, Lahaina News, August 3, 1995: 1,20.

— Mahinahina Water Plant to be commissioned, Lahaina News, August 3, 1995: 5.

— state cuts may lead to service cuts for Maui Princess, Lahaina News, August 10, 1995: 1,16.

— work on Honoapiʻilani Highway to begin, Lahaina News, August 10, 1995: 4.

— Maui County Council bill to create more parks in residential areas, Lahaina News, August 10, 1995: 6.

— two dams in West Maui dedicated, Lahaina News, August 17, 1995: 3.

— State begins planning for new school facilities, Lahaina News, September 14, 1995: 3.

— history of roads, Lahaina News, September 28, 1995: 3.

— history of roads, Lahaina News, September 28, 1995: 3.

— Ben Cayetano releases funds for Hawaii public schools and libraries, Lahaina News, October 5, 1995: 4.

— Lahaina Water Treatment Facility ground breaking held, Lahaina News, November 2, 1995: 4.

— night time park drinking ban passed, Lahaina News, November 9, 1995: 16.

— storm drain markings need repainting, Lahaina News, November 16, 1995: 2,5.

— new restrooms at D.T. Fleming Park almost completed, Lahaina News, November 23, 1995: 4.

— state to continue subsidizing Maui to Molokaʻi ferry, Lahaina News, December 14, 1995: 1,20.

— first reading of West Maui Community Plan at Maui County Council, Lahaina News, December 14, 1995: 20.

— tour bus congestion eased by security guard at Lahaina Harbor, Lahaina News, December 28, 1995: 1.

— West Maui bus services merging, Lahaina News, December 28, 1995: 3.

— surfing accident highlights need for better emergency call system, Lahaina News, January 4, 1996: 1,2.

— Honokowai to get intersection signal, Lahaina News, January 11, 1996: 1,16.

— Maui County Council approves new emergency radio system, Lahaina News, January 18, 1996: 16.

— Lahaina Bypass plans almost ready for public, Lahaina News, January 18, 1996: 16.

— Amfac/JMB Hawaii submits preliminary design plan for park mauka of West Maui Recreational Center, Lahaina News, January 25, 1996: 7.

— complaints received over parking, Lahaina News, January 25, 1996: 7.

— water storage tank construction begins, Lahaina News, February 8, 1996: 6.

— opinions from residents sought on traffic, Lahaina News, February 22, 1996: 3.

— traffic light to be installed along Honoapiʻilani Highway, Lahaina News, March 28, 1996: 4.

— Front Street Improvement Project detailed, Lahaina News, April 11, 1996: 4.

— pros and cons of airport expansion discussed, Lahaina News, May 16, 1996: 1,3.

— funds released for intersection on Honoapiʻilani Highway, Lahaina News, May 16, 1996: 6.

— new public restrooms to be installed, Lahaina News, May 23, 1996: 1,20.

— funds released for highway projects, Lahaina News, June 27, 1996: 2.

— park connected to Lahaina Recreation Center being designed, Lahaina News, June 27, 1996: 4.

— 8-inch water line broken, Lahaina News, June 27, 1996: 4.

— construction of sidewalks begin along Front Street, Lahaina News, July 4, 1996: 1,2.

— highway lane to close for 6 months for installation of sewer line, Lahaina News, July 11, 1996: 3.

— Molokaʻi ferry increases rates, Lahaina News, July 25, 1996: 1.

— traffic delays expected near Chart House, Lahaina News, August 1, 1996: 1.

— Honolua Ditch water agreement stalled, Lahaina News, August 1, 1996: 1.

— Dickenson Street to get stop signs, Lahaina News, August 8, 1996: 1.

— parents seek sidewalks for Hui Road F , Lahaina News, August 15, 1996: 1,20.

— comfort station opens at Mala Wharf, Lahaina News, August 22, 1996: 5.

— Honoapiʻilani Highway to be resurfaced, Lahaina News, August 22, 1996: 5.

— hydrogeologist Matt Hagemann works on wellhead protection program, Lahaina News, September 5, 1996: 1,2.

— Lahaina Task Force considering traffic issues, Lahaina News, September 12, 1996: 2.

— update on Front Street Improvement Project, Lahaina News, September 19, 1996: 1.

— parking lot planned for Wahie Lane, Lahaina News, September 19, 1996: 4.

— county Highways Division to begin work on Lower Honoapiʻilani Road , Lahaina News, September 26, 1996: 3.

— County Planning Director David Blane discusses changes to signage and downtown parking with Lahaina Task Force, Lahaina News, September 26, 1996: 2.

— State Department of Transportation to place signs to warn motorists following accident, Lahaina News, October 10, 1996: 1,20.

— issues with beach wall near Launiupoko discussed, Lahaina News, October 10, 1996: 3.

— installation of wastewater lines half done, Lahaina News, October 10, 1996: 5.

— plans to expand Hanakaʻoʻo Beach Park, Lahaina News, October 17, 1996: 1,20.

— restrooms to open at Mala Wharf, Lahaina News, October 24, 1996: 5.

— sidewalks improved, Lahaina News, October 31, 1996: 4.

— state to investigate areas where highway is vulnerable to ocean, Lahaina News, November 14, 1996: 1,20.

— committee considers improvements to parking at Lahaina Harbor, Lahaina News, November 14, 1996: 2.

— sea water and sand wash on Honoapi'ilani Highway, Lahaina News, November 14, 1996: 20.

— metal netting along Honoapi'ilani Highway criticized, Lahaina News, November 21, 1996: 2.

— accidents frequent at corner of Dickenson and Wainee streets, Lahaina News, November 21, 1996: 2.

— bike lanes sometimes sacrificed, Lahaina News, December 5, 1996: 3,18.

— sea wall planned for Honokowai Park, Lahaina News, December 12, 1996: 3.

— merchants critical of pause to Front Street Improvement Project work, Lahaina News, December 26, 1996: 1,14.

— highway design funds release for Honoapi'ilani Highway widening, Lahaina News, January 9, 1997: 14.

— plan to enhance bicycle safety in Pali Tunnel, Lahaina News, January 9, 1997: 2.

— Amfac/JMB Hawaii seeking public support for highway widening, Lahaina News, January 16, 1997: 1,16.

— planned widening of Honoapi'ilani Highway debated, Lahaina News, January 23, 1997: 1,16.

— mayor Linda Lingle initiating discussion on public park at North Beach, Lahaina News, January 30, 1997: 1.

— traffic mitigation to be discussed at Lahaina Civic Center, Lahaina News, January 30, 1997: 1.

— senator Roz Baker trying to restore subsidy for Moloka'i ferry service, Lahaina News, February 6, 1997: 3.

— traffic light to be installed in Honokowai, Lahaina News, February 13, 1997: 3.

— traffic issues in North Beach to be discussed by Maui Planning Commission, Lahaina News, February 20, 1997: 1.

— update on Front Street project, Lahaina News, February 27, 1997: 2.

— workers support return of ferry to Moloka'i, Lahaina News, March 13, 1997: 1,20.

— County Council working on flooding issues, Lahaina News, March 27, 1997: 1.

— plans published for widening of Honoapi'ilani Highway, Lahaina News, April 3, 1997: 3.

— highway to be resurfaced by Rimrock Paving Co., Lahaina News, July 10, 1997: 2.

— Senator Daniel Inouye seeks funding for county harbors, Lahaina News, July 24, 1997: 15.

— skateboard park proposed, Lahaina News, August 21, 1997: 1.

— skateboarding growth stymied by lack of parks, Lahaina News, September 18, 1997: 14.

— State and Army Corps seek comments on expansion of Ma'alaea Harbor, Lahaina News, September 18, 1997: 15.

— utility work continues on Front Street, Lahaina News, September 25, 1997: 2.

— Mala Wharf silt problem discussed, Lahaina News, October 2, 1997: 1,2.

— renovations of Front Street continues, Lahaina News, October 2, 1997: 3.

— residents want more information on proposal to widen highway in Ka'anapali, Lahaina News, October 16, 1997: 1,3.

— E Noa Corporation running trolley service between South and West Maui, Lahaina News, October 30, 1997: 13.

— Scott Cunningham named harbors district manager for Maui, Lahaina News, December 18, 1997: 3.

— Maui Skateboard Association to ask for skate park, Lahaina News, December 25, 1997: 1,2.

— highway to be resurfaced, Lahaina News, January 1, 1998: 2.

— Roz Baker hopes Lahaina to Moloka'i ferry a priority for upcoming legislative session, Lahaina News, January 22, 1998: 1,16.

— work begins on new pool and community center in South Maui, Lahaina News, January 22, 1998: 5.

— plans for lower road work to be considered by Maui Planning Commission, Lahaina News, February 19, 1998: 1,16.

— trolley services between West Maui and Wailea announced by Trans-Hawaiian Services, Lahaina News, March 19, 1998: 11.

— plans to widen Honoapi'ilani Highway at Ka'anapali explained, Lahaina News, March 26, 1998: 1,16.

— Trans-Hawaiian Services introducing trolley service, Lahaina News, March 26, 1998: 11.

— plans for Napili Park unveiled, Lahaina News, March 26, 1998: 2.

— panel to review proposal for Mala Wharf, Lahaina News, April 9, 1998: 1.

— trolleys now in service, Lahaina News, April 9, 1998: 13.

— Maui County Council to discuss appropriation of beach access and park land, Lahaina News, April 23, 1998: 7.

— Kekaa Drive to be detour while Honoapi'ilani Highway is expanded, Lahaina News, April 30, 1998: 1,20.

— Governor Ben Cayetano says state plans to restore Lahaina to Kaunakakai ferry, Lahaina News, May 14, 1998: 1.

— plans nearly complete for widening of Honoapi'ilani Highway in Ka'anapali, Lahaina News, May 21, 1998: 3.

— Department of Transportation plans to resurface Honoapi'ilani Highway, Lahaina News, June 4, 1998: 1,20.

— skatepark to be ready soon, Lahaina News, June 4, 1998: 3.

— Ma'alaea Harbor supplemental environmental impact statement finished, Lahaina News, June 11, 1998: 15.

— Maui Council seeking group to run skateboard park, Lahaina News, June 18, 1998: 1,20.

— plans for Lahaina-Kaunakakai ferry being considered, Lahaina News, June 25, 1998: 1,16.

— state establishing Lahaina to Ma'alaea bikeway, Lahaina News, July 2, 1998: 8.

— skateboard park to open, Lahaina News, July 23, 1998: 1,20.

— Hawaiian Cablevision to install fiber optic network, Lahaina News, July 23, 1998: 3.

— Dugied Construction to install Automated Weather Observing Systems at Kapalua-West Mui Airport, Lahaina News, July 30, 1998: 7.

— traffic signal to be installed at Honoapi'ilani Highway and Dickenson Street, Lahaina News, August 6, 1998: 7.

— highway widening to begin in October, Lahaina News, August 27, 1998: 1,20.

— plans to extend Kahului Airport runway, Lahaina News, September 3, 1998: 1.

— Keopuolani Park to open, Lahaina News, September 3, 1998: 3.

— groups want two parks closed at night to improve safety and reduce vagrancy, Lahaina News, September 24, 1998: 1,20.

— highway resurfacing project winding down, Lahaina News, October 1, 1998: 1,20.

— highway widening project begins, Lahaina News, October 29, 1998: 1.

— concern over using Amfac cane haul as detour while highway is widened, Lahaina News, November 5, 1998: 1.

— Department of Transportation updates on highway widening, Lahaina News, November 12, 1998: 1.

— West Side traffic coalition to discuss issues, Lahaina News, November 12, 1998: 3.

— highway widening project discussed, Lahaina News, November 19, 1998: 1.

— light industrial park planned for Lahaina, Lahaina News, December 31, 1998: 11.

— Lahaina-Moloka'i ferry researched, Lahaina News, January 28, 1999: 1.

— Mayor James Apana discusses ways to improve parking in Lahaina, Lahaina News, January 28, 1999: 1,16.

— residents may ask Maui Land and Pineapple to sell acres near Pohaku Park, Lahaina News, February 25, 1999: 1,16.

— lawmakers seeking funding Lahaina-Moloka'i ferry, Lahaina News, February 25, 1999: 11.

— residents critical of new utility poles installed by Maui Electric Company at Pu'ukoli'i Road, Lahaina News, March 4, 1999: 1,16.

— engineers to explain "Honokowai Park Beach Nourishment Demonstration Project", Lahaina News, March 25, 1999: 3.

— ISDN telephone service now available, Lahaina News, April 1, 1999: 13.

— Maui County to inform businesses of ADA requirements, Lahaina News, April 1, 1999: 13.

— Honokowai Park beach restoration to be held, Lahaina News, April 8, 1999: 1,16.

— Honoapi'ilani Highway issues to be discussed at community forum, Lahaina News, April 8, 1999: 1,16.

— traffic study of Honoapi'ilani Highway to be done, Lahaina News, April 15, 1999: 1,16.

— West side improvement projects target litter, Lahaina News, April 22, 1999: 1,16.

— new lifeguard tower built by community at D.T. Fleming Park, Lahaina News, May 20, 1999: 3.

— highway crew focusing on utility work, Lahaina News, June 3, 1999: 1.

— firm problems highway traffic counts, noise, Lahaina News, June 10, 1999: 3.

— results to be shared, Lahaina News, July 22, 1999: 1.

— work on Lahaina Bypass may begin in 2002, Lahaina News, July 22, 1999: 1,16.

— traffic study results to be released, Lahaina News, July 29, 1999: 1,16.

— task force attempting to find alternate routes to Lahaina, Lahaina News, August 19, 1999: 3.

— Maui County Council concerned about bicycle safety, Lahaina News, September 2, 1999: 1,20.

— County to expand Lahaina Recreation Center, Lahaina News, September 2, 1999: 3.

— Department of Transportation to hold hearings on proposed Kihei-Upcountry Maui highway project, Lahaina News, September 23, 1999: 5.

— task force studies developing new access to West Maui, Lahaina News, October 21, 1999: 1,20.

— Maui County Council to consider ways to improve busy intersection at Wainee Street and Lahainaluna Road, Lahaina News, October 21, 1999: 1,20.

— Front Street sidewalks filthy, Lahaina News, October 28, 1999: 1,20.

— Lahaina Watershed Project hoped for, Lahaina News, November 18, 1999: 1,2.

— Lahaina Watershed Project hoped for, Lahaina News, November 18, 1999: 1,2.

— Maui County Council concerned for traffic problems at new Mahanalua Nui subdivision, Lahaina News, November 25, 1999: 1,20.

— offering "Share a Holiday Feast", Lahaina News, November 25, 1999: 15.

— Eileen Williams leads country line dances, Lahaina News, November 25, 1999: 15.

— expansion of Honoapi'ilani Highway speeds up, Lahaina News, December 2, 1999: 1.

— Napilihau Road to be fixed in January, Lahaina News, December 23, 1999: 1.

— Lahainaluna High School to change traffic patterns, ease congestion, Lahaina News, December 30, 1999: 3.

— Jan Yagi-Buen discusses importance of new road to connect West and Central Maui, Lahaina News, January 20, 2000: 1,16.

— repairs to Napilihau to begin this week, Lahaina News, February 10, 2000: 1,20.

— Department of Transportation to hold meeting to discuss Paia Bypass Road, Lahaina News, February 17, 2000: 16.

— heliport planned for site of former Olowalu landfill, Lahaina News, February 24, 2000: 1,2.

— speed bumps sought following child's death, Lahaina News, February 24, 2000: 1,2.

— Maui County Council may try 4-way stop at intersection of Lahainaluna Road and Wainee Street, Lahaina News, March 9, 2000: 1,3.

— new highway lanes to open mid-April, Lahaina News, March 16, 2000: 1,16.

— Senate changes bill to require council review of proposed heliport, Lahaina News, March 23, 2000: 1,2.

— residents seek improvements to Lahainaluna Road traffic, Lahaina News, March 30, 2000: 1,2.

— Kiewit Construction Co. and Bob Siarot of Department of Transportation meet with residents to discuss highway project issues, Lahaina News, March 30, 2000: 5.

— Olowalu heliport bill dead, Lahaina News, May 4, 2000: 1,2.

— Hana Hawaii designated "Hawaii's Millennium Legacy Trail" in White House ceremony, Lahaina News, June 1, 2000: 7.

— state attempting to revive Lahaina-Moloka'i ferry, Lahaina News, June 8, 2000: 1,6.

— Hawaii Helicopters Inc. seeks permission to provide helicopter transportation from Kapalua-West Maui airport when emergency is declared, Lahaina News, June 8, 2000: 1,6.

— traffic study of Honoapi'ilani Highway completed, Lahaina News, June 29, 2000: 1,8.

— Maui County to test 4-way stop at Lahainaluna Road and Wainee Street, Lahaina News, July 13, 2000: 1.

— Maui County Council pursing extension to Dickenson Street, Lahaina News, July 27, 2000: 1,17.

— Hawaii Drought Council drafting Hawaii Drought Plan, Lahaina News, August 3, 2000: 17.

— workshops for disaster preparedness to be held, Lahaina News, August 3, 2000: 9.

— residents in path of Lahaina Bypass ask state to help alleviate past setbacks, Lahaina News, August 24, 2000: 1,15.

— County to hold meeting on plans to replace Front Street sewer line, Lahaina News, September 21, 2000: 1,6.

— coastal land trust forming, Lahaina News, September 28, 2000: 7.

— county officials seek comments from residents on sewer project on Front Street, Lahaina News, October 5, 2000: 1,15.

— Maui County Project Impact initiative to hold meeting on West Maui isolation problems, Lahaina News, October 26, 2000: 3.

— Maui County Impact Initiative to hold meeting to discuss disaster planning, Lahaina News, November 9, 2000: 6.

— Moloka'i Princess ferry to begin operation in January between Moloka'i and Maui, Lahaina News, December 28, 2000: 1,15.

— Mayor James Apana discusses parking problems in Lahaina, Lahaina News, January 25, 2001: 1.

— traffic concerns expressed at public meeting, Lahaina News, February 1, 2001: 1,22.

— Mayor James Apana unveils plan to improve parking in Lahaina, Lahaina News, February 8, 2001: 1,22.

— panel to work on issues with highway, Lahaina News, February 8, 2001: 1,22.

— State Senator Jan Yagi-Buen forms West Maui Highway Action Committee to work on traffic issues, Lahaina News, February 8, 2001: 1,22.

— Mayor James Apana to hold meetings to target traffic issues, Lahaina News, February 22, 2001: 3.

— carrying capacity study a priority of JoAnne Johnson, Lahaina News, February 22, 2001: 5.

— West Maui Highway Action Committee seeks traffic solutions, Lahaina News, March 1, 2001: 1,22.

— call to make Honoapiʻilani Highway safer, Lahaina News, March 1, 2001: 2.

— Transportation Action Committee seeking input on traffic, Lahaina News, March 1, 2001: 20.

— County Council Public Works and Transportation Committee to study traffic issues, Lahaina News, March 8, 2001: 3.

— West Side isolation panel to meet, Lahaina News, March 22, 2001: 2.

— Councilwoman JoAnne Johnson seeks building ban to fix traffic, Lahaina News, March 29, 2001: 1,18.

— West Maui Taxpayers Association to help improve traffic and County Charter, Lahaina News, April 5, 2001: 22.

— Senator Jan Yagi-Buen outlines accomplishments from 2001 session, Lahaina News, May 10, 2001: 10.

— West Maui Taxpayers Association completes study to prove highway is dangerous, Lahaina News, May 10, 2001: 3.

— residents ask about Amfac/JMB's Kaʻanapali 2020 report, Lahaina News, May 24, 2001: 1,22.

— County Council Department of Public Works to hold information meeting on plans for Lower Honoapiʻilani Road Phase IV, Lahaina News, June 7, 2001: 1.

— County Council Parks and Recreation Committee recommends county take over parks, Lahaina News, August 9, 2001: 3.

— Department of Public Works and Waste Management to hold a hearing on Environmental Assessment for Lower Honoapiʻilani Road Phase IV project, Lahaina News, August 23, 2001: 3.

— state installing highway guardrails, Lahaina News, August 30, 2001: 1.

— County Council Planning Committee to hold "Transportation Infrastructure Planning Workshop", Lahaina News, September 6, 2001: 3.

— repair of Honoapiʻilani Highway underway, Lahaina News, September 13, 2001: 3.

— residents seek funding for stake park and road improvements from Maui County Council, Lahaina News, November 8, 2001: 1,20.

— temporary highway fix for Olowalu planned, Lahaina News, November 15, 2001: 3.

— traffic devices discussed, Lahaina News, January 17, 2002: 1.

— flooding continues at Pau Nau subdivision, Lahaina News, January 17, 2002: 1,18.

— West Maui Taxpayers Association held meeting to update community on capital improvements, Lahaina News, January 24, 2002: 1,18.

— flooding along Wainee Street due to heavy rains, Lahaina News, January 31, 2002: 1,9.

— flood control projects underway, Lahaina News, February 7, 2002: 1,20.

— Lahaina Watershed Flood Control Project to be explained at public hearing, Lahaina News, February 14, 2002: 1.

— officials to explain Lahaina Watershed Flood Control Project, Lahaina News, February 21, 2002: 2.

— residents frustrated at delays to Lahaina Watershed Flood Control Project, Lahaina News, February 28, 2002: 1,20.

— boaters express concerns for Mala Wharf, Lahaina News, March 7, 2002: 1,20.

— funding released for Lahaina Small Boat Harbor, Lahaina News, April 25, 2002: 3.

— crosswalks installed by near schools, Lahaina News, May 23, 2002: 3.

— West Maui Taxpayers Association supporting highway improvement, Lahaina News, July 11, 2002: 5.

— Dick Mayer to moderate "Watersheds at Risk: A Search for Solutions", Lahaina News, July 11, 2002: 9.

— Pedestrian Safety Conference to be held, Lahaina News, August 1, 2002: 9.

— bus system to begin, Lahaina News, August 29, 2002: 2,9.

— bus system to begin, Lahaina News, September 5, 2002: 8.

— Department of Public Works and Waste Management announces that roads will be repaved, Lahaina News, September 26, 2002: 1.

— roads in West Maui to be repaved, Lahaina News, October 3, 2002: 9.

— representative Brian Blundell to push for acute care facility and roadway solutions, Lahaina News, November 14, 2002: 1,24.

— Stu Kahan to lead discussion of West Maui Transportation Plan, Lahaina News, January 23, 2003: 16.

— County Council Public Works and Traffic Committee focusing on traffic issues, Lahaina News, February 20, 2003: 1,20.

— drainage study of Lahaina Town to be conducted, Lahaina News, March 13, 2003: 1,18.

— Department of Public Works and Environmental Management to study Lahaina drainage, Lahaina News, March 20, 2003: 2.

— Maui County proposes highway and parks from Puamana to the Pali, Lahaina News, March 27, 2003: 1,20.

— plans to update Lahaina Town Master Drainage Plan presented, Lahaina News, April 3, 2003: 3.

— Lahaina gateway sign replaced, Lahaina News, May 1, 2003: 2.

— roadwork slated near Kahakuloa Town, Lahaina News, May 1, 2003: 2.

— Department of Public Works and Environmental Management to discuss flood control projects, Lahaina News, June 5, 2003: 3.

— director of the State Department of Transportation Rodney Haraga discusses improvements to transportation, Lahaina News, July 3, 2003: 1,18.

— Department of Transportation Highways Division Planning Branch to hold public hearing, Lahaina News, July 24, 2003: 1,18.

— Governor Linda Lingle indicates that work on Lahaina Bypass years away, Lahaina News, September 4, 2003: 1,20.

— Department of Public Works and Environmental Management to discuss traffic study, Lahaina News, September 25, 2003: 17.

INGAMELLS, J. LEE

— hired by Hawaiian Commercial and Sugar Co. as directory of agronomy, Lahaina News, September 2, 1999: 13.

INGRAM, BOBBY [MUSICIAN]

— interviewed, Lahaina News, June 5, 1985: 10.

— to perform at Casanova's, Lahaina News, August 15, 1990: 15.

— to perform at Villa Lounge, Lahaina News, August 13, 1992: 15.

— to perform at Pacific'O, Lahaina News, December 16, 1993: 19.

— to perform at Moose McGillycuddy's, Lahaina News, March 28, 1996: 12.

— to perform at Moose McGillycuddy's, Lahaina News, September 12, 1996: 16.

INHERIT THE WIND [PLAY]

— to be performed by Maui Community Theatre, Lahaina News, October 26, 1995: 12.

— reviewed, Lahaina News, November 9, 1995: 11.

INIKI [HURRICANE]

— looters asked to return property, damage to Maui described, Lahaina News, September 17, 1992: 1,3.

— impact on Lahaina described, Lahaina News, September 24, 1992: 6.

— benefits for victims of to be held, Lahaina News, October 1, 1992: 15.

— the brig Carthaginian survives, Lahaina News, November 12, 1992: insert4.

— Lahaina Harbor no longer needs to be dredged due to, Lahaina News, November 26, 1992: 4.

— workers at Kaʻanapali Beach Hotel deliver presents to Kauaʻi, Lahaina News, December 24, 1992: 1,4.

INITIAL RESPONSE TRAINING CENTER
— offering CPR and First Aid courses, Lahaina News, March 9, 1995: 4.

INJECTION WELLS
— Sierra Club Legal Defense Fund concerned about, Lahaina News, October 27, 1994: 5.
— Environmental Protection Agency reverses decision on, Lahaina News, December 14, 1995: 5.
— see also Environmental Protection Agency, pollution, and sewage

INJURIES AND DEATHS
— construction worker Joseph Caires Jr. injured in fall from Royal Lahaina Hotel , Lahaina Sun, March 3, 1971: 1.
— Gregory Kualaau killed at construction site near Olowalu, Lahaina Sun, March 17, 1971: 1.
— Isami Koshiyama passed away, Lahaina Sun, March 17, 1971: 3.
— Chong Chock passes away, Lahaina Sun, March 24, 1971: 5.
— Sunao Ito murdered near Front Street, Lahaina Sun, May 19, 1971: 6.
— two car accidents in west Maui, with photographs, Lahaina Sun, June 2, 1971: 4.
— Japanese seaman Toshihisa Ochi hospitalized, Lahaina Sun, July 21, 1971: 1.
— injured seaman Toshihisa Ochi has recovered, Lahaina Sun, July 28, 1971: 10.
— three people killed in automotive accident on Kahekili highway near Waihee, Lahaina Sun, August 4, 1971: 11.
— Arnubi Akini killed in automotive accident, Lahaina Sun, August 11, 1971: 11.
— Warner Weir in critical condition after near drowning, Lahaina Sun, August 18, 1971: 3.
— Maclean Chandler, tourist, dies of heart attack, Lahaina Sun, August 25, 1971: 11.
— 12th traffic death of the year reported, Lahaina Sun, August 25, 1971: 2.
— Scott Wilbourn in automobile accident, Lahaina Sun, September 1, 1971: 13.
— George Kahahane Jr injured in motorcycle crash, Lahaina Sun, September 22, 1971: 14.
— Gregorio Vinuya passes away, Lahaina Sun, September 29, 1971: 14.
— George Jones injured when his helicopter plunged into the sea during a rescue operation, Lahaina Sun, December 1, 1971: 13.
— Beoren Barr, three-year old, killed on the pali highway between Olowalu and Ma'alaea, Lahaina Sun, January 12, 1972: 7.
— Jane Chow of Hilo killed in traffic accident, Lahaina Sun, January 19, 1972: 16.
— Enrique Mallory of Paia dies in motorcycle accident, Lahaina Sun, March 15, 1972: 5.
— shark attack described, Lahaina Sun, March 22, 1972: 3.
— discussion of what to do in case of an emergency, Lahaina Sun, March 29, 1972: 5.
— Sister Leona Abella dies 10 days after being taken from the water off Napili, Lahaina Sun, April 26, 1972: 6.
— Ralph Calistro dies in boating accident in the Moloka'i Channel, Lahaina Sun, May 10, 1972: 10.
— Gary Frampton and Jocelyn Aotaki continue to recover, Lahaina Sun, June 28, 1972: 11.
— Bruce Davison Sr. recovering from the bends, Lahaina Sun, July 19, 1972: 3.
— Irene Lanoza passed away, Lahaina Sun, July 26, 1972: 11.
— John Dotson killed in Kihei in traffic accident, Lahaina Sun, September 13, 1972: 3.
— three deaths in automobile accidents described, Lahaina Sun, October 4, 1972: 15.
— Thomas Kekalia dies picking opihi, Lahaina Sun, October 11, 1972: 10.

— Maria Gutierrez dies at Seven Pools near Hana, Lahaina Sun, November 15, 1972: 3.
— two Japanese sailors, Kimuso Nakagama and Hideyuke Kamimura, were struck and killed by an automobile in Wailuku, Lahaina Sun, November 29, 1972: 9.
— Benson Akina dies following the crash of a single-engine plane at Kahana, Lahaina Sun, December 13, 1972: 15.
— shark attack at Ho'okipa, Lahaina Sun, January 17, 1973: 6.
— wreckage of F-4 flown by Lieutenant Harry Perkins and Lieutenant Jerry Provost found on Haleakala , Lahaina Sun, March 7, 1973: 6.
— drunk cyclist falls into ocean, Lahaina Sun, May 2, 1973: 3.
— Artemio Ganutisi is Maui county's ninth traffic fatality, Lahaina Sun, August 29, 1973: 15.
— Mark Skidgel attacked by shark off Puamana beach, Lahaina News, August 15, 1980: 6.
— managing poisons safely discussed, Lahaina News, September 1, 1980: 11.
— private sea and mountain rescue unit proposed for Ka'anapali, Lahaina News, July 1, 1983: 14.
— dangerous highways in West Maui discussed, Lahaina News, December 28, 1983: 2,9,11,12.
— Charlie Good saved by Loretta Miller and Eddie Nelson, Lahaina News, January 4, 1984: 4.
— Mark Blase lost in plane crash off Hana, Lahaina News, January 11, 1984: 5.
— toxic seaweed blamed for illness on Front Street, Lahaina News, January 25, 1984: 5.
— Lahaina man injured by Jet-ski, Lahaina News, March 28, 1984: 4.
— girl dies after falling into Kahoma Stream, Lahaina News, April 18, 1984: 5.
— alcohol often cause of highway deaths, Lahaina News, August 15, 1984: 3.
— State sued in death of James Limperos in crash on Honoapi'ilani Highway, Lahaina News, September 26, 1984: 10.
— crash kills cyclist William Wood, Lahaina News, June 19, 1985: 3.
— Anthony Domut killed in one-car accident on Honoapi'ilani Highway, Lahaina News, July 17, 1985: 3.
— honeymooning couple killed in auto crash near Launiupoko Park, Lahaina News, October 23, 1985: 3.
— tourist dies after jumping in front of sugar train, Lahaina News, March 18, 1987: 3.
— Mark Melle dies in car collision, Lahaina News, July 18, 1990: 4.
— traffic fatality on Honoapi'ilani Highway, Lahaina News, January 2, 1991: 4.
— motorcyclist dies, Lahaina News, January 2, 1992: 5.
— two traffic fatalities reported, Lahaina News, January 16, 1992: 5.
— search called off for missing plane, Lahaina News, January 23, 1992: 5.
— murder suicide involving Rose Marie Alconcel and Frank Alconcel Jr., Lahaina News, February 20, 1992: 1,7,8.
— homeless man drowns, Lahaina News, July 16, 1992: 4.
— unidentified man drowns off Ka'anapali Villas, Lahaina News, September 3, 1992: 4.
— teenager from Austria killed in head-on collision, Lahaina News, September 17, 1992: 3.
— search suspected for missing kayaker Joseph Tremblay, Lahaina News, March 11, 1993: 11.
— Arsenia Bumanglag killed in car accident, Lahaina News, March 18, 1993: 3,4.
— shark attacks off Wailua Bay, Lahaina News, March 18, 1993: 4.
— Lisa Feliciano dies in car accident on Honoapi'ilani Highway, Lahaina News, April 22, 1993: 3.
— traffic fatality in Olowalu, Lahaina News, May 20, 1993: 1,3.
— manager of Lahaina Monarch Building Supply Troy Reynolds killed by exploding propane cannister, Lahaina News, June 17, 1993: 1.

— Lani Carmichael and Valma Redo killed in traffic accident, Lahaina News, June 24, 1993: 8.

— David Acker and Vicki Tranilla die in motorcycle accident, Lahaina News, July 8, 1993: 6.

— body found on beach near Koa Lagoon condominiums, Lahaina News, September 2, 1993: 6.

— Charles Carl Heitz killed in automobile accident, Lahaina News, September 23, 1993: 6.

— two people killed in road accidents, Lahaina News, November 4, 1993: 3.

— family continues to search for Levette Aquino and her son Kapena last seen crossing flooded Kaua'ula Stream, Lahaina News, March 31, 1994: 1.

— James Dean Martin killed in traffic accident, Lahaina News, March 31, 1994: 5.

— two tourists drown off Ka'anapali Beach, Lahaina News, May 19, 1994: 5.

— Konrad Grond dies after boat sinks off Molokini Island, Lahaina News, August 25, 1994: 5.

— Brant Greenburg dies in apparent murder, Lahaina News, October 20, 1994: 5.

— King Kamehameha III Elementary School student hit by car at crosswalk, Lahaina News, December 22, 1994: 6.

— photograph of paramedics helping students after Sugar Cane train clipped school bus, Lahaina News, February 23, 1995: 1.

— car crash injures three, Lahaina News, March 9, 1995: 4.

— no foul play suspected in death of homeless man near Kahoma Stream Channel, Lahaina News, March 23, 1995: 3.

— girl hit crossing Honoapi'ilani Highway, Lahaina News, July 6, 1995: 1.

— Brenda Howard dies in traffic accident, Lahaina News, July 20, 1995: 2.

— Stephen King dies in motorcycle crash, Lahaina News, October 5, 1995: 4.

— surfer Ray Hayes suffers broken thighbone, Lahaina News, January 4, 1996: 1.

— two divers die , Lahaina News, April 4, 1996: 1,18.

— cocaine and heroin found in recent drug deaths, Lahaina News, April 11, 1996: 1,14.

— heroin a factor in Beau LeBallister's diving death, Lahaina News, May 16, 1996: 1,2.

— motorcycle crash kills Paul Holliday, Lahaina News, May 23, 1996: 1,3.

— death of Pollyann Van Zweden in five-car automobile accident mourned at Lahaina Intermediate School, Lahaina News, June 6, 1996: 1.

— fatal car crash on Honoapi'ilani Highway ties up police phones, Lahaina News, October 10, 1996: 4.

— memorial service planned for victims of airplane crash on Moloka'i, Lahaina News, November 7, 1996: 1.

— three injured in head-on crash, Lahaina News, July 15, 1999: 3.

— hit and run on Honoapi'ilani Highway near Puamana injures girl, Lahaina News, March 23, 2000: 3.

— two die in collision in Olowalu, Lahaina News, November 30, 2000: 3.

INK DROP PRODUCTIONS [BUSINESS]
— featured, Lahaina News, April 11, 1984: 7.

INKSTER, JULI
— golfer's career described, Lahaina News, March 6, 1985: A10.

INNER CIRCLE [MUSICAL GROUP]
— to perform at Maui Arts and Cultural Center, Lahaina News, August 11, 1994: 11.

INNER PEACE MOVEMENT
— hosting lecture by psychic Pat White, Lahaina News, October 17, 1984: 3.

INNOCENTI, KRISTEN [ARTIST]
— works displayed at Larry Dotson Gallery, Lahaina News, February 17, 1988: 18.

INOUYE, DANIEL [POLITICIAN]
— assisting with student visit to Washington DC, Lahaina Sun, February 3, 1971: 1.

— calls for return of Kaho'olawe to the State of Hawaii, Lahaina Sun, February 17, 1971: 6.

— introduces legislation to return Kaho'olawe, Lahaina Sun, May 5, 1971: 3.

— suggests federal funds for Lahaina Bypass, Lahaina News, February 17, 1988: 1,20.

— supporting bill to limit abuse of 900 numbers, Lahaina News, October 31, 1991: 4.

— announces that super computer to be built at Maui Research and Technology Park, Lahaina News, November 28, 1991: 7.

— to seek federal money to purchase land near Big Beach at Makena, Lahaina News, January 9, 1992: 5.

— to speak at Cultural Values in the Age of Technology conference, Lahaina News, March 12, 1992: 3,4.

— calls for probe of algae bloom, Lahaina News, April 16, 1992: 1,9.

— to speak to Maui Chamber of Commerce, Lahaina News, April 23, 1992: 8.

— to hold luncheon, Lahaina News, May 21, 1992: 4.

— to seek federal waiver to maintain restrictions at Kapalua-West Maui Airport, Lahaina News, June 4, 1992: 1,4.

— responds to criticisms from Rick Reed, Lahaina News, June 4, 1992: 1,4.

— criticized for sending brochure paid for by Congress, Lahaina News, June 11, 1992: 4.

— criticized by Rick Reed for lack of fiscal restraint, Lahaina News, June 25, 1992: 2.

— re-election event to be held, Lahaina News, August 20, 1992: 4.

— to hold rally, Lahaina News, August 27, 1992: 4.

— announces approval of funds to research green algae bloom, Lahaina News, October 22, 1992: 4.

— changes to rules for shipping fruits and vegetables, Lahaina News, February 25, 1993: 6.

— announces plan to establish super computer at the Research and Technology Park, Lahaina News, September 23, 1993: 6.

— seeks to change buffer around whales from 300 to 100 yards, Lahaina News, December 16, 1993: 1,20.

— honors employers for hiring disabled, Lahaina News, July 14, 1994: 13.

— seeking funding for homeless center, Lahaina News, July 24, 1997: 1,3.

— to speak at luncheon sponsored by Maui Chamber of Commerce, Lahaina News, January 29, 1998: 13.

— discusses economic impact of Department of Defense projects, Lahaina News, February 5, 1998: 2.

— to discuss economic impact of Department of Defense, Lahaina News, February 12, 1998: 13.

— to attend event at Maui Mall, Lahaina News, August 6, 1998: 14.

— to speak at West Maui AJA Veterans Club's Memorial Service, Lahaina News, May 27, 1999: 5.

— attends Memorial Day event, Lahaina News, June 3, 1999: 1,3.

— secures funding for Maui Community College, Lahaina News, September 9, 1999: 1.

— named "Man of the Century" by Maui Democratic Party, Lahaina News, December 9, 1999: 20.

— announces funding for Maui Family Support Services, Inc., Lahaina News, May 18, 2000: 7.

INOUYE, KAORU
— scored hole-in-one, Lahaina News, August 22, 1990: 9.

INOUYE, KAREN
— joins Finance Factors, Ltd., Lahaina News, October 17, 2002: 8.

INSTITUTE FOR EMERGENCY MEDICAL EDUCATION
— to hold convention, Lahaina News, November 26, 1986: 10.

INSTITUTE FOR SPIRITUAL DEVELOPMENT
— to hold "Healing Night", Lahaina News, March 30, 2000: 13.

INSTITUTE OF BODY THERAPEUTICS
— to open second branch, Lahaina News, January 8, 1986: 3.
— to offer classes on massage, Lahaina News, January 15, 1986: 3.
— to hold massage classes, Lahaina News, July 15, 1987: 3.

INSTITUTE OF REAL ESTATE MANAGEMENT
— to offer course, Lahaina News, April 3, 1991: 4.

INSURANCE
— public forum on, Lahaina News, July 9, 1986: 3.
— State proposing changes to, Lahaina News, November 28, 1991: 5.
— fire insurance rates to go down because of new fire station, Lahaina News, December 26, 1991: 1.
— fire insurance rates to go down because of new fire station, Lahaina News, January 9, 1992: 2.
— rates still affected by hurricanes Iniki and Iwa, Lahaina News, July 22, 1993: 7.
— state and insurance companies at odds over proposed insurance bill, Lahaina News, April 28, 1994: 2.
— auto insurance bill passes legislature, Lahaina News, May 18, 1995: 1,13.
— State Insurance Commissioner to speak, Lahaina News, November 21, 1996: 15.

INTEGRATED SOLID WASTE MASTER PLAN
— report completed, Lahaina News, April 8, 1993: 1.

INTERIOR DEPARTMENT [UNITED STATES GOVERNMENT]
— commits money for picnic facilities at Kamaole Beach, Lahaina Sun, March 10, 1971: 5.

INTERISLAND RESORTS [BUSINESS]
— planning to develop 470-room hotel in Lahaina, Lahaina Sun, January 20, 1971: 1.
— opens Maui Surf hotel, Lahaina Sun, July 28, 1971: 5.
— posts loss for 1981, Lahaina News, June 1, 1982: 11.
— shows loss for first quarter, Lahaina News, June 15, 1983: 11.
— sold to Fourmac Corporation, Lahaina News, February 22, 1984: 17.
— sale to Fourmac Investment Corporation delayed, Lahaina News, May 9, 1984: 13.

INTERNAL REVENUE SERVICE (IRS)
— experience being audited described, Lahaina Sun, April 11, 1973: 6.
— to expand walk-in services, Lahaina News, April 6, 1988: 3.
— services available in Wailuku, Lahaina News, June 8, 1988: 3.
— offering retirement planning seminar, Lahaina News, January 25, 1989: 16.
— to offer assistance to taxpayers, Lahaina News, November 14, 1990: 5.
— to have extended hours during tax filing season, Lahaina News, January 9, 1992: 2.
— expanding office hours, Lahaina News, April 9, 1992: 3,4.
— to hold Electronic Filing Orientation Seminar, Lahaina News, October 1, 1992: 11.
— to offer tax advice, Lahaina News, January 14, 1993: 6.
— to offer free tax assistance, Lahaina News, March 24, 1994: 8.

INTERNATIONAL AND ISRAELI FOLK DANCING FESTIVAL
— to be held, Lahaina News, July 30, 1998: 17.
— to be held, Lahaina News, August 6, 1998: 20.

INTERNATIONAL BOTTLED WATER ASSOCIATION
— awards Michael Beck Aqua awards, Lahaina News, December 15, 1994: 15.

INTERNATIONAL CATERING CONCEPTS [BUSINESS]
— awarded catering contract for Outrigger Hotels Hydrofest, Lahaina News, August 20, 1992: 12.

INTERNATIONAL CIGAR CELEBRATION
— to be held, Lahaina News, March 9, 1995: 12.
— to be held at the Ritz-Carlton, Lahaina News, April 13, 1995: 15.

INTERNATIONAL COASTAL CLEANUP
— to be held, Lahaina News, September 12, 1996: 3.

INTERNATIONAL CONFERENCE ON COLD FUSION
— held at West Maui, Lahaina News, December 23, 1993: 1,4.

INTERNATIONAL COUNCIL OF SHOPPING CENTERS
— names Whalers Village as Shopping Center of the Year, Lahaina News, April 29, 1999: 13.
— conference to be held, Lahaina News, July 1, 1999: 11.
— to be held, Lahaina News, July 8, 1999: 11.

INTERNATIONAL CULTURAL FESTIVAL
— to be part of Aloha Festivals, Lahaina News, October 8, 1998: 6.
— to be held, Lahaina News, October 7, 1999: 16.
— to be held at Lahaina Cannery Mall, Lahaina News, October 11, 2001: 17.
— to be held, Lahaina News, October 18, 2001: 16.
— to be held, Lahaina News, October 17, 2002: 18.

INTERNATIONAL FESTIVAL OF CANOES
— to be held, seeking carvers, Lahaina News, March 13, 2003: 8.
— to be held by LahainaTown Action Committee, Lahaina News, May 1, 2003: 1,3.
— to be held, Lahaina News, May 8, 2003: 1,20.
— insert included, Lahaina News, May 8, 2003: insert1-insert16.
— being held, Lahaina News, May 15, 2003: 3.
— to conclude this week, Lahaina News, May 22, 2003: 1.
— celebrated at Wharf Cinema Center, Lahaina News, June 26, 2003: 14.

INTERNATIONAL FOOD SERVICE EXECUTIVES' ASSOCIATION
— to meet at Maui Marriott Hotel , Lahaina News, August 12, 1993: 8.

INTERNATIONAL INTELLIGENCER
— publication discussed, Lahaina Times, August, 1980 volume 4 number 7: 2.

INTERNATIONAL IRISH DANCE COMPANY [TROUPE]
— to perform "Spirit of the Dance", Lahaina News, March 22, 2001: 17.

INTERNATIONAL LONGSHOREMEN'S AND WAREHOUSEMEN'S UNION (ILWU)
— discusses end of hotel strike, Lahaina Sun, December 30, 1970: 5.
— Local 142 insert included in Lahaina News, Lahaina News, April 25, 1990: B1,B2,B3,B4.
— forms Labor-Management Committee with Amfac/JMB, Lahaina News, September 9, 1993: 7.
— members demonstrate outside Maui Westin, Lahaina News, February 8, 1996: 18.
— endorses candidates, Lahaina News, November 2, 2000: 23.
— Local 142 suspends contract with Royal Lahaina Resort, Lahaina News, February 8, 2001: 3.
— Labor Relations Board investigating for unfair labor practices, Lahaina News, August 30, 2001: 1,8.
— Local 142 agrees to mediation with Kapalua Land Co., Lahaina News, February 27, 2003: 3.

INTERNATIONAL OF ADMINISTRATIVE PROFESSIONALS
— Joyce Brown elected president of No Ka Oi Chapter of, Lahaina News, May 31, 2001: 8.

INTERNATIONAL PEACE POEM PROJECT
— to sponsor poetry contest in honor of Dr. Martin Luther King's birthday, Lahaina News, January 25, 2001: 7.

INTERNATIONAL READING ASSOCIATION
— to hold convention at Grand Regency, Lahaina News, July 2, 1992: 16.

INTERNATIONAL RELATIONS
— US-Japan summit occurring soon in Honolulu, Lahaina Sun, August 30, 1972: 9.
— US-Japan summit occurring soon in Honolulu, Lahaina Sun, September 6, 1972: 1,3.
— Russian submarine sighted off of the Ka'anapali coast, Lahaina Sun, July 18, 1973: 8.

INTERNATIONAL REVENUE SERVICE
— refund checks waiting, Lahaina News, November 26, 1992: 13.

INTERNATIONAL STUDENT EXCHANGE
— seeking volunteer families, Lahaina News, September 6, 1989: 3.

INTERNATIONAL TRANSACTIONAL ANALYSIS ASSOCIATION CONFERENCE
— to be held, Lahaina News, January 21, 1999: 11.

INTERNATIONAL YEAR OF PEACE
— celebrated at Kamehameha III School, Lahaina News, December 3, 1986: 3.

INTERNET
— increased importance of, Lahaina News, June 27, 1996: 13,18.
— Kapalua Resort opens store on, Lahaina News, March 12, 1998: 11.
— WebNow.com offering seminar on, Lahaina News, April 22, 1999: 11.
— Hawaii Office of Consumer Protection warns of scams, Lahaina News, October 4, 2001: 2.
— CalendarMaui.com website launched, Lahaina News, October 18, 2001: 9.
— calendarmaui.com seeking events for website, Lahaina News, April 11, 2002: 2.

INTERNET HAWAII [BUSINESS]
— offering free online advertising, Lahaina News, November 14, 1996: 9.

INTERNMENT
— editorial supporting apology for Japanese, Lahaina News, August 3, 1988: 4.

INTERTRIBAL COUNCIL OF HAWAII
— to hold Maui Powwow, Lahaina News, May 22, 1997: 17.
— to hold Maui Powwow, Lahaina News, May 29, 1997: 16.
— to hold Maui Powwow, Lahaina News, June 4, 1998: 9.
— Hawaii-Maui Chapter to hold Powwow, Lahaina News, October 19, 2000: 20.
— to hold Powwow, Lahaina News, May 9, 2002: 16.

INTO THE WOODS [MUSICAL]
— to be performed, Lahaina News, February 6, 1991: 8,9.
— to open, Lahaina News, February 13, 1991: 9.
— to include optional dinner, Lahaina News, February 20, 1991: 9.
— dinner special to end, Lahaina News, February 27, 1991: 8,9.
— two nights remaining, Lahaina News, March 6, 1991: 11.

INU INU LOUNGE [BUSINESS]
— to feature big band music, Lahaina News, December 17, 1986: 2,12.
— renovated, Lahaina News, March 6, 1991: 14.
— music at Maui Inter-Continental Hotel, Lahaina News, January 23, 1992: 20.
— see also Maui Inter-Continental Wailea

INVESTMENT
— see business

INVESTORS CHOICE INTERNATIONAL EQUITY CAPITAL CONFERENCE
— to be held at The Westin Maui, Lahaina News, April 12, 2001: 9.

I'O [RESTAURANT]
— opens, Lahaina News, November 12, 1998: 13.
— featured, Lahaina News, July 1, 1999: 5.
— offering kama'aina special, Lahaina News, September 12, 2002: 9.

'IOLANI PALACE
— described, Lahaina News, August 1, 1983: 7,8,9.

IONA, CHARLES
— police officer to speak on alcohol and driving at West Maui Youth Center, Lahaina News, May 25, 1995: 4.

IONA CONTEMPORARY DANCE THEATRE
— to perform, Lahaina News, December 14, 1995: 15.
— to stage "Destiny", Lahaina News, June 6, 2002: 16.

IONGI, MELE
— wins tennis title, Lahaina News, July 3, 2003: 13.

IRELAND, JILL [ARTIST]
— leading workshop on acrylic painting, Lahaina News, October 29, 1998: 26.
— to give workshop on "Secrets of Acrylic Painting", Lahaina News, January 14, 1999: 13.
— wins Lahaina Poster Contest, Lahaina News, August 19, 1999: 1.
— wins Lahaina Poster Contest with "Endless Lahaina Summer", Lahaina News, August 26, 1999: 14.
— to offer courses with Art School at Kapalua, Lahaina News, February 24, 2000: 9.
— to offer acrylics painting workshop, Lahaina News, April 27, 2000: 13.
— to offer workshop on acrylic painting, Lahaina News, December 7, 2000: 24.

IRIS, NICKOLAS [MUSICIAN]
— to perform at Stella Blues Café and Deli, Lahaina News, July 8, 1993: 12.

IRONS, ANDY
— surfs at Honolua Bay, Lahaina News, February 17, 2000: 1.
— surfer wins Xbox Pipeline Masters at the Banzai Pipeline, Lahaina News, December 26, 2002: 11.

IRONS, RICK
— surfer's life discussed, Lahaina News, February 22, 1984: 6.

IRS
— see Internal Revenue Service (IRS)

IRVINE, BO [COMEDIAN]
— to perform at Comedy Club, Lahaina News, September 26, 1991: 12.
— to perform at the Sports Page for New Year's Eve, Lahaina News, January 2, 1992: 12.

IRWIN, GROVER
— named commission of Region 892 for American Youth Soccer Organization (AYSO), Lahaina News, April 16, 1998: 7.
— Regional Commissioner Grover Irwin featured, Lahaina News, August 13, 1998: 14.

IRWIN, HALE
— golfer returning to play in Kapalua International Championship, Lahaina News, June 20, 1984: 4.
— Kapalua golf pro wins U.S. Open, Lahaina News, June 27, 1990: 7.
— golfer to play at Isuzu Kapalua International, Lahaina News, October 17, 1990: 9.
— wins Ka'anapali Classic, Lahaina News, October 23, 1997: 8.
— to play in EMC Ka'anapali Classic, Lahaina News, September 23, 1999: 7.
— golfer wins Ka'anapali Classic, Lahaina News, October 26, 2000: 1.

IRWIN MORTGAGE [BUSINESS]
— Dora May joins, Lahaina News, March 18, 1999: 13.
— hires Schinook Sheen Nannauck as loan officer, Lahaina News, December 9, 1999: 15.

ISAAC, ANGELA
— joins Bank of Hawaii as executive vice president, Lahaina News, August 9, 2001: 8.

ISAACS, GREGORY [MUSICIAN]
— to perform reggae at Maui Arts and Cultural Center, Lahaina News, October 10, 1996: 16.

ISAAK, CHRIS [MUSICIAN]
— to perform at Maui Arts and Cultural Center, Lahaina News, February 11, 1999: 17.

ISBELL, ALAN
— appointed editor of Mauian Magazine, Lahaina News, October 8, 1986: 3.

ISECKE, CONRAD
— chosen as vice chairman for Maui ACLU, Lahaina Sun, January 13, 1971: 6.

ISEKE, WARREN
— names Senate page for Hiram Fong, Lahaina Sun, May 9, 1973: 7.

ISELIN, JOAN
— promoted to principal broker at Kapalua Land Company, Ltd., Lahaina News, July 11, 1991: 6.
— realtor recognized, Lahaina News, October 13, 1994: 15.

ISHAYAS ASCENSION
— course to be offered, Lahaina News, January 9, 1997: 10.

ISHII, IVAN
— participated in Maui Youth Council, Lahaina Sun, January 13, 1971: 5.

ISHIKAWA, TOSHIO
— appointed as Maui County deputy planning director, Lahaina Sun, June 2, 1971: 2.

ISLAM
— lecture on "Message from the Land of Rumi" to be held, Lahaina News, September 4, 2003: 16.

ISLAND AIR [BUSINESS]
— offering ohana travel package, Lahaina News, October 21, 1993: 11.
— increases routes, Lahaina News, August 3, 1995: 8.
— hoping to secure standard hours at Kapalua-West Maui Airport, Lahaina News, March 6, 1997: 1.
— to begin flights from Kona to Kapalua-West Maui airport, Lahaina News, September 3, 1998: 11.
— inaugurates direct service between Kapalua-West Maui Airport and Kona and Kona-Lana'i, Lahaina News, September 10, 1998: 11.
— to change hours of flight operations at Kapalua-West Maui Airport, Lahaina News, March 2, 2000: 3.
— no objections to schedule changes at public meeting, Lahaina News, March 16, 2000: 1,5.
— adds flight to Kapalua-West Maui Airport, Lahaina News, December 5, 2002: 8.
— see also Aloha Island Air [business]

ISLAND ART, POTTERY AND FRAME SHOP [BUSINESS]
— to open, Lahaina News, June 19, 2003: 8.

ISLAND BIKER, THE [BUSINESS]
— sponsoring mountain bike race, Lahaina News, January 9, 1992: 7.

ISLAND CARD SHOP [BUSINESS]
— purchased by Robert Larkin and Randall Love, Lahaina News, June 1, 1988: 19.

ISLAND COLLECTION, THE [BUSINESS]
— opens in Kihei, Lahaina News, May 23, 1991: 8.

ISLAND DESIGN CENTER [BUSINESS]
— featured, Lahaina News, April 18, 2002: 7.

ISLAND DODGE [BUSINESS]
— appoints Jim Wheeler as general sales manager, Lahaina News, March 7, 1996: 11.
— supporting Maui Food Bank's "Food Drive 2000", Lahaina News, November 16, 2000: 12.

ISLAND FISH HOUSE [RESTAURANT]
— opens following renovations, Lahaina News, December 19, 1991: 13.

ISLAND GECKO MAUI [BUSINESS]
— t-shirt business featured, Lahaina News, December 5, 1984: 22.
— to relocate to California, Lahaina News, April 22, 1987: 10.

ISLAND GLARE [MUSICAL GROUP]
— to perform at the Royal Ocean Terrace at the Royal Lahaina Resort, Lahaina News, February 20, 1991: 10.
— continues to perform at Royal Lahaina Resort, Lahaina News, April 3, 1991: 7.
— continues to perform at Royal Ocean Terrace at Royal Lahaina Resort, Lahaina News, April 24, 1991: 10.

ISLAND GROWS FESTIVAL
— to be held, Lahaina News, July 25, 2002: 18.

ISLAND HARVEST AND HUKILAU
— to be held, Lahaina News, May 28, 1998: 13.

ISLAND HOLIDAYS
— see Amfac, Royal Lahaina Hotel, Ka'anapali Hotel

ISLAND HONDA [BUSINESS]
— bringing Hondas to West Maui for test driving, Lahaina News, July 11, 1991: 6.

ISLAND IMAGES SALON
— opens new store, Lahaina News, September 28, 1988: 18.

ISLAND KIDS [BUSINESS]
— opens, Lahaina News, July 13, 1988: 2.

ISLAND LESBIAN CONNECTION
— to hold Valentine's Dance, Lahaina News, February 7, 2002: 16.
— to hold "A Happy Valentine's Dance", Lahaina News, February 6, 2003: 16.

ISLAND LIFE 101
— class to be held by Jill Engledow, Lahaina News, July 24, 2003: 2.

ISLAND LIVING [BUSINESS]
— to feature art and culture products, Lahaina News, May 16, 1984: 7.

ISLAND LOCK AND KEY [BUSINESS]
— featured, Lahaina News, November 16, 1983: 14.
— expands, Lahaina News, September 13, 1989: 6.
— now affiliated with the American Automobile Association, Lahaina News, December 31, 1992: 10.

ISLAND MAIL SERVICE CENTERS [BUSINESS]
— to open at Lahaina Square, Lahaina News, February 6, 1991: 6.

ISLAND MARINE ACTIVITIES [BUSINESS]
— to begin "Beachcomber Party Dinner Cruise", Lahaina News, February 16, 1995: 15.
— names Kris Hunter as director of research and education, Lahaina News, January 14, 1999: 11.
— appoints Joseph Mobley as research and education director, Lahaina News, October 21, 1999: 13.
— resumes Lahaina Princess Barefoot Dinner Cruises, Lahaina News, June 26, 2003: 14.

ISLAND MARINE INSTITUTE
— offering humpback whale naturalist course, Lahaina News, December 2, 1999: 6.
— offering whale watching tours, Lahaina News, December 26, 2002: 8.

ISLAND MORTGAGE CORPORATION [BUSINESS]
— changes name to Maui Island Mortgage, Lahaina News, December 12, 1991: 17.
— Jeff Reiss joins, Lahaina News, May 21, 1992: 9.
— Sam Rowe named president of, Lahaina News, December 30, 1993: 5.

ISLAND MUUMUU WORKS [BUSINESS]
— opens third store, Lahaina News, February 11, 1987: 11.

ISLAND POSSE [MUSICAL GROUP]
— to perform at World Café, Lahaina News, June 6, 1996: 15.

ISLAND PRINCESS [SHIP]
— to arrive in Lahaina Harbor, Lahaina News, November 21, 1991: 11.

ISLAND PROPERTY MANAGEMENT
— selected to provide fiscal management to Honokowai Sunrise Association of Apartment Owners, Lahaina News, September 16, 1993: 9.

ISLAND QUINTET [MUSICAL GROUP]
— to perform with pianist Grant Mack, Lahaina News, May 5, 1994: 16.

ISLAND SCUBA, INC. [BUSINESS]
— opens at Hyatt Regency, Lahaina News, December 13, 1989: 7.
— collects trash from the beach and reefs of Ka'anapali, Lahaina News, December 13, 2001: 8.

ISLAND SOAP AND CANDLE WORKS [BUSINESS]
— opens at Ma'alaea Harbor Village Shops, Lahaina News, October 26, 2000: 20.
— opens in Whalers Village, Lahaina News, November 15, 2001: 8.

ISLAND, THE
— gated golf course community, to be completed, Lahaina News, January 25, 2001: 13.
— gated golf course community holds grand opening, Lahaina News, June 14, 2001: 7.
— development featured, Lahaina News, February 7, 2002: 7.
— real estate development featured, Lahaina News, May 16, 2002: 7.
— development featured, Lahaina News, July 11, 2002: 7.

ISLAND TOGS WOMEN'S APPAREL
— opening in Whaler's Village, Lahaina Sun, November 25, 1970: 3.

ISLANDAIR [BUSINESS]
— increasing flights to West Maui, Lahaina News, March 31, 1994: 1.
— lowers fares to Moloka'i, Lahaina News, November 17, 1994: 10.

ISLANDERS, THE [MUSICAL GROUP]
— to perform at Moose McGillycuddy's, Lahaina News, July 18, 1996: 12.

ISLEN, JOAN
— receives certified residential specialist (CRS) designation, Lahaina News, February 3, 1994: 7.

ISLEN, KEITH
— selected top producer by Coldwell Banker McCormack Real Estate, Lahaina News, April 4, 1990: 6.

ISOBE, CHERLY
— names merchandising manager from POI stores, Lahaina News, January 21, 1993: 8.

ISOLATION PLANNING COMMITTEE, LAHAINA/WEST MAUI
— see Lahaina/West Maui Isolation Planning Committee

ISOM, MARIE ANNETTE [WRITER]
— author of "ADD/ADHD A Parent's Practical Guide to Attention Deficit Disorders" to visit Borders Books, Lahaina News, August 29, 2002: 20.

ISRAEL, PETER [MUSICIAN]
— to perform at Greek Zorba, Lahaina News, May 25, 1995: 12.

ISSACS, LEONARD
— life of guest at Ritz-Carlton saved by employees, Lahaina News, October 11, 2001: 1,20.

ISUZU-KAPALUA INTERNATIONAL
— results of golf tournament, Lahaina News, September 17, 1986: 4.
— golf tournament held, Lahaina News, November 12, 1986: 1,6.
— golf tournament won by Andy Bean, Lahaina News, November 19, 1986: 6,7.
— golf tournament detailed, Lahaina News, November 2, 1988: 5.
— proceeds given to Cameron Center, Lahaina News, March 29, 1989: 3.
— to be held, Lahaina News, October 18, 1989: 5.
— to be held, Lahaina News, October 25, 1989: 11.
— golf tournament begins Sunday, Lahaina News, November 1, 1989: 24.
— professional portion to begin, Lahaina News, November 8, 1989: 24.
— team announced, Lahaina News, August 1, 1990: 14.
— to be held in November, Lahaina News, October 10, 1990: 18.
— to be held at Bay Course at the Kapalua Resort, Lahaina News, October 17, 1990: 9.
— scheduled, Lahaina News, October 31, 1990: 9.
— to be held this week, Lahaina News, November 7, 1990: 14.
— see also Kapalua International Golf Tournament

ITAL ROOTS REGGAE [MUSICAL GROUP]
— to perform at World Cafe, Lahaina News, January 25, 1996: 14.

ITALIAN AMERICAN CLUB OF MAUI
— forming, Lahaina News, August 3, 1995: 4.
— officers elected, Lahaina News, August 17, 1995: 4.
— to meet, Lahaina News, January 6, 2000: 13.
— to meet, Lahaina News, March 9, 2000: 12.

ITO, ALISON
— announces changes to Kahului Airport Shuttle schedule, Lahaina News, February 16, 1995: 12.

ITO, ALVIN
— writes Landlord-Tenant Handbook, Lahaina News, August 20, 1998: 13.

ITO, SUNAO
— investigation of murder of, Lahaina Sun, May 19, 1971: 6.
— murder investigation continues, Lahaina Sun, May 26, 1971: 8.
— investigation of murder continues, Lahaina Sun, June 9, 1971: 2.

ITT SHERATON CORPORATION
— to manage Hotel Hana-Maui, Lahaina News, May 30, 1990: 6.
— partnering with Nansay International, Lahaina News, November 14, 1990: 13.

IVEY, GARNER
— elected zone chairman with the Kihei Community Association, Lahaina Sun, December 2, 1970: 4.
— Alexander & Baldwin property manager named Maui United Way campaign chairman, Lahaina News, July 2, 1986: 18.

IVEY, HELEN
— honored for volunteer efforts, Lahaina News, May 28, 1992: 7.

IWASAKI, NEIL
— Burger King employee wins Excellence in Management Award, Lahaina News, November 18, 1999: 14.

IWATAKE, YUKIYO
— named principal of King Kamehameha III Elementary School, Lahaina News, September 5, 1990: 3.

IWI
— see human remains

IYAMA, TAKESHI
— forms solar technology partnership with Jason Schwartz, Lahaina News, June 9, 1994: 12.

J

J. WALTER CAMERON CENTER
— planned rehabilitation facility seeking bids for construction, Lahaina Sun, September 1, 1971: 11.
— financing okayed, Lahaina Sun, December 8, 1971: 17.
— creation described, Lahaina Sun, November 15, 1972: 6,7.
— completed, Lahaina Sun, February 28, 1973: 10.
— now open, Lahaina Sun, March 21, 1973: 4.
— dedication ceremony conducted by Douglas Sodetani, Lahaina Sun, May 2, 1973: 10.
— Audrey Rocha Reed named new executive director, Lahaina News, May 15, 1982: 2.
— receives grant from Isuzu Kapalua International golf tournament, Lahaina News, March 16, 1988: 14.
— now accepting nominations for "outstanding executive director", Lahaina News, May 14, 1998: 7.
— receives funds from Isuzu Kapalua International, Lahaina News, March 29, 1989: 3.
— to hold bazaar, Lahaina News, August 17, 2000: 16.
— to hold bazaar, Lahaina News, August 15, 2002: 9.
— to hold bazaar, Lahaina News, August 14, 2003: 14.

J.C. PENNY [BUSINESS]
— Ace Hardware to be catalog center for, Lahaina News, March 20, 2003: 8.

J.J. ENTERPRISES [BUSINESS]
— appoints Dick Hoag as sales manager, Lahaina News, March 12, 1986: 3.
— hires Ron Morin as sales representative, Lahaina News, April 2, 1986: 3.
— awarded contract for restaurants owned by Alan Ong, Lahaina News, July 2, 1986: 3.
— becomes advertising agent for Cashback Tours, Lahaina News, March 4, 1987: 10.

J.J.'S BEACH GRILL [RESTAURANT]
— opens at 505 Front Street, Lahaina News, February 20, 1991: 7.
— to hold benefit for military couples, Lahaina News, March 27, 1991: 15.
— reviewed, Lahaina News, April 3, 1991: 6.
— raises money to bring military couples to Maui for weddings, Lahaina News, April 17, 1991: 3.
— adds new entrees, Lahaina News, June 18, 1992: 21.

J.R. MUSIC SHOP [BUSINESS]
— expands to Maui, Lahaina News, November 22, 1989: 5.

J&F MUSIC
— opens, Lahaina News, May 18, 1988: 18.

JABOOKA JUICE [RESTAURANT]
— opens, Lahaina News, December 18, 1997: 11.

JACINTO, CASSIE
— Scholar/Athlete of the Week, Lahaina News, April 19, 2001: 12.

JACINTO, TARA
— Lahainaluna High School volleyball coach discusses prospects, Lahaina News, November 14, 1991: 5,6.

JACK CROSS REALTY
— opening in Whaler's Village, Lahaina Sun, November 25, 1970: 3.

JACK HANNA'S ANIMAL ADVENTURES [TELEVISION SHOW]
— taping at Whalers Village Center Stage, Lahaina News, February 24, 2000: 14.

JACK IN THE BOX [RESTAURANT]
— first neighbor island restaurant to open in Kahului, Lahaina News, February 8, 1984: 16.

— opens in Lahaina, Lahaina News, August 20, 1986: 8.
— sponsoring Reindeer Run and Walk, Lahaina News, December 1, 1994: 9.

JACK KELLEY MEMORIAL GOLF TOURNAMENT
— results of, Lahaina News, October 22, 1998: 16.
— held, Lahaina News, September 23, 1999: 10.
— to be held by Whalers Realty to benefit St. Francis Medical Center, Lahaina News, October 19, 2000: 14.
— won by threesome from Sullivan Properties, Lahaina News, October 26, 2000: 12.
— raises money for Saint Francis Medical Center, Lahaina News, February 8, 2001: 7.

JACK MILLAR MEMORIAL SCHOLARSHIP
— received by Patrick Kamaheiwa Ross, Lahaina News, August 9, 1989: 3.

JACK MILLER AND THE BIG I BAND [MUSICAL GROUP]
— to perform at Casanova's, Lahaina News, April 17, 1991: 17.

JACK'S FAMOUS BAGELS [RESTAURANT]
— opens at West Maui Center, Lahaina News, January 1, 1998: 7.
— to hold grand opening, Lahaina News, February 12, 1998: 16.
— celebrates grand opening, Lahaina News, February 19, 1998: 3.
— changes name to Lahaina Bagel Caffe, Lahaina News, April 15, 1999: 11.

JACKSON, CAROLE
— coaching for Lahaina Swim Club, Lahaina News, July 18, 1996: 11.

JACKSON, JAMES WESLEY [COMEDIAN]
— to perform at Comedy Club, Lahaina News, September 30, 1993: 12.

JACKSON, JOHN
— promoted to senior vice president and general manager of Kahului Trucking and Storage, Inc., Lahaina News, March 6, 1991: 9.

JACKSON, JOHNNY "BANG-BANG"
— planning "Boxing Bonanza", Lahaina News, April 5, 2001: 14.

JACKSON, MARK
— joins Maui Pacific Realty Partners, Inc., Lahaina News, March 14, 1996: 10.

JACKSON, TIM
— awarded associate of the month by Maui Marriott, Lahaina News, March 12, 1992: 13.

JACOB NEIZMAN MEMORIAL GOLF TOURNAMENT
— to be held at Royal Ka'anapali North Course, Lahaina News, July 27, 1988: 3,11.

JACOBSEN, PETER
— golfer to play at Isuzu Kapalua International, Lahaina News, October 17, 1990: 9.

JACOBSON, JAKE
— comments on proposed thrillcraft corridor, Lahaina News, February 24, 1988: 1.

JACQUELINE'S ROMANCE [BUSINESS]
— to open, Lahaina News, February 17, 1994: 6.

JACQUES COUSTEAU, THE FIRST 75 YEARS [FILM]
— to be shown at Wailea, Lahaina News, March 18, 1987: 3.

JAFFE, MARC [COMEDIAN]
— to perform at Comedy Club and the Sports Page, Lahaina News, March 5, 1992: 14.

JAHNER, RICHARD
— to pay fine to state Contractors License Board, Lahaina News, March 19, 1992: 11.

J'AI ETE AU BAL (I WENT TO THE DANCE) YUM YUM YUM [FILM]
— to be shown at Maui Arts and Cultural Center, Lahaina News, May 9, 1996: 14.

JAKEWAY, LEE
— hired by Hawaiian Commercial and Sugar Co. as project engineer, Lahaina News, September 2, 1999: 13.

JAKOBSEN, CHRISTIAN
— owner of Erik's Seafood Grotto featured, Lahaina News, November 6, 1997: 6,7.
— executive chef of Erik's Seafood Grotto featured, Lahaina News, February 7, 2002: 5.
— executive chef discusses the relocation of Erik's Seafood Grotto, Lahaina News, October 10, 2002: 1,20.

JAKOBSEN, ERIK
— killed in automobile accident, Lahaina News, May 19, 1994: 3,5.

JAMBA JUICE [BUSINESS]
— collecting donations for American Cnacer Society with "Free Smoothie Morning", Lahaina News, April 18, 2002: 16.
— names managers, Lahaina News, February 27, 2003: 8.
— to open store in Lahaina, Lahaina News, March 20, 2003: 8.

JAMES AND THE GIANT PEACH [PLAY]
— to be performed as part of Maui Academy of Performing Arts' children's summer program, Lahaina News, July 16, 1998: 17.

JAMES, BONEY [MUSICIAN]
— to perform at Maui Music Festival, Lahaina News, May 7, 1998: 21.

JAMES CAMPBELL, ESTATE OF
— see Campbell, Estate of James

JAMES COLLINS BLUES BAND [MUSICAL GROUP]
— performs at World Café, Lahaina News, January 18, 1996: 12.
— to perform at World Café, Lahaina News, March 21, 1996: 12.

JAMES, GEORGE [ARTIST]
— to lead watercolor workshop, Lahaina News, May 30, 2002: 14.

JAMES, GLENN
— Pacific Disaster Center meteorologist featured, Lahaina News, July 5, 2001: 18.

JAMES, HELEN
— talk on fossilized extinct flightless birds, Lahaina News, March 23, 1988: 14.

JAMES MANNESS MEMORIAL
— to be held, Lahaina News, August 29, 1990: 4.
— Dance Marathon to be held, Lahaina News, September 12, 1991: 5.
— Dance Marathon to be held by Maui AIDS Foundation, Lahaina News, January 23, 1992: 5.
— results of Dance Marathon, Lahaina News, March 11, 1993: 15.
— "Dance Party Xtreme" to be held to support Maui AIDS Foundation, Lahaina News, March 19, 1998: 2.
— "Dance Party Xtreme" to be held by Maui AIDS Foundation, Lahaina News, February 24, 2000: 3.

JAMES, ROBERT [WRITER]
— to sign book "What Is This Called Aloha", Lahaina News, February 6, 2003: 16.

JAMES, WHITE AND ASSOCIATES CPAS, INC. [BUSINESS]
— relocates, Lahaina News, December 9, 1999: 15.

JAMES-PALMER, ROBERT KAKA'IMUA [WRITER]
— to autograph his "Maui Organic Growing Guide", Lahaina News, July 22, 1987: 3.

JAMESON'S GRILL AND BAR [RESTAURANT]
— opens, Lahaina News, May 2, 1996: 14.
— featured, Lahaina News, June 6, 1996: 7,9.
— opens, Lahaina News, October 30, 1997: 14.
— celebrating second anniversary, Lahaina News, April 30, 1998: 16.
— to hold golf tournament, Lahaina News, May 21, 1998: 15.
— wins "Best of the Award of Excellence" from Wine Spectator Magazine, Lahaina News, November 19, 1998: 13.

— to hold Winemaker's Dinner, Lahaina News, December 10, 1998: 20.
— opens new location in Maui Coast Hotel, Lahaina News, February 4, 1999: 13.
— to host magician Jordan Hahn, Lahaina News, May 11, 2000: 20.
— featured, Lahaina News, September 7, 2000: 6.

JAN AND THE ALOHA BAND
— alleged to have canceled concerts in Lahaina, Lahaina Times, August 20, 1983 volume 7 number 8: 1.

JANCKS, CHARLIE
— director of County Department of Public works and Waste Management discusses attempt to extend Dickenson Street, Lahaina News, July 27, 2000: 1,17.
— leaving position as director of Public Works and Waste Management, Lahaina News, August 31, 2000: 17.

JANE, MARTHA [COMEDIAN]
— to perform at Comedy Club, Lahaina News, August 12, 1993: 12.
— to perform at Honolulu Comedy Club, Lahaina News, October 20, 1994: 16.

JANES, LIZ [WRITER]
— to speak to the American Association of University Women, Lahaina News, March 23, 2000: 12.

JANI, LOIS
— to lead Condo Owners Forum hosted by Condominium Council of Maui, Lahaina News, June 12, 2003: 7.

JANIS, HARVEY
— wins Camera Club Council of Hawaii photo contest, Lahaina News, October 21, 1993: 8.

JANKLOWICZ, GILAD "GILL"
— to emcee Ka'anapali Aerobic Beauty Contest, Lahaina News, September 14, 1988: 11.
— star of ESPN aerobics show "Bodies in Motion" to teach at Lahaina Nautilus Center, Lahaina News, February 10, 1994: 11.

JANSSENS, GLEN
— appointed director of production services at Media Systems, Lahaina News, January 23, 1992: 12.

JAPAN
— films produced by Billy Graham on, shown in Lahaina and Kihei, Lahaina Sun, November 11, 1970: 2.
— visit described, Lahaina Sun, August 4, 1971: 9.
— high school students from visit Lahainaluna High School, Lahaina Sun, August 11, 1971: 3.
— Japanese businessmen to meet with Maui businessmen, Lahaina Sun, July 18, 1973: 6.
— rewriting history, Lahaina News, August 15, 1982: 10.
— royalty visit Maui, Lahaina News, June 26, 1985: 1,9.
— visit from royalty a top story in 1985, Lahaina News, January 8, 1986: 1.
— arts and cultural traditions featured on KHET-Channel 11, Lahaina News, September 20, 1989: 8.
— Hawaiian Airlines awarded passenger and cargo service between Honolulu and Fukuoka, Lahaina News, October 24, 1990: 7.
— non-credit class to be offered, Lahaina News, April 17, 1991: 9.
— Hawaiian Airlines begins service to Fukuoka, Lahaina News, May 23, 1991: 8.
— economic issues expected to result in reduced building activity in Maui, Lahaina News, May 21, 1992: 8.
— Na Kamali'i Nani O Lahaina Hula Halau to perform at Beach Festival and Parade at Atami, Lahaina News, August 31, 1995: 4.
— Hachioji Kuruma Ningyo and Shinnai to perform with puppets and narrative song, Lahaina News, October 3, 2002: 16.

JAPAN AIR LINES [BUSINESS]
— establishes office at Kahului Airport, Lahaina News, December 5, 1990: 4.

JAPAN GALLERY [BUSINESS]
— sponsoring Haru Endo demonstrating flower arranging, Lahaina News, October 12, 1988: 3.

JAPAN GRAND PRIX OF HAWAII, LTD. [BUSINESS]
— proposes golf course in Makena, Lahaina News, September 3, 1992: 13.
— proposes golf course in Makena, Lahaina News, September 23, 1993: 6.

JAPAN KARATE ASSOCIATION-HAWAII
— holds holiday tournament, Lahaina News, December 23, 1993: 9.

JAPAN-AMERICAN SOCIETY OF HAWAII
— to hold social event at Four Seasons Resort in Wailea, Lahaina News, June 11, 1992: 8.

JAPAN-HAWAII ASSOCIATION
— members hosted at Maui Beach Hotel, Lahaina Sun, December 1, 1971: 13.

JAPAN-HAWAII ECONOMIC COUNCIL
— Walter Dods Jr. named Hawaii chairman, Lahaina News, November 1, 1989: 8.

JAPANESE AIR TRAVEL ASSOCIATION
— members invited to join Mayor Cravalho on promotional trip to Far East, Lahaina Sun, January 6, 1971: 1.

JAPANESE CULTURAL DAY
— to be held, Lahaina News, April 30, 1992: 4.

JAPANESE CULTURAL SOCIETY OF MAUI
— sponsoring koto and shakuhachi concert, Lahaina News, May 21, 1986: 3.
— sponsoring luncheon to benefit Maui Community Arts and Cultural Center, Lahaina News, February 25, 1987: 6.
— to hold Shinnen Enkai festival, Lahaina News, January 23, 1992: 5.
— to host New Year's celebration at Maui Beach Hotel, Lahaina News, January 14, 1993: 15.
— to install new officers, Lahaina News, June 10, 1999: 17.
— to host presentation on Otsuki-Mi, Lahaina News, September 9, 1999: 12.
— to hold Nihon Bunka 30th anniversary dinner, Lahaina News, October 14, 1999: 12.
— to hold "Shinnen Enkai 2001", Lahaina News, February 1, 2001: 20.
— to hold kimono fashion show, Lahaina News, June 14, 2001: 21.
— to present "Nihon Bunka" awards, Lahaina News, November 28, 2002: 5.

JAPANESE KARAOKE SPRING FESTIVAL
— to be held by Bernice Inouye Music Studio, Lahaina News, April 4, 2002: 16.

JARREAU, AL [MUSICIAN]
— performance reviewed, Lahaina News, October 10, 1984: 17.
— to perform at Maui Arts and Cultural Center, Lahaina News, September 2, 1999: 17.
— to perform at Maui Arts and Cultural Center, Lahaina News, September 23, 1999: 13.

JARVIS, BIRNEY
— moves to Lahaina, Lahaina Sun, January 5, 1972: 18.
— joins Lahaina Sun, Lahaina Sun, January 19, 1972: 6.
— surfing experience described, Lahaina Sun, April 5, 1972: 7.

JARVIS, JANE [MUSICIAN]
— to accompany performance of "The Devil is a Woman" , Lahaina News, March 7, 1990: 13.

JARVIS, ROBERT [ARTIST]
— works displayed at Larry Dotson Gallery, Lahaina News, February 17, 1988: 18.

JASTRAM, SONTRA OLDFIELD [ARTIST]
— exhibit at Ka'anapali Beach Hotel, Lahaina Sun, December 30, 1970: 7.

JAVA JAZZ [RESTAURANT]
— featured, Lahaina News, March 20, 2003: 14.

JAVA LIVING [BUSINESS]
— to open at Limahana Place, Lahaina News, April 24, 2003: 9.
— expanding, Lahaina News, October 2, 2003: 9.

JAWS MAUI [BOOK]
— published, Lahaina News, August 21, 1997: 15.

JAXON-BEAR ELI
— to hold training sessions on freedom and human potential, Lahaina News, May 26, 1994: 16.

JAYCEES
— selling huli huli chicken as fundraiser, Lahaina Sun, December 2, 1970: 3.
— organize Sweetheart Banquet at Coconut Grove restaurant, Lahaina Sun, February 10, 1971: 6.
— planning carnival in Lahaina, Lahaina Sun, July 7, 1971: 1.
— carnival planned, Lahaina Sun, July 7, 1971: 1.
— Maui Carnival this weekend, Lahaina Sun, July 14, 1971: 5.
— District Fair planned, Lahaina Sun, August 4, 1971: 10.
— hold blood drive, Lahaina Sun, September 22, 1971: 15.
— Reverend Lewis Fry installed as president of Lahaina Jaycees, Lahaina Sun, September 29, 1971: 12.
— offer prize for best decorated house, Lahaina Sun, December 22, 1971: 4.
— lacking new members, Lahaina Sun, March 8, 1972: 8.
— to hold carnival, Lahaina Sun, July 11, 1973: 4.
— Carnival to be held at Kahului Fairgrounds, Lahaina News, June 18, 1986: 3.
— Carnival set for July 27th, Lahaina News, July 16, 1986: 3.
— Carnival to be held at the Kahului Fairgrounds, Lahaina News, July 13, 1988: 3.
— Carnival details, Lahaina News, July 20, 1988: 20.
— seeking participants for carnival, Lahaina News, May 24, 1989: 2.
— Carnival to be held, Lahaina News, May 24, 1989: 2.
— Carnival to be held at War Memorial Complex, Lahaina News, June 28, 1989: 3.
— Carnival to include demonstration of glass repair techniques, Lahaina News, July 19, 1989: 2.
— carnival to be held, Lahaina News, July 11, 1990: 15.
— Carnival to be held, Lahaina News, July 11, 1990: 15.
— Carnival to be held in July, Lahaina News, June 13, 1991: 14.
— Carnival to be held in July, Lahaina News, June 20, 1991: 12.
— 32nd annual Carnival to be held, Lahaina News, June 27, 1991: 13.
— details of 32nd annual Carnival, Lahaina News, July 11, 1991: 17.
— Carnival to be held this weekend, Lahaina News, July 18, 1991: 12.
— co-hosting carnival in Kihei, Lahaina News, March 12, 1992: 4,5.
— planning carnival, Lahaina News, May 28, 1992: 9.
— booth space available for carnival, Lahaina News, June 24, 1993: 4.
— Carnival planned, Lahaina News, July 11, 1996: 13.
— sponsoring free summer concert, Lahaina News, June 26, 1997: 16.
— Summer Jam to be held, Lahaina News, June 4, 1998: 16.
— Summer Jam to feature 'Ale'a and Pure Heart, Lahaina News, June 24, 1999: 12.
— Jaycee Summer Jam to be held, Lahaina News, June 22, 2000: 16.
— "Hawaii Jaycees Jam" to be held, Lahaina News, June 14, 2001: 21.
— Hawaii Jaycees Jam fundraiser to be held, Lahaina News, June 21, 2001: 16.
— Hawaii Jaycees Jam concert to be held, Lahaina News, July 18, 2002: 16.
— Hawaii Jaycees Jam to be held, Lahaina News, July 10, 2003: 16.
— to hold Hawaii Jaycees Jam at Maui Arts and Cultural Center, Lahaina News, July 10, 2003: 16.

JAZZ EVENING WITH THE BOBBY WATSON QUINTET, A
— to be held at Maui Arts and Cultural, Lahaina News, September 20, 2001: 16.

JAZZ ON THE BEACH
— hosted by KPOA radio station, Lahaina News, September 29, 1994: 11,12.
— continues, Lahaina News, November 3, 1994: 27.

JAZZERCISE
— organizes fundraiser for West Maui Youth Center, Lahaina News, February 15, 1984: 5.

JAZZERIE CLUB
— "Soulmates" musical to be performed at, Lahaina News, May 15, 2003: 16.

JBA PRINTING AND PROMOTIONS [BUSINESS]
— to close, Lahaina News, December 12, 2002: 8.

JCB
— signs agreement with First Hawaiian Bank, Lahaina News, October 10, 1990: 12.

JDH AND ASSOCIATES [BUSINESS]
— has lost money on Holo Honokowai apartments, Lahaina News, September 14, 1988: 1,14.
— opposed by Maui County Council and Mayor Hannibal Tavares on converting Holo Honokowai to hotel, Lahaina News, December 21, 1988: 1.
— abandons plan to make long-term rentals profitable, Lahaina News, January 4, 1989: 1.
— apply to convert Maui Park apartment to condominiums, Lahaina News, February 14, 1990: 5.

JDI LIMITED PARTNERS [BUSINESS]
— seeking to replace existing Harbor Village with new structure, Lahaina News, January 11, 2001: 1,15.
— proposing Harbor Village shopping complex, Lahaina News, June 7, 2001: 1,9.

JEFFERSON AIRPLANE
— see Jefferson Starship, The [musical group]

JEFFERSON STARSHIP, THE [MUSICAL GROUP]
— to perform at the Lahaina Civic Center, Lahaina News, October 31, 1984: 17.
— to play on Maui, Lahaina News, April 16, 1986: 8.
— cancels show, Lahaina News, April 30, 1986: 8.
— to perform at Maui Marriott Ballroom, Lahaina News, March 5, 1992: 14,15.
— featured, Lahaina News, March 12, 1992: 15.
— cancels concert, Lahaina News, March 26, 1992: 10.
— to perform at fundraiser for Eco Art, Lahaina News, April 22, 1993: 15.
— to perform, Lahaina News, April 29, 1993: 10.
— "Volunteers" to perform at Royal Lahaina Tennis Stadium, Lahaina News, April 20, 2000: 17.
— celebrating 35 years, Lahaina News, April 27, 2000: 12.
— to perform at Maui Arts and Cultural Center, Lahaina News, February 22, 2001: 17.

JEFFREY [FILM]
— Two Pumps Up to show, Lahaina News, October 5, 1995: 10.

JEFFREY T. LONG & ASSOCIATES [BUSINESS]
— chosen as architects for Kaʻanapali Hillside project, Lahaina News, September 26, 1984: 14.

JENCKS, BRADFORD
— appointed General Manager of Maui Inter-Continental Wailea, Lahaina News, April 27, 1988: 3.

JENCKS, CHARLES
— awarded Rotarian of the Year, Lahaina News, July 4, 1990: 4.
— appointed deputy director of Public Works, Lahaina News, February 27, 1991: 4.
— to be Director of County Public Works and Waste Management, Lahaina News, January 19, 1995: 4.
— sworn in as director of county Public Works and Waste Management, Lahaina News, February 9, 1995: 3.
— Public Works Director discusses Kaʻanapali Golf Course using treated water, Lahaina News, June 15, 1995: 1.
— public works director meets with community groups, Lahaina News, November 2, 1995: 1,16.
— County Public Works Director updates on Front Street Improvement Project, Lahaina News, April 3, 1997: 1.
— Public Works Director speaks on Front Street improvements, Lahaina News, August 14, 1997: 1.
— new director of land planning and community development at Maui Land and Pineapple Co., Lahaina News, October 12, 2000: 16.
— appointed to board of directors of Maui Chamber of Commerce, Lahaina News, August 2, 2001: 9.

JENKINS, BILL [ARTIST]
— carver offering services, Lahaina News, March 8, 1989: 2.

JENKINS, DAVE [MUSICIAN]
— releases "Cruisin' On Hawaiian Time" with Kapono Beamer, Lahaina News, December 15, 1994: 16.

JENKINS, JEANNETTE
— appointed national sales manager for Ritz-Carlton, Lahaina News, February 3, 1994: 7.

JENKINS, ROBERT [COMEDIAN]
— to perform at Comedy Club and the Sports Page, Lahaina News, September 24, 1992: 14,17.

JENKINS, SCOTT
— wins Hard Rock Cafe Rock 'n Roll 10K run, Lahaina News, June 6, 1996: 16.

JENNINGS, TOM [ARTIST]
— to exhibit at Hui Noʻeau Visual Arts Center, Lahaina News, July 23, 1998: 16.

JENSEN, ROCKY
— to lecture on Hawaiian topics at Maui Prince Hotel, Lahaina News, July 4, 1990: 4.

JENSON, SUSAN BELLE [ARTIST]
— art displayed at Bank of Maui, Lahaina News, October 12, 1988: 20.
— exhibiting at Old Jail Gallery, Lahaina News, December 28, 1988: 13.
— holds "Hoʻolokahi" exhibit with John Aperto, Lahaina News, March 13, 1991: 13.
— to exhibit "Maui Earthworks" at Lahaina Arts Gallery, Lahaina News, April 5, 2001: 20.

JERENE, HELEN [ARTIST]
— teaching workshops, Lahaina News, March 26, 1998: 12.
— to teach watercolor, Lahaina News, March 18, 1999: 17.
— to lead art workshops, Lahaina News, March 25, 1999: 3.

JERNIGAN, TAMMY
— astronaut to speak to Maui Girl Scouts, Lahaina News, August 15, 1991: 3.

JEROME, VANIA LEE
— to teach song classes, Lahaina News, January 3, 2002: 16.

JERONIMO, JOANNA [ARTIST]
— motivational speaker who uses Neuro-Linguistic Programming featured, Lahaina News, July 17, 1985: 1,8.
— to offer workshop on power selling, Lahaina News, February 15, 1989: 3.
— to speak at Lahaina Arts Society, Lahaina News, April 5, 1989: 17.
— reception at Wyland Galleries for, Lahaina News, December 19, 1990: 16.

JERRY BOSER MEMORIAL LONGBOARD CONTEST
— to be held, Lahaina News, May 25, 2000: 9.
— to be held, Lahaina News, May 15, 2003: 12.

JERRY LEWIS MUSCULAR DYSTROPHY TELETHON
— sent to Hawaii for the first time, Lahaina Sun, August 1, 1973: 4.
— Lahaina Square Shopping Center to host mini-telethon in support of muscular dystrophy telethon, Lahaina News, August 15, 1984: 3.
— schedule of performers, Lahaina News, August 29, 1990: 11.
— to be hosted at Lahaina Cannery Mall, Lahaina News, August 29, 1990: 3.
— breaks fundraising record, Lahaina News, September 12, 1990: 1.
— volunteers sought, Lahaina News, August 29, 1991: 3.
— to be held, Lahaina News, September 3, 1992: 4.

JESKE, SUSAN
— Miss USA World visited West Maui, Lahaina News, September 6, 1989: 1.

JET SKIS
— see thrillcrafts

JETS, THE [MUSICAL GROUP]
— to perform at Baldwin Auditorium, Lahaina News, June 17, 1987: 3.

JEWELL, GERI [COMEDIAN]
— to perform at Comedy Club and the Sports Page, Lahaina News, March 27, 1991: 12,14.
— to perform at Comedy Club and the Sports Page, Lahaina News, April 9, 1992: 19.

JEWELRY
— trends in, Lahaina News, December 12, 1990: 13.

JEWELRY PALACE
— opening in Whaler's Village, Lahaina Sun, November 25, 1970: 3.

JEWISH ARTS AND EDUCATION COUNCIL
— hosting Jewish sacred dance, Lahaina News, December 3, 1998: 20.

JEWISH CONGREGATION OF MAUI
— to hold Friday night services at Lahaina Methodist Church, Lahaina News, January 16, 1985: 3.
— hosting open houses, Lahaina News, August 21, 1985: 3.
— open house set for September 7 at Lahaina United Methodist Church Social Hall, Lahaina News, September 4, 1985: 3.
— hold Yom Kippur services at the Maui Marriott, Lahaina News, September 25, 1985: 3.
— opening new gift shop, Lahaina News, November 6, 1985: 3.
— to hold Chanukah Party, Lahaina News, November 20, 1985: 11.
— will hold Chanukah Part and Launiupoko Park, Lahaina News, December 4, 1985: 3.
— will held Shabbat services December 20, Lahaina News, December 18, 1985: 3.
— to hold Shabbat service, Lahaina News, February 19, 1986: 3.
— set to celebrate Purim, Lahaina News, March 26, 1986: 3.
— to hold Friday night service at Wailuku Union Church, Lahaina News, April 2, 1986: 3.
— celebrating Jewish Heritage Week, Lahaina News, May 7, 1986: 3.
— receipt of new Torah celebrated, Lahaina News, June 4, 1986: 3.
— to begin celebration of Rosh Hoshonah, Lahaina News, September 23, 1987: 9.
— to hold Shabbat service, Lahaina News, December 2, 1987: 3.
— to hold Shabbat service, Lahaina News, August 17, 1988: 15.
— to begin Rosh Hashanah, Lahaina News, September 7, 1988: 3.
— "L'Chaim! To Life! A Celebration of Jewish Culture and Creatvity on Maui" to be held, Lahaina News, May 22, 1997: 17.
— to host "Great Shul Gelt Affair", Lahaina News, June 25, 1998: 12.
— to hold Shabbat Services, Lahaina News, March 18, 1999: 16.
— to hold Sabbath Services, Lahaina News, August 23, 2001: 16.

JEWISH OLYMPIAN, THE
— photograph exhibit to be held at Ka'ahumanu Center, Lahaina News, February 26, 1998: 12.

JEZIERNY, GIM LIM
— new vice president of Maui Theatre, Lahaina News, April 10, 2003: 14.

JEZIERNY, TOM
— becomes president of Maui Electric Company, Lahaina News, April 4, 1990: 7.

JGL ENTERPRISES, INC [BUSINESS]
— pulls request for outfall for Napilihau Villages development, Lahaina News, June 10, 1993: 1.
— applies to Maui Planning Commission for zoning change to build townhouses, Lahaina News, November 4, 1993: 2.
— residents concerned about rezoning request at Napilihau Villages, Lahaina News, November 25, 1993: 1,3.
— project approved by Maui County Council, Lahaina News, March 24, 1994: 1,20.
— hearing to be held to determine details on development proposal by, Lahaina News, August 11, 1994: 1,3.
— hearing on proposed apartment complex in Napili finishes, Lahaina News, September 22, 1994: 6.
— waiting for recommendation on proposed apartment complex, Lahaina News, January 5, 1995: 4.
— Mark Honda recommends approval of Napilihau Villages housing project proposed by, Lahaina News, January 12, 1995: 1,16.
— plans for Napilihau Villages to come to Maui Planning Commission, Lahaina News, February 2, 1995: 4.
— Army Corps of Engineers concludes wetland in proposed development will not be regulated, Lahaina News, May 11, 1995: 2.
— wants to change plans for affordable housing project, Lahaina News, September 26, 1996: 1,18.

JIAN, YU TIAN
— Chinese healer to lecture, Lahaina News, March 27, 2003: 16.
— continues to lead lectures, Lahaina News, April 3, 2003: 16.

JIM ROSE CIRCUS
— to be held on Maui, Lahaina News, March 8, 2001: 14.

JIMMY AND THE HURRICANES [MUSICAL GROUP]
— played their last night at Blue Max, Lahaina News, May 9, 1984: 12.

JIMMY MAC AND THE KOOL KATS [MUSICAL GROUP]
— reviewed, Lahaina News, January 6, 1988: 9.
— career described, Lahaina News, May 4, 1988: 12.
— to perform at fundraiser for Lindal Lingle, Lahaina News, June 20, 1990: 5.

JIMMY THACKERY AND THE DRIVERS [MUSICAL GROUP]
— to perform at Moose McGillycuddy's, Lahaina News, February 8, 1996: 14.
— to perform at Casanova's, Lahaina News, February 20, 1997: 12.

JIN SHIN JYUTSU
— discussed as alternative healing method, Lahaina News, April 20, 1988: 20.
— workshop to be held, Lahaina News, September 16, 1999: 12.

JIVE SISTERS [MUSICAL GROUP]
— to perform at Maui Chamber of Commerce annual banquet, Lahaina News, May 10, 1989: 6.

JMB REALTY CORP. [BUSINESS]
— to purchase Amfac Inc., Lahaina News, September 14, 1988: 1,20.
— see also Amfac/JMB [business]

JOB FAIR
— to take place at Maui Community College, Lahaina News, October 11, 1989: 3.
— to be held at Ka'ahumanu Center, Lahaina News, October 3, 1990: 9.

JOBS
— how to get, Lahaina Times, August 20, 1983 volume 7 number 8: 2, 4.

JODO MISSION, LAHAINA
— temple and pagoda in Lahaina dedicated, Lahaina Sun, March 10, 1971: 1,4.
— photograph of, Lahaina Sun, September 1, 1971: 10.
— Noh performance to take place, Lahaina News, May 17, 1989: 13.
— to celebrate O-Bon Festival, Lahaina News, July 2, 1992: 4.
— to celebrate O-Bon Festival, Lahaina News, July 1, 1993: 3.
— to host floating lantern ceremony, Lahaina News, June 30, 1994: 4.
— O-Bon Festival described, Lahaina News, July 14, 1994: 2.
— celebrate 100th anniversary, Lahaina News, October 20, 1994: 5.
— to hold Floating Lantern Ceremony as part of O-Bon Festivities, Lahaina News, June 29, 1995: 4.
— to host floating lantern ceremony, Lahaina News, July 4, 1996: 2.
— holds O-Bon Festival, Lahaina News, July 18, 1996: 1.
— to hold Hanamatsuri, Lahaina News, April 2, 1998: 16.
— to hold O-Bon Festival and Floating Lanterns Ceremony, Lahaina News, June 29, 2000: 1.
— location for Lahaina Rotary Club's Fiesta and Auction, Lahaina News, May 17, 2001: 3.
— to hold O-Bon Festival, Lahaina News, June 28, 2001: 1.
— Zen Master Kono Roshi to speak, Lahaina News, February 20, 2003: 2.
— to hold O-Bon celebration, Lahaina News, July 3, 2003: 16.

JOE CANO AND DA TALK OF DA TOWN [MUSICAL GROUP]
— described, Lahaina News, August 3, 1988: 8.
— to perform at Casanova's, Lahaina News, April 10, 1991: 12.
— to perform for New Years, Lahaina News, December 24, 1992: 13.

JOE CANO AND EL GRITO [MUSICAL GROUP]
— to perform at Villa Lounge, Lahaina News, September 17, 1992: 14.

JOE SAMPLE TRIO [MUSICAL GROUP]
— to perform at Maui Arts and Cultural Center, Lahaina News, July 31, 1997: 17.

JOE, STEVE C. K.
— to offer workshops and business and investment, Lahaina News, July 6, 1988: 3,11.

JOEL GOLDFARB QUARTET [MUSICAL GROUP]
— to perform at Blackie's Bar, Lahaina News, January 16, 1992: 12.
— continues to perform at Blackie's Bar, Lahaina News, March 12, 1992: 16.
— continues to perform at Blackie's Bar, Lahaina News, June 25, 1992: 18.
— continues to perform at Kapalua Bay Hotel, Lahaina News, November 12, 1992: 19.

JOE'S BAR AND GRILL [RESTAURANT]
— opens, Lahaina News, December 7, 1995: 14.

JOEY LUM MEMORIAL GOLF FOUNDATION
— tournament to be held, Lahaina News, August 23, 2001: 12.
— to hold golf tournament, Lahaina News, August 8, 2002: 12.

JOFFREY II DANCERS [TROUPE]
— cancel Hawaii tour, Lahaina News, April 18, 1984: 5.

JOHANSEN, WAILANI [ARTIST]
— to be profiled on Hawaii Public Television, Lahaina News, June 11, 1998: 2.

JOHN BULLOCK MEMORIAL SCHOLARSHIP
— awarded to Clinton Baybayan, Lahaina News, June 5, 1997: 5.

JOHN, DEBBIE
— promoted to general manager at Galerie Lassen, Inc., Lahaina News, October 24, 1991: 8.

JOHN, ELTON [MUSICIAN]
— purchases works by Christian Riese Lassen , Lahaina News, March 20, 1991: 14.
— to perform at Blaisdell Arena in Honolulu, Lahaina News, November 25, 1999: 17.

JOHN MORIARTY JAZZ TRIO [MUSICAL GROUP]
— to perform at the Ritz-Carlton's Sunset Lounge, Lahaina News, December 31, 1992: 11.
— to perform at Ritz-Carlton, Lahaina News, January 6, 1994: 11.

JOHN NORRIS' NEW ORLEANS JAZZ [MUSICAL GROUP]
— to perform at Ka'ahumanu Shopping Center, Lahaina News, August 29, 1990: 4.

JOHN PALMER [SHIP]
— involved in conflict in Lahaina in the 1820s, Lahaina Sun, January 6, 1971: 8.

JOHN-ROGER [WRITER]
— to speak at Border Books on his book "Spiritual Warrior, The Art of Spiritual Living", Lahaina News, April 2, 1998: 16.

JOHNNY PAYCHECK AND THE WORKING MAN'S BAND [MUSICAL GROUP]
— to perform at Lahaina Civic Center, Lahaina News, May 4, 1988: 14.

JOHNSON, BOB
— director of the county Economic Development Division to speak to Kiwanis Club, Kihei Wailea, Lahaina News, May 13, 1993: 4.
— Head of Maui County Office of Economic Development featured, Lahaina News, May 27, 1993: 7.

JOHNSON, BONNIE [ARTIST]
— teaching oil painting at Kihei Community Complex, Lahaina News, April 24, 1985: 20.

JOHNSON, CATHLEEN
— appointed as senior vice president of marketing at Hawaii Visitors Bureau, Lahaina News, June 16, 1994: 10.

JOHNSON, CHASE
— earns Eagle Scout rank, Lahaina News, July 10, 2003: 2.

JOHNSON, CHRIS
— diver displays ulua caught while spear fishing, Lahaina Sun, November 18, 1970: 1.
— diver rescued by Coast Guard helicopter, Lahaina Sun, June 9, 1971: 5.

JOHNSON, CRAIG
— offering off-season training to paddlers, Lahaina News, January 2, 1992: 6.

JOHNSON, DALE
— running for Maui County Council, Lahaina News, June 1, 1980: 3.
— candidate for County Council highlighted, Lahaina News, July 15, 1980: 4.

JOHNSON, DAVID PAUL
— to serve as guest chef at A Pacific Café, Lahaina News, March 31, 1994: 15.
— chef to demonstrate making your own organic baby food, Lahaina News, May 26, 1994: 16.
— Jan Kasprzycki paints portrait of, Lahaina News, January 19, 1995: 12.
— leading cooking classes, Lahaina News, February 8, 2001: 20.
— offering cooking class "Making Tapas", Lahaina News, March 15, 2001: 20.
— opens Yakiniku Cafe, Lahaina News, April 12, 2001: 9.
— to offer class on "Baking Breads and More", Lahaina News, April 19, 2001: 16.
— to offer "Kids Kuisine" cooking class, Lahaina News, September 13, 2001: 16.
— to offer course on dim sum, Lahaina News, September 20, 2001: 17.

— chef to teach "Candy Making", Lahaina News, December 13, 2001: 17.
— to teach cooking class for Valentine's Day, Lahaina News, January 17, 2002: 16.
— chef to offer cooking demonstration at Whalers Village , Lahaina News, July 25, 2002: 21.

JOHNSON, EARVIN "MAGIC"
— conducting adult basketball clinic, Lahaina News, July 12, 1989: 1.
— to hold basketball camp, Lahaina News, July 11, 1990: 24.
— basketball player to offer "Executive Basketball Camp" with Jerry West, Lahaina News, June 6, 1991: 9.
— basketball player to hold camp, Lahaina News, August 6, 1992: 5.
— speculation on his return to the NBA, Lahaina News, September 3, 1992: 5.
— returns for basketball camp, Lahaina News, June 16, 1994: 7.
— stops by Gold's Gym, Lahaina News, December 17, 1998: 12.

JOHNSON, ERIC [MUSICIAN]
— to perform at Rhythm and Blues Mele, Lahaina News, May 17, 2001: 21.

JOHNSON, GARY
— Safeway manager to retire, Lahaina News, July 4, 1996: 5.

JOHNSON, HENRY
— planning to create a Maui chapter of the Elks Club, Lahaina Sun, August 18, 1971: 10.

JOHNSON, JACK [MUSICIAN]
— to perform at 2001 Maui Music Odyssey, Lahaina News, December 13, 2001: 17.

JOHNSON, JACQUELINE LEE
— trust fund provides grant to Maui Humane Society, Lahaina News, August 15, 2002: 9.

JOHNSON, JIM
— helping to coordinate Civil Defense volunteers, Lahaina News, May 29, 1997: 1.

JOHNSON, JOANNE [POLITICIAN]
— to seek West Side seat on County Council, Lahaina News, February 12, 1998: 1,20.
— Republican candidate has website, Lahaina News, September 10, 1998: 7.
— advocates for volunteerism, Lahaina News, May 6, 1999: 1,24.
— filed to run for West Maui set on Maui County Council, Lahaina News, July 6, 2000: 15.
— candidate for West Maui County Council, Lahaina News, November 2, 2000: 19.
— discusses plans as new member of Maui Council, Lahaina News, November 16, 2000: 1,13.
— Councilwoman elect to meet with West Maui Taxpayers Association, Lahaina News, December 21, 2000: 3.
— to speak at West Maui Taxpayers Association, Lahaina News, January 4, 2001: 1.
— to speak to West Maui Taxpayers Association, Lahaina News, January 4, 2001: 17.
— to speak to West Maui Taxpayers Association, Lahaina News, January 11, 2001: 16.
— carrying capacity study a priority of JoAnne Johnson, Lahaina News, February 22, 2001: 5.
— seeks building ban to fix traffic, Lahaina News, March 29, 2001: 1,18.
— to introduce building moratorium bill, Lahaina News, April 5, 2001: 2.
— discusses County funding for West Maui, Lahaina News, June 28, 2001: 1,22.
— encourages people to volunteer for Relay for Life, Lahaina News, July 19, 2001: 3.
— Parks and Recreation Committee recommends county take over parks, Lahaina News, August 9, 2001: 3.

— to hold informal meeting at Waihee, Lahaina News, November 8, 2001: 16.
— to hold meeting on Papalaua Wayside Park, Lahaina News, November 15, 2001: 1,18.
— to speak with West Maui Taxpayers Association, Lahaina News, January 3, 2002: 1,18.
— to speak to West Maui Taxpayers Association's Annual Meeting, Lahaina News, January 10, 2002: 2.
— to speak to West Maui Taxpayers Association's Annual Meeting, Lahaina News, January 17, 2002: 2.
— critical of mayor's budget, Lahaina News, April 11, 2002: 5.
— honors veterans, Lahaina News, May 30, 2002: 1,20.
— comments on Maui County Council, Lahaina News, July 11, 2002: 2.
— discusses government reform, Lahaina News, July 25, 2002: 1,24.
— councilmember to discuss potential campsites, Lahaina News, July 25, 2002: 2.
— cleared of ethics complaints by Board of Ethics, Lahaina News, September 5, 2002: 1,2.
— to seek second term on council, Lahaina News, September 12, 2002: 3.
— discusses Maui County Council budget issues, Lahaina News, March 13, 2003: 5.
— meets with Friends of Moku'ula at Malu'ulu O Lele Park, Lahaina News, June 26, 2003: 1.

JOHNSON, JOHNNY
— appointed director of sales for Maui Marriott Resort, Lahaina News, August 23, 1989: 6.

JOHNSON, LOUIS [MUSICIAN]
— to perform at Casanova's, Lahaina News, September 5, 1991: 18.

JOHNSON, LOUIS, JR. [COMEDIAN]
— to perform at Honolulu Comedy Club, Lahaina News, February 29, 1996: 14.

JOHNSON, MIKE "BOATS" [COMEDIAN]
— to perform at Comedy Club, Lahaina News, July 25, 1991: 10.
— to perform at Comedy Club and the Sports Page, Lahaina News, October 15, 1992: 17,18.

JOHNSON, NELSON
— police officer revives visitor at Grand Wailea Resort, Lahaina News, September 17, 1998: 18.

JOHNSON, REX
— joins Amfac/JMB Hawaii as director of special projects, Lahaina News, October 31, 1991: 10.
— State transportation director says state will maintain conditions at Kapalua airport, Lahaina News, September 10, 1992: 1.
— discusses funding issues for Lahaina Bypass, Lahaina News, August 26, 1993: 1,5.
— director of State Department of Transportation announces program aimed at drug-impaired drivers, Lahaina News, August 25, 1994: 5.

JOHNSON, ROBERT
— Maui County Economic Development appointee reviewing county's priorities, Lahaina News, April 23, 1992: 15.
— Maui County Economic Development Office Coordinator wondering about the need for Maui Visitors Bureau, Lahaina News, September 21, 1995: 10.

JOHNSON, ROCKY
— Mobile Car Care featured, Lahaina News, September 23, 1987: 1,16.

JOHNSON, RUBELLITE
— keynote speaker at opening ceremonies of Kahekili Park, Lahaina News, October 15, 1992: 3.

JOHNSON, RUSSELL
— passes CPA exam, Lahaina News, February 18, 1987: 3.
— appointed controller at Kapalua Land Company, Ltd., Lahaina News, January 23, 1992: 12.

JOHNSON-MOORE SEMINARS [BUSINESS]
— featured, Lahaina News, August 8, 1984: 14.

JOHNSTON ATOLL
— Defense Threat Reduction Agency taking public comments on cleanup of, Lahaina News, March 7, 2002: 17.
— Defense Threat Reduction Agency taking public comments on cleanup of, Lahaina News, March 14, 2002: 16.

JOHNSTON, DEAN [ARTIST]
— woodwork to be exhibited during Friday Night is Art Night, Lahaina News, June 22, 1995: 11.

JOHNSTON, DENNY [COMEDIAN]
— to perform at Comedy Club, Lahaina News, September 19, 1990: 10.

JOHNSTON, GRAHAM
— sets new world record at Lahaina Aquatic Center, Lahaina News, September 5, 2002: 13.

JOHNSTON, MIKE
— new food and beverage director at Trilogy Excursions, Lahaina News, April 24, 2003: 14.

JOHNSTON, OLLIE [ARTIST]
— Disney animator to open exhibit, Lahaina News, January 16, 1991: 13.

JOLLY ROGER PIRATES
— report on basketball team game against Maui Cactus Jack, Lahaina Sun, January 20, 1971: 7.

JONES, BETTINA [ARTIST]
— to exhibit under the Banyan Tree, Lahaina News, October 24, 1996: 15.

JONES, BETTY
— dancer to perform with Dances We Dance Company at Maui Youth Theatre, Lahaina News, January 2, 1985: 3.

JONES, BOB
— to perform at World Café, Lahaina News, July 18, 1996: 12.

JONES, EILEEN [ARTIST]
— to exhibit at Hunt Gallery, Lahaina News, July 27, 1995: 12.
— to exhibit at Old Jail Gallery, Lahaina News, March 7, 1996: 14.
— to exhibit at Lahaina Arts Society, Lahaina News, March 5, 1998: 16.

JONES, GARY
— appointed tennis director at Royal Lahaina Tennis Ranch, Lahaina News, September 26, 1991: 9.

JONES, GEORGE
— injured when his helicopter plunged into the sea during a rescue operation, Lahaina Sun, December 1, 1971: 13.

JONES, GIULIAN [COMEDIAN]
— to perform at the Sports Page, Lahaina News, June 6, 1991: 15.
— to perform at Iao Theater, Lahaina News, June 13, 1991: 13,15.

JONES, JUNE
— University of Hawai'i football coach meets with Maui coaches, Lahaina News, May 13, 1999: 1,20.
— University of Hawai'i football coach to speak to Maui Chamber of Commerce, Lahaina News, May 22, 2003: 8.
— to speak to Maui Chamber of Commerce, Lahaina News, May 29, 2003: 8.

JONES, K.C.
— basketball player interviewed while vacationing in Lahaina, Lahaina News, July 10, 1985: 4.

JONES, MAC
— representative for Drug Addiction Services of Hawaii discusses rise in use of ecstasy, Lahaina News, August 29, 1991: 1.

JONES, MEAGAN
— to discuss humpback whale songs, Lahaina News, January 18, 2001: 17.

JONES, PATSY [ARTIST]
— designed Pineapple-O-Lantern for newspaper cover, Lahaina News, October 31, 1991: 3.

JONES, TIM [COMEDIAN]
— to perform at Comedy Club and the Sports Page, Lahaina News, September 17, 1992: 13,16.
— to perform at Comedy Club, Lahaina News, September 9, 1993: 12.
— to perform at Honolulu Comedy Club, Lahaina News, October 26, 1995: 11.
— to perform at Honolulu Comedy Club, Lahaina News, November 2, 1995: 12.

JONES, TOM [MUSICIAN]
— coming to Maui, Lahaina News, November 9, 1983: 12.

JONES, TREVOR [MUSICIAN]
— now playing at Blackbeard's Restaurant, Lahaina News, May 15, 1980: 8.
— interviewed on his return to Maui, Lahaina News, October 24, 1984: 17.
— performs at Pioneer Inn, Lahaina News, April 8, 1987: 4.
— to perform for St. Patrick's Day, Lahaina News, March 15, 1989: 9.
— to perform at Pioneer Inn, Lahaina News, September 26, 1990: 10.
— to perform at Pioneer Inn , Lahaina News, March 5, 1992: 15.
— to perform at Pioneer Inn , Lahaina News, June 4, 1992: 13.
— continues to perform at Pioneer Inn, Lahaina News, July 9, 1992: 17.
— to perform at Pioneer Inn , Lahaina News, September 3, 1992: 15.
— to perform at Moondoggies, Lahaina News, November 25, 1993: 12.
— to perform at Moondoggies, Lahaina News, March 17, 1994: 9.
— to perform at Westin Maui for St. Patrick's Day, Lahaina News, March 9, 1995: 11.
— performs at Ka'anapali Kalikimaka event to benefit Maui Food Bank, Lahaina News, December 14, 2000: 3.
— to lead "A Night of Nautical Song", Lahaina News, December 6, 2001: 17.

JONES, VOLCANO [MUSICIAN]
— to perform at Casanova's, Lahaina News, September 3, 1992: 18.

JOOS, KATA [ARTIST]
— featured, Lahaina News, April 24, 1997: 10.

JORDAN, DIANA [COMEDIAN]
— to appear at the Maui Prince, Lahaina News, January 20, 1988: 18.

JORDAN, KEVIN [COMEDIAN]
— to perform at Comedy Club and the Sports Page, Lahaina News, July 30, 1992: 13,15.

JORDAN, STEVE
— to represent Toastmasters in national contest, Lahaina News, April 13, 1988: 12.

JORDAN, TODD [COMEDIAN]
— to perform at Comedy Club and the Sports Page, Lahaina News, February 27, 1991: 8,12.
— to perform at Comedy Club and the Sports Page, Lahaina News, July 16, 1992: 17,20.

JORGENSEN, CHRISTIAN HUGO
— named executive chef of the Westin Maui, Lahaina News, November 5, 1998: 17.
— chef of Tropica featured, Lahaina News, June 7, 2001: 16,17.

JORSTAD, STAN [ARTIST]
— "These Rare Lands" photograph exhibit be held at Maui Arts and Cultural Center, Lahaina News, January 13, 2000: 12.
— photographic exhibition to be held, Lahaina News, February 17, 2000: 16.

JOSEPH AND THE AMAZING TECHNICOLOR DREAMCOAT [MUSICAL]
— to be performed at the Baldwin Mini-Theatre, Lahaina News, July 23, 1992: 26.
— reviewed, Lahaina News, August 6, 1992: 11.
— continues, Lahaina News, August 13, 1992: 18.
— to be performed by Baldwin High School students, Lahaina News, January 17, 2002: 17.

JOSEPH, DAVID
— found guilty, Lahaina Sun, May 26, 1971: 6.
— receives building code violations for Banana Patch residence, Lahaina Sun, June 30, 1971: 10.
— owner of "Banana Patch" dies, Lahaina News, August 1, 1981: 6.

JOSEPH, RANDY [ARTIST]
— sculptures discussed, Lahaina News, May 29, 1985: 7.
— scuptures featured by Lahaina Art Society, Lahaina News, February 25, 1987: 3.
— use of lost wax technique featured, Lahaina News, July 8, 1987: 1,24.
— featured by Lahaina Arts Society, Lahaina News, February 24, 1988: 18.

JOSEPH, STAN
— joins Corey Pacific Leasing, Inc., Lahaina News, July 4, 1990: 7.

JOSEPHS, JAI [MUSICIAN]
— to perform at Unity Church, Lahaina News, September 13, 1989: 5.

JOSWICK, FRAN
— named executive director of Maui Friends of the Animals, Lahaina News, December 27, 1989: 5.

JOURNEY [MUSICAL GROUP]
— to perform at Maui Arts and Cultural Center, Lahaina News, October 3, 2002: 14.
— to perform at Maui Arts and Cultural Center, Lahaina News, October 10, 2002: 16.

JOURNEY TO THE ORIENT
— to be held at Lahaina Cannery Mall, Lahaina News, August 7, 2003: 14.

JOURNEYMAN JEWELERS [BUSINESS]
— reviewed, Lahaina News, October 19, 1983: 14.

JOURNEYS TO POLYNESIA
— to be held at Lahaina Cannery Mall, Lahaina News, August 8, 2002: 14.

JOY [PLAY]
— to be performed, Lahaina News, November 27, 1985: 20.
— to be performed by Maui Youth Theatre, Lahaina News, December 4, 1985: 3.

JOY, BRUGH
— to talk on healing power of touch, Lahaina News, March 9, 1988: 18.
— to present "A Re-Touch of Joy" at Akahi Farm, Lahaina News, April 5, 1989: 14.

JOY, RACHEL
— Scholar/Athlete of the Week, Lahaina News, May 23, 2002: 12.

JOYFUL NOISE QUARTET, THE [MUSICAL GROUP]
— to perform at Ka'ahumanu Shopping Center, Lahaina News, January 12, 1995: 4.

JOYFUL SOUND [MUSICAL GROUP]
— to perform at Lahaina Cannery Mall, Lahaina News, May 9, 2002: 15.

JTB HAWAII INC. [BUSINESS]
— Public Utilities Commission approves use of large tour buses, Lahaina News, December 15, 1994: 4.

JUAN SEBASTIAN DEL CANO VISITS LAHAINA [SHIP]
— visits Lahaina, Lahaina Sun, February 16, 1972: 3.

JUBB, KENDAHL JAN [ARTIST]
— to exhibit at Village Galleries, Lahaina News, May 15, 2003: 16.

JUDAISM
— congregation formed in Kahului, Lahaina News, July 12, 1989: 6.
— see also Jewish Congregation of Maui, and specific people and events

JUDGE, SHIRLEY CHONG
— named Hawaii Division Secretary of the Year, Lahaina News, May 30, 1990: 6.

JUDICIARY, HOUSE COMMITTEE ON
— to hold meeting on tort reform, Lahaina News, October 2, 1997: 15.

JUDY'S GANG [TROUPE]
— to hold fundraiser dance play, Lahaina News, June 9, 1994: 16.
— to stage "A Day in the Life of Mrs. Santa Claus", Lahaina News, December 12, 2002: 21.

JUICY'S HEALTH FOOD CAFÉ AND JUICE BAR [RESTAURANT]
— reviewed, Lahaina News, September 12, 1991: 16,18.
— wins "Da Kine Grinds" health food contest, Lahaina News, April 30, 1992: 10.

JULLIARD ENSEMBLE [MUSICAL GROUP]
— performs at Maui Community College, Lahaina Sun, July 14, 1971: 2.
— performance reviewed, Lahaina Sun, July 28, 1971: 2.
— to play on Maui, Lahaina Sun, March 7, 1973: 6.

JULY 4TH
— Ka'anapali Beach location for celebration of, Lahaina News, July 3, 1985: 1.
— parade to be held in conjunction with the Makawao Rodeo, Lahaina News, July 3, 1985: 8.
— celebrations described, Lahaina News, July 10, 1985: 1,20.
— fireworks planned to mark 100th birthday of Statue of Liberty, Lahaina News, July 2, 1986: 1,11.
— events listed, Lahaina News, July 1, 1987: 1.
— Hospice Maui to offer entertainment and fireworks, Lahaina News, June 14, 1989: 2.
— events listed, Lahaina News, June 21, 1989: 18.
— Ka'anapali Beach Operators Association to host fireworks, Lahaina News, June 21, 1989: 3.
— events described, Lahaina News, June 28, 1989: 1,17.
— events described, Lahaina News, July 12, 1989: 1,5.
— celebrations planned, Lahaina News, June 27, 1990: 9.
— Friday Night is Art Night has "Red, White and Blue" theme, Lahaina News, July 4, 1990: 17.
— events being organized, Lahaina News, June 13, 1991: 12.
— Makawao Rodeo to be held in Olinda, Lahaina News, June 20, 1991: 11.
— events being organized, Lahaina News, June 20, 1991: 9.
— events, Lahaina News, June 27, 1991: 10,14.
— Makawao Rodeo to be held, Lahaina News, June 27, 1991: 13.
— Valley Isle Road Runners to hold 5K walk/run, Lahaina News, June 27, 1991: 7.
— events, Lahaina News, July 4, 1991: 10.
— to be celebrated at Ka'anapali Resort, Lahaina News, June 25, 1992: 19.
— Maui Inter-Continental Wailea to organize benefit for Kihei Youth Center, Lahaina News, June 25, 1992: 21.
— concert to be held at Ka'anapali Resort, Lahaina News, July 2, 1992: 20,21.
— to be celebrated at Maui Sun Hotel, Lahaina News, July 2, 1992: 24.
— fireworks to be held at Ka'anapali Beach, other details, Lahaina News, July 1, 1993: 3.
— information on, Lahaina News, June 30, 1994: 3,16.
— to be held, Lahaina News, June 29, 1995: 11,12.

— to be celebrated at Ka'anapali Beach, Lahaina News, June 27, 1996: 1.

— events, Lahaina News, June 27, 1996: 15.

— events, Lahaina News, July 4, 1996: 14.

— to be celebrated at Ka'anapali Resort, Lahaina News, June 18, 1998: 16.

— to be celebrated, Lahaina News, July 2, 1998: 1,9.

— Ka'anapali Resort planning, Lahaina News, July 1, 1999: 1,16.

— Ka'anapali Resort to celebrate, Lahaina News, June 29, 2000: 3.

— events to be held, Lahaina News, June 28, 2001: 1,3.

— Pacific Whale foundation to hold "Fireworks Cruises", Lahaina News, June 28, 2001: 21.

— Ka'anapali Beach Resort Association to host events, Lahaina News, June 28, 2001: 3.

— Freedom Fest to be held by First Assembly King's Cathedral, Lahaina News, June 27, 2002: 17.

— fireworks to be held, Lahaina News, June 27, 2002: 3.

— celebrated, Lahaina News, July 11, 2002: 1.

— to be celebrated at Ka'anapali Beach Resort, Lahaina News, July 3, 2003: 1,3.

JUNE, JUST [COMEDIAN]

— to perform at Comedy Club, Lahaina News, April 25, 1990: 15.

JUNG, DAVID

— pledges that Sea Link of Hawaii will revive Moloka'i ferry, Lahaina News, November 9, 2000: 1,12.

— captain discusses Moloka'i Princess ferry beginning operation in January between Moloka'i and Maui, Lahaina News, December 28, 2000: 1,15.

JUNG, RYAN

— surfer wins Mehehune Division championship, Lahaina News, December 15, 1994: 9.

JUNG, SINLING [ARTIST]

— offering mask-making class, Lahaina News, March 13, 1991: 3.

— to conduct healing seminar for women, Lahaina News, April 17, 1991: 3,4.

— to conduct "Creative Art Mask Making" class, Lahaina News, October 17, 1991: 5.

JUNGLE BOB'S [BUSINESS]

— opens at 550 Front Street, Lahaina News, May 24, 1989: 8.

— to open store at 505 Front Street, Lahaina News, June 28, 1989: 15.

JUNGLEBOOK [PLAY]

— to be performed at Central Maui Youth Center, Lahaina News, March 20, 1991: 11.

— to be performed at Central Maui Youth Center, Lahaina News, March 27, 1991: 16.

JUNIO, ROMAN

— announces engagement of daughter Marilou Magtaan Junio and Renato Guerrero, Lahaina News, January 2, 2003: 5.

JUNIOR ACHIEVEMENT OF MAUI

— seeking volunteers from business community, Lahaina News, November 15, 1989: 8.

— new officers elected, Lahaina News, September 12, 1991: 4.

— Project Business Course begins, Lahaina News, October 24, 1991: 9.

— to honor local business executives, Lahaina News, November 7, 1991: 9.

— new board members elected, Lahaina News, April 13, 1995: 12.

— South Maui Ala Carte to be held, Lahaina News, August 14, 1997: 16.

— to be offered at Princess Nahienaena Elementary School, Lahaina News, April 16, 1998: 11.

— receives grant from McInerny Foundation, Lahaina News, December 17, 1998: 17.

— to be offered to public school children, Lahaina News, January 21, 1999: 11.

— receives donation from Alexander and Baldwin, Lahaina News, October 5, 2000: 14.

— seeks nominations for Hawaii Business Hall of Fame, Lahaina News, November 9, 2000: 18.

— launches fundraising campaign, Lahaina News, January 25, 2001: 7.

— seeks parent volunteers for classes, Lahaina News, February 14, 2002: 8.

— honors supporters, Lahaina News, May 2, 2002: 8.

JUNIOR LIFEGUARD PROGRAM

— to be offered, Lahaina News, June 5, 1997: 3.

— to be held, Lahaina News, July 10, 1997: 15.

— to be held, Lahaina News, July 17, 1997: 15.

— to offer water safety program, Lahaina News, June 11, 1998: 15.

— to be held, Lahaina News, May 2, 2002: 12.

JUNIOR NATURALIST PROGRAM

— to be hosted by Maui Ocean Center, Lahaina News, May 23, 2002: 8.

JUNIOR RYDER CUP TEAM

— West Side golfer earns spot on, Lahaina News, September 6, 2001: 12.

JUNK

— see pollution

JURASZ, SUSAN

— studying whales off West Maui, Lahaina News, April 1, 1987: 1,8,10,20.

JUSKO, DON [ARTIST]

— creates coloring book of Maui, Lahaina News, July 1, 1983: 9,10,11.

JUST ADD WATER [BUSINESS]

— opens Maui Fresh next to Hali'imaile General Store, Lahaina News, February 3, 2000: 11.

JUST BEFORE BEDTIME [PLAY]

— to perform at Iao Theatre, Lahaina News, November 13, 1997: 21.

JUVENAL AND CO. HAIR SALON [BUSINESS]

— raises money for Red Cross Relief Fund, Lahaina News, November 29, 2001: 8.

JUVENILE DIABETES RESEARCH FOUNDATION INTERNATIONAL

— to hold "Maui Walk to Cure Diabetes", Lahaina News, November 4, 1999: 7.

— to hold fundraiser at Sarento's, Lahaina News, May 24, 2001: 18.

— fundraiser held at Sarento's on the Beach, Lahaina News, September 13, 2001: 9.

— Duck Derby Races to be held at Westin Maui to benefit, Lahaina News, June 19, 2003: 8.

K

K & H KAHANA [BUSINESS]

— planning zero-lot-line housing for Honokowai, Lahaina News, February 27, 1997: 3.

KA EHU KAI [MUSICAL GROUP]

— to perform at Lahaina Cannery Mall, Lahaina News, September 4, 2003: 17.

KA HALE A KE OLA HOMELESS RESOURCE CENTER

— fundraiser to support homeless, the Maui Food Bank, and Maui Community College Counseling service, Lahaina News, February 7, 1990: 3.

— receives donation from Alexander and Baldwin, Inc., Lahaina News, March 12, 1992: 5.

— awarded gift from Maui Chapter of the Women's Council of Realtors, Lahaina News, July 8, 1993: 4.

— renames thrift shop to Homeless Treasures, Lahaina News, April 21, 1994: 9,12.

— to hold food drive, Lahaina News, July 28, 1994: 4.

— wants to build homeless rehabilitation center, Lahaina News, October 5, 2000: 1,15.

— to hold hearing on homeless shelter, Lahaina News, November 2, 2000: 1,2.

— seeking approval to build West Side Resource Center, Lahaina News, November 9, 2000: 1.

— to build homeless center, Lahaina News, December 20, 2001: 1.

— see also homeless

KA HEKILI-NUI 'AHU-MANU [KING]

— biography given, Lahaina Sun, June 14, 1972: 21.

KA HOKU MOKU MAUI [FILM]

— to begin filming in Maui, Lahaina Sun, June 7, 1972: 15.

KA 'I'IMI 'IKE

— column continues to be printed, Lahaina News, January 1, 1998: 2.

KA IMI NAAUAU O HAWAII NEI

— to hold educational benefit concert, Lahaina News, August 9, 2001: 16.

KA KUPUNA O MAUI

— to hold "Awareness Demonstration" with Nation of Hawaii and Lahaina Open Space Society, Lahaina News, October 17, 1996: 14.

— to host Aha Kupuna, Lahaina News, October 22, 1998: 20.

KA LAHUI O HAWAII

— group supporting Native Hawaiian Sovereignty to hold general election, Lahaina News, January 31, 1990: 3.

— to hold informational meeting, Lahaina News, August 1, 1990: 4.

— to hold workshop on "Project Hawaiian Justice", Lahaina News, November 11, 1999: 5.

KA LEO HANO AWARDS

— to be held to honor musicians, Lahaina News, January 3, 2002: 8.

— to hold "most popular musician" vote campaign at Borders Books, Lahaina News, June 6, 2002: 16.

— to be held at Maui Arts and Cultural Center, Lahaina News, July 11, 2002: 14.

— to honor music legends, Lahaina News, July 18, 2002: 16.

KA LIMA O MAUI

— fundraising underway, Lahaina Sun, December 6, 1972: 12,13.

— rehabilitation center's activities described, Lahaina Sun, December 20, 1972: 6.

— report on numbers of disabled peoples served, Lahaina News, January 10, 1990: 24.

— Hard Rock Cafe recycling with, Lahaina News, July 25, 1990: 1,2.

— receives grant from Alexander and Baldwin, Lahaina News, November 4, 1993: 7.

— Willie Nelson to perform for, Lahaina News, August 1, 1996: 21.

— offering free job training, Lahaina News, December 7, 2000: 16.

— to offer free job training, Lahaina News, January 4, 2001: 14.

— provides free job training, Lahaina News, February 1, 2001: 8.

— offering free job training, Lahaina News, February 8, 2001: 8.

— providing job training, Lahaina News, March 8, 2001: 8.

— providing job training, Lahaina News, April 12, 2001: 8.

— providing job training, Lahaina News, May 10, 2001: 8.

— continues to offer job training, Lahaina News, June 21, 2001: 9.

KA MANA O HAWAII

— to perform at Maui Arts and Cultural Center, Lahaina News, January 18, 1996: 12.

KA NO'EAU DANCE ACADEMY

— to host Hoolaulea, Lahaina News, June 6, 1990: 13.

KA PIKO O LELE

— Nimble Makalani Dearden appointed manager, Lahaina News, September 23, 1999: 2.

KA PO'E PILIHANA O WAIOLA

— to offer food and refreshments at King Kamehameha Day festivities, Lahaina News, June 6, 1991: 2.

KAAHUI, EDWARD

— hearing continues over firing, Lahaina Sun, September 20, 1972: 19.

KA'AHUMANU [QUEEN]

— long distance canoe race to be held, Lahaina News, August 14, 1997: 14.

— death discussed, Lahaina News, October 23, 1997: 18.

— festival to honor, Lahaina News, March 15, 2001: 18.

KA'AHUMANU CHURCH

— history and planned facelift detailed, Lahaina News, July 4, 1984: 9,10,11.

KA'AHUMANU, LAKI PU'UMAIKAI

— Harvest Chapel pastor organizes anti-drug march, Lahaina News, April 15, 1999: 1.

— Bishop's impact on Pentecostal Church of God, Lahaina News, October 12, 2000: 1,17.

— presides over blessing of Napili Park , Lahaina News, October 10, 2002: 1.

KA'AHUMANU PRESCHOOL

— to hold book sale, Lahaina News, October 31, 1990: 8.

KA'AHUMANU SHOPPING CENTER

— construction to begin, Lahaina Sun, March 15, 1972: 5.

— under construction, Lahaina Sun, April 5, 1972: 5.

— new stores to open, Lahaina Sun, May 9, 1973: 11.

— Richard Chang named general manager, Lahaina Sun, May 23, 1973: 11.

— set to open, Lahaina Sun, July 25, 1973: 6.

— featuring jazz, Lahaina News, August 29, 1990: 4.

— celebrating 17th year, Lahaina News, September 12, 1990: 9.

— to hold Bridal Fair, Lahaina News, December 26, 1990: 7.

— summer concert series scheduled, Lahaina News, August 22, 1991: 12.

— to break ground in early 1993, Lahaina News, July 30, 1992: 11.

— to celebrate 19th anniversary, Lahaina News, September 10, 1992: 4.

— groundbreaking held at, Lahaina News, March 11, 1993: 6.

— to host juried art show, Lahaina News, July 8, 1993: 12.

— celebrating 20th anniversary, Lahaina News, September 16, 1993: 18.

— keiki fingerprinting to be available at , Lahaina News, October 21, 1993: 4.

— Mall Ball begins at, Lahaina News, November 17, 1994: 18,19.

— to celebrate grand reopening, Lahaina News, March 2, 1995: 12.

— to host "Dinamation Dinosaur Exhibit", Lahaina News, August 15, 1996: 14.

— to host "Dinamation Dinosaur Exhibit", Lahaina News, September 5, 1996: 16.

— to hold keiki fingerprinting, Lahaina News, October 17, 1996: 14.

— new stores opening, Lahaina News, August 26, 1999: 14.

— opening new retail area, Lahaina News, November 11, 1999: 11.

KA'AI, NINO [MUSICIAN]

— to promote new CD "Kahuliau" at Borders Books, Lahaina News, June 17, 1999: 16.

KA'AI, SAM

— opens Sam Ka'ai's Wood Shop in Whaler's Village, Lahaina Sun, November 25, 1970: 3.

— speaking of Higgins Maddigan's reprimand for tearing down an old building, Lahaina Sun, December 16, 1970: 2.

— photograph of, at opening of Whaler's Village, Lahaina Sun, December 30, 1970: 6.

— speaks of Maui Historic Commission's approval of signs on Front Street, Lahaina Sun, May 19, 1971: 2.

— Maui Historic Commission plans for Lahaina courthouse, Lahaina Sun, April 19, 1972: 3.

— details Lahaina Canoe Club plans, Lahaina Sun, June 21, 1972: 14.

— vows to resign if new large hotel is built in Lahaina, Lahaina Sun, December 27, 1972: 4.

— steps down in protest as chair of Maui Historic Commission following approval of Bruce McNeil's condominium in Lahaina, Lahaina Sun, April 25, 1973: 3.

— discusses Lahaina canoe club, Lahaina Sun, May 16, 1973: 22.

— associated with E'ala, double-hulled canoe, Lahaina News, September 10, 1986: 1.

— photographs on board the E'ala, Lahaina News, January 7, 1987: 16.

— to lecture on Hawaiian topics at Maui Prince Hotel, Lahaina News, July 4, 1990: 4.

— to lecture at Lahaina Cannery Mall as part of Aloha Summer, Lahaina News, August 15, 1990: 15.

— participates in ceremony at Palauea Beach marking return of Kaho'olawe, Lahaina News, May 12, 1994: 1,4.

— encouraged Abraham "Snake" Ah Hee to join the crew of the Hokule'a, Lahaina News, August 3, 1995: 9.

— to lecture on Polynesian fishing, migration and voyaging, Lahaina News, March 20, 1997: 17.

— blesses the Pinnacle Ka'anapali's Kai nehe, Lahaina News, May 29, 2003: 6.

KA'AIHUE, VERONICA

— photographed mending nets, Lahaina Sun, January 6, 1971: 7.

KA'ANAPALI [TOWN]

— Maui Surf, a 12-story hotel, opens, Lahaina Sun, July 28, 1971: 5.

— 900 travel agents due to visit, Lahaina Sun, March 29, 1972: 4.

— historical photograph reproduced, Lahaina Sun, March 21, 1973: 12,13.

— sandcastle context held, Lahaina News, December, 1979: 12.

— hearing delayed on Harry Weinberg's proposed gas and food complex, Lahaina News, December 7, 1983: 5.

— Roberts Hawaii, Inc. plans to locate catamaran in, Lahaina News, March 28, 1984: 17.

— dispute over shoreline holds up jurisdiction change, Lahaina News, July 20, 1988: 1,14.

— Department of Transportation gets control of near-shore waters, Lahaina News, August 10, 1988: 18.

— Royal Court Plaza shopping center proposed, public hearing to be held, Lahaina News, November 21, 1991: 1.

— Amfac/JMB planning luxury neighborhood in, Lahaina News, October 27, 1994: 7.

— featured in "Sunless in Seatle" television show, Lahaina News, May 30, 1996: 12.

— homes available, Lahaina News, July 18, 2002: 6.

— description of real estate in, Lahaina News, October 31, 2002: 8,9.

— see also specific hotels, Whaler's Village, etc.

KA'ANAPALI 2020: MAKING IT PONO [REPORT]

— Amfac/JMB holds public meeting, Lahaina News, November 11, 1999: 1,16.

— vision for Amfac/JMB Hawaii explained, Lahaina News, January 18, 2001: 1,7.

— West Maui Taxpayers Association to hold update on, Lahaina News, May 17, 2001: 3.

KA'ANAPALI ACTIVITY CENTER

— opening in Whaler's Village, Lahaina Sun, November 25, 1970: 3.

KA'ANAPALI AEROBIC BEAUTY CONTEST

— to be held, Lahaina News, September 14, 1988: 6,10.

KA'ANAPALI AIRPORT

— expected to receive exclusive rights to operate passenger flights, Lahaina Sun, May 19, 1971: 3.

— last plane departs from, Lahaina News, January 22, 1986: 1,14.

KA'ANAPALI ALII

— to hold food and toy drive, Lahaina News, January 2, 1991: 3.

— condominium featured, Lahaina News, February 22, 2001: 6.

— development featured, Lahaina News, March 21, 2002: 6.

— development featured, Lahaina News, July 11, 2002: 6.

KA'ANAPALI BEACH

— jet skiers and parasailers harassing whales off , Lahaina News, January 20, 1988: 1.

— Maui County may do away with accessory use permits for commercial boat operators, Lahaina News, July 20, 1995: 1.

— State finds water safe from sharks off, Lahaina News, March 11, 1999: 3.

— named as "Maui's Best Beach" by Hawaii Magazine, Lahaina News, July 1, 1999: 3.

KA'ANAPALI BEACH HOTEL [BUSINESS]

— strike at, Lahaina Sun, November 11, 1970: 1,4.

— dedication of new wing, Lahaina Sun, May 12, 1971: 6.

— Jack Dettloff named new manager, Lahaina Sun, August 25, 1971: 5.

— to participate in Honoapi'ilani Highway clean up , Lahaina News, September 26, 1984: 3.

— renovations begin, Lahaina News, January 30, 1985: 3.

— dinner show "Here is Hawaii" reopens at, Lahaina News, April 16, 1986: 3.

— receives award from United Way, Lahaina News, August 20, 1986: 14.

— offering course on Hawaiiana, Lahaina News, October 29, 1986: 3.

— raises money for United Way, Lahaina News, December 3, 1986: 12.

— The Island Image opens, Lahaina News, December 17, 1986: 2.

— offers after Christmas buffet, Lahaina News, December 24, 1986: 12.

— Ka'anapali Beach Operators Association to provide free trolley service to Kapalua West Maui Airport, Lahaina News, March 25, 1987: 3.

— to hold Hawaiian Studies workshops, Lahaina News, October 21, 1987: 3.

— appoints Mark Erskine as Director of Marketing, Lahaina News, April 20, 1988: 3.

— seeking permission to expand, Lahaina News, May 11, 1988: 1.

— sold to Grosvenor Properties, Ltd., Lahaina News, July 20, 1988: 3.

— announces new kama'aina rates, Lahaina News, December 21, 1988: 12,13.

— has cut staff turnover by teaching Hawaiiana, Lahaina News, May 3, 1989: 1.

— to offer luau specials, Lahaina News, July 5, 1989: 3.

— honored for Hawaiiana program by First Lady Lynn Waihee, Lahaina News, July 5, 1989: 3.

— new luau show added, Lahaina News, July 26, 1989: 13.

— employees raise money for Maui United Way, Lahaina News, August 2, 1989: 9.

— Donald Mahoney becomes Director of Food and Beverages at, Lahaina News, October 25, 1989: 10.

— offering kama'aina rates for dinner, Lahaina News, October 25, 1989: 14.

— appoints Ben Quiseng as director of rooms, Lahaina News, November 15, 1989: 9.

— executives appointed, Lahaina News, March 21, 1990: 4.

— hotel employees visit historical places in Lahaina, Lahaina News, July 11, 1990: 1,16,18.

— to host solo hula festival "Hula Le'a O Na Keiki", Lahaina News, September 12, 1990: 18.

— appoints Patrick Ornellas as account executive, Lahaina News, October 10, 1990: 12.

— mayor-elect Linda Lingle to ask for delay in decision on proposed expansion, Lahaina News, November 14, 1990: 1.

— to hold public meeting to discuss plans, Lahaina News, December 5, 1990: 3.

— expansion approved by Maui County Planning Commission, Lahaina News, December 26, 1990: 1.

— to hold hula competition for children, Lahaina News, August 22, 1991: 10.

— proposes dormitories for workers, Lahaina News, September 12, 1991: 1.

— proposing 3-day work week for workers living in Hana and on Moloka'i, Lahaina News, September 12, 1991: 1,2.

— request to build dormitories approved by Maui County Planning Commission, Lahaina News, October 3, 1991: 5.

— to hold Hoolaulea, Lahaina News, October 17, 1991: 15,21,22.

— awarded "Employer of the Year" by Hawaii Federation of Business and Professional Women, Lahaina News, November 7, 1991: 9.

— recognized by president George Bush as 648th Daily Point of Light, Lahaina News, January 2, 1992: 5.

— employees named 648th point of light, Lahaina News, April 30, 1992: 10.

— to be closed for renovations, Lahaina News, June 25, 1992: 16.

— cancels renovation plans, Lahaina News, August 27, 1992: 3.

— promotes Cindy Balboa to account executive in the sales office, Lahaina News, September 3, 1992: 8.

— honored by George H.W. Bush as a point of light, Lahaina News, January 14, 1993: 2.

— to feature native storytellers, Lahaina News, October 14, 1993: 14.

— to host Hula O Na Keiki festival, Lahaina News, October 14, 1993: 14,15.

— employees at following diet developed at Waianae Coast Comprehensive Health Center, Lahaina News, November 25, 1993: 1,3.

— to host Hula O Na Keiki hula competition, Lahaina News, September 8, 1994: 12.

— Barry Tani Villiarimo named executive sous chef at, Lahaina News, February 16, 1995: 13.

— Cynthia Litzau Herberg appointed new executive director at, Lahaina News, March 14, 1996: 10.

— to host July 4th, Lahaina News, June 27, 1996: 1.

— hosts kukui tree planting ceremony, Lahaina News, September 19, 1996: 20.

— to manage Plantation Inn, Lahaina News, March 13, 1997: 1.

— now owns Plantation Inn, Lahaina News, May 22, 1997: 9.

— to hold Hula O Na Keiki, Lahaina News, August 14, 1997: 3.

— names Barry Villiarimo as executive chef, Lahaina News, August 21, 1997: 12.

— wins award from Hospitality and Marketing Association International, Lahaina News, April 16, 1998: 11.

— donates money to Hui O Wa'a Kaulua, Lahaina News, April 23, 1998: 2.

— to sell malasadas at Lahaina Cannery Mall to help Visitor Industry Charity Walk, Lahaina News, May 7, 1998: 21.

— hosts Lahaina Arts Society artists, Lahaina News, March 18, 1999: 13.

— to host Hawaii Junior Olympic Boxing Championships, Lahaina News, May 6, 1999: 16.

— promoting "Aloha Passport for Kids" program, Lahaina News, May 20, 1999: 13.

— Tom Muromoto appointed executive chef at, Lahaina News, November 4, 1999: 11.

— Gold List award winner in Conde Nast Traveler magazine, Lahaina News, February 24, 2000: 14.

— from Travel Industry Association of America, Lahaina News, September 21, 2000: 11.

— hosting Hula O Na Keiki, Lahaina News, October 26, 2000: 27.

— to celebrate Mardi Gras, Lahaina News, December 28, 2000: 16.

— launches new website, Lahaina News, June 28, 2001: 8.

— awarded Wanda Award with Travel Holiday Magazine, Lahaina News, July 26, 2001: 8.

— Glenn Adolpho new sales manager at, Lahaina News, October 25, 2001: 8.

— to offer all-you-can-eat buffet, Lahaina News, December 6, 2001: 9.

— to celebrate Oktoberfest, Lahaina News, October 10, 2002: 14.

— to host steel guitar music, Lahaina News, May 1, 2003: 18.

— to offer new dinner show "Kupanaha: Maui Magic for All Ages, Lahaina News, June 26, 2003: 14.

KA'ANAPALI BEACH HOTEL GOLF CLUB

— offering golf holidays, Lahaina News, April 29, 1987: 3.

— results, Lahaina News, March 10, 1994: 7.

— junior golf season begins, Lahaina News, April 6, 1995: 16.

KA'ANAPALI BEACH MINISTRY

— to hold "Hoomana O Na Lahua Apau" service, Lahaina News, November 16, 2000: 16.

— to hold "Hoomana O Na Lahui Apau", Lahaina News, November 23, 2000: 20.

— to hold Christmas Eve mass, Lahaina News, December 21, 2000: 16.

KA'ANAPALI BEACH OPERATORS ASSOCIATION

— appoints Fawcett-McDermott Associates as advertising company, Lahaina Sun, February 3, 1971: 7.

— planning a promotion for tourists, Lahaina Sun, August 25, 1971: 11.

— sponsors promotional program with Sunset Magazine, Lahaina Sun, December 1, 1971: 12.

— sponsoring Na Mele O Maui, Lahaina News, July 18, 1984: 3.

— Dana Feneck elected president, Lahaina News, January 30, 1985: 18.

— to provide free trolley service between the Ka'anapali Beach Resort and Kapalua West Maui Airport, Lahaina News, March 25, 1987: 3.

— selects Jeff Tai as Director of Marketing, Lahaina News, January 20, 1988: 3,18.

— donates to Hale Makua, Lahaina News, March 23, 1988: 3.

KA'ANAPALI BEACH PROPERTIES, INC. [BUSINESS]

— Donald "Bucky" Buchnowski joins, Lahaina News, June 1, 2000: 13.

KA'ANAPALI BEACH RESORT ASSOCIATION

— Katherine Hendler elected president of, Lahaina News, April 17, 1991: 9.

— celebrates Christmas, Lahaina News, December 11, 1997: 1.

— offering Na Mele O Maui scholarships, Lahaina News, May 7, 1998: 18.

— taking applications for Na Mele O Maui Scholarships, Lahaina News, May 6, 1999: 2.

— new management team includes Shelley Kekuna, Lahaina News, February 1, 2001: 8.

— to celebrate 4th of July, Lahaina News, July 3, 2003: 1,3.

KA'ANAPALI BEAUTY SALON [BUSINESS]

— offering sunburn care, Lahaina News, July 27, 1995: 10.

— opens at Ka'anapali Beach Hotel, Lahaina News, September 5, 1996: 22.

KA'ANAPALI BUSINESS CENTER

— opens in Westin Maui, Lahaina News, February 17, 1994: 6.

KA'ANAPALI CLASSIC

— Ray Stosik appointed tournament director, Lahaina News, June 20, 1990: 7.

— awards dinner to feature comedian Roy Firestone, Lahaina News, September 5, 1990: 7.

— enters into long-term sponsorship agreement with First Development, Inc., Lahaina News, October 31, 1990: 9.

— to take place in December, Lahaina News, November 14, 1990: 24.

— Lee Travino expected to play, Lahaina News, December 5, 1990: 8.

— golf tournament featured, Lahaina News, October 9, 1997: 16,17,18.

— to be played, Lahaina News, October 16, 1997: 1,3.

— won by Hale Irwin, Lahaina News, October 26, 2000: 1.

KA'ANAPALI DEVELOPMENT CORPORATION [BUSINESS]
— new name for Amfac/JMB, Lahaina News, October 24, 2002: 1,16.
— donates land for proposed West Maui acute care facility, Lahaina News, August 7, 2003: 1,20.

KA'ANAPALI ESTATE COFFEE [BUSINESS]
— success of, Lahaina News, January 20, 1994: 6.
— to open, Lahaina News, July 27, 1995: 10.
— staff changes, Lahaina News, July 4, 1996: 18.
— featured, Lahaina News, January 2, 1997: 1,16.
— receives Award of Merit from the Hawaii Visitors and Convention Bureau, Lahaina News, May 29, 1997: 5.
— Barbara Roth appointed vice-president of marketing and sales at, Lahaina News, July 24, 1997: 13.
— reports high coffee yield , Lahaina News, January 29, 1998: 13.
— opens new processing facility, Lahaina News, November 5, 1998: 15.
— reports on coffee harvest, Lahaina News, March 25, 1999: 13.
— has new website, Lahaina News, May 20, 1999: 13.
— Michael Harvanchik named sales and marketing manager at, Lahaina News, May 18, 2000: 16.
— names Sean Loa sales and marketing manager, Lahaina News, August 24, 2000: 14.
— closing, Lahaina News, October 4, 2001: 1,20.

KA'ANAPALI GOLF COURSES
— to use treated water, Lahaina News, June 15, 1995: 1.
— donates golf carts to Lahainaluna High School, Lahaina News, November 27, 1997: 11.
— offering Summer Junior Special, Lahaina News, July 15, 1999: 7.
— Randy Blando recognized as employee of the month, Lahaina News, August 5, 1999: 11.
— to hold community food drive, Lahaina News, October 17, 2002: 2.

KA'ANAPALI GOLF ESTATES
— Amfac/JMB chooses Whalers Realty as listing agent for, Lahaina News, November 3, 1994: 23.
— featured, Lahaina News, March 16, 2000: 10.
— development featured, Lahaina News, June 6, 2002: 7.
— featured, Lahaina News, June 13, 2002: 7.
— featured, Lahaina News, January 23, 2003: 6.

KA'ANAPALI HILLSIDE
— Jeffrey T. Long & Associates chosen as architects for development, Lahaina News, September 26, 1984: 14.
— groundbreaking for Phase IIB of development, Lahaina News, July 24, 1985: 8.
— market for development featured, Lahaina News, April 15, 1999: 10.
— update on market for development, Lahaina News, June 17, 1999: 12.
— housing development featured, Lahaina News, September 28, 2000: 12.
— development featured, Lahaina News, December 21, 2000: 12.
— houses available at development, Lahaina News, March 1, 2001: 6.

KA'ANAPALI HOTEL [BUSINESS]
— new name for Maui Hilton, Lahaina Sun, February 28, 1973: 11.
— renovations, Lahaina News, June 29, 1995: 10.

KA'ANAPALI KAI CHARTERS
— builds catamaran Teralani 2, Lahaina News, December 28, 2000: 16.

KA'ANAPALI KALIKIMAKA
— to benefit Food Bank, Lahaina News, December 3, 1998: 5.
— to support Maui Food Bank, Lahaina News, December 9, 1999: 7.

KA'ANAPALI KAU LIO RIDING STABLES [BUSINESS]
— horseback riding at, Lahaina News, June 6, 1984: 9.
— owned by Jim Bruce, closes, Lahaina News, July 18, 1991: 14.

KA'ANAPALI KLASSIC OCEAN SWIM
— results of, Lahaina News, May 30, 1990: 6.
— to be held, Lahaina News, April 24, 2003: 11.

KA'ANAPALI NORTH BEACH JOINT VENTURE
— asks Maui Planning Commission to consider request for hotel developments at North Beach, Lahaina News, March 9, 1995: 1,16.
— seeks clarification from Maui Planning Commission on project's required contributions, Lahaina News, April 13, 1995: 2.

KA'ANAPALI NORTH COURSE
— to host EMC Ka'anapali Classic, Lahaina News, October 12, 2000: 3.
— real estate development at, Lahaina News, January 17, 2002: 6.

KA'ANAPALI OCEAN RESORT
— construction begins, Lahaina News, February 8, 2001: 17.

KA'ANAPALI OWNERSHIP RESORTS
— submits new plan for time share resort at North Beach, Lahaina News, April 10, 1997: 1.

KA'ANAPALI PLANTATION
— residents play shuffle board, Lahaina News, August 8, 1990: 24.

KA'ANAPALI POINT
— surf location featured in Wetscreams [film], Lahaina Times, August, 1980 volume 4 number 7: 5.

KA'ANAPALI QUEEN [SHIP]
— catamaran arrives at Ka'anapali Beach, Lahaina News, November 28, 1996: 14.
— catamaran added to Trilogy Excursions fleet, Lahaina News, May 8, 1997: 14.

KA'ANAPALI RESORT
— receives Award for Excellence from Urban Land Institute, Lahaina News, December 31, 1986: 3.
— planning Fourth of July, Lahaina News, July 1, 1999: 1,16.

KA'ANAPALI ROYAL
— featured, Lahaina News, February 1, 2001: 7.
— development featured, Lahaina News, November 8, 2001: 7.

KA'ANAPALI SALON [BUSINESS]
— has new manager, Lahaina News, August 21, 1997: 12.

KA'ANAPALI SHORES HOTEL [BUSINESS]
— parent company changes name from Hotel Corporation of the Pacific to Aston Hotels and Resorts, Lahaina News, February 12, 1986: 3.
— and shoreline erosion, Lahaina News, August 3, 1988: 1.
— hosts Sand Castle Sundays, Lahaina News, October 19, 1988: 3.
— featured, Lahaina News, February 3, 2000: 10.
— grants a wish with Starlight Children's Foundation, Lahaina News, March 22, 2001: 8.
— supports Starlight Children's Foundation, Lahaina News, March 29, 2001: 8.
— Denise Young new resort manager at, Lahaina News, July 26, 2001: 8.
— Annual Homeowners Meeting to be held, Lahaina News, January 10, 2002: 6.
— Mark Mrantz is new general manager at, Lahaina News, October 3, 2002: 8.
— new managers at, Lahaina News, August 28, 2003: 8.

KA'ANAPALI SOUTH COURSE
— to host Maui Chamber of Commerce Golf Tournament, Lahaina News, April 29, 1999: 7.

KA'ANAPALI TAXI [BUSINESS]
— wins taxi concession at Kahului airport, Lahaina News, January 16, 1992: 8.

KA'ANAPALI TOWERS
— two 12-story condominiums planned, Lahaina Sun, May 30, 1973: 7.

KA'ANAPALI TROLLEY
— begins operation, Lahaina News, December 10, 1986: 4.

KA'ANAPALI VACATION CLUB
— plans for North Beach timeshare open to public comment, Lahaina News, October 3, 1996: 3.

KA'ANAPALI VISTA
— development is 25 years old, Lahaina News, July 4, 2002: 6.
— featured, Lahaina News, August 29, 2002: 18.

KA'ANAPALI—MAKING IT PONO
— steering committee announced, Lahaina News, November 11, 1999: 16.

KAAPANA, LEDWARD [MUSICIAN]
— to perform at Maui Prince Hotel, Lahaina News, December 26, 1990: 8.
— continues to perform at Molokini Lounge at the Maui Prince Hotel, Lahaina News, April 3, 1991: 8.
— to perform at Aloha Festivals, Lahaina News, October 10, 1991: 17.
— to perform at Bank of Hawaii Ki-Ho'alu 2000 Hawaiian Slack Key Guitar Festival, Lahaina News, May 25, 2000: 17.

KA'APANA, LEDWARD [MUSICIAN]
— to perform at Maui Arts and Cultural Center, Lahaina News, May 22, 2003: 15.
— to perform at Maui Arts and Cultural Center, Lahaina News, May 29, 2003: 16.

KA'AU CRATER BOYS, THE [MUSICAL GROUP]
— to perform a Honolua Surf, Lahaina News, June 13, 1996: 10.
— to perform last Maui concert at Maui Marriott, Lahaina News, August 21, 1997: 17.

KAAUAMO, FRANK
— taro farmer described, Lahaina Sun, July 18, 1973: 13.

KAAUAMO, HENRY
— taro farmer featured, Lahaina News, October 4, 1989: addition3,addition11.

KAAWA, MIKE [MUSICIAN]
— releases "Hwn Boy" CD, Lahaina News, June 3, 1999: 2.

KABANIAEV, NIKOLAI
— to teach ballet master class, Lahaina News, May 11, 1995: 12.

KABUKI
— to be featured in Ukiyo-e prints at Honolulu Academy of Arts, Lahaina News, January 16, 1991: 13.

KADOTANI [FAMILY]
— featured, Lahaina News, July 22, 1987: 1,11.
— saves house from fire, Lahaina News, July 12, 2001: 1,18.

KADOTANI, HATSUMI
— retires from Lahaina Public Library after 35 years, Lahaina News, September 28, 1988: 6.

KADOTANI, LEAH AND KAYLEN
— Scholar/Athlete of the Week, Lahaina News, December 5, 1996: 13.

KADOTANI, SAM "SAMMY"
— community involvement featured, Lahaina News, July 4, 1991: 8.
— "Unofficial Mayor" of Lahaina featured, Lahaina News, November 9, 2000: 1,12.

KAENA POINT [OAHU]
— as surf spot, Lahaina Times, July, 1980 volume 4 number 6: 1.

KAENAE OPEN MARKET
— to be held, Lahaina News, December 11, 1997: 18.

KAENAE SCHOOL
— described, including photographs, Lahaina Sun, March 28, 1973: 15.

KAGAWA, KEN
— named officer of Lahaina Kamaakina Fishing Association, Lahaina Sun, December 23, 1970: 1,10.

KAGE, KAZUO
— reappointed to the planning commission, Lahaina Sun, January 13, 1971: 8.

KAGEHIRO, JAN
— named Vice President of Corporate Communications at Amfac, Inc., Lahaina News, December 13, 1989: 7.

KAHAHANE, GEORGE
— named officer of Lahaina Kamaakina Fishing Association, Lahaina Sun, December 23, 1970: 11.

KAHAHANE, JOHN
— member of Lahaina Kamaakina Fishing Association, Lahaina Sun, December 23, 1970: 11.

KAHAHANE, MILDRED
— featured, Lahaina News, April 23, 1992: 18.

KAHAHANE, SHAY-ANNE
— part of royal couple for Junior Promenade at Lahainaluna High School, Lahaina News, April 9, 1998: 2.

KAHAHANE SR., FRANK
— named officer of Lahaina Kamaakina Fishing Association, Lahaina Sun, December 23, 1970: 11.

KAHAHANE-LIVED, CHARLENE
— Scholar/Athlete of the Week, Lahaina News, March 26, 1998: 6.

KAHAIALI'I FAMILY [MUSICAL GROUP]
— featured, Lahaina News, April 16, 1992: 3.
— to perform at Ka'anapali Beach Hotel, Lahaina News, July 14, 1994: 15.
— to perform at Ka'anapali Beach Hotel, Lahaina News, October 27, 1994: 18.

KAHAIALI'I, KODY
— Scholar/Athlete of the Week, Lahaina News, March 28, 2002: 10.

KAHAIALI'I, MANU [MUSICIAN]
— begins column in Lahaina News, Lahaina News, July 17, 1985: .
— lyrics reprinted, Lahaina News, May 14, 1986: 8.
— Maui trustee for Office of Hawaiian Affairs featured, Lahaina News, March 29, 1989: 2.
— to offer slack key guitar class, Lahaina News, December 26, 1991: 4.
— to lead slack key guitar classes, Lahaina News, January 2, 1992: 5.
— to be celebrated at the Maui Arts and Cultural Center, Lahaina News, October 27, 1994: 20.

KAHAIALI'I, WALTER
— Scholar/Athlete of the Week, Lahaina News, May 18, 2000: 14.

KAHAIALI'I, WILLIE [MUSICIAN]
— touring in Canada, Lahaina News, July 11, 1984: 12.
— returns from Canada, playing Whalers Pub, Lahaina News, January 16, 1985: 17.
— interviewed, Lahaina News, February 6, 1985: 17.
— still playing at Ocean House, Lahaina News, November 13, 1985: 10.
— recommended, Lahaina News, January 1, 1986: 8.
— performs with his father Manu at Royal Lahaina Resort, Lahaina News, August 9, 1989: 1.
— to perform at Old Lahaina Cafe and Luau, Lahaina News, June 27, 1990: 10.
— to perform at Casanova's, Lahaina News, August 22, 1990: 13.
— to perform at Kobe Japanese Steak House, Lahaina News, October 10, 1990: 13.
— to perform at Kobe Japanese Steak House, Lahaina News, October 17, 1990: 15.
— to perform at Beaux Art Ball, Lahaina News, June 6, 1991: 18.
— to perform at Campbell Park, sponsored by LahainaTown Action Committee, Lahaina News, October 17, 1991: 15.
— to perform during Halloween celebration, Lahaina News, October 24, 1991: 17,18.

— wins four Na Noku Hanohano awards, Lahaina News, April 23, 1992: 3.

— to perform at Compadres Mexican Bar and Grill, Lahaina News, August 20, 1992: 18.

— to perform at fundraiser for Pop Warner Association, Lahaina News, September 10, 1992: 13.

— performs at Pop Warner football benefit, Lahaina News, September 17, 1992: 13.

— performs at benefit concert for Scot T. Rotten, Lahaina News, April 1, 1993: 1.

— to perform at Maui Lu Longhouse, Lahaina News, October 7, 1993: 13.

— to perform at Compadres Mexican Bar and Grill, Lahaina News, March 3, 1994: 12.

— to perform at Compadres Mexican Bar and Grill, Lahaina News, March 17, 1994: 9.

— to perform at Compadres Mexican Bar and Grill, Lahaina News, April 28, 1994: 13.

— to perform at Ludwigs, Lahaina News, February 8, 1996: 14.

— to perform at Hula Grill, Lahaina News, February 22, 1996: 13.

— to perform at Moose McGillycuddy's, Lahaina News, May 9, 1996: 15,16.

— to perform at World Cafe, Lahaina News, June 13, 1996: 10.

— to perform at World Café, Lahaina News, July 11, 1996: 12.

— to perform at World Cafe, Lahaina News, August 8, 1996: 15.

— to perform with Amy Gilliom, Lahaina News, April 24, 1997: 11.

— to perform benefit concert for Ronald McDonald House, Lahaina News, December 11, 1997: 19.

— to perform at fundraiser for Hui O Wa'a Kaulua, Lahaina News, December 24, 1998: 13.

— to perform with Amy Hanaiali'i Gilliom, Lahaina News, December 2, 1999: 17.

— to perform at Maui Arts and Cultural Center to benefit Maui Dharma Center, Lahaina News, June 29, 2000: 21.

— to perform with Amy Hanaiali'i Gilliom at Maui Arts and Cultural Center, Lahaina News, November 30, 2000: 18.

— releases new CD "The Uncle in Me, Volume 2", Lahaina News, July 19, 2001: 15.

— releases new CD, Lahaina News, November 15, 2001: 14.

— to perform Christmas concert, Lahaina News, November 29, 2001: 17.

— to hold "Willie Kalikimaka", Lahaina News, December 6, 2001: 16.

— to perform holiday concert, Lahaina News, December 5, 2002: 19.

— to play "Willie Kalikimaka", Lahaina News, December 12, 2002: 20.

KAHAINA GATEWAY CENTER

— to be completed in October, 1990, Lahaina News, August 15, 1990: 11.

KAHAKALAU, "SISTAH" ROBI [MUSICIAN]

— to perform at Traditional Acoustic Christmas Concert, Lahaina News, January 9, 1997: 11.

— to perform at Maui Arts and Cultural Center, Lahaina News, January 16, 1997: 11.

— to perform at Maui Arts and Cultural Center, Lahaina News, March 5, 1998: 17.

— to perform at Maui Arts and Cultural Center, Lahaina News, March 12, 1998: 20.

— to perform at Live on the Beach, Lahaina News, May 21, 1998: 8.

— to perform at "Music on the Beach", Lahaina News, May 28, 1998: 12.

— to perform at Lahaina Cannery Mall's 13th anniversary commemoration, Lahaina News, March 9, 2000: 12.

— to perform at Ho'onanea Hawaiian Series, Lahaina News, March 7, 2002: 15.

— to perform at Maui Arts and Cultural Center, Lahaina News, March 14, 2002: 17.

KAHAKUI, DONNA KAHIWAOKAWAILANI "KAHI"

— paddles from Kapalua to Waikiki, Lahaina News, June 25, 1998: 1,7.

— attempting 200-mile paddle, Lahaina News, October 11, 2001: 13.

KAHAKULOA [TOWN]

— described, including photographs, Lahaina Sun, July 4, 1973: 12,13.

— portable bridge to become permanent, Lahaina News, December 14, 1988: 16.

— Planning Commission to hold hearing to review special management area permit, Lahaina News, February 7, 1990: 28.

— roadwork slated near, Lahaina News, May 1, 2003: 2.

KAHAKULOA CAMP

— Lahainaluna Voyaging Team visits, Lahaina News, December 11, 1997: 17.

KAHAKULOA HAWAIIAN CONGREGATIONAL PROTESTANT CHURCH

— to hold musical fundraiser, Lahaina News, November 6, 1997: 17.

KAHALEKULU, YONG

— selected to compete in Marriott's national teppan competition, Lahaina News, November 15, 1989: 9.

KAHALEPUNA, STERLING

— passes away, Lahaina News, September 30, 1999: 2.

KAHAN, STUART

— to lead discussion of West Maui Transportation Plan, Lahaina News, January 23, 2003: 16.

KAHANA [TOWN]

— public hearing to discuss proposed apartment complex, Lahaina Sun, January 31, 1973: 6.

— land settlement reached with Native Hawaiian families, Lahaina News, November 23, 1983: 4.

— Maui Planning Commission recommends commercial space and apartment rental units in, Lahaina News, May 6, 1987: 1.

— developer Mark Henderson Ives proposes condominium project, Lahaina News, August 9, 1989: 1.

— Maui Land and Pineapple, Co. seeking zoning change in, Lahaina News, May 30, 1990: 5.

— State and County oppose housing project in, Lahaina News, October 31, 1991: 1,3.

— County Planning Commission will not require environmental impact statement for residential project in, Lahaina News, February 6, 1992: 1.

— West Maui Planning Commission recommends converting land from agricultural to residential, Lahaina News, April 2, 1992: 6.

— residential subdivision approval recommended by Maui County Council, Lahaina News, September 3, 1992: 3.

— housing project approved for, Lahaina News, November 12, 1992: 12.

— State Land Use Commission votes to reclassify land from agricultural to urban in, Lahaina News, January 21, 1993: 4.

— funds may be available to fix drainage issue, Lahaina News, May 11, 1995: 4.

— brush fire, Lahaina News, February 5, 1998: 1.

— affordable condominiums proposed at, Lahaina News, June 20, 2002: 6.

KAHANA AND LAHAINA VIDEO [BUSINESS]

— opening second video rental store, Lahaina News, August 14, 1985: 1.

KAHANA BEACH HOTEL [BUSINESS]

— planned by Mike Resnick, Lahaina Sun, February 14, 1973: 12,13.

KAHANA BEACH RESORT CONDOMINIUM

— Aston Hotels and Resorts Hawaii now managing sales, marketing, and reservations, Lahaina News, September 14, 2000: 15.

KAHANA BRIDGE

— opens, Lahaina News, October 13, 1994: 15.

KAHANA CANOE CLUB
— wins Kahana Invitational regatta, Lahaina News, May 23, 1984: 6.
— to meet at Lahaina Civic Center, celebrating 10th anniversary, Lahaina News, January 29, 1986: 3.
— to hold fundraisers, Lahaina News, July 15, 1987: 6.
— holds fundraiser, Lahaina News, August 26, 1987: 3.
— to hold car wash and rummage sale fundraiser, Lahaina News, April 4, 1990: 3.
— to sponsor third outrigger canoe regatta race, Lahaina News, June 20, 1990: 8.
— to hold general membership meeting, Lahaina News, February 27, 1991: 6.
— to hold long distance canoe race, Lahaina News, May 15, 1991: 7.
— to host breakfast and auction, Lahaina News, March 5, 1992: 8.
— sponsoring Hotel/Resort Canoe Championship Regatta, Lahaina News, March 25, 1993: 6.
— featured, Lahaina News, May 6, 1993: 10.
— featured, Lahaina News, May 12, 1994: 6.
— to hold Maui Hotel/Resort Canoe Championship Regatta, Lahaina News, March 30, 1995: 7.
— sponsoring Regatta at Hanaka'o'o Beach Park, Lahaina News, April 11, 1996: 7.
— featured, Lahaina News, May 9, 1996: 6.
— to compete, Lahaina News, May 22, 1997: 1,13.
— featured, Lahaina News, June 4, 1998: 14.
— girls crew to compete in state championship, Lahaina News, July 9, 1998: 14.
— finishes third in AA division of Canoe racing Association State Championships, Lahaina News, August 6, 1998: 19.
— participates in Festival of Canoes Parade, Lahaina News, May 20, 1999: 1.
— upcoming season featured, Lahaina News, June 10, 1999: 6.
— rebuilding, Lahaina News, June 15, 2000: 12.
— welcomes new members, Lahaina News, March 1, 2001: 15.
— to hold workouts, Lahaina News, March 15, 2001: 11.
— to hold workouts, Lahaina News, April 5, 2001: 14.
— continues to hold workouts, Lahaina News, April 12, 2001: 14.
— featured, Lahaina News, July 5, 2001: 12.
— to hold annual general membership meeting, Lahaina News, February 21, 2002: 13.
— featured, Lahaina News, July 18, 2002: 12.
— featured, Lahaina News, June 26, 2003: 10.

KAHANA FALLS HOTEL CONDOMINIUM
— holds groundbreaking, Lahaina News, October 17, 1990: 11.

KAHANA FALLS RESORT [BUSINESS]
— opens, Lahaina News, March 19, 1992: 12.
— supporting Visitor Industry Charity Walk, Lahaina News, October 11, 2001: 9.
— to hold toy drive, Lahaina News, February 21, 2002: 8.
— honors employees, Lahaina News, April 4, 2002: 8.
— honors top employees, Lahaina News, January 23, 2003: 9.

KAHANA GATEWAY APARTMENTS
— Ronald "Ron" Wiele named resident manager, Lahaina News, January 30, 1991: 5.

KAHANA GATEWAY PROFESSIONAL BUILDING
— location of new West Maui Kidney Dialysis Center, Lahaina News, December 8, 1994: 3.

KAHANA GATEWAY SHOPPING CENTER [BUSINESS]
— to be developed by Mike Resnik, Lahaina News, November 16, 1988: 1.
— to hold recruitment fair, Lahaina News, May 9, 1990: 5.
— fitness center open by DeAnn and Gregg Steele, Lahaina News, June 20, 1991: 5.
— to open, Lahaina News, November 28, 1991: 2.
— tenants listed, Lahaina News, January 16, 1992: 9.

— hosting health fair, Lahaina News, April 16, 1992: 4.
— to hold sidewalk sale, Lahaina News, May 7, 1992: 3.
— drawing winners announced, Lahaina News, May 21, 1992: 4.
— to host Summer Fun Challenge, Lahaina News, July 9, 1992: 3.
— retains Catapult Productions, Inc., Lahaina News, September 17, 1992: 11.
— to hold drawing for prizes, Lahaina News, December 10, 1992: 3,4.
— kiosk space opening in, Lahaina News, January 5, 1995: 6.

KAHANA HARDWARE, THE [BUSINESS]
— opens, Lahaina News, January 16, 1992: 9.

KAHANA KEYES [RESTAURANT]
— reviewed, Lahaina News, September 28, 1983: 13.

KAHANA KOIN-OP LAUNDROMAT [BUSINESS]
— to open soon, Lahaina News, November 19, 1992: 5.

KAHANA OUTRIGGER
— emergency sea wall concerns residents, Lahaina News, October 14, 1993: 1.

KAHANA RIDGE
— Maui County Council's Planning Committee considering request by Corporation 3521 for development on , Lahaina News, June 8, 1995: 1,2.
— lots available, Lahaina News, April 25, 1996: 12.
— construction funded, Lahaina News, September 5, 1996: 22.
— development featured, Lahaina News, November 11, 1999: 10.
— new homes available at, Lahaina News, January 6, 2000: 10.
— Joe McKay joins as manager, Lahaina News, June 22, 2000: 8.
— Summer Home Show to be held, Lahaina News, July 6, 2000: 8.
— featured, Lahaina News, August 17, 2000: 12.
— sales surge at, Lahaina News, December 7, 2000: 18.
— sales surging, Lahaina News, July 19, 2001: 6.
— ocean view lots left, Lahaina News, July 26, 2001: 7.
— real estate featured, Lahaina News, September 13, 2001: 6.
— development featured, Lahaina News, November 8, 2001: 6.
— lots remaining, Lahaina News, February 28, 2002: 6.
— development featured, Lahaina News, April 25, 2002: 6.

KAHANA SONS [MUSICAL GROUP]
— show at Lahaina Broiler reviewed, Lahaina News, March 1, 1980: 5.

KAHANA STREAM
— stagnant water moved by rain, Lahaina News, February 2, 1995: 1.

KAHANA STREAM SILT BASIN
— to be cleaned, Lahaina News, May 26, 1994: 4.

KAHANA SUNSET
— featured, Lahaina News, May 6, 1999: 14.
— Pearl Collins becomes general manager, Lahaina News, August 16, 2001: 8.

KAHANA TERRACE [RESTAURANT]
— featuring music and new menu, Lahaina News, July 11, 1991: 16.
— featured, Lahaina News, October 1, 1998: 6.
— to offer specials for Valentine's Day, Lahaina News, February 4, 1999: 7.

KAHANA VALLEY
— Maui County Planning and Land Use Committee defers decision to rezone acres of, as part of quiet title settlement, Lahaina News, April 17, 1991: 1.

KAHANA VIDEO [BUSINESS]
— featured, Lahaina News, May 2, 1984: 17.

KAHANA VILLA
— development featured, Lahaina News, May 9, 1984: 14.

KAHANA VILLAGE
— condominium featured, Lahaina News, January 4, 2001: 12.
— featured, Lahaina News, August 2, 2001: 6.

KAHANAMOKU, MRS. DUKE
— dedicates train coach honoring Duke Kahanamoku, Lahaina Sun, January 20, 1971: 1.

KAHEKILI [PLAY]
— to be performed, Lahaina News, September 4, 1997: 16.

KAHEKILI PARK
— Dr. Rubellite Johnson keynote speaker at opening of, Lahaina News, October 15, 1992: 3.
— Amfac/JMB Hawaii allowing sunset picnickers at, Lahaina News, May 2, 1996: 3.

KAHELEKULU, YONG
— to compete at Marriott's national teppan competition, Lahaina News, November 22, 1989: 4.

KAHI KAMALI'I
— groundbreaking held for infant and child center, Lahaina News, August 22, 2002: 9.

KAHIAMOE, NANETTE PUAMANA
— named Secretary of the Year, Lahaina News, January 2, 1991: 5.

KAHIKO O HAWAII [SHOW]
— reviewed, Lahaina News, May 6, 1987: 4.

KAHLE, RICHARD
— to speak to West Maui Taxpayers Association, Lahaina News, May 11, 1988: 14.

KAHN, DAVID
— named director of sales for Hyatt Regency Maui, Lahaina News, February 5, 1986: 3.

KAHN, ERIKA [ARTIST]
— papermaker to offer lecture and workshops, Lahaina News, February 6, 1985: 3.
— to teach gyotaku at Hui No'eau Visual Arts Center, Lahaina News, July 27, 1988: 11.
— to exhibit at Village Gallery-Lahaina, Lahaina News, October 28, 1993: 10.

KAHN, ROB
— see signage

KAHOMA STREAM
— Army Corps of Engineers recommends converting part of stream to concrete channel as part of flood plan, Lahaina Sun, March 21, 1973: 1.
— flood control project to be funded by bonds, Lahaina News, February 15, 1984: 5.
— girl dies after falling into, Lahaina News, April 18, 1984: 5.
— project to tie up traffic, Lahaina News, March 4, 1987: 1.
— construction of bridge delayed, Lahaina News, January 20, 1988: 1.
— bridge construction delayed, Lahaina News, May 4, 1988: 1.
— debate concerning detour during construction of, Lahaina News, June 15, 1988: 1,14.
— Mayor Hannibal Tavares may agree to detour while rebuilt, Lahaina News, July 6, 1988: 1,24.
— bridge to reopen, Lahaina News, July 6, 1988: 11.
— floods, Lahaina News, June 7, 1989: 3,10.
— ancient Hawaiian remains while working on flood control project, Lahaina News, October 25, 1989: 3.

KAHOMA STREAM FLOOD CONTROL PROJECT
— funding clears U.S. House Committee and is sent to floor for a vote, Lahaina News, October 3, 1984: 13.
— Maui County Council passes resolution to proceed with, Lahaina News, June 25, 1986: 3.
— groundbreaking for, Lahaina News, January 14, 1987: 12.
— half finished, Lahaina News, November 18, 1987: 1.
— completed by U.S. Army Corps of Engineers, Lahaina News, June 6, 1990: 1.

KAHO'OHALAHALA, HA'AHEO
— Lahainaluna High School student wins National Leadership and Service Award, Lahaina News, April 22, 1999: 5.

KAHO'OHALAHALA, SOL [POLITICIAN]
— to hold forum, Lahaina News, September 5, 1996: 19.
— to run for 7th House District, Lahaina News, July 23, 1998: 1.
— asked to explain campaign donation, Lahaina News, January 21, 1999: 1,16.
— lawmakers seeking funding Lahaina-Moloka'i ferry, Lahaina News, February 25, 1999: 1.
— encourages residents to lobby for state funding, Lahaina News, March 4, 1999: 1,16.
— faces two challengers in race to be state Representative for District 7, Lahaina News, August 3, 2000: 5.
— candidate for State House Representative, District 7, Lahaina News, October 26, 2000: 22.
— meets with Friends of Moku'ula at Malu'ulu O Lele Park, Lahaina News, June 26, 2003: 1.

KAHO'OHANOHANO, DAVID
— running for Upcountry seat on County Council, Lahaina News, July 6, 2000: 15.

KAHO'OHANOHANO, DAVID [POLITICIAN]
— candidate for Upcountry County Council Seat, Lahaina News, November 2, 2000: 22.

KAHO'OHANOHANO, POHAKU [ARTIST]
— to teach class on weaving, Lahaina News, August 28, 1997: 10.
— to teach "Weaving Lauhala Baskets", Lahaina News, October 9, 1997: 20.
— to hold class on weaving lauhala mats, Lahaina News, January 8, 1998: 12.
— to lead lauhala weaving class, Lahaina News, February 7, 2002: 16.

KAHO'OLAWE [ISLAND]
— revegetation program, Lahaina Sun, February 10, 1971: 2.
— Daniel Inouye calls for return of to the State of Hawaii, Lahaina Sun, February 17, 1971: 6.
— Maui County Council asks for return of, Lahaina Sun, February 24, 1971: 2.
— return opposed by Marco Meyer, Lahaina Sun, March 3, 1971: 8.
— legislation introduced by Daniel Inouye to return, Lahaina Sun, May 5, 1971: 3.
— U.S. argues it needs to retain control, Lahaina Sun, June 2, 1971: 6.
— Hawaii State Chamber of Commerce supports continued use by Navy as bombing target, Lahaina Sun, July 7, 1971: 3.
— Maui Chamber of Commerce concerned with economic impact of Navy pullout, Lahaina Sun, July 21, 1971: 9.
— Mayor Cravalho and Life of the Land sue to stop bombing of, Lahaina Sun, August 4, 1971: 1,2.
— Admiral Thomas Hayward defends navy's use of, Lahaina Sun, September 15, 1971: 1.
— hearing set for lawsuit to stop the Navy's bombing of, Lahaina Sun, November 10, 1971: 1.
— issues discussed, Lahaina Sun, January 26, 1972: 6,7.
— editorial comments about return of island, Lahaina Sun, February 16, 1972: 15.
— suit against U.S. Navy dismissed, Lahaina Sun, May 24, 1972: 11.
— history of described, Lahaina Sun, January 31, 1973: 22.
— attempts to remove goats from island detailed, Lahaina Sun, February 21, 1973: 5.
— 19th century events on island detailed, Lahaina Sun, March 28, 1973: 22.
— U.S. Representative Patsy Mink joins call for return of, Lahaina Sun, August 8, 1973: 5.
— Navy kills goats with machine guns, Lahaina News, June 15, 1980: 19.

— mayor Tavares asks Navy to reduce noise of bombing, Lahaina News, December 15, 1982: 2.
— attempts to recover it described, Lahaina News, September 5, 1984: 7,8,9.
— editorial calling for a settlement, Lahaina News, September 12, 1984: 2.
— attempts to recover it described, article continued from last issue, Lahaina News, September 12, 1984: 7,8,9.
— State Senator Rick Reed urges U.S. Navy to stop bombing, Lahaina News, February 3, 1988: 4,6.
— cultural develops connected to trying to stop bombings, Lahaina News, May 18, 1988: 1,5.
— access possible through Protect Kaho'olawe Ohana, Lahaina News, May 18, 1988: 3.
— resistance to bombing of, Lahaina News, June 1, 1988: 1.
— damage to archaeological sites leads to legal fight, Lahaina News, June 8, 1988: 1.
— editorial supporting return of, Lahaina News, June 8, 1988: 2.
— Walter Ritte, Jr. skeptical of President Bush's order to halt Navy bombing on, Lahaina News, October 31, 1990: 1.
— Turstee "Frenchy" DeSoto to represent OHA on the Kaho'olawe Island Conveyance Committee, Lahaina News, November 14, 1990: 4.
— "Stillborn" to open at Maui Community Theatre, Lahaina News, December 26, 1990: 11.
— conveyance commission to hold public hearing, Lahaina News, April 24, 1991: 5.
— Conveyance commission to hold public hearing, Lahaina News, May 8, 1991: 4.
— public meeting to discuss proposed National Marine Sanctuary around, Lahaina News, August 8, 1991: 7.
— public meeting to be held on proposed Marine Sanctuary, Lahaina News, August 22, 1991: 3.
— Representative Patsy Mink favors Marine Sanctuary around, Lahaina News, September 5, 1991: 1.
— ceremony at Palauea Beach held to mark return of, Lahaina News, May 12, 1994: 1,4.
— fishing rules discussed, Lahaina News, September 29, 1994: 6.
— Lahainaluna High School Voyaging Program travels to , Lahaina News, July 8, 1999: 3.
— Lahainaluna High School students to voyage to, Lahaina News, May 4, 2000: 9.

KAHO'OLAWE COMMUNITY PLAN
— Maui Planning Commission to hold public hearing, Lahaina News, September 16, 1993: 3.

KAHO'OLAWE ISLAND CONVEYANCE COMMISSION
— to hold meeting and workshop, Lahaina News, March 12, 1992: 3.
— see also Kaho'olawe

KAHO'OLAWE ISLAND RESERVE COMMISSION
— to meet, Lahaina News, December 5, 1996: 14.
— to hold meeting on restoration plan, Lahaina News, July 17, 1997: 17.
— to review Ocean Management Plan, Lahaina News, August 21, 1997: 15.
— to detail cleanup plan, Lahaina News, May 14, 1998: 16.
— releases Open Waters Schedule, Lahaina News, January 28, 1999: 7.
— plans to be explained, Lahaina News, February 4, 1999: 1.
— to hold workshop on Ocean Management Program, Lahaina News, February 18, 1999: 12.
— Hokulani Holt-Padilla to speak on "The Cultural Heritage of Kaho'olawe", Lahaina News, October 19, 2000: 21.
— Samantha Whitecraft and Lisa Pytka to speak on "Everyday Data that Makes a Difference: Simple Data, Big Results in the Kaho'olawe Island Reserve", Lahaina News, April 3, 2003: 17.

KAHO'OLAWE: KE ALOHA KUPA'A I KA AINA
— art show to be held at Kazuma International Gallery, Lahaina News, January 9, 1997: 13.
— exhibit continues, Lahaina News, January 16, 1997: 10.

KAHUA [MUSICAL GROUP]
— to perform at Ka'anapali Beach Hotel's Tiki Courtyard, Lahaina News, February 6, 2003: 16.

KAHUA HAWAIIAN INSTITUTE
— to hold lecture on tantra, Lahaina News, September 11, 1997: 16.
— "Surf the Tantric Wave in Hawaii" to be held, Lahaina News, July 8, 1999: 13.
— plan Summer Oceanic Tantra Retreat, Lahaina News, July 13, 2000: 16.
— to hold Oceanic Tantra seminars, Lahaina News, November 30, 2000: 16.
— leading workshop "Sexual Energy and Artistic Expression", Lahaina News, November 15, 2001: 16.
— to hold "Initiation into the Tantric Heart", Lahaina News, February 14, 2002: 17.
— to hold Women's Retreat, Lahaina News, April 4, 2002: 16.

KAHUA KAI
— Whalers Realty, Inc. and Kirkland Development Company held ground breaking for, Lahaina News, January 20, 2000: 11.
— subdivision breaks ground, Lahaina News, February 10, 2000: 13.
— development includes innovative drainage system, Lahaina News, December 7, 2000: 20.
— development featured, Lahaina News, February 13, 2003: 6.

KAHULUI [TOWN]
— town plan to be unveiled, Lahaina Sun, June 16, 1971: 12.
— mayor Cravalho skeptical of development plans, Lahaina Sun, June 30, 1971: 9.
— Hawaii Wood Preserving Company given permission to build wood treating plant, Lahaina Sun, October 27, 1971: 5.
— new park planned, Lahaina Sun, March 15, 1972: 4.
— renewal plans for discussed, Lahaina Sun, July 19, 1972: 4,5.
— Wailuku-Kahului general plan discussed, Lahaina Sun, October 25, 1972: 5.
— Mayor Cravalho claims Wailuku-Kahului general plan is good, Lahaina Sun, December 27, 1972: 14.

KAHULUI AIRPORT
— United plans to bring charter passenger flights to, Lahaina Sun, January 13, 1971: 6.
— more parking planned, Lahaina Sun, July 21, 1971: 3.
— improvements to, announced, Lahaina Sun, August 18, 1971: 11.
— receives air traffic facility of the year award, Lahaina Sun, September 1, 1971: 15.
— parking limitations imposed, Lahaina Sun, September 15, 1971: 6.
— Department of Transportation opens more parking stalls, Lahaina News, December 9, 1987: 3.
— new terminal opens, Lahaina News, December 27, 1989: 5.
— map of new terminal, Lahaina News, March 12, 1992: 12.
— lawsuit challenges environmental study for expansion of, Lahaina News, October 15, 1992: 3.
— Kiewit Pacific Co. contracting firm files lawsuit against state over Terminal extension project, Lahaina News, December 23, 1993: 7.
— Sierra Club to hold update on, Lahaina News, April 9, 1998: 16.
— plans to extend runway, Lahaina News, September 3, 1998: 1.

KAHULUI AIRPORT SHUTTLE
— new schedule for, Lahaina News, February 16, 1995: 12.

KAHULUI COMMUNITY PARK
— process for creating a master development plan criticized, Lahaina Sun, January 26, 1972: 14.

KAHULUI HARBOR
— claimed by Mike Cleveland to be unfit for swimming due to pollution, Lahaina Sun, November 18, 1970: 1.
— tested for pollution, Lahaina Sun, December 16, 1970: 3.
— pollution in, discussed, Lahaina Sun, February 3, 1971: 4.
— oil spill contained, Lahaina Sun, September 8, 1971: 5.
— closed due to kona winds, Lahaina Sun, February 9, 1972: 3.
— plans for expansion, Lahaina Sun, February 9, 1972: 5.
— featured in Wetscreams [film] as surf location, Lahaina Times, August, 1980 volume 4 number 7: 5.
— improvements planned, including additional container yard, Lahaina News, October 18, 1989: 7.
— pleasure ship Regent Sea to debark, Lahaina News, September 24, 1992: 9.

KAHULUI PUBLIC LIBRARY
— works on Alcoholics Anonymous by Dick B. featured in display, Lahaina News, August 5, 1993: 5.
— features Alcoholics Anonymous display, Lahaina News, August 26, 1993: 8.

KAHULUI RAILROAD STORIES
— documentary to be shown at Bailey House, Lahaina News, June 1, 2000: 17.

KAHULUI SHELL SERVICE
— purchased by Earl Yokoyama, Lahaina News, November 21, 1990: 12.

KAHULUI TOWN TERRACE
— developer receives low-income tax credits for development of, Lahaina News, January 10, 1990: 7.

KAHULUI UNION CHURCH
— to hold bell choir, Lahaina News, December 6, 2001: 16,17.

KAHUMOKU BROTHERS, THE [MUSICAL GROUP]
— to perform at Villa Restaurant, Lahaina News, April 28, 1994: 13.
— to perform at Westin Maui, Lahaina News, September 22, 1994: 16.

KAHUMOKU, GEORGE [MUSICIAN]
— raising pigs, Lahaina News, October 13, 1994: 14.
— releases "Ho'oilina" album, Lahaina News, January 11, 1996: 13.
— releases "E Lili'u" CD, Lahaina News, August 15, 1996: 16.
— to perform at Westin Maui, Lahaina News, April 10, 1997: 9.
— to participate in Hawaiian Ki ho'alu (slack key) Workshop, Lahaina News, June 3, 1999: 17.
— to perform at opening of Mama's Ribs 'n Rotisserie, Lahaina News, July 1, 1999: 13.
— releases CD "Hymns of Hawai'i" with Daniel Ho, Lahaina News, December 9, 1999: 19.
— featured, Lahaina News, May 25, 2000: 1,14.
— to perform at Ku'u Home O Wailuku music festival, Lahaina News, October 19, 2000: 18.
— continues to perform at Hula Grill, Lahaina News, February 8, 2001: 19.
— to offer slack key workshop, Lahaina News, June 13, 2002: 15.
— to perform at Maui Arts and Cultural Center, Lahaina News, May 22, 2003: 15.
— to perform at Maui Arts and Cultural Center, Lahaina News, May 29, 2003: 16.

KAHUMOKU, KEOKI [MUSICIAN]
— to perform at Espresso Bar Courtyard, Lahaina News, October 8, 1998: 16.
— continues to perform at Espresso Bar Courtyard, Lahaina News, October 15, 1998: 17.
— continues to perform at Espresso Bar Courtyard, Lahaina News, November 12, 1998: 16.
— continues to offer classes on slack key guitar, Lahaina News, December 10, 1998: 21.

— continues to perform slack key guitar, Lahaina News, March 25, 1999: 17.
— continues to perform at Kapalua Shops, Lahaina News, April 22, 1999: 13.
— continues to perform at Kapalua Shops, Lahaina News, June 24, 1999: 13.
— continues to perform at Kapalua Shops, Lahaina News, October 21, 1999: 17.
— continues to perform at Kapalua Shops, Lahaina News, November 25, 1999: 16.
— continues to perform at Kapalua Shops, Lahaina News, March 23, 2000: 13.
— continues to perform at Kapalua Shops, Lahaina News, May 18, 2000: 20.
— continues to perform, Lahaina News, September 14, 2000: 21.
— continues to perform at Kapalua Shops, Lahaina News, December 21, 2000: 16,17.

KAI, CAROLE [MUSICIAN]
— to perform at "Local Divas in Concert", Lahaina News, September 23, 1999: 12.

KA'I HUAKA'I A ME KA LOKAHI (PROCESSION FOR UNITY)
— protest march held, Lahaina News, March 8, 2001: 2.

KAI KU ONO [RESTAURANT]
— provides shuttle service between Sugar Beach and the Maui Prince, Lahaina News, October 15, 1998: 13.
— to hold "Good Eats and Musical Treats", Lahaina News, March 11, 1999: 12.
— to hold "Good Eats and Musical Treats", Lahaina News, March 25, 1999: 17.

KAI NEHE
— development featured, Lahaina News, February 6, 2003: 6.
— featured, Lahaina News, February 13, 2003: 7.
— development featured, Lahaina News, May 29, 2003: 6.

KAI OPUA CANOE CLUB
— to hold Queen Lili'uokalani Long Distance Canoe Races, Lahaina News, August 21, 1997: 13.
— to sponsor Queen Lili'uokalani World Champion Outrigger Canoe Race, Lahaina News, August 27, 1998: 15.
— to sponsor Queen Lili'uokalani World Champion Outrigger Canoe Race, Lahaina News, September 3, 1998: 15.

KAIAHUA, EDWARD
— dies at La Jolla V.A. Medical Center, Lahaina News, April 7, 1994: 4.

KAIAHUA, KALUA
— chiropractor featured, Lahaina News, March 3, 1994: 1,2.

KAIAMA, CARL
— asks Maui Planning Commission to defer decision on condominiums due to water shortages, Lahaina Sun, May 26, 1971: 6.
— discusses drought in Maui, Lahaina Sun, August 18, 1971: 1.

KAIAMA, ROY, JR.
— retrial to be held, Lahaina News, May 28, 1992: 9.

KAIKOURA, NEW ZEALAND
— to become twin city with Lahaina, Lahaina News, April 23, 1992: 17.
— to establish sister city agreement with Lahaina, Lahaina News, November 11, 1999: 1,2.

KAIKUA'ANA NE KAIKUAHINE HULA HALAU
— to offer Christmas Recital, Lahaina News, December 23, 1999: 16.

KAILI-NUNES, RAENARD
— named queen for David Malo Day Celebration, Lahaina News, April 17, 1985: 1,20.

KAILUA HIGH SCHOOL
— band to perform, Lahaina News, March 6, 2003: 14.
— school band to perform at Lahaina Cannery Mall, Lahaina News, March 6, 2003: 16.

KAIMANA
— C. Brewer Homes neighborhood opens, Lahaina News, November 17, 1994: 10.

KAʻIMIOLA, GEORGE
— to lecture on cultural historiography, Lahaina News, December 7, 2000: 25.

KAIMIOLA, GEORGE MANULANI
— to give tour of Bailey House Museum, Lahaina News, September 6, 2001: 16.
— to lead tour at Bailey House Museum, Lahaina News, June 6, 2002: 17.
— to offer tour of Bailey House Museum, Lahaina News, August 8, 2002: 17.
— to offer "Historic Wailuku Walking Tour", Lahaina News, August 29, 2002: 20.
— offering tours of historic sites, Lahaina News, November 21, 2002: 20.

KAIMIOLA, KEOKI MANULANI
— to lead workshop on "Hawaiian Christian Heritage", Lahaina News, March 23, 2000: 12.

KAINA, ANDY [MUSICIAN]
— performance reviewed, Lahaina News, August 29, 1984: 12.

KAINA, JIMMY CEALOHALANI [MUSICIAN]
— to sing with the Maui Symphony Pops, Lahaina News, September 16, 1993: 17,18.

KAINA KOUNTRY [MUSICAL GROUP]
— performance reviewed, Lahaina News, August 29, 1984: 12.

KAISER DEVELOPMENT CORPORATION
— applies to develop shopping complex at Dickenson and Wainee, Lahaina News, September 19, 1984: 3.

KAISER PERMANENTE [BUSINESS]
— clinic to hold open house, Lahaina News, May 28, 1986: 3.
— clinic opens, Lahaina News, May 20, 1987: 3.
— renovation of Lahaina office complete, Lahaina News, April 6, 1988: 1.
— to hold open house, Lahaina News, April 24, 1991: 4.
— names Cora Tellez as Hawaii regional manager, Lahaina News, June 13, 1991: 18.
— clinic to reduce hours, Lahaina News, July 11, 1991: 4.
— to sponsor keiki run, Lahaina News, April 30, 1992: 6.
— to host cooking class by Judy Ridolfino, Lahaina News, January 15, 1998: 12.
— moves care departments from Wailuku Clinic, Lahaina News, February 27, 2003: 8.

KAIULANI, VICTORIA
— biography and political importance of princess, Lahaina News, January 1, 1981: 10.
— biography of princess, Lahaina News, November 1, 1981: 11.

KAIWI CHANNEL RELAY RACE
— results of, Lahaina News, May 24, 2001: 14.

KAIWI, CHRIS
— named general manager of Plantation House Restaurant, Lahaina News, May 8, 1991: 6.

KAJIHARA, TAKASHI
— landowner requesting zoning change, Lahaina News, July 16, 1992: 5.

KAJIHIRO, RICHARD
— arrested for burglary, Lahaina News, February 13, 1992: 1.
— indicted for burglaries, Lahaina News, March 5, 1992: 1.

KAJIURA, STEVE
— to present "The Fascinating World of Sharks" at Maui Ocean Center, Lahaina News, December 14, 2000: 20.

KAJIYAMA, KATS [WRITER]
— to sign copies of "Maui and his Magical Deeds", Lahaina News, November 20, 1997: 16.

KAKUGAWA, GLENN [MUSICIAN]
— wins Whipple Memorial Golf Tournament, Lahaina News, October 3, 1990: 6.
— to perform at B.J.'s Chicago Pizzeria, Lahaina News, October 6, 1994: 15.

KALA IKI THRIFT STORE
— opens, Lahaina News, January 11, 1989: 5.
— to open with Christmas items for sale, Lahaina News, December 6, 1989: 3.
— to hold clearance sale, Lahaina News, January 10, 1990: 24.
— to hold sale, Lahaina News, September 12, 1991: 5.
— to hold clearance sale, Lahaina News, January 16, 1992: 5.
— to open on select days, Lahaina News, June 25, 1992: 2.
— to open at Kula Hospital grounds, Lahaina News, November 7, 1996: 14.
— to feature Christmas items, Lahaina News, December 12, 1996: 8.
— open, Lahaina News, July 10, 1997: 16.
— continues to offer specials, Lahaina News, January 15, 1998: 13.
— continues to support patients at Kula Hospital, Lahaina News, October 22, 1998: 21.
— continues to raise money for hospital patients, Lahaina News, June 24, 1999: 12.
— continues to support patients, Lahaina News, March 23, 2000: 13.

KALAHUA, KALUA
— practitioner of Laʻau Lapaʻau featured, Lahaina News, August 24, 1988: 2.

KALAKAUA, DAVID [KING]
— King's trip around the world recounted, Lahaina News, August 1, 1981: 11,12.
— King's birthday to be celebrated at Banyan Tree Park, Lahaina News, November 16, 2000: 1.
— King's birthday to be celebrated at Banyan Tree Park, Lahaina News, November 23, 2000: 7.

KALAMA, DAVID
— win Hard Rock Cafe World Cup of Windsurfing, Lahaina News, May 23, 1991: 10.

KALAMA HEIGHTS RETIREMENT RESIDENCE
— to hold Christmas Craft Fair, Lahaina News, November 23, 2000: 20.

KALAMA INTERMEDIATE SCHOOL
— ukulele band to perform at Maui Prince Hotel, Lahaina News, December 19, 1991: 21.
— band to perform, Lahaina News, May 27, 1999: 12.
— musicians to stage free Christmas Concert, Lahaina News, December 14, 2000: 20.
— band to perform free concert, Lahaina News, May 29, 2003: 17.

KALAMA, LEINAʻALA HEINE [MUSICIAN]
— to perform at "Starry Night Four Hula", Lahaina News, January 29, 1998: 15.

KALAMA PARK [KIHEI]
— petition requests stop to erosion control project, Lahaina Sun, April 21, 1971: 2.
— indoor showers moved, Lahaina Sun, April 21, 1971: 2.
— petition stop to erosion control project rejected by Maui County Council, Lahaina Sun, May 12, 1971: 5.
— seniors party held, Lahaina Sun, March 14, 1973: 12.
— new playground to be developed, Lahaina News, January 9, 1992: 5.

— seeking volunteers to help develop playground, Lahaina News, January 30, 1992: 4.
— carnival to be held to raise money for playground, includes poster contest, Lahaina News, February 20, 1992: 4.
— carnival to be held, will include poster contest, Lahaina News, March 5, 1992: 4.
— playground equipment to be installed, Lahaina News, May 28, 1992: 6.
— playground equipment arrives, Lahaina News, January 14, 1993: 7.
— playground to open, Lahaina News, February 18, 1993: 7,8.
— Maui Inline Hockey Association opens rink at, Lahaina News, July 1, 1999: 7.

KALAMA PARK WHALE
— Kihei Community Association plans to reset structure, Lahaina News, March 11, 1993: 10.

KALANI HIGH SCHOOL
— updating list for 10th-year class reunion, Lahaina News, April 16, 1986: 3.

KALAOLA, LILIA
— David Malo queen, Lahaina News, April 17, 1997: 16.

KALAPA, LOWELL
— president of the Tax Foundation of Hawaii, Lahaina News, March 5, 1998: 13.
— to speak on state tax issues, Lahaina News, March 12, 1998: 16.
— to speak about taxes, Lahaina News, March 19, 1998: 11.
— president of Tax Foundation of Hawaii to speak to Maui League of Republican Women, Lahaina News, March 13, 2003: 17.

KALAPANA [MUSICAL GROUP]
— to perform at Molokini Lounge at the Maui Prince Hotel, Lahaina News, April 10, 1991: 12.
— to perform at Ho'onanea Hou Hawaiian Music series, Lahaina News, November 5, 1998: 21.
— to perform during Festival of Canoes Parade, Lahaina News, May 20, 1999: 17.
— to perform at benefit for Hawaii Firefighters, Lahaina News, September 19, 2002: 25.

KALAUPAPA
— paintings by Jim Kingwell, Lahaina News, February 6, 1997: 18.

KALAWAY, BENTLEY
— to talk "Somatic Awareness in Movement and Music: Toward Sensing and Becoming More of Who You Are", Lahaina News, September 20, 2001: 17.

KALEAKALA NATIONAL PARK
— to host night hike, Lahaina News, July 10, 1997: 17.

KALEHUA PRODUCTIONS
— to give hula performance, Lahaina News, September 10, 1998: 20.

KALEIALOHA CONDOMINIUM
— units available, Lahaina News, July 8, 1999: 10.

KALEO O KALANI [MUSICAL GROUP]
— to perform, Lahaina News, February 22, 1989: 9.
— to perform at Molokini Lounge at the Maui Prince Hotel, Lahaina News, March 13, 1991: 9.

KALEPA, ARCHIE
— saves people off Mala Wharf during hurricane Iniki, Lahaina News, September 24, 1992: 6.
— named Waterman of the Year, Lahaina News, December 8, 1994: 4.
— West Maui Water Safety Officer warns of dangers of drinking and driving, Lahaina News, February 9, 1995: 1.
— surfer to compete in Biarritz Surf Festival, Lahaina News, August 22, 1996: 12.
— teaches Lahainaluna Voyagers, Lahaina News, October 29, 1998: 11.
— West Maui Water Safety Captain visits Sacred Hearts School, Lahaina News, October 19, 2000: 1.
— recalls career as surfer, Lahaina News, January 17, 2002: 1,20.

KALEPA, DALLAS
— honored by Maui County Council for service with the Hawaii Army National Guard, Lahaina Sun, February 24, 1971: 6.

KALEPOLEPO FISHPOND
— efforts to restore, Lahaina News, May 15, 1997: 12.

KALEPOLEPO PARK
— to closed due to sewer pump improvements, Lahaina News, October 7, 1993: 5.

KALMON, RICKY [COMEDIAN]
— to perform at Comedy Club and the Sports Page, Lahaina News, February 18, 1993: 13,14.
— to perform at Comedy Club and the Sports Page, Lahaina News, February 25, 1993: 9.
— to perform at Comedy Club, Lahaina News, October 21, 1993: 16.

KALO MAN SLACK KEY [CD]
— released by Ikaika Brown, Lahaina News, July 4, 1996: 15.

KALUA PIG
— cook-off held at Royal Lahaina Resort, Lahaina News, May 31, 1989: 19.

KALUA, ZEKE
— new executive director West Maui Taxpayers Association, Lahaina News, June 21, 2001: 1,13.

KAM, BETTY LOU
— Bishop Museum Resource Specialist to present on "Early Hawaiian Books, Laws, Money and Prints: The Amazing Role of Lahainaluna and the Printing at Hale Pa'i", Lahaina News, July 20, 2000: 8.

KAM, EDEAN
— appointed director of rooms at Four Seasons Resort Wailea, Lahaina News, January 23, 1991: 5.

KAMA, JOHN
— at meeting between Hawaiian Homes Commission and The Hawaiians, Lahaina Sun, December 23, 1970: 6.

KAMA'AINA CLUBMAKERS
— owner Mike Moynahan named Western Regional Clubmaker of the year, Lahaina News, September 11, 2003: 8.

KAMA'AINA KITCHEN [RESTAURANT]
— opens at The Wharf Cinema Center, Lahaina News, October 4, 2001: 8.

KAMA'AINA LOAN [BUSINESS]
— opens, Lahaina News, March 11, 1993: 12.

KAMAE, EDDIE [MUSICIAN]
— will use grant money to preserve the music of elderly Maui musicians, Lahaina Sun, March 21, 1973: 10.
— films to be featured, Lahaina News, June 3, 1993: 3.
— to screen "The Hawaiian Way", Lahaina News, October 27, 1994: 20.
— film "Words Earth and Aloha" to be shown at Hawaiian International Film Festival, Lahaina News, November 9, 1995: 3.
— Sons of Hawaii to perform at B.J.'s Chicago Pizzeria for documentary, Lahaina News, January 7, 1999: 1,20.
— to perform with Henry Kapono, Lahaina News, November 25, 1999: 7.
— filming documentary on Lahaina, Lahaina News, December 9, 1999: 1,2.
— produces film "Sons of Hawaii—A Sound, A Band, A Legend", Lahaina News, November 9, 2000: 21.

KAMAE, EDDIE AND MYRNA
— pays tribute to role of kupuna in preserving Hawaiian culture, Lahaina News, November 5, 1998: 2.

KAMAKAHI, DAVID [MUSICIAN]
— to perform at "A Taste of Lahaina", Lahaina News, September 2, 1999: 18.

KAMAKAHI, DENNIS [MUSICIAN]
— to perform at Bankoh Kiho'alu festival, Lahaina News, June 11, 1998: 16.
— to perform at Ka'anapali Beach Hotel, Lahaina News, May 20, 1999: 15.
— to perform at "A Taste of Lahaina", Lahaina News, September 2, 1999: 18.

KAMAKAHI, GAIL
— to speak at Kilauea Military Camp, Lahaina News, October 22, 1986: 5.

KAMAKAWIWO'OLE, FRANCIS, JR.
— featured, Lahaina News, December 14, 2000: 1,17.

KAMAKAWIWO'OLE, ISRAEL [MUSICIAN]
— to perform, Lahaina News, April 25, 1996: 15.
— to perform, Lahaina News, June 27, 1996: 15.
— to perform at Alexander and Baldwin Community Fair, Lahaina News, July 4, 1996: 15.
— to perform at Maui Arts and Cultural Center, Lahaina News, April 3, 1997: 12,13.

KAMANNU, AARON
— incident where officer received a self-inflicted gunshot wound is a closed matter, Lahaina News, October 26, 1995: 1.

KAMANO, STACY
— "Baywatch Hawaii" actress signs autographs, Lahaina News, January 27, 2000: 11.
— "Baywatch Hawaii" actress to meet fans at Whalers Village, Lahaina News, July 20, 2000: 17.

KAMAOLE
— Maui Planning Commission to consider development proposals, Lahaina News, February 4, 1993: 11.
— Mayor Linda Lingle supports state obtaining beach parcel, Lahaina News, February 4, 1993: 11.
— Kenny Barr only planning commissioner to vote against request to develop land near, Lahaina News, November 25, 1993: 6.

KAMAOLE BEACH
— United States Interior Department commits money for picnic facilities, Lahaina Sun, March 10, 1971: 5.
— commercial mooring area to be installed, Lahaina News, September 24, 1992: 2.
— land exchange sought for, Lahaina News, October 22, 1992: 12.

KAMAOLE BEACH PARK II
— to be improved, Lahaina News, January 30, 1992: 4,5.
— sewage spill at, Lahaina News, January 28, 1993: 10.

KAMAOLE LAND VENTURE
— to develop resort in Kihei, Lahaina News, August 30, 1989: 5.

KAMAOLE SHOPPING CENTER
— grand opening to be held, Lahaina News, June 17, 1987: 3.

KAMAU [PLAY]
— Alani Apio's play to be read at Gallerie Ha, Lahaina News, October 31, 2002: 28.

KAMAUNU, AARON
— benefit concert to be held for injured Lahaina Police Bicycle Officer, Lahaina News, December 2, 1993: 1,4.
— benefit concert results, Lahaina News, December 9, 1993: 2.
— returns home, continuing therapy, Lahaina News, December 30, 1993: 1.
— now patrol officer, Lahaina News, August 10, 1995: 3.

KAMAUNU, KAPONO
— teaches students haka at Summer Voyaging Camp, Lahaina News, September 24, 1998: 2.

KAMAUU, HOAKALEI
— to lecture on hula at Lahaina Public Library, Lahaina News, October 5, 1988: 3.

KAMEDA, KATHY
— receives Na Honoapi'ilani Award for work on Na Mele O Maui, Lahaina News, December 6, 1989: 3.

KAMEEIAMOKU, ANALU
— to teach class on genealogy, Lahaina News, February 25, 1999: 12.

KAMEHAMEHA DAY
— see King Kamehameha Day

KAMEHAMEHA FESTIVAL
— to be held at Banyan Tree Park, Lahaina News, June 8, 2000: 3.
— held, Lahaina News, June 15, 2000: 1.

KAMEHAMEHA I [KING]
— biography of, Lahaina News, March 15, 1981: 10.
— history of, Lahaina News, May 30, 1996: 12.
— history of, Lahaina News, June 6, 1996: 14.

KAMEHAMEHA IKI PARK
— proposed location for Hawaiian cultural park, Lahaina News, November 9, 1995: 1,16.
— members of Hui O Wa'a Kaulua building hulls at , Lahaina News, February 22, 1996: 3.
— Hui O Wa'a Kaulua plans open house, Lahaina News, November 21, 1996: 1,13.
— hui leader Keola Sequiera honored, Lahaina News, January 23, 1997: 1.
— Light Bringers asked to leave, Lahaina News, March 6, 1997: 1,16.
— Light Bringers Rescue Mission given until July 4 to leave, Lahaina News, June 12, 1997: 1,2.
— Hui O Wa'a Kaulua plans canoe house and Keiki Hale at, Lahaina News, September 17, 1998: 1,32.
— groups want closed at night, Lahaina News, September 24, 1998: 1,20.
— Friends of Moku'ula member Akoni Akana discusses history of, Lahaina News, March 29, 2001: 1.

KAMEHAMEHA MIDDLE SCHOOL ORCHESTRA
— to perform at Lahaina Cannery Mall, Lahaina News, April 25, 2002: 17.

KAMEHAMEHA SCHOOLS
— plans for school discussed, Lahaina Sun, May 24, 1972: 3.
— proposal to develop "land bank" between Kamehameha Schools and the State approved, Lahaina Sun, May 31, 1972: 6.
— planning Summer Enrichment Program, Lahaina News, May 18, 1988: 18.
— alumni association to install new officers, Lahaina News, April 24, 1991: 5.
— release honor roll, Lahaina News, January 18, 1996: 4.
— alumni to meet, Lahaina News, October 16, 1997: 16.
— purchases 80 acres from Kulamalu Limited Partnership, Lahaina News, August 3, 2000: 13.
— Maui Campus accepting applications, Lahaina News, September 5, 2002: 1,3.
— planning recruitment workshops, Lahaina News, September 12, 2002: 2.
— to hold Community Open House, Lahaina News, September 19, 2002: 16.
— to hold meetings for families, Lahaina News, September 19, 2002: 25.
— to hold Community Open House, Lahaina News, September 26, 2002: 18.
— offering Career and Technical Education Scholarship program, Lahaina News, June 12, 2003: 8.
— residents rally to support traditional admissions policy, Lahaina News, September 18, 2003: 1.

KAMEHAMEHA V [KING]
— tribute paid to, Lahaina News, December 21, 2000: 1,2.

KAMELAMELA, KIEILE
— wins boxing match, Lahaina News, October 1, 1998: 20.

KAMENHOFF, WENDY [COMEDIAN]
— to perform at Comedy Club and the Sports Page, Lahaina News, June 24, 1993: 13,14.

KAMIKAWA, RAY
— former state Tax Director leading a workshop on technology taxes, Lahaina News, November 15, 2001: 8.

KAMIL'S SAAB AND VOLVO SERVICE [BUSINESS]
— opens, Lahaina News, October 22, 1992: 10.

KAMIYA, SANAE "SUNNY"
— opens Sunny-K store, Lahaina News, June 14, 2001: 8.

KAMP KUMULANI
— to sponsor play day, Lahaina News, December 19, 1991: 4.
— to be held, Lahaina News, August 7, 1997: 12.
— to be held, Lahaina News, July 23, 1998: 17.
— to be held at Napilihau Recreation Center, Lahaina News, July 1, 1999: 3.
— to be held, Lahaina News, July 15, 1999: 13.
— to be held, Lahaina News, June 7, 2001: 2.

KAMUELA'S UPCOUNTRY CONNECTION GALLERY [BUSINESS]
— to exhibit at the West Maui, Lahaina News, February 13, 1997: 14.

KANAE, DANELL
— promoted to operations manager at Kahului Walmart branch, Lahaina News, September 5, 2002: 8.

KANAHA
— history of described, Lahaina Sun, August 9, 1972: 19.
— resort apartment complex discussed, Lahaina Sun, February 7, 1973: 4.
  Environmental study planned for Kanaha, Lahaina Sun, February 28, 1973: 4,5.
— Federal Environmental Protection Agency studies proposed sewage treatment plant, Lahaina Sun, March 14, 1973: 5.
— water clearing at intake, Lahaina News, February 4, 1993: 1.

KANAHA POND
— pollution in, discussed, Lahaina Sun, February 3, 1971: 5.
— named landmark, Lahaina Sun, September 1, 1971: 7.
— impact of environmental damage on ecology discussed, Lahaina Sun, January 24, 1973: 9.

KANAHA SEWAGE PLANT
— plans criticized, Lahaina Sun, July 19, 1972: 3.

KANAHELE [FAMILY]
— to present on shell leis at Art School of Kapalua, Lahaina News, December 24, 1998: 3.
— to demonstrate Ni'ihau shell lei making, Lahaina News, January 7, 1999: 16.

KANAHELE, KEKUHI [MUSICIAN]
— to perform at "Music on the Beach", Lahaina News, February 25, 1999: 5.
— chanter, singer and hula performer to performer at Maui Arts and Cultural Center, Lahaina News, November 4, 1999: 13.

KANAHELE, MARCUS
— named co-chair of American Heart Association residential campaign, Lahaina News, January 18, 1989: 5.

KANAHELE, PUALANI
— to teach "A History of Change" workshop, Lahaina News, November 30, 1988: 3.

KANAHELE, PU'UONUA DENNIS "BUMPY"
— featured, Lahaina News, November 30, 1995: 1,12.
— to speak at Na Kupuna O Maui's "'Aha Kupuna", Lahaina News, July 16, 1998: 16.

KANAKA JAM [MUSICAL GROUP]
— to perform at Lopaka's Grill and Bar, Lahaina News, January 9, 1992: 14.

KANAZAWA, CHRIS
— appointed senior vice-president, real estate, for Amfac/JMB, Lahaina News, May 13, 1993: 6.
— president of Amfac/JMB Hawaii discusses need for new visitor project, Lahaina News, June 26, 1997: 4.

KANE [FAMILY]
— extended family featured, Lahaina Sun, August 9, 1972: 5.

KANE, DAIN [POLITICIAN]
— candidate for Wailuku-Waihee-Waikapu County Council, Lahaina News, November 2, 2000: 20.

KANE, DAWN
— new general manager of Mahana at Ka'anapali, Lahaina News, January 2, 2003: 8.

KANE, JOHN [MUSICIAN]
— to perform at B.J.'s Chicago Pizzeria, Lahaina News, March 7, 1996: 14.
— to perform at B.J.'s Chicago Pizzeria, Lahaina News, April 25, 1996: 16.
— to perform at B.J.'s Chicago Pizzeria, Lahaina News, August 29, 1996: 12.
— to perform at B.J.'s Chicago Pizzeria, Lahaina News, September 12, 1996: 16.
— to perform at B.J.'s Chicago Pizzeria, Lahaina News, January 23, 1997: 12.

KANE, LANI
— to box Dave Fried of West Maui Boxing Club, Lahaina News, July 20, 2000: 16.

KANE, MONDO [MUSICIAN]
— to perform at Maui Prince, Lahaina News, July 30, 1992: 16.

KANE, RAYMOND [MUSICIAN]
— to perform at the Maui Community Arts and Cultural Center, Lahaina News, February 20, 1991: 11.

KANEAKUA, KAI PO
— to discuss Hawaiian healing, Lahaina News, August 6, 1998: 21.
— to discuss traditional Hawaiian healing, Lahaina News, September 10, 1998: 21.

KANEALII, KELI'I "AXEL" [MUSICIAN]
— featured, Lahaina News, January 9, 1992: 10.

KANEKI, CHIEKO
— to teach non-credit Japanese class , Lahaina News, April 17, 1991: 9.

KANEKOA [MUSICAL GROUP]
— reggae-fusion-rock group to perform, Lahaina News, July 10, 2003: 16.

KANEKOA, JANELLE
— receives Aloha Award from Kapaula Bay Hotels and Villas, Lahaina News, July 11, 1991: 6.

KANEKUNI, PHYLLIS
— promoted to vice president of special services at Hill and Knowlton/Communications Pacific, Lahaina News, August 8, 1990: 6.

KANEMITSU, MYRTLE
— president of Lahaina chapter of Business and Professional Women's Organization featured, Lahaina News, September 19, 1991: 12.

KANENGISER, WILLIAM [MUSICIAN]
— to perform at Hawaii Guitar Festival, Lahaina News, June 15, 1995: 11.

KANER, JAZ [COMEDIAN]
— to perform at Comedy Club and the Sports Page, Lahaina News, December 26, 1990: 8,10.
— to perform at Honolulu Comedy Club, Lahaina News, July 28, 1994: 13.

KANESHINA, JACQUELINE
— named assistant branch manager of First Hawaiian Creditcorp's Maui Branch, Lahaina News, May 6, 1993: 9.

KANIHO, CHRIS
— former police officer becomes basketball coach, Lahaina News, January 25, 1996: 10.

KANIHO, HAROLD
— crossing guard featured, Lahaina News, May 17, 2001: 1.
— honored as "Educator of the Month" by Hula Grill, Lahaina News, June 28, 2001: 8.

KANIHO, JOHN, SR.
— passes away, Lahaina News, June 17, 1999: 15.

KANIKAPILA BOYS, THE [MUSICAL GROUP]
— to perform , Lahaina News, March 5, 1998: 16.

KANO'EAU DANCE ACADEMY
— organizing Lei Day celebration, Lahaina News, April 24, 1991: 10.
— to hold fundraiser, Lahaina News, June 6, 1991: 12.
— named Halau of the Year, Lahaina News, February 19, 1998: 2.
— succeeds at Hula O Na Keiki, Lahaina News, November 14, 2002: 1,15.
— halau wins Mokihana Hula Festival, Lahaina News, October 9, 2003: 18.

KANOUFF, MICHAEL
— benefit to be held for, Lahaina News, March 26, 1998: 13.
— benefit dance to be held for, Lahaina News, April 2, 1998: 16.

KANTNER, GEORGE [COMEDIAN]
— to perform at Maui Comedy Club, Lahaina News, August 24, 1995: 12.

KANTNER, PAUL [MUSICIAN]
— to perform at Casanova's, Lahaina News, August 1, 1991: 17.

KANU [PLAY]
— performed at Kahului Fairgrounds, Lahaina Sun, May 17, 1972: 10.
— reviewed, Lahaina Sun, May 31, 1972: 15.

KAOI-FM [RADIO STATION]
— connection to music scene discussed, Lahaina News, June 6, 1984: 12.
— anniversary party postponed, Lahaina News, June 11, 1986: 8.
— radio station celebrating 18th birthday, Lahaina News, June 13, 1991: 12.
— to begin "Earth Tracks" radio program, Lahaina News, October 17, 1991: 20.
— purchases KOAS and KKON, Lahaina News, March 12, 1992: 13.
— to celebrate birthday along with Casanova's, Lahaina News, June 25, 1992: 22.
— to host Fun Run, Lahaina News, January 9, 1997: 10.
— to feature Henry Kapono at Music on the Beach, Lahaina News, June 18, 1998: 3.
— to host Fun Run, Lahaina News, January 7, 1999: 15.
— doctor Michael Klapper to host "Sounds of Healing" radio show on, Lahaina News, January 21, 1999: 11.
— Greg Everett is new manager, Lahaina News, August 19, 1999: 14.
— "Growing Younger With Suni Rae" show added, Lahaina News, January 11, 2001: 14.
— animal expert Warrn Eckstein to host nationally syndicated talk show on, Lahaina News, April 24, 2003: 20.

KAOPALA BAY
— attempts to save reef, Lahaina News, April 29, 1993: 1.

KAPA
— process detailed, Lahaina News, December 19, 1984: 10.

KAPA, MITCH [MUSICIAN]
— to perform at Marriott Makai Bar, Lahaina News, January 16, 1992: 15.

KAPAHU FARM
— tour of taro patches to be offered, Lahaina News, October 31, 2002: 28.

KAPAHULEHUA, KAWIKA
— captain of Hokule'a to speak at Lahaina Cannery Mall, Lahaina News, July 25, 1990: 11.

KAPALUA
— preschool to refurbish, Lahaina News, July 17, 2003: 6.

KAPALUA BAY
— condominium planned near coconut grove at, Lahaina News, November 12, 1998: 1,20.
— Department of Land and Natural Resources allowed to clear old trees from, Lahaina News, June 24, 1999: 11.

KAPALUA BAY CLUB
— featured, Lahaina News, December 18, 1997: 9.

KAPALUA BAY HAWAII CORPORATION
— Peter Chang appointed vice president of hotel operations, Lahaina News, June 20, 1991: 7.

KAPALUA BAY HOTEL [BUSINESS]
— now managed by Kapalua Land Company, Lahaina News, February 1, 1984: 16.
— expansion objected to by Kapalua Villa Association, Lahaina News, January 7, 1987: 4.
— granted Special Management Permit with conditional changes, Lahaina News, January 14, 1987: 1.
— announces renovations, Lahaina News, June 24, 1987: 3.
— activity centers approved by Maui County Planning Commission, Lahaina News, September 9, 1987: 3.
— offering special deals, Lahaina News, April 13, 1988: 12.
— purchased by group of investors, Lahaina News, June 28, 1989: 7.
— appoints Keith Shibuya as group service manager, Lahaina News, October 11, 1989: 5.
— Matthew Bailey named resident manager, Lahaina News, March 7, 1990: 7.
— appoints Tim Kwock as director of sales and marketing, Lahaina News, March 21, 1990: 4.
— offering summer program for children, Lahaina News, May 30, 1990: 5.
— appoints Scott Ullrich as director of food and beverage, Lahaina News, June 6, 1990: 7.
— offering golf special for visitors, Lahaina News, October 31, 1990: 9.
— appoints Deborah Lyn Eaton as guest services manager, Lahaina News, December 5, 1990: 4.
— Barry Herbert appointed training manager, Lahaina News, December 19, 1990: 7.
— criticized for limiting access to Hawea Point, Lahaina News, September 15, 1994: 1,2.
— discusses liability issues at Hawea Point, Lahaina News, January 19, 1995: 4.
— files for bankruptcy, Lahaina News, December 21, 1995: 3.
— may be purchased by Colony Capital Inc., Lahaina News, March 28, 1996: 10.
— closes for renovations, Lahaina News, April 3, 1997: 10.
— reopens after remodeling, Lahaina News, August 21, 1997: 1.
— unveils new menu, Lahaina News, November 5, 1998: 7.
— signs lease with Beach Activities, Lahaina News, November 4, 1999: 11.
— participated in "National Groundhog Job Shadow Day", Lahaina News, March 1, 2001: 8.
— changes name to Kapalua Bay Hotel and Ocean Villas, Lahaina News, February 28, 2002: 8.
— to offer Samuel Adams Beer Dinner, Lahaina News, June 26, 2003: 20.
— see also Kapalua Bay Hotel and Ocean Villas [business]

KAPALUA BAY HOTEL AND OCEAN VILLAS [BUSINESS]

— Sarah Urquhart becomes group coordinator, Lahaina News, May 2, 1984: 17.
— to begin major redecorating program, Lahaina News, September 12, 1984: 3.
— announces staff promotions, Lahaina News, October 31, 1984: 3.
— personnel changes announced, Lahaina News, December 26, 1984: 3.
— may be sold, Lahaina News, January 23, 1985: 3.
— promotions announced , Lahaina News, January 30, 1985: 18.
— receives five stars from Fisher Annotative Travel Guide, Lahaina News, February 13, 1985: 3.
— appointments announced, Lahaina News, February 27, 1985: 3.
— sale finalized to group headed by Mark Rolfing, Lahaina News, May 29, 1985: 3.
— promotions described, Lahaina News, August 14, 1985: 8.
— promotions described, Lahaina News, August 21, 1985: 3.
— awards given to outstanding employees, Lahaina News, October 16, 1985: 20.
— ownership officially transferred to K.B.H. Co., Lahaina News, October 30, 1985: 3.
— Karl Rathgeb named general manager, Lahaina News, November 20, 1985: 11.
— Brett Huske named as director of sales, Lahaina News, January 1, 1986: 3.
— announces personnel promotions, Lahaina News, January 22, 1986: 3.
— receives five stars from Stern's Travel guides, Lahaina News, February 5, 1986: 3.
— golf operations wins awards, Lahaina News, February 5, 1986: 3.
— names Graham John Brindle as director of engineering, Lahaina News, April 2, 1986: 3.
— Loren Malencheck named advertising/media coordinator, Lahaina News, April 16, 1986: 3.
— Stan Zydel appointed general manager of, Lahaina News, December 5, 1990: 4.
— Stan Zydel appointed general manager of, Lahaina News, December 12, 1990: 6.
— Paul Gomez and Tracy White appointed assistant managers at, Lahaina News, January 16, 1991: 5.
— to be represented by Laird McNeil Wilson Advertising, Inc., Lahaina News, January 16, 1991: 5.
— appointments announced, Lahaina News, February 6, 1991: 6.
— to hold first Vintner's Dinner of 1991, Lahaina News, February 20, 1991: 9.
— Vintner's dinner reviewed, Lahaina News, February 27, 1991: 14.
— golf club recognized as one of best by Gold Digest, Lahaina News, February 27, 1991: 6.
— adds exercise facility, Lahaina News, February 27, 1991: 8.
— Lee Conching appointed regional director of sales-Eastern Region for, Lahaina News, February 27, 1991: 8.
— Aloha and Mahalo Awards announced, Lahaina News, March 27, 1991: 9.
— hosting Vintner's Dinner, Lahaina News, April 10, 1991: 8.
— Vintner's Dinner to feature De Loach Vineyards, Lahaina News, April 17, 1991: 11.
— to offer package to view the eclipse, Lahaina News, May 1, 1991: 14.
— to feature Cuvaison Winery, Lahaina News, May 8, 1991: 19.
— offering eclipse package, Lahaina News, May 15, 1991: 11.
— expands recreational program, Lahaina News, May 15, 1991: 5.
— to offer eclipse package on Navatek I, Lahaina News, May 23, 1991: 13.
— Plantation Course opens, Lahaina News, May 23, 1991: 8.
— to offer Kama'aina golf packages, Lahaina News, June 27, 1991: 7.
— Henry Richardson appointed executive chef at, Lahaina News, December 12, 1991: 16.
— to host lectures on whales by Richard Roshon, Lahaina News, January 2, 1992: 5.
— appoints Ben Quiseng as assistant manager, Lahaina News, January 23, 1992: 13.
— announces Lincoln-Mercury will sponsor Kapalua International golf tournament, Lahaina News, March 12, 1992: 10.
— to offer Easter brunch, Lahaina News, April 2, 1992: 20.
— employee awards announced, Lahaina News, April 23, 1992: 16.
— to host wine symposium, Lahaina News, April 23, 1992: 7.
— Hilton Hotels Corp. may take over management of, Lahaina News, May 7, 1992: 10.
— to exhibit "Pohaku: Through Hawaiian Eyes", Lahaina News, June 11, 1992: 5.
— Mary Zazzaro appointed national sales manager, Lahaina News, September 3, 1992: 8.
— to renovate, Lahaina News, October 22, 1992: 10.
— named a Golf Resort Winner by Golf Magazine, Lahaina News, December 17, 1992: 11.
— new directors appointed, Lahaina News, February 18, 1993: 9.
— renovations underway, Lahaina News, February 25, 1993: 6.
— employees recognized, Lahaina News, March 11, 1993: 12.
— established job hotline for applicants, Lahaina News, April 1, 1993: 8.
— names Goran Streng as executive chef, Lahaina News, April 22, 1993: 6.
— staff changes, Lahaina News, April 29, 1993: 9.
— Jeani Lund and Joe Higgins appointed directors, Lahaina News, September 16, 1993: 10.
— David Sosner appointed general manager, Lahaina News, November 18, 1993: 7.
— criticized for limiting access to Hawea Point, Lahaina News, September 15, 1994: 1,2.
— new appointments announced, Lahaina News, November 10, 1994: 13.
— to celebrate Aloha Festivals, Lahaina News, October 12, 1995: 14.
— to showcase J. Lohr Vineyard, Lahaina News, April 18, 1996: 16.
— David Sosner promoted to vice president of, Lahaina News, December 21, 2000: 14.
— new name for Kapalua Bay Hotel, Lahaina News, February 28, 2002: 8.
— recognizes employees, Lahaina News, April 18, 2002: 8.
— completes renovations, Lahaina News, September 26, 2002: 8.
— names new managers, Lahaina News, November 14, 2002: 9.
— to hold Winemaker's Dinner, Lahaina News, March 20, 2003: 16.
— Noah Bekofsky new executive chef at, Lahaina News, May 1, 2003: 8.
— Rob Shelton new general manager at, Lahaina News, September 25, 2003: 8.
— Channing Bridges new sales and marketing director at, Lahaina News, October 2, 2003: 8.
— see also Kapalua Bay Hotel [business]

KAPALUA BAY RESORT [BUSINESS]

— offering deluxe vacations to the super-rich, Lahaina News, December 28, 1983: 3,7.
— personnel changes made, Lahaina News, April 4, 1984: 13.
— receives top honors in Stern's Travel Guides, Lahaina News, May 27, 1987: 16.
— report of ongoing renovations, Lahaina News, August 12, 1987: 4.
— offering kama'aina rate for golf, Lahaina News, May 24, 1989: 8.
— Plantation golf course to open, Lahaina News, January 24, 1990: 6.
— general medical office opens at, Lahaina News, October 24, 1991: 4.
— receives "Award for Excellence" from Urban Land Institute, Lahaina News, November 18, 1993: 6.
— to host Kapalua Betsy Nagelsen Pro-Am Tennis Invitational, Lahaina News, November 24, 1994: 8.

— named one of top 50 tennis resorts, Lahaina News, July 24, 1997: 13.
— community featured, Lahaina News, September 4, 1997: 8.
— opens internet store, Lahaina News, March 12, 1998: 11.
— plans major renovation, Lahaina News, August 26, 1999: 14.
— pre-sale begins at Coconut Grove at, Lahaina News, September 16, 1999: 11.
— receives "Odyssey Award" in the category of environment from Travel Industry Association of America, Lahaina News, November 11, 1999: 11.
— to offer junior tennis camps and clinics, Lahaina News, June 26, 2003: 11.

KAPALUA BEACH
— hotel proposed for, as part of Maui Land & Pineapple Company's plans for tourist development, Lahaina Sun, May 24, 1972: 9.

KAPALUA BETSY NAGELSEN TENNIS INVITATIONAL
— to be held, Lahaina News, November 21, 1990: 24.

KAPALUA CELEBRATION OF THE ARTS
— "Keep it Hawaii" to be held at Ritz-Carlton, Lahaina News, March 20, 1997: 15.

KAPALUA GRILL AND BAR [RESTAURANT]
— reviewed, Lahaina News, June 1, 1983: 18.
— reviewed, Lahaina News, March 21, 1990: 18.
— reviewed, Lahaina News, July 4, 1991: 14.
— offering kama'aina deals, Lahaina News, October 3, 1991: 12.
— executive chef Hale Lake featured, Lahaina News, February 20, 1992: 9.
— featured, Lahaina News, August 19, 1993: 12.
— donates to West Maui Youth Center, Lahaina News, December 23, 1993: 2.

KAPALUA HOTEL
— names Douglas Stacy as director of special projects, Lahaina News, October 8, 1986: 3.

KAPALUA INTERNATIONAL GOLF TOURNAMENT
— held, featuring Arnold Palmer, Lahaina News, November 2, 1983: 7,8,9.
— approved by the Professional Golfers Association (PGA) Tour, Lahaina News, July 4, 1984: 6.
— to be sponsored by Isuzu Motors, Inc., Lahaina News, October 3, 1984: 13.
— featured, Lahaina News, November 7, 1984: 7,8,9.
— TV coverage to expand, Lahaina News, June 24, 1987: 6.
— to be held, Lahaina News, October 30, 1997: 1,18.
— see also Isuzu-Kapalua International, Lincoln-Mercury Kapalua International

KAPALUA JUNIOR TENNIS CAMPS
— to be held, Lahaina News, June 19, 2003: 13.

KAPALUA KAI SAILING, INC [BUSINESS]
— opens, Lahaina News, November 3, 1994: 23.

KAPALUA LAND COMPANY [BUSINESS]
— now managing Kapalua Bay Hotel, Lahaina News, February 1, 1984: 16.
— to develop fee simple lots at Pineapple Hill, Lahaina News, December 19, 1984: 3.
— Brian McLaughlin resigns as president of, Lahaina News, May 29, 1985: 3.
— new vice-presidents announced, Lahaina News, December 18, 1985: 3.
— requests new hotel near Kapalua Bay Golf Course, Lahaina News, October 22, 1986: 3,5.
— names Gary Gifford as president, Lahaina News, August 12, 1987: 18.
— Colin Cameron steps down as president of, Lahaina News, August 12, 1987: 18.

— signs agreement with Office of Hawaiian Affairs and Hui Alanui O Makena concerning Native Hawaiian burials disinterred, Lahaina News, August 19, 1987: 3.
— discusses housing with Hawaii Housing Authority, Lahaina News, September 16, 1987: 1,9.
— Sheri-Ann Min direct of property management at, Lahaina News, October 14, 1987: 17.
— offering golf scholarships, Lahaina News, June 8, 1988: 3.
— proceeding with new hotel, Lahaina News, June 15, 1988: 1.
— planning 3rd golf course, Lahaina News, July 6, 1988: 3.
— removes Hawaiian bones from sand dune, Lahaina News, December 7, 1988: 1,24.
— development discovers ancient Hawaiian remains, Lahaina News, January 4, 1989: 1,16.
— seeks reimbursement after Ritz-Carlton Hotel location changed due to ancient Hawaiian remains being found, Lahaina News, March 8, 1989: 1,16.
— stops studying ancient Hawaiian remains found in sand dunes, Lahaina News, March 29, 1989: 1.
— awards golf scholarships, Lahaina News, May 10, 1989: 3.
— signs agreement on reinternment of ancient Hawaiian bones, Lahaina News, September 13, 1989: 3.
— offering golf scholarship, Lahaina News, April 11, 1990: 7.
— appoints Jan Beemer as operations manager of commercial leases, Lahaina News, July 18, 1990: 7.
— Grant Imamura receives golf scholarship, Lahaina News, July 25, 1990: 14.
— William Prince appointed director of finance and accounting at, Lahaina News, January 30, 1991: 5.
— offering golf scholarships, Lahaina News, April 17, 1991: 18.
— to offer golf scholarship, Lahaina News, May 1, 1991: 4,5.
— promotes Joan Iselin to principal broker, Lahaina News, July 11, 1991: 6.
— appoints Russell Johnson as controller, Lahaina News, January 23, 1992: 12.
— Don Young promoted to executive vice president of operations at, Lahaina News, June 4, 1992: 9.
— awards golf scholarship, Lahaina News, July 16, 1992: 10.
— promotes Margaret Santos to vice president, marketing, Lahaina News, August 20, 1992: 13.
— Gary Gifford now president and chief executive officer, Lahaina News, August 27, 1992: 10.
— gives scholarship to Tiana Munar, Lahaina News, August 26, 1993: 12.
— awards tennis scholarship, Lahaina News, July 28, 1994: 6.
— promotions announced, Lahaina News, September 1, 1994: 13.
— employees honored, Lahaina News, September 15, 1994: 13.
— recognizes employees, Lahaina News, January 26, 1995: 12.
— offers tennis scholarship, Lahaina News, March 28, 1996: 7.
— awards Ryan Okamura annual gold scholarship, Lahaina News, July 18, 1996: 6.
— offering golf scholarship, Lahaina News, April 10, 1997: 16.
— offering tennis scholarship, Lahaina News, May 15, 1997: 11.
— appoints Charles Ka'upu as Hawaiian cultural advisor, Lahaina News, May 22, 1997: 9.
— Peter Sanborn appointed vice-president of marketing, Lahaina News, June 12, 1997: 15.
— students tour facilities, Lahaina News, July 17, 1997: 12.
— has new websites, Lahaina News, November 13, 1997: 11.
— Maintenance Department volunteers time at Lahaina Recreation Center, Lahaina News, February 26, 1998: 11.
— Caroline Peters Egli appointed vice president/administration, Lahaina News, April 30, 1998: 13.
— breaks ground on Kapalua Golf Academy, Lahaina News, February 11, 1999: 13.

— names Kim David Carpenter as director of Mercedes Championship, Lahaina News, March 25, 1999: 13.

— proposes single-family subdivision in Kapalua Resort area, Lahaina News, June 10, 1999: 13.

— promotes Kim David Carpenter to director of marketing and tournament operations, Lahaina News, October 28, 1999: 15.

— breaks ground on The Coconut Grove on Kapalua Bay, Lahaina News, November 11, 1999: 3.

— opens Kapalua Golf Academy and putting course, Lahaina News, March 16, 2000: 11.

— promotes Kim David Carpenter to vice president of marketing, Lahaina News, March 30, 2000: 11.

— Stephen Collins appointed golf courses superintendent, Lahaina News, March 30, 2000: 6.

— agrees to mediation with ILWU Local 142, Lahaina News, February 27, 2003: 3.

— razes the wooden residence Maka'oi'oi at the top of Pineapple Hill Road, regarded as unsafe, Lahaina News, October 9, 2003: 3.

KAPALUA MAUI CHARITIES

— distributes money to charities, Lahaina News, March 25, 1999: 2.

— silent auction to support schools, Lahaina News, December 30, 1999: 2.

— announces the charities to benefit from the PGA Mercedes Championship, Lahaina News, August 17, 2000: 7.

— names beneficiaries for next Mercedes Championship, Lahaina News, June 14, 2001: 15.

— to host Mercedes Championship, Lahaina News, March 27, 2003: 9.

— named as beneficiary of Mercedes Championships, Lahaina News, May 29, 2003: 8.

KAPALUA MAUKA

— Maui Land and Pineapple moving forward with plans for, Lahaina News, July 4, 2002: 1,20.

— Maui Planning Commission met to discuss development proposed by Maui Land and Pineapple at, Lahaina News, May 15, 2003: 1,20.

— public hearing to be held on development of, Lahaina News, July 17, 2003: 1,2.

KAPALUA MAUKA MASTER PLAN

— unveiled, Lahaina News, August 23, 2001: 1,8.

KAPALUA MUSIC ASSEMBLY

— offering violin lessons, Lahaina News, October 29, 1986: 1,20.

— presenting pianist Michael Boriskin, Lahaina News, November 4, 1987: 10.

— house tour scheduled, Lahaina News, March 8, 1989: 17.

— gives music awards to Lahaina school students, Lahaina News, June 7, 1989: 3.

KAPALUA MUSIC FESTIVAL

— details provided, Lahaina News, July 1, 1983: 6.

— to begin Friday, Lahaina News, August 1, 1984: 13.

— performances to be broadcast on Hawaii Public Radio, Lahaina News, July 24, 1985: 8.

— to be held, Lahaina News, August 6, 1986: 18.

— to be held, Lahaina News, August 12, 1987: 3.

— to be held, Lahaina News, May 25, 1988: 10.

— to be held, Lahaina News, May 31, 1989: 18,19.

— to be held, Lahaina News, May 23, 1990: 13.

— to be held, Lahaina News, June 6, 1990: 13.

— events described, Lahaina News, June 13, 1990: 15.

— to be held, Lahaina News, May 8, 1991: 19.

— tickets on sale, Lahaina News, May 15, 1991: 10.

— tickets on sale, Lahaina News, May 23, 1991: 12.

— to be held this weekend, Lahaina News, June 6, 1991: 12.

— to be held this weekend, Lahaina News, June 13, 1991: 12.

— to be held, Lahaina News, March 26, 1992: 13.

— to be held, Lahaina News, April 2, 1992: 17.

— to be held, Lahaina News, April 9, 1992: 17.

— to be held, Lahaina News, May 7, 1992: 22.

— events listed, Lahaina News, May 21, 1992: 15.

— to be held, Lahaina News, June 4, 1992: 15.

— to feature more jazz this year, Lahaina News, June 3, 1993: 12.

— to be held, Lahaina News, March 17, 1994: 10.

— to be held, Lahaina News, April 21, 1994: 15.

— featured, Lahaina News, May 26, 1994: 10.

— to be held, Lahaina News, May 25, 1995: 11,12.

— changes name to Maui Chamber Music Festival, Lahaina News, May 30, 1996: 13.

KAPALUA NATURE SOCIETY

— to hold environmental conference "Earth Maui Nature Summit", Lahaina News, August 15, 1996: 2.

— to present Richard Roshon presentation on "Man, Kayak and the Whale—A Harmonious Way of Life", Lahaina News, January 30, 1997: 11.

— to offer hikes, Lahaina News, April 17, 1997: 12.

— to offer hikes, Lahaina News, May 1, 1997: 16.

— offering hikes, Lahaina News, June 5, 1997: 16.

— continues to offer hikes, Lahaina News, June 26, 1997: 16.

— selling Norfolk pines as fundraisers, Lahaina News, December 11, 1997: 11.

— seeking volunteers for clean-up at Lipoa Point, Lahaina News, May 28, 1998: 12.

— collects Christmas trees for recycling, Lahaina News, January 27, 2000: 1.

KAPALUA OPEN TENNIS CHAMPIONSHIPS

— to begin, Lahaina News, August 27, 1986: 3.

— registration for tennis competition open, Lahaina News, August 15, 1990: 18.

— to be played Labor Day weekend, Lahaina News, August 22, 1991: 8.

— tennis competition to be held, Lahaina News, August 29, 1991: 7.

— tennis tournament to be held, Lahaina News, August 8, 2002: 13.

— to be held, Lahaina News, August 15, 2002: 12.

KAPALUA PACIFIC CENTER

— to host "Cultural Values in the age of Technology" symposium, Lahaina News, June 20, 1991: 1.

KAPALUA PLANTATION COURSE

— to host Coca-Cola Classic, Lahaina News, October 26, 1995: 6.

KAPALUA RIDGE VILLAS

— featured, Lahaina News, July 20, 2000: 12.

KAPALUA SEAFOOD FESTIVAL

— Jake Shimabukuro to perform at, Lahaina News, June 12, 2003: 18.

KAPALUA SHOPS, THE [BUSINESS]

— sponsoring auction benefit auction for Maui Community Arts and Cultural Center held in memory of Mararet Cameron, Lahaina News, September 7, 1988: 9.

— opening later, Lahaina News, October 19, 1988: 3.

— celebrating 10th anniversary, Lahaina News, March 21, 1990: 7.

— celebrating completion of renovations, Lahaina News, March 28, 1990: 16.

— scheduling Christmas festivities, Lahaina News, December 12, 1991: 6.

— continues to offer Hula Kahiko O Hawaii, Lahaina News, September 9, 1993: 12.

— to host music, Lahaina News, March 28, 2002: 20,21.

— to hold craft events, Lahaina News, May 9, 2002: 17.

— continues to feature craft and music activities, Lahaina News, June 20, 2002: 17.

— entertainment continues at, Lahaina News, October 3, 2002: 17.

— to hold Sidewalk Sale, Lahaina News, July 3, 2003: 8.

KAPALUA TENNIS CLUB
— named best retailer by Tennis Buyer's Guide magazine, Lahaina News, May 4, 1995: 8.
— to offer tennis camps, Lahaina News, February 19, 1998: 6.
— offers tennis camps, Lahaina News, March 5, 1998: 14.
— offering free lessons, Lahaina News, May 14, 1998: 14.
— to hold "Sunday Stroke of a Day" clinic, Lahaina News, November 4, 1999: 7.

KAPALUA TENNIS GARDEN
— hosting Sixth Annual Doubles Championship, Lahaina News, April 23, 1986: 4.
— appoints new tennis pros, Lahaina News, April 30, 1986: 3.
— free clinics to be offered, Lahaina News, October 28, 1999: 9.
— continues to offer clinics, Lahaina News, November 4, 1999: 7.
— to hold tennis clinics, Lahaina News, May 4, 2000: 14.

KAPALUA, THE ART SCHOOL AT
— see Art School at Kapalua, The

KAPALUA VILLAGE COURSE
— names Gary Planos as director of golf, Lahaina News, September 17, 1986: 11.
— promotes Douglas Bohn to head professional, Lahaina News, December 26, 1996: 8.

KAPALUA VILLAGE HOTEL
— claims it is built on Hawaiian burial grounds, Lahaina News, February 25, 1987: 1,20.

KAPALUA VILLAS ASSOCIATION
— opposes Kapalua Bay Hotel expansion, Lahaina News, January 7, 1987: 4.

KAPALUA WEST MAUI AIRPORT
— has been postponed indefinitely, Lahaina Sun, December 15, 1971: 5.
— Ka'anapali Beach Operators Association to provide free trolley service to Ka'anapali Beach Resort, Lahaina News, March 25, 1987: 3.
— receiving few complaints about noise, Lahaina News, July 12, 1989: 1.
— conditions to be maintained, Lahaina News, September 10, 1992: 1.
— residents drop suit to allow purchase of to move ahead, Lahaina News, October 8, 1992: 1.
— Federal Express plane skids on runway, Lahaina News, October 29, 1998: 1.
— disaster drill planned, Lahaina News, May 13, 1999: 1.

KAPALUA WINE AND FOOD SYMPOSIUM
— to be held at Kapalua Bay Hotel & Villas, Lahaina News, July 18, 1984: 3.
— opens, Lahaina News, July 25, 1984: 3.
— offered at Kapalua Resort, Lahaina News, August 7, 1985: 8.
— Guenoc Winery receives top honors at, Lahaina News, September 18, 1985: 3.
— to be held at Kapalua Bay Hotel, Lahaina News, July 9, 1986: 3.
— detailed, Lahaina News, July 20, 1988: 6.
— scheduled, Lahaina News, June 21, 1989: 3.
— to be held, Lahaina News, July 4, 1990: 13.
— to be held, Lahaina News, July 11, 1990: 15.
— plans described, Lahaina News, July 18, 1990: 9.
— to be held, Lahaina News, June 6, 1991: 13.
— to be held, Lahaina News, June 13, 1991: 12.
— details given, Lahaina News, June 20, 1991: 9.
— to be held July 19-21, Lahaina News, June 27, 1991: 12.
— to be held in July, Lahaina News, May 7, 1992: 19.
— to be held, Lahaina News, May 21, 1992: 15.
— to be held, Lahaina News, June 4, 1992: 15,16.
— details provided, Lahaina News, July 2, 1992: 22.
— details provided, Lahaina News, July 9, 1992: 17.
— to be held, Lahaina News, April 22, 1993: 15.

— details, Lahaina News, July 15, 1993: 10.
— to be held, Lahaina News, March 17, 1994: 10.
— to be held, Lahaina News, April 28, 1994: 14.
— details, Lahaina News, June 30, 1994: 14.
— details, Lahaina News, July 7, 1994: 13.
— held, Lahaina News, July 28, 1994: 14.
— to be held, Lahaina News, July 13, 1995: 11.
— to be held, Lahaina News, April 4, 1996: 13.
— to be held, Lahaina News, June 20, 1996: 13.
— to be held, Lahaina News, June 19, 1997: 9.
— details of, Lahaina News, June 26, 1997: 6.
— to be held; reservations being taken, Lahaina News, April 2, 1998: 17.
— to be held, Lahaina News, July 2, 1998: 7.
— to be held, Lahaina News, July 9, 1998: 1,20.
— to be held, Lahaina News, July 8, 1999: 2.
— to be held, Lahaina News, July 15, 1999: 1,2.
— to be held, Lahaina News, June 15, 2000: 7.
— to be held, Lahaina News, June 22, 2000: 6.
— to be held, Lahaina News, June 29, 2000: 3.
— to be held, Lahaina News, June 28, 2001: 10.
— to begin on Friday, Lahaina News, July 5, 2001: 2.
— to be held, Lahaina News, June 20, 2002: 14.
— tickets selling out, Lahaina News, July 4, 2002: 9.

KAPALUA WINE AND MUSIC FESTIVAL
— see Kapalua Wine and Food Symposium

KAPALUA-WEST MAUI AIRPORT
— debate over state purchasing, Lahaina News, May 30, 1990: 1,12.
— airport administrator to review state plan to purchase , Lahaina News, June 13, 1990: 2.
— debate continues, Lahaina News, June 20, 1990: 1.
— State likely to condemn in order to obtain it, Lahaina News, May 15, 1991: 1.
— state Office of Environmental Quality Control evaluating impact of the state buying, Lahaina News, November 7, 1991: 1.
— Councilman Dennis Nakamura to seek changes to bill to discourage lengthening of, Lahaina News, January 14, 1993: 1.
— state takes control of, Lahaina News, April 1, 1993: 1.
— state seeking input on rules for, Lahaina News, October 14, 1993: 1,4.
— rules to be maintained, Lahaina News, August 11, 1994: 4.
— Mahalo Air ending service to, Lahaina News, September 7, 1995: 3.
— Island Air seeking to secure standard hours, Lahaina News, March 6, 1997: 1.
— public hearing to be held on proposed administrative changes for, Lahaina News, April 13, 2000: 1.
— residents wary of future of, Lahaina News, April 27, 2000: 1,16.
— commentary on possible closing of, Lahaina News, November 21, 2002: 14.

KAPANALI ALOHA INSTITUTE (KAI)
— to hold classes at Malu'ulu O Lele Cultural Center, Lahaina News, April 10, 2003: 2.

KAPAU, WALTER
— editorial criticizing his not being in jail, Lahaina News, November 21, 1984: 2.

KAPAUA CLAMBAKE PRO-AM
— to be held, Lahaina News, June 12, 2003: 11.

KAPENA [MUSICAL GROUP]
— performing at Royal Lahaina Resort, Lahaina News, August 7, 1985: 10.
— to perform at Maui Marriott Resort, Makai Bar, Lahaina News, August 22, 1990: 11,13.
— to perform on the ship Stardancer, Lahaina News, February 13, 1991: 11.

— to perform at fundraiser for Pop Warner Association, Lahaina News, September 10, 1992: 13.

— to perform at Maui Onion Festival, Lahaina News, August 3, 1995: 14.

— to perform "Live on the Beach" concert, Lahaina News, October 26, 1995: 11.

— to perform on the beach, Lahaina News, September 26, 1996: 14.

— to perform "Live on the Beach", Lahaina News, June 26, 1997: 16,17.

— to perform at A Taste of Lahaina, Lahaina News, September 10, 1998: 16.

— to perform at Pineapple Jam, Lahaina News, March 25, 1999: 6.

— to perform at Golden Oldies Revue, Lahaina News, October 19, 2000: 21.

— to perform at Lahaina Marine Art Festival, Lahaina News, March 1, 2001: 21.

— to perform at Golden Oldies Revue Show, Lahaina News, September 20, 2001: 16.

— to perform at benefit for Hawaii Firefighters, Lahaina News, September 19, 2002: 25.

— to perform for annual Hawai'i Firefighters Benefit, Lahaina News, October 9, 2003: 15.

KAPILI INSTITUTE
— to offer vocal workshops, Lahaina News, January 9, 2003: 17.

— continues to offer vocal workshops, Lahaina News, January 16, 2003: 17.

KAPILI, WILLIAM
— named chairman of Maui-Moloka'i Community Development Corporation, Lahaina Sun, February 3, 1971: 3.

KAPI'OLANI CHILDREN'S MIRACLE NETWORK
— to receive proceeds from celebrity softball game, Lahaina News, May 24, 1989: 3.

— to hold Miracle Golf Tournament, Lahaina News, May 15, 1997: 11.

— Maui Marriott raises money for, Lahaina News, June 25, 1998: 11.

KAPIOLANI HULA HALAU
— to perform at Lahaina Cannery Shopping Center, Lahaina News, August 10, 1988: 3.

KAPONO, HENRY [MUSICIAN]
— central role in Hawaiian music discussed, Lahaina News, May 8, 1985: 10.

— to appear at Maui Marriott, Lahaina News, August 10, 1988: 17.

— to perform at Maui Marriott Resort, Lahaina News, January 24, 1990: 14.

— to perform at school bazaar, Lahaina News, March 14, 1990: 16.

— to perform at "Super Star Search '90", Lahaina News, June 20, 1990: 9.

— to perform at Hard Rock Cafe, Lahaina News, December 26, 1990: 8.

— to perform at Hard Rock Cafe, Lahaina News, January 2, 1991: 8.

— to perform at Molokini Lounge at the Maui Prince Hotel, Lahaina News, May 8, 1991: 21.

— performs at Studio 505, Lahaina News, August 15, 1991: 14.

— to perform at Hawaiian International Music Festival, Lahaina News, August 29, 1991: 14.

— donates memorabilia to Hard Rock Cafe, Lahaina News, November 7, 1991: 19.

— to perform with Maui Symphony Orchestra, Lahaina News, March 26, 1992: 13.

— to perform with Maui Symphony Orchestra, Lahaina News, April 9, 1992: 16,19.

— to perform at Studio 505, Lahaina News, May 14, 1992: 14.

— to perform at Plantation House Restaurant holiday show, Lahaina News, December 10, 1992: 18.

— to participate in "Celebration of the Arts" at Ritz-Carlton, Lahaina News, April 8, 1993: 9.

— to headline benefit for Hawaii's forests, Lahaina News, September 2, 1993: 12.

— performs at Celebration of the Arts, Lahaina News, March 31, 1994: 13.

— to perform at "Rainbow Within You", Lahaina News, August 11, 1994: 12.

— to perform at the Hula Grill, Lahaina News, July 20, 1995: 11.

— performs at the Maui Onion Festival, Lahaina News, August 7, 1997: 1.

— to perform at Maui Arts and Cultural Center, Lahaina News, October 23, 1997: 20.

— to perform at Lahaina ho'olaule'a, Lahaina News, April 23, 1998: 7.

— to perform at Music on the Beach, Lahaina News, June 18, 1998: 3.

— to perform, Lahaina News, June 25, 1998: 5.

— to perform with Eddie Kamae, Lahaina News, November 25, 1999: 7.

— to perform, Lahaina News, May 3, 2001: 19.

— to perform at "I Love Lahaina", Lahaina News, October 25, 2001: 15.

— to perform at the "Celebration of the Arts", Lahaina News, March 28, 2002: 17.

— to perform at Ritz-Carlton holiday tree lighting event, Lahaina News, November 28, 2002: 16.

— see also Cecilio and Kapono [musical group]

KAPONO, WAINALU
— recovering from heart surgery , Lahaina News, December 26, 1996: 5.

KAPPAS, SOTOS [MUSICIAN]
— performing at Casanova's, Lahaina News, August 26, 1999: 18.

KAPRALIK, DAVID "KAWIKA"
— onion famer featured, Lahaina News, March 21, 1990: B6.

KAPTEL ASSOCIATES [BUSINESS]
— Maui Land and Pineapple Co may give up part ownership of, owner of Ritz-Carlton , Lahaina News, August 31, 1995: 1,2.

KAPU, KE'EAUMOKU
— discusses challenges to Kaua'ula Valley, Lahaina News, April 19, 2001: 1,18.

KAPUA VILLAGE SUBDIVISION
— Maui Planning Commission Maui allowing Kapulani Estates to intervene on special management area permit for, Lahaina News, January 28, 1999: 1.

KAPUNI SNORKEL ADVENTURES [BUSINESS]
— Circuit Court ruling allows Aloha Voyages to offer tours, Lahaina News, January 13, 1988: 1,16.

— closes luau on Moloka'i, applies for new permit, Lahaina News, May 11, 1988: 10.

KAPUO [BUSINESS]
— store featured, Lahaina Sun, June 6, 1973: 3.

KARA, GENSHO
— reverend discussed new temple and pagoda at Lahaina Jodo Mission, Lahaina Sun, March 10, 1971: 1,4.

KARAOKE
— available at Maui Marriott, Lahaina News, June 21, 1989: 16.

— held at Maui Marriott Resort, Lahaina News, December 19, 1990: 12.

— Lauren Nakano to host at Maui Marriott Resort, Lahaina News, December 26, 1990: 8.

— featured at Tiger's Restaurant, Lahaina News, July 25, 1991: 13.

— competition to be held by Hawaii Stars Television Show, Lahaina News, August 26, 1993: 15.

— Lahaina Center Christmas Karaoke Competition to be held, Lahaina News, November 25, 1993: 12.

— results of Lahaina Center Karaoke Contest, Lahaina News, December 30, 1993: 10.

— Japanese Karaoke Spring Festival to be held by Bernice Inouye Music Studio, Lahaina News, April 4, 2002: 16.

KARAOKE MAUI STYLE [BUSINESS]
— opens at Lahaina Center, Lahaina News, January 30, 2003: 8.

KARAOKE STAR SEARCH
— to be held at Whalers Village, Lahaina News, August 1, 1990: 11.
— to be held at Whalers Village, Lahaina News, August 8, 1990: 13.
— over 50 people scheduled to perform, Lahaina News, August 15, 1990: 15.

KARASIK, PAUL
— to speak at sales seminar, Lahaina News, August 2, 1989: 6.

KARATE
— offered by YMCA, Lahaina News, October 5, 1988: 20.
— Japan Karate Association-Hawaii holds holiday tournament, Lahaina News, December 23, 1993: 9.
— tournament to be held, Lahaina News, July 28, 1994: 6.
— members of Lahaina Dojo to complete in Japan, Lahaina News, July 20, 1995: 7.
— students to compete against Shotokan, Lahaina News, July 24, 1997: 14.
— lessons to be offered, Lahaina News, March 26, 1998: 7.
— Festival of Kings Karate Tournament held, Lahaina News, August 12, 1999: 6.
— students from Shotokan Karate-Do advance , Lahaina News, June 27, 2002: 12.
— see also martial arts

KARINEN, LARRY
— skillful as a basketball coach for Lahainaluna, Lahaina News, January 25, 1984: 4.
— Lahainaluna High School head basketball coach featured, Lahaina News, January 23, 1985: 4.
— Lahainaluna High School basketball coach interviewed, Lahaina News, January 15, 1986: 4.
— coach interviewed about Lahainaluna basketball team, Lahaina News, January 29, 1986: 4.

KARL, JOHN
— appointed as vice president and general manager of Sheraton Maui Hotel, Lahaina News, August 28, 1985: 8.

KARMA KAFE
— to hold Thanksgiving Food Drive, Lahaina News, November 15, 2001: 2.

KAROUSEL KIDS
— theatre group to perform, Lahaina News, August 14, 1997: 16.

KARR, HOWARD
— promoted to vice chairman at First Hawaiian Bank, Lahaina News, January 30, 1992: 12.

KARTES, NANCY JO
— passes away, Lahaina News, September 4, 2003: 2.
— memorial service to be held for, Lahaina News, September 11, 2003: 2.

KASPRZYCKI, JAN [ARTIST]
— life featured, Lahaina News, November 5, 1986: 7.
— to host opening reception of "Night and Day", Lahaina News, July 19, 1989: 12.
— to exhibit at David Paul's Lahaina Grill, Lahaina News, July 1, 1993: 11.
— to exhibit at Kapalua Bay Hotel, Lahaina News, December 30, 1993: 10.
— paints portrait of David Paul Johnson, Lahaina News, January 19, 1995: 12.
— "Nightscapes" to be on display at the Maui Arts and Cultural Center, Lahaina News, October 16, 1997: 17.
— to exhibit at NaPua Gallery, Lahaina News, August 12, 1999: 16.
— to exhibit at NaPua Gallery, Lahaina News, August 10, 2000: 17.
— opens Avalene Gallery, Lahaina News, November 1, 2001: 8.

KASPRZYCKI, LISA [ARTIST]
— to exhibit at Village Gallery Contemporary, Lahaina News, April 23, 1998: 16.
— opens Avalene Gallery, Lahaina News, November 1, 2001: 8.

KASS KASS AND FOUR STARTS [MUSICAL GROUP]
— to perform at Casanova's, Lahaina News, May 13, 1993: 12.

KATER, PETER [MUSICIAN]
— pianist to perform at Unity Church, Lahaina News, March 16, 2000: 13.

KATO, KENNY
— successes at swimming competitions, Lahaina News, June 30, 1994: 6.

KATO, NAGATO [POLITICIAN]
— candidate feels Maui Council needs inspiration, Lahaina News, July 30, 1998: 1,20.

KATSUNAI, MILDRED AND ANDREW
— local teachers featured , Lahaina News, October 25, 2001: 1,18.

KATZ, IRVING
— offers workshop on "Letting Go of Negative Additions and Developing Positive Convictions", Lahaina News, March 9, 1988: 18.

KAU KAU GRILL AND BAR [RESTAURANT]
— musical line-up at Maui Marriott listed, Lahaina News, April 11, 1990: 15.
— celebrating Marriott Hotel's 70th anniversary, Lahaina News, August 21, 1997: 12.

KAUA'I [ISLAND]
— current attraction described, with photographs, Lahaina News, May 15, 1983: 7,8,9.
— Maui builders find work on, Lahaina News, April 8, 1993: 5,6.

KAUAULA LAND CO.
— proposed subdivision delayed by disagreements over Kaua'ula archaeological study, Lahaina News, April 26, 2001: 1,22.

KAUA'ULA VALLEY
— subdivision described, Lahaina Sun, January 19, 1972: 3.
— caretaker Ke'eaumoku Kapu discusses challenges to, Lahaina News, April 19, 2001: 1,18.
— historic and cultural significance of, Lahaina News, May 3, 2001: 1,22.

KAUFFMAN, CHERYL
— wins Jackpot Queen contest, Lahaina News, November 7, 1984: 3.

KAUFMAN, GREGORY
— to present at Pacific Whale Foundation, Lahaina News, March 18, 1987: 18.
— comments on proposed thrillcraft corridor, Lahaina News, February 24, 1988: 1.
— founder of Pacific Whale Foundation responds to Rick Reed's claim of unethical conduct, Lahaina News, April 4, 1990: 1.
— Pacific Whale Foundation member to lead whale watch, Lahaina News, February 20, 2003: 17.

KAUFMAN, LORI
— Princess Nahienaena Elementary School teacher preparing students for Na Mele O Maui, Lahaina News, November 30, 2000: 1,20.

KAUHANE, JUNE [UNION BARGAINER]
— connected to hotel strike, Lahaina Sun, November 11, 1970: 1.

KAUI, NORMAN KALANI
— indicted for bank robbery, Lahaina News, August 28, 1997: 1,3.

KAULANA [CATAMARAN]
— facelift completed, Lahaina News, December 30, 1987: 3.

KAUMEHEIWA, SEAN
— wins ice carving contest, Lahaina News, December 25, 1997: 7.

KAUNOA SENIOR CENTER
— offering quilting for seniors, Lahaina News, January 28, 1987: 3.
— sponsoring Liability Workshop, Lahaina News, January 18, 2001: 16.

KAUNOA SENIOR SERVICES
— Leisure Program offering classes for senior citizens, Lahaina News, February 15, 1996: 10.
— Leisure Program to provide activities, Lahaina News, February 29, 1996: 4.
— to hold seminar on nutrition, Lahaina News, October 23, 1997: 20,21.
— continues to offer nutrition program, Lahaina News, April 23, 1998: 17.
— continues to offer nutrition program, Lahaina News, June 11, 1998: 16.
— continues to offer nutrition program, Lahaina News, August 27, 1998: 17.
— to offer tips for fighting Medicare fraud, Lahaina News, September 24, 1998: 17.
— to offer nutrition program, Lahaina News, December 10, 1998: 21.
— to hold nutrition program, Lahaina News, March 25, 1999: 17.
— to hold health services, Lahaina News, May 6, 1999: 21.

KAUPU, CHARLES
— teaches teachers about Honokahua agreement, Lahaina News, March 21, 1996: 1,14.
— appointed Hawaiian cultural advisor by Kapalua Land Company, Lahaina News, May 22, 1997: 9.
— leads blessing ceremony at Pioneer Inn, Lahaina News, December 12, 2002: 3.

KAUSHAL, ADHIMAN
— to perform classical Indian music, Lahaina News, January 29, 1998: 16.

KAWA'A, LUANA
— new Hawaiian cultural advisor for Westin Maui, Lahaina News, August 1, 2002: 8.

KAWAGUCHI, ALAN
— becomes athletic director at Lahainaluna High School, Lahaina News, November 2, 1995: 7.
— Lahainaluna High School Athletic Director retires, Lahaina News, March 15, 2001: 1,22.

KAWAGUCHI, BOB
— Lahainaluna High School athletics director retires, Lahaina News, May 30, 1990: 2.
— coach featured, Lahaina News, June 6, 1996: 16.

KAWAGUCHI, BRYCE
— embarks on military career, Lahaina News, September 13, 2001: 1,18.

KAWAGUCHI, CASEY
— Scholar/Athlete of the Week, Lahaina News, March 12, 1998: 15.

KAWAGUCHI, JENNIFER
— to represent West Maui at Chrysanthemum Ball, Lahaina News, October 20, 1994: 6.
— Lahainaluna High School graduate awarded scholarship from Maui Board of Realtors, Lahaina News, June 22, 1995: 4.

KAWAGUCHI, JON
— Lahainaluna High School baseball player featured, Lahaina News, February 15, 1984: 4.

KAWAGUCHI, KENJI
— Lahainaluna graduate appointed deputy director of the Maui County Department of Parks and Recreation, Lahaina News, February 19, 1986: 3.

KAWAGUCHI, ROBERT
— appointed athletic director for Lahainaluna School, Lahaina Sun, May 12, 1971: 7.

KAWAHARA, ROBERT
— to attend National Young Leaders Conference in Washington, D.C., Lahaina News, October 17, 1991: 5.

KAWAHARA, RONALD
— fined for failing to register as a condominium hotel operator registration, Lahaina News, August 11, 1994: 7.
— awarded Maui Chamber of Commerce's T.S. Shinn Award, Lahaina News, June 26, 1997: 7.

KAWAHINEKOA [FAMILY]
— reunion detailed, Lahaina News, July 17, 1985: 20.

KAWAIAEA, MARK "MARCO"
— paddling event to raise funds for, Lahaina News, July 24, 2003: 13.

KAWAIHOA, SOL [MUSICIAN]
— to perform at Bailey House Museum, Lahaina News, August 1, 1996: 20.
— to lecture on "The History of Slack Key Guitar and Ukulele", Lahaina News, October 3, 1996: 14.
— to perform at Bailey House Museum, Lahaina News, December 5, 1996: 15.
— to lecture on slack key guitar, Lahaina News, February 27, 1997: 10.
— to lecture on "The Music and History of Slack Key", Lahaina News, March 27, 1997: 13.
— to discuss "The Music and History of Slack Key", Lahaina News, July 10, 1997: 16.
— continues to offer musical classes, Lahaina News, November 6, 1997: 16.
— continues to teach slack key guitar, Lahaina News, March 5, 1998: 16.
— to discuss "'Hawaii Aloha' and the Music and History of Slack Key", Lahaina News, March 26, 1998: 13.
— continues to present on Slack Key at Bailey House, Lahaina News, September 2, 1999: 16.
— to hold "Slack Key—The Old Way and Hawai'i Aloha", Lahaina News, January 31, 2002: 16.
— offers "Slack Key—The Old Way and Hawai'i Aloha", Lahaina News, February 28, 2002: 16.
— to present "The Old Ways and Hawai'i Aloha" at Bailey House Museum, Lahaina News, June 20, 2002: 17.
— to discuss "Kio'alu: The Old Hawaiian Way and Hawai'i Aloha", Lahaina News, October 17, 2002: 21.

KAWAI'I, ABRAHAM
— to lecture on Hawaiian bodywork, Lahaina News, July 6, 1988: 3.
— to lecture on "Huli Honua Pueoneone—The Principles of Ancient Architectural Design and Interior Design", Lahaina News, August 10, 1988: 17.

KAWAMOTO, ISAMU
— scores hole-in-one at Waiehu Golf Course, Lahaina News, October 25, 1989: 11.

KAWAMOTO, LISA
— Scholar/Athlete of the Week, Lahaina News, September 21, 2000: 7.

KAWAMURA, GEORGINA KAUI [POLITICIAN]
— Maui County budget director discusses funding research on algae blooms, Lahaina News, January 16, 1992: 3.
— County budget director to use performance measures, Lahaina News, August 3, 1995: 5.
— running for Lana'i seat of Maui County Council, Lahaina News, August 10, 2000: 3.
— candidate for Lahaina County Council, Lahaina News, November 2, 2000: 21.

KAWAMURA, TED
— teacher offers free class on fish raising, Lahaina News, April 25, 1990: 1,6.

KAWANO, PAT [POLITICIAN]
— discusses hazardous intersection in Lahaina, Lahaina News, July 11, 1990: 1.
— to speak at Democratic Century Club, Lahaina News, February 20, 1997: 11.

— County Council Chair to speak to Democratic Century Club, Lahaina News, February 19, 1998: 13.
— to become chair of Maui County Council, Lahaina News, December 24, 1998: 1.

KAWARA SOBA TAKASE [RESTAURANT]
— new Japanese soba restaurant opens, Lahaina News, March 16, 1995: 10.

KAY, SHEILA [COMEDIAN]
— to perform at Comedy Club, Lahaina News, September 16, 1993: 16.
— to perform at Maui Comedy Club, Lahaina News, May 18, 1995: 10.

KAYA, GEORGE
— appointed director of Public Works, Lahaina News, February 27, 1991: 4.
— County Public Works director discusses delay of Mahinahina bridge opening, Lahaina News, January 23, 1992: 2.
— Public Works director to be asked about sewer main Maui County Council, Lahaina News, July 16, 1992: 1.
— talked about problems persisting at Mala Wharf, Lahaina News, February 4, 1993: 1.
— leaves County Public Works and Waste Management for position at Mayor's office, Lahaina News, January 19, 1995: 4.

KAYA, JOHN
— comments on closing of Olowalu Landfill, Lahaina News, June 22, 1988: 1,12,13.
— comments on closing of Olowalu Landfill, Lahaina News, July 13, 1988: 1,20.

KAYA, MASA
— inducted into Hawaii Golf Hall of Fame, Lahaina News, April 29, 1993: 6.

KAYAKING
— see paddling

KAYTON, EDWIN [ARTIST]
— presents "A Tribute to Hula" at Maui Marriott Resort, Lahaina News, May 8, 1985: 3.
— to show sculptures at Kapalua Bay Hotel, Lahaina News, February 19, 1986: 3.
— to be artist in resident at Hawaiian Cultural Arts Expo, Lahaina News, March 4, 1993: 10.

KAZUMA INTERNATIONAL GALLERY [BUSINESS]
— to feature "Tobu: To Soar to New Heights", Lahaina News, July 7, 1994: 15.
— to exhibit "Treasures from the Palaces of Indonesia", Lahaina News, November 28, 1996: 10.

KBH COMPANY [BUSINESS]
— sells Kapalua Bay Hotel, Lahaina News, June 28, 1989: 7.

KCOM CORPORATION [BUSINESS]
— proposes 62-unit affordable housing project, Lahaina News, April 23, 1992: 3.
— plans to build affordable housing, Lahaina News, July 2, 1992: 3,4.
— public hearing to be held to consider proposed shopping center, Lahaina News, August 27, 1992: 3.
— to develop affordable rental units along Honoapiʻilani Highway, Lahaina News, January 20, 1994: 7.

KE ʻALA O KA MAILE
— to perform during "Kukahi 2003", Lahaina News, February 13, 2003: 17.

KE ALALOA O MAUI [BOOK]
— by Inez Ashdown published, Lahaina Sun, December 27, 1972: 7.

KE ANA PUEO
— history of featured in Ka ʼTimi ʼike, Lahaina News, January 23, 1997: 2.

KE AU HOU
— Maui District Task Force proposal to be discussed at public meeting, Lahaina News, December 24, 1992: 3.

KE KULA KAMALIʻI PUʻUWAI LAʻA
— Sacred Hearts School students visit Lahaina Public Library, Lahaina News, September 18, 2003: 2.

KEA LANI FOOD AND WINE MASTERS
— to offer cooking demonstrations, Lahaina News, October 5, 2000: 16.
— members of Hawaii Regional Cuisine to be featured at, Lahaina News, March 21, 2002: 16.

KEA LANI HOTEL [BUSINESS]
— hotel under construction near Wailea Resort, Lahaina News, March 20, 1991: 7.
— to partner with Avis Rent a Car, Lahaina News, June 13, 1991: 18.
— holds grand opening, Lahaina News, July 23, 1992: 21.
— Grand Chefs on Tour to be held at, Lahaina News, September 2, 1999: 16.
— restaurant Caffe Ciao featured, Lahaina News, December 2, 1999: 14,15.
— Food Network chefs to be part of "Food and Wine Masters", Lahaina News, March 16, 2000: 12.

KEAGGY, CHERI [MUSICIAN]
— to perform at the Family Life Christian Center, Lahaina News, May 14, 1998: 17.

KEAHI, CHRISTOPHER
— life described, Lahaina News, June 28, 1989: 6.
— parish priest leaves for Honolulu, Lahaina News, December 12, 1990: 4.
— reverend retires from Maria Lanakila Church, Lahaina News, July 4, 1991: 1.

KEAHI, HANNAH
— dies in pedestrian accident; memorial held for, Lahaina News, November 29, 1989: 2.

KEAHI, KAI
— Kahana Canoe Club president discusses club, Lahaina News, July 18, 2002: 12.

KEAHI, MYRON
— police seeking, Lahaina News, August 20, 1998: 9.

KEALA, DAVID [MEMBER OF THE HAWAIIAN HOMES COMMISSION]
— at meeting between Hawaiian Homes Commission and The Hawaiians, Lahaina Sun, December 23, 1970: 6.

KEALA, NONI
— Scholar/Athlete of the Week, Lahaina News, February 15, 1996: 6.

KEALAHOU CHURCH
— description and photograph, Lahaina Sun, December 2, 1970: 2.

KEALALUHI, KO [MUSICIAN]
— to perform at Lahaina Cannery Mall, Lahaina News, April 4, 2002: 17.

KEALE, MOE [MUSICIAN]
— to perform at Lahaina Cannery Shopping Center, Lahaina News, September 27, 1989: 8.

KEALE, MOSES
— selected as chair of Office of Hawaiian Affairs, Lahaina News, January 2, 1991: 3.

KEALIA NATIONAL WILDLIFE REFUGE
— hike to be led by Sierra Club, Lahaina News, October 21, 1999: 16.

KEALIA POND MIDGE STUDY
— researchers to present on, Lahaina News, November 29, 2001: 16.

KEALIA POND NATIONAL WILDLIFE REFUGE
— to offer tours, Lahaina News, December 12, 2002: 14.
— staff to hold tour, Lahaina News, August 14, 2003: 16.

KEANAE ARBORETUM
— to temporarily close, Lahaina News, July 30, 1992: 5.

KEANAE BIRD SANCTUARY
— Sierra Club leading hikes to, Lahaina News, May 20, 1999: 17.

KEANAE OPEN MARKET
— to open at Keanae Ball Park, Lahaina News, September 3, 1998: 21.
— to be held, Lahaina News, October 1, 1998: 17.
— to be held, Lahaina News, February 4, 1999: 17.
— to feature Hawaiian arts and crafts, Lahaina News, April 22, 1999: 12.

KEANAE-WAILUA [PLACE]
— featured, Lahaina Sun, July 18, 1973: 1,12,13.

KEANINI, BOBBY
— finds sea mine, Lahaina News, September 11, 1997: 2.

KEARNEY, DICK [ARTIST]
— work to be displayed at "Friday Night is Art Night", Lahaina News, August 23, 1989: 11.
— ex-NASA artist featured, Lahaina News, September 6, 1989: 11.
— celebrates first published lithographs, Lahaina News, October 25, 1989: 17.
— featured at Sunset Galleries, Lahaina News, May 23, 1990: 15.
— to show latest lithographs at Friday Night is Art Night, Lahaina News, October 24, 1990: 16.
— demonstrates painting technique to students, Lahaina News, November 14, 1990: 5.

KEATHLEY, THERESA
— to lecture on reincarnation, Lahaina News, April 17, 1997: 12.

KEATING, SCOTT
— jewelry designer to appear, Lahaina News, December 20, 1989: 4.

KEAU, CHARLIE
— archaeology class to be held at Bailey House Museum, Lahaina News, July 1, 1999: 13.

KEAUNUI, KENNETH
— performing in South America, Lahaina Sun, January 20, 1971: 7.

KEAWALA'I CONGREGATIONAL CHURCH
— to hold benefit to celebrate 155 years since founding, Lahaina News, February 18, 1987: 11.
— to hold benefit luau, Lahaina News, March 4, 1993: 12.
— to hold fundraiser for restoration, Lahaina News, March 11, 1993: 10,11.
— fundraiser successful, Lahaina News, April 8, 1993: 5.
— problems with termites, Lahaina News, October 21, 1993: 7.
— to hold luau, Lahaina News, March 12, 1998: 20.
— to hold annual benefit luau, Lahaina News, March 11, 1999: 12.
— to hold luau, Lahaina News, March 8, 2001: 16.
— choir joins Maui Brass Ensemble, Lahaina News, July 19, 2001: 16.
— to host "Aha Mele", Lahaina News, August 22, 2002: 20.

KEAWE, AUNTIE GENOA [MUSICIAN]
— to perform at the Lahaina Civic Center, Lahaina Sun, May 16, 1973: 3.
— to perform at Maui Community College Ho'olaule'a, Lahaina News, April 11, 1984: 5.
— to perform at Ka'anapali Beach Hotel Tiki Bar, Lahaina News, September 16, 1999: 14.
— to perform at lei Day Hula Festival, Lahaina News, April 20, 2000: 16.
— to perform at Ka'anapali Beach Hotel for Aloha Week, Lahaina News, October 19, 2000: 11.
— to perform at Ku'u Home O Wailuku music festival, Lahaina News, October 19, 2000: 18.
— to perform at Ka'anapali Beach Hotel, Lahaina News, March 22, 2001: 14.
— to perform at Ka'anapali Beach Hotel's Tiki Courtyard, Lahaina News, June 13, 2002: 1.

KEAWE CAMP
— former residents to reunite, Lahaina News, October 12, 2000: 6.
— residents to hold reunion, Lahaina News, October 19, 2000: 20.

KEAWE, DENNIS KANAE [ARTIST]
— to speak at Native Hawaiian Plant Society, Lahaina News, February 13, 1992: 4.

KEAWE, JOHN [MUSICIAN]
— to perform at Old Lahaina Cafe and Luau, Lahaina News, March 28, 1990: 15.
— to perform, Lahaina News, December 19, 1996: 11.
— to perform at Seascape Ma'alaea Restaurant, Lahaina News, January 20, 2000: 12.
— to perform at Ma'alaea Restaurant, Lahaina News, March 30, 2000: 12.

KEEFE, CHERYL
— hired as account coordinator for Catapult Communications Inc., Lahaina News, May 25, 1995: 10.

KEEHI MARINE
— presents Ocean Expo, Lahaina News, March 20, 1991: 7.
— presenting Ocean Expo '91, Lahaina News, April 10, 1991: 6.

KEELIKOLANI, RUTH [PRINCESS]
— political biography detailed, Lahaina News, April 15, 1981: 7,10.

KEENE, MATTHEW
— to sign copies of "Chocolate Is My Kryptonite/How To Survive the Forces of Food", Lahaina News, July 16, 1998: 16.

KEEP AMERICA BEAUTIFUL DAY
— organized, Lahaina News, April 13, 1988: 3.
— to be held, Lahaina News, April 17, 1991: 7.
— to be held, Lahaina News, April 24, 1991: 1.

KEEP, CORBIN [MUSICIAN]
— to perform at Keolahou Congregational Church, Lahaina News, November 11, 1999: 13.

KEEP HAWAII BEAUTIFUL CLEANUP DAY
— to be held, Lahaina News, April 8, 1999: 3.

KEEP IT HAWAII
— Hawaii Visitors Bureau program begins, Lahaina News, November 23, 1995: 10.
— Old Lahaina Luau receives Kahili award, Lahaina News, April 22, 1999: 11.
— awards to be given by Hawai'i Visitors and Convention Bureau, Lahaina News, May 11, 2000: 11.
— West Maui businesses win award, Lahaina News, April 18, 2002: 1,5.

KEG [RESTAURANT]
— to open on Front Street, Lahaina, Lahaina News, August 1, 1984: 14.

KEHLER VETERINARY CLINIC
— seeking permission to operate in residential district, Lahaina News, July 23, 1992: 10.

KE'IA [MUSICAL GROUP]
— featured, Lahaina News, March 25, 1987: 8.

KEIKI BARGAINS [BUSINESS]
— reviewed, Lahaina News, October 30, 1985: 7.

KEIKI CHRISTMAS KARAOKE COMPETITION
— to be held, Lahaina News, December 19, 1996: 10.
— results of, Lahaina News, January 2, 1997: 12.
— results of, Lahaina News, January 6, 2000: 2.
— to be held, Lahaina News, December 7, 2000: 23.
— Makanalani Hussey wins, Lahaina News, December 28, 2000: 3.

KEIKI FISHING TOURNAMENT
— planned, Lahaina News, August 26, 1987: 3.
— results of, Lahaina News, September 28, 2000: 9.
— Lahaina Yacht Club planning, Lahaina News, September 18, 2003: 13.
— held, Lahaina News, September 25, 2003: 1.

KEIKI HULA FESTIVAL
— Joy Pascual wins, Lahaina News, November 7, 1991: 16.
— to be held at Lahaina Cannery Mall, Lahaina News, July 15, 1999: 12.
— to be held, Lahaina News, August 24, 2000: 21.
— to be held at Lahaina Cannery Mall, Lahaina News, July 12, 2001: 17.
— to be held at Lahaina Cannery Mall, Lahaina News, July 4, 2002: 14.
— to be held, Lahaina News, July 11, 2002: 16.
— to be held at Lahaina Cannery Mall, Lahaina News, July 10, 2003: 15.

KEIKI ID FAIR
— to be held, Lahaina News, July 22, 1999: 12.

KEIKI IN THEATRE THEATRE
— drama program for children to offer "Oh the Mo'o!" musical, Lahaina News, July 22, 1999: 2.

KEIKI KARAOKE TALENT CONTEST
— to be held at Wharf Cinema Center, Lahaina News, December 9, 1999: 17.

KEIKI O KULA PRE-SCHOOL
— to hold Keiki O Kula Festival, Lahaina News, April 2, 1992: 22.
— to hold festival, Lahaina News, April 9, 1992: 8.

KEIKI O MAUI
— regatta to be held at Hanaka'o'o Beach Park, Lahaina News, June 28, 1989: 9.
— regatta to be held, Lahaina News, June 12, 1997: 12.

KEIKI ONION OLYMPICS
— to be held as part of Maui Onion Festival, Lahaina News, March 21, 1990: B7.

KEIKI PLAY MORNING
— continues to be held, Lahaina News, December 23, 1999: 17.
— continues to be held, Lahaina News, April 20, 2000: 17.

KEIKI SAND CASTLE CONTEST
— results, Lahaina News, September 22, 1994: 15.

KEIKI SONG COMPETITION
— Waihee School wins, Lahaina News, November 15, 1989: 3.

KEIKI STORYTIME
— to be held at Borders Books and Music, Lahaina News, April 22, 1999: 12.

KEIKI SURF JAM
— to be held, Lahaina News, July 13, 1995: 7.

KEIKI'S DREAM PROGRAM
— to hold "Do a Mile and Share a Smile" fundraiser, Lahaina News, June 10, 1999: 6.
— holds "Do a Mile and Share a Smile", Lahaina News, June 15, 2000: 16.
— to hold Matching Fund Drive, Lahaina News, March 20, 2003: 8.

KEIKO, TAMI
— to compete in Chrysanthemum Ball, Lahaina News, November 28, 1996: 3.

KEITER, CHRIS
— Scholar/Athlete of the Week, Lahaina News, November 28, 1996: 5.

KEITER, MARTY
— named director of golf at Kapalua at Village Course, Lahaina News, October 29, 1986: 3.
— Kapalua's director awards scholarship to Natalie Nakamura, Lahaina News, July 31, 1997: 9.

KEKA'A
— Amfac/JMB to open 10-acre open space in, Lahaina News, May 27, 1999: 3.

KEKA'A BEACH
— students clean up, Lahaina News, March 8, 2001: 3.

KEKA'A REEF
— to be studied, Lahaina News, September 18, 1997: 1.

KEKAHUNA, ANNIE
— remembered, part I, Lahaina News, October 26, 2000: 7.
— remembered, part II, Lahaina News, November 9, 2000: 6.
— remembered, part III, Lahaina News, November 23, 2000: 8.
— remembered, part IV, Lahaina News, November 30, 2000: 14.
— remembered, part V, Lahaina News, December 28, 2000: 3.
— remembered, part VI, Lahaina News, January 11, 2001: 6.
— remembered, part VII, Lahaina News, January 18, 2001: 5.
— remembered, part VIII, Lahaina News, January 25, 2001: 5.
— remembered, conclusion, Lahaina News, February 1, 2001: 2.

KEKAHUNA KAMALA
— kumu hula re-signs at Wharf Shops & Restaurants, Lahaina News, July 13, 1988: 10.

KEKALIA, THOMAS
— dies picking opihi, Lahaina Sun, October 11, 1972: 10.

KEKA'S JEEP SERENADERS [MUSICAL GROUP]
— reviewed, Lahaina News, May 30, 1984: 21.

KEKA'S TERRACE [RESTAURANT]
— opens at Sheraton Maui, Lahaina News, December 5, 1996: 8.

KEKIPI, VELMA
— running for at-large trustee of Office of Hawaiian Affairs, Lahaina News, August 15, 1984: 3.

KEKONA, KALANI [MUSICIAN]
— member of Kanaka Jam featured, Lahaina News, February 13, 1992: 18.
— to perform at L, Lahaina News, February 13, 1992: 22.

KEKONA, VIVIAN
— wins Silversword Women's Golf Club, Lahaina News, December 19, 1991: 9.
— wins Silversword Women's golf club ACE for April, Lahaina News, May 21, 1992: 12.

KEKUNA, KEN
— benefit from Self-Help Housing Corporation, Lahaina News, January 30, 1992: 3.

KEKUNA, SHELLEY
— part of new management team at Ka'anapali Beach Resort Association, Lahaina News, February 1, 2001: 8.

KELATORI, KEOLA
— pitcher featured, Lahaina News, July 2, 1998: 14.

KELAWEA CAMP
— poor water quality at, Lahaina Sun, December 9, 1970: 6.

KELAWEA MAUKA
— elderly rental project proposed by Affording Housing Corp. for, Lahaina News, November 16, 1995: 3.

KELLAM, TERRY
— discusses impact of possible limit to thrillcraft areas of activity, Lahaina News, March 30, 1988: 1.

KELLEY, CHRISTOPHER
— Maui Ocean Center to host on "The Discovery of the Ward Midget Submarine off Pearl Harbor", Lahaina News, June 26, 2003: 8.

KELLEY, MICHAEL
— Small Business Person of the Year, Lahaina News, May 26, 1994: 7.
— named Retail Entrepreneur of the Year, Lahaina News, September 25, 1997: 12.

KELLEY, RICHARD "DOC"
— chair of Outrigger Enterprises to speak to Maui Chamber of Commerce, Lahaina News, October 2, 1997: 15.
— column supporting Bank of Hawaii president Larry Johnson against bribery charges, Lahaina News, December 18, 1997: 21.

KELLEYS OF THE OUTRIGGER [BOOK]
— published on life of Roy and Estelle Kelley, Lahaina News, August 15, 1990: 11.

KELLNER, JEROME
— to present "Walk with the Titans", Lahaina News, August 31, 2000: 21.

KELLY COVINGTON BAND [MUSICAL GROUP]
— to perform at Pacific'O Restaurant, Lahaina News, September 14, 1995: 12.
— to perform at Pacific's Restaurant, Lahaina News, September 19, 1996: 18.
— see also Covington, Kelly [musician]

KELLY, DAVID [ACTOR]
— actors from Oregon Shakespeare Festival to hold classes, Lahaina News, December 15, 1994: 19.

KELLY, DON
— named director of sales at Hyatt Regency Maui, Lahaina News, July 25, 1991: 7.

KELLY, MARIAN [COMEDIAN]
— to perform at Comedy Club and the Sports Page, Lahaina News, April 2, 1992: 16,17,20.
— to perform at Honolulu Comedy Club, Lahaina News, January 25, 1996: 14.

KELLY, MARY OLSEN [WRITER]
— to sign book "Path of the Pearl: Discover Your Treasures Within", Lahaina News, November 14, 2002: 21.

KELLY, PETER
— award Certified Real Estate Brokerage Manager designation, Lahaina News, March 19, 1986: 3.

KELLY, RAINBOW
— complains of County attempts to impede his commercial activities, Lahaina Sun, January 26, 1972: 3.

KELSEY, BOB
— sells Lahaina News, Lahaina News, February 1, 1983: 8,9.
— businesses reviewed, Lahaina News, November 9, 1983: 14.
— ends column in Lahaina News, Lahaina News, September 3, 1986: 6.
— announces closing of the Lahaina Sun, Lahaina News, November 1, 1989: 1.
— moves to Oahu and is ordained in the Holy Orthodox Faith, Lahaina News, September 12, 1990: 3.

KELSEY, DONNA
— recurring column begins and is not indexed, Lahaina News, August, 1979: 8,9.

KELSEY, ROBERT
— section containing short news pieces begins and typically not indexed, Lahaina Sun, June 2, 1970: .
— work displayed at Lahaina Art Gallery, Lahaina Sun, June 2, 1971: 3.
— column in Lahaina Sun discussed, Lahaina Sun, July 26, 1972: 16,17.

KEMBLE, ROBERT
— elected to board of West Maui Taxpayers Association, Lahaina News, July 1, 1987: 3.

KEMP, MICHAEL
— appointed national sales manager at Ritz-Carlton Mauna Lani, Lahaina News, May 27, 1993: 8.

KEMPER LESNIK ORGANIZATION
— donates to Lahainaluna High School, Lahaina News, March 25, 1993: 6.

KEMPER, MICHELLE
— selected as acting executive director of Kihei Youth Center, Lahaina News, December 9, 1993: 5.

KEMPER OPEN
— see Women's Kemper Open

KEN, OMAN
— to perform "Starwheel: The Journey of the Sacred Circle", Lahaina News, February 9, 1995: 11.

KENAI HELICOPTERS
— fined for illegal landings, Lahaina News, February 1, 1984: 16.

KENDALL, LIZ
— to talk on chronobiology "The Rhythms of Life", Lahaina News, February 17, 2000: 17.
— to hold class on chronobiology, Lahaina News, March 2, 2000: 13.

KENKNIGHT, FRED [ARTIST]
— to exhibit at Village Galleries, Lahaina News, February 17, 2000: 16.
— to exhibit at Village Galleries, Lahaina News, February 15, 2001: 16.
— exhibiting at the Village Galleries, Lahaina News, March 29, 2001: 14.
— to exhibit at Village Gallery Contemporary, Lahaina News, April 4, 2002: 16.
— to exhibit at Village Galleries, Lahaina News, August 1, 2002: 21.

KENNEDY, EDWARD
— interested in Maui shrine, Lahaina Sun, August 25, 1971: 5.

KENNEDY, JOHN
— Senator Ted Kennedy backs proposed JFK memorial in Iao Valley, Lahaina Sun, December 29, 1971: 4.

KENNEDY, LORI
— selected Director of Public Relations at Four Seasons Resort Maui, Lahaina News, February 8, 1996: 6.

KENNEY, RONNY [COMEDIAN]
— to perform at Comedy Club, Lahaina News, October 3, 1991: 12.
— to perform at Comedy Club and the Sports Page, Lahaina News, May 7, 1992: 21,24.
— to perform at Comedy Club and the Sports Page, Lahaina News, May 27, 1993: 12,15.
— to perform at Maui Comedy Club, Lahaina News, August 10, 1995: 11.

KENNISON, WILLIAM
— named chair of Maui United Way Campaign, Lahaina News, January 3, 1990: 5.

KENNY G [MUSICIAN]
— to perform at Royal Lahaina Tennis Stadium, Lahaina News, September 23, 1987: 7,8.
— to perform at the Royal Lahaina Tennis Stadium, Lahaina News, October 19, 1988: 11.

KENOLIO, KOANA
— planning family reunion, Lahaina News, June 18, 1998: 2.
— family to hold reunion, Lahaina News, July 2, 1998: 8.

KENOLIO MAUKA
— to be developed by Betsill Brothers Construction, Lahaina News, October 10, 2002: 6.

KENPO DOJO
— students of successful at Festival of the Kings—Hoʻolauleʻaʻona Aliʻi—martials art tournament, Lahaina News, August 23, 2001: 12.

KENTRON HAWAII LTD [BUSINESS]
— planning hydrofoil service between Maui and Honolulu , Lahaina Sun, March 14, 1973: 5.
— see also ferries

KENTUCKY FRIED CHICKEN [RESTAURANT]
— Lahaina restaurant receives "White Glove" award for sanitation, Lahaina News, May 2, 1984: 4.

KEOHO, CHARLES
— discusses Central Pacific Dive Club adopting a reef, Lahaina News, May 9, 1990: 1.

KEOKI SOUNDS [MUSICAL GROUP]
— to perform at Hula Grill, Lahaina News, July 27, 1995: 12.

KEOLAHOU CONGREGATIONAL HAWAIIAN CHURCH
— Kihei Fine Art Shows continue to be held, Lahaina News, August 29, 2002: 21.

KEONA BANQUET
— healthcare workers to be honored at, Lahaina News, March 20, 2003: 2.

KEONE'O'IO
— see Friends of Keone'o'io

KEOPUOLANI [QUEEN]
— celebration held at Waiola Congregational Church, Lahaina News, November 15, 1980: 3.
— Hiram Bingham's discussion of her faith, Lahaina News, August 15, 1981: 11,12.
— description of her faith in 1848 monograph by Hiram Bingham, Lahaina News, January 1, 1983: 15,16.
— ceremony held at Waiola Congregational Church, Lahaina News, November 30, 1983: 7,8,9,10.
— biography of, Lahaina News, May 8, 1985: 1,9.
— tribute to be paid to, Lahaina News, September 6, 2001: 14.
— tribute to be paid to Queen at Ho'omana'o 2001, Lahaina News, September 6, 2001: 14.

KEOPUOLANI PARK
— to open, Lahaina News, September 3, 1998: 3.
— Department of Parks and Recreation begins construction on field, Lahaina News, September 28, 2000: 9.
— Walk for Juvenile Diabetes to be held at, Lahaina News, November 7, 2002: 17.

KEOUGH, FATHER CORNELIUS
— founder of mental health improvement program GROW visits Maui, Lahaina Sun, December 20, 1972: 15.

KEPA, MITCH [MUSICIAN]
— to perform at Makai Bar at Marriott, Lahaina News, January 30, 1992: 17.
— to perform at Makai Bar, Lahaina News, March 28, 1996: 13.
— to perform at Makai Bar, Lahaina News, September 19, 1996: 18.
— to perform at "Music on the Beach", Lahaina News, December 17, 1998: 21.
— to perform at "Music on the Beach", Lahaina News, December 24, 1998: 7.
— to perform at Leilani's on the Beach, Lahaina News, February 1, 2001: 19.
— performs at Westin Maui's Ono Bar and Grill, Lahaina News, July 11, 2002: 15.

KERBOX, BUZZY
— wins Oxbow World Masters Championship, Lahaina News, August 20, 1998: 15.
— wins Hana Highway Surf/MCD Surfboard Paddle Race, Lahaina News, July 27, 2000: 7.

KERBY, TERRY
— Maui Ocean Center to host on "The Discovery of the Ward Midget Submarine off Pearl Harbor", Lahaina News, June 26, 2003: 8.

KERNAHAN, EARL
— to host revival at Lahaina United Methodist Church, Lahaina News, March 2, 1988: 22.
— new pastor of Honolua United Methodist Church, Lahaina News, November 7, 1991: 4.
— reverend of Honolua United Methodist Church announces additional service, Lahaina News, January 9, 1992: 3.

KERR, JEANETTE
— golfer' career described, Lahaina News, March 6, 1985: A11.

KERSTING, HENRY
— tax shelter promoter penalized, Lahaina News, October 13, 1994: 15.

KERWOOD, SARAH
— fundraiser to be held for, Lahaina News, December 27, 2001: 1,18.
— Java Jazz to hold benefit for, Lahaina News, January 3, 2002: 2.

KESSENICH, WES
— wins Maui Marathon, Lahaina News, March 20, 1991: 5.

KESSLER, BRIAN [MUSICIAN]
— to play at Borders, Lahaina News, July 8, 1999: 12.

KESSLER, DON
— discusses possible state teacher strike, Lahaina Sun, October 13, 1971: 4.

KETOFSKY, MORTON
— to offer course "Inquiry as a Path of Spiritual Evolution", Lahaina News, January 16, 1997: 10.

KEY TO LIFE CHIROPRACTIC [BUSINESS]
— opens, Lahaina News, May 29, 1997: 5.
— to sponsor "Kids Day America", Lahaina News, May 9, 2002: 8.
— to sponsor "Kids Day America", Lahaina News, May 16, 2002: 2.

KEYES, CHARLES
— appointed vice president and manager of Bank of Hawaii's Maui Region Business Banking Center, Lahaina News, February 27, 1991: 8.
— part of new Central Pacific Bank team, Lahaina News, February 7, 2002: 8.

KEYES, JOE [COMEDIAN]
— to perform at Comedy Club and the Sports Page, Lahaina News, January 30, 1992: 17.

KEYHANI, CYRUS
— named systems manager at Marriott and Renaissance Resorts Hawaii, Lahaina News, July 10, 2003: 8.

KEYHANI, DARIUS
— Lahainaluna High School student takes a first prize in Hawaii Business Student Conference, Lahaina News, May 1, 1991: 4.
— Lahainaluna High School student receives scholarships, Lahaina News, June 6, 1991: 1.

KFVE-TV
— now available on Maui, Lahaina News, February 20, 1992: 5.

KHAC CHIENSEMBLE [MUSICAL GROUP]
— to perform Vietnamese music, Lahaina News, February 18, 1999: 13.

KHAN, USTAD SHUJAAT
— to perform classical Indian music, Lahaina News, January 29, 1998: 16.

KHET
— "Dialog" focusing on the University of Hawaii, Lahaina News, February 6, 1992: 5.

KHNL
— receives award for excellence in print advertising, Lahaina News, January 23, 1991: 5.
— ranked fourth most-watched independent television station in the United States, Lahaina News, January 30, 1992: 12.

KHONG, PETER
— promoted to manager of Japanese guest services at Westin Maui, Lahaina News, August 22, 1990: 9.
— hired by Grand Hyatt Wailea, Lahaina News, February 20, 1992: 10.

KHPR
— see Hawaii Public Radio (KHPR)

KHUA CAMP
— project to improve water and sewer lines to, Lahaina News, December 23, 1999: 3.

KI HOʻALU SLACK KEY GUITAR FESTIVAL
— slack key festival scheduled, Lahaina News, July 18, 1990: 11.
— Bankoh to sponsor, Lahaina News, May 25, 1995: 12.
— to be held, Lahaina News, June 10, 1999: 14.
— to be held, Lahaina News, May 25, 2000: 17.
— successful, Lahaina News, June 15, 2000: 3.
— to be held, Lahaina News, June 14, 2001: 21.
— to be held, Lahaina News, June 21, 2001: 17.
— to be held, Lahaina News, June 20, 2002: 17.
— to be held, Lahaina News, June 20, 2002: 3.
— held, Lahaina News, June 27, 2002: 1.
— to be held, Lahaina News, June 12, 2003: 18.
— to be held, Lahaina News, June 19, 2003: 16.

KIAHANI RESORT MANAGEMENT [BUSINESS]
— retained by Catapult Productions, Lahaina News, April 16, 1992: 14.

KIAKONA, KIMO
— comments on proposed thrillcraft corridor, Lahaina News, February 24, 1988: 1.

KIANG, KAM
— owner of Lahaina's Hop Wo Store passes away, Lahaina Sun, September 8, 1971: 13.

KIANG, SHENG-PIAO [ARTIST]
— featured at Lahaina Arts Society Upstairs Gallery, Lahaina News, April 29, 1987: 3.

KIAWE BROILER [RESTAURANT]
— offering Cajun and Creole menu, Lahaina News, May 7, 1986: 3.
— adding new menu items, Lahaina News, February 18, 1987: 11.

KIBE, RICHARD
— participated in Maui Youth Council, Lahaina Sun, January 13, 1971: 5.

KIDCARE PHOTO IDS
— can be obtained at Child Safety Day, Lahaina News, August 11, 1994: 4.

KIDNAY, JOHN
— discusses boating courses offered by Coast Guard Auxiliary, Lahaina News, November 22, 1989: 6.

KIDS A.M.
— play group to meet at Lahaina Youth Center, Lahaina News, April 24, 1997: 13.
— continues to be offered at Lahaina Youth Center, Lahaina News, May 22, 1997: 17.
— continues to host play and activity group, Lahaina News, June 26, 1997: 17.
— group for kids and parents to meet, Lahaina News, February 18, 1999: 13.
— free group for toddlers continues to be offered, Lahaina News, June 24, 1999: 13.

KID'S DAY AMERICA
— to be held, Lahaina News, May 9, 2002: 8.
— to be held at Lahaina Cannery Mall, Lahaina News, May 15, 2003: 14.
— Maui Fire Department staff attend, Lahaina News, May 22, 2003: 3.

KIDS' DAY INTERNATIONAL
— to be held, Lahaina News, April 24, 1997: 12.

KIDS IN THE ARTS EDUCATION FOR CHILDREN
— to produce "The Three Little Pigs", Lahaina News, May 8, 1997: 17.

KID'S KORNER
— feature for children introduced, Lahaina News, December 2, 1987: 12.

KIDS OF LAHAINA [THEATRE GROUP]
— beginning third season, Lahaina News, August 28, 1985: 8.

KIDSCIENCE: WATER WATCH [TELEVISION SHOW]
— to include segments on West Maui's watershed, Lahaina News, April 11, 1996: 6.

KIDSUMMER NIGHT'S DREAM, A [PLAY]
— to be performed at Maui Theatre Theatre, Lahaina News, July 20, 2000: 1,9.

KIEK, LAUREN
— Scholar/Athlete of the Week, Lahaina News, January 23, 2003: 12.

KIEK, SHANNON
— Scholar/Athlete of the Week, Lahaina News, May 2, 1996: 20.

KIEWIT PACIFIC CO. [BUSINESS]
— awarded road construction contract, Lahaina News, June 13, 1991: 18.
— contracting firm files lawsuit against state over Kahului Airport Terminal extension project, Lahaina News, December 23, 1993: 7.
— beings highway widening project, Lahaina News, October 29, 1998: 1.
— speeding expansion of Honoapiʻilani, Lahaina News, December 2, 1999: 1.
— meets with residents to discuss highway project issues, Lahaina News, March 30, 2000: 5.

KIGER, BOB
— unearthing abandoned Haiku Mill, Lahaina News, August 21, 1985: 1,20.
— advocating for bike math around Maui, Lahaina News, January 6, 1988: 1,14.
— opening Old Mill Haiku museum, Lahaina News, January 6, 1988: 1,14.

KIHEI [TOWN]
— Mana Kai condominium being built, Lahaina Sun, September 15, 1971: 5.
— plans to move school criticized, Lahaina Sun, July 5, 1972: 15.
— Maui Planning Commission rejects Anthony Arisumi's request to build affordable housing, Lahaina Sun, December 13, 1972: 3.
— retirement community for affluent elderly planned, Lahaina Sun, March 14, 1973: 12.
— featured, Lahaina Sun, August 22, 1973: 12,13,14.
— residential subdivision planned, Lahaina News, August 1, 1980: 13.
— editorial discussing recent history, Lahaina News, August 15, 1980: 2.
— rural Kihei described, Lahaina News, October 15, 1980: 13.
— new bank to open, Lahaina News, January 15, 1981: 2.
— residents question impact of proposed projects, Lahaina News, June 3, 1993: 4.
— community group may overlap functions with Kihei Youth Center, Lahaina News, October 28, 1993: 6.

KIHEI ART SHOW, THE
— to be held, Lahaina News, May 11, 2000: 21.
— held, Lahaina News, June 1, 2000: 16.
— to be held, Lahaina News, June 29, 2000: 21.
— to be held, Lahaina News, January 4, 2001: 16.
— to be held, Lahaina News, April 5, 2001: 20.
— to be held at Keolahou Church, Lahaina News, April 19, 2001: 17.
— to be held, Lahaina News, August 30, 2001: 16.
— continues to feature local artists, Lahaina News, October 4, 2001: 16.
— to be held, Lahaina News, November 29, 2001: 17.

KIHEI BOAT RAMP
— contract awarded to pave, Lahaina News, August 6, 1992: 9.

KIHEI CANOE CLUB
— sponsoring Ben Abiera Memorial, Lahaina News, May 23, 1990: 10.
— sponsoring Moki Kalanikau Regatta, Lahaina News, June 27, 1990: 6.
— wins Ben Abiera Relay, Lahaina News, June 4, 1992: 8.

— featured, Lahaina News, May 20, 1993: 6.
— to sponsor Ben Abiera Relays, Lahaina News, May 27, 1993: 9.
— holding Ka Lae Pohaku-Molokini Long Distance Race, Lahaina News, September 18, 1997: 14.
— to sponsor Kihei Shoreline Race, Lahaina News, February 18, 1999: 7.
— to celebrate "Ka 'Ohana Moana" at Maui Ocean Center as benefit, Lahaina News, May 11, 2000: 9.
— to hold Ben Abiera Memorial race, Lahaina News, May 25, 2000: 8.
— regattas continue, Lahaina News, June 29, 2000: 1,15.
— to hold practice, Lahaina News, March 15, 2001: 11.
— plans benefit races, Lahaina News, March 6, 2003: 13.

KIHEI CARNIVAL
— to be held Saturday, Lahaina News, March 19, 1992: 4.

KIHEI COLD AND SELF STORAGE [BUSINESS]
— opens, Lahaina News, May 30, 1991: 3.

KIHEI COMMERCIAL CENTER
— opens in Kihei, Lahaina News, May 30, 1991: 3.

KIHEI COMMUNITY ASSOCIATION
— to hold fundraiser, Lahaina News, August 1, 1990: 14.
— to hold general meeting, Lahaina News, November 14, 1991: 3.
— to meet; to hold grand opening for new office, Lahaina News, January 9, 1992: 5.
— to hold grand opening, Lahaina News, January 16, 1992: 4.
— hosting carnival, Lahaina News, March 12, 1992: 4,5.
— calls for improved disaster management, Lahaina News, May 28, 1992: 7.
— to hold public forum on planning for growth, Lahaina News, June 11, 1992: 8.
— to hold general membership meeting, Lahaina News, July 2, 1992: 7.
— to discuss sewage and water issues, Lahaina News, July 16, 1992: 6.
— developers to present to, Lahaina News, July 16, 1992: 7.
— sponsoring developer presentation, Lahaina News, July 30, 1992: 7.
— president Gene Thompson writes about proposed amendments to County Charter, Lahaina News, October 1, 1992: 13,14.
— considering changes charter, Lahaina News, October 29, 1992: 16.
— to meet to talk about parks, Lahaina News, November 26, 1992: 14,18.
— Carla Flood designs t-shirt for, Lahaina News, November 26, 1992: 18.
— to meet, Lahaina News, November 26, 1992: 18.
— to hold general membership meeting; Mayor Linda Lingle to speak, Lahaina News, March 11, 1993: 10.
— plans to reset the Kalama Park Whale structure, Lahaina News, March 11, 1993: 10.
— new board of directors elected, Lahaina News, March 11, 1993: 10.
— Coastal Zone Watch Committee to meet, Lahaina News, May 6, 1993: 7.
— to meet, Lahaina News, May 13, 1993: 4.
— Coastal Zone Watch Committee to meet to discuss algae problem, Lahaina News, May 27, 1993: 5.
— to review proposed developments, Lahaina News, May 27, 1993: 5.
— board actions detailed, Lahaina News, June 10, 1993: 7.
— meeting to discuss area development, Lahaina News, July 15, 1993: 5.
— to address complaint that Kihei is boring for youth, Lahaina News, August 5, 1993: 5.
— to hold meeting, Lahaina News, August 12, 1993: 6.
— vote to oppose new development until conditions met, Lahaina News, August 19, 1993: 7.
— report on last meeting, Lahaina News, August 26, 1993: 7.
— supports planning department's revisions of Kihei-Makena Community Plan, Lahaina News, August 26, 1993: 7.

— formally files a list of concerns over area's parks, Lahaina News, September 9, 1993: 5.
— to hold presentation on proposed water rate increase, Lahaina News, September 9, 1993: 5.
— to hold community meeting, Lahaina News, September 23, 1993: 6.
— lists top priorities, Lahaina News, September 30, 1993: 6.
— seeking help from Tri-Isle Main Street to develop Kihei's sense of place, Lahaina News, November 11, 1993: 6.
— to meet, Lahaina News, November 11, 1993: 6.
— president offers update on current situation, Lahaina News, December 2, 1993: 5,8.
— executive board elected, Lahaina News, December 9, 1993: 5.
— to hold Keiki Kalama Christmas Party, Lahaina News, December 9, 1993: 5.
— honoring retiring president Gene Thompson, Lahaina News, February 3, 1994: 4.
— to hold "Harvest Ball", Lahaina News, October 13, 1994: 19,20.
— hosting lawmakers to discuss legislative session, Lahaina News, May 15, 1997: 3.
— forms Save Our Shoreline action committee, Lahaina News, August 21, 1997: 9.
— to discuss "Ocean Concerns", Lahaina News, July 16, 1998: 16.
— to hold Harvest Ball, Lahaina News, October 8, 1998: 17.
— hosting Harvest Ball, Lahaina News, October 15, 1998: 16.
— to host drug-free Halloween Party, Lahaina News, October 29, 1998: 28.
— to elect new officers, Lahaina News, November 12, 1998: 16.
— to hold "Some Enchanted Evening" dance, Lahaina News, November 4, 1999: 12.
— to hold fundraiser auction and ball, Lahaina News, October 26, 2000: 14.
— to hold public forum to explain charter amendments, Lahaina News, October 10, 2002: 1.

KIHEI COMMUNITY BON DANCE
— to be held, Lahaina News, September 3, 1992: 13.
— to be held, Lahaina News, September 2, 1993: 6.

KIHEI COMMUNITY CENTER
— continues to host country dances, Lahaina News, May 7, 1998: 20.
— continues to host country dances, Lahaina News, July 30, 1998: 16.

KIHEI COMMUNITY PLAN CITIZEN'S ADVISORY COMMITTEE
— opposes restaurants between Kamaole II and III Beach Parks, Lahaina News, September 3, 1992: 13.

KIHEI DESTINATION ASSOCIATION
— to hold annual fundraising auction, Lahaina News, November 28, 1996: 11.
— annual membership luncheon to be held, Lahaina News, February 20, 1997: 11.
— Maui Visitors Bureau Executive Director Marsha Wienert to speak to, Lahaina News, June 15, 2000: 14.

KIHEI ELEMENTARY SCHOOL
— Kindergarten Class Party to be held, Lahaina News, August 27, 1992: 13.
— PTA to hold school workday, Lahaina News, December 3, 1992: 11.
— PTA to meet, Lahaina News, December 10, 1992: 9.
— PTA to hold fundraiser, Lahaina News, December 17, 1992: 13.
— air conditioners installed in portables, Lahaina News, January 14, 1993: 7.
— PTA reports membership drop, Lahaina News, January 14, 1993: 7.
— PTA to meet, Lahaina News, February 11, 1993: 7.
— to offer lunch recess mediation program, Lahaina News, February 18, 1993: 7,8.
— honor roll announced, Lahaina News, March 25, 1993: 9.
— PTA to meet, Lahaina News, April 15, 1993: 4.
— Library to hold book fair, Lahaina News, May 13, 1993: 4.

KIHUNE, HOWARD [POLITICIAN]
— councilmember would vote against proposed airport, Lahaina News, August 14, 1985: 1,20.
— councilmember announces he is running again for Maui County Council, Lahaina News, September 18, 1985: 1,20.
— councilmember seeks options for proposed airport in West Maui, Lahaina News, November 20, 1985: 1,20.
— councilmember to propose Honolua as new site for airport, Lahaina News, December 4, 1985: 1,20.
— councilmember proposes bus ban on Front Street, Lahaina News, January 15, 1986: 1.
— councilmember asks that Mahinahina acreage be single-family residences, Lahaina News, January 22, 1986: 1.
— councilmember urges new officers of Lahaina Community Swimming Pool, Inc. to organize effectively, Lahaina News, February 12, 1986: 1.
— councilmember calls for upgrading infrastructure, Lahaina News, January 21, 1987: 1.
— councilmember seeks money for infrastructure, Lahaina News, February 18, 1987: 8.
— presents wish list for West Maui to Chamber of Commerce, Lahaina News, April 20, 1988: 11.
— wants Olowalu Landfill reopened, Lahaina News, July 13, 1988: 1,20.
— discusses need for fire sprinklers, Lahaina News, August 10, 1988: 1,24.
— hopes roadside peddlers can be removed from Olowalu, Lahaina News, June 14, 1989: 1.
— proposes hotel building ban, Lahaina News, October 25, 1989: 1.
— loses council seat, Lahaina News, November 14, 1990: 7.
— selected as chair of Maui County Council, Lahaina News, January 9, 1991: 3.
— Maui County Council chair concerned that sugar plantations find affordable housing, Lahaina News, March 13, 1991: 1.
— says extension of Kahului Airport unlikely, Lahaina News, May 23, 1991: 1.
— seeks new regional park, Lahaina News, May 30, 1991: 3.
— Lahaina News clarifies that he would vote no to Wyland's appeal, Lahaina News, June 20, 1991: 2.
— criticizes lack of repairs on Front Street, Lahaina News, June 27, 1991: 3,4.
— supports regional park, Lahaina News, July 11, 1991: 1.
— opposes proposed Napili Trade Center, Lahaina News, July 25, 1991: 1.
— hopes regional park can be a gift from Maui Land and Pineapple, Lahaina News, July 25, 1991: 6.
— says that Napili Parks Committee expecting proposal on park, Lahaina News, August 15, 1991: 9.
— seeks to revise parking law, Lahaina News, December 12, 1991: 1.
— Maui County Council chair sees closing landfills as priority, Lahaina News, January 16, 1992: 1,4.

KIHUNE, JEFF
— Lahainaluna High School football coach discusses season, Lahaina News, September 3, 1998: 14.

KIHUNE, ROBERT
— Lahaina-born Admiral selected to head education and training for Navy, Lahaina News, August 20, 1992: 4.

KIHUNE, ROSE KIKINA KAPAKU
— life described, Lahaina News, April 17, 1991: 1,10.

KI'I GALLERY [BUSINESS]
— opens in Whalers Village, Lahaina News, November 15, 2001: 8.

KILLA B'Z
— wins Hyatt Regency Maui employee softball tournament, Lahaina News, June 29, 2000: 15.

KILLETT, JIM
— announce winner of Lahaina Town Action Committee poster contest, Lahaina News, November 15, 1989: 1,19.

KILLETT, JIM AND NANCY
— open art gallery, Lahaina News, May 14, 1986: 6.

KILLETT, NANCY
— recognized by Soroptimists International, Lahaina News, May 10, 2001: 1,22.

KILLGORE, CECIL
— comments on proposed thrillcraft corridor, Lahaina News, February 24, 1988: 1.

KILLION, LARRY
— discusses issues with Olowalu dump, Lahaina News, March 2, 1988: 24.

KILMER, SUSAN [ARTIST]
— featured, Lahaina News, March 14, 1990: 17.
— to exhibit at Lahaina Arts Society, Lahaina News, June 7, 2001: 19.

KILOHANA AWARDS FOR OUTSTANDING VOLUNTEERISM
— announced by Governor Ben Cayetano, Lahaina News, May 7, 1998: 18.
— ceremony to be held, Lahaina News, April 8, 1999: 12.
— Governor holds ceremony for Outstanding Volunteerism, Lahaina News, May 10, 2001: 2.

KIM, ATASHA
— Scholar/Athlete of the Week, Lahaina News, October 10, 1996: 12.

KIM, BARRY [MUSICIAN]
— to host Karaoke Star Search, Lahaina News, August 15, 1990: 15.
— to perform with Maui Symphony, Lahaina News, October 31, 1990: 14,15.
— continues to host karaoke at Lobby Bar of Maui Marriott Resort, Lahaina News, April 24, 1991: 10.
— continues to offer karaoke at Marriott, Lahaina News, August 29, 1991: 9.
— continues to offer karaoke at Marriott, Lahaina News, October 17, 1991: 16.
— hosts karaoke at Lobby Bar, Lahaina News, November 7, 1991: 18.
— continues to offer karaoke at Marriott, Lahaina News, July 2, 1992: 23,24.
— hosting "Hawaii Stars", Lahaina News, October 22, 1998: 9.
— to host "Hawaii Stars", Lahaina News, October 29, 1998: 27.

KIM, EDWARD
— promoted to vice president at Bank of Hawaii, Lahaina News, August 22, 2002: 8.

KIM, MALIA
— to donate hair to cancer patients, Lahaina News, January 16, 2003: 1,20.

KIM, PAM
— coaching for Lahaina Swim Club, Lahaina News, July 18, 1996: 11.

KIM, SIMON YOUNG [MUSICIAN]
— to perform at Maui Arts and Cultural Center, Lahaina News, January 28, 1999: 13.
— to perform at Maui Arts and Cultural Center, Lahaina News, February 4, 1999: 16.

KIM, WAN SOO
— to discuss Oriental medicine, Lahaina News, November 12, 1998: 17.

KIMATA, ALICIA
— to give free massages at Down to Earth, Lahaina News, October 15, 1998: 16.

KIMBALL, ALICE MARY
— play based on to be performed at Iao Theatre, Lahaina News, March 14, 1990: 15.

KIMES, SUSIE
— leading seminars at Maui Christian Women's Conference, Lahaina News, October 4, 2001: 18.
— to lead seminars in the Maui Christian Women's Conference, Lahaina News, October 11, 2001: 2.

KIMO BEAN COFFEE COMPANY [BUSINESS]
— opens, Lahaina News, September 10, 1998: 11.

KIMONOS
— Japanese Cultural Society of Maui to hold fashion show featuring, Lahaina News, June 14, 2001: 21.

KIMO'S [RESTAURANT]
— reviewed, Lahaina Times, July, 1980 volume 4 number 6: 3.
— schedule beach volleyball tournament with Hobie Sports, Lahaina News, October 31, 1991: 5.
— featured, Lahaina News, January 2, 1997: 6,7.
— featured, Lahaina News, March 20, 1997: 8.
— honors Princess Nahienaena School teachers, Lahaina News, June 18, 1998: 13.
— hosts students from Princess Nahienaena Elementary School, Lahaina News, February 4, 1999: 13.
— sponsors Princess Nahienaena Elementary School "Educator of the Month", Lahaina News, May 6, 1999: 11.
— softball team wins, Lahaina News, May 6, 1999: 16.
— recognizes outstanding educators at Princess Nahienaena Elementary School, Lahaina News, May 25, 2000: 6.
— recognizes outstanding educators at Princess Nahienaena Elementary School, Lahaina News, June 29, 2000: 7.
— honors firefighters of the months, Lahaina News, September 21, 2000: 19.
— recognizes educators of the month Brian Santillo, Renette Watson, Irene Tihada, and Robert Temple from Princess Nahienaena Elementary School, Lahaina News, December 21, 2000: 3.
— to hold Jerry Boser Longboarding Contest, Lahaina News, April 19, 2001: 12.
— honors educators of the month from Princess Nahienaena School, Lahaina News, July 19, 2001: 18.
— featured, Lahaina News, November 1, 2001: 14.
— announces Educators of the Month, Lahaina News, February 21, 2002: 3.
— celebrating 25th anniversary, Lahaina News, March 21, 2002: 1,20.
— joins TS Restaurants in recognizing teacher Karyn Murphy, Lahaina News, March 28, 2002: 8.
— honors Lahaina educators, Lahaina News, December 19, 2002: 2.
— to hold Jerry Boser Memorial Longboard Contest, Lahaina News, April 17, 2003: 13.
— announces "Educators of the Month", Lahaina News, May 22, 2003: 2.

KIMO'S-HOBIE LONGBOARD CONTEST
— results announced, Lahaina News, July 11, 1984: 4.

KIMO'S-HOBIE VOLLEYBALL TOURNAMENT
— held, Lahaina News, December 17, 1986: 12.

KIMURA, ALTON
— appointed assistant vice president at Bank of Hawaii, Lahaina News, February 13, 1992: 12.

KIMURA, HIDEO
— demonstrates Aikido, Lahaina Sun, December 6, 1972: 1,15,16,17,18.

KIMURA, LLOYD
— receives American Institute of CPAs/HSCPA Public Service Award, Lahaina News, May 4, 1995: 13.

KIMURA, MANABU
— to head Cancer Crusade, Lahaina News, April 15, 1982: 12.

KIMURA MICHAEL
— appointed to Maui County Planning Commission, Lahaina Sun, February 9, 1972: 3.
— first day as part of Maui County Planning Commission described, Lahaina Sun, February 16, 1972: 5.

KINARD, CHRIS
— named vice president of human resources of Amfac, Inc., Lahaina News, September 6, 1989: 2.

KINA'U MINISTRIES
— to hold Concert of the Stars, Lahaina News, July 13, 1995: 12.
— to hold benefit concert, Lahaina News, August 8, 1996: 15.
— to hold benefit concert, Lahaina News, August 15, 1996: 16.

KINCADE, CARLETON [ARTIST]
— to exhibit at Art School at Kapalua, Lahaina News, December 31, 1998: 13.
— to exhibit at Art School at Kapalua, Lahaina News, January 7, 1999: 16.

KINDER, GEORGE [WRITER]
— establishes investment business, Lahaina News, July 22, 1993: 8.
— to discuss his book "The Seven Stages of Money Maturity", Lahaina News, June 24, 1999: 12.

KINDERGARTEN DAISY GIRL SCOUTS
— plants trees at Princess Nahienaena School, Lahaina News, November 18, 1999: 15.

KINDLER, STEVE [MUSICIAN]
— to perform, Lahaina News, September 25, 1985: 10.

KINDRED, MATT
— teaching scuba classes, Lahaina Sun, January 20, 1971: 7.

KING AND I, THE [PLAY]
— to be performed by Baldwin Theatre Guild, Lahaina News, February 4, 1987: 11.

KING AND QUEEN OF HEARTS CAMPAIGN
— to benefit American Heart Association, Lahaina News, July 31, 2003: 18.

KING, B.B. [MUSICIAN]
— to perform at Maui Arts and Cultural Center, Lahaina News, October 28, 1999: 6.
— to perform at Maui Arts and Cultural Center, Lahaina News, November 4, 1999: 12.
— to perform at Maui Arts and Cultural Center, Lahaina News, March 1, 2001: 16.
— to perform at Maui Arts and Cultural Center, Lahaina News, March 8, 2001: 17.
— to perform at Maui Arts and Cultural Center, Lahaina News, November 7, 2002: 21.

KING, BETSY
— golfer wins Women's Kemper Open, Lahaina News, March 28, 1984: 6.
— golfer's career described, Lahaina News, March 6, 1985: A4.

KING, CAROLE [MUSICIAN]
— to perform at Royal Lahaina Resort Tennis Stadium, Lahaina News, February 28, 1990: 11.

KING IS SWING [SHOW]
— performed at Maui Inter-Continental Wailea Hotel, Lahaina News, June 11, 1986: 14.

KING, JEAN [POLITICIAN]
— lieutenant-governor receives public funds for her compaign, Lahaina News, September 1, 1982: 4.
— endorsed by Lahaina News, Lahaina News, September 1, 1982: 8.

KING KAHEKILI PARK
— residents to hold community beach party, Lahaina News, May 25, 1995: 4.

KING KALAKAUA'S NUTCRACKER BALLET

— to be held, Lahaina News, November 28, 2002: 16.

KING KAMEHAMEHA CELEBRATION FLORAL PARADE

— canceled following resignation of Maui Commissioner Buzz Fernandez, Lahaina News, May 4, 2000: 1,2.

KING KAMEHAMEHA DAY

— events described, Lahaina Sun, June 2, 1971: 3.
— parade planned, Lahaina Sun, May 24, 1972: 10.
— theme will be "Centennial in Flowers", Lahaina Sun, May 31, 1972: 10.
— special service to be held at Holy Innocents' Church in Lahaina, Lahaina Sun, June 6, 1973: 22.
— history and planned events of discussed, Lahaina News, March 1, 1980: 3.
— photographs of parade , Lahaina News, July 1, 1982: 3.
— celebrations planned, Lahaina News, June 6, 1984: 3.
— parade described, Lahaina News, June 13, 1984: 9,10,11.
— parade to be held June 8, Lahaina News, April 10, 1985: 9.
— parade set for June 8, Lahaina News, June 5, 1985: 9.
— parade celebrated in Lahaina, Lahaina News, June 12, 1985: 1,8,9.
— parade to be held on Front Street, Lahaina News, June 11, 1986: 1.
— celebration to take place at Maui Marriott, Lahaina News, June 3, 1987: 3.
— parade schedule described, Lahaina News, June 3, 1987: 4.
— to be celebrated at Maui Marriott, Lahaina News, June 10, 1987: 3.
— celebration scheduled, Lahaina News, April 19, 1989: 14.
— celebration described, Lahaina News, June 7, 1989: 1,12.
— winners from parade announced, Lahaina News, June 21, 1989: 10,11.
— parade to be held, Lahaina News, May 23, 1990: 5.
— events listed, Lahaina News, May 30, 1990: 11.
— parade plans detailed, Lahaina News, June 6, 1990: 11.
— parade held, Lahaina News, June 20, 1990: 1.
— Pa'u riders needed for parade , Lahaina News, January 16, 1991: 1,3.
— parade taking shape, Lahaina News, April 3, 1991: 1.
— preparations for parade, Lahaina News, May 23, 1991: 1,11.
— parade details given, Lahaina News, May 23, 1991: 11,12.
— Pacific Fleet Band to perform at parade , Lahaina News, May 30, 1991: 7.
— parade details given, Lahaina News, June 6, 1991: 11.
— parade described, Lahaina News, June 20, 1991: 3.
— Lori Sablas appointed Maui chair of parade, Lahaina News, August 1, 1991: 12.
— parade scheduled, Lahaina News, April 23, 1992: 5.
— Pacific Fleet Band planning to participate in parade, Lahaina News, May 7, 1992: 1.
— parade being planned, Lahaina News, May 7, 1992: 4.
— events listed, Lahaina News, May 21, 1992: 15.
— parade being planned, Lahaina News, May 21, 1992: 4.
— to be celebrated by Maui Marriott Resort Associates, Lahaina News, June 4, 1992: 15.
— details on parade, Lahaina News, June 11, 1992: 16.
— to be celebrated at Maui Marriott, Lahaina News, June 11, 1992: 19,20.
— Ned and Pua Lindsey to be grand marshals at parade, Lahaina News, June 11, 1992: 3.
— parade to be held, Lahaina News, April 22, 1993: 3.
— parade to be held, Lahaina News, June 10, 1993: 3.
— parade to feature canoe procession, Lahaina News, April 14, 1994: 2.
— parade being organized, Lahaina News, May 5, 1994: 2.
— to be held, Lahaina News, May 26, 1994: 11.
— details on events, Lahaina News, June 2, 1994: 3,12.
— events detailed, Lahaina News, June 9, 1994: 3.

— storefront decoration contest to be held, Lahaina News, June 9, 1994: 6.
— archery tournament to be held, Lahaina News, June 9, 1994: 9.
— event described, photographs of, Lahaina News, June 23, 1994: 3.
— parade to be held, Lahaina News, March 2, 1995: 3.
— to be held, Lahaina News, June 8, 1995: 4.
— celebration to be held on Saturday, Lahaina News, June 15, 1995: 4.
— importance of volunteers for, Lahaina News, June 15, 1995: 5.
— held, Lahaina News, June 22, 1995: 1,3.
— parade to be held, Lahaina News, April 18, 1996: 6.
— to be held, Lahaina News, May 9, 1996: 2.
— LahainaTown Action Committee seeking entries for, Lahaina News, May 23, 1996: 4.
— parade to be held on Saturday, Lahaina News, June 6, 1996: 1.
— Ho'olaule'a to be held at Kamehameha Iki Park, Lahaina News, June 6, 1996: 20.
— Waiola Church to hold service for, Lahaina News, June 6, 1996: 20.
— parade held, Lahaina News, June 13, 1996: 1.
— Westin Maui wins parade contest, Lahaina News, June 27, 1996: 15.
— parade entries sought for, Lahaina News, April 17, 1997: 1.
— parade being organized, Lahaina News, May 29, 1997: 1.
— parade to be held, Lahaina News, June 5, 1997: 1.
— parade to be held, Lahaina News, June 5, 1997: 17.
— parade winners announced, Lahaina News, June 19, 1997: 2.
— to be held, Lahaina News, May 14, 1998: 7.
— parade taking entries, Lahaina News, May 21, 1998: 9.
— parade and ho'olaule'a to be held, Lahaina News, May 28, 1998: 3.
— parade to be held, Lahaina News, June 11, 1998: 1,20.
— to be celebrated at Lahaina Cannery Mall, Lahaina News, June 11, 1998: 16.
— parade winners, Lahaina News, June 18, 1998: 9.
— parade to feature Peace Poem, Lahaina News, April 22, 1999: 5.
— parade theme to be "E Ho'omaika'i I Na Lahui" (Celebrate the Cultures), Lahaina News, April 29, 1999: 9.
— entries sought for parade, Lahaina News, May 20, 1999: 2.
— taking entries for parade, Lahaina News, May 27, 1999: 5.
— parade to be held, Lahaina News, June 10, 1999: 1,20.
— parade held, Lahaina News, June 17, 1999: 2.
— events to be held, Lahaina News, June 8, 2000: 20.
— parade planning committee to meet, Lahaina News, February 8, 2001: 1.
— to be celebrated, Lahaina News, February 15, 2001: 1,18.
— parade being planned, Lahaina News, March 1, 2001: 20.
— events to be held, Lahaina News, March 1, 2001: 22.
— being planned, Lahaina News, May 3, 2001: 1,22.
— crafters sought for, Lahaina News, May 24, 2001: 19.
— youth "Scooter Battalion" and ukulele marching band to participate , Lahaina News, May 31, 2001: 1.
— events to be held for, Lahaina News, June 7, 2001: 18.
— parade to be held, Lahaina News, June 7, 2001: 21.
— top parade entries honored, Lahaina News, June 14, 2001: 1,5.
— parade to be held, Lahaina News, April 4, 2002: 5.
— volunteers sought for parade, Lahaina News, April 11, 2002: 2.
— editorial in support of, Lahaina News, June 6, 2002: 4.
— parade to be held, Lahaina News, June 13, 2002: 1,18.
— Lahaina Cannery Mall to celebrate, Lahaina News, June 13, 2002: 14.
— parade held, Lahaina News, June 20, 2002: 1.
— parade to be planned, Lahaina News, March 20, 2003: 2.
— parade being planned, Lahaina News, April 10, 2003: 2.
— Parade planning is underway, Lahaina News, April 24, 2003: 2.
— volunteers sought for parade, Lahaina News, May 29, 2003: 18.
— help sought for parade, Lahaina News, June 5, 2003: 9.
— parade being organized, Lahaina News, June 12, 2003: 1,24.
— to be celebrated at Lahaina Cannery Mall, Lahaina News, June 12, 2003: 21.
— parade held, Lahaina News, June 19, 2003: 2.

KING KAMEHAMEHA I
— see Kamehameha I [King]

KING KAMEHAMEHA III ELEMENTARY SCHOOL
— proposed relocation, Lahaina Sun, November 25, 1970: 3.
— new classroom building under construction, Lahaina Sun, June 16, 1971: 4.
— new classrooms being constructed, Lahaina Sun, September 22, 1971: 1,14.
— move to new site will not happen soon, Lahaina Sun, December 15, 1971: 17.
— history of recounted, Lahaina Sun, June 6, 1973: 12,13.
— poetry by students, Lahaina News, March 21, 1984: 21,22,23,24.
— planning campus beautification, Lahaina News, March 6, 1985: 3.
— campus beautification project organized, Lahaina News, January 15, 1986: 3.
— collecting items for rummage sale, Lahaina News, April 30, 1986: 3.
— PTA to meet, Lahaina News, September 17, 1986: 3.
— Parent-Teacher Association reformed, Lahaina News, November 5, 1986: 4.
— PTA potluck held, Lahaina News, February 18, 1987: 10.
— planning school bazaar, Lahaina News, February 25, 1987: 3.
— bazaar planned, Lahaina News, May 20, 1987: 3.
— kindergarten registration opens, Lahaina News, August 12, 1987: 3.
— computer lab dedicated, Lahaina News, September 9, 1987: 3.
— Christmas tree fundraiser sells out, Lahaina News, October 14, 1987: 3.
— student government officers named, Lahaina News, October 21, 1987: 12.
— extends Christmas tree pre-sale, Lahaina News, November 18, 1987: 3.
— Christmas trees to arrive soon, Lahaina News, December 9, 1987: 26.
— to hold CPTA meeting, Lahaina News, January 20, 1988: 18.
— to hold International Dinner, Lahaina News, March 16, 1988: 3,14.
— Concerned Parent-Teacher Association to meet, Lahaina News, August 24, 1988: 3.
— annual Spaghetti Feed to be held, Lahaina News, September 28, 1988: 3.
— seeking adult supervisors, Lahaina News, November 30, 1988: 3.
— students ask Mayor Hannibal Tavares to support community pool, Lahaina News, March 29, 1989: 1.
— summer school starts, Lahaina News, June 7, 1989: 3.
— faces loss of loss of Vice Principal, Lahaina News, June 14, 1989: 1.
— Parents Teachers Association plans to lobby for vice principal, Lahaina News, October 11, 1989: 1.
— to hold recycling drive, Lahaina News, December 20, 1989: 3.
— receives federal funding, Lahaina News, December 27, 1989: 11.
— author Jim Trelease to speak at, Lahaina News, January 17, 1990: 5.
— Roz Baker introduces bill to give vice principal, Lahaina News, January 24, 1990: 3.
— bill to fund vice principal receives little legislative support, Lahaina News, January 31, 1990: 3.
— kindergarten pre-registration begins, Lahaina News, February 21, 1990: 4.
— pre-registration for Kindergarten to begin, Lahaina News, March 21, 1990: 3.
— Parent Teacher Association calls on parents to support educational bills, Lahaina News, March 21, 1990: 3.
— to hold spaghetti fundraiser, Lahaina News, April 4, 1990: 3.
— Roz Baker says will get a vice principal, Lahaina News, May 2, 1990: 1.
— to offer art class, Lahaina News, July 4, 1990: 3.
— principal Don Williams retires, Lahaina News, July 11, 1990: 1.
— Governor John Waihee releases money to build portables, Lahaina News, July 11, 1990: 1.

— Yukiyo Iwatake named principal, Lahaina News, September 5, 1990: 3.
— seeking adult supervisors for lunch room, Lahaina News, September 26, 1990: 6.
— accepting registration for kindergarten, Lahaina News, February 20, 1991: 3.
— seeking volunteers, Lahaina News, February 27, 1991: 1.
— Coldwell Banker McCormack Real Estate to hold car wash fundraiser for, Lahaina News, March 20, 1991: 3.
— playground to be revived, Lahaina News, April 3, 1991: 1.
— receives donation from Coldwell Banker McCormack Real Estate for playground, Lahaina News, May 1, 1991: 1.
— to hold fundraiser, funds for playground short, Lahaina News, May 15, 1991: 4.
— volunteers help build playground, Lahaina News, June 27, 1991: 1.
— seeking school aides, Lahaina News, October 10, 1991: 5.
— kitchen needs exhaust fan, Lahaina News, March 19, 1992: 1.
— new exhaust fan to be installed in cafeteria, Lahaina News, July 16, 1992: 1.
— seeking new principal and vice principal, Lahaina News, August 6, 1992: 3.
— Susan Scofield named principal, Lahaina News, August 27, 1992: 3.
— Proud Grandparents Association formed, Lahaina News, December 24, 1992: 2.
— PTA to hold beautification project, Lahaina News, February 25, 1993: 3.
— students to compete in Physical Fitness Festival, Lahaina News, March 4, 1993: 3.
— kitchen exhaust fan to be fixed, Lahaina News, March 25, 1993: 3.
— to celebrate May Day, Lahaina News, May 27, 1993: 2.
— to hold talent show, Lahaina News, June 3, 1993: 3.
— receives grant from Hyatt Regency Maui, Lahaina News, January 27, 1994: 2.
— kindergarten registration begins, Lahaina News, February 17, 1994: 4.
— principal Susan Scofield featured, Lahaina News, April 14, 1994: 1.
— student Jason Pante wins "1994 Buckle Up Hawaiian Style", Lahaina News, June 23, 1994: 5.
— kindergarten registration begins, Lahaina News, July 14, 1994: 6.
— A-Plus program meeting to be held, Lahaina News, August 11, 1994: 4.
— Richard Paul appointed as principal, Lahaina News, August 25, 1994: 1.
— described, Lahaina News, August 25, 1994: 3.
— to hold Christmas Craft Fair, Lahaina News, November 24, 1994: 6.
— holds fun run, Lahaina News, May 18, 1995: 7.
— wood treatment chemical affects classroom at, Lahaina News, January 18, 1996: 1,14.
— PTA to meet, Lahaina News, April 4, 1996: 2.
— seeking volunteers, Lahaina News, August 1, 1996: 1.
— to hold rummage sale, Lahaina News, October 10, 1996: 3.
— to hold Karnival, Lahaina News, October 24, 1996: 4.
— PTA to hold Karnival, Lahaina News, October 31, 1996: 18.
— air conditioning to be installed, Lahaina News, November 14, 1996: 3.
— to celebrate May Day, Lahaina News, May 1, 1997: 17.
— principal to head to Japan, Lahaina News, October 2, 1997: 1.
— to hold carnival, Lahaina News, November 6, 1997: 1,16.
— staging "Wishes Come True" , Lahaina News, December 11, 1997: 1.
— principal's list, Lahaina News, December 11, 1997: 17.
— to perform "Colors—we're better together", Lahaina News, April 16, 1998: 12.
— recognizes students, Lahaina News, May 7, 1998: 9.
— PTA supporting reading program, Lahaina News, June 11, 1998: 3.
— Principal's List published, Lahaina News, July 23, 1998: 9.

— new school year to begin soon, Lahaina News, July 30, 1998: 2.
— parents discuss ways of clearing out Malu'ulu O Lele Park, Lahaina News, October 15, 1998: 1,8.
— plan being developed to secure area at Malu'ulu O Lele Park, Lahaina News, October 22, 1998: 1,2.
— to hold Karnival, Lahaina News, October 22, 1998: 11.
— will have secure park area, Lahaina News, November 12, 1998: 1,20.
— Principal's List announced, Lahaina News, March 18, 1999: 8.
— students to perform at King Kamehameha Day Parade, Lahaina News, April 29, 1999: 9.
— awarded Hawaii State PTSA's Reading/Literacy Award for Great Reading Race Program, Lahaina News, May 27, 1999: 2.
— Governor Ben Cayetano releases money for electrical system at, Lahaina News, August 26, 1999: 14.
— playground toys closed pending safety review, Lahaina News, September 2, 1999: 1,20.
— to benefit from Karnival, Lahaina News, October 14, 1999: 3.
— playground must be rebuilt due to safety concerns, Lahaina News, November 4, 1999: 1,16.
— playgrounds almost ready, Lahaina News, March 2, 2000: 1,2.
— work continues on playground, Lahaina News, May 4, 2000: 1.
— preparing for May Day, Lahaina News, May 11, 2000: 19.
— May Day to be celebrated, Lahaina News, May 18, 2000: 20.
— students raise money to improvements to the playground, Lahaina News, June 1, 2000: 7.
— burials found at, Lahaina News, October 19, 2000: 2.
— Principal's List published, Lahaina News, December 7, 2000: 16.
— counselor Edson Wagatsuma organizes cross-country team at, Lahaina News, December 28, 2000: 1,15.
— principal Rick Paul featured, Lahaina News, January 18, 2001: 3.
— students earn high grades, Lahaina News, March 1, 2001: 17.
— raises money for American Heart Association, Lahaina News, March 15, 2001: 15.
— students raise money, Lahaina News, May 31, 2001: 5.
— honor roll announced, Lahaina News, June 28, 2001: 16.
— Lindsay Ball is new principal at, Lahaina News, October 4, 2001: 1,20.
— places sixth in "most lei per student" category in Memorial Day Lei contest, Lahaina News, October 11, 2001: 2.
— honor roll, Lahaina News, November 22, 2001: 16.
— to hold Christmas Art Enrichment camp, Lahaina News, December 13, 2001: 14.
— jumpers visit for "Jump Rope for Heart Day", Lahaina News, February 14, 2002: 3.
— honor roll announced, Lahaina News, March 14, 2002: 9.
— to hold May Day, Lahaina News, April 25, 2002: 2.
— to hold May Day, Lahaina News, May 2, 2002: 2.
— to hold tsunami drill, Lahaina News, May 9, 2002: 16.
— planning parent night, Lahaina News, May 23, 2002: 2.
— to hold student art contest, Lahaina News, June 6, 2002: 1,18.
— TS Restaurants bring Hawaiian entertainers to year-end assembly, Lahaina News, June 13, 2002: 1,18.
— volunteers to help repair, Lahaina News, August 1, 2002: 1.
— renovated by employees from Hyatt Regency Maui , Lahaina News, August 8, 2002: 3.
— holds assembly to honor police and firefighters, Lahaina News, September 19, 2002: 13.
— improvements planned, Lahaina News, October 3, 2002: 1,20.
— honor roll released, Lahaina News, November 21, 2002: 15.
— students to be honored at PTA meeting, Lahaina News, December 5, 2002: 14.
— Mana'o Company performs at, Lahaina News, December 26, 2002: 1.
— honor roll released, Lahaina News, February 6, 2003: 2.
— PTA to meet, Lahaina News, February 13, 2003: 3.
— PTA to meet, Lahaina News, February 20, 2003: 2.

— planning tsunami drill, Lahaina News, February 27, 2003: 9.
— honor roll announced, Lahaina News, April 24, 2003: 22.
— student Gina Carmella wins Keiki Menu Design Contest, Lahaina News, June 12, 2003: 2.
— honor roll announced, Lahaina News, June 19, 2003: 18.
— fifth graders to lead Relay for Life, Lahaina News, July 17, 2003: 3.
— classes begin, Lahaina News, August 28, 2003: 1.
— parents urged to avoid using staff parking stalls, Lahaina News, September 11, 2003: 1,18.
— to hold tsunami drill, Lahaina News, October 9, 2003: 5.

KING KEKAULIKE HIGH SCHOOL
— to hold fundraiser for boys cross country team, Lahaina News, August 26, 1999: 7.
— school band to perform at Maui Arts and Cultural Center, Lahaina News, April 13, 2000: 13.
— band to perform at Maui Arts and Cultural Center, Lahaina News, May 17, 2001: 20.
— basketball team to hold rummage sale, Lahaina News, January 17, 2002: 13.
— band to perform Spring Concert, Lahaina News, April 4, 2002: 17.
— Interact Club presents grant to Maui Youth and Family Services, Lahaina News, January 2, 2003: 18.
— band to play free Spring concert, Lahaina News, April 3, 2003: 17.

KING, KELLY
— Board of Education member expresses views on education, Lahaina News, November 17, 1994: 1,3.

KING, MARTIN LUTHER JR.
— editorial praising, Lahaina News, January 10, 1990: 8.
— see also Martin Luther King Jr. Day

KING, MIKE
— diver mentioned , Lahaina Sun, December 23, 1970: 2.

KING OF MASKS, THE [FILM]
— to be shown at Maui Arts and Cultural Center, Lahaina News, July 29, 1999: 12.

KING, SERGE KAHILI
— to present "Ancient Solutions to Modern Problems", Lahaina News, August 30, 2001: 17.

KING, STEVE [MUSICIAN]
— to perform at Bounty Music, Lahaina News, July 30, 1998: 17.

KINGMA, DAPHINE ROSE
— to offer free lecture at Maui Community College, Lahaina News, January 9, 1991: 3.
— to speak on relationships, Lahaina News, January 16, 1991: 4.

KINGS CATHEDRAL
— to host Freedom Fest, Lahaina News, June 28, 2001: 21.

KING'S CHAPEL LAHAINA, THE
— First Assembly of God opens new church, Lahaina News, April 19, 2001: 3.

KING'S CHINESE SEAFOOD RESTAURANT [RESTAURANT]
— opens at Lahaina Cannery Mall, Lahaina News, September 19, 2002: 8.

KINGSTON, MAXINE HONG [WRITER]
— new documentary on life of, Lahaina News, February 27, 1991: 14.

KINGSTON TRIO, THE [MUSICAL GROUP]
— to play at the Maui Lu Longhouse, Lahaina News, January 16, 1985: 17.
— to perform benefit concert at the Maui Inter-Continental Wailea, Lahaina News, October 31, 1990: 14.
— to hold fundraiser for Seabury Hall Financial Aid Scholarship Program, Lahaina News, May 15, 1991: 11.
— to perform at Monarch Ballroom at Hyatt Regency Maui, Lahaina News, May 23, 1991: 13.

— to perform, Lahaina News, May 30, 1991: 7.
— to perform at Maui Arts and Cultural Center, Lahaina News, November 17, 1994: 18.
— to perform at Maui Arts and Cultural Center, Lahaina News, January 13, 2000: 13.
— to perform at Maui Arts and Cultural Center, Lahaina News, January 20, 2000: 12.

KINGWELL, JIM [ARTIST]
— to exhibit at Lahaina Grill, Lahaina News, August 27, 1992: 17.
— designs Reyn Spooner shirt for Cheeseburger in Paradise, Lahaina News, August 22, 1996: 17.
— to exhibit at Island Art Collection, Lahaina News, September 19, 1996: 16.
— featured, Lahaina News, September 26, 1996: 17.
— makes appearance at Cheeseburger in Paradise, Lahaina News, October 31, 1996: 19.
— paintings of Kalaupapa, Lahaina News, February 6, 1997: 18.
— work to be featured, Lahaina News, April 10, 1997: 14.
— to lead Maui Watercolorists Association workshop, Lahaina News, September 25, 2003: 16.

KINIMAKA, JON
— attempting to expand Drug Court, Lahaina News, January 9, 2003: 1,2.

KINIMAKA, KAIMANA
— surfer featured on "Hawaiian Moving Company", Lahaina News, October 7, 1999: 1.

KINISON, SAM [COMEDIAN]
— to perform at Casanova's, Lahaina News, November 28, 1991: 18.

KINKADE, AMELIA
— to hold workshop on psychic powers at Haiku Community Center, Lahaina News, June 6, 2002: 16.

KINKADE, CARLETON [ARTIST]
— to display artwork at Art School at Kapalua, Lahaina News, March 26, 1998: 2.
— to exhibit at Village Gallery, Lahaina News, January 4, 2001: 16.
— to exhibit at The Village Galleries, Lahaina News, January 3, 2002: 17.

KINKADE, THOMAS [ARTIST]
— opens Thomas Kinkade Gallery, Lahaina News, February 24, 1994: 9.
— to present "Painter of Light" at Thomas Kinkade Gallery, Lahaina News, February 23, 1995: 11.

KINKELLA, VICKI
— appointed as leisure sales manager at Embassy Suites Resort Maui, Lahaina News, November 23, 1995: 10.

KINOSHITA, MATT
— wins Lahaina Surf Classic, Lahaina News, May 9, 1990: 7.

KINSEY, BIG DADDY [MUSICIAN]
— to perform at Maui Marriott ballroom, Lahaina News, November 7, 1996: 16.

KIPA VILLAGE
— condominium featured, Lahaina News, December 2, 1999: 12.

KIRIATY, AVI [ARTIST]
— to paint Marquesan mural, Lahaina News, July 26, 2001: 3.

KIRIN CUP
— teams to compete at Kapalua Bay golf course, Lahaina News, December 14, 1988: 18.

KIRK BANKS TOURNAMENT
— to be held at Lahaina Cannery Mall, Lahaina News, March 13, 2003: 12.

KIRK, COLETTE
— featured, Lahaina News, November 9, 1988: 2.
— expanding Lahaina Health Center's "Substance Abuse and Outpatient Alcoholism Program", Lahaina News, September 13, 1989: 4.

KIRK, IRENE
— life described, Lahaina News, April 26, 1989: 2.

KIRK, WILLIAM
— Major to speak to American Association of Retired Persons , Lahaina News, October 1, 1998: 16.

KIRKEBY, MARK
— named general manager of 505 Front Street, Lahaina News, June 20, 1991: 7.

KIRKWOOD, CHERYL
— memorial service to be held for, Lahaina News, February 20, 1997: 3.

KIRSTEN, DOROTHY [OPERA SINGER]
— performed Puccini's "Tosca" at Baldwin High School auditorium, Lahaina Sun, February 3, 1971: 8.

KISHI BUILDING
— gutted by fire, Lahaina News, November 19, 1986: 3,16.

KISHI MARKET
— closing, Lahaina Sun, April 19, 1972: 11.

KISHI, RICHARD KAZUO
— discusses closure of Animal Farm, Lahaina Sun, January 27, 1971: 5.
— criticized for signage in front of his store on Front Street, Lahaina Sun, August 4, 1971: 2.
— sentenced for crime, Lahaina News, February 1, 1983: 2.

KISHI, SHINKO
— jodo leader from Hawaii visits Maui, Lahaina Sun, October 25, 1972: 11.

KISHIDA, GAIL
— wedding to Patrick Tatsumi announced, Lahaina Sun, January 20, 1971: 3.

KISMET [PLAY]
— auditions open for Maui Community Theatre, Lahaina News, September 7, 1988: 3.

KISS ME KATE [MUSICAL]
— auditions to be held, Lahaina News, October 24, 1991: 4.
— to be performed, Lahaina News, February 6, 1992: 22.
— to open February 21, Lahaina News, February 13, 1992: 25.
— grand opening to be held, Lahaina News, February 20, 1992: 16.

KISS OF HAWAII
— to hold beach party, Lahaina News, April 23, 1998: 16.

KISTLER, NANCY
— honored for volunteer efforts, Lahaina News, May 28, 1992: 7.

KITAGAWA, LEIGHTON
— named sales manager at Maui Prince Hotel, Lahaina News, May 13, 1987: 12.

KITAGAWA, MEL
— promoted to asset manager for Maui for the Estate of James Campbell, Lahaina News, December 21, 1988: 13.

KITAGAWA MOTORS, INC. [BUSINESS]
— names Ronald Furukawa as assistant general manager, Lahaina News, March 25, 1993: 10,11.

KITCHEN AND BATH TOUR
— National Kitchen and Bath Association to host annual exhibit, Lahaina News, August 22, 1996: 9.

KITCHENS BY DESIGN [BUSINESS]
— carries products by Poggenpohl, Lahaina News, December 30, 1999: 13.
— chefs David Paul Johnson and Consuelo Bronick to teach Brazilian cuisine, Lahaina News, July 19, 2001: 16.

KITE FANTASY [BUSINESS]
— to host Beanie Baby Swap and Trade, Lahaina News, August 27, 1998: 16,17.
— to offer Pokeman Trading Session, Lahaina News, May 13, 1999: 17.

— to hold Pokeman training session, Lahaina News, June 3, 1999: 17.

— continues to hold Pokeman trading days, Lahaina News, September 2, 1999: 14.

— continues to hold Pokeman card trading sessions, Lahaina News, January 20, 2000: 13.

KITE FESTIVAL
— to be held at Napili Park, Lahaina News, March 28, 2002: 20.

KITHARA [MUSICAL GROUP]
— to perform at Seabury Hall, Lahaina News, September 24, 1992: 18.

KITMASTER SPAZ [MUSICIAN]
— to perform at Jaycees Summer Jam, Lahaina News, June 4, 1998: 16.

KITSUKE
— kimono dressing class to be held, Lahaina News, July 3, 2003: 17.

KITTY AWARDS
— top performers in Maui Community Theatre honored, Lahaina News, January 27, 1988: 1,10.

— Maui Community Theatre receives, Lahaina News, February 3, 1988: 12.

— to be presented by Maui Community Theatre, Lahaina News, January 2, 1991: 7,8.

— to be held, Lahaina News, January 16, 1991: 11,14.

— to be presented by Maui Community Theatre, Lahaina News, January 16, 1992: 18.

KITTY VINCENT SCHOLARSHIP IN THEATRE ARTS
— now open, Lahaina News, April 26, 1989: 9.

KITV 4 [BUSINESS]
— joining with AT&T Wireless collecting unused wireless phones to reduce domestic violence, Lahaina News, July 5, 2001: 9.

KIWANIS CLUB
— installing fence around Child Care Center at the old Honokowai School, Lahaina Sun, February 24, 1971: 1.

— Senator Spark Matsunaga speaks to Kahului chapter, Lahaina Sun, March 10, 1971: 3.

— awarded plaque for fundraising accomplishments, Lahaina Sun, March 24, 1971: 2.

— new officers announced, Lahaina Sun, June 23, 1971: 10.

— Ernest Okimoto installed as president, Lahaina Sun, September 29, 1971: 12.

— Jim Shefte new president of Lahaina club, Lahaina Sun, October 25, 1972: 4.

— to hold 7th annual Wine & Cheese Benefit, Lahaina News, April 18, 1984: 4.

— Shower of Stars set for August 4, Lahaina News, August 1, 1984: 13.

— grant to West Maui Youth Center, Lahaina News, November 14, 1984: 3.

— hold Wine and Cheese Tasting Benefit, Lahaina News, May 1, 1985: 3.

— play Peanut Day fundraiser, Lahaina News, June 5, 1985: 8.

— Wine and Cheese Tasting fundraiser to be held, Lahaina News, June 11, 1986: 3.

— new officers installed, Lahaina News, October 15, 1986: 3.

— to hold annual Wine and Cheese Tasting fundraiser, Lahaina News, May 20, 1987: 3.

— officers installed, Lahaina News, October 7, 1987: 3,16.

— organizing fundraiser, Lahaina News, July 26, 1989: 3.

— changes meeting time, Lahaina News, June 16, 1994: 5.

— hosting Maui Kiwanis Golf Classic at Sandalwood Golf Course, Lahaina News, August 17, 2000: 6.

— to provide keiki safety tips, Lahaina News, March 27, 2003: 16.

— Kahului chapter to hold "Sing for the Center" featuring Japanese karaoke to benefit Maui Nisei Veterans Memorial Center, Lahaina News, July 31, 2003: 18.

— to form Central Maui Club, Lahaina News, September 4, 2003: 2.

KIWANIS CLUB, KIHEI-WAILEA
— to meet at Wailuku Community Center, Lahaina News, November 14, 1991: 3.

— to hold Christmas party, Lahaina News, December 5, 1991: 4,5.

— to hold dance, Lahaina News, March 19, 1992: 4.

— to meet, Lahaina News, June 4, 1992: 7.

— to meet, Lahaina News, June 18, 1992: 15.

— to meet, Lahaina News, July 9, 1992: 7.

— to meet, Lahaina News, November 26, 1992: 18.

— to hold Christmas party, Lahaina News, December 3, 1992: 11.

— to hold "Swing into Spring" fundraiser, Lahaina News, March 25, 1993: 8.

— to host Bob Johnson, director of the county Economic Development Division, Lahaina News, May 13, 1993: 4.

— to meet, Lahaina News, May 20, 1993: 5.

— to host talk by Adele Rigg, Lahaina News, June 24, 1993: 8.

— to meet, Lahaina News, August 5, 1993: 5.

— to hold annual Installation Dinner, Lahaina News, September 30, 1993: 6.

— to host speaker Lane Fujii, Lahaina News, December 16, 1993: 6.

— to present "Swing in the Spring", Lahaina News, April 25, 1996: 17.

— to hold "Swing in the Spring" fundraiser, Lahaina News, February 27, 1997: 10.

KIWANIS CLUB, LAHAINA
— organizing Key Club at Lahainaluna High School, Lahaina Sun, January 13, 1971: 7.

— Shower of Stars show announced, Lahaina News, August 15, 1983: 3,4.

— give grant to West Maui Youth Center, Lahaina News, January 18, 1984: 5.

— to host wine-tasting fundraiser, Lahaina News, June 22, 1988: 10.

— to host Shower of Stars Talent Competition, Lahaina News, August 22, 1990: 11.

— constructs bus stop at Napilihau, Lahaina News, October 31, 1990: 7.

— to support literacy, Lahaina News, December 19, 1990: 4,5.

— "E Kokua I Na Kamali'i Christmas Festival" continues, Lahaina News, December 26, 1990: 5.

— to hold fundraiser for literacy program, Lahaina News, January 2, 1991: 4.

— new officers installed, Lahaina News, October 3, 1991: 4.

— to sponsor "Peanut Day", Lahaina News, December 19, 1991: 4.

— inducts new members, Lahaina News, May 28, 1992: 3.

— to hold Shower of Stars talent show, Lahaina News, August 13, 1992: 4.

— donates to American Red Cross, Lahaina News, September 24, 1992: 3.

— donates money to Imua Rehabilitation for equipment, Lahaina News, December 24, 1992: 24.

— to meet, Lahaina News, January 28, 1993: 4.

— to meet at Maui Marriott Hotel , Lahaina News, March 4, 1993: 4.

— donates to West Maui Little League, Lahaina News, June 10, 1993: 9.

— new officers elected, Lahaina News, June 17, 1993: 2.

— to hold installation dinner, Lahaina News, September 16, 1993: 4.

— selling Entertainment Book as fundraiser, Lahaina News, September 29, 1994: 5.

— electing new officers, Lahaina News, May 11, 1995: 2.

— to meet, Lahaina News, February 15, 1996: 12.

KIXX [MUSICAL GROUP]
— to perform at Maui Sun Hotel, Lahaina News, July 30, 1992: 15.

KIYABU, DURWIN
— promoted at Nishikawa Architects, Inc., Lahaina News, August 10, 2000: 13.

KIYONAGA, ROBIN
— former Lahainaluna High School track star studying at the University of Hawaii, Lahaina News, January 12, 1995: 7.

KLAHANI RESORTS CORPORATION
— opens travel agency, Lahaina News, March 7, 1996: 11.

KLAHANI TRAVEL [BUSINESS]
— to open, Lahaina News, December 17, 1998: 17.

KLAPER, MICHAEL
— doctor to host "Sounds of Healing" radio show on KAOI, Lahaina News, January 21, 1999: 11.

KLEEFISCH, WILLIAM BOYD
— new CEO of Maui Memorial Medical Center to speak at Maui League of Republican Women, Lahaina News, April 8, 1999: 12.
— CEO of Maui Memorial Medical Center to speak to American Association of Retired Persons, Lahaina News, September 30, 1999: 13.

KLEVEN, LORA
— report on travel/surf adventure, Lahaina News, August 17, 1995: 7.

KLHI-FM [BUSINESS]
— L.D. Reynolds joins radio station , Lahaina News, April 16, 1992: 15.
— radio station owners to contest ruling stripping control of the station from them, Lahaina News, January 6, 1994: 1,3.
— Dale and Ginny Parsons lose control of radio station following bankruptcy, Lahaina News, March 17, 1994: 1.
— radio station purchased by Lahaina Broadcasting, Co., Lahaina News, May 12, 1994: 1.
— Federal Communications Commission ruling allows sale of radio station , Lahaina News, September 8, 1994: 1.
— radio station moves to Front Street to share space with KPOA, Lahaina News, February 23, 1995: 6.
— radio station sale to Lahaina Broadcasting Co. completed, Lahaina News, March 23, 1995: 10.
— Glen Gerrard appointed program director at radio station, Lahaina News, August 24, 1995: 10.
— radio station switches to "alternative" music format, Lahaina News, July 11, 1996: 3.

KLIEGER, PAUL
— archaeologist discusses Moku'ula, Lahaina News, November 9, 1995: 3.
— to discuss research on Moku'ula , Lahaina News, May 27, 1999: 12.

KLIEN, SCOTT
— Lahaina Intermediate School student wins Geography Bee, Lahaina News, March 4, 1999: 3.

KLING, KELLY
— new sales manager at Westin Maui, Lahaina News, August 28, 2003: 8.

KLOBE, TOM [ARTIST]
— presents SFCA Retrospective for Art Maui, Lahaina News, January 13, 1988: 16.

KLOCK, DAVID
— general manager of Maui Eldorado, developer of proposed Royal Court Plaza shopping center, wants issues resolve, Lahaina News, December 26, 1991: 1,2.

KLOMPUS, LEONARD (LENNY)
— appointed sports development director at Maui Visitors Bureau, Lahaina News, June 21, 2001: 9.

KLUGH, EARL [MUSICIAN]
— to perform at Maui Arts and Cultural Center, Lahaina News, November 14, 1996: 14.

KM HATANO SCHOLARSHIP PROGRAM
— announced, Lahaina News, June 1, 1988: 19.
— to offer scholarships, Lahaina News, December 5, 1990: 5,7.
— offering scholarships, Lahaina News, December 19, 1991: 6.

— offered by Hyatt Regency, Lahaina News, January 13, 1994: 2.
— available, Lahaina News, February 22, 1996: 10.

KM HAWAII, INC. [BUSINESS]
— donates to Maui Community Arts and Cultural Center, Lahaina News, April 4, 1990: 7.

KMART [BUSINESS]
— to open on Maui, Lahaina News, June 4, 1992: 9.
— opens, Lahaina News, July 15, 1993: 6.

KMENTT, WALDEMAR (WALLY)
— engraver featured, Lahaina News, April 4, 1984: 13.
— caretake of Brig Carthaginian featured, Lahaina News, May 25, 1988: 3.

KMVI [BUSINESS]
— radio station sponsoring Bash on the Beach '89, Lahaina News, April 26, 1989: 3.
— radio station sponsoring fun run, Lahaina News, January 9, 1992: 7.
— radio station names new staff, Lahaina News, February 16, 1995: 13.

KNAPP, ANDREAS
— Westin Maui check featured on "Chef's Table" television show, Lahaina News, February 28, 1990: 24.
— Westin Maui Hotel chef creates new menu, Lahaina News, August 1, 1990: 9.

KNASTER, MIRKA [WRITER]
— to speak to Maui Authors Guild, Lahaina News, November 18, 1987: 3.

KNIGHT, DAMON [WRITER]
— to be hosted by Maui Authors Guild, Lahaina News, September 9, 1987: 3.
— Maui Authors Guild hosts workshop by, Lahaina News, October 14, 1987: 17.

KNIGHT, SONNY [MUSICIAN]
— featured, Lahaina News, August 15, 1990: 13.

KNIGHT, STACY
— wins Lahaina Coolers Las Vegas Challenge, Lahaina News, July 4, 2002: 18.

KNOW THYSELF AS SOUL FOUNDATION, THE
— to teach meditation, Lahaina News, December 4, 1997: 25.
— to offer meditation instruction, Lahaina News, October 4, 2001: 17.
— to offer meditation class, Lahaina News, February 6, 2003: 16.
— to hold meditation workshops, Lahaina News, September 25, 2003: 16.

KNOX, STEPHEN
— selected as chair of Maui Chamber of Commerce, Lahaina News, July 16, 1992: 16.

KNUPPE, H. JAMES
— organizes global air race, Lahaina News, June 18, 1992: 12.
— elected to National Housing Hall of Fame, Lahaina News, March 31, 1994: 12.
— receives Award of the Year for Design, Construction and Landscaping, Lahaina News, March 27, 1997: 10.

KNUTSON-ADOLPHO, CHERYL
— police searching for, Lahaina News, February 5, 1998: 3.

KOA [MUSICAL GROUP]
— to perform at Royal Lahaina Resort, Lahaina News, September 13, 1989: 9.
— to perform at Royal Ocean Terrace Lounge at the Royal Lahaina Resort, Lahaina News, August 29, 1990: 14.
— continues to perform at Royal Ocean Terrace at Royal Lahaina Resort, Lahaina News, March 13, 1991: 9.

KOALA BLUE [BUSINESS]
— opens; owned by Olivia Newton-John, Lahaina News, December 7, 1988: 8.

KOBAYASHI, DEWEY
— receives posthumous "Marketing Person of the Year" award from Maui Chapter of the American Marketing Association, Lahaina News, May 16, 1984: 17.

KOBAYASHI, GEORGE
— named wine and beverage director of Roy's, Lahaina News, January 30, 1992: 10.
— joins Hula Grill as wine and service manager, Lahaina News, August 18, 1994: 9.

KOBAYASHI, HARRY
— new member of Maui County Council, Lahaina Sun, December 30, 1970: 8.
— voted against improvement projects, Lahaina Sun, January 20, 1971: 1.
— reacts to number of resolutions at Maui County Council meeting, Lahaina Sun, January 20, 1971: 8.

KOBAYASHI, KALVIN
— discusses proposed heliport, Lahaina News, March 2, 1988: 24.

KOBAYASHI, NOBURU
— architect working on moderate income housing development, Lahaina Sun, December 2, 1970: 3.

KOBE JAPANESE STEAKHOUSE [RESTAURANT]
— opens with Buddhist blessing, Lahaina News, January 22, 1986: 3.
— featured, Lahaina News, September 20, 1989: 11.
— featured, Lahaina News, December 6, 1989: 14.
— featured, Lahaina News, February 14, 1990: 14.
— offering specials, Lahaina News, March 7, 1990: 13.
— to offer late night special, Lahaina News, March 14, 1990: 15.
— featured, Lahaina News, May 2, 1990: 14.
— featured, Lahaina News, August 8, 1991: 17.
— featured, Lahaina News, October 3, 1996: 6,7.
— changes to personnel, Lahaina News, January 23, 1997: 14.
— hosts Aloha Spirit Awards, Lahaina News, July 16, 1998: 13.

KOCH, LEIL
— awarded Certified Commercial Investment Member (CCIM) designation, Lahaina News, December 17, 1992: 8.
— awarded Certified International Property Specialist designation, Lahaina News, December 22, 1994: 13.

KOCHANSKI, WLADIMAR JAN [MUSICIAN]
— pianist to perform at Baldwin High School auditorium, Lahaina News, April 18, 1984: 5.

KOCHI CITY
— dancers from Japan perform at John Manjiro "Izanai Yosakoi Festival of the Future", Lahaina News, March 22, 2001: 1.

KODAMA, D.K.
— chef at Sansei Seafood Restaurant and Sushi Bar to give cooking demonstrations at Liberty House, Lahaina News, September 10, 1998: 21.
— chef taking over Fleming's on the Green, Lahaina News, February 27, 2003: 8.
— opens Vino restaurant, Lahaina News, October 2, 2003: 9.

KODAMA, SCOTT
— runner-up for Hawaii's Golden Diamond Award, Lahaina News, November 30, 1988: 3.

KODO [MUSICAL GROUP]
— shows added by Maui Philharmonic Society, Lahaina News, December 31, 1986: 3.
— drummers from Sado Island to perform, Lahaina News, January 18, 1989: 9.

KOELE LODGE
— upcountry lodge owned by Rockresorts scheduled to open next year, Lahaina News, November 29, 1989: 4.
— opens, Lahaina News, January 17, 1990: 24.

KOENIG, VANCE [MUSICIAN]
— to perform at Gerard's, Lahaina News, January 9, 1991: 7.
— continues to perform at Gerard's, Lahaina News, April 3, 1991: 7.
— continues to perform at Gerard's, Lahaina News, April 24, 1991: 10.
— to perform at Gerard's, Lahaina News, July 18, 1991: 10.

KOEPKE, CAROL
— appointed to general manager of Lahaina Shores Beach Resort, Lahaina News, January 31, 2002: 8.

KOEPPEL, GARY
— discusses Maui Marine Art Expo, Lahaina News, January 27, 1994: 8.

KOHALA [MUSICAL GROUP]
— to perform at Maui Arts and Cultural Center, Lahaina News, July 10, 2003: 16.

KOHLER, AINA
— Lahaina girl pitches no-hitter, Lahaina News, June 4, 1992: 8.
— Scholar/Athlete of the Week, Lahaina News, December 4, 1997: 13.

KOHO GRILL AND BAR [RESTAURANT]
— sponsoring Hana Relay, Lahaina News, September 5, 1990: 7.
— to open in Napili Plaza Shopping Center, Lahaina News, March 27, 1991: 9.
— to open, Lahaina News, November 7, 1991: 8.
— names Doris Quijas as general manager, Lahaina News, December 5, 1991: 13.
— George Cusick named managing partner, Lahaina News, December 12, 1991: 16.
— new location, Lahaina News, January 23, 1992: 22.
— to exhibit photographs, Lahaina News, February 6, 1992: 10,11.
— to hold Keiki Day, Lahaina News, October 26, 1995: 11.

KOHOMUA [MUSICAL GROUP]
— to perform at Lahaina Cannery Mall, Lahaina News, September 19, 2002: 23.

KOHO'OHANOHANO, POHAKU
— teaching course on lauhala basket weaving, Lahaina News, March 20, 1997: 17.

KOHRS, CONRAD
— swimming coach featured, Lahaina News, May 18, 1995: 7.

KO'IE'IE FISHPOND
— lecture to be held on, Lahaina News, October 22, 1998: 20.

KOIKE, TOSHIMICHI
— donates to Maui Community Arts and Cultural Center, Lahaina News, June 7, 1989: 8.

KOINONIA PENTECOSTAL CHURCH
— to show Christian movies with Lahaina Christian Fellowship, Lahaina News, August 23, 2001: 17.
— to show Christian movies, Lahaina News, November 22, 2001: 21.

KOJIM, HARI
— films segment of "Let's Go Fishing" at Sheraton Maui, Lahaina News, July 24, 1997: 15.

KOKO [GORILLA]
— refuge to the created from land donated by Maui Land and Pineapple Co., Lahaina News, October 5, 2000: 3.

KOKUA FUND
— fundraiser to support Mayor Arakawa Community Kokua Fund, Lahaina News, January 23, 2003: 2.

KOKUA KUPUNA BENEFIT CONCERT
— to be held, Lahaina News, February 11, 1999: 16.

KOKUA NA KEIKI
— health education program to be held, Lahaina News, June 1, 1988: 19.
— Family Asthma Program to be held, Lahaina News, July 31, 1997: 16.
— Family Asthma Program to be held at Iao School and Wailuku Pool, Lahaina News, July 2, 1998: 8.

KOKUA PROGRAM
— to offer breast and cervical cancer screening, Lahaina News, December 13, 2001: 2.

KOKUBUN, RICHARD
— accused of murder of Tom and Wendy Day, Lahaina Sun, January 19, 1972: 5.

KOKUSAI MOTORS (KM) HAWAII, INC. [BUSINESS]
— purchases Hyatt Regency Maui, Lahaina News, July 8, 1987: 3.
— celebrates acquisition of Hyatt Regency, Lahaina News, July 15, 1987: 1.
— purchases 22 acres of land in Ka'anapali formerly planned for Sea Village, Lahaina News, July 18, 1990: 7.

KOLBERT/HANSSEN/MITCHELL ARCHITECTS [BUSINESS]
— Oahu firm to renovate Lahaina Cannery Mall, Lahaina News, October 29, 1998: 13.

KOLINSKY, SUE [COMEDIAN]
— to perform at Comedy Club, Lahaina News, August 26, 1993: 16.

KOLODGY, MICK [ARTIST]
— "Masked" show to be held at Art School of Kapalua, Lahaina News, February 10, 2000: 17.

KOLOHE BOYS, THE [MUSICAL GROUP]
— to perform at Borders Books, Lahaina News, January 20, 2000: 12.

KOMET [BOAT]
— history of Carthaginian II recounted, Lahaina News, February 22, 1996: 12.

KOMIYAMA, SHUICHI
— new director of Arts Education for Children Group, Lahaina News, January 10, 2002: 14.
— to hold Maui World Music Workshops, Lahaina News, June 12, 2003: 5.

KOMOHANA HALE
— bids to build too high, Lahaina News, March 7, 1990: 1.
— people start moving into, Lahaina News, March 20, 1991: 1.

KOMULA, DENISE
— named Rookie of the Year at the Peter Burwash International's annual convention, Lahaina News, December 13, 1989: 8.

KONA BREWING CO. [BUSINESS]
— to host Maui Music Splash with Embassy Suites Resort, Lahaina News, July 18, 1996: 12.

KONA STORM [MUSICAL GROUP]
— to perform at Casanova's, Lahaina News, December 19, 1990: 13.
— to perform at Polli's Mexican Restaurant, Lahaina News, March 20, 1991: 11.

KONDO, GEORGE
— elected vice chairman of County Police Commission, Lahaina Sun, January 27, 1971: 2.

KONDO, REIKO
— honored by state for outstanding service, Lahaina Sun, July 26, 1972: 9.

KONDO, RONALD [POLITICIAN]
— speaks of proposal to dredge a swimming area in Launiupoko State Park, Lahaina Sun, November 11, 1970: 3.
— at public meeting in Lahaina, Lahaina Sun, December 23, 1970: 10.
— summarizes legislative activity, Lahaina Sun, March 31, 1971: 1.
— reflects on recent legislative session, Lahaina Sun, April 28, 1971: 6.
— urges students to work within the system, Lahaina Sun, June 23, 1971: 2.
— nominated for president of West Maui Business Association, Lahaina Sun, May 10, 1972: 5.
— details of his election campaign for 6th district of the State House, Lahaina Sun, September 20, 1972: 7.
— hired by State Health Department, Lahaina News, May 1, 1980: 8.

KONDO, SHOZO "DYKE"
— life described, Lahaina News, May 3, 1989: 2.

KONG, JAMES
— assisting in creation of Maui-Moloka'i Community Development Corporation, Lahaina Sun, February 3, 1971: 3.

KONG, KENNETH
— appointed to engineering section of the Department of Public Works by Mayor Cravalho, Lahaina Sun, January 6, 1971: 2.

KONI [MUSICAL GROUP]
— to perform at Lahaina Civic Center, Lahaina News, March 1, 2001: 20.

KONNO, DARREN
— appointed marketing manager at Lahaina Cannery Mall, Lahaina News, February 15, 2001: 8.

KONOKOWAI KAUHALE
— offers housing relief, Lahaina News, August 15, 1990: 1.

KONRAD, HOWARD [ARTIST]
— scrimshaw work discussed, Lahaina News, September 5, 1984: 14.
— owner of Lahaina Scrimshaw featured, Lahaina News, February 4, 1987: 12.

KOOL & THE GANG [MUSICAL GROUP]
— to perform, Lahaina News, March 13, 1985: 16.
— performance reviewed, Lahaina News, March 27, 1985: 12.

KOOLA [MUSICAL GROUP]
— described, Lahaina News, September 2, 1987: 7,8.

KOOP, C. EVERETT
— Surgeon General to visit Lahaina, Lahaina News, February 22, 1989: 1.
— praises restoration effort on Seaman's Hospital, Lahaina News, March 1, 1989: 1,16.

KOPROWSKI, LORI [ARTIST]
— to exhibit at Lahaina Arts Society, Lahaina News, February 6, 2003: 17.

KOREAN WAR VETERANS NATIONAL RECOGNITION DAY
— to be held, Lahaina News, May 11, 2000: 20.

KORMAN, HARVEY [COMEDIAN]
— attends Aku Memorial Celebrity Golf Tournament, Lahaina News, May 29, 1985: 4.
— to perform at Maui Arts and Cultural Center with Tim Conway, Lahaina News, December 12, 2002: 19.
— tickets on sale for show, Lahaina News, December 26, 2002: 17.

KORN, KEN
— named national sales manager at The Ritz-Carlton, Lahaina News, October 3, 1991: 7.

KORN, ULRICH
— named executive chef at Kapalua Bay Hotel, Lahaina News, March 19, 1986: 3.

KOROLUCK, BOB
— new sales manager at KLHI-FM, Lahaina News, April 23, 1992: 16.

KOSAKA, AYAKO
— life described, Lahaina News, May 10, 1989: 4.

KOSAKA, GLEN
— Maui County Council's legal advisor does not believe Holo Honokowai agreement will hold up, Lahaina News, March 22, 1989: 12.

KOSAKA, MELANIE
— Scholar/Athlete of the Week, Lahaina News, November 6, 1997: 9.

KOSENKA, JENNY
— new executive director of Art School at Kapalua, Lahaina News, April 23, 1998: 13.
— new director featured, Lahaina News, July 9, 1998: 7.

KOSHER EREV SHABBAT DINNER
— to host guest speaker Louis Goldberg, Lahaina News, January 1, 1998: 5.

KOSHIYAMA, ISAMI
— passes away, Lahaina Sun, March 17, 1971: 3.

KOTANI, OZZIE [MUSICIAN]
— to participate in Hawaiian Ki ho'alu (slack key) Workshop, Lahaina News, June 3, 1999: 17.

KOTTKE, LEO [MUSICIAN]
— to perform at Stouffer Wailea Beach Resort, Lahaina News, April 26, 1989: 9.
— to perform at Embassy Suites Resort Ballroom, Lahaina News, June 20, 1991: 8,9.
— to perform at Embassy Suites Resort Ballroom, Lahaina News, June 27, 1991: 12.
— to perform at Maui Marriott Grand Ballroom, Lahaina News, July 15, 1993: 12.
— to perform at Maui Arts and Cultural Center, Lahaina News, November 29, 2001: 15.
— to play at Maui Arts and Culture Center, Lahaina News, December 6, 2001: 16.

KOVACIC, ROBERT
— involved in car accident, Lahaina Sun, April 7, 1971: 2.

KOYAMA, ERIC
— appointed manager of The Villa restaurant, Lahaina News, August 16, 1989: 6.

KPOA MUSIC AND GIFT SHOP [BUSINESS]
— opens, Lahaina News, November 5, 1992: 8.

KPOA-FM [BUSINESS]
— radio station to open in West Maui, Lahaina News, September 12, 1984: 12.
— names Dick Warner as director of sales, Lahaina News, January 9, 1985: 3.
— radio station featured, Lahaina News, February 25, 1987: 8.
— radio station doubles its output power, Lahaina News, February 27, 1991: 8.
— radio station hosting live jazz at Maui Marriott Resort, Lahaina News, June 6, 1991: 14.
— hosting live jazz at Maui Marriott Resort's Lobby Bar, Lahaina News, June 20, 1991: 9.
— Rodger Layng joins, Lahaina News, August 1, 1991: 11.
— hires Allen "Poki" Pokipala to marketing team, Lahaina News, August 29, 1991: 4.
— to broadcast updates of PING Kapalua International Golf Tournament, Lahaina News, November 7, 1991: 5,7.
— approved for power increase, Lahaina News, December 12, 1991: 16.
— state representative Roz Baker to give weekly 5 minute updates on legislature on, Lahaina News, January 16, 1992: 3.
— increases signal power, Lahaina News, March 26, 1992: 11.
— has transitioned to jazz format, Lahaina News, May 7, 1992: 19.
— recognized by Hawaii Visitor Bureau with Kahili Award for music programming, Lahaina News, June 11, 1992: 13.
— moves to 505 Front Street, Lahaina News, August 27, 1992: 10.
— radio station offer "King for a Day" special with the Lodge at Koele, Lahaina News, June 3, 1993: 13.
— radio station installs digital production and playback equipment, Lahaina News, August 5, 1993: 7.
— radio station expands, Lahaina News, March 24, 1994: 8.
— radio station to host jazz and Hawaiian music event at Whalers Village, Lahaina News, April 14, 1994: 12.
— radio show "Midnight Party" to air in Japan, Lahaina News, June 30, 1994: 8.
— Robyn Gately appointed general sales manager, Lahaina News, July 21, 1994: 7.
— to host entertainment stage in Aloha Festivals' Annual Downtown Ho'olaule'a, Lahaina News, September 15, 1994: 14.
— radio station celebrates 10 years, Lahaina News, September 22, 1994: 12.
— hosting "Jazz on the Beach", Lahaina News, September 29, 1994: 11,12.
— to celebrate 10 years of business, Lahaina News, October 27, 1994: 20.
— Alaka'I Paleka named director of, Lahaina News, February 22, 1996: 11.
— most popular radio station on Maui, Lahaina News, March 19, 1998: 11.
— to broadcast live from Lahaina Seafood Restaurant, Lahaina News, July 27, 2000: 20.
— radio personality Charly Espina moves to, Lahaina News, January 2, 2003: 8.

KRAFT, GEORGE
— to talk on "Management of Multiple Sclerosis", Lahaina News, August 27, 1998: 16.

KRAFTSOW, GARY [WRITER]
— to sign book "Yoga for Transformation" at Borders Books, Lahaina News, September 12, 2002: 20.

KRAHN, MICHAEL [ARTIST]
— to sign Lahaina poster, Lahaina News, December 4, 1997: 19.
— wins Lahaina Poster Contest, Lahaina News, July 19, 2001: 14.
— to exhibit at Village Galleries, Lahaina News, April 18, 2002: 16.
— wins Best in Show at Lahaina Poster Contest, Lahaina News, July 24, 2003: 1,18.

KRAMER, CARLTON
— named vice president of sales and marketing for Hilo Hatties, Lahaina News, September 14, 1995: 10.

KRASNIEWSKI, STANLEY
— joins Alexander and Baldwin Properties, Lahaina News, August 20, 1998: 13.

KRATKA, ILENE [ARTIST]
— featured at Hui No'eau Visual Arts Center, Lahaina News, September 30, 1987: 3.

KRAUS, NORMAN RICHARD [ARTIST]
— sand sculptor to create European castle at Maui Surf Hotel, Lahaina News, September 26, 1984: 10.

KRAUSE, LAMBERTH AND KARI
— owners of Balloons Galore, Lahaina News, November 14, 1984: 18.

KRAZY KAMP [PLAY]
— to be performed at Theatre Theatre Maui, Lahaina News, July 25, 1996: 11,12.

KRESMAN, JACKIE [ARTIST]
— at Casay Galleries, Lahaina News, February 13, 1991: 13.

KRISHNA FESTIVAL
— held at Camp Pecusa, Lahaina Sun, April 19, 1972: 6.

KRISHNAN, RAMANATHAN (RAMESH)
— success of tennis player detailed, Lahaina News, April 25, 1984: 4.
— tennis player's success described, Lahaina News, April 25, 1984: 4.

KRISTOFFERSON, KRIS [MUSICIAN]
— performs at Kokua Kaua'i Relief Concert, Lahaina News, October 1, 1992: 3.

KROGSTAD, KERMIT FRANCIS
— dies at Maui Memorial Hospital, Lahaina News, January 2, 1991: 4.

KRUCK, BRITTANY
— Scholar/Athlete of the Week, Lahaina News, February 14, 2002: 12.

KRUCK, JENAE
— Scholar/Athlete of the Week, Lahaina News, January 17, 2002: 12.

KRUEGER, JOEHAYNE
— performing in "Joseph, and the Technicolor Dreamcoat", Lahaina News, July 30, 1992: 18.

KRUPNICK, MIKE
— discusses Certified Pest Control's new chemical free pest control method, Lahaina News, May 19, 1994: 12.

KRUPNICK, NASYA
— awarded Hannah Keahi Scholastic Achievement Award, Lahaina News, January 30, 1997: 6.

KRYSER CORP. [BUSINESS]
— disciplined by the Department of Commerce and Consumer Affairs, Lahaina News, June 9, 1994: 12.

KSM PROFESSIONAL GROUP
— sponsoring CPR class at Lahaina Intermediate School, Lahaina News, May 17, 1989: 2.
— to offer CPR classes, Lahaina News, June 14, 1989: 2.

KSSK [BUSINESS]
— radio station to air 49ers games, Lahaina News, September 16, 1999: 7.

KU, FRANCES [ARTIST]
— to lead workshop on watercolor, Lahaina News, October 24, 2002: 18.
— to lead workshop "Waves in Watercolor", Lahaina News, October 31, 2002: 29.

KU, GENESIS
— Scholar/Athlete of the Week, Lahaina News, March 1, 2001: 14.

KU KANAKA [MUSICAL]
— to be held at Maui Arts and Cultural Center, Lahaina News, September 24, 1998: 16.

KUALA'AU, GREGORY
— killed at a construction accident near Olowalu, Lahaina Sun, March 17, 1971: 1.

KUALA'AU, RON [MUSICIAN]
— to perform at Molokini Lounge at the Maui Prince Hotel, Lahaina News, January 16, 1992: 17.
— to perform at Borders Books, Lahaina News, September 16, 1999: 12.
— to perform at Borders Books, Lahaina News, September 23, 1999: 12.

KUALAPUU SCHOOL
— successful at Na Mele O Maui Song Competition, Lahaina News, December 8, 1994: 16.

KUANG, TING SHAO [ARTIST]
— work displayed at Dyansen Gallery, Lahaina News, January 27, 1988: 3.

KUBO, DUDLEY
— U.S. Soul Conservation Service engineer discusses proposed flood control measures, Lahaina News, March 6, 1991: 1,5.

KUBO, TODD
— acting postmaster at Lahaina Post Office featured, Lahaina News, August 22, 1991: 9.

KUBOTA, GARY
— to become editor of Lahaina News, Lahaina News, March 1, 1989: 1.
— Lahaina News editor to offer class on media relations, Lahaina News, September 20, 1989: 6.
— leaving Lahaina News for position at Honolulu Star Bulletin, Lahaina News, April 22, 1993: 3.

KUBOTA, ROB [COMEDIAN]
— to perform at Comedy Club and the Sports Page, Lahaina News, May 23, 1991: 11.
— to perform at Comedy Club and the Sports Page, Lahaina News, September 17, 1992: 13,16.
— to perform at Maui Comedy Club, Lahaina News, August 10, 1995: 11.

KU'E [MUSICAL GROUP]
— to perform at A Taste of Lahaina, Lahaina News, September 10, 1998: 16.

KUGLMEIER, LUDWIG
— hired by Coldwell Banker McCormack Real Estate, Lahaina News, November 19, 1992: 5.

KUHAULUA, JESS [SUMO WRESTLER]
— awarded East-West Center award , Lahaina Sun, February 9, 1972: 14.

KUHIO DAY
— see Prince Kuhio Day

KUI: THE LIFE AND MUSIC OF KUI LEE [FILM]
— to be performed, Lahaina News, May 16, 1996: 7.

KUIA, JOHN
— president of Kahana Canoe Club featured, Lahaina News, July 5, 2001: 12.

KUIHELANI HIGHWAY
— being constructed from Ma'alaea to Kahului Airport, Lahaina Sun, November 18, 1970: 1.

KUIKAHI, WAYNE [ARTIST]
— demonstrates coconut weaving at Lahaina Cannery Mall, Lahaina News, August 29, 1990: 11.

KUILIMA [BUSINESS]
— nightclub on the North Shore of Oahu discussed, Lahaina Times, July, 1980 volume 4 number 6: 3.

KUKAHIKO, EARL "CHIEF"
— grounds foreman for Lahainaluna High School retirement celebrated, Lahaina News, November 6, 1985: 3.
— founder of Lahaina Canoe Club featured, Lahaina News, June 25, 1992: 10.
— baseball coach featured, Lahaina News, May 26, 1994: 8.
— Lahainaluna High School coach featured, Lahaina News, May 2, 1996: 20.
— Lahainaluna High School softball coach discussed, Lahaina News, March 20, 1997: 13.
— to perform to Lahaina seniors, Lahaina News, May 22, 1997: 1,3.
— softball coach featured, Lahaina News, May 13, 1999: 6.
— to lead King Kamehameha Day Parade with wife Barbara, Lahaina News, June 10, 1999: 1,20.
— installed as minister at Association of Hawaiian Evangelical Churches, Lahaina News, August 3, 2000: 5.
— featured, Lahaina News, November 23, 2000: 1,6.
— awarded Outstanding Older Americans, Lahaina News, May 3, 2001: 1,22.
— Lahainaluna High School softball coach resigns, Lahaina News, February 7, 2002: 12.
— blesses renovation at Maui Medical Group-Lahaina, Lahaina News, August 1, 2002: 22.

KUKAHIKO, ELLIE
— named manager of Nanatomi Seafood and Steakhouse, Lahaina News, June 20, 1991: 5.
— new manager of Nanatomi's Restaurant, Lahaina News, August 1, 1991: 18.

KUKAHIKO, JOHN
— Reverend featured, Lahaina Sun, August 9, 1972: 9.

KUKAHIKO, ROBERT JOHN
— Scholar/Athlete of the Week, Lahaina News, May 13, 1999: 7.

KUKAHIKO, TIARA
— Scholar/Athlete of the Week, Lahaina News, February 12, 1998: 14.

KUKAHIKO, TWYLA
— Scholar/Athlete of the Week, Lahaina News, March 21, 1996: 7.

KUKALANI BEAST
— animal scaring people likely a bird, Lahaina Sun, July 25, 1973: 3.

KUKO, DENISE [ARTIST]
— photographer creates poster entitled "Compadres", Lahaina News, March 1, 1989: 16.

KULA [TOWN]
— construction of microwave relay station at, near completion, Lahaina Sun, December 23, 1970: 6.
— plan to improve water supply, Lahaina Sun, September 22, 1971: 7.
— featured, Lahaina Sun, August 8, 1973: 12,13,14.
— Pacific'O has new farm at, Lahaina News, November 29, 2001: 8.

KULA AGRICULTURE PARK
— lots available, Lahaina News, May 16, 1984: 17.

KULA BAY TROPICAL CLOTHING COMPANY [BUSINESS]
— opens, Lahaina News, January 16, 1991: 5.

KULA CLINIC
— Doctor Nicole Malia Apoliona joins, Lahaina News, August 15, 2002: 8.

KULA ELEMENTARY SCHOOL
— to hold Harvest Festival, Lahaina News, October 31, 1996: 18.

KULA HALE BAREFOOT HOP
— teenagers' dance to be held at War Memorial Gym, Lahaina Sun, April 5, 1972: 11.

KULA IKI THRIFT SHOP
— to be open Saturday, Lahaina News, August 8, 1991: 3.

KULAMALU LIMITED PARTNERSHIP
— sells 80 acres to Kamehameha Schools, Lahaina News, August 3, 2000: 13.

KULEANA
— development featured, Lahaina News, June 13, 1984: 18.

KULEANA KU'IKAHI
— community group formed to promote culture, Lahaina News, October 18, 2001: 1.
— files lawsuit over approval of Kaua'ula project, Lahaina News, November 7, 2002: 1,24.

KULEK, SIDNEY
— Lahaina-Ka'anapali & Pacific Railroad named president, Lahaina Sun, December 29, 1971: 7.

KULOLOIO, LEINA'ALA
— Educator of the Month at Kimo's Restaurant, Lahaina News, February 21, 2002: 3.

KULOLOIO, LES
— to present "The Power of Activating", Lahaina News, July 6, 2000: 17.
— to present on "Maui Ancient and Prehistoric Burials—Maui Island", Lahaina News, August 2, 2001: 17.
— to present on "Maui Ancient and Prehistoric Burials—Maui Island, Part IV", Lahaina News, November 15, 2001: 17.
— to present "Simplicity" at 'Ohana Connection, Lahaina News, August 22, 2002: 21.
— to present "When the 'Ohana Connects and Disconnects" at 'Ohana Connection, Lahaina News, April 24, 2003: 21.

KULOLOIO, LESLIE
— speaks of Protect Kaho'olawe Ohana's attempt to end bombing of Kaho'olawe, Lahaina News, May 18, 1988: 1,5.

KULULANI CHAPEL
— to hold auction fundraiser, Lahaina News, November 17, 1994: 4.

KULVINSKAS, VICTORAS
— to speak on "Survival into the 21st Century", Lahaina News, January 11, 1996: 2.

KUMON CENTER, WEST MAUI
— opens, Lahaina News, February 17, 1994: 1,4.

KUMU A O NO NA KAMALI'I
— to meet at Maui Marriott Hotel , Lahaina News, April 15, 1993: 4.

KUMU PRODUCTIONS INC. [BUSINESS]
— opens, Lahaina News, November 9, 2000: 18.

KUMULANI CHAPEL
— offering turkey, Lahaina News, November 19, 1986: 3.
— free Thanksgiving dinner, Lahaina News, November 18, 1987: 3.
— to hold Christmas service, Lahaina News, December 23, 1987: 3.
— to hold fundraiser for outreach to the Philippines, Lahaina News, August 16, 1989: 3.
— seeking donations to fund crisis hotline, Lahaina News, March 28, 1990: 3.
— to hold silent auction, Lahaina News, July 18, 1990: 3.
— preschool given money raised by Kapalua Hook-up Fishing Tournament, Lahaina News, December 19, 1990: 18.
— to host Thanksgiving dinner, Lahaina News, November 21, 1991: 3.
— to offer Christmas Eve Services, Lahaina News, December 19, 1991: 6.
— youth group to hold car wash fundraiser, Lahaina News, March 26, 1992: 4.
— to hold car wash fundraiser, Lahaina News, April 2, 1992: 3.
— Jay Carty to offer series of lectures, Lahaina News, May 27, 1993: 4.
— plans to expand preschool, Lahaina News, February 17, 1994: 4.
— hosting benefit concert for Rwanda Relief, Lahaina News, June 23, 1994: 5.
— to hold keiki services on Christmas Eve, Lahaina News, December 15, 1994: 6.
— to hold Harvest Festival, Lahaina News, October 19, 1995: 4.
— to hold Palm Sunday service, Lahaina News, March 20, 1997: 16.
— to hold "Freedom Seminars" with Erich Grieshaber, Lahaina News, November 6, 1997: 16.
— "Hooked on Jesus" summer program a success, Lahaina News, September 17, 1998: 19.
— to hold Harvest Festival, Lahaina News, October 29, 1998: 28.
— planning free Thanksgiving dinner, Lahaina News, November 18, 1999: 17.
— to hold auction, Lahaina News, November 30, 2000: 5.
— plans Kamp Kumulani, Lahaina News, May 30, 2002: 2.
— to hold Harvest Festival, Lahaina News, October 24, 2002: 21.
— to hold thanksgiving dinner, Lahaina News, November 28, 2002: 16.
— to present "If Angels Were Mortal", Lahaina News, December 19, 2002: 20.
— to host play "If Angels Were Mortals", Lahaina News, December 19, 2002: 3.
— to hold Bible school, Lahaina News, May 29, 2003: 9.

KUNA LODGE
— art exhibits for the summer announced, Lahaina Sun, May 12, 1971: 7.

KUNISHIGI, FLORANCE
— wins employee Accident Awareness Bingo at Kapalua Bay Hotel and Villas, Lahaina News, March 26, 1992: 11.

KUNITAKE, CHERYL
— chef at Woody's Oceanfront Grill, Lahaina News, March 25, 1999: 13.

KUNITOMO, JERRY
— names Maui liaison for Roz Baker, Lahaina News, February 20, 2003: 8.

KUNIYOSHI, ED
— consultant presents plan for Front Street, Lahaina News, November 21, 1990: 1.

KUNKEL, EARL
— businessman featured, Lahaina News, January 18, 1989: 2.

KUNNA, JOHN
— working to protect Pu'u Kukui Reserve, Lahaina News, July 6, 2000: 1,14.

KUNST, DAVE
— first world walker renews marriage vows in Maui, Lahaina News, January 13, 1994: 1,4.

KUNTZ, NANCY
— to present on brain development, Lahaina News, April 3, 1997: 12.

KUPAHU, HENRY [MUSICIAN]
— named Maui's Outstanding Male Older American, Lahaina News, May 25, 2000: 1,14.
— passes away, Lahaina News, February 15, 2001: 3.

KUPAU, SUMMER [WRITER]
— named student president at King Kamehameha III School, Lahaina News, October 21, 1987: 12.
— publishes "Exploring Historic Lahaina", Lahaina News, June 7, 2001: 9.

KUPO, ELIZABETH MOANI
— president of Professional Secretaries International, No Ka Oi Chapter, Lahaina News, August 15, 1990: 11.

KUPU [BOOK]
— published, Lahaina News, April 19, 1989: 9.

KUPUNAKEA
— Lahainaluna High School students remove alien plants at, Lahaina News, November 26, 1998: 6.

KURIYAMA, STANLEY
— appointed executive vice president of Alexander and Baldwin Properties, Lahaina News, January 23, 1992: 13.

KURRASCH, RICHARD
— new pastor at Lahaina United Methodist Church, Lahaina News, August 31, 2000: 15.
— new pastor at Lahaina United Methodist Church, Lahaina News, October 12, 2000: 17.

KURRY, KEVIN
— comments on plan to introduce bill to regulate tour activities, Lahaina News, November 15, 1989: 1.

KUTSCHERENKO, ALEX
— named regional group sales manager at Ruth's Chris Steak House, Lahaina News, October 11, 2001: 8.

KUTSUNAI, ANDREW
— senior class advisor to retire after 34 years, Lahaina News, September 1, 1994: 2.

KUTUNAI PHOTO STUDIO
— to take yearbook portraits for Lahainaluna High School seniors, Lahaina News, June 28, 1989: 3.

KU'U HOME O WAILUKU
— block party to be held on Market Street, Lahaina News, September 16, 1999: 12.
— music festival to be held, Lahaina News, October 19, 2000: 18.

KU'U: THE HUI ALOHA 'AINA ANTI-ANNEXATION PETITIONS
— talk to be held by Noenoe Silva, Lahaina News, August 27, 1998: 3.

KUWAHARA, CLARENCE
— named executive director of Hawaii Society of Certified Accountants, Lahaina News, October 31, 1990: 12.

KUZMA, JOHN [MUSICIAN]
— to perform at Aloha Cantina, Lahaina News, April 20, 1995: 12.

KWOCK, TIM
— appointed director of sales and marketing at Kapalua Bay Hotel, Lahaina News, March 21, 1990: 4.

KWON, RONALD
— doctor advocates to privatize Maui Memorial Hospital, Lahaina News, October 3, 1990: 1,4.

KYLE, WILLIS
— owner of Lahaina-Ka'anapali and Pacific Railroad dies, Lahaina News, September 19, 1991: 8.

KYUSHU AND TOYO CORPORATION [BUSINESS]
— planning subdivision in Kihei, Lahaina News, May 28, 1992: 6.

L

L.A. GATSBY, INC. [BUSINESS]
— buys Polli's On the Beach restaurant, Lahaina News, October 31, 1990: 11.

L&L DRIVE-INN [RESTAURANT]
— opens in Lahaina, Lahaina News, November 5, 1998: 17.

LA BELLE BOUTIQUE [BUSINESS]
— moves location, Lahaina News, January 11, 1996: 11.

LA BRETAGNA [RESTAURANT]
— chocolate reviewed, Lahaina News, May 20, 1987: 4.

LA CAGE AUX FOLLES [PLAY]
— to debut, Lahaina News, November 29, 1989: 21.

LA COM, DIANA AND WAYNE [ARTISTS]
— works to be exhibited at Village Gallery, Lahaina News, January 10, 1990: 13.
— to exhibit at Village Galleries, Lahaina News, April 20, 2000: 16.

LA DOLCE VITA [BUSINESS]
— opens in The Shops at Wailea, Lahaina News, December 12, 2002: 8.

LA FAMILIA [RESTAURANT]
— to open in old Royal Ka'anapali Restaurant site, Lahaina News, July 15, 1983: 10.
— reviewed, Lahaina News, October 5, 1983: 14.

LA FAMILIA UNIDA DE MAUI
— to celebrate Cinco de Mayo, Lahaina News, May 1, 1997: 16.

LA FOGATA [RESTAURANT]
— featured, Lahaina News, March 2, 2000: 5.

LA JOLLA, USS (SUBMARINE)
— visits Lahaina, Lahaina News, August 21, 2003: 1,20.

LA LECHE LEAGUE
— announces fall series, Lahaina News, August 27, 1986: 12.

LA MARCHINA, ROBERT [CONDUCTOR]
— conducts Honolulu Symphony at Baldwin Auditorium , Lahaina Sun, November 11, 1970: 1.

LA PEROUSE [RESTAURANT]
— has new hours, Lahaina News, June 12, 1985: 3.
— opens at Maui Inter-Continental Wailea Hotel, Lahaina News, May 21, 1986: 3.
— opens for dinner, Lahaina News, May 6, 1987: 10.
— awarded Wine Spectator Magazine's Award of Excellence, Lahaina News, November 11, 1987: 6.
— offering Vintner Dinner Series, Lahaina News, December 6, 1989: 12.
— to hold vintner dinner, Lahaina News, February 7, 1990: 13.
— representative for Les Vins George Duboeuf to visit, Lahaina News, December 19, 1990: 14.
— to feature wines from Chateau Beychevelle, Lahaina News, March 6, 1991: 13.

LA PEROUSE BAY
— Friends of Keoneʻoʻio continue to care for, Lahaina News, April 10, 2003: 21.
— see also Friends of Keoneʻoʻio

LA PEROUSE, JEAN-FRANCOIS
— navigator's visit to Maui recounted, Lahaina News, February 24, 1994: 2.

LA TASCA [RESTAURANT]
— opens, Lahaina News, December 17, 1992: 9.
— opens at Lahaina Center, Lahaina News, December 24, 1992: 10.

LAANUI, LEALOHA
— named Miss Jackpot, Lahaina News, October 23, 1997: 10.

LAʻAU LAPAʻAU
— Maʻalaea Community Garden to host workshop on, Lahaina News, February 27, 1997: 10.

LABASAN, LLOYD
— reprimand rescinded for lowering American flag following Challenger explosion, Lahaina News, March 26, 1986: 1.

LABB, JERRY
— assembles "Feast or Famine II" art show, Lahaina News, November 5, 1998: 14.

LABOR
— dispute at Pioneer Mill resolved, Lahaina Sun, June 30, 1971: 1.
— employees of Lahaina-Kaʻanapali & Pacific Railroad vote to unionize, Lahaina Sun, July 21, 1971: 9.
— Maui Land & Pineapple seeking student workers, Lahaina Sun, August 11, 1971: 11.
— West coast dock strike hurting sugar and pineapple companies, Lahaina Sun, August 18, 1971: 1.
— state teacher strike possible, Lahaina Sun, October 13, 1971: 4.
— sugar and teacher strikes in Maui are possible, Lahaina Sun, February 2, 1972: 5.
— potential strike of pineapple workers averted, Lahaina Sun, February 9, 1972: 5.
— unemployment and strikes discussed at Maui Chamber of Commerce, Lahaina Sun, February 16, 1972: 5.
— school "holiday" declared as teachers vote, Lahaina Sun, February 23, 1972: 3.
— statistics criticized by Mayor Cravalho, Lahaina Sun, March 29, 1972: 4.
— strike averted in sugar industry, Lahaina Sun, April 19, 1972: 3.
— Mayor Cravalho suggests importing agricultural workers , Lahaina Sun, April 26, 1972: 3.
— Lahaina Tree House votes to unionize, Lahaina Sun, September 20, 1972: 3.
— Maui teachers plan to walkout, Lahaina Sun, October 4, 1972: 9.
— Maui teachers vote to strike, Lahaina Sun, October 11, 1972: 3,10.
— workers walk out at Pioneer Mill, Lahaina Sun, October 18, 1972: 10.
— West Coast dock strike affecting Maui, Lahaina Sun, November 29, 1972: 3,9.
— West Coast dock strike settlement, Lahaina Sun, December 6, 1972: 7.
— hotel workers negotiating new contract, Lahaina Sun, February 28, 1973: 10,11.
— Maui teachers voting on authorizing a strike, Lahaina Sun, March 14, 1973: 10.
— teachers strike, Lahaina Sun, April 11, 1973: 1,5.
— teachers vote on arbitration plan, Lahaina Sun, April 18, 1973: 5.
— bargaining position of Hawaii State Teachers' Association described, Lahaina Sun, April 18, 1973: 5.
— teachers return to classroom after strike, Lahaina Sun, April 25, 1973: 3.
— laid-off workers appeal for help, Lahaina Sun, June 27, 1973: 4.

— Hawaiian Airlines asks union for concessions, Lahaina News, December 15, 1982: 3.
— general strike of Hawaii's public workers looms, Lahaina News, February 22, 1984: 3.
— editorial on response to United Airlines strike, Lahaina News, June 19, 1985: 2.
— cost of United Airlines strike to Maui detailed, Lahaina News, July 24, 1985: 8.
— AFI-CIO Local 5 hotel workers continuing to strike at Sheraton-Maui Hotel, Lahaina News, March 14, 1990: 2.
— insert featuring ILWU Local 142 included in Lahaina News, Lahaina News, April 25, 1990: B1,B2,B3,B4.
— workers ratify hotel contract, Lahaina News, July 4, 1990: 1.
— union members demonstrate outside Maui Westin, Lahaina News, February 8, 1996: 16.
— Royal Lahaina Resort hold rally to protest wages, Lahaina News, November 16, 2000: 7.
— ILWU Local 142 and Kapalua Land Co. agree to mediation , Lahaina News, February 27, 2003: 3.
— see also business, strikes, and specific unions

LABOR AND INDUSTRIAL RELATIONS, DEPARTMENT OF
— to begin enforcing new construction standards, Lahaina News, April 13, 1995: 12.
— has information kiosk at Lahaina Cannery Mall, Lahaina News, April 18, 1996: 8.
— seeking nominations for Laulima Awards, Lahaina News, June 12, 1997: 15.
— taking nominations for Laulima Award, Lahaina News, July 2, 1998: 12.
— to raise minimum wage, Lahaina News, December 20, 2001: 9.

LABOR DAY
— to be celebrated, Lahaina News, August 22, 2002: 17.

LABOR, DEPARTMENT OF
— adds touchscreen kiosk at Lahaina Cannery Mall, Lahaina News, June 2, 1994: 10.

LABOR LAW
— seminar to be held, Lahaina News, March 19, 1992: 10.

LABOR LAW EMPLOYERS SEMINAR
— to be held, Lahaina News, August 18, 1994: 8.
— to be held , Lahaina News, May 18, 1995: 6.
— to be held, Lahaina News, September 12, 1996: 15.
— to be held, Lahaina News, September 18, 1997: 16.
— to be held, Lahaina News, October 8, 1998: 13.
— to be held, Lahaina News, September 2, 1999: 13.
— to be held, Lahaina News, November 2, 2000: 12.
— workshop to be held, Lahaina News, May 10, 2001: 9.
— to be held at Maui Beach Hotel, Lahaina News, May 9, 2002: 8.
— to be held, Lahaina News, May 16, 2002: 8.

LABOR RELATIONS BOARD
— investigating ILWU for unfair labor practices, Lahaina News, August 30, 2001: 1,8.

LABOR SERVICES, INC. [BUSINESS]
— opens in Lahaina, Lahaina News, November 8, 1989: 5.
— offering four hours of free labor as promotion, Lahaina News, November 15, 1989: 9.

LABORTE, CHARLIE [COMEDIAN]
— to perform at Comedy Club and the Sports Page, Lahaina News, December 26, 1991: 12.

LABORTE, DOMINIQUE
— Scholar/Athlete of the Week, Lahaina News, January 10, 2002: 13.

LABORTE, ERNEST
— passes away, Lahaina News, June 17, 1999: 15.

LABRADO, DARRELL [MUSICIAN]
— to perform at "A Taste of Lahaina", Lahaina News, September 2, 1999: 18.

LABRADOR, LERA
— promoted to lease marketing representative at GECC Financial Corporation, Lahaina News, March 25, 1993: 11.

LACLERGUE, ALEXANDRA
— Scholar/Athlete of the Week, Lahaina News, April 18, 2002: 13.

LACLERGUE, RON
— general manager of Grill and Bar in Kapalua donates money to The Preschool at Kapalua, Lahaina News, February 3, 1994: 9.

LACOM, WAYNE AND DIANA [ARTISTS]
— to exhibit at Village Galleries, Lahaina News, March 9, 1995: 12.

LACRO, DENISE
— Scholar/Athlete of the Week, Lahaina News, May 30, 1996: 10.

LADERA, ANGELO
— youth soccer player accepted for F.C. Global International Soccer Training and Competition, Lahaina News, May 9, 1996: 6.

LADIES AUXILIARY OF VETERANS OF FOREIGN WARS (VFW)
— to hold annual Western Steak and Chicken Fry, Lahaina News, January 23, 2003: 16.

LADY FROM VENUS, THE
— to speak at Maui Palms Hotel, Lahaina News, July 8, 1993: 12.

LADYSMITH BLACK MAMBAZO [MUSICAL GROUP]
— to perform at Maui Arts and Cultural Center, Lahaina News, September 22, 1994: 14.

LAENUI, POKA
— to speak on Hawaiian sovereignty, Lahaina News, November 7, 1996: 15.

LAFOND, RICHARD JOSEPH, JR.
— named executive director of Maui Tomorrow, Lahaina News, August 13, 1992: 4.
— to host open mike night at Cafe Makawao, Lahaina News, June 19, 1997: 17.

LAGAZO, CHRIS
— Scholar/Athlete of the Week, Lahaina News, October 17, 1996: 12.
— named to Dean's List, Lahaina News, July 5, 2001: 5.

LAGBAS, ELIZABETH
— Scholar/Athlete of the Week, Lahaina News, June 14, 2001: 14.

LAGBAS, MYCHAEL
— Scholar/Athlete of the Week, Lahaina News, June 1, 2000: 8.

LAGOY, R. GREGORY
— discusses stress, Lahaina News, March 8, 1989: 3.
— Hospice Maui Executive Director honored as "Maui's Outstanding Executive Director for a Non-Profit Organization", Lahaina News, July 26, 2001: 8.

LAGUNERO, AL [ARTIST]
— opens gallery, Lahaina News, March 14, 1984: 4.
— work featured, Lahaina News, September 12, 1984: 13.
— to speak to Ohana Luncheon and Trade Faire, Lahaina News, April 26, 1989: 3.

LAHAINA [TOWN]
— home construction, Lahaina Sun, December 2, 1970: 3.
— photograph of waterfront, Lahaina Sun, December 9, 1970: 1.
— new gas lines installed, Lahaina Sun, December 9, 1970: 3.
— fictional history of, discussed by Higgins Maddigan, Lahaina Sun, December 23, 1970: 9.
— photograph from 1908, Lahaina Sun, December 30, 1970: 5.
— Press kit available soon, Lahaina Sun, January 13, 1971: 5.
— press kit available, Lahaina Sun, January 27, 1971: 7.
— restoration efforts discussed, Lahaina Sun, March 24, 1971: 3.

— history summarized, Lahaina Sun, July 7, 1971: 4.
— Banyan tree birthday celebration planned, Lahaina Sun, November 8, 1972: 12.
— early history recounted, Lahaina Sun, January 10, 1973: 22.
— lades of, photographed, Lahaina Sun, August 29, 1973: 12,13.
— isolationism less of an option for the town, Lahaina Sun, August 29, 1973: 3.
— current conditions celebrated, Lahaina Sun, August 29, 1973: 5.
— conditions described, Lahaina News, November, 1979: 2.
— nightlife discussed, Lahaina Times, July, 1980 volume 4 number 6: 3.
— description of nightlife, Lahaina Times, July, 1980 volume 4 number 6: 5.
— meaning of debated, Lahaina News, December 1, 1980: 10.
— description of town at 2 AM, Lahaina News, January 15, 1981: 3.
— history of, Lahaina News, February 1, 1981: 7,10.
— description from 1905, Lahaina News, May 1, 1981: 11,12.
— early history, Lahaina News, October 1, 1981: 11,12.
— history recounted, Lahaina News, September 15, 1982: 11,12.
— new recreation center and housing project planned, Lahaina News, May 15, 1983: 2.
— discussion of need for more tourists, Lahaina Times, August 20, 1983 volume 7 number 8: 1, 2.
— historic photographs of Lahaina Town, Lahaina News, January 25, 1984: 7,8,9.
— history of summarized by Bob Kelsey, Lahaina News, February 29, 1984: 8.
— retrospective of how Lahaina was in 1959, 25 years ago, Lahaina News, August 15, 1984: 7,8,9.
— description of history and current situation, Lahaina News, December 4, 1985: 1,10.
— description of history and current situation, part 2 of 3, Lahaina News, December 11, 1985: 1,12,13.
— description of history and current situation, part 3 of 3, Lahaina News, December 18, 1985: 1,10,11.
— Charles O'Neal gives impressions after living in Lahaina five years, Lahaina News, March 5, 1986: 9.
— county and Army Corps of Engineers agree to ease traffic bottleneck, Lahaina News, April 8, 1987: 1.
— described as mini United States, Lahaina News, July 1, 1987: 4.
— study expected to be completed, Lahaina News, April 16, 1992: 3.
— to become twin city with Kaikoura, New Zealand, Lahaina News, April 23, 1992: 17.
— founding of, Lahaina News, April 23, 1992: B3,B4.
— history of, Lahaina News, April 23, 1992: B5.
— improvement plan goes to mayor Linda Lingle and Maui Council, Lahaina News, December 24, 1992: 3.
— police report that arrests are up, Lahaina News, March 24, 1994: 1.
— history of, Lahaina News, February 1, 1996: 10.
— history of printing at, Lahaina News, February 8, 1996: 12.
— biographies of John Manjiro and Joseph Heco, shipwrecked in mid-19 century, Lahaina News, February 8, 1996: 13.
— history of , Lahaina News, May 8, 1997: 2,18.
— gateway sign installed, Lahaina News, July 17, 1997: 1.
— anti-crime patrols walking, Lahaina News, June 17, 1999: 1,20.
— to establish sister city agreement with Kaikoura, New Zealand, Lahaina News, November 11, 1999: 1.
— Eddie Kamae filming documentary on, Lahaina News, December 9, 1999: 1,2.
— cruise ships to arrive at, Lahaina News, December 30, 1999: 13.
— history of the 1960s, part I, Lahaina News, February 24, 2000: 8.
— history of the 1960s, part I, Lahaina News, March 9, 2000: 4.
— history of the 1960s, part III, Lahaina News, April 6, 2000: 14.
— history of the 1960s, part IV, Lahaina News, April 20, 2000: 2.
— jeweler June Sarkin recalls Lahaina of the 1960s, Lahaina News, June 7, 2001: 3.

— Tom Hansen offers memories of, Part I, Lahaina News, August 2, 2001: 5.
— Tom Hansen offers memories of, Part I, Lahaina News, August 9, 2001: 5.
— Tom Hansen offers memories of, Part III, Lahaina News, August 16, 2001: 5.
— see also Front Street

LAHAINA ACTION COMMITTEE
— see LahainaTown Action Committee

LAHAINA ACUPUNCTURE AND MASSAGE CENTER [BUSINESS]
— featured, Lahaina News, October 10, 1984: 18.

LAHAINA ALOHA PATROL
— invites local politicians on evening patrol, Lahaina News, September 11, 2003: 2.

LAHAINA AMPHITHEATRE
— plans for housing development may jeopardize, Lahaina News, May 30, 1990: 1.

LAHAINA APPLIANCE, CO. [BUSINESS]
— opens, Lahaina News, December 19, 1990: 7.

LAHAINA AQUATIC CENTER
— groundbreaking ceremony held, Lahaina News, March 27, 1991: 1.
— to open, Lahaina News, April 16, 1992: 8.
— to hold grand opening, Lahaina News, July 2, 1992: 3.
— opens, Lahaina News, August 13, 1992: 1.
— new hours set, Lahaina News, August 27, 1992: 3.
— holds grand opening, Lahaina News, August 27, 1992: 7.
— waiting for equipment for chlorine system, Lahaina News, October 1, 1992: 3.
— playground equipment ordered, Lahaina News, April 29, 1993: 2.
— to be closed for Hawaii State Age Group Swimming Championships, Lahaina News, July 22, 1993: 9.
— expands hours, Lahaina News, June 9, 1994: 6.
— to host USSA Western Zone Age Group Swimming Championships, Lahaina News, July 21, 1994: 6.
— United States Swimming Association Western Zone Championship to be held at, Lahaina News, August 11, 1994: 6.
— results of Swimming Association Western Zone Championships, Lahaina News, August 25, 1994: 1.
— human waste found in pool, Lahaina News, December 1, 1994: 1.
— to bo closed to install non-slip surface, Lahaina News, May 18, 1995: 4.
— will not close for resurfacing, Lahaina News, May 25, 1995: 4.
— swimmers to meet at, Lahaina News, July 17, 1997: 14.
— hosts students on survival training, Lahaina News, November 27, 1997: 5.
— being used by Lahainaluna High School swimming program, Lahaina News, February 12, 1998: 14.
— temporary skateboard park established near, Lahaina News, March 26, 1998: 1.
— Maui Water Polo to practice at, Lahaina News, April 9, 1998: 15.
— proposed site for skateboard park, Lahaina News, April 16, 1998: 3.
— offering programs, Lahaina News, July 23, 1998: 15.
— to offer lessons, Lahaina News, November 26, 1998: 15.
— to close for swim meet, Lahaina News, October 7, 1999: 9.
— Valley Isle Masters Swimmers holds workouts at, Lahaina News, December 28, 2000: 6.
— to be closed for lifeguard training, Lahaina News, February 15, 2001: 13.
— to hold classes, Lahaina News, April 5, 2001: 14.
— offering swimming lessons, Lahaina News, May 10, 2001: 15.
— Senior Lifeguard Jack Spottswood featured, Lahaina News, July 12, 2001: 1,20.

— Texam Graham Johnston breaks two master swim world records at, Lahaina News, September 20, 2001: 13.
— to close for training, Lahaina News, March 7, 2002: 13.
— to hold free swimming lessons, Lahaina News, July 4, 2002: 13.
— to offer free swimming classes, Lahaina News, July 25, 2002: 15.
— Graham Johnston sets new world record at, Lahaina News, September 5, 2002: 13.
— to hold "Evening Splash", Lahaina News, February 27, 2003: 13.

LAHAINA ARMORY PARK
— to have playground added, Lahaina News, November 2, 1988: 1.

LAHAINA ART AND FRAME [BUSINESS]
— Jim Nash awarded certification by the Professional Picture Framers Association, Lahaina News, June 6, 1991: 17.

LAHAINA ART GALLERIES [BUSINESS]
— new Majime and Oshino Okuda display opens, Lahaina Sun, December 16, 1970: 3.
— featuring four artists in "The Age of Light" show, Lahaina News, July 26, 1989: 11.
— wins Pineapple Award for best Halloween display, Lahaina News, November 21, 1991: 11.
— hosting Ocean Art Festival, Lahaina News, January 9, 1992: 10.
— opening in Wailea Shopping Village, Lahaina News, August 5, 1993: 7.
— to host benefit for The Art School at Kapalua, Lahaina News, November 2, 1995: 11,12.
— to hold benefit for the Art School at Kapalua, Lahaina News, December 21, 1995: 14.
— featuring "Festival of Art and Flowers", Lahaina News, November 13, 1997: 21.
— to open new gallery, Lahaina News, July 29, 1999: 11.
— to open new flagship location, artists attending listed, Lahaina News, September 18, 2003: 14.
— to host local artists during "Friday Night is Art Night", Lahaina News, October 9, 2003: 18.

LAHAINA ART GLASS [BUSINESS]
— studio featured, Lahaina News, October 31, 1996: 21.

LAHAINA ARTS CENTER
— Galleries celebrates 20th anniversary, Lahaina News, February 13, 1985: 11.
— Galleries to hold first workshop of 1985, Lahaina News, February 20, 1985: 3.

LAHAINA ARTS SOCIETY
— displays work of James Warren, Lahaina Sun, November 18, 1970: 4.
— board of directors announced, Lahaina Sun, January 13, 1971: 7.
— organizing Beaux Arts Ball, Lahaina Sun, January 27, 1971: 2.
— offering free classes, Lahaina Sun, June 2, 1971: 7.
— creating plans for old Lahaina courthouse, Lahaina Sun, January 19, 1972: 16.
— photographs of summer education program, Lahaina Sun, August 2, 1972: 19.
— displays summarized, Lahaina News, November, 1979: 6.
— sponsors sandcastle contest, Lahaina News, December, 1979: 12.
— to hold benefit art auction, Lahaina News, January 15, 1982: 16.
— annual art scholarship offered, Lahaina News, April 15, 1982: 10.
— lease not renewed in Court House, Lahaina News, May 1, 1982: 2.
— hosts photography exhibit of Gary LaVarack's work, Lahaina News, May 2, 1984: 3.
— activities detailed, Lahaina News, November 21, 1984: 10.
— to hold craft fair, Lahaina News, January 23, 1985: 3.
— grants scholarships, Lahaina News, May 15, 1985: 20.
— offering classes at West Maui Youth Center, Lahaina News, May 22, 1985: 3.

— featuring "Butterfly Hula", Lahaina News, February 4, 1999: 16.

— to hold art fair, Lahaina News, May 6, 1999: 20.

— to hold classes, Lahaina News, May 6, 1999: 21.

— to hold 37th birthday party, Lahaina News, May 20, 1999: 1.

— officers installed, Sherrie Barnhard elected president of, Lahaina News, July 1, 1999: 3.

— to hold fairs, Lahaina News, August 12, 1999: 16.

— clashing with Lahaina Town Action Committee on use of Banyan Tree Park, Lahaina News, August 26, 1999: 1,20.

— to hold arts and crafts fairs, Lahaina News, November 18, 1999: 17.

— to host "Vision, Expression, Spirit" exhibit, Lahaina News, December 9, 1999: 17.

— continues to hold arts and crafts fairs at Banyan Tree, Lahaina News, December 9, 1999: 20.

— featuring artwork by Sherri Weiner, Russell Gourdine, and Putu Fisher, Lahaina News, December 9, 1999: 21.

— providing scholarships, Lahaina News, February 17, 2000: 15.

— awards scholarships, Lahaina News, May 11, 2000: 9.

— to offer classes to children, Lahaina News, May 18, 2000: 21.

— seeking board members, Lahaina News, May 25, 2000: 6.

— to hold free art classes, Lahaina News, June 1, 2000: 17.

— Peggy Robertson recounts origin of, Lahaina News, July 27, 2000: 19.

— welcomes new artists, Lahaina News, August 10, 2000: 8.

— invites new members, Lahaina News, August 17, 2000: 8.

— continues to hold arts and crafts fairs beneath the Banyan Tree, Lahaina News, January 25, 2001: 16.

— accepting entries for its High School Art and Senior High School Award Exhibit, Lahaina News, February 1, 2001: 17.

— offers free art classes for children, Lahaina News, February 15, 2001: 17.

— continues to offer free classes for children, Lahaina News, March 1, 2001: 21.

— to offer free art classes for children, Lahaina News, March 22, 2001: 17.

— to offer art classes, Lahaina News, May 10, 2001: 21.

— holds scholarship reception, Lahaina News, May 17, 2001: 16.

— Charles Lyon and Susan Kilmer to exhibit at, Lahaina News, June 7, 2001: 19.

— continues to offer art classes for children, Lahaina News, June 14, 2001: 21.

— offering free classes for children, Lahaina News, July 26, 2001: 17.

— offering free art classes, Lahaina News, August 23, 2001: 17.

— installs new officers, Lahaina News, August 23, 2001: 2.

— staging "The Power of Art", Lahaina News, November 1, 2001: 16.

— "The Power of Art" to be held, Lahaina News, November 8, 2001: 16.

— Mike Carroll is featured artist at, Lahaina News, December 6, 2001: 3.

— to offer free art classes for children, Lahaina News, December 20, 2001: 16.

— to hold arts and crafts fairs, Lahaina News, December 27, 2001: 16.

— showing "The Power of Art", Lahaina News, January 17, 2002: 17.

— sponsoring "Peace Mural Painting Day", Lahaina News, April 18, 2002: 17.

— accepting artwork from high school seniors for scholarship competition, Lahaina News, May 2, 2002: 2.

— to celebrate 40th anniversary, Lahaina News, May 9, 2002: 14.

— presents scholarships, Lahaina News, May 23, 2002: 2.

— to offer Outreach Art Program, Lahaina News, May 30, 2002: 3.

— continues to offer classes, Lahaina News, June 27, 2002: 16.

— continues to hold arts and crafts fairs at Banyan Tree Park, Lahaina News, July 11, 2002: 16.

— to hold art classes for children, Lahaina News, July 11, 2002: 17.

— Outreach Arts Programs continues, Lahaina News, August 22, 2002: 20.

— Outreach Arts Programs continues, Lahaina News, September 12, 2002: 20.

— to hold juried show "Celebrating Coastal and Shoreline Trees of Maui", Lahaina News, October 31, 2002: 24.

— to hold reception for "Celebrating Coastal and Shoreline Trees of Maui", Lahaina News, November 7, 2002: 20.

— continues to hold arts and crafts fairs at Banyan Tree Park, Lahaina News, November 21, 2002: 20.

— invites entries for "Coastal and Shoreline Trees", Lahaina News, December 26, 2002: 14.

— continues to hold arts and crafts fairs at Banyan Tree Park, Lahaina News, January 23, 2003: 16.

— Project Graduation to hold silent auction fundraiser, Lahaina News, February 13, 2003: 2.

— to award scholarships, Lahaina News, March 27, 2003: 14.

— continues to hold arts and crafts fairs at Banyan Tree Park, Lahaina News, April 10, 2003: 20.

— to feature artists Mark Murphy and Charlie Lyon, Lahaina News, May 1, 2003: 14.

— announces winners of Senior High School Scholarship Program, Lahaina News, May 22, 2003: 14.

— continues to hold arts and crafts fairs at Banyan Tree Park, Lahaina News, May 22, 2003: 16.

— to resume art classes, Lahaina News, July 10, 2003: 14.

— continues to offer art classes, Lahaina News, August 28, 2003: 17.

— continues to hold arts and crafts fairs at Banyan Tree Park, Lahaina News, September 18, 2003: 16.

— to award scholarships, Lahaina News, October 9, 2003: 18.

LAHAINA AUTO BODY AND PAINT [BUSINESS]

— opens, Lahaina News, December 26, 1996: 8.

LAHAINA AUTO CLASSIC

— to be held at West Maui Youth Center, Lahaina News, November 4, 1987: 3.

LAHAINA AUTOMOTIVE AND TOWING

— cited for lot full of junk cars, Lahaina News, July 9, 1986: 1,14.

LAHAINA BAGEL CAFFE [RESTAURANT]

— new name for Jack's Famous Bagels, Lahaina News, April 15, 1999: 11.

LAHAINA BANYAN TREE HOʻOLAULEʻA

— Aloha Festivals seeking crafters for, Lahaina News, August 28, 2003: 5.

LAHAINA BAPTIST CHURCH

— offered free child care so mothers could shop, Lahaina Sun, December 9, 1970: 4.

— Azusa Pacific College Dynamics Chorale perform, Lahaina Sun, June 16, 1971: 3.

— to hold Christmas service, Lahaina News, December 23, 1987: 3.

— to hold youth camp, Lahaina News, June 22, 1988: 2.

— to hold "Mid Summer's Night Sing", Lahaina News, August 10, 1988: 17.

— offering camp, Lahaina News, May 3, 1989: 3,4.

— to hold vacation Bible schools, Lahaina News, July 5, 1989: 3.

— to hold auction, Lahaina News, January 24, 1990: 5.

— to hold auction to benefit West Maui Youth summer camps, Lahaina News, January 31, 1990: 2.

— to hold auction, Lahaina News, February 7, 1990: 2.

— to hold seminar on parenting, Lahaina News, March 14, 1990: 3.

— women's mission group sponsoring Arts and Crafts Fair, Lahaina News, December 5, 1990: 3.

— training people willing to teach conversational English, Lahaina News, December 12, 1990: 4.

— to hold auction fundraiser for Youth Fund, Lahaina News, February 6, 1991: 3.

— to hold Hawaiian luau, Lahaina News, June 20, 1991: 3.

— to hold luau, Lahaina News, June 27, 1991: 4.

— to offer Bible school, Lahaina News, June 27, 1991: 4.

— youth group returns from youth camp in Oklahoma , Lahaina News, August 8, 1991: 5.

— to hold craft fair, Lahaina News, November 14, 1991: 2.

— deadline for craft fair approaching, Lahaina News, November 21, 1991: 3.

— to hold craft fair, Lahaina News, December 5, 1991: 4.

— sponsoring Christmas Cantata, Lahaina News, December 19, 1991: 5.

— conducting Vacation Bible School, Lahaina News, July 2, 1992: 4.

— women's mission group to hold Craft Fair, Lahaina News, October 15, 1992: 3.

— to hold Craft and Gift Fair, Lahaina News, December 3, 1992: 3.

— installs Craig Webb as new pastor, Lahaina News, February 2, 1995: 4.

— to hold Bible school, Lahaina News, June 29, 1995: 4.

— to hold "The Wild and Wonderful Good News Stampede", Lahaina News, June 26, 1997: 3.

— to hold "Mt. Extreme: The Ultimate Good News Challenge", Lahaina News, June 24, 1999: 2.

— to hold "Mt. Extreme: The Ultimate Good News Challenge", Lahaina News, July 1, 1999: 3.

— Mt. Extreme: Ultimate Good News Adventure Vacation Bible School held, Lahaina News, August 12, 1999: 8.

— Youth Group selling kalula turkeys to fund College Scholarship Fund, Lahaina News, November 18, 1999: 15.

— Youth Group to sell kalua turkeys, Lahaina News, November 25, 1999: 15.

— to hold Christmas Eve service, Lahaina News, December 23, 1999: 16.

— Youth Ministry to hold Spaghetti Dinner, Lahaina News, February 24, 2000: 17.

— choir to perform "A Christmas Cantata", Lahaina News, December 6, 2001: 16.

— to host Marriage and Family Enrichment Weekends by Phil and Susy Downer, Lahaina News, February 28, 2002: 5.

— holds canned food drive for Light Bringers, Lahaina News, January 23, 2003: 2.

— to present "Walk thru The Old Testament", Lahaina News, May 29, 2003: 9.

LAHAINA BEAD SHOP [BUSINESS]
— opens, Lahaina News, April 28, 1994: 9.

LAHAINA BED AND BREAKFAST
— see Old Lahaina House

LAHAINA BOOK EMPORIUM
— to celebrate one year anniversary, Lahaina News, January 7, 1999: 13.

LAHAINA BOOSTERS CLUB
— to hold kalua pig fundraiser, Lahaina News, February 13, 1991: 20.

LAHAINA BROADCASTING CO. [BUSINESS]
— purchases KLHI FM-101 following Dale Parsons losing asset, Lahaina News, May 12, 1994: 1.

— Federal Communications Commission ruling allows sale of KLHI to, Lahaina News, September 8, 1994: 1.

— completes purchase of KLHI-FM 101, Lahaina News, March 23, 1995: 10.

— Janet Sharon appointed accounts manager, Lahaina News, May 4, 1995: 13.

— Bernard Clark joins, Lahaina News, March 27, 1997: 10.

— acquires radio stations, Lahaina News, April 29, 1999: 13.

— changes name to Pacific Radio Group, Lahaina News, November 4, 1999: 11.

LAHAINA BROILER KARAOKE BAR [RESTAURANT]
— remodeled, Lahaina Sun, January 27, 1971: 2.

— reviewed, Lahaina News, December 28, 1988: 6.

— hosted by Tony Dee, Lahaina News, November 7, 1991: 16.

— continues to offer karaoke, Lahaina News, March 12, 1992: 17.

— to hold anniversary party, Lahaina News, September 24, 1992: 15,16.

LAHAINA BUSINESS AND PROFESSIONAL WOMEN'S CLUB
— rummage sale held, Lahaina Sun, April 21, 1971: 3.

— hosts county planner Chris Hart, Lahaina Sun, April 18, 1973: 4.

— to hold Easter Bake Sale, Lahaina News, March 26, 1986: 3.

— new officers installed, Lahaina News, June 22, 1988: 2.

— new officers installed, Lahaina News, June 21, 1989: 6.

— officers elected, Lahaina News, July 4, 1990: 7.

— selling Entertainment Book as fundraiser, Lahaina News, September 16, 1993: 3.

— to sell Entertainment Book to raise money for scholarship fund, Lahaina News, September 14, 1995: 11.

— selling Entertainment Book to fund scholarships, Lahaina News, October 5, 1995: 10.

— to sell Entertainment Book, Lahaina News, August 22, 1996: 4.

LAHAINA BUSINESS PARK
— industrial zoning request for is up for final approval, Lahaina News, May 9, 1996: 8.

— lots available at, Lahaina News, May 25, 2000: 11.

— construction begins at, Lahaina News, July 20, 2000: 13.

— construction of continues, Lahaina News, September 14, 2000: 15.

— construction of buildings to begin, Lahaina News, January 11, 2001: 13.

— Jerome Metcalfe proposes theme park for, Lahaina News, January 18, 2001: 14.

— lots available, Lahaina News, February 22, 2001: 8.

LAHAINA BYPASS
— proposed, Lahaina News, July 30, 1986: 1,11.

— public hearing set for October, Lahaina News, September 3, 1986: 16.

— options considered by Mayor Tavares, Lahaina News, October 1, 1986: 1.

— state recommends widening instead, Lahaina News, October 29, 1986: 1,5.

— upper route receives tentative approval by mayor's traffic committee, Lahaina News, December 3, 1986: 1.

— editorial in support of mauka route, Lahaina News, December 3, 1986: 2.

— account of project provided, Lahaina News, December 10, 1986: 1,14.

— call for citizen support of, Lahaina News, December 10, 1986: 1,14.

— editorial to Governor Waihee asking for support of, Lahaina News, December 10, 1986: 2.

— mayor Tavares calls on residents to lobby for, Lahaina News, December 31, 1986: 12.

— update on possible plans, Lahaina News, March 18, 1987: 1,7.

— State offers additional option, Lahaina News, June 3, 1987: 1.

— State chooses Alternate A-II , Lahaina News, July 15, 1987: 1.

— delays explained, Lahaina News, September 2, 1987: 1.

— first hearing set, Lahaina News, October 14, 1987: 1.

— discussed by representative Bill Pfeil, Lahaina News, October 21, 1987: 11.

— hearing to be held at Civic Center, Lahaina News, October 28, 1987: 20.

— results from public hearing at Lahaina Civic Center, Lahaina News, November 4, 1987: 1.

— editorial in support of, Lahaina News, November 18, 1987: 2.

— Department of Transportation to speed up construction of, Lahaina News, January 20, 1988: 1.

LAHAINA CANNERY SHOPPING CENTER [BUSINESS]

— to feature multi-ethnic performance, Lahaina News, August 1, 1990: 11.

— to host Jerry Lewis Muscular Dystrophy Telethon, Lahaina News, August 29, 1990: 3.

— to host Festival of Trees, Lahaina News, December 19, 1990: 3.

— introduces Kama'aina card, Lahaina News, February 6, 1991: 3.

— to celebrate 4th anniversary with Ho'ike Maui festival of Hawaiian life and culture, Lahaina News, March 6, 1991: 11.

— Ho'ike Maui festival continues, Lahaina News, March 13, 1991: 8.

— presenting body building and bikini contest, Lahaina News, May 15, 1991: 4.

— results of Body Building and Bikini Contest announced, Lahaina News, May 30, 1991: 4.

— to host karaoke contest, Lahaina News, December 5, 1991: 4.

— to celebrate 5th anniversary and hold pineapple festival, Lahaina News, March 12, 1992: 7.

— pineapple baking contest won by Mitchum, Lahaina News, April 23, 1992: 16.

— karaoke contest winners announced, Lahaina News, June 11, 1992: 3.

— hosts ice carving competition, Lahaina News, December 3, 1992: 1.

— to host Children's Day, Lahaina News, September 8, 1994: 12.

— to host children's craft and fun fair, Lahaina News, September 22, 1994: 15.

— to celebrate eighth year, Lahaina News, March 23, 1995: 11.

— celebrates 8th year, Lahaina News, March 30, 1995: 11,12.

— to host Kid's Day, Lahaina News, September 14, 1995: 11.

— celebrating Halloween, Lahaina News, October 26, 1995: insert5.

— hosting pineapple carving contest, Lahaina News, November 9, 1995: 12.

— sponsors "Celebration of Youth and the Arts", Lahaina News, January 18, 1996: 4.

— Children's Fair to be offered by Hawaii Association for the Education of Young Children, Lahaina News, January 25, 1996: 4.

— to host hula show, Lahaina News, February 22, 1996: 14.

— to hold keiki fingerprinting, Lahaina News, October 17, 1996: 14.

— hosts Bishop Museum's "Na Mamo, Today's Hawaiian People" exhibit, Lahaina News, October 17, 1996: 5.

— to host jazz concerts, Lahaina News, February 20, 1997: 10.

— to celebrate 10th anniversary, Lahaina News, March 13, 1997: 17.

— celebrates 10th anniversary, Lahaina News, March 20, 1997: 16.

— sponsoring keiki essay contest, Lahaina News, June 5, 1997: 15.

— Summer Flower Fair to be held, Lahaina News, July 10, 1997: 17.

— to hold Wood Carving Competition, Lahaina News, October 2, 1997: 18.

— to hold "Shoot for the Stars Talent Competition", Lahaina News, October 30, 1997: 16.

— sponsoring holiday events, Lahaina News, December 4, 1997: 24.

— celebrating 11 years, Lahaina News, March 12, 1998: 8.

— offering "Safety Kids' Day", Lahaina News, May 21, 1998: 13.

— results of lei making contest, Lahaina News, May 21, 1998: 13.

— to be renovated, Lahaina News, June 11, 1998: 13.

— offers McGruff coloring contest, Lahaina News, June 11, 1998: 2.

— to host Ice Carving Competition, Lahaina News, June 11, 1998: 2.

— to host "Tropical Fruit Festival, Lahaina News, July 9, 1998: 17.

— to hold Children's Fair, Lahaina News, July 23, 1998: 16.

— Kolbert/Hanssen/Mitchell Architectures of Oahu to lead renovations of, Lahaina News, October 29, 1998: 13.

— to host Festival of Hula, Lahaina News, January 28, 1999: 5.

— celebrates completion of renovation, Lahaina News, February 4, 1999: 5.

— new stores to open, Lahaina News, April 8, 1999: 11.

— continues to offer keiki hula shows, Lahaina News, July 8, 1999: 12.

— planning "Hawaii Traditions" month, Lahaina News, August 5, 1999: 12.

— to hold Hawaii cooking demonstrations, Lahaina News, August 26, 1999: 16.

— commemorating 13th anniversary, Lahaina News, March 9, 2000: 12.

— to host 'ukulele contest, Lahaina News, April 6, 2000: 14.

— holds Millennium Essay Contest, Lahaina News, May 11, 2000: 17.

— to host Mother's Day activities, Lahaina News, May 11, 2000: 20.

— holds Lei Making Contest, Lahaina News, May 18, 2000: 8.

— to host Job Fair, Lahaina News, July 6, 2000: 16.

— continues to feature Polynesian dancing, Lahaina News, July 6, 2000: 17.

— celebrating "Hawaii Traditions", Lahaina News, August 10, 2000: 16.

— to hold "Hawaiian Tradition" demonstrations, Lahaina News, August 17, 2000: 1.

— results of "Bingo All the Way" , Lahaina News, January 18, 2001: 14.

— Valentine's Day to be celebrated at, Lahaina News, February 8, 2001: 20.

— Darren Konno appointed marketing manager at, Lahaina News, February 15, 2001: 8.

— turns 14, Lahaina News, March 22, 2001: 8.

— holds "Count the Grains of Rice" contest, Lahaina News, April 12, 2001: 8.

— to celebrate Lei Day, Lahaina News, April 26, 2001: 17.

— to host Kamehameha Day events, Lahaina News, June 7, 2001: 20.

— to host Island Style Jazz Festival, Lahaina News, June 21, 2001: 14.

— to host "Maui Made Product Show", Lahaina News, July 26, 2001: 17.

— to hold Coffee Festival, Lahaina News, August 2, 2001: 9.

— to hold "That's My Baby" and "That's My Toddler" contest, Lahaina News, September 20, 2001: 16,17.

— to host Santa, Lahaina News, December 6, 2001: 14.

— Donald Andrus wins grand prize in "Jingle Balls Rock" promotion at, Lahaina News, January 3, 2002: 8.

— to host hula festival, Lahaina News, January 17, 2002: 14.

— planning 15th anniversary, Lahaina News, February 28, 2002: 14.

— to celebrate Lei Day, Lahaina News, May 16, 2002: 18.

— restaurants at Pineapple Court featured, Part I, Lahaina News, June 6, 2002: 8,9.

— restaurants at Pineapple Court featured, Part I, Lahaina News, June 13, 2002: 8,9.

— to hold "Journeys to Polynesia", Lahaina News, August 8, 2002: 14.

— to hold "HI-Tech Fair", Lahaina News, September 12, 2002: 20.

— plans "That's My Baby!" contest, Lahaina News, September 19, 2002: 17.

— to hold "Cannery Kids Night", Lahaina News, October 24, 2002: 21.

— to offer "Cannery Kids Night", Lahaina News, October 31, 2002: 29.

— planning holiday events, Lahaina News, December 5, 2002: 2.

— to host pictures with Santa, Lahaina News, December 12, 2002: 20.

— to hold holiday activities, Lahaina News, December 19, 2002: 17.

— to hold Festival of Hula, Lahaina News, January 16, 2003: 14.

— to celebrate Chinese New Year, Lahaina News, January 30, 2003: 14.

— to host drum festival, Lahaina News, February 20, 2003: 16.

— to celebrate 16th anniversary, Lahaina News, March 20, 2003: 9.

— to hold yo-yo contest, Lahaina News, April 10, 2003: 10.

— to celebrate 16th anniversary, Lahaina News, April 10, 2003: 14.

— to host Kids Day America, Lahaina News, May 15, 2003: 14.

— to hold "Summer Show", Lahaina News, June 19, 2003: 14.

— to hold "Summer Show", Lahaina News, June 26, 2003: 16.

— Keiki Hula Festival to be held at, Lahaina News, July 10, 2003: 15.

— to host Journey to the Orient, Lahaina News, August 7, 2003: 14.

LAHAINA CANOE CLUB

— obtains new outrigger canoes, Lahaina Sun, June 7, 1972: 7.

— planning new canoe shed, Lahaina Sun, June 21, 1972: 14.

— committed to preservation of Hawaiian culture, Lahaina Sun, August 30, 1972: 9.

— new canoes launched, Lahaina Sun, September 20, 1972: 10.

— victorious in canoe races, Lahaina Sun, July 11, 1973: 20.

— hold fourth annual restaurant canoe race, Lahaina News, May 9, 1984: 4.

— begins season, Lahaina News, March 13, 1985: 7.

— acquires new Hawaiian Rocket canoe, Lahaina News, May 22, 1985: 4.

— to hold breakfast fundraiser, Lahaina News, August 28, 1985: 4.

— keiki division to hold breakfast fundraiser, Lahaina News, October 16, 1985: 3.

— fundraiser has been rescheduled, Lahaina News, November 6, 1985: 3.

— to hold general membership meeting, Lahaina News, January 15, 1986: 3.

— activities set, Lahaina News, April 9, 1986: 3.

— to hold general meeting, Lahaina News, January 28, 1987: 3.

— meeting postponed due to bad weather, Lahaina News, February 4, 1987: 11.

— to hold general meeting, Lahaina News, March 4, 1987: 3.

— to hold annual breakfast, Lahaina News, April 8, 1987: 20.

— junior women take state title, Lahaina News, August 12, 1987: 6.

— Women's Moloka'i Crew thanks businesses for support, Lahaina News, October 28, 1987: 3.

— general membership meeting, Lahaina News, February 17, 1988: 18.

— to host annual Eggs Benedict Breakfast, Lahaina News, April 6, 1988: 20.

— to hold Keiki O Maui Canoe Regatta, Lahaina News, June 15, 1988: 6.

— to hold practices, Lahaina News, March 8, 1989: 3.

— to hold fundraiser, Lahaina News, April 5, 1989: 3.

— looking for volunteers, Lahaina News, September 20, 1989: 24.

— to hold 10th Annual Restaurant Canoe Race, Lahaina News, May 2, 1990: 6.

— sponsoring Keiki O Maui Regatta, Lahaina News, June 13, 1990: 8.

— to hold annual general meeting, Lahaina News, February 13, 1991: 20.

— to hold auction, Lahaina News, March 27, 1991: 8.

— attempting to locate charter members, Lahaina News, May 30, 1991: 1.

— planning 20th anniversary, Lahaina News, June 6, 1991: 2,7.

— celebrates 20 years, Lahaina News, June 27, 1991: 4.

— founder Earl Kukahiko featured, Lahaina News, June 25, 1992: 10.

— hires new coach; begins recruiting, Lahaina News, April 22, 1993: 7.

— to hold Restaurant Race, Lahaina News, April 29, 1993: 6.

— to begin 1994 season, Lahaina News, January 27, 1994: 6.

— featured, Lahaina News, May 5, 1994: 8.

— Senior Masters crew featured, Lahaina News, July 7, 1994: 6.

— coach Tim Garcia featured, Lahaina News, May 11, 1995: 7.

— paddling season to begin, Lahaina News, February 22, 1996: 7.

— to hold Restaurant Canoe Races, Lahaina News, April 18, 1996: 12.

— featured, Lahaina News, April 25, 1996: 9.

— to hold benefit breakfast, Lahaina News, July 25, 1996: 13.

— to participate in Restaurant Race, Lahaina News, May 1, 1997: 16.

— featured, Lahaina News, May 15, 1997: 11.

— to hold "Restaurant Races", Lahaina News, April 30, 1998: 15.

— focusing on rebuilding, Lahaina News, May 28, 1998: 6.

— hosting Honokohau Race, Lahaina News, March 18, 1999: 14.

— Paul "Buff" Weaver joins, Lahaina News, June 3, 1999: 14.

— to hold Restaurant Races, Lahaina News, May 4, 2000: 14.

— optimistic about season, Lahaina News, June 22, 2000: 13.

— raises money with breakfast at Leilani's on the Beach, Lahaina News, April 5, 2001: 2.

— to hold annual Restaurant Race, Lahaina News, April 19, 2001: 13.

— to hold Restaurant Race, Lahaina News, April 26, 2001: 15.

— to hold Restaurant Races, Lahaina News, May 3, 2001: 15.

— to hold Restaurant Races, Lahaina News, May 3, 2001: 20.

— hosts Keiki O Maui regatta, Lahaina News, June 21, 2001: 1.

— featured, Lahaina News, June 21, 2001: 12.

— celebrating 30th year, Lahaina News, August 16, 2001: 1.

— featured, Lahaina News, July 4, 2002: 12.

— to hold Restaurant Races, Lahaina News, April 10, 2003: 10.

— featured, Lahaina News, June 19, 2003: 12.

LAHAINA CARDINALS [BASEBALL TEAM]

— results of season given, Lahaina News, July 9, 1986: 4.

LAHAINA CARPET AND INTERIORS [BUSINESS]

— featured, Lahaina News, May 30, 1984: 20.

— featured, Lahaina News, August 29, 2002: 14.

LAHAINA CARTAGE COMPANY [BUSINESS]

— new name for Maui Go-For Service, Lahaina News, April 22, 1993: 6.

LAHAINA CENTER

— chooses Sofos Realty as property management company, Lahaina News, June 20, 1990: 7.

— over half of the space has been leased at, Lahaina News, January 30, 1991: 5.

— to hold Superbowl Supersavings, Lahaina News, January 23, 1992: 4.

— Linda Patton and Cheryl Stay win St. Patrick's Day Lahaina Center, Lahaina News, April 16, 1992: 15.

— Fashion/Dance Extravaganza featuring Miss Hawaii Heather Hays, Lahaina News, May 7, 1992: 19.

— to host Christmas Karaoke Contest , Lahaina News, November 26, 1992: 22,23.

— hosting Christmas entertainment, Lahaina News, December 17, 1992: 2,4.

— Aloha Festival Essay Contest held, Lahaina News, November 11, 1993: 3.

— scheduling events, Lahaina News, December 9, 1993: 11.

— opens Hale Kahiko, Lahaina News, January 23, 1997: 16.

— looking for artists and crafters, Lahaina News, April 20, 2000: 2.

— continues to offer Aloha Friday Keiki Hula shows, Lahaina News, February 21, 2002: 16.

— continues to hold Keiki Hula Shows, Lahaina News, June 26, 2003: 20.

LAHAINA CHILD CARE CENTER

— received to ceremonial flags from the Lahaina Community Action Program, Lahaina Sun, June 16, 1971: 12.

LAHAINA CHRISTIAN FELLOWSHIP

— free concert with Paul Clark, Lahaina News, February 17, 1988: 18.

— to sponsor Bible teaching, Lahaina News, September 14, 1988: 15.

— to hold "Da Last Blast" party, Lahaina News, August 14, 1997: 2.

LAHAINA CINEMAS THEATER [BUSINESS]

— theatres reviewed, Lahaina News, March 1, 1989: 6.

— hosts Summer Pals program, Lahaina News, August 22, 2002: 14.

LAHAINA CITIZENS ADVISORY COMMITTEE

— focuses on environmental problems, Lahaina News, July 23, 1992: 12.

— to hold final meetings, Lahaina News, October 29, 1992: 6.

— meet to discuss regional issues, Lahaina News, January 19, 1995: 1,16.

— resists County plans for Napili Regional Park, Lahaina News, May 11, 1995: 6.

LAHAINA CIVIC AND RECREATION CENTER
— construction begins on first phase, Lahaina Sun, December 23, 1970: 10.
— should be completed soon, includes photographs, Lahaina Sun, November 10, 1971: 11.
— to get new chain link fence, Lahaina News, May 30, 1984: 22.
— construction scheduled to make it handicapped accessible, Lahaina News, September 12, 1984: 3.
— to hold "Open Gym", Lahaina News, December 28, 2000: 16.
— gymnasium to close for upgrades, Lahaina News, August 14, 2003: 12.

LAHAINA CIVIC CENTER AMPHITHEATER
— audience size limited and no alcohol allowed at, Lahaina News, October 16, 1985: 1.

LAHAINA CLINIC
— Maui Medical Group has new services and equipment, Lahaina News, November 19, 1998: 3.

LAHAINA CLUB, THE
— raises money for Lahainaluna High School to install ceiling fans, Lahaina News, April 3, 2003: 1,20.

LAHAINA COBBLER [BUSINESS]
— opens, Lahaina News, December 10, 1986: 3.

LAHAINA COMMUNITY ACTION PROGRAM
— presents two ceremonial flags to Lahaina Child Care Center, Lahaina Sun, June 16, 1971: 12.
— organizing wholesale buying club for food, Lahaina Sun, August 9, 1972: 7.

LAHAINA COMMUNITY PLAN
— debated by Maui County Council, Lahaina News, September 14, 1983: 7.
— okayed by County Council Planning Committee, heading to public hearing, Lahaina News, September 28, 1983: 5.
— discussed in feature article, Lahaina News, October 5, 1983: 7,8,9.
— residents support plan, Lahaina News, November 9, 1983: 3,4.
— on Maui County Council agenda for December 2, Lahaina News, November 16, 1983: 6.
— passed by Maui County Council planning committee, Lahaina News, November 23, 1983: 4,5.
— approved by Maui County Council and sent to major for signature, Lahaina News, December 21, 1983: 7.
— signed by mayor Tavares, is now law, Lahaina News, February 1, 1984: 12.
— West Side condo managers seek amendment to, Lahaina News, September 30, 1987: 1.
— residents seek revision of, Lahaina News, May 10, 1989: 1.
— to be reviewed by committee of citizens, Lahaina News, June 21, 1989: 3.
— set to be revised by Maui County, Lahaina News, February 20, 1991: 1.
— Maui County Council's planning committee plans to reactivate citizen's advisory committee, Lahaina News, March 20, 1991: 1.
— revisions sought to add more parks, Lahaina News, May 21, 1992: 1.
— debates over fate of Mala Wharf, Lahaina News, October 15, 1992: 1.
— advisory committee designates land at North Beach to park, Lahaina News, October 29, 1992: 1.
— advisory committee rejects Olowalu Park, Lahaina News, October 29, 1992: 1.
— advisory committee rejects shopping center proposed by Weinberg Foundation, Lahaina News, October 29, 1992: 3.
— almost completed, Lahaina News, December 3, 1992: 1,3.
— Maui Planning Commission to hold public hearing, Lahaina News, September 16, 1993: 3.

LAHAINA COMMUNITY PLAN CITIZEN ADVISORY COMMITTEE
— vote to designate Camp Pecusa as beach park fails at, Lahaina News, October 15, 1992: 1.
— defers decisions on vertical takeoff aircrafts and proposed residential community near Kihei Elementary School, Lahaina News, October 29, 1992: 17.
— moves to erase dormant project districts, Lahaina News, November 5, 1992: 3.
— designates area near Mala Wharf for small boat harbor, Lahaina News, November 5, 1992: 4.
— drafts letter to Amfac/JMB concerning Puʻukoliʻi Village project, Lahaina News, December 24, 1992: 4.

LAHAINA COMMUNITY SWIMMING POOL
— to hold membership drive, pushing for public pool in Lahaina, Lahaina News, January 29, 1986: 3.
— elect officers, Lahaina News, February 12, 1986: 1.
— to hold annual membership meeting, Lahaina News, March 4, 1987: 3.
— campaign for swimming pool, Lahaina News, March 23, 1988: 1.
— continues attempts to build pool, Lahaina News, May 18, 1988: 1.
— receives surplus money from Greater Lahaina Reunion, Lahaina News, June 8, 1988: 3.
— architect's conceptual drawing of, Lahaina News, July 18, 1990: 1.
— construction begins, Lahaina News, January 16, 1991: 1.
— attempts to reduce costs, Lahaina News, February 20, 1991: 1.
— breaks ground, Lahaina News, March 20, 1991: 1.
— photo of groundbreaking ceremony, Lahaina News, November 7, 1991: 3.
— opening this summer, Lahaina News, March 5, 1992: 8.
— see also swimming pools

LAHAINA COMMUNITY THANKSGIVING
— service to be held, Lahaina News, November 28, 1996: 10.

LAHAINA COMPREHENSIVE HEALTH CENTER
— opens, Lahaina News, July 23, 1986: 1,3.
— continues to offer HIV counseling and testing, Lahaina News, June 24, 1999: 13.
— continues to offer HIV Counseling and Testing Clinic, Lahaina News, September 14, 2000: 21.
— continues to offer free HIV counseling and testing, Lahaina News, December 28, 2000: 16.
— offering HIV Counseling and Testing Clinics, Lahaina News, November 14, 2002: 21.

LAHAINA COOLERS [RESTAURANT]
— opens in Dickenson Square, Lahaina News, March 8, 1989: 17.
— reviewed, Lahaina News, April 19, 1989: 8.
— to hold Beach Party, Lahaina News, May 3, 1989: 8.
— reviewed, Lahaina News, July 19, 1989: 13.
— featured, Lahaina News, November 15, 1989: 15.
— planning special Valentine's Day, Lahaina News, January 24, 1990: 12.
— serving heart-shaped pizzas for Valentine's Day, Lahaina News, February 7, 1990: 13.
— reviewed, Lahaina News, May 16, 1990: 12.
— adopts new menu, Lahaina News, August 8, 1990: 14,24.
— to hold Blue Marlin Bash, Lahaina News, September 19, 1990: 10.
— sponsors Historic 5K Lahaina Run/Walk, Lahaina News, September 26, 1990: 14.
— to hold Lahaina Coolers Historic Fun Run, Lahaina News, October 3, 1990: 1.
— sponsoring run touring historic sites of Lahaina, Lahaina News, October 10, 1990: 24.
— to present laser show for Halloween, Lahaina News, October 31, 1990: 13.
— offering Christmas dinner, Lahaina News, December 19, 1990: 14.

— adds to menu, Lahaina News, January 30, 1991: 7.
— to hold Beach Party Weekend, Lahaina News, May 15, 1991: 10.
— changes menu, Lahaina News, July 25, 1991: 11.
— to host Blue Marlin Bash, Lahaina News, September 5, 1991: 9.
— seeking volunteers for Historic Fun Run, Lahaina News, September 12, 1991: 3.
— sponsoring Historic Fun Run, Lahaina News, September 12, 1991: 6.
— looking for volunteers for Fun Run, Lahaina News, September 19, 1991: 3.
— Historic Fun Run detailed, Lahaina News, September 19, 1991: 6,7.
— to expand, Lahaina News, March 12, 1992: 11,12.
— promotes John Hearne to general manager, Lahaina News, July 23, 1992: 17.
— to host Blue Marlin Bash, Lahaina News, September 10, 1992: 17.
— seeking volunteers for Historic Fun Run, Lahaina News, October 1, 1992: 3.
— Historic Fun Run to occur at start of Aloha Festival, Lahaina News, October 8, 1992: 4.
— to offer laser show for Halloween, Lahaina News, October 29, 1992: 19.
— featured, Lahaina News, November 5, 1992: 18.
— celebrates fourth anniversary, Lahaina News, March 11, 1993: 12.
— to host Beach Party Weekend, Lahaina News, May 13, 1993: 10.
— to hold goodbye party for crew of Kelea, Lahaina News, June 17, 1993: 15.
— to hold Historic Fun Run, seeking volunteers, Lahaina News, September 16, 1993: 14.
— to host Blue Marlin Bash, Lahaina News, September 16, 1993: 17.
— to hold Blue Marlin Bash, Lahaina News, September 23, 1993: 11.
— to hold Historic Fun Run, Lahaina News, October 7, 1993: 7.
— Historic Fun Run results, Lahaina News, October 21, 1993: 13.
— featuring German beer for Octoberfest, Lahaina News, October 21, 1993: 15.
— celebrates five years, Lahaina News, April 21, 1994: 9.
— hosts Beach Party Weekend, Lahaina News, May 19, 1994: 15.
— to host "Blue Marlin Bash", Lahaina News, September 22, 1994: 15.
— to host Historic Lahaina Fun Run, Lahaina News, October 13, 1994: 10.
— photograph of Lahaina Historic Fun Run, Lahaina News, October 20, 1994: 8.
— staging "Coolers Cabaret", Lahaina News, December 8, 1994: 16.
— to host "Coolers Cabaret", Lahaina News, December 15, 1994: 17.
— celebrates 6th birthday, Lahaina News, April 20, 1995: 11.
— to host Historic Fun Run/Walk, Lahaina News, October 19, 1995: 6.
— sold by Gail Coe and Nicholai Mathison, Lahaina News, October 26, 1995: 1,16.
— to hold Christmas dinner, Lahaina News, December 21, 1995: 14.
— celebrating Mother's Day, Lahaina News, May 2, 1996: 10.
— featured, Lahaina News, December 5, 1996: 7,9.
— featured, Lahaina News, March 4, 1999: 5.
— Stacy Knight wins Las Vegas Challenge, Lahaina News, July 4, 2002: 18.
— Ken Hultquist wins Las Vegas Challenge, Lahaina News, August 8, 2002: 18.

LAHAINA COOLERS HISTORIC FUN RUN
— to be held, Lahaina News, October 17, 1996: 15.
— to be held, Lahaina News, October 17, 1996: 2.
— to be held, Lahaina News, October 24, 1996: 12.

LAHAINA COOLERS LAS VEGAS CHALLENGE
— preliminary round held, Lahaina News, September 5, 2002: 18.

LAHAINA CRIME WATCH
— patrol expanding, Lahaina News, February 22, 2001: 1,3.

LAHAINA DELI [RESTAURANT]
— robbed, Lahaina Sun, December 8, 1971: 17.

LAHAINA DIVERS [BUSINESS]
— Lynn Laymon contributes footage to music video, Lahaina News, November 1, 1989: 24.
— begins environmental program, Lahaina News, July 25, 1990: 7.
— to open second store, Lahaina News, December 19, 1990: 7.
— purchases Central Pacific Divers, Lahaina News, May 1, 1991: 7.
— to offer trainings to persons with handicaps with Handicapped Scuba Association, Lahaina News, July 4, 1991: 5.
— to offer trainings to persons with handicaps with Handicapped Scuba Association, Lahaina News, August 15, 1991: 4.
— to include Elite Dive, Lahaina News, November 7, 1991: 7.
— to include "elite dive" in charter schedule, Lahaina News, December 5, 1991: 19.
— owner Kim Roberts seeks artificial reef for Puamana , Lahaina News, January 2, 1992: 3.
— adds new charter boat, Lahaina News, April 1, 1993: 8.
— publishes dive map, Lahaina News, August 5, 1993: 8.
— opens new headquarters, Lahaina News, September 16, 1993: 10.
— to offer dive trip to Molokini, Lahaina News, June 23, 1994: 11.
— to host reef cleanup, Lahaina News, September 29, 1994: 5.
— to sponsor reef clean-up, Lahaina News, October 19, 1995: 4.
— seeking divers to help with reef cleanup, Lahaina News, September 5, 1996: 19.
— Laura Scott joins, Lahaina News, June 26, 1997: 14.

LAHAINA ELEMENTARY SCHOOL
— construction of new grade school begins, Lahaina News, October 21, 1987: 1.
— receives money from State for construction, Lahaina News, May 15, 1991: 1.

LAHAINA EXPRESS [BUSINESS]
— expands transportation service, Lahaina News, March 24, 1994: 8.

LAHAINA FARMER'S MARKET
— to be held, Lahaina News, October 13, 1994: 6.
— to be held at Wharf Cinema Center, Lahaina News, August 10, 2000: 17.
— to be held at Wharf Cinema Center, Lahaina News, August 31, 2000: 21.

LAHAINA FASHIONS [BUSINESS]
— complaint filed against by Maui Planning Commission and Maui County Council for selling from display booths, Lahaina News, October 9, 1985: 3.
— sold to Kaupo Ranch, Lahaina News, February 7, 2002: 8.

LAHAINA FEDERAL CREDIT UNION [BUSINESS]
— annual membership meeting, Lahaina Sun, February 17, 1971: 4.
— to hold annual general meeting, Lahaina News, March 11, 1999: 11.

LAHAINA FIRE STATION
— see Fire and Ambulance Station, Lahaina

LAHAINA FISH COMPANY [BUSINESS]
— requesting special license to have music and entertainment, Lahaina News, October 24, 1990: 4.

LAHAINA FISH MARKET
— sold to Patrick Ballenger, Lahaina Sun, January 31, 1973: 13.

LAHAINA FISHING SUPPLY [BUSINESS]
— has new owners, Lahaina News, July 2, 1992: 16,18.

LAHAINA FLORIST [BUSINESS]
— described, Lahaina News, October 11, 1989: 12.

LAHAINA FOREIGN CARS [BUSINESS]
— featured, Lahaina News, September 12, 1984: 14.

LAHAINA FORT
— historical marker for, discussed , Lahaina Sun, December 16, 1970: 6.

LAHAINA FOUNDATION GALLERY [BUSINESS]
— to open, Lahaina News, April 10, 1991: 6.

LAHAINA GIRLS MENEHUNE LEAGUE
— basketball team to hold tryouts, Lahaina News, November 4, 1999: 7.

LAHAINA GRILL [RESTAURANT]
— see David Paul's Lahaina Grill [restaurant]

LAHAINA GROWN [MUSICAL GROUP]
— to perform at Borders Books, Lahaina News, May 25, 2000: 18.

LAHAINA HAIRSTYLISTS [BUSINESS]
— to donate $1 from each job to Salvation Army, Lahaina News, November 28, 1990: 3.
— donating $1 per job to Salvation Army, Lahaina News, December 5, 1990: 5.
— purchased by Dee Merriles, Lahaina News, June 13, 1991: 9.
— to close, Lahaina News, December 26, 1996: 8.

LAHAINA HARBOR
— ocean floor studied in anticipation of building new small boat harbor, Lahaina Sun, November 18, 1970: 4.
— tested for pollution, Lahaina Sun, December 16, 1970: 3.
— construction of new docking facility, Lahaina Sun, December 30, 1970: 8.
— criticism of plan to move showers at Lahaina small boat harbor outside, Lahaina Sun, April 21, 1971: 4.
— request for federal funds turned down, Lahaina Sun, October 13, 1971: 1.
— plan for in Lahaina given go-ahead, Lahaina Sun, March 29, 1972: 3.
— safety concerns over electric conduit, Lahaina Sun, August 2, 1972: 22.
— described in large pull-out section, Lahaina News, March 1, 1983: 7,8,9,10.
— painted by Gorham Gilman in 1850s, Lahaina News, January 11, 1984: 7,8,9.
— to be dredged, Lahaina News, May 11, 1988: 3.
— permit to expand sought, Lahaina News, July 27, 1988: 1.
— bids soon to be let for fuel tank , Lahaina News, October 19, 1988: 1,24.
— channel closed for maintenance dredging, Lahaina News, November 9, 1988: 1.
— no bids to run fuel station, Lahaina News, December 7, 1988: 6.
— Native Hawaiian Plant Shop to hold cleanup, Lahaina News, February 8, 1989: 3.
— issues with fuel pollution discussed, Lahaina News, April 19, 1989: 1,13.
— improvements include new Harbormaster's Office, Lahaina News, April 19, 1989: 13.
— dedication ceremony planned, Lahaina News, April 26, 1989: 1.
— Maui Oil Company to provide fuel as stop-gap measure, Lahaina News, July 5, 1989: 1.
— editorial urging state to fund refueling facility, Lahaina News, July 5, 1989: 8.
— Local Motion Boogie Board Bash held, Lahaina News, August 2, 1989: 6.
— to get automated fueling area, Lahaina News, October 18, 1989: 1.
— contract awarded to build automated fueling facility, Lahaina News, November 22, 1989: 28.
— taker proposed to refuel boats, Lahaina News, January 3, 1990: 3.
— fuel tanker would need permit, Lahaina News, January 10, 1990: 1.
— R.I. Namba Construction, Inc. awarded contract by Department of Transportation to remove abandoned pipes in Lahaina Harbor, Lahaina News, January 24, 1990: 6.
— sewage and waste oil dumping facilities planned, Lahaina News, May 23, 1990: 7.
— state refuses to open public restroom facility on 24-hour basis, Lahaina News, June 27, 1990: 3.
— Sea Princess scheduled to arrive, Lahaina News, October 10, 1990: 11.
— Atlantis Submarines to begin operating in, Lahaina News, October 10, 1990: 8.
— passenger ships to arrive, Lahaina News, November 21, 1990: 11,12.
— cruise ships to arrive, Lahaina News, January 9, 1991: 5.
— passenger ships Vistafjor and Crown Odyssey set to arrive, Lahaina News, January 23, 1991: 5.
— Crown Odyssey scheduled to debark, Lahaina News, January 30, 1991: 4.
— Crown Odyssey scheduled to debark, Lahaina News, February 6, 1991: 6.
— Royal Viking Sky to debark, Lahaina News, March 13, 1991: 7.
— Pacific Princess to debark, Lahaina News, March 20, 1991: 6.
— Pacific Princess to debark, Lahaina News, March 27, 1991: 9.
— Pacific Princess to debark, Lahaina News, April 10, 1991: 6.
— Pacific Princess to debark, Lahaina News, April 17, 1991: 9.
— Pacific Princess to debark, reception planned, Lahaina News, May 1, 1991: 7.
— Pacific Princess to debark, reception planned, Lahaina News, May 8, 1991: 6.
— Royal Viking ship to arrive, Lahaina News, May 15, 1991: 8.
— Royal Viking ship to arrive, Lahaina News, June 6, 1991: 6.
— Royal Viking Sky ship to arrive, Lahaina News, June 13, 1991: 10.
— state Legislature authorizes money for improvements of, Lahaina News, July 18, 1991: 1.
— sewage dump linked to inaction of harbors division, Lahaina News, August 8, 1991: 1.
— fueling facility to be constructed, Lahaina News, August 8, 1991: 1,4.
— State harbors official Dave Parsons reviews lack of restrooms, Lahaina News, August 22, 1991: 1.
— State Harbors division demonstrates that sewage pump works, Lahaina News, August 29, 1991: 1.
— bathroom still under construction, Lahaina News, September 26, 1991: 1.
— New Amsterdam [ship] to arrive, Lahaina News, September 26, 1991: 9.
— Island Princess to arrive, Lahaina News, October 10, 1991: 7.
— fueling facility nearing completion, Lahaina News, October 17, 1991: 1.
— sales booths moved to make way for underground electrical and telephone lines, Lahaina News, February 20, 1992: 3.
— The Rotterdam to arrive, Lahaina News, March 5, 1992: 9.
— The Rotterdam ship to arrive, Lahaina News, March 12, 1992: 13.
— Saga Fjord scheduled to debark, Lahaina News, March 26, 1992: 10.
— to be dredged, Lahaina News, March 26, 1992: 3.
— Saga Fjord scheduled to debark, Lahaina News, April 2, 1992: 12.
— Royal Odyssey to dock, Lahaina News, April 9, 1992: 12.
— State rules changing for small boat harbors, Lahaina News, April 23, 1992: 5.
— Pacific Princess to debark, Lahaina News, May 7, 1992: 10.
— algae spreading into, Lahaina News, May 14, 1992: 1.
— being studied by Army Corps of Engineers, Lahaina News, May 28, 1992: 1.
— State Department of Transportation awards contract to Jacky Dugied to repair wharf at, Lahaina News, May 28, 1992: 4.
— cruise ship Asuka Yokohama to debark, Lahaina News, July 2, 1992: 12.
— dredging to begin, Lahaina News, September 10, 1992: 3.
— pleasure ship Island Princess to debark, Lahaina News, October 1, 1992: 10.
— Island Princess to debark, Lahaina News, October 22, 1992: 10.
— Island Princess to debark, Lahaina News, October 29, 1992: 13.
— Royal Odyssey to debark, Lahaina News, November 26, 1992: 13.

— no longer needs to be dredged due to hurricane Iniki, Lahaina News, November 26, 1992: 4.

— Royal Odyssey to debark, Lahaina News, December 3, 1992: 4.

— Mala boaters allowed to use during dredging, Lahaina News, January 21, 1993: 3.

— ship Canberra to debark, Lahaina News, February 11, 1993: 11.

— pleasure ship "Maxim Gorky" to debark, Lahaina News, March 25, 1993: 10.

— pleasure ship Regent Sun to debark, Lahaina News, April 8, 1993: 6.

— pleasure ship Fair Princess to debark, Lahaina News, April 15, 1993: 6.

— pleasure ship Sagafjord to debark, Lahaina News, May 13, 1993: 6.

— pleasure ship Sagafjord to debark, Lahaina News, May 20, 1993: 7.

— update on issues, Lahaina News, June 17, 1993: 9.

— Kona Storm of 1980 reunion to take place, Lahaina News, October 7, 1993: 2.

— pleasure ship Fair Princess to debark, Lahaina News, October 21, 1993: 11.

— officials want surfers out of the entrance to, Lahaina News, February 10, 1994: 1,2.

— update on changes, Lahaina News, April 7, 1994: 7.

— Pacific West Fuels to rebuild fueling facility, Lahaina News, April 28, 1994: 4.

— Maui County Board of Water Supply to replace water line that serves, Lahaina News, July 21, 1994: 3.

— complaints of buses idling at, Lahaina News, September 1, 1994: 3.

— project to increase water pressure and improve fire protection to begin, Lahaina News, February 9, 1995: 1.

— bill required to allow passengers to download, Lahaina News, April 27, 1995: 1,16.

— surf stairway proposed, Lahaina News, June 22, 1995: 1,16.

— bill to establish inter-island ferry service approved by Governor Ben Cayetano, Lahaina News, June 22, 1995: 4.

— surfer stairs supported by Maui Council's Parks and Recreation Committee, Lahaina News, July 6, 1995: 3.

— legal protection sought for surfer stairway at, Lahaina News, July 27, 1995: 4.

— tour bus congestion eased by security guard at, Lahaina News, December 28, 1995: 1.

— boat days, Lahaina News, January 25, 1996: 12.

— boat days for, Lahaina News, February 22, 1996: 11.

— update urged in master plan, Lahaina News, March 14, 1996: 3.

— access for surfers considered, Lahaina News, June 13, 1996: 1,16.

— plan for surfer steps progresses, Lahaina News, September 26, 1996: 1,5.

— committee considers improvements to parking at, Lahaina News, November 14, 1996: 2.

— cruise ships to arrive, Lahaina News, December 12, 1996: 13.

— oil response team forming, Lahaina News, April 17, 1997: 3.

— Maui Princess to return following renovation, Lahaina News, April 17, 1997: 7.

— oil spill response team forming, Lahaina News, May 8, 1997: 14.

— volunteers clean up, Lahaina News, May 8, 1997: 3.

— Adopt-A-Harbor Program started by Division of Boating and Ocean Recreation branch of Department of Land and Natural Resources, Lahaina News, May 22, 1997: 9.

— access for surfers to be finished in mid-August, Lahaina News, July 10, 1997: 9.

— ships to debark, Lahaina News, October 2, 1997: 15.

— Hawai'iloa to visit, Lahaina News, October 2, 1997: 17.

— task force to make visits for cruise ships easier, Lahaina News, October 9, 1997: 1,3.

— cruise ships discussed by Chuck Penque, Lahaina News, October 23, 1997: 1,2.

— cruise ships to arrive, Lahaina News, November 13, 1997: 11.

— cruise ships scheduled to visit, Lahaina News, March 26, 1998: 11.

— cruise ships scheduled to visit, Lahaina News, April 2, 1998: 13.

— cruise ships scheduled to visit, Lahaina News, April 16, 1998: 11.

— cruise ships scheduled to visit, Lahaina News, April 30, 1998: 13.

— holds clean-up day, Lahaina News, April 30, 1998: 15.

— cruise ships scheduled to visit, Lahaina News, May 7, 1998: 15.

— volunteers from LahainaTown Action Committee paint loading dock, Lahaina News, May 7, 1998: 18.

— cruise ships scheduled to visit, Lahaina News, May 14, 1998: 13.

— proposal still being considered for surfer steps at, Lahaina News, August 6, 1998: 1,20.

— plan for cruise ship pier unveiled, Lahaina News, August 20, 1998: 1,20.

— cruise ships to return to, Lahaina News, August 20, 1998: 13.

— list of boats to arrive, Lahaina News, August 27, 1998: 13.

— cruise ships to return September 14, Lahaina News, September 10, 1998: 11.

— cruise ships to return to, Lahaina News, September 17, 1998: 13.

— cruise ships to return to, Lahaina News, September 24, 1998: 13.

— ship schedule for October, Lahaina News, October 1, 1998: 13.

— cruise ships to return, Lahaina News, October 8, 1998: 13.

— Boat Days scheduled, Lahaina News, October 22, 1998: 17.

— ships to arrive, Lahaina News, November 5, 1998: 17.

— cruise ships to arrive, Lahaina News, November 26, 1998: 13.

— recycling depot established, Lahaina News, December 3, 1998: 10.

— top charter boats for 1998 at, Lahaina News, April 1, 1999: 15.

— ships to debark, Lahaina News, June 24, 1999: 11.

— cruise ships to debark, Lahaina News, September 30, 1999: 11.

— cruise ships to arrive at, Lahaina News, December 23, 1999: 13.

— improves undertaken by State and volunteers, Lahaina News, April 6, 2000: 3.

— cruise ships to arrive at, Lahaina News, April 20, 2000: 13.

— USS Port Royal to debark at, Lahaina News, July 27, 2000: 19.

— cruise ships to visit, Lahaina News, September 21, 2000: 16.

— cruise and military ships to visit, Lahaina News, September 28, 2000: 1.

— cruise ships to visit, Lahaina News, November 2, 2000: 12.

— military and cruise ships to arrive, Lahaina News, November 16, 2000: 12.

— cruise ships to visit, Lahaina News, November 30, 2000: 12.

— cruise ships to visit, Lahaina News, December 28, 2000: 16.

— cruise ships to arrive at, Lahaina News, March 8, 2001: 8.

— cruise ships to arrive at, Lahaina News, March 29, 2001: 8.

— cruise ships to arrive at, Lahaina News, April 26, 2001: 8.

— state to repair harbor dock, Lahaina News, May 10, 2001: 1.

— cruise ships arriving, Lahaina News, August 30, 2001: 9.

— cruise ships to visit, Lahaina News, December 20, 2001: 9.

— major changes planned for, Lahaina News, March 14, 2002: 1,2.

— cruise ships to arrive, Lahaina News, March 14, 2002: 8.

— cruise ships to arrive, Lahaina News, April 11, 2002: 9.

— busy schedule for cruise ships, Lahaina News, April 25, 2002: 8.

— cruise ships to visit, Lahaina News, October 3, 2002: 8.

— boating community comments on proposed rules and user fees, Lahaina News, October 10, 2002: 1,2.

— cruise ships to visit, Lahaina News, November 28, 2002: 8.

— cruise ships to visit, Lahaina News, December 5, 2002: 8.

— cruise ships to visit, Lahaina News, December 12, 2002: 8.

— cruise ships to visit, Lahaina News, April 24, 2003: 14.

— cruise ships to visit, Lahaina News, May 8, 2003: 8.

— Amateur Surfing Association held qualifying contest at, Lahaina News, June 5, 2003: 13.

LAHAINA HEALTH CENTER

— Hawaiian Dredging & Construction begins work on, Lahaina News, February 6, 1985: 3.

— to hold seminar on pregnancy, Lahaina News, December 3, 1998: 11.

— to offer seminar on pregnancy, Lahaina News, December 3, 1998: 20.

LAHAINA HEALTH CLUB
— expands, Lahaina News, December 27, 1989: 5.

LAHAINA HISTORIC DISTRICT
— rules ignored by many shop owners on Front Street, Lahaina News, September 2, 1987: 1.
— county to begin enforcing codes in, Lahaina News, June 3, 1993: 7.
— fines to be assessed for cheap signage and roving salespeople, Lahaina News, October 21, 1993: 5.
— Maui County Cultural Resources Commission wants idling buses to be ticketed, Lahaina News, May 11, 1995: 1,6.

LAHAINA HISTORIC DISTRICT ARCHITECTURAL STYLE BOOK
— Winter and Company awarded production to , Lahaina News, September 4, 2003: 1,8.

LAHAINA HONGWANJI MISSION
— see Hongwanji Mission

LAHAINA HONOLUA SENIOR CITIZENS CLUB
— president Mae Fujiwara featured, Lahaina News, June 28, 2001: 1,22.

LAHAINA HOTEL [BUSINESS]
— design approved by Maui Historical Commission, Lahaina Sun, November 11, 1970: 3.
— for sale, Lahaina News, December 15, 1981: 7.
— opens, Lahaina News, May 3, 1989: 4.
— reviewed, Lahaina News, December 13, 1989: 23.
— renovated, Lahaina News, December 27, 1989: 4.
— restorations complete, Lahaina News, February 28, 1990: 4.
— for sale, Lahaina News, September 9, 1993: 6,7.

LAHAINA IMPROVEMENT ASSOCIATION
— name changed from Lahaina Retail Committee, Lahaina Sun, June 9, 1971: 7.
— criticizes location of Lahaina-Ka'anapali & Pacific Railroad terminal in Lahaina, Lahaina Sun, July 21, 1971: 1.
— Tim Mitchell elected chairman, Lahaina Sun, December 8, 1971: 8.
— looking for new members, Lahaina Sun, March 22, 1972: 4.
— results of last meeting discussed, Lahaina Sun, April 26, 1972: 9.

LAHAINA INN
— proposed by Interisland Resorts and C.W. Brooks, Lahaina Sun, January 20, 1971: 1.
— selected as romantic inn by American Historical Inns, Lahaina News, May 11, 1995: 10.

LAHAINA INTERFAITH FOOD EFFORT (LIFE)
— seeks food and money for the poor, Lahaina News, December 10, 1992: 3.

LAHAINA INTERMEDIATE SCHOOL
— groundbreaking held, Lahaina News, October 26, 1983: 5.
— open house, Lahaina News, September 18, 1985: 3.
— public hearing to discuss rules, Lahaina News, October 16, 1985: 20.
— wins Na Mele O Maui School Song Festival, Lahaina News, November 13, 1985: 1,3.
— open house at, Lahaina News, September 10, 1986: 3.
— class officers elected, Lahaina News, October 15, 1986: 3.
— to hold fundraiser, Lahaina News, October 14, 1987: 3.
— Parent Teacher Association to meet, Lahaina News, December 2, 1987: 3.
— surveys parents, Lahaina News, December 9, 1987: 3.
— Parent-Teaching meeting set, Lahaina News, February 17, 1988: 18.
— Parent week to be held this week, Lahaina News, March 16, 1988: 1.
— surveys parents concerning vandalism, graffiti, Lahaina News, March 30, 1988: 1.
— to host Invitational Volleyball Tournament, Lahaina News, March 30, 1988: 20.
— to hold International Pot Luck, Lahaina News, May 25, 1988: 10.
— Parent Teacher Student Association to hold luau, Lahaina News, September 28, 1988: 18.
— Parent Teacher Student Association to hold luau, Lahaina News, October 19, 1988: 14.
— lists academic awards for 2nd quarter, Lahaina News, February 15, 1989: 13.
— Parents Teachers Students Association to hold fundraiser, Lahaina News, October 11, 1989: 3.
— conducting parents workshops, Lahaina News, October 11, 1989: 3.
— Parents Teachers Students Association to hold luau, Lahaina News, October 18, 1989: 4.
— to hold parents workshops, Lahaina News, October 18, 1989: 4.
— luau was successful, Lahaina News, November 22, 1989: 3.
— to hold spring concert, Lahaina News, May 30, 1990: 5.
— registration to begin for Fall semester, Lahaina News, August 22, 1990: 5.
— to hold fundraiser luau, Lahaina News, September 19, 1990: 4,5.
— to hold fundraiser luau, Lahaina News, October 10, 1990: 6.
— holding general meeting of Parents Teachers Students association, Lahaina News, November 14, 1990: 3.
— girls basketball team competes in tournament, Lahaina News, December 12, 1990: 3.
— Parent Teacher Student Association celebrating the Filipino community, Lahaina News, March 6, 1991: 5.
— results volleyball team, Lahaina News, May 1, 1991: 7.
— students host program to honor Mark and Debbie Ferrari, Lahaina News, May 8, 1991: 2.
— honor roll announced, Lahaina News, May 8, 1991: 4.
— to pilot School Community Based Management program, Lahaina News, September 26, 1991: 1.
— to teach about dangers of drug abuse, Lahaina News, November 7, 1991: 4.
— parents to meet, Lahaina News, December 5, 1991: 4.
— students Kawehi Lindsey and Wendy Calio to perform "Students Staying Straight", Lahaina News, May 14, 1992: 3.
— to host School/Community-Based Management conference, Lahaina News, August 20, 1992: 9.
— parents interested in Lions-Quest Skills for Adolescence Program to meet, Lahaina News, October 29, 1992: 3.
— girls basketball takes second place at St. Anthony Intermediate School Basketball Tournament, Lahaina News, November 26, 1992: 11.
— submits plan to become SCBM school, Lahaina News, January 21, 1993: 3.
— begins School Community Based Management program, Lahaina News, March 4, 1993: 1.
— to host Scholastic Book Fair, Lahaina News, March 4, 1993: 4.
— seeking funds to participate in solar energy race, Lahaina News, March 25, 1993: 2.
— sins model solar energy car competition, Lahaina News, April 22, 1993: 2.
— to celebrate May Day, Lahaina News, April 29, 1993: 2.
— receives funds to plan joint cafeteria with Princess Nahienaena Elementary School, Lahaina News, May 6, 1993: 1.
— Diane Dennis is new principal, Lahaina News, August 26, 1993: 4.
— coordinating youth transportation with West Maui Youth Center, Lahaina News, October 7, 1993: 3.
— holds student recognition assembly, Lahaina News, December 2, 1993: 4.
— community offers incentive, Lahaina News, December 9, 1993: 3.
— principal Diane Dennis featured, Lahaina News, April 21, 1994: 1,2.
— to hold community planting/work day, Lahaina News, May 26, 1994: 4.
— update on PTSA members, Lahaina News, June 23, 1994: 2.
— recognition award ceremony held, Lahaina News, July 7, 1994: 2.
— Vance Yatsushiro appointed principal, Lahaina News, August 25, 1994: 1.
— Parent Teacher Student Association to meet, Lahaina News, October 13, 1994: 6.

— begins "Wednesday is Tutor Day in Lahaina" tutoring program, Lahaina News, January 31, 2002: 1,18.

— to hold "Parent Week", Lahaina News, February 28, 2002: 16.

— announces "Partners in Living and Learning Renaissance" students, Lahaina News, February 28, 2002: 9.

— to host volleyball tourney, Lahaina News, April 11, 2002: 12.

— has improved in last 10 years, Lahaina News, April 18, 2002: 1,18.

— band flourishing under Mark Gilmore, Lahaina News, April 25, 2002: 1.

— held "Multi-Cultural Day", Lahaina News, May 9, 2002: 3.

— students honored, Lahaina News, May 9, 2002: 9.

— to hold "Partners in Living and Learning Renaissance", Lahaina News, May 16, 2002: 1.

— students honored for reading achievement, Lahaina News, June 13, 2002: 1,18.

— to hold Dance-a-thon fundraiser, Lahaina News, August 8, 2002: 5.

— to hold Dance-a-thon fundraiser, Lahaina News, August 15, 2002: 9.

— Marsha Nakamura new principal at, Lahaina News, August 29, 2002: 1,22.

— launches effort to improve library, receives donation from Bendon Family Foundation, Lahaina News, September 5, 2002: 3.

— principal Marsha Nakamura discusses innovative programs at, Lahaina News, October 17, 2002: 1,24.

— Partners in Living and Learning Program holds "Reward Day", Lahaina News, November 7, 2002: 1.

— "Reward Day" held, Lahaina News, November 14, 2002: 16.

— honor roll released, Lahaina News, December 5, 2002: 15.

— honor roll released, Lahaina News, March 6, 2003: 18.

— principal Marsha Nakamura discusses school, Lahaina News, April 10, 2003: 3.

— groups seeking to improve, Lahaina News, April 17, 2003: 3.

— holds volleyball tournament, Lahaina News, April 24, 2003: 1,22.

— seeking suggestions to improve, Lahaina News, April 24, 2003: 2.

— students enrolled in Partners in Living and Learning Renaissance Program treated to reward day, Lahaina News, May 8, 2003: 1.

— students competed in Vocational Industry Clubs of America skills challenge, Lahaina News, May 15, 2003: 1,20.

— message from principal Marsha Nakamura, Lahaina News, May 15, 2003: 9.

— technology coordinator Rob Siarot discusses programs at, Lahaina News, May 22, 2003: 1,18.

— honor roll announced, Lahaina News, June 12, 2003: 15.

— graduate Desiree Sumajit receives Principal's Award, Lahaina News, June 26, 2003: 8.

— program to enhance unity among students, Lahaina News, August 14, 2003: 1,20.

— reminders from, Lahaina News, August 14, 2003: 2.

— to host Parent Week, Lahaina News, September 11, 2003: 1,5.

LAHAINA INTERPRETIVE PLAN

— LahainaTown Action Committee, Hui O Wa'a Kaulua, and Friends of Moku'ula working on, Lahaina News, August 5, 1999: 1,16.

LAHAINA JACKPOT FISHING TOURNAMENT

— 567.2 pound marlin breaks record at, Lahaina News, November 7, 1984: 3.

— to be held this week, Lahaina News, October 30, 1985: 3.

— won by Wet N' Wild from Honolulu, Lahaina News, November 6, 1985: 1.

— to be held, Lahaina News, October 29, 1986: 6.

— largest catch scheduled, black marlin, Lahaina News, November 5, 1986: 1.

— results announced, Lahaina News, November 26, 1986: 8,9.

— results, Lahaina News, November 8, 1989: 8.

— wahine tournament has record number of participants, Lahaina News, November 15, 1989: 28.

— wahine tournament scheduled, Lahaina News, April 11, 1990: 7.

— results, Lahaina News, August 1, 1990: 3,14.

— to be held, Lahaina News, October 10, 1990: 24.

— to be held, Lahaina News, October 31, 1990: 9.

— results, Lahaina News, November 14, 1990: 9.

— results of, Lahaina News, November 10, 1994: 9.

— results; Marlin Mischief wins, Lahaina News, October 31, 1996: 1,3.

— results of, Lahaina News, October 30, 1997: 1,8.

— results of, Lahaina News, November 6, 1997: 9.

— results of, Lahaina News, October 29, 1998: 19.

— results of, Lahaina News, November 2, 2000: 9.

LAHAINA JEWELRY FANTASY [BUSINESS]

— opens, Lahaina News, June 29, 2000: 16.

LAHAINA JOB JUNCTION

— job fair to be held, Lahaina News, January 16, 1991: 4.

— to be held, Lahaina News, January 23, 1992: 4.

— to be held, Lahaina News, January 30, 1992: 3.

LAHAINA JODO MISSION

— see Jodo Mission, Lahaina

LAHAINA JUNIOR TENNIS CLUB

— to hold Christmas Tree Recycling Project, Lahaina News, December 21, 2000: 7.

— recycling Christmas Trees, Lahaina News, December 28, 2000: 6.

LAHAINA JUNIOR TENNIS PROGRAM

— awarded grant from United States Tennis Association, Lahaina News, November 19, 1998: 15.

LAHAINA KAMAAKINA FISHING ASSOCIATION

— created, Lahaina Sun, December 23, 1970: 1.

— hope to secure state bounty on sharks, Lahaina Sun, December 23, 1970: 11.

— studying ways to alleviate pollution in Lahaina harbor, Lahaina Sun, December 23, 1970: 11.

LAHAINA KAYAK AND SURF CLUB

— to host fun day, Lahaina News, January 21, 1987: 10.

— sponsoring events, Lahaina News, April 15, 1987: 12.

LAHAINA KINGDOM HALL OF JEHOVAH'S WITNESSES

— residents of Pu'unoa Place opposing development plans of, Lahaina News, March 14, 2002: 3.

LAHAINA LINGERIE [BUSINESS]

— opens, Lahaina News, October 21, 1999: 13.

LAHAINA LIQUOR [BUSINESS]

— featured, Lahaina News, February 8, 1984: 16.

LAHAINA LITTLE CHIEFS PEE WEE

— football team to complete in Maui Bowl games, Lahaina News, November 23, 1988: 5.

LAHAINA MACADAMIA NUT & COFFEE CO. [BUSINESS]

— featured, Lahaina News, June 26, 1985: 20.

LAHAINA MARDI GRAS

— to be held at Lahaina Civic Center, Lahaina News, February 10, 1988: 9.

— to be held at Lahaina Civic Center, Lahaina News, February 15, 1989: 9.

LAHAINA MARINE ART FESTIVAL

— Kapena to perform at, Lahaina News, March 1, 2001: 21.

LAHAINA MARKET PLACE

— discussed by Higgins Maddigan, Lahaina Sun, December 23, 1970: 9.

— request for children's zoo rejected, Lahaina Sun, April 21, 1971: 3.

— Lahaina Tree Garden restaurant now open, Lahaina Sun, July 14, 1971: 4.

— photographs of, Lahaina News, July 15, 1981: 16.

— renovations planned, Lahaina News, April 11, 1984: 17.

— featured, Lahaina News, April 18, 1984: 17.

— changes detailed, Lahaina News, April 10, 1985: 1,7.

LAHAINA MEMORIAL AMPHITHEATRE
— grand opening held, Lahaina Sun, August 9, 1972: 10.
— Barangay Fold Dancers and Nishizaki Dance Team participate in opening ceremony, Lahaina Sun, August 16, 1972: 9.

LAHAINA MERCHANTS COMMITTEE
— to host "There's a Party on Front Street", Lahaina News, July 4, 1996: 14,15.
— to hold "There's a Party on Front Street", Lahaina News, July 25, 1996: 13.
— sponsoring concierge party, Lahaina News, July 25, 1996: 2.

LAHAINA METHODIST CHURCH
— to hold annual bazaar and children's fair, Lahaina News, February 25, 1987: 3.

LAHAINA MUSIC AND CRAFT FESTIVAL
— to be held at Lahaina Civic Center, Lahaina News, August 9, 1989: 12.

LAHAINA NATURAL FOODS [BUSINESS]
— reviewed, Lahaina News, June 1, 1983: 15.
— featured, Lahaina News, March 7, 1984: 17.
— closed at the end of 1985, Lahaina News, January 8, 1986: 1.

LAHAINA NAUTILUS CENTER [BUSINESS]
— value of equipment in rehabilitation discussed, Lahaina News, July 30, 1986: 4.
— fitness club opens in Lahaina, Lahaina News, February 3, 1988: 12.
— extends introductory offer, Lahaina News, February 10, 1988: 11.
— offering new classes, Lahaina News, April 20, 1988: 11.
— offers yoga, Lahaina News, June 22, 1988: 3.
— adding acupuncturist, Lahaina News, July 13, 1988: 10.
— adds hours and staff, Lahaina News, September 14, 1988: 15.
— offering Hellerwork sessions, Lahaina News, September 21, 1988: 20.
— Ginger Ikenberry new massage therapist at, Lahaina News, October 5, 1988: 3.
— offering noon aerobics, Lahaina News, November 9, 1988: 12.
— to offer free facials, Lahaina News, December 21, 1988: 17.
— celebrates first year, Lahaina News, January 25, 1989: 2.
— to hold hula classes, Lahaina News, March 1, 1989: 3.
— sunset aerobics to be offered, Lahaina News, March 22, 1989: 13.
— offering hula lessons, Lahaina News, June 7, 1989: 6.
— sports massage seminar to be held, Lahaina News, August 2, 1989: 6.
— expanding, Lahaina News, October 11, 1989: 5.
— workshop offered for aerobics instructors, Lahaina News, November 8, 1989: 24.
— offering aerobic certification program, Lahaina News, November 22, 1989: 5.
— expands facilities, Lahaina News, March 21, 1990: 7.
— to offer aerobics classes, Lahaina News, May 13, 1993: 7.
— state considering legal action against, Lahaina News, October 13, 1994: 1,8.
— Office of Consumer Protection to not act against, Lahaina News, October 27, 1994: 8.

LAHAINA NEIGHBORHOOD PLAYGROUP
— established, Lahaina News, October 1, 1986: 5.

LAHAINA NEWS [BUSINESS]
— staff described, Lahaina News, August, 1979: 2.
— Bob Kelsey hired as editor, Lahaina News, March 1, 1980: 13.
— celebrates first year, current challenges described, Lahaina News, June 15, 1980: 6.
— equipment upgraded, Lahaina News, May 1, 1981: 2.
— goals of newspaper discussed, Lahaina News, May 15, 1981: 2.
— details of last 10 years of publication, Lahaina News, June 1, 1981: 10,11.
— pressure to support hotel industry described, Lahaina News, September 1, 1981: 2.
— Christian values of, Lahaina News, October 1, 1981: 2.
— financial situation not positive, Lahaina News, February 1, 1982: 2.
— celebrates 3 years, Lahaina News, June 1, 1982: 1.
— endorses Jean King for lieutenant governor, Lahaina News, September 15, 1982: 8.
— editorial supporting mayor Tavares, Lahaina News, October 15, 1982: 3.
— sold to Bill and Nancy Worth, Lahaina News, February 1, 1983: 8,9.
— new owners Bill and Mary Worth discuss their values, Lahaina News, February 15, 1983: 11.
— announces that it is becoming a weekly publication, Lahaina News, August 15, 1983: 2.
— begins a regular column on Art, Lahaina News, September 21, 1983: 12.
— operations described, Lahaina News, February 15, 1984: 7,8,9.
— criticized by Bishop Museum for use of photograph, Lahaina News, March 7, 1984: 2.
— paper turns six, Lahaina News, June 6, 1984: 2.
— Kim Ball ends sports column, Lahaina News, October 17, 1984: 4.
— most comics strips are removed from publication following a redesign, Lahaina News, October 24, 1984: 2.
— series begins written by students at Lahainaluna High School, Lahaina News, January 30, 1985: .
— printing now being done by Maui News rather than Hawaii Hochi in Honolulu, Lahaina News, March 20, 1985: 2.
— to change distribution system, reduce number mailed, Lahaina News, June 5, 1985: 1.
— Manu Kahaiali'i begins column, Lahaina News, July 17, 1985: .
— introduces monthly column "At the Harbor", Lahaina News, August 21, 1985: 9.
— top stories of 1985 reviewed, Lahaina News, January 8, 1986: 1,20.
— Fur & Feathers columnist Janetha Brooksby moves off island, will continue to write column, Lahaina News, April 23, 1986: 8.
— sold to Colin Cameron and Mary Cameron Stanford, Lahaina News, August 27, 1986: 1.
— Bob Kelsey ends his "Second Opinion" column, Lahaina News, September 3, 1986: 6.
— now being mailed to residences in West Maui, Lahaina News, November 19, 1986: 1.
— cartoons by "RR" begin publication in, Lahaina News, January 21, 1987: 12.
— begins monthly feature on Chinese Horoscope, Lahaina News, January 28, 1987: 6.
— begins feature "Tips for Tourists"; will not automatically be indexed otherwise, Lahaina News, February 11, 1987: 9,10.
— begins column by Dr. John Briley on medicine, will not be generally indexed unless relevant to Maui, Lahaina News, March 25, 1987: 10.
— Furs and Feathers column starts again, printed sporadically, Lahaina News, May 27, 1987: 12.
— Bill O'Connor stops writing "Dining & Entertainment" section, Lahaina News, December 9, 1987: 8.
— to begin series on healing, Lahaina News, April 6, 1988: 1.
— Bill O'Connor to stop writing the entertainment and sports columns, Lahaina News, April 13, 1988: 11,12.
— names Gary Kubota as new editor, Lahaina News, March 1, 1989: 1.
— former editor Bill Worth moves from Maui, Lahaina News, May 17, 1989: 6.
— hires Richard Adena as advertising sales representative, Lahaina News, May 31, 1989: 15.
— offering free advertising space to promote jobs for youths, Lahaina News, June 7, 1989: 7.
— to publish special Aloha Week souvenir edition, Lahaina News, September 13, 1989: 1.

— Louise Rockett to begin writing "West Maui People" column, Lahaina News, May 16, 1990: 1.

— to publish weekly report on crime in West Maui, Lahaina News, May 23, 1990: 1.

— to begin publishing cartoons by Mikel Mesh, Lahaina News, January 23, 1991: 1.

— to begin selling copies, Lahaina News, August 22, 1991: 1.

— personnel changes, Lahaina News, September 10, 1992: 9.

— Mark Percell begins writing "West Maui Views" column, Lahaina News, December 3, 1992: 4.

— Gary Kubota leaving for position at Honolulu Star Bulletin, Lahaina News, April 22, 1993: 3.

— promotes Mark Vieth to editor of, Lahaina News, June 17, 1993: 2.

— closes production office, Lahaina News, August 5, 1993: 4.

— "The Wine Press" column begins, not usually indexed, Lahaina News, September 16, 1993: 16.

— recent hires announced, Lahaina News, December 1, 1994: 13.

— Craig Nalette named to sales staff, Lahaina News, January 26, 1995: 13.

— electronic edition discussed, Lahaina News, August 3, 1995: 8.

— sold by West Maui News Corp. to group from West Maui, Lahaina News, November 23, 1995: 1,2.

— Lynn Britton appointed as new manager, Lahaina News, November 23, 1995: 1,2.

— receives Watershed Kokua Award from West Maui Watershed Advisory Committee, Lahaina News, November 23, 1995: 3.

— discontinues television listings, Lahaina News, December 28, 1995: 3.

— "Up Front Lahaina" article begins, offers short updates on events, etc., Lahaina News, January 18, 1996: 3.

— begins "Scholar Athlete of the Week" column, Lahaina News, January 25, 1996: 11.

— Ka 'I'imi 'Ike column begins, not always indexed, Lahaina News, March 7, 1996: 2.

— joins Made in Hawaii, Lahaina News, March 21, 1996: 4.

— "Destinations" column begins appearing, Lahaina News, April 11, 1996: 10,11.

— Ka 'I'imi 'Ike column continues, Lahaina News, May 2, 1996: 6.

— accessible at http://www.maui.net/~mauiduck, Lahaina News, June 6, 1996: 1.

— "Smart Nutrients" column begins, Lahaina News, June 20, 1996: 6.

— Art Parts column published, not otherwise indexed, Lahaina News, September 26, 1996: 17.

— "West Maui Movie Capsule" column begins, not otherwise indexed, Lahaina News, October 10, 1996: 18.

— Entertainment section becomes calendar rather than paragraph entries, generally not indexed, Lahaina News, November 7, 1996: 16.

— top stories of previous year, Lahaina News, January 2, 1997: 1,2.

— "Smart Shopper" column begins, not otherwise indexed, Lahaina News, February 13, 1997: 5,6,7.

— "You Asked For It" column begins, responding to reader questions, not always indexed, Lahaina News, February 20, 1997: 3.

— "Historical Highlights" offers transcriptions by Barbara Sharp, Lahaina News, May 22, 1997: 2.

— website named "Outstanding Education-Related Site" by the Education Index, Lahaina News, May 22, 1997: 6.

— hosting speech by president of the Tax Foundation of Hawaii Lowell Kalapa, Lahaina News, March 5, 1998: 13.

— "On the Party Line" column begins, Lahaina News, April 16, 1998: 5.

— "Up Front Lahaina" column continues, Lahaina News, July 16, 1998: 3.

— Maui County responds to "Hawaii Environment and Health News" insert, Lahaina News, September 17, 1998: 3.

— "On the Party Line" column continues, not typically indexed, Lahaina News, November 12, 1998: 2.

— editor wins HPA Pa'i Award, Lahaina News, April 15, 1999: 1.

— Lahainaluna High School students shadow Mae McCarter, Lahaina News, April 29, 1999: 13.

— begins to publish obituaries, Lahaina News, June 17, 1999: 15.

— has new website, Lahaina News, June 24, 1999: 11.

— "Healing Word" column by Michael Klaper begins, not usually indexed, Lahaina News, October 21, 1999: 7.

— changes include expanded coverage and four-color cover, Lahaina News, May 18, 2000: 1.

— writers win awards from Society of Professional Journalism-Hawaii Chapter, Lahaina News, June 22, 2000: 1,15.

— Obden Newspapers, Inc. to purchase from Maui Chronicle, Inc., Lahaina News, October 5, 2000: 1,15.

— wins award from the Society of Professional Journalists-Hawaii Chapter in business reporting category, Lahaina News, June 28, 2001: 22.

— wins Pa'i Awards from Hawaii Publishers Association, Lahaina News, May 1, 2003: 1.

— wins Community Reporting category in Excellence in Journalism Awards from Society of Professional Journalists-Hawaii Chapter, Lahaina News, June 19, 2003: 1,20.

LAHAINA OPEN SPACE SOCIETY (LOSS)

— to focus on preserving open space at Ka'anapali North Beach, Lahaina News, September 26, 1996: 2.

— to hold "Awareness Demonstration" with Nation of Hawaii and Ka Kupuna O Maui, Lahaina News, October 17, 1996: 14.

— to hold meeting, Lahaina News, January 2, 1997: 10.

— to hold meeting to discuss culturally significant areas with Na Kapula O Maui and Nation of Hawaii, Lahaina News, February 27, 1997: 11.

— to hold meeting with Na Kapula O Maui, Lahaina News, April 10, 1997: 12.

— to meet with Na Kupuna O Maui, Lahaina News, July 17, 1997: 16.

— to meet at Malu'ulu O Lele Cultural Center, Lahaina News, September 25, 1997: 16.

— continues to meet, Lahaina News, October 2, 1997: 20.

— to meet at Malu'ulu O Lele Cultural Center, Lahaina News, October 9, 1997: 20.

— continues to meet, not always indexed, Lahaina News, October 16, 1997: 16.

— continues to meet, Lahaina News, January 22, 1998: 12.

— demonstrates against the Launiupoko housing project, Lahaina News, March 5, 1998: 3.

— to hold event with Kahana Canoe Club, Lahaina News, April 23, 1998: 17.

— receives nonprofit status, Lahaina News, August 20, 1998: 7.

— to hold annual meeting, Lahaina News, December 3, 1998: 11.

— to hold annual meeting at Malu'ulu O Lele Cultural Center, Lahaina News, December 10, 1998: 11.

— to meet at Malu'ulu O Lele Cultural Center, Lahaina News, June 3, 1999: 16.

LAHAINA ORCHID SOCIETY

— to be held at Lahaina Shopping Center, Lahaina News, November 14, 1984: 3.

— to hold Fall show, Lahaina News, November 20, 1985: 3.

— hosting orchid show at Lahaina Shopping Center, Lahaina News, May 7, 1986: 3.

— Fall Orchid Show scheduled, Lahaina News, November 12, 1986: 3.

— to present show, Lahaina News, November 18, 1987: 3.

— spring show scheduled, Lahaina News, May 3, 1989: 4.

— hosting Thanksgiving show, Lahaina News, November 15, 1989: 5.

— to hold Mother's Day show, Lahaina News, May 8, 1991: 3.

— purpose and activities described, Lahaina News, June 20, 1991: 1,14.

— to hold Thanksgiving show, Lahaina News, November 21, 1991: 3.

— to host Valentine's Day show, Lahaina News, February 6, 1992: 4.

— to hold Valentine's Day show, Lahaina News, February 13, 1992: 18.
— exhibit scheduled, Lahaina News, April 23, 1992: 5.
— Mother's Day Show and Sale scheduled, Lahaina News, April 30, 1992: 4.
— to display at Whalers Village, Lahaina News, July 2, 1992: 3.
— to hold summer show with Maui Orchid Society, Lahaina News, July 7, 1994: 13.
— to hold show, Lahaina News, May 8, 1997: 16.
— to exhibit at Lahaina Cannery Mall, Lahaina News, February 5, 1998: 12,13.
— see also Maui Orchid Society, orchids

LAHAINA OUTDOOR CIRCLE
— discusses plans for banyan tree in Lahaina, Lahaina Sun, February 3, 1971: 7.

LAHAINA PLAYGROUP
— to offer playgroup for children, Lahaina News, July 18, 1996: 12.
— to meet, Lahaina News, August 29, 1996: 10.
— meets at Launiupoko Wayside Park, Lahaina News, July 30, 1998: 16.
— to meet, Lahaina News, September 10, 1998: 20.
— to be held, Lahaina News, March 4, 1999: 12.

LAHAINA POLICE DEPARTMENT
— see police

LAHAINA POP WARNER ASSOCIATION
— holds luau fundraiser, Lahaina News, September 20, 1989: 24.
— fundraiser a success, Lahaina News, October 11, 1989: 6.
— football team to hold first day of practice, Lahaina News, August 1, 1990: 14.
— to hold fundraiser; teams photographed, Lahaina News, September 5, 1990: 11,12,13,14.
— to hold fundraiser at Sacred Hearts School, Lahaina News, September 12, 1990: 16.
— described, Lahaina News, November 21, 1990: 2.
— featured, Lahaina News, September 5, 1991: 11,12,13,14.
— registration open for football players, Lahaina News, August 22, 1996: 12.
— to hold Christmas Tree Sale, Lahaina News, November 28, 1996: 6.
— hopes to use War Memorial Stadium, Lahaina News, July 31, 1997: 1.
— to hold registration, Lahaina News, June 18, 1998: 14.
— to present concert with Baba B, Merv Oana and guests, Lahaina News, October 15, 1998: 15.
— to hold benefit concert, Lahaina News, November 4, 1999: 1.
— Toddy Lilikoi seeks community support for Pop Warner league, Lahaina News, June 22, 2000: 1,15.
— begins season, Lahaina News, September 5, 2002: 1.
— to hold registration, Lahaina News, July 10, 2003: 13.
— Kale Casco hoping to bring unity to, Lahaina News, July 17, 2003: 1,20.

LAHAINA POSTER CONTEST
— being held, Lahaina News, August 15, 1996: 17.
— entries to be displayed at Lahaina Arts Society, Lahaina News, July 13, 2000: 16.
— to be sponsored by Lahaina Town Action Committee, Lahaina News, May 24, 2001: 2.
— to be held, Lahaina News, June 21, 2001: 14.
— Michael Krahn wins, Lahaina News, July 19, 2001: 14.

LAHAINA PRE-SCHOOL
— sponsoring book fair, Lahaina News, January 30, 1992: 3.

LAHAINA PRESS KIT
— deemed successful, Lahaina Sun, April 14, 1971: 6.

LAHAINA PRINTSELLERS [BUSINESS]
— tenant of Seamen's Hospital, Lahaina News, February 29, 1984: 11.
— opening in new location, Lahaina News, March 30, 1988: 20.

— wins award from DECOR Magazine, Lahaina News, May 11, 1988: 3.
— leases Hale Aloha, Lahaina News, May 25, 1988: 1.
— offering tours of new location, Lahaina News, June 1, 1988: 3.
— offers gift certificate drawing, Lahaina News, June 22, 1988: 3.
— to open at Hale Aloha, Lahaina News, July 27, 1988: 11.
— opening fourth gallery, Lahaina News, June 28, 1989: 7.
— opens fourth Maui gallery, Lahaina News, June 13, 1990: 7.
— donates antique to Maui Historical Society benefit auction, Lahaina News, July 25, 1990: 6.
— opens new store at Lahaina Cannery, Lahaina News, August 29, 1990: 13.
— to hold rare book sale, Lahaina News, November 21, 1990: 16.
— appoints Lisa-Anne Raney as office manager, Lahaina News, May 1, 1991: 7.
— opens new gallery at Grand Hyatt Resort, Lahaina News, December 12, 1991: 16.
— to demonstrate copperplate map-making, Lahaina News, January 23, 1992: 18.
— to release limited edition of Stephen Strickland's latest intaglio work, Lahaina News, December 30, 1993: 10,11.
— exhibiting "Classical Studies in the Traditional Manner", Lahaina News, February 24, 1994: 9.
— opens in Kapalua Shops, Lahaina News, January 26, 1995: 12.

LAHAINA PRISON
— see Hale Pa'ahao

LAHAINA PROVISION COMPANY [RESTAURANT]
— reviewed, Lahaina News, December 24, 1992: 14.

LAHAINA PUBLIC CHARTER SCHOOL FOR THE PERFORMING ARTS
— state rejects funding for, Lahaina News, February 24, 2000: 1,2.

LAHAINA PUBLIC LIBRARY
— showing films on Easter Island and whaling, Lahaina Sun, December 9, 1970: 4.
— story hour held, Lahaina Sun, June 30, 1971: 12.
— plan to move Lahaina library protested, Lahaina Sun, January 19, 1972: 6.
— discussion of process to discuss possible move, Lahaina Sun, February 2, 1972: 15.
— petition circulated calling for stop in plan to move branch, Lahaina Sun, March 1, 1972: 3.
— exhibits watercolors of Hawaiian medicinal herbs by Nils Larsen, Lahaina Sun, March 29, 1972: 14.
— proposed move opposed, Lahaina Sun, April 5, 1972: 3.
— further debate over potential relocation of, Lahaina Sun, April 26, 1972: 3.
— proposed move discussed, Lahaina Sun, May 10, 1972: 20.
— proposed relocation debated, Lahaina Sun, May 17, 1972: 5.
— public meeting to discuss proposed relocation, Lahaina Sun, May 31, 1972: 6.
— relocation approved by Maui County Council, Lahaina Sun, May 31, 1972: 6.
— Oletha Davenport Williams retires from, Lahaina Sun, June 14, 1972: 4.
— State representative Ron Kondo pledges to keep the library in current location, Lahaina Sun, June 14, 1972: 5.
— reflection on value of the library, Lahaina Sun, August 2, 1972: 23.
— cutting hours due to budget shortfalls, Lahaina Sun, September 6, 1972: 10.
— featured, Lahaina News, August 28, 1985: 1,9.
— celebrates 30th birthday, Lahaina News, March 5, 1986: 1.
— computerized check-out system completed, Lahaina News, August 6, 1986: 1,10.
— summer reading kicks off with clowns, Lahaina News, June 10, 1987: 3.

— to hold storytelling and film events, Lahaina News, July 1, 1987: 3.

— hosting summer films, Lahaina News, July 8, 1987: 3,16.

— sets Summer Fun Film schedule, Lahaina News, July 15, 1987: 3.

— librarian Nancy Shim promoted to Program Coordinator for all Maui Public Libraries, Lahaina News, July 15, 1987: 3.

— offers Toddler Theatre, Lahaina News, August 26, 1987: 3.

— Toddler Theatre at, Lahaina News, September 2, 1987: 3.

— to hold Toddler Theatre, Lahaina News, October 7, 1987: 3.

— hosts guitar demo by Ken Emerson, Lahaina News, November 11, 1987: 11.

— Friends of the Lahaina Public Library hold book sale, Lahaina News, April 20, 1988: 6.

— offering seminar on improving cashier sales skills, Lahaina News, July 6, 1988: 3.

— implements new hours, Lahaina News, September 7, 1988: 3.

— Hatsumi Kadotani retires after 35 years, Lahaina News, September 28, 1988: 6.

— to host lecture on hula by Hoakalei Kamauu, Lahaina News, October 5, 1988: 3.

— closed for holidays, Lahaina News, November 9, 1988: 3,12.

— Marcia Nakama and Beth Stewart join the staff, Lahaina News, June 28, 1989: 1.

— to offer program on international folkdance, Lahaina News, November 8, 1989: 6.

— holds free story hour for children, Lahaina News, December 13, 1989: 4.

— new site proposed, Lahaina News, March 14, 1990: 1.

— legislature authorizes funds for new, Lahaina News, June 13, 1990: 1.

— Friends of the Lahaina Public Library to hold book sale, Lahaina News, July 11, 1990: 4.

— Friends of the Lahaina Public Library to hold book sale, Lahaina News, July 11, 1990: 4.

— to be closed for day of staff development, Lahaina News, October 10, 1990: 7.

— to be closed for election, Lahaina News, October 31, 1990: 7.

— offers puppet show, Lahaina News, January 2, 1991: 3.

— funds sought for, Lahaina News, January 23, 1991: 1.

— State funding likely according to Representative Joe Souki, Lahaina News, February 6, 1991: 1.

— announces new hours, Lahaina News, June 6, 1991: 3.

— Friends of the Lahaina Public Library to be formed, Lahaina News, July 11, 1991: 5.

— Friends of the Lahaina Public Library to hold book sale, Lahaina News, August 1, 1991: 3.

— need for new building discussed, Lahaina News, September 26, 1991: 1,3.

— to sponsor "Hawaiian Royalty" storytelling by Woody Fern, Lahaina News, October 3, 1991: 5.

— sponsoring toddler reading, Lahaina News, November 21, 1991: 4.

— to hold annual book sale, Lahaina News, August 13, 1992: 4.

— new site being considered, Lahaina News, September 10, 1992: 3.

— Maui County Cultural Resources Commission calls for library to be remodeled, Lahaina News, October 8, 1992: 1.

— results of children's children reading contest, Lahaina News, October 22, 1992: 3.

— to host public session for Roz Baker, Lahaina News, February 25, 1993: 2.

— librarian threatened, Lahaina News, March 18, 1993: 4.

— to show "Waco, the Big Lie", Lahaina News, September 16, 1993: 3,4.

— state seeking new site for, Lahaina News, August 17, 1995: 1,16.

— dispute over land near, Lahaina News, October 26, 1995: 1,16.

— hours to stay the same, Lahaina News, January 4, 1996: 4.

— changes digital cataloging system, Lahaina News, July 18, 1996: 1.

— to offer Young Adult Summer Reading , Lahaina News, June 5, 1997: 3.

— offering summer reading program, Lahaina News, June 12, 1997: 16.

— to offer painting activity, Lahaina News, August 7, 1997: 12.

— to celebrate National Children's Book Week, Lahaina News, November 13, 1997: 20.

— summer schedule, Lahaina News, June 18, 1998: 2.

— summer schedule, Lahaina News, June 25, 1998: 2.

— holds Summer Reading program, Lahaina News, July 2, 1998: 8.

— to change hours, Lahaina News, September 10, 1998: 6.

— to be re-roofed, Lahaina News, October 22, 1998: 15.

— celebrating Children's Book Week, Lahaina News, November 12, 1998: 17.

— to celebrate Children's Book Week, Lahaina News, November 12, 1998: 8.

— residents seek modified hours for, Lahaina News, November 26, 1998: 3.

— to host pilot Kathy O'Brien, Lahaina News, June 10, 1999: 17.

— Lieutenant Governor Mazie Hirono takes up issues, Lahaina News, June 17, 1999: 1,20.

— to host children's event with pilot Kathy O'Brien, Lahaina News, June 17, 1999: 16.

— to host presentation on soil and water conservation, Lahaina News, July 1, 1999: 12.

— Mr. Kenn to perform magic and comedy, Lahaina News, July 8, 1999: 13.

— librarian Peggy Robertson discusses changes in library hours, Lahaina News, November 11, 1999: 5.

— residents unhappy about new hours, Lahaina News, February 3, 2000: 1,16.

— book drop to be unavailable during renovations, Lahaina News, February 17, 2000: 16.

— Willie K and Amy Hanaiali'i Gilliom to play free concert at, Lahaina News, May 25, 2000: 20.

— Diane Ferlatte to present "Have I Got a Story to Tell" at , Lahaina News, June 15, 2000: 17.

— Ki-Ho'alu 2000 Hawaiian Slack Key Guitar Festival, Lahaina News, June 15, 2000: 3.

— Lord MacMillan Hughes donates portrait of King David Kalakaua to, Lahaina News, December 14, 2000: 2.

— John Clark is new librarian, Lahaina News, January 25, 2001: 1,20.

— tax forms available at, Lahaina News, March 1, 2001: 10.

— to host summer reading programs, Lahaina News, June 7, 2001: 2.

— to host summer reading programs, Lahaina News, June 14, 2001: 19.

— hosting community party, Lahaina News, July 5, 2001: 3.

— to offer internet workshop, Lahaina News, September 27, 2001: 3.

— Santa to visit, Lahaina News, December 12, 2002: 21.

— has new display featuring artist George Allan, Lahaina News, January 9, 2003: 18.

— Bobbie Dee Best is new branch manager, Lahaina News, May 1, 2003: 1,18.

— to host Summer Reading Program with puppet and mask show "The Continuing Adventures of Maui the Trickster", Lahaina News, June 5, 2003: 17.

— to display paintings by Belinda Ling, Lahaina News, July 17, 2003: 16.

— to hold "Story Time", Lahaina News, September 4, 2003: 2.

— accepting applications for student helper position, Lahaina News, October 2, 2003: 8.

LAHAINA PUBLIC SCHOOL

— hosting program for Tsunami Awareness Month, Lahaina News, April 12, 2001: 1.

— author Gill McBarnet reads to children, Lahaina News, April 12, 2001: 22.

— approves rebuilding bell tower at Hale Aloha, Lahaina News, November 12, 1992: insert1,insert4.
— volunteer ambassadors sent to New Zealand and Fiji, Lahaina News, November 12, 1992: insert3.
— to hold poster signing fundraiser, Lahaina News, December 31, 1992: 5.
— to hold poster signing fundraiser, Lahaina News, January 14, 1993: 2,3.
— to hold benefit poster signing, Lahaina News, January 21, 1993: 4.
— blesses start of research project to restore Moku'ula Island and Lake Mokuhinia, Lahaina News, February 4, 1993: 3.
— includes 4-page insert in issue, Lahaina News, May 13, 1993: insert 1,insert2,insert3,insert4.
— to plant coconut trees at Campbell Park, Lahaina News, March 10, 1994: 4.
— begins work improving Campbell Park, Lahaina News, March 31, 1994: 5.
— holds annual membership, Lahaina News, April 21, 1994: 20.
— hires former Pioneer Mill general manager Keoki Freeland, Lahaina News, November 3, 1994: 1,6.
— seeking compromise concerning tourist buses, Lahaina News, February 16, 1995: 1,3.
— to hold annual meeting, Lahaina News, April 20, 1995: 6.
— installs bell at Hale Aloha Church, Lahaina News, February 8, 1996: 1.
— history of Carthaginian, Lahaina News, February 22, 1996: 12.
— wins Maui Historical Society award for restoring Hale Aloha Bell Tower, Lahaina News, May 16, 1996: 6.
— spruce up three public telephones, Lahaina News, July 4, 1996: 2.
— historic documents being transcribed by Barbara Sharp, Lahaina News, April 10, 1997: 1,20.
— holds mahalo for Jim Luckey, Lahaina News, April 10, 1997: 3.
— reprints historical documents transcribed by Barbara Sharp, Lahaina News, April 24, 1997: 2,14.
— brochure lists historic sites, Lahaina News, September 18, 1997: 7.
— to hold "Breakfast in the Prison" annual meeting, Lahaina News, March 26, 1998: 5.
— to hold annual meeting, Lahaina News, April 2, 1998: 16.
— to manage Old Lahaina Courthouse, Lahaina News, February 25, 1999: 1,2.
— to hold annual meeting, Lahaina News, May 6, 1999: 20.
— Keoki Freeland to review projects and goals, Lahaina News, May 13, 1999: 3.
— Carthaginian rigging repaired, Lahaina News, March 15, 2001: 1.
— volunteers restore Carthaginian's gangplank, Lahaina News, May 3, 2001: 3.
— to hold Chinese Moon Festival, Lahaina News, September 27, 2001: 1.
— research director Barbara Sharp featured, Lahaina News, December 13, 2001: 1,18.
— to hold Winter Solstice Festival with Wo Hing Society, Lahaina News, December 20, 2001: 1,18.
— to celebrate Chinese New Year, Lahaina News, January 31, 2002: 14.
— to host Neil Hannahs from Bishop Estate at annual meeting, Lahaina News, April 25, 2002: 1.
— to work with police to address crime problems, Lahaina News, August 22, 2002: 1,2.
— director Keoki Freeland discusses replacing the Carthaginian, Lahaina News, September 12, 2002: 1,24.
— to hold Chinese Moon Celebration, Lahaina News, September 19, 2002: 1,22.
— to celebrate Chinese New Year, Lahaina News, January 23, 2003: 1,20.
— Alan Arakawa to be guest speaker at annual breakfast meeting, Lahaina News, March 20, 2003: 1.

— to sink Carthaginian II and replace with new vessel, Lahaina News, July 31, 2003: 1,2.
— to hold Chinese Moon Festival, Lahaina News, September 11, 2003: 14.

LAHAINA RETAIL COMMITTEE
— meeting to discuss business climate in Lahaina, Lahaina Sun, December 16, 1970: 3.
— organizational structure described, Lahaina Sun, December 16, 1970: 3.
— meeting announced, Lahaina Sun, January 6, 1971: 2.
— described, Lahaina Sun, January 20, 1971: 5.
— prioritizes improvement of off-street parking, Lahaina Sun, February 10, 1971: 1.
— planning promotion campaign for Lahaina, Lahaina Sun, February 24, 1971: 1.
— plans membership drive, Lahaina Sun, March 31, 1971: 2.
— looking into holding the Lahaina Whaling Spree in 1972, Lahaina Sun, May 26, 1971: 1.
— changing name to Lahaina Improvement Association, Lahaina Sun, June 9, 1971: 7.
— see also West Maui Business Association

LAHAINA SCRIMSHAW FACTORY [BUSINESS]
— featured, Lahaina News, September 5, 1984: 14.
— featured, Lahaina News, February 4, 1987: 12.
— former partner Thomas Peden dies, Lahaina News, March 21, 1990: 2.

LAHAINA SEAFOOD RESTAURANT AND MARKET [RESTAURANT]
— opens, Lahaina News, July 20, 2000: 14.
— KPOA to be broadcast live from, Lahaina News, July 27, 2000: 20.

LAHAINA SENIOR CITIZEN CLUB
— planning a trip to Kaua'i, Lahaina Sun, April 21, 1971: 8.

LAHAINA SHINGON MISSION
— to hold O Bon Festival, Lahaina News, June 20, 2002: 1.

LAHAINA SHOE AND LUGGAGE REPAIR COMPANY
— likely to receive permission to open, Lahaina News, July 9, 1992: 3.

LAHAINA SHOPPING CENTER
— celebrates 18 years, Lahaina News, March 15, 1983: 11.
— hosting Lahainaluna school bazaar, Lahaina News, February 26, 1986: 3.
— stores destroyed by fire, Lahaina News, June 3, 1987: 1.
— to promote gift certificates, Lahaina News, March 19, 1992: 4.
— offering Las Vegas vacation as prize, Lahaina News, July 16, 1992: 3,4.
— offering interisland vacation as part of Spring Sale, Lahaina News, February 25, 1993: 2.
— to be renovated, Lahaina News, October 20, 1994: 10.
— begins renovation project, Lahaina News, July 20, 1995: 10.
— Maui County Council rejects sign for, Lahaina News, May 23, 1996: 3.

LAHAINA SHOPPING CENTER BUSINESSMEN'S ASSOCIATION
— new officers selected, Lahaina Sun, February 24, 1971: 8.

LAHAINA SHORES BEACH RESORT
— Carol Koepke appointed general manager of, Lahaina News, January 31, 2002: 8.
— see also McNeil Construction Company

LAHAINA SHORES HOTEL [BUSINESS]
— State investigating landscaping work done at, Lahaina News, November 5, 1992: 1,4.

LAHAINA SHORES RESTAURANT [BUSINESS]
— to open at 505 Front Street, Lahaina News, September 26, 1990: 9.

LAHAINA SHORES SALON [BUSINESS]
— featured, Lahaina News, October 26, 1983: 14.

LAHAINA SHORES SHOPPING CENTER
— apparently sold to Lawrence McNeil Construction, Lahaina News, October 10, 1984: 3.

LAHAINA SHORES VILLAGE [BUSINESS]
— development featured, Lahaina News, May 23, 1984: 18.
— featured, Lahaina News, June 6, 1984: 13.
— featured, Lahaina News, June 13, 1984: 17.
— editorial supporting improvements at Lahaina Shores Village, Lahaina News, June 13, 1984: 2.
— featured, Lahaina News, June 20, 1984: 14.
— only bid to purchase was too low and not accepted, Lahaina News, August 29, 1984: 3.
— for sale again, Lahaina News, June 12, 1985: 3.
— to be auctions at the Federal Bankruptcy Court, Lahaina News, July 17, 1985: 3.
— sold again, Lahaina News, August 7, 1985: 8.
— sold to John Kean and Dick Farley, Lahaina News, September 25, 1985: 3.
— changes name back to Whalers Market Place, Lahaina News, October 16, 1985: 3.

LAHAINA SOUND STUDIO [BUSINESS]
— featured, Lahaina News, February 17, 1988: 7.
— used by the group Soft Touch, not Hapa, as reported in previous edition, Lahaina News, March 2, 1988: 22.
— recording studio at Lahaina Square Shopping Center, Lahaina News, September 20, 1989: 9.

LAHAINA SQUARE SHOPPING CENTER
— to host mini-telethon in support of Jerry Lewis muscular dystrophy telethon, Lahaina News, August 15, 1984: 3.

LAHAINA STATION
— concession opens in rail car, Lahaina News, December 19, 1984: 14.

LAHAINA SUMMER JUNIOR OPEN TENNIS TOURNAMENT
— to be held, Lahaina News, August 3, 2000: 3.

LAHAINA SUN [BUSINESS]
— "Tiny Bubbles" section by A. Bodoya and C. Honey begins June 2, 1971 and is not indexed, Lahaina Sun, June 2, 1971: .
— first birthday of the newspaper, Lahaina Sun, November 3, 1971: 1,2,3.
— Jack Seabern named advertising manager, Lahaina Sun, December 15, 1971: 6.
— Jarvis Birney joins staff, Lahaina Sun, January 19, 1972: 6.
— Tom Curran joins the journalism staff, Lahaina Sun, June 28, 1972: 19.
— columnist Robert Kelsey's work discussed, Lahaina Sun, July 26, 1972: 16,17.
— Don Graydon, publisher and editor, moves to East San Jose Sun, Lahaina Sun, August 16, 1972: 5.
— Sue Beving joins reporting staff, Lahaina Sun, August 16, 1972: 5.
— praised by Hawaii Business magazine, Lahaina Sun, September 6, 1972: 21.
— Russ Williams joins staff as a reporter, Lahaina Sun, February 14, 1973: 4.
— production process detailed, Lahaina Sun, March 28, 1973: 12,13.
— moving location and changing name to Maui Sun, Lahaina Sun, July 25, 1973: 21.
— will use airplane instead of barge to bring printed paper from Honolulu, Lahaina Sun, August 15, 1973: 6.
— closing, Lahaina News, November 1, 1989: 1.

LAHAINA SURF [BUSINESS]
— low income housing described, Lahaina Sun, January 19, 1972: 3.
— inquiries concerning apartment, received by Hale Mahaolu, Lahaina Sun, April 26, 1972: 15.
— first families moving into apartments, Lahaina Sun, November 29, 1972: 5.
— Amfac representative C. Earl Stoner responds to criticisms of apartment project, Lahaina Sun, January 31, 1973: 7.
— distributing 30-gallon bags of wood chips, Lahaina News, March 16, 1995: 4.

LAHAINA SURF CLASSIC
— presented by Local Motion, Lahaina News, April 25, 1990: 12.

LAHAINA SURF TENANTS ASSOCIATION
— to hold rummage sale, Lahaina News, November 7, 1991: 4.
— to hold rummage sale, Lahaina News, November 21, 1991: 3.
— to host rummage sale, Lahaina News, April 16, 1992: 4.
— to hold Christmas Rummage sale, Lahaina News, November 30, 1995: 4.

LAHAINA SWIM CLUB
— to attend swim meet in Hilo, Lahaina News, March 17, 1994: 6.
— featured, Lahaina News, July 18, 1996: 11.
— featured, Lahaina News, March 27, 1997: 6.
— featured, Lahaina News, November 6, 1997: 8.
— places eighth in state meet, Lahaina News, January 7, 1999: 14.
— featured, Lahaina News, June 24, 1999: 6.
— to hold rummage sale, Lahaina News, October 14, 1999: 12.
— competes in Hawaii Short Course Age Group Swimming Championships, Lahaina News, February 10, 2000: 9.
— raises money for West Maui Youth Center, Lahaina News, June 15, 2000: 12.
— results of competition, Lahaina News, June 15, 2000: 12.
— succeeding in competitions, Lahaina News, June 28, 2001: 15.
— featured, Lahaina News, August 22, 2002: 10.
— successful in tournament, Lahaina News, June 26, 2003: 1,2.

LAHAINA SWIM TEAM
— successes detailed, Lahaina News, November 2, 2000: 8.

LAHAINA TASK FORCE
— being created by Planning Department, Lahaina News, June 20, 1996: 14.
— discusses issues, Lahaina News, August 1, 1996: 2.
— committee considering traffic issues, Lahaina News, September 12, 1996: 2.
— County Planning Director David Blane discusses changes to signage and downtown parking, Lahaina News, September 26, 1996: 4.
— to recommend county office for Lahaina, Lahaina News, November 28, 1996: 1,2.
— recommends additional parking, Lahaina News, January 9, 1997: 3,14.
— editorial in support of, Lahaina News, July 17, 1997: 4.

LAHAINA TENNIS ASSOCIATION
— receives grant from United States Tennis Association's Star Search Grant, Lahaina News, May 21, 1998: 14,15.

LAHAINA TENNIS CLUB
— accepting entries for Christmas tournament, Lahaina Sun, December 16, 1970: 3.
— to hold potluck, Lahaina News, September 30, 1987: 3.
— to host Lahaina Junior Novice Tournament, Lahaina News, November 2, 1988: 3,18.
— to host youth program, Lahaina News, September 6, 1989: 3.
— to hold Summer Tennis Camp, Lahaina News, July 11, 1996: 11.
— founder Shigesh Wakida ready to retire, Lahaina News, April 27, 2000: 1,2.
— to meet, Lahaina News, October 19, 2000: 9.

LAHAINA TIMES [BUSINESS]
— sending reporters to international destinations, Lahaina Times, July, 1980 volume 4 number 6: 1.
— "On the Fairway" column by Roger Fredericks begins, is not otherwise indexed, Lahaina News, March 28, 1996: 7.
— "Car Care" column with Jim Lytte begins, is not otherwise indexed, Lahaina News, April 18, 1996: 14.

LAHAINA TOWN ANTIQUES & VINTAGE CLOTHING COMPANY [BUSINESS]
— opens, Lahaina News, February 20, 1991: 7.

LAHAINA TOWN CRIME WATCH
— representative Laki Ka'ahumanu to speak at community meeting focusing on reducing crime in Lahaina, Lahaina News, July 18, 2002: 1.
— meeting to establish, Lahaina News, August 1, 2002: 1,24.

LAHAINA TOWN OPERATORS' ASSOCIATION
— working to improve Lahaina Town, Lahaina News, December 11, 1985: 24.

LAHAINA TOWNE ANTIQUES [BUSINESS]
— to open, Lahaina News, December 19, 1990: 7.

LAHAINA TOWNE BAZAAR [BUSINESS]
— cited for allowing vendors to do business in parking lot, Lahaina News, December 17, 1992: 1,2.
— injunction may stop use of parking lot by vendors, Lahaina News, December 31, 1992: 3.
— to be torn down, Lahaina News, February 25, 1993: 2,3.

LAHAINA TOWNE COSTUME [BUSINESS]
— featured, Lahaina News, August 17, 1988: 2,3.

LAHAINA TOWNE TUXEDO [BUSINESS]
— opens, Lahaina News, March 27, 1997: 10.

LAHAINA TRADE CENTER
— new businesses open in, Lahaina News, September 8, 1994: 10.

LAHAINA TRAIL
— C. Brewer Properties to permit access to, Lahaina News, August 6, 1992: 9.

LAHAINA TREE GARDEN [RESTAURANT]
— now open in Lahaina Market Place, Lahaina Sun, July 14, 1971: 4.

LAHAINA TREEHOUSE [RESTAURANT]
— workers vote to unionize, Lahaina Sun, September 20, 1972: 3.
— reopens, Lahaina News, May 8, 1991: 22.

LAHAINA UNITED METHODIST CHURCH
— celebrates 90th anniversary, Lahaina News, December 10, 1986: 3,16.
— Earl Kernahan to host revival, Lahaina News, March 2, 1988: 22.
— to hold yard sale, Lahaina News, April 16, 1992: 4.
— to hold yard sale, seeking donations, Lahaina News, April 23, 1992: 5.
— to hold bazaar, Lahaina News, October 14, 1993: 5.
— to hold Vacation Bible School, Lahaina News, August 18, 1994: 5.
— to hold bazaar, Lahaina News, October 13, 1994: 7.
— to celebrate centennial, Lahaina News, November 30, 1995: 4.
— to celebrate 100 years, Lahaina News, February 1, 1996: 4.
— celebrating centennial, Lahaina News, February 8, 1996: 4.
— to hold centennial celebration, Lahaina News, November 21, 1996: 14.
— offering preschool year-round, Lahaina News, July 22, 1999: 3.
— Children of the Rainbow Nursery holds graduation ceremony, Lahaina News, June 15, 2000: 1.
— Richard Kurrasch is new pastor of, Lahaina News, October 12, 2000: 17.
— Tongan congregation selling plate lunches to benefit building fund, Lahaina News, October 11, 2001: 16.

LAHAINA UNITED PENTECOSTAL CHURCH
— to hold yard sale, Lahaina News, November 6, 1997: 14.

LAHAINA UPHOLSTERY AND FLOORING [BUSINESS]
— featured, Lahaina News, March 28, 1984: 17.

LAHAINA VENTURES [BUSINESS]
— Bruce McNeil-owned company declares bankruptcy, Lahaina News, December 15, 1981: 7.
— trustees named, Lahaina News, January 4, 1984: 5.

LAHAINA VISITOR CENTER
— likely to be approved, Lahaina News, December 15, 1994: 3.
— LahainaTown Action Committee holds grand opening for, Lahaina News, April 13, 1995: 1,20.
— featured, Lahaina News, April 20, 1995: 4.
— seeking volunteers, Lahaina News, December 14, 1995: 18.
— celebrates first year, Lahaina News, March 14, 1996: 4.
— plans for Lahaina-Kaunakakai ferry being considered, Lahaina News, August 6, 1998: 1.
— plans to be presented to Maui County Cultural Resources, Lahaina News, August 20, 1998: 2.
— Cultural Resources Commission to consider plan for, Lahaina News, August 27, 1998: 1,20.
— residents attempt to intervene in application to build, Lahaina News, September 3, 1998: 1,24.
— Cultural Resources Commission seeks information on, Lahaina News, September 10, 1998: 1,24.
— training volunteers, Lahaina News, June 24, 1999: 5.
— to answer visitor's pressing questions, Lahaina News, April 20, 2000: 1,20.
— opens at Old Lahaina Courthouse, Lahaina News, July 12, 2001: 16.
— opens at Old Lahaina Courthouse, Lahaina News, July 19, 2001: 16.

LAHAINA WASTEWATER RECLAMATION FACILITY
— expansion blessing set, Lahaina News, February 5, 1986: 3.
— difficulties at, Lahaina News, April 22, 1993: 1,3.
— Sierra Club Legal Defense Fund concerned about proposed injection wells at, Lahaina News, October 27, 1994: 5.

LAHAINA WATER COMPANY [BUSINESS]
— opens, Lahaina News, November 5, 1992: 8.
— to provide new water system, Lahaina News, November 18, 1993: 5.

LAHAINA WATER TAXI SERVICE [BUSINESS]
— featured, Lahaina News, February 22, 1984: 17.

LAHAINA WATER TREATMENT FACILITY
— ground breaking held, Lahaina News, November 2, 1995: 4.

LAHAINA WATER WORKS SPORTING GOODS [BUSINESS]
— purchased by Mark Rolfing and Doug Stacey, to be renamed West Maui Sports and Fishing Supply, Lahaina News, July 9, 1992: 13.

LAHAINA WATERSHED FLOOD CONTROL PROJECT
— informational meeting to be held on, Lahaina News, July 19, 1989: 1.
— U.S. Soil Conservation Servicing looking to move outlet of proposed, Lahaina News, May 8, 1991: 1.
— Puamana Community Association to sue county and state for inadequate environmental assessment on Lahaina Flood Control Project, Lahaina News, July 18, 1991: 1.
— U.S. Soil Conservation Service investigating alternative flood control for, Lahaina News, October 10, 1991: 12.
— Modified Alterative Plan to be discussed in public hearing, Lahaina News, November 7, 1991: 4.
— State and federal officials leaning against preparing an Environmental Impact Statement, Lahaina News, November 28, 1991: 1,4.
— assessment released, Lahaina News, March 5, 1992: 1,4.
— deadline set for ruling on whether to require Environmental Impact Assessment for Lahaina Watershed project, Lahaina News, April 30, 1992: 4.
— public input sought, Lahaina News, February 17, 2000: 1,2.

— to be explained at public hearing, Lahaina News, February 14, 2002: 1.

— residents frustrated at delays to, Lahaina News, February 28, 2002: 1,20.

— draft Environmental Impact Statement to be discussed, Lahaina News, June 12, 2003: 14.

LAHAINA WELDING [BUSINESS]
— flooded by Kahoma Stream, Lahaina News, June 7, 1989: 3.

LAHAINA WESTERN GUN CLUB
— range opens, Lahaina News, April 2, 1998: 15.

LAHAINA WHALING FESTIVAL
— planning discussed, Lahaina Sun, March 17, 1971: 1.

LAHAINA WHALING SPREE
— planning discussed, Lahaina Sun, February 3, 1971: 2.

— now called Lahaina Whaling Festival, Lahaina Sun, February 17, 1971: 1,8.

— canceled for 1971, Lahaina Sun, March 31, 1971: 1.

— Lahaina Retail Committee looking into holding in 1972, Lahaina Sun, May 26, 1971: 1.

LAHAINA YACHT CLUB
— names officers, Lahaina Sun, December 23, 1970: 8.

— results of first ocean race, Lahaina Sun, March 1, 1972: 8.

— looking for a Jackpot Queen to preside over festivities, Lahaina News, October 17, 1984: 3.

— organizes Spring Wahine Fishing Tournament, Lahaina News, April 9, 1986: 3.

— organizes Sauza Cup boat race, Lahaina News, July 29, 1987: 6.

— to hold summer regatta, Lahaina News, July 5, 1989: 2.

— to hold Bud Cup Regatta, Lahaina News, August 23, 1989: 5.

— to hold Bud Cup Regatta, Lahaina News, August 30, 1989: 24.

— to hold race, Lahaina News, May 9, 1990: 3.

— raises funds for scholarships, Lahaina News, May 9, 1990: 5.

— Vince Firazzo wins race, Lahaina News, March 27, 1991: 8.

— to host races, Lahaina News, May 23, 1991: 10.

— hosting Keiki Fishing Tournament, Lahaina News, August 29, 1991: 7.

— sponsoring Keiki Fishing tournament, Lahaina News, September 5, 1991: 24.

— sponsoring Keiki Fishing tournament, Lahaina News, September 12, 1991: 6.

— results of Keiki fishing tournament, Lahaina News, September 26, 1991: 24.

— commodore Mark Robinson featured, Lahaina News, September 26, 1991: 8.

— sponsors Lana'i fishing tournament with Ma'alaea Boating and Fishing Club, Lahaina News, October 3, 1991: 8.

— elects new officers, Lahaina News, December 26, 1991: 5.

— to host Keiki Fishing Tournament, Lahaina News, September 10, 1992: 8.

— to celebrate opening of sailing season, Lahaina News, February 9, 1995: 3.

— Golf Tournament raises money for Maui Memorial Hospital, Lahaina News, October 26, 1995: 5.

— to receive grant from Roy Disney following his victory in Victoria-Maui yacht race, Lahaina News, August 8, 1996: 1,20.

— results of Keiki Fishing Tournament, Lahaina News, September 19, 1996: 12.

— awards scholarships to Lahainaluna High School students, Lahaina News, June 26, 1997: 2.

— Governor Ben Cayetano awards funds from Sport Tourism Program to, Lahaina News, July 31, 1997: 9,15.

— to host "Chili Cook-off", Lahaina News, May 14, 1998: 16.

— Keiki Fishing Tournament to be held, Lahaina News, September 3, 1998: 15.

— Keiki Fishing Tournament to be held, Lahaina News, September 10, 1998: 15.

— Keiki Fishing Tournament draws over 100 contestants, Lahaina News, September 24, 1998: 1.

— Wahine Jackpot Tournament to be held, Lahaina News, October 15, 1998: 3.

— to hold Spring Wahine Fishing Tournament, Lahaina News, April 8, 1999: 7.

— to hold Keiki Fishing Tournament, Lahaina News, September 2, 1999: 9.

— Keiki Fishing Tournament to be held, Lahaina News, September 9, 1999: 7.

— results of Spring Wahine tournament, Lahaina News, May 11, 2000: 15.

— Keiki Fishing Tournament held, Lahaina News, September 21, 2000: 1.

— results of Keiki Fishing Tournament, Lahaina News, September 28, 2000: 8.

— to hold Spring Wahine Fishing Tournament, Lahaina News, April 12, 2001: 15.

— to hold Spring Wahine Fishing Tournament, Lahaina News, April 19, 2001: 13.

— to hold Spring Wahine Fishing Tournament, Lahaina News, April 26, 2001: 15.

— to hold Keiki Fishing Tournament, Lahaina News, September 20, 2001: 13.

— Wahine Jackpot Tournament results, Lahaina News, November 1, 2001: 13.

— to hold Wahine fishing tournament, Lahaina News, May 9, 2002: 13.

— Keiki Fishing Tournament to be held, Lahaina News, August 29, 2002: 11.

— Jackpot Fishing Tournament won by Jeni-K, Lahaina News, August 7, 2003: 13.

— planning Keiki Fishing Tourney, Lahaina News, September 18, 2003: 13.

— held Keiki Fishing Tournament, Lahaina News, October 2, 2003: 13.

LAHAINA YOUTH CENTER
— "Hearts and Saddles" fundraiser for to be held at Embassy Suites Hotel, Lahaina News, February 17, 1994: 11.

LAHAINA YOUTH CONTRACT FOOTBALL BOOSTER CLUB
— to hold rummage sale, Lahaina News, February 20, 1997: 10.

LAHAINA-HONOLUA SENIOR CITIZENS CLUB
— concerned with cost of building new power lines, Lahaina News, March 19, 1992: 3.

— ILWU Business Agent Joe Franco to speak to, Lahaina News, February 7, 2002: 3.

LAHAINA-KA'ANAPALI AND PACIFIC RAILROAD [BUSINESS]
— robbery staged for tourists, Lahaina Sun, November 18, 1970: 4.

— robbery of, staged for tourists, Lahaina Sun, November 18, 1970: 4.

— discuss ways to bring more tourists to Lahaina, Lahaina Sun, November 25, 1970: 3.

— requested to create line to proposed Lahaina Inn, Lahaina Sun, January 20, 1971: 1.

— founder A.W. McKelvey resigns, Lahaina Sun, April 14, 1971: 1.

— report on passengers and miles travelled since opening, Lahaina Sun, April 21, 1971: 7.

— new engine arrives, Lahaina Sun, July 14, 1971: 5.

— location of terminal near Lahaina criticized, Lahaina Sun, July 21, 1971: 1.

— working with Lahaina Improvement Association to improve passenger experience, Lahaina Sun, July 28, 1971: 1,12.

— photograph of engine, Lahaina Sun, September 8, 1971: 7.

— basketball team to compete in Maui Interscholastic League, Lahaina News, December 13, 1989: 8.

— success of students described, Lahaina News, December 20, 1989: 6.

— basketball team has good start to the season, Lahaina News, January 10, 1990: 5.

— wrestling and basketball teams featured, Lahaina News, January 24, 1990: 8.

— reunion of class of 1970 planned, Lahaina News, February 7, 1990: 2.

— vice president investigating egg-throwing incident, Lahaina News, February 7, 1990: 3.

— basketball team in state tournament, Lahaina News, February 7, 1990: 8.

— track team featured, Lahaina News, February 14, 1990: 11.

— baseball team photographed, Lahaina News, February 28, 1990: 5.

— track team results, Lahaina News, February 28, 1990: 6.

— receives donation from Moore Foundation and Department of Education, Lahaina News, March 7, 1990: 3.

— girls basketball begins season, Lahaina News, March 7, 1990: 9.

— carnival to start, Lahaina News, March 21, 1990: 3.

— baseball team begins season well, Lahaina News, March 21, 1990: 9.

— sports at, Lahaina News, March 28, 1990: 12.

— update on sports teams, Lahaina News, April 4, 1990: 4.

— update on sports teams, Lahaina News, April 18, 1990: 7.

— to hold Spring Concert, Lahaina News, April 25, 1990: 3.

— basketball team photo; updates on sports, Lahaina News, April 25, 1990: 8,9.

— wins state tennis tournament, Lahaina News, May 2, 1990: 5.

— students to compete in Plymouth-AAA Troubleshooting contest, Lahaina News, May 16, 1990: 5.

— requesting portable classrooms to replace building destroyed by fire, Lahaina News, May 23, 1990: 1,6.

— students given free ride on Atlantis submarine, Lahaina News, May 23, 1990: 5,6.

— graduates recognized, photographed, Lahaina News, June 6, 1990: 2,8,9,10.

— receives third place for outstanding state student council, Lahaina News, June 6, 1990: 3.

— scholarship winners named, Lahaina News, June 13, 1990: 5.

— state to build new classrooms, Lahaina News, June 27, 1990: 1.

— seniors asked to take yearbook pictures, Lahaina News, June 27, 1990: 5.

— to hold pep rally; yearbook portrait deadline coming up, Lahaina News, August 22, 1990: 4.

— deadline for photos for yearbook nears, Lahaina News, August 29, 1990: 4.

— to hold kalua pig sale; update on sports, Lahaina News, October 3, 1990: 6.

— still waiting for portables, Lahaina News, October 10, 1990: 1.

— sports updates, Lahaina News, October 10, 1990: 18,24.

— to hold homecoming, John Marciel and Mitzie Colon to preside, Lahaina News, October 17, 1990: 5,6.

— football and volleyball updates, Lahaina News, October 17, 1990: 8.

— parents to meet, Lahaina News, October 24, 1990: 4.

— booster club to meet, Lahaina News, October 31, 1990: 9.

— volleyball team to play Baldwin High School, Lahaina News, October 31, 1990: 9.

— varsity football team listed, Lahaina News, November 7, 1990: 14.

— looking for soccer coach, Lahaina News, November 14, 1990: 10.

— to hold open house, Lahaina News, November 14, 1990: 3.

— portables constructed, Lahaina News, November 21, 1990: 1.

— basketball pre-season tournament to be held, Lahaina News, November 21, 1990: 24.

— looking for soccer coach, Lahaina News, November 21, 1990: 24.

— report cards available, Lahaina News, November 21, 1990: 3.

— facilities evaluated, Lahaina News, November 28, 1990: 1,2.

— to hold open house, Lahaina News, November 28, 1990: 3.

— to hold campus cleanup, Lahaina News, December 5, 1990: 3.

— to participate in Close Up Foundation Citizen Bee, Lahaina News, December 5, 1990: 5.

— booster club to meet, Lahaina News, December 5, 1990: 8.

— pre-season basketball tournament to be held, Lahaina News, December 5, 1990: 8.

— to hold Swim-A-Thon, Lahaina News, December 12, 1990: 20.

— basketball team did well at its invitational, Lahaina News, December 19, 1990: 24.

— 10th graders perform well in mathematics but poorly in reading, Lahaina News, January 2, 1991: 1.

— wrestling results from Kona Invitational, Lahaina News, January 2, 1991: 16.

— Swim-A-Thon fundraiser successful, Lahaina News, January 2, 1991: 16.

— basketball team to compete against Seabury Hall, Lahaina News, January 16, 1991: 20.

— basketball team to play Moloka'i High School, Lahaina News, January 23, 1991: 16.

— report cards sent, Lahaina News, February 6, 1991: 3.

— basketball to play; tennis team's prospects discussed by coach Shigesh Wakida, Lahaina News, February 13, 1991: 20.

— to survey students regarding summer school, Lahaina News, February 13, 1991: 4.

— honor roll announced, Lahaina News, February 20, 1991: 4,5.

— athletic department to hold a bazaar, Lahaina News, February 27, 1991: 6.

— boys tennis team beats Mission Viejo High School, Lahaina News, February 27, 1991: 6.

— tennis teams beat Seabury Hall, Lahaina News, March 6, 1991: 5.

— Maui District winner of Maui Trial Tournament, Lahaina News, March 13, 1991: 3.

— tennis team results, Lahaina News, March 13, 1991: 7.

— to hold Junior Promenade, Lahaina News, March 27, 1991: 3,4.

— organizing "Spring Fling", Lahaina News, April 3, 1991: 4.

— concert band to present Annual Spring Concert, Lahaina News, April 10, 1991: 3.

— scholarships give to students of, Lahaina News, April 24, 1991: 1.

— honor roll announced, Lahaina News, May 1, 1991: 3,4.

— receives money from State for construction, Lahaina News, May 15, 1991: 1.

— Booster Club to meet, to hold golf tournament fundraiser, Lahaina News, May 15, 1991: 7.

— to hold commencement exercises, Lahaina News, May 30, 1991: 3.

— graduates and scholarship recipients listed, Lahaina News, June 6, 1991: 10.

— seniors portraits to be shot, Lahaina News, August 8, 1991: 3.

— must pick up homeroom assignments, Lahaina News, August 22, 1991: 3.

— seniors reminded to have portraits taken, Lahaina News, August 29, 1991: 3.

— class of 1966 holds reunion, Lahaina News, August 29, 1991: 3.

— State estimates that student population at will double, Lahaina News, September 5, 1991: 1.

— to celebrate 160 years, Lahaina News, September 12, 1991: 1.

— sports described, Lahaina News, September 26, 1991: 9.

— football team to play, Lahaina News, October 10, 1991: 8.

— president of Booster Club Eugene Perry featured, Lahaina News, October 17, 1991: 3.

— homecoming events organized, Lahaina News, October 17, 1991: 4,5.

— teacher Art Fillazar featured, Lahaina News, November 7, 1991: 3.

— report cards to be issued, Lahaina News, November 14, 1991: 3.

— volleyball coach discusses prospects, Lahaina News, November 14, 1991: 5,6.

— student Chalon Allen finalist for Hearst Foundation Youth Senate Program, Lahaina News, November 21, 1991: 3.

— honor roll listed, Lahaina News, December 5, 1991: 11.

— to hold Christmas concert, Lahaina News, December 12, 1991: 19.

— alumni basketball tournament to be held, Lahaina News, December 12, 1991: 4.

— planning events for Christmas, Lahaina News, December 12, 1991: 8.

— to compete in Distributive Educational Clubs of America (DECA) competition, Lahaina News, January 23, 1992: 5.

— basketball team in first place, Lahaina News, January 30, 1992: 8.

— principal Henry Ariyoshi receives check from McDonald's, Lahaina News, February 6, 1992: 5.

— students are finalists in National Golden Key Art Competition, Lahaina News, February 13, 1992: 7.

— sports updates, Lahaina News, March 5, 1992: 8.

— Japanese Club to hold Bake n' Rummage sale, Lahaina News, March 12, 1992: 3.

— wins Foodland's "Shop for a Better Education" banner contest., Lahaina News, March 12, 1992: 4.

— Boost Club planning fundraisers, Lahaina News, March 12, 1992: 9.

— athletics department to hold bazaar, Lahaina News, March 19, 1992: 3.

— student group returns from trip to Washington, D.C., Lahaina News, April 2, 1992: 21.

— concert band to perform, Lahaina News, April 9, 1992: 16.

— junior prom to be held, Lahaina News, April 9, 1992: 5.

— police called to halt three disruptive students, Lahaina News, May 7, 1992: 3.

— to hold golf tournament, Lahaina News, May 21, 1992: 11,12.

— graduating class featured, Lahaina News, June 11, 1992: 23,24,25,26.

— incoming seniors reminded to get their pictures taken, Lahaina News, July 9, 1992: 4.

— registration underway for Fall, Lahaina News, July 23, 1992: 5,7.

— class of 1982 celebrating 10 year reunion, Lahaina News, July 30, 1992: 4.

— registration continues, Lahaina News, August 13, 1992: 4.

— football team to begin season, Lahaina News, August 20, 1992: 8.

— updates on sports, Lahaina News, September 24, 1992: 13.

— results of SAT test to be distributed, Lahaina News, October 22, 1992: 4.

— football team wins, Lahaina News, October 22, 1992: 8.

— football season ends, Lahaina News, November 5, 1992: 12.

— results for golf team, Lahaina News, November 12, 1992: 8.

— band concert to be held, Lahaina News, December 10, 1992: 16.

— to hold parent orientation, Lahaina News, December 10, 1992: 4.

— wins girls softball opener, Lahaina News, December 17, 1992: 11.

— wrestling team competes, Lahaina News, December 24, 1992: 8.

— student Josh Perry seeking Maui Interscholastic League Wrestling title, Lahaina News, December 31, 1992: 6.

— fire code violations fewer this year, Lahaina News, January 14, 1993: 1,3.

— results of sports competitions, Lahaina News, January 21, 1993: 7.

— update on sports, Lahaina News, January 28, 1993: 6.

— report cards ready, Lahaina News, February 4, 1993: 4.

— update on basketball team, Lahaina News, February 4, 1993: 6.

— update on sports, Lahaina News, February 11, 1993: 8.

— update on sports at, Lahaina News, February 18, 1993: 7.

— hosting Vocational Education Showcase, Lahaina News, February 25, 1993: 2.

— win league wrestling tournament, other updates on sports, Lahaina News, February 25, 1993: 4.

— to hold "Spring Fling Bazaar", Lahaina News, March 4, 1993: 3.

— to host fundraiser, Lahaina News, March 4, 1993: 5.

— selected by Academy of Travel and Tourism for two-year program, Lahaina News, March 18, 1993: 3.

— to hold "Spring Fling Bazaar", Lahaina News, March 18, 1993: 3.

— receives donation from Kemper Lesnik Organization, Lahaina News, March 25, 1993: 6.

— update on sports, Lahaina News, March 25, 1993: 6.

— students participate in History Day, Lahaina News, April 8, 1993: 3.

— to hold campus clean-up, Lahaina News, April 8, 1993: 3.

— report cards to be sent out, Lahaina News, April 8, 1993: 3.

— update on Lahainaluna High School tennis, Lahaina News, April 8, 1993: 8.

— participates in Mock Trial competition, Lahaina News, April 15, 1993: 3.

— concert band to perform, Lahaina News, April 15, 1993: 3.

— Panama Tevaga captures gold in long jump, Lahaina News, May 6, 1993: 10.

— Lane Fujii named as general manager of Maui Stingrays, Lahaina News, May 6, 1993: 11.

— class of 1973 to hold reunion, Lahaina News, May 6, 1993: 4.

— Booster Club to meet, Lahaina News, May 6, 1993: 4.

— events, Lahaina News, May 20, 1993: 2,3.

— Boarding Department chooses new president, Lahaina News, June 3, 1993: 3.

— graduating class photos and details, Lahaina News, June 3, 1993: 9,10,11.

— graduation held, Lahaina News, June 10, 1993: 1.

— Football Boosters to sell Kalua pig as fundraiser, Lahaina News, June 10, 1993: 4.

— publishes newsletter, Lahaina News, June 24, 1993: 4.

— issues reminders to students, Lahaina News, July 22, 1993: 3,4.

— class of 1978 to celebrate reunion, Lahaina News, September 9, 1993: 3.

— looking for coaches, Lahaina News, September 16, 1993: 11.

— class of 1978 to celebrate reunion, Lahaina News, September 16, 1993: 4.

— football team wins first game, Lahaina News, September 23, 1993: 8.

— class of 1974 to hold reunion, Lahaina News, October 7, 1993: 3.

— to celebrate homecoming, Lahaina News, October 14, 1993: 4.

— class of 1978 to celebrate reunion, Lahaina News, October 21, 1993: 3.

— students offered financial planning course, Lahaina News, October 21, 1993: 4.

— principal Henry "Bruno" Ariyoshi receives award from Milken Family Foundation National Educator Award, Lahaina News, October 28, 1993: 1,12.

— fire inspector finds code violations at, Lahaina News, November 4, 1993: 1,3.

— to hold 12-hour marathon to promote "drug and alcohol free celebration", Lahaina News, November 18, 1993: 8.

— concert band to represent Hawaii in France, needs support, Lahaina News, November 25, 1993: 3.

— Maui Interscholastic League in wrestling to begin, Lahaina News, November 25, 1993: 8.

— basketball team stronger from transfers, Lahaina News, December 2, 1993: 10.

— concert band to represent Hawaii in France, needs support, Lahaina News, December 2, 1993: 3.

— to present annual Christmas Concert, Lahaina News, December 9, 1993: 11.

— shut down early due to lack of running water, Lahaina News, December 9, 1993: 2.

— soccer team prospects discussed, Lahaina News, December 9, 1993: 7.

— alumni to compete, Lahaina News, December 9, 1993: 8.

— team to rebuild after Shelley Garcia's final season, Lahaina News, December 16, 1993: 10.

— student Buddy Perry named to state high school all-star squad, Lahaina News, December 16, 1993: 11.

— to hold 50th class reunion, Lahaina News, December 23, 1993: 2.

— to hold West Maui Marathon Madness, Lahaina News, January 13, 1994: 4.

— Shelley Garcia key to softball success, Lahaina News, January 13, 1994: 6.

— softball team wins playoff game, Lahaina News, February 3, 1994: 9.

— softball team wins championship, Lahaina News, February 10, 1994: 11.

— to celebrate 25th anniversary of David Malo Day, Lahaina News, February 10, 1994: 3.

— to hold Spring Fling Bazaar, Lahaina News, February 17, 1994: 4.

— report on basketball team, Lahaina News, February 17, 1994: 8.

— "Spring Fling '94" postponed, Lahaina News, February 24, 1994: 4.

— basketball team finishes second in Maui Interscholastic League, Lahaina News, February 24, 1994: 6.

— honor roll announced, Lahaina News, March 3, 1994: 4.

— baseball and basketball teams featured, Lahaina News, March 3, 1994: 7,10.

— principal Henry Ariyoshi collects Milken Family Foundation National Educator Award, Lahaina News, March 10, 1994: 4.

— student Stephen Lucas wins wrestling title, Lahaina News, March 10, 1994: 6.

— Deidre Rocket named to Maui All-Star team, Lahaina News, March 17, 1994: 7.

— seeking alumni to help with David Malo Day, Lahaina News, March 31, 1994: 3.

— "Spring Fling Bazaar" to be held, Lahaina News, March 31, 1994: 4.

— report on wrestling coach Neil Nakata, Lahaina News, March 31, 1994: 7,8.

— Spring Fling Bazaar to be held, Lahaina News, April 7, 1994: 4.

— sports teams featured, Lahaina News, April 7, 1994: 6.

— class of 1984 to hold reunion, Lahaina News, April 14, 1994: 3.

— students to participate in DECA Career Development Conference in Detroit, Lahaina News, April 21, 1994: 5.

— update on sports results, Lahaina News, April 21, 1994: 7.

— update on sports results, Lahaina News, April 28, 1994: 6.

— honor roll announced, Lahaina News, May 5, 1994: 2.

— report on sports activities, Lahaina News, May 5, 1994: 8.

— to hold awards ceremony, Lahaina News, May 19, 1994: 5.

— class of 1974 to hold reunion, Lahaina News, May 26, 1994: 4.

— student Kapena Lum wins national award in physical education, Lahaina News, May 26, 1994: 8,9.

— Randy Arakawa and Melba Santella to head the Class of 1994, Lahaina News, June 2, 1994: 1.

— update on successful athletic year, Lahaina News, June 2, 1994: 5.

— photographs of graduating class, Lahaina News, June 2, 1994: 6,7.

— to hold freshman orientation, Lahaina News, June 23, 1994: 5.

— senior class reminded to have yearbook portraits taken, Lahaina News, June 30, 1994: 4.

— to participate in Project Graduation, Lahaina News, August 18, 1994: 1,2.

— described, Lahaina News, August 25, 1994: 3.

— football team featured, Lahaina News, August 25, 1994: 8.

— senior class advisor Andrew Kutsunai to retire after 34 years, Lahaina News, September 1, 1994: 2.

— varsity football team featured, Lahaina News, September 1, 1994: 8,9.

— Parent Teacher Student Association to hold general membership, Lahaina News, September 8, 1994: 5.

— update on cross country team, Lahaina News, September 15, 1994: 9.

— Parent Teacher Student Association consider upcoming election, Lahaina News, September 22, 1994: 1,2.

— update on football team, Lahaina News, September 22, 1994: 8,9.

— update on sports, Lahaina News, October 6, 1994: 9.

— update on football team, Lahaina News, October 13, 1994: 11.

— wins Maui County Fair's School Spirit Competition, Lahaina News, October 20, 1994: 5.

— update on football team, Lahaina News, October 20, 1994: 9.

— girls softball team featured, Lahaina News, October 27, 1994: 10.

— Homecoming Parade held, Lahaina News, October 27, 1994: 8.

— update on football results, Lahaina News, November 3, 1994: 21.

— Athletic Department to hold kalua pig sale, Lahaina News, November 3, 1994: 4.

— report cards to be ready, Lahaina News, November 10, 1994: 7.

— results of football championship game, Lahaina News, November 10, 1994: 8.

— Project Graduation donates turkeys to the needy, Lahaina News, November 24, 1994: 3.

— update on Maui Interscholastic League, Lahaina News, November 24, 1994: 8.

— updates from, Lahaina News, December 1, 1994: 7.

— wrestling team featured, Lahaina News, December 1, 1994: 8.

— honor roll announced, Lahaina News, December 8, 1994: 7.

— football players and coach named to Maui Interscholastic League All-Star Football team, Lahaina News, December 8, 1994: 9.

— students attend Traffic Safety Project Graduation Conference, Lahaina News, December 15, 1994: 6.

— update on athletics, Lahaina News, December 22, 1994: 6.

— girls soccer team featured, Lahaina News, December 22, 1994: 7.

— Project Graduation participates in Traffic Safety Week, Lahaina News, December 29, 1994: 2.

— class of 1970 to hold reunion, Lahaina News, January 5, 1995: 4.

— update on Interscholastic League Boys Soccer, Lahaina News, January 5, 1995: 7.

— to hold dance fundraiser, Lahaina News, January 26, 1995: 14.

— update on sports teams, Lahaina News, January 26, 1995: 8.

— impact of death of student Justin Bacalso discussed, Lahaina News, February 16, 1995: 8.

— update on wrestling team, Lahaina News, February 16, 1995: 8,9.

— prospects for girls basketball team discussed, Lahaina News, February 23, 1995: 7.

— paint over graffiti, Lahaina News, March 2, 1995: 1.

— results of History Day, Lahaina News, March 16, 1995: 2.

— basketball coach George Nunes retiring, Lahaina News, March 16, 1995: 6.

— update on girls basketball team, Lahaina News, March 16, 1995: 6.

— update on sports events, Lahaina News, March 23, 1995: 7.

— members of Project Graduation to meet on Oahu, Lahaina News, April 6, 1995: 4.

— basketball team successful, Lahaina News, April 13, 1995: 9.

— update on baseball team, Lahaina News, April 13, 1995: 9.

— concert band to perform, Lahaina News, April 27, 1995: 11.

— report on sports, Lahaina News, April 27, 1995: 7.

— update on sports events, Lahaina News, May 4, 1995: 8.

— students recognized, Lahaina News, May 11, 1995: 2.

— baseball team defeated, Lahaina News, May 11, 1995: 7.

— students win Hawaii History Day contest, Lahaina News, May 18, 1995: 1,16.

— holds athletics awards banquet, Lahaina News, May 18, 1995: 7.

— Buddy Perry and Spring Eubank honored as top athletes, Lahaina News, May 25, 1995: 5.

— principal Henry Ariyoshi to retire, Lahaina News, June 1, 1995: 1,3.

— pictures of graduating class, Lahaina News, June 1, 1995: 2,5.

— commencement exercises to be held, Lahaina News, June 1, 1995: 3.

— to hold football benefit, Lahaina News, June 8, 1995: 4.

— Project Graduation held, Lahaina News, June 22, 1995: 2.

— graduate Jennifer Kawaguchi receives scholarship from Maui Board of Realtors, Lahaina News, June 22, 1995: 4.

— class of 1975 to hold 20-year reunion, Lahaina News, June 29, 1995: 4.

— athletic director Derrick Montalvo to retire, Lahaina News, June 29, 1995: 7.

— honor roll announced, Lahaina News, July 6, 1995: 4.

— announces summer projects, Lahaina News, July 20, 1995: 4.

— 1980 reunion to be held, Lahaina News, July 27, 1995: 4.

— students earn national traffic safety honors, Lahaina News, August 3, 1995: 2.

— Booster Club to hold general membership meeting, Lahaina News, August 17, 1995: 4.

— report on football team, Lahaina News, August 17, 1995: 7.

— Booster Club to hold general membership meeting, Lahaina News, August 24, 1995: 4.

— update of football, Lahaina News, August 24, 1995: 6.

— students pick up trash along Lahainaluna Road, Lahaina News, August 31, 1995: 3.

— Michael Nakano is new principal of, Lahaina News, August 31, 1995: 3.

— lack athletic director, Lahaina News, August 31, 1995: 3.

— class of 1980 to hold reunion, Lahaina News, August 31, 1995: 4.

— to join School/Community-Based Management (SCBM) system, Lahaina News, August 31, 1995: 4.

— report on football team, Lahaina News, August 31, 1995: 6.

— football team ties against Pearl City, Lahaina News, September 7, 1995: 4.

— football team begins Maui Interscholastic League, Lahaina News, September 14, 1995: 7.

— football team coaches discuss team, Lahaina News, September 21, 1995: 7.

— football teams loses to Maui High, Lahaina News, September 28, 1995: 7.

— volleyball coach Lisa Kanhai featured, Lahaina News, October 5, 1995: 6.

— Traffic Safety Team to hold rummage sale, Lahaina News, October 12, 1995: 6.

— update on volleyball team, Lahaina News, October 12, 1995: 9.

— Ryan Casco and Kim-Ann Young are Homecoming King and Queen, Lahaina News, October 19, 1995: 1,2.

— homecoming to be celebrated, Lahaina News, October 19, 1995: 2.

— running team featured, Lahaina News, October 19, 1995: 6.

— to offer program on computers and networking, Lahaina News, November 2, 1995: 1.

— Alan Kawaguchi becomes athletic director, Lahaina News, November 2, 1995: 7.

— results of varsity football league, Lahaina News, November 2, 1995: 7.

— varsity basketball program featured, Lahaina News, November 9, 1995: 6.

— Parent Teacher Student Association to meet, Lahaina News, November 16, 1995: 4,5.

— update on softball team, Lahaina News, November 23, 1995: 7.

— honor roll, Lahaina News, December 7, 1995: 2.

— wrestling team featured, Lahaina News, December 7, 1995: 6.

— Traffic Safety Team supporting "Lights on For Life", Lahaina News, December 14, 1995: 4.

— update on girls soccer program, Lahaina News, December 21, 1995: 9.

— boys basketball team to host tournament, Lahaina News, December 21, 1995: 9.

— girls softball team discussed, Lahaina News, December 28, 1995: 7.

— Traffic Safety Team to hold bicycle safety training, Lahaina News, January 4, 1996: 4.

— student Brad Fujii takes first place in conservation awareness contest, Lahaina News, January 4, 1996: 4.

— coach Matt Edris featured, Lahaina News, January 11, 1996: 6.

— archives project to begin, Lahaina News, January 18, 1996: 1,14.

— update on softball team, Lahaina News, January 18, 1996: 6.

— former police officer Chris Kaniho becomes basketball coach, Lahaina News, January 25, 1996: 10.

— Project Graduation to sold huli-huli chicken sale, Lahaina News, February 15, 1996: 10.

— students accepted at Massachusetts Institute of Technology, Lahaina News, February 15, 1996: 10.

— Traffic Safety Team to hold training, Lahaina News, February 15, 1996: 10.

— basketball coach Jody Klein featured, Lahaina News, February 22, 1996: 7.

— golf program featured, Lahaina News, March 7, 1996: 7.

— students win medallions at Hawaii State DECA Career Development Conference, Lahaina News, March 21, 1996: 2.

— track team and coach featured, Lahaina News, March 21, 1996: 7.

— Traffic Safety Team to hold "Strides for Safety", Lahaina News, April 11, 1996: 6.

— agriculture at, Lahaina News, April 18, 1996: 1,18.

— update on athletics, Lahaina News, April 25, 1996: 9.

— PTSA to meet, Lahaina News, May 2, 1996: 18.

— athletics department holds banquet, Lahaina News, May 23, 1996: 6.

— graduating class featured, Lahaina News, May 30, 1996: 1,4,6,7.

— valuable artifacts gifted by Robinetta Tompkin March missing, Lahaina News, June 27, 1996: 5.

— debate over uniforms continues, Lahaina News, July 11, 1996: 1,16.

— editorial on student uniforms, Lahaina News, July 11, 1996: 4.

— football team to host kalua pig ticket, Lahaina News, July 18, 1996: 12.

— class of 1981 to hold reunion, Lahaina News, July 18, 1996: 13.

— Traffic Safety Team receives award, Lahaina News, July 18, 1996: 2.

— parents vote on school uniform policy, Lahaina News, July 25, 1996: 1.

— yearbook photos to be taken, Lahaina News, July 25, 1996: 12.

— class of 1981 to hold reunion, Lahaina News, July 25, 1996: 12.

— to hold orientation, Lahaina News, August 22, 1996: 5.

— opens football season, Lahaina News, August 29, 1996: 6.

— football team highlighted, Lahaina News, September 5, 1996: 15.

— update on football program, Lahaina News, September 12, 1996: 18.

— cross country team featured, Lahaina News, October 3, 1996: 12.

— seeking coaches, Lahaina News, October 3, 1996: 13.

— volleyball teams featured, Lahaina News, October 10, 1996: 13.

— Class of 1977 to hold reunion, Lahaina News, October 10, 1996: 14.

— football coach Eric Sodetani featured, Lahaina News, October 24, 1996: 1,13.

— Project Graduation to sell Glenn's Gourmet Sweetbread as fundraiser, Lahaina News, October 24, 1996: 4.

— participates in Get the Drift and Bag It, Lahaina News, October 31, 1996: 5.

— update on upcoming basketball season at, Lahaina News, November 21, 1996: 7.

— softball team featured, Lahaina News, November 28, 1996: 5.

— wrestling team featured, Lahaina News, December 19, 1996: 17.

— basketball team featured, Lahaina News, January 16, 1997: 6.

— girl's soccer team featured, Lahaina News, January 23, 1997: 7.

— soccer team featured, Lahaina News, February 13, 1997: 13.

— softball team to compete in state title, Lahaina News, February 13, 1997: 13.

— NFL all-stars speak to, Lahaina News, February 13, 1997: 3.

— issues with scheduling graduation, Lahaina News, February 20, 1997: 1,16.

— swim team featured, Lahaina News, February 27, 1997: 6.

— Academy of Travel and Tourism participates in voyaging project, Lahaina News, March 6, 1997: 2.

— women's basketball team featured, Lahaina News, March 13, 1997: 13.

— has waiver to move graduation date, Lahaina News, March 27, 1997: 1.

— baseball coach Randy Montalvo featured, Lahaina News, March 27, 1997: 7.

— students to give free walking tours of Old Lahaina Town, Lahaina News, April 3, 1997: 1.

— to hold Junior Promenade, Lahaina News, April 3, 1997: 13.

— golf team featured, Lahaina News, April 10, 1997: 16.

— readying for David Malo Day, Lahaina News, April 10, 1997: 3.

— to hold David Malo Day, Lahaina News, April 17, 1997: 1,16.

— to give last tour of Lahaina Town, Lahaina News, April 17, 1997: 13.

— band to perform Spring Concert, Lahaina News, April 17, 1997: 13.

— tennis team featured, Lahaina News, April 17, 1997: 5.

— Sal Saribay Jr and Hazel Bumanglag named as United States National Award Winners in Business Education, Lahaina News, April 17, 1997: 7.

— Traffic Safety Team recognized by Governor Ben Cayetano for volunteerism, Lahaina News, April 24, 1997: 1.

— school band to play, Lahaina News, April 24, 1997: 12.

— surf team featured, Lahaina News, May 1, 1997: 1.

— track team featured, Lahaina News, May 1, 1997: 15.

— learning about Hawaiian culture, Lahaina News, May 1, 1997: 2.

— wins Maui Interscholastic Surf Championship, Lahaina News, May 15, 1997: 11.

— to hold fundraiser plant sale, Lahaina News, May 15, 1997: 12.

— student success, Lahaina News, May 15, 1997: 2.

— commencement to be held, Lahaina News, May 22, 1997: 6.

— agriculture department to hold plant sale, Lahaina News, May 29, 1997: 17.

— graduating class, Lahaina News, May 29, 1997: 6,7,8,9.

— top athletes honored, Lahaina News, June 5, 1997: 15.

— students win scholarships, Lahaina News, June 19, 1997: 2.

— sends reminders to students and parents, Lahaina News, August 14, 1997: 2.

— football team to begin season, Lahaina News, August 28, 1997: 7.

— football team featured, Lahaina News, September 4, 1997: 14.

— football team featured, Lahaina News, September 11, 1997: 14.

— results of football play, Lahaina News, September 18, 1997: 14.

— football team featured, Lahaina News, October 2, 1997: 16.

— football team featured, Lahaina News, October 9, 1997: 10.

— girls volleyball team featured, Lahaina News, October 16, 1997: 14.

— homecoming celebration concludes, Lahaina News, October 23, 1997: 3.

— report on football team, Lahaina News, October 23, 1997: 8.

— boys volleyball team featured, Lahaina News, October 23, 1997: 9.

— football team can seal title, Lahaina News, October 30, 1997: 6.

— cross country team featured, Lahaina News, October 30, 1997: 7.

— team celebrates winning Maui Interscholastic League, Lahaina News, November 6, 1997: 2.

— football team playing for Neighbor Island title, Lahaina News, November 13, 1997: 1,3.

— teams prepare for post-season, Lahaina News, November 13, 1997: 8,9.

— football team wins Maui Interscholastic League, Lahaina News, November 20, 1997: 1,12.

— girls softball and basketball teams to hold Thanksgiving Kalua turkey sale, Lahaina News, November 20, 1997: 17.

— defeats Kaua'i Interscholastic Federation champion Kaimea, Lahaina News, November 27, 1997: 1,9.

— to honor football players, Lahaina News, December 4, 1997: 1.

— softball coach Earle Kukahiko featured, Lahaina News, December 4, 1997: 12.

— players from football team dominates MIL All-Star team, Lahaina News, December 4, 1997: 13.

— wrestling team featured, Lahaina News, December 11, 1997: 16.

— honor roll students listed, Lahaina News, December 11, 1997: 17.

— honoring football team, Lahaina News, December 11, 1997: 3.

— senior Pedro Haro-Arvizu named an alternate to Senate Youth Program, Lahaina News, December 18, 1997: 14.

— helps Kapalua Nature Society with decorating Norfolk pines, Lahaina News, December 18, 1997: 14.

— basketball team featured, Lahaina News, December 18, 1997: 16.

— basketball team featured, Lahaina News, December 25, 1997: 8.

— voyaging students learn sailing legends, Lahaina News, January 22, 1998: 2.

— girls soccer team featured, Lahaina News, January 22, 1998: 6.

— boys soccer team featured, Lahaina News, January 29, 1998: 6.

— football team needs home field, Lahaina News, February 5, 1998: 6.

— update on softball team, Lahaina News, February 5, 1998: 7.

— swimming program featured, Lahaina News, February 12, 1998: 14.

— class of 1978 to hold reunion, Lahaina News, February 19, 1998: 2.

— softball team featured, Lahaina News, February 19, 1998: 6.

— swimming teams featured, Lahaina News, February 19, 1998: 6.

— wrestling team wins titles, Lahaina News, February 26, 1998: 1.

— holds "Brown Bag to Stardom Talent Contest", Lahaina News, February 26, 1998: 2.

— trainer Suzanne Nagy featured, Lahaina News, February 26, 1998: 6.

— update on sports teams, Lahaina News, March 5, 1998: 15.

— to hold kalua pig sale, Lahaina News, March 5, 1998: 17.

— report on sports teams, Lahaina News, March 12, 1998: 15.

— second quarter honor roll announced, Lahaina News, March 12, 1998: 19.

— results of student essay contest, Lahaina News, March 19, 1998: 1.

— new head coach Neal Fujiwara featured, Lahaina News, March 19, 1998: 6,7.

— girls basketball team featured, Lahaina News, April 2, 1998: 14.

— girl tennis team featured, Lahaina News, April 9, 1998: 14,15.

— preparing for junior prom and Malo Day, Lahaina News, April 9, 1998: 2.

— golf team featured, Lahaina News, April 16, 1998: 6,7.

— girls basketball team featured, Lahaina News, April 16, 1998: 7.

— to celebrate David Malo Day, Lahaina News, April 23, 1998: 1,20.

— softball team featured, Lahaina News, April 23, 1998: 14.

— update on teams, Lahaina News, April 23, 1998: 14.

— students honored, Lahaina News, April 30, 1998: 13.

— track teams featured, Lahaina News, April 30, 1998: 14.

— surf team featured, Lahaina News, May 7, 1998: 10.

— basketball team defends Maui Interscholastic League championship, Lahaina News, May 7, 1998: 10.

— student Sal Saribay, Jr. receives National Leadership and Service award, Lahaina News, May 7, 1998: 18.

— concert band to offer Spring Concert at Sheraton Maui, Lahaina News, May 7, 1998: 20.

— update on girls basketball and other sports, Lahaina News, May 21, 1998: 14.

— publishes honor roll for third quarter, Lahaina News, May 21, 1998: 6.

— class of 1978 to hold reunion, Lahaina News, May 28, 1998: 3.

— Athletic Awards Banquet to be held, Lahaina News, May 28, 1998: 6.

— graduating class pictured, Lahaina News, June 4, 1998: 5,6,7.

— class of 1978 to hold reunion, Lahaina News, June 4, 1998: 9.

— update on sports, Lahaina News, June 11, 1998: 15.

— class of 1978 to hold reunion, Lahaina News, June 11, 1998: 2.

— class of 1978 to hold reunion, Lahaina News, June 18, 1998: 2.

— Lisa Arcangel named Maui Interscholastic League's Co-Female Prep Athlete of the Year, Lahaina News, June 25, 1998: 7.

— School Academy of Travel and Tourism Program is visited by the National Academy Foundation president John Ferrandino, Lahaina News, June 17, 1999: 8.

— Voyaging Program travels to Kahoʻolawe, Lahaina News, July 8, 1999: 3.

— class to schedule portraits, Lahaina News, July 15, 1999: 5.

— attendance policy, Lahaina News, July 29, 1999: 2,3.

— to hold registration, Lahaina News, July 29, 1999: 3.

— to use "Baby Think It Over" parenting dolls, Lahaina News, August 5, 1999: 3.

— class of 1969 to hold reunion, invites other years, Lahaina News, August 5, 1999: 3.

— registration for football underway, Lahaina News, August 5, 1999: 7.

— class of 1969 to hold reunion, Lahaina News, August 12, 1999: 1,16.

— Athletic Department to receive grant from the 2000 Mercedes golf Championships, Lahaina News, August 12, 1999: 3.

— voyaging students sail from Moʻolele to Molokaʻi, Lahaina News, August 26, 1999: 1.

— football team featured, Lahaina News, September 2, 1999: 8.

— student Jessica Nohara competes in Kapalua Fun Swim Challenge, Lahaina News, September 23, 1999: 1.

— football team featured, Lahaina News, September 23, 1999: 6.

— report on success of football, Lahaina News, September 30, 1999: 6.

— update on football, Lahaina News, October 7, 1999: 9.

— Homecoming Parade set, Lahaina News, October 14, 1999: 5.

— volleyball team featured, Lahaina News, October 14, 1999: 6.

— has hosted Maui Interscholastic League Cross Country Lahaina Open, Lahaina News, October 14, 1999: 7.

— cross country team featured, Lahaina News, October 21, 1999: 8.

— Tiare Lawrence and King Kamana Helekahi are homecoming king and queen, Lahaina News, October 28, 1999: 3.

— athletic trainer Jonathan Conrad featured, Lahaina News, October 28, 1999: 8.

— softball team featured, Lahaina News, November 25, 1999: 8.

— football season ends with banquet, Lahaina News, December 2, 1999: 8.

— to hold yard sale for victims of earthquake in Taiwan, Lahaina News, December 9, 1999: 19.

— to host Lahainaluna Invitational Basketball Tournament, Lahaina News, December 9, 1999: 9.

— new coaches of junior varsity, Lahaina News, December 23, 1999: 8.

— to change traffic patterns, ease congestion, Lahaina News, December 30, 1999: 3.

— seeking community input on proposed change to student drop-off system, Lahaina News, January 13, 2000: 5.

— receives money for computer learning center, Lahaina News, January 27, 2000: 1,16.

— parents' night slated, Lahaina News, February 3, 2000: 16.

— wrestling team featured, Lahaina News, February 3, 2000: 6.

— students learn food service operations at Hyatt Regency Maui, Lahaina News, February 10, 2000: 15.

— forms Lahainaluna Historical Preservation Committee, Lahaina News, February 10, 2000: 15.

— soccer team featured, Lahaina News, February 10, 2000: 6.

— swimming team featured, Lahaina News, February 17, 2000: 6.

— Administrative Building grounds received a facelift, Lahaina News, February 24, 2000: 1,3.

— parents night a success, Lahaina News, February 24, 2000: 2.

— implements program to recognize students, Lahaina News, February 24, 2000: 3.

— tennis team featured, Lahaina News, February 24, 2000: 6.

— needs help to prepare for computer lab, Lahaina News, March 9, 2000: 1,16.

— baseball team featured, Lahaina News, March 16, 2000: 6.

— upcoming events at, Lahaina News, March 23, 2000: 3.

— girls basketball team successful, Lahaina News, March 23, 2000: 6.

— senior Audrey Mae Alvarez awarded scholarship to Hawaii Pacific University, Lahaina News, March 30, 2000: 3.

— Ben Cayetano releases funds for, Lahaina News, March 30, 2000: 5.

— students mentoring Big Brothers/Big Sisters After School Mentoring Program, Lahaina News, April 13, 2000: 2.

— track and field team featured, Lahaina News, April 13, 2000: 6.

— junior prom to be held; William Louis Kamika Gundaker and Noelani Rhonda-May Frances Rickard are king and queen, Lahaina News, April 20, 2000: 14.

— golfing team featured, Lahaina News, April 27, 2000: 6.

— students to voyage to Kahoʻolawe, Lahaina News, May 4, 2000: 9.

— teams to hold Kalua Pig Sale, Lahaina News, May 11, 2000: 1.

— preparing new computer lab, Lahaina News, May 25, 2000: 1,14.

— school year winding down, Lahaina News, May 25, 2000: 3.

— to hold Athletic Awards Banquet, Lahaina News, May 25, 2000: 8.

— graduation ceremony to be held, Lahaina News, June 1, 2000: 1,6.

— surf team featured, Lahaina News, June 1, 2000: 8.

— recognizes best student athletes, Lahaina News, June 8, 2000: 14.

— silent auction to support surf team, Lahaina News, June 8, 2000: 15.

— reunion held in Las Vegas, Lahaina News, June 8, 2000: 17.

— pictures of graduating class, Lahaina News, June 8, 2000: 7,8,9.

— Student Council places second in Outstanding Student Council Award Recognition (OSCAR) program, Lahaina News, June 29, 2000: 7.

— mandatory meeting of football team to be held, Lahaina News, July 27, 2000: 7.

— memories from 1967 of, Lahaina News, August 3, 2000: 15.

— increased support for Hawaiian culture at, Lahaina News, August 10, 2000: 5.

— 1980 reunion to be held, Lahaina News, August 17, 2000: 16.

— history of food at, Lahaina News, August 17, 2000: 8.

— memories of 1970s and 1980s recounted, Lahaina News, August 24, 2000: 16.

— yearbooks ready, Lahaina News, August 31, 2000: 17.

— football team featured, Lahaina News, August 31, 2000: 6.

— Maui Electric, Co. to install solar lights, Lahaina News, September 14, 2000: 11.

— Alan Yamamoto new Head Custodian, Lahaina News, September 21, 2000: 1,6.

— cross-country girls team featured, Lahaina News, September 28, 2000: 8.

— to hold kalua pig fundraiser, Lahaina News, September 28, 2000: 8.

— girls volleyball team featured, Lahaina News, October 5, 2000: 8.

— School Academy of Travel and Tourism club elects officers, Lahaina News, October 19, 2000: 2.

— PTSA raises money for school, Lahaina News, October 19, 2000: 2.

— football team to play Maui High, Lahaina News, October 26, 2000: 10.

— EAST lab to hold open house, Lahaina News, October 26, 2000: 29.

— football player Lawrence Torres injured in game, Lahaina News, October 26, 2000: 4.

— to celebrate homecoming, Lahaina News, November 2, 2000: 3.

— football team exceeds expectations, Lahaina News, November 9, 2000: 8.

— Future Club created, Lahaina News, November 16, 2000: 1,2.

— Foundation Golf Tournament to be held, Lahaina News, November 16, 2000: 11.

— students unveil Environmental and Spatial Technology (EAST) Lab, Lahaina News, November 16, 2000: 13.

— women's softball team featured, Lahaina News, November 23, 2000: 10.

— Foundation Golf Tournament to be held, Lahaina News, November 23, 2000: 11.

— Football Awards Banquet held, Lahaina News, November 30, 2000: 7.

— cheerleaders competing, Lahaina News, December 7, 2000: 12.
— basketball team featured, Lahaina News, December 14, 2000: 14.
— wrestling team to compete, Lahaina News, December 14, 2000: 14.
— wrestling team featured, Lahaina News, December 21, 2000: 6.
— basketball team featured, Lahaina News, January 11, 2001: 9.
— to hold car wash to support boarders, Lahaina News, January 18, 2001: 2.
— swim team wins meet, Lahaina News, January 18, 2001: 8.
— swimming team featured, Lahaina News, January 25, 2001: 8.
— PTSA seeks new members, Lahaina News, February 1, 2001: 17.
— boy soccer team successful, Lahaina News, February 8, 2001: 14.
— asks students to return medical equipment, Lahaina News, February 8, 2001: 14.
— girl soccer team successful, Lahaina News, February 15, 2001: 12.
— EAST students celebrate conference win, Lahaina News, March 8, 2001: 1,18.
— Athletic Director Alan Kawaguchi retires, Lahaina News, March 15, 2001: 1,22.
— Future Club holds annual softball tournament, Lahaina News, March 15, 2001: 11.
— results of girls varsity basketball team, Lahaina News, March 22, 2001: 12.
— Future Club to hold annual softball tournament, Lahaina News, March 22, 2001: 2.
— Distributive Education Clubs (DECA) of America chapter attends Hawaii State Conference, Lahaina News, March 29, 2001: 2.
— Beverly Behrmann and students research history of, Lahaina News, May 3, 2001: 1,22.
— Agriculture Program to hold a plant sale for Mother's Day, Lahaina News, May 10, 2001: 3.
— to celebrate David Malo Day, Lahaina News, May 17, 2001: 1.
— baseball team featured, Lahaina News, May 17, 2001: 14.
— Athletic Department offering sports physicals, Lahaina News, May 17, 2001: 15.
— to hold Senior Ball, Lahaina News, May 17, 2001: 3.
— Brian Garcia wins Patsy Mink Congressional Art Award, Lahaina News, May 24, 2001: 1,22.
— football team to hold golf tournament, Lahaina News, May 24, 2001: 15.
— takes third place at AAA/Ford Student Auto Skills contest, Lahaina News, May 24, 2001: 9.
— class of 2001 to graduate, Lahaina News, May 31, 2001: 3.
— graduation held; class photographs, Lahaina News, June 7, 2001: 1,9,10,11.
— Academy of Travel and Tourism graduate class pictured, Lahaina News, June 7, 2001: 8.
— Parent Community Networking Center Facilitator Tonata Sakalia featured, Lahaina News, June 14, 2001: 1,9.
— hosts Youth Football Clinic, Lahaina News, June 14, 2001: 16.
— honors outstanding athletes, Lahaina News, June 14, 2001: 16.
— wins "Outstanding Student Council" award, Lahaina News, June 14, 2001: 2.
— to hold Youth Football Clinic, Lahaina News, July 5, 2001: 12.
— to hold Youth Football Clinic, Lahaina News, July 12, 2001: 13.
— honor roll announced, Lahaina News, July 19, 2001: 18.
— football featured, Lahaina News, July 26, 2001: 1,20.
— football practices to be held, Lahaina News, August 2, 2001: 13.
— student Kristal Wimmer-Kunitomo admitted to University of Southern California medical school, Lahaina News, August 9, 2001: 1,20.
— conducting tryouts for volleyball teams, Lahaina News, August 23, 2001: 13.
— class of 1972 to hold reunion, Lahaina News, August 23, 2001: 2.
— varsity football team featured, Lahaina News, August 30, 2001: 12.
— Class of 1972 to hold reunion, Lahaina News, August 30, 2001: 16.
— message from principal Michael Nakano, Lahaina News, September 6, 2001: 2.

— mentoring program helps students, Lahaina News, September 13, 2001: 1,18.
— students respond to September 11th attack, Lahaina News, September 20, 2001: 1,18.
— Rick Brooks is new basketball coach, Lahaina News, September 20, 2001: 1,18.
— football team featured, Lahaina News, September 20, 2001: 12.
— Booster Club to hold kalua pig sale, Lahaina News, September 20, 2001: 13.
— Al Dasugo becomes coach of basketball team, Lahaina News, September 27, 2001: 12.
— Booster Club to hold kalua pig sale, Lahaina News, September 27, 2001: 13.
— boys varsity volleyball team featured, Lahaina News, October 4, 2001: 12.
— Booster Club to hold kalua pig sale, Lahaina News, October 4, 2001: 13.
— PTSA to meet, Lahaina News, October 4, 2001: 2.
— football team featured, Lahaina News, October 11, 2001: 12.
— cross country program featured, Lahaina News, October 11, 2001: 12.
— Student Council plans sign-waving, Lahaina News, October 11, 2001: 3.
— homecoming to be celebrated, Lahaina News, October 18, 2001: 1,20.
— cheerleading team featured, Lahaina News, October 18, 2001: 12.
— Academy of Travel and Tourism students learn about Polynesian navigation, Lahaina News, October 18, 2001: 3.
— students named to Wendy's High School Heisman Program, Lahaina News, October 25, 2001: 13.
— celebrating homecoming, Lahaina News, November 1, 2001: 1.
— class of 1972 to hold reunion, Lahaina News, November 1, 2001: 2.
— Brodie Yazaki is unofficial mascot of, Lahaina News, November 1, 2001: 3.
— football team defeats Maui High, Lahaina News, November 8, 2001: 1,20.
— football team defeats Maui High, Lahaina News, November 8, 2001: 13.
— football team wins Maui Interscholastic League, Lahaina News, November 15, 2001: 1,18.
— Foundation to hold golf fundraiser, Lahaina News, November 15, 2001: 1,18.
— student participates in foreign exchange in Japan, Lahaina News, November 22, 2001: 1,22.
— football team featured, Lahaina News, November 22, 2001: 10.
— Foundation to hold golf fundraiser, Lahaina News, November 22, 2001: 11.
— football team to hold Awards Banquet, Lahaina News, November 29, 2001: 13.
— Foundation to hold golfing tournament, Lahaina News, November 29, 2001: 13.
— football team to be honored for Maui Interscholastic League championship season, Lahaina News, December 6, 2001: 12.
— Honor Roll released, Lahaina News, December 20, 2001: 10.
— EAST Lab raising money to attend an EAST conference in Arkansas, Lahaina News, December 20, 2001: 11.
— softball team featured, Lahaina News, December 20, 2001: 12.
— girls soccer team featured, Lahaina News, December 27, 2001: 12.
— Future Club holds a driving safety rally, Lahaina News, December 27, 2001: 3.
— soccer team featured, Lahaina News, January 3, 2002: 12.
— basketball team featured, Lahaina News, January 10, 2002: 12.
— Hilo Hatties contributes to Foundation, Lahaina News, January 24, 2002: 8.
— swimming team featured, Lahaina News, January 31, 2002: 12.
— wrestling team featured, Lahaina News, February 7, 2002: 12.

— Athletic Booster Club offering scholarships, Lahaina News, March 13, 2003: 13.

— to hold kalua pig sale fundraiser, Lahaina News, March 13, 2003: 13.

— class of 1978 to hold reunion, Lahaina News, March 13, 2003: 2.

— marketing students win awards from Distributive Education Clubs of America, Lahaina News, March 20, 2003: 1,20.

— baseball team featured, Lahaina News, March 20, 2003: 12.

— to offer basketball clinic, Lahaina News, March 20, 2003: 12.

— Athletic Booster Club to offer scholarship, Lahaina News, March 20, 2003: 12.

— honor roll released, Lahaina News, March 20, 2003: 18.

— girls basketball team featured, Lahaina News, March 27, 2003: 12.

— basketball team featured, Lahaina News, March 27, 2003: 13.

— announces students of the month, Lahaina News, March 27, 2003: 2.

— basketball program to hold clinic, Lahaina News, April 3, 2003: 12.

— representative Brian Blundell hosts student at State Capitol, Lahaina News, April 3, 2003: 2.

— PTSA seeks volunteers, Lahaina News, April 3, 2003: 3.

— to hold David Malo Day, Lahaina News, April 10, 2003: 1,24.

— softball program featured, Lahaina News, April 10, 2003: 10.

— Parent Information Night to be held, Lahaina News, April 10, 2003: 2.

— auction to benefit Booster Band Club, Lahaina News, April 10, 2003: 9.

— students compete in state agricultural competition, Lahaina News, April 17, 2003: 1,18.

— girls swim team featured, Lahaina News, April 17, 2003: 12.

— basketball program featured, Lahaina News, April 17, 2003: 13.

— to hold basketball clinics, Lahaina News, April 24, 2003: 11.

— held Junior Promenade, Lahaina News, April 24, 2003: 3.

— student Alexa Lasco to attend Presidential Classroom program, Lahaina News, May 1, 2003: 1,18.

— tennis team featured, Lahaina News, May 1, 2003: 12.

— student Joshua Peters to attend People Student Ambassador Program, Lahaina News, May 8, 2003: 1.

— golf tournament to be held, Lahaina News, May 8, 2003: 12.

— Athletic Department to hold awards dinner, Lahaina News, May 15, 2003: 12.

— to conduct physical exams, Lahaina News, May 15, 2003: 13.

— to hold golf tournament, Lahaina News, May 15, 2003: 13.

— honor roll announced, Lahaina News, May 15, 2003: 18.

— track and field team featured, Lahaina News, May 22, 2003: 12.

— to hold athletics banquet, Lahaina News, May 22, 2003: 13.

— band seeking alumni to play at graduation, Lahaina News, May 22, 2003: 3.

— class of 2003 photographed, Lahaina News, May 29, 2003: 1,2,3,5.

— class of 2003 graduates, Lahaina News, June 5, 2003: 1.

— teacher Penny Wakida to retire, Lahaina News, June 5, 2003: 1,2.

— Athletic Department awards dinner held, Lahaina News, June 5, 2003: 12.

— Sargent's Fine Art awards scholarships to students from, Lahaina News, June 12, 2003: 17.

— honor roll announced, Lahaina News, July 10, 2003: 18.

— students travel to Kona to learn about Hawaiian culture, Lahaina News, July 17, 2003: 1.

— football clinic to be held, Lahaina News, July 17, 2003: 12.

— students experience Makali'i, Lahaina News, July 24, 2003: 3.

— to offer water polo classes, Lahaina News, July 31, 2003: 13.

— Tongan community donates rock wall fronting cafeteria, Lahaina News, July 31, 2003: 3.

— class of 1973 donates to Foundation, Lahaina News, July 31, 2003: 9.

— football team to play Kahuku, Lahaina News, August 14, 2003: 13.

— student attends national Future Farmers of America conference, Lahaina News, August 14, 2003: 2.

— to play Kahuku, Lahaina News, August 21, 2003: 12.

— to hold orientation, Lahaina News, August 21, 2003: 5.

— football team featured, Lahaina News, August 28, 2003: 12.

— forming bowling team, Lahaina News, September 4, 2003: 12.

— Kekoa Mowat and Dennis Harmon contributing to success of football team, Lahaina News, September 11, 2003: 12.

— Food Service Program hosts Cafe Sauvage chef Dean Luis, Lahaina News, September 11, 2003: 9.

— teachers learn about Hawaiian culture, Lahaina News, September 18, 2003: 1,20.

— Booster Club to hold annual kalua pig fundraiser, Lahaina News, September 18, 2003: 12.

— volleyball team featured, Lahaina News, September 25, 2003: 12.

— Booster Club to hold annual kalua pig fundraiser, Lahaina News, September 25, 2003: 13.

— class of 2004 conducts community service project, Lahaina News, October 2, 2003: 1.

— Booster Club to hold annual kalua pig fundraiser, Lahaina News, October 2, 2003: 12.

— girls volleyball team featured, Lahaina News, October 2, 2003: 12.

— counselor Keenan Reader featured, Lahaina News, October 9, 2003: 1,2.

— bowling team featured, Lahaina News, October 9, 2003: 12.

— students participate in Hawaiian culture program at the University of Hawai'i at Manoa, Lahaina News, October 9, 2003: 3.

LAHAINALUNA HIGH SCHOOL FOUNDATION

— to support Lahainaluna High School, Lahaina News, October 5, 2000: 2.

— receives grant from anonymous local donor, Lahaina News, September 20, 2001: 2.

— Foundation starts library program, Lahaina News, November 21, 2002: 1,2.

— Foundation starts library program, Lahaina News, December 5, 2002: 16.

— Foundation providing books to library, Lahaina News, December 19, 2002: 2.

— Foundation providing books to library, Lahaina News, January 9, 2003: 18.

— Foundation providing books to library, Lahaina News, January 16, 2003: 2.

— Diane Delos Reyes appointed new director, Lahaina News, April 10, 2003: 15.

— offering scholarships, Lahaina News, June 12, 2003: 1,2.

— holds scholarship banquet, Lahaina News, June 12, 2003: 17.

— Plantation House to hold fundraiser scholarship program, Lahaina News, July 10, 2003: 3.

— library to hold forum with teens, Lahaina News, September 18, 2003: 1.

LAHAINALUNA HIGH SCHOOL LIBRARY

— history and conditions described, Lahaina News, November 1, 1980: 1.

— early history recounted, Lahaina News, May 15, 1981: 16.

— may get a new library, Lahaina News, February 14, 1990: 1.

— State budget does not include funding for swimming pool and library, Lahaina News, December 19, 1990: 1.

— ceramics students to display work in school's library, Lahaina News, May 4, 1995: 2.

— state releases funds for library at, Lahaina News, December 18, 1997: 14.

— PTSA seeks more books for the library, Lahaina News, January 14, 1999: 1.

— staff affirm need for new library, Lahaina News, December 7, 2000: 1,2.

— library project to begin, Lahaina News, August 23, 2001: 1,8.

— breaks ground on new library, Lahaina News, October 18, 2001: 1,20.

— new library ready to open, Lahaina News, September 5, 2002: 1,2.

— benefactor Harlow Wright tours library, Lahaina News, May 22, 2003: 9.

— holds panel on ways to support teens, Lahaina News, October 2, 2003: 3.

LAHAINALUNA HISTORICAL PRESERVATION COMMITTEE

— awarded grant from O.I. Moore Foundation, Lahaina News, April 4, 1996: 2.

— formed at Lahainaluna High School, Lahaina News, February 10, 2000: 15.

LAHAINALUNA INTERMEDIATE SCHOOL

— particulate in "5-4-Life" walk-a-thon, Lahaina News, January 2, 1991: 2.

— to hold ice cream benefit, Lahaina News, September 17, 1992: 3.

— cultural clubs featured, Lahaina News, November 18, 1993: 2.

— girls basketball team in running for league title, Lahaina News, February 24, 1994: 6.

— to hold volleyball invitational tournament, Lahaina News, April 14, 1994: 7.

— students visit Ka'anapali Classic Stay in School Junior Golf Clinic, Lahaina News, November 2, 1995: 2.

— PTSA to hold forums for year-round schooling, Lahaina News, October 29, 1998: 11.

LAHAINALUNA ROAD

— schools to stagger schedule to ease congestion on, Lahaina News, March 18, 1999: 1.

LAHAINALUNA SINGS [RECORD]

— to go on sale for Christmas season, Lahaina Sun, December 6, 1972: 5.

LAHAINALUNA SURF TEAM

— seeking donations for silent auction, Lahaina News, May 22, 1997: 13.

LAHAINALUNA TRAVEL ACADEMY

— recognizes first six graduating seniors, Lahaina News, June 16, 1994: 5.

LAHAINALUNA VOYAGING TEAM

— visits Kahakuloa Camp, Lahaina News, December 11, 1997: 17.

— meets with Pua Lindsey, Lahaina News, March 12, 1998: 19.

LAHAINALUNA VOYAGING WATER SAFETY PROGRAM

— held at Lahaina Aquatic Center, Lahaina News, November 27, 1997: 5.

LAHAINALUNA WEIGHTLIFTING CLUB

— to demonstrate, Lahaina News, May 13, 1999: 17.

LAHAINATOWN ACTION COMMITTEE

— trying to sign new members, Lahaina News, September 14, 1988: 3.

— planning to meet S.S. Monterey on arrival in Lahaina, Lahaina News, September 21, 1988: 20.

— editorial supporting work of, Lahaina News, October 19, 1988: 4.

— sponsoring poster contest, Lahaina News, November 23, 1988: 3.

— planning to hang Christmas lights, Lahaina News, November 30, 1988: 3.

— greets S.S. Monterey, Lahaina News, December 28, 1988: 3.

— chooses Joyce Schaunaman's "Lahaina Harbor" for commemorative poster, Lahaina News, January 4, 1989: 3.

— to host Pomare Properties chairman Jim Romig at Longhi's, Lahaina News, January 25, 1989: 1.

— appoints Jeri Bostwick as public relations director, Lahaina News, January 25, 1989: 16.

— to host "Art Night", Lahaina News, March 15, 1989: 2.

— Mayor Hannibal Tavares to speak to, Lahaina News, March 29, 1989: 3.

— begins "Friday Night is Art Night", Lahaina News, June 14, 1989: 17.

— planning Halloween contest, Lahaina News, September 13, 1989: 1.

— extends deadline for art contest, Lahaina News, October 11, 1989: 11.

— participating in Aloha Week, Lahaina News, October 11, 1989: 3.

— winner of poster contest announced, Lahaina News, November 15, 1989: 1,19.

— chooses Connie Sutherland as chair, Lahaina News, January 17, 1990: 4.

— Linda Lingle to speak to, Lahaina News, January 24, 1990: 6.

— chooses work by George Allen for 1990 poster, Lahaina News, February 21, 1990: 14.

— to organize "Taste of Lahaina", Lahaina News, March 28, 1990: 3.

— opposes permanent activities booth, Lahaina News, April 11, 1990: 1,6.

— seek to preserve roadways from expansion, Lahaina News, August 8, 1990: 1.

— to hold contest for art for annual poster, Lahaina News, September 26, 1990: 5.

— architect Robert Fox speaks at quarterly meeting, Lahaina News, September 26, 1990: 9.

— selects Marion Freeman as artist of annual poster, Lahaina News, November 21, 1990: 1.

— David Allaire becomes chair, Lahaina News, January 9, 1991: 5.

— to meet, Lahaina News, January 23, 1991: 3.

— Theo Morrison appointed executive director of, Lahaina News, January 30, 1991: 5.

— concerned that Hare Krishna group granted to operate in Banyan Tree area, Lahaina News, February 6, 1991: 1.

— unveiling annual poster at South Seas Trading Post, Lahaina News, February 6, 1991: 3.

— organizes greeting passengers from passenger ships, Lahaina News, March 20, 1991: 6.

— to hold art contest for students, Lahaina News, April 24, 1991: 2,4.

— to hold Art Night celebration, Lahaina News, May 15, 1991: 11.

— to organize "Tuesday Is a Taste of Lahaina", Lahaina News, July 18, 1991: 10.

— begins planning Halloween costume contest, Lahaina News, August 22, 1991: 8.

— sponsoring "Once is not Enough Trash Bash", Lahaina News, September 12, 1991: 3.

— to hold Lahaina poster contest, Lahaina News, September 12, 1991: 3.

— poster contest deadline next month, Lahaina News, September 12, 1991: 8.

— hosting costume contest, Lahaina News, September 19, 1991: 3.

— poster contest continues, Lahaina News, September 19, 1991: 8.

— to hold reception for poster contest, Lahaina News, October 10, 1991: 4.

— announces Stephen Burr as winner of poster contest, Lahaina News, October 31, 1991: 13.

— creates telephone tree to deal with rolling blackouts, Lahaina News, November 28, 1991: 6.

— continues to sponsor "Tuesday Is a Taste of Lahaina", Lahaina News, December 12, 1991: 21.

— to hold annual town meeting, Lahaina News, January 23, 1992: 4.

— chair James Duckworth featured, Lahaina News, March 5, 1992: 3.

— to ask permission to close Front Street for two summer events, Lahaina News, April 2, 1992: 3.

— newspaper correction regarding permit request, Lahaina News, April 9, 1992: 5.

— seeking longer parking hours along Front Street, Lahaina News, May 21, 1992: 1.

— seeks better review of sewage issues, Lahaina News, August 6, 1992: 1,3.

— to hold poster competition, Lahaina News, October 8, 1992: 2.

— Laura Ospanik wins poster contest, Lahaina News, October 29, 1992: 20.

— to hold open house, Lahaina News, November 26, 1992: 13.

— to hold open house, Lahaina News, December 3, 1992: 4.

— seeking nonprofit group to benefit from Taste of Lahaina event, Lahaina News, January 28, 1993: 4.

— seeks more bikeways, Lahaina News, February 4, 1993: 3.

— Fran Peart Mitsumura elected chairperson, Lahaina News, February 18, 1993: 4.

— videotapes activity of time share booth, Lahaina News, March 11, 1993: 3.

— opposes timeshare sales practices, Lahaina News, March 25, 1993: 4.

— to hold poster design contest, Lahaina News, September 9, 1993: 12.

— dealing nearing for poster contest, Lahaina News, September 16, 1993: 3.

— Arlene Marcoe Anthony wins poster contest, Lahaina News, September 30, 1993: 4.

— to hold public meeting with Maui Police Department, Lahaina News, October 7, 1993: 3.

— raises $20,000 from "A Taste of Lahaina", Lahaina News, October 14, 1993: 14.

— plans benefit for injured bicycle officers, Lahaina News, November 18, 1993: 1.

— to hold town meeting with Linda Lingle, Lahaina News, January 13, 1994: 2.

— new board members elected, Lahaina News, January 27, 1994: 3.

— receives grant to support Art Night, Lahaina News, February 17, 1994: 2.

— Ruth Nakamura Griffith hired as assistant to the director, Lahaina News, April 14, 1994: 3.

— challenges legality of vending in historic district, Lahaina News, April 28, 1994: 1.

— seeking artists to facilitate "Art in Action" projects, Lahaina News, May 5, 1994: 15.

— accepting reservations to use banner space on Front Street, Lahaina News, May 19, 1994: 16.

— seeking artists for "Art in Action" project, Lahaina News, May 26, 1994: 15.

— Marcoe to sign posters for, Lahaina News, June 30, 1994: 12.

— to act as mediator between county and merchants regarding Front Street improvements, Lahaina News, July 28, 1994: 1,16.

— visitor's center to open, Lahaina News, August 11, 1994: 1,3.

— "A Taste of Lahaina" to be held soon, Lahaina News, August 11, 1994: 11.

— to hold annual Lahaina Poster Competition, Lahaina News, August 25, 1994: 15.

— discusses end of impasse with One World, One Family over t-shirt vending, Lahaina News, September 8, 1994: 1.

— results of store decoration contest, Lahaina News, November 10, 1994: 7.

— update on latest activities, Lahaina News, November 17, 1994: 2.

— Cultural Resources Commission recommends approval of request to renovate rooms at Old Courthouse by, Lahaina News, December 8, 1994: 1.

— results of poster contest to be announced, Lahaina News, December 8, 1994: 16.

— Lahaina Visitor Center at Old Lahaina Courthouse likely to be approved, Lahaina News, December 15, 1994: 3.

— receives approval of Lahaina Visitor Center from Maui County Council, Lahaina News, January 12, 1995: 1.

— Mark DeColibus becomes new president, Lahaina News, January 26, 1995: 3.

— skeptical of plans for strip mall near swimming pool, Lahaina News, March 16, 1995: 3.

— holds grand opening of Lahaina Visitors Center, Lahaina News, April 13, 1995: 1,20.

— gives grant to maintain double-hulled canoe Moʻolele, Lahaina News, May 4, 1995: 4.

— seeking sponsors for Taste of Lahaina, Lahaina News, June 15, 1995: 2.

— to hold Art Night celebration, Lahaina News, June 29, 1995: 11.

— sponsors needed for Taste of Lahaina, Lahaina News, June 29, 1995: 4.

— to hold poster contest to feature local artist, Lahaina News, July 13, 1995: 2.

— beginning to plan Halloween bash, Lahaina News, July 13, 1995: 2.

— seeking submissions for poster competition, Lahaina News, August 3, 1995: 16.

— seeking submissions for poster competition, Lahaina News, August 10, 1995: 11,12.

— seeking volunteers for A Taste of Lahaina, Lahaina News, August 24, 1995: 4.

— seeking artists for Halloween face painting, Lahaina News, October 12, 1995: 14.

— seeking recipes for second edition of "A Taste of Lahaina", Lahaina News, October 19, 1995: 9.

— seeking recipes for A Taste of Lahaina Cookbook, Lahaina News, October 26, 1995: 12.

— seeking recipes for A Taste of Lahaina Cookbook, Lahaina News, November 2, 1995: 12.

— volunteers important to, Lahaina News, November 9, 1995: 2.

— to help establish Hawaiian canoe park, Lahaina News, November 30, 1995: 1,12.

— seeking volunteers for Lahaina Visitor Center, Lahaina News, December 14, 1995: 18.

— seeking nominations for Lahaina Kokua Award, Lahaina News, December 21, 1995: 6.

— seeking nominations for Lahaina Kokua Award, Lahaina News, December 28, 1995: 2.

— to hold annual meeting, Lahaina News, January 18, 1996: 4.

— holds annual meeting, Kokua Awards given, Lahaina News, January 25, 1996: 4.

— honors Jim Luckey with Lahaina Kokua Award, Lahaina News, February 8, 1996: 1,16.

— to erect gateway signs, Lahaina News, February 8, 1996: 2.

— marketing meeting to be held, Lahaina News, March 7, 1996: 11.

— update on, Lahaina News, June 13, 1996: 2.

— seeking volunteers for "A Taste of Lahaina", Lahaina News, July 25, 1996: 13.

— poster contest being held, Lahaina News, August 8, 1996: 17.

— reception for poster contest to be held, Lahaina News, September 5, 1996: 21.

— to form task force to work on problem with drug dealers, Lahaina News, September 12, 1996: 1.

— planning walking tour of old Lahaina Town, Lahaina News, October 17, 1996: 4.

— update on local issues, Lahaina News, December 12, 1996: 2.

— to hold annual meeting, Lahaina News, January 9, 1997: 2.

— to hold annual dinner, Lahaina News, January 16, 1997: 1.

— trying to remove brochure racks on Front Street, Lahaina News, January 16, 1997: 5.

— Keola Sequeira receives Kokua award from, Lahaina News, January 23, 1997: 1.

— impact on Lahaina described, Lahaina News, April 24, 1997: 3.

— seeking historical information on Front Street, Lahaina News, May 15, 1997: 2.

— seeking dock for cruise ships, Lahaina News, June 5, 1997: 1.

— to hold poster contest, Lahaina News, June 19, 1997: 2.

— results of poster contest, Lahaina News, July 31, 1997: 12.

— to hold meetings, Lahaina News, July 31, 1997: 13.

— offering booths for Halloween, seeking volunteers, Lahaina News, October 16, 1997: 2,9.
— Mayor Linda Lingle tells residents to lobby for county's share of Transit Accommodations Tax, Lahaina News, January 15, 1998: 1,16.
— holds annual meeting, Lahaina News, January 15, 1998: 2.
— welcomes cruise ship, Lahaina News, January 29, 1998: 2.
— helps organize WhaleFest, Lahaina News, March 5, 1998: 8.
— organizing greetings for cruise ships visiting Lahaina Harbor, Lahaina News, April 2, 1998: 13.
— president of Waldron Steamship Committee Bill Thayer to speak to, Lahaina News, April 23, 1998: 1.
— volunteers paint Lahaina Harbor loading dock, Lahaina News, May 7, 1998: 18.
— filling booths for "A Taste of Lahaina", Lahaina News, July 9, 1998: 7.
— accepting entries for Lahaina Poster Competition, Lahaina News, July 30, 1998: 7.
— taking entries for Lahaina Poster Competition, Lahaina News, August 6, 1998: 7.
— entries to poster competition to be displayed, Lahaina News, August 13, 1998: 16.
— to receive grant for "In Celebration of Canoes", Lahaina News, August 20, 1998: 8.
— taking applications for booths for Halloween, Lahaina News, October 8, 1998: 17.
— host walking tour to discuss possible locations for Lahaina Visitor Center and Restroom Complex, Lahaina News, October 8, 1998: 2.
— abandons plans to build visitor center at Lahaina Public Library, Lahaina News, December 10, 1998: 1,2.
— to host new Mayor James "Kimo" Apana, Lahaina News, January 7, 1999: 3.
— Executive Director Theo Morrison may leave, Lahaina News, March 25, 1999: 1,20.
— editorial in support of, Lahaina News, March 25, 1999: 4.
— may return to Old Lahaina Courthouse, Lahaina News, April 1, 1999: 1,20.
— Lyons Naone is new president of, Lahaina News, April 8, 1999: 3.
— Lisa Dirks hired as events coordinator, Lahaina News, June 10, 1999: 15.
— to hold poster competition, Lahaina News, June 24, 1999: 2.
— asks to use Banyan Tree Park, Lahaina News, July 1, 1999: 1,16.
— accepting applications for "A Taste of Lahaina", Lahaina News, July 1, 1999: 11.
— poster competition to be held, Lahaina News, July 8, 1999: 5.
— applications accepted for poster contest, Lahaina News, July 29, 1999: 3.
— working on Lahaina Interpretive Plan, Lahaina News, August 5, 1999: 1,16.
— clashing with Lahaina Arts Society on use of Banyan Tree Park, Lahaina News, August 26, 1999: 1,20.
— seeking volunteers for A Taste of Lahaina, Lahaina News, August 26, 1999: 9.
— seeking volunteers for A Taste of Lahaina, Lahaina News, September 2, 1999: 7.
— seeking recipes for "A Taste of Lahaina Cookbook III", Lahaina News, October 14, 1999: 5.
— looking for new location for "A Taste of Lahaina", Lahaina News, November 25, 1999: 1.
— to hold annual meeting recognizing town helpers, Lahaina News, January 6, 2000: 1.
— to hold annual meeting; Marsha Wienert to speak to, Lahaina News, January 13, 2000: 1.
— president Theo Morrison discusses issues brought to Maui County Cultural Resources Commission, Lahaina News, January 13, 2000: 1,16.

— seeking artists to participate in Ocean Art Festival during WhaleFest, Lahaina News, February 17, 2000: 15.
— to publish "A Taste of Lahaina Cookbook III", Lahaina News, February 24, 2000: 3.
— hosting art and culture courses, Lahaina News, April 20, 2000: 2.
— seeks site for "A Taste of Lahaina", Lahaina News, May 11, 2000: 1,8.
— to host "In Celebration of Canoes" festival, Lahaina News, May 11, 2000: 6.
— to hold Lahaina Poster Contest, Lahaina News, May 18, 2000: 7.
— to hold Lahaina Poster Contest, Lahaina News, June 22, 2000: 6.
— poster contest winners announced, Lahaina News, July 13, 2000: 3.
— improving Kamehameha Iki Park, Lahaina News, July 13, 2000: 3.
— identifies "sump" area by Lahaina Aquatic Center as site for special events, Lahaina News, July 27, 2000: 1.
— to hold candidate forum at Old Lahaina Courthouse, Lahaina News, August 3, 2000: 1.
— accepting application for "A Taste of Lahaina", Lahaina News, August 3, 2000: 5.
— to hold candidates forum, Lahaina News, August 10, 2000: 1.
— seeking artists for Halloween, Lahaina News, October 19, 2000: 1.
— coordinating holiday festivities, Lahaina News, November 30, 2000: 1.
— to hold Festival of Art and Flowers, Lahaina News, November 30, 2000: 16.
— Jim Lucky to speak to, Lahaina News, January 11, 2001: 3.
— Jim Lucky to speak to, Lahaina News, January 18, 2001: 1.
— to hold Annual Town Meeting at the Old Courthouse, recognizes volunteers, Lahaina News, January 25, 2001: 1,20.
— seeking volunteers for Lahaina Visitor Center, Lahaina News, May 17, 2001: 17.
— to sponsor Lahaina Poster Contest, Lahaina News, May 24, 2001: 2.
— to hold town meeting, Lahaina News, April 4, 2002: 1,20.
— seeks input from residents on future of Lahaina, Lahaina News, April 11, 2002: 1,20.
— to hold annual Lahaina Poster Competition, Lahaina News, May 30, 2002: 2.
— to hold poster contest, Lahaina News, June 20, 2002: 5.
— Ronaldo Macedo wins poster contest, Lahaina News, July 18, 2002: 17.
— to work with police to address crime problems, Lahaina News, August 22, 2002: 1,2.
— seeking volunteers to prepare wreaths for Front Street, Lahaina News, November 28, 2002: 2.
— to host annual lighting of the Banyan Tree, Lahaina News, December 5, 2002: 2.
— to hold lighting ceremony at Banyan Tree Park, Lahaina News, December 12, 2002: 3.
— to hold town meeting, Lahaina News, January 2, 2003: 3.
— Waikiki Improvement Association President Rick Egged to speak to, Lahaina News, January 2, 2003: 3.
— seeking volunteers to take down Christmas wreaths, Lahaina News, January 2, 2003: 3.
— to hold Town Meeting, Lahaina News, January 9, 2003: 1,2.
— honors residents, Lahaina News, January 16, 2003: 1,20.
— Ronaldo Macedo wins Lahaina Poster contest, Lahaina News, February 6, 2003: 2.
— to host Lahaina Poster Contest, Lahaina News, May 22, 2003: 2.
— poster contest deadline approaching, Lahaina News, June 26, 2003: 22.
— Erin Dertner wins Lahaina Poster Contest, Lahaina News, July 24, 2003: 9.

LAHUIOKALANI CONGREGATIONAL CHURCH
— hosting Christmas concert by Na Mele Ohana Choir, Lahaina News, December 21, 2000: 16.

LA'IA, BU [COMEDIAN]
— to run for governor as Green Party candidate, Lahaina News, August 6, 1998: 17.
— looking for comedians, Lahaina News, June 19, 2003: 14.
— seeking comedians in comedy search, Lahaina News, June 26, 2003: 20.

LAINA CRATER
— featured, Lahaina Times, August, 1980 volume 4 number 7: 1.

LAIRD MCNEIL WILSON ADVERTISING, INC. [BUSINESS]
— to represent Kapalua Bay Hotel and Villas, Lahaina News, January 16, 1991: 5.

LAIRD, ROBBIE [ARTIST]
— to exhibit at Village Galleries Maui, Lahaina News, May 10, 2001: 20.
— to exhibit at Village Gallery Contemporary, Lahaina News, February 20, 2003: 16.

LAKAHI CORPORATION
— activities to help the poor detailed, Lahaina Sun, June 21, 1972: 4.

LAKE, DAVID
— mayor Hannibal Tavares awards certificate of merit to, Lahaina News, September 10, 1986: 3.
— rewarded by mayor, Lahaina News, February 11, 1987: 11.
— police officer to speak on drug use, Lahaina News, February 23, 1995: 2.

LAKE, HALE
— executive chef at Kapalua Grill and Bar featured, Lahaina News, February 20, 1992: 9.

LAKOTA SIOUX INDIAN DANCE THEATRE [TROUPE]
— to perform at Maui Arts and Cultural Center, Lahaina News, October 10, 1996: 14.

LALETIN, CHRIS
— praises Visitor Industry Training and Education Center, Lahaina News, September 5, 1991: 4.
— restaurant manager honored, Lahaina News, February 8, 1996: 6.

LALLY, JANICE
— to lecture on art in Australia, Lahaina News, August 27, 1992: 6.

LAM, "BUTCH"
— new Lahaina police captain, Lahaina News, January 26, 1995: 1,20.

LAM, NORA [WRITER]
— to speak, Lahaina News, November 4, 1993: 3.

LAMARCHINA, ROBERT
— to be guest conductor of Maui Symphony , Lahaina News, October 9, 1997: 20.

LAMAS, PETER
— make-up consultant to present, Lahaina News, April 22, 1999: 12.

LAMBERT, DANIEL
— joins The Gas Company, Lahaina News, October 3, 1990: 9.

LAMBERT, JENNY [ARTIST]
— to exhibit at Banyan Tree Gallery, Lahaina News, June 30, 1994: 13.

L'AMOUR BRIDAL SALON [BUSINESS]
— bought by GP Enterprise, Lahaina News, July 3, 2003: 8.

LAMPKIN, MONTE RAY
— arrested for parole violation, Lahaina Sun, March 24, 1971: 1,8.

LANA'I [ISLAND]
— Lana'i Company proposes housing and tourist projects for Lana'i, Lahaina Sun, December 29, 1971: 6.
— development plans detailed, Lahaina Sun, September 20, 1972: 3.
— sailing to island detailed, Lahaina Sun, January 24, 1973: 15.
— Castle & Cooke planning resort on, Lahaina News, October 19, 1983: 14.
— featured, Lahaina News, October 3, 1984: 7,8,9.
— described, Lahaina News, February 5, 1986: 1,12,13.

LANA'I CANOE CLUB
— sponsoring Pineapple Festival Canoe, Lahaina News, August 20, 1998: 15.

LANA'I CORPORATION [BUSINESS]
— proposes housing and tourist projects for Lana'i, Lahaina Sun, December 29, 1971: 6.
— proposes development plan for Lana'i, Lahaina Sun, January 17, 1973: 3.
— development plan criticized, Lahaina Sun, February 28, 1973: 11.
— offering special rates to Hawaii residents, Lahaina News, June 13, 1996: 6.

LANA'I HIGH AND ELEMENTARY SCHOOL
— PTSA to hold fundraiser, Lahaina News, June 13, 1996: 11.
— to hold fundraiser, Lahaina News, June 20, 1996: 12.

LANCASTER, BURT [ACTOR]
— attends Aku Memorial Celebrity Golf Tournament, Lahaina News, May 29, 1985: 4.

LAND
— see ceded land, development, Hawaiian Homes Commission, Hawaiians, property, real estate

LAND AND CONSTRUCTION COMPANY [BUSINESS]
— apparent low bidder for low and moderate housing project in Paia, Lahaina Sun, March 10, 1971: 5.

LAND AND NATURAL RESOURCES, STATE DEPARTMENT OF (DLNR)
— proposes rules governing the use of state parks, Lahaina Sun, July 21, 1971: 11.
— to hold public hearings on fishing management, Lahaina News, April 22, 1987: 10.
— to hold public hearing, Lahaina News, July 22, 1987: 3.
— to hold public hearings on proposed commercial mooring, Lahaina News, August 26, 1987: 3.
— signs agreement on reinternment of ancient Hawaiian bones, Lahaina News, September 13, 1989: 3.
— to hold hearings on land use issues, Lahaina News, November 22, 1989: 3.
— deployed fish aggregating devices, Lahaina News, January 3, 1990: 28.
— reviewing longline fishing rules, Lahaina News, April 25, 1990: 1,5.
— to give plants away in celebration of Arbor Week, Lahaina News, November 7, 1990: 5.
— warns that aquifer depletion may require water management area, Lahaina News, November 28, 1990: 1,2.
— to re-institute voluntary Fish Buoy Card reporting system, Lahaina News, January 2, 1991: 16.
— to deploy fish aggregating devices, Lahaina News, May 23, 1991: 10.
— to consider proposed Kapunakea Preserve, Lahaina News, January 9, 1992: 3.
— to hold public meeting to discuss rules affecting Molokini Shoals, Lahaina News, April 2, 1992: 4,5.
— to hold hearing on Molokini, Lahaina News, April 9, 1992: 7.
— opens Kula and Kahikinui State Forest Reserves, Lahaina News, June 11, 1992: 6.
— to become responsible for small harbors, Lahaina News, July 9, 1992: 9.
— Bill Paty to stay as chairperson, Lahaina News, December 31, 1992: 20.
— to hold public information meeting on proposed conservation district, Lahaina News, January 27, 1994: 3.
— taking comments on hunting preserve, Lahaina News, September 29, 1994: 5.
— Mike Wilson likely to be approved as head of, Lahaina News, January 5, 1995: 2.

— may pursue state park at Honolua Bay, Lahaina News, January 26, 1995: 1,20.

— to expand licensing requirements for anglers, Lahaina News, December 12, 1996: 22.

— seeking to develop a recreational fishing license system, Lahaina News, January 23, 1997: 3.

— approves Lahaina Arts Society's return to Old Lahaina Courthouse, Lahaina News, December 18, 1997: 1.

— to hold public hearing on proposed changes to Hawaii State Park System rules, Lahaina News, June 18, 1998: 16.

— to discuss South Maui beach issues, Lahaina News, July 16, 1998: 15.

— to hold meeting to discuss management strategies, Lahaina News, February 25, 1999: 12.

— allowed to clear old trees at Kapalua Bay, Lahaina News, June 24, 1999: 11.

— increases fees for fishing, Lahaina News, September 2, 1999: 14.

— state begins camping fees, Lahaina News, December 7, 2000: 16.

— seeking participants for Youth Conservation Corps 2001 summer program, Lahaina News, April 19, 2001: 2.

— explains fishing regulations, Lahaina News, August 9, 2001: 8.

— to set new minimum legal sizes for fishing, Lahaina News, July 4, 2002: 1.

— to hold hearings on Maui Land and Pineapple application for land use within Conservation District, Lahaina News, August 1, 2002: 8.

— to hold public hearing on land use within Conservation District, Lahaina News, August 8, 2002: 8.

— to hold hearings on Hawaii Administrative Rules for State Historic Preservation District, Lahaina News, August 22, 2002: 9.

— to hold public hearings on lay net regulations, Lahaina News, September 19, 2002: 5.

— includes Makila Road in state inventory of historic places , Lahaina News, March 27, 2003: 3.

LAND USE AND CODES ADMINISTRATION, MAUI COUNTY

— Maui County Cost of Government Commission recommendations improvements for, Lahaina News, October 15, 1980: 10.

LAND USE COMMISSION, STATE

— land reclassified to allow Sokan Hawaii, Inc. to build golf courses, Lahaina News, November 21, 1990: 12.

— to hold public hearing on Amfac, Inc.'s request to reclassify agricultural land, Lahaina News, December 5, 1990: 3.

— public hearing scheduled to consider Amfac's request to reclassify agricultural land, Lahaina News, December 12, 1990: 4.

— to hold public hearing on proposal to develop 200 residential lots, Lahaina News, November 21, 1991: 2.

— to meet concerning Ma'alaea, Lahaina News, July 30, 1992: 5.

— votes to reclassify land from agricultural to urban in Kahana, Lahaina News, January 21, 1993: 4.

— to meet at Maui Marriott Hotel , Lahaina News, March 4, 1993: 3.

— to decide on proposed Pu'ukoli'i Village, Lahaina News, March 25, 1993: 3.

— considering allowing Wailea Ranch to be developed, Lahaina News, November 25, 1993: 6.

— elects new officers, Lahaina News, September 22, 1994: 6.

— commercial park planned in West Maui, Lahaina News, February 16, 1995: 3.

— to hold public hearing, Lahaina News, April 8, 1999: 1.

— to hold public hearing on reclassifying land from agriculture to urban use for Kahului Airport expansion, Lahaina News, April 15, 1999: 13.

— to discuss issue of developing agricultural lands, Lahaina News, December 26, 2002: 1,18.

— meeting to consider development of agriculture lands on slope between Lahaina and Olowalu, Lahaina News, April 17, 2003: 1,18.

LAND USE RESEARCH FOUNDATION

— participates in "Partners in Planning" symposium, Lahaina News, December 28, 1988: 12.

— executive director Dan Davidson promotes Developer's Agreement Bill, Lahaina News, March 23, 1995: 3.

LANDAVAZO, YVONNE

— appointed regional director of public relations at Four Seasons Resort, Lahaina News, July 9, 1998: 12.

LANDGRAFF, LIBERT

— appointed to task force to consider disinterring ancient Hawaiian remains, Lahaina News, January 4, 1989: 1,16.

LANDLORD-TENANT HANDBOOK [BOOK]

— written by Alvin Ito, Lahaina News, August 20, 1998: 13.

LANDRETH, SONNY [MUSICIAN]

— to perform at Maui Arts and Cultural Center, Lahaina News, September 26, 1996: 16.

LANDSCAPE INDUSTRY COUNCIL OF HAWAII

— to hold landscape employee training workshop, Lahaina News, February 16, 1995: 6.

— to sponsor employee training workshop on pruning landscape plants, Lahaina News, June 1, 1995: 10.

LANDTEC, INC. [BUSINESS]

— unveils plan for Napili project, Lahaina News, June 19, 2003: 1,18.

LANE, ED [ARTIST]

— to exhibit "Exuberance II", Lahaina News, February 25, 1999: 12.

LANEY, LEROY

— economist discusses Maui's economic outlook, Lahaina News, August 19, 1999: 13.

— to discuss local economy, Lahaina News, September 20, 2001: 9.

— economist to speak to Maui Chamber of Commerce, Lahaina News, September 18, 2003: 9.

LANGA, SANFORD

— lawyer and member of panel discussing hippies on Maui, Lahaina Sun, December 2, 1970: 1.

— lawyer discusses place of hippies on Maui, Lahaina Sun, December 16, 1970: 7.

— director for Maui ACLU, Lahaina Sun, January 13, 1971: 6.

LANGLEY 'UKULELE ENSEMBLE [MUSICAL GROUP]

— visits Maui from British Columbia, Canada, Lahaina News, August 10, 2000: 14.

LANI [BUSINESS]

— apparel store opens, Lahaina News, January 28, 1999: 11.

LANI'S BY DAY/ALEX'S BY NIGHT [RESTAURANT]

— opens, Lahaina News, August 18, 1994: 15.

LANI'S PANCAKE COTTAGE [RESTAURANT]

— reviewed, Lahaina News, March 1, 1983: 14.

LANOZA, ROY, JR.

— Scholar/Athlete of the Week, Lahaina News, October 4, 2001: 13.

LANPHERE, DON [MUSICIAN]

— to perform at Blackie's Bar, Lahaina News, December 24, 1992: 15.

— to perform at Blackie's Bar, Lahaina News, December 31, 1992: 11,12.

LANTING, FRANS [ARTIST]

— to teach photography, Lahaina News, August 21, 1997: 1.

LAPALE, TINA

— wins California Golden Gloves junior welterweight division, Lahaina News, April 8, 1999: 7.

LAPPERT'S ICE CREAM [BUSINESS]

— purchased by Pele's Hawaiian Partners, Lahaina News, September 13, 1989: 6.

— donates to local schools, Lahaina News, May 1, 1991: 4.

LAPULE MA KE KAI
— Sundays at the Sea event held by Kane O Maui Jaycees, Lahaina News, May 9, 1984: 5.

LARGE APPLIANCES PICK-UP AND RECYCLING PROGRAM
— to be held, Lahaina News, September 2, 1999: 15.

LARGE TELESCOPE TOPICAL MEETING
— to be held at Hyatt Regency Maui, Lahaina News, August 13, 1992: 12.

LARGENT, STEVE
— football player plays at golf benefit for Lahainaluna athletic department, Lahaina News, May 2, 1984: 6.

LARK [PLAY]
— performed by Honolulu Theatre for Youth, Lahaina Sun, February 21, 1973: 5.

LARK QUARTET [MUSICAL GROUP]
— performance presented by Maui Philharmonic Society, Lahaina News, February 17, 1994: 12.

LARRY DOTSON GALLERY [BUSINESS]
— opens, Lahaina News, May 13, 1987: 3.
— featuring Jane and Linus Chao, Lahaina News, January 27, 1988: 3.
— featuring Robert Jarvis, Dorothy Saar, and Kristen Innocenti, Lahaina News, February 17, 1988: 18.
— reception for Lorraine E'drie and Paula Heinz, Lahaina News, March 2, 1988: 22.
— to feature Julie Patten, Lahaina News, March 16, 1988: 14.
— featuring Dotson's works, Lahaina News, June 22, 1988: 10.
— features paintings of Digant, Lahaina News, August 3, 1988: 3.

LARRY LIBRES FISHING AND DIVING TOURNAMENT
— to be held, Lahaina News, August 12, 1999: 7.

LARSEN, GAIL
— opens "Speakers Hawaii", Lahaina News, April 3, 1991: 4.

LARSEN, GRANGER
— wins Open Mini Grom Division of NSSA Nationals, Lahaina News, July 19, 2001: 1.

LARSEN, WESLEY
— wins Shapers Pohai Na Keiki Nalu titles, Lahaina News, June 25, 1998: 7.

LARSON, CHARLES
— Admiral to speak to Navy League, Lahaina News, May 28, 1992: 6.
— Admiral to speak to Navy League, Lahaina News, June 18, 1992: 15.
— Admiral to speak to Navy League, Lahaina News, July 2, 1992: 6.
— report on Admiral's speech to Navy League, Lahaina News, July 16, 1992: 6.

LARSON, CURTIS [ARTIST]
— to exhibit at Upstairs Gallery , Lahaina News, June 7, 1989: 3.
— sculptor featured at Village Gallery Contemporary, Lahaina News, August 22, 1996: 17.
— to exhibit at Village Gallery-Contemporary, Lahaina News, October 24, 1996: 15.

LARSON, DOYLENE
— home destroyed by fire, Lahaina Sun, December 30, 1970: 1.

LARSON, NICOLETTE [MUSICIAN]
— to perform at Casanova's, Lahaina News, May 2, 1990: 15.

LARUSSO, KIM [FARMER]
— critical of Maui County Water Master Plan, Lahaina Sun, January 26, 1972: 8.

LAS VEGAS
— Hawaiian Airlines, Inc to triple service between Honolulu and, Lahaina News, October 20, 1994: 13.

LASCO, ALEXA
— Lahainaluna High School student to attend Presidential Classroom program, Lahaina News, May 1, 2003: 1,18.

LASSEN [MUSICAL GROUP]
— to hold benefit for Eric MacCammond, Lahaina News, March 7, 1996: 13.

LASSEN, CHRIS
— surfer pictured, Lahaina Times, August, 1980 volume 4 number 7: 1.
— surfer featured in Wetscreams [film], Lahaina Times, August, 1980 volume 4 number 7: 5.

LASSEN, CHRISTIAN RIESE [ARTIST]
— art located at the Hyatt, Lahaina Times, July, 1980 volume 4 number 6: 1, 4.
— sells painting for record amount, Lahaina News, April 13, 1988: 3.
— to debut new paintings at "Friday Night is Art Night", Lahaina News, August 23, 1989: 9.
— opening new gallery in Lahaina, Lahaina News, October 24, 1990: 6.
— work purchased by Nikki Sixx of Motley Crew, Lahaina News, April 3, 1991: 10.
— returns from Japan, Lahaina News, June 13, 1991: 16.
— begins "Meet the Artist" series, Lahaina News, August 22, 1991: 13.
— presents painting to Princess Dalal of Saudi Arabia, Lahaina News, October 10, 1991: 16.
— partnering with The Pacific Whale Foundation to create marine museum in West Maui, Lahaina News, January 2, 1992: 5.
— to create poster for Hawaiian Tropic Bikini Contest, Lahaina News, March 12, 1992: 21.
— to open new gallery, Lahaina News, March 26, 1992: 10.
— flies to Florida to work on painting, Lahaina News, April 23, 1992: 25,29.
— signs contract with Disney for three original paintings, Lahaina News, February 3, 1994: 6.
— selected by Evander Holyfield to create a painting commemorating his fight against Michael Moorer., Lahaina News, April 28, 1994: 13.

LASSEN, DELORES
— named top producer by Coldwell Banker McCormack Real Estate, Lahaina News, October 24, 1991: 8.
— named top producer of third quarter by Coldwell Banker McCormack, Lahaina News, November 14, 1991: 8.

LASSEN, WALTER
— veteran recalls attack on Pearl Harbor, Lahaina News, June 25, 1998: 1,3.

LASSITER, MIKE [MUSICIAN]
— to perform at Makai Bar, Lahaina News, March 28, 1996: 13.
— to perform at Makai Bar, Lahaina News, September 19, 1996: 18.

LASSITER, ROCKY
— police officer's car sinks into hole created by water main break, Lahaina News, August 29, 1984: 3.

LAST CHANCE AUTO ROUNDUP
— to support American Lung Association, Lahaina News, December 28, 2000: 16.

LAST MINUTE BAND [MUSICAL GROUP]
— to perform at Lahaina Civic Center, Lahaina News, March 15, 2001: 20.

LAST NIGHT AT BALLYHOO, THE [PLAY]
— to be performed at Seabury Hall, Lahaina News, February 17, 2000: 16.
— Seabury Hall students performing, Lahaina News, February 24, 2000: 16.

LASZLO, JOHN [DOCTOR]
— to talk on smoking and lung cancer, Lahaina News, June 12, 1985: 3.

LATASCA [RESTAURANT]
— opens, Lahaina News, April 1, 1993: 12.

LATATUDES AND ADATUDES [BUSINESS]
— to open at Limahana Place, Lahaina News, April 24, 2003: 9.

LATHROP, TONY
— bike lanes sometimes sacrificed for infrastructure projects, Lahaina News, December 5, 1996: 3,18.

LATTER DAY SAINTS
— sponsoring "Pacific Festival", Lahaina News, November 23, 1988: 3,5.

LAU, ELIZABETH
— joins Design Interiors and Upholstery, Lahaina News, October 24, 1990: 6.

LAU, KILA
— jazz instructor teaches dance classes, Lahaina News, September 15, 1980: 8.

LAU, RON [TEACHER]
— position on strike discussed, Lahaina Sun, April 11, 1973: 5.

LAUB, PAUL AND CONNIE
— to purchase property on Front Street, Lahaina News, March 25, 1993: 11.
— pull out of plans to purchase site on Front Street, Lahaina News, July 22, 1993: 1.

LAUGHING WILD [PLAY]
— to be performed by Maui Community Theatre/OnStage, Lahaina News, June 24, 1993: 13.

LAULE'A
— homes available at, Lahaina News, June 27, 1996: 12.

LAUNDRY AND BOURBON [PLAY]
— comedy to be performed, Lahaina News, April 23, 1992: 25.

LAUNIUPOKO ASSOCIATES
— employee Jim Riley discusses plans for lands owned in Lahaina and Olowalu, Lahaina News, July 20, 2000: 15.

LAUNIUPOKO BEACH PARK
— site where Pioneer Mill disposes of waste water, Lahaina Sun, November 11, 1970: 1.
— proposal to dredge a swimming area in, Lahaina Sun, November 11, 1970: 3.
— erosion control wall built at, Lahaina Sun, November 11, 1970: 3.
— ocean swimming area being constructed, Lahaina Sun, December 23, 1970: 11.
— featured, Lahaina Times, October, 1980 volume 4 number 9: 1.
— seaplane crashes on beach near, Lahaina News, April 23, 1986: 1.
— money authorized to develop children's wading pool, Lahaina News, July 2, 1992: 9.
— Keiki Surf Jam held at, Lahaina News, July 28, 1994: 7.
— vandalized, Lahaina News, December 21, 1995: 5.
— swimming lessons for babies being held at, Lahaina News, January 4, 1996: 1,2.
— shore erosion noted at, Lahaina News, May 30, 1996: 1,14.
— threatened by shore erosion, Lahaina News, September 5, 1996: 1.
— Lahaina Bypass extended to, Lahaina News, January 23, 1997: 1.
— groups seek to preserve, Lahaina News, March 12, 1998: 1,17.
— Lahaina Intermediate School students treated to party at, Lahaina News, May 14, 1998: 3.
— fire started in sugar cane field burns at, Lahaina News, August 26, 1999: 1.
— memorial service for September 11th victims held at, Lahaina News, September 20, 2001: 3.
— real estate at featured, Lahaina News, July 31, 2003: 6.

LAU'OHO [MUSICAL GROUP]
— to perform at "Music on the Beach", Lahaina News, January 28, 1999: 5.

LAUPER, CINDY [MUSICIAN]
— vacations on island, Lahaina News, March 6, 1985: 7.

LAUREL BURCH SECRET JUNGLE [BUSINESS]
— opens, Lahaina News, September 10, 1992: 9.

LAURENCE BUFFET DANCE STUDIO
— to perform "Moments of Dance '98, with a Baroque Extravaganza", Lahaina News, February 19, 1998: 12.

LAURIE, GREG
— to speak to The Harvest Crusades, Lahaina News, July 17, 2003: 1,20.

LAVARACK, GARY [ARTIST]
— photography exhibit at Lahaina Arts Society's Old Jail Gallery, Lahaina News, May 2, 1984: 3.
— interviewed and work discussed, Lahaina News, May 2, 1984: 7.

LAVERY, ALEX
— promoted to director of operations at Cheeseburger in Paradise, Inc, Lahaina News, June 30, 1994: 9.

LAW DAY
— panel organized to celebrate, Lahaina Sun, April 28, 1971: 3.

LAW WEEK
— to be held, Lahaina News, May 1, 1991: 3.
— to be held with theme "Struggle for Justice", Lahaina News, April 30, 1992: 4.

LAWAI'A [MUSICAL GROUP]
— to perform at fundraiser for Pop Warner Association, Lahaina News, September 10, 1992: 13.

LAWFUL HAWAIIAN GOVERNMENT
— to hold a Convention of Legislature, Lahaina News, June 15, 2000: 16.

LAWRENCE, JAMIE [MUSICIAN]
— participated in Maui Youth Council, Lahaina Sun, January 13, 1971: 5.
— to perform at Stouffer Wailea, Lahaina News, May 13, 1993: 12.
— to perform at Borders Books and Music, Lahaina News, December 20, 2001: 16.

LAWRENCE, JOHN
— house suffers storm damage, Lahaina Sun, December 30, 1970: 1.

LAWRENCE, MIKE
— director of health hoping to reform health care, Lahaina News, December 22, 1994: 3.

LAWRENCE, MISCHELLE
— project manager at The Vintage at Ka'anapali, Lahaina News, May 18, 2000: 10.

LAWRENCE, RICK [ARTIST]
— featured, Lahaina News, April 17, 1997: 10.

LAWRENCE, SHARON
— turned down as member of Maui Planning Commission, Lahaina News, December 28, 1983: 3.
— leaving Maui, Lahaina News, December 17, 1986: 1,20.

LAWS
— Mayor Cravalho seeks reforms of, Lahaina Sun, January 6, 1971: 1.
— ruling expected on ant-hitchhiking law, Lahaina Sun, February 17, 1971: 3.
— Judge S. George Fukuoka discusses why trials can be slow, Lahaina Sun, April 14, 1971: 2.
— legal aid available in Wailuku, Lahaina Sun, June 23, 1971: 12.
— Public Defender Council discussed, Lahaina Sun, July 14, 1971: 3.
— rules governing the use of state parks proposed by the Department of Land and Natural Resources, Lahaina Sun, July 21, 1971: 11.

— Mayor Cravalho orders Maui County jail to be closed due to condition, Lahaina Sun, August 25, 1971: 2.
— treatment of prisoners at Maui County jail criticized, Lahaina Sun, August 25, 1971: 9.
— State Law Enforcement Officials Conference held at Maui Hilton Hotel, Lahaina Sun, September 1, 1971: 15.
— law to prohibit surfboard racks on bicycles introduced in Maui County Council, Lahaina Sun, September 8, 1971: 13.
— discussion of what to do if you are arrested, Lahaina Sun, October 27, 1971: 13.
— hashish smugglers arrested, Lahaina Sun, October 27, 1971: 6.
— Maui County Council studies changes to railroad laws, Lahaina Sun, October 27, 1971: 6.
— signs posted warning patrons not to purchase alcohol for minors, Lahaina Sun, November 10, 1971: 1.
— Maui Police Chief Abraham Aiona asks for jay-walking ordinance, Lahaina Sun, November 10, 1971: 13.
— Maui county court system reorganized to confirm to rest of the state, Lahaina Sun, January 19, 1972: 9.
— commentary on law and prison rehabilitation, Lahaina Sun, March 1, 1972: 13.
— Mayor Elmer Cravalho supports new penal code, Lahaina Sun, March 22, 1972: 5.
— opposition to proposed bill requiring surety bond, Lahaina Sun, August 23, 1972: 3.
— courts criticized for cost of photocopying, Lahaina Sun, October 4, 1972: 21.
— woman complains of civil rights violations in Maui Memorial Hospital psychiatric ward, Lahaina Sun, November 8, 1972: 4.
— Board of Adjustments and Appeals acquires reputation as efficient and reasonable, Lahaina Sun, December 6, 1972: 4.
— Hawaii Legal Services Project reports it handled 800 civil cases, Lahaina Sun, May 9, 1973: 11.
— advice on choosing a lawyer, Lahaina News, April 15, 1980: 15.
— further reflections on hiring a lawyer, Lahaina News, May 1, 1980: 12.
— landlord and tenant conflicts discussed, Lahaina News, July 1, 1980: 12.
— further discussion of landlord and tenant rights, Lahaina News, July 15, 1980: 11.
— further discussion of landlord and tenant rights, Lahaina News, August 1, 1980: 11.
— mayor urges police and judges to act on leash laws, Lahaina News, April 15, 1982: 12.
— leash law citations up, Lahaina News, May 1, 1982: 10.
— mayor Tavares urges dough drunk driving laws, Lahaina News, May 1, 1982: 6.
— liquor laws changed, Lahaina News, July 15, 1982: 4.
— Hawaii Land Reform Act declared unconstitutional, Lahaina News, April 15, 1983: 2,11,15.
— Hawaii Land Reform Act declared unconstitutional, Lahaina News, February 22, 1984: 17.
— U.S. Supreme Court rules that landholders can be forced to sell leases to homeowners, Lahaina News, June 6, 1984: 3.
— editorial on U.S. Supreme Court ruling that landholders can be forced to sell leases to homeowners, Lahaina News, June 13, 1984: 2.
— State advisory committee proposes to limit or ban water activities from Ka'anapali beaches, Lahaina News, August 1, 1984: 3.
— driver's license exams and road tests now available two days a week at Lahaina Civic Center, Lahaina News, August 15, 1984: 3.
— driver's license exams and road tests available Lahaina Civic Center every week day, Lahaina News, September 5, 1984: 3.
— editorial critical of federal court ruling allowing for handbilling, Lahaina News, January 16, 1985: 2.
— editorial criticizing worker's compensation, Lahaina News, March 27, 1985: 2.

— community says jet ski rules will not work, Lahaina News, May 1, 1985: 1,20.
— editorial praising state Supreme Court ruling undermining leasehold property, Lahaina News, August 7, 1985: 2.
— handicapped must obtain new parking placard, Lahaina News, August 21, 1985: 3.
— Maui Community College offering non-credit courses on legal planning, Lahaina News, September 25, 1985: 3.
— Abe Aiona asks for law to allow County to haul away junk automobiles, Lahaina News, October 9, 1985: 8.
— proposal to eliminate written test for people re-licensing, Lahaina News, October 16, 1985: 3.
— editorial supporting seatbelt law, Lahaina News, November 27, 1985: 2.
— public hearing set concerning safety inspections of vehicles, Lahaina News, January 29, 1986: 3.
— hope expressed that government will clarify legislation concerning x-rated videos, Lahaina News, February 12, 1986: 1.
— editorial criticizing small penalty for Wholesale Produce Dealers Association of Hawaii admitting to price fixing, Lahaina News, April 23, 1986: 2.
— Maui Planning Commissions approves new courthouse, Lahaina News, April 30, 1986: 1.
— editorial criticizing court rulings concerning traffic accidents and sexual abuse, Lahaina News, May 21, 1986: 2.
— editorial on tort reform, Lahaina News, August 13, 1986: 2.
— drinking age raised to 21, Lahaina News, October 1, 1986: 12.
— Council to discuss bill related to peddling, Lahaina News, October 15, 1986: 8.
— motorists to no longer receive renewal notices, Lahaina News, November 26, 1986: 3.
— Maui Police Department to conduct roadblocks, Lahaina News, December 17, 1986: 2.
— mediation workshops held, Lahaina News, January 7, 1987: 3.
— anti-slander legislation introduced, Lahaina News, February 11, 1987: 3.
— smoking banned in work places, Lahaina News, September 30, 1987: 3.
— citations given for illegal beach activities , Lahaina News, October 14, 1987: 1,2.
— caller identification improvements to be used to find nuisance callers, Lahaina News, November 11, 1987: 6.
— Maui Senior Law Fair to host Caroline Richardson, Lahaina News, June 1, 1988: 19.
— new shoreline rules, Lahaina News, August 23, 1989: 3.
— no-fault insurance law to be reviewed, Lahaina News, February 6, 1991: 4.
— county law forbids loud music from cars and trucks, Lahaina News, March 6, 1991: 1.
— Lahaina has lowest rate of seat belt use, Lahaina News, March 27, 1991: 3.
— road tests to be only given on Tuesdays and Wednesdays, Lahaina News, July 11, 1991: 5.
— Maui County Bar Association president Ray Wimberley wants to speed up processing of legal documents, Lahaina News, January 23, 1992: 5.
— new phone number for road test appointments, Lahaina News, March 5, 1992: 4.
— labor law seminar to be held, Lahaina News, March 19, 1992: 10.
— officials to enforce fire regulations at local schools, Lahaina News, March 26, 1992: 1,4.
— commercial drivers not in the new system have been downgraded, Lahaina News, April 9, 1992: 13.
— challenge to per diem judges, Lahaina News, April 16, 1992: 5.
— Maui County Council drops bill banning animal slaughter in residential neighborhoods, Lahaina News, July 2, 1992: 4.

— new car lemon law changed, Lahaina News, October 29, 1992: 9.

— Maui Job Service Employer committee to host seminar on labor law, Lahaina News, March 25, 1993: 11.

— new penalty for unregistered cars, Lahaina News, August 19, 1993: 4.

— Chamber of Commerce of Hawaii publishes manual on Labor and Employment Law, Lahaina News, September 16, 1993: 9,10.

— West Maui Taxpayers Association seeks change to Samaritan Law, Lahaina News, December 30, 1993: 1,3.

— targets timeshare signage, Lahaina News, June 23, 1994: 1.

— seminar to be offered on labor law, Lahaina News, August 4, 1994: 9.

— Labor Law Employer Seminar to be held, Lahaina News, August 18, 1994: 8.

— wage and hour laws seen as minefield to employers, Lahaina News, September 8, 1994: 10.

— tax shelter promoter Henry Kersting penalized, Lahaina News, October 13, 1994: 15.

— state representatives seek input on criminal law, Lahaina News, October 13, 1994: 5.

— Maui County Council working on legislation to curb drinking at park, Lahaina News, October 20, 1994: 1.

— legal firm Mybeck and Mybeck offers protection for intellectual property, Lahaina News, December 22, 1994: 12.

— Maui County Council passes ordinance to prohibit drinking in parks, Lahaina News, December 22, 1994: 2.

— aerial fireworks curbed but unlimited firecrackers allowed, Lahaina News, June 29, 1995: 1,2.

— ordinance would ban businesses talk through doorways, Lahaina News, July 6, 1995: 1.

— new liquor rules being considered, Lahaina News, December 5, 1996: 1.

— value of restitution, Lahaina News, March 13, 1997: 2.

— no-fault reform discussed in House and Senate, Lahaina News, March 27, 1997: 2.

— attorneys offering free legal advice, Lahaina News, May 1, 1997: 16.

— late traffic fines to be accepted, Lahaina News, July 17, 1997: 6.

— Joseph Souki discusses need to reduce lawsuit abuse, Lahaina News, September 11, 1997: 12.

— Sierra Club and Maui Tomorrow to hold workshop explaining environmental, Lahaina News, September 11, 1997: 17.

— Labor Law Employer Seminar to be held, Lahaina News, May 10, 2001: 9.

— labor law developments to be discussed, Lahaina News, October 17, 2002: 8.

— developments in labor law to be discussed, Lahaina News, October 24, 2002: 8.

— workshop to cover copyright protection, Lahaina News, August 21, 2003: 8.

LAWSON, VIRGINIA
— named officer for Lahaina Yacht Club, Lahaina Sun, December 23, 1970: 8.

LAWTON, UMEMURA AND YAMAMOTO [ARCHITECTS]
— working on expansion of Maui Surf Hotel, Lahaina News, June 5, 1985: 3.

LAWYER, ROBERT
— police searching for, Lahaina News, March 12, 1998: 2.

LAYING ON HANDS
— discussed as alternative healing method, Lahaina News, May 4, 1988: 1,15,16.

LAYLA [CATAMARAN]
— runs aground, Lahaina News, August 16, 1989: 1.

LAYMON, LYNN
— contributes footage to music video, Lahaina News, November 1, 1989: 24.

— publishes "Underwater Videographer's Handbook", Lahaina News, January 7, 1993: 4.

LAYNE, MCAVOY
— to perform Mark Twain's Letters from the Sandwich Islands at Iao Theatre, Lahaina News, July 25, 1991: 13,14.

LAYNG, RODGER
— joins KPOA-FM, Lahaina News, August 1, 1991: 11.

LAYTON, ROBERT [COMIC BOOK WRITER]
— X-Factor comic book writer and artist to appear, Lahaina News, December 25, 1985: 3.

LAYTON, ROBERT [REALTOR]
— opens Ho'oli Hale real estate company, Lahaina News, August 28, 1985: 8.

LAZELL, BILL
— to speak at AARP meeting, Lahaina News, October 28, 1987: 3.

— to offer seminar on aging, Lahaina News, February 15, 1989: 3.

LAZINSKY, NICK [COMEDIAN]
— to perform at Comedy Club and the Sports Page, Lahaina News, November 26, 1992: 22,26.

LAZY J'S [MUSICAL GROUP]
— to perform at Lopaka's Grill and Bar, Lahaina News, March 26, 1992: 18.

— changes name to Swing Shift, Lahaina News, April 9, 1992: 22.

LBC [BUSINESS]
— offers door to door service to the Philippines, Lahaina News, July 16, 1992: 16.

LE CLASSIQUE [BUSINESS]
— opens in Whalers Village, Lahaina News, February 21, 1990: 5.

LE LECHE LEAGUE INTERNATIONAL
— meets on Maui to discuss breastfeeding, Lahaina Sun, December 1, 1971: 5.

— meeting held in Waikiki, Lahaina Sun, February 9, 1972: 14.

LE MAIRE, ELLEN
— named reservations manager at the Four Seasons Resort Wailea, Lahaina News, December 17, 1992: 8.

LEACH, CHRISTOPHER [MUSICIAN]
— performs at Friday Night is Art Night, Lahaina News, April 25, 1990: 17.

LEACH, MARGARET [ARTIST]
— "Postcards from Maui" to be held at Viewpoints Gallery, Lahaina News, December 24, 1998: 13.

— to hold reception at Viewpoints Gallery, Lahaina News, September 21, 2000: 20.

LEADER OF THE PACK [MUSICAL]
— to open at Maui Community Theatre, Lahaina News, July 30, 1992: 13.

— continues, Lahaina News, August 6, 1992: 13.

— continues, Lahaina News, August 27, 1992: 18.

LEAGUE OF WOMEN VOTERS
— registering young eligible voters, Lahaina Sun, September 29, 1971: 14.

— to meet, Lahaina News, October 24, 1990: 4.

LEAHY, HATTIE
— died of natural causes, Lahaina News, February 25, 1993: 2.

LEAL, MARK
— running for Board of Education, Lahaina News, August 6, 1998: 14.

LEARY, TIMOTHY
— appearance at The Maui Bluebird reviewed, Lahaina News, December, 1979: 5,13.

LEA'S OCEAN CUISINE [RESTAURANT]
— opens, Lahaina News, July 2, 1998: 12.

LEASEHOLD
— see property

LEASH LAWS
— debate continues, Lahaina Sun, November 24, 1971: 1,11.

LEBLANC, LENNY [MUSICIAN]
— to perform at Kahului Elementary School, Lahaina News, October 1, 1992: 18.

LEBUSE, SUZZI [ARTIST]
— reception to be held at Ruth's Chris Steakhouse, Lahaina News, August 5, 1999: 12.

LECLERC, WANDA
— to begin working at the Art School at Kapalua, Lahaina News, April 4, 2002: 14.

LEDBETTER, TRAVIS
— Scholar/Athlete of the Week, Lahaina News, March 8, 2001: 12.

LEE, ALBERT [COMEDIAN]
— to perform at Comedy Club and the Sports Page, Lahaina News, March 13, 1991: 8,11.
— to perform at Comedy Club, Lahaina News, January 2, 1992: 10.
— to perform at Comedy Club and the Sports Page, Lahaina News, December 31, 1992: 12,14.

LEE, ALICE [POLITICIAN]
— editorial critical of, Lahaina News, January 18, 1989: 4.
— announces that Maui County Council to sponsor conferences on affordable housing, Lahaina News, April 10, 1991: 4.
— to speak to Maui Chamber of Commerce's West Maui committee, Lahaina News, May 8, 1991: 6.
— announces plan to seek re-election, Lahaina News, April 2, 1992: 5,6.
— conveys request from Maui Zoo to build a playground, Lahaina News, July 9, 1992: 5.
— named "Local Official of the Year-Western Region" by the National Association of Home Builders, Lahaina News, December 10, 1992: 10.
— to chair Maui County Council, Lahaina News, December 1, 1994: 7.
— hosting event, Lahaina News, September 10, 1998: 7.

LEE, AMY
— passes away, Lahaina News, February 13, 1997: 2.

LEE, BILLY [ARTIST]
— to display work, Lahaina News, January 13, 1988: 3.
— exhibition at 505 Front Street, Lahaina News, February 24, 1988: 18.
— to exhibit sand sculptures, Lahaina News, September 28, 1988: 18.
— interview with, Lahaina News, October 5, 1988: 6.
— wins sandcastle contest, Lahaina News, December 7, 1988: 16.
— demonstrates sand sculptor techniques, Lahaina News, October 4, 1989: 3.
— to sand sculpture classes, Lahaina News, February 20, 1991: 3,4.
— sand sculpture work featured, Lahaina News, July 2, 1998: 8.
— to teach sand sculpting at Whalers Village, Lahaina News, July 27, 2000: 18.
— to teach sand sculpting at Whalers Village, Lahaina News, August 10, 2000: 16.
— continues to teach sand sculpting, Lahaina News, August 17, 2000: 16.
— teaches sand sculpting, Lahaina News, November 2, 2000: 12.
— continues to teach sand sculpting, Lahaina News, November 30, 2000: 17.
— continues to teach sand sculpting, Lahaina News, March 1, 2001: 20.
— continues to offer sand sculpting, Lahaina News, May 31, 2001: 17.

LEE, BUD [MUSICIAN]
— to perform at Sir Wilfred's, Lahaina News, July 2, 1992: 26.
— to perform at Sir Wilfred's, Lahaina News, November 12, 1992: 22.
— to perform at Sir Wilfred's, Lahaina News, January 28, 1993: 16.

LEE, DAVID [ARTIST]
— life recounted, Lahaina News, August 1, 1981: 7.
— to exhibit at David Lee Gallery, Lahaina News, July 25, 2002: 20.

LEE, GEORGE
— tennis player career discussed, Lahaina News, September 5, 1984: 4.
— tennis player moving to Honolulu to pursue career, Lahaina News, October 2, 1985: 4.

LEE, GEORGE [MUSICIAN]
— to perform at Moose McGillycuddy's, Lahaina News, February 21, 1990: 13.

LEE GEORGE BAND [MUSICAL GROUP]
— reviewed, Lahaina News, February 21, 1990: 14.

LEE, JACK [MUSICIAN]
— bagpiper to perform, Lahaina News, November 28, 2002: 15.

LEE, JACKIE
— discusses closure of Shoreline Transportation, Lahaina News, December 16, 1987: 1.

LEE, JACQUELINE [ARTIST]
— to exhibit at Hui No'eau Visual Arts Center, Lahaina News, July 4, 2002: 17.

LEE, JOHNNY [MUSICIAN]
— playing on Maui, Lahaina News, November 13, 1985: 10.

LEE, JUDITH
— disputes failing road test, Lahaina News, May 6, 1993: 3.

LEE, KEKAPA [MUSICIAN]
— featured, Lahaina News, December 28, 1988: 2.
— reverend attends groundbreaking ceremony for Lahaina Aquatic Center, Lahaina News, March 27, 1991: 1.
— reverend at Waiola Church featured, Lahaina News, January 9, 1992: 3.
— gospel hymns on new music release, Lahaina News, April 2, 1998: 18.
— wins Na Hoku award, Lahaina News, May 21, 1998: 1,20.
— moving from Waiola Church to position in Oahu, Lahaina News, October 14, 1999: 1,2.
— farewell concert to be held at Westin Maui, Lahaina News, October 21, 1999: 16.

LEE, KEONI
— bus driver for Sacred Hearts School featured, Lahaina News, September 26, 2002: 1,20.

LEE, MICHAEL
— appointed as director of sales and marketing at Westin Maui, Lahaina News, September 2, 1999: 13.

LEE, SOLOMON
— named commander of the Lahaina District of the Maui Police Department, Lahaina News, April 10, 1985: 9.
— police captain tells Banyan Tree Square Preservation Committee that drug crackdown needed, Lahaina News, May 22, 1985: 1.
— police captain's initiatives against drugs and vagrancy detailed, Lahaina News, July 3, 1985: 1,9.
— editorial supporting police captain, Lahaina News, July 3, 1985: 2.

LEE, TERRY
— founder of Elite Properties featured, Lahaina News, October 31, 1991: 3.

LEEBRICK, KARL
— lieutenant colonel reflects on character of president Harry Truman, Lahaina Sun, January 3, 1973: 14.

LEECH, TONI AND MICHAEL
— open Zoolu's Grille and Bar restaurant, Lahaina News, October 7, 1999: 6,7.

LEED, MELVEEN [MUSICIAN]
— performs to benefit American Cancer Society, Lahaina News, August 13, 1986: 3.
— performs at benefit concert for Na Mele O Maui, Lahaina News, December 24, 1986: 12.
— to perform at Maui Arts and Cultural Center, Lahaina News, December 10, 1998: 21.
— to perform at "Local Divas in Concert", Lahaina News, September 23, 1999: 12.
— to perform at Hale Makua Foundation's 'Ohana Luau , Lahaina News, August 1, 2002: 18.
— to perform at New Year's Eve Dinner at Ka'anapali Beach Hotel, Lahaina News, December 26, 2002: 15.
— Hale Makua Foundation to hold 'Ohana Luau, Lahaina News, July 17, 2003: 14.
— to perform at Hale Makua Foundation's 'Ohana Luau, Lahaina News, July 24, 2003: 17.

LEEPER, CRAIG
— named regional manager of South Maui for Aston Hotels and Resorts, Lahaina News, December 12, 1990: 6.

LEETEG, EDGAR [ARTIST]
— work featured, Lahaina News, April 15, 1981: 11.

LEGAL AID SOCIETY
— offering legal aid in Wailuku, Lahaina Sun, June 23, 1971: 12.
— to offer workshops, Lahaina News, July 8, 1993: 3,4.
— to host Neighborhood Legal Clinic, Lahaina News, July 20, 1995: 5.
— sponsoring Neighborhood Legal Clinic with Hawaii Lawyers Care, Lahaina News, September 21, 1995: 4.
— starts volunteer program, Lahaina News, December 14, 1995: 19.
— to investigate housing discrimination, Lahaina News, January 31, 2002: 8.
— to offer training on consumer law issues, Lahaina News, July 18, 2002: 8.
— Ryker Wada hired as complaint analyst, Lahaina News, April 17, 2003: 8.

LEGEND OF THE SEAS, THE [SHIP]
— arrives at Lahaina Harbor, Lahaina News, April 24, 1997: 16.

LEGENDS
— story of Maui , Lahaina Sun, December 29, 1971: 10.
— The Twin Waters of Life described, Lahaina Sun, August 16, 1972: 15.

LEGENDS OF THE BAY
— surfing contest held, Lahaina News, March 4, 1999: 7.
— surf contest to be held at Honolua Bay, Lahaina News, February 6, 2003: 13.

LEHMANN, KARL [ARTIST]
— to lead slide show on tribal cultures of New Guinea, Lahaina News, January 31, 2002: 16.
— photographer to narrate "Wildlife of South Africa Slide Show", Lahaina News, March 21, 2002: 17.
— photographer to lead "Wildlife of South Africa Slide Show", Lahaina News, July 17, 2003: 17.
— to display "Namibia, Wildlife and the Skeleton Coast Slide Show", Lahaina News, October 2, 2003: 16,18.

LEHR, DIANA [ARTIST]
— work featured at Serata d'Arta, Lahaina News, October 1, 1986: 12.
— exhibiting at Village Galleries, Lahaina News, June 20, 1990: 13.
— to exhibit at Village Galleries, Lahaina News, January 5, 1995: 12.
— featured, Lahaina News, January 19, 1995: 12.
— to exhibit works at The Village Gallery, Lahaina News, January 21, 1999: 13.

— to exhibit at Village Gallery Contemporary, Lahaina News, January 28, 1999: 12.
— to exhibit at The Village Gallery Contemporary, Lahaina News, February 24, 2000: 16.

LEHRING, ADOLF [ARTIST]
— works exhibited at Lahaina Galleries, Lahaina News, January 30, 1991: 9.

LEHUA [MUSICAL GROUP]
— to perform at Lahaina Cannery Mall, Lahaina News, March 14, 2002: 17.

LEHUA, FALESESEGI
— wins Lahaina Cannery Mall's Father's Day Contest, Lahaina News, June 26, 1997: 3.

LEI CAFÉ [RESTAURANT]
— reviewed, Lahaina News, March 2, 1988: 3.
— featured, Lahaina News, June 8, 1988: 9.

LEI DAY
— lei contest to be held at Maui Inter-Continental Wailea Hotel, Lahaina News, April 24, 1985: 7.
— events held at Royal Lahaina Resort, Kapalua Shops, Lahaina News, April 27, 1988: 6.
— at Royal Lahaina Resort; Maui Inter-Continental Wailea Hotel, Lahaina News, April 26, 1989: 7,13.
— events to be held at Maui Inter-Continental Wailea, Royal Lahaina Resort, Lahaina News, April 25, 1990: 15.
— to be held at Ka'anapali Beach, Lahaina News, April 25, 1990: 16.
— to take place at Royal Lahaina Resort Tennis Stadium, Lahaina News, April 17, 1991: 12.
— schedule described, Lahaina News, May 1, 1991: 14.
— to be held as part of Aloha Festival, Lahaina News, October 14, 1993: 16.
— to be held, Lahaina News, April 25, 1996: 16.
— Hula Festival to feature Genoa Keawe, Lahaina News, April 20, 2000: 16.
— Lahaina Cannery Mall to celebrate, Lahaina News, April 26, 2001: 17.
— Hula Festival to be a tribute to Myra English, Lahaina News, April 26, 2001: 20.
— to be celebrated, Lahaina News, May 3, 2001: 20.
— to be celebrated at Lahaina Cannery Mall, Lahaina News, May 2, 2002: 16.
— to be celebrated at Lahaina Cannery Mall, Lahaina News, May 16, 2002: 18.
— to be held at Lahaina Cannery Mall, Lahaina News, April 24, 2003: 21.
— to be celebrated, Lahaina News, May 1, 2003: 16.
— held at Lahaina Cannery Mall, Lahaina News, May 15, 2003: 8.
— see also hula

LEIGH, WAYNE
— discusses Kapi'olani Children's Miracle Network, Lahaina News, June 25, 1998: 11.

LEILANI'S ON THE BEACH [RESTAURANT]
— reviewed, recipes shared, Lahaina News, July 9, 1986: 8.
— featured, Lahaina News, July 29, 1987: 7.
— event to support skateboard park, Lahaina News, April 30, 1998: 1,10.
— hosting fundraiser for proposed skateboard park, Lahaina News, May 7, 1998: 19.
— to hold benefit for Maui lifeguards, Lahaina News, May 27, 1999: 7.
— Paul "Buff" Weaver running, Lahaina News, June 3, 1999: 14.
— to hold benefit for Maui lifeguards, Lahaina News, June 10, 1999: 7.
— to hold pancake breakfast fundraiser for lifeguards, Lahaina News, June 24, 1999: 12.

— names Patrol Officer Mike Casicas as "Police Officer of the Month, Lahaina News, April 13, 2000: 2.

— names Richard Dods as "Police Office of the Month", Lahaina News, June 29, 2000: 7.

— recognizes Lahainaluna High School teachers Tisha McGlaughlin and Brian Kelly as "Educators of the Month", Lahaina News, July 27, 2000: 19.

— honor police officer Terry Nakooka, Lahaina News, September 21, 2000: 19.

— rallies to help worker Mike Manning suffering from health issue, Lahaina News, September 21, 2000: 3.

— recognizes Lahainaluna High School "Teachers of the Month" Art Watkins, Tisha McGlaughlin, and Romana Domingo, Lahaina News, October 26, 2000: 14.

— honors Leo Delatori and Lynn Kahoʻohalahala as educators of the month, Lahaina News, December 21, 2000: 15.

— Lahaina Canoe Club raises money with breakfast at, Lahaina News, April 5, 2001: 2.

— honors Lahainaluna High School Joanne Dennis, Barbie Otomo and Dennis Sasai, Lahaina News, April 19, 2001: 2.

— honors Ed Bartholomew and Anne Goff as educators of the month, Lahaina News, June 14, 2001: 8.

— celebrates 19th anniversary, Lahaina News, August 2, 2001: 9.

— honors educators, Lahaina News, November 1, 2001: 2.

— Detective Lloyd Yamashita honored by, Lahaina News, November 29, 2001: 2.

— names Lisa Tomita as police officer of the month, Lahaina News, February 14, 2002: 2.

— honors Harridean Ambrose, Michael Sado, and Joann Yamamoto as educators of the month, Lahaina News, March 7, 2002: 5.

— honors teachers Sidney Yee, Shanda Arume and Stephen Pisacano, Lahaina News, July 11, 2002: 9.

— names Sheila Kimura as Police Officer of the Month, Lahaina News, March 20, 2003: 2.

— to celebrate 21st anniversary with "Stevie Guitar's Summer Solstice Surf and Song Celebration", Lahaina News, June 19, 2003: 15.

— hosts luncheon for participants in Junior Lifeguard Program, Lahaina News, July 10, 2003: 13.

LEISURE SCIENTISTS, THE [MUSICAL GROUP]

— to perform at Longhi's, Lahaina News, August 13, 1998: 18.

— releases new CD, Lahaina News, December 17, 1998: 24.

LEITCH, MARY

— passes away, Lahaina News, September 30, 1999: 2.

LELAND, TOM

— to lecture on Schizophrenia, Lahaina News, October 3, 1991: 5.

LELAULU, LELEI

— to speak on "Smart Growth, Native Practices and Common Sense", Lahaina News, June 8, 2000: 16.

LELE

— see Lahaina

LEMAHIEU, PAUL

— State Superintendent to speak to E Komo Mai Club, Lahaina News, October 7, 1999: 16.

LEMAR, CINDY

— impact on Mala recounted, Lahaina News, June 21, 2001: 1,13.

— discusses difficulties with cleanup-project at Mala Wharf, Lahaina News, July 25, 2002: 1,24.

LEMARCA, DIANNA

— Scholar/Athlete of the Week, Lahaina News, October 26, 2000: 12.

LEMMEL, BETH

— appointed manager of Benetton, Lahaina News, February 6, 1991: 7.

LEMONGRASS [RESTAURANT]

— opens, Lahaina News, May 27, 1999: 11.

— featured, Lahaina News, August 5, 1999: 5.

LEMURIA [SPECULATIVE PLACE]

— discussed, Lahaina Sun, August 15, 1973: 19.

LEN THE BARBER [BUSINESS]

— featured, Lahaina News, February 15, 1984: 14.

LEND ME A TENOR [PLAY]

— auditions to be held, Lahaina News, January 9, 1997: 10.

— featured, Lahaina News, March 6, 1997: 11.

LENNON, JOHN [MUSICIAN]

— art work featured , Lahaina News, July 29, 1987: 1,17.

— Wharf Cinema Center celebrating artwork of, Lahaina News, December 21, 1995: 14.

LENT

— service to be held at Emmanuel Lutheran Church, Lahaina News, February 19, 1998: 13.

— service to be held by Emmanuel Lutheran Church, Lahaina News, February 21, 2002: 17.

LENT, CAROL

— to offer vegetarian cooking classes, Lahaina News, February 13, 1997: 11.

— to offer vegetarian cooking classes, Lahaina News, March 6, 1997: 10.

LEO A DALEY [BUSINESS]

— presents plan for Lahaina Harbor, Lahaina News, August 20, 1998: 1,20.

LEOIKI

— Native Hawaiian on whaling ship in 1825, Lahaina Sun, January 6, 1971: 8.

LEOLA'S FAMILY FUNWEAR [BUSINESS]

— dealing with flooding, Lahaina News, December 12, 1990: 1.

LEONARD, BRETT

— Scholar/Athlete of the Week, Lahaina News, May 28, 1998: 6.

LEONARD, CHRISTY

— wins Miss Hawaii USA, Lahaina News, June 1, 2000: 1.

— Miss Hawaii attended Sacred Hearts School, Lahaina News, February 15, 2001: 1,18.

LEONARD, DAVID

— to present "Sex, Gravity and Immortality" with Constantine Darling, Lahaina News, November 2, 2000: 25.

LEONARD, JULIE

— to offer workshop on making journals, Lahaina News, February 6, 1992: 4.

LEONARD, KATHLEEN

— owner of Fleming's on the Greens open to holding fundraisers, Lahaina News, April 11, 2002: 8.

LEONG, CHIU [ARTIST]

— work displayed alongside Ira Ono's, Lahaina News, January 4, 1984: 10.

LEONG, DEBYE

— wins map drawing contest from Wharf Cinema Center, Lahaina News, July 23, 1998: 13.

LEONG, GWEN

— named conference services manager at Four Seasons Resort Wailea, Lahaina News, November 12, 1992: 12.

LEONG, HANI

— life in Lahaina recounted, Lahaina News, May 31, 1989: 5.

LEONG, PETER

— appointed by mayor Tavares as County Director of Finance, Lahaina News, September 15, 1980: 7.

LEONG, TIM

— hired by Gima Yoshimori Miyabara Deguchi Architects, Inc., Lahaina News, November 28, 1991: 10.

LEPAGE, THOMAS
— Supreme Court of Hawaii issues restraining order against, Lahaina News, November 22, 2001: 8.

LERGER, LIA
— Maui's Teen Miss represents Maui at Miss Universe Gala, Lahaina News, May 28, 1998: 3.

LES TOOTS [BUSINESS]
— nightclub reviewed, Lahaina News, March 5, 1986: 12.

LESSIN, ALEXANDER [DOCTOR]
— to offer workshops on "Humanistic Psychology, Becoming Your Best", Lahaina News, June 19, 1985: 3.

LESSING, DORIS [WRITER]
— work reviewed, Lahaina News, July 17, 1985: 11.

LESTER, JAY
— named officer for Lahaina Yacht Club, Lahaina Sun, December 23, 1970: 8.

LETOFSKY, MORTON
— Diamond Approach group to present, Lahaina News, September 24, 1998: 17.

LETTERS TO THE EDITOR
— letters to the editor become more common with this issue and are not comprehensively indexed, Lahaina Sun, June 16, 1971: 2.

LEUKEMIA AND LYMPHONY SOCIETY
— to hold Light the Night Walk, Lahaina News, August 22, 2002: 9.
— seeking participants for Light the Night Walk, Lahaina News, September 12, 2002: 2.
— to hold Light the Night Walk, Lahaina News, September 19, 2002: 5.
— to hold Maui Light the Night Walk fundraiser, Lahaina News, October 17, 2002: 14.

LEUNG, H. [ARTIST]
— Chinese landscape painter to exhibit at Friday Night is Art Night, Lahaina News, March 5, 1992: 18.
— to exhibit at Lahaina Galleries, Lahaina News, February 11, 1993: 14,15.

LEUNG, H. AND THOMAS [ARTISTS]
— to exhibit at Lahaina Galleries, Lahaina News, February 24, 1994: 9.

LEUNG, THOMAS [ARTIST]
— Chinese landscape painter to exhibit at Friday Night is Art Night, Lahaina News, March 5, 1992: 18.

LEVAL, RENDEALL
— appointed Maui SQN Commander of the Civil Air Patrol, Lahaina News, October 1, 1992: 3.

LEVEY, JOEL AND MICHELLE [WRITERS]
— to discuss book "Living in Balance", Lahaina News, July 13, 2000: 16.

LEVINSKY, ELLEN [ARTIST]
— featherworks featured at Lahaina Arts Society, Lahaina News, December 9, 1987: 26.
— to exhibit at Lahaina Art Society, Lahaina News, April 7, 1994: 12.
— to demonstrate "humu papa", Lahaina News, August 15, 1996: 17.
— to offer feather art workshop, Lahaina News, February 18, 1999: 13.
— to demonstrate featherwork, Lahaina News, September 23, 1999: 12.
— to exhibit at Lahaina Arts Society, Lahaina News, March 16, 2000: 12.
— to exhibit "Feather Fantasies" at Lahaina Arts Gallery, Lahaina News, April 5, 2001: 20.
— to hold workshop "Make A Feather Picture", Lahaina News, August 14, 2003: 17.

LEW, BRIAN
— joins Westin Maui's sales teams, Lahaina News, September 5, 1991: 6.
— named "Manager of the Quarter" at the Westin Maui, Lahaina News, February 18, 1993: 9.

LEWIN, BARRY
— new general manager at Hyatt Regency Maui Resorts and Spa, Lahaina News, December 7, 2000: 19.

LEWIN, JOHN
— Health Director recommends people who have received blood transfusions get tested for AIDS, Lahaina News, April 1, 1987: 3.
— State health director to speak to Hawaii Pacific Gerontological Society, Lahaina News, September 5, 1991: 3.

LEWIN, NICK [COMEDIAN]
— to perform at Comedy Club and the Sports Page, Lahaina News, February 20, 1991: 9,11.

LEWIN, TALIA
— Scholar/Athlete of the Week, Lahaina News, February 6, 2003: 12.

LEWIS, ALAN AND BRENDA
— win certificate from Gallery Pacifica, Lahaina News, November 7, 2002: 22.

LEWIS, BRAD
— description of surfer, Lahaina Times, October, 1980 volume 4 number 9: 1.

LEWIS, DICK [ARTIST]
— to exhibit at Kihei Art Gallery, Lahaina News, March 15, 1989: 2.
— show continues at Glassman Galleries, Lahaina News, March 21, 1990: 14.
— to end show at Glassman Galleries, Lahaina News, April 4, 1990: 14.

LEWIS, JERRY [ENTERTAINER]
— attends Aku Memorial Celebrity Golf Tournament, Lahaina News, May 29, 1985: 4.

LEWIS, JOHN [MUSICIAN]
— to perform at Longhi's to perform with Ricardo Dioso, Lahaina News, November 25, 1999: 6.

LEWIS, LINDA
— appointed as community development officer at Bank of Hawaii, Lahaina News, November 28, 2002: 8.

LEWIS, MIKE [MUSICIAN]
— to perform at Blackie's Bar, Lahaina News, June 17, 1993: 14.

LEWIS, RAMSEY [MUSICIAN]
— to perform at Embassy Suites Hotel Ballroom, Lahaina News, January 16, 1991: 10.
— to be guest soloist for Maui Symphony's "Jazz Jazz and More Jazz Concert", Lahaina News, January 23, 1991: 7.

LEWIS, RICHARD
— to talk on "Luminous Leadership—A New Paradigm for a New Humanity", Lahaina News, August 28, 2003: 17.

LEWIS, STEPHEN [WRITER]
— co-author of "Sanctuary: The Path to Consciousness" to lecture on Quantum Energetic Balancing, Lahaina News, June 6, 2002: 16.

LEXUS OF MAUI [BUSINESS]
— to open, Lahaina News, January 21, 1993: 9.
— opens showroom on Maui, Lahaina News, July 7, 1994: 8.

LEYKIS, TOM
— talk show host to broadcast from Hard Rock Cafe, Lahaina News, February 5, 1998: 1,16.

LIBERMAN, JACOB [WRITER]
— to sign copies of "Wisdom from an Empty Mind", Lahaina News, August 9, 2001: 16.
— to speak on "Unconditional Acceptance: A new way of seeing, a new way of being" at 'Ohana Connection, Lahaina News, April 10, 2003: 21.

LIBERTY HOUSE [BUSINESS]
— opening in Whaler's Village, Lahaina Sun, November 25, 1970: 3.
— will open in new shopping center in Lahaina, Lahaina Sun, December 1, 1971: 1.

— expansion at Ka'ahumanu Center completed, Lahaina News, May 1, 1980: 8.

— to open in Lahaina Center, Lahaina News, September 12, 1990: 10.

— to open in Kihei, Lahaina News, November 28, 1991: 7.

— reopens following renovations, Lahaina News, November 3, 1994: 23.

LIBRARIES

— closed August 9th for Library Institute Day, Lahaina News, August 7, 1985: 8.

— Lahaina Library featured, Lahaina News, August 28, 1985: 1,9.

— Lahaina library celebrates 30th birthday, Lahaina News, March 5, 1986: 1.

— Lahaina Library closes temporarily, Lahaina News, July 2, 1986: 18.

— services for disabled discussed, Lahaina News, February 11, 1987: 3.

— Maui Public Libraries to be closed for Memorial Day, Lahaina News, May 23, 1990: 5.

— parking discussed at Maui County Library Advisory Commission, Lahaina News, November 16, 1995: 3.

— closed for Martin Luther King Jr. Day, Lahaina News, January 13, 2000: 12.

— bookmobile to stop at Princess Nahienaena Elementary School, Lahaina News, September 21, 2000: 21.

— bookmobile to stop at Princess Nahienaena Elementary School, Lahaina News, September 28, 2000: 16.

— bookmobile to stop at Princess Nahienaena Elementary School, Lahaina News, October 19, 2000: 21.

— Maui Bookmobile to make stops in West Maui, Lahaina News, August 1, 2002: 9.

— see also Lahaina Public Library, Lahainaluna High School Library, Maui Friends of the Library, other specific libraries

LIBRARY ADVISORY COMMISSION

— to hold public meeting, Lahaina News, November 9, 1995: 4.

LIBRARY, MAUI PUBLIC

— offering dial-a-story service, Lahaina News, February 6, 1992: 3.

LIBUTTI, FRANK

— commanding general of Marine Forces Pacific to speak at Maui Tropical Plantation, Lahaina News, November 18, 1999: 16.

LICENSING EXECUTIVES SOCIETY

— to meet at Hyatt Regency Maui, Lahaina News, September 13, 1989: 1.

LICHTENHAHN, DUTCH

— appointed director of security at Kapalua Bay Hotel and Villas, Lahaina News, February 6, 1991: 6.

LIEDING, CHRIS [ARTIST]

— to offer class on sculpture, Lahaina News, October 29, 1998: 28.

LIEM, T.P.

— proposes mansion near Kapalua Bay Hotel, Lahaina News, August 2, 1989: 3.

— residents oppose mansion sought by, Lahaina News, November 1, 1989: 3.

— group files petition opposing proposed mansion, Lahaina News, December 6, 1989: 1.

— County corporate counsel rules that mansion does not require special management area permit, Lahaina News, January 24, 1990: 28.

— mansion proposed by raises concern for open space, Lahaina News, January 31, 1990: 1,3.

— opposition to proposed mansion grows, Lahaina News, February 14, 1990: 1.

— Mayor Hannibal Tavares condemns proposed mansion on Hawea Point, Lahaina News, February 21, 1990: 1.

— appears to have resolved conflict with Friends of Hawea Point over development of mansion, Lahaina News, November 28, 1990: 3,4.

— proposed home said to limit access to Hawea Point, Lahaina News, September 29, 1994: 1,3.

LIERLY, JEAN

— director West Maui Youth Center updates on programs, Lahaina News, June 13, 1996: 3.

— now administrative coordinator of Maui Interfaith Volunteer Caregivers, Lahaina News, January 22, 1998: 2.

LIEURANCE, ANDY

— promoted to vice president and general manager of Maui operations of Chaney, Brooks and Co., Lahaina News, December 1, 1994: 13.

LIFE FORCE ASSOCIATES

— to hold lectures on healing, Lahaina News, December 25, 1985: 3.

LIFE OF THE LAND

— searching for sources of pollution, Lahaina Sun, November 18, 1970: 1.

— meeting scheduled at Kahului Library, Lahaina Sun, January 6, 1971: 8.

— report on pollution in Maui, Lahaina Sun, February 3, 1971: 5.

— sought fine for Wailea Land Corporation for development activities, Lahaina Sun, February 10, 1971: 2.

— complaint against Wailea Land Corporation dismissed, Lahaina Sun, March 24, 1971: 5.

— present at seminar on ecology and the future of Maui , Lahaina Sun, April 7, 1971: 1.

— sued by E.T. Ige Construction for damages, Lahaina Sun, June 2, 1971: 5.

— suit brought by E.T. Ige Construction is dropped, Lahaina Sun, June 9, 1971: 5.

— criticizes planned power plant, Lahaina Sun, July 21, 1971: 12.

— attempts to upgrade waters in Ma'alaea Bay to Class AA, Lahaina Sun, July 28, 1971: 11.

— sues to stop bombing of Kaho'olawe, Lahaina Sun, August 4, 1971: 1,2.

— to hold meeting at Maui Community College, Lahaina Sun, August 4, 1971: 2.

— opens office in Wailuku, Lahaina Sun, October 20, 1971: 14.

— discussed in editor's commentary, Lahaina Sun, October 27, 1971: 11.

— accuses mayor Cravalho of conflict of interest in Wailea development, Lahaina Sun, July 5, 1972: 3.

— recommends changing flight patterns to reduce aircraft noise pollution, Lahaina Sun, September 27, 1972: 5.

— questions land grading projects, Lahaina Sun, October 4, 1972: 27.

— offers to purchase Dole pineapple operation in Moloka'i, Lahaina Sun, October 18, 1972: 5.

— attempts to control tourism growth, Lahaina Sun, November 15, 1972: 4.

— questions legality of County Planning Commission, Lahaina Sun, January 31, 1973: 6.

LIFE OF THE PARTY [PLAY]

— reviewed, Lahaina News, May 29, 1997: 14.

LIFEFEST MAUI

— to be held at Wailea Resort, Lahaina News, September 11, 2003: 9.

LIFEGUARD

— prepared for winter surf, Lahaina News, January 29, 1998: 1,2.

— junior lifeguard program to be held, Lahaina News, May 29, 2003: 12.

LIFOU ISLAND DANCE THEATRE

— to perform at Maui Arts and Cultural Center, Lahaina News, September 12, 2002: 21.

LIGGET, JOE

— educational activities described, Lahaina Sun, July 25, 1973: 14.

— collects canned goods for homeless, Lahaina News, October 25, 2001: 2.

— collecting canned goods for the homeless, Lahaina News, December 6, 2001: 2.

— continues to discussions of the Bible with Reverend Rumboa, Lahaina News, December 27, 2001: 16.

— distributed bags to the needy, Lahaina News, January 10, 2002: 3.

— Chez Paul to host benefit for, Lahaina News, January 24, 2002: 9.

— to hold "Sports Night", Lahaina News, April 4, 2002: 13.

— thanks Mike Tyson for donating money to organization, Lahaina News, May 9, 2002: 12.

— continues to hold Bible reading meetings, Lahaina News, July 4, 2002: 17.

— to distribute bags of food to the needy, Lahaina News, August 22, 2002: 16.

— continues to hold Bible study meetings, Lahaina News, October 17, 2002: 21.

— establishes emergency fund for Nelson Lopez, Lahaina News, October 17, 2002: 3.

— accepting canned foods, Lahaina News, January 2, 2003: 5.

— accepting canned foods, Lahaina News, January 9, 2003: 18.

— Lahaina Baptist Church holds canned food drive for, Lahaina News, January 23, 2003: 2.

— joins forces with Centro Cristiano Betel to help Spanish-speaking residents, Lahaina News, February 20, 2003: 3.

— accepting donations of canned foods, Lahaina News, February 27, 2003: 9.

— to hold fundraiser, Lahaina News, April 17, 2003: 2.

— offering assistance to Spanish population, Lahaina News, August 7, 2003: 5.

LIGHT THE NATION [TELEVISION SHOW]
— to be aired on Akaku: Maui Community Television, Lahaina News, October 14, 1999: 12.

LIGHT THE NIGHT WALK
— participants sought for, Lahaina News, August 22, 2002: 9.

— seeking participants, Lahaina News, September 12, 2002: 2.

LIGHTHOUSES
— exhibit by Love Dean, Lahaina News, April 10, 1991: 12.

— exhibit continues, Lahaina News, April 17, 1991: 17,18.

LIHIKAI SCHOOL
— PTA to hold bazaar, Lahaina News, February 5, 1998: 13.

— takes first place in Foodland's Shop for Better Education Banner contest, Lahaina News, April 9, 1998: 13.

LILI INDUSTRIAL LAUNDRY [BUSINESS]
— opens, Lahaina News, November 14, 1996: 9.

LILIKOI, EDDIE
— hosting karaoke at Embassy Suites Resort, Lahaina News, March 30, 1995: 11.

LILIKOI, TODDY
— seeks community support for Pop Warner league, Lahaina News, June 22, 2000: 1,15.

LILIʻUOKALANI [QUEEN]
— death and burial recounted, Lahaina News, March 1, 1981: 7,10.

— handwritten letter reprinted, Lahaina News, June 1, 1981: 15.

— centennial of overthrow to be commemorated, Lahaina News, January 7, 1993: 4.

— musical tribute "He Poʻai Aloha—Encircled with Love" to be performed, Lahaina News, March 30, 2000: 12.

— Heʻui Cultural Arts Festival to celebrate, Lahaina News, September 27, 2001: 2.

LILLEDAL, TOM
— front street merchant not happy about proposed improvements to Front Street, Lahaina News, September 8, 1994: 1,7.

LILLIE, LEWIS
— report on basketball player, Lahaina Sun, January 20, 1971: 7.

LILLY, JOHN C.
— memorial service held for doctor to be held on Pacific Whale Foundation's Ocean Spirit catamaran, Lahaina News, January 3, 2002: 16.

LILLY, P.A.
— representative from Harbors Division discusses issue of people living on boats in Lahaina harbor, Lahaina Sun, December 30, 1970: 4.

— representative from Harbors Division discusses construction of new docking facility, Lahaina Sun, December 30, 1970: 8.

LILY [PLAY]
— to be performed by Bryna Weiss at Maui Arts and Cultural Center, Lahaina News, November 7, 1996: 14.

LILY CAI CHINESE DANCE COMPANY [TROUPE]
— to perform at Maui Arts and Cultural Center, Lahaina News, January 30, 2003: 17.

— to perform at Maui Arts and Cultural Center, Lahaina News, February 6, 2003: 16.

LIM FAMILY [MUSICAL GROUP]
— family to perform at "Music on the Beach", Lahaina News, March 25, 1999: 7.

LIMAHANA PLACE
— stores to open, Lahaina News, April 17, 2003: 8.

— grand opening to be held, Lahaina News, April 24, 2003: 9.

LIMPEROS, JAMES
— killed in automobile accident, Lahaina News, June 27, 1984: 3.

LIN WA [SHIP]
— described, Lahaina Sun, July 11, 1973: 21.

LINARES, VINCENT RYAN [POLITICIAN]
— to serve as Patsy Mink's Washington intern, Lahaina News, January 14, 1993: 3.

— candidate for Board of Education, Lahaina News, October 26, 2000: 23.

LINCOLN DAY
— Republicans to hold dinner, Lahaina News, February 14, 1990: 3.

LINCOLN, GREGORY [ARTIST]
— to help celebrate 40th anniversary of Lahaina Arts Society, Lahaina News, May 9, 2002: 14.

LINCOLN, LYNN
— new loan officer at Home Financial Services, Inc., Lahaina News, March 25, 1993: 10.

LINCOLN-MERCURY [BUSINESS]
— will sponsor Kapalua International golf tournament, Lahaina News, March 12, 1992: 10.

LINCOLN-MERCURY KAPALUA INTERNATIONAL
— Fred Couples wins, Lahaina News, November 10, 1994: 1.

— golf tournament to be held, Lahaina News, November 7, 1996: 1,20.

— being held, Lahaina News, November 6, 1997: 5.

— see also Kapalua International Golf Tournament

LINDAN, PATRICK [POLITICIAN]
— appointed by governor John Waihee to Maui District School Advisory Council, Lahaina News, August 1, 1991: 3.

— to run for Maui County Council, Lahaina News, May 5, 1994: 3.

— helping to set up anti-crime network, Lahaina News, December 15, 1994: 1,20.

LINDBERGH, CHARLES
— watches designed by to be produced, Lahaina News, July 25, 1991: 10.

LINDEMANS WINES [BUSINESS]
— to hold fundraiser for Pacific Whale Foundation, Lahaina News, July 7, 1994: 16.

LINDLEY, DAVID [MUSICIAN]
— to perform at Embassy Suites Resort, Lahaina News, August 15, 1991: 12.

LINDSAY, BARRIE
— to talk on "Living Your Joy Now" at 'Ohana Connection breakfast, Lahaina News, May 1, 2003: 17.

LINDSAY, JOHN
— mayor of New York visits Honolulu for National League of Cities convention, Lahaina Sun, December 8, 1971: 6.

LINDSEY [FAMILY]
— history discussed, Lahaina News, July 29, 1987: 1,17.

LINDSEY BUILDING AND CO. [BUSINESS]
— sponsoring home construction workshop with First Federal Savings, Lahaina News, June 11, 1992: 6.

LINDSEY, ED [POLITICIAN]
— archaeologist discusses local sites, Lahaina News, March 12, 1998: 1,17.
— to hold public meeting, Lahaina News, June 11, 1998: 17.
— to hold "Acts of Aloha Weekends", Lahaina News, September 3, 1998: 18.
— campaign for Mayor detailed, Lahaina News, September 10, 1998: 7.

LINDSEY, ED AND PUANANI
— Maui Cultural Lands non-profit featured, Lahaina News, August 21, 2003: 3.

LINDSEY, LOKELANI [POLITICIAN]
— says that Lahainaluna High School may be a new library, Lahaina News, February 14, 1990: 1.
— to hold fundraiser to support mayoral candidacy, Lahaina News, June 20, 1990: 5.
— candidate profiled, Lahaina News, September 19, 1990: 2,6,7.
— Maui District School superintendent to propose sites for new Kihei elementary school, Lahaina News, October 15, 1992: 12.
— to conduct public meeting on proposed Kihei elementary school, Lahaina News, October 29, 1992: 17.
— resets date for picking location of South Maui school, Lahaina News, January 14, 1993: 7.
— party to be held for, Lahaina News, February 18, 1993: 4.

LINDSEY, MARY HELEN
— to represent Lahaina District at sovereignty convention, Lahaina News, February 4, 1999: 1.

LINDSEY, NED
— named officer of Lahaina Kamaakina Fishing Association, Lahaina Sun, December 23, 1970: 11.
— native Hawaiian and family featured, Lahaina News, October 4, 1989: addition5,addition11.
— featured, Lahaina News, November 1, 1989: 13.
— resident passes away, Lahaina News, March 14, 1996: 1,2.

LINDSEY, NED AND PUA
— to be grand marshals at King Kamehameha Day parade, Lahaina News, June 11, 1992: 3.

LINDSEY, PUA
— to be honored at Hula O Na Keiki, Lahaina News, September 25, 1997: 7.
— meets with Lahainaluna Voyaging, Lahaina News, March 12, 1998: 19.
— to lead King Kamehameha Day Parade, Lahaina News, June 13, 2002: 1,18.

LINDSEY, ROSE
— member of Lahaina Kamaakina Fishing Association, Lahaina Sun, December 23, 1970: 11.

LINDSEY, WAINALU RASHAAN
— family seeking donations to help with medical costs, Lahaina News, June 18, 1998: 2.

LINEN CLOSET [BUSINESS]
— opens, Lahaina News, September 17, 1986: 11.

LING, BELINDA [ARTIST]
— paintings to be displayed at Lahaina Public Library, Lahaina News, July 17, 2003: 16.

LING, JOHN
— lecture hosted by Pacific Whale Foundation, Lahaina News, December 13, 1989: 4.

LINGLE, LINDA [POLITICIAN]
— files to run for re-election for Maui County Council, Lahaina News, July 18, 1984: 3.
— holds fundraiser, Lahaina News, September 2, 1987: 3.
— comments on legality of special use permit to Aloha Voyages for commercial tourist operation, Lahaina News, November 18, 1987: 1,11,12.
— speaks of decision to evict Lahaina Arts Society from Old Lahaina Courthouse, Lahaina News, January 27, 1988: 1.
— discusses whether developers should pay impact fees, Lahaina News, March 9, 1988: 1.
— speaks to pool advocates, Lahaina News, March 30, 1988: 20.
— discusses future of proposed swimming pool, Lahaina News, August 17, 1988: 1.
— to speak at West Maui Realtors Association, Lahaina News, September 14, 1988: 15.
— discusses proposed swimming pool, Lahaina News, October 26, 1988: 1,24.
— to hold fundraiser at Maui Tropical Plantation, Lahaina News, September 6, 1989: 24.
— to speak to Lahaina Town Action Committee, Lahaina News, January 24, 1990: 6.
— supports community pool, Lahaina News, February 21, 1990: 2.
— running for mayor, Lahaina News, February 21, 1990: 2.
— to hold dinner with Pat Saiki, Lahaina News, March 28, 1990: 4.
— to hold fundraiser featuring Jimmy Mac and the Kool Kats, Lahaina News, June 20, 1990: 5.
— to open mayoral campaign, Lahaina News, July 25, 1990: 6.
— candidate profiled, Lahaina News, September 12, 1990: 1,4,6.
— to speak to Lahaina Kiwanis at Pioneer Inn, Lahaina News, September 19, 1990: 5.
— to hold rallies, Lahaina News, September 26, 1990: 7.
— to hold rally at Kalama Park, Lahaina News, October 3, 1990: 3.
— to speak to Lahaina Rotary Club, Lahaina News, October 31, 1990: 7.
— mayor-elect to ask for delay in decision on Ka'anapali Beach Hotel proposed expansion, Lahaina News, November 14, 1990: 1.
— mayor begins to put cabinet together, Lahaina News, November 14, 1990: 1.
— proposes hotel development moratorium, Lahaina News, November 28, 1990: 1.
— selecting people for her cabinet, Lahaina News, December 19, 1990: 1.
— mayor assigns low priority to building hotels, Lahaina News, January 2, 1991: 1.
— appoints members of West Maui Advisory Committee, Lahaina News, January 2, 1991: 3.
— inauguration scheduled, Lahaina News, January 2, 1991: 3.
— sworn in as mayor, Lahaina News, January 9, 1991: 1.
— mayor's appointment of Cyrus Chan criticized, Lahaina News, January 9, 1991: 1,5.
— stops permits for buildings that require additional water from aquifer, Lahaina News, January 9, 1991: 3.
— selecting administration, Lahaina News, January 16, 1991: 2,9.

— major attends Maui Contractors Association annual banquet, Lahaina News, January 23, 1991: 5.

— board and commission appointments listed, Lahaina News, February 20, 1991: 5,8.

— opposes proposal to make county conform to state plans for planned housing projects, Lahaina News, March 13, 1991: 1.

— to lead March of Dimes walk, Lahaina News, March 13, 1991: 5.

— proposes $181 million budget for Maui County, Lahaina News, March 20, 1991: 3.

— attends groundbreaking ceremony for Lahaina Aquatic Center, Lahaina News, March 27, 1991: 1.

— disagrees with Joseph Conant, executive director of state Housing Finance and Development Corporation, on implications of legislation, Lahaina News, April 3, 1991: 1.

— participating in Girl Scout program were scouts watch women executives in action, Lahaina News, April 10, 1991: 3.

— request for water source development funds from legislature likely, Lahaina News, April 17, 1991: 1.

— proposes to eliminate property taxes on Hawaiian Home lands, Lahaina News, April 17, 1991: 18.

— opposes parks bill, Lahaina News, April 17, 1991: 3.

— proclaims April as "National Cable Month", Lahaina News, April 17, 1991: 3.

— creates Advisory Committee on bikeways, Lahaina News, April 17, 1991: 4.

— creates recycling/composting program, Lahaina News, April 24, 1991: 4,5.

— proposes reducing property tax rate, Lahaina News, May 1, 1991: 1.

— to speak to Hawaii Association of Public Works conference, Lahaina News, May 15, 1991: 8.

— to speak to annual meeting of West Maui Taxpayers Association, Lahaina News, May 23, 1991: 3.

— names Allan Sparks to Charter Commission, Lahaina News, May 23, 1991: 4.

— appoints Guy Haywood as Corporation Counsel, Lahaina News, May 23, 1991: 6.

— opposition to transferring state parks to county lessens, Lahaina News, June 13, 1991: 3.

— signs County budget, Lahaina News, June 27, 1991: 6.

— releases rules for watching the solar eclipse, Lahaina News, June 27, 1991: 6.

— supports regional park, Lahaina News, July 11, 1991: 1.

— rejects subsidized bus system, Lahaina News, August 8, 1991: 7.

— speaks of limited country trash pickup in Lahaina, Lahaina News, August 15, 1991: 1.

— concerned about rapid seaweed growth, Lahaina News, August 22, 1991: 1,3.

— endorses limiting number of hostess bars to twelve, Lahaina News, September 12, 1991: 4.

— approves new water rates, Lahaina News, September 12, 1991: 5.

— to speak at Maui Historic Commission's final meeting, Lahaina News, September 19, 1991: 3.

— requests more sidewalks and parks, Lahaina News, October 3, 1991: 1.

— editorial praising, Lahaina News, October 3, 1991: 9.

— seeks to build affordable housing, Lahaina News, October 10, 1991: 1.

— signs proclamation announcing Domestic Violence Awareness Month, Lahaina News, October 17, 1991: 11.

— creates Beach Access Advisory Committee, Lahaina News, November 21, 1991: 4.

— names people to citizen advisory committees, Lahaina News, November 21, 1991: 6.

— to interview Maui News editor Nora Cooper, Lahaina News, November 28, 1991: 2.

— allowing homeless to relocate from Ma'alaea beach, Lahaina News, December 19, 1991: 6,7.

— sees closing of landfills as a priority, Lahaina News, December 26, 1991: 1.

— announces Maui County to fund research on algae bloom problem, Lahaina News, January 2, 1992: 1.

— appoints committee to study transportation alternatives, Lahaina News, January 2, 1992: 5.

— approves Napili Trade Center, Lahaina News, January 16, 1992: 4.

— announces grant for shelter for homeless, Lahaina News, February 6, 1992: 4.

— says state recommendations to reduce algae bloom premature, Lahaina News, March 12, 1992: 1.

— opposes moving shore permitting to County Councils, Lahaina News, March 19, 1992: 1.

— presents budget to Maui County, Lahaina News, March 26, 1992: 3.

— honors Bill "Kosuo" Azeka, Lahaina News, March 26, 1992: 5.

— proposes to provide money to promote small business, Lahaina News, April 16, 1992: 13.

— to speak to Maui Contractors Association general meeting, Lahaina News, April 16, 1992: 14.

— proclaims Professional Secretaries Week, Lahaina News, April 23, 1992: 8.

— asked by Rick Reed to clear algae from beaches, Lahaina News, April 30, 1992: 1.

— announces recycling grant, Lahaina News, May 21, 1992: 4.

— to speak to Maui Chamber of Commerce, Lahaina News, May 21, 1992: 8.

— states pool in Kihei not a priority, Lahaina News, June 25, 1992: 7.

— names Helen Christman to Liquor Control Commission, Lahaina News, July 23, 1992: 10.

— submits beach access plan, Lahaina News, July 23, 1992: 10.

— critical of Lahaina News stories on sewage problems, Lahaina News, July 30, 1992: 1.

— forms advisory committee to advice on beach access, Lahaina News, August 20, 1992: 4.

— to meet with William Carroll, appealing firing from Department of Public Works, Lahaina News, August 27, 1992: 1.

— signs bill exempting churches from paying for road improvements, Lahaina News, September 10, 1992: 4.

— denies UPW grievance over firing of William Carroll, Lahaina News, September 24, 1992: 6.

— to hold public meeting on county budget, Lahaina News, October 8, 1992: 2.

— attends public meeting on Maui County budget, Lahaina News, October 22, 1992: 1.

— sued by former county employee William Carroll, Lahaina News, November 26, 1992: 1.

— defends county Managing Director Richard Haake, Lahaina News, December 31, 1992: 3.

— signs property tax bills, Lahaina News, January 14, 1993: 4.

— supports state obtaining Kamaole beach parcel, Lahaina News, February 4, 1993: 11.

— to host Maui Catholic Charities Executive Director Charles Ridings, Lahaina News, February 4, 1993: 16.

— submits nominations to various boards and commissions, Lahaina News, February 18, 1993: 4.

— sends nominees to Maui County Council, Lahaina News, February 25, 1993: 5.

— disagrees with Howard Tagomori on funding Kihei substation, Lahaina News, March 11, 1993: 10.

— sewage treatment priority in budget, Lahaina News, March 18, 1993: 1,4.

— talks about West Maui Projects, Lahaina News, April 1, 1993: 1.

— to lead bike ride through Lahaina Town, Lahaina News, April 22, 1993: 3.

— signs proclamation recognizing National Be Kind to Animals Week, Lahaina News, May 6, 1993: 1.

— appoints new members to West Maui Advisory Committee, Lahaina News, July 15, 1993: 2.

— to host Mayor's Ball, Lahaina News, August 12, 1993: 6.

— interviewed, Lahaina News, August 19, 1993: 1,3.

— part two of interview with, Lahaina News, August 26, 1993: 2,3.

— third installment of interview, Lahaina News, September 2, 1993: 3.

— invites comments on county budget, Lahaina News, September 16, 1993: 3.

— appoints new members to West Maui Advisory Committee, Lahaina News, September 16, 1993: 3.

— meets with Lightbringers Rescue Mission, other non-profit organizations, Lahaina News, September 30, 1993: 3,4.

— begins recruitment for county boards, commissions, and advisory committees, Lahaina News, October 14, 1993: 4.

— hears concerns from timeshare resale worker, Lahaina News, December 16, 1993: 1,4.

— to attend LahainaTown Action committee town meeting, Lahaina News, January 13, 1994: 2.

— talks about funding to improve Front Street, Lahaina News, January 27, 1994: 1,2.

— to have open telephone lines, Lahaina News, February 10, 1994: 4.

— to speak at Republican Party's Lincoln Day Dinner, Lahaina News, February 17, 1994: 12.

— unveils budget requests, Lahaina News, March 24, 1994: 1,20.

— proclaims April as "Child Abuse Prevention Month", Lahaina News, April 14, 1994: 3.

— to host open telephone line, Lahaina News, April 21, 1994: 5.

— begins re-election campaign, Lahaina News, June 9, 1994: 6.

— attends opening of Planet Hollywood restaurant, Lahaina News, July 7, 1994: 1,3.

— seeks support for Olowalu camping areas, Lahaina News, July 14, 1994: 5.

— Mayor seeks volunteers to fill Board of Variances and Appeals vacancy, Lahaina News, September 8, 1994: 5.

— begins holding county budget meetings, Lahaina News, September 15, 1994: 6.

— seeking new board member for Board of Variances and Appeals, Lahaina News, September 15, 1994: 6.

— seeking resident for county boards, Lahaina News, October 13, 1994: 7.

— members of Maui County Council hold unannounced meeting to criticize, Lahaina News, October 20, 1994: 1.

— office extends deadline for Board and Commission appointments, Lahaina News, November 24, 1994: 6.

— continues to have open telephone line for constituents, Lahaina News, December 22, 1994: 6.

— seeks funding for Maui Community College and state mental health services, Lahaina News, January 26, 1995: 6.

— releases nominations to fill vacancies, Lahaina News, February 9, 1995: 3.

— met with Lahainaluna High School Traffic Safety Team, Lahaina News, March 16, 1995: 4.

— more officers proposed in budget, Lahaina News, March 23, 1995: 1,16.

— to headline "Rainbow of Dreams" fundraiser, Lahaina News, March 30, 1995: 6.

— critical of Governor Ben Cayetano cutting funds for Front Street, Lahaina News, June 1, 1995: 1,12.

— says that funding still short for Front Street Improvement Project, Lahaina News, June 8, 1995: 1.

— to speak at Maui Visitors Bureau, Lahaina News, June 29, 1995: 10.

— nominates Richard Bissen as County Prosecuting Attorney, Lahaina News, July 27, 1995: 4.

— Mayor to hold budget meeting, Lahaina News, August 31, 1995: 4.

— to hold meeting on budget, Lahaina News, September 14, 1995: 6.

— not convinced on need to split Public Works and Waste Management Department, Lahaina News, October 5, 1995: 3.

— seeking volunteers to serve on county boards and commissions, Lahaina News, October 19, 1995: 4.

— seeking volunteers for county boards and commissions, Lahaina News, October 26, 1995: 2.

— residents to have open telephone line to, Lahaina News, January 11, 1996: 2.

— Robbie Ann Kane appointed coordinator for county's Office of Economic Development, Lahaina News, January 18, 1996: 4.

— appoints citizen's task force to recommend rules for Lahaina's historic district, Lahaina News, February 15, 1996: 11.

— visits Princess Nahienaena School, Lahaina News, April 18, 1996: 3.

— to be keynote speaker at Maui Visitor Bureau's annual general meeting, Lahaina News, June 13, 1996: 11.

— meets with West Maui Taxpayers Association, Lahaina News, July 25, 1996: 2.

— continues to host open telephone line, Lahaina News, August 22, 1996: 15.

— mayor initiating discussion on public park at North Beach, Lahaina News, January 30, 1997: 1.

— continues to hold open telephone line, Lahaina News, January 30, 1997: 10.

— updates on possible open space at North Beach, Lahaina News, February 13, 1997: 1.

— new police to focus on visitor industry, Lahaina News, February 27, 1997: 1,16.

— budget, Lahaina News, March 20, 1997: 1,20.

— to speak at Maui Visitors Bureau, Lahaina News, June 19, 1997: 3.

— to hold meeting on use of War Memorial Stadium, Lahaina News, August 7, 1997: 1.

— thanks residents for living with construction during Front Street improvements, Lahaina News, August 14, 1997: 1.

— discusses gubernatorial race at Lahaina Rotary meeting, Lahaina News, September 4, 1997: 1,2.

— seeking board members, Lahaina News, September 25, 1997: 6.

— seeking board members, Lahaina News, October 2, 1997: 18.

— to speak to West Maui Soroptimists, Lahaina News, October 2, 1997: 21.

— asks public to make budget requests, Lahaina News, October 2, 1997: 21.

— forming Commission on Children and Youth, Lahaina News, October 9, 1997: 9.

— to take budget requests from the public, Lahaina News, October 16, 1997: 1,16.

— county to hire special counsel to advise Maui Planning Commission, Lahaina News, November 13, 1997: 1.

— extends application deadline for county boards and commissions, Lahaina News, November 20, 1997: 2.

— to speak at town meeting, Lahaina News, January 8, 1998: 1.

— tells residents to lobby for county's share of TAT money, Lahaina News, January 15, 1998: 1,16.

— speaks against hotel room tax increase, Lahaina News, February 12, 1998: 13.

— nominates residents to serve on county commissions, Lahaina News, February 12, 1998: 3.

— to speak to Maui Chamber of Commerce, Lahaina News, March 12, 1998: 11.

— to speak to Maui Chamber of Commerce and HMAA, Lahaina News, March 19, 1998: 11.

— unveils proposed budget, Lahaina News, March 19, 1998: 3.

— to speak at Maui Chamber of Commerce meeting, Lahaina News, March 26, 1998: 11.

— to speak to Maui Chamber of Commerce Installation Banquet, Lahaina News, May 7, 1998: 15.

— to speak to the Maui Chamber of Commerce, Lahaina News, May 14, 1998: 17.

— opens campaign headquarters, Lahaina News, July 16, 1998: 9.

— campaigns on Front Street, Lahaina News, November 5, 1998: 15.

— to flip the switch on the Banyan Tree, Lahaina News, December 10, 1998: 8.

— gubernatorial candidate to speak to Maui Chamber of Commerce, Lahaina News, January 31, 2002: 8.

— holds Birthday Bash fundraiser, Lahaina News, June 20, 2002: 20.

— to appear in three events on Maui, Lahaina News, July 4, 2002: 20.

— gubernatorial platform summarized, Lahaina News, July 11, 2002: 1,20.

— names Harold Hardcastle as honorary chairman, Lahaina News, September 5, 2002: 5.

— discusses gubernatorial campaign, Lahaina News, October 17, 2002: 1,17.

— Governor to speak at luncheon, Lahaina News, December 19, 2002: 8.

— appoints Nelson Befitel as director of Department of Labor and Industrial Relations, Lahaina News, December 19, 2002: 8.

— Governor announces search for Hawaii's best exporters, Lahaina News, June 5, 2003: 8.

— Roz Baker critical of for not signing helicopter air ambulance bill, Lahaina News, July 3, 2003: 2.

— Governor to speak to West Maui Taxpayers Association, Lahaina News, July 10, 2003: 9.

— Governor forms Maui Advisory Committee, Lahaina News, July 17, 2003: 9.

— to speak to joint meeting of West Maui Taxpayers Association and West Maui Improvement Foundation, Lahaina News, July 24, 2003: 2.

— to hold "Talk Story" community forum, Lahaina News, July 31, 2003: 2.

— to hold "Talk Story" community forum, Lahaina News, August 7, 2003: 1,18.

— releases funding for capital improvement fund for public school projects, Lahaina News, August 14, 2003: 1.

— held "Talk Story", Lahaina News, August 14, 2003: 1,20.

LINK CORPORATION
— purchases Cannon's International Business College, Lahaina News, April 2, 1992: 13.

LINN, GAIL
— stars in television show "Hawaii in Style", Lahaina News, November 8, 1989: 5.

LINNELL, ANN AND JOHN
— owners of physical therapy office featured, Lahaina News, October 1, 1986: 9.

LINNELL, JOHN [MUSICIAN]
— releases record, Lahaina News, December 16, 1987: 15.

LINSKY, JEFF [MUSICIAN]
— to perform as part of Atherton Performing Arts Series, Lahaina News, June 6, 1996: 15.

LION DANCE
— to be held at Wo Hing Temple, Lahaina News, March 13, 1985: 3.
— planned for Lahaina Cannery, Lahaina News, February 17, 1988: 18.
— to be performed at Wharf Shopping Center, Lahaina News, January 24, 1990: 14.
— to be held at Wharf Cinema Center, Lahaina News, January 24, 1990: 5.

LION DANCERS [TROUPE]
— to attend Chinese New Year celebration in West Maui, Lahaina News, February 20, 1991: 8.
— to perform during Chinese New Year, Lahaina News, January 30, 1992: 16.

LION IN WINTER, THE [PLAY]
— to be performed by Maui Community Theatre, Lahaina Sun, November 15, 1972: 10.
— to be performed by Maui Academy of Performing Arts, Lahaina News, January 19, 1995: 11.

LION'S CLUBS OF MAUI
— organizes free glaucoma detection clinic, Lahaina Sun, February 24, 1971: 3.
— Lahaina chapter hosts blood drive, Lahaina Sun, March 10, 1971: 3.
— new officers announced, Lahaina Sun, June 23, 1971: 10.
— annual Pancake Breakfast fundraiser to be held, Lahaina News, August 20, 1986: 3.
— to hold benefit golf tournament, Lahaina News, February 17, 1994: 8.

LIONS-QUEST SKILLS FOR ADOLESCENCE PROGRAM
— parents to meet, Lahaina News, October 29, 1992: 3.
— to meet, Lahaina News, November 5, 1992: 3.

LIPOA POINT
— Kapalua Nature Society seeking volunteers for clean-up at, Lahaina News, May 28, 1998: 12.

LIPOSUCTION
— seminar held, Lahaina News, April 22, 1987: 3.

LIPSHER, JULIAN
— named health educator, Lahaina Sun, April 18, 1973: 4.

LIQUID BLUE [MUSICAL GROUP]
— to perform at Moose McGillycuddy's, Lahaina News, August 22, 1996: 16.

LIQUOR
— license cost to increase, Lahaina News, November 4, 1993: 7.
— new rules being considered, Lahaina News, December 5, 1996: 1.
— license rules under review, Lahaina News, January 2, 1997: 1.

LIQUOR CONTROL COMMISSION
— Outlawing films in restaurants and bars, Lahaina Times, June, 1980 volume 4 number 5: 1,10.
— meeting set to discuss limits to number of liquor licenses in Lahaina, Lahaina News, April 4, 1984: 5.
— to hold public meeting on proposed amendments, Lahaina News, March 6, 1991: 5.

LIQUOR CONTROL, DEPARTMENT OF
— offers to review regulations with licensee employees, Lahaina News, August 1, 1991: 4.

LISELL, DAWN [ACTOR]
— actors from Oregon Shakespeare Festival to hold classes, Lahaina News, December 15, 1994: 19.

LITERACY
— Lahaina Baptist Church training people willing to teach conversational English, Lahaina News, December 12, 1990: 4.
— Kiwanis to support, Lahaina News, December 19, 1990: 4,5.

LITERACY CHAMPIONS CAMPAIGN
— GTE Hawaiian Tel to sponsor, Lahaina News, September 2, 1999: 16.

LITERACY OUTREACH PROJECT
— moves into new office, Lahaina News, March 1, 2001: 10.

LITTER BUGS ME!
— clean-up to be held, Lahaina News, July 4, 1990: 3.
— Children of Honokohau paint trash receptacles part of, Lahaina News, May 24, 2001: 8.
— to be held, Lahaina News, July 12, 2001: 1.
— to be held, Lahaina News, July 19, 2001: 16.

LITTLE CHARLIE AND THE NIGHTCATS [MUSICAL GROUP]
— to perform at Casanova's, Lahaina News, August 21, 1997: 18.

LITTLE FOXES, THE [PLAY]
— performed by Maui Community Theatre, Lahaina News, April 1, 1987: 3.

LITTLE GRASS SHACK [RESTAURANT]
— opens, Lahaina News, April 1, 1993: 8.

LITTLE LEAGUE
— see West Maui Little League

LITTLE MAKANA
— County seeking access to, Lahaina News, October 6, 1994: 1,2.

LITTLE MERMAID, THE [PLAY]
— to be performed at Iao Theatre, Lahaina News, July 4, 1991: 14.

LITTLE MISS OF AMERICA PAGEANT
— to be held, Lahaina News, May 15, 1997: 13.

LITTLE NIGHT MUSIC, A [PLAY]
— to be performed by Maui Academy of Performing Arts, Lahaina News, February 24, 1994: 11.

LITTLE, RICH [COMEDIAN]
— to perform at Hyatt Regency, Lahaina News, December 28, 1983: 7.
— to perform on Maui, Lahaina News, August 15, 1984: 13.
— editorial praising the performer, Lahaina News, August 15, 1984: 2.

LITTLE SHOP OF HORRORS [PLAY]
— to be performed by Maui Community Theatre, Lahaina News, August 10, 1988: 7.
— to be performed by Rogers Productions' Professional Theatre, Lahaina News, January 19, 1995: 11.

LIU, E. LEE [POLITICIAN]
— council member asks for input on proposed Mahinahina airport, Lahaina News, October 2, 1985: 3.

LIU, EDWIN
— member of FCC discusses cable industry, Lahaina Sun, December 23, 1970: 6.

LIVE TONIGHT AT THE GLOBE! #5 [PLAY]
— comedy to be performed at Seabury Hall, Lahaina News, March 5, 1992: 16.

LIVEX CORP. [BUSINESS]
— Japanese firm to purchase 118 unites of Sands of Kahana from Honfed Bank, Lahaina News, September 12, 1990: 10.

LIVING CONDITIONS
— strange situations described, Lahaina Times, September, 1980 volume 4 number 8: 2.

LIVING REEF
— part of Amfac, Inc.'s development plans, Lahaina News, September 21, 1988: 1.

LIVING THE VISION [RADIO SHOW]
— begins on Sunday on KHEI, Lahaina News, September 18, 1985: 3.

LIZADA, CAESAR
— awarded employee of the year by Media Systems, Lahaina News, January 13, 1988: 16.

LJUBIC, MARKO
— Scholar/Athlete of the Week, Lahaina News, January 6, 2000: 6.

LOA, SEAN
— named sales and marketing manager at Ka'anapali Estate Coffee, Lahaina News, August 24, 2000: 14.

LOBSTER COVE, THE [RESTAURANT]
— opens, Lahaina News, June 11, 1992: 13.

LOCAL
— meaning of term discussed, Lahaina News, June 1, 1981: 4.

LOCAL BOYS, THE [MUSICAL GROUP]
— new to Maui music scene, Lahaina News, March 12, 1986: 8.

LOCAL CONNECTION, THE [TROUPE]
— to dance at Ka'anapali Beach Hotel, Lahaina News, July 31, 1985: 7.

LOCAL EXCHANGE TRADING SYSTEM [L.E.T.S.]
— to hold workshop on improving business, Lahaina News, February 27, 1991: 8.

LOCAL FOOD [RESTAURANT]
— opens for take-out food, Lahaina News, August 22, 1990: 9.

LOCAL GRINDS
— contest to be held at Ka'ahumanu Center, Lahaina News, September 17, 1992: 18.

LOCAL MOTION [BUSINESS]
— to host surf competition, Lahaina News, November 22, 1989: 9.
— named "Hawaii Apparel of the Year - Export Market" by the Hawaiian Fashion Industry Association, Lahaina News, July 25, 1990: 7.
— to open next to Hard Rock Café, Lahaina News, October 10, 1990: 11.
— to open at Lahaina Center, Lahaina News, December 5, 1990: 4.
— sponsoring Lahaina Surf Classic, Lahaina News, May 1, 1991: 7.
— sponsoring Lahaina Surf Classic, Lahaina News, April 30, 1992: 6.
— wins best Halloween window display contest, Lahaina News, November 5, 1992: 16.
— to present Lahaina Surf Classics, Lahaina News, May 5, 1994: 8.
— to co-sponsor Lahaina Surf Classic with MCD Surfwear, Lahaina News, May 19, 1994: 8.
— surfer Tom Curren to visit store, Lahaina News, November 3, 1994: 21.
— presents Lahaina Surf Classic, Lahaina News, April 20, 1995: 10.
— summer surf season begins, Lahaina News, June 1, 1995: 6.

LOCATIONS REAL ESTATE [BUSINESS]
— names Kenneth Smith as top-selling salesperson, Lahaina News, October 24, 1991: 9.
— testing system allowing remote access to images of properties, Lahaina News, February 24, 1994: 10.

LOCKHEED MISSILES AND SPACE COMPANY [BUSINESS]
— proposes installing pulsed ruby laser at Mt. Haleakala observatory, Lahaina Sun, March 8, 1972: 3.

LODGE AT KOELE
— see Koele Lodge

LODGE MAUI
— to hold "Rusty Nail Night", Lahaina News, September 11, 1997: 16.

LOEB, LISA [MUSICIAN]
— to perform at Maui Arts and Cultural Center, Lahaina News, June 5, 2003: 15.

LOERO, RICHARD
— Ka'anapali Coffee featured, Lahaina News, January 2, 1997: 1,16.

LOEW, ALLISON
— joins Coldwell Banker McCormack Real Estate, Lahaina News, February 24, 1988: 3.

LOGGINS, KENNY [MUSICIAN]
— performance reviewed, Lahaina News, November 21, 1984: 17.
— performance in Honolulu reviewed , Lahaina News, September 18, 1985: 10.
— to perform on Maui, Lahaina News, April 16, 1986: 8.
— tour of islands detailed, Lahaina News, April 30, 1986: 8.
— performance reviewed, Lahaina News, May 14, 1986: 12.
— to perform at Royal Lahaina Tennis Stadium, Lahaina News, March 12, 1992: 15.
— to perform at Royal Lahaina Tennis Stadium, Lahaina News, March 19, 1992: 14.
— to perform at Maui Arts and Cultural Center, Lahaina News, February 4, 1999: 17.
— to perform at Maui Arts and Cultural Center, Lahaina News, February 11, 1999: 16.

LOGO SHOP, THE [BUSINESS]
— opens at Westin Maui Hotel, Lahaina News, August 29, 1990: 8.

LOHMAN, PAUL
— new principal of Sacred Hearts School, Lahaina News, August 31, 2000: 1,15.

LOKAHI PACIFIC [BUSINESS]
— fishing co-op established on Maui, Lahaina Sun, August 4, 1971: 1,11.
— beginning commercial production of shrimp, Lahaina Sun, September 1, 1971: 15.
— electing new board of directors, Lahaina Sun, November 17, 1971: 12.
— receives funding from federal Office of Economic Opportunity, Lahaina Sun, November 24, 1971: 13.
— offices being set up in Kihei, Lahaina Sun, December 1, 1971: 13.
— new board of directors announced, Lahaina Sun, December 8, 1971: 17.
— awarded corporation charter for American Taxpayer's Marine Aquaculture Research Corporation, Lahaina Sun, August 23, 1972: 7.
— receives grant from federal government, Lahaina Sun, April 11, 1973: 10.
— to hold "Spring Craft Fair", Lahaina News, March 13, 1991: 14.
— to hold "Spring Craft Fair", Lahaina News, March 20, 1991: 11.
— sponsoring Spring Craft Fair, Lahaina News, March 5, 1992: 4,5.
— purchases apartment building to provide affordable housing, Lahaina News, June 17, 1993: 6.

LOKELANI CONSTRUCTION COMPANY [BUSINESS]
— chooses Jeffrey T. Long & Associates as architects for Ka'anapali Hillside, Lahaina News, September 26, 1984: 14.

LOKELANI INTERMEDIATE SCHOOL
— Marion Muller named principal, Lahaina News, September 10, 1992: 11.
— hosting study night, Lahaina News, October 22, 1992: 12.
— sponsoring AIDS education event, Lahaina News, October 29, 1992: 17.
— showers inadequate, Lahaina News, December 3, 1992: 10.
— to hold Christmas Fair, Lahaina News, December 3, 1992: 11.
— to hold carwash fundraiser, Lahaina News, December 10, 1992: 9.
— new picnic tables installed, Lahaina News, December 31, 1992: 8.
— begins membership drive, Lahaina News, February 11, 1993: 6.
— to hold study night for students, Lahaina News, March 11, 1993: 10.
— honor roll announced, Lahaina News, March 11, 1993: 11.
— to hold song festival, Lahaina News, May 6, 1993: 7.
— Song Festival held, Lahaina News, May 13, 1993: 5.
— to hold slam dunk contest, Lahaina News, May 20, 1993: 5.
— honor roll announced, Lahaina News, May 20, 1993: 5.
— PTSA to hold dinner and silent auction, Lahaina News, May 27, 1993: 5.
— honor roll announced, Lahaina News, July 15, 1993: 5.
— looking for volunteer computer experts, Lahaina News, October 28, 1993: 6.
— to hold craft fair, Lahaina News, October 28, 1993: 6.
— PTSA to meet, Lahaina News, November 11, 1993: 6.
— band to perform at Maui Arts and Cultural Center, Lahaina News, April 29, 1999: 17.

LOKELANI ROOM [RESTAURANT]
— reviewed, Lahaina News, January 10, 1990: 12.
— holds trivia contest, Lahaina News, January 24, 1990: 13.
— featured, Lahaina News, July 30, 1992: 15.
— Arnold DeClercq appointed new manager of, Lahaina News, November 10, 1994: 13.

LOKETO [MUSICIAN]
— to perform at Casanova's, Lahaina News, July 23, 1992: 25.

LOKO MAUI [BUSINESS]
— to renovate 744 Front Street, Lahaina News, March 28, 2002: 3.

LONE STAR [PLAY]
— comedy to be performed, Lahaina News, April 23, 1992: 25.

LONG, ART [ARTIST]
— joins Lahaina Gallery, Lahaina News, March 15, 1983: 6.

LONG, BARBARA
— discusses issue of road conditions in Lahaina, Lahaina Sun, January 13, 1971: 7.
— see also leash laws

LONG, CARY [COMEDIAN]
— to perform at Comedy Club, Lahaina News, February 13, 1992: 18,23.

LONG DISTANCE/USA-SPRINT
— changes in personnel announced, Lahaina News, May 27, 1993: 8.

LONG, EDWARD
— honored by Muscular Dystrophy Association with Personal Achievement Award, Lahaina News, July 18, 2002: 18.

LONG, GAYLE
— to offer course on business, Lahaina News, June 13, 1996: 11.

LONG, HOWIE
— visits Planet Hollywood, Lahaina News, April 10, 1997: 16.

LONG, JONNY [MUSICIAN]
— to perform at Maui Arts and Cultural Center, Lahaina News, February 1, 2001: 21.
— to perform at , Lahaina News, February 8, 2001: 20.

LONG, STEVE
— homeless veteran dies, Lahaina News, January 20, 1994: 1,2.

LONG, TONY
— named officer for Lahaina Yacht Club, Lahaina Sun, December 23, 1970: 8.
— discusses planned Lahaina Whaling Spree, Lahaina Sun, February 3, 1971: 2.

LONGHAIRS
— see hippies

LONGHI, BOB
— Total Experience party described, Lahaina News, September 28, 1983: 7,8,9.
— becomes part owner of Golden State Warriors, Lahaina News, December 3, 1986: 6.
— to host cooking show on Hawaiian Cablevision's Maui Today Channel 6, Lahaina News, May 11, 1995: 12.
— unveils "Longhi's—Recipes and Reflections From Maui's Most Opinionated Restaurateur", Lahaina News, March 19, 1998: 12.
— celebrates 65th birthday, autographs his book, Lahaina News, April 2, 1998: 8.

LONGHI, CHARLES
— on Dean's list at Berklee College of Music, Lahaina News, July 1, 1987: 10.

LONGHI GALLERY [BUSINESS]
— to open at Old Wailuku Town, Lahaina News, October 13, 1994: 19.

LONGHI, SALLY
— art collection to be exhibited at Longhi's restaurant, Lahaina News, April 9, 1992: 21.

LONGHI'S [RESTAURANT]
— chocolate reviewed, Lahaina News, May 20, 1987: 4.
— Tom Hall to perform at, Lahaina News, June 22, 1988: 7.
— to host Hemp Seed Feast and Hemp Expo, Lahaina News, July 20, 1995: 5.
— to host Hemp Seed Feast and Hemp Expo, Lahaina News, August 3, 1995: 4.

— holds Gourmet Hemp Seed Feast and Help Clothing Show held, Lahaina News, October 5, 1995: 10.

— to host benefit show "The Sounds of Christmas", Lahaina News, December 4, 1997: 17.

— receives Five Star Diamond Award from American Academy of Hospitality Sciences, Lahaina News, September 17, 1998: 13.

— to open at second location, Lahaina News, June 10, 1999: 13.

— receives Academy of Hospitality Sciences Five Diamond Award, Lahaina News, September 23, 1999: 11.

— to host "Music for Youth" benefit, Lahaina News, December 30, 1999: 18.

— Willie Nelson to perform at concert to benefit Maui Cancer Institute Alliance, Lahaina News, November 23, 2000: 2.

— West Maui Breast Cancer Benefit held, Lahaina News, January 18, 2001: 6.

LONGHI'S PIZZERIA AND DELICATESSEN [RESTAURANT]

— to open next to Kaiser Clinic, Lahaina News, February 13, 1985: 13.

— purchased by Julie and David Salvucchi and Andrew Still, Lahaina News, March 9, 1988: 4.

LONGLINE FISHING

— public hearing held, Lahaina News, January 30, 1991: 1.

— longline fishing moratorium recommended by task force, Lahaina News, February 20, 1991: 20.

— controls sought for, Lahaina News, February 27, 1991: 1.

— Western Pacific Regional Fishery Management Council upholds longline limits, Lahaina News, May 23, 1991: 5.

— see also fishing

LONGLINE TASK FORCE

— to hold public hearing, Lahaina News, January 23, 1991: 1,16.

LONGS DRUGS [BUSINESS]

— opens first store in Maui opens at the Maui Mall in Kahului, Lahaina Sun, December 8, 1971: 16.

— granted permit to fill in wetlands for Retail Business Center, Lahaina News, November 28, 1990: 8.

— to open in Kihei, Lahaina News, November 28, 1991: 3,4.

— third store on Maui opens, Lahaina News, November 28, 1991: 7.

LONGYEAR, WILLIAM

— Exhibit at Lahaina Art Society Gallery, Lahaina Sun, March 3, 1971: 6.

LOO, MARK

— named Maui Marriott's Regional Salesman of the Quarter, Lahaina News, May 23, 1990: 8.

LOOK HOMEWARD ANGEL [PLAY]

— to be performed by Baldwin Performing Arts Center, Lahaina News, March 9, 1995: 12.

LOOKING HORSE, ARVOL

— chief to speak at the Eddie Tam Assembly Hall, Lahaina News, November 29, 2001: 17.

LOOMIS, PHYLLIS [ARTIST]

— work displayed at Lahaina Art Society gallery, Lahaina Sun, April 19, 1972: 6.

LOOMIS, RICHARD

— saved Sister Leona Abella after she was swept off a rock near Napili, Lahaina Sun, April 12, 1972: 9.

LOOSE SHOES BLUES BAND [MUSICAL GROUP]

— to perform at Polli's On the Beach, Lahaina News, October 17, 1990: 17.

— to perform on the ship Stardancer, Lahaina News, February 20, 1991: 11.

LOOSE TIES [MUSICAL GROUP]

— to perform, Lahaina News, March 31, 1994: 16.

LOPAKA'S BAR AND GRILL [RESTAURANT]

— to close, be replaced by teen cantina, Lahaina News, September 2, 1993: 6.

LOPES, BRIANNE

— wins talent show, Lahaina News, February 11, 1993: 15.

LOPEZ, ABEL

— diagnosed with terminal cancer, Lahaina News, May 22, 2003: 3.

LOPEZ, GERRY

— participating in longboard surfing contest, Lahaina Times, June, 1980 volume 4 number 5: 9.

— one of Maui's main surf stars, Lahaina Times, July, 1980 volume 4 number 6: 1.

— surfer described as never coming to Lahaina, Lahaina Times, July, 1980 volume 4 number 6: 3.

— surfer wins Longboard Surf Contest, Lahaina Times, August 20, 1983 volume 7 number 8: 2.

LOPEZ, LUIS

— appointed Assistant Controller at Maui Marriott, Lahaina News, April 20, 1988: 13.

LOPEZ, MARCOS

— appointed director of Engineering at Hyatt Regency Maui, Lahaina News, December 30, 1987: 3.

LOPEZ, NANCY

— golfer participates in Women's Kemper Open, Lahaina News, March 14, 1984: 20.

— golfer's career described, Lahaina News, March 6, 1985: A8.

LOPEZ, NELSON

— fundraiser to be held at Compadres Bar and Grill for, Lahaina News, January 12, 1995: 10.

LOPEZ, SEVERINO

— honored by Pioneer Mill for years of service, Lahaina Sun, April 7, 1971: 6.

LOPIANETSKY, JOHN

— named regional manager for Ruth's Chris Steak House, Lahaina News, May 31, 2001: 8.

LORD, JACK [ARTIST]

— work described, Lahaina News, July 1, 1981: 12.

LORDAHL, JO ANN

— to speak on "Reconnecting the Healing Circle" at 'Ohana Connection, Lahaina News, August 15, 2002: 17.

LORELLEI/SINGH KAUR BIRTHDAY BENEFIT CONCERT

— to be held, Lahaina News, January 1, 1998: 16.

LORENCE, PENNY

— demonstrates aerobics to older adults, Lahaina News, October 19, 2000: 8.

LORENZO, RANDY [MUSICIAN]

— to perform at Lahaina Cannery Mall, Lahaina News, September 4, 1997: 16.

— to perform at Bankoh Kiho'alu festival, Lahaina News, June 11, 1998: 16.

LORRAINE'S ORCHIDS [BUSINESS]

— opens, Lahaina News, December 12, 1996: 13.

LOS ANGELES CHAMBER BALLET [TROUPE]

— presented by Maui Philharmonic Society, Lahaina News, January 6, 1994: 12.

LOS ANGELES RAIDERETTES [TROUPE]

— to perform at the Wharf Cinema Center, Lahaina News, February 6, 1992: 17.

LOS CHAMUYEROS [MUSICAL GROUP]

— Argentine Tango band to perform at Hapa's, Lahaina News, February 27, 2003: 17.

LOS LOBOS [MUSICAL GROUP]
— to perform at Casanova's, Lahaina News, January 30, 1992: 21.
— to perform at Maui Arts and Cultural Center, Lahaina News, September 25, 1997: 17.
— to perform at Maui Arts and Cultural Center, Lahaina News, October 9, 1997: 21.

LOST AND LAST
— to be held, Lahaina News, March 12, 1998: 20.

LOST AT LAST [MUSICAL GROUP]
— to perform, Lahaina News, January 15, 1998: 12.

LOST GENERATION [FILM]
— presented by Baptist Mission, Lahaina Sun, November 17, 1971: 12.

LOST HORIZON NIGHT CLUB [BUSINESS]
— refurbished, Lahaina News, July 9, 1986: 14.

LOST IN YONKERS [PLAY]
— to be performed at Maui Arts and Cultural Center, Lahaina News, October 12, 1995: 13.

LOST WORLD ARTS GALLERY [BUSINESS]
— hosting presentation on the interior of Papua New Guinea, Lahaina News, December 10, 1998: 20.
— "Wildlife of Madagascar Slide Show" to be held, Lahaina News, June 20, 2002: 16,18.
— to hold Tribal Cultures of New Guinea slide show, Lahaina News, September 5, 2002: 17.

LOTTERY
— suggested by Representative Harold Duponte, Lahaina Sun, February 17, 1971: 7.
— State Representative Bill Pfeil expresses opposition to, Lahaina News, June 22, 1988: 20.

LOTUS GALLERY [BUSINESS]
— to hold reception for Alexandra Morrow and Heyoehkah Merrifield, Lahaina News, February 13, 1991: 13.

LOUCHE, SUZY
— chosen as a volunteer of the year by Hawaii State Theatre Council, Lahaina News, August 8, 1990: 4.

LOUCKS, SUSIE [COMEDIAN]
— to perform at Comedy Club and the Sports Page, Lahaina News, November 12, 1992: 18.

LOUIE, DEAN
— Cafe Sauvage chef featured, Lahaina News, April 4, 2002: 9.

LOUIE LOUIE [MUSICIAN]
— scheduled to perform at grade opening of Hard Rock Cafe , Lahaina News, July 4, 1990: 14.

LOUIS LATOUR [BUSINESS]
— featured winery at Bay Club restaurant's Winemaker's Dinner, Lahaina News, September 25, 2003: 16.

LOUIS VUITTON, HAWAII, INC [BUSINESS]
— to open store at Whalers Village, Lahaina News, June 18, 1992: 10.

LOUNSBURY, FRED
— named director of engineering at Marriott Hotel, Lahaina News, January 18, 1989: 5.

LOVE BOUTIQUE [BUSINESS]
— to hold merchandizing party, Lahaina News, October 28, 1993: 11.

LOVE, DAVIS, III
— golfer to play at Isuzu Kapalua International, Lahaina News, October 17, 1990: 9.
— golfer to play at Lincoln-Mercury Kapalua International, Lahaina News, October 23, 1997: 8.
— wins Lincoln-Mercury Kapalua International, Lahaina News, November 13, 1997: 1.

LOVE, KATHERINE [ARTIST]
— to exhibit at Hui No'eau Visual Arts Center, Lahaina News, July 4, 2002: 17.

LOVE LETTERS [PLAY]
— to be performed by Marcia and Jack Seabern, Lahaina News, February 6, 1992: 4.
— postponed, Lahaina News, February 13, 1992: 18.
— to be performed by Maui Community Theatre/OnStage, Lahaina News, July 15, 1993: 12.
— to be performed at Herb and Scott Rogers Professional Theatre, Lahaina News, February 9, 1995: 11.
— reviewed, Lahaina News, February 16, 1995: 14.

LOVE LIES [MUSICAL GROUP]
— featured, to perform at Moose McGillycuddy's, Lahaina News, March 16, 1995: 11.
— to perform at Moose McGillycuddy's, Lahaina News, December 21, 1995: 14.
— featured, Lahaina News, December 28, 1995: 9.

LOVE, MIKE [MUSICIAN]
— to perform with Endless Summer Beach Band, Lahaina News, February 28, 1990: 11.

LOVEIN, MATTHEW [ARTIST]
— to exhibit at Village Galleries, Lahaina News, January 5, 1995: 12.

LOVE'S [RESTAURANT]
— closes, Lahaina News, February 1, 1982: 4.

LOW, JIMMY
— assistant manager of Kapaula West Maui Airport says there are few noise complaints, Lahaina News, July 12, 1989: 1.

LOWE, PAUL
— spiritual teacher to speak, Lahaina News, August 29, 2002: 21.
— to lead spiritual workshop, Lahaina News, September 5, 2002: 16.

LOWELL, REBECCA [ARTIST]
— to exhibit watercolor art at Maui Ocean Center, Lahaina News, May 21, 1998: 17.

LOWELL, VIRGINIA
— State Librarian asked to rework Lahaina Public Library's hours, Lahaina News, June 17, 1999: 1,20.

LOWEN, ALAN
— to conduct seminars on success in business, Lahaina News, December 6, 1989: 5.

LOWENTHAL, PHIL
— public defender member of panel discussing hippies on Maui, Lahaina Sun, December 2, 1970: 1.
— public defender discusses place of hippies on Maui, Lahaina Sun, December 16, 1970: 7.
— public defender director for Maui ACLU, Lahaina Sun, January 13, 1971: 6.

LOWMAN, BETINA
— interviewed, Lahaina Sun, March 15, 1972: 9.

LOWREY, RUSSELL [ARTIST]
— to exhibit at Village Galleries, Lahaina News, January 21, 1993: 14.

LOWSON AND ASSOCIATES [BUSINESS]
— update on development at "The Old Lahaina Store", Lahaina News, April 24, 2003: 6.

LOWSON, JAMES "MAC"
— to propose alternate redistricting plan for state district, Lahaina News, June 27, 1991: 1.
— vice chair of Maui Advisory Committee criticizes redistricting law, Lahaina News, July 25, 1991: 2,4.
— named to Liquor Control Commission by Mayor Linda Lingle, Lahaina News, September 3, 1992: 3.

— confirmed as Liquor Control commissioner, Lahaina News, October 22, 1992: 4.

— becomes president of Lahaina Rotary Club, Lahaina News, July 20, 2000: 8.

LOWSON, LAURIE

— realtor featured, Lahaina News, April 29, 1999: 12.

— receives Certified Residential Specialist (CRN) designation, Lahaina News, June 12, 2003: 8.

LOWSON, SHERI MORRISON

— appointed by mayor Linda Lingle as executive assistant, Lahaina News, March 6, 1991: 7.

LOYD, KEN [ARTIST]

— to demonstrate oil painting and Village Gallery Contemporary, Lahaina News, April 20, 2000: 16.

LOZANO, LEONARDO

— listed in Who's Who Among Students in American Universities and Colleges, Lahaina News, March 12, 1992: 3.

LUANA'S [BUSINESS]

— marks 25th anniversary, Lahaina News, June 24, 1987: 4.

— closes, Lahaina News, July 9, 1998: 1,9.

LUAU

— availability on Maui, Lahaina News, February 27, 1997: 11.

LUAUS RESTAURANT [RESTAURANT]

— featured, Lahaina News, April 3, 1997: 6.

— closes, Lahaina News, August 28, 1997: 12.

LUBBERS, BERNIE "RUBBERS" [COMEDIAN]

— to perform at Comedy Club and the Sports Page, Lahaina News, June 20, 1991: 8.

LUBEL, AL [COMEDIAN]

— to perform at Comedy Club, Lahaina News, May 9, 1990: 17.

LUCARELLI, DAVID

— owner of Hop Tomato Italian Bistro and Brewery plans to assemble world record pizza, Lahaina News, April 19, 2001: 1,9.

LUCAS, STEPHEN

— Lahainaluna High School student wrestler wins division at Aloha Games, Lahaina News, June 25, 1992: 10.

— Lahainaluna High School student wins wrestling title, Lahaina News, March 10, 1994: 6.

LUCE, CLARE BOOTHE

— former member of Congress to address Maui Chamber of Commerce, Lahaina Sun, November 1, 1972: 10.

— compares Nixon and Cravalho, Lahaina Sun, November 15, 1972: 3.

LUCKEY, JIM

— named manager of Lahaina Restoration Foundation, Lahaina Sun, October 25, 1972: 1.

— working on exhibits for Lahaina Restoration Foundation, Lahaina Sun, May 2, 1973: 13.

— general manager of Lahaina Restoration Foundation discusses potential for Hale Aloha, Lahaina News, April 9, 1986: 1,16.

— receives Ten Sun Shinn Award from Chamber of Commerce, Lahaina News, June 10, 1987: 1.

— head of Lahaina Restoration Foundation to speak at AARP, Lahaina News, January 6, 1988: 3.

— executive director of Lahaina Restoration Foundation to speak to the American Association of Retired People, Lahaina News, February 28, 1990: 3.

— to join Elizabeth Anderson on tours of local cemeteries, Lahaina News, April 3, 1991: 3.

— service recognized by Lahaina Restoration Foundation, Lahaina News, December 10, 1992: 3.

— travels to Fiji representing the Lahaina Restoration Foundation, Lahaina News, May 13, 1993: insert1,insert2.

— presents update of archaeological study of Malu'ulu O Lele Park, Lahaina News, May 4, 1995: 5.

— honored by LahainaTown Action Committee with Lahaina Kokua Award, Lahaina News, February 8, 1996: 1,16.

— retirement celebrated, Lahaina News, December 19, 1996: 1,28.

— Lahaina Restoration Foundation holds mahalo for, Lahaina News, April 10, 1997: 3.

— to speak to LahainaTown Action Committee, Lahaina News, January 11, 2001: 3.

— to speak to LahainaTown Action Committee, Lahaina News, January 18, 2001: 1.

LUCKEY, TYLER

— Scholar/Athlete of the Week, Lahaina News, June 22, 2000: 12.

LUCKY LUCK'S HAWAIIAN GOURMET COOKBOOK [BOOK]

— reviewed, Lahaina Sun, June 28, 1972: 15.

LUDER, JOSEPH

— president-elect for Lahaina Restoration Foundation, Lahaina News, November 12, 1992: insert2.

— passes away, memorial to be held, Lahaina News, May 21, 1998: 3.

— services planned for, Lahaina News, June 11, 1998: 3.

LUDWIG'S OF MAUI [BUSINESS]

— nightclub soundproofs building, Lahaina News, January 5, 1995: 4.

— nightclub to reopen under new ownership, Lahaina News, December 14, 1995: 16,17.

— vandalism at nightclub may be vendetta, Lahaina News, February 15, 1996: 1.

LUECHOW, ALF

— to present "Why fear when I am here" at 'Ohana Connection, Lahaina News, September 25, 2003: 17.

LUIGI'S [BUSINESS]

— to feature disco, Lahaina News, January 23, 1992: 18,19.

LUM, ALLYN

— director of sales at Napili Kai Beach Club, Lahaina News, January 15, 1998: 11.

— joins The Wright Company LLC, Lahaina News, April 4, 2002: 8.

LUM, DOUGLAS

— to be guest chef at David Paul's Lahaina Grill, Lahaina News, March 28, 1996: 12,13.

LUM, KAPENA

— Lahainaluna High School student wins national award in physical education, Lahaina News, May 26, 1994: 8,9.

LUM, TERRI

— offering workshop on foster parenting, Lahaina News, October 24, 1991: 5.

LUMANIA

— evidence and character of mythical place discussed, Lahaina Times, June, 1980 volume 4 number 5: 2,4.

LUMBER

— possible future discussed, Lahaina Sun, June 13, 1973: 22,23.

LUMPY'S AND COMPANY [RESTAURANT]

— opens, Lahaina News, October 24, 1996: 9.

LUNA, B. MARTIN

— elected head of Easter Seal Society of Maui, Lahaina Sun, June 28, 1972: 11.

LUNA, GLENDA

— receives letter from mayor Hannibal Tavares for saving children from apartment fire, Lahaina News, August 1, 1990: 2.

LUNDEEN, MICHELE [MUSICIAN]

— blues singer to perform with local band Spontaneous Combustion, Lahaina News, August 22, 2002: 19.

LUNDQUIST, DAWN [ARTIST]
— to exhibit at Beach Front Gallery, Lahaina News, April 5, 1989: 17.
— featured at Lahaina Arts Society's Old Jail Gallery, Lahaina News, May 16, 1990: 13.
— to exhibit at Seaside Fine Arts, Lahaina News, August 24, 1995: 12.

LUNES, DRELYNNE
— Lahainaluna High School student finalist in National Golden Key Art Competition, Lahaina News, February 13, 1992: 7.

LUNEY, E. LOY
— member of Maui County Council, Lahaina Sun, December 30, 1970: 8.

LUNG ASSOCIATION
— to sell Entertainment '93 coupon books, Lahaina News, November 26, 1992: 4.
— selling Entertainment book, Lahaina News, December 31, 1992: 5.

LUNG, JOSEPH AKONE TAM
— named to Vanderbilt University Dean's List, Lahaina News, June 17, 1999: 15.
— marketer to speak at "Preparing Maui for the Future", Lahaina News, October 7, 1999: 13.

LUNG, MARIA LI
— Biology professor to speak at "Preparing Maui for the Future", Lahaina News, October 7, 1999: 13.

LUNSFORD, SUSANNE
— opens branch of Old Republic Title and Escrow, Lahaina News, July 30, 1998: 13.

LUPUS SUPPORT GROUP
— to meet, Lahaina News, December 26, 2002: 16.

LUTEY, SCOTT KEALOHA
— chef at Sea House Restaurant, Lahaina News, August 6, 1998: 10,11.
— Napili Kai Beach Club chef wins Sam Choy Poke Contest, Lahaina News, October 22, 1998: 17.
— prize-winning Poke recipe, Lahaina News, November 5, 1998: 7.

LUTGEN, TOM
— appointed library director at the Maui Research and Technology Center, Lahaina News, September 24, 1998: 13.

LUTY, GWEN
— receives "Aloha Spirit Award", Lahaina News, July 18, 1990: 7.

LYALL, MAGGIE
— joins Faught and Miyashiro Advertising, Inc., Lahaina News, August 12, 1993: 9.

LYLE, SANDY
— golfer wins Kapalua International Championship of Golf, Lahaina News, November 14, 1984: 4.

LYNDAL'S BURNING [MUSICAL GROUP]
— to perform at Moose McGillycuddy's, Lahaina News, October 20, 1994: 16.

LYNN, DEBRA [MUSICIAN]
— singer to perform at Keawalai Church, Lahaina News, March 30, 2000: 12.
— to perform at Sandcastle Restaurant, Lahaina News, June 29, 2000: 20.
— member of Maui Light Opera Company to perform at Va Bene Italian Beachside Grill, Lahaina News, May 30, 2002: 16.

LYNNE, JANINA
— to lead writer's workshop, Lahaina News, January 2, 1992: 5.

LYNNE, LISA [MUSICIAN]
— harpist to perform with George Tortorelli, Lahaina News, May 28, 1998: 12.

LYON ARBORETUM
— featured, Lahaina News, June 13, 1996: 6.

LYON, CHARLIE [ARTIST]
— to exhibit at Lahaina Arts Society, Lahaina News, June 7, 2001: 19.
— to exhibit at Lahaina Arts Society, Lahaina News, May 1, 2003: 14.
— to exhibit at Lahaina Arts Society, Lahaina News, May 15, 2003: 17.

LYON, LESLIE CONNELL AND CHARLES [WRITERS]
— publish "Surf Clowns: Seven Mental Missions", Lahaina News, May 18, 2000: 1,6.

LYONS, DWIGHT
— doctor supports stand-alone surgery center, Lahaina News, June 30, 1994: 1.

LYONS, MICHAEL, II
— to head United Way Maui's fundraising campaign, Lahaina News, August 8, 1984: 3.
— named chair of Maui Economic Development Board, Lahaina News, October 8, 1992: 8.
— to be honored at Boy Scouts Distinguished Citizen Dinner, Lahaina News, June 10, 1999: 15.

LYTLE, JIM
— to speak to American Association of Retired Persons, Lahaina News, January 27, 2000: 13.

M

M. BUTTERFLY [PLAY]
— to be performed by OnStage at Iao Theatre, Lahaina News, November 26, 1992: 21.

MA'ALAEA [TOWN]
— proposed power plant discussed, Lahaina Sun, May 19, 1971: 1,6.
— work expected to start on boat harbor, Lahaina Sun, December 29, 1971: 16.
— conditions of small boat harbor and local stores troubling, Lahaina Sun, March 14, 1973: 15.
— Alexander and Baldwin has development plans for, Lahaina News, January 2, 1992: 5.
— community association to meet, Lahaina News, June 18, 1992: 14.
— Alexander and Baldwin proposes new road, Lahaina News, June 18, 1992: 15.
— C. Brewer Properties seeking to reclassify c. 20,000 acres of land in Ma'alaea, Lahaina News, July 9, 1992: 6,7.
— Triangle Partnership to ask for permit extension, Lahaina News, July 16, 1992: 7.
— C. Brewer Properties proposes 169-acre development, Lahaina News, July 23, 1992: 10.
— Alexander and Baldwin to hold public meeting to explain proposed development in, Lahaina News, August 13, 1992: 9.
— Alexander and Baldwin Properties proposed project called premature, Lahaina News, September 3, 1992: 12.
— community association seeks sewage plant, Lahaina News, December 31, 1992: 8.
— Maui Electric, Inc. hopes to expand power plant at, Lahaina News, February 25, 1993: 5.
— community garden featured, Lahaina News, April 8, 1993: 4.
— joins national Main Street Association, Lahaina News, April 29, 1993: 5.
— Sierra Club to produce video on value of, Lahaina News, July 31, 1997: 15.
— Maui Ocean Center nearing completion, Lahaina News, December 4, 1997: 21.
— beach cleanup held, Lahaina News, June 18, 1998: 15.
— Maui Surfrider Foundation attempting to preserve Ma'alaea Pipeline, Lahaina News, August 12, 1999: 14.

MA'ALAEA BOAT AND FISHING CLUB
— to hold fundraiser, Lahaina News, March 27, 1997: 6.

MA'ALAEA COMMUNITY ASSOCIATION
— seek environmental impact statement for Alexander and Baldwin's proposed project, Lahaina News, June 25, 1992: 6.
— to meet to discuss proposed zoning changes, Lahaina News, July 16, 1992: 7.
— opposes expansion of commercial boating at Ma'alaea Harbor, Lahaina News, July 16, 1992: 7.
— to become member of Ma'alaea Boat and Fishing Club, Lahaina News, July 23, 1992: 10.
— calls Alexander and Baldwin Properties proposed project premature, Lahaina News, September 3, 1992: 12.
— to meet to discuss C. Brewer Properties proposal, Lahaina News, November 19, 1992: 5.
— to meet, Lahaina News, December 24, 1992: 7.
— Marshall Smith elected as president of, Lahaina News, January 21, 1993: 11.
— to hold meeting, Lahaina News, February 18, 1993: 8.
— opposes bill to transfer Condominium Management Education Fund to general fund, Lahaina News, February 25, 1993: 5.
— to hold fundraiser, Lahaina News, April 8, 1993: 5.
— to meet, Lahaina News, April 15, 1993: 4.
— garden equipment stolen, Lahaina News, July 1, 1993: 5.
— to intervene in Maui Electric Company's proposal to expand plant, Lahaina News, July 1, 1993: 5.
— supports Planning Department's version of Kihei-Makena Community plan, Lahaina News, September 16, 1993: 5.
— considering speed bumps on Hale Kai Street, Lahaina News, September 30, 1993: 6.
— to meet, Lahaina News, January 8, 1998: 12.
— to hold annual meeting, Lahaina News, January 15, 1998: 13.

MA'ALAEA COMMUNITY GARDEN
— to hold board meeting, Lahaina News, September 19, 1996: 15.
— to host workshop on La'au Lapa'au, Lahaina News, February 27, 1997: 10.
— continues to hold workshops, Lahaina News, July 9, 1998: 17.
— offering classes, Lahaina News, August 6, 1998: 17.
— class on home composting to be held, Lahaina News, March 30, 2000: 12.
— to offer home composting workshop, Lahaina News, October 5, 2000: 16.
— to sponsor home composting workshop, Lahaina News, April 10, 2003: 2.
— to host home composting workshop, Lahaina News, June 5, 2003: 9.
— composting workshop to be held, Lahaina News, July 17, 2003: 16.

MA'ALAEA GRILL [RESTAURANT]
— opens at Ma'alaea Harbor Village, Lahaina News, December 13, 2001: 8.

MA'ALAEA HARBOR
— tested for pollution, Lahaina Sun, December 16, 1970: 3.
— work expected to start on Ma'alaea boat harbor, Lahaina Sun, December 29, 1971: 16.
— no longer has Coast Guard ship, Lahaina News, October 31, 1990: 1,3.
— public meeting to discuss improvements to be held, Lahaina News, February 20, 1991: 5.
— sponsors Lana'i fishing tournament with Lahaina Yacht Club, Lahaina News, October 3, 1991: 8.
— Department of Transportation awards Jacky Dugied contract to repair comfort station at, Lahaina News, January 23, 1992: 12.
— to be renovated, Lahaina News, January 30, 1992: 4.
— federal funds appropriated for projects at, Lahaina News, June 25, 1992: 8.

— expansion to begin soon, Lahaina News, July 2, 1992: 7.
— meeting to be held over plans, Lahaina News, December 3, 1992: 10.
— meeting to be held to discuss plans by U.S. Army Corps of Engineers, Lahaina News, December 10, 1992: 9.
— concerns raised, Lahaina News, December 17, 1992: 13.
— Department of Transportation awards contract to pave parking areas at Ma'alaea Boat Harbor, Lahaina News, May 6, 1993: 7.
— new plan to be discussed, Lahaina News, August 26, 1993: 8.
— boat explodes, Lahaina News, November 4, 1993: 6.
— state firm on plans to increase number of outside permits allowed, Lahaina News, December 2, 1993: 5.
— State and Army Corps seek comments on expansion of, Lahaina News, September 18, 1997: 15.
— benefit reggae bash to be held, Lahaina News, December 18, 1997: 18.
— Pacific Whale Foundation adds new catamaran "Ocean Spirit", Lahaina News, January 1, 1998: 13.
— comments sought on expansion of, Lahaina News, May 28, 1998: 6.
— supplemental environmental impact statement finished, Lahaina News, June 11, 1998: 15.
— meeting to be held on supplemental environmental impact statement, Lahaina News, June 18, 1998: 15.
— sailing course, Lahaina News, November 5, 1998: 19.
— Save Ma'alaea Surf Rally to be held, Lahaina News, February 25, 1999: 6.
— Save Ma'alaea Surf Rally to be held, Lahaina News, March 4, 1999: 7.
— Maui Surfrider Foundation attempting to preserve Ma'alaea Pipeline from expansion of, Lahaina News, August 12, 1999: 14.
— Save Ma'alaea Defense Fund to challenge, Lahaina News, August 26, 1999: 2.
— Maui Surfrider Foundation to discuss expansion of, Lahaina News, March 30, 2000: 3.
— Hawaii Watercolor Society to paint boats at , Lahaina News, June 6, 2002: 16.

MA'ALAEA HARBOR VILLAGE
— plans to be discussed, Lahaina News, September 26, 1996: 15.
— construction begins, Lahaina News, October 14, 1999: 11.
— Arisumi Brothers Inc. building, Lahaina News, February 17, 2000: 13.
— Ma'alaea Grill opens at, Lahaina News, December 13, 2001: 8.

MABELLE, SALLY [MUSICIAN]
— to lead singing workshop, Lahaina News, February 20, 2003: 16.

MAC CONTRACTING INC. [BUSINESS]
— awarded contract to fixed courts at Malu'ulu O Lele Park, Lahaina News, March 16, 1995: 4.

MACARTHUR, HELEN
— awarded Certified Residential Special (CRS) designation, Lahaina News, December 10, 1992: 10.

MACARTHUR, ROGER
— promoted to senior vice president and branch manager of First Hawaiian Bank at Kahului, Lahaina News, December 20, 1989: 4.
— to receive Distinguish Citizen recognition from the Boy Scouts, Lahaina News, May 16, 2002: 3.

MACBETH [PLAY]
— to be performed by Maui Youth Theatre, Lahaina News, August 23, 1989: 4.
— tickets are on sale, Lahaina News, September 6, 1989: 3.
— schedule, Lahaina News, September 13, 1989: 5.
— to include backstage tour, Lahaina News, September 20, 1989: 3.

MACCAMMOND, ERIC
— benefit planned for, Lahaina News, November 9, 1995: 4.
— benefit to be held by Lahaina Arts Society to support fight against cancer, Lahaina News, August 28, 1997: 10.

MACCHI/JENCKS DESIGN GROUP [BUSINESS]
— formed, Lahaina News, August 27, 1992: 10.

MACCLUER, DOUG
— Maui Land & Pineapple plantation manager comments on loss of topsoil near Honolua Bay, Lahaina News, January 31, 1990: 1.

MACCONCEPTS [BUSINESS]
— to offer free seminar on graphics software, Lahaina News, February 28, 1990: 4.

MACDONALD, HAROLD [MUSICIAN]
— to perform at Pioneer Inn , Lahaina News, April 2, 1992: 19.
— to perform at Pioneer Inn , Lahaina News, July 9, 1992: 17.

MACDONALD, JERRY
— owner of Buzz's donates to help renovate Queen Theater, Lahaina Sun, February 17, 1971: 2.
— reflects on restaurant business in Lahaina, Lahaina News, December 24, 1998: 1,16.

MACDONALD, KATHLEEN [ARTIST]
— "Postcards from Maui" to be held at Viewpoints Gallery, Lahaina News, December 24, 1998: 13.
— to hold reception at Viewpoints Gallery, Lahaina News, September 21, 2000: 20.

MACDONALD, LAURIE
— pro skateboarder living in Maui, Lahaina Times, June, 1980 volume 4 number 6: 1.
— skateborder pictured, Lahaina Times, August, 1980 volume 4 number 7: 1.

MACDONALD, STEPHEN
— promoted to sales manager at Lahaina News, Lahaina News, September 10, 1992: 9.

MACDOWELL, JEAN
— selected as Outstanding Older Americans of Maui County, Lahaina News, May 25, 1988: 10,12.

MACEDO, RONALDO [ARTIST]
— wins Lahaina Poster Contest, Lahaina News, September 21, 1995: 4.
— to exhibit at Lahaina Galleries, Lahaina News, May 21, 1998: 16.
— to demonstrate painting at Festival of Art and Flowers, Lahaina News, November 19, 1998: 5.
— to exhibit at Art School at Kapalua, Lahaina News, February 4, 1999: 9.
— to visit Lahaina Galleries, Lahaina News, June 24, 1999: 12.
— to unveil new original paintings, Lahaina News, August 16, 2001: 17.
— wins Lahaina Poster Contest, Lahaina News, July 18, 2002: 17.
— wins LahainaTown Action Committee's Lahaina Poster contest, Lahaina News, February 6, 2003: 2.

MACHADO, ELIZABETH "MOANI"
— earns Certified Professional Secretary rating, Lahaina News, January 18, 1996: 10.
— Hawaii Federation of Business and Professional Women's Clubs names state young careerist, Lahaina News, November 14, 1996: 8.
— wins first place in Business and Professional Women's competition, Lahaina News, July 17, 1997: 13.

MACHADO, LINDA
— to talk on "Impact of Emotional/Behavioral Disorders on Families", Lahaina News, April 24, 2003: 20.

MACHIAS [SHIP]
— ship owned by Aloha Voyages travels to Moloka'i, Lahaina News, November 18, 1987: 12.

MACHIDA, GERALD [POLITICIAN]
— candidacy for State Senate featured, Lahaina News, October 22, 1986: 1,5,16.

MACHIDA, HINAE
— to compete in Chrysanthemum Ball, Lahaina News, November 28, 1996: 3.

MACINTOSH
— see computers, specific businesses

MACK, BILL [ARTIST]
— to exhibit at Lahaina Galleries, Lahaina News, February 17, 1994: 11.

MACK, GRANT [MUSICIAN]
— pianist to perform with Island Quintet, Lahaina News, May 5, 1994: 16.

MACK, MARTY MIM
— participant of March of Dimes interviewed, Lahaina Sun, January 24, 1973: 6.

MACKAY, MARK [ARTIST]
— work published as poster for Earthtrust, Lahaina News, February 6, 1992: 11.

MACMASTER, NATALIE [MUSICIAN]
— to perform at Maui Arts and Cultural Center, Lahaina News, April 26, 2001: 21.
— to perform at Maui Arts and Cultural Center, Lahaina News, May 3, 2001: 20.

MACNET COMPUTER CENTER [BUSINESS]
— opens in Wailuku, Lahaina News, July 24, 1997: 13.
— opens, Lahaina News, July 31, 1997: 13.
— relocates, Lahaina News, April 8, 1999: 11.

MACPHEE, ANGUS
— discusses attempts to recover Kaho'olawe, Lahaina News, September 12, 1984: 8.

MACQUIRE, BROOKS [MUSICIAN]
— to perform at Cheeseburger in Paradise, Lahaina News, September 26, 1996: 16.

MACY'S THANKSGIVING DAY PARADE
— Old Lahaina Luau to run first float from Hawai'i at, Lahaina News, November 9, 2000: 18.
— audition hula dancer to perform at, Lahaina News, August 16, 2001: 9.
— auditions held for, Lahaina News, August 23, 2001: 1.

MAD CLOAK [PLAY]
— auditions to be held for, Lahaina News, August 7, 2003: 17.
— auditions to be held for, Lahaina News, August 14, 2003: 16.
— playwright Pat Matsumoto to unveil new play, Lahaina News, September 18, 2003: 18.
— to open, Lahaina News, September 25, 2003: 1,2.
— to debut, Lahaina News, September 25, 2003: 16.

MAD DOG DRUMMERS OF MU [MUSICAL GROUP]
— to perform at Casanova's to celebrate new album "Unleashed", Lahaina News, May 26, 1994: 16.
— to perform at Casanova's, Lahaina News, January 12, 1995: 12.
— to host drumming workshop with Paul Daniel , Lahaina News, July 20, 1995: 12.

MAD HATTER CONCERT AND DANCE
— to be held at Westin Maui, Lahaina News, September 7, 1988: 3.

MADALINE MICHAELS GALLERY [BUSINESS]
— begins participation in Friday Night is Art Night, Lahaina News, October 31, 1990: 16.

MADALIPAY, MARINO
— Scholar/Athlete of the Week, Lahaina News, January 27, 2000: 7.

MADAMBA, JUSTA
— passes away, Lahaina News, March 30, 2000: 3.

MADDIGAN, HIGGINS

— businessman reprimanded for tearing down an old building, Lahaina Sun, December 16, 1970: 2.
— businessman elected vice chairman of Lahaina Retail Board, Lahaina Sun, December 16, 1970: 3.
— businessman discusses Lahaina Market Place, Lahaina Sun, December 23, 1970: 9.
— businessman proposes public luaus, Lahaina Sun, January 13, 1971: 5.
— businessman discusses planned Lahaina Whaling Spree, Lahaina Sun, February 3, 1971: 2.
— businessman withdraws request for children's petting zoo in Lahaina Market, Lahaina Sun, May 12, 1971: 5.

MADE IN MAUI

— trade show held, Lahaina News, June 15, 1983: 7,8,9.
— Trade Council promoting products made in Maui, Lahaina News, July 22, 1987: 3.
— trade show to be held, Lahaina News, August 13, 1992: 4,12.
— Trade Council appoints Don "Swanie" Swanson as chair of "Operation Awareness" subcommittee, Lahaina News, February 18, 1993: 9,10.
— Lahaina News joins, Lahaina News, March 21, 1996: 4.
— benefits small businesses, Lahaina News, August 1, 1996: 15.
— featured, Lahaina News, August 1, 1996: 9,10,11,16.

MADHU THOMPSON

— to talk on "The Nature of Man According to Vedanta", Lahaina News, January 9, 2003: 17.

MADWOMAN OF CHAILLOT, THE [PLAY]

— to be performed by Maui Community Theatre, Lahaina Sun, August 15, 1973: 4.

MAEHARA, ICHIRO

— appointed director of county's parks and recreation, Lahaina Sun, January 6, 1971: 2.
— discusses plan to move showers at Lahaina small boat harbor, Lahaina Sun, May 12, 1971: 4.
— discusses improvements to Honokowai County Park, Lahaina Sun, June 2, 1971: 1.

MAFI-WILLIAMS, LORRAINE [ARTIST]

— to hold workshop on Australian aboriginal traditions, Lahaina News, June 11, 1992: 6.

MAFILEO, LATU POPI

— Tongan storyteller to present at Hui No'eau Visual Arts Center, Lahaina News, October 31, 1990: 17.

MAGAOAY, ERNEST

— promoted to branch manager of Lana'i Branch of First Hawaiian Bank, Lahaina News, October 3, 1990: 9.

MAGEE, CHRIS [CARTOONIST]

— wins Hawaii Publisher Association award, Lahaina News, April 13, 1995: 4.

MAGIC MAUI, THE BEST OF THE ISLAND [BOOK]

— in third printing, Lahaina News, December 28, 1988: 13.

MAGIC THEATRE

— see Maui Myth and Magic Theatre

MAGICAL MAUI INTERNATIONAL MUSIC AND CRAFT FESTIVAL

— Marty Dread to perform at, Lahaina News, April 4, 1996: 15.

MAGID, AVI

— Rabbi to speak on "Hebrew-Hawaiian Connection: A Unity of Traditions, Values and Practices", Lahaina News, April 10, 1997: 13.

MAGID, SHAYNA BAECKER [ARTIST]

— to exhibit at Hawaiian Wedding Certificates, Lahaina News, July 14, 1994: 15.

MAGNUSSON, CHEYNE

— surfer featured, Lahaina News, December 14, 1995: 10.
— surfer featured, Lahaina News, June 7, 2001: 14.

MAGOON, ORVILLE

— owner of Guenoc Winery to be at Maui Prince Hotel, Lahaina News, September 13, 1989: 5.

MAGUIRE, BROOKS [MUSICIAN]

— performs at Cheeseburger in Paradise, Lahaina News, September 1, 1994: 15.
— continues to perform at Cheeseburger in Paradise, Lahaina News, May 4, 1995: 16.
— to perform from new CD "Pieces of a Dream", Lahaina News, August 19, 1999: 16.

MAHALO AIRLINES [BUSINESS]

— to begin service between Oahu and Kaua'i, Lahaina News, September 30, 1993: 8.
— offers $10 fares, Lahaina News, October 14, 1993: 8.
— offering cheap flights, Lahaina News, October 21, 1993: 9,11.
— slashes interisland fares, Lahaina News, December 9, 1993: 6.
— attempt to fly into Kapalua-West Maui Airport limited by berm bordering runway, Lahaina News, March 23, 1995: 1,16.
— studying impact of flights on Maui Lands and Pineapple Co fields, Lahaina News, April 6, 1995: 1,2.
— ending service to Kapalua-West Maui airport, Lahaina News, September 7, 1995: 3.
— partners with Mahalo Air in West Maui, Lahaina News, June 27, 1996: 13.
— celebrates joint venture with Hawaiian Airlines, Lahaina News, July 4, 1996: 3.
— files for chapter 11 bankruptcy, Lahaina News, July 31, 1997: 1.

MAHANA [TOWN]

— seawall planned at, Lahaina News, February 27, 1985: 3.

MAHANA AT KA'ANAPALI, THE [BUSINESS]

— condominium featured, Lahaina News, July 11, 1984: 15.
— receives "Best Housekeeping Property of the Year" award from Aston Hotels & Resorts, Lahaina News, May 8, 1991: 6.
— to be managed by Henrik Rasmussen, Lahaina News, August 2, 2001: 8.
— real estate featured, Lahaina News, August 9, 2001: 6.
— featured, Lahaina News, August 1, 2002: 6.
— Demi Yamamoto joins as front office manager, Lahaina News, October 31, 2002: 6.
— Dawn Kane new general manager, Lahaina News, January 2, 2003: 8.
— announces new appointments, Lahaina News, May 8, 2003: 8.

MAHANALUA NUI

— Maui County Council concerned for traffic problems at, Lahaina News, November 25, 1999: 1,20.

MAHARAJA, SRILA BHAKTIVEDANTA NARAYANA

— to speak, Lahaina News, May 13, 1999: 17.

MAHARISHI MAHESH YOGI

— practitioners to meet, Lahaina News, October 19, 2000: 20.

MAHELE O MAUI [NOVEL]

— reviewed, Lahaina News, March 21, 1984: 7.

MAHER, LEO

— stroke specialist to talk on "Reducing Your Risk Factors for Stroke", Lahaina News, December 13, 2001: 16.
— doctor to discuss preventable risk factors for strokes, Lahaina News, May 16, 2002: 16.

MAHINAHINA [TOWN]

— residents do not want proposed airport in, Lahaina News, May 22, 1985: 1,11.
— Maui County Planning Commission approves airport in, Lahaina News, June 12, 1985: 1.

— County Planning Commission to review shoreline setback variance for drainage project, Lahaina News, May 16, 1990: 5.

— site work on desedimentation basin begins, Lahaina News, September 15, 1994: 6.

— Water Treatment Plant almost completed at, Lahaina News, May 25, 1995: 1.

— Maui Land and Pineapple questions ability of Judge Bertram to hear application for development, Lahaina News, February 25, 1999: 1,16.

— see also airports

MAHINAHINA BEACH CONDOMINIUM [BUSINESS]
— featured, Lahaina News, April 8, 1999: 10.
— pets allowed, Lahaina News, August 16, 2001: 6.

MAHINAHINA BRIDGE
— reopening delayed, Lahaina News, March 5, 1992: 1.

MAHINAHINA STREAM
— drainage channel and desilting basin authorized, Lahaina News, April 5, 1989: 1.

MAHINAHINA SURF [BUSINESS]
— request for variance to allow more units turned down, Lahaina Sun, August 1, 1973: 3.

MAHINAHINA WATER PLANT
— to be commissioned, Lahaina News, August 3, 1995: 5.

MAHOE, HAZEL
— discusses financial situation at West Maui Youth Center, Lahaina News, July 15, 1983: 7,8,9.

MAHOE, PUA
— to speak on "Talking Aloha" at a 'Ohana Connection breakfast, Lahaina News, December 6, 2001: 17.

MAHONEY, BRENDAN
— named manager of the quarter by Maui Marriott, Lahaina News, May 26, 1994: 7.
— named executive chef at Maui Marriott, Lahaina News, November 12, 1998: 13.

MAHONEY, DONALD
— becomes Director of Food and Beverage at Ka'anapali Beach Hotel, Lahaina News, October 25, 1989: 10.

MAI TAIS [RESTAURANT]
— opens at The Shops at Wailea, Lahaina News, August 16, 2001: 8.

MAIDEN, MICHAEL [ARTIST]
— to appear at Wyland Galleries, Lahaina News, September 6, 2001: 16.

MAIELUA FAMILY
— reunion to be held, Lahaina News, June 1, 2000: 7.

MAIELUA, JESSICA
— Scholar/Athlete of the Week, Lahaina News, April 29, 1999: 6.

MAIELUA, PATRICIA
— challenging county claim to land ownership, Lahaina News, December 9, 1987: 1,17.

MAIELUA, SOLOMON NUKUHIWA
— planning family reunion, Lahaina News, June 18, 1998: 2.
— family to hold reunion, Lahaina News, July 2, 1998: 8.

MAIL ROOM, THE [BUSINESS]
— featured, Lahaina News, August 7, 1985: 11.

MAIL SERVICES PLUS [BUSINESS]
— opens, Lahaina News, December 3, 1992: 4.

MAILANEN, PETER SHAWN
— dies in vehicle accident, Lahaina News, January 2, 1991: 4.

MAILANI AND LEI [MUSICAL GROUP]
— to perform at Hawaii Jaycee Summer Jam, Lahaina News, June 22, 2000: 16.

MAILHOLT, TERRI LYNN WONG
— Mrs. Hawaii to attend Lahaina Cannery Sidewalk Sale, Lahaina News, July 6, 1988: 11.
— competes at Mrs. Hawaii pageant, Lahaina News, December 7, 1988: 2.

MAIMIOLA, GEORGE MANULANI
— to discuss Hawaiian artifacts at Bailey House Museum, Lahaina News, September 16, 1999: 12.

MAITHER, BRIAN
— president of Rotary Club of Lahaina, Lahaina News, June 27, 1990: 8.
— life celebrated, Lahaina News, August 29, 1996: 1.

MAJOR MARINE TOURS, INC. [BUSINESS]
— acquires Windjammer Cruises , Lahaina News, January 20, 1994: 7.

MAJURO
— Salvation Army raising funds to help, following typhoon, Lahaina News, December 26, 1990: 5.

MAKAHA SONS OF NI'IHAU [MUSICAL GROUP]
— to play at Royal Lahaina Resort, Lahaina News, September 4, 1985: 10.
— to play at Royal Lahaina Resort on New Year's Eve, Lahaina News, December 4, 1985: 8.
— to perform at "Year of the Hawaiian" concert, Lahaina News, May 27, 1987: 3.
— to perform, Lahaina News, February 15, 1989: 9.
— to perform at the Maui Marriott Ballroom, Lahaina News, December 10, 1992: 17.
— to perform at Hula Grill, Lahaina News, August 24, 1995: 12.
— to perform at "Music on the Beach", Lahaina News, March 26, 1998: 12.
— to perform at Hale Makua annual Ohana Luau, Lahaina News, June 3, 1999: 16.
— to perform at "A Taste of Lahaina", Lahaina News, September 2, 1999: 18.
— to perform at Maui Arts and Cultural Center, Lahaina News, June 28, 2001: 21.
— to perform at Ho'onanea Hawaiian Series, Lahaina News, March 7, 2002: 15.
— to perform at Maui Arts and Cultural Center, Lahaina News, March 14, 2002: 17.
— to perform at "Ho'ala Ka Ike", Lahaina News, November 14, 2002: 18.
— to perform at "Freedom Fest", Lahaina News, July 3, 2003: 17.

MAKAHIKI
— set for December 1 at Lahaina Civic Center, Lahaina News, November 27, 1985: 3.

MAKAHIKI MASKED BALL
— to be held at Maui Marriott, Lahaina News, December 26, 1990: 8.
— to be held at Maui Marriott, Lahaina News, January 2, 1991: 8.

MAKAI BAR [RESTAURANT]
— musical line-up listed at Maui Marriott, Lahaina News, April 11, 1990: 15.
— musical groups listed at Maui Marriott, Lahaina News, May 2, 1990: 15.
— to hold a Cinco de Mayo celebration, Lahaina News, April 28, 1994: 13.
— closing, Lahaina News, July 27, 2000: 20.

MAKAI MASSAGE AND BODYWORK [BUSINESS]
— opens at Napili Kai Beach Resort, Lahaina News, April 11, 2002: 8.

MAKALI'I [CANOE]
— Lahainaluna High School Voyaging Program visit, Lahaina News, August 8, 2002: 2.
— Lahainaluna High School students experience, Lahaina News, July 24, 2003: 3.

MAKANA
— Alexander and Baldwin planning subdivision in Paia, Lahaina News, May 8, 1991: 6.

MAKANA, MAYLA [WRITER]
— author of "Love, Tears and Laughter" to visit Borders Books, Lahaina News, October 11, 2001: 17.

MAKANI COFFEE SHOP [RESTAURANT]
— to feature Oktoberfest food, Lahaina News, October 2, 1985: 9.

MAKANI LTD [BUSINESS]
— presents workshops on people collecting Hawaiiana, Lahaina News, February 28, 1990: 3.

MAKANI SANDS
— development featured [name corrected in July 4 issue], Lahaina News, June 27, 1984: 15.

MAKANI SANITARY LANDFILL
— new hours for landfill, Lahaina News, December 26, 1991: 4.
— Maui County Council Member Vince Bagoyo fears dumping will increase after closure of, Lahaina News, April 2, 1992: 6.

MAKA'OI'OI
— Kapalua Land Company razes the wooden residence at the top of Pineapple Hill Road, regarded as unsafe, Lahaina News, October 9, 2003: 3,4.

MAKAUKAU HULA HALAU
— re-signs at Wharf Shops & Restaurants, Lahaina News, July 13, 1988: 10.
— raises money for Hawaiian Studies scholarships, Lahaina News, December 12, 1996: 1.

MAKAWAO [TOWN]
— rodeo held, Lahaina Sun, June 28, 1972: 4,5.
— new intermediate school planned, Lahaina Sun, February 14, 1973: 10.
— housing development planned, Lahaina Sun, February 14, 1973: 5.
— "Surfer's Paradise" (film) to be shown there, Lahaina Times, July, 1980 volume 4 number 6: 1.
— Upcountry Fair to be held, Lahaina News, June 6, 1991: 12,13.
— rodeo held, Lahaina News, July 10, 1997: 1.
— voted a top arts location by AmericanStyle Magazine, Lahaina News, June 10, 1999: 13.

MAKAWAO RODEO
— to be held this weekend., Lahaina News, July 3, 1985: 8.
— to take place over July 4th weekend, Lahaina News, June 24, 1987: 3.
— concert planned following, Lahaina News, July 1, 1987: 3.
— described, Lahaina News, July 1, 1987: 6.
— to be held in Olinda, Lahaina News, June 20, 1991: 11.
— to be held, Lahaina News, June 27, 1991: 13.
— details given, Lahaina News, July 4, 1991: 13.
— parade route for, Lahaina News, July 2, 1992: 20.
— to be held, Lahaina News, July 2, 1992: 25.
— to be held, Lahaina News, July 1, 1993: 8.
— Parade to be held at Makawao Town, Lahaina News, June 29, 2000: 20.
— to be held, Lahaina News, June 26, 2003: 10.

MAKAWAO TOURING CHOIR [MUSICAL GROUP]
— to hold benefit concert, Lahaina News, June 10, 1987: 3.

MAKE-A-WISH FOUNDATION
— Lauren Rankin visits Hyatt Regency Maui as part of, Lahaina News, February 16, 1995: 6.
— Pacific Whale Foundation hosts 100th child, Lahaina News, November 9, 2000: 11.

MAKEKAU, CHARLES
— union bargainer involved in hotel strike, Lahaina Sun, November 11, 1970: 1.
— president of Maui chapter of The Hawaiians meeting with Richard Paglinawan of Hawaiian Homes Commission, Lahaina Sun, December 16, 1970: 3.
— president of Maui chapter of The Hawaiians meeting with Hawaiian Homes Commission, Lahaina Sun, December 23, 1970: 6.

MAKENA
— Japanese company Seibu Group purchases land, Lahaina Sun, July 11, 1973: 3.
— film Koyaanisqatsi to be shown as fundraiser for efforts to save Big Beach, Lahaina News, November 16, 1983: 5.
— Japan Grand Prix proposes golf course in, Lahaina News, September 3, 1992: 13.
— Wai'olu Condominium project approved in, Lahaina News, October 1, 1992: 14.
— Japan Grand Prix of Hawaii, Ltd. proposes golf course in, Lahaina News, September 23, 1993: 6.
— see also Big Beach

MAKENA BEACH
— tested for pollution, Lahaina Sun, December 16, 1970: 3.
— tourist beaten, Lahaina Sun, March 15, 1972: 3.
— recent attacks at, discussed, Lahaina Sun, April 19, 1972: 1,7.
— hippies cleared from, Lahaina Sun, April 26, 1972: 20.

MAKENA COMMUNITY ASSOCIATION
— to meet with Maui County water board for assistance in water service, Lahaina News, October 8, 1992: 7.
— to meet with Grand Prix officials to discuss proposed golf course, Lahaina News, October 22, 1992: 13.
— approves golf course proposed by Grand Prix Hawaii, Lahaina News, November 5, 1992: 13.
— to meet, Lahaina News, October 7, 1993: 5.
— officers elected, Lahaina News, November 18, 1993: 5.

MAKENA GOLF COURSE
— offering special rates, Lahaina News, August 5, 1987: 3.
— to hold benefit walk for Industry Charity Walk, Lahaina News, April 30, 1992: 7.
— hosting "Stan Sheriff Invitational", Lahaina News, November 19, 1998: 15.

MAKENA HOMEOWNERS ASSOCIATION
— asks to move a water line , Lahaina News, July 9, 1992: 7.
— asks for more police patrols, Lahaina News, December 10, 1992: 8.
— to sell t-shirts, Lahaina News, December 10, 1992: 9.
— to meet, Lahaina News, January 28, 1993: 10.

MAKENA RESORT
— names Charles "Alan" Alamida as operations manager, Lahaina News, November 28, 1990: 8.

MAKI EUROPEAN [BUSINESS]
— opens, Lahaina News, April 7, 1994: 10.

MAKILA LAND CO. [BUSINESS]
— ordered by Commission on Water Resource Management to halt drilling in lands above Lahaina, Lahaina News, January 24, 2002: 1,18.
— protests against water drilling continue, Lahaina News, January 31, 2002: 1,9.

MAKILA ROAD
— included by State Department Land and Natural Resources in state inventory of historic places, Lahaina News, March 27, 2003: 3.
— Hawaiians gather to commemorate designation as an historic site, Lahaina News, April 3, 2003: 1.

MAKING MEMORIES BREAST CANCER FOUNDATION
— working with Aston Hotels and Resorts Hawaii to grant family wish, Lahaina News, October 26, 2000: 20.

MAKK, A.B. [ARTIST]
— to exhibit at Sargent's Fine Art, Lahaina News, July 25, 2002: 22.

MAKK, AMERICO, EVA, AND A.B. [ARTISTS]
— featured at Lahaina Galleries, Lahaina News, August 22, 1990: 14.

MAKK, EVA [ARTIST]
— to exhibit at Sargent's Fine Art, Lahaina News, July 25, 2002: 22.

MAKK FAMILY [ARTISTS]
— to exhibit at Sargent's Fine Art, Lahaina News, March 18, 1999: 17.
— to exhibit at Sargent's Fine Art, Lahaina News, March 25, 1999: 16.

MAKUAOLE, ESTER
— Living treasure featured on Hawaii Public Television, Lahaina News, November 14, 1991: 22.

MALA WHARF
— tested for pollution, Lahaina Sun, December 16, 1970: 3.
— plans to improve wharf, Lahaina Sun, August 25, 1971: 10,12.
— redevelopment plan discussed, Lahaina Sun, September 29, 1971: 1.
— development plans denied by State Department of Land and Natural Resources, Lahaina Sun, December 8, 1971: 1.
— demolition delayed, Lahaina Sun, December 15, 1971: 1.
— history described, Lahaina Sun, February 21, 1973: 15.
— conflict over shoreline near, Lahaina News, June 10, 1987: 1.
— developer to hold public meeting, Lahaina News, June 17, 1987: 3.
— plans to repair loading docks at, Lahaina News, July 13, 1988: 2.
— to be renovated, Lahaina News, June 28, 1989: 3.
— state plans to fix, Lahaina News, August 2, 1989: 1.
— state completes study of, Lahaina News, February 7, 1990: 1.
— boat launch to be repaved by Hoʻokano Paving Co., Lahaina News, February 28, 1990: 3.
— Rick Reed attacks state's refusal to unveil recommendations before meeting, Lahaina News, March 14, 1990: 1.
— editorial critical of state's refusal to unveil recommendations before meeting, Lahaina News, March 14, 1990: 24.
— plans to demolish being reconsidered, Lahaina News, March 21, 1990: 3.
— to be site of Ole Longboard Classic surfing competition, Lahaina News, April 25, 1990: 12.
— legislature authorizes funds for renovations, Lahaina News, June 13, 1990: 1.
— pollution detected at, Lahaina News, December 26, 1990: 1.
— fence creating parking issues, Lahaina News, December 17, 1992: 3.
— problems persist, Lahaina News, February 4, 1993: 1.
— residents frustrated at slowness of improvements, Lahaina News, February 11, 1993: 4.
— temporarily fixed by volunteers , Lahaina News, February 25, 1993: 3.
— Roz Baker asks that Mala Wharf dredging to speed up, Lahaina News, March 11, 1993: 2.
— dredging to begin next month, Lahaina News, April 15, 1993: 1.
— funds sought for bathrooms at, Lahaina News, June 10, 1993: 3,4.
— Stuart Kahan says it is still too shallow, Lahaina News, June 17, 1993: 1.
— work planned by American Divers, Inc., Lahaina News, June 24, 1993: 1.
— work resumes, Lahaina News, September 2, 1993: 1.
— clean-up coordinated by Community Work Day, Lahaina News, January 27, 1994: 3.
— to have bathrooms installed, Lahaina News, August 4, 1994: 1.
— police fear wharf improvements to attract "undesirables", Lahaina News, November 17, 1994: 3.
— launching ramp to be replaced, Lahaina News, April 27, 1995: 5.
— work on comfort station to begin, Lahaina News, June 22, 1995: 2.
— boat ramp to be improved, Lahaina News, November 9, 1995: 1.
— state to dredge, Lahaina News, January 11, 1996: 2.
— update urged in master plan, Lahaina News, March 14, 1996: 3.
— restrooms to open, Lahaina News, October 10, 1996: 5.
— restrooms to open, Lahaina News, October 24, 1996: 5.
— restroom to open, Lahaina News, November 21, 1996: 1.
— graffiti covered at, Lahaina News, March 20, 1997: 2.
— adopted by Mala Wharf Fishing and Recreation Association as part of Adopt-A-Harbor campaign, Lahaina News, August 14, 1997: 15.
— silt problem discussed, Lahaina News, October 2, 1997: 1,2.

— panel to review proposal for, Lahaina News, April 9, 1998: 1.
— dredging to begin, Lahaina News, May 27, 1999: 5.
— boat catches fire at, Lahaina News, February 15, 2001: 9.
— boaters express concerns, Lahaina News, March 7, 2002: 1,20.
— difficulties with cleanup-project , Lahaina News, July 25, 2002: 1,24.

MALA WHARF FISHING AND RECREATION ASSOCIATION
— elections scheduled, Lahaina News, October 1, 1992: 3.
— to meet, Lahaina News, April 1, 1993: 3.
— to meet, Lahaina News, April 29, 1993: 2.
— seeking place for bones uncovered at Mala Wharf, Lahaina News, May 6, 1993: 1.
— president Stuart Kahan says Mala Wharf still too shadow, Lahaina News, June 17, 1993: 1.
— holds "Anything Goes Tournament", Lahaina News, July 8, 1993: 9.
— to host "Anything Goes" Fishing Tournament, Lahaina News, October 6, 1994: 9.
— adopts Mala Wharf as part of Adopt-A-Harbor campaign, Lahaina News, August 14, 1997: 15.
— to meet to discuss improvements, Lahaina News, September 11, 1997: 1.

MALA WHARF PARK
— receives money from State, Lahaina News, May 15, 1991: 1.
— grass beginning to grow, Lahaina News, November 26, 1992: 3.

MALACHOWSKI, ANDREW
— arrested for theft of jewelry, Lahaina Sun, May 9, 1973: 3.

MALAFU, LAVI
— lei maker on Front Street featured, Lahaina News, May 4, 1988: 3.

MALAMA AINA
— community to clean-up Maui County, Lahaina News, January 22, 1998: 12.

MALAMA E NA KEIKI O NA PUʻŪWAI HEMOLELE
— Sacred Hearts to offer summer program, Lahaina News, June 6, 2002: 5.

MALAMA NA KEIKI PRESCHOOL
— to hold Book Fair, Lahaina News, December 2, 1987: 3.

MALAMA NA MAKUA A KEIKI
— to hold used CD sale, Lahaina News, August 3, 2000: 16.

MALAMA ULA CANOE CLUB
— to hold benefit gift and craft fair, Lahaina News, December 17, 1998: 24.
— to host "Lahaina Gift and Craft Fair", Lahaina News, January 21, 1999: 12.
— to hold gift and craft fair, Lahaina News, February 18, 1999: 12.
— to hold Lahaina Gift and Craft Fair, Lahaina News, June 3, 1999: 16.
— to hold gift and craft fair fundraiser, Lahaina News, June 24, 1999: 12.
— to hold Kihei Sea Fest '99, Lahaina News, July 29, 1999: 12.

MALAMALA, SIONE
— Scholar/Athlete of the Week, Lahaina News, September 18, 2003: 12.

MALANI BILYEU [MUSICAL GROUP]
— to perform at Gabel's, Lahaina News, January 2, 1991: 8.
— to perform at Gabel's, Lahaina News, January 23, 1991: 8.
— continues to perform at Gabel's, Lahaina News, March 6, 1991: 14.

MALATHION [PESTICIDE]
— editorial opposing its use on Maui, Lahaina News, January 2, 1985: 2.

MALCOM, DON
— economist discusses need to evolve to stay attractive visitors, Lahaina News, December 17, 1998: 1,28.

MALENCHEK, LOREN
— named advertising/media coordinator at Kapalua Bay Hotel & Villas, Lahaina News, April 16, 1986: 3.
— named advertising director at Kapalua Advertising Company, Lahaina News, April 29, 1987: 6.

MALIA, AUNTIE [MUSICIAN]
— featured at Hyatt Regency Maui, Lahaina News, April 8, 1987: 3.

MALIKO ESTATE
— development featured, Lahaina News, May 16, 1984: 18.

MALIKO ROPING CLUB
— to hold rodeo, Lahaina News, April 10, 1991: 5.

MALINO [MUSICAL GROUP]
— to perform at Wharf Cinema Center, Lahaina News, August 29, 2002: 17.

MALINOWSKI, TERRY
— speaks to Maui Alzheimer's Support Group, Lahaina News, June 8, 1988: 14.

MALKOFF, STEPHEN [ARTIST]
— to paint Banyan Tree, Lahaina News, August 15, 2002: 2.

MALL BALL
— to be held as benefit for the American Cancer Society, Lahaina News, December 1, 1994: 16.

MALLEA, LOLA [ARTIST]
— featured, Lahaina News, August 15, 1996: 17.

MALLOTT, KENNY
— doctor to offer free screenings for skin cancer, Lahaina News, May 8, 1997: 5.

MALO [MUSICAL GROUP]
— concert announced, Lahaina Sun, November 22, 1972: 2.
— show reviewed, Lahaina Sun, December 6, 1972: 6.

MALO, DAVID
— biography detailed, Lahaina Sun, September 13, 1972: 17.
— life recounted, Lahaina News, April 15, 1983: 9.
— photographs of David Malo Day celebration, Lahaina News, May 1, 1983: 10.
— religious tolerance encouraged by, Lahaina News, April 11, 1990: B8.
— impact on Hawaiian history discussed, Lahaina News, April 17, 1997: 16.
— see also David Malo Day

MALO, MAKIA
— Hawaiian storyteller to present at Hui No'eau Visual Arts Center, Lahaina News, October 31, 1990: 17.
— to tell stories as part of Talking Island Tour, Lahaina News, October 22, 1992: 16.

MALONE, MARK ANTHONY
— new director of catering and convention services at Ritz-Carlton, Lahaina News, September 14, 2000: 16.

MALONE, TOM [MUSICIAN]
— to perform at Blackie's Bar, Lahaina News, August 8, 1990: 11.

MALONEY, KATHRYN
— joins Hale Alii Realty Inc., Lahaina News, April 9, 1992: 12.

MALUHIA AT WAILEA
— reservations are under way for, Lahaina News, August 31, 2000: 11.
— PRM Realty Group breaks ground on project, Lahaina News, October 26, 2000: 19.

MALUHIA COUNTRY RANCHES [BUSINESS]
— to hold open house, Lahaina News, October 7, 1999: 13.
— holds prize drawings, Lahaina News, November 11, 1999: 11.
— featured, Lahaina News, January 27, 2000: 11.

MALUNA KAI ESTATES
— featured, Lahaina News, February 27, 2003: 6.

MALU'ULU O LELE CULTURAL CENTER
— as location for children's events, Lahaina News, September 21, 1983: 9.
— "An Evening with Kids of Lahaina" to be presented, Lahaina News, October 31, 1984: 3.
— to hold meeting on adult day care, Lahaina News, June 10, 1987: 18.
— accepting applicants for Adult Day Care program, Lahaina News, July 1, 1987: 3.
— needs volunteers for Work Day, Lahaina News, August 26, 1987: 3.
— looking for cooks to teach classes, Lahaina News, December 12, 1990: 4.
— to offer life drawing classes, Lahaina News, April 3, 1991: 10.
— to hold Scotty K Spam Bakeoff, Lahaina News, May 1, 1991: 1.
— to hold art classes, Lahaina News, May 1, 1991: 4.
— hosting craft classes, Lahaina News, December 5, 1991: 4.
— offering craft classes, Lahaina News, December 12, 1991: 6.
— renovations of, Lahaina News, January 30, 1992: 6.
— ballet lessons to be held at, Lahaina News, February 20, 1992: 3.
— to offer courses, Lahaina News, April 23, 1992: 4.
— to hold hula course, Lahaina News, May 7, 1992: 3,4.
— outreach aid Stephanie Rivera available for senior citizens, Lahaina News, June 4, 1992: 4.
— offering courses in ula, acting, and movement therapy, Lahaina News, August 27, 1992: 3.
— Fall program to begin, Lahaina News, September 10, 1992: 3.
— begins classes, Lahaina News, January 21, 1993: 4.
— to hold classes, Lahaina News, January 28, 1993: 4.
— offering Hawaiian culture classes, Lahaina News, April 13, 1995: 4.
— to hold discussion "Spiritual Solutions and the New Civilization", Lahaina News, September 14, 1995: 6.
— sponsoring "Spiritual Solutions and the New Civilization", Lahaina News, November 23, 1995: 4.
— Moanaliha Uwekoolani discusses Dennis "Bumpy" Kanahele, Lahaina News, November 30, 1995: 1,12.
— to host "Peace Friday", Lahaina News, March 27, 1997: 12.
— to host Noenoe Silva speaking on Ku'e: The Hui Aloha 'Aina Anti-Annexation Petitions, Lahaina News, August 27, 1998: 3.
— groups want closed at night, Lahaina News, September 24, 1998: 1,20.
— Hui Kako'o 'Aina Ho'opulapula to hold meeting at, Lahaina News, October 11, 2001: 20.
— Kapanali Aloha Institute (KAI) to hold classes at, Lahaina News, April 10, 2003: 2.

MALU'ULU O LELE PARK
— historical marker for, discussed , Lahaina Sun, December 16, 1970: 6.
— projects desired by West Maui Business Association, Lahaina Sun, December 23, 1970: 2.
— history detailed, Lahaina News, May 2, 1984: 8,9,10.
— tennis courts to be named after tennis player Shigeto "Shigesh" Wakida, Lahaina News, April 9, 1986: 3.
— Maui County Cultural Resources Commission grants permit to clean up, Lahaina News, June 25, 1992: 2.
— homeless evicted from near, Lahaina News, March 18, 1993: 1.
— archaeologists find potential building, Lahaina News, April 22, 1993: 1,3.
— update on archaeological dig, Lahaina News, May 6, 1993: 3.
— update on archaeological dig, Lahaina News, May 13, 1993: insert1,insert4.
— archaeological study almost done, Lahaina News, April 14, 1994: 2.
— police have no solution to stop drinking at, Lahaina News, July 21, 1994: 1,16.
— Maui County Council to examine problem of drinking in, Lahaina News, July 28, 1994: 4.
— problem of drinking at, Lahaina News, August 4, 1994: 2.

— Maui County Council working on legislation to curb drinking at park, Lahaina News, October 20, 1994: 1.

— Maui County Council supports ban of drinking at, Lahaina News, December 8, 1994: 1.

— Maui County Council passes ordinance to prohibit drinking in parks, Lahaina News, December 22, 1994: 2.

— tennis courts to be fixed, Lahaina News, March 16, 1995: 4.

— update on archaeological study given by James Luckey, Lahaina News, May 4, 1995: 5.

— project to replace backstop damages archaeological wall, Lahaina News, August 3, 1995: 1,5.

— baseball may move from so that Hawaiians can better study and protect the island, Lahaina News, October 5, 1995: 1,16.

— users asked not to play softball, Lahaina News, November 16, 1995: 1,20.

— monument to be erected by Friends of Moku'ula, Lahaina News, January 11, 1996: 1,16.

— fence erected, softball season will not be played at, Lahaina News, January 11, 1996: 1,16.

— cultural park on J. Kalani English's agenda, Lahaina News, January 16, 1997: 1,2.

— parents of children at King Kamehameha III Elementary School discuss ways of clearing out, Lahaina News, October 15, 1998: 1,8.

— plan being developed to give King Kamehameha III Elementary School secure area in, Lahaina News, October 22, 1998: 1,2.

— Friends of Moku'ula begin work removing park, Lahaina News, November 19, 1998: 1,20.

— results of archaeological studies, Lahaina News, May 27, 1999: 1,16.

— Susan Lebo surveys, Lahaina News, May 27, 1999: 16.

— coed soccer to be held at, Lahaina News, June 24, 1999: 7.

— shopping center proposed near, Lahaina News, September 23, 1999: 1,3.

— restoration plans progressing, Lahaina News, January 4, 2001: 1,15.

MAMAIJA, PAT
— Samoan storyteller to present at Hui No'eau Visual Arts Center, Lahaina News, October 31, 1990: 17.

MAMA'S FISH HOUSE [RESTAURANT]
— featured, Lahaina News, April 4, 1996: 12.
— featured, Lahaina News, February 6, 1997: 6,7,8.
— receives "Mom and Pop Business Survivor" award, Lahaina News, December 2, 1999: 13.

MAMA'S ORIGINAL MAUI PIZZA [RESTAURANT]
— opens on Front Street, Lahaina News, March 15, 1982: 5.
— reviewed, Lahaina News, April 15, 1983: 14.
— coloring contest begins, Lahaina News, April 18, 1984: 4.
— coloring contest winners announced, Lahaina News, May 23, 1984: 4.
— coloring contest winners named, Lahaina News, July 3, 1985: 8.

MAMA'S RIBS 'N ROTISSERIE
— opens at Napili Plaza, Lahaina News, July 1, 1999: 13.

MAME [PLAY]
— to be performed by Maui Youth Theatre, Lahaina News, December 14, 1988: 5.

MAMORU AND AIKO TAKITANI FOUNDATION
— awards scholarship to Lahainaluna High School student, Lahaina News, May 23, 2002: 2.
— Lahainaluna High School student Kealani Gomez-Poland wins scholarship, Lahaina News, May 22, 2003: 2.

MAN FOR ALL SEASONS, A [PLAY]
— to be performed by Maui Community Theatre, Lahaina News, November 7, 1991: 21.
— grand finale to be held, Lahaina News, November 14, 1991: 22.
— to be presented by Maui Community Theatre, Lahaina News, November 28, 1991: 18.

MAN OF LA MANCHA [PLAY]
— to be performed by Baldwin Theatre Guild, Lahaina News, August 5, 1993: 11.
— to be performed, Lahaina News, August 12, 1993: 14.

MANA WAKA [FILM]
— to be presented by Queen Te Arikinui Dame Te Atairangikaahu at Hale Pa'ahao, Lahaina News, August 1, 1991: 18.

MANA—THE MAGIC SPEAR [FILM]
— shown at Family Film Festival, Lahaina Sun, January 27, 1971: 2.

MANAGEMENT ADVISORY SERVICES, INC [BUSINESS]
— conducting seminar on developing flagging skills, Lahaina News, October 25, 1989: 10.

MANAGEMENT CONSULTANTS OF HAWAII, INC. [BUSINESS]
— appoints Dave Ferguson as executive vice president, Lahaina News, June 24, 1993: 10.

MANA'O COMPANY [MUSICAL GROUP]
— to perform at Maui County Fair, Lahaina News, October 3, 1991: 12.
— performs at King Kamehameha III Elementary School, Lahaina News, December 26, 2002: 1.

MANA'O NANI 'O MAUI [BUSINESS]
— seeking products to include in its catalogue, Lahaina News, February 20, 1985: 7.
— featured, Lahaina News, February 27, 1985: 9.

MANAWAHI [SHIP]
— account of, including sinking, Lahaina Sun, August 22, 1973: 1,3.

MANAWAITI, DENNIS [MUSICIAN]
— to perform at Westin Maui, Lahaina News, April 16, 1992: 18.

MANDEL, HARVEY [MUSICIAN]
— to perform at World Cafe, Lahaina News, July 10, 1997: 18.

MANDEL, HOWIE
— to perform at The Westin Maui, Lahaina News, April 22, 1993: 14.

MANDEL, STEFAN PAYNE [ARTIST]
— opens gallery, Lahaina News, July 5, 2001: 8.

MANDEVILLE, KIANA
— hired by Westin Maui as sales manager, Lahaina News, January 16, 2003: 8.

MANDOLPH, RANDOLPH
— play "Get Off With Me" to be performed by Maui Community Theatre, Lahaina News, July 25, 1990: 11.

MANDOLPH, ROBERT [DANCER]
— tap dancer to hold workshops, Lahaina News, September 6, 1989: 3.

MANELE BAY HOTEL
— owned by Rockresorts; scheduled to open next year, Lahaina News, November 29, 1989: 4.
— names Mark McGuffie as general manager, Lahaina News, October 10, 1991: 7.

MANGANESE
— see sea mining

MANGLAYLAY, SHERYL
— Scholar/Athlete of the Week, Lahaina News, May 3, 2001: 14.

MANGO [MUSICAL GROUP]
— releases album "Romancing the Islands", Lahaina News, December 25, 1985: 8.

MANGO CAFE AND PIE SHOP [RESTAURANT]
— opens at Sheraton Maui, Lahaina News, December 5, 1996: 8.
— featured, Lahaina News, December 19, 1996: 18.

MANGO JONES'S [RESTAURANT]
— opens, Lahaina News, January 17, 1990: 4.
— reviewed, Lahaina News, February 21, 1990: 6.

MANGO LINE DESIGNS [BUSINESS]
— creates balloon decorations, Lahaina News, November 12, 1998: 13.

MANGO MANOR
— rental receives complaints, Lahaina News, May 13, 1993: 1,3.

MANHATTAN RHYTHM KINGS [MUSICAL GROUP]
— to perform for Maui Philharmonic Society, Lahaina News, October 3, 1990: 12.
— to perform at Stouffer Wailea Beach Resort, Lahaina News, October 10, 1990: 14.
— to open Maui Philharmonic season, Lahaina News, October 17, 1990: 17.

MANHATTAN TRANSFER [MUSICAL GROUP]
— to perform at Maui Arts and Cultural Center, Lahaina News, September 10, 1998: 21.
— to perform at Maui Arts and Cultural Center, Lahaina News, October 22, 1998: 20.

MANJIRO FESTIVAL
— to be held, Lahaina News, March 13, 2003: 3.

MANJIRO, JOHN
— featured, Lahaina News, February 8, 1996: 13.
— honored by festival, Lahaina News, March 11, 1999: 1,16.
— Yosakoi Festival to be held, Lahaina News, March 11, 1999: 1,16.
— Yosakoi Festival to be held to honor, Lahaina News, March 9, 2000: 3.
— "Izanai Yosakoi Festival of the Future" to include parade, Lahaina News, March 8, 2001: 3.

MANN, HERBIE [MUSICIAN]
— to perform at Hyatt Regency Maui, Lahaina News, May 19, 1994: 15.

MANN, JANET
— to present on bottlenose dolphins in Shark Bay, Australia, Lahaina News, November 25, 1999: 16.

MANN, JIM [WRITER]
— wrote book directed to hippies, Lahaina Sun, December 9, 1970: 6.
— participated in Maui Youth Council, Lahaina Sun, January 13, 1971: 5.
— connected to Maui County Committee on Ecology, Lahaina Sun, January 20, 1971: 6.
— discusses hippie brochure, Lahaina Sun, January 27, 1971: 2.

MANNATECH
— to meet, Lahaina News, November 12, 1998: 16.

MANO KELA [BOAT]
— places second in Big Island Invitational Marlin Tournament, Lahaina News, October 3, 1990: 6.

MANOLA, GLEN [MUSICIAN]
— to perform at Borders Books, Lahaina News, September 16, 1999: 13.
— to perform at Borders Books, Lahaina News, October 21, 1999: 16.

MANTIAGO, JERRY
— receives Hobie scholarship, Lahaina News, June 11, 1992: 3.

MANTIS ECO-CARE [BUSINESS]
— offering workshops on home composting, Lahaina News, August 7, 1997: 12.
— to offer workshop on home composting, Lahaina News, January 15, 1998: 12.

MANTON, SPIKE [COMEDIAN]
— to perform at Comedy Club and the Sports Page, Lahaina News, May 1, 1991: 14,16.

MANU-PAE
— story described, Lahaina Sun, April 11, 1973: 14.

MANY ADVENTURES OF SNOW WHITE, THE [PLAY]
— to be performed by Maui Academy of Performing Arts, Lahaina News, February 1, 2001: 21.

MANY FLAVORS OF MAUI, THE [BOOK]
— published by volunteers of Maui Memorial Hospital Auxiliary, Lahaina News, February 26, 1986: 3.
— to be sold at Nagasako's Super Market, Lahaina News, March 26, 1986: 3.

MANZANO, ALEXANDER
— dies in motorcycle accident, Lahaina News, January 2, 1992: 5.

MAORI
— dancers to perform at Aston's Kamaole Sands-Maui, Lahaina News, June 6, 1990: 13.
— Queen Te Arikinui Dame Te Atairangikaahu to present the film "Mana Waka" at Hale Pa'ahao, Lahaina News, August 1, 1991: 18.

MAPES, LOWELL [ARTIST]
— show at Village Gallery, Lahaina News, December 31, 1986: 3.
— to appear at Village Gallery, Lahaina News, January 3, 1990: 15.
— to exhibit at Friday Night is Art Night, Lahaina News, June 27, 1990: 11.
— reception to held at Village Galleries, Lahaina News, August 1, 1990: 13.
— to exhibit, Lahaina News, December 19, 1996: 25.
— to exhibit "Travels" at Village Gallery, Lahaina News, May 31, 2001: 16.

MAPFUMO, THOMAS [MUSICIAN]
— to perform at Casanova's, Lahaina News, August 27, 1992: 18.

MAQUIRE, BROOKS [MUSICIAN]
— to perform at Aloha Cantina, Lahaina News, February 17, 1994: 11.
— continues to perform at Aloha Cantina, Lahaina News, September 1, 1994: 15.
— to perform at Cheeseburger in Paradise, Aloha Cantina, Lahaina News, April 6, 1995: 11,12.

MARA III, VEDERINE EDWARD
— sentenced for murder of Monica Pagasian, Lahaina Sun, November 17, 1971: 6.

MARAN, DAVID
— appointed general manager of Starbucks at Lahaina Cannery Mall, Lahaina News, October 10, 2002: 8.

MARATHON CAFE
— show to benefit Baldwin High School, Lahaina News, September 3, 1992: 14.
— to hold M Judy Ridolfino fundraiser, Lahaina News, June 15, 1995: 11.

MARATHON CAFE IX
— to be held, Lahaina News, June 11, 1998: 17.
— to be held, Lahaina News, June 18, 1998: 16.

MARATHON CAFE X
— to be held by Judy Ridolfino, Lahaina News, June 17, 1999: 9.

MARATHON CAFE XI (LIGHTNING STRIKES)
— to be held, Lahaina News, June 15, 2000: 17.
— to be held, Lahaina News, June 22, 2000: 16.

MARATHON CAFE XIII (SPIES)
— comedy dance play show to be held, Lahaina News, June 14, 2001: 20.
— to be held, Lahaina News, June 21, 2001: 16.

MARC RESORTS GROUP
— now managing Maui Eldorado Resort, Lahaina News, June 27, 1991: 7.

MARCEAU, MARCEL [PERFORMER]
— to perform at Maui Arts and Cultural Center, Lahaina News, November 8, 2001: 17.

MARCELLO [ARTIST]
— to exhibit at Lahaina Galleries, Lahaina News, February 18, 1999: 12.

MARCH FOR JESUS
— to be held, Lahaina News, May 20, 1999: 16.

MARCH OF DIMES
— held on Maui, Lahaina Sun, May 10, 1972: 21.
— fundraiser underway, Lahaina Sun, December 13, 1972: 6.
— Marty Mim Mack to visit Maui in support of fundraiser, Lahaina Sun, January 10, 1973: 3.
— walkathon, Lahaina Sun, January 17, 1973: 1,6.
— Marty Mim Mack interviewed, Lahaina Sun, January 24, 1973: 6.
— $41,370 in total pledges, Lahaina Sun, January 24, 1973: 7.
— march set for January 25, Lahaina News, January 22, 1986: 3.
— fundraiser scheduled, Lahaina News, January 7, 1987: 3.
— WalkAmerica Walk/Run scheduled, Lahaina News, January 24, 1990: 28.
— walk scheduled, Lahaina News, March 6, 1991: 5.
— to be held, Lahaina News, March 13, 1991: 3,5.
— to conduct training session for seminar leaders for "BABIES + YOU", Lahaina News, April 17, 1991: 7.
— awards scholarships to Maui Community College nursing students, Lahaina News, January 30, 1992: 5.
— to hold WalkAmerica event, Lahaina News, April 14, 1994: 7.
— to hold WalkAmerica, Lahaina News, April 11, 1996: 13.
— to hold WalkAmerica '97, Lahaina News, April 3, 1997: 13.
— to hold WalkAmerica, Lahaina News, April 2, 1998: 2.
— NFL players to compete in charity basketball for, Lahaina News, April 20, 2000: 16.
— announces Danny Agsalog as chair of Maui WalkAmerica 2001, Lahaina News, March 1, 2001: 10.
— Maui WalkAmerica 2001 to raise money for, Lahaina News, April 12, 2001: 20.

MARCH, ROBINETTA TOMPKIN
— looking for missing valuable artifacts gifted to Lahainaluna High School, Lahaina News, June 27, 1996: 5.

MARCHELLO, KELLI
— Scholar/Athlete of the Week, Lahaina News, November 14, 1996: 12.
— tennis player is rated USTA #3 Girls 14 player, Lahaina News, July 16, 1998: 15.
— tennis player featured, Lahaina News, August 26, 1999: 6.

MARCI, ANITA [ARTIST]
— to lead workshop on textural watercolors, Lahaina News, November 7, 2002: 16.
— to hold workshops on watercolors, Lahaina News, November 14, 2002: 17.
— to offer watercolor workshops, Lahaina News, January 30, 2003: 3.
— to lead course on "Comprehending Color", Lahaina News, February 27, 2003: 2.
— to lead course on "Comprehending Color", Lahaina News, April 3, 2003: 16.
— to teach "Textural Techniques" at The Art School at Kapalua, Lahaina News, April 24, 2003: 16.
— to hold painting workshop, Lahaina News, June 26, 2003: 9.
— to host watercolor workshop, Lahaina News, August 7, 2003: 15.
— to hold watercolor workshop series "Stellar Still Life", Lahaina News, October 2, 2003: 2.

MARCIEL, DAVID
— police officer offers tips to reduce crime, Lahaina News, November 15, 1989: 3.

MARCINIAK, ROXANNE
— crowned Maui Onion Queen, Lahaina News, August 6, 1992: 3.

MARCOE [ARTIST]
— painting wins LahainaTown Action Committee poster contest, Lahaina News, June 23, 1994: 11.
— to sign posters for LahainaTown Action Committee, Lahaina News, June 30, 1994: 12.
— demonstrating pastels, Lahaina News, July 14, 1994: 15.

MARCOLIN, JOSEPH [ARTIST]
— to present at Maui Marine Expo, Lahaina News, January 13, 1988: 16.

MARCO'S GELATO D'ITALIA [RESTAURANT]
— reviewed, Lahaina News, January 18, 1984: 13.

MARCO'S RISTORANTE AND BAR [RESTAURANT]
— reviewed, Lahaina News, October 26, 1983: 12,14.
— now open late night, Lahaina News, June 11, 1986: 3.
— chocolate reviewed, Lahaina News, May 20, 1987: 4.

MARCOTTE, ROGER
— running for mayor, Lahaina Sun, September 13, 1972: 5.

MARCUS, DANIEL
— wins Dracula's Dash 8K run, Lahaina News, November 8, 1989: 4.
— runner wins Hard Rock Cafe Rock n' Roll 10K run, Lahaina News, July 2, 1992: 12.

MARCUS JOHNSON TRIO [MUSICAL GROUP]
— to perform at Longhi's Restaurant, Lahaina News, September 19, 1996: 18.

MARDI GRAS
— to be held by Big Brothers/Big Sisters, Lahaina News, January 31, 1990: 2.
— scheduled, Lahaina News, February 7, 1990: 2.
— to be held at The Villa Restaurant, Lahaina News, February 14, 1990: 15.
— scheduled for Lahaina Civic Center, Lahaina News, February 21, 1990: 13.
— to be celebrated at Westin Maui's Villa Restaurant, Lahaina News, February 6, 1991: 13.
— Maui Hotel Association to hold fundraiser for Big Brothers/Big Sisters, Lahaina News, February 13, 1992: 19.
— Garden Restaurant at the Kapalua Bay Hotel to have special menu, Lahaina News, February 13, 1992: 19.
— Willie K to perform at, Lahaina News, February 20, 1992: 12.
— to be celebrated, Lahaina News, February 20, 1992: 3.
— to be held, Lahaina News, February 18, 1993: 4.
— fundraiser to be held by Big Brothers/Big Sisters, Lahaina News, February 25, 1993: 8.
— Big Brothers/Big Sisters to hold annual benefit, Lahaina News, February 3, 1994: 4.
— restaurants participating in, Lahaina News, March 3, 1994: 11.
— Maui Symphony Orchestra to hold masked ball, Lahaina News, February 2, 1995: 12.
— masked ball to be held by Maui Symphony Orchestra, Lahaina News, February 16, 1995: 15.
— Big Brothers/Big Sisters to hold fundraiser during, Lahaina News, February 16, 1995: 16.
— to be celebrated at Ka'anapali Beach Hotel, Lahaina News, December 28, 2000: 16.

MARDI GRAS OF THE PACIFIC
— see Halloween

MARGARET CAMERON SCHOLARSHIP
— available to music students from Maui Philharmonic Society, Lahaina News, February 22, 1989: 13.
— recipients announced, Lahaina News, May 24, 1989: 3.

MARGARET FOLLETT HASKINS SCHOLARSHIP FUND
— awarded to Maui Community College students, Lahaina News, July 26, 2001: 5.

MARGARITA'S BEACH CANTINA [RESTAURANT]
— new name for Polli's On the Beach, Lahaina News, March 27, 1991: 9.

MARIA BENITEZ SPANISH DANCE COMPANY [TROUPE]
— to perform, Lahaina News, September 21, 1988: 3.

MARIA LANAKILA CATHOLIC CHURCH
— to hold bazaar at Sacred Hearts School, Lahaina News, March 6, 1985: 3.
— changes mass schedule, Lahaina News, August 28, 1985: 3.
— announces changes to Catholic services, Lahaina News, May 28, 1986: 3.
— reverend Christopher Keahi retires from, Lahaina News, July 4, 1991: 1.
— appoints Arsene Daenen as new priest, Lahaina News, July 11, 1991: 4.
— father Marisi Palepale installed as pastor, Lahaina News, March 5, 1992: 3,4.
— to hold fundraiser, Lahaina News, August 19, 1993: 4.
— donates food to Lightbringers Rescue Mission, Lahaina News, December 2, 1993: 4.
— planning major renovation, Lahaina News, May 19, 1994: 5.
— Hapa to hold benefit concert, Lahaina News, September 29, 1994: 11.
— to hold rummage sale, Lahaina News, November 17, 1994: 4.
— renovations to begin, Lahaina News, April 27, 1995: 3.
— finds time capsule from 1928, Lahaina News, May 11, 1995: 1.
— renovations continue, Lahaina News, August 17, 1995: 1.
— to be rededicated following renovations, Lahaina News, December 7, 1995: 1,20.
— choir to perform at Wharf Cinema Center, Lahaina News, December 21, 1995: 14.
— Joseph Bukowski III new pastor, Lahaina News, September 10, 1998: 1,24.
— Father Raphael Smulders retiring to St. Patrick's on Oahu, Lahaina News, October 29, 1998: 21.
— to hold Palm Sunday masses, Lahaina News, March 25, 1999: 7.
— Filipino Catholic Club to hold dinner dance fundraiser, Lahaina News, September 23, 1999: 12.
— to hold Easter service, Lahaina News, April 20, 2000: 8.
— Sisters of St. Francis leaving, Lahaina News, June 8, 2000: 1,7.
— holds Service of Light, Lahaina News, September 27, 2001: 6.
— warns people of fake requests for donations, Lahaina News, July 18, 2002: 3.
— Father Joseph Bukoski remembered, Lahaina News, September 19, 2002: 18.
— hosting programs by Hui Malama Learning Center, Lahaina News, February 27, 2003: 9.
— bids farewell to Father William Petrie and Father James McDonough, Lahaina News, June 19, 2003: 2.

MARIA MULDAUR BAND, THE [MUSICAL GROUP]
— to perform at Hawaiian Islands Rhythm and Blues Mele, Lahaina News, May 14, 1998: 18.

MARIA-HAUMANI, MARY SANTA
— to present on "Sex: Safe, Safer, Safest", Lahaina News, February 15, 2001: 16,17.

MARIANI, RUSSELL
— to speak on nutrition and dietary practices, Lahaina News, May 16, 1996: 11.

MARIANO, BENIEDEAN BULOSAN
— resident makes Dean's List at Seattle Pacific University, Lahaina News, May 24, 2001: 2.

MARIE, ANNA
— speaks about her business success, Lahaina News, July 24, 1985: 1,20.

MARIE CALLENDER'S [RESTAURANT]
— featured, Lahaina News, November 4, 1987: 7,8.
— featured, Lahaina News, June 15, 1988: 10.
— reviewed, Lahaina News, October 12, 1988: 8.
— reviewed, Lahaina News, February 15, 1989: 11.
— reviewed, Lahaina News, May 3, 1989: 11.
— reviewed, Lahaina News, August 2, 1989: 16.
— featured, Lahaina News, November 1, 1989: 13.
— featured, Lahaina News, January 3, 1990: 13.
— announces new menu, Lahaina News, March 26, 1992: 14.
— featured, Lahaina News, September 24, 1992: 17.

MARIJUANA
— Cravalho discusses laws associated with, Lahaina Sun, January 20, 1971: 2.
— Dave Evans record song "Operation Green Harvest" on cultivation of, Lahaina Times, July, 1980 volume 4 number 6: 1.

MARINE ART FESTIVAL
— to be held at Lahaina Cannery Mall, Lahaina News, March 6, 1997: 13.

MARINE ART TOURS
— tour of homes to be offered, Lahaina News, December 12, 1991: 24,25.

MARINE CORPS
— celebrated by Navy League of the United States, Lahaina News, November 5, 1986: 16.
— Marine Corps Private Jamie Ficarra completes basic training at the Marine Corps Recruit Depot, Lahaina News, March 1, 2001: 10.

MARINE MAMMAL PROTECTION, STATE
— seeking help to monitor seals, Lahaina News, September 24, 1998: 17.

MARINE OPTION PROGRAM
— students from to conduct survey of Molokini Crater with Pacific Whale Foundation, Lahaina News, July 22, 1987: 3,10.
— coordinator Donna Liddicote-Brown to present on limu, Lahaina News, May 3, 2001: 21.

MARINE PATROL
— bill may move from Department of Public Safety to Department of Land and Natural Resources, Lahaina News, February 23, 1995: 1,4.
— to be abolished, Lahaina News, August 3, 1995: 5.

MARINE RESEARCH CONSULTANTS
— study finds no long-term effect of sediment runoff into Honolua Bay, Lahaina News, August 15, 1990: 1.

MARINO, DOMINICK
— president of Maui Contractors Association introduces "Maui Building Guide 1993", Lahaina News, February 25, 1993: supplement3.

MARINO, TOM
— completed exam and is now CPA, Lahaina News, March 12, 1986: 12.

MARK, GORDON [MUSICIAN]
— to perform at "The Art of the Solo 'Ukulele", Lahaina News, March 28, 2002: 19.

MARK MORRIS DANCE GROUP [TROUPE]
— to perform at Maui Arts and Cultural Center, Lahaina News, November 9, 2000: 25.
— to perform at Maui Arts and Cultural Center, Lahaina News, November 16, 2000: 16.

MARK OF DIMES
— to hold Maui WalkAmerica 2001, Lahaina News, March 29, 2001: 2.

MARK TWAIN TONIGHT!
— Hal Holbrook to present at Maui Arts and Cultural Center, Lahaina News, March 23, 2000: 12.

MARKET CAFE [RESTAURANT]
— reviewed, Lahaina News, October 8, 1992: 14.

MARKEY, JULIE
— becomes secretary for the Maui Chamber of Commerce, Lahaina Sun, July 11, 1973: 4.

MARKOWITZ, GARY [ARTIST]
— to exhibit at Sargent's Fine Art, Lahaina News, November 9, 2000: 22.
— to exhibit at Art School at Kapalua, Lahaina News, November 30, 2000: 5.
— to exhibit at Art School at Kapalua, Lahaina News, December 14, 2000: 20.

MARKS, DREW [COMEDIAN]
— to perform at Honolulu Comedy Club, Lahaina News, July 28, 1994: 13.

MARKS, HELEN
— to speak to Maui Christian Women's Club, Lahaina News, September 10, 1992: 3.

MARKS, RICHARD
— sheriff of Kalaupapa to speak to Rotary Club of Lahaina, Lahaina News, January 25, 1989: 5.

MARLEY, BOB [MUSICIAN]
— tribute to be held, Lahaina News, February 22, 2001: 16.

MARLEY, DAMIAN "JR. GONGE" [MUSICIAN]
— to headline "Boy Marley Tribute and Benefit Concert", Lahaina News, February 24, 2000: 15.

MARLEY, JULIAN [MUSICIAN]
— to headline "Boy Marley Tribute and Benefit Concert", Lahaina News, February 24, 2000: 15.

MARLEY, ZIGGY [MUSICIAN]
— to perform at Lahaina Civic Center, Lahaina News, September 28, 1988: 9.
— to perform at "Reggae in the Country '98", Lahaina News, March 26, 1998: 13.
— to perform , Lahaina News, April 2, 1998: 17.
— to perform with Melody Makers, Lahaina News, April 9, 1998: 16.
— to perform at Maui Arts and Cultural Center, Lahaina News, July 1, 1999: 14.
— to perform at "Reggae in the Country", Lahaina News, August 5, 1999: 13.

MARRIAGES
— John Stewart and Ida Uncapher marry, Lahaina Sun, March 17, 1971: 2.
— examples of polygamous marriage in Maui, Lahaina Times, October, 1980 volume 4 number 9: 4.
— listed in new section, not otherwise indexed, Lahaina News, January 9, 1992: 13.
— opinions on same-sex sought, Lahaina News, February 8, 1996: 3.

MARRIN, D.L. "WEST"
— to present "Changing Our Perception of Water", Lahaina News, September 27, 2001: 17.

MARRIOTT AND RENAISSANCE RESORTS HAWAII
— appoints Paul Chicoine as area director of marketing sales, Lahaina News, August 26, 1999: 13.

MARRIOTT HAWAII BUSINESS COUNCIL
— donates to Maui Community College, Lahaina News, May 18, 2000: 9.

MARRIOTT INTERNATIONAL
— presents Leadership Excellence to Stan Engeldorf, Lahaina News, July 4, 2002: 8.

MARRIOTT LOBBY BAR AND SUSHI [RESTAURANT]
— featured, Lahaina News, July 2, 1998: 6,7.

MARRIOTT VACATION CLUB INTERNATIONAL
— to open Maui Ocean Club sales center, Lahaina News, August 21, 2003: 8.

MARS
— glass tunnels photographed on, Lahaina News, June 29, 2000: 18.
— concern over photos, Lahaina News, July 27, 2000: 18.

MARSALIS, WYNTON [MUSICIAN]
— to perform at Hyatt Regency Hotel Grand Ballroom, Lahaina News, March 12, 1986: 8.
— career described, in anticipation of his performance, Lahaina News, March 19, 1986: 12.

MARSH, ARIEL
— Scholar/Athlete of the Week, Lahaina News, October 29, 1998: 18.

MARSHALL, DON
— named division manager for Monarch Building Supply, Lahaina News, July 25, 1990: 7.

MARSHALL, GARRY
— to speak at Maui Writers Conference, Lahaina News, September 3, 1998: 16.

MARSHALL, STEPHEN
— Ritz-Carlton is new executive chef, Lahaina News, April 6, 2000: 9.

MARSHALL, STEWART [ARTIST]
— recent paintings exhibited at Village Gallery Lahaina, Lahaina News, April 19, 1989: 3.

MARTIAL ARTS
— featured as youth activity, Lahaina News, December 16, 1987: 1,16.
— shown at Royal Lahaina Resort, Lahaina News, August 16, 1989: 7.
— Randy Casko School of Tae Kwon-Do did well at recent tournament, Lahaina News, September 6, 1989: 1.
— Festival of Kings Karate Tournament to be held, Lahaina News, July 27, 2000: 6.
— International Zen Dojo of Maui to hold fundraiser, Lahaina News, September 14, 2000: 9.
— Master Koichi Tohei confirms higher ranking for Maui Ki-Aikido teachers, Lahaina News, March 29, 2001: 12.
— Tae Kwon-Do students earn black belts, Lahaina News, July 12, 2001: 12.
— students at Kenpo Dojo successful at Festival of the Kings—Hoʻolauleʻaʻona Aliʻi—martials art tournament, Lahaina News, August 23, 2001: 12.
— Kurt Miyajima to teach, Lahaina News, January 10, 2002: 16.
— classes to be offered, Lahaina News, October 3, 2002: 2.
— Maui Ki-Aikido to offer course, Lahaina News, August 21, 2003: 12.
— T'ai Chi Maui to hold demonstration, Lahaina News, September 4, 2003: 17.
— Christopher Curtis to talk on "Principles of Aikido", Lahaina News, September 4, 2003: 17.
— Maui Kenpo Doho offering free judo classes, Lahaina News, September 11, 2003: 12.

MARTIAL ARTS SPECTACULAR
— to be held, Lahaina News, February 18, 1999: 7.

MARTIN AND MACARTHUR [BUSINESS]
— to open, Lahaina News, August 20, 1998: 13.

MARTIN, BEN
— elected race director at Maui County Hawaiian Canoe Association, Lahaina News, April 8, 1999: 7.

MARTIN, BILLY [ACTOR]
— resident of West Maui featured, Lahaina News, May 27, 1987: 8.

MARTIN, BRAD LEE
— fined for damaging silversword plants at Haleakala National Park, Lahaina Sun, September 1, 1971: 15.

MARTIN, CHRISTY
— member of Invasive Species Committee to present "Alien Species In Our Backyard", Lahaina News, November 8, 2001: 17.

MARTIN, DICK [COMEDIAN]
— praises the Maui Hilton, Lahaina Sun, January 13, 1971: 7.

MARTIN, DOLORES
— conflict with Maui Historic Commission over retail properties she rents, Lahaina Sun, June 21, 1972: 3.

MARTIN, DON "KAMOI" [ENTERTAINER]
— local resident featured, Lahaina News, February 15, 1989: 2.
— host of Sheraton Luau, Lahaina News, August 16, 1989: 13.
— Hawaiian storytelling session to be held, Lahaina News, August 3, 1995: 16.

MARTIN, DON "UNCLE"
— passed away, Lahaina News, March 20, 1997: 3.

MARTIN, DONALD
— becomes manager of Wailuku Sugar Company, Lahaina Sun, June 7, 1972: 14.

MARTIN, J. GARY
— proposes apartment building, Lahaina News, November 14, 1990: 3,4.

MARTIN, JERRY
— directing Maui Symphony Opera Gala, Lahaina News, February 18, 1987: 10.

MARTIN, JOAN
— joins First Hawaii Title, Lahaina News, June 28, 2001: 8.

MARTIN LAWRENCE GALLERIES [BUSINESS]
— to host party, Lahaina News, August 29, 2002: 20.

MARTIN LUTHER KING JR. DAY
— editorial in support of, Lahaina News, April 20, 1988: 2.
— Jan Dapitan named coordinator of, Lahaina News, December 28, 1988: 3.
— events described, Lahaina News, January 16, 1991: 4.
— peace walk to be held, Lahaina News, January 14, 1993: 3.
— International Peace Poem Project to sponsor poetry contest in honor of, Lahaina News, January 25, 2001: 7.
— statewide poetry contest to be held to commemorate, Lahaina News, January 30, 2003: 2.
— statewide poetry contest to be held to commemorate, Lahaina News, January 30, 2003: 2.
— Lahainaluna High School student Kira Sabini is finalist in Peace Poetry Contest, Lahaina News, May 8, 2003: 2.

MARTIN, MAHINA
— executive director of Hui O Wa'a Kaulua, Lahaina News, March 29, 2001: 1,9.

MARTIN, RON
— to offer course on retail manager's skills, Lahaina News, April 30, 1998: 13.

MARTIN, ULI
— pastry chef joins Kapalua Bay Hotel, Lahaina News, November 19, 1992: 5.

MARTINAGE, MICHAEL
— promoted to transient sales manager at Hyatt Regency Maui, Lahaina News, June 4, 1992: 9.

MARTINEZ, LUPE
— to compete in Moscow at International Peace Marathon, Lahaina News, June 28, 1989: 9.

MARTINEZ, PETER
— Light Bringers offering assistance to Spanish population, Lahaina News, August 21, 2003: 2.

MARTORELLI, ROBERT
— work featured, Lahaina News, August 2, 1989: 17.

MARTY DREAD
— see Dread, Marty

MARTY DREAD AND CULTURE SHOCK [MUSICAL GROUP]
— to perform at Moose McGillycuddy's, Lahaina News, October 31, 1991: 14.
— to perform at Studio 505, Lahaina News, November 28, 1991: 15.
— to perform at Longhi's, Lahaina News, January 30, 1992: 16.
— featured, Lahaina News, February 6, 1992: 16.
— continues to perform at Studio 505, Lahaina News, June 4, 1992: 14.
— to perform at Casanova's, Lahaina News, December 24, 1992: 18.
— continues to perform at Studio 505, Lahaina News, December 31, 1992: 14.
— to perform on The Pride of Maui, Lahaina News, February 11, 1993: 14.
— to perform at James Manness Memorial Dance-A-Thon, Lahaina News, February 18, 1993: 13.
— continues to perform at Studio 505, Lahaina News, July 1, 1993: 11.
— continues to perform at Studio 505, Lahaina News, September 23, 1993: 11.
— to perform at Blue Tropix, Lahaina News, February 3, 1994: 12.

MARTY DREAD AND POSITIVE FORCE [MUSICAL GROUP]
— to perform at Makai Bar Maui Marriott Resort, Lahaina News, May 26, 1994: 11.

MARTY DREAD AND SLY DOG [MUSICAL GROUP]
— to perform at Borders Books, Lahaina News, July 15, 1999: 12.

MARTY DREAD BIRTHDAY BASH
— to be held at Maui Brews, Lahaina News, June 4, 1998: 16.

MARUI/O'NEILL MAUI INVITATIONAL
— Robby Naish wins surfing competition, Lahaina News, April 18, 1984: 6.
— boardsailing tournament to be held, Lahaina News, March 28, 1990: 9.
— windsurfing contest continues, Lahaina News, April 3, 1991: 16.

MARUMOTO, BARBARA [POLITICIAN]
— introduces bill to remove excise tax on residential rentals, Lahaina News, February 21, 1990: 3.

MARVIN, LEE [ACTOR]
— visits Maui, Lahaina Sun, March 22, 1972: 4.

MARY ANNE FITCH REALTY ASSOCIATES HAWAII
— merges with Coldwell Banker Island Properties, Lahaina News, January 20, 2000: 10.

MARZETTI, GIOVANNI
— Scholar/Athlete of the Week, Lahaina News, April 29, 1999: 6.

MARZO, CLAY
— surfer competes in National Scholastic Surfing Association's Summer Spray-Offs, Lahaina News, July 6, 2000: 1,14.
— surfer featured, Lahaina News, July 26, 2001: 12.
— surfer preparing for national surf title, Lahaina News, April 11, 2002: 12.
— surfer to compete in , Lahaina News, July 25, 2002: 14.
— surfer to represent Hawaii at international surfing contest, Lahaina News, April 3, 2003: 12.

MASON, DAVE [MUSICIAN]
— to perform at Casanova's, Lahaina News, December 19, 1990: 12,13.
— to perform at Maui Arts and Cultural Center, Lahaina News, July 15, 1999: 14.
— concert rescheduled, Lahaina News, July 29, 1999: 12.

MASON, GEORGE
— Pacific Business News editor advocates for private sector running public services, Lahaina News, September 29, 1994: 1,2.

MASON, GLENN
— architect makes recommendations for Old Courthouse, Lahaina News, November 7, 1996: 1,20.
— preparing plan to restore Old Lahaina Courthouse, Lahaina News, November 14, 1996: 2.

MASONIC TEMPLE
— to meet, Lahaina News, June 15, 2000: 17.

MASQUE OF BEAUTY AND THE BEST, THE [PLAY]
— Maui Youth Theatre to open, Lahaina News, November 9, 1988: 12.

MASS TRANSIT
— editorial in support of, Lahaina News, November 22, 1989: 24.

MASTER CLASS [PLAY]
— to be performed by Maui OnStage, Lahaina News, January 25, 2001: 16.
— to be performed by Maui OnStage, Lahaina News, February 1, 2001: 20.

MASTERS AT KA'ANAPALI HILLSIDE, THE
— Tom Soeten Realty and Iwado Realty named principal brokers for, Lahaina News, December 22, 1994: 13.
— featured, Lahaina News, December 23, 1999: 12.
— development featured, Lahaina News, August 3, 2000: 12.
— condominium featured, Lahaina News, January 18, 2001: 12.
— real estate development featured, Lahaina News, January 17, 2002: 6.
— development featured, Lahaina News, July 4, 2002: 7.
— development featured, Lahaina News, August 1, 2002: 7.
— featured, Lahaina News, August 29, 2002: 19.
— new listings at, Lahaina News, November 21, 2002: 6.
— featured, Lahaina News, January 2, 2003: 7.
— featured, Lahaina News, March 6, 2003: 7.

MASTERS GALLERY [BUSINESS]
— opens at Ma'alaea Shopping Center, Lahaina News, November 30, 2000: 12.

MASTERS, LESLIE [ARTIST]
— to exhibit at Lahaina Arts Society, Lahaina News, April 10, 2003: 20.

MASUDA, WILLIAM
— lecture on "Living Positively with Buddha", Lahaina News, March 27, 1985: 3.

MASUMOTO, HAROLD
— appointed to task force to consider disinterring ancient Hawaiian remains, Lahaina News, January 4, 1989: 1,16.

MASUMOTO, PAT
— develops manual called "The Hawaiian-Style Belly Laugh", Lahaina News, December 21, 1995: 15.
— speaker to present "The Hawaiian Style Belly Laugh", Lahaina News, August 15, 1996: 14.
— highlighted on "Maui Women Making a Difference", Lahaina News, March 7, 2002: 5.
— to teach "Laughter Aerobics", Lahaina News, November 28, 2002: 17.
— to hold auditions for her play "Mad Cloak", Lahaina News, August 7, 2003: 17.
— play "Mad Cloak" to open , Lahaina News, September 25, 2003: 1,2.

MATAAFA, ANNA
— Maui's Young Miss America represents Maui at Miss Universe Gala, Lahaina News, May 28, 1998: 3.

MATAAFA, GINA BELLA
— wins HMSA's "Name the 5-a-Day Fruits" contest, Lahaina News, December 9, 1999: 11.
— first grader wins "Name the 5 A Day Friends" contest, Lahaina News, March 23, 2000: 1.

MATAAFA, SOPHIE
— resident circulation petition asking for overpass on Honoapi'ilani Highway, Lahaina News, December 29, 1994: 1.
— circulates petition to request Amfac/JMB to plant and irrigate former Pioneer Mill sugar fields , Lahaina News, April 20, 2000: 1,8.
— receives scholarship to meets Erin Brokovich, Lahaina News, July 3, 2003: 9.

MATEO, DANNY [POLITICIAN]
— councilman to be sworn in Friday, Lahaina News, July 18, 2002: 2.
— councilmember to discuss Iao Aquifer, Lahaina News, September 4, 2003: 8.

MATERIAL THINGS [BUSINESS]
— opens, Lahaina News, March 16, 1995: 10.

MATHEOS, CARLOS
— to offer tango classes, Lahaina News, June 17, 1993: 16.

MATHER, LINDA
— named public relations manager for Maui Visitors Bureau, Lahaina News, September 16, 1993: 10.

MATHIAS, ZANE AND BETH
— to take photographs at the Olympics in Barcelona, Lahaina News, July 23, 1992: 16.

MATLOCK, ED
— fundraiser for, Lahaina News, November 9, 1988: 12.

MATSON NAVIGATION COMPANY [BUSINESS]
— expanded services to Big Island and Kaua'i, Lahaina News, July 4, 1991: 4.
— to refund money to businesses due to rate dispute, Lahaina News, April 9, 1992: 12.

MATSUDA, FUJIO
— director in public meeting in Wailuku with State Department of Transportation to discuss needs, Lahaina Sun, December 2, 1970: 1.

MATSUDA, MARK
— joins civil engineering firm Otomo Engineering Inc., Lahaina News, September 5, 2002: 8.

MATSUDE, HECTOR
— director of pesticide monitoring program warns of misuse of pesticides in the State, Lahaina News, February 27, 1985: 2.

MATSUI, BRENT
— featured in Sports Illustrated after pitching one-hitter for Lahaina Cardinals, Lahaina News, July 18, 1991: 1.
— Scholar/Athlete of the Week, Lahaina News, September 12, 1996: 18.

MATSUI, KEIKO [MUSICIAN]
— to perform at Maui Music Festival, Lahaina News, April 22, 1999: 3.
— to perform at Maui Music Festival, Lahaina News, May 13, 1999: 8.
— receives standing ovation at Maui Music Festival, Lahaina News, June 3, 1999: 2.

MATSUI, ZUKE
— reappointed to the planning commission, Lahaina Sun, January 13, 1971: 8.
— Maui Planning Commission chairman criticized, Lahaina Sun, August 1, 1973: 3.

MATSUMOTO, HAROLD
— State planning director favors Launiupoko for site of boat marina, Lahaina News, August 1, 1991: 1.

MATSUMOTO, PAT
— artist to exhibit at Hui No'eau Visual Arts Center, Lahaina News, August 13, 1998: 16.
— playwright to unveil new play "Mad Cloak", Lahaina News, September 18, 2003: 18.

MATSUMOTO, RICHARD
— to manage Seawatch Restaurant, Lahaina News, November 18, 1993: 7.

MATSUMOTO, SUKEICHI
— owner of Chevron Service Station featured, Lahaina Sun, March 29, 1972: 17.

MATSUMOTO, WADE
— scores hole-in-one at Waiehu Golf Course, Lahaina News, October 25, 1989: 11.

MATSUNAGA, SPARK [POLITICIAN]
— assisting with student visit to Washington DC, Lahaina Sun, February 3, 1971: 1.
— discusses current political situation, Lahaina Sun, March 10, 1971: 3.
— recommends that the U.S. recognizes Red China, Lahaina Sun, March 17, 1971: 3.
— asks for federal study of Philippine guerrillas, Lahaina Sun, March 17, 1971: 5.
— tribute to be held on Memorial Day, Lahaina News, May 23, 1990: 1.

MATSUOKA, RURIKO
— awarded manager of the quarter by Westin Maui, Lahaina News, December 1, 1994: 13.

MATT YEE IN MAKE THE YULETIDE GAY [PLAY]
— to be presented by Maui AIDS Foundation, Lahaina News, December 18, 1997: 18.

MATTHEWS, AMY "KITTY"
— joins Pacific Radio Group, Lahaina News, December 20, 2001: 9.

MATTHEWS, WALTER
— inspires author to reflect on meaning of life, Lahaina Sun, August 15, 1973: 5.

MATTILA, DAVID
— director of whale rescue for the Center of Coastal Studies to talk on "Whale Rescue—The Freeing of Entangled Whales", Lahaina News, February 7, 2002: 17.

MATTILA, KRISTINE
— new director of sales at Royal Lahaina Resort, Lahaina News, December 4, 1985: 3.

MATTOS, JOANN
— appointed branch manager of Maui office of Home Financial Services, Inc., Lahaina News, March 6, 1991: 9.

MAU, HOWARD
— becomes temporary district engineer of the highway division of the state's Department of Transportation, Lahaina News, October 9, 1985: 1,20.

MAUGA, RUSS [MUSICIAN]
— to perform at A Taste of Lahaina, Lahaina News, September 11, 1997: 13.

MAUI
— stories about, Lahaina News, March 28, 1984: 9,10,11.

MAUI - THE DEMIGOD [PLAY]
— to be performed at Maui Community College, Lahaina News, June 11, 1992: 21.

MAUI : WHEN DOES THE MADNESS END? [VIDEO]
— to be shown on television, Lahaina News, September 26, 1990: 7.

MAUI, A MURDER MYSTERY [FILM]
— extras wanted, Lahaina News, October 4, 1989: 1.

MAUI, A PARADISE GUIDE [BOOK]
— 3rd edition published by Paradise Publications, Lahaina News, April 27, 1988: 3.

MAUI A.J.A. VETERANS
— see A.J.A. Veterans Club

MAUI AADVANTAGE PASSPORT
— successful, Lahaina News, December 15, 1994: 15.

MAUI ACADEMY OF PERFORMING ARTS, THE
— presenting "Ho'olako: Hawaiian Legends", Lahaina News, October 7, 1987: 3.
— selling season tickets, Lahaina News, June 13, 1990: 18.
— "The Hobbit" to be performed at, Lahaina News, July 4, 1990: 15.
— new name for Maui Youth Theatre, Lahaina News, July 4, 1990: 16.
— to perform "Pieces VIII", Lahaina News, July 18, 1990: 11.
— performing "Pieces VII - Beyond the Best of Broadway", Lahaina News, July 25, 1990: 11.
— to present "Pieces VIII - Beyond the Best of Broadway", Lahaina News, August 1, 1990: 11.
— names Stephanie Sheppard as director of development, Lahaina News, August 15, 1990: 7.
— registration has started for Fall, Lahaina News, September 12, 1990: 8.
— to hold fundraiser at Bailey House Museum, Lahaina News, September 12, 1990: 8,9.
— sponsoring Garden Party fundraiser, Lahaina News, September 19, 1990: 3,5.
— hosting Garden Party at Bailey House Museum, Lahaina News, September 26, 1990: 5.
— to perform "Wiley and the Hairy Man", Lahaina News, October 10, 1990: 14.
— raises more than $20,000 at Garden Party, Lahaina News, October 10, 1990: 3.
— facing financial issues, Lahaina News, November 14, 1990: 1.
— to present "Scrooge", Lahaina News, November 21, 1990: 13.
— selling poster by Cynthia Conrad as fundraiser, Lahaina News, November 21, 1990: 13.
— to hold winter break classes, Lahaina News, December 19, 1990: 6.
— to hold classes during winter break, Lahaina News, December 26, 1990: 5.
— presenting "Hulihia Hawaii", Lahaina News, January 2, 1991: 8.
— Keali'i Reichel to perform, Lahaina News, January 9, 1991: 8.
— to perform "The Apple Tree", Lahaina News, April 24, 1991: 11.
— season tickets on sale, Lahaina News, May 15, 1991: 10.
— season tickets on sale, Lahaina News, May 23, 1991: 12.
— to perform "Who's Afraid of Virginia Woolf", Lahaina News, June 6, 1991: 15.
— to offer acting session for children, Lahaina News, June 6, 1991: 17.
— offering Summer Theatre Arts series, Lahaina News, July 11, 1991: 14.
— to perform "Pieces", a concert of dances, Lahaina News, August 1, 1991: 18.
— Joe and Barbara Tanaka to host fashion show fundraiser for, Lahaina News, August 1, 1991: 3.
— to perform "Pieces", a concert of dances, Lahaina News, August 8, 1991: 14.
— scholarships available from, Lahaina News, August 8, 1991: 4.
— registration begins for Summer Session III classes, Lahaina News, August 15, 1991: 3.
— to hold auditions for "The Death and Life of Sherlock Holmes", Lahaina News, August 29, 1991: 3.
— to perform "Robin Goodfellow", Lahaina News, September 19, 1991: 16,22.
— hosts 3rd Annual Garden Party, Lahaina News, September 19, 1991: 8.
— renting Halloween costumes, Lahaina News, October 17, 1991: 6.
— to stage "Kiss Me Kate" and "The Boys Next Door", Lahaina News, October 24, 1991: 4.
— to perform "Aladdin", Lahaina News, November 28, 1991: 18.
— to perform "The Boys Next Door", Lahaina News, January 9, 1992: 14.

— seeking donations for community patron drive, Lahaina News, January 30, 1992: 5.
— to hold auditions for "Ozma of Oz", Lahaina News, March 5, 1992: 5.
— to hold auditions for mystery production, Lahaina News, April 2, 1992: 6.
— receives grant from Robert E. Black Memorial, Lahaina News, April 23, 1992: 8.
— to perform "The Maui Murders" , Lahaina News, May 28, 1992: 18.
— to hold auditions for Pieces X dance concert, Lahaina News, June 18, 1992: 4.
— "Pieces X" continues, Lahaina News, August 6, 1992: 13.
— to offer singing lessons, Lahaina News, August 20, 1992: 4.
— to offer singing lessons, Lahaina News, September 10, 1992: 4.
— to hold dance workshop, Lahaina News, September 24, 1992: 6.
— to perform "The Grapes of Wrath", Lahaina News, October 15, 1992: 18.
— to offer drama classes, Lahaina News, December 31, 1992: 5.
— to perform "The Nerd", Lahaina News, January 14, 1993: 12.
— to hold workshop, Lahaina News, March 11, 1993: 16.
— to hold acting workshops, Lahaina News, March 25, 1993: 16.
— to hold tribute to Michael and Linda Takita, Lahaina News, March 25, 1993: 16.
— to hold "Pieces XI , Lahaina News, June 24, 1993: 15.
— to perform "Pieces XI", Lahaina News, August 19, 1993: 14.
— to hold Garden Party, Lahaina News, September 2, 1993: 12.
— to hold auditions for youth performing troupe, Lahaina News, October 14, 1993: 15.
— renting costumes, Lahaina News, October 14, 1993: 16.
— to perform "Narnia", Lahaina News, December 2, 1993: 15.
— offering theatre classes, Lahaina News, December 30, 1993: 11,12.
— to perform "The Arkansaw Bear", Lahaina News, February 24, 1994: 12.
— to perform "In Search of Animals" for young children, Lahaina News, April 28, 1994: 15.
— receives grant from Alexander and Baldwin Foundation, Lahaina News, June 23, 1994: 12.
— to hold auditions for "Pieces XII", Lahaina News, July 7, 1994: 15.
— "Sum'r Playing" to be performed, Lahaina News, July 28, 1994: 13.
— offering creative drama class taught by Molli Fleming, Lahaina News, October 13, 1994: 20.
— offering Theatre in the Schools touring plays, receives grant from McInerny Foundation, Lahaina News, November 3, 1994: 27, 28.
— announces States of Youth presentations, Lahaina News, November 3, 1994: 27,28.
— to offer gift wrapping as fundraiser, Lahaina News, December 15, 1994: 19.
— spring classes begin, Lahaina News, January 5, 1995: 12.
— to receives funds from benefit hair styling event, Lahaina News, February 9, 1995: 10.
— to hold theater workshops, Lahaina News, March 9, 1995: 12.
— producing new theatre experience, Lahaina News, April 13, 1995: 16.
— to offer courses for youth, Lahaina News, August 31, 1995: 12.
— to rent Halloween costumes, Lahaina News, October 12, 1995: 15.
— to offer classes, Lahaina News, December 28, 1995: 8.
— to host "Tintypes" celebration of American music, Lahaina News, March 14, 1996: 12,13.
— to perform "Three Fairy Tales", Lahaina News, April 11, 1996: 13.
— planning The Garden Party, Lahaina News, August 29, 1996: 10.
— to hold spring dance and drama classes, Lahaina News, January 2, 1997: 11.
— starting spring dance and drama classes, Lahaina News, January 9, 1997: 10.
— to host drama workshops, Lahaina News, March 20, 1997: 16.
— to hold Spring Recital '97, Lahaina News, May 22, 1997: 16.

— students to present "Spring Dance Extravaganza", Lahaina News, May 14, 1998: 17.
— to hold youth theater dancing programs, Lahaina News, June 4, 1998: 9.
— to offer youth theater classes, Lahaina News, September 10, 1998: 21.
— Don Quixote to be performed by, Lahaina News, May 25, 2000: 18.
— to present "Dance Extravaganza Spring 2001", Lahaina News, May 24, 2001: 20.
— to hold "Annie Jr." musical, Lahaina News, August 2, 2001: 16.
— to hold Garden Party, Lahaina News, September 13, 2001: 16.
— to hold Spring Dance Extravaganza, Lahaina News, May 16, 2002: 16.
— to hold Pieces XX at Maui Arts and Cultural Center, Lahaina News, August 1, 2002: 20.
— to begin fall schedule, Lahaina News, August 22, 2002: 21.
— to hold Garden Party, Lahaina News, September 12, 2002: 20,21.
— to perform "Phantom", Lahaina News, May 8, 2003: 16.
— to present "Pieces XXI: Musicals, Movies and More", Lahaina News, July 31, 2003: 17.
— to hold Garden Party, Lahaina News, August 21, 2003: 2.

MAUI ACADEMY OF TRAVEL AND TOURISM
— see Academy of Travel and Tourism

MAUI ACTION [MAGAZINE]
— published by Activity Owners Association, Lahaina News, January 31, 1990: 5.

MAUI ACTIVITIES MALL
— internet site available, Lahaina News, April 30, 1998: 13.

MAUI ADULT DAY CARE CENTER
— may expand in Lahaina, Lahaina News, February 4, 1987: 3.
— announces satellite facility, Lahaina News, June 3, 1987: 3.
— opens in West Maui, Lahaina News, July 13, 1988: 2.
— grand opening to be held, Lahaina News, August 17, 1988: 3.
— has room, Lahaina News, April 5, 1989: 3.
— described, Lahaina News, April 26, 1989: 13.
— looking for volunteers, Lahaina News, June 14, 1989: 3.
— Mayor Tavares visits, Lahaina News, December 27, 1989: 11.
— to be dedicated, Lahaina News, March 11, 1999: 11.
— named as beneficiary of Mercedes Championships, Lahaina News, May 29, 2003: 8.

MAUI ADULT SCHOOL
— offering courses in conversational Japanese, Lahaina Sun, February 16, 1972: 17.

MAUI ADVENTIST SCHOOL
— to hold open house, Lahaina News, April 23, 1998: 16.
— to hold open house, Lahaina News, May 14, 1998: 16.

MAUI ADVISORY COMMITTEE
— see Governor's Maui Advisory Committee

MAUI AFFORDABLE HOUSING ALLIANCE
— to offer workshop on self-help housing, Lahaina News, June 14, 1989: 3.
— to hold public meeting, Lahaina News, December 13, 1989: 1.

MAUI AIDS FOUNDATION
— formed, Lahaina News, April 23, 1986: 1,16.
— to hold benefit, Lahaina News, July 8, 1987: 3.
— to hold fundraiser at Hamburger Mary's, Lahaina News, July 22, 1987: 10.
— board to meet, Lahaina News, September 9, 1987: 3.
— to offer trainings, Lahaina News, March 16, 1988: 14.
— to hold penny drive, Lahaina News, April 20, 1988: 6.
— sponsoring support group, Lahaina News, April 27, 1988: 6.
— sponsoring support groups, Lahaina News, June 1, 1988: 28.
— support groups meeting, Lahaina News, June 8, 1988: 13.

— Hawaiian entertainers to perform in support of, Lahaina News, July 13, 1988: 6.

— to host dance marathon benefit, Lahaina News, August 10, 1988: 3,16.

— sponsoring support groups, Lahaina News, September 7, 1988: 14.

— support group to meet, Lahaina News, September 28, 1988: 18.

— support groups sponsored at Hospice Maui, Lahaina News, October 5, 1988: 3,20.

— opens office and drop-in center, Lahaina News, November 9, 1988: 12.

— seeking volunteers to provide support, Lahaina News, January 25, 1989: 5.

— offering training sessions; hosting Upcountry Auction, Lahaina News, February 15, 1989: 5.

— seeking part-time director, Lahaina News, March 15, 1989: 14.

— to hold "Common Cents" fundraiser, Lahaina News, April 5, 1989: 5,6.

— organizing AIDS '89 program, Lahaina News, May 3, 1989: 4.

— planning dance marathon, Lahaina News, July 26, 1989: 3.

— organizing dance marathon fundraiser, Lahaina News, September 27, 1989: 2.

— to hold fundraiser, Lahaina News, October 4, 1989: 3.

— benefit dance marathon to be held, Lahaina News, October 11, 1989: 3.

— seeking ticket donations to provide to those infected with HIV, Lahaina News, July 25, 1990: 6.

— conducting volunteer training, Lahaina News, August 22, 1990: 4.

— to train volunteers, Lahaina News, August 29, 1990: 4.

— sponsoring workshop "Healing Our Lives", Lahaina News, September 5, 1990: 4.

— seeking office furniture and office equipment, Lahaina News, September 26, 1990: 7.

— seeking office furniture and office equipment, Lahaina News, October 3, 1990: 3.

— case manager and volunteer coordinator added to staff, Lahaina News, December 5, 1990: 5.

— to hold premier of "Longtime Companion" as fundraiser, Lahaina News, December 26, 1990: 11.

— opens new office, Lahaina News, January 9, 1991: 3.

— to hold orientation for volunteers, Lahaina News, January 16, 1991: 4.

— to hold James Manness Memorial Dance Marathon, Lahaina News, February 6, 1991: 8.

— to hold dance marathon, Lahaina News, February 13, 1991: 9.

— to hold public informational meeting, Lahaina News, March 13, 1991: 5.

— to train volunteers, Lahaina News, April 17, 1991: 7.

— sponsoring hotline for teens, Lahaina News, May 1, 1991: 3.

— sponsoring special AIDS Hotline for teens, Lahaina News, May 8, 1991: 3.

— sponsoring "Girl's Night Out", Lahaina News, June 13, 1991: 6.

— to hold fashion show fundraiser, Lahaina News, November 14, 1991: 15.

— fundraiser held at Club D-Lite, Lahaina News, November 21, 1991: 14,15.

— to hold James Manness Memorial Dance-a-thon, Lahaina News, January 23, 1992: 5.

— to hold dance-a-thon fundraiser, Lahaina News, January 30, 1992: 4.

— to hold James Manness Memorial Dance-a-thon, Lahaina News, February 6, 1992: 19.

— seeking volunteer beauty experts, Lahaina News, August 13, 1992: 9.

— seeking volunteer beauty experts, Lahaina News, August 20, 1992: 15.

— to hold benefit "Look Great, Feel Great", Lahaina News, August 20, 1992: 20.

— "Look Good, Feel Great" fundraiser a success, Lahaina News, September 3, 1992: 13.

— to hold James Manness Memorial Dance-A-Thon, Lahaina News, February 11, 1993: 7.

— to host "Look Good, Feel Great" fundraiser, Lahaina News, August 12, 1993: 6.

— to hold fundraiser "Look Good, Feel Great", Lahaina News, September 16, 1993: 8.

— to hold volunteer training, Lahaina News, October 21, 1993: 3,4.

— to host Dance-A-Thon fundraiser, Lahaina News, March 10, 1994: 4.

— offering volunteer training, Lahaina News, April 7, 1994: 4.

— seeking volunteers for "Common Cents Penny Drive", Lahaina News, May 26, 1994: 5.

— Kathi Murakami crowned as "Penny Queen", Lahaina News, July 7, 1994: 4.

— Look Good, Feel Great fundraiser held, Lahaina News, August 11, 1994: 4.

— "Look Good, Feel Great" to be held, Lahaina News, August 18, 1994: 16.

— to offer HIV/AIDS Educator training with American Red Cross, Lahaina News, September 1, 1994: 7.

— to hold James Manness Memorial Dance-a-thon on theme of "March Forth!", Lahaina News, March 2, 1995: 12.

— to speak to West Maui Youth Center, Lahaina News, May 11, 1995: 2.

— to hold D.E. Eastman Look Good, Feel Great fundraiser, Lahaina News, August 17, 1995: 6.

— to offer volunteer training program, Lahaina News, October 12, 1995: 6.

— to hold James Manness Memorial Dance-A-Thon, Lahaina News, March 14, 1996: 13.

— to hold "D's Dazzling Fantasy Show and Dance" fundraiser, Lahaina News, June 20, 1996: 12.

— to begin free volunteer training course, Lahaina News, September 26, 1996: 15.

— to hold meeting on Maui AIDS-Related Services (MARS), Lahaina News, November 14, 1996: 15.

— to host James Manness Memorial Dance-A-Thon, Lahaina News, February 27, 1997: 10.

— to hold D.E. Eastman Look Good, Feel Great Family Day, Lahaina News, August 14, 1997: 17.

— offering volunteer training, Lahaina News, September 25, 1997: 17.

— seeking volunteers, Lahaina News, December 11, 1997: 11.

— presents "Matt Yee in Make the Yuletide Gay", Lahaina News, December 18, 1997: 18.

— receives grant from James and Abigail Campbell Foundation, Lahaina News, January 15, 1998: 5.

— to hold James Manness Memorial "Dance Party Xtreme", Lahaina News, March 19, 1998: 2.

— to host James Manness Memorial "Dance Party Xtreme", Lahaina News, March 26, 1998: 2.

— to hold James Manness Memorial "Dance Party Xtreme", Lahaina News, April 2, 1998: 2.

— to host Paradise Bike Ride, Lahaina News, May 7, 1998: 21.

— seeking volunteers, Lahaina News, May 21, 1998: 9.

— offering free training program, Lahaina News, June 4, 1998: 16.

— Eastman, D.E. "Look Good, Feel Great" event to benefit , Lahaina News, August 20, 1998: 17.

— seeking volunteers, Lahaina News, October 29, 1998: 15.

— to hold Book Fair at Walden Books, Lahaina News, November 5, 1998: 21.

— moves main office, Lahaina News, November 5, 1998: 8.

— to hold Book Fair, Lahaina News, December 3, 1998: 21.

— to hold James Manness Memorial Dance Party, Lahaina News, February 4, 1999: 9.

— to hold Foundation Dance Party, Lahaina News, March 11, 1999: 13.

— James Manness Memorial Dance Party to be held, Lahaina News, March 18, 1999: 8.

— to hold James Manness Memorial "Dance Party Xtreme", Lahaina News, May 13, 1999: 15.

— appoints two new staff, Lahaina News, May 13, 1999: 15.

— to hold "Sex, Dating and Relationships" discussion group, Lahaina News, May 13, 1999: 17.

— to hold James Manness Memorial "Dance Party Xtreme", Lahaina News, May 20, 1999: 16.

— to hold "Sex, Dating and Relationships" discussion group, Lahaina News, June 3, 1999: 2.

— to hold Dance Riot III, Lahaina News, July 29, 1999: 12.

— to hold "D.E. Eastman Look Good, Feel Great" benefit, Lahaina News, August 12, 1999: 3.

— planning "Maui Pride 2000", Lahaina News, August 19, 1999: 16.

— to hold Halloween costume party, Lahaina News, October 28, 1999: 16.

— continues to offer "Sex, Dating and Relationships" meeting, Lahaina News, December 2, 1999: 16.

— to hold James Manness Memorial "Dance Party Xtreme" to be held, Lahaina News, February 24, 2000: 3.

— to hold James Manness Memorial "Dance Party Xtreme" to be held, Lahaina News, March 30, 2000: 12.

— to hold Maui HIV Conference, Lahaina News, March 30, 2000: 13.

— to hold Maui HIV Conference, Lahaina News, April 6, 2000: 16.

— offering "Gender Minorities Training", Lahaina News, May 11, 2000: 20.

— to hold D.E. Eastman—Look Good, Feel Great, Lahaina News, August 24, 2000: 20.

— to hold "Gay and Bisexual Men's Kahului Coffee Klutch", Lahaina News, November 30, 2000: 17.

— planning "2001 Dance Party Xtreme", Lahaina News, November 30, 2000: 17.

— coordinating Bridges Youth Group meeting, Lahaina News, December 7, 2000: 25.

— to offer "Gay and Bisexual Men's Monthly Hike", Lahaina News, January 4, 2001: 16.

— coordinating events, Lahaina News, February 1, 2001: 20.

— continues to offer "Gay and Bisexual Men's Monthly Hike", Lahaina News, March 1, 2001: 20.

— to present "Understanding HIV/AIDS in the Hawaiian Community", Lahaina News, March 8, 2001: 17.

— to host "Understanding HIV/AIDS in the Hawaiian Community", Lahaina News, March 15, 2001: 20.

— to hold James Manness Memorial Dance Odyssey fundraiser, Lahaina News, April 12, 2001: 17.

— "The Maui HIV Conference—Enhancing Quality of Life for Persons with HIV AIDS" to be held, Lahaina News, April 12, 2001: 21.

— to hold James Manness Memorial Dance Odyssey fundraiser, Lahaina News, April 19, 2001: 16.

— coordinating events, Lahaina News, May 3, 2001: 20.

— to hold hike and coffee events, Lahaina News, May 31, 2001: 16.

— to hold "Dance Riot—Maui Gay Pride 2001", Lahaina News, June 21, 2001: 16.

— offering "Gay and Bisexual Men's Kick Boxing Class", Lahaina News, July 12, 2001: 16.

— continues to organize events, Lahaina News, September 20, 2001: 16.

— to hold volunteer training, Lahaina News, October 11, 2001: 16.

— to hold "La'i Wahine" workshop for transgender community, Lahaina News, November 1, 2001: 16.

— to coordinate events, Lahaina News, November 29, 2001: 17.

— to hold "A Gay and Bisexual Men's Coffee Klutch", Lahaina News, November 29, 2001: 17.

— seeking volunteers for James Manness Memorial "United We Dance" benefit, Lahaina News, January 3, 2002: 2.

— to hold James Manness Memorial "United We Dance" benefit, Lahaina News, January 10, 2002: 16.

— to hold James Manness Memorial benefit, Lahaina News, April 11, 2002: 2.

— to hold James Manness Memorial benefit dance party, Lahaina News, April 25, 2002: 16.

— to hold "The Art of Living—Everything you need to create your own paradise", Lahaina News, June 20, 2002: 16.

— to hold Halloween Dance, Lahaina News, October 24, 2002: 21.

— offering HIV counseling and testing, Lahaina News, March 6, 2003: 17.

— hosting weekly meetings with Asian and Pacific Islanders Support Network, Lahaina News, March 6, 2003: 17.

— Asian and Pacific Islander Support Network to hold weekly meetings, Lahaina News, March 20, 2003: 17.

— members learn hula, Lahaina News, April 3, 2003: 17.

— offering HIV counseling and testing, Lahaina News, May 22, 2003: 17.

— to hold testing day in conjunction with National HIV Testing Day, Lahaina News, June 19, 2003: 9.

— to hold "Art-Cetera" silent auction fundraiser, Lahaina News, July 31, 2003: 5.

— to hold "Art-Cetera" silent auction fundraiser, Lahaina News, August 7, 2003: 16.

MAUI AIDS RELATED SERVICES (MARS)
— to hold meeting, Lahaina News, July 11, 1996: 13.

MAUI AIR CONDITIONING COMPANY [BUSINESS]
— new name of Lahaina Refrigeration & Services, Inc., Lahaina News, December 26, 1990: 7.

MAUI AIR, INC. [BUSINESS]
— offering cheap tickets to Honolulu, Lahaina Sun, July 14, 1971: 1.

— sold to Bob Nielson, owner of Island Air Transfer, Lahaina Sun, July 19, 1972: 10.

MAUI ALGAE BLOOM TASK FORCE
— concerned with additional planned sewage injection wells, Lahaina News, March 26, 1992: 1,4.

MAUI ALZHEIMER'S SUPPORT GROUP
— hosting talk by Terry Malinowski, Lahaina News, June 8, 1988: 14.

— to host speech by Tom Bodden, Lahaina News, April 9, 1992: 8.

MAUI AMENITIES [BUSINESS]
— featured, Lahaina News, January 4, 1996: 13.

MAUI AND LANA'I [BOOK]
— published by Dona Early, Lahaina News, April 13, 1995: 13.

MAUI ANIMAL ALOHA CENTER
— seeking volunteers, Lahaina News, November 5, 1992: 4.

MAUI ANIMAL SHELTER AND ADOPTION CENTER
— to host Dog Day Afternoon, Lahaina News, April 23, 1992: 8.

MAUI APPLE USERS SOCIETY
— see computers

MAUI AQUATICS
— to offer swimming classes, Lahaina News, March 1, 2001: 15.

— Lahaina Aquatic Center offering swimming lessons, Lahaina News, May 10, 2001: 15.

— offering swimming lessons, Lahaina News, January 10, 2002: 13.

— to offer swimming lessons, Lahaina News, January 17, 2002: 13.

— continues to offer swimming lessons, Lahaina News, February 28, 2002: 13.

— to offer year-round swimming lessons, Lahaina News, October 3, 2002: 13.

— offering swimming lessons, Lahaina News, October 10, 2002: 13.

— offering swimming lessons, Lahaina News, October 17, 2002: 11.

— continues to offer swimming programs, Lahaina News, October 31, 2002: 10.

— offering swimming programs, Lahaina News, December 19, 2002: 11.

— continues to hold swimming lessons, Lahaina News, January 23, 2003: 13.

— continues to offer swimming lessons, Lahaina News, February 13, 2003: 13.

— continues to offer swimming lessons, Lahaina News, February 20, 2003: 12.

— continues to offer swimming lessons, Lahaina News, February 27, 2003: 13.

— continues to offer swimming lessons, Lahaina News, March 20, 2003: 12.

— continues to offer swimming lessons, Lahaina News, March 27, 2003: 13.

— offering swimming lessons with Maui County, Lahaina News, April 3, 2003: 12.

— to hold swimming lessons, Lahaina News, April 24, 2003: 11.

— continues to offer swimming lessons, Lahaina News, May 8, 2003: 12.

— continues to offer swimming lessons, Lahaina News, May 22, 2003: 13.

— continues to hold swimming lessons, Lahaina News, June 19, 2003: 12.

— continues to offer swimming programs, Lahaina News, July 17, 2003: 12.

— continues to offer swimming programs, Lahaina News, July 31, 2003: 13.

— continues to offer swimming programs, Lahaina News, September 18, 2003: 13.

— offering swimming lessons, Lahaina News, September 25, 2003: 13.

— offering swimming lessons, Lahaina News, October 2, 2003: 12.

MAUI ART AND CREATIVE PEOPLE [BOOK]
— to be presented, Lahaina News, July 9, 1986: 3.

MAUI ARTS AND CULTURAL CENTER
— see Maui Community Arts and Cultural Center

MAUI ARTS AND MUSIC ASSOCIATION (MAMA)
— accepts Steve Okerlund for career development, Lahaina News, May 14, 1992: 17.

— to begin first local talent showcase, Lahaina News, June 25, 1992: 19.

— seeking funding from Maui County Council seeking funding from Maui County Council, Lahaina News, February 11, 1993: 4.

— accepting tapes from musical performers, Lahaina News, July 28, 1994: 15.

MAUI ARTS SOCIETY
— to feature photographs by Randy Miller, Theresa Young and Deanna Benatovich, Lahaina News, June 6, 2002: 17.

MAUI ASSOCIATION ALLIED TRADE SHOW
— trade booths available, Lahaina News, September 5, 1996: 22.

MAUI ASSOCIATION FOR FAMILY AND COMMUNITY EDUCATION
— seeking exhibitors for Maui County Fair Homemakers' Exhibits, Lahaina News, August 18, 1994: 5.

— to host Maui County Fair Homemakers' Section Exhibits, Lahaina News, August 8, 1996: 18.

— organizing Homemaker Section Exhibits for Maui County Fair, Lahaina News, August 20, 1998: 8.

— seeking residents to participate in Maui County Fair Homemakers exhibits, Lahaina News, September 14, 2000: 19.

MAUI ASSOCIATION OF CONDOMINIUM OWNERS (MACO)
— activities described, Lahaina News, September 1, 1980: 13.

— names William Wilson as vice-president, Lahaina News, July 1, 1981: 8.

MAUI ASSOCIATION OF RETARDED CITIZENS (MARC)
— fundraiser set at Hyatt Regency Hotel, Lahaina News, January 18, 1984: 5.

— proposed group home fails due to land use laws, Lahaina News, May 16, 1984: 5.

— Lahaina Day Activities Center Program described, Lahaina News, October 17, 1984: 7,8.

— open Hale Lahaina residential house, Lahaina News, November 20, 1985: 3.

— to hold fundraiser titled "Sweet Dreams—A Delectable Dessert Experience", Lahaina News, May 21, 1986: 3.

— now called ARC of Maui, Lahaina News, February 22, 2001: 2.

MAUI AUTHORS GUILD
— to hold organizational meeting at Kahului Library, Lahaina News, February 20, 1985: 3.

— to meet, Lahaina News, March 6, 1985: 3.

— to discuss how to prepare material for magazine submissions, Lahaina News, June 5, 1985: 9.

— demonstrate "teacherless writing class", Lahaina News, July 31, 1985: 7.

— to hold workshop on "The Business of Writing", Lahaina News, September 25, 1985: 3.

— Kaui Goring to speak, Lahaina News, October 30, 1985: 3.

— Jane Wilkins Pultz of Press Pacifica to speak to, Lahaina News, January 1, 1986: 3.

— award Margo Berdeshevsky and Niles Szwed first place in writing contest, Lahaina News, May 14, 1986: 3.

— Foster Hull featured speaker for, Lahaina News, December 3, 1986: 12.

— to meet, Lahaina News, December 31, 1986: 3.

— to host talks by Kate Wilhelm and Damon Knight, Lahaina News, September 9, 1987: 3.

— Maggie Morgan Doran wins writing contest, Lahaina News, June 22, 1988: 10.

— see also Maui Writers Guild

MAUI AVIATORS LLC [BUSINESS]
— expands its flight line, Lahaina News, August 17, 2000: 14.

MAUI BALLET AND DANCE SCHOOL
— to hold open auditions, Lahaina News, March 24, 1994: 16.

— to hold summer dance activity camp, Lahaina News, March 31, 1994: 16.

— planning summer dance activity, Lahaina News, July 21, 1994: 12.

— to offer summer program, Lahaina News, July 28, 1994: 14.

MAUI BASH 2001
— to be held at Maui Arts and Cultural, Lahaina News, August 23, 2001: 17.

MAUI BEACH AND TENNIS CLUB
— opens, Lahaina News, September 27, 1989: 4.

MAUI BEACH HOTEL
— to host breakfasts organized by Power Women of Maui, Lahaina News, July 8, 1987: 3.

— to host New Year's celebration by Japanese Cultural Society, Lahaina News, January 14, 1993: 15.

— continues to offer "Open Mike Singing", Lahaina News, December 24, 1998: 12.

MAUI BEAR HUGS
— presents teddy bears to Maui Fire Department, Lahaina News, May 24, 2001: 10.

MAUI BEER CO. [BUSINESS]
— to present Black Uhuru at Maui Tropical Plantation, Lahaina News, April 14, 1994: 12.
— Whale Ale selected as People's Choice at The Great Hawaiian Beer Festival, Lahaina News, August 4, 1994: 9.

MAUI BELL [BUSINESS]
— nightclub reviewed, Lahaina News, March 5, 1986: 12.

MAUI BICYCLE CLUB
— prepared bike path plan, Lahaina Sun, February 7, 1973: 12.

MAUI BIG BOOK [BUSINESS]
— hires additional staff, Lahaina News, December 13, 2001: 8.

MAUI BLUES BAND [MUSICAL GROUP]
— to perform at Taco Jo's Cantina, Lahaina News, October 7, 1993: 12.

MAUI BOARD OF REALTORS
— hold golf tournament in honor of Ralph Yagi, Lahaina News, October 5, 1988: 3.
— to hold informational meeting on projects planned for upcoming year, Lahaina News, March 14, 1990: 5,6.
— to help homeless, Lahaina News, April 17, 1991: 3.
— to publish Real Estate Guide, accepting advertisements, Lahaina News, August 8, 1991: 7.
— offers suggestions to solve affordable homes shortage, Lahaina News, December 5, 1991: 14,32.
— awards scholarship to Jennifer Kawaguchi, Lahaina News, June 22, 1995: 4.
— offering scholarships, Lahaina News, January 25, 1996: 4.
— building new facility at Maui Business Park, Lahaina News, May 25, 2000: 11.
— announces Graduate Realtors Institute (GRI) graduating class, Lahaina News, December 7, 2000: 21.
— completes construction of office, Lahaina News, February 22, 2001: 8.
— to host Presidential Scholarship Golf Tournament, Lahaina News, March 29, 2001: 13.
— to hold Presidential Scholarship Golf Tournament, Lahaina News, April 5, 2001: 14.
— to hold Presidential Scholarship Golf Tournament, Lahaina News, April 12, 2001: 14.
— to hold Presidential Scholarship Golf Tournament, Lahaina News, April 19, 2001: 13.
— awards scholarships, Lahaina News, May 31, 2001: 7.
— president Laurie Smith Lowson discusses market, Lahaina News, October 11, 2001: 6.
— announces new officers and directors, Lahaina News, October 25, 2001: 8.
— changes name to Realtors Association of Maui, Lahaina News, August 8, 2002: 8.

MAUI BOARD OF WATER SUPPLY
— see Water Supply, Board of

MAUI BOAT AND YACHT CLUB
— to hold race, Lahaina News, August 10, 1995: 7.

MAUI BOOKING AND TRAVEL SERVICES [BUSINESS]
— featured, Lahaina News, December 28, 1983: 16.

MAUI BRASS ENSEMBLE [MUSICAL GROUP]
— to perform, Lahaina News, January 13, 1994: 8.
— joins Keawala'I Congregational Church choir, Lahaina News, July 19, 2001: 16.

MAUI BREWS [RESTAURANT]
— to host Marty Dred Birthday Bash, Lahaina News, June 4, 1998: 16.
— hosting benefit concert for arts scholarships in memory of Eric Mac-Cammond, Lahaina News, August 5, 1999: 14.
— to host "World Dance Day", Lahaina News, December 9, 1999: 20.

— Singles in Paradise hosting mixer at, Lahaina News, February 3, 2000: 12.
— featured, Lahaina News, November 2, 2000: 6,7.

MAUI BROCHURE [BUSINESS]
— purchased by Maui Circulation, Lahaina News, June 27, 1991: 9.

MAUI BROTHERS VOLLEYBALL CLUB
— to host annual tournament, Lahaina News, August 18, 1994: 7.

MAUI BROWN SISTERS [MUSICAL GROUP]
— to perform, Lahaina News, February 8, 1996: 14.

MAUI BUDDHIST COUNCIL
— sponsoring O-Bon festival, Lahaina News, July 4, 1991: 3.

MAUI BUNS [BUSINESS]
— opens at the Wharf, Lahaina News, December 23, 1987: 3.

MAUI BUSINESS AND PROFESSIONAL WOMEN
— see Business and Professional Women's Clubs of Maui

MAUI BUSINESS AND TECHNOLOGY CENTER
— Pali Tech attracted by super-computer at, Lahaina News, August 20, 1992: 12.

MAUI BUSINESS COUNCIL
— pro-business political action group formed, Lahaina News, April 27, 1988: 1.

MAUI BUSINESS DIRECTORY
— to be published, Lahaina News, September 17, 1992: 11.

MAUI BUSINESS PARK
— Maui Board of Realtors building new facility at, Lahaina News, May 25, 2000: 11.

MAUI BUSINESS PROFESSIONAL WOMEN'S CLUB
— to hold Scholarship Fashion Show and Auction, Lahaina News, November 9, 2000: 18.

MAUI CACTUS JACK
— basketball team to play University of Alaska basketball team in February, Lahaina Sun, January 20, 1971: 7.
— report on basketball game against Jolly Roger Pirates, Lahaina Sun, January 20, 1971: 7.

MAUI CALLS
— celebration held at Maui Arts and Cultural Center, Lahaina News, August 15, 1996: 16.
— celebration held at Maui Arts and Cultural Center, Lahaina News, August 22, 1996: 12.
— wine tasting event to be held, Lahaina News, August 6, 1998: 10.
— to be held at Maui Arts and Cultural Center, Lahaina News, August 17, 2000: 16.

MAUI CAMERA CLUB
— to meet, Lahaina News, August 1, 2002: 18.
— to meet, Lahaina News, August 8, 2002: 17.

MAUI CANCER INSTITUTE ALLIANCE
— Willie Nelson to perform at concert at Longhi's for, Lahaina News, November 23, 2000: 2.

MAUI CANOE AND KAYAK CLUB
— Chart House Racing Series to be held, Lahaina News, January 7, 1999: 15.
— races to be held, Lahaina News, January 21, 1999: 7.
— series resumes, Lahaina News, January 28, 1999: 7.
— series continues, Lahaina News, February 4, 1999: 15.
— competing, Lahaina News, March 2, 2000: 6.
— season to finish with Great Kahakuloa Championship race at Kahului Harbor, Lahaina News, April 6, 2000: 7.
— fourth leg of Hurricane Ocean Racing Series to be held, Lahaina News, February 22, 2001: 12.
— to hold Hurricane/Eyecatcher Race Series, Lahaina News, January 10, 2002: 13.

— Hurricane/Eye Catcher Racing Series to be held, Lahaina News, January 17, 2002: 12.
— series continues, Lahaina News, January 31, 2002: 13.
— series continues, Lahaina News, March 7, 2002: 13.
— continues, Lahaina News, March 14, 2002: 13.
— race series continues, Lahaina News, March 28, 2002: 11.
— continues, Lahaina News, April 11, 2002: 12.

MAUI CANOE SAILING ASSOCIATION
— takes first place in Moloka'i-to-Oahu crossing, Lahaina News, November 7, 1990: 14.

MAUI CARPENTER'S UNION
— picket outside Benihana restaurant, Lahaina News, May 3, 1989: 1.

MAUI CARPET AND DRAPERY [BUSINESS]
— to hold reopen, Lahaina News, July 15, 1999: 11.
— selected as representative for CarpetsPlus of America, Lahaina News, August 19, 1999: 14.

MAUI CATHOLIC CHARITIES
— to hold Hand-in-Hand auction, Lahaina News, January 24, 1990: 5.
— to hold food drive, Lahaina News, May 23, 1990: 5.
— collecting food for Food Bank of Maui, Lahaina News, May 30, 1990: 5.
— holds fundraiser for homeless, Lahaina News, December 26, 1990: 4.
— to hold fundraiser for homeless, Lahaina News, January 2, 1991: 4.
— to hold fundraiser for homeless, Lahaina News, January 16, 1991: 4.

MAUI CENTER FOR ATTITUDINAL HEALING
— opens new store, Lahaina News, September 14, 1988: 3.
— to host workshop on health and increasing awareness, Lahaina News, December 14, 1988: 5.
— needs space for meetings, Lahaina News, March 1, 1989: 2.
— to hold facilitator/volunteer training, Lahaina News, March 1, 1989: 3.
— to offer workshop on coping with tragedy, Lahaina News, May 17, 1989: 2.
— to hold workshop "Love is Eternal", Lahaina News, September 20, 1989: 3.

MAUI CENTER FOR INDEPENDENT LIVING
— needs help, Lahaina News, April 10, 1985: 3.
— offers free workshop for attendants for disabled persons, Lahaina News, June 18, 1986: 3.
— to co-host forum entitled "The Americans with Disabilities Act", Lahaina News, September 26, 1990: 7.
— selling Moloka'i bread as fundraiser, Lahaina News, October 9, 1997: 9.
— selling bread for fundraiser, Lahaina News, October 16, 1997: 9.

MAUI CHAMBER BUSINESS EXPO
— see Business Expo and Food Fair

MAUI CHAMBER MUSIC
— festival to be held, Lahaina News, May 30, 1996: 13.
— to perform Baroque concert at Holy Innocents Church, Lahaina News, October 24, 1996: 14,15.
— to host baroque concert, Lahaina News, November 7, 1996: 15.
— to perform, Lahaina News, March 20, 1997: 16.
— festival to be held, Lahaina News, June 5, 1997: 17.
— festival to be held at Sacred Hearts Church, Lahaina News, June 12, 1997: 16.
— festival opens tonight, Lahaina News, June 12, 1997: 9.
— to be perform, Lahaina News, March 5, 1998: 16.
— festival to be held, Lahaina News, May 28, 1998: 1.
— festival to be held, Lahaina News, June 4, 1998: 16.
— festival to begin concert series, Lahaina News, May 27, 1999: 13.
— festival to be held, Lahaina News, June 3, 1999: 16.
— festival to include Maui Symphony Orchestra performing "Romance and Virtuosity", Lahaina News, June 8, 2000: 20.
— festival to be held, Lahaina News, June 7, 2001: 20.

MAUI CHAMBER OF COMMERCE
— helps prepare booklet for hippies, Lahaina Sun, December 9, 1970: 6.
— invited to visit the Far East with Mayor Cravalho, Lahaina Sun, January 6, 1971: 2.
— studying creation of job bank, Lahaina Sun, May 5, 1971: 5.
— discusses problem of hippies in Maui, Lahaina Sun, May 19, 1971: 8.
— admits that it represents the businessman's point of view, Lahaina Sun, December 1, 1971: 12.
— seeking to use money put aside in 1904 to combat bubonic plague for different purposes, Lahaina Sun, March 1, 1972: 3.
— report on activities, Lahaina Sun, May 31, 1972: 6.
— does not support moratorium on large buildings, Lahaina Sun, February 28, 1973: 6.
— stands against a proposed building moratorium, Lahaina Sun, March 7, 1973: 5.
— requests ability to use trust set aside for bubonic plague, Lahaina Sun, July 4, 1973: 3.
— work of Investigation and Complaints Committee described, Lahaina Sun, July 18, 1973: 3.
— approves creation of Maui dollars, Lahaina Sun, July 18, 1973: 6.
— opposes elimination of mandatory tour stops, Lahaina Sun, August 1, 1973: 3.
— Maui Dollars received, Lahaina Sun, August 8, 1973: 6.
— Maui Dollar found to have a typographic error, Lahaina Sun, August 22, 1973: 4.
— organizes Made in Maui trade show, Lahaina News, June 15, 1983: 7.
— featured, Lahaina News, January 18, 1984: 7,8,9.
— Biennial Policy Convention to be held at Maui Beach Hotel, Lahaina News, May 16, 1984: 17.
— co-sponsor island-wide clean-up, Lahaina News, December 5, 1984: 3.
— holds 75th annual meeting, Lahaina News, June 19, 1985: 3.
— begins membership directory, Lahaina News, October 23, 1985: 20.
— to hold Auction and fundraiser at Maui Lu Resort-Longhouse, Lahaina News, October 30, 1985: 3.
— asks for bypass around Lahaina, Lahaina News, June 4, 1986: 3.
— Jack Miller receives T.S. Shinn Award, Lahaina News, July 2, 1986: 3.
— to hold general membership meeting, Lahaina News, July 30, 1986: 3.
— West Maui Committee to meet, Lahaina News, November 12, 1986: 3.
— lobbies for improvements to West Maui, Lahaina News, February 18, 1987: 1.
— appoints Gregory McAnally as executive director, Lahaina News, March 25, 1987: 12.
— to hold annual meeting, Lahaina News, May 13, 1987: 3.
— awards Jim Luckey the Ten Sun Shinn Award, Lahaina News, June 10, 1987: 1.
— names James Wagoner as president, Lahaina News, June 17, 1987: 3.
— holds fundraiser, Lahaina News, October 7, 1987: 3.
— to hold membership meeting, Lahaina News, December 2, 1987: 3.
— hosting informational meeting "Garbage to Energy for Maui County", Lahaina News, January 13, 1988: 16.
— hosts meeting on sea bed mining, Lahaina News, January 13, 1988: 16.
— sponsoring West Maui General Membership meeting, Lahaina News, February 10, 1988: 11.
— to hold membership meeting, Lahaina News, March 2, 1988: 12,22.
— sponsoring public seminar on marijuana eradication, Lahaina News, March 2, 1988: 3.
— to offer small business seminar, Lahaina News, March 9, 1988: 3.

— West Maui Committee to meet, Lahaina News, April 13, 1988: 12.
— plans seminar on good management practices, Lahaina News, May 11, 1988: 14.
— to meet, Lahaina News, July 13, 1988: 3,10.
— sponsoring candidate breakfast, Lahaina News, October 19, 1988: 14.
— to host "Business After Hours", Lahaina News, November 2, 1988: 3.
— sponsoring event on projecting profits and cash flow with U.S. Small Business Administration, Lahaina News, February 15, 1989: 14.
— holds membership meeting, Lahaina News, February 15, 1989: 3.
— offering seminar for small businesses, Lahaina News, March 8, 1989: 3.
— to honor Persons of the Year with Small Business Administration, Lahaina News, April 5, 1989: 15.
— to include jazz music at annual banquet, Lahaina News, May 10, 1989: 6.
— sponsoring food and beverage seminar, Lahaina News, May 17, 1989: 9.
— moves offices following fire, Lahaina News, May 17, 1989: 9.
— awards T.S. Shinn award to Joan McKelvey, Lahaina News, June 28, 1989: 1.
— seeking donations to rebuild its building, Lahaina News, June 28, 1989: 7.
— offering workshop on patents, trademarks, and copyrights, Lahaina News, August 9, 1989: 3.
— returns home, Lahaina News, August 9, 1989: 4.
— to host Honolulu Mayor Frank Fasi, Lahaina News, August 30, 1989: 5.
— to dedicate new offices, Lahaina News, September 6, 1989: 2.
— sponsoring panel discussion of labor shortage, Lahaina News, October 4, 1989: 5.
— mixer planned, Lahaina News, January 17, 1990: 4.
— Governor John Waihee to speak to, Lahaina News, January 31, 1990: 5.
— opposes increase in general excise tax to build mass transit system on Oahu, Lahaina News, March 28, 1990: 7.
— to hold early bird networking meeting, Lahaina News, April 18, 1990: 5.
— to hold annual business administration awards luncheon, Lahaina News, April 18, 1990: 5.
— to hold policy convention, Lahaina News, April 25, 1990: 7.
— to hold Maui Chamber Business Expo, Lahaina News, May 16, 1990: 6.
— to host Business Expo, Lahaina News, May 30, 1990: 6.
— to hold Business Before Hours breakfast, Lahaina News, June 13, 1990: 7.
— to hold luncheon on business outlook, Lahaina News, July 25, 1990: 7.
— to hold candidate forum, Lahaina News, August 22, 1990: 9.
— Wayne Hedani appointed as president, Lahaina News, August 29, 1990: 8.
— to hold political forums, Lahaina News, September 5, 1990: 4.
— sponsoring golf outing, Lahaina News, September 12, 1990: 11.
— meets with Ed Hirata about Kapalua-West Maui Airport, Lahaina News, October 3, 1990: 1.
— sponsoring golf tournament, Lahaina News, October 3, 1990: 6.
— sponsoring golf outing, Lahaina News, October 10, 1990: 18.
— to hold "Business Before Hours", Lahaina News, November 14, 1990: 11.
— to hold quarterly general meeting, Lahaina News, December 19, 1990: 7.
— Mark Stormon to speak at quarterly general membership luncheon, Lahaina News, February 6, 1991: 6.
— to host Mark Stormon at general membership luncheon, Lahaina News, February 20, 1991: 7.

— West Maui committee to sponsor Business Outlook Forum, Lahaina News, March 6, 1991: 10.
— West Maui committee to sponsor Business Outlook Forum, Lahaina News, March 13, 1991: 7.
— hosts presentations on business outlook, Lahaina News, March 20, 1991: 6.
— organizes "Business After Hours" with Makena Clubhouse Restaurant, Lahaina News, March 20, 1991: 6.
— to meet Maui County Administration at general membership breakfast, Lahaina News, April 17, 1991: 9.
— to host speaker Alice Lee, Lahaina News, May 8, 1991: 6.
— to hold Business Before Hours meeting, Lahaina News, May 15, 1991: 8.
— to hold Business Before Hours meeting, Lahaina News, May 30, 1991: 3.
— to hold 81st annual banquet, Lahaina News, June 27, 1991: 7.
— to hold Business After Hours, Lahaina News, July 4, 1991: 4.
— continues to present Business After Hours, Lahaina News, July 11, 1991: 6.
— to hold Business After Hours, Lahaina News, July 18, 1991: 6.
— to host "Business After Hours" at Maui Schooner Resort, Lahaina News, August 22, 1991: 4.
— continues to offer Business After Hours, Lahaina News, September 12, 1991: 4.
— continues to offer Business After Hours meetings, Lahaina News, October 24, 1991: 8.
— Bank of Hawaii chief economist David Ramsour to speak to, Lahaina News, February 13, 1992: 12.
— to promote "Maui Trade Dollars", Lahaina News, March 19, 1992: 9.
— organizing Business Expo and Food Fair, Lahaina News, April 16, 1992: 15.
— Business Expo and Food Fair scheduled, Lahaina News, April 23, 1992: 16.
— to host mayor Linda Lingle, Lahaina News, May 21, 1992: 8.
— to host event "Set Sail for the Junior Business After Hours", Lahaina News, June 4, 1992: 9.
— to host "Set Sail for the Junior Business After Hours", Lahaina News, June 11, 1992: 14.
— annual banquet scheduled, Lahaina News, June 18, 1992: 10.
— to hold annual banquet, Lahaina News, June 18, 1992: 15.
— selects Stephen Knox as chair, Lahaina News, July 16, 1992: 16.
— general membership to be held at Marie Callender's Restaurant, Lahaina News, August 6, 1992: 8.
— offering entrepreneurial training, Lahaina News, September 3, 1992: 8.
— continues to hold buffet breakfasts, Lahaina News, September 10, 1992: 9.
— receives donation from Maui Trade Dollar Association, Lahaina News, September 17, 1992: 11.
— West Maui committee to hold general meeting, Lahaina News, October 1, 1992: 11.
— to host "Business After Hours", Lahaina News, January 14, 1993: 6.
— to host Business After Hours, Lahaina News, February 11, 1993: 11.
— to hold meeting on outlook, Lahaina News, February 11, 1993: 11.
— issues 1993 dollar, Lahaina News, February 18, 1993: 9.
— introduces "Made in Maui" sticker, Lahaina News, March 11, 1993: 12.
— to host talk by Pat Saiki, Lahaina News, March 25, 1993: 11.
— to host marketing seminar, Lahaina News, April 15, 1993: 7.
— continues to offer Business After Hours, Lahaina News, April 15, 1993: 7.
— to hold annual banquet, Lahaina News, June 17, 1993: 12.
— offering marketing seminar, Lahaina News, July 22, 1993: 7.
— to hold quarterly general membership, Lahaina News, July 22, 1993: 7.

— to offer seminar on marketing, Lahaina News, August 19, 1993: 13.

— continues to hold "Business After Hours", Lahaina News, August 19, 1993: 13.

— publishes manual on Labor and Employment Law, Lahaina News, September 16, 1993: 9,10.

— offering seminar on telephone marketing, Lahaina News, September 23, 1993: 7.

— West Maui Committee to hold general membership meeting, Lahaina News, December 2, 1993: 9.

— to sponsor Bridal Faire at Westin Maui, Lahaina News, January 6, 1994: 11,12.

— to host George Kinder presenting on retiring, Lahaina News, January 13, 1994: 5.

— West Maui Committee to host seminar "Staying Alive Until '85", Lahaina News, February 17, 1994: 6.

— offering marketing seminar, Lahaina News, March 17, 1994: 8.

— to sponsor Scans Symposium III, Lahaina News, March 31, 1994: 9.

— offering "Marketing Magic" workshop, Lahaina News, May 12, 1994: 10.

— continues to hold "business after hours" events, Lahaina News, May 12, 1994: 10.

— offers workshops on marketing, Lahaina News, June 2, 1994: 10.

— to hold annual banquet, Lahaina News, June 30, 1994: 8.

— to hold forum "Focus on the Economy", Lahaina News, July 21, 1994: 7.

— to hold forum "Focus on the Economy", Lahaina News, July 28, 1994: 9.

— to hold "Focus on the Economy" forum, Lahaina News, August 4, 1994: 9.

— hosting Sgt. Moses Kane at next "Good Morning Maui" gathering, Lahaina News, September 15, 1994: 13.

— continues to host "Business After Hours", Lahaina News, October 20, 1994: 13.

— to hold quarterly meeting, Lahaina News, October 27, 1994: 14,15.

— continues to offer "Business After Hours", Lahaina News, November 10, 1994: 13.

— hosing "Good Morning Maui—Take 2", Lahaina News, January 12, 1995: 6.

— West Maui Committee meets, Lahaina News, January 26, 1995: 12.

— West Maui Committee to hold Business and Economic Outlook Forum, Lahaina News, February 2, 1995: 7.

— to host "The Morning After—So You Thought Your Love Affair Would Never End", Lahaina News, February 2, 1995: 7.

— West Maui Committee focuses on future of agriculture, Lahaina News, February 16, 1995: 12.

— hosting "Business After Hours" at Compadres Mexican Bar and Grill, Lahaina News, February 16, 1995: 12.

— organizing Irish "Business After Hours" for St. Patrick's Day, Lahaina News, March 16, 1995: 10.

— to participate in Long Distance/USA-Spring Membership Calling Plan, Lahaina News, March 30, 1995: 10.

— to honor small business award winners, Lahaina News, April 13, 1995: 12.

— to hold "End of Season Tax Relaxer", Lahaina News, April 27, 1995: 10.

— to hold forum on worker's compensation, Lahaina News, May 25, 1995: 10.

— offering workshop on reducing workers' compensation costs, Lahaina News, June 22, 1995: 10.

— to hold annual banquet, Lahaina News, June 29, 1995: 10.

— sponsoring "Breakfast with your Legislator", Lahaina News, July 20, 1995: 10.

— to host "Disaster in Paradise" emergency planning on Maui-Take 2, Lahaina News, September 14, 1995: 10.

— to host "Finding and Qualifying for Venture Capital Funds", Lahaina News, October 12, 1995: 12.

— sponsoring workshop on "Funding Opportunities for Small Businesses", Lahaina News, October 26, 1995: 10.

— State Finance Director Earl Anzai to speak, Lahaina News, November 2, 1995: 2.

— offering workshop on online business, Lahaina News, March 21, 1996: 10.

— to host technology training programs, Lahaina News, April 18, 1996: 8,9.

— to host Business After Hours, Lahaina News, April 25, 1996: 14.

— invites public to choose artwork for Business Directory, Lahaina News, July 18, 1996: 13.

— to host "It's the Economy!" workshop, Lahaina News, August 1, 1996: 20.

— to offer seminar on substance abuse policy, Lahaina News, September 26, 1996: 15.

— to visit Costco, Lahaina News, October 17, 1996: 15.

— to hold Business Expo and Food Fair, Lahaina News, November 21, 1996: 14.

— offering Business After Hours networking session, Lahaina News, January 9, 1997: 10.

— receives from state Employment Training Fund, Lahaina News, May 22, 1997: 9.

— awards Ronald Kawahara the T.S. Shinn Award, Lahaina News, June 26, 1997: 7.

— to offer retail training program, Lahaina News, August 14, 1997: 12.

— to hold "Business After Hours", Lahaina News, August 14, 1997: 12.

— hosting "Cafeteria Plan Seminar", Lahaina News, September 18, 1997: 12.

— chair of Outrigger Enterprises Richard "Doc" Kelley to speak to, Lahaina News, October 2, 1997: 15.

— to honor Al Boteilho and Mercer "Chubby" Vicens, Lahaina News, October 16, 1997: 12.

— offering "Business After Hours" meeting, Lahaina News, November 13, 1997: 11.

— releases trade dollar, Lahaina News, December 11, 1997: 21.

— Senator Daniel Inouye to speak at luncheon sponsored by, Lahaina News, January 29, 1998: 13.

— sponsoring morning breakfast with Mayor Linda Lingle, Lahaina News, March 12, 1998: 11.

— planning tax revolt, Lahaina News, March 26, 1998: 1.

— continues to hold "Business After Hours", Lahaina News, April 16, 1998: 12.

— to hold "Wine, Dine and Fine Music" fundraiser, Lahaina News, April 16, 1998: 12.

— to host Installation Banquet with Mayor Linda Lingle as guest speaker, Lahaina News, May 7, 1998: 15.

— to hold "Memories of Old Wailuku", Lahaina News, May 7, 1998: 20.

— new officers named, Lahaina News, June 4, 1998: 13.

— to hold "Summer Party", Lahaina News, June 11, 1998: 13.

— to hold Home Show, Lahaina News, June 25, 1998: 11.

— to host training on how to use the internet, Lahaina News, July 16, 1998: 13.

— "Business After Hours" continues to be held, Lahaina News, September 10, 1998: 11.

— to feature talk by Thomas Schwab on stocks, Lahaina News, October 8, 1998: 13.

— Vicky Cayetano to speak to at "Entrepreneur and Humanitarian Luncheon", Lahaina News, October 15, 1998: 13.

— to hold "Business After Hours" at Costco, Lahaina News, October 22, 1998: 17.

— to collect presents for the Children's Advocacy Center of Maui, Lahaina News, December 10, 1998: 9.

— continues to hold "Business After Hours", Lahaina News, February 11, 1999: 16.

— continues to hold "Business After Hours", Lahaina News, March 18, 1999: 13.
— continues to hold "Business After Hours", Lahaina News, April 15, 1999: 11.
— to offer course on restaurant management, Lahaina News, April 15, 1999: 11.
— to hold installation banquet, Lahaina News, May 6, 1999: 15.
— to hold golf tournament, Lahaina News, May 6, 1999: 17.
— continues to hold "Business After Hours", Lahaina News, May 13, 1999: 13.
— Kevin Baptist incoming chair, Lahaina News, May 20, 1999: 13.
— continues to hold "Business After Hours", Lahaina News, October 21, 1999: 13.
— releases annual Maui Trade Dollar, Lahaina News, November 4, 1999: 11.
— Fundraising Golf Tournament to be held, Lahaina News, April 27, 2000: 6.
— to hold "We Love Palauea Party" with Sierra Club, Lahaina News, May 4, 2000: 14.
— to hold annual "Breakfast with the Mayor", Lahaina News, March 8, 2001: 8.
— to hold fundraiser golf course, Lahaina News, April 26, 2001: 14.
— to hold Golf Tournament, Lahaina News, May 3, 2001: 15.
— honors Cesar Gaxiola with Aloha Award, Lahaina News, June 21, 2001: 2.
— Charles Jencks appointed to board of directors of, Lahaina News, August 2, 2001: 9.
— to hold "In Success! Together We Stand" panel discussion, Lahaina News, October 11, 2001: 9.
— gubernatorial candidate Linda Lingle to speak, Lahaina News, January 31, 2002: 8.
— to hold "Business After Hours", Lahaina News, February 7, 2002: 8.
— gubernatorial candidate D. G. "Andy" Anderson to speak to, Lahaina News, March 28, 2002: 15.
— to hold annual Installation Luncheon, Lahaina News, May 30, 2002: 8.
— golf tournament to support, Lahaina News, August 22, 2002: 11.
— to speak to Alan Arakawa, Lahaina News, February 20, 2003: 9.
— Mayor Arakawa to speak to, Lahaina News, February 27, 2003: 8.
— releases message concerning airport traffic rules, Lahaina News, March 6, 2003: 8.
— to hold Business After Hours at Outback Steakhouse, Lahaina News, April 17, 2003: 8.
— to hold Business After Hours, Lahaina News, May 8, 2003: 8.
— to hold Business After Hours, Lahaina News, May 15, 2003: 8.
— to host University of Hawai'i football coach June Jones, Lahaina News, May 22, 2003: 8.
— to hold "Business After Hours", Lahaina News, June 12, 2003: 8.
— to hold "Business After Hours", Lahaina News, July 10, 2003: 8.
— to hold "Business After Hours", Lahaina News, September 4, 2003: 8.
— economist Leroy Laney to speak to, Lahaina News, September 18, 2003: 9.
— to hold Employment Law Seminar, Lahaina News, October 2, 2003: 8.
— continues to hold "Business After Hours", Lahaina News, October 9, 2003: 8.

MAUI CHANNEL SWIM
— swimmer Bill Nelson required help, Lahaina News, September 14, 1983: 4.
— to be held, Lahaina News, September 3, 1998: 15.

MAUI CHEFS AND COOKS ASSOCIATION
— to hold food fair "The Chef and the Maui Child", Lahaina News, May 14, 1998: 17.
— to hold "The Chef and the Maui Child", Lahaina News, May 21, 1998: 16.

MAUI CHEFS PRESENT
— to feature local chefs, Lahaina News, August 21, 2003: 14.
— to be held, Lahaina News, August 28, 2003: 1,2.
— to be held, Lahaina News, September 4, 2003: 14.

MAUI CHEMICAL AND PAPER PRODUCTS [BUSINESS]
— establishes Kawasaki Scholarship, Lahaina News, May 6, 1999: 2.

MAUI CHESS CLUB
— see chess

MAUI CHILDBIRTH AND FAMILY EDUCATION
— to hold classes, Lahaina News, January 9, 1992: 3.
— offering infant care classes, Lahaina News, February 6, 1992: 5.
— to offer parenting workshops, Lahaina News, August 20, 1992: 4.
— to hold classes on childbirth preparation, Lahaina News, February 24, 1994: 4.
— to offer breastfeeding class, Lahaina News, June 5, 1997: 16.
— to begin courses, Lahaina News, September 4, 1997: 17.
— starting infant care series, Lahaina News, February 12, 1998: 17.
— to hold classes, Lahaina News, May 7, 1998: 21.
— to offer care classes, Lahaina News, June 18, 1998: 16.
— to hold classes, Lahaina News, June 25, 1998: 12.
— continues to offer classes, Lahaina News, August 27, 1998: 17.
— begins infant care classes, Lahaina News, September 17, 1998: 28.
— offering classes, Lahaina News, February 4, 1999: 9.
— to offer classes, Lahaina News, June 17, 1999: 15.
— continues to hold childbirth preparation classes, Lahaina News, August 19, 1999: 15.
— continues to offer preparation classes, Lahaina News, December 30, 1999: 15.
— to offer infant CPR class, Lahaina News, January 24, 2002: 16.

MAUI CHILDBIRTH EDUCATION ASSOCIATION
— see Maui Childbirth and Family Education

MAUI CHILDREN'S COALITION
— to hold public legislative forum, Lahaina News, January 25, 1996: 4.

MAUI CHINESE CLUB
— to celebrate Chinese New Year, Lahaina Sun, February 9, 1972: 15.
— Danny Fong becomes president, Lahaina Sun, May 31, 1972: 10.

MAUI CHIP [BUSINESS]
— Aloha Airlines to offer collector cans of potato chips, Lahaina News, July 26, 1989: 6.

MAUI CHIPS
— history described, Lahaina Sun, August 11, 1971: 9.
— possible future discussed, Lahaina Sun, June 13, 1973: 13.

MAUI CHORAL ARTS ASSOCIATION
— recruiting adult singers, Lahaina News, September 18, 2003: 16.
— recruiting adult singers, Lahaina News, September 25, 2003: 17.
— seeking adult singers, Lahaina News, October 2, 2003: 16.

MAUI CHOREOGRAPHER'S FORUM
— to host composition workshop, Lahaina News, March 12, 1992: 22.
— to perform at Maui Community Theatre, Lahaina News, April 9, 1992: 22.
— offering dance demonstration, Lahaina News, August 20, 1992: 4.

MAUI CHRISTIAN ACADEMY
— students seeking help to attend Presidential Inauguration, Lahaina News, October 24, 1984: 3.

MAUI CHRISTIAN MINISTERS ASSOCIATION
— opposition to gambling, Lahaina Sun, March 17, 1971: 3.
— considering creating a youth hostel, Lahaina Sun, April 14, 1971: 1.
— studying plan for transient housing, Lahaina Sun, May 12, 1971: 2.

MAUI CHRISTIAN WOMEN'S CLUB
— to hold brunch, Lahaina News, October 9, 1985: 8.
— to hold luncheon, Lahaina News, January 16, 1991: 3.
— to hold "Spring Fling Brunch", Lahaina News, March 20, 1991: 3.
— to hold "Bouquets in May Brunch", Lahaina News, May 8, 1991: 4.

— to hold brunch, Lahaina News, June 13, 1991: 4.

— to hold brunch, Lahaina News, August 15, 1991: 3.

— Gayle Shufeldt to speak at brunch, Lahaina News, October 10, 1991: 5.

— to hold Country Faire Brunch, Lahaina News, November 14, 1991: 2.

— to hold Great Escape Brunch, Lahaina News, May 14, 1992: 3.

— to hold Back to School Brunch, Lahaina News, September 10, 1992: 3.

— to hold brunch, Lahaina News, November 12, 1992: 4,5.

— to hold brunch on theme "Love Make the World Go Round", Lahaina News, February 11, 1993: 4.

— to host speaker Kats Enoki, Lahaina News, March 11, 1993: 3.

— to hold fashion brunch, Lahaina News, September 9, 1993: 3.

— to hold "What's in the Basket" brunch, Lahaina News, October 14, 1993: 5.

— to hold fashion show, Lahaina News, July 14, 1994: 6.

— to hold "Small Fry Brunch", Lahaina News, November 10, 1994: 7.

— to hold "April Showers Brunch", Lahaina News, April 13, 1995: 4.

— to offer "Queen for a Day Brunch", Lahaina News, May 11, 1995: 2.

— to hold "Gaining Knowledge" brunch, Lahaina News, August 10, 1995: 4.

— to hold "Return Engagement Brunch", Lahaina News, September 14, 1995: 6.

— to hold "Holiday Sparkle Brunch", Lahaina News, December 14, 1995: 18.

— to hold "Love Boat Aloha Style", Lahaina News, February 8, 1996: 4.

— to host "It's for the Birds" brunch, Lahaina News, March 14, 1996: 11.

— to hold "Glorious Days of Summer" brunch, Lahaina News, July 11, 1996: 13.

— to hold Pre-Christmas Brunch, Lahaina News, November 14, 1996: 15.

— to hold "Joy of Christmas Brunch", Lahaina News, December 12, 1996: 8,9.

— to hold "Fresh Start Brunch", Lahaina News, January 9, 1997: 10.

— to host "Spring Fever" luncheon, Lahaina News, March 13, 1997: 16.

— to hold "May Day Luncheon", Lahaina News, May 15, 1997: 12.

— to host "A Tisket A Tasket Luncheon", Lahaina News, June 12, 1997: 17.

— to hold "Summer Picnic Brunch", Lahaina News, August 14, 1997: 16.

— to hold Thanksgiving Luncheon, Lahaina News, November 13, 1997: 20.

— to hold "Christmas Spirit Luncheon", Lahaina News, December 11, 1997: 19.

MAUI CHRISTIAN WOMEN'S CONFERENCE

— Susie Kimes leading seminars at, Lahaina News, October 4, 2001: 18.

MAUI CHURCH OF RELIGIOUS SCIENCE

— moves services to Wailuku, Lahaina News, November 23, 1988: 3.

MAUI CINDERELLA SCHOLARSHIP PAGEANT

— to be held, Lahaina News, March 7, 2002: 16.

MAUI CIRCULATION, INC [BUSINESS]

— bought Maui Brochure, Lahaina News, June 27, 1991: 9.

MAUI CITIZENS PREPAREDNESS COUNCIL

— to meet, Lahaina News, March 11, 1999: 12.

— to meet, Lahaina News, June 3, 1999: 16.

— to present on natural food sources as part of Y2K preparation, Lahaina News, June 17, 1999: 16.

— to discuss Y2K gardens, Lahaina News, September 16, 1999: 12.

— to hold meeting on Y2K concerns, Lahaina News, November 25, 1999: 16.

MAUI CLASSIC CHAMPIONSHIP

— basketball tournament won by Jolly Roger Pirates, Lahaina Sun, January 27, 1971: 7.

MAUI CLASSIC CRUISERS

— to hold Car Show at Azeka Place II, Lahaina News, September 26, 2002: 16.

MAUI CLASSICAL MUSIC FESTIVAL

— to be held, Lahaina News, May 29, 2003: 1,18.

— to be held at Maui Arts and Cultural Center, Lahaina News, June 5, 2003: 17.

MAUI CLEAN AIR COALITION

— to meet, Lahaina News, September 4, 1997: 16.

MAUI CLOTHING CO. [BUSINESS]

— featured, Lahaina News, November 24, 1994: 9.

MAUI COASTAL LAND TRUST

— to hold discussion on land trusts, Lahaina News, March 29, 2001: 8.

— awarded grant from Atherton Family Foundation, Lahaina News, May 3, 2001: 8.

— signs up its first Founder's Circle member, Lahaina News, May 31, 2001: 7.

— to hold fundraiser "Buy Back the Beach", Lahaina News, March 7, 2002: 14.

— to hold "Buy Back the Beach" fundraiser, Lahaina News, March 14, 2002: 17.

— appoints Dale Bonar as executive director, Lahaina News, July 4, 2002: 2.

— "Buy Back the Beach" benefit luau to be held, Lahaina News, January 16, 2003: 2.

— to hold fundraiser, Lahaina News, January 23, 2003: 18.

— to hold luau benefit, Lahaina News, January 30, 2003: 2.

MAUI COASTAL PRESERVATION TRUST

— appoints leadership, Lahaina News, February 8, 2001: 2.

MAUI COFFEE COMPANY [BUSINESS]

— expanding, Lahaina News, November 19, 1998: 13.

MAUI COFFEE ROASTERS [RESTAURANT]

— to hold "Open Mic Night", Lahaina News, November 18, 1999: 16.

MAUI COLON HEALTH CENTER

— to host lecture, Lahaina News, April 29, 1993: 5.

— to hold lectures, Lahaina News, May 13, 1993: 4,5.

MAUI COMEDY CLUB [BUSINESS]

— looking for talent, Lahaina News, August 17, 1988: 10.

— to close, Lahaina News, September 14, 1988: 11,13.

MAUI COMMERCIAL BOATERS AND OCEAN AFFILIATED TRANSPORTATION ASSOCIATION [MCBOAT]

— parasailers withdraw from, Lahaina News, June 1, 1988: 19.

MAUI COMMUNITY ARTS AND CULTURAL CENTER

— to hold fundraiser at the estate of Pundy Yokouchi, Lahaina News, October 16, 1985: 3,20.

— Japanese Cultural Society sponsoring luncheon to benefit, Lahaina News, February 25, 1987: 6.

— receives donation from Alexander & Baldwin, Lahaina News, April 22, 1987: 10.

— to hold "A Day of Wine and Racing" fundraiser, Lahaina News, November 18, 1987: 3.

— fundraising for proposed center, Lahaina News, February 10, 1988: 3.

— auction in memory of Margaret Cameron to be held, Lahaina News, September 7, 1988: 9.

— receives donation from Harold K.L. Castle Foundation, Lahaina News, November 23, 1988: 3.

— fundraiser held, Lahaina News, February 15, 1989: 13.

— benefit to be held at Embassy Suites Resort Kaʻanapali, Lahaina News, February 22, 1989: 1.
— receives donation from Maui Land and Pineapple, Lahaina News, April 19, 1989: 1.
— to receive proceeds from City Bank Helps Maui Invitational Golf Tournament, Lahaina News, April 26, 1989: 13.
— receives check from golf tournament organized by City Bank, Lahaina News, May 31, 1989: 3.
— receives donation from Toshimichi Koike, Lahaina News, June 7, 1989: 8.
— names Thom Wyand as assistant director, Lahaina News, July 26, 1989: 3.
— fundraising efforts continue, Lahaina News, October 11, 1989: 8.
— fundraising lagging, Lahaina News, November 1, 1989: 2.
— Soroptimists International to hold benefit dinner for, Lahaina News, March 21, 1990: 14.
— receives donation from KM Hawaii, Inc, owners of Hyatt Regency Hotel, Lahaina News, April 4, 1990: 7.
— to break ground, Lahaina News, June 20, 1990: 11.
— ground breaking ceremony to be held, Lahaina News, June 27, 1990: 12.
— ground breaking ceremony to be held, Lahaina News, July 4, 1990: 1,13.
— foundations donate towards construction of, Lahaina News, September 12, 1990: 8.
— seeking additional funds from state, Lahaina News, March 13, 1991: 5.
— to host presentation by Pamille Berg "Art, Craft, & Architecture", Lahaina News, April 3, 1991: 10.
— decides to build Center in phases, Lahaina News, April 17, 1991: 7.
— friends of Masaru "Pundy" Yokouchi offer money to, Lahaina News, August 1, 1991: 5.
— names Thom Weyand as executive director, Lahaina News, October 24, 1991: 8.
— Bill Fisher and Christina Cowan join, Lahaina News, October 31, 1991: 10.
— hires G. Todd Vaules as technical director, Lahaina News, February 13, 1992: 13.
— construction begins, Art Vento hired as project manager, Lahaina News, March 19, 1992: 9.
— Bill Fisher named interim director of, Lahaina News, June 18, 1992: 10.
— to hold Christmas Pau Hana Party, Lahaina News, December 10, 1992: 17.
— construction continues, Lahaina News, December 24, 1992: 9.
— to hold Paniolo party, Lahaina News, March 25, 1993: 15,16.
— opening ceremony being planned, Lahaina News, February 24, 1994: 12.
— Rusty Conway hired as technical director, Lahaina News, March 24, 1994: 8.
— seeking local entertainers for opening festival, Lahaina News, March 31, 1994: 16.
— opening reception planned, Lahaina News, April 21, 1994: 16.
— grand opening planned, Lahaina News, May 5, 1994: 11.
— to hold grand opening this weekend, Lahaina News, May 12, 1994: 11.
— pictures from grand opening, Lahaina News, May 19, 1994: 6.
— receives money from Harry and Jeanette Weinberg Foundation, Lahaina News, May 26, 1994: 5.
— receives grant from Harry and Jeanette Weinberg Foundation, Lahaina News, November 17, 1994: 6.
— box office now open, Lahaina News, January 12, 1995: 12.
— to host "Legends of Hawaiian Music: Da Bunch", Lahaina News, January 12, 1995: 12.
— Seiha Hogaku Kai Japanese Classical Music Association to hold benefit concert for, Lahaina News, January 26, 1995: 16.

— new appointments announced, Lahaina News, March 9, 1995: 6.
— to celebrate first birthday, Lahaina News, May 4, 1995: 14.
— to host "Celebrating the Artist in Us" exhibit, Lahaina News, May 4, 1995: 16.
— offering free tours, Lahaina News, May 4, 1995: 4.
— offering alternative movies, Lahaina News, July 27, 1995: 12.
— to show original Batman movie, Lahaina News, August 24, 1995: 12.
— to offer "Critic's Choice Film Series", Lahaina News, August 31, 1995: 12.
— Critic's Choice Film Series continues, Lahaina News, September 14, 1995: 12.
— concert featuring Gregory Isaacs and Marty Dread canceled, Lahaina News, September 28, 1995: 11.
— to show "The Vampire Show: A Tribute to Bela Lugosi", Lahaina News, October 12, 1995: 15.
— to host "The Mythology of Angels", Lahaina News, December 14, 1995: 15.
— offering art seminar, Lahaina News, December 28, 1995: 8.
— to host Critic's Choice Film Series, Lahaina News, March 28, 1996: 14.
— to present celebration of "Maui Calls", Lahaina News, August 15, 1996: 16.
— events listed, Lahaina News, January 23, 1997: 10.
— continues to show films, Lahaina News, May 15, 1997: 12.
— "Celebrating Christian Endeavor in the Islands" to be held, Lahaina News, May 22, 1997: 16.
— offers usher training, Lahaina News, June 19, 1997: 16.
— hosting "Maui Calls", Lahaina News, August 14, 1997: 16.
— Hoʻonanea Hou Hawaiian Music Series to be held, Lahaina News, September 18, 1997: 13.
— kicks off Hoʻonanea Hou Hawaiian Music Series, Lahaina News, September 25, 1997: 16.
— to hold Artisan Gift Gallery, Lahaina News, December 4, 1997: 24.
— Mark Nerenhausen resigns as director, Lahaina News, December 11, 1997: 21.
— seeking business sponsors for Extreme Sports Expo, Lahaina News, December 11, 1997: 21.
— Christina Cowan named acting general manager at, Lahaina News, December 25, 1997: 11.
— to hold usher training, Lahaina News, May 7, 1998: 21.
— Christina Cowan new president, Lahaina News, July 16, 1998: 13.
— hosting "Learning Across the Curriculum: A Summer Institute for Teachers", Lahaina News, July 23, 1998: 17.
— to hold "Ring in the Holidays with Good Cheer", Lahaina News, November 26, 1998: 17.
— appoints Karen Fischer as managing director, Lahaina News, December 3, 1998: 17.
— Pamela Dodson joins, Lahaina News, March 25, 1999: 13.
— to hold "Maui Calls" benefit, Lahaina News, August 19, 1999: 16.
— to hold "Bubbles and Boxes" benefit, Lahaina News, November 11, 1999: 12.
— to conduct usher training, Lahaina News, February 10, 2000: 17.
— to hold "City Bank helps Maui" benefit golf tournament, Lahaina News, April 5, 2001: 14.
— receives grant from Wailea Realty Corp., Lahaina News, April 19, 2001: 9.
— Colleen Furukawa new grants manager, Lahaina News, August 16, 2001: 8.
— Hokulani Holt-Padilla joins, Lahaina News, September 6, 2001: 9.
— to show "Ghost World", Lahaina News, November 22, 2001: 20.
— to hold usher training, Lahaina News, February 7, 2002: 16.

MAUI COMMUNITY COLLEGE
— discussion of college curriculum, Lahaina Sun, December 30, 1970: 4.
— drug abuse conference to be held at, Lahaina Sun, February 24, 1971: 1.

— holds seminars on ecology, Lahaina Sun, March 17, 1971: 2.
— faculty back Robert Brunish as new provost, Lahaina Sun, April 14, 1971: 3.
— likely provost Robert Brunish offers ideas for the college, Lahaina Sun, April 21, 1971: 5.
— Candidates for provost position described, Lahaina Sun, April 28, 1971: 1,8.
— student protest concerning proposed Code of Conduct, Lahaina Sun, April 28, 1971: 1,8.
— controversy over new student center, Lahaina Sun, May 12, 1971: 3.
— update on provost search, Lahaina Sun, May 19, 1971: 1.
— 14-foot koa-wood tiki dedicated, Lahaina Sun, May 19, 1971: 5.
— provost selection will occur soon, Lahaina Sun, June 2, 1971: 2.
— receives federal grants for student aid, Lahaina Sun, June 2, 1971: 8.
— H. Glen Fishback appointed new provost, Lahaina Sun, June 16, 1971: 1.
— history instructor Tim Head receives undergraduate teaching award, Lahaina Sun, June 23, 1971: 12.
— federal student loan funds received, Lahaina Sun, August 18, 1971: 11.
— receives National Institutes of Health grant, Lahaina Sun, August 25, 1971: 2.
— Maui County Council recommends it become a four-year college, Lahaina Sun, October 20, 1971: 15.
— receives state funds for furniture and equipment, Lahaina Sun, November 10, 1971: 6.
— UH president Cleveland discusses possibility of college becoming 4-year, Lahaina Sun, December 8, 1971: 15.
— editorial comments on college becoming 4-year, Lahaina Sun, December 8, 1971: 2.
— flea market to be held, Lahaina Sun, December 15, 1971: 8.
— open house held, Lahaina Sun, April 19, 1972: 14.
— films on spiritual leader Chiranjiva shown, Lahaina Sun, September 20, 1972: 10.
— University of Hawai'i President Cleveland speaks, Lahaina Sun, November 8, 1972: 3.
— reaccredited, Lahaina Sun, March 14, 1973: 11.
— counselor Stephen Francis reinstated with back pay, Lahaina Sun, April 11, 1973: 4.
— to hold conference "Spirit of Health—Ethics of an Emerging World", Lahaina News, October 1, 1982: 3.
— receives grant for computer equipment, Lahaina News, March 1, 1983: 6.
— tuition lowered by Board of Regents, Lahaina News, May 1, 1983: 3.
— hosts workshop on Maui's cultural resources, Lahaina News, June 1, 1983: 3.
— to host Ho'olaule'a, Lahaina News, April 11, 1984: 5.
— non-credit courses in fall begin next week, Lahaina News, August 29, 1984: 3.
— offering college-level courses in Lahaina, Lahaina News, January 2, 1985: 3.
— to hold Ho'olaule'a, Lahaina News, April 24, 1985: 12.
— offering non-credit class on the financial health of your business, Lahaina News, July 3, 1985: 3.
— offering non-credit courses on legal planning, Lahaina News, September 25, 1985: 3.
— registration for second semester classes begin, Lahaina News, December 11, 1985: 3.
— registration for Fall begins, Lahaina News, August 6, 1986: 3.
— offering four-year degrees in West Maui, Lahaina News, November 19, 1986: 3.
— courses for Spring semester detailed, Lahaina News, January 14, 1987: 4.
— College Scholarship Fee Waiver Forms received, Lahaina News, March 25, 1987: 18.
— to hold graduation at Royal Lahaina Resort, Lahaina News, May 13, 1987: 3.
— to host performance of "The Dream of Kitamura", Lahaina News, May 27, 1987: 16.
— sponsoring financial security seminar, Lahaina News, January 27, 1988: 3.
— offering workshops, Lahaina News, February 10, 1988: 11.
— offering car clinic, Lahaina News, February 24, 1988: 18.
— will inspect cars for free, Lahaina News, May 4, 1988: 14.
— hosts Dorothy Pyle speaking on Maui sugar industry, Lahaina News, June 1, 1988: 19.
— to host Glen Grant speaking on "Grabbing Your Audience: Training for Interpretation Techniques" at Maui Community College, Lahaina News, July 6, 1988: 17.
— to host preservation workshop for historical papers and photos, Lahaina News, July 27, 1988: 11.
— to offer classes at Lahaina Intermediate School, Lahaina News, August 3, 1988: 12.
— offering certificate in Management Program, Lahaina News, September 7, 1988: 14.
— Office of Community Services offering certificate in Management Program, Lahaina News, September 7, 1988: 14.
— offering workshop "Burma: The Golden Land", Lahaina News, September 21, 1988: 3,20.
— to host lecture on historic preservation, Lahaina News, October 5, 1988: 3.
— offering workshops on finding and writing grants, Lahaina News, October 19, 1988: 14.
— Jay Polmar to offer speedreading classes at, Lahaina News, November 2, 1988: 11.
— offering cashier training, Lahaina News, November 23, 1988: 3.
— offering car clinic, Lahaina News, November 23, 1988: 5.
— offering certificate to interpret Maui for tourists, Lahaina News, January 25, 1989: 6.
— to offer career development courses, Lahaina News, February 22, 1989: 13.
— to offer course on copyrights, trademarks, and patent law, Lahaina News, February 22, 1989: 3.
— Office of Community Services offering courses, Lahaina News, March 8, 1989: 16.
— offering courses on customer service, Lahaina News, March 8, 1989: 3.
— offering business courses, Lahaina News, March 29, 1989: 14.
— offering basic Japanese for the tourist industry, Lahaina News, April 12, 1989: 3.
— Fashion Technology Department to hold show, Lahaina News, April 26, 1989: 12.
— offering courses on real estate, Lahaina News, April 26, 1989: 3.
— offering class on child care businesses, Lahaina News, May 17, 1989: 9.
— offering course on business stress, Lahaina News, August 16, 1989: 6.
— Fall classes begin, Lahaina News, August 23, 1989: 3.
— to offer seminar "Resolving Conflicts in the Workplace", Lahaina News, August 23, 1989: 6.
— offering course on the "Art of Window Display", Lahaina News, August 30, 1989: 5.
— to perform "Dracula: The Musical?", Lahaina News, September 27, 1989: 3.
— students produce news magazine for television, Lahaina News, November 29, 1989: 22.
— offering courses on business skills, marketing, problem solving, paralegal skills, Lahaina News, December 6, 1989: 5.
— to offer course on kayak surfing, Lahaina News, December 6, 1989: 7.

— Summer school registration begins, Lahaina News, March 18, 1999: 16.

— library to hold fundraiser, Lahaina News, March 18, 1999: 17.

— library to hold fundraiser, Lahaina News, March 25, 1999: 16.

— library to hold book fair, Lahaina News, April 8, 1999: 12,13.

— holds reentry workshop, Lahaina News, April 22, 1999: 11.

— culinary team places second in competition, Lahaina News, April 22, 1999: 11.

— presents "Happy Hour", Lahaina News, May 6, 1999: 20.

— to offer a Masters of Education degree, Lahaina News, May 20, 1999: 16.

— to offer Retail Industry Training in Excellence [RITE] course, Lahaina News, June 17, 1999: 13.

— early registration for Fall 1999 to begin, Lahaina News, June 17, 1999: 16.

— offering new degree in marine science, Lahaina News, June 24, 1999: 12.

— looking for high school students to intern as computer lab assistants, Lahaina News, July 8, 1999: 11.

— promoting computer science degree, Lahaina News, August 12, 1999: 16.

— Senator Daniel Inouye secures funding for, Lahaina News, September 9, 1999: 1.

— registration underway, Lahaina News, January 6, 2000: 12,13.

— Criminal Justice Club to hold Fun Run, Lahaina News, January 6, 2000: 7.

— to host workshop on propagation and sale of threatened and endangered plants, Lahaina News, January 27, 2000: 12.

— offers course for retail workers, Lahaina News, February 17, 2000: 14.

— offering Bachelor of Arts in Business Administration, Lahaina News, March 9, 2000: 13.

— to host "Quality is Free" business workshop, Lahaina News, March 23, 2000: 12.

— to offer Bachelor of Arts in Liberal Studies, Lahaina News, March 23, 2000: 12.

— offering expanded slate of summer courses, Lahaina News, April 20, 2000: 2.

— summer studies planned, Lahaina News, May 11, 2000: 9.

— to offer Bachelor of Arts in Hawaiian Studies, Lahaina News, May 18, 2000: 20.

— to hold annual Telethon fundraiser, Lahaina News, November 16, 2000: 16.

— spring semester to begin, Lahaina News, November 23, 2000: 21.

— Criminal Justice Club to hold fun run, Lahaina News, January 4, 2001: 9.

— offering scholarships for auto programs, Lahaina News, February 15, 2001: 12.

— Educational Opportunity Center to hold free college entry workshop, Lahaina News, May 31, 2001: 17.

— offering massage therapy program, Lahaina News, July 12, 2001: 9.

— to hold "Strategies for Success for High School Seniors", Lahaina News, May 2, 2002: 17.

— offering University of Hawai'i degree in psychology, Lahaina News, May 2, 2002: 17.

— Maui Language Institute expanding program to address needs of native English speakers, Lahaina News, May 2, 2002: 2.

— recruiting students for dental assistant certification program, Lahaina News, May 23, 2002: 17.

— to hold information session on Psychology bachelor of arts degree, Lahaina News, June 20, 2002: 16.

— Maui Language Institute offering summer program, Lahaina News, June 20, 2002: 18.

— Provost's Golf Tournament raises $30,000, Lahaina News, July 18, 2002: 12.

— recruiting instructors for Fall semester, Lahaina News, July 25, 2002: 9.

— to hold driver education instructor course, Lahaina News, August 15, 2002: 8.

— receives grant for rural development and job training, Lahaina News, September 19, 2002: 8.

— Educational Opportunity Center receives U.S. Department of Education grant, Lahaina News, October 17, 2002: 14.

— new faculty appointed, Lahaina News, November 14, 2002: 8.

— new scholarship program targets Hawaiian students, Lahaina News, December 12, 2002: 14.

— to hold information session, Lahaina News, December 19, 2002: 8.

— Nursing Program recruiting students, Lahaina News, January 2, 2003: 8.

— receives grant from Alexander and Baldwin Foundation, Lahaina News, January 30, 2003: 8.

— to hold College Fair, Lahaina News, April 3, 2003: 18.

— to hold College Fair, Lahaina News, April 10, 2003: 15.

— to host biotechnology enrichment program, Lahaina News, May 1, 2003: 8.

— Culinary Arts Department to offer coffee workshop with Hawaii Coffee Association, Lahaina News, July 17, 2003: 8.

— to hold informational session on Sustainable Technology, Building Maintenance and Architectural AutoCAD, Lahaina News, August 21, 2003: 16.

— to host Watershed Forum, Lahaina News, September 4, 2003: 18.

— see also Business and Industrial Development Services

MAUI COMMUNITY CORRECTIONAL CENTER

— Law Librarian Sandy Wada wins Maui County Bar Association's Liberty Bell Award, Lahaina News, November 30, 2000: 5.

MAUI COMMUNITY MENTAL HEALTH CENTER

— seeking donations for homeless, Lahaina News, October 24, 1990: 9.

MAUI COMMUNITY SCHOOL FOR ADULTS

— sponsoring low impact aerobics, Lahaina News, October 7, 1993: 7.

— offering step aerobics with YMCA, Lahaina News, December 2, 1993: 10.

— sponsoring parenting course, Lahaina News, February 10, 1994: 4.

— seeking literacy tutors, Lahaina News, August 24, 1995: 4.

MAUI COMMUNITY THEATRE

— looking for props for upcoming production of "Auntie Mame", Lahaina Sun, August 2, 1972: 9.

— celebrates 50 years, Lahaina Sun, August 16, 1972: 19.

— casting underway for "My Fair Lady", Lahaina Sun, January 24, 1973: 10.

— performs Follies, Lahaina News, January 4, 1984: 10.

— to perform "Morning at Seven", Lahaina News, May 2, 1984: 5.

— to hold fundraiser, Lahaina News, October 17, 1984: 3.

— featured, including hope to rebuild after fire, Lahaina News, October 24, 1984: 7,8,9.

— raises $12,000, Lahaina News, November 21, 1984: 3.

— H. Neil Whiting named director of, Lahaina News, February 20, 1985: 3.

— upcoming activities described, Lahaina News, February 5, 1986: 8.

— performing "You Can't Take It With You", Lahaina News, April 2, 1986: 3.

— performing "Annie Get your Gun", Lahaina News, January 14, 1987: 3.

— performing Lillian Hellman's "The Little Foxes", Lahaina News, April 1, 1987: 3.

— to hold general membership meeting, Lahaina News, April 22, 1987: 10.

— Kitty Vincent Scholarship now available from, Lahaina News, May 6, 1987: 3.

— seeking directors and plays for upcoming season, Lahaina News, June 10, 1987: 3.

— to present "Come Back to the Five and Dime Jimmy Dean, Jimmy Dean", Lahaina News, June 10, 1987: 3.

— to perform "The Foreigner" by Larry Shue, Lahaina News, August 12, 1987: 3.

— Annual Variety Show, Lahaina News, August 19, 1987: 3.

— presenting "The Foreigner", Lahaina News, September 16, 1987: 3.

— "The Foreigner" reviewed, Lahaina News, October 7, 1987: 4.

— to perform "42nd Street", Lahaina News, January 27, 1988: 3.

— to perform "Ain't Misbehavin'", Lahaina News, February 24, 1988: 18.

— to hold auditions for "Vanities", Lahaina News, March 9, 1988: 17.

— accepting applications for Kitty Vincent scholarship, Lahaina News, March 23, 1988: 3.

— to hold auditions for "Fifth of July", Lahaina News, April 6, 1988: 3.

— sponsoring acting workshop, Lahaina News, April 27, 1988: 6.

— to hold auditions for "Fools", Lahaina News, May 11, 1988: 14.

— may be evicted from Iao Theatre, Lahaina News, May 18, 1988: 8.

— "Fifth of July" to open, Lahaina News, June 1, 1988: 19.

— Rita Whitford is Managing Director (newspaper correction), Lahaina News, June 1, 1988: 7.

— review of Neil Simon play "Fools", Lahaina News, July 6, 1988: 7.

— to perform "Little Shop of Horrors", Lahaina News, August 10, 1988: 7.

— to hold general meeting, Lahaina News, August 17, 1988: 15.

— auditions open for "Kismet", Lahaina News, September 7, 1988: 3.

— to produce "Crimes of the Heart", Lahaina News, September 21, 1988: 20.

— Cheri Pluta has lead role in "Kismet", Lahaina News, November 9, 1988: 9.

— to host holiday variety show, Lahaina News, December 14, 1988: 9.

— to perform "Same Time Next Year", Lahaina News, January 4, 1989: 3.

— Kitty Awards to be presented, Lahaina News, January 4, 1989: 7.

— performs "Fiddler on the Roof", Lahaina News, January 25, 1989: 9.

— to hold auditions for "Biloxi Blues", Lahaina News, February 22, 1989: 3.

— performs "Same Time Next Year", Lahaina News, March 1, 1989: 9.

— Neil Simon's "Biloxi Blues" opens, Lahaina News, April 26, 1989: 9.

— to hold fundraiser at Maui Marriott Resort, Lahaina News, June 28, 1989: 3.

— fundraiser held at Maui Marriott Ballroom, Lahaina News, July 5, 1989: 12.

— to hold fundraising gala at Maui Marriott Resort, Lahaina News, July 12, 1989: 3.

— cast set for "Amadeus", Lahaina News, August 2, 1989: 9.

— to hold auditions for "Dracula", Lahaina News, August 16, 1989: 3.

— to perform "La Cage Aux Folles", Lahaina News, November 22, 1989: 12.

— to perform "Oklahoma", Lahaina News, March 7, 1990: 13.

— to perform "Oklahoma", Lahaina News, March 21, 1990: 13.

— to perform "Hair", Lahaina News, June 27, 1990: 12.

— to hold Cocktail Sunset Sail fundraiser, Lahaina News, August 22, 1990: 4.

— Board of Trustees seeking volunteers, Lahaina News, August 29, 1990: 4.

— to perform "Rebecca", Lahaina News, September 5, 1990: 16.

— to hold auditions for "Stillborn", Lahaina News, September 26, 1990: 5.

— to perform the musical "Sugar", Lahaina News, November 14, 1990: 15.

— to perform "Stillborn", Lahaina News, December 19, 1990: 13.

— selling 1991 season tickets, Lahaina News, December 26, 1990: 11.

— selling 1991 season tickets, Lahaina News, January 2, 1991: 8.

— selling 1991 season tickets, Lahaina News, January 9, 1991: 8.

— to host Kitty Awards, Lahaina News, January 16, 1991: 11,14.

— to perform "Cabaret", Lahaina News, January 23, 1991: 4.

— to perform "Beyond Therapy", Lahaina News, January 23, 1991: 8.

— to perform "Cabaret", Lahaina News, February 20, 1991: 11.

— presents improvisational comedy, Lahaina News, April 17, 1991: 18.

— to host improvisation comedy, Lahaina News, April 24, 1991: 14.

— to perform "Tribute" by Scotty Templeton, Lahaina News, May 1, 1991: 18.

— to present "Marathon Cafe II", Lahaina News, June 6, 1991: 17.

— sponsoring stage performance with Richard Hatch, Lahaina News, June 20, 1991: 11,12.

— hosting Mark Twain 5K fundraiser with Valley Isle Road Runners Association, Lahaina News, July 25, 1991: 9.

— to perform "Play On", Lahaina News, August 15, 1991: 15.

— to perform "A Man for All Seasons", Lahaina News, November 7, 1991: 21.

— to present "Return of the Greater Tuna", Lahaina News, December 12, 1991: 25.

— to hold auditions for "Evita", Lahaina News, January 2, 1992: 5.

— to present Kitty Awards, Lahaina News, January 16, 1992: 18.

— to perform "Ili'ili", Lahaina News, February 6, 1992: 4.

— to hold auditions for "Evita", Lahaina News, March 5, 1992: 5.

— to perform "Evita", Lahaina News, May 7, 1992: 24,26.

— to perform "Driving Miss Daisy", Lahaina News, June 18, 1992: 21,22.

— to hold benefit Fun Walk/Run "Da Doo Ron Run", Lahaina News, July 23, 1992: 15.

— to hold benefit walk/run "Da Doo Ron Run", Lahaina News, August 6, 1992: 5.

— to perform "Who Needs Sneeds", Lahaina News, December 17, 1992: 22.

— to perform "Social Security", Lahaina News, January 28, 1993: 15.

— to perform "As Is", Lahaina News, February 4, 1993: 15.

— needs items for rummage sale, Lahaina News, September 16, 1993: 18.

— holds fundraiser at Blue Tropix, Lahaina News, February 17, 1994: 9.

— to hold auditions for "Under the Star Gladness", Lahaina News, June 9, 1994: 16.

— to hold benefit showing classic film comedies, Lahaina News, March 30, 1995: 12.

— to perform "I Hate Hamlet", Lahaina News, June 22, 1995: 12.

— Amy Gilliom to host benefit for, Lahaina News, September 5, 1996: 18.

— to produce "Extremities", Lahaina News, January 30, 1997: 11.

— to perform "The Shadow Box", Lahaina News, April 17, 1997: 13.

— to hold auditions for "How the Other Half Loves", Lahaina News, August 21, 1997: 17.

— to hold auditions for "How the Other Half Loves", Lahaina News, August 28, 1997: 10.

— season to begin with "How the Other Half Loves", Lahaina News, October 2, 1997: 21.

— to host "How the Other Half Loves", Lahaina News, October 9, 1997: 20.

— still performing "How the Other Half Dies", Lahaina News, October 16, 1997: 16.

— to hold auditions for "A Hawaiian Kine Christmas Carol", Lahaina News, October 23, 1997: 20.

— to produce "Private Lives", Lahaina News, January 8, 1998: 12.

— to perform "Love! Valour! Compassion!", Lahaina News, February 12, 1998: 16.

— to hold auditions for "Company", Lahaina News, April 16, 1998: 12.

— to perform Stephen Sondheim's "Company", Lahaina News, May 28, 1998: 13.

— to perform "The Odd Couple", Lahaina News, October 15, 1998: 16.
— celebrating Iao Theater's 70th birthday, Lahaina News, November 12, 1998: 16.
— to hold auditions for "Da Mayah", Lahaina News, December 3, 1998: 20.
— to perform "I Do! I Do!", Lahaina News, December 10, 1998: 20.
— to hold auditions for "One Flew Over the Cuckoo's Next", Lahaina News, February 18, 1999: 12.
— to perform "Cabaret", Lahaina News, March 4, 1999: 12.
— offering summer acting classes, Lahaina News, May 6, 1999: 2.
— to offer adult acting classes, Lahaina News, November 25, 1999: 15.
— to perform "A Wailuku Christmas", Lahaina News, December 9, 1999: 20.
— to produce The Beauty Queen of Leenane, Lahaina News, January 27, 2000: 12.
— to perform "5th of July", Lahaina News, June 1, 2000: 16.

MAUI COMMUNITY THEATRE PLAYHOUSE
— destroyed by fire, Lahaina News, September 26, 1984: 3.

MAUI COMMUNITY THEATRE/MAUI ONSTAGE
— to perform "Laughing Wild", Lahaina News, June 24, 1993: 13.
— to perform "Love Letters", Lahaina News, July 15, 1993: 12.
— looking for volunteers, Lahaina News, August 12, 1993: 14.
— to perform "Gin Game", Lahaina News, August 26, 1993: 13.
— to hold auditions for "Once On This Island", Lahaina News, September 9, 1993: 11.
— to perform "Once On This Island", Lahaina News, November 25, 1993: 11.
— see also Maui OnStage

MAUI COMMUNITY WEEK DAY
— "Tony and Denise's Talent Showcase" to benefit, Lahaina News, March 21, 2002: 16.

MAUI COMPREHENSIVE REHABILITATION CENTER
— adds new hotline, Lahaina News, December 31, 1992: 20.

MAUI CONDO AND RECREATION GUIDE [BOOK]
— published by Canon and Eger Publications, Lahaina News, July 17, 1985: 3.

MAUI CONFERENCE ON QUALITY GROWTH
— content detailed, Lahaina Sun, December 20, 1972: 5.

MAUI CONTRACTORS ASSOCIATION
— invites participants to Building Materials Expo, Lahaina News, February 17, 1988: 3,18.
— organizes Building and New Products Trade Show, Lahaina News, August 16, 1989: 6.
— has volunteered to help fix a home used as refuge for children, Lahaina News, August 30, 1989: 5.
— publishes Building and Remodeling Directory, Lahaina News, August 30, 1989: 5.
— helping fix Maui Youth and Family Shelter in Paia, Lahaina News, September 13, 1989: 1.
— Women's Auxiliary to hold Christmas bazaar, Lahaina News, October 25, 1989: 2.
— to hold annual installation banquet, Lahaina News, November 29, 1989: 4.
— installs new officers, Lahaina News, December 13, 1989: 7.
— holds meeting, Lahaina News, February 21, 1990: 5.
— projects planned for the 1990s, directory of companies, Lahaina News, February 28, 1990: supplement.
— association with Maui Correctional Center's Workline Program discussed, Lahaina News, February 28, 1990: supplement17,supplement18.
— selling booth space for New Products Show, Lahaina News, March 28, 1990: 7.

— copies of tabloid list of projects still available, Lahaina News, April 4, 1990: 7.
— selling booth space for New Products Show, Lahaina News, April 11, 1990: 2.
— to mee with State Senator Mike Crozier, Lahaina News, July 25, 1990: 7.
— critical of State efforts to build affordable homes, Lahaina News, August 8, 1990: 6.
— to hold candidate forum, Lahaina News, August 22, 1990: 9.
— Joe Donaghy becomes president, Lahaina News, January 9, 1991: 5.
— holds annual banquet, Lahaina News, January 23, 1991: 5.
— projects planned for the 1990s, directory of companies, Lahaina News, February 27, 1991: supplement.
— association with Maui Correctional Center's Workline Program discussed, Lahaina News, February 27, 1991: supplement16,supplement17.
— to hold general membership meeting, Lahaina News, March 13, 1991: 7.
— booths still available at Building Material Product Show, Lahaina News, May 30, 1991: 3.
— to hold Building Material Product Show, Lahaina News, June 6, 1991: 6.
— to host presentation by water department, Lahaina News, August 15, 1991: 6.
— to hold general membership meeting, Lahaina News, August 22, 1991: 4.
— to hold general membership meeting at Maui Palms Longhouse, Lahaina News, October 24, 1991: 8.
— offering CPR classes, Lahaina News, October 24, 1991: 8,9.
— building products trade show to be held, Lahaina News, October 24, 1991: 9.
— to hold annual golf tournament, Lahaina News, November 21, 1991: 9.
— Al Boteilho elected president, Lahaina News, November 28, 1991: 6.
— to hold annual golf tournament, Lahaina News, November 28, 1991: 8.
— offers suggestions to solve affordable homes shortage, Lahaina News, December 5, 1991: 14,32.
— new officers announced, Lahaina News, December 19, 1991: 13.
— organizing petition calling for speeder processing of building permits, Lahaina News, January 23, 1992: 11.
— to hold monthly seminars to address contractor needs, Lahaina News, January 23, 1992: 11,12.
— to hold general meeting, Lahaina News, February 13, 1992: 12.
— seeking advertising for upcoming consumer tabloid, Lahaina News, February 13, 1992: 12.
— Joe Souki to speak to, Lahaina News, March 12, 1992: 12,13.
— to hold Annual Building and New Products Show, Lahaina News, April 2, 1992: 12.
— to offer CPR/First Aid classes, Lahaina News, April 9, 1992: 13.
— to hold general meeting, Lahaina News, April 23, 1992: 16.
— to hold event on time management, Lahaina News, June 4, 1992: 9.
— Building and Products Expo Show to be held, Lahaina News, June 4, 1992: 9.
— to hold Products Expo Show, Lahaina News, June 25, 1992: 13,14,15.
— schedules general membership meeting, Lahaina News, August 20, 1992: 4.
— to hold Installation Banquet, Lahaina News, November 26, 1992: 20.
— Marie Kimmey to speak, Lahaina News, February 11, 1993: 11.
— to hold OSHA-approved CPR training, Lahaina News, February 18, 1993: 10.
— publishes "Maui Building Guide 1993", Lahaina News, February 25, 1993: supplement.

— Building and New Product show scheduled, Lahaina News, April 29, 1993: 9.
— to meet to discuss Kahului Harbor Master Plan, Lahaina News, May 20, 1993: 7.
— to hold general membership, Lahaina News, August 26, 1993: 10.
— to hold general membership meeting, Lahaina News, September 23, 1993: 7.
— to meet, Lahaina News, February 17, 1994: 6.
— to hold general membership meeting, Lahaina News, January 18, 1996: 10.
— hosting Storm Water and Urban Runoff Seminar, Lahaina News, February 22, 1996: 10.
— moves to new location, Lahaina News, November 14, 1996: 8.
— Home Show to be held, Lahaina News, June 19, 1997: 16.
— Home Show to be held, Lahaina News, June 19, 1997: 6.
— to hold yard sale, Lahaina News, July 31, 1997: 16.
— to hold Home Show, Lahaina News, June 25, 1998: 11.
— to hold yard sale, Lahaina News, August 13, 1998: 13.
— to hold Home Show, Lahaina News, June 19, 2003: 8.
— to hold Home Show, Lahaina News, June 26, 2003: 20.

MAUI CONTRACTORS WOMEN'S AUXILIARY
— to hold garage sale for Ronald McDonald House, Lahaina News, April 13, 2000: 12.
— to hold garage sale to support heart transplant patients Matthew McCall and Daphne Kawaiaea, Lahaina News, April 18, 2002: 16.
— to hold garage sale, Lahaina News, April 3, 2003: 8.

MAUI CORRECTIONAL CENTER
— association with Maui Contractors Association discussed, Lahaina News, February 28, 1990: supplement17,supplement18.
— association with Maui Contractors Association discussed, Lahaina News, February 27, 1991: supplement16,supplement17.

MAUI COUNCIL OF THE NAVY LEAGUE
— Navy Admiral Ronald Hays to speak to, Lahaina News, January 22, 1986: 3.
— to host Rear Admiral Alfred Manning at luncheon, Lahaina News, April 23, 1986: 3.
— James Robert Richards "sailor of the quarter" for, Lahaina News, November 12, 1986: 3.
— honors machinist Laredo Bell, Lahaina News, September 2, 1987: 3.

MAUI COUNTY
— audit of financial records planned, Lahaina Sun, October 6, 1971: 3.
— building in Wailuku completed ahead of schedule, Lahaina Sun, November 10, 1971: 12.
— accused of violating charter with auditing contract, Lahaina Sun, December 1, 1971: 1,11.
— automobile registrations mixed up and delayed, Lahaina Sun, January 5, 1972: 13.
— vote to be held on extending term of mayor to 4 years, Lahaina Sun, April 19, 1972: 14.
— studying feasibility of pick paths, Lahaina Sun, May 10, 1972: 21.
— budgeting procedures criticized by Maui Justice Foundation, Lahaina Sun, June 21, 1972: 10.
— Permanent Ordinances of the County of Maui printed, Lahaina Sun, June 28, 1972: 21.
— new office building described, including photographs, Lahaina Sun, July 5, 1972: 6.
— new building opens, Lahaina Sun, August 23, 1972: 19.
— mayor Cravalho reacts to charge by Allen Barr against County Council, Lahaina Sun, August 30, 1972: 10.
— four-year terms for councilmen and mayor will not be voted on, Lahaina Sun, September 20, 1972: 3.
— faulty vending machines at new building discussed, Lahaina Sun, October 11, 1972: 9.
— control over quonset huts on beach between Kahului and Wailuku, Lahaina Sun, November 22, 1972: 19.

— sued by residents of Piihana for flooding damage, Lahaina Sun, December 20, 1972: 14.
— budget is $15.8 million, Lahaina Sun, March 7, 1973: 6.
— public hearing on budget sparsely attended, Lahaina Sun, March 28, 1973: 3.
— receives federal money from Revenue Sharing Act, Lahaina Sun, April 11, 1973: 3.
— revised budget has additional $2.2 million, Lahaina Sun, June 6, 1973: 5.
— Marilyn Moniz, new prosecuting attorney added to staff, Lahaina News, May 1, 1980: 14.
— selling bonds, Lahaina News, July 15, 1980: 10.
— Council overturns mayor's veto of budget, Lahaina News, July 15, 1980: 10.
— issues with budget discussed, Lahaina News, July 15, 1980: 7.
— receives funding from federal housing funds, Lahaina News, September 1, 1980: 10.
— proposal to convert to biennial budget studied, Lahaina News, October 15, 1980: 4.
— property tax reform called for by mayor Tavares, Lahaina News, January 15, 1981: 11.
— Honokowai-Napili-Kapalua Taxpayers Association critical of taxes, Lahaina News, May 1, 1981: 16.
— taking over property tax valuation, assessment, and collection from the state, Lahaina News, July 1, 1981: 8.
— found negligent in operation of Olowalu Landfill, Lahaina News, April 15, 1987: 1,9.
— opposes new mooring permits, Lahaina News, July 22, 1987: 10.
— bans off-hour dumping at landfills, Lahaina News, August 5, 1987: 3.
— budget provides capital improvement funds to West Maui, Lahaina News, August 3, 1988: 1,24.
— declared a nuclear-free zone, Lahaina News, June 21, 1989: 1.
— considering offering pilot after school program, Lahaina News, January 10, 1990: 1.
— budget for West Maui projects detailed, Lahaina News, April 4, 1990: 1.
— Lee Dodson appointed budget director, Lahaina News, December 5, 1990: 3.
— unfurls new flag, Lahaina News, December 26, 1990: 5.
— Linda Lingle sworn in as mayor, Lahaina News, January 9, 1991: 1.
— Brian Miskae selected as planning director, Lahaina News, January 16, 1991: 2.
— Guy Haywood selected as deputy planning director, Lahaina News, January 16, 1991: 2,9.
— Stephanie Aveiro selected as director of Department of Human Concerns, Lahaina News, January 16, 1991: 9.
— Henry Oliva selected as deputy director of Department of Human Concerns, Lahaina News, January 16, 1991: 9.
— liquor control director to investigate fight, Lahaina News, January 23, 1991: 3.
— grants from available to non-profit groups, Lahaina News, January 30, 1991: 4.
— set to revise Lahaina Community Plan, Lahaina News, February 20, 1991: 1.
— board and commission appointments by mayor Linda Lingle listed, Lahaina News, February 20, 1991: 5.
— to hold public hearing on allowing swap meet in Wailuku, Lahaina News, March 6, 1991: 7.
— mayor Linda Lingle proposes $181 million budget, Lahaina News, March 20, 1991: 3.
— deadline to file appeals with Board of Taxation Review coming up, Lahaina News, April 3, 1991: 3.
— to hold hearing on property tax system, Lahaina News, May 1, 1991: 1.

— parks director Chermaine Tavares exploring potential sites for park in Napili, Lahaina News, May 8, 1991: 1.

— planning public meeting on Napili Trade Center, Lahaina News, May 8, 1991: 1.

— Guy Haywood appointed Corporation Counsel, Lahaina News, May 23, 1991: 6.

— head of recycling says Maui should recycle more, Lahaina News, June 20, 1991: 1,3.

— Edyln Taniguchi appointed assistant treasurer, Lahaina News, June 20, 1991: 7.

— Planning Director calls for new approach to land usage, Lahaina News, November 28, 1991: 1.

— satellite office available at Lahaina Civic Center, Lahaina News, December 5, 1991: 4.

— offering grants to non-profits, Lahaina News, December 5, 1991: 5.

— transportation committee proposes trolley system for Maui, Lahaina News, December 12, 1991: 1.

— searching for Maui Country Economic Development Coordinator, Lahaina News, December 12, 1991: 3,5.

— bill proposes creating non-profit hospital, Lahaina News, December 12, 1991: 6.

— grants for non-profits available from, Lahaina News, December 12, 1991: 7.

— panel recommends approval of Herbert Horita's project in Kihei, Lahaina News, December 19, 1991: 17.

— to fund research on algae bloom problem, Lahaina News, January 2, 1992: 1.

— Prosecutor Larry Butrick says prosecuting homicides is first priority, Lahaina News, January 9, 1992: 1.

— Mayor's Advisory Committee on the homeless to hold meeting, Lahaina News, March 12, 1992: 5.

— passes law excepting Hawaiian homesteaders from county property tax, mayor Lingle likely to sign, Lahaina News, March 26, 1992: 12.

— hearings on budget set, Lahaina News, April 2, 1992: 1.

— to purchase water from Amfac/JMB following landslide, Lahaina News, May 21, 1992: 1.

— claims to not own polluted ditch at Honokowai Stream, Lahaina News, June 25, 1992: 2.

— offering driver's license services in Kihei on Saturdays, Lahaina News, July 9, 1992: 7.

— "Government on Wheels" to offer services, Lahaina News, July 16, 1992: 5.

— to mail survey about property status, Lahaina News, July 16, 1992: 8.

— to send survey on residential exemptions at condominiums, Lahaina News, July 23, 1992: 3.

— kills bill to control noise from roosters, Lahaina News, July 23, 1992: 3.

— killed a bill to outlaw slaughtering animals for food in residential areas, Lahaina News, July 23, 1992: 3.

— passes bill to help fund Ukumehame Public Shooting Range, Lahaina News, July 23, 1992: 3.

— passes bill for conditional permit for shoe repair shop in Lahaina, Lahaina News, July 23, 1992: 3,4.

— passes bill to allow Maui Land and Pineapple to build employee housing, Lahaina News, July 23, 1992: 4.

— mobile services rescheduled, Lahaina News, July 23, 1992: 4.

— proposed amendments to charter listed, Lahaina News, July 23, 1992: 6.

— mobile services scheduled for Upcountry and North Shore, Lahaina News, August 6, 1992: 3.

— to hold public hearings on applying to Community Block Grant Program, Lahaina News, October 8, 1992: 9.

— offering some services in Kihei, Lahaina News, November 12, 1992: 11.

— parks department to pursue park in Napili, Lahaina News, November 19, 1992: 1.

— reviews emergency plans, Lahaina News, December 3, 1992: 4.

— Government on Wheels bus temporarily closed, Lahaina News, December 24, 1992: 5.

— money received from Federal Transportation Authority to support new Transportation Coordinator position, Lahaina News, December 31, 1992: 20.

— bond issue awarded, Lahaina News, February 18, 1993: 5.

— to hold hearings on budget, Lahaina News, March 25, 1993: 3.

— hosting Lahaina Historic District workshop, Lahaina News, May 20, 1993: 2.

— to offer licensing services at Lahaina satellite office, Lahaina News, August 5, 1993: 4.

— concerns over maximum tax program, Lahaina News, August 12, 1993: 1,15.

— Economic Development, Tourism and Environment Committee to hold workshop on ocean resource management, Lahaina News, November 11, 1993: 3.

— Mayor Linda Lingle signs bill to allow fire departments to use volunteers, Lahaina News, December 2, 1993: 1.

— Mayor Linda Lingle unveils budget requests, Lahaina News, March 24, 1994: 1,20.

— says that Front Street improvements will be done quickly, Lahaina News, July 14, 1994: 1,20.

— Mayor Linda Lingle not convinced on need to split Public Works and Waste Management Department, Lahaina News, October 5, 1995: 3.

— funding "Art of Trash" exhibit, Lahaina News, February 1, 1996: 12.

— increases grants to West Side groups, Lahaina News, August 22, 1996: 2.

— accepting budget requests, Lahaina News, September 19, 1996: 1.

— residents need to fill county boards, Lahaina News, September 19, 1996: 4.

— trying to remove brochure racks on Front Street, Lahaina News, January 16, 1997: 5.

— mayor Linda Lingle's budget discussed, Lahaina News, March 20, 1997: 1,20.

— budget earmarks funding for West Maui projects, Lahaina News, June 19, 1997: 1.

— seeking input for Napili park, Lahaina News, December 18, 1997: 1,2.

— update on races for seats and mayor, Lahaina News, February 26, 1998: 3.

— mayor Linda Lingle unveils proposed budget, Lahaina News, March 19, 1998: 3.

— looking for location for homeless resource center, Lahaina News, May 7, 1998: 1,20.

— offering Learn to Swim program, Lahaina News, June 18, 1998: 15.

— disaster management plan discussed, Lahaina News, July 16, 1998: 1.

— Sheraton Maui must obtain permits to keep steel pilings, Lahaina News, August 20, 1998: 3.

— seeking volunteers for county panels, Lahaina News, December 3, 1998: 11.

— recruiting for residents to serve on county panels, Lahaina News, December 10, 1998: 11.

— residents make budget requests to new county administration, Lahaina News, January 21, 1999: 1,16.

— budget proposed, Lahaina News, March 18, 1999: 1.

— sending tax property assessments, Lahaina News, March 18, 1999: 8.

— to inform businesses of ADA requirements, Lahaina News, April 1, 1999: 13.

— Overall Economic Development Plan to be discussed, Lahaina News, April 8, 1999: 11.

MAUI COUNTY CODE
— available on the internet, Lahaina News, October 22, 1998: 15.

MAUI COUNTY COMMISSION ON CULTURE AND THE ARTS
— to sponsor concert of local musicians in Wailuku, Lahaina News, July 30, 1992: 18.
— sponsoring free concerts, Lahaina News, August 20, 1992: 22.
— compiling cultural directory, Lahaina News, December 26, 2002: 1.

MAUI COUNTY COMMITTEE ON ECOLOGY
— projects described, Lahaina Sun, January 20, 1971: 6.

MAUI COUNTY COMMITTEE ON THE STATUS OF WOMEN
— seeks nominations for Circle of Women Awards, Lahaina News, March 1, 1989: 5.
— announces Circle of Women Awards, Lahaina News, March 22, 1989: 13.
— sponsoring talk by Amanda Smith, Lahaina News, October 11, 1989: 3.
— sponsoring Women's Conference, Lahaina News, October 3, 1990: 3.
— to hold Women's Conference, Lahaina News, October 10, 1990: 6.
— to host "Equality Day" Celebration, Lahaina News, August 20, 1992: 4.
— to highlight Pat Masumoto and Marie Smith on "Maui Women Making a Difference", Lahaina News, March 7, 2002: 5.
— to hold Women's Health Fair, Lahaina News, June 20, 2002: 18.
— celebrating Women's Health Month, Lahaina News, August 28, 2003: 5.

MAUI COUNTY COMMUNITY PARTNERSHIP
— to offer grants, Lahaina News, January 27, 2000: 13.
— to offer grants, Lahaina News, January 25, 2001: 17.

MAUI COUNTY COMMUNITY TELEVISION, INC. [BUSINESS]
— Daria Palmer to be general manager, Lahaina News, February 4, 1993: 10.

MAUI COUNTY CORPORATION COUNSEL
— to decide fate of beach access in Napili, Lahaina News, December 19, 1991: 1.

MAUI COUNTY COUNCIL
— considering emergency powers for Mayor, Lahaina Sun, December 23, 1970: 1,5.
— public meeting in Wailuku with State Department of Transportation to public meeting scheduled, Lahaina Sun, December 30, 1970: 8.
— discussed improvement projects, Lahaina Sun, January 13, 1971: 2.
— meeting to discuss overriding a veto by Mayor Cravalho, Lahaina Sun, January 13, 1971: 6.
— approves shops at the Maui Eldorado condominium, Lahaina Sun, January 13, 1971: 6.
— approves $14 million for sewers and buildings, Lahaina Sun, January 20, 1971: 1.
— asked Maui Historic Commission to create rules for signage, Lahaina Sun, January 20, 1971: 1.
— overrides Mayor Cravalho's veto concerning apartment zoning, Lahaina Sun, January 20, 1971: 6.
— chambers damaged by rain, Lahaina Sun, January 20, 1971: 6.
— meeting schedule for January 29, Lahaina Sun, January 27, 1971: 4.
— approves $2.22 million for new building, Lahaina Sun, February 3, 1971: 8.
— approvers $2.22 million for county building in Wailuku, Lahaina Sun, February 10, 1971: 6.
— asks for return of Kaho'olawe, Lahaina Sun, February 24, 1971: 2.
— proposal to create a Committee on Environmental Control within, Lahaina Sun, February 24, 1971: 6.
— seeks change in route for electric power poles, Lahaina Sun, March 3, 1971: 1,2.
— capital improvement projects detailed, Lahaina Sun, March 3, 1971: 1,8.
— meeting to discuss proposed rules planned, Lahaina Sun, March 17, 1971: 5.
— building in Wailuku under construction (includes photographs), Lahaina Sun, April 14, 1971: 3.
— meet on Lana'i, Lahaina Sun, April 28, 1971: 4.
— studying law to ban peddling, Lahaina Sun, May 12, 1971: 4.
— budget approved, Lahaina Sun, June 9, 1971: 1,8.
— approves funds for capital improvement projects, Lahaina Sun, June 23, 1971: 3.
— budget signed by mayor Cravalho, Lahaina Sun, June 30, 1971: 12.
— committee system criticized by Joe Bulgo, Lahaina Sun, July 7, 1971: 1,2.
— accepts gift of 12-acres of land from Alexander & Baldwin, Inc., Lahaina Sun, July 14, 1971: 10.
— announces no property tax increase for the year, Lahaina Sun, October 20, 1971: 14.
— news from meeting, Lahaina Sun, October 20, 1971: 15.
— recommends that Maui Community College become a four-year institution, Lahaina Sun, October 20, 1971: 15.
— studies changes to railroad laws to mandate warning signals, Lahaina Sun, October 27, 1971: 6.
— accused of ignoring charter , Lahaina Sun, November 24, 1971: 4.
— endorses Maui United Fund drive, Lahaina Sun, December 8, 1971: 8.
— County Attorney claims audit is legal, Lahaina Sun, January 5, 1972: 13.
— section devoted to Council business begins in Lahaina Sun, Lahaina Sun, January 12, 1972: .
— handing of money has improved, Lahaina Sun, January 12, 1972: 15.
— publishes sewage master plan, Lahaina Sun, January 19, 1972: 10.
— to hold meeting to discuss operating budget and capital improvement projects, Lahaina Sun, March 8, 1972: 12.
— pared budget presented to, Lahaina Sun, March 8, 1972: 3.
— supports cockfighting, Lahaina Sun, March 8, 1972: 5.
— debate over tourism at budget hearing, Lahaina Sun, March 29, 1972: 7.
— contract for new sewer system questioned, Lahaina Sun, April 12, 1972: 15.
— moving into new complex in Wailuku, Lahaina Sun, April 26, 1972: 10.
— okays budget for next fiscal year, Lahaina Sun, June 21, 1972: 5.
— request to study feasibility of broadcasting council meetings deferred, Lahaina Sun, January 10, 1973: 3.
— criticized for secrecy, Lahaina Sun, January 10, 1973: 9.
— county commission membership changes detailed, Lahaina Sun, January 17, 1973: 10.
— Goro Hokama elected chair, Lahaina Sun, January 17, 1973: 7.
— studying stray dogs, expansion of Honoapi'ilani highway, and rise in telephone rates, Lahaina Sun, May 9, 1973: 7.
— members described, includes photographs, Lahaina Sun, May 30, 1973: 1,12,13.
— debates fairness of paying to expand water supply for a tourist development, Lahaina Sun, July 4, 1973: 4.
— meeting with large agenda finished, Lahaina Sun, July 18, 1973: 3.
— questions firm creating Maui Dollars, Lahaina Sun, August 1, 1973: 3.
— approves ballot measures to increase Council power, Lahaina News, July 15, 1980: 10.
— Maui County Cost of Government Commission makes recommendations to improve the County Land Use and Codes Administration, Lahaina News, October 15, 1980: 10.

— mayor comments on policy regarding appointing people to multiple boards, Lahaina News, January 1, 1981: 1.

— passes bill to require public disclosure of county official finances, Lahaina News, October 15, 1982: 2.

— to hold public hearing on real property tax, Lahaina News, May 1, 1983: 10.

— approves variable real property tax rate, Lahaina News, May 15, 1983: 2,3.

— budget approved, Lahaina News, May 15, 1983: 6.

— budget fight ended, Lahaina News, June 15, 1983: 6.

— debates Lahaina Community Plan, Lahaina News, September 14, 1983: 7.

— supplemental budget submitted, Lahaina News, October 19, 1983: 6.

— planning committee passes Lahaina Community Plan, Lahaina News, November 23, 1983: 4,5.

— budget passes, Lahaina News, February 1, 1984: 7.

— budget to be discussed at informal meeting at Lahaina Civic Center, Lahaina News, April 4, 1984: 3.

— to retain control of Old Court House, Lahaina News, May 2, 1984: 4.

— cuts budget of Maui County Visitors Association, Lahaina News, May 16, 1984: 17.

— Revenue Sharing Committee disburses money to local nonprofit organizations, Lahaina News, June 13, 1984: 3.

— Mayor Tavares wants part of budget surplus to go to Maui County Visitors Association, Lahaina News, September 26, 1984: 14.

— co-sponsor island-wide clean-up, Lahaina News, December 5, 1984: 3.

— committee asks for swimming pool for Lahaina to be built sooner, Lahaina News, February 20, 1985: 1,7.

— files complaint against Lahaina Fashions, Inc. to stop selling from display booths, Lahaina News, October 9, 1985: 3.

— holds public hearing on proposed airport in West Maui, Lahaina News, November 13, 1985: 1,20.

— supports deposits on bottles and cans, Lahaina News, November 13, 1985: 3.

— to consider proposed airport in Mahinahina on January 6, Lahaina News, December 25, 1985: 3.

— Council approves airport in Mahinahina, Lahaina News, February 26, 1986: 1,16.

— waiting for mayor's opinion on proposed airport at Mahinahina, Lahaina News, March 19, 1986: 1.

— approves proposed airport at Mahinahina, lawsuits likely, Lahaina News, March 26, 1986: 1,12.

— to hold hearing on budget at Lahaina Civic Center, Lahaina News, April 2, 1986: 3.

— to receive portion of state's hotel room tax, Lahaina News, April 23, 1986: 3.

— passes resolution to proceed with Kahoma Flood Control Project, Lahaina News, June 25, 1986: 3.

— grants available from, Lahaina News, July 16, 1986: 3.

— to hold budget meeting, Lahaina News, April 1, 1987: 3.

— agrees with Army Corps of Engineers to ease traffic bottleneck in Lahaina, Lahaina News, April 8, 1987: 1.

— to hold hearing regarding budget, Lahaina News, March 30, 1988: 20.

— welcoming testimony on amendments to charter, Lahaina News, March 30, 1988: 20.

— public hearing described, Lahaina News, April 6, 1988: 11.

— to hold hearing on proposed land exchange to realign Lower Honoapi'ilani Road, Lahaina News, June 1, 1988: 19,20.

— reads bill relating to the Kahoma Stream detour, Lahaina News, September 7, 1988: 20.

— approves condemnation of Luakini Street for conversion to parking lot, Lahaina News, October 26, 1988: 1.

— fight conversion of Holo Honokowai to hotel, Lahaina News, December 21, 1988: 1.

— seeks input on fairgrounds relocation, Lahaina News, March 8, 1989: 16.

— budget hearing set, Lahaina News, May 3, 1989: 3.

— to hold hearings on fire code, Lahaina News, July 5, 1989: 3.

— to hold public hearing on traffic, beaches, Lahaina News, July 26, 1989: 3.

— holds public hearing on beach access, Lahaina News, August 9, 1989: 3.

— to hold hearing on land use standards for Kapalua project, Lahaina News, September 27, 1989: 1.

— set to approve development of Ritz-Carlton hotel, Lahaina News, October 11, 1989: 1.

— proposes property tax relief, Lahaina News, November 1, 1989: 3.

— may overturn ban on permanent activities booth, Lahaina News, April 11, 1990: 1,6.

— examining dangerous road crossings, Lahaina News, September 5, 1990: 1.

— passes resolution in support of recycling, reuse, and source reduction, Lahaina News, September 26, 1990: 6,7.

— panel to study proposed light industrial site at Napili, Lahaina News, October 24, 1990: 1.

— proposes ban on tour buses from Baker Street, Lahaina News, November 21, 1990: 4.

— delays confirmation of Cyrus Chan, Lahaina News, February 20, 1991: 3.

— to hold public hearing on proposed development in Napili, Lahaina News, March 20, 1991: 1.

— to hold public hearing on proposed development in Napili, Lahaina News, April 10, 1991: 1.

— to sponsor conferences on affordable housing, Lahaina News, April 10, 1991: 4.

— considers designating loading zone on Front Street, Lahaina News, April 24, 1991: 1.

— considers limiting parking on Dickenson Street, Lahaina News, April 24, 1991: 1.

— mayor Linda Lingle signs bill creating recycling/composting program, Lahaina News, April 24, 1991: 4,5.

— rejects William Crockett as Maui Charter Commissioner, Lahaina News, May 8, 1991: 8.

— passes bill to reduce property tax, Lahaina News, May 23, 1991: 1.

— to hold public meeting on budget, Lahaina News, August 29, 1991: 3.

— postpones voting on proposed Napili Trade Center, Lahaina News, September 5, 1991: 3.

— votes against extending Kahului Airport runway, Lahaina News, September 12, 1991: 11.

— to be closed this week due to staffing shortages, Lahaina News, September 19, 1991: 3.

— to vote on Napili Trade Center, Lahaina News, October 3, 1991: 5.

— approves Napili Trade Center, Lahaina News, December 26, 1991: 3.

— approves development in Kihei proposed by Herbert Horita Development, Lahaina News, December 26, 1991: 4.

— unsuccessful recovering money lost in state airport building revenues, Lahaina News, January 2, 1992: 5.

— reading bill to allow zero lot line subdivisions for affordable housing, Lahaina News, January 9, 1992: 9.

— Goro Hokama announces retirement from Dole Food Co., Lahaina News, January 16, 1992: 3.

— Planning and Economic Development Committee schedules meeting on proposed Wailea 670 project, Lahaina News, January 30, 1992: 4.

— may rewrite rules on the use of public facilities for craft fairs, Lahaina News, February 13, 1992: 3.

— may except Hawaiian homesteaders from paying county property taxes, Lahaina News, February 20, 1992: 3.

— to vote on several West Maui bills, Lahaina News, April 2, 1992: 3.

— questions why additional $100,000 submitted to the county, Lahaina News, April 2, 1992: 3.

— may provide money to promote small business, Lahaina News, April 16, 1992: 13.

— bills exempting churches from taxes thought to be unconstitutional, Lahaina News, April 30, 1992: 3.

— passes budget, Lahaina News, June 11, 1992: 3.

— proposal to limit terms of to be discussed, Lahaina News, June 18, 1992: 4.

— drops bill banning animal slaughter in residential neighborhoods, Lahaina News, July 2, 1992: 4.

— meeting to discuss real estate taxes and Upcountry high school, Lahaina News, July 2, 1992: 4.

— considering bill to create Ukumehame Public Shooting Range, Lahaina News, July 9, 1992: 3,4.

— to ask Public Works director George Kaya about sewer main, Lahaina News, July 16, 1992: 1.

— members advocate for economic diversification, Lahaina News, July 23, 1992: 7.

— may pass bill requiring county to pay for road improvements for church developments, Lahaina News, July 23, 1992: 9.

— passes property tax exemption for churches, Lahaina News, August 13, 1992: 4.

— asked to restore funds to West Maui Youth Center, Lahaina News, August 27, 1992: 1.

— to hold hearing on proposed zoning changes, Lahaina News, September 10, 1992: 11.

— votes to approve Wailea 670 development, Lahaina News, September 24, 1992: 2.

— approves shoe and luggage repair shop on Wainee Street, Lahaina News, October 1, 1992: 9.

— Wailea 670 proposal passes final reading, Lahaina News, October 8, 1992: 7.

— votes to eliminate subcommittee reviewing Kahului Airport extension, Lahaina News, October 22, 1992: 4.

— to consider proposed shopping center in Honokowai , Lahaina News, February 11, 1993: 3.

— to hold public meeting on budget, Lahaina News, April 1, 1993: 4.

— to meet, Lahaina News, April 15, 1993: 3.

— residents want more police and firefighters, Lahaina News, April 15, 1993: 4.

— Planning Committee to hold public meeting on proposed golf course Upcountry, Lahaina News, April 29, 1993: 3.

— hearing on property taxes to be held, Lahaina News, April 29, 1993: 3.

— approves zoning change from agriculture to residential for project near Kahana Gateway, Lahaina News, June 24, 1993: 4.

— Tom Morrow to be recommended as vice chair of, Lahaina News, September 9, 1993: 1,12.

— elects new vice chairman, Lahaina News, September 23, 1993: 3.

— supports Kihei Public Library, Lahaina News, November 11, 1993: 6.

— lawyers plan to challenge Planning Committee's decision concerning Napilihau Villages, Lahaina News, March 10, 1994: 1,3.

— hearings planned for budget, Lahaina News, March 17, 1994: 3.

— approves JGL project, Lahaina News, March 24, 1994: 1,20.

— to hold public meeting on budget, Lahaina News, March 24, 1994: 7.

— Planning Committee to hold public meeting, Lahaina News, June 2, 1994: 3.

— to consider issue of t-shirt vending by the Banyan Tree, Lahaina News, July 14, 1994: 5.

— to examine drinking in Malu'ulu O Lele Park, Lahaina News, July 28, 1994: 4.

— members hold unannounced meeting to criticize Mayor Linda Lingle, Lahaina News, October 20, 1994: 1.

— working on legislation to curb drinking at park, Lahaina News, October 20, 1994: 1.

— to vote on drinking in parks, Lahaina News, November 17, 1994: 1,24.

— supports of drinking at Malu'ulu O Lele Park, Lahaina News, December 8, 1994: 1.

— passes ordinance to prohibit drinking in parks, Lahaina News, December 22, 1994: 2.

— approves creation of Lahaina Visitor Center, Lahaina News, January 12, 1995: 1.

— wants to reduce county liability for recreational facilities, Lahaina News, February 16, 1995: 1,3.

— residents request funds for Light Bringers Mission at Budget Committee hearing, Lahaina News, April 6, 1995: 1,3.

— holds public meeting in West Maui, Lahaina News, April 13, 1995: 2.

— considers banning drinking in Honokowai Park, Lahaina News, May 18, 1995: 3.

— Parks and Recreation Committee to discuss regulating drinking in county parks, Lahaina News, May 25, 1995: 4.

— to discuss Pioneer Mill's plan for strip mall, Lahaina News, June 1, 1995: 3.

— Planning Committee to hold meetings to discuss West Maui Community Plan, Lahaina News, July 6, 1995: 5.

— residents at public meeting on West Maui Community Plan urge slow growth, Lahaina News, July 13, 1995: 1,16.

— budget director Georgina Kawamura says county programs to use performance measures, Lahaina News, August 3, 1995: 5.

— bans people in store entrances from calling out to pedestrians, Lahaina News, August 10, 1995: 1,2,16.

— bans on park drinking and hawking pass first reading at, Lahaina News, August 24, 1995: 1,16.

— to seek share of traffic tickets, Lahaina News, August 24, 1995: 7.

— Mayor Linda Lingle hosts discussion of budget, Lahaina News, September 28, 1995: 1,12.

— to discuss bird poisoning at hotels, Lahaina News, September 28, 1995: 3.

— Charles Fletcher speaks on need to protect beaches, Lahaina News, October 12, 1995: 1,16.

— to discuss bird poisoning at hotels, Lahaina News, October 12, 1995: 3.

— supports Hawaiian cultural park, Lahaina News, November 9, 1995: 1,16.

— changes position on shopping center proposed by Amfac/JMB Hawaii , Lahaina News, November 23, 1995: 1,12.

— to hold public meeting on West Maui Community Plan, Lahaina News, November 23, 1995: 6.

— holds public hearing on West Maui Community Plan, Lahaina News, December 7, 1995: 1,20.

— first reading of West Maui Community Plan at, Lahaina News, December 14, 1995: 20.

— defers amendments to West Maui Community Plan, Lahaina News, December 21, 1995: 1,16.

— cuts funds for wastewater re-use line, Lahaina News, December 21, 1995: 1,16.

— still seeking end to hawking, Lahaina News, February 1, 1996: 1,14.

— takes final action on West Maui Community Plan, Lahaina News, February 29, 1996: 1,2.

— budget hearing to be held, Lahaina News, April 4, 1996: 2.

— holds public hearing on budget requests, Lahaina News, April 11, 1996: 1,3.

MAUI COUNTY COUNCIL OF COMMUNITY ASSOCIATIONS

MAUI COUNTY DANCE BAND
— to perform at Fall dance at Grand Hyatt Wailea, Lahaina News, October 10, 1991: 21.

MAUI COUNTY DATA BOOK
— published, Lahaina News, February 24, 1994: 4.
— published, Lahaina News, March 30, 1995: 10.
— published, Lahaina News, October 30, 1997: 13.

MAUI COUNTY DEPARTMENT OF HUMAN CONCERNS
— see Housing and Human Concerns, Department of

MAUI COUNTY DEPARTMENT OF PARKS AND RECREATION
— see Parks and Recreation, Maui County Department of

MAUI COUNTY FAIR
— request to submit possible themes, Lahaina Sun, June 9, 1971: 2.
— events detailed, Lahaina Sun, October 13, 1971: 1.
— police turned away people wearing tank tops, Lahaina Sun, October 20, 1971: 6.
— directors named for 1972 Fair, Lahaina Sun, November 10, 1971: 6.
— details, Lahaina Sun, October 4, 1972: 4,5.
— photographs and parade winners, Lahaina Sun, October 11, 1972: 7.
— Maui County fair to be held, Lahaina Sun, July 4, 1973: 21.
— planning has begun, Lahaina Sun, August 29, 1973: 15.
— bird and bunny exhibits described, Lahaina News, October 1, 1980: 7.
— plans for 59th annual, Lahaina News, October 1, 1981: 16.
— details provided, Lahaina News, August 15, 1982: 10.
— details provided, Lahaina News, September 15, 1982: 15.
— opens, Lahaina News, October 3, 1984: 13.
— set for October 10, Lahaina News, October 9, 1985: 3.
— photo contest announced, Lahaina News, July 2, 1986: 18.
— sign up for parade, Lahaina News, August 27, 1986: 3.
— seeking competitors, Lahaina News, September 3, 1986: 3.
— feature talent contents, seeking entertainers, Lahaina News, July 29, 1987: 3.
— deadline to participate nearing, Lahaina News, August 12, 1987: 18.
— seeking submissions of produce, Lahaina News, September 9, 1987: 3.
— opens, Lahaina News, September 23, 1987: 9.
— described, Lahaina News, September 30, 1987: 3.
— events described, Lahaina News, October 7, 1987: 1.
— to be held, Lahaina News, September 28, 1988: 1.
— events listed, Lahaina News, October 5, 1988: 1.
— to be held, Lahaina News, May 31, 1989: 3.
— organized, Lahaina News, September 20, 1989: 3.
— to hold Healthy Baby contest, Lahaina News, October 4, 1989: 2.
— to take place at War Memorial Complex, Lahaina News, September 19, 1990: 5.
— to be held, Lahaina News, September 26, 1990: 6.
— to be held; has shuttle; schedule for, Lahaina News, October 3, 1990: 5.
— record attendance at, Lahaina News, October 17, 1990: 6.
— repays loan from Maui County, Lahaina News, December 19, 1990: 6.
— to be held, Lahaina News, September 12, 1991: 18.
— scheduled, Lahaina News, September 26, 1991: 1,13.
— events detailed, Lahaina News, September 26, 1991: 17.
— details, Lahaina News, October 3, 1991: 18.
— to be held at the War Memorial complex, Lahaina News, October 1, 1992: 18.
— to feature island chefs, Lahaina News, September 30, 1993: 13.
— featured, Lahaina News, October 7, 1993: 11.
— Association announces scholarship recipient, Lahaina News, June 30, 1994: 4.
— to be held, Lahaina News, July 21, 1994: 11,12.
— to hold preliminary contests for karaoke competition, Lahaina News, July 28, 1994: 13.

— registration forms ready, Lahaina News, July 28, 1994: 14.
— holds preliminary competition for karaoke contest, Lahaina News, August 25, 1994: 14.
— registration forms ready, Lahaina News, August 25, 1994: 16.
— to include cooking contests, Lahaina News, September 1, 1994: 16.
— booths available, Lahaina News, September 1, 1994: 7.
— pre-sale tickets available, Lahaina News, September 15, 1994: 16.
— held, Lahaina News, October 6, 1994: 1,14.
— Lahainaluna High School wins School Spirit Competition, Lahaina News, October 20, 1994: 5.
— organizational meeting to be held, Lahaina News, June 27, 1996: 15.
— chairs to meet, Lahaina News, July 11, 1996: 12.
— planning, Lahaina News, August 22, 1996: 15.
— karaoke contest to be held, Lahaina News, September 19, 1996: 15.
— livestock and poultry exhibit applications being accepted, Lahaina News, September 18, 1997: 17.
— to be held, Lahaina News, October 2, 1997: 10.
— Parade to be sponsored by AAAAA Rent-A-Space, Lahaina News, July 9, 1998: 7.
— to be held, Lahaina News, August 20, 1998: 8.
— to be held, Lahaina News, August 27, 1998: 9.
— to be held, Lahaina News, September 3, 1998: 8.
— to be held, Lahaina News, August 12, 1999: 8.
— to be held, Lahaina News, August 26, 1999: 14.
— spaces are available in the parade, Lahaina News, September 14, 2000: 6.
— opens, Lahaina News, September 28, 2000: 7.
— to open, Lahaina News, July 12, 2001: 16.
— seeking corporate sponsors, Lahaina News, August 2, 2001: 8.
— trailer now open weekdays, Lahaina News, August 16, 2001: 16,17.
— to be held, Lahaina News, October 4, 2001: 18.
— seeking corporate sponsors, Lahaina News, April 25, 2002: 8.
— Association appoints Joe Pontanilla as chair of Better Living Tent, Lahaina News, July 4, 2002: 2.
— trailer opened in the Maui Memorial Gym parking lot, Lahaina News, August 15, 2002: 9.
— applications for parade available, Lahaina News, August 22, 2002: 9.
— to be held, Lahaina News, September 19, 2002: 13.
— Mayor James Apana announces start of county's recruitment drive for county boards, commissions and committees, Lahaina News, October 17, 2002: 14.
— to be held, Lahaina News, May 8, 2003: 2.

MAUI COUNTY FARM BUREAU
— sponsoring "Most Creative Use of Broccoli" recipe contest, Lahaina News, May 24, 1989: 17.
— Recipe Contest to be held, Lahaina News, June 6, 1990: 14.

MAUI COUNTY GENERAL PLAN
— public hearing scheduled to discuss, Lahaina News, May 1, 1991: 1.

MAUI COUNTY GOVERNMENT
— said to be the worst offender in ocean dumping, Lahaina Sun, November 18, 1970: 1.

MAUI COUNTY HAWAIIAN CANOE ASSOCIATION
— competitions to be held, Lahaina News, May 19, 1994: 8.
— regatta ends, Lahaina News, July 27, 1995: 6.
— completes regatta season, Lahaina News, July 18, 1996: 6.
— regatta season opens, Lahaina News, June 5, 1997: 12.
— won by Hawaiian Canoe Club, Lahaina News, July 24, 1997: 15.
— hosting Ocean Relay Race, Lahaina News, April 23, 1998: 14,15.
— offering scholarships, Lahaina News, June 10, 1999: 15.
— offering scholarships, Lahaina News, June 24, 1999: 7.
— long distance racing season continues, Lahaina News, August 19, 1999: 7.
— to hold summer regattas, Lahaina News, June 1, 2000: 9.
— in-shore regattas conclude, Lahaina News, July 20, 2000: 6.
— long distance season to begin, Lahaina News, August 10, 2000: 7.

MAUI COUNTY HISTORIC COMMISSION
— approves closure of Front Street for Friday Night is Art Night, Lahaina News, May 30, 1990: 1.

MAUI COUNTY IMMIGRANT SERVICES
— organizing summer basketball league, Lahaina News, July 26, 1989: 2.

MAUI COUNTY IMPACT INITIATIVE
— to hold meeting to discuss disaster planning, Lahaina News, November 9, 2000: 6.

MAUI COUNTY ISSUES [NEWSPAPER]
— begins publication, Lahaina Sun, September 27, 1972: 5.

MAUI COUNTY JAIL
— officially closed, Lahaina Sun, January 12, 1972: 8.

MAUI COUNTY JOB FAIR
— to be held at Maui Community College, Lahaina News, May 7, 1998: 20.

MAUI COUNTY LIQUOR CONTROL
— inspector reprimanded for incident, Lahaina News, May 30, 1991: 1.

MAUI COUNTY LIQUOR CONTROL COMMISSION
— see Liquor Control Commission

MAUI COUNTY MEDICAL SOCIETY
— sponsoring free diabetes tests, Lahaina Sun, December 2, 1970: 1.
— continues breast cancer screening program, Lahaina News, March 15, 1981: 14.

MAUI COUNTY NEWS
— television program on Akaku: Maui Community Television seeks reporters, Lahaina News, February 1, 2001: 17.
— local TV news program to be shown on Akaku: Maui Community Television, Lahaina News, March 8, 2001: 16.

MAUI COUNTY OFFICE OF ECONOMIC DEVELOPMENT
— see Economic Development, Maui County Office of (OED)

MAUI COUNTY OFFICE ON AGING
— see Aging, Maui County Office of

MAUI COUNTY OVERALL ECONOMIC DEVELOPMENT PLAN
— to be updated, Lahaina News, December 17, 1998: 17.

MAUI COUNTY PHARMACISTS ASSOCIATION
— condemns doctors dispensing drugs by themselves, Lahaina Sun, May 12, 1971: 1,3.

MAUI COUNTY PLANNING DEPARTMENT
— see Planning Department, Maui County

MAUI COUNTY PRIVATE INDUSTRY COUNCIL
— Mel Gowing appointed to, Lahaina News, February 22, 1984: 17.

MAUI COUNTY PROJECT IMPACT
— initiative to hold meeting on West Maui isolation problems, Lahaina News, October 26, 2000: 3.
— to hold meeting to discuss disaster planning, Lahaina News, November 16, 2000: 16.
— residents express concern for isolation, Lahaina News, November 23, 2000: 1,6.
— fair to be held on theme of "Ready, Set, Safe!", Lahaina News, April 5, 2001: 20.

MAUI COUNTY REFUSE
— pick-up service expands, Lahaina News, May 21, 1992: 4.

MAUI COUNTY SALARY COMMISSION
— to meet, Lahaina News, February 6, 1992: 4.

MAUI COUNTY SCANS ADVISORY COMMITTEE
— to hold symposium, Lahaina News, March 18, 1993: 6.

MAUI COUNTY SENIOR CITIZEN'S FAIR
— see Senior Citizens Fair

MAUI COUNTY SHOOTERS ASSOCIATION
— to form, Lahaina News, April 15, 1987: 12.

MAUI COUNTY SUMMER BASKETBALL LEAGUE
— results detailed, Lahaina News, August 28, 1985: 4.

MAUI COUNTY TAXI ASSOCIATION
— to oppose de-regulation of taxis, Lahaina News, July 10, 1985: 1.

MAUI COUNTY TENNIS CHAMPIONSHIP
— to be held at Kapalua Tennis Garden to be held at Kapalua Tennis Garden, Lahaina News, June 12, 1985: 20.

MAUI COUNTY TRAFFIC SAFETY COUNCIL
— students appointed, Lahaina Sun, January 12, 1972: 5.
— turns down request for stop sign, Lahaina News, September 17, 1992: 8.

MAUI COUNTY TRI-ISLE COMPREHENSIVE HEALTH PLANNING COUNCIL
— elects A. Duane Black as first chair, Lahaina Sun, January 24, 1973: 7.

MAUI COUNTY VETERANS COUNCIL
— to hold service for Memorial Day, Lahaina News, May 21, 1992: 4.

MAUI COUNTY VISITORS ASSOCIATION
— optimistic that tourism will increase, Lahaina News, May 15, 1980: 13.
— budget cut by Maui County Council, Lahaina News, May 16, 1984: 17.
— editorial criticizing cut in budget by Maui County Council, Lahaina News, May 16, 1984: 2.
— editorial supporting additional funding, Lahaina News, October 3, 1984: 2.
— editorial against government intervention in, Lahaina News, November 28, 1984: 2.
— becomes part of Hawaii Visitors Bureau, Lahaina News, July 24, 1985: 2.

MAUI COUNTY WASTEWATER DIVISION
— reports more spills in county than the six previous years , Lahaina News, October 29, 1992: 1.

MAUI COUNTY WOMEN'S CONFERENCE
— deadline for entry in the art and craft display September 10, Lahaina News, August 28, 1985: 3.
— to meet at Maui Community College, Lahaina News, September 11, 1985: 3,20.
— theme for conference to be "Empowering Women into the New Millennium", Lahaina News, June 14, 2001: 2.

MAUI COUNTY WORK DAY PROGRAM
— cleanup set for July 26, Lahaina News, July 9, 1986: 14.

MAUI COUNTY YOUTH CONNECTIONS
— Guide to Youth Activities and Programs published, Lahaina News, June 19, 1997: 2.
— guide to youth activities now available, Lahaina News, May 14, 1998: 7.
— guide published, Lahaina News, May 21, 1998: 9.

MAUI COUNTY YOUTH CONTACT CENTER
— proposal discussed in editorial, Lahaina Sun, March 31, 1971: 8.

MAUI COUNTY ZOO
— Zoo Fest '86 scheduled, Lahaina News, March 12, 1986: 3.

MAUI COUNTY'S JUNIOR FIREFIGHTER AWARD
— recipients honored, Lahaina News, May 4, 2000: 2.

MAUI CRAFT II
— to be held by Lahaina Arts Society, Lahaina News, November 30, 1988: 3.

MAUI CRAFTS AND MINIATURE SHOW
— to be held at Lahaina Arts Society, Lahaina News, December 7, 1995: 14.

MAUI CRAFTS GUILD
— organization described, Lahaina News, May 9, 1984: 10.
— at Hyatt Regency Maui, Lahaina News, August 3, 1988: 6.
— celebrates seventh year, Lahaina News, February 28, 1990: 24.
— announces recipient of scholarship, Lahaina News, June 11, 1992: 3,4.
— artists to be showcased, Lahaina News, June 18, 1992: 21.
— to hold shows, Lahaina News, February 9, 1995: 11.
— to host artist shows, Lahaina News, February 16, 1995: 16.

MAUI CRIME STOPPERS
— see Crime Stoppers

MAUI CULTURAL COMMISSION
— to meet to consider requests, Lahaina News, July 9, 1992: 4.

MAUI CULTURAL DAY
— to be held, Lahaina News, May 1, 1991: 17.

MAUI CULTURAL LANDS
— featured, Lahaina News, August 21, 2003: 3.

MAUI DANCE COUNCIL
— sponsoring jazz and African classes, Lahaina News, December 12, 1991: 7.
— presenting performance by MaBiba Baegne and Fred Simpson, Lahaina News, April 28, 1994: 15.
— accepting applications for summer workshop, Lahaina News, April 28, 1994: 15.
— to hold concert, Lahaina News, May 30, 1996: 2.
— to hold "Spring Dance Bash", Lahaina News, April 29, 1999: 17.
— hosting pot luck social, Lahaina News, February 24, 2000: 17.

MAUI DANCE SPIRIT
— to be held at Tradewinds Gymnastics Dojo, Lahaina News, December 7, 2000: 25.

MAUI DATA BOOK AND NEWCOMERS GUIDE
— published, Lahaina News, April 3, 1997: 10.

MAUI DHARMA CENTER
— offering classes on Tibetan Buddhism, Lahaina News, January 9, 1997: 11.
— to sponsor teachings by Dagmo Sakya, Lahaina News, January 23, 1997: 10.

MAUI DIABETES CONFERENCE
— to be held, Lahaina News, October 26, 2000: 14.

MAUI DIRECT EMBROIDERY COMPANY [BUSINESS]
— moves to larger location, Lahaina News, October 31, 1990: 11.

MAUI DISPOSAL CO. INC. [BUSINESS]
— acquired by Horizon Waste Services, Inc., Lahaina News, April 20, 2000: 13.

MAUI DISTRICT HIGH
— School Music Festival to be held at Maui High School Gymnatorium, Lahaina News, May 6, 1987: 3.
— School Music Festival to be held, Lahaina News, May 11, 2000: 20.

MAUI DISTRICT SCHOOL ADVISORY COUNCIL
— to meet, Lahaina News, February 20, 1997: 10.

MAUI DIVE SHOP [BUSINESS]
— to open at Kahana Gateway, Lahaina News, July 18, 1990: 7.
— moves to expanded location, Lahaina News, March 26, 1992: 10.
— adds new store, Lahaina News, May 28, 1992: 12.
— boat engines sabotaged, Lahaina News, March 14, 1996: 3.
— opens in Kapalua Shops, Lahaina News, March 21, 1996: 10.
— offers diving experience for terminally ill young man, Lahaina News, November 18, 1999: 14.
— adds new ship, Maka Koa, Lahaina News, July 13, 2000: 14.
— opens new location, Lahaina News, November 23, 2000: 16.

MAUI DIVERS [BUSINESS]
— returns to Lahaina Town, Lahaina News, June 19, 1997: 7.

MAUI DRUG COURT
— Lahaina Rotary Club to hold benefit to support, Lahaina News, July 19, 2001: 1,5.
— concert to be held to support, Lahaina News, July 26, 2001: 16.
— graduates of program, Lahaina News, October 25, 2001: 2.
— Jon Kinimaka attempt to expand, Lahaina News, January 9, 2003: 1,2.

MAUI E-TICKET [BOAT]
— tri-hulled ship begins operation, Lahaina News, November 21, 1990: 11.
— to begin commercial operation, Lahaina News, May 8, 1991: 6.

MAUI EASTER SEAL SOCIETY
— see Easter Seal Society of Maui

MAUI ECO-ADVENTURES [BUSINESS]
— to lead hikes in Maunalei Arboretum, Lahaina News, October 14, 1999: 7.
— offering hikes in Maunalei Arboretum, Lahaina News, October 28, 1999: 9.
— leading hikes into Maunalei Arboretum, Lahaina News, November 25, 1999: 9.
— to lead hikes into Maunalei Arboretum, Lahaina News, December 23, 1999: 9.
— rewarding visitor industry employees with special rates to Africa, Lahaina News, April 5, 2001: 9.

MAUI ECO-DIRECTORY MAP AND GUIDE
— searching for environmentally concerned businesses, Lahaina News, May 19, 1994: 13.
— searching for appropriate businesses, Lahaina News, July 28, 1994: 8.
— published, Lahaina News, January 25, 1996: 3.
— accepting applications for next edition, Lahaina News, March 7, 1996: 11.

MAUI ECONOMIC CONCERNS OF THE COMMUNITY
— Maui Republican Party to host executive director Charles Ridings, Lahaina News, November 4, 1999: 13.
— intends to break ground on West Side Resource Center for homeless, Lahaina News, March 8, 2001: 1,18.
— executive director Charles Ridings awarded "Maui's Outstanding Executive Director of a Non-Profit Organization", Lahaina News, July 25, 2002: 2.

MAUI ECONOMIC DEVELOPMENT BOARD (MEDB)
— formed to promote jobs, Lahaina News, June 1, 1983: 15.
— conference on Cultural Values described, Lahaina News, June 4, 1992: 3.
— study backs runway extension at Kahalui airport, Lahaina News, July 30, 1992: 7.
— Michael Lyons named chair of, Lahaina News, October 8, 1992: 8.
— to host grantsmanship training program, Lahaina News, August 22, 1996: 15.
— receives grant from Hawaii Community Foundation, Lahaina News, September 25, 1997: 12.
— to offer "Fundraising Basics" workshop, Lahaina News, May 28, 1998: 13.
— to stage Maui County Products and Trade Show, Lahaina News, October 15, 1998: 13.
— Jeanne Skog named interim president and CEO of, Lahaina News, January 21, 1999: 11.
— Jeanne Skog named president and CEO of, Lahaina News, February 25, 1999: 11.
— to hold "Excite Camp" to expose girls to technology, Lahaina News, July 19, 2001: 9.

MAUI ECONOMIC OPPORTUNITY [BUSINESS]
— receives Head Start funding from federal Department of Health, Education and Welfare, Lahaina Sun, February 17, 1971: 5.
— non-profit seeks funds to recover from fire, Lahaina News, February 7, 1990: 1.

— to hold workplace training, Lahaina News, March 7, 1996: 11.

— to provide transportation services to disabled persons, Lahaina News, October 2, 1997: 15.

— receives Kellogg Foundation grant, Lahaina News, July 8, 1999: 5.

— headquarters to be dedicated, Lahaina News, August 5, 1999: 11.

— to offer small business training course, Lahaina News, October 28, 1999: 15.

— receives grant from U.S. Department of Labor to train migrant farm workers, Lahaina News, February 24, 2000: 14.

— offering business course, Lahaina News, August 31, 2000: 14.

— offering entrepreneurial course, Lahaina News, September 7, 2000: 18.

— Enlace Hispano (Hispanic Link) program to be held, Lahaina News, May 30, 2002: 2.

— launches Utility Assistance Program, Lahaina News, June 13, 2002: 2.

— to host Affordable Housing Conference, Lahaina News, May 1, 2003: 8.

— to hold Affordable Housing Conference, Lahaina News, May 8, 2003: 8.

— workshop on intellectual property and patent to be held at, Lahaina News, May 15, 2003: 8.

— to present "Making Affordable Housing A Reality: The Successful Vermont Model", Lahaina News, July 17, 2003: 8.

MAUI ELDORADO

— developer of proposed Royal Court Plaza shopping center wants issues resolve, Lahaina News, December 26, 1991: 1,2.

— reaches agreement with Royal Court Corp. to develop upscale shopping center, Lahaina News, March 12, 1992: 12.

— development featured, Lahaina News, February 20, 2003: 7.

— development featured, Lahaina News, March 6, 2003: 6.

— development featured, Lahaina News, June 26, 2003: 7.

MAUI ELDORADO MANAGEMENT CORPORATION

— files for bankruptcy, Lahaina Sun, June 7, 1972: 4.

— bankruptcy details provided, Lahaina Sun, June 21, 1972: 5.

MAUI ELDORADO RESORT

— names Edward Hoffman as manager, Lahaina News, January 17, 1990: 24.

— being managed by Marc Resorts Group, Lahaina News, June 27, 1991: 7.

— Matt Swartz new general manager at, Lahaina News, April 27, 2000: 11.

— featured, Lahaina News, April 4, 2002: 6.

— development featured, Lahaina News, July 25, 2002: 6.

— development featured, Lahaina News, August 8, 2002: 7.

MAUI ELECTRIC COMPANY [BUSINESS]

— plans for underground wiring in Front Street, Lahaina Sun, December 9, 1970: 7.

— responding to major storm hitting Lahaina, Lahaina Sun, December 30, 1970: 1.

— criticized for power poles, Lahaina Sun, January 20, 1971: 5.

— completing new transmission line from Kahului to Lahaina, Lahaina Sun, January 20, 1971: 8.

— seeking 25 acres of land at Ma'alaea for generation plant, Lahaina Sun, January 20, 1971: 8.

— new route for poles is considered, Lahaina Sun, January 27, 1971: 1.

— approved to run power poles along highway, Lahaina Sun, February 3, 1971: 1.

— resists alternate routes for electric power poles, Lahaina Sun, March 3, 1971: 1,2.

— route of power poles discussed, Lahaina Sun, March 10, 1971: 5.

— reduces rates in Hana to conform with rest of the island, Lahaina Sun, March 17, 1971: 2.

— will not put power poles on central Maui highway, Lahaina Sun, March 31, 1971: 1,8.

— seeks permission to build an electric generation plant near Ma'alaea, Lahaina Sun, May 12, 1971: 1,8.

— proposed plant in Ma'alaea discussed, Lahaina Sun, May 19, 1971: 1,6.

— given go-ahead to install diesel generators near Kealia Pond, Lahaina Sun, July 14, 1971: 4.

— given approval to start work on power plant near Ma'alaea, Lahaina Sun, August 4, 1971: 1,3.

— electric generating station near Kealia Pond nears completion, Lahaina Sun, December 8, 1971: 8.

— requests permission to install power poles along Kula Road, Lahaina Sun, May 31, 1972: 10.

— given permission to install new diesel generators, Lahaina Sun, November 29, 1972: 4,5.

— researching use of windmills in Ma'alaea, Lahaina News, April 15, 1980: 13.

— asks for rate hike, Lahaina News, May 15, 1983: 11.

— electricity rates fall, Lahaina News, September 11, 1985: 3.

— bills drop due to lower fuel prices, Lahaina News, January 15, 1986: 3.

— drops rates, Lahaina News, September 16, 1987: 3.

— raises rates, Lahaina News, November 18, 1987: 18.

— rates fall, Lahaina News, May 18, 1988: 18.

— responds to possible development of geothermal, Lahaina News, January 17, 1990: 14.

— Tom Jezierny becomes president of, Lahaina News, April 4, 1990: 7.

— prices rise, Lahaina News, November 21, 1990: 3.

— prices rise, Lahaina News, December 19, 1990: 5.

— to raise rates, Lahaina News, May 30, 1991: 3.

— to raise rates, Lahaina News, October 17, 1991: 6.

— encourages customers to use less electricity during peak times, Lahaina News, November 7, 1991: 6.

— requesting rate 17% increase, Lahaina News, November 21, 1991: 28.

— Lahaina Town Action Committee creates telephone tree to deal with rolling blackouts, Lahaina News, November 28, 1991: 6.

— proposes increase in electrical rates, Lahaina News, January 9, 1992: 2.

— plans to build 20 megawatt unit, Lahaina News, January 23, 1992: 13.

— to reduce price of electricity due to fuel prices, Lahaina News, February 13, 1992: 3.

— bills to decrease, Lahaina News, March 12, 1992: 3.

— adopts new computerized customer service system, Lahaina News, April 2, 1992: 6.

— explains power outage at Olowalu, Lahaina News, April 9, 1992: 5.

— to hold information meeting, Lahaina News, June 18, 1992: 4.

— to hold workshop "MECO in Our Community", Lahaina News, July 2, 1992: 4.

— reviewing two sites for future growth, Lahaina News, October 1, 1992: 14.

— Kihei-Makena Community Advisory Committee turns down request for electric plant, Lahaina News, October 22, 1992: 13.

— hopes to expand the Ma'alaea power plant, Lahaina News, February 25, 1993: 5.

— negotiations continue for site of new power plant, Lahaina News, May 6, 1993: 6,7.

— Ma'alaea Community Association to intervene in proposal to expand plant, Lahaina News, July 1, 1993: 5.

— offering rebate on purchase of fluorescent lights, Lahaina News, September 16, 1993: 9.

— promoting fluorescent bulbs, Lahaina News, October 7, 1993: 6.

— to pay damages, Lahaina News, November 4, 1993: 6.

— anticipates customer savings from programs to improve efficiency, Lahaina News, December 30, 1993: 1,12.

— CF Savers program ends, Lahaina News, April 21, 1994: 12.

— installs new polls on Front Street, Lahaina News, June 6, 1996: 2.

— to offer rebates for water heaters, Lahaina News, September 5, 1996: 18.

— to raise electricity rates, Lahaina News, November 14, 1996: 9.

— gives Sheraton Maui rebate check for efficiency, Lahaina News, April 3, 1997: 10.

— gives away high-efficiency showerheads, Lahaina News, April 24, 1997: 7.

— Solar Water Heating Fair to be held, Lahaina News, September 25, 1997: 3.

— asks Public Utilities Commission to increase electric rates, Lahaina News, January 29, 1998: 13.

— Microenterprise Division to offer business loans, Lahaina News, September 3, 1998: 11.

— offering microloans, Lahaina News, September 17, 1998: 13.

— allowed to raise rates, Lahaina News, January 7, 1999: 13.

— residents critical of new utility poles at Puʻukoliʻi Road, Lahaina News, March 4, 1999: 1,16.

— to offer internet billing, Lahaina News, July 29, 1999: 11.

— announces Energy Efficiency Awards, Lahaina News, September 9, 1999: 11.

— Maui County Council Economic Development Committee to discuss Integrated Resource Plan, Lahaina News, July 20, 2000: 14.

— to install solar light at Lahainaluna High School, Lahaina News, September 14, 2000: 11.

— signs agreement with Mayor James Apana support solar roofs, Lahaina News, September 19, 2002: 8.

MAUI ELECTRIC JAZZ [MUSICAL GROUP]

— to perform at Studio 505, Lahaina News, September 19, 1991: 16.

MAUI ENTERPRISE FORUM, THE

— to be held, Lahaina News, February 7, 2002: 8.

MAUI ESTATE PLANNING COUNCIL

— new officers elected, Lahaina News, March 31, 1994: 9.

MAUI EXECUTIVES ASSOCIATION

— business to business organization welcoming new members, Lahaina News, January 31, 2002: 8.

— welcoming new members, Lahaina News, March 28, 2002: 21.

— continues to meet, Lahaina News, May 23, 2002: 17.

— continues to meet, Lahaina News, July 4, 2002: 17.

— continues to meet, Lahaina News, August 29, 2002: 21.

— continues to meet, Lahaina News, January 2, 2003: 17.

MAUI FAMILY COMMUNITY LEADERSHIP

— sponsoring workshops on fundraising by Ramona Mullahey, Lahaina News, April 19, 1989: 13.

MAUI FAMILY REUNION

— to hold seminars to train counselors, Lahaina News, October 2, 1985: 9.

— hosts "Let's Talk" program for fathers and sons, Lahaina News, April 16, 1986: 3.

MAUI FAMILY SUPPORT SERVICES

— organizes program for mothers and their pre-adolescent daughters, Lahaina News, June 4, 1986: 3.

— hosting program on how fathers can talk to their sons, Lahaina News, June 11, 1986: 3.

— to hold fund-raiser dress sale, Lahaina News, April 9, 1992: 4.

— Daniel Inouye announces funding for, Lahaina News, May 18, 2000: 7.

— sponsoring Napili Plaza Arts and Crafts Fair, Lahaina News, May 25, 2000: 18.

— sponsoring Napili Plaza Arts and Crafts Fair, Lahaina News, June 8, 2000: 20,21.

— sponsoring Napili Plaza Arts and Crafts Fair, Lahaina News, July 27, 2000: 20.

— named beneficiary of the Napili Plaza Craft Fair, Lahaina News, August 24, 2000: 19.

— receives state funds for early childhood center on Maui, Lahaina News, October 12, 2000: 19.

— to hold 20th anniversary celebration, Lahaina News, October 19, 2000: 20.

— begins capital campaign to build center, Lahaina News, November 9, 2000: 11.

MAUI FARM DAY

— to be held, Lahaina News, July 9, 1992: 13.

MAUI FARM, THE [BUSINESS]

— to break ground, Lahaina News, July 2, 1992: 18.

— names Paula Ambre as executive director, Lahaina News, November 5, 1992: 8.

— Donna Vida named Program Director, Lahaina News, March 4, 1993: 12.

— to offer tours, Lahaina News, February 27, 2003: 17.

MAUI FARMERS MARKET

— to be held at Kahului Shopping Center, Lahaina News, March 20, 1997: 17.

— to be held at Kahului Shopping Center, Lahaina News, April 17, 1997: 13.

— continues to be held at Kahului Shopping Center, Lahaina News, June 5, 1997: 17.

MAUI FILIPINO COMMUNITY COUNCIL

— to hold Miss Maui Filipina Pageant, Lahaina News, June 19, 2003: 16.

MAUI FILIPINO FIESTA

— details of events, Lahaina Sun, February 9, 1972: 14.

MAUI FILIPINO FILM FESTIVAL

— to be held, Lahaina News, January 26, 1995: 15,16.

MAUI FILM FESTIVAL

— to show "Traveler", Lahaina News, July 17, 1997: 17.

— to be held, Lahaina News, September 11, 1997: 16.

— to show "Atlantis", Lahaina News, September 25, 1997: 17.

— continues, Lahaina News, October 2, 1997: 21.

— to show "Ulee's Gold", Lahaina News, October 16, 1997: 17.

— to show "Young Poisoner's Handbook", Lahaina News, October 23, 1997: 21.

— to screen "Young Poisoner's Handbook", Lahaina News, October 30, 1997: 16.

— to show "Love! Valour! Compassion!", Lahaina News, October 30, 1997: 16.

— to show "Box of Moonlight", Lahaina News, November 6, 1997: 17.

— to show "When the Cat's Away", Lahaina News, November 20, 1997: 17.

— to show "She's So Lovely", Lahaina News, November 20, 1997: 17.

— showing "She's So Lovely", Lahaina News, November 27, 1997: 12.

— to show "Gabbeh", Lahaina News, November 27, 1997: 13.

— to show "Madame Butterfly", Lahaina News, December 4, 1997: 25.

— to show "Year of the Horse", Lahaina News, December 11, 1997: 18.

— to show "Baraka", Lahaina News, December 18, 1997: 18.

— to show "Funny", Lahaina News, December 25, 1997: 13.

— to show "Funny", Lahaina News, January 1, 1998: 16.

— to show "The End of Violence", Lahaina News, January 1, 1998: 16.

— to show "Mon Homme", Lahaina News, January 8, 1998: 12.

— to show "Mouth to Mouth", Lahaina News, January 22, 1998: 13.

— to show "The Full Monty", Lahaina News, February 19, 1998: 13.

— to show "Fast, Cheap and Out of Control", Lahaina News, March 5, 1998: 17.

— to show "The Tango Lesson", Lahaina News, March 12, 1998: 21.

— to host Oscar Party, Lahaina News, March 19, 1998: 12.

— to show "Kundun", Lahaina News, March 19, 1998: 13.

— to show film "Live Flesh", Lahaina News, April 16, 1998: 13.

— to show "Mindwalk", Lahaina News, April 23, 1998: 17.

— to show "Love and Death on Long Island", Lahaina News, April 30, 1998: 16,17.

— to show "Great Expectations", Lahaina News, April 30, 1998: 17.

— to show "Mrs. Dalloway", Lahaina News, May 21, 1998: 16.

— to show "Sliding Doors", Lahaina News, May 28, 1998: 13.

— to show "Shooting Fish", Lahaina News, June 11, 1998: 16,17.

— to show "Deja Vu", Lahaina News, June 18, 1998: 16.

— to show "The Real Blonde", Lahaina News, June 25, 1998: 13.

— to show "Wild Man Blues", Lahaina News, July 2, 1998: 16.

— to show "Artemesia", Lahaina News, July 9, 1998: 17.

— to show "Titanic", Lahaina News, August 13, 1998: 16.

— to show "I Love You Don't Touch Me", Lahaina News, August 13, 1998: 16.

— to show "The Opposite of Sex", Lahaina News, August 20, 1998: 17.

— to show "Paniolo O Hawaii—Cowboys of the Far West", Lahaina News, August 27, 1998: 16.

— to show "Last Days of Disco", Lahaina News, August 27, 1998: 17.

— to show "Lawrence of Arabia", Lahaina News, September 3, 1998: 20.

— to show "Beyond Silence", Lahaina News, September 10, 1998: 20.

— to show "The Land Girls", Lahaina News, September 17, 1998: 25.

— to show "Gandhi", Lahaina News, November 19, 1998: 16.

— to show "Beyond Silence", Lahaina News, November 19, 1998: 17.

— to show "Billy's Hollywood Screen Kiss", Lahaina News, November 19, 1998: 17.

— to show "Passion in the Desert", Lahaina News, November 26, 1998: 16.

— to show "The Mighty", Lahaina News, December 10, 1998: 21.

— to show "The Saltmen of Tibet", Lahaina News, December 17, 1998: 25.

— to show "The Imposters", Lahaina News, December 24, 1998: 12.

— to show "The Knowledge of Healing", Lahaina News, February 11, 1999: 17.

— to show "Gods and Monsters", Lahaina News, February 18, 1999: 13.

— to show "Central Station", Lahaina News, March 4, 1999: 13.

— to show "Down in the Delta", Lahaina News, March 11, 1999: 12.

— to show "Little Voice", Lahaina News, March 25, 1999: 17.

— to show "Dancemaker", Lahaina News, June 24, 1999: 12.

— to show "Spike and Mike's Classic Festival of Animation", Lahaina News, June 24, 1999: 13.

— to show "Lovers of the Arctic Circle", Lahaina News, July 15, 1999: 13.

— to show "Besieged", Lahaina News, July 22, 1999: 13.

— to show "The Loss of Sexual Innocence", Lahaina News, July 29, 1999: 13.

— to show "The Castle", Lahaina News, August 5, 1999: 12.

— to show "The Red Violin", Lahaina News, August 12, 1999: 17.

— to show "Three Seasons, Lahaina News, August 19, 1999: 16,17.

— to show "Buena Vista Social Club", Lahaina News, August 26, 1999: 16.

— to show "Run Lola Run", Lahaina News, August 26, 1999: 17.

— to show "Get Real", Lahaina News, September 9, 1999: 13.

— to show "Moloka'i: The Story of Father Damien", Lahaina News, September 16, 1999: 13.

— to show "Tea with Mussolini", Lahaina News, September 23, 1999: 13.

— to show "Twin Falls Idaho", Lahaina News, October 21, 1999: 17.

— to show "Autumn Tale", Lahaina News, October 28, 1999: 17.

— to show "My Life So Far", Lahaina News, November 4, 1999: 13.

— to show "Mumford", Lahaina News, November 11, 1999: 13.

— to show "The Dinner Game", Lahaina News, November 18, 1999: 17.

— to show "Harold and Maude", Lahaina News, November 25, 1999: 16.

— to show "Train of Life", Lahaina News, January 13, 2000: 13.

— to show "The Straight Story", Lahaina News, January 20, 2000: 13.

— to show "The Limey", Lahaina News, February 10, 2000: 17.

— to show "Princess Mononoke", Lahaina News, February 17, 2000: 16.

— to show "Some Fish Can Fly", Lahaina News, February 17, 2000: 17.

— to show "Cradle Will Rock", Lahaina News, March 2, 2000: 13.

— to show "Naturally Native", Lahaina News, May 11, 2000: 21.

— to show "Me, Myself and I", Lahaina News, May 18, 2000: 21.

— to be held, Lahaina News, June 1, 2000: 7.

— to show "The Big Buzz", Lahaina News, June 15, 2000: 17.

— to show "Gimme Shelter", Lahaina News, September 7, 2000: 20.

— to be held, Lahaina News, September 14, 2000: 1,2,18.

— to show "Mad About Mambo", Lahaina News, September 14, 2000: 21.

— to show "Butterfly (La Lengua de las Mariposas)", Lahaina News, September 21, 2000: 21.

— to show "Orfeu", Lahaina News, October 5, 2000: 17.

— to show "Love and Sex", Lahaina News, October 5, 2000: 17.

— to show "Five Senses", Lahaina News, October 19, 2000: 21.

—FirstLight 2000 to be held, Lahaina News, December 21, 2000: 1,9.

— to hold "First Light 2000: Academy Screenings on Maui", Lahaina News, December 28, 2000: 8.

— to show "Loving Jezebel", Lahaina News, February 8, 2001: 21.

— to show "An Everlasting Piece", Lahaina News, February 22, 2001: 17.

— showing "Wonder Boys", Lahaina News, March 15, 2001: 20.

— to show "Tomcats", Lahaina News, March 22, 2001: 17.

— to show "Price of Milk", Lahaina News, May 17, 2001: 21.

— to show "Venus Beauty Institute", Lahaina News, May 24, 2001: 21.

— to be held, Lahaina News, June 7, 2001: 21.

— to be held, Lahaina News, June 14, 2001: 21.

— to show "Calle 54", Lahaina News, August 23, 2001: 16.

— to show "Grateful Dawg", Lahaina News, December 27, 2001: 17.

— to show "Innocence", Lahaina News, January 3, 2002: 17.

— to show "Sidewalks of New York", Lahaina News, January 10, 2002: 17.

— to show "Better Than Sex", Lahaina News, January 17, 2002: 17.

— to show "The Independent", Lahaina News, January 24, 2002: 17.

— to show "Happy Accidents", Lahaina News, February 7, 2002: 17.

— to show "Cool and Crazy", Lahaina News, February 14, 2002: 17.

— to show "Kandahar", Lahaina News, February 28, 2002: 17.

— to screen "Metropolis", Lahaina News, April 18, 2002: 16.

— to show "Stolen Summer", Lahaina News, May 23, 2002: 17.

— underway, Lahaina News, June 13, 2002: 16.

— to show "Dogtown", Lahaina News, June 20, 2002: 17.

— to show "The Fast Runner", Lahaina News, July 18, 2002: 17.

— to show "Sex With Strangers", Lahaina News, July 25, 2002: 21.

— to show "Late Marriage", Lahaina News, August 1, 2002: 21.

— to show "Monsoon Wedding" and "Kissing Jessica Stein", Lahaina News, August 15, 2002: 16.

— to show "The Believer", Lahaina News, August 22, 2002: 21.

— to show "Stolen Summer", Lahaina News, August 29, 2002: 20.

— to show "Dogtown and Z-Boys", Lahaina News, August 29, 2002: 20.

— to show "Sunshine State", Lahaina News, September 12, 2002: 21.

— to show "Lovely and Amazing", Lahaina News, September 19, 2002: 25.

— to show "Sex and Lucia", Lahaina News, September 26, 2002: 17.

— to show "Tadpole", Lahaina News, October 3, 2002: 17.

— to show "Full Frontal", Lahaina News, October 10, 2002: 17.

— to show "Crop Circles", Lahaina News, October 24, 2002: 20.

— to show "Satin Rouge", Lahaina News, October 24, 2002: 21.

— to show "Mostly Martha", Lahaina News, November 14, 2002: 21.

— to show "Ayurveda: The Art of Being", Lahaina News, November 21, 2002: 21.

— to show "Me Without You", Lahaina News, December 5, 2002: 21.

— to show "Antwone Fisher", Lahaina News, December 12, 2002: 21.

— to hold "FirstLight: Academy Screenings on Maui", Lahaina News, December 26, 2002: 14.

— to show "On Guard", Lahaina News, February 13, 2003: 17.

— to show "Standing in the Shadows of Motown", Lahaina News, February 27, 2003: 16.

— to show "Talk to Her", Lahaina News, February 27, 2003: 16.

— to show "Frida", Lahaina News, March 6, 2003: 17.

— to show "Pleasure and Pain: Ben Harper On Tour", Lahaina News, March 27, 2003: 16.

— to show "Lost in La Mancha", Lahaina News, April 3, 2003: 17.

— to show "Divine Intervention", Lahaina News, April 10, 2003: 21.

— to show "Nicholas Nickelby", Lahaina News, April 17, 2003: 17.

— to show "All the Real Girls", Lahaina News, April 24, 2003: 21.

— to show "Frida", Lahaina News, May 1, 2003: 16.

— to show "Laurel Canyon", Lahaina News, May 8, 2003: 17.

— to show "Nowhere in Africa", Lahaina News, May 15, 2003: 17.

— to show "Talk to Her", Lahaina News, May 22, 2003: 16.

— schedule at Wailea and the Maui Arts and Cultural Center, Lahaina News, June 12, 2003: 22.

— to show "Nowhere in Africa", Lahaina News, July 3, 2003: 16.

— to show "L'Auberge Espagnole", Lahaina News, July 10, 2003: 17.

— to show "Rivers and Tides", Lahaina News, July 24, 2003: 17.

— to show "Winged Migration", Lahaina News, July 31, 2003: 17.

— to show "Auyrveda", Lahaina News, August 7, 2003: 17.

— to show "Respiro", Lahaina News, August 21, 2003: 17.

— to show "The Guys", Lahaina News, September 4, 2003: 17.

— to show "House of Fools", Lahaina News, September 25, 2003: 17.

— to show "Winged Migration", Lahaina News, October 2, 2003: 17.

— to show "Camp", Lahaina News, October 2, 2003: 17.

— to show "The Holy Land", Lahaina News, October 9, 2003: 17.

MAUI FILM/VIDEO GROUP

— to host video production workshops for teens, Lahaina News, July 1, 1987: 3.

— to meet at Maui Community College, Lahaina News, July 29, 1987: 3.

— to hold general meeting, Lahaina News, June 22, 1988: 10.

MAUI FIRE DEPARTMENT

— see Fire Department, Maui

MAUI FISHPOND ASSOCIATION

— to discuss restoring ancient Ko'ie'ie fishpond, Lahaina News, April 20, 2000: 16.

MAUI FOOD BANK

— fundraiser to support, Lahaina News, February 7, 1990: 3.

— Maui Catholic Charities to hold drive for, Lahaina News, May 23, 1990: 5.

— to launch canned food drive, Lahaina News, March 5, 1992: 5.

— food drive scheduled, Lahaina News, March 12, 1992: 13.

— drive underway, Lahaina News, March 26, 1992: 3.

— to hold benefit at Napili Plaza, Lahaina News, April 16, 1992: 22.

— fraudulent requests for contributions reported, Lahaina News, May 7, 1992: 3.

— drive to be held, Lahaina News, March 4, 1993: 7.

— to hold canned food drive, Lahaina News, April 22, 1993: 3.

— to hold food drive, Lahaina News, May 6, 1993: 4.

— sponsoring food safety class, Lahaina News, September 9, 1993: 5.

— to hold Turkey Shoot for Turkeys with Valley Isle Sport Shooters, Lahaina News, November 18, 1993: 8.

— to hold "Bid on a Brighter Future Art Auction", Lahaina News, March 17, 1994: 4.

— begins "Check Out Hunger", Lahaina News, November 20, 1997: 2.

— Ka'anapali Kalikimaka to benefit, Lahaina News, December 3, 1998: 5.

— Maui Medical Group to collect food for, Lahaina News, December 10, 1998: 9.

— to be supported by Ka'anapali Kalikimaka, Lahaina News, December 9, 1999: 7.

— receives donation from Wailea Community Association, Lahaina News, May 18, 2000: 8.

— Ka'anapali Kalikimaka event to benefit, Lahaina News, December 14, 2000: 3.

— receives donation from Wailea Community Association, Lahaina News, July 12, 2001: 8.

— to hold food drive, Lahaina News, December 13, 2001: 1,20.

— receives donation from Harry and Jeanette Weinberg Foundation, Inc., Lahaina News, December 27, 2001: 10.

— to distribute food boxes, Lahaina News, March 21, 2002: 2.

— to hold food drive at Lahaina Cannery Mall, Lahaina News, April 25, 2002: 16.

— to distribute boxes, Lahaina News, May 16, 2002: 3.

— Hawaii Artisan Events at Renaissance Wailea Beach Resort to support, Lahaina News, July 25, 2002: 21.

— Hawaii Artisan Events to benefit, Lahaina News, August 8, 2002: 17.

— receives grant from Alexander and Baldwin Foundation, Lahaina News, October 10, 2002: 8.

— receives donation from Realtors Association of Maui, Lahaina News, January 9, 2003: 9.

— editorial in support of, Lahaina News, March 6, 2003: 4.

— collecting donations, Lahaina News, March 20, 2003: 2.

— to collect donations, Lahaina News, March 27, 2003: 9.

MAUI FREEDOM JAM

— concert to benefit for Maui United Way to be held, Lahaina News, October 11, 2001: 1,20.

MAUI FRESH [BUSINESS]

— opened by Maui Pineapple Company, Ltd, Lahaina News, January 13, 2000: 11.

MAUI FRIENDS OF THE ANIMALS

— dog wash fundraiser to benefit Pet Adoption Home Building Fund, Lahaina News, October 12, 1988: 3.

— sponsoring "Pose Your Pets With Santa", Lahaina News, December 7, 1988: 16.

— to hold benefit at La Familia Restaurant, Lahaina News, February 22, 1989: 13.

— to hold dog wash fundraiser, Lahaina News, April 19, 1989: 14.

— names Fran Joswick as executive director, Lahaina News, December 27, 1989: 5.

MAUI FRIENDS OF THE LIBRARY

— to hold book sale, Lahaina News, April 13, 1988: 4.

— beginning membership drive, Lahaina News, December 12, 1990: 3.

— donates funds to local libraries, Lahaina News, May 13, 1999: 15.

MAUI FUDGE AND ICE CREAM

— to be represented by Entrekin/Zucco Advertising, Lahaina News, November 22, 1989: 5.

MAUI FUMIGATION

— wins award for best exhibit at Building and New Products Trade Show, Lahaina News, August 16, 1989: 6.

MAUI GARDEN CLUB

— to meet, Lahaina News, January 11, 1996: 2.

MAUI GAS SERVICES

— opens, Lahaina News, May 11, 1988: 3.

— new hires listed, Lahaina News, June 21, 1989: 6.

— Richard Frandsen promoted to senior vice president-operations, Lahaina News, August 1, 1990: 7.

MAUI GATEWAY
— offering internet services for homes, Lahaina News, December 3, 1998: 17.
— owners George and Paige Fontaine present check to Hale Kau Kau program at St. Theresa's Church, Lahaina News, January 14, 1999: 11.

MAUI GENEALOGICAL SOCIETY
— to hold fundraiser, Lahaina News, July 12, 1989: 3.

MAUI GIFT BASKETS [BUSINESS]
— hoping to expand, Lahaina News, March 12, 1986: 3.

MAUI GIRL FRIDAY
— acquires Telecheck Hawaii, Lahaina Sun, March 31, 1971: 5.

MAUI GIRLS SOFTBALL ASSOCIATION
— fastpitch league play underway, Lahaina News, May 11, 2000: 14.

MAUI GO KARTERS ASSOCIATION
— to hold race, Lahaina News, October 7, 1999: 9.

MAUI GOLD MANUFACTURING [BUSINESS]
— engraver Waldemar Kmentt featured, Lahaina News, April 4, 1984: 13.

MAUI GOLF AND SPORTS PARK
— to open at Ma'alaea Triangle, Lahaina News, October 10, 2002: 8.

MAUI GOURMET CAFE AND EATERY, THE [RESTAURANT]
— reviewed, Lahaina News, February 2, 1995: 11.

MAUI GRAND PRIX
— results detailed, Lahaina News, November 14, 1984: 4.

MAUI GREEN COALITION
— to hold meeting, Lahaina News, March 28, 1990: 4.

MAUI GREEN PARTY
— see Green Party

MAUI GYMNASTICS CENTER
— to hold "Summer Saulting Spectacular", Lahaina News, June 26, 1997: 17.

MAUI GYMNASTICS INVITATIONAL
— to be held, Lahaina News, December 31, 1998: 13.
— to be held, Lahaina News, January 7, 1999: 14.
— to be held, Lahaina News, January 4, 2001: 9.

MAUI HARDWOODS, INC
— expanding, Lahaina Sun, July 18, 1973: 4.

MAUI HARVEST
— supporting homeless, Lahaina News, April 25, 1990: 5.
— to distribute food with Salvation Army, Lahaina News, July 25, 1991: 5.

MAUI HAWAII BALLROOM DANCE ASSOCIATION
— see Hawaii Ballroom Dance Association

MAUI HIGH PERFORMANCE COMPUTING CENTER
— to offer workshop "Getting Wired for Business", Lahaina News, May 18, 1995: 6.
— Eugene Bal II named as director of, Lahaina News, December 12, 1996: 13.
— to improve computing, Lahaina News, January 29, 1998: 13.

MAUI HIGH SCHOOL
— history and current situation discussed, Lahaina Sun, December 8, 1971: 17.
— Mayor Cravalho announces it will be used for youth-oriented activities, Lahaina Sun, May 31, 1972: 14.
— class of 1973 to hold reunion, Lahaina News, August 13, 1992: 4.
— Cheerleaders Booster Club to hold dance benefit, Lahaina News, December 10, 1992: 17.
— class of 1974 to hold reunion, Lahaina News, May 19, 1994: 6.
— Class of 1979 to hold reunion, Lahaina News, October 1, 1998: 16.
— class of 1979 to hold reunion, Lahaina News, October 8, 1998: 16.

— Band to perform, Lahaina News, March 16, 2000: 13.
— successful at Na Mele O Maui, Lahaina News, December 20, 2001: 14.
— band to perform at Maui Arts and Cultural Center, Lahaina News, March 6, 2003: 17.
— Library to hold "Community Leaders Call to Action Meeting", Lahaina News, September 25, 2003: 5.

MAUI HILTON HOTEL
— praised by comedian Dick Martin, Lahaina Sun, January 13, 1971: 7.
— Jack Pugh appointed new manager, Lahaina Sun, July 28, 1971: 10.
— renamed to Maui Ka'anapali hotel, Lahaina Sun, February 28, 1973: 11.
— Hotel Corporation of the Pacific takes over management of, Lahaina News, August 31, 1983: 14.

MAUI HISTORIC COMMISSION
— approves design for new Lahaina Hotel, Lahaina Sun, November 11, 1970: 3.
— argument with Ken Russell concerning shop sign, Lahaina Sun, November 18, 1970: 3.
— argument with Ken Russell concerning shop sign, Lahaina Sun, November 25, 1970: 1,2.
— reprimands Higgins Maddigan for tearing down an old building, Lahaina Sun, December 16, 1970: 2.
— commends West Maui Business Association for work on seawall area, Lahaina Sun, December 16, 1970: 3.
— resolves argument with Ken Russell concerning shop sign, Lahaina Sun, January 13, 1971: 1,2.
— approves plan for construction of 470-room Lahaina Inn, Lahaina Sun, January 20, 1971: 1.
— rejects request to fly a banner on Front Street, Lahaina Sun, February 17, 1971: 4.
— seeking to control peddling in Lahaina, Lahaina Sun, March 17, 1971: 1.
— rejects request to paint portrait of Queen Lili'uokalani in front of Queen Theatre, Lahaina Sun, March 17, 1971: 5.
— requests funds from Maui County Council to purchase Hawaiian artifacts, Lahaina Sun, April 21, 1971: 2.
— okays highway markers indicating "Historical Lahaina", Lahaina Sun, April 21, 1971: 4.
— requests ban on peddling in the Lahaina historic district, Lahaina Sun, April 21, 1971: 7.
— approve signs on Front Street, Lahaina Sun, May 19, 1971: 2.
— Clarence Peters named to commission, Lahaina Sun, May 19, 1971: 2.
— studying rules for signage, Lahaina Sun, May 19, 1971: 5.
— planning sidewalk in Lahaina historic district, Lahaina Sun, May 19, 1971: 7.
— criticized in letter to the editor, Lahaina Sun, June 16, 1971: 2.
— decisions include banning nearly-nude wooden carvings and other objects outside Front Street merchant, Lahaina Sun, July 21, 1971: 10.
— okays repainting of Tong Society building, Lahaina Sun, August 18, 1971: 8.
— decisions listed, Lahaina Sun, August 18, 1971: 8.
— Chris Hart assumes expanded duties, Lahaina Sun, September 15, 1971: 1.
— Warren Hinton critical of signage at Lahaina small boat harbor, Lahaina Sun, October 20, 1971: 15.
— results of meeting described, Lahaina Sun, December 15, 1971: 6.
— opposes illegal parking signs in Lahaina, Lahaina Sun, February 16, 1972: 13.
— discusses Banyan Tree Courtyard, Lahaina Sun, March 15, 1972: 5.
— plans for Lahaina courthouse, Lahaina Sun, April 19, 1972: 3.

— recommends denying permit for sandwich board signs, Lahaina Sun, May 17, 1972: 7.

— conflict with landlord Dolores Martin, Lahaina Sun, June 21, 1972: 3.

— pushing for strict adherence to rules on appearance of store windows, Lahaina Sun, July 19, 1972: 7.

— preparing for battle on location of new Lahaina small boat harbor, Lahaina Sun, October 18, 1972: 12.

— topics at meeting detailed, Lahaina Sun, January 17, 1973: 7.

— expected to discuss large building in Lahaina planned by McNeil Construction Company i, Lahaina Sun, March 7, 1973: 5.

— approves resort shopping center in Lahaina proposed by Bruce McNeil, Lahaina Sun, March 21, 1973: 3.

— no longer has power to regulate signage in downtown Lahaina, Lahaina Sun, May 9, 1973: 3.

— urges citizens to take pride in Lahaina Town, Lahaina News, December 11, 1985: 1,24.

— sponsoring lecture by Pualani Kanahele entitled "Daces and Worship of Pele", Lahaina News, February 5, 1986: 3.

— supports proposed renovations of Pioneer inn, Lahaina News, February 26, 1986: 1.

— to meet at Lahaina Civic Center, Lahaina News, June 18, 1986: 3.

— to reconstruct Gate House at Hale Pa'ahao, Lahaina News, July 23, 1986: 1.

— backs more parking, Lahaina News, August 27, 1986: 12.

— regular meeting to be held, Lahaina News, November 19, 1986: 16.

— approves plan to renovate Hale Pa'ahao, Lahaina News, January 21, 1987: 3.

— approves sidewalks, Lahaina News, March 25, 1987: 12.

— approves expansion of parking at Burger King on Front Street, Lahaina News, May 27, 1987: 1.

— approves renovation of Queen Theatre on Front Street, Lahaina News, May 27, 1987: 1.

— approves Triplex theatre at The Wharf Shops and Restaurant, Lahaina News, November 18, 1987: 3.

— activities over past year recounted, Lahaina News, December 30, 1987: 13.

— to hold meeting to discuss widening of Wainee Street, Lahaina News, September 20, 1989: 1.

— to hold meeting on widening of Wainee Street, Lahaina News, October 18, 1989: 2.

— could be reconstituted, Lahaina News, December 13, 1989: 36.

— and controversy over activities booth permit, Lahaina News, April 18, 1990: 1.

— rejects after-the-fact request for mural by Wyland, Lahaina News, March 20, 1991: 1.

— decision against Wyland mural to be appealed by Waikiki Traders, Lahaina News, May 1, 1991: 4.

— to review proposed commercial building, Lahaina News, July 18, 1991: 5.

— to meet to consider proposed commercial building, Lahaina News, July 25, 1991: 5.

— recommends widening Luakini Street, Lahaina News, August 8, 1991: 1.

— to host mayor Linda Lingle at final meeting, Lahaina News, September 19, 1991: 3.

MAUI HISTORIC DEVELOPMENT COMMITTEE
— adopts a statement of purpose, Lahaina Sun, August 29, 1973: 15.

MAUI HISTORICAL MUSEUM
— seeking volunteers, Lahaina News, August 11, 1994: 4.

MAUI HISTORICAL SOCIETY
— to hold a garden party in Wailuku, Lahaina Sun, July 7, 1971: 5.

— exhibit at Lahaina Library, Lahaina News, May 8, 1985: 3.

— hosting exhibits and hikes for grand opening of Bailey House Museum, Lahaina News, October 14, 1987: 3.

— sponsors talk on fossilized extinct flightless birds, Lahaina News, March 23, 1988: 14.

— Cynthia Conrad donates art to Bailey Art Project, Lahaina News, June 1, 1988: 19.

— to hold annual meeting; Lynn Ann Davis to present on Bishop Museum visual collections, Lahaina News, February 8, 1989: 3.

— organizing book sale, Lahaina News, April 12, 1989: 3.

— sponsors display at Lahaina Public Library, Lahaina News, January 24, 1990: 2.

— Mayor Hannibal Tavares plans to appoint members to new Maui County Cultural Resources Commission, Lahaina News, February 21, 1990: 3.

— to hold benefit auction; antiques donated, Lahaina News, July 25, 1990: 6.

— to hold Preservation Conference, Lahaina News, October 17, 1991: 9.

— sponsoring tours of the Bailey House, Lahaina News, November 14, 1991: 3.

— to host Maui Heritage Series, Lahaina News, May 21, 1992: 4.

— to hold a cake sale, Lahaina News, November 12, 1992: 22.

— to hold Hawaiian Craft Fair, Lahaina News, November 12, 1992: 5.

— to offer "Legends of Pele", Lahaina News, December 10, 1992: 17.

— seeking nominations for Preservation Awards, Lahaina News, August 12, 1993: 15.

— presenting "Talking Island Festival", Lahaina News, October 14, 1993: 16.

— to hold Hawaiian Crafts Fair, Lahaina News, October 28, 1993: 11.

— to host Preservation Conference, Lahaina News, May 11, 1995: 2.

— Maui Visitors Bureau Executive Director Marsha Wienert to speak to, Lahaina News, May 18, 1995: 4.

— seeking nominations for Preservation Awards, Lahaina News, March 7, 1996: 10.

— seeking volunteers, Lahaina News, April 25, 1996: 6.

— to hold Preservation Conference, Lahaina News, May 2, 1996: 16,18.

— to hold Hawaiiana classes, Lahaina News, January 16, 1997: 10.

— president Linda Decker to give lecture "What did Edward Bailey See?", Lahaina News, June 12, 1997: 17.

— seeking volunteers for Bailey House Museum, Lahaina News, January 29, 1998: 16.

— offering cultural classes, Lahaina News, October 1, 1998: 8.

— to hold annual meeting, Lahaina News, July 15, 1999: 12.

— Bailey House Museum to host "Talk History With Victoria", Lahaina News, December 19, 2002: 20.

— publishes book "Water of Kama—The Story of the Bailey House Site", Lahaina News, June 12, 2003: 18.

MAUI HOLOKU BALL
— to be held at Outrigger Wailea Resort, Lahaina News, September 9, 1999: 12.

MAUI HOMELESS RESOURCE CENTER
— Maui Homeless Resource Center food drive to be held by Jack in the Box and Maui Jaycees, Lahaina News, July 8, 1993: 4.

— see also homeless

MAUI HORSE OWNERS ASSOCIATION
— discussed, Lahaina Sun, March 24, 1971: 1,8.

MAUI HORSE SHOW ASSOCIATION
— to hold first annual meeting, Lahaina News, December 5, 1990: 8.

— to hold first meeting at Eddie Tam Center, Lahaina News, December 19, 1990: 24.

MAUI HOTEL ASSOCIATION
— Chris von Imhof elected president of, Lahaina News, August 12, 1987: 18.

— opens new office, Lahaina News, January 20, 1988: 3.

— quarterly general membership meeting to be held, Lahaina News, September 28, 1988: 3.

— holds seminar on new OSHA standards, Lahaina News, October 19, 1988: 3.

— to hold Charity Ball, Lahaina News, September 13, 1989: 5.

— to hold Charity Ball, Lahaina News, September 27, 1989: 11.

— sponsoring seminar on environmental planning, Lahaina News, March 14, 1990: 5.

— contracted with Maui Recycling Group, Lahaina News, May 2, 1990: 2.

— to hold Visitor Industry Charity Walk, Lahaina News, May 16, 1990: 5.

— to hold Trade Fair, Lahaina News, September 5, 1990: 6.

— accepting reservations for booth space at Trade Fair, Lahaina News, September 12, 1990: 11.

— taking booth reservations for Trade Fair, Lahaina News, September 26, 1990: 9.

— to hold Trade Fair, Lahaina News, October 3, 1990: 9.

— to organize Hotel Trade Show, Lahaina News, October 10, 1990: 11,12.

— to hold Trade Fair at Royal Lahaina Resort Alii Ballroom, Lahaina News, October 17, 1990: 11,12.

— to hold open house, Lahaina News, October 24, 1990: 6.

— to hold Trade Fair, Lahaina News, October 24, 1990: 7.

— to hold Charity Ball, Lahaina News, November 14, 1990: 3.

— to hold Kupunas Christmas Dinner, Lahaina News, December 12, 1990: 4.

— Environmental Committee collects recycling, Lahaina News, February 13, 1991: 5.

— to hold Visitor Industry Charity Walk, Lahaina News, April 17, 1991: 18.

— to hold Visitor Industry Charity Walk, Lahaina News, May 15, 1991: 5.

— executive director Lynn Britton says hotels are in trouble, Lahaina News, November 7, 1991: 1.

— new officers selected, Lahaina News, June 18, 1992: 11.

— Lynn Britton resigns as president, Lahaina News, November 5, 1992: 9.

— Terryl Vencl named executive director, Lahaina News, February 11, 1993: 11.

— Charity Walk to be held, Lahaina News, May 18, 1995: 7.

— donates defibrillators to county Fire Department, Lahaina News, December 18, 1997: 13.

— booth space available, Lahaina News, August 13, 1998: 13.

— booths available for Trade Fair, Lahaina News, August 20, 1998: 13.

— donates to Maui Ocean Center food drive, Lahaina News, November 8, 2001: 9.

— to hold golf fundraiser to benefit Maui Academy of Travel Tourism, Lahaina News, October 10, 2002: 13.

MAUI HOTEL ASSOCIATION ALLIED MEMBERS

— to hold 3rd annual Trade Fair, Lahaina News, August 1, 1991: 11.

— organizing trade fair, Lahaina News, August 8, 1991: 8.

— to hold Trade Fair, Lahaina News, August 15, 1991: 6.

— to hold Trade Fair, Lahaina News, September 5, 1991: 6.

— Trade Fair to be held this week, Lahaina News, September 19, 1991: 6.

— to hold Trade Fair, Lahaina News, August 27, 1992: 10.

— to hold Trade Fair, booths available, Lahaina News, October 7, 1993: 5.

— to hold Trade Fair, booths available, Lahaina News, October 14, 1993: 9.

— to hold trade fair, Lahaina News, September 1, 1994: 12.

— to hold Trade Fair, Lahaina News, September 15, 1994: 13.

— to hold trade fair, Lahaina News, September 29, 1994: 5.

— to hold annual Trade Fair, Lahaina News, September 14, 1995: 10.

— Trade Fair to be held, Lahaina News, September 4, 1997: 12.

— Trade Fair to be held, Lahaina News, September 25, 1997: 12.

— to hold trade fair, Lahaina News, July 22, 1999: 11.

— booth spaces at trade fair available, Lahaina News, August 5, 1999: 11.

MAUI HUI MALAMA

— offering volunteer training for literacy program, Lahaina News, April 16, 1986: 3.

— expanding educational outreach, Lahaina News, May 27, 1987: 1.

— offering English classes to immigrants, Lahaina News, July 15, 1987: 12.

— offers second language training, Lahaina News, February 24, 1988: 3.

— to train language tutors, Lahaina News, March 16, 1988: 15.

— offering free training for tutors, Lahaina News, March 29, 1989: 14.

— looking for volunteer tutors, Lahaina News, June 7, 1989: 2.

— Lynn Waihee to support adult literacy program, Lahaina News, March 7, 1990: 3.

— looking for part-time Japanese-English language tutors, Lahaina News, August 1, 1990: 4.

— to offer training to reading tutors, Lahaina News, January 2, 1991: 3,4.

— receives funds to improve handicap accessibility of building , Lahaina News, February 18, 1993: 10.

MAUI HUMANE SOCIETY

— appealing for donations, Lahaina Sun, August 16, 1972: 11.

— Third annual Walk for Animals benefit set for May 5, Lahaina News, May 2, 1984: 4.

— to hold "Walk for Animals" event, Lahaina News, May 1, 1985: 8.

— "Walk for Animals" raises $5,881, Lahaina News, May 29, 1985: 3.

— to hold benefit showing of "Lethal Weapon 2", Lahaina News, June 28, 1989: 3.

— to hold fair, Lahaina News, May 9, 1990: 16.

— to hold fundraiser at Stouffer Wailea Beach Resort, Lahaina News, November 7, 1990: 11.

— to hold fundraiser "Just Desserts" at Stouffer Wailea Beach Resort, Lahaina News, November 14, 1990: 14.

— to hold annual meeting, offer dog obedience training, Lahaina News, February 6, 1991: 3.

— receives national recognition, Lahaina News, March 13, 1991: 3.

— to hold yard sale fundraiser, Lahaina News, July 18, 1991: 4.

— to hold yard sale, seeking donations, Lahaina News, July 25, 1991: 4.

— to hold dog obedience training classes, Lahaina News, September 26, 1991: 6,7.

— to hold fundraiser at Stouffer Wailea Beach Resort, Lahaina News, October 3, 1991: 13.

— to control pet population, Lahaina News, October 17, 1991: 3.

— launches annual membership drive, Lahaina News, February 6, 1992: 4.

— offers incentives to spay/neuter your pets, Lahaina News, February 6, 1992: 5.

— offering spay/neuter program, Lahaina News, February 13, 1992: 4.

— re-establishes health program for animals adopted from the animal shelter, Lahaina News, March 19, 1992: 3.

— to hold Just Desserts fundraiser, Lahaina News, January 28, 1993: 10.

— to hold dog obedience classes, Lahaina News, March 11, 1993: 11.

— to hold feline photo contest, Lahaina News, June 24, 1993: 8.

— to show "Free Willy" as fundraiser, Lahaina News, July 1, 1993: 5.

— to hold dog obedience classes, Lahaina News, July 15, 1993: 5.

— to hold "poi dog" contest, Lahaina News, August 19, 1993: 7.

— to hold yard sale, Lahaina News, August 26, 1993: 8.

— to hold Thanksgiving Walk, Lahaina News, November 18, 1993: 5.

— to hold membership meeting, Lahaina News, January 27, 1994: 3.

— to host annual "Poi Cat Contest", Lahaina News, April 28, 1994: 5.

— Maui Onion Festival to benefit, Lahaina News, August 4, 1994: 12,13.
— to hold open house, Lahaina News, December 8, 1994: 3.
— to hold "mobile adoption" at Lahaina Cannery Mall, Lahaina News, February 23, 1995: 2.
— to hold "Just Desserts" benefit, Lahaina News, March 23, 1995: 11.
— publishing "Pet of the Week", not otherwise indexed, Lahaina News, March 23, 1995: 7.
— to hold do obedience classes, Lahaina News, March 30, 1995: 6.
— to hold t-shirt design contest, Lahaina News, July 6, 1995: 11.
— having open house, Lahaina News, December 14, 1995: 19.
— to hold "Just Desserts" fundraiser, Lahaina News, March 14, 1996: 13.
— to hold Dog Day Afternoon, Lahaina News, May 2, 1996: 18.
— to celebrate Adopt-A-Cat Month, Lahaina News, June 27, 1996: 14,15.
— holds "More than Just Desserts" fundraiser, Lahaina News, April 3, 1997: 7.
— to hold "Dog Day Afternoon" event, Lahaina News, June 19, 1997: 16.
— benefit to be held, Lahaina News, September 18, 1997: 16.
— to hold Dog Day Afternoon fundraiser, Lahaina News, October 9, 1997: 20.
— to hold "Walk for the Animals", Lahaina News, November 6, 1997: 17.
— selling calendars as a fundraiser, Lahaina News, November 20, 1997: 2.
— to hold obedience classes for dogs, Lahaina News, December 25, 1997: 3.
— to hold obedience classes, Lahaina News, January 1, 1998: 13.
— encourages people to spay pets, Lahaina News, January 29, 1998: 9.
— to hold "More Than Just Desserts" fundraiser, Lahaina News, May 21, 1998: 16.
— to hold obedience classes for dogs, Lahaina News, July 16, 1998: 16.
— to hold obedience classes, Lahaina News, January 14, 1999: 13.
— encourages people to spay and neuter pets, Lahaina News, January 28, 1999: 12.
— to hold "Dog Day Afternoon", Lahaina News, March 18, 1999: 16.
— to hold photo contest for calendar, Lahaina News, April 29, 1999: 14.
— to hold "More Than Just Desserts" benefit, Lahaina News, May 6, 1999: 7.
— to offer dog training classes, Lahaina News, June 3, 1999: 16.
— hosting Adopt-a-Cat month, Lahaina News, June 3, 1999: 2.
— making operational changes due to budget shortfall, Lahaina News, July 8, 1999: 5.
— caring for abused dogs, Lahaina News, July 29, 1999: 1.
— Matthew Minford is "employee of the year", Lahaina News, August 19, 1999: 14.
— Maui Mall to hold Halloween Pet Costume Contest to benefit, Lahaina News, October 28, 1999: 16.
— cuts in support funding leads to change hours of operation, Lahaina News, November 4, 1999: 5.
— to hold "Walk for the Animals", Lahaina News, November 18, 1999: 16.
— to hold obedience classes, Lahaina News, January 6, 2000: 13.
— to offer obedience classes, Lahaina News, March 23, 2000: 13.
— to hold sunset cruise fundraiser, Lahaina News, April 13, 2000: 12.
— to offer dog training classes, Lahaina News, June 15, 2000: 17.
— to hold "Walk for Orphaned Animals", Lahaina News, October 19, 2000: 9.
— to hold "Walk for Orphaned Animals", Lahaina News, October 26, 2000: 12.
— recognizes local businesses for their support, Lahaina News, February 22, 2001: 8.

— to hold a pet photo contest for calendar, Lahaina News, May 3, 2001: 16.
— holds "Animal Aloha Program" fundraiser with Maui restaurants, Lahaina News, May 3, 2001: 9.
— sale of works by Val Baldwin at Axum Pacifica Gallery to support, Lahaina News, July 26, 2001: 16.
— to hold "Walk for Orphaned Animals 2001", Lahaina News, October 11, 2001: 16.
— hosting "Walk for Orphaned Animals" fundraiser, Lahaina News, October 18, 2001: 2.
— to hold "Walk for Orphaned Animals 2001", Lahaina News, October 25, 2001: 17.
— to open Cat Building, Lahaina News, November 8, 2001: 17.
— to hold benefit auction at The Shops at Wailea, Lahaina News, December 20, 2001: 16.
— offering Paintball Tournament fundraiser, Lahaina News, January 10, 2002: 13.
— to hold Mascot Competition, Lahaina News, January 10, 2002: 16.
— to hold Paintball Tournament, Lahaina News, January 17, 2002: 13.
— to hold annual meeting, Lahaina News, January 17, 2002: 16.
— to hold "Dog Day Afternoon", Lahaina News, March 7, 2002: 16.
— to host craft and gift fair, Lahaina News, April 18, 2002: 16.
— to host "Be Kind to Animals Week", Lahaina News, May 2, 2002: 16.
— to hold "Maui's Best Craft and Gift Fair", Lahaina News, May 30, 2002: 16.
— to hold "More than Just Desserts" fundraiser, Lahaina News, June 27, 2002: 16.
— to hold "Maui's Best Craft and Gift Fair", Lahaina News, July 25, 2002: 20.
— receives bequest from the trust fund of the late Jacqueline Lee Johnson, Lahaina News, August 15, 2002: 9.
— to host Walk for Orphaned Animals, Lahaina News, October 10, 2002: 13.
— to hold Walk for Orphaned Animals, Lahaina News, October 17, 2002: 11.
— to hold annual meeting, Lahaina News, January 16, 2003: 16.
— to hold 50th Anniversary open house, Lahaina News, February 27, 2003: 17.
— to hold "Dog Day Afternoon", Lahaina News, March 6, 2003: 16.
— announces new hours, Lahaina News, April 3, 2003: 3.

MAUI IMUA REHABILITATION CENTER
— sponsoring Menehune Madness Parade and Bed Race, Lahaina News, March 13, 1991: 8.

MAUI INC. MAGAZINE [BUSINESS]
— sponsoring Conference on Business and the Environment, Lahaina News, February 6, 1991: 7.
— sponsoring design contest for students, Lahaina News, November 14, 1991: 9.

MAUI INDUSTRIAL ARTS FAIR
— set for February 21 and 22, Lahaina News, February 12, 1986: 3.
— results described, Lahaina News, March 5, 1986: 18.

MAUI INLINE HOCKEY ASSOCIATION
— opens rink at Kalama Park, Lahaina News, July 1, 1999: 7.
— hosts youth pick-up games, Lahaina News, July 8, 1999: 6.
— to host youth pick-up games, Lahaina News, July 15, 1999: 7.

MAUI INTER-CONTINENTAL HOTEL WAILEA [BUSINESS]
— renovations completed, Lahaina News, November 1, 1982: 7.
— to hold bi-weekly luaus, Lahaina News, May 30, 1984: 22.
— sushi bar opens, Lahaina News, June 13, 1984: 3.
— promotions announced, Lahaina News, July 11, 1984: 14.
— luaus now only on Thursdays, Lahaina News, September 12, 1984: 3.

— featuring Kenney and Peters with Frank Withalm playing big band tunes, Lahaina News, December 5, 1984: 14.

— hosting Maui Marine Art Expo, Lahaina News, January 30, 1985: 10.

— spa opens at, Lahaina News, June 4, 1986: 3.

— appoints James Purdy as director of sales, Lahaina News, June 11, 1986: 14.

— sponsors "100 Holes of Golf" fundraiser for Easter Seal Society, Lahaina News, June 18, 1986: 3.

— Thanksgiving celebrations occurring at, Lahaina News, November 19, 1986: 3.

— brunch moved to Lokelani Ballroom, Lahaina News, November 26, 1986: 10.

— receives Award of Excellence from Travel/Holiday, Lahaina News, December 31, 1986: 3.

— to show film by Jacques Cousteau, Lahaina News, March 11, 1987: 18.

— to hold May Day Lei Contest, Lahaina News, April 22, 1987: 10.

— introduces special menu, Lahaina News, April 29, 1987: 6.

— to feature "Wonderful World of Curry", Lahaina News, June 24, 1987: 3.

— celebrates Valentine's Day, Lahaina News, February 10, 1988: 11.

— appoints Bradford Jencks as General Manager, Lahaina News, April 27, 1988: 3.

— to host Symphony of Chocolates to benefit Maui Family YMCA, Lahaina News, May 11, 1988: 14.

— receives M&D Award from Medical Meetings Magazine, Lahaina News, October 19, 1988: 3.

— sold to affiliate of Kenchiku Shiryo Kenkyusha Co., and J.C. West, Lahaina News, December 7, 1988: 6,16.

— receives Four-Diamond Award from American Automobile Association, Lahaina News, January 18, 1989: 5.

— to host Lei Day celebration, Lahaina News, April 26, 1989: 7.

— featuring curries by executive chef Richard Reynolds, Lahaina News, August 2, 1989: 9.

— to host curry night, Lahaina News, August 8, 1990: 13,16.

— to present dinner show featuring music from "South Pacific", Lahaina News, January 2, 1991: 8.

— musical group Union Pacific to perform at Inu Inu Lounge, Lahaina News, February 20, 1991: 11.

— to host Mayor's Ball, Lahaina News, May 1, 1991: 16.

— to host Oktoberfest, Lahaina News, October 3, 1991: 13.

— denied permit to take in outside laundry, Lahaina News, March 19, 1992: 4.

— to organize benefit for Kihei Youth Center, Lahaina News, June 11, 1992: 8.

— to host benefit for Kihei Youth Center, Lahaina News, June 18, 1992: 14,15.

— presents bridal fashion show, Lahaina News, September 9, 1993: 5.

— see also Kiawe Broiler [restaurant]

MAUI INTERFACE CORP. [BUSINESS]
— marketing two-acre homesites at The Plantation Estate, Lahaina News, November 7, 1990: 7.

MAUI INTERFAITH VOLUNTEER CAREGIVERS
— Jean Lierly now administrative coordinator, Lahaina News, January 22, 1998: 2.

MAUI INTERNATIONAL DANCE, ARTS AND CRAFTS FESTIVAL
— held, Lahaina Sun, August 1, 1973: 11.

MAUI INTERNATIONAL SHORT FILM FESTIVAL
— to be held, Lahaina News, September 6, 2001: 16.

MAUI INTERSCHOLASTIC LEAGUE BASKETBALL
— report on league results, Lahaina Sun, January 20, 1971: 7.

MAUI INVASIVE SPECIES COMMITTEE
— attempts to stop ivy gourd from spreading, Lahaina News, March 30, 2000: 3.

MAUI INVITATIONAL BASKETBALL TOURNAMENT
— to be headlined by Arkansas, Lahaina News, June 27, 1991: 7.

— Arizona State University beats Maryland, Lahaina News, December 1, 1994: 9.

— UCLA Bruins to play in, Lahaina News, November 16, 1995: 9.

— college basketball tournament to be held, Lahaina News, November 9, 2000: 10.

— will not be impacted by renovation to Lahaina Civic Center Gymnasium, Lahaina News, August 21, 2003: 12.

MAUI ISLAND COFFEE [BUSINESS]
— opens at The Wharf Cinema Center, Lahaina News, November 26, 1992: 13.

MAUI ISLAND DUAL SPORT
— opens, Lahaina News, February 22, 1996: 11.

MAUI ISLAND FORMULA [BUSINESS]
— begins selling beauty product line, Lahaina News, October 17, 1990: 11.

MAUI ISLAND MORTGAGE [BUSINESS]
— expands by hiring Cynthia Loughman as loan officer, Lahaina News, July 25, 1990: 7.

— new name for Island Mortgage Corporation, Lahaina News, December 12, 1991: 17.

MAUI ISLANDER HOTEL [BUSINESS]
— seeking zoning changes, Lahaina News, December 19, 1996: 12.

— now being managed by Aston Hotels and Resorts, Lahaina News, April 2, 1998: 1,9.

— reservations department wins Lei Day Lei Making contest, Lahaina News, May 14, 1998: 7.

— begins renovations, Lahaina News, October 1, 1998: 13.

— Ohana Hotels to take over management of, Lahaina News, April 19, 2001: 9.

MAUI JACKS
— playing University of Hawai'i basketball team, Lahaina Sun, February 24, 1971: 7.

MAUI JAMDOWN 2000
— to be held, Lahaina News, July 13, 2000: 18.

— to be held, Lahaina News, July 20, 2000: 16.

MAUI JAPANESE CHAMBER OF COMMERCE
— new officers installed, Lahaina News, October 17, 1991: 9.

— to host Arthur Alexander, president of Japan Economic Institute of America, Lahaina News, August 5, 1993: 7.

MAUI JAPANESE CULTURAL SOCIETY
— to host "Traditions in Fashion II", Lahaina News, June 16, 1994: 12.

MAUI JAZZ FESTIVAL
— to be held in Ka'anapali, Lahaina News, July 25, 1990: 11.

— details of, Lahaina News, August 8, 1990: 17.

— to be held in Ka'anapali, Lahaina News, August 29, 1990: 10.

— schedule listed, Lahaina News, September 5, 1990: 15.

— to be held, Lahaina News, May 15, 1997: 7.

— see also Hawaii International Jazz Festival

MAUI JAZZ SOCIETY
— sponsoring Dizzy Gillespie at Maui Prince Hotel, Lahaina News, March 6, 1991: 14.

— to host Dizzy Gillespie, Lahaina News, April 24, 1991: 11.

— sponsoring performance by Ayana at Casanova's, Lahaina News, June 13, 1991: 13.

— to host festival, Lahaina News, April 23, 1992: 27.

— to hold festival, performers listed, Lahaina News, April 30, 1992: 15.

— president Phil Rivera featured, Lahaina News, June 25, 1992: 18.

— hosting saxophonist Tito Puente at Hyatt Regency Maui, Lahaina News, December 24, 1992: 15.

— to host Maui Jazz Festival, Lahaina News, August 26, 1993: 15.

— to host Maui Jazz Festival, Lahaina News, August 26, 1993: 8.

— Gabe Baltazar to receive Legends of Jazz Award, Lahaina News, June 24, 1999: 14.

MAUI JIM SUNGLASSES [BUSINESS]

— featured, Lahaina News, October 19, 1988: 2.

— chosen as official sunglass for Super Bowl XXIII, Lahaina News, January 25, 1989: 17.

— acquired by RLI Vision Corp. of Peoria, Illinois, Lahaina News, December 12, 1996: 13.

— featured, Lahaina News, March 20, 1997: 1.

— holds sales contest, Lahaina News, December 4, 1997: 21.

MAUI JOB JUNCTION

— to be held at Maui Community College, Lahaina News, September 26, 1990: 9.

— to be held, Lahaina News, August 22, 1991: 4.

— to be held, Lahaina News, September 5, 1991: 6.

MAUI JUNIOR DAVIS CUP

— Dean Shimada and Brooke Gannon most valuable players, Lahaina News, July 19, 1989: 5.

MAUI JUNIOR GOLF ASSOCIATION

— recognizes members for scholastic achievement, Lahaina News, October 23, 1997: 18.

MAUI JUNIOR MISS PAGEANT

— Gloria Ancheta named winner, Lahaina Sun, July 26, 1972: 15.

MAUI JUSTICE FOUNDATION

— criticized for targeting mayor Cravalho, Lahaina Sun, December 1, 1971: 11.

— questions qualifications of Kase Higa for district court, Lahaina Sun, January 19, 1972: 7.

— critical of Mayor Cravalho, Lahaina Sun, April 19, 1972: 10.

— critical of budgeting procedures of Maui County, Lahaina Sun, June 21, 1972: 10.

— accuses mayor Cravalho of conflict of interest in Wailea development, Lahaina Sun, July 5, 1972: 3.

MAUI KA PU'UWAI

— to be held at Ritz-Carlton, Lahaina News, September 25, 2003: 1.

MAUI KA'ANAPALI CLASSIC

— see Ka'anapali Classic

MAUI KA'ANAPALI VILLAS

— restaurant damaged by fire, Lahaina News, April 24, 1985: 20.

— Mike Sands appointed general manager, Lahaina News, June 19, 1997: 6.

MAUI KAI

— development featured, Lahaina News, March 23, 2000: 10.

— condominium featured, Lahaina News, September 7, 2000: 16.

— ocean front units available at, Lahaina News, November 2, 2000: 10.

— development featured, Lahaina News, April 17, 2003: 6.

— development featured, Lahaina News, June 12, 2003: 6.

— units available at, Lahaina News, October 2, 2003: 6.

MAUI KAI RESORT, THE

— Paul Gomez appointed general manager, Lahaina News, July 24, 1997: 13.

MAUI KAYAK AND CANOE CLUB

— to hold Kahana Canoe Club Kayak race, Lahaina News, March 13, 1991: 7.

— to sponsor racing with Compadre Mexican Bar and Grill, Lahaina News, January 21, 1993: 7.

— co-sponsoring Compadres Kayak Racing series, Lahaina News, February 24, 1994: 6.

— participates in Compadres Racing Series, Lahaina News, February 2, 1995: 6.

— to present third leg of Compadres Kayak Racing Series, Lahaina News, February 23, 1995: 7.

— to hold fourth leg of Compadres Kayak Racing Series, Lahaina News, March 16, 1995: 6.

— to hold fourth leg of Chart House Kayak Racing Series, Lahaina News, February 22, 1996: 7.

— series to begin, Lahaina News, December 26, 1996: 7.

— series continues, Lahaina News, January 2, 1997: 10.

— Kihei Shoreline Race to be held, Lahaina News, January 30, 1997: 7.

— racing series continues, Lahaina News, January 15, 1998: 7.

— continues to offer Chart House Kayak and Canoe Racing series, Lahaina News, January 14, 1999: 6.

— featured, Lahaina News, February 27, 2003: 12.

MAUI KENPO DOJO

— featured, Lahaina News, October 26, 2000: 10.

MAUI KIDS & CO. [BUSINESS]

— opens at Lahaina Center, Lahaina News, May 23, 1990: 8.

MAUI KOKUA SERVICES, INC. [BUSINESS]

— publishes directory of community services, Lahaina News, July 25, 1990: 6.

— to hold fundraiser whale watch, Lahaina News, April 23, 1992: 7.

— seeking volunteers, Lahaina News, January 7, 1993: 4.

— seeking volunteers, Lahaina News, January 14, 1993: 3.

— needs suicide/crisis volunteers, Lahaina News, February 25, 1993: 3.

— to hold volunteer orientation, Lahaina News, March 25, 1993: 4.

— adds employee assistance program, Lahaina News, February 22, 1996: 11.

— to hold whale watch fund-raiser, Lahaina News, February 22, 1996: 14.

— to hold 20th anniversary meeting, Lahaina News, August 8, 1996: 15.

— seeking volunteers for Crisis Helpline, Lahaina News, August 22, 1996: 5.

— to hold "A Whale of Day" benefit, Lahaina News, February 20, 1997: 10.

— to hold luau as fundraiser, Lahaina News, September 11, 1997: 16.

— board to meet, Lahaina News, August 6, 1998: 21.

— to hold annual meeting, Lahaina News, August 12, 1999: 17.

— to hold benefit whale watch, Lahaina News, March 2, 2000: 13.

MAUI KUMAMOTO KENJIN KAI

— to hold New Year's Celebration, Lahaina News, February 13, 2003: 16.

MAUI LAGER BEER [BUSINESS]

— Rudie Cashen hired by, Lahaina News, September 2, 1987: 3.

— closes, Lahaina News, November 14, 1990: 11.

MAUI LAND AND PINEAPPLE [BUSINESS]

— permission sought from to drill test wells behind Napili, Lahaina Sun, November 11, 1970: 3.

— given permission to build golf course north of Honolua Bay, Lahaina Sun, November 18, 1970: 3.

— owns land where highway will be constructed, Lahaina Sun, November 18, 1970: 4.

— delays repair to sewage line due to canning season, Lahaina Sun, December 9, 1970: 2.

— 270 homes planned in Alaeloa, Lahaina Sun, January 27, 1971: 1,2.

— proposes public beach as part of Maui Pine development in West Maui, Lahaina Sun, February 24, 1971: 1,8.

— public beach proposed as part of development, Lahaina Sun, February 24, 1971: 1,8.

— expected to give land to United States International University once merger with Mauna Olu College is completed, Lahaina Sun, March 10, 1971: 1.

— planning 3000 hotel rooms in West Maui, Lahaina Sun, April 21, 1971: 1,8.

— to relocate an old dump away from the ocean, Lahaina Sun, December 8, 1971: 1.

— decision on proposed housing project in Napilihau deferred by Maui Planning Commission, Lahaina Sun, December 15, 1971: 7.

— personnel changes, Lahaina Sun, January 12, 1972: 1.

— seeks permit to discharge water into Kahului Harbor, Lahaina Sun, March 29, 1972: 4.

— revenues down for 1971, Lahaina Sun, April 26, 1972: 3.

— affirms that Kahului cannery will stay open, Lahaina Sun, May 31, 1972: 3.

— will partner with Los Angeles firm in Honolua resort project near Napili, Lahaina Sun, September 20, 1972: 3.

— income dropped for 1972, Lahaina Sun, March 7, 1973: 11.

— unimpressive financial year, Lahaina Sun, April 25, 1973: 3.

— change to plan for Napili, Lahaina Sun, May 9, 1973: 7.

— Kapalua development needs new partners, Lahaina Sun, June 20, 1973: 3.

— to donate land for beach part at Honokahua, Lahaina Sun, June 20, 1973: 3.

— earnings rose for last six months, Lahaina Sun, August 22, 1973: 6.

— profits up for 1979, Lahaina News, March 15, 1980: 13.

— earnings up, Lahaina News, June 1, 1980: 13.

— net loss means no dividend, Lahaina News, November 15, 1981: 5.

— reports a loss, mainly from losses at Kapalua Bay Hotel, Lahaina News, November 15, 1982: 13.

— lost money in 1982, Lahaina News, March 15, 1983: 11.

— shows profit, Lahaina News, November 2, 1983: 14.

— reaches land settlement in Kahana with Native Hawaiian families, Lahaina News, November 23, 1983: 4.

— reports profits for 1983, Lahaina News, February 15, 1984: 14.

— withdraws from agreement to lease land for West Maui airstrip discussed, Lahaina News, April 11, 1984: 4.

— land sought from by Hawaiian Airlines for land for West Maui airport, Lahaina News, April 25, 1984: 3.

— earnings increased sharply for first quarter, Lahaina News, May 9, 1984: 13.

— profits increased for first half of the year, Lahaina News, August 8, 1984: 14.

— plan to build shopping center along Honoapi'ilani Highway, Lahaina News, January 30, 1985: 3.

— donates land in Napili, perhaps for fire station, Lahaina News, March 22, 1989: 1.

— donates to Maui Community Arts and Cultural Center, Lahaina News, April 19, 1989: 1.

— donation towards construction of community center in Kahului, Lahaina News, October 18, 1989: 7.

— plantation manager comments on loss of topsoil near Honolua Bay, Lahaina News, January 31, 1990: 1.

— public hearing on plans to restore burial site at Honokahua, Lahaina News, April 18, 1990: 3.

— seeking zoning change in Kahana, Lahaina News, May 30, 1990: 5.

— receives special management area permit for golf clubhouse, Lahaina News, August 1, 1990: 7.

— to start employee housing program, Lahaina News, October 31, 1990: 1.

— share owned by Harry Weinberg donated to foundation, Lahaina News, November 14, 1990: 11.

— performance mixed, Lahaina News, November 14, 1990: 13.

— willing to give land for potential park in Napili, Lahaina News, May 8, 1991: 1.

— Howard Kihune hopes will donate land for park, Lahaina News, July 25, 1991: 6.

— sponsoring design contest for students, Lahaina News, November 14, 1991: 9.

— to give The Nature Conservancy easement of native forest at Pu'u Kukui, Lahaina News, February 13, 1992: 4.

— donates towards construction of homeless shelter, Lahaina News, March 26, 1992: 5.

— self-help employee housing almost finished, Lahaina News, June 25, 1992: 2.

— to build catch basin to stem runoff concerns, Lahaina News, July 16, 1992: 9.

— Maui County to allow to build housing for employees, Lahaina News, July 23, 1992: 4.

— announces contractor to redevelop Ka'ahumanu Center, Lahaina News, August 20, 1992: 13.

— asked to donate land for a park in Napili, Lahaina News, September 24, 1992: 1.

— appoints Fred Trotter III as director, Lahaina News, December 3, 1992: 4.

— permit for proposed residential development approved by Maui Planning Commission, Lahaina News, May 27, 1993: 3.

— postpones project to repair Honolua Ditch, Lahaina News, June 10, 1993: 1.

— appoints announced, Lahaina News, May 19, 1994: 13.

— may swap land with state for park in Honolua Bay, Lahaina News, January 26, 1995: 1,20.

— Mahalo Airlines studying impact of flights on fields of, Lahaina News, April 6, 1995: 1,2.

— new appointments announced, Lahaina News, May 18, 1995: 6.

— may give up part ownership of Kaptel Associations, owner of Ritz-Carlton, Lahaina News, August 31, 1995: 1,2.

— to provide more water to Honokohau Valley, Lahaina News, September 21, 1995: 1.

— finalizes agreement to provide more water to Honokohau Stream Department of Water Supply, Lahaina News, September 28, 1995: 1,12.

— may purchase reclaimed water from Public Works and Waste Management Department, Lahaina News, October 12, 1995: 3.

— temporary trail created at Slaughterhouse Beach, Lahaina News, November 9, 1995: 1,16.

— parcel proposed for Napili Regional Park, Lahaina News, February 27, 1997: 1.

— offers pineapple tours, Lahaina News, June 19, 1997: 16.

— to develop resort in Kapalua with Yarmouth Capital Partners II, Lahaina News, July 10, 1997: 12.

— discusses future planning of West Maui, Lahaina News, July 24, 1997: 13.

— criticized for wastewater violations, Lahaina News, October 2, 1997: 1,2.

— Maui Planning Commission may deny housing project proposed by, Lahaina News, August 13, 1998: 1.

— manager of Pu'u Kukui Watershed Randy Bartlett discusses threats to ecosystem, Lahaina News, December 10, 1998: 3.

— to hold blessing for new trail at Slaughterhouse Beach in February, Lahaina News, January 28, 1999: 3.

— questions ability of Judge Bertram to hear application for development, Lahaina News, February 25, 1999: 1,16.

— to pull Tibouchina plants in the Pu'u Kukui Watershed, Lahaina News, September 30, 1999: 12.

— builds stairs down to Slaughterhouse Beach, Lahaina News, October 21, 1999: 14.

— provides land for a refuge for Koko the gorilla, Lahaina News, October 5, 2000: 3.

— Charles Jencks appointed new director of land planning and community development at, Lahaina News, October 12, 2000: 16.

— to hold public meeting on expansion of Kapalua Resort, Lahaina News, June 20, 2002: 9.

— moving forward with plans for Kapalua Mauka, Lahaina News, July 4, 2002: 1,20.

— breaks ground on Kapua Village subdivision , Lahaina News, August 1, 2002: 8.

— Maui Planning Commission met to discuss development at Kapalua Mauka proposed by, Lahaina News, May 15, 2003: 1,20.

MAUI LANDS AND HOMES, INC. [BUSINESS]

— opens office in West Maui, Lahaina News, April 3, 1991: 4.

MAUI LANGUAGE INSTITUTE

— to offer classes on English Second Language, Lahaina News, January 3, 2002: 16.

— to offer English Second Language classes, Lahaina News, February 7, 2002: 16.

MAUI LANI

— Grand Fairways North residential development opens at, Lahaina News, August 26, 1999: 13.

— donating to public schools for each unit sold, Lahaina News, March 23, 2000: 11.

MAUI LANI FAMILY DAY AND CONCERT ON THE GREENS

— to be held, Lahaina News, May 6, 1999: 8.

MAUI LANI HOMES [BUSINESS]

— designing homes, Lahaina News, October 8, 1998: 13.

MAUI LEAGUE OF REPUBLICAN WOMEN

— see League of Women Voters

MAUI LEARNING CENTER

— planning "Triple Whammy Summer School", Lahaina News, June 22, 2000: 6.

MAUI LEATHER AND PALMWOOD FURNISHINGS [BUSINESS]

— opens, Lahaina News, July 20, 2000: 14.

— celebrates grand opening, Lahaina News, December 28, 2000: 16.

MAUI LEATHERNECKS

— to host car wash, Lahaina News, April 23, 1992: 7.

— Marine Corps veterans announces annual activities, Lahaina News, May 4, 1995: 4.

MAUI LEGAL AID SOCIETY

— see Legal Aid Society

MAUI LIFE EXPO

— to be held, Lahaina News, October 8, 1992: 2.

— to be held at Lahaina Square Shopping Center, Lahaina News, October 22, 1992: 4.

MAUI LIVE POETS SOCIETY

— events to be held, Lahaina News, December 14, 1995: 14.

— begins work on world's longest poem, Lahaina News, June 20, 1996: 3.

— to hold poetry readings, Lahaina News, August 1, 1996: 20.

— to hold poetry readings, Lahaina News, August 8, 1996: 14.

— to meet, Lahaina News, December 5, 1996: 15.

— to hold open reading, Lahaina News, December 12, 1996: 8.

— hosting poetry program for kids, Lahaina News, April 10, 1997: 13.

— creating Peace Poem, Lahaina News, June 18, 1998: 16.

— continues to meet, Lahaina News, June 25, 1998: 12.

— to hold readings, Lahaina News, September 10, 1998: 20.

— continues to meet, Lahaina News, December 17, 1998: 24.

— continues to meet at Borders Books, Lahaina News, February 18, 1999: 12.

— continues to meet, Lahaina News, April 1, 1999: 16.

— continues to meet, Lahaina News, May 6, 1999: 20.

— continues to meet, Lahaina News, October 21, 1999: 16.

— continues to offer open poetry readings, Lahaina News, December 2, 1999: 16.

— Maui Peace Poem project growing, Lahaina News, November 2, 2000: 1,13.

— to meet, Lahaina News, May 16, 2002: 16.

— continues to meet, Lahaina News, May 23, 2002: 16.

MAUI LONG TERM CARE PARTNERSHIP

— supporting long-term care programs, Lahaina News, January 9, 2003: 8.

MAUI LONGBOARDS [BUSINESS]

— opens, Lahaina News, February 1, 1996: 11.

MAUI LU RESORT

— to hold Aloha Mele Luncheon, Lahaina News, September 1, 1981: 16.

MAUI LU-WOW [RESTAURANT]

— opens, Lahaina News, April 4, 1996: 9.

— reviewed, Lahaina News, July 4, 1996: 12.

MAUI LUPUS SUPPORT GROUP

— continues to meet, Lahaina News, July 25, 2002: 2.

MAUI MADE PRODUCT SHOW

— to be held, Lahaina News, July 20, 2000: 16.

— to be held at Lahaina Cannery Mall, Lahaina News, July 26, 2001: 17.

MAUI MADRIGAL [MUSICAL GROUP]

— to hold "Singing for the Seasons", Lahaina News, December 13, 2001: 16.

MAUI MAINTENANCE ENGINEERS ASSOCIATION

— elects new officers, Lahaina News, February 15, 1989: 13.

— elect officers, Lahaina News, March 7, 1990: 7.

— to hold drive to support Maui Youth and Family Services Shelter, Lahaina News, April 11, 1990: 3.

— to hold seminar on electrical troubleshooting, Lahaina News, April 11, 1990: 5.

— offering seminar on plumbing, Lahaina News, June 20, 1990: 7.

— donates to Visitor Industry Training and Education Center, Lahaina News, November 28, 1990: 8.

— new officers announced, Lahaina News, February 20, 1991: 7.

— new officers named, Lahaina News, March 12, 1992: 13.

— gives grant to Maui Community College Visitor Industry Training and Education Center (VITEC), Lahaina News, April 2, 1992: 13.

— names new officers, Lahaina News, April 15, 1993: 7.

— held annual election of officers, Lahaina News, July 7, 1994: 9.

MAUI MALE REVUE COMMITTEE

— male strip show to benefit algae cleanup, Lahaina News, April 22, 1993: 3.

MAUI MALL [BUSINESS]

— under construction, Lahaina Sun, June 23, 1971: 11.

— announces "Festival of the Bands" competition, Lahaina News, October 24, 1984: 3.

— to be renovated, Lahaina News, March 4, 1993: 8.

— to celebrate re-opening, Lahaina News, June 17, 1993: 3,10.

— Megaplex Cinemas opens, Lahaina News, May 6, 1999: 10.

— to hold grand reopening, Lahaina News, November 25, 1999: 16.

— launches new website, Lahaina News, July 5, 2001: 9.

— to hold "Sea Fest 2001" boat show, Lahaina News, July 26, 2001: 16.

— to show film "Step Into Liquid", Lahaina News, August 7, 2003: 12.

MAUI MARATHON

— to be held, Lahaina News, March 9, 1988: 4.

— registration begins, Lahaina News, January 17, 1990: 5.

— to be held, Lahaina News, February 14, 1990: 12.

— begins Saturday, Lahaina News, March 7, 1990: 8.

— to be held, Lahaina News, March 2, 1995: 6.

— to be held, Lahaina News, February 8, 1996: 10.

— to be held, Lahaina News, March 7, 1996: 1,4.

— to be held, Lahaina News, February 27, 1997: 6.

— Valley Isle Road Runners Association seeking volunteers to help with, Lahaina News, March 13, 1997: 13.

— to be held, Lahaina News, March 5, 1998: 14.

— won by Aaron Pierson, Lahaina News, March 19, 1998: 1.

— won by Mari Tanigawa, Lahaina News, March 19, 1998: 2.

— to be held, Lahaina News, January 7, 1999: 15.

— to be held, Lahaina News, March 18, 1999: 20.

— raised money for local charities, Lahaina News, June 24, 1999: 7.

— video featured on Akaku: Maui Community Television, Lahaina News, July 8, 1999: 6.

— nearly sold out, Lahaina News, December 9, 1999: 9.

— sold out, Lahaina News, January 13, 2000: 7.

— to be held, Lahaina News, March 16, 2000: 3.

— raised money for local charities, Lahaina News, August 10, 2000: 7.

— almost full, Lahaina News, January 18, 2001: 9.

— almost full, Lahaina News, February 1, 2001: 14.

— to include fundraiser for young girl with a severe seizure disorder, Lahaina News, March 8, 2001: 13.

— to be held, Lahaina News, March 15, 2001: 11.

— raised money for local charities, Lahaina News, May 17, 2001: 15.

— held, Lahaina News, July 5, 2001: 13.

— planning underway, Lahaina News, April 18, 2002: 12.

— training for to begin, Lahaina News, May 9, 2002: 12.

— to be held, Lahaina News, June 20, 2002: 12.

— to raise funds for young kidney transplant recipient, Lahaina News, September 5, 2002: 13.

— to be held, Lahaina News, September 19, 2002: 12.

— Sports Authority receives award for best aid station at, Lahaina News, October 17, 2002: 11.

— entry forms available, Lahaina News, November 21, 2002: 11.

— entry forms available, Lahaina News, December 19, 2002: 11.

MAUI MARINE ART EXPO

— hosted by Maui Inter-Continental Wailea, Lahaina News, January 30, 1985: 10.

— student poster contest them is "Malama Maui Ma'ema'e", Lahaina News, January 29, 1986: 3.

— Jean-Michel Cousteau appearing at, Lahaina News, March 4, 1987: 8.

— to be held at Maui Inter-Continental Wailea hotel, Lahaina News, January 13, 1988: 16.

— features Cousteau movies, Lahaina News, February 3, 1988: 4.

— opened, Lahaina News, February 10, 1988: 3.

— returning to Wailea, Lahaina News, January 25, 1989: 16.

— to be held, Lahaina News, January 24, 1990: 14.

— opens at Lahaina Center, Lahaina News, January 31, 1990: 15.

— attended by mayor Hannibal Tavares, Lahaina News, February 14, 1990: 5.

— Jean-Michael Cousteau to appear, Lahaina News, February 28, 1990: 12.

— to be held at Stouffers Resort, Lahaina News, January 23, 1991: 9.

— continues at Stouffers Resort, Lahaina News, February 6, 1991: 12.

— continues at Stouffers Resort, Lahaina News, February 13, 1991: 13.

— open at Stouffer Wailea Beach Resort, Lahaina News, February 20, 1991: 12.

— extended, Lahaina News, March 20, 1991: 13,14.

— to be held at Stouffer Wailea Beach Resort, Lahaina News, January 23, 1992: 20.

— details given, Lahaina News, January 30, 1992: 19,21.

— to be held, Lahaina News, January 28, 1993: 14.

— to be held, Lahaina News, February 11, 1993: 15.

— to be held at Foundation Gallery, Lahaina News, February 18, 1993: 14.

— Jean-Michel Cousteau to speak at, Lahaina News, February 25, 1993: 5.

— to be held at Kea Lani Resort, Lahaina News, January 6, 1994: 12.

— to be held, Lahaina News, January 20, 1994: 12.

— featured, Lahaina News, January 27, 1994: 8.

— to be held, Lahaina News, November 17, 1994: 19.

— to open, Lahaina News, February 2, 1995: 12.

— Jean-Michel Cousteau to present at, Lahaina News, February 16, 1995: 16.

MAUI MARKET APPAREL, GIFT, AND JEWELRY SHOW

— to be held at Lahaina Civic Center, Lahaina News, March 29, 1989: 14.

— to be held, Lahaina News, April 4, 1990: 7.

MAUI MARKETPLACE

— to hold ho'olaule'a, Lahaina News, October 8, 1998: 16.

MAUI MARKING DEVICE, A [BUSINESS]

— owners featured, Lahaina News, April 11, 2002: 8.

MAUI MARRIAGE ENCOUNTER GROUP

— to host Marriage Day celebration, Lahaina News, February 10, 1994: 4.

MAUI MARRIOTT RESORT [BUSINESS]

— Bruce Curtis new manager on Maui, Lahaina News, July 1, 1981: 8.

— offering free valet parking for handicapped persons, Lahaina News, July 11, 1984: 3.

— names Brad Snyder as resident manager, Lahaina News, June 19, 1985: 8.

— appoints Richard Deleonardis as director of conventions and catering, Lahaina News, June 19, 1985: 8.

— receives 4 diamond rating from the American Automobile Association {AAA}, Lahaina News, August 14, 1985: 3.

— receives award from Hotel Sales and Marketing Association International, Lahaina News, October 30, 1985: 3.

— new parking lot opens, Lahaina News, December 10, 1986: 3.

— names Scot Hamilton as director of sales, Lahaina News, February 18, 1987: 3.

— appoints Adele Samson as senior sales manager, Lahaina News, March 4, 1987: 10.

— names Scott Hamilton as director of marketing, Lahaina News, May 6, 1987: 10.

— appoints Robert Ekman as director of sales, Lahaina News, May 20, 1987: 3.

— offers kama'aina package, Lahaina News, September 9, 1987: 3.

— receives award, Lahaina News, October 14, 1987: 3.

— donates computer to Baldwin High School, Lahaina News, April 13, 1988: 12.

— appoints Luis Lopez as Assistant Controller, Lahaina News, April 20, 1988: 13.

— appoints John McCallom as Director of Human Resources, Lahaina News, April 20, 1988: 13.

— Bill Countryman appointed director of Food and Beverage, Lahaina News, April 20, 1988: 13.

— highly rated by Corporate Meetings and Incentives magazine, Lahaina News, June 22, 1988: 11.

— to feature karaoke, Lahaina News, August 3, 1988: 12.

— ballroom features music of Gershwin, Lahaina News, September 7, 1988: 6.

— Fred Lounsbury named director of engineering, Lahaina News, January 18, 1989: 5.

— promotes Margaret Smith to sales manager, Lahaina News, June 28, 1989: 7.

— entertainment listed, Lahaina News, March 21, 1990: 13.

— entertainment listed, Lahaina News, March 28, 1990: 18.

— part of reorganization of Marriott Hotels, Resorts & Suites, Lahaina News, September 12, 1990: 10.

— raises $1500 from Halloween Bash for the American Heart Association, Lahaina News, November 28, 1990: 3.

— names Paul Toner as director of sales, Lahaina News, August 15, 1991: 6.

— promotes Chuck Brady to director of corporate sales, Lahaina News, August 15, 1991: 6.

— Glen Goto awarded manager of the quarter, Lahaina News, August 22, 1991: 4.

— offering health classes, Lahaina News, October 10, 1991: 3.

— names Scott Sibley as executive chef, Lahaina News, October 24, 1991: 8.

— recognizes employees Tanya Cress, Paul Toner, and Darnell Criste, Lahaina News, November 7, 1991: 8.

— to host Eco-Fair, Lahaina News, December 12, 1991: 5.

— employee awards announced, Lahaina News, February 6, 1992: 10.

— employee awards announced, Lahaina News, February 6, 1992: 11.

— director of corporate sales Chuck Brady named manager of the year, Lahaina News, March 5, 1992: 10.

— awards Tim Jackson associate of the month, Lahaina News, March 12, 1992: 13.

— to celebrate King Kamehameha Day, Lahaina News, June 4, 1992: 15.

— employee awards announced, Lahaina News, July 30, 1992: 12.

— honors employees, Lahaina News, February 4, 1993: 9.

— recognized by American Automobile Association, Lahaina News, February 18, 1993: 10.

— changes in personnel announced, Lahaina News, April 22, 1993: 6.

— awarded with Four Diamond accommodation rating by American Automobile Association (AAA), Lahaina News, February 10, 1994: 6.

— employees recognized, Lahaina News, March 31, 1994: 12.

— employees receive training in Certified Meeting Professional (CMP) certification program, Lahaina News, March 31, 1994: 9.

— employees recognized, Lahaina News, April 21, 1994: 12.

— holds thank you barbeque for employees after large convention, Lahaina News, May 12, 1994: 10.

— wins President's Award from Marriott International, Lahaina News, May 19, 1994: 13.

— employees recognized, Lahaina News, May 26, 1994: 7.

— employees awarded, Lahaina News, September 22, 1994: 13.

— Crystal Zhou new assistant chief engineer at, Lahaina News, September 22, 1994: 13.

— awarded Gold Key and Golf Platter awards from Meetings and Conventions and Incentive Travel magazines, Lahaina News, October 6, 1994: 11.

— Tadd Warner and Jeff Browning new managers at, Lahaina News, October 27, 1994: 15.

— employees honored, Lahaina News, October 27, 1994: 15.

— employees honored, Lahaina News, December 22, 1994: 13.

— honors employees, Lahaina News, February 9, 1995: 6.

— honors employees, Lahaina News, April 13, 1995: 12.

— announces promotions, Lahaina News, April 27, 1995: 10.

— honors employees, Lahaina News, June 1, 1995: 10.

— honors employees, Lahaina News, July 20, 1995: 10.

— honors employees, Lahaina News, August 17, 1995: 10.

— new staff hired, Lahaina News, October 12, 1995: 12.

— employees honored, Lahaina News, November 9, 1995: 10.

— donates turkeys to Light Bringers, Lahaina News, November 30, 1995: 4.

— to hold Na Mele O Maui and 'Opio Song Competition, Lahaina News, December 7, 1995: 15.

— employees honored, Lahaina News, December 14, 1995: 16.

— employees honored, Lahaina News, December 28, 1995: 10,12.

— employees honored, Lahaina News, January 25, 1996: 12.

— employees honored, Lahaina News, February 1, 1996: 11.

— restaurant manager Chris Laletin honored, Lahaina News, February 8, 1996: 6.

— named hotel of the year by Marriott International, Lahaina News, March 7, 1996: 11.

— employees honored, Lahaina News, March 7, 1996: 11.

— employees honored, Lahaina News, April 18, 1996: 9.

— associates honored, Lahaina News, May 9, 1996: 8.

— associates honored, Lahaina News, June 27, 1996: 12.

— hosting fundraiser for Lahaina's Arts Education for Children Group, Lahaina News, July 31, 1997: 6.

— awarded Four-Diamond accommodation rating by the American Automobile Association (AAA), Lahaina News, March 5, 1998: 13.

— Julie Gates is new director of sales, Lahaina News, April 2, 1998: 13.

— workers help employees who are battling cancer, Lahaina News, April 2, 1998: 3.

— new members of sales team announced, Lahaina News, February 25, 1999: 11.

— workers to help improve Lahainaluna High School grounds, Lahaina News, August 5, 1999: 11.

— hired Mark Barnes and Margaret Laletin, Lahaina News, September 2, 1999: 13.

— renovations completed, Lahaina News, January 25, 2001: 14.

— collects trash from the beach and reefs of Ka'anapali, Lahaina News, December 13, 2001: 8.

— to host safety classes, Lahaina News, February 21, 2002: 9.

— new buffets now available, Lahaina News, August 1, 2002: 11.

— Bill Countryman new general manager at, Lahaina News, May 8, 2003: 8.

— Cyrus Keyhani named systems manager, Lahaina News, July 10, 2003: 8.

MAUI MARSHALS, THE

— to host Aloha State Games at Ukumehame Firing Range, Lahaina News, June 4, 1998: 15.

MAUI MASTERS SWIM CLUB

— begins to practice at Lahaina Aquatic Center, Lahaina News, September 24, 1992: 13.

— continues evening swim workouts, Lahaina News, January 27, 1994: 6.

— to host benefit swim, Lahaina News, March 23, 1995: 7.

— to hold Ka'anapali Klassic, Lahaina News, May 11, 1995: 7.

— to hold Ka'anapali Klassic, Lahaina News, May 2, 1996: 18.

— to hold Maui Roughwater Swim Race, Lahaina News, October 3, 1996: 13.

— Maui Roughwater Swim Race to be held, Lahaina News, October 9, 1997: 21.

— to hold Ka'anapali Klassic Ocean Swim, Lahaina News, April 30, 1998: 17.

— donates to West Maui Youth Center, Lahaina News, June 11, 1998: 9.

— to hold Ka'anapali Klassic Ocean Swim, Lahaina News, April 8, 1999: 7.

— Kapalua Fun Swim Challenge to support turtle conservation, Lahaina News, June 1, 2000: 9.

— to hold Kapalua Fun Swim Challenge, Lahaina News, June 8, 2000: 14.

— to hold Maui Roughwater Swim Race, Lahaina News, October 12, 2000: 9.

— to hold Maui Roughwater Swim Race, Lahaina News, October 19, 2000: 9.

MAUI MATSURI

— Japanese street festival to be held, Lahaina News, June 6, 2002: 16.

— street festival to be held, Lahaina News, February 20, 2003: 17.

— annual Japanese street festival to be held, Lahaina News, May 29, 2003: 16.

MAUI MAUI STEAK AND SEAFOOD [RESTAURANT]

— opens in former Lahaina Broiler space, Lahaina News, December 12, 1996: 12.

— to hold "Ladies Luncheon", Lahaina News, February 13, 1997: 11.

MAUI MEADOWS

— recent fire displaces eight people, Lahaina News, August 22, 1996: 5.

MAUI MEADOWS HOMEOWNERS ASSOCIATION

— formed, requests buffer from Wailea 670 development, Lahaina News, August 27, 1992: 13.

— advocates to improve community, Lahaina News, April 1, 1993: 6,7.

— seeking members, Lahaina News, May 20, 1993: 5.
— to hold annual meeting, Lahaina News, November 25, 1993: 6.
— residents express main concerns, Lahaina News, December 9, 1993: 5.

MAUI MEDICAL GROUP, INC. [BUSINESS]
— clinic opening in evenings, Lahaina News, September 23, 1987: 3.
— now affiliated with Phycor, Inc., Lahaina News, September 18, 1997: 12.
— to collect food for the Maui Food Bank, Lahaina News, December 10, 1998: 9.
— renovating Lahaina Clinic, Lahaina News, April 4, 2002: 3.
— Sumathi McGregor joins Obstetrician-Gynecologist staff, Lahaina News, May 23, 2002: 8.
— Earl Kukahiko leads blessing of renovations at, Lahaina News, August 1, 2002: 22.
— plans diabetes education classes, Lahaina News, February 20, 2003: 17.
— to hold diabetes education classes, Lahaina News, April 10, 2003: 20.
— to hold Diabetes Education Classes, Lahaina News, June 19, 2003: 16.
— to hold Diabetes Education Classes, Lahaina News, July 17, 2003: 17.
— to hold classes on diabetes, Lahaina News, August 7, 2003: 16.
— to hold diabetes classes, Lahaina News, August 14, 2003: 16.
— Eugene Chen appointed to General Surgery department, Lahaina News, August 14, 2003: 8.

MAUI MEDICAL SOCIETY
— sponsors Diabetes Detection Drive, Lahaina Sun, December 1, 1971: 12.

MAUI MEMORIAL HOSPITAL
— converts to new rate system, Lahaina Sun, July 5, 1972: 9.
— seeking to expand, Lahaina Sun, July 26, 1972: 9.
— data on patient care provided, Lahaina Sun, January 24, 1973: 7.
— will not station a doctor during peak emergency hours, Lahaina Sun, January 31, 1973: 6.
— nursing home planned, Lahaina Sun, March 14, 1973: 13.
— offers workshops on coping with cancer, Lahaina News, March 4, 1987: 10.
— Doctor Ronald Kwon advocates to privatize, Lahaina News, October 3, 1990: 1,4.
— Dr. Mahmood Mirzai passes away, Lahaina News, December 12, 1991: 6.
— raising rates, Lahaina News, January 16, 1992: 5.
— state legislature considering autonomy for, Lahaina News, February 20, 1992: 3.
— may change rates, Lahaina News, March 5, 1992: 5.
— hope to expand hospital and parking area, Lahaina News, March 24, 1994: 7.
— Stereotactic Mammographic Unit opens, Lahaina News, October 3, 1996: 18.
— auxiliary to hold fundraising sale, Lahaina News, November 28, 1996: 11.
— celebrates retirement of Dr. Marion Hanlon, Lahaina News, March 12, 1998: 11.
— marketing committee collecting historical data, Lahaina News, July 8, 1999: 11.

MAUI MEMORIAL HOSPITAL AUXILIARY
— publishes "The Many Flavors of Maui" cookbook as fundraiser, Lahaina News, February 26, 1986: 3.

MAUI MEMORIAL MEDICAL CENTER
— to open sleep disorder unit, Lahaina News, August 10, 2000: 1.
— opens new parking lots, Lahaina News, April 26, 2001: 8.
— Social Work Services Department to present "Redirecting Children's Behavior", Lahaina News, November 1, 2001: 2.

— to add complementary and alternative care providers, Lahaina News, January 17, 2002: 1,18.
— Foundation receives grant from Alexander and Baldwin Foundation, Lahaina News, May 23, 2002: 8.
— to celebrate 50th anniversary, Lahaina News, May 30, 2002: 2.
— to celebrate 50th anniversary, Lahaina News, June 6, 2002: 16.
— adds new radiation therapy procedure, Lahaina News, June 27, 2002: 8.
— receives accreditation, Lahaina News, November 7, 2002: 8.
— to offer tests for Peripheral Vascular Disease (PVD), Lahaina News, September 18, 2003: 2.
— to offer tests for Peripheral Vascular Disease (PVD), Lahaina News, September 25, 2003: 9.

MAUI MEMORIAL MEDICAL CENTER FOUNDATION
— to recognize heroes of health care, Lahaina News, February 17, 2000: 15.
— sponsoring "Learn How to Increase Your income and Reduce Taxes", Lahaina News, April 27, 2000: 13.
— West Maui Breast Cancer Benefit held at Longhi's, Lahaina News, January 18, 2001: 6.
— to hold Keola Awards, Lahaina News, May 10, 2001: 9.

MAUI MEMORIAL PARK
— donates to printing of hippie brochure, Lahaina Sun, January 27, 1971: 2.

MAUI MEMORIES [BUSINESS]
— to open, Lahaina News, July 11, 1990: 6.

MAUI MENTAL HEALTH ASSOCIATION
— creation of, discussed, Lahaina Sun, February 9, 1972: 14.
— hosting stress reduction seminar, Lahaina News, January 2, 1985: 3.
— to hold golf tournament fundraiser, Lahaina News, June 10, 1993: 9.

MAUI MENTAL HEALTH SERVICE
— Edgar Auerswald named head of, Lahaina Sun, February 2, 1972: 14.

MAUI METROPOLITAN MUSEUM
— going out of business, to hold sale, Lahaina News, June 17, 1999: 16.

MAUI MEX FOODS, INC. [BUSINESS]
— building commissary kitchen at La Familia Village, Lahaina News, July 25, 1984: 14.

MAUI MIATA CLUB
— continues to meet, Lahaina News, November 19, 1998: 16.
— to hold whale watching land cruise, Lahaina News, March 11, 1999: 12.
— to meet, Lahaina News, April 8, 1999: 12.

MAUI MIKE'S TROPHIES AND AWARDS [BUSINESS]
— moves location, Lahaina News, November 30, 1995: 10.

MAUI MILITARY MUSEUM
— displays military past, Lahaina News, May 17, 2001: 1,22.
— to open at Napili Plaza, Lahaina News, May 24, 2001: 10.
— curator Alan DeCoite to host Christian Home Educators, Lahaina News, January 24, 2002: 1,2.
— celebrating first anniversary, Lahaina News, May 2, 2002: 16.
— must leave its current position, Lahaina News, June 5, 2003: 1,2.

MAUI MINI MISS AMERICAN STARLET
— Taylor Jean Trout wins beauty pageant, Lahaina News, March 15, 2001: 1.

MAUI MISSION SCHOOL
— offering kindergarten classes, Lahaina News, November 26, 1986: 10.
— to hold reunion, Lahaina News, April 1, 1999: 16.

MAUI MIXERS
— Square Dance Club to hold dance, Lahaina News, October 8, 1998: 16.
— to hold square dance, Lahaina News, December 17, 1998: 24.

— continues to offer square dancing, Lahaina News, January 28, 1999: 13.

— to hold square dance, Lahaina News, April 1, 1999: 16.

— square dancing continues to be held, Lahaina News, June 3, 1999: 17.

— to hold square dances, Lahaina News, July 29, 1999: 12.

— continues to hold square dancing, Lahaina News, October 7, 1999: 17.

— continues to hold dances, Lahaina News, December 30, 1999: 16.

MAUI MODEL RAILROAD HISTORICAL SOCIETY

— to hold public exhibit, Lahaina News, May 1, 1991: 3.

— presenting public exhibit, Lahaina News, May 8, 1991: 3.

MAUI MOMENTS

— photo gallery opens, Lahaina News, December 24, 1986: 8.

MAUI MONEY GAME

— created by Mike Farrell, featured, Lahaina News, January 15, 1986: 7.

MAUI MONKEY [BUSINESS]

— registers trademark, Lahaina News, May 26, 1994: 7.

— Sacred Hearts School students to visit store to learn about business, Lahaina News, September 14, 2000: 16.

MAUI MOTORCYCLE CLUB

— sponsoring moto-cross championship, Lahaina Sun, July 19, 1972: 14.

MAUI MOUNTAIN BIKE ADVENTURES [BUSINESS]

— featured, Lahaina News, February 13, 1992: 9.

— to hold grand opening, Lahaina News, May 21, 1992: 8.

MAUI MOUNTAIN BIKE CLUB

— seeking members, Lahaina News, January 7, 1993: 4.

— holds "Poli Poli Mountain Bike Challenge", Lahaina News, July 10, 1997: 14.

MAUI MULTI-CULTURAL ORGANIZATION

— sponsoring Multi-Cultural Fair, Lahaina News, January 18, 1996: 4.

— calendar available at County Building, Lahaina News, March 1, 2001: 10.

— "The Faces and Food of Maui" calendar available, Lahaina News, February 14, 2002: 2.

MAUI MUNCHIES [RESTAURANT]

— featured, Lahaina News, August 22, 1991: 11.

MAUI MURDERS, THE [PLAY]

— to be performed by Maui Academy of Performing Arts, Lahaina News, May 28, 1992: 18.

MAUI MUSCLE FITNESS CENTER

— opens, Lahaina News, January 4, 1996: 6.

MAUI MUSCLE SPORTS CLUB-KAHANA [BUSINESS]

— to open, Lahaina News, March 9, 2000: 11.

MAUI MUSIC FESTIVAL

— to be held at Baldwin Auditorium and War Memorial Gym, Lahaina Sun, April 19, 1972: 10.

— to be held, Lahaina News, July 6, 1995: 10.

— to be held, Lahaina News, August 17, 1995: 12.

— to be held, Lahaina News, August 24, 1995: 12.

— to be held, Lahaina News, August 31, 1995: 11.

— details, Lahaina News, August 15, 1996: 18.

— held, Lahaina News, August 29, 1996: 1.

— details of, Lahaina News, August 29, 1996: 14.

— tickets on sale, Lahaina News, April 23, 1998: 2.

— to include Keiko Matsui, the Braxton Brothers, and Spyro Gyra, Lahaina News, April 22, 1999: 3.

— spots available for food vendors, Lahaina News, May 13, 1999: 13.

— details, Lahaina News, May 13, 1999: 8.

— to be held, Lahaina News, May 11, 2000: 24.

— to be held at Ka'anapali Resort, Lahaina News, May 25, 2000: 21.

— to be held, Lahaina News, June 27, 2002: 1,2.

— to benefit Montessori School of Maui, Lahaina News, October 9, 2003: 14.

MAUI MUSIC ODYSSEY

— concert to benefit Surfrider Foundation, Lahaina News, December 13, 2001: 1,8.

MAUI MYTH AND MAGIC THEATRE

— offering courses, Lahaina News, February 18, 1987: 10.

— to open, Lahaina News, July 22, 1999: 11.

— to hold benefit for Arts Education for Children Group's summer programs, Lahaina News, May 4, 2000: 1.

— to teach youth drama, Lahaina News, June 15, 2000: 6.

— to teach drama to youth, Lahaina News, June 22, 2000: 17.

— to present hula shows, Lahaina News, November 2, 2000: 24.

— John Young new general manager of, Lahaina News, May 9, 2002: 8.

— changes to Maui Theatre, Lahaina News, July 25, 2002: 8.

MAUI 'N ME [BUSINESS]

— purchased by Laura Stice, Lahaina News, February 27, 1991: 8.

MAUI NEI

— A Journey Through Lahaina's Past wins Certificate of Commendation from American Association for State and Local History, Lahaina News, July 24, 2003: 8.

MAUI NEI HULA FESTIVAL

— held in Japan, Lahaina News, September 7, 2000: 19.

MAUI NET [BUSINESS]

— connecting local businesses to internet, Lahaina News, August 3, 1995: 8.

— adds new dial-up telephone lines, Lahaina News, February 26, 1998: 11.

— adds new dial-in telephone numbers, Lahaina News, April 2, 1998: 13.

— warns companies of hackers, Lahaina News, July 1, 1999: 11.

MAUI NEWS [NEWSPAPER]

— sued by George Ferreira Jr., Lahaina Sun, February 17, 1971: 5.

— owner of purchases Lahaina News, Lahaina News, August 27, 1986: 1.

— Leimomi Hussey awarded Player of the Year, Lahaina News, May 27, 1987: 16.

MAUI NISEI VETERANS MEMORIAL CENTER

— Kiwanis Club of Kahului to hold "Sing for the Center" featuring Japanese karaoke to benefit, Lahaina News, July 31, 2003: 18.

MAUI NO KA OI: OHANA BASH

— to be held, Lahaina News, April 17, 2003: 18.

MAUI NON-PROFIT DIRECTORS

— Mayor James Apana to speak at Legislative Breakfast, Lahaina News, November 29, 2001: 17.

— new board members and officers installed, Lahaina News, January 3, 2002: 2.

MAUI NORMAN K. TAMANAHA HAWAIIAN MARATHON AND CYCLE RACE

— described, Lahaina Sun, April 12, 1972: 21.

MAUI NUI BOTANICAL GARDENS

— to hold fundraiser "Ho'olaule'a o Na 'Opio o Na Moku", Lahaina News, May 3, 2001: 20.

— to hold native tree giveaway, Lahaina News, October 24, 2002: 14.

— to give away native trees, Lahaina News, October 31, 2002: 14.

MAUI NUI-MADE PRODUCTS FESTIVAL

— Maui County Office of Economic Development seeking vendors for, Lahaina News, July 3, 2003: 8.

— Office of Economic Development seeking vendors for, Lahaina News, July 10, 2003: 8.

— to be held at Lahaina Cannery Mall, Lahaina News, July 24, 2003: 8.

MAUI NURSES SCHOLARSHIP FOUNDATION
— to receive funds from Maui Tennis Loves Nurses Mixed Doubles Tournament, Lahaina News, November 2, 1988: 5.
— to hold tennis and golf tournament, Lahaina News, November 8, 2001: 13.

MAUI OCEAN ACADEMY
— forms windsurfing team, Lahaina News, April 18, 1996: 12.

MAUI OCEAN CENTER
— proposed, Lahaina News, October 12, 1988: 1,14.
— public hearing to be held at Lahaina Public Library, Lahaina News, October 26, 1988: 3.
— moves business to Lahaina, Lahaina News, July 5, 1989: 4.
— Amfac, Inc. puts project on hold, Lahaina News, June 13, 1990: 1.
— proposed park may lure eco-tourists, Lahaina News, March 3, 1994: 6.
— nearing completion, Lahaina News, December 4, 1997: 21.
— to hold public opening, Lahaina News, March 12, 1998: 11.
— to open, Lahaina News, March 12, 1998: 24.
— adds four baby scalloped hammerhead sharks, Lahaina News, January 7, 1999: 15.
— Jean-Michel Cousteau to visit, Lahaina News, January 21, 1999: 13.
— to hold slide show on spinner dolphins, Lahaina News, February 18, 1999: 12.
— to host "Eye-to-eye with the Whales" slide show, Lahaina News, February 18, 1999: 13.
— seeking volunteers, Lahaina News, March 4, 1999: 13.
— tiger shark doing well at, Lahaina News, May 6, 1999: 18.
— flagtail tilefish added to collection, Lahaina News, June 17, 1999: 13.
— to extend hours, Lahaina News, July 8, 1999: 11.
— hold orientation for volunteers, Lahaina News, October 21, 1999: 13.
— sharks featured in "Baywatch Hawaii", Lahaina News, December 2, 1999: 13.
— offering information and interactive displays on humpback whales, Lahaina News, December 9, 1999: 15.
— to offer course on marine mammals for school children, Lahaina News, December 23, 1999: 7.
— offering "Fishy Families" marine education program, Lahaina News, February 3, 2000: 13.
— awarded Certificate of Merit in the Attraction Category from Hawai'i Visitors and Convention Bureau, Lahaina News, May 4, 2000: 13.
— hosts Maui Country's Junior Firefighter Award, Lahaina News, May 4, 2000: 2.
— to celebrate "Ka 'Ohana Moana" as benefit for Kihei Canoe Club, Lahaina News, May 11, 2000: 9.
— offering "Keiki Ocean Activities", Lahaina News, May 25, 2000: 6.
— holding volunteer training program, Lahaina News, June 15, 2000: 17.
— to hold "Sea Talks" marine life series, Lahaina News, July 20, 2000: 17.
— announces new appointments, Lahaina News, October 12, 2000: 16.
— establishes aquarium at Kahului Airport, Lahaina News, November 9, 2000: 20.
— to hold Kama'aina Appreciation Day, Lahaina News, November 23, 2000: 20.
— to host talk by Steve Kajiura on "The Fascinating World of Sharks", Lahaina News, December 14, 2000: 20.
— to host archaeologist James Sinclair, Lahaina News, March 1, 2001: 16.
— Hannah Bernard appointed education director, Lahaina News, April 19, 2001: 8.
— to host Dale Zarrella presenting "Sea Talk", Lahaina News, June 21, 2001: 17.
— inviting public to watch rice coral procreate, Lahaina News, July 19, 2001: 9.
— to support intern program with University of Hawaii, Lahaina News, August 9, 2001: 9.
— new employees at, Lahaina News, September 6, 2001: 9.
— hosting "Sea Talk" events, Lahaina News, October 18, 2001: 9.
— to hold Kama'aina Appreciation Day, Lahaina News, November 22, 2001: 8.
— Monique Faulkner new food and beverage director, Lahaina News, December 6, 2001: 9.
— collects trash from the beach and reefs of Ka'anapali, Lahaina News, December 13, 2001: 8.
— hosted members of the New York Mayor's Office of Emergency Management, Lahaina News, December 20, 2001: 9.
— Reef Cafe reopens, Lahaina News, January 10, 2002: 8.
— celebrating 4th anniversary, Lahaina News, February 28, 2002: 8.
— to celebrate 4th birthday, Lahaina News, March 7, 2002: 16.
— seeking volunteers, Lahaina News, April 4, 2002: 16.
— to host Earth Day clean-up, Lahaina News, May 2, 2002: 8.
— to premiere "Hawaii's Ocean Realm", Lahaina News, May 23, 2002: 16.
— to host Junior Naturalist Program, Lahaina News, May 23, 2002: 8.
— continues to hold "Family Fun Day", Lahaina News, May 30, 2002: 16.
— continues to hold "Family Fun Day", Lahaina News, June 13, 2002: 16.
— presents Hawai'i Nature Center with results of fundraiser, Lahaina News, June 20, 2002: 8.
— announces new summer hours, Lahaina News, July 4, 2002: 8.
— watch live coral spawn at, Lahaina News, July 11, 2002: 16.
— to show "Save Ma'alaea: A Cry for Help", Lahaina News, August 22, 2002: 1,24.
— Tapani Vuori new merchandise director at, Lahaina News, August 29, 2002: 14.
— to hold food drive, Lahaina News, December 12, 2002: 2.
— supporting turtle research, Lahaina News, December 19, 2002: 9.
— Stephen Parker is new director of marketing, Lahaina News, January 23, 2003: 9.
— to hold "Sea of Love" Valentine's Dinner, Lahaina News, February 13, 2003: 16.
— Samantha Whitecraft to present "E Holo Mua—Kaho'olawe Ocean Resources Monitoring and Management" as part of Sea Talks Series, Lahaina News, May 22, 2003: 2.
— to host talk by Christopher Kelley and Terry Kerby on "The Discovery of the Ward Midget Submarine off Pearl Harbor", Lahaina News, June 26, 2003: 8.
— to offer Camp Kaimana, Lahaina News, July 17, 2003: 16.
— continues to hold Sea Life workshop, Lahaina News, July 24, 2003: 16.
— to hold "Sex in the Sea Week", Lahaina News, July 24, 2003: 8.
— offering Camp Kaimana, Lahaina News, July 31, 2003: 16.
— to host "Totally Tubular Tunnel Sleepover", Lahaina News, August 7, 2003: 16.
— Kate Zolezzi new general manager, Lahaina News, August 14, 2003: 8.
— celebrating Coastweek, Lahaina News, September 18, 2003: 8.
— to offer talk on "Mating Behavior in Whitetip Reef Sharks", Lahaina News, September 25, 2003: 17.

MAUI OCEAN CLUB
— to open sales center, Lahaina News, August 21, 2003: 8.

MAUI OCEAN SWIM CLUB
— to hold Ka'anapali Klassic Ocean Swim, Lahaina News, May 16, 1990: 7.
— to host Maui Rough-Water Swim, Lahaina News, October 17, 1990: 7.
— to hold Ka'anapali Klassic Ocean Swim, Lahaina News, May 15, 1991: 7.
— to hold Maui Rough-Water Swim, Lahaina News, October 10, 1991: 8.

MAUI OCEANFRONT INN
— to be renovated, Lahaina News, December 21, 2000: 13.

MAUI OHANA KEIKI FREE FISHING TOURNAMENT
— to be held by Lahaina Yacht Club, Lahaina News, September 4, 1997: 15.

MAUI OIL COMPANY [BUSINESS]
— to provide fuel at Lahaina Harbor as stop-gap measure, Lahaina News, July 5, 1989: 1.

MAUI OKINAWA KENJIN KAI
— to hold annual bazaar, Lahaina News, May 6, 1999: 20.
— to hold Okinawan Festival, Lahaina News, August 22, 2002: 9.

MAUI OKINAWAN FESTIVAL
— see Okinawan Festival

MAUI ONION
— history of on Maui, Lahaina News, March 21, 1990: B3.

MAUI ONION [SHIP]
— wins Bud Cup Regatta, Lahaina News, September 13, 1989: 24.

MAUI ONION COOK-OFF
— scheduled, Lahaina News, March 15, 1989: 14.
— to be held, Lahaina News, July 8, 1993: 10,11.

MAUI ONION FESTIVAL
— events detailed, Lahaina News, March 21, 1990: B1,B2,B3,B4,B5,B6,B7,B8.
— raises money, Lahaina News, April 4, 1990: 16.
— to be held, Lahaina News, June 13, 1991: 12.
— to be held, Lahaina News, June 20, 1991: 9.
— to be held at Whaler's Village, Lahaina News, June 27, 1991: 12.
— details given, Lahaina News, July 4, 1991: 12.
— cook-off to be held at Whalers Village; volunteers needed, Lahaina News, July 4, 1991: 3.
— details given, Lahaina News, July 11, 1991: 10.
— onion eating contest won by Paul Payne, Lahaina News, July 25, 1991: 12.
— to be held, Lahaina News, May 28, 1992: 4.
— seeking pageant participants, Lahaina News, June 11, 1992: 3.
— to open July 24th, Lahaina News, June 11, 1992: 5.
— contestants sought for Festival Queen Pageant, Lahaina News, June 18, 1992: 4.
— contestants sought for Festival Queen Pageant, Lahaina News, July 2, 1992: 4.
— chefs sought to compete in Maui Onion Cook-Off, Lahaina News, July 9, 1992: 20.
— seeking contestants for Queen Pageant, Lahaina News, July 9, 1992: 4,5.
— details provided, Lahaina News, July 16, 1992: 18.
— to start on Friday, Lahaina News, July 23, 1992: 19.
— Roxanne Marciniak crowned queen, Lahaina News, August 6, 1992: 3.
— to be held, Lahaina News, July 22, 1993: 10.
— to be held; includes cook-off and eating contest, Lahaina News, July 14, 1994: 15.
— to be held, Lahaina News, July 28, 1994: 12.
— events detailed; to benefit Maui Humane Society, Lahaina News, August 4, 1994: 12,13,14.
— booths available for, Lahaina News, July 13, 1995: 5.
— details, Lahaina News, August 3, 1995: 13,14,,15.
— to be held; to produce cookbook, Lahaina News, August 1, 1996: 1,8,14.
— to be held at Whalers Village, Lahaina News, July 24, 1997: 3.
— to be held, Lahaina News, July 31, 1997: 7.
— winners of recipe contest announced, Lahaina News, August 21, 1997: 9.
— to be held, Lahaina News, July 23, 1998: 7.
— to be held, Lahaina News, July 30, 1998: 9.
— results of competitions at, Lahaina News, August 6, 1998: 8.
— to be held, Lahaina News, May 20, 1999: 13.
— to be held, Lahaina News, July 8, 1999: 11.
— to be held, Lahaina News, July 22, 1999: 11.
— applications for recipe contest available, Lahaina News, July 22, 1999: 5.
— to be held, Lahaina News, July 29, 1999: 1,16.
— to be held, Lahaina News, July 27, 2000: 3.
— to be held, Lahaina News, August 3, 2000: 17.
— recipe contest winners to appear on Fox's Hawai'i's Kitchen, Lahaina News, August 17, 2000: 15.
— to be held, Lahaina News, July 12, 2001: 15.
— to be held, Lahaina News, August 2, 2001: 9.
— to be held, Lahaina News, August 16, 2001: 8.
— to be held, Lahaina News, July 18, 2002: 14.
— to be held at Whalers Village, Lahaina News, July 25, 2002: 19.
— to be held, Lahaina News, August 1, 2002: 2,11.
— organized, recipe contest to be held, Lahaina News, July 24, 2003: 18.
— to be held, Lahaina News, July 31, 2003: 14.
— held, Lahaina News, August 21, 2003: 8.

MAUI ONSTAGE
— to perform "M. Butterfly" at Iao Theatre, Lahaina News, November 26, 1992: 21.
— to perform Guys and Dolls, Lahaina News, March 11, 1993: 16.
— to perform "Nunsense", Lahaina News, March 18, 1993: 12.
— to perform "Noises Off", Lahaina News, April 27, 1995: 11.
— to perform Terrence McNally's play "Master Class", Lahaina News, January 25, 2001: 16.
— to perform comedy "Art", Lahaina News, April 12, 2001: 20.
— to present "The Garden Behind the Moon", Lahaina News, November 1, 2001: 17.
— to perform "The Garden Behind The Moon" based on book by Howard Pyle, Lahaina News, November 8, 2001: 18.
— to present "The Garden Behind the Moon", Lahaina News, December 13, 2001: 14.
— to hold auditions for "You Can't Take it With You", Lahaina News, December 27, 2001: 14.
— to perform "All in the Timing" comedy, Lahaina News, January 31, 2002: 16.
— to hold "HOT L BALTIMORE", Lahaina News, April 11, 2002: 16.
— to perform "HOT L BALTIMORE", Lahaina News, May 30, 2002: 16.
— performing "Tartuffe: Born Again", Lahaina News, February 27, 2003: 18.
— to perform "Tartuffe: Born Again", Lahaina News, March 6, 2003: 16.
— to hold auditions for musical "Sweet Charity", Lahaina News, April 10, 2003: 20.
— to perform "Two Rooms", Lahaina News, May 15, 2003: 14.
— to perform Lee Blessing's play "Two Rooms", Lahaina News, May 22, 2003: 16.
— to perform "Two Rooms", Lahaina News, May 29, 2003: 17.
— to hold "Sweet Charity" musical, Lahaina News, June 26, 2003: 21.
— to perform "Sweet Charity", Lahaina News, July 3, 2003: 16.
— to hold "Auditions at the Iao", Lahaina News, August 14, 2003: 16.
— seeks volunteer for next production "WIT", Lahaina News, September 25, 2003: 9.
— to begin theatre season with "WIT", Lahaina News, October 2, 2003: 18.

MAUI ORCHID SOCIETY
— to hold show, Lahaina News, July 8, 1987: 3.
— to hold exhibit at Maui Prince Hotel, Lahaina News, February 7, 1990: 14.

— to hold floral exhibition at Maui Prince Hotel, Lahaina News, April 11, 1990: 18.

— to hold show, Lahaina News, February 6, 1991: 3.

— to celebrate 50th anniversary, Lahaina News, March 20, 1991: 3.

— to exhibit at Maui Prince Hotel, Lahaina News, April 9, 1992: 7,8.

— to hold summer show with Lahaina Orchid Society, Lahaina News, July 7, 1994: 13.

— to hold monthly meeting, Lahaina News, March 12, 1998: 20.

— to hold "Giant Easter Show", Lahaina News, April 2, 1998: 17.

— to hold Easter show, Lahaina News, April 9, 1998: 16.

— to hold show for Mother's Day, Lahaina News, May 7, 1998: 20.

— to meet, Lahaina News, June 18, 1998: 16.

— continues to meet, Lahaina News, August 20, 1998: 17.

— to meet, Lahaina News, April 15, 1999: 13.

— continues to meet, Lahaina News, August 12, 1999: 16.

— to meet at Wailuku Community Center, Lahaina News, September 16, 1999: 13.

— Thanksgiving Day Show to be held, Lahaina News, November 18, 1999: 16.

— master orchid grower Gabe Greenwood to talk to, Lahaina News, March 16, 2000: 13.

— to hold Easter Show at Ka'ahumanu Shopping Center, Lahaina News, April 20, 2000: 8.

MAUI ORGANIC GARDENING GUIDE [BOOK]

— published by Oasis Maui, Lahaina News, April 1, 1987: 3.

MAUI ORIGINAL PANCAKE AND STEAK HOUSE [RESTAURANT]

— opens, Lahaina News, October 3, 1991: 7.

— reviewed, Lahaina News, October 17, 1991: 18,19.

— hosts performance by marimbist Nachiko Maekane, Lahaina News, May 13, 1987: 14.

— Summer Music Camp announced, Lahaina News, June 3, 1987: 3.

— music camp to offer free public concerts, Lahaina News, August 12, 1987: 3.

— opens new season on the theme of Maui Magic, Lahaina News, September 2, 1987: 3.

— fundraising, Lahaina News, February 3, 1988: 3.

— presents Murray Louis Dance Company, Lahaina News, April 20, 1988: 11.

— Kolleen Wheeler appointed president of, Lahaina News, April 20, 1988: 13.

— hosts fundraiser themed "The Big Chill", Lahaina News, June 8, 1988: 8,14.

— to host Hartford Ballet, Lahaina News, September 28, 1988: 18.

— presenting film "Tales of Hoffman", Lahaina News, October 19, 1988: 14.

— to offer Merry Magic Christmas show, Lahaina News, November 16, 1988: 9.

— received grant from Oceanic Cablevision, Lahaina News, December 28, 1988: 3.

— presents Swedish Chamber Orchestra, Lahaina News, January 18, 1989: 9.

— receives grant from National Endowment for the Arts, Lahaina News, January 25, 1989: 16.

— Margaret Cameron Scholarship available to music students from, Lahaina News, February 22, 1989: 13.

— to host benefit concert by Brothers Cazimero, Lahaina News, February 22, 1989: 9.

— to hold benefit at Hali'imaile General Store, Lahaina News, April 5, 1989: 17.

— looking for places to house Long Island Youth Symphony, Lahaina News, May 10, 1989: 3.

— accepting applications for summer music institute, Lahaina News, June 14, 1989: 10.

— seeking artwork for front cover of season program, Lahaina News, August 16, 1989: 3.

— sponsoring "Big Chill II" fundraiser, Lahaina News, October 11, 1989: 8.

— to hold Black and White Ball, Lahaina News, November 1, 1989: 13.

— to present Ballet Hispanico, Lahaina News, November 8, 1989: 6.

— to host Black and White Ball, Lahaina News, November 15, 1989: 14.

— presenting national tour of "1940's Radio Hour", Lahaina News, March 14, 1990: 15.

— to sponsor event with Billy Taylor Trio, Lahaina News, April 25, 1990: 15.

— to hold brunch and fashion show fundraiser, Lahaina News, May 30, 1990: 11.

— first event to feature Manhattan Rhythm Kings, Lahaina News, October 3, 1990: 12.

— to present performance by Honolulu Symphony, Lahaina News, November 28, 1990: 9.

— presents Weslia Whitfield at Stouffer Wailea Beach Resort, Lahaina News, January 16, 1991: 10,11.

— presents Michael Greenfield at Stouffer Wailea Beach Resort, Lahaina News, January 16, 1991: 10,11.

— to perform with The Ohio Ballet, Lahaina News, February 13, 1991: 9.

— to host fashion show fundraiser at Four Seasons Resort, Lahaina News, April 17, 1991: 12.

— to feature performance by Tziganka, a Russian Gypsy company, Lahaina News, October 17, 1991: 20.

— to offer dance classes, Lahaina News, October 24, 1991: 4.

— presents the Tchaikovsky Chamber Orchestra, Lahaina News, November 7, 1991: 21.

— to present Honolulu Symphony at Grand Ballroom of the Four Seasons Resort-Wailea, Lahaina News, January 9, 1992: 12.

— to present jazz and pop vocals, Lahaina News, January 23, 1992: 18.

— to present "From Porter to Puccini", Lahaina News, February 6, 1992: 22.

— names Sandra McGuinness as executive director, Lahaina News, March 12, 1992: 12,13.

— making scholarships available, Lahaina News, March 19, 1992: 6.

— seeking performing artists interested in providing educational services, Lahaina News, August 20, 1992: 4.

— to perform Mozart and others, Lahaina News, December 3, 1992: 18.

— seeking young artists, corporate sponsors, Lahaina News, September 30, 1993: 13.

— to present Jackie Dankworth and the Alec Dankworth Quartet, Lahaina News, October 28, 1993: 11.

— to feature harp music by Alfredo Rolando Ortiz, Lahaina News, December 2, 1993: 15.

— presents Los Angeles Chamber Ballet, Lahaina News, January 6, 1994: 12.

— to host Los Angeles Chamber Ballet, Lahaina News, January 20, 1994: 12.

— to present Lark Quartet, Lahaina News, February 17, 1994: 12.

— to present Glenn Miller Orchestra, Lahaina News, April 14, 1994: 12.

— to offer scholarships, Lahaina News, May 26, 1994: 5.

— presenting Combattimento Consort Amsterdam, Lahaina News, October 13, 1994: 20.

— to present Ballet Concierto de Puerto Rico, Lahaina News, March 23, 1995: 11,12.

— elects new officers and directors, Lahaina News, July 27, 1995: 2.

— to begin 54th season, Lahaina News, October 12, 1995: 14.

— to host Eroica Trio, Lahaina News, February 20, 1997: 11.

— to hold benefit concert, Lahaina News, October 23, 1997: 20.

MAUI OUTDOOR CIRCLE
— to hold holiday program, Lahaina News, December 2, 1999: 16.

MAUI PACIFIC CENTER
— conference to be held, Lahaina News, August 12, 1993: 4.
— to hold "The Role of Business Associations in Pacific Island Economic Growth", Lahaina News, September 23, 1999: 11.
— to host "The Role of Business Associations in Pacific Island Economic Growth", Lahaina News, November 4, 1999: 11.
— developing plans to identify and respond to risks to West Maui, Lahaina News, February 10, 2000: 1,20.
— hosting Maui County Project Impact initiative to consider West Maui isolation problems, Lahaina News, October 26, 2000: 3.
— receives grant the Alexander and Baldwin Foundation, Lahaina News, February 8, 2001: 2.
— to host "Smart Growth for Our Communities—Envisioning Maui County in 2020", Lahaina News, September 27, 2001: 9.
— West Maui Disaster Plan ready, Lahaina News, November 22, 2001: 1,22.

MAUI PANIOLO DANCE ASSOCIATION
— to hold dances, Lahaina News, November 14, 1996: 14.
— to hold dance, Lahaina News, December 5, 1996: 14.
— continues to offer country-western dance, Lahaina News, September 4, 1997: 17.
— continues to offer country-western dance, Lahaina News, November 13, 1997: 21.
— continues to hold country dancing, Lahaina News, December 23, 1999: 16.
— to celebrate National Dance Week, Lahaina News, April 12, 2001: 17.
— to hold dances, Lahaina News, April 19, 2001: 16,17.
— continues to hold free country dance lessons, Lahaina News, October 31, 2002: 29.
— continues to offer dance lessons, Lahaina News, January 30, 2003: 16.
— continues to offer lessons, Lahaina News, May 1, 2003: 17.
— continues to hold free country dance lessons, Lahaina News, June 19, 2003: 17.
— continues to offer lessons, Lahaina News, August 7, 2003: 17.

MAUI PANIOLO POSSE
— donates money to West Maui Youth Center, Lahaina News, March 31, 1994: 14.
— continues to present country-western dancing, Lahaina News, June 30, 1994: 15.
— continues to offer country western dancing, Lahaina News, August 11, 1994: 11.
— continues to offer country western dancing, Lahaina News, August 25, 1994: 14.
— continues to offer country western dancing, Lahaina News, October 13, 1994: 20.
— continues to offer country-western lessons and dances, Lahaina News, December 15, 1994: 18.
— continues to host dances, Lahaina News, February 16, 1995: 15.
— continues to hold country-western dancing activities, Lahaina News, May 11, 1995: 12.
— continues to offer dancing lessons, Lahaina News, August 10, 1995: 11.
— to hold Country-western line dances, Lahaina News, December 21, 1995: 14.
— to hold line dances, Lahaina News, April 17, 1997: 12.
— continues to hold line dancing, Lahaina News, May 1, 1997: 16.
— to offer classes on line dancing, Lahaina News, June 12, 1997: 16.
— featured, Lahaina News, July 31, 1997: 3.
— continues to offer western dance lessons, Lahaina News, November 9, 2000: 24.

— to hold Country Western dance, Lahaina News, November 29, 2001: 17.
— continues to offer dance courses, Lahaina News, January 17, 2002: 16.
— continues to hold Country Western dance, Lahaina News, June 27, 2002: 17.

MAUI PARK
— to get air conditioning, Lahaina News, December 12, 1990: 6.
— William Arter named general manager of, Lahaina News, January 30, 1991: 5.
— Castle Group, Inc. acquires management contract for, Lahaina News, July 25, 1996: 7.
— converting to long-term condominium rentals, Lahaina News, February 3, 2000: 11.
— condominiums for sale at, Lahaina News, June 29, 2000: 11.
— to hold reopening, Lahaina News, October 5, 2000: 13.

MAUI PARKINSON'S SUPPORT GROUP
— to meet, Lahaina News, April 22, 1993: 4.
— to meet, Lahaina News, July 19, 2001: 17.
— support group continues to meet, Lahaina News, October 25, 2001: 17.
— to meet, Lahaina News, April 18, 2002: 17.
— continues to meet, Lahaina News, August 15, 2002: 17.
— continues to meet, Lahaina News, September 5, 2002: 17.
— has new West Maui chapter, Lahaina News, March 6, 2003: 2.

MAUI PAYLESS DRUG STORE [BUSINESS]
— opening, once called Pay 'N Save, Lahaina News, June 17, 1993: 12.

MAUI PEACE ACTION
— to organize protest war in Iraq, Lahaina News, February 13, 2003: 18.
— to distribute Maui Peace Portrait postcards, Lahaina News, March 6, 2003: 2.
— to hold discussion on Mideast issues, Lahaina News, April 17, 2003: 16.
— to hold discussion of the Middle East, Lahaina News, April 24, 2003: 20.
— to show film on weapons inspections in Iraq, Lahaina News, May 22, 2003: 16.
— to show film "Living in Conflict" by Mikayala Mickelberg, Lahaina News, June 5, 2003: 16.
— to host talk by Dr. Helen Caldicott, Lahaina News, June 19, 2003: 16.
— to show "The War Against the Third World: What I've Learned About U.S. Foreign Policy", Lahaina News, August 28, 2003: 5.
— to show "On the Beach", Lahaina News, September 25, 2003: 18.

MAUI PEACE POEM
— growing globally, Lahaina News, November 2, 2000: 1,13.

MAUI PETROLEUM
— to get new fuel take at Lahaina Harbor, Lahaina News, October 19, 1988: 24.

MAUI PHILHARMONIC SOCIETY
— Jose Romero elected president, Lahaina Sun, May 2, 1973: 11.
— to hold wine and cheese concert, Lahaina News, September 26, 1984: 3.
— presenting Rossini's opera "La Cenerentola", Lahaina News, December 5, 1984: 14.
— scholarship fund details announced, Lahaina News, March 19, 1986: 3.
— begins "friends" campaign, Lahaina News, December 31, 1986: 12.
— adds additional performances of "Kodo", Lahaina News, December 31, 1986: 3.
— to perform at Baldwin Auditorium, Lahaina News, April 22, 1987: 10.

MAUI PINEAPPLE COMPANY [BUSINESS]

— objects to proposed condominiums connected to Napili light industrial complex, Lahaina News, March 6, 1991: 1,10.
— to offer Hawaiian Pineapple Plantation tours, Lahaina News, January 23, 1997: 11.
— opens Maui Fresh next to Hali'imaile General Store, Lahaina News, January 13, 2000: 11.
— gates access to Punalau or "Windmills Beach", Lahaina News, April 5, 2001: 1.
— continues to offer tours, Lahaina News, January 2, 2003: 17.
— continues to offer tours, Lahaina News, January 30, 2003: 16.
— Howard Nager is new vice president of fresh sales and marketing, Lahaina News, October 9, 2003: 8.

MAUI PINEAPPLE DESSERT AND SUSHI COOKING CONTEST

— to be held as part of Pineapple Festival, Lahaina News, August 30, 2001: 9.

MAUI PINEAPPLE FESTIVAL

— to be held, Lahaina News, July 4, 1996: 14.
— to be held, Lahaina News, August 13, 1998: 17.
— to be held, Lahaina News, August 20, 1998: 16.
— to be held on Lana'i, Lahaina News, July 1, 1999: 12.
— to be held, Lahaina News, August 12, 1999: 16.
— to be held, Lahaina News, August 19, 1999: 15.
— to be held, Lahaina News, August 2, 2001: 18.
— to be held, Lahaina News, August 16, 2001: 14,20.
— Maui Pineapple Dessert and Sushi Cooking Contest to be held, Lahaina News, August 30, 2001: 9.

MAUI PINEAPPLE PLANTATION [BUSINESS]

— offering tours, Lahaina News, February 28, 2002: 16.
— offering tours, Lahaina News, March 7, 2002: 17.
— continues to offer tours, Lahaina News, March 28, 2002: 21.
— continues to offer tours, Lahaina News, June 20, 2002: 17.
— continues to offer tours, Lahaina News, September 5, 2002: 17.
— continues to offer tours, Lahaina News, April 10, 2003: 21.
— continues to offer tours, Lahaina News, June 26, 2003: 20.
— continues to offer tours, Lahaina News, August 28, 2003: 17.

MAUI PINOY CHEFS

— to offer cooking demonstrations, Lahaina News, August 27, 1998: 16.

MAUI PLANTATION

— to be connected to Lahaina and Ka'anapali by shuttle operated by Roberts Hawaii, Lahaina News, December 19, 1984: 24.

MAUI PLAYERS [BAND]

— playing at Piero's, Lahaina Times, September, 1980 volume 4 number 8: 2, 3.

MAUI POLICE DEPARTMENT

— see police

MAUI POLO CLUB

— begins its Fall 1985 season, Lahaina News, September 18, 1985: 4.
— to host George Manoa Sr. Memorial Invitational Tournament, Lahaina News, June 17, 1999: 7.

MAUI POLYNESIAN TAHITI FETE

— to be held as part of the Aloha Festivals, Lahaina News, August 10, 2000: 16.
— to be held at Maui Memorial Gymnasium, Lahaina News, August 9, 2001: 17.
— to be held, Lahaina News, August 7, 2003: 17.

MAUI POP WARNER FEDERATION

— see Lahaina Pop Warner Association

MAUI PORTUGUESE CHAMBER OF COMMERCE

— to host mayoral candidate forum, Lahaina News, September 17, 1986: 11.

— offering college scholarships, Lahaina News, April 15, 1987: 12.
— Mayor-elect James Apana to meet with, Lahaina News, November 26, 1998: 16.

MAUI POWER STATION, THE [MUSICAL GROUP]

— to perform at Maui Inter-Continental Resort, Lahaina News, June 23, 1994: 12.

MAUI POWWOW

— to be held by Intertribal Council of Hawaii, Lahaina News, June 4, 1998: 9.

MAUI PRESS, THE [NEWSPAPER]

— to begin publication in September, Lahaina News, September 12, 1991: 9.

MAUI PRINCE HOTEL [BUSINESS]

— opens, Lahaina News, August 6, 1986: 3.
— offering kama'aina package, Lahaina News, October 15, 1986: 3.
— hosts fundraiser for Maui Symphony, Lahaina News, September 9, 1987: 3.
— George Paoa to perform at, Lahaina News, December 30, 1987: 3.
— comedy show at, Lahaina News, January 20, 1988: 18.
— to host Oktoberfest, Lahaina News, September 21, 1988: 3.
— to host lectures by photographer and naturalist Richard Roshon, Lahaina News, January 25, 1989: 18.
— hosting Santa at Keiki Luncheon, Lahaina News, December 13, 1989: 6.
— featuring series on Hawaiian lectures, Lahaina News, July 4, 1990: 4.
— offering Big Band music, Lahaina News, June 20, 1991: 10.
— hosting Vintner's Dinner, focusing on wines of Australia, Lahaina News, July 11, 1991: 15.
— to host "Joy of Seafood", Lahaina News, July 18, 1991: 10.
— offering Big Band and swing music, Lahaina News, August 8, 1991: 13,14.
— offering kama'aina rates, Lahaina News, August 8, 1991: 8.
— offering brunch, Lahaina News, September 12, 1991: 17.
— becomes member of Preferred Hotels and Resorts Worldwide and Leading Hotels of the World, Lahaina News, September 12, 1991: 4.
— chef Roger Dikon to pair Scharffenberger Cellars' wine with dinner, Lahaina News, December 5, 1991: 23.
— featuring Mele Ohana daily, Lahaina News, December 5, 1991: 26.
— to host exhibit by Maui Orchid Society, Lahaina News, April 9, 1992: 7,8.
— cuts staff, Lahaina News, September 3, 1992: 8.
— hosting food and wine seminar, Lahaina News, September 24, 1992: 18.
— appoints Cindy Lynne Smith as director of sales and marketing, Lahaina News, June 30, 1994: 9.
— expands, Lahaina News, April 13, 1995: 12.

MAUI PRINCESS [SHIP]

— bill required to allow to passengers to debark at Lahaina Harbor, Lahaina News, April 27, 1995: 1,16.
— state cuts may lead to cuts, Lahaina News, August 10, 1995: 1,16.
— Sea Link of Hawaii, Inc plans to suspend ferry service, Lahaina News, September 19, 1996: 8.
— former Lahaina-Moloka'i ferry now tourist ship, Lahaina News, May 1, 1997: 14.
— to hold "Full Moon Boogie", Lahaina News, July 10, 1997: 15.

MAUI PROFESSIONAL PHOTOGRAPHERS' ASSOCIATION

— photographer staging print exhibit at Lahaina Gallery Mall, Lahaina News, March 30, 2000: 12.
— to hold seminar on Photoshop 5.5, Lahaina News, September 21, 2000: 20.
— names Terry Rowe as Professional Photographer of the Year, Lahaina News, January 4, 2001: 14.

MAUI PSYCHOLOGICAL ASSOCIATES
— opened by Paul Beljan, Lahaina News, March 27, 1997: 10.

MAUI PUBLISHING CO. [BUSINESS]
— helps prepare booklet for hippies, Lahaina Sun, December 9, 1970: 6.

MAUI QUILTERS GUILD
— to exhibit at Lahaina Cannery Mall, Lahaina News, February 4, 1999: 17.

MAUI REACH TO RECOVERY PROGRAM
— mastectomies to meet at Cameron Center, Lahaina News, July 24, 1985: 8.

MAUI RECYCLING GROUP
— sponsoring Hawaii Materials Exchange to encourage reuse of material, Lahaina News, November 18, 1993: 6.
— offering information on recycling at condominiums, Lahaina News, November 24, 1994: 6.
— to hold home composting workshop, Lahaina News, December 12, 1996: 8.
— Rick Woodford re-elected president of, Lahaina News, August 14, 1997: 2.
— publishes "Your Recycling Guide", Lahaina News, January 15, 1998: 5.
— promotes recycling, Lahaina News, March 12, 1998: 18.
— Wilma Nakamura new executive director, Lahaina News, July 17, 2003: 8.

MAUI RECYCLING SERVICE [BUSINESS]
— expands to Lahaina, Lahaina News, January 23, 1992: 13.
— featured, Lahaina News, February 6, 1992: 10.
— receives grant to provide pick-up service, Lahaina News, June 16, 1994: 4,5.
— to recycle motor oil, Lahaina News, June 6, 1996: 15.

MAUI REDEVELOPMENT AGENCY
— to hold "Wailuku Growth by Design Workshop", Lahaina News, February 25, 1999: 11.
— updating plans to revitalize Wailuku Town, Lahaina News, January 6, 2000: 11.

MAUI RELIGIOUS SCIENCE CENTER
— to discuss "Conversations with God", Lahaina News, May 21, 1998: 16.
— continues to discuss "Conversations with God", Lahaina News, August 27, 1998: 17.

MAUI REMEMBERS: A LOCAL HISTORY [BOOK]
— book by Bren Bailey and Gail Bartholomew published, Lahaina News, November 3, 1994: 9.

MAUI REPORTER [NEWSPAPER]
— suspends publication, Lahaina News, January 15, 1983: 4,5.

MAUI REPORTERS ASSOCIATION
— organized, with Larry Ross as interim chairman, Lahaina Sun, April 5, 1972: 4.

MAUI REPUBLICAN PARTY
— see Republican Party

MAUI RESEARCH AND TECHNOLOGY CENTER
— attracting start-ups, Lahaina News, March 19, 1992: 12.
— dedication ceremony scheduled, Lahaina News, May 7, 1992: 4.
— Maui Software tenant at, Lahaina News, July 9, 1992: 14.
— launches JASON Project with Department of Education, Lahaina News, April 13, 1995: 12.
— to offer "Legal Matters for Technology Startups", Lahaina News, April 13, 1995: 4.
— to host "Creating and Visualizing Your Strategy", Lahaina News, June 27, 1996: 14.
— to offer workshop "Starting a Venture in Hawaii", Lahaina News, August 7, 1997: 5.

— marketing workshop to be held at, Lahaina News, October 2, 1997: 15.
— to hold workshop on "Buying Or Selling A Business", Lahaina News, October 9, 1997: 21.
— offering workshop on business start-up, Lahaina News, December 18, 1997: 21.
— to hold "Consciousness of the Earth Festival", Lahaina News, April 30, 1998: 16.
— ThermoTrex opening research office at, Lahaina News, June 4, 1998: 13.
— to offer workshop on "Opportunities in Exporting", Lahaina News, June 18, 1998: 13.
— to host "Developing Your Extended Team", Lahaina News, June 25, 1998: 11.
— to offer "First Course in Fund-Raising", Lahaina News, September 17, 1998: 29.
— to host "Tying Into Hawaii's Growth Industries", Lahaina News, March 4, 1999: 12.
— to host "Increasing Value While Cutting Costs", Lahaina News, March 18, 1999: 13.
— to hold workshops on creating health and wellness tourism business plans, Lahaina News, March 29, 2001: 8.

MAUI RESEARCH AND TECHNOLOGY PARK
— super computer to be built at, Lahaina News, November 28, 1991: 7.
— featured, Lahaina News, December 12, 1991: 15.
— Pamela Tumpap promoted to assistant manager, Lahaina News, June 18, 1992: 10.
— holds dedication ceremony, Lahaina News, August 11, 1994: 7.

MAUI RETAIL INDUSTRY CONFERENCE
— to be held, Lahaina News, May 8, 1997: 1.
— to be held, Lahaina News, June 3, 1999: 13.
— to be held at Westin Maui, Lahaina News, June 10, 1999: 13.

MAUI ROADWAY PARK
— dragster competes at, Lahaina News, June 6, 1991: 5.

MAUI ROSE SINGLES SOCIETY
— to host inaugural dance at Maui Inter-Continental Wailea, Lahaina News, October 31, 1991: 15.

MAUI ROSE, THE [RESTAURANT]
— featured, Lahaina News, March 12, 1992: 20.

MAUI ROUGHWATER SWIM RACE
— scheduled, Lahaina News, September 20, 1989: 24.
— to be held by Maui Masters Swim Club, Lahaina News, October 3, 1996: 13.

MAUI ROYAL BALL
— canceled, Lahaina News, October 29, 1992: 20.

MAUI SAILBOARD CLUB
— membership expands, Lahaina News, November 26, 1986: 12.

MAUI SAILING CANOE ASSOCIATION
— to hold interisland cruise, Lahaina News, October 10, 1991: 8.
— to hold interisland cruise, Lahaina News, October 17, 1991: 4.
— to hold interisland cruise, Lahaina News, October 24, 1991: 6.
— interisland cruise to be held this weekend, Lahaina News, October 31, 1991: 5.
— wins Na Hoko Kai race, Lahaina News, August 27, 1992: 7,9.

MAUI SAILS [BUSINESS]
— moves into Triangle Square, Lahaina News, June 27, 1996: 12.

MAUI SANCTUARY
— to offer Ocean User's Workshop on rules, Lahaina News, November 14, 2002: 2.

MAUI SANDCASTLE CONTEST
— see sand castle

MAUI SANDS
— development featured, Lahaina News, May 2, 1984: 18.

MAUI SCENTS [BUSINESS]
— described, Lahaina News, March 16, 1988: 7.

MAUI SCHOLASTIC SURF CHAMPIONSHIPS
— may be held at Lahaina Harbor or Hoʻokipa Beach Park, Lahaina News, April 20, 2000: 16.

MAUI SCHOOL OF BUSINESS AND ADVANCED LEARNING
— offering business courses, Lahaina News, February 25, 1999: 11.

MAUI SCHOOL SCIENCE FAIR
— set for February 21 and 22, Lahaina News, February 12, 1986: 3.

MAUI SCRAP METAL IMPORTS
— waiting for equipment to shred metal, Lahaina News, November 9, 1988: 1.
— has received metal shredding machine, Lahaina News, August 9, 1989: 1.
— presents donation to Kihei School, Lahaina News, September 16, 1993: 5,8.

MAUI SEA KAYAKING CLUB
— to participate in "Get the Drift and Bag It", Lahaina News, October 14, 1993: 7.

MAUI SEA SPREE
— to take place at Kahana Beach Park, Lahaina News, May 18, 1995: 7.

MAUI SENIOR CITIZENS
— to hold Karaoke "sing alone" Festival, Lahaina News, September 17, 1986: 3.

MAUI SENIOR LAW FAIR
— to host Caroline Richardson, Lahaina News, June 1, 1988: 19.

MAUI SHADE SHOP [BUSINESS]
— described, Lahaina News, May 15, 1983: 11.

MAUI SHRIMP AQUACULTURE PROJECT
— described, Lahaina Sun, January 20, 1971: 4.

MAUI SHRINERS CLUB
— meeting at Royal Lahaina Hotel, Lahaina News, February 1, 1982: 10.
— to participate in King Kamehameha Day parade, Lahaina News, May 24, 2001: 16.
— Maui Shrine Club to participate in King Kamehameha Day parade, Lahaina News, May 24, 2001: 16.

MAUI SIERRA CLUB
— see Sierra Club

MAUI SILKSCREEN DESIGNS [BUSINESS]
— featured, Lahaina News, July 18, 1984: 14.
— purchased by Ray Rogers, Lahaina News, May 29, 1985: 3.

MAUI SKATE PARK ASSOCIATION
— seeks volunteers, Lahaina News, June 24, 1999: 3.
— seeking volunteers, Lahaina News, July 15, 1999: 7.
— seeking volunteers, Lahaina News, July 22, 1999: 6.
— seeks volunteers, Lahaina News, August 5, 1999: 7.
— see also skateboarding

MAUI SKATEBOARD ASSOCIATION
— holds contest, Lahaina News, August 11, 1994: 6.
— to ask for skate park, Lahaina News, December 25, 1997: 1,2.
— planning benefit for skateboard park, Lahaina News, April 16, 1998: 3.
— to hold fundraiser to support proposed skateboard park, Lahaina News, May 14, 1998: 17.
— to hold fundraiser to support proposed skateboard park, Lahaina News, May 21, 1998: 16.

MAUI SKI CO. [BUSINESS]
— open second location, Lahaina News, December 31, 1992: 10.

MAUI SLACK KEY WORKSHOP
— students taught by slack key musicians, Lahaina News, June 26, 2003: 3.

MAUI SMALL BUSINESS DEVELOPMENT CENTER
— see Small Business Development Center

MAUI SOFTWARE [BUSINESS]
— active at Maui Research and Development Center, Lahaina News, July 9, 1992: 14.

MAUI SOIL AND WATER CONSERVATION DISTRICTS
— sponsor seminar on conservation, Lahaina Sun, June 9, 1971: 7.

MAUI SONS AND DAUGHTERS OF NISEI VETERANS
— to present documentary programs on Akaku: Maui Community Television, Lahaina News, March 26, 1998: 2.

MAUI SOUTH SEAS HOTEL
— planned development in Kahana, Lahaina Sun, November 11, 1970: 4.

MAUI SPACE SURVEILLANCE COMPLEX
— to hold tours, Lahaina News, October 23, 1997: 20.
— Amos Technical Conference to discuss system, Lahaina News, August 26, 1999: 14.

MAUI SPECIAL LEARNING CENTER
— presents Family Fun Day at Seabury Hall, Lahaina News, June 8, 1988: 13.

MAUI SPORTING GOODS
— donates money to Lahaina Pop Warner, Lahaina News, December 11, 1997: 17.

MAUI STAND FOR CHILDREN RALLY
— to be held, Lahaina News, May 30, 1996: 2.

MAUI STINGRAYS
— to hold charity game for Hui Malama Learning Center, Lahaina News, November 9, 1995: 6.
— to hold contest for bat technicians, Lahaina News, July 17, 1997: 14.
— baseball team to help raise funds for Children's Advocacy Center, Lahaina News, November 6, 1997: 14.

MAUI STYLE [BUSINESS]
— now owned by Tracy Flanagan and Nancy Goode, Lahaina News, June 13, 1991: 9.

MAUI STYLE WRESTLING CLUB
— to hold practices, Lahaina News, March 24, 1994: 12.
— announces first dual meet, Lahaina News, April 7, 1994: 6.
— clubs hold first competition, Lahaina News, May 4, 1995: 8.
— youth wrestling program to begin, Lahaina News, March 26, 1998: 16.
— tournament held at Jimmie H. Greig Gymnasium, Lahaina News, May 10, 2001: 1.
— to teach children, Lahaina News, April 4, 2002: 12.
— to teach children, Lahaina News, April 11, 2002: 12.

MAUI SUBSTANCE ABUSE TRAINING COLLABORATIVE
— seeking counselors, Lahaina News, June 1, 2000: 7.

MAUI SUDBURY SCHOOL
— to hold open house, Lahaina News, February 26, 1998: 13.
— to hold open house, Lahaina News, April 23, 1998: 17.

MAUI SUGAR PLANTATION FESTIVAL
— to be held at Alexander and Baldwin Sugar Museum, Lahaina News, August 14, 2003: 14.

MAUI SUMMER JAMBOREE
— to be held at Maui War Memorial Stadium, Lahaina News, June 13, 1991: 14.
— to be held at the Maui Arts and Cultural Center, Lahaina News, June 19, 1997: 16.
— to be held, Lahaina News, June 25, 1998: 12.

MAUI SUMMER JOB FAIR
— to be held, Lahaina News, May 16, 1990: 5.

MAUI SUN [BUSINESS]
— Thom Weyand becomes managing editor, Lahaina News, November 1, 1981: 6.
— editorial on closing of, Lahaina News, January 15, 1982: 2,5.
— newspaper to hold talent show, Lahaina News, September 10, 1992: 19.

MAUI SUN HOTEL [BUSINESS]
— offering "Alert Cab" program, Lahaina News, December 26, 1991: 4.
— Jay Yamaguchi appointed executive chef, Lahaina News, January 30, 1992: 10.
— to host "Bridal Affair", Lahaina News, January 30, 1992: 4.
— to offer Fright Night for Halloween, Lahaina News, October 1, 1992: 17.
— to host international film festival, Lahaina News, November 12, 1992: 22.
— to hold talent contest this weekend, Lahaina News, November 19, 1992: 9.
— cancels music pending completion of renovations, Lahaina News, January 14, 1993: 6.
— to be managed by Hawaii Pacific Resorts, Lahaina News, January 20, 1994: 6.

MAUI SUNSET GRILL AND BAR [RESTAURANT]
— opens in former location of Moondoggies, Lahaina News, April 6, 1995: 11.

MAUI SURF HOTEL [BUSINESS]
— opening, includes photographs, Lahaina Sun, June 16, 1971: 5.
— opening, Lahaina Sun, July 28, 1971: 5.
— to host Maui Easter Seal fashion show fundraiser, Lahaina Sun, April 18, 1973: 10.
— close to being sold, Lahaina News, January 18, 1984: 14.
— Hemmeter Investment Co. agrees to purchase, Lahaina News, November 21, 1984: 3.
— renovations may close hotel, Lahaina News, February 13, 1985: 3.
— permit for 200-room addition, Lahaina News, March 27, 1985: 20.
— closing for renovations, Lahaina News, April 17, 1985: 3.
— Christopher Hemmeter revealed expansion plans for, Lahaina News, June 5, 1985: 3.
— work on renovations and addition begins, Lahaina News, June 25, 1986: 3.

MAUI SURF OHANA
— announces Hawaii Amateur Surfing Association series, Lahaina News, October 10, 2002: 13.
— announces Hawaii Amateur Surfing Association series, Lahaina News, November 14, 2002: 11.

MAUI SURF RESORT
— offering kama'aina Christmas party special, Lahaina News, December 4, 1985: 3.

MAUI SURFER GIRLS
— surfing school offering classes, Lahaina News, April 4, 2002: 13.

MAUI SURFING ASSOCIATION
— to hold surfing instruction certification program, Lahaina News, July 19, 2001: 12.

MAUI SWAP MEET
— described, Lahaina News, October 10, 1984: 6.
— to be held at Kahului Fairgrounds, Lahaina News, July 24, 1985: 8.
— described, Lahaina News, January 9, 1992: 8.

MAUI SWIM CLUB
— results of competition, Lahaina News, April 7, 1994: 6.
— seeking participants, Lahaina News, August 20, 1998: 15.

MAUI SWING DANCE SOCIETY
— to hold swing dance, Lahaina News, March 2, 2000: 12.

MAUI SYMPHONY CHORUS
— seeking singers, Lahaina News, February 13, 1997: 11.
— continues rehearsals, Lahaina News, June 3, 1999: 16.
— rehearses at Kahului Baptist Church, Lahaina News, October 5, 2000: 17.
— to hold choral music concert, Lahaina News, May 9, 2002: 16.

MAUI SYMPHONY, FRIENDS OF THE
— appoints James French as musical director, Lahaina News, January 2, 1992: 5.
— prepare for new season, Lahaina News, September 24, 1992: 4.

MAUI SYMPHONY ORCHESTRA
— season announced, Lahaina News, September 18, 1985: 3.
— to perform at 4th of July, Lahaina News, July 2, 1986: 1.
— presents an opera gala, Lahaina News, February 18, 1987: 10.
— present a Wailea Starlight Concert, Lahaina News, April 1, 1987: 3.
— to sponsor "A Symphony of Green" for July 4th, Lahaina News, June 24, 1987: 3.
— seeking private sponsors, Lahaina News, July 8, 1987: 24.
— fundraiser held at Maui Prince Hotel, Lahaina News, September 9, 1987: 3.
— 1987-1988 season begins, Lahaina News, September 16, 1987: 3.
— presenting "An Opera Gala", Lahaina News, March 9, 1988: 17, 18.
— to present Wailea Starlight Concert, Lahaina News, April 13, 1988: 13.
— to perform on July 4th, Lahaina News, June 15, 1988: 12.
— presents pops concert, Lahaina News, October 19, 1988: 3.
— to present starlight concert, Lahaina News, April 5, 1989: 14.
— officers named, Lahaina News, June 21, 1989: 3.
— schedule announced, Lahaina News, August 30, 1989: 3.
— announces 1989-1990 season, Lahaina News, September 6, 1989: 9.
— to perform Bach, Lahaina News, September 27, 1989: 2.
— to perform at Ka'anapali Beach Hotel, Lahaina News, November 8, 1989: 6.
— to perform with William Ransom, Lahaina News, November 22, 1989: 12.
— to perform Winter Classics Concert, Lahaina News, January 10, 1990: 12.
— to perform French masters, Lahaina News, January 17, 1990: 12.
— to perform Opera Gala, Lahaina News, February 28, 1990: 11.
— to host Opera Gala, Lahaina News, March 7, 1990: 13.
— to perform Opera Gala, Lahaina News, March 14, 1990: 15.
— to present season finale, Lahaina News, April 11, 1990: 15.
— finale to be performed, Lahaina News, April 18, 1990: 11.
— to present Wailea Starlight Concert, Lahaina News, September 12, 1990: 16.
— to begin 12th season, Lahaina News, September 26, 1990: 10.
— 23th season opens, Lahaina News, October 3, 1990: 11,12.
— to perform with violinist Benny Kim, Lahaina News, October 31, 1990: 14,15.
— to perform with Benny Kim, Lahaina News, November 7, 1990: 11.
— Wendell Warrington to be guest conductor for Christmas Concert, Lahaina News, December 5, 1990: 14.
— to include Ramsey Lewis as guest soloist for "Jazz Jazz and More Jazz Concert", Lahaina News, January 23, 1991: 7.
— presents Winter Classics Concert, Lahaina News, February 6, 1991: 9.
— to perform "Opera Gala V", Lahaina News, March 6, 1991: 17.
— to hold "Opera Gala V", Lahaina News, March 13, 1991: 14.
— to present "Maui Pops Concert", Lahaina News, March 27, 1991: 12.
— to perform "Maui Pops Concert" at Wailea Shopping Village, Lahaina News, April 17, 1991: 14,17.

MAUI TENANTS ADVISORY BOARD
— attempt to secure affordable housing, Lahaina Sun, May 12, 1971: 7.

MAUI TENNIS CLUB ESTATES
— condominium planned by Rand Hawaii Ltd., Lahaina Sun, January 27, 1971: 3.

MAUI, THE LAST HAWAIIAN PLACE [BOOK]
— author Robert Wenkam autographing copies at the Lahaina Restoration Foundation, Lahaina Sun, November 18, 1970: 2.

MAUI, THE LAST PLACE [BOOK]
— reviewed, Lahaina Sun, January 20, 1971: 5.

MAUI THEATRE
— to hold Maui Fairytale Theatre, Lahaina News, December 24, 1992: 18.
— to hold "A KidSummer Night's Dream", Lahaina News, July 20, 2000: 1,9.
— new name for Maui Myth and Magic Theatre, Lahaina News, July 25, 2002: 8.
— Gim Lim Jezierny new vice president, Lahaina News, April 10, 2003: 14.
— to host Mother's Day matinee of 'Ulalena, Lahaina News, May 1, 2003: 8.
— to host Mother's Day matinee of 'Ulalena, Lahaina News, May 8, 2003: 18.
— offers kama'aina rate for 'Ulalena show, Lahaina News, July 3, 2003: 8.
— free hula shows to be held at, Lahaina News, July 10, 2003: 17.

MAUI THEATRE COUNCIL
— newly formed, to hold meeting, Lahaina News, May 26, 1994: 11.
— to hold "Maui Celebrates Theatre" party, Lahaina News, July 7, 1994: 15.

MAUI THEATRE INVITATIONAL
— to be held, Lahaina News, February 20, 1992: 4.
— to hold workshops, Lahaina News, March 19, 1992: 4.
— to hold workshop called "The Next Stage", Lahaina News, April 2, 1992: 5.

MAUI TIBETAN BUDDHIST CENTER
— fundraiser to be held by Rodney K. and his Mumbo Jumbo Band, Lahaina News, October 10, 1991: 4.
— to host Tibetan New Year Gala, Lahaina News, February 25, 1999: 13.
— to celebrate Tibetan New Year, Lahaina News, March 4, 1999: 12.

MAUI TO GO ARTS AND CRAFTS
— to host Joelle C demonstrating printmaking, Lahaina News, April 26, 2001: 20.

MAUI TODAY
— photoadvertising channel names Barbara Brensinger as programming and sales coordinator, Lahaina News, June 13, 1991: 9.
— television channel receives awards, Lahaina News, April 23, 1992: 15.
— television channel receives Award of Merit from Pele Awards, Lahaina News, April 21, 1994: 12.

MAUI TOMORROW, THE
— to host "Designing our Communities", Lahaina News, April 16, 1992: 5.
— names Richard Joseph Lafond Jr. as executive director, Lahaina News, August 13, 1992: 4.
— environmental group critical of lack of access to Hawea Point, Lahaina News, September 29, 1994: 1,3.
— to hold Jungle Journey I hike, Lahaina News, January 5, 1995: 4.
— to lead "Jungle Journey II" hike, Lahaina News, February 2, 1995: 4.
— to hold "Designing Our Community" forum, Lahaina News, October 19, 1995: 4.

— board to discuss water issues, Lahaina News, September 19, 1996: 15.
— to hold workshop on Hawaii's environmental laws, Lahaina News, September 11, 1997: 17.
— to hold "We Love Palauea Party" with Sierra Club, Lahaina News, April 6, 2000: 16.

MAUI TOY WORKS [BUSINESS]
— opens in Whalers Village, Lahaina News, February 6, 2003: 8.

MAUI TOYOTA [BUSINESS]
— turns 22, Lahaina News, May 22, 1997: 6.

MAUI TRADE DOLLAR
— popular, Lahaina News, June 11, 1992: 13.
— expands promotion, Lahaina News, July 23, 1992: 17.
— Association donates to Maui Chamber of Commerce, Lahaina News, September 17, 1992: 11.
— 1993 edition available, Lahaina News, January 21, 1993: 9.
— 1994 edition available now, Lahaina News, February 17, 1994: 6.
— new on to be introduced, Lahaina News, December 5, 1996: 6.

MAUI TRAILER BOAT CLUB
— to meet, Lahaina News, May 28, 1992: 8.
— to meet, Lahaina News, December 24, 1992: 8.
— to meet to discuss whale sanctuary, Lahaina News, September 30, 1993: 4.
— to hold fundraiser, Lahaina News, March 27, 1997: 6.

MAUI TRANSLATORS [BUSINESS]
— offering free emergency telephone translation assistance, Lahaina News, July 24, 1985: 8.
— featured, Lahaina News, September 11, 1985: 7.

MAUI TREASURES [BUSINESS]
— thrift store opens, Lahaina News, January 6, 1994: 7.

MAUI TRIATHLON
— results, Lahaina News, August 8, 1990: 7.

MAUI TRIBE PRODUCTIONS
— to sponsor statewide song contest , Lahaina News, November 29, 2001: 14.

MAUI TROPICAL PLANTATION
— offers talk story on history of plantation camps, Lahaina News, August 24, 1988: 14.
— site of Hoe Down organized by Rotary Clubs of Maui to host to raise funds for Children's Advocacy Center, Lahaina News, October 17, 1990: 6.
— to celebrate 10 years of business, Lahaina News, October 27, 1994: 20.

MAUI TWINS
— Maui Botanical Gardens to hold meeting of, Lahaina News, February 5, 1998: 12.

MAUI UNITED FUND DRIVE
— donation by employees of Pioneer Mills, Lahaina Sun, December 30, 1970: 4.
— endorsed by Maui County Council, Lahaina Sun, December 8, 1971: 8.
— report on fundraising, Lahaina Sun, October 4, 1972: 22.
— Under-12 Hurricanes raising money to represent Hawaii in regional championship, Lahaina News, May 16, 2002: 12.

MAUI UNITED WAY
— see United Way

MAUI USA, INC. [BUSINESS]
— to begin construction of Kahana Ridge water tank and pipeline, Lahaina News, October 5, 1995: 4.
— Kahana Ridge featured, Lahaina News, June 25, 1998: 10.

MAUI VACATIONS CLUB
— to open Off-Site Broker Preview Center, Lahaina News, October 31, 2002: 6.

MAUI VEGETABLE GROWER'S COOPERATIVE ASSOCIATION [BUSINESS]
— featured, Lahaina News, January 30, 1985: 18.

MAUI VETERANS CENTER
— to hold an open house, Lahaina News, November 8, 1989: 3.
— sponsoring seminar on Post Traumatic Stress Disorder, Lahaina News, February 4, 1993: 4.
— Department of Veterans Affairs representative to visit, Lahaina News, March 18, 1999: 16.

MAUI VISITORS ASSOCIATION
— seeks funds to market Maui to tourists, Lahaina News, January 9, 1991: 1,5.

MAUI VISITORS BUREAU
— Dana Reneck elected chairman, Lahaina News, September 10, 1986: 3.
— focuses on upscale visitors, Lahaina News, January 21, 1987: 5.
— to sponsor Maui Classic NCAA pre-season basketball tournament, Lahaina News, August 17, 1988: 15.
— new members announced, Lahaina News, June 13, 1991: 9.
— to advertise in Midwestern and Eastern cities, Lahaina News, April 9, 1992: 12.
— to meet, Lahaina News, July 16, 1992: 4.
— executive director of Maui branch Roger Dubin nearly ousted, Lahaina News, April 1, 1993: 3.
— using artwork from Robert Lyn Nelson in current campaign, Lahaina News, May 20, 1993: 7.
— trying to appeal to visitor lifestyles, Lahaina News, June 10, 1993: 6.
— to host live music at Kahului Airport, Lahaina News, September 30, 1993: 7.
— to make materials available to travel agent terminals, Lahaina News, December 16, 1993: 7.
— presenting live Hawaiian entertainment at Kahului Airport, Lahaina News, May 19, 1994: 16.
— to promote movie production on Maui, Lahaina News, June 9, 1994: 12.
— to hold annual general membership meeting, Lahaina News, July 28, 1994: 8.
— to hold annual general meeting, Lahaina News, August 4, 1994: 9.
— to hold annual general membership meeting, Lahaina News, August 18, 1994: 8.
— executive director Roger Dubin resigns, Lahaina News, September 1, 1994: 13.
— offering Maui AAdvantage Passport with American Airlines, Inc., Lahaina News, October 6, 1994: 11.
— Marsha Wienert named executive director, Lahaina News, October 6, 1994: 7.
— Marsha Weinert claims that Japanese visitor numbers are inaccurate, Lahaina News, February 23, 1995: 6.
— Mayor Linda Lingle to speak at annual general meeting of, Lahaina News, June 29, 1995: 10.
— new leadership installed, Lahaina News, July 20, 1995: 10.
— Maui County Economic Development Office Coordinator Robert Johnson wondering about the value of, Lahaina News, September 21, 1995: 10.
— considers crime as top priority , Lahaina News, January 25, 1996: 1,16.
— mayor Linda Lingle to be keynote speaker, Lahaina News, June 13, 1996: 11.
— announces new board of directors, Lahaina News, September 19, 1996: 8.
— Lydee Felipe Ritchie is new public relations manager, Lahaina News, October 10, 1996: 8.
— expects rise in visitors due to additional flights, Lahaina News, November 21, 1996: 1.
— promoting Maui to Southern California, Lahaina News, March 6, 1997: 3.
— unveils marketing plan, Lahaina News, September 18, 1997: 1.
— launches shopping campaign, Lahaina News, January 8, 1998: 11.
— expects tourism to increase, Lahaina News, January 22, 1998: 3.
— funding from Maui County Council sought for, Lahaina News, April 9, 1998: 1,9.
— Mayor Linda Lingle to speak at membership meeting, Lahaina News, June 11, 1998: 13.
— targeting teenagers and couples in marketing efforts, Lahaina News, January 20, 2000: 1,16.
— Executive Director Marsha Wienert to speak to Kihei Destination Association, Lahaina News, June 15, 2000: 14.
— Executive Director Marsha Wienert optimistic about visitor industry, Lahaina News, July 6, 2000: 1,14.
— Toni Rojas appointed director of sales, Lahaina News, March 15, 2001: 8.
— to publish a Recreation Sites Handbook, other changes announced, Lahaina News, June 21, 2001: 9.
— to hold annual General Membership Meeting, Lahaina News, November 29, 2001: 8.
— to hold membership meeting, Lahaina News, December 6, 2001: 17.

MAUI VOCAL
— community chorus offering Hawaiian music, Lahaina News, June 30, 1994: 15.
— Community Chorus to meet, Lahaina News, September 19, 1996: 15.

MAUI VOLLEYBALL ASSOCIATION
— formed, Lahaina News, June 27, 1996: 16.

MAUI WAENA INTERMEDIATE SCHOOL
— band to offer free concert, Lahaina News, May 20, 1999: 17.
— band to offer Spring concert, Lahaina News, May 23, 2002: 16.

MAUI WAR MEMORIAL CENTER
— track affected by wind, Lahaina Sun, May 26, 1971: 7.
— stadium almost finished, needs to be used, Lahaina Sun, June 2, 1971: 7.
— stadium opening, Lahaina Sun, September 8, 1971: 12.

MAUI WATER POLO
— to practice at Lahaina Aquatics Center, Lahaina News, April 9, 1998: 15.
— practice continues to be held, Lahaina News, June 18, 1998: 15.
— continues to practice, Lahaina News, July 9, 1998: 15.

MAUI WATERCOLORISTS ASSOCIATION
— to meet, Lahaina News, September 5, 2002: 17.
— to host artist Kim Wilson, Lahaina News, November 14, 2002: 20.
— to paint at Ho'okipa Beach Park, Lahaina News, November 28, 2002: 17.
— to hold plein air paint-out, Lahaina News, December 26, 2002: 17.
— to paint at D.T. Fleming Beach Park, Lahaina News, March 13, 2003: 17.
— Phil Sabado to lead watercolor workshop, Lahaina News, March 20, 2003: 16.
— celebrating one-year anniversary, Lahaina News, May 8, 2003: 14.
— to hold plein air painting, Lahaina News, June 5, 2003: 16,17.
— to hold juried art exhibitions, Lahaina News, August 14, 2003: 18.
— to paint at D.T. Fleming Beach Park, Lahaina News, August 21, 2003: 17.

MAUI WATERGEAR [BUSINESS]
— Ka'ahumanu Center, Lahaina News, August 26, 1999: 14.

MAUI WEATHER TODAY
— television weather program airing in West Maui, Lahaina News, September 16, 1993: 4.

MAUI WEDDING ASSOCIATION
— to hold Bridal Faire, Lahaina News, March 2, 2000: 11.

MAUI WEDDING CONNECTION [BUSINESS]
— to open at Limahana Place, Lahaina News, April 24, 2003: 9.

MAUI WEDDING FAIRE
— to be held, Lahaina News, January 9, 1991: 3.
— to be held, Lahaina News, January 16, 1991: 4.

MAUI WESTIN
— see Westin Maui Hotel [business]

MAUI WET SEAL [BUSINESS]
— opens at Lahaina Center, Lahaina News, October 3, 1990: 9.

MAUI WHALEWATCHERS
— to meet, Lahaina News, April 18, 1984: 5.
— to hold last event of the season, Lahaina News, May 9, 1984: 5.
— to meet, Lahaina News, January 2, 1985: 3.
— to meet at Wo Hing Temple, Lahaina News, January 9, 1985: 3.
— offering moonlight cruise, Lahaina News, May 1, 1985: 4.
— to meet at Wo Hing Temple, Lahaina News, January 29, 1986: 3.
— to meet, Lahaina News, January 14, 1987: 3.
— membership meeting at Lahaina Civic Center, Lahaina News, February 11, 1987: 11.
— hosting lecture by Roy Nickerson, Lahaina News, February 25, 1987: 3.
— to meet at Artful Dodger, Lahaina News, January 13, 1988: 3.

MAUI WOMEN MAKING A DIFFERENCE
— Pat Masumoto and Marie Smith highlighted on, Lahaina News, March 7, 2002: 5.

MAUI WOMEN'S FELLOWSHIP
— to hold "New Horizon Luncheon", Lahaina News, January 15, 1998: 13.
— to hold "The Love Luncheon", Lahaina News, February 12, 1998: 16.
— to hold "Wearing of the Green", Lahaina News, March 12, 1998: 20.
— to hold "April in Maui" luncheon, Lahaina News, April 9, 1998: 17.
— to hold "Spring Bonnet Luncheon", Lahaina News, May 14, 1998: 16.

MAUI WORLD MUSIC WORKSHOPS
— to be held, Lahaina News, June 12, 2003: 5.
— to be held, Lahaina News, June 26, 2003: 22.

MAUI WOWI SMOOTHIE STAND [RESTAURANT]
— opens, Lahaina News, January 30, 2003: 9.

MAUI WRITERS CONFERENCE
— to be held at the Ritz-Carlton, Lahaina News, September 2, 1993: 2.
— to be held at Ritz-Carlton, Lahaina News, June 9, 1994: 13.
— speaker line-up changed, Lahaina News, August 4, 1994: 16.
— to feature Terry Anderson as keynote speaker, Lahaina News, August 25, 1994: 14.
— to be held, Lahaina News, September 1, 1994: 15.
— seeking artwork for official program, Lahaina News, January 19, 1995: 12.
— to be held, Lahaina News, July 27, 1995: 4.
— to be held, Lahaina News, July 11, 1996: 10.
— to offer kama'aina rate, Lahaina News, July 31, 1997: 9.
— Garry Marshall to speak at, Lahaina News, September 3, 1998: 16.
— to be held at Grand Wailea Resort, Lahaina News, June 17, 1999: 13.
— to be held, national authors to attend, Lahaina News, August 19, 1999: 2.
— screenwriting competition to be held, Lahaina News, May 25, 2000: 16.
— Youth Writers Competition won by Corey Samuels, Lahaina News, September 14, 2000: 8.
— to be held, Lahaina News, February 1, 2001: 16.
— to be held, Lahaina News, May 23, 2002: 2.

MAUI WRITERS GUILD
— to meet at Maui Coffee Roasters, Lahaina News, September 10, 1992: 4.
— to host Ellen Pelissero, Lahaina News, February 18, 1993: 4.
— to meet, Lahaina News, June 24, 1993: 4.
— to host talk by Diane Fairechild, Lahaina News, July 22, 1993: 4.
— sponsoring writing contest, Lahaina News, March 17, 1994: 4.
— to hold meeting at Tropical Provision Bookstore, Lahaina News, November 24, 1994: 10.
— upcoming events of, Lahaina News, December 1, 1994: 14.
— to host State Senator Avery Chumbley and Jeff Swartz, Lahaina News, June 27, 1996: 14.
— to meet at Borders Books, Lahaina News, September 18, 1997: 17.
— Rita Goldman to discuss copy editing and proofreading at, Lahaina News, November 5, 1998: 20,21.
— see also Maui Authors Guild

MAUI WRITERS RETREAT
— accepting submission, Lahaina News, July 8, 1999: 5.

MAUI YMCA
— planning a program at Camp Keanae, Lahaina News, May 1, 1980: 7.

MAUI YOGA SHALA
— offer creative movement classes, Lahaina News, February 13, 2003: 16.
— to offer programs for children, Lahaina News, March 20, 2003: 16.
— offering kids creative movement classes, Lahaina News, April 10, 2003: 21.

MAUI YOUNG BUDDHIST ASSOCIATION
— to hold resume and interviewing workshop, Lahaina News, March 24, 1994: 8.

MAUI YOUNG BUSINESS ROUNDTABLE
— to meet, Lahaina News, July 25, 2002: 9.
— to hold membership drive, Lahaina News, January 9, 2003: 3.
— seeking members, Lahaina News, January 16, 2003: 8.
— to hold general membership meeting, Lahaina News, March 13, 2003: 8.
— to hold membership drive, Lahaina News, August 7, 2003: 8.

MAUI YOUTH AMBASSADORS
— chosen, to visit the USSR, Lahaina News, May 27, 1987: 16.
— works featured at Territorial Savings Building, Lahaina News, July 8, 1987: 3.
— video showing trip to USSR, Lahaina News, October 28, 1987: 3.
— to hold fundraiser, Lahaina News, March 23, 1988: 14.
— seeking new candidates, Lahaina News, May 11, 1988: 14.
— hosting dance, Lahaina News, May 25, 1988: 12.
— host visiting Soviet dancers, Lahaina News, July 20, 1988: 11.
— presenting works by local artists, Lahaina News, September 28, 1988: 18.
— to hold benefit at Stouffers Wailea Beach Hotel, Lahaina News, February 15, 1989: 20.
— to hold "Maui to Moscow '90" fundraiser, Lahaina News, April 4, 1990: 13.
— to host "Friday Night is Art Night" fundraiser, Lahaina News, May 12, 1994: 4.
— to hold art fundraiser, Lahaina News, May 26, 1994: 14.
— to offer a recycling drop box, Lahaina News, June 30, 1994: 4.
— presents scholarships, Lahaina News, July 21, 1994: 4.
— to hold arts and crafts fair in conjunction with Muscular Dystrophy Association Telethon, Lahaina News, August 25, 1994: 5.
— operating recycling drop box, Lahaina News, September 22, 1994: 6.

MAUI YOUTH AND FAMILY SERVICES
— offering class for parents with children from previous marriages, Lahaina News, October 1, 1986: 5.
— planning "safe place" for West Maui Youth, Lahaina News, November 19, 1986: 1,7.
— notes lack of foster homes, Lahaina News, November 18, 1987: 1,8.
— offers drug education plan, Lahaina News, July 6, 1988: 11.

— performing "The Christmas Nightingale", Lahaina News, November 29, 1989: 18.

— offering mini-series of shows, Lahaina News, November 29, 1989: 21.

— to hold auditions for "South Pacific", Lahaina News, November 29, 1989: 36.

— seeks help from Maui County, Lahaina News, January 3, 1990: 1,3.

— to hold auditions for "Bye Bye Birdie", Lahaina News, March 14, 1990: 3.

— to perform "Octette Bridge Club", Lahaina News, May 30, 1990: 11.

— to host Foreign Film Festival, Lahaina News, June 6, 1990: 13.

— hosting Foreign Film Festival , Lahaina News, June 13, 1990: 15.

— changes name to Maui Academy of Performing Arts, Lahaina News, July 4, 1990: 16.

MAUI ZENDO

— looking for "Aquarius family" to conduct community-service projects, Lahaina Sun, December 8, 1971: 8.

MAUI ZOO

— to host Zoo Fest, Lahaina News, March 27, 1991: 15.

— seeking to build a playground, Lahaina News, July 9, 1992: 5.

— seeking performers for Zoofest, Lahaina News, February 17, 1994: 12.

— performers sought for Zoofest, Lahaina News, February 24, 1994: 12.

MAUI ZOOLOGICAL SOCIETY

— new board of directors installed, Lahaina News, December 23, 1993: 3.

— giraffes from Moloka'i delivered to, Lahaina News, April 1, 1999: 8.

MAUI-LANA'I CONNECTION

— reunion to be held, Lahaina News, October 30, 1997: 17.

MAUI-MOLOKA'I COMMUNITY DEVELOPMENT CORPORATION

— directors named, Lahaina Sun, February 3, 1971: 3.

— controversies during first two weeks, Lahaina Sun, February 10, 1971: 1.

— change in leadership, Lahaina Sun, February 17, 1971: 2.

— issues with board of directors and employees, Lahaina Sun, March 3, 1971: 2.

MAUI!

— opens for business on the internet, Lahaina News, January 5, 1995: 6.

MAUI/LANA'I ISLANDS BURIAL COUNCIL

— Erik Fredericksen recommends to preserve pre-contact burial site, Lahaina News, December 17, 1998: 1,28.

MAUIAINA MAGAZINE

— to hold "Ohana Luncheon and Trade Fair", Lahaina News, June 18, 1998: 16.

MAUIAN HOTEL [BUSINESS]

— Nane Aluli named general manager of, Lahaina News, April 27, 2000: 11.

MAUIAN MAGAZINE [BUSINESS]

— appointed Alan Isbell as editor, Lahaina News, October 8, 1986: 3.

— for sale, Lahaina News, June 14, 1989: 7.

MAUIFEST

— to be held to benefit Hana Canoe Club, Lahaina News, September 18, 2003: 18.

MAUIIKAMALO [PLAY]

— to be performed at Maui Arts and Cultural Center, Lahaina News, May 28, 1998: 13.

MAUI'S BEST CRAFT FAIR

— to be held, Lahaina News, July 10, 1997: 16.

MAUI'S GAY ASIAN PACIFIC ISLANDER SUPPORT NETWORK

— to hold karaoke night, Lahaina News, July 19, 2001: 16.

MAUI'S SONS AND DAUGHTERS OF THE 442

— president Leonard Oka interviewed, Lahaina News, May 21, 1992: 3.

MAUK, VERN [ARTIST]

— visits Maui, Lahaina News, April 18, 1990: 12.

MAULIN, MARILYN

— president of Soroptimists International featured, Lahaina News, August 9, 1989: 4.

MAUNA OLU COLLEGE

— sends gift to school in South Vietnam, Lahaina Sun, January 6, 1971: 1.

— expected to announce merger with United States International University, Lahaina Sun, February 17, 1971: 1,2.

— merger discussed, faculty and student react, Lahaina Sun, March 3, 1971: 1,5.

— merger okayed by Board of Trustees, Lahaina Sun, March 10, 1971: 1,6.

— Commencement held, Lahaina Sun, April 28, 1971: 4.

— transfer finalized, Lahaina Sun, May 5, 1971: 1.

— graduation ceremony, Lahaina Sun, May 19, 1971: 4.

— receives federal grants for student aid, Lahaina Sun, June 2, 1971: 8.

MAUNALEI ARBORETUM

— Maui Eco-Adventures to lead hikes to, Lahaina News, October 14, 1999: 7.

— Maui Eco-Adventures to lead hikes in, Lahaina News, October 28, 1999: 9.

— hikes to be led by Maui Eco-Adventures, Lahaina News, December 23, 1999: 9.

MAUNALOA [MOLOKA'I]

— impact of pineapple closure on, Lahaina Sun, October 18, 1972: 4,5.

MAUNAOLU YOUTH CENTER

— added as a United Way agency, Lahaina News, August 7, 1985: 8.

MAUVAIS, JAQUELYNN [ARTIST]

— watercolors to be shown at Provenance Gallery, Lahaina News, October 26, 1988: 16.

MAX, PETER [ARTIST]

— works described, Lahaina News, March 7, 1990: 16.

MAX SHERLEY & ASSOCIATES [BUSINESS]

— collecting books to send to soldiers in operation desert shield, Lahaina News, October 17, 1990: 6.

— to send donated items to Hawaii military participating Operation Desert Storm, Lahaina News, January 23, 1991: 1.

MAXIMINIO, FABIO

— to teach Capoeira, Lahaina News, January 3, 2002: 17.

MAXWELL, CHARLES KAULUWEHI

— new president of Aboriginal Lands of Hawaiian Ancestry (ALOHA) described, Lahaina Sun, July 11, 1973: 14,15.

— files as candidate for OHA, Lahaina News, August 15, 1980: 6.

— to speak on Hawaii Public Television on legacy of Dr. Martin Luther King, Jr., Lahaina News, January 10, 1990: 2.

— to host KNUI live from DC, Lahaina News, September 12, 1991: 5.

— discusses ancient history of humpback whales, Lahaina News, March 18, 1999: 3.

— to discuss biology and behavior of sharks, Lahaina News, July 8, 1999: 13.

— concerned about preserving archaeological sites at Palauea, Lahaina News, November 23, 2000: 17.

— to speak on "Respect for the 'aumakua—the importance of sharks to Hawaiians", Lahaina News, April 25, 2002: 17.

— to discuss significance of Haleakala, Lahaina News, July 31, 2003: 16.

MAY DAY
— celebration at Kam III School, Lahaina Sun, April 28, 1971: 3.
— photograph, Lahaina Sun, May 5, 1971: 1.
— celebrated, Lahaina Sun, May 5, 1971: 2.
— lei contest to be held at Maui-Intercontinental Wailea, Lahaina News, April 23, 1986: 3.
— Central Maui Youth Center to hold fundraiser, Lahaina News, April 27, 1988: 6.
— to be held at Lahaina Intermediate School, Lahaina News, April 29, 1993: 2.
— to be celebrated at King Kamehameha III School, Lahaina News, May 27, 1993: 2.
— to be celebrated at Ka'anapali Beach Hotel, Lahaina News, April 28, 1994: 13.
— to be celebrated at Lahaina Cannery Mall, Lahaina News, April 27, 1995: 5.
— celebration held, Lahaina News, May 25, 1995: 1,16.
— to be celebrated, Lahaina News, May 1, 1997: 17.
— held, Lahaina News, May 8, 1997: 1,16.
— to be celebrated, Lahaina News, April 30, 1998: 16.
— celebrated at Princess Nahienaena Elementary School, Lahaina News, May 7, 1998: 1.
— to be celebrated, Lahaina News, April 29, 1999: 16.
— celebrated, Lahaina News, May 6, 1999: 1,24.
— Lahaina-Honolua Senior Citizen's Club holds show, Lahaina News, May 6, 1999: 3.
— Princess Nahienaena to celebrate, Lahaina News, May 13, 1999: 1.
— to be celebrated at Princess Nahienaena Elementary School, Lahaina News, May 13, 1999: 16.
— King Kamehameha III Elementary School preparing for, Lahaina News, May 11, 2000: 19.
— celebrated by Lahaina Intermediate School, Lahaina News, June 1, 2000: 1.
— celebrated at King Kamehameha III School, Lahaina News, May 31, 2001: 1.
— to be observed by Outrigger Wailea Resort, Lahaina News, April 25, 2002: 17.
— celebration held, Lahaina News, May 23, 2002: 1.
— celebrated at Wharf Cinema Center, Lahaina News, May 30, 2002: 18.
— to be held at Westin Maui, Lahaina News, April 24, 2003: 16.
— events planned at Westin Maui Hotel, Lahaina News, April 24, 2003: 21.
— to be celebrated at Wailea Marriott, Lahaina News, April 24, 2003: 21.
— to be celebrated, Lahaina News, May 1, 2003: 16.
— see also Lei Day

MAY, DORA
— joins Irwin Mortgage, Lahaina News, March 18, 1999: 13.

MAY, JIM [WRITER]
— storyteller to visit Makawao Public Library, Lahaina News, March 27, 2003: 17.

MAYALL, JOHN [MUSICIAN]
— to perform at Casanova's, Lahaina News, March 13, 1991: 11.
— to perform at Hawaiian Islands Rhythm and Blues Mele, Lahaina News, May 6, 1999: 21.
— to perform at Hawaiian Islands Rhythm and Blues Mele, Lahaina News, May 13, 1999: 17.
— to perform, Lahaina News, May 20, 1999: 14.
— to perform, Lahaina News, May 20, 1999: 16.
— to perform at Maui Arts and Cultural Center, Lahaina News, January 4, 2001: 17.
— to perform, Lahaina News, January 16, 2003: 15.

MAYBERRY, JACK [COMEDIAN]
— to perform at Comedy Club and the Sports Page, Lahaina News, December 5, 1990: 9,14.

MAYEDA, DANIEL
— receives certificate for dental implant surgery, Lahaina News, January 30, 1991: 5.
— re-elected Second Vice-President of the American Academy of Cosmetic Dentistry, Lahaina News, June 4, 1992: 9.
— installed as president of American Academy of Cosmetic Dentistry, Lahaina News, June 8, 1995: 10.

MAYER, DICK
— Maui Community College instructor appointed to Maui Planning Commission, Lahaina Sun, September 20, 1972: 14.
— professor of economics to attend workshop on development organized by Manuel Moniz, Lahaina News, July 1, 1993: 1,12.
— to moderate "Watersheds at Risk: A Search for Solutions", Lahaina News, July 11, 2002: 9.

MAYER, REBECCA
— producing Maui Music Festival, Lahaina News, July 6, 1995: 10.

MAYES, JIM
— search called off for missing plane piloted by, Lahaina News, January 23, 1992: 5.

MAYHEW, J.D. [ARTIST]
— etchings discussed, Lahaina News, February 27, 1985: 11.
— to exhibit at Foundation Galleries, Lahaina News, January 30, 1992: 16.

MAYO, FRED
— manager of The Whaler on Ka'anapali Beach, Lahaina News, July 6, 2000: 9.

MAYOR EDDIE TAM MEMORIAL CENTER
— funds requested to improve, Lahaina Sun, February 17, 1971: 7.

MAYOR HANNIBAL TAVARES COMMUNITY CENTER
— see Tavares Center

MAYOR'S BALL
— to benefit Maui Symphony, Lahaina News, July 27, 1988: 3.
— to be held at Maui Inter-Continental Wailea, Lahaina News, January 3, 1990: 16.
— to be held, Lahaina News, January 24, 1990: 14.
— to be held at Maui Inter-Continental Wailea, Lahaina News, May 1, 1991: 16.
— to be held, Lahaina News, May 15, 1991: 12.
— to be held, Lahaina News, July 30, 1992: 15.
— to be held, Lahaina News, August 6, 1992: 12,13.
— to be held, Lahaina News, August 12, 1993: 6.
— to be held, Lahaina News, August 19, 1993: 7.
— to be held, Lahaina News, August 12, 1999: 17.
— to be held, Lahaina News, August 19, 1999: 14.

MAYOR'S ECONOMIC SUMMIT
— held, considers ideas for Lahaina , Lahaina News, November 4, 1999: 1,3.

MAYOR'S INVITATIONAL ART SHOW
— The Mystery of Moloka'i is theme of, Lahaina News, August 10, 1995: 12.

MAYOR'S WEST MAUI ADVISORY COMMITTEE
— see West Maui Advisory Committee to the Mayor

MAYS, WILLIE
— baseball player participates in Legends of Baseball game, Lahaina News, December 26, 1984: 4.

MAZATLAN
— discussed as a destination, Lahaina Times, July, 1980 volume 4 number 6: 2.

MAZZARELLA, ED
— to speak at Surfrider Foundation meeting, Lahaina News, January 4, 2001: 15,16,17.

MB APPLIANCE [BUSINESS]
— opens, Lahaina News, September 5, 1990: 6.

MB FURNISHERS, INC. [BUSINESS]
— moves to new location, Lahaina News, April 29, 1993: 9.

MCANALLY, GREGORY
— appointed executive director of Maui Chamber of Commerce, Lahaina News, March 25, 1987: 12.

MCATEER, DAVID
— member of Ralph Nader's team gives public talks, Lahaina Sun, March 3, 1971: 6.

MCBARNET, GIL [WRITER]
— story "The Whale Who Wanted to be Small" printed, biography described, Lahaina News, December 25, 1985: 1.
— signing books at Upstart Crow and Company Bookstore and Coffeeshop, Lahaina News, November 19, 1986: 16.
— publishes "The Wonderful Journey" , Lahaina News, January 21, 1987: 10.
— to sign books at The Whalers Book Shoppe, Lahaina News, December 9, 1987: 26.
— publishes "Fountains of Fire", Lahaina News, December 23, 1987: 3.
— publishes "The Goodnight Gecko", Lahaina News, December 5, 1991: 6.
— to speak at Maui Writers Guild, Lahaina News, April 15, 1999: 13.
— reads to children at Lahaina Public School, Lahaina News, April 12, 2001: 22.

MCBRIDE, DOUG
— selected as artistic director for Theatre Theatre Maui's production of Noel Coward's "Hay Fever", Lahaina News, February 9, 1995: 11.

MCCABE, ROBERT
— appointed co-editor of Maui Press with Terrie Elliker, Lahaina News, February 13, 1992: 12.
— named editor of South Maui Times, Lahaina News, March 20, 1997: 2.

MCCALL, MIDGE
— boat decorations described, Lahaina Sun, June 6, 1973: 14.
— designer's life and work described, Lahaina News, August 21, 1985: 7.

MCCALLOM, JOHN
— appointed Director of Human Resources at Maui Marriott, Lahaina News, April 20, 1988: 13.

MCCANN, MIKA [ARTIST]
— to exhibit at Lahaina Arts Society, Lahaina News, January 28, 1993: 14.
— to exhibit at Lahaina Arts Society, Lahaina News, March 5, 1998: 16.

MCCARTHY, BOB
— organizing Aloha Friday Fair and Farmers Market organized by, Lahaina News, October 5, 1995: 4.

MCCARTHY, JESSE
— Scholar/Athlete of the Week, Lahaina News, August 27, 1998: 15.

MCCARTHY, KATIE
— Scholar/Athlete of the Week, Lahaina News, March 15, 2001: 11.

MCCARTHY, THELMA [MUSICIAN]
— to perform at Kapalua Bay Hotel, Lahaina News, August 29, 1990: 14.

MCCARTHY, THUMPER
— resident featured, Lahaina News, August 10, 1988: 2.

MCCARTHY, TIM
— named general manager at Compadres in Lahaina, Lahaina News, December 12, 1991: 16.

MCCARTNEY, DONNA
— to speak on "Nurture and Care for the Caretaker", Lahaina News, December 2, 1993: 4.

MCCLAIN, MOLLY [ARTIST]
— to lead workshop on "How Different Backgrounds Change the Painting", Lahaina News, April 24, 2003: 20.

MCCLEAN, DICK
— golfer qualifies for U.S. Open Golf Championship, Lahaina News, May 27, 1987: 6.
— wins IBA Cup/Tournament of Champions, Lahaina News, December 19, 1991: 9.
— wins Aloha Section, PGA Stroke Play Championship, Lahaina News, August 13, 1992: 6.
— wins GTE Hawaiian Tel Hall of Fame Championship, Lahaina News, May 27, 1993: 10.

MCCLELLAND, CHIP
— businessman and volunteer featured, Lahaina News, January 2, 1992: 8.

MCCLURE, MIKE
— preparation for Maui Marathon discussed, Lahaina News, March 23, 1988: 16.

MCCLURE, YUKIKO
— promoted to catering/conference services manager at The Westin Maui, Lahaina News, March 8, 2001: 8.

MCCLUSKY, USS [SHIP]
— sailors to volunteer for community service, Lahaina News, September 4, 1985: 3.
— photograph of sailors volunteering for community service, Lahaina News, September 11, 1985: 1.

MCCONNELL, AMANDA OPSHAL [ARTIST]
— displaying art at Old Lahaina Court House, Lahaina News, November 4, 1987: 3.

MCCORD [FAMILY]
— growing Christmas trees in Kula, Lahaina News, December 12, 1984: 7,8,9.

MCCORD, RICHARD [WRITER]
— author of "The Chain Gang" to speak at Borders, Lahaina News, March 4, 1999: 12.

MCCORMACK, MIKE
— part of partnership purchasing Embassy Suites Resort, Lahaina News, August 6, 1992: 6.

MCCORMACK REALTY [BUSINESS]
— opening in Whaler's Village, Lahaina Sun, November 25, 1970: 3.
— see also Coldwell Banker McCormack Real Estate [business]

MCCORRISTON, WILLIAM
— Hawaiian Airlines executive promises that company will stand by airstrip promises, Lahaina News, October 23, 1985: 1,20.

MCCOY, HAROLD
— to speak on "Power of the Focused Mind" at 'Ohana Connection, Lahaina News, November 28, 2002: 17.
— to speak on "Power of the Focused Mind" at 'Ohana Connection, Lahaina News, November 28, 2002: 17.

MCCOY, SCOTT
— new executive director of West Maui Youth Center, Lahaina News, August 19, 1993: 4.

MCCOY TRAVEL AND CRUISE CENTER [BUSINESS]
— opens "Cruise Headquarters" department, Lahaina News, April 6, 1995: 6.

MCCUTCHEON, STANLEY
— attorney speaks to illegal occupation of Hawaii, Lahaina Sun, January 17, 1973: 1.

MCD SURFWEAR [BUSINESS]
— to co-sponsor Lahaina Surf Classic with Local Motion, Lahaina News, May 19, 1994: 8.

MCDERMOTT, JOHN [WRITER]
— publishes "Kelleys of the Outrigger", Lahaina News, August 15, 1990: 11.

MCDONAGH, DIANE
— joins Atlantis Submarines as sales representative, Lahaina News, April 2, 1992: 12.
— named sales manager for passenger submarine operations at Atlantis Submarines, Lahaina News, March 25, 1993: 10.

MCDONALD, BOB
— elected treasurer of Lahaina Retail Board, Lahaina Sun, December 16, 1970: 3.
— named officer for Lahaina Yacht Club, Lahaina Sun, December 23, 1970: 8.

MCDONALD, CAITLIN
— Scholar/Athlete of the Week, Lahaina News, October 1, 1998: 14.
— Lahainaluna High School senior featured, Lahaina News, December 12, 2002: 1,22.

MCDONALD, JAMES
— chef's apprentice places first in Seafood Festival Competition, Lahaina News, August 1, 1991: 11.
— executive chef of I'o featured, Lahaina News, July 1, 1999: 5.
— chef of Pacific'O leads cooking demonstration, Lahaina News, December 21, 2000: 14.
— executive chef of Pacific'O featured, Lahaina News, September 13, 2001: 14,15.
— chef wins "A Taste of Morrad", Lahaina News, November 15, 2001: 8.

MCDONALD, KELLY [COMEDIAN]
— to perform at Comedy Club, Lahaina News, August 22, 1990: 13.

MCDONALD, KIM [ARTIST]
— to visit Sargent's Fine Art, Lahaina News, June 27, 2002: 16.
— to be featured at Sargent's Fine Art, Lahaina News, April 10, 2003: 23.

MCDONALD, MICHAEL [MUSICIAN]
— to perform at Maui Music Festival, Lahaina News, April 30, 1998: 1.

MCDONALD, RONALD [CLOWN]
— to participate in Taste of Lahaina, Lahaina News, August 27, 1992: 3.

MCDONALD, SHERRI CARDEN [WRITER]
— publishes "The Spiritual Guide for the Really Busy Person", Lahaina News, January 2, 2003: 8.

MCDONALD'S [RESTAURANT]
— to open in Lahaina Farmer's Market, Lahaina Sun, August 22, 1973: 6.
— opening new restaurant in Lahaina, Lahaina News, August 1, 1982: 4.
— opens in Lahaina, Lahaina News, June 15, 1983: 6.
— grand opening in Lahaina, Lahaina News, July 1, 1983: 3.
— selling coupon books with Halloween Gift Certificates, Lahaina News, October 2, 1985: 3,9.
— gives check to Lahainaluna High School principal Henry Ariyoshi, Lahaina News, February 6, 1992: 5.
— honors Erlinda Rosario with "Partners in Paradise" award, Lahaina News, July 5, 2001: 9.
— wraps up McExtra Cash and Car Giveaway, Lahaina News, November 8, 2001: 8.
— collecting donations for Guam typhoon victims, Lahaina News, January 9, 2003: 9.

MCDONOUGH, JAMES
— Father bids farewell to Maria Lanakila Church and Sacred Hearts Museum, Lahaina News, June 19, 2003: 2.

MCELFRESH, CHERYL [ARTIST]
— to exhibit at Lahaina Arts Society, Lahaina News, January 9, 2003: 3.

MCELFRESH, SAM
— passes away, Lahaina News, January 19, 1995: 4.

MCELFRESH, THELMA
— awarded Woman of Distinction by Soroptimists International, Lahaina News, April 2, 1992: 4.

MCFARLIN, STEVE "SPANKY" [COMEDIAN]
— to perform at Honolulu Comedy Club, Lahaina News, April 11, 1996: 12.

MCGARVEY, THOM
— consultant to Sing Out Maui youth singing group, Lahaina Sun, November 1, 1972: 9.

MCGEHEE, LENDA [ARTIST]
— to exhibit at Village Gallery-Lahaina, Lahaina News, September 2, 1993: 11.

MCGILL, SCOTT
— chef at Kimo's featured, Lahaina News, November 1, 2001: 14.

MCGILLEN, TOM [COMEDIAN]
— to perform at Comedy Club, Lahaina News, July 25, 1990: 11.
— to perform at Comedy Club, Lahaina News, September 19, 1991: 16.
— to perform at Comedy Club and the Sports Page, Lahaina News, October 22, 1992: 14,16,18.

MCGOWAN, PATRICK [ARTIST]
— sculptures to be displayed at Viewpoints Gallery, Lahaina News, April 8, 1999: 12.

MCGOWAN-MAHOE DEVELOPMENT COMPANY [BUSINESS]
— building the Kahana Sunset condominium between Ka'anapali and Napili, Lahaina Sun, July 7, 1971: 3.

MCGREGOR, SUMATHI
— joins Maui Medical Group's Obstetrician-Gynecologist staff, Lahaina News, May 23, 2002: 8.

MCGREW, STEVE [COMEDIAN]
— to perform at Comedy Club, Lahaina News, June 20, 1990: 11.
— to perform at Comedy Club, Lahaina News, October 10, 1991: 14.
— to perform at Comedy Club and the Sports Page, Lahaina News, August 27, 1992: 14,15,17.
— to perform at Honolulu Comedy Club, Lahaina News, November 9, 1995: 12.

MCGUFFEY, HELEN
— arthritis sufferer featured, Lahaina News, April 2, 1992: 3.

MCGUFFIE, MARK
— named general manager of Manele Bay Hotel, Lahaina News, October 10, 1991: 7.

MCGUINNESS, PAT [ARTIST]
— to participate in "Four by Four Equals" show, Lahaina News, February 2, 1995: 10.

MCGUINNESS, SANDRA
— named executive director of The Maui Philharmonic Society, Lahaina News, March 12, 1992: 12,13.

MCGUIRE, BROOKS [MUSICIAN]
— to perform at Pioneer Inn , Lahaina News, June 4, 1992: 13.
— to perform at Moondoggies, Lahaina News, November 25, 1993: 12.

MCINERNEY, BOB
— receives "Pro of the Year Award" from the Hawaii division of the United States Professional Tennis Association, Lahaina News, September 10, 1998: 14.

MCINERNY FOUNDATION
— awards grant to The Art School at Kapalua, Lahaina News, March 22, 2001: 9.
— provides grant to the Art School at Kapalua, Lahaina News, April 4, 2002: 14.
— awards grant to Hui Malama Learning Center, Lahaina News, October 17, 2002: 14.

MCKAY, JOE
— real estate manager joins Kahana Ridge, Lahaina News, June 22, 2000: 8.

MCKAY, PRAKASH
— to give talk on "Dealing with Grief in Children", Lahaina News, March 27, 2003: 17.

MCKAY, RUTH
— president of Soroptimists International and West Maui Taxpayers Association featured, Lahaina News, January 11, 1989: 2.
— named president of West Maui Taxpayers Association, Lahaina News, July 12, 1989: 3.
— elected District Director at Soroptimist regional conference, Lahaina News, May 23, 1990: 6.

MCKELVEY [FAMILY]
— joins celebration of Lahaina Ka'anapali and Pacific Railroad's 30th birthday, Lahaina News, June 22, 2000: 3.

MCKELVEY, A.W. "MAC"
— resigns from Lahaina-Ka'anapali & Pacific Railroad, Lahaina Sun, April 14, 1971: 1.
— ashes scattered, Lahaina News, August 18, 1994: 1.

MCKELVEY, ANGUS
— weds Gretchen Schneider at Sugar Cane Train's Ka'anapali Station, Lahaina News, November 16, 2000: 15.

MCKELVEY, JOAN
— speaks of merchants organizing to advocate for changes in Lahaina , Lahaina News, August 24, 1988: 1.
— receives T.S. Shinn award from the Maui Chamber of Commerce, Lahaina News, June 28, 1989: 1.
— announce winner of Lahaina Town Action Committee poster contest, Lahaina News, November 15, 1989: 1,19.
— to receive Woman of Distinction Award from Soroptimists International, Lahaina News, May 23, 1991: 4.
— owner of South Seas Trading Post featured, Lahaina News, December 26, 1991: 7.
— sells South Seas Trading Post, Lahaina News, September 28, 2000: 1,14.

MCKELVEY, MRS. A.W.
— vice president of Lahaina Art Society, Lahaina Sun, January 13, 1971: 7.

MCKEOWN, TOM
— named "Volunteer of the Year" by Mercedes Championship, Lahaina News, November 14, 2002: 11.

MCKIM, BRIAN [COMEDIAN]
— to perform at Comedy Club, Lahaina News, September 19, 1990: 10.
— to perform at Comedy Club, Lahaina News, September 26, 1991: 12.

MCKINLEY HIGH SCHOOL
— reunion scheduled for class of 1972, Lahaina News, March 12, 1992: 4.

MCKINLEY, STUART
— Hawaii Government Employees Association official to speak to Democratic Century Club, Lahaina News, November 20, 1997: 17.

MCKINZIE, EDITH
— to present on Hawaiian chants, Lahaina News, April 11, 1990: 3.

MCKOWN, DAVID
— appointed account executive at Destination Maui, Inc., Lahaina News, April 18, 1990: 5.

MCKOY, JAMES
— rheumatologist to speak at Kaiser's Wailuku Clinic, Lahaina News, January 8, 1998: 12.
— to speak on Fibromyalgia, Lahaina News, February 18, 1999: 12.
— doctor to discuss lupus, Lahaina News, June 10, 1999: 17.
— to talk on "Living Well with Lupus", Lahaina News, October 19, 2000: 20.
— to lecture on "How to Manage Your Arthritis Before it Manages You", Lahaina News, March 27, 2003: 16.
— doctor to present lecture on "Living Well with Arthritis", Lahaina News, October 9, 2003: 5.

MCKUEN, ROD
— to perform in "Soulmates, A Rock Opera", Lahaina News, August 21, 2003: 18.

MCLAUGHLIN, BRIAN
— resigns as president of Kapalua Land Company, Lahaina News, May 29, 1985: 3.

MCLAUGHLIN, SHAWN
— discusses improvements to S-turns Park, Lahaina News, March 17, 1994: 1.

MCLEAN, JIM [COMEDIAN]
— to perform at Honolulu Comedy Club, Lahaina News, October 27, 1994: 18.

MCLEMORE, JIM
— frontman for Jimmy Mac and the Kool Kats now a father, Lahaina News, September 21, 1988: 9.

MCLEOD, JERRY
— named president of Monarch Building Supply, Inc., Lahaina News, July 8, 1993: 8.

MCMAHON, BRAD
— named sales director for Upper Deck Hawaiian Winter league, Lahaina News, June 18, 1992: 10.

MCMICHAEL, DON [ARTIST]
— work displayed at Dolphin Galleries, Lahaina News, February 10, 1988: 3.

MCMILLAN, DON [COMEDIAN]
— to perform at Comedy Club and the Sports Page, Lahaina News, July 1, 1993: 11.

MCNAMARA, GARRETT
— wins tow-in contest with Brazilian Rodrigo Resende, Lahaina News, January 10, 2002: 3.

MCNAMARA, KATHLEEN
— assistant chief psychology service of U.S. Veterans Administration to speak to women veterans and servicewomen, Lahaina News, May 18, 1995: 4.

MCNEIL, BRUCE
— receives approval for resort shopping center in Lahaina, Lahaina Sun, March 21, 1973: 3.
— given go-ahead to build large apartment-hotel in Lahaina, Lahaina Sun, April 11, 1973: 4.
— brisk sales expected of planned condominium in Lahaina, Lahaina Sun, April 18, 1973: 3.

MCNEIL CONSTRUCTION COMPANY [BUSINESS]
— proposing large high-rise in Lahaina, Lahaina Sun, January 3, 1973: 11.
— company owner amazed by controversy over proposed building in Lahaina, Lahaina Sun, January 10, 1973: 4.
— Maui County Council studying ways to stall proposed McNeil Building in Lahaina, Lahaina Sun, January 24, 1973: 4.

— conflict over proposed building continues, Lahaina Sun, January 31, 1973: 4,5.

— editorial comments on proposed large building in Lahaina, Lahaina Sun, February 7, 1973: 8.

— planned building expected to be on Maui Historic Commission agenda, Lahaina Sun, March 7, 1973: 5.

— construction of large apartment-hotel on schedule, Lahaina Sun, May 2, 1973: 3.

MCNISH, BRUCE
— promoted to director of operations at The Westin Maui, Lahaina News, April 8, 1993: 6.

MCNULTY, JIM [ARTIST]
— to demonstrate floral design, Lahaina News, November 16, 1995: 15.

MCOUAT, OONA [MUSICIAN]
— to perform at Keolahou Congregational Church, Lahaina News, November 11, 1999: 13.

MCPHEE, IRENE AND BARRY
— owners of inflatable tour boat company featured, Lahaina News, April 26, 2001: 1,9.

MCPHERSON, MICHAEL [WRITER]
— to give farewell reading at Artful Dodger Feed and Read, Lahaina News, July 27, 1988: 11.

MCSWEENEY, DAN
— studying whales off West Maui, Lahaina News, April 1, 1987: 1,8,10,20.

— discuss status of whales in the Pacific, Lahaina News, May 11, 1988: 1,12,13.

MCVAY, DAVID
— playing high school basketball, Lahaina Sun, January 20, 1971: 7.

MDG SUPPLY INC. [BUSINESS]
— mayor's ownership in, part of accusation of conflict of interest, Lahaina Sun, July 5, 1972: 3,4.

— plans to move out of Kahului before area renewal, Lahaina Sun, July 19, 1972: 4,5.

ME AND THE BOYS [MUSICAL GROUP]
— featured, Lahaina News, April 19, 1989: 12.

MEADOWCRAFT, JAN
— elected president of American Lung Association, Lahaina News, May 14, 1998: 7.

MEADOWGOLD'S HEALTHY BABY CONTEST
— to be held, Lahaina News, September 26, 1990: 6.
— entry forms available, Lahaina News, October 3, 1990: 3.

MEADOWS, DWAYNE
— to talk on "Hawaii's Year-round Whales and Dolphins", Lahaina News, March 13, 2003: 16.

MEANS, DIANE ALBA
— offering instruction on Feng Shui, Lahaina News, December 2, 1999: 6.

— to present on Feng Shui, Lahaina News, March 30, 2000: 12.

— to lead workshop on Feng Shui, Lahaina News, October 12, 2000: 20.

— continues to teach workshops on Feng Shui, Lahaina News, January 18, 2001: 16.

— to offer "Feng Shui—Practical Applications for Everyday Living", Lahaina News, February 1, 2001: 20.

— to teach Feng Shui, Lahaina News, October 4, 2001: 16.

— to hold "Romance Your Home" course, Lahaina News, June 20, 2002: 16.

— to lead "Feng Shui for Small Business", Lahaina News, October 31, 2002: 6.

— to present on Feng Shui, Lahaina News, May 15, 2003: 17.

MEARNS, BARBARA
— moves yoga classes to Lahaina, Lahaina News, May 5, 1994: 3.

MEDCHECK OF MAUI, INC. [BUSINESS]
— to answer health questions at Lahaina Shopping Center, Lahaina News, August 1, 1991: 4.

— to offer testing at Lahaina Pharmacy, Lahaina News, September 19, 1991: 8.

— continues health testing, Lahaina News, October 10, 1991: 4.

— scheduling testing for diabetes and cholesterol, Lahaina News, November 21, 1991: 3.

— continues to offer medical testing, Lahaina News, December 12, 1991: 6.

— continues free medical testing, Lahaina News, January 30, 1992: 4.

— continues to offer health services, Lahaina News, September 10, 1992: 3.

— continues to conduct health checks, Lahaina News, January 26, 1995: 6.

— continues to perform health checks, Lahaina News, May 11, 1995: 2.

— continues to offer health checks, Lahaina News, July 11, 1996: 13.

— continues offering health checks, Lahaina News, September 12, 1996: 15.

MEDDINGS, LUCILLE
— former president of the Kihei Community Association, Lahaina Sun, December 2, 1970: 4.

MEDEIROS, ART
— Haleakala National Park biologist to talk on ecosystem conservation, Lahaina News, June 12, 1997: 16.

— biologist to talk on "Wiliwili Forest Conservation at Pu'uokali Lava Flows: A Piece of Near Pre-Contact , Lahaina News, September 4, 2003: 17.

MEDEIROS, DONALD
— Maui County hires as traffic coordinator, Lahaina News, January 24, 2002: 8.

MEDEIROS, JOSEPH
— chairman of county board of adjustments and appeals asks if people are being treated properly, Lahaina Sun, September 27, 1972: 22.

MEDEMA, KEN [MUSICIAN]
— to perform at Hope Chapel, Lahaina News, March 14, 1996: 13.

MEDIA SERVICES [BUSINESS]
— appoints Glen Janssens and Jim Skoog, Lahaina News, January 23, 1992: 12.

MEDIA SYSTEMS, INC. [BUSINESS]
— featured, Lahaina News, September 7, 1988: 2,13.

— honors employees, Lahaina News, June 13, 1990: 7.

— announces new appointments, Lahaina News, June 27, 1990: 8.

— Zane and Beth Mathias to photograph Olympics in Barcelona, Lahaina News, July 23, 1992: 16.

— appoints Jonathan Weston as production department manager, Lahaina News, April 13, 1995: 12.

— announces employees of the year, Lahaina News, February 13, 2003: 8.

— new employees announced, Lahaina News, September 18, 2003: 8.

MEDIATION SERVICES OF MAUI, INC. [BUSINESS]
— to train mediators, Lahaina News, March 1, 1989: 3.

— sponsoring discussion at Lahaina Public Library, Lahaina News, April 23, 1992: 5.

— sponsoring "Mediate, Don't Litigate" workshop, Lahaina News, September 16, 1993: 8.

— to hold basic training session, Lahaina News, September 8, 1994: 5.

— to offer mediation training, Lahaina News, March 6, 1997: 10.

MEDIC FOUR
— featured article, Lahaina News, January 2, 1985: 6,7,8.

MEDICINE
— see health

MEDINA, RICK [POLITICIAN]
— details of his election campaign for 7th district of the State House, Lahaina Sun, September 27, 1972: 4.
— Maui Council candidate profiled, Lahaina News, September 15, 1980: 2.
— plans to give property tax relief to owners, Lahaina News, March 27, 1991: 1,10.
— critical of Mayor Linda Lingle, Lahaina News, October 20, 1994: 1.

MEDITATION
— course to be offered, Lahaina News, December 19, 1996: 10.
— instruction to be held, Lahaina News, May 3, 2001: 21.
— representatives of Sant Thakar Singh to teach, Lahaina News, January 3, 2002: 17.

MEECHAN, COLLEEN [ARTIST]
— to exhibit at The Village Galleries, Lahaina News, December 2, 1999: 16.
— to exhibit at Village Galleries, Lahaina News, May 18, 2000: 20.

MEEKO, JOE [POWERLIFTER]
— wins Maui International Powerlifting Championships, Lahaina News, March 13, 1985: 4.

MEETINGS & CONVENTIONS MAGAZINE
— gives Gold Key Award to Westin Maui Hotel, Lahaina News, August 29, 1990: 8.

MEHAU, LARRY
— suing Rick Reed for accusing him of being the godfather of organized crime in Hawaii, Lahaina News, December 5, 1991: 4.
— loses libel suit brought against Rick Reed, Lahaina News, February 13, 1992: 3.
— headed for a new trial involving Rick Reed, Lahaina News, August 20, 1992: 4.

MEI, STEVE [ARTIST]
— to exhibit at Sunset Galleries, Lahaina News, May 2, 1990: 17.

MELANDER-MAGOON, KAREN [MUSICIAN]
— presented by Maui Symphony Orchestra, Lahaina News, January 6, 1994: 12.

MELASHENKO, JOE
— to become pastor of Seventh-day Adventist Church, Lahaina News, January 23, 1991: 3.

MELE HO'IKE
— to perform with Hula Ku'i, Lahaina News, February 4, 1999: 17.

MELE O MAKENA
— Hawaiian Music Festival to be held, Lahaina News, July 25, 1990: 11.
— Hawaiian music festival to be held, Lahaina News, June 13, 1991: 13.
— to be held July 27, Lahaina News, June 20, 1991: 10,11.
— to be held July 27, Lahaina News, June 27, 1991: 13.
— 3rd annual festival to be held, Lahaina News, July 11, 1991: 15.
— to be held, Lahaina News, July 18, 1991: 12.
— details given, Lahaina News, July 25, 1991: 13.

MELE OHANA [MUSICAL GROUP]
— to perform at The Maui Prince, Lahaina News, November 7, 1991: 18.
— featured daily at Maui Prince, Lahaina News, December 5, 1991: 26.
— to perform at Molokini Lounge, Maui Prince, Lahaina News, June 18, 1992: 21.

MELICHAR, JON [COMEDIAN]
— to perform at Comedy Club and the Sports Page, Lahaina News, March 20, 1991: 10.
— to perform at Comedy Club and the Sports Page, Lahaina News, March 19, 1992: 14,15.

MELLE, MARK
— gallery employee dies in car collision, Lahaina News, July 18, 1990: 4.

MELLO, BECKY [MUSICIAN]
— reviewed, Lahaina News, December, 1979: 5.

MELVA, AUNTY
— to teach lei making, Lahaina News, June 14, 2001: 20.
— to teach lei making, Lahaina News, June 21, 2001: 16.
— continues to teach lei making, Lahaina News, July 5, 2001: 16.

MELVIN, GEORGE
— arranged sending gift from Mauna Olu College to school in South Vietnam, Lahaina Sun, January 6, 1971: 1.

MEMORIAL DAY
— to be celebrated, Lahaina News, May 24, 1989: 11.
— events plan, including tribute to U.S. Senator Spark Matsunaga, Lahaina News, May 23, 1990: 1.
— events described, Lahaina News, May 21, 1992: 4.
— celebrations; poppies to be sold, Lahaina News, May 25, 1995: 3,4.
— to be celebrated, Lahaina News, May 22, 1997: 1.
— to include festival and jazz concert, Lahaina News, May 20, 1999: 1,20.
— celebrations to be held, Lahaina News, May 27, 1999: 1.
— events scheduled, Lahaina News, May 27, 1999: 1,16.
— service to be held, Lahaina News, May 18, 2000: 9.
— West Maui A.J.A. Veterans Club to hold service, Lahaina News, May 25, 2000: 6.
— West Maui AJA Veterans Club to hold service, Lahaina News, May 23, 2002: 2.
— services held, Lahaina News, May 30, 2002: 1,20.
— Brigadier General Clarence Merton Agena speaks to West Maui AJA Veterans Club for, Lahaina News, May 29, 2003: 1,18.

MEMORY WALK
— to be held to benefit Alzheimer Association, Lahaina News, September 11, 1997: 2.

MENDELSSOHN STRING QUARTET
— presented by Maui Philharmonic Society, Lahaina News, November 30, 1988: 16.

MENDES, ERNEST, JR.
— resident of Waihee featured, Lahaina Sun, July 4, 1973: 15.

MENDEZ, LEILANI SHARPE [MUSICIAN]
— to perform at benefit concert for Piilani School of Hula, Lahaina News, August 23, 1989: 3.
— to perform at Old Lahaina Cafe and Luau, Lahaina News, February 28, 1990: 11.

MENEHUNE BASKETBALL LEAGUE
— see basketball

MENEHUNE FOREST GALLERY AND GIFT [BUSINESS]
— opens, Lahaina News, June 27, 1996: 12.

MENEHUNE MADNESS PARADE AND BED RACE
— sponsored by Maui Imua Rehabilitation Center, Lahaina News, March 13, 1991: 8.

MENOR, SELBERIO
— appointed by mayor Tavares as Civil Defense Administrator, Lahaina News, August 15, 1980: 10.
— Civil Defense administrator advises to prepare for winter storms, Lahaina News, December 26, 1991: 4.

MENTAL HEALTH
— call for reform in psychiatric law, Lahaina Sun, November 8, 1972: 4.
— issues with mental health services discussed, Lahaina Sun, November 15, 1972: 4.
— law under review by Mental Health Association of Hawaii, Lahaina Sun, December 13, 1972: 4.

MENTAL HEALTH ASSOCIATION
— first gathering of the association, Lahaina Sun, March 15, 1972: 5.
— to present recommendations on mentally ill criminal offenders, Lahaina News, May 21, 1992: 4.

MENTAL HEALTH KOKUA
— to hold whale watch benefit, Lahaina News, March 1, 2001: 20.
— to hold whale watch fundraiser, Lahaina News, February 13, 2003: 2.
— to offer whale watch fundraiser, Lahaina News, February 20, 2003: 17.

MENUDO [MUSICAL GROUP]
— to perform at the War Memorial Gym, Lahaina News, September 11, 1985: 9.

MEO
— opening new base at Cameron Center, Lahaina News, August 12, 1999: 16.

MERCADO, HAZEL
— graduates with honors from Air Academy in Vancouver, Washington, Lahaina News, July 29, 1999: 3.

MERCEDES CHAMPIONSHIP
— to be held at The Plantation Course, Lahaina News, November 12, 1998: 15.
— tickets available, Lahaina News, December 10, 1998: 19.
— David Duval wins, Lahaina News, January 14, 1999: 3.
— raised $180,000 for local nonprofit groups, Lahaina News, January 28, 1999: 11.
— Nancy Cross appointed tournament director for, Lahaina News, April 6, 2000: 7.
— raises money for local non-profits, Lahaina News, August 24, 2000: 19.
— golf tournament to be held in Kapalua, Lahaina News, December 28, 2000: 1,7.
— to be held, Lahaina News, January 4, 2001: 1,8.
— to be held, players listed, Lahaina News, January 11, 2001: 1,8.
— supports charities, Lahaina News, May 17, 2001: 9.
— proceeds from distributed to local charities, Lahaina News, May 31, 2001: 9.
— beneficiaries for next tournament named, Lahaina News, June 14, 2001: 15.
— named Wilma Brown Vorfield as "Bank of America Charity Cup Volunteer of the Year", Lahaina News, June 28, 2001: 11.
— to be held at Kapalua's Plantation Course, Lahaina News, January 3, 2002: 1,13.
— raises money for local charities, Lahaina News, April 11, 2002: 3.
— seeking applications for tournament beneficiaries, Lahaina News, May 9, 2002: 3.
— beneficiaries named, Lahaina News, July 18, 2002: 13.
— tickets on sale, Lahaina News, August 15, 2002: 12.
— names Tom McKeown "Volunteer of the Year", Lahaina News, November 14, 2002: 11.
— to be held, Lahaina News, January 2, 2003: 2.
— golf tournament to be held, Lahaina News, January 9, 2003: 13.
— Ernie Els wins golf tournament, Lahaina News, January 16, 2003: 12.
— to be hosted by Kapalua Maui Charities, Inc., Lahaina News, March 27, 2003: 9.
— names Kapalua Maui Charities as beneficiary, Lahaina News, May 29, 2003: 8.
— tickets on sale for, Lahaina News, September 11, 2003: 12.

MERCER, DAVID
— to lead seminar on legal issues faced by condominiums, Lahaina News, October 22, 1992: 12.

MERCHANT, NATALIE [MUSICIAN]
— to perform at Alexander and Baldwin Amphitheatre, Lahaina News, February 11, 1999: 17.
— to perform at Maui Arts and Cultural Center, Lahaina News, March 11, 1999: 13.
— to perform at Maui Arts and Cultural Center, Lahaina News, March 18, 1999: 16.
— to perform at Maui Arts and Cultural Center, Lahaina News, December 27, 2001: 15.
— to perform at Maui Arts and Cultural Center, Lahaina News, January 24, 2002: 16.

MERCI, ANITA [ARTIST]
— to lead "Tropical Technique in Watercolor", Lahaina News, June 5, 2003: 16.

MERCY AIR HELICOPTER AMBULANCE
— popular exhibit at Public Safety Awareness Day, Lahaina News, July 6, 1995: 1.

MEREDITH, KIM CHAR [MUSICIAN]
— to perform at Borders Books from new release "Give and Take", Lahaina News, June 19, 2003: 16.

MEREDITH, REX [COMEDIAN]
— to perform at Comedy Club, Lahaina News, November 14, 1991: 17.
— to perform at Comedy Club and the Sports Page, Lahaina News, February 11, 1993: 13,15.
— to perform at Comedy Club, Lahaina News, February 24, 1994: 11.
— to perform at Honolulu Comedy Club, Lahaina News, February 15, 1996: 13.

MERIKA AND SASCHA [MUSICAL GROUP]
— to perform at Borders Books, Lahaina News, June 24, 1999: 12.

MERLIN, ERIC
— captain of Leaky Teaky [ship] featured, Lahaina Sun, August 29, 1973: 14.

MERRIFIELD, HEYOEHKAH [ARTIST]
— reception to be held at Lotus Gallery, Lahaina News, February 13, 1991: 13.
— exhibiting at Lotus Gallery, Lahaina News, February 20, 1991: 12.

MERRIFIELD, VALERIE [MUSICIAN]
— harpist to perform, Lahaina News, October 25, 1989: 2.

MERRILES, DEE
— purchases Lahaina Hairstylists, Lahaina News, June 13, 1991: 9.

MERRILL, CATHERINE
— to lead figurative ceramic sculpture workshop at Hui No'eau Visual Arts Center, Lahaina News, March 21, 2002: 16.

MERRILL LYNCH [BUSINESS]
— presenting workshop on "Investment Strategies Update", Lahaina News, October 1, 1998: 13.
— hosting seminar on taxes, Lahaina News, August 26, 1999: 13.

MERRILL, MARK
— wins division at Hawaii State Open Junior Championship in golf, Lahaina News, September 6, 1989: 5.

MERRIMAN, PETER
— chef planning restaurant at Ma'alaea Harbor Village, Lahaina News, November 5, 1998: 17.
— chef hosts Whalers Village monthly cooking demonstration, Lahaina News, November 14, 2002: 21.
— chef to give cooking demonstrations, Lahaina News, December 12, 2002: 21.

MERRIMAN, ROBERT
— running Coldwell Banker Island Properties real estate information center at Grand Wailea Resort, Lahaina News, March 16, 2000: 11.

MERRITT, KIERA
— successful at junior miss pageant, Lahaina News, December 5, 2002: 14.

MERRY CHRISTMAS, MISS CRABTREE [PLAY]
— to be performed by Theatre Theatre Maui, Lahaina News, December 17, 1998: 1.

MERRY KEANAE CHRISTMAS, A
— to be held, Lahaina News, November 26, 1998: 16.

MERSEBERG, KIMO
— kahu to retire, Lahaina News, May 20, 1999: 17.
— retirement service held for, Lahaina News, June 10, 1999: 15.

MERUK, ALEX
— long-time resident of Lahaina dies at 92, Lahaina News, June 15, 1983: 6.

MERWIN, WILLIAM [POET]
— reading works at the Artful Dodger, Lahaina News, December 9, 1987: 26.
— to speak at Borders Books, Lahaina News, December 24, 1998: 12.
— poet to read from "Folding Cliffs" collection, Lahaina News, April 13, 2000: 12.

MESCH, BEVERLY
— director of Women Helping Women discusses shelter, Lahaina News, April 15, 1987: 1,19.

MESH, MIKEL [ARTIST]
— cartoonist raises money for environmental causes, Lahaina News, July 4, 1990: 5.
— cartoonist to begin publishing cartoons in Lahaina News, Lahaina News, January 23, 1991: 1.

MESSARA, MARK
— general counsel for Surfrider Foundation on green algae problem, Lahaina News, November 5, 1992: 1.

MESSENJAH [MUSICAL GROUP]
— to perform benefit concert for Iao School Renaissance Education Foundation, Lahaina News, October 28, 1993: 10.

MESSIAH, THE [MUSIC]
— sing-a-long to be performed, Lahaina News, November 27, 1985: 3.
— sing-along to be performed at Saint Anthony Church, Lahaina News, November 28, 1990: 4.
— to be performed by Maui Symphony Orchestra, Lahaina News, December 2, 1993: 15.
— to be performed at Castle Theatre, Lahaina News, November 17, 1994: 19.
— to be performed by Maui Symphony Orchestra, Lahaina News, December 8, 1994: 16.
— to feature soprano Carmen Pelton, Lahaina News, December 15, 1994: 16.
— Maui Symphony Orchestra to hold auditions for, Lahaina News, November 9, 1995: 12.
— to be held, Lahaina News, December 7, 1995: 16.
— to be performed, Lahaina News, December 14, 1995: 14,15.
— to be performed at Maui Arts and Cultural Center, Lahaina News, December 12, 1996: 8.

MESSIANIC SERVICE
— to be held, Lahaina News, August 6, 1998: 20.

MESSINA, JIM [MUSICIAN]
— concert reviewed, Lahaina News, September, 1979: 4.

MESTAS, R.J.
— memorial service to be held for, Lahaina News, August 7, 2003: 5.

MESTON, KELLY
— returns money found by banyan tree to owner, Lahaina Sun, May 26, 1971: 3.

METAPHYSICAL LUNCHEON
— see 'Ohana Luncheon

METCALF, THOMAS [ARTIST]
— to exhibit at Lahaina Arts Society, Lahaina News, January 11, 2001: 3.
— to exhibit at Lahaina Arts Society, Lahaina News, January 31, 2002: 14.
— featured artist at Lahaina Arts Society, Lahaina News, February 7, 2002: 16.

METCALF, WAYNE
— State Insurance Commissioner to speak, Lahaina News, November 21, 1996: 15.

METCALFE, JEROME
— planning theme park in Lahaina Business Park, Lahaina News, January 18, 2001: 14.

METROPOLITAN ART GALLERY [BUSINESS]
— to open, Lahaina News, March 7, 1990: 7.
— opens, Lahaina News, March 21, 1990: 14.
— holds grand opening, Lahaina News, March 28, 1990: 18.
— personnel changes at, Lahaina News, December 24, 1992: 10.

METZ, JASON [TENNIS PLAYER]
— begins residence as tennis pro at Maui Marriott, Lahaina News, December 26, 1984: 3.

MEUNIER, ED
— named officer for Lahaina Yacht Club, Lahaina Sun, December 23, 1970: 8.

MEWES [PLAY]
— to be shown on Akaku cablevision, Lahaina News, January 8, 1998: 12.
— to be performed at Lahaina Cannery Mall, Lahaina News, August 20, 1998: 8.

MEXICO
— trip to, described, Lahaina Sun, March 24, 1971: 6.
— travel to described, Lahaina News, October, 1979: 7,12.

MEYER, HENRY
— at meeting between Hawaiian Homes Commission and The Hawaiians, Lahaina Sun, December 23, 1970: 6.

MEYER, MARCO [POLITICIAN]
— proposes solution to waste water from Pioneer Mill, Lahaina Sun, November 25, 1970: 1.
— member of Maui County Council, Lahaina Sun, December 30, 1970: 8.
— introduces resolution to add surfing to high school curriculum, Lahaina Sun, January 20, 1971: 7.
— opposes return to Kaho'olawe to the State of Hawaii, Lahaina Sun, March 3, 1971: 8.
— asks for law aimed at slow drivers, Lahaina Sun, September 22, 1971: 7.

MEYERSON, KENNETH
— attacked while sleeping in his car, Lahaina Sun, June 23, 1971: 12.

MIATA CLUB
— to meet, Lahaina News, July 30, 1998: 17.
— to meet, Lahaina News, August 6, 1998: 20.
— continues to meet, Lahaina News, January 14, 1999: 13.
— continues to meet, Lahaina News, June 10, 1999: 17.

MICE
— population increasing in Kihei and Makena, Lahaina Sun, August 4, 1971: 10.

MICHAELS, AL
— sportscaster visits Maui, Lahaina Sun, December 27, 1972: 7.

MICHEL, HANS
— farmer wants county to pay for land usage, Lahaina News, February 4, 1993: 2.

MICHELOB MASTERS SAILBOARD
— regatta series accepting entries, Lahaina News, April 25, 1990: 12.

MICHIMOTO, RYAN
— Scholar/Athlete of the Week, Lahaina News, May 25, 2000: 8.
— wins Evans scholarship, Lahaina News, August 30, 2001: 3.

MICK TAYLOR BAND, THE [MUSICAL GROUP]
— to perform at Casanova's, Lahaina News, August 29, 1990: 11.

MICKEY, BARBARA
— Maui Youth and Family Services representative speaks of lack of foster homes, Lahaina News, November 18, 1987: 1,8.

MICRO GAIA, INC. [BUSINESS]
— building microalgae production facility at the Maui Research and Technology Park, Lahaina News, February 24, 2000: 13.
— to open at Maui Research and Technology Park, Lahaina News, October 12, 2000: 16.

MICRONESIA
— delegates to meet in Hana to discuss the future of the Trust Territory, Lahaina Sun, September 29, 1971: 1,13.
— diplomatic conference is underway, Lahaina Sun, October 6, 1971: 11.
— diplomatic conference ending, Lahaina Sun, October 13, 1971: 15.
— talks concerning trusteeship of Micronesia continuing, Lahaina Sun, October 20, 1971: 12.
— issues connected to trust territory status apparently resolved, Lahaina Sun, April 26, 1972: 11.
— discussion of changes in, Lahaina Sun, May 17, 1972: 15.

MICRONESIA [FILM]
— shown at Lahaina Library, Lahaina Sun, May 5, 1971: 3.

MID-PACIFIC AIRLINES [BUSINESS]
— reports a loss, Lahaina News, September 1, 1981: 5.
— post profit for third quarter, Lahaina News, November 1, 1981: 5.
— requests permission to use proposed airstrip at Mahinahina, Lahaina News, December 14, 1983: 2.
— offering low-priced tours of Neighbor Islands, Lahaina News, June 13, 1984: 12.
— plans to introduce air cargo operations, Lahaina News, June 13, 1984: 3.
— flights between Honolulu and West Maui planned, Lahaina News, June 20, 1984: 3.
— interisland flight promotion begins, Lahaina News, June 20, 1984: 3.
— purchases additional YS-11 aircraft, Lahaina News, August 8, 1984: 14.
— plans to launch inter-island cargos service, Lahaina News, October 24, 1984: 4.
— will intervene in hearing to change district boundary for airport in West Maui, Lahaina News, November 21, 1984: 3.
— express parcel service begins, Lahaina News, December 26, 1984: 3.
— changes fair structure to make all seats the same price, Lahaina News, January 2, 1985: 3.
— announces fare offer, Lahaina News, June 26, 1985: 20.
— to service Kapalua-West Maui airport, Lahaina News, March 11, 1987: 3.
— announces special fairs, Lahaina News, May 13, 1987: 14.
— reduces interisland fares, Lahaina News, November 18, 1987: 3.

MIDAS, JOHN [COMEDIAN]
— to perform at Comedy Club and the Sports Page, Lahaina News, November 7, 1990: 10.
— to perform at Comedy Club and the Sports Page, Lahaina News, April 1, 1993: 12.

MIDLIFE CLARITY: EPIPHANIES FROM GROWN-UP GIRLS [BOOK]
— book launch to be held at Borders Books, Lahaina News, June 27, 2002: 17.

MIDSON, BRIAN
— Hawai'i Undersea Research Lab to lead virtual tour of Lo'ihi, Lahaina News, November 9, 2000: 25.

MIDSUMMER NIGHT'S BALL, A
— to be held by Lahaina Arts Society, Lahaina News, July 18, 1996: 10.

MIDSUMMER NIGHT'S DREAM, A [PLAY]
— to be performed at Hui No'eau Visual Arts Center, Lahaina News, July 30, 1992: 18.

MIDWIFERY
— discussed as alternative healing method, Lahaina News, May 4, 1988: 15.

MIKADO [MUSICAL]
— Gilbert and Sullivan to be performed, Lahaina News, July 13, 1995: 11,12.
— to be performed at Maui Arts and Cultural Center, Lahaina News, October 19, 1995: 9.

MIKAMI, JO ANN
— named account executive at Starr Seigle McCombs, Inc., Lahaina News, October 11, 1989: 5.

MILBOURN, JESSICA
— Scholar/Athlete of the Week, Lahaina News, March 9, 2000: 6.
— awarded Mamoru and Aiko Takitani Foundation scholarship, Lahaina News, May 17, 2001: 10.

MILES, BUDDY
— guitarist to perform at Partners, Lahaina News, October 26, 1988: 9,16.

MILES, DAVID
— owner of Hop Tomato Italian Bistro and Brewery plans to assemble world record pizza, Lahaina News, April 19, 2001: 1,9.

MILES, RICK
— van damaged by golf ball, Lahaina Sun, February 24, 1971: 1.

MILITARY
— Air force unit leaving Maui, Lahaina Sun, May 19, 1971: 1.
— number of military families in Hawaii increases, Lahaina Sun, October 27, 1971: 12.
— editorial discussing Maui County Council's vote to keep nuclear ships from anchoring off Lahaina, Lahaina News, April 18, 1984: 2.
— pilot jettisons disarmed bombs after falling ill, Lahaina News, September 19, 1984: 3.
— former destroyer escort sailors planning reunion, Lahaina News, November 18, 1987: 3.
— receives approval for relay Mirror Experiment, Lahaina News, December 16, 1987: 15.
— large exercise to be conducted off West Maui, Lahaina News, June 23, 1994: 1,16.
— women veterans and servicewomen to meet, Lahaina News, May 18, 1995: 4.
— Rita Silva seeking information on women who served in, Lahaina News, September 26, 1996: 1.
— Maui residents participate in live fire training at Schofield Barracks, Lahaina News, May 13, 1999: 15.

MILK CARTON BOAT RACE
— results, Lahaina Sun, July 25, 1973: 11.

MILKEN FAMILY FOUNDATION NATIONAL EDUCATOR AWARD
— principal Henry Ariyoshi collects, Lahaina News, March 10, 1994: 4.

MILL KALUA TITA
— to be held on July 4th, Lahaina News, June 28, 1989: 1.

MILL VALLEY ISLE
— Leilani Roseline Re crowned, Lahaina News, January 20, 1994: 4.

MILLAR [FAMILY]
— founders of Napili Kai Beach Club award scholarships, Lahaina News, June 5, 1997: 15.

MILLAR, DOROTHY
— becomes first female Rotarian in Lahaina, Lahaina News, December 2, 1987: 1.

MILLAR, JACK
— awarded "Small Businessman of the Year" in Hawaii for 1971, Lahaina Sun, June 2, 1971: 8.

MILLAR, RANDALL [ARTIST]
— to participate in "Four by Four Equals" show, Lahaina News, February 2, 1995: 10.

MILLER, AMY
— appointed director of Honolua United Methodist Preschool, Lahaina News, March 10, 1994: 4.

MILLER, BAIRD
— threatens to resign from Maui Historic Commission over activities booth permit controversy, Lahaina News, April 18, 1990: 1.

MILLER, BART
— career at Pioneer Inn celebrated, Lahaina News, February 15, 1983: 7.
— former manager of the Pioneer Inn and supporter of local music praised, Lahaina News, October 16, 1985: 10.

MILLER, CARLY
— Scholar/Athlete of the Week, Lahaina News, May 17, 2001: 14.

MILLER, CLIFFORD
— to meet with veterans to discuss benefits, Lahaina News, May 21, 1998: 9.

MILLER, CONNIE FRANCIS
— named to Maui County Committee on the Status of Women, Lahaina News, August 20, 1992: 15.

MILLER, DENNIS [COMEDIAN]
— to perform at Hyatt Regency Maui for New Year's Eve, Lahaina News, December 5, 1991: 23.

MILLER, EASSIE
— named superintendent of wastewater treatment plant, Lahaina News, October 8, 1986: 3.

MILLER, ED
— native of Kapingamarangi, described, Lahaina Sun, May 10, 1972: 15.

MILLER, GEORGE
— case manager at Maui Community Mental Health Center discusses homeless, Lahaina News, October 24, 1990: 1,8,9.

MILLER, GLEN
— appointed director of marketing at Westin Maui, Lahaina News, December 6, 1989: 5.
— appointed Director of Marketing at Westin Maui, Lahaina News, December 13, 1989: 7.
— director of marketing at Westin Maui named "1990 Director of Marketing by Westin Hotels and Resorts", Lahaina News, April 10, 1991: 6.

MILLER, JACK
— receives T.S. Shinn Award from Maui Chamber of Commerce, Lahaina News, July 2, 1986: 3.

MILLER, JEROME
— named assistant state director for American Association of Retired Persons, Lahaina News, July 6, 1988: 11.

MILLER, JOHN
— calls for more voices to support education, Lahaina News, January 21, 1993: 10.
— state House Resolution recognizes volunteer efforts, Lahaina News, April 29, 1993: 5.

— Parent Teacher Association legislative liaison urges volunteerism, Lahaina News, August 26, 1993: 7.
— to run for house or senate, Lahaina News, November 25, 1993: 7.
— named as director of advertising of KEI TV59, Lahaina News, October 13, 1994: 15.

MILLER, KAIPO
— becomes principal of Princess Nahienaena Elementary School, Lahaina News, August 2, 2001: 1,20.
— principal of Princess Nahienaena Elementary School featured, Lahaina News, October 10, 2002: 1,20.

MILLER, KENNETH P.
— pastor to speak at United Methodist Churches, Lahaina Sun, June 23, 1971: 9.

MILLER, LOIS JEANNE [ARTIST]
— Kihei Arts Council presenting show by, Lahaina News, April 18, 1990: 12.
— to exhibit at Banyan Tree Gallery, Lahaina News, May 13, 1993: 11.

MILLER, RANDALL [ARTIST]
— to speak for Church of God, Lahaina News, February 24, 1988: 18.
— to give course on camera maintenance, Lahaina News, May 24, 1989: 3.
— to exhibit at Lahaina Arts Society Gallery, Lahaina News, July 30, 1998: 17.
— to exhibit photographs at Maui Arts Society, Lahaina News, June 6, 2002: 17.

MILLER, RENEE
— promoted at Maui Youth and Family Services, Lahaina News, January 25, 2001: 14.

MILLER, RON
— DJ to host disco at Casanova's, Lahaina News, April 24, 1991: 11.

MILLER, SUSANA
— to lead Argentine tango classes, Lahaina News, July 10, 2003: 17.

MILLER, WARREN
— film "Endless Winter" to be shown, Lahaina News, March 21, 1996: 13.
— "Snowriders" film to be shown, Lahaina News, February 27, 1997: 7.
— "Snowriders II" to be shown, Lahaina News, February 26, 1998: 13.
— snowboard adventure film "Freeriders" to be shown, Lahaina News, January 14, 1999: 12.
— film "Fifty" to be shown, Lahaina News, January 13, 2000: 12.
— latest film "Ride" to be shown at the Maui Arts and Cultural Center, Lahaina News, January 4, 2001: 17.
— film "Ride" to be shown, Lahaina News, January 11, 2001: 3.
— film "Cold Fusion" to be shown, Lahaina News, January 3, 2002: 17.
— film "Storm" to be shown, Lahaina News, January 9, 2003: 17.

MILLIGAN, DENNIS
— house suffers storm damage, Lahaina Sun, December 30, 1970: 1.

MILLIKIN, JENI
— appointed public relations manager at Kapalua Bay Hotel and Villas, Lahaina News, February 6, 1991: 6.

MILLINGTON, JUNE AND JEAN
— to perform at Maui Arts and Cultural Center, Lahaina News, April 2, 1998: 17.

MILLINGTON, SAMUEL
— named new executive director of the Hui Malama Learning Center, Lahaina News, March 9, 2000: 5.

MILLS, BILL
— purchases Maui Lani project from Alexander & Baldwin, Lahaina News, December 27, 1989: 5.
— purchases land from Blackfield Hawaii Corp., Lahaina News, December 27, 1989: 5.

MILLS, DEBORAH
— to talk on "Remembering Our Divine Consciousness", Lahaina News, January 16, 2003: 16.

MILNER, MICHAEL
— nearly-nude carvings and other objects banned from outside the shop of, Lahaina Sun, July 21, 1971: 10.

MIN, JOHN E.
— appointed as vice chair of Housing Finance and Development Corp. by Governor Ben Cayetano, Lahaina News, August 31, 1995: 10.
— Planning Director to speak to Haiku Community Association, Lahaina News, May 23, 2002: 17.

MIN, SHERI-ANN
— promoted to director of property management at Kapalua Land Company, Lahaina News, October 14, 1987: 17.

MINA, MICHAEL
— guest chef to cook at Roy's Kahana Bar and Grill, Lahaina News, July 22, 1993: 12.

MINA, VINCENT
— Ma'alaea Community Garden member to offer workshop on "How to Grow Soil", Lahaina News, May 28, 1998: 12.
— to speak on "Our Relationship to Body and Soil Health" at 'Ohana Connection breakfast, Lahaina News, May 22, 2003: 17.

MINAMI, LAWRENCE
— named Maui's Outstanding Older American, Lahaina News, July 25, 1991: 6.
— resident featured, Lahaina News, February 8, 1996: 7.

MINAMI, RAYNOR
— Department of Education inspector discusses unsafe playground at King Kamehameha III Elementary School, Lahaina News, November 4, 1999: 1,16.

MIND INTERNATIONAL
— research organization searching for Atlantis featured, Lahaina Times, August, 1980 volume 4 number 7: 2.

MIND JOGGERS SUPPORT GROUP
— to be coordinated by Alzheimer's Association, Lahaina News, January 25, 2001: 17.

MIND'S EYE INTERIORS [BUSINESS]
— expands showroom, Lahaina News, November 5, 1992: 8.

MING COURT [RESTAURANT]
— welcomes Chinese New Year, Lahaina News, February 13, 1985: 3.
— offering a Christmas bonus to diners, Lahaina News, October 30, 1985: 3.
— offers new lunch service, Lahaina News, August 27, 1986: 13.

MING YUEN CHINESE [RESTAURANT]
— celebrates anniversary, Lahaina News, November 14, 1984: 3.
— hosting lei day singles party, Lahaina News, April 23, 1992: 30.

MINK, JOHN
— husband of Patsy Mink discusses need for better services veterans, Lahaina News, May 28, 1998: 1,16.

MINK, PATSY [POLITICIAN]
— US representative to talk on civil liberties, Lahaina Sun, February 24, 1971: 7.
— discusses Hawaii's failure to request historic preservation funds from the Interior Department, Lahaina Sun, December 8, 1971: 1.
— US representative sues federal government for information on nuclear testing, Lahaina Sun, April 26, 1972: 21.
— US representative details of 1972 election, Lahaina Sun, September 27, 1972: 6.
— US representative commends veterans for complaining about Veterans Administration services to Maui, Lahaina Sun, December 20, 1972: 7.
— campaigns in West Maui, Lahaina News, September 3, 1986: 1.
— to hold fundraiser, Lahaina News, August 22, 1990: 4.
— to hold fundraiser, Lahaina News, August 29, 1990: 4.
— sworn in as representative, Lahaina News, January 9, 1991: 4.
— favors Marine Sanctuary around Kaho'olawe, Lahaina News, September 5, 1991: 1.
— praised by National Council of Senior Citizens, Lahaina News, March 12, 1992: 3.
— announces federal funding for elderly housing complex in Kahului, Lahaina News, October 15, 1992: 8.
— to visit Maui, Lahaina News, October 22, 1992: 4.
— announces that Vincent Ryan Linares will serve as Washington office intern, Lahaina News, January 14, 1993: 3.
— says Davis-Bacon Act to be suspended, Lahaina News, March 4, 1993: 8.
— holds meeting, speaks of National Park system, Lahaina News, June 17, 1993: 4.
— discusses likely end of federal price support program for sugar, Lahaina News, December 8, 1994: 12,13.
— appoints Lloyd Sodetani as delegate to White House Conference on Small Business, Lahaina News, December 22, 1994: 13.
— seeks federal study of proposed North Beach development, Lahaina News, May 4, 1995: 5.
— wins primary election, Lahaina News, September 26, 1996: 3.
— announces that U.S. Department of Justice increases funding for police, Lahaina News, January 9, 1997: 14.
— succeeds in maintaining U.S. Sugar Program, Lahaina News, July 31, 1997: 13.
— to speak at Memorial Day Service, Lahaina News, May 14, 1998: 1.
— to speak to A.J.A. Veterans Club, Lahaina News, May 21, 1998: 9.
— Lahainaluna High School student Brian Garcia wins Patsy Mink Congressional Art Award, Lahaina News, May 24, 2001: 1,22.
— staff to include Maui resident Hideo Abe, Lahaina News, June 14, 2001: 2.
— reports on federal money to help fund Lahaina Recreation Center Expansion Project, Lahaina News, July 4, 2002: 2.
— reports that U.S. Army Honolulu Engineers District project to restore eroded areas along Honoapi'ilani Highway, Lahaina News, July 11, 2002: 1.

MINKOWSKI, STEVEN [ARTIST]
— to present "Views of Maui and Lana'i" to Hui No'eau Visual Arts Center , Lahaina News, June 15, 1988: 14.

MINNESOTA
— former residents to reunite at Kalama Park, Lahaina News, February 20, 1992: 4.
— for residents now living on Maui to hold reunion, Lahaina News, February 20, 1997: 10.
— reunion to be held, Lahaina News, February 26, 1998: 13.
— reunion to be held, Lahaina News, February 25, 1999: 13.

MINOAKA [MUSICAL GROUP]
— to sign new CD at Borders Books, Lahaina News, March 16, 2000: 12.

MIRACLE ON FRONT STREET [PLAY]
— to be performed by Kids of Lahaina, Lahaina News, December 18, 1985: 3.

MIRACLE WORKER, THE [PLAY]
— continues at Baldwin Theatre Guild, Lahaina News, January 24, 1990: 14.

MIRACLES BOOKERY [BUSINESS]
— to hold open house, Lahaina News, September 18, 1997: 16.
— to hold "One Canoe, Earth" art show, Lahaina News, October 12, 2000: 20.
— to hold "Read, Speak and Be Seen: Open Mike for Open Minds", Lahaina News, September 19, 2002: 25.
— to hold open mike nights, Lahaina News, October 31, 2002: 29.

MIRECOURT PIANO TRIO [MUSICAL GROUP]
— to perform at St. Anthony Church Center, Lahaina News, March 12, 1986: 3.

MIRONOUE, HIROKI [ARTIST]
— to hold workshop on watercolors, Lahaina News, September 14, 1988: 13.

MIRZAI, MAHMOOD
— surgeon at Maui Memorial Hospital passes away, Lahaina News, December 12, 1991: 6.

MISCHELLE ECOLE DE BALLET MAUI
— to open, Lahaina News, September 21, 1988: 20.
— to begin classes at Malu'ulu O Lele Cultural Center, Lahaina News, September 28, 1995: 11.
— to begin fall session, Lahaina News, September 26, 1996: 15.
— to hold dance extravaganza, Lahaina News, June 5, 1997: 16.
— to begin spring session, Lahaina News, March 18, 1999: 8.

MISCOVICH, SCOTT
— Ohana Physicians Group offering free physical examinations, Lahaina News, September 10, 1998: 6.

MISHIMA, BETH
— Scholar/Athlete of the Week, Lahaina News, December 14, 2000: 14.

MISKAE, BRIAN
— selected as Maui County planning director, Lahaina News, January 16, 1991: 2.
— County Planning Director discusses likely citation for owners of mural painted by Wyland, Lahaina News, February 13, 1991: 1.
— Maui County Planning Director calls for new approach to land usage, Lahaina News, November 28, 1991: 1.
— Maui County Planning Director asks Kihei-Makena Community Plan Advisory Panel to focus on Kihei proper, Lahaina News, November 26, 1992: 15.
— says is not bound by advice from Kihei-Makena citizen advisory group, Lahaina News, January 14, 1993: 7.
— disagrees with project districts plan in Kihei, Lahaina News, January 28, 1993: 10.
— disagrees with north-south collector road, Lahaina News, January 28, 1993: 10.
— supports Kihei Residents Against Aina Lea (KRAAL), Lahaina News, July 15, 1993: 5.

MISNER, DON
— director of engineering at Ka'anapali Beach Hotel hosts students, Lahaina News, January 29, 1998: 9.

MISS AMERICAN STARLET SCHOLARSHIP PAGEANT
— to be held, Lahaina News, February 28, 2002: 16.

MISS GAY MOLOKA'I PAGEANT
— editorial criticizing mayor Tavares' attempt to halt, Lahaina News, October 16, 1985: 2.

MISS HAWAII
— Lisa Morton vying for, Lahaina News, June 10, 1993: 2.

MISS HAWAII SCHOLARSHIP PAGEANT
— reigning Miss Valley Isle Leilani Roseline Re to represent Maui, Lahaina News, March 17, 1994: 3.

MISS HAWAII USA
— Christy Leonard wins, Lahaina News, June 1, 2000: 1.

MISS KALUA TITA
— won by Shirnette Kalua, Lahaina News, July 16, 1986: 3.
— to take place at Royal Lahaina Resort with Pig-a-thon, Lahaina News, June 24, 1987: 3.

MISS KE ALA O KA MALAMALAMA PAGEANT
— drag queen pageant to be held, Lahaina News, April 10, 2003: 20.

MISS KEIKI HULA
— Keana Caramer named, Lahaina News, July 26, 2001: 5.

MISS LAHAINA PAGEANT
— to be held; applications being accepted, Lahaina News, May 9, 1990: 2.
— Miss Hawaii USA Leimomi Bacalso to participate in, Lahaina News, May 23, 1990: 5.
— finalists to complete at Lahaina Cannery Shopping Center, Lahaina News, May 30, 1990: 11.
— details, Lahaina News, June 6, 1990: 3.
— supplement, Lahaina News, June 13, 1990: B1,B2,B3,B4,B5,B6,B7,B8.
— won by Sydney Iaukea, Lahaina News, June 27, 1990: 3.
— applications now being accepted, Lahaina News, May 23, 1991: 3,4.
— insert and information on, Lahaina News, June 6, 1991: 1,B1,B2,B3,B4.
— to be held Saturday, Lahaina News, June 13, 1991: 4.
— results, Lahaina News, June 27, 1991: 1.

MISS MAUI
— Lisa Morton crowned as, Lahaina News, February 4, 1993: 3.

MISS MAUI EX'CEL PAGEANT
— begins, Lahaina News, May 7, 1998: 20.

MISS MAUI FILIPINA PAGEANT
— announced, Lahaina Sun, March 15, 1972: 1.
— to be held, Lahaina News, July 22, 1987: 3.
— to be held, Lahaina News, April 17, 1997: 13.
— to be held, Lahaina News, March 26, 1998: 13.
— to be held at Ka'ahumanu Center, Lahaina News, April 16, 1998: 12.
— finals to be held, Lahaina News, July 23, 1998: 17.
— to be held, Lahaina News, April 15, 1999: 12.
— to be held, Lahaina News, June 20, 2002: 16.
— to be held, Lahaina News, June 19, 2003: 16.

MISS MAUI PAGEANT
— to be held at Baldwin Auditorium, Lahaina News, March 29, 1989: 14.
— to be held, Lahaina News, November 1, 1989: 6.
— won by Nadine Tabandera, Lahaina News, February 13, 1991: 1,8.
— to be held at Maui Sun Hotel, Lahaina News, January 23, 1992: 4.
— to be held, Lahaina News, October 22, 1998: 15.
— application deadline, Lahaina News, September 25, 2003: 9.

MISS PUERTO RICO
— contest to be held on Maui, Lahaina Sun, June 20, 1973: 9.

MISS TITA CONTEST
— to occur during 4th of July celebrations, Lahaina News, July 2, 1986: 1.

MISS VALLEY ISLE CELESTINA HENNESSEY
— organizing fundraiser for needy children, Lahaina News, December 21, 1995: 14.

MISS VALLEY SCHOLARSHIP PAGEANT
— applications being accepted, Lahaina News, July 4, 1991: 3.
— applications being accepted, Lahaina News, July 18, 1991: 5.

MISSIONARIES
— interacting with whalers in Lahaina in the 1820s, Lahaina Sun, January 6, 1971: 8.
— environmentalists and Christians compared, Lahaina Sun, February 21, 1973: 1,10,11,12,13.

MISSIONARIES, THE [MUSICAL GROUP]
— featured, Lahaina News, November 5, 1992: 14.
— to perform at Moose McGillycuddy's, Lahaina News, March 11, 1993: 13.
— continue to perform at Longhi's, Lahaina News, May 20, 1993: 9.
— continue to perform at Longhi's, Lahaina News, June 24, 1993: 13,14.
— continues to perform at Moose McGillycuddy's, Lahaina News, December 16, 1993: 19.

— continues to perform at Moose McGillycuddy's, Lahaina News, June 2, 1994: 12.
— pictured; to perform at Moose McGillycuddy's, Lahaina News, May 4, 1995: 16.
— continues to perform at Moose McGillycuddy's, Lahaina News, January 25, 1996: 14.
— continue perform at World Cafe, Lahaina News, March 28, 1996: 12.
— featured, Lahaina News, July 18, 1996: 14.
— to perform at Moose McGillycuddy's, Lahaina News, September 19, 1996: 18.
— to perform at Moose McGillycuddy's, Lahaina News, January 9, 1997: 12.
— to perform at Moose McGillycuddy's, Lahaina News, June 5, 1997: 9.

MISTER, TERI
— to talk on "The Art of Manifestation" at 'Ohana Connection, Lahaina News, May 8, 2003: 17.

MITCHELL, DAVID
— named store manager at Monarch Building Supply, Lahaina News, April 24, 1991: 7.
— passes away, Lahaina News, May 24, 2001: 3.

MITCHELL, DOROTHY
— ceremony to honor, Lahaina News, April 24, 2003: 2.

MITCHELL, EDMUND "THE MACHINE"
— places 30th in Bankoh Kayak Challenge, Lahaina News, May 26, 1994: 9.
— wins second leg of Compadres Kayak Racing Series , Lahaina News, February 16, 1995: 9.
— wins third leg of Compadres Kayak Racing Series, Lahaina News, March 2, 1995: 6.

MITCHELL, HARRY
— discusses value of Hawaiian herbal medicine, Lahaina News, April 27, 1988: 1,17.
— pays homage to son James Kimo Mitchell who died on Kaho'olawe, Lahaina News, June 1, 1988: 1.

MITCHELL, JODY [ARTIST]
— to teach class in lei making, Lahaina News, January 30, 1992: 5.
— to offer workshops on lei making, Lahaina News, February 6, 1992: 4.

MITCHELL, KELLY
— appointed manager of Aston Kahana Reef, Lahaina News, September 16, 1999: 11.

MITCHELL, MUFFY
— Planning Coastal Zone Management Coordinator discusses archaeological map of Maui, Lahaina News, December 1, 1981: 16.

MITCHELL, STEVE
— owner of Coats of Arms International featured, Lahaina News, September 14, 1988: 2.

MITCHELL, THOMAS
— named president of Elite Properties, Lahaina News, November 21, 1991: 11.

MITCHELL, TIMOTHY
— discusses planned Lahaina Whaling Spree, Lahaina Sun, February 3, 1971: 2.
— elected chairman of Lahaina Improvement Association, Lahaina Sun, December 8, 1971: 8.
— head of Lahaina Restoration Foundation resigns, Lahaina Sun, August 23, 1972: 3.
— see also Maui Historic Commission

MITCHELL, TOM [ARTIST]
— photographs featured at Lahaina Arts Society, Lahaina News, December 9, 1987: 26.

MITSUMURA, FRAN PEART
— appointed branch manager of First Federal Savings and Loan, Lahaina News, October 29, 1992: 13.
— elected chairperson of LahainaTown Action Committee, Lahaina News, February 18, 1993: 4.

MITTENDORFF, G.E.
— Naval Captain discusses Kaho'olawe, Lahaina News, May 18, 1988: 1,5.

MITTLEMAN, STEVE [COMEDIAN]
— to perform at Comedy Club and the Sports Page, Lahaina News, June 24, 1993: 13.

MIURA, MARVIN [POLITICIAN]
— announces candidacy for Maui County mayor, Lahaina News, July 11, 1990: 2.
— candidate profiled, Lahaina News, September 19, 1990: 7,14.

MIYABUCHI, JON
— appointed sales manager at PrimeCo Personal Communications L.P., Lahaina News, July 10, 1997: 12.

MIYAGUCHI, GAYLE
— to hold class on making 'Uli'uli, Lahaina News, September 2, 1999: 17.

MIYAJIMA, KURT
— to teach Chi Gung and Tai Chi, Lahaina News, January 10, 2002: 16.
— continues to offer courses on Ghi Gung and Tai Chi, Lahaina News, January 31, 2002: 17.
— continues to teach Chi Gung and Tai Chi, Lahaina News, August 15, 2002: 17.
— to talk on "Tai Chi/Chi Gung and Breathing", Lahaina News, May 29, 2003: 17.

MIYAKO [ISLAND]
— performers from to stage "Koenkai—An Evening of Music and Dance of Miyakojima", Lahaina News, March 9, 2000: 12.

MIYAMOTO, CRAIG
— elected secretary of the South Pacific District of the Public Relations Society of America, Lahaina News, November 28, 1990: 8.

MIYAMOTO, NOBORU
— member of Lahaina Kamaakina Fishing Association, Lahaina Sun, December 23, 1970: 11.

MIYAMOTO, OWEN
— state's airport administrator suggests more direct flights are likely, Lahaina News, January 1, 1983: 2.
— to speak to Maui Hotel Association, Lahaina News, September 28, 1988: 3.
— airport administrator to review state plan to purchase Kapalua-West Maui airport, Lahaina News, June 13, 1990: 2.
— Airports Administrator awarded Engineer of the Year by the Hawaii Council of Engineering Society, Lahaina News, March 13, 1991: 7.

MIYAMURA, HENRY
— to conduct the Hawaii Youth Symphony, Lahaina News, March 7, 2002: 16.

MIYASAKI, TAKEO
— retires from Post Office after 90 years, Lahaina Sun, December 16, 1970: 6.

MIYASAKI, TATSU
— named officer of Lahaina Kamaakina Fishing Association, Lahaina Sun, December 23, 1970: 11.

MIYASHIRA, DONNA
— named food and beverage controller of Four Seasons Resort, Lahaina News, September 12, 1991: 4.

MIYAZONO, FLOYD
— named deputy director of Department of Parks and Recreation, Lahaina News, June 21, 1989: 3.
— County parks deputy director discusses proposed Lahaina amphitheatre, Lahaina News, May 30, 1990: 1.

MIZPA HISPANIC CHURCH
— to hold meeting on "Hispanics in Maui", Lahaina News, August 2, 2001: 1,20.

MIZROCH, SALLY
— discusses fluke I.D. research, Lahaina News, February 1, 1996: 1,14.

MIZUMOTO, LANCE
— promoted to vice president of Kihei Branch of First Hawaiian Bank, Lahaina News, May 29, 1997: 5.

MIZUNO, TEISHA
— Scholar/Athlete of the Week, Lahaina News, May 7, 1998: 10.

MIZUNO, TYSON
— Scholar/Athlete of the Week, Lahaina News, June 21, 2001: 12.

MOANA TERRACE [RESTAURANT]
— featured, Lahaina News, February 18, 1993: 15.

MOBERG, JIM
— joins Century 21 First Pacific Properties, Lahaina News, August 1, 1991: 11.

MOBILE CAR CARE [BUSINESS]
— featured, Lahaina News, September 23, 1987: 1,16.

MOBLEY, JOSEPH
— to talk about dolphin language communication, Lahaina News, March 20, 1985: 7.
— appointed research and education director at Island Marine, Lahaina News, October 21, 1999: 13.

MOBY DICK [NOVEL]
— read as background for Whaler's Village, Lahaina Sun, December 16, 1970: 5.

MOBY DICK'S [RESTAURANT]
— described, Lahaina News, August 26, 1987: 12.

MOBY GRAPE [MUSICAL GROUP]
— to perform at Moose McGillycuddy's, Lahaina News, August 25, 1994: 14.

MOCA SCHOOL OF NEW WORLD DANCE
— to perform, Lahaina News, January 23, 1997: 10.
— to offer swing dancing lessons, Lahaina News, January 30, 1997: 10.

MODERN MANDOLIN QUARTET, THE [MUSICAL GROUP]
— to perform at Hawaii Guitar Festival, Lahaina News, June 15, 1995: 11.

MOFFAT, RILEY
— to present on "Surveying the Mahele", Lahaina News, June 19, 1997: 17.

MOFFATT, TOM
— discusses reasons for larger concerts being canceled, Lahaina News, March 26, 1992: 10.

MOFFETT, WILLIAM "BUZ"
— offering window-tinting service, Lahaina News, March 30, 1995: 10.

MOGILNER, VICTORIA
— to present on "Oriental Facial Regeneration and Ways to Love and Nurture", Lahaina News, May 15, 2003: 17.

MOHALA GOLF TOURNAMENT
— to benefit Punana Leo O Lahaina, Lahaina News, February 28, 2002: 13.
— to be held, Lahaina News, April 4, 2002: 13.

MOHLER, JULIE
— promoted to convention services manager at Westin Maui Hotel, Lahaina News, May 30, 1990: 6.

MOKIAO, KEKUHI
— Scholar/Athlete of the Week, Lahaina News, October 18, 2001: 12.

MOKIHANA HULA FESTIVAL
— won by Maui halau Kano'eau Dance Academy, Lahaina News, October 9, 2003: 18.

MOKU, MARY
— at meeting between Hawaiian Homes Commission and The Hawaiians, Lahaina Sun, December 23, 1970: 6.
— Reverend gives blessing at Pihana heiau before archaeologists begin work, Lahaina Sun, August 25, 1971: 8.

MOKUHINIA
— plan to restore Front Street includes proposal to restore, Lahaina News, November 21, 1990: 1.
— described, study planned, Lahaina News, November 12, 1992: 3,insert2,insert3.
— possible restoration to be studied, Lahaina News, January 28, 1993: 4.

MOKULE'IA BEACH
— Slaughterhouse Trail to be fixed, Lahaina News, May 23, 1996: 1,18.

MOKULELE HIGHWAY
— plans to widen, Lahaina News, March 11, 1993: 10.

MOKU'ULA
— Friends of Moku'ula Island organizing to restore; history of, Lahaina News, December 19, 1991: 3.
— described, Lahaina News, November 12, 1992: insert3.
— possible restoration of island to be studied, Lahaina News, January 28, 1993: 4.
— blessing held at start of project, Lahaina News, February 4, 1993: 3.
— Maui Cultural Resources Commission recommends land swap to preserve, Lahaina News, May 11, 1995: 1,6.
— project to replace backstop damages archaeological wall on, Lahaina News, August 3, 1995: 1,5.
— digging near should be supervised, Lahaina News, August 10, 1995: 1.
— Friends of hoping to protect island, Lahaina News, September 28, 1995: 1,12.
— archaeologist Paul Klieger discusses, Lahaina News, November 9, 1995: 3.
— article in both Hawaiian and English, Lahaina News, June 20, 1996: 2.
— English translation of story from previous week, Lahaina News, June 27, 1996: 3.
— second part of article in Hawaiian, Lahaina News, July 4, 1996: 2.
— second part of article translated into English, Lahaina News, July 11, 1996: 2.
— third part of article, in Hawaiian, Lahaina News, July 18, 1996: 2.
— third part of article translated into English, Lahaina News, July 25, 1996: 2.
— update on recent projects, Lahaina News, August 1, 1996: 2.
— Friends of Moku'ula receives grant to begin restoring, Lahaina News, October 1, 1998: 1,20.
— project to unearth old capital may begin in 2001, Lahaina News, September 30, 1999: 1,16.
— World Archaeological Congress discusses importance of, Lahaina News, January 27, 2000: 1,16.
— Sacred Sites International Foundation discusses importance of, Lahaina News, January 27, 2000: 1,16.
— Eagle Scout improves, Lahaina News, August 16, 2001: 3.
— see also Friends of Moku'ula, The

MOLER, PRISCILLA
— president of West Maui Youth Center rejects request by Lingle administration to vacate, Lahaina News, August 6, 1992: 1,3.

MOLIERE
— Baldwin Theatre Guild to perform "The Imaginary Invalid", Lahaina News, May 23, 1990: 13.

MOLINA, AUNTY MARY
— scholarship at Maui Community College offered in honor of , Lahaina News, September 21, 1988: 20.

MOLINA, CHRISTINA
— Scholar/Athlete of the Week, Lahaina News, February 29, 1996: 6.

MOLINA, KEITH
— Scholar/Athlete of the Week, Lahaina News, August 13, 1998: 15.

MOLINA, MANUEL
— discussed as potential mayoral candidate, Lahaina Sun, June 28, 1972: 6,7.

MOLINA, MIKE [POLITICIAN]
— candidate for Makawao-Haiku-Paia Council Seat did not respond to survey from Lahaina News, Lahaina News, November 2, 2000: 22.
— meets with Friends of Moku'ula at Malu'ulu O Lele Park, Lahaina News, June 26, 2003: 1.

MOLINA, TREICIA
— Scholar/Athlete of the Week, Lahaina News, May 21, 1998: 14.

MOLINARO, URSULA [WRITER]
— holds reading at Artful Dodger, Lahaina News, September 30, 1987: 3.

MOLINERO, FELIX-NUNEZ [ARTIST]
— to exhibit at Metropolitan Art Gallery, Lahaina News, March 28, 1990: 18.

MOLLY B'S [RESTAURANT]
— opens on Front Street, Lahaina News, April 18, 1990: 5.
— featured, Lahaina News, May 23, 1990: 14.

MOLOKA'I [ISLAND]
— moderate income housing development on, Lahaina Sun, December 2, 1970: 3.
— hiking trip described, Lahaina Sun, September 1, 1971: 3.
— account of a visit to, Lahaina Sun, February 2, 1972: 6,7.
— approval asked to convert ranch to African safari, Lahaina Sun, March 8, 1972: 3.
— unfair treatment of criticized, Lahaina Sun, April 26, 1972: 3.
— editorial on possible futures, Lahaina Sun, October 18, 1972: 3.
— impact of pineapple closure on, Lahaina Sun, October 18, 1972: 4,5.
— University of Hawai'i researches studying economic future of, Lahaina Sun, January 24, 1973: 10.
— new newspaper, Lahaina Sun, February 21, 1973: 3.
— oil refinery proposed, Lahaina Sun, June 6, 1973: 15.
— possible future of island discussed, Lahaina Sun, June 13, 1973: 5.
— travel to described, Lahaina News, March 1, 1980: 10.
— Mayor Tavares dedicates elderly housing project, Lahaina News, July 1, 1980: 6.
— Mayor Tavares creates task force to advise on economic development, Lahaina News, August 1, 1980: 10.
— Plant Materials Center threatened with closure, Lahaina News, October 1, 1980: 4.
— desire to be a separate county, Lahaina News, May 1, 1982: 3.
— Louisiana Land & Exploration Co. purchases 7,000 acres from Moloka'i Ranch, Lahaina News, November 9, 1983: 5.
— described, Lahaina News, February 5, 1986: 1,12,13.
— editorial supporting self-governance, Lahaina News, April 29, 1987: 2.
— residents commute to Maui to work, Lahaina News, January 13, 1988: 1.
— Moloka'i Memorial Athletic Scholarship Fund established, Lahaina News, November 15, 1989: 3.
— Goodfellow Brothers, Inc. general contractor for major capital improvements on, Lahaina News, July 4, 1991: 4.
— featured, Lahaina News, May 9, 1996: 13,14.
— memorial service planned for victims of airplane crash on, Lahaina News, November 7, 1996: 1.
— workers support return of ferry, Lahaina News, March 13, 1997: 1,20.
— captain David Jung pledges that Sea Link of Hawaii will revive ferry, Lahaina News, November 9, 2000: 1,12.
— ferry operation to begin with Maui, Lahaina News, December 28, 2000: 1,15.
— Moloka'i shuttle service returns, Lahaina News, May 10, 2001: 8.

MOLOKA'I CHAMBER OF COMMERCE
— Henry Keawe Ayau Jr. elected president of, Lahaina News, August 13, 1992: 12.

MOLOKA'I FERRY
— may become self-supporting, Lahaina News, June 8, 1988: 1,20.
— increases rates, Lahaina News, July 25, 1996: 1.

MOLOKA'I MUSIC FESTIVAL
— scheduled, Lahaina News, September 12, 1990: 16.
— to be held in September, Lahaina News, June 20, 1991: 12.
— details, Lahaina News, September 12, 1991: 18.

MOLOKA'I PRINCESS [SHIP]
— Moloka'i shuttle service returns, Lahaina News, May 10, 2001: 8.
— expanding schedule, Lahaina News, May 24, 2001: 1,22.

MOLOKA'I RANCH
— hosts students, Lahaina News, September 1, 1994: 7.

MOLOKINI [ISLAND]
— U.S. Navy to remove unexploded bombs found near shore of, Lahaina News, August 10, 1988: 17.
— Department of Land and Natural Resources to hold public meeting to discuss rules affecting, Lahaina News, April 2, 1992: 4,5.
— Department of Land and Natural Resources to hold public meeting to discuss rules affecting, Lahaina News, April 9, 1992: 7.

MOLOKINI LOUNGE
— to hold cooking seminar, Lahaina News, April 2, 1992: 5.

MOLOKINI SHOALS MARINE LIFE CONSERVATION DISTRICT
— U.S. Navy to remove unexploded bombs found in, Lahaina News, August 10, 1988: 17.

MOLONEY, C. TIMOTHY
— named administrator for Maui Memorial Hospital, Lahaina News, January 2, 1991: 5.

MOLTZAU, RALPH
— reappointed to the Board of Adjustments and Appeal, Lahaina Sun, January 13, 1971: 8.
— named plantations manager for Maui Land & Pineapple, Lahaina Sun, May 19, 1971: 4.

MOMENTUS TRAINING
— to be held, Lahaina News, March 4, 1999: 12.

MOMIX [TROUPE]
— to offer "Millennial Space Show", Lahaina News, October 14, 1999: 13.
— to present "Millennial Space Show", Lahaina News, October 21, 1999: 17.
— to perform at Maui Arts and Cultural Center, Lahaina News, April 10, 2003: 20.

MOMOA, JASON
— "Baywatch Hawaii" actor to meet fans at Whalers Village, Lahaina News, July 20, 2000: 17.

MOMSEN, ROSE
— to lecture on quilting, Lahaina News, March 12, 1998: 21.

MONAHAN, WILLIAM [POLITICIAN]
— announces that he will not run for office, Lahaina News, July 15, 1982: 9.

MONARCH BUILDING SUPPLY [BUSINESS]
— appoints new officers, Lahaina News, May 6, 1987: 3.
— names Don Marchall as division manager, Lahaina News, July 25, 1990: 7.
— names Jerry McLeod as president, Lahaina News, July 8, 1993: 8.

MONDALE, WALTER
— editorial praising for choice of Geraldine Feraro as Vice-Presidential running mate, Lahaina News, July 18, 1984: 2.

MONDAVI, ROBERT
— winemaker to attend "Dinner with the Mondavi's" at Plantation House restaurant, Lahaina News, November 10, 1994: 16.

MONDAY NIGHT CLASS [BOOK]
— reviewed, Lahaina Sun, January 13, 1971: 6.

MONDEN, ROBERT [POLITICIAN]
— meets with Lahaina Citizen Advisory Committee, Lahaina News, January 19, 1995: 1,16.

MONEY
— postal orders recommended, Lahaina Sun, December 15, 1971: 1.
— seminar on planned giving sponsored by the American Red Cross, Lahaina News, April 23, 1992: 7.

MONIZ, MANUEL "JUNIOT" [POLITICIAN]
— discusses West Maui Youth Center occupying Honokahua School rent free, Lahaina Sun, May 5, 1971: 6.
— to hold workshop on development, Lahaina News, July 1, 1993: 1,12.

MONIZ, MARILYN
— new prosecuting attorney added to Maui County staff, Lahaina News, May 1, 1980: 14.
— speaks to Banyan Tree Square Preservation Committee, Lahaina News, March 19, 1986: 1.

MONIZ, PIA
— receives Kapalua's golf scholarship, Lahaina News, July 19, 1989: 5.

MONIZ, STACEY
— to speak to League of Republican Women, Lahaina News, September 30, 1999: 13.
— executive director of Women Helping Women describes agency, Lahaina News, October 17, 2002: 16.

MONIZ-KAHO'OHANOHANO, MARILYN
— County Parks Director speaks of improvements, Lahaina News, April 20, 1988: 11.
— to speak at pro-life rally, Lahaina News, January 18, 1989: 3,5.

MONK SEALS
— seen near Kapalua Bay Club, Lahaina News, April 2, 1992: 4.
— observed in Ka'anapali waters, Lahaina News, March 4, 1993: 1.
— visitors told to avoid monk seals in Molokini Inlet, Lahaina News, October 2, 1997: 17.
— agencies offer tips on protecting, Lahaina News, February 11, 1999: 1,6.

MONOGRAMS PLUS [BUSINESS]
— opens at Wharf Cinema Center, Lahaina News, December 12, 1990: 6.

MONSQUEDA, PERGENTINO
— Navy Hospitalman graduates from Basic Hospital Corps School, Lahaina News, August 30, 2001: 2.

MONTALVO, DERRICK
— Lahainaluna High School athletics director featured, Lahaina News, January 16, 1992: 7.
— Lahainaluna High School athletic director to retire, Lahaina News, June 29, 1995: 7.

MONTALVO, RANDY
— Lahainaluna High School baseball coach featured, Lahaina News, March 5, 1992: 8.
— may play in Hawaii Winter Baseball League, Lahaina News, September 1, 1994: 9.
— will play in Hawaii Winter Baseball League, Lahaina News, October 6, 1994: 9.
— Lahainaluna High School baseball coach featured, Lahaina News, March 27, 1997: 7.

MONTALVO, SUZETTE
— varsity cheerleading advisor featured, Lahaina News, February 20, 1992: 6.

MONTBLANC [BUSINESS]
— boutique opens, Lahaina News, July 5, 2001: 9.

MONTELEONE, NOEL [MUSICIAN]
— to perform at Pioneer Inn , Lahaina News, August 20, 1992: 18.
— to perform at Pioneer Inn , Lahaina News, September 10, 1992: 17.

MONTEREY, S.S. [SHIP]
— sailing to Honolulu, Lahaina News, August 17, 1988: 6.
— arrives in Lahaina, Lahaina News, December 28, 1988: 3.

MONTESSORI SCHOOL
— gala fundraiser to be held, Lahaina News, March 27, 1991: 14.
— gala to be held at Four Seasons Resort Wailea, Lahaina News, April 3, 1991: 8.
— to hold Children's Fair, Lahaina News, October 31, 1991: 4.
— to hold gala fundraiser, Lahaina News, March 18, 1993: 8.
— Hale O Keiki to hold wine auction and tasting, Lahaina News, October 13, 1994: 20.
— gala to be held, Lahaina News, March 13, 1997: 16.
— gala to benefit Montessori schools, Lahaina News, February 15, 2001: 16.
— to hold Music Fest fundraiser, Lahaina News, September 6, 2001: 15.
— Willie Nelson to perform at Music Fest, Lahaina News, September 13, 2001: 16.
— Willie Nelson to perform at Music Fest, Lahaina News, October 17, 2002: 20.
— to hold gala fundraiser, Lahaina News, February 6, 2003: 16.
— Willie Nelson to play benefit concert for, Lahaina News, October 9, 2003: 14.

MONTGOMERY, CAROLE [COMEDIAN]
— to perform at Comedy Club, Lahaina News, October 3, 1990: 11.
— to perform at Comedy Club and the Sports Page, Lahaina News, December 19, 1990: 12.
— Community work featured, Lahaina News, July 18, 1991: 9.

MONTGOMERY GALLERY [BUSINESS]
— reviewed, Lahaina News, October 30, 1985: 11.

MONTIZOR, FRANK [DANCE]
— to attend Mayor's Ball, Lahaina News, August 12, 1999: 17.

MONTLUZIN, SCOTT DE
— joins staff at Art School at Kapalua, Lahaina News, February 22, 1996: 14.

MONTOYA, JEFF
— Lahainaluna junior successful golfer, Lahaina News, May 6, 1987: 6.

MONTOYA, NANCY
— named lead broker for Piilani Village, Lahaina News, February 11, 1993: 11.

MONTOYA, NANCY AND MIKE
— featured, Lahaina News, December 3, 1998: 16.

MONTOYA, WARREN
— opening the Whaling Spree, Lahaina News, December 23, 1999: 13.

MO'OKIHA [CANOE]
— being assembled by Hui O Wa'a Kaulua, Lahaina News, March 7, 1996: 2.
— work continues, Lahaina News, April 4, 1996: 2.
— designer discusses inspiration, Lahaina News, May 2, 1996: 6.
— work to resume on canoe resumes, Lahaina News, March 26, 1998: 1,16.

— Leon Sterling to work on , Lahaina News, May 7, 1998: 1,17.

— Hui O Wa'a Kaulua to begin lashing, Lahaina News, March 11, 1999: 12.

MO'OLELE [CANOE]

— completes summer enrichment program, Lahaina News, August 6, 1986: 10.

— meeting of interested people to be held, Lahaina News, September 8, 1994: 5.

— receives grant from Lahaina Town Action Committee, Lahaina News, May 4, 1995: 4.

MOOMIN SHOP [BUSINESS]

— to open at Wharf Cinema Center, Lahaina News, April 30, 1998: 16.

— holds grant opening, Lahaina News, May 7, 1998: 15.

MOOMINS, THE

— children's show to be broadcast, Lahaina News, December 3, 1998: 17.

MOON, CAITLIN

— Scholar/Athlete of the Week, Lahaina News, November 19, 1998: 15.

MOON, DICKIE

— TS Restaurants vice president featured, Lahaina News, March 1, 2001: 1,24.

MOON, JADE

— visits Old Lahaina Cafe and Luau, Lahaina News, October 11, 1989: 9.

MOON, MEREDITH

— to lecture on Jungian psychology, Lahaina News, October 24, 1984: 4.

MOON, PETER [MUSICIAN]

— to perform "Morning at Seven", Lahaina News, August 1, 1984: 12.

— performance reviewed, Lahaina News, August 8, 1984: 12.

— to play in Maui in legitimate event, Lahaina News, December 3, 1986: 8.

— to play free concert at Lahaina Cannery Shopping Center, Lahaina News, December 21, 1988: 9.

— to perform at Hawaii Guitar Festival, Lahaina News, June 15, 1995: 11.

MOON, RICHARD "DICK"

— promoted to senior vice president at T S Restaurants, Lahaina News, February 3, 1994: 7.

MOONBOW BOUTIQUE [BUSINESS]

— to hold benefit for Save Our Seas, Lahaina News, August 10, 1988: 16.

MOONDOGGIES BAR AND RESTAURANT [BUSINESS]

— opens in Lahaina, Lahaina News, March 19, 1992: 16.

— to host "Here's Johnny Party" for Carson's retirement, Lahaina News, May 21, 1992: 17.

— celebrating one year, Lahaina News, February 25, 1993: 9.

— receiving noise complaints, attempting to limit, Lahaina News, November 11, 1993: 1,3.

— reviewed, Lahaina News, November 3, 1994: 25.

— to hold benefit for Surfrider Foundation, Lahaina News, November 23, 2000: 6.

MOONLIGHT MO'OLELO

— "Chicken Skin" storytelling to be held at Ritz-Carlton, Lahaina News, October 12, 2000: 19.

— to feature "Voyages From ... Voyage To", Lahaina News, November 9, 2000: 24.

— continues to be held at Ritz-Charlton, Lahaina News, December 7, 2000: 24.

— to be held at Ritz-Carlton on theme of "Life as a Paniolo (Hawaiian cowboy)", Lahaina News, February 8, 2001: 18.

MOORE, BRUCE

— becomes business support specialist for Lahaina Complex, Lahaina News, August 15, 2002: 1,20.

— discusses school improvements in Lahaina, Lahaina News, September 25, 2003: 1,2.

MOORE FOUNDATION

— donates to Lahainaluna High School, Lahaina News, March 7, 1990: 3.

MOORE, GENE

— job search coach featured, Lahaina News, March 14, 2002: 8.

MOORE, JOE

— attends movie at International Film Festival Week, Lahaina News, January 9, 1992: 12.

— to perform in "The Duke" at Maui Arts and Cultural Center, Lahaina News, September 29, 1994: 12.

MOORE, LANI

— wins golf tournament, Lahaina News, October 3, 1990: 7.

MOORE, LAWRENCE CLARK [ALSO KNOWN AS GARTH GIDEON]

— arrested for parole violation, Lahaina Sun, March 24, 1971: 1,8.

MOORE, LESLIE

— named general manager of Kapalua Hotel & Villas, Lahaina News, October 24, 1984: 3.

MOORE, MEG

— receives "Professional Awareness" award from Coldwell Banker McCormack Real Estate, Lahaina News, April 21, 1994: 12.

— named regional director of the Maui Board of Realtors, Lahaina News, October 27, 1994: 15.

MOORE, MICHAEL

— owner of Old Lahaina Cafe and Luau hoping to change parking laws, Lahaina News, December 12, 1991: 1.

MOORE, P.J. [ARTIST]

— to exhibit at Lahaina Art Society, Lahaina News, April 7, 1994: 12.

MOORE, TIM

— part-owner of Old Lahaina Cafe and Luau to attend public policy conference in Washington, D.C., Lahaina News, June 15, 1995: 10.

— receives U.S. Small Business Administration Annual Small Business Award, Lahaina News, May 23, 1996: 4.

— discusses economy, Lahaina News, April 16, 1998: 1,16.

MOORHEAD, EILEEN [WRITER]

— to read from her book "The Pretzel Family", Lahaina News, January 13, 2000: 12.

MOOSE MCGILLYCUDDY'S [RESTAURANT]

— reviewed, Lahaina News, March 29, 1989: 8.

— reviewed, Lahaina News, May 31, 1989: 20.

— featured, Lahaina News, September 27, 1989: 11.

— featured, Lahaina News, January 17, 1990: 10.

— Venus to perform, Lahaina News, February 7, 1990: 13.

— to hold toy drive, Lahaina News, November 26, 1992: 4.

— to celebrate 10th anniversary, Lahaina News, February 11, 1993: 3.

— loses lawsuit against musical group Sun King, Lahaina News, March 4, 1999: 11.

MORAN, MARC [COMEDIAN]

— to perform at Honolulu Comedy Club, Lahaina News, August 18, 1994: 15.

— to perform at Honolulu Comedy Club, Lahaina News, August 25, 1994: 14.

MORCA DANCE THEATRE

— to perform Flamenco, Lahaina News, January 15, 1986: 10.

MORE, ROGER

— elected chair of board for Hawaii Public Radio, Lahaina News, July 30, 1992: 12.

MOREA PARADISE
— to paint faces as fundraiser for Youth Ambassadors of America, Lahaina News, June 7, 1989: 9.

MORELL, BARRY [OPERA SINGER]
— performed Puccini's "Tosca" at Baldwin High School auditorium, Lahaina Sun, February 3, 1971: 8.

MORENO, CARLOS
— Scholar/Athlete of the Week, Lahaina News, December 6, 2001: 12.

MORENO, FERNANDO
— Scholar/Athlete of the Week, Lahaina News, December 27, 2001: 12.

MOREWOOD, TONY [COMEDIAN]
— to perform at Comedy Club and the Sports Page, Lahaina News, August 6, 1992: 11,13.

MOREY, SEAN [COMEDIAN]
— to perform at Comedy Club, Lahaina News, February 28, 1990: 11.
— to perform at Comedy Club and the Sports Page, Lahaina News, February 4, 1993: 13,15.
— to be hosted by Honolulu Comedy Club, Lahaina News, June 23, 1994: 11.

MORGAN, ALANA
— to discuss Feng Shui, Lahaina News, June 20, 2002: 17.

MORGAN, CRAIG AND CIMI [BUSINESS]
— open Ka'anapali business Center in Westin Maui, Lahaina News, February 17, 1994: 6.

MORGAN, NEAL "POPPY"
— passes away, Lahaina News, February 20, 1997: 1,16.

MORGAN STANLEY [BUSINESS]
— to hold "Live the Good Life", Lahaina News, November 22, 2001: 8.

MORGAN, TEDDY [MUSICIAN]
— to perform at Casanova's, Lahaina News, April 3, 1997: 11.

MORGANNA, TIARA ALANA
— to talk on "Exploring Sexuality and Love—A Workshop for Young Adults", Lahaina News, October 2, 2003: 17.

MORI, RUSSELL
— largest fish ever caught from shoreline anywhere in Hawaii immortalized in Gyotaku-style print, Lahaina News, July 4, 1990: 9.

MORIHARA, DAVID [POLITICIAN]
— asks the county if school bus system could be used for mass transit, Lahaina News, September 26, 1991: 1,3.

MORINOUE, HIROKI [ARTIST]
— woodblocks to be exhibited, Lahaina News, January 24, 1990: 14.
— to teach workshop on monoprints, Lahaina News, August 29, 1990: 13.
— to offer workshop on woodblocks, Lahaina News, April 10, 1991: 13.
— to exhibit at Maui Arts and Cultural Center, Lahaina News, November 8, 2001: 16.
— to teach "Playing with Mud, Textures and Color", Lahaina News, November 8, 2001: 16.

MORIS, ANDRE [DANCER]
— offering classes, Lahaina News, September 5, 1990: 4.
— to hold dance classes, Lahaina News, September 12, 1990: 8.

MORISAKI, LANNY
— member of Maui County Council, Lahaina Sun, December 30, 1970: 8.
— assists in conflict over signage, Lahaina Sun, January 13, 1971: 1,2.
— voted against improvement projects, Lahaina Sun, January 20, 1971: 1.

MORITA, CLYDE
— describes agriculture as major source of air pollution, Lahaina Sun, February 17, 1971: 1.
— setting up permanent air pollution testing station in Wailuku, Lahaina Sun, February 17, 1971: 1.

MORITA, JAY-ME
— Scholar/Athlete of the Week, Lahaina News, May 31, 2001: 13.

MORITA, PAT [ACTOR]
— to host Senior Citizens Fair, Lahaina News, November 4, 1993: 3.
— makes surprise entrance at King Kamehameha III School assembly, Lahaina News, November 23, 1995: 3.

MORIYAMA, COREY
— appointed manager of human resource development at Amfac, Inc., Lahaina News, October 17, 1990: 12.

MORMONS
— pageant held at Pulehu, Lahaina News, July 22, 1987: 10.

MORNING AT SEVEN [PLAY]
— to be performed by Maui Community Theatre, Lahaina News, May 2, 1984: 5.

MORPHIC RESONANCE [MUSICAL GROUP]
— to perform, Lahaina News, June 13, 2002: 14.
— to perform, Lahaina News, June 20, 2002: 17.
— continues to perform at Whalers Village, Lahaina News, July 11, 2002: 17.

MORRELL, DAVID
— vice president of Pioneer Mill, Co. named chairman of Maui United Way Pacesetter Campaign, Lahaina News, August 1, 1991: 3,4.
— appointed vice-president of diversified services at Hawaiian Commercial and Sugar Company, Lahaina News, October 24, 1996: 9.

MORRELL, MALIA
— selected for Maui All-Star swim team, Lahaina News, March 14, 1990: 11.

MORRELL, MARTI
— memorialized, Lahaina News, December 5, 1991: 1,3.

MORRIS, JOAN
— teaches water jogging, Lahaina News, February 18, 1999: 7.
— leads water aerobics class, Lahaina News, November 18, 1999: 7.

MORRIS, MAVERICK
— wins Lahaina Library's Summer Reading Program, Lahaina News, September 12, 1991: 3.

MORRIS RESORT INTERIORS [BUSINESS]
— new name for Rattan Concepts, Lahaina News, July 26, 2001: 8.

MORRIS, TRICIA
— senior loan officer at Maui Island Mortgage featured, Lahaina News, July 25, 1991: 7.
— owner of Premiere Mortgage discusses clauses in mortgages, Lahaina News, March 13, 2003: 7.

MORRISH, TOM
— president of Lahaina-Ka'anapali & Pacific Railroad speaks to West Maui Business Association regarding tourism in Lahaina, Lahaina Sun, December 9, 1970: 4.

MORRISON, MICHAEL
— to lead discussion of health awareness, Lahaina News, September 30, 1999: 13.

MORRISON, SHANNON
— to lead watercolor workshop "Painting Forms in Nature", Lahaina News, August 14, 2003: 16.

MORRISON, SHERI
— leaving as executive director of West Maui Taxpayers Association, Lahaina News, February 25, 1987: 20.
— leaving West Maui Taxpayers Association, Lahaina News, March 18, 1987: 2.

MORRISON, THEO [ARTIST]
— named president of Lahaina Arts Society, Lahaina News, March 21, 1990: 4.
— hired as arts coordinator at Malu'ulu O Lele Cultural Center, Lahaina News, November 14, 1990: 16.
— hired as arts coordinator at Malu'ulu O Lele Cultural Center, Lahaina News, November 21, 1990: 16,17.
— appointed executive director of Lahaina Town Action Committee, Lahaina News, January 30, 1991: 5.
— teaches art of basketry, Lahaina News, March 17, 1994: 10.
— executive director of LahainaTown Action Committee discusses opening of visitor's center, Lahaina News, August 11, 1994: 1,3.
— works with LahainaTown Action Committee, Lahaina News, April 24, 1997: 3.
— to speak to the American Association of Retired Persons, Lahaina News, August 27, 1998: 9.
— Executive Director may leave LahainaTown Action Committee, Lahaina News, March 25, 1999: 1,20.

MORROW, ALEXANDRA [ARTIST]
— reception to be held at Lotus Gallery, Lahaina News, February 13, 1991: 13.
— exhibiting at Lotus Gallery, Lahaina News, February 20, 1991: 12.
— to host watercolor class, Lahaina News, September 1, 1994: 15.

MORROW, TOM [POLITICIAN]
— calls Mayor Tavares a czar, Lahaina News, February 17, 1988: 1,20.
— to hold fund-raiser, Lahaina News, August 20, 1992: 4.
— to be recommended as vice chair of the Maui County Council, Lahaina News, September 9, 1993: 1,12.
— concerned about impact of sea wall fronting Napili Sunset Resort, Lahaina News, July 7, 1994: 1,7.
— new chair of Planning Committee, Lahaina News, January 5, 1995: 4.
— councilman met with Lahaina Citizen Advisory Committee members, Lahaina News, March 16, 1995: 2.
— agrees to send light industrial park sent back to Planning Committee, Lahaina News, March 28, 1996: 1,16.
— to hold public meeting, Lahaina News, October 10, 1996: 15.
— memorial held for, Lahaina News, November 14, 1996: 3.

MORTGAGES
— guide to, Lahaina News, November 16, 2000: 9.
— discussion of clauses in, Lahaina News, March 13, 2003: 7.
— see also real estate

MORTIMER, ANN
— lecture on "Clay and the Inner Voyage—A Personal Perspective", Lahaina News, February 6, 1985: 3.

MORTON, LISA
— crowned as Miss Maui, Lahaina News, February 4, 1993: 3.
— participating in Miss Hawaii competition, Lahaina News, June 10, 1993: 2.

MORTON, PETER
— owner of Hard Rock Cafe talks about recycling program, Lahaina News, July 25, 1990: 1,2.
— recognized for helping American Cancer Society fundraiser, Lahaina News, August 1, 1990: 4.

MORTON, RANDY
— named general manager of Four Seasons Resort Maui, Lahaina News, April 27, 1995: 10.

MOSELEY, NANCY [ARTIST]
— to teach jewelry making for children, Lahaina News, July 14, 1994: 15.

MOSER, STEVEN
— to hold fundraiser to send medical supplies to Nicaragua, Lahaina News, October 26, 1988: 17.
— new chief medical officer at Maui Memorial Medical Center, Lahaina News, June 20, 2002: 8.

MOSEULA, DORIS
— Scholar/Athlete of the Week, Lahaina News, December 21, 2000: 6.

MOSGROVE, JOHN
— architect opens shop, Lahaina News, October 1, 1992: 11.
— architect opens office at the Kahana Gateway Professional Building, Lahaina News, November 26, 1992: 13.

MOSQUITOES
— number of, Lahaina Times, October, 1980 volume 4 number 9: 1.
— becoming more numerous in Lahaina, Lahaina News, June 25, 1992: 1.

MOSS, HALSEY [ARTIST]
— exhibiting at 20th Century Masters Gallery, Lahaina News, February 27, 1991: 13.

MOSS, NIKKI [ARTIST]
— to be featured at Lahaina Arts Society, Lahaina News, March 28, 2002: 22.

MOSSMAN, BOYD
— judge to rule if Aloha Voyage can be granted a special use permit to operate tourist operation, Lahaina News, November 18, 1987: 1,11,12.
— judge reelected as president of Maui County Council of the Boy Scouts of America, Lahaina News, February 13, 1991: 5.

MOSUELA, DORIS [ARTIST]
— work to exhibited, Lahaina News, May 15, 1991: 4.

MOTELEWSKI, TRACY
— awarded first place for Residential Gross Commission Income as Prudential sales associates, Lahaina News, August 31, 2000: 11.
— named Prudential Real Estate Affiliates Chairman's Circle, Lahaina News, October 4, 2001: 8.

MOTHER HICKS [PLAY]
— to be performed by Maui Youth Theatre, Lahaina News, October 12, 1988: 9.

MOTHERS
— work and fulfillment described, Lahaina News, May 8, 1985: 1,8.

MOTHERS AGAINST DRUNK DRIVING (MADD)
— meet to discuss how to reduce drunk driving during graduation, Lahaina News, April 4, 1984: 3.
— presents Outstanding Law Enforcement Awards, Lahaina News, June 18, 1998: 2.
— seeking speakers for Youth Victim Impact Panel Program, Lahaina News, September 10, 1998: 6.
— seeking volunteers, Lahaina News, September 2, 1999: 15.
— seeking volunteers, Lahaina News, July 6, 2000: 6.
— seeking volunteer speakers for Youth Alcohol Impact Panel Program, Lahaina News, August 10, 2000: 8.
— seeking volunteers to speak for Youth Alcohol Impact Panel Program, Lahaina News, June 28, 2001: 11.

MOTHER'S DAY
— children's supplement features, Lahaina News, April 23, 1986: A,B,C,D.
— children sharing thoughts, Lahaina News, April 27, 1988: 7,8,9,10.
— essay writing contest organized by Westin Maui, Lahaina News, May 4, 1988: 14.
— shopping hints, Lahaina News, May 3, 1989: 14,15,16,17,18.
— letters, poems, ideas, Lahaina News, May 10, 1989: 9,10,11,16.
— Lahaina News to publish special gift guide, Lahaina News, April 11, 1990: 5.
— gift guide, Lahaina News, May 2, 1990: 7,8,9,10,11,12.

— specials described, Lahaina News, May 9, 1990: 14,15,19,22.
— gift guide, Lahaina News, May 1, 1991: 8,9,10,11,12,13.
— gift guide, Lahaina News, May 8, 1991: 1,9,10,11,12,18.
— specials, Lahaina News, May 7, 1992: 20.
— Royal Lahaina Resort contest results announced, Lahaina News, May 14, 1992: 3.
— events to be held, Lahaina News, April 29, 1993: 3.
— events to be held, Lahaina News, May 6, 1993: 18,19.
— winners of Lahaina Shopping Center giveaway announced, Lahaina News, June 3, 1993: 3.
— events, Lahaina News, May 5, 1994: 4,15,16.
— to be celebrated, Lahaina News, May 11, 1995: 11.
— celebrated, Lahaina News, May 2, 1996: 10,15.
— Lahaina Cannery to hold "Queen for a Day" competition, Lahaina News, May 9, 1996: 16.
— events to be held, Lahaina News, May 1, 1997: 2,8,9.
— contest winner announced, Lahaina News, May 15, 1997: 3.
— Maui Orchid Society to hold show for, Lahaina News, April 30, 1998: 17.
— to be celebrated at the Lahaina Cannery, Lahaina News, April 30, 1998: 17.
— Lahaina Cannery Mall to hold contest, Lahaina News, May 7, 1998: 20.
— restaurants offering special meals, Lahaina News, May 7, 1998: 8.
— to be celebrated at Lahaina Cannery Mall, Lahaina News, May 6, 1999: 20.
— events scheduled, Lahaina News, May 6, 1999: 9.
— restaurants to offer special meals, Lahaina News, May 4, 2000: 7.
— Lahaina Cannery Mall to host activities, Lahaina News, May 11, 2000: 20.
— Champagne Brunch to be held at Ka'anapali Beach Hotel, Lahaina News, May 3, 2001: 10.
— to be celebrated at Lahaina Cannery Mall, Lahaina News, May 10, 2001: 20.
— events to be held, Lahaina News, May 9, 2002: 16.
— to be celebrated, Lahaina News, May 8, 2003: 14.

MOTO, BRIAN
— appointed first deputy corporation counsel for the County of Maui, Lahaina News, February 7, 2002: 8.

MOTOR VEHICLES AND LICENSING, DIVISION OF
— opens new office, Lahaina News, May 28, 1992: 12.
— reschedules mobile licensing service, Lahaina News, July 30, 1992: 3,4.
— new office to be opened, Lahaina News, September 24, 1992: 3.
— to offer road exams on Saturdays, Lahaina News, November 23, 2000: 7.
— announces new hours, Lahaina News, March 8, 2001: 2.
— to add additional day of Motor Vehicle Registration, Lahaina News, April 26, 2001: 2.
— new hours, Lahaina News, July 4, 2002: 2.
— to establish Maui Mall Service Center, Lahaina News, May 8, 2003: 8.

MOTORCYCLES
— Maui County Council approves recreational site, Lahaina Sun, September 1, 1971: 12.
— Maui Motorcycle Club sponsoring moto-cross championship, Lahaina Sun, July 19, 1972: 14.

MOUFFE, DAVID [ARTIST]
— to display at Banyan Tree Gallery, Lahaina News, March 9, 1995: 11.

MOULLE, PIERRE
— chef demonstrates culinary talents at Kea Lani Hotel, Lahaina News, October 7, 1999: 16.

MO'UNGA, LOIENI
— Scholar/Athlete of the Week, Lahaina News, October 24, 1996: 12.

MOUNTAIN SLOPE WATER
— to conduct water testing and clinic, Lahaina News, August 23, 2001: 16.

MOVEMENT ARTS CENTER
— to host Congolese drum and dance classes, Lahaina News, November 5, 1998: 20.

MOVIES
— see films, specific films and actors

MOVING
— tips on how to move, Lahaina News, May 15, 1981: 10.

MOWAT, KEKOA
— contributing to success of Lahainaluna High School football , Lahaina News, September 11, 2003: 12.

MOYAD, MARK
— to speak on role of nutrition in reducing cancer risk, Lahaina News, October 19, 2000: 11.

MOYNAHAN, MIKE
— owner of Kama'aina Clubmakers named Western Regional Clubmaker of the year, Lahaina News, September 11, 2003: 8.

MOYNAHAN, PETE
— CEO of C. Brewer Homes, Inc. speaks about issues with proposed Villages of Leiali'i, Lahaina News, December 29, 1994: 1,3.

MOZART, WOLFGANG AMADEUS [MUSICIAN]
— 200th anniversary of the death of to be commemorated, Lahaina News, January 16, 1991: 11.
— to be performed by Maui Symphony Orchestra, Lahaina News, October 15, 1992: 18.

MOZLEY, JIM
— Amfac vice president discusses Amfac redefining its development goals, Lahaina News, January 2, 1991: 1.

MR. AND MS. MAUI ONION PAGEANT
— to be held, Lahaina News, March 14, 1990: 3.

MR. SUB [RESTAURANT]
— to open in Napili, Lahaina News, December 19, 1991: 13.

MR. SUNSHINE [MUSICAL GROUP]
— to perform at Casanova's, Lahaina News, January 16, 1992: 18.

MR. WINE [BUSINESS]
— opens, Lahaina News, June 24, 1993: 9.
— to hold Pacific Luau, Lahaina News, May 29, 1997: 16.

MRANTZ, MARK
— new general manager at Aston Ka'anapali Shores, Lahaina News, October 3, 2002: 8.

MRS. HAWAII PAGEANT
— Terri Lynn Mailholt competes at pageant, Lahaina News, December 7, 1988: 2.
— promoted by Sherry Barbier and Verna Boonstra, Lahaina News, April 23, 1992: 4.
— scheduled, Lahaina News, April 23, 1992: 5,7.
— Jackie Allaire to compete, Lahaina News, May 21, 1992: 4.
— tickets available, Lahaina News, June 4, 1992: 14.
— tickets available, Lahaina News, June 11, 1992: 18.
— Colleen Nagasako as Lahaina contestant, Lahaina News, June 11, 1992: 3.
— Sherry Collins crowned, Lahaina News, June 18, 1992: 4.
— to be held, Lahaina News, April 29, 1993: 2.
— to be held at Ka'anapali Beach Hotel, Lahaina News, June 3, 1993: 3.
— pageant canceled, Lahaina News, June 17, 1993: 2.
— Sharon Weddle to represent Hawaii, Lahaina News, August 4, 1994: 4.
— entry forms available, Lahaina News, January 12, 1995: 4.

MS. ANNUAL JACKPOT BEAUTY PAGEANT
— held, Lahaina News, October 15, 1986: 3.

MU [ROCK GROUP]
— to play in Maui, Lahaina Sun, May 30, 1973: 11.

MUCH ADO ABOUT NOTHING [PLAY]
— to be performed at Hui Noʻeau Visual Arts Center , Lahaina News, July 21, 1994: 12.
— featured, Lahaina News, July 28, 1994: 15.

MUELLER, FED [ARTIST]
— antiques donated to Honolulu Academy of Arts to be exhibited, Lahaina News, August 15, 1990: 17.

MUELLER, JACK AND ROMELDA
— given Pejcha Award for community service, Lahaina News, December 2, 1993: 8.

MUELLER, MARION
— confirmed as vice principal of Lahainaluna High School, Lahaina News, August 22, 1990: 4.

MUELLER, NED [ARTIST]
— offering outdoor figure and landscape painting workshop, Lahaina News, April 12, 2001: 11.

MUKAISU, TERUO
— resident of Wainee Village discusses future, Lahaina News, August 1, 1990: 1,6.

MULDAUR, MARIA [MUSICIAN]
— to perform at Embassy Suites Resort, Lahaina News, May 30, 1991: 7.
— to perform at "Hawaiian Islands Rhythm and Blues Mele", Lahaina News, May 21, 1998: 17.
— blues singer to perform with Red Hot Bluesiana Band at Royal Lahaina Resort, Lahaina News, October 3, 2002: 14.

MULHOLLAND, MIKE
— joins First Hawaiian Bank as loan officer, Lahaina News, November 14, 2002: 8.

MULKEY, DAVE
— new manager of Lahaina Ace Hardware, Lahaina News, April 3, 1997: 10.

MULL, BILL [ARTIST]
— photographer to give slide show, Lahaina News, March 6, 1997: 10.

MULLAHEY, RAMONA
— to present workshops on fundraising, Lahaina News, April 19, 1989: 13.
— to offer workshop on "Fundraising Strategies: Defining Your Market", Lahaina News, April 19, 1989: 3,13.

MULLANE, ROBERT
— to lecture on "Coastal Processes in Maui", Lahaina News, September 16, 1999: 13.

MULLANY, MITCH [COMEDIAN]
— to perform at Comedy Club, Lahaina News, August 8, 1991: 12.

MULLER, BERNARD [CHEF]
— chef at Marriott reviewed, Lahaina News, March 6, 1985: 4.

MULLER, JENNIFER [DANCER]
— to perform for Maui Philharmonic Society, Lahaina News, October 14, 1993: 16.

MULLER, MARION
— named principal of Lokelani Intermediate School, Lahaina News, September 10, 1992: 11.

MULLINS, JOHN
— renting Animal Farm, Lahaina Sun, January 27, 1971: 1,5.

MULLINS, VIRGINIA
— given eviction notice for "Animal Farm" house, Lahaina Sun, February 24, 1971: 7.

MULTI-ETHNIC CULTURAL CELEBRATION
— to be held March 8 at Baldwin High School, Lahaina News, February 26, 1986: 3.

MULTICULTURAL FESTIVAL
— to be held at Lihikai School, Lahaina News, March 26, 1992: 5.

MUMFORD, KATHLEEN
— discusses proposed swimming pool, Lahaina News, March 23, 1988: 1.

MUNAR, TIANA
— receives scholarship from Kapalua Land Co., Lahaina News, August 26, 1993: 12.

MUNCH, EDVARD [ARTIST]
— show to open at Honolulu Academy of Arts, Lahaina News, September 12, 1990: 19.

MUNDO, RAND
— to discuss reflexology, Lahaina News, January 14, 1999: 13.

MUNEO YAMAMOTO CONTRACTOR
— awarded contract to repair wharf at Lahaina Harbor, Lahaina News, November 18, 1987: 3.

MUNNELLY, MIKE [COMEDIAN]
— to perform at Comedy Club, Lahaina News, September 30, 1993: 12.

MUNSON, R.W.
— to present to Napilihau Campaign Recycle Maui on recycling, Lahaina News, June 20, 1991: 3.

MUNTAL, J.P.
— Hawaii Public Radio person to speak on "Maui Hiroshima-Nagasaki Interfaith Peace Prayer Day", Lahaina News, July 30, 1998: 16.
— to speak on "Maui Hiroshima-Nagasaki Interfaith Peace Prayer Day", Lahaina News, August 6, 1998: 20.

MUR ROBLES, VIVIAN
— hired by Grand Hyatt Wailea, Lahaina News, February 20, 1992: 10.

MUR, VIVIAN
— appointed vice president for Maui Chapter's Hotel Sales and Marketing Association, Lahaina News, October 3, 1990: 9.

MURAKAMI, PAT
— discusses installation of guardrails in Wahikuli Park, Lahaina Sun, August 18, 1971: 3.

MURAKAMI, RALPH
— to replace Roy Hirose as Maui Deputy District Superintendent, Lahaina News, January 30, 1992: 12.
— named as superintendent for Maui District Schools, Lahaina News, January 14, 1993: 3.
— Maui District Superintendent discusses study survey revealing drug use habits, Lahaina News, December 23, 1993: 1,3.

MURAMATSU, MASUMI
— to speak "Humor in Leadership: Reflections of a Simultaneous Interpreter", Lahaina News, November 30, 2000: 17.

MURAMOTO, JEROME
— catches 567.2 pound marlin at Jackpot tournament, Lahaina News, November 7, 1984: 3.

MURAOKA, LENORE
— golfer participates in Women's Kemper Open, Lahaina News, March 14, 1984: 21.

MURASHIGE, GEORGE
— appointed to County Planning Commission, Lahaina Sun, January 13, 1971: 8.

MURATA, TERRY HOLOKAI [ARTIST]
— to offer courses for Lahaina Arts Society, Lahaina News, November 4, 1987: 10.

MURAYAMA, MILTON [WRITER]
— to read from "All I Asking For Is My Body", Lahaina News, May 21, 1992: 18.
— to read at Hui No'eau Visual Arts Center, Lahaina News, May 28, 1992: 18.

MURAYAMA, SHIGETO
— discusses Board of Water Supply plans, Lahaina Sun, January 20, 1971: 1.

MURDOCK, COLIN
— discusses Maui Electric Company's new transmission line, Lahaina Sun, January 20, 1971: 8.
— represents Maui Electric Company's opposition to alternate route for electric poles, Lahaina Sun, March 3, 1971: 2.
— appointed to the Small Business Administration District Advisory Council for Hawaii, Lahaina Sun, April 14, 1971: 6.
— see also Maui Electric Company

MURDOCK, DAVID
— dedicates recreational complex on Lana'i, Lahaina News, January 20, 1988: 3.

MUROMOTO, THOMAS
— appointed executive chef at Ka'anapali Beach Hotel, Lahaina News, November 4, 1999: 11.
— chef wins A Taste of Lahaina, Lahaina News, September 26, 2002: 9.

MURPHY, BOB
— golfer to defend Ka'anapali Classic title, Lahaina News, October 19, 1995: 12.

MURPHY, HELEN
— passes away, her life remembered, Lahaina News, April 29, 1987: 4.

MURPHY, KARYN
— Educator of the Month at Kimo's Restaurant, Lahaina News, February 21, 2002: 3.
— teacher recognized by Kimo's Restaurant, Lahaina News, March 28, 2002: 8.

MURPHY, MARCIA
— Westin Maui "Manager of the Second Quarter", Lahaina News, September 22, 1994: 13.

MURPHY, MARK [ARTIST]
— to exhibit at Lahaina Arts Society, Lahaina News, May 1, 2003: 14.

MURPHY, MARY [ARTIST]
— to help celebrate 40th anniversary of Lahaina Arts Society, Lahaina News, May 9, 2002: 14.
— to exhibit at Lahaina Arts Society, Lahaina News, May 15, 2003: 17.

MURPHY-GOODE WINERY [BUSINESS]
— featured at The Prince Court Restaurant, Lahaina News, May 15, 1991: 12.

MURRAY, ALLAN [COMEDIAN]
— to perform at Comedy Club, Lahaina News, March 7, 1990: 13.
— to perform at Comedy Club and the Sports Page, Lahaina News, November 28, 1991: 14,15.

MURRAY, BETSY LOPES
— participant in Makawao Rodeo, Lahaina News, July 4, 1984: 6.

MURRAY LOUIS DANCE COMPANY [TROUPE]
— to perform with Maui Philharmonic Society, Lahaina News, April 20, 1988: 11.

MURRAY, PETER
— named senior director of marketing and planning for Discovery Airways, Lahaina News, November 1, 1989: 8.

MURRAY, RICHARD AND BETSY
— volunteers at Lahaina Baptist Church featured, Lahaina News, November 21, 2002: 1,2.

MUSASHI JAPANESE CUISINE [RESTAURANT]
— reviewed, Lahaina News, April 13, 1988: 6.
— reviewed, Lahaina News, August 17, 1988: 8.
— reviewed, Lahaina News, November 30, 1988: 8.
— reviewed, Lahaina News, February 22, 1989: 8.
— reviewed, Lahaina News, June 21, 1989: 15.
— featured, Lahaina News, October 18, 1989: 11.
— featured, Lahaina News, January 31, 1990: 12.
— featured, Lahaina News, April 23, 1992: 28.

MUSCLE CLASSIC MAUI
— to be held, Lahaina News, June 5, 1997: 16.

MUSCULAR DYSTROPHY ASSOCIATION
— Telethon to be held at Lahaina Cannery Shopping Center, Lahaina News, August 26, 1987: 3.
— Bowling against Dystrophy fundraiser to be held, Lahaina News, February 6, 1992: 4.
— to hold benefit auction, Lahaina News, July 23, 1992: 7.
— Maui Youth Ambassadors to hold craft fair in conjunction with Telethon, Lahaina News, August 25, 1994: 5.
— offering support groups, Lahaina News, December 30, 1999: 15.
— honors Edward Long with Personal Achievement Award, Lahaina News, July 18, 2002: 18.

MUSHROOMS, MAGIC
— allegedly sourced in Red China, Lahaina Times, August, 1980 volume 4 number 7: 2, 6.

MUSIC
— Honolulu Symphony plays Beethoven at Baldwin Auditorium, Lahaina Sun, November 11, 1970: 1.
— Seabury Hall Chapel Choir performing at Holy Innocents' Church, Lahaina Sun, November 11, 1970: 4.
— Review of Honolulu Symphony's presentation of Beethoven's music, Lahaina Sun, November 18, 1970: 3.
— events in Maui reviewed, Lahaina Sun, March 10, 1971: 2.
— performance by Hawaii Brass Ensemble and Chamber Singers perform at Baldwin High School, Lahaina Sun, March 17, 1971: 1.
— Lahainaluna High School Concert Band performance set, Lahaina Sun, April 7, 1971: 8.
— bell concert to be held at Lahaina Methodist Church, Lahaina Sun, April 7, 1971: 8.
— Hawaii Youth Symphony and Junior Orchestra to perform at Ka'anapali Beach Hotel, Lahaina Sun, April 14, 1971: 2.
— ukulele lessons held weekly at Kam III School by Masami Hironaka, Lahaina Sun, April 14, 1971: 6.
— concert of Bach's works presented at Maui Community College, Lahaina Sun, April 14, 1971: 8.
— pianist Walter Hautzig offers recital at Baldwin Auditorium, Lahaina Sun, April 21, 1971: 2.
— student bands to play on Lana'i, Lahaina Sun, April 21, 1971: 8.
— Azusa Pacific College Dynamics Chorale perform at Lahaina Baptist Mission, Lahaina Sun, June 16, 1971: 3.
— Maui Philharmonic Society conducting a fund drive, Lahaina Sun, August 4, 1971: 1.
— traditional Japanese music concert at the Lahaina Jodo Mission, Lahaina Sun, August 11, 1971: 5.
— flute concert by Elliot Weisgarber at Lahaina Jodo Mission, Lahaina Sun, August 18, 1971: 5.
— Maui Philharmonic Society has raised $7000, Lahaina Sun, September 15, 1971: 4.
— Pianist Mischa Dichter to play at Baldwin Auditorium, Lahaina Sun, October 20, 1971: 13.
— programs for the spring announced, Lahaina Sun, October 20, 1971: 13.
— reviewed in editorial, Lahaina Sun, October 27, 1971: 2.
— Maui Philharmonic Society requests funds from Maui County, Lahaina Sun, November 10, 1971: 13.

— grant from Maui Council to subsidize school concerts, Lahaina Sun, December 22, 1971: 7.

— Maui Philharmonic Society receives funds from Maui County, Lahaina Sun, January 12, 1972: 5.

— free concert offered by Hawaii Youth Symphony at Sheraton Maui Hotel, Lahaina Sun, January 26, 1972: 13.

— USC Chamber Singers perform at Baldwin Auditorium, Lahaina Sun, February 2, 1972: 14.

— violin recital to begin Maui Filipino Fiesta, Lahaina Sun, February 9, 1972: 14.

— Honolulu Symphony Orchestra performing Cinderella, Lahaina Sun, February 23, 1972: 8.

— Diamond Head Crater Celebration plans described, Lahaina Sun, March 8, 1972: 9.

— Song Of Norway by Edvard Grieg to be performed at Iao Theatre, Lahaina Sun, March 15, 1972: 5.

— Honolulu Symphony Orchestra performing Peter and the Wolf, with narration in pidgin, Lahaina Sun, March 15, 1972: 9.

— County Department of Parks and Recreation offering ukulele classes, Lahaina Sun, March 29, 1972: 11.

— pianist Gary Graffman to play, Lahaina Sun, April 5, 1972: 5.

— Haiku Boggie Festival held, Lahaina Sun, April 5, 1972: 8.

— Maui District Music Festival to be held at Baldwin Auditorium and War Memorial Gym, Lahaina Sun, April 19, 1972: 10.

— "Music From the 4th Stream" to be held at Baldwin High School, Lahaina Sun, April 19, 1972: 6.

— "The Me Nobody Knows" to be performed at St. Anthony High School, Lahaina Sun, May 10, 1972: 14.

— details of "The Me Nobody Knows", Lahaina Sun, May 17, 1972: 10.

— Sing Out Maui chorus to perform at Baldwin High School Auditorium, Lahaina Sun, June 14, 1972: 14.

— review of event at Queen Theatre, Lahaina Sun, August 2, 1972: 14.

— Aloha Week luau scheduled at the old Lahaina prison, Lahaina Sun, October 4, 1972: 14.

— rock bands play at Maui Community College, Lahaina Sun, October 11, 1972: 11.

— Honolulu Symphony Orchestra to hold free open rehearsals, Lahaina Sun, October 11, 1972: 19.

— Honolulu Symphony Orchestra to hold free open rehearsals, Lahaina Sun, October 11, 1972: 22.

— singer Emma Veary performs on Maui, Lahaina Sun, November 22, 1972: 22.

— Rolling Stones play in Honolulu, Lahaina Sun, January 31, 1973: 5.

— Eddie Kamae will use grant money to preserve the music of elderly Maui musicians, Lahaina Sun, March 21, 1973: 10.

— fiddle music at Baldwin auditorium reviewed, Lahaina Sun, March 21, 1973: 7.

— Tuna de Caminos [group] to play traditional Spanish music at Maui Community College, Lahaina Sun, March 28, 1973: 11.

— falsetto singing at Lahaina Civic Center, Lahaina Sun, April 11, 1973: 11.

— Elizabeth Cole and Frank Tavares to perform at Maui Community College, Lahaina Sun, April 18, 1973: 10.

— Genoa Keawe to perform at the Lahaina Civic Center, Lahaina Sun, May 16, 1973: 3.

— rock group Mu to play in Maui, Lahaina Sun, May 30, 1973: 11.

— chanter George Naope to perform at Baldwin High School, Lahaina Sun, August 22, 1973: 5.

— Tom Petty and the Heartbreakers reviewed, Lahaina News, May 1, 1980: 4.

— review of Zuproc [band], Lahaina Times, June, 1980 volume 4 number 5: 3.

— surf music in 1980, Lahaina Times, June, 1980 volume 4 number 5: 3.

— review of Dancer (band), Lahaina Times, June, 1980 volume 4 number 5: 3.

— Dave Evans record song "Operation Green Harvest" on cultivation of marijuana, Lahaina Times, July, 1980 volume 4 number 6: 1.

— "Seed to Seed" discussed, Lahaina Times, July, 1980 volume 4 number 6: 8.

— Drug Bust Song by Danny Paradise, Lahaina Times, August, 1980 volume 4 number 7: 1.

— Cecilio And Kapono playing in Lahaina, Lahaina Times, September, 1980 volume 4 number 8: 2, 3.

— review of Razor, Lahaina Times, October, 1980 volume 4 number 9: 4.

— Tokyo String Quartet to play at St. Anthony's Church Center, Lahaina News, October 15, 1982: 12.

— Honolulu Brass Quintet to play, Lahaina News, August 1, 1983: 10.

— situation in Maui described, Lahaina News, August 15, 1983: 12.

— Merrell Fankhauser releases an album, Lahaina Times, August 20, 1983 volume 7 number 8: 1.

— status of the amphitheatre as a location, Lahaina Times, August 20, 1983 volume 7 number 8: 1.

— bands in the 1960s playing free concerts, Lahaina Times, August 20, 1983 volume 7 number 8: 1.

— concert scene in Maui discussed, Lahaina Times, August 20, 1983 volume 7 number 8: 1.

— problems with a concert that did not occur, Lahaina Times, August 20, 1983 volume 7 number 8: 1, 2.

— La Familia Restaurant playing live music, Lahaina News, October 12, 1983: 12.

— review of upcoming Halloween events, Lahaina News, October 26, 1983: 14.

— Tom Jones to play on Maui, Lahaina News, November 9, 1983: 12.

— Honolulu Symphony performs, Lahaina News, March 28, 1984: 4.

— Maui Community College Ho'olaule'a to feature, Lahaina News, April 11, 1984: 5.

— Hawaiian Appreciation Songfest planned, Lahaina News, May 23, 1984: 5.

— West Maui Youth Center sponsors first teen disco show, Lahaina News, July 18, 1984: 4.

— Maui Symphony Orchestra to perform at Gala Concert, Lahaina News, September 19, 1984: 3.

— KPOA-FM 93 will begin airing jazz music, Lahaina News, October 10, 1984: 17.

— general discussion of music in West Maui, Lahaina News, January 9, 1985: 17.

— discussion of improved financial situation of industry in Lahaina, Lahaina News, January 23, 1985: 17.

— recounting of a week of music in Honolulu, Lahaina News, January 30, 1985: 17.

— update on changes to venues, Lahaina News, February 20, 1985: 12.

— criticism of Longhi's charging $5 cover, Lahaina News, March 6, 1985: 7.

— description of difficulty in bringing bands to Maui, Lahaina News, March 13, 1985: 16.

— summary of schedule at Maui Community College's Ho'olaule'a, Lahaina News, April 24, 1985: 12.

— Hawaii Chamber Orchestra to perform Bach and Handel, Lahaina News, June 5, 1985: 8.

— jazz playing at Maui Lu, Lahaina News, June 12, 1985: 10.

— review of music celebrating Kamehameha Day, Lahaina News, June 26, 1985: 10.

— July 4th week events described, Lahaina News, July 3, 1985: 10.

— Ka'anapali venues attempting to draw locals, Lahaina News, July 10, 1985: 10.

— advice on where to find live music, Lahaina News, July 17, 1985: 10.

— upcoming Hawaiian music events detailed, Lahaina News, July 31, 1985: 10.

— request for readers to say what they want to see in music in West Maui, Lahaina News, August 14, 1985: 10.

— callers complain about local music scene, Lahaina News, August 21, 1985: 10.

— Longhi's reopens, Lahaina News, August 28, 1985: 10.

— song about Salvation Army Thrift Store, Lahaina News, August 28, 1985: 7.

— Makaha Sons of Ni'ihau to play at Royal Lahaina Resort, Lahaina News, September 4, 1985: 10.

— Maui Symphony Orchestra season announced, Lahaina News, September 18, 1985: 3.

— concern expressed that music scene is in decline, Lahaina News, October 16, 1985: 10.

— editorial criticizing changes in policy at the Lahaina Civic Center which will make concerts less viable, Lahaina News, October 16, 1985: 2.

— police Captain Lee's proposal to limit number of tickets and alcohol sale at Lahaina Civic Center criticized, Lahaina News, October 23, 1985: 10.

— Halloween events listed, Lahaina News, October 30, 1985: 10.

— review of Halloween events, Lahaina News, November 6, 1985: 10.

— praise for KAOI-FM, Lahaina News, November 20, 1985: 8.

— few events on Maui, Lahaina News, December 4, 1985: 8.

— Christmas events detailed, Lahaina News, December 18, 1985: 8.

— Morca Dance Theatre to perform Flamenco, Lahaina News, January 15, 1986: 10.

— discussion of music scene at beginning of 1986, Lahaina News, January 15, 1986: 8.

— description of improvements in the music scene, Lahaina News, January 22, 1986: 8.

— Prazak String Quartet to perform at St. Anthony's Church Center, Lahaina News, January 29, 1986: 3.

— Hawaiian steel guitar described, Lahaina News, February 5, 1986: 10.

— opera to be broadcast by Hawaii Public Radio and Hawaii Opera Theatre, Lahaina News, February 12, 1986: 3.

— history of service charges, Lahaina News, February 26, 1986: 8.

— Mirecourt Piano Trio to perform at St. Anthony Church Center, Lahaina News, March 12, 1986: 3.

— Ohana Concert to feature Olomana and Kalapana, Lahaina News, April 2, 1986: 8.

— Zoofest reviewed, Lahaina News, April 9, 1986: 8.

— Honolulu Boys' Choir to perform at Lahaina Civic Center, Lahaina News, April 30, 1986: 3.

— Maui Philharmonic to perform Schubert Octet, Lahaina News, May 14, 1986: 3.

— koto and shakuhachi concert to be held, Lahaina News, May 21, 1986: 3.

— future of in Maui seen as bleak, Lahaina News, May 28, 1986: 4.

— Norman Calvin Franco hoping to create a marching band, Lahaina News, July 23, 1986: 3.

— local scene updates, Lahaina News, July 30, 1986: 7.

— Fifth annual Kapalua Music Festival to be held, Lahaina News, August 6, 1986: 18.

— Jimmy Buffett to perform at Royal Lahaina Tennis Stadium, Lahaina News, August 13, 1986: 8.

— Concord String Quartet opens Maui Philharmonic Society's season, Lahaina News, August 27, 1986: 12,13.

— lessons to be offered by Joan Hayden, Lahaina News, September 17, 1986: 3.

— review of summer events, Lahaina News, September 24, 1986: 8.

— Concord String Quartet to play, Lahaina News, October 1, 1986: 12.

— Bettine Ware and Richard Patterson to perform classical music at Makawao Union Church, Lahaina News, October 8, 1986: 5.

— update on music scene in West Maui, Lahaina News, October 8, 1986: 8.

— Na Mele O Maui scheduled, Lahaina News, November 5, 1986: 1,16.

— changes in availability of jazz in Lahaina described, Lahaina News, November 5, 1986: 8.

— fake Peter Moon concert rips off customers, Lahaina News, December 3, 1986: 8.

— local gift ideas for the holiday season, Lahaina News, December 17, 1986: 8.

— Musicfest at La Familia, Lahaina News, December 24, 1986: 3.

— Mike Warner ends his column with Lahaina News, Lahaina News, December 31, 1986: 8.

— Chicago Brass to perform at Wailea Shopping Village, Lahaina News, February 11, 1987: 11.

— life of a bodyguard for rock stars described, Lahaina News, February 11, 1987: 8,12.

— Maui Symphony presents an opera gala, Lahaina News, February 18, 1987: 10.

— Royal Hawaiian Resort to feature Hawaiian concert, Lahaina News, May 13, 1987: 14.

— "Year of the Hawaiian" concert to be held, Lahaina News, May 27, 1987: 3.

— John Linnell releases single "The Dream Lives On", Lahaina News, December 16, 1987: 15.

— conditions on Maui discussed, Lahaina News, January 20, 1988: 8.

— vocal workshop to be held at Unity Church, Lahaina News, April 6, 1988: 20.

— Na Mele O Na Kupuna (songs of the elderly) published, Lahaina News, June 8, 1988: 13.

— Mendelssohn String Quartet presented by Maui Philharmonic Society, Lahaina News, November 30, 1988: 16.

— drummers from Sado Island to perform, Lahaina News, January 18, 1989: 9.

— Chinese classical and folk music to be performed, Lahaina News, February 8, 1989: 5.

— Big Band sound returns to Maui Inter-Continental Wailea Hotel, Lahaina News, February 22, 1989: 13.

— Margaret Cameron Scholarship available to music students from Maui Philharmonic Society, Lahaina News, February 22, 1989: 13.

— April events detailed, Lahaina News, April 5, 1989: 9.

— school bands to perform at Maui High School auditorium, Lahaina News, May 3, 1989: 12.

— concert set for Dickenson Square, Lahaina News, June 21, 1989: 1.

— Sheraton Maui to offer series, Lahaina News, July 26, 1989: 6.

— reflections on Woodstock, Lahaina News, August 16, 1989: 16.

— "Jazz in Hawaii" to be shown on television, Lahaina News, September 20, 1989: 16.

— Na Mele O Maui, a Hawaiian song celebration, scheduled for Ka'anapali Beach Resort, Lahaina News, September 20, 1989: 3.

— Lahaina Sound recording studio at Lahaina Square Shopping Center, Lahaina News, September 20, 1989: 9.

— non-denominational gospel concert to be held, Lahaina News, January 17, 1990: 12.

— Maui Community College to host music of old Hawaii, Lahaina News, January 17, 1990: 12.

— Hyatt Regency events listed, Lahaina News, March 21, 1990: 14.

— Reggae Sunsplash '90 to be held at War Memorial Stadium, Lahaina News, May 9, 1990: 18.

— Maui District High School Music Festival to be held, Lahaina News, May 9, 1990: 5.

— Kapalua Music Festival to be held, Lahaina News, May 23, 1990: 13.

— Dixieland brass band to participate in Kamehameha Day Parade, Lahaina News, June 6, 1990: 11.

— Ki Ho 'Alu slack key guitar festival to be held, Lahaina News, July 11, 1990: 15.

— Ki Ho 'Alu slack key guitar festival to be held, Lahaina News, July 18, 1990: 11.

— Mele O Makena Hawaiian Music Festival to be held, Lahaina News, July 25, 1990: 11.
— Maui Jazz Festival to be held, Lahaina News, July 25, 1990: 11.
— Festival of the Bands to be held at Maui Mall, Lahaina News, August 8, 1990: 13.
— Ki Ho 'Alu slack key guitar festival to be held at Ala Moana Park Oahu, Lahaina News, August 8, 1990: 17.
— Billboard Song Contest to be presented by Kentucky Fried Chicken, Lahaina News, August 8, 1990: 5.
— Moloka'i Music Festival scheduled, Lahaina News, September 12, 1990: 16.
— disco music at Casanova's, Lahaina News, October 24, 1990: 15.
— Festival of the Bands scheduled for Maui Mall, Lahaina News, November 7, 1990: 12.
— details for Festival of the Bands, Lahaina News, November 21, 1990: 15.
— "The Kingdom Song" cantata to be performed, Lahaina News, December 12, 1990: 4.
— Lahainaluna High School concert band to present Annual Spring Concert, Lahaina News, April 10, 1991: 3.
— Hawaiian Jam Music Festival to be held at Maui Prince Hotel, Lahaina News, May 1, 1991: 16,18.
— Kapalua Music Festival to be held, Lahaina News, May 8, 1991: 19.
— Mele O Makena Hawaiian music festival to be held, Lahaina News, June 13, 1991: 13.
— more jazz to be expected on Maui, Lahaina News, June 13, 1991: 18.
— Maui Prince offering Big Band music, Lahaina News, June 20, 1991: 10.
— Moloka'i Music Festival to be held in September, Lahaina News, June 20, 1991: 12.
— El Crab Catcher hosting musicians to try out new material, Lahaina News, June 27, 1991: 13.
— jazz featured at Maui Marriott Resort's Lobby Bar, Lahaina News, July 11, 1991: 11.
— 3rd annual Mele O Makena festival to be held, Lahaina News, July 11, 1991: 15.
— Maui Prince offering Big Band music, Lahaina News, July 11, 1991: 15.
— Villa Restaurant at Westin Maui to feature cabaret lounge, Lahaina News, July 18, 1991: 9.
— Embassy Suites Resorts to hold "Maui Summer Music Splash", Lahaina News, July 25, 1991: 10.
— Ka'anapali Beach Hotel hosting "Beat the Heat" event, Lahaina News, August 8, 1991: 12.
— Hawaiian International Music Festival to be held at the Maui War Memorial Stadium, Lahaina News, August 8, 1991: 14.
— "Maui Summer Music Splash" detailed, Lahaina News, August 15, 1991: 12.
— Ka'ahumanu Center to offer free summer concerts, Lahaina News, August 15, 1991: 15.
— Studio 505 to feature jazz, Lahaina News, September 26, 1991: 14.
— fundraiser for local children's charities to be held at Maui Marriott Resort, Lahaina News, October 10, 1991: 14.
— slack key festival sponsored by Bank of Hawaii, Lahaina News, October 17, 1991: 17.
— Steve Sargenti critical of liquor commission rules concerning performance, Lahaina News, December 19, 1991: 1.
— Friends of the Maui Symphony appoints James French as musical director, Lahaina News, January 2, 1992: 5.
— reasons for larger concerts being canceled discussed, Lahaina News, March 26, 1992: 10.
— 11th annual Kapalua Music Festival to be held, Lahaina News, March 26, 1992: 13.
— "Arica and Friends" concert to benefit Maui County children's Advocacy Center, Lahaina News, April 9, 1992: 21.

— Foothill College Fanfairs Vocal Jazz Ensemble to perform, Lahaina News, April 16, 1992: 22.
— Maui District Intermediate Music Festival to be held, Lahaina News, April 23, 1992: 30.
— Maui District High School Music Festival to be held, Lahaina News, May 7, 1992: 24.
— Trash Bash to held, Lahaina News, May 14, 1992: 3.
— Lahaina Cannery Mall to hold karaoke contest, Lahaina News, May 21, 1992: 17.
— "Maui Juice Fest, Summer Blastoff Concert" to be held, Lahaina News, June 11, 1992: 22.
— Oli Exhibition seeking kumu hula to participate, Lahaina News, July 2, 1992: 6,7.
— Hui No'eau Visual Arts Center to present "County Jam", Lahaina News, July 16, 1992: 22.
— harpist Maria Casale to perform at St. Anthony Church Center, Lahaina News, July 16, 1992: 22.
— Maui County Commission on Culture and the Arts sponsoring free concerts, Lahaina News, August 20, 1992: 22.
— A Journey Through Rhythm to be held, Lahaina News, August 27, 1992: 6.
— Kupuna Ukulele Serenaders to perform at Annual Senior Citizens' Fair, Lahaina News, September 10, 1992: 3.
— benefits for victims of hurricane Iniki to be held, Lahaina News, October 1, 1992: 15.
— Kokua Kaua'i Relief Concert held, Lahaina News, October 1, 1992: 3.
— "The Art of the Chanter" to be held at Maui High School Gymnatorium, Lahaina News, October 22, 1992: 18.
— "The Art of the Chanter" to be held at Maui High School Gymnatorium, Lahaina News, October 29, 1992: 20.
— Broadcast Music, Inc (BMI) to enforce music copyright laws on Maui, Lahaina News, November 12, 1992: 1,17.
— clarification of copyright law, Lahaina News, November 19, 1992: 3.
— slack key to be featured at Ka'anapali Beach Hotel, Lahaina News, December 24, 1992: 15.
— live music expands in Lahaina, Lahaina News, February 4, 1993: 13.
— Haleakala Chamber Music Society to present The Haleakala Chamber Players, Lahaina News, February 4, 1993: 15.
— The Pride of Maui to host Reggae Cruise, Lahaina News, February 11, 1993: 14.
— Maui Beach Hotel to feature karaoke, Lahaina News, February 11, 1993: 16.
— ensemble from Australia to perform, Lahaina News, February 25, 1993: 11.
— Reggae Festival to be held, Lahaina News, February 25, 1993: 9.
— song festival to be held at Lokelani Intermediate School, Lahaina News, May 6, 1993: 7.
— Lokelani Intermediate Song Festival held, Lahaina News, May 13, 1993: 5.
— Kapalua Music Festival to feature more jazz this year, Lahaina News, June 3, 1993: 12.
— Henry Allen teaching steel guitar as part of Folk Arts Apprenticeship Award, Lahaina News, July 1, 1993: 2.
— benefit concert to be held for homeless, Lahaina News, August 19, 1993: 15.
— harpist Erik Perglund and Scott Perkins to perform, Lahaina News, December 30, 1993: 12.
— Na Mele O Maui song competition to be held, Lahaina News, March 3, 1994: 12.
— Spring Equinox Music and Crafts Festival to be held, Lahaina News, March 10, 1994: 16.
— KPOA to host jazz and Hawaiian music event at Whalers Village, Lahaina News, April 14, 1994: 12.
— Seabury Hall to present spring concert, Lahaina News, April 14, 1994: 12.

— Maui Visitors Bureau presenting live Hawaiian entertainment at Kahului Airport, Lahaina News, May 19, 1994: 16.

— Bach to be featured at Kapalua Music Festival, Lahaina News, May 26, 1994: 10.

— KPOA Radio to offer "Jazz on the Beach", Lahaina News, June 16, 1994: 11.

— Hawaii Guitar Festival to be held, Lahaina News, June 16, 1994: 12.

— Kenny Endo Taiko drummers to perform, Lahaina News, June 23, 1994: 11.

— "Jazz on the Beach" continues at Whalers Village, Lahaina News, August 4, 1994: 16.

— "Garden of Be" being performed at Kahana Gateway, Lahaina News, August 11, 1994: 10.

— People Helping People concert to be held, Lahaina News, August 18, 1994: 16.

— World Independence Afro-Pop and Jazz Festival to be held, Lahaina News, August 18, 1994: 16.

— Hawaiian International Film Festival to present Hawaiian music concert, Lahaina News, October 27, 1994: 20.

— Maui Academy of Performing Arts offering jazz workshop by Jeff Hendrix, Lahaina News, January 5, 1995: 12.

— fundraiser to be held for Nelson Lopez, Lahaina News, January 12, 1995: 10.

— "I Have a Dream" festival to be held at Lahaina Civic Center, Lahaina News, January 12, 1995: 10.

— West African Dance and Drum Workshop to be held, Lahaina News, January 12, 1995: 12.

— "Legends of Hawaiian Music: Da Bunch" to perform at Maui Arts and Cultural Center, Lahaina News, January 12, 1995: 12.

— Laurie DeVito to teach Jazz dance master class, Lahaina News, January 26, 1995: 16.

— Dixieland Jazz Festival to be held, Lahaina News, February 16, 1995: 15.

— Pacific and Asian Affairs Council to present "Blowing Zen", Lahaina News, February 16, 1995: 15.

— Ho'omau Hawaiian Music Festival to be held, Lahaina News, February 16, 1995: 16.

— KPOA personality Alaka'i Paleka hosts karaoke, Lahaina News, February 23, 1995: 10.

— Dixieland Jazz Festival to be held, Lahaina News, February 23, 1995: 11.

— "Blowing Zen" to be presented, Lahaina News, February 23, 1995: 12.

— Maui Community College sponsoring choir festival, Lahaina News, March 23, 1995: 12.

— "Sounds of the Big Band Era" to be held at Maui Lu Resort, Lahaina News, March 30, 1995: 12.

— new noise rules may keep bar music off streets, Lahaina News, April 13, 1995: 3.

— loud music compared ot sound of surf, Lahaina News, April 20, 1995: 1,16.

— Maui High School bands to perform at Maui Arts and Cultural Center, Lahaina News, April 20, 1995: 12.

— Bankoh Ki-ho'alu Slack Key Guitar Festival to be held, Lahaina News, May 25, 1995: 12.

— guitar masters to perform at Hawaii Guitar Festival, Lahaina News, June 15, 1995: 11.

— Maui Music Festival, Lahaina News, July 6, 1995: 10.

— Daniel Paul and the Mad Dog Drummers of Mu to host drumming workshop, Lahaina News, July 20, 1995: 12.

— Blues Night to be held at Moose McGillycuddy's, Lahaina News, August 17, 1995: 12.

— Blues Night to be held at Moose McGillycuddy's, Lahaina News, August 24, 1995: 12.

— Maui Music Festival to be held, Lahaina News, August 31, 1995: 11.

— creating electronic music with Ensoniq to be held at Bounty Music, Lahaina News, October 12, 1995: 15.

— Early Music Maui to perform at Boar's Head Christmas Feast, Lahaina News, December 14, 1995: 15.

— Hiroshi Uta wins first place in Kamehameha Iki Park Festival nose flute contest, Lahaina News, January 11, 1996: 16.

— Damon Williams wins Brown Bags to Stardom Contest, Lahaina News, April 4, 1996: 1,18.

— concert honoring Uncle Kalua Kaiahua to held, Lahaina News, May 2, 1996: 16.

— youth ukulele contest to be held at Hula Grill, Lahaina News, June 6, 1996: 15.

— Youth Ukulele Contest to be held at Hula Grill, Lahaina News, June 13, 1996: 10.

— National Youth Choir of Great Britain seeking rooms for visit, Lahaina News, July 18, 1996: 3.

— Maui Chamber Musicians to perform Baroque concert, Lahaina News, October 24, 1996: 14,15.

— Entertainment section becomes calendar rather than paragraph entries, generally not indexed, Lahaina News, November 7, 1996: 16.

— "One" concert to be held, Lahaina News, November 21, 1996: 14.

— Lahaina Cannery Mall to host jazz concerts, Lahaina News, February 13, 1997: 11.

— "The Lahaina Elvis" to perform, Lahaina News, April 24, 1997: 13.

— Nakayama Minyo-Kai Hawaii Shibu to celebrate 20th anniversary with recital, Lahaina News, May 8, 1997: 16.

— Bankoh Kiho'alu, Slack Key Guitar Festival to be held, Lahaina News, June 12, 1997: 16.

— Hula Grill to host Youth Ukulele Contest, Lahaina News, June 19, 1997: 16.

— youth ukulele contest to be held, Lahaina News, June 26, 1997: 9,16.

— Ho'onanea Hou Hawaiian Music Series to be held at Maui Arts and Cultural Center, Lahaina News, September 18, 1997: 13.

— Maui Arts and Cultural Center kicks off Ho'onanea Hou Hawaiian Music Series, Lahaina News, September 25, 1997: 16.

— Na Mele O Maui to be held at Ka'anapali, Lahaina News, November 27, 1997: 1,9.

— Early Music Maui to hold "Boar's Head Feast", Lahaina News, December 4, 1997: 24.

— Gaither Homecoming Musical Spectacular to be held at Aston Wailea Resort, Lahaina News, February 5, 1998: 13.

— "Hawaiian Music and Crafts Festival" to be held at Lahaina Cannery Mall, Lahaina News, February 26, 1998: 12.

— jazz benefit to be held at Maui Arts and Cultural Center, Lahaina News, February 26, 1998: 13.

— Maui Chamber Music Festival to be held, Lahaina News, March 5, 1998: 16.

— Maui Business and Professional Women's Club presents "The Beamer Family—Hawaiiana in Concert", Lahaina News, March 5, 1998: 16.

— Maui District School Music Festival to be held, Lahaina News, April 9, 1998: 17.

— Maui District School Music Festival to be held, Lahaina News, April 16, 1998: 12.

— tickets on sale for Maui Music Festival, Lahaina News, April 23, 1998: 2.

— Hawaiian Islands Rhythm and Blues Mele to be held, Lahaina News, May 14, 1998: 18.

— Na Hoku Awards held, Lahaina News, May 21, 1998: 1,20.

— Waiakea Intermediate School Ukulele Band to perform, Lahaina News, May 21, 1998: 16.

— Hawaiian Islands Rhythm and Blues Mele to be held, Lahaina News, May 28, 1998: 12.

— Bankoh Kiho'alu festival, Lahaina News, June 4, 1998: 17.

— Maui Summer Jam to be held, Lahaina News, June 18, 1998: 17.

— ukulele contest to be held at Hula Grill, Lahaina News, June 25, 1998: 5.

— Halau Maui Nui Bash: A Celebration of Hawaiian Music to benefit Punana Leo o Maui building fund, Lahaina News, October 18, 2001: 1.
— The Shops at Wailea to offer live entertainment, Lahaina News, November 1, 2001: 17.
— "E Ho'oulu Aloha—To Grow in Love" fundraiser for Bailey House Museum to be held, Lahaina News, November 8, 2001: 15.
— E Ho'oulu Aloha—To Grow in Love concert to be held, Lahaina News, November 15, 2001: 16.
— "Voices Rock Ka'anapali" concert to be held, Lahaina News, December 13, 2001: 1,18.
— 2001 Maui Music Odyssey to be held, Lahaina News, December 13, 2001: 17.
— "Christmas A Capella" to be held, Lahaina News, December 20, 2001: 16.
— "Voices Rock Ka'anapali" to be held, Lahaina News, December 27, 2001: 14.
— "Year End Rockin' Blues Mele" to be held, Lahaina News, December 27, 2001: 16.
— classic rock concert "Voices Rock Ka'anapali" to be held at Ka'anapali Resort, Lahaina News, January 3, 2002: 1,18.
— Ka Leo Hano Awards to be held to honor musicians, Lahaina News, January 3, 2002: 8.
— "Voices Rock Ka'anapali" concert to be held, Lahaina News, January 10, 2002: 1,18.
— "Voices Rock Ka'anapali" held, Lahaina News, January 24, 2002: 14.
— Hawaiian Islands Winter Rhythm and Blues Mele to held, Lahaina News, January 31, 2002: 16.
— "A Spring Fling" to be held, Lahaina News, March 14, 2002: 17.
— "Celebration of the Arts" to feature Hawaiian culture, Lahaina News, March 28, 2002: 17.
— "The Art of the Solo 'Ukulele" to be held at the Maui Arts and Cultural Center, Lahaina News, March 28, 2002: 19.
— "Bomb-Diggity 2" to be held at Maui Arts and Cultural Center, Lahaina News, March 28, 2002: 20.
— "The HeArt of Music" to be held at the Maui Arts and Cultural Center, Lahaina News, April 18, 2002: 17.
— Ukulele Festival to be held at Lahaina Cannery Mall, Lahaina News, April 25, 2002: 14.
— Hawaiian Islands Rhythm and Blues Mele to be held, Lahaina News, April 25, 2002: 15.
— Rhythm and Blues Mele to be held, Lahaina News, May 9, 2002: 17.
— industry reception to be held Hapa's, Lahaina News, May 16, 2002: 16.
— violinist Chee Yun to perform, Lahaina News, May 16, 2002: 16,17.
— "A Walk Down Abbey Road" celebration of the Beatles to be held, Lahaina News, June 13, 2002: 17.
— Ki ho'alu Slack Key Festival to be held, Lahaina News, June 20, 2002: 17.
— Ki ho'alu Slack Key Festival to be held, Lahaina News, June 20, 2002: 3.
— Maui Summer Music Festival to be held at Lahaina Civic Center Amphitheater, Lahaina News, June 27, 2002: 1,2.
— Taiko Festival to be held, Lahaina News, June 27, 2002: 16.
— Ka Leo Hano Awards to be held at Maui Arts and Cultural Center, Lahaina News, July 11, 2002: 14.
— Hawaii Jaycees Jam concert to be held, Lahaina News, July 18, 2002: 16.
— Keawala'i Congregational Church to host 'Aha Mele", Lahaina News, August 22, 2002: 20.
— San Jose Taiko and Hanayui to perform at Maui Arts and Cultural Center, Lahaina News, October 3, 2002: 17.
— Na Mele O Maui to hold Keiki and 'Opio Song Competition, Lahaina News, October 17, 2002: 15.
— International Cultural Festival to be held, Lahaina News, October 17, 2002: 18.

— "E Ho'oulu Aloha: To Grow in Love" benefit for Bailey House to be held , Lahaina News, November 21, 2002: 18.
— bagpiper Jack Lee to perform, Lahaina News, November 28, 2002: 15.
— work of Edna Pualani Farden Bekeart featured, Lahaina News, December 12, 2002: 1,22.
— St. Lawrence String Quartet to perform at the Maui Arts and Cultural Center, Lahaina News, January 30, 2003: 16.
— Festival of Drums to be held at Lahaina Cannery Mall, Lahaina News, February 13, 2003: 14.
— Lahaina Cannery Mall to host drum festival, Lahaina News, February 20, 2003: 16.
— benefit to be held for Maya and Shandra, Lahaina News, February 27, 2003: 16.
— Argentine Tango band Los Chamuyeros to perform at Hapa's, Lahaina News, February 27, 2003: 17.
— Slack Key Guitar and Junior Ukulele Festival to be held, Lahaina News, February 27, 2003: 18.
— CD "JOURNEY HOME—Lost Love Letters in the Sand" release party to be held, Lahaina News, March 13, 2003: 16.
— Maui No Ka Oi: Ohana Bash to be held, Lahaina News, April 17, 2003: 18.
— Maui District High School Music Festival to be held, Lahaina News, May 8, 2003: 14.
— Rhythm and Blues Mele to be held at Maui Arts and Cultural Center, Lahaina News, May 8, 2003: 17.
— performances at International Festival of Canoes, Lahaina News, May 8, 2003: insert12,insert13.
— Maui Classic Music Festival to be held, Lahaina News, May 29, 2003: 1,18.
— Ki Hoalu Slack Key Guitar Festival to be held, Lahaina News, June 12, 2003: 18.
— Lahaina Cannery Mall to hold "Summer Show", Lahaina News, June 19, 2003: 14.
— Nassau Suffolk Performing Arts to hold workshops and concerts, Lahaina News, June 26, 2003: 17,18.
— students taught by slack key musicians, Lahaina News, June 26, 2003: 3.
— Friends of Moku'ula to hold benefit concert, Lahaina News, July 10, 2003: 1,20.
— Hawaii International Jazz Festival to be held, Lahaina News, July 24, 2003: 14.
— weekly slack key guitar concerts to be held at Ritz-Carlton, Lahaina News, September 18, 2003: 3.
— Masters of Hawaiian Slack Guitar concerts to be held at Ritz-Carlton, Lahaina News, October 2, 2003: 2.
— note: simple listing of musical venues or acts are not always indexed, Lahaina News, , 2999: .

MUSIC MAN [MUSICAL]
— auditions to be held, Lahaina News, December 25, 1985: 3.
— to be performed by Maui Youth Theatre, Lahaina News, February 26, 1986: 3.
— to be performed in March, Lahaina News, February 26, 1986: 3.

MUSIC OF MORGAN MANNER [PERFORMANCE]
— to be held at Maui Inter-Continental Wailea, Lahaina News, January 9, 1985: 3.

MUSICAL CABARET [SHOW]
— presented at Maui Prince Hotel, Lahaina News, October 7, 1987: 3.

MUSIK, ZSUZSI EVERS [ARTIST]
— paintings to be shown at Artful Dodger, Lahaina News, July 27, 1988: 10.

MUSSELWHITE, CHARLIE [MUSICIAN]
— reviewed, Lahaina News, April 11, 1984: 14.
— to perform at Blue Max, Lahaina News, February 19, 1986: 8.

MUSTPHA, GAEL [WRITER]
— to sign copies of "Hula Girl" at Waldenbooks, Lahaina News, October 26, 2000: 28.

MUTUAL BENEFIT GRAND MASTERS TENNIS TOURNAMENT
— held at the Hyatt Regency, Lahaina News, April 25, 1984: 4.

MUZIJEVIC, PEDJA [MUSICIAN]
— pianist to perform in a Maui Symphony Orchestra concert, Lahaina News, February 3, 1994: 12.

MY AUNTIE'S PLACE [RESTAURANT]
— reviewed, Lahaina News, November 9, 1988: 6.

MY FAIR LADY [MUSICAL]
— to be performed at Maui Academy of Performing Arts, Lahaina News, October 6, 1994: 15.
— reviewed, Lahaina News, October 13, 1994: 17.

MY LITTLE GRASS SHACK IN KEALAKEKUA, HAWAII [SONG]
— history and popularity described, Lahaina News, August 7, 1985: 20.

MY NAME IS ALICE [PLAY]
— opens at Iao Theatre, Lahaina News, September 5, 1991: 18.
— opens Friday, Lahaina News, September 12, 1991: 18.
— performed by Maui Community Theatre, Lahaina News, September 26, 1991: 17.

MYBECK, WALTER
— running for Board of Education, Lahaina News, August 6, 1998: 14.

MYERS, A. MAURICE
— president of Aloha Airgroup resigns, Lahaina News, January 6, 1994: 5.

MYERS ADVERTISING INC. [BUSINESS]
— selected by Lahaina Cannery Shopping Center, Lahaina News, December 28, 1988: 13.
— receives awards from Westin Fairs Association, Lahaina News, March 6, 1991: 10.
— retained by Coldwell Banker McCorack Real Estate, Lahaina News, March 27, 1991: 10.
— hires Irene Brown as account manager, Lahaina News, May 31, 2001: 8.

MYERS, JEAN
— receives award for excellence in advertising at Pele Awards, Lahaina News, May 9, 1990: 8.

MYERS, PAUL
— elected chairman of Lahaina Retail Board, Lahaina Sun, December 16, 1970: 3.
— discusses renovation of Whale's Tale restaurant, Lahaina Sun, January 27, 1971: 3.
— discusses press kit for Lahaina, Lahaina Sun, January 27, 1971: 7.
— discusses planned Lahaina Whaling Spree, Lahaina Sun, February 3, 1971: 2.

MYERS, WILLIAM (BILL) [POLITICIAN]
— Scholar/Athlete of the Week, Lahaina News, November 7, 1996: 12.
— candidate for Board of Education, Lahaina News, October 26, 2000: 25.

MYLES, LARRY [COMEDIAN]
— to perform at Comedy Club and the Sports Page, Lahaina News, May 14, 1992: 14,17.
— to perform at Comedy Club, Lahaina News, January 20, 1994: 11.
— to perform at Honolulu Comedy Club, Lahaina News, February 29, 1996: 14.

MYTHOLOGY
— see legends

MYTHOLOGY OF ANGELS, THE
— to be presented, Lahaina News, December 14, 1995: 15.

N

NA ALA HELE TRAIL AND ACCESS PROGRAM
— to improve Old Lahaina Pali Trail, Lahaina News, June 13, 1996: 10.
— to work on Old Lahaina Pali Trail, Lahaina News, July 11, 1996: 12.
— to work on Old Lahaina Pali Trail, Lahaina News, November 14, 1996: 14.
— seeking volunteers to work on trails, Lahaina News, January 16, 1997: 10.
— seeking volunteers, Lahaina News, February 13, 1997: 11.
— trail program seeking volunteers, Lahaina News, July 10, 1997: 16.
— to improve trail, Lahaina News, September 11, 1997: 16.
— to work on Old Lahaina Pali Trail, Lahaina News, December 25, 1997: 13.
— to improve Old Lahaina Pali Trail, Lahaina News, July 23, 1998: 17.
— to lead a hike to Waiakoa Loop Trail, Lahaina News, May 30, 2002: 16.

NA HALE O MAKENA
— holds groundbreaking ceremony, Lahaina News, December 7, 2000: 21.

NA HOALOHA O LELE
— fundraiser for halau at Old Lahaina Cafe, Lahaina News, October 26, 1988: 16.
— group formed to oppose widening of Wainee Street, Lahaina News, October 11, 1989: 1.
— to hold meeting, Lahaina News, January 3, 1990: 28.
— wins group Auana division at Mokihana Hula Festival, Lahaina News, October 10, 1990: 7.
— organizing Lei Day celebration, Lahaina News, April 24, 1991: 10.

NA HOKU AWARDS
— held, Lahaina News, May 21, 1998: 1,20.

NA HOKUPA [MUSICAL GROUP]
— to perform at Molokini Lounge at the Maui Prince Hotel, Lahaina News, February 27, 1991: 12.

NA HONU WEST MAUI SOCCER CLUB
— seeking sponsors, Lahaina News, January 25, 2001: 9.

NA KAI EWALU CANOE CLUB
— sponsoring long distance race, Lahaina News, August 19, 1999: 7.

NA KAI OLA
— offering Hawaiian language classes, Lahaina News, April 25, 1996: 6.

NA KAMALIʻI NANI O LAHAINA HULA HALAU
— to perform at Beach Festival and Parade at Atami, Japan, Lahaina News, August 31, 1995: 4.
— return from Japan, Lahaina News, September 21, 1995: 16.
— to perform at Festival of Hula, Lahaina News, January 10, 2002: 15.

NA KAMALIʻI O KE AKUA
— to hold One Pitch Men's Mixed Softball Tournament, Lahaina News, August 19, 1999: 6.
— attends Tahiti Fete on Oahu, Lahaina News, March 27, 2003: 3,18.
— to perform at May Day Fest, Lahaina News, April 24, 2003: 16.

NA KAMALIʻI TE MEA O TE ATUA
— to perform keiki-style Tahitian shows, Lahaina News, July 27, 2000: 21.
— continues to perform, Lahaina News, September 21, 2000: 21.
— Tahitian shows to be held, Lahaina News, April 12, 2001: 21.
— wins tree decorating contest at Lahaina Cannery Mall, Lahaina News, January 10, 2002: 8.
— hula dancers to perform at King Kamehameha Day, Lahaina News, June 13, 2002: 14.

NA KEIKI HOʻOKUKU UKULELE
— to be held at Hula Grill, Lahaina News, June 21, 2001: 14.

NA KEIKI O KA MOANA
— sponsoring Ka'anapali Biathlon, Lahaina News, March 4, 1993: 5.
— hosting Maui Westside 2K Ocean Sprint, Lahaina News, March 3, 1994: 7.
— to hold Ka'anapali Biathlon, Lahaina News, May 19, 1994: 9.

NA KUPUNA O HAWAI'I NEI
— sponsoring conference to discuss issues, Lahaina News, February 21, 2002: 1.
— meeting of Hawaiians sponsored by, Lahaina News, February 28, 2002: 3.

NA KUPUNA O MAUI
— to hold meeting on Hawaiian Sovereignty, Lahaina News, September 26, 1996: 14.
— to hold meeting to discuss culturally significant areas with Nation of Hawaii and Lahaina Open Space Society, Lahaina News, February 27, 1997: 11.
— to hold meeting with Lahaina Open Space Society, Lahaina News, April 10, 1997: 12.
— to meet with Lahaina Open Space Society, Lahaina News, May 29, 1997: 16.
— to meet with Lahaina Open Space Society, Lahaina News, July 17, 1997: 16.
— to demonstrate against annexation, Lahaina News, October 9, 1997: 20.
— to meet to discuss issues, Lahaina News, October 30, 1997: 16.
— demonstrates against the Launiupoko housing project, Lahaina News, March 5, 1998: 3.
— to hold vigil to oppose proposed Villages of Leiali'i, Lahaina News, March 19, 1998: 13.
— begins vigil opposing Villages of Leiali'i, Lahaina News, March 26, 1998: 12.
— to hold event with Kahana Canoe Club, Lahaina News, April 23, 1998: 17.
— encourages Hawaiians to elect delegates to Native Hawaiian Convention, Lahaina News, November 5, 1998: 2.
— to host He'ui Cultural Arts Festival, Lahaina News, August 5, 1999: 12.
— visits Mahanalua Nui Subdivision with Maui County Council Public Works and Water Committee, Lahaina News, November 25, 1999: 1.
— planning overnight vigil asking for divine guidance and spiritual unity, Lahaina News, January 6, 2000: 1.
— He'ui Cultural Arts Festivals to be held at Banyan Tree Park, Lahaina News, March 16, 2000: 12.
— He'ui Cultural Arts Festival celebrates first anniversary, Lahaina News, August 3, 2000: 1.
— He'ui Cultural Arts Festivals continue to be held, Lahaina News, November 23, 2000: 21.
— demonstrates at Wahikuli State Park against the proposed Villages of Leiali'i, Lahaina News, December 14, 2000: 1.
— He'ui Cultural Arts Festivals continue, Lahaina News, January 18, 2001: 16.
— leading charge to stage convention to protect rights, Lahaina News, April 12, 2001: 1,24.
— to hold meeting, Lahaina News, May 3, 2001: 2.
— kupuna to meet at "Aha Kuka O Na Kupuna O Maui—Let Us Come Together to Address the Attacks Against Native Hawaiian Entitlements", Lahaina News, May 24, 2001: 3.
— to hold arts and crafts fairs, Lahaina News, November 29, 2001: 17.
— to hold arts and crafts fairs, Lahaina News, December 27, 2001: 16.
— to hold fair at Banyan Tree Park, Lahaina News, January 17, 2002: 16.
— to hold demonstration against Arakaka 2 lawsuit, Lahaina News, August 8, 2002: 5.
— to raise concerns for bill to force sale of Queen's personal land holdings, Lahaina News, August 29, 2002: 3.
— continues to hold arts and crafts fairs at Banyan Tree Park, Lahaina News, November 21, 2002: 20.
— continues to hold arts and crafts fairs at Banyan Tree Park, Lahaina News, January 23, 2003: 16.
— continues to hold arts and crafts fairs at Banyan Tree Park, Lahaina News, April 10, 2003: 20.

NA KUPUNA O MAUI HE'UI CULTURAL ARTS FESTIVAL
— to be held, Lahaina News, July 29, 1999: 11.
— to be held at Banyan Tree Park, Lahaina News, August 26, 1999: 17.
— to be held at Banyan Tree Park, Lahaina News, October 14, 1999: 12.
— "He 'Ui Cultural Arts Festivals" held at Banyan Tree Park, Lahaina News, October 21, 1999: 14.
— see also He'ui Cultural Arts Festival

NA LEO HO'OULU [MUSICAL GROUP]
— performs at Wharf Cinema Center for Aloha Friday, Lahaina News, January 6, 1994: 12.

NA LEO KAKO'O O MAUI
— hosting golf tournament as fundraiser, Lahaina News, January 28, 1999: 7.
— to host tournament at Sandalwood Golf Course, Lahaina News, February 4, 1999: 15.
— to hold golf tournament fundraiser, Lahaina News, February 1, 2001: 15.
— to host golf tournament fundraiser, Lahaina News, February 15, 2001: 13.
— to hold golf fundraiser, Lahaina News, February 13, 2003: 12.

NA LEO O NA WAHINE: WOMEN'S VOICES
— to be shown on Akaku: Maui Community Television, Lahaina News, May 25, 2000: 18.

NA LEO O NANAIKAPONO
— to perform Hawaiian songs, Lahaina News, March 12, 1998: 21.

NA LEO O WAIOLA
— sponsoring Christmas holiday performances, Lahaina News, December 17, 1986: 2.

NA LEO PILIMEHANA [MUSICAL GROUP]
— to perform at Maui Community College Ho'olaule'a, Lahaina News, April 11, 1984: 5.
— to perform at Maui Arts and Cultural Center, Lahaina News, March 6, 1997: 12.
— to perform at "Live on the Beach", Lahaina News, July 24, 1997: 16.
— to perform at Maui Arts and Cultural Center, Lahaina News, November 13, 1997: 21.
— to perform at Alexander and Baldwin Community Fair, Lahaina News, August 27, 1998: 17.
— to perform at Maui Arts and Cultural Center, Lahaina News, November 26, 1998: 17.
— to perform at Maui Arts and Cultural Center, Lahaina News, December 3, 1998: 11.
— to perform at Maui Arts and Cultural Center, Lahaina News, March 22, 2001: 14.
— to perform at Maui Arts and Cultural Center, Lahaina News, March 29, 2001: 17.
— to perform at Maui Arts and Cultural Center, Lahaina News, April 5, 2001: 21.
— to perform at Ka'anapali Beach Hotel dance party, Lahaina News, April 10, 2003: 8.
— to be held at Ka'anapali Beach Hotel, Lahaina News, April 17, 2003: 17.
— to perform at Ka'anapali Beach Hotel, Lahaina News, April 24, 2003: 20.

NA LIMA PAEPAE O LELE
— to establish Hawaiian immersion charter school, Lahaina News, August 26, 1999: 1,20.
— supporting Hawaiian Language Immersion through Punana Leo o Lahaina program, Lahaina News, April 6, 2000: 1,2.

NA MAKAʻALA VOLUNTEER COASTAL MONITORING TEAM
— seeking volunteers to monitor nearshore waters, Lahaina News, July 4, 1996: 5.

NA MEA HAWAII STORE [BUSINESS]
— opens, Lahaina News, December 7, 2000: 1,22.
— opens store at Lahaina Cannery Mall, Lahaina News, November 29, 2001: 8.

NA MEA HULA O MAUI
— to perform at Lahaina Cannery Mall, Lahaina News, March 30, 2000: 13.

NA MELE KEIKI O KA AINA [CONCERT]
— rescheduled by Kihei Youth Center, Lahaina News, November 6, 1985: 3.

NA MELE O MAUI
— festival to be held in September, Lahaina Sun, August 29, 1973: 15.
— 1981 event organized, Lahaina News, November 1, 1981: 16.
— set for November, Lahaina News, July 18, 1984: 3.
— 1984 event reviewed, Lahaina News, November 14, 1984: 7,8,9.
— music, dance, and culture festival held, Lahaina News, October 30, 1985: 1,20.
— events scheduled, Lahaina News, November 6, 1985: 1.
— Lahaina Intermediate School wins School Song Festival, Lahaina News, November 13, 1985: 1,3.
— festival scheduled, Lahaina News, November 5, 1986: 1,16.
— results, Lahaina News, November 12, 1986: 1, 11.
— Michael White appointed chairman, Lahaina News, February 11, 1987: 3.
— offers scholarships, Lahaina News, April 22, 1987: 10.
— gives scholarships to local students, Lahaina News, May 27, 1987: 3.
— annual event to begin, Lahaina News, November 18, 1987: 1,4.
— offering scholarships, Lahaina News, May 18, 1988: 2.
— events detailed, Lahaina News, October 26, 1988: 3.
— Hawaiian Arts and Crafts exhibits to take place at Royal Lahaina Resort, Lahaina News, November 2, 1988: 18.
— organizer Betsy Hinau featured, Lahaina News, November 2, 1988: 2.
— detailed, Lahaina News, November 2, 1988: 6.
— results of Keiki Song Competition, Lahaina News, November 16, 1988: 13.
— Hawaiian song celebration scheduled for Kaʻanapali Beach Resort, Lahaina News, September 20, 1989: 3.
— scheduled for the Kaʻanapali Beach Resort, Lahaina News, October 4, 1989: 3.
— scholarships from helping students study Hawaiiana, Lahaina News, November 1, 1989: 13.
— to begin, Lahaina News, November 8, 1989: 10.
— Waihee School wins Keiki Song Competition, Lahaina News, November 15, 1989: 3.
— school song competition to be held, Lahaina News, October 24, 1990: 15.
— song competition to be held, Lahaina News, October 31, 1990: 13.
— to feature Keiki Song Competition, Lahaina News, November 7, 1990: 10.
— event detailed, Lahaina News, November 14, 1990: 14.
— Keiki contest results, Lahaina News, November 28, 1990: 4.
— to award scholarships, Lahaina News, June 13, 1991: 5,6.
— awarding scholarships, Lahaina News, June 20, 1991: 3.
— to be held in April, Lahaina News, March 12, 1992: 16.
— featured, Lahaina News, March 26, 1992: 3.

— to take place Friday and Saturday, Lahaina News, April 2, 1992: 1,16.
— winners announced, Lahaina News, April 9, 1992: 4,5.
— Hana School wins, Lahaina News, April 16, 1992: 19.
— festival details, Lahaina News, March 18, 1993: 9.
— announces scholarship recipients, Lahaina News, August 5, 1993: 4.
— song competition to be held, Lahaina News, March 3, 1994: 12.
— song competition details, Lahaina News, March 10, 1994: 16.
— announces scholarship recipients, Lahaina News, June 23, 1994: 5.
— to be held, Lahaina News, November 24, 1994: 10.
— results of, Lahaina News, December 8, 1994: 1,16.
— contest to be held, Lahaina News, December 7, 1995: 15.
— to offer scholarships, Lahaina News, May 9, 1996: 14.
— to feature student art, Lahaina News, November 21, 1996: 15.
— to be held at Maui Marriott Resort, Lahaina News, November 28, 1996: 1,2,11.
— to be held, Lahaina News, December 5, 1996: 14.
— results of, Lahaina News, December 12, 1996: 5.
— offering scholarships, Lahaina News, May 15, 1997: 2.
— announces scholarships, Lahaina News, August 21, 1997: 6.
— to be held, Lahaina News, November 20, 1997: 10.
— to be held at Kaʻanapali, Lahaina News, November 27, 1997: 1,9.
— to be held, Lahaina News, December 4, 1997: 1.
— festival to be held, Lahaina News, November 26, 1998: 1.
— to be held, Lahaina News, December 3, 1998: 1,6.
— Keiki and ʻOpio Song Competition to be held, Lahaina News, December 10, 1998: 11.
— applications being taken for scholarships, Lahaina News, May 6, 1999: 2.
— to discuss future of scholarships, Lahaina News, August 5, 1999: 12.
— to be held, Lahaina News, December 2, 1999: 1,20.
— song competition to be held, Lahaina News, December 9, 1999: 1.
— to be held, Lahaina News, November 23, 2000: 1,3.
— song competition returns, Lahaina News, November 30, 2000: 2.
— results of, Lahaina News, December 7, 2000: 6.
— results of student art competition, Lahaina News, December 14, 2000: 8.
— scholarships available, Lahaina News, February 8, 2001: 2.
— awards scholarship to Leila Diego, Lahaina News, May 17, 2001: 17.
— song competition to be held, Lahaina News, November 29, 2001: 1,14.
— song competition to be held, Lahaina News, November 29, 2001: 14.
— to be held, Lahaina News, December 6, 2001: 17.
— Maui High School successful at, Lahaina News, December 20, 2001: 14.
— to award scholarships, Lahaina News, March 7, 2002: 5.
— to hold Keiki and ʻOpio Song Competition, Lahaina News, October 17, 2002: 15.
— celebrating 30 years, Lahaina News, November 28, 2002: 1,3.
— song contest celebrating 30 years, Lahaina News, December 5, 2002: 17.
— held, Lahaina News, December 12, 2002: 9.
— seeking applicants for scholarships, Lahaina News, March 6, 2003: 2.
— Krista Alvarado wins scholarship from, Lahaina News, May 15, 2003: 2.

NA MELE O NA KUPUNA [BOOK]
— published, Lahaina News, June 8, 1988: 13.

NA MELE PANA [MUSICAL GROUP]
— performs traditional Hawaiian songs at Baldwin High School, Lahaina News, November 4, 1987: 10.

NA MOKU AUPUNI O KOʻOLAU HUI
— holding Hoʻolauleʻa, Lahaina News, July 31, 1997: 16.
— to hold farmer's market, Lahaina News, October 30, 1997: 17.

NA 'OIWI [MUSICAL GROUP]
— to perform at "Music on the Beach", Lahaina News, July 23, 1998: 9.
— to perform at Ka'anapali Beach Hotel, Lahaina News, January 11, 2001: 1.

NA PALE O KE KAI
— seeking volunteers to monitor oceans, Lahaina News, January 16, 1997: 5.

NA PALOLA NUI [MUSICAL GROUP]
— to perform at Hula Grill, Lahaina News, November 24, 1994: 11.
— to perform at the Hula Grill, Lahaina News, July 20, 1995: 11,12.
— to perform at Hula Grill, Lahaina News, February 15, 1996: 13.
— to perform at Hula Grill, Lahaina News, April 4, 1996: 15.
— to perform at Hula Grill, Lahaina News, August 29, 1996: 12.

NA PO'E KOKUA
— forms to assist native Hawaiians in housing matters, Lahaina News, July 2, 1992: 4.
— non-profit group to hold fundraiser at Pacific'O, Lahaina News, May 24, 2001: 3.

NA PUA MAKAMAE O WAIOLA
— to hold benefit at Ruth's Chris Steak House, Lahaina News, November 26, 1998: 16.
— after-school Hawaiian immersion program starting, Lahaina News, December 3, 1998: 11.
— immersion program to begin, Lahaina News, December 10, 1998: 11.
— to form, Lahaina News, December 17, 1998: 12.

NA PUA O KAPIOLANI
— hula studio to celebrate the legacy of Aunty Emma Kapiolani Farden Sharpe, Lahaina News, February 14, 2002: 14,17.

NA WAHINE E KAUHI A KAMA
— to hold Kulolo Sale, Lahaina News, June 24, 1999: 2.

NA WAHINE O KE KAI
— Outrigger Canoe Championship to be held, Lahaina News, September 21, 1995: 7.
— to be held, Lahaina News, September 19, 1996: 13.
— Outrigger Canoe Championship to be held, Lahaina News, June 18, 1998: 15.
— Outrigger Canoe Championships Bankoh to be held, Lahaina News, September 23, 1999: 7.
— Outrigger Canoe Championship to be held, Lahaina News, September 21, 2000: 8.

NA WAIHO'OLU'U O KE ANUENUE [MUSICAL GROUP]
— to perform from their new CD "Together" at Borders Book, Lahaina News, October 28, 1999: 16.

NA-MELE-O-HANA [GROUP]
— perform at Kahului Shopping Center, Lahaina Sun, April 26, 1972: 10.

NA'AUAO [MUSICAL GROUP]
— to perform at "Music on the Beach", Lahaina News, November 19, 1998: 17.

NA'AUAO, SEAN [MUSICIAN]
— releases new CD "Neutralize It", Lahaina News, August 31, 2000: 22.
— to perform at Lahaina Cannery Mall's 16th anniversary, Lahaina News, March 20, 2003: 9.

NABAVI, PARIS
— appointed director of food and beverage at Kapalua Bay Hotel and Villas, Lahaina News, December 10, 1992: 10.

NABORS, JIM [MUSICIAN]
— to perform with Maui Symphony Orchestra, Lahaina News, December 14, 2000: 20.

NACHOS GRANDE [RESTAURANT]
— opens, Lahaina News, January 6, 2000: 11.

NACHTIGALL, PAUL
— director of marine mammal research program to discuss methods for testing dolphin and whale hearing, Lahaina News, November 7, 2002: 3.
— to speak on "Studying Hearing in Dolphins and Whales", Lahaina News, November 14, 2002: 17.

NACUA, DWIGHT
— West Maui Business Association manager resigns, Lahaina Sun, October 11, 1972: 8.

NADAMA [MUSICIAN]
— to perform from "Heart to Heart" CD, Lahaina News, February 11, 1999: 16.

NADAMA AND SHASTROS [MUSICIANS]
— to perform at Maui Yoga Shala, Lahaina News, July 25, 2002: 20.

NADER'S RAIDERS
— challenge increase in airline fares, Lahaina Sun, July 25, 1973: 3.

NADINE'S MUSIC [BUSINESS]
— opens, Lahaina News, December 24, 1986: 12.

NAE'OLE, CLIFFORD
— named Hawaiian cultural advisor for Ritz-Carlton, Lahaina News, April 16, 1998: 11.
— to speak at Bailey House on "Honokahua Preservation and Hawaiian Unification", Lahaina News, November 4, 1999: 13.
— to hold "Moonlight Mo'olelo" at Ritz-Carlton, Lahaina News, September 21, 2000: 1,6.

NAE'OLE, IOKEPA
— to present "The Link Between Land and Sea" at The Nature Conservancy, Lahaina News, September 6, 2001: 16.

NAGAMINE CAMERA & PHOTO SHOP [BUSINESS]
— to open branch in Whaler's Village, Lahaina News, July 25, 1984: 14.

NAGAMINE PHOTO [BUSINESS]
— featured, Lahaina News, August 15, 1984: 14.

NAGAMINE, RALPH
— County Public Works deputy director discusses delay of Mahinahina bridge opening, Lahaina News, January 23, 1992: 2.
— head of Land Use and Codes Division of Public Works speaks of need to bring Lahaina buildings up to code, Lahaina News, August 5, 1993: 1,12.

NAGAO, MAMORI
— promoted to assistant vice president to vice president of Maui region, Lahaina News, June 20, 1990: 7.

NAGAO, TRACY
— Scholar/Athlete of the Week, Lahaina News, October 22, 1998: 19.

NAGAOKA, RICK
— director of sales at Renaissance Wailea Beach Resort, Lahaina News, February 7, 2002: 8.

NAGASAKO [FAMILY]
— featured; store closing, Lahaina News, October 26, 2000: 6.

NAGASAKO, JESSICA
— Scholar/Athlete of the Week, Lahaina News, November 14, 1996: 12.

NAGASAKO, MARTINA
— wins Lahaina Intermediate School "Outstanding Student of 1998", Lahaina News, July 2, 1998: 2.

NAGASAKO, MASAO
— in memoriam, Lahaina News, October 2, 1985: 1,20.

NAGASAKO SUPERMARKET [BUSINESS]
— fire and theft reported, Lahaina News, April 15, 1980: 7.
— featured, Lahaina News, July 25, 1984: 14.

NAGASAKO, THUMPER
— to compete in X Games IX, Lahaina News, July 31, 2003: 13.

NAGASAKO VARIETY STORE [BUSINESS]
— featured, Lahaina News, December 19, 1996: 23.
— supermarket to close, Lahaina News, October 16, 1997: 1,3.
— closes after 28 years, Lahaina News, October 19, 2000: 1,7.

NAGASAKO-PETERSON, PATTY [POLITICIAN]
— see Peterson, Patty Nagasako [politician]

NAGASKO BUILDING
— history of, Lahaina News, July 31, 1985: 1.

NAGEL, RAY
— to speak at Maui United Way annual meeting, Lahaina News, February 20, 1985: 7.

NAGER, HOWARD
— vice president of fresh sales and marketing at Maui Pineapple Co., Lahaina News, October 9, 2003: 8.

NAGLE, SUZY
— store manager at Tiffany and Co., Lahaina News, September 15, 1994: 12.

NAGOURNEY, JON [MUSICIAN]
— to perform at Blackie's Bar, Lahaina News, March 14, 1990: 15.
— to perform at Blackie's Bar with Brian Como Quartet, Lahaina News, March 21, 1990: 13.

NAHIENAENA
— life recounted, Lahaina News, December 31, 1986: 1,20.
— education described, Lahaina News, April 12, 1989: S5.

NAI'A PROPERTIES [BUSINESS]
— names Myke Capps as "Employee of the Year", Lahaina News, April 25, 2002: 8.
— names Willie Nelson resident manager of the year, Lahaina News, January 23, 2003: 9.
— honors top employees, Lahaina News, January 23, 2003: 9.

NAIHE, LOPAKA [MUSICIAN]
— to perform at Lahaina Cannery Mall, Lahaina News, September 4, 1997: 17.

NAIL STOP [BUSINESS]
— opens, Lahaina News, February 24, 1994: 10.

NAISH, ROBBY
— surfer wins O'Neill Invitational, Lahaina News, April 18, 1984: 6.

NAKAGAWA, DEREK
— to perform in "Mad Cloak", Lahaina News, September 18, 2003: 18.

NAKAGAWA, FRANCIS
— potluck dinner to be held for at Maria Lanakila Church, Lahaina News, December 19, 1991: 4,5.
— farewell dinner to be held, Lahaina News, December 26, 1991: 3.

NAKAGAWA, LINDA
— boxer featured, Lahaina News, February 10, 1994: 11.

NAKAI, GLYNNIS
— lecturing on Kealia Pond National Wildlife Refuge, Lahaina News, June 3, 1999: 16.

NAKALELE POINT
— police seeking help identifying body found at, Lahaina News, July 18, 1996: 1.
— access closed, Lahaina News, December 12, 1996: 2.

NAKAMA, MARCIA
— joins staff at Lahaina Public Library, Lahaina News, June 28, 1989: 1.

NAKAMOTO, DENNIS
— appointed environmental health specialist for Maui, Lahaina Sun, December 16, 1970: 3.
— discusses pollution in Kahului Harbor, Lahaina Sun, February 3, 1971: 5.
— resigns to accept a position in Honolulu, Lahaina Sun, April 14, 1971: 2.

NAKAMOTO, STUART
— leading workshop on Computerized Cost of Production, Lahaina News, October 25, 2001: 8.

NAKAMOTO, TOMIO "LOLI"
— photographer to be honored at Wharf Cinema Center, Lahaina News, October 2, 1997: 11.
— photographical retrospective opens, Lahaina News, October 9, 1997: 1,2.
— photographer's life recounted, Lahaina News, June 14, 1989: 1,4.

NAKAMURA, CHARLOTTE WADA
— receives University of Hawai'i Distinguished Alumni Award, Lahaina News, December 9, 1999: 11.

NAKAMURA, DENNIS
— named golf manager at Bay Golf Course, Lahaina News, November 26, 1986: 12.
— named head professional for Kapalua Resort's Village course, Lahaina News, January 16, 1991: 5.
— files to run for Maui County Council, Lahaina News, July 30, 1992: 4.
— hopes to work on water issues, Lahaina News, November 12, 1992: 4.
— to seek changes to bill to discourage lengthening of Kapalua-West Maui airport, Lahaina News, January 14, 1993: 1.
— to recommend Tom Morrow as vice chair of the Maui County Council, Lahaina News, September 9, 1993: 1,12.
— to work for West Maui school complex, Lahaina News, September 23, 1993: 2.
— discuss possible solution to timeshare issue, Lahaina News, March 10, 1994: 1.
— featured with Dennis Nakamura the educator, Lahaina News, March 17, 1994: 2.
— featured with Dennis Nakamura the politician, Lahaina News, March 17, 1994: 2.
— wins County Council seat, but loses vote in West Maui, Lahaina News, November 17, 1994: 24.
— meets with West Maui residents, Lahaina News, April 6, 1995: 3.
— cuts turkey at Light Bringers Thanksgiving Dinner, Lahaina News, December 7, 1995: 2.
— state Campaign Spending Commission to review West Maui Councilman campaign expenditures, Lahaina News, November 7, 1996: 1,3.
— criticized for campaign spending, Lahaina News, November 7, 1996: 3.
— candidate for West Maui County Council did not respond to survey from Lahaina News , Lahaina News, November 2, 2000: 19.

NAKAMURA, DWIGHT
— named bishop of Jodo sect of Buddhism in Hawaii, Lahaina News, September 28, 1983: 5.

NAKAMURA, HARUKI
— reappointed to Board of Water Supply, Lahaina Sun, January 13, 1971: 8.

NAKAMURA, HOWARD
— discusses new 12-story building in Ka'anapali, Lahaina Sun, November 11, 1970: 4.
— meeting with North Short Improvement Association in Paia, Lahaina Sun, December 30, 1970: 5.
— involved in conflict over signage, Lahaina Sun, January 13, 1971: 2.
— discusses plans for banyan tree in Lahaina, Lahaina Sun, February 3, 1971: 7.
— studying impact of Nixon's economic policies on Maui, Lahaina Sun, December 1, 1971: 13.
— critical of environmentalists, Lahaina Sun, February 21, 1973: 1,10,11,12,13.
— named vice president of Alexander and Baldwin Hawaii, Lahaina News, August 16, 1989: 6.

NAKAMURA, KIMPEI [ARTIST]
— to hold two-day workshop on ceramics, Lahaina News, July 25, 1990: 13.

NAKAMURA, MARSHA
— new principal at Lahaina Intermediate School, Lahaina News, August 29, 2002: 1,22.
— Lahaina Intermediate School principal discusses innovative programs at, Lahaina News, October 17, 2002: 1,24.
— principal of Princess Nahienaena Elementary School reports on school, Lahaina News, February 13, 2003: 5.
— message from, Lahaina News, March 6, 2003: 3.
— Lahaina Intermediate School principal discusses school, Lahaina News, April 10, 2003: 2.
— message from Lahaina Intermediate School principal, Lahaina News, May 15, 2003: 9.

NAKAMURA, NATALIE
— receives golf scholarship from Kapalua Land Company, Lahaina News, July 31, 1997: 9.

NAKAMURA, WILMA
— new executive director at Maui Recycling Group, Lahaina News, July 17, 2003: 8.

NAKANO, LAUREN
— to host karaoke, Lahaina News, July 4, 1990: 15.
— continues to offer karaoke at Maui Marriott Resort's Lobby Bar, Lahaina News, March 20, 1991: 9.

NAKANO, MICHAEL
— named principal of Maui High School, Lahaina News, April 9, 1992: 4.
— new principal of Lahainaluna High School, Lahaina News, August 31, 1995: 3.
— Lahainaluna High School fights cancer, Lahaina News, September 28, 2000: 1,14.
— message from Lahainaluna High School principal, Lahaina News, September 6, 2001: 2.
— principal discusses Lahainaluna High School, Lahaina News, October 24, 2002: 1,16.

NAKAO, TAKAICHI [ARTIST]
— work discussed, Lahaina Sun, March 8, 1972: 7.

NAKAOKA, JESSIE [MUSICIAN]
— to perform at Maui Lu Longhouse, Lahaina News, June 25, 1992: 21.

NAKASHIMA, JAYSON
— Kalama Intermediate School student is honorary Mayor for Day, Lahaina News, November 9, 2000: 11.

NAKASONE, ROB [POLITICIAN]
— mayoral candidate supported by former Maui mayor Elmer Cravalho, Lahaina News, November 15, 1982: 2.
— did not attend public hearing on proposed airport in Mahinahina, Lahaina News, January 29, 1986: 1.
— councilman absent from meeting to decide on proposed airport in Mahinahina, Lahaina News, March 12, 1986: 1.
— reason for voting for airport explained, Lahaina News, March 26, 1986: 1.
— editorial critical of for changing mind concerning proposed airport in Mahinahina, Lahaina News, April 2, 1986: 2.
— to seek reelection, Lahaina News, July 7, 1994: 4.

NAKATA, HARUKO
— honored for service, Lahaina News, March 13, 2003: 1.

NAKATA, NEIL
— Lahainaluna High School wrestling coach featured, Lahaina News, December 12, 1991: 4.
— Lahainaluna High School wrestling coach discusses current season, Lahaina News, March 31, 1994: 7,8.

NAKATA, NICHOLAS
— part of royal couple for Junior Promenade at Lahainaluna High School, Lahaina News, April 9, 1998: 2.
— Scholar/Athlete of the Week, Lahaina News, February 4, 1999: 15.

NAKATANI, AL AND JANE
— educators to speak on consequences of human denigration, Lahaina News, September 9, 1999: 12.

NAKAYAMA MINYO-KAI HAWAII SHIBU [TROUPE]
— to celebrate 20th anniversary, Lahaina News, May 8, 1997: 16.
— to perform at Maui Arts and Cultural Center, Lahaina News, September 18, 2003: 16.

NAKI, LANI AND CAROLINE
— celebrate 50th anniversary at Harvest Chapel, Lahaina News, July 4, 2002: 1.

NAKIHEI, ROBERT
— assisting in creation of Maui-Moloka'i Community Development Corporation, Lahaina Sun, February 3, 1971: 3.

NAKOA, KALANI
— appointed national sales manager at the Westin Maui, Lahaina News, February 18, 1993: 9.
— new sales and marketing director at Hyatt Regency Maui Resort and Spa, Lahaina News, May 1, 2003: 8.

NAKOOKA, DONALD
— police officer dies after shooting himself, Lahaina News, December 13, 2001: 3.

NAKOOKA, JESSE [MUSICIAN]
— to perform at the Sheraton Maui, Lahaina News, May 23, 1984: 9.10.11.
— to perform at Maui Sun Hotel, Lahaina News, January 23, 1992: 19.

NAKOOKA, TERRY
— police officer honored by Leilani's on the Beach, Lahaina News, September 21, 2000: 19.

NALEIEHA REGATTA
— to be held, Lahaina News, June 19, 1997: 14,15.

NALEPA, CHARLIE
— new president of Lahaina Rotary Club, Lahaina News, July 11, 1991: 4.
— West Maui Taxpayers Association to hold thank you party for, Lahaina News, June 25, 1992: 2.

NALETTE, CRAIG
— named to Lahaina News sales staff, Lahaina News, January 26, 1995: 13.
— named sales manager at Lahaina News, Lahaina News, November 12, 1998: 13.
— installed as minister at Association of Hawaiian Evangelical Churches, Lahaina News, August 3, 2000: 5.

NALU [MUSICAL GROUP]
— featured, Lahaina News, May 24, 1989: 16.

NAMIBIA, WILDLIFE AND THE SKELETON COAST SLIDE SHOW
— to be held, Lahaina News, May 16, 2002: 17.

NAMIKI, JUN [MUSICIAN]
— to perform at Maui Beach Hotel, Lahaina News, October 2, 2003: 16.

NANATOMI SEAFOOD AND STEAKHOUSE [BUSINESS]
— reviewed, Lahaina News, April 27, 1988: 13.
— Ellie Kukahiko named manager of, Lahaina News, June 20, 1991: 5.
— reviewed, Lahaina News, August 1, 1991: 18.

NANI PACIFICA [BUSINESS]
— featured, Lahaina News, July 11, 1984: 14.

NANNAUCK, SCHINOOK SHEEN
— joins Irwin Mortgage as loan officer, Lahaina News, December 9, 1999: 15.

NANNY'S KITCHEN
— opens, Lahaina News, August 14, 1997: 18.

NANOD, LANCE
— track coach featured, Lahaina News, March 26, 1992: 8.

NANSAY INTERNATIONAL
— partnering with ITT Sheraton Corporation, Lahaina News, November 14, 1990: 13.

NAONE, KAPIOHOOKALANI LYONS
— to teach class on Hawaiian Warriors, Lahaina News, January 11, 1996: 2.
— teaching a class on heiau, Lahaina News, July 24, 1997: 17.
— to teach class on "The Hawaiian Warrior", Lahaina News, October 30, 1997: 17.
— to lead class on "The Hawaiian Warrior", Lahaina News, July 2, 1998: 17.
— to speak at Maui Ocean Center, Lahaina News, October 8, 1998: 6.
— to hold class on "The Hawaiian Warrior", Lahaina News, February 4, 1999: 17.
— new president of LahainaTown Action Committee, Lahaina News, April 8, 1999: 3.
— discusses proposed Harbor Village, Lahaina News, October 14, 1999: 1.
— participates in King Kamehameha Festival, Lahaina News, June 15, 2000: 1.
— to discuss "The Hawaiians' Approach to Conservation", Lahaina News, May 24, 2001: 20.
— to teach class on Hawaiian Moon Calendar at Bailey House, Lahaina News, September 27, 2001: 17.

NA'OPE, GEORGE
— hula competition to pay tribute, Lahaina News, October 8, 1998: 1.

NAPA AUTO PARTS [BUSINESS]
— to become an oil collection site, Lahaina News, April 22, 1999: 5.

NAPELA, CHARLIE
— appointed executive director of West Maui Taxpayers Association, Lahaina News, March 25, 1987: 12.

NAPILI
— State pledges support to resolve water contamination issue in, Lahaina Sun, November 11, 1970: 1,3.
— access to clean water discussed, Lahaina Sun, February 3, 1971: 4.
— large condominium project begins, Lahaina Sun, January 5, 1972: 6.
— groundbreaking ceremonies for low and moderate income housing, Lahaina Sun, April 12, 1972: 11.
— new hotels planned, Lahaina Sun, May 30, 1973: 6.
— seventy-two new homes expected in the coming year, Lahaina News, April 1, 1983: 10.
— repairs to dam almost finished, Lahaina News, March 14, 1990: 28.
— ground breaking ceremony for fire and ambulance station, Lahaina News, May 9, 1990: 5.
— more fundraising needed for fire station, Lahaina News, May 30, 1990: 1.
— Bank of Hawaii to provide interim financing for Fire and Ambulance Station, Lahaina News, August 1, 1990: 4.
— proposed light industrial complex at Rainbow Ranch opposed by some residents, Lahaina News, August 15, 1990: 1,3.
— public meeting on proposed light industrial project, Lahaina News, August 22, 1990: 1,3.
— disagreement continues over proposed light industrial project, Lahaina News, August 29, 1990: 1.
— hearing scheduled to discuss proposed light industrial project, Lahaina News, September 19, 1990: 14.

— hearing to consider light industrial project, Lahaina News, September 26, 1990: 7.
— controversy over proposed light industrial area continues, Lahaina News, October 3, 1990: 20.
— Maui County Council panel appears undecided, Lahaina News, October 10, 1990: 1.
— hearing concerning proposed light industrial project to be held, Lahaina News, October 17, 1990: 1.
— Maui County Council panel to study proposed light industrial site, Lahaina News, October 24, 1990: 1.
— Maui County Council to discuss proposed light industrial park, Lahaina News, November 14, 1990: 3.
— children can design and paint murals on new bus stop, Lahaina News, November 21, 1990: 17.
— decision on proposed light industrial park deferred, Lahaina News, November 21, 1990: 4.
— residents discuss creating beach access, Lahaina News, January 9, 1991: 1.
— children seen leaving area before fire above Lahainaluna High School, Lahaina News, January 9, 1991: 4.
— plans for proposed industrial park changed by new developer, Richard Takase, Lahaina News, February 20, 1991: 1.
— Maui County Council to hold public meeting on proposed industrial park, Lahaina News, February 27, 1991: 5.
— Maui Pineapple Company objects to proposed condominiums connected to light industrial complex, Lahaina News, March 6, 1991: 1,10.
— Fireman's Ball to raise money for Fire and Ambulance Station, Lahaina News, March 6, 1991: 11.
— public hearing on development to be held, Lahaina News, March 20, 1991: 1.
— West Maui Taxpayers Association sponsoring grand opening ceremonies for Fire and Ambulance Safety Facility, Lahaina News, March 27, 1991: 3.
— Maui County Council to hold public hearing on proposed industrial park, Lahaina News, April 10, 1991: 1.
— Napili Gardens townhouse project proposed, Lahaina News, April 10, 1991: 1.
— Maui County Council Public Works Committee to consider improvements to public beach at, Lahaina News, April 24, 1991: 1.
— Maui County parks director Chermaine Tavares exploring potential sites for park in, Lahaina News, May 8, 1991: 1.
— site inspection for possible locations of country park, Lahaina News, May 23, 1991: 4.
— hearing on Napili Trade Center canceled, Lahaina News, May 30, 1991: 3.
— Maui County Council Planning and Economic Development Committee to hold meeting on proposed Napili Trade Center, Lahaina News, June 6, 1991: 3.
— hearing to discuss Napili Trade Center scheduled, Lahaina News, June 13, 1991: 4.
— public meeting to be held on watershed, Lahaina News, July 4, 1991: 3.
— Trade Center opposed by Howard Kihune, Lahaina News, July 25, 1991: 1.
— Maui County Council vote on Trade Center will be close, Lahaina News, August 22, 1991: 1,5.
— Maui County Council postpones voting on proposed Napili Trade Center, Lahaina News, September 5, 1991: 3.
— vote on proposed Trade Center delayed by Maui County Council, Lahaina News, September 26, 1991: 4.
— Trade Center to be voted on by Maui County Council, Lahaina News, October 3, 1991: 5.
— Trade Center likely to be approved by Maui Council, mayor Linda Lingle may veto, Lahaina News, October 17, 1991: 3.

— developer of proposed Trade Center promises contribution to community, Lahaina News, November 14, 1991: 11.

— Trade Center approved by Maui County Council, Lahaina News, December 26, 1991: 3.

— Subway Sandwiches opens, Lahaina News, January 2, 1992: 8.

— mayor Linda Lingle approves Trade Center, Lahaina News, January 16, 1992: 4.

— regional ball park to be created, Lahaina News, March 19, 1992: 8.

— First Hawaiian Bank opening branch in, Lahaina News, June 25, 1992: 16.

— Maui County still pursuing developing a park in, Lahaina News, June 25, 1992: 2.

— residents urge maintaining parks before adding more, Lahaina News, September 3, 1992: 3.

— Maui Land and Pineapple, Co. asked to donate land for park in, Lahaina News, September 24, 1992: 1.

— JGL Enterprise applies to Maui Planning Commission for zoning change to build townhouses in, Lahaina News, November 4, 1993: 2.

— Department of Health notified Board of Water Supply of water contamination in Napili, Lahaina News, May 30, 1996: 3.

— Al and Pat Kwiecinski donates defibrillator to fire station, Lahaina News, July 11, 1996: 1,6.

— beach wall needs to be monitored, Lahaina News, December 19, 1996: 1,28.

— Maui County Office on Aging canvassing neighborhoods to identify older adult residents, Lahaina News, April 23, 1998: 16.

— brothers send holiday toys to Montserrat, Lahaina News, December 31, 1998: 1.

— water wells to be cleaned in, Lahaina News, September 9, 1999: 1,16.

— wild boar frequenting neighborhood, Lahaina News, September 30, 1999: 1,16.

— real estate developments featured, Lahaina News, June 7, 2001: 6.

— new condo construction in, Lahaina News, August 23, 2001: 7.

NAPILI BAY CIVIC IMPROVEMENT DISTRICT COMMITTEE

— Maui County Planning Department reviewing possible abolition of, Lahaina News, December 13, 1989: 36.

NAPILI BEACH

— change to public right-of-way proposed, Lahaina Sun, October 27, 1971: 14.

NAPILI BEACH RESORT ASSOCIATION

— names Lisa Nuyen as director of marketing, Lahaina News, August 26, 1999: 3.

NAPILI CANOE CLUB

— to meet at Hanaka'o'o Beach Park, Lahaina News, January 29, 1986: 3.

— to hold general meeting, Lahaina News, April 2, 1986: 3.

— gearing up for 1987 racing season, Lahaina News, January 21, 1987: 10.

— sponsors first canoe racing regatta, Lahaina News, May 6, 1987: 3.

— to participate in pre-season regatta, Lahaina News, May 18, 1988: 18.

— places second in Kamehameha-Hilo race, Lahaina News, August 16, 1989: 24.

— to hold kayak races, Lahaina News, February 20, 1991: 20.

— seeking paddlers, Lahaina News, February 20, 1992: 6.

— wins Hana race, Lahaina News, May 7, 1992: 14.

— wins Kamehameha Day regatta, Lahaina News, June 18, 1992: 13.

— loses Maui County Hawaiian Canoe Association regatta championship, Lahaina News, June 25, 1992: 9.

— takes second place in state finals, Lahaina News, August 6, 1992: 1,4.

— wins women's portion of Dutchie Kino Memorial Long Distance Canoe Race, Lahaina News, August 13, 1992: 6.

— win three canoe races, Lahaina News, August 20, 1992: 6.

— featured, Lahaina News, May 13, 1993: 8.

— held invitational canoe race in memory of Laurie Dolan, Lahaina News, May 27, 1993: 10.

— dominates division at Hawaiian Canoe Association state championship, Lahaina News, August 12, 1993: 10.

— results of latest races, Lahaina News, August 19, 1993: 8.

— results of race, Lahaina News, August 18, 1994: 7.

— to host Dougie Tihada Memorial Regatta, Lahaina News, July 6, 1995: 7.

— success at state paddling competition, Lahaina News, August 17, 1995: 7.

— to hold car wash to raise money, Lahaina News, March 21, 1996: 6.

— plans rebuild, Lahaina News, May 16, 1996: 13.

— featured, Lahaina News, July 11, 1996: 10.

— needs donations to replace stolen wheels from canoe trailer, Lahaina News, September 12, 1996: 18.

— Moloka'i, Lahaina News, October 17, 1996: 1.

— featured, Lahaina News, May 29, 1997: 13.

— upcoming races, Lahaina News, September 25, 1997: 14.

— featured, Lahaina News, June 18, 1998: 14.

— competes in Dougie T. Tihada Regatta, Lahaina News, July 9, 1998: 15.

— plans opening day, Lahaina News, March 18, 1999: 2.

— seeking members, Lahaina News, March 25, 1999: 16.

— being led by Greg Heneghan, Lahaina News, June 17, 1999: 6.

— to hold opening day meeting, Lahaina News, March 16, 2000: 7.

— featured, Lahaina News, June 29, 2000: 14.

— Maui County Hawaiian Canoe Association summer regattas continue, Lahaina News, July 6, 2000: 13.

— compete at State championships, Lahaina News, August 17, 2000: 6.

— wins second long distance race, Lahaina News, August 24, 2000: 8.

— to hold opening day, welcoming paddlers, Lahaina News, March 15, 2001: 11.

— featured, Lahaina News, June 28, 2001: 14.

— races in Kihei Canoe Club regatta, Lahaina News, July 12, 2001: 13.

— invites paddlers, Lahaina News, March 21, 2002: 13.

— featured, Lahaina News, June 20, 2002: 12.

— planning opening day events, Lahaina News, April 3, 2003: 12.

— to hold practices, Lahaina News, April 17, 2003: 13.

— to hold practices, Lahaina News, April 24, 2003: 11.

— to present Dougie Tihada Memorial Regatta at Hunakao'o Beach Park (Canoe Beach), Lahaina News, July 3, 2003: 12.

NAPILI CROSS COUNTRY TEAM

— holds practices at Napili Park, Lahaina News, August 22, 2002: 10.

— seeking runners, Lahaina News, October 10, 2002: 13.

— competed in West Maui Kids Track practice meet, Lahaina News, February 27, 2003: 12.

NAPILI FIRE AND AMBULANCE STATION

— see Fire and Ambulance Station, Napili

NAPILI KAI BEACH CLUB [RESTAURANT]

— fire caused by electrical short, Lahaina News, May 30, 1984: 22.

— retains Baney & Associates Inc. as advertising firm, Lahaina News, July 25, 1984: 14.

— manager Dorothy Millar selected to lead campaign to develop fire station, Lahaina News, May 31, 1989: 1.

— appoints Mike Walters as food and beverage manager, Lahaina News, October 10, 1991: 6.

— featured, Lahaina News, November 28, 1991: 3.

— presenting Napili Kai Youth Foundation Invitational golf tournament, Lahaina News, January 9, 1992: 7.

— children perform Hawaiian songs and dances at Sea House Restaurant, Lahaina News, January 30, 1992: 18.

— featuring Napili Kai Foundation Dinner Show, Lahaina News, March 5, 1992: 14.

— continues to host children performing Hawaiian songs and dances, Lahaina News, May 14, 1992: 15,16.

— continues to offer dinner show, Lahaina News, November 5, 1992: 16.

— appoints James Shefte as vice president and general manager, Lahaina News, May 20, 1993: 7.

— completing renovations, Lahaina News, September 30, 1993: 8.

— announces Napili Kai Youth Foundation Invitational Golf Tournament, Lahaina News, December 16, 1993: 11.

— adds wedding services, Lahaina News, February 24, 1994: 10.

— to hold hoolaulea for Aloha Festival, Lahaina News, October 13, 1994: 18.

— to host Youth Foundation Golf Tournament, Lahaina News, January 11, 1996: 6.

— featured, Lahaina News, April 4, 1996: 5,6.

— Millar family presents scholarships, Lahaina News, July 18, 1996: 3.

— Sea House Restaurant renovations completed, Lahaina News, November 28, 1996: 14.

— voted at top ten by Travel and Leisure magazine, Lahaina News, March 11, 1999: 11.

— changes name to Napili Kai Beach Resort, Lahaina News, June 3, 1999: 13.

NAPILI KAI BEACH RESORT [BUSINESS]

— wins Pele "Awards of Merit" from Honolulu Advertising Federation, Lahaina News, March 1, 2001: 8.

NAPILI KAI FOUNDATION

— to hold fundraising fair, Lahaina News, November 1, 1989: 6.

— children to entertain , Lahaina News, May 30, 1990: 11.

— continues to hold dinner show at Napili Kai Beach Club, Lahaina News, May 21, 1992: 17.

— Dinner Show continues, Lahaina News, July 9, 1992: 21.

— awards scholarships, Lahaina News, August 27, 1992: 4.

— members of to visit Disneyland, Lahaina News, June 19, 1997: 17.

— announces winners of J.C. Millar Memorial Scholarships, Lahaina News, July 16, 1998: 13.

— awards J.C. Millar Memorial Scholarships, Lahaina News, September 14, 2000: 11.

— children to stage Polynesian Hula Show, Lahaina News, March 22, 2001: 16.

— to stage Polynesian Hula Show, Lahaina News, May 10, 2001: 20.

— to stage Polynesian Hula Show, Lahaina News, May 24, 2001: 20.

— celebrating 36 years, Lahaina News, March 21, 2002: 14.

— awards scholarships to college students, Lahaina News, July 4, 2002: 5.

— to hold Polynesian Dinner Show, Lahaina News, June 19, 2003: 17.

— to hold Polynesian Dinner Show, Lahaina News, September 4, 2003: 17.

NAPILI KAI YOUTH FOUNDATION

— Invitational Gold Tournament to be held, Lahaina News, January 2, 1997: 5.

NAPILI MAI [MUSICAL GROUP]

— to perform at Old Lahaina Cafe and Luau, Lahaina News, July 25, 1990: 11.

NAPILI MARKET, THE [BUSINESS]

— to hold grand opening, Lahaina News, January 16, 1992: 4.

— to celebrate first anniversary, Lahaina News, January 14, 1993: 2.

— to hold grand opening, Lahaina News, January 21, 1993: 4,5.

NAPILI PARK ADVISORY COMMITTEE

— to hold public meeting on proposed park, Lahaina News, July 11, 1991: 2.

— expecting proposal on park, Lahaina News, August 15, 1991: 9.

NAPILI PLACE

— winners from Tenth Anniversary Celebration announced, Lahaina News, April 4, 2002: 8.

NAPILI PLAZA

— to hold grand opening, Lahaina News, January 14, 1993: 2.

— to hold "Winter Festival, Lahaina News, December 10, 1998: 8.

— celebrating Easter, Lahaina News, April 1, 1999: 2.

— Maui Family Support Services, Inc. named beneficiary of Craft Fair, Lahaina News, August 24, 2000: 19.

— Craft Fair to be held, Lahaina News, September 21, 2000: 20.

— Craft Fair continues, Lahaina News, December 7, 2000: 16.

— hosting Winter Festival, Lahaina News, December 6, 2001: 14.

— planning Winter Festival, Lahaina News, December 13, 2001: 16.

— celebrating 10 years, Lahaina News, March 7, 2002: 8.

— to celebrate 10th anniversary, Lahaina News, March 14, 2002: 16.

— to hold Winter Festival 2002, Lahaina News, December 12, 2002: 18.

NAPILI PRESCHOOL

— registration begins, Lahaina News, July 9, 1986: 3.

— sponsoring book fair, Lahaina News, January 30, 1992: 3.

NAPILI REGIONAL PARK

— Lahaina Citizen Advisory Committee resists County plans for, Lahaina News, May 11, 1995: 6.

— Maui Land and Pineapple, Co. owns proposed parcel for, Lahaina News, February 27, 1997: 1.

— in Linda Lingle's budget, Lahaina News, March 20, 1997: 1,20.

— Maui County seeking input, Lahaina News, December 18, 1997: 1,2.

— Maui County Council to hold meeting to discuss, Lahaina News, March 5, 1998: 1.

— plans for unveiled, Lahaina News, March 26, 1998: 2.

— plans taking shape, Lahaina News, April 16, 1998: 1.

— Maui Country to act on plans, Lahaina News, April 23, 1998: 1,20.

— Parks Department to show final plans for, Lahaina News, June 18, 1998: 7.

— work to begin later this year, Lahaina News, June 25, 1998: 1,16.

— residents urged to keep lobbying for, Lahaina News, November 5, 1998: 1.

— Maui Planning Commission to discuss, Lahaina News, December 3, 1998: 20.

— residents urged to keep lobbying for, Lahaina News, December 3, 1998: 7.

— approved by Maui Planning Commission, Lahaina News, December 17, 1998: 3.

— ground breaking held, Lahaina News, June 3, 1999: 1.

— County Parks Department to discuss access, Lahaina News, June 17, 1999: 3.

— County Council to discuss access ideas, Lahaina News, June 24, 1999: 1,16.

— access from Kohi Street appears best for county, Lahaina News, July 8, 1999: 1,16.

— County plans path through Honokeana to, Lahaina News, February 3, 2000: 1.

— construction of phase I soon to be completed, Lahaina News, June 1, 2000: 1,6.

— phase I complete, almost ready for kids, Lahaina News, August 24, 2000: 1,15.

— first phase completed, Lahaina News, August 31, 2000: 8.

— to open, Lahaina News, November 30, 2000: 1,20.

— editorial urging that access issues be resolved, Lahaina News, December 14, 2000: 4.

— Maui County secures pedestrian access to, Lahaina News, December 28, 2000: 1,15.

— construction begins for pedestrian access to, Lahaina News, July 4, 2002: 1,20.

— Reverend Laki Ka'ahumanu presides over blessing of, Lahaina News, October 10, 2002: 1.

— access to be dedicated, Lahaina News, October 10, 2002: 3.

NAPILI RIDGE

— real estate development featured, Lahaina News, August 12, 1999: 12.
— development featured, Lahaina News, February 20, 2003: 6.

NAPILI ROAD

— repairs to begin this week, Lahaina News, February 10, 2000: 1,20.

NAPILI SHORES

— development featured, Lahaina News, June 20, 1984: 15.
— development featured, Lahaina News, July 25, 1984: 15.
— development celebrates 20th anniversary, Lahaina News, March 19, 1992: 11.

NAPILI SUNSET RESORT

— Councilman Thomas Morrow concerned about impact of sea wall fronting, Lahaina News, July 7, 1994: 1,7.

NAPILI SURF

— complex connected to new Napili-Honokowai sewage line, Lahaina News, March 12, 1986: 12.

NAPILI SURFRIDERS

— wrestling team successful, Lahaina News, May 30, 2002: 12.

NAPILI TRADE CENTER

— project out to bid, Lahaina News, November 26, 1992: 12.
— not meeting county building codes, Lahaina News, June 29, 1995: 1.

NAPILI VILLAGE CENTER

— proposed, conceptual drawing printed, Lahaina News, June 24, 1999: 1,11.

NAPILI VILLAS

— to be developed, Lahaina News, December 14, 2000: 10.
— featured, Lahaina News, April 5, 2001: 7.
— opens on-site sales office, Lahaina News, May 17, 2001: 7.
— groundbreaking held for, Lahaina News, July 12, 2001: 7.
— Phase II featured, Lahaina News, November 29, 2001: 7.
— featured, Lahaina News, March 21, 2002: 7.
— Phase III to be finished soon, Lahaina News, May 30, 2002: 7.
— development featured, Lahaina News, July 25, 2002: 7.
— sales at, Lahaina News, November 21, 2002: 7.
— featured, Lahaina News, January 16, 2003: 7.
— development featured, Lahaina News, March 20, 2003: 7.

NAPILIHAU

— Maui County Planning Commission defers decision for low and moderate income housing in, Lahaina Sun, July 28, 1971: 2.
— decision on proposed housing project in Napilihau deferred by Maui Planning Commission, Lahaina Sun, December 15, 1971: 7.
— Maui Planning Commission approves second phase of housing project, Lahaina Sun, January 5, 1972: 6.
— housing development for low and moderate income families will be constructing, Lahaina Sun, March 22, 1972: 14.
— 13.5 acre housing project planned, Lahaina News, August 15, 1982: 6.
— planned shopping center approved by Maui County Planning Commission, Lahaina News, August 28, 1985: 3.
— investment real estate opportunities, Lahaina News, June 14, 2001: 6.

NAPILIHAU CAMPAIGN RECYCLE MAUI

— R. W. Munson to present to on recycling, Lahaina News, June 20, 1991: 3.

NAPILIHAU COMMUNITY ASSOCIATION

— seeking recreational park, Lahaina News, August 8, 1990: 1.
— to hold homeowners' meeting, Lahaina News, September 12, 1991: 3.
— to meet, Lahaina News, October 7, 1993: 3.

NAPILIHAU JOINT VENTURES

— has reservations for first phase, Lahaina News, August 3, 1995: 4.

NAPILIHAU PLAY GROUP

— support group for families with children formed, Lahaina News, April 1, 1999: 16.
— offered at Napilihau Recreation Center, Lahaina News, May 6, 1999: 20.

NAPILIHAU TOWNHOUSES

— ground breaking for, Lahaina News, September 4, 1997: 9.

NAPILIHAU VILLAGES

— hearing to be held on drainage plan for, Lahaina News, May 6, 1993: 4.
— request for outfall at Kaopala Bay pulled, Lahaina News, June 10, 1993: 1.
— residents concerned about JGL Enterprises' rezoning request at, Lahaina News, November 25, 1993: 1,3.
— Army Corps of Engineers releases preliminary report on, Lahaina News, February 16, 1995: 5.
— Maui Council to re-examine, Lahaina News, October 24, 1996: 1,20.
— first phase of construction begins, Lahaina News, April 17, 1997: 2.
— Supreme Court pulls permit for, Lahaina News, November 13, 1997: 1,3.
— Maui Planning Commission to consider proposed, Lahaina News, March 5, 1998: 1,20.
— plans for future phases withdrawn, Lahaina News, April 16, 1998: 1,16.

NARCISSUS QUEEN PAGEANT

— Chinese Chamber of Commerce searching for contestants for, Lahaina News, August 8, 1990: 5.

NARDIN, DOYA [WRITER]

— to sign new book at Kihei Community Center, Lahaina News, October 17, 1991: 7.

NARNIA [MUSICAL]

— to be performed by Maui Academy of Performing Arts, Lahaina News, December 2, 1993: 15.
— details of production, Lahaina News, December 9, 1993: 10.
— to be performed by Maui Academy of Performing Arts, Lahaina News, August 1, 2002: 20.

NARROW GAUGE IN A KINGDOM: THE HAWAIIAN RAILROAD COMPANY, 1878-1897 [BOOK]

— reviewed, Lahaina Sun, April 5, 1972: 15.

NARUKAMI THE THUNDERGOD [PLAY]

— kabuki play performed at Baldwin high school, Lahaina Sun, February 14, 1973: 11.

NASH, JIM

— awarded certification by the Professional Picture Framers Association, Lahaina News, June 6, 1991: 17.

NASH, SUE [ARTIST]

— to exhibit at Viewpoints Gallery, Lahaina News, April 30, 1992: 18.
— to demonstrate printmaking at The Villages Galleries, Lahaina News, January 21, 1999: 12.
— to exhibit at the Village Galleries, Lahaina News, January 20, 2000: 12.

NASKA PUBLIC HOUSING

— plans to phase out, Lahaina Sun, March 24, 1971: 2.

NASSAU SUFFOLK PERFORMING ARTS

— to hold workshops and concerts, Lahaina News, June 26, 2003: 17,18.

NAT WHITON DRILLING [BUSINESS]

— studying density of ocean floor off Lahaina, Lahaina Sun, November 18, 1970: 4.

NATAFGY, SAMMY

— new general manager of Rusty Harpoon restaurant, Lahaina News, November 14, 2002: 8.

NATALE, NICHOLAS
— concert to be held to benefit, Lahaina News, September 24, 1998: 16.

NATALIE COLE [SINGER]
— to perform on Maui, Lahaina News, July 4, 1984: 14.

NATION OF HAWAII
— Moanaliha Uwekoolani discusses leadership of Dennis "Bumpy" Kanahele, Lahaina News, November 30, 1995: 1,12.
— to hold meeting on Hawaiian Sovereignty, Lahaina News, September 26, 1996: 14.
— to hold "Awareness Demonstration" with Lahaina Open Space Society and Ka Kupuna O Maui, Lahaina News, October 17, 1996: 14.
— to hold meeting to discuss culturally significant areas with Na Kapula O Maui and Lahaina Open Space Society, Lahaina News, February 27, 1997: 11.

NATIONAL ACADEMY FOUNDATION
— president John Ferrandino visits Lahainaluna High School Academy of Travel and Tourism Program, Lahaina News, June 17, 1999: 13.

NATIONAL ASSOCIATION OF COUNTIES, WESTERN INTERSTATE REGION
— Goro Hokama announces will meet on Maui, Lahaina News, May 1, 1991: 4.

NATIONAL ASSOCIATION OF DRUG STORES
— to hold convention at the Grand Hyatt Wailea, Lahaina News, April 2, 1992: 12.
— to hold convention at the Grand Hyatt Wailea, Lahaina News, April 23, 1992: 15.

NATIONAL ASSOCIATION OF MINIATURE ENTHUSIASTS (NAME)
— to host show exhibit at Embassy Suites Resort, Lahaina News, March 5, 1992: 4.

NATIONAL ASSOCIATION OF MINIATURE ENTHUSIASTS [NAME]
— to host exhibit at Embassy Suites Resort, Lahaina News, March 12, 1992: 4.

NATIONAL ASSOCIATION OF STATE CREDIT UNION SUPERVISORS
— to hold convention at Maui Marriott, Lahaina News, September 9, 1993: 7.

NATIONAL AUCTION GROUP [BUSINESS]
— to auction David and Leslie Manthel's Olinda Vista Equestrian Estate, Lahaina News, January 28, 1999: 11.

NATIONAL BEEF COOK-OFF
— Carole Enmark to participate, Lahaina News, July 30, 1992: 4.

NATIONAL BOYS CHOIR OF MELBOURNE [MUSICAL GROUP]
— to perform at the Wharf Cinema Shops and Restaurants, Lahaina News, September 13, 1989: 5.

NATIONAL CANCER INSTITUTE
— probing high breast cancer rates in Hawaii, Lahaina News, April 11, 1996: 1,16.
— to study high rate of breast cancer in Hawaii, Lahaina News, April 25, 1996: 1,18.

NATIONAL COUNCIL OF SENIOR CITIZENS
— praises Congresswoman Patsy Mink, Lahaina News, March 12, 1992: 3.

NATIONAL DANCE WEEK
— to be celebrated by Maui Paniolo Dance Association, Lahaina News, April 12, 2001: 17.

NATIONAL DEFENSE CENTER OF EXCELLENCE FOR RESEARCH IN OCEAN SCIENCES (CEROS)
— to hold informational meeting, Lahaina News, October 29, 1998: 13.

NATIONAL EMERGENCY MEDICAL SERVICES WEEK
— to hold open house, Lahaina News, May 13, 1999: 16.

NATIONAL FILM BOARD OF CANADA
— films shown at Maui Community College, Lahaina Sun, July 5, 1972: 10.

NATIONAL FRAUD INFORMATION CENTER
— provides tips on understanding fraud, Lahaina News, October 22, 1998: 17.

NATIONAL GEOGRAPHIC
— review of article on Maui, Lahaina Sun, April 14, 1971: 5.

NATIONAL GUARD
— training to respond to riots, Lahaina Sun, December 16, 1970: 1,4.
— target range flooded out, Lahaina News, December 13, 1989: 3.
— participate in hurricane exercise, Lahaina News, September 15, 1994: 2.

NATIONAL HONOR SOCIETY
— Lahainaluna High School students inducted into, Lahaina News, June 6, 2002: 1,20.

NATIONAL KITCHEN AND BATH ASSOCIATION
— to hold tour of West Maui homes, Lahaina News, October 10, 1996: 8.
— "Great Kitchen and Bath Tour" to be held, Lahaina News, October 15, 1998: 13.

NATIONAL MARINE FISHERIES SERVICE
— agents to watch for whale violations, Lahaina News, March 13, 1997: 1,20.
— Marine Mammal Health and Stranding Response Program untangles humpback whale, Lahaina News, March 6, 2003: 2.
— finds dead turtle tied up near Mala Wharf, Lahaina News, August 14, 2003: 1,20.

NATIONAL MARINE SANCTUARIES PRESERVATION ACT
— supports Hawaii sanctuary, Lahaina News, October 10, 1996: 5.

NATIONAL MOBILE SHARPENING SERVICE (BUSINESS)
— purchased by Mike and Andrew Marynowski, Lahaina News, April 29, 1993: 9.

NATIONAL NETWORK AGAINST RESORT AND GOLF COURSE DEVELOPMENT
— Japanese anti-golf course group visits Maui, Lahaina News, January 30, 1992: 5.

NATIONAL OCEANIC AND ATMOSPHERIC ADMINISTRATION (NOAA)
— holds public meeting on proposed marine sanctuary around Kaho'olawe, Lahaina News, September 5, 1991: 1.
— to hold public meeting on Hawaii Islands Humpback Whale National Marine Sanctuary, Lahaina News, March 11, 1993: 8.
— to hold public meeting, Lahaina News, June 23, 1994: 1,16.
— draft plan for sanctuary to be released soon, Lahaina News, January 5, 1995: 1.
— plans progressing for Hawaiian Islands Humpback Whale National Marine Sanctuary, Lahaina News, April 20, 1995: 3.
— Sanctuaries and Reserves Division to hold meeting, Lahaina News, August 24, 1995: 4.
— to present draft plan for Hawaiian Islands National Humpback Whale Sanctuary, Lahaina News, September 21, 1995: 1,16.
— seeking advice on sanctuary plan, Lahaina News, February 15, 1996: 10.
— studying algae growth, Lahaina News, July 24, 1997: 3.
— launches a new web page, Lahaina News, December 18, 1997: 17.
— to hold public meeting on Northwestern Hawaiian Islands Coral Reef Ecosystem, Lahaina News, April 4, 2002: 5.
— to review plan for Hawaiian Islands Humpback Whale National Marine Sanctuary, Lahaina News, May 2, 2002: 1,18.
— see also Hawaiian Islands Humpback Whale National Marine Sanctuary

NATIONAL PARK SERVICE
— plans to create wilderness area in Haleakala, Lahaina Sun, October 20, 1971: 12.

NATIONAL PTA REFLECTIONS AWARDS
— Lahaina complex students among winners at, Lahaina News, March 7, 2002: 1,18.

NATIONAL PUBLIC RADIO (NPR)
— may be opening station on Maui, Lahaina News, February 1, 1984: 3.

NATIONAL REGISTRY OF NATURAL LANDMARKS
— names Kanaha Pond as landmark, Lahaina Sun, September 1, 1971: 7.

NATIONAL RELIGIOUS CONGRESS
— West Maui students to attend, Lahaina News, February 19, 1998: 3.

NATIONAL SAFE BOATING WEEK
— to be held on theme of "Boat Smart! Boat Safe!", Lahaina News, May 15, 2003: 13.

NATIONAL SCHOOL LUNCH DAY
— celebrated, Lahaina News, October 24, 1990: 5.

NATIONAL SECRETARIES WEEK
— to be celebrated, Lahaina News, April 18, 1990: 3.

NATIONAL SLEEP AWARENESS WEEK
— to be held, Lahaina News, March 27, 2003: 8.

NATIONAL WEATHER SERVICE
— responds to recent flooding, Lahaina Sun, February 3, 1971: 1.

NATIONAL WILDLIFE FEDERATION
— seeking to convince the Environmental Protection Agency to prepare a full environmental impact statement on proposed sewage treatment center, Lahaina Sun, January 31, 1973: 10.

NATIONAL YOUTH CHOIR OF GREAT BRITAIN
— seeking rooms for visit, Lahaina News, July 18, 1996: 3.

NATIONALIST CHINESE COUNSEL GENERAL
— plans to visit Maui, Lahaina Sun, May 24, 1972: 10.

NATIVE HAWAIIAN ADVISORY COUNCIL
— to hold workshop on political processes, Lahaina News, October 30, 1997: 17.
— to hold workshop on political processes, Lahaina News, November 6, 1997: 16.

NATIVE HAWAIIAN AUTONOMY ACT
— hearing to be held to discuss, Lahaina News, January 29, 1998: 1,2.

NATIVE HAWAIIAN CONVENTION
— Na Kupuna O Maui encourages Hawaiians to elect delegates to, Lahaina News, November 5, 1998: 2.
— delegates to be chosen for, Lahaina News, January 14, 1999: 12.

NATIVE HAWAIIAN DATA BOOK, THE [BOOK]
— published, Lahaina News, January 5, 1995: 1,3.
— published by Office of Hawaiian Affairs, Lahaina News, August 21, 1997: 9.

NATIVE HAWAIIAN EDUCATION ACT
— Senate Committee on Indian Affairs to hold hearings on reauthorizing, Lahaina News, November 25, 1999: 1.

NATIVE HAWAIIAN LIBRARY PROJECT
— provides Hawaiiana videos, Lahaina News, April 12, 1989: S13.
— lectures on Hawaiian Herbal Medicine and Lomilomi to be held, Lahaina News, August 22, 1991: 3.
— to hold quilting project, Lahaina News, February 25, 1993: 3.

NATIVE HAWAIIAN OCEAN ACTIVITIES
— operating E'ala, a double-hulled canoe, Lahaina News, September 10, 1986: 1.

NATIVE HAWAIIAN PLANT SHOP [BUSINESS]
— to host cleanup party at Lahaina Harbor, Lahaina News, February 8, 1989: 3.

NATIVE HAWAIIAN PLANT SOCIETY
— to hold monthly meeting at Maui Botanical Garden, Lahaina News, May 3, 1989: 4.
— to host artists Dennis Kanae Keawe and Patrick Horimoto, Lahaina News, February 13, 1992: 4.
— to hold hike to Red Hill, Lahaina News, March 25, 1993: 9.
— to host presentation on "Pu'u Kukui Watershed", Lahaina News, November 7, 1996: 14.
— to host presentation on plants and birds on Midway Atoll, Lahaina News, February 24, 2000: 16.
— to meet, Lahaina News, February 15, 2001: 16.

NATIVE TREE GIVEAWAY
— to be held, Lahaina News, October 31, 2002: 29.

NATIVE VIBE [MUSICAL GROUP]
— to perform at Longhi's, Lahaina News, November 16, 1995: 15.
— to perform, Lahaina News, December 28, 1995: 8.
— to perform at Maui Music Festival, Lahaina News, August 29, 1996: 14.

NATSU MATSURI
— Japanese Summer Festival to be held, Lahaina News, June 15, 2000: 16.

NATURE CONSERVANCY OF HAWAII, THE
— receives donation from Fred Baldwin Memorial Foundation, Lahaina News, December 26, 1990: 4,5.
— Valerie Cartwright Bays named Maui Project Development Coordinator, Lahaina News, October 10, 1991: 5.
— calls on government to help save endangered species, Lahaina News, November 14, 1991: 1.
— partnering with Amfac/JMB on pilot program to protect native forests above Honokowai, Lahaina News, January 16, 1992: 1.
— Maui Land and Pineapple, Co. to give easement of native forest at Pu'u Kukui to, Lahaina News, February 13, 1992: 4.
— receives pennies from Princess Nahienaena students, Lahaina News, May 9, 1996: 1,18.
— to hold hike into Waikamoi Preserve, Lahaina News, June 20, 1996: 13.
— to host hike in Waikamoi Preserve, Lahaina News, March 13, 1997: 17.
— to hold "Run for the Rain Forest", Lahaina News, June 11, 1998: 15.
— to offer Wet Side hike in Haleakala National Park, Lahaina News, March 15, 2001: 20.
— Iokepa Nae'ole to present "The Link Between Land and Sea" at, Lahaina News, September 6, 2001: 16.
— to celebrate National Trails Day, Lahaina News, June 5, 2003: 16.

NATURE'S COVE
— opens, Lahaina News, December 3, 1986: 11.

NATURE'S NECTAR [BUSINESS]
— opens, Lahaina News, February 4, 1993: 9.

NATURE'S TRAIL [BUSINESS]
— opens, Lahaina News, September 26, 2002: 8.

NATUROPATHIC MEDICINE
— discussed as alternative healing method, Lahaina News, May 4, 1988: 15,16.

NATWICK, GRIM [ARTIST]
— commemorated at Circle Gallery, Lahaina News, November 7, 1990: 13.

NAUTILUS CENTER [BUSINESS]
— see Lahaina Nautilus Center [business]

NAVA, AARON
— Scholar/Athlete of the Week, Lahaina News, November 21, 1996: 6.

NAVA, LYN
— Country Western Dance to be held to benefit, Lahaina News, November 18, 1993: 3.

NAVA, RICK
— appointed board member of Media Systems, Lahaina News, May 31, 1989: 15.
— Lahaina Rotary Club planning community projects, Lahaina News, July 24, 2003: 1,18.

NAVARRETTE, JESSICA CAMPOS
— graduates from College of Notre Dame, Lahaina News, June 17, 1999: 15.
— graduates from College of Notre Dame, Lahaina News, June 24, 1999: 2.

NAVATEK II [SHIP]
— to begin operations, Lahaina News, March 17, 1994: 8.
— offering food service, Lahaina News, May 5, 1994: 14.
— Clayton Murohayashi named president , Lahaina News, May 26, 1994: 7.
— offering whale watch cruise, Lahaina News, January 5, 1995: 12.
— United States Coast Guard decides not to charge captain of after the boat hit a reef, Lahaina News, February 23, 1995: 2.
— to hold whale watches, Lahaina News, January 18, 1996: 10.
— breaks free of moorings, Lahaina News, January 9, 1997: 14.
— encouraging students to volunteer in community, Lahaina News, May 22, 1997: 2.
— returns to Ma'alaea Harbor, Lahaina News, February 3, 2000: 11.
— Sunset Odyssey Dinner Cruise featured, Lahaina News, April 6, 2000: 8,9.

NAVY LEAGUE OF THE UNITED STATES
— Maui Council hosted "Sailor of the Quarter", Lahaina News, September 25, 1985: 3.
— celebrates United States Marine Corps, Lahaina News, November 5, 1986: 16.
— to meet, Lahaina News, April 22, 1987: 10.
— awards grant to Baldwin high school student Andrew Osorno, Lahaina News, February 3, 1988: 3.
— Maui Council announces events, Lahaina News, May 25, 1988: 12.
— to host Admiral Charles Larson, Lahaina News, May 28, 1992: 6.
— David Glazier to speak to, Lahaina News, January 29, 1998: 8.
— to hold forum on terrorism at Pioneer Inn, Lahaina News, February 21, 2002: 9.

NAVY, UNITED STATES
— open house aboard the fleet tender Bryce Canyon, Lahaina Sun, February 24, 1971: 1.
— details of attempts to raise the U.S.S. Bluegill, Lahaina News, November 16, 1983: 7,8,9,10.
— State House of Representative passes resolution concerning sound tests by, Lahaina News, April 2, 1998: 1,9.
— Lahainaluna High School students tour nuclear submarine USS San Francisco, Lahaina News, December 10, 1998: 15.
— to describe proposed grid of sonar-based sound transmitters, Lahaina News, August 19, 1999: 15.
— destroyer U.S.S. O'Kane to offer public tour, Lahaina News, February 10, 2000: 3.
— three ships to debark at Lahaina Harbor, Lahaina News, June 22, 2000: 6.
— opposition mounts to plan to use LFA sonar, Lahaina News, July 27, 2000: 1,17.
— USS Port Royal to debark at Lahaina Harbor, Lahaina News, July 27, 2000: 19.
— residents planning campaign against sonar, Lahaina News, April 19, 2001: 3.
— sailors clean Hanaka'o'o Beach Park, Lahaina News, March 20, 2003: 1,3.

NAY, JIMMY
— golf tournament to be held for, Lahaina News, December 28, 1995: 12.

NAYA, SEIJI
— director of the state Department of Business, Economic Development and Tourism to discuss economy, Lahaina News, October 18, 2001: 9.
— director of the state Department of Business, Economic Development and Tourism to discuss economy, Lahaina News, October 25, 2001: 17.

NAYLOR, HOWARD
— installed as president of Kiwanis Club , Lahaina News, October 7, 1987: 3,16.
— elected to Lieutenant Governor of Kiwanis' Hawaii division, Lahaina News, May 16, 1990: 6.

NAYLOR, ROGER [COMEDIAN]
— to perform at Comedy Club and the Sports Page, Lahaina News, March 19, 1992: 14,15.

NAZARIAN, WILLIAM
— State Securities Commissioner orders Sasha international Trading Co. to cease and desist investment scam, Lahaina News, May 18, 1995: 6.

NE JAME, ADELE
— to read poetry, Lahaina News, October 31, 1996: 18.

NEAR, HOLLY [MUSICIAN]
— to perform, Lahaina News, October 30, 1997: 16.

NEEDHAM, PIN
— lecture hosted by Pacific Whale Foundation, Lahaina News, December 13, 1989: 4.

NEEDLEWORK SHOP, THE [BUSINESS]
— opens, Lahaina News, February 15, 2001: 8.
— to teach needlework, Lahaina News, August 2, 2001: 16.
— to hold "Needlework in Progress" sessions, Lahaina News, August 15, 2002: 17.
— continues to hold "Needlework in Progress", Lahaina News, August 29, 2002: 21.

NEES, MICHAEL [ARTIST]
— to exhibit at the Art School at Kapalua, Lahaina News, September 28, 2000: 17.
— to exhibit at the Art School at Kapalua, Lahaina News, October 5, 2000: 16.

NEFF, LESLIE
— to present "Discover the Purpose of the Life" workshop with Sally Rasor Good and Gary Barclay, Lahaina News, January 19, 1995: 4.

NEIGHBOR ISLANDS MANAGEMENT CONFERENCE
— held at the Royal Lahaina Hotel, Lahaina Sun, March 3, 1971: 3.

NEIGHBORHOOD GRANTS OF MAUI PROGRAM
— accepting applications, Lahaina News, May 18, 2000: 7.

NEIZMAN, IKAIKA
— Scholar/Athlete of the Week, Lahaina News, October 5, 2000: 9.
— named to Hawaii All-State Football team, Lahaina News, February 14, 2002: 1,20.

NEIZMAN, JACOB
— passes away, his life remembered, Lahaina News, April 29, 1987: 6.
— Jacob Neizman Memorial Golf Tournament to be held at Royal Ka'anapali North Course, Lahaina News, July 27, 1988: 3,11.

NEIZMAN, JOY AND JAMES "KIMO"
— response to death of child featured, Lahaina News, February 13, 2003: 1,20.

NEIZMAN, KENNY [ARTIST]
— work described, Lahaina News, September, 1979: 6.
— life to be celebrated, Lahaina News, March 20, 2003: 1,20.

NEIZMAN, SHYLOE
— Scholar/Athlete of the Week, Lahaina News, June 17, 1999: 7.

NEKOMOTO, ROBERT

— discusses laws connected to air pollution, Lahaina Sun, February 17, 1971: 1,5.

NELSEN, JANE

— to speak on parenting, Lahaina News, April 24, 2003: 2.

NELSON, BONNIE

— appointed chair of Lahaina Yacht Club Victoria-Maui Race, Lahaina News, June 12, 1997: 12.

NELSON, CHERYL

— Scholar/Athlete of the Week, Lahaina News, January 13, 2000: 6.

NELSON, DON

— reflects on career in NBA, Lahaina News, May 30, 1996: 10.

NELSON, DWIGHT

— to speak on the next millennium at Seventh Day Adventist Church, Lahaina News, June 3, 1999: 16.

NELSON, HAYWOOD [ENTERTAINER]

— visits Maui, Lahaina News, September 24, 1986: 1,14.

NELSON, JOHN ALLEN [ACTOR]

— attends Celebrity Chefs fundraiser at Benihana, Lahaina News, October 24, 1990: 17.

NELSON, JOHN "EDDY"

— receives Sustained Superior Performance Award from the Hawaii Department of Social Services and Housing, Lahaina News, July 10, 1985: 8.
— housing manager's life described, Lahaina News, June 21, 1989: 4,5.
— to be fired from Piilani Housing, Lahaina News, December 5, 1990: 1,2.
— Mitsuo Shito responds to firing of, Lahaina News, December 19, 1990: 1,4.

NELSON, KEITH [COMEDIAN]

— to perform at Comedy Club, Lahaina News, January 2, 1992: 10.

NELSON, MARY RUTH "PAT"

— to present workshops at Maui Community College's Business Training Program, Lahaina News, October 31, 1990: 12.
— to hold workshops through Maui Community College, Lahaina News, November 14, 1990: 13.
— named top producer for August by Coldwell Banker McCormack Real Estate, Lahaina News, October 3, 1991: 7.
— named top lister by Coldwell Banker McCormack Real Estate, Lahaina News, October 24, 1991: 8.

NELSON, MIKE

— engineer discusses Pioneer Mill dumping pollution into the ocean, Lahaina Sun, November 25, 1970: 4.
— engineer representative to the Hawaiian Sugar Planters' Association's Environmental Standards Committee, Lahaina Sun, November 25, 1970: 4.
— to give art demonstration, Lahaina News, August 5, 1999: 12.

NELSON, PAUL

— appointed as vice president of engineering and construction at Amfac, Lahaina News, November 22, 1989: 5.

NELSON, RICHARD [ARTIST]

— to speak to Lahaina Arts Society, Lahaina News, March 4, 1987: 8.
— creates painting of Haleakala Ranch, Lahaina News, June 14, 1989: 18.
— to conduct classes at Malu'ulu O Lele Cultural Center, Lahaina News, February 20, 1991: 5.

NELSON, ROBERT AND UILANI [ARTISTS]

— to exhibit at Lahaina Galleries, Lahaina News, March 5, 1992: 18.

NELSON, ROBERT LYN [ARTIST]

— work discussed, Lahaina News, October 5, 1983: 12.
— paintings featured at Marine Art Expo '84, Lahaina News, February 8, 1984: 17.
— to appear at Maui Marine Art Expo, Lahaina News, March 13, 1985: 7,24.
— to exhibit at Maui Marine Art Expo, Lahaina News, March 12, 1986: 3.
— life and works described, Lahaina News, May 24, 1989: 10.
— completes triptych, Lahaina News, September 27, 1989: 9.
— to host poster signing to benefit Pacific Whale Foundation, Lahaina News, February 28, 1990: 13.
— to appear at Lahaina Galleries, Lahaina News, October 31, 1990: 16.
— opens showroom, Lahaina News, April 22, 1993: 6.
— to hold fundraiser for Little League, Lahaina News, May 13, 1993: 8.
— artwork being used by Maui Visitors Bureau, Lahaina News, May 20, 1993: 7.
— to open new gallery, Lahaina News, March 31, 1994: 14.
— publishes new book, Lahaina News, August 11, 1994: 12.
— to open studios in Monterey, Lahaina News, October 20, 1994: 16.
— to offer "Marine Life Drawing" class, Lahaina News, February 4, 1999: 16.

NELSON, SKY

— expresses resistance to proposed airport in West Maui, Lahaina News, May 22, 1985: 1,11.
— Lahainaluna High School varsity basketball coach discusses season, Lahaina News, November 9, 1995: 6.
— Lahainaluna High School coach to offer basketball camp, Lahaina News, August 15, 1996: 13.

NELSON, TESS [ARTIST]

— guest artist at Sunset Galleries, Lahaina News, May 30, 1990: 12.

NELSON, TRACY

— to perform at the Valley Isle Big Blues Mele, Lahaina News, May 15, 1997: 13.

NELSON, WALT

— evangelist to speak to Lahaina Seventh-day Adventist Church, Lahaina News, December 7, 1995: 3.

NELSON, WILLIE [MUSICIAN]

— purchases homes on Maui, Lahaina News, March 1, 1983: 4.
— review of concert in Maui, Lahaina News, January 25, 1984: 12.
— ticket sales in Maui progressing, Lahaina News, February 1, 1984: 14.
— sick at recent performance in Maui, Lahaina News, February 22, 1984: 14.
— second show canceled, Lahaina News, March 21, 1984: 14.
— tickets refunded for canceled performance, Lahaina News, May 9, 1984: 12.
— to perform, Lahaina News, February 12, 1986: 8.
— concert reviewed, Lahaina News, April 2, 1986: 8.
— makes surprise appearance at Keg Boathouse restaurant, Lahaina News, January 21, 1987: 3.
— to perform at Royal Lahaina Resort Tennis Stadium, Lahaina News, January 17, 1990: 12.
— to perform for Ka Lima O Maui, Lahaina News, August 1, 1996: 21.
— playing benefit concert for Ka Lima O Maui, Lahaina News, August 8, 1996: 16.
— to perform at Maui Arts and Cultural Center to benefit Maui Dharma Center, Lahaina News, June 29, 2000: 21.
— to perform benefit concert for Maui Dharma Center, Lahaina News, July 13, 2000: 17.
— to perform at benefit concert for Maui Cancer Institute Alliance at Longhi's restaurant, Lahaina News, November 23, 2000: 2.
— to perform fundraiser for Maui Cancer Institute Alliance, Lahaina News, November 30, 2000: 17.
— to perform at Montessori School Music Fest, Lahaina News, September 13, 2001: 16.
— to perform at "In the Spirit of Unity, a Maui County Thanksgiving", Lahaina News, November 15, 2001: 1,18.

— to perform at Montessori Music Fest, Lahaina News, October 17, 2002: 20.

— named resident manager of the year by Nai'a Properties, Lahaina News, January 23, 2003: 9.

— to play benefit concert for Montessori School of Maui, Lahaina News, October 9, 2003: 14.

NELSON-IWATA, JANET

— named president of Concierge Aloha People of Service, Lahaina News, July 13, 1988: 10.

NENE

— attempts to establish in Haleakala, Lahaina Sun, August 11, 1971: 11.

— Haleakala National Park to host presentation by Cathleen Hodges on, Lahaina News, August 28, 1997: 10,11.

— Friends of Haleakala National Park offering "Adopt-A-Nene" program, Lahaina News, November 27, 1997: 13.

— living near county water plant, Lahaina News, July 2, 1998: 1,20.

NEPTUNE UNDERWATER ADVENTURES [BUSINESS]

— system allows divers to talk on the sea floor, Lahaina News, September 7, 2000: 18.

NERD, THE [PLAY]

— to be performed by Maui Academy of Performing Arts, Lahaina News, January 14, 1993: 12.

— performances continue, Lahaina News, January 28, 1993: 15.

NERENHAUSEN, MARK

— resigning as director of Maui Arts and Cultural Center, Lahaina News, December 11, 1997: 21.

NESBIT, SID

— architect of Pohailani resort submits plans, Lahaina Sun, March 28, 1973: 3.

NESS, ROBERT

— to present to the American Association of Retired People, Lahaina News, December 21, 1988: 13.

NETTLESHIP, RUTH

— named sales and advertising coordinator for Napili Kai Beach Club Resort, Lahaina News, October 2, 1985: 9.

NETWORK OF VOLUNTEER LEADERS

— to offer course for volunteer coordinators, Lahaina News, July 5, 2001: 17.

NEUBAUER, DEANE

— inviting input on University of Hawai'i Strategic Plan, Lahaina News, March 7, 2002: 16.

NEUTEUFEL, WERNER

— named general manager of Hyatt Regency Maui, Lahaina News, March 25, 1987: 12.

NEVADA BOB'S GOLF & TENNIS [BUSINESS]

— sponsoring Royal Lahaina Open Tennis Tournament, Lahaina News, March 30, 1988: 3.

— to open at Lahaina Cannery Shopping Center, Lahaina News, August 10, 1988: 17.

NEW AGE FAIRE

— held, Lahaina News, November 11, 1987: 6.

NEW BLOOD [MUSICAL GROUP]

— to perform at Moose McGillycuddy's, Lahaina News, May 20, 1993: 19.

— to perform at Moose McGillycuddy's, Lahaina News, June 17, 1993: 14.

NEW ENGLAND

— design based on proposed for Front Street, Lahaina Sun, August 4, 1971: 1,3.

NEW ENGLAND NEW VAUDEVILLE REVUE [TROUPE]

— to perform at Iao Theatre, Lahaina News, February 13, 1992: 22.

NEW FREEDOM CIRCUIT RIDERS

— to hold revival services, Lahaina News, March 19, 1998: 12.

NEW HARMONY

— to hold wellness event, Lahaina News, October 31, 1996: 18.

— continues to offer First Saturday Event, Lahaina News, January 30, 1997: 10.

— First Saturday event to be held, Lahaina News, December 4, 1997: 24.

— Wellness and Rejuvenation Center to hold hands-on wellness techniques event, Lahaina News, January 29, 1998: 17.

— First Saturday event to be held, Lahaina News, July 2, 1998: 16.

— First Saturday event to be held, Lahaina News, January 28, 1999: 13.

— First Saturday Event to be held, Lahaina News, April 1, 1999: 16.

NEW HEBRIDES

— lots sold in by Amalgamated Land, Inc., Lahaina Sun, April 7, 1971: 5.

— sale of property criticized, Lahaina Sun, May 19, 1971: 2.

— independence may mean that Hawaiian investment is lost, Lahaina News, August 1, 1980: 13.

NEW LIFE CHRISTIAN CHURCH

— establishes itself in Lahaina, Lahaina News, October 1, 1992: 3.

NEW MOON TRAVELING MAGIC SHOW

— to perform at Maui Arts and Cultural Center, Lahaina News, November 20, 1997: 17.

— to be perform, Lahaina News, November 27, 1997: 12.

NEW ORLEANS

— Children's supplement features, Lahaina News, May 16, 1984: A,B,C,D.

NEW RIDERS OF THE PURPLE SAGE [MUSICAL GROUP]

— to perform at Casanova Restaurant, Lahaina News, December 1, 1994: 15.

NEW SHANGHAI CIRCUS

— see Shanghai Circus, New

NEW WORLD GUITAR TRIO [MUSICAL GROUP]

— featured, Lahaina News, November 17, 1994: 17.

NEW YEAR'S

— resolutions listed, Lahaina News, January 1, 1986: 1,10.

— editorial with wishes for New Year, Lahaina News, January 1, 1986: 2.

— Orient Express restaurant to celebrate Thai new year, Lahaina News, April 16, 1986: 1.

— events detailed, Lahaina News, December 28, 1988: 1.

— messages, Lahaina News, December 28, 1988: 4,6.

— alternatives to drinking alcohol described, Lahaina News, December 27, 1989: 1,3.

— Japanese-style described, Lahaina News, December 27, 1989: 3.

— events detailed, Lahaina News, December 27, 1989: 6,10,17,18,19.

— events, Lahaina News, December 12, 1990: 3,10,14.

— events, Lahaina News, December 19, 1990: 14.

— Dennis Miller to perform at Hyatt Regency Maui, Lahaina News, December 5, 1991: 23.

— events described, Lahaina News, December 26, 1991: 16,17,18.

— events described, Lahaina News, January 2, 1992: 12,14.

— events listed, Lahaina News, December 24, 1992: 13.

— events listed, Lahaina News, December 31, 1992: 13.

— events detailed, Lahaina News, December 23, 1993: 10,11,12.

— events, Lahaina News, December 30, 1993: 11.

— events, Lahaina News, December 29, 1994: 7,8.

— Hyatt Regency Maui to hold dance party, Lahaina News, December 21, 1995: 14.

— First Night Maui to be held, Lahaina News, December 28, 1995: 8.

— events to be held, Lahaina News, December 28, 1995: 8.

— events, Lahaina News, December 26, 1996: 11.

— First Night Maui seeking vendors and volunteers, Lahaina News, October 30, 1997: 2.

— First Night Maui to be held, Lahaina News, December 25, 1997: 13.

— First Night Maui celebration to be held, Lahaina News, December 17, 1998: 12.

— First Night Maui to be held, Lahaina News, December 31, 1998: 12.

— Maui planning events for the year 2000, Lahaina News, June 17, 1999: 1.

— events to be held, Lahaina News, December 23, 1999: 10,11.

— to be celebrated, Lahaina News, December 30, 1999: 1.

— The Swing Thing to be held at Embassy Vacation Resort, Lahaina News, December 30, 1999: 3.

— see also First Night Maui

NEW YORK
— travel to described, Lahaina Sun, February 9, 1972: 18.

NEW YORK CITY, USS [SUBMARINE]
— nuclear-powered submarine visits Lahaina , Lahaina News, June 13, 1984: 12.

NEW YORK EXPRESS ROLLER DANCE COMPANY [TROUPE]
— to perform, Lahaina News, February 2, 1995: 10.

NEW YORK GOURMET CAFE AND CATERING [RESTAURANT]
— opens, Lahaina News, October 12, 1995: 12.

— to hold free swap meet, Lahaina News, March 14, 1996: 10.

NEW YORK STYLE HUSTLE AND DANCE PARTY
— continues to be held, Lahaina News, June 26, 2003: 20.

NEW ZEALAND
— trip to, described, Lahaina Sun, April 5, 1972: 19.

— earlier article criticized , Lahaina Sun, April 19, 1972: 9.

— travel to, described, Lahaina Sun, December 13, 1972: 22,23.

— description of winter spent in, Lahaina Sun, May 30, 1973: 9.

— "Waiora" play to be performed at Iao Theater, Lahaina News, September 16, 1999: 13.

— "Te Ao Tawhito/Te Ao Hou (Old Worlds/New Worlds)" exhibit to be held, Lahaina News, February 1, 2001: 20.

NEWLIN, TOREY
— missing, Lahaina News, February 28, 2002: 1,2.

— family increases reward for tips on disappearance of, Lahaina News, March 7, 2002: 2.

NEWMAN, JOHN
— opens local franchise of Rainbow International Carpet Care and Restoration Specialists, Lahaina News, June 12, 1997: 15.

NEWNAN, CRAIG
— passes away, Lahaina News, June 24, 1999: 5.

NEWSPAPERS
— new newspaper promised for Maui, Lahaina Sun, May 17, 1972: 6.

— Jack Stephens and James Franklin affirm desire to produce new newspaper on Maui, Lahaina Sun, May 24, 1972: 9.

— New newspaper issues second edition, Lahaina Sun, June 21, 1972: 3.

— new newspaper issues third edition, Lahaina Sun, July 19, 1972: 3.

— new paper suing county officials, Lahaina Sun, August 9, 1972: 5.

— status of freedom of the press on Maui discussed, Lahaina Sun, September 27, 1972: 18,19.

— Maui County Issues begins publication, Lahaina Sun, September 27, 1972: 5.

— New Newspaper sued, Lahaina Sun, October 18, 1972: 10.

— attitudes towards New Newspaper discussed, Lahaina Sun, November 8, 1972: 3.

— publishers of New Newspaper sue councilman Joe Bulgo, Lahaina Sun, December 6, 1972: 5.

— national trend attacking reporting discussed, Lahaina Sun, January 3, 1973: 6.

— response to story concerning national trend attacking reporting, Lahaina Sun, January 17, 1973: 8.

— new paper in Moloka'i, Lahaina Sun, February 21, 1973: 3.

— politicians attempting to break up joint operation of Honolulu's daily newspapers, Lahaina News, March 15, 1980: 6.

— Thom Weyand becomes managing editor of Maui Sun, Lahaina News, November 1, 1981: 6.

— editorial on closing of the Maui Sun, Lahaina News, January 15, 1982: 2,5.

— Maui Reporter suspects publication, Lahaina News, January 15, 1983: 4,5.

— Lahaina News sold to Bill and Nancy Worth, Lahaina News, February 1, 1983: 8,9.

— summary of events from 1986, Lahaina News, January 7, 1987: 1,16.

NEWTON, NICOLE
— hired by Westin Maui as director of catering and conference services, Lahaina News, January 16, 2003: 8.

NEWTON, SMOKEY [ARTIST]
— work featured, Lahaina News, February 15, 1981: 14.

NEWTON, WAYNE [MUSICIAN]
— to perform, Lahaina News, April 6, 2000: 16.

NEWTON-JOHN, OLIVIA [SINGER]
— company opens Koala Blue store in Lahaina, Lahaina News, December 7, 1988: 8.

NEXT [MUSICAL GROUP]
— to perform at Royal Ocean Terrace Lounge at the Royal Lahaina Resort, Lahaina News, June 20, 1990: 9,11.

— to perform at Royal Ocean Terrace Lounge at the Royal Lahaina Resort, Lahaina News, September 19, 1990: 11.

NFL ALUMNI ASSOCIATION
— co-hosting a booth at Maui County Fair, Lahaina News, September 14, 1995: 3.

— hold fundraiser for Big Brothers/Big Sisters, Lahaina News, November 16, 1995: 15.

NG, CHRIS [TENNIS PLAYER]
— representing Hawaii at Olympic Qualifying Tournament, Lahaina News, May 16, 1984: 6.

NGUYEN, ANNIE
— Miss Lahaina to compete in Miss Hawaii Teen Pageant, Lahaina News, May 25, 2000: 1.

NIAMI, BILL
— co-skipper wins Victoria-to-Maui race, Lahaina News, July 18, 1984: 7.

NICARAGUA
— Steven Moser to show "Coverup—The Iran-Contra Affair" to raise funds for, Lahaina News, October 26, 1988: 17.

NICE, SHIRLEY [WRITER]
— author of "Speaking for Impact" to visit Borders Books, Lahaina News, August 26, 1999: 17.

NICHOLS, NORMA
— to lecture on "Image of Women in American Art", Lahaina News, May 30, 1984: 22.

NICKEL, TIMOTHY AND NANCY LEROI [MUSICIANS]
— to perform, Lahaina News, June 18, 1992: 22.

NICKELE, GARY
— new president of Amfac/JMB, Lahaina News, March 15, 2001: 9.

NICKELS, BARBARA JOY [ARTIST]
— work displayed at Sir Wilfred's, Lahaina News, June 17, 1987: 3.

NICKENS, WAYNE [DOCTOR]
— to speak at Lahaina Civic Center on "Depression and the Holidays", Lahaina News, December 5, 1984: 3.
— to speak on sleep disturbances at Lahaina Civic Center, Lahaina News, December 19, 1984: 24.
— forms Foundation for National Education on Alcoholism and Drug Abuse, Lahaina News, June 19, 1985: 3.
— book on alcoholism entitled "Not Guilty, Not Crazy" reviewed, Lahaina News, July 31, 1985: 1,20.

NICKERSON, ROY
— lecture for Maui Whalewatchers, Lahaina News, February 25, 1987: 3.
— to speak to Maui Whale Watchers, Lahaina News, March 11, 1987: 3.
— returns to Lahaina to become historian for Lahaina Restoration Foundation, Lahaina News, April 3, 1991: 1.

NICK'S AQUA SPORTS
— opens at Hyatt Regency Maui, Lahaina News, February 10, 1988: 11.
— sponsoring reef cleanup, Lahaina News, September 7, 1988: 14.

NICK'S FISHMARKET
— to open, Lahaina News, August 20, 1998: 13.

NICOLAS, GWENDOLYN
— named Hawaii Secretary of the Year by Professional Secretaries International, Lahaina News, June 13, 1991: 18.

NIDLE, SHELDON [WRITER]
— to lecture, Lahaina News, July 27, 1995: 12.

NIEHAUS, DAVID
— receives contract to renovate former Maui County Police headquarters, Lahaina News, September 6, 1989: 2.

NIELSON, BOB
— owner of Island Air Transfer buys Maui Air, Lahaina Sun, July 19, 1972: 10.

NIEMAN, LEONARDO [ARTIST]
— featured at Center Art Gallery, Lahaina News, February 24, 1988: 18.

NIGHT LIFE
— veracity of Lahaina Times' account discussed, Lahaina Times, September, 1980 volume 4 number 8: 1, 2, 3.

NIGHT OF THE WHALE
— to be held as part of WhaleFest '97, Lahaina News, March 13, 1997: 1,3.

NIGHT OUT AT THE CENTER
— concert series held by Maui Community College and the Maui Arts and Cultural Center to finish, Lahaina News, July 13, 1995: 12.

NIGHT SLYDE [MUSICAL GROUP]
— to perform at Moose McGillycuddy's, Lahaina News, November 9, 1995: 12.

NIGHT, SONNY [MUSICIAN]
— to perform at Swan Court, Hyatt Regency Maui, Lahaina News, September 19, 1996: 18.

NIGHTENGALE, JOHN
— director of proposed Maui Ocean Center discusses plans, Lahaina News, October 12, 1988: 1,14.

NIGHTINGALE, THE [PLAY]
— to be performed by the Maui Academy of Performing Arts, Lahaina News, July 20, 1995: 12.
— reviewed, Lahaina News, July 27, 1995: 11.

NIGHTMARE IN HAWAII [FILM]
— reviewed, Lahaina News, July, 1979: 5.

NII, ANDY
— Maui district school superintendent spoke to parents regarding move of Kam III elementary school , Lahaina Sun, November 25, 1970: 3.

NI'IHAU [ISLAND]
— described, Lahaina News, June 1, 1981: 11,12.
— featured, Lahaina News, December 7, 1983: 7,8,9.
— lei makers to visit The Art School at Kapalua, Lahaina News, December 31, 1998: 5.

NIKHILANANDA, NICK [POLITICIAN]
— candidate for East Maui County Council, Lahaina News, November 2, 2000: 16,17.

NIKKO RESTAURANT [RESTAURANT]
— to host Japanese Culture Night, Lahaina News, September 19, 1996: 18.

NILSSON, MARK
— appointed artist liaison for Foundation Galleries, Lahaina News, September 12, 1991: 4.

NINO, LEO [COMEDIAN]
— to perform at Comedy Club and the Sports Page, Lahaina News, October 8, 1992: 10.

NIP, AL
— organizes Lahainaluna High School teachers to learn about Hawaiian culture, Lahaina News, September 18, 2003: 1,20.

NISEI PROJECT
— to be staged by Covenant Dance Theatre, Lahaina News, July 10, 2003: 17.

NISEI VETERANS MEMORIAL CENTER
— hosting "Tobu—To Soar to New Heights—Three Generations", Lahaina News, July 28, 1994: 14.
— Alexander and Baldwin Foundation awards grant to, Lahaina News, June 19, 2003: 8.

NISHIJIMA, HERB
— Kapalua Senior Golf Course Superintendent featured, Lahaina News, July 16, 1998: 1,14,15.

NISHIJO [FAMILY]
— wins shopping spree at Lahaina Center, Lahaina News, June 25, 1992: 22.

NISHIKAWA ARCHITECTS [BUSINESS]
— opens, Lahaina News, December 19, 1990: 7.
— moves location, Lahaina News, December 3, 1998: 17.
— promotes Durwin Kiyabu and Dennis Harmon, Lahaina News, August 10, 2000: 13.

NISHIKAWA, LANE [PERFORMER]
— to perform "I'm on a Mission from Buddha", Lahaina News, March 9, 2000: 12.
— play "When We Were One" to be previewed at Maui Arts and Cultural Center, Lahaina News, December 7, 2000: 24.
— to hold performance classes, Lahaina News, September 20, 2001: 17.
— to teach acting class, Lahaina News, September 27, 2001: 17.
— "When We Were One" to be performed, Lahaina News, March 21, 2002: 16.
— play "We Were Brothers" to be performed, Lahaina News, October 31, 2002: 22.
— to hold auditions for "All That is Sacred", Lahaina News, March 6, 2003: 17.

NISHIKI, WAYNE [POLITICIAN]
— political activities criticized, Lahaina News, May 15, 1980: 2.
— profiled by Bob Kelsey, Lahaina News, January 1, 1981: 13.
— update on legal challenges, Lahaina News, December 1, 1982: 2.
— councilman asks booking agents to not sell thrillcraft rides, Lahaina News, March 16, 1988: 1.
— wants traffic signals at Honoapi'ilani Highway and Dickenson, Lahaina News, July 4, 1990: 1.

— Maui Council member calls for volunteers for Citizens Advisory Committees, Lahaina News, August 1, 1991: 4.

— concerned over shorelines structures, plantings by Sheraton Maui, Lahaina News, August 15, 1991: 1.

— concerned over who controls Kapalua airport, Lahaina News, September 19, 1991: 2.

— announces intention to run for Congress to unseat Daniel Inouye, Lahaina News, October 24, 1991: 3.

— responds to attacks by fellow Democrats, Lahaina News, June 11, 1992: 6.

— ousted from Democratic Party for supporting Rick Reed, Lahaina News, June 18, 1992: 4.

— reinstated by Democratic Party, Lahaina News, July 2, 1992: 3.

— seeks council to discuss new hotels at North Beach, Lahaina News, October 26, 1995: 3.

— member of Maui County Council supports bill authorizing settling claims even when county attorneys recommend against it, Lahaina News, August 13, 1998: 3.

— files for reelection, Lahaina News, July 27, 2000: 8.

— candidate for South Maui County Council, Lahaina News, November 2, 2000: 18.

NISHINO, MARK

— appointed assistant vice president of Kahului Branch of Central Pacific Bank, Lahaina News, March 15, 2001: 8.

NISHIYAMA, KRISTINE

— listed in Who's Who Among Students in American Universities and Colleges, Lahaina News, March 12, 1992: 3.

NISHIYAMA, PATTY

— member of Na Kupuna O Maui to discuss issues, Lahaina News, August 2, 2001: 3.

NISHIZAKI DANCE TEAM [TROUPE]

— participate in opening of Lahaina Amphitheatre, Lahaina Sun, August 16, 1972: 9.

NISHIZAKI, ERNEST

— named general manager of Sheraton Maui Hotel, Lahaina News, July 25, 1984: 14.

NISSAN CUP WORLD CHAMPIONSHIP OF GOLF

— to be played at Kapalua, Lahaina News, October 23, 1985: 4.

NISSAN WAILEA PRO TENNIS CLASSIC

— to be held, Lahaina News, October 17, 1990: 8.

NITRITES

— found in water off Maui, Lahaina News, August 22, 1991: 1,20.

NITTA, GENE

— comments on proposed thrillcraft corridor, Lahaina News, February 24, 1988: 1.

NITTA, GEORGE "MANJU"

— to teach baseball, Lahaina News, January 13, 2000: 7.

NITTAKU INVESTMENT, INC. [BUSINESS]

— may no longer manage Pioneer Inn, Lahaina News, March 18, 1993: 1,4.

NIXON, RICHARD [POLITICIAN]

— travels to China after two-day stay in Oahu, Lahaina Sun, February 23, 1972: 13.

— U.S. president meets with Japan's Prime Minister in Honolulu, Lahaina Sun, September 6, 1972: 3,5.

NO DEADWOOD BIG BAND [MUSICAL GROUP]

— to play at Whalers Village, Lahaina News, June 15, 1988: 14.

NO DOUBT [MUSICAL GROUP]

— to perform at Maui Arts and Cultural Center, Lahaina News, April 23, 1998: 17.

— to perform at Maui Arts and Cultural Center, Lahaina News, April 30, 1998: 16.

— to perform at the Alexander and Baldwin Amphitheatre, Lahaina News, October 5, 2000: 17.

— to perform at Maui Arts and Cultural Center, Lahaina News, October 19, 2000: 22.

— to perform at Maui Arts and Cultural Center, Lahaina News, October 26, 2000: 27,28.

NO HONOAPI'ILANI AWARD

— presented to Eleanor Sommerville and Kathy Kameda, Lahaina News, December 6, 1989: 3.

NO KA OI DELI INC. [RESTAURANT]

— opens, Lahaina News, August 21, 1997: 12.

NO KAI OLA

— to hold Hawaiian language and hula classes, Lahaina News, May 9, 1996: 14.

NO SURRENDER [MUSICAL GROUP]

— to perform at Moose McGillycuddy's, Lahaina News, December 8, 1994: 16.

NOA NOA [BUSINESS]

— opens at Lahaina Center, Lahaina News, April 18, 1990: 5.

— holds grand opening, Lahaina News, June 27, 1990: 8.

— opens second location in Lahaina, Lahaina News, December 26, 1990: 7.

— expands to mainland, Lahaina News, June 27, 1991: 9.

NOBRIGA, DAVID "BUDDY"

— discusses West Maui watershed plans, Lahaina Sun, September 29, 1971: 4.

— honored by Boy Scouts of America for service, Lahaina News, February 13, 1991: 4,5.

— to receive Distinguish Citizen recognition from the Boy Scouts, Lahaina News, May 16, 2002: 3.

NOCHE FLAMENCA [PERFORMERS]

— to perform flamenco at the Maui Arts and Cultural Center, Lahaina News, January 10, 2002: 17.

— to perform at Maui Arts and Cultural Center, Lahaina News, January 17, 2002: 16.

NOE, ROBERT A

— IRS District Director to lecture on taxes, Lahaina News, January 13, 1994: 5.

NOELANI [CONDOMINIUM]

— featured, Lahaina News, September 5, 1984: 15.

NOHARA, GAVIN

— completes Marine Corp training, Lahaina News, August 1, 2002: 9.

NOHARA, JESSICA

— Scholar/Athlete of the Week, Lahaina News, June 12, 1997: 13.

— sets record for 100-meter freestyle, Lahaina News, May 7, 1998: 10.

— swimmer successful, Lahaina News, November 18, 1999: 8.

— leads Lahaina Swim Club to success at Maui County Age Group Swim Meet, Lahaina News, October 26, 2000: 12.

NOHARA, MATTHEW

— takes second place in Patsy Mink's Second Congressional District Art Contest, Lahaina News, May 21, 1998: 1.

NOHARA, WES

— vice chair of the West Maui Soil and Water Conservation District discusses interim fix for flooding and dust issues, Lahaina News, December 14, 2000: 1,17.

NOID, BENJAMIN

— to speak on natural killer cells and hormones, Lahaina News, March 14, 2002: 2.

— to speak on natural killer cells and hormones, Lahaina News, March 21, 2002: 16.

NOISE
— residents of Wahikuli complain of noise from dirt bikes, Lahaina News, June 6, 1990: 1.
— Maui County attempting to restrict high levels of from boom boxes, Lahaina News, June 6, 1990: 1,3.

NOISE COMPATIBILITY PROGRAM
— at Kahului Airport, to be discussed, Lahaina News, November 1, 1989: 6.

NOISES OFF [PLAY]
— to be performed by Maui OnStage/Maui Academy of Performing Arts, Lahaina News, April 27, 1995: 11.

NOJIMA, SANFORD
— appointed assistant to the general manager at Makena Resort, Lahaina News, January 23, 1992: 13.

NOLAN, DENNIS [WRITER]
— to speak "Cross the Bridge to Dreams", Lahaina News, June 4, 1998: 17.

NOLAN, FERNANDO
— graduates from International Air Academy, Lahaina News, January 20, 1988: 3.

NOLAN-KAHAHANE, DALINA
— appointed as reservation manager at Trilogy Excursions, Lahaina News, September 22, 1994: 13.

NOLAND, BROTHER
— see Brother Noland [musician]

NOMURA, KEN
— Lahaina Intermediate School principal transfers to Lahikai, Lahaina News, November 29, 2001: 1.

NONNENMACHER, CHRISTINE [ARTIST]
— photographer to teach, Lahaina News, May 13, 1999: 16.

NOODLE CAFE [RESTAURANT]
— featured, Lahaina News, May 4, 2000: 6.

NORCROSS, ZOE
— to discuss beach erosion in talk on "Maui's Dynamic Beaches", Lahaina News, October 9, 2003: 3.

NORFOLK, BOBBY
— storyteller to appear at Makawao Public Library, Lahaina News, June 24, 1999: 12.

NORFOLK, SHERRY
— storyteller to appear at Lahaina Public Library, Lahaina News, June 17, 1999: 17.

NORIMOTO, AKEMI
— to represent Westin Maui and Kaua'i in Asian sector, Lahaina News, June 24, 1993: 10.

NORIMOTO, ARLYNNE
— named Manager of the First Quarter by Westin Maui, Lahaina News, June 1, 1995: 10.

NORMAN, GREG
— golfer wins Kapalua International Championship of Golf, Lahaina News, November 9, 1983: 4.

NORMAN POWERS DANCE PRODUCTIONS
— to hold dance at Auntie Aloha's Hawaiian Hut, Lahaina News, August 10, 2000: 16,17.

NORR, NANCY [ARTIST]
— opens working painting studio on Front Street, Lahaina News, March 20, 1991: 7.
— to visit Sargent's Fine Arts, Lahaina News, March 6, 2003: 16,17.
— to exhibit at Sargent's Fine Art, Lahaina News, August 28, 2003: 17.
— to exhibit at Sargent's Fine Art, Lahaina News, September 4, 2003: 16.

NORRIS, NEAL
— interviewed, Lahaina Sun, March 8, 1972: 15.

NORTH AMERICAN SECURITIES ADMINISTRATORS ASSOCIATION
— offers tips for online investing, Lahaina News, September 20, 2001: 9.

NORTH BEACH
— area to be developed by Amfac, Inc. and Tobishima Corp., Lahaina News, January 1, 1986: 3.
— Amfac/JMB holds groundbreaking for park at, Lahaina News, January 16, 1992: 3.
— Lahaina Citizen Advisory Committee requests part at, Lahaina News, June 9, 1994: 1.
— Maui Planning Commission to consider request for hotel development at, Lahaina News, March 9, 1995: 1,16.
— party being held by residents hoping to preserve, Lahaina News, March 30, 1995: 6.
— Army Corps of Engineers studying wetlands at, Lahaina News, April 6, 1995: 1,16.
— Congresswoman Patsy Mink seeks federal study of development proposed for , Lahaina News, May 4, 1995: 5.
— Mayor's West Maui Advisory Committee holds informational hearing, Lahaina News, May 11, 1995: 1,16.
— testimony heard opposing beach at, Lahaina News, August 24, 1995: 3.
— night access for divers an issue, Lahaina News, April 18, 1996: 7.
— Amfac/JMB Hawaii holds public meeting on proposed time share at, Lahaina News, October 24, 1996: 3.
— Amfac/JMB Hawaii seeking approval for traffic mitigation plan at, Lahaina News, December 5, 1996: 1,20.
— mayor Linda Lingle initiating discussion on public park at, Lahaina News, January 30, 1997: 1.
— hawkbill turtles may be nesting at, Lahaina News, January 30, 1997: 1,16.
— mayor Linda Lingle updates on possible open space at, Lahaina News, February 13, 1997: 1.
— Land Use Committee to tour area of proposed development, Lahaina News, April 17, 1997: 3.
— Maui Planning Commission to consider traffic issues in , Lahaina News, June 12, 1997: 3.
— Mayor and council to discuss, Lahaina News, July 10, 1997: 1.
— Maui Planning Commission to discuss Amfac Maui's application for Special Management Area at, Lahaina News, July 10, 1997: 16.
— issues to be discussed at Planning Commission meeting, Lahaina News, July 17, 1997: 1.
— Maui Planning Commission to tour, Lahaina News, August 7, 1997: 3.
— issues connected to development proposed by Amfac Maui and Ka'anapali Ownership Resorts, Lahaina News, August 14, 1997: 1.
— resolution heard supporting creation of beach park, Lahaina News, August 21, 1997: 9.
— Mayor Linda Lingle announces new agreement between Maui County and Amfac, Lahaina News, September 25, 1997: 2,3.
— Maui Planning Commission to discuss agreement, Lahaina News, November 6, 1997: 1,13.
— county to hire special counsel to advise Maui Planning Commission, Lahaina News, November 13, 1997: 1.
— hearing officer recommends construction permit for, Lahaina News, January 8, 1998: 1,2.

NORTH BEACH GRILLE [RESTAURANT]
— opens, Lahaina News, March 11, 1993: 14.
— featured, Lahaina News, April 15, 1993: 11.
— finalist for Embassy Suites Restaurant of the Year competition, Lahaina News, March 30, 1995: 11.
— featured, Lahaina News, June 1, 2000: 15.
— featured, Lahaina News, March 6, 2003: 9.

NORTH BEACH PARK
— Roselle Bailey blesses , Lahaina News, January 24, 2002: 3.

NORTH BEACH PROJECT
— Maui County Planning Commission grants intervenor status to groups, Lahaina News, June 1, 1988: 1.

NORTH SHORE PADDLE
— race to be held, Lahaina News, August 22, 2002: 10.

NORTH SHORT IMPROVEMENT ASSOCIATION
— meeting in Paia, Lahaina Sun, December 30, 1970: 5.

NORTHWEST AIRLINES [BUSINESS]
— enters into deal with Hawaiian Airlines, Lahaina News, December 26, 1990: 7.

NORTHWEST HAWAIIAN ISLANDS MANAGEMENT PLAN
— draft created by local fisherman Isaac Harp, Lahaina News, August 17, 2000: 1,20.

NORTHWESTERN HAWAIIAN ISLANDS CORAL REEF ECOSYSTEM
— Bill Clinton signs Executive Order to establish, Lahaina News, January 4, 2001: 2.
— National Oceanic and Atmosphere Administration (NOAA) to hold meeting on, Lahaina News, April 4, 2002: 5.
— National Oceanic and Atmosphere Administration (NOAA) to hold meeting on, Lahaina News, April 11, 2002: 16.

NORTHWESTERN HAWAIIAN ISLANDS CORAL REEF ECOSYSTEM RESERVE
— hearing to be set to discuss, Lahaina News, December 14, 2000: 9.

NORTHWESTERN MUTUAL LIFE INSURANCE [BUSINESS]
— sells Maui Inter-Continental Hotel Wailea, Lahaina News, December 7, 1988: 6.
— to offer financial seminar, Lahaina News, June 10, 1999: 13.

NORWEST MORTGAGE OF HAWAII
— offers home financing options, Lahaina News, December 28, 2000: 13.

NOTTAGE, PETER
— appointed as senior vice president-construction and development at McCormack Properties, Inc., Lahaina News, April 9, 1992: 12.

NOU NOUS, THE [CARTOON STRIP]
— will begin publishing in Lahaina News, Lahaina News, January 23, 1991: 1.

NOVAK-CLIFFORD, ANTHONY [ARTIST]
— photographer featured, Lahaina News, April 15, 1993: 6.
— certified as Advanced Master Black and White Printer, Lahaina News, September 10, 1998: 11.
- see also Anthony Novak-Clifford Photography [business]

NOWA, IRIS [ARTIST]
— to exhibit at Norr Studios, Lahaina News, March 2, 1995: 12.

NOWELL, JOHNITA
— accepted as a candidate in the Certified Real Estate Brokerage Manager Management Certification Program, Lahaina News, November 18, 1999: 13.

NOXON, JAMES
— teaching class on MIDI, Lahaina News, November 13, 1997: 20.

NOYES, MARTHA
— to present "Plants in Hawaiian Medicine", Lahaina News, May 17, 2001: 20.

NUDITY
— on beaches discussed, Lahaina Sun, June 16, 1971: 10.

NUI NO KE OLA PONO
— Kokua Program offering health screenings to Native Hawaiian and Pacific Islander women, Lahaina News, August 1, 2002: 9.

NUMEROLOGY
— workshop to be held, Lahaina News, July 6, 1995: 5.

NUNES, GEORGE
— Lahainaluna coach praised, Lahaina News, February 4, 1987: 6.
— Lahainaluna High School basketball coach featured, Lahaina News, February 8, 1989: 2.
— Lahainaluna High School basketball coach featured, Lahaina News, November 28, 1991: 8.
— Lahainaluna High School basketball coach discusses upcoming year, Lahaina News, December 2, 1993: 10.
— basketball coach retiring, Lahaina News, March 16, 1995: 6.

NUNES, KEONE
— to lecture on "Kakau Uhi", Lahaina News, June 5, 2003: 9.

NUNG
— see Vietnam War

NUNSENSE [PLAY]
— ends Maui Youth Theatre's season, Lahaina News, May 25, 1988: 7.
— to be performed by Maui Community Theatre/OnStage, Lahaina News, December 10, 1992: 17.
— to be performed by Maui OnStage, Lahaina News, March 18, 1993: 12.
— featured, Lahaina News, March 25, 1993: 13,16.
— final shows to be held, Lahaina News, April 8, 1993: 12.
— to be performed at the Maui Arts and Culture Center, Lahaina News, March 9, 1995: 10.

NUNSENSE II: THE SECOND COMING [PLAY]
— to performed by Maui Community Theatre, Lahaina News, March 31, 1994: 16.
— performed by Maui Community Theatre/Maui OnStage, Lahaina News, April 7, 1994: 11.
— to be performed by Maui Community Theatre/Maui OnStage, Lahaina News, April 21, 1994: 16.

NURSING
— University of Hawai'i School of Nursing to hold information session, Lahaina News, October 24, 1990: 2.

NUTCRACKER, THE [BALLET]
— to be performed at Baldwin Auditorium, Lahaina News, December 6, 1989: 12.
— to be performed by the Maui Academy of Performing Arts, Lahaina News, November 26, 1992: 26.
— to open, Lahaina News, December 3, 1992: 18.
— to be performed at Maui Community Theatre, Lahaina News, December 19, 1996: 11.
— to be performed by West Hawaii Dance Theatre, Lahaina News, September 10, 1998: 21.
— to be performed by West Hawaii Dance Theatre, Lahaina News, December 10, 1998: 9.

NUTS [PLAY]
— to be performed Maui's 2nd Circuit Court, Lahaina News, May 23, 1991: 16.

NUYEN, LISA
— named director of marketing for Ka'anapali Beach Resort Association, Lahaina News, August 26, 1999: 3.
— appointed director sales and marketing by PRM Realty Group, Lahaina News, February 1, 2001: 8.

NYE, BILL
— to perform at environmental conference "Earth Maui Nature Summit", Lahaina News, August 15, 1996: 2.

O

O-BON FESTIVAL
— organized by Maui Buddhist Association, Lahaina Sun, May 31, 1972: 6.
— planned by Lahaina Jodo Mission, Lahaina News, June 21, 1989: 5.
— photographs of, Lahaina News, July 12, 1989: 7.
— service and dance planned, Lahaina News, August 15, 1990: 6.
— to be held, Lahaina News, June 13, 1991: 4.
— to be held at Pu'unene Nichiren Mission, Lahaina News, June 20, 1991: 3.
— continues, sponsored by Maui Buddhist Council, Lahaina News, July 4, 1991: 3.
— to be held this weekend, Lahaina News, July 11, 1991: 5.
— to take place at Makawao Hongwanji Mission, Lahaina News, July 18, 1991: 5.
— Lahaina Hongwanji Mission to hold service, Lahaina News, August 1, 1991: 3.
— service to be held at Wailuku Shingon Mission, Lahaina News, August 8, 1991: 3.
— to be held, Lahaina News, July 2, 1992: 4.
— to be held, Lahaina News, September 3, 1992: 13.
— to be held, Lahaina News, July 1, 1993: 3.
— to be held in Kihei community, Lahaina News, September 2, 1993: 6.
— described, Lahaina News, July 14, 1994: 2.
— to be held by Lahaina Jodo Mission, Lahaina News, June 29, 1995: 4.
— to be held by Lahaina Hongwanji Mission, Lahaina News, July 13, 1995: 5.
— to be hosted by Lahaina Hongwanji Mission, Lahaina News, August 1, 1996: 21.
— to be held at Azeka Place Shopping Center, Lahaina News, August 29, 1996: 11.
— festival to be held, Lahaina News, July 30, 1998: 1,20.
— practices to be held, Lahaina News, June 10, 1999: 16.
— practices to be held, Lahaina News, June 17, 1999: 17.
— held, Lahaina News, August 5, 1999: 1,16.
— to be held by Lahaina Hongwanji Mission, Lahaina News, July 20, 2000: 8.
— held, Lahaina News, July 27, 2000: 3.
— to be held by Jodo Mission, Lahaina News, June 28, 2001: 1.
— to be held, Lahaina News, July 5, 2001: 17.
— to be held by Hongwanji Mission, Lahaina News, August 2, 2001: 3.
— Lahaina Hongwanji Mission to hold practice for, Lahaina News, June 6, 2002: 17.
— to be held, Lahaina News, June 20, 2002: 1.
— to be held, Lahaina News, July 4, 2002: 16.
— dance practices to be held at Lahaina Hongwanji Mission, Lahaina News, June 12, 2003: 21.
— practice to be held at Lahaina Shingon Mission, Lahaina News, June 19, 2003: 17.
— festivals to be held, Lahaina News, June 26, 2003: 1.
— celebration held, Lahaina News, July 10, 2003: 1.
— to be held by Lahaina Hongwanji Mission, Lahaina News, July 31, 2003: 18.

O.I. MOORE FOUNDATION
— awards grant to Lahainaluna Historical Preservation Committee, Lahaina News, April 4, 1996: 2.

OAHU CONVENTION CENTER
— seen as positive for neighbor islands as well, Lahaina News, December 15, 1994: 14.

OAHU SELF-HELP HOUSING CORPORATION
— accepting applications for people to build their own homes, Lahaina News, August 2, 1989: 1.

OAKES, STEPHANIE
— community benefit to be held for, Lahaina News, November 5, 1998: 14.

OATO, VERNON
— named human resources director at West Maui Hotel, Lahaina News, June 6, 1991: 6.

OBAYASHI HAWAII CORPORATION [BUSINESS]
— purchases land in Ka'anapali, Lahaina Sun, August 1, 1973: 4.
— to begin sale of increment B of Waiehu Terrace, Lahaina News, January 9, 1992: 9.
— offering program for remaining homes in Waiehu Terrace Increment B development, Lahaina News, December 9, 1993: 6.

OBITUARIES
— begin to be printed in Lahaina News, Lahaina News, June 17, 1999: 15.

O'BRIEN, JIM
— to hold seminar on "Quality Management for Managers and Professionals", Lahaina News, August 20, 1998: 13.

O'BRIEN, PAT
— visits Maui and drinks at Rusty Harpoon bar, Lahaina Sun, February 9, 1972: 3.

O'CALLAGHAN, BRIAN
— studying whales off West Maui, Lahaina News, April 1, 1987: 1,8,10,23.

OCCUPATIONAL SAFETY, DEPARTMENT OF
— reminds employers to post OSHA form, Lahaina News, February 24, 1994: 10.

OCEAN ACTIVITIES CENTER OF MAUI
— purchases Hotel Lana'i, Lahaina News, October 17, 1984: 3.
— purchased by Mike and Pamela Salzer, Lahaina News, February 28, 2002: 8.

OCEAN ADORNMENTS [BUSINESS]
— opening, Lahaina News, May 9, 1990: 8.

OCEAN ARTS FESTIVAL
— to be held, Lahaina News, January 23, 1991: 9.
— to be held at Lahaina Galleries, Lahaina News, January 20, 1994: 10,11.
— LahainaTown Action Committee seeking artists to participate in, Lahaina News, February 17, 2000: 15.
— artists sought for, Lahaina News, February 28, 2002: 3.
— to be held, Lahaina News, March 14, 2002: 14.
— to be held, Lahaina News, March 6, 2003: 3.
— to be held to celebrate return of the whales, Lahaina News, March 13, 2003: 14.

OCEAN CONSERVANCY
— to hold International Coastal Cleanup, Lahaina News, October 2, 2003: 5.

OCEAN EXCITEMENT
— jet ski reported in violation of new rules, Lahaina News, October 12, 1988: 1,20.

OCEAN EXPO
— presented by Keehi Marine, Lahaina News, March 20, 1991: 7.
— to be held, Lahaina News, April 3, 1991: 4.
— presented by Keehi Marine, Lahaina News, April 10, 1991: 6.

OCEAN RECREATION COUNCIL OF HAWAII, THE (TORCH)
— to conduct whalewatching tour as fundraiser, Lahaina News, March 12, 1986: 12.
— spring meeting to be held, Lahaina News, March 11, 1987: 3.

— hosts meeting on sea bed mining, Lahaina News, January 13, 1988: 16.

— promotes protection of coral reefs, Lahaina News, December 19, 1996: 13.

OCEAN RECREATION MANAGEMENT PLAN

— discussed, Lahaina News, October 7, 1987: 1.

— discussed, Lahaina News, February 3, 1988: 1,24.

— editorial critical of, Lahaina News, February 24, 1988: 2.

— being reworked in response to criticism, Lahaina News, March 23, 1988: 1.

— being reworked by Harbor Division, Lahaina News, March 30, 1988: 1.

— public meeting to be held, Lahaina News, May 25, 1988: 10.

— criticized by Chris Hart, Maui planning director, Lahaina News, November 23, 1988: 1,16.

OCEAN USERS ENFORCEMENT WORKSHOP

— to focus on marine laws, Lahaina News, November 13, 1997: 9.

— to be held, Lahaina News, November 1, 2001: 1.

— to discuss rules, Lahaina News, November 14, 2002: 2.

OCEANFRONT MARKETPLACE [BUSINESS]

— featured, Lahaina News, May 23, 2002: 7.

— featured, Lahaina News, July 18, 2002: 7.

OCEANHOUSE, INC.[BUSINESS]

— proposes two-story office building, Lahaina News, March 20, 1991: 1.

OCEANHOUSE RESTAURANT [RESTAURANT]

— featured, Lahaina News, July 10, 1985: 7.

OCEANIC CABLEVISION

— see cablevision, Hawaiian Cablevision [business]

OCEANIC INDEPENDENCE [SHIP]

— taken out of service until May 1, Lahaina News, January 15, 1983: 2.

OCEANIT LABORATORIES

— chosen for algae cleanup, Lahaina News, July 4, 1996: 3.

— working on algae control, Lahaina News, September 5, 1996: 4.

OCEANS

— black coral diving described, Lahaina Sun, April 25, 1973: 7.

— Navy seeking to raise U.S.S. Bluegill to move it further off shore, Lahaina News, October 12, 1983: 3,5.

— use remains controversial topic, Lahaina News, September 21, 1988: 1,15.

— state to add extra ocean patrols, Lahaina News, November 8, 1989: 1.

— marine educators inviting proposals for workshops, papers, and exhibits for conference in Hilo, Lahaina News, March 14, 1990: 3.

— State Department of Transportation proposes new rules for ocean recreation areas, Lahaina News, September 12, 1990: 1.

— reef cleanup scheduled, Lahaina News, September 12, 1990: 8.

— conflicts between thrillcrafts and people swimming and fishing recounted; areas of activity suggested, Lahaina News, October 17, 1990: 1,10.

— concern for safety after U.S. Coast Guard cutter Cape Corwin decommissioned, Lahaina News, October 31, 1990: 1.

— Richard Roshon to offer series of lectures "The Sea and Its Species", Lahaina News, November 14, 1990: 5.

— lifeguards provided with jet skis, Lahaina News, October 24, 1991: 1.

— recounting storms, ocean swells, Lahaina News, May 19, 1994: 2.

— bill may move Marine Patrol from Department of Public Safety to Department of Land and Natural Resources, Lahaina News, February 23, 1995: 1,4.

— battle between sharks and young humpback whale seen, Lahaina News, April 20, 1995: 1,16.

— Na Pale O Ke Kai seeking volunteers to monitor oceans, Lahaina News, January 16, 1997: 5.

— Sea Grant at University of Hawai'i to track sediment, Lahaina News, September 4, 1997: 15.

— workshop to be held for ocean users, Lahaina News, November 13, 1997: 20.

— Ocean Users Enforcement Workshops to be held, Lahaina News, November 13, 1997: 9.

— Year of the Ocean to be celebrated, Lahaina News, January 8, 1998: 7.

— lifeguards prepared for winter surf, Lahaina News, January 29, 1998: 1,2.

— County to teach ocean safety and awareness, Lahaina News, August 19, 1999: 6.

— state and federal regulatory agencies to hold workshop on guidelines for viewing sea mammals and turtles, Lahaina News, November 18, 1999: 3.

— guest speakers from Sustainable Seas Expedition to discuss deep sea exploratory dives, Lahaina News, January 13, 2000: 5.

— "Exploring Hawaii's Coral Reefs" published by Pacific Whale Foundation, Lahaina News, August 24, 2000: 7.

— see also thrill crafts

OCEANS ALIVE

— educational program to debut at Club Lana'i, Lahaina News, December 27, 1989: 5.

OCHI, TOSHIHISA

— Japanese seaman hospitalized, Lahaina Sun, July 21, 1971: 1.

— injured seaman has recovered, Lahaina Sun, July 28, 1971: 10.

O'CONNELL, PAT

— surfer featured, Lahaina News, February 9, 1995: 7.

O'CONNOR, BILL

— begins as sports writer for Lahaina News, Lahaina News, October 31, 1984: 4.

— writing for "Dining & Entertainment" section discussed, Lahaina News, December 9, 1987: 8.

— to stop writing the entertainment column, Lahaina News, April 13, 1988: 11,12.

— to stop writing the sports column, Lahaina News, April 13, 1988: 12.

O'CONNOR, BRIAN AND RITA

— to teach dancing at Aloha Ballroom Dance Academy, Lahaina News, May 1, 2003: 17.

O'CONNOR, CHRISTY

— to play at EMC Ka'anapali Classic, Lahaina News, July 15, 1999: 6.

O'CONNOR, DAN [WRITER]

— to speak on new book "Spice: An Island Intrigue", Lahaina News, November 7, 2002: 20.

O'CONNOR, DONALD [PERFORMER]

— to perform in benefit for Maui Community Theatre OnStage, Lahaina News, February 18, 1993: 13.

— to perform, Lahaina News, March 4, 1993: 9.

O'CONNOR, ERIN [COMEDIAN]

— to perform at Comedy Club and the Sports Page, Lahaina News, March 5, 1992: 14.

— to perform at Comedy Club and the Sports Page, Lahaina News, December 10, 1992: 15,17.

— to perform at Comedy Club, Lahaina News, May 26, 1994: 11.

O'CONNOR, PETER

— named executive assistant manager/director of food and beverages at Hyatt Regency Maui, Lahaina News, April 18, 1996: 8.

O'CONNOR, RITA

— to teach samba, Lahaina News, July 10, 2003: 17.

— to hold Samba Latin Dance workshops, Lahaina News, July 17, 2003: 17.

OCTETTE BRIDGE CLUB [PLAY]
— to be performed by Maui Youth Theatre, Lahaina News, May 30, 1990: 11.

ODA, CHRIS
— spearheaded drive for King Kamehameha III School to have a vice-principal, Lahaina News, May 16, 1990: 1,10.

ODA, MALINO
— wins division at Hilo Junior Summer Open, Lahaina News, September 3, 1992: 6.
— becomes highest ranked junior tennis player from Maui, Lahaina News, February 2, 1995: 6.
— tennis player featured, Lahaina News, June 5, 1997: 13.

ODA, MAYUMI [ARTIST]
— to lecture, Lahaina News, April 10, 1985: 3.

ODC/SAN FRANCISCO DANCE COMPANY [TROUPE]
— to perform, Lahaina News, October 12, 1988: 3.

ODD COUPLE, THE [PLAY]
— performed by Maui Community Theatre, Lahaina News, February 1, 1981: 16.
— to be performed by Maui Community Theatre, Lahaina News, October 15, 1998: 16.
— to be performed, Lahaina News, October 22, 1998: 20.

ODES, CARY [COMEDIAN]
— to perform at Comedy Club, Lahaina News, February 7, 1990: 13.
— to perform at Comedy Club and the Sports Page, Lahaina News, February 27, 1991: 8,12.
— to perform at Comedy Club and the Sports Page, Lahaina News, March 12, 1992: 15,18.

ODETTE'S [BUSINESS]
— featured, Lahaina News, September 26, 1984: 14.

ODUSA [SHIP]
— is first to arrive in Maui in Victoria-Maui race, Lahaina Sun, July 19, 1972: 1.

OFF CENTER [PUBLICATION]
— distributed by Maui Arts & Cultural Center, Lahaina News, February 21, 1990: 5.

OFFERGELD, JEAN-MARC [ARTIST]
— featured artist at Lahaina Arts Society, Lahaina News, March 7, 2002: 16.

OFFICE MART
— celebrates grand opening, Lahaina News, April 24, 1997: 10.

OFFICE OF COMMUNITY SERVICES, MAUI COMMUNITY COLLEGE
— see Maui Community College

OFFICE OF ECONOMIC DEVELOPMENT
— see Economic Development, Maui County Office of

OFFICE OF ECONOMIC DEVELOPMENT, MAUI COUNTY OFFICE OF
— forms Business Advocacy Task Force to work with Mayor Alan Arakawa, Lahaina News, May 1, 2003: 8.

OFFICE OF HAWAIIAN AFFAIRS
— see Hawaiian Affairs, Office of

OFFICE OLYMPICS
— to be organized by Lung Association, Lahaina News, June 5, 1997: 17.

OGATA, EDDIE
— surfer competes in National Scholastic Surfing Association's Summer Spray-Offs, Lahaina News, July 6, 2000: 1,14.

OGATA, PAUL [COMEDIAN]
— to perform at Comedy Club and the Sports Page, Lahaina News, June 4, 1992: 13.

OGAWA, SUSAN [ARTIST]
— to offer workshops on shibori, Lahaina News, July 17, 1997: 17.
— to offer course on shibori, Lahaina News, July 24, 1997: 16.

OGDEN NEWSPAPERS INC [BUSINESS]
— to purchase Lahaina News from Maui Chronicle Inc., Lahaina News, October 5, 2000: 1,15.

OH THE MO'O [MUSICAL]
— to be performed by Theatre Theatre Maui, Lahaina News, July 22, 1999: 2.

'OHANA CONNECTION
— Randy Christmam to present "Energize Your Eyes", Lahaina News, May 23, 2002: 16.

OHANA COUNCIL OF THE HAWAIIAN KINGDOM
— to meet, Lahaina News, December 2, 1993: 4.

OHANA FLORALS AND GIFTS
— opens in Lahaina Cannery Mall, Lahaina News, July 31, 2003: 8.

OHANA HAWAIIAN COFFEE
— opens, Lahaina News, March 2, 2000: 11.

OHANA HOTELS [BUSINESS]
— to take over management of Maui Islander Hotel, Lahaina News, April 19, 2001: 9.

OHANA LUAU
— fundraiser for Hale Makua Foundation to be held, Lahaina News, July 5, 2001: 15.

OHANA LUNCHEON AND TRADE FAIRE
— to meet , Lahaina News, February 24, 1988: 18.
— to host talk by Pacific Whale Foundation, Lahaina News, March 29, 1989: 14.
— Al Lagunero to speak, Lahaina News, April 26, 1989: 3.
— to feature Steve "Swami" Bhaerman, Lahaina News, January 3, 1990: 16.

OHANA PHYSICIANS GROUP
— to offer free physical examinations to school children, Lahaina News, September 3, 1998: 8.

OHANA RANCH ESTATES
— to hold meeting, Lahaina News, September 5, 1996: 22.

OHANA SAVERS
— alliance formed, Lahaina News, March 27, 1997: 10.
— loyalty program created, Lahaina News, December 9, 1999: 15.

O'HARA, DOROTHY
— elected secretary of the Kihei Community Association, Lahaina Sun, December 2, 1970: 4.

OHASHI, TSUGIO
— proposes master plan for bike paths on Maui, Lahaina Sun, February 7, 1973: 12.

OHATA, ROBERT
— discusses moderate income housing on Maui and Moloka'i, Lahaina Sun, December 2, 1970: 3.

OHE'O GULCH
— Friends of Haleakala National Park to hold service trip to, Lahaina News, August 29, 2002: 15.

OHIO BALLET
— to perform with Maui Philharmonic , Lahaina News, February 13, 1991: 9.

OHM, PAUL
— named assistant director of food and beverages for Hyatt Regency Maui, Lahaina News, May 9, 1996: 8.

OHR, JUDI
— Lahaina Sun columnist is an author of the Whole Earth Cook Book, Lahaina Sun, June 28, 1972: 19.

OHTA, HERB
— ukulele virtuoso will play at Baldwin auditorium, Lahaina Sun, April 11, 1973: 11.

OIHANA PROPERTY MANAGEMENT & SALES, INC. [BUSINESS]
— sponsoring Condominium Conference and Trade Show, Lahaina News, October 3, 1990: 9.
— Judy Anderson joins staff as office manager of bookkeeping department, Lahaina News, October 3, 1990: 9.
— sponsoring Condominium Conference and Trade Show, Lahaina News, October 10, 1990: 12.
— sponsoring Condominium Conference and Trade Show, Lahaina News, October 17, 1990: 12.
— sponsoring Condominium Conference and Trade Show, Lahaina News, October 24, 1990: 7.
— Condominium Conference and Trade show to be held November 10th, Lahaina News, October 31, 1990: 12.
— to hold Condominium Conference and Trade Show next week, Lahaina News, November 7, 1990: 7.

OISHI, CARRELL
— acting district superintendent of schools assures that seniors will graduate, Lahaina Sun, April 18, 1973: 5.

'OIWI: A NATIVE HAWAIIAN JOURNAL
— authors to present on works published in, Lahaina News, June 28, 2001: 20.

OKA, LEONARD
— son of member of 100th Battalion discusses veterans, Lahaina News, May 21, 1992: 3.

OKADA [FAMILY]
— tennis playing family featured, Lahaina News, November 18, 1993: 8.

OKADA, DIANE
— former Lahainaluna High School athlete doing well at University of Redlands, Lahaina News, May 15, 1991: 7.
— named co-player of the year in women's tennis for Big West Conference, Lahaina News, May 6, 1993: 10.

OKADA, JEAN
— to tour mainland this summer, Lahaina News, July 18, 1991: 7.
— tennis player receives scholarship offers, Lahaina News, December 26, 1991: 11.
— wins Kona Spring Junior Open, Lahaina News, June 18, 1992: 12.
— named to NCAA 1996 All-American team, Lahaina News, June 20, 1996: 10.
— wins Wilson Kapalua Open, Lahaina News, September 4, 1997: 1.
— tennis player wins Satellite Tournament in England, Lahaina News, February 26, 1998: 1.
— wins USTA Challenger title in California, Lahaina News, April 30, 1998: 15.
— now ranked Number 114 in world doubles, Lahaina News, July 30, 1998: 15.

OKADA, JEAN AND DIANE
— named to 1994 Big West Conference all-conference tennis team, Lahaina News, May 19, 1994: 9.

OKADA, STEVEN
— wins Boys 18 Singles division in Lahaina Juniors tournament, Lahaina News, August 8, 1990: 7.
— wins Wailuku Junior Summer Open tennis, Lahaina News, August 22, 1991: 8.

OKAHIRO, GIICHI
— former Pioneer Mill employee discusses history of West Maui, Lahaina Sun, August 29, 1973: 7.

OKAMOTO, AYAKO
— golfer's career described, Lahaina News, March 6, 1985: A10.

OKAMOTO, BRIDGETTE
— appointed public relations manager at Westin ?Maui, Lahaina News, January 30, 2003: 8.

OKAMOTO, LYNN
— named marketing director for Lahaina Cannery Shopping Center, Lahaina News, March 4, 1987: 10.
— joins Estate of James Campbell, Lahaina News, May 24, 1989: 8.
— appointed marketing manager for Whalers Village, Lahaina News, October 10, 1991: 6.

OKAMURA, RON
— new principal at Kihei School featured, Lahaina News, September 2, 1993: 6.

OKANEKU, RANDAL
— speaks of Austin, Tsutsumi and Associates undertaking island-wide survey of traffic, Lahaina News, August 24, 1988: 1.

OKAZU YAN [BUSINESS]
— retail store to close, Lahaina News, July 15, 1983: 10.

OKEN, ALAN
— astrologer to give workshop, Lahaina News, June 12, 1985: 3.

OKERLUND, STEVE [MUSICIAN]
— accepted by Maui Arts and Music Association for career development, Lahaina News, May 14, 1992: 17.

OKIMOTO, ARIET
— Scholar/Athlete of the Week, Lahaina News, April 30, 1998: 15.

OKIMOTO, CARY
— appointed Director of Sales-Asia for Aston Hotels and Resorts, Lahaina News, May 21, 1992: 9.

OKIMOTO, DENNIS
— named senior vice president of Wailea Resort Company, Inc, Lahaina News, January 30, 1992: 10,11.

OKIMOTO, HUMIO
— president of West Maui AJA Veterans Club discusses student visit to Washington DC, Lahaina Sun, February 3, 1971: 1.

OKINAWA
— dancers and musicians to perform at Baldwin High School, Lahaina News, March 4, 1987: 8.

OKINAWAN FESTIVAL
— to be held, Lahaina News, June 7, 2001: 20.
— to be held, Lahaina News, June 7, 2001: 20.
— to be held by Maui Okinawa Kenjin Kai, Lahaina News, August 22, 2002: 9.

OKLAHOMA [PLAY]
— to be formed by Maui Community Theatre, Lahaina News, March 7, 1990: 13.
— to be performed by Maui Community Theatre, Lahaina News, March 21, 1990: 13.
— concludes, Lahaina News, March 28, 1990: 18.

OKTOBERFEST
— Makani Coffee Shop to feature food for, Lahaina News, October 2, 1985: 9.
— fundraiser by Maui Youth Theatre , Lahaina News, October 8, 1986: 3.
— to be held at Maui Prince Hotel, Lahaina News, September 21, 1988: 3.
— to be held at Maui Inter-Continental Wailea, Lahaina News, October 3, 1991: 13.
— to be held this weekend, Lahaina News, October 17, 1991: 17.
— to be held at Makena Resort, Lahaina News, October 15, 1992: 16.
— to be held, Lahaina News, October 22, 1992: 18.
— to be held at Ka'anapali Beach Hotel, Inter-Continental Resort, Lahaina News, September 30, 1993: 12,13.
— to be celebrated, Lahaina News, October 10, 1996: 15.
— to be held, Lahaina News, October 17, 1996: 14.

— beers made in Hawaii to be featured, Lahaina News, October 2, 1997: 9.

— to be held at Inu Inu , Lahaina News, October 23, 1997: 20.

— to be sponsored by Sheraton Maui and Sheraton Maui, Lahaina News, October 14, 1999: 11.

— sail to be held, Lahaina News, October 4, 2001: 9.

— Maui Symphony Orchestra to celebrate, Lahaina News, October 10, 2002: 14,16,17.

— to be held at Ka'anapali Beach Hotel, Lahaina News, October 17, 2002: 20.

OKUBA, SUZANNE
— crowned queen of Chrysanthemum Ball, Lahaina News, December 9, 1993: 2.

OKUBO, ED
— county housing director discusses bids to build Komohana Hale, Lahaina News, March 7, 1990: 1.

— Maui County housing coordinator says housing project near West Maui ball field nearing completion, Lahaina News, December 12, 1990: 1.

OKUBO, EDWIN
— Housing Administrator asserts county claim to ownership of land parcel, Lahaina News, December 9, 1987: 1,17.

— Housing Administrator discusses impact of housing and the lack of highways on Maui's economy, Lahaina News, December 9, 1987: 1,20.

OKUDA, MAJIME
— new exhibit of paintings opens in Lahaina Art Gallery, Lahaina Sun, December 16, 1970: 3.

OKUDA, OSHINO
— paintings exhibited at Lahaina Art Gallery, Lahaina Sun, December 16, 1970: 3.

OKUMURA, NELSON
— named general chairman of Scout-O-Rama, Lahaina News, March 13, 1991: 5.

OLD CANNERY [BUILDING]
— to be razed, Lahaina News, March 7, 1984: 3.

OLD KINE PHOTOS [BUSINESS]
— featured, Lahaina News, September 21, 1983: 14.

OLD LAHAINA BOOK EMPORIUM [BUSINESS]
— opens, Lahaina News, July 16, 1998: 1,20.

— moves to larger location, Lahaina News, February 10, 2000: 14.

— holds grand reopening, Lahaina News, February 17, 2000: 16.

OLD LAHAINA CAFE AND LUAU [RESTAURANT]
— reviewed, Lahaina News, April 20, 1988: 3.

— celebrates second anniversary, Lahaina News, July 6, 1988: 6.

— reviewed, open for lunch, Lahaina News, August 10, 1988: 8.

— to celebrate Thanksgiving Hawaiian style, Lahaina News, November 23, 1988: 8.

— reviewed, Lahaina News, March 22, 1989: 8.

— reviewed, Lahaina News, July 5, 1989: 13.

— featured, Lahaina News, October 11, 1989: 9.

— featured, Lahaina News, December 13, 1989: 21.

— featuring Hawaiian group Hookanies, Lahaina News, February 21, 1990: 13.

— to feature Leilani Sharpe Mendez, Lahaina News, February 28, 1990: 11.

— featured, Lahaina News, April 18, 1990: 10.

— Travel Marketing Company advertising agent for, Lahaina News, August 8, 1990: 6.

— ranked in top 500 in nation for independently-owned food service establishments, Lahaina News, September 26, 1990: 12.

— receives Kahili Award from the Hawaii Visitors Bureau, Lahaina News, December 5, 1990: 9.

— recognized by Restaurant Hospitality, Lahaina News, July 4, 1991: 4.

— has new menu, Lahaina News, March 5, 1992: 17.

— receives award from Hawaii Visitors Bureau, Lahaina News, May 21, 1992: 8.

— receives Kahili Awards from the Hawaii Visitors Bureau, Lahaina News, June 18, 1992: 17.

— reviewed, Lahaina News, August 20, 1992: 19.

— turns seven years old, Lahaina News, July 8, 1993: 7.

— hoping to move, Lahaina News, September 12, 1996: 1.

— to perform at Aloha Festival, Lahaina News, October 10, 1996: 15.

— to have new location, Lahaina News, November 20, 1997: 15.

— celebrates grand opening, Lahaina News, May 21, 1998: 9.

— featured, Lahaina News, May 28, 1998: 11.

— honored with "Keep It Hawai'i" Kahili award, Lahaina News, April 22, 1999: 11.

— partners open "The Feast at Lele", Lahaina News, May 6, 1999: 15.

— honored with a "Keep It Hawai'i" Kahili Award, Lahaina News, April 20, 2000: 13.

— dancers rehearse for Macy's Thanksgiving Day Parade, Lahaina News, November 9, 2000: 1.

— to run float at Macy's Thanksgiving Day Parade, the first ever from Hawai'i, Lahaina News, November 9, 2000: 18.

— dancers to participate in Macy's Thanksgiving Day Parade, Lahaina News, December 7, 2000: 1,22.

— to honor Queen Ka'ahumanu, Lahaina News, March 15, 2001: 18.

— auditions for Macy's Thanksgiving Day Parade, Lahaina News, August 23, 2001: 1.

— members to participate in Macy's Thanksgiving Day Parade, Lahaina News, November 22, 2001: 9.

— benefit to be held at The Friends of Moku'ula, Lahaina News, January 31, 2002: 2.

— Kalani Ho takes management position at, Lahaina News, September 26, 2002: 3.

— to perform at Macy's parade, Lahaina News, November 21, 2002: 12.

— performing free hula shows, Lahaina News, April 3, 2003: 17.

— to offer shows at Queen's Stage at Queen Ka'ahumanu Center, Lahaina News, May 8, 2003: 17.

OLD LAHAINA CENTER
— fences off shortcuts to property, Lahaina News, April 29, 1999: 1.

— theater to open at, Lahaina News, July 8, 1999: 11.

— to offer hula show, Lahaina News, August 17, 2000: 16.

OLD LAHAINA COURTHOUSE
— to remain in county hands, Lahaina News, May 2, 1984: 4.

— Maui County Planning Department operating a satellite office at, Lahaina News, August 6, 1986: 18.

— to be renovated, Lahaina News, January 27, 1988: 1.

— Lahaina Arts Society allowed to stay, Lahaina News, February 10, 1988: 1.

— being restored, Lahaina News, November 26, 1992: 1.

— site of proposed Lahaina Visitor Center, Lahaina News, December 15, 1994: 3.

— importance to Lahaina discussed, Lahaina News, April 13, 1995: 20.

— Mayor Linda Lingle names task force to decide renovations and future of, Lahaina News, June 29, 1995: 4.

— Task Force considers use of Courthouse, Lahaina News, July 27, 1995: 4.

— Task Force to meet, Lahaina News, August 3, 1995: 4.

— Task Force favors museum for Old Courthouse, Lahaina News, August 17, 1995: 1,2,16.

— Lahaina Courthouse Task Force favors museum for, Lahaina News, August 17, 1995: 1,2,16.

— Task Force continues to consider use of courthouse, Lahaina News, September 14, 1995: 1,16.

— Task Force exploring possibility of creating museum for building, Lahaina News, October 12, 1995: 1,16.
— Task Force seeking public input, Lahaina News, November 2, 1995: 16.
— Task Force ready to report, Lahaina News, December 14, 1995: 1,20.
— ready to report, Lahaina News, December 14, 1995: 1,20.
— funding proposed for, Lahaina News, February 15, 1996: 3.
— money for improvements in Mayor Linda Lingle's budget, Lahaina News, March 21, 1996: 1,14.
— architect Glenn Mason makes recommendations for renovation of, Lahaina News, November 7, 1996: 1,20.
— to be restored, Lahaina News, February 13, 1997: 2.
— Lahaina Arts Society returning to, Lahaina News, December 11, 1997: 1,2.
— to close for renovation, Lahaina News, January 15, 1998: 1.
— renovation underway, Lahaina News, May 7, 1998: 17.
— renovation almost finished, Lahaina News, December 3, 1998: 1.
— to be managed by Lahaina Restoration Foundation, Lahaina News, February 25, 1999: 1,2.
— LahainaTown Action Committee may return to, Lahaina News, April 1, 1999: 1,20.
— Mayor and Council differ over rent for, Lahaina News, July 1, 1999: 1,16.
— traces of old courthouse found during archaeological study, Lahaina News, August 12, 1999: 1,20.

OLD LAHAINA HOUSE
— operating as a bed and breakfast, Lahaina News, July 11, 1996: 2.
— bed and breakfast to fight county fines, Lahaina News, July 18, 1996: 3.
— update on legal struggle, Lahaina News, August 1, 1996: 3.

OLD LAHAINA LUAU DANCERS
— to perform at Reflections of Old Lahaina Luau and Concert benefit, Lahaina News, August 19, 1999: 18.

OLD LAHAINA LUAU/ALOHA MIXED PLATE [BUSINESS]
— personnel changes announced, Lahaina News, October 28, 1999: 15.

OLD LAHAINA PALI TRAIL
— volunteers work to improve, Lahaina News, July 17, 1997: 16.
— volunteers sought, Lahaina News, November 27, 1997: 13.

OLD LAHAINA PRISON
— see Hale Pa'ahao

OLD LAHAINA TOWN ART FAIRE
— organizers Buck Rogers and Rachel Rogers interviewed, Lahaina Sun, May 23, 1973: 8.

OLD LAHAINA TOWNE COOKIES [RESTAURANT]
— featured, Lahaina News, August 15, 1983: 11.

OLD LAHAINA TRAIL
— may be restored, Lahaina News, June 7, 1989: 3.

OLD MILL HAIKU
— to open as National Historic Place and Tree Museum, Lahaina News, January 6, 1988: 1,14.

OLD PRISON
— see Hale Pa'ahao

OLD REPUBLIC TITLE AND ESCROW [BUSINESS]
— opens branch in Lahaina, Lahaina News, July 30, 1998: 13.

OLDE MARKET STREET BOOK EMPORIUM
— to exhibit vintage books, Lahaina News, May 22, 1997: 16.

OLDE WAILUKU GALLERY [BUSINESS]
— to hold children's coloring contest, Lahaina News, September 1, 1994: 16.
— to hold children's coloring contest, Lahaina News, September 15, 1994: 16.

OLDENBURG, DORIS
— appointed general manager of Aston Waikiki Beach Tower, Lahaina News, January 23, 1991: 5.

OLDS, TOM [ARTIST]
— to exhibit at Van Dorland Gallery, Lahaina News, August 1, 1991: 17.

OLE LONGBOARD CLASSIC
— results, Lahaina News, August 25, 1994: 9.
— to be held, Lahaina News, September 3, 1998: 1,24.

OLE SURFBOARDS [BUSINESS]
— owner Bob "Ole" Olson featured, Lahaina News, August 18, 1994: 6.

OLEANNA [PLAY]
— to be performed at Maui Community Theatre, Lahaina News, August 31, 1995: 12.
— reviewed, Lahaina News, September 14, 1995: 11.

O'LEARY, BRIAN
— astronomer and former astronaut to speak at Unity Church of Maui, Lahaina News, January 9, 1991: 3.
— NASA scientist to speak to Alaya Unlimited's Ohana Luncheon, Lahaina News, May 16, 1996: 10.

O'LEARY, GEORGE
— brings Hawaiian troupe to Arizona for two weeks, Lahaina News, February 27, 1991: 3.

OLENA AT KEHALANI
— SCD International celebrates grand opening of, Lahaina News, July 12, 2001: 8.

'OLI AND HAWAIIAN FALSETTO FESTIVAL
— to be held, Lahaina News, September 5, 1991: 18.

OLIDA POLO FIELD
— to host polo, Lahaina News, May 8, 1997: 16.

OLIM, JOHN
— named Customer Services manager for Aloha Airlines in Maui, Lahaina News, April 13, 1988: 3.

OLINDA [TOWN]
— farming described, Lahaina Sun, July 11, 1973: 12.

OLINDA HONOR CAMP
— prisoners working on local highway projects, Lahaina Sun, November 18, 1970: 4.
— honor camp programs described, funding uncertain, Lahaina Sun, July 11, 1973: 12,13.
— Maui Chamber of Commerce wants honor camp to remain, Lahaina Sun, July 18, 1973: 3.
— Maui Chamber of Commerce has taken no action, Lahaina Sun, July 25, 1973: 4.

OLINDA VISTA EQUESTRIAN
— to be auction by National Auction Group, Lahaina News, January 28, 1999: 11.

OLINDA-KULA CONSERVATION DISTRICT
— receives conservation award, Lahaina News, December 26, 1996: 8.

OLIVA, HENRY
— selected as Maui County deputy director of Department of Human Concerns, Lahaina News, January 16, 1991: 9.
— Parks Director discusses parcel proposed for Napili Regional Park, Lahaina News, February 27, 1997: 1.

OLIVEIRA, JOYLYNN
— to present "The Cultural Importance of Whales in Hawaii", Lahaina News, June 8, 2000: 21.

OLIVER, BILL [MUSICIAN]
— to perform at Maui Community College in support of the environment, Lahaina News, March 20, 1991: 11.

OLIVER, STEPHANIE STOKES [WRITER]
— to read from her book "Daily Cornbread", Lahaina News, October 7, 1999: 16.

OLIVIERA, ELMAR [MUSICIAN]
— to perform with Maui Symphony Orchestra, Lahaina News, October 14, 1999: 12,13.

OLOMANA [MUSICAL GROUP]
— performs at Royal Lahaina Resort, Lahaina News, August 7, 1985: 10.
— performing at Nanatomi's, Lahaina News, November 18, 1987: 3,18.
— to perform at Maui Prince Hotel, Lahaina News, July 26, 1989: 13.
— to perform at Hawaiian concert, Lahaina News, August 16, 1989: 3.
— to perform at Aha Mele Luau, Lahaina News, September 20, 1989: 3.
— to perform for New Year's Eve, Lahaina News, December 26, 1990: 8,10.
— to perform at Stouffer Wailea Beach Resort, Lahaina News, January 2, 1991: 8.
— to perform at Molokini Lounge at the Maui Prince Hotel, Lahaina News, April 17, 1991: 12.
— to perform at "Music on the Beach", Lahaina News, April 23, 1998: 6.

OLOWALU [TOWN]
— shore front tested for pollution, Lahaina Sun, December 16, 1970: 3.
— location of Teen Challenge, a program for Maui youth, Lahaina Sun, January 27, 1971: 6.
— contractor responds to Maui County Planning Commission report on proposed apartment building , Lahaina Sun, April 19, 1972: 10.
— Teen Challenge's rehabilitation facility described, Lahaina Sun, August 16, 1972: 7.
— brush fire spreads, Lahaina News, July 16, 1986: 3.
— construction of Ukumehame Firing Range to begin, Lahaina News, September 7, 1988: 1.
— Maui Ocean Center proposed, Lahaina News, October 12, 1988: 1,14.
— roadside peddlers may be removed from, Lahaina News, June 14, 1989: 1.
— power outage explained, Lahaina News, April 9, 1992: 5.
— landfill closes, Lahaina News, December 17, 1992: 1.
— road to be widened, Lahaina News, January 7, 1993: 1.
— Mayor Linda Lingle seeks support for camping in, Lahaina News, July 14, 1994: 5.
— Alan Arakawa urges administration to purchase land at, Lahaina News, January 22, 1998: 1,16.
— archaeologist Erik Fredericksen recommends preserving pre-contact burial site at Olowalu, Lahaina News, December 17, 1998: 1,28.
— state probing public land status, Lahaina News, April 27, 2000: 1,16.
— brush fire near Olowalu Transfer Station, Lahaina News, January 25, 2001: 2.
— temporary highway fix planned, Lahaina News, November 15, 2001: 3.
— shark warning signs posted at, Lahaina News, August 8, 2002: 1,20.

OLOWALU DUMP
— odor caused by broken sludge-drying pond, Lahaina News, January 23, 1985: 3.
— may close soon, Lahaina News, March 2, 1988: 1,24.

OLOWALU ELUA ASSOCIATIONS [BUSINESS]
— changes to subdivision triggers hearing, Lahaina News, October 3, 2002: 1,20.

OLOWALU GENERAL STORE
— lease acquired by Al Covic, Lahaina News, August 11, 1994: 7.

OLOWALU LANDFILL
— county found negligent in operation of, Lahaina News, April 15, 1987: 1,9.
— to be closed to commercial users, Lahaina News, June 22, 1988: 1,12,13.
— closes, Lahaina News, July 6, 1988: 1.
— Howard Kihune wants reopening of, Lahaina News, July 13, 1988: 1,20.
— fumes to be reduced, Lahaina News, September 20, 1989: 1.
— to close, Lahaina News, May 28, 1992: 4.
— closure delayed, Lahaina News, July 2, 1992: 1.
— almost closed, Lahaina News, August 19, 1993: 4.

OLOWALU RECYCLING CENTER
— now taking appliances, Lahaina News, August 22, 1996: 4.

OLOWALU RESIDENTIAL CONVENIENCE CENTER
— opens following closure of Olowalu landfill, Lahaina News, July 30, 1992: 3.

OLOWALU TRANSFER STATION
— recycling now available at, Lahaina News, July 10, 1997: 1.
— to hold "Amnesty Day", Lahaina News, March 15, 2001: 20.

OLSON, BOB "OLE"
— surfboard shaper featured, Lahaina News, November 16, 1983: 4.
— surfboard maker featured, Lahaina News, December 4, 1985: 4.
— surfboard shaper's career discussed further, Lahaina News, January 1, 1986: 4.
— surfboard maker featured, Lahaina News, October 24, 1991: 3.
— owner of Ole Surfboards featured, Lahaina News, August 18, 1994: 6.
— surfer concerned changes to harbor will ruin "Thousand peaks" surf spot, Lahaina News, October 27, 1994: 6.
— owner of Ole Longboard Classic featured, Lahaina News, August 21, 1997: 13.
— surfboard shaper to be honored, Lahaina News, August 12, 1999: 7.

OLSON, HARRY
— architect working on moderate income housing development, Lahaina Sun, December 2, 1970: 3.

OLSON, STORRS
— talk on fossilized extinct flightless birds, Lahaina News, March 23, 1988: 14.

OLSON, TOMI [ARTIST]
— work displayed at Lahaina Art Society gallery, Lahaina Sun, April 19, 1972: 6.

OLYMPICS
— gymnasts , Lahaina News, January 2, 1997: 11.
— gymnasts meet at Lahaina Civic Center, Lahaina News, January 9, 1997: 6.

OMAHA, USS [SUBMARINE]
— visits Lahaina, Lahaina News, June 21, 1989: 1.

OMAR, STEVE
— discusses fate of people living at the "Animal Farm", Lahaina Sun, February 3, 1971: 6.
— editorial on work of Project Marxen UFO Committee, Lahaina Sun, April 11, 1973: 8,9.
— discusses existence of UFOs, Lahaina Sun, August 1, 1973: 19.
— recounts storm at sea, Lahaina News, April 10, 1997: 17.
— surfer featured, Lahaina News, June 5, 1997: 1,8.
— trip to the Himalayas recounted, part I, Lahaina News, November 14, 2002: 14.
— trip to the Himalayas recounted, part II, Lahaina News, November 28, 2002: 18.

OMBUSDMAN
— office described, Lahaina Sun, June 23, 1971: 11.
— representative will be on Maui to accept complaints, Lahaina Sun, July 19, 1972: 11.
— importance of discussed, Lahaina Sun, January 31, 1973: 8.

OMEGA [SHIP]
— wins Victoria-Maui International Yacht Race, Lahaina News, July 20, 1988: 12.

OMI [MUSICIAN]
— to perform at Borders Books, Lahaina News, November 22, 2001: 20.

OMNI THEATRE
— purchased by Kurisu & Perfus real estate company, Lahaina News, March 28, 1990: 7.

OMORI, MASAO
— participates in groundbreaking for Kahoma Stream Flood Control Project, Lahaina News, January 14, 1987: 12.
— owner of Hawaii Omori Corporation passes away, Lahaina News, July 7, 1994: 4.

OMPOY, TRACY
— named director of magical moments at the Maui Marriott Resort, Lahaina News, March 21, 1996: 10.

OMWAKE, MARY
— reverend discusses travel to Italy for the "Association for Global New Thought Synthesis Dialogue 2001", Lahaina News, July 12, 2001: 16.

ON THE PARTY LINE
— column continues to be printed, not typically indexed, Lahaina News, November 12, 1998: 2.

ONAGA, GERALD
— named chairman of Building Industry Association of Hawaii's Remodelers Council, Lahaina News, March 6, 1991: 10.

ONCE ON THIS ISLAND [PLAY]
— auditions being held by Maui Community Theatre/OnStage, Lahaina News, September 9, 1993: 11.
— to be performed by Maui Community Theatre/Maui OnStage, Lahaina News, November 25, 1993: 11.

ONCE UPON A MATTRESS [PLAY]
— to be performed by Baldwin Theatre Guild, Lahaina News, November 7, 1991: 20.
— to be performed by Baldwin Theatre Guild, Lahaina News, November 14, 1991: 15.
— opening Saturday, Lahaina News, November 14, 1991: 22.

ONCE UPON A SHOE [PLAY]
— to be performed by Theatre Theatre Maui, Lahaina News, July 23, 1998: 16.

ONE DAY SIGNS [BUSINESS]
— opens, Lahaina News, November 28, 1991: 7.

ONE FLEW OVER THE CUCKOO'S NEST [PLAY]
— to be performed at Iao Theatre, Lahaina News, April 8, 1999: 12.
— to conclude, Lahaina News, April 22, 1999: 12.

ONE FOUNDATION [MUSICAL GROUP]
— to perform at A Taste of Lahaina, Lahaina News, September 10, 1998: 16.

ONE WORLD [MUSICAL]
— to be staged by Arts Education for Children Group (AECG), Lahaina News, July 18, 2002: 14.

ONE WORLD, ONE FAMILY [BUSINESS]
— application to sell t-shirts in Lahaina incomplete, Lahaina News, May 19, 1994: 4.
— hearing scheduled for request to sell t-shirts, Lahaina News, May 26, 1994: 4.

— denied request to sell t-shirts, Lahaina News, June 2, 1994: 1,16.
— discusses end of impasse with LahainaTown Action Committee, Lahaina News, September 8, 1994: 1.

ONE-HOUR PHOTO [BUSINESS]
— opens at the Maui Marriott, Lahaina News, June 22, 1988: 3.
— opens, Lahaina News, December 25, 1997: 11.

O'NEAL, JOHN
— to present "Exploring the African American and Local Cultures Through the Story Circle", Lahaina News, June 16, 1994: 12.
— to perform "The Writings of Junebug Jabbo Jones" after , Lahaina News, June 23, 1994: 12.

O'NEILL MAUI INVITATIONAL
— see Marui/O'Neill Maui Invitational

O'NEILL, MIKE
— CEO of Bank of Hawaii to speak, Lahaina News, March 27, 2003: 8.

ONEMAUISTORY
— celebration of Maui culture to be held, Lahaina News, September 1, 1994: 14.

ONG, ERIC
— realtor discusses properties on West Side, Lahaina News, February 22, 2001: 7.

ONION
— see Maui onion

ONION COOKOFF
— see Maui Onion Cookoff

ONION FESTIVAL
— see Maui Onion Festival

ONION OLYMPICS
— to be held at Whalers Village, Lahaina News, March 21, 1990: 3.

ONIZUKA MEMORIAL COMMITTEE
— hosts visit by astronaut Guy Gardner, Lahaina News, May 24, 1989: 3.

ONO, IRA [ARTIST]
— work displayed alongside Chiu Leong's, Lahaina News, January 4, 1984: 10.
— to give workshop on trash art, Lahaina News, January 23, 1992: 5.

ONO, RAYMOND
— promoted to branch manager by First Hawaiian Bank, Lahaina News, January 24, 1990: 6.
— becomes branch manager at Kahului, Lahaina News, March 7, 1990: 7.

ONO, SANFORD "SANDY"
— promoted to crude oil grader for PRI International Australia, Lahaina News, March 6, 1991: 9.

ONO, YOKO [ARTIST]
— exhibits John Lennon's work at Dyansen Gallery, Lahaina News, June 17, 1987: 3.
— discusses art of John Lennon, Lahaina News, July 29, 1987: 1,17.
— returns to Maui for UNICEF fundraiser, Lahaina News, July 13, 1988: 1,11.

ONUMA, DENNIS
— appointed director of restaurants by Sheraton Maui, Lahaina News, September 23, 1999: 11.

OOKLA THE MOC [MUSICAL GROUP]
— to perform at Lahaina Civic Center Amphitheater with Alpha Bloody, Lahaina News, February 18, 1999: 12.

OPEN DOORS
— hosting Faith Promise Dinner, Lahaina News, October 31, 1996: 18.

OPEN MIKE SINGING
— to be offered at Maui Beach Hotel, Lahaina News, August 13, 1998: 17.

OPERA
— Puccini's "Tosca" performed at Baldwin High School auditorium, Lahaina Sun, February 3, 1971: 8.

OPERATION: CHILD SAFE
— to be implemented, Lahaina News, January 6, 1994: 1.

OPPENHEIMER, HANK
— working to protect Pu'u Kukui Reserve, Lahaina News, July 6, 2000: 1,14.

OPTIMYSTICS, THE [MUSICAL GROUP]
— to perform at Pioneer Inn, Lahaina News, September 19, 1991: 16.
— continues to perform at Pioneer Inn, Lahaina News, December 5, 1991: 23.
— continue to perform at Pioneer Inn, Lahaina News, January 9, 1992: 11.
— to perform at Moose McGillycuddy's, Lahaina News, November 3, 1994: 27.

ORANGE JULIUS [RESTAURANT]
— adds pita sandwiches to menu, Lahaina News, March 5, 1998: 7.
— opens in Lahaina Cannery Mall, Lahaina News, November 25, 1999: 13.

ORCHID SOCIETY
— see Lahaina Orchid Society, Maui Orchid Society

ORCHIDS
— exhibition at Lahaina-Ka'anapali & Pacific Railroad terminal, Lahaina Sun, April 21, 1971: 3.
— Lahaina Orchid Society to meet, Lahaina Sun, May 19, 1971: 6.
— Fall Orchid Show scheduled, Lahaina News, November 12, 1986: 3.
— show to be held at Lahaina Shopping Center, Lahaina News, November 14, 1991: 2.

ORDONEZ, ASHELY
— Scholar/Athlete of the Week, Lahaina News, November 29, 2001: 13.

OREGON SHAKESPEAREAN FESTIVAL [TROUPE]
— to perform at Maui Youth Theatre, Lahaina News, November 2, 1988: 3.

ORESCAN, STEPHEN
— attacked while camping at Makena Beach, Lahaina Sun, March 22, 1972: 3.

ORESTEIN, MICHAEL [COMEDIAN]
— to perform at Maui Comedy Club, Lahaina News, June 29, 1995: 12.

ORIENT EXPRESS [RESTAURANT]
— reviewed, Lahaina News, May 2, 1984: 15.
— to celebrate Thai new year, Lahaina News, April 16, 1986: 1.

ORIENTAL MEDICINE
— discussed as alternative healing method, Lahaina News, May 4, 1988: 16.

ORIGINAL MAUI SWEET BAKED HAM COMPANY [BUSINESS]
— opens, Lahaina News, July 12, 1989: 4.

ORIGINAL PANCAKE HOUSE
— to open at Lahaina Center, Lahaina News, December 5, 1990: 4.

ORIGINAL RED DIRT SHIRT [BUSINESS]
— opens, Lahaina News, June 12, 1997: 15.

ORIKASA, WARREN
— installed as president of Maui Japanese Chamber of Commerce, Lahaina News, October 17, 1991: 9.

ORLECK, ROBERT [COUNTY ATTORNEY]
— argues that anti-hitchhiking law is constitutional, Lahaina Sun, February 17, 1971: 3.

ORNELLAS, PATRICK
— appointed account executive at Ka'anapali Beach Hotel, Lahaina News, October 10, 1990: 12.

ORONSAY [SHIP]
— passenger liner arrives in Lahaina, Lahaina Sun, June 6, 1973: 9.

ORR, JAMES [WRITER]
— to attend Maui Writers Conference, Lahaina News, July 27, 1995: 4.

ORR, NANCY [ARTIST]
— Jim Belushi purchases art of, Lahaina News, February 24, 1994: 9.
— benefit to be held for, Lahaina News, November 25, 1999: 20.
— receiving treatment for breast cancer, Lahaina News, December 2, 1999: 6.

ORTIZ, ALFREDO ROLANDO [MUSICIAN]
— to play harp, Lahaina News, December 2, 1993: 15.

ORTIZ, ENRIQUE
— new director for American Red Cross, Lahaina News, July 25, 2002: 2.

ORTIZ, PETER
— epidemiologist featured, Lahaina News, February 6, 1992: 3.

ORTMANN, J.P.
— thanked for helping improve school facilities in Kihei, Lahaina News, June 24, 1993: 7.

OSATO, SHARON
— named manager of American Savings Bank's Lahaina branch, Lahaina News, May 18, 1995: 6.

OSBORNE, TIM [MUSICIAN]
— to perform at Polli's Mexican Restaurant, Lahaina News, December 19, 1990: 13.
— to perform at Polli's Mexican Restaurant, Lahaina News, January 2, 1991: 8.
— to perform at Villa Lounge, Lahaina News, August 13, 1992: 15.

OSBOURNE, OZZY [MUSICIAN]
— performance in Honolulu reviewed, Lahaina News, June 27, 1984: 12.

OSBURN, CHRIS [MUSICIAN]
— to perform at Mom's at Maui Mall, Lahaina News, March 30, 2000: 13.

O'SHEA, MICHAEL
— Scholar/Athlete of the Week, Lahaina News, May 14, 1998: 15.

OSHIRO, CHASE
— Governor Ben Cayetano presents Hawaii Youth Medal of Honor for volunteerism to, Lahaina News, September 17, 1998: 18,19.

OSHIRO, NORMAN
— to present "True Health" at 'Ohana Connection breakfast, Lahaina News, July 26, 2001: 17.

OSKIE RICE POLO CUP
— to be held at Maui Polo Club's arena, Lahaina News, May 13, 1987: 12.

OSORNO, ANDREW
— student receives grant from Maui Chapter of the Navy League of the United States, Lahaina News, February 3, 1988: 3.

OSPANIK, LAURA [ARTIST]
— wins Lahaina Town Action Committee poster contest, Lahaina News, October 29, 1992: 20.

OSSOFSKY, JACK
— to present on issues connected to aging, Lahaina News, November 23, 1988: 5.

OSTLER, ALYCE
— chef cooks restaurant-quality meals for customers, Lahaina News, October 19, 2000: 16.

O'SULLIVAN, DAN [COMEDIAN]
— to perform at The Sports Page, Lahaina News, November 21, 1990: 15.

OTAHEITE POLYNESIAN CLOTHING
— opening in Whaler's Village, Lahaina Sun, November 25, 1970: 3.

OTHELLO [PLAY]
— to be performed at Honolulu Theatre for Youth, Lahaina News, March 21, 2002: 16.

OTOMO ENGINEERING INC. [BUSINESS]
— Mark Matsuda joins firm, Lahaina News, September 5, 2002: 8.

OTOMO, JANA
— Scholar/Athlete of the Week, Lahaina News, July 30, 1998: 15.

OTOMO, LAYNE
— received Eagle scout award, Lahaina Sun, June 30, 1971: 4.

OTOMO, STACY
— engineer opens office in Wailuku, Lahaina News, March 5, 1992: 9,10.

OTOMO, TARA
— Scholar/Athlete of the Week, Lahaina News, February 8, 2001: 14.

OTSUKA [ARTIST]
— to appear at Lahaina Galleries, Lahaina News, June 17, 1999: 16.

OTSUKI, TAMAYO [COMEDIAN]
— to perform at Comedy Club and the Sports Page, Lahaina News, March 13, 1991: 8,11.

OTSUKI-MI
— Japanese Cultural Society to host presentation on, Lahaina News, September 9, 1999: 12.

OUCHI, KIMMIE
— wins Wailuku Junior Open [tennis], Lahaina News, August 16, 1989: 7.
— wins Wailuku Junior Summer Open tennis, Lahaina News, August 22, 1991: 8.

OUCHI, WILLIAM
— to speak on "Looking to the Future: The Role of Education", Lahaina News, August 6, 1998: 17.
— to speak on "Looking to the Future: The Role of Education", Lahaina News, August 13, 1998: 16.

OUR MAUI [BOOK]
— created by seventh graders, Lahaina News, January 6, 1994: 12.

OUR TOWN [PLAY]
— to be performed by Maui OnStage/Maui Academy of Performing Arts, Lahaina News, January 12, 1995: 12.
— auditions to be held by Maui OnStage/Maui Academy of Performing Arts, Lahaina News, January 19, 1995: 11.
— to be performed, Lahaina News, March 16, 1995: 12.
— reviewed, Lahaina News, March 23, 1995: 11.

OURA, KAREY ANNE
— takes over Edward Jones office, Lahaina News, June 19, 2003: 8.

OUTBACK STEAKHOUSE [RESTAURANT]
— opening in Kahana, Lahaina News, April 2, 1998: 8.
— to open on Sunday, Lahaina News, April 23, 1998: 9.
— featured, Lahaina News, May 7, 1998: 6,7.
— offers call-ahead seating and curbside take away, Lahaina News, August 2, 2001: 8.
— supporting Red Cross Disaster Relief Fund, Lahaina News, October 11, 2001: 9.
— featured, Lahaina News, November 7, 2002: 14,15.

OUTDOOR CIRCLE
— meeting announced, Lahaina Sun, November 3, 1971: 14.

OUTER ISLAND SURFBOARDS [BUSINESS]
— business described, Lahaina News, August 19, 1987: 6.

OUTFIELD [MUSICAL GROUP]
— to play at the Lahaina Civic Center, Lahaina News, August 27, 1986: 8.

OUTRIGGER CANOE CLUB
— ironwoman team captures first place, Lahaina News, September 9, 1993: 8.
— wins channel race, Lahaina News, October 15, 1998: 15.

OUTRIGGER ENTERPRISES, INC [BUSINESS]
— buying Maui Inter-Continental Resort, to rename Outrigger Wailea Resort, Lahaina News, January 21, 1999: 11.

OUTRIGGER WAILEA RESORT [BUSINESS]
— to manage Royal Lahaina Resort, Lahaina News, March 21, 1990: 4.
— acquires Hawaiiana Resorts condominium resort operations, Lahaina News, March 31, 1994: 9.
— new name of Maui Inter-Continental Resort following purchase by Outrigger Enterprises, Inc., Lahaina News, January 21, 1999: 11.
— announces staff changes, Lahaina News, September 7, 2000: 18.
— to take over management of Royal Kahana Resort, Lahaina News, March 22, 2001: 8.
— to observe Mei Day, Lahaina News, April 25, 2002: 17.
— Romeo Paet named executive chef at, Lahaina News, July 4, 2002: 8.

OUTSTANDING OLDER AMERICANS
— 23 Maui County residents nominated for award, Lahaina News, June 5, 1985: 8.
— awards ceremony to be held, Lahaina News, April 30, 1992: 4.
— nominations sought, Lahaina News, March 24, 1994: 7.
— nominations sought for, Lahaina News, March 7, 1996: 10.
— candidates announced, Lahaina News, May 2, 1996: 16.
— awards ceremony to be held, Lahaina News, October 30, 1997: 2.
— musician Henry Kupahu named Maui's Outstanding Male Older American, Lahaina News, May 25, 2000: 1,14.
— awards announced, Lahaina News, July 10, 2003: 9.

OUTSTANDING OLDER AMERICANS OF MAUI COUNTY
— nominations sought for, Lahaina News, March 18, 1999: 8.

OUTSTANDING VOLUNTEER AWARDS
— nominations sought for, Lahaina News, December 30, 1993: 2.

OVER THE EDGE [MUSICAL GROUP]
— to perform at Moose McGillycuddy's, Lahaina News, February 13, 1992: 19.

OVER THE RAINBOW MAUI [BUSINESS]
— opens, Lahaina News, June 1, 2000: 14.

OVEREATERS ANONYMOUS
— to meet, Lahaina News, September 23, 1999: 12.
— to meet, Lahaina News, April 20, 2000: 17.
— to meet at Haiku Elementary School, Lahaina News, June 8, 2000: 21.
— continues to meet, Lahaina News, September 28, 2000: 17.
— to hold weekend retreat, Lahaina News, October 5, 2000: 16.
— to hold public forum, Lahaina News, January 11, 2001: 3.
— continues to be held, Lahaina News, April 19, 2001: 17.
— continues to meet, Lahaina News, July 5, 2001: 16.
— continues to meet, Lahaina News, September 6, 2001: 16.

OVERTHROW
— discussion of U.S. involvement in overthrow of the Hawaiian monarchy, Lahaina News, July 15, 1981: 11,12.
— anniversary to be observed, Lahaina News, January 14, 1993: 3,12.

OVERTON, RICK [COMEDIAN]
— to perform at Maui Comedy Club, Lahaina News, August 17, 1995: 12.

OVERVOLD, ROBBIE [ARTIST]
— interior designer to offer class on shopping for furniture, Lahaina News, January 30, 1992: 5.

OVISSI [ARTIST]
— to exhibit at the Metropolitan Art Gallery, Lahaina News, August 1, 1991: 17.

OWEN, JENNIFER [ARTIST]
— to offer kiln firing class, Lahaina News, April 17, 1991: 15.

OWEN, RENA
— Maori actress to host acting workshop, Lahaina News, July 9, 1998: 7.
— New Zealand actress to lead acting workshop, Lahaina News, July 23, 1998: 8.

OWENS, GREG
— chiropractor opens new practice, Lahaina News, May 29, 1997: 5.

OXBOW WORLD MASTERS CHAMPIONSHIP
— won by Buzzy Kerbox, Lahaina News, August 20, 1998: 15.

OZMA OF OZ: A TALE OF THE TIMES [PLAY]
— auditions scheduled by Maui Academy of Performing Arts, Lahaina News, March 5, 1992: 5.
— to be performed by Maui Academy of Performing Arts, Lahaina News, April 16, 1992: 22.
— performances continue, Lahaina News, April 23, 1992: 26,30.

P

P R MAUI [BUSINESS]
— resuming business on Maui, Lahaina News, September 30, 1993: 8.

PA'ANI PILI [MUSICAL GROUP]
— to perform at B.J.'s Chicago Pizzeria, Lahaina News, November 14, 1996: 16.

PACHECO, ZACH
— Scholar/Athlete of the Week, Lahaina News, September 11, 1997: 14.

PACIFIC AEROSPACE MUSEUM
— to formally open, Lahaina News, August 8, 1991: 8.

PACIFIC AND ASIAN AFFAIRS COUNCIL
— to present "Blowing Zen", Lahaina News, February 16, 1995: 15.

PACIFIC ARCHITECTURE AND ENVIRONMENTAL PLANNING CO. [BUSINESS]
— opens, Lahaina News, March 2, 1995: 7.

PACIFIC ARTS FESTIVAL COMMITTEE
— accepting applications for people to represent Hawaii at the Festival of the Pacific Arts in New Caledonia, Lahaina News, May 16, 1984: 5.

PACIFIC BAD BOYS [MUSICAL GROUP]
— to perform at "Year of the Hawaiian" concert, Lahaina News, May 27, 1987: 3.
— to perform at Maui Lu Resort on New Year's Eve with Brother Noland, Lahaina News, January 2, 1992: 12.

PACIFIC BASIN DEVELOPMENT CONFERENCE
— speakers scheduled; to be held in Wailea, Lahaina News, August 17, 1988: 15.

PACIFIC BASIN TRAVEL SYSTEMS, INC. [BUSINESS]
— building Maui South Seas Hotel, Lahaina Sun, November 11, 1970: 4.
— financial troubles, leading to stoppage in construction of hotel in Kahana, Lahaina Sun, May 12, 1971: 2.

PACIFIC BREWING
— to distribute Maui Lager Beer in state, Lahaina News, May 20, 1987: 3.
— see also Maui Lager Beer

PACIFIC BUSINESS NEWS
— now managed by Rod Smith, Lahaina News, April 2, 1992: 12.
— editor George Mason advocates for private sector running public services, Lahaina News, September 29, 1994: 1,2.
— article expresses need for reform of state laws, Lahaina News, June 18, 1998: 13.

PACIFIC CAFE [RESTAURANT]
— to hold birthday party to benefit American Cancer Society, Lahaina News, July 27, 2000: 15.

PACIFIC CAFE HONOKOWAI, A [RESTAURANT]
— opens in Honokowai, Lahaina News, November 12, 1998: 13.
— to hold opening, Lahaina News, November 19, 1998: 13.
— featured, Lahaina News, December 3, 1998: 8.

PACIFIC CENTER CONFERENCE
— to be held, Lahaina News, May 21, 1992: 4.

PACIFIC CENTER OF PHOTOGRAPHY
— to hold "Worlds Within Worlds" exhibition, Lahaina News, January 3, 2002: 3.

PACIFIC COAST MORTGAGE CORPORATION
— seeks permit to build office building in Lahaina, Lahaina News, May 29, 1985: 3.

PACIFIC CONSTRUCTION CO., LTD. [BUSINESS]
— co-sponsoring ODC/San Francisco dance company performance, Lahaina News, October 12, 1988: 3.
— to change name to Fletcher Pacific Construction Co., Ltd., Lahaina News, June 13, 1991: 18.

PACIFIC DISASTER CENTER
— Glenn James meteorologist featured, Lahaina News, July 5, 2001: 18.

PACIFIC DIVE SERVICES, INC. [BUSINESS]
— opens, Lahaina News, February 21, 1990: 5.

PACIFIC DIVING SCHOOL
— opens, Lahaina News, September 6, 1989: 2.

PACIFIC FLEET BAND [MUSICAL GROUP]
— to perform, Lahaina News, March 16, 1995: 11.

PACIFIC GRILL [RESTAURANT]
— offering ohana brunch, Lahaina News, July 11, 1991: 17.

PACIFIC IMAGES FILM FESTIVAL
— to be held, Lahaina News, July 17, 1997: 16.

PACIFIC IMAGING CENTER [BUSINESS]
— to hold open house, Lahaina News, April 6, 1995: 6.
— to offer computer courses, Lahaina News, July 27, 1995: 10.
— to offer computer courses, Lahaina News, August 31, 1995: 10.

PACIFIC INSTITUTE
— to hold "Investment in Excellence in the '90s", Lahaina News, October 13, 1994: 15.

PACIFIC INTERNATIONAL SPORTS CONFERENCE AND EXPO (PISCES)
— conference to focus on lifestyle sports industry, Lahaina News, October 8, 1998: 15.

PACIFIC ISLAND CONFERENCE
— to be held, Lahaina News, June 9, 1994: 6.

PACIFIC ISLAND IMAGES FILM FESTIVAL
— to be held at Maui Arts and Cultural Center, Lahaina News, August 1, 1996: 20.
— to be held at Maui Community College, Lahaina News, July 10, 1997: 17.

PACIFIC ISLANDS WILDLIFE REFUGES
— photographs taken at on display, Lahaina News, June 12, 2003: 14.

PACIFIC JET SKI RENTALS [BUSINESS]
— continues operation during whale season, Lahaina News, January 9, 1992: 1.
— halts operation following temporary restraining order, Lahaina News, January 23, 1992: 1.
— operations halted until court hearing, Lahaina News, January 23, 1992: 3.

PACIFIC MANAGEMENT BASIN
— managing agent for Paniolo Hale, Lahaina News, November 21, 1990: 12.

PACIFIC MARINE OF HONOLULU
— awarded contract to build mooring in West Maui, Lahaina News, January 6, 1988: 3.

PACIFIC MARITIME ACADEMY OF HONOLULU
— to offer Ocean & Motorboat Operators course, Lahaina News, February 12, 1986: 3.
— offering licensure courses for Ocean or Motorboat Operator, Lahaina News, February 4, 1987: 3.

PACIFIC MASTERS SWIMMING CHAMPIONSHIPS
— to be held, Lahaina News, June 12, 1997: 13.

PACIFIC MUSEUMS, INC. [BUSINESS]
— to design and build new exhibit at Whalers Village Shopping Center, Lahaina News, February 20, 1991: 7.

PACIFIC OCEAN RESEARCH FOUNDATION
— sponsors Light Tackle Tan & Release Tournament, Lahaina News, August 8, 1990: 7.
— helping to protect gamefish, Lahaina News, September 21, 1995: 7.

PACIFIC OVERTURE
— to hold public concert "Three Nights Only: A Celebration of Sondheim", Lahaina News, November 3, 1994: 27.

PACIFIC PRINCESS [SHIP]
— to arrive at Lahaina Harbor, Lahaina News, January 9, 1991: 5.

PACIFIC RADIO GROUP, INC. [BUSINESS]
— new name of Lahaina Broadcasting Company, Lahaina News, November 4, 1999: 11.
— introduces website, Lahaina News, March 2, 2000: 11.
— Amy "Kitty" Matthews joins, Lahaina News, December 20, 2001: 9.

PACIFIC RESOURCES INC. [BUSINESS]
— earnings up, Lahaina News, June 1, 1980: 13.
— earnings reported for second quarter, Lahaina News, August 15, 1981: 16.
— plans coal shipment facility in Oregon, Lahaina News, September 15, 1981: 16.
— Profits increase, Lahaina News, November 15, 1981: 16.
— to sponsor energy education workshop, Lahaina News, October 8, 1992: 7.

PACIFIC RIM BUSINESS BROKERS
— opens in Wailuku, Lahaina News, July 25, 1991: 7.

PACIFIC SOUND MACHINE [MUSICAL GROUP]
— to perform on Halloween, Lahaina News, October 22, 1998: 7.

PACIFIC SUNWEAR [BUSINESS]
— Ka'ahumanu Center, Lahaina News, August 26, 1999: 14.

PACIFIC TREASURES [PERFORMANCE]
— puppet show to be performed at Lahaina Cannery Shopping Center, Lahaina News, May 9, 1990: 5.

PACIFIC TSUNAMI WARNING CENTER
— staff to discuss tsunamis, Lahaina News, April 1, 1999: 2.

PACIFIC VISIONS [BUSINESS]
— reviewed, Lahaina News, December 7, 1988: 8.

PACIFIC VOYAGING SOCIETY
— to participate in Taro Festival, Lahaina News, March 21, 1996: 13.

PACIFIC WHALE FOUNDATION
— sets whalewatch, Lahaina News, February 8, 1984: 5.
— announces "Aloha to the Whales" cruise, Lahaina News, May 16, 1984: 5.
— will conduct "Welcome Home the Whales Whalewatch", Lahaina News, November 21, 1984: 3.
— to offer workshop for water users, Lahaina News, December 19, 1984: 3.
— Whale Day celebration, Lahaina News, March 27, 1985: 3.
— to host "Welcome Home the Whales", Lahaina News, November 27, 1985: 3.
— celebration scheduled, Lahaina News, April 9, 1986: 3.
— releases new whale watching guide, Lahaina News, November 5, 1986: 3.
— holds fundraiser at Stouffer Wailea Resort, Lahaina News, November 5, 1986: 3.
— studying whales off West Maui, Lahaina News, April 1, 1987: 1,8,10,20.
— supporting research on Maui, Lahaina News, April 8, 1987: 1,10.
— to conduct survey of Molokini Crater with students from the Marine Option Program, Lahaina News, July 22, 1987: 3,10.
— organizes "Get the Drift and Bag it", Lahaina News, October 14, 1987: 17.
— to hold fundraiser "A Seven Course Symphony—A Rhapsody in Food", Lahaina News, November 18, 1987: 18.
— planning Whale Day 88, Lahaina News, April 20, 1988: 6.
— Dr. Paul Forestall to lecture on whales, Lahaina News, March 8, 1989: 17.
— representatives to speak at Ohana Luncheon and Trade Faire, Lahaina News, March 29, 1989: 14.
— providing free boat rides, Lahaina News, July 26, 1989: 3.
— submits petition to stop slaughter of dolphins in driftnets submitted to Congressman Daniel Akaka, Lahaina News, October 18, 1989: 3.
— sponsoring lectures by Dr. John Ling and Dr. Pin Needham, Lahaina News, December 13, 1989: 4.
— to hold Whale Day celebration, Lahaina News, April 10, 1991: 10,12.
— partnering with Christian Riese Lassen to create marine museum in West Maui, Lahaina News, January 2, 1992: 5.
— seeking volunteers to help with Whale Day/Earth Day, Lahaina News, April 23, 1992: 7.
— to hold Whale Day, Lahaina News, April 22, 1993: 4.
— awarded grant from Environmental Protection Agency, Lahaina News, July 15, 1993: 5.
— Lindemans Wines to hold fundraiser for, Lahaina News, July 7, 1994: 16.
— opens store and Marine Resource Center, Lahaina News, November 17, 1994: 10.
— seeking volunteers for Earth Day/Whale Day, Lahaina News, January 26, 1995: 6.
— to participate in "Year of the Sea Turtle", Lahaina News, October 12, 1995: 6.
— to hold Welcome Home the Whales Celebration Cruises, Lahaina News, November 23, 1995: 4.
— to host whale count, Lahaina News, February 22, 1996: 10.
— to celebrate return of humpback whales, Lahaina News, November 28, 1996: 10.
— seeking volunteers for whale count, Lahaina News, February 27, 1997: 10.
— to host Whale Day '97, Lahaina News, March 6, 1997: 11.
— sponsoring Whale Week, Lahaina News, March 13, 1997: 16.
— Keiki Day to be held, Lahaina News, July 10, 1997: 17.
— to hold Keiki Day, Lahaina News, July 17, 1997: 16.
— looking for volunteers to help with Great American Fish Count, Lahaina News, August 21, 1997: 15.
— adds new catamaran "Ocean Spirit" at Ma'alaea Harbor, Lahaina News, January 1, 1998: 13.

— to present "The Great Maui Whale Festival Symposium: Wild Whales in Our Midst", Lahaina News, January 31, 2002: 16.

— Irene Bowie is new marketing manager, Lahaina News, February 7, 2002: 8.

— begins Maui Marine CORE (Conserving Ocean Resources through Education) program, Lahaina News, April 11, 2002: 2.

— to celebrate Earth Day, Lahaina News, April 18, 2002: 17.

— continues to provide Whale Information Station at the McGregor Point scenic overlook, Lahaina News, April 25, 2002: 16.

— continues to host Seaside Stories, Lahaina News, July 11, 2002: 16.

— to hold snorkeling tours, Lahaina News, July 18, 2002: 16.

— to hold Dolphin Sand Sculpture Contest, Lahaina News, August 1, 2002: 20.

— continues to hold snorkeling tours, Lahaina News, August 8, 2002: 16.

— Wild Whale and Dolphin Research Project underway, Lahaina News, August 22, 2002: 22.

— to offer snorkeling tours of free fish, Lahaina News, August 29, 2002: 20.

— to hold Keiki Ocean Discovery Time., Lahaina News, September 19, 2002: 24.

— continues to run reef station at Kahekili Park, Lahaina News, October 10, 2002: 16.

— to offer Marine Mammal Naturalist Training Course, Lahaina News, November 7, 2002: 21.

— to show IMAX movie, Lahaina News, November 14, 2002: 17.

— to hold Keiki Ocean Discovery Time., Lahaina News, November 21, 2002: 20.

— naturalist to give talk on humpback whales, Lahaina News, December 12, 2002: 21.

— to offer "Family Full Moon Tidepool Exploration", Lahaina News, December 19, 2002: 20.

— continues to staff Whale Information Station at McGregor Point, Lahaina News, December 26, 2002: 17.

— to hold whale watching tours, Lahaina News, January 9, 2003: 17.

— to hold whale watching cruise, Lahaina News, January 23, 2003: 16.

— to hold Run for the Whales, Lahaina News, February 6, 2003: 13.

— to hold Whale Day Celebration, Lahaina News, February 13, 2003: 14.

— to hold Keiki Ocean Discovery Time, Lahaina News, February 20, 2003: 17.

— seeking volunteers for Great Whale Count, Lahaina News, February 20, 2003: 18.

— to hold Family Ocean Discovery Series at Borders Books and Music, Lahaina News, February 27, 2003: 16.

— seeking volunteers for Great Whale Count, Lahaina News, February 27, 2003: 9.

— to host a Family Whalewatch and Sing-a-long with Uncle Wayne, Lahaina News, March 13, 2003: 16.

— to hold family whale watch, Lahaina News, March 20, 2003: 16.

— continues to run Coral Reef Information Station at Ulua Beach, Lahaina News, May 15, 2003: 17.

— continues to offer "Seaside Stories", Lahaina News, July 31, 2003: 16.

— to hold coral reef tours at Kahekili Park (Airport Beach), Lahaina News, August 7, 2003: 16.

— Wild Dolphin Sand Sculpture Contest to be held at Keawakapu Beach, Lahaina News, August 7, 2003: 16.

— continues to offer "Seaside Stories", Lahaina News, October 2, 2003: 16.

PACIFIC WINGS AIRLINES [BUSINESS]

— to start new flights between Honolulu and Moloka'i, Lahaina News, September 24, 1998: 13.

— enters code share relationship with Aloha Airlines, Lahaina News, September 23, 1999: 11.

— expanding service at Waimea/Kohala Airport, Lahaina News, January 20, 2000: 11.

— new flights starting, Lahaina News, February 24, 2000: 14.

— increases Lana'i flights, Lahaina News, January 4, 2001: 14.

PACIFICA ARTS & GRAPHICS [BUSINESS]

— opens in Makawao, Lahaina News, February 20, 1991: 7.

PACIFIC'O [RESTAURANT]

— opens, Lahaina News, August 5, 1993: 10.

— to feature jazz, Lahaina News, April 21, 1994: 15.

— awarded first place at last year's "A Taste of Lahaina" in fish and seafood division, Lahaina News, August 4, 1994: 20.

— featured, Lahaina News, October 2, 1997: 6,7,8.

— featured, Lahaina News, December 7, 2000: 7.

— featured, Lahaina News, September 13, 2001: 14,15.

— has new farm in Kula, Lahaina News, November 29, 2001: 8.

— new kitchen opens, Lahaina News, January 17, 2002: 8.

— receives Judges Award at A Taste of Lahaina, Lahaina News, September 26, 2002: 9.

— adds new menu items, Lahaina News, December 5, 2002: 8.

— offering space for parties, Lahaina News, February 27, 2003: 8.

PACKARD, MICHAEL

— appointed vice president of residential property management division of Chaney, Brooks and Co., Lahaina News, March 31, 1994: 12.

— helps Chaney, Brooks and Company expand on Maui, Lahaina News, February 24, 2000: 13.

PACOPAE, JAMES

— testifies in favor of expanding Ka'anapali Resort, Lahaina News, December 21, 1995: 1.

PADDLING

— clubs on Maui planning a competition, Lahaina Sun, April 11, 1973: 3.

— opening of season described, Lahaina Sun, May 2, 1973: 4.

— new Lahaina Canoe Club described, Lahaina Sun, May 16, 1973: 22.

— races set for Kamehameha Day, Lahaina Sun, May 30, 1973: 3.

— Kaiwi Channel race to be held, Lahaina News, September 24, 1986: 6.

— outrigger canoe race sponsored by Surf Sports, Lahaina News, April 5, 1989: 3.

— photographs from regatta, Lahaina News, July 26, 1989: 7.

— state competition planned, Lahaina News, July 26, 1989: 7.

— Napili Canoe Club places second in Kamehameha-Hilo race, Lahaina News, August 16, 1989: 24.

— Maui-Moloka'i canoe regatta to be held, Lahaina News, September 13, 1989: 1.

— Great Polli's Pali Outrigger Canoe Race scheduled, Lahaina News, February 7, 1990: 9.

— Great Polli's Pali Outrigger Canoe Race to be held, Lahaina News, February 14, 1990: 12.

— Great Polli's Pali Outrigger Canoe Race scheduled, Lahaina News, February 21, 1990: 9.

— canoe season gearing up; canoe clubs described, Lahaina News, April 18, 1990: 7.

— Napili Invitational to be held, Lahaina News, May 9, 1990: 7.

— outrigger canoe season to begin, Lahaina News, May 16, 1990: 7.

— Hoomanao Challenge to be held, Lahaina News, May 23, 1990: 9.

— outrigger season begins, Lahaina News, June 6, 1990: 6.

— Lahaina Canoe Club sponsoring Keiki O Maui Regatta, Lahaina News, June 13, 1990: 8.

— Doug Tihada Memorial Regatta to be held, Lahaina News, July 4, 1990: 6.

— Napili Sophomore Women crew photographed, Lahaina News, July 11, 1990: 11.

— results from the season so far, Lahaina News, July 11, 1990: 8.

— Maui County finals to take place, Lahaina News, July 18, 1990: 6.

— results of John Lake Regatta, Lahaina News, August 1, 1990: 3.

— Moloka'i-to-Oahu long distance race to be held, Lahaina News, August 8, 1990: 7.
— results of the Steinlager Hawaiian Canoe Racing State Championship regatta, Lahaina News, August 15, 1990: 18.
— Moloka'i-to-Oahu outrigger race to be held, Lahaina News, October 3, 1990: 6.
— Napili Invitational canoe race scheduled at Hanaka'o'o Beach Park, Lahaina News, May 8, 1991: 6.
— Kahana Canoe Club to hold long distance canoe race, Lahaina News, May 15, 1991: 7.
— Ho'omana'o Challenge to be held, Lahaina News, May 23, 1991: 10.
— Ben Abiera Memorial Relays to be held, Lahaina News, May 23, 1991: 10.
— Maui Sailing Canoe Association to hold interisland cruise, Lahaina News, October 10, 1991: 8.
— offered off-season training by Craig Johnson, Lahaina News, January 2, 1992: 6.
— season begins, Lahaina News, January 30, 1992: 8.
— Napili Canoe Club seeking paddlers, Lahaina News, February 20, 1992: 6.
— canoe races begin, Lahaina News, April 23, 1992: 23.
— Napili Canoe Club wins races at Kahana Invitational Outrigger Canoe Race, Lahaina News, May 21, 1992: 11.
— Ben Abiera Relay Canoe Race to be held, Lahaina News, May 28, 1992: 9.
— Kihei Canoe Club wins, Lahaina News, June 4, 1992: 7.
— results of Kamehameha Day regatta, Lahaina News, June 11, 1992: 11.
— Napili Canoe Club wins Kamehameha Day regatta, Lahaina News, June 18, 1992: 13.
— Napili Canoe Club loses Maui County Hawaiian Canoe Association regatta championship, Lahaina News, June 25, 1992: 9.
— Napili Canoe Club captures Tihada canoe regatta, Lahaina News, July 2, 1992: 12.
— Moki Kalanikau Maui County Hawaiian Canoe Association regatta results, Lahaina News, July 9, 1992: 7.
— Napili Canoe Club to compete in John M. Lake regatta, Lahaina News, July 16, 1992: 10.
— Hawaiian Canoe Club wins John M. Lake regatta, Lahaina News, July 23, 1992: 14.
— canoe racing improving on Maui, Lahaina News, July 30, 1992: 8.
— Napili Canoe Club takes second place in state finals, Lahaina News, August 6, 1992: 1,4.
— Maui Sailing Canoe Association wins Na Hoko Kai race, Lahaina News, August 27, 1992: 7,9.
— Napili is 11th in Moloka'i-Oahu race, Lahaina News, October 1, 1992: 8.
— Pana Manu Canoe Club of Australia wins Bankoh Moloka'i Hoe outrigger canoe race, Lahaina News, October 15, 1992: 10.
— Compadres Kayak Racing Series to continue, Lahaina News, April 1, 1993: 4.
— Rory Frampton wins Compadres Kayak Racing Series, Lahaina News, April 8, 1993: 8.
— state championships to be held at Hanaka'o'o Beach Park, Lahaina News, June 3, 1993: 6.
— results of Ho'omana'o 1993, Lahaina News, June 10, 1993: 8.
— Regatta season to open, Lahaina News, June 10, 1993: 9.
— results from Maui County Hawaiian Canoe Association in-shore regatta, Lahaina News, June 17, 1993: 8.
— results of second Maui County Hawaiian Canoe Association regatta, Lahaina News, June 24, 1993: 11.
— update on regatta season, Lahaina News, July 8, 1993: 9.
— latest regatta results, Lahaina News, July 15, 1993: 7,8.
— Napili Canoe Club dominates races, Lahaina News, August 26, 1993: 12.

— results of Moloka'i Channel Race, Lahaina News, September 16, 1993: 11.
— Napili Canoe Club to compete in Na Wahine O Ke Kai, Lahaina News, September 23, 1993: 9.
— results of Na Wahine O Ke Kai, Lahaina News, September 30, 1993: 9.
— racing series to open, Lahaina News, January 20, 1994: 8.
— Compadres Kayak Racing series continues, Lahaina News, January 27, 1994: 6.
— results of Compadres Kayak Racing Series, Lahaina News, February 17, 1994: 7,8.
— Compadres Kayak Racing series continues, Lahaina News, February 24, 1994: 6.
— Compadres Kayak Racing fourth leg to be held, Lahaina News, March 10, 1994: 6.
— Compadres Kayak Racing fourth leg results, Lahaina News, March 17, 1994: 6.
— Compadres Kayak Racing fifth leg to be held, Lahaina News, March 24, 1994: 12.
— Edmund Mitchell wins fifth leg of Compadres Kayak Racing Series, Lahaina News, March 31, 1994: 7.
— Compadres Kayak Racing series continues, Lahaina News, April 7, 1994: 6.
— results of Compadres Kayak Racing Series, Lahaina News, April 21, 1994: 6.
— update on Compadres Kayak Racing Series, Lahaina News, April 28, 1994: 7.
— Edmund Mitchell places 30th in Bankoh Kayak Challenge, Lahaina News, May 26, 1994: 9.
— Napili Canoe Club results, Lahaina News, June 16, 1994: 6.
— Dougie Tihada Memorial Canoe Regatta to be held, Lahaina News, July 7, 1994: 7.
— State Championship Regatta to be held, Lahaina News, August 4, 1994: 6.
— results of state championship, Lahaina News, August 11, 1994: 6.
— Queen Lili'uokalani Canoe Race, Lahaina News, September 1, 1994: 9.
— Kahana Canoe Club to hold Maui Hotel/Resort Canoe Championship Regatta, Lahaina News, March 30, 1995: 7.
— results of races, Lahaina News, April 27, 1995: 7.
— Napili Canoe Club successful, Lahaina News, May 4, 1995: 8.
— Kahana Canoe Club hosts pre-season regatta, Lahaina News, May 11, 1995: 7.
— Bankoh Kayak Challenge to take place, Lahaina News, May 18, 1995: 7.
— Hawaiian Canoe Club continues to dominate, Lahaina News, June 29, 1995: 7.
— Napili Canoe Club to host Dougie Tihada Memorial Regatta, Lahaina News, July 6, 1995: 7.
— two West Maui clubs in running for runner-up slot of Maui County Hawaiian Canoe Association regatta, Lahaina News, July 13, 1995: 7.
— Maui County Hawaiian Canoe Association regatta ends, Lahaina News, July 27, 1995: 6.
— Great Kahakuloa Race to be held, Lahaina News, August 10, 1995: 7.
— Napili Canoe Club teams win gold, Lahaina News, August 17, 1995: 7.
— Offshore No. 1 wins Bankoh Na Wahine O Ke Kai, Lahaina News, September 28, 1995: 7.
— LahainaTown Action Committee to help establish Hawaiian canoe park, Lahaina News, November 30, 1995: 1,12.
— Chart House Kayak Racing series to be held, Lahaina News, January 25, 1996: 10.
— Chart House Kayak Racing series continues, Lahaina News, February 1, 1996: 6.

— John Stuart featured, Lahaina News, February 8, 1996: 11.

— Chart House Kayak Racing series continues, Lahaina News, February 8, 1996: 11.

— report on Chart House Kayak Racing, Lahaina News, February 15, 1996: 7.

— Lahaina Canoe Club paddling season to begin, Lahaina News, February 22, 1996: 7.

— importance of Polynesian ocean-voyaging discussed, Lahaina News, March 7, 1996: 1,16.

— Chart House Kayak Racing series continues, Lahaina News, March 7, 1996: 7.

— Jeannie Gonzales and Derek Vinuya featured, Lahaina News, April 4, 1996: 17.

— history of in Maui, Lahaina News, April 18, 1996: 13.

— results of Naleieha Regatta , Lahaina News, June 27, 1996: 16.

— crews compete In State Championship Regatta, Lahaina News, August 1, 1996: 19.

— Na Wahine O Ke Kai to be held, Lahaina News, September 19, 1996: 13.

— Hui O Wa'a Kaulua plans open house at Kamehameha Iki Park, Lahaina News, November 21, 1996: 1,13.

— Hui O Wa'a Kaulua featured, Lahaina News, December 5, 1996: 1.

— Maui Kayak Club series to begin, Lahaina News, December 26, 1996: 7.

— results of Hanaka'o'o Triangle Race, Lahaina News, January 9, 1997: 6.

— youth program started by Sierra Club, Lahaina News, January 16, 1997: 6.

— Eyecatcher Ho'omana'o Challenge to be held, Lahaina News, May 22, 1997: 1.

— Maui County Hawaiian Canoe Association regatta to open, Lahaina News, May 29, 1997: 12.

— Aston Ka'anapali Shores Sailing Canoe Regatta to be held, Lahaina News, May 29, 1997: 12.

— Keiki O Maui regatta to be held, Lahaina News, June 12, 1997: 12.

— Naleieha Regatta to be held, Lahaina News, June 19, 1997: 14,15.

— summer regattas, Lahaina News, June 26, 1997: 1,13.

— Hawaiian Canoe Racing Association's state races to begin, Lahaina News, July 31, 1997: 14.

— Queen Ka'ahumanu long distance canoe race to be held, Lahaina News, August 14, 1997: 14.

— Kai Opua Canoe Club to hold Queen Lili'uokalani Long Distance Canoe Races, Lahaina News, August 21, 1997: 13.

— Hawai'iloa to visit Maui, Lahaina News, September 18, 1997: 9.

— Hale O Lono race, Lahaina News, October 2, 1997: 16.

— Bankoh Moloka'i Hoe to be held, Lahaina News, October 9, 1997: 11.

— Bankoh Moloka'i Hoe won by Outrigger Australia 2 team, Lahaina News, October 16, 1997: 15.

— Keola Sequeira featured, Lahaina News, October 16, 1997: 6.

— Chart House Kayak Racing Series to begin, Lahaina News, January 8, 1998: 6.

— Kahana Canoe Club hosts second leg of Chart House Kayak and Canoe Racing series, Lahaina News, January 29, 1998: 7.

— Chart House Kayak Racing Series continues, Lahaina News, February 12, 1998: 15.

— Chart House Kayak Racing Series continues, Lahaina News, February 19, 1998: 6.

— Chart House Kayak Racing Series continues, Lahaina News, March 12, 1998: 15.

— Chart House Kayak Racing Series continues, Lahaina News, March 19, 1998: 7.

— Chart House Kayak Racing Series continues, Lahaina News, March 26, 1998: 7.

— Maui County Hawaiian Canoe Association hosting Ocean Relay Race, Lahaina News, April 23, 1998: 14,15.

— canoe festival to be held, Lahaina News, May 7, 1998: 1.

— "In Celebration of Canoes" to be held, Lahaina News, May 21, 1998: 1,20.

— "Festival of Canoes" to be held, Lahaina News, May 28, 1998: 1.

— Team Makakoa places second in Eyecatcher Ho'omana'o Challenge Outrigger Sailing Canoe Race, Lahaina News, May 28, 1998: 1,16.

— Na Wahine O Ke Kai Outrigger Canoe Championship to be held, Lahaina News, June 18, 1998: 15.

— Maui County Hawaiian Canoe Association regatta continues, Lahaina News, July 2, 1998: 15.

— final leg of Maui County Hawaiian Canoe Association in-shore regatta season, Lahaina News, July 16, 1998: 5.

— Derrick Vinuya representing Hawaii at International World Sprints Championships, Lahaina News, August 13, 1998: 15.

— Bankoh Moloka'i Hoe canoe race to be held, Lahaina News, October 8, 1998: 15.

— Outrigger Canoe Club wins channel race, Lahaina News, October 15, 1998: 15.

— Maui Kayak and Canoe Club continues to offer Chart House Kayak and Canoe Racing series, Lahaina News, January 14, 1999: 6.

— Ben Martin elected race director at Maui County Hawaiian Canoe Association, Lahaina News, April 8, 1999: 7.

— Canoe Beach ready for competition, Lahaina News, April 29, 1999: 15.

— "In Celebration of Canoes" festival to be held, Lahaina News, May 6, 1999: 19.

— Derek Vinuya and Elizabeth Dolezal compete in Starbucks Solo Kayak and Canoe World Championship, Lahaina News, June 10, 1999: 2.

— season ends, Lahaina News, July 29, 1999: 6.

— Bankoh Na Wahine O Ke Kai Outrigger Canoe Championships to be held, Lahaina News, September 23, 1999: 7.

— Bankoh Hinano Moloka'i Hoe Outrigger Championship to be held, Lahaina News, October 7, 1999: 9.

— Kihei Canoe Club to hold Ben Abiera Memorial race, Lahaina News, May 25, 2000: 8.

— Maui County Hawaiian Canoe Association to hold summer regattas, Lahaina News, June 1, 2000: 9.

— summer season continues, Lahaina News, June 15, 2000: 13.

— Lahaina Canoe Club optimistic about season, Lahaina News, June 22, 2000: 13.

— Kihei Canoe Club to hold Moki Kalanikau Regatta, Lahaina News, June 29, 2000: 15.

— Maui County Hawaiian Canoe Association long distance season to begin, Lahaina News, August 10, 2000: 7.

— paddler Derek Vinuya wins medals at World Outrigger Sprint Championships, Lahaina News, September 7, 2000: 14.

— Na Wahine O Ke Kai Outrigger Canoe Championship to be held, Lahaina News, September 21, 2000: 8.

— Aston Ka'anapali Shores Hawaiian Sailing Canoe Regatta to be held, Lahaina News, September 28, 2000: 9.

— Maui Canoe and Kayak Club featured, Lahaina News, January 18, 2001: 8.

— Hard Rock Cafe Puamana to Canoe Beach event held, Lahaina News, January 18, 2001: 8.

— "Fun in the Sun 2001" races to be held at Hoaloha Park, Lahaina News, March 8, 2001: 13.

— results of Kaiwi Channel Relay Race, Lahaina News, May 24, 2001: 14.

— Lahaina Canoe Club hosts Keiki O Maui regatta, Lahaina News, June 21, 2001: 1.

— Maui County Hawaiian Canoe Association results, Lahaina News, August 2, 2001: 12.

— Maui paddlers successful at Hawaiian Canoe Racing Association, Lahaina News, August 16, 2001: 1,18.

— now a Maui Interscholastic League sport, Lahaina News, February 14, 2002: 12.

— featured, Lahaina News, February 27, 2003: 12.

— International Festival of Canoes to be held by LahainaTown Action Committee, Lahaina News, May 1, 2003: 1,3.

— International Festival of Canoes insert included, Lahaina News, May 8, 2003: insert1-insert16.

— Team Maui wins race, Lahaina News, May 29, 2003: 13.

— see also Kahana Canoe Club

PADGETT, DAVE

— comments on proposed thrillcraft corridor, Lahaina News, February 24, 1988: 1.

PADILLA, HOKULANI

— to lecture on traditional hula at Maui Community College, Lahaina News, November 18, 1987: 3.

— to lecture at Bailey House Museum on "Hawaiian Language and Social Structure", Lahaina News, February 8, 1996: 4.

PADON, JOHN [COMEDIAN]

— to perform at Comedy Club, Lahaina News, February 21, 1990: 13.

— to perform at Comedy Club and the Sports Page, Lahaina News, March 6, 1991: 11,13.

— to perform at Comedy Club and the Sports Page, Lahaina News, August 27, 1992: 14,15,17.

PADUA, ARMAND

— leaves position as deputy director of the Department of Parks and Recreation, Lahaina News, July 8, 1993: 4.

PAE, RANGA [MUSICAL GROUP]

— to perform at Wellness Fair, Lahaina News, September 6, 2001: 14.

PAET, ROMEO

— named executive chef at Outrigger Wailea Resort, Lahaina News, July 4, 2002: 8.

PAGADUAN, DESIREE

— named secretary of the year by the Maui No Ka Oi Chapter of Professional Secretaries International, Lahaina News, February 13, 1992: 13.

PAGAN BABIES, THE [MUSICAL GROUP]

— to perform at Casanova's, Lahaina News, August 15, 1991: 15.

PAGAN, HELEN HARRIET KAPAAU

— queen of Aloha Week, Lahaina News, August 30, 1989: 1.

PAGDILAO, KEISHA

— Scholar/Athlete of the Week, Lahaina News, July 26, 2001: 13.

PAGDILAO, NICOMEDES AND MERCEDES

— file civil suit for traffic accident, Lahaina News, December 26, 1991: 8.

PAGDILAO, TASHA

— Scholar/Athlete of the Week, Lahaina News, February 17, 2000: 7.

PAGE NAVIGATION SCHOOL

— merges with Houston Marine Training Services, Lahaina News, December 3, 1986: 3,11.

PAGE, RANDALL

— county prosecuting attorney plans to refile felony theft charges against Arata "Ralph" Yoshitake, Lahaina News, August 20, 1992: 3.

PAGLINAWAN, RICHARD

— Hawaiian Homes Commission representative meets with Charles Makekau of The Hawaiians, Lahaina Sun, December 16, 1970: 3.

— at meeting between Hawaiian Homes Commission and The Hawaiians, Lahaina Sun, December 23, 1970: 6.

PAHINUI BROTHERS [MUSICAL GROUP]

— to perform at Aulani Ballroom at Maui Inter-Continental Resort, Lahaina News, January 23, 1992: 18.

PAHINUI, CYRIL [MUSICIAN]

— to launch slack key concert series, Lahaina News, October 9, 2003: 14.

PAHINUI, MARTIN [MUSICIAN]

— to perform at Ka'anapali Beach Hotel, Lahaina News, May 20, 1999: 15.

PAHK, IVAN

— new executive chef at Sansei Seafood Restaurant, Lahaina News, May 4, 2000: 13.

PAHUKOA, ERLAND [MUSICIAN]

— to perform at Borders Books from new CD "He Mana'o O Keanae", Lahaina News, September 16, 1999: 12.

PAHUKOA, HARRY III

— being sought by police, Lahaina News, March 5, 1998: 2.

PAIA [TOWN]

— new sugar cane technology installed at plantation near, Lahaina Sun, December 2, 1970: 1,4.

— North Short Improvement Association meeting in, Lahaina Sun, December 30, 1970: 5.

— low and moderate housing project planned, Lahaina Sun, March 10, 1971: 5.

— sand removed from Baldwin Beach Park, Lahaina Sun, May 26, 1971: 1,8.

— low and medium income housing project nears completion, Lahaina Sun, June 7, 1972: 5.

— featured, Lahaina Sun, August 15, 1973: 12,13,14,15.

— Stores going out of business, Lahaina Times, June, 1980 volume 4 number 5: 1.

— Alexander and Baldwin planning subdivision in Paia, Lahaina News, May 8, 1991: 6.

— two-story restaurant planned for, Lahaina News, March 19, 1992: 10.

PAIA BYPASS ROAD

— Department of Transportation to hold meeting to discuss, Lahaina News, February 17, 2000: 16.

PAIA MAIN STREET ASSOCIATION

— to hold Christmas party, Lahaina News, December 10, 1998: 9.

PAIA MILL

— to be closed by Hawaiian Commercial and Sugar, Co., Lahaina News, September 21, 2000: 16.

PAIA SCHOOL

— takes first place in Foodland's Shop for Better Education Banner contest, Lahaina News, April 9, 1998: 13.

PAIA TOWN HISTORICAL PHOTO EXHIBIT

— to be held, Lahaina News, June 20, 1996: 13.

PAIEA [MUSICAL GROUP]

— to be performed at Maui Arts and Cultural Center, Lahaina News, October 14, 1999: 12.

PAINE WEBBER [BUSINESS]

— vice president to hold seminar on public investment, Lahaina News, July 26, 1989: 6.

PAKI MAUI RESORT [BUSINESS]

— to be operated by Classic Small Hotels & Resorts, Lahaina News, September 12, 1990: 10.

— now being managed Aston Hotels and Resorts Hawaii, Lahaina News, September 14, 2000: 15.

— Scott Dougherty appointed general manager, Lahaina News, September 28, 2000: 13.

PALAKIKO, KU'ULEI (DANNY BOY)

— to offer free conversational Hawaiian language classes at Waiola Church Hale 'Ai, Lahaina News, October 9, 2003: 5.

PALAKIKO, MEGHAN

— Scholar/Athlete of the Week, Lahaina News, May 22, 2003: 12.

PALANK, JIM
— represents Westin Maui to wholesale sector, Lahaina News, March 31, 1994: 12.
— promoted to Director of Sales of Westin Maui, Lahaina News, November 9, 1995: 10.

PALAUEA
— historic park proposed in, Lahaina News, October 15, 1992: 12.
— Hawaiian group asks panel to protect archaeological sites at, Lahaina News, October 29, 1992: 16.
— group calls for park at, Lahaina News, November 5, 1992: 13.
— Maui Planning Commission conducting site inspection at, Lahaina News, May 18, 2000: 11.

PALAUEA BEACH
— County Council's Land Use Committee cleans plan for residential project near, Lahaina News, September 7, 2000: 17.
— Maui Planning Commission approves project at, Lahaina News, November 23, 2000: 17.
— Hawaiians concerned about preserving archaeological sites at, following approval of residential project at, Lahaina News, November 23, 2000: 17.

PALAZZI GALLERY WEST [BUSINESS]
— begins art education program, Lahaina News, June 11, 1992: 6.

PALEKA, ALAKAʻI [ENTERTAINER]
— presenter featured, Lahaina News, October 10, 1991: 15.
— KPOA personality hosts karaoke, Lahaina News, February 23, 1995: 10.
— named director of KPOA, Lahaina News, February 22, 1996: 11.
— to hold karaoke challenge, Lahaina News, August 13, 1998: 16.

PALEPALE, MARISI
— father installed as pastor of Catholic community of West Maui, Lahaina News, March 5, 1992: 3,4.
— Maria Lanakila Church community says goodbye to Father, Lahaina News, June 18, 1998: 1,6.

PALI, BRYAN
— Scholar/Athlete of the Week, Lahaina News, May 10, 2001: 14.

PALI, ERIC
— wins Flag of Honor from the Food and Beverage Institute of the Republic of China, Lahaina News, September 27, 1989: 5.

PALI KAI BRANCH
— to move, Lahaina News, September 26, 1991: 9.

PALI KAI REALTORS
— cited for outstanding service by the International Relocation Network, Lahaina News, March 5, 1992: 10.

PALI TECH
— attracted by super-computer available at Maui Business and Technology Center, Lahaina News, August 20, 1992: 12.

PALI TUNNEL
— plan to enhance bicycle safety in, Lahaina News, January 9, 1997: 2.

PALISOUL, PHIL [COMEDIAN]
— to perform at Comedy Club and the Sports Page, Lahaina News, November 19, 1992: 9,12.

PALLESEN, CAROL
— plans book making workshops, Lahaina News, January 24, 2002: 16,17.

PALM COURT [RESTAURANT]
— offering cuisines of a different country each evening, Lahaina News, February 26, 1986: 3.

PALM, GARRY [ARTIST]
— watercolor artist to exhibit, Lahaina News, February 20, 2003: 16.

PALM, OLAF [ARTIST]
— to exhibit at Village Gallery, Lahaina News, May 27, 1999: 12.

PALM TREES DESIGNS
— opens, Lahaina News, November 1, 1989: 9.

PALMER, ARNOLD
— golfer plays at Kapalua International Tournament of Golf, Lahaina News, November 2, 1983: 7.
— golfer to compete at GTE Kaʻanapali Classic, Lahaina News, October 12, 1988: 13.

PALMER, BRUCE
— to discuss the Age of the Dinosaurs, Lahaina News, October 26, 1988: 3,16.

PALMER, DARIA
— to be general manager of Maui County Community Television, Inc, Lahaina News, February 4, 1993: 10.
— leaves Maui Ocean Center, Lahaina News, August 27, 1998: 13.

PALOLO [MUSICAL GROUP]
— to perform at World Café, Lahaina News, July 25, 1996: 13.
— to perform at "Live on the Beach", Lahaina News, May 22, 1997: 15.

PALOMINO, ANNA
— to lead workshop on Native landscaping, Lahaina News, March 6, 1997: 10.

PALS PROGRAM
— see Summer Play and Learn Series (PALS) program

PALUSKY, EARL
— awarded Certified Residential Specialist designation, Lahaina News, August 14, 1997: 12.

PAN PACIFIC MASTERS SWIMMING CHAMPIONSHIP
— to be held, Lahaina News, July 11, 1996: 11.

PANAMA DANCERS [PERFORMERS]
— to perform, Lahaina News, February 24, 1988: 3.

PANAMUNA RIGGEROOS [SHIP]
— wins Kaiwi Channel outrigger canoe championship, Lahaina News, October 1, 1998: 9.

PANCAKE COTTAGE [RESTAURANT]
— reviewed, Lahaina News, January 1, 1981: 16.

PANCHO AND LEFTY'S CANTINA AND RESTAURANTE [RESTAURANT]
— reviewed, Lahaina News, October 7, 1987: 7.
— wins first place in Christmas decorating contest, Lahaina News, December 27, 1989: 2.
— reopens, Lahaina News, September 12, 1996: 15.
— hosts classes in Retail Industry Training in Excellence, Lahaina News, January 8, 1998: 11.
— celebrates 15 years, Lahaina News, August 1, 2002: 11.
— to celebrate Cinco De Mayo, Lahaina News, May 1, 2003: 14.
— to celebrate 16 years, Lahaina News, August 14, 2003: 18.
— celebrates 16th anniversary, Lahaina News, October 9, 2003: 8.

PANDA EXPRESS [RESTAURANT]
— opens, Lahaina News, May 7, 1992: 10.
— opens second location, Lahaina News, November 17, 1994: 10.

PANDANUS CLUB, THE [MUSICAL GROUP]
— to perform at fundraiser to Piʻilani School of Hula, Lahaina News, September 14, 1988: 11.
— to perform at Molokini Lounge at the Maui Prince Hotel, Lahaina News, February 13, 1991: 11.
— to perform at Molokini Lounge at the Maui Prince Hotel, Lahaina News, May 23, 1991: 14.
— to perform at Kaʻanapali Beach Hotel's Tiki Courtyard, Lahaina News, October 24, 2002: 22.

PANEY, JANICE
— appointed Kihei branch manager for First Hawaiian Bank, Lahaina News, January 16, 1991: 5.

PANG, ALVIN
— thanked for help in creating program for low and middle income housing, Lahaina Sun, January 20, 1971: 3.

PANG, LORRIN
— discusses "Lung Disease on Maui: Past, Present and Future", Lahaina News, May 10, 2001: 20.
— District Health Officer to speak on GMOs, Lahaina News, August 7, 2003: 2.

PANG, MICHAEL
— kumu hula to premiere "Paiea", Lahaina News, October 7, 1999: 17.

PANG, MILTON
— appointed as manager of Sound of the Falls Restaurant, Lahaina News, July 8, 1993: 8.

PANG, TYLUN
— hired by Westin Maui, Lahaina News, September 22, 1994: 13.

PANIOLO HALE
— to be managed by Pacific Management Basin, Lahaina News, November 21, 1990: 12.

PANIOLO SPURS [MUSICAL]
— to be performed by Honolulu Theatre for Youth, Lahaina News, February 16, 1995: 15.

PANTE, JASON
— King Kamehameha III Elementary School student wins "1994 Buckle Up Hawaiian Style", Lahaina News, June 23, 1994: 5.

PAOA, GEORGE [MUSICIAN]
— performance reviewed, Lahaina News, December 5, 1984: 21.
— to play at Lahaina Canoe Club, Lahaina News, January 16, 1985: 17.
— to perform at Maui Prince Hotel, Lahaina News, December 30, 1987: 3.
— to play at Maui Prince, Lahaina News, February 10, 1988: 9.
— new album, Lahaina News, July 11, 1990: 13.
— to host free Polynesian show at Wailea Shopping Village, Lahaina News, October 31, 1990: 14.
— to perform at Maui Lu Resort, Lahaina News, March 23, 1995: 11.

PAPAKEA BEACH RESORT [BUSINESS]
— featured, Lahaina News, March 7, 1984: 18.
— featured, Lahaina News, July 18, 1984: 15.
— sponsoring Rossini's opera "La Cenerentola", performed by the Maui Philharmonic Society, Lahaina News, December 5, 1984: 14.
— featured, Lahaina News, August 15, 2002: 7.

PAPALAUA BEACH PARK
— becomes official county camping site, Lahaina News, March 28, 2002: 5.

PAPALAUA WAYSIDE PARK
— campsite to be developed at, Lahaina News, June 8, 1995: 5.
— may be ready for public camping soon, Lahaina News, July 13, 1995: 2.
— JoAnne Johnson to hold meeting on, Lahaina News, November 15, 2001: 1,18.

PAPANIKOLAS, SUZY [ARTIST]
— to exhibit at Village Gallery Contemporary, Lahaina News, April 27, 2000: 12.
— to exhibit at Village Gallery Contemporary, Lahaina News, March 13, 2003: 16.

PAPAYA
— possible future discussed, Lahaina Sun, June 13, 1973: 10,12.
— record production in May, Lahaina Sun, June 27, 1973: 7.
— production in Paia discussed, Lahaina Sun, August 15, 1973: 12,13.

PAPAYA ADMINISTRATIVE COMMITTEE
— plan to meet on Maui, Lahaina Sun, May 24, 1972: 10.

PAPERBACKS PLUS [BUSINESS]
— opens, Lahaina News, March 21, 1996: 11.
— to hold grand opening, Lahaina News, May 23, 1996: 2.

PAPILLON HAWAIIAN HELICOPTERS [BUSINESS]
— fined for illegal landings, Lahaina News, February 1, 1984: 16.
— faces minor charges, requests special use permit, Lahaina News, November 7, 1984: 3.
— seeks to extend special use permit, Lahaina News, September 13, 1989: 1.
— seeking renewal of operation permit, Lahaina News, January 10, 1990: 24.
— no longer authorized to fly out of West Maui, Lahaina News, January 24, 1990: 4.
— operating permit to be discussed, Lahaina News, May 30, 1990: 5.
— announces new prices, Lahaina News, May 26, 1994: 7.

PAPOHAKU RANCHLANDS
— development featured, Lahaina News, February 29, 1984: 18.
— development featured, Lahaina News, April 11, 1984: 18.

PAPYRUS [BUSINESS]
— opens, Lahaina News, May 29, 1997: 5.

PAQUETTE, DAVID [MUSICIAN]
— returning to play piano at Pioneer Inn , Lahaina News, November 30, 1983: 12.
— to perform on Maui, Lahaina News, August 15, 1984: 12.
— final performance at Pioneer Inn, Lahaina News, October 16, 1985: 10.
— performs in Lahaina, interviewed, Lahaina News, November 19, 1986: 8.
— interviewed, Lahaina News, March 23, 1988: 6.
— jazz pianist to perform at Pioneer Inn, Lahaina News, October 18, 2001: 15.
— to play at Pioneer Inn, Lahaina News, October 25, 2001: 16.

PARADE OF HOMES
— to be held at Honolulu Country Club, Lahaina News, March 28, 1990: 6.
— to be held, Lahaina News, June 12, 1997: 16.
— to be held, Lahaina News, March 29, 2001: 8.
— deadline soon to add your property to, Lahaina News, June 28, 2001: 8.
— to be held, Lahaina News, October 4, 2001: 8.

PARADISE FRUIT [RESTAURANT]
— opens in Rainbow Mall, Lahaina News, December 19, 1991: 13.

PARADISE ISLAND PRODUCTIONS [BUSINESS]
— releases first single by Jennifer Anne Hughes, Lahaina News, October 11, 1989: 4.

PARADISE PUBLICATIONS
— publishes third edition of "Maui, a Paradise Guide", Lahaina News, April 27, 1988: 3.
— announces Best Bet awards, Lahaina News, November 21, 1990: 13.

PARADISE RIDES
— to be held, Lahaina News, June 24, 1999: 7.
— to be held, Lahaina News, July 1, 1999: 7.
— bicycle ride to benefit Hawaii AIDS organizations, Lahaina News, January 25, 2001: 9.
— to benefit AIDS organizations, Lahaina News, February 1, 2001: 14.
— volunteer needed for, Lahaina News, April 26, 2001: 15.
— volunteers sought for, Lahaina News, May 3, 2001: 15.

PARADISE SPORTSWEAR [BUSINESS]
— opens Original Red Dirt Shirt store, Lahaina News, June 12, 1997: 15.
— opens new Original Red Dirt Shirt store, Lahaina News, August 14, 1997: 12.

PARADISE TELEVISION NETWORK
— begins "Maui, On-Line", Lahaina News, January 26, 1995: 13.
— offering "Maui, On-Line", Lahaina News, March 2, 1995: 11,12.
— introduces computer on-line service, Lahaina News, July 20, 1995: 10.
— wins Aegis Award for an in-room video for The Westin Maui, Lahaina News, July 26, 2001: 8.

PARADISE USED CARS [BUSINESS]
— disciplined by the Department of Commerce and Consumer Affairs, Lahaina News, June 9, 1994: 12.

PARAGLIDING
— becoming more popular on Maui, Lahaina News, February 6, 1997: 12.

PARAGON AIR
— reducing kama'aina rates, Lahaina News, June 19, 1997: 6.
— has kama'aina rate, Lahaina News, October 9, 1997: 14.

PARAMMAHANSA YOGANANDA
— meditation sessions based on teachings of, Lahaina News, December 13, 2001: 17.

PARAQUAT
— mayor Tavares opposes use of pesticide, Lahaina News, August 7, 1985: 1.
— pesticide under scrutiny by federal Drug Enforcement Administration, Lahaina News, August 7, 1985: 1,9.

PARASAILING
— described, Lahaina News, October 31, 1984: 4.
— parasailers withdraw from Maui Commercial Boaters and Ocean Affiliated Transportation Association [MCBOAT], Lahaina News, June 1, 1988: 19.

PARENT COMMUNITY NETWORK CENTER (PCNC)
— Karen Waggoner and Sandy Kilbride return as coordinators, Lahaina News, September 16, 1993: 8.

PARENTING
— workshop on to be held, Lahaina News, February 4, 1993: 11.
— workshop to be held by Diana Geddes Day, Lahaina News, February 16, 1995: 6.
— Positive Parenting and Support classes being offered, Lahaina News, November 20, 1997: 2.
— "The Parent Line" established, Lahaina News, August 13, 1998: 9.

PARENTS
— support group to meet, Lahaina News, April 17, 1997: 12.
— offering parenting classes, Lahaina News, March 19, 1998: 2.
— teaching positive parenting, Lahaina News, July 13, 2000: 17.
— to discuss parenting techniques, Lahaina News, July 20, 2000: 16.
— continues to hold discussions on parenting techniques, Lahaina News, August 10, 2000: 17.
— continues to offer support to parents, Lahaina News, October 12, 2000: 21.
— continues to offer advice on parenting, Lahaina News, April 5, 2001: 21.
— continues to offer videos and discussions on parenting techniques, Lahaina News, May 24, 2001: 21.
— continues to meet, Lahaina News, August 2, 2001: 16.
— continues to hold discussions on parenting techniques, Lahaina News, August 30, 2001: 16.
— continues to offer support of parenting techniques, Lahaina News, November 22, 2001: 21.
— continues to meet, Lahaina News, May 23, 2002: 17.

PARENTS AND CHILDREN TOGETHER (PACT)
— opens new office in Maui, Lahaina News, June 21, 2001: 2.

PARENTS ANONYMOUS OF HAWAII
— to meet at Waiola Church, Lahaina News, October 3, 1991: 4.
— to hold meeting, Lahaina News, May 26, 1994: 5.
— results announced of poster contest, Lahaina News, October 19, 1995: 2.

PARENTS FOR DRUG PREVENTION
— group forming, Lahaina News, September 3, 1998: 8.

PARENTS FOR JUSTICE
— seeking people harmed by Maui Family Court or Maui Family Lawyers, Lahaina News, July 5, 2001: 5.

PARENTS SUPPORTING DRUG PREVENTION AND EDUCATION IN OUR SCHOOLS
— to meet, Lahaina News, May 28, 1998: 12.

PARENTS SUPPORTING PARENTS
— organization to meet, Lahaina News, April 3, 1991: 4.

PARENTS TEACHERS ASSOCIATION OF KING KAMEHAMEHA III ELEMENTARY SCHOOL
— see King Kamehameha III Elementary School

PARK, DAVE [COMEDIAN]
— to perform at Comedy Club and the Sports Page, Lahaina News, March 26, 1992: 13,16.

PARK, SAM [ARTIST]
— to exhibit at Gallerie Hawaii, Lahaina News, July 26, 2001: 16.

PARKER, DAVE [COMEDIAN]
— to perform at Comedy Club, Lahaina News, December 9, 1993: 11.
— to perform at Comedy Club, Lahaina News, December 16, 1993: 19.
— to perform at Comedy Club, Lahaina News, December 30, 1993: 11.

PARKER, JAN [ARTIST]
— to exhibit at Lahaina Galleries, Lahaina News, June 25, 1998: 12.
— to appear at Lahaina Galleries, Lahaina News, April 1, 1999: 16.
— to visit Lahaina Galleries, Lahaina News, September 4, 2003: 15.

PARKER, SISTA MONICA [MUSICIAN]
— see Sista Monica Parker [musician]

PARKER, STEPHEN
— new director of marketing at Maui Ocean Center, Lahaina News, January 23, 2003: 9.

PARKING
— off-street parking priority of Lahaina Retail Committee, Lahaina Sun, February 10, 1971: 1.
— off street parking in Lahaina planned, Lahaina Sun, March 17, 1971: 6.
— West Maui Business Association proposes off-street, Lahaina Sun, March 31, 1971: 3.
— overnight ban questioned, Lahaina Sun, May 19, 1971: 7.
— letter to the editor expressing concerns, Lahaina Sun, June 16, 1971: 3.
— more parking for Kahului airport, Lahaina Sun, July 21, 1971: 3.
— situation in Lahaina discussed, Lahaina Sun, August 4, 1971: 3.
— West Maui Business Association hiring lawyer to help with parking issues, Lahaina Sun, August 11, 1971: 11.
— Mayor Cravalho discusses plans for off-street parking in Lahaina, Lahaina Sun, September 15, 1971: 1.
— time limits set, Lahaina Sun, October 6, 1971: 15.
— editorial discusses recent developments, Lahaina Sun, October 6, 1971: 2.
— possible off-street parking sites studied, Lahaina Sun, October 13, 1971: 12.
— new parking in Lahaina, Lahaina Sun, November 10, 1971: 1.
— work expected to begin soon in facilities, Lahaina Sun, January 12, 1972: 7.
— signs in Lahaina criticized, Lahaina Sun, January 19, 1972: 6.
— first parking lot opens in Lahaina, Lahaina Sun, June 7, 1972: 6.
— dedication program details provided, Lahaina Sun, June 21, 1972: 3.
— second parking lot in Lahaina expected soon, Lahaina Sun, July 19, 1972: 7.
— work on off-street parking in Lahaina continues, Lahaina Sun, August 30, 1972: 10.
— plan to reduce parking on Front Street proposed, Lahaina News, June 25, 1986: 1.
— law passed prohibiting parking in parts of West Maui, Lahaina News, June 25, 1986: 3.
— editorial supporting new plan, Lahaina News, August 6, 1986: 2.

— being considered by Maui County Council committees, Lahaina News, August 6, 1986: 3.
— plan for Lahaina sent for study, Lahaina News, August 27, 1986: 11.
— Maui Historic Commission backs more, Lahaina News, August 27, 1986: 12.
— merchants offer views on proposed ban, Lahaina News, September 17, 1986: 1,5.
— Whaler's Village plan discussed, Lahaina News, October 8, 1986: 4.
— plan for Lahaina seen as defective, Lahaina News, October 25, 1989: 1,4.
— Mayor James Apana discusses problems in Lahaina, Lahaina News, January 25, 2001: 1.
— see also infrastructure

PARKINSON'S DISEASE
— see Maui Parkinson's Support Group

PARKS
— State Parks administrator Joseph Souza announces plans to condemn private land to create a state park in Makena area, Lahaina Sun, October 13, 1971: 3.
— activities for fall detailed, Lahaina Sun, September 13, 1972: 11.
— popularity described, Lahaina News, November 1, 1980: 4.
— Maui County spent over half a million dollars in improvements, Lahaina News, March 1, 1982: 12.
— West Maui Taxpayers Association seeks more, Lahaina News, November 1, 1989: 1.
— editorial supporting more parks, Lahaina News, November 1, 1989: 10.
— proposal to ban nudity in, Lahaina News, November 15, 1989: 2.
— mayor Linda Lingle's opposition to transferring state parks to county lessens, Lahaina News, June 13, 1991: 3.
— police officers to patrol, Lahaina News, August 4, 1994: 2.
— corrections to July 21 story regarding source of funding, Lahaina News, August 4, 1994: 4.
— Maui County Council to vote on drinking in, Lahaina News, November 17, 1994: 1,24.
— community help sought for S-Turn Park, Lahaina News, July 27, 1995: 3.
— Maui County Council bill to create more parks in residential areas, Lahaina News, August 10, 1995: 6.
— night time park drinking ban passed, Lahaina News, November 9, 1995: 16.
— vandalism reported, Lahaina News, December 21, 1995: 5.
— permit offices to be closed to participate in Parks and Recreation District Challenge, Lahaina News, July 1, 1999: 7.

PARKS AND AGRICULTURE COMMITTEE, MAUI COUNTY COUNCIL
— to consider bill on commercial ocean recreational activity, Lahaina News, August 14, 2003: 12.

PARKS AND RECREATION COMMITTEE
— to consider access to Eddie Tam Memorial Center, Lahaina News, November 20, 1997: 16.

PARKS AND RECREATION, MAUI COUNTY DEPARTMENT OF
— changes phone number, Lahaina News, October 23, 1985: 20.
— sponsoring art classes with Lahaina Arts Society, Lahaina News, July 22, 1987: 3.
— offers after-school program, Lahaina News, August 3, 1988: 3.
— organizing summer basketball league, Lahaina News, July 26, 1989: 2.
— to hold meeting on proposed swimming pool, Lahaina News, March 28, 1990: 4.
— to hold coaching seminars, Lahaina News, May 2, 1990: 6.
— hiring for summer programs, Lahaina News, May 23, 1990: 3.
— district supervisor Marian Feenstra safety and irrigation top priorities for parks, Lahaina News, August 4, 1994: 1,4.

— starting "Family Nites", Lahaina News, July 18, 1996: 6.
— to hold "Family Nites", Lahaina News, August 1, 1996: 20.
— hosting "Family Nites", Lahaina News, August 8, 1996: 14.
— starting "Wahine Slowpitch Softball Night", Lahaina News, May 15, 1997: 11.
— setting up Mountainball League, Lahaina News, May 15, 1997: 11.
— to offer Ha'aheo Program, Lahaina News, June 5, 1997: 3.
— to hold "Youth Activity Days", Lahaina News, July 17, 1997: 14.
— to hold hearing on park access, Lahaina News, November 13, 1997: 21.
— organizing "Ladies Softball Nite", Lahaina News, May 14, 1998: 14.
— to show final plans for Napili Park, Lahaina News, June 18, 1998: 7.
— bringing back "Family Nights" at Lahaina Civic Center gym, Lahaina News, July 30, 1998: 15.
— postpones "Family Nights" due to construction in Lahaina Civic Center gym, Lahaina News, August 6, 1998: 20.
— residents urged to keep lobbying for Napili Park, Lahaina News, November 5, 1998: 1.
— softball registration soon, Lahaina News, January 21, 1999: 7.
— sponsoring family nights, Lahaina News, June 24, 1999: 12.
— sponsoring family nights, Lahaina News, July 1, 1999: 12.
— begins volleyball registration, Lahaina News, March 30, 2000: 6.
— to hold meeting for basketball league, Lahaina News, May 4, 2000: 14.
— seeking input on events at beaches, Lahaina News, August 24, 2000: 3.
— make regulate surf schools, Lahaina News, September 14, 2000: 1,24.
— to hold "Open Gym Activities", Lahaina News, September 21, 2000: 9.
— begins construction of field at Keopuolani Park, Lahaina News, September 28, 2000: 9.
— co-ed volleyball league forming, Lahaina News, March 22, 2001: 13.
— to build Veterans Memorial, Lahaina News, May 24, 2001: 16.
— space available for Summer Learn to Swim and Junior Lifeguard Programs, Lahaina News, June 7, 2001: 15.
— space available for Summer Learn to Swim and Junior Lifeguard Programs, Lahaina News, June 14, 2001: 15.
— to hold swim lessons, Lahaina News, July 12, 2001: 13.
— to recondition turf at War Memorial Football Stadium, Lahaina News, February 21, 2002: 13.
— starting volleyball league, Lahaina News, March 7, 2002: 13.
— forming volleyball league, Lahaina News, March 14, 2002: 13.
— to hold free Open Gym nights, Lahaina News, April 18, 2002: 12.
— to hold Junior Lifeguard Program, Lahaina News, May 2, 2002: 12.
— to hold youth swimming programs, Lahaina News, June 6, 2002: 13.
— to update "Maui County Youth Connections", Lahaina News, September 19, 2002: 5.
— to close permit offices, Lahaina News, April 3, 2003: 17.
— to hold Summer PALS Program, Lahaina News, April 24, 2003: 2.
— to hold swimming and junior lifeguard programs, Lahaina News, May 1, 2003: 13.
— to hold swimming and junior lifeguard programs, Lahaina News, May 8, 2003: 12.
— to hold swimming and junior lifeguard programs, Lahaina News, May 22, 2003: 13.

PARKS, ROSE
— volunteering at Maui Memorial Auxiliary, Lahaina News, April 12, 2001: 2.

PAROLA, SHIRLEY TONG [WRITER]
— to sign copies of "Remembering Diamondhead", Lahaina News, March 16, 2000: 12.

PARRIS, JAZZLYN [RADIO HOST]
— show reviewed, Lahaina News, April 10, 1985: 12.

PARROTT, ALICE KAGAWA
— selected as artist-in-residence, Lahaina Sun, September 15, 1971: 13.

PARSON, ALAN [MUSICIAN]
— to perform in "A Walk Down Abbey Road" celebration of the Beatles, Lahaina News, June 13, 2002: 17.

PARSON, GINNY
— attends Royal Lahaina's Suspects Murder Mystery Dinner Theater, Lahaina News, September 30, 1993: 13.

PARSONS, BILL
— Maui's only competitor in Mr. and Ms. Maui Body Builders Competition, Lahaina News, November 23, 1983: 6.

PARSONS, DALE AND GINNY
— KLHI radio station owners to contest ruling stripping control of the station from them, Lahaina News, January 6, 1994: 1.
— ownership of KLHI-FM following bankruptcy goes to trial, Lahaina News, January 13, 1994: 1.
— lose KLHI following bankruptcy, Lahaina News, March 17, 1994: 1.

PARSONS, DAVE
— comments on proposed thrillcraft corridor, Lahaina News, February 24, 1988: 1.
— State Boating Manager rejects banning thrillcraft, Lahaina News, April 27, 1988: 1.
— State harbors official reviews lack of restrooms, Lahaina News, August 22, 1991: 1.

PARSONS, HEATHER SECORD
— to discuss "Let's Bring More Heaven to Earth", Lahaina News, July 20, 2000: 17.

PARSONS-UXB JOINT VENTURE
— to hold small business fair, Lahaina News, October 18, 2001: 9.

PARTON AND BURTON [BUSINESS]
— law firm created by John Parton and Carolyn Burton, Lahaina News, May 1, 1991: 7.

PARTY DOLLS [MUSICAL GROUP]
— to perform at Longhi's, Lahaina News, January 9, 1991: 7.
— to perform at Longhi's, Lahaina News, February 27, 1991: 8.
— continue to perform at Longhi's, Lahaina News, April 10, 1991: 10.
— continue to perform at Longhi's, Lahaina News, May 1, 1991: 14.
— continues to perform at Casanova's, Lahaina News, June 13, 1991: 13.
— continues to perform at Moose McGillycuddy's, Lahaina News, July 25, 1991: 10,12.

PARTY OF ONE, A [TROUPE]
— to be performed at Maui Prince, Lahaina News, February 3, 1988: 3.
— to perform at Maui Prince Hotel, Lahaina News, May 30, 1991: 10.
— continues to perform at Molokini Lounge at the Maui Prince Hotel, Lahaina News, June 6, 1991: 14,15.

PARTY PANTRY [BUSINESS]
— opens another store, Lahaina News, June 1, 1981: 5.
— will occupy half of new building at Lahainaluna Road and Wainee Street, Lahaina News, July 17, 1985: 3.

PARTYGRAMS [BUSINESS]
— Jonathan Eden purchases, Lahaina News, February 4, 1999: 13.

PASCALE, CATHLEEN
— hired as controller for Chadwick Hawaii Group, Inc., Lahaina News, December 5, 1991: 12,13.

PASCUA, MITCHELL
— Scholar/Athlete of the Week, Lahaina News, February 28, 2002: 12.

PASCUAL, AUDIE
— appointed branch manager at Finance Factors, Ltd., Lahaina News, April 18, 1996: 8.

PASCUAL, EDWIN
— co-valedictorian at Lahainaluna High School with Kevin Yamada, Lahaina News, June 18, 1986: 1,16.

PASCUAL, JOY
— receives perpetual Pookela award from Mike White, general manager of Ka'anapali Beach Hotel for winning Keiki Hula Festival, Lahaina News, November 7, 1991: 16.

PASCUAL, LESTER
— chef at North Beach Grille featured, Lahaina News, June 1, 2000: 15.

PASCUAL, MACARIO [ARTIST]
— donates recent artwork "Sakada Immigrants" to State of Hawaii, Lahaina News, January 21, 1987: 10,11.
— work to be exhibited in Makawao, Lahaina News, June 21, 1989: 9.
— painting selected for next year's Art Maui poster, Lahaina News, April 3, 1991: 10.
— Scholar/Athlete of the Week, Lahaina News, March 28, 1996: 7.
— to exhibit at Village Gallery, Lahaina News, February 15, 2001: 16.
— to exhibit at Village Gallery, Lahaina News, November 22, 2001: 15.
— to exhibit at Village Galleries, Lahaina News, March 27, 2003: 14.

PASSAGE TO INDIA, A [RESTAURANT]
— opens at Wharf Cinema Center, Lahaina News, September 7, 1995: 8.

PAT PAULINE AND DA US GUYS [MUSICAL GROUP]
— to perform at Lahaina Cannery and Lopaka's, Lahaina News, May 9, 1990: 17,18.

PATA, PUEO [MUSICIAN]
— to perform at Lahaina Cannery Mall, Lahaina News, December 2, 1999: 17.

PATANELLI, KAREN
— named Host of the Year at Westin Maui, Lahaina News, September 26, 1990: 9.

PATAO, VERNON PATAOL
— competes in Olympics in Barcelona, Lahaina News, August 20, 1992: 1.
— to be guest on Mayor Linda Lingle's radio show on KLHI, Lahaina News, August 27, 1992: 6.
— life after the Olympics, Lahaina News, September 3, 1992: 6.

PATCH
— see People Attentive to Children (PATCH)

PATHWALKER, ARAYA [ARTIST]
— to teach art classes at Art School at Kapalua, Lahaina News, June 1, 2000: 7.
— to lead class on making pendant ornaments, Lahaina News, December 7, 2000: 24.
— to exhibit at Lahaina Arts Society's Banyan Tree Gallery, Lahaina News, September 25, 2003: 18.
— to exhibit at Banyan Tree Gallery, Lahaina News, October 9, 2003: 16.

PATRIOT [SHIP]
— United States Line recently launches, Lahaina News, January 4, 2001: 14.

PATSY MINK CONGRESSIONAL ART AWARD
— Lahainaluna High School student Brian Garcia wins, Lahaina News, May 24, 2001: 1,22.

PATTEN, DICK VAN [ACTOR]
— to star in Dick Van Patten Celebrity Challenge, Lahaina News, November 27, 1997: 13.

PATTEN, JULIE [ARTIST]
— to be featured at Larry Dotson Gallery, Lahaina News, March 16, 1988: 14.

PATTERSON, JIM
— developer proposes Lighthouse Building as retail development, Lahaina News, November 7, 1990: 1.
— of Plantation Inn, planning to build office building, Lahaina News, July 11, 1991: 6.
— developer asks for extension of special management area permit, Lahaina News, May 28, 1992: 4.

PATTERSON, JIM [COMEDIAN]
— to perform at Comedy Club and the Sports Page, Lahaina News, October 1, 1992: 15,17.

PATTON, TATIANA
— named Manager of the Quarter by Stouffer Renaissance Wailea Beach Resort, Lahaina News, June 1, 1995: 10.

PATY, WILLIAM
— director of Department of Land and Natural Resources reviewing longline fishing rules, Lahaina News, April 25, 1990: 1,5.
— to stay as chairperson of the Department of Land and Natural Resources (DLNR), Lahaina News, December 31, 1992: 20.

PAU HANA INN
— holds fundraiser for Friends of Father Damien, Lahaina News, September 2, 1987: 3.

PAUL, DANIEL [MUSICIAN]
— to host drumming workshop with the Mad Dog Drummers of Mu , Lahaina News, July 20, 1995: 12.

PAUL, DAVID
— chef at Lahaina Grill featured, Lahaina News, August 8, 1991: 18.
— Lahaina Grill voted "Best Maui Restaurant" by Honolulu Magazine, Lahaina News, January 11, 1996: 14.

PAUL, DAVID AND PETER
— The Barbarian Brothers to appear at Lahaina Center, Lahaina News, July 23, 1992: 3.

PAUL, RICHARD
— appointed principal at King Kamehameha III Elementary School, Lahaina News, August 25, 1994: 1.
— King Kamehameha III Elementary School principal featured, Lahaina News, January 18, 2001: 3.
— honored as "Educator of the Month" by Hula Grill, Lahaina News, June 28, 2001: 8.

PAULL, DENNI
— new assistant director of marketing Trilogy Excursions, Lahaina News, April 12, 2001: 8.

PAULO, MICHAEL
— Jazz musician to play with Junior Maile, Lahaina News, August 16, 2001: 16.

PAULSON, JOCELYN
— exploring her roots at Lahainaluna High School, Lahaina News, April 12, 2001: 1,24.

PAUMANA
— townhouse featured, Lahaina News, April 12, 2001: 7.

PAUPU, PATTY
— Lahainaluna High School softball coach featured, Lahaina News, November 21, 1991: 8.

PAUVERT, JACQUES
— new chef at JJ's Beach Grill changes menu, Lahaina News, June 18, 1992: 20.

PA'UWELA POINT
— Sierra Club organizing hike to, Lahaina News, October 12, 2000: 20.

PAVAO, DENNIS [MUSICIAN]
— to perform at Old Lahaina Cafe and Luau, Lahaina News, July 11, 1990: 15.
— to perform at Maui County Zoological and Botanical Gardens, Lahaina News, February 29, 1996: 14.
— to perform at B.J.'s Chicago Pizzeria, Lahaina News, June 11, 1998: 7.
— to perform at Music on the Beach, Lahaina News, October 22, 1998: 9.
— to perform at Festival of Pacific Island Arts and Culture, Lahaina News, May 20, 1999: 8.

— to perform at Reflections of Old Lahaina Luau and Concert benefit, Lahaina News, August 19, 1999: 18.
— passes away, Lahaina News, January 24, 2002: 3.

PAVILION RESTAURANT [RESTAURANT]
— to reopen, Lahaina News, June 13, 1991: 10.

PAW MATES [BUSINESS]
— in home pet service available, Lahaina News, November 17, 1994: 10.

PAY 'N SAVE [BUSINESS]
— opens first store on Maui, Lahaina News, October 19, 1983: 14.

PAYNE, DUSTIN
— surfer featured, Lahaina News, July 26, 2001: 12.
— surfer clinches United States Surfing Federation Championships in Oceanside, California, Lahaina News, August 15, 2002: 13.

PEACE CELEBRATION DAY
— to be held at D.T. Fleming Beach Park, Lahaina News, April 30, 1998: 16.

PEACE ELDERS JAMBOREE
— to be held on Valentine's Day, Lahaina News, February 6, 1992: 4.

PEACE FRIDAY
— to be held, Lahaina News, May 22, 1997: 17.
— to be held at Malu'ulu O Lele Cultural Center, Lahaina News, May 29, 1997: 16.

PEACE POEM
— to be part of King Kamehameha Day Parade, Lahaina News, June 3, 1999: 2.

PEACE RALLY
— focused on Persian Gulf crisis, Lahaina News, January 9, 1991: 4.

PEACEMOVES MAUI
— benefit concert and art auction to be held, Lahaina News, July 24, 1985: 10.
— to hold benefit concert, Lahaina News, October 28, 1987: 3.
— sues Air Force over laser experiment, Lahaina News, January 6, 1988: 3.
— to hold benefit dance, Lahaina News, July 6, 1988: 17.

PEACOCK, THE [RESTAURANT]
— purchased by Gandor Corporation of Texas, Lahaina News, August 8, 1984: 14.
— reviewed, Lahaina News, January 13, 1988: 9.
— opens as Ristorante la Scala, Lahaina News, August 23, 1989: 13.

PEALE, NORMAN VINCENT
— to speak at Maui Rotary Club luncheon, Lahaina News, January 10, 1990: 6.

PEANUT DAYS
— to be held at Whalers Village Shopping Center, sponsored by Lahaina Kiwanis Club, Lahaina News, December 26, 1991: 4.

PEARCE, JOSEPH CHILTON
— to give lectures entitled "Magical Child Matures" and "Human Development and Meditation", Lahaina News, October 9, 1985: 3.

PEARL CONNECTION [BUSINESS]
— opens, Lahaina News, May 30, 1990: 6.
— moves location, Lahaina News, November 28, 1996: 14.

PEARL HARBOR
— Tom Hansen comments on, Lahaina News, December 7, 2000: 17.
— survivor Andy Antosik living in Puamana, Lahaina News, December 6, 2001: 1,18.

PEARL JAM [MUSICAL GROUP]
— to perform at War Memorial Gym, Lahaina News, September 3, 1992: 18.
— to perform, Lahaina News, September 10, 1992: 18.
— to perform, Lahaina News, September 17, 1992: 18.
— to perform this week, Lahaina News, September 24, 1992: 14.

— to perform at Maui Arts and Cultural Center, Lahaina News, February 12, 1998: 17.

— to begin worldwide tour at the Maui Arts and Cultural Center, Lahaina News, February 19, 1998: 13.

PEARLS FOR YOU [BUSINESS]
— featured, Lahaina News, February 22, 1989: 2.

PEARSON, DURK
— nutritionist to speak at Stouffer Wailea Beach Resort, Lahaina News, March 19, 1992: 4.

PEARSON, RON [COMEDIAN]
— to perform at Comedy Club, Lahaina News, July 8, 1993: 11.

PEART, FRANCES
— appointed branch manager of First Interstate Bank in Lahaina, Lahaina News, May 29, 1985: 3.
— new president of Soroptimists International of West Maui, Lahaina News, August 15, 1991: 6.
— bank manager featured, Lahaina News, April 30, 1992: 4.

PECK, JOHN
— chef joins Fish and Game Brewing Company, Lahaina News, April 8, 1999: 11.

PEDDLING
— Maui Historic Commission seeking to control, Lahaina Sun, March 17, 1971: 1.
— ban requested by Maui Historic Commission, Lahaina Sun, April 21, 1971: 7.
— law proposed, Lahaina Sun, May 12, 1971: 4.
— prohibited by Maui County Council, Lahaina Sun, July 21, 1971: 9.

PEDEN, THOMAS [ARTIST]
— scrimshaw work discussed, Lahaina News, September 5, 1984: 14.
— former partner in Lahaina Scrimshaw dies, Lahaina News, March 21, 1990: 2.

PEDESTRIAN SAFETY CONFERENCE
— to be held, Lahaina News, August 1, 2002: 9.
— to be held at Ka'anapali Beach Hotel, Lahaina News, August 15, 2002: 9.

PEDIGO, BECKY [COMEDIAN]
— to perform at Honolulu Comedy Club, Lahaina News, January 11, 1996: 14.

PEE WEE BASEBALL
— discussed, Lahaina Sun, February 17, 1971: 7.

PEENSTRA, MARIAN
— suggests West Maui parks should have youth programs, Lahaina News, February 10, 1994: 1.

PEEPLES, NIA
— to perform, Lahaina News, November 30, 1988: 7,9.

PEGASUS SCHOOL OF HYPNOSIS
— to hold Beginning Hypnosis Class, Lahaina News, July 25, 2002: 21.

PEKING ACROBATS [TROUPE]
— to perform, Lahaina News, January 13, 1988: 16.
— to perform, Lahaina News, January 20, 1994: 12.

PELLEGRINO, HOKUAO
— to demonstrate poi making at Bailey Museum, Lahaina News, July 25, 2002: 21.

PELTON, CARMEN
— soprano to perform with Maui Symphony Orchestra, Lahaina News, October 20, 1994: 15.
— soprano to perform Handel's "Messiah", Lahaina News, December 15, 1994: 16.

PENCE, MARTIN
— judge leading County Civil Service hearing on Joseph Abreu complaint, Lahaina Sun, January 26, 1972: 5.

PENDLETON, CHRIS [COMEDIAN]
— to perform at Comedy Club and the Sports Page, Lahaina News, June 11, 1992: 18,21.

PENDRAGON, BARBARA
— appointed as sales manager at Media Systems, Inc, Lahaina News, January 30, 1992: 10.

PENETRATORS, THE [MUSICAL GROUP]
— praised by Mick Fleetwood, Lahaina News, June 14, 1989: 16.
— to perform at Studio 505, Lahaina News, February 6, 1992: 17.
— to perform at Studio 505, Lahaina News, February 13, 1992: 19.

PENGUIN PALACE BOOGIE BAND [MUSICAL GROUP]
— playing at Longhi's, Lahaina News, May 13, 1987: 8.
— to perform at Longhi's, Lahaina News, May 27, 1987: 3.
— to perform at Moose McGillycuddy's, Lahaina News, July 19, 1989: 14.
— to perform at Moose McGillycuddy's, Lahaina News, March 21, 1990: 13.
— to perform at Longhi's, Lahaina News, April 4, 1990: 13.
— to perform at Moose McGillycuddy's, Lahaina News, April 18, 1990: 11.
— to perform at Longhi's, Lahaina News, November 28, 1990: 9.
— to perform at Longhi's, Lahaina News, January 23, 1991: 8.
— continues to perform at Longhi's, Lahaina News, March 27, 1991: 12.
— continues to perform at Longhi's, Lahaina News, April 24, 1991: 7.
— continues to perform at Moose McGillycuddy's, Lahaina News, June 20, 1991: 8.
— continues to perform at Moose McGillycuddy's, Lahaina News, September 12, 1991: 13.

PENHALLOW, DAVID [WRITER]
— will sign copies of "After the Ball", Lahaina News, August 31, 2000: 20.

PENNARIO, LEONARD [MUSICIAN]
— to perform with Maui Symphony Orchestra, Lahaina News, February 4, 1993: 14.

PENNER, JONATHAN [WRITER]
— presentation at Artful Dodger Feed "N Read, Lahaina News, September 2, 1987: 3.

PENNINGTON, ALEXIS
— Scholar/Athlete of the Week, Lahaina News, August 21, 1997: 13.

PENNINGTON, HOWARD
— discusses Moloka'i ferry, Lahaina News, June 8, 1988: 1.

PENQUE, CHUCK
— discusses cruise ships in Lahaina Harbor, Lahaina News, October 23, 1997: 1,2.

PEOPLE ATTENTIVE TO CHILDREN (PATCH)
— to hold seminar to support daycare, Lahaina News, December 6, 1989: 3.
— to hold workshop on running a home child-care business, Lahaina News, July 18, 1990: 3.
— to offer child care, Lahaina News, December 19, 1991: 5.
— offering child care, Lahaina News, January 2, 1992: 4.
— to present workshop for family child care providers, Lahaina News, February 13, 1992: 4.
— to hold conflict management workshop, Lahaina News, May 7, 1992: 6.
— to discuss value of intergenerational connections, Lahaina News, April 22, 1993: 4.
— to hold conference "Family Child Care Into the Limelight", Lahaina News, April 21, 1994: 5.
— offering classes for those caring for children, Lahaina News, March 21, 1996: 2.
— to host Park Play Day, Lahaina News, November 21, 1996: 15.
— to host session on child care, Lahaina News, January 9, 1997: 10,11.

— continues to hold infant/child CPR class, Lahaina News, November 13, 1997: 20.

— offering child care, Lahaina News, May 7, 1998: 18.

— continues to offer classes for child care providers, Lahaina News, September 17, 1998: 18.

— "Play Days" to be held, Lahaina News, November 26, 1998: 17.

— to hold free classes with Arts Education for Children Group, Lahaina News, May 27, 1999: 13.

— to inspect child safety seats, Lahaina News, November 16, 2000: 17.

PEOPLE HELPING PEOPLE
— concert to be held, Lahaina News, August 18, 1994: 16.

PEOPLE OPPOSED TO THE WHALE SANCTUARY (POWS)
— attempts to stop creation of whale sanctuary, Lahaina News, July 13, 1995: 3.

PEOPLES, DAVID
— golfer to compete in Kapalua International Tournament, Lahaina News, November 7, 1991: 7.

PEOPLE'S GUIDE TO MEXICO [BOOK]
— reviewed, Lahaina Sun, August 22, 1973: 4.

PEOPLES OF THE ISLAND WORLD [FILM]
— shown at Lahaina Library, Lahaina Sun, May 5, 1971: 3.

PEOPLE'S POTTERY [BUSINESS]
— to hold benefit for breast cancer research, Lahaina News, September 20, 2001: 9.

PEPPI'S LAHAINA GAME ROOM
— opens in Lahaina, Lahaina Sun, April 5, 1972: 17.

PERCELL, MARK
— begins writing "West Maui Views" for Lahaina News, Lahaina News, December 3, 1992: 4.

— to resign as executive director of West Maui Taxpayers Association, Lahaina News, February 3, 1994: 1.

— discusses issues connected to affordable housing , Lahaina News, February 3, 1994: 2.

— discusses county projects to ease housing needs, Lahaina News, October 22, 1998: 3.

PERCY, HELEN
— doctor featured, Lahaina News, February 20, 1997: 1,2.

PERDUE, JACKSON [COMEDIAN]
— to perform at Comedy Club, Lahaina News, May 2, 1990: 15.

PERELLO, JAYME
— to present "The Social Ocean", Lahaina News, August 17, 2000: 17.

PEREZ, ALBERT
— named "Environmentalist of the Year" by Safe Solutions, Lahaina News, December 5, 1991: 6.

PEREZ, KAPI
— appointed manager of Chris' Smokehouse, Lahaina News, August 1, 1990: 7.

PERFECT PETS [BUSINESS]
— expands, Lahaina News, December 28, 1995: 12.

PERFORMING ARTS, THE MAUI ACADEMY OF
— see Maui Academy of Performing Arts, The

PERKINS, BILL [MUSICIAN]
— performs at Sam's Upstairs, Lahaina News, August 16, 1989: 17.

— to perform at Blackie's Bar, Lahaina News, August 15, 1990: 15,16.

— to perform at Blackie's Bar, Lahaina News, August 29, 1991: 9,12.

— to perform at Blackie's Bar, Lahaina News, June 10, 1993: 10.

— to perform at Blackie's Bar, Lahaina News, June 17, 1993: 14.

PERKINS, ELROY
— report on basketball player, Lahaina Sun, January 20, 1971: 7.

PERMANENT ORDINANCES OF THE COUNTY OF MAUI [BOOK]
— printed, Lahaina Sun, June 28, 1972: 21.

PERREIRA, BRADY
— Lahainaluna High School student now playing with the University of Hawai'i Rainbows, Lahaina News, April 30, 1992: 6.

— number two starting pitcher for Western Athletic Conference Champion University of Hawaii Rainbow baseball team, Lahaina News, May 21, 1992: 11.

PERREIRA, JOCELYN
— Tri-Isle Main Street coordinator speaks of importance of small business, Lahaina News, August 5, 1993: 1,3.

PERREIRA, LEIMOMI
— to organize statewide canoe championship, Lahaina News, March 1, 1981: 15.

PERREIRA, NOLAN
— appointed by mayor Linda Lingle as executive assistant, Lahaina News, March 6, 1991: 7.

— to speak to Maui Contractors Association, Lahaina News, May 15, 1991: 8.

PERREIRA, PAMY
— awarded scholarships by Hyatt Regency Maui to study at Maui Community College, Lahaina News, July 1, 1987: 10.

PERRELLO, JAYME
— to discuss how marine animals protect themselves with Lena Gervan, Lahaina News, May 25, 2000: 19.

PERRI, TISH
— recognized by Soroptimists International, Lahaina News, May 10, 2001: 1,22.

PERRY, BUDDY
— Lahainaluna High School student named to state high school all-star squad, Lahaina News, December 16, 1993: 11.

PERRY, C.S. [ARTIST]
— wins Lahaina Poster Contest, Lahaina News, September 19, 1996: 16.

PERRY, EUGENE
— president of Lahainaluna High School's Booster Club featured, Lahaina News, October 17, 1991: 3.

PERRY, GLENN
— Amfac promotes to general manager of Ka'anapali Beach Hotel, Lahaina News, December 18, 1985: 3.

PERRY, JAMES
— promoted to president and chief operating officer of Dillingham Construction Corporation, Lahaina News, March 18, 1993: 6.

PERRY, JOHN
— post office employee rebuked for lowering the flag to half-staff following Challenger explosion, Lahaina News, February 26, 1986: 1,16.

PERRY, JOSH
— Lahainaluna High School student seeking Maui Interscholastic League Wrestling title, Lahaina News, December 31, 1992: 6.

PERRY, SUE [ARTIST]
— showing paintings at Old Jail Gallery, Lahaina News, October 3, 1984: 13.

— featured at Lahaina Arts Society Upstairs Gallery, Lahaina News, July 6, 1988: 11.

— to speak to Maui chapter of Business and Professional Women, Lahaina News, October 25, 1989: 10.

— to visit Lahaina Galleries, Lahaina News, September 11, 2003: 15.

— to visit Lahaina Galleries, Lahaina News, October 9, 2003: 17.

PERRY, TERRY [ARTIST]
— showing photographs at Old Jail Gallery, Lahaina News, October 3, 1984: 13.

PERSIAN GULF WAR
— see Gulf War

PERSONA, WILLIAM [ARTIST]
— clown paintings exhibited, Lahaina News, May 15, 1980: 9.

PERSONS, JANIS
— to interpret astrology, Lahaina News, May 29, 2003: 16.
— to offer hypnosis class, Lahaina News, July 31, 2003: 16.
— to teach astrology, Lahaina News, August 28, 2003: 16.

PESCHIERA, PAUL
— appointed vice chairman of American Hotel and Motel Association Condominium Committee, Lahaina News, December 3, 1986: 3.
— appointed vice-president of industry affairs at Aston Hotels and Resorts, Lahaina News, February 4, 1987: 9.
— reappointed vice-chairman of American Hotel and Motel Association's Condominium Committee, Lahaina News, January 6, 1988: 3.

PET SHOP [BUSINESS]
— to hold Pet Costume Parade, Lahaina News, October 23, 1997: 20.

PETER BURWASH INTERNATIONAL
— Junior Tennis Camp to begin, Lahaina News, July 17, 1985: 3.
— tennis professionals to offer free tennis clinics, Lahaina News, May 31, 1989: 3.
— to host tennis tournament, Lahaina News, May 15, 1991: 7.

PETER, LAURENCE [WRITER]
— discusses Peter Principle at Baldwin High School, Lahaina Sun, June 16, 1971: 9.

PETER MOON BAND, THE [MUSICAL GROUP]
— to perform in Lahaina, Lahaina News, September 28, 1983: 6.
— to perform benefit concert for Lahaina Rotary Club, Lahaina News, May 1, 1985: 3.
— performing at Lahaina Civic Center Amphitheaatre, Lahaina News, August 7, 1985: 20.
— to perform at Whalers Village, Lahaina News, March 21, 1990: 13.
— to perform at Casanova's, Lahaina News, April 18, 1990: 11.
— to perform at Maui Marriott's Makai Bar, Lahaina News, December 5, 1990: 9.
— to perform at Molokini Lounge at the Maui Prince Hotel, Lahaina News, March 6, 1991: 13.
— to perform at Makai Bar at Maui Marriott, Lahaina News, April 17, 1991: 11.
— to perform at Maui Marriott's Makai Bar, Lahaina News, August 29, 1991: 9.
— to perform at Ka'anapali Resort, Lahaina News, October 17, 1991: 9.

PETER PAN [PLAY]
— to be performed by Maui Youth Theatre, Lahaina News, June 18, 1986: 3.
— to be performed by Maui Academy of Performing Arts, Lahaina News, February 16, 1995: 15.
— reviewed, Lahaina News, March 2, 1995: 10.
— to be performed at Maui Arts and Cultural Center, Lahaina News, July 24, 2003: 15.
— to be performed by Maui Academy of Performing Arts, Lahaina News, July 31, 2003: 16.

PETER STUYVESANT TRAVEL ALOHA CLASSIC
— Wavesailing World Championships to be held, Lahaina News, October 12, 1988: 13.
— scheduled at Ho'okipa Beach Park, Lahaina News, October 17, 1991: 4.
— insert included, Lahaina News, November 3, 1994: 13,14,15,18,19,20.
— won by Bjorn Dunkerbeck, Lahaina News, November 17, 1994: 1.

PETERS, ANGELA
— female player on Lahaina Chiefs Midget football team featured, Lahaina News, October 29, 1998: 18.

PETERS, CHANELL LEHUANANI
— takes job at Alaska Airlines, Lahaina News, August 19, 1999: 13,14.

PETERS, CLARENCE
— named to Maui Historic Commission, Lahaina Sun, May 19, 1971: 2.

PETERS, JOSHUA
— Lahainaluna High School student to attend People Student Ambassador Program, Lahaina News, May 8, 2003: 1.

PETERSEN, J. LARS
— named general manager of KFC-Hawaii, Lahaina News, April 9, 1992: 12.

PETERSON, HOLLY
— chef from Mondavi Vineyard discusses wine and food, Lahaina News, November 30, 1988: 16.
— head chef at Robert Mondavi Winery to prepare gala wine tasting dinner, Lahaina News, November 1, 1989: 13.

PETERSON, PATTY NAGASAKO [POLITICIAN]
— to be a delegate to the National Federation of Republican Women's Convention, Lahaina News, September 25, 1997: 6.
— participants in LahainaTown Action Committee forum, Lahaina News, August 17, 2000: 3.
— candidate for State House Representative, District 8, Lahaina News, October 26, 2000: 21.
— running for Hawaii Representative District 10 seat, Lahaina News, September 19, 2002: 3,20.

PETERSON SIGN COMPANY [BUSINESS]
— to open at Limahana Place, Lahaina News, April 24, 2003: 9.

PETIT, RICHARD [ARTIST]
— to present at Maui Marine Expo, Lahaina News, January 13, 1988: 16.

PETRIE, WILLIAM
— Father bids farewell to Maria Lanakila Church and Sacred Hearts Museum, Lahaina News, June 19, 2003: 2.

PETRONIO, STEPHEN
— dance company to perform "Not Garden", Lahaina News, February 18, 1999: 12.

PETROSSIAN, VAL
— joins Hilo Hatties Fashion Center as buyer, Lahaina News, January 28, 1993: 8.

PETRUS, JIM
— named general manager of Grand Hyatt Wailea Resort and Spa, Lahaina News, January 23, 1991: 5.

PETS
— animal massage therapy workshop to be held, Lahaina News, February 8, 1996: 4.
— can be photographed at Pet's Discount , Lahaina News, November 23, 2000: 20.
— see also Maui Humane Society, Valley Isle Kennel Club

PET'S DISCOUNT MAUI [BUSINESS]
— opens, Lahaina News, August 20, 1998: 13.
— offering "Santa Claws" pet photography, Lahaina News, November 23, 2000: 20.

PETTIT, RICHARD [ARTIST]
— watercolorist's work featured, Lahaina News, March 13, 1985: 15.
— to sign poster at Maui Marine Art Expo, Lahaina News, March 19, 1992: 18.

PEYTON, WALTER
— football player celebrates opening of Chili's Restaurant, Lahaina News, September 12, 1991: 15.

PFEIFFER, ROBERT J.
— editorial on president of Alexander & Baldwin calling Maui the most anti-business county in Hawaii, Lahaina News, September 19, 1984: 2.
— continues as chairman and chief executive officer of Alexander and Baldwin, Lahaina News, November 7, 1990: 8.
— selected Kama'aina of the Year by Historic Hawaii Foundation, Lahaina News, November 21, 1990: 11.

PFEIL, BILL [POLITICIAN]
— interviewed, Lahaina News, November 21, 1984: 7,8,9.
— against death penalty, Lahaina News, January 30, 1985: 3.
— preparing resolution on motorized water vehicles, Lahaina News, March 20, 1985: 7.
— editorial on his having a traffic ticket fixed, Lahaina News, October 2, 1985: 2.
— proposes legislators should not be immune from arrest, Lahaina News, January 29, 1986: 1.
— lists bills he will introduce at legislature, Lahaina News, March 12, 1986: 1.
— does not expect session on tort reform, Lahaina News, July 9, 1986: 1.
— announces re-election campaign, Lahaina News, July 16, 1986: 3.
— unhappy about tort reform bill, Lahaina News, July 30, 1986: 8.
— reacts to tort bill, Lahaina News, August 6, 1986: 18.
— candidacy for State Representative featured, Lahaina News, October 29, 1986: 1,10.
— opposes spraying of marijuana plants with glyphosate, Lahaina News, December 10, 1986: 3.
— invites public to opening of legislature in Honolulu, Lahaina News, January 14, 1987: 3.
— announces Department of Health will work to improve waste water treatment, Lahaina News, February 25, 1987: 6.
— to hold brown back luncheon at Lahaina Civic Center, Lahaina News, March 11, 1987: 18.
— Brown bag meeting with constituents described, Lahaina News, March 25, 1987: 1,20.
— to hold public "brownbag", Lahaina News, June 17, 1987: 3.
— public "brownbag" with Rick Reed described, Lahaina News, June 24, 1987: 1.
— discusses Lahaina bypass, Lahaina News, October 21, 1987: 11.
— organizes meeting with Maui residents with Rick Reed, Lahaina News, December 9, 1987: 3.
— meeting with constituency, Lahaina News, January 27, 1988: 3.
— provides legislative report, Lahaina News, February 3, 1988: 20.
— Legislative report, Lahaina News, February 10, 1988: 3.
— Legislative Report on bills, Lahaina News, February 17, 1988: 20.
— comments on proposed thrillcraft corridor, Lahaina News, February 24, 1988: 1.
— to hold brown bag with State Senator Rick Reed, Lahaina News, February 24, 1988: 18.
— reports on new bills on law enforcement, Lahaina News, March 2, 1988: 15.
— reports on Tourist Accommodations Tax, Lahaina News, March 16, 1988: 15.
— comments on status of Ocean Recreation Management Plan, Lahaina News, March 23, 1988: 1.
— discusses golf course legislation, Lahaina News, March 23, 1988: 10.
— discusses Aloha Voyages' hope to offer tours to Moloka'i, Lahaina News, March 30, 1988: 1.
— reports on possible improvement to access to government, Lahaina News, April 6, 1988: 4.
— discusses workers compensation reform, Lahaina News, April 20, 1988: 13.
— reports on attempts to develop affordable housing, Lahaina News, April 27, 1988: 24.
— to meet with constituents, Lahaina News, April 27, 1988: 6.
— legislative report focuses on thrillcraft issue, Lahaina News, May 4, 1988: 18.
— account of public meeting, Lahaina News, May 11, 1988: 1,4.
— reports on proposed legislation for parasailing, Lahaina News, May 11, 1988: 11.
— reports on positive results of State Legislative session, Lahaina News, May 18, 1988: 15.
— provides opinion on Lahaina Bypass, Lahaina News, May 25, 1988: 20.
— summarizes condominium bills from current legislative session, Lahaina News, June 1, 1988: 28.
— expresses opposition to state lottery, Lahaina News, June 22, 1988: 20.
— editorial commenting on, Lahaina News, July 6, 1988: 4.
— retiring from politics, Lahaina News, July 6, 1988: 4.

PFLEGER, MICHAEL
— to speak on "Poverty, Substance Abuse, Violence and the Churches' Response", Lahaina News, January 7, 1999: 16.

PHANTOM [MUSICAL]
— to be performed by Maui Academy of Performing Arts, Lahaina News, May 8, 2003: 16.

PHANTOM TOLLBOOTH, THE [PLAY]
— auditions to be held, Lahaina News, May 27, 1993: 5.
— to be performed at Iao Theatre, Lahaina News, August 5, 1993: 11.

PHAT FOR YOUR SOUL [MUSICAL GROUP]
— to perform at World Café, Lahaina News, August 29, 1996: 12.

PHILIPPINE MARKETING GROUP
— created by Bank of Hawaii, Lahaina News, December 15, 1994: 15.

PHILIPPINE WEEK
— celebrated, Lahaina Sun, June 9, 1971: 7.

PHILIPPINES
— politicians from visit Maui, Lahaina Sun, March 10, 1971: 3.
— Spark Matsunaga requests study of guerillas in, Lahaina Sun, March 17, 1971: 5.
— travel agents from, to visit Maui, Lahaina Sun, August 4, 1971: 8.

PHILLIPS, JAN [WRITER]
— author of "Marry Your Muse" to lead workshop, Lahaina News, April 15, 1999: 12.

PHILLIPS, MARY WALKER [ARTIST]
— fiber artist to lecture at Hui No'eau, Lahaina News, March 13, 1985: 24.

PHILLIPS, PEGGY
— nutritionist to speak at Down to Earth, Lahaina News, December 31, 1998: 12.
— to discuss "Personal Purification—Space Cleaning for Body, Home and Office", Lahaina News, June 22, 2000: 17.

PHILLIPS, THOMAS
— named policeman of the year, Lahaina News, June 1, 1980: 15.
— appointed Maui police chief, Lahaina News, August 6, 1998: 7.

PHILLIPS, TOM
— Maui police chief discusses staff shortages, Lahaina News, October 19, 2000: 1,7.

PHIPPS, BILL [ACTOR]
— missing a scrapbook with material from his career, Lahaina Sun, December 27, 1972: 3.

PHIPPS, SANDY
— promoted to sales account executive at Westin Maui Hotel, Lahaina News, April 11, 1990: 5.

PHOENIX ORGANIZATIONAL CONSULTING SERVICES
— announces search for "Most Disorganized Home Office on Maui" announces search for "Most Disorganized Home Office on Maui", Lahaina News, January 27, 1994: 5.

PHOENIX, UNIVERSITY OF
— students in Human Services Program support local student organizations, Lahaina News, January 3, 2002: 2.
— to host "Business After Hours", Lahaina News, January 10, 2002: 8.
— to offer Bachelor of Science in Criminal Justice Administration, Lahaina News, July 4, 2002: 2.

PHOTO/GRAPHIC CAR SHOW-OFF
— to be held at Ka'ahumanu Center, Lahaina News, May 27, 1993: 15.
— to be held this week, Lahaina News, June 17, 1993: 16.

PHU THO HAO
— sent donations, Lahaina Sun, January 6, 1971: 2.

PHYSICAL THERAPY CARE, LTD.
— expands offices, Lahaina News, August 3, 1988: 3.

PICKARD, CHARLIE
— Lahainaluna High School graduate remembered, Lahaina News, June 19, 2003: 1,20.

PICKENS, TRENT [ARTIST]
— to exhibit at Village Galleries, Lahaina News, March 22, 2001: 16.

PICTURES OF PARADISE
— art gallery renewed, Lahaina News, November 15, 1982: 15.

PIDGLEY, STEVEN
— nominated by Successful Meetings magazine for convention service manager of the year, Lahaina News, March 26, 1992: 10.

PIE, WILLIAM
— connection to local music described, Lahaina News, July 6, 1988: 2.
— has video stolen showing Kiefer Sutherland and Julia Roberts at private party, Lahaina News, September 19, 1991: 1,2.
— resolves court case with Inside Edition television show over video of Kiefer Sutherland and Julia Roberts, Lahaina News, November 28, 1991: 4.
— promoter and production manager featured, Lahaina News, January 23, 1992: 15.

PIECE OF MAUI, A
— opens at Wharf Cinema Center, Lahaina News, March 15, 2001: 9.

PIECES V [CONCERT]
— auditions to be held, Lahaina News, June 10, 1987: 3.

PIECES VII [PLAY]
— auditions to be held by Maui Youth Theatre, Lahaina News, June 7, 1989: 5.

PIECES VIII [PLAY]
— to be performed by Maui Academy of Performing Arts, Lahaina News, July 18, 1990: 11.

PIECES X [PLAY]
— to be performed by Maui Academy of Performing Arts, Lahaina News, July 30, 1992: 16.

PIECES XI [PERFORMANCE]
— auditions to be held, Lahaina News, June 24, 1993: 15.
— to be performed by Maui Academy of Performing Arts, Lahaina News, August 19, 1993: 14.

PIECES XII [DANCE CONCERT]
— to be performed, Lahaina News, August 18, 1994: 14.
— reviewed, Lahaina News, August 25, 1994: 13.

PIECES XIX
— dance concert to be held, Lahaina News, August 2, 2001: 16.

PIECES XVI
— to be held at Maui Academy of Performing Arts, Lahaina News, July 16, 1998: 17.
— to be held, Lahaina News, July 23, 1998: 16.

PIECES XVII
— to be held at Maui Arts and Cultural Center, Lahaina News, July 15, 1999: 13.

PIECES XX
— to be held at Maui Arts and Cultural Center, Lahaina News, August 1, 2002: 20.

PIECES XXI: MUSICALS, MOVIES AND MORE
— to be presented by Maui Academy of Performing Arts, Lahaina News, July 31, 2003: 17.

PIERESON, STEVE [MUSICIAN]
— to perform at "Year End Rockin' Blues Mele", Lahaina News, December 27, 2001: 16.

PIFER, JAMES
— reverend discusses Ka'ahumanu Church, Lahaina News, July 4, 1984: 10,11.

PIHANA HEIAU
— archaeological work at, Lahaina Sun, August 25, 1971: 8.

PIIHANA HOUSING PROJECT
— concerned about future flooding damage, Lahaina Sun, April 19, 1972: 11.

PIILANI HOUSING
— Social Service Aide John Nelson to be fired , Lahaina News, December 5, 1990: 1,2.

PI'ILANI SCHOOL OF HULA
— to compete in California, Lahaina News, September 21, 1988: 2,15.
— to hold fundraiser at Ka'anapali Beach Hotel, Lahaina News, September 28, 1988: 6.
— benefit concert held for, Lahaina News, August 23, 1989: 3.

PIILANI VILLAGE
— four homes left at, Lahaina News, May 29, 1997: 18.
— featured, Lahaina News, September 18, 1997: 8.

PIILANI VILLAGE SHOPPING CENTER
— Lydee Ritchie appointed public/tenant relations manager at, Lahaina News, March 15, 2001: 8.
— plans grand opening, Lahaina News, March 15, 2001: 9.

PILOBOLUS [TROUPE]
— to perform at Baldwin Auditorium, Lahaina News, March 13, 1991: 11.
— dance troupe to perform, Lahaina News, April 20, 1995: 12.

PILTZ, MAYNARD
— member of the Hawaiian Homes Commission at meeting between Hawaiian Homes Commission and The Hawaiians, Lahaina Sun, December 23, 1970: 6.

PINCKEL, DAVID [MUSICIAN]
— to perform at Maui Arts and Cultural Center, Lahaina News, April 3, 2003: 15.

PINCKNEY, DARRELL
— to fight Jesus Salud at Makawao Gym, Lahaina News, September 5, 1991: 24.

PINEAPPLE
— festival to be held at Ka'ahumanu Center, Lahaina News, August 25, 1994: 16.
— industry outlook positive, Lahaina News, July 13, 1995: 10.
— see also Maui Land and Pineapple [business], Maui Pineapple Plantation [business], etc.

PINEAPPLE AMBLE
— to be held, Lahaina News, July 22, 1999: 6.
— Haiku Flower Festival to begin, Lahaina News, August 5, 1999: 7.
— begins, Lahaina News, August 12, 1999: 7.

PINEAPPLE CARVING CONTEST
— to be held at Lahaina Cannery Mall, Lahaina News, November 9, 1995: 12.

PINEAPPLE COURT
— Lahaina Cannery Mall restaurants featured, Part I, Lahaina News, June 6, 2002: 8,9.
— Lahaina Cannery Mall restaurants featured, Part I, Lahaina News, June 13, 2002: 8,9.

PINEAPPLE GROWERS ASSOCIATION OF HAWAII
— to hold pineapple tasting, Lahaina News, June 2, 1994: 12.

PINEAPPLE HAWAII [BUSINESS]
— opening in Whaler's Village, Lahaina Sun, November 25, 1970: 3.

PINEAPPLE HILL [RESTAURANT]
— reviewed, Lahaina News, September 16, 1987: 7.
— featured, Lahaina News, July 20, 1988: 10.
— reviewed, Lahaina News, December 28, 1988: 10.
— reviewed, Lahaina News, June 28, 1989: 16.
— renovations completed, Lahaina News, October 4, 1989: 9.
— featured, Lahaina News, January 10, 1990: 10.
— reviewed, Lahaina News, July 4, 1991: 11.
— closing, Lahaina News, November 7, 1996: 3.
— Maui County Cultural Resources Commission held meeting to discuss razing historic home of D.T. Fleming (Maka'oi'oi), Lahaina News, May 8, 2003: 1,18.

PINEAPPLE JAM FEST
— to be held, Lahaina News, March 18, 1999: 17.

PINEAPPLE JUBILEE
— to be held at Lahaina Cannery Mall, Lahaina News, February 22, 2001: 16.

PINNACLE KA'ANAPALI, THE
— development featured, Lahaina News, February 8, 2001: 6.
— homesites featured, Lahaina News, July 26, 2001: 6.
— featured, Lahaina News, September 20, 2001: 7.
— featured, Lahaina News, November 15, 2001: 7.
— featured, Lahaina News, December 20, 2001: 7.
— work continues on, Lahaina News, March 7, 2002: 7.
— featured, Lahaina News, April 11, 2002: 7.
— featured, Lahaina News, May 2, 2002: 7.
— development featured, Lahaina News, March 20, 2003: 6.

PINOCCHIO [PLAY]
— to be performed by Maui Youth Theatre, Lahaina News, June 15, 1988: 10.
— to be performed by Maui Academy of Performing Arts, Lahaina News, July 22, 1999: 12.

PIONEER INN [BUSINESS]
— rules from 1901 reprinted, Lahaina Sun, January 27, 1971: 2.
— manager Mike Stevenson plans to leave, Lahaina Sun, April 19, 1972: 11.
— potentially sold to Alan Freeland, Lahaina Sun, May 2, 1973: 4.
— history of, Lahaina News, July 1, 1981: 15.
— mentioned in article in the National Enquirer, Lahaina News, August 1, 1982: 7.
— history and myths described, Lahaina News, February 15, 1983: 7,8,9,10.
— renovation plans to be shown, Lahaina News, February 19, 1986: 1.
— Maui Historic Commission supports proposed renovations, Lahaina News, February 26, 1986: 1.
— grounds to be caretaken by Lahaina Restoration Foundation, Lahaina News, February 18, 1987: 10.
— to be renovated, Lahaina News, February 25, 1987: 1,11.
— history of, Lahaina News, February 25, 1987: 1,11.
— to feature Trevor and Rene; Blue Mango, Lahaina News, February 28, 1990: 11.
— restaurant reviewed, Lahaina News, March 14, 1990: 14.
— entertainment listed, Lahaina News, March 14, 1990: 15.
— events listed, Lahaina News, March 21, 1990: 13.
— musical line-up listed, Lahaina News, April 11, 1990: 15.

— offering show recreating whaling days, Lahaina News, May 23, 1990: 13.
— to celebrate 130th birthday, Lahaina News, June 20, 1990: 3.
— new management possible, Lahaina News, March 18, 1993: 1,4.
— bar and restaurant to be renovated, Lahaina News, June 3, 1993: 1.
— selects Noel Young to oversee renovations, Lahaina News, September 16, 1993: 9.
— restaurant reopens following renovations, Lahaina News, December 2, 1993: 11.
— reduces staff, Lahaina News, December 16, 1993: 2.
— to be renovated, Lahaina News, September 18, 1997: 1,12.
— to join Best Western chain, Lahaina News, September 18, 1997: 1,12.
— Howard Lennon discusses renovations of, Lahaina News, September 18, 1997: 12.
— celebrating 100 years, Lahaina News, January 18, 2001: 1,15.
— jazz pianist David Paquette to perform at, Lahaina News, October 18, 2001: 15.
— David Paquette to perform at, Lahaina News, November 1, 2001: 16.
— celebrates 100 years, Lahaina News, December 6, 2001: 3.
— celebrated 100 years, Lahaina News, December 13, 2001: 1.
— celebrated 100 years, Lahaina News, January 17, 2002: 3.
— Navy League of the United States Maui Council to hold forum on terrorism at, Lahaina News, February 21, 2002: 9.
— receives Best Western's Director's Award, Lahaina News, February 28, 2002: 8.
— installs time capsule, Lahaina News, December 12, 2002: 1,3.

PIONEER MILL [BUSINESS]
— facing problem of disposing waste water, Lahaina Sun, November 11, 1970: 1.
— discussed possible locations for Kamehameha III elementary school, Lahaina Sun, November 25, 1970: 3.
— plans to dump pollution in the ocean until 1974, Lahaina Sun, November 25, 1970: 4.
— production record set, Lahaina Sun, December 23, 1970: 3.
— criticized for dumping waste water into ocean at Launiupoko, Lahaina Sun, February 3, 1971: 5.
— labor dispute resolved, Lahaina Sun, June 30, 1971: 1.
— request to discharge waste water into the ocean postponed, Lahaina Sun, September 8, 1971: 5.
— smell from Mill's waste water should subside after sugar cane harvest completed, Lahaina Sun, November 17, 1971: 5.
— given permission to discharge waste water into ocean, Lahaina Sun, November 24, 1971: 6.
— announces results of 1971 growing season, Lahaina Sun, February 2, 1972: 9.
— claims that Moloka'i Joe Warren stole try-pot, Lahaina Sun, March 1, 1972: 7.
— attempting to neutralize stench of settlement pond, Lahaina Sun, August 9, 1972: 12.
— workers walk out, Lahaina Sun, October 18, 1972: 10.
— to trade land with the State of Hawaii for sewage treatment plant, Lahaina Sun, January 31, 1973: 10.
— manager John Siemer criticizes "freeloaders", Lahaina Sun, May 23, 1973: 5.
— apologizes for smoke pollution from can burning, Lahaina News, November 2, 1983: 5.
— David Paquette [musician] returning to play piano at, Lahaina News, November 30, 1983: 12.
— workers laid off because of lack of water, Lahaina News, October 10, 1984: 3.
— to cut sugar production, Lahaina News, September 3, 1986: 1,2.
— David Shankel becomes power systems superintendent, Lahaina News, June 17, 1987: 3.

— installs shining star for holiday, Lahaina News, December 28, 1988: 1.
— celebrating 130th birthday, Lahaina News, July 11, 1990: 4,5.
— fire at, Lahaina News, January 30, 1991: 4.
— plans to burn and harvest cane, Lahaina News, September 12, 1991: 3.
— reschedules cane burning, Lahaina News, September 19, 1991: 3.
— blamed for increase in mosquitoes, Lahaina News, July 16, 1992: 9.
— Keoki Freeland resigns as vice president and general manager, Lahaina News, September 1, 1994: 1,5.
— planning to use cane to produce energy, Lahaina News, May 4, 1995: 1,20.
— Maui County Council to discuss plan for strip mall, Lahaina News, June 1, 1995: 3.
— to begin cane burning, Lahaina News, June 8, 1995: 4.
— coffee harvest expected, Lahaina News, November 2, 1995: 10.
— prospects for using cane to generate energy not feasible , Lahaina News, January 11, 1996: 3.
— to begin harvesting sugar, Lahaina News, May 2, 1996: 18.
— future of explored at conference, Lahaina News, February 12, 1998: 1,20.
— future plans discussed, Lahaina News, March 11, 1999: 1,11.
— financial outlook unfavorable, Lahaina News, March 11, 1999: 11.
— taking steps to control dust, Lahaina News, June 24, 1999: 1.
— former manager worried about flooding after plantation closes, Lahaina News, July 15, 1999: 1,2.
— trying to reduce dust at Pu'ukoli'i, Lahaina News, August 12, 1999: 3.
— Wainee Village homes to be demolished by Amfac Land Co., Lahaina News, August 19, 1999: 1,20.
— editorial urging the sugar plant to be preserved, Lahaina News, December 21, 2000: 4.
— community meeting to be held to discuss demolition of, Lahaina News, September 20, 2001: 1,18.
— residents want smokestack preserved from demolition, Lahaina News, September 27, 2001: 1,8.
— Environmental Protection Agency finds elevated levels of arsenic and lead near, Lahaina News, June 12, 2003: 1,2.
— see also sugarcane

PIONEER MILL FEDERAL CREDIT UNION [BUSINESS]
— annual meeting announced, Lahaina Sun, January 13, 1971: 5.
— changes name to West Maui Community Federal Credit Union, Lahaina News, November 16, 2000: 12.

PIONEER PRINTERS [BUSINESS]
— appoints Richard Adena as account manager, Lahaina News, December 26, 1990: 7.

PIPER, ANN [ARTIST]
— work to be featured at The Art School of Kapalua, Lahaina News, November 8, 2001: 18.

PIRATES OF PENZANCE, THE [MUSICAL]
— to be performed by Maui Academy of Performing Arts, Lahaina News, July 8, 1993: 10.

PIRINGER, BONNIE
— photographed at Whaler's Village, Lahaina Sun, February 3, 1971: 7.

PISANO, JOHN [MUSICIAN]
— to perform at Hawai'i Guitar Festival, Lahaina News, June 12, 1997: 17.

PIT CRATER
— featured, Lahaina Times, August, 1980 volume 4 number 7: 1.

PITCHER, RHONDA
— to present on herbs and nutrition at Hawaiian Moons Market, Lahaina News, March 4, 1999: 12.

PITRE, JOHN [ARTIST]
— attends Friday Night is Art Night, Lahaina News, July 25, 1990: 9,13.
— to exhibit at Wyland Galleries, Lahaina News, August 22, 1991: 13.
— to exhibit at Wyland Gallery, Lahaina News, March 24, 1994: 15.
— to exhibit at Wyland Galleries, Lahaina News, August 11, 1994: 12.
— to visit Wyland Gallery, Lahaina News, April 22, 1999: 12.

PITTA, MARK [COMEDIAN]
— to perform at Comedy Club and the Sports Page, Lahaina News, May 20, 1993: 9,10.

PITTENGER, BENJAMIN ARTHUR
— joins Tateishi and Apo law firm, Lahaina News, February 6, 1991: 6.

PITTMAN, KATRINA
— to offer lecture on transcendental meditation, Lahaina News, July 8, 1993: 4.

PITZER, FRANCES
— to talk on "Creative Wellness" at 'Ohana Connection, Lahaina News, November 21, 2002: 21.

PIZZA FEAST
— at Inter-Continental Hotel Wailea, Lahaina News, January 27, 1988: 3.

PIZZA FRESH AND CAFE [RESTAURANT]
— opens, Lahaina News, May 28, 1992: 11.
— opens, Lahaina News, July 16, 1992: 16.
— featured, Lahaina News, March 18, 1993: 11.

PIZZA HUT [RESTAURANT]
— to begin free delivery in Lahaina, Lahaina News, March 14, 1990: 6.
— to open new location, Lahaina News, July 21, 1994: 7.

PIZZA PATIO [RESTAURANT]
— to offer Chicago-style pizza, Lahaina News, January 17, 1990: 24.

PIZZA PEOPLE OF NAPILI [RESTAURANT]
— opens at Napili Plaza, Lahaina News, December 1, 1994: 15.
— opens second outlet, Lahaina News, January 4, 1996: 14.

PIZZARAMA [RESTAURANT]
— opens, Lahaina News, August 31, 2000: 14.

PIZZO, RAY AND DIANE [ARTISTS]
— to demonstrate fused glass technique at Sea Side Fine Art, Lahaina News, May 25, 1995: 12.

PLANET HOLLYWOOD [RESTAURANT]
— to open, Lahaina News, August 12, 1993: 7.
— opens, Lahaina News, January 20, 1994: 6.
— opens; ceremony attended by Mayor Linda Lingle Sylvester Stallone, and Arnold Schwarzenegger, Lahaina News, July 7, 1994: 1,3.
— Front Street merchants concerned about special treatment for, Lahaina News, July 7, 1994: 3.
— contractor fined for using unlicensed workers, Lahaina News, July 21, 1994: 1.
— reviewed, Lahaina News, July 21, 1994: 11.
— contractor Shrader and Martinez Construction Inc. denied chance to change plea , Lahaina News, September 15, 1994: 5.
— hosts supermodels of the world, Lahaina News, September 22, 1994: 15.
— to hold "Night at the Oscars", Lahaina News, March 23, 1995: 11.
— to host "Oscarama", Lahaina News, March 20, 1997: 16.
— new menu items, Lahaina News, September 4, 1997: 7.
— Arnold Schwarzenegger visits, Lahaina News, January 29, 1998: 9.
— U.S. Olympic Women's Hockey Team to visit, Lahaina News, March 5, 1998: 7.

PLANET HOPE
— seeking computer instructors to help homeless, Lahaina News, March 11, 1999: 2.

PLANET JUICE AND JAVA [RESTAURANT]
— opens, Lahaina News, July 25, 1996: 7.
— reviewed, Lahaina News, August 1, 1996: 17.

PLANET SAVIORS [BUSINESS]
— selling non-toxic paint, Lahaina News, October 27, 1994: 15.

PLANNED FAMINE
— students to participate in World's Visions' event, Lahaina News, May 28, 1992: 4.

PLANNED PARENTHOOD
— Women's Health Day to be held, Lahaina News, April 9, 1986: 3.
— to hold program on how fathers can talk to their sons, Lahaina News, June 11, 1986: 3.
— organizing Women's Health Day, Lahaina News, October 1, 1986: 12.

PLANNERS, ARCHITECTS, AND LANDSCAPE ARCHITECTS OF MAUI [PALM]
— to host student tour, Lahaina News, March 16, 1988: 15.

PLANNING
— editorial praising planning in Ka'anapali, Lahaina News, September 14, 1988: 4.
— Maui no better than other places, Lahaina News, December 28, 1988: 12.
— "Partners in Planning" symposium held in Wailea, Lahaina News, December 28, 1988: 12.
— public hearing on Maui County General Plan, Lahaina News, July 18, 1990: 4.

PLANNING AND ECONOMIC COMMITTEE, MAUI COUNTY COUNCIL
— to review proposed 670 Wailea project, Lahaina News, July 9, 1992: 7.

PLANNING AND ECONOMIC DEVELOPMENT COMMITTEE, MAUI COUNTY COUNCIL
— to hold meeting on proposed Napili Trade Center, Lahaina News, June 6, 1991: 3.
— recommends approval of request to allow show making and repair shop, Lahaina News, July 9, 1992: 3.

PLANNING AND ECONOMIC DEVELOPMENT, STATE DEPARTMENT OF
— requests proposals for energy conservation projects, Lahaina News, June 18, 1986: 3.

PLANNING AND LAND USE COMMITTEE, MAUI COUNTY
— to hold hearing concerning proposed light industrial project to be held, Lahaina News, October 17, 1990: 1.
— defers decision to rezone acres of Kahana Valley as part of quiet title settlement, Lahaina News, April 17, 1991: 1.
— approves Maui Land and Pineapple Co plan for Honokohau, Lahaina News, September 21, 1995: 1,16.

PLANNING COMMISSION, MAUI COUNTY
— gives permission to Maui Land & Pineapple to build golf course in a state conversation district, Lahaina Sun, November 18, 1970: 3.
— defers decision by Custom Builders, Ltd. to rezone land in Napili, Lahaina Sun, November 18, 1970: 3.
— approves request by Wailea Land Corp to develop area on Maui's south shore, Lahaina Sun, December 2, 1970: 2.
— considers Maui Electric's request to build power plant near Ma'alaea, Lahaina Sun, May 12, 1971: 1,8.
— concerned about threat to fish ponds from hotel development on Moloka'i, Lahaina Sun, May 26, 1971: 6.
— okayed rezoning for housing in Lahaina, Lahaina Sun, June 2, 1971: 6.
— projects approved by, discussed, Lahaina Sun, August 11, 1971: 1,3.
— okays extension of wharf facilities, Lahaina Sun, August 25, 1971: 11.
— recommends Concrete Industries Maui be allowed to move to a site near Honokowai Stream, Lahaina Sun, October 27, 1971: 11.

— defers decision on proposed housing project in Napilihau, Lahaina Sun, December 15, 1971: 7.
— approves second phase of housing project in Napilihau, Lahaina Sun, January 5, 1972: 6.
— tightens zoning regulations, Lahaina Sun, June 28, 1972: 19.
— account of contentious meeting, Lahaina Sun, August 2, 1972: 3.
— Dick Mayer appointed to, Lahaina Sun, September 20, 1972: 14.
— denies rezoning request in Kihei, Lahaina Sun, November 8, 1972: 5.
— considers Lana'i Corporation's development proposal for Lana'i , Lahaina Sun, January 17, 1973: 3.
— legality of questioned by Life of the Land, Lahaina Sun, January 31, 1973: 6.
— turns down Sharon Lawrence as member, Lahaina News, December 28, 1983: 3.
— approves two shoreline management area permits, Lahaina News, July 4, 1984: 7.
— approves rezoning for two shopping complexes, Lahaina News, September 26, 1984: 3.
— approves airport in Mahinahina, Lahaina News, June 12, 1985: 1.
— limits Harry Weinberg's plan for shopping development in Ka'anapali, Lahaina News, June 12, 1985: 1.
— approves shopping center in Napilihau, Lahaina News, August 28, 1985: 3.
— files complaint against Lahaina Fashions, Inc. to stop selling from display booths, Lahaina News, October 9, 1985: 3.
— approves shopping center proposed by Harry Weinberg, Lahaina News, January 15, 1986: 3.
— approves new courthouse, Lahaina News, April 30, 1986: 1.
— approves plan for more housing, Lahaina News, October 1, 1986: 11.
— publishes continuance of meeting for Special Management Area hearing connected to Kapalua Bay Hotel, Lahaina News, November 26, 1986: 15.
— considering zoning changes, Lahaina News, February 18, 1987: 10.
— orders Environmental Impact Statement for Ka'anapali development, Lahaina News, March 18, 1987: 3.
— recommends commercial space and apartment rental units in Kahana, Lahaina News, May 6, 1987: 1.
— approves stand on Ka'anapali Beach, Lahaina News, May 27, 1987: 1.
— approves more housing in West Maui, Lahaina News, September 9, 1987: 1.
— approves off-site parking stalls, activity centers, Lahaina News, September 9, 1987: 3.
— grants permit for apartment complex in Mahinahina, Lahaina News, March 2, 1988: 13.
— conducting public hearing over expansion of Ka'anapali Resort, Lahaina News, May 11, 1988: 1.
— grants intervenor status to groups concerning North Beach Project, Lahaina News, June 1, 1988: 1.
— to hold public hearings on proposed projects, Lahaina News, November 15, 1989: 2.
— to hold workshop on proposed zoning ordinances, Lahaina News, February 7, 1990: 28.
— to hold hearing to review special management area permit in Kahakuloa, Lahaina News, February 7, 1990: 28.
— to review shoreline setback variance for Mahinahina drainage project, Lahaina News, May 16, 1990: 5.
— defers request by Andrew DeMello for special use permit, Lahaina News, November 14, 1990: 4.
— to review Ka'anapali Beach Hotel request to expand, Lahaina News, December 12, 1990: 1.
— approves expansion of Ka'anapali Beach Hotel, Lahaina News, December 26, 1990: 1.

— critical of Fantasy Island Activity and Tours, Inc.'s erecting activities booths, Lahaina News, March 7, 1990: 1.

— to hold public hearing on General Plan, Lahaina News, August 15, 1990: 6.

— to hold public meeting on design study for Lahaina town, Lahaina News, October 17, 1990: 5.

— to hold meeting to plan to improve Front Street, Lahaina News, November 7, 1990: 4.

— to hold public meeting on Front Street improvements, Lahaina News, November 14, 1990: 3.

— produces draft of Country Town Design Guidelines, Lahaina News, December 26, 1990: 5.

— in conflict with Maui County Public Works Department over treatment of historic roads, Lahaina News, July 25, 1991: 1.

— concerned over shorelines structures, plantings by Sheraton Maui, Lahaina News, August 15, 1991: 1.

— to provide list of historic sites in West Maui, Lahaina News, October 1, 1992: 1.

— sponsoring seminar by Charles Eley on Hawaii Model Energy Code, Lahaina News, January 14, 1993: 3.

— to meet to discuss Kihei-Makena Community Plan, Lahaina News, July 15, 1993: 5.

— creating a Lahaina Task Force, Lahaina News, June 20, 1996: 14.

— permits oceanfront building without public review, Lahaina News, October 17, 2002: 1,17.

— to prepare master plan for relocating Honoapi'ilani Highway, Lahaina News, October 31, 2002: 1,30.

— to consider request from Doug White to build residence over storm drainage culvert, Lahaina News, September 18, 2003: 1,20.

PLANOS, GARY

— named director of golf at Kapalua at Village Course, Lahaina News, September 17, 1986: 11.

— names director of golf at Kapalua Bay Hotel and Resort, Lahaina News, January 24, 1990: 6.

PLANTATION CAMPS

— talk story on history of, Lahaina News, August 24, 1988: 14.

PLANTATION CHRISTMAS [PLAY]

— to be presented at Kapalua Shops, Lahaina News, December 16, 1993: 18.

PLANTATION CLUB ESTATES

— ground breaking ceremony held, Lahaina News, May 28, 1992: 12.

PLANTATION ESTATES, THE

— sells 30 lots for $69 million, Lahaina News, September 26, 1990: 9.

— majority of owners Japanese nationals, Lahaina News, September 26, 1990: 9.

— Maui Interface Corp. marketing two-acre homesites at, Lahaina News, November 7, 1990: 7.

— additional 40 homesites offered, Lahaina News, September 19, 1991: 6.

PLANTATION HOUSE [RESTAURANT]

— to open, owned by Roy Dunn, Michael Hooks, and Michael Smith, Lahaina News, April 24, 1991: 7.

— Alex Stanislaw becomes head chef, Lahaina News, May 1, 1991: 7.

— names Chris Kaiwi as general manager and Buck Florian as manager, Lahaina News, May 8, 1991: 6.

— Alan Usler becomes sommelier, Lahaina News, September 12, 1991: 4.

— celebrates anniversary, Lahaina News, June 4, 1992: 14.

— holds 1st anniversary party, Lahaina News, July 23, 1992: 26.

— reviewed, Lahaina News, August 6, 1992: 14.

— hosting fundraiser for Big Brothers/Big Sisters, Lahaina News, March 18, 1993: 12.

— appoints Arnold DeClercq as restaurant manager, Lahaina News, June 3, 1993: 7.

— to offer "A Midsummer Night's Fare", Lahaina News, June 17, 1993: 14.

— featured, Lahaina News, August 26, 1993: 14.

— provided food for King Kamehameha III Elementary School students taking SAT, Lahaina News, April 18, 1996: 6.

— to hold vintner dinner with wines of Shafer Vineyards, Lahaina News, August 8, 1996: 16.

— to host winemakers, Lahaina News, November 6, 1997: 16.

— to hold "A Mid Summer's Night Wine Dinner", Lahaina News, August 10, 2000: 5.

— to hold charity feast for Lahainaluna High School Foundation, Lahaina News, June 27, 2002: 14,18.

— featured, Lahaina News, December 19, 2002: 16.

— establishes scholarship for Lahainaluna High School culinary students, Lahaina News, January 2, 2003: 1,20.

— to hold fundraiser for Lahainaluna High School Foundation's scholarship program, Lahaina News, July 10, 2003: 3.

PLANTATION INN [BUSINESS]

— Gerard's French restaurant reopens, Lahaina News, September 2, 1987: 3.

— recent changes detailed, Lahaina News, October 14, 1987: 4.

— addition planned, Lahaina News, July 27, 1988: 20.

— expands, Lahaina News, February 20, 1991: 7.

— Jim Patterson planning to build office building, Lahaina News, July 11, 1991: 6.

— to be managed by Ka'anapali Beach Hotel, Lahaina News, March 13, 1997: 1.

— now owned by Ka'anapali Beach Hotel, Lahaina News, May 22, 1997: 9.

PLANTS

— orchid show scheduled at Lahaina Shopping Center, Lahaina News, May 7, 1986: 3.

PLAY IT AGAIN SAM [PLAY]

— presented by Baldwin Theatre Guild, Lahaina News, March 18, 1987: 18.

PLAY ON [PLAY]

— to be performed by Maui Community Theatre, Lahaina News, August 15, 1991: 15.

PLAY TO LEARN TOYS [BUSINESS]

— opens, Lahaina News, December 12, 2002: 8.

PLAYER, GARY

— golfer leading Senior PGA Ka'anapali Classic, Lahaina News, October 15, 1992: 10.

PLAYING ON THE PLANET [BUSINESS]

— new gallery opens, Lahaina News, November 28, 1991: 7.

PLAYTIME RENTALS

— engines of six jet boats damaged, Lahaina Sun, August 25, 1971: 9.

PLEASANT HAWAIIAN HOLIDAYS

— names Gary Hogan as president, Lahaina News, June 24, 1993: 10.

PLUMBO, FRANCO [CHEF]

— to visit Maui, Lahaina Sun, January 31, 1973: 11.

PLUMERIA RESALE BOUTIQUE

— raising money for Hospice Maui, Lahaina News, August 12, 1999: 14.

PLUMFIELD ART SCHOOL

— showing film "Safari Night", Lahaina News, December 5, 1990: 14.

PLUTA, CHERI

— has lead role in Maui Community Theatre's "Kismet", Lahaina News, November 9, 1988: 9.

PLUTA, JOSEPH

— honored by University of Hawaii, Lahaina News, May 23, 1996: 4.

— message from West Maui Taxpayers Association president, Lahaina News, August 29, 2002: 5.

POCKET COOLER, THE
— beverage insulation product being manufactured on Maui, Lahaina News, July 12, 1989: 4.

POE, JOY
— to hold lecture on "Women Artists" for Lahaina Arts Society, Lahaina News, October 12, 1995: 6.

POETRY
— by Bryan di Salvatore, Lahaina Sun, May 19, 1971: 3.
— Citizens of the Sun by Bryan di Salvatore, Lahaina Sun, June 23, 1971: 5.
— by Eloise Clarke, Lahaina Sun, February 16, 1972: 7.
— The Big Island by Jim Mann, Lahaina Sun, March 22, 1972: 17.
— by students of Kamehameha III Elementary School, Lahaina News, March 21, 1984: 21,22,23,24.
— Poetry in Paradise sponsoring convention, Lahaina News, April 13, 1988: 3,12.
— Poetry in Paradise announces contest, Lahaina News, July 20, 1988: 3.
— poems now being accepted for contest by Sparrowgrass Poetry Forum in West Virginia, Lahaina News, January 17, 1990: 5.
— Sparrowgrass Poetry Forum offering awards, Lahaina News, June 6, 1991: 5.
— Peace Poetry contest results, Lahaina News, June 14, 2001: 17.
— Gallerie Ha to host "Sound Out 5", Lahaina News, September 4, 2003: 16.

POETRY FESTIVAL
— held at Princess Nahienaena Elementary School, Lahaina News, March 15, 2001: 14.

POGNI, STEVE
— opens new business Soap Opera, Lahaina News, October 14, 1999: 11.
— accepted by the National Registry of Who's Who, Lahaina News, January 13, 2000: 11.

POHAI KEALOHA HULA HALAU
— to perform at Lahaina Cannery Shopping Center, Lahaina News, August 24, 1988: 3.
— staging weekly keiki hula show at Hale Kahiko, Lahaina News, April 3, 1997: 12.
— to perform, Lahaina News, April 10, 1997: 12.
— to perform at Hale Kahiko, Lahaina News, June 22, 2000: 16.

POHAILANI
— planning proceeds on resort, Lahaina Sun, March 28, 1973: 3.
— to be sold and residents displaced, Lahaina News, July 2, 1986: 1,11.
— real estate development featured, Lahaina News, November 22, 2001: 6.

POHAKU [MUSICAL GROUP]
— reviewed, Lahaina News, March 7, 1990: 16.

POHAKU PARK
— now called S-turns Park, Lahaina News, March 17, 1994: 1.
— to be improved, Lahaina News, April 6, 1995: 3.
— plague to honor Andrea Heath-Blundell and Brian Maither , Lahaina News, October 9, 1997: 1,3.
— residents may ask Maui Land and Pineapple to sell acres near, Lahaina News, February 25, 1999: 1,16.
— see also S-Turns Park

POHINAHINA—BOY FROM THE SUN [FILM]
— shown at Family Film Festival, Lahaina Sun, January 27, 1971: 2.

POI
— contaminated, blamed for outbreak of dysentery in 1970, Lahaina Sun, January 27, 1971: 1.

POI DOG SHOW
— to be held, Lahaina News, June 6, 1991: 3.

POI FACTORY
— protests of plans to convert to The Haven restaurant, Lahaina News, September 1, 1980: 7.

POINTER SISTERS [MUSICAL GROUP]
— performing in Honolulu but not Maui, Lahaina News, March 28, 1984: 14.

POIRIER, DICK
— Office of State Planning representative hears testimony on the Hawaiian Islands Humpback Whale National Sanctuary, Lahaina News, March 24, 1994: 2.

POKEMAN
— Kite Fantasy continues to host trading sessions, Lahaina News, June 24, 1999: 13.
— trading day held at Kite Fantasy, Lahaina News, September 2, 1999: 14.

POKIPALA, ALLAN "POKI"
— hired by KPOA, Lahaina News, August 29, 1991: 4.

POLAND, BRYAN "DE BRIS" [ARTIST]
— to exhibit at Lahaina Arts Society, Lahaina News, August 31, 1995: 12.

POLICE
— roadblocks during New Year's weekend announced, Lahaina Sun, December 30, 1970: 4.
— budget requests, Lahaina Sun, January 20, 1971: 8.
— Maui Police Department request new radio communications system, Lahaina Sun, February 10, 1971: 2.
— forms chapter of State of Hawaii Organization of Police Officers, Lahaina Sun, February 17, 1971: 5.
— hosts Maui Community College students at picnic, Lahaina Sun, May 5, 1971: 1.
— picnic with Maui Community College students described, Lahaina Sun, May 12, 1971: 1.
— Lahaina Retail Committee hoping police will be nicer to tourists, Lahaina Sun, May 26, 1971: 5.
— looking for suspects in attack, Lahaina Sun, June 23, 1971: 12.
— concern that police telephone is busy, Lahaina Sun, June 30, 1971: 1.
— criticized proposing that they only warn tourists who violate Lahaina parking laws, Lahaina Sun, July 28, 1971: 1.
— discuss complaints about dune buggy rentals, Lahaina Sun, July 28, 1971: 1,9.
— Abraham Aiona announces a restructuring of the department, Lahaina Sun, August 11, 1971: 11.
— studying recent fires in Lahaina, Lahaina Sun, September 1, 1971: 1.
— State Law Enforcement Officials Conference held at Maui Hilton Hotel, Lahaina Sun, September 1, 1971: 15.
— organized crime discussed at Hawaii State Conference of Law Enforcement Officials, Lahaina Sun, September 8, 1971: 15.
— install new radio repeater station, Lahaina Sun, September 15, 1971: 6.
— stop fire near Baldwin High School, Lahaina Sun, October 6, 1971: 1.
— turned away people wearing tank tops at County Fair, Lahaina Sun, October 20, 1971: 6.
— discussion of what to do if the police arrest you, Lahaina Sun, October 27, 1971: 13.
— police station requested beside Lahaina Civic Recreation Center, Lahaina Sun, November 10, 1971: 11.
— oppose law against slow drivers, Lahaina Sun, November 10, 1971: 13.
— new picnic with Maui Community College students planned , Lahaina Sun, November 17, 1971: 12.
— issue connected to use of special funds has been resolved, Lahaina Sun, November 17, 1971: 14.

— no solution to drinking at Maluʻulu O Lele Park, Lahaina News, July 21, 1994: 1,16.

— say that traffic congestion to continue, Lahaina News, August 18, 1994: 1.

— offering crime prevention seminars, Lahaina News, September 29, 1994: 10.

— preparing for Halloween, Lahaina News, October 6, 1994: 3.

— seek volunteers for anti-crime network, Lahaina News, October 20, 1994: 1,6.

— investigating death of visitor, Lahaina News, October 20, 1994: 5.

— fear wharf improvements to attract "undesirables", Lahaina News, November 17, 1994: 3.

— thank community for making Halloween safe, Lahaina News, December 1, 1994: 3.

— to receive funding for community police officers, Lahaina News, December 29, 1994: 2.

— Lanny Tihada appointed new deputy chief, Lahaina News, December 29, 1994: 3.

— Sgt. Leeland Scott is new supervisor for Crime Reduction Unit, Lahaina News, January 5, 1995: 3.

— "Butch" Lam new Lahaina captain, Lahaina News, January 26, 1995: 1,20.

— Business Education Alert Training (BEAT) promoted, Lahaina News, February 2, 1995: 3.

— West Maui Community Policing (WMCOP) to meet, Lahaina News, February 2, 1995: 3.

— Maui Police Department to install emergency call boxes, Lahaina News, February 16, 1995: 1,3.

— more officers proposed in Mayor Linda Lingle's budget, Lahaina News, March 23, 1995: 1,16.

— discusses motorcycle parking, Lahaina News, March 23, 1995: 2.

— community meeting to be held, Lahaina News, May 4, 1995: 5.

— closer to ticketing buses on Wharf Street, Lahaina News, May 18, 1995: 1,16.

— "Aloha Patrol" to remind merchants of code violations, Lahaina News, May 18, 1995: 2.

— West Maui to get two more community officers, Lahaina News, May 25, 1995: 1,16.

— to hold Keiki Safe Day, Lahaina News, June 29, 1995: 4.

— offer advice on road safety, Lahaina News, July 6, 1995: 4.

— Community Oriented Policing Program to meet, Lahaina News, August 3, 1995: 4.

— to discuss community policing efforts, Lahaina News, September 7, 1995: 2.

— using peddling rule to target drug dealer, Lahaina News, September 21, 1995: 3.

— begin program at Lahaina Intermediate School to teach students about police work, Lahaina News, October 19, 1995: 1,2.

— incident where officer received a self-inflicted gunshot wound is a closed matter, Lahaina News, October 26, 1995: 1.

— seeking community input, Lahaina News, November 2, 1995: 3.

— community policing expanding, Lahaina News, November 16, 1995: 2.

— to focus on gang activity, Lahaina News, December 21, 1995: 1.

— expanding community policing program in West Maui, Lahaina News, February 15, 1996: 2.

— community meeting to be held, Lahaina News, March 7, 1996: 3.

— community policing praised at Community Oriented Policing Program, Lahaina News, March 21, 1996: 1,4.

— Citizens' Patrol to begin soon, Lahaina News, March 28, 1996: 3.

— to hold public meeting, Lahaina News, April 4, 1996: 2.

— seeking public comments, Lahaina News, May 9, 1996: 4.

— Citizens' Patrol having an impact, Lahaina News, May 16, 1996: 3.

— public meeting to be held, Lahaina News, June 6, 1996: 15.

— Citizens Patrol deterring crime on beaches, Lahaina News, June 6, 1996: 6.

— calling snarled after car crash, Lahaina News, June 13, 1996: 1.

— to meet with community, Lahaina News, June 13, 1996: 10.

— warn of scam with soliciting contributions, Lahaina News, July 18, 1996: 2.

— seeking witnesses connected to remains found at Nakalele Point, Lahaina News, July 25, 1996: 1.

— Citizen Patrol having impact, Lahaina News, August 15, 1996: 1.

— reaction to gunshots at Weinberg Court Apartments, Lahaina News, August 22, 1996: 1,20.

— rave party at Honolua Bay squashed, Lahaina News, September 5, 1996: 1.

— short-handed, seeking citizens to lobby, Lahaina News, September 19, 1996: 1.

— requests for more police a top budget request, Lahaina News, September 26, 1996: 1,18.

— fatal car crash on Honoapiʻilani Highway ties up police phones, Lahaina News, October 10, 1996: 4.

— Citizen Patrol may expand, Lahaina News, October 17, 1996: 1.

— additional patrols has impact, Lahaina News, November 21, 1996: 1,20.

— to meet with community, Lahaina News, December 19, 1996: 4.

— to hold meeting, Lahaina News, January 2, 1997: 10.

— U.S. Department of Justice increases funding for, Lahaina News, January 9, 1997: 14.

— Liquor Control commissioners approves tougher laws, Lahaina News, January 16, 1997: 3.

— seeking information on recent robberies, Lahaina News, January 30, 1997: 3.

— West Maui Cycle and Sports to donate bikes to, Lahaina News, February 13, 1997: 3.

— mayor Linda Lingle discusses focus on visitor industry, Lahaina News, February 27, 1997: 1,16.

— to teach basics to resort workers, Lahaina News, March 20, 1997: 1.

— want citizen's patrols on Front Street, Lahaina News, April 24, 1997: 1,16.

— Citizens' Patrol program to begin at Front Street, Lahaina News, July 17, 1997: 1.

— Citizen's Patrol needs volunteers, Lahaina News, October 16, 1997: 9.

— set ground rules for Halloween, Lahaina News, October 30, 1997: 1.

— Maui County Citizens' Patrol begins, Lahaina News, November 6, 1997: 1,13.

— warm of phone call scams, Lahaina News, January 1, 1998: 13.

— seek help in identifying counterfeited money suspect, Lahaina News, January 8, 1998: 3.

— seeking David Pico, Jr., Lahaina News, January 29, 1998: 8.

— searching for fugitive Cheryl Knutson-Adolpho, Lahaina News, February 5, 1998: 3.

— looking for fugitive George Keliʻiaukai Hoʻokano, Lahaina News, February 19, 1998: 2.

— seeking Anthony G. Balgas Jr., Lahaina News, February 26, 1998: 2.

— searching for Robert Lawyer, Lahaina News, March 12, 1998: 2.

— to offer free child seat inspections, Lahaina News, April 23, 1998: 16.

— plan to monitor Banyan Tree Park, Lahaina News, June 11, 1998: 1,20.

— officers receive Outstanding Law Enforcement Award from Mothers Against Drunk Driving, Lahaina News, June 18, 1998: 2.

— seeking help to solve the murder of Raymond Ramos, Jr., Lahaina News, July 9, 1998: 1.

— Visitor Oriented Policing Program (VOPP) formed, Lahaina News, July 23, 1998: 1,20.

— volunteer patrols organized, Lahaina News, August 6, 1998: 3.

— Thomas Phillips appointed police chief, Lahaina News, August 6, 1998: 7.

— takes zero tolerance to Front Street violations, Lahaina News, August 20, 1998: 1.

— seeking Myron Keahi Sr. for burglary, Lahaina News, August 20, 1998: 9.

— Charles Hall appointed deputy chief of police, Lahaina News, September 3, 1998: 8.

— offering "Citizens Police Academy" program, Lahaina News, October 29, 1998: 15.

— reminders for Halloween, Lahaina News, October 29, 1998: 22.

— injured in chase, Lahaina News, October 29, 1998: 3.

— warns of scams, Lahaina News, November 5, 1998: 8.

— reminding people to buckle up their children, Lahaina News, December 3, 1998: 11.

— warns public of scam seeking contributions for "Hawaii Most Wanted Magazine", Lahaina News, January 21, 1999: 2.

— seeking identity of jewelry thief, Lahaina News, January 21, 1999: 3.

— Lahaina News to assist in RATH (Reduce Auto Theft in Hawaii) program, Lahaina News, March 18, 1999: 8.

— to be rated by the Commission on Accreditation for Law Enforcement Agencies, Lahaina News, May 13, 1999: 15.

— to teach merchants about shoplifting, fraud, etc., Lahaina News, May 13, 1999: 2.

— Senator Jan Yagi-Buen discusses tax reforms and funding for Maui, Lahaina News, May 20, 1999: 2.

— asking for help in death of Robert French, Lahaina News, May 27, 1999: 1,16.

— vacancies at, Lahaina News, June 10, 1999: 15.

— anti-crime patrols walking Lahaina Town, Lahaina News, June 17, 1999: 1,20.

— officers honored for saving lives, Lahaina News, June 17, 1999: 3.

— officer killed while directing traffic, Lahaina News, August 12, 1999: 1,20.

— unveil Speed Monitoring Trailer to show driver's speed, Lahaina News, August 26, 1999: 3.

— Dallas police officer Bridget Wilson honored at Pioneer Inn, Lahaina News, September 9, 1999: 3.

— plans roadblocks throughout September, Lahaina News, September 23, 1999: 1.

— looking for vandals of Children's Garden Preschool, Lahaina News, October 21, 1999: 6.

— trying to locate Patrick Vegas, wanted for terroristic threatening, Lahaina News, October 28, 1999: 13.

— Maui Police Captain Wayne Ribao discusses concerns with residents, Lahaina News, January 20, 2000: 1.

— Sandalwood Restaurant to hold "Maui Bear Hugs Den" to collect bears for police officers to comfort traumatized children, Lahaina News, June 8, 2000: 17.

— officers transferred from Visitor Oriented Policing Program, Lahaina News, August 24, 2000: 1.

— officer Michael Casicas resigns in frustration, Lahaina News, October 12, 2000: 1,24.

— Maui police chief Tom Phillips discusses staff shortages, Lahaina News, October 19, 2000: 1,7.

— looking for drivers who do not buckle up their children, Lahaina News, November 23, 2000: 7.

— forms Highway Incident Traffic Team to deal with highway closures, Lahaina News, April 5, 2001: 1,24.

— 56th Recruit Class graduated, Lahaina News, November 29, 2001: 2.

— police officer Charles Hirata honored with Alaka'i Award , Lahaina News, December 13, 2001: 2.

— officer Donald Nakooka lies after shooting himself, Lahaina News, December 13, 2001: 3.

— traffic devices discussed, Lahaina News, January 17, 2002: 1.

— Maui Police Department to be assessed by Commission on Accreditation for Law Enforcement Agencies, Inc., Lahaina News, April 4, 2002: 5.

— targeting drug dealers, Lahaina News, August 8, 2002: 1,9.

— to work with groups to address crime problems, Lahaina News, August 22, 2002: 1,2.

— recruit class graduates, Lahaina News, September 12, 2002: 8.

— Crime Stoppers celebrates 22 years, Lahaina News, October 31, 2002: 21.

— Tivoli Faaumu named Maui's "Top Cop", Lahaina News, November 28, 2002: 1,2.

— upgrades phone system, Lahaina News, April 24, 2003: 21.

— Mayor Alan Arakawa to attend grand opening of Wailuku Police Resource Center, Lahaina News, July 24, 2003: 8.

— seeking information on motor vehicle crash, Lahaina News, October 2, 2003: 1.

— see also Aiona, Abraham

POLICE [MUSICAL GROUP]

— to perform on Maui, Lahaina News, March 7, 1984: 9,10,11.

POLICE OFFICERS ASSOCIATION OF HAWAII

— Maui chapter formed, Lahaina Sun, December 16, 1970: 1.

— seeking to represent state's policemen, Lahaina Sun, December 16, 1970: 1.

POLITICS

— situation on Maui described, Lahaina Sun, March 22, 1972: 19.

— Mayor Cravalho discusses Maui, Lahaina Sun, March 22, 1972: 21.

— current conditions in Maui discussed, Lahaina Sun, September 20, 1972: 4,5.

— David Asai discusses people's fear of opposing county administration, Lahaina Sun, September 27, 1972: 5.

— importance of citizen participation challenged, Lahaina Sun, December 20, 1972: 9.

— editorial critical of financial disclosure rules, Lahaina Sun, March 14, 1973: 8.

— reflection on disconnection between people in Hawaii and the federal government, Lahaina Sun, March 14, 1973: 9.

— role of lobbying in political process discussed, Lahaina Sun, March 28, 1973: 9.

— difficulties in obtaining financial disclosure records for state politicians detailed, Lahaina Sun, April 11, 1973: 8.

— editorial on Maui County scheming to support McNeil's construction of large apartment-hotel in Lahaina, Lahaina Sun, May 2, 1973: 9.

— Jimmy Carter's reelection discussed, Lahaina News, January 15, 1980: 2.

— results of 1980 election discussed, Lahaina News, December 1, 1980: 1.

— discussion of Reagan's mandate, Lahaina News, December 15, 1980: 3.

— National Taxpayers Union claim Congressional delegation spends considerable amount, Lahaina News, November 1, 1982: 2.

— Clayton Hee begins regular column in Lahaina News, will not always be indexed, Lahaina News, February 15, 1983: 2.

— summary of 1983 legislative session, Lahaina News, May 15, 1983: 2.

— editorial praising mayor Tavares for attending meeting on pollution in West Maui, Lahaina News, September 7, 1983: 2.

— editorial criticizing closed meetings, Lahaina News, November 30, 1983: 2.

— Legislature reconvenes, Representative Clayton Hee begins newspaper column, Lahaina News, February 1, 1984: 4.

— editorial critical of attempts to make Maui nuclear-free, Lahaina News, March 21, 1984: 2.

— Clayton Hee provides summary of 1984 legislative session, Lahaina News, June 13, 1984: 7.

— editorial on value of judges as check, Lahaina News, August 1, 1984: 2.

— editorial on charter changes on November ballot, Lahaina News, September 5, 1984: 2.

— editorial on strengths and weaknesses of Mondale and Reagan, Lahaina News, October 31, 1984: 2.

— editorial discussion on election results , Lahaina News, November 14, 1984: 2.

— editorial urging lawmakers to fix worker's compensation, Lahaina News, January 9, 1985: 2.

— editorial advocating for more power at the counties, Lahaina News, January 16, 1985: 2.

— editorial supporting "home rule" where counties are given more power, Lahaina News, January 23, 1985: 2.

— editorial critical of governor George Ariyoshi, Lahaina News, January 30, 1985: 2.

— Lahaina students attend the Election '84 Youth Inaugural Conference in Washington DC, Lahaina News, January 30, 1985: 3.

— State Representative Bill Pfeil reports, Lahaina News, April 10, 1985: 1,6.

— editorial critical of State legislature, Lahaina News, May 1, 1985: 2.

— editorial criticizing U.S. support of apartheid South Africa, Lahaina News, August 28, 1985: 2.

— editorial criticizing judiciary probes, Lahaina News, September 11, 1985: 2.

— editorial on current Democratic Party in Hawai'i, Lahaina News, December 4, 1985: 2.

— editorial on potential successes of current legislative session, Lahaina News, February 5, 1986: 2.

— Democratic Party to meet on Maui, Lahaina News, March 5, 1986: 3.

— Bill Eger announces candidacy for mayoral race, Lahaina News, March 12, 1986: 12.

— voter registration to take place in Lahaina, Lahaina News, July 16, 1986: 3.

— editorial critical of Democratic party, Lahaina News, August 20, 1986: 2.

— Andy Anderson and John Waihee attend ceremony for Research and Technology Park, Lahaina News, October 8, 1986: 1.

— coverage of mayoral election, Lahaina News, October 15, 1986: 1,5.

— State Senate race featured, Lahaina News, October 22, 1986: 1,5,16.

— candidacy for State Representative featured, Lahaina News, October 29, 1986: 1,10,11.

— people around the world unite for peace, Lahaina News, December 31, 1986: 3.

— RESULTS, a political awareness group, to meet in Wailuku, Lahaina News, February 4, 1987: 11.

— editorial on increase to salaries for legislators, Lahaina News, February 18, 1987: 2.

— legislators to meet with senior citizens, Lahaina News, March 18, 1987: 18.

— editorial supporting public input in development projects, Lahaina News, June 17, 1987: 2.

— Democrats to hold straw poor for presidential preference, Lahaina News, March 2, 1988: 22.

— editorial review of Fourteenth Legislative session, Lahaina News, May 18, 1988: 2.

— candidates for West Maui council to debate, Lahaina News, August 10, 1988: 17.

— candidates to debate again, Lahaina News, August 24, 1988: 14.

— Democrats open campaign headquarters, Lahaina News, September 14, 1988: 11.

— Dukakis campaign looking for volunteers, Lahaina News, September 21, 1988: 20.

— editorial critical of Alice Lee's apparent failure to meet residency requirements, Lahaina News, October 12, 1988: 4.

— Maui Chamber of Commerce sponsoring candidate breakfast, Lahaina News, October 19, 1988: 14.

— Rosalyn Baker and Don Dela Cruz featured, Lahaina News, October 26, 1988: 1,14,15.

— Joe Souki and Pat Elf featured, Lahaina News, November 2, 1988: 1,14,15.

— walk-in absentee voting organized, Lahaina News, November 2, 1988: 3.

— editorial opposing pay increases for public officials, Lahaina News, April 19, 1989: 4.

— attempts to create computer bulletin board for public information, Lahaina News, July 26, 1989: 3.

— meeting concerning use of initiative process in land-use issues, Lahaina News, September 13, 1989: 3.

— editorial approving of improving access to public information, Lahaina News, September 27, 1989: 12.

— public to meet state and county political figures at Kihei Community Center, Lahaina News, November 1, 1989: 6.

— Legislative timetable for 1990 session given, Lahaina News, December 27, 1989: 32.

— Rick Reed says state bills to allow for initiative measures are dead, Lahaina News, February 7, 1990: 28.

— legislature starts Hawaii Area-Wide Information Access Network to improve access, Lahaina News, February 21, 1990: 28.

— legislators planning meeting sponsored by West Maui Taxpayers Association, Lahaina News, February 21, 1990: 4.

— resident can now fax testimony to legislature, Lahaina News, March 14, 1990: 3.

— editorial challenging finding of survey on excise tax increase, Lahaina News, March 28, 1990: 10.

— campaign spending criticized, Lahaina News, May 2, 1990: 1.

— state legislators receive mixed review, Lahaina News, May 9, 1990: 1.

— editorial urging attendance at a public meeting to review legislative session, Lahaina News, May 16, 1990: 14.

— open house with lawmakers to discuss legislative session, Lahaina News, May 16, 1990: 5.

— voter registration begins, Lahaina News, June 27, 1990: 5.

— voter registration, Lahaina News, August 1, 1990: 5.

— number of registered voters increases, Lahaina News, August 15, 1990: 6.

— Maui County Council of Community Associations to present mayoral candidates, Lahaina News, August 15, 1990: 6.

— voter registration up, Lahaina News, August 29, 1990: 4.

— Republican candidates to appear on Hawaii Public Television's "Dialog" , Lahaina News, August 29, 1990: 4.

— voter registration up 11%, Lahaina News, September 19, 1990: 4.

— editorial urging people to vote in the primary election, Lahaina News, September 19, 1990: 8.

— Maui League of Republican Women to meet, Lahaina News, October 24, 1990: 4.

— walk-in absentee voting to be conducted, Lahaina News, October 31, 1990: 7.

— preview of legislative session to be broadcast on KHET/11, Lahaina News, January 2, 1991: 3.

— Roz Baker appraises State budget, Lahaina News, January 16, 1991: 1,9.

— update on contact information for Maui representatives, Lahaina News, January 23, 1991: 4.

— no-fault insurance law to be reviewed, Lahaina News, February 6, 1991: 4.

— Joe Souki discusses upcoming 1991 legislative session, Lahaina News, February 6, 1991: 4.

— Rick Reed calling for term limits, Lahaina News, March 13, 1991: 3.

— Frontline special to air on Iran Hostages and President Reagan, Lahaina News, April 10, 1991: 14.

— funds for Lahaina likely, Lahaina News, April 17, 1991: 1.

— mayor Linda Lingle opposes parks bill, Lahaina News, April 17, 1991: 3.

— legislature funds building projects, including Lahaina Bypass, Lahaina News, May 15, 1991: 1.

— Rick Reed claims reapportionment is a joke, Lahaina News, May 15, 1991: 1.

— Rick Reed continues criticism of redistricting plan, Lahaina News, May 30, 1991: 1.

— State Reapportionment Commission responds to criticism to redistricting proposal, Lahaina News, June 13, 1991: 1.

— reapportionment hearing set, Lahaina News, June 13, 1991: 5.

— Hawaii State Reapportionment Commission to hold hearing, Lahaina News, June 20, 1991: 3.

— James "Mac" Lowson to propose alternate redistricting plan, Lahaina News, June 27, 1991: 1.

— residents criticize redistricting plan, Lahaina News, July 4, 1991: 1,7.

— Maui County Republican Party to meet, Lahaina News, July 4, 1991: 3.

— Coalition for Auto Insurance Reform lobbying for reduced car insurance premiums, Lahaina News, July 4, 1991: 6,7.

— James Lowson, vice chair of Maui Advisory Committee. criticizes redistricting law, Lahaina News, July 25, 1991: 2,4.

— Republican Party objects to Russell Blair from becoming state Senator due to reapportionment, Lahaina News, November 7, 1991: 1,9.

— Maui County Charter Commission considering replacing office of the mayor with appointed city manager., Lahaina News, November 14, 1991: 1.

— lieutenant governor Ben Cayetano asked by Republican Party to void appointment of senators not chosen by voters due to reapportionment, Lahaina News, January 2, 1992: 1.

— lieutenant governor Ben Cayetano responds to request to prevent Russell Blair from assuming senatorial seat, Lahaina News, January 9, 1992: 2.

— legislative schedule printed, Lahaina News, January 16, 1992: 4.

— Senate and House Directories for Hawaii State Legislature, Lahaina News, January 23, 1992: 2,3.

— Foster Hull and Leina'ala Teruya Drummond declare as Republican candidates, Lahaina News, February 13, 1992: 3.

— funds from legislature limited this year, Lahaina News, February 20, 1992: 3.

— expect abortion to be an issue in upcoming election, Lahaina News, April 30, 1992: 1.

— legislature approves funds for West Maui projects, Lahaina News, May 7, 1992: 1,6.

— delegates selected for national Democratic Convention, Lahaina News, July 2, 1992: 4.

— upcoming election discussed, Lahaina News, July 9, 1992: 8.

— candidates featured, Lahaina News, July 23, 1992: 12.

— county studies about Lahaina remain unimplemented, Lahaina News, August 13, 1992: 1,3.

— Kihei Community Association to sponsors candidate meeting, Lahaina News, August 13, 1992: 9.

— forum to be held for District 11 candidates, Lahaina News, September 10, 1992: 11.

— primary election to take place, Lahaina News, September 17, 1992: 3.

— candidates for House District 11 discuss education, Lahaina News, September 17, 1992: 7.

— results of primaries, Lahaina News, September 24, 1992: 2.

— West Maui Taxpayers Association to hold candidate forum, Lahaina News, October 8, 1992: 2.

— candidates forum to be held in West Maui, Lahaina News, October 15, 1992: 3.

— candidates discuss issues at forum, Lahaina News, October 22, 1992: 3.

— general election to be held next week, Lahaina News, October 29, 1992: 3.

— meet the candidates event to take place Upcountry, Lahaina News, October 29, 1992: 4.

— Hawaiian Cablevision to offer free shows to support Bill Clinton's inauguration, Lahaina News, January 14, 1993: 12.

— directory of Senators and Representatives, Lahaina News, January 28, 1993: 11.

— Maui legislators split on Governor John Waihee's decision to order special session of state Legislature, Lahaina News, July 8, 1993: 1.

— Hawaii Federation of Democratic Women publishing cookbook, Lahaina News, September 23, 1993: 3.

— West Maui lawmakers meet with residents prior to 1994 session, Lahaina News, January 13, 1994: 1,2.

— state and insurance companies at odds over proposed insurance bill, Lahaina News, April 28, 1994: 2.

— funding for improvements to Princess Nahienaena Elementary School approved, Lahaina News, May 5, 1994: 1.

— Roz Baker and Mike White to offer legislative update, Lahaina News, May 5, 1994: 2.

— community forum with Roz Baker and Mike White held, Lahaina News, May 19, 1994: 1,20.

— Roz Baker, Joe Tanaka, Joe Souki, and Avery Chumbley to hold forum, Lahaina News, May 19, 1994: 6.

— legislature criticized for eliminating position of deputy director of environmental health, Lahaina News, May 26, 1994: 1,20.

— update on candidates, Lahaina News, June 9, 1994: 6.

— update on candidates, Lahaina News, June 30, 1994: 4.

— Rock the Vote committee hoping to sign up voters, Lahaina News, July 7, 1994: 4.

— businesses support "Rock the Vote", Lahaina News, July 14, 1994: 12,13.

— update on status of local candidates, Lahaina News, July 14, 1994: 6.

— Maui County attempting to increase voter participation, Lahaina News, July 14, 1994: 6.

— importance of voting discussed, Lahaina News, July 28, 1994: 3.

— Roz Baker to sit on education committee, Lahaina News, July 28, 1994: 4.

— "Make Kids Count in '94" to hold candidates forum, Lahaina News, August 18, 1994: 5.

— race between Roz Baker and Jan Yagi Buen detailed, Lahaina News, September 8, 1994: 2.

— complaints over political signs received, Lahaina News, September 8, 1994: 2.

— candidates Suzanne Radcliffe and Chris Halford left off the ballots, Lahaina News, September 15, 1994: 1,4.

— impact of economy of voter turnout discussed by Leroy Laney of First Hawaiian Bank, Lahaina News, September 15, 1994: 4.

— overview of candidates, Lahaina News, September 15, 1994: supplement1,supplement2,supplement3,supplement4.

— precinct officials complain of campaigning too close to polling sites, Lahaina News, September 22, 1994: 1.

— Maui County Council of Community Associations to hold candidate forum, Lahaina News, September 29, 1994: 5.

— Maui Chamber of Commerce to host candidate forum, Lahaina News, October 6, 1994: 7.

— primary candidates call for election reform, Lahaina News, October 13, 1994: 1,8.

— Maui Chamber of Commerce to host candidate forum, Lahaina News, October 13, 1994: 15.

— West Maui Taxpayers Association to hold candidates forum, Lahaina News, October 13, 1994: 4.

— West Maui Taxpayers Association and Maui Chamber of Commerce to hold second candidate's forum, Lahaina News, November 3, 1994: 4.

— analysis of voters, Lahaina News, November 17, 1994: 1.

— update on status of bills, Lahaina News, March 9, 1995: 1,16.

— updates on legislative session, Lahaina News, March 30, 1995: 3.

— election 2000 updates, Lahaina News, July 27, 2000: 8.

— candidate forum to be held at Old Lahaina Courthouse, Lahaina News, August 3, 2000: 1.

— LahainaTown Action Committee to hold candidates forum, Lahaina News, August 10, 2000: 1.

— summary of upcoming elections, Lahaina News, August 10, 2000: 1,15.

— battle for Lana'i seat on the Maui County Council featured, Lahaina News, August 10, 2000: 3.

— deadline to register to vote soon, Lahaina News, August 17, 2000: 1.

— absentee ballots requests available, Lahaina News, August 17, 2000: 3.

— Akaku: Maui Community Television to host "Talk Politics", Lahaina News, August 24, 2000: 3.

— election 2000 updates, Lahaina News, August 31, 2000: 8.

— special election to be held for seats on the Office of Hawaiian Affairs board of trustees, Lahaina News, September 14, 2000: 3.

— West Maui Taxpayers Association to host "Candidates Night 2000", Lahaina News, September 28, 2000: 3.

— West Maui Taxpayers Association held "Candidates Night 2000", Lahaina News, October 12, 2000: 1,24.

— Board of Education contest featured, Lahaina News, October 12, 2000: 6.

— candidates for State House Representative, District 8, Lahaina News, October 26, 2000: 21.

— candidates for State House Representative, District 7, Lahaina News, October 26, 2000: 22.

— candidates for Board of Education, Lahaina News, October 26, 2000: 23,25.

— candidates for East Maui County Council, Lahaina News, November 2, 2000: 16.

— candidates for South Maui County Council, Lahaina News, November 2, 2000: 18.

— candidates for West Maui County Council, Lahaina News, November 2, 2000: 19.

— candidates for Wailuku-Waihee-Waikapu County Council, Lahaina News, November 2, 2000: 20.

— candidates for Lahaina County Council, Lahaina News, November 2, 2000: 21.

— candidates for Upcountry County Council Seat, Lahaina News, November 2, 2000: 22.

— candidates for Makawao-Haiku-Paia Council Seat, Lahaina News, November 2, 2000: 22.

— candidates for Kahului County Council Seat, Lahaina News, November 2, 2000: 23.

— Kalama Intermediate School student Jayson Nakashima is honorary Mayor for Day, Lahaina News, November 9, 2000: 11.

— Hawaiians to protest court case challenging Article XII of Hawaii State Constitution, Lahaina News, February 1, 2001: 1,22.

— calls for Hawaiian Constitution Convention , Lahaina News, April 12, 2001: 1,24.

— state Reapportionment Commission to meet, Lahaina News, September 27, 2001: 3.

— County offering deputy voter registrar training, Lahaina News, May 9, 2002: 2.

— candidate filing deadline approaching, Lahaina News, July 18, 2002: 2.

— West Maui Taxpayers Association to host candidates' forum, Lahaina News, September 12, 2002: 1,22.

— Roz Baker and Brian Blundell hold a community forum, Lahaina News, December 19, 2002: 1.

— lawmakers to investigate Child Protective Services, Lahaina News, July 31, 2003: 1,2.

POLITICS OF ECOLOGY [BOOK]

— book by James Ridgeway, reviewed, Lahaina Sun, December 16, 1970: 2.

POLLACK, WILLIAM [WRITER]

— author of "Real Boys" to lead training seminar, Lahaina News, October 3, 2002: 9.

POLLI'S ON THE BEACH [RESTAURANT]

— hires Vic Miller as general manager, Lahaina News, August 26, 1987: 3.

— sold to L.A. Gatsby, Inc., Lahaina News, October 31, 1990: 11.

— changes name to Margarita's Beach Cantina, Lahaina News, March 27, 1991: 9.

POLLOCK, KERRY [COMEDIAN]

— to perform at Warren and Annabelle's, Lahaina News, October 28, 1999: 16.

— to perform at Warren and Annabelle's magic club, Lahaina News, October 31, 2002: 24.

— to perform at Warren and Annabelle's magic club, Lahaina News, November 7, 2002: 20.

POLLUTION

— sources in West Maui sought, Lahaina Sun, November 18, 1970: 1.

— discussed by sugar plantations, Lahaina Sun, November 25, 1970: 4.

— water pollution discussed, Lahaina Sun, December 30, 1970: 6.

— discussed in opinion piece, Lahaina Sun, January 13, 1971: 7.

— discussed, Lahaina Sun, February 3, 1971: 4,5.

— cars example of pollution on Maui, Lahaina Sun, February 3, 1971: 5.

— surveillance of harbor pollution , Lahaina Sun, February 3, 1971: 5.

— problem of solid waste in Hawaii discussed, Lahaina Sun, February 3, 1971: 5.

— concern of Maui County's approach to pollution, Lahaina Sun, February 10, 1971: 2.

— agriculture described as major source of air pollution in Maui, Lahaina Sun, February 17, 1971: 1,5.

— Hearing on air quality conducted by the State Health Department, Lahaina Sun, March 10, 1971: 8.

— complaint of dust from Maui Concrete & Aggregates, Lahaina Sun, April 7, 1971: 4.

— situation in Kahului harbor discussed in editorial by Sam Goo, Lahaina Sun, April 14, 1971: 8.

— Warwick Armstrong speaks of its ongoing importance, Lahaina Sun, May 5, 1971: 5.

— plans to flush polluted water from Lahaina small boat harbor, Lahaina Sun, May 26, 1971: 2.

— water samples taken in Lahaina show high levels of fecal coliform, Lahaina Sun, May 26, 1971: 2.

— ban on phosphate soaps studied, Lahaina Sun, June 2, 1971: 1,8.

— brackish water released by Pioneer Mill, Lahaina Sun, June 23, 1971: 9.

— solid waste management techniques discussed, Lahaina Sun, June 30, 1971: 12.

— tests show dangerously high levels of fecal coliforms, Lahaina Sun, July 28, 1971: 10.

— smell from Pioneer Mill noted, Lahaina Sun, September 8, 1971: 5.

— oil spill in Kahului Harbor, Lahaina Sun, September 8, 1971: 5.

— Pioneer Mill's request to discharge waste water into the ocean postponed, Lahaina Sun, September 8, 1971: 5.

— State Health Department plans to issue decision on Pioneer's request to discharge waste water, Lahaina Sun, October 13, 1971: 15.

— smell from waste water should subside after sugar cane harvest completed, Lahaina Sun, November 17, 1971: 5.

— sugar cane companies impact less, Lahaina Sun, November 24, 1971: 11.

— Pioneer Mill given permission to discharge waste water into ocean, Lahaina Sun, November 24, 1971: 6.

— Maui Land & Pineapple to relocate an old dump away from the ocean, Lahaina Sun, December 8, 1971: 1.

— Richard Marland, the State's top environmental specialist, says there is no need for sugar companies to change their cane burning practices, Lahaina Sun, December 15, 1971: 1,8.

— environmental study underway for new power plant near Kealia Pond, Lahaina Sun, January 12, 1972: 1.

— new rules are a concern for sugar and pineapple industries, Lahaina Sun, January 19, 1972: 9.

— film on pollution in Kaneohe Bay to be shown by Lahaina Outdoor Circle , Lahaina Sun, March 8, 1972: 9.

— Maui Land & Pineapple seeks permit to discharge water into Kahului Harbor, Lahaina Sun, March 29, 1972: 4.

— Pioneer Mill waste water discussed, Lahaina Sun, May 24, 1972: 3.

— discussion of burning sugar cane, Lahaina Sun, June 7, 1972: 5.

— Pioneer Mill attempting to neutralize stench of settlement pond, Lahaina Sun, August 9, 1972: 12.

— concern over impact on tourism of waste water created by Pioneer Mill, Lahaina Sun, August 30, 1972: 17.

— Maui County priorities criticized, Lahaina Sun, November 8, 1972: 19.

— air pollution discussed, Lahaina Sun, November 8, 1972: 7.

— concern for noise pollution from jets flying over Wailuku and Kahului, Lahaina Sun, November 29, 1972: 12.

— rules controlling agricultural burning to be tightened, Lahaina Sun, January 3, 1973: 10.

— courthouse said to not be to blame for harbor pollution, Lahaina Sun, January 17, 1973: 7.

— issues with sewage by Mala wharf discussed, Lahaina Sun, February 7, 1973: 18,19.

— current and future sewage systems discussed, Lahaina Sun, February 28, 1973: 4,5.

— Makena beach clean-up planned, Lahaina Sun, March 28, 1973: 1.

— Environmental Protection Agency increases funding to fight water pollution in Hawaii, Lahaina Sun, April 25, 1973: 11.

— oil spill in Kahului, Lahaina Sun, May 30, 1973: 3.

— smaller garbage cans to replace large drums currently in use, Lahaina Sun, June 6, 1973: 19.

— State Department of Health seeking input, Lahaina Sun, June 20, 1973: 3.

— changes in air pollution regulations will improve air quality, Lahaina Sun, June 27, 1973: 12,13.

— junk cars removed, Lahaina News, May 1, 1980: 14.

— abandon boats in West Maui discussed, Lahaina News, August 1, 1980: 3.

— police paying more attention to highway littering, Lahaina News, October 15, 1980: 4.

— police cracking down on litter, Lahaina News, January 1, 1981: 1.

— Maui County plans to produce electricity from refuse, Lahaina News, February 15, 1982: 8.

— plans to produce electricity from refuse moves ahead, Lahaina News, April 15, 1982: 8.

— Mary County exploring ways to convert trash to energy, Lahaina News, February 15, 1983: 6.

— abandoned cars an issue in Maui, Lahaina News, July 1, 1983: 7.

— editorial criticizing pollution in Hawaii, Lahaina News, August 1, 1983: 2.

— mysterious gas reported on Front Street, Lahaina News, August 15, 1983: 3.

— on Maui, Lahaina News, August 31, 1983: 2,7,8,9,10.

— discussed in feature article, Lahaina News, September 7, 1983: 7,8,9,10.

— air quality tested in Lahaina, Lahaina News, September 14, 1983: 7.

— Citizens for a Healthy Environment (CHEM) hold meeting at Lahaina Civic Center, Lahaina News, September 21, 1983: 5,6.

— EBD [pesticide], used on pineapples, banned by the EPA, Lahaina News, October 5, 1983: 14.

— editorial concerning raw sewage off Ka'anapali, Lahaina News, October 12, 1983: 2.

— pond at Pioneer Mill tested, Lahaina News, October 12, 1983: 4.

— landslide dirties Lahaina water supply, Lahaina News, October 19, 1983: 5,6.

— more sewage spills in Ka'anapali, Lahaina News, October 26, 1983: 3.

— open residential burning banned, Lahaina News, October 26, 1983: 5.

— Pioneer Mill apologizes for smoke pollution from cane burning, Lahaina News, November 2, 1983: 5.

— pesticide DBCP may be banned, Lahaina News, November 23, 1983: 16.

— underground fire at Olowalu dump reported, Lahaina News, December 14, 1983: 7.

— PBCP ban is delayed by the FDA, Lahaina News, January 11, 1984: 14.

— trash plan offered, Lahaina News, February 1, 1984: 7.

— sewage spilled off Ka'anapali Golf Course, Lahaina News, May 2, 1984: 5.

— abandoned cars and other junk in Lahaina, Lahaina News, May 9, 1984: 7,8,9.

— editorial on responses to story on abandoned vehicles, Lahaina News, May 16, 1984: 2.

— litter campaign to begin, Lahaina News, February 6, 1985: 3.

— litter campaign detailed, Lahaina News, February 13, 1985: 1.

— editorial on pesticides found in wells, Lahaina News, March 20, 1985: 2.

— community clean-up day set for April 27, Lahaina News, April 17, 1985: 3.

— editorial supporting banning of DBCP, Lahaina News, April 24, 1985: 2.

— Maui clean-up day set for April 27, Lahaina News, April 24, 1985: 20.

— editorial challenging finding of Department of Agriculture on its failure to monitor pesticide use, Lahaina News, May 8, 1985: 2.

— editorial opposing government's plan to spray paraquat to eradicate marijuana, Lahaina News, July 10, 1985: 2.

— Community Work Day set for July 27, Lahaina News, July 10, 1985: 3.

— meeting of Safe Solutions group opposing pesticides, Lahaina News, July 31, 1985: 7.

— pesticide paraquat under scrutiny by federal Drug Enforcement Administration, Lahaina News, August 7, 1985: 1,9.

— "Get the Drift and Bag it" set for October 20, Lahaina News, October 9, 1985: 8.

— federal Environmental Protection Agency asked to help solve odor from Lahaina sewage treatment plant, Lahaina News, October 23, 1985: 3.

— results of beach clean-up reported, Lahaina News, November 6, 1985: 3.

— community work day to be held November 23, Lahaina News, November 20, 1985: 11.

— sewage spill in Ka'anapali Golf Course lagoon, Lahaina News, December 25, 1985: 3.

— mayor Tavares proposes plan, Lahaina News, March 5, 1986: 1.

— editorial on mayor's interest in sewage, Lahaina News, March 5, 1986: 2.

— sewage hookup now available at Napili-Honokowai, Lahaina News, March 5, 1986: 3.

— Jim Caslin finds WWII unexploded mine while diving for lobsters, Lahaina News, April 2, 1986: 1.

— editorial asking for new litter laws, Lahaina News, May 14, 1986: 2.

— buy-back program for abandoned cars begins, Lahaina News, January 16, 1992: 5.

— vehicle buy-back program successful, Lahaina News, March 19, 1992: 3.

— DBCP found in well in Napili, Lahaina News, March 26, 1992: 4.

— fears dumping will increase once Makani Landfill closes, Lahaina News, April 2, 1992: 6.

— injection wells approved, Lahaina News, April 9, 1992: 1,13.

— Olowalu transfer station delayed, Lahaina News, April 16, 1992: 1.

— phone books to be recycled, Lahaina News, May 28, 1992: 3.

— motor oil drop-off program continues, Lahaina News, May 28, 1992: 7.

— wastewater spilled at Hawaiian Homes Pump Station, Lahaina News, May 28, 1992: 9.

— Maui County claims to not own polluted ditch at Honokowai Stream, Lahaina News, June 25, 1992: 2.

— State puts injection wells on hold, Lahaina News, June 25, 1992: 2.

— Olowalu landfill closure delayed, Lahaina News, July 2, 1992: 1.

— annual highway cleanup to be held, Lahaina News, July 9, 1992: 4.

— Ma'alaea Community Association to respond to trash problem, Lahaina News, July 23, 1992: 10.

— Algae Bloom Task Force expected to issue report, Lahaina News, July 30, 1992: 3.

— closure of Olowalu landfill leads to new drop off facility, Lahaina News, July 30, 1992: 3.

— freshwater algae blocks resident's toilet and sink, Lahaina News, July 30, 1992: 4.

— Maui County plans to reuse Kihei effluent, Lahaina News, July 30, 1992: 6,7.

— Kihei Recycling Center to re-open, Lahaina News, August 27, 1992: 13.

— debris problem in Kahoma Stream flood control project to be addressed, Lahaina News, September 10, 1992: 3.

— ocean clean-up planned, Lahaina News, September 24, 1992: 3.

— Maui County Recycling Coordinator Dr. Hana Steel updates on recycling, Lahaina News, September 24, 1992: 4.

— Get the Drift and Bag It to be held, Lahaina News, September 24, 1992: 6.

— pollution studies for West Maui's near shore waters, Lahaina News, November 12, 1992: 1,2.

— call for state action to keep shores clean, Lahaina News, November 12, 1992: 2.

— Olowalu landfill closes, Lahaina News, December 17, 1992: 1.

— solution needed for oil dumping in Lahaina Harbor, Lahaina News, December 17, 1992: 28.

— sewage spill reported, Lahaina News, January 7, 1993: 4.

— State House Speaker Joe Souki supports bill to increase pressure to remove algae, Lahaina News, January 21, 1993: 1.

— algae study nears completion, Lahaina News, January 21, 1993: 1.

— State Senator Russell Blair calls for solution to algae problem, Lahaina News, January 21, 1993: 10.

— State Department of Health to study algae, Lahaina News, January 28, 1993: 1.

— sewage spill at Kamaole Beach Park II, Lahaina News, January 28, 1993: 10.

— Kahana Gateway Shopping Center becomes recycling drop off point, Lahaina News, January 28, 1993: 4.

— water at Kanaha intake is clearing, Lahaina News, February 4, 1993: 1.

— Mark Percell claims algae removal bill has defects, Lahaina News, February 4, 1993: 2.

— sewage spills into Kapunakea Drainage Ditch, Lahaina News, February 4, 1993: 3.

— Maui likely to get fined for sewage issues, Lahaina News, February 11, 1993: 1,3.

— panel sponsored by Sierra Club to discuss algae issues, Lahaina News, February 11, 1993: 7.

— Department of Public Works to hold meeting to discuss wastewater, Lahaina News, February 18, 1993: 8.

— County and state officials to discuss algae, Lahaina News, March 4, 1993: 3.

— algae cleanup bill dies in committee, Lahaina News, March 11, 1993: 2.

— Public Works Department to survey condominiums about presence of algae , Lahaina News, March 11, 1993: 3.

— Rick Reed introduces resolution to clean algae from beaches, Lahaina News, March 25, 1993: 3.

— Kihei Community Association supports addressing algae issues, Lahaina News, April 1, 1993: 6.

— county report calls for increased recycling, Lahaina News, April 8, 1993: 1.

— drainage plan for development to send runoff into Kaopala Bay, Lahaina News, April 15, 1993: 1.

— wastewater pump stations improved, Lahaina News, April 15, 1993: 4.

— seaweed accumulation survey coming sent to hotels, condominiums, and apartments, Lahaina News, April 29, 1993: 2,3.

— muddy waters seen near Lahaina Broiler, Lahaina News, May 13, 1993: 3.

— Kihei Community Association addresses, Lahaina News, May 20, 1993: 4.

— Environmental Protection Agency continues to work on algae growth, Lahaina News, May 27, 1993: 1.

— algae meeting to be held by Kihei Community Association, Lahaina News, May 27, 1993: 5.

— phone books to be recycled, Lahaina News, June 3, 1993: 3.

— Tetra Tech Inc. begins dye test to determine fate of effluent from injection wells, Lahaina News, July 1, 1993: 3.

— algae cleanup hampered by lack of beach access, Lahaina News, July 1, 1993: 6.

— Eve Clute calls phosphorus as key to algae growth, Lahaina News, July 8, 1993: 3.

— Olowalu landfill almost closed, Lahaina News, August 19, 1993: 4.

— residents seek state probe of Kaopala Bay, Lahaina News, August 26, 1993: 1.

— wastewater spilled at Lahaina Wastewater Treatment Facility, Lahaina News, August 26, 1993: 4.

— deputy director of the Department of Health Bruce Anderson wants larger ocean study, Lahaina News, September 2, 1993: 1,12.

— resort managers say silt near coastal waters drawing visitor complaints, Lahaina News, September 9, 1993: 1.

— concern expressed for agricultural run-off, Lahaina News, September 16, 1993: 3.

— Maui Sea Kayaking Club to participate in "Get the Drift and Bag It", Lahaina News, October 14, 1993: 7.

— Eve Clute receives grant to study algae, Lahaina News, November 4, 1993: 3.

— Menehune Shores to remove algae from beaches, Lahaina News, November 4, 1993: 6.

— Hawaii Materials Exchange to encourage reuse of material, Lahaina News, November 18, 1993: 6.

— trash a top health concern in Lahaina, Lahaina News, December 9, 1993: 1,12.

— Hazardous Waste operations and Emergency Response Refresher Training Course to be held, Lahaina News, January 6, 1994: 5.

— cost to clean beaches estimated at $1 million, Lahaina News, February 3, 1994: 1.

— community meeting to be held on runoff and soil erosion in West Maui, Lahaina News, February 3, 1994: 4.

— runoff and soil erosion are concerns, Lahaina News, February 17, 1994: 3.

— state supporting recycling, Lahaina News, July 9, 1998: 12.

— "Litter Bugs Me" to be held, Lahaina News, July 16, 1998: 1.

— large appliance pick-up to be held, Lahaina News, August 27, 1998: 9.

— "Get the Drift and Bag It" to be held, Lahaina News, September 10, 1998: 18.

— pesticide workshop to be held, Lahaina News, March 25, 1999: 13.

— Environmental Protection Agency warns that injection well flow may increase, Lahaina News, April 15, 1999: 1,16.

— Pioneer Mill taking steps to control dust, Lahaina News, June 24, 1999: 1.

— landfill fee enacted, Lahaina News, June 24, 1999: 11.

— "Litter Bugs Me" to be held by Community Work Day Program, Lahaina News, July 15, 1999: 1.

— Pioneer Mill trying to reduce dust at Puʻukoliʻi, Lahaina News, August 12, 1999: 3.

— appliances to be recycled, Lahaina News, September 2, 1999: 15.

— water wells in Napili and Honokahua to be cleaned as a result of a legal settlement , Lahaina News, September 9, 1999: 1,16.

— American Lung Association to hold seminar on indoor air quality, Lahaina News, September 9, 1999: 13.

— "Get the Drift and Bag It" planned, Lahaina News, September 9, 1999: 5.

— drivers find unusual junk during cleanup during Get the Drift and Bag It, Lahaina News, September 23, 1999: 1.

— vice president of Kaʻanapali Estate Coffee Kimo Falconer discusses terrace system in former sugar lands, Lahaina News, November 11, 1999: 1,3.

— Amnesty Days at the dump, Lahaina News, December 30, 1999: 15.

— "Restaurant Waste Minimization and Pollution Prevention Training" to be held, Lahaina News, April 27, 2000: 11.

— county to pick-up unwanted appliances, Lahaina News, September 14, 2000: 19.

— telephone books to be recycled, Lahaina News, October 12, 2000: 19.

— Hawaii Pollution Prevention Information Project attempts to reduce, Lahaina News, November 9, 2000: 1,12.

— wastewater spilled along Lahainaluna Road, Lahaina News, December 14, 2000: 8.

— Central Maui Landfill and Olowalu Transfer Station to hold "Amnesty Day", Lahaina News, March 15, 2001: 20.

— Amfac/JMB responds to resident concern for dust, Lahaina News, April 26, 2001: 1,22.

— Community Work Day to hold "Drop and Swap" paint exchange, Lahaina News, April 26, 2001: 2.

— according to Pacific Whale Foundation, cigarette butts seen as problem on Maui beaches, Lahaina News, June 21, 2001: 2.

— landfills to have free days on Sundays, Lahaina News, June 28, 2001: 5.

— county to pick-up unwanted appliances, Lahaina News, July 5, 2001: 5.

— algae creating problems, Lahaina News, July 26, 2001: 2.

— Mayor Apana announces that recycling will continue, Lahaina News, July 26, 2001: 8.

— free days to be held at landfills, Lahaina News, September 13, 2001: 16.

— Department of Public Works and Waste Management to collect hazardous waste, Lahaina News, September 20, 2001: 2.

— Department of Public Works and Waste Management to hold Household Hazardous Waste Drop-off Program, Lahaina News, October 18, 2001: 2.

— county to collect bulky trash items, Lahaina News, October 25, 2001: 3.

— Maui County to pick up bulky items, Lahaina News, November 29, 2001: 3.

— Maui Marriott Resort and Ocean Club, Maui Ocean Center, and Island Scuba collect trash from the beach and reefs of Kaʻanapali, Lahaina News, December 13, 2001: 8.

— Great Hawaii Cleanup to be held, Lahaina News, April 25, 2002: 5.

— Community Work Day to hold "Litter Bugs Me", Lahaina News, July 11, 2002: 3.

POLMAR, JAY

— to offer classes on speedreading at Maui Community College, Lahaina News, November 2, 1988: 11.

POLO IN THE COUNTRY

— to be held at Olinda Outdoor Polo Field, Lahaina News, November 6, 1997: 16.

POLYNESIAN HAWAIIANS [ORGANIZATION]

— fundraising luau at Aloha Restaurant in Kahului, Lahaina Sun, October 27, 1971: 12.

POLYNESIAN INVESTMENT COMPANY [BUSINESS]

— plan to build 52-unit condominium near Honokowai and Napili, Lahaina Sun, June 23, 1971: 3.

POLYNESIAN PRAISE [MUSICAL GROUP]

— to perform at Kaʻahumanu Center, Lahaina News, August 15, 1991: 15.

POLYNESIAN SHORES [CONDOMINIUM]

— featured, Lahaina News, July 4, 1984: 19.

POMARE PROPERTIES CORPORATION [BUSINESS]

— chairman Jim Romig to speak to LahainaTown Action Committee, Lahaina News, January 25, 1989: 1.

— purchases lease to shopping center from Harry Weinberg, Lahaina News, May 24, 1989: 9.

— renamed to Romig Properties Corporation, Lahaina News, August 27, 1992: 10.

POMEGRANATES IN THE SUN

— now represented by Grapevine Productions, Lahaina News, January 23, 1992: 12.

POMERANTZ, RENNIE [ARTIST]

— featured at Lahaina Arts Society Upstairs Gallery, Lahaina News, July 6, 1988: 11.

PONO PACIFIC LAND MANAGEMENT

— seeking participants for Youth Conservation Corps 2001 summer program, Lahaina News, April 19, 2001: 2.

PONTANILLA, JOSEPH

— named Maui island manager at GTE Hawaiian Tel, Lahaina News, May 6, 1993: 9.

— named to Maui island manager of GTE Hawaiian Tel, Lahaina News, May 20, 1993: 7.

POOKELA [MUSICAL GROUP]

— to headline Valentine's Day show, Lahaina News, February 13, 1992: 18.

POʻOKELA CHURCH

— to hold bazaar, Lahaina News, September 5, 1996: 18.

— to hold bazaar, Lahaina News, August 28, 1997: 11.

— to hold bazaar, Lahaina News, September 4, 1997: 16.

POʻOKELA PROGRAM

— Lahainaluna High School mentoring program helps students, Lahaina News, September 13, 2001: 1,20.

POPA CHUBBY BAND [MUSICAL GROUP]

— to perform, Lahaina News, September 11, 1997: 17.

POPDAN, TOM

— Lahainaluna High School swim coach discusses win, Lahaina News, February 21, 2002: 13.

POPE, DEBORAH

— of Hawaii Museums Association to talk at Bailey House Museum, Lahaina News, September 3, 1998: 21.

— to present on "Cultural Preservation and Tourism: Strange Bedfellows or Natural Partners", Lahaina News, September 10, 1998: 20.

POPE, LAURA
— Scholar/Athlete of the Week, Lahaina News, January 29, 1998: 6.

POPPINS, PENGUINS, PIGS—A CHILDREN'S PLAY BY THE SHOWBIZ KIDS [PLAY]
— to be performed at Lahaina Cannery Mall, Lahaina News, May 23, 2002: 17.

POPULATION
— of Maui County, Lahaina Sun, December 23, 1970: 8.
— comparison of population of Maui County towns, 1960 and 1970, Lahaina Sun, December 23, 1970: 8.
— Maui county projected to have 52,000 residents by 1977, Lahaina Sun, January 31, 1973: 11.
— Hawaii's population nearing 1 million, Lahaina News, December 1, 1980: 10.
— racial diversity in Hawaii described, Lahaina News, January 15, 1981: 10.
— demographic changes noted, Lahaina News, May 1, 1982: 6.
— growing in Hawaii, Lahaina News, November 15, 1982: 11.
— race and longevity discussed, Lahaina News, January 1, 1983: 3.
— increased on Maui by 8.4 percent from 1980 to 1982, Lahaina News, July 11, 1984: 3.

POQUETTE, JIM
— catches 875-pound marling, Lahaina News, April 17, 1985: 20.

PORNOGRAPHY
— Alex de Renzy [director] visits Lahaina, Lahaina Sun, December 29, 1971: 15.
— editorial opposing pornography but opposing police crackdown, Lahaina News, October 23, 1985: 2.
— editorial on politics of, Lahaina News, July 16, 1986: 2.

PORTER, DAVID
— BYU coach to lead tennis clinic, Lahaina News, January 9, 2003: 12.

PORTER, LISA [MUSICIAN]
— to hold release party for CD "Lisa", Lahaina News, December 9, 1999: 22.
— harpist performs, Lahaina News, December 27, 2001: 16.

PORTUGAL
— Somos Amigos festival to celebrate Portuguese heritage, Lahaina News, September 14, 2000: 17.

PORTUGUESE CHAMBER OF COMMERCE
— awards scholarships to Maui County students, Lahaina News, May 23, 1984: 3.

POST, JILL
— discusses possible eviction of Maui Community Theatre from Iao Theatre, Lahaina News, May 18, 1988: 8.

POST OFFICE
— two employees retire after 90 years, Lahaina Sun, December 16, 1970: 6.
— amount of junk mail criticized, Lahaina Sun, February 21, 1973: 9.
— new Lahaina post office opens, Lahaina News, November 1, 1980: 15.
— mailing dates for holidays set, Lahaina News, November 6, 1985: 3.
— changes hours, Lahaina News, February 17, 1988: 3.
— to change Saturday hours, Lahaina News, August 9, 1989: 3.
— expands hours for Christmas, Lahaina News, December 13, 1989: 4.
— to extend hours, Lahaina News, December 12, 1990: 4.
— holiday hours, Lahaina News, December 3, 1992: 3.
— may move, Lahaina News, February 13, 1997: 1.
— plans to relocate discussed, Lahaina News, February 27, 1997: 1.
— planning new downtown office, Lahaina News, February 19, 1998: 1,16.
— Jane Agawa retires from, Lahaina News, November 7, 2002: 1.

POSTERS UNLIMITED [BUSINESS]
— opening at Kahana Gateway Shopping Center, Lahaina News, November 12, 1992: 12.
— hosting keiki fingerpainting and stencil printing, Lahaina News, December 30, 1993: 11.

POTHAST, LARRY
— to conduct seminar on association management, Lahaina News, July 2, 1992: 19.

POTHOLES
— patched, Lahaina Sun, January 27, 1971: 1.
— see also infrastructure

POTTHOFF, SUE
— promoted at Faught & Miyahsiro Advertising, Lahaina News, February 25, 1987: 3.

POTTS, DAMIAN
— Lahainaluna High School student finishes second in state's cross country meet, Lahaina News, November 28, 1990: 7,20.
— Lahainaluna High School student cross country champ, Lahaina News, December 5, 1991: 18.

POTTS, LES
— new song, Lahaina Times, August, 1980 volume 4 number 7: 1.

POTTS, NORMA JEAN [ARTIST]
— to exhibit at Lahaina Arts Society, Lahaina News, September 12, 2002: 21.

POULSON, ARITA
— low bidder on proposed school building in Kihei, Lahaina News, May 28, 1992: 12.

POULSON, SALLY [RESIDENT]
— met with mayor Cravalho regarding water and telephone service, Lahaina Sun, December 9, 1970: 1.

POUND 4 POUND [MUSICAL GROUP]
— to perform at "A Taste of Lahaina", Lahaina News, September 2, 1999: 18.

POWELL, PETER AND MADELINE [ARTISTS]
— to exhibit at Viewpoints Gallery, Lahaina News, January 9, 1991: 8.

POWER HEALTH CENTER OF MAUI
— to open, Lahaina News, March 29, 1989: 14.
— reviewed, Lahaina News, April 5, 1989: 2.
— offering free hypnosis demonstration, Lahaina News, June 7, 1989: 2.

POWER PLANT
— proposed plant in Ma'alaea discussed, Lahaina Sun, May 19, 1971: 1,6.
— Ma'alaea plant opposed in public meeting, Lahaina Sun, May 26, 1971: 1,8.
— plant near Kealia Pond opposed at hearing, Lahaina Sun, June 9, 1971: 6.
— ruling on Ma'alaea plant expected July 6, Lahaina Sun, June 23, 1971: 1.
— Maui County Council asking for caution, Lahaina Sun, June 30, 1971: 12.
— Maui Chamber of Commerce supports building near Ma'alaea, Lahaina Sun, July 7, 1971: 3.
— diesel generator approved for location near Kealia Pond, Lahaina Sun, July 14, 1971: 4.
— acreage of power plant reduced, Lahaina Sun, July 21, 1971: 1,12.
— criticism of in Ma'alaea, Lahaina Sun, September 1, 1971: 2.
— electric generating station near Kealia Pond nears completion, Lahaina Sun, December 8, 1971: 8.
— environmental study underway for new power plant near Kealia Pond, Lahaina Sun, January 12, 1972: 1.

POWER POLES
— detract from external appearance of Pub Tiki, Lahaina Sun, May 31, 1972: 19.

POWER, STEVEN [ARTIST]
— to visit Wyland Galleries, Lahaina News, April 25, 2002: 16.

POWERFUL WOMEN OF MAUI
— to hold networking event, Lahaina News, May 27, 1987: 3.
— hosting seminar on successful relationships, Lahaina News, July 8, 1987: 16.
— to hold breakfasts at Maui Beach Hotel, Lahaina News, July 8, 1987: 3.

POWERHOUSE BAR AND GRILL [RESTAURANT]
— reviewed, Lahaina News, September 5, 1991: 15,16.
— offering happy hour for Halloween, Lahaina News, October 31, 1991: 13.

POWERS, BARBARA
— appointed store manager for Hilo Hatties, Lahaina News, December 23, 1999: 13.

POWERS, BEVERLY
— career from actress to minister detailed, Lahaina News, March 15, 1989: 2.
— appointed pastor at Sheraton Hotel, Lahaina News, April 10, 1991: 4.

POWERS, NORMAN [DANCER]
— offers dancing lessons at Dance Time of Hawaii, Lahaina News, October 28, 1999: 15.

POWERS, PATRICK
— named account manager for Sprint Hawaii, Lahaina News, November 4, 1999: 11.

PR MAUI [BUSINESS]
— representing reggae group "Common Sense", Lahaina News, March 19, 1992: 11.

PRADZYNSKI, THOMAS [ARTIST]
— to exhibit at Dolphin Galleries, Lahaina News, August 8, 2002: 16.

PRAVER, TORI
— Scholar/Athlete of the Week, Lahaina News, March 20, 2003: 12.

PRAYER DAY OBSERVANCE
— encouraged by Mayor Hannibal Tavares, Lahaina News, April 26, 1989: 12.

PRAYER RAVE
— concert to be held, Lahaina News, December 17, 1998: 24.

PRAZAK STRING QUARTET [MUSICAL GROUP]
— to perform at St. Anthony's Church Center, Lahaina News, January 29, 1986: 3.

PRE-SCHOOL
— value of, Lahaina News, May 17, 1989: 1.

PREBLE, DUANE [ARTIST]
— to offer art workshops for young students, Lahaina News, April 24, 1985: 7.

PREGILL, CAROL
— new executive director of the Retail Merchants of Hawaii, Lahaina News, August 24, 2000: 14.

PRELLER, ARNO
— Christian Scientist to talk on "Health Care Through Prayer", Lahaina News, October 14, 1993: 7.

PREMIER VIDEO [BUSINESS]
— to open, Lahaina News, July 22, 1993: 8.

PREMIERE MORTGAGE [BUSINESS]
— opens, Lahaina News, November 25, 1999: 13.

PRESCHOOL AT KAPALUA
— to refurbish, Lahaina News, July 17, 2003: 6.

PRESCHOOL OPEN DOORS PROJECT
— accepting applications, Lahaina News, June 2, 1994: 3.

PRESCHOOL, THE
— Ron LaClergue donates money to, Lahaina News, February 3, 1994: 9.

PRESERVATION AWARDS
— nominations sought for, Lahaina News, January 16, 1985: 3.
— Maui Historical Society seeking nominations for, Lahaina News, March 7, 1996: 10.

PRESTON, BILLY [MUSICIAN]
— to perform at Casanova's, Lahaina News, July 18, 1990: 11.

PRESTON, MILTON
— organ recipient featured, Lahaina News, April 22, 1993: 4,16.

PRETZELMAKER [RESTAURANT]
— recently added shave ice to menu, Lahaina News, April 4, 2002: 18.

PREY, DICK [ARTIST]
— to exhibit "Notations and Re-illustrations", Lahaina News, January 14, 1999: 13.

PREY, RICHARD [ARTIST]
— exhibit of photography to be held at Territorial Savings and Loan Association, Lahaina News, May 23, 1991: 17.

PRICE, JONA-MARIE
— promoted to president of Christian Riese Lassen's publishing company, Lahaina News, October 31, 1990: 12.
— president of Galerie Lassen featured, Lahaina News, October 3, 1991: 3.

PRICE, WARREN
— Attorney General seeks reversal of judge's decision to allowed continued operation of thrillcrafts, Lahaina News, January 16, 1992: 1.

PRICECOSTCO [BUSINESS]
— see Costco

PRIDE, CHARLIE [MUSICIAN]
— to perform on Maui, Lahaina News, August 15, 1984: 12.
— upcoming performance, Lahaina News, October 31, 1984: 17.
— performance reviewed, Lahaina News, November 14, 1984: 17.

PRIMECO HAWAII [BUSINESS]
— expanding digital wireless network coverage, Lahaina News, February 12, 1998: 13.
— personnel changes, Lahaina News, July 16, 1998: 13.

PRIMECO HAWAII HEALTH AND FITNESS FAIR
— to be held, Lahaina News, May 21, 1998: 13.

PRIMITIVE MAN AND HIS ART [ART EXHIBIT]
— featuring New Guinea ancestral masks and statues, to be held, Lahaina News, February 12, 1986: 3.

PRINCE CLASSICS, THE [MUSICAL GROUP]
— to perform at Maui Prince Hotel, Lahaina News, December 19, 1991: 22.
— to perform at the Molokini Lounge at the Maui Prince Hotel, Lahaina News, January 30, 1992: 18.

PRINCE, CONNIE [ARTIST]
— to hold "Art is Fun" show at Lahaina Arts Society, Lahaina News, October 8, 1998: 16.

PRINCE COURT, THE [RESTAURANT]
— to hold wine tasting reception for Byron Vineyard and Winery, Lahaina News, February 20, 1991: 11.
— to hold wine tasking from Zilliken Winery of Germany, Lahaina News, August 29, 1991: 12.
— to feature wines from Zilliken Winery of Germany, Lahaina News, September 5, 1991: 18.
— to host Italian wine dinner, Lahaina News, June 11, 1992: 21.

PRINCE FAIRY FOOT [PLAY]
— performed by Baldwin Performing Arts Learning Center, Lahaina News, December 14, 1995: 15.

PRINCE, JORDAN
— boy survives harrowing sail on canoe, Lahaina News, May 18, 2000: 3.

PRINCE KUHIO DAY
— activities described, Lahaina News, March 25, 1987: 4.
— to be celebrated, Lahaina News, March 20, 1997: 17.

PRINCE, LORETTA
— reunited with sons after 14 years, Lahaina News, November 29, 1989: 2.

PRINCE, WILLIAM
— appointed director of finance and accounting at Kapalua Land Company, Lahaina News, January 30, 1991: 5.

PRINCESS NAHIENAENA ELEMENTARY SCHOOL
— seeking adult supervisors, Lahaina News, November 30, 1988: 3.
— Concerned Parents and Teachers of Princess Nahienaena School worried about walk to school, Lahaina News, February 15, 1989: 1.
— presenting workshop on social issues of youth, Lahaina News, December 26, 1990: 4.
— to host workshop on social issues of youth, Lahaina News, January 2, 1991: 4.
— implements Adopt-a-student program, Lahaina News, February 20, 1991: 3.
— student to participate in drug education program displaying art work, Lahaina News, May 8, 1991: 1.
— update on recent activities, Lahaina News, February 6, 1992: 7.
— delegation from testifies before state finance committee, Lahaina News, March 5, 1992: 6.
— wins Foodland's "Shop for a Better Education" banner contest., Lahaina News, March 12, 1992: 4.
— receives funds to plan joint cafeteria with Lahaina Intermediate School, Lahaina News, May 6, 1993: 1.
— honor roll announced, Lahaina News, January 6, 1994: 3.
— principal Sandra Shawhan-Royster featured, Lahaina News, April 28, 1994: 1,16.
— funding for improvements to approved, Lahaina News, May 5, 1994: 1.
— described, Lahaina News, August 25, 1994: 3.
— Senator Avery Chumbley says funding for new cafeteria still possible, Lahaina News, April 27, 1995: 5.
— new cafeteria to be built, Lahaina News, December 21, 1995: 6.
— offering preschool classes, Lahaina News, February 1, 1996: 4.
— celebrates Valentine's Day, Lahaina News, February 22, 1996: 4.
— new principal Edwina Wilson Snyder to hold public meeting, Lahaina News, April 4, 1996: 2.
— donates pennies to The Nature Conservancy, Lahaina News, May 9, 1996: 1,18.
— expresses thanks to supporters, Lahaina News, June 13, 1996: 5.
— PTA to meet, Lahaina News, December 12, 1996: 9.
— students earn high marks, Lahaina News, June 19, 1997: 2.
— funds released for cafeteria, Lahaina News, June 19, 1997: 2.
— to hold open house, Lahaina News, September 25, 1997: 16.
— receives grant from GTE Hawaiian Tel Phone Book Recycling Contest, Lahaina News, November 20, 1997: 2.
— to host "treecycling" event, Lahaina News, January 1, 1998: 1.
— to hold "treecycling" event, Lahaina News, January 8, 1998: 12.
— seeking reading buddies, Lahaina News, March 12, 1998: 18.
— to offer summer program, Lahaina News, April 2, 1998: 2.
— to offer Junior Achievement Program, Lahaina News, April 16, 1998: 11.
— playground equipment assembled at, Lahaina News, August 6, 1998: 19.
— receives state funds for new play court, Lahaina News, October 22, 1998: 15.
— to recycle Christmas trees, Lahaina News, December 24, 1998: 1.
— staggered schedule may be unfeasible, Lahaina News, March 25, 1999: 1.
— results of Poetry Festival, Lahaina News, March 25, 1999: 9.
— Kimo's Restaurant sponsoring "Educator of the Month" program, Lahaina News, May 6, 1999: 11.
— student Jason Bilog finalist at Hawaii State Geography Bee, Lahaina News, June 10, 1999: 15.
— PTA works to improve school, Lahaina News, September 30, 1999: 3.
— to recycle trees, Lahaina News, December 23, 1999: 7.
— to recycle trees, Lahaina News, December 30, 1999: 15.
— celebrates May Day, Lahaina News, May 11, 2000: 1.
— Kimo's Restaurant recognizes outstanding educators at, Lahaina News, May 25, 2000: 6.
— to host Hawaiian Immersion program, Lahaina News, June 29, 2000: 1,8.
— bookmobile to visit, Lahaina News, September 21, 2000: 21.
— Hawaiian Language Immersion Program to begin, Lahaina News, September 28, 2000: 1,14.
— bookmobile to visit, Lahaina News, September 28, 2000: 16.
— parents visit during open house, Lahaina News, October 12, 2000: 2.
— students volunteer at Toys for Tots, Lahaina News, December 21, 2000: 1,15.
— holds Poetry Festival, Lahaina News, March 15, 2001: 14.
— celebrates career of Principal Edwina Wilson Snyder, Lahaina News, June 7, 2001: 1,22.
— Kimo's restaurant honors educators of the month, Lahaina News, July 19, 2001: 18.
— Kaipo Miller becomes principal of, Lahaina News, August 2, 2001: 1,20.
— holds open house for parents, Lahaina News, September 27, 2001: 2.
— participates in "Phone Call to the Deep" scientific research expedition, Lahaina News, November 22, 2001: 17.
— workshops to prepare children for Kindergarten, Lahaina News, March 7, 2002: 1,2.
— held "Cafe U.S.A." annual breakfast program, Lahaina News, March 28, 2002: 3.
— mediators to patrol playgrounds of, Lahaina News, May 9, 2002: 1,20.
— librarian Marylyn Barboza featured, Lahaina News, May 16, 2002: 1,20.
— PTA to hold golf tournament to benefit, Lahaina News, October 3, 2002: 2.
— principal Kaipo Miller featured, Lahaina News, October 10, 2002: 1,20.
— golf tournament to support, Lahaina News, October 10, 2002: 13.
— considering modified calendar, Lahaina News, October 17, 2002: 1.
— PTA to hold "Tee it up for Technology" golf fundraiser, Lahaina News, October 17, 2002: 11.
— considering changes to calendar, Lahaina News, October 31, 2002: 1,30.
— Community-Based Management Council encouraging participation, Lahaina News, November 7, 2002: 1.
— not enough teachers vote to support change in school schedule, Lahaina News, December 5, 2002: 1,22.
— dedicates new playground, Lahaina News, February 6, 2003: 1,20.
— principal Marsha Nakamura reports on school, Lahaina News, February 13, 2003: 5.
— students held May Day Celebration, Lahaina News, June 12, 2003: 15.
— A+ Program available at, Lahaina News, August 7, 2003: 2.
— Parent Community Network Center (PCNC) featured, Lahaina News, August 21, 2003: 1.

PRINCETON REVIEW OF HAWAII
— helping students to prepare for SAT, Lahaina News, December 30, 1999: 15.

PRINCEVILLE AIRWAYS
— adding roundtrip flights between Honolulu and new Kapalua-West Maui Airport, Lahaina News, February 18, 1987: 10,11.
— raises fares, Lahaina News, October 28, 1987: 3.
— special fares for Hawaii residents, Lahaina News, February 24, 1988: 18.
— announces midnight flight between Honolulu and Kahului, Lahaina News, March 16, 1988: 15.
— renamed Aloha IslandAir, Inc., Lahaina News, June 22, 1988: 3.

PRINE, JOHN [MUSICIAN]
— to perform at Maui Arts and Cultural Center, Lahaina News, October 10, 2002: 17.
— to perform at Maui Arts and Cultural Center, Lahaina News, October 17, 2002: 21.

PRINTING
— history of printing in Hawaii discussed, Lahaina Sun, January 5, 1972: 14.
— history of printing in Hawaii described, Lahaina News, March 15, 1983: 7,8,9.

PRINTS PACIFIC
— presents workshops on people collecting Hawaiiana, Lahaina News, February 28, 1990: 3.

PRIOR, TIM
— new environmental health specialist for water, Lahaina Sun, May 26, 1971: 2.

PRISCILLA'S MAUI MAUI [BUSINESS]
— opens, Lahaina News, December 28, 1995: 10.

PRISON GATEHOUSE
— see Hale Paahao

PRITCHETT, DAVID
— promoted to head professional at Kapalua Village Course, Lahaina News, January 11, 1996: 6.

PRIVATE LIVES [PLAY]
— to be performed by Maui Community Theatre, Lahaina News, January 8, 1998: 12.
— comedy to be performed by Maui Community Theatre, Lahaina News, January 22, 1998: 12.
— to close, Lahaina News, February 5, 1998: 12.

PRM REALTY GROUP [BUSINESS]
— breaks ground on "Maluhia at Wailea" project, Lahaina News, October 26, 2000: 19.

PRO BOWL
— results detailed, Lahaina News, February 6, 1985: 4.
— held in Honolulu, Lahaina News, February 11, 1987: 1,6.
— to take place in Honolulu, Lahaina News, January 6, 1988: 12.
— photographs from, Lahaina News, February 17, 1988: 6.
— will remain in Hawaii for next five years, Lahaina News, December 31, 1992: 7.

PROCKETTE, ALLEN
— fundraiser held for, Lahaina News, April 23, 1998: 16.

PRODUCT LIABILITY TASK FORCE
— continues to grow, Lahaina News, November 29, 1989: 4.

PRODUCTS EXPO SHOW
— to be held, Lahaina News, June 25, 1992: 13,14,15.

PROFESSIONAL BOWLERS ASSOCIATION
— to host fundraiser for Big Brothers/Big Sisters, Lahaina News, November 23, 1988: 5.

PROFESSIONAL GOLF ASSOCIATION, ALOHA SECTION
— to play in tournament on Lana'i, Lahaina News, March 12, 1992: 9.

PROFESSIONAL GOLFERS ASSOCIATION (PGA)
— approves Kapalua International Tournament of Golf, Lahaina News, July 4, 1984: 6.

PROFESSIONAL SECRETARIES INTERNATIONAL, WEST MAUI CHAPTER
— No Ka Oi Chapter holds meeting at Sheraton Maui, Lahaina News, March 21, 1984: 5.
— to offer annual seminar, Lahaina News, January 20, 1988: 18.
— West Maui chapter forming, Lahaina News, June 27, 1990: 8.
— West Maui Chapter to meet, Lahaina News, October 24, 1990: 6.
— holds Executive Day's Luncheon, Lahaina News, November 21, 1990: 11.
— to meet, Lahaina News, November 28, 1990: 8.
— to hold general membership meeting, Lahaina News, January 30, 1991: 5.
— to hold general membership meeting, Lahaina News, February 27, 1991: 8.
— to offer seminar on standing up to public opinion, Lahaina News, April 17, 1991: 9.
— to meet, Lahaina News, May 30, 1991: 3.
— new officers installed, Lahaina News, August 15, 1991: 6.
— to hold car wash, Lahaina News, September 26, 1991: 6.
— Desiree Pagaduan named secretary of the year by the Maui No Ka Oi Chapter, Lahaina News, February 13, 1992: 13.
— new officers selected, Lahaina News, July 2, 1992: 18.
— new officers selected, Lahaina News, July 9, 1992: 13.
— to hold reception, Lahaina News, July 25, 1996: 13.
— to hold meeting, Lahaina News, September 19, 1996: 15.

PROFESSIONALL [BUSINESS]
— nail salon opens at Lahaina Cannery Mall, Lahaina News, June 24, 1999: 11.

PROJECT AWARE (AQUATIC WORLD AWARENESS, RESPONSIBILITY AND EDUCATION)
— to host Ocean Conservancy International Cleanup Day, Lahaina News, August 21, 2003: 2.

PROJECT BALLET THEATRE [TROUPE]
— to perform, Lahaina News, March 7, 2002: 17.
— to perform, Lahaina News, March 14, 2002: 16.

PROJECT BEACON (BILINGUAL EDUCATION AND CAREER OPPORTUNITIES FOR NEIGHBOR ISLANDS)
— grant supporting University of Hawai'i students received, Lahaina News, May 3, 2001: 2.

PROJECT GRADUATION
— Lahainaluna High School to participate in, Lahaina News, August 18, 1994: 1,2.
— receives donation from Lahaina Rotary Club, Lahaina News, April 6, 1995: 4.
— to hold planning meeting, Lahaina News, October 5, 1995: 4.
— Ho'olaule'a 97 to benefit , Lahaina News, November 6, 1997: 17.
— to hold informational meeting, Lahaina News, October 25, 2001: 2.
— to be held by Lahainaluna High School, Lahaina News, January 30, 2003: 1,20.

PROJECT IMPACT MAUI COUNTY
— discusses traffic issues, Lahaina News, February 1, 2001: 1,22.
— to focus on disaster planning, Lahaina News, April 26, 2001: 2.

PROJECT KAHO'OLAWE OHANA
— attempts to recover it described, Lahaina News, September 5, 1984: 7,8,9.
— attempts to recover it described, article continued from last issue, Lahaina News, September 12, 1984: 7,8,9.

PROJECT KAKO'O: SUPPORTIVE PARENTING
— volunteers sought for demonstration project, Lahaina News, June 18, 1998: 2.

PROJECT PO'OKELA
— celebrating 10th anniversary of tree planting ceremony, Lahaina News, September 5, 1996: 19.

PROJECT REEFKEEPER
— to conduct workshop on coral reefs, Lahaina News, July 15, 1993: 3.
— to host workshops on coral reef conservation, Lahaina News, July 21, 1994: 4.

PROJECT S.E.A.-LINK
— offering marine naturalist training to high school students, Lahaina News, April 12, 2001: 20.
— to hold "Dive In to Earth Day", Lahaina News, April 19, 2001: 14.
— recruiting divers for "Great American Fish Count 2001", Lahaina News, July 5, 2001: 1.
— organizing "Great American Fish Count 2001", Lahaina News, July 19, 2001: 17.
— offering "Coral Reef Ecology for Teachers" course, Lahaina News, November 1, 2001: 16.
— executive director Liz Foote to speak at Maui Ocean Center, Lahaina News, July 25, 2002: 21.
— to conduct reef evaluation, Lahaina News, July 10, 2003: 1,20.
— Trilogy Excursions supports Adopt-a-Reef Program, Lahaina News, October 2, 2003: 5.
— to conduct reef field survey, Lahaina News, October 9, 2003: 5.

PROJECT SAFE PLACE
— opens first site in West Maui, Lahaina News, December 10, 1986: 16.

PROMISES [DOCUMENTARY]
— to be shown at the Maui Arts and Cultural Center, Lahaina News, April 25, 2002: 17.

PROPANE
— being sold by Air Liquide America, Lahaina News, February 26, 1998: 11.

PROPERTY
— sale of land at Kahului Harbor announced, Lahaina Sun, October 20, 1971: 5.
— land difficult to purchase because of prices, Lahaina Sun, March 21, 1973: 6,7.
— Seibu Group of Japan purchases areas near Ulupalakua, Lahaina Sun, July 11, 1973: 3.
— land ownership as barrier to county project, Lahaina News, December 9, 1987: 1,17.
— dispute over shoreline in Ka'anapali holds up jurisdiction change, Lahaina News, July 20, 1988: 1,14.
— West Maui Taxpayers Association encourages discussion of leasehold, Lahaina News, April 6, 2000: 13.
— West Maui Taxpayers Association forms committee to pursue leasehold reform, Lahaina News, June 15, 2000: 9.
— leasehold issues featured, Lahaina News, July 27, 2000: 11.
— leasehold discussed, Lahaina News, September 7, 2000: 17.
— West Maui Taxpayers Association seeks input on leasehold issue, Lahaina News, October 19, 2000: 15.
— see also development, infrastructure, real estate

PROPST, EMMANUEL
— Scholar/Athlete of the Week, Lahaina News, November 15, 2001: 12.

PROSECUTING ATTORNEY'S OFFICE, COUNTY
— to be headed by Larry Butrick, Lahaina News, April 17, 1991: 7.

PROSTITUTION
— interview with a retired prostitute, Lahaina News, August 15, 1980: 3.

PROTECT KAHO'OLAWE OHANA
— trying to stop bombing of Kaho'olawe , Lahaina News, May 18, 1988: 1,5.
— planning to visit Kaho'olawe, Lahaina News, January 30, 1991: 4.

PROTECT MA'ALAEA COALITION
— to meet, Lahaina News, February 13, 1992: 4.
— benefit to be held for at Compadres Mexican Bar and Grill, Lahaina News, August 25, 1994: 14.

PROTECTION AND ADVOCACY AGENCY
— to hold meetings to determine service priorities, Lahaina News, July 31, 1997: 16.

PROUD GRANDPARENTS ASSOCIATION
— receives First Lady's Outstanding Volunteer Award from Lynne Waihee, Lahaina News, April 28, 1994: 3.

PROUD HAWAIIAN SOCIETY
— to hold first general meeting at Waiola Church, Lahaina News, December 14, 1995: 18.
— put fence around Princess Nahienaena School's Preschool/Special Education classroom, Lahaina News, August 21, 1997: 9.

PROUD, MELISSA
— surfer successful, Lahaina News, January 9, 1997: 1,6.

PROVENANCE GALLERY [BUSINESS]
— to hold reception for Michelle De'Alberich, Lahaina News, February 15, 1989: 14.

PROWLER [MUSICAL GROUP]
— performing at Moose McGillycuddy's, Lahaina News, May 2, 1990: 15.
— to perform at Moose McGillycuddy's, Lahaina News, August 1, 1990: 11.

PRUDENTIAL LOCATIONS, INC. [BUSINESS]
— Ken Smith named salesperson of the month, Lahaina News, February 8, 1996: 6.

PRUDENTIAL REAL ESTATE AFFILIATES CHAIRMAN'S CIRCLE
— Tracy Motelewski named to, Lahaina News, October 4, 2001: 8.

PRUDENTIAL SECURITIES [BUSINESS]
— found to have duped Hawaii investors, Lahaina News, October 28, 1993: 7.
— investors misled by need to file, Lahaina News, December 15, 1994: 15.

PRUDENTIAL-BACHE SECURITIES [BUSINESS]
— opens new office, Lahaina News, June 22, 1988: 3.

PRUETT, BOB
— to coach a team at the Hula Bowl, Lahaina News, January 16, 2003: 13.

PRUZYNSKI, JOANNE
— elected vice president of the Kihei Community Association, Lahaina Sun, December 2, 1970: 4.

PRYOR, CHRISTOPHER
— to cycle across four Hawaiian Islands to benefit HIV/AIDS service agencies, Lahaina News, July 12, 2001: 12.

PRYOR, FRED
— to offer seminar on "Conflict Management and Confrontation Skills", Lahaina News, October 17, 2002: 8.
— to offer seminar on "Conflict Management and Confrontation Skills", Lahaina News, October 24, 2002: 8.

PS ... YOUR CAT IS DEAD [PLAY]
— to be performed at Iao Theatre, Lahaina News, October 3, 1991: 18.

PSALTY AND FRIENDS SHOW
— to be performed, Lahaina News, August 21, 1997: 16.

PSYCHEDELIC WET [FILM]
— shown at Lahaina Library, Lahaina Sun, August 18, 1971: 2.

PSYCHIC FAIR
— to be held at Maui Beach Hotel, Lahaina News, July 27, 1988: 11.
— to be held at Maui Beach Hotel, Lahaina News, January 25, 1989: 5.
— to be held by Alaya Unlimited, Lahaina News, May 25, 1995: 12.

— to be held, Lahaina News, July 27, 1995: 12.

— to be held, Lahaina News, November 14, 1996: 15.

— to be held, Lahaina News, January 23, 1997: 10.

— to be held, Lahaina News, March 6, 1997: 11.

PSYCHOTHERAPISTS

— to meet at International Transactional Analysis Association Conference, Lahaina News, January 21, 1999: 11.

PSYCHOTIC TOURIST [MUSICAL GROUP]

— to perform at Moose McGillycuddy's, Lahaina News, May 1, 1991: 14.

PTA

— fundraising drive began, Lahaina Sun, March 10, 1971: 8.

PUAMANA

— impacting flood control for Wainee Street, Lahaina News, October 31, 1991: 1.

— artificial reef sought for Puamana by resident Kim Roberts, Lahaina News, January 2, 1992: 3.

— residents blocked from beach by rocks, Lahaina News, April 22, 1993: 3.

— development featured, Lahaina News, June 7, 2001: 7.

— real estate featured, Lahaina News, August 9, 2001: 7.

— real estate developments at, Lahaina News, January 17, 2002: 7.

— sales strong at, Lahaina News, March 14, 2002: 7.

— real estate development featured, Lahaina News, May 9, 2002: 7.

— Maui County proposes highway and parks from the Pali to, Lahaina News, March 27, 2003: 1,20.

— development featured, Lahaina News, April 10, 2003: 19.

— fast track affordable housing slated above, Lahaina News, July 24, 2003: 1,18.

PUAMANA BEACH

— Mark Skidgel attacked by shark, Lahaina News, August 15, 1980: 6.

PUAMANA COMMUNITY ASSOCIATION

— cited for operating an illegal hotel, Lahaina News, July 15, 1983: 7,20.

— to sue county and state for inadequate environmental assessment on Lahaina Flood Control Project, Lahaina News, July 18, 1991: 1.

PUAMANA RESORT

— begins recycling program, Lahaina News, July 16, 1992: 4.

PUAMELIA OCEANFRONT

— development featured, Lahaina News, March 21, 1984: 18.

PUB TIKI

— power poles in front criticized for affecting external appearance, Lahaina Sun, May 31, 1972: 19.

PUBLIC DEFENDER BILL

— ACLU recommends that Governor Burns veto, Lahaina Sun, May 19, 1971: 8.

PUBLIC EMPLOYEES' HEALTH FUND

— state senators to discuss changes in, Lahaina News, June 21, 2001: 9.

PUBLIC HEARINGS AND MEETINGS

— with state legislators, Lahaina Sun, December 9, 1970: 4.

— Maui's state legislators in Lahaina, Lahaina Sun, December 23, 1970: 10.

— North Short Improvement Association meeting in Paia, Lahaina Sun, December 30, 1970: 5.

— Life of the Land meeting scheduled, Lahaina Sun, January 6, 1971: 8.

— summary of meeting at Kahului library to talk about island ecology, Lahaina Sun, January 13, 1971: 1,2.

— hearing concerning omnibus housing bill, Lahaina Sun, February 17, 1971: 8.

— meeting to discuss, Lahaina Sun, March 24, 1971: 1,2.

— Naska public housing will be phased out, Lahaina Sun, March 24, 1971: 2.

— State Office of Consumer Protection public meeting to hear complaints, Lahaina Sun, April 14, 1971: 5.

— Army Corps of Engineers hold public meeting to discuss water needs of Maui, Lahaina Sun, May 12, 1971: 6.

— public housing tenants to meet, Lahaina Sun, May 12, 1971: 7.

— discussing Maui Electric Company's request for new power plant near Kealia Pond, Lahaina Sun, May 19, 1971: 1.

— Army Corps of Engineers hold public meeting to discuss water needs of Maui, Lahaina Sun, May 26, 1971: 8.

— to discuss proposed changes to welfare law, Lahaina Sun, June 9, 1971: 3.

— challenge proposed welfare changes, Lahaina Sun, June 16, 1971: 1.

— to discuss traffic problems in west Maui scheduled, Lahaina Sun, June 23, 1971: 1.

— to explain inspections of hospitals and medical facilities, Lahaina Sun, June 23, 1971: 2.

— concerning redevelopment plan for North Wailuku, Lahaina Sun, June 30, 1971: 12.

— Army Corps of Engineers to hold public meeting to discuss ship harbor for Ma'alaea Bay., Lahaina Sun, July 7, 1971: 10.

— State Board of Agriculture holds annual public hearing, Lahaina Sun, September 15, 1971: 13.

— Hawaiian Homes Commission schedules public hearing, Lahaina Sun, September 29, 1971: 12.

— proposal to make Front Street one way, Lahaina Sun, October 6, 1971: 1.

— requested to discuss beach access, Lahaina Sun, October 27, 1971: 14.

— Maui County Council requests, to discuss air quality, Lahaina Sun, January 12, 1972: 5.

— to discuss Nixon's Phase II wage-price regulation, Lahaina Sun, February 9, 1972: 5.

— Maui County Council to hold meeting to discuss operating budget and capital improvement projects, Lahaina Sun, March 8, 1972: 12.

— discussion of West Maui plan, Lahaina Sun, March 22, 1972: 3.

— ineffectiveness of criticized, Lahaina Sun, July 19, 1972: 22.

— claimed to have impact on government, Lahaina Sun, December 6, 1972: 5.

— importance of citizen participation challenged, Lahaina Sun, December 20, 1972: 9.

— to discuss tourism development in Wailea, Lahaina Sun, January 10, 1973: 11.

— public seeking more house lots, Lahaina Sun, February 7, 1973: 4.

— on proposed natural area reserve south of Makena, Lahaina Sun, March 14, 1973: 3.

— limiting use of conservation districts, Lahaina Sun, March 21, 1973: 11.

— on Maui County budget sparsely attended, Lahaina Sun, March 28, 1973: 3.

— attempt to draw citizens into discussion of transportation problems, Lahaina Sun, May 9, 1973: 3.

— in Wailuku to discuss air pollution, Lahaina Sun, May 30, 1973: 10.

— on unit pricing and dating of foods to be held, Lahaina Sun, May 30, 1973: 10.

— to consider underwater observatory along Lahaina shoreline, Lahaina Sun, June 6, 1973: 11.

— against pornography, Lahaina News, July 15, 1980: 7.

— anger of locals expressed at meeting with police department, Lahaina News, August 1, 1980: 4.

— to be held at Lahaina Civic Center on airport, harbor, and highway programs, Lahaina News, September 21, 1983: 14.

— Citizens for a Healthy Environment (CHEM) hold meeting on pollution at Lahaina Civic Center, Lahaina News, September 21, 1983: 5,6.

— concerning airport and Lahaina Community Plan, Lahaina News, October 12, 1983: 14.

— to discuss new county sign ordinance set, Lahaina News, October 12, 1983: 6.

— airstrip hearing rescheduled, Lahaina News, November 2, 1983: 6.

— U.S. Army Corps of Engineers to discuss small boat harbors on Maui, Lahaina News, February 1, 1984: 12.

— on proposed whale sanctuary to be held, Lahaina News, February 15, 1984: 5.

— to discuss Maui County budget, Lahaina News, April 4, 1984: 3.

— set with Maui County Liquor Control Commission to discuss limits to number of liquor licenses in Lahaina, Lahaina News, April 4, 1984: 5.

— on the future of Lahaina, Lahaina News, November 27, 1985: 3.

— announced to consider rezoning proposals, Lahaina News, July 16, 1986: 3.

PUBLIC RELATIONS SOCIETY-HAWAII

— awards Koa Anvil to Hill and Knowlton/Skinner Communications, Lahaina News, August 20, 1992: 12.

PUBLIC RESOURCES FOR JOBS (PRO JOBS)

— endorses Rick Reed and Peter Young, Lahaina News, September 17, 1986: 3,11.

PUBLIC SAFETY AWARENESS DAY

— held, Lahaina News, July 6, 1995: 1.

PUBLIC UTILITIES COMMISSION, STATE (PUC)

— hearing request from Hawaiian Telephone Company to increase rates, Lahaina Sun, December 2, 1970: 2.

— hearing request from Hawaiian Telephone Company to increase rates, Lahaina Sun, December 9, 1970: 7.

— public hearing poorly attended, Lahaina Sun, December 23, 1970: 4.

— studying interisland hydrofoil proposal, Lahaina Sun, November 24, 1971: 6.

— affirms approval of major rate increase by Hawaiian Telephone Company, Lahaina Sun, December 22, 1971: 16.

— Charles Arakaki appointed to, Lahaina Sun, January 26, 1972: 14.

— to hold public hearing on proposed increase in electricity rates, Lahaina News, January 9, 1992: 2.

— to require integrated resource plan, Lahaina News, March 26, 1992: 6.

— approves JTB Hawaii Inc's request to use large tour buses, Lahaina News, December 15, 1994: 4.

PUBLIC WORKS AND ENVIRONMENTAL MANAGEMENT, MAUI COUNTY DEPARTMENT OF

— new name of Department of Public Works, Lahaina News, December 5, 2002: 8.

— to study Lahaina drainage, Lahaina News, March 20, 2003: 2.

— work on Kahekili Highway begins, Lahaina News, April 17, 2003: 2.

— to discuss flood control project, Lahaina News, June 5, 2003: 3.

— to discuss flood control project, Lahaina News, June 12, 2003: 14.

— to discuss traffic study, Lahaina News, September 25, 2003: 17.

PUBLIC WORKS AND TRAFFIC COMMITTEE, MAUI COUNTY COUNCIL

— focusing on traffic issues, Lahaina News, February 20, 2003: 1,20.

PUBLIC WORKS AND WASTE MANAGEMENT, MAUI COUNTY DEPARTMENT OF

— chooses Wahikuli Terrace Park as site for Waste Water Pump No. 3, Lahaina News, March 17, 1994: 1,16.

— Mayor Linda Lingle not convinced on need to split, Lahaina News, October 5, 1995: 3.

— having hard time selling reclaimed water, Lahaina News, October 12, 1995: 3.

— to pick-up unwanted appliances, Lahaina News, September 21, 2000: 19.

— honors firms and individuals pollution control, Lahaina News, October 5, 2000: 14.

— to hold wastewater pretreatment training courses, Lahaina News, April 5, 2001: 8.

— to hold a hearing on Environmental Assessment for Lower Honoapi'ilani Road Phase IV project, Lahaina News, August 23, 2001: 3.

— to collect hazardous waste, Lahaina News, September 20, 2001: 2.

— to hold Household Hazardous Waste Drop-off Program, Lahaina News, October 18, 2001: 2.

— to pick up bulky items, Lahaina News, December 6, 2001: 2.

— announces that roads will be repaved, Lahaina News, September 26, 2002: 1.

PUBLIC WORKS AND WATER COMMITTEE, MAUI COUNTY COUNCIL

— to gather more information on proposed expansion of sewer system, Lahaina News, April 23, 1992: 1.

— to examine Lahainaluna Road issues, Lahaina News, September 10, 1998: 1.

— visits Mahanalua Nui Subdivision with Na Kupuna O Maui, Lahaina News, November 25, 1999: 1.

PUBLIC WORKS DEPARTMENT, MAUI COUNTY

— responds to recent flooding, Lahaina Sun, February 3, 1971: 1.

— to continue to push to widen Wainee Street, Lahaina News, October 25, 1989: 1,4.

— unveils Lahaina traffic plan, Lahaina News, November 7, 1990: 1.

— moves baseyard and offices in Lahaina, Lahaina News, June 6, 1991: 3.

— in conflict with Maui County Planning Department over treatment of historic roads, Lahaina News, July 25, 1991: 1.

— waiting for Teen Challenge to act to get buildings rebuilt, Lahaina News, August 15, 1991: 1.

— alleges Sheraton Maui landscaping within the shoreline, Lahaina News, September 12, 1991: 1.

— announces refuse pickup schedule, Lahaina News, January 2, 1992: 4.

— announces landfill schedule, Lahaina News, January 2, 1992: 5.

— to hold public meeting on delay of Mahinahina Bridge widening, Lahaina News, January 9, 1992: 1.

— sending survey to help improve procedures and services, Lahaina News, April 23, 1992: 8.

— awards contracts for highway projects, Lahaina News, July 23, 1992: 4.

— announces resurfacing of Hauoli Street to take place, Lahaina News, December 31, 1992: 8.

— to survey condominiums about presence of algae , Lahaina News, March 11, 1993: 3.

— to hold information meetings on upcoming major projects, Lahaina News, February 24, 1994: 4.

— centralizing recycling bins at Olowalu Transfer Station, Lahaina News, March 24, 1994: 6.

— proposes changes to Soil Erosion and Sedimentation Control Ordinance, Lahaina News, January 9, 1997: 10.

— Director Charles Jencks updates on Front Street Improvement Project, Lahaina News, April 3, 1997: 1.

— to hold information meeting on plans for Lower Honoapi'ilani Road Phase IV, Lahaina News, June 7, 2001: 1.

PUBLIC WORKS, MAUI COUNTY COUNCIL COMMITTEE ON

— Maui County Council to study Honoapi'ilani highway development, Lahaina News, April 22, 1987: 3.

— approves realignment of Lower Honoapi'ilani Road, Lahaina News, May 6, 1987: 1.

— seeking input on hazardous intersection, Lahaina News, July 11, 1990: 1.

— to consider improvements to public beach at Napili, Lahaina News, April 24, 1991: 1.

— to address road hazard at corner of Dickenson Street and Honoapi'ilani Highway, Lahaina News, May 8, 1991: 1.

— criticized for lack of repairs on Front Street, Lahaina News, June 27, 1991: 3,4.

— to discuss request to remove large rocks at Black Rock, Lahaina News, February 5, 1998: 3.

— to visit Harbor Village site , Lahaina News, May 24, 2001: 22.

PUCK, TEDDY AU
— Scholar/Athlete of the Week, Lahaina News, July 5, 2001: 12.

PUCKETT, RANDY [ARTIST]
— work displayed at Dolphin Galleries, Lahaina News, February 10, 1988: 3.

— to exhibit at Foundation Galleries, Lahaina News, February 20, 1992: 15.

— to hold reception at Foundation Galleries, Lahaina News, February 20, 1992: 17.

PUENTE, TITO [MUSICIAN]
— to perform at Hyatt Regency Maui, sponsored by Maui Jazz Society, Lahaina News, December 24, 1992: 15.

— to perform, Lahaina News, December 31, 1992: 12.

— featured, Lahaina News, January 7, 1993: 9,10.

PUERTO RICO
— travel to described, Lahaina News, January 15, 1980: 10.

PUESCHEL, JOE
— discusses Lahaina Whaling Festival, Lahaina Sun, February 17, 1971: 1.

— honored for volunteer work, Lahaina News, June 9, 1994: 5.

— remembered, Lahaina News, June 16, 1994: 1.

PUGH, JACK
— project director for planned condominium, Lahaina Sun, January 27, 1971: 3.

— appointed new manager of Maui Hilton Hotel, Lahaina Sun, July 28, 1971: 10.

PUKALANI [TOWN]
— Maui County Planning Commission okays rezoning for development, Lahaina Sun, August 4, 1971: 1,3.

— described, Lahaina Sun, July 11, 1973: 13,14.15.

PUKALANI BYPASS
— Phase II begins, Lahaina News, September 24, 1992: 4.

PUKALANI HIGHLANDS PARTNERS
— stop work when bones uncovered, Lahaina News, January 30, 1992: 5.

PUKALANI TERRACE CENTER
— elects new board, Lahaina News, April 15, 1993: 7.

— Santa to visit, Lahaina News, November 17, 1994: 19.

PULA, VICTORIA
— to lead "Talk (Hawaiian) History with Victoria" at Bailey House, Lahaina News, September 20, 2001: 16.

— to speak to Bailey House Museum, Lahaina News, January 17, 2002: 16.

— to discuss Hawaiian history at Bailey House Museums, Lahaina News, February 14, 2002: 16.

— offering tours of Bailey House, Lahaina News, March 7, 2002: 17.

— to speak on Hawaiian history at Bailey House Museum, Lahaina News, September 19, 2002: 24.

— to present "Talk History with Victoria" at Bailey House, Lahaina News, October 10, 2002: 17.

PULEHU
— experimental papaya cultivation project initiated by Alexander & Baldwin, Lahaina Sun, May 5, 1971: 5.

PULLAN, WILLOW [MUSICIAN]
— to hold workshop on children's song and dance, Lahaina News, June 6, 1991: 15.

— to hold workshop on children's song and dance, Lahaina News, June 13, 1991: 13.

PULTZ, JANE WILKINS
— of Press Pacifica to speak to Maui Authors' Guild, Lahaina News, January 1, 1986: 3.

PUNALAU BEACH
— Maui Pineapple Co gates access to , Lahaina News, April 5, 2001: 1.

PUNANA LEO O LAHAINA
— Hawaiian Language Preschool dedicated, Lahaina News, May 25, 1988: 1,14.

— Hawaiian Language Immersion Preschool planned, Lahaina News, August 15, 1996: 14.

— preschool may begin soon, Lahaina News, December 12, 1996: 1,21.

— opening in the summer, Lahaina News, May 28, 1998: 3.

— ready for students, Lahaina News, October 29, 1998: 3.

— benefit to be held at Avalon Restaurant, Lahaina News, December 10, 1998: 11,17.

— opens, Lahaina News, January 14, 1999: 1,16.

— enrollment to begin, Lahaina News, February 25, 1999: 5.

— to hold Ho'omau benefit concert, Lahaina News, March 11, 1999: 13.

— to hold opening enrollment, Lahaina News, February 17, 2000: 15.

— supporting Hawaiian Language Immersion, Lahaina News, April 6, 2000: 1,2.

— expanding Immersion Program, Lahaina News, May 18, 2000: 1,6.

— holds first graduation, Lahaina News, August 3, 2000: 1,20.

— Hawaiian Language Immersion Preschool has openings, Lahaina News, October 5, 2000: 7.

— to hold registration, Lahaina News, February 22, 2001: 2.

— to hold registration, Lahaina News, March 1, 2001: 10.

— planning open house, Lahaina News, March 8, 2001: 17.

— celebrates graduation, Lahaina News, July 5, 2001: 1.

— successful, Lahaina News, July 12, 2001: 1,18.

— applications accepted for preschool, Lahaina News, August 30, 2001: 3.

— space available at, Lahaina News, September 6, 2001: 1.

— Mohala Gold Tournament to benefit, Lahaina News, February 28, 2002: 13.

— to hold open enrollment, Lahaina News, February 28, 2002: 5.

— Ho'omau benefit concert to be held for, Lahaina News, March 14, 2002: 15.

— to hold "Ho'omau 2002" fundraiser, Lahaina News, March 21, 2002: 16.

— Hawaiian Language Immersion preschool featured, Lahaina News, April 11, 2002: 1,20.

— perform at Waiola Church, Lahaina News, July 4, 2002: 1,20.

— to hold open house, Lahaina News, March 13, 2003: 1.

— to hold Ho'omau 2003 fundraiser, Lahaina News, March 20, 2003: 17.

— Hawaiian language school featured, Lahaina News, July 3, 2003: 1,3.

— preschool to hold open enrollment, Lahaina News, July 17, 2003: 5.

— opens new year, Lahaina News, August 14, 2003: 3.

PUNANA LEO O MAUI
— benefit concert for Hawaiian Language Preschool, Lahaina News, August 3, 1988: 3.

— holds bazaar, Lahaina News, May 10, 1989: 3.

— fashion show benefit to be held, Lahaina News, August 14, 1997: 16.

— Hawaiian Language Preschool to be held, Lahaina News, August 13, 1998: 17.

— fashion show to be held, Lahaina News, August 20, 1998: 16.

— Halau Maui Nui Bash: A Celebration of Hawaiian Music to benefit building fund, Lahaina News, October 18, 2001: 1.

PUNANA LEO O MAUI
— to hold benefit concert, Lahaina News, March 14, 1996: 13.

PURDY, EBEN
— see Maui Tenants Advisory Board

PURDY, JAMES
— appointed direct of sales of Inter-Continental Wailea Hotel, Lahaina News, June 11, 1986: 14.

PURE HEART [MUSICAL GROUP]
— to perform at Jaycees Summer Jam, Lahaina News, June 4, 1998: 16.
— to perform at A Taste of Lahaina, Lahaina News, September 10, 1998: 16.
— to perform at Borders Books, Lahaina News, June 24, 1999: 12.
— to perform at "A Taste of Lahaina", Lahaina News, September 2, 1999: 18.

PURE IMAGE POOLS
— to distribute Chloromatic Hawaii products, Lahaina News, June 9, 1994: 12.

PURIM
— Jewish Congregation to hold potluck, Lahaina News, February 27, 1985: 3.

PURNELL, NANETTE NAPOLEON
— to offer workshops on studying cemeteries and gravestones, Lahaina News, August 17, 1988: 3,14.

PURPLEHEART PUPPETS
— to perform "The Pacific Passage", Lahaina News, January 16, 1992: 3.

PURPUS, TERRY
— faces jail time and fine for killing nene, Lahaina News, November 27, 1997: 1.

PUTT, BOB
— longtime resident to move back to Oregon, Lahaina News, November 7, 1990: 2.

PU'U KANI [MUSICAL GROUP]
— to perform at Molokini Lounge at the Maui Prince Hotel, Lahaina News, February 20, 1991: 11.

PU'U KEKA'A
— Hawaiians to perform blessing at, Lahaina News, June 26, 1997: 1.
— vigil held at, Lahaina News, January 13, 2000: 1,16.

PU'U KUKUI
— Maui Land and Pineapple, Co. to give The Nature Conservancy easement of native forest at, Lahaina News, February 13, 1992: 4.
— efforts made to protect, Lahaina News, July 6, 2000: 1,14.

PU'U KUKUI CRATER
— Terry Rowe photographs rare species in, Lahaina News, July 26, 2001: 1.

PU'U KUKUI WATERSHED
— threatened, Lahaina News, December 10, 1998: 3.
— presentation on to be held at Ritz-Carlton, Lahaina News, September 16, 1999: 1.
— Youth for Environmental Service volunteers to pull Tibouchina plants in , Lahaina News, September 30, 1999: 12.

PU'U OLAI - LA PEROUSE BAY STATE PARK AND RESERVE AREA
— planned, Lahaina Sun, June 9, 1971: 3.

PU'UKOLI'I [TOWN]
— decline of town detailed, Lahaina Sun, December 13, 1972: 16,17.
— Amfac/JMB Hawaii plans 1600 units in, Lahaina News, September 3, 1992: 3.
— residents concerned about impact of Amfac/JM project near, Lahaina News, December 10, 1992: 3.
— Lahaina Community Plan Citizen Advisory Committee drafts letter to Amfac/JMB concerning Village project, Lahaina News, December 24, 1992: 4.
— Amfac proposes development in, Lahaina News, January 28, 1993: 3.
— reactions to Amfac/JMB proposed project, Lahaina News, February 18, 1993: 1.

— proposed development site raises traffic and housing issues, Lahaina News, March 11, 1993: 1,4.
— reunion to be held, Lahaina News, February 4, 1999: 9.
— reunion to be held, Lahaina News, May 20, 1999: 15.
— camp to hold reunion, Lahaina News, June 24, 1999: 2.

PU'UKOLI'I VILLAGE
— part of Amfac, Inc.'s development plans, Lahaina News, September 21, 1988: 1.
— state Land Use Commission to meet, Lahaina News, March 25, 1993: 3.
— work to begin on, Lahaina News, June 20, 1996: 2.
— senior center to be developed at, Lahaina News, August 8, 1996: 1.

PU'UNENE
— location of new sewage plant, Lahaina News, July 23, 1992: 11.

PU'UNOA BEACH
— luxury condominium development planned for Lahaina, Lahaina News, March 7, 1984: 17.
— development featured, Lahaina News, April 25, 1984: 14.

PU'UNOA PLACE
— residents opposing development plans by Lahaina Kingdom Hall of Jehovah's Witnesses, Lahaina News, March 14, 2002: 3.

PU'UPIHA CEMETERY
— eroding, Lahaina News, April 15, 1983: 6.
— police officer Mike Casicas planning community project to clean up, Lahaina News, March 17, 1994: 3.

PYEWACKET [BOAT]
— may break Victoria-Maui race record, Lahaina News, July 11, 1996: 1.
— wins Victoria-Maui race, Lahaina News, July 18, 1996: 7.
— Roy Disney's yacht first monohull to break eight days, Lahaina News, July 17, 1997: 15.

PYLE, CARTER
— house suffers storm damage, Lahaina Sun, December 30, 1970: 1.

PYLES, TOM
— discusses opening of Adult Care Center in West Maui, Lahaina News, July 13, 1988: 2.

PYTKA, LISA
— to speak on "Everyday Data that Makes a Difference: Simple Data, Big Results in the Kaho'olawe Island Reserve", Lahaina News, April 3, 2003: 17.

Q

QUAGGA [MUSICAL GROUP]
— to perform at Sir Wilfred's, Lahaina News, July 2, 1992: 26.
— to perform at Sir Wilfred's, Lahaina News, November 12, 1992: 22.

QUANTAS AIRLINES [BUSINESS]
— donates tickets to Arthritis Foundation for fundraiser, Lahaina News, August 19, 1993: 15.

QUANTUM ENERGETIC BALANCING
— presentation to be held, Lahaina News, April 11, 2002: 17.
— to be discussed, Lahaina News, May 16, 2002: 17.

QUAYLE, DAN [POLITICIAN]
— attends opening of Ruth's Chris Steak House, Lahaina News, August 6, 1998: 2.

QUAYLE, ELIZABETH
— reflects on living on Maui, Lahaina News, June 29, 2000: 10.
— realtor describes living on Maui, Lahaina News, December 28, 2000: 12.

QUEEN ELIZABETH II [SHIP]
— large cruise ship visits Lahaina, Lahaina News, April 9, 1986: 1.

QUEEN KAʻAHUMANU CENTER
— to hold musical concert, Lahaina News, October 4, 2001: 16.
— to feature music, Lahaina News, October 11, 2001: 16.
— entertainment to be held, Lahaina News, November 29, 2001: 16.
— to hold festival celebrating Queen Kaʻahumanu, Lahaina News, March 14, 2002: 16.

QUEEN KAʻAHUMANU FESTIVAL
— to be held, Lahaina News, March 13, 1997: 16.
— to be held, Lahaina News, March 20, 1997: 16.
— to be held, Lahaina News, March 18, 1999: 16.
— to be held, Lahaina News, March 13, 2003: 20.

QUEEN LILIʻUOKALANI CANOE RACE
— to be held, Lahaina News, September 1, 1994: 9.

QUEEN LILIʻUOKALANI CHILDREN'S CENTER
— to host "The Legend of the Laughing Gecko" with Hui O Waʻa Kaulua, Lahaina News, February 3, 2000: 12.

QUEEN THEATRE
— renovations planned, Lahaina Sun, February 17, 1971: 2.
— request to paint portrait of Queen Liliʻuokalani rejected by Maui Historic Commission, Lahaina Sun, March 17, 1971: 5.
— criticized for showing pornographic films, Lahaina Sun, March 17, 1971: 5.
— to be renovated, Lahaina News, October 28, 1987: 1,20.

QUESTAS, ELARIO
— 102-year old "Cutie Pie" featured, Lahaina News, June 8, 1988: 6.
— life featured, Lahaina News, October 4, 1989: 4.
— Honokohau resident to turn 109, Lahaina News, August 3, 1995: 5.
— celebrates 112th birthday, Lahaina News, August 20, 1998: 7.
— Honokohau Valley resident passes away at 112, Lahaina News, February 11, 1999: 1,6.

QUICKSILVER [BUSINESS]
— sponsors Amateur Surfing Association qualifying surfing contest at Lahaina Harbor, Lahaina News, June 5, 2003: 13.

QUIGLEY, GLENN
— Kahana Sunset general manager concerned about JGL Enterprises' rezoning request at Napilihau Villages, Lahaina News, November 25, 1993: 1,3.

QUIJAS, DORIS
— named general manager of Koho Grill, Lahaina News, December 5, 1991: 13.

QUIKSILVER BOARDRIDERS CLUB
— presents "Harbor Contest-Malama o Ke Kai", Lahaina News, May 14, 1998: 14.
— Harbor Contest-Malala o ke Kai delayed, Lahaina News, May 21, 1998: 14.
— presents "Harbor Contest-Malama o Ke Kai", Lahaina News, June 4, 1998: 14.
— Hui O Lahaina Ocean Festival to be held, Lahaina News, September 24, 1998: 1.

QUILL, MARTIN
— discusses Na Hale O Makena development, Lahaina News, December 7, 2000: 21.

QUILLAN, JOSEPH [ARTIST]
— featured at Lahaina Galleries, Lahaina News, August 29, 1990: 13.
— featured at Lahaina Galleries, Lahaina News, March 19, 1992: 18.
— featured at Lahaina Galleries, Lahaina News, October 22, 1992: 17.

QUILT-MAKING
— mistakenly reported in Lahaina News as being offered, Lahaina News, August 3, 1988: 3.

QUILTER'S CORNER [BUSINESS]
— to offer classes, Lahaina News, September 14, 2000: 20.
— closing after 21 years, Lahaina News, October 12, 2000: 16.

QUILTS 'N FABRIC [BUSINESS]
— opens, Lahaina News, February 8, 2001: 8.

QUILTS 'N KITCHEN [BUSINESS]
— holds grant opening, Lahaina News, April 16, 1998: 11.

QUINLAN, DENNIS
— appointed sales manager at Embassy Suites Resort Maui, Lahaina News, August 14, 1997: 12.

QUINN, ANTHONY [ACTOR]
— artwork exhibited at Center Arts Galleries-Hawaii, Lahaina News, February 4, 1987: 3.
— to promote an exhibit of his work at Center Art Gallery, Lahaina News, October 19, 1988: 3.

QUINN, BRIAN
— named sales manager at Westin Maui Hotel, Lahaina News, March 21, 1990: 4.
— joins Westin Maui's sales teams, Lahaina News, September 5, 1991: 6.

QUIRIT, LARRY
— new chef at Grand Wailea Resort Hotel and Spa, Lahaina News, November 23, 2000: 16.

QUIRK, NOREEN [ARTIST]
— jewelry designs to be exhibited at Maui Crafts Guild, Lahaina News, February 2, 1995: 12.

QUISENBERRY, WALTER [STATE HEALTH DIRECTOR]
— discusses water contamination issues at Napili, Lahaina Sun, November 11, 1970: 1,3.
— discusses access to clean water in Napili, Lahaina Sun, February 3, 1971: 4.
— State Director of Health clears most fish for market, Lahaina Sun, June 23, 1971: 11.

QUISENG, BEN
— appointed director of rooms, Lahaina News, November 15, 1989: 9.
— appointed assistant manager at The Kapalua Villa, Lahaina News, January 23, 1992: 13.

R

R.I. NAMBA CONSTRUCTION, INC. [BUSINESS]
— awarded contract by Department of Transportation to remove abandoned pipes in Lahaina Harbor, Lahaina News, January 24, 1990: 6.

R&R UNDERWATER [BUSINESS]
— opens, Lahaina News, August 14, 1997: 12.

RAʻA, TAROʻO [SAILOR]
— visits Maui, Lahaina Sun, February 21, 1973: 7.

RABANAL, EPI
— appointed Sales Manager at Westin Maui, Lahaina News, February 3, 1988: 3.
— promoted to director of sales and marketing at Royal Lahaina Resort, Lahaina News, June 8, 1995: 10.

RABANAS, MILTON [MUSICIAN]
— to perform at Maui Prince, Lahaina News, July 30, 1992: 16.
— to perform at Molokini Lounge at the Maui Prince Hotel, Lahaina News, August 13, 1992: 17.
— to perform at Molokini Lounge at the Maui Prince Hotel, Lahaina News, December 24, 1992: 17.

RABASA, HERMINA
— mayor Hannibal Tavares awards certificate of merit to, Lahaina News, September 10, 1986: 3.

RACE AND TRACK PERFORMANCE SHOW
— to be held at Kaʻahumanu Center, Lahaina News, June 13, 1991: 6.

RACE UNITY DAY
— to be held at Kamaole III Park, Lahaina News, June 11, 1998: 16.

RACISM
— Maui lodge of the Elk's Club attempting to change "whites only" policy of national organization, Lahaina Sun, May 16, 1973: 4.

RADCLIFFE, DONALD
— reports on arrests of illegal aliens, Lahaina News, October 19, 1995: 3.

RADIATORS, THE [MUSICAL GROUP]
— to perform at Maui Arts and Cultural Center, Lahaina News, January 7, 1999: 17.
— to perform at Maui Arts and Cultural Center, Lahaina News, January 14, 1999: 12.

RADIO
— Radio station proposed, Lahaina Sun, July 28, 1971: 2,11.
— shortwave radio time channel described, Lahaina Sun, December 1, 1971: 14.
— FM radio reception improves, Lahaina Sun, December 1, 1971: 6.
— situation of stations on Maui described, Lahaina Sun, May 24, 1972: 15.
— newscaster Dan Richards fired from KNUI, Lahaina Sun, August 2, 1972: 5.
— announcer Bill Thompson complains on the air about radio management, Lahaina Sun, January 10, 1973: 7.
— KNUI fires disk jockey Buck Buchanan, Lahaina Sun, February 14, 1973: 4.
— "Hawaii Calls" to be broadcast from Maui Surf Hotel, Lahaina Sun, May 9, 1973: 11.
— FM station planned for Maui, Lahaina Sun, July 11, 1973: 7.
— KNUI has been sold to Harwell Shepherd, Lahaina Sun, July 25, 1973: 4.
— KNUI sold to Tom Elkins and Norma Phegley Craig, Lahaina News, September 15, 1980: 13.
— new FM station planned, Lahaina News, December 7, 1983: 14.
— National Public Radio (NPR) may be opening station on Maui, Lahaina News, February 1, 1984: 3.
— Media Update, Maui performs survey of listening habits, Lahaina News, February 22, 1984: 17.
— KHPR receives grant for transmitter on Haleakala, Lahaina News, August 8, 1984: 3.
— West Maui to have a radio station, named KPOA, Lahaina News, September 12, 1984: 12.
— KLHI to cover Halloween parade live, Lahaina News, October 24, 1984: 3.
— Lahaina radio stations described, Lahaina News, October 31, 1984: 18.
— KWPR-FM delays starting broadcasting, Lahaina News, January 30, 1985: 3.
— KLHI installs dish, can now bring ABC Contemporary News to Maui, Lahaina News, February 6, 1985: 3.
— description of local radio stations, Lahaina News, February 13, 1985: 12.
— KHUI begins new classical music show, Lahaina News, September 4, 1985: 8.
— praise for KAOI-FM, Lahaina News, November 20, 1985: 8.
— KAOI anniversary party postponed, Lahaina News, June 11, 1986: 8.
— KPOA featured, Lahaina News, February 25, 1987: 8.
— Barry Shannon and Kathy Collins to host "Maui Mornings" on FM 101, Lahaina News, March 18, 1987: 18.
— FM 101 to play "Mother and Child Reunion" randomly throughout the week, Lahaina News, May 6, 1987: 3.
— industry in West Maui described, Lahaina News, April 20, 1988: 7.
— competition between discussed, Lahaina News, April 27, 1988: 16.
— Carmen Adams featured, Lahaina News, June 1, 1988: 7.

— Gary Johnson's show "Traffic Jazz" now called "21 Degrees North", Lahaina News, August 17, 1988: 3.
— KAOI sponsoring "Spare Change for Christmas", Lahaina News, December 21, 1988: 12.
— FM 101 hopes to overturn rejection of permit to build radio tower in Ulupalakua, Lahaina News, March 28, 1990: 1.
— Chuck Gardner sells share of KPOA FM to Chuck Bergson, Lahaina News, April 11, 1990: 5.
— Ron Vaught named general manager of KMUI radio, Lahaina News, September 12, 1990: 11.
— KPOA-FM doubles its output power, Lahaina News, February 27, 1991: 8.
— seeking to improve audience share, Lahaina News, April 2, 1992: 12.
— KPOA moves to 505 Front Street, Lahaina News, August 27, 1992: 10.
— KLHI station owners to contest ruling stripping control of the station from them, Lahaina News, January 6, 1994: 1,3.
— ownership of KLHI-FM following bankruptcy goes to trial, Lahaina News, January 13, 1994: 1.
— ham radio class to be offered, Lahaina News, May 26, 1994: 5.
— KPOA radio show "Midnight Party" to air in Japan, Lahaina News, June 30, 1994: 8.
— KMVI names new staff, Lahaina News, February 16, 1995: 13.
— KLHI switches to "alternative" music format, Lahaina News, July 11, 1996: 3.
— FM 101 opens, Lahaina News, July 25, 1996: 2.
— see also specific radio stations

RADIO SHACK [BUSINESS]
— featured, Lahaina News, July 4, 1984: 17.

RADNER, ROGENE
— selected Distinguished Toastmaster, Lahaina News, September 3, 1992: 11.

RAFFETTO, SHACKLEY
— to explain Maui Drug Court, Lahaina News, July 20, 2000: 1,9.

RAFFLES [RESTAURANT]
— wins award for fine dining, Lahaina News, March 12, 1986: 12.
— reopening at Stouffer Wailea Beach Resort, Lahaina News, December 23, 1993: 7.

RAHN, CATHERINE [ARTIST]
— to exhibit at Elizabeth Doyle Gallery, Lahaina News, April 13, 2000: 12.

RAINBOW ART GALLERY [BUSINESS]
— opens at Lahaina Center, Lahaina News, May 23, 1990: 8.

RAINBOW INTERNATIONAL CARPET CARE AND RESTORATION SPECIALISTS
— John Newman opens local franchise, Lahaina News, June 12, 1997: 15.

RAINBOW MARKET [BUSINESS]
— opens, Lahaina News, March 25, 1993: 11.

RAINBOW OF DREAMS
— fundraiser for Friends of Children's Advocacy Center to be headlined by Mayor Linda Lingle, Lahaina News, March 30, 1995: 6.

RAINBOW RANCH [BUSINESS]
— horseback riding at, Lahaina News, June 6, 1984: 8,9.
— proposed site of light industrial complex in Napili, Lahaina News, August 15, 1990: 1.
— Napili Village Center proposed, conceptual drawing printed, Lahaina News, June 24, 1999: 1,11.

RAINBOW WITHIN YOU
— art festival to be held at Ritz-Carlton, Lahaina News, August 24, 1995: 11.

RAINBOWS END
— equine rescue and retirement facility receives award, Lahaina News, October 1, 1998: 8.

RAINE, CHRIS [COMEDIAN]
— to perform at Comedy Club and the Sports Page, Lahaina News, June 17, 1993: 14.

RAITT, BONNIE [MUSICIAN]
— to perform at Royal Lahaina Tennis Stadium, Lahaina News, September 13, 1989: 8.
— to perform at Royal Lahaina Tennis Stadium, Lahaina News, September 20, 1989: 8.
— to perform at Maui Arts and Cultural Center, Lahaina News, March 5, 1998: 17.
— to perform, Lahaina News, March 12, 1998: 21.

RAKUTARO [RESTAURANT]
— featured, Lahaina News, November 7, 1996: 6,7.

RALPH, JACKIE
— presents "Relationship 101" workshop at Unity Church of Maui, Lahaina News, May 18, 1988: 18.
— to hold "Happiness 101" workshop at Unity Church, Lahaina News, April 12, 1989: 3.

RALSTON, DENNIS [TENNIS PLAYER]
— to hold clinics, Lahaina News, July 17, 1985: 3.

RALSTON, RICK
— owner of Crazy Shirts featured, Lahaina News, January 7, 1987: 4.

RAMALES, MARK
— Scholar/Athlete of the Week, Lahaina News, September 26, 1996: 12.

RAMELB, FELICIANO
— pleads not guilty in traffic deaths, Lahaina News, January 4, 1984: 5.
— sentencing set, Lahaina News, June 27, 1984: 3.
— sentenced to 5 years for negligent homicide, Lahaina News, August 15, 1984: 3.

RAMELB, NADINE [ARTIST]
— to exhibit watercolors at Art School at Kapalua, Lahaina News, September 24, 1998: 17.
— to exhibit at the Art School at Kapalua, Lahaina News, October 1, 1998: 16.
— to offer watercolor workshop, Lahaina News, December 10, 1998: 20.
— opens watercolorist studio, Lahaina News, December 21, 2000: 14.
— to lead watercolor workshop for Hawaii Watercolor Society, Lahaina News, October 3, 2002: 17.

RAMOS DRAFTING SERVICE [BUSINESS]
— offering services, Lahaina News, July 23, 1998: 13.

RAMOS, RAYMOND JR.
— police seeking help to solve murder of, Lahaina News, July 9, 1998: 1.

RAMSAY, JIM
— offering reward for arrest of people responsible for killing Hawaiian ducks, Lahaina News, September 20, 1989: 3.

RAMSOUR, DAVID
— Bank of Hawaii chief economist to speak to Maui Chamber of Commerce, Lahaina News, February 13, 1992: 12.

RAND, VALERIE
— named sales manager of Four Seasons Resort in Wailea, Lahaina News, November 7, 1990: 8.

RANDOLPH, WILLIE [COMEDIAN]
— to perform at Comedy Club, Lahaina News, June 27, 1991: 12.
— to perform at Comedy Club and the Sports Page, Lahaina News, June 25, 1992: 18,21.

RANDY HANSEN BAND [MUSICAL GROUP]
— to play at Partners, Lahaina News, October 26, 1988: 9,16.

RANE, JEANNIE ROBERTS [ARTIST]
— featured at Larry Dodson Gallery, Lahaina News, March 30, 1988: 20.

RANGANKETAN [MUSICAL GROUP]
— to perform at Ka'ahumanu Center, Lahaina News, February 25, 1993: 12.

RANGER, DAN
— manager of Sugar Cane Train leaves, Lahaina News, May 15, 1983: 6.

RANIS, CHEYENNE
— Scholar/Athlete of the Week, Lahaina News, March 7, 1996: 7.

RANKIN, LAUREN
— visits Hyatt Regency Maui as part of Make-A-Wish Foundation, Lahaina News, February 16, 1995: 6.

RANKIN-CHAPMAN, KEN
— becomes captain with Hawaii Helicopters, Lahaina News, June 6, 1990: 7.

RANNEY, KEITH
— to talk "Somatic Awareness in Movement and Music: Toward Sensing and Becoming More of Who You Are", Lahaina News, September 20, 2001: 17.

RANSOM, WILLIAM [MUSICIAN]
— to perform with Maui Symphony Orchestra, Lahaina News, November 8, 1989: 6.
— to perform with Maui Symphony Orchestra, Lahaina News, November 22, 1989: 12.

RANSON, ROBYN AND ALLAN
— owners of Westside Natural Foods and Deli featured, Lahaina News, July 5, 2001: 1,8.

RAPA NUI
— becomes sister-island to Maui, Lahaina News, May 28, 1998: 1.

RAPP, KATARINA [ARTIST]
— featured, Lahaina News, January 16, 1997: 13.

RASMUSSEN, HENRIK
— to manage Mahana at Ka'anapali, Lahaina News, August 2, 2001: 8.

RATHGEB, KARL
— named general manager of Kapalua Bay Hotel and Villas, Lahaina News, November 20, 1985: 11.

RATKOWSKI, ROB [ARTIST]
— offering class on photographing artwork, Lahaina News, May 9, 1990: 20.
— to present "Hawaii's Underground Giant Kazumura", Lahaina News, July 10, 2003: 16.

RATTAN ART GALLERY [BUSINESS]
— reopens, Lahaina News, May 1, 1980: 19.

RATTAN CONCEPTS [BUSINESS]
— changes name to Morris Resort Interiors, Lahaina News, July 26, 2001: 8.

RAU, DAVID
— named head golf professional at Kapalua's Village Course, Lahaina News, May 16, 2002: 8.

RAVEN [SHIP]
— breaks mooring, Lahaina News, February 2, 1995: 1.

RAVEN, GLADYS [PRESIDENT OF LAHAINA OUTDOOR CIRCLE]
— discusses plans for banyan tree in Lahaina, Lahaina Sun, February 3, 1971: 7.

RAVEN THE HUNGRY [PLAY]
— to be performed by Honolulu Youth Theatre, Lahaina News, February 27, 1985: 3.

RAW SILK [MUSICAL GROUP]
— reviewed, Lahaina News, December 13, 1989: 22.

RAWLS, LOU [MUSICIAN]
— to perform in Honolulu, praised for his telethon supporting the United Negro College Fund , Lahaina News, December 19, 1984: 21.
— to perform at Maui Arts and Cultural Center, Lahaina News, April 15, 1999: 12.

RAY, GREG [COMEDIAN]
— to perform at Comedy Club, Lahaina News, December 5, 1991: 22.
— to perform at Comedy Club, Lahaina News, November 11, 1993: 12.

RAY, SONDRA [WRITER]
— to offer workshop on "Unlimited Life", Lahaina News, March 13, 1997: 16.
— author of "Healing and Holiness" to discuss sacred relationships, Lahaina News, December 12, 2002: 20.

RAYMOND, STANLEY
— becomes industrial relations director for Lihue Plantation Company, Lahaina Sun, July 21, 1971: 3.

RAZOR [MUSICAL GROUP]
— review of, Lahaina Times, October, 1980 volume 4 number 9: 4.

RE, LEILANI ROSELINE
— crowned as Mill Valley Isle, Lahaina News, January 20, 1994: 4.
— reigning Miss Valley Isle to represent Maui in Miss Hawaii Scholarship Pageant, Lahaina News, March 17, 1994: 3.

READER, KEENAN
— Lahainaluna High School counselor featured, Lahaina News, October 9, 2003: 1,2.

READER'S DIGEST [PUBLICATION]
— review of coverage of Hawaii in January , Lahaina Sun, January 27, 1971: 2.

REAL ESTATE
— plans to limit speculation on moderate income housing development, Lahaina Sun, December 2, 1970: 3.
— rezoning controversy in Spreckelsville, Lahaina Sun, June 9, 1971: 6.
— description of current situation in Maui compared to the mainland, Lahaina Sun, March 1, 1972: 16.
— impact of speculation described, Lahaina News, July, 1979: 18.
— the section "This Week's Featured Property" begins to focus on individual units, which are not typically indexed, Lahaina News, August 1, 1984: .
— Holo Honokowai accepting applications from renters, Lahaina News, August 19, 1987: 3.
— top lister awards announced, Lahaina News, October 18, 1989: 7.
— realtors active on committees, Lahaina News, December 27, 1989: 5.
— prices up, Lahaina News, March 14, 1990: 5.
— top realtors named, Lahaina News, May 9, 1990: 8.
— Maui Community College to offer courses for agents, Lahaina News, June 6, 1990: 5,7.
— Hawaii State Real Estate Appraisal Board to offer courses, Lahaina News, March 27, 1991: 9,10.
— condominium prices stable, Lahaina News, September 12, 1991: 11.
— concerns raised about timeshare sales techniques, Lahaina News, September 3, 1992: 9.
— Certified Commercial Investment Member (CIIM) designations awarded, Lahaina News, November 26, 1992: 19,20.
— lease market rebounding, Lahaina News, February 11, 1993: 11.
— update on current situation, Lahaina News, April 29, 1993: 7.
— new computer system allows remote access to images of properties, Lahaina News, February 24, 1994: 10.
— update on market, Lahaina News, August 10, 1995: 10.

— Multiple Listing Service now available, Lahaina News, August 10, 1995: 10.
— update on market, Lahaina News, September 28, 1995: 10.
— update focusing on return of Japanese buyers, Lahaina News, October 19, 1995: 7.
— current situation of, Lahaina News, November 16, 1995: 10.
— update on current market, Lahaina News, December 21, 1995: 12.
— update on current market, Lahaina News, January 25, 1996: 12,13.
— importance of seeking advice on mortgages, Lahaina News, February 29, 1996: 12.
— update on current market, Lahaina News, March 28, 1996: 11.
— Hawaii Real Estate Research and Education Center to offer seminars on, Lahaina News, April 18, 1996: 8.
— update on current market, Lahaina News, April 25, 1996: 13.
— update on current market, Lahaina News, May 23, 1996: 17.
— update on current market, Lahaina News, May 23, 1996: 17.
— homes available at Laule'a, Lahaina News, June 27, 1996: 12.
— update on current market, Lahaina News, June 27, 1996: 9.
— update on current market, Lahaina News, July 25, 1996: 6.
— update on current market, Lahaina News, August 22, 1996: 8.
— market improving, Lahaina News, September 26, 1996: 8.
— update on current market, Lahaina News, October 24, 1996: 8.
— update on current situation, Lahaina News, December 5, 1996: 6,18.
— update on current market situation, Lahaina News, December 26, 1996: 9.
— Maui Community College to offer Real Estate Pre-Licensing Course, Lahaina News, January 16, 1997: 10.
— impact of California on local market, Lahaina News, January 30, 1997: 14.
— sales boom at the Ka'anapali Alii, Lahaina News, April 17, 1997: 6.
— update on current market situation, Lahaina News, April 24, 1997: 6.
— price of oceanfront unit reduced, Lahaina News, May 8, 1997: 12.
— trends in condominium sales, Lahaina News, May 15, 1997: 6.
— Whaler Condominium featured, Lahaina News, May 22, 1997: 8.
— four homes left at Piilani Village, Lahaina News, May 29, 1997: 18.
— Kahana Ridge construction almost completed, Lahaina News, June 5, 1997: 14.
— Amfac Maui opens Ke Alii Subdivision, Lahaina News, June 12, 1997: 14.
— prices dropping at Ka'anapali Hillside, Lahaina News, June 19, 1997: 12.
— Sakamoto Properties featured, Lahaina News, June 26, 1997: 12.
— editorial on continued problems with, Lahaina News, July 10, 1997: 4.
— Sands of Kahana featured, Lahaina News, July 10, 1997: 8.
— beach front property available, Lahaina News, July 17, 1997: 8.
— Pu'u Hale featured, Lahaina News, July 24, 1997: 8.
— sales activity increases, Lahaina News, August 14, 1997: 8.
— Maui For Sale By Owner Assistance Program opens, Lahaina News, August 14, 1997: 9.
— luxury home in Napili featured, Lahaina News, August 21, 1997: 8.
— Paki Maui units available, Lahaina News, August 28, 1997: 14.
— Kapalua Resort community featured, Lahaina News, September 4, 1997: 8.
— The Masters condominium project featured, Lahaina News, September 11, 1997: 8.
— Piilani Village featured, Lahaina News, September 18, 1997: 8.
— Kahana Ridge construction almost completed, Lahaina News, September 25, 1997: 8.
— time for renters to invest, Lahaina News, October 9, 1997: 14.
— Maui Eldorado featured, Lahaina News, October 16, 1997: 8.
— options at Kapalua detailed, Lahaina News, October 23, 1997: 14.
— Kahana Sunset featured, Lahaina News, October 30, 1997: 12.
— Mahinahina Beach Condominiums featured, Lahaina News, November 6, 1997: 12.

— Wahikuli Homestead featured, Lahaina News, November 13, 1997: 10.
— Kahana Ridge construction completed, Lahaina News, November 20, 1997: 14.
— Ke Alii Subdivision nearing completion, Lahaina News, November 27, 1997: 10.
— update on available houses , Lahaina News, December 4, 1997: 20.
— update on current market, Lahaina News, December 11, 1997: 20.
— update on sales at Kapalua Resort, Lahaina News, December 18, 1997: 20.
— Mahinahina Beach Condominiums featured, Lahaina News, December 25, 1997: 10.
— Ka'anapali Hillside featured, Lahaina News, January 1, 1998: 14.
— Kahana Ridge featured, Lahaina News, January 8, 1998: 10.
— Whaler On Ka'anapali Beach selling well, Lahaina News, January 15, 1998: 10.
— update on projected market, Lahaina News, January 22, 1998: 10.
— update on current market, Lahaina News, January 29, 1998: 12.
— Hololani development featured, Lahaina News, February 5, 1998: 10.
— Sands of Kahana featured, Lahaina News, February 12, 1998: 12.
— Monte D. Fitts Realtors discusses current sales, Lahaina News, February 19, 1998: 10.
— townhouses available through Whalers Realty, Lahaina News, February 26, 1998: 10.
— update on current market, Lahaina News, March 5, 1998: 12.
— Whalers Realty celebrates 22nd anniversary, Lahaina News, March 12, 1998: 10.
— oceanfront opportunities described, Lahaina News, March 19, 1998: 10.
— update on current market, Lahaina News, March 26, 1998: 10,11.
— Maui Kai Condominium featured, Lahaina News, April 2, 1998: 12.
— Kahana Sunset featured, Lahaina News, April 9, 1998: 12.
— high-end beach property featured, Lahaina News, April 16, 1998: 10.
— update on current market, Lahaina News, April 23, 1998: 12.
— Kahana Ridge featured, Lahaina News, April 30, 1998: 12.
— The Mahana at Ka'anapali featured, Lahaina News, May 7, 1998: 14.
— partial ownership of house at Kai Ala Place available, Lahaina News, May 14, 1998: 12.
— oceanfront properties available, Lahaina News, May 21, 1998: 12.
— advantage of purchasing over renting, Lahaina News, May 28, 1998: 10.
— Kapalua Resort featured, Lahaina News, June 4, 1998: 12.
— Mahinahina Beach featured, Lahaina News, June 11, 1998: 12.
— home ownership discussed, Lahaina News, June 18, 1998: 12.
— 107 Halelo Street featured, Lahaina News, July 9, 1998: 12.
— home for sale in Pineapple Hill, Lahaina News, July 16, 1998: 12.
— Puamana planned unit featured, Lahaina News, July 23, 1998: 12.
— Kapalua Resort featured, Lahaina News, July 30, 1998: 12.
— Ka'anapali Hillside featured, Lahaina News, August 6, 1998: 16.
— market is perfect for first time buyers , Lahaina News, August 13, 1998: 12.
— Ka'anapali Hillside featured, Lahaina News, September 3, 1998: 10.
— properties in Ka'anapali featured, Lahaina News, September 10, 1998: 10.
— Kapalua Golf Villas featured, Lahaina News, September 17, 1998: 12.
— Kahana Ridge houses under construction, Lahaina News, October 1, 1998: 12.
— home ownership discussed, Lahaina News, October 8, 1998: 12.
— Mahinahina Beach featured, Lahaina News, October 15, 1998: 12.
— Ka'anapali Vistas featured, Lahaina News, October 29, 1998: 12.
— home on Ironwood Lane featured, Lahaina News, November 5, 1998: 16.

— Kuleana Condominiums featured, Lahaina News, November 12, 1998: 12.
— Sands of Kahana featured, Lahaina News, November 19, 1998: 12.
— Whaler on Ka'anapali Beach featured, Lahaina News, November 26, 1998: 12.
— rebate offered for Kahana Ridge, Lahaina News, December 10, 1998: 16.
— Whalers Realty Inc. featured, Lahaina News, December 17, 1998: 16.
— Kapalua condominiums featured, Lahaina News, December 31, 1998: 10.
— The Masters at Ka'anapali Hillside featured, Lahaina News, January 7, 1999: 12.
— shared ownership available at Sands of Kahana, Lahaina News, January 14, 1999: 10.
— Ka'anapali Royal Condominium featured, Lahaina News, January 21, 1999: 10.
— Mike Montoya of Whalers Realty reflects on moving to Maui, Lahaina News, January 28, 1999: 10.
— Kahana Ridge development featured, Lahaina News, February 4, 1999: 12.
— Ka'anapali Golf Estates featured, Lahaina News, February 11, 1999: 12.
— update on open houses, Lahaina News, February 18, 1999: 10.
— appeal of housing in Maui, Lahaina News, February 25, 1999: 10.
— Kapalua featured, Lahaina News, March 4, 1999: 10.
— shared ownership available at Sands of Kahana, Lahaina News, March 11, 1999: 10.
— Ka'anapali Alii Condominiums featured, Lahaina News, March 18, 1999: 12.
— Whalers Realty to hold "Art, Sushi, and Open House" party, Lahaina News, March 25, 1999: 12.
— Ka'anapali Hillside featured, Lahaina News, April 15, 1999: 10.
— Ka'anapali Hillside featured, Lahaina News, April 22, 1999: 10.
— Kahana Sunset featured, Lahaina News, May 6, 1999: 14.
— The Masters at Ka'anapali featured, Lahaina News, May 13, 1999: 12.
— indicators discussed, Lahaina News, May 20, 1999: 12.
— update on Kahana Ridge, Lahaina News, May 27, 1999: 10.
— Maui Kai featured, Lahaina News, June 10, 1999: 12.
— update on Ka'anapali Hillside, Lahaina News, June 17, 1999: 12.
— importance of location discussed, Lahaina News, June 24, 1999: 10.
— Kaleialoha Condominium units available, Lahaina News, July 8, 1999: 10.
— Positano Villa featured, Lahaina News, July 15, 1999: 10.
— Kahana Ridge featured, Lahaina News, July 22, 1999: 10.
— Ka'anapali Hillside featured, Lahaina News, August 5, 1999: 10.
— Napili Ridge featured, Lahaina News, August 12, 1999: 12.
— Ka'anapali Golf Estates featured, Lahaina News, August 19, 1999: 13.
— Sands of Kahana featured, Lahaina News, August 26, 1999: 12.
— Pineapple Hill featured, Lahaina News, September 2, 1999: 12.
— Kahana Ridge featured, Lahaina News, September 16, 1999: 10.
— pre-sale begins at Coconut Grove at Kapalula Bay, Lahaina News, September 16, 1999: 11.
— Ka'anapali Beach featured, Lahaina News, September 30, 1999: 10.
— Royal Kahana featured, Lahaina News, October 7, 1999: 12.
— open house at Maluhia Country Ranches to be held, Lahaina News, October 7, 1999: 13.
— Kapalua Golf Villa featured, Lahaina News, October 14, 1999: 10.
— time share resales available at The Whaler, Lahaina News, October 28, 1999: 14.
— update on market, Lahaina News, November 4, 1999: 10.
— Kanaha Ridge featured, Lahaina News, November 11, 1999: 10.
— changes in the market discussed, Lahaina News, November 18, 1999: 13.

REAL ESTATE COMMISSION

REAL ESTATE MAUI STYLE

REAL ESTATE SCAMS

REAL EXPERIENCE ANTI-TOBACCO YOUTH SUMMIT
— to be held, Lahaina News, July 24, 2003: 2.

REAL PEOPLE [TELEVISION SHOW]
— episode filmed in Lahaina, Lahaina News, October 12, 1983: 7,8,9.

REALTORS ASSOCIATION OF MAUI (RAM)
— new name for Maui Board of Realtors, Lahaina News, August 8, 2002: 8.
— donates to Maui Food Bank, Lahaina News, January 9, 2003: 9.
— awards scholarships, Lahaina News, June 26, 2003: 15.
— to hold Presidential Scholarship golf tournament, Lahaina News, July 31, 2003: 13.

REARDON, MICHAEL [ACTOR]
— presents "The Gospel According to Mark", Lahaina News, October 30, 1985: 3.
— to perform, Lahaina News, October 26, 1988: 16.

REASER, DON
— named general manager of Royal Lahaina Resort, Lahaina News, July 25, 1991: 7.

REAUX, JAMES
— new chef at the Westin Maui featured, Lahaina News, November 14, 1991: 18,19.
— chef wins first place at Taste of Lahaina, Lahaina News, October 15, 1992: 16.
— Westin Maui's Executive Chef wins Lahaina Cannery's Pineapple Cook-off, Lahaina News, April 15, 1993: 10.
— chef creates "Magic Mui Memories" dinner, Lahaina News, June 24, 1993: 13,14.

REAUX, JENNIFER
— appointed sales manager at Westin Maui, Lahaina News, January 26, 1995: 13.

REAVES-PHILLIPS, SANDRA [MUSICIAN]
— to perform at Baldwin Auditorium, Lahaina News, March 23, 1988: 3.
— performs at Baldwin Auditorium, Lahaina News, March 21, 1990: 13.

REBECCA [PLAY]
— to be performed at Maui Community Theatre, Lahaina News, September 5, 1990: 16.

REBIRTHING
— as healing method, Lahaina News, April 13, 1988: 20.

RECEIVES DONATION FROM HARRY AND JEANETTE WEINBERG FOUNDATION
— donates to Food Bank, Lahaina News, December 27, 2001: 10.

RECREATION
— projects desired by West Maui Business Association, Lahaina Sun, December 23, 1970: 2.
— editorial criticizing jet skis, Lahaina News, May 7, 1986: 2.
— new patrol boat helping enforce ski boat rules, Lahaina News, May 7, 1986: 3.

RECYCLING OFFICE
— running Used Motor Oil Curbside Pick-up Pilot Project, Lahaina News, January 15, 1998: 5.

RED AND WHITE SONGFEST
— committee seeking singers, Lahaina News, March 31, 1994: 16.
— committee looking for singers, Lahaina News, April 21, 1994: 16.

RED BULL CLIFF DIVING LANA'I CONTEST
— to be held, Lahaina News, August 29, 2002: 11.

RED CROSS
— disaster training offered, Lahaina News, August 6, 1986: 3.
— offering advanced lifesaving courses, Lahaina News, April 29, 1987: 3.
— sponsoring "Single Superstars Beach Olympics" to raise money for San Francisco earthquake relief, Lahaina News, November 8, 1989: 24.
— students donate to fund, Lahaina News, September 27, 2001: 1,18.
— "Spirit of Aloha Cut-A-Thon" to support Disaster Relief Fund, Lahaina News, October 18, 2001: 9.
— "Art from the Heart" benefit to be held, Lahaina News, April 11, 2002: 14.

RED FIRECRACKER, GREEN FIRECRACKER [FILM]
— to be shown at Maui Arts and Cultural Center, Lahaina News, April 25, 1996: 17.

RED HOT CHILI PEPPERS [MUSICAL GROUP]
— to perform at War Memorial Stadium, Lahaina News, March 26, 1992: 16.
— concert canceled, to hold second concert in Honolulu, Lahaina News, April 9, 1992: 22.

RED HOT LOUISIANA BAND [MUSICAL GROUP]
— to perform at Casanova's, Lahaina News, September 17, 1992: 17.

RED LANTERN CHINESE SEAFOOD [RESTAURANT]
— opens, Lahaina News, August 7, 1997: 6,7.
— to begin Sunday Night Jazz, Lahaina News, December 18, 1997: 8.

RED LOBSTER [RESTAURANT]
— to open, Lahaina News, August 12, 1993: 7.
— closes Front Street location, Lahaina News, April 13, 1995: 5.

RED PALMS ESTATE [BUSINESS]
— offering space for holiday parties, Lahaina News, November 28, 1996: 14.
— development featured, Lahaina News, March 14, 2002: 6.

RED PALMS I.E. [BUSINESS]
— new art store opens, Lahaina News, November 28, 1996: 13.
— to hold Christmas in Lahaina arts and craft sale, Lahaina News, November 20, 1997: 17.

RED RIDING IN THE HOOD [MUSICAL]
— to be performed as part of Theatre Theatre summer youth workshop, Lahaina News, July 20, 1995: 11.

RED ROSE, THE [PLAY]
— performed at Maui Academy of Performing Arts, Lahaina News, November 3, 1994: 26.

RED SHOW, THE [FILM]
— to be shown at Maui Youth Theatre, Lahaina News, September 14, 1988: 15.

REDDINGTON, DAN [COMEDIAN]
— to perform at Comedy Club and the Sports Page, Lahaina News, February 13, 1991: 9,11.
— to perform at the Sports Page for New Year's Eve, Lahaina News, January 2, 1992: 12.

REDSTONE, KENNY
— to speak on Maui's medicinal plants, Lahaina News, October 1, 1998: 16.

REECE, KIM TAYLOR [ARTIST]
— featured, Lahaina News, June 13, 1990: B5.

REED, AUDREY ROCHA
— new executive director for J. Walter Cameron Center, Lahaina News, May 15, 1982: 2.

REED, HELEN
— to raise cancer awareness, Lahaina News, March 17, 1994: 4.
— recounts African safari, Lahaina News, December 3, 1998: 17.

REED, HELEN AND ROB
— recount visit to Antarctica, Part I, Lahaina News, July 18, 2002: 1,9.

REED, RICK [POLITICIAN]
— endorsed by Public Resources for Jobs (Pro Jobs), Lahaina News, September 17, 1986: 3,11.
— candidacy for State Senate featured, Lahaina News, October 22, 1986: 1,5,16.

— opens satellite offices following win, Lahaina News, December 3, 1986: 3.

— to speak to American Association of Retired Persons, Lahaina News, December 31, 1986: 12.

— to draft Senate resolution to study health impact of cane burning, Lahaina News, March 4, 1987: 3.

— to hold brown back luncheon at Lahaina Civic Center, Lahaina News, March 11, 1987: 18.

— proposes health care facility for West Maui, Lahaina News, March 11, 1987: 3.

— Brown bag meeting with constituents described, Lahaina News, March 25, 1987: 1,20.

— allocates money to projects in West Maui, Lahaina News, April 15, 1987: 12.

— to hold public "brownbag", Lahaina News, June 17, 1987: 3.

— public "brownbag" with Bill Pfeil described, Lahaina News, June 24, 1987: 1.

— editorial opposing his views on homosexuality, Lahaina News, August 5, 1987: 2.

— organizes meeting with Maui residents with Bill Pfeil, Lahaina News, December 9, 1987: 3.

— concerned with speed limits for thrillcraft, Lahaina News, January 27, 1988: 3.

— urges U.S. Navy to stop bombing Kahoʻolawe, Lahaina News, February 3, 1988: 4.

— opposes jet skis off shore, Lahaina News, February 17, 1988: 17.

— comments on proposed thrillcraft corridor, Lahaina News, February 24, 1988: 1.

— introduces bill to repair Mala Wharf, Lahaina News, February 24, 1988: 18.

— to hold brown bag with State Representative Bill Pfeil, Lahaina News, February 24, 1988: 18.

— decides not to run for U.S. Congress, Lahaina News, April 20, 1988: 6.

— to meet with constituents, Lahaina News, April 27, 1988: 6.

— account of public meeting, Lahaina News, May 11, 1988: 1,4.

— made floor leader by Republican state senators, Lahaina News, July 20, 1988: 3.

— to hold "pre-session" public meeting, Lahaina News, December 21, 1988: 17.

— supports Millyard bypass route for Lahaina Bypass, Lahaina News, January 11, 1989: 1,20.

— told of plight of Holo Honokowai residents, Lahaina News, January 11, 1989: 20.

— reports on Senate bills to ban thrillcraft, Lahaina News, February 8, 1989: 14.

— update on Senate, Lahaina News, February 15, 1989: 14.

— to hold public meeting, Lahaina News, February 22, 1989: 1.

— reports on Ocean Recreation Management Plan to ban jet skis, Lahaina News, March 15, 1989: 14.

— reports on proposed pay raises, Lahaina News, April 19, 1989: 14.

— seeks explanation for green algae off West Maui, Lahaina News, August 23, 1989: 1.

— critical of state's support of West Maui, Lahaina News, September 13, 1989: 3.

— hoping to increase affordability of housing, Lahaina News, January 3, 1990: 1.

— says state bills to allow for initiative measures are dead, Lahaina News, February 7, 1990: 28.

— attacks state's refusal to unveil recommendations for Mala Wharf before meeting, Lahaina News, March 14, 1990: 1.

— accuses Pacific Whale Foundation founder Gregory Kaufman of unethical behavior, Lahaina News, April 4, 1990: 1.

— to seek reelection, Lahaina News, July 4, 1990: 3.

— criticizes advertisement as violent, Lahaina News, November 14, 1990: 5.

— appraises State budget, Lahaina News, January 16, 1991: 9.

— speaks of reform to unemployment compensation, Lahaina News, January 23, 1991: 1.

— calling for term limits, Lahaina News, March 13, 1991: 3.

— claims reapportionment is a joke, Lahaina News, May 15, 1991: 1.

— continues criticism of redistricting plan, Lahaina News, May 30, 1991: 1.

— urges lobbying to support construction of restrooms at Mala Wharf Park, Lahaina News, June 6, 1991: 1.

— requests probe to determine if local government complying with Clean Water Act, Lahaina News, September 19, 1991: 1.

— being sued by Larry Mehau, who was accused of being the godfather of organized crime in Hawaii, Lahaina News, December 5, 1991: 4.

— wins libel suit brought by Larry Mehau, Lahaina News, February 13, 1992: 3.

— asks mayor Linda Lingle to clear algae from beaches, Lahaina News, April 30, 1992: 1.

— to hold fundraiser, run for U.S. Senate, Lahaina News, May 21, 1992: 4.

— critical of Senator Inouye's record, Lahaina News, June 4, 1992: 1,4.

— to hold fundraiser, Lahaina News, June 11, 1992: 3.

— Wayne Nishiki ousted from Democratic Party for supporting, Lahaina News, June 18, 1992: 4.

— critical of senator Daniel Inouye's lack of fiscal restraint, Lahaina News, June 25, 1992: 2.

— holds dinner with former Senator Hiram Fong and Senator Phil Gramm, Lahaina News, August 13, 1992: 11.

— fundraiser planned by old Fireman's Ball committee, Lahaina News, August 13, 1992: 3.

— headed for a new trial involving Larry Mehau, Lahaina News, August 20, 1992: 4.

— seeking funding for facilities in Kihei, Lahaina News, January 28, 1993: 10.

— introduces bills to fund improvements of Kihei public schools, Lahaina News, February 11, 1993: 7.

— introduces resolution to clean algae from beaches, Lahaina News, March 25, 1993: 3.

REED, ROY ALLEN [MUSICIAN]

— celebrating 4th year as hair care expert, Lahaina News, December 27, 1989: 5.

— to perform at Longhi's, Lahaina News, February 21, 1990: 13.

— fundraiser to be held for, Lahaina News, March 24, 1994: 7.

REEF CAFE [RESTAURANT]

— reopens at Maui Ocean Center, Lahaina News, January 10, 2002: 8.

REEF ENVIRONMENTAL EDUCATION FOUNDATION (REEF)

— seeks to support reef preservation, Lahaina News, January 25, 2001: 15.

— to hold REEF Week, Lahaina News, February 1, 2001: 17.

— to hold fish identification seminar, Lahaina News, December 6, 2001: 13.

REEF WEEK

— to be held by Reef Environmental Education Foundation (REEF), Lahaina News, February 1, 2001: 17.

REEFS

— cleanup sponsored by Hyatt Regency Maui and Nicks Aqua Sports, Lahaina News, September 7, 1988: 14.

— protection outlined at Earth Maui Nature Summit, Lahaina News, September 4, 1997: 1,2.

REESE, KIM TAYLOR [ARTIST]

— appeared at Good Image Gallery, Lahaina News, September 5, 1990: 17.

REESER, DAN
— to be honored by the Sierra Club, Lahaina News, November 4, 1999: 12.

REEVES, DAVID
— named conference services manager at Four Seasons Resort Wailea, Lahaina News, December 12, 1991: 16.

REEVES, JAMES LEE [COMEDIAN]
— to perform at Comedy Club and the Sports Page, Lahaina News, April 23, 1992: 25,27.
— to perform at Comedy Club and the Sports Page, Lahaina News, March 11, 1993: 13,15.

REEVES, RALPH
— named officer for Lahaina Yacht Club, Lahaina Sun, December 23, 1970: 8.
— editorial response to criticism from, Lahaina Sun, February 7, 1973: 6.
— reflects on decline of Lahaina, Lahaina Sun, March 7, 1973: 8.

REEVES, SHERI
— teaching marine art class, Lahaina News, October 8, 1998: 17.

REFLECTIONS OF OLD LAHAINA LUAU AND CONCERT
— benefit to be held for The Friends of Moku'ula, Lahaina News, August 19, 1999: 18.
— to be held, Lahaina News, August 26, 1999: 8.

REFORESTATION PROJECT
— information session to be held, Lahaina News, February 24, 2000: 16.

REFORM PARTY OF HAWAII
— no longer affiliated with the National Reform Party, Lahaina News, May 18, 2000: 17.

REGENBAUM, DAVID
— to speak on conducting annual membership meetings, Lahaina News, January 28, 1993: 8.

REGGAE EXPLOSION
— to be held at Maui Arts and Cultural Center, Lahaina News, October 3, 1996: 14.

REGGAE FESTIVAL
— to be held, Lahaina News, February 25, 1993: 9.
— to be held, Lahaina News, March 4, 1993: 9.

REGGAE SUNSPLASH
— to be held at War Memorial Stadium, Lahaina News, May 9, 1990: 18.
— to be held, Lahaina News, May 16, 1990: 11.
— to be held at Maui Tropical Plantation, Lahaina News, May 19, 1994: 16.

REGIS HAIR SALON [BUSINESS]
— to hold "Clip for Cure", Lahaina News, October 8, 1998: 17.
— to hold "Clips for a Cure" to benefit Regis Foundation for Breast Cancer Research, Lahaina News, October 26, 2000: 28.

REGULATORY AGENCIES, DEPARTMENT OF
— conducts public hearing on cable TV, Lahaina Sun, December 2, 1970: 2.
— conducts public hearing on cable TV, Lahaina Sun, December 9, 1970: 6.

REHABILITATION HOSPITAL OF THE PACIFIC
— forms Maui Comprehensive Rehabilitation Center with Hale Makua, Lahaina News, June 18, 1992: 4.
— expand medical team on Maui, Lahaina News, February 1, 2001: 8.

REHAK, MARY ANN
— general manager of Gerard's discusses restaurant, Lahaina News, September 21, 1988: 10.

REICHEL, KEALI'I [MUSICIAN]
— comments on newly dedicated Hawaiian Language Preschool, Punana Leo, Lahaina News, May 25, 1988: 1,14.
— to lecture on Hawaiian topics at Maui Prince Hotel, Lahaina News, July 4, 1990: 4.
— to perform at the Maui Academy of Performing Arts, Lahaina News, January 9, 1991: 8.
— organizing performance of chants at Iao Theatre, Lahaina News, February 17, 1994: 12.
— to perform at Maui Lu Resort, Lahaina News, February 9, 1995: 11.
— to teach Hawaiian history class, Lahaina News, April 13, 1995: 4.
— to perform in "Tales of Maui", Lahaina News, August 17, 1995: 11.
— performs at telethon, Lahaina News, November 2, 1995: 12.
— featured, Lahaina News, January 18, 1996: 13.
— tops list of nominees for Na Hoku Hanohano awards, Lahaina News, April 18, 1996: 16.
— to perform benefit for Punana Leo O Maui, Lahaina News, August 1, 1996: 21.
— to perform as part of "A Lei For All Seasons", Lahaina News, August 8, 1996: 14,15.
— to perform at benefit concert for Kina'u Ministries, Lahaina News, August 15, 1996: 16.
— to perform at SeaWatch Restaurant's "Another Starry Night for Hula", Lahaina News, February 6, 1997: 14.
— to perform at A Taste of Lahaina, Lahaina News, September 4, 1997: 3.
— to support release of CD by Damon Williams, Lahaina News, January 1, 1998: 1,3.
— to perform at Carnegie Hall, Lahaina News, January 29, 1998: 17.
— to perform at Carnegie Hall, Lahaina News, February 5, 1998: 13.
— to perform at A Taste of Lahaina, Lahaina News, September 10, 1998: 16.
— to perform at Maui Arts and Cultural Center, Lahaina News, February 4, 1999: 5.
— to perform at Reflections of Old Lahaina Luau and Concert benefit, Lahaina News, August 19, 1999: 18.
— to perform at "Reflections of Old Lahaina", Lahaina News, August 26, 1999: 8.
— to perform three Maui shows, Lahaina News, February 3, 2000: 1.
— to perform "Kukahi 2000", Lahaina News, February 10, 2000: 18.
— to perform at Ka'ahumanu Center, Lahaina News, November 16, 2000: 17.
— to be featured at "The Art of the Chanter", Lahaina News, January 11, 2001: 3.
— to perform at Maui Arts and Cultural Center, Lahaina News, February 8, 2001: 21.
— to perform at Maui Arts and Cultural Center as part of Ho'onanea Hawaiian Series, Lahaina News, February 15, 2001: 16.
— to perform at "I Love Lahaina", Lahaina News, October 25, 2001: 15.
— performs at "I Love Lahaina", Lahaina News, November 8, 2001: 3.
— to lead "Na Mele Hakukole—Chants and Songs of Ridicule", Lahaina News, January 17, 2002: 15.
— to perform at Maui Arts and Cultural Center, Lahaina News, February 7, 2002: 17.
— to perform at Maui Arts and Cultural Center, Lahaina News, February 14, 2002: 15,16.
— to stage Kukahi 2003, Lahaina News, February 13, 2003: 17.

REIFURTH, LAWRENCE
— Hawaii State Insurance Commissioner delays decision on Hawaii Insurance Bureau's workers' compensation filings, Lahaina News, September 1, 1994: 12.

REIKI
— practitioners to meet, Lahaina News, August 8, 2002: 17.

REILLEY'S STEAKS AND SEAFOOD [RESTAURANT]
— opens, Lahaina News, August 26, 1993: 10.
— names Michael Gardner as executive chef, Lahaina News, March 9, 1995: 6.
— to hold Pacific Luau, Lahaina News, May 29, 1997: 16.
— featured, Lahaina News, January 7, 1999: 9.

REINECKE, KURT [POLITICIAN]
— announces candidacy for state senator for 5th district, Lahaina News, April 4, 1990: 2.
— candidate profiled, Lahaina News, September 5, 1990: 1,8.

REINSTATED HAWAIIAN GOVERNMENT
— to hold educational meetings, Lahaina News, September 20, 2001: 16.
— to hold educational talks, Lahaina News, October 11, 2001: 16.
— to hold "Vigil for Justice and Peace" at Kamehameha Iki Park, Lahaina News, November 8, 2001: 3.
— continues to hold meetings, Lahaina News, November 15, 2001: 16.
— continues to meet, Lahaina News, January 17, 2002: 16.

REISCHL, ERIK [MUSICIAN]
— pianist performs at Longhi's benefit for musically inclined youth, Lahaina News, February 6, 1997: 3.
— to perform on Maui, Lahaina News, January 29, 1998: 8.

REISS, JEFF
— joins Island Mortgage Corporation, Lahaina News, May 21, 1992: 9.

REITH, DIRK
— opens concession in rail car at Lahaina station, Lahaina News, December 19, 1984: 14.

RELAY FOR LIFE
— to be held, Lahaina News, July 20, 2000: 15.
— to be held by American Cancer Society, Lahaina News, May 31, 2001: 2.
— American Cancer Society to hold, Lahaina News, July 5, 2001: 5.
— seeking volunteers, Lahaina News, July 19, 2001: 3.
— American Cancer Society to hold, Lahaina News, June 6, 2002: 5.
— teams sought for, Lahaina News, July 4, 2002: 5.
— to honor cancer survivors, Lahaina News, July 25, 2002: 1,3.
— held, Lahaina News, August 1, 2002: 1.
— to be held, Lahaina News, November 28, 2002: 5.
— teams to hold car wash, Lahaina News, March 13, 2003: 2.
— to be held, Lahaina News, March 27, 2003: 2.
— to be held at Kihei, Lahaina News, April 3, 2003: 16.
— to benefit American Cancer Society, Lahaina News, April 3, 2003: 18.
— to be held, Lahaina News, June 26, 2003: 1,2.
— to be led by fifth graders from King Kamehameha III Elementary School, Lahaina News, July 17, 2003: 3.
— held, Lahaina News, July 24, 2003: 2.

RELENTLESS [MUSICAL GROUP]
— to perform at Moose McGillycuddy's with Willie Haukaloa, Lahaina News, December 26, 1991: 12.
— to perform at Studio 505, Lahaina News, January 30, 1992: 17.

RELIGION
— Episcopalians meet on Maui, Lahaina Sun, October 11, 1972: 7.
— survey of religious preferences released, Lahaina Sun, April 25, 1973: 11.
— Kekua Ola church in Kahana to resume services, Lahaina Sun, May 9, 1973: 10.
— missionaries from Youth With a Mission come to Maui, Lahaina News, January 18, 1984: 10.
— Shabbat service scheduled, Lahaina News, August 20, 1986: 15.
— Jewish Ceremonies held, Lahaina News, October 1, 1986: 12.
— Eucharist ministers commissioned, Lahaina News, December 24, 1986: 3.
— prospects for Year of the Rabbit detailed, Lahaina News, December 31, 1986: 1,,9.
— Shabbot service to be held, Lahaina News, January 21, 1987: 3.
— Jews celebrate Passover, Lahaina News, March 30, 1988: 20.
— High Holiday services to be held, Lahaina News, September 24, 1992: 3.
— Kamp Kumulani 2000—Discover God's Plan, Lahaina News, July 20, 2000: 8.

REMAINS
— Historical Preservation Division to hold public meetings on rules for handling ancient burials, Lahaina News, January 26, 1995: 2.
— discovered at D.T. Fleming Park, Lahaina News, September 7, 1995: 1.

REMER, JANE
— to speak at Arts Education Forum, Lahaina News, March 5, 1998: 16.

RENA CHING HULA TROUPE
— performance at Kahului Shopping Center reviewed, Lahaina Sun, June 21, 1972: 17.

RENAISSANCE PSYCHIC FAIRE
— see Psychic Fair

RENAISSANCE WAILEA BEACH RESORT
— Rick Nagaoka new director of sales at, Lahaina News, February 7, 2002: 8.
— to hold Hawaii Artisan Events, Lahaina News, April 4, 2002: 17.

RENATA [MUSICAL GROUP]
— to perform at Pacific'o Restaurant, Lahaina News, September 26, 1996: 16.

RENNIE HARRIS PUREMOVEMENT
— to perform "Rome and Jewels", Lahaina News, October 11, 2001: 16.

RENT
— rules and regulations discussed, Lahaina Sun, April 14, 1971: 8.
— public housing rent increases 50%, Lahaina Sun, July 14, 1971: 4.
— Impact on Stores in Paia, Lahaina Times, June, 1980 volume 4 number 5: 1.
— reason for business failure, Lahaina Times, October, 1980 volume 4 number 9: 1.

RENTAL HOUSING TRUST FUND
— to take applications for low-interest rate loans, Lahaina News, September 28, 1995: 2.

REPLINGER, RAP [ENTERTAINER]
— remembered, Lahaina News, February 1, 1984: 14.

REPOGLE, ADAM
— wins Ho'okipa Classic memorial surf meet, Lahaina News, January 19, 1995: 6.

REPOLLO, DESMON AND STEVE [MUSICIANS]
— continue to perform Makai Bar at Marriott, Lahaina News, May 14, 1992: 17.

REPOLLO, STEVE ANTONE [MUSICIAN]
— to perform at Marriott Makai Bar, Lahaina News, December 19, 1991: 19.
— to perform at Makai Bar Maui Marriott Resort, Lahaina News, April 21, 1994: 15.

REPRESENT YOUTH OUTREACH
— group formed to help young people, Lahaina News, March 28, 2002: 1,20.
— to hold fundraiser at Java Jazz, Lahaina News, April 4, 2002: 16,17.
— to hold fundraiser at Java Jazz, Lahaina News, May 16, 2002: 2.
— grand opening of facility to be held, Lahaina News, September 12, 2002: 1,22.
— seeking volunteers, Lahaina News, June 12, 2003: 2.

REPUBLICAN PARTY

— annual convention held in Kahului Armory, Lahaina Sun, April 28, 1971: 4.
— meets in Kahului, Lahaina Sun, May 26, 1971: 6.
— Paul Elkins elected as party chairman, Lahaina Sun, October 20, 1971: 5.
— platform announced, Lahaina Sun, May 17, 1972: 11.
— Maui chairman Paul Elkins accuses mayor Cravalho of conflict of interest in Wailea development, Lahaina Sun, July 5, 1972: 3.
— Paul Elkins to seek party nomination for mayoral race, Lahaina Sun, July 19, 1972: 9.
— Diana Hansen, running against Patsy Mink, to campaign in Maui, Lahaina Sun, July 26, 1972: 11.
— Maui County to hold its annual convention, Lahaina News, July 9, 1986: 3.
— to host Lincoln Day dinner, Lahaina News, February 8, 1989: 5.
— women to meet, Lahaina News, September 20, 1989: 3.
— to hold Lincoln Day dinner, Lahaina News, February 14, 1990: 3.
— to meet, Lahaina News, July 4, 1991: 3.
— to meet, Lahaina News, August 1, 1991: 4.
— to meet, Lahaina News, August 8, 1991: 3.
— Foster Hull elected chair of Maui, Lahaina News, August 29, 1991: 4.
— western region leaders to meet at Maui Inter-Continental Wailea hotel, Lahaina News, September 19, 1991: 3,8.
— regional conference to be held, Lahaina News, September 26, 1991: 7.
— regional conference to be held this week, Lahaina News, October 10, 1991: 4.
— district chair objects to Russell Blair becoming state Senator due to reapportionment, Lahaina News, November 7, 1991: 1,9.
— to hold monthly meeting at Civil Defense Room of the County Building, Lahaina News, November 7, 1991: 9.
— seeking to oust of Senator Russell Blair, Lahaina News, November 21, 1991: 1.
— asks lieutenant governor Ben Cayetano to void appointment of senators not chosen by voters due to reapportionment, Lahaina News, January 2, 1992: 1.
— starting candidate search, Lahaina News, January 30, 1992: 1,28.
— pro-life supporters hope party will oppose abortion, Lahaina News, February 6, 1992: 1.
— to meet; Lincoln Day Dinner scheduled, Lahaina News, February 6, 1992: 4.
— Foster Hull and Leina'ala Teruya Drummond declare as candidates, Lahaina News, February 13, 1992: 3.
— to meet, Lahaina News, March 5, 1992: 4.
— to hold monthly meeting, Lahaina News, May 7, 1992: 6.
— to hold monthly meeting, Lahaina News, July 9, 1992: 5.
— to hold meeting, Lahaina News, August 13, 1992: 4.
— to hold candidate night, Lahaina News, August 20, 1992: 4.
— to meet, Lahaina News, April 15, 1993: 3.
— to hold annual Lincoln Day Dinner, Lahaina News, February 17, 1994: 12.
— to celebrate Abraham Lincoln's birthday, Lahaina News, February 16, 1995: 6.
— to meet, Lahaina News, January 29, 1998: 16.
— to hold convention at Lihikai School, Lahaina News, March 11, 1999: 12.
— Boyd Kleefisch CEO of Maui Memorial Medical Center to speak at Maui League of Republican Women, Lahaina News, April 8, 1999: 12.
— to hold luau fundraiser, Lahaina News, October 14, 1999: 13.
— establishes phone line for upcoming events, Lahaina News, October 21, 1999: 14.
— to hold luau fundraiser, Lahaina News, October 21, 1999: 16.
— to host executive director of Maui Economic Concerns of the Community Inc. Charles Riding, Lahaina News, November 4, 1999: 13.
— to hold precinct caucus meetings, Lahaina News, February 10, 2000: 16.
— to hold Sweetheart Dance, Lahaina News, February 10, 2000: 16.
— new leadership in Maui County, Lahaina News, July 6, 2000: 15.
— to host Candidate's night, Lahaina News, July 27, 2000: 8.
— to hold "Meet Our Candidates Night", Lahaina News, August 10, 2000: 3.
— candidates pictured, Lahaina News, October 26, 2000: 32.
— to hold fundraiser, Lahaina News, September 5, 2002: 5.
— to hold monthly social event, Lahaina News, February 20, 2003: 17.
— president of Tax Foundation of Hawaii Lowell Kalapa to speak to Maui League of Republican Women, Lahaina News, March 13, 2003: 17.
— to hold County Convention, Lahaina News, March 20, 2003: 3.
— to hold district meetings, Lahaina News, May 22, 2003: 16.

REPUBLICAN WOMEN'S CLUB

— to meet, Lahaina News, May 23, 1990: 6.

RESCUE 911 [TELEVISION SHOW]

— records episode on Maui, Lahaina News, October 29, 1992: 17.

RESCUE ME MAUI

— calendar published by firefighters, Lahaina News, April 13, 1995: 12.
— calendar features firefighters, Lahaina News, April 20, 1995: 11.

RESCUES

— rescue called off after two men hike out safely, Lahaina Sun, April 21, 1971: 3.
— Lawrence Peterson [tourist] missing, Lahaina Sun, April 28, 1971: 3.
— black coral divers Bob Carey and Chris Johnson rescued by Coast Guard helicopter, Lahaina Sun, June 9, 1971: 5.
— Michael Davis rescued from the ocean, Lahaina Sun, July 28, 1971: 10.
— five young people rescued on open 16-foot boat, Lahaina Sun, September 29, 1971: 1.
— man rescued from ocean, Lahaina Sun, November 17, 1971: 12.
— helicopter crashes in ocean attempting to rescue two Australian seamen, Lahaina Sun, November 24, 1971: 1.
— practice mine discovered, Lahaina Sun, February 9, 1972: 3.
— Crew of trimaran Far Horizons rescued, Lahaina Sun, February 23, 1972: 3.
— Sister Leona Abella rescued after being swept off a rock near Napili, Lahaina Sun, April 12, 1972: 9.
— four hikers get lost in Haleakala Crater, Lahaina Sun, May 17, 1972: 11.

RESEARCH AND TECHNOLOGY PARK

— to be blessed, Lahaina News, October 1, 1986: 5.

RESIDENCY LAWS

— criticized as restricting working producers from coming to Hawaii, Lahaina Sun, February 10, 1971: 4.

RESNICK, MIKE

— developer planning to build Kahana Beach hotel, Lahaina Sun, February 14, 1973: 12,13.
— to develop Kahana Gateway, Lahaina News, November 16, 1988: 1.

RESORTS PACIFICA [BUSINESS]

— rental manager for Ka'anapali Royal condominiums, Lahaina News, October 18, 1989: 7.

RESOURCES UNLIMITED [BUSINESS]

— renamed Maui Silkscreen Designs, Lahaina News, July 18, 1984: 14.

RESPICIO, ROLAND

— Scholar/Athlete of the Week, Lahaina News, December 30, 1999: 9.

RESSER, DONALD

— to present on Haleakala National Park acquisitions, Lahaina News, October 7, 1999: 16.

RESTA, PIERO [ARTIST]
— reviewed, Lahaina News, August 1, 1983: 12.
— to unveil sculpture, Lahaina News, January 17, 1990: 12.

RESTAURANT AT THE END OF THE UNIVERSE, THE [PLAY]
— to be performed by Baldwin Theatre Guild, Lahaina News, April 21, 1994: 16.

RESTAURANT INDUSTRY SERVICE EXCELLENCE (RISE)
— program to be offered, Lahaina News, May 6, 1999: 15.
— to hold job training course, Lahaina News, March 16, 2000: 13.

RESTAURANT RACE
— to be held at Hanaka‘o‘o Beach Park, Lahaina News, May 1, 1991: 7.

RESTAURANT SERVICE PROFESSIONAL
— training for restaurant workers to be held, Lahaina News, May 4, 2000: 13.
— classes offered, Lahaina News, May 11, 2000: 11.
— course continues, Lahaina News, May 18, 2000: 16.

RETAIL
— see business, real estate, tourism, and specific businesses

RETAIL COMMITTEE
— prepares press kit, Lahaina Sun, December 23, 1970: 8.

RETAIL INDUSTRY TRAINING IN EXCELLENCE (RITE)
— to hold training course, Lahaina News, December 11, 1997: 21.
— course to be offered at Maui Community College, Lahaina News, June 17, 1999: 13.

RETAIL MAP
— two-page map of Maui with retail advertising, typically on pages 6 and 7, begins with this issue and is not indexed, Lahaina Sun, June 16, 1971: .

RETIREMENT PLANNING FOR YOUNG ADULTS
— to be held by F. Dennis DeStefano, Lahaina News, July 12, 2001: 9.

RETRIBUTION [MUSICAL GROUP]
— featured, Lahaina News, March 24, 1994: 13.

RETTINGHOUSE, GAIA
— to talk on "Receptive Writing" at ‘Ohana Connection, Lahaina News, October 9, 2003: 17.

RETURN OF THE GREATER TUNA [PLAY]
— to be performed by Maui Community Theatre, Lahaina News, December 12, 1991: 25.
— to be performed by Maui Community Theatre, Lahaina News, December 19, 1991: 22.
— to finish this week, Lahaina News, December 26, 1991: 15.

RETURN OF THE NENE [FILM]
— shown at Family Film Festival, Lahaina Sun, January 27, 1971: 2.

RETURN WITNESS PROGRAM
— department of the prosecuting attorney looking for help with, Lahaina News, June 5, 1985: 9.

REUNION [MUSICAL GROUP]
— to perform at Lahaina Civic Center, Lahaina News, January 24, 1990: 28.

REVERE, ALAN [ARTIST]
— jewelry showcased, Lahaina News, December 16, 1987: 15.

REVERSADE, GERARD
— to help Maui Community Arts and Cultural Center, Lahaina News, February 20, 1992: 17.

REX PETERSON GALLERY [BUSINESS]
— opens, Lahaina News, December 12, 1996: 24.

REYES, DIANE DELOS
— recognized by Soroptimists International, Lahaina News, May 10, 2001: 1,22.

REYES, ENRIQUE
— chef of La Fogata featured, Lahaina News, March 2, 2000: 5.

REYNOLDS ALUMINUM RECYCLING CO. [BUSINESS]
— paying higher prices for aluminum cans, Lahaina News, February 5, 1986: 3.
— reports on recycling totals for past year, Lahaina News, April 20, 1988: 6.
— to hold contest to encourage recycling, Lahaina News, May 24, 1989: 6.
— to offer free child identification kits, Lahaina News, October 4, 1989: 3.
— to pay for aluminum cans, Lahaina News, August 1, 1991: 5.
— continues recycling program, Lahaina News, August 8, 1991: 4.
— continues recycling aluminum cans, Lahaina News, December 12, 1991: 7.

REYNOLDS, L.D.
— radio announcer joins KLHI-FM, Lahaina News, April 16, 1992: 15.

REYNOLDS, LESLIE
— "Mr. Hypnotist" performs Las Vegas-style hypnosis show, Lahaina News, July 19, 2001: 14.
— "Mr. Hypnotist" to perform at Royal Lahaina Resort, Lahaina News, August 23, 2001: 15.

REYNOLDS, RICHARD
— named executive chef at Inter-Continental Hotel, Lahaina News, March 19, 1986: 3.

REYNOLDS, TROY
— manager of Lahaina Monarch Building Supply killed by exploding propane cannister, Lahaina News, June 17, 1993: 1.

REYS, GLENN
— veteran's experience discussed, Lahaina Sun, October 18, 1972: 6,7.

REZENTS, ERNEST
— chair of Maui County Arborist Committee discusses rejection of art fairs at Banyan Tree Park, Lahaina News, September 9, 1999: 1,16.

REZIN [MUSICAL GROUP]
— to perform at Compadres, Lahaina News, April 23, 1998: 18.

RHODES, MINDY [MUSICIAN]
— to perform at Blue Lagoon, Lahaina News, October 30, 1997: 15.

RHYTHM KINGS, THE [MUSICAL GROUP]
— to perform at Casanova's, Lahaina News, September 12, 1990: 18.
— to perform at Casanova's, Lahaina News, November 14, 1990: 15.
— to perform at Longhi's, Lahaina News, February 13, 1991: 11.
— photograph of, Lahaina News, February 27, 1991: 12.

RIBAO, WAYNE
— Maui Police Captain discusses concerns with residents, Lahaina News, January 20, 2000: 1.

RIBBENS, DAVID
— chef featured, Lahaina News, December 4, 1997: 16.

RICARDO, BENNIE [COMEDIAN]
— to perform at Comedy Club, Lahaina News, July 4, 1991: 10.

RICCO'S [RESTAURANT]
— reviewed, Lahaina News, January 1, 1981: 16.
— reviewed, Lahaina News, January 4, 1984: 13.
— wins best pizza in western United States with "Bleu Hawaii" pizza, Lahaina News, December 5, 1990: 14.

RICE, JERRY
— and other NFL players to compete in charity basketball game for March of Dimes, Big Brothers/Big Sisters, and Easter Seals, Lahaina News, April 20, 2000: 16.

RICE, SUSAN [COMEDIAN]
— to perform at Honolulu Comedy Club, Lahaina News, February 15, 1996: 13.

RICHARD BONHOMME, USS [SHIP]
— to visit Lahaina, Lahaina News, February 18, 1999: 11.

RICHARD DANSKIN GALLERIES [BUSINESS]
— open, Lahaina News, July 4, 1990: 7.

RICHARDS, DAN [NEWSCASTER]
— fired from KNUI, Lahaina Sun, August 2, 1972: 5.

RICHARDS, DAVID [ARTIST]
— watercolorist to exhibit at The Art School at Kapalua, Lahaina News, March 4, 1999: 12.
— to exhibit at Lahaina Arts Society, Lahaina News, September 2, 1999: 17.

RICHARDS, EMIL [MUSICIAN]
— performance reviewed, Lahaina News, July 18, 1984: 12.
— to play at Blackie's Bar, Lahaina News, July 13, 1988: 7.
— extends stay at Blackies Bar, Lahaina News, July 27, 1988: 11.
— to play at Blackie's Bar, Lahaina News, July 19, 1989: 11.
— to perform at Blackie's Bar, Lahaina News, March 28, 1990: 15.
— to perform at Blackie's Bar, Lahaina News, August 8, 1991: 12.
— to perform at Blackie's Bar, Lahaina News, January 23, 1992: 16,22.
— to perform at Blackie's Bar, Lahaina News, June 18, 1992: 18,19.
— to perform at Blackie's Bar, Lahaina News, July 8, 1993: 11.
— to perform at The Bay Club at the Kapalua Bay Hotel, Lahaina News, August 28, 2003: 15.

RICHARDS, WILLIAM
— missionary in Maui in 1820s, Lahaina Sun, January 6, 1971: 8.
— history of early missionary, Lahaina News, June 4, 1986: 1,16.

RICHARDSON, CAROLINE
— to speak to Maui Senior Law Fair, Lahaina News, June 1, 1988: 19.

RICHARDSON, HENRY "CLAY"
— chef promoted to executive sous chef, Lahaina News, May 9, 1990: 9.
— appointed executive chef for Kapalua Bay Hotel and Villas, Lahaina News, December 12, 1991: 16.

RICHARDSON, RICH [ARTIST]
— to exhibit at The Art School at Kapalua, Lahaina News, November 5, 1998: 9.

RICHARDSON, ROBERT
— will not be renewed as judge, Lahaina News, September 1, 1980: 6.

RICHARDSON, WILLIAM
— chief justice to speak at the annual meeting of the Lahaina Restoration Foundation, Lahaina Sun, February 24, 1971: 1.

RICHESIN, CARMIE
— named Maui chairman of "Citizens for America" lobbying group, Lahaina News, February 1, 1984: 3.

RICHTER, BILL
— to join rededication of peace park at Kamaole III, Lahaina News, February 8, 1996: 4.

RICHY, BARBARA
— to offer workshop on "Training Intensive in Energy Healing and Mastery", Lahaina News, April 10, 1997: 12.

RICKARD, GENA RAY
— participant in Makawao Rodeo, Lahaina News, July 4, 1984: 6.

RICKARD, KAHOLO
— former Lahainaluna High School student named most valuable player on the University of Hawai'i baseball team, Lahaina News, June 10, 1999: 7.

RICKARD, RHONDA-MAY FRANCES
— Lahainaluna High School prom queen, Lahaina News, April 20, 2000: 14.

RID DIRT SHIRT STORE [BUSINESS]
— opening at The Wharf Cinema Center, Lahaina News, September 27, 2001: 9.

RIDDIM, HAKA [MUSICIAN]
— to perform at Borders Books, Lahaina News, July 29, 1999: 12.

RIDDLE KING RELAYS
— to benefit Special Olympics, Lahaina News, March 13, 1985: 7.

RIDE [FILM]
— Warren Miller film to be shown at the Maui Arts and Cultural Center, Lahaina News, January 4, 2001: 17.

RIDENOUR, DANA [ARTIST]
— to visit Diamond Head Gallery, Lahaina News, May 22, 2003: 16.

RIDGWAY, DAVID [ARTIST]
— featured at Old Jail Gallery, Lahaina News, March 4, 1987: 8.

RIDICULE [FILM]
— to be shown at Maui Arts and Cultural Center, Lahaina News, April 24, 1997: 13.

RIDINGS, CHARLES
— Maui Catholic Charities official to speak to Lahaina Rotary Club, Lahaina News, June 11, 1992: 3.
— executive director of Maui Economic Concerns of the Community Inc. to speak to Maui Republican Party, Lahaina News, November 4, 1999: 13.
— discusses proposal for West Side Resource Center, Lahaina News, November 23, 2000: 1,19.
— Executive Director of Maui Economic Concerns of the Community discusses plans to break ground on West Side Resource Center for homeless, Lahaina News, March 8, 2001: 1,18.
— discusses homeless rehabilitation center, Lahaina News, December 20, 2001: 1.
— executive director of Maui Economic Concerns of the Community awarded "Maui's Outstanding Executive Director of a Non-Profit Organization", Lahaina News, July 25, 2002: 2.

RIDOLFINO, JUDY [DANCER]
— to perform, Lahaina News, February 4, 1993: 15.
— to host "That's What I Like" revue, Lahaina News, February 6, 1997: 15.
— Marathon Cafe VIII to be held, Lahaina News, June 12, 1997: 17.
— Marathon Cafe VIII to be held, Lahaina News, June 19, 1997: 16.
— to hold Marathon Cafe VIII, Lahaina News, June 26, 1997: 16.
— to offer cooking class for Kaiser Permanente, Lahaina News, January 15, 1998: 12.
— to hold "Marathon Cafe IX", Lahaina News, June 11, 1998: 17.
— to hold "I Just Wanna Be Happy", Lahaina News, January 28, 1999: 13.
— to hold fundraiser, Lahaina News, June 10, 1999: 17.
— to hold Marathon Cafe X, Lahaina News, June 17, 1999: 9.
— to attend Mayor's Ball, Lahaina News, August 12, 1999: 17.
— to feature "What Do you Wanna Be?", Lahaina News, January 27, 2000: 13.
— to offer "What Do You Wanna Be?", Lahaina News, February 3, 2000: 13.
— to perform "Tap 2000: Tap Into America's Hearts to Keep Our Children Safe", Lahaina News, May 18, 2000: 21.
— to present "Escapade", Lahaina News, January 25, 2001: 6.
— to present "Escapade", Lahaina News, February 1, 2001: 16,20.
— to offer dance performance at Queen Ka'ahumanu Center, Lahaina News, May 10, 2001: 19.
— to hold annual dance show "You Should Be Dancing", Lahaina News, January 31, 2002: 17.
— dance troupe to stage "Dancing from A to Z", Lahaina News, February 6, 2003: 15.

RIEDY, MATT [COMEDIAN]
— to perform at Comedy Club and the Sports Page, Lahaina News, July 16, 1992: 17,20.

RIEHL, DAVID
— married at Nautilus Center, Lahaina News, January 4, 1989: 2.

RIFLE RANGE
— meeting to discuss plan, Lahaina Sun, January 27, 1971: 7.

RIGER'S RESTAURANT [RESTAURANT]
— features karaoke, Lahaina News, July 25, 1991: 13.

RIGG, ADELE
— to speak to Kihei-Wailea Kiwanis Club, Lahaina News, June 24, 1993: 8.

RIGHT TIME, THE [BOOK]
— Barbara Sharp publishes third Lahaina mystery novel, Lahaina News, June 27, 2002: 5.

RIGHTEOUS BROTHERS [MUSICAL GROUP]
— to perform on Maui, Lahaina News, August 15, 1984: 12.

RILEY, JIM
— Launiupoko Associates employee discusses plans for lands owned in Lahaina and Olowalu, Lahaina News, July 20, 2000: 15.

RILEY, LU ANNE
— promoted to vice president of Gilbert and Associates, Lahaina News, April 25, 2002: 8.

RILEY, TIM [ARTIST]
— to exhibit paintings at The Art School at Kapalua, Lahaina News, December 13, 2001: 17.

RIMPAC
— to be held, Lahaina News, June 23, 1994: 1,16.

RIMROCK PAVING CO. [BUSINESS]
— receives award to resurface highway, Lahaina News, July 10, 1997: 2.

RINGLEIN, MARK
— named general manager of Aloha Cantina, Lahaina News, October 6, 1994: 11.

RINKER, LAURIE
— golfer's career described, Lahaina News, March 6, 1985: A10.

RINPOCHE, TAI SITU
— Buddhist leader to visit, Lahaina News, May 29, 1985: 3.
— Buddhist teacher to speak, Lahaina News, March 2, 1995: 3.

RIO DE JANEIRO [BUSINESS]
— beauty salon opens, Lahaina News, January 9, 1992: 8.

RIOS, CONNIE
— to discuss Hawaiian spiritual practices, Lahaina News, November 1, 2001: 17.

RIPE TOMATOES, THE [MUSICAL GROUP]
— to perform at Kobe Japanese Steak House, Lahaina News, January 16, 1992: 12.
— to perform at Kobe Japanese Steak House, Lahaina News, January 30, 1992: 18.
— to perform at Kobe Japanese Steak House, Lahaina News, February 20, 1992: 15.
— featured, Lahaina News, March 5, 1992: 14.
— continue to perform at Studio 505, Lahaina News, April 30, 1992: 13.
— continues to perform at Moose McGillycuddy's, Lahaina News, July 16, 1992: 17.
— continue to perform at Longhi's, Lahaina News, October 29, 1992: 19.
— to perform at Blue Tropix, Lahaina News, March 25, 1993: 13.
— to perform at Blue Tropix, Lahaina News, April 29, 1993: 11.
— continues to perform at Blue Tropix, Lahaina News, July 1, 1993: 11.
— continues to perform at Compadres Mexican Bar and Grill, Lahaina News, February 17, 1994: 11.

RIPLEY, RIP [ENTERTAINER]
— magician's career featured, Lahaina News, March 25, 1987: 1.

RIPPEE, ROBERT
— named associate director of sales at Hyatt Regency Maui, Lahaina News, March 9, 1995: 6.

RISKA, SUSAN
— named to on-site management team of Sofos Realty Corporation, Lahaina News, July 18, 1991: 6.

RISTORANTE LA SCALA [RESTAURANT]
— opens, Lahaina News, August 23, 1989: 13.

RITCHIE, LYDEE
— appointed public/tenant relations manager at Piilani Village Shopping Center, Lahaina News, March 15, 2001: 8.

RITCHIE'S ROASTED NUTS
— Page Dahms wins Gummy Bear contest organized by, Lahaina News, September 25, 1985: 1.

RITTE, WALTER, JR.
— skeptical of President Bush's order to halt Navy bombing on Kaho'olawe, Lahaina News, October 31, 1990: 1.

RITTE, WALTER LEE, SR.
— ordered to report to prison, Lahaina News, March 5, 1992: 5.

RITTER, JULIAN [ARTIST]
— works displayed at Hui No'eau Visual Arts Center, Lahaina News, September 7, 1988: 14.

RITTER, MICHAEL "TEX"
— offering swimming lessons at Lahaina Aquatic Center, Lahaina News, October 24, 2002: 11.

RITZ-CARLTON HOTEL [BUSINESS]
— development discovers ancient Hawaiian remains, Lahaina News, January 4, 1989: 1,16.
— decision delayed to allow development after bones found, Lahaina News, February 8, 1989: 1,20.
— to be relocated after ancient Hawaiian remains found, Lahaina News, March 8, 1989: 1,16.
— site to moved following ancient Hawaiian bones being found, Lahaina News, April 26, 1989: 1.
— likely to win lawmakers' approval, Lahaina News, October 11, 1989: 1.
— Urban Design Review Board approves design, Lahaina News, December 6, 1989: 28.
— correction on previous story on occupancy of, Lahaina News, December 20, 1989: 3.
— seeking special management area permit, Lahaina News, January 10, 1990: 24.
— groundbreaking scheduled, Lahaina News, November 28, 1990: 8.
— groundbreaking scheduled, Lahaina News, December 5, 1990: 4.
— breaks ground, Lahaina News, December 12, 1990: 1.
— Jeremy Sosner appointed director of sales and marketing, Lahaina News, May 23, 1991: 8.
— Sandra Fewer appointed public relations director at, Lahaina News, August 22, 1991: 4.
— Ken Korn named national sales manager, Lahaina News, October 3, 1991: 7.
— appoints Donald Welsh as vice president of sales and marketing, Lahaina News, October 10, 1991: 7.
— John Toner appointed general manager, Lahaina News, July 23, 1992: 16.
— opens, Lahaina News, September 24, 1992: 8.
— Leigh Drewry appointed sales manager, Lahaina News, September 24, 1992: 9.
— to post signs indicating water safety, Lahaina News, November 19, 1992: 1.
— commended by Governor John Waihee for service and leadership, Lahaina News, December 31, 1992: 10.
— Noboru Takanoa appointed director of Asia and Pacific Sales, Lahaina News, December 31, 1992: 10.
— Nicholas Clayton becomes general manager of, Lahaina News, February 18, 1993: 10.
— video projector missing, Lahaina News, April 22, 1993: 3.

— opens sales office in Honolulu, Lahaina News, May 6, 1993: 9.

— foundation cracking from soil movement, Lahaina News, June 3, 1993: 1.

— to hold Viva Italia buffet, Lahaina News, June 3, 1993: 13.

— Hawaii Carpenters Union form informational picket lines in front of, Lahaina News, September 2, 1993: 2.

— appointments announced, Lahaina News, August 4, 1994: 9.

— to host "A Rainbow Within You", Lahaina News, August 18, 1994: 15.

— details of "Celebration of the Arts", Lahaina News, April 6, 1995: 10,11.

— to restructure debt to avoid foreclosure, Lahaina News, May 25, 1995: 10.

— Maui Land and Pineapple Co may give up part ownership of, Lahaina News, August 31, 1995: 1,2.

— holds "Tree of Lights" tree lighting ceremony, Lahaina News, November 30, 1995: 11.

— Heide Denecke appointed sales manager, Lahaina News, December 26, 1996: 8.

— staff changes at, Lahaina News, November 13, 1997: 11.

— names Clifford Nae'ole Hawaiian cultural advisor, Lahaina News, April 16, 1998: 11.

— to host big band concert and dance, Lahaina News, May 7, 1998: 16.

— hosting festival on Hawaiian art and culture, Lahaina News, March 18, 1999: 9.

— receives a best service award from Travel and Leisure Magazine, Lahaina News, June 10, 1999: 13.

— to host winemaker dinner featuring chef Craig Connole, Lahaina News, July 15, 1999: 13.

— to host dinner featuring wine from Chateau Trimbach, Lahaina News, August 19, 1999: 16.

— ranked third in world by Travel and Leisure magazine, Lahaina News, October 21, 1999: 13.

— to host winemakers dinner with Grgich Hills Cellars, Lahaina News, November 11, 1999: 12.

— Stephen Marshall is new executive chef, Lahaina News, April 6, 2000: 9.

— hula performances slated throughout "Celebration of the Arts 2000", Lahaina News, April 20, 2000: 1.

— hosting "Celebration of the Arts", Lahaina News, April 20, 2000: 3.

— serving champagne Sunday brunch, Lahaina News, July 6, 2000: 7.

— Mark Anthony Malone is new director of catering and convention services at, Lahaina News, September 14, 2000: 16.

— hosting "Moonlight Mo'olelo", Lahaina News, September 21, 2000: 1,6.

— to host "Chicken Skin" stories at Beach House Lawn, Lahaina News, October 12, 2000: 19.

— managers earn designation of Certified Meeting Professionals, Lahaina News, November 9, 2000: 18.

— is Hawai'i State Award of Excellence "Golden Lei" winner, Lahaina News, November 23, 2000: 16.

— plans tree-lighting ceremony, Lahaina News, November 30, 2000: 16.

— to hold Moonlight Mo'olelo on theme of "Life as a Paniolo (Hawaiian cowboy)", Lahaina News, February 8, 2001: 18.

— to host "Celebration of the Arts", Lahaina News, April 5, 2001: 17,24.

— to host "Celebration of the Arts", Lahaina News, April 12, 2001: 1,11.

— Steven Sampson appointed director of sales and marketing at, Lahaina News, May 24, 2001: 8.

— employees save life of guest, Lahaina News, October 11, 2001: 1,20.

— to host "Celebration of the Arts", Lahaina News, April 4, 2002: 3.

— to hold Hawaii International Film Festival, Lahaina News, November 7, 2002: 18.

— to host auction of antiques, Lahaina News, November 14, 2002: 9.

— Joe Jelasquez new director of sales and marketing at, Lahaina News, February 27, 2003: 8.

— John Zaner appointed manager of culinary division at, Lahaina News, April 3, 2003: 8.

— to host "Celebration of the Arts", Lahaina News, April 17, 2003: 3.

— Javier Cano new general manager at, Lahaina News, April 24, 2003: 14.

— employees receive designations, Lahaina News, May 22, 2003: 8.

— names new directors, Lahaina News, July 10, 2003: 8.

— to launch cultural series, Lahaina News, August 21, 2003: 9.

— to offer cultural series "Mai Ka Pu'uwai", Lahaina News, August 28, 2003: 5.

— to offer weekly slack key guitar concerts, Lahaina News, September 18, 2003: 3.

RIVALS, THE [PLAY]
— to be performed by Baldwin Theatre Guild, Lahaina News, November 3, 1994: 28.

RIVERA, PHIL [MUSICIAN]
— to perform at Gerard's, Lahaina News, June 6, 1990: 13.

— to perform at Gerard's, Lahaina News, June 27, 1990: 12.

— to perform at Gerard's, Lahaina News, January 9, 1991: 7.

— continues to perform at Gerard's, Lahaina News, April 3, 1991: 7.

— continues to perform at Gerard's, Lahaina News, April 24, 1991: 10.

— featured, Lahaina News, June 25, 1992: 18.

RIVERA, STEPHANIE
— Outreach aid for senior citizens available at Malu'ulu O Lele Cultural Center, Lahaina News, June 4, 1992: 4.

— to direct senior citizens to services, Lahaina News, June 11, 1992: 4,8.

— outreach aide continues to meet the elderly at Lahaina Civic Center, Lahaina News, July 16, 1992: 4.

RIVERS, ARIANA
— Scholar/Athlete of the Week, Lahaina News, September 20, 2001: 12.

RIVERS, PHIL [MUSICIAN]
— to perform at Gerard's, Lahaina News, July 18, 1991: 10.

RIVERS, STELLA [ARTIST]
— to exhibit at Art School at Kapalua, Lahaina News, August 19, 1999: 17.

RIZZI, TONY [MUSICIAN]
— to perform at Blackie's Bar, Lahaina News, April 18, 1990: 11.

ROAD AND TRACK PERFORMANCE CENTER [BUSINESS]
— to hold photo contest, Lahaina News, May 15, 1991: 4.

ROADS
— see infrastructure

ROARING TWENTIES (MUSICAL GROUP)
— featured, Lahaina News, April 16, 1992: 16.

ROBB-DELORIA, SUE
— Lahaina Canoe Club paddler featured, Lahaina News, May 15, 1997: 11.

ROBBER BRIDEGROOM, THE [PLAY]
— to be presented by Baldwin Theatre Guild, Lahaina News, October 28, 1993: 11.

ROBBIE WILSON SALON [BUSINESS]
— to sponsor fashion show to benefit Koko the Gorilla, Lahaina News, October 9, 1997: 21.

— to hold benefit for Koko the Gorilla, Lahaina News, October 16, 1997: 16.

ROBBINS, JOHN
— author of "Diet for a New America" to speak, Lahaina News, January 30, 1992: 5.

ROBERSON, JUSTIN
— Y2K Hoʻokipa Classic to be held in memory of, Lahaina News, December 30, 1999: 9.

ROBERT, GARY
— installed as chairman of Lahaina Corps of the Salvation Army, Lahaina News, February 20, 1985: 3.

ROBERT LYN NELSON STUDIOS
— to expand, Lahaina News, February 24, 1994: 9.

ROBERT STEMMLER VINEYARDS
— Kapalua Bay Hotel and Villas's Vintner's Dinner, Lahaina News, February 20, 1991: 9.

ROBERTO THE CLOWN
— to perform at Lahaina Center, Lahaina News, April 16, 1992: 17.

ROBERTS, ANNE
— to lecture on distant healing, Lahaina News, February 20, 1997: 11.

ROBERTS, DAWN [ARTIST]
— to exhibit at Village Gallery Contemporary, Lahaina News, March 11, 1999: 12.

ROBERTS HAWAII TOURS [BUSINESS]
— plans to locate catamaran in Kaʻanapali, Lahaina News, March 28, 1984: 17.
— expands to Big Island, Lahaina News, July 11, 1984: 14.
— beginning shuttle service between Lahaina, Kaʻanapali, and Maui Plantation, Lahaina News, December 19, 1984: 24.
— proposes limiting taxi licenses, Lahaina News, March 5, 1986: 1,20.
— in conflict with Shoreline Transportation over buses in West Maui, Lahaina News, November 12, 1986: 1,8.
— ordered to cease route in West Maui between Kaʻanapali and Lahaina Town, Lahaina News, July 8, 1987: 1.
— editorial critical of company, Lahaina News, July 8, 1987: 2.
— sued by Shoreline Transportation for unfair trade practices, Lahaina News, June 22, 1988: 1.
— supports Aloha Week, Lahaina News, September 6, 1989: 1.

ROBERTS, HOWARD [MUSICIAN]
— to perform at Blackie's Bar, Lahaina News, August 1, 1991: 14.

ROBERTS, JULIA [ACTOR]
— visits Maui, Lahaina News, July 25, 1990: 1.
— visits West Maui, Lahaina News, August 15, 1990: 15.
— has video stolen showing her and Kiefer Sutherland at private party, Lahaina News, September 19, 1991: 1,2.
— William Pie and Inside Edition television show resolve court case of video showing Kiefer Sutherland and, Lahaina News, November 28, 1991: 4.

ROBERTS, KAI
— to lead Argentine tango workshop, Lahaina News, October 10, 2002: 16.

ROBERTS, KIM
— resident seeks artificial reef for Puamana, Lahaina News, January 2, 1992: 3.

ROBERTS, LYNDA
— named public relations liaison, Lahaina News, November 21, 1990: 12.

ROBERTS, RICK [MUSICIAN]
— interviewed, Lahaina News, October 3, 1984: 12.

ROBERTSON, PEGGY [ARTIST]
— librarian discusses changes to library hours, Lahaina News, November 11, 1999: 5.
— leads protest of changes to library hours, Lahaina News, February 10, 2000: 3.
— creates "Discarded But Still Valuable—2000 Years of Knowledge" from old encyclopedia, Lahaina News, April 5, 2001: 1.
— to exhibit at Karma Kafe, Lahaina News, January 31, 2002: 18.

ROBERTSON, REED
— qualified for AP Scholar Award, Lahaina News, December 20, 2001: 2.

ROBERTSON, RON [COMEDIAN]
— to perform at Comedy Club and the Sports Page, Lahaina News, December 26, 1991: 12.

ROBERTSON, VICTORIA JEWELL [ARTIST]
— to offer courses with Art School at Kapalua, Lahaina News, February 24, 2000: 9.

ROBERTSON-LORANT, LAURIE [WRITER]
— to present on "Herman Melville and Pacific Islands History", Lahaina News, June 5, 2003: 17.

ROBIA, KALEI
— Scholar/Athlete of the Week, Lahaina News, December 17, 1998: 18.

ROBIA, KALEIMAILE
— Lahainaluna High School named a U.S. National Award Winner in Business Education, Lahaina News, June 17, 1999: 15.

ROBILOTTA, GARY PATRICK [MUSICIAN]
— performing benefit concert for Hui Malama Learning Center, Lahaina News, September 13, 2001: 3.

ROBIN, CRAIG
— joins Synchromic Studios, Lahaina News, May 9, 1996: 8.
— joins Maui County Office of Economic Development, Lahaina News, January 15, 1998: 11.

ROBIN GOODFELLOW [PLAY]
— to be performed by The Maui Academy of Performing Arts, Lahaina News, September 19, 1991: 16,22.

ROBIN HOOD [MUSICAL]
— opens Friday at Old Lahaina Prison, Lahaina News, July 16, 1992: 17.

ROBINSON, DARREN
— deadlifts 702 pounds, Lahaina News, July 1, 1999: 7.
— power lifter successful, Lahaina News, November 18, 1999: 9.

ROBINSON, ED [ARTIST]
— to speak on Hawaii marine life, Lahaina News, April 10, 2003: 21.

ROBINSON, FRANK
— baseball player participates in Legends of Baseball game, Lahaina News, December 26, 1984: 4.

ROBINSON, JEFF
— life of surfer featured, Lahaina Sun, May 9, 1973: 22.

ROBINSON, KIMBERLY
— missing, police looking for, Lahaina News, March 26, 1992: 4.

ROBINSON, MARK
— Lahaina Yacht Club commodore featured, Lahaina News, September 26, 1991: 8.

ROBINSON, MICHAEL [MUSICIAN]
— to perform, Lahaina News, January 3, 1990: 14.

ROBINSON, TERRIE
— choreographer to hold dance workshops, Lahaina News, July 17, 1997: 9.

ROBINSON, TONY [COMEDIAN]
— to perform at Comedy Club and the Sports Page, Lahaina News, July 2, 1992: 21,24.

ROBOTICS
— children's supplement features, Lahaina News, January 23, 1985: A,B,C,D.

ROBYN HELZNER TRIO [MUSICAL GROUP]
— to perform at "L'Chaim Unplugged! - The Soul of Jewish Music", Lahaina News, May 28, 1998: 13.

ROCHA, BOBBIE
— benefit concert at Blue Tropix held for, Lahaina News, November 3, 1994: 25.

ROCHE, DAVID
— named manager of research and development by Amfac, Inc, Lahaina News, August 16, 1989: 6.

ROCHE, JOHN
— appointed manager of Aloha Activities Center, Lahaina News, February 4, 1987: 11.

ROCHE, SHANNON
— Scholar/Athlete of the Week, Lahaina News, June 10, 1999: 7.

ROCHE, THOMAS
— joins PAC/Asia Realty and Development Incorp., Lahaina News, October 29, 1992: 13.
— passes away, Lahaina News, August 7, 2003: 3.

ROCHE, TOM
— named resident rental manager of Kaʻanapali Royal, Lahaina News, November 15, 1989: 9.
— joins Chaney Brooks, Lahaina News, October 31, 1991: 10.

ROCHELEAU, JOHN
— Salvation Army co-director featured, Lahaina News, May 14, 1992: 3.

ROCHELEAU, MARY
— Salvation Army co-director featured, Lahaina News, May 14, 1992: 3.

ROCK BOTTOM REMAINDERS [MUSICAL GROUP]
— to perform at the Maui Writers Conference, Lahaina News, June 9, 1994: 13.

ROCK THE VOTE
— committee hoping to sign up voters, Lahaina News, July 7, 1994: 4.

ROCK-N-ROLL [RESTAURANT]
— opens at The Shops at Wailea, Lahaina News, August 16, 2001: 8.

ROCKER, TOMMY [MUSICIAN]
— to perform at Moose McGillycuddy's, Lahaina News, November 7, 1991: 14,15.
— to perform at Moose McGillycuddy's, Lahaina News, November 14, 1991: 15.
— to perform at Cheeseburger in Paradise, Lahaina News, April 9, 1998: 17.

ROCKETT, DAVE
— Lahainaluna High School soccer coach recognized, Lahaina News, March 25, 1993: 5,6.

ROCKETT, LOUISE
— to begin writing "West Maui People" column for Lahaina News, Lahaina News, May 16, 1990: 1.
— nomination to the Maui Planning Commission voted down by Maui County Council, Lahaina News, March 24, 1994: 1,20.
— columnist leaves Lahaina News, Lahaina News, August 4, 1994: 3.

ROCKRESORTS [BUSINESS]
— scheduled to open to resorts, Lahaina News, November 29, 1989: 4.
— names Rick Brunette as director of food and beverage, Lahaina News, December 20, 1989: 4.

ROCKWELL INTERNATIONAL CORPORATION
— awarded contract to operate "Star Wars" military site on Maui, Lahaina News, July 4, 1990: 7.

ROCKWELL, NORMAN [ARTIST]
— work on display at Hyatt Regency Hotel, Lahaina News, August 1, 1983: 10.

ROCKWELL POWER SYSTEMS
— to locate in Kihei, Lahaina News, June 6, 1991: 4.

ROCKWELL, RICK [COMEDIAN]
— to perform at Honolulu Comedy Club, Lahaina News, January 18, 1996: 12.

ROCKY HORROR PICTURE SHOW [FILM]
— shown at Lahaina Civic Center, Lahaina News, February 29, 1984: 4.
— to be shown, Lahaina News, October 31, 1996: 18.

ROCKY HORROR PICTURE SHOW [PLAY]
— to be performed by Maui OnStage and One On One, Lahaina News, October 1, 1992: 18.
— to be performed, Lahaina News, October 8, 1992: 10,11,12.
— to be performed at Maui Community College, Lahaina News, October 28, 1993: 11.

RODEO
— preparations for at Makawao, Lahaina Sun, June 30, 1971: 5.
— held at Makawao, Lahaina Sun, June 28, 1972: 4,5.
— Makawao Rodeo to be held, Lahaina News, June 26, 2003: 10.

RODGERS, JIMMIE [MUSICIAN]
— to perform at 1950s concert, Lahaina News, August 23, 1989: 3.

RODNEY K. AND HIS MUMBO JUMBO BAND
— to hold fundraiser for Maui Tibetan Center, Lahaina News, October 10, 1991: 4.

RODRIGUES, AL
— running for mayor, Lahaina Sun, September 13, 1972: 4.

RODRIGUES, CECILIO [MUSICIAN]
— to perform at Casanova's, Lahaina News, May 23, 1991: 16.

RODRIGUEZ-PANTOJA, RICARDO
— charged with manslaughter in death of police officer Gene Williams, Lahaina News, August 19, 1999: 1.

ROGENE OF HAWAII, LTD [BUSINESS]
— design company featured, Lahaina News, March 21, 1984: 17.

ROGER, JOHN
— critical of unequal property tax system, Lahaina Sun, October 25, 1972: 3.

ROGERS AND HAMMERSTEIN
— "Carousel" to be performed by Baldwin Theatre Guild, Lahaina News, January 5, 1995: 12.

ROGERS, BUCK
— organizer of Old Lahaina Town Art Faire interviewed, Lahaina Sun, May 23, 1973: 8.

ROGERS, DANE
— Scholar/Athlete of the Week, Lahaina News, March 13, 2003: 12.

ROGERS, GLENN
— promoted to executive vice-president of Alexander and Baldwin, Inc., Lahaina News, July 24, 1997: 13.

ROGERS, GLYN WOOD
— opens boutique at The Wharf Cinema Center, Lahaina News, April 30, 1992: 10.

ROGERS, JEFF
— new Maui Regional PTA Director, Lahaina News, August 14, 2003: 1,20.

ROGERS, JIMMY [MUSICIAN]
— to perform at Maui Marriott's ballroom, Lahaina News, October 17, 1996: 16.

ROGERS, JOHN [COMEDIAN]
— to perform at Comedy Club, Lahaina News, February 24, 1994: 11.

ROGERS, KENNY [MUSICIAN]
— planning first performance in Honolulu, Lahaina News, October 8, 1986: 8.
— to perform at Hula Bowl, Lahaina News, January 1, 1998: 1.

ROGERS, MARSHA [ARTIST]
— featured, Lahaina News, September 5, 1996: 21.

ROGERS PRODUCTIONS PROFESSIONAL THEATRE SERIES
— to be held, Lahaina News, January 5, 1995: 10.

ROGERS, RACHEL
— organizer of Old Lahaina Town Art Faire interviewed, Lahaina Sun, May 23, 1973: 8.

ROGERS, RAY
— purchases Maui Silkscreen Designs, Lahaina News, May 29, 1985: 3.

ROGERS-AREGGER, SUSAN [ARTIST]
— to lead paper-dying and collage workshop, Lahaina News, April 5, 2001: 18.
— to hold workshop on paper-dying and collage, Lahaina News, April 12, 2001: 21.

ROGERSON, KEN [COMEDIAN]
— to perform at Comedy Club and the Sports Page, Lahaina News, May 14, 1992: 14,17.
— to perform at Comedy Club, Lahaina News, January 20, 1994: 11.

ROGGENBACK, SHIRLEY [MUSICIAN]
— performance to be hosted by Calvary Chapel, Lahaina News, January 5, 1995: 12.

ROHLFING, PATRICIA
— promoted to senior vice president, Lahaina News, January 30, 2003: 8.

ROJAS, TONI
— appointed director of sales at Maui Visitors Bureau, Lahaina News, March 15, 2001: 8.

ROLAND, BILL
— mediator featured, Lahaina News, April 9, 1992: 3.

ROLFING
— discussed as alternative healing method, Lahaina News, April 20, 1988: 1,20.

ROLFING, DEBI
— completes International Real Estate courses, Lahaina News, October 6, 1994: 11.

ROLFING, FRED
— lawyer discusses Aloha Voyages' hope to offer tours to Moloka'i, Lahaina News, January 13, 1988: 1,16.

ROLFING, MARK
— receives "Marketing Person of the Year" award from Maui Chapter of the American Marketing Association, Lahaina News, May 16, 1984: 17.
— heading group purchasing Kapalua Bay Hotel & Villas, Lahaina News, May 29, 1985: 3.
— becomes color commentator at NBC, Lahaina News, October 14, 1987: 17.
— signs contract with NBC Sports, Lahaina News, January 25, 1989: 13.
— Isuzu Kapalua International Golf Tournament chairman discusses Isuzu Motors no longer being title sponsor, Lahaina News, November 14, 1990: 11,12.
— to host golf television show on KITV , Lahaina News, December 29, 1994: 5.
— appointed to Hawaii Tourism Authority Board of Directors, Lahaina News, October 15, 1998: 13.
— inducted into the Hawaii Golf Hall of Fame, Lahaina News, April 13, 2000: 1.

ROLFING REALTY [BUSINESS]
— receives certified real estate brokerage manager designation, Lahaina News, June 30, 1994: 9.

ROLFING SPORTS [BUSINESS]
— Sherel Gallagher Stosik named general manager, Lahaina News, January 24, 1990: 6.

ROLLING STONES, THE [BAND]
— play in Honolulu, Lahaina Sun, January 31, 1973: 5.

ROMAINE, JOHN [ARTIST]
— featured artist at Lahaina Arts Society, Lahaina News, December 19, 2002: 19.

ROMAN, DENI
— to hold Yoga Flexibility Workshops, Lahaina News, February 15, 2001: 13.
— leading class on yoga flexibility, Lahaina News, March 15, 2001: 20.

ROME AND JEWELS
— Rennie Harris Puremovement to perform, Lahaina News, October 11, 2001: 16.

ROMEO AND JULIET [PLAY]
— to be performed at Wailea Shopping Village, Lahaina News, September 12, 1990: 18.

ROMERO, JOSE
— elected president of Maui Philharmonic Society, Lahaina Sun, May 2, 1973: 11.

ROMIG, JIM
— chairman of Pomare Properties to speak to LahainaTown Action Committee, Lahaina News, January 25, 1989: 1.
— named chair of Retail Merchants of Hawaii, Lahaina News, September 24, 1992: 9.

RONALD A. KAWAHARA & CO. [BUSINESS]
— merges with Aus Certified Public Accountancy Corp., Lahaina News, August 15, 1990: 11.

RONALD K. BROWN AND EVIDENCE [TROUPE]
— to perform at Maui Arts and Cultural Center, Lahaina News, November 7, 2002: 20.

RONALD MCDONALD CHILDREN'S CHARITIES
— accepting grant applications, Lahaina News, October 17, 1991: 7.

RONALD MCDONALD HOUSE
— first organizational meeting held, Lahaina News, February 29, 1984: 4.
— Maui Contractors Women's Auxiliary to hold garage sale for, Lahaina News, April 13, 2000: 12.
— to benefit from Hula Bowl, Lahaina News, January 18, 2001: 9.

RONNI JUSTIN ON THE CHAPMAN STICK [MUSICAL GROUP]
— to perform at Molokini Lounge at the Maui Prince Hotel, Lahaina News, March 20, 1991: 10.

ROOM, THE [MUSICAL GROUP]
— to perform at benefit concert at Maui Brews, Lahaina News, August 5, 1999: 14.

ROOMMATE FINDERS OF MAUI [BUSINESS]
— featured, Lahaina News, December 21, 1983: 16.

ROONEY, JOHN
— member of the Coastal Geology Group to discuss "Historical Changes and Future Beach Preservation Along West Maui and Kihei Shorelines", Lahaina News, June 6, 2002: 17.

ROONEY, MICKEY [PERFORMER]
— to perform in benefit for Maui Community Theatre OnStage, Lahaina News, February 18, 1993: 13.
— to perform, Lahaina News, March 4, 1993: 9.

ROOSEVELT HIGH SCHOOL
— playing baseball games on Maui, Lahaina Sun, February 24, 1971: 7.

ROOSTERS
— complaints of noise from, Lahaina News, April 9, 1992: 1,13.

ROOTS NATTY ROOTS [MUSICAL GROUP]
— to perform at Casanova's, Lahaina News, December 10, 1992: 17.
— to perform at Longhi's, Lahaina News, April 29, 1993: 11.
— to perform at Longhi's, Lahaina News, October 21, 1993: 16.

ROSCO WRIGHT TRIO [MUSICAL GROUP]
— to perform at Pacific'O, Lahaina News, December 16, 1993: 19.

ROSE, JIM
— to bring circus to Maui, Lahaina News, March 8, 2001: 14.

ROSE ROSELINSKY, LOOSE IN WAILUKU AGAIN! [PLAY]
— to be performed at Iao Theatre, Lahaina News, January 7, 1999: 16.

ROSEBERRY, MATTHEW
— Scholar/Athlete of the Week, Lahaina News, February 15, 2001: 13.

ROSEHILL, MAHELA
— retired Kamehameha Schools educator to give talk "From the Mountains to the Sea—Life on an Ahupua'a", Lahaina News, February 7, 2002: 16.

ROSELANI ICE CREAM [BUSINESS]
— presents grant to Maui Community College Culinary Arts Department, Lahaina News, December 19, 2002: 8.

ROSELINSKY, ROSE
— to perform "It's About Time", Lahaina News, January 1, 1998: 16,17.
— to perform "It's About Time", Lahaina News, January 8, 1998: 12.

ROSEN, PETER [MUSICIAN]
— to perform at Borders Books, Lahaina News, August 19, 1999: 16.

ROSENTHAL, DON
— organizing West Maui Youth Athletic Association's youth basketball league, Lahaina News, December 30, 1993: 8.
— creator of West Maui Youth Athletic Association featured, Lahaina News, December 28, 1995: 7.
— basketball coach featured, Lahaina News, January 2, 1997: 5.
— featured, Lahaina News, December 21, 2000: 1,15.
— West Maui Youth Basketball Commissioner discusses new season, Lahaina News, December 28, 2000: 6.

ROSENTHAL, PHILLIP
— youth athlete featured, Lahaina News, January 25, 1996: 11.

ROSHI, KONO
— Zen Master to speak, Lahaina News, February 20, 2003: 2.

ROSHON, RICHARD [ARTIST]
— plan kayak trip around Maui, Lahaina News, June 12, 1985: 4.
— kayak trip around Maui described, Lahaina News, July 17, 1985: 4.
— photographer's career described, Lahaina News, July 23, 1986: 4.
— photographer's work shown at First Hawaiian Bank, Lahaina News, November 19, 1986: 16.
— kayaking around Maui, Lahaina News, May 13, 1987: 3.
— featured, Lahaina News, May 20, 1987: 6.
— to give lectures at Maui Prince Hotel, Lahaina News, January 25, 1989: 18.
— to exhibit at Maui Prince Hotel, Lahaina News, March 15, 1989: 2.
— to exhibit photographs, Lahaina News, February 21, 1990: 14.
— photographer to offer series of lectures "The Sea and Its Species", Lahaina News, November 14, 1990: 5.
— photographer to speak at Maui Prince Hotel, Lahaina News, December 19, 1990: 15.
— to offer lectures on whales at Kapalua Bay Hotel and Villas, Lahaina News, December 12, 1991: 5.
— to lecture on whales, Lahaina News, December 19, 1991: 6.
— to lecture on whales, Lahaina News, January 2, 1992: 5.
— to lecture on whales , Lahaina News, November 26, 1992: 23.
— to lecture at Kapalua Bay Hotel, Lahaina News, December 31, 1992: 12.
— to present "Man, Kayak and the Whale—Harmonious Way of Life" , Lahaina News, February 6, 1997: 14.
— shares experiences at sea, Lahaina News, February 13, 1997: 1,2,10.
— continues to present on whales, Lahaina News, February 27, 1997: 10.
— to share experiences at sea, Lahaina News, February 12, 1998: 1.
— to present "Man, Kayak and the Whale—A Harmonious Way of Life", Lahaina News, February 19, 1998: 12.
— to discuss environment, Lahaina News, December 6, 2001: 1,18.
— to lead talk on "Man, Kayak and a Whale", Lahaina News, January 3, 2002: 16.
— to speak on "Man, Kayak and the Whale", Lahaina News, January 10, 2002: 17.
— continues to present "Man, Kayak and the Whale", Lahaina News, February 14, 2002: 17.

ROSS, BETH
— elected as new president of American Association of Retired Persons, Lahaina News, December 22, 1994: 6.

ROSS, COLLEEN [ARTIST]
— featured, Lahaina News, March 21, 1990: 16,17.

ROSS, DON
— praised for work organizing James Taylor concert, Lahaina News, February 12, 1986: 8.

ROSS, JOHN [COMEDIAN]
— to perform at Maui Marriott Resort, Lahaina News, April 4, 1990: 13.

ROSS, LILIA
— demonstrating use of paring knives, Lahaina News, June 24, 1999: 13.

ROSS, LORENZO
— named catering sales manager at Hyatt Regency Maui, Lahaina News, August 17, 1995: 10.

ROSS, LOUISE
— president of Napilihau Community Association talks of proposed light industrial project, Lahaina News, August 22, 1990: 1,3.
— nominated by Mayor Linda Lingle to Maui Planning Commission, Lahaina News, May 19, 1994: 5,6.
— receives preliminary approval from Maui County Council to replace Edwina Smythe on Maui Planning Commission, Lahaina News, June 9, 1994: 1.
— appointed to Maui Planning Commission, Lahaina News, June 23, 1994: 5.
— advocating for park in Napili, Lahaina News, January 1, 1998: 1,2.

ROSS, PATRICK KAMAHEIWA
— receives Jack Millar Memorial Scholarship, Lahaina News, August 9, 1989: 3.

ROSS, PEGGY
— critical of native Hawaiian leadership, Lahaina Sun, June 7, 1972: 3.
— plans to run for Mayor of Maui County, Lahaina Sun, June 21, 1972: 3.
— challenges County ordinance against political signs, Lahaina Sun, August 2, 1972: 9.

ROSS, REBECCA
— opens Elite Mortgage, Lahaina News, May 11, 2000: 11.

ROSSEAU, JACQUELINE
— discusses issues connected to new marine sanctuary, Lahaina News, June 24, 1993: 1.

ROSSI, JOSEPH
— seeks Maui County Council permission to operate flower shop from their home, Lahaina News, July 23, 1992: 10.
— request to rezone area in Kihei denied, Lahaina News, October 22, 1992: 13.

ROTARY CLUB
— Lahaina chapter elects officers, Lahaina News, June 27, 1984: 3.
— Lahaina chapter awards checks to local groups for projects, Lahaina News, July 3, 1985: 3.
— new officers installed, Lahaina News, July 30, 1986: 3.
— held assembly, service plans announced, Lahaina News, August 20, 1986: 3,14.

— funding polio immunizations around the world, Lahaina News, March 16, 1988: 3.

— to hold hoe-down to benefit Maui Youth Theatre, Lahaina News, November 9, 1988: 3.

— donate proceeds of Rotary Hoe Down to Maui Youth Theatre, Lahaina News, December 21, 1988: 12.

— to hold nighttime golf tournament, Lahaina News, December 21, 1988: 12.

— Richard Mark, sheriff of Kalaupapa, to speak, Lahaina News, January 25, 1989: 5.

— to hold hoedown fundraiser for Maui Youth Theatre, Lahaina News, September 27, 1989: 11.

— to hold hoedown fundraiser for Maui Youth Theatre, Lahaina News, October 25, 1989: 8.

— raises money at hoe down to help Maui Youth Theatre, Lahaina News, November 15, 1989: 9.

— officers elected, Lahaina News, July 4, 1990: 4.

— to hold Hoedown to raise money for Friends of the Children's Advocacy Center of Maui, Lahaina News, September 26, 1990: 7.

— to host Hoe Down to raise funds for Children's Advocacy Center, Lahaina News, October 17, 1990: 6.

— Hoe Down to be held, Lahaina News, October 24, 1990: 4.

— Hoe Down to be held, Lahaina News, October 31, 1990: 7,8.

— Hoedown to include barbecue steak and chicken dinner, Lahaina News, November 7, 1990: 4,5.

— Hoedown a success, Lahaina News, November 28, 1990: 4.

— to hold annual Chinese Dinner and Auction fundraiser, Lahaina News, April 3, 1991: 6.

— sponsoring Keiki Halloween Parade, Lahaina News, October 17, 1991: 6.

— to present a rock and roll party, Lahaina News, November 14, 1991: 21.

— to hold fundraiser for environmental projects, Lahaina News, November 21, 1991: 19.

— to hold annual Chinese dinner and auction at the Wo Hing Temple, Lahaina News, April 23, 1992: 5.

— to hold benefit dinner/auction for scholarships, Lahaina News, April 30, 1992: 4.

— to hold conference at Maui Sun hotel, Lahaina News, January 14, 1993: 7.

— to hold golf fundraiser, Lahaina News, January 14, 1993: 9.

— awards scholarships, Lahaina News, May 20, 1993: 2.

— to host fundraiser for scholarship fund, Lahaina News, May 20, 1993: 2,3.

— fundraiser attended by more than 150 people, Lahaina News, May 27, 1993: 1.

— to hold food drive, Lahaina News, November 20, 1997: 1.

— to hold "Monte Carlo Night", Lahaina News, March 2, 2000: 13.

— Yee Chiat Tay awarded Rotary Foundation Academic-Year Ambassadorial Scholarship, Lahaina News, September 25, 2003: 3.

ROTARY CLUB, KAHULUI

— names Bill Baldwin as employer of the year, Lahaina News, January 8, 1998: 11.

ROTARY CLUB, KEPA'A

— names scholarship after chef Greg Gaspar, Lahaina News, September 2, 1999: 13.

ROTARY CLUB, KIHEI-WAILEA

— head of Republican Party Terry Walker to speak to, Lahaina News, June 18, 1992: 14.

— to hold luncheon, Lahaina News, July 9, 1992: 7.

— to meet, Lahaina News, November 26, 1992: 18.

— to hold golf tournament fundraiser, Lahaina News, February 25, 1993: 5.

— to host golf tournament, Lahaina News, March 4, 1993: 5.

— to meet, Lahaina News, July 22, 1993: 6.

— to hold golf tournament honoring Pat Miramontez, Lahaina News, February 24, 1994: 6.

— to hold gift drive for needy children, Lahaina News, December 13, 2001: 16.

ROTARY CLUB, LAHAINA

— John Siemer installed as new president, Lahaina Sun, July 28, 1971: 10.

— to hold benefit concert with Peter Moon Band, Lahaina News, May 1, 1985: 3.

— sponsoring Halloween parade, Lahaina News, October 23, 1985: 3.

— presents Lanny Thada with Vocational Service Award, Lahaina News, February 4, 1987: 3.

— to sponsor Chinese dinner, Lahaina News, June 10, 1987: 3.

— Awards Lori Gomez, Lahainaluna High School teacher, Vocational Service Award, Lahaina News, May 11, 1988: 14.

— new officers installed, Lahaina News, July 12, 1989: 6.

— selling tickets to annual scholarship auction, Lahaina News, March 14, 1990: 2.

— to hold Chinese dinner and auction, Lahaina News, April 4, 1990: 3.

— Chinese Dinner and Auction fundraiser featured, Lahaina News, April 11, 1990: 18.

— fundraiser successful, Lahaina News, April 25, 1990: 3.

— installs Brian Maither as president, Lahaina News, June 27, 1990: 8.

— to host Linda Lingle, Lahaina News, October 31, 1990: 7.

— holds fundraiser for scholarships, Lahaina News, March 6, 1991: 3.

— annual dinner and auction a success, Lahaina News, April 17, 1991: 1,3.

— Charlie Nalepa new president of, Lahaina News, July 11, 1991: 4.

— raises $600 for Big Brothers/Big Sisters at Bowlathon, Lahaina News, August 29, 1991: 7.

— to host Maui Catholic Charities official Charles Ridings, Lahaina News, June 11, 1992: 3.

— to host baseball player Dave Dravecky, Lahaina News, June 11, 1992: 6.

— donates to West Maui Little League, Lahaina News, July 8, 1993: 1.

— donates funds to West Maui Little League, Lahaina News, July 8, 1993: 4.

— new officers elected, Lahaina News, August 5, 1993: 4.

— welcomes exchange students from Japan, Lahaina News, August 26, 1993: 4.

— Rick Nava inducted as member, Lahaina News, September 23, 1993: 3.

— to sponsor Scholarship Scramble golf tournament, Lahaina News, January 20, 1994: 9.

— helps local youth programs, Lahaina News, February 17, 1994: 4.

— new members announced, Lahaina News, March 24, 1994: 7.

— Lisa Kushi inducted as new member, Lahaina News, April 28, 1994: 4.

— Pancho Villa Fiesta to be held, Lahaina News, May 5, 1994: 4.

— Bruce Raney inducted, Lahaina News, June 2, 1994: 3.

— awards scholarships to Lahainaluna High School students, Lahaina News, June 2, 1994: 3.

— gives grant to West Maui Little League, Lahaina News, July 14, 1994: 9.

— inducts Ronald Ellstrom, Lahaina News, August 4, 1994: 4.

— clean up Lahaina House as a service project, Lahaina News, December 1, 1994: 7.

— contributing to Rose Parade float, Lahaina News, December 29, 1994: 2.

— donates to Lahainaluna High School's Project Graduation, Lahaina News, April 6, 1995: 4.

— to hold Pancho Villa Fiesta and Auction, Lahaina News, April 20, 1995: 6.

— provides scholarships to Lahainaluna High School students, Lahaina News, June 1, 1995: 2.

— Chuck Bergson begins as president, Lahaina News, July 13, 1995: 5.

— to meet, Lahaina News, October 12, 1995: 6.

— provides grant to Maui Youth and Family Services, Lahaina News, December 7, 1995: 3.

— to meet, Lahaina News, January 4, 1996: 4.

— announces Scholarship Scramble tournament, Lahaina News, February 8, 1996: 11.

— to hold Scholarship Scramble Golf Tournament, Lahaina News, March 7, 1996: 7.

— to hold Scholarship Scramble Golf Tournament, Lahaina News, March 21, 1996: 6.

— scholarships awarded, Lahaina News, May 9, 1996: 14.

— spruce up three public telephones, Lahaina News, July 4, 1996: 2.

— continues to meet, Lahaina News, October 3, 1996: 15.

— to host Scholarship Scramble Golf Tournament, Lahaina News, January 9, 1997: 6.

— to hold Scholarship Scramble Golf Tournament, Lahaina News, January 16, 1997: 6.

— meeting canceled, Lahaina News, April 24, 1997: 13.

— presents "Young Person of the Year" award to Karen Ancheta, Lahaina News, May 1, 1997: 3.

— awards scholarships to Lahainaluna High School students, Lahaina News, June 5, 1997: 15.

— to hold Fiesta and Auction, Lahaina News, June 19, 1997: 16.

— Linda Lingle discusses gubernatorial race, Lahaina News, September 4, 1997: 1,2.

— to hold Scholarship Scramble at Ka'anapali Golf Course, Lahaina News, January 1, 1998: 12.

— continues to meet, Lahaina News, January 8, 1998: 12.

— to hold Scholarship Scramble at Ka'anapali Golf Course, Lahaina News, January 15, 1998: 1.

— holds Fiesta and auction to support student scholarships, Lahaina News, May 7, 1998: 2.

— to hold Fiesta and Auction at Lahaina Jodo Mission, Lahaina News, May 14, 1998: 1.

— Fiesta event successful, Lahaina News, May 28, 1998: 2.

— awards scholarships, Lahaina News, June 4, 1998: 5.

— to hold "Scholarship Scramble" golf tournament, Lahaina News, December 10, 1998: 19.

— to hold "Scholarship Scramble", Lahaina News, December 17, 1998: 19.

— to hold "Scholarship Scramble" golf tournament, Lahaina News, December 24, 1998: 8.

— to hold "Scholarship Scramble" golf tournament, Lahaina News, January 14, 1999: 7.

— to meet, Lahaina News, March 18, 1999: 17.

— to hold Fiesta and Auction, Lahaina News, May 13, 1999: 15.

— Fiesta and Auction to include bullets recovered from the Battle of Gettysburg, Lahaina News, May 20, 1999: 1,20.

— continues to meet, Lahaina News, May 27, 1999: 13.

— donates to American Youth Soccer Organization, Lahaina News, July 8, 1999: 6.

— looking for families for a student exchange from Japan, Lahaina News, October 28, 1999: 13.

— holds Halloween Parade with Soroptimists International, Lahaina News, November 4, 1999: 1,3.

— to sponsor youth program, Lahaina News, November 4, 1999: 5.

— to recognize Grant Butler, Lahaina News, January 13, 2000: 3.

— to hold "Scholarship Scramble" at Ka'anapali Golf Course, Lahaina News, January 13, 2000: 7.

— to hold Fiesta and Auction at Lahaina Jodo Mission, Lahaina News, May 18, 2000: 20.

— held Fiesta and Auction, Lahaina News, May 25, 2000: 3.

— awards scholarships, Lahaina News, June 1, 2000: 3.

— continues to meet, Lahaina News, July 13, 2000: 17.

— Mac Lowson new president of, Lahaina News, July 20, 2000: 8.

— continues to meet, Lahaina News, December 7, 2000: 25.

— continues to meet, Lahaina News, April 19, 2001: 16.

— to hold Fiesta and Auction, Lahaina News, May 3, 2001: 2.

— to hold Fiesta and Auction, Lahaina News, May 10, 2001: 2.

— Fiesta and Auction held at Lahaina Jodo Mission, Lahaina News, May 17, 2001: 3.

— new officers announced, Lahaina News, June 14, 2001: 5.

— awards scholarships, Lahaina News, June 28, 2001: 2.

— to hold meeting to form a morning Rotary Club, Lahaina News, June 28, 2001: 5.

— to hold benefit to support Maui Drug Court, Lahaina News, July 19, 2001: 1,5.

— to hold benefit to support Maui Drug Court, Lahaina News, July 26, 2001: 14.

— continues to meet, Lahaina News, April 4, 2002: 16.

— to hold annual Fiesta and Action, Lahaina News, May 2, 2002: 16.

— to hold Scholarship Scramble Golf Tournament, Lahaina News, June 13, 2002: 3.

— to hold "Scholarship Scramble" fundraiser, Lahaina News, June 20, 2002: 12.

— recognizes Grant Butler for service, Lahaina News, September 12, 2002: 2.

— to support exchange program, Lahaina News, March 13, 2003: 2.

— offering Student Exchange Program to Kobe, Japan, Lahaina News, March 20, 2003: 2.

— to hold auction fundraiser, Lahaina News, March 20, 2003: 3.

— to hold auction fundraiser, Lahaina News, March 27, 2003: 9.

— awards scholarships, Lahaina News, June 5, 2003: 1,3.

— to hold Scholarship Scramble golf tournament, Lahaina News, June 5, 2003: 12.

— continues to meet, Lahaina News, June 5, 2003: 17.

— to hold "Scholarship Scramble" golf tournament, Lahaina News, June 12, 2003: 11.

— to hold "Scholarship Scramble" golf tournament, Lahaina News, June 19, 2003: 13.

— president Rick Nava planning community projects, Lahaina News, July 24, 2003: 1,18.

— former president Thomas Roche passes away, Lahaina News, August 7, 2003: 3.

ROTARY CLUB, LAHAINA SUNRISE

— meets, Lahaina News, August 9, 2001: 16,17.

— to meet, Lahaina News, September 6, 2001: 16.

— plants bougainvillea along Honoapi'ilani Highway, Lahaina News, October 4, 2001: 3.

— to meet, Lahaina News, January 10, 2002: 17.

— meets, Lahaina News, January 10, 2002: 9.

— to host basketball game, Lahaina News, June 6, 2002: 12.

— to meet at Pioneer Inn's Snug Harbor Parlor, Lahaina News, May 22, 2003: 17.

— continues to meet, Lahaina News, August 14, 2003: 17.

ROTARY CLUB, UPCOUNTRY

— to hold "Taste of the Tropics" benefit, Lahaina News, September 26, 1996: 14.

— to host airplane captain Al Haynes, Lahaina News, April 2, 1998: 16.

— to celebrate 5th anniversary, Lahaina News, February 17, 2000: 17.

ROTARY FOUNDATION

— to hold annual fundraiser "Monte Carlo Night", Lahaina News, March 15, 2001: 2.

ROTARY INTERNATIONAL

— names Rina Chung as recipient of Rotary Ambassadorial Scholarship, Lahaina News, January 6, 1994: 2.

ROTARY MOONLIGHT GOLF TOURNAMENT

— to be held, Lahaina News, April 25, 1990: 12.

ROTH, BARBARA
— appointed vice-president of marketing and sales at Ka'anapali Estate Coffee, Lahaina News, July 24, 1997: 13.

ROTH, ERIC [WRITER]
— to attend Maui Writers Conference, Lahaina News, July 27, 1995: 4.

ROTHENBERG, MICHAEL [WRITER]
— to read poetry at Artful Dodger, Lahaina News, September 14, 1988: 13.

ROTTEN, SCOTTY [MUSICIAN]
— to perform at Polli's On the Beach, Lahaina News, October 31, 1990: 14.
— to perform at El Crab Catcher, Lahaina News, July 18, 1991: 9.
— to perform at Kobe Japanese Steak House, Lahaina News, October 3, 1991: 12.
— featured, Lahaina News, November 7, 1991: 14,15.
— to perform at Compadres Mexican Bar and Grill, Lahaina News, December 12, 1991: 19.
— to perform at Compadres, Lahaina News, March 12, 1992: 18.
— to perform at Cheeseburgers in Paradise, Lahaina News, January 6, 1994: 11.
— continues to perform at Aloha Cantina, Lahaina News, September 1, 1994: 15.
— continues to perform at Aloha Cantina, Lahaina News, September 22, 1994: 16.
— continues to perform at Aloha Cantina, Lahaina News, October 27, 1994: 19.
— to perform at Moose McGillycuddy's, Lahaina News, March 14, 1996: 12.
— to retire from performing, Lahaina News, May 4, 2000: 5.

ROUART, MADELEINE
— to show post-impressionist watercolors, Lahaina News, February 22, 1989: 3.

ROUGH ROAD ENDURANCE RACE
— to be held, Lahaina News, December 17, 1992: 10,11.
— to be held, Lahaina News, December 31, 1992: 7.

ROUGH-WATER SWIM
— race to be sponsored by Maui Ocean Swim Club, Lahaina News, October 10, 1991: 8.

ROUSE, JIM [POLITICIAN]
— running for Hawaii Representative District 10 seat, Lahaina News, September 19, 2002: 20.
— to speak to Maui Democratic Country Club, Lahaina News, October 3, 2002: 1.

ROWAN, DAN [ENTERTAINER]
— arrives in Lahaina after sailing from Los Angeles, Lahaina Sun, April 28, 1971: 1.

ROWE, SAM
— named president of Island Mortgage Corp., Lahaina News, December 30, 1993: 5.

ROWE, TERRY [ARTIST]
— named Professional Photographer of the Year by the Maui Professional Photographers' Association, Lahaina News, January 4, 2001: 14.
— photographs rare species in Pu'u Kukui crater, Lahaina News, July 26, 2001: 1.

ROWING
— see paddling

ROY ALLEN REED BAND [MUSICAL GROUP]
— performing at Longhi's, Lahaina News, March 21, 1990: 14.

ROYAL BALL
— to be held at Maui Marriott Resort, Lahaina News, October 25, 1989: 14.

ROYAL CHRISTMAS AT THE BALDWIN MANOR, A [TOUR]
— fundraiser for American Cancer Society, Lahaina News, December 11, 1985: 9.

ROYAL COURT CORP. [BUSINESS]
— proposed shopping center criticized, Lahaina News, December 26, 1991: 1,2.
— reaches agreement with Maui Eldorado to develop upscale shopping center, Lahaina News, March 12, 1992: 12.

ROYAL FIVE ORCHESTRA [MUSICAL GROUP]
— to perform at The Maui Prince, Lahaina News, August 22, 1991: 12.

ROYAL HAWAIIAN AIR SERVICE
— Royal Hawaiian Air Service expected to receive exclusive rights to operate passenger flights Ka'anapali airport, Lahaina Sun, May 19, 1971: 3.
— introduces new kama'aina fares, Lahaina News, September 12, 1984: 3.
— offering flight tours of Maui, Lahaina News, September 26, 1984: 14.
— suing Maui Land & Pineapple for breach of contract over land for airport, Lahaina News, January 2, 1985: 3.
— going out of business, Lahaina News, May 28, 1986: 3.

ROYAL HAWAIIAN AIRLINES [BUSINESS]
— last plane to depart from Ka'anapali airstrip, Lahaina News, January 22, 1986: 1,14.

ROYAL HAWAIIAN CARRIAGES
— county law does not allow horse-drawn carriages, Lahaina News, February 13, 1992: 1,6.

ROYAL HAWAIIAN CRUISES
— Bruce DeYoung appointed general manager of Maui vessels, Lahaina News, September 4, 1997: 12.

ROYAL HAWAIIAN HOTEL
— advertising campaign wins national competition, Lahaina Sun, February 10, 1971: 2.

ROYAL HAWAIIAN RESORT
— to feature Hawaiian concert, Lahaina News, May 13, 1987: 14.

ROYAL KA'ANAPALI 10K RUN
— to be held on Royal Ka'anapali Golf Course, Lahaina News, June 12, 1985: 20.

ROYAL KA'ANAPALI NORTH GOLF COURSE
— to host West Maui Youth Center Invitational Golf Tournament, Lahaina News, May 29, 1985: 3.

ROYAL KA'ANAPALI REALTY
— opens at Honokowai Marketplace, Lahaina News, August 15, 2002: 8.

ROYAL KAHANA CONDOMINIUM
— featured, Lahaina News, April 4, 1984: 14.
— featured, Lahaina News, June 6, 1984: 14.
— development featured, Lahaina News, July 13, 2000: 12.

ROYAL KAHANA RESORT
— Outrigger Hotels and Resort to take over management of, Lahaina News, March 22, 2001: 8.

ROYAL KEIKI TENNIS CLUB
— organized for children, Lahaina News, August 14, 1985: 4.

ROYAL LAHAINA HOTEL [BUSINESS]
— Strike at, Lahaina Sun, November 11, 1970: 1,4.
— 12-story addition nearing completion, Lahaina Sun, November 11, 1970: 4.
— 12-story, 350-room addition opens, Lahaina Sun, February 24, 1971: 6.
— construction worker Joseph Caires Jr. injured in fall , Lahaina Sun, March 3, 1971: 1.
— dedication of addition to the hotel, Lahaina Sun, May 12, 1971: 6.
— receives Four Diamond Award of Excellence, Lahaina News, May 2, 1984: 17.

ROYAL LAHAINA KALUA PIG COOK-OFF
— to be held, Lahaina News, May 27, 1987: 16.

ROYAL LAHAINA LUAU
— reviewed, Lahaina News, August 12, 1987: 9.

ROYAL LAHAINA OPEN TENNIS TOURNAMENT
— organized, Lahaina News, February 4, 1987: 9.
— sponsored by Nevada Bob's, Lahaina News, March 30, 1988: 3.
— begins, Lahaina News, April 6, 1988: 6.

ROYAL LAHAINA RESORT [BUSINESS]
— Thea Shelton joins as sales manager, Lahaina News, January 30, 1985: 18.
— names Fraught & Miyashiro Advertising to handle food and beverage advertising, Lahaina News, January 8, 1986: 3.
— wins awards from Restaurant Hospitality magazine, Lahaina News, November 4, 1987: 3.
— hosting kalua pig cook-off, Lahaina News, May 31, 1989: 19.
— to be managed by Outrigger Hotels Hawaii, Lahaina News, March 21, 1990: 4.
— to host Hawaii High School Tennis Championships, Lahaina News, March 28, 1990: 9.
— musical line-up listed, Lahaina News, April 4, 1990: 13.
— to again be managed by Hawaiian Hotels and Resorts, Lahaina News, May 23, 1991: 8.
— names Don Reason as general manager, Lahaina News, July 25, 1991: 7.
— scheduling a twice weekly hula show, Lahaina News, February 13, 1992: 18.
— improvements planned, Lahaina News, April 9, 1992: 20.
— changes culinary department, Lahaina News, February 18, 1993: 9.
— to host Suspects Murder Mystery Dinner Theater, Lahaina News, September 23, 1993: 10.
— recognizes employees, Lahaina News, September 30, 1993: 8.
— to feature a life-size gingerbread house, Lahaina News, November 25, 1993: 12.
— begins "Adopt a Keiki" program to help needy children, Lahaina News, December 16, 1993: 2.
— new positions created, Lahaina News, April 21, 1994: 12.
— begins holiday season with Valley isle Symphony, Lahaina News, November 24, 1994: 11.
— history of, Lahaina News, January 26, 1995: 4.
— Mary Blackwell named sales manager, Lahaina News, March 9, 1995: 6.
— Laurence Fabrao named assistant front manager at, Lahaina News, March 9, 1995: 6.
— Epi Rabanal promoted to director of sales and marketing at, Lahaina News, June 8, 1995: 10.
— Brian Thomas promoted to head tennis professional, Lahaina News, June 29, 1995: 10.
— Michael Ako named new manager, Lahaina News, August 3, 1995: 8.
— to hold "Adopt A Keiki" program, Lahaina News, November 30, 1995: 4.
— hosting Wild Alaskan Salmon Festival, Lahaina News, July 4, 1996: 13.
— hold rally to protest wages, Lahaina News, November 16, 2000: 7.
— seek new contract, Lahaina News, February 1, 2001: 3.
— ILWU Local 142 suspends contract with, Lahaina News, February 8, 2001: 3.
— workers walk out, Lahaina News, February 15, 2001: 8.

ROYAL LAHAINA TENNIS RANCH
— Cari Buck chosen as new head professional at, Lahaina News, May 9, 1990: 8.
— appoints Gary Jones as tennis director, Lahaina News, September 26, 1991: 9.

— to offer customer service seminar, Lahaina News, October 24, 1991: 9.
— continues to offer after-school clinics, Lahaina News, November 25, 1999: 9.

ROYAL LAHAINA TENNIS STADIUM
— Crosby, Stills, and Nash to perform at, Lahaina News, March 20, 1991: 9.

ROYAL OCEAN TERRACE LOUNGE [RESTAURANT]
— featured, Lahaina News, June 24, 1987: 9.
— musical line-up listed, Lahaina News, April 11, 1990: 15.
— musical groups listed, Lahaina News, May 2, 1990: 15.
— nominated as one of "Hawaii's Best Restaurants" by readers of Aloha Magazine, Lahaina News, June 3, 1993: 13.
— featured, Lahaina News, March 6, 1997: 6,14.

ROYAL PACIFIC BANK
— correction: have not yet been approved to sell stock, Lahaina News, September 24, 1992: 3.

ROYAL PACIFIC BANK [BUSINESS]
— to keep staff and management of First Interstate Bank, Lahaina News, January 9, 1992: 2.
— hopes to open in Fall, Lahaina News, July 16, 1992: 16.

ROYAL SHAKESPEARE COMPANY [TROUPE]
— to give workshops, Lahaina News, January 9, 1992: 5.

ROYCE, SHIRLEY [ARTIST]
— work displayed at Lahaina Art Gallery, Lahaina Sun, July 28, 1971: 11.

ROYCE, W. T.
— representative from Maui Land & Pineapple discusses proposed public beach in West Maui, Lahaina Sun, February 24, 1971: 1.

ROY'S [RESTAURANT]
— expanding to Maui, Lahaina News, October 10, 1990: 11.
— to hold grand opening, benefit for Lahaina Arts Society, Lahaina News, May 28, 1992: 3.
— to celebrate second anniversary, Lahaina News, March 6, 2003: 8.

ROY'S KAHANA BAR AND GRILL [RESTAURANT]
— opens at Kahana Gateway shopping center, Lahaina News, January 16, 1992: 8.
— George Kobayashi named wine and beverage director, Lahaina News, January 30, 1992: 10.
— featured, Lahaina News, January 30, 1992: 20.
— celebrating second anniversary, Lahaina News, January 27, 1994: 8.

ROY'S NICOLINA RESTAURANT [RESTAURANT]
— to host four renowned female chefs, Lahaina News, April 20, 1995: 11.
— hosts "The Roy's Stars of Tomorrow", Lahaina News, September 3, 1998: 11.

ROZANSKI, WALTER
— security guard extinguishes fire at Gazebo Restaurant, Lahaina News, November 7, 1990: 4.

ROZENBERG, JOHN
— producing Maui Music Festival, Lahaina News, July 6, 1995: 10.

RUBBENS FORD BAND, THE [MUSICAL GROUP]
— to perform at Hawaiian Islands Rhythm and Blues Mele, Lahaina News, May 14, 1998: 18.

RUBENSTEIN, MICHAEL
— Scholar/Athlete of the Week, Lahaina News, August 9, 2001: 13.

RUBIN, NANCY SHIPLEY
— to present "Freedom and the Power to Change", Lahaina News, April 6, 1988: 3.
— to offer workshops on art, Lahaina News, November 23, 1988: 5.

RUBINE, NAOMI [ARTIST]
— develops weaving kit, Lahaina News, November 1, 1982: 10.

RUBLIENKAR, BRUCE
— memorial service to be held for, Lahaina News, April 18, 2002: 5.

RUBY'S DINER [RESTAURANT]
— featured, Lahaina News, December 5, 2002: 9.
— Miguel Vazquez named top employee for 2002, Lahaina News, January 2, 2003: 9.
— Jean Coppers hired as restaurant manager, Lahaina News, January 16, 2003: 8.
— offering kama'aina discount, Lahaina News, June 26, 2003: 14.

RUDNER, RITA [COMEDIAN]
— to perform at Grand Wailea on New Year's Eve, Lahaina News, December 30, 1993: 10.

RUDOSKY, JIM
— named president of Cooperative Marketing Group, Lahaina News, August 27, 1992: 10.

RUFF, HOWARD
— to present lecture "Invest in Your Child", Lahaina News, March 30, 1995: 10.

RUGGLES, CLIVE
— to discuss "Ancient Hawaiian Astronomy", Lahaina News, June 13, 2002: 17.
— to speak on "Ancient Hawaiian Astronomy", Lahaina News, June 20, 2002: 16.

RUIS, JR. ANTONE
— at meeting between Hawaiian member of the Hawaiian Homes Commission and The Hawaiians, Lahaina Sun, December 23, 1970: 6.

RUIZ, KEOKI [MUSICIAN]
— to perform at Villa Restaurant, Lahaina News, September 23, 1993: 11.

RUMBOA, REVEREND
— to hold Bible study with Light Bringers Rescue Mission, Lahaina News, March 29, 2001: 17.

RUN FOR THE LITTLES
— fun run benefitting Big Brothers and Big Sisters, Lahaina News, February 20, 1985: 3.
— raised $3000 for Maui's Big Brothers/Big Sisters, Lahaina News, March 20, 1985: 7.

RUNDGREN, TODD [MUSICIAN]
— new album "Nearly Human" reviewed, Lahaina News, August 30, 1989: 16.
— to perform in "A Walk Down Abbey Road" celebration of the Beatles, Lahaina News, June 13, 2002: 17.

RUNNING
— Bud Light Haleakala "Run to the sun" marathon to be held, Lahaina News, August 23, 1989: 5.
— Dracula Dash to be held, Lahaina News, October 11, 1989: 24.
— Keiki Dash to be held, Lahaina News, October 11, 1989: 24.
— Dracula Dash still accepting registrations, Lahaina News, October 25, 1989: 11.
— Chart House/Gas Company fun run scheduled, Lahaina News, February 7, 1990: 9.
— fun run to be held at Westin Maui, Lahaina News, February 21, 1990: 9.
— Chart House/Gas Company 10K fun run to be held, Lahaina News, April 4, 1990: 5.
— Chart House/Gas Company 10K fun run to be held, Lahaina News, April 11, 1990: 7.
— Iao Valley 10K scheduled, Lahaina News, April 11, 1990: 7.
— Na Holo Wahine to be held, Lahaina News, May 9, 1990: 7.
— Lahaina Coolers Historic Fun Run to be held, Lahaina News, October 3, 1990: 1.
— Dracula's Dash registrations being accepted, Lahaina News, October 10, 1990: 18.
— Lahaina Coolers Historic Fun Run results, Lahaina News, October 24, 1990: 12.
— results of Festival of Running, Lahaina News, December 5, 1990: 20.
— Maui Community College Criminal Justice Club to host Fun Run, Lahaina News, December 26, 1990: 14.
— Steve Borowski named race director of Ironman Triathlon World Championship, Lahaina News, January 16, 1991: 20.
— Chart House/The Gas Company 10K to be held, Lahaina News, March 6, 1991: 5.
— Wes Kessenich wins Maui Marathon, Lahaina News, March 20, 1991: 5.
— Tedeschi 10K to be organized by Valley Isle Road Runners' Association, Lahaina News, May 23, 1991: 10.
— Terry Fox 10K Run to be held, Lahaina News, August 15, 1991: 4.
— Dracula's Dash to be held, Lahaina News, October 17, 1991: 4.
— Salvation Army to hold fun run, Lahaina News, November 7, 1991: 7.
— 5K run sponsored by Subway Sandwiches, Lahaina News, November 21, 1991: 9.
— Surfer Joe's Grill and Bar to hold Santa Claus 10K run, Lahaina News, December 19, 1991: 8,9.
— sponsored by KMVI Radio and Maui Community College Criminal Justice Club, Lahaina News, January 9, 1992: 7.
— Maui Triathlon to be held this weekend, Lahaina News, April 2, 1992: 8.
— Chart House/Gas Company 10K fun run to be benefit Big Brothers/Big Sisters, Lahaina News, April 9, 1992: 11.
— Chart House/Gas Company 10K fun run to be benefit Big Brothers/Big Sisters, Lahaina News, April 16, 1992: 10.
— Lahaina Hard Rock Café sponsoring 10K run, Lahaina News, May 21, 1992: 11.
— Tedeschi Vineyards to hold 10K Scenic Run, Lahaina News, May 21, 1992: 12.
— Midnight Marathon to be held, Lahaina News, June 18, 1992: 12.
— Hana Relay race to be held, Lahaina News, September 10, 1992: 8.
— Valley Isle Road Runners Association hosting annual Haleakala Run to the Sun, Lahaina News, September 24, 1992: 11,13.
— Hana Relay rescheduled, Lahaina News, October 1, 1992: 7,8.
— Dan Marcus wins Lahaina Coolers 5K, Lahaina News, October 22, 1992: 8.
— Maui Marathon to be held, Lahaina News, March 11, 1993: 9.
— Troy Barboza Law Enforcement Torch Run to be held, Lahaina News, May 13, 1993: 8.
— Haleakala Run to the Sun to be held, Lahaina News, August 12, 1993: 10.
— Valley Isle Roadrunners to host Hana Relay, Lahaina News, September 9, 1993: 9.
— Terry Fox Run held, Lahaina News, September 16, 1993: 11.
— Lahaina Coolers Historic Fun Run to be held, Lahaina News, October 7, 1993: 7.
— Reindeer Walk and Run for Arthritis to be held, Lahaina News, November 18, 1993: 12.
— Harbor to Harbor run to be held, Lahaina News, November 18, 1993: 12.
— to support Arthritis Foundation, Lahaina News, November 25, 1993: 10.
— Maui Community College Criminal Justice Fun Run to be held, Lahaina News, December 30, 1993: 8.
— West Maui School Complex to host West Maui Marathon Madness, Lahaina News, January 20, 1994: 9.
— Maui Marathon to be held, Lahaina News, March 10, 1994: 6.
— Chart House/Gas Co. Run/Walk to be held, Lahaina News, March 31, 1994: 7.
— Na Holo Wahine Run to be held, Lahaina News, April 28, 1994: 7.
— Tedeschi Vineyards to host 10K Run/Walk, Lahaina News, May 19, 1994: 8,9.

— Summer's Here! Biathlon/Relay to be held, Lahaina News, June 16, 1994: 7.

— Harbor to Harbor road race held, Lahaina News, October 27, 1994: 11.

— Reindeer Run and Walk to be held, Lahaina News, December 1, 1994: 9.

— Aluminum Man/Woman biathlon to be held, Lahaina News, December 15, 1994: 8.

— Aluminum Man/Woman biathlon to be held, Lahaina News, December 22, 1994: 6.

— Maui Marathon to be held, Lahaina News, March 2, 1995: 6.

— Aluminum Woman/Man Series Triathlon to be held, Lahaina News, April 20, 1995: 10.

— Hawaii Ultra Runners Team (HURT) and Valley Isle Road Runner's Association to host Run to the Sun, Lahaina News, September 28, 1995: 7.

— Lahaina Coolers to host Historic Fun Run/Walk, Lahaina News, October 19, 1995: 6.

— Valley Isle Road Runners Association and Maui Community College Criminal Justice Club to hold Fun Run, Lahaina News, January 4, 1996: 6.

— Hard Rock Cafe to host 10K, Lahaina News, May 23, 1996: 2.

— Westin Maui fields team for Hana Relay Race, Lahaina News, October 10, 1996: 9.

— 5K Reindeer Run and Walk to be held, Lahaina News, December 5, 1996: 15.

— Fun Run sponsored by KAOI radio and Maui Community College's Criminal Justice Club, Lahaina News, January 2, 1997: 10.

— Maui Marathon to be held, Lahaina News, February 27, 1997: 6.

— Chart House hosting Fun Run and Walk, Lahaina News, March 13, 1997: 13.

— Hard Rock Cafe 10K run to be held, Lahaina News, May 22, 1997: 13.

— Matthew Holton wins Hard Rock Cafe 10K Rock 'n Roll Run, Lahaina News, June 5, 1997: 13.

— Maui Marathon to be held, Lahaina News, March 5, 1998: 14.

— Chart House 5K/10K Fun Run and Walk to benefit Big Brothers/Big Sisters, Lahaina News, April 2, 1998: 1.

— First Hawaiian Bank Troy Barboza Law Enforcement Torch Run to be held, Lahaina News, April 2, 1998: 15.

— Chart House 10K won by Jeff Sanders, Lahaina News, April 16, 1998: 1.

— Earth Maui Nature Summit 5K Run held, Lahaina News, June 18, 1998: 1.

— "Aluminum Man Not-so-serious Series" biathlon to be held, Lahaina News, January 14, 1999: 7.

— "Aluminum Man Not-so-serious Series" biathlon to be held, Lahaina News, January 21, 1999: 7.

— "Run for the Whales" to be held, Lahaina News, February 18, 1999: 7.

— Maui Tacos 5K Fun Run/Walk to be held, Lahaina News, March 4, 1999: 7.

— Chart House 5K/10K Fun Run/Walk to be held, Lahaina News, March 11, 1999: 7.

— Maui Tacos 5K Fun Run/Walk to be held, Lahaina News, March 18, 1999: 14.

— Chart House to host 5K/10K Fun Run/Walk, Lahaina News, March 25, 1999: 14.

— First Hawaiian Bank Troy Barboza Law Enforcement Torch Run to be held for Special Olympics, Lahaina News, April 1, 1999: 15.

— First Hawaiian Bank Troy Barboza Law Enforcement Torch Run to be held for Special Olympics, Lahaina News, April 8, 1999: 7.

— Valley Isle Road Runner to hold Na Holo Wahine 5K Run/Walk, Lahaina News, May 6, 1999: 17.

— Maui Community College Criminal Justice Club to hold Fun Run, Lahaina News, January 6, 2000: 7.

— First Hawaiian Bank Troy Barboza Law Enforcement Run to benefit Special Olympics, Lahaina News, March 30, 2000: 6.

— Kapalua Earth Maui 5K Fun Run to be held, Lahaina News, May 18, 2000: 14.

— Maui Community College Criminal Justice Club to hold fun run, Lahaina News, January 4, 2001: 9.

— mile run race to be held, Lahaina News, March 14, 2002: 13.

— Maui Tacos hosting 5K Fun Run/Walk, Lahaina News, August 22, 2002: 11.

— Valley Isle Road Runners strong at championships, Lahaina News, October 31, 2002: 11.

— exercises held for youth at Napili Park, Lahaina News, December 5, 2002: 11.

— training to be held, Lahaina News, December 19, 2002: 11.

— cross country teams seeking runners, Lahaina News, August 7, 2003: 13.

— participates sought for cross country team, Lahaina News, August 14, 2003: 13.

— cross country teams seeking runners, Lahaina News, August 21, 2003: 12.

— Maui Tacos to hold 5K Fun Run/Walk, Lahaina News, August 28, 2003: 13.

RUSKIN, IAN

— to perform in play on life of Harry Bridges, Lahaina News, October 11, 2001: 14.

RUSS FREEMAN AND THE RIPPINGTONS [MUSICAL GROUP]

— to perform at Maui Music Festival, Lahaina News, August 31, 1995: 11.

— to perform at Maui Music Festival, Lahaina News, August 8, 1996: 16.

RUSSELL, DAVE

— studio engineer discusses Lahaina Sound Studio, Lahaina News, February 17, 1988: 7.

— studio engineer at Lahaina Sound discusses recording, Lahaina News, September 20, 1989: 9.

RUSSELL, KEN

— owner of Four Winds Men's Hair Styling Shop wants to hang wooden sign in front of his shop, Lahaina Sun, November 18, 1970: 3.

— conflict with Maui Historic Commission over signage for his shop, Lahaina Sun, November 25, 1970: 1,2.

— granted permission to erect wooden sign in front of his shop, Lahaina Sun, January 13, 1971: 1,2.

RUSSELL, WILLIAM

— named vice president of American Savings Bank, Lahaina News, June 27, 2002: 8.

RUSTY HARPOON, THE [RESTAURANT]

— to hold softball tournament fundraiser for Lahaina Pop Warner Football Association, Lahaina News, November 9, 1988: 12.

— featured, Lahaina News, January 23, 1992: 21.

— now has sushi bar, Lahaina News, January 18, 1996: 12.

— Sammy Natafgy new general manager, Lahaina News, November 14, 2002: 8.

RUTH'S CHRIS STEAK HOUSE [RESTAURANT]

— lease signed, Lahaina News, March 19, 1998: 11.

— opening soon, Lahaina News, July 23, 1998: 13.

— opening attended by Dan Quayle, Lahaina News, August 6, 1998: 2.

— featured, Lahaina News, September 3, 1998: 6,7.

— to hold "Wine Wonders from Down Under", Lahaina News, October 22, 1998: 20.

— hosting "The Wines of Chateau Potelle", Lahaina News, November 5, 1998: 7.

— to hold "An Evening With Mr. Wine, Trav Duro Jr.", Lahaina News, December 3, 1998: 21.

— opening in South Maui, Lahaina News, December 14, 2000: 18.

— John Lopianetsky named regional manager at, Lahaina News, May 31, 2001: 8.

— names Alex Kutscherenko as regional group sales manager, Lahaina News, October 11, 2001: 8.

— featured, Lahaina News, January 3, 2002: 14.

RYAN COMPANY, THE, INC. [BUSINESS]

— new name for Aloha International Employment Services, Lahaina News, March 26, 1992: 11.

RYAN, JACKIE [MUSICIAN]

— to perform at Blackie's Bar, Lahaina News, October 10, 1991: 14.

— to perform at Casanova's; sponsored by Maui Jazz Society, Lahaina News, October 17, 1991: 20.

RYAN, KAY

— recognized as "Big Sister of the Year", Lahaina News, May 29, 1997: 3.

RYAN, LINDA

— to offer cooking classes, Lahaina News, January 23, 1985: 3.

RYDER, LEI'OHU [MUSICIAN]

— to offer singing classes, Lahaina News, August 13, 1998: 16.

— singing class to be held, Lahaina News, April 1, 1999: 17.

— to perform at Reflections of Old Lahaina Luau and Concert benefit, Lahaina News, August 19, 1999: 18.

— to perform new music at Borders Books, Lahaina News, July 13, 2000: 16.

— to perform at Ku'u Home O Wailuku music festival, Lahaina News, October 19, 2000: 18.

RYDER, TONY [ARTIST]

— to lead workshop on "Drawing the Features of the Face", Lahaina News, February 7, 2002: 17.

— continues to teach "Portrait Painting in Oil", Lahaina News, February 14, 2002: 17.

S

S-TURN PARK

— funds available for improvement, Lahaina News, March 17, 1994: 1.

— permits sought for improvements, Lahaina News, July 21, 1994: 3.

— community help sought for, Lahaina News, July 27, 1995: 3.

— changes at, Lahaina News, February 15, 1996: 2.

— nearly completed, Lahaina News, December 12, 1996: 5.

— dedicated, Lahaina News, December 26, 1996: 1.

S. H. KRESS AND COMPANY [BUSINESS]

— announces plans to close stores in Hawaii, Lahaina News, November 15, 1980: 16.

SÁMONTE, KALEI

— to teach dancing at The Art School at Kapalua, Lahaina News, September 26, 2002: 18.

— to teach dance classes at the Art School of Kapalua, Lahaina News, October 3, 2002: 18.

SAAIMAN, HETTIE [ARTIST]

— to be featured at Lahaina Arts Society, Lahaina News, August 30, 2001: 17.

— offering "Paint with Inks" art workshop, Lahaina News, September 6, 2001: 16.

— to hold "Paint with Ink" workshop, Lahaina News, February 21, 2002: 16.

— to exhibit at Village Galleries, Lahaina News, May 15, 2003: 16.

SAAR, DOROTHY [ARTIST]

— works displayed at Larry Dotson Gallery, Lahaina News, February 17, 1988: 18.

SABADO, PHILIP [ARTIST]

— work featured at Lahaina Art Society's Old Jail Gallery, Lahaina News, August 17, 1988: 14.

— chosen as Mele Artist, Lahaina News, November 1, 1989: 7.

— to be guest artist at Old Jail Gallery, Lahaina News, November 7, 1990: 13.

— to teach art classes, Lahaina News, June 9, 1994: 16.

— to hold summer art classes, Lahaina News, June 22, 1995: 12.

— to leading watercolor workshop for Maui Watercolorists Association, Lahaina News, March 20, 2003: 16.

— to hold workshop for Maui Watercolorists Association, Lahaina News, June 12, 2003: 20.

SABAS, MIKE

— playing high school basketball, Lahaina Sun, January 20, 1971: 7.

SABAS, MYRNA

— police officer honored for saving lives, Lahaina News, June 17, 1999: 3.

SABATINE, LUCAS

— Scholar/Athlete of the Week, Lahaina News, September 24, 1998: 14.

SABINI, KIRA

— Lahainaluna High School student finalist at Dr. Martin Luther King Jr. Peace Poetry Contest, Lahaina News, May 8, 2003: 2.

SABLAS, LORI

— appointed Maui chair for the King Kamehameha Day Parade, Lahaina News, August 1, 1991: 12.

— director of Po'okela program featured, Lahaina News, June 4, 1992: 3.

SACCHETTI, ALLEN

— wins Pennsylvania Lottery, Lahaina News, December 21, 1995: 6.

SACCONE, MIKE [COMEDIAN]

— to perform at Comedy Club and the Sports Page, Lahaina News, January 9, 1991: 7.

— to perform at Maui Comedy Club, Lahaina News, May 11, 1995: 12.

SACHI, KARLA [ARTIST]

— to display at Seaside Fine Art, Lahaina News, May 27, 1999: 12.

— to sign copies of "Turtle Songs", Lahaina News, June 10, 1999: 17.

SACK N SAVE [BUSINESS]

— accepting competitor coupons, Lahaina News, March 23, 1995: 10.

SACRED GARDENS FARM

— market to be held at Wharf Cinema Center, Lahaina News, October 26, 2000: 28.

— to hold Flower and Food Fairs, Lahaina News, December 14, 2000: 20.

— to hold Flower and Food Fairs, Lahaina News, April 19, 2001: 16.

SACRED HEARTS SCHOOL

— kept open after fire, Lahaina Sun, August 25, 1971: 1.

— fire at being studied by fire department, Lahaina Sun, August 25, 1971: 1,3.

— reopens after fire, Lahaina Sun, September 1, 1971: 5.

— raising funds to rebuild after fire, Lahaina Sun, October 20, 1971: 1.

— fundraising continues, Lahaina Sun, October 27, 1971: 1.

— fundraising continues, Lahaina Sun, November 10, 1971: 4.

— work done to prepare site for new classrooms, Lahaina Sun, January 19, 1972: 6.

— plans for new classrooms approved by Maui Historic Commission, Lahaina Sun, January 19, 1972: 9.

— update on fire investigation and recovery, Lahaina Sun, February 23, 1972: 5.

— construction of new classrooms begins, Lahaina Sun, March 15, 1972: 4.

— new building will be blessed in August, Lahaina Sun, June 21, 1972: 11.

— new classrooms in use, Lahaina Sun, September 6, 1972: 22.

— planning Hawaiian Appreciation Songfest, Lahaina News, May 23, 1984: 5.

— announces they will participate in Federal lunch program, Lahaina News, September 4, 1985: 8.

— celebrating Catholic School Week, Lahaina News, February 5, 1986: 3.

— to hold annual bazaar, Lahaina News, March 12, 1986: 3,12.

— accepting applications for next year, Lahaina News, July 23, 1986: 14.

— orientation for parents to be offered, Lahaina News, September 17, 1986: 11.

— holds candy fundraiser, Lahaina News, November 19, 1986: 3.

— calendar sale fundraiser underway, Lahaina News, November 26, 1986: 12.

— honor roll listed, Lahaina News, December 24, 1986: 8.

— planning their annual bazaar, Lahaina News, February 18, 1987: 10.

— to hold annual bazaar, Lahaina News, March 4, 1987: 8.

— lists honor students, Lahaina News, May 6, 1987: 10.

— Parents Teachers Guild to meet, Lahaina News, September 23, 1987: 3.

— bazaar planned, Lahaina News, March 2, 1988: 3.

— bazaar to take place, Lahaina News, March 9, 1988: 1,20.

— to offer free lunches to students, Lahaina News, August 17, 1988: 15.

— library to hold book fair, Lahaina News, December 7, 1988: 16.

— bazaar fundraiser successful, Lahaina News, April 26, 1989: 12.

— students raise money for victims of San Francisco earthquake, Lahaina News, November 1, 1989: 6.

— to hold bazaar and fundraiser, Lahaina News, December 27, 1989: 11.

— to sponsor public drug informational meeting, Lahaina News, January 17, 1990: 5.

— to organize bazaar, Lahaina News, January 24, 1990: 5.

— looking for auction items for fundraiser, Lahaina News, February 21, 1990: 2.

— bazaar a success, Lahaina News, March 28, 1990: 18.

— purchases new school bus with donations, Lahaina News, September 26, 1990: 8.

— scholars listed, Lahaina News, November 28, 1990: 4.

— principal's list announced, Lahaina News, February 6, 1991: 3.

— accepting applications, Lahaina News, February 20, 1991: 3.

— holds peace vigil at Banyan Tree, poems reprinted, Lahaina News, February 27, 1991: 4.

— students make flag pins to send to troops, Lahaina News, March 6, 1991: 1.

— receives donation of computers from Safeway, Lahaina News, March 6, 1991: 3.

— holds bazaar at Maria Lanakila Catholic Church, Lahaina News, March 6, 1991: 4.

— to hold bazaar, Lahaina News, March 13, 1991: 1.

— to hold "Focuses On Its Future" meeting, Lahaina News, May 8, 1991: 4.

— festival winners announced, Lahaina News, December 19, 1991: 5.

— scholars announced, Lahaina News, December 19, 1991: 6.

— to hold bazaar, Lahaina News, February 6, 1992: 3.

— bazaar to be held, Lahaina News, March 5, 1992: 3.

— bazaar featured, Lahaina News, March 12, 1992: 3.

— bazaar a success, Lahaina News, March 26, 1992: 4.

— honor roll recipients listed, Lahaina News, July 9, 1992: 4.

— announces policy for free and reduced price lunch, Lahaina News, August 27, 1992: 3.

— Sister Lina and Wendy Abbott new teachers at Sacred Hearts School, Lahaina News, September 24, 1992: 3.

— new playground equipment installed, Lahaina News, October 1, 1992: 3.

— announces honor roll, Lahaina News, November 26, 1992: 4.

— releases honor roll, Lahaina News, February 11, 1993: 4.

— Bazaar begins, Lahaina News, March 4, 1993: 2.

— Bazaar to be held, Lahaina News, March 11, 1993: 3,4.

— Parent Teacher Guild elects officers, Lahaina News, September 23, 1993: 3.

— honor roll announced, Lahaina News, November 11, 1993: 3.

— to hold annual rummage sale, seeking donations, Lahaina News, February 3, 1994: 4.

— to hold bazaar, Lahaina News, March 10, 1994: 2.

— honor roll, Lahaina News, June 16, 1994: 4.

— described, Lahaina News, August 25, 1994: 3.

— to hold bazaar, Lahaina News, February 23, 1995: 2.

— seeking items for bazaar, Lahaina News, March 2, 1995: 3.

— bazaar to be held this weekend, Lahaina News, March 9, 1995: 4.

— announces fourth quarter honor roll, Lahaina News, June 22, 1995: 5.

— receives new backboards, Lahaina News, January 11, 1996: 2.

— bazaar to be held, Lahaina News, February 29, 1996: 10,11.

— petting zoo at bazaar photographed, Lahaina News, March 14, 1996: 3.

— bazaar held, Lahaina News, May 16, 1996: 1.

— to host Maui Chamber Music Festival, Lahaina News, May 30, 1996: 13.

— seventh-graders participate in Kapalua Nature Society hike, Lahaina News, February 13, 1997: 2.

— bazaar to be held, Lahaina News, March 6, 1997: 2.

— thanks the community, Lahaina News, May 15, 1997: 14.

— to host "Aloha Fun Days" with Arts Education for Children group, Lahaina News, June 26, 1997: 3.

— successful at spelling bee, Lahaina News, February 12, 1998: 8.

— to hold bazaar, Lahaina News, March 5, 1998: 3.

— to hold bazaar, Lahaina News, March 12, 1998: 1.

— Wolf Cubs learn about bike safety, Lahaina News, April 2, 1998: 1.

— recognizes students, Lahaina News, May 7, 1998: 9.

— student honor roll, Lahaina News, November 19, 1998: 10.

— students raise money for UNICEF, Lahaina News, November 19, 1998: 10.

— announces second quarter honor roll, Lahaina News, February 4, 1999: 9.

— students successful at spelling contest, Lahaina News, February 11, 1999: 1.

— bazaar to be held, Lahaina News, March 11, 1999: 1.

— honor roll announced, Lahaina News, June 10, 1999: 9.

— student honor roll published, Lahaina News, November 18, 1999: 14.

— student honor roll published, Lahaina News, February 17, 2000: 8.

— to hold bazaar, Lahaina News, March 2, 2000: 1.

— bazaar begins Friday, Lahaina News, March 9, 2000: 3.

— Sisters of St. Francis leaving, Lahaina News, June 8, 2000: 1,7.

— account of the fire and rebuilding, Lahaina News, June 15, 2000: 1,15.

— Paul Lohman new principal, Lahaina News, August 31, 2000: 1,15.

— students to visit Maui Monkey store to learn about business, Lahaina News, September 14, 2000: 16.

— St. Francis Day held, pets invited, Lahaina News, October 12, 2000: 1,11.

— offering after-school programs, Lahaina News, October 12, 2000: 11.

— West Maui Water Safety Captain Archie Kalepa visits, Lahaina News, October 19, 2000: 1.

— honor roll for first quarter announced, Lahaina News, November 16, 2000: 7.
— second quarter honor roll announced, Lahaina News, February 1, 2001: 16.
— students shine in spelling bee, Lahaina News, February 15, 2001: 1.
— bazaar to be held, Lahaina News, March 8, 2001: 1,18.
— to hold May Day/Hawaiian Studies Program, Lahaina News, May 10, 2001: 3.
— honor roll announced, Lahaina News, June 14, 2001: 10.
— Bonnie Wojdyla is new principal, Lahaina News, July 19, 2001: 1,20.
— renovations completed, Lahaina News, August 9, 2001: 1,20.
— holds blessing for Early Learning Center, Lahaina News, August 23, 2001: 3.
— honors Saint Francis of Assisi, Lahaina News, October 11, 2001: 1.
— linking classes with internet, Lahaina News, November 29, 2001: 9.
— to hold annual bazaar, Lahaina News, December 20, 2001: 2.
— student designs t-shirt for upcoming bazaar, Lahaina News, February 7, 2002: 9.
— bazaar to be held, Lahaina News, February 21, 2002: 2.
— students busy with charity projects, Lahaina News, February 28, 2002: 1,18.
— to hold 30th annual bazaar, Lahaina News, February 28, 2002: 3.
— honor roll announced, Lahaina News, February 28, 2002: 9.
— bazaar to be held, Lahaina News, March 7, 2002: 3,20.
— to hold Summer School Program, Lahaina News, May 2, 2002: 2.
— to offer summer program Malama e na Keiki o na Puʻūwai Hemolele, Lahaina News, June 6, 2002: 5.
— uniforms can now be ordered, Lahaina News, August 1, 2002: 9.
— uniforms can now be ordered, Lahaina News, August 15, 2002: 16.
— featured, Lahaina News, September 19, 2002: 1,26.
— bus driver Keoni Lee featured, Lahaina News, September 26, 2002: 1,20.
— honor roll released, Lahaina News, November 14, 2002: 17.
— students raise money for diabetes research, Lahaina News, December 19, 2002: 3.
— annual bazaar to be held, Lahaina News, February 27, 2003: 1,20.
— results of t-shirt design contest, Lahaina News, February 27, 2003: 9.
— bazaar to be held, Lahaina News, March 6, 2003: 1,20.
— students recognized for superior fitness, Lahaina News, March 27, 2003: 1,18.
— Susan Hendricks new principal, Lahaina News, July 3, 2003: 1,18.
— offering summer program, Lahaina News, July 3, 2003: 9.
— to offer summer program, Lahaina News, July 10, 2003: 3.
— Early Learning Center open for registration, Lahaina News, August 28, 2003: 2.
— receives proceeds from A Taste of Lahaina, Lahaina News, September 25, 2003: 14.

SACRED SITES INTERNATIONAL FOUNDATION
— discusses importance of Mokuʻula, Lahaina News, January 27, 2000: 1,16.

SADLICKA, DONNA
— soprano to perform with Hawaii Opera Theatre, Lahaina News, May 4, 1995: 14.

SADO, MICHAEL
— honored as educator of the month by Leilani's on the Beach, Lahaina News, March 7, 2002: 5.

SAENG'S THAI CUISINE [RESTAURANT]
— opens, Lahaina News, April 2, 1992: 18.
— featured, Lahaina News, December 3, 1992: 17.

SAFE COMMUNITY GROUP
— to meet, Lahaina News, September 17, 1998: 1,32.
— to meet, Lahaina News, September 24, 1998: 16.
— working to address problems, Lahaina News, January 17, 2002: 1,20.
— to hold free keiki car seat inspection, Lahaina News, February 27, 2003: 16.

SAFE SOLUTIONS
— group opposed to pesticides to meet, Lahaina News, July 31, 1985: 7.
— benefit concert for Maui Lu Resort, Lahaina News, September 18, 1985: 3.

SAFECO INSURANCE COMPANY [BUSINESS]
— to meet at Four Seasons Resort, Lahaina News, May 20, 1993: 7.

SAFETY
— Fire safety program announced, Lahaina News, October 15, 1980: 10.
— Mickey Weems saved from ocean by cruise ship Independence, Lahaina News, February 8, 1984: 3.
— disaster training offered, Lahaina News, August 6, 1986: 3.
— need for more lifeguards, Lahaina News, April 4, 1990: 1,8.
— Ritz-Carlton to post signs indicating water safety, Lahaina News, November 19, 1992: 1.
— lifeguards warned of dangerous surf, Lahaina News, October 21, 1993: 1,2.
— Weinberg Court Apartment fire hydrant system has locks on it, Lahaina News, January 19, 1995: 1.
— training held with simulated plane crash, Lahaina News, February 8, 1996: 3.
— County to teach ocean safety and awareness, Lahaina News, August 19, 1999: 6.
— preparing for hurricane season to be discussed, Lahaina News, May 11, 2000: 11.

SAFETY, DEPARTMENT OF
— to abolish Marine Patrol, Lahaina News, August 3, 1995: 5.

SAFETY EQUIPMENT DISTRIBUTORS ASSOCIATION
— to meet at Hyatt Regency Maui, Lahaina News, July 9, 1992: 14.
— convention to be held, Lahaina News, July 16, 1992: 16.

SAFEWAY [BUSINESS]
— opening store in Maui Mall, Lahaina News, November 1, 1981: 5.
— opening set, Lahaina News, August 31, 1983: 14.
— sues state over decision on importing milk, Lahaina News, February 29, 1984: 17.
— editorial praising lawsuit, Lahaina News, March 7, 1984: 2.
— State changes regulations for fresh milk to make importation more difficult, Lahaina News, March 28, 1984: 17.
— editorial supporting attempt to import milk, Lahaina News, March 28, 1984: 2.
— files suit that "shelf life" law interferes with interstate commerce, Lahaina News, July 4, 1984: 18.
— opening in Lahaina Cannery Shopping Center, Lahaina News, January 14, 1987: 12.
— photographs from opening, Lahaina News, January 21, 1987: 1.
— Santa to visit, Lahaina News, December 19, 1990: 6.
— "Apples for Students" program donates computers to Sacred Hearts School, Lahaina News, March 6, 1991: 3.
— praised for donating computers to local schools, Lahaina News, March 20, 1991: 5.
— begins home delivery service, Lahaina News, June 27, 1991: 9.
— selling "Santa Dollars", Lahaina News, December 5, 1991: 4.
— resumes aluminum recycling with BFI Waste Systems, Lahaina News, October 12, 1995: 6.
— offering "Valentine Express" speedy check-out, Lahaina News, February 22, 1996: 11.
— manager Gary Johnson to retire, Lahaina News, July 4, 1996: 5.
— scrip fundraiser successful, Lahaina News, January 14, 1999: 3.
— donates to the Boys and Girls Club, Lahaina News, January 3, 2002: 8.

SAFFERY, NANI
— reverend blesses newly renovated Kapalua Shops, Lahaina News, April 18, 1990: 5.

SAFFREY, EUGENE
— mayor Hannibal Tavares awards certificate of merit to, Lahaina News, September 10, 1986: 3.

SAFIAN, JOHN
— assisting Doylene Larson, who lost her house in a fire, Lahaina Sun, December 30, 1970: 1.

SAIKI, PAT [POLITICIAN]
— to speak to Maui Chamber of Commerce, Lahaina News, March 25, 1993: 11.
— gubernatorial candidate to appear, Lahaina News, November 18, 1993: 3.
— to speak at Republican Party's Lincoln Day Dinner, Lahaina News, February 17, 1994: 12.
— seeks end to favoritism among politicians, Lahaina News, March 3, 1994: 1,3.
— begins campaign for governor as a Republican, Lahaina News, June 2, 1994: 3.
— opens office for election campaign, Lahaina News, June 16, 1994: 5.

SAILBOARDS MAUI [BUSINESS]
— expands, Lahaina News, March 2, 1995: 7.

SAILING
— sail of catamaran Tom Cat described, Lahaina Sun, December 8, 1971: 7.
— Peter Fonda's yacht loses three of its small boats, Lahaina Sun, February 2, 1972: 5.
— Spanish schooner Juan Sebastian del Cano visits Lahaina, Lahaina Sun, February 16, 1972: 3.
— Chilean Navy's training schooner Esmeralda drops anchor off Lahaina, Lahaina Sun, March 1, 1972: 5.
— new Coast Guard regulations in force, Lahaina Sun, March 8, 1972: 8.
— trip to Lana'i detailed, Lahaina Sun, January 24, 1973: 15.
— description of voyage to Tahiti, Lahaina Sun, January 24, 1973: 18,19.
— life of J. Gordon Gibson detailed, Lahaina Sun, March 7, 1973: 14.
— Flying Cloud [ship] described, Lahaina Sun, March 21, 1973: 14,15.
— Gerry N [ship] sinks off of Maui, crew survives, Lahaina Sun, April 11, 1973: 15.
— Michael Gohr, owner of Tanqueray II, described, Lahaina Sun, May 30, 1973: 14.
— Midge McCall's boat decorations described, Lahaina Sun, June 6, 1973: 14.
— visiting yachts not welcome in harbor, Lahaina Sun, June 20, 1973: 7.
— purchasing a boat described, Lahaina Sun, July 4, 1973: 9.
— race from Olowalu to Lahaina won by Bill Crawford, Lahaina Sun, July 11, 1973: 9.
— overdue ship with Ross and Betty Cobb arrives in Maui, Lahaina Sun, July 25, 1973: 4.
— damage caused by electrolysis, Lahaina Sun, July 25, 1973: 9.
— trip planned around Cape Horn, Lahaina Sun, August 8, 1973: 15.
— Honolulu-Hanalei Bay yacht race described, Lahaina Sun, August 8, 1973: 9.
— account of burning of the catamaran Manawahi, Lahaina Sun, August 22, 1973: 1,3.
— report on yacht races held by Lahaina Yacht Club, Lahaina Sun, August 22, 1973: 7.
— race from Lahaina to Oahu recounted, Lahaina Sun, August 29, 1973: 6.
— conditions described, Lahaina News, July, 1979: 15.
— catamaran races, Lahaina News, September, 1979: 12.
— The "From the Rat Bench" column begins with short entries connected to sailing, boats, etc. It is not generally indexed., Lahaina News, December, 1979: 7.

— "broiler boat" trimaran has been sold, Lahaina News, April 15, 1980: 8.
— abandon boats in West Maui discussed, Lahaina News, August 1, 1980: 3.
— Charley wins Victoria-to-Maui race, Lahaina News, July 18, 1984: 7,8,9.
— description of trip from Hawaii to Tahiti, Lahaina News, January 22, 1986: 4.
— Victoria to Maui yacht race described, Lahaina News, July 2, 1986: 4.
— America's Cup results, Lahaina News, February 4, 1987: 10.
— update on America's Cup, Lahaina News, April 1, 1987: 6.
— Hawaiian Electric supporting Hawaii effort for America's Cup, Lahaina News, August 5, 1987: 6.
— Maui Sailing Canoe Association wins race, Lahaina News, August 29, 1990: 7.
— sloop Admiral Nevelosky to compete in Bud Cup Regatta, Lahaina News, August 29, 1990: 7.
— San Diego-Maui yacht race held, Lahaina News, June 20, 1991: 4.
— Hoomanao Challenge results announced, Lahaina News, June 18, 1992: 12.
— Keahi Ho to offer lessons, Lahaina News, June 10, 1993: 9.
— biennial Victoria-Maui International Yacht Race to be held, Lahaina News, July 7, 1994: 7.
— keiki course to be offered by Lahaina Yacht Club, Lahaina News, July 28, 1994: 6.
— Steinlager Ho'omana'o sailing canoe race to be held, Lahaina News, May 25, 1995: 5.
— Victoria-Maui Yacht Race to be held, Lahaina News, June 20, 1996: 10.

SAINT ANTHONY CHURCH
— to hold "Messiah" sing-along, Lahaina News, November 28, 1990: 4.

SAINT ANTHONY HIGH SCHOOL
— to hold reunion for class of 1969, Lahaina News, August 9, 1989: 3.
— to hold bazaar, Lahaina News, April 25, 1990: 3.
— basketball tournament scheduled, Lahaina News, December 5, 1990: 8.
— to play in basketball tournament, Lahaina News, December 12, 1990: 20.

SAINT FRANCIS MEDICAL CENTER
— Jack Kelley Memorial Golf Tournament raises money for, Lahaina News, February 8, 2001: 7.

SAISON DES BRIDES [BUSINESS]
— opens, Lahaina News, May 25, 1995: 10.
— to hold holiday sale, Lahaina News, December 26, 1996: 10.

SAITO, WARD
— joins Kapalua Realty, Lahaina News, February 4, 1987: 11.

SAKAI, KAZUICHI "KAZU"
— honored by Boy Scouts of America for service, Lahaina News, February 13, 1991: 4,5.

SAKALIA, TONATA
— Lahainaluna High School student accepted into United States Collegiate Wind Band, Lahaina News, April 9, 1992: 6.
— Parent Community Networking Center Facilitator featured, Lahaina News, June 14, 2001: 1,9.

SAKAMOTO, ANN
— new residential loan officer joins Bank of Hawaii, Lahaina News, November 21, 2002: 9.

SAKAMOTO, CLYDE
— appointed Provost of Maui Community College [first part placed incorrect on page], Lahaina News, May 1, 1991: 5.
— Maui Community College provost announces increased assistance to Maui County residents, Lahaina News, August 11, 1994: 4.

SAKAMOTO, KYLE
— part of new Central Pacific Bank team, Lahaina News, February 7, 2002: 8.

SAKAMOTO PROPERTIES, INC [BUSINESS]
— recognized by Who's Who in Luxury Real Estate, Lahaina News, May 1, 1997: 12.

SAKAMOTO, ROY AND BETTY
— honored by Governor Ben Cayetano, Lahaina News, July 9, 1998: 1.

SAKUMA, YOSHI
— promoted to manager of Maui/Kauaʻi Foodland division, Lahaina News, July 14, 1994: 13.

SAKURAS, THE [MUSICAL GROUP]
— perform at Maui Palms, Lahaina News, January 9, 1992: 14.
— to perform at Maui Palms, Lahaina News, February 20, 1992: 18.
— continues to perform at Maui Palms, Lahaina News, June 4, 1992: 18.

SAL GODINEZ QUARTET [MUSICAL GROUP]
— to perform at Blackie's Bar, Lahaina News, January 30, 1991: 7.
— to perform at Blackie's Bar, Lahaina News, June 13, 1991: 13.

SAL GODINEZ QUINTET [MUSICAL GROUP]
— to perform at Blackie's Bar, Lahaina News, August 22, 1990: 13.

SALAZAR, JORGE
— awarded contract to build mooring in West Maui, Lahaina News, January 6, 1988: 3.

SALAZAR, OWANA [MUSICIAN]
— to perform at Lahaina Cannery Mall's 16th anniversary, Lahaina News, March 20, 2003: 9.
— wins Island Contemporary Album of the Year for "Wahine Slack 'n' Steel", Lahaina News, July 10, 2003: 20.
— to perform at Lahaina Center, Lahaina News, September 18, 2003: 15.

SALOONATICS, THE [MUSICAL GROUP]
— to perform at Moose McGillycuddy's, Lahaina News, December 31, 1992: 12.
— to perform at Compadres Mexican Bar and Grill, Lahaina News, February 11, 1993: 13.

SALSMAN, JOEL [MUSICIAN]
— pianist to perform and give lessons, Lahaina News, October 15, 1998: 9.

SALUD, JESUS
— to fight Darrell Pinckney at Makawao Gym, Lahaina News, September 5, 1991: 24.

SALUTE TO AMERICA
— to be held at Kaʻanapali Hotel, Lahaina News, June 27, 1984: 3.
— to be held at Hyatt Regency Maui, Lahaina News, June 26, 1985: 3.

SALVADOR, ANTHONY
— Lahainaluna High School graduate honored at Universal Technical Institute, Lahaina News, December 12, 1991: 5.

SALVADOR, ELY
— receives Managing Director's Award at Westin Maui, Lahaina News, October 13, 1994: 15.

SALVATION ARMY
— recent activity in Maui recounted, Lahaina News, March 15, 1981: 15.
— Eva den Hartog to speak at meeting of, Lahaina News, April 15, 1981: 15.
— senior citizens dinner offered for Thanksgiving, Lahaina News, November 15, 1981: 16.
— Lieutenant Jeffrey Martin will take over Maui Salvation Army, Lahaina News, February 15, 1982: 2.
— recognition dinner held, Lahaina News, March 15, 1982: 10.
— activities praised, Lahaina News, December 1, 1982: 3.
— kettle drive begins, Lahaina News, November 23, 1983: 5.

— Salvation Army Week held, Lahaina News, May 9, 1984: 5.
— Gary Robert installed as chairman of Lahaina Corps, Lahaina News, February 20, 1985: 3.
— offering free bible school., Lahaina News, July 10, 1985: 3.
— Christmas campaign begins, Lahaina News, November 27, 1985: 3,20.
— to hold spring sale fundraiser, Lahaina News, May 21, 1986: 3.
— expands services, plans fund campaign, Lahaina News, June 18, 1986: 1.
— to hold Vacation Bible School, Lahaina News, July 9, 1986: 3.
— opening Thrift Store, Lahaina News, October 8, 1986: 5.
— to hold coloring contest, Lahaina News, April 8, 1987: 3.
— to host church sermons, Lahaina News, September 9, 1987: 3.
— accepting applications for Christmas Food, Lahaina News, December 7, 1988: 16.
— sponsoring essay contest on the meaning of Easter, Lahaina News, March 15, 1989: 2.
— seeking donations to help victims of Hurricane Hugo, Lahaina News, October 11, 1989: 3.
— looking for volunteers, Lahaina News, November 22, 1989: 1.
— accepting applications for food baskets, Lahaina News, November 22, 1989: 3.
— to hold Vacation Bible School, Lahaina News, March 21, 1990: 3.
— to hold Evangelistic Campaign, Lahaina News, May 23, 1990: 5.
— to hold annual Evangelistic Campaign, Lahaina News, May 30, 1990: 5.
— proposes homeless shelter, Lahaina News, July 18, 1990: 4.
— to hold Basketball Mini Camp, Lahaina News, July 25, 1990: 14.
— plans for homeless shelter put on hold, Lahaina News, August 1, 1990: 1.
— seeking help for Philippine earthquake disaster, Lahaina News, August 1, 1990: 5.
— donates clothes stolen from, Lahaina News, September 26, 1990: 1.
— to receive $1 donation from Lahaina Hair Stylists per job, Lahaina News, December 5, 1990: 5.
— raising funds to help Majuro following typhoon, Lahaina News, December 26, 1990: 5.
— organizing basketball camps, Lahaina News, July 11, 1991: 7.
— to distribute food with Maui Harvest, Lahaina News, July 25, 1991: 5.
— sponsoring workshops on women's health, Lahaina News, August 29, 1991: 3.
— to offer workshops on women's health, Lahaina News, September 5, 1991: 3.
— to host series on women's health, Lahaina News, September 12, 1991: 3.
— seminars on women's health continue, Lahaina News, September 19, 1991: 3.
— to hold revival meeting, Lahaina News, November 7, 1991: 4.
— to hold fun run, Lahaina News, November 7, 1991: 7.
— to hold fun run, Lahaina News, November 14, 1991: 4.
— beginning Christmas donation drive, Lahaina News, December 12, 1991: 3.
— to hold Christmas brunch, Lahaina News, December 17, 1992: 4.
— to hold Christmas Brunch, Lahaina News, December 24, 1992: 4.
— wants to offer interim shelters for homeless, Lahaina News, December 31, 1992: 1.
— begins capital campaign, Lahaina News, January 28, 1993: 10.
— receives donation from GTE Hawaiian Tel, Lahaina News, July 8, 1993: 7.
— to open thrift store, Lahaina News, July 22, 1993: 6.
— accepting Christmas Basket Applications, Lahaina News, November 11, 1993: 3.
— accepting Christmas Basket Applications, Lahaina News, November 18, 1993: 3.
— thanks holiday supporters, Lahaina News, March 31, 1994: 3.

— Thrift Store has new warehouse, Lahaina News, November 3, 1994: 4.

— taking applications for Christmas Boxes, Lahaina News, December 8, 1994: 3.

— accepting donations for victims of Oklahoma City Federal Building bombing, Lahaina News, May 4, 1995: 4.

— asking people to adopt a family for Christmas, Lahaina News, November 30, 1995: 2.

— organizing help for families, Lahaina News, December 21, 1995: 3.

— seeking donations for Christmas, Lahaina News, December 12, 1996: 1,2.

— accepting donations for Christmas Baskets, Lahaina News, November 27, 1997: 8.

— holding "Santa's Workshop and Christmas Food Box", Lahaina News, December 11, 1997: 11.

— adopts "Zero Tolerance" stand towards drug use and dealing, Lahaina News, November 26, 1998: 9.

— to help Foodland with "Share a Holiday Feast" program, Lahaina News, November 18, 1999: 15.

— to hold "Lokahi Back to School" program to support needy students, Lahaina News, June 8, 2000: 17.

— to hold "Angel Tree" program, Lahaina News, November 30, 2000: 5.

— seeks volunteers and donations, Lahaina News, December 7, 2000: 23.

— needs volunteers for holiday season, Lahaina News, December 14, 2000: 1.

— to hold concert fundraiser, Lahaina News, December 20, 2001: 3.

— leader Richard Hieb sent to Arizona, Lahaina News, February 7, 2002: 1,20.

SALVATION ARMY WEEK
— to be held, Lahaina News, May 15, 1991: 4.

SAM CHOY [RESTAURANT]
— Lahainaluna High School tour, Lahaina News, December 10, 1998: 15.

SAM CHOY POKE FESTIVAL
— won by Donna Williams-Crane, Lahaina News, September 30, 1999: 5.

SAM CHOY'S KAHULUI [RESTAURANT]
— opens, Lahaina News, January 29, 1998: 16.

SAM CHOY'S LAHAINA RESTAURANT AND BIG ALOHA BREWERY
— opens, Lahaina News, December 17, 1998: 17.

SAM KA'AI'S WOOD SHOP [BUSINESS]
— opening in Whaler's Village, Lahaina Sun, November 25, 1970: 3.

SAMARPAN, JOEL
— to present "Tantra of the Heart", Lahaina News, October 4, 2001: 17.

SAME TIME NEXT YEAR [PLAY]
— to be performed by Maui Community Theatre, Lahaina News, January 4, 1989: 3.

— performed by Maui Community Theatre, Lahaina News, March 1, 1989: 9.

SAME-SEX MARRIAGE
— opinions sought, Lahaina News, February 8, 1996: 3.

SAMOA
— travel to described, Lahaina News, August, 1979: 7,15.

SAMOAN JUSTICE [TELEVISION SHOW]
— explores killing at a birthday party on Oahu, Lahaina News, January 10, 1990: 24.

SAMPLE, JOE [MUSICIAN]
— to perform at Maui Arts and Cultural Center, Lahaina News, August 7, 1997: 12.

SAMPSON, BRENDA
— chair of Sacred Heart's Bazaar featured, Lahaina News, March 12, 1992: 3.

SAMPSON, PETER [MAGICIAN]
— to headline fundraiser for International Diabetes Youth Camp, Lahaina News, August 27, 1992: 14.

SAMPSON, STEVEN
— appointed director of sales and marketing at Ritz-Carlton, Lahaina News, May 24, 2001: 8.

SAM'S BEACHSIDE GRILL [RESTAURANT]
— featured, Lahaina News, January 21, 1987: 4.

— opens, Lahaina News, February 11, 1987: 11.

— opening celebrations, Lahaina News, April 22, 1987: 8.

— publishes promotional brochure, Lahaina News, July 8, 1987: 24.

— featured, Lahaina News, August 3, 1988: 7.

— reviewed, Lahaina News, October 5, 1988: 8.

— reviewed, Lahaina News, January 4, 1989: 8.

— reviewed, Lahaina News, April 5, 1989: 8.

— reviewed, Lahaina News, May 24, 1989: 15.

— reviewed, Lahaina News, September 13, 1989: 9.

— featured, Lahaina News, December 27, 1989: 16.

SAM'S UPSTAIRS [RESTAURANT]
— now open, Lahaina News, March 29, 1989: 20.

— Soroptimists International to hold fundraiser at, Lahaina News, July 26, 1989: 13.

SAMSON, ADELE
— appointed sales manager by Maui Marriott, Lahaina News, March 4, 1987: 10.

SAMUDIO, KAMUELA
— to portray David Malo at Lahainaluna High School pageant, Lahaina News, April 29, 1999: 3.

SAMUEL ADAMS [BUSINESS]
— Beer Dinner to be held at Grand Wailea, Lahaina News, August 21, 1997: 17.

— Summer Ale to be featured on evening cruise, Lahaina News, May 21, 1998: 17.

— to host dinner at Kapalua Bay Hotel, Lahaina News, June 26, 2003: 20.

SAMUELSON, GORDON [MUSICIAN]
— jazz trio performs at Taco Jo's, Lahaina News, February 17, 1994: 11.

SAN DIEGO, JOHN
— police chief to retire, Lahaina News, April 1, 1981: 6.

SAN DIEGO-MAUI YACHT RACE
— results, Lahaina News, July 4, 1991: 7.

SAN FRANCISCO
— sperm whale skeleton purchased from whalery in, Lahaina Sun, November 25, 1970: 1.

— city described, Lahaina Sun, February 16, 1972: 18.

SAN FRANCISCO OPERA [TROUPE]
— performs "Cosi fan Tutte", Lahaina News, October 7, 1987: 3.

— singers to perform at Maui Arts and Cultural Center, Lahaina News, March 8, 2001: 16.

SAN FRANCISCO OPERA CENTER
— gala concert to be held, Lahaina News, March 11, 1999: 12.

SAN FRANCISCO, USS [SUBMARINE]
— Lahainaluna High School students tour nuclear submarine, Lahaina News, December 10, 1998: 15.

SAN JOSE TAIKO AND HANAYUI [MUSICAL GROUP]
— to perform at Maui Arts and Cultural Center, Lahaina News, October 3, 2002: 17.

SAN LUIGI VERO CUOIO [BUSINESS]
— opens at The Shops at Kapalua, Lahaina News, October 6, 1994: 11.

SANBORN, PETER
— Amfac properties manager discusses Whaler's village, Lahaina Sun, December 16, 1970: 5.
— Amfac properties manager discusses planned American Society of Travel Agents convention, Lahaina Sun, July 7, 1971: 2.
— Amfac properties manager named to Maui Chamber of Commerce board of directors, Lahaina Sun, August 4, 1971: 10.
— appointed vice-president of marketing at Kapalua Land Company, Lahaina News, June 12, 1997: 15.

SANCHEZ, ROLANDO [MUSICIAN]
— to perform at Casanova's, Lahaina News, January 16, 1991: 11.

SANCIN, JOHN [MUSICIAN]
— reviewed, Lahaina News, May 1, 1980: 5.

SANCTUARY ADVISORY COUNCIL
— Hawaiian Islands Humpback Whale National Marine Sanctuary selects individuals to serve on, Lahaina News, September 3, 1998: 17.

SAND
— removal halted, Lahaina Sun, May 12, 1971: 1,8.
— removed from Baldwin Beach Park, Lahaina Sun, May 26, 1971: 1,8.
— suit brought by E.T. Ige Construction against Life of the Land is dropped, Lahaina Sun, June 9, 1971: 5.
— State Board of Land and Natural Resources approves removal of sand dunes in Kihei, Lahaina Sun, August 9, 1972: 24.

SAND SCULPTURE
— contest will take place November 25th, Lahaina News, November 21, 1984: 3.
— contest to be held December 1, Lahaina News, November 27, 1985: 20.
— ninth annual contest to be held, Lahaina News, November 27, 1985: 20.
— contest to be held, Lahaina News, November 23, 1988: 3.
— contest to be held at Kamaole Beach, Lahaina News, November 21, 1990: 3.
— keiki contest to be held at Royal Lahaina Resort, Lahaina News, August 10, 1995: 4.
— contest to be held, Lahaina News, August 17, 1995: 4.
— Wild Dolphin Sand Sculpture Contest to be held by Pacific Whale Foundation at Keawakapu Beach, Lahaina News, August 7, 2003: 16.

SANDAL SHOP, THE [BUSINESS]
— owner Clyde Shimabukuro to retire, Lahaina News, August 8, 1991: 9.

SANDALS, ETC. [BUSINESS]
— opening at Wharf Cinema, Lahaina News, September 26, 1990: 9.

SANDALWOOD
— golf course opens, Lahaina News, December 5, 1991: 19.

SANDALWOOD RESTAURANT [RESTAURANT]
— to hold "Maui Bear Hugs Den" to collect bears for police officers to comfort traumatized children, Lahaina News, June 8, 2000: 17.

SANDCASTLE [RESTAURANT]
— to host "Deb and Jer's Sandcastle Broadway Dinner Theater Revue", Lahaina News, June 29, 2000: 20.
— to host "Deb and Jer's Sandcastle Broadway Dinner Theater Revue", Lahaina News, July 6, 2000: 16.

SANDERS, JEFF
— top Maui finisher at Gatorade Ironman Triathlon held on Big Island, Lahaina News, November 11, 1993: 8.
— wins Windward Triathlon, Lahaina News, August 25, 1994: 9.
— wins 10K Chart House run, Lahaina News, April 16, 1998: 1.
— Maui's top finisher in XTERRA World Championship triathlon, Lahaina News, November 4, 1999: 7.

SANDERSON, BRYANT
— David Malo king, Lahaina News, April 17, 1997: 16.

SANDERVAL, RENE [COMEDIAN]
— to perform at Comedy Club and the Sports Page, Lahaina News, November 12, 1992: 18.

SANDOVAL, ARTURO [MUSICIAN]
— to perform at Maui Arts and Cultural Center, Lahaina News, March 27, 1997: 13.

SANDPIPER GRILL AND CLUB
— to open at Aston Kamaole Sands-Maui, Lahaina News, October 31, 1990: 11,12.

SANDS, MIKE
— appointed general manager at Maui Ka'anapali Villas, Lahaina News, June 19, 1997: 6.
— promoted at Aston Hotels and Resorts Hawaii, Lahaina News, January 11, 2001: 14.

SANDS OF KAHANA
— Honfed Bank to sell 118 units to Livex Corp. of Japan, Lahaina News, September 12, 1990: 10.
— shared ownership available at, Lahaina News, July 1, 1999: 10.
— shared ownership units available, Lahaina News, October 21, 1999: 12.
— featured, Lahaina News, April 6, 2000: 12.
— featured, Lahaina News, July 27, 2000: 10.
— featured, Lahaina News, September 21, 2000: 14.
— shared ownership available at, Lahaina News, November 16, 2000: 8.
— featured, Lahaina News, January 11, 2001: 12.
— featured, Lahaina News, June 28, 2001: 6.
— featured, Lahaina News, August 23, 2001: 6.
— development featured, Lahaina News, October 18, 2001: 6.
— development featured, Lahaina News, May 30, 2002: 6.
— development featured, Lahaina News, September 19, 2002: 6.
— development featured, Lahaina News, May 1, 2003: 6.
— development featured, Lahaina News, June 26, 2003: 6.

SANDS, SALLY SEFTON [ACTOR]
— to hold workshop for Maui Community Theatre, Lahaina News, April 27, 1988: 6.

SANDS, STEPHEN [ARTIST]
— exhibit at office of mayor's office, Lahaina News, February 12, 1986: 3.
— signing at Maria Lanakila Church, Lahaina News, April 8, 1987: 12.
— works featured by Lahaina Arts Society, Lahaina News, January 13, 1988: 3.

SANDWICH ISLAND PUBLISHING
— publishes "Best of Maui", Lahaina News, August 7, 1997: 5.
— publishes "Furby Training Guide", Lahaina News, December 24, 1998: 11.

SANDWICH ISLANDS
— history of name detailed, Lahaina Sun, July 21, 1971: 8.

SANFORD, CLAIRE [ARTIST]
— presents metal workshop at Hui No'eau Visual Arts Center, Lahaina News, February 27, 1991: 13.

SANFORD, MARY CAMERON
— named to board of Maui Land and Pineapple, Co. Inc., Lahaina News, June 25, 1992: 16.

SANO, EVELYN
— teaching Ikebana, Lahaina News, May 20, 1999: 16.

SANSEI SEAFOOD RESTAURANT AND SUSHI BAR [RESTAURANT]
— opens in Kapalua Shops, Lahaina News, April 4, 1996: 8.
— featured, Lahaina News, March 20, 1997: 7.

— rated highest in state in food category by Zagat Hawai'i Restaurant Survey, Lahaina News, June 10, 1999: 13.
— Ivan Pahk new executive chef at, Lahaina News, May 4, 2000: 13.
— featured, Lahaina News, March 1, 2001: 18.
— staff changes at, Lahaina News, November 1, 2001: 8.
— promotions announced, Lahaina News, October 24, 2002: 8.
— to hold Halloween event, Lahaina News, October 31, 2002: 28.

SANT THAKAR SINGH
— representatives of to teach meditation, Lahaina News, March 11, 1999: 13.
— representatives to teach inner light and sound meditation, Lahaina News, August 24, 2000: 20.
— representatives to offer free meditation instruction, Lahaina News, February 15, 2001: 17.

SANTA
— arriving at Maui Inter-Continental Wailea this weekend, Lahaina News, December 18, 1985: 3.

SANTA CLAUS PARADE
— to be held December 15, Lahaina News, December 5, 1984: 3.

SANTA CRUZ STEEL [MUSICAL GROUP]
— to perform at Casanova's, Lahaina News, November 7, 1991: 20.

SANTANA [MUSICAL GROUP]
— concert on Oahu reviewed, Lahaina News, December, 1979: 4.
— planning to come to Maui, Lahaina News, July 15, 1983: 12.
— to perform at Royal Lahaina Tennis Stadium, Lahaina News, May 8, 1991: 19.

SANTANA, CARLOS [MUSICIAN]
— to perform at Royal Lahaina Tennis Stadium, Lahaina News, February 18, 1993: 13.
— to perform, Lahaina News, February 25, 1993: 9.
— to perform at Royal Lahaina Tennis Stadium, Lahaina News, March 4, 1993: 10,11.
— to perform at Maui Arts and Cultural Center, Lahaina News, April 25, 1996: 17.
— to perform at Maui Arts and Cultural Center, Lahaina News, December 18, 1997: 19.
— to perform, Lahaina News, December 25, 1997: 12.

SANTELLA, ARTERO
— passes away, Lahaina News, May 1, 2003: 3.

SANTELLA, EMIL
— name mistakenly left off Lahainaluna High School Honor Roll list, Lahaina News, March 2, 1988: 22.

SANTILLO, BRIAN
— recognized as educator of the month by Kimo's Restaurant, Lahaina News, December 21, 2000: 3.

SANTOS, BARBARA [WRITER]
— to write "Maui Onion Cookbook", Lahaina News, August 1, 1996: 14.
— to sign copies of "The Maui Onion Cookbook", Lahaina News, May 15, 1997: 12.

SANTOS, LEAH
— receives Wo Hing Society of Lahaina scholarship, Lahaina News, August 7, 2003: 2.

SANTOS, MARGARET
— promoted to director of marketing for Kapalua Land Co., Lahaina News, April 30, 1986: 3.
— promoted to vice president, marketing at Kapalua Land Company, Ltd., Lahaina News, August 20, 1992: 13.

SANTOS, VELMA [POLITICIAN]
— position on strike discussed, Lahaina Sun, April 11, 1973: 5.
— Maui County Council members visit Rainbow Ranch, Lahaina News, August 15, 1990: 1.
— candidate profiled, Lahaina News, September 19, 1990: 1.

— appointed to Real Property Tax Review Board, Lahaina News, March 12, 1992: 5.
— to be honored by Maui League of Republican Women, Lahaina News, March 11, 1999: 13.
— to be honored by Maui League of Republican Women, Lahaina News, March 18, 1999: 16.

SARASIN, DOE [ARTIST]
— to exhibit ceramics, Lahaina News, July 25, 1990: 13.
— to appear at Sunset Galleries, Lahaina News, October 10, 1990: 16.

SARENTO'S ON THE BEACH [RESTAURANT]
— to reopen following renovations, Lahaina News, April 26, 2001: 8.
— to hold fundraiser for Juvenile Diabetes Research Foundation International, Lahaina News, May 24, 2001: 18.
— fundraiser held for Juvenile Diabetes Research Foundation International, Lahaina News, September 13, 2001: 9.

SARGENT, DICK [ARTIST]
— opens gallery, Lahaina News, May 26, 1994: 14.

SARGENT, ROCKY
— piloting boat in America's Cup, Lahaina News, March 18, 1987: 6.

SARGENT, STEVE [MUSICIAN]
— to perform at Taco Jo's Cantina, Lahaina News, September 16, 1993: 16.

SARGENTI, STEVE [MUSICIAN]
— critical of liquor commission rules concerning performance, Lahaina News, December 19, 1991: 1.
— to perform at Pioneer Inn , Lahaina News, June 4, 1992: 13.

SARGENTI, STEVE AND KATHY [MUSICIANS]
— to perform at El Crab Catcher, Lahaina News, October 31, 1991: 14.
— continues to perform at El Crab Catcher, Lahaina News, December 19, 1991: 21.

SARGENT'S FINE ART [BUSINESS]
— opens new gallery in Maui Marriott, Lahaina News, November 29, 2001: 8.
— awards scholarship to Lahainaluna High School student, Lahaina News, June 27, 2002: 5.
— promoted Kim Smith to vice president , Lahaina News, August 8, 2002: 8.
— to host "World Peace Artist", Lahaina News, March 20, 2003: 15.
— gallery awards scholarships to Lahainaluna High School students, Lahaina News, June 12, 2003: 17.
— Victor Bregeda to exhibit, Lahaina News, July 10, 2003: 17.

SARIBAY, RYAN
— Scholar/Athlete of the Week, Lahaina News, September 10, 1998: 15.

SARIBAY, SAL, JR.
— Scholar/Athlete of the Week, Lahaina News, April 16, 1998: 7.
— Lahainaluna High School student receives National Leadership and Service award, Lahaina News, May 7, 1998: 18.

SARKIN, JUNE
— jeweler recalls Lahaina of the 1960s, Lahaina News, June 7, 2001: 3.

SASADA, CRAIG
— named golf professional at Kapalua's Plantation Course, Lahaina News, March 21, 2002: 13.

SATCHIDANADA
— Swami to speak, Lahaina News, January 30, 1997: 2.

SATIRE
— possible future discussed, Lahaina Sun, June 13, 1973: 19.

SATO, ED
— coach discussed, Lahaina Sun, February 17, 1971: 7.

SATO, HERBERT
— named general manager of Lahaina Cannery Shopping Center, Lahaina News, February 18, 1987: 3.

SATO, JOANNE
— promoted to loan officer at GECC Financial Corp, Lahaina News, July 7, 1994: 9.

SATO, TADASHI [ARTIST]
— work praised by Robert Kelsey, Lahaina Sun, April 7, 1971: 6.
— commissioned to create mosaic mural at Lahaina Civic Center, Lahaina Sun, July 7, 1971: 11.
— will create a mural in Lahaina, Lahaina Sun, January 19, 1972: 18.

SATO'S TROPICAL FISHES
— business described, Lahaina Sun, January 3, 1973: 5.

SATTERFIELD, JANA
— promoted to marketing manager at Anheuser-Busch, Lahaina News, October 2, 2003: 8.

SATTLER, KAY [ARTIST]
— to exhibit at Village Gallery-Lahaina, Lahaina News, October 21, 1993: 15.

SAUNDERS, LAREN
— Scholar/Athlete of the Week, Lahaina News, November 25, 1999: 8.

SAUNDERS, SUSIE
— named assistant vice president and branch manager at First Hawaiian Creditcorp, Lahaina News, July 25, 1991: 7.

SAUZA CUP YACHT RACE
— organized by Lahaina Yacht Club, Lahaina News, July 29, 1987: 6.
— to be held, Lahaina News, June 22, 1988: 3.
— won by M1, photographed, Lahaina News, August 3, 1988: 3.

SAVAGE HAIR AND BODY TREATMENTS [BUSINESS]
— to open, Lahaina News, December 2, 1999: 16.

SAVE MA'ALAEA BENEFIT
— to be held at Hard Rock Cafe, Lahaina News, February 4, 1999: 16.

SAVE MA'ALAEA DEFENSE FUND
— to challenge expansion of Ma'alaea Harbor, Lahaina News, August 26, 1999: 2.

SAVE MA'ALAEA SURF RALLY
— to be held at Ma'alaea Harbor, Lahaina News, February 25, 1999: 6.
— to be held, Lahaina News, March 4, 1999: 7.

SAVE MA'ALAEA: A CRY FOR HELP [FILM]
— documentary to be shown to support Surfrider Foundation, Lahaina News, March 28, 2002: 1,20.
— to be shown by Maui Ocean Center, Lahaina News, August 22, 2002: 1,24.

SAVE MA'ALAEA: A CRY FOR HELP [FILM]
— to be shown by Surfrider Foundation, Lahaina News, February 20, 2003: 16.

SAVE THE CHILDREN RELAY
— seeking volunteers, Lahaina News, January 17, 1990: 5.
— Veryfind Products to sponsor relay, Lahaina News, February 7, 1990: 3.
— fundraiser to be held, Lahaina News, April 18, 1990: 7.
— to be held, Lahaina News, April 25, 1990: 12.

SAVE THE WHALES INTERNATIONAL
— campaigning to end whaling, Lahaina News, February 24, 1988: 18.
— volunteer work described, Lahaina News, March 23, 1988: 3.
— offering lectures, Lahaina News, January 18, 1989: 3.
— hosts lecture at Ka'anapali Beach Hotel, Lahaina News, March 1, 1989: 5.
— seeking volunteers for Whale Spree festival, Lahaina News, January 16, 1991: 3,4.

SAVOU, LAUMANA AND TUI
— improve church grounds at Sacred Hearts Mission, Lahaina News, March 26, 1998: 5.

SAWADA, HARUYUKI [MUSICIAN]
— trumpeter performs at Blackie's, Lahaina News, September 6, 1989: 9.

SAX, EDDIE [COMEDIAN]
— to perform at Comedy Club and the Sports Page, Lahaina News, June 3, 1993: 13.
— to perform at Comedy Club, Lahaina News, December 9, 1993: 11.

SAX QUARTET [MUSICAL GROUP]
— to perform at Makawao Union Church, Lahaina News, November 2, 1988: 9.

SAXTON, SANDY
— restaurant owner featured, Lahaina News, December 21, 1988: 2.

SAYLES, DAN
— named Broker-in-Charge at Kehalani C. Brewer Homes, Lahaina News, February 1, 1996: 11.

SCANS SYMPOSIUM III
— to be sponsored by Maui Chamber of Commerce, Lahaina News, March 31, 1994: 9.

SCARLET FIRE [MUSICAL GROUP]
— to perform at Paia Community Center, Lahaina News, March 18, 1993: 12.
— to perform at Moose McGillycuddy's, Lahaina News, September 28, 1995: 11.

SCAROLES VILLAGE PIZZERIA [RESTAURANT]
— reviewed, Lahaina News, May 30, 1990: 12.
— to hold golf tournament to benefit Lightbringers Rescue Mission, Lahaina News, March 24, 1994: 12.

SCARTISSUE: THE LEGEND OF FRANKENSTEIN [PLAY]
— to be performed by Maui Youth Theatre, Lahaina News, March 16, 1988: 14.

SCD INTERNATIONAL [BUSINESS]
— holds grant opening for Olena at Kehalani project, Lahaina News, July 12, 2001: 8.

SCENTCHIPS MAUI [BUSINESS]
— home fragrance company opens in Lahaina Cannery Mall, Lahaina News, December 13, 2001: 9.

SCENTUOUS SHOP MAUI [BUSINESS]
— featured, Lahaina News, October 12, 1983: 14.

SCHAFF, LAVENDA
— to present "Tara Pilgrimage to India" with Amira Segal, Lahaina News, September 13, 2001: 16,17.

SCHAMEL, DENA
— trucker and swimsuit contestant featured, Lahaina News, July 1, 1987: 1.

SCHAR, BOB
— football player to speak at Nautilus Center, Lahaina News, July 13, 1988: 10.

SCHARFFENBERGER CELLARS
— chef Roger Dikon to pair dinner with wine from, Lahaina News, December 5, 1991: 23,26.

SCHATZKIN, PAUL
— coordinating 4th of July fireworks, Lahaina News, May 2, 1984: 5.
— comments on proposed thrillcraft corridor, Lahaina News, February 24, 1988: 1.
— joins Shearson Lehman Brothers, Lahaina News, December 5, 1990: 4.
— joins Shearson Lehman Brothers, Lahaina News, December 12, 1990: 6.

SCHAUNAMAN, JOYCE [ARTIST]
— "Lahaina Harbor" chosen by Lahaina Town Action Committee for commemorative poster, Lahaina News, January 4, 1989: 3.

SCHEFCIK, LARRY
— appointed general manager at Cutter Jeep Eagle Maui, Lahaina News, November 14, 1996: 9.

SCHELLEMANS, FRANCIS
— associate pastor at Maria Lanakila Catholic Church retires, Lahaina News, March 22, 2001: 3.

SCHIEBELHUT, JOHN
— treasurer of Lahaina Art Society, Lahaina Sun, January 13, 1971: 7.

SCHIFFER, MONICA
— promoted at Aston Hotels and Resorts Hawaii, Lahaina News, January 11, 2001: 14.

SCHLEA, ALIYA
— Scholar/Athlete of the Week, Lahaina News, February 18, 1999: 7.

SCHLEA, BRENT
— surfing featured, Lahaina News, November 29, 2001: 12.

SCHLICKENMEYER, CHRIS
— winner of longboard surfing contest, Lahaina Times, June, 1980 volume 4 number 5: 9.

SCHLOSSER, MARK
— captain of winning vessel in Victoria-Maui race discusses experience, Lahaina News, July 16, 1986: 4.

SCHMEECKLE, JOE [ARTIST]
— to exhibit at Maui Sculpture Gallery, Lahaina News, July 30, 1992: 18.

SCHMIDT, BRIAN [COMEDIAN]
— to perform at Comedy Club and the Sports Page, Lahaina News, April 23, 1992: 25,27.

SCHMIDT, DAWN
— local student enrolls at Oklahoma State University, Lahaina News, October 24, 2002: 14.

SCHMIDT, WARD
— candidate for County Council highlighted, Lahaina News, July 1, 1980: 17.
— critical of police arresting nude sunbathers, Lahaina News, September 1, 1980: 7.

SCHNABEL, SNEH VICTORIA
— to give talk on "Love's Own Truths", Lahaina News, October 11, 2001: 17.

SCHOLARSHIP FASHION SHOW AND AUCTION
— to be held by Maui Business Professional Women's Club, Lahaina News, November 9, 2000: 18.

SCHOLARSHIPS
— Fujitsu Asian Scholarship Program now available, Lahaina News, August 1, 1991: 4,5.
— Wally Yonamine Foundation Scholarship is due, Lahaina News, August 8, 1991: 3,4.
— available from the Maui Academy of Performing Arts, Lahaina News, August 8, 1991: 4.
— March of Dimes awards to Maui Community College nursing students, Lahaina News, January 30, 1992: 5.
— Napili Kai Foundation awards J.C. Millar Memorial Scholarships, Lahaina News, September 14, 2000: 11.
— Na Mele O Maui to offer, Lahaina News, February 8, 2001: 2.
— Na Mele O Maui awards scholarship to Leila Diego, Lahaina News, May 17, 2001: 17.

SCHOOL-COMMUNITY BASED MANAGEMENT (SCBM)
— Councilmember Jim Gallagher featured, Lahaina News, August 12, 1993: 2.
— council seeking new members, Lahaina News, September 10, 1998: 1.
— council alters school schedule, Lahaina News, September 17, 1998: 18.

SCHOOLS
— enrollment figures for beginning of school year, Lahaina Sun, September 1, 1971: 12.
— pre-school at Kapalua to hold auction fundraiser, Lahaina News, April 24, 1985: 7,20.
— see also specific schools

SCHOTTEN, YIZHAK [MUSICIAN]
— to be musical director of Kapalua Music Festival, Lahaina News, May 28, 1992: 14.
— to perform at Maui Chamber Music Festival, Lahaina News, June 12, 1997: 1,9.

SCHROEDER, JENNY
— appointed general manager at Chaney, Brooks and Company, Lahaina News, November 23, 2000: 16.

SCHRUIFF, STEPHANIE
— appointed room service manager at Kapalua Bay Hotel and Villas, Lahaina News, February 6, 1991: 6.

SCHUBERT OCTET [MUSICAL PIECE]
— to be performed by Maui Philharmonic, Lahaina News, May 14, 1986: 3.

SCHULER HOMES [BUSINESS]
— homes in Wailuku built by set to open in 1993, Lahaina News, June 25, 1992: 16.
— files to offer common stock to public, Lahaina News, November 25, 1993: 7.

SCHULER, JAMES
— outlines plans for future housing developments, Lahaina News, April 2, 1992: 11.
— receives entrepreneur of the year award, Lahaina News, July 2, 1992: 16.

SCHULZ, UWE
— discusses proposed swimming pool, Lahaina News, March 23, 1988: 1.
— local architect featured, Lahaina News, October 26, 1988: 2.
— architect helping to restore historic Lahaina featured, Lahaina News, June 18, 1992: 3.

SCHUMAN, ROBERT
— Exhibit at Lahaina Art Society Gallery, Lahaina Sun, March 3, 1971: 6.

SCHUSSER, BETSY
— doctor opens Aloha Family Practice Clinic, Lahaina News, August 26, 1999: 13.

SCHUSTER, FRANK
— appointed director of Wailea Community Association, Lahaina News, April 1, 1993: 7.

SCHUSTER, MICHAEL [PERFORMER]
— puppeteer to perform at Maui Arts and Cultural Center, Lahaina News, December 13, 2001: 17.

SCHWARTZ, JASON [POLITICIAN]
— candidate for Maui County Council featured, Lahaina News, August 13, 1992: 11.
— executive director of Maui Arts and Music Associates, Lahaina News, February 11, 1993: 4.
— forms solar technology partnership with Takeshi Iyama, Lahaina News, June 9, 1994: 12.

SCHWARZ, TARA
— herbalist to present at Down to Earth, Lahaina News, May 8, 2003: 16.

SCHWARZENEGGER, ARNOLD
— attends opening of Planet Hollywood restaurant, Lahaina News, July 7, 1994: 1,3.
— visits Planet Hollywood, Lahaina News, January 29, 1998: 9.
— to host Lana'i Pine Hawaii Pacific Target Shoot, Lahaina News, October 22, 1998: 20.

SCIENCE
— Relay Mirror Experiment approved , Lahaina News, December 16, 1987: 15.

SCIENCE AND INDUSTRIAL ARTS FAIR
— to be held, Lahaina News, February 13, 1992: 4.

SCIENCE CARNIVAL
— to be held, sponsored by Maui Chamber of Commerce, Maui Mall, and Bishop Museum, Lahaina News, May 1, 1991: 4.
— details, Lahaina News, May 8, 1991: 4,8.

SCIENCE CITY
— Haleakala Observatories news featured, Lahaina News, February 20, 2003: 2.

SCOFIELD, SUSAN
— named principal of King Kamehameha III School, Lahaina News, August 27, 1992: 3.
— King Kamehameha III principal featured, Lahaina News, April 14, 1994: 1.

SCOPES MONKEY TRIAL
— "Inherit the Wind" to be performed by Maui Community Theatre, Lahaina News, October 26, 1995: 12.

SCORE
— Maui Chapter to hold "How to Start Your Own Business", Lahaina News, June 5, 1997: 17.
— members receive high score from national business organization, Lahaina News, July 17, 1997: 12.

SCOTT, BILL [COMEDIAN]
— to perform at Comedy Club and the Sports Page, Lahaina News, April 1, 1993: 12.
— to perform at Honolulu Comedy Club, Lahaina News, January 18, 1996: 12.

SCOTT BROTHERS [BUSINESS]
— painting company reviewed, Lahaina News, July 16, 1986: 14.

SCOTT, LAURA
— joins Lahaina Divers, Lahaina News, June 26, 1997: 14.

SCOTT, PHIL [ENGINEER]
— discusses pollution from sugar plantations, Lahaina Sun, November 25, 1970: 4.

SCOTT, SUSAN [WRITER]
— to discuss treating marine injuries in "All Things Considered", Lahaina News, May 11, 2000: 21.

SCOTTY K SPAM BAKEOFF
— to be held at Maluʻulu O Lele Cultural Center, Lahaina News, May 1, 1991: 1.

SCOUT-O-RAMA
— to be held by Boy Scouts at Kaʻahumanu Center, Lahaina News, April 4, 1990: 3.
— to be held, Lahaina News, April 10, 1991: 4.

SCRABBLE
— competition to be held at Embassy Suites, Lahaina News, April 30, 1998: 16.

SCREAMING VOLCANO [MUSICAL GROUP]
— to perform at Moose McGillycuddy's, Lahaina News, July 8, 1993: 11.

SCRIPTWRITING SCHOOL OF MAUI
— to hold workshop, Lahaina News, September 15, 1994: 15.

SCROOGE [PLAY]
— to be presented by Maui Youth Theatre, Lahaina News, November 21, 1984: 3.
— to be presented by Maui Academy of Performing Arts, Lahaina News, November 21, 1990: 13.
— continues, Lahaina News, December 5, 1990: 9.

SCUBA
— classes to be offered at Skin Diving Hawaii, Lahaina Sun, January 20, 1971: 7.

SCULLY, MIKE [WRITER]
— to attend Maui Writers Conference, Lahaina News, August 19, 1999: 2.

SCULPTURE GARDEN SANCTUARY
— created by Bruce Turnbull, Anna Good, and Steve Turnbull, Lahaina News, October 24, 1996: 15.

SCURO, JOSEPH
— attorney to speak, Lahaina News, July 18, 1996: 13.

SEA BREEZE [BUSINESS]
— planning renovations, Lahaina News, August 23, 1989: 3.

SEA CADET
— program seen as alternative to dropping out, Lahaina News, May 22, 1985: 9.

SEA EXPLORER SHIP 120
— class to meet at St. Theresa's Church, Lahaina News, August 21, 1997: 15.

SEA FAIR
— boat show to be held, Lahaina News, July 25, 2002: 20.

SEA GRANT EXTENSION, UNIVERSITY OF HAWAII
— to hold workshop on whale watching, Lahaina News, October 9, 1985: 3.
— to offer workshop on aquaculture, Lahaina News, April 25, 1996: 6.
— to track sediment, Lahaina News, September 4, 1997: 15.

SEA HABITAT
— see underwater observatory

SEA HOUSE [RESTAURANT]
— reviewed, Lahaina News, February 21, 1990: 12.
— reviewed, Lahaina News, September 5, 1991: 17.
— reviewed, Lahaina News, April 30, 1992: 17.
— featured, Lahaina News, November 12, 1992: 21.
— renovations complete, Lahaina News, November 28, 1996: 14.
— featured, Lahaina News, August 6, 1998: 10,11.
— to host Stone Creek Wine Maker Dinner, Lahaina News, July 8, 1999: 12.
— to hold Stone Creek Wine Maker Dinner, Lahaina News, July 15, 1999: 12.
— Mike Gallagher named executive chef, Lahaina News, July 29, 1999: 3.
— appoints Verna Biga as Food and Beverages director, Lahaina News, August 26, 1999: 13.
— chef Michael Gallagher introduces new menu at, Lahaina News, November 11, 1999: 11.
— featured, Lahaina News, October 5, 2000: 6.
— featured, Lahaina News, December 6, 2001: 9.
— to open, Lahaina News, November 28, 2002: 8.

SEA LINK OF HAWAII [BUSINESS]
— plans to suspend Maui Princess ferry service, Lahaina News, September 19, 1996: 8.
— plans to revive Molokaʻi ferry, Lahaina News, November 9, 2000: 1,12.
— Molokaʻi Princess expanding schedule, Lahaina News, May 24, 2001: 1,22.
— to support "Great American Fish Count 2001", Lahaina News, July 12, 2001: 16.
— expands Molokaʻi Ferry service, Lahaina News, July 26, 2001: 9.

SEA MINING
— controversy over mining leases continue, Lahaina News, July 6, 1988: 1,12.
— discussion sponsored by Blue Ocean Preservation Society, Lahaina News, April 26, 1989: 3.

SEA PRINCESS [SHIP]
— scheduled to arrive at Lahaina Harbor, Lahaina News, October 10, 1990: 11.
— arriving in Lahaina Harbor, Lahaina News, October 17, 1990: 11.
— to anchor off Lahaina on November 5th, Lahaina News, October 31, 1990: 12.
— merchants and volunteers assigned to greet the ship, Lahaina News, November 7, 1990: 7.
— Boat Day to be held on November 24th, Lahaina News, November 14, 1990: 11.
— scheduled to stop at Lahaina, Lahaina News, November 28, 1990: 8.

SEA SAILS
— hosts lecture on whales at Ka'anapali Beach Hotel, Lahaina News, March 1, 1989: 5.

SEA SIDE FINE ART [BUSINESS]
— to demonstrate fused glass technique of Ray and Diane Pizzo, Lahaina News, May 25, 1995: 12.

SEA VILLAGE
— see Hawaiian Sea Village

SEA WALLS
— in West Maui, discussed, Lahaina News, August 3, 1988: 1,18.

SEA-BED MINING
— editorial opposing, Lahaina News, September 30, 1987: 2.

SEABERN, JACK
— named advertising manager of Lahaina Sun, Lahaina Sun, December 15, 1971: 6.

SEABERN, MARCIA AND JACK
— to perform "Love Letters", Lahaina News, February 6, 1992: 4.

SEABOURN LEGEND [SHIP]
— to debark at Lahaina Harbor, Lahaina News, May 8, 1997: 14.

SEABREEZE CARPET CLEANING [BUSINESS]
— featured, Lahaina News, September 7, 1983: 14.

SEABURY CRAFT FAIR
— to take place, Lahaina News, May 6, 1987: 3.

SEABURY DANCE ENSEMBLE
— to offer "Dance Showcase 2001", Lahaina News, March 8, 2001: 16.

SEABURY HALL
— school begins fund drive, Lahaina News, January 22, 1986: 3.
— hosts Shakespearean Show, Lahaina News, January 25, 1989: 16.
— to show animation films, Lahaina News, February 22, 1989: 3.
— to hold open house, Lahaina News, January 30, 1991: 4.
— "The Voice of the Prairie" continues, Lahaina News, January 30, 1992: 21.
— to host Craft Fair, Lahaina News, February 13, 1992: 4.
— to hold craft fair, Lahaina News, March 12, 1992: 5.
— to host craft fair, Lahaina News, April 23, 1992: 8.
— to present "The Boyfriend", Lahaina News, November 5, 1992: 17.
— Performing Arts Department to perform "Brighton Beach Memoirs", Lahaina News, February 16, 1995: 16.
— to hold Craft Fair, Lahaina News, May 9, 1996: 16.
— to hold school reunion, Lahaina News, June 20, 1996: 12.
— to hold Craft Fair, Lahaina News, May 8, 1997: 16.
— to hold craft fair, Lahaina News, April 30, 1998: 17.
— Craft Fair to be held, Lahaina News, May 7, 1998: 20.
— to hold art fair, Lahaina News, May 6, 1999: 20.
— to host play "Fellow Travelers: Two Cold War Conspiracy Tales", Lahaina News, November 4, 1999: 12.
— performing arts students to stage "Story Theater", Lahaina News, December 2, 1999: 16.
— to hold "The Last Night at Ballyhoo", Lahaina News, February 17, 2000: 16.
— students performing "The Last Night at Ballyhoo", Lahaina News, February 24, 2000: 16.

— to perform "The World Goes 'Round", Lahaina News, April 13, 2000: 12.
— students to perform "Step by Step", Lahaina News, April 27, 2000: 12.
— to hold Craft Fair, Lahaina News, May 11, 2000: 20.
— two seniors win Paul Wood Performing Arts Awards, Lahaina News, July 6, 2000: 5.
— to perform C.P. Taylor's "And a Nightingale Sang", Lahaina News, February 15, 2001: 16.
— to hold Craft Fair, Lahaina News, May 10, 2001: 20.
— craft fair to be held, Lahaina News, May 9, 2002: 16.
— to perform "Side Shows", Lahaina News, May 16, 2002: 16.
— craft fair to be held, Lahaina News, May 8, 2003: 15.
— "Side Shows: A Festival of One-Act Plays" to be held, Lahaina News, May 15, 2003: 16.

SEABURY HALL CHAPEL CHOIR
— performing at Holy Innocents' Church, Lahaina Sun, November 11, 1970: 4.

SEABURY HALL COUNTRY FAIR
— to be held, Lahaina News, April 6, 1988: 20.

SEABURY HALL CRAFT FAIR
— held, Lahaina News, May 21, 1986: 7.
— to be held, Lahaina News, May 1, 1991: 18.

SEABURY HALL DANCE PROGRAM
— to perform "Step by Step", Lahaina News, April 25, 2002: 16.

SEABURY HALL PERFORMING ARTS
— concludes its season, Lahaina News, April 16, 1992: 22.
— to offer "The Crucible", Lahaina News, January 21, 1993: 15.
— presents "Live! Tonight! At the Globe! #7: Space!", Lahaina News, October 13, 1994: 20.

SEAMAN'S CEMETERY
— graves to be relocated for widening of Wainee Street, Lahaina News, November 16, 1988: 1.

SEAMEN'S HOSPITAL
— to be restored, Lahaina News, January 1, 1981: 7.
— photographs of, Lahaina News, July 15, 1981: 8.
— dedicated after restoration, Lahaina News, June 15, 1982: 1.
— Lahaina Printsellers as tenant of, Lahaina News, February 29, 1984: 11.
— renovations detailed, Lahaina News, February 29, 1984: 9,10.
— restoration efforts praised by Surgeon General C. Everett Koop, Lahaina News, March 1, 1989: 1,16.

SEAN THE JUGGLER [ENTERTAINER]
— featured, Lahaina News, March 21, 1990: 15.

SEAQUEST
— catamaran destroyed by high surf, Lahaina News, January 8, 1998: 1.

SEARCH FOR SIGNS OF INTELLIGENT LIFE IN THE UNIVERSE [PLAY]
— to be performed at Studio H'Poko, Lahaina News, April 15, 1993: 9.

SEARCH FOR TALENT
— presented by Exchange Club of Maui, Lahaina News, April 27, 1988: 6.

SEARS [BUSINESS]
— will open in new shopping center in Lahaina, Lahaina Sun, December 1, 1971: 1.

SEASCAPE MA'ALAEA RESTAURANT [RESTAURANT]
— to offer "Old Man and the Sea" event, Lahaina News, June 15, 2000: 16.

SEASIDE FINE ART [BUSINESS]
— opens, Lahaina News, April 6, 1995: 12.

SEASONAL FARM WORKERS PROGRAM
— seeking to bring unemployed from Moloka'i to Maui, Lahaina News, December 2, 1987: 1.

SEASONS [RESTAURANT]
— featured, Lahaina News, January 9, 1992: 13.

SEATRIZ, AURELIA
— community work featured, Lahaina News, July 18, 1991: 3.

SEATTLE
— described, Lahaina Sun, January 26, 1972: 18.

SEAVIEW [SHIP]
— breaks free of mooring in the Lahaina Roadstead, Lahaina News, January 23, 2003: 1.

SEAWATCH RESTAURANT [RESTAURANT]
— to host dinner featuring wine from Chalone Vineyard , Lahaina News, June 23, 1994: 12.
— to feature jazz pianist Brian Cuomo, Lahaina News, August 18, 1994: 16.
— to host "Another Starry Night for Hula", Lahaina News, February 6, 1997: 14.

SEAWEED
— scientists discuss problems with, Lahaina News, March 7, 1996: 1,4.
— see also pollution

SEAWEST DESIGNS [BUSINESS]
— Shanelle Evans joins as account executive, Lahaina News, March 14, 1990: 6.

SECOND HAND ROSE DINNER
— to be held at Hui No'eau Visual Arts Center, Lahaina News, September 12, 1991: 5.

SECORD, HEATHER [MUSICIAN]
— to perform at Borders Books, Lahaina News, March 23, 2000: 13.

SECORD-PARSONS, HEATHER
— to talk on "Elemental Spirals, Feng Shui and Phi", Lahaina News, March 8, 2001: 16.

SECRET GARDEN, THE [PLAY]
— to be performed at Maui Academy of Performing Arts, Lahaina News, September 29, 1994: 12.
— to be performed by Maui Academy of Performing Arts, Lahaina News, November 24, 1994: 11.
— featured, Lahaina News, December 8, 1994: 15.

SECRETARIES WEEK
— to be held, Lahaina News, February 16, 1995: 13.
— value of laughter in the workplace, Lahaina News, April 6, 1995: 6.

SECRETARIO, PHILBERT
— member of Lahaina Kamaakina Fishing Association, Lahaina Sun, December 23, 1970: 11.

SECRETARY DAY
— Hawaiian Airlines to hold drawing for trips to Las Vegas, Lahaina News, April 10, 1991: 3.
— drawing for Hawaiian Airlines tickets to be held, Lahaina News, April 17, 1991: 7.
— Fashion Show to be held by Soroptimist International, Lahaina News, April 12, 2001: 8.
— Fashion Show to be held by Soroptimist International, Lahaina News, April 19, 2001: 17.

SECRETS, THE [BAND]
— success at Moose's, Lahaina Times, August 20, 1983 volume 7 number 8: 2.

SECTION, THE [MUSICAL GROUP]
— to perform at Moose McGillycuddy's, Lahaina News, November 2, 1995: 12.
— to perform at World Café, Lahaina News, February 29, 1996: 14.

— continues to perform at World Cafe, Lahaina News, April 11, 1996: 12.
— continues to perform at Moose McGillycuddy's, Lahaina News, May 23, 1996: 2.
— to perform at World Cafe, Lahaina News, June 13, 1996: 10.

SEDDON, KAREN
— project manager discusses Front Street construction, Lahaina News, March 16, 1995: 1,4.
— project manager for Front Street Improvement Project meets with community groups, Lahaina News, November 2, 1995: 1,16.
— Front Street improvements probably to finish next month, Lahaina News, May 15, 1997: 1.

SEEBACH, DAVID [MAGICIAN]
— to perform with Maui Philharmonic Society, Lahaina News, November 16, 1988: 9.

SEEGER, DICK [ARTIST]
— featured, Lahaina News, March 18, 1987: 4.

SEEGER, GUENTER
— chef to participate in Kapalua Wine Symposium, Lahaina News, July 15, 1993: 10.

SEGAL, AMIRA
— to present "Tara Pilgrimage to India" with Lavenda Schaff, Lahaina News, September 13, 2001: 16,17.

SEHRING, ADOLPH [ARTIST]
— to exhibit at Galerie Lassen, Lahaina News, March 31, 1994: 14.

SEIBU HAWAII
— settles conflict with Hui Alanui O Makena over Makena road closure, Lahaina News, July 29, 1987: 2.

SEIBU LIONS
— Japanese baseball team to be hosted by Maui Prince Hotel, Lahaina News, January 30, 1992: 9.

SEIGO CORPORATION [BUSINESS]
— laundry service to open, Lahaina News, July 11, 1990: 6.

SEIHA HOGAKU KAI JAPANESE CLASSICAL MUSIC ASSOCIATION
— to hold benefit concert for Maui Arts and Cultural Center, Lahaina News, January 26, 1995: 16.

SEINO, MICHAEL
— wins Lahainaluna Golf Tournament, Lahaina News, May 30, 1984: 4.

SEINO SANDRA
— working to implement program helping to find missing children, Lahaina News, January 6, 1994: 1.

SEIZANKAI [MUSICAL GROUP]
— to perform at Maui Arts and Cultural Center, Lahaina News, September 11, 1997: 16.

SEKI, RAE
— appointed as director of new Tiffany and Co.in Wailea, Lahaina News, September 21, 2000: 16.

SELF-DEFENSE
— seminar to be held on, Lahaina News, July 14, 1994: 6.

SELF-HELP HOUSING CORPORATION
— benefits local home-owners, Lahaina News, January 30, 1992: 3.

SELF-HELP HOUSING CORPORATION [BUSINESS]
— work described, Lahaina News, July 4, 1991: 9.
— finishes Kapalua Self-Help Housing Project, Lahaina News, July 22, 1993: 1.
— seeking more self-help housing, Lahaina News, July 20, 1995: 2.
— seeks families interested in building their own homes, Lahaina News, October 29, 1998: 15.
— recruiting families for Kihei Project, Lahaina News, April 22, 1999: 11.

SELIGMAN, NINA [ARTIST]
— to exhibit, Lahaina News, August 6, 1998: 9.

SELIN, MARJO
— "Fitness and Muscle Classic" to be held, Lahaina News, April 30, 1998: 16.

SELKEN, SARAH
— wins Lahaina Yacht Club Spring Wahine Tournament, Lahaina News, May 8, 1991: 1.

SELLARS, STAN [COMEDIAN]
— to perform at Comedy Club, Lahaina News, August 19, 1993: 15.

SEN JU SUCHI BAR [RESTAURANT]
— featured, Lahaina News, June 2, 1994: 11.

SENATE, U.S.
— earmarks funds to address native Hawaiian housing problems, Lahaina News, December 14, 2000: 8.

SENIOR CARE MANAGEMENT MAUI [BUSINESS]
— offering care management service for seniors, Lahaina News, June 28, 2001: 9.
— provides support for senior, Lahaina News, July 19, 2001: 9.

SENIOR CITIZENS CLUB, LAHAINA-HONOLUA
— to hold silent auction, Lahaina News, April 3, 2003: 17.

SENIOR CITIZENS DAY
— program announced, Lahaina Sun, May 19, 1971: 3.

SENIOR CITIZENS FAIR
— to be held at War Memorial Gym, Lahaina News, July 4, 1990: 3.
— to be held after being postponed due to hurricane Iniki, Lahaina News, October 29, 1992: 7.
— to be hosted by Pat Morita, Lahaina News, November 4, 1993: 3.
— to be held; featuring Grandparent/Grandchild Look A Like Contest, Lahaina News, October 23, 1997: 21.
— to be held on Halloween, Lahaina News, October 29, 1998: 24.
— to be held on Halloween, Lahaina News, October 29, 1998: 24.
— to be held, Lahaina News, October 26, 2000: 28.
— to be held, Lahaina News, October 18, 2001: 2.

SENIOR FESTIVAL
— performing "Driving Miss Daisy", Lahaina News, July 2, 1992: 26.

SENIOR MANAGEMENT CONFERENCE
— to be held at Westin Maui, Lahaina News, September 13, 1989: 4.

SENIOR MEDICATION MANAGEMENT AND WELLNESS PROGRAM
— nurse Linda Decker to discuss medications, Lahaina News, November 2, 2000: 25.

SENIOR STROLL
— to be held, Lahaina News, February 12, 1998: 17.

SENIORS
— seminar on estate planning to be held, Lahaina News, May 10, 1989: 3.
— seminar on long-term care insurance to be offered, Lahaina News, June 7, 1989: 2.
— ceramics classes popular for, Lahaina News, June 28, 1989: 11.
— Maui Community College to offer classes on computers, Lahaina News, August 16, 1989: 3.
— elderly care in crisis, Lahaina News, September 6, 1989: 1.
— editorial calling for better planning on Maui, Lahaina News, September 6, 1989: 12.
— services listed, Lahaina News, September 20, 1989: 4.
— free legal advice offered to, Lahaina News, October 18, 1989: 3.
— Celebration of Aging to be held, Lahaina News, November 1, 1989: 6.
— to receive help with taxes from American Association of Retired Persons, Lahaina News, March 7, 1990: 3.
— services available from Maui County, Lahaina News, October 3, 1996: 14.

SEPTEMBER 11TH
— memorial service held at Launiupoko Beach Park, Lahaina News, September 20, 2001: 3.
— editorial call to support victims of, Lahaina News, September 20, 2001: 4.
— art event to benefit victims of, Lahaina News, October 4, 2001: 17.
— memorial to be held, Lahaina News, August 29, 2002: 8.

SEQUEIRA, KEOLA
— president of Hui O Wa'a Kaulua supports Hawaiian cultural park at Kamehameha Iki Park, Lahaina News, November 9, 1995: 1,16.
— canoe builder featured, Lahaina News, October 3, 1996: 1.
— receives LahainaTown Action Committee Kokua award, Lahaina News, January 23, 1997: 1.
— canoe building resigns from Hui O Wa'a Kaulua, Lahaina News, June 12, 1997: 1.
— to speak on canoe building, Lahaina News, October 2, 1997: 21.
— canoe builder featured, Lahaina News, October 16, 1997: 6.

SEQUEIRA, PETER
— congratulated for his retirement from Pioneer Mill, Lahaina Sun, February 24, 1971: 1.
— honored by Pioneer Mill for years of service, Lahaina Sun, April 7, 1971: 6.
— services planned for, Lahaina News, June 18, 1998: 3.

SERA, KAITLAN
— Scholar/Athlete of the Week, Lahaina News, September 6, 2001: 12.

SERA, KAITLAN AND KELLEEN
— tennis players featured, Lahaina News, August 8, 2002: 12.

SERA, KELLEEN
— Scholar/Athlete of the Week, Lahaina News, August 23, 2001: 13.

SERRANO, EDMUND "EDDIE"
— passes away, Lahaina News, August 19, 1999: 15.

SERRANO, HECTOR [MUSICIAN]
— to perform at Maui AIDS Foundation's James Manness Memorial "Dance Party Xtreme", Lahaina News, March 26, 1998: 2.

SERRANO, JUSTIN
— Scholar/Athlete of the Week, Lahaina News, October 31, 1996: 15.

SERRANO, NOELLE
— Scholar/Athlete of the Week, Lahaina News, February 19, 1998: 6.

SERVCO PACIFIC, INC. [BUSINESS]
— to hold job fair, Lahaina News, September 21, 2000: 16.

SERVICES CORPS OF RETIRED EXECUTIVES (SCORE)
— seeking volunteers, Lahaina News, September 16, 1993: 3.
— looking for new members, Lahaina News, August 27, 1998: 13.
— to be held by the Office of Economic Development, Lahaina News, July 10, 2003: 8.
— branch coming to Maui, Lahaina News, August 21, 2003: 8.
— to open branch on Maui, Lahaina News, September 4, 2003: 8.
— volunteers to provide small business counseling, Lahaina News, September 18, 2003: 9.

SESAME STREET
— to appear at Lahaina Cannery, Lahaina News, April 21, 1994: 16.

SESHADRI, KARTIK [MUSICIAN]
— to perform at Maui Arts and Cultural Center, Lahaina News, March 7, 2002: 16.

SESKEVICS, ABBY
— competes for Hawaii Swim Team-Lahaina, Lahaina News, December 31, 1992: 7.

SESSING JANICE
— National Oceanic and Atmospheric Agency representative hears testimony on the Hawaiian Islands Humpback Whale National Sanctuary, Lahaina News, March 24, 1994: 2.

SEVEN SEA CRUISES [BUSINESS]
— to offer sight-seeing trips to Moloka'i, Lahaina News, July 2, 1998: 3.

SEVENTH WAVE [MUSICAL GROUP]
— hosted by Artful Dodger Feed and Read, Lahaina News, March 18, 1987: 18.

SEVENTH-DAY ADVENTIST CHURCH
— celebrates 100th year in Hawaii, Lahaina News, November 27, 1985: 20.
— Joe Melashenko to become new pastor, Lahaina News, January 23, 1991: 3.
— to hold quit smoking clinic, Lahaina News, November 14, 1991: 2.
— to hold four-evening seminar, Lahaina News, January 2, 1992: 5.
— churches to hold Sabbath on Saturday, Lahaina News, November 18, 1993: 3.
— to host Bible school, Lahaina News, June 6, 1996: 15.
— Vegetarian Food Fair to be held, Lahaina News, May 7, 1998: 21.
— to host "Next Millennium Seminar—Your Future on the Eve of 2000", Lahaina News, June 17, 1999: 16.

SEVENTH-DAY ADVENTIST CHURCH, KAHULUI
— to hold discussion on "Practical Christianity in a Changing World", Lahaina News, November 7, 2002: 20.

SEVENTH-DAY ADVENTIST CHURCH, KIHEI
— raising money to build new church, Lahaina News, December 3, 1998: 11.

SEVENTH-DAY ADVENTIST CHURCH, LAHAINA
— offering undersea bible adventure, Lahaina News, May 1, 2003: 2.
— to hold summer bible program, Lahaina News, May 8, 2003: 2.

SEVENTH-DAY ADVENTIST CHURCHES
— hosting cooking demonstration for low-cholesterol, low-fat dishes, Lahaina News, March 28, 1990: 4.

SEVERNS, MIKE [WRITER]
— author of "Molokini: Hawaii's Island Marine Sanctuary" to talk at Natural Selections Coffee Co., Lahaina News, January 9, 2003: 17.

SEVERSON, JOHN
— 50-year-old sailboarder featured, Lahaina News, May 30, 1984: 4.
— interviewed, Lahaina News, May 4, 1988: 6,7.

SEW SPECIAL FASHION SHOW
— to be held, Lahaina News, August 8, 1990: 4.

SEWAGE, SEWERS
— line broken in Kahului harbor, Lahaina Sun, November 18, 1970: 1.
— county to end ocean dumping of, Lahaina Sun, December 9, 1970: 2.
— request for treatment plants in Lahaina, central Maui and Kihei, Lahaina Sun, December 9, 1970: 2.
— outfalls tested for pollution, Lahaina Sun, December 16, 1970: 3.
— as potential source of irrigation water, Lahaina Sun, December 23, 1970: 11.
— projects desired by West Maui Business Association, Lahaina Sun, December 23, 1970: 2.
— treatment plant approved by Maui County Council, Lahaina Sun, January 20, 1971: 1.
— treatment plant proposed, Lahaina Sun, March 10, 1971: 1,8.
— condition of Kahului Harbor discussed in editorial, Lahaina Sun, March 10, 1971: 8.
— public meetings proposed, Lahaina Sun, March 17, 1971: 1.
— plant proposed for West Maui, Lahaina Sun, March 31, 1971: 1,8.
— petition requesting sewage system in Lahaina submitted to Maui County Council, Lahaina Sun, April 21, 1971: 4.
— update of current projects, Lahaina Sun, April 28, 1971: 3.
— federal money awarded for sewage treatment system for Wailuku and Kahului, Lahaina Sun, May 19, 1971: 1.
— federal money sought for sewer system, Lahaina Sun, June 9, 1971: 3.
— repairs planned, Lahaina Sun, July 21, 1971: 9.

— construction of new system begins soon, Lahaina Sun, November 10, 1971: 1.
— construction of treatment plant underway, Lahaina Sun, December 8, 1971: 5.
— sewage master plan published, Lahaina Sun, January 19, 1972: 10.
— sewer plan criticized and discussed, Lahaina Sun, February 2, 1972: 3.
— raw sewage discharged in Kahului, Lahaina Sun, April 12, 1972: 10.
— contract for new sewer system questioned, Lahaina Sun, April 12, 1972: 15.
— planned Kanaha Sewage Plant criticized, Lahaina Sun, July 19, 1972: 3.
— Environmental Protection Agency requiring more complete review of Wailuku-Kahului sewer plant, Lahaina Sun, August 9, 1972: 5.
— environmental impact statement being studied, Lahaina Sun, September 20, 1972: 22.
— federal Environmental Protection Agency allows bids for new treatment facility to be advertised, Lahaina Sun, November 1, 1972: 13.
— bids received for Wailuku-Kahului sewer system, environmental concerns persist, Lahaina Sun, January 17, 1973: 3.
— laws being twisted to support Wailuku sewer project, Lahaina Sun, January 17, 1973: 9.
— alternatives to Kanaha Pond discussed, Lahaina Sun, January 31, 1973: 9.
— issues with sewage by Mala wharf discussed, Lahaina Sun, February 7, 1973: 18,19.
— criticism of proposed Wailuku-Kahului sewage plant at Kahana, Lahaina Sun, February 14, 1973: 3.
— Wailuki-Kahului sewage treatment system debated in public meetings, Lahaina Sun, February 21, 1973: 3.
— system detailed, Lahaina Sun, February 28, 1973: 1,4,5.
— missing chart ranking potential treatment sites discussed, Lahaina Sun, March 7, 1973: 9.
— system for Paia to be studied, Lahaina Sun, March 14, 1973: 11.
— Federal Environmental Protection Agency studies proposed sewage treatment plant at Kanaha, Lahaina Sun, March 14, 1973: 5.
— site for Wailuku-Kahului treatment plant approved by the Environmental Protection Agency, Lahaina Sun, May 23, 1973: 3.
— Kihei sewage disposal plant receives another approval, Lahaina Sun, July 11, 1973: 6.
— Mayor Tavares discusses sewer fee, Lahaina News, July 1, 1980: 6.
— Lahaina plant opened, Lahaina News, July 15, 1980: 6.
— dumping sewage in manholes no longer legal, Lahaina News, August 1, 1980: 7.
— fees discussed, Lahaina News, October 1, 1980: 13.
— mayor Tavares requests pause in proposed water treatment facility, Lahaina News, April 15, 1981: 14.
— bids requested for Napili-Honokowai sewage system, Lahaina News, April 15, 1982: 11.
— editorial criticizing cost of settling legal fight over sewers, Lahaina News, January 25, 1984: 2.
— mayor Tavares proposes plan, Lahaina News, March 5, 1986: 1.
— Napili Surf complex connected to, Lahaina News, March 12, 1986: 12.
— more wells planned despite algae growth, Lahaina News, March 19, 1992: 1.
— Maui Algae Bloom Task Force concerned with additional planned sewage injection wells, Lahaina News, March 26, 1992: 1,4.
— injection wells approved, Lahaina News, April 9, 1992: 1.
— Maui County public works director George Kaya denies spill, Lahaina News, April 16, 1992: 3.
— expansion of sewers delayed, Lahaina News, April 23, 1992: 1.
— correction from last issue: injection wells in fact approved, Lahaina News, April 30, 1992: 3.
— Environmental Protection Agency warns state Department of Health that wastewater system needs to be operational, Lahaina News, May 7, 1992: 3.

— divers call for halt to injection wells, Lahaina News, June 11, 1992: 1.

— gas smell near Maui Hard Rock Café, Lahaina News, July 2, 1992: 3.

— Robert Adams' fight to end smell from Kihei Wastewater Treatment Plant likely successful, Lahaina News, July 2, 1992: 8.

— Environmental Protection Agency wants bidding for injection well study , Lahaina News, July 2, 1992: 9.

— Ka'anapali sewage line has problems, Lahaina News, July 9, 1992: 1,8.

— poor upkeep at Lahaina Pump Station alleged, Lahaina News, July 16, 1992: 1.

— Maui County Council to ask Public Works director George Kaya about sewer main, Lahaina News, July 16, 1992: 1.

— retired chemist Eassie Miller comments on lack of effort to resolve issues with sewer lines, Lahaina News, July 23, 1992: 1.

— history of issues traced to 1987, Lahaina News, July 23, 1992: 1.

— new plant to be at Pu'unene, Lahaina News, July 23, 1992: 11.

— Mayor Linda Lingle critical of Lahaina News stories on problems, Lahaina News, July 30, 1992: 1.

— Maui County plans to reuse Kihei effluent, Lahaina News, July 30, 1992: 6,7.

— merchants seek better review of, Lahaina News, August 6, 1992: 1,3.

— county employee requests probe, Lahaina News, August 6, 1992: 3.

— County plans to videotape Front Street sewer line, Lahaina News, August 13, 1992: 4.

— union and Lahaina News editor advocate for reinstatement of William Carroll, who criticized wastewater facilities, Lahaina News, August 20, 1992: 1,3,16.

— problems revealed by video, Lahaina News, August 27, 1992: 1.

— main sewer feed pipe to be replaced by Selland Construction, Lahaina News, August 27, 1992: 4.

— Environmental Protection Agency forbids more injection wells, Lahaina News, September 3, 1992: 1.

— another spill occurs at Mala Wharf, Lahaina News, September 10, 1992: 1.

— spill at Mala Wharf probed by West Maui Taxpayers Association, Lahaina News, September 17, 1992: 1.

— Public Works department working on South Maui wastewater plan, Lahaina News, October 1, 1992: 13,14.

— bids to develop Lahaina Wastewater Treatment Facility low, Lahaina News, October 22, 1992: 10.

— number of spills in Maui County surpasses the six previous years , Lahaina News, October 29, 1992: 1.

— October issue of "Environment Hawaii" magazine will focus on issue of, Lahaina News, October 29, 1992: 3.

— spill reported on South Kihei Road, Lahaina News, November 19, 1992: 5.

— spill reported at Kilohana Drive, Lahaina News, November 26, 1992: 18.

— comments by West Maui Taxpayers Association, Lahaina News, January 21, 1993: 3.

— Maui likely to get fined for , Lahaina News, February 11, 1993: 1,3.

— update on issues, Lahaina News, February 25, 1993: 5.

— need to consider rules discussed in "Maui Building Guide 1993", Lahaina News, February 25, 1993: supplement14.

— county described as short-sighted, Lahaina News, March 4, 1993: 7.

— treatment high priority in Mayor Linda Lingle's budget, Lahaina News, March 18, 1993: 1,4.

— developers may have to reuse effluent, Lahaina News, March 18, 1993: 7.

— state approves expansion of Lahaina Wastewater Reclamation Facility, Lahaina News, March 25, 1993: 1.

— spill along Honoapi'ilani Highway, Lahaina News, March 25, 1993: 3.

— another spill into lagoon at Ka'anapali Resort reported, Lahaina News, April 1, 1993: 4.

— spill on Halama Street reported, Lahaina News, April 1, 1993: 7.

— fee to increase in Central Maui, Lahaina News, June 24, 1993: 4.

— spill on Kenolio Road, Lahaina News, July 1, 1993: 5.

— spill on South Kihei Road, Lahaina News, September 16, 1993: 8.

— spill at Lahaina Wastewater Reclamation Facility, Lahaina News, October 7, 1993: 3.

— pump station to be moved away from surf, Lahaina News, October 28, 1993: 1,12.

— spill along Honoapi'ilani Highway caused by pump failure, Lahaina News, November 25, 1993: 3.

— spills a top health concern in Lahaina, Lahaina News, December 9, 1993: 1,12.

— spill close to old Ka'anapali Airstrip, Lahaina News, February 17, 1994: 4.

— Wahikuli Terrace Park chosen as site for Waste Water Pump No. 3 by Department of Public Works and Waste Management, Lahaina News, March 17, 1994: 1,16.

— waste water line replacement along Honoapi'ilani Highway planned, Lahaina News, April 7, 1994: 4.

— improvements to system to affect traffic, Lahaina News, April 14, 1994: 1.

— meeting held concerning relocation of Lahaina Wastewater Pump Station No. 3, Lahaina News, May 12, 1994: 4.

— effluent sent into reservoir used to irrigate pineapple fields, Lahaina News, May 19, 1994: 1.

— wastewater transmission line replacement project resuming, Lahaina News, May 19, 1994: 6.

— Wahikuli residents oppose proposal to relocate pump station, Lahaina News, May 26, 1994: 1,20.

— Draft Environmental Assessment for proposed Lahaina Wastewater Pump Station 3 available, Lahaina News, July 21, 1994: 4.

— wastewater line replacement project finished, Lahaina News, August 18, 1994: 5.

— Environmental Protection Agency intends to issue more permits for injection wells, Lahaina News, October 6, 1994: 1.

— Sierra Club Legal Defense Fund concerned about proposed injection wells, Lahaina News, October 27, 1994: 5.

— human waste found in Lahaina Aquatic Center pool, Lahaina News, December 1, 1994: 1.

— Environmental Protection Agency to hold hearings on injection wells, Lahaina News, January 26, 1995: 6.

— Environmental Protection Agency hosts meetings on injection wells at Lahaina Wastewater Reclamation Facility, Lahaina News, February 9, 1995: 2.

— editorial opposing injection wells and supporting reclamation, Lahaina News, February 9, 1995: 3.

— work begins on pump station at Wahikuli Terrace Park, Lahaina News, March 23, 1995: 2.

— Ka'anapali Golf Course to use treated water, Lahaina News, June 15, 1995: 1.

— treatment plant improved, Lahaina News, August 31, 1995: 1,2.

— new treatment plant operational, Lahaina News, August 31, 1995: 7.

— proposed pump station in Wahikuli on schedule, Lahaina News, September 7, 1995: 2.

— highway lane to close for 6 months for installation of sewer line, Lahaina News, July 11, 1996: 3.

— Environmental Protection Agency warns that injection well flow may increase, Lahaina News, April 15, 1999: 1,16.

— County to hold meeting on plans to replace Front Street sewer line, Lahaina News, September 21, 2000: 1,6.

— county officials seek comments from residents on sewer project on Front Street, Lahaina News, October 5, 2000: 1,15.

— see also pollution

SEWARD, ROGER [COMEDIAN]
— to perform at Comedy Club and the Sports Page, Lahaina News, December 12, 1991: 20,21.

SEX ABUSE INTERVENTIONS, INC. [BUSINESS]
— sex abuse counseling available from, Lahaina News, December 13, 1989: 4.
— to hold workshop on campus safety, Lahaina News, July 17, 1997: 17.

SEXUAL ASSAULT CRISIS CENTER
— looking for volunteers, Lahaina News, September 28, 1983: 5,6.
— services described, Lahaina News, May 16, 1984: 9,10,11,12.

SEXUAL RESPONSIBILITY HAWAII
— to challenge sexual perversity, permissiveness and irresponsibility, Lahaina News, October 8, 1986: 3.
— Mike Gabbard spokesman for, Lahaina News, October 8, 1986: 3.

SGT. LEISURE [BUSINESS]
— expands, Lahaina News, October 29, 1992: 13.

SHABBAT
— services held, Lahaina News, December 3, 1986: 12.

SHACHU, SEIHA HOGAKU-KAI MIYAZAKI
— to perform Japanese folk music, Lahaina News, September 16, 1999: 12.

SHADIAN, MANER [ARTIST]
— work to be shown at Lahaina Arts Society's Old Jail Gallery, Lahaina News, September 28, 1988: 3.

SHADOW BOX, THE [PLAY]
— to be performed by Maui Community Theatre, Lahaina News, April 17, 1997: 13.
— to be performed at Iao Theater, Lahaina News, April 24, 1997: 12.
— run continues, Lahaina News, May 1, 1997: 16.
— reviewed, Lahaina News, May 1, 1997: 18.
— continues, Lahaina News, May 8, 1997: 16.

SHAGGY AND RAYVON [MUSICAL GROUP]
— to perform at Maui Summer Jam, Lahaina News, June 18, 1998: 17.

SHAKERS, THE [MUSICAL GROUP]
— to perform at Blue Tropix, Lahaina News, October 26, 1995: 11.

SHAKESPEARE, WILLIAM [WRITER]
— to be performed at Seabury Hall, Lahaina News, March 12, 1992: 21.
— "A Midsummer Night's Dream" to be performed at Hui No'eau Visual Arts Center, Lahaina News, July 30, 1992: 18.
— plays to be performed by Studio H'Poko, Lahaina News, August 13, 1992: 14,18.
— adaptations of to be performed in "Live Tonight, at the Bloge!", Lahaina News, April 1, 1993: 15.
— to be performed at Seabury Hall, Lahaina News, April 8, 1993: 11,12.
— "Twelfth Night" to be performed, Lahaina News, May 6, 1993: 19.
— "Shakespeare Under the Stars" to be performed by Studio H'Poko, Lahaina News, August 5, 1993: 11.
— to be performed by Studio H'Poko, Lahaina News, August 12, 1993: 14.
— birthday to be celebrated by Maui Academy of Performing Arts, Lahaina News, April 21, 1994: 16.
— "Much Ado About Nothing" to be performed by Studio H'Poko, Lahaina News, July 7, 1994: 15.
— actors from Oregon Shakespeare Festival to hold classes on, Lahaina News, December 15, 1994: 19.

SHALIT, LINDA
— appointed director of marketing of Ka'anapali Beach Resource Association, Lahaina News, December 30, 1993: 5,6.

SHALIT, STEVE
— appointed managing director of Westin Maui Hotel, Lahaina News, April 10, 1991: 6.
— elected chair of Maui Hotel Association, Lahaina News, June 18, 1992: 11.

SHANER, JANET [ARTIST]
— to exhibit at Lahaina Art Society show, Lahaina News, July 15, 1993: 12.

SHANGHAI CIRCUS, NEW [TROUPE]
— to perform at Maui Arts and Cultural Center, Lahaina News, March 2, 2000: 13.
— to perform at Maui Arts and Cultural Center, Lahaina News, March 8, 2001: 16.
— to perform at Maui Arts and Cultural Center, Lahaina News, February 28, 2002: 17.
— to perform at Maui Arts and Cultural Center, Lahaina News, March 6, 2003: 14.
— to perform at Maui Arts and Cultural Center, Lahaina News, March 6, 2003: 14.

SHANKARA [MUSICAL GROUP]
— releases new CD, Lahaina News, August 28, 2003: 16.

SHANNON, BARRY
— to co-host "Maui Mornings" on FM 101, Lahaina News, March 18, 1987: 18.

SHANNON, RANDY
— named head professional at Kapalua Bay Course, Lahaina News, August 23, 1989: 5.

SHANTI NILAYA
— organization described, Lahaina News, February 1, 1981: 2.

SHAOLIN ARTS SOCIETY
— to perform at Lahaina Cannery Mall, Lahaina News, January 23, 2003: 14.

SHAOLIN WARRIORS [TROUPE]
— to perform at Maui Arts and Cultural Center, Lahaina News, March 28, 2002: 21.

SHAPERS OF MA'ALAEA [BUSINESS]
— to open at Ma'alaea Harbor Village, Lahaina News, February 17, 2000: 13.

SHAPERS, THE [BUSINESS]
— to host Pohai Na Keiki Nalu, Lahaina News, July 4, 1996: 15.
— to host Pohai Na Keiki Nalu, Lahaina News, July 11, 1996: 12.
— results of contest, Lahaina News, July 18, 1996: 11.

SHAPIRO, GERRI
— opens Herbalife health nutrition center, Lahaina News, September 30, 1999: 11.

SHARK, BUD [ARTIST]
— to offer class in printmaking, Lahaina News, March 12, 1992: 21.

SHARK PIT
— surfing spot reviewed, Lahaina Sun, January 3, 1973: 18,19.

SHARKS
— bounty on, hoped for by Lahaina Kamaakina Fishing Association, Lahaina Sun, December 23, 1970: 11.
— around Maui, Lahaina Sun, January 17, 1973: 18.
— seen off beaches between Ka'anapali and Honokowai, Lahaina Sun, March 7, 1973: 5.
— Sightings, Lahaina Times, June, 1980 volume 4 number 5: 1.
— sightings in Lahaina Harbor, Lahaina Times, September, 1980 volume 4 number 8: 1.
— attack canoe off Lahaina, Lahaina Times, September, 1980 volume 4 number 8: 1, 7.
— appropriateness of hunt debated, following death of Marti Morrell, Lahaina News, December 5, 1991: 9.
— hunt for shark called off, Lahaina News, December 19, 1991: 11.
— legislative bill seeks eradication of, Lahaina News, February 13, 1992: 1,6.
— "The Great White Shark: Lonely Lord of the Sea" to be shown, Lahaina News, February 20, 1992: 16.
— Joe Souki backs shark hunting bill, Lahaina News, April 16, 1992: 1.

— study required before hunt, Lahaina News, June 18, 1992: 6.

— no hunt to be undertaken following shark attack, Lahaina News, March 25, 1993: 4.

— sighted off South Maui, Lahaina News, August 5, 1993: 5.

— Hawaiian ideas of, Lahaina News, November 7, 1996: 2.

— warning signs posted at Olowalu, Lahaina News, August 8, 2002: 1,20.

SHARKS, THE [MUSICAL GROUP]

— to perform at Moose McGillycuddy's, Lahaina News, March 6, 1991: 11.

— to perform at Moose McGillycuddy's, Lahaina News, August 1, 1991: 14.

— to perform at Moose McGillycuddy's, Lahaina News, September 5, 1991: 9.

SHARKTOOTH BREWERY AND STEAKHOUSE [RESTAURANT]

— opens at Ka'ahumanu Center, Lahaina News, January 4, 1996: 14.

— to offer bear at Oktoberfest, Lahaina News, October 2, 1997: 9.

SHARP, BARBARA [WRITER]

— publishes reprint of 1853 journal by William Mitchell Stenson, Lahaina News, July 4, 1991: B2,B3.

— receives thanks for volunteer work, Lahaina News, June 11, 1992: 4.

— transcribing historic documents from Lahaina Restoration Foundation, Lahaina News, April 10, 1997: 1,20.

— Lahaina Restoration Foundation research director featured, Lahaina News, December 13, 2001: 1,18.

— publishes third Lahaina mystery novel "The Right Time", Lahaina News, June 27, 2002: 5.

SHARP ENTERPRISES [BUSINESS]

— creates CD-ROM virtual tour of Maui, Lahaina News, June 28, 2001: 9.

SHARP, STUART [ARTIST]

— to exhibit at Village Gallery-Contemporary, Lahaina News, February 20, 1997: 13.

— to appear at Village Gallery Contemporary, Lahaina News, April 1, 1999: 16.

— to exhibit on Village Gallery Contemporary, Lahaina News, April 6, 2000: 16.

— to exhibit at Village Gallery Contemporary, Lahaina News, January 11, 2001: 3.

— to exhibit at Village Gallery Contemporary, Lahaina News, March 14, 2002: 16.

SHARPE, "AUNTIE" EMMA KAPIOLANI FARDEN [ENTERTAINER]

— performing in South America, Lahaina Sun, January 20, 1971: 7.

— nominated for national fellowship, Lahaina News, October 5, 1983: 10.

— to perform at the Sheraton Maui, Lahaina News, May 23, 1984: 9.10.11.

— career detailed, Lahaina News, February 13, 1985: 1,6,7.

— remembered, Lahaina News, August 19, 1987: 1,20.

— remembered, Lahaina News, August 19, 1987: 1,20.

— Kapiolani Hula Halau to perform at Lahaina Cannery Shopping Center, Lahaina News, August 10, 1988: 3.

— celebrates birthday; life recounted, Lahaina News, September 14, 1988: 9.

— celebrates 85th birthday, Lahaina News, September 13, 1989: 11.

— planning garage sale to support her Kapiolani Hula Halau, Lahaina News, May 9, 1990: 5.

— celebrates 86th birthday, Lahaina News, September 12, 1990: 17.

— hula dancer remembered, Lahaina News, September 26, 1991: 2.

— celebration of life of kumu hula to be held, Lahaina News, October 31, 1991: 3.

— tribute at Maui Lu Longhouse, Lahaina News, September 17, 1992: 16.

— legacy to be celebrated by Na Pua O Kapiolani Hula Studio, Lahaina News, February 14, 2002: 14,17.

SHARPE, BARBARA

— Lahaina Restoration Foundation researcher discusses history of whaling, Lahaina News, July 28, 1994: 3.

SHARPE, EMMA FARDEN

— see Sharpe, "Auntie" Emma Kapiolani Farden

SHARPER IMAGE [BUSINESS]

— opens in Whalers Village, Lahaina News, January 4, 1989: 10.

— holds weekly auctions, Lahaina News, September 20, 1989: 9.

— to hold auction to benefit Napili Fire and Ambulance Station, Lahaina News, December 26, 1990: 8.

SHATNER, WILLIAM

— to star in Dick Van Patten Celebrity Challenge, Lahaina News, November 27, 1997: 13.

SHAVE ICE [BOOK]

— written by Tom Stevens, Lahaina News, June 21, 1989: 7.

SHAW, OLA

— to lead West Maui Christian Men's Camp, Lahaina News, September 19, 2002: 19.

SHAW, SANDY

— nutritionist to speak at Stouffer Wailea Beach Resort, Lahaina News, March 19, 1992: 4.

SHAWHAN-ROYSTER, SANDRA

— principal of Nahienaena Elementary School featured, Lahaina News, April 28, 1994: 1,16.

SHAWN, B.B. [MUSICIAN]

— to perform at Hawai'i Guitar Festival, Lahaina News, June 12, 1997: 17.

— to perform at Hawai'i Guitar Festival, Lahaina News, June 12, 1997: 18.

SHAY, CLAUDIA

— discusses self-help housing project, Lahaina News, July 4, 1991: 9.

SHAY, MAURA

— manager of Westin Maui's Japanese guest services featured, Lahaina News, January 16, 1992: 8.

SHAYE, SAUL

— to lecture on holistic health and healing, Lahaina News, January 9, 1985: 3.

SHEARMAN, NANCY [ARTIST]

— to offer collage workshop at Hui No'eau Visual Arts Center, Lahaina News, March 7, 2002: 16.

SHEBS, LAURIE

— becomes member of American Chiropractic Association, Lahaina News, June 29, 1995: 10.

SHEEHAN, PATTY

— golfer's career described, Lahaina News, March 6, 1985: A10.

SHEELEY, JENNA

— Scholar/Athlete of the Week, Lahaina News, June 24, 1999: 6.

SHEELEY, JERROLD "CAPPY"

— paddler featured, Lahaina News, June 20, 1996: 7.

— career featured, Lahaina News, July 17, 1997: 3.

— joins Lowson and Associates, Lahaina News, March 30, 2000: 10.

SHEFTE, JAMES

— appointed vice president and general manager of Napili Kai Beach Club, Lahaina News, May 20, 1993: 7.

SHELDON, SABRINA

— Scholar/Athlete of the Week, Lahaina News, June 28, 2001: 14.

SHELL [BUSINESS]

— gas station opens, Lahaina News, July 16, 1998: 13.

— stations awarded Winning Combination Program Award from Shell Oil , Lahaina News, May 22, 2003: 8.

SHELL VACATIONS [BUSINESS]
— to open Off-Site Broker Preview Center, Lahaina News, October 31, 2002: 6.
— sales managers named, Lahaina News, December 12, 2002: 8.

SHELTERS
— need help, Lahaina News, November 22, 1989: 1.

SHELTON, JACK
— seeking donations for American Lung Association, Lahaina News, February 17, 1988: 3.
— to participate in TransAmerica Bicycle Trek to benefit American Lung Association, Lahaina News, March 16, 1988: 3.
— unable to complete bike trek due to job obligations, Lahaina News, April 6, 1988: 3.

SHELTON, ROB
— playground committee chair at King Kamehameha III School speaks of playground renovations, Lahaina News, April 3, 1991: 1.
— Lahainaluna High School Foundation to hold fundraiser, Lahaina News, November 15, 2001: 1,18.
— named new general manager of The Kapalua Villas, Lahaina News, September 25, 2003: 8.

SHELTON, THEA
— joins Royal Lahaina Resort as sales manager, Lahaina News, January 30, 1985: 18.
— appointed director of sales of Ka'anapali Beach Hotel, Lahaina News, August 5, 1987: 3.

SHEPHERD, SHIRLEY [ARTIST]
— works exhibited at Kula Lodge, Lahaina Sun, May 5, 1971: 3.
— art show at Lahaina Art Society gallery, Lahaina Sun, December 1, 1971: 13.

SHEPPARD, STEPHANIE
— activities in West Maui described, Lahaina News, June 20, 1990: 2.
— named director of development at Maui Academy of Performing Arts, Lahaina News, August 15, 1990: 7.

SHER, MIKE
— general manager of Hard Rock Cafe discusses Thanksgiving dinner for homeless and elderly, Lahaina News, November 7, 1991: 19.

SHERATON LUAU
— reopens, Lahaina News, August 16, 1989: 13.
— featured, Lahaina News, March 28, 1990: 14.

SHERATON MAUI HOTEL [BUSINESS]
— not affected by ILWU hotel strike, Lahaina Sun, November 11, 1970: 1.
— beach area tested for pollution, Lahaina Sun, December 16, 1970: 3.
— develops program to increase job awareness and skill development, Lahaina News, December 1, 1981: 7.
— Jesse Nakooka and Auntie Emma Sharpe to perform, Lahaina News, May 23, 1984: 9.10.11.
— names Ernest Nishizaki as general manager, Lahaina News, July 25, 1984: 14.
— Steven Holden named vice president and general manager , Lahaina News, September 19, 1984: 14.
— appoints John Karl as vice president and general manager, Lahaina News, August 28, 1985: 8.
— renovated, Lahaina News, August 6, 1986: 3.
— Luau Grounds refurbished, Lahaina News, September 3, 1986: 3.
— essay contest for Mom of the Year, Lahaina News, April 29, 1987: 3.
— luau featured, Lahaina News, October 25, 1989: 15.
— offering food credit to guests staying more than five days, Lahaina News, October 25, 1989: 8.
— to hold new nightly luaus, Lahaina News, July 4, 1990: 7.
— to host luau organized by Sam and Sharon Ako, Lahaina News, July 18, 1990: 12.
— Maui County Planning Department concerned over shorelines structures, plantings by, Lahaina News, August 15, 1991: 1.
— Maui County Public Works Department alleges landscaped within shoreline, Lahaina News, September 12, 1991: 1.
— to close for renovations, Lahaina News, January 19, 1995: 10.
— breaks ground on redevelopment, Lahaina News, May 18, 1995: 6.
— Department of Health investigating runoff from construction site at, Lahaina News, July 11, 1996: 1.
— alters footpath to Black Rock, Lahaina News, August 8, 1996: 2.
— announces new appointments, Lahaina News, August 22, 1996: 5.
— reopening with new restaurants, Lahaina News, November 7, 1996: 8,15.
— ready for soft reopening, Lahaina News, November 14, 1996: 1,20.
— new restaurants open, Lahaina News, December 5, 1996: 8.
— receives rebate from Maui Electric Company for energy efficiency, Lahaina News, April 3, 1997: 10.
— reopens after renovations, Lahaina News, April 10, 1997: 1,18.
— Hari Kojima films segment of "Let's Go Fishing" at, Lahaina News, July 24, 1997: 15.
— to host "Christmas Teen Dance", Lahaina News, December 18, 1997: 19.
— "Christmas Teen Dance" seeking chaperones, Lahaina News, December 25, 1997: 12.
— big waves have eroded beaches in front of, Lahaina News, February 12, 1998: 1,3.
— Maui County Council grants emergency Special Management Area, Lahaina News, April 30, 1998: 1,20.
— must obtain permits to keep steel pilings, Lahaina News, August 20, 1998: 3.
— to remove steel pilings, Lahaina News, September 3, 1998: 1,24.
— Maui County Council to inspect Pu'u Keka'a at, Lahaina News, April 1, 1999: 1,20.
— to sponsor Oktoberfest with Teralani catamaran, Lahaina News, October 14, 1999: 11.
— employees raise money for Visitor Industry Charity Walk, Lahaina News, May 18, 2000: 16.
— to hold "Sizzling Summer Saturdays", Lahaina News, July 20, 2000: 16.
— workers win Housekeeping Olympics, Lahaina News, September 21, 2000: 11.
— restaurant promotes Gerald Bahouth to general manager, Lahaina News, January 16, 2003: 9.
— introduces students to hospitality industry, Lahaina News, February 13, 2003: 9.
— featured, Lahaina News, June 5, 2003: 14.

SHERGOLD, CRAIG
— boy with incurable tumor hopes to receive enough get well cards to get into the Guinness Book of World Records, Lahaina News, April 11, 1990: 3.

SHERMAN, DAVO [ARTIST]
— see Davo [artist]

SHERMAN, NANCY
— named as executive director of Theatre Theatre Maui, Lahaina News, October 13, 1994: 7.

SHERO-MARUYAMA, PATRICK
— service to be held for, Lahaina News, August 6, 1998: 20.

SHIBAO, GILBERT
— running Lahaina Pop Warner football, Lahaina News, September 26, 2002: 12.

SHIBAO, KA'EO KIYOKO
— wins Cinderella Miss Division, Lahaina News, April 11, 2002: 3.

SHIBATA, MYLES
— appointed manager of Westin Kaua'i, Lahaina News, August 30, 1989: 5.

SHIBUYA, KEITH
— appointed group service manager at Kapalua Bay Hotel, Lahaina News, October 11, 1989: 5.

SHIELD, JAN [PROFESSOR]
— presentations at Old Jail Gallery, Lahaina News, July 31, 1985: 11.

SHIELDS, BEVERLY
— awarded First Lady's Outstanding Volunteer Service Award, Lahaina News, May 2, 1990: 4.

SHIELDS, BROOKE [ACTOR]
— to perform in "Vagina Monologues", Lahaina News, February 7, 2002: 16.

SHIELDS, JACKIE
— promoted to head of shipping at Lahaina Printsellers, Lahaina News, May 16, 1990: 6.

SHIGELLOSIS
— see dysentery

SHIKUMA, RAE
— county water director quits, Lahaina News, December 26, 1991: 5.
— appointed deputy director of the state Commission on Water Resource Management, Lahaina News, February 6, 1992: 4.

SHIM, LOREN
— new general manager at The Whaler on Ka'anapali Beach, Lahaina News, July 31, 2003: 8.

SHIM, NANCY [LIBRARIAN]
— work at Lahaina Library featured, Lahaina News, August 28, 1985: 1,9.
— promoted to Program Coordinator for all Maui Public Libraries, Lahaina News, July 15, 1987: 3.

SHIMABAKURO, GARY
— Laulima Hawaii President to speak to Maui Chamber of Commerce, Lahaina News, February 20, 1997: 11.

SHIMABUKURO, CLYDE
— owner of Clyde's Shoes and The Sandal Shop to retire, Lahaina News, August 8, 1991: 9.

SHIMABUKURO, JAKE [MUSICIAN]
— to perform at "The Art of the Solo 'Ukulele", Lahaina News, March 28, 2002: 19.
— to perform at Kapalua Seafood Festival, Lahaina News, June 12, 2003: 18.
— to perform at Kapalua Seafood Festival, Lahaina News, June 26, 2003: 16.
— to perform at Kapalua Seafood Festival, Lahaina News, July 10, 2003: 14.

SHIMABUKURO, ROBERT
— candidate for Maui Council discusses positions, Lahaina Sun, August 23, 1972: 9.

SHIMADA, DEAN
— most valuable player on Maui Junior Davis Cup Team, Lahaina News, July 19, 1989: 5.

SHIMOMURA, KEVIN
— wins World Junior Masters Golf Championships, Lahaina News, August 31, 2000: 6.

SHIMOZONO, JIM
— appointed general manager of Amfac Maui, Lahaina News, April 25, 1996: 12.

SHINER, SANDRA
— psychotherapist to speak at Business and Professional Women's monthly luncheon, Lahaina News, October 24, 1996: 14.
— psychotherapist to speak at Business and Professional Women, Lahaina News, October 24, 1996: 14.

SHINN, T.S. "UNCLE"
— mayor Cravalho may join him in visit to mainland China, Lahaina Sun, November 24, 1971: 1.

SHINNEN ENKAI
— celebration to be held, Lahaina News, January 16, 1992: 5.
— to be held by Japanese Cultural Society, Lahaina News, January 9, 2003: 16.

SHINTANI, TERRY
— employees at Ka'anapali Beach Hotel following diet developed by, Lahaina News, November 25, 1993: 1,3.

SHINYAMA, BRANDI
— to compete in Chrysanthemum Ball, Lahaina News, November 28, 1996: 3.

SHIPPING
— barge rate challenged, Lahaina Sun, August 4, 1971: 1,2.
— Matson container ship bringing emergency supplies from Canada is delayed, Lahaina Sun, September 29, 1971: 13.

SHIRELLES, THE [MUSICAL GROUP]
— to perform to benefit Hawaii Firefighters Association, Lahaina News, November 13, 1997: 21.

SHIRO MORI QUARTET [MUSICAL GROUP]
— to perform at Blackie's Bar, Lahaina News, January 31, 1990: 13.
— to perform at Blackie's Bar, Lahaina News, April 11, 1990: 15.
— to perform at Blackie's Bar, Lahaina News, May 2, 1990: 15.
— to perform at Blackie's Bar, Lahaina News, October 24, 1990: 15.

SHIRO MORI QUINTET [MUSICAL GROUP]
— to perform at Blackie's Bar, Lahaina News, June 6, 1991: 14.

SHIROHARA, NOBU
— appointed president of CM Holding Corporation, Lahaina News, November 5, 1992: 8.

SHISHIDO, MILES
— to disxcuss "Japanese Gardens and Values", Lahaina News, September 17, 1992: 8.

SHITO, MITSUO
— responds to firing of John "Eddy" Nelson, Lahaina News, December 19, 1990: 1,4.

SHO CHIKU BAI FESTIVAL
— to be held, Lahaina News, June 23, 1994: 11.

SHOCK WAVE STUDIO [BUSINESS]
— featured, Lahaina News, February 13, 1985: 13.

SHOEBOX SCULPTURE EXHIBITION
— to be held at Maui Arts and Cultural Center, Lahaina News, December 5, 2002: 20.

SHOGREN, ANN
— joins Physical Therapy Care, Lahaina News, May 31, 1989: 15.

SHOPE, RICHARD [ARTIST]
— to perform "Mars, Mime, and Mythology", Lahaina News, June 22, 1995: 12.

SHOPS AT WAILEA, THE
— opening, Lahaina News, November 30, 2000: 12.
— more stores open at, Lahaina News, January 4, 2001: 14.
— grand opening held, Lahaina News, March 15, 2001: 8.
— continues to hold "WOW! Wailea On Wednesday—A Festival of the Arts", Lahaina News, July 19, 2001: 17.
— continues to hold "WOW! Wailea On Wednesday—A Festival of the Arts", Lahaina News, September 6, 2001: 17.
— to offer live entertainment, Lahaina News, November 1, 2001: 17.
— continues to offer "WOW—Wailea On Wednesdays", Lahaina News, February 7, 2002: 17.
— offering music, Lahaina News, December 19, 2002: 20.

SHOPSHEAR, CHRIS
— dubbed ugliest bartender of Maui in fundraiser for American Cancer Society, Lahaina News, January 18, 1989: 3.

SHORELINE EROSION
— in West Maui, discussed, Lahaina News, August 3, 1988: 1,18.
— see also sea walls

SHORELINE TRANSPORTATION [BUSINESS]
— begins island-wide bus service, Lahaina News, June 4, 1986: 3.
— in conflict with Roberts Tours and Transportation fight over buses in West Maui, Lahaina News, November 12, 1986: 1,8.
— acquires new buses, Lahaina News, May 20, 1987: 10.
— declares bankruptcy, Lahaina News, July 22, 1987: 1.
— goes out business, Lahaina News, December 16, 1987: 1.
— sues Roberts Tours and Transportation for unfair trade practices, Lahaina News, June 22, 1988: 1.

SHORT, BO [MUSICIAN]
— to perform at Greek Zorba, Lahaina News, May 25, 1995: 12.

SHORTRIDGE, STEPHEN CHARLES [ARTIST]
— to exhibit at Gallerie Hawaii, Lahaina News, January 9, 2003: 17.

SHORTY, GUITAR [MUSICIAN]
— to perform at Maui Arts and Cultural Center, Lahaina News, August 1, 1996: 21.

SHOSTAKOVICH STRING QUARTET [MUSICAL GROUP]
— to perform at St. Anthony Church, Lahaina News, February 14, 1990: 15.

SHOTOKAN KARATE-DO
— students from advance , Lahaina News, June 27, 2002: 12.

SHOW OF STARS
— to be held at Maui Arts and Cultural Center, Lahaina News, August 13, 1998: 16.

SHOWCASE [PERFORMANCE]
— to be performed by Brigham Young University-Hawaii, Lahaina News, May 16, 1996: 10.

SHOWER OF STARS TALENT CONTEST
— to be held at Lahaina Cannery Mall, Lahaina News, August 1, 1990: 11.
— main competition to be held, Lahaina News, August 8, 1990: 13.
— presented by Lahaina Kiwanis Club, Lahaina News, August 22, 1990: 11.
— Lahaina Kiwanis Club to hold talent show, Lahaina News, August 13, 1992: 4.
— Taylor Jean Trout succeeds at, Lahaina News, August 28, 2003: 3.

SHOWMAKER, JOHN [ARTIST]
— to exhibit at Village Gallery, Lahaina News, November 1, 2001: 16.

SHRADER AND MARTINEZ CONSTRUCTION INC. [BUSINESS]
— fined for using unlicensed workers when building Planet Hollywood, Lahaina News, July 21, 1994: 1.
— Planet Hollywood contractor denied chance to change plea , Lahaina News, September 15, 1994: 5.

SHRIMP
— aquaculture project described, Lahaina Sun, January 20, 1971: 4.

SHRINER'S HOSPITAL
— to hold Onion Sale for Patient Transportation fund, Lahaina News, April 29, 1999: 16.

SHTAM, ALEX
— Scholar/Athlete of the Week, Lahaina News, October 30, 1997: 6.

SHULER HOMES, INC. [BUSINESS]
— earnings report, Lahaina News, August 5, 1993: 7.
— announces top producers, Lahaina News, August 15, 2002: 8.

SHULMAN, EVAN [MUSICIAN]
— featured, Lahaina News, January 16, 1992: 12.

SHULTZ, MARK
— Captain of the Year at Lahaina Harbor, Lahaina News, February 17, 1994: 8.

SHUMANN, WOLFGANG
— recounts experience fall of Berlin wall, Lahaina News, January 17, 1990: 5.

SIAROT, ROBERT
— engineer details alternatives for easing traffic issues, Lahaina News, May 21, 1986: 1,11.
— Maui Distinct Engineer describes state priorities for Lahaina, Lahaina News, August 20, 1992: 3.
— Highway Division's chief engineer for Maui says locations for new emergency phones not selected yet, Lahaina News, June 1, 1995: 12.
— updates on highway widening, Lahaina News, November 12, 1998: 1.
— Department of Transportation meets with residents to discuss highway project issues, Lahaina News, March 30, 2000: 5.
— Lahaina Intermediate School teacher honored by TS Restaurants, Lahaina News, June 13, 2002: 5.
— Lahaina Intermediate School technology coordinator discusses programs, Lahaina News, May 22, 2003: 1,18.

SIBLEY, SCOTT
— named executive chef at Maui Marriott, Lahaina News, October 24, 1991: 8.
— chef at Maui Marriott Resort featured, Lahaina News, October 31, 1991: 16,17.
— chef featured, Lahaina News, August 1, 1996: 6,7.

SIDDHA MEDITATION
— to be demonstrated at Maui Community College, Lahaina News, January 2, 1985: 3.

SIDE SHOWS [PLAY]
— to be performed at Seabury Hall Performance Studio, Lahaina News, May 17, 2001: 20.
— to be performed at Seabury Hall, Lahaina News, May 16, 2002: 16.

SIDEWALK
— planned in Lahaina historic district, Lahaina Sun, May 19, 1971: 7.

SIEGFRIED, MAGGIE [MUSICIAN]
— to perform at Borders Books, Lahaina News, July 15, 1999: 13.
— to perform at Borders Books, Lahaina News, October 7, 1999: 16.
— to perform at Borders Books, Lahaina News, June 15, 2000: 16.

SIEMER, JOHN
— manager of Pioneer Mill discusses problem of water disposal at Pioneer Mill, Lahaina Sun, November 11, 1970: 1.
— manager of Pioneer Mill is new president of Lahaina Rotary Club, Lahaina Sun, July 28, 1971: 10.
— manager of Pioneer Mill criticizes "freeloaders", Lahaina Sun, May 23, 1973: 5.

SIERRA CLUB
— criticizes strict new camping rules, Lahaina Sun, December 29, 1971: 18.
— sponsor Jim Boll speaking on "The Different Desert: New Mexico's White Sands National Monument", Lahaina News, May 27, 1987: 3.
— to meet , Lahaina News, June 24, 1987: 3.
— showing "Beautiful are the People of Hawaii" at meeting, Lahaina News, July 22, 1987: 10.
— honors Hui Alanui O Makena as Conservationists of the Year, Lahaina News, November 11, 1987: 11.
— opposes thrillcraft use, Lahaina News, August 10, 1988: 16.
— suing to stop thrillcrafts, Lahaina News, December 21, 1988: 1.
— sponsoring climb to "Wailuku Cross", Lahaina News, April 10, 1991: 4.
— sponsoring climb to Wailuku Cross, Lahaina News, April 17, 1991: 7.

— organizing hike to Moku Mana bird sanctuary, Lahaina News, May 1, 1991: 5.

— to lead hike to Hanaula Summit, Lahaina News, May 15, 1991: 4.

— to eradicate gorse and replant native plants, Lahaina News, June 13, 1991: 6.

— leading hike of Old Lahaina Trail, Lahaina News, August 6, 1992: 9.

— hosting Hoʻo Kaulana Hawaii Annual Art Showing, Lahaina News, February 25, 1993: 9.

— prepared to serve county notice to stop violating the Clean Water Act, Lahaina News, July 15, 1993: 1,3.

— Legal Defense Fund has not served notice to the county, Lahaina News, December 30, 1993: 3.

— to meet, Lahaina News, December 29, 1994: 2.

— to hold meeting, Lahaina News, January 12, 1995: 4.

— to hold meeting, Lahaina News, January 19, 1995: 4.

— to host pool hike, Lahaina News, May 16, 1996: 10.

— to train hike leaders, Lahaina News, February 6, 1997: 15.

— to hold benefit whale watch cruise, Lahaina News, February 27, 1997: 10,11.

— teams to explore East Maui streams, Lahaina News, June 5, 1997: 16.

— to help clean Hoʻokipa Beach Park, Lahaina News, July 10, 1997: 17.

— to produce video on value of Maʻalaea, Lahaina News, July 31, 1997: 15.

— holding "Skyline Trail Star Hike", Lahaina News, July 31, 1997: 16.

— to hold workshop on Hawaii's environmental laws, Lahaina News, September 11, 1997: 17.

— to hold "Palauea Beach Party", Lahaina News, March 26, 1998: 13.

— to offer hike at Maʻalaea Bay, Lahaina News, March 26, 1998: 7.

— to hold "Palauea Beach Party", Lahaina News, April 2, 1998: 16.

— to hold update on Kahului Airport, Lahaina News, April 9, 1998: 16.

— to hold whale watch benefit, Lahaina News, April 9, 1998: 17.

— hosting benefit for Adopt-a-Buoy program, Lahaina News, April 16, 1998: 12.

— to show film "In God's Hand", Lahaina News, April 16, 1998: 13.

— to show film "The Stream That Built a Town", Lahaina News, April 16, 1998: 13.

— to hold "Keep Hawaii Beautiful Day", Lahaina News, April 23, 1998: 16.

— opens environmental education office, Lahaina News, February 18, 1999: 12.

— offering beach hike, Lahaina News, March 4, 1999: 12.

— to hold "Malama Kahakai", Lahaina News, April 22, 1999: 12.

— planning a hike to Wailua Iki, Lahaina News, May 6, 1999: 20.

— to host hike into Waikamoi Forest, Lahaina News, June 10, 1999: 17.

— to lead hike to Kealia National Wildlife Refuge, Lahaina News, October 21, 1999: 16.

— leading hike into Iao Valley, Lahaina News, October 28, 1999: 16.

— to hold Coastal Heritage Day, Lahaina News, October 28, 1999: 6.

— to honor Mary Evanson and Dan Reeser, Lahaina News, November 4, 1999: 12.

— to host Hana Cave Tour, Lahaina News, November 4, 1999: 12.

— planning Banana Poka service trip, Lahaina News, December 9, 1999: 20.

— to hold "Vision 2000" meeting, Lahaina News, January 27, 2000: 12.

— to hold service trip to Waihou Springs Trail, Lahaina News, February 3, 2000: 13.

— leading hike to Maʻalaea Kiʻipohaku, Lahaina News, February 10, 2000: 16.

— to hold beach cleanup at Hamoa/Koki, Lahaina News, February 24, 2000: 16.

— to hold Kanaio Reserve Native Plant Hike, Lahaina News, March 9, 2000: 12.

— to hold Full Moon Pali Hike, Lahaina News, March 16, 2000: 12.

— to hold "We Love Palauea Party" with Maui Tomorrow, Lahaina News, April 6, 2000: 16.

— planning hike to Hanaʻula/Kealaloa Ridge, Lahaina News, May 25, 2000: 19.

— National Stream Clean-up Day to focus on Iao Stream, Lahaina News, June 8, 2000: 20.

— to hold Wailua Iki Water Hike, Lahaina News, June 15, 2000: 16.

— to hold hike to Polipoli , Lahaina News, June 22, 2000: 16.

— holding star watch with Harriet Witt-Miller, Lahaina News, July 27, 2000: 20.

— to hold tour of Piʻilani Heiau and National Botanical Garden at Kahanu, Lahaina News, August 3, 2000: 16.

— to hold hike to Makapipi Water, Lahaina News, August 10, 2000: 16.

— organizing hike to Paʻuwela Point shoreline, Lahaina News, October 12, 2000: 20.

— to hold hike to Waikamoi/Makawao Forest, Lahaina News, October 26, 2000: 28.

— organizing project to pull alien pine seedlings, Lahaina News, December 14, 2000: 20.

— to hold Annual Meeting, Lahaina News, January 11, 2001: 3.

— to hold hike over the rough lava of the King's Highway, Lahaina News, January 11, 2001: 3.

— to organize bird watching with Lance Tanino, Lahaina News, January 25, 2001: 16.

— to lead hike to Native Hawaiian petroglyphs, Lahaina News, February 8, 2001: 20.

— to hold hike to Waihee Ridge, Lahaina News, February 22, 2001: 16.

— plans snorkel outing at Kahekili Park, Lahaina News, March 8, 2001: 16.

— planning hike in Kanaio to the Tibetan Buddhist Retreat Center, Lahaina News, March 15, 2001: 20.

— to hold hike to Kealia National Wildlife Refuge, Lahaina News, April 12, 2001: 20.

— to celebrate Earth Day with "We Love the Gardens Day", Lahaina News, April 19, 2001: 16.

— to hold coastal clean-up, Lahaina News, April 26, 2001: 20.

— offering Maui Cave Adventure at Kaʻeleku Caverns, Lahaina News, May 3, 2001: 20.

— to hold Oheo Service Trip, Lahaina News, May 10, 2001: 20.

— hiking to Papaʻanea Reservoir, Lahaina News, May 24, 2001: 20.

— organizing work on archaeological sites, Lahaina News, July 5, 2001: 16.

— to hold clean-up at Pauwela Point, Lahaina News, July 19, 2001: 16.

— to hold anniversary clinic, Lahaina News, August 2, 2001: 2.

— to hold Hana Cave tour at Kaʻeleku Caverns, Lahaina News, September 20, 2001: 17.

— to lead hike to Puʻu Mahoe, Lahaina News, September 27, 2001: 16.

— to hold "Earth-in-Space Adventure benefit, Lahaina News, July 4, 2002: 18.

— to host "Earth-in-Space Adventure" with writer Harriet Witt, Lahaina News, July 11, 2002: 16.

— planning hike to Waikamoi Stream, Lahaina News, July 25, 2002: 20.

— honors Lucienne DeNaie, Lahaina News, October 3, 2002: 9.

— to hold hike to Keoneʻoʻio (La Perouse Bay), Lahaina News, December 12, 2002: 21.

SIFTON, CLIFF

— discusses shrimp aquaculture project, Lahaina Sun, January 20, 1971: 4.

SIGEL, JAY

— wins EMC2 Kaʻanapali Classic, Lahaina News, October 29, 1998: 32.

SIGMUND, ERIC

— to lecture on fulfillment, Lahaina News, December 14, 1988: 16.

— to discuss "Hoʻoponopono: A Traditional Hawaiian Practice for Setting Relationships Right", Lahaina News, January 21, 1999: 11.

SIGN LANGUAGE
— interpreter workshop to be held, Lahaina News, October 21, 1987: 3.

SIGN SOLUTIONS [BUSINESS]
— awarded Jaiom Berger Aluminum Man perpetual trophy, Lahaina News, April 12, 2001: 14.

SIGNAGE
— conflict between Maui Historic Commission and Ken Russell, Lahaina Sun, November 18, 1970: 3.
— conflict between Maui Historic Commission and Ken Russell, Lahaina Sun, November 25, 1970: 1.
— conflict between Maui Historic Commission and Ken Russell, Lahaina Sun, January 13, 1971: 1,2.
— rules studied, Lahaina Sun, May 19, 1971: 5.
— political signs banned on Maui, Lahaina Sun, May 26, 1971: 1.
— bumper sticker law may be unconstitutional, Lahaina Sun, June 2, 1971: 1.
— Maui Historic Commission decides on new rules, Lahaina Sun, June 23, 1971: 1.
— new signs approved, Lahaina Sun, June 30, 1971: 8.
— Maui County Council works committee recommends removing stop sign on Pu'unene Ave., Lahaina Sun, November 17, 1971: 14.
— Foodland likely has only revolving sign in Maui, Lahaina Sun, December 15, 1971: 15.
— correcting earlier story, Lahaina Shell station also has a revolving sign, Lahaina Sun, December 22, 1971: 2.
— State rejects highway markers in Lahaina, Lahaina Sun, January 12, 1972: 15.
— illegal parking signs in Lahaina may be removed, Lahaina Sun, February 16, 1972: 13.
— sandwich sign business in Lahaina criticized, Lahaina Sun, May 10, 1972: 3.
— Maui Historic Commission recommends denying permit for sandwich board signs, Lahaina Sun, May 17, 1972: 7.
— walking billboards debated, Lahaina Sun, June 21, 1972: 3.
— installed on Front Street despite Maui Historic Commission's objection, Lahaina Sun, June 28, 1972: 4.
— defies Maui Historic Commission ruling, Lahaina Sun, July 19, 1972: 7.
— rules against political signs challenged by Peggy Ross, Republican candidate for mayor, Lahaina Sun, August 2, 1972: 9.
— requests for signs on Front Street debated, Lahaina Sun, August 23, 1972: 5.
— ordinance banning political signs ruled unconstitutional, Lahaina Sun, November 1, 1972: 5.
— Maui Historical Commission no longer has power to regular, Lahaina Sun, May 9, 1973: 3.
— law proposed to give Maui Historic Commission specific controls, Lahaina Sun, May 23, 1973: 4.

SILKS IN PARADISE [BUSINESS]
— opens at Lahaina Center, Lahaina News, October 17, 1990: 11.

SILLIMAN, RON [POET]
— at Artful Dodger's Feed'N'Read, Lahaina News, February 10, 1988: 11.

SILVA, ANNA [MUSICIAN]
— to sing with the Maui Symphony Pops, Lahaina News, September 16, 1993: 17,18.

SILVA, CHARLIE
— awarded Makana O Maui Award for June, Lahaina News, October 10, 1990: 12.

SILVA, JACUELINE
— Billabong Pro Maui competition held, Lahaina News, December 19, 2002: 1,12.

SILVA, MARIO
— boxer plans to return, Lahaina Sun, February 16, 1972: 5.
— boxer scheduled fight in Maui, Lahaina Sun, February 23, 1972: 13.

SILVA, NOENOE
— to speak on petitions opposing annexation, Lahaina News, August 27, 1998: 3.

SILVA, WENDALL
— becomes executive director of State Foundation on Culture and the Arts , Lahaina News, January 31, 1990: 14.

SILVER CLOUD LIMO [BUSINESS]
— described, Lahaina News, March 2, 1988: 8.

SILVER DIFFUSER
— used by Pioneer Mill, Lahaina Sun, December 2, 1970: 1.
— installed at sugar cane plantation near Paia, Lahaina Sun, December 2, 1970: 1,4.

SILVER JUBILEE DAY
— food booths offered, Lahaina News, May 23, 1984: 5.

SILVER LININGS [BUSINESS]
— opens in Lahaina Cannery Mall, Lahaina News, September 13, 2001: 8.

SILVERSWORD GOLF COURSE
— groundbreaking for, Lahaina News, October 1, 1986: 5.

SILVERSWORD WOMEN'S GOLF CLUB
— to hold invitational tournament, Lahaina News, November 9, 1988: 3.
— results, Lahaina News, August 1, 1990: 14.
— results, Lahaina News, September 3, 1992: 6.

SIMIEN, TERRANCE
— Zydeco master to perform at Maui Arts and Cultural Center, Lahaina News, February 20, 2003: 17.

SIMON, ABBY [MUSICIAN]
— plays at Baldwin Auditorium with Honolulu Symphony, Lahaina Sun, November 11, 1970: 1.

SIMON, JOSE [COMEDIAN]
— to perform at Comedy Club and the Sports Page, Lahaina News, April 30, 1992: 13,15.
— to perform at Maui Comedy Club, Lahaina News, August 17, 1995: 12.

SIMON, MARK
— new director of marketing for Four Seasons Resort Maui, Lahaina News, June 14, 2001: 8.

SIMONE, CAROLE [WRITER]
— author of "Goddess of 5th Avenue" to speak at Borders Books, Lahaina News, March 7, 2002: 16.

SIMONE-ALLEMANN, ANASTASIA
— wins "Most Original" lei, Lahaina News, May 20, 1999: 15.

SIMONS, CLARENCE ALFRED "SI"
— Lahaina Rotary Club member honored on 95th birthday, Lahaina News, November 23, 1995: 4.
— memorialized, Lahaina News, November 7, 1996: 9.
— passes away, Lahaina News, December 18, 1997: 1,2.

SIMONS, MICHAEL
— certified public accountant acquires accounting practice of Thomas Marino, Lahaina News, January 9, 1992: 8.

SIMONSEN, VALERIE
— to discuss homeopathy, Lahaina News, March 18, 1999: 16.
— to explain First Aid Hypnotherapy, Lahaina News, April 22, 1999: 13.
— to speak on hepatitis, Lahaina News, October 14, 1999: 13.
— to talk on "Holiday Blues Busters", Lahaina News, November 4, 1999: 13.
— to talk "We Live On What We Pour Out", Lahaina News, July 13, 2000: 16,17.

SIMPICH JR, FREDERICK
— presents on Hawaii's uncelebrated immigrants for the Lahaina Restoration Foundation, Lahaina Sun, March 15, 1972: 10.

SIMPLE PLEASURES [RESTAURANT]
— opened in summer, Lahaina News, December 11, 1997: 10.

SIMPSON, FRED [DANCER]
— performance hosted by Maui Dance Council, Lahaina News, April 28, 1994: 15.

SIMS, PAT [ARTIST]
— quilter's detailed, Lahaina News, April 10, 1997: 2.

SINATRA, FRANK [MUSICIAN]
— to perform at Aloha Stadium, Lahaina News, July 9, 1986: 3.

SINCLAIR, JAMES
— to speak on "Shipwreck Treasures" at Maui Ocean Center, Lahaina News, March 1, 2001: 16.

SINDBAD [BUSINESS]
— opens, Lahaina News, July 22, 1993: 7.

SINDELAR, JOEY
— wins Kapalua Challenge golf tournament, Lahaina News, November 25, 1999: 9.

SING, JIMMY TAN
— diver recovered black coral trees off of Maui, Lahaina Sun, December 23, 1970: 2.

SING OUT MAUI
— youth singing group from Maui described, Lahaina Sun, November 1, 1972: 9.

SING, TRACEY TAM
— to discuss research on Moku'ula , Lahaina News, May 27, 1999: 12.

SINGER, DENNIS
— surfer featured in Wetscreams [film], Lahaina Times, August, 1980 volume 4 number 7: 5.
— featured in Surfer magazine, Lahaina Times, October, 1980 volume 4 number 9: 2.

SINGER, EUGENE
— honored by the Tag and Label Manufacturers Institute, Inc., Lahaina News, April 16, 1992: 14.

SINGER, HERSH
— to speak to American Marketing Association's Maui Chapter, Lahaina News, February 20, 1985: 3.

SINGER, JOHN
— flautist to participate in "Blowing Zen" presentation, Lahaina News, February 23, 1995: 12.

SINGER, LIZ [ARTIST]
— to exhibit Banyan Tree Gallery, Lahaina News, February 11, 1993: 14.
— to offer drawing workshop at Art School at Kapalua, Lahaina News, February 17, 2000: 8.
— to offer drawing workshop at The Art School at Kapalua, Lahaina News, January 25, 2001: 16.

SINGH, SANT THAKAR
— to teach meditation, Lahaina News, March 18, 1999: 16.
— representatives to offer meditation classes, Lahaina News, August 19, 1999: 17.
— representatives of to offer free meditation instruction, Lahaina News, May 23, 2002: 16.

SINGLES IN PARADISE [BUSINESS]
— hosting mixer, Lahaina News, February 3, 2000: 12.
— opens, Lahaina News, February 10, 2000: 15.

SINSKEY, ROBERT
— winemaker to host event at Plantation House Restaurant, Lahaina News, September 3, 1998: 20.

SINTON, JOHN
— offering lecture on Haleakala's past and future volcanic activity, Lahaina News, October 9, 1997: 21.
— to speak on Haleakala, Lahaina News, October 16, 1997: 16.

SIR WILFRED'S COFFEE SHOP [RESTAURANT]
— celebrating grand opening, Lahaina News, June 17, 1987: 3.
— features jazz music, Lahaina News, January 9, 1992: 14.
— to celebrate 20 years, Lahaina News, January 16, 1997: 14.
— sponsors chess tournament, Lahaina News, April 1, 1999: 8.
— to hold chess tournament, Lahaina News, November 9, 2000: 24.
— to hold chess tournament, Lahaina News, September 12, 2002: 21.
— to hold chess tournament, Lahaina News, September 19, 2002: 24.
— celebrating 25 years, Lahaina News, January 16, 2003: 8.
— to host chess tournament, Lahaina News, February 13, 2003: 16.

SISGOLD, STEVE [WRITER]
— to teach workshop on manifestation, Lahaina News, February 6, 1997: 14.
— to offer "Living in Passion and Purpose" workshop, Lahaina News, June 19, 1997: 16.
— to lead workshop "Re-Creation 1999—Preparing for the New Millennium", Lahaina News, December 31, 1998: 13.
— to premiere documentary "Holocaust In My Body", Lahaina News, January 11, 2001: 2.

SISTA MONICA PARKER [MUSICIAN]
— to perform at Casanova's, Lahaina News, April 25, 1996: 17.
— to perform at Maui Brews, Lahaina News, September 28, 2000: 2.
— to perform at Maui Brews, Lahaina News, September 28, 2000: 2.

SISTER ANTOINETTE
— featured, Lahaina News, May 1, 1997: 1,18.

SISTERS OF ST. FRANCIS
— leaving the Maria Lanakila Church parish and Sacred Hearts School, Lahaina News, June 8, 2000: 1,7.

SIXX, NIKKI [MUSICIAN]
— purchases work by Christian Riese Lassen, Lahaina News, April 3, 1991: 10.

SKAGGS, RICKY [MUSICIAN]
— to perform at Lahaina Civic Auditorium, Lahaina News, September 3, 1992: 15.
— to perform at Lahaina Civic Auditorium, Lahaina News, September 10, 1992: 17.

SKATEBOARDING
— discussed, Lahaina Times, June, 1980 volume 5 number 5: 1.
— plan for park postponed, Lahaina News, November 18, 1993: 5.
— illegal on roadways, Lahaina News, March 2, 1995: 3.
— temporary park to be established near Lahaina Aquatic Center, Lahaina News, March 26, 1998: 1.
— benefit planned for park, Lahaina News, April 16, 1998: 3.
— event to support park, Lahaina News, April 30, 1998: 1.
— editorial in favor of park, Lahaina News, May 7, 1998: 4.
— efforts to create park continue, Lahaina News, May 14, 1998: 8.
— pros support skate park, Lahaina News, May 21, 1998: 1,20.
— part to be ready, Lahaina News, June 4, 1998: 3.
— Maui Council seeking group to run skateboard park, Lahaina News, June 18, 1998: 1,20.
— park needs to secure insurance, Lahaina News, July 9, 1998: 1.
— skateboard park to open, Lahaina News, July 23, 1998: 1,20.
— fundraiser for park to be held, Lahaina News, August 13, 1998: 1.
— benefit for skate park postponed, Lahaina News, August 20, 1998: 1,20.
— West Maui Youth Center advocates expanding park, Lahaina News, September 10, 1998: 2.
— West Maui Skate Park hours, Lahaina News, September 17, 1998: 3.
— Hi-Tech Skate Challenge to be held at Keopuolani Skate Park, Lahaina News, January 21, 1999: 7.

— skate park to be torn down, Lahaina News, September 7, 2000: 15.
— Split's professional skateboard team to demonstrate at Keopuolani Park, Lahaina News, March 1, 2001: 15.
— see also Maui Skate Park Association, West Maui Skate Park

SKELTON, ELIZABETH LAU
— becomes Maui district representative for National Federation of Independent Business (NFIB), Lahaina News, January 7, 1993: 7.

SKELTON, RED [ENTERTAINER, ARTIST]
— at Hyatt's Center Art Gallery, Lahaina News, July 23, 1986: 14.
— visit to Center Art Gallery successful, Lahaina News, July 30, 1986: 3.

SKI THE OUTER LIMITS [FILM]
— reviewed, Lahaina Sun, August 18, 1971: 2.

SKILLINGS, LES
— present at public meeting on ecology, Lahaina Sun, January 13, 1971: 2.

SKIM HAWAII
— plans skimboarding contest at Makena's "Big Beach", Lahaina News, May 16, 2002: 13.

SKIN DEEP TATTOOING [BUSINESS]
— featured, Lahaina News, July 15, 1983: 11.
— celebrates 20 years, Lahaina News, February 1, 1996: 11.

SKINNER COMMUNICATIONS [BUSINESS]
— moved to new location, Lahaina News, December 19, 1984: 24.
— to represent Backstage Productions, Lahaina News, August 8, 1990: 6.

SKINNER, DAN [ARTIST]
— to exhibit for Lahaina Arts Society, Lahaina News, October 31, 1991: 13.
— to exhibit at Lahaina Arts Society, Lahaina News, November 7, 1991: 14.

SKINNER, GEORJA
— owner of Skinner Communications featured, Lahaina News, November 16, 1988: 2.
— owner of Skinner Communications featured, Lahaina News, December 5, 1991: 3.
— sees increase in industry for Maui, Lahaina News, December 3, 1992: 4.

SKIPPERS SEAFOOD AND CHOWDER HOUSE [RESTAURANT]
— reviewed, Lahaina News, May 1, 1983: 14.

SKOG, JEANNE
— named interim president and CEO of Maui Economic Development Board, Lahaina News, January 21, 1999: 11.
— named president and CEO of Maui Economic Development Board, Lahaina News, February 25, 1999: 11.

SKOOG, JIM
— named director of audio visual services at Media Systems, Lahaina News, January 23, 1992: 12.

SKRIMSTAD, NANCY [ARTIST]
— to hold "Unique Holiday Cards" workshop at Hui No'eau Visual Arts Center, Lahaina News, November 30, 2000: 17.
— to exhibit at Hui No'eau Visual Arts Center, Lahaina News, June 28, 2001: 20.

SLACK KEY FESTIVAL
— to be held at Maui Inter-Continental Wailea, sponsored by Bank of Hawaii, Lahaina News, October 24, 1991: 22.

SLACK KEY GUITAR AND JUNIOR UKULELE FESTIVAL
— to be held at Lahaina Cannery Mall, Lahaina News, April 6, 2000: 14.
— to be held at Lahaina Cannery Mall, Lahaina News, February 27, 2003: 18.

SLACK SAX [MUSICAL GROUP]
— performing concert at Ka'anapali Beach Hotel, Lahaina News, January 2, 1985: 16.

SLAGLE, BRYAN [GEMOLOGIST]
— visiting Lahaina, Lahaina News, June 27, 1984: 14.

SLAM HOUNDS, THE [MUSICAL GROUP]
— to perform at Moose McGillycuddy's, Lahaina News, February 22, 1996: 13.

SLAMMIN' BABES, THE [MUSICAL GROUP]
— to perform at Maui Arts and Cultural Center, Lahaina News, April 2, 1998: 17.

SLASH [MUSICIAN]
— Guns N' Roses guitarist vacations in West Maui, Lahaina News, May 14, 1992: 15.

SLATER, JACKIE [FOOTBALL PLAYER]
— career to date discussed, Lahaina News, February 8, 1984: 6.

SLAUGHTERHOUSE BEACH
— Maui Council seeking safer path to, Lahaina News, February 2, 1995: 1,16.
— trail to may be improved, Lahaina News, July 6, 1995: 1,12.
— fence eliminates two access trails, Lahaina News, October 26, 1995: 1,16.
— temporary trail created, Lahaina News, November 9, 1995: 1,16.
— blessing to be held for new trail in February, Lahaina News, January 28, 1999: 3.
— accessible with stairs created by Maui Land and Pineapple, Lahaina News, October 21, 1999: 14.

SLAUGHTERHOUSE TRAIL
— to be fixed, Lahaina News, May 23, 1996: 1,18.

SLAVA'S SNOWSHOW
— clown troupe to perform, Lahaina News, December 27, 2001: 17.

SLAVINSKY, ELAINE
— receives Ruth Kemble Award for Volunteer Service from Hawai'i Nurses' Association, Lahaina News, June 7, 2001: 8.

SLEEK PHYSIQUE CONTEST
— to be held, Lahaina News, April 16, 1992: 4.

SLOAN, MARTHA KIYOMI
— promoted to assistant vice president, Lahaina News, October 1, 1992: 10.

SLOM, SAM [POLITICIAN]
— to speak at event hosted by Lahaina News and West Maui Taxpayers Association, Lahaina News, October 9, 1997: 14.
— to speak, Lahaina News, October 16, 1997: 12.
— to speak, Lahaina News, October 23, 1997: 1,15.
— speaks to West Maui Taxpayers Association, Lahaina News, November 6, 1997: 1,13.
— critical of State's economic policies, Lahaina News, August 26, 1999: 1,20.

SLY DOG [MUSICAL GROUP]
— to perform at Moose McGillycuddy's, Lahaina News, August 8, 1996: 16.
— to perform at Haiku Ho'olaule'a Flower Festival, Lahaina News, May 29, 1997: 17.
— to perform at Maui Summer Jam, Lahaina News, June 18, 1998: 17.

SMALL BUSINESS ADMINISTRATION, U.S.
— offers loans to businesses who suffered storm damage, Lahaina Sun, February 17, 1971: 4.
— to answer questions about possible support for Wailuku, Lahaina Sun, November 22, 1972: 4.
— sponsoring event on projecting profits and cash flow, Lahaina News, February 15, 1989: 14.
— to host seminar on financial statements, Lahaina News, April 5, 1989: 14.

— to honor Persons of the Year with Maui Chamber of Commerce, Lahaina News, April 5, 1989: 15.

— sponsoring food and beverage seminar, Lahaina News, May 17, 1989: 9.

— loan officer to visit Maui, Lahaina News, March 26, 1992: 10.

— to honor small business award winners with Maui Chamber of Commerce, Lahaina News, April 13, 1995: 12.

— seeking nominations for Small Business Person of the Year award, Lahaina News, September 4, 1997: 1`2.

— to honor award winners, Lahaina News, April 23, 1998: 13.

— to hold awards luncheon, Lahaina News, April 30, 1998: 16.

— warns owners for 2000 computer malfunction, Lahaina News, June 25, 1998: 11.

— seeking nominations for Small Business Person of the Year awards, Lahaina News, September 17, 1998: 13.

— seeking nominations for Small Business Person of the Year awards, Lahaina News, September 24, 1998: 13.

— warns of Y2K issues, Lahaina News, October 29, 1998: 20.

— to host courses on internet access, Lahaina News, January 21, 1999: 11.

— urges people to take Y2K seriously, Lahaina News, April 1, 1999: 3.

— announces Small Business Person of the Year Awards for Hawaii, Lahaina News, April 29, 1999: 13.

— giving free copies of Quickbooks to small businesses, Lahaina News, August 19, 1999: 14.

— seeking nominations for Small Business Person of the Year award, Lahaina News, October 26, 2000: 20.

— to announce winners at SBA Small Business Awards, Lahaina News, March 22, 2001: 8.

— posts resources to website, Lahaina News, October 4, 2001: 8.

— honors top performers, Lahaina News, November 7, 2002: 8.

— Ombudsman Michael Berrera accepting comments on federal regulatory enforcement, Lahaina News, January 23, 2003: 8.

— Ombudsman Michael Berrera accepting comments on federal regulatory enforcement, Lahaina News, January 30, 2003: 8.

SMALL BUSINESS DEVELOPMENT CENTER

— to open, Lahaina News, January 24, 1990: 6.

— opens at Maui Community College, Lahaina News, May 1, 1991: 7.

— offering session on "Starting a Venture in Hawaii", Lahaina News, October 27, 1994: 15.

— to offer sessions for small businesses, Lahaina News, November 10, 1994: 13.

— to sponsor workshops, Lahaina News, November 17, 1994: 10.

— offering workshop on using MauiLink and the internet, Lahaina News, December 1, 1994: 13.

— offering class on internet, Lahaina News, December 15, 1994: 14.

— to host workshop on starting a venture in Hawaii, Lahaina News, January 12, 1995: 6.

— offering "Entrepreneurial Marketing" workshop, Lahaina News, January 26, 1995: 13.

— to hold entrepreneurial marketing workshop, Lahaina News, April 6, 1995: 6.

— offering "Developing Business Plans and Proposals" workshop, Lahaina News, April 13, 1995: 12.

— to sponsor workshop on starting a business, Lahaina News, June 8, 1995: 10.

— hosting workshop on marketing strategy, Lahaina News, March 21, 1996: 10.

— UH Hilo Network to present on business uses for the internet, Lahaina News, November 21, 1996: 15.

SMALL BUSINESS HAWAII

— organizing to oppose increase in General Excise Tax, Lahaina News, February 5, 1998: 1.

SMALL BUSINESS HAWAII CONFERENCE

— to be held on Oahu with theme "Small Business in the '90s", Lahaina News, December 20, 1989: 4.

SMALL BUSINESS REGULATORY REVIEW BOARD

— state seeking nominations for, Lahaina News, July 2, 1998: 12.

SMALL STORE, THE [BUSINESS]

— opens, Lahaina News, March 11, 1993: 12.

SMART GROWTH FOR OUR COMMUNITIES— ENVISIONING MAUI COUNTY IN 2020

— conference to be held, Lahaina News, August 23, 2001: 9.

SMELTZER, STEVEN [ARTIST]

— sculptor featured, Lahaina News, September 19, 1996: 17.

— opens Avalene Gallery, Lahaina News, November 1, 2001: 8.

SMITH, AMANDA

— to speak to the Maui County Committee on the Status of Women, Lahaina News, October 11, 1989: 3.

SMITH, ANDREA [ARTIST]

— work and life described, Lahaina News, September 7, 1983: 12.

— featured, Lahaina News, August 30, 1989: 10.

— opens art show at Lahaina Galleries, Lahaina News, December 6, 1989: 13.

— exhibits at Lahaina Galleries, Lahaina News, December 12, 1990: 12.

— to exhibit at Gallery Ka'anapali, Lahaina News, December 19, 1991: 19.

— to speak at Alaya Unlimited Ohana Luncheon, Lahaina News, January 12, 1995: 11.

— featured, Lahaina News, October 10, 1996: 17.

— to exhibit at Lahaina Galleries, Lahaina News, January 21, 1999: 12.

— to visit Lahaina Galleries with son Matthew, Lahaina News, July 1, 1999: 2.

— to exhibit at Lahaina Galleries, Lahaina News, March 22, 2001: 16.

— to lead seminar on "Square One", Lahaina News, March 21, 2002: 16.

— to visit Sargent's Fine Art, Lahaina News, August 29, 2002: 16.

— to exhibit at The Art School at Kapalua, Lahaina News, December 5, 2002: 18.

— to exhibit paintings at The Art School at Kapalua, Lahaina News, December 26, 2002: 16.

— to lead workshop for Maui Watercolorists Association, Lahaina News, July 17, 2003: 16.

SMITH, BOB

— chair of Mayor's West Maui Advisory Committee reflects on term, Lahaina News, January 5, 1995: 1.

SMITH, BOB AND LESLIE

— political work described, Lahaina News, May 11, 1988: 3.

SMITH, CECILE

— general manager of Lahaina-Ka'anapali & Pacific Railroad featured, Lahaina Sun, August 23, 1972: 14.

SMITH, CHARLOTTE

— appointed to national Disability's Community Partnership Program, Lahaina News, February 25, 1993: 5.

SMITH, CINDY LYNNE

— appointed as director of sales and marketing at Maui Prince Hotel, Lahaina News, June 30, 1994: 9.

SMITH, DALE

— to open Maui Muscle Sports Club-Kahana, Lahaina News, March 9, 2000: 11.

SMITH, ED

— to speak on education to Lahaina Complex Site-Based Council , Lahaina News, October 19, 1995: 4.

— Lieutenant General of U.S. Army Pacific Command to speak on homeland security, Lahaina News, May 16, 2002: 2.

SMITH, HOWARD
— drowns, Lahaina News, July 16, 1992: 4.

SMITH, JEFFREY
— affiliate of Sleep Disorder Clinic to speak at Maui Memorial Medical Center, Lahaina News, July 3, 2003: 16.

SMITH, KENNETH
— named top-selling salesperson at Locations Real Estate, Lahaina News, October 24, 1991: 9.

SMITH, KIM
— promoted to vice president of Sargent's Fine Art, Lahaina News, August 8, 2002: 8.

SMITH, LISA [MUSICIAN]
— to present "Gypsies, Paniolos and Classical Guitarists" at Lahaina Public Library, Lahaina News, January 4, 1989: 3.
— to perform at Baldwin High School Auditorium, Lahaina News, April 8, 1993: 12.

SMITH, LYNNE [ARTIST]
— to exhibit at Village Galleries, Lahaina News, April 20, 1995: 11.

SMITH, MARGARET [COMEDIAN]
— promoted to sales manager at Maui Marriott Resort, Lahaina News, June 28, 1989: 7.
— to perform at Comedy Club and the Sports Page, Lahaina News, May 21, 1992: 13,17.

SMITH, MARIE
— highlighted on "Maui Women Making a Difference", Lahaina News, March 7, 2002: 5.

SMITH, MARILYN
— offering golf clinic, Lahaina News, February 18, 1987: 3.

SMITH, MARSHALL
— elected as Ma'alaea Community Association president, Lahaina News, January 21, 1993: 11.

SMITH, MATTHEW [ARTIST]
— painting unveiled at Chadwick Hawaii Jewelers, Lahaina News, October 1, 1998: 13.
— to unveil painting at Chadwick Hawaii Jewelers, Lahaina News, October 15, 1998: 16.
— to exhibit at Lahaina Galleries, Lahaina News, January 21, 1999: 12.
— to exhibit at Lahaina Galleries, Lahaina News, March 22, 2001: 16.
— to visit Sargent's Fine Art, Lahaina News, August 21, 2003: 9.

SMITH, MATTHEW AND ANDREA [ARTISTS]
— to visit Lahaina Galleries, Lahaina News, February 12, 1998: 17.

SMITH, MICHAEL
— to open Plantation House Restaurant, Lahaina News, April 24, 1991: 7.

SMITH, NICOLE
— to discuss "Instinctive Feng Shui", Lahaina News, June 6, 2002: 17.

SMITH, ROD
— now managing Pacific News, Lahaina News, April 2, 1992: 12.

SMITH, SAM
— appointed operations manager at Entrekin/Zucco Advertising, Lahaina News, May 23, 1990: 8.

SMITH, STEVE [COMEDIAN]
— to perform at Comedy Club, Lahaina News, June 27, 1991: 12.
— to perform at Comedy Club and the Sports Page, Lahaina News, June 25, 1992: 18,21.
— to perform at Maui Comedy Club, Lahaina News, August 24, 1995: 12.

SMITH, TERESA [ARTIST]
— to lead a painting workshop, Lahaina News, May 24, 2001: 20.

SMITH, UA
— offering class on hula, Lahaina News, May 3, 2001: 21.

SMITH, VERNON
— president of North Short Improvement Association, Lahaina Sun, December 30, 1970: 5.

SMITH, W.A.S.
— becomes provost of Maunaolu campus of United States International University, Lahaina Sun, January 12, 1972: 4.

SMITH, WILLIAM O.
— life of the man who planted the banyan tree detailed, Lahaina Sun, April 18, 1973: 12,13.

SMITHSON, BO [COMEDIAN]
— to perform at Comedy Club and the Sports Page, Lahaina News, April 29, 1993: 10,11.

SMOKEY WILSON AND HIS BAND FROM MARS [MUSICAL GROUP]
— to perform at Maui Arts and Cultural Center, Lahaina News, November 6, 1997: 17.

SMOKING
— Maui County Council passes anti-smoking laws, Lahaina News, December 18, 1997: 14.

SMOTHERS BROTHERS [ENTERTAINERS]
— to perform at Hyatt Regency Grand Ballroom, Lahaina News, November 28, 1984: 17.
— to perform at Hyatt Regency Grand Ballroom, Lahaina News, December 19, 1984: 21.

SMS CONSULTING [BUSINESS]
— to conduct county satisfaction survey, Lahaina News, August 14, 2003: 9.

SMULDERS, RAPHAEL
— Maria Lanakila Church Father retiring to St. Patrick's on Oahu, Lahaina News, October 29, 1998: 21.

SMYTHE, DUKE
— awarded Levi-James Kahahane Scholastic Achievement Award, Lahaina News, January 30, 1997: 6.

SMYTHE, EDWINA
— planning commissioner talks about volunteerism, Lahaina News, May 24, 1989: 4,5.
— chairing Aloha Week, Lahaina News, August 30, 1989: 1.
— shoots a hole-in-one, Lahaina News, January 30, 1991: 16.

SMYTHE, JULAYNE [ARTIST]
— to teach traditional Hawaiian basketry, Lahaina News, April 3, 1991: 10.

SNAITH, DAVID
— leading seminar on "Magic of Healing", Lahaina News, January 7, 1999: 16.

SNAKES
— Department of Land and Natural Resources looking for, Lahaina News, December 11, 1997: 11.
— sea snake found at Waiehu, Lahaina News, December 10, 1998: 19.

SNIEGOWSKI, CHESTER
— director for Maui ACLU, Lahaina Sun, January 13, 1971: 6.

SNIEGOWSKI, PATTIE
— director for Maui ACLU, Lahaina Sun, January 13, 1971: 6.

SNOW WHITE AND THE SEVEN (DORKS) DWARFS [PLAY]
— to be performed by Theatre Theatre Maui, Lahaina News, July 14, 1994: 15.
— to be performed by Theatre Theatre Maui, Lahaina News, July 21, 1994: 2.

SNOWBIRD [BOAT]
— runs aground following stormy weather, Lahaina News, January 2, 1991: 1.

SNOWRIDERS [FILM]
— Warren Miller's film to be shown, Lahaina News, February 27, 1997: 7.

SNUBA
— technology introduced , Lahaina News, April 20, 1988: 6.

SNUG HARBOR [RESTAURANT]
— restaurant at Pioneer Inn featured, Lahaina News, April 5, 2001: 10,11.

SNYDER, APRYLLSA
— offer puppet show at Lahaina Public Library, Lahaina News, January 2, 1991: 3.

SNYDER, BRAD
— named resident manager at Maui Marriott Resort, Lahaina News, June 19, 1985: 8.

SNYDER, DON
— basketball player missed playing for Maui Cactus Jack, Lahaina Sun, January 20, 1971: 7.

SNYDER, EDWINA WILSON
— new principal of Princess Nahienaena Elementary School to hold meeting, Lahaina News, April 4, 1996: 2.
— Princess Nahienaena Elementary School celebrates career of, Lahaina News, June 7, 2001: 1,22.

SNYDER, KRISTINE [MUSICIAN]
— to perform, Lahaina News, September 26, 2002: 16,17.
— to perform at The Shops at Wailea, Lahaina News, May 15, 2003: 16.

SOAP OPERA [BUSINESS]
— opens, Lahaina News, October 14, 1999: 11.

SOARES, DONNA
— manager of Wharf Shops and Restaurants named Woman of the Year by Business and Professional Women's Club of Lahaina, Lahaina News, January 25, 1989: 17.

SOARES, WILLIAM "BUTCH" [POLITICIAN]
— retires from Pioneer Mill after almost 50 years, Lahaina Sun, June 9, 1971: 7.
— announces candidacy for Maui Council, Lahaina News, August 1, 1990: 4,5.
— to hold fundraiser, Lahaina News, August 15, 1990: 6.
— candidate profiled, Lahaina News, September 12, 1990: 6,7.
— candidate for Maui County Council featured, Lahaina News, August 13, 1992: 11.
— Republican candidate for Maui County Council to speak at Lahaina Kiwanis Club breakfast, Lahaina News, August 13, 1992: 4.
— to hold fundraiser, Lahaina News, September 10, 1992: 3.

SOBAJE, HELEN [ARTIST]
— to exhibit at Lahaina Arts Society, Lahaina News, September 2, 1999: 17.

SOCCER
— youth program to begin, Lahaina News, December 19, 1991: 9.
— games continue, Lahaina News, July 2, 1992: 13.
— youth league begins in West Maui, Lahaina News, July 2, 1992: 15.
— youth league continues, awaiting uniforms, Lahaina News, July 9, 1992: 12.
— update on league play, Lahaina News, July 30, 1992: 8.
— results of West Maui Youth Association league, Lahaina News, August 6, 1992: 6.
— Kihei Kool Kats win Friendship Tourney, Lahaina News, December 3, 1992: 7.
— result of games, Lahaina News, November 4, 1993: 9.
— clinic to be held, Lahaina News, July 28, 1994: 6.
— West Maui American Soccer Organization (AYSO) to hold camp, Lahaina News, August 10, 1995: 7.
— popularity of surging, Lahaina News, September 14, 1995: 7.
— youth player Angelo Ladera accepted for F.C. Global International Soccer Training and Competition, Lahaina News, May 9, 1996: 6.

— popularity grows, Lahaina News, August 29, 1996: 6.
— annual general membership meeting to be held, Lahaina News, January 16, 1997: 14.
— American Youth Soccer Organization to hold registrations for, Lahaina News, May 8, 1997: 15.
— registration continues, Lahaina News, May 15, 1997: 11.
— registration successful, Lahaina News, August 14, 1997: 14.
— Irwin Grover named commission of Region 892 for American Youth Soccer Organization (AYSO), Lahaina News, April 16, 1998: 7.
— West Maui American Youth Soccer Organization (AYSO) to hold registration, Lahaina News, May 7, 1998: 10.
— camp to be held for children, Lahaina News, July 9, 1998: 15.
— season ends, Lahaina News, November 12, 1998: 14.
— coed scrimmages to be held at Malu'ulu O Lele Park, Lahaina News, February 4, 1999: 15.
— Hawaii Youth Soccer Association teams featured, Lahaina News, February 11, 1999: 14,15.
— coed soccer scrimmages to be held, Lahaina News, February 25, 1999: 6.
— Maui youth accepted to National Soccer Academy, Lahaina News, February 25, 1999: 7.
— AYSO registration underway, Lahaina News, April 29, 1999: 7.
— registration underway, Lahaina News, May 13, 1999: 6.
— West Maui AYSO soccer league has openings, Lahaina News, July 22, 1999: 11.
— World Cup Soccer increases popularity of, Lahaina News, September 30, 1999: 6.
— Chaos wins Maui AYSO league with perfect record, Lahaina News, October 28, 1999: 7.
— popularity of, Lahaina News, January 13, 2000: 6.
— Lahainaluna High School team featured, Lahaina News, February 10, 2000: 6.
— West Maui American Youth Soccer Organization Regional Commission warns of lack of volunteers for upcoming season, Lahaina News, March 2, 2000: 6.
— registration underway, Lahaina News, May 18, 2000: 15.
— West Maui AYSO league continues to expand, Lahaina News, September 21, 2000: 7.
— Soccerfest to complete 2000 season, Lahaina News, November 16, 2000: 10.
— Na Honu West Maui Soccer Club seeking sponsors, Lahaina News, January 25, 2001: 9.
— Na Honu West Maui Soccer Club seeking sponsors, Lahaina News, February 1, 2001: 14.
— team to travel to Honolulu for tournament, Lahaina News, March 1, 2001: 14.
— American Youth Soccer Association to hold registration, Lahaina News, May 17, 2001: 14.
— AYSO to hold registration, Lahaina News, May 24, 2001: 15.
— Major League Soccer to hold camps, Lahaina News, July 19, 2001: 12.
— league play to be held, Lahaina News, August 2, 2001: 13.
— results of AYSO season, Lahaina News, September 13, 2001: 12.
— AYSO Lahaina teams successful, Lahaina News, November 15, 2001: 12.
— AYSO registration to begin, Lahaina News, May 9, 2002: 12.
— West Maui American Youth Soccer Organization (AYSO) registration to begin, Lahaina News, May 16, 2002: 13.
— camp to be held, Lahaina News, August 1, 2002: 15.
— West Maui American Youth Soccer Organization (AYSO) featured, Lahaina News, August 29, 2002: 10.
— Kirk Banks Tournament to be held in Honolulu, Lahaina News, March 13, 2003: 12.
— AYSO to hold final sign-up, Lahaina News, June 12, 2003: 11.
— Owen Ueno is new commissioner for West Maui American Youth Soccer Organization (AYSO), Lahaina News, September 18, 2003: 12.

SOCHACZEWSKI, PAUL SPENCER
— to discuss his book "Redheads", Lahaina News, June 22, 2000: 16.

SOCIAL SECURITY [PLAY]
— to be performed by Maui Community Theatre, Lahaina News, January 28, 1993: 15.
— Maui Community Theatre to hold auditions, Lahaina News, February 4, 1993: 16.
— to be performed at Maui Community Theatre Onstage, Lahaina News, April 22, 1993: 14.

SOCIETY OF INCENTIVE TRAVEL UNIVERSITY
— to hold convention at Grand Hyatt Wailea Resort, Lahaina News, June 4, 1992: 9.
— to hold conference, Lahaina News, June 11, 1992: 14.
— to hold conference, Lahaina News, June 18, 1992: 10.

SOCIETY OF PROFESSIONAL JOURNALISTS-HAWAII CHAPTER
— writers at Lahaina News win awards from Hawaii Chapter, Lahaina News, June 22, 2000: 1,15.
— Lahaina News wins in business reporting category, Lahaina News, June 28, 2001: 22.
— Lahaina News wins Community Reporting award from, Lahaina News, June 19, 2003: 1,20.

SOCKHOP AND CRAFTS FAIR
— rescheduled, Lahaina News, July 20, 1995: 12.

SODER, LORNA
— coordinating milk drive for Pakkred Babies' Home outside Bangkok, Thailand, Lahaina News, November 1, 2001: 3.

SODETANI, DOUGLAS
— served as master of ceremony for Mayor Carvalho's second inauguration ceremony, Lahaina Sun, January 6, 1971: 2.
— named chairman of State Real Estate Commission, Lahaina Sun, March 3, 1971: 3.
— receives Honorary Lifetime Trustee award by the National Association of Realtors, Lahaina News, October 10, 1996: 8.

SODETANI, ERIC
— Lahainaluna football coach featured, Lahaina News, October 24, 1996: 1,13.

SODETANI, LLOYD
— appointed by Patsy Mink as delegate to White House Conference on Small Business, Lahaina News, December 22, 1994: 13.

SODOMA, SALLY DANIELS
— to direct "Some Like It Hot" for Maui Community Theatre, Lahaina News, August 22, 1990: 4.

SOFOS REALTY CORPORATION [BUSINESS]
— chosen as property management company for Lahaina Center, Lahaina News, June 20, 1990: 7.
— Susan Riska and Craig Swift named to on-site management team, Lahaina News, July 18, 1991: 6.

SOFT TOUCH [MUSICAL GROUP]
— featured, Lahaina News, July 22, 1987: 7,9.
— featured, Lahaina News, May 10, 1989: 17.
— to perform at Maui Marriott Resort, Lahaina News, November 15, 1989: 14.
— featured, Lahaina News, November 28, 1991: 14.
— to perform at Makai Bar, Lahaina News, March 28, 1996: 13.
— to perform at Makai Bar, Lahaina News, September 19, 1996: 18.

SOFTBALL
— celebrity game to be held, Lahaina News, August 12, 1987: 3.
— Wahine Kukini Softball Tournament, Lahaina News, July 18, 1991: 7.
— Wahine Kukini Softball Tournament scheduled, Lahaina News, July 25, 1991: 9.
— Wahine Kukini Softball Tournament to be held this weekend, Lahaina News, August 8, 1991: 6.
— league to hold organizational meeting, Lahaina News, September 10, 1992: 8.
— standings for West Maui United States Slo-Pitch Softball Association, Lahaina News, November 9, 1995: 6.
— Cherokee Ohana II wins season, Lahaina News, November 30, 1995: 7.
— USSSA Softball League of West Maui to meet, Lahaina News, December 7, 1995: 3.
— registration has begun, Lahaina News, January 11, 1996: 6.
— update on league play, Lahaina News, September 19, 1996: 13.
— Lahainaluna High School team featured, Lahaina News, November 28, 1996: 5.
— Maui Stingrays team participate in clinic, Lahaina News, December 5, 1996: 12.
— registration underway, Lahaina News, January 9, 1997: 6.
— registration underway, Lahaina News, January 16, 1997: 6.
— league play held, Lahaina News, April 10, 1997: 16.
— Lahaina Ladybugs featured, Lahaina News, April 24, 1997: 5,14.
— West Maui Parks and Recreation Department starting night league, Lahaina News, May 15, 1997: 11.
— West Maui USSSA league begins, Lahaina News, June 5, 1997: 13.
— update on league play, Lahaina News, June 19, 1997: 13.
— update on league play, Lahaina News, October 30, 1997: 6.
— league play ends, Lahaina News, December 11, 1997: 17.
— registration ending, Lahaina News, January 22, 1998: 7.
— Hawaii Junior Olympics Softball Association to hold free clinic, Lahaina News, February 19, 1998: 12.
— USSSA games held in Lahaina, Lahaina News, February 19, 1998: 6.
— USSSA scores, Lahaina News, March 5, 1998: 15.
— USSSA results, Lahaina News, March 26, 1998: 7.
— update on league action, Lahaina News, April 9, 1998: 15.
— results of recent play, Lahaina News, April 30, 1998: 15.
— update on USSSA league play, Lahaina News, May 21, 1998: 15.
— Ladies Softball Nite to be held, Lahaina News, May 21, 1998: 15.
— teams to meet, Lahaina News, June 11, 1998: 15.
— league registration underway, Lahaina News, July 30, 1998: 15.
— local scores, Lahaina News, August 27, 1998: 15.
— results of recent games, Lahaina News, September 3, 1998: 15.
— scores from recent games, Lahaina News, September 10, 1998: 15.
— latest scores, Lahaina News, September 24, 1998: 14.
— results of recent games, Lahaina News, October 1, 1998: 15.
— latest scores, Lahaina News, November 5, 1998: 19.
— local scores, Lahaina News, November 26, 1998: 15.
— league forming, Lahaina News, December 3, 1998: 19.
— West Maui USSSA to hold organizational meeting, Lahaina News, December 10, 1998: 19.
— deadline approach for teams to register, Lahaina News, January 14, 1999: 7.
— West Maui USSSA results, Lahaina News, March 11, 1999: 7.
— softball coach Earle Kukahiko featured, Lahaina News, May 13, 1999: 6.
— Maui Girls Softball Association holds awards ceremony, Lahaina News, June 10, 1999: 6,7.
— champions determined, Lahaina News, June 24, 1999: 7.
— results of recent games, Lahaina News, September 9, 1999: 7.
— West Maui USSSA game to be held, Lahaina News, September 16, 1999: 7.
— recent games, Lahaina News, September 23, 1999: 7.
— recent games, Lahaina News, September 30, 1999: 6.
— Bulletproof leads league standings, Lahaina News, October 21, 1999: 9.
— USSSA league games held, Lahaina News, October 28, 1999: 9.
— recent USSSA games, Lahaina News, November 18, 1999: 8.

— results of USSSA league play, Lahaina News, November 25, 1999: 9.

— team Bulletproof wins USSSA league, Lahaina News, December 2, 1999: 9.

— league forming, Lahaina News, December 9, 1999: 9.

— registration underway, Lahaina News, January 13, 2000: 7.

— fastpitch league play underway, Lahaina News, May 11, 2000: 14.

— league forming, Lahaina News, May 18, 2000: 15.

— results of league play, Lahaina News, June 1, 2000: 9.

— results of USSSA action, Lahaina News, September 14, 2000: 9.

— results of USSSA action, Lahaina News, September 21, 2000: 9.

— update on scores, Lahaina News, September 28, 2000: 9.

— results from USSSA action, Lahaina News, October 12, 2000: 9.

— update on USSSA league play, Lahaina News, October 19, 2000: 9.

— results of USSSA action, Lahaina News, October 26, 2000: 12.

— results of league play, Lahaina News, November 9, 2000: 10.

— results of league play, Lahaina News, November 23, 2000: 11.

— results of USSSA league play, Lahaina News, November 30, 2000: 6.

— registration for Lahaina Girls softball to begin, Lahaina News, March 8, 2001: 13.

— to hold registration, Lahaina News, August 2, 2001: 13.

— registration underway, Lahaina News, August 9, 2001: 13.

— Lahainaluna High School team featured, Lahaina News, December 20, 2001: 12.

— West Maui USSSA league to start, Lahaina News, January 24, 2002: 13.

— Lahaina Girls Fastpitch Softball program featured, Lahaina News, May 2, 2002: 12.

— co-ed program to begin, Lahaina News, June 6, 2002: 12.

— co-ed program to begin, Lahaina News, June 20, 2002: 12.

— Lahaina Girls Softball team wins Maui Invitational Softball Tournament, Lahaina News, July 4, 2002: 12.

— co-ed program to begin, Lahaina News, July 11, 2002: 12.

— USSSA league forming, Lahaina News, August 1, 2002: 14.

— USSSA league forming, Lahaina News, January 23, 2003: 13.

— USSSA league forming, Lahaina News, January 30, 2003: 13.

— results of Lahainaluna High School league play, Lahaina News, February 20, 2003: 1.

— Lahaina Girls Softball to hold clinics, Lahaina News, March 6, 2003: 12.

— coed games to be held, Lahaina News, May 8, 2003: 12.

— coed league forming, Lahaina News, May 15, 2003: 13.

— coed league forming, Lahaina News, May 22, 2003: 13.

— Lahaina Girls team wins tournament, Lahaina News, July 17, 2003: 12.

SOHO TOO GALLERY & LOFT [BUSINESS]
— reviewed, Lahaina News, July 2, 1986: 12.

SOICHI, CLARENCE
— honorary mayor of Lahaina featured, Lahaina News, August 15, 1991: 11.

SOIL CONSERVATION SERVICE, U.S.
— investigating alternative flood control for Lahaina Watershed Project, Lahaina News, October 10, 1991: 12.

— working on Puamana flood control design, Lahaina News, October 31, 1991: 1.

— Maui County Council to help with flooding issues, Lahaina News, March 27, 1997: 1.

SOKAN HAWAII, INC. [BUSINESS]
— allowed to reclassify land to build golf courses, Lahaina News, November 21, 1990: 12.

— proposes golf course in Waihee, Lahaina News, December 19, 1991: 7.

SOLAR WATER HEATING FAIR
— to be held, Lahaina News, September 25, 1997: 3.

SOLDIERS OF LIGHT
— to perform at Hawaii Baptist Academy, Lahaina News, May 29, 1997: 16.

SOLDWISCH, SCOTT
— Lahainaluna High School pitching coach featured, Lahaina News, April 2, 1992: 8.

SOLI, GAYLORD [ARTIST]
— to visit Sargent's Fine Arts, Lahaina News, March 6, 2003: 16.

SOLID WASTE DIVISION, MAUI COUNTY
— proposals to be made for new county laws on recycling, Lahaina News, January 4, 1996: 3.

— offering Large Appliance Recovery project, Lahaina News, March 7, 1996: 10.

SOMA, CHARLES
— doctor to discuss osteoarthritis, Lahaina News, March 14, 2002: 17.

— Orthopedic surgeon to lecture on arthritis, Lahaina News, October 24, 2002: 21.

— Orthopedic surgeon to lecture on arthritis, Lahaina News, November 28, 2002: 17.

SOME LIKE IT HOT [PLAY]
— auditions to be held, Lahaina News, August 22, 1990: 4.

SOMERVILLE, JIM
— named director of tennis at Aston Kamaole Sands, Lahaina News, May 1, 1991: 7.

SOMMERVILLE, ELEANOR
— receives Na Honoapi'ilani Award for work on Na Mele O Maui, Lahaina News, December 6, 1989: 3.

SOMOS AMIGOS
— "We Are Friends" street festival to be held, Lahaina News, August 3, 2000: 5.

— festival to celebrate Portuguese heritage, Lahaina News, September 14, 2000: 17.

SON SEEKER, THE [BOAT]
— begins operation in Ma'alaea, Lahaina News, January 24, 1990: 9.

SONEDA, SHINJI
— meeting with Mayor Cravalho, Lahaina Sun, December 23, 1970: 4.

SONG FOR A NISEI FISHERMAN, A [PLAY]
— to be performed by Maui Community College, Lahaina News, June 6, 1984: 3.

SONG'S ORIENTAL KITCHEN [RESTAURANT]
— opens third location, Lahaina News, November 12, 1992: 12.

SONKIN, KEN [COMEDIAN]
— to perform at Comedy Club, Lahaina News, February 21, 1990: 13.

— to perform at Honolulu Comedy Club, Lahaina News, April 25, 1996: 16.

SONS OF HAWAII [MUSICAL GROUP]
— to perform at celebration of life of Manu Kahaiali'i, Lahaina News, October 27, 1994: 20.

— to perform at B.J.'s Chicago Pizzeria, Lahaina News, September 4, 1997: 2.

— to perform in Lahaina for documentary, Lahaina News, January 7, 1999: 1,20.

— to perform at Reflections of Old Lahaina Luau and Concert benefit, Lahaina News, August 19, 1999: 18.

SONS OF HAWAII: A SOUND, A BAND, A LEGEND [FILM]
— produced by Eddie Kamae, Lahaina News, November 9, 2000: 21.

SONTAG, SHERRY [WRITER]
— to discuss book "Blindman's Bluff", Lahaina News, February 4, 1999: 16.

SOON, NICK
— owner of Kaupo store featured, Lahaina Sun, June 6, 1973: 3.

SORO, SUZY [COMEDIAN]
— to perform at Comedy Club and the Sports Page, Lahaina News, December 3, 1992: 14,18.
— to perform at Comedy Club, Lahaina News, November 11, 1993: 12.

SOROPTIMISTS INTERNATIONAL
— to hold first Lahaina Christmas Dinner Dance, Lahaina News, December 15, 1981: 6.
— awards announced, Lahaina News, May 23, 1984: 17.
— women honored for advancing the status of women, Lahaina News, June 6, 1984: 3.
— new officers installed, Lahaina News, July 4, 1984: 4.
— awards announced, Lahaina News, December 12, 1984: 3.
— to hold Sweetheart's Ball, Lahaina News, January 30, 1985: 3.
— awards Stephanie Higa training scholarship , Lahaina News, May 15, 1985: 3.
— new officers elected, Lahaina News, May 29, 1985: 3.
— fund-raising cruise set for September 14, Lahaina News, August 28, 1985: 3.
— to hold sunset cruise about the Prince Kuhio, Lahaina News, September 11, 1985: 20.
— mayor Tavares signs proclamation naming October 1-8, 1985 as Soroptimist Week, Lahaina News, October 2, 1985: 7.
— sponsoring Halloween parade, Lahaina News, October 23, 1985: 3.
— selling See's candy as Christmas fundraiser, Lahaina News, November 13, 1985: 3,7.
— Sweethearts Ball fundraiser planned, Lahaina News, February 5, 1986: 3.
— held Easter Egg hunt, Lahaina News, March 26, 1986: 3.
— name new officers, Lahaina News, June 25, 1986: 3.
— honor women in Women Helping Women Program, Lahaina News, July 2, 1986: 3.
— raising money selling holiday candy, Lahaina News, October 22, 1986: 3.
— plant trees for Arbor Day, Lahaina News, November 12, 1986: 6.
— to hold annual Sweetheart's Ball Dinner Dance, Lahaina News, February 4, 1987: 11.
— to send delegates to Founder Region Conference, Lahaina News, April 22, 1987: 3.
— honor Joyce Horikawa, Lahaina News, May 20, 1987: 17.
— to host author Alan Cohen, Lahaina News, June 10, 1987: 18.
— to hold fashion show to commemorate the Greater Lahaina Reunion, Lahaina News, June 17, 1987: 3.
— sells See's candy as fundraiser, Lahaina News, October 14, 1987: 3.
— purchases medical equipment with money raised from Sweethearts' Ball, Lahaina News, October 28, 1987: 12.
— planning Sweethearts Ball, Lahaina News, January 27, 1988: 3.
— Sweethearts Ball fundraiser for Maui Special Olympics, Lahaina News, February 10, 1988: 11.
— donates equipment to Lahaina Emergency Ambulance Service, Lahaina News, March 16, 1988: 3.
— scholarships announced, Lahaina News, March 16, 1988: 3.
— sponsoring Maui Special Olympics Area Track and Field Games, Lahaina News, March 30, 1988: 14.
— selling candy as fundraiser, Lahaina News, October 12, 1988: 3.
— candy sale almost complete, Lahaina News, November 9, 1988: 12.
— planning Sweethearts Ball fundraiser, Lahaina News, January 4, 1989: 3.
— president Ruth McKay featured, Lahaina News, January 11, 1989: 2.
— new officers installed, Lahaina News, July 5, 1989: 3.
— to hold fundraiser at Sam's Upstairs, Lahaina News, July 26, 1989: 13.
— raise money at "An Evening In Casablanca" held at Sam's Upstairs, Lahaina News, August 16, 1989: 17.
— gives money to Maui Youth and Family Shelter, Lahaina News, September 20, 1989: 1.
— scholarships available from, Lahaina News, January 17, 1990: 5.
— sponsoring Sweetheart's Ball to benefit Special Olympics, Lahaina News, January 31, 1990: 13.
— sponsoring golf tournament fundraiser, Lahaina News, February 28, 1990: 6.
— hosting benefit dinner for Maui Community Arts and Cultural Center, Lahaina News, March 21, 1990: 14.
— sponsoring benefit golf tournament, Lahaina News, March 21, 1990: 8.
— to hold Benefit Partners Golf Tournament, Lahaina News, March 28, 1990: 9.
— members return from International Convention, Lahaina News, July 25, 1990: 3.
— hosts Easter Egg hunt, Lahaina News, March 20, 1991: 3.
— to hold Easter egg hunt, Lahaina News, March 27, 1991: 3.
— donates medical equipment to Maui Memorial Hospital, Lahaina News, March 27, 1991: 9.
— photograph from Easter egg hunt, Lahaina News, April 10, 1991: 4.
— to give Woman of Distinction Award to Joan McKelvey, Lahaina News, May 23, 1991: 4.
— Fran Peart installed as president, Lahaina News, August 15, 1991: 6.
— sponsoring Keiki Halloween Parade, Lahaina News, October 17, 1991: 6.
— to hold health classes, Lahaina News, November 14, 1991: 2.
— sponsoring free classes on breast self-examination, Lahaina News, November 21, 1991: 3.
— to hold Sweetheart's Ball, Lahaina News, January 23, 1992: 16.
— awards Thelma McElfresh Woman of Distinction award, Lahaina News, April 2, 1992: 4.
— gives grant to Lahainaluna High School library, Lahaina News, April 16, 1992: 4.
— to hold benefit for Mardi Gras, Lahaina News, February 4, 1993: 4.
— to hold Family Christmas dinner, Lahaina News, December 9, 1993: 11.
— recognizes Lahainaluna High School student Micah Hu, Lahaina News, May 26, 1994: 3.
— provides grant to purchase stereo tactic mammographic unit, Lahaina News, December 8, 1994: 3.
— holds Easter egg hunt, Lahaina News, April 20, 1995: 1.
— raises money at auction during "A Taste of Lahaina", Lahaina News, October 12, 1995: 6.
— to meet, Lahaina News, February 15, 1996: 12.
— donates to Maui Memorial Hospital, Lahaina News, March 28, 1996: 3.
— to meet, Lahaina News, June 13, 1996: 11.
— to hold benefit auction, Lahaina News, September 5, 1996: 5.
— installs new officers, Lahaina News, September 12, 1996: 3.
— to meet, Lahaina News, April 17, 1997: 13.
— continues to meet, Lahaina News, July 10, 1997: 16.
— Mayor Linda Lingle to speak to, Lahaina News, October 2, 1997: 21.
— continues to meet, Lahaina News, September 24, 1998: 17.
— sponsoring scholarships, Lahaina News, November 19, 1998: 20.
— to hold whale watch on Prince Kuhio, Lahaina News, March 11, 1999: 12.
— recognizing achievement of county residents, Lahaina News, March 18, 1999: 8.
— supporting Arts Education for Children Group, Lahaina News, March 25, 1999: 6.
— presents Summer Music Camp Showcase, Lahaina News, July 8, 1999: 2.
— gives grant to Arts Education for Children Group, Lahaina News, July 22, 1999: 5.

— awards Lynn Ho "Woman of Distinction", Lahaina News, August 12, 1999: 9.
— holds Halloween Parade with Lahaina Rotary Club, Lahaina News, November 4, 1999: 1,3.
— to hold "Gala Casino Night", Lahaina News, January 27, 2000: 12.
— continues to meet, Lahaina News, February 24, 2000: 17.
— awards scholarship to Yee Chiat Tay, Lahaina News, June 22, 2000: 6.
— continues to meet, Lahaina News, August 3, 2000: 17.
— new officers installed, Lahaina News, August 3, 2000: 5.
— participated in American Cancer Society's Relay for Life 2000, Lahaina News, August 10, 2000: 8.
— thanks supporters of silent auction, Lahaina News, September 21, 2000: 18.
— to hold "Holiday Dinner Train" fundraiser on the Sugar Cane Train, Lahaina News, December 7, 2000: 24.
— to hold Secretary's Day Fashion Show, Lahaina News, April 5, 2001: 9.
— honors leaders at luncheon, Lahaina News, April 12, 2001: 3.
— recognizes Diane Delos Reyes, Nancy Killett, and Tish Perri, Lahaina News, May 10, 2001: 1,22.
— continues to meet, Lahaina News, July 26, 2001: 17.
— continues to meet, Lahaina News, August 23, 2001: 17.
— installs new officers, Lahaina News, August 30, 2001: 2.
— planning "Whale Mania Maui" benefit, Lahaina News, January 10, 2002: 9.
— continues to meet, Lahaina News, March 7, 2002: 17.
— to hold "Whale Mania Maui, An Awesome Art Adventure", Lahaina News, March 14, 2002: 5.
— to hold Easter Egg Hunt, Lahaina News, March 21, 2002: 15.
— to hold Secretary's Day Fashion Show, Lahaina News, April 18, 2002: 8.
— to hold Whale Mania Maui charity art event, Lahaina News, May 16, 2002: 14.
— planning "Whale Mania Maui", Lahaina News, May 23, 2002: 1,3.
— names Kim Willis as "Soroptimist of the Year", Lahaina News, June 27, 2002: 1,2.
— continues to meet, Lahaina News, July 11, 2002: 17.
— to auction whales from Whale Mania Maui program, Lahaina News, February 6, 2003: 3.
— auctions Whale Mania Maui whales, Lahaina News, March 20, 2003: 3.
— to hold Easter Egg Hunt, Lahaina News, April 17, 2003: 2.
— continues to meet, Lahaina News, June 12, 2003: 21.

SORVINO, PAUL
— to star in Dick Van Patten Celebrity Challenge, Lahaina News, November 27, 1997: 13.

SOSNER, DAVID
— appointed general manager of the Kapalua Villas, Lahaina News, November 18, 1993: 7.
— promoted to vice president of Kapalua Club and Villas, Lahaina News, December 21, 2000: 14.

SOSNER, JEREMY
— appointed director of sales and marketing at Ritz-Carlton Hotel, Lahaina News, May 23, 1991: 8.

SOUKI, JOSEPH [POLITICIAN]
— urges that buses for the elderly remain in operation, Lahaina Sun, March 7, 1973: 5.
— holds fundraiser, Lahaina News, September 28, 1988: 18.
— featured, Lahaina News, November 2, 1988: 1,14.
— seeks money for Lahaina Bypass, Lahaina News, December 13, 1989: 1,3.
— comments on bill to fund vice principal position at King Kamehameha III School, Lahaina News, January 31, 1990: 3.

— says funding for community pool doubtful, Lahaina News, February 7, 1990: 1,3.
— discusses upcoming 1991 legislative session, Lahaina News, February 6, 1991: 1.
— evaluates legislative session, Lahaina News, May 15, 1991: 1.
— plans to review medical care in West Maui, Lahaina News, January 2, 1992: 1,2.
— to speak to Maui Contractors Association general meeting, Lahaina News, March 12, 1992: 12,13.
— things rise in cost for A-Plus After School program still a good deal, Lahaina News, March 19, 1992: 3.
— supports shark hunting bill, Lahaina News, April 16, 1992: 1.
— discusses funds approved by legislature, Lahaina News, May 7, 1992: 1.
— selected as House Speaker, Lahaina News, November 12, 1992: 4.
— State House Speaker supports bill to increase pressure to remove algae, Lahaina News, January 21, 1993: 1.
— discusses legislative concerns, Lahaina News, January 28, 1993: 1,5.
— seeking input on criminal laws, Lahaina News, October 13, 1994: 5.
— to hold hearing on legalizing gambling, Lahaina News, September 14, 1995: 6.
— to speak at Maui County Century Club, Lahaina News, December 14, 1995: 19.
— discusses upcoming legislative session, Lahaina News, December 28, 1995: 1,12.
— discusses state House budget, Lahaina News, April 4, 1996: 2.
— wins primary election, Lahaina News, September 26, 1996: 3.
— discusses upcoming legislative session, Lahaina News, November 14, 1996: 7.
— to speak at Democratic Century Club, Lahaina News, December 12, 1996: 8.
— editorial critical of, Lahaina News, January 30, 1997: 4.
— discusses need to reduce lawsuit abuse, Lahaina News, September 11, 1997: 12.
— seeks funding for Lahaina hospital, Lahaina News, February 18, 1999: 1.
— participants in LahainaTown Action Committee forum, Lahaina News, August 17, 2000: 3.
— candidate for State House Representative, District 8, Lahaina News, October 26, 2000: 21.
— to head House Transportation Committee, Lahaina News, December 7, 2000: 3.

SOUL JAHS [MUSICAL GROUP]
— to perform at the Maui Arts and Cultural Center with Third World, Lahaina News, March 25, 1999: 16.

SOUL PROVIDERS [MUSICAL GROUP]
— to perform at Moose McGillycuddy's, Lahaina News, June 20, 1996: 12.

SOULMATE [MUSICAL]
— to be performed at Jazzerie Club, Lahaina News, May 15, 2003: 16.

SOULMATES, A ROCK OPERA [MUSICAL]
— to be performed at Maui Arts and Cultural Center, Lahaina News, August 21, 2003: 18.

SOUND OF MAUI, THE [MUSICAL GROUP]
— featured, Lahaina News, August 9, 1989: 11.
— to perform at the Napili Kai Beach Club, Lahaina News, January 9, 1992: 11.
— to perform at Sea House Restaurant, Lahaina News, February 13, 1992: 20.
— to perform at Sea House Restaurant, Lahaina News, March 11, 1993: 15.
— to perform at Sea House Restaurant, Lahaina News, September 23, 1993: 11.

SOUND OF MUSIC, THE [MUSICAL]
— auditions being held at Baldwin Mini Theatre, Lahaina News, August 10, 1995: 12.

SOUND OF THE FALLS, THE [RESTAURANT]
— Supper Club offering French culinary adventure at Westin Maui, Lahaina News, November 7, 1990: 10,11.
— Supper Club offering "Bienvenue En France" , Lahaina News, November 21, 1990: 13,15.
— recognized by The Best of Hawaii, Lahaina News, July 18, 1991: 6.
— featuring world seafood, Lahaina News, September 3, 1992: 16.
— receives Award of Excellence from the Wine Spectator magazine, Lahaina News, November 19, 1992: 5.
— featured, Lahaina News, February 25, 1993: 11.
— featured, Lahaina News, November 11, 1993: 10.
— presenting Mediterranean food, Lahaina News, February 24, 1994: 11.
— to feature South American food, Lahaina News, September 29, 1994: 12.
— sommelier Charles Fredy to select wine at, Lahaina News, October 20, 1994: 13.

SOUND, THE [MUSICAL GROUP]
— to perform at Hale Hokulani, Lahaina News, February 27, 2003: 16.

SOUNDS, KEOKI [MUSICIAN]
— to perform at the Hula Grill, Lahaina News, July 20, 1995: 11.

SOUNDWAVE [MUSICAL GROUP]
— vocal jazz ensemble from Vancouver to perform, Lahaina News, May 30, 1991: 10.
— to perform at Kaʻahumanu Center, Lahaina News, June 6, 1991: 15.

SOUP NUTZ AND JAVA JAZZ
— hosting fundraiser for West Maui Garden Academy, Lahaina News, August 16, 2001: 3.
— event to benefit West Maui Garden Academy, Lahaina News, August 23, 2001: 16.

SOUSA, KEOKI
— leading workshop on Laʻau Lapaʻau, Lahaina News, November 4, 1999: 12.
— to offer "Traditional Hawaiian Healing Practices", Lahaina News, October 5, 2000: 17.
— to present "Hawaiian History of Iao Valley", Lahaina News, March 14, 2002: 17.
— to talk on "To Heal the Nation: Hoʻoponopono Ea", Lahaina News, November 14, 2002: 21.

SOUTH AMERICA
— experiences of two Maui women in, Lahaina Sun, November 29, 1972: 5.
— travel to described, Lahaina News, March 15, 1980: 10.

SOUTH MAUI CONDOMINIUM COUNCIL
— to hold workshop on Federal Disabilities Act, Lahaina News, January 9, 1992: 5.
— to offer seminar "Almost Free Legal Advice", Lahaina News, June 4, 1992: 7.
— to organize seminar on legal issues, Lahaina News, October 8, 1992: 7.
— to organize seminar on why boards get sued, Lahaina News, October 15, 1992: 12.
— hosting seminar on legal issues for condominiums, Lahaina News, October 22, 1992: 12.
— to take role more seriously, Lahaina News, April 29, 1993: 5.
— to hold seminar on insurance, Lahaina News, July 8, 1993: 6.
— sponsoring "Mediate, Don't Litigate" workshop, Lahaina News, September 16, 1993: 8.
— to hold legal seminar, Lahaina News, October 28, 1993: 7.
— sponsoring roundtable of landscaping, Lahaina News, January 13, 1994: 5.
— sponsoring "Ocean Accidents vs. Condo Associations", Lahaina News, October 6, 1994: 7.
— to hold membership luncheon, Lahaina News, March 23, 1995: 10.

SOUTH MAUI TIMES [BUSINESS]
— Robert McCabe named editor of, Lahaina News, March 20, 1997: 2.

SOUTH MAUI WASTEWATER MASTER PLAN
— to be created, Lahaina News, October 1, 1992: 13,14.

SOUTH MAUI WEEKLY [BUSINESS]
— Joseph Sugarman purchases controlling interest in newspaper, Lahaina News, November 25, 1999: 13.

SOUTH PACIFIC [MUSICAL]
— to be performed by Maui Youth Theatre, Lahaina News, November 29, 1989: 36.
— auditions to be held, Lahaina News, December 6, 1989: 12.
— to open, Lahaina News, January 31, 1990: 12.
— opens, Lahaina News, February 7, 1990: 13.
— continues, Lahaina News, February 21, 1990: 13.
— continues, Lahaina News, February 28, 1990: 11.
— auditions to be held by Maui Community Theatre, Lahaina News, April 10, 1997: 12.
— to be performed by Maui Community Theatre, Lahaina News, May 29, 1997: 17.
— to open, Lahaina News, June 5, 1997: 16.
— reviewed, Lahaina News, June 12, 1997: 8.
— reviewed, Lahaina News, June 19, 1997: 8.

SOUTH PACIFIC KAYAKS AND OUTFITTERS
— co-sponsoring Compadres Kayak Racing series, Lahaina News, February 24, 1994: 6.

SOUTH PHILLY STEAKS AND FRIENDS [RESTAURANT]
— opens at Lahaina Cannery Mall, Lahaina News, March 21, 2002: 8.

SOUTH SEAS TRADING POST [BUSINESS]
— hosting garden party for Lahaina Town Action Committee, Lahaina News, February 6, 1991: 3.
— owner Joan McKelvey featured, Lahaina News, December 26, 1991: 7.
— relocating, Lahaina News, April 29, 1993: 8,9.
— Joan McKelvey sells, Lahaina News, September 28, 2000: 1,14.

SOUZA, ALBERT [MAINTENANCE SUPERVISOR]
— discussing end of ocean dumping of sewage by county, Lahaina Sun, December 9, 1970: 2.

SOUZA, ALLAN
— rewarded by mayor, Lahaina News, February 11, 1987: 11.

SOUZA, JOE
— liquor control director to investigate fight, Lahaina News, January 23, 1991: 3.

SOUZA, JOHN
— Haiku resident featured, Lahaina Sun, July 25, 1973: 12.

SOUZA, JOSEPH ALAN
— announces plans to condemn private land to create a state park in Makena area, Lahaina Sun, October 13, 1971: 3.
— awarded Heroism Medal by the Boy Scouts of America, Lahaina News, November 12, 1992: 10,11.

SOVEREIGNTY
— see Hawaiian Sovereignty

SOVIET UNION
— Maui-Moscow mural unveiled, Lahaina News, October 19, 1988: 18.

SOVIET/HAWAIIAN-HEART TO HEART EXCHANGE
— looking for volunteers, Lahaina News, June 7, 1989: 2.

SPACE SURVEILLANCE
— tours available at facility , Lahaina News, February 12, 1998: 2.

SPALDING, SIMON [MUSICIAN]
— chanteyman and fiddler to perform, Lahaina News, October 13, 1994: 18.

SPANGLER, KIM
— to offer "The Secrets of Investing in a Chaotic Market", Lahaina News, March 15, 2001: 8.

SPANISH
— Light Bringers offering assistance to, Lahaina News, August 7, 2003: 5.

SPANKY [COMEDIAN]
— to perform at Comedy Club and the Sports Page, Lahaina News, May 23, 1991: 11.
— to perform at Comedy Club and the Sports Page, Lahaina News, April 16, 1992: 17.
— to perform at Comedy Club and the Sports Page, Lahaina News, November 19, 1992: 9,12.
— to perform at Comedy Club, Lahaina News, April 28, 1994: 14.

SPARKS, ALLAN
— named to Charter Commission by mayor Linda Lingle, Lahaina News, May 23, 1991: 4.

SPARKS, RUSSELL
— education specialist at Department of Land and Natural Resources to speak on "Fisheries Management in Hawaii", Lahaina News, November 22, 2001: 20.
— to present "Hawaii's Near Shore Fishing Regulation—Past, Present and Future", Lahaina News, April 24, 2003: 21.

SPARKS, STEVE [MUSICIAN]
— tribute to be held for, Lahaina News, August 7, 2003: 5.

SPATS PASSION DANCE COMPANY [BUSINESS]
— to premiere at Hyatt Regency Maui, Lahaina News, June 13, 1984: 12.

SPATS TRATTORIA [RESTAURANT]
— to hold beach party, Lahaina News, June 17, 1987: 3.
— nightclub reviewed, Lahaina News, May 23, 1991: 18.
— nightclub at Hyatt Regency Maui, Lahaina News, January 2, 1992: 11.
— now offering wine tasting, Lahaina News, February 6, 1992: 17.
— to offer live jazz, Lahaina News, February 13, 1992: 19.
— to feature wines from Signorello Vineyards, Lahaina News, March 26, 1992: 13.
— renovations continue, Lahaina News, April 9, 1992: 13.
— renovations continue, Lahaina News, April 16, 1992: 15.
— changing menu, Lahaina News, March 11, 1993: 14.
— changes name to Trattoria, Lahaina News, June 2, 1994: 11.
— to host fundraiser for victims of Hurricane Marilyn, Lahaina News, October 19, 1995: 9.
— to feature Mediterranean cuisine, Lahaina News, April 25, 1996: 16.

SPEAK OUT
— television show on Akaku: Maui Community Television, Lahaina News, February 26, 1998: 13.

SPEAKERS HAWAII [BUSINESS]
— opens, to highlight Hawaii-based speakers, Lahaina News, April 3, 1991: 4.

SPEAKIN' EASY IN CHICAGO [SHOW]
— to be performed at The Performing Arts Learning Center, Lahaina News, March 19, 1992: 17.

SPECIAL EFX [MUSICAL GROUP]
— to perform at Maui Zoo Botanical Gardens, Lahaina News, June 21, 1989: 17.

SPECIAL FAIR DAY
— to be held, Lahaina News, August 29, 1996: 11.

SPECIAL OLYMPICS
— seeking sponsors, Lahaina News, May 7, 1986: 3.
— to hold first organizational meeting, Lahaina News, January 7, 1987: 3.
— basketball tournament to be held, Lahaina News, January 14, 1987: 3.
— to hold organizational meeting, Lahaina News, January 21, 1987: 3.
— competitors resting between events, Lahaina News, February 4, 1987: 11.
— committee planning games, Lahaina News, February 4, 1987: 3.
— committee to meet, Lahaina News, February 11, 1987: 11.
— to hold track and field event, Lahaina News, April 1, 1987: 12.
— fundraiser planned at Maui Prince Hotel, Lahaina News, April 15, 1987: 12.
— seeking volunteers, Lahaina News, September 30, 1987: 3.
— to be supported by Sweethearts Ball fundraiser, Lahaina News, February 10, 1988: 11.
— Area Track and Field Games sponsored by Soroptimists International, Lahaina News, March 30, 1988: 14.
— looking for coaches, Lahaina News, December 6, 1989: 7.
— positive impact of, Lahaina News, January 24, 1990: 1,3.
— contestants in Honolulu listed, Lahaina News, February 7, 1990: 28.
— seeks volunteers for track and field competition, Lahaina News, March 21, 1990: 2.
— results, Lahaina News, April 4, 1990: 5.
— Tony Barbosa marathon to support, Lahaina News, April 25, 1990: 12.
— police sponsoring marathon in honor of Troy Barbosa, Lahaina News, May 2, 1990: 6.
— celebration of at Westin Maui, Lahaina News, July 4, 1990: 4.
— Lahaina Nautilus to allow Olympians to practice, Lahaina News, October 24, 1990: 4.
— seeking volunteer coaches, Lahaina News, September 12, 1991: 3.
— sponsoring tennis clinic, Lahaina News, October 3, 1991: 8.
— seeking volunteers, Lahaina News, October 10, 1991: 5.
— to hold yard sale, Lahaina News, October 17, 1991: 5.
— to hold yard sale, Lahaina News, October 24, 1991: 4.
— to hold winder awards banquet, Lahaina News, December 5, 1991: 5.
— Winter Games to be held on Oahu, Lahaina News, January 2, 1992: 2.
— Area Spring Games to be held, Lahaina News, March 26, 1992: 8.
— to hold Area Spring Games this weekend, Lahaina News, April 2, 1992: 8.
— Troy Barboza Law Enforcement Torch Run to benefit, Lahaina News, May 7, 1992: 14.
— to hold yard sale, Lahaina News, May 7, 1992: 4.
— to hold yard sale, Lahaina News, June 4, 1992: 4.
— car show to benefit , Lahaina News, June 11, 1992: 6.
— benefit to be held, Lahaina News, June 18, 1992: 4.
— Olympian Aaron Hayman featured, Lahaina News, July 23, 1992: 3.
— coaches needed, Lahaina News, September 17, 1992: 8.
— to meet, Lahaina News, September 24, 1992: 6.
— to host Area Fall Games, Lahaina News, November 12, 1992: 5.
— to hold Christmas Awards Banquet, Lahaina News, December 10, 1992: 9.
— to hold volunteer training program, Lahaina News, February 18, 1993: 7.
— Area Spring Games to be held, Lahaina News, April 1, 1993: 5.
— to hold Winter Area Games, Lahaina News, December 9, 1993: 2.
— to hold Spring games, Lahaina News, March 17, 1994: 6.
— registration begins for winter sports, Lahaina News, September 14, 1995: 7.
— to host Maui Area Winter Games, Lahaina News, November 16, 1995: 8.
— receives grant from Harry and Jeanette Weinberg Foundation, Lahaina News, December 14, 1995: 19.
— winter sports season registration begins, Lahaina News, August 22, 1996: 12.

— winter sports season underway, Lahaina News, September 19, 1996: 13.

— to hold Maui Area Winter Games, Lahaina News, October 31, 1996: 15.

— to hold Spring Area Games, Lahaina News, April 10, 1997: 16.

— seeking volunteers for upcoming games, Lahaina News, April 23, 1998: 15.

— Ashworth Kapalua Clambake Pro-Am Invitational to raise money for, Lahaina News, July 2, 1998: 15.

— Ashworth Kapalua Clambake Pro-Am Golf Tournament raises money for, Lahaina News, August 5, 1999: 7.

— First Hawaiian Bank Troy Barboza Law Enforcement Run to benefit, Lahaina News, March 30, 2000: 6.

— to benefit from First Hawaiian Bank Barboza Law Enforcement Torch Run, Lahaina News, April 6, 2000: 7.

— competition to be held, Lahaina News, October 12, 2000: 9.

— spring games to be held, Lahaina News, April 5, 2001: 14.

— spring games continue, Lahaina News, April 19, 2001: 13.

— to hold bowling competition, Lahaina News, October 11, 2001: 12.

SPECTOR, CINDY
— recognized for 10 years of service to the Salvation Army, Lahaina News, March 15, 1982: 10.

SPECTOR, JENNIFER
— Lahainaluna High School student to compete in National DECA Career Development Conference, Lahaina News, May 18, 1988: 14.

SPECTRACOLOR HAWAII PRINTING AND IMAGING [BUSINESS]
— purchases five-color printing press, Lahaina News, June 29, 2000: 16.

SPEED READING
— sessions offered for seniors, Lahaina News, October 19, 1988: 18.

SPELLING BEE
— to be held, Lahaina News, March 3, 1994: 4.

SPENCE, KAREN [RADIO PERSONALITY
— as source of sports information, Lahaina News, January 21, 1987: 6.

SPENCER, JOHNNY [MUSICIAN]
— performing concert at Ka'anapali Beach Hotel, Lahaina News, January 2, 1985: 16.

SPENCER, RANDY
— to manage Seawatch Restaurant, Lahaina News, November 18, 1993: 7.

SPENCERCLIFF CORP.
— sold to Nittaku Enterprise Company, a Japanese restaurant company, Lahaina News, June 11, 1986: 3.

SPIDER
— black widow found in Lahaina, Lahaina News, November 11, 1999: 5.

SPINDEN, KEITH
— named executive chef at Hyatt Regency, Lahaina News, December 30, 1993: 6.

SPIRIT [MUSICAL GROUP]
— to perform at Casanova's, Lahaina News, November 7, 1990: 11.

SPIRIT IN THE BODY
— concert to be performed at Maui Arts and Cultural Center, Lahaina News, July 24, 2003: 16.

SPIRIT OF AMERICA [MARCHING BAND]
— to perform in Lahaina, Lahaina News, July 8, 1987: 24.

SPIRIT OF THE DANCE [TROUPE]
— to perform at Maui Arts and Cultural Center, Lahaina News, March 13, 2003: 17.

— to perform at Maui Arts and Cultural Center, Lahaina News, March 20, 2003: 16.

SPIRIT OF THE WEST [BUSINESS]
— fine art and collectibles shop opens, Lahaina News, January 5, 1995: 12.

SPIRIT OF UNITY TOUR
— to be held, Lahaina News, September 3, 1998: 21.

SPIRITUAL WARRIOR [MUSICAL GROUP]
— to perform at Studio 505, Lahaina News, February 4, 1993: 13.

— to perform at Longhi's, Lahaina News, November 25, 1993: 12.

— to appear on Hot Hawaiian Nights, Lahaina News, June 22, 1995: 11.

SPIROFF, KORY
— becomes owner of Domino's Pizza, Lahaina News, December 19, 1991: 13.

SPLASH OF BROADWAY, A [REVUE]
— continues at Westin Maui, Lahaina News, December 5, 1991: 22,23.

SPLASH! [BUSINESS]
— opens at Lahaina Center, Lahaina News, May 23, 1990: 8.

SPONTANEOUS COMBUSTION [MUSICAL GROUP]
— to perform at Moose McGillycuddy's, Lahaina News, March 21, 1996: 12.

SPOONER, AMY
— wins Amateur Public Links Championship, Lahaina News, July 2, 1998: 15.

— wins U.S. Amateur Public Links Championship, Lahaina News, July 16, 1998: 1.

SPORTS
— high school results tend to appear on page 7 of the Lahaina Sun and not comprehensively indexed, Lahaina Sun, : .

— results of high school games, Lahaina Sun, March 10, 1971: 7.

— boxing match between Joe Frazier and Muhammad Ali discussed, Lahaina Sun, March 17, 1971: 7.

— results, Lahaina Sun, March 17, 1971: 8.

— Maui Classic discussed, Lahaina Sun, March 24, 1971: 7.

— high school results, Lahaina Sun, March 24, 1971: 7.

— swimming courses offered at War Memorial Center, Lahaina Sun, June 23, 1971: 2.

— Rusty Harpoon-Windsock Bicycle Race planned for July 4, Lahaina Sun, June 30, 1971: 3.

— horse racing will begin at Kahului Fairgrounds, Lahaina Sun, August 4, 1971: 8.

— tennis courts to open at the Royal Lahaina Hotel, Lahaina Sun, August 4, 1971: 8.

— Lahaina Tennis Tourney announced, Lahaina Sun, August 11, 1971: 11.

— surfing meet held at Ho'okipa Park, Lahaina Sun, October 27, 1971: 6.

— Lahaina Canoe Club opening soon, Lahaina Sun, December 22, 1971: 18.

— Lahaina Tennis Club Christmas Tournament is underway, Lahaina Sun, December 22, 1971: 18.

— High School track meet set for March, Lahaina Sun, January 5, 1972: 7.

— Bud Grant, Minnesota Vikings head coach offers clinic, Lahaina Sun, January 12, 1972: 8.

— boxer Ruben Navarro breaks training in Lahaina, Lahaina Sun, January 19, 1972: 8.

— Lahainaluna High School wrestling team defeat St. Anthony High School, Lahaina Sun, February 2, 1972: 15.

— Mario Silva planning comeback in boxing, Lahaina Sun, February 16, 1972: 5.

— football camp organized by L.A. quarterback Roman Gabriel , Lahaina Sun, March 22, 1972: 5.

— marathoner Bob Getzen interviewed, Lahaina Sun, March 22, 1972: 9.

— County baseball stadium expected to be finished next year, Lahaina Sun, April 12, 1972: 14.

— boxing held at Maui War Memorial Gym, Lahaina Sun, April 19, 1972: 19.

— Mayor Cravalho objects to request for skydiving drop zone, Lahaina Sun, May 10, 1972: 5.

— footrace against the Lahaina-Kaʻanapali & Pacific Railroad planned, Lahaina Sun, May 10, 1972: 5.

— construction of public swimming pool at Lahainaluna High School approved, Lahaina Sun, June 14, 1972: 3.

— Golf clubhouse to be constructed in Wailea, Lahaina Sun, June 14, 1972: 9.

— Maui Senior Basketball League begins, Lahaina Sun, June 28, 1972: 19.

— Victoria-Maui race to begin, Lahaina Sun, June 28, 1972: 3.

— rodeo held at Makawao, Lahaina Sun, June 28, 1972: 4,5.

— Victoria-Maui race underway, Lahaina Sun, July 5, 1972: 7.

— "Odusa" is first to arrive in Victoria-Maui yacht race, Lahaina Sun, July 19, 1972: 1.

— moto-cross race held, Lahaina Sun, August 2, 1972: 22.

— "Cherokee" wins Victoria-Maui yacht race, Lahaina Sun, August 2, 1972: 4.

— Lanaʻi to Lahaina Inter-Island Relay to be held, Lahaina Sun, August 9, 1972: 10.

— licenses for deer on Kauaʻi issued, Lahaina Sun, August 16, 1972: 10.

— girl's softball described, Lahaina Sun, August 23, 1972: 22.

— tennis players advocate for new courts in Lahaina, Lahaina Sun, September 20, 1972: 22.

— County Council might support new tennis courts in Lahaina, Lahaina Sun, September 27, 1972: 14.

— dojo leader Shinko Kishi visits Maui, Lahaina Sun, October 25, 1972: 11.

— horse show planned for Makawao, Lahaina Sun, October 25, 1972: 7.

— Aikido demonstration held on Maui, Lahaina Sun, December 6, 1972: 1,15,16,17,18.

— popularity of darts increases, Lahaina Sun, December 6, 1972: 3.

— Norman K. Tamanaha Marathon set, Lahaina Sun, March 28, 1973: 4.

— new clubhouse opens in Wailea golf course, Lahaina Sun, May 2, 1973: 10.

— race track opposed, Lahaina Sun, May 23, 1973: 10.

— Go-carts used at old Punene airstrip, Lahaina Sun, May 23, 1973: 6.

— new hunting licenses required, Lahaina Sun, June 27, 1973: 3.

— diver Chip Bahouth's routine described, Lahaina Sun, July 4, 1973: 11.

— hunting seasons for rams opens , Lahaina Sun, July 4, 1973: 7.

— results of recent canoe competition, Lahaina Sun, July 11, 1973: 20.

— diving off Maui described, Lahaina Sun, August 1, 1973: 1,9.

— hand gliding on Maui described, Lahaina Sun, August 1, 1973: 5.

— kite-flying record set by Dick Eipper, Lahaina Sun, August 22, 1973: 4.

— Sunfish yacht race organized by Lahaina Yacht Club, Lahaina Sun, August 29, 1973: 3.

— report on local league play, Lahaina News, September, 1979: 12.

— report on local league play, Lahaina News, October, 1979: 12.

— softball results, Lahaina News, November, 1979: 13.

— results of 7 mile run, Lahaina News, March 1, 1980: 14.

— Special Olympics held at Maui Memorial Swimming Pool, Lahaina News, April 1, 1980: 13.

— ordinance prohibiting roller skates and skateboards , Lahaina News, August 1, 1980: 10.

— Almaden Grand Masters Tennis Tournament held, Lahaina News, October 15, 1980: 3.

— Royal Hawaiian World Soccer Crown to be held in Honolulu, Lahaina News, February 15, 1981: 16.

— statewide canoe championship organized, Lahaina News, March 1, 1981: 15.

— description of horseback ride to the Haleakala crater, Lahaina News, May 15, 1981: 11,12.

— Amfac Resorts no longer sponsoring Island Holidays pro tennis classic, Lahaina News, July 15, 1981: 5.

— Hanshin Tigers baseball team trains in Maui, Lahaina News, February 15, 1983: 6.

— Kapalua Open golf tournament expands, Lahaina News, February 15, 1983: 6.

— yacht clubs install new officers, Lahaina News, March 1, 1983: 10.

— Women's Kemper Open begins, Lahaina News, March 1, 1983: 6.

— Maui High School student Eugene Fontanilla wins Maui Marathon, Lahaina News, March 15, 1983: 6.

— Lahainaluna High School captured two state tennis doubles titles, Lahaina News, April 1, 1983: 6.

— Women's Kemper Open scheduled, Lahaina News, July 1, 1983: 6.

— editorial objecting to jet skis, Lahaina News, July 15, 1983: 2.

— West Maui's Little League All-Stars win state title, Lahaina News, August 15, 1983: 3.

— more detailed coverage begins with this issue but is typically not indexed, Lahaina News, August 31, 1983: 3.

— swimmer Bill Nelson required help during Maui Channel Swim, Lahaina News, September 14, 1983: 4.

— Napili women lose Na Wahine O Ke Kai paddling race, Lahaina News, September 28, 1983: 4.

— World Holiday Tennis Challenge set for August, Lahaina News, September 28, 1983: 5.

— windsurfer Matt Schweitzer featured, Lahaina News, October 19, 1983: 4.

— Kapalua International Championship of Golf begins in November, Lahaina News, October 26, 1983: 4.

— Arnold Palmer plays at Kapalua International Tournament of Golf, Lahaina News, November 2, 1983: 7,8,9.

— Greg Norman wins Kapalua International Championship of Golf, Lahaina News, November 9, 1983: 4.

— Bill Parsons Maui's only competitor in Mr. and Ms. Maui Body Builders Competition, Lahaina News, November 23, 1983: 6.

— Honolulu Marathon discussed, Lahaina News, December 14, 1983: 6.

— Waiakea Invitational Wrestling Tournament held at UH Hilo, Lahaina News, January 11, 1984: 4.

— Maui Triathlon results, Lahaina News, January 18, 1984: 4.

— meeting to discuss jet-ski rules set, Lahaina News, February 8, 1984: 3.

— contributed $6 million to Maui economy in 1983, Lahaina News, March 7, 1984: 4,5.

— college coaches attend Nike promotion at Stouffer's Wailea Hotel, Lahaina News, March 7, 1984: 6.

— Women's Kemper Open results, Lahaina News, March 14, 1984: 15,16,17,18,19,20,21,22,23.

— Lahainaluna High School competes in State tennis tournament, Lahaina News, March 28, 1984: 5.

— Lahainaluna tennis teams win both state high school doubles, Lahaina News, April 4, 1984: 4.

— Grand Masters Invitational Tennis Tournament begins at Hyatt Regency, Lahaina News, April 11, 1984: 3.

— Dale Eggeling to represent Royal Kaʻanapali Golf Courses as touring pro, Lahaina News, April 11, 1984: 5.

— NFL stars participate in benefit for Lahainaluna High School Athletic Department, Lahaina News, April 18, 1984: 6.

— success of tennis player Krishnan Ramanathan detailed, Lahaina News, April 25, 1984: 4.

— annual Champagne Polo Brunch to be held, Lahaina News, May 23, 1984: 3.

— U.S. wins Nissan Cup world Championship of Golf, Lahaina News, November 13, 1985: 4.

— Joseph M. Pagan fastpitch tournament set to begin November 28, Lahaina News, November 20, 1985: 11.

— Mark O'Meara wins Isuzu Kapalua International golf tournament, Lahaina News, November 20, 1985: 4.

— hiking MacGregor's Point recounted, Lahaina News, November 27, 1985: 7.

— surfboard maker Bob Olson (Ole) featured, Lahaina News, December 4, 1985: 4.

— Fourth Annual Kapalua/Betsy Nagelsen Pro-Am Invitational to be held, Lahaina News, December 11, 1985: 4.

— Kahuku to defend its wrestling championship, Lahaina News, December 11, 1985: 9.

— tennis courts at Malu'ulu O Lele Park to be named after tennis player Shigesh Wakida, Lahaina News, December 18, 1985: 4.

— Wailea's Blue Course ranked by Golf Digest Magazine, Lahaina News, January 1, 1986: 3.

— Lahaina juniors win trophies at Hilo Junior Winter Tennis Tournament, Lahaina News, January 8, 1986: 3.

— Lahainaluna High School basketball coach Larry Karinen interviewed, Lahaina News, January 15, 1986: 4.

— Larry Karinen interviewed about Lahainaluna basketball team, Lahaina News, January 29, 1986: 4.

— update on Lahainaluna High School sports, Lahaina News, February 5, 1986: 22.

— Pro Bowl sells out, will be played in Honolulu at least until 1990, Lahaina News, February 12, 1986: 4.

— end of Lahaina Basketball League described, Lahaina News, February 26, 1986: 4.

— basketball coach Luke Higgins interviewed, Lahaina News, February 26, 1986: 4.

— Lahainaluna High School basketball discussed, Lahaina News, March 12, 1986: 10,11.

— canoe clubs begin new season, Lahaina News, March 19, 1986: 18.

— Lahainaluna High School wrestling team featured, Lahaina News, March 19, 1986: 4.

— tennis classes offered by Royal Keiki Tennis Club, Lahaina News, March 26, 1986: 3.

— nation baseball season discussed, Lahaina News, March 26, 1986: 4.

— martial arts competition "Friday Night at the Fights" held at Maui Marriott Hotel, Lahaina News, April 2, 1986: 4.

— Aloha Basketball Classic to be played on Maui, Lahaina News, April 9, 1986: 4.

— Aloha Classic basketball game stopped due to leaky room at War Memorial Stadium, Lahaina News, April 16, 1986: 4.

— Fourth Annual Martial Arts Tournament to be held at Lahaina Civic Center, Lahaina News, April 23, 1986: 3.

— Kapalua Tennis Garden hosting Sixth Annual Doubles Championship, Lahaina News, April 23, 1986: 4.

— popularity of tennis discussed, Lahaina News, April 30, 1986: 4.

— popularity of martial arts discussed, Lahaina News, May 7, 1986: 4.

— Aku Cup to be held in May, Lahaina News, May 14, 1986: 4.

— details on recent events, Lahaina News, June 4, 1986: 4.

— Celebrity Softball Classic set for July, Lahaina News, June 11, 1986: 14.

— Kimo's/Hobie Longboard contest planned, Lahaina News, June 11, 1986: 4.

— "100 Holes of Golf" fundraiser for Easter Seal Society sponsored by Wailea Golf Club and Maui Inter-Continental Hotel, Lahaina News, June 18, 1986: 3.

— results of Lahaina Cardinals baseball team's season given, Lahaina News, July 9, 1986: 4.

— summary of events coming up in the Fall, Lahaina News, August 20, 1986: 4.

— Kapalua Open Tennis Tournament to begin, Lahaina News, August 27, 1986: 3.

— running event up Haleakala described, Lahaina News, August 27, 1986: 4.

— surfing contest held at Ho'okipa Beach Park, Lahaina News, September 10, 1986: 3.

— events over Labor Day described, Lahaina News, September 10, 1986: 4.

— polo season opens, Lahaina News, September 17, 1986: 11.

— Sailboards Maui Grand Prix International to be held, Lahaina News, September 17, 1986: 11.

— Silversword golf course groundbreaking held, Lahaina News, October 1, 1986: 5.

— rule son watching football games, Lahaina News, October 1, 1986: 6.

— events in October detailed, Lahaina News, October 8, 1986: 6.

— Maui Special Olympics reorganizing, Lahaina News, October 15, 1986: 3.

— windsurfing swap meet held, Lahaina News, October 15, 1986: 3.

— swap meet for windsurfers held, Lahaina News, November 5, 1986: 3.

— Isuzu-Kapalua International Golf Tournament held, Lahaina News, November 12, 1986: 1,6.

— Sky Ranch Air Services looking to start hand gliding service, Lahaina News, December 17, 1986: 12.

— Kimo's-Hobie Volleyball tournament held, Lahaina News, December 17, 1986: 12.

— visit by ESPN's Roger Twibell recounted, Lahaina News, December 24, 1986: 6.

— editorial supporting new seniors golf tournament, Lahaina News, January 7, 1987: 2.

— water walking equipment obtained by Lahaina Beach Center, Lahaina News, January 7, 1987: 3.

— coaching kids' basketball featured, Lahaina News, January 7, 1987: 6.

— residents predict NFL playoff outcomes, Lahaina News, January 14, 1987: 6.

— radio personality Karen Spence featured, Lahaina News, January 21, 1987: 6.

— Lahainaluna sports successful, Lahaina News, February 4, 1987: 6.

— Royal Lahaina Open Tennis Tournament organized, Lahaina News, February 4, 1987: 9.

— Pro Bowl held in Honolulu, Lahaina News, February 11, 1987: 1,6.

— Marilyn Smith offering golf clinic, Lahaina News, February 18, 1987: 3.

— report on tennis tournament attended by Lahaina athletes, Lahaina News, March 4, 1987: 6.

— Lahainaluna basketball team to play in state championships, Lahaina News, March 11, 1987: 6.

— windsurf swap meet planned, Lahaina News, April 8, 1987: 3.

— Lahainaluna High School win state-wide girls tennis tournament, Lahaina News, April 15, 1987: 6,17.

— Lahainaluna High School girls basketball team in state tournament, Lahaina News, April 22, 1987: 6.

— predictions on NBA finals from West Maui residents, Lahaina News, June 10, 1987: 4.

— tennis events on Maui described, Lahaina News, June 17, 1987: 6.

— Maui Classic tournament planned, Lahaina News, July 1, 1987: 6.

— triathlon held, Lahaina News, July 8, 1987: 4.

— paddling season ends, Lahaina News, July 22, 1987: 6.

— Lahaina Canoe Club junior women take state title, Lahaina News, August 12, 1987: 6.

— Pop Warner football league described, Lahaina News, August 19, 1987: 6.

— Rainbow football report on KHNL/13 described, Lahaina News, August 19, 1987: 6.

— Hyatt Regency Maui loses Celebrity Softball Game, Lahaina News, September 2, 1987: 3.

— events summarized, Lahaina News, September 9, 1987: 10.

— gymnastics lessons to be offered by YMCA, Lahaina News, September 16, 1987: 3.

— local events described, Lahaina News, October 7, 1987: 10.

— Pop Warner football league schedule, Lahaina News, October 7, 1987: 16.

— Aloha Classic Windsurfing Championship held, Lahaina News, October 14, 1987: 17.

— Pop Warner football league to hold games, Lahaina News, October 14, 1987: 3.

— Major league baseball discussed, Lahaina News, October 14, 1987: 6.

— Pop Warner football league to hold games, Lahaina News, October 21, 1987: 12.

— tennis program to be held at Lahaina Tennis Court, Lahaina News, October 21, 1987: 3.

— Hawaiian Airlines Maui Classic Basketball Tournament to be held at the Lahaina Civic Center, Lahaina News, October 21, 1987: 6.

— Hawaiian Airlines Maui Classic Basketball Tournament seeking volunteers, Lahaina News, October 28, 1987: 12.

— Festival of Running in Wailea canceled, Lahaina News, October 28, 1987: 12.

— Moloka'i-Oahu paddling race described, Lahaina News, October 28, 1987: 6.

— Ike Sugano wins the Lahaina Jackpot fishing tournament, Lahaina News, November 4, 1987: 1.

— West Maui Youth Athletic Association has basketball sign-ups, Lahaina News, November 4, 1987: 10.

— Hawaiian Airlines Maui Basketball Classic to offer shuttles for attendees, Lahaina News, November 11, 1987: 11.

— Pop Warner football league schedule, Lahaina News, November 11, 1987: 6.

— Hawaiian Airlines Maui Basketball Classic detailed, Lahaina News, November 18, 1987: 10.

— West Maui Youth Athletic Association basketball sign-ups continued, Lahaina News, November 18, 1987: 18.

— Valley Isle Road Runners to hold track meet, Lahaina News, December 2, 1987: 3.

— basketball coaches needed, Lahaina News, December 9, 1987: 26.

— photographs from Hawaiian Airlines Maui Basketball Classic, Lahaina News, December 9, 1987: 6.

— Tae Kwon-Do as activity for youth, Lahaina News, December 16, 1987: 1,16.

— Hawaiian Airlines Maui Basketball Classic recap, Lahaina News, December 16, 1987: 6.

— national highlights of previous year recounted, Lahaina News, December 30, 1987: 12.

— Valley Isle Road Runners Association to hold track meet, Lahaina News, January 6, 1988: 3.

— Midget Basketball schedule announced, Lahaina News, January 13, 1988: 16.

— West Maui Youth Athletic Association basketball games held, Lahaina News, January 20, 1988: 18.

— Midget Basketball teams complete season, Lahaina News, February 10, 1988: 11.

— West Maui Youth Athletic Association baseball sign-ups begin, Lahaina News, March 16, 1988: 15.

— Lahaina Intermediate School to host Invitational Volleyball Tournament, Lahaina News, March 30, 1988: 20.

— Royal Lahaina Open Tennis Tournament now sponsored by Nevada Bob's, Lahaina News, March 30, 1988: 3.

— connection to jazz for some professionals, Lahaina News, April 6, 1988: 6.

— sailboarding race across Moloka'i channel to be held , Lahaina News, April 13, 1988: 1,11.

— State Boating Manager Dave Parsons rejects banning thrillcraft, Lahaina News, April 27, 1988: 1.

— editorial supporting ban of jet skis, Lahaina News, April 27, 1988: 2.

— paddling described, Lahaina News, July 27, 1988: 14.

— Pop Warner football league sign-up begins, Lahaina News, July 27, 1988: 3.

— Pop Warner football league to hold benefit luau, Lahaina News, August 17, 1988: 3.

— Cycle to the Sun to be held, Lahaina News, August 24, 1988: 12.

— Wailea Speed Crossing windsurfing race to be held, Lahaina News, August 24, 1988: 12.

— review of activities at Lahainaluna High School, Lahaina News, October 12, 1988: 12.

— Peter Stuyvesant Travel Aloha Classic Wavesailing World Championships to be held, Lahaina News, October 12, 1988: 13.

— adult tennis classes to be held, Lahaina News, October 12, 1988: 20.

— Dracula Dash 8K run organized, Lahaina News, October 12, 1988: 3.

— festival of running set, Lahaina News, November 2, 1988: 18.

— Rusty Harpoon Restaurant to hold softball tournament fundraiser for Lahaina Pop Warner Football Association, Lahaina News, November 9, 1988: 12.

— Scott Kodama runner-up for Hawaii's Golden Diamond Award, Lahaina News, November 30, 1988: 3.

— Aloha Relay planned, Lahaina News, December 28, 1988: 3.

— Lahainaluna High School win Maui Interscholastic League title, Lahaina News, February 15, 1989: 1.

— aerobics competition to be held, Lahaina News, April 12, 1989: 3.

— results of Spring Wahine Tournament, Lahaina News, May 10, 1989: 3.

— Tedeschi 10K run scheduled, Lahaina News, May 24, 1989: 2.

— celebrity softball game to benefit Children's Miracle Network Telethon, Lahaina News, May 24, 1989: 3.

— Valley Isle Road Runners Association to host Maui Biathlon, Lahaina News, June 28, 1989: 9.

— Royal Ka'anapali 5K/10K run scheduled, Lahaina News, July 26, 1989: 2.

— summer basketball league being organized, Lahaina News, July 26, 1989: 2.

— Local Motion Boogie Board Bash held at Lahaina Harbor, Lahaina News, August 2, 1989: 6.

— Peter Stuyvesant Travel Aloha Classic to be held at Ho'okipa Beach Park, Lahaina News, August 2, 1989: 6.

— martial arts shown at Royal Lahaina Resort, Lahaina News, August 16, 1989: 7.

— Hawaii Aerobics Championship to be held at Maui Marriott Resort, Lahaina News, August 23, 1989: 5.

— "Wake Cycle to the Sun" to be held, Lahaina News, August 30, 1989: 24.

— winners of state aerobics competition photographed, Lahaina News, September 6, 1989: 5.

— Hana Relay scheduled, Lahaina News, September 13, 1989: 24.

— contest to broadcast inning of baseball open to under-18s, Lahaina News, September 13, 1989: 3.

— Lahaina Waves youth soccer undefeated, Lahaina News, November 1, 1989: 24.

— Moloka'i Memorial Athletic Scholarship Fund established, Lahaina News, November 15, 1989: 3.

— Maui Interscholastic League hosting state cross country championships, Lahaina News, November 15, 1989: 6.

— scuba diving seminar sponsored by Kama'aina Dive Club, Lahaina News, November 22, 1989: 3.

— intramural results, Lahaina News, December 27, 1989: 9.

— University of Hawai'i Wahine Volleyball to play University of California-Irvine at Wailuku War Memorial Gym, Lahaina News, October 3, 1991: 8.

— classes available in karate and Tae Kwan Do, Lahaina News, October 10, 1991: 8.

— Peter Stuyvesant Travel Aloha Classic windsurfing contest to be held this week, Lahaina News, October 24, 1991: 6.

— Hobie Sports and Kimo's Restaurant schedule beach volleyball tournament , Lahaina News, October 31, 1991: 5.

— beach volleyball tournament to be held, Lahaina News, November 7, 1991: 5.

— photograph of Lahaina Little Chiefs, Lahaina News, November 21, 1991: 9.

— Lahainaluna High School wrestling team to compete, Lahaina News, December 5, 1991: 19.

— teen weight training offered, Lahaina News, December 26, 1991: 11.

— Lahainaluna High School wrestling team wins at Kona Invitational Tournament, Lahaina News, December 26, 1991: 11,12.

— yoga to be offered, Lahaina News, December 26, 1991: 24.

— Lahainaluna High School wrestling team to compete against Hana, Lahaina News, January 2, 1992: 6.

— teen weight training offered at the YMCA, Lahaina News, January 2, 1992: 6.

— mountain bike race to be held from Kaupo to Keokea, Lahaina News, January 9, 1992: 7.

— War Memorial Track and Football Stadium now open, Lahaina News, January 23, 1992: 5.

— West Maui Youth Center softball team wins division, Lahaina News, January 23, 1992: 7.

— Maui Girls Softball Association begins registration, Lahaina News, January 23, 1992: 8.

— Japanese baseball team Seibu Lions to be hosted by Maui Prince Hotel, Lahaina News, January 30, 1992: 9.

— instructor Roger Bacon discusses value of martial arts, Lahaina News, February 6, 1992: 8.

— Superkids on Maui to take place, Lahaina News, February 6, 1992: 9.

— senior stroll to take place at the War Memorial Stadium, Lahaina News, February 6, 1992: 9.

— Lahainaluna High School to offer coaches clinic, Lahaina News, February 13, 1992: 10.

— mountain biking featured, Lahaina News, February 13, 1992: 9.

— to be celebrated at Makai Bar, Lahaina News, February 20, 1992: 12.

— Little League practices begin, Lahaina News, February 20, 1992: 16.

— stadium proposed behind Lahaina Civic Center, Lahaina News, February 20, 1992: 6.

— developers planning to build baseball stadium, Lahaina News, March 5, 1992: 3.

— Hard Rock Cafe to host World Cup of Windsurfing, Lahaina News, March 12, 1992: 10.

— Valley Isle Archery and Hunting Club to compete in Aloha State Archers Association's Hunters and Field Championships, Lahaina News, March 12, 1992: 9.

— regional ball park to be created in Napili, Lahaina News, March 19, 1992: 8.

— Maui Challenge triathlon to be held, Lahaina News, March 19, 1992: 8.

— World Cup of Windsurfing canceled, Lahaina News, March 26, 1992: 8.

— National Horseshow Pitchers Association contest held, Lahaina News, March 26, 1992: 8.

— trap shooting featured, Lahaina News, April 9, 1992: 10.

— Hawaii Horseshoe Pitchers Association tournament scheduled, Lahaina News, April 16, 1992: 10.

— Lahainaluna High School results, Lahaina News, April 16, 1992: 10.

— Ka'anapali Classic ocean swim to be held, Lahaina News, April 23, 1992: 22.

— teen weight training to be offered, Lahaina News, April 30, 1992: 6.

— ultimate frisbee games to be held, Lahaina News, April 30, 1992: 6.

— Memorial Softball Tournament to be held, Lahaina News, May 21, 1992: 12.

— Keiki Triathlon to be held, Lahaina News, May 21, 1992: 12.

— boxers Glenn Carvalho and Chris Gomes win at Hawaii Junior Olympic Championships, Lahaina News, May 21, 1992: 12.

— Lahaina youth train for Olympics, Lahaina News, May 28, 1992: 8.

— Lahaina Plebes Athletic Association to hold reunion, Lahaina News, May 28, 1992: 8.

— water polo team to practice, Lahaina News, May 28, 1992: 8.

— recreation opportunities in South Maui listed, Lahaina News, May 28, 1992: 9.

— South Maui recreation events to be held, Lahaina News, June 4, 1992: 8.

— South Maui recreation events to be held, Lahaina News, June 11, 1992: 11.

— Brad McMahon named sales director for Upper Deck Hawaiian Winter league, Lahaina News, June 18, 1992: 10.

— fight between Evander Holyfield and Larry Holmes to be televised, Lahaina News, June 18, 1992: 13.

— Master Holland's Tang Soo Do offered at Valley Isle Fitness Center, Lahaina News, June 18, 1992: 13.

— slow pitch league results given, Lahaina News, July 2, 1992: 13.

— county Department of Parks and Recreation to sponsor ultimate frisbee games, Lahaina News, July 9, 1992: 12.

— Maui County Council considering bill to create Ukumehame Public Shooting Range, Lahaina News, July 9, 1992: 3,4.

— Maui Ikaika Bodybuilding Competition to be held, Lahaina News, July 9, 1992: 7.

— results from slow pitch league, Lahaina News, July 9, 1992: 7.

— Hawaii Horseshow Pitching Association to hold tournament, Lahaina News, July 9, 1992: 7.

— martial arts classes to be offered at Master Holland's Tang Soo Do, Lahaina News, July 9, 1992: 7.

— Hawaii Horseshow Pitching Association to hold tournament, Lahaina News, July 16, 1992: 11.

— karate competition results, Lahaina News, July 30, 1992: 9.

— martial arts tournament to be held, Lahaina News, August 13, 1992: 6.

— students advance in Tae Kwon Do, Lahaina News, August 13, 1992: 6.

— flag football league to begin, Lahaina News, September 10, 1992: 8.

— Koho Grill offers live and delayed football, Lahaina News, September 17, 1992: 13.

— Pop Warner results, Lahaina News, September 17, 1992: 4.

— local results, Lahaina News, October 1, 1992: 8.

— Hawaii Horseshow Pitching Association to hold tournament, Lahaina News, October 15, 1992: 10.

— results of gymnastics competition, Lahaina News, November 5, 1992: 10.

— final drag races of the year to be held, Lahaina News, November 12, 1992: 9.

— results of drag racing competition, Lahaina News, November 26, 1992: 6.

— Gerry Asper and Lisa Stone win gold at Paradise Cup Bodybuilding Championship, Lahaina News, December 3, 1992: 6.

— fundraiser to be held to send team to Western Region Gymnastics Championship, Lahaina News, December 10, 1992: 6.

— triathletes talk about competing, Lahaina News, December 24, 1992: 8.

— Maui Raiders Softball team recruiting, Lahaina News, December 24, 1992: 8.

— Brady Perreira to play baseball in Japan, Lahaina News, December 31, 1992: 6.

— results of gymnastics competition, Lahaina News, January 21, 1993: 6.

— girls softball games to be held, Lahaina News, January 21, 1993: 7.

— results of Lahainaluna High School competitions, Lahaina News, January 21, 1993: 7.

— promotions announced Casco's Tae Kwon-Do of Lahaina, Lahaina News, January 28, 1993: 7.

— updates on Lahainaluna High School wrestling, Lahaina News, February 4, 1993: 6.

— Bud Light Triathlon to hold race at Ka'anapali, Lahaina News, February 11, 1993: 1.

— results of Compadres Kayak Racing series, Lahaina News, February 11, 1993: 8.

— Maui Challenge Triathlon, Lahaina News, February 11, 1993: 9.

— Seibu Lions to be hosted by Maui Prince Hotel, Lahaina News, February 11, 1993: 9.

— drag racing season begins, Lahaina News, February 18, 1993: 6.

— wrestlers sent to state competition, Lahaina News, March 4, 1993: 5.

— drag races to be held, Lahaina News, March 4, 1993: 5.

— Ka'anapali Biathlon to begin, Lahaina News, March 11, 1993: 8.

— Edmund Mitchell wins Hanaka'o'o Triangle Race, Lahaina News, March 11, 1993: 9.

— Grave Digger is top eliminator in drag racing, Lahaina News, March 11, 1993: 9.

— umpire clinic to be held, Lahaina News, March 11, 1993: 9.

— kayaking and swimming affected by strong winds, Lahaina News, March 18, 1993: 5.

— Maui Challenge Triathlon to be held, Lahaina News, March 18, 1993: 5.

— Maui Milkcap Championship Tournament scheduled, Lahaina News, March 18, 1993: 5.

— drag racing to be held, Lahaina News, April 1, 1993: 5.

— Ulupalakua Ranch Tri-Ranch Rodeo to be held, Lahaina News, April 1, 1993: 5.

— Bud Light Triathlon Series to end on Maui, Lahaina News, April 29, 1993: 6.

— Valley Isle Road Runners to hold Youth Awards Banquet, Lahaina News, April 29, 1993: 7.

— Milk Cap Classic competition to be held, Lahaina News, April 29, 1993: 7.

— Ka'ahumanu Center Milkcap Summer Slamma to benefit Big Brothers/Big Sisters, Lahaina News, May 27, 1993: 10.

— drag racing to be held on Memorial Day, Lahaina News, May 27, 1993: 10.

— Bob Craver named race director for Maui Bud Light Triathlon Championship, Lahaina News, June 3, 1993: 6.

— results of Bankoh Kayak Challenge, Lahaina News, June 3, 1993: 6.

— Maui Ikaika Bodybuilding Championship to be held, Lahaina News, June 17, 1993: 9.

— soccer scholarships available, Lahaina News, June 17, 1993: 9.

— Keiki Day Milkcap Slam Tournament to be held, Lahaina News, June 24, 1993: 12.

— International Squash Association to open squash court, Lahaina News, July 1, 1993: 8.

— Maui County Immigrant Services accepting team registration for annual league , Lahaina News, July 15, 1993: 8.

— umpire clinic to be held, Lahaina News, July 22, 1993: 9.

— volunteers needed for triathlon, Lahaina News, July 22, 1993: 9.

— Island Biker to hold Pineapple Scramble, Lahaina News, August 19, 1993: 9.

— umpire clinic to be held, Lahaina News, August 19, 1993: 9.

— drag racing to resume, Lahaina News, August 26, 1993: 12.

— Lae Ula O Kai Canoe Club competes in ironwoman competition, Lahaina News, September 2, 1993: 8.

— Diane Burgevin to compete in Maui Channel Swim, Lahaina News, September 2, 1993: 8.

— Terry Fox Run to be held, Lahaina News, September 2, 1993: 9.

— Outrigger Canoe Club ironwoman team captures first place, Lahaina News, September 9, 1993: 8.

— triathletes to compete, Lahaina News, September 23, 1993: 1,3,8.

— cowboy action shoot to be held, Lahaina News, September 23, 1993: 8.

— results of Maui Bud Light Triathlon Series Championship, Lahaina News, September 30, 1993: 1,15.

— results of Maui Bud Light Triathlon Series Championship, Lahaina News, September 30, 1993: 10.

— Valley Isle Timing Association to host drag racing, Lahaina News, September 30, 1993: 9.

— karate to be taught to children, Lahaina News, October 14, 1993: 10,11.

— World Cup windsurfing to be held, Lahaina News, October 28, 1993: 8.

— kick boxing seminar to be held, Lahaina News, November 4, 1993: 8,9.

— Valley Isle timing Association to end racing season, Lahaina News, November 4, 1993: 9.

— free karate classes, Lahaina News, November 4, 1993: 9.

— Jeff Sanders top Maui finisher at Gatorade Ironman Triathlon held on Big Island, Lahaina News, November 11, 1993: 8.

— drag racing season results, Lahaina News, November 18, 1993: 12.

— West Maui American Youth Soccer Organization to hold post-season meeting, Lahaina News, December 2, 1993: 10.

— Japan Karate Association-Hawaii holds holiday tournament, Lahaina News, December 23, 1993: 9.

— Lahaina Nautilus Center to hold aerobics workshop, Lahaina News, February 3, 1994: 9.

— skateboarder Kea Eubank wins contest on Oahu, Lahaina News, February 3, 1994: 9.

— boxer Linda Nakagawa featured, Lahaina News, February 10, 1994: 11.

— Robert "Wally Gator" Bouchard featured, Lahaina News, February 17, 1994: 7.

— drag racing season opening, Lahaina News, February 17, 1994: 8.

— Mauna Kea Snowboard Champions to be held, Lahaina News, March 3, 1994: 10.

— results of Compadres Kayak Racing Series, Lahaina News, March 3, 1994: 10.

— Tae Kwon Do black belts awarded, Lahaina News, March 17, 1994: 6.

— umpire clinic to be held, Lahaina News, March 17, 1994: 6.

— drag racing to be held this weekend, Lahaina News, March 17, 1994: 7.

— Chiemsee Windsurfing World Cup to be held, Lahaina News, March 17, 1994: 7.

— Aluminum Man biathlon to be held, Lahaina News, March 24, 1994: 12.

— King's Trail Biathlon to be held by Na Keiki O Ka Moana, Lahaina News, April 7, 1994: 6.

— update on wrestling, Lahaina News, April 14, 1994: 6.

— drag racing to be held, Lahaina News, April 21, 1994: 6,7.

— Lahaina Rugby Club featured, Lahaina News, April 28, 1994: 6.

— Aluminum Man/Woman triathlon to be held, Lahaina News, May 12, 1994: 6.

— Ka'anapali Biathlon to be held, Lahaina News, May 12, 1994: 6,7.

— new black belts awarded, Lahaina News, May 12, 1994: 7.

— drag racing to be held over Memorial Day, Lahaina News, May 12, 1994: 7.

— Maui In-Line Hockey association begins registration, Lahaina News, May 26, 1994: 8.

— Kamehameha Day Archery Tournament held, Lahaina News, June 9, 1994: 9.

— Kalani Ho finalist for Robert Matsumoto Maui Interscholastic League Sportsmanship award, Lahaina News, June 16, 1994: 7.

— Lahaina Ladybugs win softball championship, Lahaina News, June 23, 1994: 7.

— soccer camp to be held, Lahaina News, June 23, 1994: 7.

— Bowlathon to be held, Lahaina News, July 21, 1994: 6.

— soccer being played, Lahaina News, July 21, 1994: 6.

— spring board diving course to be held by YMCA, Lahaina News, July 28, 1994: 6.

— in-line hockey opening game, Lahaina News, August 4, 1994: 7.

— Maui Skateboard Association holds contest, Lahaina News, August 11, 1994: 6.

— Aluminum Man/Woman biathlon to be held, Lahaina News, September 8, 1994: 6.

— Lahaina athletes Jeff Sanders and Chris Tang prepare for Ironman Triathlon, Lahaina News, September 22, 1994: 9.

— snowboarding night sponsored by Hi-Tech Sports to be held at Maui Marriott, Lahaina News, October 13, 1994: 11.

— Peter Stuyvesant Travel Aloha Classic competition to be held, Lahaina News, October 27, 1994: 11.

— clay shooting range to open, Lahaina News, October 27, 1994: 14.

— insert included for Peter Stuyvesant Travel Aloha Classic , Lahaina News, November 3, 1994: 13,14,15,18,19,20.

— softball league to hold informational meeting, Lahaina News, December 15, 1994: 8.

— Lahaina Rugby Club plays, Lahaina News, December 15, 1994: 9.

— Lahaina Dojo of the Japan Karate Association-Hawaii to hold tournament, Lahaina News, December 29, 1994: 5.

— Maui Masters Swim Club to hold New Year's Resolution Swim, Lahaina News, December 29, 1994: 5.

— youths achieve black belts, Lahaina News, January 26, 1995: 8.

— water aerobics to be held by YMCA, Lahaina News, January 26, 1995: 8.

— Celebrity Sports Challenge NFL All-Stars vs. Maui Police Department Charity Basketball Game, Lahaina News, January 26, 1995: 9.

— Maui Superkids to hold American Lung Association, Lahaina News, February 2, 1995: 6.

— Westside Sporting Clays opens, Lahaina News, February 16, 1995: 9.

— results of West Maui softball games, Lahaina News, February 23, 1995: 7.

— update on Maui Interscholastic League Wrestling Championship, Lahaina News, March 2, 1995: 6.

— Tai Chi Chuan class opens, Lahaina News, March 9, 1995: 7.

— Lahaina "Hot Shots" Soccer Team holds car wash, Lahaina News, March 23, 1995: 2.

— Lahaina karate students to host Japanese champions, Lahaina News, April 6, 1995: 7.

— Maui Style Wrestling Club to practice, Lahaina News, April 6, 1995: 7.

— State Track and Field Championships to be held, Lahaina News, April 13, 1995: 9.

— umpire Steve "Specs" Ashfield featured, Lahaina News, April 20, 1995: 10.

— Hobie Hawaii, Hula Grill and Maui Marriott to hold first Dig Me Beach Classic Volleyball Tournament, Lahaina News, April 20, 1995: 10.

— Maui Sea Spree to take place at Kahana Beach Park, Lahaina News, May 18, 1995: 7.

— American Youth Soccer Organization registration begins, Lahaina News, May 25, 1995: 5.

— roller hockey summer league sign-ups begin, Lahaina News, May 25, 1995: 5.

— Maui County Junior Lifeguard Program to be held, Lahaina News, May 25, 1995: 5.

— Lahaina Dojo of the Japan Karate Association to hold benefit car wash, Lahaina News, June 15, 1995: 2.

— soccer registration continues, Lahaina News, June 22, 1995: 6.

— junior lifeguard program starting, Lahaina News, June 22, 1995: 6.

— Tracey Gleason participates in triathlon, Lahaina News, June 22, 1995: 6.

— Maui Team Competition to be held, Lahaina News, June 29, 1995: 7.

— Maui County Junior Lifeguard Program to be held, Lahaina News, July 6, 1995: 7.

— members of Lahaina Dojo to complete in Japan, Lahaina News, July 20, 1995: 7.

— registration for lifeguard training begins, Lahaina News, July 20, 1995: 7.

— Tae Kwon Do promoted, Lahaina News, August 3, 1995: 9.

— co-ed softball league begins, Lahaina News, August 3, 1995: 9.

— soccer season to begin, Lahaina News, September 7, 1995: 4.

— Maui Triathlon Championship to be held, Lahaina News, September 7, 1995: 4.

— softball standings, Lahaina News, October 5, 1995: 6.

— Maui Family Support Services to hold fundraiser for Maui Stingrays, Lahaina News, October 5, 1995: 6.

— NRA Basic Safety Pistol Course to be offered, Lahaina News, October 5, 1995: 6.

— Maui Muscle Fitness Center opens, Lahaina News, November 30, 1995: 7.

— NRA Basic Pistol Safety Course to be held, Lahaina News, November 30, 1995: 7.

— softball season to not be played Mahu'ulu O Lele Park, Lahaina News, January 11, 1996: 1,16.

— Maui Gymnastics Invitational to be held, Lahaina News, January 11, 1996: 6.

— boys awarded black belts , Lahaina News, February 1, 1996: 7.

— Maui Hat Draw Ultimate Frisbee Tournament to be held, Lahaina News, February 22, 1996: 7.

— gateball featured, Lahaina News, April 11, 1996: 7.

— history of paddling in Maui, Lahaina News, April 18, 1996: 13.

— Marjo Selin's Muscle Classic to be held, Lahaina News, May 16, 1996: 12.

— discussion of muscle workout, Lahaina News, May 16, 1996: 14.

— Maui American Youth Soccer Organization begins registration, Lahaina News, June 6, 1996: 16.

— West Maui Youth Baseball to sponsor Slow Pitch Softball Tournament, Lahaina News, June 13, 1996: 11.

— Samalia Berger semifinalist in "Teen Magazine's 1997 Athlete of the Year" program, Lahaina News, June 20, 1996: 10.

— kickboxing tournament to be held, Lahaina News, June 20, 1996: 10.

— Maui Volleyball Association formed, Lahaina News, June 27, 1996: 16.

— kickboxing tournament to be held, Lahaina News, June 27, 1996: 16.

— deadline for softball season nearing, Lahaina News, July 18, 1996: 6.

— softball registration extended, Lahaina News, July 25, 1996: 12.

— triathletes to participate in Kona Ironman, Lahaina News, August 8, 1996: 13.

— karate goodwill tournament to be held, Lahaina News, August 15, 1996: 12.

— Alfred Huang to lead Tai Chi exercises, Lahaina News, September 26, 1996: 12.

— polo tournament to be held at Olinda Outdoor Polo Field to benefit Maui Animal Aloha Center, Lahaina News, October 10, 1996: 12.

— West Maui American Youth Soccer Organization season to end soon, Lahaina News, October 31, 1996: 17.

— paragliding becoming more popular on Maui, Lahaina News, February 6, 1997: 12.

— boxing on Maui, Lahaina News, March 20, 1997: 13.

— indoor polo season to begin, Lahaina News, March 27, 1997: 13.

— polo being played Upcountry, Lahaina News, April 17, 1997: 12.

— boxing on Maui, Lahaina News, May 1, 1997: 15.

— American Youth Soccer Organization to hold registrations for, Lahaina News, May 8, 1997: 15.

— update on baseball and softball at Lahaina Recreation Center, Lahaina News, May 22, 1997: 13.

— kickboxing to be held, Lahaina News, May 22, 1997: 16.

— Tyson vs. Holyfield II to be available via pay per view, Lahaina News, June 26, 1997: 16.

— Maui Gymnastics Center to hold "Summer Saulting Spectacular", Lahaina News, June 26, 1997: 17.

— softball and mountain ball seasons begin, Lahaina News, July 10, 1997: 14.

— Chiselers Dive Tournament to be held, Lahaina News, August 7, 1997: 11.

— skateboarding growth stymied by lack of parks, Lahaina News, September 18, 1997: 14.

— softball results, Lahaina News, October 2, 1997: 16.

— soccer referees trained, Lahaina News, October 9, 1997: 9.

— West Maui Parks looking for women's basketball teams, Lahaina News, December 11, 1997: 17.

— Maui Gymnastics Invitation to be held, Lahaina News, January 1, 1998: 17.

— importance of coaches as role models, Lahaina News, January 8, 1998: 6.

— Maui Gymnastics Invitation to be held, Lahaina News, January 8, 1998: 7.

— "The Jewish Olympian" photograph exhibit to be held at Ka'ahumanu Center, Lahaina News, February 26, 1998: 12.

— Lahaina boxers to compete in South Carolina, Lahaina News, February 26, 1998: 7.

— U.S. Olympic Women's Hockey Team to visit Planet Hollywood, Lahaina News, March 5, 1998: 7.

— Helen Giragosian offering karate lessons, Lahaina News, March 12, 1998: 15.

— youth wrestling program to begin, Lahaina News, March 26, 1998: 16.

— Maui Water Polo to practice at Lahaina Aquatics Center, Lahaina News, April 9, 1998: 15.

— boxers to compete, Lahaina News, May 14, 1998: 14.

— Maui Water Polo practice to be held at Lahaina Aquatics Center, Lahaina News, May 28, 1998: 6.

— masters to teach martial arts, Lahaina News, June 25, 1998: 6.

— Youth Coach Certification Program held, Lahaina News, July 30, 1998: 15.

— athletes of the year discussed, Lahaina News, August 13, 1998: 14.

— Gold's Gym hosting "Westside Boxing Club", Lahaina News, September 24, 1998: 15.

— windsurfing world championship to be held, Lahaina News, November 5, 1998: 19.

— martial artists pass black belt examination, Lahaina News, December 3, 1998: 18.

— West Maui Powerlifters featured, Lahaina News, February 11, 1999: 15.

— Martial Arts Spectacular to be held, Lahaina News, February 18, 1999: 7.

— Martial Arts Spectacular to be held, Lahaina News, February 25, 1999: 7.

— Volunteer Center of Maui County to honor coaches, Lahaina News, February 25, 1999: 7.

— "Hawaiian Diving Adventures" to begin third season on television, Lahaina News, February 25, 1999: 7.

— students take black belt test, Lahaina News, March 25, 1999: 14.

— Darren Robinson sets powerlifting record, Lahaina News, March 25, 1999: 14.

— coed water polo practice to be held, Lahaina News, March 25, 1999: 14.

— state boxing championship to be held at the Westin Maui, Lahaina News, March 25, 1999: 15.

— update on boxing matches, Lahaina News, April 1, 1999: 14.

— powerlifters hoist trophy, Lahaina News, April 1, 1999: 14.

— Lahaina Pony Baseball Team to hold Portuguese sausage benefit, Lahaina News, April 1, 1999: 15.

— baseball clinic to be held by University of Hawaii baseball players, Lahaina News, April 1, 1999: 15.

— American Youth Soccer Organization to begin summer season, Lahaina News, April 15, 1999: 6.

— Ka'anapali Beach Hotel to host Hawaii Junior Olympic Boxing Championships, Lahaina News, May 6, 1999: 16.

— coed soccer to be played, Lahaina News, May 20, 1999: 6.

— Derek Vinuya and Elizabeth Dolezal compete in Starbucks Solo Kayak and Canoe World Championship, Lahaina News, June 10, 1999: 2.

— results of state weightlifting championships, Lahaina News, June 17, 1999: 7.

— Kapalua Villas offering mountain hikes, Lahaina News, June 24, 1999: 7.

— "Hawaiian Diving Adventures" to begin third season on television, Lahaina News, June 24, 1999: 7.

— Darren Robinson deadlifts 702 pounds, Lahaina News, July 1, 1999: 7.

— powerlifters set record, Lahaina News, July 22, 1999: 11.

— local wrestler Thomas Fevella, Jr. wins three medals at national competition, Lahaina News, July 29, 1999: 1,3.

— Festival of the Kings Karate Championships held, Lahaina News, August 12, 1999: 6.

— West Maui Powerlifters win brackets at AAU contest, Lahaina News, August 26, 1999: 6.

— Maui Inline Hockey Association new Mite Division, Lahaina News, August 26, 1999: 7.

— Darren Robinson wins national "Raw" title, Lahaina News, September 16, 1999: 6.

— West Maui USSSA softball game to be held, Lahaina News, September 16, 1999: 7.

— Maui Go Karters Association to hold race, Lahaina News, October 7, 1999: 9.

— water polo course to be offered, Lahaina News, November 4, 1999: 7.

— water aerobics program promotes health, Lahaina News, November 18, 1999: 7.

— Hawaii State Kart Racing Championship to be held, Lahaina News, November 18, 1999: 8.

— Maui Extreme Triathlon results, Lahaina News, November 18, 1999: 8.

— West Maui Powerlifters set records, Lahaina News, November 18, 1999: 9.

— update on powerlifters competition, Lahaina News, December 9, 1999: 9.

— new coaches of junior varsity at Lahainaluna High School, Lahaina News, December 23, 1999: 8.

— Maui Gymnastics Invitational Meet to be held, Lahaina News, December 23, 1999: 9.

— Maui Gymnastics Invitational Meet to be held, Lahaina News, January 6, 2000: 7.

— Umpire's Clinic to be held, Lahaina News, March 9, 2000: 6.

— West Side lifters shatter state records, Lahaina News, March 9, 2000: 7.
— members of Team Maui powerlifters compete at AAU State Powerlifting Championship, Lahaina News, March 23, 2000: 6.
— Umpire's Clinic to be held, Lahaina News, March 23, 2000: 6.
— registration for volleyball begins at West Maui Parks and Recreation, Lahaina News, March 30, 2000: 6.
— results of Muscle Factory PL Championships, Lahaina News, April 13, 2000: 7.
— Maui Aikido-Ki Society opens dojo, Lahaina News, May 11, 2000: 14.
— West Maui Powerlifters competing in the 2000 WABDL Hawaii Invitational Bench Press and Deadlift Championships, Lahaina News, June 22, 2000: 12.
— karate students promoted, Lahaina News, June 29, 2000: 15.
— Festival of Kings Karate Tournament to be held, Lahaina News, July 27, 2000: 6.
— Maui Invitational Water Polo Tournament to be held, Lahaina News, August 3, 2000: 7.
— Maui Inline Hockey Association to hold registration, Lahaina News, August 17, 2000: 6.
— Maui cheerleaders to exhibit, Lahaina News, September 21, 2000: 20.
— West Maui Parks and Recreation to begin "Open Gym Activities", Lahaina News, September 28, 2000: 9.
— cheerleading developing as a sport, Lahaina News, October 12, 2000: 8.
— Maui Kenpo Dojo featured, Lahaina News, October 26, 2000: 10.
— Lahainaluna High School cheerleaders competing, Lahaina News, December 7, 2000: 12.
— Maui Gymnastics Invitational Meet to be held, Lahaina News, January 4, 2001: 9.
— Hawaii lifters defend title, Lahaina News, March 22, 2001: 13.
— Jackson, Johnny "Bang-Bang" planning "Boxing Bonanza", Lahaina News, April 5, 2001: 14.
— weightlifters compete in Waimanalo, Lahaina News, April 26, 2001: 15.
— results of track team competition, Lahaina News, May 24, 2001: 14.
— results of wrestling competition, Lahaina News, May 31, 2001: 12.
— Designer Body Maui Muscle and Physique Championship to be held, Lahaina News, May 31, 2001: 16.
— boxing match to be held, Lahaina News, July 5, 2001: 13.
— Bang-Bang Boxing Productions plans amateur boxing event, Lahaina News, July 12, 2001: 13.
— kiteboarding to be taught at Maui Sailing Center, Lahaina News, July 19, 2001: 13.
— soccer camp for children to be held, Lahaina News, July 26, 2001: 13.
— hunting licenses available, Lahaina News, July 26, 2001: 13.
— hunting licenses available, Lahaina News, August 2, 2001: 13.
— special education teacher Joe Balagitao Jr. moves from Baldwin High School to Lahainaluna High School, Lahaina News, August 30, 2001: 1,8.
— local weight lifters compete in Bench Press and Deadlift State Championships, Lahaina News, September 20, 2001: 13.
— Hawaiian Islands Natural Bodybuilding and Fitness Championships to be held, Lahaina News, September 27, 2001: 13.
— Hawaiian Islands Natural Bodybuilding and Fitness Championships to be held, Lahaina News, October 4, 2001: 13.
— "King of Fast Pitch Softball" Eddie Feigner to appear at charity softball game, Lahaina News, October 25, 2001: 13.
— Pop Warner cheerleaders heading to regional contest, Lahaina News, November 1, 2001: 12.
— skimboarders to perform on Oahu, Lahaina News, December 13, 2001: 13.
— Hula Bowl to be held, Lahaina News, December 27, 2001: 12.

— International Skimboarding Championships to be held at Sandy Beach, Lahaina News, December 27, 2001: 13.
— "Knockouts at Kalama" to be held, Lahaina News, January 10, 2002: 13.
— Garrett McNamara wins tow-in contest with Brazilian Rodrigo Resende, Lahaina News, January 10, 2002: 3.
— "Knockouts at Kalama" to be held, Lahaina News, January 17, 2002: 13.
— Bang-Bang Boxing planning open house, Lahaina News, February 21, 2002: 13.
— West Style Wrestling to welcome children, Lahaina News, March 21, 2002: 13.
— Hawaii State World Bench Press and Deadlift (WABDL) Championships to be held at Lahaina Civic Center, Lahaina News, April 25, 2002: 13.
— Skim Hawaii plans skimboarding contest at Makena's "Big Beach", Lahaina News, May 16, 2002: 13.
— Maui residents set records at Lahaina powerlifting contest, Lahaina News, May 30, 2002: 13.
— North Shore Paddle race to be held, Lahaina News, August 22, 2002: 10.
— Red Bull Cliff Diving Lana'i contest to be held, Lahaina News, August 29, 2002: 11.
— stock car races scheduled, Lahaina News, September 5, 2002: 13.
— kiteboarders to compete at Ho'okipa, Lahaina News, September 19, 2002: 12.
— Hawaiian Islands Natural Bodybuilding and Fitness Championships to be held at Maui Arts and Cultural Center, Lahaina News, October 3, 2002: 13.
— Napili Cross Country Team seeking runners, Lahaina News, October 10, 2002: 13.
— Georg Woodman to offer Judo classes, Lahaina News, November 7, 2002: 10.
— table tennis club forming, Lahaina News, November 21, 2002: 11.
— water polo featured, Lahaina News, December 12, 2002: 10.
— West Maui Table Tennis Club formed by Craig Volentine, Lahaina News, December 12, 2002: 10.
— gymnasts to compete, Lahaina News, January 2, 2003: 13.
— West Maui Kids Track Championships to be held, Lahaina News, February 13, 2003: 13.
— West Maui Kids Track Championships to be held, Lahaina News, February 20, 2003: 12.
— Napili Cross Country Team competed in West Maui Kids Track practice meet, Lahaina News, February 27, 2003: 12.
— West Maui Kids Track Championships to be held, Lahaina News, February 27, 2003: 13.
— West Maui Kids Track Championships held, Lahaina News, March 13, 2003: 1.
— West Maui Kids Track Championships held, Lahaina News, March 20, 2003: 13.
— West Maui Kids Track to hold practices, Lahaina News, May 1, 2003: 12.
— West Maui Track Club seeking athletes, Lahaina News, May 29, 2003: 12.
— girls water polo plays, Lahaina News, May 29, 2003: 12.
— West Maui Track Club seeking young athletes, Lahaina News, June 12, 2003: 11.
— to present "Na Mea Pa'ani Kahiko O Na 'Oiwi O Hawaii—The Ancient Sports of Native Hawaiians", Lahaina News, June 12, 2003: 21.
— water polo lessons to be offered, Lahaina News, June 19, 2003: 12.
— West Maui Track Club seeking young athletes, Lahaina News, June 19, 2003: 12.
— coed softball to be held, Lahaina News, June 26, 2003: 10.
— Lahainaluna High School to offer water polo classes, Lahaina News, July 31, 2003: 13.

— Maui Ki-Aikido to offer course, Lahaina News, August 21, 2003: 12.
— Valley Isle Road Runners preparing for cross country season, Lahaina News, September 4, 2003: 12.
— see also specific sports

SPORTS AUTHORITY [BUSINESS]
— receives award for best aid station at Maui Marathon, Lahaina News, October 17, 2002: 11.

SPORTS CLUB KAHANA
— offering specials, Lahaina News, October 19, 2000: 9.
— offering free week access to club to Maui residents, Lahaina News, October 26, 2000: 12.

SPORTS PRO HAWAII, INC [BUSINESS]
— participates in Adopt-A-Highway program, Lahaina News, October 17, 1991: 7.

SPORTS SHINKO SCHOLARSHIP AND GOLF TOURNAMENT
— to be held, Lahaina News, July 13, 2000: 7.

SPORTZ & CO.
— offering comedy workshop, Lahaina News, May 15, 1991: 13.

SPOTTS, PEGGY
— gymnast teaching at Malu'ulu O Lele Cultural Center, Lahaina News, February 19, 1986: 4.

SPOTTSWOOD, JACK
— Lahaina Aquatic Center Senior Lifeguard featured, Lahaina News, July 12, 2001: 1,20.

SPRAGUE, PETER [MUSICIAN]
— to perform at Blackie's Bar, Lahaina News, July 4, 1991: 10,13.

SPRECKELSVILLE [TOWN]
— rezoning controversy, Lahaina Sun, June 9, 1971: 6.
— seawall proposed at by Sugar Cove Condominium and Cyrus Monroe, Lahaina News, May 28, 1992: 5.

SPREITER, JANET [ARTIST]
— painter to exhibit at Lahaina Arts Society, Lahaina News, June 5, 2003: 18.

SPRING STAGES OF YOUTH BASIC
— to begin, Lahaina News, January 26, 1995: 14,15.

SPRING WIND QUINTET [MUSICAL GROUP]
— to perform at Maui Arts and Cultural Center, Lahaina News, May 3, 2001: 20.

SPRINGER, CATHLEEN
— homeopath to give health care presentation, Lahaina News, March 5, 1998: 17.
— to discuss history of homeopathy, Lahaina News, March 12, 1998: 21.
— to hold workshop on wellness, Lahaina News, April 23, 1998: 17.
— to present on homeopathic medicine, Lahaina News, June 25, 1998: 12.
— to speak on homeopathy, Lahaina News, November 12, 1998: 13.

SPRINKLE, ANNA
— King Kamehameha III Elementary School teacher honored by TS Restaurants, Lahaina News, June 13, 2002: 5.

SPRINT HAWAII [BUSINESS]
— lowers inter-island rate, Lahaina News, July 17, 1997: 12.
— opens store, Lahaina News, July 30, 1998: 13.
— acquires PrimeCo Personal Communication's PCS license and operations, Lahaina News, February 4, 1999: 13.
— program collecting used wireless phones to benefit Easter Seals of Hawaii, Lahaina News, July 4, 2002: 8.

SPUDS MACKENZIE
— to appear at Maui Inter-Continental Wailea's Inu Inu Lounge, Lahaina News, May 25, 1988: 12.

SPYRO GYRA [MUSICAL GROUP]
— to perform at Maui Music Festival, Lahaina News, April 22, 1999: 3.

ST. ANTHONY HIGH SCHOOL
— defeated by Lahainaluna in basketball, Lahaina Sun, January 27, 1971: 7.
— to be site of statewide track meet, Lahaina News, April 25, 1990: 9.
— to hold Hoolaulea, Lahaina News, July 30, 1992: 18.
— to hold Christmas Bazaar, Lahaina News, November 17, 1994: 4.
— grade school to hold bazaar, Lahaina News, January 12, 1995: 4.
— to hold Christmas Bazaar, Lahaina News, November 7, 1996: 14.
— grade school to hold Fun Daze Bazaar, Lahaina News, January 2, 1997: 11.
— to hold Fun Daze Bazaar, Lahaina News, January 16, 1997: 10.
— to hold silent auction, Lahaina News, February 6, 1997: 14,15.
— to honor alumni, Lahaina News, February 12, 1998: 17.
— to hold Junior Senior School Dinner Auction, Lahaina News, February 11, 1999: 16,17.
— band to perform, Lahaina News, May 6, 1999: 21.
— Junior Senior High School Ho'olaule'a to be held, Lahaina News, June 27, 2002: 15.

ST. CLAIR, MARY BAXTER [ARTIST]
— to exhibit at Sargent's Fine Art, Lahaina News, October 17, 2002: 22.

ST. FRANCIS DAY
— held at Sacred Hearts School, pets invited, Lahaina News, October 12, 2000: 1,11.

ST. FRANCIS MEDICAL CENTER
— John E. "Jack" Kelley golf tournament to benefit, Lahaina News, September 11, 1997: 16.
— Jack Kelley Memorial Golf Tournament to raise money for, Lahaina News, September 10, 1998: 19.
— receives donation from Whalers Realty Inc., Lahaina News, May 18, 2000: 11.
— bone marrow donor registry to conduct registration, Lahaina News, August 14, 2003: 16.

ST. JOHN, JOHN [ARTIST]
— opens gallery in Lahaina, Lahaina Sun, December 23, 1970: 4.
— letter to the editor concerning feelings towards the hippies, Lahaina Sun, February 10, 1971: 8.
— mural to be destroyed to make way for development, Lahaina Sun, January 12, 1972: 7.

ST. JOHN, LORETTA [MUSICIAN]
— to perform at the Sandalwood, Lahaina News, September 16, 1993: 18.

ST. JOHN'S EPISCOPAL CHURCH
— to hold moonlight walk, Lahaina News, March 13, 1997: 16,17.
— to hold Spring Art Fair, Lahaina News, May 1, 1997: 16.
— to introduce its labyrinth, Lahaina News, July 2, 1998: 16.

ST. JOHN'S KULA FESTIVAL
— to be held, Lahaina News, September 27, 2001: 15.

ST. JOSEPH SCHOOL
— to hold annual feast and fundraiser, Lahaina News, April 12, 1989: 3.
— to hold Christmas Craft Bazaar, Lahaina News, November 14, 1996: 14.
— to hold Christmas Craft Bazaar, Lahaina News, November 20, 1997: 16.
— to hold Christmas Craft Fair and Bazaar, Lahaina News, November 18, 1999: 16.
— to hold Christmas Craft Fair, Lahaina News, November 16, 2000: 16.

ST. LAWRENCE STRING QUARTET [MUSICAL GROUP]
— to perform at the Maui Arts and Cultural Center, Lahaina News, January 30, 2003: 16.

ST. MARIA GORETTI TOUR CHOIR [MUSICAL GROUP]
— to perform at Maria Lanakila Church, Lahaina News, July 17, 1985: 3.

ST. MARTIN, TED
— basketball player to hold free throw contest, Lahaina News, November 22, 1989: 9.
— beaten by Curt Hold in free throw competition, Lahaina News, December 13, 1989: 8.

ST. PATRICK'S DAY
— celebrations on Lahaina-Ka'anapali & Pacific Railroad described, Lahaina Sun, March 22, 1972: 21.
— celebrated at Hyatt Regency Maui, Lahaina News, March 4, 1987: 10.
— to be celebrated at Maui Marriott's Makai Bar, Lahaina News, March 14, 1990: 15.
— events for, Lahaina News, March 13, 1991: 9.
— buffet to be offered at Maui Inter-Continental Resort, Lahaina News, March 12, 1992: 18.
— parade to be held, Lahaina News, February 17, 1994: 11.
— Reilley's Food and Sprits seeking participants for, Lahaina News, February 24, 1994: 11.
— parade details, Lahaina News, March 10, 1994: 16.
— parade to be held, Lahaina News, March 9, 1995: 11.
— events detailed, Lahaina News, March 16, 1995: 12.
— parade to be held, Lahaina News, March 14, 1996: 12.
— results of parade competition, Lahaina News, March 28, 1996: 13.
— seeking volunteers for parade, Lahaina News, January 15, 1998: 5.
— seeking volunteers for parade, Lahaina News, January 22, 1998: 5.
— parade to be held, Lahaina News, March 12, 1998: 18.

ST. THERESA'S CHURCH
— complains about drainage problems, Lahaina News, July 9, 1992: 6.
— receives grant from owners of Maui Gateway, Lahaina News, January 14, 1999: 11.

STACY, DOUGLAS
— named director of special projects at Kapalua Hotel, Lahaina News, October 8, 1986: 3.

STACY, HOLLIS
— golfer's career described, Lahaina News, March 6, 1985: A10.

STADIUM
— at Maui War Memorial Center opening, Lahaina Sun, September 8, 1971: 12.
— see also Maui War Memorial Center

STAKEOUT [RESTAURANT]
— reviewed, Lahaina News, July, 1979: 2.

STALLINGS, JIM [ARTIST]
— featured, Lahaina News, January 30, 1997: 13.
— opens gallery, Lahaina News, March 25, 1999: 16.
— painting to live music of San Diego Symphony, Lahaina News, March 30, 2000: 1.

STALLINGS-ALAILIMA, SIONNA
— Scholar/Athlete of the Week, Lahaina News, November 28, 1996: 5.
— Scholar/Athlete of the Week, Lahaina News, June 5, 1997: 13.

STALLONE, SYLVESTER
— attends opening of Planet Hollywood restaurant, Lahaina News, July 7, 1994: 1,3.

STALLWORTH, ISAAC "BUD"
— basketball player career detailed, Lahaina News, November 28, 1984: 4.
— basketball player attempts to re-enter professional basketball recounted, Lahaina News, December 25, 1985: 4.

STAMPEDE FEVER [FILM]
— shown at Lahaina Library, Lahaina Sun, August 18, 1971: 2.

STAMPS
— two missionary stamps recently sold, Lahaina News, December 1, 1980: 3.

STANCIN, JOHN [ARTIST]
— work displayed at Lahaina Art Gallery, Lahaina Sun, June 2, 1971: 3.

STANDARD ELECTRIC
— to install traffic light on Kuihelani Highway, Lahaina News, June 14, 1989: 3.

STANFIELD'S WEST MAUI FLORAL [BUSINESS]
— opens, Lahaina News, July 2, 1992: 17.

STANFORD, VERNE
— to become managing director of the Maui Community Arts and Cultural Center, Lahaina News, August 23, 1989: 6.

STANISLAW, ALEXANDER JOHN, JR.
— becomes head chef at Plantation House Restaurant, Lahaina News, May 1, 1991: 7.
— chef featured, Lahaina News, September 5, 1996: 8.

STANLEY, KIRK [ARTIST]
— featured, Lahaina News, September 9, 1993: 10,11.

STANT, EMERSON
— sentenced for killing his wife at Kahului airport, Lahaina Sun, March 21, 1973: 10.

STAR, LANI [MUSICIAN]
— to offer vocal workshops, Lahaina News, January 9, 2003: 17.
— to perform at Mandala's, Lahaina News, August 21, 2003: 16.

STAR MARKETS [BUSINESS]
— to open at Maui Mall shopping center, Lahaina Sun, April 5, 1972: 10.
— to open in Honokowai, Lahaina News, May 14, 1998: 13.
— grand opening held, Lahaina News, August 13, 1998: 13.
— John Fujieki named chairman of the board, Lahaina News, August 23, 2001: 9.

STAR QUEST
— talent contest underway, Lahaina News, February 20, 2003: 17.
— Lahainaluna High School students win final, Lahaina News, February 27, 2003: 3.

STAR TREK [TELEVISION SHOW]
— convention to take place in Waikiki, Lahaina News, October 3, 1990: 12.

STAR-SPANGLED GIRL, THE [PLAY]
— to be performed at Maui Community Theatre, Lahaina News, October 7, 1999: 16.
— to be performed at Iao Theater, Lahaina News, October 14, 1999: 12.
— to conclude, Lahaina News, October 21, 1999: 16.

STARBORN [MUSICAL GROUP]
— played at musical festival, Lahaina News, May 2, 1984: 14.

STARBUCKS COFFEE [RESTAURANTS]
— to open, Lahaina News, March 18, 1999: 1,20.
— Green Team seeking volunteers to help clean Baby Beach, Lahaina News, October 12, 2000: 1.
— to hold "Coffee Experience" contest, Lahaina News, November 2, 2000: 12.
— adopts stretch of Honoapi'ilani Highway, Lahaina News, November 30, 2000: 3.
— "Give a Gift, Receive a Latte" program held, Lahaina News, December 14, 2000: 18.
— opens at Lahaina Cannery Mall, Lahaina News, April 11, 2002: 9.
— David Maran appointed general manager at Lahaina Cannery Mall, Lahaina News, October 10, 2002: 8.
— sponsors local canoe races, Lahaina News, February 27, 2003: 13.

STARDANCER [SHIP]
— to offer disco music, Lahaina News, February 27, 1991: 12.

STARK, MICHAEL [ARTIST]
— to display at Banyan Tree Gallery, Lahaina News, March 9, 1995: 11.

STARK, SUSANNE [ARTIST]
— to be featured at Lahaina Arts Society, Lahaina News, March 28, 2002: 22.
— to be featured at Lahaina Art Society, Lahaina News, March 6, 2003: 17.

STARLIGHT CHILDREN'S FOUNDATION
— grants a wish with Aston Ka'anapali Shores, Lahaina News, March 22, 2001: 9.

STARQUEST: A GALACTIC GOOD NEWS ADVENTURE
— to be held at Lahaina Baptist Church, Lahaina News, July 2, 1998: 8.

STARR BROTHERS CIRCUS
— to perform at Wailuku War Memorial, Lahaina News, December 24, 1998: 12.

STARR SEIGLE MCCOMBS, INC. [BUSINESS]
— wins Gold EFFIE Award for Kentucky Fried Chicken campaign, Lahaina News, October 17, 1990: 12.
— announces promotion of employees, Lahaina News, November 14, 1990: 13.

STARS OF MAUI N CONCERT
— to benefit Kahakuloa Hawaiian Congregational Protestant Church, Lahaina News, November 13, 1997: 20.

STARS OF THE MOSCOW BALLET
— to perform, Lahaina News, November 14, 1996: 14.

STARTING A BUSINESS IN MAUI COUNTY
— guide prepared by Maui County, Lahaina News, June 25, 1998: 11.
— guide published, Lahaina News, July 23, 1998: 13.

STARWOOD HOTELS AND RESORTS [BUSINESS]
— Karen Schulz Hughes appointed new director of sales and marketing at, Lahaina News, May 31, 2001: 8.
— to expand Westin Ka'anapali Ocean Resort Villas, Lahaina News, April 4, 2002: 8.

STATE ALGAE BLOOM TASK FORCE
— to hold final meeting, Lahaina News, June 4, 1992: 4.

STATE DIRECTORY
— insert in September 27, 1989 edition, Lahaina News, : .

STATE FARM INSURANCE COMPANY [BUSINESS]
— to hold Child Safety Day and Bike Safety Rodeo, Lahaina News, May 16, 2002: 16.

STATE FILM INDUSTRY BRANCH
— appoints Robert Enrietto as production development manager, Lahaina News, March 13, 1991: 7.

STATE FOUNDATION ON CULTURE AND THE ARTS
— seeking volunteers to purchase art, Lahaina News, October 10, 1990: 7.
— seeking volunteers to purchase art, Lahaina News, October 17, 1990: 6.
— selects two pieces from Art Maui for State's public collection, Lahaina News, April 3, 1991: 10.
— selects works from Art Maui '92, Lahaina News, April 23, 1992: 29.
— to hold grant workshop, Lahaina News, August 29, 2002: 15.

STATE HARBORS DIVISION
— see Harbors Division, State

STATE HISTORICAL PRESERVATION CONFERENCE
— suggestions offered for making historic districts work better, Lahaina News, June 14, 2001: 1,22.

STATE LAND USE COMMISSION
— see Land Use Commission, State

STATE OF HAWAII
— pledges support for Napili due to water contamination, Lahaina Sun, November 11, 1970: 1.
— proposal to dredge a swimming area in Launiupoko State Park, Lahaina Sun, November 11, 1970: 3.
— working on highway projects on Maui, Lahaina Sun, November 18, 1970: 1.
— criticized for slow speed of donating land to Haleakala National Park, Lahaina Sun, April 7, 1971: 2.
— summary of funds received from, Lahaina Sun, April 28, 1971: 6.
— to trade land with Pioneer Mill for sewage treatment plant, Lahaina Sun, January 31, 1973: 10.
— governor's committee claims Hawaii unsympathetic to business, Lahaina News, February 8, 1984: 16.
— Lahainaluna High School swimming pool and library not included in budget, Lahaina News, December 19, 1990: 1.
— establishes information office at Kahului Shopping Center, Lahaina News, September 26, 1991: 7.
— may withdraw support for Hawaiian Islands National Marine Sanctuary, Lahaina News, November 4, 1993: 1,3.
— introduces "Getting Down to Business" website, Lahaina News, August 28, 1997: 12.

STATE OF HAWAII DATA BOOK [BOOK]
— available, Lahaina News, September 15, 1994: 13.
— published, Lahaina News, September 24, 1998: 13.
— now available from Department of Business, Economic Development and Tourism, Lahaina News, December 7, 2000: 19.
— published, Lahaina News, November 1, 2001: 8.

STATE OF HAWAII ORGANIZATION OF POLICE OFFICERS
— chapter formed, Lahaina Sun, February 17, 1971: 5.

STATE PARK AT MAKENA (SPAM)
— marks 10-year struggle to make Big Beach a state park, Lahaina News, July 8, 1993: 6.

STATE PLANNING, OFFICE OF
— accepting applications for marine and coastal zone management advisory, Lahaina News, September 21, 1995: 4.
— seeking input on controlling polluted runoff, Lahaina News, January 18, 1996: 4.

STATE REAL ESTATE COMMISSION
— Douglas Sodetani named as chair, Lahaina Sun, March 3, 1971: 3.
— to present seminar on condominium management, Lahaina News, April 10, 1991: 6.

STATE SECURITIES COMMISSIONER
— orders Sasha international Trading Co. to cease and desist investment scam, Lahaina News, May 18, 1995: 6.

STATE TRANSPORTATION DEPARTMENT
— studying possible sites for a ferry landing on Maui, Lahaina Sun, October 13, 1971: 14.

STATEHOOD
— parade set for Front Street for August 18th, Lahaina News, July 18, 1984: 3.
— editorial on impact of Statehood, Lahaina News, August 15, 1984: 2.
— celebration plans detailed, Lahaina News, August 15, 1984: 3.
— retrospective of how Lahaina was in 1959, 25 years ago, Lahaina News, August 15, 1984: 7,8,9.
— celebrations described, Lahaina News, August 15, 1984: 7,8,9.

STATEWIDE TRANSPORTATION IMPROVEMENT PROGRAM (STIP)
— Department of Transportation to hold meeting on, Lahaina News, May 22, 2003: 3.

STERMITZ, TOM
— to lead class on Argentine Tango, Lahaina News, October 2, 2003: 16.

STETSON, DALE
— named general manager of Maui Eldorado Resort, Lahaina News, October 6, 1994: 11.

STEVE LOWRY QUARTET [MUSICAL GROUP]
— continues to perform at Blackie's Bar, Lahaina News, May 30, 1991: 7.
— continues to perform at Blackie's Bar, Lahaina News, July 11, 1991: 11.
— continues to perform at Blackie's Bar, Lahaina News, December 19, 1991: 20.

STEVE LOWRY QUINTET [MUSICAL GROUP]
— to perform at Blackie's Bar, Lahaina News, January 16, 1991: 10.

STEVE "O"
— to perform at Comedy Club, Lahaina News, July 4, 1991: 10.

STEVENS, ADELINE [WRITER]
— stories about Maui written by, Lahaina News, March 28, 1984: 9,10,11.

STEVENS, JO ANN [ARTIST]
— to exhibit at The Kapalua Shops, Lahaina News, November 12, 1992: 19.
— work exhibited at Lahaina Arts Society, Lahaina News, January 18, 1996: 12.
— featured, Lahaina News, January 9, 1997: 13.
— to exhibit at Lahaina Arts Society, Lahaina News, March 4, 1999: 12.
— to exhibit at Lahaina Arts Society, Lahaina News, January 3, 2002: 15.
— to exhibit "From the Mountains to the Sea" at Lahaina Arts Society, Lahaina News, January 10, 2002: 16.

STEVENS, PHIL [MUSICIAN]
— see Ke'ia [musical group]

STEVENS, TOM [WRITER]
— "Shave Ice" collection described, Lahaina News, June 21, 1989: 7.
— satirical essays reviewed, Lahaina News, September 20, 1989: 5.

STEVENSON, MIKE
— discussed proposal for public luaus, Lahaina Sun, January 13, 1971: 5.
— discusses remodeling of Lahaina Broiler, Lahaina Sun, January 27, 1971: 2.
— discusses planned Lahaina Whaling Spree, Lahaina Sun, February 3, 1971: 2.
— discusses Lahaina Whaling Festival, Lahaina Sun, February 17, 1971: 1.

STEWARD, BETH
— joins staff at Lahaina Public Library, Lahaina News, June 28, 1989: 1.

STEWART, FRANK [POET]
— presenting at the Artful Dodger, Lahaina News, September 16, 1987: 3.

STEWART, JANET
— to sign copies of "'Ohana O Janet Stewart", Lahaina News, December 10, 1998: 20.

STEWART, JANET [ARTIST]
— completes painting to celebrate Lahainaluna High School's 160 years, Lahaina News, September 12, 1991: 1.
— to be featured at Wyland Galleries, Lahaina News, March 2, 1995: 11.
— to exhibit at Wyland Galleries, Lahaina News, March 16, 1995: 12.

STEWART, JIMMY [MUSICIAN]
— guitarist to perform at Blackie's Bar, Lahaina News, December 7, 1988: 11.

STEWART, JOHN
— marries Ida Kailakanoa, Lahaina Sun, March 17, 1971: 2.

STEWART, KEN
— report on basketball player, Lahaina Sun, January 20, 1971: 7.

STEWART, SCOTT
— role as manager of Teen Challenge described, Lahaina News, August 29, 1984: 7,8,9.

STEWART, SCOTT [MUSICIAN]
— to perform with Maui Symphony Orchestra, Lahaina News, March 30, 1995: 11.

STEWART, VALENTINA
— named Maui Lawyer of the Year by the Maui County Bar Association, Lahaina News, May 11, 2000: 9.

STEWART-PACIFIC-ERICKSON
— awarded contract to pave section of highway, Lahaina Sun, November 18, 1970: 1.

STICE, LAURA
— purchases Maui 'N Me, Lahaina News, February 27, 1991: 8.

STICKLAND, STEVE [ARTIST]
— to demonstrate intaglio, Lahaina News, June 3, 1993: 13.

STILLBORN [PLAY]
— Maui Community Theatre to hold auditions, Lahaina News, September 26, 1990: 5.
— Maui Community Theater to perform, Lahaina News, December 19, 1990: 13.
— to open, Lahaina News, December 26, 1990: 11.
— to be performed at Iao Theatre, Lahaina News, January 2, 1991: 8.

STILLMAN, GUY
— member of Lahaina Kamaakina Fishing Association, Lahaina Sun, December 23, 1970: 11.

STILLS, STEPHEN [MUSICIAN]
— opens night club Studio 505, Lahaina News, September 5, 1991: 9.

STILLWATER, MICHAEL [MUSICIAN]
— to perform at Iao Congregational Church, Lahaina News, December 12, 1991: 25.

STILLWELL, KENNETH [ARTIST]
— work discussed, Lahaina News, January 16, 1985: 10.

STINSON, DAVID [MUSICIAN]
— releases tape, Lahaina News, December 13, 1989: 4.

STOCKTON, DAVE
— golfer to play at Maui Ka'anapali Classic, Lahaina News, September 19, 1996: 13.

STODD, RUSSELL
— doctor claims Maui needs more hospital beds, Lahaina News, September 5, 1990: 1,9.

STOMP [MUSICAL GROUP]
— to perform at Maui Arts and Cultural Center, Lahaina News, December 7, 2000: 25.
— to perform at Maui Arts and Cultural Center, Lahaina News, December 14, 2000: 20.

STONE, LISA
— wins gold at Paradise Cup Bodybuilding Championship, Lahaina News, December 3, 1992: 6.

STONE, MYRNA
— appointed sales manager at Real Estate Maui Style, Lahaina News, July 28, 1994: 9.

STONE, PATRICIA
— to discuss Berman Report, Lahaina News, March 15, 1989: 1.

STONE SOUP [PLAY]
— to be performed by Maui Academy of Performing Arts, Lahaina News, October 26, 1995: 12.

STONE TEMPLE PILOTS [MUSICAL GROUP]
— to perform at Maui Arts and Cultural Center, Lahaina News, December 19, 1996: 24.
— to perform at Maui Arts and Cultural Center, Lahaina News, December 26, 1996: 11.
— to perform, Lahaina News, January 2, 1997: 10.

STONE, TOM
— to present "Na Mea Pa'ani Kahiko O Na 'Oiwi O Hawaii—The Ancient Sports of Native Hawaiians", Lahaina News, June 12, 2003: 21.

STOPPARD AND FEVDEAU [COMEDIANS]
— to perform at Seabury Hall, Lahaina News, August 14, 1997: 16.
— to perform at Studio H'Poko, Lahaina News, August 21, 1997: 16.
— complete their performances, Lahaina News, August 28, 1997: 10.

STORM [FILM]
— Warren Miller film to be shown, Lahaina News, January 9, 2003: 17.
— to be shown, Lahaina News, January 16, 2003: 16.

STORM, HYEMEYOHSTS (WOLF)
— American Indian teacher leads "Earth Teaching" events, Lahaina News, May 7, 1998: 20.

STORMON, MARK
— Bishop Museum Eclipse Project Manager to speak to Maui Chamber of Commerce, Lahaina News, February 6, 1991: 6.
— to speak to Maui Chamber of Commerce, Lahaina News, February 20, 1991: 7.

STORY, CRAIG
— benefit sail to be held for, Lahaina News, September 7, 2000: 1,2.

STORY, LIZ [MUSICIAN]
— to perform at Stouffer Wailea Beach Resort, Lahaina News, May 31, 1989: 21.
— to perform in Makawao, Lahaina News, October 31, 1990: 14.

STORY OF LAHAINA [BOOKLET]
— published by the Lahaina Restoration Foundation, Lahaina Sun, December 20, 1972: 14.

STORY OF SUGAR [TELEVISION SHOW]
— to be shown on local television, Lahaina Sun, April 7, 1971: 6.

STORY, ROB
— wins prize at Maui Home Show, Lahaina News, July 16, 1998: 13.

STOSIK, RAY
— tournament director of GTE Ka'anapali Classic, Lahaina News, June 20, 1990: 7.

STOSIK, SHEREL GALLAGHER
— appointed general manager of Rolfing Sports, Lahaina News, January 24, 1990: 6.

STOUFFER WAILEA BEACH RESORT [BUSINESS]
— offering kama'aina rate, Lahaina News, July 11, 1984: 3.
— receives five diamond rating from the American Automobile Association, Lahaina News, February 20, 1985: 7.
— renovations planned, Lahaina News, December 4, 1985: 3.
— announces promotions in management, Lahaina News, March 12, 1986: 3.
— appoints John Bruns as assistant general manager, Lahaina News, May 28, 1986: 3.
— Lost Horizon Night Club refurbished, Lahaina News, July 9, 1986: 14.
— receives award from World Tennis magazine, Lahaina News, July 30, 1986: 3.
— hosts La Confrerie de la Chaine Des Rotisseurs, Lahaina News, August 20, 1986: 3.
— holds fundraiser for Pacific Whale Foundation, Lahaina News, November 5, 1986: 3.
— celebrates 10 year anniversary, Lahaina News, September 28, 1988: 3.

— hosting Maui Marine Art Expo, Lahaina News, February 20, 1991: 12.
— hosting Maui Humane Society fundraiser, Lahaina News, October 3, 1991: 13.
— announces new appointments, Lahaina News, April 16, 1992: 13,14.
— receives award from Conde Nast Traveler, Lahaina News, November 19, 1992: 5.
— Raffles to reopen, Lahaina News, December 23, 1993: 7.
— changes name to Wailea Resort, Lahaina News, May 23, 1996: 16.
— to change name to Wailea Resort, Lahaina News, May 23, 1996: 16.

STOUGHTON, JAMES
— mayor Hannibal Tavares awards certificate of merit to, Lahaina News, September 10, 1986: 3.

STOUT, ROGER
— Maui Global Communications discusses importance of internet to Maui businesses, Lahaina News, August 3, 1995: 8.

STOW, STEVEN DONALD
— machete attacker has new charges added, Lahaina News, May 2, 1996: 1,22.

STOWELL, JERRY
— to discuss humpback whale migration, Lahaina News, January 9, 2003: 1.

STRADA, LA [FILM]
— to be shown at Lahaina library, Lahaina News, February 27, 1985: 3.

STRAIGHT, DONALD
— appointed vice president of flight operations at Hawaiian Airlines, Lahaina News, February 3, 1994: 7.

STRANGE, CURTIS
— pro golfer fishes with Mark Rolfing, Lahaina News, December 21, 1988: 13.

STRASEN, LEANN [ARTIST]
— quilter to exhibit at Lahaina Cannery Mall, Lahaina News, February 4, 1999: 17.

STRASSER, DENNIS [ARTIST]
— has two paintings on display at the county administration building removed by mayor Tavares , Lahaina News, August 15, 1983: 6.
— featured in two national juried exhibitions, Lahaina News, May 16, 1984: 4.
— featured, Lahaina News, October 10, 1984: 10.
— Lahainaluna coach praised, Lahaina News, February 4, 1987: 6.

STRATTON, GEORGE [WRITER]
— to speak to Maui Authors Guild, Lahaina News, November 18, 1987: 3.

STRAZAR, MARIE
— to discuss "Managing Museum Collections", Lahaina News, February 12, 1998: 16.
— to speak on "Managing Museum Collections", Lahaina News, August 27, 1998: 16.

STREET BIKERS UNITED
— to exhibit motorcycles at Lahaina Cannery Mall, Lahaina News, November 2, 1995: 11.

STREET LEGAL [MUSICAL GROUP]
— to perform at Moose McGillycuddy's, Lahaina News, January 9, 1992: 10.
— to perform at Studio 505, Lahaina News, July 16, 1992: 17.

STREET SOUNDS [MUSICAL GROUP]
— to perform at Maui Arts and Cultural Center, Lahaina News, April 1, 1999: 17.
— to perform at Maui Arts and Cultural Center, Lahaina News, April 8, 1999: 12.

STREETWALKER [MUSICAL GROUP]
— to perform at Polli's On the Beach, Lahaina News, November 21, 1990: 15.

STRENG, GORAN
— named as new executive chef at Kapalua Bay Hotel and Villas, Lahaina News, April 22, 1993: 6.

STRICKLAND, STEPHEN [ARTIST]
— to demonstrate copperplate map-making at Lahaina Printsellers, Lahaina News, January 23, 1992: 18.
— to offer intaglio demonstrations at Lahaina Printsellers, Lahaina News, March 26, 1992: 18.
— to demonstrate intaglio, Lahaina News, October 8, 1992: 12.
— to exhibit at Lahaina Printsellers, Lahaina News, December 31, 1992: 12.
— intaglio work to be released, Lahaina News, March 24, 1994: 15.
— to demonstrate intaglio, Lahaina News, May 26, 1994: 15.
— to demonstrate copperplate engravings, Lahaina News, January 19, 1995: 12.

STRIKES
— Ka'anapali Hotel strike enters second month, Lahaina Sun, November 11, 1970: 1,4.
— strike continues at Royal Lahaina and Ka'anapali hotels, Lahaina Sun, November 18, 1970: 2.
— strike continues at Royal Lahaina and Ka'anapali hotels, Lahaina Sun, November 25, 1970: 1.
— hotel strike enters third month, Lahaina Sun, December 9, 1970: 3.
— Governor Burns announces a tentative agreement to end the strike at the Royal Lahaina and Ka'anapali Beach Hotels, Lahaina Sun, December 23, 1970: 2.
— hotel strike at Ka'anapali Beach and Royal Lahaina Hotels ends, Lahaina Sun, December 30, 1970: 5.
— see also business, ILWU, labor

STRING CHEESE INCIDENT, THE [MUSICAL GROUP]
— to perform, Lahaina News, December 27, 2001: 17.
— to perform at Lahaina Civic Center, Lahaina News, January 31, 2002: 15.
— Friends of clean area near Pu'u Piha Cemetery, Lahaina News, February 21, 2002: 15.
— Torey Newlin missing after attending, Lahaina News, February 28, 2002: 1,2.

STROCK, CHERYL AND ARDEN
— named general manager of 5A Rent-a-Space, Lahaina News, September 12, 1991: 4.

STRONG, STEVEN
— doctor at Kaiser Permanente retires, Lahaina News, June 6, 1996: 3.

STUART, DONALD [ARTIST]
— to lead metal workshop at Hui No'eau Visual Arts Center, Lahaina News, March 28, 2002: 20.

STUART, JOHN
— kayaker featured, Lahaina News, February 8, 1996: 11.

STUART, MIMI [ARTIST]
— to exhibit at Sargent's Fine Art, Lahaina News, August 15, 2002: 16.

STUDENTS STAYING STRAIGHT
— student group to perform at request of White House Conference for a Drug Free America, Lahaina News, March 30, 1988: 14.
— to host overnight lock-in at Lahainaluna High School, Lahaina News, January 25, 1989: 16,17.
— drug and alcohol free program to host annual lock-in, Lahaina News, April 28, 1994: 5.

STUDIO 505 [RESTAURANT]
— opens, Lahaina News, June 20, 1991: 5.
— opens, Lahaina News, August 15, 1991: 14.
— co-owner and musician Stephen Stills at opening, Lahaina News, September 5, 1991: 9.
— offering disco dance music, Lahaina News, November 21, 1991: 16.
— presents check to Hale Makua, Lahaina News, January 2, 1992: 5.

— to open early for youth, Lahaina News, January 21, 1993: 13.
— Budweiser Girls will be on hand for Super Bowl, Lahaina News, January 28, 1993: 13.

STUDIO BLUE
— nightclub opens, Lahaina News, August 22, 1996: 12.

STUDIO ELAN VITAL [BUSINESS]
— opens, Lahaina News, July 11, 1991: 14.

STUDIO H'POKO
— to perform plays of Shakespeare, Lahaina News, August 13, 1992: 14,18.
— to perform "Search for Signs of Intelligent Life in the Universe", Lahaina News, April 15, 1993: 9.
— to perform "Much Ado About Nothing", Lahaina News, July 7, 1994: 15.
— presents "The Tempest", Lahaina News, August 20, 1998: 16.

STUDLEY, JONATHAN
— new chef at Kula Lodge, Lahaina News, December 7, 1995: 14.

STUMPF, JOE
— to offer marketing seminar, Lahaina News, February 13, 1992: 12.

STURGEON, JAYNE
— to speak on Tarot cards, Lahaina News, August 15, 1984: 3.
— offering writers' workshop in Kihei, Lahaina News, August 15, 1984: 3.

STURGEON, THEODORE
— science fiction writer to appear in Maui, Lahaina News, April 15, 1983: 6.
— offering writers' workshop in Kihei, Lahaina News, August 15, 1984: 3.

STURTZ, MERRY
— to lead workshop on "Peaceful Parenting", Lahaina News, March 13, 2003: 16.

SUBCONTRACTORS ASSOCIATION OF HAWAII
— to hold conference, Lahaina News, July 14, 1994: 12.

SUBMARINE TOURS
— editorial raising concerns for plans to offer, Lahaina News, April 22, 1987: 2.
— editorial support senator Rick Reed's concerns for proposed, Lahaina News, May 27, 1987: 2.

SUBMARINES
— mini-submarine being constructed in Lahaina, Lahaina Sun, January 19, 1972: 7.

SUBWAY SANDWICHES [RESTAURANT]
— opening at the Wharf, Lahaina News, December 13, 1989: 7.
— celebrating 25th birthday, Lahaina News, June 6, 1990: 7.
— opens fifth store on Maui, Lahaina News, October 3, 1991: 7.
— sponsoring 5K run, Lahaina News, November 21, 1991: 9.
— organizing 5K run near Wailuku Industrial Park, Lahaina News, November 28, 1991: 24.
— opens in Napili, Lahaina News, January 2, 1992: 8.
— expanding rapidly on Maui, Lahaina News, January 23, 1992: 11.
— Napili location purchased by Joe and Suki Cho, Lahaina News, August 22, 2002: 8.

SUDBURY MAUI SCHOOL
— to meet, Lahaina News, July 29, 1999: 12.

SUDDEN RUSH [MUSICAL GROUP]
— to perform at Live on the Beach, Lahaina News, October 23, 1997: 20.

SUDO, PHIL [WRITER]
— to speak at Borders Books, Lahaina News, September 23, 1999: 12.
— author of "Zen Guitar" and "Zen Computer" to speak at Maui Writers Guild, Lahaina News, October 21, 1999: 17.

SUETOS, CASSIE
— Scholar/Athlete of the Week, Lahaina News, December 28, 2000: 7.

SUFI
— to hold camp, Lahaina News, October 7, 1999: 16.

SUFISM AND THE INNER MUSIC: MUSIC, DISCOURSE AND MORE
— to be held, Lahaina News, August 30, 2001: 16.

SUGAR
— said to be second worst offender in ocean dumping, Lahaina Sun, November 18, 1970: 1.
— Silver Diffuser installed near Paia, Lahaina Sun, December 2, 1970: 1.
— consumption of in the United States, Lahaina Sun, February 10, 1971: 7.
— public tour of HC&S sugar mill offered, Lahaina Sun, March 31, 1971: 3.
— film on sugar production to be shown on local television, Lahaina Sun, April 7, 1971: 6.
— free tours of HC&S sugar offered, Lahaina Sun, June 9, 1971: 5.
— condition of the industry discussed, Lahaina Sun, August 11, 1971: 8.
— problems with finding adequate storage, Lahaina Sun, September 1, 1971: 1,16.
— history of described, Lahaina Sun, September 1, 1971: 7.
— piling up in Kahului due to west coast dock strike, Lahaina Sun, September 22, 1971: 10.
— mayor Cravalho claims that sugar lands are under-assessed, Lahaina Sun, September 29, 1971: 5.
— representatives from Maui attend Congress of the International Society of Sugarcane Technologists in Louisiana, Lahaina Sun, October 20, 1971: 11.
— production totals announced, Lahaina Sun, October 20, 1971: 5.
— production process and history described, includes photographs, Lahaina Sun, November 3, 1971: 12,13.
— Hawaiian Sugar Technologists Conference to be held in Waikiki, Lahaina Sun, November 10, 1971: 6.
— industry not profitable enough, Lahaina Sun, November 24, 1971: 11.
— 1971 harvest ending, Lahaina Sun, November 24, 1971: 6.
— movement of sugar can between Oahu and neighbor islands halted to control sugar cane smut, Lahaina Sun, December 1, 1971: 12.
— Neighbor Island Conference of the Hawaiian Sugar Planters' Association held at Royal Lahaina Hotel, Lahaina Sun, December 8, 1971: 5.
— can burning discussed, Lahaina Sun, December 15, 1971: 1,8.
— Richard Marland, the State's top environmental specialist, says there is no need for sugar companies to change their cane burning practices, Lahaina Sun, December 15, 1971: 1,8.
— economic issues discussed, Lahaina Sun, December 15, 1971: 16.
— strake averted, Lahaina Sun, April 19, 1972: 3.
— federal funds sought to combat the spread of fungus that threatens crops, Lahaina Sun, April 26, 1972: 10.
— Bank of Hawaii expects profits from sugar to increase, Lahaina Sun, May 10, 1972: 5.
— industry situation described, Lahaina Sun, May 31, 1972: 3.
— discussion of burning sugar cane, Lahaina Sun, June 7, 1972: 5.
— new method of irrigation to be installed, Lahaina Sun, June 28, 1972: 14.
— rock removal plant being tested, Lahaina Sun, September 13, 1972: 14.
— mechanical harvester developed, Lahaina Sun, October 25, 1972: 4.
— cane fires disrupt traffic, Lahaina Sun, November 15, 1972: 9.
— changes proposed to irrigation system, Lahaina Sun, November 22, 1972: 7.
— to remain a major industry, Lahaina Sun, May 2, 1973: 3.

— cost of production rising, Lahaina Sun, May 23, 1973: 11.
— cane processing involving a dry cleaner described, Lahaina Sun, May 30, 1973: 15.
— possible future discussed, Lahaina Sun, June 13, 1973: 6,7.
— production described, including photographs, Lahaina Sun, June 20, 1973: 10,11.
— war with artificial sweeteners may suffer setbacks, Lahaina Sun, July 11, 1973: 3.
— editorial on financial situation of industry, Lahaina News, March 1, 1982: 2.
— future is glum, Lahaina News, January 1, 1983: 4.
— industry in moral struggle to survive, Lahaina News, September 7, 1983: 14.
— opinion on cane burning, Lahaina News, July 16, 1986: 6.
— Pioneer Mill to cut production, Lahaina News, September 3, 1986: 1,2.
— Maui Community College hosts Dorothy Pyle speaking on Maui industry, Lahaina News, June 1, 1988: 19.
— American Sugar Alliance - International Sweetener Symposium to be held, Lahaina News, August 6, 1992: 6.
— cane burning fees to rise, Lahaina News, October 7, 1993: 1.
— residents want green harvest for cane, Lahaina News, October 7, 1993: 1.
— issues discussed, Lahaina News, February 3, 1994: 1,2.
— federal price support program may end, Lahaina News, December 8, 1994: 1,12.
— Amfac/JMB plans to reorganize operations, including Pioneer Mill, Lahaina News, December 8, 1994: 12.
— Hawaiian Commercial and Sugar Co. to increase efficiency, Lahaina News, January 19, 1995: 10.
— industry outlook negative, Lahaina News, July 13, 1995: 10.
— Patsy Mink succeeds in maintaining U.S. Sugar Program, Lahaina News, July 31, 1997: 13.

SUGAR [MUSICAL]
— to be performed by Maui Community Theatre, Lahaina News, November 14, 1990: 15.
— to be performed at Iao Theatre, Lahaina News, November 28, 1990: 10.

SUGAR ACT
— Senator Spark Matsunaga discusses value of, Lahaina Sun, March 10, 1971: 3.

SUGAR CANE DAYS
— results of, Lahaina News, September 18, 1997: 2.

SUGAR CANE TRAIN
— received funding for turntable, Lahaina News, December 3, 1986: 12.
— commemorates 5 millionth passenger, Lahaina News, April 11, 1996: 1.
— to hold Christmas event, Lahaina News, November 30, 2000: 16.
— see also Lahaina-Ka'anapali and Pacific Railroad [business]

SUGAR MUSEUM
— introduces annual pass, Lahaina News, January 9, 2003: 9.
— to hold Maui Sugar Plantation Festival, Lahaina News, August 14, 2003: 14.

SUGARCANE
— production record set, Lahaina Sun, December 23, 1970: 3.
— television commercial filmed at Lahaina, Lahaina Sun, December 30, 1970: 7.
— editorial urging cane burning study be done properly, Lahaina News, February 25, 1987: 2.
— see also cane burning

SUGARMAN, JOSEPH
— to give lecture "Never Leave Home Without It", Lahaina News, November 30, 2000: 17.

SUKEROKU: FLOWER OF EDO
— Kabuki comedy to be performed as benefit for victims of earthquake in Kobe, Lahaina News, March 23, 1995: 12.

SULLIVAN, MARK "SULLY" [MUSICIAN]
— to perform at Pineapple Hill, Lahaina News, March 13, 1991: 8.
— to perform at Pineapple Hill, Lahaina News, March 20, 1991: 9.
— continues to perform at Pineapple Hill, Lahaina News, April 10, 1991: 9.
— president of Foodland honored by Chamber of Commerce, Lahaina News, April 24, 1991: 7.
— continues to perform at Pineapple Hill, Lahaina News, April 24, 1991: 7.

SULLIVAN, PAT
— property owner abandons attempt to rezone following community resistance, Lahaina News, July 20, 1995: 1,16.

SULLIVAN PROPERTIES, INC. [BUSINESS]
— featured, Lahaina News, December 13, 2001: 6,7.

SULTANOV, ALEXEI [MUSICIAN]
— to perform with Maui Symphony Orchestra, Lahaina News, January 31, 1990: 13.
— to perform at St. Anthony's Church, Lahaina News, February 7, 1990: 13.
— to perform at Maui Marriott Ballroom, Lahaina News, October 10, 1990: 14.
— to perform at Maui Marriott Ballroom, Lahaina News, October 17, 1990: 15.

SUMMER
— programs offered, Lahaina News, May 27, 1999: 5.
— activities planned, Lahaina News, May 18, 2000: 19.

SUMMER FLOWER FAIR
— to be held, Lahaina News, July 17, 1997: 16.

SUMMER FUN [PROGRAM]
— details announced for 1971, Lahaina Sun, June 16, 1971: 9.

SUMMER FUN CENTERS
— to open at Lahaina Civic Center, Lahaina News, June 15, 1983: 6.

SUMMER MUSIC ENRICHMENT CAMP
— to be offered, Lahaina News, July 23, 1998: 17.

SUMMER MUSIC FESTIVAL
— being held at Royal Lahaina Hotel, Lahaina News, July 24, 1985: 10.

SUMMER PLAY AND LEARN SERIES (PALS) PROGRAM
— registration open, Lahaina News, May 16, 1990: 3.
— accepting children, Lahaina News, July 4, 1990: 3.
— response to is good, Lahaina News, July 25, 1990: 1.
— looking for volunteers for the summer, Lahaina News, August 1, 1990: 4.
— to hold talent contest, Lahaina News, August 15, 1990: 7.
— to be held, Lahaina News, May 8, 1991: 3,4.
— program to begin, Lahaina News, May 30, 1991: 3.
— program to be held, Lahaina News, June 6, 1991: 3.
— to host talent show, Lahaina News, July 25, 1991: 13.
— registration for summer program begins, Lahaina News, June 11, 1992: 5.
— summer program to begin, Lahaina News, June 18, 1992: 14,15.
— offering recreational and art activities, Lahaina News, July 2, 1992: 7.
— seeking recreation leaders, Lahaina News, September 30, 1993: 4.
— registration opens for, Lahaina News, May 4, 1995: 4.
— taking employment applications for summer 1999, Lahaina News, March 11, 1999: 11.
— to be offered, Lahaina News, May 6, 1999: 20.
— program held at Lahaina Cinemas Theater, Lahaina News, August 22, 2002: 14.

SUMMER PROGRAMS
— listed, Lahaina News, June 5, 1997: 3.

SUMMER SHOW
— to be held at Lahaina Cannery Mall, Lahaina News, June 26, 2003: 16.

SUMMER STOCK FOR KIDS
— performing arts workshop for youth to be held, Lahaina News, June 1, 1995: 2.

SUMMER YOUTH EMPLOYMENT PROGRAM
— accepting applications, Lahaina News, May 16, 1984: 17.

SUMMER YOUTH FAIR
— to be held, Lahaina News, May 22, 1997: 6.

SUMMIT AT KA'ANAPALI, THE
— development featured, Lahaina News, August 24, 2000: 10.
— West Maui Development Co. announces new development, Lahaina News, October 12, 2000: 15.
— breaks ground, Lahaina News, December 14, 2000: 10.
— featured, Lahaina News, April 5, 2001: 6.
— real estate, Lahaina News, May 31, 2001: 6.
— development featured, Lahaina News, September 20, 2001: 6.
— featured, Lahaina News, October 25, 2001: 6.
— real estate development releases Phase II, Lahaina News, March 7, 2002: 6.
— Phase II featured, Lahaina News, April 18, 2002: 6.
— Phase II released, Lahaina News, June 13, 2002: 6.
— development featured, Lahaina News, August 8, 2002: 6.
— Phase III nearly sold out, Lahaina News, October 17, 2002: 6.
— development featured, Lahaina News, November 28, 2002: 6.
— development featured, Lahaina News, April 10, 2003: 18.
— sales doing well at the final phase of, Lahaina News, June 5, 2003: 7.
— development featured, Lahaina News, July 3, 2003: 7.
— featured, Lahaina News, September 4, 2003: 7.

SUMNER, GEORGE [ARTIST]
— works displayed at Provenance Gallery, Lahaina News, February 17, 1988: 18.
— to exhibit at Foundation Galleries, Lahaina News, January 30, 1992: 16.

SUM'R PLAYING [PLAY]
— to be performed by Maui Academy of Performing Arts, Lahaina News, July 28, 1994: 13,14.

SUN DAY [BUSINESS]
— opens, Lahaina News, July 22, 1993: 7.

SUN KING [MUSICAL GROUP]
— to perform at Moose McGillycuddy's, Lahaina News, January 16, 1992: 12.
— to perform at Casanova's, Lahaina News, January 30, 1992: 21.
— featured; played in Kuwait during Gulf War, Lahaina News, March 26, 1992: 13.
— to perform at Longhi's, Lahaina News, August 19, 1993: 15.
— continues to perform at Inu Inu Lounge at Maui Inter-Continental Resort, Lahaina News, March 3, 1994: 12.
— continues to perform at Moose McGillycuddy's, Lahaina News, July 7, 1994: 14.
— to perform at Ludwigs, Lahaina News, January 25, 1996: 14.
— wins lawsuit against Moose McGillycuddy's, Lahaina News, March 4, 1999: 11.

SUNDANCE [MUSICAL GROUP]
— to perform at Casanova's, Lahaina News, April 3, 1991: 8.
— to perform at Casanova's, Lahaina News, May 30, 1991: 10.
— to perform at Moose McGillycuddy's, Lahaina News, January 30, 1992: 17.

SUNDERMAN, MARILYN [WRITER]
— to appear at "Past Lives, Present Joy", Lahaina News, April 8, 1999: 13.

SUNDLOW, TOM & HARA [ARCHITECTS]
— preparing plans for Kihei sewage treatment plant, Lahaina Sun, December 9, 1970: 2.

SUNDRAM [ARTIST]
— guest artist at Metropolitan Art Gallery, Lahaina News, February 27, 1991: 13.
— Australian artist exhibiting at Lahaina Cannery Mall, Lahaina News, January 6, 1994: 12.

SUNGLASS ASSOCIATION OF AMERICA
— met at the Wailea Hotel, awards Michael Jackson "Shady Personality of 1984" award, Lahaina News, November 7, 1984: 2.

SUNHILD PUPPETS
— offer free performances, Lahaina Sun, November 29, 1972: 11.

SUNKING [MUSICAL GROUP]
— continues to perform at Moose McGillycuddy's, Lahaina News, December 30, 1993: 11.

SUNLESS IN SEATTLE
— television show features Ka'anapali, Lahaina News, May 30, 1996: 12.

SUNNE [CLOWN]
— at Lahaina Public Library, Lahaina News, June 10, 1987: 3.

SUNNY-K [BUSINESS]
— opens in Kukui Mall Shopping Center, Lahaina News, June 14, 2001: 8.

SUNRISE CAFÉ
— now open, Lahaina News, September 3, 1986: 3.

SUNSET CLUB
— West Maui AJA Veterans Auxiliary to hold backed good and rummage sale, Lahaina News, April 2, 1992: 4.
— to meet, Lahaina News, April 1, 1993: 4.
— to hold rummage sale, Lahaina News, April 15, 1993: 3.
— to hold rummage and baked goods sale, Lahaina News, April 14, 1994: 3.

SUNSET GALLERIES [BUSINESS]
— to host Lahaina's Artist Guild, Lahaina News, July 25, 1990: 13.
— to hold reception for Roman Czerwinski, Dick Kearney, Sherri Reeve, and Doe Sarasin, Lahaina News, December 12, 1991: 19.

SUNSET MAGAZINE
— spends 10 days shooting in Maui for a promotional program, Lahaina Sun, December 1, 1971: 12.

SUNSET ODYSSEY DINNER CRUISE
— featured, Lahaina News, April 6, 2000: 8,9.

SUNSET SERENADING
— to be held at Lahaina Center, Lahaina News, November 29, 2001: 16.

SUNSETS AND SAND DOLLARS
— beach party to be held to benefit Friends of the Children's Justice Center, Lahaina News, July 24, 2003: 5.
— to be held to benefit Friends of the Children , Lahaina News, July 31, 2003: 5.

SUNSHINE HELICOPTERS [BUSINESS]
— pilots recognized for safety, Lahaina News, April 20, 2000: 13.

SUNSHINE OF HAWAII RENT-A-CAR
— expanding to Oahu, Lahaina News, August 2, 1989: 6.

SUNYA'S FLOWERS AND PLANTS [BUSINESS]
— opens in The Shops at Kapalua Resort, Lahaina News, October 15, 1992: 7,8.

SUPER SITES [BUSINESS]
— building websites, Lahaina News, March 25, 1999: 13.

SUPERBOWL
— account of game, won by San Francisco 49'ers, Lahaina Sun, December 30, 1970: 5.
— discussed by John Page , Lahaina Sun, January 13, 1971: 4.
— report on results, Lahaina Sun, January 20, 1971: 7.
— events, Lahaina News, January 23, 1992: 16.

SUPERBOWL SUPERSAVINGS
— to be held at Lahaina Center, Lahaina News, January 23, 1992: 4.

SUPERCAMP
— summer camp opens on the Big Island, Lahaina News, June 15, 1983: 10.

SUPERKIDS
— games to benefit American Lung Association, Lahaina News, February 11, 1999: 15.

SUPERWHALE [BUSINESS]
— expands to Oahu, Lahaina News, May 17, 1989: 9.

SUPERWHALE CHILDREN'S BOUTIQUES
— opens at Whalers Village, Lahaina News, March 20, 1991: 7.
— to close, Lahaina News, March 12, 1998: 11.
— changes business to supply school uniforms, Lahaina News, August 26, 1999: 13.

SUPPA, RON
— creator of "Rocky" to hold seminar, Lahaina News, March 30, 1995: 12.

SUPREME COURT
— pulls permit for Napilihau Villages, Lahaina News, November 13, 1997: 1,3.

SURDUL, BETH [ARTIST]
— to appear at "Friday Night is Art Night", Lahaina News, August 23, 1989: 9.

SURF-PSYCHO-SEXY [MUSICAL GROUP]
— to perform at Moose McGillycuddy's, Lahaina News, November 3, 1994: 27.
— to perform at Moose McGillycuddy's, Lahaina News, October 17, 1996: 16.

SURFER [MAGAZINE]
— history described, Lahaina Sun, February 21, 1973: 18,19.
— Jackie Dunn on cover of, Lahaina Times, July, 1980 volume 4 number 6: 1.
— discusses Kaena Point as a surf spot, Lahaina Times, July, 1980 volume 4 number 6: 1.

SURFER'S PARADISE [FILM]
— containing footage of longboard surf competition at Maia Wharf, Lahaina Times, June, 1980 volume 4 number 5: 9.
— Laurie Macdonald featured in, Lahaina Times, July, 1980 volume 4 number 6: 1.

SURFING
— proposed for high school sports, Lahaina Sun, January 20, 1971: 7.
— situation in Maui described, Lahaina Sun, January 5, 1972: 3.
— photograph and poem, Lahaina Sun, January 5, 1972: 8.
— report of conditions at Honolua Bay, Lahaina Sun, February 23, 1972: 18.
— latest conditions described, Lahaina Sun, March 1, 1972: 18.
— interview with Neil Norris, Lahaina Sun, March 8, 1972: 15.
— Makai Surf Supplies is closing, Lahaina Sun, March 29, 1972: 16.
— Frank Carlson featured, Lahaina Sun, April 5, 1972: 6.
— Birney Jarvis featured, Lahaina Sun, April 5, 1972: 7.
— local scene described, Lahaina Sun, May 10, 1972: 17.
— Lightning Bolt design of surf boards, Lahaina Sun, September 27, 1972: 17.
— winter conditions described, Lahaina Sun, October 11, 1972: 17.
— Maui Surfing Association formed, Lahaina Sun, October 18, 1972: 10.

— conditions at Sunset discussed, Lahaina Sun, October 18, 1972: 17.

— value of Maui Surf Association discussed, Lahaina Sun, October 25, 1972: 17.

— cause of waves discussed, Lahaina Sun, November 8, 1972: 19.

— discussion of surfers underestimating the size of the wave, Lahaina Sun, November 15, 1972: 12,13.

— not possible with tsunamis, Lahaina Sun, November 29, 1972: 22.

— discussion of jerk straps, Lahaina Sun, December 27, 1972: 18,19.

— Shark Pit [surfing spot] reviewed, Lahaina Sun, January 3, 1973: 18,19.

— value of surf report discussed, Lahaina Sun, January 10, 1973: 18,19.

— purchasing a new surfboard discussed, Lahaina Sun, January 31, 1973: 18,19.

— conflicts between surfers described, Lahaina Sun, February 28, 1973: 18,19.

— locations in North Maui described, Lahaina Sun, March 21, 1973: 18,19.

— surfboard design discussed, Lahaina Sun, April 18, 1973: 22.

— Steve Sayre's trip to Africa described, Lahaina Sun, April 25, 1973: 22.

— competition between Leeward Community College and Maui Community College described, Lahaina Sun, May 2, 1973: 22.

— life of Jeff Robinson featured, Lahaina Sun, May 9, 1973: 22.

— advice for beginners, Lahaina Sun, May 23, 1973: 22.

— competitions planned, Lahaina Sun, June 20, 1973: 17.

— tips on learning how to surf, Lahaina Sun, July 25, 1973: 20.

— early history of, described, Lahaina Sun, August 1, 1973: 20.

— design changes discussed, Lahaina Sun, August 8, 1973: 20.

— summer spots reviewed, Lahaina Sun, August 15, 1973: 20.

— summer spots reviewed, Lahaina Sun, August 22, 1973: 20.

— advice on caring for a surfboard, Lahaina Sun, August 29, 1973: 20.

— conditions described, Lahaina News, July, 1979: 13.

— summer conditions described, Lahaina News, August, 1979: 12,13.

— report on conditions on Kaua'i, Lahaina News, September, 1979: 11.

— September conditions described, Lahaina News, October, 1979: 11.

— conditions at Honolua Bay described, Lahaina News, November, 1979: 11,12.

— social status of surfers described, Lahaina News, December, 1979: 11.

— reflection on surfing in the 1970s, Lahaina News, January 15, 1980: 11.

— different styles described, Lahaina News, March 1, 1980: 11.

— powerful surf described, Lahaina News, April 1, 1980: 10.

— Roy Graham sues Random House Publishers for publishing a picture of him on "The Holiday Guide to Hawaii", Lahaina News, April 15, 1980: 13.

— annual long board contest held, Lahaina News, May 1, 1980: 15.

— equipment options discussed, Lahaina News, May 15, 1980: 15.

— Conditions on Maui, Lahaina Times, June, 1980 volume 4 number 5: 1.

— Maui Surfing Association, Lahaina Times, June, 1980 volume 4 number 5: 1.

— Longboard surf contest at Maia wharf, Lahaina Times, June, 1980 volume 4 number 5: 9.

— report on summer locations, Lahaina News, June 1, 1980: 11.

— Waimea Bay as surf spot, Lahaina Times, July, 1980 volume 4 number 6: 1.

— Kaena Point as surf spot, Lahaina Times, July, 1980 volume 4 number 6: 1.

— surfers congregating at Kimo's (nightclub), Lahaina Times, July, 1980 volume 4 number 6: 3.

— 1980 Expression Session, Lahaina Times, July, 1980 volume 4 number 6: 7.

— Kaena Point as surf spot, Lahaina Times, July, 1980 volume 4 number 6: 7.

— lack of life guards discussed, Lahaina News, July 1, 1980: 13.

— report of conditions around Maui, Lahaina Times, August, 1980 volume 4 number 7: 1.

— review of conditions, Lahaina Times, September, 1980 volume 4 number 8: 1, 6.

— Town and Country Surf Contest, Lahaina Times, September, 1980 volume 4 number 8: 6.

— Hurricane surf in Florida, Lahaina Times, September, 1980 volume 4 number 8: 6.

— violence towards reporters who publicize surf spots , Lahaina Times, October, 1980 volume 4 number 9: 1, 2.

— World Unity Surf Context, Lahaina Times, October, 1980 volume 4 number 9: 2.

— limited coverage of Maui in surf magazines, Lahaina Times, October, 1980 volume 4 number 9: 2.

— Maui covered in Wave-Rider magazine, Lahaina Times, October, 1980 volume 4 number 9: 2.

— Hawaii Surf and Sea magazine soon to be published, Lahaina Times, October, 1980 volume 4 number 9: 2.

— children starting to, Lahaina Times, August 20, 1983 volume 7 number 8: 1, 2.

— discussion of surfer girls, Lahaina Times, August 20, 1983 volume 7 number 8: 2.

— Maui Boys Surf Contest held at Lahaina Breakwall, Lahaina Times, August 20, 1983 volume 7 number 8: 2.

— tips, Lahaina Times, August 20, 1983 volume 7 number 8: 3.

— Maui surf spots evaluated, Lahaina News, February 20, 1985: 1,6.

— Kimo's-Hobie Longboard Contest to be held once conditions are right., Lahaina News, July 3, 1985: 4.

— display to be located in Cannery Shopping Center, Lahaina News, November 26, 1986: 6.

— Tony Mardian of Mr. Hobie purchases old surfboard once owned by Duke Kahanamoku, Lahaina News, November 26, 1986: 6.

— upcoming events described, Lahaina News, August 26, 1987: 6.

— upcoming events on Maui summarized, Lahaina News, March 2, 1988: 6.

— results of Native Action Surf Contest, Lahaina News, August 9, 1989: 20.

— Local Motion to host competition, Lahaina News, November 22, 1989: 9.

— Billabong Pro to be held, Lahaina News, December 6, 1989: 7.

— women compete at Sunset Beach Sunwear Women's Pro, Lahaina News, December 13, 1989: 8.

— competitions to be held on Sunset Beach, Oahu, Lahaina News, December 20, 1989: 6.

— Local Motion presenting Lahaina Surf Classic, Lahaina News, April 25, 1990: 12.

— Ole Longboard Classic to be held at Mala Wharf, Lahaina News, April 25, 1990: 12.

— Ole Longboard Classic to be held, Lahaina News, May 2, 1990: 5,6.

— Lahaina Surf Classic held, Lahaina News, May 9, 1990: 4.

— Matt Kinoshita wins Lahaina Surf Classic, Lahaina News, May 9, 1990: 7.

— Local Motion to sponsor Lahaina Surf Classic, Lahaina News, May 1, 1991: 7.

— Hard Rock Café to sponsor World Cup of, Lahaina News, December 5, 1991: 19.

— fate of beach access in Napili to be decided by Maui County Corporation Counsel, Lahaina News, December 19, 1991: 1.

— Hobie Sports' Surf Classic to be held, Lahaina News, January 23, 1992: 8.

— Local Motion sponsoring Lahaina Surf Classic, Lahaina News, April 30, 1992: 6.

— Lahaina Surf Class to be held, Lahaina News, May 7, 1992: 14.

— Nancy Emerson to reopening school of, Lahaina News, November 26, 1992: 2.

— Kimo's restaurant to hold Jerry Boser Longboarding Contest, Lahaina News, April 19, 2001: 12.

— Cheyne Magnusson featured, Lahaina News, June 7, 2001: 14.

— Maui surfers win Crazy Shirts/Town and Country Hawaii Amateur Surfing Association State Championships, Lahaina News, June 28, 2001: 15.

— NSSA Nationals held in Southern California, Lahaina News, July 12, 2001: 13.

— Maui Surfing Association to hold surfing instruction certification program, Lahaina News, July 19, 2001: 12.

— Kimo's Longboard Contest and Jerry Boser Memorial contest to be held, Lahaina News, August 16, 2001: 12.

— West Fest Summer Jam including surf contest, Lahaina News, September 6, 2001: 13.

— Billabong Girls World Champion Tour to be held at Honolua Bay, Lahaina News, October 11, 2001: 13.

— final event the Association of Surfing Professionals' World Championship Tour to be held, Lahaina News, October 18, 2001: 13.

— tow-in contest slated at Jaws, Lahaina News, November 1, 2001: 13.

— Billabong Girls World Champion Tour to be held at Honolua Bay, Lahaina News, November 22, 2001: 1.

— tow in contest slated at Jaws, Lahaina News, November 22, 2001: 11.

— Layne Beachley wins fourth world surfing title, Lahaina News, December 6, 2001: 1.

— Layne Beachley wins fourth world surfing title, Lahaina News, December 13, 2001: 12.

— Hawaiian Longboard Federation season to begin, Lahaina News, February 28, 2002: 13.

— Maui Surfer Girls to offer classes, Lahaina News, April 4, 2002: 13.

— Clay Marzo preparing for national surf title, Lahaina News, April 11, 2002: 12.

— Kimo's /Jerry Boser Memorial Longboard Contest to be held, Lahaina News, May 23, 2002: 12.

— competitions scheduled, Lahaina News, June 20, 2002: 13.

— Aston No Ka Oi competition held as part of Hawaiian Longboard Federation's 2002 Steinlager Series, Lahaina News, July 4, 2002: 12.

— Maui Surf Ohana announces Hawaii Amateur Surfing Association series, Lahaina News, October 10, 2002: 13.

— Hawaiian Longboard Federation launches website, Lahaina News, November 7, 2002: 11.

— Billabong Pro Maui tournament to be held, Lahaina News, December 5, 2002: 1.

— Vespa Trails held at Honolua Bay, Lahaina News, December 12, 2002: 11.

— Surfrider Foundation sponsoring Ho'okipa Surf Class in Memory of Justin Roberson, Lahaina News, January 2, 2003: 13.

— Legends of the Bay contest held at Honolua Bay, Lahaina News, February 6, 2003: 13.

— Hui O Pohaku-Westside Maui Longboard contest held, Lahaina News, February 20, 2003: 1.

— to compete at Ho'okipa Beach Park, Lahaina News, March 27, 2003: 13.

— Kimo's Jerry Boser Memorial Longboard Contest to be held, Lahaina News, April 10, 2003: 10.

— Hawaiian Longboard Federation to hold series, Lahaina News, April 10, 2003: 11.

— Kimo's to hold Jerry Boser Memorial Longboard Contest, Lahaina News, April 17, 2003: 13.

— Jerry Boser Memorial Longboard Contest to be held, Lahaina News, May 15, 2003: 12.

— Local Motion contest to be held, Lahaina News, May 22, 2003: 12.

— Amateur Surfing Association held qualifying contest at Lahaina Harbor, Lahaina News, June 5, 2003: 13.

— Kim Ball advocates to add surfing to school sports, Lahaina News, July 31, 2003: 12.

SURFING MAUI [FILM]
— Maui musicians on, Lahaina Times, June, 1980 volume 4 number 5: 3.

SURFRIDER ENTERPRISES PHOTO SHOP
— opening in Whaler's Village, Lahaina Sun, November 25, 1970: 3.

SURFRIDER FOUNDATION
— to battle algae problem in coastal waters, Lahaina News, November 5, 1992: 1.

— contact information provided, Lahaina News, November 12, 1992: 4.

— to do something about algae in Maui waters, Lahaina News, December 10, 1992: 3.

— to form a chapter in Lahaina, Lahaina News, April 15, 1993: 3.

— Wind Sail and Surf to hold raffle to support, Lahaina News, March 7, 1996: 6.

— to help clean Ho'okipa Beach Park, Lahaina News, July 10, 1997: 17.

— Maui chapter featured, Lahaina News, March 18, 1999: 7.

— revived on Maui, Lahaina News, May 20, 1999: 7.

— attempting to preserve Ma'alaea Pipeline, Lahaina News, August 12, 1999: 14.

— editorial in favor of saving Ma'alaea Pipeline, Lahaina News, August 19, 1999: 4.

— planning benefit for Save Ma'alaea Defense Fund, Lahaina News, August 19, 1999: 8.

— to hold "End of Summer Celebration and Surf Bash Concert", Lahaina News, August 26, 1999: 2.

— "End of Summer Celebration and Surf Bash Concert" held, Lahaina News, September 2, 1999: 15.

— to meet concerning future plans for Ho'okipa Beach Park, Lahaina News, February 17, 2000: 1.

— to hold meeting on protecting beaches, Lahaina News, February 17, 2000: 17.

— to discuss issues such as Ma'alaea Harbor expansion, Lahaina News, March 30, 2000: 3.

— to hold public meeting on issues, Lahaina News, June 22, 2000: 1.

— Foodland to help raise money for, Lahaina News, August 24, 2000: 19.

— seeks members, Lahaina News, August 31, 2000: 7.

— to hold benefit part at the Hard Rock Cafe, Lahaina News, October 19, 2000: 20.

— to hold benefit at Hard Rock Cafe, Lahaina News, November 9, 2000: 7.

— A Night with Friends of Surfrider benefit to be held at Moondoggies Maui, Lahaina News, November 23, 2000: 6.

— to host Ed Mazzarella from the national body, Lahaina News, January 4, 2001: 15,16,17.

— to hold public meeting, Lahaina News, May 3, 2001: 21.

— editorial in support of, Lahaina News, July 19, 2001: 4.

— Maui Music Odyssey concert to benefit, Lahaina News, December 13, 2001: 1,8.

— documentary "Save Ma'alaea: A Cry for Help" to be shown on Akaku: Maui Community Television, Lahaina News, July 11, 2002: 12.

— sponsoring Ho'okipa Surf Class in Memory of Justin Roberson, Lahaina News, January 2, 2003: 13.

— planning beach cleanups, Lahaina News, May 1, 2003: 2.

SURIANO, TONY
— to hold conference on chemical dependency, Lahaina News, June 10, 1987: 18.

SUSAN G. KOMEN BREAST CANCER FOUNDATION
— awards grant to Community Clinic of Maui, Lahaina News, October 17, 2002: 14.

SUSHI GO! [RESTAURANT]
— celebrating first year of business, Lahaina News, February 15, 2001: 8.

SUSPECTS MURDER MYSTERY DINNER THEATER
— to be hosted by Royal Lahaina Resort, Lahaina News, September 23, 1993: 10.

SUSTAINABLE SEAS EXPEDITION
— guest speakers from to discuss deep sea exploratory dives, Lahaina News, January 13, 2000: 5.

SUSTAINABLE TOURISM STUDY
— consultants to explain, Lahaina News, September 18, 2003: 8.

SUTHERLAND, CHARLES "CHUCK" [ARTIST]
— featured, Lahaina News, April 3, 1997: 14.
— passes away, Lahaina News, March 16, 2000: 5.
— tributes paid to, Lahaina News, March 23, 2000: 3.
— research boat is named after, Lahaina News, February 15, 2001: 1,18.

SUTHERLAND, CONNIE
— named chair of Lahaina Town Action Committee, Lahaina News, January 17, 1990: 4.

SUTHERLAND, KIEFER [ACTOR]
— visits Maui, performs with Carpe Diem at Tiger's Den, Lahaina News, July 25, 1990: 1.
— visits West Maui, Lahaina News, August 15, 1990: 15.
— has video stolen showing he and Julia Roberts at private party, Lahaina News, September 19, 1991: 1,2.
— William Pie and Inside Edition television show resolve court case of video showing Julia Roberts and, Lahaina News, November 28, 1991: 4.

SUTHERLAND, NANCY
— featured, Lahaina News, August 27, 1998: 2.

SUTHERLAND, ROBERT
— named to Environmental Standards Committee of the Hawaiian Sugar Planters' Association, Lahaina Sun, March 24, 1971: 5.

SUTTON, HAL
— to play in Mercedes Championship, Lahaina News, January 11, 2001: 8.

SUWA, JACK
— dismisses concern for misuse of pesticides, Lahaina News, February 27, 1985: 2.

SUYAMA, COLLEEN
— to rewrite zoning laws, Lahaina News, April 5, 1989: 1,16.

SUZUKI, SHOKAI
— appointed minister at Lahaina for Hongwanji Mission, Lahaina News, July 5, 1989: 1.

SWAN, AMY
— leading support group "Practical Discipline for Parents", Lahaina News, September 13, 2001: 16.
— to speak on special needs children, Lahaina News, November 8, 2001: 16.

SWAN COURT [RESTAURANT]
— featured; visited by Donald Trump and Marla Maples, Lahaina News, January 16, 1992: 14.
— to close for renovations, Lahaina News, April 2, 1992: 12.
— repens following renovations, Lahaina News, May 7, 1992: 10.
— featured, Lahaina News, February 3, 2000: 5.
— to hold wine dinner with Robert Mondavi, Lahaina News, August 31, 2000: 20.

SWANBERG, DENNIS "THE SWAN" [COMEDIAN]
— to perform at Lahaina Baptist Church, Lahaina News, December 30, 1999: 17.

SWANN, JEFFREY [MUSICIAN]
— pianist to perform at Maui Arts and Cultural Center, Lahaina News, May 18, 1995: 11.

SWANS
— killed by dogs at Embassy Suites Resort, Lahaina News, February 11, 1993: 4.

SWANSON, DAVID [MUSICIAN]
— to perform, Lahaina News, December 24, 1998: 12.

SWANSON, DON "SWANIE"
— files papers to run in 11th Representative District, Lahaina News, July 2, 1992: 6.
— appointed chair of "Operation Awareness" subcommittee of the Made in Maui Trade Council, Lahaina News, February 18, 1993: 9,10.

SWANSON, GARY [ARTIST]
— to appear at Lahaina Galleries, Lahaina News, May 9, 1990: 21.

SWANSON, GAYLE [MUSICIAN]
— to perform at benefit concert at Maui Brews, Lahaina News, August 5, 1999: 14.

SWANSON, JANE BRADLEY [ARTIST]
— to exhibit at Lahaina Art Society show, Lahaina News, July 15, 1993: 12.
— to exhibit at The Art Center of Maui, Lahaina News, September 24, 1998: 13.

SWAP MEET
— beginning at corner of Dickenson and Wainee, Lahaina News, July 15, 1987: 3.

SWARTZ, MATT
— new general manager of the Maui Eldorado Resort, Lahaina News, April 27, 2000: 11.

SWATCH WATCHES
— new designs to be shown, Lahaina News, October 17, 1991: 6.

SWEDISH CHAMBER ORCHESTRA
— presented by Maui Philharmonic Society, Lahaina News, January 18, 1989: 9.

SWEENEY, CHARLES
— donates to Maui Community College for visitor industry training, Lahaina News, April 4, 1990: 6.

SWEENEY DEVELOPMENT
— to request operating a Children's Activity Center in Kea Lani Hotel, Lahaina News, July 16, 1992: 7.

SWEENEY, MICHELE
— concierge accepted into Les Clefs D'Or, Lahaina News, May 9, 1990: 8.

SWEENEY, SHAWN
— promoted to general manager at Kea Lani Hotel, Lahaina News, January 29, 1998: 13.

SWEENEY TODD [MUSICAL]
— to be performed by Maui Community Theatre/Maui OnStage, Lahaina News, October 14, 1993: 16.

SWEET CHARITY [MUSICAL]
— to be staged by Maui OnStage, Lahaina News, April 10, 2003: 20.
— to be performed by Maui OnStage, Lahaina News, June 26, 2003: 21.
— to be performed by Maui OnStage, Lahaina News, July 3, 2003: 16.
— continues to be performed, Lahaina News, July 10, 2003: 16.

SWEET EDITION [MUSICAL GROUP]
— to perform at The Wharf Cinema Center, Lahaina News, December 17, 1992: 20.

SWEET HOME MAUI [BUSINESS]
— opens in Lahaina Cannery Mall, Lahaina News, June 14, 2001: 8.

SWEET HONEY IN THE ROCK [MUSICAL GROUP]
— to perform, Lahaina News, July 20, 1995: 12.
— to perform, Lahaina News, December 4, 1997: 25.
— to perform at Maui Arts and Cultural Center, Lahaina News, December 7, 2000: 24.

SWEET NOTHINGS [BUSINESS]
— to open at Wharf Cinema Center, Lahaina News, January 10, 1990: 6.

SWEETHEART BANQUET
— organized by Lahaina Jaycees at Coconut Grove restaurant, Lahaina Sun, February 10, 1971: 6.

SWEETHEART'S BALL
— report on Soroptimist fundraiser, Lahaina News, February 1, 1984: 3.
— to feature Terry Head and Gisela, Lahaina News, February 8, 1984: 12.
— begin organized by Soroptimists International, Lahaina News, January 30, 1985: 3.
— set for February 22, Lahaina News, February 5, 1986: 3.
— Soroptimists International purchases medical equipment with money raised from, Lahaina News, October 28, 1987: 12.
— Soroptimists International fundraiser for Maui Special Olympics, Lahaina News, February 10, 1988: 11.
— fundraiser planned, Lahaina News, January 4, 1989: 3.
— described, Lahaina News, January 25, 1989: 9.
— to be held by Soroptimists International, Lahaina News, January 17, 1990: 5.
— to be held, Lahaina News, January 24, 1990: 14.
— to be held to benefit Special Olympics, Lahaina News, January 31, 1990: 13.
— scheduled to take place at Embassy Suites Hotel, Lahaina News, February 7, 1990: 13.
— to be held, Lahaina News, January 30, 1991: 7.
— to be held, Lahaina News, February 6, 1991: 8.
— to be held by Soroptimist International, Lahaina News, January 23, 1992: 16.
— to be held, Lahaina News, February 6, 1992: 17.
— to be held, Lahaina News, February 13, 1992: 18.

SWENSON, DOUG
— to lead Yoga Awareness Workshop, Lahaina News, January 16, 2003: 16.

SWIFT, CRAIG
— named to on-site management team of Sofos Realty Corporation, Lahaina News, July 18, 1991: 6.

SWIM-A-THON
— to be held by Lahainaluna High School, Lahaina News, December 12, 1990: 20.

SWIMMING
— lessons offered by American Red Cross, Lahaina News, June 20, 1990: 8.
— Maui Ocean Swim Club to hold Ka'anapali Klassic Ocean Swim, Lahaina News, May 15, 1991: 7.
— Ka'anapali Classic ocean swim to be held, Lahaina News, April 30, 1992: 6.
— Olympic Club wins Maui Channel Swim, Lahaina News, September 10, 1992: 8.
— Age Group Swimming Season begins, Lahaina News, November 5, 1992: 12.
— Maui named as site of the Western Zone Age Group Swimming Championships, Lahaina News, December 17, 1992: 10.
— Abby Seskevics competes for Hawaii Swim Team-Lahaina, Lahaina News, December 31, 1992: 7.
— Maui Masters Swim Club taking new members, Lahaina News, December 31, 1992: 7.
— Hawaii Swim Club-Lahaina improves, Lahaina News, January 14, 1993: 8.
— competition to be held by county Department of Parks and Recreation, Lahaina News, January 28, 1993: 7.

— Department of Parks and Recreation to hold Swim Meet, Lahaina News, February 4, 1993: 6.
— Maui Ocean Swim Club to hold Ka'anapali Klassic, Lahaina News, May 13, 1993: 7.
— competition to be held at Lahaina Aquatic Center, Lahaina News, August 19, 1993: 9.
— Maui County Age Group Swimming Short Course season to be held, Lahaina News, October 14, 1993: 10.
— results of Mayor's Open Relay Meet, Lahaina News, October 21, 1993: 12,13.
— third meeting of the Maui County Short Course Swimming scheduled, Lahaina News, October 28, 1993: 8.
— members of Hawaii Swim Club-Lahaina qualify for State Short Course Championships, Lahaina News, November 4, 1993: 9.
— YMCA to offer lessons, Lahaina News, December 9, 1993: 8.
— New Years' Resolution Swim to take place, Lahaina News, January 6, 1994: 8.
— Maui Westside 2K Ocean Sprint to be held, Lahaina News, March 3, 1994: 7.
— Lahaina Swim Club to attend swim meet in Hilo, Lahaina News, March 17, 1994: 6.
— Maui Ocean Swim Club to hold Ka'anapali Klassic Ocean Swim, Lahaina News, April 28, 1994: 7.
— Coach Soichi Sakamoto Invitational swimming meet held, Lahaina News, June 9, 1994: 9.
— Blackrock 2000 Challenge to be held, Lahaina News, June 16, 1994: 7.
— Maui Swim Club wins statewide title, Lahaina News, June 23, 1994: 7.
— results of junior competitions, Lahaina News, June 30, 1994: 6.
— Western Zone Championships to be held, Lahaina News, August 4, 1994: 7.
— United States Swimming Association Western Zone Championship to be held at Lahaina Aquatic Center, Lahaina News, August 11, 1994: 6.
— results of Swimming Association Western Zone Championships, Lahaina News, August 25, 1994: 1.
— Maui Swim Club-Lahaina members are top finishers, Lahaina News, May 25, 1995: 5.
— Maui Masters Swim Club presents Black Rock Challenge, Lahaina News, June 22, 1995: 6.
— Hawaii State Long Course Swimming Championships to be held, Lahaina News, August 10, 1995: 7.
— youth program to meet, Lahaina News, November 16, 1995: 8.
— Pan Pacific Masters Swimming Championship to be held, Lahaina News, July 11, 1996: 11.
— Long Course season begins, Lahaina News, May 22, 1997: 13.
— Pac Pacific Masters Swimming Championships to be held, Lahaina News, June 12, 1997: 13.
— swimmers to meet at Lahaina Aquatic Center, Lahaina News, July 17, 1997: 14.
— Lahaina Swim Club members quality for Western Zone Swimming Championships, Lahaina News, July 31, 1997: 14.
— Maui Channel Swim to be held, Lahaina News, August 28, 1997: 6.
— Lahaina Swim Club featured, Lahaina News, November 6, 1997: 8.
— Maui Masters Swim Club to hold annual "Swim For Your Heart", Lahaina News, February 19, 1998: 12.
— class for toddlers, Lahaina News, July 16, 1998: 5.
— Lahaina swimmers to compete in state championships, Lahaina News, July 23, 1998: 14,15.
— Lahaina Aquatics Center offering synchronized swimming, Lahaina News, July 30, 1998: 7.
— Maui Channel Swim to be held, Lahaina News, September 3, 1998: 15.
— Mau Swim Club-Lahaina seeking participants, Lahaina News, September 3, 1998: 15.

— Lahaina Aquatic Center members compete , Lahaina News, December 17, 1998: 18.

— workouts to be held, Lahaina News, February 25, 1999: 7.

— Ka'anapali Klassic Ocean Swim to be held, Lahaina News, April 1, 1999: 15.

— Lahainaluna High School student Jessica Nohara competes in Kapalua Fun Swim Challenge, Lahaina News, September 23, 1999: 1.

— Kihei Aquatic and Community Center selected as site for Western Zone Age Group Swimming Championship, Lahaina News, October 7, 1999: 9.

— Lahaina Swim Club featured, Lahaina News, December 9, 1999: 8.

— Lahaina Swim Club competes in Hawaii Short Course Age Group Swimming Championships, Lahaina News, February 10, 2000: 9.

— Maui Masters Swim Club to hold Maui Roughwater Swim Race, Lahaina News, October 12, 2000: 9.

— Jessica Nohara leads Lahaina Swim Club to success at Maui County Age Group Swim Meet, Lahaina News, October 26, 2000: 12.

— Lahainaluna High School team successful, Lahaina News, February 22, 2001: 12.

— Valley Isle Masters Swimmers to hold workouts at Lahaina Aquatic Center, Lahaina News, March 1, 2001: 15.

— classes being offered by county Department of Parks and Recreation, Lahaina News, June 28, 2001: 15.

— Western Zones Open Water Race to be held at Kamaole Beach Park, Lahaina News, August 2, 2001: 13.

— Valley Isle Masters Swimmers to hold Roughwater Swim Race, Lahaina News, September 27, 2001: 13.

— Maui Aquatics offering swimming lessons, Lahaina News, January 10, 2002: 13.

— class offered by Maui Aquatics, Lahaina News, January 24, 2002: 13.

— Lahainaluna High School team featured, Lahaina News, January 31, 2002: 12.

— Maui Aquatics offering swimming lessons, Lahaina News, April 18, 2002: 13.

— Department of Parks and Recreation to hold youth programs, Lahaina News, June 6, 2002: 13.

— Lahaina Swim Club wins state title, Lahaina News, January 16, 2003: 12.

— Maui Aquatics continues to offer swimming lessons, Lahaina News, January 16, 2003: 13.

— Lahaina Swim Club successful in tournament, Lahaina News, June 26, 2003: 1,2.

— Rich Wiseman to compete in Masters Swimming competition, Lahaina News, July 24, 2003: 12.

— see also community swimming pool, Lahaina Community Swimming Pool, Inc

SWIMMING POOL SUPPLY SERVICE

— opened by Eddie and Mary Kanohokula, Lahaina News, July 4, 1990: 7.

SWIMMING POOLS

— upgraded from phase 5 to phase 2 of Lahaina Recreation Center, Lahaina News, March 6, 1985: 16.

— supporters told to raise money, Lahaina News, May 1, 1985: 20.

— Mayor Hannibal Tavares may veto funding for, Lahaina News, August 17, 1988: 1.

— Maui County Finance Committee declines funds to study, Lahaina News, October 26, 1988: 1,24.

— 505 Front Street to raise funds for with wishing pool, Lahaina News, October 26, 1988: 17.

— supporters to fight Mayor Hannibal Tavares' rejection, Lahaina News, November 30, 1988: 1.

— backers meet, Lahaina News, March 15, 1989: 1.

— Maui County may move forward with development of, Lahaina News, July 19, 1989: 3.

— funding doubtful, Lahaina News, February 7, 1990: 1,3.

— Maui County parks director to speak on proposal for, Lahaina News, March 21, 1990: 3.

— Maui County parks director Charmaine Tavares confident of funding for, Lahaina News, April 4, 1990: 1.

— panel to discuss proposed, Lahaina News, April 11, 1990: 1.

— construction bids may go out in January, Lahaina News, April 18, 1990: 1,16.

— Mayor Tavares signs County budget including funding for, Lahaina News, June 27, 1990: 5.

— initial plans created, Lahaina News, July 11, 1990: 1.

— Amfac, Inc. to submit revised offer to help develop, Lahaina News, August 8, 1990: 1.

— public meeting to be held, Lahaina News, October 17, 1990: 5.

— see also Lahaina Community Swimming Pool

SWIMWEAR HAWAII [BUSINESS]

— opens, Lahaina News, August 19, 1999: 13.

SWINDLE, ORSON [POLITICIAN]

— to speak at Republican Party's Lincoln Day Dinner, Lahaina News, February 17, 1994: 12.

SWING IS KING [MUSICAL SHOW]

— returns to Maui Inter-Continental Wailea, Lahaina News, January 15, 1986: 10.

SWING KINGS, THE [MUSICAL GROUP]

— to perform at Maui Brews, Lahaina News, October 15, 1998: 17.

— to perform at Maui Brews, Lahaina News, March 4, 1999: 13.

— to perform at Embassy Suites, Lahaina News, March 11, 1999: 12.

SWING SHIFT [MUSICAL GROUP]

— to perform at Lopaka's Grill and Bar, Lahaina News, April 9, 1992: 22.

SWING THING, THE [MUSICAL]

— to be performed for New Years, Lahaina News, December 30, 1999: 3.

SWINGING JOHNSONS [MUSICAL GROUP]

— to perform at World Café, Lahaina News, September 12, 1996: 16.

SWISHER, LYNN

— named vice president of Hawaiian Commercial and Sugar Co., Lahaina News, December 26, 2002: 8.

SWOERS, ED

— new position at Hyatt Regency Maui, Lahaina News, July 31, 1985: 7.

SYDNEY, SUSANNE

— Maui County candidate profiled, Lahaina News, September 1, 1980: 4.

— running for Maui County Council, Lahaina News, February 15, 1984: 6.

SYKES, JUDY

— named realtor of the year, Lahaina News, December 26, 1990: 7.

SYLVA, ADELAIDE KUAMU

— life recounted, Lahaina News, May 3, 2001: 17.

SYLVA, FRANK AND ADELAIDE

— holds luau for wedding anniversary, Lahaina News, April 19, 2001: 5.

— part II of feature, Lahaina News, April 26, 2001: 11.

— first meeting described, Lahaina News, May 10, 2001: 16,17.

— story of their relationship, Lahaina News, May 17, 2001: 11.

SYLVA, RENE

— to lecture on "The Endangered Native Plant Species of Hawaii", Lahaina News, August 15, 1996: 15.

SYLVAN LEARNING CENTER

— now enrolling students, Lahaina News, June 21, 1989: 3.

— students raising funds for Muscular Dystrophy Association, Lahaina News, August 16, 1989: 3.

— director Stacia Andagan featured, Lahaina News, July 9, 1992: 13.

— moves to Wailuku Industrial Park, Lahaina News, April 15, 1993: 7.

— to hold seminars, Lahaina News, July 31, 1997: 16.

SYMPHONY OF CHOCOLATES

— to be held at Maui Inter-Continental Wailea, Lahaina News, April 24, 1985: 20.

SYNCHROMIC STUDIOS [BUSINESS]

— Craig Robin joins as director of operations, Lahaina News, May 9, 1996: 8.

SYNERGY DESIGN [BUSINESS]

— wins Honolulu Advertising Federation Pele Award, Lahaina News, May 18, 2000: 16.

SYSTEMS BY DESIGN [BUSINESS]

— to become a Macintosh dealer, Lahaina News, December 16, 1993: 7.

SZAKACS, SHANE

— wins karaoke competition, Lahaina News, July 13, 2000: 9.

T

T-SHIRT FACTORY [BUSINESS]

— opens store in Wharf Cinema Center, Lahaina News, December 12, 1996: 13.

— opens in Lahaina Cannery Mall, Lahaina News, September 30, 1999: 11.

— opens store in Whalers Village, Lahaina News, March 20, 2003: 8.

T.S. SHINN SERVICE AWARD

— given to Don Aus, Lahaina News, September 28, 1988: 2.

TABACO, ROBERT

— Scholar/Athlete of the Week, Lahaina News, October 23, 1997: 9.

TABANDERA, NADINE

— wins Miss Maui Pageant, Lahaina News, February 13, 1991: 1,8.

TABANDERA, NATASHA

— Miss Maui featured, Lahaina News, June 6, 1991: 1.

TABISOLA, JIMMY

— employee recognized by Westin Maui, Lahaina News, January 23, 1992: 13.

TABORA, ROY GONZALEZ [ARTIST]

— to exhibit at Wyland Galleries, Lahaina News, July 2, 1992: 22.

— to exhibit at Wyland Galleries, Lahaina News, July 9, 1992: 20.

— to exhibit at Wyland Galleries, Lahaina News, July 13, 1995: 11.

— to visit Pictures Plus, Lahaina News, July 18, 2002: 16.

TADAO, SHERLYN

— Scholar/Athlete of the Week, Lahaina News, July 6, 2000: 12.

TAE KWON-DO

— see martial arts

TAGOMORI, HOWARD

— Deputy Police Chief requests more officers to fight drugs, Lahaina News, September 10, 1986: 1.

— Maui Police Chief discusses issues faced by drug addicts, Lahaina News, November 23, 1988: 1,16.

— disagrees with Mayor Linda Lingle on funding Kihei substation, Lahaina News, March 11, 1993: 10.

— police chief discusses funding for community police officers, Lahaina News, December 29, 1994: 2.

TAGUPA, KIMO

— receives "Aloha Award" at Kapalua Hotel, Lahaina News, December 12, 1991: 20.

TAHAURI, JILL

— to teach lei making, Lahaina News, July 13, 2000: 17.

TAHITI

— travel to described, Lahaina News, July, 1979: 12,16.

— shows to be held at Wharf Cinema Center, Lahaina News, August 8, 2002: 16.

TAHITI FETE

— to be held at Lahaina Cannery Mall, Lahaina News, August 17, 1995: 11,12.

— to be held, Lahaina News, August 12, 1999: 16.

— to be held at Lahaina Cannery Mall, Lahaina News, April 26, 2001: 20.

— to be held, Lahaina News, April 11, 2002: 15.

— to be held at Lahaina Cannery Mall, Lahaina News, April 3, 2003: 17.

— see also Aloha Festivals

TAI CHI

— see martial arts

TAI, JEFF

— selected Director of Marketing for Ka'anapali Beach Operators Association, Lahaina News, January 20, 1988: 3,18.

TAI, JEFF AND LEO

— featured, Lahaina News, July 27, 1988: 2.

TAI KOH [RESTAURANT]

— reviewed, Lahaina News, April 11, 1984: 15.

TAIKO

— drum performance to be held at Lahaina Cannery Mall, Lahaina News, August 19, 1999: 9.

— Maui Taiko to perform at Lahaina Cannery Mall, Lahaina News, August 19, 1999: 9.

— drummers to perform at Banyan Tree Park, Lahaina News, November 23, 2000: 7.

— Taiko Festival Maui to be held, Lahaina News, May 3, 2001: 20.

— festival to be held, Lahaina News, June 27, 2002: 16.

— San Jose Taiko and Hanayui to perform at Maui Arts and Cultural Center, Lahaina News, October 3, 2002: 17.

— Taiko Festival to be held at Maui Arts and Cultural Center, Lahaina News, June 26, 2003: 20.

— Watanabe Taiko Drummers to perform at Lahaina Cannery Mall as part of "Journey to the Orient", Lahaina News, August 7, 2003: 1,14.

TAILOR OF PANAMA [FILM]

— to be shown at Maui Arts and Cultural Center, Lahaina News, July 19, 2001: 17.

TAJ MAHAL [MUSICIAN]

— to perform at Casanova's, Lahaina News, April 23, 1992: 30.

— to perform at Casanova's, Lahaina News, April 30, 1992: 16.

— to perform at Casanova's, Lahaina News, May 26, 1994: 16.

TAKABUKI, ANNE

— promoted to vice president at Wailea Resort Company, Ltd., Lahaina News, July 2, 1992: 17.

TAKACS STRING QUARTET

— to perform, Lahaina News, April 13, 1988: 3.

TAKAGAKI, KOUHEI [ARTIST]

— to exhibit at Lahaina Cannery Mall, Lahaina News, February 3, 2000: 12.

TAKAHAMA, KIICHI

— police officer urges cyclists to protect their bicycles from theft, Lahaina Sun, January 20, 1971: 8.

— police officer discusses planned Lahaina Whaling Spree, Lahaina Sun, February 3, 1971: 2.

TAKAHASHI, ALVIN

— Betsill Brothers Construction appoints as principal broker, Lahaina News, July 19, 2001: 9.

TAKAHASHI, DONN
— named general manager of Maui Prince Hotel, Lahaina News, October 1, 1992: 10,11.

TAKAHASHI, HIDEO "PAKALA"
— member of the "Lost Battalion" honored, Lahaina News, August 22, 2002: 3.

TAKAHASHI, TENEY
— rejoins Amfac/JMB Hawaii as senior vice president for real estate division, Lahaina News, May 11, 1995: 10.

TAKAKI, DONALD
— president of Island Movers, Inc. to join Hawaiian Airlines board of directors, Lahaina News, March 19, 1992: 10.

TAKANA, KAKUEI
— Japan's Prime Minister meets with President Nixon in Honolulu, Lahaina Sun, September 6, 1972: 3,5.

TAKANO, NOBORU
— appointed director of Asia and Pacific Sales for the Ritz-Carlton, Lahaina News, December 31, 1992: 10.

TAKASE, RICHARD
— plans for proposed industrial park at Napili changed by new developer, Lahaina News, February 20, 1991: 1.
— developer of proposed Napili Trade Center promises contribution to community, Lahaina News, November 14, 1991: 11.

TAKASHIMA, KENNY "TOP SHAPE"
— remembered, Lahaina News, July 19, 2001: 1,20.
— captain passes away, Lahaina News, July 19, 2001: 20.

TAKATSUKA, LIKICHI
— retires from Post Office after 90 years, Lahaina Sun, December 16, 1970: 6.

TAKAYAMA, MONICA
— completes Accredited Master Professional Pet Sitter Course, Lahaina News, December 24, 1998: 11.

TAKAYESU, JAMES
— comments on commission's decision to stop Kapuni Snorkel Adventure from offering luau on Moloka'i, Lahaina News, May 11, 1988: 10.

TAKE HOME MAUI DELI, THE [RESTAURANT]
— offering gift packs, Lahaina News, December 19, 1991: 23.
— featured, Lahaina News, May 14, 1992: 16.

TAKE OFF POUNDS SENSIBLY (TOPS)
— to meet at Kaunoa Senior Center, Lahaina News, June 24, 1999: 13.
— members continue to meet, Lahaina News, July 29, 1999: 12.

TAKEDA, SUSAN
— promoted to vice president at the Bank of Hawaii, Lahaina News, October 27, 1994: 15.

TAKEMOTO, MICHAEL [ARTIST]
— interviewed, Lahaina News, January 29, 1986: Art-1,Art-2,Art-3,Art-4.
— to explain ink brush technique, Lahaina News, October 17, 2002: 20.

TAKEUCHI, GEORGE
— discusses plans for underground wiring in Front Street, Lahaina Sun, December 9, 1970: 7.
— see also West Maui Business Association

TAKEUCHI, SUMI
— passed away, Lahaina Sun, March 29, 1972: 9.

TAKEYESU, JAMES
— County Corporation Counsel to speak at Maui League of Republican Women, Lahaina News, March 11, 1999: 12.

TAKISHITA, ANDRA
— named wedding coordinator at Hyatt Regency Maui, Lahaina News, February 22, 1996: 11.

TAKITA, LINDA
— to perform in "I do, I do" with her husband Michael Takita, Lahaina News, January 8, 1986: 3.
— Maui Youth Theatre director seeks help from Maui County, Lahaina News, January 3, 1990: 1.
— executive artistic director of Maui Academy of Performing Arts discusses institution's financial issues, Lahaina News, November 14, 1990: 1.

TAKITA, MICHAEL
— to perform in "I do, I do" with his wife Linda Takita, Lahaina News, January 8, 1986: 3.

TAKITA, MICHAEL AND LINDA
— tribute to be held by Maui Academy of Performing Arts, Lahaina News, March 25, 1993: 15.

TAKITANI, ANTHONY
— to discuss automobile insurance with Democratic Century Club, Lahaina News, January 22, 1998: 13.

TAKITANI, ERNEST
— owner of Queen Theater involved in renovations, Lahaina Sun, February 17, 1971: 2.

TAKITANI, HENRY [POLITICIAN]
— state senator at public meeting in Lahaina, Lahaina Sun, December 23, 1970: 10.

TAKSIM TRIO [MUSICAL GROUP]
— to perform at Maui Arts and Cultural Center, Lahaina News, March 25, 1999: 16.

TAL, LEO
— appointed Director of Public Relations for Wharf Shops and Restaurants, Lahaina News, May 11, 1988: 14.

TALBOT, SINA
— purchases For Shear Hair Design, Lahaina News, November 9, 1995: 10.

TALENT CONTEST
— held at Baldwin Auditorium, Lahaina News, March 1, 1980: 14.
— to be held at Lahaina Cannery Mall, Lahaina News, August 30, 2001: 16.

TALES FROM THE RING OF FIRE [PERFORMANCE]
— to be performed by Peter and Dana Marshall at Pu'unene Clubhouse, Lahaina News, January 16, 1985: 3.

TALES OF HOFFMAN [FILM]
— to be presented by Maui Philharmonic Society, Lahaina News, October 19, 1988: 14.

TALES OF MAUI [PLAY]
— to be performed at Maui Arts and Cultural Center, Lahaina News, August 17, 1995: 11.

TALISMAN [MUSICAL GROUP]
— to perform at the Maui Inter-Continental Wailea, Lahaina News, October 24, 1984: 3.

TALK OF DA TOWN, THE [MUSICAL GROUP]
— to perform at Longhi's, Lahaina News, April 11, 1990: 15.
— to perform at Longhi's, Lahaina News, April 18, 1990: 11.
— to perform at Royal Ocean Terrace Lounge at the Royal Lahaina Resort, Lahaina News, May 9, 1990: 18.
— to perform at Casanova's, Lahaina News, September 5, 1990: 15.
— to perform at Longhi's, Lahaina News, March 20, 1991: 9.
— to perform at Longhi's, Lahaina News, May 30, 1991: 7.
— continues to perform at Longhi's, Lahaina News, August 8, 1991: 13.
— continues to perform at Longhi's, Lahaina News, November 7, 1991: 14.

TALKING ISLAND TOUR
— to be held at Ka'anapali Beach Hotel, Lahaina News, October 22, 1992: 16.

TALKING STORIES [TROUPE]
— theater group to hold fundraiser, Lahaina News, June 12, 2003: 21.
— to hold acting workshop, Lahaina News, October 9, 2003: 16.

TAM, EDDIE
— police officer discusses brochure to deter hippies from coming to Maui, Lahaina Sun, December 9, 1970: 1,6.
— biography of police officer, Lahaina News, March 2, 1995: 2.

TAM, GEORGE
— Indicted for felony theft, Lahaina News, October 15, 1982: 2.

TAMANGO'S URBAN TAP [TROUPE]
— to perform "In Full Cycle", Lahaina News, March 20, 2003: 17.
— to perform, Lahaina News, March 27, 2003: 16.

TAMAYO [COMEDIAN]
— to perform at Maui Marriott Hotel, Lahaina News, January 7, 1993: 11.
— to perform at Maui Marriott Hotel, Lahaina News, January 14, 1993: 13.

TAMAYO, RANDY
— Lahainaluna High School basketball player featured, Lahaina News, March 12, 1986: 9.

TAMGATAILOA, LEO
— captures third place at Wood Carving Competition, Lahaina News, August 6, 1998: 7.

TAMING OF THE SHREW [PLAY]
— to be performed by Maui Youth Theatre, Lahaina News, July 29, 1987: 3.
— Shakespeare to be performed by Maui Youth Theatre, Lahaina News, September 2, 1987: 3.

TAN LAHAINA COMPANY [BUSINESS]
— opens, Lahaina News, November 12, 1986: 3.

TANABE, BARBARA
— to become chairman of the board of Hawaii Visitors Bureau, Lahaina News, July 7, 1994: 9.

TANAKA, ANN
— named retail trainer at Crazy Shirts, Lahaina News, May 13, 1993: 6.

TANAKA, CASEY
— named Outstanding Youth Competitor at JKA Hawaii Maui Dojo Goodwill Invitational Tourney, Lahaina News, December 10, 1992: 6.

TANAKA, JOANNE
— to present "Ways to Feel Better", Lahaina News, February 22, 2001: 16.

TANAKA, JOE [POLITICIAN]
— announces run for Maui County Council, Lahaina News, March 5, 1986: 20.
— organizes golf tournament to benefit Maui Youth Theatre, Lahaina News, October 14, 1987: 3.
— spearheads display of dinosaur replicas, Lahaina News, August 24, 1988: 9.
— to host fashion show with wife Barbara to benefit The Maui Academy of Performing Arts, Lahaina News, August 1, 1991: 3.
— takes out papers to run for 9th District House Seat, Lahaina News, June 25, 1992: 2.

TANAKA, KIM
— Scholar/Athlete of the Week, Lahaina News, April 18, 1996: 13.

TANAKA, KIMBERLY
— wins East Kaua'i Juniors tournament, Lahaina News, August 15, 1991: 4.

TANAKA, ROBERT
— consulting on Kahana residential project, Lahaina News, February 6, 1992: 1.

TANG, CHRIS
— completed Kona Ironman Triathlon, Lahaina News, October 27, 1994: 11.

TANG SOO DO MARTIAL ARTS CLUB
— training offered by Ron Holland, Lahaina News, September 25, 1985: 4.

TANGEN, SYLVIA
— Working on virtual Encyclopedia of Maui, Lahaina Sun, February 17, 1971: 3.

TANIGAWA, MARI
— wins Maui Marathon, Lahaina News, March 19, 1998: 2.

TANIGUCHI, EDYLN
— appointed assistant treasurer for Maui County, Lahaina News, June 20, 1991: 7.

TANINO, LANCE
— to lead bird watching trip with Sierra Club, Lahaina News, January 25, 2001: 16.

TANTRA
— Kahua Hawaiian Institute to hold lecture on, Lahaina News, September 11, 1997: 16.

TANTRA SYMPOSIUM
— to be held at Lea Lani Resort, Lahaina News, July 15, 1993: 5.

TANVEER, ANJUN
— named food and beverage director at Embassy Suites Resort, Lahaina News, March 14, 1996: 10.

TAPASWAN LUMBER COMPANY [BUSINESS]
— expanding to Maui from the Big Island, Lahaina News, April 22, 1987: 10.

TAPAT, JEANETTE
— crowned Miss Maui Filipina, 1972, Lahaina Sun, March 15, 1972: 1.

TARGET RANGE
— flooded out, Lahaina News, December 13, 1989: 3.

TARLOW, PETER
— to speak on "Creating a Safe Community", Lahaina News, April 27, 2000: 1.
— to speak on "Creating Safe Communities in Economically Challenging Times" at Maui Community College, Lahaina News, April 27, 2000: 13.

TARNOFF, STEVEN
— to support Jack Kelley Memorial Golf Tournament, Lahaina News, September 16, 1999: 6.

TARO FESTIVAL
— to be held, Lahaina News, March 21, 1996: 13.

TARTUFFE [PLAY]
— to be performed by Baldwin Theatre Guild, Lahaina News, April 30, 1992: 14.
— continues at Baldwin Mini Theatre, Lahaina News, May 14, 1992: 18.
— continues, Lahaina News, May 21, 1992: 18.

TARTUFFE: BORN AGAIN [PLAY]
— to be performed by Maui OnStage, Lahaina News, February 27, 2003: 18.

TASCA RISTORANTE [BUSINESS]
— reviewed, Lahaina News, August 22, 1991: 14.

TASHI LHUNPO MONKS
— to visit Maui, Lahaina News, December 26, 2002: 3.
— to visit Maui, Lahaina News, January 2, 2003: 14.

TASHOMBE AND FRIENDS [MUSICIANS]
— performance reviewed, Lahaina News, April 4, 1984: 12.

TASHOMBE, FULTON [MUSICIAN]
— to perform at Maui Marriott, Lahaina News, May 3, 1989: 12.
— to perform at Villa Lounge, Lahaina News, July 2, 1992: 21.
— to perform at Villa Lounge, Lahaina News, August 13, 1992: 15.

TASK FORCE ON THE OLD LAHAINA COURTHOUSE
— see Old Lahaina Courthouse

TASTE OF LAHAINA, A
— restaurants participating in, Lahaina News, December 5, 1990: 9.
— to be held, Lahaina News, August 27, 1992: 3.
— to be held at Lahaina Center parking lot, Lahaina News, September 10, 1992: 17.
— to be held, Lahaina News, September 10, 1992: 4.
— details for, Lahaina News, September 17, 1992: 15.
— results, Lahaina News, October 1, 1992: 3.
— reservations being accepted, Lahaina News, May 27, 1993: 3.
— details of, Lahaina News, August 18, 1994: 2.
— to be held, Lahaina News, September 15, 1994: 14.
— featured, Lahaina News, September 15, 1994: 3.
— held, Lahaina News, September 22, 1994: 1.
— police report that no arrests made, Lahaina News, October 6, 1994: 3.
— seeking sponsors, Lahaina News, June 15, 1995: 2.
— registration begins, Lahaina News, July 13, 1995: 5.
— beneficiaries set, Lahaina News, July 20, 1995: 5.
— to be held, Lahaina News, August 17, 1995: 12.
— volunteers sought for, Lahaina News, August 24, 1995: 4.
— details of, Lahaina News, September 7, 1995: insert1,insert2,insert 3,insert4,insert5,insert6,insert7,insert8.
— reviewed, Lahaina News, September 14, 1995: 2.
— results of, Lahaina News, September 21, 1995: 1,12.
— Soroptimists International raises money during, Lahaina News, October 12, 1995: 6.
— raises money, Lahaina News, November 2, 1995: 2.
— LahainaTown Action Committee seeking volunteers for, Lahaina News, July 25, 1996: 13.
— planning underway, Lahaina News, August 8, 1996: 4.
— to feature top chefs, Lahaina News, August 29, 1996: 1.
— to be held this weekend, Lahaina News, September 12, 1996: 1,7,8,9,12,13,14.
— results, Lahaina News, September 19, 1996: 3.
— update on bachelor auction, Lahaina News, October 3, 1996: 2.
— to be held at Lahaina Cannery Mall, Lahaina News, July 17, 1997: 6.
— to be held, Lahaina News, July 31, 1997: 17.
— to feature Brothers Cazimero and Keali'i Reichel, Lahaina News, September 4, 1997: 3.
— over 25,000 people expected, Lahaina News, September 11, 1997: 1.
— results of, Lahaina News, September 18, 1997: 1,2.
— discussion to move it to Front Street, Lahaina News, September 25, 1997: 1.
— couple buys kitchen at auction, Lahaina News, October 2, 1997: 15.
— this year's theme is "... Beached in Paradise", Lahaina News, August 13, 1998: 2.
— to be held, Lahaina News, August 27, 1998: 1.
— to be held; looking for volunteers, Lahaina News, September 3, 1998: 8,21.
— Keali'i Reichel to perform at, Lahaina News, September 10, 1998: 16.
— musicians listed, Lahaina News, September 10, 1998: 16.
— held, Lahaina News, September 24, 1998: 2.
— being organized, Lahaina News, November 19, 1998: 2.

— LahainaTown Action Committee accepting applications for, Lahaina News, July 1, 1999: 11.
— LahainaTown Action Committee seeking volunteers for, Lahaina News, August 26, 1999: 9.
— food contest to be held, Lahaina News, September 23, 1999: 11.
— LahainaTown Action Committee to hold cookbook competition, Lahaina News, October 14, 1999: 5.
— looking for new location, Lahaina News, November 25, 1999: 1.
— LahainaTown Action Committee seeks site for, Lahaina News, May 11, 2000: 1,8.
— Maui County finds a location for, Lahaina News, June 22, 2000: 1,15.
— officials evaluate proposed site for, Lahaina News, June 29, 2000: 1,8.
— seeking volunteers, Lahaina News, August 24, 2000: 19.
— details on music to be scheduled for, Lahaina News, August 31, 2000: 19.
— details of, Lahaina News, September 7, 2000: 1,8,9,10.
— held, Lahaina News, September 14, 2000: 18,19.
— held successfully, Lahaina News, September 21, 2000: 10.
— booths available, Lahaina News, August 16, 2001: 2.
— to be held, Lahaina News, August 30, 2001: 14.
— to be held, Lahaina News, September 6, 2001: 1,18,20.
— Willie K performed at, Lahaina News, September 13, 2001: 1.
— to be planned, Lahaina News, August 15, 2002: 14.
— to begin, Lahaina News, August 22, 2002: 16,18.
— to support Lahaina Youth Contact Football Booster Club (LYCFBC), Lahaina News, August 29, 2002: 16.
— National Honor Society to benefit from, Lahaina News, September 5, 2002: 15.
— "Maui Chefs Present...." to be held at Hyatt Regency Maui, Lahaina News, September 5, 2002: 9.
— details of, Lahaina News, September 12, 2002: 15,16,17.
— results of, Lahaina News, September 26, 2002: 9.
— to be held Lahaina Recreation Center Park II, Lahaina News, August 21, 2003: 14.
— to feature "Keiki Fun Zone", Lahaina News, August 28, 2003: 9.
— to be held, Lahaina News, September 4, 2003: 14.
— to be held, details of, Lahaina News, September 11, 2003: 1,3.
— proceeds given to Sacred Hearts School, Lahaina News, September 25, 2003: 14.
— results listed, Lahaina News, September 25, 2003: 14.

TASTE OF SOUTH MAUI
— to benefit Kihei Youth Center, Lahaina News, July 24, 1997: 16.
— to be held by Kihei Youth Center, Lahaina News, July 22, 1999: 12.
— to benefit Kihei Youth Center, Lahaina News, July 27, 2000: 20.

TATE, DONNELL "ANDY"
— appointed International Game Fish Association (IGFA) representative, Lahaina News, July 15, 1999: 7.

TATEISHI AND APO [BUSINESS]
— promotes April Goo to legal assistant, Lahaina News, June 6, 1991: 6.
— law corporation hires new lawyers, Lahaina News, February 3, 1994: 7.

TATEYAMA, CANDIS
— wins scholarship from Wailea Community Association, Lahaina News, September 16, 1993: 8.

TATSUMI, PATRICK
— wedding to Gail Kishida announced, Lahaina Sun, January 20, 1971: 3.

TATTOOING
— described, Lahaina News, September 15, 1981: 13.

TATUS, CHRIS
— named Front Office Manager at Maui Marriott, Lahaina News, December 16, 1987: 3.

TAU'A, KELI'I
— Hokule'a sailor to present "The Spirit the Wa'a Brings Forth", Lahaina News, November 23, 2000: 21.

TAUB, ROBERT
— pianist to perform at Maui Arts and Cultural Center, Lahaina News, April 13, 1995: 16.

TAUKEIAHO, SELETI
— Eagle Scout organizing book drive, Lahaina News, May 28, 1992: 4.

TAVARES, CHARMAINE [POLITICIAN]
— Maui County parks director considers offering pilot after school program, Lahaina News, January 10, 1990: 1.
— Maui County parks director to speak on proposal for community swimming pool, Lahaina News, March 21, 1990: 3.
— confident that swimming pool fill be funded, Lahaina News, April 4, 1990: 1.
— County parks director seeks to redo D.T. Fleming Park, Lahaina News, February 20, 1991: 1.
— Maui County parks director exploring potential sites for park in Napili, Lahaina News, May 8, 1991: 1.
— Maui County parks director to meet with vendors concerning craft fairs at the Lahaina Center, Lahaina News, July 9, 1992: 3.
— county parks director says proposal to develop natatorium at Kalama Park "not completely dead", Lahaina News, November 26, 1992: 18.
— County Parks Director may prohibit drinking at Malu'ulu O Lele Park, Lahaina News, October 28, 1993: 3,4.
— county Parks Director talks about pre-construction at D.T. Fleming Beach Park, Lahaina News, March 9, 1995: 4.
— County Parks Director proposes double the park land, Lahaina News, July 13, 1995: 4.
— to kick-off campaign for Maui County Council, Lahaina News, July 25, 1996: 13.
— candidate for Upcountry County Council Seat, Lahaina News, November 2, 2000: 22.

TAVARES, HANNIBAL [POLITICIAN]
— defends request for more police officers, Lahaina News, May 1, 1980: 14.
— mayor meets with people in Hana, Lahaina News, June 15, 1980: 19.
— mayor cancels plans to attend National Conference of Mayors, Lahaina News, June 15, 1980: 19.
— mayor interviewed by Bob Kelsey, Lahaina News, July 1, 1980: 2,3.
— mayor discusses changes to sewage fees, Lahaina News, July 1, 1980: 6.
— mayor dedicates Moloka'i elderly housing project, Lahaina News, July 1, 1980: 6.
— mayor denies police request for more money, Lahaina News, July 15, 1980: 7.
— mayor makes citizen's arrest, Lahaina News, August 15, 1980: 7.
— mayor to propose anti-pornography ordinance, Lahaina News, October 1, 1980: 13.
— mayor major endorses program where victims of crime are flown back to Hawaii, Lahaina News, December 1, 1980: 11.
— mayor requests pause in proposed water treatment facility, Lahaina News, April 15, 1981: 14.
— mayor supports County Office of Immigrant Services, Lahaina News, June 1, 1981: 8.
— mayor urges Maui Council to create residential condominium project in Lahaina, Lahaina News, July 15, 1982: 3.
— mayor reveals paving plan, Lahaina News, October 1, 1982: 2.
— mayor Lahaina News editorial supporting, Lahaina News, October 15, 1982: 3.
— major asks Navy to reduce noise of bombing Kaho'olawe, Lahaina News, December 15, 1982: 2.
— mayor writes President Reagan regarding Native Hawaiian Study Commission, Lahaina News, April 15, 1983: 6.
— mayor signs Lahaina Community Plan, Lahaina News, February 1, 1984: 12.
— mayor asks hotel industry for support lobbying legislature to allow counties more taxing authority, Lahaina News, April 18, 1984: 17.
— mayor arguing with West Maui Taxpayers Association regarding property taxes, Lahaina News, May 9, 1984: 2,3.
— mayor Mayor's 16th Invitational Art Exhibit to be held, Lahaina News, May 16, 1984: 7.
— mayor seeks Australian support in dealing with Australian sailor charged with crimes, Lahaina News, July 11, 1984: 3.
— mayor creates committee to encourage more filming on Maui, Lahaina News, July 25, 1984: 15.
— mayor wants part of budget surplus to go to Maui County Visitors Association, Lahaina News, September 26, 1984: 14.
— mayor criticizes helicopter companies for excessive noise, Lahaina News, February 6, 1985: 3.
— mayor fights use of malathion to eliminate fruit flies, Lahaina News, March 27, 1985: 3,20.
— mayor opposes use of paraquat, writes to President Reagan, Lahaina News, August 7, 1985: 1.
— mayor appoints citizen's committee to promote public education on dangers of drugs, Lahaina News, August 21, 1985: 3.
— mayor honors former teacher Ruthie Hawk, Lahaina News, March 12, 1986: 12.
— mayor asks for jet ski control, Lahaina News, April 16, 1986: 3.
— mayor asks Army Corps of Engineers to reduce scope of Kahoma Stream Flood Control project, Lahaina News, May 14, 1986: 3.
— mayor opposes use of paraquaot to eradicate marijuana, Lahaina News, June 11, 1986: 14.
— mayor ad hoc committee makes recommendations regarding Honoapi'ilani Highway, Lahaina News, June 25, 1986: 1,16.
— mayor awards certificates of merit, Lahaina News, September 10, 1986: 3.
— mayor begins program recognizing outstanding youth, Lahaina News, October 1, 1986: 12.
— mayor calls on residents to lobby for Lahaina Bypass, Lahaina News, December 31, 1986: 12.
— mayor opposes moratorium on development, Lahaina News, March 4, 1987: 1.
— mayor reaffirms ban on use of public park for Miss Gay Moloka'i Beauty Pageant, Lahaina News, March 4, 1987: 3.
— mayor budget issued, Lahaina News, March 25, 1987: 2.
— mayor to honor Maui youth, Lahaina News, October 14, 1987: 17.
— mayor presents "Outstanding Youth" awards, Lahaina News, December 16, 1987: 3,15.
— mayor called a czar by councilman Tom Morrow, Lahaina News, February 17, 1988: 1,20.
— mayor to address American Association of Retired Persons, Lahaina News, March 2, 1988: 22.
— mayor announces scholarships and summer jobs, Lahaina News, April 27, 1988: 6.
— mayor may agree to detour while Kahoma bridge rebuilt, Lahaina News, July 6, 1988: 1,24.
— mayor comments on 4000 housing units planned for West Maui, Lahaina News, November 2, 1988: 1,24.
— Mayor to fight conversion of Holo Honokowai to hotel, Lahaina News, December 21, 1988: 1.
— mayor supports purchasing Holo Honokowai, Lahaina News, January 4, 1989: 1.
— Mayor to speak at pro-life rally, Lahaina News, January 18, 1989: 3,5.
— mayor intervenes in standoff over human remains found at Honokahua, Lahaina News, March 1, 1989: 1,16.
— mayor to speak to Lahaina Town Action Committee, Lahaina News, March 29, 1989: 3.

— mayor plans to improve infrastructure, Lahaina News, April 5, 1989: 1,16.

— mayor supports widening of Wainee Street, Lahaina News, November 15, 1989: 1.

— mayor to sign new property tax bill, Lahaina News, December 13, 1989: 4.

— mayor visits Maui Adult Day Care Center, Lahaina News, December 27, 1989: 11.

— mayor attends Maui Marine Art Expo, Lahaina News, February 14, 1990: 5.

— mayor condemns proposed mansion on Hawea Point, Lahaina News, February 21, 1990: 1.

— mayor proposes to ban bicycle tour operations on county highways, Lahaina News, February 21, 1990: 1.

— mayor proposes new law to speed up building permits, Lahaina News, March 7, 1990: 7.

— mayor seeks larger budget, Lahaina News, March 21, 1990: 1.

— mayor proposed budget to be discussed at public hearing, Lahaina News, March 28, 1990: 3.

— mayor supports funding for swimming pool, Lahaina News, May 9, 1990: 2.

— mayor saluted by Republican Party of Maui County, Lahaina News, May 16, 1990: 5.

— mayor signs County budget, including money for swimming pool, Lahaina News, June 27, 1990: 5.

— mayor congratulates winners of Keiki Fishing Derby, Lahaina News, August 1, 1990: 1.

— mayor sends letter to Glenda Luna thanking her for saving children from apartment fire, Lahaina News, August 1, 1990: 2.

— mayor honored at gala function, Lahaina News, December 26, 1990: 5.

— mayor services to be held for, Lahaina News, January 22, 1998: 1.

TAVARES, JAMES

— to offer help for sick plants , Lahaina News, May 20, 1993: 3.

— to speak on common landscape problems, Lahaina News, May 16, 1996: 11.

TAVARES, LAWRENCE

— speaking of National Guard's riot training, Lahaina Sun, December 16, 1970: 1,4.

TAVARES, MEL

— member of Lahaina Kamaakina Fishing Association, Lahaina Sun, December 23, 1970: 11.

TAVARES CENTER

— dedicated, Lahaina News, September 24, 1998: 7.

TAX FOUNDATION OF HAWAII

— releases report, Lahaina News, October 23, 1997: 15.

TAX REVIEW COMMISSION

— to hold public information meeting, Lahaina News, October 17, 1996: 14.

TAXATION, STATE DEPARTMENT OF

— to help with taxes, Lahaina News, September 16, 1999: 11.

— to help residents with taxes, Lahaina News, September 23, 1999: 11.

— to offer help with taxes, Lahaina News, October 28, 1999: 17.

— to hold tax incentive workshop, Lahaina News, March 9, 2000: 12.

— to hold workshop, Lahaina News, November 21, 2002: 9.

— to hold workshop, Lahaina News, November 28, 2002: 8.

— to hold tax workshops, Lahaina News, July 31, 2003: 8.

— to hold tax workshops, Lahaina News, August 7, 2003: 8.

TAXES

— no property tax increase this year, Lahaina Sun, October 20, 1971: 14.

— unchanged for Maui County, Lahaina Sun, November 3, 1971: 11.

— Maui condominiums being used as tax loopholes by absentee owners, Lahaina Sun, February 7, 1973: 9.

— sightseeing and transportation company assets seized by the Internal Revenue Service, Lahaina Sun, May 23, 1973: 3.

— property assessments challenged, Lahaina Sun, May 23, 1973: 4.

— Honokowai-Napili-Kapalua Taxpayers Association comments on, Lahaina News, May 15, 1980: 6.

— West Maui homeowners lose challenge to 1983 property taxes, Lahaina News, October 26, 1983: 3.

— Lahaina home owners appeal property tax assessments, Lahaina News, December 7, 1983: 6.

— mayor Tavares changes mind, supports variable tax rate for real estate, Lahaina News, February 1, 1984: 7.

— editorial support of variable hotel tax, Lahaina News, March 21, 1984: 2.

— hotel tax discussed, Lahaina News, March 21, 1984: 4,5.

— editorial complaining of, Lahaina News, April 11, 1984: 2.

— Mayor Tavares asks hotel industry for support lobbying legislature to allow counties more taxing authority, Lahaina News, April 18, 1984: 17.

— editorial criticizing property tax as regressive, Lahaina News, May 9, 1984: 2,3.

— editorial criticizing property tax, Lahaina News, May 30, 1984: 3.

— editorial on tax reform, Lahaina News, November 7, 1984: 2.

— editorial on raising General Excise Tax, Lahaina News, February 6, 1985: 2.

— West Maui Taxpayers Association to talk about highway, Lahaina News, March 27, 1985: 1.

— editorial complaining about tax rate, Lahaina News, April 24, 1985: 2.

— editorial on President Reagan's tax reform plan, Lahaina News, June 5, 1985: 2.

— editorial supporting counties having taxing authority, Lahaina News, November 13, 1985: 2.

— editorial calling for room tax and not excise tax, Lahaina News, January 29, 1986: 2.

— seminar on "Legal Tax Avoidance" to be held at Lahaina Civic Center, Lahaina News, March 12, 1986: 12.

— editorial critical of property taxes, Lahaina News, April 9, 1986: 2.

— property tax increase upsets Wahikuli residents, Lahaina News, April 16, 1986: 1.

— Maui County to receive portion of state's hotel room tax, Lahaina News, April 23, 1986: 3.

— property tax deadline August 20, Lahaina News, August 13, 1986: 3.

— clinic offered to seniors, Lahaina News, February 18, 1987: 3,10.

— property owners urged to check their property assessment, Lahaina News, March 22, 1989: 13.

— editorial complaining about, Lahaina News, June 28, 1989: 12.

— alternate methods to calculate property taxes considered, Lahaina News, August 30, 1989: 3.

— Maui County Council proposes property tax relief, Lahaina News, November 1, 1989: 3.

— property taxes increase, Lahaina News, November 8, 1989: 1.

— editorial supporting need for relief, Lahaina News, November 8, 1989: 14.

— new property tax affects 14,500 homeowners, Lahaina News, December 13, 1989: 4.

— editorial opposing increase in general excise tax to fund mass transit on Oahu, Lahaina News, March 7, 1990: 23.

— elderly to receive help from American Association of Retired Persons, Lahaina News, March 7, 1990: 3.

— property tax appeals increase, Lahaina News, April 25, 1990: 1,3.

— editorial urging property tax reform, Lahaina News, April 25, 1990: 18.

— property tax reform likely, Lahaina News, June 6, 1990: 1.

— reduced property taxes sought, Lahaina News, June 20, 1990: B12.

— property tax rollback likely, Lahaina News, July 11, 1990: 2.

— property tax reform may cause issues for homeowners, Lahaina News, July 25, 1990: 1,6.

— property tax deferral available, Lahaina News, August 22, 1990: 1.

— Goro Hokama proposes new real property tax relief, Lahaina News, September 5, 1990: 4.

— little response to property tax deferral program, Lahaina News, October 31, 1990: 1.

— State looking for residents whose refund checks were returned, Lahaina News, November 14, 1990: 4.

— IRS taking tax questions over the phone, Lahaina News, December 19, 1990: 5.

— Mayor Hannibal Tavares asks Council to consider property tax amendments, Lahaina News, December 26, 1990: 5.

— IRS offering in-person assistance, Lahaina News, January 30, 1991: 4.

— deadline to file appeals with Board of Taxation Review coming up, Lahaina News, April 3, 1991: 3.

— IRS to offer services, Lahaina News, April 10, 1991: 3.

— Maui County to hold hearing on property tax system, Lahaina News, May 1, 1991: 1.

— deadline for filing, Lahaina News, August 1, 1991: 4.

— refunds from the IRS should be available now, Lahaina News, September 12, 1991: 5.

— property tax changes seem likely, Lahaina News, October 24, 1991: 12.

— Velma Santos appointed to Real Property Tax Review Board, Lahaina News, March 12, 1992: 5.

— Internal Revenue Service expanding office hours, Lahaina News, April 9, 1992: 3,4.

— more tax revenues expected from condominiums, Lahaina News, September 10, 1992: 1.

— property tax likely to be rolled back, Lahaina News, October 1, 1992: 9.

— bill to roll back property tax assessments heading for final reading, Lahaina News, October 8, 1992: 9.

— Mayor Linda Lingle signs tax bills, Lahaina News, January 14, 1993: 4.

— Internal Revenue Service to offer advice, Lahaina News, January 14, 1993: 6.

— advice from the IRS discussed in "Maui Building Guide 1993", Lahaina News, February 25, 1993: supplement15.

— assistance to be offered by IRS, Lahaina News, May 13, 1993: 7.

— increase proposed to fund school facilities, Lahaina News, December 30, 1993: 7.

— preparation seminar to be held, Lahaina News, January 6, 1994: 6.

— due soon, Lahaina News, February 17, 1994: 6.

— new federal laws apply, Lahaina News, March 17, 1994: 8.

— wealthy hit hardest by tax changes, Lahaina News, April 7, 1994: 10.

— changes for real estate investors, Lahaina News, April 14, 1994: 10.

— new rules for charitable giving, Lahaina News, May 5, 1994: 10.

— tax exemption for cruise ships may end, Lahaina News, February 2, 1995: 2.

— Real Property taxes due soon, Lahaina News, February 2, 1995: 4.

— residents oppose increases to, Lahaina News, March 16, 1995: 1,4.

— help available to Maui seniors for filing, Lahaina News, September 19, 1996: 4.

— Governor Ben Cayetano signs bill to target delinquent taxes, Lahaina News, July 10, 1997: 2.

— Mayor Linda Lingle speaks against hotel room tax increase, Lahaina News, February 12, 1998: 13.

— Lowell Kalapa to speak on, Lahaina News, March 19, 1998: 11.

— members of Maui Chamber of Commerce planning tax revolt, Lahaina News, March 26, 1998: 1.

— IRS extending hours for last minute filers, Lahaina News, April 9, 1998: 1.

— personal income tax cut has support, Lahaina News, May 14, 1998: 1,20.

— reform to be sought in upcoming legislative session, Lahaina News, June 18, 1998: 1,20.

— cigarette tax to increase, Lahaina News, July 9, 1998: 12.

— State tax cut takes effect in January, Lahaina News, December 31, 1998: 1.

— "Property Tax Reduction" scam reported, Lahaina News, January 14, 1999: 11.

— workshop to cover, Lahaina News, March 11, 1999: 13.

— Maui County sending property assessments, Lahaina News, March 18, 1999: 8.

— residents ask County to tighten belt instead of raising, Lahaina News, April 1, 1999: 1,20.

— hearing on property tax rate hike to be held, Lahaina News, May 13, 1999: 2.

— Merrill Lynch hosting seminar on, Lahaina News, August 26, 1999: 13.

— confusion over tax exchange discussed, Lahaina News, January 13, 2000: 11.

— tax incentive workshop to be held, Lahaina News, March 9, 2000: 12.

— Maui County Council taking comments on real property rates, Lahaina News, April 13, 2000: 11.

— Lori Feroldi of L&F Tax Services to take questions, Lahaina News, January 11, 2001: 14.

— Lori Feroldi of L&F Tax Services to take questions, Lahaina News, January 18, 2001: 14.

— forms available from Lahaina Public Library, Lahaina News, March 1, 2001: 10.

— property tax assessment process flawed, Lahaina News, May 17, 2001: 8.

— Janis Casco and Valentina Stewart Watson to hold "The Tax Relief Act of 2001" seminar, Lahaina News, December 13, 2001: 16.

TAXIS

— request to Maui County Council to increase fares, Lahaina Sun, November 29, 1972: 10.

— taxi drivers to oppose de-regulation, Lahaina News, July 10, 1985: 1.

— oppose limited taxi licenses, Lahaina News, March 5, 1986: 1,20.

TAXPAYER'S ASSOCIATION, WEST MAUI

— see West Maui Taxpayers Association

TAY, JING

— Scholar/Athlete of the Week, Lahaina News, January 30, 2003: 12.

TAY, YEE CHIAT

— awarded scholarship from Soroptimists International, Lahaina News, June 22, 2000: 6.

— awarded Rotary Foundation Academic-Year Ambassadorial Scholarship, Lahaina News, September 25, 2003: 3.

TAY, YEE NING

— Scholar/Athlete of the Week, Lahaina News, May 23, 1996: 6.

TAYLOR, BONITA

— rabbi to conduct Jewish High Holiday services, Lahaina News, September 12, 1996: 15.

— rabbi to conduct Rosh Hashanah and Yom Kippur, Lahaina News, September 25, 1997: 17.

— rabbi to speak on "Jonah's Tale: A Story of Personal Transformation", Lahaina News, October 2, 1997: 20.

TAYLOR, JAMES [MUSICIAN]

— to perform at Royal Lahaina Tennis Stadium, Lahaina News, February 5, 1986: 16.

TAYLOR, JOHN [MUSICIAN]

— to perform at Pioneer Inn , Lahaina News, October 22, 1992: 14.

— to perform at Taco Jo's Cantina, Lahaina News, September 16, 1993: 16.

TAYLOR, KARA [ARTIST]
— to exhibit at Hui Noʻeau Visual Arts Center, Lahaina News, July 1, 1999: 13.

TAYLOR, KARIN
— promoted to secretary/treasurer of Sargent's Fine Art, Lahaina News, August 8, 2002: 8.

TAYLOR, LYNN [ARTIST]
— discusses tie-dying, Lahaina Sun, April 21, 1971: 6.

TAYLOR, MARK [COMEDIAN]
— to perform at Comedy Club and the Sports Page, Lahaina News, December 3, 1992: 14,18.

TAYLOR, ROBERT [ARTIST]
— to exhibit "Flora, Fauna, and Other Friends" watercolors, Lahaina News, October 27, 1994: 19.

TAYLOR, TRACY [ARTIST]
— to offer watercolor workshop, Lahaina News, September 12, 2002: 21.

TAYLOR, WILLIAM
— elected zone chairman with the Kihei Community Association, Lahaina Sun, December 2, 1970: 4.

TB9 [FILM]
— snowboarding movie to be shown, Lahaina News, November 23, 2000: 20.

TCBY [RESTAURANT]
— reviewed, Lahaina News, March 1, 1989: 8.
— reviewed, Lahaina News, June 7, 1989: 12.
— adds frozen yogurt shake, Lahaina News, February 6, 1991: 8.

TCHAIKOVSKY CHAMBER ORCHESTRA
— presented by the Maui Philharmonic Society, Lahaina News, November 7, 1991: 21.

TE AO TAWHITO/TE AO HOU (OLD WORLDS/NEW WORLDS)
— exhibit to be held, Lahaina News, February 1, 2001: 20.

TE TIARE PATITIFA
— to perform at Dances of Tahiti, Lahaina News, April 17, 2003: 16.

TE VAKA [MUSICAL GROUP]
— to perform at Maui Arts and Cultural Center, Lahaina News, September 13, 2001: 16.
— to perform at Maui Arts and Cultural Center, Lahaina News, May 9, 2002: 14.
— visits Lahainaluna High School, Lahaina News, May 16, 2002: 9.

TE WAKA HIUA [DANCERS]
— to perform at Aston's Kamaole Sands-Maui, Lahaina News, June 6, 1990: 13.

TEACHING
— U.S. Office of Education approves grants to train teachers, Lahaina Sun, January 27, 1971: 4.

TEAM MAKAKOA
— places second in Eyecatcher Hoʻomanaʻo Challenge Outrigger Sailing Canoe Race, Lahaina News, May 28, 1998: 1,16.

TEAMWORK COMMUNICATIONS, INC. [BUSINESS]
— finalists for Pele Award for Best Television Program produced in Hawaii, Lahaina News, March 24, 1994: 8.

TECH SURF SPORTS AND SHAPERS
— owner Kim Ball featured, Lahaina News, February 20, 1997: 6.

TECHNICAL ADVISORY COMMITTEE ON GROUNDWATER PROTECTION
— formed, Lahaina News, August 5, 1987: 3.

TECHNOLOGY
— computer classes to be held for parents, Lahaina News, November 13, 1985: 3.
— Computer and Electronics Fair to be held at Maui High School Gym, Lahaina News, November 13, 1985: 3.
— super computer to be built at Maui Research and Technology Park, Lahaina News, November 28, 1991: 7.
— fiber optic complex to be built on Maui, Lahaina News, December 17, 1992: 8.
— wireless telephone packages, Lahaina News, October 17, 1996: 8,9,18.
— HI-Tech Fair to be held at Lahaina Cannery, Lahaina News, September 12, 2002: 9.

TECHNOVENTURES SPACE ADVENTURE
— "A journey to the Stars" to open, Lahaina News, August 8, 2002: 16.
— "A Journey to the Stars" to open at Queen Kaʻahumanu Center, Lahaina News, August 15, 2002: 16.

TEDESCHI VINEYARDS [BUSINESS]
— debuts Maui Blush, Lahaina News, December 3, 1986: 11.
— releases beaujolais-style wine, Lahaina News, December 24, 1986: 3.
— wins medals, Lahaina News, December 9, 1987: 3.
— offering free guided tours, Lahaina News, September 28, 1988: 3.
— sets release day for 1988 Maui Nouveau Beaujolais, Lahaina News, October 19, 1988: 17.
— releases new wine for Valentine's Day called Rose Ranch Cuvée, Lahaina News, February 15, 1989: 3.
— releases Maui Nouveau wine, Lahaina News, November 21, 1990: 15.
— selling "Eclipse" red wine, Lahaina News, July 4, 1991: 4.
— offering Christmas gift packs, Lahaina News, December 19, 1991: 23.
— to hold 10K Scenic Run, Lahaina News, May 21, 1992: 12.
— releases 1992 Maui Nouveau, Lahaina News, November 26, 1992: 26.
— to host trade show, Lahaina News, March 11, 1993: 12.
— to host 10K Run/Walk, Lahaina News, May 19, 1994: 8,9.
— celebrating 20th anniversary, Lahaina News, January 12, 1995: 11,12.
— to host Maui County Agricultural Trade Show and Sampling, Lahaina News, April 22, 1999: 12.
— to hold Ulupalakua Thing, Lahaina News, April 17, 2003: 8.

TEE TO PIN [BUSINESS]
— wins kiosk contest at Kaʻahumanu Center, Lahaina News, May 14, 1998: 13.

TEEN CHALLENGE
— program for Maui youth, Lahaina Sun, January 27, 1971: 6.
— youth rehabilitation center seeks support for fund drive, Lahaina Sun, January 5, 1972: 14.
— rehabilitation facility in Olowalu described, Lahaina Sun, August 16, 1972: 7.
— program , Lahaina News, August 29, 1984: 7,8,9.
— to celebrate national Teen Challenge week, Lahaina News, November 16, 1988: 14.
— drug rehabilitation program to hold "Jug-A-Thon" fundraiser, Lahaina News, March 13, 1991: 7.
— recovering from fire that destroyed buildings, Lahaina News, March 27, 1991: 1,5.
— celebrates 20th anniversary, Lahaina News, July 25, 1991: 4.
— hampered by fire at dorm, Lahaina News, August 8, 1991: 1.
— needs to act to get buildings rebuilt, Lahaina News, August 15, 1991: 1.
— still waiting to rebuild destroyed dormitories, Lahaina News, August 29, 1991: 1.
— services decrease due to lack of housing, Lahaina News, October 10, 1991: 2.
— public hearing on plan to rebuild dormitories, Lahaina News, October 31, 1991: 1.
— nearing approval of permits to rebuild, Lahaina News, November 14, 1991: 11.
— construction of new complex may begin soon, Lahaina News, November 28, 1991: 2.

— facility needs water well, Lahaina News, September 17, 1992: 3.
— facilities being painted by West Maui Condominium Managers, Lahaina News, December 3, 1992: 3.
— close to opening new dormitory, Lahaina News, December 10, 1992: 4.
— program plans to expand, Lahaina News, May 13, 1993: 1.
— dorm is ready to be occupied but lacks adequate fire protection, Lahaina News, July 22, 1993: 1.
— history of, Lahaina News, January 20, 1994: 3.
— to hold annual Jog-A-Thon, Lahaina News, March 10, 1994: 7.
— expands outreach programs, Lahaina News, July 14, 1994: 3.
— to hold Jog-A-Thon, Lahaina News, March 9, 1995: 7.
— benefit performance to be held for, Lahaina News, March 16, 1995: 12.
— to beautify campus by planting orchids, Lahaina News, August 10, 1995: 3.
— clears property, Lahaina News, August 24, 1995: 7.
— celebrates 25 years, Lahaina News, May 2, 1996: 19.
— featured, Lahaina News, September 19, 1996: 1,20.

TEENAGE MUTANT NINJA TURTLE
— Michelangelo to appear at Lahaina Fun Factory, Lahaina News, July 11, 1990: 2.

TEICHOTZ, MARC [MUSICIAN]
— to perform with Maui Symphony Orchestra, Lahaina News, November 17, 1994: 19.

TEJERO, NERIO
— wins "Santa's Treasure Chest" promotion, Lahaina News, January 15, 1998: 11.

TELECHECK HAWAII
— acquired by Maui Girl Friday, Lahaina Sun, March 31, 1971: 5.

TELECOMMUNICATIONS
— legislation to make it easier for small companies to enter market , Lahaina News, June 20, 1990: 1,14.

TELEPHONE
— telephone books distributed, Lahaina Sun, March 31, 1971: 5.
— rates increasing, Lahaina Sun, April 14, 1971: 8.
— rate increases discussed, Lahaina Sun, May 31, 1972: 11.
— Maui will soon be able to dial directly to other Hawaiian Islands, the mainland, Canada, and Mexico, Lahaina Sun, February 7, 1973: 11.
— public hearing on proposed rate increases sparsely attended, Lahaina Sun, April 25, 1973: 10.
— comparison of 1955 and 1973 Maui telephone directories, Lahaina Sun, April 25, 1973: 15.
— new rates announced, Lahaina Sun, June 27, 1973: 6.
— bills jump 93.4%, Lahaina News, January 15, 1983: 11.
— Hawaiian Telephone requests rate hike, Lahaina News, June 1, 1983: 15.
— editorial criticizing rate hike, Lahaina News, October 10, 1984: 2.
— mobile phone service upgraded, Lahaina News, March 4, 1987: 10.
— new service reduces long distance calls to state offices, Lahaina News, September 6, 1989: 1.
— cellular telephones now available, Lahaina News, January 24, 1990: 6.
— cellular phone planned for Papawai Lookout, Lahaina News, June 6, 1991: 3.
— Coast Guard discourages use of cellular phones for emergencies, Lahaina News, August 8, 1991: 4.
— Coast Guard discourages use of cellular phones for emergencies, Lahaina News, August 15, 1991: 3.
— new phone book being delivered, recycling begins, Lahaina News, June 11, 1992: 5.
— fiber optics system proposed, Lahaina News, June 18, 1992: 10.
— Long Distance/USA-Sprint receives approval for interisland outbound services, Lahaina News, January 26, 1995: 13.

— rates would rise with request filed by GTE Hawaiian Tel, Lahaina News, June 8, 1995: 10.
— GTE Hawaiian Telephone seeking increase in rates, Lahaina News, November 30, 1995: 10.
— scams with pagers, Lahaina News, November 14, 1996: 8.
— Sprint Hawaii lowers inter-island rate, Lahaina News, July 17, 1997: 12.
— PrimeCo Hawaii expanding digital wireless network coverage, Lahaina News, February 12, 1998: 13.
— AT&T one-rate wireless service available, Lahaina News, August 20, 1998: 13.

TELEPHONE BOOKS
— to be recycled, Lahaina News, October 12, 2000: 19.

TELEVISION
— Department of Regulatory Agencies conducts public hearing on, Lahaina Sun, December 2, 1970: 2.
— Department of Regulatory Agencies conducts public hearing on, Lahaina Sun, December 9, 1970: 6.
— expansion of facilities, Lahaina Sun, December 23, 1970: 6.
— Hawaiian Cable Vision Corporation hoping to expand cable services in Lahaina, Lahaina Sun, December 23, 1970: 6.
— commercial on Hawaiian sugar cane filmed at Lahaina, Lahaina Sun, December 30, 1970: 7.
— Hawaiian Cable Vision Corporation improves FM radio reception on Maui, Lahaina Sun, December 1, 1971: 6.
— cable TV in Maui described, Lahaina Sun, July 5, 1972: 21.
— decision on microwave relay for cable TV on Haleakala delayed, Lahaina Sun, August 16, 1972: 9.
— Comtec Inc requests antenna on Haleakala, Lahaina Sun, September 27, 1972: 7.
— services expanded in West Maui, Lahaina Sun, November 29, 1972: 19.
— updates to cable system delayed due to west coast dock strike, Lahaina Sun, December 13, 1972: 4.
— Channel 8 cable TV station delayed, Lahaina Sun, June 6, 1973: 22.
— free HBO offered to West Maui for four day trial, Lahaina News, May 1, 1980: 13.
— satellite news conference held between Maui and London, Lahaina News, July 15, 1982: 4.
— editorial complaint about number of advertisements following M*A*S*H, Lahaina News, May 1, 1983: 2.
— special research projects of grade 4 and 5 students featured on channel 7, Lahaina News, July 25, 1984: 15.
— Lahaina News begins publishing a multi-page listing of television shows and movies, which is not indexed, Lahaina News, October 10, 1984: .
— Cinemax available on Maui, Lahaina News, February 5, 1986: 24.
— interview with David Weiss of Satellite Systems about satellite dishes, Lahaina News, February 5, 1986: 4.
— Daniels & Associates to purchase Hawaiian Cable Vision Co., Lahaina News, March 11, 1987: 1.
— Soviet news program to air on Discovery Channel, Lahaina News, May 25, 1988: 10.
— listings change, Lahaina News, September 28, 1988: 1.
— cable costs to rise, Lahaina News, February 8, 1989: 1.
— complaint over charging structure for HBO and other services, Lahaina News, January 23, 1992: 1,4.
— KHNL ranked fourth most-watched independent television station in the United States, Lahaina News, January 30, 1992: 12.
— KFVE-TV now available on Maui, Lahaina News, February 20, 1992: 5.
— community access channel to begin, Lahaina News, August 6, 1992: 3.
— Maui-based station to open, Lahaina News, October 15, 1992: 3.
— cable TV rates to be regulated, Lahaina News, October 15, 1992: 4,5.

— Domino's Pizza sponsoring team league, Lahaina News, October 4, 1989: 6.

— Junior Novice Tennis tournament to be held, Lahaina News, October 11, 1989: 6.

— Nissan Wailea Pro Tennis Classic scheduled, Lahaina News, October 25, 1989: 11.

— Aloha Airlines Junior Tennis Championships to be held, Lahaina News, October 25, 1989: 11.

— state junior competition to culminate in Aloha Airlines Junior Tennis Championships, Lahaina News, November 1, 1989: 24.

— Aloha Airlines Junior Tennis Championships to be held, Lahaina News, November 22, 1989: 8.

— Ryan Ideta's success recounted, Lahaina News, November 29, 1989: 5.

— Junior Davis Cup Team selected, Lahaina News, November 29, 1989: 5.

— Aloha Airlines Junior Tennis Championships to be held, Lahaina News, December 6, 1989: 7.

— Denise Komula named Rookie of the Year at the Peter Burwash International's annual convention, Lahaina News, December 13, 1989: 8.

— Ryan Ideta candidate for U.S. National Team, Lahaina News, January 3, 1990: 10.

— Lahainaluna High School prospects described, Lahaina News, February 7, 1990: 9.

— Lahaina Junior Tennis Tournament to be held, Lahaina News, February 14, 1990: 12.

— Royal Lahaina Tennis Ranch selected as training center by United States Tennis Association, Lahaina News, February 21, 1990: 9.

— Roy Brunson named head professional at Royal Lahaina Tennis Ranch, Lahaina News, March 21, 1990: 4.

— Hawaii High School Tennis Championships to be held at Royal Lahaina Resort, Lahaina News, March 28, 1990: 9.

— National Tennis Rating Program clinic to be held, Lahaina News, March 28, 1990: 9.

— Lahainaluna High School wins tennis tournament, Lahaina News, May 2, 1990: 5.

— Kapalua Jr. Vet/Senior Championship to be held, Lahaina News, May 16, 1990: 7.

— Kapalua Resort to offer camp, Lahaina News, May 23, 1990: 9.

— Lahaina wins Junior Davis Cup, Lahaina News, May 23, 1990: 9,10.

— results of Kapalua Jr. Vets/Senior Championship, Lahaina News, May 30, 1990: 6.

— Shigesh Wakida to hold clinic, Lahaina News, June 6, 1990: 6.

— results of Peter Burwash International "No Champs" tournament, Lahaina News, June 6, 1990: 6.

— Maui Jr. Davis Club Team gives awards of excellence, Lahaina News, June 20, 1990: 8.

— results of Junior Sectionals held at Punahou, Lahaina News, June 27, 1990: 7.

— McCormack Wailea Open tournament to be held, Lahaina News, June 27, 1990: 7.

— results of Maui County Tennis Championship listed, Lahaina News, July 4, 1990: 6.

— Junior Summer Circuit tournament to be held, Lahaina News, July 11, 1990: 9.

— Junior Summer Circuit tournament to be held, Lahaina News, July 18, 1990: 6.

— fundraiser for members of Maui's Jr. Davis Cup Team, Lahaina News, July 25, 1990: 14.

— Steven Okada wins Boys 18 Singles division in Lahaina Juniors tournament, Lahaina News, August 8, 1990: 7.

— registration for Kapalua Open begins, Lahaina News, August 15, 1990: 18.

— Shigesh Wakida to hold clinic, Lahaina News, September 5, 1990: 7.

— Jean Okada and Kim Harvey runners-up at women's doubles at Kapalua Open, Lahaina News, September 12, 1990: 1.

— Nissan Wailea Pro Tennis Classic to be held, Lahaina News, October 17, 1990: 8.

— Lahaina Junior Tennis to hold car wash fundraiser, Lahaina News, November 14, 1990: 10.

— Kapalua Betsy Nagelsen Tennis Invitational to be held, Lahaina News, November 21, 1990: 24.

— new schedule introduced at Royal Lahaina Tennis Ranch, Lahaina News, December 5, 1990: 8.

— Women's Kemper Open to be held, Lahaina News, January 2, 1991: 16.

— Lahaina Junior Open to be held, Lahaina News, January 16, 1991: 20.

— Wailuku Jr. Winter Open Tennis Tournament held, Lahaina News, February 27, 1991: 6.

— Lunas defend state championship, Lahaina News, March 27, 1991: 8.

— Lahainaluna High School team successful, Lahaina News, April 3, 1991: 16.

— Hawaii High School State Tennis Championships to be held at Royal Lahaina Tennis Ranch, Lahaina News, April 17, 1991: 10.

— Lahainaluna High School doubles team successful, Lahaina News, April 24, 1991: 6.

— Wailea Tennis Club to offer free clinic, Lahaina News, April 24, 1991: 6.

— Kapalua Jr. Vet./Senior Championship to be held, Lahaina News, May 1, 1991: 7.

— Wailea Tennis Club to offer free clinic, Lahaina News, May 1, 1991: 7.

— Kapalua Resort to offer camp for adults, Lahaina News, May 8, 1991: 6.

— Kapalua Jr. Vet./Senior Championship to be held, Lahaina News, May 8, 1991: 6.

— Kapalua Jr. Vet./Senior Championship to be held at Tennis Garden, Lahaina News, May 15, 1991: 7.

— Peter Burwash International to host tennis tournament, Lahaina News, May 15, 1991: 7.

— National Tennis Month begins, Lahaina News, June 6, 1991: 9.

— summer camp for children to be offered at Maui Marriott, Lahaina News, June 13, 1991: 17.

— Ryan Ideta and Steven Okada win age divisions, Lahaina News, June 20, 1991: 4.

— Maui Marriott offering tennis camp, Lahaina News, June 27, 1991: 7.

— Maui Marriott offering tennis camp, Lahaina News, July 11, 1991: 7.

— Kapalua Open to be held on Labor Day, Lahaina News, August 15, 1991: 4.

— Steven Okada and Kimmie Ouchi win Wailuku Junior Summer Open tennis, Lahaina News, August 22, 1991: 8.

— Kapalua Open to be held, Lahaina News, August 29, 1991: 7.

— Lahaina Junior Tennis Program begins, Lahaina News, September 19, 1991: 7.

— Nissan Tennis Circuit to stop at Wailea, Lahaina News, October 24, 1991: 6.

— Lahaina Junior Tennis Program to offer classes for beginners, Lahaina News, November 7, 1991: 7.

— Lahaina juniors win Lahaina Junior Novice tournament, Lahaina News, November 14, 1991: 4.

— Ryan Ideta and Jean Okada win respective divisions, Lahaina News, December 5, 1991: 19.

— tennis pro Cari Buck featured, Lahaina News, December 19, 1991: 8.

— Lahaina Junior Tennis Program to offer classes for beginners, Lahaina News, December 19, 1991: 9.

— Jean Okada receives scholarship offers, Lahaina News, December 26, 1991: 11.

— Lahaina Junior Tennis Program to offer classes for beginners, Lahaina News, January 30, 1992: 9.

— Women's Kemper Open to be held, Lahaina News, January 30, 1992: 9.

— Lahainaluna High School tennis team to play at Lahaina Civic Center, Lahaina News, February 6, 1992: 9.

— Wailea Tennis Club to hold kickoff party for USTA adult league players, Lahaina News, February 13, 1992: 10.

— Wailea Tennis Club to hold kickoff party for USTA adult league players, Lahaina News, February 20, 1992: 6.

— results of Lahaina Junior Open announced, Lahaina News, March 5, 1992: 8.

— USTA League Tennis sign up begins, Lahaina News, March 5, 1992: 8.

— Smally Kailihiwa Memorial Tennis Scholarship Tournament to be held, Lahaina News, April 9, 1992: 11.

— Ryan Ideta and Jean Okada win state singles titles, Lahaina News, April 23, 1992: 22.

— 35 and older tournament to be held, Lahaina News, April 30, 1992: 6,7.

— "No Champs" tournament to be held, Lahaina News, May 21, 1992: 11.

— camps to be held at Kapalua Resort, Lahaina News, May 28, 1992: 9.

— Kapalua Resort to hold camp, Lahaina News, June 4, 1992: 8.

— Jean Okada wins Kona Spring Junior Open, Lahaina News, June 18, 1992: 12.

— teachers at Kapalua Land Company, Ltd. Become certified members of the United States Professional Tennis Association, Lahaina News, July 2, 1992: 13.

— Beach and Tennis Club to offer Kids' Summer Tennis Kamp, other clinics offered, Lahaina News, July 16, 1992: 11.

— Pro-Am Tennis Invitational to be held, Lahaina News, August 13, 1992: 6.

— results of Lahaina Junior Summer Open, Lahaina News, August 20, 1992: 10.

— results of Hilo Junior Summer Open, Lahaina News, August 20, 1992: 8.

— Malino Oda wins division at Hilo Junior Summer Open, Lahaina News, September 3, 1992: 6.

— registration underway for Wailea Junior/Senior Vets Championship, Lahaina News, October 29, 1992: 12.

— Betsy Nagelsen Pro-Am Invitational to be held, Lahaina News, October 29, 1992: 12.

— Maui Nurses Mixed Doubles Tennis Tournament to be held, Lahaina News, November 5, 1992: 12.

— results of Lahaina Tennis Club Tournament, Lahaina News, November 12, 1992: 8,9.

— Wailea Tennis Club named one of 50 greatest tennis resorts by Tennis Magazine, Lahaina News, December 17, 1992: 11.

— United States Tennis Association Adult Tennis forming, Lahaina News, February 11, 1993: 9.

— Wells Park tennis courts renamed "Smally" Kalihiwa Tennis Courts, Lahaina News, February 25, 1993: 3.

— Joseph Bedoya Jr new tennis professional at Hyatt Regency Maui, Lahaina News, March 25, 1993: 6.

— adult camp to be held, Lahaina News, April 22, 1993: 8.

— clinic to be held, Lahaina News, April 29, 1993: 6.

— Diane Okada named co-player of the year in women's tennis for Big West Conference, Lahaina News, May 6, 1993: 10.

— Royal Lahaina Resort and Peter Burwash International begin Junior Excellence Program, Lahaina News, May 27, 1993: 9.

— Kapalua Open to be held, Lahaina News, June 10, 1993: 9.

— dates changed for Wailea Open Tennis Tournament, Lahaina News, June 24, 1993: 12.

— finals of Japan Prince Cup National Tennis Tournament to be held, Lahaina News, July 8, 1993: 9.

— Kapalua Open to be held, Lahaina News, July 22, 1993: 9.

— Kapalua Open to be held, Lahaina News, September 2, 1993: 9.

— United States Tennis Association Satellite Circuit to hold final round, Lahaina News, November 4, 1993: 9.

— Lahaina women amongst finalists at USTA Team Tennis Championship, Lahaina News, November 11, 1993: 3.

— Wailea Tennis Club to host Junior/Senior Veterans Tennis Tournament, Lahaina News, November 11, 1993: 8.

— teams from Stanford University and the University of Hawai'i to play, Lahaina News, November 25, 1993: 10.

— Wailea Tennis Club to host Wailea Tennis Fest, Lahaina News, December 2, 1993: 10.

— results of Aloha Airlines Junior Tennis Championships, Lahaina News, December 9, 1993: 8.

— Shigesh Wakida honored for work with young athletes, Lahaina News, December 23, 1993: 8.

— Adult Tennis League now forming, Lahaina News, February 10, 1994: 11.

— Makena Tennis Club to hold tournament, Lahaina News, March 10, 1994: 7.

— clinic to be held at Kapaula Resort, Lahaina News, April 28, 1994: 7.

— Jr. Vet/Senior Championship to be held at The Tennis Club at Kapalua, Lahaina News, May 5, 1994: 8.

— Kapalua Tennis camp to be held, Lahaina News, June 9, 1994: 9.

— Wailea Open Tennis Championship to be held, Lahaina News, June 16, 1994: 7.

— Lahaina Tennis Club to hold Lahaina Open tennis tournament, Lahaina News, July 28, 1994: 6.

— results of Lahaina Junior Tennis Summer Open, Lahaina News, August 11, 1994: 6.

— Jean Okada wins open single Kapalua Open Tennis Championships, Lahaina News, September 22, 1994: 9.

— Kapalua Betsy Nagelsen Pro-Am Tennis Invitational to be held at Kapalu Resort, Lahaina News, November 24, 1994: 8.

— Whales Alive Celebrity Tennis Party to include Lloyd, Beau, and Jeff Bridges, Lahaina News, November 24, 1994: 8.

— Prince Racquet Sports Company to host fundraiser, Lahaina News, December 8, 1994: 9.

— Malino Oda becomes highest ranked junior tennis player from Maui, Lahaina News, February 2, 1995: 6.

— results of Lahainaluna High School team competition , Lahaina News, March 9, 1995: 7.

— courts at Malu'ulu O Lele Park to be fixed, Lahaina News, March 16, 1995: 4.

— Kapalua tennis club to hold Junior Veteran/Senior Champions, Lahaina News, May 11, 1995: 7.

— Kim Wilson featured, Lahaina News, July 6, 1995: 7.

— Hawaii team captures gold at Zone Championship, Lahaina News, August 24, 1995: 6.

— Johan Carlsson and Jean Okada defended titles at Wilson Kapalua Open, Lahaina News, September 14, 1995: 7.

— Betsy Nagelsen Pro-Am Invitational to be held, Lahaina News, November 23, 1995: 6.

— United States Tennis Association Adult Tennis League forming, Lahaina News, February 8, 1996: 11.

— Lahainaluna High School girls team featured, Lahaina News, February 29, 1996: 6.

— Sylvia Ng Perpetual Award presented, Lahaina News, April 18, 1996: 12.

— Kapalua Tennis Club to hold Jr. Vet./Senior Championships, Lahaina News, May 9, 1996: 16.

— Jean Okada named to NCAA 1996 All-American team, Lahaina News, June 20, 1996: 10.

— Lahaina Tennis Club to hold Summer Tennis Camp, Lahaina News, July 11, 1996: 11.

— Wilson Kapalua Open to be held, Lahaina News, August 22, 1996: 1.

— Kapalua Betsy Nagelsen Tennis Invitational to be held, Lahaina News, October 3, 1996: 13.

— teacher Shigesh Wakida featured, Lahaina News, October 17, 1996: 13.

— Kapalua Betsy Nagelsen Tennis Invitational to be held, Lahaina News, November 28, 1996: 10.

— Maui United States Tennis Association Senior Tennis League formed, Lahaina News, January 30, 1997: 7.

— Junior Vet./Senior Tennis Championship to be held, Lahaina News, May 1, 1997: 17.

— Kapalua Tennis Club to hold Summer Junior Tennis Program, Lahaina News, May 15, 1997: 11.

— Kapalua Tennis Club offering tennis camps, Lahaina News, May 22, 1997: 13.

— registration underway for Maui Open Tennis Tournament, Lahaina News, July 10, 1997: 14.

— Kapalua Tennis Club to hold workshop, Lahaina News, August 14, 1997: 14.

— Kapalua Tennis Club's Summer Junior Tennis Program, Lahaina News, August 21, 1997: 13.

— players may receive NTRP rating, Lahaina News, August 21, 1997: 13.

— Kapalua Open to be held, Lahaina News, August 28, 1997: 7.

— Jean Okada wins Wilson Kapalua Open, Lahaina News, September 4, 1997: 1.

— Kapalua Tennis Club named Club of the Year by Hawaii Pacific Section of the United States Tennis Association, Lahaina News, December 4, 1997: 13.

— USTA team captain meeting to be held, Lahaina News, January 15, 1998: 7.

— Shigesh Wakida to offer free tennis program, Lahaina News, April 30, 1998: 15.

— Junior Veteran/Senior Tennis Championships to be held, Lahaina News, April 30, 1998: 15.

— results of Kapalua Junio Vet/Senior Tennis Championship, Lahaina News, May 14, 1998: 15.

— training to be offered at Kapalua Tennis Club, Lahaina News, June 25, 1998: 7.

— Kapalua Tennis Club to offer training for kids, Lahaina News, July 9, 1998: 15.

— Wailuku Summer Junior Open tennis tournament to be held, Lahaina News, July 16, 1998: 15.

— Kapalua Tennis Club to offer training for kids, Lahaina News, July 16, 1998: 15.

— Wailuku Summer Junior Open tennis tournament to be held, Lahaina News, July 23, 1998: 15.

— Kapalua Tennis Club to offer training for kids, Lahaina News, July 23, 1998: 15.

— USTA/Hawaii Pacific Section to host games, Lahaina News, August 20, 1998: 15.

— Bob McInerney receives "Pro of the Year Award" from the Hawaii division of the United States Professional Tennis Association, Lahaina News, September 10, 1998: 14.

— Lahaina Junior Tennis Program awarded grant from United States Tennis Association, Lahaina News, November 19, 1998: 15.

— Lahaina Winter Junior Open to be held, Lahaina News, January 7, 1999: 15.

— Maui USTA Senior Tennis League to be held, Lahaina News, January 14, 1999: 7.

— Maui USTA Senior Tennis League to begin play, Lahaina News, February 4, 1999: 15.

— USTA women's tennis team formed, Lahaina News, February 18, 1999: 7.

— PBI Mixed Doubles Tennis Tournament to be held, Lahaina News, February 25, 1999: 7.

— Tennis Magazine names Kapalua Resort as one of greatest tennis resorts, Lahaina News, March 11, 1999: 7.

— Royal Lahaina Junior Summer Tennis Camps to be held, Lahaina News, May 27, 1999: 7.

— camps to be held at Royal Lahaina, Lahaina News, June 10, 1999: 7.

— Kapalua Tennis Summer Junior Tennis Program set, Lahaina News, June 24, 1999: 6.

— Royal Lahaina Junior Summer Tennis Camps to be held, Lahaina News, June 24, 1999: 7.

— camps to be held at Royal Lahaina, Lahaina News, July 8, 1999: 6.

— ailing tennis legend Shigesh Wakida teaching children about character, Lahaina News, August 5, 1999: 1,6.

— Adult League Sectional Championships to be played, Lahaina News, August 19, 1999: 7.

— Royal Lahaina Tennis Ranch to hold clinics, Lahaina News, September 9, 1999: 7.

— teams raising money, Lahaina News, September 9, 1999: 7.

— Royal Lahaina Tennis Ranch to hold clinics, Lahaina News, September 16, 1999: 7.

— Royal Lahaina Tennis Ranch to hold clinics, Lahaina News, October 7, 1999: 9.

— Kapalua Tennis welcoming tennis enthusiasts, Lahaina News, November 18, 1999: 8.

— Kapalua Tennis offering "Sunday Stroke of the Day" clinics, Lahaina News, November 25, 1999: 9.

— Lahainaluna High School team featured, Lahaina News, February 24, 2000: 6.

— Royal Lahaina Tennis Ranch to hold Junior After-School Clinics, Lahaina News, February 24, 2000: 6.

— West Maui Junior Team competes, Lahaina News, March 30, 2000: 7.

— Shigesh Wakida held Prince Fun Tennis Tournament, Lahaina News, July 13, 2000: 6.

— Lahaina Summer Junior Open Tennis Tournament to be held, Lahaina News, August 3, 2000: 3.

— results of Wilson Kapalua Open, Lahaina News, September 14, 2000: 10.

— Wayne Bryan and Greg Patton to host clinics, Lahaina News, October 26, 2000: 11.

— free clinics to be offered by Wayne Bryan and Greg Patton, Lahaina News, November 2, 2000: 9.

— Kapalua Junior Tennis Program continues work of Shigesh Wakida, Lahaina News, November 30, 2000: 6.

— National Open Junior Tournament to be held, Lahaina News, December 7, 2000: 12.

— Kapalua Tennis Garden and Village Tennis Center to hold National Open, Lahaina News, February 1, 2001: 14.

— USTA tournament to be held at Kapalua, Lahaina News, February 8, 2001: 14.

— Wailea Tennis Club offering free clinics, Lahaina News, May 17, 2001: 15.

— Lahaina Tennis Club continues, Lahaina News, November 8, 2001: 12.

— Shigeto "Shigesh" Wakida Tennis Courts to be repaired, Lahaina News, November 29, 2001: 13.

— Lahaina Junior Tennis Club recycling trees, Lahaina News, December 27, 2001: 1.

— Ala Hou Counseling Center offering mental health counseling services, Lahaina News, January 10, 2002: 2.

— Kapalua's Tennis Garden to offer junior tennis event, Lahaina News, February 14, 2002: 13.

— Kapalua Junior Vet/Senior Tennis Championships to be held, Lahaina News, May 2, 2002: 12.
— Kapalua Open Tennis Championships to be held, Lahaina News, August 8, 2002: 13.
— teams quality for United States Tennis Association National Championships, Lahaina News, September 5, 2002: 12.
— teams preparing for league play, Lahaina News, November 28, 2002: 12.
— teams preparing for league play, Lahaina News, December 19, 2002: 11.
— BYU coach David Porter to lead clinic, Lahaina News, January 9, 2003: 12.
— Kapalua Junior Tennis Camps to be held, Lahaina News, June 19, 2003: 13.
— Kapalua Resort to offer junior tennis camps and clinics, Lahaina News, June 26, 2003: 11.
— Mele Iongi wins Hawaii Pacific Section Junior Sectional Championship, Lahaina News, July 3, 2003: 13.
— Maui team competes in Adult National Championships, Lahaina News, September 25, 2003: 12.

TENNIS ANYONE [BUSINESS]
— opens, Lahaina News, May 28, 1992: 11,12.

TENNIS GARDEN
— to offer junior tennis event, Lahaina News, February 14, 2002: 13.

TENNIS MAGAZINE
— names Kapalua Resort as one of greatest tennis resorts, Lahaina News, March 11, 1999: 7.

TENUTA, JUDY [COMEDIAN]
— to perform at Westin Maui Valley Isle Ballroom, Lahaina News, April 28, 1994: 12.

TERADA, AMY
— appointed director of domestic travel industry sales for the Ritz-Carlton, Lahaina News, November 18, 1993: 7.

TERADA, JOHN
— Hawaii Lupus Foundation representative to discuss "Living With Lupus", Lahaina News, March 27, 2003: 16.
— to speak at Lupus Foundation, Lahaina News, April 17, 2003: 16.
— to speak on "Living with Lupus", Lahaina News, May 29, 2003: 9,16.

TERAIN, DAISA
— to talk on "Indoor Air Pollution is Making You Sick", Lahaina News, June 26, 2003: 21.

TERALANI CHARTERS [BUSINESS]
— offering vintage sail from Ka'anapali Beach, Lahaina News, December 8, 1994: 16.
— to sponsor Oktoberfest with Sheraton Maui, Lahaina News, October 14, 1999: 11.
— to hold Oktoberfest Sail, Lahaina News, October 4, 2001: 9.

TERMITES
— presence on Maui described, Lahaina Sun, April 7, 1971: 2.

TERRA PACIFIC DEVELOPMENT, CO. LLC [BUSINESS]
— named as project developer for The Vintage at Ka'anapali, Lahaina News, June 8, 2000: 11.

TERRACE RESTAURANT [RESTAURANT]
— updates menu, Lahaina News, October 20, 1994: 16.

TERREBONNE, NANCY [ARTIST]
— to exhibit at Lahaina Arts Society, Lahaina News, June 5, 1997: 18.

TERREBONNE, NANCY AND ROBERT
— to exhibit at Lahaina Arts Society, Lahaina News, July 4, 1996: 14.

TERREBONNE, ROBERT [ARTIST]
— to exhibit at Lahaina Arts Society, Lahaina News, June 5, 1997: 18.
— to exhibit at Lahaina Arts Society Gallery, Lahaina News, July 30, 1998: 17.

TERRITORIAL SAVINGS AND LOANS [BUSINESS]
— to hold seminars on trust, Lahaina News, March 11, 1993: 12.
— to host seminar on trusts, Lahaina News, March 18, 1993: 6.

TERRY, AL
— receives Bill Kohne Big Brothers/Big Sisters award, Lahaina News, April 12, 1989: 5.

TERRY FOX RUN
— to be held at Wailea Shopping Village, Lahaina News, September 5, 1990: 5.
— raises more than $3700, Lahaina News, September 19, 1990: 18.
— to be held, Lahaina News, September 10, 1992: 8.
— to be held, Lahaina News, September 2, 1993: 9.
— run to be held, Lahaina News, August 15, 1996: 12.
— to be held to benefit Cancer Research Center of Hawaii, Lahaina News, October 8, 1998: 15.
— "Day of Hope" fundraiser for American Cancer Society to be held, Lahaina News, October 19, 2000: 18.
— run to be held to support cancer research, Lahaina News, October 11, 2001: 13.
— Four Seasons Resort Maui to host run for cancer research, Lahaina News, October 11, 2001: 13.

TERRY, MICHAEL
— vice president and general manager of Amfac/JMB's Maui Real Estate Division, Lahaina News, October 27, 1994: 7.

TERUYA, CHRISTINE KONG
— details of his election campaign for 7th district of the State House, Lahaina Sun, September 27, 1972: 4.

TERZIS, GEORGE [MUSICIAN]
— to perform to grade 6 social studies class at Lokelani Intermediate, Lahaina News, December 17, 1992: 13.

TESHIMA, MORITO
— provides details on annual meeting of Pioneer Mill Federal Credit Union meeting, Lahaina Sun, January 13, 1971: 5.

TESORO HAWAII [BUSINESS]
— raises money for American Red Cross, Lahaina News, October 4, 2001: 9.

TESTER, KEITH
— Lahaina Restoration Foundation chairman discussed annual report, Lahaina Sun, March 10, 1971: 6.

TETRA TECH INC. [BUSINESS]
— begins dye test to determine fate of effluent from injection wells, Lahaina News, July 1, 1993: 3.
— report on green algae growth discussed, Lahaina News, July 8, 1993: 3.
— apparently failed to find dye placed into injection wells, Lahaina News, December 9, 1993: 1.

TEVAGA, MARVIN
— to preside over Lahainaluna High School homecoming, Lahaina News, November 2, 2000: 3.

TEVAGA, PANAMA
— named to 1992 Maui Interscholastic League Volleyball All-Star Team, Lahaina News, December 3, 1992: 7.
— captures gold in long jump, Lahaina News, May 6, 1993: 10.

TEXEIRA, CATHERINE [MUSICIAN]
— to sing with the Maui Symphony Pops, Lahaina News, September 16, 1993: 17,18.

TEXEIRA, RED
— artwork discussed, Lahaina Sun, April 28, 1971: 5.

THACKERY, JIMMY [MUSICIAN]
— to perform at Casanova's, Lahaina News, February 20, 1997: 12.
— blues guitar player to perform at Hapa's, Lahaina News, September 25, 2003: 15.

THAI CHEF
— reviewed, Lahaina News, March 7, 1990: 12.

THAILAND
— travel to, Lahaina Times, October, 1980 volume 4 number 9: 1, 4.

THANKSGIVING
— Hoolaulea details announced, Lahaina Sun, November 17, 1971: 12.
— Hoolaulea celebrated at Baldwin House, Lahaina Sun, November 22, 1972: 10.
— activities for children, Lahaina News, November 14, 1984: !,B,C,D.
— special meals to be offered at some restaurants, Lahaina News, November 20, 1985: 11.
— children's supplement features, Lahaina News, November 27, 1985: A,B,C,D.
— Westin Maui offering take-out turkey, Lahaina News, November 18, 1987: 3.
— Kumulani Chapel offering free Thanksgiving dinner, Lahaina News, November 18, 1987: 3.
— specials detailed, Lahaina News, November 16, 1988: 3,5.
— events, Lahaina News, November 23, 1988: 3,6.
— Maui Inter-Continental Wailea to host dinner, Lahaina News, October 25, 1989: 8.
— Kumulani Chapel to offer free dinners, Lahaina News, November 15, 1989: 3.
— interfaith dinner to be offered at Old Lahaina Prison, Lahaina News, November 15, 1989: 5.
— Hawaiian elements described, Lahaina News, November 22, 1989: 14.
— interfaith dinner to be held at Old Lahaina Prison, Lahaina News, November 22, 1989: 3.
— events described, Lahaina News, November 14, 1990: 2,4,18.
— events and specials, Lahaina News, November 21, 1990: 3,16,18.
— dinners to be served at Hard Rock Cafe , Lahaina News, December 5, 1990: 3,5.
— Maui Marriott to offer luau, Lahaina News, November 14, 1991: 16.
— events and food availability detailed, Lahaina News, November 21, 1991: 20,21.
— interfaith services to be held, Lahaina News, November 21, 1991: 5.
— restaurant specials, Lahaina News, November 28, 1991: 17.
— Annual Turkey Giveaway to be held, Lahaina News, November 12, 1992: 5.
— events listed, Lahaina News, November 19, 1992: 3,14.
— events, Lahaina News, November 26, 1992: 4,25.
— events, Lahaina News, November 11, 1993: 13,14,15.
— featuring Turkey-to-go dinner special, Lahaina News, November 18, 1993: 1.
— events, Lahaina News, November 25, 1993: 3,11.
— dining guide, Lahaina News, November 17, 1994: 14,15,16.
— interfaith services to be held, Lahaina News, November 17, 1994: 4.
— events, restaurants, Lahaina News, November 16, 1995: 11,12,13,14.
— events, Lahaina News, November 16, 1995: 4.
— events, Lahaina News, November 14, 1996: 8.
— events, Lahaina News, November 21, 1996: 1,8,9,10,11.
— restaurants featured, Lahaina News, November 13, 1997: 16,17,18.
— restaurants featured, Lahaina News, November 20, 1997: 6,7,8,9,10.
— restaurant offerings, Lahaina News, November 12, 1998: 6,7.
— restaurant offerings, Lahaina News, November 19, 1998: 6,7,8.
— West Maui Ecumenical Thanksgiving to be held, Lahaina News, November 18, 1999: 17.
— restaurants, Lahaina News, November 18, 1999: 6.
— events held, Lahaina News, November 25, 1999: 16.
— restaurant offerings, Lahaina News, November 16, 2000: 6.
— events to be held, Lahaina News, November 23, 2000: 20.
— "In the Spirit of Unity, a Maui County Thanksgiving", Lahaina News, November 15, 2001: 1,18.

— Gemini catamaran sailing for, Lahaina News, November 15, 2001: 10.
— Karma Kafe to hold food drive, Lahaina News, November 15, 2001: 2.
— restaurants offering special menus for, Lahaina News, November 15, 2001: 9,10.
— Macy's Thanksgiving Day Parade to be held, Lahaina News, November 22, 2001: 1,9.
— Hale Hokulani to hold free dinner, Lahaina News, November 22, 2001: 20.
— service to be held, Lahaina News, November 21, 2002: 16.
— events to be held, Lahaina News, November 28, 2002: 16.
— see also Maui Invitational

THAT'S MY BABY
— contest to be held at Lahaina Cannery Mall, Lahaina News, September 26, 2002: 18.

THAT'S WHAT I LIKE [REVUE]
— Judy Ridolfino to lead, Lahaina News, January 30, 1997: 12.

THAVONSOUK, THEP [ARTIST]
— work displayed at Old Jail Gallery, Lahaina News, August 8, 1984: 3.

THAYER, BILL
— president of Waldron Steamship Committee to speak to Lahaina Town Action Committee, Lahaina News, April 23, 1998: 1.
— owner of Waldron Steamship Co. Ltd. To speak to Lahaina Town Meeting, Lahaina News, January 24, 2002: 1,2.

THAYER, JAMES AND BLACK, CPAS [BUSINESS]
— to hold open house, Lahaina News, January 21, 1993: 9.

THC [MUSICAL GROUP]
— to perform at Moose McGillycuddy's, Lahaina News, July 11, 1996: 12.
— to perform at World Cafe, Lahaina News, December 5, 1996: 16.

THEATRE
— Waiakoa Theatre to become real estate office, Lahaina Sun, January 5, 1972: 4.
— Maui Community Theatre casting for upcoming "Auntie Mame", Lahaina Sun, May 31, 1972: 11.
— events described, Lahaina News, September 9, 1987: 9.
— Kitty Awards honor top performers in Maui Community Theatre, Lahaina News, January 27, 1988: 1,10.
— Noh performance to take place at Lahaina Jodo Mission, Lahaina News, May 17, 1989: 13.
— actors from Oregon's Shakespearean Festival to tour Maui, Lahaina News, November 22, 1989: 4.
— Oregon Shakespeare Festival actors offering workshop, Lahaina News, November 29, 1989: 21.
— Royal Shakespeare Company to give workshops, Lahaina News, January 9, 1992: 5.
— season tickets available for shows by Herb and Scott Rogers Productions, Inc., Lahaina News, December 15, 1994: 19.
— actors from Oregon Shakespeare Festival to hold classes, Lahaina News, December 15, 1994: 19.
— Rogers Productions Professional Theatre Series to be held, Lahaina News, January 5, 1995: 10.
— festival of one-act plays "Brave Acts" to be held, Lahaina News, June 8, 1995: 12.
— "West Maui Players" company forming, Lahaina News, January 10, 2002: 14.
— see also Senior Festival

THEATRE THEATRE MAUI
— group to be formed, Lahaina News, March 5, 1992: 3.
— presents "1959 Pink Thunderbird", Lahaina News, April 23, 1992: 25.

— open summer children's theatre program, Lahaina News, May 7, 1992: 4.

— registration for summer children's theatre now open, Lahaina News, May 14, 1992: 3.

— registration open for summer children's program, Lahaina News, May 21, 1992: 4.

— summer youth program registration ending soon, Lahaina News, May 28, 1992: 4.

— accepting students for summer youth program, Lahaina News, May 27, 1993: 4.

— 1994 Youth Summer Production Workshop to be held, Lahaina News, May 12, 1994: 3.

— provides scholarship to participate in Snow White and the Seven (Dorks) Dwarfs, Lahaina News, July 14, 1994: 6.

— names Nancy Sherman as executive director, Lahaina News, October 13, 1994: 7.

— seeking original stage play and director for upcoming theatre productions, Lahaina News, November 10, 1994: 16.

— to hold Summer Stock for Kids, a performing arts workshop for youth, Lahaina News, June 1, 1995: 2.

— offering summer options for youth, Lahaina News, May 23, 1996: 15.

— to perform "Krazy Kamp", Lahaina News, July 25, 1996: 11,12.

— offering summer stock for kids, Lahaina News, June 5, 1997: 3.

— begins "Summer Stock for Kids" workshop, Lahaina News, June 12, 1997: 2.

— to offer summer classes, Lahaina News, July 10, 1997: 17.

— to perform "Against the Tide", Lahaina News, July 17, 1997: 16.

— to teach television production skills to youth, Lahaina News, May 7, 1998: 16.

— to perform "Merry Christmas, Miss Crabtree", Lahaina News, December 17, 1998: 1.

— summer program offered, Lahaina News, May 27, 1999: 5.

— to hold drama classes, Lahaina News, April 20, 2000: 14.

— offering creative drama classes for young performers, Lahaina News, June 8, 2000: 19.

— scholarships available for summer drama workshop, Lahaina News, March 29, 2001: 2.

— to offer summer drama program, Lahaina News, May 24, 2001: 18.

— to hold registration for summer drama program, Lahaina News, May 31, 2001: 14.

— "Tom Sawyer" to be performed, Lahaina News, July 12, 2001: 3.

— offers scholarships for summer program, Lahaina News, April 25, 2002: 5.

— to offer summer drama program, perform "Happy Daze" musical, Lahaina News, June 6, 2002: 14.

— to stage "Happy Daze", Lahaina News, July 25, 2002: 17.

— to hold summer program, Lahaina News, May 8, 2003: 2,3.

— to hold summer program, Lahaina News, May 22, 2003: 2.

THEO H. DAVIES [BUSINESS]
— photo exhibit to be displayed at Lahaina Cannery Mall, Lahaina News, January 16, 1997: 14.

THERMOTREX [BUSINESS]
— opening research office at Maui Research and Technology Center, Lahaina News, June 4, 1998: 13.

THEY BECAME WHAT THEY BEHELD [BOOK]
— reviewed by Charles Foster, Lahaina Sun, December 23, 1970: 8.

THIBAUT, ROB
— restaurant owner featured, Lahaina News, December 21, 1988: 2.

— co-owner of T.S. Restaurants of Hawaii passes away, services planned, Lahaina News, May 7, 1998: 1,3,17.

— services held for, Lahaina News, May 14, 1998: 20.

THICKE, ALAN [ENTERTAINER]
— attends Aku Memorial Celebrity Golf Tournament, Lahaina News, May 29, 1985: 4.

THIRD HEAVEN SPA AND GIFTS [BUSINESS]
— opens at Napili Plaza, Lahaina News, March 1, 2001: 8.

THIRD WORLD [MUSICAL GROUP]
— to play at Lahaina Civic Center, Lahaina News, February 27, 1985: 12.

— to perform, Lahaina News, March 6, 1985: 7.

— power goes out at concert, no refunds offered, Lahaina News, March 20, 1985: 12.

— to perform at the Maui Arts and Cultural Center with Soul Jahs, Lahaina News, March 25, 1999: 16.

THIS IS HAWAII [PERFORMANCE]
— reviewed, Lahaina News, November 1, 1981: 12.

THODEN, WAYNE AND JOLAINE
— to teach gymnastics at West Maui Carden Academy, Lahaina News, January 23, 2003: 13.

THOENE, PETER
— appointed senior sales manager at Stouffer Wailea Beach Resort, Lahaina News, August 6, 1992: 8.

THOM, CHARLIE
— to perform Karuk Indian purification ceremony, Lahaina News, February 18, 1999: 12.

THOMA, JEAN PIERRE [MUSICIAN]
— to perform at Borders Books, Lahaina News, July 22, 1999: 12.

THOMAS, BRIAN
— promoted to head tennis professional at the Royal Lahaina Resort, Lahaina News, June 29, 1995: 10.

THOMAS, DAVID
— reelected as president of Maui Marriott Resort, Lahaina News, November 26, 1986: 3.

— head of Media Systems featured, Lahaina News, September 7, 1988: 2,13.

THOMAS, FRANK [ARTIST]
— Disney animator to open exhibit, Lahaina News, January 16, 1991: 13.

THOMAS, JACK [COMEDIAN]
— to perform at Comedy Club and the Sports Page, Lahaina News, October 29, 1992: 18,22.

THOMAS, JANELLA
— Lahainaluna High School student receives scholarship from Maui Youth Ambassadors, Lahaina News, July 21, 1994: 4.

THOMAS KINKADE GALLERY [BUSINESS]
— adds new employees, Lahaina News, May 26, 1994: 14.

— to host Business After Hours, Lahaina News, November 16, 1995: 5.

THOMAS, LINDA
— Holy Innocents' Preschool Headmaster featured, Lahaina News, May 10, 2001: 1,22.

THOMAS, MARTY
— finalist of Bud Surf Tour Qualifying Series, Lahaina News, May 26, 1994: 9.

THOMAS, MORVEN
— moves offices, Lahaina News, February 18, 1987: 10.

THOMAS, RAY [COMEDIAN]
— to perform at Comedy Club, Lahaina News, August 29, 1991: 10.

— to perform at Comedy Club and the Sports Page, Lahaina News, July 23, 1992: 20,23.

THOMAS, RUSSELL
— executive sous chef at Ritz-Carlton featured, Lahaina News, May 2, 1996: 7,8.

THOMETZ, SEVAN [MUSICIAN AND ARTIST]
— to perform at Moose McGillycuddy's, Lahaina News, April 7, 1994: 12.

— to exhibit at Mana Kai Resort, Lahaina News, November 17, 1994: 19.

THOMPSON, BERRY [COMEDIAN]
— to perform at Comedy Club, Lahaina News, October 24, 1991: 20.

THOMPSON, DALE
— appointed as director of Maui Marriott Galerie Lassen, Lahaina News, July 7, 1994: 9.

THOMPSON, DANNY
— to perform with Richard Thompson, Lahaina News, April 6, 2000: 16.

THOMPSON, DEBRA
— named director of food and beverage operations at Royal Lahaina Hotel, Lahaina News, October 10, 1984: 3.
— Amfac employee honored at Pacesetter Breakfast, Lahaina News, May 6, 1987: 10.

THOMPSON, GARY
— opens Clean and Green Landscape Services, Lahaina News, January 29, 1998: 13.

THOMPSON, GENE
— retiring from Kihei Community Association, Lahaina News, February 3, 1994: 4.

THOMPSON, JOHN
— named ticketing manager for Atlantis Submarines, Lahaina News, November 28, 1991: 7.

THOMPSON, LEONARD
— wins August Coldwell Banker Burnet Classic, Lahaina News, September 10, 1998: 15.

THOMPSON, NAINOA
— speaks to conference at Ka'anapali Beach Hotel on importance of Polynesian ocean-voyaging canoes, Lahaina News, March 7, 1996: 1,16.
— to speak at benefit for Hui O Wa'a Kaulua, Lahaina News, June 20, 2002: 2.
— to speak at Hawaii State Association of Counties Conference, Lahaina News, June 20, 2002: 5.

THOMPSON, PAULA
— named Director of Public Relations at Westin Maui, Ka'anapali, Lahaina News, January 13, 1988: 16.
— joins Lahaina office of Pali Kai Realtors, Lahaina News, October 25, 1989: 10.
— joins Chaney Brooks, Lahaina News, October 31, 1991: 10.

THOMPSON, PEGGY [ARTIST]
— wins LahainaTown Action Committee poster contest, Lahaina News, July 13, 2000: 3.
— to exhibit at Lahaina Arts Society, Lahaina News, April 10, 2003: 20.

THOMPSON, RICHARD [MUSICIAN]
— to perform at Casanova's, Lahaina News, March 20, 1997: 14.
— to perform at Maui Arts and Cultural Center, Lahaina News, March 30, 2000: 13.
— to perform with jazz bassist Danny Thompson, Lahaina News, April 6, 2000: 16.

THOMPSON, TRAVIS
— county Finance director discusses rise in tax revenues from condominiums, Lahaina News, September 10, 1992: 1.
— West Maui Taxpayers Association, Lahaina News, August 12, 1993: 1,15.

THREE CROWNS [BUSINESS]
— jewelry store opens, Lahaina News, May 28, 1998: 11.

THREE DOG NIGHT [MUSICAL GROUP]
— to play at Lahaina Civic Center, Lahaina News, May 2, 1984: 14.
— performance reviewed, Lahaina News, May 16, 1984: 14.

THREE FAIRY TALES [PLAY]
— to be performed by Maui Academy of Performing Arts, Lahaina News, April 11, 1996: 13.

THREE OF HEARTS [MUSICAL GROUP]
— reviewed, Lahaina News, September 16, 1987: 8,9.

THREE PLUS [MUSICAL GROUP]
— to perform from their new CD "Three Plus 4U", Lahaina News, April 18, 2002: 15.
— to perform at union event for Labor Day, Lahaina News, August 22, 2002: 17.
— to perform at Maui No Ka Oi: Ohana Bash, Lahaina News, April 17, 2003: 18.

THREE SCOOPS OF ALOHA [MUSICAL GROUP]
— to perform at Old Lahaina Cafe and Luau, Lahaina News, February 7, 1990: 13.
— to perform at Molokini Lounge at the Maui Prince Hotel, Lahaina News, March 27, 1991: 14.

THREE WISHES [PLAYS]
— to be performed at Seabury Hall, Lahaina News, October 1, 1992: 17,18.

THRILLCRAFTS
— editorial to ban use of, Lahaina News, April 11, 1984: 2.
— State proposes to ban from Ka'anapali, Lahaina News, August 1, 1984: 3.
— State proposes to ban from Ka'anapali, Lahaina News, August 1, 1984: 3.
— editorial supporting banning of, Lahaina News, August 8, 1984: 2.
— proposed ban may be unconstitutional, Lahaina News, January 23, 1985: 3.
— community says rules will not work, Lahaina News, May 1, 1985: 1,20.
— editorial opposing, Lahaina News, May 8, 1985: 2.
— skier Scott Carpenter saves woman from drowning, Lahaina News, July 10, 1985: 3.
— editorial in support of regulatory bill, Lahaina News, March 11, 1987: 2.
— bill to regulate in state legislature, Lahaina News, March 11, 1987: 3.
— residents call for banning of, Lahaina News, August 10, 1988: 1,16.
— hearing set, Lahaina News, September 7, 1988: 1.
— editorial critical of State's decision not to ban, Lahaina News, October 5, 1988: 4.
— new rules in effect; riders reported to Maui police and Department of Transportation, Lahaina News, October 12, 1988: 1,20.
— West Maui Taxpayers Association supports ban of, Lahaina News, December 21, 1988: 1.
— bill to ban advances in House of Representatives, Lahaina News, March 8, 1989: 1.
— Roz Baker's bill dies in the legislature, Lahaina News, March 29, 1989: 1.
— issue updated, Lahaina News, June 28, 1989: 1.
— state proposes banning, Lahaina News, October 25, 1989: 3.
— hearing set to discuss banning of, Lahaina News, November 1, 1989: 2.
— ban scheduled to take effect, Lahaina News, December 13, 1989: 1,3.
— opponents of rally, Lahaina News, January 3, 1990: 28.
— legislators seek ban, Lahaina News, January 24, 1990: 28.
— Roz Baker confident of ban, Lahaina News, February 21, 1990: 4.
— ban close to passing legislature, Lahaina News, April 25, 1990: 2.
— Governor John Waihee signs bill banning, Lahaina News, July 11, 1990: 2.
— State Department of Transportation proposes rules allowing for, Lahaina News, September 12, 1990: 1.
— conflicts with people swimming and fishing recounted; areas of activity suggested, Lahaina News, October 17, 1990: 1,10.
— threatening whales swimming near shore, Lahaina News, February 27, 1991: 1.

— allowed to operate again off Ka'anapali, Lahaina News, May 30, 1991: 1.
— state representative Roz Baker to seek tighter laws on ban of, Lahaina News, January 9, 1992: 1.
— Attorney General seeks reversal of judge's decision to allowed continued operation of, Lahaina News, January 16, 1992: 1.
— operations of Pacific Jet Ski Rentals halted until court hearing, Lahaina News, January 23, 1992: 3.
— restraining order against use lifted, Lahaina News, February 6, 1992: 7.

THULE
— mythical place discussed, Lahaina Times, June, 1980 volume 4 number 5: 2.

THUNDER IN THE TROPICS
— Bang-Bang Boxing Productions to hold, Lahaina News, June 27, 2002: 12.

THURBER, JIM
— to discuss New Testament, Lahaina News, May 15, 1997: 12.

THURSTON, CRAIG AND LOUISE
— farmers in Olinda described, Lahaina Sun, July 11, 1973: 12.

TIAN-JIAN, YU
— to talk on "Self Healing, Self-Enlightenment", Lahaina News, March 27, 2003: 17.

TIBET
— lamas from Drepung Loseling Monastery to perform, Lahaina News, July 20, 1995: 12.
— "Heart and Soul" music benefit to help children refugees in India, Lahaina News, May 31, 2001: 17.
— "Heart and Soul" music benefit to help children refugees in India, Lahaina News, June 7, 2001: 20.

TIBETAN BUDDHIST SOCIETY
— sponsoring sacred dance and devotional chanting, Lahaina News, October 12, 1988: 20.

TIBETAN NEW YEAR
— celebration to be held at Dharma Center, Lahaina News, March 5, 1998: 16.

TICE, MASSIE
— begins distributing ACTS coupon book, Lahaina News, September 14, 1988: 14.

TIFFANY AND CO. [BUSINESS]
— opens, Lahaina News, September 15, 1994: 12.
— hosting benefit for American Cancer Society, Lahaina News, April 29, 1999: 2.
— open store at The Shops at Wailea, Lahaina News, July 8, 1999: 11.
— appoints Rae Seki as director of new store in Wailea, Lahaina News, September 21, 2000: 16.

TIFFANY LEE AND COMPANY [MUSICAL GROUP]
— to perform at benefit concert at Maui Brews, Lahaina News, August 5, 1999: 14.

TIGER'S RESTAURANT [RESTAURANT]
— Tropical Gangster to perform at, Lahaina News, July 11, 1990: 15.
— receives award for remodeling, Lahaina News, February 27, 1991: 8.
— holds grand opening, Lahaina News, July 25, 1991: 7.
— features karaoke, Lahaina News, August 15, 1991: 15.
— continues to offer karaoke, Lahaina News, September 5, 1991: 9.

TIHADA, DOUGIE
— career described, Lahaina News, March 22, 1989: 2.

TIHADA, IRENE
— recognized as educator of the month by Kimo's Restaurant, Lahaina News, December 21, 2000: 3.
— volunteer featured, Lahaina News, December 27, 2001: 1,18.

TIHADA, LANNY
— career as coach of Lahainaluna High School football team described, Lahaina News, September 4, 1985: 4.
— receives Vocational Service Award from Lahaina Rotary Club, Lahaina News, February 4, 1987: 3.
— career of Lahainaluna High School coach featured, Lahaina News, December 14, 1988: 14,18.
— police officer discusses pro-active approach to crime, Lahaina News, December 16, 1993: 1,4.
— coach and police officer moving from Lahaina to Moloka'i, Lahaina News, May 19, 1994: 1,20.
— appointed new deputy police chief, Lahaina News, December 29, 1994: 3.

TIKI CAFE [RESTAURANT]
— opens, Lahaina News, October 15, 1992: 16.

TIKI TERRACE [RESTAURANT]
— featured, Lahaina News, July 1, 1987: 9.
— reviewed, Lahaina News, May 25, 1988: 9.
— featured, Lahaina News, September 28, 1988: 8.
— wins A Taste of Lahaina, Lahaina News, September 26, 2002: 9.

TILAK
— to speak at Kapila Institute, Lahaina News, February 6, 2003: 16.

TILBURG, HANS KONRAD VAN
— to speak on "Wrecks to the Northwest: Our Maritime Legacy in the Hawaiian Archipelago", Lahaina News, March 6, 2003: 2.

TILT DANCE COMPANY [TROUPE]
— beginning new dance program, Lahaina News, October 29, 1998: 15.
— to begin new dance program, Lahaina News, November 5, 1998: 8.

TIMBOY, MARCIA [ARTIST]
— to lead Symbolic Image Making workshop, Lahaina News, December 7, 2000: 9.
— to lead Symbolic Image Making workshop, Lahaina News, December 14, 2000: 8.
— to lead Symbolic Image Making Workshop at The Art School at Kapalua, Lahaina News, October 18, 2001: 17.

TIME MAGAZINE
— employees participate in volunteer projects on the West Side, Lahaina News, February 10, 2000: 1,20.

TIMES, MIKE
— forms Represent Youth Outreach to help young people, Lahaina News, March 28, 2002: 1,20.
— to operate Represent Youth Outreach, Lahaina News, September 12, 2002: 22.

TIMESHARES
— pros and cons discussed, Lahaina News, December 1, 1981: 4,5.
— salespeople on Front street banned, Lahaina News, December 15, 1981: 2.
— limits put on selling, Lahaina News, May 15, 1982: 2.
— concerned raised by West Maui Taxpayers Association, Lahaina News, February 25, 1993: 7.
— Roz Baker seeks sanity in time share industry, Lahaina News, May 13, 1993: 1,3.
— new rules go into effect, Lahaina News, July 10, 1997: 1.

TIMMERMANS BROTHERS [MUSICAL GROUP]
— to perform at Longhi's Restaurant, Lahaina News, July 24, 1997: 7.

TIMMERMAN'S JAZZ ENSEMBLE [MUSICAL GROUP]
— to perform at Whalers Village, Lahaina News, December 14, 2000: 20.

TINA TUNES [MUSICAL GROUP]
— to perform at Borders Books, Lahaina News, August 26, 1999: 16.

TINTYPES [PERFORMANCE]
— last weekend of at Maui Academy of Performing Arts, Lahaina News, March 28, 1996: 14.

TINY BUBBLES
— section by A. Bodoya and C. Honey begins June 2, 1971 and is not indexed, Lahaina Sun, June 2, 1971: .

TIPPING
— discussion of, Lahaina Times, August 20, 1983 volume 7 number 8: 2.

TIRRELL, BARBARA [ACTRESS]
— to perform, Lahaina News, November 23, 1988: 14.
— to perform, Lahaina News, December 7, 1988: 11.

TITO'S TACOS
— changes name to Maui Tacos, Lahaina News, January 6, 1994: 6.

TITRA, STEPHEN [PERFORMER]
— to entertain at Maui Arts and Cultural Center, Lahaina News, January 26, 1995: 16.

TO RAISE A NATION [BOOK]
— author Mary Cooke visits Maui, Lahaina Sun, March 17, 1971: 3.

TOASTMASTERS
— new club formed, Lahaina News, October 3, 1984: 13.
— West Maui Whalers Toastmasters Club to meet, Lahaina News, October 31, 1984: 3.
— West Maui Whalers Toastmasters featured, Lahaina News, March 2, 1988: 13.
— to send Steve Jordan to national contest, Lahaina News, April 13, 1988: 12.
— to hold annual membership, Lahaina News, July 30, 1992: 4.
— West Maui Whalers to meet, Lahaina News, September 30, 1993: 4.
— Kihei chapter to meet, Lahaina News, August 1, 1996: 20.
— offering storytelling workshop, Lahaina News, September 25, 1997: 16.
— to hold "Tellabration (Evening of Storytelling)", Lahaina News, November 13, 1997: 21.
— continue to meet, Lahaina News, July 30, 1998: 16.
— continues to meet, Lahaina News, April 1, 1999: 16.
— Nancy Chaplick appointed area governor for Maui, Lahaina News, September 23, 1999: 5.
— holding a public speaking seminar, Lahaina News, June 15, 2000: 16.
— forming West Side club, Lahaina News, September 12, 2002: 2.
— to form club on West Side, Lahaina News, October 17, 2002: 14.
— to hold demonstration meeting, Lahaina News, January 9, 2003: 18.
— new group to meet, Lahaina News, March 6, 2003: 2.
— to start club at Lahaina Civic Center, Lahaina News, May 15, 2003: 18.

TOASTMASTERS, KIHEI
— to meet at Seiler's Real Estate School, Lahaina News, September 26, 1996: 15.
— to meet, Lahaina News, August 30, 2001: 17.
— continues to meet, Lahaina News, November 8, 2001: 17.
— continues to meet, Lahaina News, November 22, 2001: 20.
— continues to meet, Lahaina News, January 24, 2002: 17.
— continues to meet, Lahaina News, February 21, 2002: 17.
— continues to meet, Lahaina News, July 25, 2002: 21.
— continues to meet, Lahaina News, November 14, 2002: 21.
— continues to meet, Lahaina News, November 21, 2002: 21.

TOASTMASTERS, LAHAINA
— to hold demonstration meeting, Lahaina News, January 2, 2003: 5.
— continue to meet, Lahaina News, August 14, 2003: 16.
— continues to meet, Lahaina News, October 9, 2003: 16.

TOASTMASTERS, NO KA OI
— continues to meet, Lahaina News, August 6, 1998: 20.
— continues to meet, Lahaina News, December 24, 1998: 12.

TOASTMASTERS, UPCOUNTRY
— newly formed group to meet, Lahaina News, May 1, 1997: 17.
— continues to meet, Lahaina News, March 4, 1999: 13.

TOASTMASTERS, WEST MAUI WHALERS
— officers elected, Lahaina News, April 5, 1989: 3.
— new officers installed, Lahaina News, June 28, 1989: 7.
— new officers elected, Lahaina News, June 27, 1990: 8.
— sponsoring International Youth Leadership Program, Lahaina News, March 6, 1991: 3,4.
— sponsors Youth Leadership Program, Lahaina News, April 17, 1991: 3.
— continues to meet, Lahaina News, December 31, 1992: 4.
— see also Toastmasters

TOBISHIMA [BUSINESS]
— to develop North Beach with Amfac, Inc., Lahaina News, January 1, 1986: 3.

TOCHIANA, MAYNARD
— appointed chair of Wailea Destination Association of Maui, Lahaina News, March 19, 1992: 10.

TODAY SHOW, THE [TELEVISION SHOW]
— to feature segment on Maui, Lahaina News, November 21, 1991: 1.

TODDLER THEATRE
— offered by Lahaina Library, Lahaina News, August 26, 1987: 3.

TOGASHI, KIRK
— director of West Maui Youth Center featured, Lahaina News, January 23, 1992: 3.

TOGETHER EVERYONE ACHIEVES MORE {TEAM}
— workshop held at Maui Community College, Lahaina News, February 3, 1988: 3.

TOGO'S [RESTAURANT]
— reviewed, Lahaina News, December 15, 1980: 16.
— reviewed, Lahaina News, November 23, 1983: 15.

TOGUSHI, CHARLES
— state education superintendent announces site for Upcountry high school, Lahaina News, February 20, 1992: 4.

TOKUNA, GERALD
— architect for new Weinberg shopping center, Lahaina News, November 9, 1988: 1.

TOKUNAGA, BARNEY
— member of Maui County Council, Lahaina Sun, December 30, 1970: 8.
— reacts to number of resolutions at Maui County Council meeting, Lahaina Sun, January 20, 1971: 8.

TOKUNAGA, BERNARD
— Baldwin High School principal discusses accreditation, Lahaina Sun, September 13, 1972: 3.

TOKYO STRING QUARTET [MUSICAL GROUP]
— to perform at Maui Arts and Cultural Center, Lahaina News, February 3, 2000: 13.

TOKYOSPHERE [MUSICAL GROUP]
— to perform at Saint Anthony Church Center, Lahaina News, January 30, 1991: 7.

TOLBERT, CHRIS
— wins karaoke competition, Lahaina News, July 13, 2000: 9.

TOLEDO, GERTRUDE KAPIOLANI
— murder case recounted, Part I, Lahaina News, August 30, 2001: 5.
— murder case recounted, Part II, Lahaina News, September 6, 2001: 5.
— murder case recounted, Part III, Lahaina News, September 13, 2001: 5.
— murder case recounted, Part IV, Lahaina News, September 27, 2001: 5.

TOLEDO, HAMILTON
— promoted at Aston Hotels and Resorts Hawaii, Lahaina News, January 11, 2001: 14.

TOLEDO, JOANNE "NONIE"
— named Regional Sales Director for Long Distance/USA Sprint, Lahaina News, May 6, 1993: 9.

TOM, ALLEN
— now lead onsite coordinator for Hawaii humpback whale sanctuary, Lahaina News, February 9, 1995: 16.

TOM AND TIM [MUSICAL GROUP]
— to perform at Polli's Mexican Restaurant, Lahaina News, March 13, 1991: 11.
— continues to perform at Polli's Mexican Restaurant, Lahaina News, April 24, 1991: 11.

TOM CAT [BOAT]
— abandoned off Maui, Lahaina Sun, July 5, 1972: 9.

TOM, DICK
— actor in Charlie Chan movies visits Lahaina, Lahaina Sun, January 6, 1971: 6.

TOM, DOUG
— director of Office of State Planning for Coastal Zone Management discusses property and vegetation line on beaches, Lahaina News, July 11, 1991: 1,9.
— Coastal Management chief to speak, Lahaina News, October 31, 1991: 4.

TOM SAWYER [PLAY]
— to be performed by Theatre Theatre Maui, Lahaina News, July 12, 2001: 3.

TOMA, DAVID
— police officer who inspired Baretta speaks to Lahainaluna High School, Lahaina News, November 20, 1985: 12.

TOMA, GAIL [ARTIST]
— to hold workshop on creating egg baskets, Lahaina News, March 6, 1991: 16.

TOMAS, KATHLEEN
— Scholar/Athlete of the Week, Lahaina News, September 25, 2003: 12.

TOMAS, NELSON
— Lahaina student at Seattle Pacific University to leave for mission to South Africa, Lahaina News, July 18, 2002: 18.

TOMASO, ANNE
— winner of 1980 Maui Women's Surfing Championship, Lahaina Times, June, 1980 volume 4 number 5: 1.

TOMEI, "ROMEO" ROBERT [ARTIST]
— to be featured at Elizabeth Doyle Gallery, Lahaina News, March 2, 2000: 12.
— abstract painter to appear at Sargent's Fine Art, Lahaina News, December 7, 2000: 24.

TOMMY BAHAMA [BUSINESS]
— opens, Lahaina News, December 28, 2000: 16.
— Emporium opens at The Shops at Wailea, Lahaina News, January 25, 2001: 14.
— grand opening held, Lahaina News, February 1, 2001: 9.
— Tropical Cafe and Emporium to hold benefit for breast cancer research, Lahaina News, September 20, 2001: 9.
— to open at Whalers Village, Lahaina News, April 25, 2002: 8.
— golf tournament to benefit United Way, Lahaina News, June 19, 2003: 12.

TOMODACHI STRUMMERS, THE [MUSICAL GROUP]
— to perform at Maui Prince Hotel, Lahaina News, December 19, 1991: 21.

TOMONO, BARBARA [ARTIST]
— to demonstrate fabric design techniques, Lahaina News, September 26, 1990: 13.

TOMOSO, JOHN
— named Maui County Administrator of Child and Family Service, Lahaina News, June 4, 1992: 9.

TONER, JOCELYN
— Scholar/Athlete of the Week, Lahaina News, October 15, 1998: 15.

TONER, JOHN
— appointed general manager of the Ritz-Carlton, Lahaina News, July 23, 1992: 16.
— named vice president of Ko Olina Resort Association, Lahaina News, May 23, 2002: 8.

TONER, PAUL
— named director of sales for Maui Marriott, Lahaina News, August 15, 1991: 6.
— named director of sales of Hyatt Regency Maui, Lahaina News, April 29, 1993: 9.

TONG, KIM
— appointed sales manager at Ka'anapali Beach Hotel, Lahaina News, September 6, 1989: 2.

TONG, RODNEY
— promoted to Japanese Guest Services Manager, Lahaina News, December 10, 1992: 10.

TONG SOCIETY
— Maui Historic Commission okays repainting of the building, Lahaina Sun, August 18, 1971: 8.
— photograph of building, Lahaina Sun, November 10, 1971: 5.

TONGA
— arts and crafts exhibited at Upstairs Gallery at Lahaina Arts Society, Lahaina News, October 25, 1989: 14.
— arts and crafts exhibited, Lahaina News, November 8, 1989: 13.

TONGAN COMMUNITY
— donates rock wall fronting Lahainaluna High School cafeteria, Lahaina News, July 31, 2003: 3.

TONS OF FUN [BUSINESS]
— opens, offering options for parties, Lahaina News, January 3, 2002: 8.

TONY N' TINA'S WEDDING [PLAY]
— to be performed at Hyatt Regency Maui, Lahaina News, October 24, 2002: 18.
— to be performed, Lahaina News, November 7, 2002: 20.
— featured, Lahaina News, November 21, 2002: 17.
— to be performed, Lahaina News, November 28, 2002: 17,18.
— being held at Hyatt Regency Maui, Lahaina News, December 12, 2002: 18.
— continues, Lahaina News, December 26, 2002: 17.
— continues, Lahaina News, February 20, 2003: 17.
— continues run, Lahaina News, March 27, 2003: 17.

TONY NOVAK-CLIFFORD PHOTOGRAPHY [BUSINESS]
— receives Pele award, Lahaina News, March 2, 1995: 7.

TOOLS, THE [MUSICAL GROUP]
— to play at the Santa Claus Parade, Lahaina News, December 5, 1984: 14.

TOPAZ GOLDSMITH AND GALLERY [BUSINESS]
— to display gemstones from Afghanistan, Lahaina News, January 14, 1993: 14.

TOPERICH, SASHA [MUSICIAN]
— to perform at "L'Chaim Unplugged! - The Soul of Jewish Music", Lahaina News, May 28, 1998: 13.

TORCHIANA, CATHY BRIGHT
— joins Longhi Gallery as director of special projects, Lahaina News, October 27, 1994: 15.
— Wailea Golf Club LPGA Teaching Professional named to 50 Top Teachers by Golf for Women magazine, Lahaina News, February 28, 2002: 13.

TORGESON, MARK
— participates in X-Games, Lahaina News, June 12, 2003: 10.

TORME, STEVE MARCH [MUSICIAN]
— to perform at Kea Lani Hotel, Lahaina News, November 18, 1999: 15.
— to perform at Kea Lani Hotel, Lahaina News, November 25, 1999: 18.

TORRENCE, JACKIE [STORYTELLER]
— to appear at St. Anthony's Church Center, Lahaina News, January 16, 1985: 3.

TORREY, JACK
— hired as systems and field engineer by Aloha Business Systems, Lahaina News, October 17, 1990: 12.

TORTILLA FLATS [RESTAURANT]
— reviewed, Lahaina News, December 15, 1980: 16.
— opens second location, Lahaina News, April 25, 1984: 13.

TORTORELLI, GEORGE [MUSICIAN]
— to perform with Lisa Lynne, Lahaina News, May 28, 1998: 12.

TOSCA [OPERA]
— performed at Baldwin High School auditorium, Lahaina Sun, February 3, 1971: 8.
— reviewed, Lahaina Sun, February 17, 1971: 6.

TOTALLY HAWAIIAN [BUSINESS]
— opens, Lahaina News, February 24, 1994: 10.

TOTTO, CHARLES
— State Consumer Advocate sees issue with rising electricity costs, Lahaina News, January 23, 1992: 1.

TOUCH [MUSICAL GROUP]
— show at The Blue Max reviewed, Lahaina News, January 15, 1980: 5.

TOUCH OF GOLD, A [MUSICAL GROUP]
— to perform at Maui Prince Hotel's Molokini Lounge, Lahaina News, January 30, 1991: 7.

TOUCH OF HOPE
— women's ministry to hold conference, Lahaina News, May 15, 1991: 5.
— to hold women's conference, Lahaina News, May 30, 1991: 3.

TOURISM
— inconvenienced by hotel strike, Lahaina Sun, November 11, 1970: 1.
— Japanese to Maui, promoted by Mayor Cravalho, Lahaina Sun, January 6, 1971: 2.
— visits increase to 392,000 for 1970, Lahaina Sun, February 17, 1971: 5.
— Rate of Japanese tourism to Maui increases, Lahaina Sun, March 3, 1971: 6.
— number of new hotel rooms completed is less than expected, Lahaina Sun, March 17, 1971: 7.
— New York office of Hawaii Visitors Bureau said to have no promotional material on Maui, Lahaina Sun, April 7, 1971: 1.
— debated at seminar on ecology and the future of Maui, Lahaina Sun, April 7, 1971: 1,8.
— number of visitors to Maui increases, Lahaina Sun, July 21, 1971: 8.
— dune buggy rentals criticized, Lahaina Sun, July 28, 1971: 1,9.
— visitor rate Is down in June, Lahaina Sun, August 18, 1971: 11.
— promotion being developed by Ka'anapali Beach Operators Association, Lahaina Sun, August 25, 1971: 11.

— has fallen off in the first half of the year, Lahaina Sun, September 22, 1971: 10.
— national promotion program beginning soon, Lahaina Sun, October 6, 1971: 3.
— poor reviews of Maui hotels, Lahaina Sun, October 27, 1971: 1.
— hotel occupancy high in October, Lahaina Sun, October 27, 1971: 6.
— September was busy, Lahaina Sun, November 24, 1971: 6.
— visitor count to Maui for October announced, Lahaina Sun, December 15, 1971: 1.
— ocean liner President Wilson docks in Kahului Harbor, Lahaina Sun, December 22, 1971: 16.
— tourist industry payroll grows, Lahaina Sun, December 29, 1971: 5.
— Lana'i Company proposes housing and tourist projects for Lana'i, Lahaina Sun, December 29, 1971: 6.
— Maui County to spend $30,000 in promotion, Lahaina Sun, January 5, 1972: 4.
— Hawaii is popular resort destination, Lahaina Sun, January 5, 1972: 4.
— personnel changes at Maui Land & Pineapple will not affect development, Lahaina Sun, January 12, 1972: 1.
— experience of "hypothetical traveler" described, Lahaina Sun, February 16, 1972: 7.
— numbers grew last year, Lahaina Sun, February 16, 1972: 9.
— hotel bookings heavy this semester, Lahaina Sun, March 8, 1972: 3.
— increases sharply, Lahaina Sun, March 15, 1972: 5.
— Lahaina Improvement Association concerned that tourists are being given too many tickets, Lahaina Sun, March 22, 1972: 4.
— 900 travel agents due to visit Ka'anapali, Lahaina Sun, March 29, 1972: 4.
— Travel agents visit Maui, Lahaina Sun, April 12, 1972: 7.
— and future of Hawaii's economy discussed, Lahaina Sun, April 19, 1972: 20.
— gala night for visiting travel agents, Lahaina Sun, April 19, 1972: 3.
— artist John St. John has left Maui due to lack of support for art in Lahaina, Lahaina Sun, April 19, 1972: 6.
— number of tourists visiting Maui increased, Lahaina Sun, April 26, 1972: 11.
— Wailea Tourist plan outlined, Lahaina Sun, April 26, 1972: 9.
— Japanese visitors sought, Lahaina Sun, May 10, 1972: 3.
— Wailea Tourist plan criticized, Lahaina Sun, May 10, 1972: 3.
— Bank of Hawaii expects industry to increase , Lahaina Sun, May 10, 1972: 5.
— Confrontation between State Board of Education and Hawaii State Teachers Association, Lahaina Sun, May 24, 1972: 11.
— description of tourists in Lahaina, Lahaina Sun, May 31, 1972: 21.
— report on Maui statistics for April 1972, Lahaina Sun, June 14, 1972: 14.
— impact on Front Street, Lahaina Sun, June 14, 1972: 6,7.
— record number of tourists in 1971, Lahaina Sun, July 5, 1972: 15.
— reflection on travelling away from Maui, Lahaina Sun, July 19, 1972: 19.
— story of a tourist couple, Lahaina Sun, July 26, 1972: 22.
— children diving for coins tossed by tourists off pier in Lahaina, Lahaina Sun, July 26, 1972: 9.
— value of for Maui questioned, Lahaina Sun, August 23, 1972: 17.
— situation in Lahaina discussed, Lahaina Sun, August 23, 1972: 3.
— concern over waste water created by Pioneer Mill, Lahaina Sun, August 30, 1972: 17.
— students fight planned project in Wailea, Lahaina Sun, October 11, 1972: 19.
— possible plans to make Kahului airport an international airport discussed, Lahaina Sun, October 18, 1972: 11.
— increasing on Maui, Lahaina Sun, November 1, 1972: 10.
— criticism of advertising featuring Haleakala, Lahaina Sun, November 15, 1972: 19.

— Life of the Land attempts to control tourism growth, Lahaina Sun, November 15, 1972: 4.

— Ka'anapali resort area announces new promotional campaign, Lahaina Sun, December 13, 1972: 14,15.

— construction of large hotel in Lahaina set to begin, Lahaina Sun, December 13, 1972: 5.

— over 2 million tourists visited Hawaii so far this year, Lahaina Sun, December 27, 1972: 10.

— cruise ships visit Lahaina, Lahaina Sun, December 27, 1972: 10.

— numbers of tourists in Maui described, Lahaina Sun, January 3, 1973: 3.

— hotel occupancy rate up, Lahaina Sun, January 10, 1973: 10.

— rebounded in 1972, Lahaina Sun, January 17, 1973: 11.

— tourist spending expected to be higher than military in 1973, Lahaina Sun, February 21, 1973: 5.

— up for January 1973, Lahaina Sun, March 7, 1973: 10.

— sail boats along beach in Ka'anapali described, Lahaina Sun, May 9, 1973: 15.

— issues on Maui discussed, Lahaina Sun, May 16, 1973: 1,12,13.

— passenger liner Oronsay arrives in Lahaina, Lahaina Sun, June 6, 1973: 9.

— possible future discussed, Lahaina Sun, June 13, 1973: 14,15.

— Diver Chip Bahouth's routine described, Lahaina Sun, July 4, 1973: 11.

— increased in June from last year, Lahaina Sun, August 15, 1973: 7.

— visitor count for Maui down, Lahaina News, April 15, 1980: 13.

— experience of cruise ships described, Lahaina News, June 15, 1980: 15.

— bus trip to Hana described, Lahaina News, August 1, 1980: 5.

— slumping, Lahaina News, November 1, 1980: 10.

— people of Hawaii vacation out of state, Lahaina News, November 1, 1980: 10.

— Interisland Resorts Ltd. breaks ground on employee housing project, Lahaina News, December 1, 1980: 16.

— visitors guide to West Maui, Lahaina News, December 1, 1980: 7.

— value of travel sales discussed, Lahaina News, May 15, 1981: 8,9.

— advice on talking to tourists, Lahaina News, August 1, 1981: 10.

— Sears reports that 20% of its business at Ala Moana Shopping Center is from tourists, Lahaina News, September 15, 1981: 5.

— Maui Association of Condominium Owners sends "Maui Condo and Recreation Guide" booklet to travel agents, Lahaina News, November 1, 1981: 16.

— Hawaii has a high rate of foreign tourists, Lahaina News, November 1, 1981: 5.

— number of visitors to Maui down from last year, Lahaina News, November 15, 1981: 5.

— pros and cons of timeshares discussed, Lahaina News, December 1, 1981: 4,5.

— Japanese tourists crucial for Hawaii in 1981, Lahaina News, December 15, 1981: 7.

— up for March 1982, Lahaina News, May 15, 1982: 2.

— visitor count rises, Lahaina News, June 15, 1982: 3.

— Hawaii Tropical Plantation planned for Wailuku, Lahaina News, June 15, 1982: 3.

— advice to tourists for avoiding crime, Lahaina News, July 15, 1982: 2,6.

— "Hawaii on Parade" marketing plan dropped, Lahaina News, July 15, 1982: 3.

— promotion ideas suggested in Japan-Hawaii Economic Council, Lahaina News, August 15, 1982: 4.

— thank you letter from mayor for article with warnings for tourists, Lahaina News, September 15, 1982: 13.

— Maui visitor count up, Lahaina News, September 15, 1982: 2.

— increases, Lahaina News, October 15, 1982: 11.

— Sheraton Maui at Ka'anapali to undergo renovations, Lahaina News, December 1, 1982: 11.

— hotel rates and occupancy compared across country, Lahaina News, December 1, 1982: 2.

— response to ad in Fortune Magazine positive, Lahaina News, January 1, 1983: 4.

— visitor count up 33% for November, Lahaina News, January 15, 1983: 11.

— Oceanic Independence [ship] taken out of service until May 1, Lahaina News, January 15, 1983: 2.

— Maui visitor count up, Lahaina News, February 1, 1983: 13.

— head of Marriott hotel chain pleased with performance of Maui locations, Lahaina News, February 15, 1983: 10.

— hotel occupancy rate rises, Lahaina News, February 15, 1983: 6.

— visitors spending less, Lahaina News, March 15, 1983: 11.

— County requests halt to jet-ski operators, Lahaina News, March 15, 1983: 6.

— visitors decline in January, Lahaina News, April 1, 1983: 11.

— Haleakala crater closed to horses due to drought, Lahaina News, July 15, 1983: 7.

— Japanese tourism increased, Lahaina News, August 31, 1983: 14.

— rose on Maui in August, Lahaina News, October 19, 1983: 14.

— Kapalua Resort offering deluxe vacations to the super-rich, Lahaina News, December 28, 1983: 3,7.

— Maui County Visitors Association and Hawaii Visitors Bureau feuding over jurisdiction, Lahaina News, January 4, 1984: 10.

— 72 conventions scheduled for Maui in 1984, Lahaina News, February 8, 1984: 3.

— rose in 1983, Lahaina News, February 22, 1984: 17.

— hotel tax discussed, Lahaina News, March 21, 1984: 4,5.

— has increased since last year, Lahaina News, May 2, 1984: 17.

— February visitor count up from previous year, Lahaina News, May 23, 1984: 17.

— Maui visitor count up in first four months, Lahaina News, July 18, 1984: 3.

— visitor count in May up from last year, Lahaina News, August 1, 1984: 13.

— editorial of smoke from cane fires scaring tourists, Lahaina News, August 8, 1984: 2.

— editorial on rise of Ka'anapali as a competitor to Waikiki, Lahaina News, August 29, 1984: 2.

— featured article on what to do in September in Lahaina, Lahaina News, September 19, 1984: 7,8,9.

— Maui business people meet to discuss Japanese tourism, Lahaina News, September 26, 1984: 14.

— Kapalua employees receive recognition awards, Lahaina News, October 3, 1984: 13.

— feature article seeing Maui by helicopter, Lahaina News, November 28, 1984: 7,8,9.

— best growth since 1976, Lahaina News, December 26, 1984: 3.

— editorial opposing increasing taxes on tourism, Lahaina News, January 9, 1985: 2.

— set record last year, Lahaina News, January 23, 1985: 3.

— dumb questions tourists ask, Lahaina News, February 6, 1985: 7,8,9.

— visitor totals up, Lahaina News, February 27, 1985: 3.

— editorial on response to United Airlines strike, Lahaina News, June 19, 1985: 2.

— Maui County Visitors Association becomes part of Hawaii Visitors Bureau, Lahaina News, July 24, 1985: 2.

— Upcountry Maui promoted, Lahaina News, August 14, 1985: 3.

— increased in July compared to last year, Lahaina News, August 28, 1985: 3.

— information on cruise lines to be provided at Cruise Party at Sheraton Maui Hotel, Lahaina News, September 25, 1985: 3.

— Lahaina Parasail, Inc seeks permit to moor a permanent platform off Lahaina, Lahaina News, October 9, 1985: 8.

— the process of using a travel agent described, Lahaina News, January 1, 1986: 7.

— editorial responding to Frank Blackwell of the Maui Visitors Bureau complaining that low fares will be bring lower quality tourists, Lahaina News, January 8, 1986: 2.

— editorial praising crackdown on Roberts of Hawaii buses, Lahaina News, March 19, 1986: 2.

— Queen Elizabeth II [ship] visits Lahaina, Lahaina News, April 9, 1986: 1.

— mayor Tavares says county should control shoreline to control jet skis, Lahaina News, April 16, 1986: 3.

— Maui County to receive portion of state's hotel room tax, Lahaina News, April 23, 1986: 3.

— increase explained with fall of U.S. dollar and rise of terrorism in Europe, Lahaina News, April 30, 1986: 1.

— editorial opposing American Hawaii Cruises dumping raw sewage into harbors, Lahaina News, June 18, 1986: 2.

— visitors given faulty used cars, Lahaina News, July 16, 1986: 1.

— editorial supporting changing how tourism is marketed, Lahaina News, July 30, 1986: 2.

— shore water rules affect operators, Lahaina News, August 27, 1986: 11.

— pedal boats proposed, Lahaina News, September 3, 1986: 3.

— discussion of noise abatement for helicopter tour companies, Lahaina News, September 24, 1986: 3.

— Banyan Square Association seeking to market south end of Front Street, Lahaina News, October 1, 1986: 1,2,11.

— discussion of nude beaches on Maui, Lahaina News, December 24, 1986: 18.

— Maui's reputation for nude beaches, Lahaina News, February 11, 1987: 1,10.

— "Tips for Tourists" column begins, will not automatically be indexed otherwise, Lahaina News, February 11, 1987: 9,10.

— comments on strategies to increase, Lahaina News, February 18, 1987: 4.

— tips for tourists, Lahaina News, April 8, 1987: 9,12.

— editorial raising concerns for plans to offer submarine tours, Lahaina News, April 22, 1987: 2.

— Excel Charters adds third vessel to fishing charter operations, Lahaina News, May 6, 1987: 3.

— proposed submarine tour operation to be discussed, Lahaina News, June 10, 1987: 3.

— dining and entertainment section features local companies, Lahaina News, June 10, 1987: 7,8,9.

— proposed Atlantis submarine criticized, Lahaina News, June 17, 1987: 1,20.

— dining and entertainment section features local companies, Lahaina News, June 17, 1987: 7,8,9,10.

— proposed Atlantis submarine rejected, Lahaina News, June 24, 1987: 1.

— "Explore the Orient" cruise show presented by Ka'anapali Travel, Lahaina News, July 8, 1987: 16.

— bicycle adventure down Haleakala described, Lahaina News, July 29, 1987: 4.

— conflict over legality of special use permit to Aloha Voyages for commercial tourist operation, Lahaina News, November 18, 1987: 1,11,12.

— reduced rate applies at Amfac hotels in Los Angeles and San Francisco, Lahaina News, December 16, 1987: 15.

— Department of Transportation accepting permits for commercial activities in shore waters near Ka'anapali, Lahaina News, August 10, 1988: 3.

— likened to goose that lays golden eggs; situation detailed, Lahaina News, September 7, 1988: 1.

— attempts to market Maui discussed, Lahaina News, February 22, 1989: 1,13.

— importance of ocean safety, Lahaina News, May 17, 1989: 1.

— Maui Chamber of Commerce sponsoring food and beverage seminar, Lahaina News, May 17, 1989: 9.

— may face problems, Lahaina News, July 19, 1989: 3.

— Grand Hyatt Wailea Resort and Spa scheduled to open in 1990, Lahaina News, August 2, 1989: 6.

— cruises available, Lahaina News, December 27, 1989: 12.

— groups lobby to regulate tour desks, Lahaina News, February 14, 1990: 3.

— tour operators debate proposed legislation, Lahaina News, February 28, 1990: 1.

— feeling that islands are becoming too commercial, Lahaina News, July 18, 1990: 1.

— passenger ships to arrive, including Sea Princess and Royal Viking Sky, Lahaina News, November 21, 1990: 11,12.

— visitor count is down, Lahaina News, December 12, 1990: 6.

— occupancy rate falls, Lahaina News, February 6, 1991: 1.

— drops in Maui County, Lahaina News, March 6, 1991: 10.

— may pick up in second half of year, Lahaina News, March 27, 1991: 10.

— Aloha R & R program announced by governor John Waihee, Lahaina News, March 27, 1991: 9.

— likely strong for summer, Lahaina News, June 6, 1991: 1.

— Michael White appointed to Governor's Tourism Council , Lahaina News, August 8, 1991: 11.

— activity desk operations to be investigated by the state, Lahaina News, October 17, 1991: 1.

— businesses take down signs soliciting time shares, Lahaina News, November 21, 1991: 1,10.

— visitor count is up, Lahaina News, November 28, 1991: 7.

— Hawaii Visitors Bureau official Joseph Collins says changes needed to increase, Lahaina News, December 5, 1991: 1,16.

— State officials predict good outlook for economy due to strong Japanese visitor market and low interest rates, Lahaina News, January 23, 1992: 5.

— increased numbers from West Coast, Lahaina News, January 30, 1992: 11.

— Maui Chamber of Commerce to promote "Maui Trade Dollars", Lahaina News, March 19, 1992: 9.

— hotel occupancy improves, Lahaina News, April 2, 1992: 12.

— A Hawaiian European Connection offering courtesy phones for German speakers, Lahaina News, April 30, 1992: 11.

— upscale resorts less important, Lahaina News, June 11, 1992: 13.

— merchants annoyed at tour guides leading tourists to stores that "grease the palm" of the drivers, Lahaina News, August 13, 1992: 12.

— guests at Lokelani Condominiums complain about smell of algae, Lahaina News, December 3, 1992: 3.

— hotels expect slow year, Lahaina News, December 31, 1992: 10.

— Japanese travelers expected to level, Lahaina News, January 21, 1993: 8.

— legislators crack down on timeshare sales practices, Lahaina News, March 25, 1993: 1.

— LahainaTown Action Committee opposes timeshare sales practices, Lahaina News, March 25, 1993: 4.

— president of Aloha Resorts International Mark Wan comments on industry, Lahaina News, June 3, 1993: 8.

— law to ban sale of activities below cost to deter timeshares, Lahaina News, July 1, 1993: 1,12.

— State Director of Business/Economic Development and Tourism Mufi Hannemann speaks to business and visitor industry leaders, Lahaina News, July 1, 1993: 7.

— slumps in Lahaina, Lahaina News, August 5, 1993: 1,12.

— tour drivers/guies to receive professional certification, Lahaina News, August 26, 1993: 10.

— resort managers say silt near coastal waters drawing visitor complaints, Lahaina News, September 9, 1993: 1.

— Hawaii Tourism Authority considering requests to promote tourism, Lahaina News, March 25, 1999: 13.

— Hawaii Tourism Authority considering requests to promote tourism, Lahaina News, April 1, 1999: 13.

— cruise ships slated to arrive, Lahaina News, April 15, 1999: 11.

— Maui visitor arrivals up, Lahaina News, May 6, 1999: 1.

— residents say environment and culture are crucial, Lahaina News, July 22, 1999: 1,16.

— Maui Hotel Association Allied Members to hold trade fair, Lahaina News, July 22, 1999: 11.

— visitor arrivals up, Lahaina News, August 12, 1999: 13.

— Maui voted "World's Best Island" by Travel and Leisure Magazine, Lahaina News, September 2, 1999: 1.

— Maui is "Best Island in the World" according to Conde Naste Traveler, Lahaina News, September 9, 1999: 10.

— visitor days and arrivals are up slightly, Lahaina News, September 9, 1999: 11.

— visitor arrivals up, Lahaina News, October 7, 1999: 13.

— training for restaurant workers to be held, Lahaina News, October 21, 1999: 13.

— cruise ships to debark, Lahaina News, October 28, 1999: 15.

— arrivals down from last year, Lahaina News, November 11, 1999: 11.

— cruise ship Statendam to debark, Lahaina News, November 25, 1999: 13.

— cruise ships to arrive at Lahaina Harbor, Lahaina News, December 23, 1999: 13.

— cruise ships to arrive at Lahaina Harbor, Lahaina News, December 30, 1999: 13.

— to be held at Keanae Ball Park, Lahaina News, December 30, 1999: 17.

— arrivals down, Lahaina News, January 6, 2000: 11.

— Maui Visitors Bureau targeting teenagers and couples in marketing efforts, Lahaina News, January 20, 2000: 1,16.

— arrivals increase, Lahaina News, May 18, 2000: 16.

— Marsha Wienert optimistic about visitor industry, Lahaina News, July 6, 2000: 1,14.

— catamaran "Shangri-La" to offer charters, Lahaina News, July 27, 2000: 14.

— arrivals reach record pace, Lahaina News, August 10, 2000: 14.

— state releases report on Hawaii's visitor industry capacity, Lahaina News, August 10, 2000: 14.

— merchant Clay "Duke" Gatchell launches campaign to greet cruise ships, Lahaina News, August 31, 2000: 1,15.

— visitor arrivals dip, Lahaina News, September 14, 2000: 16.

— cruise and military ships to visit, Lahaina News, September 28, 2000: 1.

— visitor arrivals are steady, Lahaina News, October 12, 2000: 16.

— cruise ships visiting Lahaina Harbor, Lahaina News, November 2, 2000: 12.

— visitor arrivals down in October, Lahaina News, December 7, 2000: 19.

— visitor numbers are increasing, Lahaina News, January 4, 2001: 1.

— United States Line recently launches cruise ship Patriot, Lahaina News, January 4, 2001: 14.

— arrives increased, Lahaina News, February 8, 2001: 8.

— cruise ships to arrive at Lahaina Harbor, Lahaina News, February 8, 2001: 8.

— arrivals up overall, Lahaina News, May 10, 2001: 9.

— arrivals up, Lahaina News, June 7, 2001: 8.

— forecast of growth, Lahaina News, July 12, 2001: 8.

— Maui is "World's Best Island" in Travel + Leisure magazine, Lahaina News, July 19, 2001: 18.

— Annual Visitor Research Report published, Lahaina News, August 23, 2001: 9.

— AskAboutMaui.com website launched, Lahaina News, October 4, 2001: 8.

— cruise ships arrive with increased security, Lahaina News, October 11, 2001: 1,20.

— cruise ships to visit, Lahaina News, November 1, 2001: 8.

— Maui is "Best Island in the World" in Condé Nast Traveler Readers' Choice Awards Poll, Lahaina News, November 8, 2001: 9.

— Boat Days to be held, Lahaina News, November 22, 2001: 8.

— Mansel Blackford to lecture on "Fragile Paradise—The Impact of Tourism on Maui, 1959-2000", Lahaina News, December 20, 2001: 16.

— to visit Lahaina Harbor, Lahaina News, December 20, 2001: 9.

— to visit Lahaina Harbor, Lahaina News, January 10, 2002: 8.

— cruise ships to visit, Lahaina News, January 10, 2002: 8.

— visitor count declines in January, Lahaina News, February 28, 2002: 8.

— Hawaii Tourism Authority and the Office of Economic Development to present tourism program at Maui Community College , Lahaina News, June 13, 2002: 5.

— Department of Business, Economic Development and Tourism seeks input on Sustainable Tourism Study, Lahaina News, September 26, 2002: 8.

— state seeking input for Sustainable Tourism Study, Lahaina News, October 3, 2002: 8.

— grants awarded by Hawaii Tourism Authority, Lahaina News, October 24, 2002: 8.

— cruise ships to visit, Lahaina News, March 27, 2003: 8.

— cruise ships to visit, Lahaina News, April 10, 2003: 14.

— Maui County Council Parks and Agriculture Committee to consider bill on commercial ocean recreational activity, Lahaina News, August 14, 2003: 12.

— cruise ship visitor numbers increase, Lahaina News, September 11, 2003: 8.

— consultants to explain Sustainable Tourism Study, Lahaina News, September 18, 2003: 8.

TOWER OF POWER [MUSICAL GROUP]
— performance reviewed, Lahaina News, May 16, 1984: 14.

TOWILL CORPORATION
— seeking to use treated sewage for irrigation, Lahaina Sun, December 23, 1970: 11.

— construction of sewage system, Lahaina Sun, March 10, 1971: 8.

— reports on sewage system for West Maui, Lahaina Sun, March 31, 1971: 1,8.

TOWNCRIERS, THE [MUSICAL GROUP]
— to perform at Moondoggies with Benny Collins Uyetake, Lahaina News, July 9, 1992: 17.

TOWNSLEY, HUGH
— doctor elected zone chairman with the Kihei Community Association, Lahaina Sun, December 2, 1970: 4.

— doctor to manage cancer prevention study, Lahaina News, August 1, 1982: 10.

TOY STORE, THE [BUSINESS]
— moves to new location, Lahaina News, October 22, 1998: 17.

TOYAMA, BENJAMIN
— labor leader opposes Maui banning nuclear-powered ships, Lahaina News, October 10, 1984: 2.

TOYOTA [BUSINESS]
— has best record for Hawaii's "Lemon List", Lahaina News, January 9, 1991: 3.

TOYS
— Christmas ideas, Lahaina News, December 19, 1990: 17,18.

TOYS FOR TOTS
— run to be held, Lahaina News, December 7, 1988: 16,24.

— sponsored by Fantasy Islands Activities and Tours, Inc., Lahaina News, November 22, 1989: 3.

— to be held at Trans/Pacific Restaurants, Lahaina News, November 17, 1994: 4.
— holiday parade to be held, Lahaina News, December 8, 1994: 3.
— parade described, Lahaina News, December 15, 1994: 1,7.
— distributing toys, Lahaina News, December 7, 1995: 3.
— drive continues, Lahaina News, December 14, 1995: 18.
— bikers collect toys for, Lahaina News, December 14, 1995: 8.
— drive to be held at Lahaina Cannery Mall, Lahaina News, November 26, 1998: 16.
— collection donations, Lahaina News, December 3, 1998: 11.
— Princess Nahienaena Elementary School students volunteer at, Lahaina News, December 21, 2000: 1,15.

TOZIER, ADRIENNE
— wins grand prize at Whalers Village's "Back for More?" contest, Lahaina News, March 28, 2002: 9.

TPG (THE PERCUSSION GROUP CINCINNATI)
— to join the Maui Symphony Orchestra, Lahaina News, March 15, 2001: 20.

TRADE COMMISSION, U.S. FEDERAL
— provides advice on Internet auctions, Lahaina News, March 2, 2000: 11.

TRADEWINDS DOJO
— to hold deep yoga, Lahaina News, December 21, 2000: 7.

TRADEWINDS GALLERY [BUSINESS]
— opens, Lahaina News, August 9, 1989: 13.

TRADEWINDSURF
— windsurfing club to meet, Lahaina News, May 13, 1987: 3.

TRAFFIC
— one-way traffic proposed for Front Street, Lahaina Sun, July 7, 1971: 1,9.
— Councilman Marco Meyer asks for law aimed at slow drivers, Lahaina Sun, September 22, 1971: 7.
— Maui County Council recommends increasing speed limit on Honoapi'ilani Highway, Lahaina Sun, October 6, 1971: 1.
— decision on changing speed limit is deferred, Lahaina Sun, October 20, 1971: 15.
— police oppose law against slow drivers, Lahaina Sun, November 10, 1971: 13.
— jay-walking ordinance receives initial approval, Lahaina Sun, November 24, 1971: 12.
— Paul Myers proposes horse-drawn streetcars in Lahaina , Lahaina Sun, March 8, 1972: 5.
— editorial discussion of current situation, Lahaina Sun, May 17, 1972: 19.
— final design for first traffic signal in West Maui, Lahaina Sun, September 27, 1972: 10.
— disrupted by cane fires, Lahaina Sun, November 15, 1972: 9.
— traffic violations by those under 18 now to be handled in district court, Lahaina Sun, November 29, 1972: 11.
— current issues in Hawaii discussed, Lahaina Sun, November 29, 1972: 17.
— first stop light will be installed in 1973, Lahaina Sun, December 20, 1972: 15.
— signs changed so drivers must stop before turning right, Lahaina Sun, February 28, 1973: 3.
— driving conditions on Maui discussed, Lahaina Sun, February 28, 1973: 9.
— West Maui Ad Hoc Committee on Traffic seeks roller skate ban, Lahaina News, April 15, 1980: 13.
— road widening near Kamehameha III school completed, Lahaina News, October 1, 1980: 4.
— part 1 of a series of editorials criticizing current conditions of, Lahaina News, January 4, 1984: 2.

— part 2 of a series of editorials criticizing current conditions of, Lahaina News, January 11, 1984: 2.
— highway safety improved in 1983, Lahaina News, February 8, 1984: 7.
— editorial complaining about, Lahaina News, July 23, 1986: 2.
— eased with opening of cane haul road, Lahaina News, November 5, 1986: 16.
— county and Army Corps of Engineers agree to ease bottleneck in Lahaina, Lahaina News, April 8, 1987: 1.
— Honoapi'ilani Highway traffic delayed, Lahaina News, May 13, 1987: 3.
— new laws come into effect, Lahaina News, August 26, 1987: 3.
— survey results released, Lahaina News, December 14, 1988: 1,24.
— witnesses sought following accident, Lahaina News, February 6, 1991: 3.
— increases 9% in West Maui, Lahaina News, July 18, 1991: 1.
— longer parking hours sought by LahainaTown Action Committee, Lahaina News, May 21, 1992: 1.
— new speed limit set for parts of Piilani Highway, Lahaina News, November 19, 1992: 5.
— slows because of sewer line replacement, Lahaina News, March 11, 1993: 2.
— traffic jams on Honoapi'ilani Highway should not last longer than July 30, Lahaina News, July 14, 1994: 1.
— community seeks overpass on Honoapi'ilani Highway, Lahaina News, December 29, 1994: 1.
— issues discussed, Lahaina News, March 9, 1995: 3.
— opinions from residents sought on, Lahaina News, February 22, 1996: 3.
— mitigation to be discussed at Lahaina Civic Center, Lahaina News, January 30, 1997: 1.
— issues in North Beach to be discussed by Maui Planning Commission, Lahaina News, February 20, 1997: 1.
— police forms Highway Incident Traffic Team to deal with highway closures, Lahaina News, April 5, 2001: 1,24.
— West Maui Taxpayers Association completes study to prove highway is dangerous, Lahaina News, May 10, 2001: 3.
— see also infrastructure

TRAFFIC COMMITTEE
— mayor seeking input into issues, Lahaina News, April 5, 2001: 22.

TRAFFIC SAFETY TEAM
— Lahainaluna High School team wins national safety honors, Lahaina News, August 3, 1995: 2.

TRAINING CENTER
— to hold courses in CPR and first aid, Lahaina News, March 14, 1996: 11.
— to offer CPR classes, Lahaina News, November 13, 1997: 20.

TRAMP [FILM]
— to be shown at Kihei School Auditorium, Lahaina News, April 22, 1993: 15.

TRANS AIR [BUSINESS]
— begins daily passenger service between Moloka'i and Honolulu, Lahaina News, June 29, 1995: 10.

TRANS HAWAII-MAUI, INC. [BUSINESS]
— awarded contract for Kahului Airport, Lahaina News, December 28, 1995: 10.

TRANS-HAWAIIAN SERVICES, INC. [BUSINESS]
— trolley services between West Maui and Wailea announced, Lahaina News, March 19, 1998: 11.
— introducing trolley service, Lahaina News, March 26, 1998: 11.
— trolleys now in service, Lahaina News, April 9, 1998: 13.

TRANS/PACIFIC RESTAURANTS
— to participate in Toys for Tots, Lahaina News, November 17, 1994: 4.

TRANSCENDENTAL MEDITATION
— practiced on Maui, Lahaina Sun, September 13, 1972: 7.
— Katrina Pittman to offer lecture on, Lahaina News, July 8, 1993: 4.
— talk on to be held at West Maui Youth Center Computer Room, Lahaina News, October 22, 1998: 21.

TRANSIENTS
— see hippies

TRANSIT ACCOMMODATIONS TAX
— Linda Lingle tells residents to lobby for county's share of, Lahaina News, January 15, 1998: 1,16.

TRANSPACIFIC YACHT RACE
— won by Windward Passage, Lahaina Sun, July 28, 1971: 8.
— Roy Disney's yacht first monohull to break eight days, Lahaina News, July 17, 1997: 15.

TRANSPORTATION
— public meeting in Wailuku with State Department of Transportation to discuss needs, Lahaina Sun, December 2, 1970: 1.
— Kentron Hawaii proposes interisland hydrofoil, Lahaina Sun, September 1, 1971: 15.
— ferry planned between Maui, Moloka'i, and Lana'i, Lahaina News, March 7, 1984: 17.
— Royal Hawaiian Carriages hopes to begin operation in Lahaina, Lahaina News, February 13, 1992: 1,6.
— bus service discussed, Lahaina News, April 18, 1996: 17.

TRANSPORTATION ACTION COMMITTEE
— seeking input on traffic, Lahaina News, March 1, 2001: 20.

TRANSPORTATION, STATE COMMISSION OF
— to hold public information meeting, Lahaina News, May 18, 1988: 1.

TRANSPORTATION, STATE DEPARTMENT OF
— to study Honoapi'ilani Highway bypass around Lahaina, Lahaina News, July 4, 1984: 18.
— studying Lahaina Bypass, Lahaina News, July 30, 1986: 11.
— to hold public meetings on proposed safety inspection rules, Lahaina News, January 21, 1987: 10.
— plans to move Carthaginian, Lahaina News, June 3, 1987: 1.
— to develop computerized transportation system, Lahaina News, July 22, 1987: 3.
— performing road tests, Lahaina News, August 19, 1987: 3.
— to hold public hearings on changes to Lahaina Boat Harbor, Lahaina News, October 28, 1987: 12.
— to hold public hearings on rules for aviation, Lahaina News, October 28, 1987: 3.
— opens more parking at Kahului Airport, Lahaina News, December 9, 1987: 3.
— to hold public meetings on rules of airports and small boat harbors, Lahaina News, January 13, 1988: 16.
— to speed up Lahaina Bypass and road widening, Lahaina News, January 20, 1988: 1.
— comments on Aloha Voyages' request for water use permit, Lahaina News, February 3, 1988: 1,23.
— hears testimony regarding rates changes at harbor and new rules for ocean use, Lahaina News, February 3, 1988: 3.
— accepting applications for off-shore mooring permits, Lahaina News, March 2, 1988: 22.
— considers limiting thrillcraft to four locations, Lahaina News, March 30, 1988: 1.
— seeking community groups to clean up state highways and harbors, Lahaina News, April 27, 1988: 6.
— to hold meeting on Ocean Recreation Management Plan, Lahaina News, May 25, 1988: 10.
— dispute over shoreline in Ka'anapali holds up jurisdiction change, Lahaina News, July 20, 1988: 1,14.

— gets control of near-shore waters off Ka'anapali, Lahaina News, August 10, 1988: 18.
— accepting permits for commercial activities in shore waters near Ka'anapali, Lahaina News, August 10, 1988: 3.
— releases traffic study, Lahaina News, December 14, 1988: 1,24.
— seeking volunteers to provide transportation to elderly and handicapped, Lahaina News, February 15, 1989: 5,13.
— to hold public hearing on results regulating tour aircraft operations, Lahaina News, May 24, 1989: 2.
— to begin renovations to Mala Wharf, Lahaina News, June 28, 1989: 3.
— awareness campaign on hazards of drunk driving, Lahaina News, November 29, 1989: 36.
— awards security contract to C & C Electrical contractors, Lahaina News, December 20, 1989: 4.
— assures West Maui Taxpayers Association that Lahaina Bypass development will continue, Lahaina News, January 17, 1990: 24.
— awards contract to R.I. Namba Construction to remove abandoned pines, Lahaina News, January 24, 1990: 6.
— contract to improve Ma'alaea Boat Harbor awarded to Bernard W. Despins & Despins General Construction, Inc., Lahaina News, August 15, 1990: 11.
— proposes new rules for ocean recreation areas, Lahaina News, September 12, 1990: 1.
— Notice of Public Hearing, Lahaina News, September 12, 1990: 27.
— moving forward with plans to buy Kapalua-West Maui airport, Lahaina News, December 5, 1990: 1.
— to hold hearing on Kahului Airport, Lahaina News, December 19, 1990: 5,6.
— awards Pacific Construction Co., Ltd. to improve Keolani Place, Lahaina News, December 19, 1990: 7.
— to hold hearing on Kahului Airport, Lahaina News, December 26, 1990: 5.
— to hold public hearing on Kahului Airport , Lahaina News, January 2, 1991: 3.
— awards contract to repair shed at Kahului Harbor to Walter Y. Arakaki, Lahaina News, January 9, 1991: 5.
— reminds commercial drivers to renew licenses, Lahaina News, January 30, 1991: 4.
— awards contract to Hawaiian Bitumuls and Paving Co. to resurface North Kihei Road, Lahaina News, February 27, 1991: 8.
— studying where to relocate residents displaced by Lahaina Bypass, Lahaina News, March 13, 1991: 1.
— awards road construction contract to Kiewit Pacific Co., Lahaina News, June 13, 1991: 18.
— seeking groups to participate in Adopt-A-Hawaii program, Lahaina News, August 1, 1991: 5.
— Sports Pro Hawaii, Inc. and GTE Hawaiian Tel have participated in Adopt-A-Highway program, Lahaina News, October 17, 1991: 7.
— awards contracts for services at Maui harbors, Lahaina News, October 31, 1991: 10.
— awards contracts for services at Maui harbors, Lahaina News, November 7, 1991: 9.
— to hold public hearing on Draft Environmental Impact Statement for Kahului Airport Master Plan, Lahaina News, November 7, 1991: 9.
— awards contract to Jacky Dugied to repair comfort station at Ma'alaea boat harbor, Lahaina News, January 23, 1992: 12.
— awards contracts for work at Lana'i Airport, Lahaina News, January 30, 1992: 12.
— Adopt-A-Highway program expands, Lahaina News, February 13, 1992: 4.
— director Rex Johnson to conduct dedication ceremony for new terminal at Kahului airport, Lahaina News, February 20, 1992: 10.
— to hold public hearing on rules governing small harbors, Lahaina News, May 7, 1992: 3.

— awards contract to Jacky Dugied to repair wharf at Lahaina Boat Harbor, Lahaina News, May 28, 1992: 4.

— to hold meeting on new fuel handling procedures at public airports, Lahaina News, July 2, 1992: 4.

— to complete Environmental Impact Statement for Kahului Airport Master Plan, Lahaina News, July 30, 1992: 5.

— awards contract to replace Hoolawa Bridge on the Hana Highway, Lahaina News, August 27, 1992: 4.

— awards contract to modify Moloka'i Airport, Lahaina News, October 1, 1992: 11.

— announces resurfacing of Haleakala Crater Road to begin, Lahaina News, November 5, 1992: 4,5.

— announces work to begin on Hoolawa Bridge, Lahaina News, December 24, 1992: 5.

— to hold hearing on Statewide Master Plan for Bikeways, Lahaina News, January 14, 1993: 3.

— to hold public meeting on Statewide Transportation Program, Lahaina News, January 21, 1993: 4.

— to hold public meeting on bikeways plan, Lahaina News, January 21, 1993: 4.

— awards contract to pave parking areas at Ma'alaea Boat Harbor, Lahaina News, May 6, 1993: 7.

— to hold meeting on operating motor vehicles at public airports and airport noise, Lahaina News, June 24, 1993: 4.

— awards contract to E.T. Ige Construction for boat ramp at Kahului Harbor, Lahaina News, July 8, 1993: 4.

— awards contract for resurfacing parts of Mokulele Highway, Lahaina News, September 30, 1993: 6.

— to improve intersection of Honoapi'ilani Highway, Lahaina News, December 30, 1993: 3.

— fees for motor vehicle safety inspections to increase, Lahaina News, April 28, 1994: 4,5.

— approves money to widen Ka'anapali Parkway, Lahaina News, August 18, 1994: 5.

— sponsoring program aimed at drug-impaired drivers, Lahaina News, August 25, 1994: 5.

— to hold meeting on Kahului Airport Noise Compatibility Program, Lahaina News, December 15, 1994: 7.

— considering options for new harbor, Lahaina News, August 3, 1995: 1,20.

— to discuss Lahaina Bypass, Lahaina News, May 9, 1996: 3.

— announces that Honoapi'ilani Highway to be resurfaced, Lahaina News, August 22, 1996: 5.

— to place signs to warn motorists following accident, Lahaina News, October 10, 1996: 1,20.

— issues with beach wall near Launiupoko discussed, Lahaina News, October 10, 1996: 3.

— Environmental Impact Statement for widening of Honoapi'ilani Highway completed, Lahaina News, April 3, 1997: 3.

— awards Rimrock Paving Co. to resurface highway, Lahaina News, July 10, 1997: 2.

— to hold hearing on highway widening, Lahaina News, March 19, 1998: 1,16.

— plans to resurface Honoapi'ilani Highway, Lahaina News, June 4, 1998: 1,20.

— to hold hearings on proposed Kihei-Upcountry Maui highway project, Lahaina News, September 23, 1999: 5.

— holding meeting on issues for aviation community, Lahaina News, October 14, 1999: 13.

— to hold public meeting for Paia Bypass Road, Lahaina News, February 17, 2000: 16.

— Bob Siarot meets with residents to discuss highway project issues, Lahaina News, March 30, 2000: 5.

— to hold public hearing on administrative rules, Lahaina News, August 3, 2000: 17.

— to discuss interim improvements to Honoapi'ilani Highway, Lahaina News, May 17, 2001: 1.

— to hold hearings on airport rules, Lahaina News, September 6, 2001: 17.

— to hold public meeting on consolidating administrative rules , Lahaina News, February 21, 2002: 17.

— to hold information meeting on improvements to Piilani Highway, Lahaina News, March 21, 2002: 16.

— to hold public hearings on updating bicycle master plan, Lahaina News, April 25, 2002: 17.

— to hold meeting on Statewide Transportation Improvement Program (STIP), Lahaina News, May 22, 2003: 3.

— seeks companies that qualify as Disadvantaged Business Enterprises (DBE), Lahaina News, June 5, 2003: 8.

— director Rodney Haraga discusses improvements to transportation, Lahaina News, July 3, 2003: 1,18.

— Highways Division Planning Branch to hold public hearing, Lahaina News, July 24, 2003: 1,18.

— seeking input on transportation projects, Lahaina News, July 31, 2003: 5.

— holds public forum, Lahaina News, August 7, 2003: 1,18.

— to discuss Lahaina Bypass, Lahaina News, August 21, 2003: 1.

TRASH BASH
— to be held, Lahaina News, May 14, 1992: 3.

TRASK JR., DAVID
— criticizers The Hawaiians, Lahaina Sun, February 10, 1971: 8.

TRATTORIA [RESTAURANT]
— new name for The Spats, Lahaina News, June 2, 1994: 11.

TRATTORIA HAIKU [RESTAURANT]
— featured, Lahaina News, April 2, 1998: 6,7.

TRATTORIA II BUCANIERE [RESTAURANT]
— adds breakfast, Lahaina News, October 17, 1996: 16.

TRAVEL
— baggage inspection soon to be available on Maui, Kaua'i and the Big Island, Lahaina Sun, January 3, 1973: 10.

TRAVEL AND LEISURE [MAGAZINE]
— votes Napili Kai Beach Club as top ten, Lahaina News, March 11, 1999: 11.

— Maui is "World's Best Island" in, Lahaina News, July 19, 2001: 18.

TRAVEL HOLIDAY MAGAZINE
— honors Ka'anapali Beach Hotel with Wanda Award, Lahaina News, July 26, 2001: 8.

TRAVEL INDUSTRY ASSOCIATION OF AMERICA
— Ka'anapali Beach Hotel's CD "E Ho'omau I Ka Po'okela" wins cultural heritage award, Lahaina News, September 21, 2000: 11.

TRAVEL INDUSTRY MANAGEMENT, SCHOOL OF
— picnic planned, Lahaina News, April 26, 1989: 3.

TRAVEL MARKETING COMPANY [BUSINESS]
— to be advertising agent for Old Lahaina Cafe and Luau, Lahaina News, August 8, 1990: 6.

TRAVEL MASTERS [BUSINESS]
— now associated with Ask Mr. Foster Associates, Lahaina News, November 4, 1987: 10.

TRAVEL PLAZA TRANSPORTATION INC. [BUSINESS]
— see JTB Hawaii Inc.

TRAVEL WRITERS
— see American Society of Travel Writers

TRAVELING MINI-SCIENCE CARNIVAL
— to be held at Ka'ahumanu Center, Lahaina News, July 16, 1998: 2.

TRAVELODGE
— to be converted to office and shopping complex, Lahaina News, June 5, 1985: 1.

TRAVINO, LEE
— golfer scheduled to play at GTE Ka'anapali Classic, Lahaina News, December 5, 1990: 8.

TRAVIS, RANDY [MUSICIAN]
— to perform at Royal Lahaina Tennis Stadium, Lahaina News, May 21, 1992: 16.
— to perform at Royal Lahaina Tennis Stadium, Lahaina News, May 28, 1992: 14,16.
— to perform this Sunday, Lahaina News, June 11, 1992: 18.
— bought a meal for the homeless, Lahaina News, July 2, 1992: 4.

TREADWELL, FOREST
— wins senior men's division of Cycle to the Sun, Lahaina News, September 17, 1992: 4.

TREASURE ISLAND [BUSINESS]
— opens at Lahaina Cannery Mall, Lahaina News, July 11, 2002: 8.

TREE CHEERS
— to be held at The Wharf Cinema Center, Lahaina News, December 19, 2002: 20.

TREE GARDEN RESTAURANT AND BAR
— loses its license due to financial difficulties, Lahaina Sun, January 19, 1972: 7.

TREECYCLING DAY
— to be organized by Maui County, Lahaina News, December 28, 2000: 2.

TREES
— Eucalyptus trees cut down, Lahaina Sun, April 7, 1971: 6.

TRELEASE, JIM [WRITER]
— to speak at Kamehameha III School, Lahaina News, January 17, 1990: 5.
— to lecture at King Kamehameha III School on importance of reading aloud, Lahaina News, January 24, 1990: 4.

TREMBLAY, JOSEPH
— search suspected for missing kayaker, Lahaina News, March 11, 1993: 11.

TREMBLEY, LISA-GAY [COMEDIAN]
— to perform at Honolulu Comedy Club, Lahaina News, November 23, 1995: 11,12.

TREMEWEN, IAN [ARTIST]
— work featured, Lahaina News, August 1, 1981: 4.
— work to be exhibited at Village Gallery, Lahaina News, August 1, 1984: 13.
— work discussed, Lahaina News, August 15, 1984: 13.
— career described, spends half his year in Australia, Lahaina News, August 14, 1985: 7.
— works to be featured at The Village Gallery, Lahaina News, August 12, 1987: 3.
— work on display at Village Gallery, Lahaina News, September 6, 1989: 4.
— to exhibit at Village Galleries, Lahaina News, August 15, 1991: 16.
— to exhibit at Village Gallery, Lahaina News, August 11, 1994: 12.
— watercolorist to exhibit at Village Gallery Contemporary, Lahaina News, February 8, 2001: 11.
— to exhibit at Village Gallery, Lahaina News, February 8, 2001: 20.

TREVOR AND RENE [MUSICAL GROUP]
— to perform at Pioneer Inn, Lahaina News, April 18, 1990: 11.

TRI-ISLAND BASKETBALL TOURNAMENT
— schedule, Lahaina Sun, February 24, 1971: 7.

TRI-ISLE RESOURCE CONSERVATION AND DEVELOPMENT PROJECT
— approved by U.S. Department of Agriculture, Lahaina Sun, May 5, 1971: 1.
— council to pinpoint Hawaiian division of lands, Lahaina News, August 28, 1997: 1,3.

TRI-STAR RESTAURANT GROUP
— George Gomes Jr. becomes corporate chef with, Lahaina News, December 14, 2000: 18.

TRIAL OF GOLDILOCKS, THE [PLAY]
— to be performed by Maui Academy of Performing Arts, Lahaina News, September 9, 1993: 11.

TRIANGLE SQUARE FACTORY STORES
— first building completed, Lahaina News, September 29, 1994: 10.

TRIBUTE [PLAY]
— to be performed by Maui Community Theatre, Lahaina News, May 8, 1991: 21.
— continues, Lahaina News, May 15, 1991: 12.
— performances continue, Lahaina News, May 23, 1991: 16.

TRIDENT TECHNOLOGIES [BUSINESS]
— trains firefighters on Sea Patch/ProgMag kit, Lahaina News, November 30, 2000: 12.

TRILLING, STEVE [COMEDIAN]
— to perform at Comedy Club and the Sports Page, Lahaina News, January 9, 1991: 7.

TRILOGY EXCURSIONS [BUSINESS]
— hired Gilbert and Associations Advertising Agency, Lahaina News, September 4, 1985: 3.
— celebrates 20th anniversary, Lahaina News, October 21, 1993: 11.
— appoints Dalina Nolan-Kahahane as reservation manager, Lahaina News, September 22, 1994: 13.
— rated best activity on Maui, Lahaina News, September 5, 1996: 22.
— sponsoring whale watch trip with Light Bringers Rescue Mission, Lahaina News, March 5, 1998: 17.
— announces new appointments, Lahaina News, May 14, 1998: 13.
— adds rigid aluminum inflatable vessel to fleet, Lahaina News, July 9, 1998: 12.
— adds new pavilion at Manale Bay, Lahaina News, October 29, 1998: 20.
— offering Whale Watch Programs, Lahaina News, January 14, 1999: 11.
— to offer "Discover Lana'i Sunset Sail", Lahaina News, May 20, 1999: 13.
— "Discover Lana'i Sunset Sail" leaves later, Lahaina News, June 3, 1999: 13.
— Chris Walsh appointed as new operations general manager at, Lahaina News, September 9, 1999: 11.
— creates Research and Development Division, Lahaina News, September 30, 1999: 11.
— named Tour and Activity Vendor of the Year by Classic Custom Vacations, Lahaina News, November 18, 1999: 13.
— Hawaii Wildlife Fund to certify employees as naturalists, Lahaina News, August 10, 2000: 14.
— acquires a new catamaran, Lahaina News, August 24, 2000: 14.
— names Robin Kragness as office manager, Lahaina News, April 5, 2001: 9.
— Denni Paull new assistant director of marketing, Lahaina News, April 12, 2001: 8.
— now offers Discover Kayaking Adventure, Lahaina News, January 17, 2002: 8.
— whale watching trips to be led by Jean-Michel Cousteau, Lahaina News, March 14, 2002: 5.
— offering kama'aina special rate, Lahaina News, June 20, 2002: 8.
— offering kama'aina rate, Lahaina News, February 20, 2003: 8.
— Mike Johnston new food and beverage director, Lahaina News, April 24, 2003: 14.
— Mike Jones promoted to Scuba Manager-Safety Manager-Quality Assurance position, Lahaina News, May 15, 2003: 8.
— supports Project S.E.A.-Link's Adopt-a-Reef Program, Lahaina News, October 2, 2003: 5.

TRINITY EPISCOPAL CHURCH
— to hold Christmas Prelude Crafts Fair, Lahaina News, November 14, 1991: 3.
— to hold Christmas Prelude Crafts Fair, Lahaina News, November 21, 1991: 4.
— to hold Hoʻoaloha Kolepa Golf Tournament, Lahaina News, March 19, 1992: 8.
— to hold rummage sale, Lahaina News, May 21, 1992: 4.
— to hold craft fair, Lahaina News, July 16, 1992: 6.
— to hold rummage sale, Lahaina News, August 27, 1992: 13.
— to hold rummage sale, Lahaina News, April 15, 1993: 4.

TRIP TO THE TOY SHOP [BALLET]
— to be performed at Lahaina Methodist Church, Lahaina News, June 3, 1987: 3.

TRIPP, NICCI
— chef to offer "Making Delicious Pasta", Lahaina News, May 17, 2001: 20.

TRIPSICHORE YOGA THEATRE [TROUPE]
— London group to perform at Maui Arts and Cultural Center, Lahaina News, February 8, 2001: 18.
— Yoga Dance Troupe to perform at Maui Arts and Cultural Center, Lahaina News, April 11, 2002: 16.

TROJAN SEED COMPANY [BUSINESS]
— developing corn variety in Maui, Lahaina Sun, May 31, 1972: 4.

TRONO, ISMAEL [ARTIST]
— to hold watercolor classes, Lahaina News, September 19, 1996: 16.

TROPE, LOU
— chef featured, Lahaina News, August 1, 1996: 6,7.

TROPIC PROVISIONS BOOKSTORE AND COFFEE SHOP [BUSINESS]
— opens, Lahaina News, August 18, 1994: 15.
— now offering evening events, Lahaina News, November 3, 1994: 26.

TROPIC TEMPTATIONS [BUSINESS]
— destination management company has new management, Lahaina News, November 16, 2000: 12.

TROPICA [RESTAURANT]
— opens at the Westin Maui, Lahaina News, December 28, 2000: 16.
— featured, Lahaina News, February 1, 2001: 10.
— featured, Lahaina News, June 7, 2001: 16,17.
— featured, Lahaina News, May 1, 2003: 9.

TROPICAL ARTWARE-MAUI
— opens in Wharf Shopping Center, Lahaina News, November 29, 1989: 4.

TROPICAL ARTWARE-MAUI [BUSINESS]
— expanding, Lahaina News, August 5, 1993: 7.

TROPICAL COURTYARD [BUSINESS]
— to host hula show, Lahaina News, October 15, 1998: 16.

TROPICAL FRUIT FESTIVAL
— to be held at Lahaina Cannery Mall, Lahaina News, July 9, 1998: 17.
— to be held at Lahaina Cannery Mall, Lahaina News, July 16, 1998: 16.

TROPICAL GANGSTER [MUSICAL GROUP]
— to perform at Tiger Restaurant, Lahaina News, July 11, 1990: 15.

TROPICAL GARDENS OF MAUI
— opening in Iao in March, Lahaina News, February 18, 1987: 10.

TROPICAL HEAT [MUSICAL GROUP]
— performance reviewed, Lahaina News, September 5, 1984: 12.

TROPICAL JEWELERS [BUSINESS]
— opens, Lahaina News, January 23, 2003: 8.

TROPICAL KIDS [BUSINESS]
— opens at Wharf Cinema Center, Lahaina News, June 24, 1999: 11.

TROPICAL PRODUCTS PACKING CO. [BUSINESS]
— seeking special use permit, Lahaina News, September 10, 1992: 4.

TROPICAL RHYTHMS [MUSICAL GROUP]
— to perform at Inu Inu Lounge, Lahaina News, March 31, 1994: 15.
— to perform at Moose McGillycuddy's, Lahaina News, November 3, 1994: 27.

TROPICANA [BUSINESS]
— opens at The Shops at Kapalua, Lahaina News, October 6, 1994: 11.

TROTTER, FRED
— appointed to Longs board of directors, Lahaina News, August 23, 1989: 6.
— appointed director of Maui Land and Pineapple, Lahaina News, December 3, 1992: 4.

TROTTIER, TOM [SCULPTOR]
— work featured, Lahaina News, January 15, 1986: 11.

TROUBLE IN PARADISE [MUSICAL GROUP]
— to perform at Keg Boathouse, Lahaina News, July 8, 1987: 24.

TROUT, TAYLOR JEAN
— wins Maui Mini Miss American Starlet beauty pageant, Lahaina News, March 15, 2001: 1.
— succeeds in Talent Competition, Lahaina News, August 28, 2003: 3.

TROY BARBOZA LAW ENFORCEMENT TORCH RUN
— to benefit Special Olympics, Lahaina News, May 7, 1992: 14.
— to be held, Lahaina News, April 2, 1998: 15.
— to benefit Special Olympics, Lahaina News, April 6, 2000: 7.

TRUDEAU, HELEN BARROW
— to lead creative dance class, Lahaina News, May 1, 1997: 16.

TRUDEAU, PIERRE-ELLIOT
— Canadian Prime Minister leaves Maui after week-long trip in Kihei, Lahaina Sun, May 2, 1973: 4.

TRUDELL, JOHN
— American Indian poet to speak at Maui Community College, Lahaina News, February 17, 2000: 16.

TRUE WEST [PLAY]
— to be performed by Independent Theatre Inc., Lahaina News, July 29, 1999: 12.
— to be performed, Lahaina News, August 5, 1999: 12.

TRUMAN, HARRY [PRESIDENT]
— character recalled by Lieutenant Col. Karl Leebrick, Lahaina Sun, January 3, 1973: 14.

TRUMP, DONALD
— visits Maui, Lahaina News, November 7, 1991: 1.
— visits Swan Court restaurant at Hyatt Regency Maui, proposes to Marla Maples, Lahaina News, January 16, 1992: 14.

TRUSTY, JEANNE
— Betsill Brothers Construction appoints as director of marketing communications, Lahaina News, July 19, 2001: 9.

TRUTHAN, ED [MUSICIAN]
— to perform at Aloha Cantina, Lahaina News, February 17, 1994: 11.
— performs at Cheeseburger in Paradise, Lahaina News, September 1, 1994: 15.

TRYGSTAD, ANNE
— supporting long-term care programs, Lahaina News, January 9, 2003: 8.

TS RESTAURANTS [BUSINESS]
— promotions announced, Lahaina News, March 9, 1995: 6.
— joins Kimo's Restaurant in recognizing teacher Karyn Murphy, Lahaina News, March 28, 2002: 9.
— honors teaches Anna Sprinkle and Robert Siarot, Lahaina News, June 13, 2002: 5.
— recognized for community service by the National Restaurant Association, Lahaina News, January 23, 2003: 8.

TSE, CHRISTIAN
— jewelry to be featured at Hutton's Fine Jewelers, Lahaina News, January 25, 2001: 16.

TSHOMBE, FULTON [MUSICIAN]
— to perform at Villa Lounge, Lahaina News, September 17, 1992: 14.

TSUBAKI, KERRI
— crowned queen at Chrysanthemum Ball, Lahaina News, January 21, 1999: 2.

TSUHA, KALEI
— storyteller to offer "Tales of the Sea", Lahaina News, November 5, 1998: 20.

TSUKANO, SHIRLEY
— appointed sales manager-kama'aina market for Aston Hotels and Resorts, Lahaina News, July 2, 1992: 18.
— appointed sales manager-kama'aina market for Aston Hotels and Resorts, Lahaina News, July 9, 1992: 14.

TSUKIYAMA, DONALD
— appointed to state position of Public Defender, Lahaina Sun, November 24, 1971: 6.

TSUNAMI
— warning leads to evacuation, Lahaina News, May 14, 1986: 1,20.
— editorial praising Civil Defense's response, Lahaina News, May 14, 1986: 2.
— history of, Lahaina News, December 1, 1994: 2.

TSUNAMI [BUSINESS]
— dance club at Grand Hyatt Wailea, Lahaina News, January 2, 1992: 12.

TSUTSUI, VALERIE
— calls for criminal probe of son's drug death, Lahaina News, April 11, 1996: 14.

TSUTSUMI, MATSATO
— develops world's first pineapple planting machine, Lahaina Sun, May 31, 1972: 5.

TSUZUKI, RON
— comments on delay of Lahaina Bypass, Lahaina News, August 17, 1988: 1,20.

TUBERCULOSIS
— Testing program, Lahaina Sun, January 6, 1971: 2.

TUCSON ARIZONA BOYS CHOIR
— sponsored by Maui Philharmonic Society, Lahaina News, April 1, 1987: 12.

TUELL, R.J. "DICK"
— elected chairman of Maui Republican Party, Lahaina News, May 14, 1986: 3.

TUIKOLOVATU, AISEA
— Tongan journalist on Maui, Lahaina News, December 17, 1986: 2.
— resident featured, Lahaina News, August 3, 1988: 2.

TUIPULOTU, LITEA
— successes at swimming competitions, Lahaina News, June 30, 1994: 6.

TULLY, BILL [ARTIST]
— to exhibit at Lahaina Arts Society Gallery, Lahaina News, April 9, 1998: 16.
— to be featured at Art School at Kapalua, Lahaina News, April 8, 1999: 12.
— to exhibit "Trees 2000", Lahaina News, September 14, 2000: 20.

TUMBLEWEEDS [PLAY]
— to be performed by Maui Youth Theatre, Lahaina News, August 6, 1986: 3.

TUMPAP, PAMELA
— promoted to assistant manager of Maui Research and Technology Park, Lahaina News, June 18, 1992: 10.
— assistant program manager for Maui Research and Technology Center speaks on business plans, Lahaina News, October 26, 1995: 10.

TUNA CLUB
— featured, Lahaina News, August 14, 2003: 13.

TUPULUA, LEROY
— arrested for robbery, Lahaina News, April 2, 1992: 5.

TURNAUCKAS, ROBERT
— named catering manager of the first quarter, Lahaina News, May 23, 1990: 8.

TURNBULL, BRUCE [ARTIST]
— described at home in Waihee, Lahaina Sun, July 4, 1973: 14.
— book Who Am I Alone? reviewed, Lahaina News, November 1, 1980: 14.
— education discussed, Lahaina News, October 16, 1985: 11.
— honored for bronze sculpture at the War Memorial Complex, Lahaina News, September 19, 1990: 13.
— wood carver to be featured at Lahaina Galleries, Lahaina News, June 18, 1992: 19.
— creates Sculpture Garden Sanctuary , Lahaina News, October 24, 1996: 15.

TURNBULL, STEVE
— wood carver to be featured at Lahaina Galleries, Lahaina News, June 18, 1992: 19.
— creates Sculpture Garden Sanctuary , Lahaina News, October 24, 1996: 15.

TURNER, ARGENTINA [MUSICIAN]
— to perform at Casanova's, Lahaina News, July 2, 1992: 26.
— to perform at Moose McGillycuddy's, Lahaina News, November 3, 1994: 27.
— continues to perform at Moose McGillycuddy's, Lahaina News, March 2, 1995: 11.

TURNER, ROBERT [ARTIST]
— to present at Hui No'eau Visual Arts Center, Lahaina News, March 27, 1985: 3.

TURNER, TINA [SINGER]
— performance in Honolulu reviewed , Lahaina News, January 8, 1986: 8.

TURTLE, TIM
— diver displays ulua caught while spear fishing, Lahaina Sun, November 18, 1970: 1.
— diver mentioned , Lahaina Sun, December 23, 1970: 2.

TURTLES
— decline of population discussed, Lahaina News, May 24, 1989: 5.
— Pacific Whale Foundation to participate in "Year of the Sea Turtle", Lahaina News, October 12, 1995: 6.
— plagued by tumors, Lahaina News, May 9, 1996: 1,3.
— hawkbill turtles may be nesting at North Beach, Lahaina News, January 30, 1997: 1,16.
— freed from net, Lahaina News, September 7, 2000: 3.
— Hawaiian Sea Turtle Stranding Network expands, Lahaina News, September 7, 2000: 3.
— Maui Ocean Center researching, Lahaina News, December 19, 2002: 9.
— found tied up near Mala Wharf, Lahaina News, August 14, 2003: 1,20.

TU'UA, TAULIA MARIE
— Scholar/Athlete of the Week, Lahaina News, May 2, 1996: 20.
— graduates from Lewis and Clark College, Lahaina News, July 5, 2001: 5.

TWA AMBASSADOR [MAGAZINE]
— to feature history of Lahaina, Lahaina Sun, March 29, 1972: 9.

TWAIN, MARK
— Letters from the Sandwich Islands to be performed at Iao Theatre by McAvoy Layne, Lahaina News, July 25, 1991: 13,14.
— Baldwin Theatre Guild to perform "Big River", music based on the writings of, Lahaina News, August 1, 1991: 18.

TWELVE DAYS OF CHRISTMAS, HAWAIIAN STYLE
— local version, Lahaina News, December 19, 1984: 7,8,9.

TWINS/TRIPLETS GATHERING
— to be held, Lahaina News, May 17, 2001: 20.

TWITCHEL, BOB
— surfer featured, Lahaina Times, August, 1980 volume 4 number 7: 3, 4.

TWITCHELL, BOBBY
— Scholar/Athlete of the Week, Lahaina News, March 27, 2003: 12.

TWO FOR TEA [BUSINESS]
— matchmaking company opens, Lahaina News, November 5, 1992: 8.

TWO LEFT FEET DANCE CLUB
— to meet, Lahaina News, April 1, 1999: 17.
— continues to meet, Lahaina News, June 3, 1999: 17.
— to teach the Swing, Lahaina News, August 12, 1999: 17.

TWO NIGHTS AND A MATINEE [PRODUCTION]
— to be performed at Iao Theater, Lahaina News, May 22, 1997: 16.

TWO OF HEARTS [MUSICAL GROUP]
— to perform at Swan Court, Hyatt Regency Maui, Lahaina News, September 19, 1996: 18.

TWO PUMPS UP
— showing film "Jeffrey", Lahaina News, October 5, 1995: 10.

TWO ROOMS [PLAY]
— to be held at Maui OnStage, Lahaina News, May 15, 2003: 14.
— Lee Blessing's play to be performed by Maui OnStage, Lahaina News, May 22, 2003: 16.
— to be performed at Maui OnStage, Lahaina News, May 29, 2003: 17.

TYLER, LEE [WRITER]
— to sign copies of "The Teed-Off Ghost, A Hawaiian Golf Mystery", Lahaina News, May 2, 2002: 17.

TYLER, WILLIE [COMEDIAN]
— to perform at Comedy Club, Lahaina News, August 29, 1991: 10.
— to perform at Comedy Club, Lahaina News, August 12, 1993: 12.

TYSON, MIKE [BOXER]
— director of Light Bringers Rescue Mission Victor Bellaros thanks for donating money to organization, Lahaina News, May 9, 2002: 12.

TZIGANKA [MUSICAL GROUP]
— Russian Gypsy company to perform, Lahaina News, October 17, 1991: 20.

U

U-HAUL [BUSINESS]
— featured, Lahaina News, January 22, 1998: 11.

U.S. ARMY CORPS OF ENGINEERS
— see Army Corps of Engineers, U.S.

U.S. MARINE HOSPITAL
— historical marker for, discussed , Lahaina Sun, December 16, 1970: 6.

U.S. NAVY
— two destroyers visit Lahaina, Lahaina Sun, February 10, 1971: 6.
— to remove unexploded bombs from shore near Molokini, Lahaina News, August 10, 1988: 17.
— see also Kaho'olawe

U.S.O. SHOW
— to be performed at Baldwin Theatre Guild's Mini-Theatre, Lahaina News, January 1, 1986: 3.

UA'U
— public urged to look out for endangered Hawaiian dark-rumped petrel, Lahaina News, November 13, 1985: 7.

UB40 [MUSICAL GROUP]
— to perform at War Memorial Stadium, Lahaina News, May 2, 1990: 15.
— to perform at Maui Arts and Cultural Center, Lahaina News, October 7, 1999: 16.

UDALL, STEWART
— former interior secretary to support repatriation for native Hawaiians, Lahaina Sun, March 21, 1973: 3.

UEBERROTH, JOHN
— resigns as president of Hawaiian Airlines and HAL Inc., Lahaina News, July 22, 1993: 8.

UEMAE, WAYNE
— new deputy director of the Maui County Public Works Department, Lahaina Sun, September 22, 1971: 10.

UENO, OWEN
— new commissioner for West Maui American Youth Soccer Organization (AYSO), Lahaina News, September 18, 2003: 12.

UENO, TRINA
— Scholar/Athlete of the Week, Lahaina News, February 10, 2000: 7.

UEOKA, ARTHUR
— Maui County Attorney accused of ignorance of constitutional principles, Lahaina Sun, June 28, 1972: 3.
— censured by Maui Reporters Association, Lahaina Sun, July 5, 1972: 4.

UEOKA, MEYER
— member of panel discussing hippies on Maui, Lahaina Sun, December 2, 1970: 1.
— attorney discusses place of hippies on Maui, Lahaina Sun, December 16, 1970: 7.
— asked to dismiss charges against hitchhikers, Lahaina Sun, February 10, 1971: 1.
— attorney discusses new hitchhiking rules, Lahaina Sun, May 26, 1971: 3.
— attorney discusses County Attorney's Office, Lahaina Sun, January 12, 1972: 18.
— elected to chair facilities committee of Board of Education, Lahaina News, January 9, 1991: 3.
— opposing condom vending machines on public school campuses, Lahaina News, May 23, 1991: 4.
— urges new Board of Education to rethink position on controversial issues, Lahaina News, December 1, 1994: 1.
— to be honored at Boy Scouts Distinguished Citizen Dinner, Lahaina News, June 10, 1999: 15.
— candidate for Board of Education, Lahaina News, October 26, 2000: 25.

UFO PARASAIL [BUSINESS]
— announces winner of "Kama'aina Getaway", Lahaina News, June 24, 1999: 11.
— owner Greg Vander-Laan announces result of "SendMeToMaui.com" Hula Bowl Sweepstakes, Lahaina News, June 14, 2001: 9.

UFONIA [MUSICAL GROUP]
— to perform at Makawao Union Church, Lahaina News, July 10, 2003: 17.

UFOS
— editorial on work of Project Marxen UFO Committee discussed, Lahaina Sun, April 11, 1973: 8,9.
— speculation on whether they are real, Lahaina Sun, June 27, 1973: 5.

— continued discussion of whether they are real, Lahaina Sun, July 4, 1973: 5.
— discussed, including stories on Maui, Lahaina Sun, July 11, 1973: 5.
— Birney Jarvis recounts seeing, Lahaina Sun, July 25, 1973: 3.
— discussion of evidence, Lahaina Sun, August 1, 1973: 19.
— Xian International events held in Lahaina last year recounted, Lahaina Sun, August 8, 1973: 19.
— report of landings in Haleakala, Lahaina Sun, August 29, 1973: 11.

UGALE, NESTOR
— Scholar/Athlete of the Week, Lahaina News, November 7, 1996: 12.

UKULELE
— Hula Grill to host youth contest, Lahaina News, June 19, 1997: 16.

UKULELE FESTIVAL
— to be held at Lahaina Cannery Mall, Lahaina News, April 25, 2002: 14.
— to be held at Maui Mall as part of Aloha Festivals, Lahaina News, October 9, 2003: 17.

UKUMEHAME
— traffic disrupted by cane fires, Lahaina Sun, November 15, 1972: 9.
— police seek funds for pistol firing range at, Lahaina News, November 21, 1990: 1.

UKUMEHAME PUBLIC SHOOTING RANGE
— construction to begin, Lahaina News, September 7, 1988: 1.
— dedicated, Lahaina News, August 1, 1990: 4.
— bill to create being considered by Maui County Council, Lahaina News, July 9, 1992: 3,4.
— Maui County passes bill to help fund, Lahaina News, July 23, 1992: 3.

'ULALENA [PLAY]
— to be performed at Maui Theatre, Lahaina News, November 21, 2002: 9.
— to be performed at Maui Theatre for Mother's Day, Lahaina News, May 1, 2003: 8.
— to be performed at Maui Theatre for Mother's Day, Lahaina News, May 8, 2003: 18.

'ULALENA [TROUPE]
— to perform in Washington, D.C., Lahaina News, November 28, 2002: 8.
— to perform in Washington, D.C., Lahaina News, December 5, 2002: 1,22.

ULLRICH, SCOTT
— appointed director of food and beverage at Kapalua Bay Hotel, Lahaina News, June 6, 1990: 7.

ULLSTEN, OLA
— former prime minister of Sweden to speak at Conference on Business and the Environment, Lahaina News, February 6, 1991: 7.

ULRICH, DAVID
— named first executive director of Hui No'eau Visual Arts Center, Lahaina News, January 30, 1991: 9.

ULTIMATE COSMETIC STUDIO [BUSINESS]
— featured, Lahaina News, November 2, 1983: 14.

ULUA BEACH
— water samples tested, no evidence of contamination, Lahaina News, November 18, 1993: 5.
— "Ocean Discovery Day for Families" to be held at, Lahaina News, February 18, 1999: 13.
— Pacific Whale Foundation offers free Coral Reef Information Station at, Lahaina News, June 21, 2001: 16.
— Pacific Whale Foundation continues to run Coral Reef Information Station at, Lahaina News, May 15, 2003: 17.

ULUA: THE MUSICAL [MUSICAL]
— to be performed at Maui Arts and Cultural Center, Lahaina News, July 24, 2003: 16.

ULUPALAKUA RANCH
— to host Maui County Agricultural Trade Show and Sampling, Lahaina News, April 11, 1996: 6.

ULUPALAKUA THING
— to be held, Lahaina News, April 17, 2003: 8.
— to be held at Ulupalakua Ranch and Tedeschi Winery, Lahaina News, April 24, 2003: 15.

UMBOUR, MARSHA [ARTIST]
— to exhibit at Village Galleries, Lahaina News, January 25, 1996: 14.

UMIDI, BART
— appointed executive chef at Westin Maui, Lahaina News, February 20, 2003: 8.

UNA THE MAGICAL CLOWN
— to celebrate release of children's video "Magical Universe", Lahaina News, September 12, 2002: 20.

UNCAPHER, IDA KAILAKANOA
— photograph of, Lahaina Sun, December 23, 1970: 9.
— marries John Stewart, Lahaina Sun, March 17, 1971: 2.

UNCLE DADDY [MUSICAL GROUP]
— to reviewed, Lahaina News, June 28, 1989: 17.

UNCLE WAYNE
— see Watkins, Wayne "Uncle" [musician]

UNCOMMON GROUND [PLAY]
— to be performed at Iao Theatre, Lahaina News, January 14, 1993: 14,15.

UNDER A MAUI ROOF [BOOK]
— published, Lahaina News, November 17, 1994: 18.

UNDER THE STAR OF GLADNESS [PLAY]
— Maui Community Theatre to hold auditions for, Lahaina News, June 9, 1994: 16.
— Maui Community Theatre to hold auditions for, Lahaina News, June 16, 1994: 12.
— to be performed at Iao Theatre, Lahaina News, September 1, 1994: 16.

UNDERTOW [MUSICAL GROUP]
— to perform at Moose McGillycuddy's, Lahaina News, November 9, 1995: 12.

UNDERWATER OBSERVATORY
— proposed for Lahaina, Lahaina Sun, June 6, 1973: 11.
— fate to be decided September 28, Lahaina Sun, June 13, 1973: 27.
— planning has begun, Lahaina Sun, July 18, 1973: 4.

UNDERWATER SYMPHONY [FILM]
— to be shown at Maui Ocean Center, Lahaina News, February 22, 1989: 13.

UNEMORI, MOTOHISA (MORI)
— details of his election campaign for 7th district of the State House, Lahaina Sun, September 27, 1972: 4.

UNICEF
— to receive donations from Hyatt Regency, Lahaina News, May 6, 1993: 18.
— fundraiser to be held at St. John's Episcopal Church, Lahaina News, October 22, 1998: 20.
— Sacred Hearts students raise money for, Lahaina News, November 19, 1998: 10.

UNION PACIFIC [MUSICAL GROUP]
— to perform at Inu Inu Lounge at Maui Inter-Continental Wailea, Lahaina News, February 20, 1991: 11.
— continues to perform at Inu Inu Lounge at Maui Inter-Continental Wailea, Lahaina News, April 17, 1991: 14.
— continues to perform at Inu Inu Lounge at Maui Inter-Continental Wailea, Lahaina News, April 24, 1991: 11.

— groundbreaking ceremony for lunar ranging station on Haleakala, Lahaina Sun, March 21, 1973: 4.

— editorial criticizing legislature for failure to hire Cecil Mackey as president, Lahaina News, June 19, 1985: 2.

— School of Nursing to hold information session, Lahaina News, October 24, 1990: 2.

— signs cooperative agreement with Chaminade University, Lahaina News, October 31, 1990: 7.

— classes now available on Maui through interactive television, Lahaina News, June 20, 1991: 3,4.

— alumni to hold tailgate party for UH-Utah game, Lahaina News, October 17, 1991: 4.

— featured on "Dialog" on KHET, Lahaina News, February 6, 1992: 5.

— Eve Chute receives "Maui Regents Award", Lahaina News, May 28, 1992: 4.

— Cooperative Extension agent James Tavares to offer advice on sick plants, Lahaina News, January 14, 1993: 2.

— Committee for the Preservation and Study of Hawaiian Language, Art and Culture to offer grants, Lahaina News, September 16, 1993: 4.

— tennis team to play Stanford University, Lahaina News, November 25, 1993: 10.

— Alumni Association to sponsor Green and White Spring Game, Lahaina News, April 21, 1994: 6.

— Alumni Association seeking entries for Distinguished Alumni Award, Lahaina News, October 8, 1998: 2.

— School of Medicine seeks applicants, Lahaina News, November 5, 1998: 8.

— alumni awards announced, Lahaina News, November 12, 1998: 7.

— Center on Maui to discuss new degrees, Lahaina News, December 10, 1998: 20.

— football coach June Jones meets with Maui coaches, Lahaina News, May 13, 1999: 1,20.

— Na Koa Football Club Invitational Golf Tournament to be held, Lahaina News, July 1, 1999: 7.

— to present on interdisciplinary Masters of Education, Lahaina News, September 9, 1999: 12.

— College of Education offering classes on Maui, Lahaina News, October 5, 2000: 7.

— football team to play on Maui, Lahaina News, November 23, 2000: 11.

— increases to tuition to be explained, Lahaina News, January 25, 2001: 16.

— explains tuition increase, Lahaina News, February 1, 2001: 21.

— School of Social Work offering program, Lahaina News, April 19, 2001: 17.

— to hold meetings on programs offered, Lahaina News, June 28, 2001: 20.

— offering new degrees through distance learning, Lahaina News, July 19, 2001: 16.

— to offer new programs on Maui, Lahaina News, August 9, 2001: 16.

— Accountancy degree to be offered, Lahaina News, September 13, 2001: 9.

— Bachelor of Arts in Business Administration to be offered at University Center, Lahaina News, November 8, 2001: 8.

— to offer Accounting Degree at Maui Community College, Lahaina News, November 29, 2001: 8.

— Master of Business Administration to be offered at Maui Community College, Lahaina News, February 21, 2002: 8.

— Deane Neubauer invites input on Strategic Plan, Lahaina News, March 7, 2002: 16.

— College of Education offering certificates, Lahaina News, September 12, 2002: 20.

— to offer statewide Rehabilitation Counselor Education program, Lahaina News, October 31, 2002: 29.

— to hold informational meeting on degree in Hawaiian Studies, Lahaina News, February 20, 2003: 16.

— now offering Hawaiian Studies degree at Maui Community College, Lahaina News, May 15, 2003: 16.

UNIVERSITY OF HAWAII ALUMNI ASSOCIATION

— holds membership drive, Lahaina News, September 7, 1988: 3,5.

— to support UH football team in San Diego, Lahaina News, September 21, 1988: 3.

UNIVERSITY OF HAWAII AT MANOA

— to offer upper and graduate-level Education courses on Maui, Lahaina News, March 28, 1990: 3.

— to hold business and travel industry management courses on Maui, Lahaina News, April 25, 1990: 7.

— Lahainaluna High School students participate in Hawaiian culture program at, Lahaina News, October 9, 2003: 3.

UNIVERSITY OF HAWAII CENTER-MAUI

— to offer Masters of Accounting program, Lahaina News, October 9, 2003: 16.

UNIVERSITY OF HAWAII RAINBOWS

— to play pre-season game, Lahaina News, November 22, 1989: 9.

— basketball team to host tournament at Lahaina Civic Center, Lahaina News, December 6, 1989: 7.

UNIVERSITY OF HAWAII SEA GRANT EXTENSION

— see Sea Grant Extension, University of Hawaii

UNWIN, CHRIS [WRITER]

— to conduct watercolor workshop at The Art School at Kapalua, Lahaina News, February 15, 2001: 16.

UP WITH PEOPLE [TROUPE]

— to perform musical production of "The Festival", Lahaina News, October 31, 1996: 18,19.

UPCOUNTRY COMMUNITY CENTER

— to host auction to benefit East Maui Animal Refuge Center, Lahaina News, November 17, 1994: 6.

— to host luau to benefit Jesus Is Alive Church Building Fund, Lahaina News, March 11, 1999: 12.

UPCOUNTRY FAIR

— planned, Lahaina News, June 1, 1981: 8.

— to be held in June, Lahaina News, May 15, 1982: 6.

— to be held at the Eddie Tam Memorial Complex, Lahaina News, June 6, 1990: 13.

— to be held in Makawao, Lahaina News, June 6, 1991: 12,13.

— to be held, Lahaina News, June 11, 1992: 22.

— to be held, Lahaina News, May 30, 1996: 2.

— to be held at Eddie Tam Memorial Park, Lahaina News, June 6, 1996: 15.

— to be held, Lahaina News, June 11, 1998: 16.

UPCOUNTRY GARDEN CLUB

— to meet, Lahaina News, July 16, 1992: 5.

— to hold meeting, Lahaina News, October 29, 1992: 3.

— to meet, Lahaina News, February 11, 1993: 5.

— to hold monthly meeting, Lahaina News, August 18, 1994: 16.

— see also Maui Garden Club

UPCOUNTRY NIGHTS WOMEN'S DANCE CLUB

— offering lessons, Lahaina News, February 4, 1999: 16.

UPCOUNTRY SQUARE DANCE CLUB

— to hold classes, Lahaina News, January 26, 1995: 16.

UPCOUNTRY SQUARES

— hoedown organized at Pukalani Elementary School, Lahaina News, April 5, 1989: 3.

— organizing hoedown at Pukalani Elementary School, Lahaina News, May 3, 1989: 4.

UPCOUNTRY SWIMMING POOL

— opens, Lahaina News, June 6, 1996: 15.

UPCOUNTRY TOUR OF HOMES
— to be held, Lahaina News, December 4, 1997: 24.

UPCOUNTRY YOUTH CENTER
— to hold holiday dance, Lahaina News, December 15, 1994: 18,19.

UPPER DECK COMPANY, THE [BUSINESS]
— signs sponsorship deal with Hawaiian Winter League, Lahaina News, April 30, 1992: 11.

UPPER DECK HAWAIIAN WINTER LEAGUE
— season canceled, Lahaina News, July 16, 1992: 4.

UPPER ROOM MUSIC AND BOOKSTORE [BUSINESS]
— featured, Lahaina News, May 16, 1984: 17.

UPSTART CROW AND COMPANY BOOKSTORE AND COFFEESHOP [BUSINESS]
— to hold author signing for Gill McBarnet, Lahaina News, November 19, 1986: 16.

URA, TAKASHI
— appointed new guest service manager at The Westin Maui, Lahaina News, March 8, 2001: 8.

URASENKE MAUI DOKO KAI
— to hold Hatsudate, Lahaina News, January 10, 2002: 16.

URAYAZA, STEPHEN
— wins vacation at "A Taste of Lahaina", Lahaina News, October 21, 1999: 7.

URBAN BUSH WOMEN
— dancers to perform, Lahaina News, May 1, 1997: 17.
— dance troupe to perform, Lahaina News, May 15, 1997: 12.

URBAN DESIGN REVIEW BOARD
— approves design of proposed Ritz-Charlton Hotel, Lahaina News, December 6, 1989: 28.

URBAN LAND INSTITUTE
— gives "Award for Excellence" to Kapalua Resort, Lahaina News, November 18, 1993: 6.

URGE, THE [MUSICAL GROUP]
— to perform at Moose McGillycuddy's, Lahaina News, December 26, 1990: 8.
— to perform at Moose McGillycuddy's, Lahaina News, January 23, 1991: 7.
— continues to perform at Moose McGillycuddy's, Lahaina News, March 13, 1991: 8.

URQUHART, SARAH
— becomes group coordinator for Kapalua Bay Hotel & Villas, Lahaina News, May 2, 1984: 17.

USLER, ALAN
— joins Plantation House as sommelier, Lahaina News, September 12, 1991: 4.

USO SHOW [PERFORMANCE]
— nostalgic show to be performed at Baldwin Mini-Theatre, Lahaina News, January 9, 1985: 3.

USSR
— Maui County Youth Ambassadors to visit, Lahaina News, May 27, 1987: 16.

UTA, HIROSHI
— wins first place in Kamehameha Iki Park Festival nose flute contest, Lahaina News, January 11, 1996: 16.

UTILITIES
— proposed rate increases sought, Lahaina Sun, December 23, 1970: 4.

UVALLE, JOEY
— attacked by three men, Lahaina Sun, April 5, 1972: 3.
— memorial held at Canoe Beach, Lahaina News, September 5, 1991: 7.

UWEKOOLANI, MOANALIHA
— discusses Dennis "Bumpy" Kanahele at meeting at Malu'ulu O Lele Cultural Center, Lahaina News, November 30, 1995: 1,12.

UYEDA, JAIANE
— Scholar/Athlete of the Week, Lahaina News, April 4, 2002: 12.

UYETAKE, BEN
— entertainment coordinator for Sacred Heart's Bazaar featured, Lahaina News, March 12, 1992: 3.

UYETAKE, BENNY COLLINS [MUSICIAN]
— featured, Lahaina News, May 10, 1989: 17.
— new recording featured, Lahaina News, May 28, 1992: 14.
— to perform at Moondoggies, Lahaina News, July 9, 1992: 17.
— to perform at B.J.'s Chicago Pizzeria, Lahaina News, October 6, 1994: 15.
— to perform at B.J.'s Chicago Pizzeria, Lahaina News, October 10, 1996: 16.
— to perform at B.J.'s Chicago Pizzeria, Lahaina News, May 22, 1997: 15.
— to perform at B.J.'s Chicago Pizzeria, Lahaina News, September 25, 1997: 13.
— to perform at Aloha Mixed Plate, Lahaina News, July 22, 1999: 14.

V

VA BENE ITALIAN BEACHSIDE GRILL
— Mauro Gramuglia new assistant sous chef at, Lahaina News, February 7, 2002: 8.
— to host operatic performance by Debra Lynn and Jerry Eiting, Lahaina News, May 30, 2002: 16.
— to host Debra Lynn and Jerry Eiting of the Maui Light Opera Company, Lahaina News, June 6, 2002: 17.
— featured, Lahaina News, October 10, 2002: 9.

VAGABOND PLAYERS, THE [TROUPE]
— continue to perform at Whalers Village, Lahaina News, March 12, 1992: 16.
— to perform during holidays, Lahaina News, November 19, 1992: 13.

VAGHN, MICHAEL
— employee honored by financial services firm Edward Jones, Lahaina News, November 2, 2000: 12.

VAGINA MONOLOGUES, THE [PLAY]
— to be held, Lahaina News, January 31, 2002: 17.
— performance to include Brooke Shields, Amy J. Carle and Michelle Shay, Lahaina News, February 7, 2002: 16.
— Teri Hatcher to perform in, Lahaina News, May 22, 2003: 14.
— Teri Hatcher to perform in, Lahaina News, May 29, 2003: 16.

VAIHI [MUSICAL GROUP]
— to perform at Borders Books, Lahaina News, October 14, 1999: 12.

VAIL, JOHN
— named to Defender Council, Lahaina Sun, July 7, 1971: 9.
— discusses role of Public Defender Council, Lahaina Sun, July 14, 1971: 3.
— casts deciding vote to appoint Donald Tsukiyama as Public Defender, Lahaina Sun, November 24, 1971: 6.

VAKALAHI, AKI
— Scholar/Athlete of the Week, Lahaina News, October 2, 2003: 12.

VALDEZ, JEFF [COMEDIAN]
— to perform at Comedy Club and the Sports Page, Lahaina News, July 2, 1992: 21,24.

VALENCIA, JOANNE [ARTIST]
— to exhibit at Lahaina Arts Society Gallery, Lahaina News, April 9, 1998: 16.

VALENTINE, SAINT
— biography of, Lahaina News, February 14, 1990: 6.

VALENTINE'S DAY
— celebrated in Lahaina, Lahaina News, February 11, 1987: 4.
— shopping and activities listed, Lahaina News, February 8, 1989: 6,13.
— meal specials, Lahaina News, February 6, 1991: 13.
— events, Lahaina News, February 13, 1991: 14.
— dining choices for, Lahaina News, February 6, 1992: 21.
— dining choices for, Lahaina News, February 13, 1992: 24,25.
— to be celebrated at Lahaina Coolers, Lahaina News, February 4, 1993: 13.
— to be celebrated, Lahaina News, February 11, 1993: 14.
— featured, Lahaina News, February 10, 1994: 6,10.
— to be held at Four Seasons Resort Wailea, Lahaina News, January 26, 1995: 16.
— to be celebrated, Lahaina News, February 9, 1995: 11.
— Lahaina Cannery Mall to sponsor contest, Lahaina News, January 29, 1998: 9.
— to be celebrated at Maui Dharma Center, Lahaina News, February 5, 1998: 13.
— Napili Plaza to celebrate, Lahaina News, February 11, 1999: 16.
— events to be held, Lahaina News, February 11, 1999: 17.
— to be celebrated, Lahaina News, February 11, 1999: 7.
— to be celebrated at Lahaina Cannery Mall, Lahaina News, February 10, 2000: 16.
— restaurant offers, Lahaina News, February 8, 2001: 10.
— Hawaii Ballroom Dance Association to hold ball, Lahaina News, February 8, 2001: 18.
— Lahaina Cannery Mall to celebrate, Lahaina News, February 8, 2001: 20.
— events to be held, Lahaina News, February 7, 2002: 14.
— Lahaina Cannery Mall to celebrate with "Flower Drum Song", Lahaina News, February 7, 2002: 2.
— Maui Paniolo Dance to hold dance, Lahaina News, February 14, 2002: 16.

VALLEJO [MUSICAL GROUP]
— to perform at The Westin Maui, Lahaina News, December 7, 2000: 26.

VALLEY AUTOMATED FUELS, INC
— awarded contract to build automated fueling facility at Lahaina Harbor , Lahaina News, November 22, 1989: 28.

VALLEY ISLE
— "Get the Drift and Bag It" to clean beaches at, Lahaina News, September 13, 2001: 1.

VALLEY ISLE ARCHERY CLUB
— to host tournament, Lahaina News, May 30, 1990: 6.

VALLEY ISLE BALLROOM
— renovation completed, Lahaina News, December 18, 1997: 8.

VALLEY ISLE BIG BLUES MELE, THE
— Tracy Nelson to perform, Lahaina News, May 15, 1997: 13.
— to be held, Lahaina News, May 22, 1997: 17.
— to be held, Lahaina News, May 29, 1997: 16.

VALLEY ISLE BUSINESS AWARDS
— honors Napili businessman and Lahaina family, Lahaina News, October 17, 1996: 1,20.

VALLEY ISLE CHECKERED FLAG ASSOCIATION
— to hold Motorcross Race, Lahaina News, September 12, 1984: 3.

VALLEY ISLE DISPOSAL [BUSINESS]
— begins operation, Lahaina News, June 17, 1999: 13.

VALLEY ISLE DRY CLEANERS [BUSINESS]
— to open, Lahaina News, February 4, 1993: 9.

VALLEY ISLE FITNESS CENTER [BUSINESS]
— to open soon, Lahaina News, September 29, 1994: 16.
— opens third location, Lahaina News, May 4, 1995: 13.

VALLEY ISLE KENNEL CLUB
— to hold AKC dog shows, Lahaina News, October 26, 2000: 28.
— to host "Meet the Breeds", Lahaina News, September 18, 2003: 13.

VALLEY ISLE LIGHTING [BUSINESS]
— becomes client of Entrekin/Zucco Advertising, Lahaina News, August 29, 1990: 8.

VALLEY ISLE LUXURY LIMOUSINES [BUSINESS]
— opens, Lahaina News, May 10, 1989: 6.

VALLEY ISLE MARINE CENTER
— wins state contract for patrol boats, Lahaina News, April 16, 1986: 3.
— to hold boat show, Lahaina News, June 18, 1992: 4.
— new retail boat showroom opens, Lahaina News, October 7, 1999: 14.

VALLEY ISLE MASTERS SWIMMERS
— to hold workouts, Lahaina News, January 7, 1999: 15.
— seeking swimmers, Lahaina News, January 28, 1999: 7.
— to hold Ka'anapali Klassic Ocean Swim, Lahaina News, April 15, 1999: 6.
— to organize events, Lahaina News, January 13, 2000: 7.
— to hold annual benefit for American Heart Association, Lahaina News, February 10, 2000: 9.
— to hold annual benefit "Swim For Your Heart", Lahaina News, February 24, 2000: 6.
— to hold Ka'anapali Klassic Ocean Swim, Lahaina News, April 27, 2000: 6.
— Ka'anapali Klassic Ocean Swim competition to be held, Lahaina News, May 4, 2000: 14.
— to hold Ka'anapali Klassic Ocean Swim, Lahaina News, May 11, 2000: 14.
— holds workouts at Lahaina Aquatic Center, Lahaina News, December 28, 2000: 6.
— to hold workouts at Lahaina Aquatic Center, Lahaina News, January 18, 2001: 9.
— to hold workouts at Lahaina Aquatic Center, Lahaina News, February 1, 2001: 14.
— to be held to benefit American Heart Association, Lahaina News, February 22, 2001: 13.
— to host "Swim for Your Heat", Lahaina News, March 1, 2001: 14.
— to hold adult swim program, Lahaina News, April 5, 2001: 14.
— to hold workouts, Lahaina News, April 12, 2001: 14.
— to hold Ka'anapali Klassic Ocean Swim, Lahaina News, May 3, 2001: 14.
— to hold Ka'anapali Klassic Ocean Swim, Lahaina News, May 10, 2001: 15.
— to hold Roughwater Swim Race, Lahaina News, September 27, 2001: 13.
— Ka'anapali Klassic Ocean Swim to benefit The Boys and Girls Club of West Maui, Lahaina News, April 25, 2002: 5.
— to hold 18th annual Ka'anapali Klassic Ocean Swim to benefit The Boys and Girls Club, Lahaina News, May 2, 2002: 12.
— to hold Roughwater Swim Race, Lahaina News, September 19, 2002: 11.
— to hold Ka'anapali Klassic Ocean Swim, Lahaina News, April 24, 2003: 11.

VALLEY ISLE MOTORS [BUSINESS]
— Bowlathon to be held with first prize from, Lahaina News, August 8, 1991: 6.
— one of nations outstanding Ford dealerships, Lahaina News, April 13, 1995: 12.
— president James Falk II receives Maui County's 2000 Entrepreneurial Success Award, Lahaina News, June 1, 2000: 14.

VALLEY ISLE RESORT FRONT DESK
— holds open house, Lahaina News, August 11, 1994: 7.

VALLEY ISLE ROAD RUNNERS ASSOCIATION

— to hold track meet, Lahaina News, January 6, 1988: 3.
— entries due soon for 10K Iao Valley Race, Lahaina News, April 13, 1988: 13.
— sponsoring runs in May, Lahaina News, May 4, 1988: 3,14.
— to hold All Comers Track Meet, Lahaina News, June 1, 1988: 19.
— to hold "Maui Mile" run, Lahaina News, June 22, 1988: 2.
— to hold Teen Challenge Maui Benefit 5K/10K, Lahaina News, August 23, 1989: 5.
— to hold Hana Relays, Lahaina News, August 23, 1989: 5.
— to hold Teen Challenge Maui Benefit 5K/10K, Lahaina News, August 30, 1989: 24.
— to hold "Dracula Dash" costume run, Lahaina News, October 18, 1989: 5.
— to hold Christmas party, Lahaina News, November 22, 1989: 8.
— to hold Christmas party, Lahaina News, November 29, 1989: 5.
— sponsor races in January, Lahaina News, December 27, 1989: 9.
— to hold fun run, Lahaina News, February 14, 1990: 12.
— sponsoring track meet, Lahaina News, May 2, 1990: 6.
— sponsoring an all-comers track meet, Lahaina News, May 9, 1990: 7.
— pre-registration for Tedeschi 10K, Lahaina News, May 23, 1990: 10.
— to hold meet, Lahaina News, July 4, 1990: 6.
— to hold meet, Lahaina News, July 11, 1990: 8.
— to host Biathlon, Lahaina News, July 18, 1990: 6.
— organizes Hana Relay, Lahaina News, September 19, 1990: 18.
— to hold "All Comers Track Meet", Lahaina News, October 3, 1990: 7.
— to hold Turkey Trot, Lahaina News, November 14, 1990: 24.
— to hold 10K Iao Valley run, Lahaina News, April 17, 1991: 10.
— to host Tedeschi 10K, Lahaina News, May 23, 1991: 10.
— to host Tedeschi 10K, Lahaina News, May 30, 1991: 4.
— to hold 5K walk/run on July 4th, Lahaina News, June 27, 1991: 7.
— hosing Mark Twain 5K fundraiser for Maui Community Theatre, Lahaina News, July 25, 1991: 9.
— to hold Haleakala Run to the Sun, Lahaina News, August 15, 1991: 4.
— to hold "Haleakala Run to the Sun", Lahaina News, August 29, 1991: 7.
— sponsoring Haleakala Run to the Sun, Lahaina News, September 12, 1991: 6.
— to hold Turkey Trot, Lahaina News, October 24, 1991: 6.
— organizing "Turkey Trot", Lahaina News, November 7, 1991: 7.
— to host 10K Iao run, Lahaina News, April 23, 1992: 22.
— to hold No Holo Wahine 5K, Lahaina News, April 30, 1992: 6.
— hosting annual Haleakala Run to the Sun, Lahaina News, September 24, 1992: 11,13.
— to host 5K run with Subway, Lahaina News, December 3, 1992: 7.
— to hold 1993 Iao 10K run, Lahaina News, April 22, 1993: 7.
— to hold "Beat the Heat" run, Lahaina News, July 8, 1993: 9.
— to host Hana Relay, Lahaina News, September 9, 1993: 9.
— to host Na Holo Wahine Run on Mother's Day, Lahaina News, May 11, 1995: 7.
— holds Hana Relays, Lahaina News, September 14, 1995: 7.
— to host harbor to harbor run, Lahaina News, October 17, 1996: 12.
— seeking volunteers to help with Maui Marathon, Lahaina News, March 13, 1997: 13.
— annual Harbor to Harbor run, Lahaina News, November 6, 1997: 9.
— to hold Na Holo Wahine 5K Run/Walk, Lahaina News, May 6, 1999: 17.
— to hold 10K run at Iao Valley, Lahaina News, July 13, 2000: 7.
— strong at championships, Lahaina News, October 31, 2002: 11.
— preparing for cross country season, Lahaina News, September 4, 2003: 12.
— cross country team featured, Lahaina News, October 9, 2003: 13.

VALLEY ISLE SPORTS SHOOTERS CLUB

— to hold Turkey Shoot for Turkeys with Maui Community Food Bank, Lahaina News, November 18, 1993: 8.
— to offer NRA Basic Safety Pistol Course, Lahaina News, October 5, 1995: 6.

VALLEY ISLE SPORTS/INDUSTRIAL REHABILITATION CENTER

— opens in West Maui, Lahaina News, June 18, 1986: 3.

VALLEY ISLE SWIM MASTERS SWIM CLUB

— raises money for West Maui Youth Center, Lahaina News, June 15, 2000: 12.

VALLEY ISLE SYMPHONY

— Orchestra to hold fund-raiser, Lahaina News, June 16, 1994: 11.
— to perform at Royal Lahaina Resort, Lahaina News, November 24, 1994: 11.

VALLEY ISLE TIMING ASSOCIATION (VITA)

— offering scholarships for auto programs, Lahaina News, February 15, 2001: 12.
— held second race at Maui Raceway Park, Lahaina News, March 29, 2001: 12.
— to hold drag races, Lahaina News, April 12, 2001: 14.
— drag races set, Lahaina News, April 19, 2001: 13.
— to hold drag racing event, Lahaina News, July 19, 2001: 13.
— to hold races, Lahaina News, August 9, 2001: 13.
— to hold drag races, Lahaina News, September 20, 2001: 13.
— to hold fundraiser for American Red Cross, Lahaina News, October 4, 2001: 13.
— drag racing to be held, Lahaina News, October 18, 2001: 13.
— to hold races, Lahaina News, November 15, 2001: 13.
— to hold races, Lahaina News, August 8, 2002: 13.
— to hold races at a Maui Raceway Park, Lahaina News, August 15, 2002: 12.
— to hold races at a Maui Raceway Park, Lahaina News, September 19, 2002: 12.

VALLEY ISLE TRIATHLON

— held on Wailea, Lahaina News, May 23, 1984: 6.

VALLEY ISLE VOTER'S ALLIANCE (VIVA)

— created by Kihei Residents Against Aina Lea (KRAAL), Lahaina News, January 6, 1994: 7.
— registers with State Campaign Spending Commission, Lahaina News, April 21, 1994: 5.
— to meet, Lahaina News, February 12, 1998: 16.

VALLEY, NINA [ARTIST]

— watercolors displayed by Lahaina Arts Society, Lahaina News, September 7, 1988: 14.
— to paint watercolors at Tropical Artware, Lahaina News, March 7, 1990: 15.

VAN DER LINDEN, LOUIS

— passed away while vacationing in Amsterdam, Lahaina Sun, August 18, 1971: 11.

VAN DORPE, ROBERT

— describes Amfac's planned Hawaiian Sea Village, Lahaina News, April 17, 1985: 1,8,9.
— project manager speaks of plans for Hawaiian Sea Village, Lahaina News, November 8, 1989: 1.

VAN HORN, KEITH [FOOTBALL PLAYER]

— interviewed during visit to Maui, Lahaina News, April 8, 1987: 6.

VAN SETERS, JACQUES

— named general manager of Stouffer Wailea Beach Resort, Lahaina News, October 8, 1992: 8.

VAN STORY, CHAD

— indicted for bank robbery, Lahaina News, August 28, 1997: 1,3.

VAN ZWALENBERG, JAY
— Maui district librarian proposes new site for Lahaina Public Library, Lahaina News, March 14, 1990: 1.

VAN ZWEDEN, POLLYANN
— death mourned at Lahaina Intermediate School, Lahaina News, June 6, 1996: 1.
— teacher killed by drunk driver remembered, Lahaina News, January 23, 1997: 2,13.

VANDALS, THE [MUSICAL GROUP]
— to perform at Maui Arts and Cultural Center, Lahaina News, April 30, 1998: 16.

VANDER-VELDE, EDWARD [ARTIST]
— to exhibit with Lahaina Arts Society, Lahaina News, July 30, 1992: 14.
— to participate in "Four by Four Equals" show, Lahaina News, February 2, 1995: 10.

VANDER-VELDE, HENRY [ARTIST]
— work described, Lahaina News, October 15, 1980: 2.
— biography of, Lahaina News, October 1, 1981: 7,10.
— works on exhibit at Old Court House, Lahaina News, January 15, 1982: 8.

VANDERBERG, JUSTIN
— found guilty of murder, Lahaina News, May 13, 1993: 4.

VANDERLAAN, GREG
— launches prototype vessel, Lahaina News, February 21, 2002: 8.

VANDERSCHOOT, ARI
— poster selected by Foundation Galleries, Lahaina News, December 19, 1991: 21.

VANDERVEEN, LOET [ARTIST]
— sculptor to exhibit at Dolphin Gallery, Lahaina News, March 15, 1989: 13.

VANDERVOORT, CHRIS
— Winner of junior division of World Unity Surf Context, Lahaina Times, October, 1980 volume 4 number 9: 2.
— photo of surfer, Lahaina Times, October, 1980 volume 4 number 9: 4.

VANNATTA, CHUCKY
— surfer featured in Wetscreams [film], Lahaina Times, August, 1980 volume 4 number 7: 5.
— surfer featured, Lahaina Times, September, 1980 volume 4 number 8: 6.

VANNOY, GLEN
— developer requests to increase number of liquor licenses in Lahaina, Lahaina News, February 29, 1984: 17.
— developer building commercial structure at corner of Lahainaluna Road and Wainee Street, Lahaina News, July 17, 1985: 3.

VARES, GLEN
— former Lahaina radio personality at "A Taste of Lahaina", Lahaina News, September 19, 1996: 1.

VARGO, J. DANIELLE [WRITER]
— to autograph copies of "Immortal Eyes", Lahaina News, May 7, 1998: 20.

VASARELY, VICTOR [ARTIST]
— to exhibit at Circle Gallery, Lahaina News, September 10, 1992: 22.

VASU [ARTIST]
— leading course on healing art, Lahaina News, January 31, 2002: 18.

VATERLAUS, GARY
— to offer "An Overview of End Times", Lahaina News, February 15, 2001: 16.

VAUGHN, CYNTHIA [NURSE]
— speaking at Osteoporosis Forum, Lahaina News, February 5, 1986: 3.

VAUGHN, MICHAEL
— named to Goldman Sachs Blue Chip Council, Lahaina News, July 8, 1999: 11.
— Edward Jones employee honored for service with A.F. McKenzie Achievement award, Lahaina News, July 18, 2002: 8.

VAUGHN, STEVIE RAY [MUSICIAN]
— opens for the Police in concert in Maui, Lahaina News, March 7, 1984: 10.

VAUGHT, RON
— named general manager of KMUI radio, Lahaina News, September 12, 1990: 11.
— resigns from KMVI radio to join TV MAUI Magazine, Lahaina News, October 13, 1994: 15.

VAULES, G. TODD
— hired as technical director for the Maui Community Arts and Cultural Center, Lahaina News, February 13, 1992: 13.

VAZQUEZ, MIQUEL
— named top employee of the year by Ruby's Diner, Lahaina News, January 2, 2003: 9.

VEARY, EMMA [MUSICIAN]
— performs on Maui, Lahaina Sun, November 22, 1972: 22.
— to perform at big band event at Ritz-Carlton, Lahaina News, May 7, 1998: 16.

VEGA, PEPE AND KIKO
— launches Maui Catering Consultants, Lahaina News, July 5, 2001: 9.

VEGETARIAN FOOD FESTIVAL
— to be held, Lahaina News, April 29, 1993: 3.
— to be held, Lahaina News, February 29, 1996: 14.
— to be held at Wailuku Community Center, Lahaina News, April 24, 1997: 13.

VELASQUEZ, JOE
— new director of sales and marketing at Ritz-Carlton, Lahaina News, February 27, 2003: 8.

VELDE, EDWARD VANDER
— see Vander-Velde, Edward [artist]

VELUPILLAI, SASI
— psychic palmist to speak, Lahaina News, October 26, 1988: 17.

VELVETEEN RABBIT, THE [PLAY]
— to be performed by Maui Youth Theatre, Lahaina News, March 2, 1988: 12.
— opens, Lahaina News, March 23, 1988: 14.

VENCL, TERRYL
— named executive director of Maui Hotel Association, Lahaina News, February 11, 1993: 11.
— to be guest on "Maui Talks—Tourism", Lahaina News, March 18, 1999: 13.

VENDREL-RUDD, NANCI
— joins The Realty Team, Lahaina News, January 16, 1991: 5.

VENTO, ART
— hired as project manager for Maui Community Arts and Cultural Center, Lahaina News, March 19, 1992: 9,10.

VENTURA, GEORGE
— details of his election campaign for 7th district of the State House, Lahaina Sun, September 27, 1972: 4.

VENTURA, JOSEPH
— dies, Lahaina News, August 2, 1989: 2.
— Lahainaluna High School student recognized for academic achievements at the University Technical Institute, Lahaina News, June 11, 1992: 4.

VENTURA, PAULA AND JOE
— political work described, Lahaina News, May 18, 1988: 3.
— update; account of Joe's failing health, Lahaina News, October 5, 1988: 2.

VENTURA, PEGGY
— Animal Control officer pictured, Lahaina News, May 26, 1994: 5.

VENTURA, SCOTT
— Aqua Blue Maui creates abalone shell laminate, Lahaina News, February 11, 1999: 13.

VENTURY, JOHN
— elected zone chairman with the Kihei Community Association, Lahaina Sun, December 2, 1970: 4.

VENTURY, TIFFANY
— wins Christmas Card contest, Lahaina News, December 31, 1992: 4.

VENUS [MUSICAL GROUP]
— reviewed, Lahaina News, March 29, 1989: 9.
— to perform at Moose McGillycuddy's, Lahaina News, February 7, 1990: 13.
— to perform at Tiger Restaurants, Lahaina News, April 18, 1990: 11.
— to perform at Moose McGillycuddy's, Lahaina News, April 25, 1990: 15.

VENUS, SPEAROUS
— expresses resistance to proposed airport in West Maui, Lahaina News, May 22, 1985: 1,11.

VENUS SWIMWEAR
— holds photo shoot in West Maui, Lahaina News, September 8, 1994: 12.

VERBIEST, CLAIRE [ARTIST]
— to offer workshops at The Art School at Kapalua, Lahaina News, January 9, 2003: 15.

VERDERY, BENJAMIN [MUSICIAN]
— chair of Yale University School of Music Guitar Department to perform with master pupils at Keawala'i Congregational Church, Lahaina News, August 16, 2001: 16.
— guitarist to hold master class, Lahaina News, August 15, 2002: 16.
— guitarist to hold Maui Master Class, Lahaina News, July 17, 2003: 18.

VERDY, BEN [GUITARIST]
— to perform in West Maui, Lahaina News, April 1, 1987: 1,9.

VERGARA, CHARLA [ARTIST]
— owner of Maui Sand Art Co. demonstrates technique, Lahaina News, March 30, 1995: 12.

VERICHECK-MAUI
— providing free check verification, Lahaina News, May 23, 2002: 8.

VERITY, HENRY
— selected as controller of the Maui Marriott Resort, Lahaina News, May 6, 1993: 9.

VERIZON HAWAII HALL OF FAME CHAMPIONSHIP AND PRO-AM
— to benefit Kapalua Junior Golf, Lahaina News, April 26, 2001: 15.

VERIZON WIRELESS [BUSINESS]
— opens new store, Lahaina News, December 27, 2001: 8.

VERMEY, RICHARD
— surfer dies, Lahaina News, November 22, 1989: 28.
— memorial fund to be applied to education of son, Lahaina News, November 29, 1989: 36.
— memorial held, Lahaina News, December 6, 1989: 2.

VERSNEL, JULIE
— editor of "Women and Guns" magazine to speak to Rotary Club of Lahaina, Lahaina News, June 17, 1993: 2.

VERYFIND PRODUCTS-SAVE THE CHILDREN
— relay to take place, Lahaina News, February 7, 1990: 3.

VETERANS
— health issues faced, Lahaina Sun, October 11, 1972: 12.
— plight of discussed, Lahaina Sun, October 18, 1972: 6,7.
— few solutions apparent, Lahaina Sun, October 25, 1972: 6.
— problems persist, Lahaina Sun, November 1, 1972: 7.
— Hawaii has fewest VA offices, Lahaina Sun, November 8, 1972: 19.
— counsellor from Honolulu here to answer questions, Lahaina Sun, November 15, 1972: 4.
— Congresswoman Patsy Mink commends veterans for complaining about Veterans Administration services on Maui, Lahaina Sun, December 20, 1972: 7.
— Mayor Cravalho establishes Jobs for Veterans Task Force, Lahaina Sun, April 25, 1973: 11.
— Veterans Administration to reduce disability benefits, Lahaina News, May 23, 1990: 1,6.
— Lightbringers Rescue Mission calls for help for Vietnam veterans, Lahaina News, January 27, 1994: 1,3.
— Educational Opportunity Center supporting, Lahaina News, February 24, 1994: 4.
— Veterans Services Division benefits counselor to visit Maui, Lahaina News, May 12, 1994: 4.
— AJA Club elects new officers, Lahaina News, August 17, 1995: 4.
— connection of Marines to Maui described, Lahaina News, June 24, 1999: 5.
— Vietnam veterans to meet, Lahaina News, September 9, 1999: 13.
— Veterans Affairs continue to hold meeting, Lahaina News, September 16, 1999: 13.
— Help Disabled War Veterans introducing program offering computers, Lahaina News, October 21, 1999: 14.
— Korean War Veterans National Recognition Day to be held, Lahaina News, May 11, 2000: 20.
— County Department of Parks and Recreation to build Veterans Memorial, Lahaina News, May 24, 2001: 16.
— VA Benefits and Services Workshop to be held, Lahaina News, March 14, 2002: 17.
— Hideo "Pakala" Takahashi of the "Lost Battalion" honored, Lahaina News, August 22, 2002: 3.
— Vietnam Veterans of Maui to hold picnic, Lahaina News, September 11, 2003: 16.

VETERANS AFFAIRS, U.S. DEPARTMENT OF
— services available for women veterans, Lahaina News, October 3, 1996: 14.
— warns of incorrect information on the internet, Lahaina News, March 26, 1998: 2.
— Clifford Miller to meet with veterans to discuss benefits, Lahaina News, May 21, 1998: 9.
— representative to visit Maui Vet Center, Lahaina News, March 18, 1999: 16.
— official to visit Maui Vet Center, Lahaina News, April 8, 1999: 13.
— to explain benefits, Lahaina News, May 13, 1999: 16.
— representative continues to offer informational visits, Lahaina News, October 21, 1999: 17.
— official continues to consult, Lahaina News, April 6, 2000: 17.
— continues to visit Maui Vet Center, Lahaina News, July 20, 2000: 17.
— to hold workshop on VA benefits, Lahaina News, August 7, 2003: 2.
— to offer workshops to veterans, Lahaina News, August 14, 2003: 17.

VETERANS CENTER, MAUI COUNTY
— see Maui Veterans Center

VETERANS DAY
— holiday closings listed, Lahaina News, November 1, 1989: 6.

VETERANS OF FOREIGN WARS LADIES AUXILIARY
— to meet, Lahaina News, April 16, 1992: 5.

VEZZANI, DAN
— owner of Dan's Frame and Art featured, Lahaina News, October 3, 1984: 14.

VICAR, ANTHONY
— Scholar/Athlete of the Week, Lahaina News, April 15, 1999: 6.

VICENS, MERCER "CHUBBY"
— to be honored by Maui Chamber of Commerce, Lahaina News, October 16, 1997: 12.

VICIOUS FISHES [MUSICAL GROUP]
— to perform at Moose McGillycuddy's, Lahaina News, September 5, 1991: 9.
— continues to perform at Moose McGillycuddy's, Lahaina News, October 3, 1991: 12.
— continues to perform at Moose McGillycuddy's, Lahaina News, November 28, 1991: 14.

VICTORIA [CITY]
— yacht race from, sponsored by the Lahaina Yacht Club, Lahaina Sun, December 23, 1970: 8.
— Victoria-Maui race underway, Lahaina Sun, July 5, 1972: 7.
— Victoria-Maui sailing race underway, Lahaina News, July 6, 2000: 13.

VICTORIA S. AND BRADLEY L. GEIST FOUNDATION
— awards grant to Hui Malama Learning Center for "Family Literacy—Family Strengthening Model Demonstration Initiative", Lahaina News, March 15, 2001: 8.

VICTORIA-MAUI YACHT RACE
— "Odusa" is first to arrive from Victoria, Lahaina Sun, July 19, 1972: 1.
— volunteers for final luau sought, Lahaina Sun, July 19, 1972: 10.
— Canadian navy vessel St. Anthony to arrive on Maui to celebrate end of race, Lahaina Sun, July 19, 1972: 14.
— "Cherokee" wins race, Lahaina Sun, August 2, 1972: 4.
— won by Charley, skipped by Bill Niami and Ron Boyd, Lahaina News, July 18, 1984: 7.
— described, Lahaina News, July 2, 1986: 4.
— 1986 race begins, Lahaina News, July 9, 1986: 1.
— editorial on success of, Lahaina News, July 16, 1986: 2.
— captain Mark Schlosser discusses victory, Lahaina News, July 16, 1986: 4.
— to take begin, Lahaina News, June 15, 1988: 1.
— publicity to be handled by Diana Gardiner, Lahaina News, June 22, 1988: 2.
— ends, Lahaina News, July 20, 1988: 12.
— scheduled, Lahaina News, June 27, 1990: 6.
— won by Knightrider and Captain Sid Halls, Lahaina News, July 25, 1990: 14,20.
— results, Lahaina News, July 30, 1992: 9.
— Pyewacket may break race record, Lahaina News, July 11, 1996: 1.
— Pyewacket wins, Lahaina News, July 18, 1996: 7.
— Bonnie Nelson appointed chair of, Lahaina News, June 12, 1997: 12.
— to be held, Lahaina News, July 9, 1998: 14.
— Grand Illusion wins, Lahaina News, July 13, 2000: 1.
— results of competition, Lahaina News, July 13, 2000: 6.
— results, Lahaina News, August 10, 2000: 12.

VICTORIAN CHRISTMAS HOUSE
— to be opened by Hui No'eau Visual Arts Center, Lahaina News, November 28, 1990: 10.

VICTORINO, LISETTE
— police seeking, Lahaina News, November 5, 1998: 11.

VICTORINO, MICHAEL [POLITICIAN]
— running for Board of Education, Lahaina News, August 6, 1998: 14.
— appointed to Hawaii Property Insurance Association, Lahaina News, August 27, 1998: 13.
— Board of Education candidate shares ideas, Lahaina News, October 22, 1998: 1,2.
— candidate for Wailuku-Waihee-Waikapu County Council, Lahaina News, November 2, 2000: 20.

VICTORY [BUSINESS]
— store opens at Wharf Cinema Center, Lahaina News, April 22, 1993: 6.

VICTORY CHRISTIAN ACADEMY
— wins "Festival of Wreaths" contest, Lahaina News, December 31, 1992: 5.

VIDA, DONNA
— named Program Director for Maui Farm, Inc, Lahaina News, March 4, 1993: 12.

VIDEO
— rental stores opening, Lahaina News, August 14, 1985: 1,9.

VIDEO EXPRESS [BUSINESS]
— one of many video rental stores in West Maui, Lahaina News, August 14, 1985: 1.

VIDEO JUNCTION [BUSINESS]
— one of many video rental stores in West Maui, Lahaina News, August 14, 1985: 1.

VIDEOLAND AND TV [BUSINESS]
— moves, Lahaina News, March 12, 1992: 13.

VIENNA CHOIR BOYS
— to perform at Maui Arts and Cultural Center, Lahaina News, October 28, 1999: 17.

VIERRA, ANTHONY
— former superintendent of parks featured, Lahaina News, April 4, 2002: 1,20.

VIERRA, LEOLA
— Lahaina merchant dealing with flooding, Lahaina News, December 12, 1990: 1.

VIERRA, PHIL
— discusses recent flooding, Lahaina Sun, February 3, 1971: 1.

VIETH, MARK
— promoted to editor of Lahaina News, Lahaina News, June 17, 1993: 2.
— Lahaina News editor discusses purchase of paper by Ogden Newspapers, Inc., Lahaina News, October 5, 2000: 1,15.

VIETNAM VETERAN TRAVELING MEMORIAL WALL
— on display, reactions to, Lahaina News, January 28, 1987: 1,16.

VIETNAM VETERANS OF MAUI COUNTY
— dedicating Vietnam Veteran Traveling Memorial Wall, Lahaina News, January 14, 1987: 3.
— to host national conference on the Big Island, Lahaina News, November 2, 1988: 16.
— seeking boats to serve as escorts during canoe race, Lahaina News, August 30, 1989: 1.
— will be crossing Maui-Moloka'i channel, Lahaina News, September 6, 1989: 1.
— complete Moloka'i-Maui canoe crossing, Lahaina News, September 27, 1989: 1.
— to hold general membership meeting, Lahaina News, August 1, 1991: 3.
— to hold general membership meeting, Lahaina News, September 26, 1991: 6.
— to hold general membership meeting, Lahaina News, October 31, 1991: 5.
— to meet at Wailuku Community Center, Lahaina News, November 7, 1991: 9.
— to hold general membership meeting, Lahaina News, November 28, 1991: 4.

— to hold general membership meeting, Lahaina News, December 5, 1991: 5.

— to meet possible Veterans Center and VA Hospital, Lahaina News, February 6, 1992: 4.

— to meet, Lahaina News, April 2, 1992: 6.

— to hold general membership meeting, Lahaina News, May 7, 1992: 6.

— to hold meeting, Lahaina News, June 4, 1992: 4.

— to meet, Lahaina News, October 1, 1992: 4.

— to meet, Lahaina News, November 5, 1992: 5.

— to meet, Lahaina News, July 4, 1996: 14.

— to meet, Lahaina News, July 25, 1996: 13.

— to meet, Lahaina News, October 31, 1996: 19.

— to meet, Lahaina News, September 9, 1999: 13.

— to meet, Lahaina News, February 10, 2000: 17.

— to meet, Lahaina News, March 9, 2000: 13.

— to host Easter Egg Hunt and Picnic, Lahaina News, April 20, 2000: 16.

— to hold picnic on Labor Day, Lahaina News, August 31, 2000: 20.

— to observe National POW MIA Day, Lahaina News, September 14, 2000: 20.

— to hold Veterans Day Parade, Lahaina News, November 9, 2000: 24.

— new officers elected, Lahaina News, December 14, 2000: 8.

— to meet at Maui Tropical Plantation, Lahaina News, January 11, 2001: 3.

— continues to meet, Lahaina News, March 15, 2001: 20.

— to meet, Lahaina News, September 13, 2001: 17.

— continues to meet, Lahaina News, October 11, 2001: 17.

— to meet, Lahaina News, April 18, 2002: 17.

— continues to meet, Lahaina News, November 14, 2002: 21.

— to hold general membership meeting, Lahaina News, April 10, 2003: 20.

— to hold picnic, Lahaina News, September 11, 2003: 16.

VIETNAM WAR

— school in, sent gift from Mauna Olu College, Lahaina Sun, January 6, 1971: 1,2.

— protested by Mauna Olu College, Lahaina Sun, January 6, 1971: 2.

— student letters sent to Tong Duc Thang concerning American POWs, Lahaina Sun, January 13, 1971: 8.

— faculty at Maui Community College urge troops to withdraw, Lahaina Sun, February 24, 1971: 1.

— Elmer Cravalho recommends United States withdrawal, Lahaina Sun, March 3, 1971: 6.

— Dennis Fujii congratulated by Maui County Council for role in war, Lahaina Sun, March 10, 1971: 4.

— discussion of guilt of Lieutenant William Calley, Lahaina Sun, April 7, 1971: 4.

— Charles Kalani is killed in action, Lahaina Sun, January 12, 1972: 16.

— current situation debated in editorials, Lahaina Sun, May 17, 1972: 20,21.

— discussion of news coverage, Lahaina Sun, January 24, 1973: 14.

— Air Force Major Lauren Lengyel's experience as prisoner of war described, Lahaina Sun, May 16, 1973: 5.

VIEWPOINTS GALLERY [BUSINESS]

— opens, Lahaina News, November 7, 1990: 7.

— has opened, Lahaina News, November 21, 1990: 12.

— presenting "Design Elements" exhibition, Lahaina News, January 30, 1991: 9.

— to hold reception for "Too Grand (2000)", Lahaina News, December 23, 1999: 17.

— to exhibit "Be Kind" featuring works by Diana Dorenzo, Lahaina News, June 8, 2000: 20.

VIGLIONE, GENE [POLITICIAN]

— to hold rally, Lahaina News, September 17, 1992: 3.

— named director of The Lightbringers, Lahaina News, November 26, 1992: 4.

VILA, CARMELITO

— named Motor Vehicle and Driver Licensing manager, Lahaina News, November 10, 1994: 13.

VILANTE, MICHELLE

— to speak on "What Do You Hunger For?" at 'Ohana Connection breakfast, Lahaina News, June 5, 2003: 17.

VILLA TERRACE [RESTAURANT]

— Westin Maui restaurant featured, Lahaina News, September 26, 1991: 15.

— distinct from Villa Restaurant, Lahaina News, October 10, 1991: 4.

VILLA, THE [RESTAURANT]

— Eric Koyama appointed manager, Lahaina News, August 16, 1989: 6.

— to celebrate Mardi Gras, Lahaina News, February 6, 1991: 13.

— featuring food and wine from the Pacific Northwest, Lahaina News, April 10, 1991: 9.

— to feature food and wine from the Pacific Northwest, Lahaina News, April 17, 1991: 11.

— offering food and wine from the Pacific Northwest, Lahaina News, April 24, 1991: 7.

— to open Cabaret Lounge, Lahaina News, May 23, 1991: 11.

— to open Cabaret Lounge at Westin Maui, Lahaina News, May 30, 1991: 7.

— continues to host cabaret, Lahaina News, August 8, 1991: 13.

— continues to offer Braodway-style cabaret, Lahaina News, September 5, 1991: 10.

— distinct from Villa Terrace, Lahaina News, October 10, 1991: 4.

— featured, Lahaina News, May 28, 1992: 17.

— new menu features Hawaiian food, Lahaina News, September 30, 1993: 11,12.

— employees recognized, Lahaina News, December 30, 1993: 5.

VILLAGE CINEMA [BUSINESS]

— closes, Lahaina News, September 24, 1986: 1.

VILLAGE GALLERIES [BUSINESS]

— opens third location, Lahaina News, January 4, 1989: 9.

— presents recent paintings from Stewart Marshall, Lahaina News, April 19, 1989: 3.

— opens at Whalers Village, Lahaina News, November 14, 1996: 17.

— to hold group show "In the Garden", Lahaina News, September 6, 2001: 17.

VILLAGE GALLERY CONTEMPORARY [BUSINESS]

— to hold "Summer Fun" art show, Lahaina News, June 1, 2000: 17.

— to hold group show, Lahaina News, May 17, 2001: 20.

— to hold "The Abstract" exhibit, Lahaina News, October 4, 2001: 16.

— to hold "Works on Paper", Lahaina News, November 8, 2001: 16.

— to hold "Art of Hawaii" exhibit, Lahaina News, August 14, 2003: 9.

— to host work in abstract art, Lahaina News, October 2, 2003: 16.

VILLAGE TENNIS CENTER, THE

— to offer junior tennis event, Lahaina News, February 14, 2002: 13.

VILLAGES OF LEIALI'I

— proposed development involving conveyed ceded lands to be considered, Lahaina News, September 17, 1992: 3.

— map of; lottery to be held in summer, Lahaina News, October 8, 1992: 1,10.

— project criticized for lacking affordable housing, Lahaina News, January 20, 1994: 4.

— Housing Finance and Development Corp. approves money to purchase ceded land for housing development, Lahaina News, August 18, 1994: 3.

— project continuing despite legal challenge from Office of Hawaiian Affairs, Lahaina News, December 1, 1994: 4,5.

— issues continue, Lahaina News, December 29, 1994: 1,3.

— Self-Help Housing Corporation seeking more self-help housing at, Lahaina News, July 20, 1995: 2.

— draft Environmental Assessment for proposed, Lahaina News, August 24, 1995: 2.
— project cleared by Office of Environmental Quality Control, Lahaina News, December 7, 1995: 3.
— state can build homes at, Lahaina News, April 18, 1996: 1,18.
— Hawaiians demonstrate against, Lahaina News, December 14, 2000: 1,17.

VILLALON, CHARLES
— County Zoning Instructor discusses enforcement of historic district rules, Lahaina News, August 16, 2001: 1,9.

VILLAREN, ALAN [MUSICIAN]
— to perform at Maui Prince, Lahaina News, July 30, 1992: 16.
— to perform at Molokini Lounge at the Maui Prince Hotel, Lahaina News, August 13, 1992: 17.
— to perform at Molokini Lounge at the Maui Prince Hotel, Lahaina News, December 24, 1992: 17.

VILLARMIA, CERIACO
— passes away, aged 101, Lahaina Sun, January 12, 1972: 17.

VILLAS AT KENOLIO
— real estate development featured, Lahaina News, October 4, 2001: 7.
— development featured, Lahaina News, August 22, 2002: 6.

VILLAVERDE, ANNA GREGO
— born in 1886, passes away, Lahaina Sun, February 2, 1972: 9.

VILLIARIMO, BARRY TANI
— named executive sous chef at Ka'anapali Beach Hotel, Lahaina News, February 16, 1995: 13.
— named executive chef at Ka'anapali Beach Hotel, Lahaina News, August 21, 1997: 12.

VILORIA, NELIE
— receives United States National Award, Lahaina News, May 13, 1993: 3.
— Lahainaluna High School student receives scholarship from Maui Youth Ambassadors, Lahaina News, July 21, 1994: 4.

VINCENS, MERCER "CHUBBY"
— promoted to vice president of Maui office of Alexander and Baldwin Properties, Inc., Lahaina News, February 3, 1994: 7.

VINCENT, DALE
— kayaker may compete in Kanaka Ikaika Race, Lahaina News, September 12, 1984: 4.
— plan kayak trip around Maui, Lahaina News, June 12, 1985: 4.
— kayak trip around Maui described, Lahaina News, July 17, 1985: 4.

VINO [RESTAURANT]
— D.K. Kodama opens, Lahaina News, October 2, 2003: 9.

VINTAGE AT KA'ANAPALI, THE
— Ka'anapali development breaks ground, Lahaina News, March 9, 2000: 11.
— Terra Pacific Development, Co. LLC named as project developer for, Lahaina News, June 8, 2000: 11.
— development featured, Lahaina News, July 5, 2001: 6.
— featured, Lahaina News, July 19, 2001: 7.
— development featured, Lahaina News, February 14, 2002: 6.
— luxury homes available at, Lahaina News, June 6, 2002: 6.

VINTNER DINNER SERIES
— to be held at La Perouse, Lahaina News, March 29, 1989: 3,14.
— returns to La Perouse, Lahaina News, October 3, 1990: 12.
— to be held at Kapalua Bay Hotel, Lahaina News, October 24, 1990: 13.
— to feature wine from Sonoma wineries, Lahaina News, November 14, 1990: 14,15.

VINUYA, DEREK
— padder featured, Lahaina News, April 4, 1996: 17.
— representing Hawaii at International World Sprints Championships, Lahaina News, August 13, 1998: 15.

— competes in Starbucks Solo Kayak and Canoe World Championship, Lahaina News, June 10, 1999: 2.
— paddler featured, Lahaina News, March 2, 2000: 6.
— paddler wins medals at World Outrigger Sprint Championships, Lahaina News, September 7, 2000: 14.

VINUYA, GREGORIO
— passes away, Lahaina Sun, September 29, 1971: 14.

VIOLENCE
— hippies accused of being cause of, Lahaina Sun, December 16, 1970: 7.

VIOLENCE HOTLINE
— set up, Lahaina News, November 9, 1988: 12,20.

VIPASSANA
— meditation session to be offered, Lahaina News, January 2, 1997: 10.

VISCOTT, DAVID
— radio personality to lecture at Unity Church, Lahaina News, December 7, 1988: 16.

VISION OF THE SEAS [SHIP]
— to visit Lahaina Harbor, Lahaina News, September 23, 1999: 11.

VISIONS OF HAWAII
— Lahaina Cannery Mall to host art classes by, Lahaina News, April 16, 1998: 13.
— to offer sculpture courses, Lahaina News, May 7, 1998: 20.
— to offer free sculpture orientation classes, Lahaina News, June 11, 1998: 17.
— to offer sculpture classes, Lahaina News, August 6, 1998: 7.

VISIT OLD LAHAINA TOWN [BROCHURE]
— published by J.J. Enterprises, Lahaina News, May 14, 1986: 3.

VISITOR INDUSTRY CHARITY WALK
— to be held, sponsored by Hawaii Hotel Association, Lahaina News, May 8, 1985: 3.
— set for May 18, Lahaina News, May 15, 1985: 3,8.
— announced for March 31, Lahaina News, March 26, 1986: 3.
— 8th annual set for May 17, Lahaina News, May 14, 1986: 3.
— planned, Lahaina News, May 13, 1987: 3.
— to hold Charity Ball, Lahaina News, July 27, 1988: 11.
— to be held; sponsored by Hawaii Hotel Association, Lahaina News, April 26, 1989: 1.
— success, Lahaina News, May 17, 1989: 7.
— to be held by Maui Hotel Association, Lahaina News, April 17, 1991: 18.
— looking for volunteer walkers, Lahaina News, April 24, 1991: 4.
— results, Lahaina News, June 6, 1991: 4.
— to hold fundraiser, Lahaina News, May 13, 1993: 3.
— to be held, Lahaina News, April 28, 1994: 9.
— Sheraton Maui employees raise money for, Lahaina News, May 18, 2000: 16.
— to be held, Lahaina News, May 17, 2001: 8.
— Kahana Falls Resort to support, Lahaina News, October 11, 2001: 9.
— to be held, Lahaina News, May 8, 2003: 8.
— to be held, Lahaina News, May 15, 2003: 16.

VISITOR INDUSTRY TRAINING AND EDUCATION CENTER (VITEC)
— offering courses, Lahaina News, February 22, 1989: 3.
— to hold workshop on food decorating, Lahaina News, March 8, 1989: 16,17.
— to hold workshop with Sam Horn, Lahaina News, April 5, 1989: 15.
— offering courses on customer service, Lahaina News, April 19, 1989: 13.
— to offer bartender training, Lahaina News, April 26, 1989: 12.
— offering courses for managers in hospitality industry, Lahaina News, October 25, 1989: 10.
— to offer seminar on upselling, Lahaina News, November 8, 1989: 5.

— offering classes on computers, coping with stress, and career development for women, Lahaina News, November 29, 1989: 36.
— offers workshop on helping Japanese visitors and on upselling, Lahaina News, December 6, 1989: 5.
— offering travel industry management courses, Lahaina News, July 11, 1990: 6.
— receives good reviews, Lahaina News, September 5, 1991: 4.
— to hold basic CPR and first aid class, Lahaina News, September 14, 1995: 6.

VISITOR ORIENTED POLICING PROGRAM
— formed, Lahaina News, July 23, 1998: 1,20.

VITAFLEX
— course on to be held, Lahaina News, June 10, 1999: 16.

VITAL, ÉLAN [ARTIST]
— work with Andrew Annenberg featured, Lahaina News, February 27, 1997: 14,16.
— to exhibit at Addi Galleries, Lahaina News, February 24, 1994: 9.
— featured, Lahaina News, April 21, 1994: 14.
— featured, Lahaina News, September 12, 1996: 17.

VITALE, JAMES
— to speak to Central Maui Diabetes Support Group on footcare and diabetes, Lahaina News, January 16, 1991: 4.

VITAMIN WORLD [BUSINESS]
— opening at , Lahaina News, August 26, 1999: 14.

VITEC
— see Visitor Industry Training and Education Center (VITEC)

VIVA JAZZ
— to be performed by Maui Philharmonic Society, Lahaina News, February 11, 1993: 15.

VLAEVA, NADEJA "NADIA" [MUSICIAN]
— pianist to perform, Lahaina News, March 20, 1997: 18.
— to perform, Lahaina News, November 12, 1998: 17.

VOCATIONAL EDUCATION WEEK
— to be held at Ka'ahumanu Center, Lahaina News, February 18, 1993: 4,5.

VOCATIONAL INDUSTRY CLUBS OF AMERICA
— sponsors skills challenge where Lahaina Intermediate School students compete, Lahaina News, May 15, 2003: 1,20.

VOGELE, BOB
— supervisor of West Maui Youth Center, Lahaina Sun, January 6, 1971: 7.

VOGUE [MAGAZINE]
— photo shoot in Lahaina, Lahaina Sun, October 20, 1971: 1,2.
— review of photoshoot on Maui, Lahaina Sun, January 12, 1972: 6.
— reviewed, Lahaina Sun, February 16, 1972: 8.

VOICE OF THE PRAIRIE, THE [PLAY]
— to be performed at Seabury Hall, Lahaina News, January 16, 1992: 18.
— continues at Seabury Hall, Lahaina News, January 30, 1992: 21.

VOICE OF THE PROPHET [PLAY]
— performed in Kahului by members of the Baha'i, Lahaina Sun, January 13, 1971: 2.

VOICES OF NATIVE AMERICA
— to be held at Maui Arts and Cultural Center, Lahaina News, October 9, 1997: 20.

VOICES OF THE RAINFOREST
— theme for films at Castle Theatre, Lahaina News, January 18, 1996: 13.

VOICES PROJECT
— featured, Lahaina News, August 28, 2003: 1,18.

VOICES ROCK KA'ANAPALI
— concert to be held, Lahaina News, December 13, 2001: 1,18.
— to be held, Lahaina News, December 27, 2001: 14.

VOICESTREAM [BUSINESS]
— opens, Lahaina News, April 26, 2001: 8.

VOLCANO CRATERS [BUSINESS]
— opens, Lahaina News, April 22, 1993: 6.

VOLCANO JONES [MUSICAL GROUP]
— to perform at Casanova's, Lahaina News, October 29, 1992: 20.
— to perform at Moose McGillycuddy's, Lahaina News, May 16, 1996: 10.

VOLENTINE, CRAIG
— creates West Maui Table Tennis Club, Lahaina News, December 12, 2002: 10.

VOLLEYBALL
— Hawaiian Airlines Wahine Volleyball Classic to be played, Lahaina News, September 5, 1990: 7.
— Lahainaluna High School team to play, Lahaina News, September 26, 1990: 14.
— Compadres Volleyball Classic to be held, Lahaina News, August 20, 1992: 10.
— University of Hawaii Wahine team to play at War Memorial Gym, Lahaina News, September 10, 1992: 8.
— University of Hawaii Wahine team to play at War Memorial Gym, Lahaina News, September 17, 1992: 4.
— Panama Tevaga named to 1992 Maui Interscholastic League Volleyball All-Star Team, Lahaina News, December 3, 1992: 7.
— Maui Brothers Volleyball Club to host annual tournament, Lahaina News, August 18, 1994: 7.
— University of Hawaii Wahine Volleyball to play against UC Irvine at War Memorial Gym, Lahaina News, August 25, 1994: 9.
— update on Maui Interscholastic League, Lahaina News, September 22, 1994: 8.
— results of "Dig Me" Beach Volleyball Classic, Lahaina News, May 4, 1995: 8.
— Eyecatcher Maui Invitational Beach Volleyball Championship, Lahaina News, March 1, 2001: 15.
— Department of Parks and Recreation hosting co-ed volleyball league, Lahaina News, March 29, 2001: 12.
— Lahaina Intermediate School holds tournament, Lahaina News, May 10, 2001: 14.
— Lahaina Intermediate School holds tournament, Lahaina News, May 24, 2001: 14.
— Lahaina Intermediate School hosting PTSA Invitational Volleyball Tournament, Lahaina News, June 7, 2001: 15.
— Parks and Recreation Department starting league, Lahaina News, March 7, 2002: 13.
— Department of Parks and Recreation forming league, Lahaina News, March 14, 2002: 13.
— coed team forming, Lahaina News, August 8, 2002: 13.
— coed league forming, Lahaina News, August 15, 2002: 12.
— coed league forming, Lahaina News, February 20, 2003: 13.
— coed league forming, Lahaina News, February 27, 2003: 13.

VOLUNTEER CENTER OF MAUI COUNTY
— to honor coaches, Lahaina News, February 25, 1999: 7.

VOLUNTEER COASTAL MONITORING TEAM
— to hold meeting and training, Lahaina News, September 14, 1995: 6.

VOLUNTEER LEGAL SERVICES HAWAII
— to hold "Organizational Management and Responsibilities", Lahaina News, March 22, 2001: 17.
— offering workshop for non-profits, Lahaina News, March 29, 2001: 16.
— to hold workshops on "Building Organizational Resources and Strategic Planning", Lahaina News, April 18, 2002: 17.

VOLUNTEER SERVICES OFFICE, STATE
— sponsoring Liability Workshop, Lahaina News, January 18, 2001: 16.

VOLUNTEERS
— County ordinance proposed to encourage volunteerism, Lahaina News, December 15, 1981: 16.
— showcase held at Ka'anapali Beach Hotel, Lahaina News, September 12, 1991: 3.

VON IMHOF, CHRIS
— elected president of Maui Hotel Association, Lahaina News, August 12, 1987: 18.

VON PHUL, PHILIP AND GINI
— art displayed at Lahaina Art Society Gallery, Lahaina Sun, January 20, 1971: 3.

VON TEMPSKY, ARMINE [WRITER]
— publishes "Born In Paradise", Lahaina News, May 22, 1985: 3.

VON TEMPSKY, FRANCIE
— to direct "Pieces XI", Lahaina News, June 24, 1993: 15.

VON TEMPSKY, LYNN
— leads yoga, Lahaina News, August 23, 2001: 13.

VORFELD, BOB
— retires as manager of Pioneer Mill, Lahaina News, March 18, 1987: 2,3.

VORFIELD, WILMA BROWN
— named "Bank of America Charity Cup Volunteer of the Year" by Mercedes Championship, Lahaina News, June 28, 2001: 11.

VOYAGING CAMP
— held, Lahaina News, September 24, 1998: 2.

VUORI, TAPANI
— new merchandise director at Maui Ocean Center, Lahaina News, August 29, 2002: 14.

W

W. T. CHANG CONTRACTORS, INC. [BUSINESS]
— building erosion control wall built at Launiupoko State Park, Lahaina Sun, November 11, 1970: 3.
— constructing ocean pool at Launiupoko State Park, Lahaina Sun, December 23, 1970: 11.

W.F.P. RECORDS
— produces song to honor Desert Shield, Lahaina News, January 2, 1991: 4.

WAAL, ARTHUR, JR.
— son of Lahaina's first postmaster visits Lahaina, Lahaina News, July 19, 2001: 2.

WADA, RYKER
— hired as complaint analyst by Legal Aid Society of Hawaii, Lahaina News, April 17, 2003: 8.

WADA, SANDY
— Maui Community Correctional Center Law Librarian wins Maui County Bar Association's Liberty Bell Award, Lahaina News, November 30, 2000: 5.

WADE, ELVIS [MUSICIAN]
— to stage "Aloha Again from Hawaii—A Tribute to Elvis", Lahaina News, August 14, 2003: 17.

WAGATSUMA, EDSON
— King Kamehameha III Elementary School counselor organizes cross-country team, Lahaina News, December 28, 2000: 1,15.

WAGNER, BOB
— UH head football coach to attend banquet, Lahaina News, February 11, 1993: 9.

WAGNER, JASON, JR.
— Lahainaluna High School junior named Century III Sylvan Scholar, Lahaina News, February 2, 1995: 4.

WAGNER, TERRY
— Lahainaluna High School graduate completes Field Medical Service Technician Course, Lahaina News, May 31, 2001: 2.

WAGONER, JAMES
— named president of Maui Chamber of Commerce, Lahaina News, June 17, 1987: 3.

WAGSTAFF, ROBERT [ARTIST]
— to appear at Hawaii Nature Center Gift Shop, Lahaina News, August 5, 1999: 12.
— to lead goauche painting demonstration, Lahaina News, October 24, 2002: 20.

WAHATSU, KINEYA
— to celebrate anniversary of teaching nagauta and shamisen in Hawaii, Lahaina News, September 12, 1990: 19.

WAHIKULI [TOWN]
— boat launch proposed, Lahaina Sun, December 23, 1970: 1.
— house lots to be sold, Lahaina Sun, October 6, 1971: 15.
— auction of housing lots delayed, Lahaina Sun, September 27, 1972: 1.
— proposed housing project expanded to 4,200 units , Lahaina News, July 11, 1991: 1.
— housing development delayed at, Lahaina News, January 16, 1992: 3.
— mix of affordable housing may change at development at, Lahaina News, June 4, 1992: 1.

WAHIKULI STATE PARK
— guardrail to be installed, Lahaina Sun, August 18, 1971: 3.
— expansion planned, Lahaina Sun, June 14, 1972: 3.
— Laura Johnson and Steve Scott married underwater off of, Lahaina News, January 21, 1987: 8.
— Na Kupuna O Maui stages demonstration at, Lahaina News, December 14, 2000: 1.

WAHIKULI TERRACE PARK
— residential development in Lahaina, Lahaina Sun, December 2, 1970: 3.
— discussion of eligibility to receive federal subsidies, Lahaina Sun, April 14, 1971: 6.
— first family moves into development, Lahaina Sun, September 15, 1971: 11.
— chosen as site for Waste Water Pump No. 3, Lahaina News, March 17, 1994: 1,16.

WAHINE O KULA HOSPITAL AUXILIARY
— members honored with Public Service Excellence Awards, Lahaina News, April 29, 1987: 3.

WAIAKEA INTERMEDIATE SCHOOL
— ukulele band to perform, Lahaina News, May 14, 1998: 17.

WAIAKOA LOOP TRAIL
— Na Ala Hele Trails and Access Program to hold hike to, Lahaina News, May 30, 2002: 16.

WAIAKOA THEATRE
— to become a real estate office, Lahaina Sun, January 5, 1972: 4.

WAIANAPANAPA PARK
— papayas stolen and plants damaged, Lahaina Sun, January 5, 1972: 7.

WAIEHU
— sea snake found at, Lahaina News, December 10, 1998: 19.

WAIEHU GOLF COURSE
— under construction, Lahaina News, November 15, 2001: 13.

WAIEHU KOU 2
— Hawaiian Homelands development featured, Lahaina News, August 17, 2000: 13.

WAIEHU TERRACE
— sale of increment B to begin, Lahaina News, January 9, 1992: 9.
— sales begin, Lahaina News, January 14, 1993: 4.

WAIHEE [TOWN]
— tested for pollution, Lahaina Sun, December 16, 1970: 3.
— described, Lahaina Sun, July 4, 1973: 14,15.

WAIHEE, JOHN [POLITICIAN]
— attends ceremony for Research and Technology Park, Lahaina News, October 8, 1986: 1.
— puts relocation of Hawaiian remains on hold, Lahaina News, December 28, 1988: 1.
— Governor to visit Lahaina, Lahaina News, March 8, 1989: 1.
— visits Lahaina, Lahaina News, March 22, 1989: 1,20.
— expected to support proposed community pool, Lahaina News, May 3, 1989: 5.
— signs seasonal ban on thrillcrafts, Lahaina News, June 28, 1989: 1.
— to speak to Maui Chamber of Commerce, Lahaina News, January 31, 1990: 5.
— to speak to Maui Chamber of Commerce, Lahaina News, February 7, 1990: 5.
— to kick off campaign, Lahaina News, April 25, 1990: 3.
— releases money to build portables at King Kamehameha III School, Lahaina News, July 11, 1990: 1.
— attends gala function honoring mayor Hannibal Tavares, Lahaina News, December 26, 1990: 5.
— governor seeking money for housing project, Lahaina News, January 16, 1991: 1.
— governor releases funds for Upcountry Community Center, Lahaina News, August 1, 1991: 5.
— proposes funding to deal with extinctions, Lahaina News, February 13, 1992: 4.
— to speak at Business and Environment Conference, Lahaina News, March 12, 1992: 12.
— to speak to Maui Chamber of Commerce, Lahaina News, July 16, 1992: 16.
— tours Maui Research and Technology Center, Lahaina News, July 30, 1992: 10.
— Pro Bowl will remain in Hawaii for next five years, Lahaina News, December 31, 1992: 7.
— to join Hawaii Visitors Bureau in Germany, Lahaina News, October 21, 1993: 11.
— releases funds for infrastructure improvements for Front Street, Lahaina News, February 10, 1994: 3.
— releases funds to install a traffic light on Honoapi'ilani Road, Lahaina News, February 24, 1994: 1.
— management plan for whale sanctuary will not be ready to be signed by, Lahaina News, November 3, 1994: 8.

WAIHEE, LYNNE
— to support Maui Hui Malama's adult literacy program, Lahaina News, March 7, 1990: 3.
— honors volunteers, Lahaina News, April 30, 1992: 18.

WAIHEE SCHOOL
— to hold alumni golf tournament, Lahaina News, April 17, 1991: 10.

WAIHEE VALLEY
— featured article on, Lahaina News, October 26, 1983: 7,8,9.

WAIKAMOI PRESERVE
— "Wet Side Hike" to be held at, Lahaina News, May 16, 2002: 16.

WAIKIKI, NELSON
— member of Lahaina Kamaakina Fishing Association, Lahaina Sun, December 23, 1970: 11.

WAIKIKI TRADERS [BUSINESS]
— applies for after-the-fact permit for mural painted by Wyland, Lahaina News, March 6, 1991: 7.
— given 15 days to appeal Maui Planning Department rejection of Wyland mural, Lahaina News, April 10, 1991: 1.
— appeals decision against Wyland mural, Lahaina News, May 1, 1991: 4.

WAIKIKI WEDDING [FILM]
— to be shown at Maui Arts and Cultural Center, Lahaina News, August 15, 1996: 14.

WAILEA
— project described, Lahaina Sun, September 15, 1971: 12.
— Planning Commission okays relocation of road away from shoreline, Lahaina Sun, June 14, 1972: 9.
— opposition to development discussed, Lahaina Sun, July 5, 1972: 5.
— discussion of mayor Cravalho's relationship with area of, Lahaina Sun, July 19, 1972: 19.
— students fight planned tourist project, Lahaina Sun, October 11, 1972: 19.
— resort project debated at Kihei school, Lahaina Sun, January 24, 1973: 3.
— tourist project approved by Planning Commission, Lahaina Sun, January 31, 1973: 3.
— Pacific Colony tourist project is being planned, Lahaina Sun, March 7, 1973: 10.
— zoning changes approved for resort project, Lahaina Sun, April 11, 1973: 3.
— proposed development Wailea 670 recommended for approval, Lahaina News, February 6, 1992: 5.
— "An Evening in Wailea" to be held, Lahaina News, December 26, 2002: 16.

WAILEA 670
— development to be discussed, Lahaina News, June 4, 1992: 7.
— referred to Maui County Council's Planning and Economic Development Committee, Lahaina News, July 9, 1992: 7.
— request to develop golf courses passes first reading, Lahaina News, August 27, 1992: 13.
— Maui Meadows Homeowners Association requests buffer from, Lahaina News, August 27, 1992: 13.
— nears approval, Lahaina News, September 24, 1992: 2.
— proposal passes final reading at Maui County Council, Lahaina News, October 8, 1992: 7.
— now called Wailea Ranch, Lahaina News, November 25, 1993: 6.

WAILEA ARTS BUFFET
— to be held, Lahaina News, July 1, 1987: 3.

WAILEA COMMUNITY ASSOCIATION
— to hold seminar on being a board member, Lahaina News, June 25, 1992: 7.
— to hold seminar on being a board member, Lahaina News, July 2, 1992: 7.
— accepting applications for scholarship, Lahaina News, March 25, 1993: 8.
— Frank Schuster appointed director of, Lahaina News, April 1, 1993: 7.
— accepting applications for scholarships, Lahaina News, May 20, 1993: 5.
— presents scholarship to Candis Tateyama, Lahaina News, September 16, 1993: 8.
— to offer scholarships, Lahaina News, May 28, 1998: 3.
— offering scholarships, Lahaina News, June 4, 1998: 9.
— awards scholarships, Lahaina News, August 12, 1999: 8.

— donates funds to Maui Food Bank, Lahaina News, May 18, 2000: 8.

— donates to Maui Community Food Bank, Lahaina News, July 12, 2001: 8.

WAILEA DESTINATION ASSOCIATION

— announces officers for 1993, Lahaina News, January 28, 1993: 8.

— elects officers, Lahaina News, January 20, 1994: 7.

— announces winners of Travel Journalism competition, Lahaina News, July 14, 1994: 13.

— announces new officers, Lahaina News, January 26, 1995: 13.

— new officers appointed, Lahaina News, January 18, 1996: 10.

— to hold Celebration of Aloha, Lahaina News, October 10, 1996: 14.

WAILEA DEVELOPMENT CORPORATION

— receives rezoning approval for resort project, Lahaina Sun, April 11, 1973: 3.

WAILEA GOLF CLUB [BUSINESS]

— sponsors "100 Holes of Golf" fundraiser for Easter Seal Society, Lahaina News, June 18, 1986: 3.

— offering instruction, Lahaina News, July 17, 1997: 14.

— Carol Garlock and Diane Driscoll-Miller join, Lahaina News, August 19, 1999: 14.

— hosting PGA Match Play Championship, Lahaina News, September 9, 1999: 7.

— receives national and state honors, Lahaina News, January 20, 2000: 7.

— to hold annual Junior Golf Class, Lahaina News, August 30, 2001: 12.

— to hold fundraiser for American Red Cross, Lahaina News, October 4, 2001: 13.

— LPGA Teaching Professional Cathy Torchiana named to 50 To Teachers by Golf for Women magazine, Lahaina News, February 28, 2002: 13.

WAILEA HO'OLAULE'A

— to be held in October, Lahaina News, June 20, 1991: 10.

— to be held in October, Lahaina News, July 4, 1991: 13.

— 5th annual to be held, Lahaina News, July 11, 1991: 15.

— to be held, Lahaina News, August 8, 1991: 13.

— to be held in October, Lahaina News, September 12, 1991: 17.

WAILEA HOU

— private school to open, Lahaina News, April 29, 1999: 14.

WAILEA JEWELRY [BUSINESS]

— opens at The Shops at Wailea, Lahaina News, January 25, 2001: 14.

WAILEA KAI [SHIP]

— to hold sunset cruise out of Ma'alaea Harbor, Lahaina News, November 21, 2002: 20.

WAILEA KAI CHARTERS

— see Ocean Activities Center

WAILEA LAND CORPORATION

— requests permission to develop area on Maui's south shore, Lahaina Sun, December 2, 1970: 2.

— fine recommended for due to development activities, Lahaina Sun, February 10, 1971: 2.

— complaint by Life of the Land dismissed, Lahaina Sun, March 24, 1971: 5.

— names David Carter as president, Lahaina Sun, May 30, 1973: 11.

WAILEA OPEN TENNIS CHAMPIONSHIPS

— to be held, Lahaina News, June 24, 1999: 7.

WAILEA RANCH

— proposal to develop considered by Land Use Commission, Lahaina News, November 25, 1993: 6.

— formerly known as Wailea 670, Lahaina News, November 25, 1993: 6.

WAILEA REALTY CORPORATION [BUSINESS]

— offering tours of Wailea's private homes, Lahaina News, May 23, 1996: 16.

— offering free tours of private houses, Lahaina News, May 23, 1996: 16.

— awards grant to Maui Arts and Cultural Center, Lahaina News, April 19, 2001: 9.

WAILEA RESORT COMPANY [BUSINESS]

— hires Entrekin/Zucco Advertising Agency, Lahaina News, September 13, 1989: 6.

— Dennis Okimoto named senior vice president of, Lahaina News, January 30, 1992: 10,11.

— promotes Anne Takabuki to vice president, Lahaina News, July 2, 1992: 17.

— hoping to build new clubhouse, Lahaina News, July 9, 1992: 7.

— seeking extension of Special Management Area Use Permit for new office building, Lahaina News, August 6, 1992: 9.

— files civil suit against environmental impact statement for proposed Kihei Elementary School, Lahaina News, August 20, 1992: 15.

— promotions announced, Lahaina News, March 31, 1994: 12.

— name changed from Stouffer Wailea Resort, Lahaina News, May 23, 1996: 16.

— celebrating Whale Week, Lahaina News, March 13, 1997: 16.

WAILEA SHOPPING VILLAGE

— presenting film series, Lahaina News, January 7, 1987: 3.

— Chicago Brass to perform, Lahaina News, February 11, 1987: 11.

— to continue free movies, Lahaina News, April 29, 1987: 3.

— continues film series, Lahaina News, November 11, 1987: 6.

— continues film series, Lahaina News, March 9, 1988: 17.

— to offer free Polynesian show, Lahaina News, October 31, 1990: 14.

— features Hawaiian entertainment, Lahaina News, January 30, 1992: 19.

— to celebrate 15th anniversary, Lahaina News, June 18, 1992: 15.

— to hold Christmas celebration, Lahaina News, December 17, 1992: 13.

— to feature Polynesian show, Lahaina News, March 11, 1993: 15.

— to host "Made in Maui" display, Lahaina News, October 21, 1993: 8.

— to host "Wailea's Celebration of Aloha", Lahaina News, October 6, 1994: 7.

WAILEA TENNIS CLUB

— named one of 50 greatest tennis resorts by Tennis Magazine, Lahaina News, December 17, 1992: 11.

WAILEA TOUR OF HOMES

— fundraiser for Hospice Maui to be held, Lahaina News, March 5, 1992: 4.

WAILING SOULS [MUSICAL GROUP]

— to perform at Lahaina Civic Center Amphitheater, Lahaina News, August 6, 1998: 15.

— to perform, Lahaina News, August 13, 1998: 16.

— to perform, Lahaina News, August 20, 1998: 16.

WAILUKU [TOWN]

— site of permanent air pollution testing station, Lahaina Sun, February 17, 1971: 1.

— redevelopment plan discussed, Lahaina Sun, July 14, 1971: 1.

— Department of Housing and Urban Development provides funds for North Wailuku General Neighborhood Renewal, Lahaina Sun, December 29, 1971: 17.

— Maui County wants Alexander & Baldwin land near Maui Memorial Gym, Lahaina Sun, January 19, 1972: 9.

— criticisms of proposed renewal project discussed, Lahaina Sun, June 28, 1972: 9.

— redevelopment plans criticized, Lahaina Sun, October 4, 1972: 3.

— Wailuku-Kahului general plan discussed, Lahaina Sun, October 25, 1972: 5.
— federal Small Business Administration to answer questions about possible support, Lahaina Sun, November 22, 1972: 4.
— tension between Maui Redevelopment Agency and Wailuku residents has subsided, Lahaina Sun, December 13, 1972: 4.
— Mayor Cravalho claims Wailuku-Kahului general plan is good, Lahaina Sun, December 27, 1972: 14.
— redevelopment program in lull, Lahaina Sun, February 28, 1973: 3.
— housing subdivision proposed, Lahaina Sun, May 23, 1973: 5.
— non-compliance with federal financing regulations leads to withholding of development funds for, Lahaina News, February 6, 1992: 4.
— financial companies offering money to rehabilitate, Lahaina News, October 15, 1992: 8.
— Maui Redevelopment Agency updating plans to revitalize, Lahaina News, January 6, 2000: 11.
— State Housing and Community Development Corporation of Hawaii (HCDCH) awards tax credit for affordable rentals in, Lahaina News, June 19, 2003: 7.
— Police Resource Center to open, Lahaina News, July 24, 2003: 8.

WAILUKU AGRIBUSINESS
— using inmates to pick pineapples, Lahaina News, August 27, 1992: 10.

WAILUKU CHRISTMAS, A [MUSICAL]
— to be performed by Maui Community Theatre, Lahaina News, December 9, 1999: 20.

WAILUKU COURTHOUSE
— likely soon to be owned by Maui County, Lahaina News, January 2, 1991: 4.

WAILUKU CROSS
— Sierra Club sponsoring climb to, Lahaina News, April 17, 1991: 7.

WAILUKU GATEWAY BEAUTIFICATION PROJECT
— groundbreaking held, Lahaina News, September 24, 1992: 6.

WAILUKU HONGWANJI
— see Hongwanji Mission

WAILUKU MAIN STREET ASSOCIATION
— to hold welcome for military, Lahaina News, June 6, 1991: 4.
— to hold Flag Day celebration, Lahaina News, June 13, 1991: 6.
— sponsoring Christmas ornament decoration contest, Lahaina News, December 5, 1991: 6.
— requests multi-story parking structure, Lahaina News, July 23, 1992: 7.
— to hold meeting on crime, Lahaina News, May 12, 1994: 4.
— sponsoring Christmas contests, Lahaina News, November 17, 1994: 4.

WAILUKU PUBLIC LIBRARY
— to sell old records, Lahaina News, September 8, 1994: 5.
— features challenged books display, Lahaina News, October 3, 1996: 14.
— hosting poetry program for kids, Lahaina News, April 10, 1997: 13.
— to be closed for termite treatment, Lahaina News, December 26, 2002: 16.

WAILUKU SAND DUNE
— state archaeologist Theresa Donham to speak on, Lahaina News, February 13, 1997: 11.

WAILUKU SUGAR COMPANY [BUSINESS]
— problems with pollution, Lahaina Sun, November 25, 1970: 4.
— report on production for 1970, Lahaina Sun, December 23, 1970: 4.
— described, Lahaina Sun, May 31, 1972: 3.
— Donald Martin becomes manager, Lahaina Sun, June 7, 1972: 14.

WAILUKU SUMMER JUNIOR OPEN
— tennis tournament to be held, Lahaina News, July 16, 1998: 15.

WAILUKU TOWN CHRISTMAS PARADE
— scheduled for December 15, Lahaina News, December 12, 1984: 3.

WAILUKU TOWNE CENTER
— spaces available for lease, Lahaina News, November 3, 1994: 23.

WAILUKU UNION CHURCH
— to hold "Huli Au (Time of Change)", Lahaina News, February 8, 2001: 20.

WAILUKU VINEYARD
— redevelopment plans criticized, Lahaina Sun, October 25, 1972: 1,14.

WAILUKU-KAHULUI GENERAL PLAN, CITIZENS ADVISORY COMMITTEE ON THE
— approves development plan, Lahaina Sun, July 19, 1972: 7.

WAILUKU-KAHULUI RECLAMATION FACILITY
— operator William Carroll charges that County is not pursuing reclamation aggressively, Lahaina News, May 14, 1992: 1.

WAILUKU-ROYAL LANES BOWLING ALLEY [BUSINESS]
— new name of Aloha Lanes; to hold benefit dance for Salvation Army, Lahaina News, August 22, 1990: 13.

WAIMEA [PLACE]
— featured as tourist destination, Lahaina News, July 11, 1996: 6,7.

WAIMEA BAY (OAHU)
— as surf spot, Lahaina Times, July, 1980 volume 4 number 6: 1.

WAINEE CHURCH
— historical marker for, discussed , Lahaina Sun, December 16, 1970: 6.

WAINEE OFFICE BUILDING
— proposed, Lahaina News, July 1, 1999: 11.

WAINEE PARK
— Amfac/JMB Hawaii break ground at expansion of, Lahaina News, June 22, 2000: 6.

WAINEE STREET
— widening of controversial, Lahaina News, November 16, 1988: 1,20.

WAINEE VILLAGE
— future of inhabitants uncertain, Lahaina News, August 1, 1990: 1,6.
— plans for Lahainaluna rental project to be submitted to Maui County Council, Lahaina News, January 12, 1995: 2.
— residents critical of project proposed by Affordable Housing Corp. at, Lahaina News, February 23, 1995: 1.

WAIOHU, PILIKILAOMANA
— discusses situation of native Hawaiian leadership, Lahaina Sun, June 7, 1972: 3.

WAIOHU, PRISCILLA
— reunited with adopted uncle Louis Wong, Lahaina News, August 1, 1983: 6.

WAIOHU, WILLIAM
— to represent Lahaina on state burial council, Lahaina News, August 13, 1998: 1,20.

WAIOLA [PLACE]
— history of detailed, Lahaina News, September 1, 1981: 11.

WAIOLA CHURCH
— to be demolished, Lahaina News, December 24, 1986: 12.
— to hold public meeting to discuss proposed changes at Campbell Park, Lahaina News, July 16, 1992: 3.
— to hold meeting to discuss projects, Lahaina News, July 23, 1992: 5.
— to host observation of the 1893 overthrow, Lahaina News, January 14, 1993: 3.
— commemoration of 1893 Overthrow described, Lahaina News, January 28, 1993: 3.
— to host music of Christmas, Lahaina News, December 16, 1993: 18.
— to hold Hawaiian language classes, Lahaina News, May 26, 1994: 4.
— to host Christmas performances, Lahaina News, December 15, 1994: 17.

— to celebrate the Psalms, Lahaina News, May 25, 1995: 12.
— Proud Hawaiian Society to meet at, Lahaina News, December 14, 1995: 18.
— to celebrate 175th anniversary, seeking information on history, Lahaina News, July 18, 1996: 10.
— breaks ground on Hale Wai, Lahaina News, August 28, 1997: 5.
— celebrating 175 years, Lahaina News, May 14, 1998: 17.
— rummage sale to be held, Lahaina News, November 5, 1998: 1.
— Kekapa Lee moving to position in Oahu, Lahaina News, October 14, 1999: 1,2.
— to host Roselle Bailey as part of Hawaiian Culture Series , Lahaina News, February 3, 2000: 12,13.
— celebrates 180 years, Lahaina News, July 31, 2003: 1,20.
— celebrates 180 years, Lahaina News, August 21, 2003: 2.
— offering free conversational Hawaiian language classes, Lahaina News, September 18, 2003: 2.
— to offer conversational Hawaiian language classes, Lahaina News, October 2, 2003: 2.

WAIOLANI
— housing development sells out, Lahaina News, May 27, 1993: 7,8.

WAIORA [PLAY]
— to be performed at Iao Theater, Lahaina News, September 16, 1999: 13.

WAIPAHU HIGH SCHOOL
— reunion scheduled for class of 1967, Lahaina News, March 12, 1992: 4.

WAIT UNTIL DARK [PLAY]
— to be performed by Maui Community Theatre, Lahaina Sun, June 13, 1973: 27.
— details of production provided, Lahaina Sun, June 20, 1973: 8.
— to be performed at Iao Theater, Lahaina News, November 18, 1999: 16.
— being held be Maui Community Theatre, Lahaina News, November 25, 1999: 16.

WAITHE, TOM
— named director of rooms at the Four Seasons Hotel in Tokyo, Lahaina News, April 16, 1992: 14.

WAITING FOR THE PARADE [PLAY]
— to be performed by Baldwin Theatre Guild, Lahaina News, January 14, 1993: 15.
— to be performed by Baldwin Theatre Guild, Lahaina News, January 21, 1993: 15.

WAKE [MAGAZINE]
— sponsoring "Wake Cycle to the Sun", Lahaina News, August 30, 1989: 24.

WAKIDA, PENNY
— discusses Theatre Theatre upcoming summer program, Lahaina News, May 8, 2003: 3.
— Lahainaluna High School teacher to retire, Lahaina News, June 5, 2003: 1,2.

WAKIDA, SHIGETA "SHIGESH"
— awarded Pan-American Tennis Award, Lahaina Sun, December 15, 1971: 14.
— tennis player featured, Lahaina News, April 11, 1984: 6.
— tennis player attending U.S. Open but not playing, Lahaina News, August 29, 1984: 4.
— tennis player career detailed, Lahaina News, June 5, 1985: 4.
— tennis player receives The American Sportsman Award, Lahaina News, December 11, 1985: 4.
— tennis courts at Malu'ulu O Lele to be named after, Lahaina News, April 9, 1986: 3.
— tennis player featured, Lahaina News, June 15, 1988: 7.
— life described, Lahaina News, July 5, 1989: 4.

— editorial thanking him for coaching Lahainaluna High School tennis, Lahaina News, May 2, 1990: 18.
— tennis player made Honorary Member of the United States Professional Tennis Registry, Lahaina News, June 13, 1990: 8.
— tennis coach at Lahainaluna High School successful, Lahaina News, April 3, 1991: 16.
— honored for work with young athletes, Lahaina News, December 23, 1993: 8.
— Lahainaluna High School tennis coach discusses chances, Lahaina News, March 24, 1994: 12.
— tennis teacher featured, Lahaina News, October 17, 1996: 13.
— to offer free tennis program, Lahaina News, April 30, 1998: 15.
— ailing tennis legend teaching children about character, Lahaina News, August 5, 1999: 1,6.
— tennis player ready to retire, Lahaina News, April 27, 2000: 1,2.
— teaching tennis, Lahaina News, June 22, 2000: 13.
— teaching tennis, Lahaina News, June 29, 2000: 15.
— held Prince Fun Tennis Tournament, Lahaina News, July 13, 2000: 6.
— passes away, Lahaina News, May 10, 2001: 1,22.
— memorial delivered for, Lahaina News, May 17, 2001: 1,22.

WALDECK, GLENN [MUSICIAN]
— to perform at Maui Community College in support of the environment, Lahaina News, March 20, 1991: 11.

WALDENBOOKS [BUSINESS]
— to hold book fair fundraiser, Lahaina News, April 6, 1988: 3.
— opening in Kihei, Lahaina News, August 2, 1989: 6.
— to hold Book Fair for Maui AIDS Foundation, Lahaina News, November 5, 1998: 21.
— to open in Whalers Village, Lahaina News, July 29, 1999: 11.
— opens at Whalers Village, Lahaina News, October 7, 1999: 13.

WALDORF SCHOOL
— to organize support for victims of the earthquake in Kobe, Japan, Lahaina News, February 16, 1995: 6.
— to hold Christmas Faire, Lahaina News, December 4, 1997: 24.
— to hold open house, Lahaina News, March 12, 1998: 20.
— to hold "Adult Waldorf Education" summer conference, Lahaina News, July 16, 1998: 16.
— to begin adult education program, Lahaina News, September 17, 1998: 28.
— to host open house, Lahaina News, March 11, 1999: 12.
— to hold "A Night to Remember" retro dance, Lahaina News, April 15, 1999: 12.
— to hold "Lei Day Hula Festival", Lahaina News, April 29, 1999: 16.
— to hold Christmas Faire, Lahaina News, December 2, 1999: 16.
— to host open house, Lahaina News, March 16, 2000: 12.

WALDRON STEAMSHIP COMMITTEE
— president Bill Thayer to speak to LahainaTown Action Committee, Lahaina News, April 23, 1998: 1.

WALES & CO. JEWELERS [BUSINESS]
— to host champagne reception, Lahaina News, March 14, 1990: 15.

WALK DOWN ABBEY ROAD, A
— musical celebration to be held, Lahaina News, June 13, 2002: 17.

WALK FOR ANIMALS
— Maui Humane Society benefit set for May 5, Lahaina News, May 2, 1984: 4.
— to be held by Maui Humane Society, Lahaina News, May 1, 1985: 8.

WALK FOR JUVENILE DIABETES
— to be held at Keopuolani Park, Lahaina News, November 7, 2002: 17.
— to be held, Lahaina News, November 14, 2002: 20.

WALK FOR MULTIPLE SCLEROSIS
— to be held, Lahaina News, March 18, 1999: 8.
— to be held, Lahaina News, April 1, 1999: 8.

WALK FOR PEACE
— planned from Paia to Kahului, Lahaina Sun, January 26, 1972: 14.
— planned for Saturday, Lahaina Sun, February 2, 1972: 8.
— rescheduled due to weather, Lahaina Sun, February 9, 1972: 15.

WALK FOR THE CURE FOR MULTIPLE SCLEROSIS
— to be held, Lahaina News, June 18, 1998: 16.

WALK OF ALOHA
— held, Lahaina News, March 8, 2001: 1,20.

WALK-RUN
— Heart Foundation organizing, Lahaina News, February 20, 1985: 3.

WALKAMERICA
— kick-off breakfast to be held, Lahaina News, January 7, 1993: 4.
— to be held, Lahaina News, April 3, 1997: 13.
— to benefit March of Dimes, Lahaina News, April 2, 1998: 2.
— Danny Agsalog to chair, Lahaina News, March 1, 2001: 10.

WALKER, ALAN
— leases Hale Aloha, Lahaina News, May 25, 1988: 1.
— honored by Cable Advertising Bureau Conference, Lahaina News, May 6, 1993: 9.

WALKER, JERRY JEFF [MUSICIAN]
— to perform at Casanova's, Lahaina News, December 19, 1990: 12.
— to perform at Casanova's, Lahaina News, December 26, 1990: 11.

WALKER, MARK
— named Maui agent for Soderholm Sales and Leasing, Inc., Lahaina News, March 5, 1992: 10.

WALKER, PENNY
— performing in South America, Lahaina Sun, January 20, 1971: 7.

WALKER, PHILLIP [MUSICIAN]
— to perform at Studio Blue nightclub, Lahaina News, August 22, 1996: 12.

WALKER, RICHARD
— businessman featured, Lahaina News, May 7, 1992: 10.

WALKER, STEVEN
— joins Alexander and Baldwin Properties, Lahaina News, February 10, 2000: 14.

WALKER, TERRY
— head of Republican Party to speak to Kihei-Wailea Rotary Club, Lahaina News, June 18, 1992: 14.

WALKING CO., THE [BUSINESS]
— opens store, Lahaina News, February 22, 2001: 8.

WALKING TOURS OF HAWAII
— Larry O'Boyle to offer self-guided historical walking tour of Lahaina, Lahaina News, January 22, 1998: 5.

WALL, ROGER
— promoted to executive vice president at Foodland, Lahaina News, February 9, 1995: 6.

WALLACE, CHARLES
— Scholar/Athlete of the Week, Lahaina News, May 30, 2002: 12.

WALLACE, GEORGE [COMEDIAN]
— to perform at the Maui Marriott, Lahaina News, June 22, 1995: 11.

WALLACE THEATRE CORP. [BUSINESS]
— plans Maui's biggest movie house, Lahaina News, July 9, 1998: 12.
— opens Maui Mall Megaplex Cinemas, Lahaina News, May 6, 1999: 10.

WALLS, MADGE
— American Heart Association board chair announces beginning of "Neighbor-Neighbor" Campaign", Lahaina News, January 24, 1990: 2.
— to discuss book "Real Estate Principles and Practices, Hawaii Supplement", Lahaina News, June 25, 1998: 11.

WALSH, CHRIS
— appointed as new operations general manager at Trilogy Excursions, Lahaina News, September 9, 1999: 11.

WALSH, DENNIS
— appointed publications editor for Alexander and Baldwin, Lahaina News, August 30, 1989: 5.

WALSH, IAN
— surfer competes in National Scholastic Surfing Association's Summer Spray-Offs, Lahaina News, July 6, 2000: 1,14.

WALSH, JIM
— Hawaii Cocoa managing partner envisions Hawaii as "Switzerland of the Pacific", Lahaina News, May 3, 1989: 1.

WALTERS, JOHN PAUL [MUSICIAN]
— to hold interactive musical "There's No Such Thing As Away", Lahaina News, January 20, 2000: 12.

WALTERS, MIKE
— named food and beverage manager at Napili Kai Beach Club, Lahaina News, October 10, 1991: 6.

WALTON, DIANNA AND STEVE
— Scholar/Athlete of the Week, Lahaina News, April 27, 2000: 6.

WALTON, LINDA
— promoted to Maui agency manager for Avis Rent-A-Car, Lahaina News, March 27, 1991: 9.

WALTON, STEVAN
— chiropractor contributes to national poll, Lahaina News, March 25, 1999: 13.

WAMPANOAG [TRIBE]
— activities and information for children in pull-out section, Lahaina News, November 9, 1983: A,B,C,D.

WANG, DANIEL [ARTIST]
— works shown at Maui Inter-Continental Wailea, Lahaina News, August 8, 1984: 3.

WANG, MARK
— president of Aloha Resorts International comments on tourism industry, Lahaina News, June 3, 1993: 8.

WAPNER, JOSEPH
— "The People's Court" judge to attend Maui County Crime Stoppers 10th anniversary celebration, Lahaina News, April 16, 1992: 4.

WAR [MUSICAL GROUP]
— coming to Maui, Lahaina News, December 7, 1983: 12.
— to perform at Casanova's, Lahaina News, February 13, 1991: 11.
— to perform at Maui Arts and Cultural Center, Lahaina News, October 26, 1995: 12.
— concert canceled, Lahaina News, November 2, 1995: 12.
— to perform, Lahaina News, March 28, 1996: 14.

WAR MEMORIAL CENTER
— bids to construct baseball stadium will be opened, Lahaina Sun, November 17, 1971: 4.

WAR MEMORIAL STADIUM
— has leaky roof, Lahaina News, April 16, 1986: 4.
— Mayor Linda Lingle to hold meeting on use of, Lahaina News, August 7, 1997: 1.
— pact reached over use of by sports leagues, Lahaina News, August 14, 1997: 3.

WAR MEMORIAL TRACK AND FOOTBALL STADIUM
— now open, Lahaina News, January 23, 1992: 5.

WARD, BARBARA [ARTIST]
— work exhibited, Lahaina News, June 21, 1989: 3.
— to exhibit at Village Galleries Maui, Lahaina News, May 7, 1998: 20.
— to exhibit at Village Galleries, Lahaina News, October 10, 2002: 17.

WARD, DAVID [DANCER]
— offering class, Lahaina News, May 5, 1994: 16.
— to offer DanceQuake '99, Lahaina News, May 13, 1999: 16.
— to offer "Graceful Edge" concert, Lahaina News, September 16, 1999: 12.

WARD, ELAINE
— contestant in Mrs. Hawaii USA pageant, Lahaina News, June 4, 1992: 4.
— passes away, Lahaina News, September 16, 1999: 3.

WARDAIR CANADA [BUSINESS]
— airline to begin direct flights between Kahului airport and Vancouver, British Columbia, Lahaina News, October 9, 1985: 3.

WARES, JUDITH [ARTIST]
— to teach printmaking to children, Lahaina News, July 1, 1987: 3.

WARHOL, ANDY [ARTIST]
— reflection on death of, Lahaina News, March 11, 1987: 12.

WARING, BILL
— named creative merchandising director at Hilo Hatties Fashion Centers, Lahaina News, May 7, 1992: 10.

WARNECKE, JOHN CARL
— former employer of Edward Beall, architect of Whaler's Village, Lahaina Sun, December 16, 1970: 5.

WARNER BROTHERS
— auditioning for new "Wonder Woman" show, Lahaina News, January 1, 1998: 13.

WARNER BROTHERS STUDIO STORE [BUSINESS]
— to open on Front Street, Lahaina News, March 27, 1997: 1,10.

WARNER, DAVID [ARTIST]
— to exhibit at "Friday Night is Art Night", Lahaina News, January 24, 1990: 15.

WARNER, DICK
— named director of sales for KPOA-FM, Lahaina News, January 9, 1985: 3.

WARNER, PAUL [PIANIST]
— recent recordings discussed, Lahaina News, January 15, 1980: 5.

WARREN AND ANNABELLE [TROUPE]
— to perform magic theatre at Ruth's Chris Steakhouse, Lahaina News, January 21, 1999: 11.

WARREN AND ANNABELLE'S [BUSINESS]
— magic nightclub opens in Lahaina Center, Lahaina News, May 13, 1999: 13.
— piano bar opens, Lahaina News, September 9, 1999: 11.
— hosted magic fundraiser for Alzheimer's Association, Lahaina News, February 3, 2000: 11.
— adding Family Show, Lahaina News, May 25, 2000: 16.
— resumes Family Show, Lahaina News, May 31, 2001: 8.
— awards college scholarships, Lahaina News, August 30, 2001: 9.

WARREN, DAVID [ARTIST]
— to teach non-credit class on public speaking, Lahaina News, February 5, 1986: 3.
— to teach art classes, Lahaina News, February 11, 1987: 3.
— featured at Hui No'eau Visual Arts Center, Lahaina News, September 30, 1987: 3.
— to exhibit for Lahaina Arts Society, Lahaina News, October 31, 1991: 13.
— to exhibit at Lahaina Arts Society, Lahaina News, November 7, 1991: 14.

WARREN, JAMES [ARTIST]
— work displayed at the Lahaina Art Society showroom, Lahaina Sun, November 18, 1970: 4.
— work featured, Lahaina News, July 15, 1980: 5.
— donate prints to Lahaina Arts Society Scholarship Fund, Lahaina News, May 13, 1987: 3.
— to exhibit at Wyland Galleries, Lahaina News, September 30, 1993: 12.
— to appear at Wyland Galleries, Lahaina News, September 6, 2001: 16.

WARREN, MOLOKA'I JOE
— charged with stealing a try-pot, claiming ownership based on ancestral right, Lahaina Sun, March 1, 1972: 7.
— treatment of disabled veterans criticized, Lahaina Sun, March 8, 1972: 8.
— now working on the Big Island, Lahaina Sun, March 29, 1972: 9.

WARREN, STEVE
— files papers to run for South Maui set on the County Council, Lahaina News, May 18, 2000: 17.

WARREN UNEMORI ENGINEERING, INC. [BUSINESS]
— selected to work on highway connecting South Maui and the Upcountry, Lahaina News, October 15, 1992: 7.

WARRINGTON, WENDELL [MUSICIAN]
— career described, Lahaina News, December 30, 1987: 11.
— to conduct Maui Symphony's Christmas Concert, Lahaina News, December 5, 1990: 14.
— featured, Lahaina News, March 19, 1992: 13.
— musical director of "oneMAUIstory", Lahaina News, August 18, 1994: 15.
— teaches students with Theatre Theatre Maui, Lahaina News, June 15, 2000: 1,7.
— to direct Theatre Theatre Maui summer drama program, Lahaina News, May 24, 2001: 18.

WARSHAUER, KRATRINA AND BRONNER
— owners of D-Lite hold fundraiser for Maui AIDS Foundation, Lahaina News, November 21, 1991: 14,15.

WARWICK, DIONNE [MUSICIAN]
— to perform, Lahaina News, May 6, 1999: 20.
— to perform at Maui Arts and Cultural Center, Lahaina News, May 6, 1999: 9.

WASANA JAKEWAY
— benefit dance held for, Lahaina News, December 17, 1986: 12.

WASHBURN, KATE
— manager of Olympic Torch Relay vacations on Maui, Lahaina News, October 3, 1984: 4.

WASHINGTON, D.C.
— to be visited by students, Lahaina Sun, February 3, 1971: 1.
— report on student fieldtrip to, Lahaina Sun, April 21, 1971: 8.

WASHINGTON, MIGUEL [COMEDIAN]
— to perform at Comedy Club and the Sports Page, Lahaina News, October 15, 1992: 17,18.

WASHINGTON SOCIETY OF CPAS
— to hold convention, Lahaina News, November 5, 1992: 9.

WASHIO, KINEYA
— to celebrate anniversary of Kineya Wahatsu's teaching nagauta and shamisen in Hawaii, Lahaina News, September 12, 1990: 19.

WASSERMAN, ROB [MUSICIAN]
— to perform with fellow Grateful Dead member Bob Weir, Lahaina News, January 3, 1990: 16.

WASTEWATER RECLAMATION DIVISION, COUNTY
— to hold public meeting to relocate Lahaina Wastewater Pump Station No. 3, Lahaina News, October 14, 1993: 4.

WATANABE, EDWARD SEIYA
— new president of West Maui AJA Veterans Club, Lahaina News, August 3, 2000: 5.

WATANABE, HIROO
— names branch manager of First Federal Savings and Loan, Lahaina News, December 11, 1985: 9.

WATANABE ING AND KAWASHIMA [BUSINESS]
— Asia Pacific Consulting Group, Lahaina News, July 4, 1991: 4.

WATANABE TAIKO DRUMMERS [MUSICAL GROUP]
— to perform at Lahaina Cannery Mall as part of "Journey to the Orient", Lahaina News, August 7, 2003: 1,14.

WATANABE, WAYNE
— promoted to captain at Lahaina Fire Station, Lahaina News, May 1, 1985: 8.

WATANABE, WINSTON AND MIDORI
— proposing park for Honokohau, Lahaina News, August 24, 1995: 1,16.
— beach front property too expensive for county, Lahaina News, September 21, 1995: 3.

WATCH-N-SEE [BUSINESS]
— opens at Lahaina Center, Lahaina News, October 17, 1990: 11.
— celebrating arrival of Gucci line of watches, Lahaina News, November 21, 1991: 11.
— opens, Lahaina News, December 25, 1997: 11.
— features Yves St. Laurent watches, Lahaina News, September 24, 1998: 13.

WATER
— problem of disposing of faced by Pioneer Mill, Lahaina Sun, November 11, 1970: 1.
— projects desired by West Maui Business Association, Lahaina Sun, December 23, 1970: 2.
— access to clean water in Napili, Lahaina Sun, February 3, 1971: 4.
— new well proposed for Napili, Lahaina Sun, February 3, 1971: 4.
— surveillance of harbor pollution , Lahaina Sun, February 3, 1971: 5.
— photographs of waterfalls on road to Hana, Lahaina Sun, February 10, 1971: 5.
— public education effort undertaken by Baldwin Highschool students, Lahaina Sun, February 17, 1971: 6.
— programs planned for Kihei and Makena, Lahaina Sun, March 3, 1971: 3.
— contract to drill new well at Napili awarded to Layne International, Lahaina Sun, April 14, 1971: 8.
— shortage impacting housing projects, Lahaina Sun, May 26, 1971: 6.
— Army Corps of Engineers hold public meeting to discuss water needs of Maui, Lahaina Sun, May 26, 1971: 8.
— Life of the Land attempts to upgrade waters in Ma'alaea Bay to Class AA, Lahaina Sun, July 28, 1971: 11.
— drought plaguing Maui, Lahaina Sun, August 18, 1971: 1.
— improvements to Iao stream undertaken, Lahaina Sun, August 18, 1971: 11.
— drought on Maui continues, Lahaina Sun, September 1, 1971: 1,16.
— water use restrictions relaxed in Hana and Kula, Lahaina Sun, September 15, 1971: 4.
— Honolua Watershed Project discussed, Lahaina Sun, September 22, 1971: 1.
— plan to improve supply at Kula, Lahaina Sun, September 22, 1971: 7.
— call for bids for one-million-gallon water tank for Honokowai-Napili system, Lahaina Sun, September 29, 1971: 1.
— West Maui watershed plans discussed, Lahaina Sun, September 29, 1971: 4.
— rainfall below average, Lahaina Sun, October 20, 1971: 11.
— geological report on West Maui water, Lahaina Sun, November 3, 1971: 11.
— record low rainfall, Lahaina Sun, November 17, 1971: 5.
— Ige Construction Company lowest bidder for one-million-gallon water storage tank in Napili, Lahaina Sun, December 8, 1971: 1.
— Maui County Water Master Plan approved, Lahaina Sun, January 26, 1972: 8.
— work nearly finished on 1.5 million gallon Wahikuli water reservoir, Lahaina Sun, March 15, 1972: 11.
— history of Wai-Ha-ha-ke, a stream near Ka'anapali, Lahaina Sun, May 31, 1972: 17.

— County Water Board rules to be reviewed, Lahaina Sun, July 5, 1972: 11.
— realtors fight proposed rule changes, Lahaina Sun, July 26, 1972: 3.
— fluoridation debated, Lahaina Sun, July 26, 1972: 9.
— legend of The Twin Waters of Life described, Lahaina Sun, August 16, 1972: 15.
— Wailuku had lowest rainfall in 70 years , Lahaina Sun, September 6, 1972: 10.
— public meetings to be held, Lahaina Sun, November 22, 1972: 11.
— history of Wailea discussed, Lahaina Sun, November 29, 1972: 14.
— well dug in Napili, Lahaina Sun, February 7, 1973: 10.
— ancient prophecies discussed, Lahaina Sun, May 30, 1973: 22.
— new wells to improve West Maui supply, Lahaina Sun, June 27, 1973: 15.
— line from Makawao to Pukalani will make housing development possible, Lahaina Sun, June 27, 1973: 3.
— Arthur Ueoka claims it is unfair that the County pay to expand water supply for Alexander & Baldwin development, Lahaina Sun, July 4, 1973: 4.
— new rules and regulations discussed, Lahaina Sun, July 18, 1973: 3.
— limited supply threatening developments in Kihei, Lahaina Sun, July 25, 1973: 3.
— shortage in Haleakala crater, Lahaina Sun, July 25, 1973: 3.
— Mayor Cravalho intervenes in supply problems, Lahaina Sun, August 1, 1973: 3.
— changes to regulations in West Maui, Lahaina News, September 15, 1980: 6.
— Maui County researching costs of pumping water, Lahaina News, July 1, 1981: 11.
— bids open for upcountry water system, Lahaina News, October 15, 1982: 11.
— drinking water now safe in Lahaina without boiling, Lahaina News, November 2, 1983: 6.
— Kapalua Water Co. wants to charge more for water, Lahaina News, November 2, 1983: 6.
— safe drinking water to become more available, Lahaina News, February 1, 1984: 5,7.
— hearing on use of near-shore waters to be held at Lahaina Civic Center, Lahaina News, April 17, 1985: 3.
— drilling expected to increase availability of, Lahaina News, October 1, 1986: 12.
— issues over previous year recounted, Lahaina News, December 30, 1987: 13.
— Department of Transportation accepting permits for commercial activities in shore waters near Ka'anapali, Lahaina News, August 10, 1988: 3.
— demand to outpace supply, Lahaina News, May 10, 1989: 1.
— importance of ocean safety, Lahaina News, May 17, 1989: 1.
— water source assessment fees criticized, Lahaina News, June 21, 1989: 1.
— treatment plant scheduled to be built near Lahainaluna High School, Lahaina News, December 27, 1989: 11.
— state accepting applications for commercial operator's permit, Lahaina News, February 14, 1990: 5.
— fees may be reduced for West Maui, Lahaina News, March 28, 1990: 1.
— need for more lifeguards, Lahaina News, April 4, 1990: 1,8.
— aquifer nearing limit, may require water management area, Lahaina News, November 28, 1990: 1,2.
— conference to be held at Hawaii State Capitol, Lahaina News, January 2, 1991: 4.
— public hearing to discuss rate, Lahaina News, May 15, 1991: 6.
— public meeting to be held on Napili watershed, Lahaina News, July 4, 1991: 3.
— public hearing to discuss rates, Lahaina News, July 11, 1991: 3.

— public meeting to be held on Lahaina Watershed, Lahaina News, July 18, 1991: 4.

— new rates proposed, Lahaina News, August 1, 1991: 3.

— Amfac may face new rules due to TCP, Lahaina News, September 5, 1991: 1,2.

— new rates approved, Lahaina News, September 12, 1991: 5.

— public hearing on Modified Alterative Plan for Lahaina Watershed, Lahaina News, November 7, 1991: 4.

— meeting to be held to discuss Modified Alternative Plan for the Lahaina Watershed, Lahaina News, November 14, 1991: 2.

— Maui County identify people failing to comply to mandatory cutbacks, Lahaina News, November 28, 1991: 5.

— county water director Rae Shikuma quits, Lahaina News, December 26, 1991: 5.

— restrictions lifted in Upcountry, Lahaina News, January 2, 1992: 5.

— exemptions sought for proposed assessment fee, Lahaina News, January 23, 1992: 5.

— David Craddick appointed county director, Lahaina News, January 30, 1992: 5.

— assessment of Lahaina Watershed project in Puamana released, Lahaina News, March 5, 1992: 1,4.

— shortage in upcountry likely, Lahaina News, March 12, 1992: 5.

— Department of Water Supply asking people to conserve, Lahaina News, April 9, 1992: 1.

— cutbacks still in force, Lahaina News, April 16, 1992: 1.

— Board of Water Supply may revise fees, Lahaina News, April 23, 1992: 8.

— Water board to review assessments, Lahaina News, April 30, 1992: 12.

— source cut off by landslide, Lahaina News, May 14, 1992: 1.

— Maui County to purchase water from Amfac/JMB following landslide, Lahaina News, May 21, 1992: 1.

— problem with muddy water resolved, Lahaina News, May 28, 1992: 4.

— restrictions continue Upcountry, Lahaina News, June 4, 1992: 4.

— Makena Homeowners Association asks to move a water line, Lahaina News, July 9, 1992: 7.

— shortages in Lahaina continue, Lahaina News, July 16, 1992: 3.

— current shortage tied to bad estimates from the 1970s, Lahaina News, July 16, 1992: 6.

— David Craddick explains water assessment proposal, Lahaina News, July 30, 1992: 6.

— Honokohau farmers concerned about, Lahaina News, August 20, 1992: 1.

— aquifer lower due to changes in land use on Wailuku slopes, Lahaina News, August 20, 1992: 14.

— Maui County Council chair concerned about source assessment proposed by water board, Lahaina News, September 24, 1992: 6,7.

— Maui County Water Board may exempt churches from water source assessment, Lahaina News, October 8, 1992: 3.

— new line installed in Makena, Lahaina News, October 29, 1992: 17.

— cleaner water to go to Kelawea Mauka, Lahaina News, October 29, 1992: 3.

— Dennis Nakamura hoping to work on problems with, Lahaina News, November 12, 1992: 4.

— Maui County Water Board director David Craddick to ask for water rebate, Lahaina News, December 17, 1992: 1.

— service to Wahikuli improves, Lahaina News, December 24, 1992: 1.

— Board of Water Supply to hold public meeting, Lahaina News, February 11, 1993: 5.

— hearing to be held on source fees, Lahaina News, April 8, 1993: 3.

— new meter fee approved, Lahaina News, April 22, 1993: 2.

— Wendy Wiltse selected Watershed Project coordinator for West Maui, Lahaina News, July 8, 1993: 1,4.

— Sierra Club prepared to serve county notice to stop violating the Clean Water Act, Lahaina News, July 15, 1993: 1,3.

— problems in Lahaina likely to continue for years, Lahaina News, August 5, 1993: 1,12.

— political issues discussed, Lahaina News, August 26, 1993: 3.

— reservoir above Lahaina Wastewater Reclamation Facility being fixed, Lahaina News, September 9, 1993: 3.

— state agencies sponsoring public meeting on coastal, Lahaina News, September 9, 1993: 3.

— West Maui Watershed Advisory Committee to meet, Lahaina News, September 16, 1993: 4.

— West Maui Watershed Advisory Committee to begin meeting, Lahaina News, September 30, 1993: 1,15.

— West Maui water safe, Lahaina News, November 11, 1993: 1,3.

— residents advised to boil water due to turbidity, Lahaina News, February 3, 1994: 4.

— workshop "Drinking Water and Wastewater in West Maui: Now and Future" to be held, Lahaina News, May 12, 1994: 1.

— discussion of ways to conserve, Lahaina News, May 26, 1994: 2.

— Water Director David Craddick says water notices will not be needed, Lahaina News, June 9, 1994: 1.

— poor quality of seen as threat, Lahaina News, December 15, 1994: 1,20.

— drinking water quality expected to improve, Lahaina News, April 27, 1995: 1,16.

— new treatment plant almost ready, Lahaina News, May 25, 1995: 1.

— Mahinahina Water Plant to be commissioned, Lahaina News, August 3, 1995: 5.

— Department of Water Supply finalizes agreement with Maui Land and Pineapple Co to provide more water to Honokohau Stream, Lahaina News, September 28, 1995: 1,12.

— Water Resource Commission and U.S. Geological Survey studying West Maui's water situation, Lahaina News, October 5, 1995: 1,16.

— Public Works having hard time selling reclaimed water, Lahaina News, October 12, 1995: 3.

— Lahaina Water Treatment Facility ground breaking held, Lahaina News, November 2, 1995: 4.

— West Maui Watershed Advisory Committee holds Kokua Award ceremony, Lahaina News, November 16, 1995: 4.

— Honokohau Valley residents want better treatment by Water Department, Lahaina News, March 28, 1996: 1,2.

— opinions of resident sought, Lahaina News, April 18, 1996: 4.

— report on West Maui Watershed, Lahaina News, June 20, 1996: 1,2.

— West Maui Watershed Project Advisory Committee to meet, Lahaina News, July 18, 1996: 1,16.

— Board of Water Supply encouraging water conservation, Lahaina News, July 18, 1996: 3.

— contamination discussed, Lahaina News, August 1, 1996: 24.

— minerals in drinking water, Lahaina News, August 8, 1996: 12.

— lead in, Lahaina News, August 29, 1996: 16.

— recycling conference to be held, Lahaina News, September 5, 1996: 19.

— Honolua Ditch Agreement discussed, Lahaina News, October 3, 1996: 1.

— contaminated wells tied to pineapple pesticide, Lahaina News, November 21, 1996: 3,18.

— Board of Water Supply to hold public hearing, Lahaina News, May 8, 1997: 16.

— "West Maui Watershed Owner's Manual" teaches ways to protect West Maui, Lahaina News, July 31, 1997: 1.

— rate a concern for condominiums, Lahaina News, August 7, 1997: 5.

— new water plant has solved problems, Lahaina News, September 11, 1997: 3.

— improvements to end problems with, Lahaina News, December 4, 1997: 1.

— Board of Water Supply trucking water into Honokohau Valley, Lahaina News, July 23, 1998: 1,20.
— State finds water off Ka'anapali Beach safe from sharks, Lahaina News, March 11, 1999: 3.
— Department of Water Supply to send Water Quality Report, Lahaina News, October 14, 1999: 5.
— Honokohau Valley residents asked to improve drinking water system, Lahaina News, October 28, 1999: 1,2.
— commentary on current situation, Lahaina News, May 17, 2001: 5.
— community objects to drilling above Lahaina, Lahaina News, January 31, 2002: 1,9.
— Dick Mayer to moderate "Watersheds at Risk: A Search for Solutions", Lahaina News, July 11, 2002: 9.
— Department of Water Supply asks residents to conserve water, Lahaina News, June 19, 2003: 9.
— residents helping to monitor reefs through Great Annual Fish Count, Lahaina News, August 14, 2003: 5.
— councilmember Danny Mateo to discuss Iao Aquifer, Lahaina News, September 4, 2003: 8.
— residents asked to conserve, Lahaina News, October 9, 2003: 5.

WATER ACTIVITIES AND VACATION ENTERTAINMENT, INC [BUSINESS]
— operators Wili Baronet and Robert Hunzikar indicted on theft and racketeering charges, Lahaina News, October 6, 1994: 11.

WATER BED
— described, Lahaina Sun, February 9, 1972: 13.

WATER CRAFT
— see thrillcrafts

WATER GARDENS OF HAWAII [BUSINESS]
— opens, Lahaina News, February 6, 1991: 6.

WATER MAN [BUSINESS]
— opens plant in Kahului Industrial complex, Lahaina News, November 11, 1987: 11.

WATER OF KAMA—THE STORY OF THE BAILEY HOUSE SITE [BOOK]
— published by the Maui Historical Society, Lahaina News, June 12, 2003: 18.

WATER POLLUTION CONTROL ADVISORY BOARD, FEDERAL
— praises Maui for progressive planning, Lahaina Sun, June 16, 1971: 1.

WATER POLO
— class to be offered, Lahaina News, June 26, 2003: 10.
— clinics to be held, Lahaina News, July 10, 2003: 13.
— clinics continue to be held, Lahaina News, July 17, 2003: 12.

WATER RESOURCE MANAGEMENT, STATE COMMISSION ON
— studying West Maui's water situation, Lahaina News, October 5, 1995: 1,16.
— proposed rules to include Hawaiian water rights, Lahaina News, June 27, 1996: 5.
— orders Makila Land Co. to halt drilling in lands above Lahaina, Lahaina News, January 24, 2002: 1,18.

WATER SPORTS AND NEW PRODUCTS EXPO
— to be held, Lahaina News, August 7, 1997: 11.
— to be held, Lahaina News, August 14, 1997: 16.
— to be held, Lahaina News, April 16, 1998: 7.
— to be held, Lahaina News, April 23, 1998: 16,17.

WATER SUPPLY, BOARD OF
— plans for 1971, Lahaina Sun, January 20, 1971: 1.
— proposes new water rates, Lahaina News, August 1, 1991: 3.
— new rates approved, Lahaina News, September 12, 1991: 5.
— to replace water line that serves Lahaina Harbor, Lahaina News, July 21, 1994: 3.

— asks chemical companies to pay for contaminated wells in Napili, Lahaina News, May 30, 1996: 3.
— to hold public hearing, Lahaina News, May 8, 1997: 16.
— trucking water into Honokohau Valley, Lahaina News, July 23, 1998: 1,20.
— plans to improve water and sewer lines to, Lahaina News, December 23, 1999: 3.
— to hold public meeting on budget, Lahaina News, June 15, 2000: 17.
— to hold public meetings, Lahaina News, October 11, 2001: 2.
— to hold hearing on amending Water System Development Fee, Lahaina News, October 18, 2001: 17.

WATER SUPPLY, DEPARTMENT OF
— finalizes agreement with Maui Land and Pineapple Co to provide more water to Honokohau Stream, Lahaina News, September 28, 1995: 1,12.
— losing plant operators due to low pay scale, Lahaina News, November 16, 1995: 1,20.
— Honokohau Valley residents want better treatment by, Lahaina News, March 28, 1996: 1,2.
— seeking to draw more water from Maui Land and Pineapple Co. Honolua Ditch, Lahaina News, August 1, 1996: 1,5.
— to clean DBCP-tainted well, Lahaina News, January 16, 1997: 3.
— to offer public tours, Lahaina News, July 8, 1999: 13.
— to send Water Quality Report, Lahaina News, October 14, 1999: 5.
— asks residents to conserve water, Lahaina News, June 19, 2003: 9.
— asks residents to conserve water, Lahaina News, October 9, 2003: 5.

WATERFRONT RESTAURANT [RESTAURANT]
— reviewed, Lahaina News, January 20, 1988: 7.
— reviewed, Lahaina News, July 18, 1991: 11.

WATERHOUSE, WILLIAM
— could have become the king of Hawaii, Lahaina News, March 15, 1981: 13.

WATERS, SCOTT
— named computer art director for Grapevine Productions, Lahaina News, June 6, 1991: 6.

WATERSHED
— protection workshop to be held, Lahaina News, July 26, 2001: 9.

WATERSHED MANAGEMENT ADVISORY COMMITTEE
— prepares products, Lahaina News, July 12, 2001: 9.

WATERSTORE, THE
— employees pass Water Quality Association's Certified Water Specialist test, Lahaina News, January 1, 1998: 15.

WATERWORKS [BUSINESS]
— featured, Lahaina News, July 24, 1985: 11.

WATKINS, WAYNE "UNCLE" [MUSICIAN]
— to perform at the Maui Arts and Cultural Center, Lahaina News, December 15, 1994: 19.
— to appear on Akaku Maui Community Television, Lahaina News, July 13, 1995: 11.
— Uncle Wayne Show to appear on Akaku Maui Community Television, Lahaina News, July 13, 1995: 11.
— to offer story time at Borders Books, Lahaina News, September 9, 1999: 13.
— to kick off "Uncle Wayne's Kids Club", Lahaina News, May 11, 2000: 16.

WATSON, BOBBY
— Lahainaluna football coach featured, Lahaina News, October 21, 1993: 12.
— Lahainaluna High School football coach honored, Lahaina News, December 9, 1993: 8.
— football coach worthy of coach of the year, Lahaina News, December 18, 1997: 17.

WATSON, EKEKELA
— Scholar/Athlete of the Week, Lahaina News, October 11, 2001: 12.

WATSON, PATRICIA [MUSICIAN]
— featured, Lahaina News, October 31, 1991: 12.
— to perform at Kapalua Bay Hotel, Lahaina News, November 12, 1992: 19.
— releases new CD, Lahaina News, February 18, 1993: 12.
— to perform at Longhi's, Lahaina News, November 25, 1993: 12.
— performs anthems at baseball game in Toronto, Lahaina News, October 30, 1997: 14.
— sings national anthems at Toronto Blue Jays game, Lahaina News, October 29, 1998: 15.
— to perform "We Love the Humpback Whale" at Borders Books, Lahaina News, May 18, 2000: 20.
— qualifies for finals of Lahaina Coolers Las Vegas Challenge, Lahaina News, September 5, 2002: 18.

WATSON, RENETTE
— recognized as educator of the month by Kimo's Restaurant, Lahaina News, December 21, 2000: 3.

WATSON, ROBERT [ARTIST]
— to appear at "Friday Night is Art Night", Lahaina News, February 14, 1990: 17.

WAVE VIDEO [BUSINESS]
— one of many video rental stores in West Maui, Lahaina News, August 14, 1985: 1.
— opened despite damage from leak, Lahaina News, October 18, 1989: 7.
— expands, Lahaina News, January 16, 1991: 5.

WAVE WARRIORS [MUSICAL GROUP]
— to perform at Moose McGillycuddy's, Lahaina News, May 30, 1991: 7.

WAYNE, JEFF [COMEDIAN]
— to perform at Comedy Club, Lahaina News, May 30, 1990: 11.
— to perform at Comedy Club and the Sports Page, Lahaina News, June 20, 1991: 8.
— to perform at Comedy Club and the Sports Page, Lahaina News, September 10, 1992: 17,19.

WAYNE, WATKINS
— to sing at Makawao Public Library, Lahaina News, July 10, 2003: 17.

WAYNE'S CARPET [BUSINESS]
— opens in Dickenson Square, Lahaina News, May 23, 1990: 8.

WAYS AND MEANS, SENATE COMMITTEE ON
— to hold public hearing on State Budget, Lahaina News, December 29, 1994: 2.

WE WERE BROTHERS [PLAY]
— to be performed at Maui Arts and Cultural Center, Lahaina News, October 31, 2002: 22.
— to be performed at Hyatt Regency Maui, Lahaina News, November 7, 2002: 20.

WEAD, ROB
— expanding self-hypnosis services, Lahaina News, September 27, 1989: 5.

WEASAK
— celebration to be held, Lahaina News, May 26, 1994: 4,5.

WEATHER
— major storm hits Lahaina, Lahaina Sun, December 30, 1970: 1,2.
— photographs of snow on Haleakala, Lahaina Sun, January 13, 1971: 1,3.
— drought appears to have ended, Lahaina Sun, December 29, 1971: 14.
— Charles Fullerton discusses cloud seeding as method for weather control, Lahaina Sun, January 12, 1972: 2.
— kona winds whip Lahaina, Lahaina Sun, February 2, 1972: 5.

— kona winds force closure of Kahului Harbor, Lahaina Sun, February 9, 1972: 3.
— kona winds result in minimal damage, Lahaina Sun, March 8, 1972: 3.
— Hurricane Diana threatens the islands, Lahaina Sun, August 23, 1972: 1.
— sun flares observed , Lahaina Sun, August 30, 1972: 5.
— discussion of seasons in Maui, Lahaina Sun, September 13, 1972: 9.
— rainfall around Maui detailed, Lahaina Sun, April 18, 1973: 11.
— storm in Kihei Heights described, Lahaina News, January 15, 1980: 3.
— intense rain reported in West Maui, Lahaina News, October 23, 1985: 1,7.
— gale-force winds hit Lahaina, Lahaina News, January 11, 1989: 1,13.
— hurricane Fernanda expected, Lahaina News, August 19, 1993: 1,16.
— recounting storms, ocean swells, Lahaina News, May 19, 1994: 2.
— tropical storm Delores moves towards Transpacific Yacht Race, Lahaina News, July 10, 1997: 15.
— see also flooding

WEATHERSPOON, KELLY
— performing in South America, Lahaina Sun, January 20, 1971: 7.

WEAVER, DICK
— named chair of the Institute of Real Estate Management's Alpha Committee, Lahaina News, November 14, 1990: 11.

WEAVER, PAUL "BUFF"
— joins Lahaina Canoe Club, Lahaina News, June 3, 1999: 14.

WEBB, BRANDON
— Scholar/Athlete of the Week, Lahaina News, April 2, 1998: 14.

WEBB, CHARLES
— joins The Realty Team, Lahaina News, September 26, 1990: 9.

WEBB, CRAIG
— new pastor installed at Lahaina Baptist Church, Lahaina News, February 2, 1995: 4.
— Reverend to lead Christmas services, Lahaina News, December 10, 1998: 9.

WEBB, KEN
— steps down as Captain, Lahaina Sun, July 11, 1973: 4.

WEBBER, ANDREW LLOYD
— "Joseph, and the Technicolor Dreamcoat" being performed, Lahaina News, July 30, 1992: 18.

WEBER, JIM [MUSICIAN]
— to perform at Lahaina Baptist Church, Lahaina News, May 15, 1997: 12.

WEBER, TINA
— description of surfer, Lahaina Times, August 20, 1983 volume 7 number 8: 2.

WEBSTER, JOY
— elected president of West Maui Business Network, Lahaina News, November 22, 1989: 5.

WEBSTER, RICHARD
— benefit to be held for, Lahaina News, December 4, 1997: 25.
— benefit concert to be held for, Lahaina News, December 11, 1997: 18.

WEDDING FAIRE
— to be held by Maui Chamber of Commerce at Westin Maui Resort, Lahaina News, December 31, 1992: 5.
— to be held, Lahaina News, January 7, 1993: 3.
— to be held, Lahaina News, January 14, 1993: 3.

WEDDLE, SHARON
— to represent Hawaii at Mrs. International Pageant, Lahaina News, August 4, 1994: 4.

WEDNESDAY IS TUTORING DAY
— director Pat Endsley discusses program, Lahaina News, April 10, 2003: 1.

WEDNESDAY MORNING PLEIN-AIR PAINTING GROUP
— to exhibit, Lahaina News, February 27, 1997: 13,16.

WEED, SUSAN
— to speak on how "Menopause Can Change Your Life", Lahaina News, January 16, 2003: 2.

WEEKEND NEIGHBOR ISLAND BIKE TREK
— to be held, Lahaina News, August 24, 1995: 6.

WEEPING BANYAN TREE BAR [RESTAURANT]
— restaurant at Hyatt Regency musical line-up listed, Lahaina News, April 11, 1990: 15.
— featured, Lahaina News, January 21, 1993: 13.

WEFLEN, JULIE
— woman abducted in Spokane reported see in West Maui, Lahaina News, May 30, 1990: 20.

WEGNER, CAROLOS
— competing at USA Boxing State Championship, Lahaina News, February 11, 1999: 15.

WEIGHT WATCHERS
— to meet, Lahaina News, January 4, 1996: 4.
— moves meetings to Sacred Hearts Church library, Lahaina News, January 18, 1996: 4.
— to meet, Lahaina News, February 22, 1996: 12.
— group to meet, Lahaina News, July 17, 2003: 17.
— group meets at Kaiser Lahaina Annex, Lahaina News, July 31, 2003: 17.

WEIGHTLIFTING
— competition held in Reno, Nevada, Lahaina News, December 14, 2000: 15.

WEINBERG COURT APARTMENT
— fire hydrant system has locks on it, Lahaina News, January 19, 1995: 1.

WEINBERG FOUNDATION
— provides money to Maui Arts and Cultural Center, Lahaina News, May 26, 1994: 5.

WEINBERG, HARRY
— purchases large property on Front Street, Lahaina Sun, June 9, 1971: 4.
— plan to build gas station and fast food restaurants at Kekaa Drive opposed by Amfac, Lahaina News, September 14, 1983: 5.
— increases holdings in Alexander & Baldwin, Lahaina News, January 4, 1984: 14.
— swaps land in Honokowai with Alexander & Baldwin for land in Lihue, Kaua'i, Lahaina News, April 4, 1984: 13.
— proposes new shopping complex in Lahaina, Lahaina News, September 12, 1984: 3.
— planning commission approves rezoning for shopping complex, Lahaina News, September 19, 1984: 3.
— plans for fast food, fast gas shopping plaza limited, Lahaina News, May 15, 1985: 1.
— planned shopping development in Ka'anapali limited by Maui County Planning Commission, Lahaina News, June 12, 1985: 1.
— receives approval for shopping center, Lahaina News, January 15, 1986: 3.
— Lahaina shopping complex nears completion, Lahaina News, September 30, 1987: 3.
— breaks ground for new shopping center, Lahaina News, November 9, 1988: 1.
— sells lease to shopping center to Pomare Corporation, Lahaina News, May 24, 1989: 9.
— foundation given property, Lahaina News, November 14, 1990: 11.

WEINERT, MARSHA [MUSICIAN]
— to be honored by Maui League of Republican Women, Lahaina News, March 11, 1999: 13.
— to be honored by Maui League of Republican Women, Lahaina News, March 18, 1999: 16.
— to speak to Lahaina Town Action Committee, Lahaina News, January 6, 2000: 1.

WEIR, BOB [MUSICIAN]
— to perform with fellow Grateful Dead member Rob Wasserman, Lahaina News, January 3, 1990: 16.

WEIR, GEORGE
— to speak at the Institute of Real Estate Management luncheon, Lahaina News, June 13, 1991: 10.

WEIR, WARNER
— in critical condition after near drowning, Lahaina Sun, August 18, 1971: 3.
— released from hospital, Lahaina Sun, August 25, 1971: 11.

WEISER, KURT [ARTIST]
— works displayed at Hui No'eau Visual Arts Center, Lahaina News, April 22, 1987: 10.

WEISGRAM, JOHN ROBERT
— Maui Staff Sergeant wins "Spot What's Hot" contest sponsored by KHNL/13, Lahaina News, November 14, 1990: 4.

WEISS
— workshop scheduled, Lahaina News, November 18, 1987: 3.

WEISS, DAVID
— interviewed about rise of television satellite dishes, Lahaina News, February 5, 1986: 4.

WEISS, MIMI
— to hold summer sessions on successful living, Lahaina News, June 8, 1988: 3.

WELCH, JOHN
— benefit concert held for, Lahaina News, November 4, 1993: 2.

WELFARE
— new rules proposed, Lahaina Sun, April 7, 1971: 6.
— finger-printing of welfare recipients requested by Councilman Joe Bulgo, Lahaina Sun, June 2, 1971: 6.
— hearing on proposed changes to the law, Lahaina Sun, June 9, 1971: 3.
— proposed changes challenged in public hearing, Lahaina Sun, June 16, 1971: 1.
— hearing to create a one-year residency law, Lahaina Sun, August 25, 1971: 11.
— residency law supported at Kahului hearing, Lahaina Sun, September 15, 1971: 1.
— residency requirement may be challenged in court, Lahaina Sun, October 20, 1971: 5.
— recipients claim to be treated unfairly, Lahaina Sun, March 15, 1972: 3.
— situation in Maui discussed, Lahaina Sun, August 16, 1972: 3.
— recipients critical of new system, Lahaina Sun, November 22, 1972: 3.

WELLNESS FAIR
— to be held at Lahaina Cannery Mall, Lahaina News, September 6, 2001: 14.

WELLS, BILL
— designs game inspired by hippie brochure, Lahaina Sun, February 24, 1971: 3,4,5.

WELLS, JUNIOR [MUSICIAN]
— to perform at Maui Arts and Cultural Center, Lahaina News, February 29, 1996: 14.

WELSH, DONALD
— appointed vice president of sales and marketing for The Ritz-Carlton Hotel, Lahaina News, October 10, 1991: 7.

WELTY, GARY [CARTOONIST]
— begins contributed to the Lahaina News, Lahaina News, October 24, 1984: 2.

WENDELL, EDDIE
— hits a hole in one at Ka'anapali North Course, Lahaina News, October 2, 1985: 4.

WENDY'S [RESTAURANT]
— to open in Lahaina, Lahaina News, January 1, 1983: 2.
— to open on Maui, Lahaina News, September 12, 1990: 10.
— seeking special management use permit to build restaurant at Maui Mall Shopping Center, Lahaina News, August 20, 1992: 4.
— to open in Kahului, Lahaina News, October 1, 1992: 4.

WENK, TIMOTHY
— magician to perform at Maui schools, focusing on recycling, Lahaina News, January 6, 1994: 3.

WENKAM, ROBERT [WRITER]
— autographing book "Maui, the Last Hawaiian Place", Lahaina Sun, November 18, 1970: 2.

WERNER, CRAIG
— chiropractor buys office, Lahaina News, February 16, 1995: 12.

WERRET, CHRIS
— engines of six Playtime Rentals jet boats of damaged, Lahaina Sun, August 25, 1971: 9.

WEST, BONNIE
— new branch sales manager at American Savings Bank's Lahaina Branch, Lahaina News, March 29, 2001: 8.

WEST COAST WHALE RESEARCH FOUNDATION
— Jim Darling and Meagan Jones to discuss humpback whale songs, Lahaina News, January 18, 2001: 17.
— names research boat after Charles B. Sutherland, Lahaina News, February 15, 2001: 1,18.

WEST FEST SUMMER JAM
— to be organized by churches, Lahaina News, August 2, 2001: 2.
— music festival to be held, Lahaina News, August 9, 2001: 1,20.
— to be held, Lahaina News, August 23, 2001: 14.
— held, Lahaina News, August 30, 2001: 1.

WEST HAWAII DANCE THEATRE
— to present "Gaite Parisienne", Lahaina News, March 23, 1995: 12.
— to perform with Infinity Ballet Company at Maui Arts and Cultural Center, Lahaina News, January 16, 1997: 10.
— to perform "Meeting of the Spirits" ballet, Lahaina News, January 22, 1998: 12.
— to perform selections from "The Nutcracker Ballet", Lahaina News, November 19, 1998: 16.
— to hold "The Nutcracker", Lahaina News, December 3, 1998: 21.
— to perform "Ballet 2000", Lahaina News, January 27, 2000: 12.

WEST, JERRY
— basketball player to offer "Executive Basketball Camp" with Magic Johnson, Lahaina News, June 6, 1991: 9.
— basketball player to hold camp, Lahaina News, August 6, 1992: 5.

WEST, LESLIE
— named officer for Lahaina Yacht Club, Lahaina Sun, December 23, 1970: 8.
— died in a boating accident off Kamaiki Point, Lahaina News, September 15, 1982: 15.

WEST MAUI
— named one of top U.S. hotel in Laura McKenzie's Travel Report Awards, Lahaina News, February 16, 1995: 13.
— residents choose people with who had greatest impact, Lahaina News, December 30, 1999: 1,20.

WEST MAUI A.J.A. VETERANS CLUB
— see A.J.A. Veterans Club

WEST MAUI ACADEMY OF DANCE
— to offer classes, Lahaina News, November 14, 1990: 4.

WEST MAUI ACUTE CARE FEASIBILITY STUDY
— says West Maui does not need hospital, Lahaina News, August 24, 1995: 1,16.

WEST MAUI ADULT DAY CARE CENTER
— see Maui Adult Day Care Center

WEST MAUI ADVISORY COMMITTEE TO THE MAYOR
— holds meeting at Lahaina Intermediate School, Lahaina News, January 9, 1991: 1.
— supports mayor Linda Lingle's proposed budget, Lahaina News, March 27, 1991: 1.
— taken out P.O. Box for community input, Lahaina News, April 10, 1991: 3.
— accepting suggestions to P.O. Box, Lahaina News, April 17, 1991: 7.
— can be contacted through post office box, Lahaina News, July 23, 1992: 4.
— Mayor Linda Lingle appoints new members, Lahaina News, July 15, 1993: 2.
— disbanded, Lahaina News, January 5, 1995: 1.
— established, Lahaina News, March 16, 1995: 1.
— endorses Bikeways Maui, Lahaina News, April 13, 1995: 1,20.
— Amfac/JMB to discuss plans for North Beach with, Lahaina News, April 27, 1995: 5.
— holds informational hearing concerning proposed North Beach development, Lahaina News, May 11, 1995: 1,16.
— asks Amfac/JMB about proposed projects, Lahaina News, May 11, 1995: 16.
— needs two new members, Lahaina News, June 22, 1995: 4.
— to discuss beach access, Lahaina News, October 17, 1996: 4.
— to hold meeting, Lahaina News, November 14, 1996: 15.
— new members being recruited, Lahaina News, January 9, 1997: 1.
— to meet, Lahaina News, January 16, 1997: 10.
— to hold meeting to discuss local issues, Lahaina News, May 11, 2000: 8.
— Mayor Alan Arakawa pledges to act on advice from West Maui Advisory Committee, Lahaina News, September 4, 2003: 1,20.
— see also Mayor's West Maui Advisory Committee

WEST MAUI AIRPORT
— see Kapalua West Maui Airport

WEST MAUI AJA WOMEN'S AUXILIARY SUNSET CLUB
— to hold garage sale, Lahaina News, October 24, 1996: 14.

WEST MAUI AMERICAN YOUTH SOCCER ORGANIZATION (AYSO)
— season to end soon, Lahaina News, October 31, 1996: 17.
— featured, Lahaina News, August 29, 2002: 10.
— see also soccer

WEST MAUI ATHLETIC ASSOCIATION
— needs coaches, Lahaina News, December 16, 1987: 15.
— selling candy as fundraiser, Lahaina News, December 23, 1987: 3.

WEST MAUI BREAST CANCER BENEFIT
— held at Longhi's, Lahaina News, January 18, 2001: 6.

WEST MAUI BUDDHIST COUNCIL
— holding "Buddha Day", Lahaina News, April 3, 1997: 12.
— to celebrate Hanamatsuri (Buddha's Birthday), Lahaina News, April 11, 2002: 1.

WEST MAUI BUSINESS ASSOCIATION
— discuss ways to bring more tourists to Lahaina, Lahaina Sun, November 25, 1970: 3.
— discussed issues connected to hippies on Maui, Lahaina Sun, December 2, 1970: 1.

— meeting with executives of the Lahaina-Ka'anapali & Pacific Railroad regarding tourism, Lahaina Sun, December 9, 1970: 4.

— submits list of desired projects to Mayor Cravalho, Lahaina Sun, December 23, 1970: 2.

— meeting of Retail Committee scheduled, Lahaina Sun, December 30, 1970: 4.

— Mayor Cravalho responds to improvement recommendations from, Lahaina Sun, December 30, 1970: 8.

— criticized for hippie brochure, Lahaina Sun, January 20, 1971: 5.

— meets with Mayor Cravalho, Lahaina Sun, March 17, 1971: 6.

— proposes off-street parking in Lahaina, Lahaina Sun, March 31, 1971: 3.

— new officers announced, Lahaina Sun, June 23, 1971: 10.

— concerned about proposed interisland ferry system docking at Lahaina, Lahaina Sun, September 22, 1971: 4.

— does not take stand on proposed interisland ferry, Lahaina Sun, January 12, 1972: 7.

— supports rules of Maui Historic Commission, Lahaina Sun, February 9, 1972: 14.

— Ron Kondo nominated as president for, Lahaina Sun, May 10, 1972: 5.

— manager Dwight Nacua resigns, Lahaina Sun, October 11, 1972: 8.

— fundraising efforts detailed, Lahaina Sun, January 17, 1973: 7.

WEST MAUI BUSINESS NETWORK

— Joy Webster elected president of, Lahaina News, November 22, 1989: 5.

WEST MAUI CARDEN ACADEMY

— fundraiser to be held at Soup Nutz and Java Jazz, Lahaina News, August 16, 2001: 3.

— to hold open house, Lahaina News, August 23, 2001: 1.

— to host after-school arts program, Lahaina News, September 13, 2001: 2.

— planning open house, Lahaina News, October 25, 2001: 3.

— accepting applications for preschool program, Lahaina News, November 8, 2001: 2.

— to hold "Casino Nights" fundraiser, Lahaina News, November 22, 2001: 3.

— to hold open house, Lahaina News, March 21, 2002: 9.

— to hold May Day Ho'olaule'a benefit, Lahaina News, May 9, 2002: 3.

— to hold ho'olaule'a fundraiser, Lahaina News, May 16, 2002: 16.

— planning summer camps, Lahaina News, May 8, 2003: 2,3.

WEST MAUI CHRISTIAN MEN'S CAMP

— to hold "Full Moon Campout", Lahaina News, November 6, 1997: 17.

— to be held, Lahaina News, October 22, 1998: 15.

— to be held at Honolua Field, Lahaina News, October 7, 1999: 3.

— to be held, Lahaina News, August 31, 2000: 16.

— to be held, Lahaina News, September 13, 2001: 2.

— Sam Huddleston to speak at, Lahaina News, September 20, 2001: 3.

— to be held, Lahaina News, September 27, 2001: 16.

— to be held, Lahaina News, September 26, 2002: 18.

— to be held, Lahaina News, September 18, 2003: 5.

WEST MAUI CIVIL DEFENSE TEAM

— see Civil Defense Agency, Maui County

WEST MAUI COMMUNITY CENTER

— needs help, Lahaina News, August 17, 1995: 2.

WEST MAUI COMMUNITY PLAN

— Maui Planning Commission defers vote on, Lahaina News, September 23, 1993: 1,5.

— Maui Land and Pineapple wants Napili Regional Park moved near Kapalua/West Maui Airport in, Lahaina News, November 18, 1993: 1,3.

— Maui County Council Planning Committee to tour key sites of , Lahaina News, June 29, 1995: 1.

— to be discussed at hearing, Lahaina News, July 6, 1995: 1,12.

— residents at public meeting urge slow growth, Lahaina News, July 13, 1995: 1,16.

— Maui Council continues to consider, Lahaina News, July 20, 1995: 1,16.

— protection of discussed in hearings on, Lahaina News, August 10, 1995: 6.

— testimony heard, Lahaina News, August 24, 1995: 3.

— Maui County Planning Committee to discuss, Lahaina News, September 7, 1995: 2.

— passed by Maui County Council's Planning Committee, Lahaina News, October 19, 1995: 1,2.

— Maui County Council to hold public meeting on, Lahaina News, November 23, 1995: 6.

— Maui County Council holds public hearing on, Lahaina News, December 7, 1995: 1,20.

— first reading at Maui County Council, Lahaina News, December 14, 1995: 20.

— amendments deferred by Maui County Council, Lahaina News, December 21, 1995: 1,16.

— close to completion, Lahaina News, February 1, 1996: 4.

— Maui County Council takes final action, Lahaina News, February 29, 1996: 1,2.

WEST MAUI COMMUNITY VOICES PROJECT (CVP)

— to publish directory of services, Lahaina News, November 1, 2001: 1,9.

— Resource Directory booklet published, Lahaina News, May 2, 2002: 3.

WEST MAUI CONDOMINIUM MANAGERS' ASSOCIATION

— to meet, Lahaina News, November 21, 1991: 11.

— to meet at Kahana Terrace Restaurant, Lahaina News, December 5, 1991: 13.

— new officers announced, Lahaina News, January 2, 1992: 9.

— to support Teen Challenge, Lahaina News, July 9, 1992: 9.

WEST MAUI CONSORTIUM FOR TEACHING ASIA AND THE PACIFIC IN THE SCHOOLS (CTAPS)

— offering workshop, Lahaina News, March 18, 1999: 2.

WEST MAUI CROONERS

— seeking new members, Lahaina News, September 17, 1986: 11.

WEST MAUI CUB SCOUTS

— see Cub Scouts

WEST MAUI CULTURAL COUNCIL

— sponsors foreign films, Lahaina News, December 24, 1986: 8.

— organizing art classes, Lahaina News, December 19, 1990: 5.

— to hold adult art classes, Lahaina News, December 26, 1990: 5.

— to hold adult art classes, Lahaina News, January 2, 1991: 4.

— sponsoring course for youth on acting, Lahaina News, November 21, 1991: 4.

WEST MAUI CYCLE AND SPORTS

— to donate bikes to police, Lahaina News, February 13, 1997: 3.

WEST MAUI CYCLES [BUSINESS]

— to hold Honolua Bay Mountain Bike Classic, Lahaina News, March 24, 1994: 12.

— to open at Limahana Place, Lahaina News, April 24, 2003: 9.

WEST MAUI DAY CARE

— fixed by West Maui Soroptimist International and Lahaina Kiwanis Club, Lahaina News, January 30, 1992: 5.

WEST MAUI DEVELOPMENT CO. [BUSINESS]

— announces "The Summit at Ka'anapali" new development , Lahaina News, October 12, 2000: 15.

WEST MAUI SOIL AND WATER CONSERVATION DISTRICT
— promoting need for Lahaina Watershed Project, Lahaina News, November 18, 1999: 1,2.
— vice chair Wes Nohara discusses interim fix for flooding and dust issues, Lahaina News, December 14, 2000: 1,17.

WEST MAUI SOIL AND WATER CONSERVATION SERVICE
— urges residents to lobby for flood control project, Lahaina News, July 26, 1989: 1.

WEST MAUI SOROPTIMISTS
— see Soroptimists International

WEST MAUI SPORTS AND FISHING SUPPLY [BUSINESS]
— new name of Lahaina Water Works Sporting Goods, Lahaina News, July 9, 1992: 13.
— featured; changes location, Lahaina News, June 19, 1997: 15.

WEST MAUI TABLE TENNIS CLUB
— table tennis club forming, Lahaina News, November 21, 2002: 11.

WEST MAUI TAXPAYERS ASSOCIATION
— hold annual meeting, Lahaina News, March 14, 1984: 3.
— claims condominiums overtaxed, Lahaina News, April 11, 1984: 17.
— disappointed at Maui Land & Pineapple withdrawing from West Maui airstrip agreement, Lahaina News, April 11, 1984: 4.
— arguing with Mayor Tavares regarding property taxes, Lahaina News, May 9, 1984: 2,3.
— to hold annual general meeting, Lahaina News, March 13, 1985: 3.
— fundraising to oppose proposed Mahinahina airport, Lahaina News, July 3, 1985: 1.
— retains lawyer Boyce Brown to help fight proposed airport in West Maui, Lahaina News, August 21, 1985: 1.
— asks court to delay Mahinahina airport, Lahaina News, October 9, 1985: 1.
— pays for notice of public hearing on proposed airport, Lahaina News, January 22, 1986: 16.
— to hold annual meeting, Lahaina News, May 7, 1986: 3.
— elect new officers, Lahaina News, June 25, 1986: 3.
— wants halt to development, Lahaina News, November 26, 1986: 1.
— Lahaina News corrects story from previous week, Lahaina News, December 3, 1986: 1.
— Sheri Morrison leaving as executive director of, Lahaina News, February 25, 1987: 20.
— Charlie Nalepa appointed executive director, Lahaina News, March 25, 1987: 12.
— loses challenge with the Hawaii State Supreme over airport zoning, Lahaina News, May 6, 1987: 3.
— to hold annual meeting, Lahaina News, May 20, 1987: 3.
— to hold annual general meeting, Lahaina News, May 27, 1987: 1.
— Jan Wise and Robert Kemble elected to board, Lahaina News, July 1, 1987: 3.
— to hold annual meeting, Lahaina News, May 11, 1988: 14.
— directors elected, Lahaina News, June 1, 1988: 1.
— president Ruth McKay featured, Lahaina News, January 11, 1989: 2.
— wants to build fire station, Lahaina News, March 22, 1989: 1.
— to host comedian Bill Dana, Lahaina News, May 17, 1989: 2.
— Ruth McKay named as president, Lahaina News, July 12, 1989: 3.
— to hold Halloween costume contest, Lahaina News, September 27, 1989: 3.
— seeks more parks, Lahaina News, November 1, 1989: 1.
— supports building fire station in Napili, Lahaina News, November 1, 1989: 5.
— assured by Department of Transportation that Lahaina Bypass will continue, Lahaina News, January 17, 1990: 24.
— to meet with Maui's state legislators, Lahaina News, February 14, 1990: 2.
— supports alternate ways to access West Maui, Lahaina News, February 21, 1990: 1.
— hosting meeting by legislators, Lahaina News, February 21, 1990: 4.
— supports countywide source assessment fee for water, Lahaina News, March 28, 1990: 1.
— to discuss Amfac, Inc.'s plans for West Maui at annual meeting, Lahaina News, May 30, 1990: 5.
— to hold fundraiser for Napili Fire and Ambulance Station, Lahaina News, August 8, 1990: 4.
— to hold political forums, Lahaina News, September 5, 1990: 4.
— to hold political forums, Lahaina News, September 12, 1990: 8.
— to host fundraiser at Benihana's for Napili Fire and Ambulance Station, Lahaina News, September 19, 1990: 4.
— to host political forum, Lahaina News, September 19, 1990: 5.
— to hold forum for political candidates, Lahaina News, September 26, 1990: 7.
— to host Celebrity Chef Dinner at Benihana, Lahaina News, October 10, 1990: 6.
— to hold political election forum, Lahaina News, October 10, 1990: 6.
— cancels political forum, Lahaina News, October 17, 1990: 5.
— to hold public meeting to discuss upcoming bazaar, Lahaina News, November 7, 1990: 5.
— opposes use of federal money to purchase Kapalua-West Maui Airport, Lahaina News, January 23, 1991: 1.
— supports keeping beach access the "Little Makaha" surfing site, Lahaina News, January 23, 1991: 3.
— sponsoring grand opening ceremonies for Napili Fire and Ambulance Safety Facility, Lahaina News, March 27, 1991: 3.
— raising money for Napili Fire and Ambulance Station, Lahaina News, May 23, 1991: 1.
— conducting poll on extending Kahului Airport runway, Lahaina News, January 9, 1992: 1.
— divided on whether to lengthen Kahului Airport runway, Lahaina News, March 5, 1992: 1.
— to host senator Rick Reed and representative Roz Baker, Lahaina News, May 14, 1992: 3.
— to hold meeting, Lahaina News, May 21, 1992: 4.
— reschedules talk by Senator Rick Reed, Lahaina News, May 28, 1992: 4.
— to hold thank you party for Charlie Nalepa, Lahaina News, June 25, 1992: 2.
— to keep calendar of events for Maui, Lahaina News, July 23, 1992: 5.
— probes sewage spill at Mala Wharf, Lahaina News, September 17, 1992: 1.
— creates events calendar, Lahaina News, November 12, 1992: 4.
— role of organization described, Lahaina News, December 31, 1992: 2.
— has created events calendar, Lahaina News, January 28, 1993: 4.
— president Mark Percell claims algae removal bill has defects, Lahaina News, February 4, 1993: 2.
— creates running event calendar, Lahaina News, March 11, 1993: 4.
— to hold annual meeting, Lahaina News, April 29, 1993: 3.
— to hold annual meeting; update on organization activities, Lahaina News, May 6, 1993: 4.
— report on annual meeting, Lahaina News, May 20, 1993: 3.
— priorities laid out by president elect Andrea Heath-Blundell, Lahaina News, June 3, 1993: 2,15.
— publishes four page supplement in Lahaina News, Lahaina News, August 5, 1993: A1,A2,A3,A4.
— county Finance Director Travis Thompson to meet with , Lahaina News, August 12, 1993: 1,15.
— president Mark Percell asks that parks be fixed before the Maui Bud Light Triathlon Series Championship is held, Lahaina News, September 2, 1993: 1.

— to hold "Night of the Great Pumpkin Masquerade Ball", Lahaina News, October 14, 1993: 13,14.

— seeks change to Samaritan Law, Lahaina News, December 30, 1993: 1,3.

— Mark Percell to resign as executive director, Lahaina News, February 3, 1994: 1.

— Mac Lowson appointed interim president, Lahaina News, April 21, 1994: 1.

— to hold annual meeting, Lahaina News, June 16, 1994: 4.

— update on status of organization, Lahaina News, June 30, 1994: 1,20.

— updates on priorities, Lahaina News, September 8, 1994: 3.

— to hold candidate forum, Lahaina News, October 13, 1994: 4.

— to hold candidate forum, Lahaina News, October 27, 1994: 8.

— sponsors candidate forum, Lahaina News, November 3, 1994: 1,7.

— to hold second candidate's forum with Maui Chamber of Commerce, Lahaina News, November 3, 1994: 4.

— to sponsor pollution prevention seminar, Lahaina News, November 10, 1994: 4.

— to hold pollution prevention seminar, Lahaina News, November 24, 1994: 6.

— report on activities over the year, Lahaina News, December 8, 1994: 5.

— sponsors seminar on reducing pollution, Lahaina News, December 15, 1994: 2.

— updates on organizational goals, Lahaina News, January 12, 1995: 3.

— to install emergency call boxes with Maui Police Department, Lahaina News, February 16, 1995: 1,3.

— begins program to help local merchants, Lahaina News, March 23, 1995: 10.

— updates on local issues, to hold annual meeting, Lahaina News, May 11, 1995: 4.

— to celebrate 22nd anniversary, Lahaina News, May 25, 1995: 4.

— new board elected to, Lahaina News, June 8, 1995: 3.

— supports bans on park drinking and hawking, Lahaina News, August 24, 1995: 1,16.

— opposes legalization of gambling, Lahaina News, September 21, 1995: 2.

— participate in seaweed removal, Lahaina News, November 9, 1995: 4.

— to host tax planning seminar, Lahaina News, November 16, 1995: 5.

— to hold tax planning seminar, Lahaina News, November 30, 1995: 4.

— lists priorities for year, Lahaina News, January 18, 1996: 2.

— supports bus service, Lahaina News, April 18, 1996: 17.

— update on activities, Lahaina News, April 18, 1996: 2.

— expresses concerns to Mayor Linda Lingle, Lahaina News, July 25, 1996: 2.

— updates on local development issues, Lahaina News, August 22, 1996: 2.

— to hold annual meeting, Lahaina News, September 12, 1996: 2.

— to hold annual meeting, Lahaina News, September 19, 1996: 15.

— wants to pay youth groups to clean seaweed from beaches, Lahaina News, October 10, 1996: 1.

— to hold politics forum, Lahaina News, October 10, 1996: 2.

— update on organization, Lahaina News, October 24, 1996: 15.

— update on projects and issues, Lahaina News, November 7, 1996: 5.

— S-Turn Park dedicated, Lahaina News, December 26, 1996: 1.

— advocacy described, Lahaina News, April 17, 1997: 1,16.

— to host talk by Sam Slom, Lahaina News, October 9, 1997: 14.

— hosting speech by president of the Tax Foundation of Hawaii Lowell Kalapa, Lahaina News, March 5, 1998: 13.

— to help remove beach algae, Lahaina News, June 25, 1998: 1.

— receives grant to clean up algae on the beach, Lahaina News, July 2, 1998: 8.

— seeking participants to help clean algae from beaches, Lahaina News, July 30, 1998: 3.

— seeking non-profit groups to help clean algae, Lahaina News, August 20, 1998: 8.

— seeking help to clean beaches , Lahaina News, August 27, 1998: 9.

— hosting candidates night, Lahaina News, October 8, 1998: 7.

— organizes volunteers to remove algae, Lahaina News, October 15, 1998: 1.

— to hold candidates forum, Lahaina News, October 29, 1998: 1.

— to host Bob Siarot, Lahaina News, November 12, 1998: 7.

— reconstituted, new officers announced, Lahaina News, April 1, 1999: 8.

— has new website, Lahaina News, June 3, 1999: 2.

— discusses Hawaii Helicopter proposal with Senator Jan Yagi-Buen, Lahaina News, September 16, 1999: 1.

— website includes news, Lahaina News, September 23, 1999: 5.

— to hold annual meeting, Lahaina News, November 11, 1999: 3.

— reports that a crosswalk will be pointed, Lahaina News, December 23, 1999: 1.

— focused on lease-to-fee issue, Lahaina News, December 30, 1999: 1,2.

— sets goals for 2000, Lahaina News, March 23, 2000: 5.

— encourages discussion of leasehold conversion, Lahaina News, April 6, 2000: 13.

— finds emergency response in Lahaina effective, Lahaina News, April 27, 2000: 3.

— represented on Mayor's West Maui Advisory Committee, Lahaina News, May 11, 2000: 8.

— forms committee to pursue leasehold reform, Lahaina News, June 15, 2000: 9.

— focus on leasehold issues, Lahaina News, July 27, 2000: 11.

— to host "Candidates Night 2000", Lahaina News, September 28, 2000: 3.

— hosting political forum, Lahaina News, October 5, 2000: 3.

— seeks input on leasehold issue, Lahaina News, October 19, 2000: 15.

— elects new officers, Lahaina News, March 1, 2001: 9.

— to help improve traffic and County Charter, Lahaina News, April 5, 2001: 22.

— identifies issues during meeting with Mayor Apana, Lahaina News, April 26, 2001: 10.

— forum to update on "Ka'anapali 2020", Lahaina News, May 17, 2001: 2.

— Zeke Kalua new executive director, Lahaina News, June 21, 2001: 1,13.

— editorial in support of, Lahaina News, June 21, 2001: 4.

— campaigning for 24-hour acute care facility, Lahaina News, November 29, 2001: 1,20.

— to host JoAnne Johnson, Lahaina News, January 3, 2002: 1,18.

— held meeting to update community on capital improvements, Lahaina News, January 24, 2002: 1,18.

— advocates for Acute Care Facility, Lahaina News, March 21, 2002: 5.

— to hold discussion on acute care facility, Lahaina News, May 2, 2002: 2.

— to hold meeting on establishing acute care facility in West Maui, Lahaina News, May 9, 2002: 16.

— holds meeting on need for acute care facility, Lahaina News, May 16, 2002: 1,20.

— supporting improving highway, Lahaina News, July 11, 2002: 5.

— editorial in support of campaign for Acute Care Facility, Lahaina News, August 15, 2002: 4.

— message from president Joseph Pluta, Lahaina News, August 29, 2002: 5.

— message from president Joseph Pluta, Lahaina News, September 5, 2002: 20.

— to host candidates' forum, Lahaina News, September 12, 2002: 1,22.

— to hold annual meeting, Lahaina News, January 2, 2003: 5.

— to host Maui County Planning Director Mike Foley, Lahaina News, January 9, 2003: 3.

— program to hold registration, Lahaina News, November 7, 2002: 11.
— program to begin 19th season, Lahaina News, January 9, 2003: 12.
— see also basketball

WEST MAUI YOUTH CENTER
— described, Lahaina Sun, January 6, 1971: 7.
— can occupy Honokahua School rent free, Lahaina Sun, May 5, 1971: 6.
— seeking donations, Lahaina Sun, June 2, 1971: 3.
— seeking local aid, Lahaina Sun, November 24, 1971: 6.
— closes, Lahaina Sun, February 28, 1973: 10.
— State approves lease of land for, Lahaina News, May 15, 1981: 7.
— opens December 1, 1981, Lahaina News, December 1, 1981: 16.
— Ray DeMellon elected president, Lahaina News, July 15, 1982: 3.
— funding needs, Lahaina News, July 15, 1983: 7,8,0.
— groundbreaking held for new building, Lahaina News, January 25, 1984: 10.
— fundraiser organized by Jazzercise, Lahaina News, February 15, 1984: 5.
— annual general meeting to be held, Lahaina News, June 20, 1984: 3.
— to hold summer dance, Lahaina News, June 20, 1984: 3.
— offering swimming lessons, Lahaina News, July 4, 1984: 7.
— sponsors first teen disco show, Lahaina News, July 18, 1984: 4.
— new building described, Lahaina News, August 8, 1984: 7,8,9.
— receives grant from Lahaina Kiwanis Club, Lahaina News, November 14, 1984: 3.
— cutting programs due to budget, Lahaina News, March 6, 1985: 1.
— editorial urging support of, Lahaina News, March 13, 1985: 2.
— new center set to open, Lahaina News, April 3, 1985: 1.
— offering art classes by Lahaina Arts Society, Lahaina News, May 22, 1985: 3.
— Invitational Golf Tournament to be held at Royal Ka'anapali North Golf Course, Lahaina News, May 29, 1985: 3.
— to hold dances, Lahaina News, April 9, 1986: 3.
— general membership meeting to be held, Lahaina News, June 18, 1986: 3.
— to hold 4th of July dance, Lahaina News, July 2, 1986: 18.
— open, Lahaina News, July 9, 1986: 3.
— to hold rummage sale, Lahaina News, August 6, 1986: 3.
— announces end of summer dance, Lahaina News, August 27, 1986: 13.
— to hold Valentine's Dance, Lahaina News, February 4, 1987: 11.
— to hold huli huli chicken fundraiser, Lahaina News, April 1, 1987: 12.
— to hold annual meeting, Lahaina News, June 17, 1987: 3.
— to hold annual meeting, Lahaina News, June 24, 1987: 3.
— receives money from Maui Chapter of Hawaii Hotel Association, Lahaina News, August 5, 1987: 3.
— to host benefit football tournament, Lahaina News, August 5, 1987: 3.
— receives donation of weightlifting equipment from Hyatt Regency Maui, Lahaina News, November 11, 1987: 11.
— to hold basketball team sign-ups, Lahaina News, November 11, 1987: 6.
— holds annual meeting, Lahaina News, June 22, 1988: 3.
— receives donation from Amfac, Inc. from golf fundraiser, Lahaina News, July 13, 1988: 2,3.
— needs basketball coaches, Lahaina News, September 14, 1988: 15.
— to hold annual general meeting, Lahaina News, May 10, 1989: 3.
— planning summer dance, camping trip, Lahaina News, August 2, 1989: 2.
— receives donation from Greater Lahaina Reunion, Lahaina News, December 27, 1989: 11.
— Lahaina Baptist Church to hold auction to support summer camp, Lahaina News, January 31, 1990: 2.
— to hold annual general meeting, Lahaina News, May 30, 1990: 5.

— to hold annual general membership meeting, Lahaina News, June 20, 1991: 3.
— director Kirk Togashi featured, Lahaina News, January 23, 1992: 3.
— general membership meeting scheduled, Lahaina News, June 4, 1992: 8.
— switching to summer schedule, Lahaina News, June 11, 1992: 4.
— general membership meeting scheduled, Lahaina News, June 18, 1992: 4.
— to hold general membership meeting, Lahaina News, June 25, 1992: 2.
— rejects request by Lingle administration to vacate, Lahaina News, August 6, 1992: 1,3.
— hoping to meet with Maui County Council concerning facilities, Lahaina News, August 13, 1992: 3.
— requests funds be restored by Maui County Council, Lahaina News, August 27, 1992: 1.
— to offer programs for youth, Lahaina News, August 27, 1992: 9.
— future of use of facilities discussed, Lahaina News, September 24, 1992: 2.
— to hold fundraisers to finance recreational programs, Lahaina News, October 8, 1992: 3.
— offering workshops, Lahaina News, December 31, 1992: 4.
— annual meeting to be held, Lahaina News, August 5, 1993: 4.
— new board elected, Lahaina News, August 19, 1993: 4.
— inmate from Maui County Correction Center to speak, Lahaina News, December 9, 1993: 2.
— seeking volunteers for summer activities, Lahaina News, May 26, 1994: 4.
— announces summer activity schedule, Lahaina News, June 9, 1994: 9.
— offer free art activities, Lahaina News, November 10, 1994: 16.
— to offer free art classes, Lahaina News, January 5, 1995: 4.
— Hawaii Drug Free Month to be held, Lahaina News, February 9, 1995: 3.
— to hold car wash fundraiser, Lahaina News, February 16, 1995: 6.
— continues to organize activities, Lahaina News, February 23, 1995: 7.
— mural painted at, Lahaina News, March 9, 1995: 4.
— to hold activities, Lahaina News, March 30, 1995: 6.
— representatives from Maui AIDS Foundation to speak to, Lahaina News, May 11, 1995: 2.
— Kathy Harris and Norma Toia of Maui AIDS Foundation speaks to, Lahaina News, May 18, 1995: 4.
— to host police officer Charles Iona speaking on alcohol and driving, Lahaina News, May 25, 1995: 4.
— seeking donation of computer, Lahaina News, June 1, 1995: 2.
— holds annual meeting, Lahaina News, August 24, 1995: 4.
— to hold annual meeting, Lahaina News, August 31, 1995: 4.
— to hold annual meeting, Lahaina News, September 7, 1995: 2.
— to hold rummage sale, Lahaina News, October 26, 1995: 2.
— offering art classes, Lahaina News, October 26, 1995: 2.
— to open Friday nights, Lahaina News, November 2, 1995: 2.
— to open Friday nights, Lahaina News, November 16, 1995: 5.
— art classes offered to children, Lahaina News, November 30, 1995: 11.
— offering free art classes, Lahaina News, December 7, 1995: 16.
— basketball team discussed, Lahaina News, January 4, 1996: 3.
— community garden established, Lahaina News, January 11, 1996: 3.
— new programs added, Lahaina News, February 8, 1996: 1.
— offering summer options for youth, Lahaina News, May 23, 1996: 15.
— services updated, Lahaina News, June 13, 1996: 3.
— events, Lahaina News, July 18, 1996: 10.
— to hold open house, Lahaina News, September 5, 1996: 18.
— burglary and vandalism at facility, Lahaina News, December 12, 1996: 4.

— to hold Mele Kalikimaka Dance, Lahaina News, December 12, 1996: 8.

— seeking community assistance, Lahaina News, May 29, 1997: 2.

— offering summer programs, Lahaina News, June 5, 1997: 3.

— seeking donations of school supplies for needy families, Lahaina News, August 28, 1997: 5.

— seeking volunteers, Lahaina News, November 20, 1997: 2.

— to host "Youth Appreciation Day", Lahaina News, December 4, 1997: 24.

— has wish list for holiday season, Lahaina News, December 18, 1997: 14.

— seeking help, Lahaina News, December 25, 1997: 3.

— offering activities for young people, Lahaina News, January 15, 1998: 3.

— opens computer room, Lahaina News, March 5, 1998: 2.

— offering test preparation classes, Lahaina News, March 12, 1998: 2.

— advocates expanding West Maui Skate Park, Lahaina News, September 10, 1998: 2.

— to hold surf contest and festival at Launiupoko Beach Park, Lahaina News, December 3, 1998: 7.

— planning after-school bus, Lahaina News, December 17, 1998: 3.

— holds Youth Appreciation Day, Lahaina News, March 11, 1999: 5.

— to honor youth role models, Lahaina News, March 18, 1999: 16.

— receives money for computers, Lahaina News, May 13, 1999: 2.

— seeking community support, Lahaina News, August 26, 1999: 5.

— to hold "West Maui Ohana New Year's Celebration", Lahaina News, September 2, 1999: 3.

— to host discussion of "Facts of Life for Teens", Lahaina News, September 23, 1999: 12.

— to host "Evening Fun at W.M.Y.C.", Lahaina News, September 23, 1999: 12,13.

— to hold "Maui's Best Craft and Gift Show", Lahaina News, May 18, 2000: 20.

— to host Maui Myth and Magic Theatre teaching youth drama, Lahaina News, June 15, 2000: 6.

WEST OAHU COLLEGE
— offering weekend college on Maui, Lahaina News, February 5, 1986: 3.

WEST SIDE CABLE
— purchases Hawaiian Cable Vision, Lahaina News, May 27, 1987: 16.

WEST SIDE HELIPORT
— see heliport

WEST SIDE NATURAL FOODS [BUSINESS]
— featured, Lahaina News, December 16, 1987: 9.

WEST SIDE POSSE
— to plan teen activities, Lahaina News, May 26, 1994: 1,4.

WEST SIDE RESOURCE CENTER
— plan discussed by Charlie Ridings, Lahaina News, November 23, 2000: 1,19.

WESTERN PACIFIC REGIONAL FISHERY MANAGEMENT COUNCIL (WESTPAC)
— extends closure of longline fishing, Lahaina News, September 12, 1991: 6.

— approves longline fishing restrictions, Lahaina News, October 14, 1993: 11.

— expected to overturn longlining rules, Lahaina News, January 6, 1994: 8.

WESTERN SLOPE WATER
— sponsoring Hawai'i's entry in the America's Cup challenge, Lahaina News, July 29, 1999: 11.

WESTERN STATES YOUTH SERVICE NETWORK
— honors Gail Gnazzo, Lahaina News, December 6, 1989: 28.

WESTERN UNION [BUSINESS]
— holds seminar on electronic mail, Lahaina News, June 5, 1985: 8.

WESTERN ZONES OPEN WATER RACE
— to be held at Kamaole Beach Park, Lahaina News, August 2, 2001: 13.

WESTIN KA'ANAPALI OCEAN RESORT VILLAS
— to expand, Lahaina News, April 4, 2002: 8.

WESTIN MAUI HOTEL [BUSINESS]
— offering take-out turkey, Lahaina News, November 18, 1987: 3.

— employees from Moloka'i interviewed, Lahaina News, January 13, 1988: 1.

— appoints Epi Rabanal as Sales Manager, Lahaina News, February 3, 1988: 3.

— offering films, lectures, and tours, Lahaina News, February 3, 1988: 4.

— guarantees 55-minute lunch, Lahaina News, March 9, 1988: 17.

— hosted luau for employees from Moloka'i, Lahaina News, March 16, 1988: 3.

— organizing Mother's Day essay writing contest, Lahaina News, May 4, 1988: 14.

— to hold "Mad Hatter" concert and dance, Lahaina News, September 7, 1988: 3.

— offering cooking demonstrations, Lahaina News, September 14, 1988: 13.

— gameshow Win, Lose or Draw to tape segments, Lahaina News, November 30, 1988: 16.

— refurbishing Haleakala Ballroom, Lahaina News, September 13, 1989: 6.

— appoints Debbie hunt as director of public relations, Lahaina News, September 20, 1989: 6.

— adds to staff, Lahaina News, November 8, 1989: 5.

— may be sold, Lahaina News, March 14, 1990: 5.

— names Brian Quinn as sales manager, Lahaina News, March 21, 1990: 4.

— results of blood drive, Lahaina News, March 28, 1990: 3.

— offering free car rental with room bookings, Lahaina News, March 28, 1990: 6.

— Sandy Phipps promoted to sales account executive, Lahaina News, April 11, 1990: 5.

— honors employees, Lahaina News, April 18, 1990: 5.

— honors employees, Lahaina News, May 30, 1990: 6.

— promotes Julie Mohler to convention services manager, Lahaina News, May 30, 1990: 6.

— including English as a second language training, Lahaina News, July 11, 1990: 6.

— chef Andreas Knapp creates new menu, Lahaina News, August 1, 1990: 9.

— employees complete course in housekeeping techniques, Lahaina News, August 8, 1990: 6.

— promotes Peter Khong to manager of Japanese guest services, Lahaina News, August 22, 1990: 9.

— receives Gold Key Award from Meetings & Conventions magazine, Lahaina News, August 29, 1990: 8.

— hosting Senior Management Conference, Lahaina News, September 12, 1990: 12.

— employees to clean highway, Lahaina News, September 12, 1990: 9.

— begins "Heart at Work" program, Lahaina News, October 17, 1990: 12.

— Darcy Ambrosio is first graduate of apprenticeship program, Lahaina News, October 24, 1990: 6.

— Sound of the Falls Supper Club offering French culinary adventure at , Lahaina News, November 7, 1990: 10,11.

— recognizes employees, Lahaina News, December 26, 1990: 7.

— adds the catamaran The Gemini to offerings, Lahaina News, February 6, 1991: 8.

— promotes Herb Yuen to director of conference services, Lahaina News, March 13, 1991: 7.

— to feature foods from the Pacific Northwest, Lahaina News, April 3, 1991: 7.

— appoints Steve Shalit as managing director, Lahaina News, April 10, 1991: 6.

— appoints Julia Gajcak as director of public relations for Westin Maui Hotel, Lahaina News, April 10, 1991: 6.

— awarded four diamonds from the American Automobile Association, Lahaina News, June 6, 1991: 6.

— names Vernon Oato as human resources director, Lahaina News, June 6, 1991: 6.

— receives Play it Safe International, Lahaina News, June 13, 1991: 10.

— named a top meeting property by Meeting and Conventions Magazine, Lahaina News, September 12, 1991: 4.

— Matthew Hart promoted to manager, Lahaina News, September 19, 1991: 6.

— food promotion to celebrate Fall harvest, Lahaina News, November 14, 1991: 15.

— new chef James Reaux featured, Lahaina News, November 14, 1991: 18,19.

— to offer Fall Harvest celebration, Lahaina News, November 21, 1991: 16.

— hosts Aloha Show, Lahaina News, January 9, 1992: 11.

— manager of Japanese guest services Maura Shay featured, Lahaina News, January 16, 1992: 8.

— receives Four Diamond Award from the American Automobile Association, Lahaina News, January 30, 1992: 12.

— promotions and hirings announced, Lahaina News, February 6, 1992: 10.

— director of romance Pat Gleeson featured, Lahaina News, February 13, 1992: 11.

— hosts of the month announced, Lahaina News, April 16, 1992: 15.

— honors employees, Lahaina News, June 4, 1992: 9.

— honors Martina Hildorfer as manager of the quarter, Lahaina News, July 2, 1992: 16.

— employees finish Dale Carnegie training course, Lahaina News, July 9, 1992: 14.

— hosts of the month announced, Lahaina News, July 9, 1992: 14.

— employee awards announced, Lahaina News, July 23, 1992: 16.

— employees honored, Lahaina News, August 13, 1992: 12.

— recognizes Terry Hanley as "Manager of the Second quarter", Lahaina News, August 27, 1992: 11.

— recognized for excellence by Corporate and Incentive magazine, Lahaina News, October 1, 1992: 11.

— presents Braille menus, Lahaina News, October 15, 1992: 16.

— appoints Yvonne Cablay as director of marketing, Lahaina News, December 3, 1992: 4.

— appoints Robert Howell as director of sales, Lahaina News, December 17, 1992: 8.

— employee awards announced, Lahaina News, December 31, 1992: 10.

— promotions announced, manager of the quarter announced, Lahaina News, January 14, 1993: 6.

— completes temporary rock wall, Lahaina News, January 21, 1993: 4.

— employee awards announced, Lahaina News, January 21, 1993: 8,9.

— employees recognized, Lahaina News, February 11, 1993: 12.

— monitoring attempts to stop beach erosion, Lahaina News, February 11, 1993: 4.

— Bruce McNish promoted to director of operations, Lahaina News, April 8, 1993: 6.

— to remove temporary beachfront wall, Lahaina News, April 22, 1993: 3.

— employees honored, Lahaina News, April 29, 1993: 9.

— recognized as top employer, Lahaina News, July 15, 1993: 6.

— awarded Gold Key Award by Meeting and Conventions Magazine, Lahaina News, September 16, 1993: 10.

— restructured, Lahaina News, November 4, 1993: 7.

— employees awarded, Lahaina News, November 18, 1993: 7.

— to hold Bridal Faire, sponsored by Maui Chamber of Commerce, Lahaina News, January 6, 1994: 11,12.

— employees honored, Lahaina News, March 3, 1994: 6.

— holds thank you barbeque for employees after large convention, Lahaina News, May 12, 1994: 10.

— creates Westin Kids Club, Lahaina News, June 16, 1994: 12.

— employees recognized, Lahaina News, June 30, 1994: 9.

— names Karen Demarke as "Manager of the First Quarter", Lahaina News, June 30, 1994: 9.

— awarded Successful Meeting Magazine Pinnacle Award, Lahaina News, July 14, 1994: 12.

— holds "Take Your Child to Work Day", Lahaina News, July 28, 1994: 9.

— appointments announced, Lahaina News, July 28, 1994: 9.

— receives "most improved results" from United Way, Lahaina News, August 18, 1994: 5.

— employees honored, Lahaina News, August 18, 1994: 9.

— awards Marcia Murphy "Manager of the Second Quarter", Lahaina News, September 22, 1994: 13.

— employees honored, Lahaina News, September 22, 1994: 13.

— hires Tylun Pang, Lahaina News, September 22, 1994: 13.

— employees honored, Lahaina News, October 6, 1994: 11.

— receives Platinum Partner Award, Lahaina News, October 13, 1994: 15.

— announces hosts of the month, Lahaina News, December 1, 1994: 13.

— chosen as top destination by Conde Nast Traveler, Lahaina News, December 15, 1994: 15.

— to offer Vegetarian alternatives, Lahaina News, December 15, 1994: 16,17.

— Stephanie Sera and Cynthia Mayer appointed, Lahaina News, December 22, 1994: 13.

— Jennifer Reaux joins as sales manager, Lahaina News, January 26, 1995: 13.

— promotions announced, Lahaina News, February 9, 1995: 6.

— hosts of the month announced, Lahaina News, February 16, 1995: 13.

— awarded Four-Diamonds by American Automobile Association, Lahaina News, February 23, 1995: 6.

— employees recognized, Lahaina News, March 9, 1995: 6.

— receives award from Corporate Meetings and Incentives Magazine, Lahaina News, March 30, 1995: 10.

— employees honored, Lahaina News, May 11, 1995: 10.

— holds take your children to work day, Lahaina News, June 29, 1995: 3.

— honors employees, Lahaina News, July 20, 1995: 10.

— employees honored, Lahaina News, July 27, 1995: 10.

— names Lynn Britton as catering sales manager, Lahaina News, August 3, 1995: 8.

— hosts honored, Lahaina News, August 17, 1995: 10.

— Lani Ahloy named as manager of the second quarter, Lahaina News, August 24, 1995: 10.

— honors employees, Lahaina News, September 14, 1995: 10.

— hosts of the month named, Lahaina News, October 12, 1995: 12.

— promotes Jim Palank to Director of Sales, Lahaina News, November 9, 1995: 10.

— employees honored, Lahaina News, November 23, 1995: 10.

— Keiki Kamp to be held, Lahaina News, November 23, 1995: 4.

— new staff announced, Lahaina News, December 14, 1995: 16.

— employees honored, Lahaina News, December 28, 1995: 10.

— employees honored, Lahaina News, January 11, 1996: 11.

— union members demonstrate, Lahaina News, February 8, 1996: 18.

— Matthew Hart named general manager of, Lahaina News, February 22, 1996: 11.

— hosts honored, Lahaina News, March 7, 1996: 11.

WESTPAC

— join Westin Maui's executive team, Lahaina News, March 21, 1996: 10.

— employees honored, Lahaina News, April 18, 1996: 9.

— new appointments announced, Lahaina News, September 19, 1996: 8.

— fields team for Hana Relay Race, Lahaina News, October 10, 1996: 9.

— recognizes employees, Lahaina News, October 24, 1996: 9.

— names hosts of the month, Lahaina News, November 14, 1996: 8.

— renovation of Valley Isle Ballroom completed, Lahaina News, December 18, 1997: 8.

— has two new managers, Lahaina News, July 22, 1999: 11.

— appoints Michael Lee as director sales and marketing, Lahaina News, September 2, 1999: 13.

— replacing beds with "Heavenly Beds", Lahaina News, September 9, 1999: 11.

— hosting "Aloha Friday Luncheon Show", Lahaina News, May 25, 2000: 19.

— plans improvement project, Lahaina News, August 24, 2000: 11.

— Roger Huldi named Director of Outlets, Lahaina News, October 5, 2000: 14.

— Vallejo to perform at, Lahaina News, December 7, 2000: 26.

— new restaurant, Tropica, opening, Lahaina News, December 28, 2000: 16.

— staff changes announced, Lahaina News, February 1, 2001: 8.

— announces staff changes, Lahaina News, March 8, 2001: 8.

— hosting investor conference, Lahaina News, April 12, 2001: 9.

— to hold job expo, Lahaina News, April 26, 2001: 9.

— holds Job Shadow Day program, Lahaina News, February 14, 2002: 8.

— Luana Kawa'a new Hawaiian cultural advisor, Lahaina News, August 1, 2002: 8.

— hires Kiana Mandeville and Nicole Newton, Lahaina News, January 16, 2003: 8.

— new sales managers, Lahaina News, January 23, 2003: 8.

— appoints Bridgette Okamoto as public relations manager, Lahaina News, January 30, 2003: 8.

— appoints Bart Umidi as new executive chef, Lahaina News, February 20, 2003: 8.

— to hold May Day events, Lahaina News, April 24, 2003: 21.

— to celebrate May Day, Lahaina News, May 1, 2003: 16.

— Kelly Kling new sales manager at, Lahaina News, August 28, 2003: 8.

— to open "Heavenly Spa", Lahaina News, September 25, 2003: 8.

WESTPAC

— Council to consider longline fishing moratorium, Lahaina News, February 20, 1991: 20.

WESTSIDE COPY AND GRAPHICS [BUSINESS]

— opens, Lahaina News, June 29, 1995: 10.

— purchased by Danny Giesen and Kathy Rosen, Lahaina News, October 10, 1996: 8.

WESTSIDE GARDEN CENTER [BUSINESS]

— opening, Lahaina News, January 14, 1993: 6.

— offering bonsai classes, Lahaina News, November 11, 1993: 3.

— offering bonsai classes, Lahaina News, November 18, 1993: 3.

WESTSIDE NATURAL FOODS AND DELI [BUSINESS]

— to open, Lahaina News, May 20, 1999: 16.

— owners Robyn and Allan Ranson featured, Lahaina News, July 5, 2001: 1,8.

WESTSIDE WELLNESS-COMPLETE CHIROPRACTIC

— doctor Jason Grindley joins, Lahaina News, August 15, 2002: 8.

WET SEAL [BUSINESS]

— using recycled paper bags, Lahaina News, January 16, 1991: 5.

WETSCREAMS [FILM]

— reviewed, Lahaina Times, August, 1980 volume 4 number 7: 5.

WEXLER, HASKELL

— to participate in the Hawaii International Film Festival on Oahu, Lahaina News, November 12, 1992: 22.

WEYAND, THOM

— becomes managing editor of Maui Sun, Lahaina News, November 1, 1981: 6.

— named executive director at Maui Community Arts and Cultural Center, Lahaina News, October 24, 1991: 8.

WHALE AID II

— rally to take place, Lahaina News, March 8, 1989: 7.

WHALE CENTER OF THE PACIFIC

— to host presentations, Lahaina News, February 6, 1997: 15.

— continues to hold slide presentations, Lahaina News, February 20, 1997: 10,11.

— to hold presentations, Lahaina News, February 27, 1997: 11.

— offers free whale slide presentation, Lahaina News, March 13, 1997: 16.

— to host talks, Lahaina News, March 20, 1997: 16.

— to offer slide presentations, Lahaina News, April 17, 1997: 12.

— continues to offer presentations, Lahaina News, June 12, 1997: 16.

WHALE DAY

— 6th annual celebration to be held, Lahaina News, April 9, 1986: 3.

— planned, Lahaina News, April 20, 1988: 6.

— to be held with Earth Day on April 22, Lahaina News, April 5, 1989: 18.

— events detailed, Lahaina News, April 19, 1989: 9.

— festival to be held, Lahaina News, March 14, 1996: 11.

— to be held, Lahaina News, March 21, 1996: 13.

— to be celebrated, Lahaina News, February 24, 2000: 1.

— celebration to include Na Hoku Winners, Lahaina News, February 13, 2003: 14.

WHALE DISCOVERY

— presented at Whalers Village, Lahaina News, March 16, 1995: 12.

WHALE MANIA MAUI

— being held, Lahaina News, March 14, 2002: 5.

— to be held by Soroptimists International, Lahaina News, May 23, 2002: 1,3.

— Soroptimists International to hold, Lahaina News, July 25, 2002: 18.

— artist Guy Buffet to paint for, Lahaina News, August 15, 2002: 14.

— growing in popularity, Lahaina News, August 29, 2002: 15.

— Hyatt Regency Maui joins, Lahaina News, September 19, 2002: 13.

— underway, whale statue on display at Mahina Surf, Lahaina News, November 7, 2002: 18.

— Soroptimists International program successful, Lahaina News, January 2, 2003: 1,20.

— successful, Lahaina News, January 9, 2003: 18.

— Soroptimist International to auction whales from Whale Mania Maui program, Lahaina News, February 6, 2003: 3.

— whales to be sold, Lahaina News, March 6, 2003: 1,20.

— whales to be sold, Lahaina News, March 13, 2003: 2.

— auctioned by Soroptimist International, Lahaina News, March 20, 2003: 3.

WHALE OF A DIAPER SERVICE [BUSINESS]

— opens, Lahaina News, April 4, 1990: 6.

WHALE SANCTUARY

— management plan not to be ready in time for Governor Waihee to approve it, Lahaina News, November 3, 1994: 8.

WHALE SPREE FESTIVAL

— sponsored by Whalers Village, Lahaina News, January 31, 1990: 4,13.

— continues, Lahaina News, February 7, 1990: 13.

— featured, Lahaina News, February 14, 1990: 18,19.

— continues, Lahaina News, February 21, 1990: 1,13.

— update on shops, Lahaina Sun, March 24, 1971: 8.

— grand opening, Lahaina Sun, May 5, 1971: 3.

— dedication ceremony described, Lahaina Sun, May 12, 1971: 6.

— Amfac planning movie house-retail store complex, Lahaina Sun, August 30, 1972: 11.

— sold by Amfac to Campbell Estate, Lahaina News, July 15, 1980: 6.

— renovation work begins, Lahaina News, September 15, 1982: 2.

— major expansion plans, Lahaina News, May 1, 1983: 11.

— expanding, Lahaina News, November 30, 1983: 14.

— fashion show set for July 4, Lahaina News, July 3, 1985: 20.

— renovation has resulted in increase in sales, Lahaina News, August 14, 1985: 3.

— results of renovation featured, Lahaina News, February 19, 1986: A,B,C,D.

— expands parking, Lahaina News, November 5, 1986: 3.

— hosts Polynesian Revue, Lahaina News, June 8, 1988: 13.

— expanding, Lahaina News, July 27, 1988: 1.

— to commemorate golden age of whaling with Whaling Spree, Lahaina News, January 11, 1989: 6,9.

— upcoming entertainment detailed, Lahaina News, March 8, 1989: 6.

— holds fish cutting competition, Lahaina News, July 5, 1989: 10.

— planning art festival, Lahaina News, November 1, 1989: 6.

— to dedicate a new pavilion, Lahaina News, November 22, 1989: 5.

— offering "Whale Spree" activities, Lahaina News, November 29, 1989: 22.

— launches Holiday Shopping Spree promotion, Lahaina News, December 13, 1989: 6.

— sponsoring Whale Spree, Lahaina News, January 31, 1990: 4,13.

— hosting Karaoke Star Search, Lahaina News, August 8, 1990: 13.

— evening events described, Lahaina News, September 12, 1990: 16.

— to hold Saturday Night Auction, Lahaina News, September 26, 1990: 10.

— to hold "Saturday Night Auctions", Lahaina News, October 10, 1990: 14.

— to host "Saturday Night Auction", Lahaina News, October 17, 1990: 15.

— to hold fundraiser for Napili Fire and Ambulance Station, Lahaina News, December 5, 1990: 9.

— to hold third Annual Whale Spree, Lahaina News, January 23, 1991: 7.

— new whale exhibit to be designed, Lahaina News, February 20, 1991: 7.

— to host biathlon, Lahaina News, August 8, 1991: 6.

— appoints Lynn Okamoto as marketing manager, Lahaina News, October 10, 1991: 6.

— to add new complex, Lahaina News, December 5, 1991: 12.

— to begin month-long celebration of return of humpback whales, Lahaina News, February 13, 1992: 18.

— scheduling a twice weekly hula show, Lahaina News, February 13, 1992: 18.

— feature hula shows twice a week, Lahaina News, March 12, 1992: 17.

— to celebrate return of the whales, Lahaina News, March 24, 1994: 7.

— employee changes, Lahaina News, November 9, 1995: 10.

— new stores open, Lahaina News, November 30, 1995: 10.

— to expand, Lahaina News, April 25, 1996: 12.

— new shops open, Lahaina News, June 5, 1997: 2.

— Ostrander-Chu appointed as advertising agency for, Lahaina News, December 18, 1997: 21.

— new stores added, Lahaina News, January 7, 1999: 13.

— to host French Festival, Lahaina News, October 21, 1999: 13.

— continue to offer Hawaiian entertainment, Lahaina News, October 21, 1999: 17.

— continues to hold "Hot Nights", Lahaina News, June 8, 2000: 21.

— continues to offer "Hot Nights", Lahaina News, October 26, 2000: 28,29.

— continues to offer "Hot Nights" entertainment, Lahaina News, January 4, 2001: 16.

— hosting "Sizzlin' Summer Games", Lahaina News, June 14, 2001: 18.

— preparing for Maui Onion Festival, Lahaina News, July 12, 2001: 15.

— new shops open, Lahaina News, November 15, 2001: 8.

— to feature Japanese folk dance and cooking demonstrations, Lahaina News, April 18, 2002: 16.

— to hold "Art in the Village", Lahaina News, March 27, 2003: 14.

— new tenants at, Lahaina News, August 28, 2003: 8.

WHALER'S VILLAGE MUSEUM

— described, Lahaina News, January 6, 1988: 4.

— discussed by Lewis Eisenberg, Lahaina News, April 27, 1988: 3.

— featured in Whale Spree Festival insert, Lahaina News, February 13, 1991: B8.

— has new self-guided audio tour, Lahaina News, June 29, 2000: 11.

— continues to offer "Hot Nights", Lahaina News, September 7, 2000: 20.

— upgrades theatre, Lahaina News, May 16, 2002: 8.

WHALES

— skeleton of sperm whale to be displayed at Whaler's Village, Lahaina Sun, November 25, 1970: 1.

— capturing live whales described, Lahaina Sun, December 15, 1971: 18.

— exhibit to be installed on Carthaginian II, Lahaina Sun, May 2, 1973: 5,13.

— Ed Jenkins designing whale exhibit, Lahaina Sun, June 20, 1973: 4.

— historic New England whaleboat acquired by Lahaina Restoration Foundation, Lahaina Sun, July 11, 1973: 3.

— sanctuary studied, Lahaina News, August 15, 1980: 6.

— season opens, Lahaina News, December 15, 1980: 10.

— described, Lahaina News, November 15, 1981: 11.

— whaling ban approved by International Whaling Commission, Lahaina News, August 15, 1982: 4.

— discussion of whale hunt, Lahaina News, January 1, 1983: 3.

— described off Lahaina, Lahaina News, March 1, 1983: 9.

— Maui whale count begins, Lahaina News, April 1, 1983: 6.

— first whale seen in Maui waters, Lahaina News, November 16, 1983: 6.

— state-wide sanctuary proposed, Lahaina News, November 23, 1983: 4.

— Maui Whale Watchers meeting set, Lahaina News, January 18, 1984: 5.

— Pacific Whale Foundation's whalewatch set, Lahaina News, February 8, 1984: 5.

— public hearing on proposed sanctuary to be held, Lahaina News, February 15, 1984: 5.

— sanctuary plan proposed, opposed, Lahaina News, February 22, 1984: 4,5.

— legislative committee asks governor to veto proposed sanctuary, Lahaina News, March 21, 1984: 17.

— Third Annual Whale Day celebrated, Lahaina News, March 21, 1984: 4.

— Maui Whale Watchers to meet, Lahaina News, April 18, 1984: 5.

— developments in research techniques, Lahaina News, April 18, 1984: 9,10,11.

— recent research discussed, Lahaina News, April 25, 1984: 7,8,9.

— editorial praising Governor Ariyoshi for vetoing proposed whale sanctuary, Lahaina News, July 18, 1984: 2.

— first whale sighted, Lahaina News, October 17, 1984: 9.

— whalewatch season begins, Lahaina News, October 31, 1984: 3.

— history and update on current status of, Lahaina News, March 13, 1985: 1,12,13.

— research of Debbie Glockner-Ferrari and Mark Ferrari featured, Lahaina News, March 13, 1985: 11.

— People Opposed to the Whale Sanctuary (POWS) attempts to stop creation of whale sanctuary, Lahaina News, July 13, 1995: 3.

— public meeting to be held on Hawaiian Islands Humpback Whale National Marine Sanctuary, Lahaina News, November 23, 1995: 1,12.

— humpback whale season delayed, Lahaina News, December 28, 1995: 1.

— Whales Alive Conference to be held, Lahaina News, January 11, 1996: 2.

— Navatek II to hold whale watches, Lahaina News, January 18, 1996: 10.

— fluke I.D. research discussed, Lahaina News, February 1, 1996: 1,14.

— researchers to share finding, Lahaina News, February 8, 1996: 7.

— National Oceanic and Atmospheric Association seeking advice on sanctuary plan, Lahaina News, February 15, 1996: 10.

— update on recent research, Lahaina News, February 29, 1996: 1,16.

— studying death of male humpback whale, Lahaina News, February 29, 1996: 1,2.

— sanctuary plans still being drafted, Lahaina News, April 11, 1996: 3.

— Pacific Whale Foundation to celebrate return of, Lahaina News, November 28, 1996: 10.

— Whales Alive to host Celebration of Whales Conference, Lahaina News, January 16, 1997: 10.

— National Marine Fisheries Service agents to watch for whale violations, Lahaina News, March 13, 1997: 1,20.

— Governor Ben Cayetano accepts whale sanctuary for five years, Lahaina News, June 12, 1997: 12.

— Maui Nui Explorer has whale sighting, Lahaina News, October 2, 1997: 18.

— Whales Alive Conference to be held, Lahaina News, January 8, 1998: 7.

— Dirk Younkerman to present on, Lahaina News, April 9, 1998: 16.

— pygmy whale beached, Lahaina News, May 21, 1998: 1.

— humpback whale sightings logged, Lahaina News, March 11, 1999: 1,16.

— Pacific Whale Foundation reports first sighting, Lahaina News, October 7, 1999: 1.

— state and federal regulatory agencies to hold workshop on guidelines for viewing sea mammals and turtles, Lahaina News, November 18, 1999: 3.

— Pacific Whale Foundation's director of research Robin Baird to speak on whale tagging, Lahaina News, January 27, 2000: 13.

— Pacific Whale Foundation looking for volunteers for Great Whale Count, Lahaina News, February 10, 2000: 2.

— details of Pacific Whale Foundation's Great Whale Count, Lahaina News, February 17, 2000: 3.

— Dr. Hannah Bernard to speak on "Humpback Whales: The Most Watchable Whales", Lahaina News, March 9, 2000: 1.

— Joylynn Oliveira to present "The Cultural Importance of Whales in Hawaii", Lahaina News, June 8, 2000: 21.

— Whalers Village Museum has new self-guided audio tour, Lahaina News, June 29, 2000: 11.

— workshop to cover responsible viewing of humpback whales, Lahaina News, December 7, 2000: 1.

— Hawaiian Islands Humpback Whale National Marine Sanctuary funds whale research, Lahaina News, January 11, 2001: 3.

— Whitlow Au of Marine Mammal Research Program to speak on "Acoustic Recording of Humpback Whales", Lahaina News, February 8, 2001: 20.

— count planned by Pacific Whale Foundation, Lahaina News, February 15, 2001: 14.

— rules to be covered at Ocean Users Workshop, Lahaina News, November 1, 2001: 1.

— Ocean Arts Festival, Lahaina News, March 14, 2002: 14.

— newborn humpback whale sighted, Lahaina News, December 26, 2002: 12.

— Jerry Stowell to discuss humpback whale migration, Lahaina News, January 9, 2003: 1.

— National Marine Fisheries Service Marine Mammal Health and Stranding Response Program untangles humpback whale, Lahaina News, March 6, 2003: 2.

— see also Pacific Whale Foundation

WHALES ALIVE CONFERENCE

— conference panel says issues shortchanged by media, Lahaina News, February 1, 1996: 3.

— Celebration of Whales Conference, Lahaina News, January 16, 1997: 10.

— to be held, Lahaina News, January 8, 1998: 7.

— to be held, Lahaina News, January 15, 1998: 12.

WHALES ALIVE INTERNATIONAL

— presents "The Celebration of Whales", Lahaina News, January 6, 1994: 7.

WHALE'S TAKE

— to host Breeze Brothers, Lahaina News, July 4, 1990: 15.

WHALE'S TALE [RESTAURANT]

— undergoing extensive remodeling, Lahaina Sun, January 27, 1971: 3.

— reviewed, Lahaina News, February 15, 1983: 14.

— renovated by new owners, Lahaina News, February 7, 1990: 5.

— Breeze Brothers to appear, Lahaina News, March 28, 1990: 18.

— featured, Lahaina News, August 2, 2001: 14.

WHALE'S TALE, A [POEM]

— printed, Lahaina News, December 21, 1988: 1,16.

WHALEWATCHERS

— see Maui Whalewatchers

WHALING

— U.S. whaling industry ending, Lahaina Sun, March 10, 1971: 2.

— sailors' harsh life described, Lahaina News, June 19, 1985: 1,9.

WHALING PARTY

— dinner and show held at Pioneer Inn, Lahaina News, May 30, 1990: 9.

WHALING SPREE [BUSINESS]

— Whaler's Village to commemorate golden age of whaling, Lahaina News, January 11, 1989: 6,9.

— history of celebration described, Lahaina News, October 6, 1994: 4.

— Warren Montoya to open, Lahaina News, December 23, 1999: 13.

WHALLEY, ROB [MUSICIAN]

— to hold benefit concert for Harvest Chapel, Lahaina News, April 20, 1995: 6.

— to perform, Lahaina News, May 27, 1999: 12.

WHARF CINEMA CENTER

— changes to shopping area detailed, Lahaina News, December 3, 1986: 1,10.

— to give away movie passes for Memorial Day weekend, Lahaina News, May 24, 1989: 3.

— to hold Sidewalk Sale, Lahaina News, June 13, 1991: 6.

— to hold Sidewalk Sale, Lahaina News, June 20, 1991: 3.

— to hold sidewalk sale, Lahaina News, August 15, 1991: 3.

— restaurants detailed, Lahaina News, December 12, 1991: 22,23.

— to host Arthritis Foundation telethon, Lahaina News, March 12, 1992: 19.

— four new restaurants open in, Lahaina News, August 13, 1992: 12.

— results of karaoke contest, Lahaina News, November 10, 1994: 7.

— to hold sidewalk sale, Lahaina News, August 8, 1996: 15.

— planning Keiki Karaoke Talent Contest, Lahaina News, December 9, 1999: 17.

— to host Aloha Festivals, Lahaina News, October 2, 2003: 2.

WHARF FLOWERS [BUSINESS]

— featured, Lahaina News, June 15, 1988: 6.

WHARF SHOPPING CENTER
— selected shops featured, Lahaina News, August 29, 1984: 14.
— collecting donations for less fortunate families, Lahaina News, December 5, 1984: 14.
— announces new tenants, Lahaina News, June 26, 1985: 3,20.

WHARF SHOPS AND RESTAURANTS
— appoints Leo Tal as Director of Public Relations, Lahaina News, May 11, 1988: 14.
— to host fashion show, Lahaina News, August 10, 1988: 3.
— celebrates 10 year anniversary, Lahaina News, September 28, 1988: 1,20.
— still celebrating 10th anniversary, Lahaina News, November 16, 1988: 13.
— Holiday Theatre to open at, Lahaina News, January 25, 1989: 1.

WHAT'S HAPPENING NOW! [TELEVISION SHOW]
— star Haywood Nelson visits Maui, Lahaina News, September 24, 1986: 1,14.

WHAT'S THE SCOOP [RESTAURANT]
— reviewed, Lahaina News, September 28, 1983: 14.

WHAT'S UPCOUNTRY ON MAUI [PUBLICATION
— seeking participation from local businesses, Lahaina News, October 23, 1985: 20.

WHEELCHAIR GETAWAYS [RESTAURANT]
— opens, Lahaina News, February 3, 2000: 11.

WHEELER, BRUCE
— bookstore manager featured, Lahaina News, April 19, 1989: 2.

WHEELER, CURT
— general manager of Ruth's Chris Steak House, Lahaina News, July 30, 1998: 13.

WHEELER, JIM
— appointed general sales manager at Island Dodge, Lahaina News, March 7, 1996: 11.

WHEELER, KOLLEEN
— appointed president of Maui Philharmonic Society, Lahaina News, April 20, 1988: 13.

WHEELING FOR MAUI'S HUNGRY
— benefit basketball game to be held, Lahaina News, November 28, 1984: 3.

WHEN WE WERE KINGS
— documentary to be shown, Lahaina News, May 29, 1997: 17.

WHEN WE WERE ONE [PLAY]
— Lane Nishikawa's to be previewed at Maui Arts and Cultural Center, Lahaina News, December 7, 2000: 24.
— to be performed, Lahaina News, March 21, 2002: 16.

WHERE THE BOYS ARE [PERFORMANCE]
— competition to be held at Iao Theatre, Lahaina News, June 30, 1994: 15.
— finals to be held, Lahaina News, July 7, 1994: 15,16.

WHIPPLE, DARLENE
— president of Nai'a Properties, Inc. listed in Who's Who, Lahaina News, August 21, 1997: 12.

WHISKEY JONES [MUSICAL GROUP]
— performance reviewed, Lahaina News, September 19, 1984: 12.

WHITE, ANNE [BUSINESS OWNER]
— All Lahaina Lock featured, Lahaina News, May 23, 1984: 17.

WHITE, CECILIA
— performs in "Mad Cloak", Lahaina News, September 25, 2003: 2.

WHITE, DOUG
— Maui Planning Commission to consider request to build house along Front Street, Lahaina News, February 27, 2003: 1,2.

WHITE, DOUG [MUSICIAN]
— see Doug White musical groups

WHITE, GERRY
— sales manager for Comprehensive Financial Services, Lahaina News, December 30, 1993: 6.

WHITE HOUSE CONFERENCE ON AGING
— to be held, Lahaina News, August 25, 1994: 5.

WHITE HOUSE/BLACK MARKET [BUSINESS]
— to open at Whalers Village, Lahaina News, February 13, 2003: 8.

WHITE, KEN
— hired by Honolulu Publishing of Maui, Lahaina News, March 20, 1991: 7.

WHITE, LAUREL
— to hold grand opening for Bikram Yoga Maui, Lahaina News, October 31, 2002: 28.

WHITE, MICHAEL
— appointed chairman of 15th annual Na Mele O Maui, Lahaina News, February 11, 1987: 3.
— named to Hawaii Tourism Marketing Council, Lahaina News, August 1, 1991: 11.
— appointed to Governor's Tourism Council , Lahaina News, August 8, 1991: 11.
— receives UH Distinguished Alumni Award, Lahaina News, May 21, 1992: 4.

WHITE, MIKE [POLITICIAN]
— Ka'anapali Beach Hotel general manager sees teaching Hawaiiana as a way to reduce staff turnover, Lahaina News, May 3, 1989: 1.
— Ka'anapali Beach Hotel general manager discusses proposed expansion, Lahaina News, December 26, 1990: 1.
— general manager of Ka'anapali Beach Hotel presents perpetual Pookela award to Joy Pascual for Keiki Hula Festival, Lahaina News, November 7, 1991: 16.
— to head Maui United Way fundraising campaign, Lahaina News, May 27, 1993: 4.
— may run for State House of Representatives, Lahaina News, December 9, 1993: 12.
— looking to support tourism, regulate timeshares, Lahaina News, December 23, 1993: 1,3.
— updates residents on legislative session, Lahaina News, March 3, 1994: 1,2.
— talks to students via lumaphone, Lahaina News, March 24, 1994: 7.
— to offer legislative update, Lahaina News, May 5, 1994: 2.
— community forum held, Lahaina News, May 19, 1994: 1,20.
— announces that funds released for improvements at Princess Nahienaena Elementary School, Lahaina News, August 18, 1994: 5.
— to hold community forum, Lahaina News, January 5, 1995: 4.
— hold public meeting, Lahaina News, March 16, 1995: 1,4.
— reports that insurance company moving along, Lahaina News, April 27, 1995: 5.
— to hold community forum with Roz Baker, Lahaina News, January 4, 1996: 4.
— says that funds released for intersection on Honoapi'ilani Highway, Lahaina News, May 16, 1996: 6.
— holds fundraiser, Lahaina News, June 27, 1996: 14.
— Ka'anapali Beach Hotel to manage Plantation Inn, Lahaina News, March 13, 1997: 1.
— encourages retailers to take interest in government, Lahaina News, May 22, 1997: 1.
— reports that money released for schools, Lahaina News, February 12, 1998: 8.
— not seeking reelection, Lahaina News, July 23, 1998: 6.
— announces release of money for Princess Nahienaena Elementary School, Lahaina News, October 22, 1998: 15.

WHITE OAK DANCE PROJECT
— to perform with Mikhail Baryshnikov, Lahaina News, October 19, 2000: 20.

WHITE, PAT
— to lecture for Inner Peace Movement, Lahaina News, October 17, 1984: 3.

WHITE, PETER [MUSICIAN]
— to perform at Maui Music Festival, Lahaina News, August 15, 1996: 18.
— to perform at Maui Music Festival, Lahaina News, May 18, 2000: 19.

WHITE, TRACY
— appointed assistant manager at The Kapalua Villas, Lahaina News, January 16, 1991: 5.

WHITECRAFT, SAMANTHA
— to speak on "Everyday Data that Makes a Difference: Simple Data, Big Results in the Kahoʻolawe Island Reserve", Lahaina News, April 3, 2003: 17.
— to present "E Holo Mua—Kahoʻolawe Ocean Resources Monitoring and Management" as part of Maui Ocean Center's Sea Talks Series, Lahaina News, May 22, 2003: 2.

WHITEFEATHER, CAROLYNNE
— to present "Personal Visual Language as Essential for Literacy", Lahaina News, July 18, 2002: 17.

WHITEHEAD, JOHN
— to speak to Concerned Women for America conference, Lahaina News, October 18, 1989: 3.

WHITEHEAD, LAWRENCE
— search for missing kayaker called off, Lahaina News, April 10, 1991: 4.

WHITEHEAD, PETER
— cult leaders impact and death described, Lahaina News, June 1, 2000: 5.

WHITENER, KEN [HYPNOTIST]
— to perform at Honolulu Comedy Club, Lahaina News, February 2, 1995: 11.

WHITFIELD, WESLIA [MUSICIAN]
— performance at Stouffer Wailea Beach Resort presented by Maui Philharmonic Society and Alexander and Baldwin, Lahaina News, January 16, 1991: 10,11.

WHITFORD, RITA
— selected as Poʻokea volunteer of the year by Hawaii State Theatre Council, Lahaina News, July 25, 1990: 6.
— to perform in "Diamond Lil—Country Living", Lahaina News, May 9, 1996: 14.

WHITING, H. NEIL
— named director of Maui Community Theater, Lahaina News, February 20, 1985: 3.

WHITLEY, PHILIP
— to talk on "The Causes of Health", Lahaina News, April 19, 2001: 17.
— to talk on "The Triad of Health", Lahaina News, November 8, 2001: 17.
— chiropractor to discuss "Network and NET in Action" at ʻOhana Connection breakfast, Lahaina News, July 4, 2002: 16.

WHITTAKER, ROGER [MUSICIAN]
— to perform at Maui Arts and Cultural Center, Lahaina News, September 16, 1999: 13.

WHITTEMORE, LINDA [ARTIST]
— "First Things First" exhibit at Village Gallery, Lahaina News, November 8, 2001: 14.
— to offer printing demonstration, Lahaina News, November 14, 2002: 20.

WHITWORTH, KATHY
— golfer participates in Women's Kemper Open, Lahaina News, March 14, 1984: 14.
— golfer's career described, Lahaina News, March 6, 1985: A5.

WHO AM I ALONE? [BOOK]
— reviewed, Lahaina News, November 1, 1980: 14.

WHO NEEDS SNEEDS [PLAY]
— to be performed by Maui Community Theatre, Lahaina News, December 17, 1992: 22.

WHOLE EARTH COOK BOOK [BOOK]
— Judi Ohr, Maui resident, is an author of, Lahaina Sun, June 28, 1972: 19.

WHOLE PEOPLE OF GOD
— to hold curriculum workshop, Lahaina News, April 3, 1997: 13.

WHOLESALE PRODUCE DEALERS ASSOCIATION OF HAWAII
— admits to price fixing, Lahaina News, April 23, 1986: 2.

WHO'S AFRAID OF VIRGINIA WOOLF [PLAY]
— to be performed at Baldwin Mini-Theatre, Lahaina News, May 23, 1991: 12.
— to be performed by Maui Academy of the Performing Arts, Lahaina News, June 6, 1991: 15.
— to be performed at Baldwin Mini-Theatre, Lahaina News, June 13, 1991: 14.

WHO'S HAPPY NOW [PLAY]
— to be performed by Maui Community Theatre, Lahaina News, August 8, 1984: 3.

WIDOW TO WIDOW
— support group to meet, Lahaina News, January 29, 1986: 3.

WIELE, RONALD "RON"
— named resident manager for Kahana Gateway apartments, Lahaina News, January 30, 1991: 5.

WIENERT, MARSHA
— named executive director of Maui Visitors Bureau, Lahaina News, October 6, 1994: 7.
— Maui Visitors Bureau Executive Director to speak at Maui Historical Society Preservation , Lahaina News, May 18, 1995: 4.
— Maui Visitors Bureau Executive Director to speak to Kihei Destination Association, Lahaina News, June 15, 2000: 14.
— optimistic about visitor industry, Lahaina News, July 6, 2000: 1,14.

WIGGLESTON, JOE
— Scholar/Athlete of the Week, Lahaina News, April 27, 2000: 7.

WIGZELL, KIM
— wins wrestling at the Central European championships, Lahaina News, March 21, 1990: 8.

WIKI-WIKI PIZZA [RESTAURANT]
— expands service, Lahaina News, June 14, 1989: 7.

WILBOURN, SCOTT
— in automobile accident, Lahaina Sun, September 1, 1971: 13.

WILCOX, LORN [CHIROPRACTOR]
— business featured, Lahaina News, November 21, 1984: 18.

WILD CHILD [MUSICAL GROUP]
— to perform at Moose McGillycuddy's, Lahaina News, April 10, 1991: 10.
— to perform at Moose McGillycuddy's, Lahaina News, June 13, 1991: 13.
— continues to perform at Moose McGillycuddy's, Lahaina News, August 8, 1991: 12.

WILD DOLPHIN SAND SCULPTURE CONTEST
— to be held by Pacific Whale Foundation at Keawakapu Beach, Lahaina News, August 7, 2003: 16.

WILD HORSES: THE IAO CALENDAR MALE REVIEW
— to be held, Lahaina News, April 10, 1997: 13.

WILD ON WATER AWARDS
— to be held, Lahaina News, March 21, 2002: 17.

WILD WILD PIZZA AND SPORTS BAR [BUSINESS]
— purchased by Rob and Susan Penny, Lahaina News, April 17, 1991: 9.
— offering discount to kama'aina, Lahaina News, July 1, 1993: 11.

WILDER, KATHRYN [WRITER]
— to offer class on writing at The Art School at Kapalua, Lahaina News, September 27, 2001: 3.
— to teach writing, Lahaina News, October 4, 2001: 16.
— to hold course on writing, Lahaina News, October 31, 2002: 12.

WILDER, ROBERT JAY
— joins Pacific Whale Foundation, Lahaina News, September 9, 1999: 11.
— to speak at Maui Ocean Center and sign book "Listening to the Sea: the Politics of Improving Environmental Protection", Lahaina News, February 10, 2000: 16.
— from the Pacific Whale Foundation to lecture on "Listening to the Sea: The Politics of Improving Environmental Protection", Lahaina News, February 22, 2001: 17.

WILEY AND THE HAIRY MAN [PLAY]
— to be performed by Maui Academy of Performing Arts, Lahaina News, October 10, 1990: 14.
— to open, Lahaina News, October 17, 1990: 17.
— opening October 26th, Lahaina News, October 24, 1990: 15.

WILEY, GEORGE [RESIDENT]
— discusses poor water quality, Lahaina Sun, December 9, 1970: 6.

WILEY, SANDEE
— appointed administrative assistant for Chadwick Hawaii Group, Inc., Lahaina News, January 16, 1992: 9.

WILHELM, KATE [WRITER]
— to be hosted by Maui Authors Guild, Lahaina News, September 9, 1987: 3.
— Maui Authors Guild hosts workshop by, Lahaina News, October 14, 1987: 17.

WILHELM, PUANANI
— Hawaiian Language Immersion Program officer discusses Hawaiian Immersion program, Lahaina News, March 28, 2002: 1,20.

WILHELM, RAY
— Baldwin High School student helping Bears succeed this season, Lahaina News, October 29, 1992: 10.
— recognized as MIL Basketball Player of the Year, Lahaina News, March 25, 1993: 6.

WILKINSON, WILL AND TASHINA
— to speak at Ohana Luncheon and Trade Fair, Lahaina News, September 12, 1996: 15.

WILLIAM SHAKESPEARE [PLAY]
— performed by Honolulu Theatre for Youth at Baldwin Auditorium, Lahaina Sun, February 10, 1971: 8.
— to be performed, Lahaina Sun, February 24, 1971: 7.

WILLIAMS, ABRAHAM
— reverend discusses Queen Keopuolani, Lahaina News, November 30, 1983: 8.

WILLIAMS, ANN
— joins Whalers Realty, Lahaina News, July 25, 2002: 9.

WILLIAMS, BEVERLY
— installed as president of Hawaii Federation of Business and Professional Women's Clubs, Lahaina News, May 22, 1985: 3.

WILLIAMS, DAMON [MUSICIAN]
— qualifies for finals of "Stars Under the Stars", Lahaina News, August 17, 1995: 12.
— Lahainaluna High School senior wins Oceanic "Road to Fame" Talent Search, Lahaina News, November 23, 1995: 12.
— wins Brown Bags to Stardom Contest, Lahaina News, April 4, 1996: 1,18.

— career featured, Lahaina News, October 30, 1997: 18.
— celebrates release of CD "Love Is All", Lahaina News, January 1, 1998: 3.
— to perform at Maui Arts and Cultural Center, Lahaina News, January 8, 1998: 13.
— to perform at Maui Arts and Cultural Center, Lahaina News, January 15, 1998: 12.
— to perform at Jaycees Summer Jam, Lahaina News, June 4, 1998: 16.
— to perform at Longhi's, Lahaina News, July 2, 1998: 18.

WILLIAMS, DAVE [CONTRACTOR]
— discussed issues connected to hippies on Maui, Lahaina Sun, December 2, 1970: 1.

WILLIAMS, DON
— principal of King Kamehameha III School discusses teacher shortage, Lahaina News, June 8, 1988: 1,20.
— principal of King Kamehameha III School discusses problems faced by education, Lahaina News, January 18, 1989: 1,13.
— meets with Governor Waihee during visit, Lahaina News, March 22, 1989: 1.
— King Kamehameha III School principal faces loss of Vice Principal, Lahaina News, June 14, 1989: 1.
— King Kamehameha III School principal retires, Lahaina News, July 11, 1990: 1.

WILLIAMS, DOROTHY
— president of Maui Meadows Homeowner Association discusses plans, Lahaina News, April 1, 1993: 6,7.

WILLIAMS, ED
— discusses gas line along Front Street, Lahaina Sun, February 17, 1971: 3.
— windsurfer lost overnight, found in morning, Lahaina News, July 27, 2000: 7.

WILLIAMS, EILEEN
— to teach country line dancing, Lahaina News, August 20, 1998: 17.

WILLIAMS, GENE
— police officer killed while directing traffic, Lahaina News, August 12, 1999: 1,20.
— Ricardo Rodriguez-Pantoja charged with manslaughter in death of police officer, Lahaina News, August 19, 1999: 1.

WILLIAMS, HOPE
— named director of catering and convention services at Hyatt Regency Maui, Lahaina News, January 11, 1996: 11.

WILLIAMS, JERRY [ARTIST]
— to discuss role of artist in environmental movement, Lahaina News, February 7, 1990: 14.

WILLIAMS, KELLER [MUSICIAN]
— to perform at Royal Lahaina Resort, Lahaina News, January 17, 2002: 14.
— to perform at Royal Lahaina Resort, Lahaina News, February 7, 2002: 15.

WILLIAMS, OLETHA DAVENPORT
— librarian retires from Lahaina Public Library, Lahaina Sun, June 14, 1972: 4.

WILLIAMS, RICKY
— to compete in Hooters Hula Bowl, Lahaina News, January 21, 1999: 7.
— plays at the Hooters Hula Bowl, Lahaina News, January 28, 1999: 1.

WILLIAMS, RONALD
— appointed regional general manager of Maui and Oahu at Atlantis Submarines, Lahaina News, March 7, 1996: 11.
— assumes chief operating officer at Atlantis Adventures, Lahaina News, April 5, 2001: 9.

WILLIAMS, ROSS
— finalist of Bud Surf Tour Qualifying Series, Lahaina News, May 26, 1994: 9.

WILLIAMS, RUSS [REPORTER]
— joins staff at Lahaina Sun, Lahaina Sun, February 14, 1973: 4.

WILLIAMS, STEVE
— First Hawaiian Bank Senior Vice President to supervise Maui region , Lahaina News, January 6, 2000: 11.

WILLIAMS-CRANE, DONNA
— wins Sam Choy Poke Festival, Lahaina News, September 30, 1999: 5.
— wins "Best in Show" award at Sam Choy Poke Contest, Lahaina News, December 27, 2001: 10.

WILLIAMSON, BILL [SPOKESPERSON]
— discusses new gas line in Lahaina, Lahaina Sun, December 9, 1970: 3.

WILLIAMSON, JAMES
— appointed president of Aloha IslandAir, Lahaina News, March 21, 1990: 4.

WILLIE AND LOBO [MUSICAL GROUP]
— to perform at World Cafe, Lahaina News, February 8, 1996: 14.
— to perform at Maui Music Festival, Lahaina News, August 29, 1996: 14.

WILLIE K. [MUSICIAN]
— see Kahaiali'i, Willie [musician]

WILLIS, ELAINE
— Foundation for Wellness founder to speak at Unity Church, Lahaina News, June 28, 2001: 20.

WILLIS, JOCELYN
— to travel to Japan to study with sponsorship of the Foundation for Study in Hawaii and Abroad, Lahaina News, June 5, 1985: 20.

WILLIS, KIM
— life coach featured, Lahaina News, November 1, 2001: 1,9.
— named as "Soroptimist of the Year", Lahaina News, June 27, 2002: 1,2.

WILLOWS, TOM
— appointed assistant manager at Hilo Hatties Lahaina store, Lahaina News, September 26, 1990: 9.

WILLY WONKA CHOCOLATE FACTORY
— may open location in Lahaina, Lahaina News, May 3, 1989: 1.

WILMORE, LARRY [COMEDIAN]
— to perform at Comedy Club, Lahaina News, May 16, 1990: 11.
— to perform at Comedy Club and the Sports Page, Lahaina News, May 6, 1993: 15,17.
— to perform at Comedy Club and the Sports Page, Lahaina News, May 13, 1993: 10.

WILSEY, LIN [ARTIST]
— wins prize at Lahaina Shopping Center, Lahaina News, December 29, 1994: 2.

WILSON, AL [MUSICIAN]
— to perform at Golden Oldies Revue, Lahaina News, October 19, 2000: 21.

WILSON, BRENDA
— joins JJ Enterprises, Lahaina News, February 4, 1987: 11.

WILSON, BRIDGET
— Dallas police officer honored at Pioneer Inn, Lahaina News, September 9, 1999: 3.

WILSON, DIANA
— offers workshops on managing stress, Lahaina News, September 18, 1985: 3.

WILSON, DONNETTE-GENE [ARTIST]
— to conduct tie and dye workshop, Lahaina News, July 11, 1990: 18.

WILSON, JAMEY
— tennis pro offers advice, Lahaina News, June 19, 1997: 13.

WILSON, JAY [ARTIST]
— reception at Village Gallery, Lahaina News, November 1, 1989: 13.

WILSON KAPALUA OPEN
— results, Lahaina News, September 14, 2000: 10.

WILSON, KIM
— tennis player featured, Lahaina News, July 6, 1995: 7.

WILSON, KIM [ARTIST]
— to present "Finding Inspiration in the Void" workshop, Lahaina News, November 14, 2002: 20.

WILSON, KIM [MUSICIAN]
— to perform a benefit concert for the Hawaii Conservation Association, Lahaina News, June 5, 1997: 9.

WILSON, LOIS [ARTIST]
— to exhibit at Banyan Tree Gallery, Lahaina News, August 26, 1993: 16.
— to exhibit at Banyan Tree Gallery, Lahaina News, February 3, 1994: 11.
— exhibiting at Lahaina Art Society, Lahaina News, February 24, 1994: 11.
— to exhibit at Lahaina Art Society, Lahaina News, February 24, 1994: 9.
— featured artist at Lahaina Arts Society "Unity in Diversity" exhibit, Lahaina News, November 9, 1995: 12.
— to teach Impressionist Plein Air Color Workshop, Lahaina News, September 18, 1997: 16.
— to be featured at Kahana Bar and Grill, Lahaina News, June 25, 1998: 13.

WILSON, MICHAEL
— discusses need to save threatened ecosystems, Lahaina News, August 29, 1996: 3.

WILSON, MIKE
— likely to be approved as head of the state Department of Land and Natural Resources, Lahaina News, January 5, 1995: 2.

WILSON, SMOKEY [MUSICAL GROUP]
— to perform at Maui Arts and Cultural Center, Lahaina News, November 6, 1997: 17.

WILSON, SUZANNE
— account of sailing adventure, Lahaina Sun, June 9, 1971: 2.

WILSON, WILLIAM
— named vice-president of Maui Association of Condominium Owners, Lahaina News, July 1, 1981: 8.

WILSON-SNYDER, EDWINA
— Princess Nahienaena Elementary School principal greets parents at open house, Lahaina News, October 12, 2000: 3.

WILT, JOHN
— hopes to bring back Police Reserve Program, Lahaina News, December 2, 1993: 1.
— Maui Community College professor honored, Lahaina News, May 25, 2000: 6.

WILTSE, WENDY
— selected Watershed Project coordinator for West Maui, Lahaina News, July 8, 1993: 1,4.
— watershed development coordinator, says that resorts, residents, and boaters also contribute to run-off and algae, Lahaina News, August 11, 1994: 1.
— supporting storm drain stenciling project, Lahaina News, October 13, 1994: 3.
— discusses status of algae clean-up study, Lahaina News, June 15, 1995: 3.
— West Maui Watershed Coordinator says County needs to move quickly on basins, Lahaina News, June 22, 1995: 1,16.

— West Maui Watershed coordinator discusses plan to help watershed, Lahaina News, September 21, 1995: 2.

— discusses need for solution to seaweed problem, Lahaina News, October 5, 1995: 3.

WIMBERLY ALLISON TONG AND GOO [BUSINESS]
— success at designing hotels, Lahaina News, November 23, 2000: 15.

WIMBERLY, WHISENAND, ALLISON, TONG AND GOO [BUSINESS]
— architectural firm creating plans to renovate Pioneer Inn, Lahaina News, February 19, 1986: 1.

WIMMER-KUNITOMO, KRISTAL
— Scholar/Athlete of the Week, Lahaina News, October 8, 1998: 14.

— Lahainaluna High School student admitted to University of Southern California medical school, Lahaina News, August 9, 2001: 1,20.

WIN, LOSE OR DRAW [GAMESHOW]
— to tape segments at Westin Maui, Lahaina News, November 30, 1988: 16.

— to tape at Westin Maui, Lahaina News, December 7, 1988: 1.

— recorded on Maui, Lahaina News, January 18, 1989: 12.

WINCHELL, TOM [ARTIST]
— to exhibit at Miracles Bookery, Lahaina News, April 13, 2000: 12.

WIND IN THE WILLOWS, THE [PLAY]
— to be performed by Maui Youth Theatre, Lahaina News, April 1, 1987: 3.

WIND SAIL AND SURF
— to hold raffle to support Surfrider Foundation, Lahaina News, March 7, 1996: 6.

WINDJAMMER [SHIP]
— described, Lahaina News, July 17, 1997: 15.

WINDJAMMER CRUISES [BUSINESS]
— acquired by Major Marine Tours, Inc., Lahaina News, January 20, 1994: 7.

— to offer new cruise , Lahaina News, October 2, 1997: 17.

— to offer Champagne Brunch Cruise, Lahaina News, April 30, 1998: 9.

— offering Champagne Brunch Cruise, Lahaina News, May 20, 1999: 13.

— offering Champagne Brunch Cruise, Lahaina News, May 4, 2000: 13.

WINDJAMMER CRUISES, OAHU [BUSINESS]
— suspends operations; not affiliated with Windjammer Cruises, Maui, Lahaina News, May 21, 1998: 13.

WINDLEY, LARRY
— black coral diver and historian featured, Lahaina News, September 1, 1994: 4.

WINDSURFING
— Budweiser Slalom event to be held, Lahaina News, August 27, 1986: 3.

— Fred Haywood described, Lahaina News, September 3, 1986: 4.

— competition held from Molokini to Wailea, Lahaina News, September 2, 1987: 3.

— clinic to be held, Lahaina News, October 3, 1990: 6.

— Aloha Classic to take place at Hoʻokipa Beach, Lahaina News, October 10, 1991: 8.

— windsurfer rescued by Coast Guard, Lahaina News, August 12, 1993: 6.

— Steve Fisher sails from Los Angeles to Maui, Lahaina News, September 11, 1997: 1,5.

— Aloha Classic to be held, Lahaina News, October 30, 1997: 16.

— world championship to be held, Lahaina News, November 5, 1998: 19.

WINE
— French beaujolais nouveau to arrive from France, Lahaina News, November 16, 1988: 5.

— festivals held at Maui hotels, Lahaina News, August 23, 1989: 8.

— Orville Magoon, owner of Guenoc Winery, to be at Maui Prince Hotel, Lahaina News, September 13, 1989: 5.

— Holly Peterson, head chef at Robert Mondavi Winery to prepare gala wine tasting dinner, Lahaina News, November 1, 1989: 13.

— representative for Les Vins George Duboeuf to be at La Perouse, Lahaina News, December 19, 1990: 14.

— Ruth's Chris Steak House to hold "Wine Wonders from Down Under", Lahaina News, October 22, 1998: 20.

— see also food and drinks

WINE & CHEESE BENEFIT
— Kiwanis Club to hold 7th annual, Lahaina News, April 18, 1984: 4.

WINE SPECTATOR MAGAZINE
— Jameson's Grill and Bar wins "Best of the Award of Excellence" from, Lahaina News, November 19, 1998: 13.

WINE SYMPOSIUM
— to be held at Kapalua , Lahaina News, July 6, 1988: 11.

WINEMAKER'S DINNER
— featuring wine from Chalk Hill, Lahaina News, June 5, 2003: 16.

WINERT, JOHN
— promoted to senior account manager at Kaiser Permanente, Lahaina News, April 14, 1994: 10.

WINERT, MARSHA
— to serve as state's tourism liaison, Lahaina News, June 12, 2003: 8.

WINFREY, VICKI
— owner of Roommate Finders of Maui featured, Lahaina News, December 21, 1983: 16.

WINSTON, GEORGE [MUSICIAN]
— to perform, Lahaina News, July 18, 1996: 12.

— to perform, Lahaina News, July 2, 1998: 16,17.

— to perform at Maui Arts and Cultural Center, Lahaina News, July 9, 1998: 16.

— to perform at Maui Arts and Cultural Center, Lahaina News, July 6, 2000: 16.

— to perform at Maui Arts and Cultural Center, Lahaina News, July 4, 2002: 15.

— to perform at Maui Arts and Cultural Center, Lahaina News, July 11, 2002: 16.

WINTER AND COMPANY
— Colorado firm awarded contract for production of Lahaina Historic District Architectural Style Book, Lahaina News, September 4, 2003: 1,8.

WINTER FESTIVAL
— to be held at Napili Plaza, Lahaina News, December 12, 2002: 18.

WINTERS, MATT
— Scholar/Athlete of the Week, Lahaina News, October 17, 1996: 12.

— Scholar/Athlete of the Week, Lahaina News, May 15, 1997: 11.

WIRAMANAYAKE, ROSEMARIE
— appointed executive housekeeper at Four Seasons Resort, Lahaina News, April 21, 1994: 12.

WIRELESS WORLD [BUSINESS]
— opens second retail location, Lahaina News, September 5, 2002: 8.

WISCHEMANN, DAVID
— killed in action in Vietnam, Lahaina Sun, November 22, 1972: 7.

WISE, ANITA [COMEDIAN]
— to perform at Comedy Club and the Sports Page, Lahaina News, March 4, 1993: 9,12.

WISE, JAN
— elected to board of West Maui Taxpayers Association, Lahaina News, July 1, 1987: 3.

WISE OWL VIDEO [BUSINESS]
— opens, Lahaina News, April 1, 1993: 8.

WISE WOMEN
— groups forming in Kihei, Wailuku Heights, and Upcountry, Lahaina News, June 25, 1998: 2.

WISEMAN, JENNIFER
— to compete in Masters Swimming competition, Lahaina News, July 24, 2003: 12.

WISEMAN, STEVEN [MUSICIAN]
— to play at Keawala'i Congregational Church, Lahaina News, January 17, 2002: 16.

WIT [PLAY]
— to be performed by Maui OnStage, Lahaina News, September 25, 2003: 9.
— Maui OnStage to begin theatre season with, Lahaina News, October 2, 2003: 18.
— to begin theatre season with "WIT", Lahaina News, October 9, 2003: 16.

WITCZAK, JAMES
— appointed as sales manager at Media Systems, Inc, Lahaina News, January 30, 1992: 10.

WITHALM, FRANK [MUSICIAN]
— performing big band tunes at the Maui Inter-Continental Wailea, Lahaina News, December 5, 1984: 14.

WITHAM, GENE
— enforcement agent for National Marine Fisheries Serice comments on thrillcraft corridor, Lahaina News, February 24, 1988: 1,20.

WITT-MILLER, HARRIET
— to speak at Maui Community College, Lahaina News, June 17, 1993: 3.
— to present "Family Night Under the Stars", Lahaina News, July 21, 1994: 12.
— writer and astrologer to speak, Lahaina News, March 6, 1997: 10,11.
— astronomy writer and lecturer to lead star-gazing event, Lahaina News, May 20, 1999: 16.
— to present "The Earth-in-space Walk", Lahaina News, March 22, 2001: 16.
— astronomer to speak on "Earth in Space Trail", Lahaina News, November 15, 2001: 16.
— astronomer to offer "Family Night Under the Stars", Lahaina News, October 31, 2002: 29.
— hosts "Family Night Under the Stars", Lahaina News, January 2, 2003: 17.
— to host "Family Night Under the Stars", Lahaina News, January 9, 2003: 16.

WIZ, THE [MUSICAL]
— to be performed by Baldwin Theatre Guild, Lahaina News, October 21, 1987: 12.
— to be performed at Kahului Community Center Playhouse, Lahaina News, July 2, 1992: 25,26.
— to be performed at Baldwin Performing Arts Learning Center, Lahaina News, January 23, 2003: 17.
— to be performed at Baldwin Performing Arts Learning Center, Lahaina News, January 30, 2003: 14.

WIZARD [SHIP]
— moonlight sails reviewed, Lahaina News, April 6, 1988: 4.

WIZARD OF OZ, THE [MUSICAL]
— to be performed at Baldwin High School Performing Arts Learning Center, Lahaina News, April 20, 1995: 12.
— to open, Lahaina News, April 27, 1995: 12.

— performances continue, Lahaina News, May 4, 1995: 16.
— to be performed at Arts Education for Children Group, Lahaina News, July 19, 2001: 3.

WO HING MUSEUM
— Lahaina's newest museum, Lahaina News, January 4, 1984: 7,8,9.
— historical documents found in, Lahaina News, December 30, 1999: 1,20.

WO HING SOCIETY OF LAHAINA
— wins Historic Hawaii Preservation Award with Lahaina Restoration Foundation, Lahaina News, April 17, 1985: 3.
— to hold Chinese Moon Festival, Lahaina News, September 27, 2001: 1.
— to hold Winter Solstice Festival with Lahaina Restoration Foundation, Lahaina News, December 20, 2001: 1,18.
— to celebrate Chinese New Year, Lahaina News, January 31, 2002: 14.
— to hold Chinese Moon Celebration, Lahaina News, September 19, 2002: 1,22.
— to celebrate Chinese New Year, Lahaina News, January 23, 2003: 1,20.
— organization reformed, Lahaina News, April 24, 2003: 1.
— presents scholarship to Leah Santos, Lahaina News, August 7, 2003: 2.
— to host Chinese Moon Festival, Lahaina News, August 28, 2003: 3.
— to teach Chinese history at Moon Festival, Lahaina News, September 4, 2003: 3.
— to hold Chinese Moon Festival, Lahaina News, September 11, 2003: 14.

WO HING TEMPLE
— update on renovations, Lahaina News, July 25, 1984: 7,8,9.
— reopens, Lahaina News, December 19, 1984: 3.
— featured, including discussion of its lion symbol, Lahaina News, January 9, 1985: 7,8,9.
— to hold Lion Dance, Lahaina News, March 13, 1985: 3.
— plans to open Chinese plate lunch, Lahaina News, December 23, 1987: 3.
— to host fundraiser for Lahaina Rotary Club, Lahaina News, March 2, 1988: 22.
— to host Rotary Club dinner and auction, Lahaina News, April 23, 1992: 4.
— to be base for police bicycle patrols, Lahaina News, June 11, 1992: 1.
— restored, Lahaina News, February 15, 1996: 12.
— to celebrate Chinese New Year, Lahaina News, January 30, 2003: 2.

WOFA [TROUPE]
— to perform dances, rhythms and music of Guinea at Maui Arts and Cultural Center, Lahaina News, April 6, 2000: 17.

WOFFINDEN, L.B.
— selected president of Better Business Bureau of Hawaii, Lahaina News, June 4, 1992: 9.

WOJDYLA, BONNIE
— setting goals as principal of Sacred Hearts School, Lahaina News, July 19, 2001: 1,20.

WOLD, MARILYN [ARTIST]
— to present at Hui No'eau Visual Arts Center, Lahaina News, June 22, 1988: 10.

WOLF, FRED [COMEDIAN]
— to perform at Comedy Club and the Sports Page, Lahaina News, May 28, 1992: 14,16.

WOLF, MORRIS
— to present "Forty Years Changing the Paradigm" at 'Ohana Connection breakfast, Lahaina News, June 27, 2002: 17.

WOLF TALES [PLAY]
— to be performed by Maui Academy of Performing Arts, Lahaina News, July 17, 1997: 17.
— to be performed by Maui Academy of Performing Arts, Lahaina News, July 24, 1997: 16.

WOLFE, DAVID
— to discuss "The Sunfood Diet", Lahaina News, March 2, 2000: 13.

WOLFE, JUSTIN
— Scholar/Athlete of the Week, Lahaina News, October 3, 2002: 13.

WOLFGRAM, CAROLE DUNCAN
— appointed as mortgage loan officer at Kahului branch of Island Mortgage, Lahaina News, September 16, 1993: 10.
— appointed as branch manager at Lahaina Office of First Federal Savings and Loans, Lahaina News, August 24, 1995: 10.

WOLFSON, CARL [COMEDIAN]
— to perform at Comedy Club at Maui Marriott Resort, Lahaina News, November 15, 1989: 17.
— to perform at Comedy Club, Lahaina News, September 26, 1990: 10.
— to perform at Comedy Club and the Sports Page, Lahaina News, January 21, 1993: 14.
— to perform at Honolulu Comedy Club, Lahaina News, October 20, 1994: 16.
— to perform at Honolulu Comedy Club, Lahaina News, March 14, 1996: 12.

WOLSZTYNIAK, JOSEPH
— discusses Bed and Breakfast settlement, Lahaina News, August 29, 1996: 1,2.

WOMAN FAR WALKING [PLAY]
— to be performed by Maori author Witi Ihimaera, Lahaina News, September 27, 2001: 16.

WOMEN HELPING WOMEN
— shelter operated by featured, Lahaina News, April 15, 1987: 1,18.
— organization spreads to West Maui, Lahaina News, December 21, 1988: 14.
— offers free counseling services, Lahaina News, April 12, 1989: 3.
— concerned about funding cuts to shelter services, Lahaina News, January 14, 1993: 3.
— to open Lahaina office, Lahaina News, April 1, 1993: 4.
— Benetton to hold clothing drive to support, Lahaina News, April 22, 1993: 3.
— to hold benefit auction, Lahaina News, September 2, 1993: 2.
— to hold fundraiser dance, Lahaina News, June 23, 1994: 12.
— shelter holds fundraiser with local restaurants, Lahaina News, June 13, 1996: 14.
— support group to meet, Lahaina News, February 13, 1997: 11.
— support group to meet, Lahaina News, February 27, 1997: 11.
— to host support group, Lahaina News, March 6, 1997: 10.
— to offer volunteer training, Lahaina News, March 13, 1997: 16.
— continues to hold support group, Lahaina News, May 22, 1997: 16.
— continues to hold support group meetings, Lahaina News, June 19, 1997: 17.
— to hold "Full Moon Boogie" fundraiser, Lahaina News, September 18, 1997: 16.
— continues to meet, not always indexed, Lahaina News, October 16, 1997: 17.
— to hold fundraiser at Planet Hollywood Maui, Lahaina News, December 11, 1997: 8.
— continues to meet, Lahaina News, December 25, 1997: 13.
— continues to meet, Lahaina News, March 12, 1998: 20.
— continues to meet, Lahaina News, April 2, 1998: 17.
— support group to hold, Lahaina News, March 25, 1999: 17.
— continues to meet, Lahaina News, August 12, 1999: 17.
— featured, Lahaina News, November 25, 1999: 14.

— to hold "High Tea" benefit, Lahaina News, April 13, 2000: 12.
— continues to meet, Lahaina News, July 6, 2000: 16.
— to hold Domestic Violence Health Symposium, Lahaina News, September 14, 2000: 7.
— to offer Domestic Violence Health Symposium, Lahaina News, September 21, 2000: 19.
— continues to meet, Lahaina News, May 17, 2001: 20.
— continues to meet, Lahaina News, August 30, 2001: 17.
— continues to meet, Lahaina News, October 11, 2001: 17.
— executive director Stacey Moniz describes agency, Lahaina News, October 17, 2002: 16.

WOMEN IN LEADERSHIP
— conference continues at Maui Community College, Lahaina News, October 23, 1985: 20.

WOMEN IN SMALL BUSINESS COMMITTEE
— US. Small Business Administration offering workshop, Lahaina News, September 12, 1996: 15.

WOMEN IN TECHNOLOGY
— to hold gender Equity Workshop for Educators and Industry, Lahaina News, July 20, 2000: 17.

WOMEN OF MAUI
— to hold luncheon celebrating the life of Rev. Martin Luther King, Lahaina News, January 24, 2002: 16.

WOMEN'S AGLOW FELLOWSHIP
— to meet at Ka'anapali Beach Hotel, Lahaina News, January 21, 1987: 11.
— meeting at Peacock Restaurant, Lahaina News, July 22, 1987: 10.
— Diana Elles to speak at, Lahaina News, August 19, 1987: 3.
— to meet, Lahaina News, September 23, 1987: 9.

WOMEN'S CONFERENCE
— to be held on Maui, Lahaina News, July 30, 1986: 3.
— to be held, Lahaina News, September 22, 1994: 6.
— held, Lahaina News, October 19, 1995: 3.
— to be held on theme of "Mentoring Youth", Lahaina News, October 10, 1996: 14.

WOMEN'S HEALTH AWARENESS FAIR
— to be held by Hui No Ke Ola Pono, Lahaina News, August 2, 2001: 2.
— to be held, Lahaina News, July 11, 2002: 16.

WOMEN'S HEALTH DAY
— organized by Hawaii Planned Parenthood, Lahaina News, October 1, 1986: 12.

WOMEN'S HEALTH MONTH
— to be held, Lahaina News, August 31, 2000: 8.
— to include "Facts of Life for Teen Girls", Lahaina News, September 7, 2000: 21.
— to be held by Maui County Committee on the Status of Women, Lahaina News, September 4, 2003: 18.

WOMEN'S KEMPER OPEN
— players and results, Lahaina News, March 14, 1984: 15,16,17,18,19, 20,21,22,23.
— editorial summary of, Lahaina News, March 14, 1984: 2.
— won by Betsy King, Lahaina News, March 28, 1984: 6.
— featured in special supplement, Lahaina News, March 6, 1985: A1, A2,A3,A4,A5,A6,A7,A8,A9,!10,A11,A12.
— Jane Blalock wins, Lahaina News, March 20, 1985: 1,4.
— moving to Princeville, Kaua'i, Lahaina News, March 20, 1985: 2.
— to be held, Lahaina News, February 7, 1990: 9.

WONG, CHARLES MIRIAM
— sister and former Sacred Hearts School principal passes away, Lahaina News, January 8, 1998: 1,2.

WONG, LOUIS
— reunited with adopted niece Priscilla Waiohu, Lahaina News, August 1, 1983: 6.

WONG, SISTER CHARLES MIRIAM
— featured, Lahaina News, April 7, 1994: 1,2.

WONG, WESLEY
— purchase of collection of Hawaiian artifacts sought by Maui Historic Commission, Lahaina Sun, April 21, 1971: 2.
— former forester honored by Conservation Council, Lahaina Sun, June 6, 1973: 22.

WOO, NEAL
— project coordinator says governor Waihee administration seeking money for housing project, Lahaina News, January 16, 1991: 1.

WOOD, KENNETH
— elected zone chairman with the Kihei Community Association, Lahaina Sun, December 2, 1970: 4.
— to discuss conservation of Hawaii's rare and endangered flora, Lahaina News, May 14, 1998: 16.

WOOD, PATRICIA [ARTIST]
— to exhibit at Hui No'eau Visual Arts Center, Lahaina News, July 1, 1999: 13.

WOODARD, JIMMY [COMEDIAN]
— to perform at Comedy Club, Lahaina News, November 21, 1990: 13.

WOODFORD, LUCAS
— wins novice division of the MBX state qualifier, Lahaina News, April 4, 1990: 5.

WOODFORD, RICK
— appointed chief operating officer for CW Restaurant Consultants, Inc., Lahaina News, December 12, 1991: 16.
— re-elected president of Maui Recycling Group, Lahaina News, August 14, 1997: 2.

WOODMAN, GEORG
— to offer Judo classes, Lahaina News, November 7, 2002: 10.
— teaching martial arts, Lahaina News, January 9, 2003: 12.
— to teach martial arts at Hongwanji Mission, Lahaina News, January 16, 2003: 13.
— continues to teach martial arts, Lahaina News, February 13, 2003: 13.

WOODS, LYNNE
— joins Coldwell Banker McCormack Real Estate, Lahaina News, September 5, 1991: 6.
— offering class on office etiquette, Lahaina News, March 13, 2003: 8.

WOODS, TIGER
— to play at Mercedes Championship, Lahaina News, December 17, 1998: 19.
— to play at Kapalua Tournament, Lahaina News, December 24, 1998: 9.
— plays at Mercedes Championships, Lahaina News, January 14, 1999: 1.
— to play at PGA Mercedes tournament, Lahaina News, December 23, 1999: 1,15.
— to compete in Mercedes Championship golf tournament, Lahaina News, December 28, 2000: 1,7.
— to play in Mercedes Championship, Lahaina News, January 11, 2001: 8.

WOODS, WILLIAM
— appointed branch manager for Coldwell Banker McCormack Real Estate, Lahaina News, October 31, 1990: 12.

WOODSOCK BAR
— moved from Ka'anapali airport to boatyard, Lahaina News, March 5, 1986: 3.

WOODWARD, DICK
— drag racer featured, Lahaina News, January 21, 1993: 6.

WOODY'S OCEANFRONT GRILL [RESTAURANT]
— changed from Aloha Cantina, Lahaina News, December 10, 1998: 1.
— opens, Lahaina News, February 4, 1999: 13.
— Cheryl Kunitake chef, Lahaina News, March 25, 1999: 13.
— featured, Lahaina News, January 6, 2000: 5.

WOOLEY, CHUCK
— to give pr, Lahaina News, October 17, 1996: 14.

WOOLWORTH [BUSINESS]
— plans to open in Lahaina Center, Lahaina News, October 10, 1990: 11.
— grand opening in Lahaina Town Center scheduled, Lahaina News, March 6, 1991: 6.
— Cea Arnold wins prize at, Lahaina News, March 6, 1991: 6.

WORDEN, U.S.S. [SHIP]
— to make three-day stop at Lahaina, Lahaina News, August 22, 1991: 3.

WORK OPTIONS RESOURCE [BUSINESS]
— offers scheduling services, Lahaina News, June 24, 1993: 9.

WORKERS COMPENSATION
— editorial hopeful that regulations can be improved, Lahaina News, August 21, 1985: 2.
— discussed by Bill Pfeil, Lahaina News, April 20, 1988: 13.

WORLD AIDS DAY
— service to be held, Lahaina News, November 25, 1999: 17.
— to be observed, Lahaina News, November 30, 2000: 16.
— to be observed, Lahaina News, November 29, 2001: 17.
— to be observes, Lahaina News, November 28, 2002: 5.

WORLD ARCHAEOLOGICAL CONGRESS
— discusses importance of Moku'ula, Lahaina News, January 27, 2000: 1,16.

WORLD CAFE [RESTAURANT]
— opens, Lahaina News, December 15, 1994: 17.
— opens, Lahaina News, April 6, 1995: 11.
— to take over space from Blue Tropix, Lahaina News, October 3, 1996: 1,18.
— to open nightclub, Lahaina News, October 24, 1996: 9.
— to hold Christmas toy drive, Lahaina News, December 19, 1996: 2.

WORLD DANCE DAY
— to be held at Maui Brews, Lahaina News, December 9, 1999: 20.

WORLD FOOD DAY
— event televised, Lahaina News, October 14, 1987: 3.

WORLD GOES 'ROUND, THE [PLAY]
— to be performed at Seabury Hall, Lahaina News, April 13, 2000: 12.

WORLD GYM [BUSINESS]
— opens in Lahaina, Lahaina News, June 6, 1990: 5.

WORLD IN A BOX, THE [FILM]
— documentary to be shown on Hawaii Public Television, Lahaina News, December 12, 2002: 16.

WORLD INDEPENDENCE AFRO-POP AND JAZZ FESTIVAL
— to be held, Lahaina News, August 18, 1994: 16.
— to be held, Lahaina News, August 25, 1994: 15,16.

WORLD MENTAL HEALTH DAY
— to host presentation "An Invitation to Celebrate: Women and Mental Health", Lahaina News, October 3, 1996: 15.

WORLD OF JACQUES YVES COUSTEAU [FILM]
— shown at the Lahaina Library, Lahaina Sun, November 11, 1970: 4.

WORLD ON ICE [SHOW]
— offered free by Aloha Airlines, Lahaina News, July 29, 1987: 3.

WORLD PEACE DAY
— event discussed, Lahaina Sun, April 26, 1972: 7.

WORLD UNITY SURF CONTEST
— report of, Lahaina Times, October, 1980 volume 4 number 9: 1.

WORLD VISIONS
— to raise awareness of famine, Lahaina News, February 18, 1993: 4.

WORLD WAR II
— Maui described during, Lahaina News, December 5, 1991: 1,16.
— "Maui During World War II" exhibit opens at Old Courthouse, Lahaina News, May 7, 1992: 22.
— 100th Battalion featured, Lahaina News, May 21, 1992: 3.
— photograph and memorabilia exhibit to be held at Old Courthouse, Lahaina News, May 21, 1992: 4.
— impact on Maui described, Lahaina News, September 9, 1993: 2.

WORLD WRESTLING FEDERATION
— to offer pay-per-view Summerslam, Lahaina News, August 26, 1993: 16.

WORLD YOUTH BASKETBALL TOURNAMENT
— to be held, Lahaina News, July 24, 2003: 13.

WORLD YOUTH DAY
— Lahaina teens to attend, Lahaina News, August 8, 2002: 1,3.

WORLD'S FAIR, 1984
— Children's supplement features, Lahaina News, May 16, 1984: A,B,C,D.

WORLDS WITHIN WORLDS
— digital photography exhibition to be held, Lahaina News, January 10, 2002: 17.

WORLEY, KATHY [REALTOR]
— top salesperson for Pali Kai Inc., Lahaina News, May 15, 1985: 8.

WORLEY, ROBIN
— to exhibit "Haute Trash", Lahaina News, April 2, 1998: 16.

WORRELL, MILES
— to manage Lahaina branch of Compadres Mexican Bar and Grill, Lahaina News, January 9, 1991: 5.

WORTH, BILL
— former editor of Lahaina News moves from Maui, Lahaina News, May 17, 1989: 6.

WORTH, BILL AND NANCY
— purchase Lahaina News, Lahaina News, February 1, 1983: 8,9.
— statement of their editorial values, Lahaina News, February 15, 1983: 11.

WORTH, NANCY
— to talk about peace mission to Soviet Union, Lahaina News, February 11, 1987: 3.
— account of visit to Russia, Lahaina News, February 18, 1987: 1,20.
— to speak to American Association of University Women (AAUW), Lahaina News, March 11, 1987: 18.

WRESTLING
— Maui Style Wrestling Program featured, Lahaina News, May 25, 2000: 8.
— Napili Surfriders team successful, Lahaina News, May 30, 2002: 12.

WRIGHT, HARLOW
— donates to Friends of the Lahainaluna Endowment Fund, Lahaina News, May 22, 2003: 9.

WRIGHT, HOLLY
— personal trainer offering fitness classes at the Art School at Kapalua, Lahaina News, November 9, 2000: 10.
— offers ball fitness classes at The Art School at Kapalua, Lahaina News, February 22, 2001: 13.

WRIGHT, JAMES
— promoted at Maui Youth and Family Services, Lahaina News, January 25, 2001: 14.

WRIGHT, JAYDE
— surfer featured, Lahaina News, November 30, 1983: 4.

WRIGHT, LEIPUA
— Scholar/Athlete of the Week, Lahaina News, August 6, 1998: 19.

WRIGHT, TED
— basketball player playing against Jolly Roger Pirates, Lahaina Sun, January 20, 1971: 7.

WRITING
— poems being accepted by Sparrowgrass Poetry Forum, Lahaina News, September 12, 1990: 9.
— Hollywood's Famous Poets Society to hold contest, Lahaina News, August 25, 1994: 14.
— Maui Live Poets Society begins work on world's longest poem, Lahaina News, June 20, 1996: 3.
— "Peace Poem" begins, Lahaina News, July 4, 1996: 1.
— Art of Storytelling with Shamisen Music to be held, Lahaina News, August 8, 1996: 16.
— script consultants Cheeah and Fairoh Carolingian to hold workshop, Lahaina News, January 2, 1997: 11.
— script consultants Cheeah and Fairoh Carolingian to hold workshop, Lahaina News, January 30, 1997: 10.
— workshops to be held, Lahaina News, November 15, 2001: 2.

WRITINGS OF JUNEBUG JABBO JONES, THE [PLAY]
— to be performed by John O'Neal, Lahaina News, June 23, 1994: 12.

WU TANG CLAN [MUSICAL GROUP]
— to perform at The Big Mele, Lahaina News, July 31, 1997: 16.

WUKELIC, MARTI
— to teach course on restaurant management for Maui Chamber of Commerce, Lahaina News, April 29, 1999: 13.

WUNDER, ARNOLD KELI'I
— appointed marketing representative in Xerox Hawaii's Maui Division Office, Lahaina News, September 17, 1998: 13.

WYAND, THOM
— named as assistant director for the Maui Community Arts and Cultural Center, Lahaina News, July 26, 1989: 3.

WYCLIFFE GORDON QUARTET [MUSICAL GROUP]
— to perform, Lahaina News, November 7, 2002: 21.
— to perform at Maui Arts and Cultural Center, Lahaina News, November 14, 2002: 20.

WYLAND GALLERIES [BUSINESS]
— shows planned, Lahaina News, January 30, 1991: 9.
— summer show scheduled, Lahaina News, August 8, 1991: 12.
— opens new gallery at Anchor Cove Shopping Center, Lahaina News, August 8, 1991: 8.
— to present annual Christmas show, Lahaina News, December 19, 1991: 19.
— to hold Christmas show, Lahaina News, December 26, 1991: 12.
— to close galleries on Kaua'i until 1993, Lahaina News, September 24, 1992: 9.
— opening new galleries in Waikiki, Lahaina News, October 15, 1992: 8.
— to host All Artist Show, Lahaina News, February 24, 1994: 9.
— to host "All Artist Show", Lahaina News, September 5, 2002: 17.

WYLAND, ROBERT [ARTIST]
— shows original oils at Dolphin Gallery, Lahaina News, November 14, 1984: 3.
— featured at Larry Dodson Gallery, Lahaina News, March 30, 1988: 20.
— hosts Christmas party, Lahaina News, December 13, 1989: 25.
— unveils new piece at Front Street Gallery, Lahaina News, September 5, 1990: 17.
— paints Whaling Walls in Japan and Australia, Lahaina News, October 31, 1990: 16,17.

— to begin three-island tour, Lahaina News, December 26, 1990: 12.

— mural causes controversy as potential advertisement, Lahaina News, January 30, 1991: 1,3.

— County to cite owners of wall painted by, Lahaina News, February 13, 1991: 1.

— Waikiki Traders applies for after-the-fact permit for mural painted by, Lahaina News, March 6, 1991: 7.

— paint splattered on mural, Lahaina News, March 13, 1991: 1.

— after-the-fact request for mural rejected by Maui Historic Commission, Lahaina News, March 20, 1991: 1.

— hearing to appeal Maui County Planning and Land Use Committee decision set, Lahaina News, May 23, 1991: 1.

— future of mural in Lahaina to be discussed at Maui County Council, Lahaina News, May 30, 1991: 1.

— Maui County Council likely to reject appeal to allow mural, Lahaina News, June 13, 1991: 1.

— plans new mural for Lahaina, Lahaina News, June 13, 1991: 1.

— lawyer asks some Maui County Council members to recuse themselves from deciding on fate of mural due to bias, Lahaina News, June 27, 1991: 1.

— opens new gallery in Anchor Cove Shopping Center, Lahaina News, July 4, 1991: 4.

— public meeting set on future of mural, Lahaina News, July 18, 1991: 5.

— debate over status of public mural continues, Lahaina News, August 15, 1991: 8.

— considering appealing decision on mural, Lahaina News, September 12, 1991: 11.

— mural on Front Street to be taken down, relocated, Lahaina News, November 28, 1991: 1.

— plans to dismantle mural, Lahaina News, January 2, 1992: 4.

— fine may be assessed on owner of building with mural by, Lahaina News, January 9, 1992: 3.

— continues to dismantle mural, Lahaina News, January 23, 1992: 28.

— begins painting mural in Long Beach, California, Lahaina News, April 30, 1992: 18.

— paints largest mural in the world in Long Beach, California, Lahaina News, May 28, 1992: 1.

— completes mural at Long Beach Convention and Entertainment Center, Lahaina News, May 28, 1992: 18.

— to premier first book, "The Art of Wyland", Lahaina News, June 11, 1992: 18.

— to unveil new pieces at Wyland Galleries, Lahaina News, February 25, 1999: 12.

— to appear at Wyland Galleries, Lahaina News, December 21, 2000: 17.

— to introduce new series of oil paintings, Lahaina News, December 20, 2001: 17.

— opens Wyland Galleries at The Shops at Wailea, Lahaina News, April 18, 2002: 8.

— to sign copies of new book "Wyland, Artist of the Sea", Lahaina News, December 19, 2002: 20.

WYLIE, DOUG [ARTIST]

— exhibiting at Wyland Galleries, Lahaina News, February 20, 1991: 12.

— to demonstrate sculpture techniques at Wyland Galleries, Lahaina News, March 26, 1992: 18.

— to be guest artist at Wyland Galleries, Lahaina News, March 26, 1992: 3.

WYLIE, GEORGE

— house suffers storm damage, Lahaina Sun, December 30, 1970: 1.

— letter to the editor congratulating the Lahaina Sun on being established, Lahaina Sun, January 27, 1971: 4.

— concern for water quality, Lahaina Sun, May 5, 1971: 5.

X

XEROX HAWAII [BUSINESS]

— Gage Beerer appointed marketing representative for Maui, Lahaina News, June 21, 2001: 9.

XIAN INTERNATIONAL

— organization described, Lahaina Sun, July 18, 1973: 14.

— governance structure detailed, Lahaina Sun, August 22, 1973: 19.

XOCHIMOKI [MUSICAL AND DANCE GROUP]

— to perform at Malu'ulu O Lele Cultural Center, Lahaina News, January 9, 1985: 3.

XTC

— see drugs

Y

Y2K

— U.S. Small Business Administration urges people to take seriously, Lahaina News, April 1, 1999: 3.

— Maui Citizens Preparedness Council to hold presentation, Lahaina News, June 3, 1999: 16.

Y2TECH MAUI

— classes set, Lahaina News, June 5, 2003: 9.

— classes set, Lahaina News, June 12, 2003: 14.

YACHTING

— see boating

YACKS, MARY

— promoted to district manager at Coffee Partners Hawaii, Lahaina News, September 19, 2002: 8.

YADAO, SHERYLN SINCO

— Queen of Junior Promenade court, Lahaina News, May 31, 2001: 3.

YAFFE, JAMES

— play "Cliffhanger" to be staged at Maui Arts and Cultural Center, Lahaina News, June 20, 2002: 15.

YAGI MEMORIAL SCHOLARSHIP

— awarded to two Maui Community College students, Lahaina News, December 7, 1988: 16.

YAGI, RALPH

— golf tournament held by Maui Board of Realtors in honor, Lahaina News, October 5, 1988: 3.

YAGI, THOMAS

— to receive Honorary Doctor of Humane Letters from the University of Hawaii, Lahaina News, December 31, 1992: 5.

YAGI-BUEN, JAN [POLITICIAN]

— to run for State Senate, Lahaina News, December 9, 1993: 1,12.

— race with Roz Baker detailed, Lahaina News, September 8, 1994: 2.

— candidate schedules fundraiser, Lahaina News, June 11, 1998: 9.

— Business Action Team supporting, Lahaina News, September 3, 1998: 18.

— lawmakers seeking funding Lahaina-Moloka'i ferry, Lahaina News, February 25, 1999: 11.

— discusses tax reforms and funding for Maui, Lahaina News, May 20, 1999: 1,2.

— forming task force to study alternate route to Lahaina, Lahaina News, August 12, 1999: 1.

— discusses work done by task force studying new access to West Maui, Lahaina News, October 21, 1999: 1,20.

— discusses importance of new road to connect West and Central Maui, Lahaina News, January 20, 2000: 1,16.

— forms West Maui Highway Action Committee to work on traffic issues, Lahaina News, February 8, 2001: 1,22.

— Senator outlines accomplishments from 2001 session, Lahaina News, May 10, 2001: 10.

— pushing for new locker rooms for Lahainaluna High School, Lahaina News, February 28, 2002: 1,2.

YAKINIKU CAFÉ [RESTAURANT]

— opens, Lahaina News, April 12, 2001: 9.

YAKINIKU LAHAINA [RESTAURANT]

— opens in Wharf Cinema Center, Lahaina News, February 17, 2000: 14.

YAMA [RESTAURANT]

— opens, Lahaina News, April 22, 1999: 11.

YAMADA, EMMA [MEMBER OF THE HAWAIIAN HOMES COMMISSION]

— at meeting between Hawaiian Homes Commission and The Hawaiians, Lahaina Sun, December 23, 1970: 6.

YAMADA, KEVIN

— co-valedictorian at Lahainaluna High School with Edwin Pascual , Lahaina News, June 18, 1986: 1,16.

YAMADA, MEIJI

— to speak on Buddhist Studies, Lahaina News, April 6, 2000: 16.

YAMADA, SHIGE [ARTIST]

— reception at Village Gallery, Lahaina News, November 1, 1989: 13.

— to exhibit at Hui No'eau Visual Arts Center, Lahaina News, December 7, 2000: 24.

YAMADA, ZACHARY

— Lahainaluna High School student wins Lahaina Arts Society, Lahaina News, May 23, 1990: 5.

YAMAGUCHI, DORIS

— sworn in as councilmember following her husband's death, Lahaina Sun, July 11, 1973: 4.

YAMAGUCHI, JAY

— appointed executive chef at the Maui Sun, Lahaina News, January 30, 1992: 10.

YAMAGUCHI, YONETO [COUNCIL]

— member of Maui County Council, Lahaina Sun, December 30, 1970: 8.

— elected president of Hawaii Association of Counties, Lahaina Sun, January 12, 1972: 17.

— dies, leaving vacancy on Maui County Council, Lahaina Sun, June 27, 1973: 3.

YAMAMOTO, ALAN

— new Head Custodian at Lahainaluna High School, Lahaina News, September 21, 2000: 1,6.

YAMAMOTO, DARYL

— Maui County Clerk updates on status of new community plan, Lahaina News, January 5, 1995: 4.

YAMAMOTO, DEMI

— joins Mahana at Ka'anapali, Lahaina News, October 31, 2002: 6.

YAMAMOTO INVITATIONAL

— track meet trials to be held, Lahaina News, March 28, 1990: 12.

YAMAMOTO, JOANN

— honored as educator of the month by Leilani's on the Beach, Lahaina News, March 7, 2002: 5.

YAMAMOTO, SATOKI

— Lahainaluna High School coach receives The American Sportsman Award, Lahaina News, December 11, 1985: 4.

YAMAMOTO STORE

— described, Lahaina Sun, May 24, 1972: 1,18,19.

YAMANOUE, KAZUO [ARTIST]

— wins Lahaina Cannery Mall ice carving contest, Lahaina News, December 1, 1994: 1.

YAMASAKA, MAMORU [POLITICIAN]

— discusses delays in Lahaina Bypass schedule, Lahaina News, December 27, 1989: 32.

YAMASAKI, CAROLYN

— joins Hawaiian Trust Co. Ltd as vice president and senior financial services officer, Lahaina News, August 18, 1994: 9.

YAMASAKI, MAMORU [POLITICIAN]

— plan for public meetings, Lahaina Sun, December 9, 1970: 4.

— at public meeting in Lahaina, Lahaina Sun, December 23, 1970: 10.

— concerned over how Civil Air Patrol is spending money, Lahaina Sun, February 28, 1973: 4.

— introduces bills relevant to West Maui, including community swimming pool, Lahaina News, February 28, 1990: 1.

— says that mayor Linda Lingle's request for water source development funds from legislature likely, Lahaina News, April 17, 1991: 1.

— farewell celebration to be held following retirement, Lahaina News, August 27, 1992: 6.

— to lead Child and Family Service fundraising campaign, Lahaina News, December 15, 1994: 6,7.

YAMASAKI, SHANE

— wins Kapalua Land Company, Ltd. Golf scholarship, Lahaina News, July 18, 1991: 7.

YAMASHIGE, ERIC H.

— appointed as vice president of Ronald M. Fukumoto Engineering Inc., Lahaina News, June 30, 1994: 9.

YAMASHIRO, IOLANI

— teaching violin in summer program offered by Arts Education for Children Group, Lahaina News, May 14, 1998: 2.

— to teach violin, Lahaina News, June 18, 1998: 7.

YAMASHIRO, JANE

— to attend international Salzburg Seminar on "Community Leadership and Policy Change", Lahaina News, November 29, 2001: 1.

YAMAUCHI, MACK

— named officer of Lahaina Kamaakina Fishing Association, Lahaina Sun, December 23, 1970: 11.

— political activities featured, Lahaina News, November 25, 1999: 6.

YAMAUCHI, SCOTT

— promoted to vice president of operations for Amfac Garden Hawaii, Lahaina News, April 4, 1990: 7.

YAMAUCHI, TAKEO

— appearing in court on charges of smuggling and possession of counterfeit money, Lahaina Sun, December 27, 1972: 10.

YAMAUCHI-AU KOI, MANDY

— cheerleader for Los Angeles Raider featured, Lahaina News, October 12, 1988: 2.

— to perform with Los Angeles Raiderettes, Lahaina News, February 6, 1992: 17.

YANAGIDA, LISA

— named "Employee of the Quarter" by Maui Youth and Family Services, Lahaina News, January 11, 2001: 14.

YANAGISAKO, DAVID [ARTIST]

— photographer's work displayed at Lahaina Arts Society's Old Jail Gallery, Lahaina News, October 23, 1985: 20.

YANNEIL, ROSEMARY KUULEI

— to appear in Who's Who in American Women, Lahaina News, May 1, 1985: 4.

YANNELL, JOHN

— Aqua Blue Maui creates abalone shell laminate, Lahaina News, February 11, 1999: 13.

YANNETY, JOE [COMEDIAN]
— to perform at Comedy Club and the Sports Page, Lahaina News, November 21, 1991: 15.

YAP, BLOSSOM
— to present to Na Hoaloha O Lele, Lahaina News, January 3, 1990: 28.

YAP, SLOAN
— resident graduates from U.S. Coast Guard Recruit Training Center, Lahaina News, November 18, 1999: 15.

YARA, ROBERT
— seeks consistency in requirement to import milk to Oahu, which would include Maui, Lahaina News, April 17, 1985: 2.

YARBOROUGH, TAWNY [HULA DANCER]
— to perform at "Hula Leʻa O Na Keiki", Lahaina News, September 19, 1990: 10.

YARMOUTH CAPITAL PARTNERS II
— to develop resort in Kapalua with Maui Land and Pineapple, Lahaina News, July 10, 1997: 12.

YASUI, BYRON [MUSICIAN]
— to perform at "The Art of the Solo ʻUkulele", Lahaina News, March 28, 2002: 19.

YATES, MAKAʻALA
— to talk on "Lomilomi Practice and Hawaiian Healing", Lahaina News, March 6, 2003: 17.

YATSUSHIRO, VANCE
— appointed principal at Lahaina Intermediate School, Lahaina News, August 25, 1994: 1.
— Lahaina Intermediate School principal leaves position, Lahaina News, May 13, 1999: 1.

YAZAKI, BRODIE
— Scholar/Athlete of the Week, Lahaina News, September 23, 1999: 6.

YAZAWA, ALBERT
— new medical director at Kula Hospital and Clinic, Lahaina News, August 16, 2001: 8.

YEAR OF THE BIBLE
— benefit concert to be held, Lahaina News, August 1, 1984: 13.

YEAR OF THE CHINESE
— celebrations planned, Lahaina News, February 15, 1989: 6.

YEAR OF THE HAWAIIAN
— begins, Lahaina News, December 31, 1986: 3.

YEAR OF THE OCEAN
— to be celebrated, Lahaina News, January 8, 1998: 7.

YEE, JOE
— custom lure maker featured, Lahaina News, March 14, 1990: 7,28.

YEE, SIDNEY [ARTIST]
— to conduct workshops, Lahaina News, June 12, 1985: 20.
— Lahainaluna High School art teacher receives fellowship to study at Kennedy Center in Washington DC, Lahaina News, June 26, 1985: 3.
— work and teaching featured, Lahaina News, September 4, 1985: 1.
— Lahainaluna High School art teacher retires, Lahaina News, August 29, 2002: 1,22.

YELLOW BOAT, THE [PLAY]
— to be performed by Metro Theater Company, Lahaina News, May 16, 1996: 10.

YELLOW PAGES
— sending advertising that could be confused with Hawaiian Telephone billing notices, Lahaina News, September 13, 1989: 4.

YEN, FLORA CHOW [ARTIST]
— brush painting and calligraphy exhibited, Lahaina News, March 12, 1986: 3.
— to teach course on Chinese brush painting, Lahaina News, August 8, 1990: 15.

YENNETTY, JOE [COMEDIAN]
— to perform at Comedy Club, Lahaina News, January 24, 1990: 14.

YESTERDAY [MUSICAL GROUP]
— to perform at Maui Arts and Cultural Center, Lahaina News, June 22, 2000: 17.

YI YI (AND A ONE AND A TWO) [FILM]
— to be shown at Maui Arts and Cultural Center, Lahaina News, February 15, 2001: 17.

YIN-FAH, YAP
— details prospects for Year of the Rabbit, Lahaina News, December 31, 1986: 1,9.

YMCA
— sponsoring after-school program, Lahaina News, October 1, 1980: 7.
— Mayor Tavares declares YMCA week, Lahaina News, February 1, 1981: 16.
— After-school activities announced, Lahaina News, September 1, 1982: 10.
— chocolate fundraiser held, Lahaina News, March 14, 1984: 8.
— offers program at Camp Keanae, Lahaina News, July 4, 1984: 7.
— offering afterschool program for children K-6, Lahaina News, January 30, 1985: 3.
— offering Wellness Education Program, Lahaina News, February 6, 1985: 3.
— offering starter fitness program, Lahaina News, February 13, 1985: 3.
— offering fitness programs, Lahaina News, May 15, 1985: 8,20.
— summer day camp registration begins, Lahaina News, May 22, 1985: 3.
— launches fundraiser to build new facility, Lahaina News, May 29, 1985: 3.
— offers swim and fitness classes, Lahaina News, June 19, 1985: 3.
— sports and Hawaiiana camps at Camp Keanae open for registration, Lahaina News, July 17, 1985: 3.
— accepting reservations for Camp Keanae, Lahaina News, August 21, 1985: 3.
— offers first aid and gymnastics classes, Lahaina News, August 28, 1985: 3.
— offering gym classes, Lahaina News, February 5, 1986: 3.
— offering course for first responders, Lahaina News, February 26, 1986: 3.
— to hold Spring Break Day Camp, Lahaina News, March 12, 1986: 12.
— offering first responder course, Lahaina News, April 16, 1986: 3.
— to offer program for pregnant women, Lahaina News, April 30, 1986: 3.
— Summer Day Camp program announced, Lahaina News, June 4, 1986: 3.
— infant and beginning swim classes planned, Lahaina News, June 11, 1986: 3.
— offering starter fitness classes, Lahaina News, July 2, 1986: 18.
— offering prenatal and postpartum exercise classes, Lahaina News, July 2, 1986: 3.
— to hold Hawaiiana and Sports camps, Lahaina News, July 9, 1986: 3.
— offering summer day camp, Lahaina News, July 30, 1986: 3.
— Afterschool Child Care program accepting applicants, Lahaina News, August 20, 1986: 14.
— offering Holiday Fun Club, Lahaina News, August 20, 1986: 3.
— offers Holiday Fun Club, Lahaina News, August 27, 1986: 13.
— offers low impact aerobics classes, Lahaina News, September 10, 1986: 3.
— offering "first responder" first aid course, Lahaina News, September 24, 1986: 3.

— offering Discover Maui Holiday Fun Club, Lahaina News, October 1, 1986: 5.
— offering swimming and gymnastics lessons, Lahaina News, October 29, 1986: 3.
— offering swim classes, Lahaina News, November 26, 1986: 12.
— offering swimming lessons, Lahaina News, December 3, 1986: 11.
— selling Christmas trees, Lahaina News, December 3, 1986: 11.
— holds holiday camp, Lahaina News, December 17, 1986: 2.
— offering swimming lessons, Lahaina News, January 14, 1987: 3.
— year-round swimming lessons to be offered, Lahaina News, February 4, 1987: 11.
— offering first responder course, Lahaina News, February 4, 1987: 11.
— offering swimming lessons, Lahaina News, March 4, 1987: 10.
— begins "Fantastic Gymnastics" for children, Lahaina News, April 1, 1987: 3.
— begins kihei gymnastics, Lahaina News, April 29, 1987: 3.
— offering course on 35mm cameras, Lahaina News, May 13, 1987: 3.
— low impact aerobics class offered, Lahaina News, May 27, 1987: 3.
— to offer all-day child care, Lahaina News, June 10, 1987: 18.
— offering summer gymnastics program, Lahaina News, June 10, 1987: 3.
— to hold Hawaiiana Camp, Lahaina News, July 8, 1987: 3.
— to hold course on photography, Lahaina News, July 22, 1987: 3.
— gymnastics lessons to be offered, Lahaina News, July 29, 1987: 3.
— accepting applications for Hawaiiana and Sports camps, Lahaina News, July 29, 1987: 3.
— offering swimming lessons, Lahaina News, October 7, 1987: 16.
— offering swimming lessons, Lahaina News, November 4, 1987: 3.
— to sell Christmas trees, Lahaina News, December 9, 1987: 26.
— to offer swimming lessons, Lahaina News, December 9, 1987: 3.
— offering gymnastics classes, Christmas day camp, Lahaina News, December 16, 1987: 3.
— to host New Year's Overnighter, Lahaina News, December 30, 1987: 3.
— offering gymnastics classes, Lahaina News, January 27, 1988: 3.
— offering aerobics classes, Lahaina News, February 3, 1988: 3.
— offers swimming lessons, Lahaina News, March 2, 1988: 12.
— summer day camp registration begins, Lahaina News, May 18, 1988: 18.
— offering summer swimming, Lahaina News, June 22, 1988: 3.
— offers summer day camp, Lahaina News, July 20, 1988: 3.
— offers low impact aerobics, Lahaina News, August 3, 1988: 3.
— accepting registrations for after-school program, Lahaina News, August 10, 1988: 17.
— offers swimming lessons, Lahaina News, September 14, 1988: 13.
— offering low-impact aerobics, Lahaina News, September 21, 1988: 3.
— offers karate class, Lahaina News, October 5, 1988: 20.
— swim lessons offered, Lahaina News, November 2, 1988: 3.
— to hold Christmas Day Camp, Lahaina News, December 14, 1988: 16.
— hosting overnighter, Lahaina News, December 28, 1988: 13.
— holds swimming lessons, Lahaina News, January 11, 1989: 5.
— offering low-impact aerobics, Lahaina News, January 18, 1989: 5.
— offering swimming and gymnastics lessons, Lahaina News, March 8, 1989: 17.
— to hold Fun Club, Lahaina News, March 22, 1989: 13.
— to hold gymnastics and swimming classes, Lahaina News, April 5, 1989: 14.
— accepting applications for Summer Day Camp, Lahaina News, April 26, 1989: 3.
— to offer swimming lessons at the Napili Surf; gymnastics lessons, Lahaina News, June 14, 1989: 2.
— summer camps offered, Lahaina News, July 12, 1989: 6.
— accepting registrations for summer camp in Keanae, Lahaina News, August 2, 1989: 3.

— registration for Summer Day Camp program, Lahaina News, August 9, 1989: 3.
— offering after-school program, Lahaina News, August 30, 1989: 3.
— swimming lessons offered for young children, Lahaina News, September 13, 1989: 3.
— offering swim classes, Lahaina News, September 27, 1989: 3.
— offering swimming lessons, Lahaina News, November 1, 1989: 6.
— to offer swimming classes, Lahaina News, November 8, 1989: 3.
— offering gymnastics classes, Lahaina News, January 24, 1990: 8.
— registration open for gymnastics classes, Lahaina News, March 14, 1990: 11.
— offering swimming lessons, Lahaina News, March 21, 1990: 8.
— offering gymnastics classes, Lahaina News, June 20, 1990: 8.
— expanding gymnastics program, Lahaina News, July 4, 1990: 6.
— to hold swimming lessons, Lahaina News, August 8, 1990: 4.
— expanding gymnastics program, Lahaina News, August 29, 1990: 7.
— offering swim lessons, Lahaina News, September 19, 1990: 4.
— offering swim classes for infants and toddlers, Lahaina News, September 26, 1990: 5,6.
— Saturday swim lessons to be held, Lahaina News, October 10, 1990: 7.
— to hold swimming lessons, Lahaina News, October 24, 1990: 4.
— swimming lessons to be held, Lahaina News, October 31, 1990: 8.
— offering Christmas day camp program, Lahaina News, December 26, 1990: 4.
— offering swimming lessons, Lahaina News, February 20, 1991: 8.
— swim lessons offered, Lahaina News, February 27, 1991: 6.
— beginning swim classes at the El Crab Catcher Pool, Lahaina News, March 6, 1991: 3.
— opening new facility, Lahaina News, April 24, 1991: 5.
— swim lessons to be held, Lahaina News, May 15, 1991: 4.
— announces summer schedule, Lahaina News, May 15, 1991: 5,6.
— registration open for day program, Lahaina News, May 30, 1991: 3.
— day program to be held, Lahaina News, June 6, 1991: 3.
— swim classes to be held at El Crab Catcher, Lahaina News, June 27, 1991: 7.
— offering swim lessons, Lahaina News, July 11, 1991: 7.
— to offer swim lessons, Lahaina News, August 15, 1991: 4.
— offering Thanksgiving morning aerobics, Lahaina News, November 21, 1991: 9.
— offering movement exploration classes, Lahaina News, December 5, 1991: 5.
— offering baby care classes, Lahaina News, December 5, 1991: 5.
— continues to offer classes on baby care, Lahaina News, December 12, 1991: 6.
— offering swimming lessons, Lahaina News, December 19, 1991: 9.
— to offer water aerobics, Lahaina News, December 26, 1991: 24.
— offering "Teen Power Pump and Wild Workout", Lahaina News, January 9, 1992: 5.
— to hold Kid's Night Out, Lahaina News, February 6, 1992: 5.
— to hold Kid's Night Out, Lahaina News, February 13, 1992: 4.
— sponsoring workshops for aerobics instructors, Lahaina News, March 12, 1992: 10.
— offering water aerobics, Lahaina News, September 3, 1992: 6.
— to hold Swim-A-Thon, Lahaina News, November 26, 1992: 2,6.
— to offer classes for toddlers, Lahaina News, December 31, 1992: 7.
— begins swim program, Lahaina News, February 18, 1993: 6.
— to offer water safety course, Lahaina News, February 25, 1993: 3.
— offering water aerobics, Lahaina News, April 29, 1993: 7.
— offering water safety course, Lahaina News, May 6, 1993: 11.
— summer programs announced, Lahaina News, May 6, 1993: 4.
— to hold Smorgasboard Sports Camp, Lahaina News, July 8, 1993: 9.
— offering water aerobics classes, Lahaina News, September 16, 1993: 11.
— hosting Swim-A-Thon, Lahaina News, September 16, 1993: 14.

— to offer water aerobics classes, Lahaina News, November 18, 1993: 8,12.

— offering step aerobics with Maui Community School for Adults, Lahaina News, December 2, 1993: 10.

— to hold country western dance to benefit the homeless shelter and Project Angel Tree, Lahaina News, December 2, 1993: 4.

— to offer swimming program, Lahaina News, January 20, 1994: 9.

— offering aerobics classes, Lahaina News, February 3, 1994: 9.

— offering summer day camp, Lahaina News, April 28, 1994: 4.

— to hold swim program, Lahaina News, June 23, 1994: 7.

— to hold spring board diving course, Lahaina News, July 28, 1994: 6.

— to hold water aerobics, Lahaina News, January 26, 1995: 8.

— presents Lahaina Spring Break Learn to Swim, Lahaina News, March 23, 1995: 7.

— to hold swimming lessons, Lahaina News, June 8, 1995: 6.

— to hold Lahaina Learn to Swim program, Lahaina News, September 28, 1995: 7.

— to hold Learn to Swim Program, Lahaina News, February 15, 1996: 7.

— to hold swim program, Lahaina News, June 27, 1996: 16.

— to offer swimming classes, Lahaina News, January 16, 1997: 6.

— to hold "Family Night", Lahaina News, September 18, 1997: 16.

— offering extensive variety of activities, Lahaina News, July 8, 1999: 6.

— events scheduled, Lahaina News, July 15, 1999: 7.

— may take over management of West Maui skatepark, Lahaina News, September 16, 1999: 1,16.

— offering programs, Lahaina News, July 12, 2001: 13.

— offering athletic programs, Lahaina News, September 27, 2001: 13.

YO-YO

— exhibition to be held, Lahaina News, July 25, 1996: 13.

— demonstration and contest to be held, Lahaina News, August 22, 1996: 15.

— contest to be held, Lahaina News, April 10, 2003: 10.

— demonstrations to be held, Lahaina News, April 17, 2003: 13.

— workshops to be held by Boys and Girls Club of West Maui, Lahaina News, May 29, 2003: 16.

— workshops continue to be held, Lahaina News, June 19, 2003: 16.

— Jennifer Baybrook to lead retreat, Lahaina News, July 17, 2003: 18.

— workshops continue to be held, Lahaina News, July 24, 2003: 16.

— workshops continue to be held, Lahaina News, September 4, 2003: 16.

YODA, RONALD

— named senior vice president and chief financial officer at Alexander and Baldwin, Lahaina News, September 26, 1990: 9.

YOGA

— taught by Barbara Means, Lahaina News, October 17, 1996: 3.

— to be held at Tradewinds Gymnastics Dojo, Lahaina News, November 30, 2000: 17.

— Lynn von Tempsky to lead classes, Lahaina News, August 23, 2001: 13.

— Doug Swenson to lead awareness workshop, Lahaina News, January 16, 2003: 16.

— to be offered at The Art School at Kapalua, Lahaina News, August 21, 2003: 18.

— Ateeka to offer class for golfers at The Art School at Kapalua, Lahaina News, September 18, 2003: 13.

YOHN, TODD [COMEDIAN]

— to perform at Comedy Club, Lahaina News, September 15, 1994: 14.

YOKOUCHI, MASARU "PUNDY"

— sells land to KM Hawaii, Inc originally planned as site for Sea Village, Lahaina News, July 18, 1990: 7.

— awarded honorary degree by the University of Hawai'i at Manoa, Lahaina News, May 23, 1991: 8.

— friends of offer money to Maui Community Arts and Cultural Center, Lahaina News, August 1, 1991: 5.

— honored by Association of Fundraising Professionals, Lahaina News, November 28, 2002: 8.

YOKOYAMA, BOB

— thanked for help in creating program for low and middle income housing, Lahaina Sun, January 20, 1971: 3.

YOKOYAMA, EARL

— purchases Kahului Shell Service, Lahaina News, November 21, 1990: 12.

YOM KIPPER

— services to be held by Jewish Congregation of Maui, Lahaina News, September 24, 1998: 17.

YOOS, JACK

— local Santa Claus featured, Lahaina News, December 12, 1991: 17.

YOSAKOI DANCE [TROUPE]

— to perform at John Manjiro Izanai Yosakoi Festival, Lahaina News, March 13, 2003: 3.

YOSHIMASU, EDWARD [GENERAL]

— promoted to brigadier general, Lahaina Sun, March 24, 1971: 2.

YOSHIMI, HELEN

— to speak at conference on assisted living, Lahaina News, June 27, 1996: 15.

YOSHIMOTO, HAMI

— discusses Kiwanis Club at Lahainaluna High School, Lahaina Sun, January 13, 1971: 7.

YOSHIMURA JEWELERS [BUSINESS]

— moves to Ka'anapali, Lahaina News, December 29, 1994: 6.

YOSHINO, OWEN [ARTIST]

— work of Lahainaluna High School student praised, Lahaina News, May 10, 1989: 3.

YOSHIOKA, ALAN

— chosen as a volunteer of the year by Hawaii State Theatre Council, Lahaina News, August 8, 1990: 4.

YOSHIOKA, HARUYO

— says that outbreak of dysentery is contained, Lahaina Sun, January 27, 1971: 1.

YOSHITAKE, ARATA "RALPH"

— charged with multiple thefts, Lahaina News, July 30, 1992: 3.

— plans to refile felony theft charges against, Lahaina News, August 20, 1992: 3.

YOSHIZAWA, ERIC

— named chairman of Scout-O-Rama, Lahaina News, March 14, 1990: 6.

YOU CAN'T TAKE IT WITH YOU [PLAY]

— performed by Maui Community Theatre, Lahaina News, April 2, 1986: 3.

— to be performed at Seabury Hall, Lahaina News, November 5, 1998: 20.

— to be performed by Maui OnStage, Lahaina News, December 27, 2001: 14.

YOU GOTTA HAVE A GIMMICK! [PLAY]

— to be performed by Baldwin Theatre Guild, Lahaina News, April 15, 1993: 12.

YOU SHOULD BE DANCING

— Judy Ridolfino to hold annual dance show, Lahaina News, January 31, 2002: 17.

YOUNG ADULT CONFERENCE

— organized by United Church of Christ, Lahaina News, July 11, 1990: 4.

YOUNG AMERICANS [ENTERTAINERS]
— hold shows at Baldwin High School auditorium, Lahaina News, February 8, 1984: 3.

YOUNG AND THE RESTLESS, THE [TELEVISION SHOW]
— filmed in Maui, Lahaina News, November 14, 1990: 3,4.

YOUNG BLOODS [MUSICAL GROUP]
— performance reviewed, Lahaina News, November 28, 1984: 17.

YOUNG BROTHERS [BUSINESS]
— increase to barge rate challenged, Lahaina Sun, August 4, 1971: 1,2.
— purchased by Hawaiian Electric Industries, Inc, Lahaina News, October 8, 1986: 3.
— to provide grants to charitable organizations with Hawaiian Tug and Barge, Lahaina News, August 30, 2001: 9.
— awarding grants with Hawaiian Tug and Barge to non-profit community organizations, Lahaina News, June 20, 2002: 8.
— now accepting grant applications for Community Gift Giving Program, Lahaina News, June 26, 2003: 14.

YOUNG, CAROLINE [ARTIST]
— to exhibit at Royal Art Gallery, Lahaina News, March 6, 1991: 16.

YOUNG, DENISE
— new resort manager at Aston Ka'anapali Shores, Lahaina News, July 26, 2001: 8.

YOUNG, DON
— appointed director of resort operations for Kapalua Land Company, Lahaina News, May 29, 1985: 3.
— promoted to executive vice president of operations at Kapalua Land Company, Ltd., Lahaina News, June 4, 1992: 9.

YOUNG, HOLLY [ARTIST]
— sculptor to appear at Lahaina Galleries, Lahaina News, December 17, 1998: 24.

YOUNG, JESSIE COLIN [MUSICIAN]
— played at musical festival, Lahaina News, May 2, 1984: 14.

YOUNG, JOHN
— new general manager of Maui Myth and Magic Theatre, Lahaina News, May 9, 2002: 8.

YOUNG, NANCY [ARTIST]
— featured at Lahaina Arts Society, Lahaina News, April 15, 1987: 12.
— featured at Village Gallery, Lahaina News, August 16, 1989: 3.
— featured, Lahaina News, August 30, 1989: 11.
— produces Maui Marathon poster, Lahaina News, March 7, 1990: 8.

YOUNG, NEIL [MUSICIAN]
— reviewed, Lahaina Sun, March 8, 1972: 18.
— Live Rust reviewed, Lahaina News, March 1, 1980: 4.

YOUNG, NOEL
— selected to oversee Pioneer Inn renovations, Lahaina News, September 16, 1993: 9.

YOUNG PEOPLE
— see hippies, youth

YOUNG, PETER
— endorsed by Public Resources for Jobs (Pro Jobs), Lahaina News, September 17, 1986: 3,11.

YOUNG STEVE [MUSICIAN]
— to perform at Iao Theatre, Lahaina News, March 16, 1995: 12.

YOUNG, THERESA [ARTIST]
— to participate in "Four by Four Equals" show, Lahaina News, February 2, 1995: 10.
— to exhibit at Lahaina Arts Society Gallery, Lahaina News, July 30, 1998: 17.
— to exhibit photographs at Maui Arts Society, Lahaina News, June 6, 2002: 17.

YOUNG, TIMOTHY
— appointed Vice President and manager of Bank of Hawaii's real estate investment banking unit, Lahaina News, October 11, 2001: 9.

YOUNG, WALLY
— member of Lahaina Kamaakina Fishing Association, Lahaina Sun, December 23, 1970: 11.

YOUNGER, JUDY
— to discuss "Loving Your Intuition", Lahaina News, April 25, 2002: 17.

YOUNGERS, SID [COMEDIAN]
— to perform at Comedy Club and the Sports Page, Lahaina News, November 28, 1990: 9,10.

YOUNKERMAN, DIRK
— to offer presentation on whales at Hale Kohola Museum, Lahaina News, January 29, 1998: 16.
— to present on whales, Lahaina News, February 5, 1998: 13.
— continues to present on whales, Lahaina News, March 5, 1998: 16.
— continues to offer presentations on whales, Lahaina News, April 9, 1998: 16.

YOUR RECYCLING GUIDE [BOOK]
— published, Lahaina News, January 15, 1998: 5.

YOURS MINE AND AURAS [BUSINESS]
— planning 20-year reunion, Lahaina News, April 25, 2002: 5.

YOUTH
— Lahaina youth group forming, Lahaina Sun, February 7, 1973: 7.
— services need volunteers to help, Lahaina News, June 28, 1989: 1.
— summer programs described, Lahaina News, June 28, 1989: 4,5.
— see also Maui Youth Theatre, West Maui Youth Center, specific sports, etc.

YOUTH ACTIVITY FAIR
— to be held, Lahaina News, October 10, 1996: 14.
— to be held, Lahaina News, March 5, 1998: 17.
— to be held, Lahaina News, March 12, 1998: 20.

YOUTH ADVISORY COUNCIL
— Mayor Linda Lingle appoints Karen Ancheta to, Lahaina News, January 25, 1996: 4.

YOUTH AMBASSADORS OF AMERICA
— to hold garage sale, Lahaina News, June 15, 1988: 14.
— Morea Paradise to paint faces as fundraiser for, Lahaina News, June 7, 1989: 9.

YOUTH APPRECIATION DAY
— to be held, Lahaina News, November 20, 1997: 1.
— held at West Maui Youth Center, Lahaina News, March 11, 1999: 5.

YOUTH CONSERVATION CORPS
— Pono Pacific Land Management and Department of Land and Natural Resources recruiting for, Lahaina News, April 19, 2001: 2.

YOUTH CONTACT CENTER
— begins operation at Kahului airport, Lahaina Sun, June 23, 1971: 1.

YOUTH FOR CHRIST/USA
— Tiffany Hunt to participate in national internship program, Lahaina News, May 10, 2001: 2.

YOUTH FOR ENVIRONMENTAL SERVICE
— to pull Tibouchina plants in the Pu'u Kukui Watershed, Lahaina News, September 30, 1999: 12.
— planning Recycling and Education Drive, Lahaina News, October 7, 1999: 16.
— "Great Youth Earth Mele" to be held, Lahaina News, April 13, 2000: 12.
— planning "Youth Vision 2001", Lahaina News, November 2, 2000: 24.
— to meet, Lahaina News, November 9, 2000: 25.

YOUTH FOR UNDERSTANDING INTERNATIONAL EXCHANGE PROGRAM
— launches summer recruitment, Lahaina News, July 22, 1987: 3.

YOUTH HOSTEL
— proposed for transients, Lahaina Sun, April 14, 1971: 1.

YOUTH INTERNATIONAL [BUSINESS]
— opens at the Lahaina Center, Lahaina News, November 7, 1990: 7.

YOUTH PROGRAMS
— two new programs announced in West Maui, Lahaina Sun, October 20, 1971: 14.
— funding sought by residents, Lahaina News, October 23, 1997: 1,2.

YOUTH RELAY FOR LIFE
— held, Lahaina News, March 13, 2003: 9.

YOUTH SUMMER MUSIC CAMP
— summer program offered, Lahaina News, May 27, 1999: 5.

YOUTH UKULELE PLAYERS CONTEST
— to be held, Lahaina News, June 26, 1997: 9.
— winners announced, Lahaina News, July 23, 1998: 3.

YOUTH VISION
— community development project to conduct leadership camp, Lahaina News, March 28, 2002: 5.

YOUTH VISION 2001
— to be held, Lahaina News, March 29, 2001: 3.

YOUTH WITH A MISSION [MUSICAL GROUP]
— to perform at Ka'ahumanu Center, Lahaina News, October 22, 1998: 20.

YU-GI-OH
— Hard Rock Café to host event to support Big Brothers/Big /Sisters of Maui, Lahaina News, April 3, 2003: 3.

YUEN, HERB
— promoted to director of conference services at Westin Maui, Lahaina News, March 13, 1991: 7.
— named director of conference services by Westin Maui, Lahaina News, November 14, 1991: 8.

YUK YUK KOMEDY KABARETS
— to open location in Lahaina, Lahaina News, March 30, 1988: 6.

YUM YUM TREE [RESTAURANT]
— to open in Lahaina Cannery Mall, Lahaina News, July 21, 1994: 7.

YUN, CHEE [MUSICIAN]
— to perform, Lahaina News, May 16, 2002: 16,17.

YURIKA FOODS [BUSINESS]
— featured, Lahaina News, August 31, 1983: 14.

YVEL [ARTIST]
— to exhibit at Hutton's Fine Jewelers, Lahaina News, February 22, 2001: 16.

Z

ZACHARY, DIANE
— facilitates Maui County Project Impact public hearing, Lahaina News, November 23, 2000: 1,6.

ZACHRY, RUFUS "RUDY"
— new pastor at Lahaina Baptist Church, Lahaina News, September 23, 1987: 3.
— reverend featured, Lahaina News, May 28, 1992: 3.

ZACK, DENISE
— planning to build preschool, Lahaina News, July 11, 1991: 6.

ZACK, TRAVIS
— Scholar/Athlete of the Week, Lahaina News, November 5, 1998: 18.

ZAMECNIK, JADRAN [ARTIST]
— to exhibit at Lahaina Arts Society Gallery, Lahaina News, September 3, 1998: 21.

ZANCHI, JUDITH
— appointed sales manager of Stouffer's Wailea Beach Resort, Lahaina News, October 4, 1989: 5.

ZANDRANDO, JOHN [MUSICIAN]
— to play at Blackie's Bar, Lahaina News, February 14, 1990: 15.
— to perform at Blackie's Bar, Lahaina News, February 21, 1990: 13.

ZANE, CLIFFORD
— scores hold-in-one at Waiehu Municipal Golf Course, Lahaina News, January 2, 1991: 16.

ZANER, JOHN
— executive chef to manage culinary division at the Ritz-Carlton, Lahaina News, April 3, 2003: 8.

ZANGRANDO, JOHN [MUSICIAN]
— to perform at Longhi's Restaurant, Lahaina News, September 19, 1996: 18.

ZANY, BOB [COMEDIAN]
— to perform at Comedy Club and the Sports Page, Lahaina News, December 10, 1992: 15,17.
— to perform at Comedy Club, Lahaina News, May 26, 1994: 11.

ZARATE, IOKEPA
— graduates from U.S. Coast Guard Recruit Training Center, Lahaina News, April 25, 2002: 5.

ZARRELLA, DALE [ARTIST]
— releases lithograph, Lahaina News, August 11, 1994: 12.
— sculptor to exhibit at Lahaina Galleries, Lahaina News, January 15, 1998: 13.
— to demonstrate wood carving techniques, Lahaina News, October 15, 1998: 16.
— to exhibit at Lahaina Galleries, Lahaina News, November 19, 1998: 16.
— sculptor to appear at Lahaina Galleries, Lahaina News, November 26, 1998: 16.
— sculptor to appear at Lahaina Galleries, Lahaina News, December 17, 1998: 24.
— to present "Sea Talk" at Maui Ocean Center, Lahaina News, June 21, 2001: 17.
— sculptor to visit Lahaina Galleries, Lahaina News, September 18, 2003: 16.

ZAUGG, JEFFREY "HULK"
— reflects on life on Maui, Lahaina News, October 2, 2003: 1,20.

ZAZZARO, MARY
— appointed national sales manager for Kapalua Bay Hotel and Villas, Lahaina News, September 3, 1992: 8.

ZEFF, STEVEN
— from Center for Whale Studies, to discuss Southern Ocean wildlife, Lahaina News, February 6, 2003: 17.

ZEPHYROS QUINTET [MUSICAL GROUP]
— to perform at Maui Arts and Cultural Center, Lahaina News, November 1, 2001: 16.

ZERNACK, NANNA
— to offer tango classes, Lahaina News, June 17, 1993: 16.

ZERO [MUSICAL GROUP]
— Grateful Dead spin-off band to perform , Lahaina News, February 11, 1999: 9.

ZEUG, MARK
— names Hawaii correspondent for sugar journal, Lahaina News, May 24, 1989: 8.

ZHOU, CRYSTAL
— new assistant chief engineer at Maui Marriott, Lahaina News, September 22, 1994: 13.

ZIGGY MARLEY AND THE MELODY MAKERS [MUSICAL GROUP]
— to perform, Lahaina News, April 2, 1998: 17.

ZIMMER, LAYTON
— Holy Innocents' Episcopal Church reverend discusses "community food basket" program, Lahaina News, January 31, 2002: 3.

ZIMMERMAN, MARIKA
— selected as Hawaii finalist for America's favorite Pre-Teen Contest, Lahaina News, August 23, 1989: 4.

ZIMMERMAN, SHELDON
— lands biggest marlin to date, Lahaina News, September 25, 2003: 13.

ZINK, DARBY [ARTIST]
— opening Plumfield Art Center, Lahaina News, July 25, 1990: 13.

ZIONDRA, ALIA
— presents "Thresholds of Faith: The Harmonics of Conscious Choice", Lahaina News, December 31, 1998: 13.
— talks on "Thresholds of Faith: The Harmonics of Conscious Choice", Lahaina News, January 7, 1999: 16.

ZOLEZZI, KATE
— new general manager at Maui Ocean Center, Lahaina News, August 14, 2003: 8.

ZONING
— decision to rezone for new housing deferred, Lahaina Sun, March 10, 1971: 2.
— approval to subdivide 34 acres in Alaeloa, Lahaina Sun, April 14, 1971: 2.

ZONTA CLUB OF MAUI
— announces availability of "Young Women in Public Affairs" scholarship, Lahaina News, March 2, 1995: 3.
— holding "Hidden Gardens of Maui II", Lahaina News, September 18, 1997: 16.

ZOO
— request for children's zoo in Lahaina Market rejected, Lahaina Sun, April 21, 1971: 3.
— request for children's petting zoo in Lahaina Market withdrawn, Lahaina Sun, May 12, 1971: 5.
— County seeking land between Wailuku and Kahului for, Lahaina Sun, January 12, 1972: 1.
— see also Maui Zoo

ZOO ADVISORY COMMITTEE
— meeting set, Lahaina Sun, November 24, 1971: 12.
— first phase of Maui zoo should be completed by Christmas, Lahaina Sun, December 1, 1971: 4.

ZOO STORY, THE [PLAY]
— to be performed by Maui Community College, Lahaina News, October 28, 1993: 11.

ZOO, THE [MUSICAL GROUP]
— to play, fronted by Mick Fleetwood , Lahaina News, May 31, 1989: 21.

ZOOFEST
— 1986 event scheduled for March 29 at Maui County Zoo, Lahaina News, March 12, 1986: 3.
— reviewed, Lahaina News, April 9, 1986: 8.
— 1987 event planned, Lahaina News, April 8, 1987: 20.
— to be held, Lahaina News, March 23, 1988: 3,14.
— to be held to support Maui Philharmonic Society, Lahaina News, April 11, 1990: 2.
— to be held at Maui Zoo, Lahaina News, March 27, 1991: 15.
— to be held, Lahaina News, April 16, 1992: 4.
— seeking performers, Lahaina News, February 17, 1994: 12.
— to be held by Maui Philharmonic Society, Lahaina News, March 31, 1994: 16.

ZOOLU'S GRILLE AND BAR [RESTAURANT]
— opens, Lahaina News, October 7, 1999: 6,7.

Z'S RISTORANTE
— to feature local artwork, Lahaina News, October 21, 1987: 3.

ZUK, DOUG
— chef joins Fish and Game Brewing Company, Lahaina News, April 8, 1999: 11.

ZUPROC [MUSICAL BAND]
— reviewed, Lahaina News, May 15, 1980: 4.

ZWEEDYK, JAMES
— chair of Building Industry Association's Hawaii Renaissance program, Lahaina News, February 28, 1990: 4.

ZYDECO, BUCKWHEAT [MUSICIAN]
— to perform at Maui Arts and Cultural Center, Lahaina News, March 23, 2000: 12.

ZYDEL, STAN
— appointed general manager of The Kapalua Villas, Lahaina News, December 5, 1990: 4.
— named general manager of The Kapalua Villas, Lahaina News, December 12, 1990: 6.

ZZ TOP [MUSICAL BAND]
— play at Blaisdell Center in Honolulu, Lahaina News, October 15, 1980: 11.

www.ingramcontent.com/pod-product-compliance
Lightning Source LLC
Chambersburg PA
CBHW052128020426

42334CB00023B/2636